PENGUIN

THE PENGUIN TV COMPANION

Jeff Evans was born in South Wales and educated at the University of Reading. A freelance journalist, he specializes in writing not only about television, but also travel and beer, having edited eight editions of the Campaign for Real Ale's best-selling annual *Good Beer Guide*. Among his other works are the award-winning *Good Bottled Beer Guide* and *Midsomer Murders: The Making of an English Crime Classic*. He has also contributed to many TV and radio programmes, newspapers and magazines, including the *Radio Times*. He is married with two sons and lives in Newbury.

The Penguin TV Companion

Jeff Evans

PENGUIN BOOKS

PENGUIN BOOKS

Published by the Penguin Group
Penguin Books Ltd, 80 Strand, London WC2R 0RL, England
Penguin Group (USA) Inc., 375 Hudson Street, New York, New York 10014, USA
Penguin Group (Canada), 90 Eglinton Avenue East, Suite 700, Toronto, Ontario, Canada M4P 2Y3
(a division of Pearson Penguin Canada Inc.)
Penguin Ireland, 25 St Stephen's Green, Dublin 2, Ireland (a division of Penguin Books Ltd)
Penguin Group (Australia), 250 Camberwell Road, Camberwell, Victoria 3124, Australia
(a division of Pearson Australia Group Pty Ltd)
Penguin Books India Pvt Ltd, 11 Community Centre, Panchsheel Park, New Delhi – 110 017, India
Penguin Group (NZ), 67 Apollo Drive, Mairangi Bay, Auckland 1310, New Zealand
(a division of Pearson New Zealand Ltd)
Penguin Books (South Africa) (Pty) Ltd, 24 Sturdee Avenue, Rosebank, Johannesburg 2196, South Africa

Penguin Books Ltd, Registered Offices: 80 Strand, London WC2R 0RL, England

www.penguin.com

First published in 2001
Second edition published 2003
This updated third edition published 2006
1

Set in 7/8.5pt PostScript Antigua
Typeset by Rowland Phototypesetting Ltd, Bury St Edmunds, Suffolk
Printed in Finland by WS Bookwell

ISBN-13: 978-0-141-02424-0
ISBN-10: 0-141-02424-0

Contents

Introduction

It's been three years since the last edition of *The Penguin TV Companion* and, boy, what a lot has happened. We're used to seeing television programmes come and go, and actors taking, and sadly leaving, the stage, but these are fast-moving times in the industry. Digital television, a relative newcomer that still hasn't totally displaced the old analogue technology, is already beginning to sound old hat, now that high-definition broadcasts have started. The cathode ray tube and its bulky boxes have given way to flat-screen plasma sets, and DVD recorders – not just players – are now fixtures in many homes.

On screen the charming individuality of the ITV regional companies has largely been superseded by the corporate uniformity of ITV plc, and new channels open up every week, it seems. In the 1960s, BBC-3 was merely a topical satire show. Today its near-namesake, BBC 3, is a digital channel that targets the younger end of the adult audience. There's also BBC 4, for the more cultured viewer, and similar digital extensions of the ITV and Channel 4 brands. But I recognize that most people are not too concerned about how or where they watch television. For most viewers, it's the quality of the programming that counts and the last few years have introduced some firm favourites: *Little Britain, Bleak House, Lost, State of Play, Desperate Housewives* and many more. There have also been some total duffers, of course, and the over-reliance on the B-list celebrity and the reality show are driving many viewers to reach for the remote control. To reflect this, there have been some important additions to *The Penguin TV Companion*.

Most notably, you will see that each programme entry now features a star rating. As you would expect, this is an indicator of how entertaining, influential and well produced the programme is, but I don't think it right that readers should just take my word for it. That's why these ratings have been compiled by taking into account the published views of numerous critics and authors over the years, as well as my own personal opinions. It would be disingenuous of me to suggest that I have seen every programme featured in this book. Some were screened when I was too young to pay them much attention; others were broadcast decades before I was born. But other informed reviewers have seen them, and described them in print, so it is appropriate that their wisdom and reflections should be taken into consideration.

The other major development in this edition is the inclusion of DVD information. More than ever, it is now possible to get hold of episodes of programmes that are deemed long past their broadcasting shelf-life and view them in your own home. So, if a programme is available on DVD at the time of going to press, I say so, and I also include the name of the studio distributing it. Armed with this information, viewers should be able to seek out long-lost favourites and, perhaps, even compare notes with the book.

After three years, it should only be expected that the book be fully revised, updated and expanded, and I can assure you that this is very much the case. Scores of new programmes have been added, taking the number featured to over 2,200, far more than you'll find in any other publication covering British television in general. There are also many more entries for actors and behind-the-scenes contributors, and existing entries have also been significantly expanded. It all amounts to what I hope can be seen as the most comprehensive survey of television in Britain in its first 70 years.

Unless someone finds a way for the human race to regenerate like Doctor Who, I shan't be around to mark the next 70 years and the mind boggles as to how far the technology will have advanced by then. You can be sure, however, that high-definition television, plasma screens and DVD recorders will be no more than quaint museum pieces when the 140th anniversary of British television is celebrated.

The Entries

As stated above, there are now more than 2,200 programmes featured in this greatly expanded book. They are listed with their country of origin, production company, UK channel and transmission dates. (Although digital channels now have sizeable audiences, it is still through terrestrial channels that most viewers will encounter programmes first, so channel and date information is based on screenings on BBC 1 and 2, ITV 1, Channel 4 and five.) Original American transmission dates are included for American series. Cast lists highlighting the regular characters follow, then major production credits, centring on creators, writers and producers of programmes. Each programme's description covers the general concept, the main storylines, character details and a good dose of trivia – the sort of facts that you could easily live without, but would prefer not to. Entries now also include information about DVD availability and star ratings have been given to all programmes. There are a maximum of four stars awarded. In simplistic terms, they signify the following:

✱✱✱✱ Essential viewing/TV landmark

✱✱✱ Highly recommended

✱✱ Average, competent fare, with some good moments

✱ Not so good/of curiosity value only

I was tempted to have a fifth category, that of no stars, but soon realized that a programme bad enough to drop off the scale must be worth watching, if only for curiosity value! There are also around 1,500 entries for TV stars and behind-the-scenes contributors. Each person's primary television work has been highlighted (with major character parts identified), though film and theatre credits (falling outside the brief) have largely been ignored. Real names and dates of birth have been provided where obtainable, though some performers are famously shy about their ages and others, understandably, prefer to have their privacy respected in such matters.

So what is and isn't included? I have established, over the years I have worked on this book, that any attempt to lay down hard-and-fast ground-rules is sure to end in dissatisfaction. It is possible, for instance, to restrict programme entries to those that have attracted the most viewers, based on audience ratings. Except that this instantly precludes programmes on 'minority' channels like BBC 2, Channel 4 and five. Would the book be complete without *Big Brother, M*A*S*H* or *The Office*? Based on the ratings charts, it would also rule out children's programmes and other daytime offerings. Other options would have been to consider including only award-winning programmes, peak-hour programming or UK-produced programmes, but these formats would fall down in similar ways. Consequently, I have adopted a loose set of criteria for the programmes featured in this book. These involve general acclaim, historical significance, biggest audiences, cult status and nostalgia value.

The programmes cover all fields: dramas, documentaries, situation comedies, variety shows, current affairs series, children's favourites, quiz shows, panel games, sports programmes, soap operas, mini-series and important one-off plays. US TV movies, however, have not been included. As a result, the following pages are a tribute to the good, the bad and the sometimes very ugly moments in TV's past. You will find everything, from the most critically acclaimed to the most cruelly derided, and even some programmes you may just have forgotten.

The entries for people are similarly based on those who have contributed most, or enjoyed most success, in television's first seven decades. They include actors, comedians, presenters, writers, producers, executives and even the brilliant engineers who made television possible in the first place. To complete the picture, there are also entries for television companies and explanations of some of the technical terms that confront the viewer on a day-to-day basis as each programme's credits roll by.

The use of small capitals for a programme name within entries indicates that there is a separate entry for the programme elsewhere in the book.

The Research

Researching and updating this book has been great fun. It has also proved rather frustrating at times. For instance, while there has been no shortage of information about American programmes, vintage British television is shrouded in obscurity. The main reason for this is the fact that most US programmes (pre-videotape) were captured on film and therefore have been preserved. British programmes in the 1940s and 1950s mainly went out live and any primitive recordings which were made, together with episodes of 1960s classics like *Doctor Who* and *Steptoe and Son*, were famously wiped as an economy and space-saving measure by the BBC in the 1970s. As a result, the detail unearthed about early British programmes is inevitably rather thinner than for American contemporaries.

Programmes are listed with their first and last transmission dates. Only the original transmissions (not repeats) have been charted. Programmes shown on BBC Television before the advent of BBC 2 (and therefore BBC 1) in 1964 have the channel listing 'BBC' only. However, some transmission dates have proved difficult to track down. Often, overseas programmes screened on ITV have not been fully networked, meaning that they have been seen only in some areas. The regions have also transmitted episodes out of sequence, sometimes years apart, and it does not follow that the region offering the first ever transmission of a programme will also be the first to show the last episode. As a result, the dates listed here for some overseas entries shown on ITV are informed estimates, but any corrections to these dates would be happily received. All programme details have been updated to March 2006, but some information may be even more recent.

It has always been my intention to include a good selection of tables, facts and bits of intriguing general information by way of appendices at the end of *The Penguin TV Companion*, but pressure on pages has not made this possible. However, readers may be interested in a related book now available called *Evans' TV Trivia* (published by Collins). This has given me the opportunity to put together a whole collection of TV lists, facts, dates, quotes and anecdotes – anything from *Countdown*'s celebrity lexicographers and *Mr Benn*'s disguises to a table of spin-offs and sequels, and how *Jeux Sans Frontières* was translated in various languages.

Acknowledgements

To produce a book of the scope and scale of *The Penguin TV Companion*, a writer needs more than a little help. I would particularly like to thank Jacqueline Kavanagh and Jeff Walden at the BBC Written Archives Centre for their assistance, and the numerous other librarians, press officers and agents who have answered my many queries. Gratitude is also due to Sheena Vigors at the National Museum of Photography, Film and Television in Bradford, and the team at the British Film Institute in London, as well as the various studios and distributors who supplied me with DVDs. I am especially indebted to my wife, Jacquie, not only for allowing me to spend most of my waking hours in front of a computer, or hidden away in a corner of some library, but also for contributing to the research herself in previous years.

Always conscious that 'the truth is out there', I have made every effort to ensure the accuracy of the information in these pages. However, without looking for an excuse for errors and omissions, there are so many facts and figures in this book that it would be a miracle if all were totally correct. If you know better, your comments will be more than welcome. To everyone who contacted me after previous editions, my thanks once again. As I've said many times before, this book is a labour of love for me, and it is gratifying to hear that so many people share my fascination with TV nostalgia. I hope that anyone seeking an answer to some nagging TV query – who played . . . ?, what was the name of . . . ?, when did . . . ? – will find it here. I hope, too, that anyone casually browsing will be drawn nostalgically back into the golden days of television and enjoy, like me, many fond memories.

Happy viewing!

Jeff Evans

Bibliography

The information in this book has been obtained from many, many sources and primarily from the programmes themselves, from press releases and from the invaluable weekly listings magazines *Radio Times* and *TV Times*. Other facts and figures have been unearthed from official websites, and from programme producers and actors' agents, who have kindly helped with inquiries. The Internet Movie Database (*www.imdb.com*) has been a useful point of reference. Scores of books have also been consulted and the most helpful general publications have been listed below.

Magazines and Annuals

Encyclopaedia Britannica
Look-In
Radio Times
Television & Radio, IBA, various editions
TV Times

Books

Baily, Kenneth (ed.): *The Television Annual*, Odhams, various editions

Brandt, George (ed.): *British Television Drama in the 1980s*, Cambridge University Press, 1993

Brooks, Tim: *The Complete Directory to Prime Time TV Stars*, Ballantine Books, 1987

Brooks, Tim, and Earle Marsh: *The Complete Directory to Prime Time Network and Cable TV Shows*, Ballantine Books, 2003

Brown, Les: *Les Brown's Encyclopedia of Television*, Visible Ink, 1992

Cain, John: *The BBC: 70 Years of Broadcasting*, BBC Books, 1992

Castleman, Harry, and Walter J. Podrazik: *Harry and Wally's Favorite TV Shows*, Prentice Hall Press, 1989

Cherry, Simon: *ITV: The People's Channel*, Reynolds & Hearn, 2005

Cooke, Alistair: *Masterpieces*, Bodley Head, 1982

Cornell, Paul, Martin Day and Keith Topping: *The Guinness Book of Classic British TV*, Guinness Publishing, 1996

Coward, Simon, Richard Down and Christopher Perry: *The Kaleidoscope British Independent Television Drama Research Guide 1955–2005* (5 vols.), Kaleidoscope Publishing, 2005

Crowther, Bruce, and Mike Pinfold: *Bring Me Laughter*, Columbus Books, 1987

Crystal, David (ed.): *The Cambridge Biographical Encyclopedia*, Cambridge University Press, 1998

Davis, Anthony: *TV's Greatest Hits*, Boxtree, 1988

Donovan, Paul: *The Radio Companion*, Grafton, 1992

Down, Richard, and Christopher Perry: *The British Television Drama Research Guide*, Kaleidoscope Publishing, 1997

—: *The British Television Music & Variety Research Guide*, Kaleidoscope Publishing, 1997

Down, Richard, Richard Marson and Christopher Perry: *The British Television Children's Research Guide*, Kaleidoscope Publishing, 1999

Editors of *TV Guide*: *TV Guide Guide to TV*, Barnes & Noble, 2004

Fane-Saunders, Kilmeny (ed.): *Radio Times Guide to Films*, BBC Books, 2004

Fischer, Stuart: *Kids' TV: The First 25 Years*, Facts on File, 1983

Fulton, Roger: *The Encyclopedia of TV Science Fiction*, Boxtree, 1995

Gambaccini, Paul, and Rod Taylor: *Television's Greatest Hits*, Network Books, 1993

Garner, Joe: *Stay Tuned*, Andrews McMeel, 2002

Gearing, Brian, and Phil McNeil (eds.): *Seventy Years of BBC Sport*, André Deutsch, 1999

Grade, Lew: *Still Dancing*, Fontana, 1987

Greenfield, Jeff: *Television: The First Fifty Years*, Crescent Books, 1981

Halliwell, Leslie, and Philip Purser: *Halliwell's Television Companion*, Granada, 1986

Harbord, Jane, and Jeff Wright: *40 Years of British Television*, Boxtree, 1992

Hayward, Anthony: *The Guinness Who's Who of Soap Operas*, Guinness Publishing, 1995

Hayward, Anthony and Deborah: *TV Unforgettables*, Guinness Publishing, 1993

Hayward, Anthony, *et al.*: *Who's Who on Television*, various editions

Hill, Tom (ed.): *Nick at Nite's Classic TV Companion*, Simon & Schuster, 1996

Home, Anna: *Into the Box of Delights*, BBC Books, 1993

Housham, David, and John Frank-Keyes: *Funny Business*, Boxtree, 1992

Hunter, Allan (ed.): *Chambers Film & TV Handbook*, Chambers, 1991

Jarvis, Peter: *Teletalk*, BBC Television Training, 1991

Javna, John: *Cult TV*, St Martin's Press, 1985

—: *The Best of Science Fiction TV*, Harmony Books, 1987

—: *The Best of TV Sitcoms*, Harmony Books, 1988

Jeffries, Stuart: *Mrs Slocombe's Pussy*, Flamingo, 2001

Kingsley, Hilary: *Soap Box*, Macmillan, 1988

Kingsley, Hilary, and Geoff Tibballs: *Box of Delights*, Macmillan, 1989

Lasswell, Mark: *Fifty Years of Television*, Crown, 2002

Lewis, Richard: *The Encyclopedia of Cult Children's TV*, Allison & Busby, 2001

Lewisohn, Mark: *Radio Times Guide to TV Comedy*, BBC Worldwide, 2003

Marschall, Rick: *The Golden Age of Television*, Bison Books, 1987

McGown, Alistair, and Mark J. Docherty: *The Hill and Beyond*, BFI, 2003

McNeil, Alex: *Total Television*, Penguin, 1996

Miall, Leonard: *Inside the BBC*, Weidenfeld & Nicolson, 1994

Morton, Alan: *The Complete Directory to Science Fiction, Fantasy and Horror Television Series*, Other Worlds Books, 1997

Passingham, Kenneth: *The Guinness Book of TV Facts and Feats*, Guinness, 1984

Penney, Edmund F.: *The Facts on File Dictionary of Film and Broadcast Terms*, Facts on File, 1991

Postgate, Oliver: *Seeing Things*, Pan, 2001

Preston, Mike: *Tele-Tunes*, Mike Preston Music, various editions

Roberts, David (ed.): *British Hit Singles and Albums*, Guinness World Records, 2005

Rogers, Dave: *The ITV Encyclopedia of Adventure*, Boxtree, 1988
Sachs, John, and Piers Morgan: *Secret Lives*, Blake Publishing, 1991
Sangster, Jim, and Paul Condon: *TV Heaven*, Collins, 2005
Schwartz, David, Steve Ryan and Fred Wostbrock: *The Encyclopedia of TV Game Shows*, Facts on File, 1995
Sheridan, Simon: *The A–Z of Classic Children's Television*, Reynolds & Hearn, 2004
Simpson, Paul (ed.): *The Rough Guide to Cult TV*, Rough Guides, 2002
Taylor, Rod: *The Guinness Book of Sitcoms*, Guinness Publishing, 1994
Terrace, Vincent: *The Ultimate TV Trivia Book*, Faber and Faber, 1991
Tibballs, Geoff. *The Golden Age of Children's Television*, Titan Books, 1991
—: *The Boxtree Encyclopedia of TV Detectives*, Boxtree, 1992
Vahimagi, Tise: *British Television*, Oxford University Press, 1994
Walker, John (ed.): *Halliwell's Who's Who in the Movies*, HarperCollins, 2003
—: *Halliwell's Film, Video & DVD Guide*, HarperCollins, 2005
Wheen, Francis: *Television*, Century, 1985
Woolery, George W.: *Children's Television: The First Thirty-Five Years* (2 vols.), Scarecrow Press, 1983 and 1985

To my dad, Roy Evans (1925–2004).
Greatly missed.

A for Andromeda/The Andromeda Breakthrough ✳✳

UK (BBC) Science Fiction. BBC 1961/1962

John Fleming	**Peter Halliday**
Prof. Reinhart	**Esmond Knight**
Dr Geers	**Geoffrey Lewis**
Prof. Madeleine Dawnay	**Mary Morris**
Christine/Andromeda	**Julie Christie** *(A for)* **Susan Hampshire** *(Breakthrough)*
Dennis Bridger	**Frank Windsor**
Dr Hunter	**Peter Ducrow**
Harvey John	**Murray-Scott**
Judy Adamson	**Patricia Kneale**
Major Quadring	**Jack May**
Harries	**John Nettleton**
J. M. Osborne	**Noel Johnson**
Gen. Vandenberg	**Donald Stewart**
Minister of Science	**Ernest Hare**
Prime Minister	**Maurice Hedley**
Minister of Defence Burdett	**David King**
Kaufman	**John Hollis**
Egon	**Peter Henchie**
Prof. Neilson	**Walter Gotell** *(Breakthrough)*
Mlle Gamboule	**Claude Farel** *(Breakthrough)*
Col. Salim	**Barry Linehan** *(Breakthrough)*
Dr Abu Zeki	**David Saire** *(Breakthrough)*
President of Azaran	**Arnold Yarrow** *(Breakthrough)*

Writers **Fred Hoyle, John Elliot**
Producers **Michael Hayes, Norman James** *(A for Andromeda)*, **John Elliot** *(Breakthrough)*

● ***A beautiful girl is created by a sinister alien computer.***

In 1970 (nine years into the future), a new giant radio telescope in the Yorkshire Dales, managed by Professor Reinhart, picks up a series of signals from the direction of the constellation Andromeda which have taken 200 years to reach Earth. Working through the messages, brilliant scientist John Fleming concludes that they form plans for a highly sophisticated computer. In a top-secret project, sponsored by the government and hidden away at Thorness on a remote Scottish island, he follows the alien instructions and builds the machine. A battle then begins for the use of its powers between good and bad scientists, government agencies and the Swiss business cartel, Intel, headed by the evil Kaufman.

Through collaboration with devious biologist Madeleine Dawnay, the computer succeeds in developing an embryo, based on the biological blueprint of Christine, a lab assistant it electrocutes. The embryo rapidly blossoms into a replica of the girl (though blonde not brunette, as Christine had been) and is given the name of Andromeda. Unfortunately, the replica girl is mentally linked to the corrupt machine and becomes its agent. It isn't until the conscientious Fleming draws her warmer, more human emotions to the fore that she is able to break free from her computer master.

In a sequel series, *The Andromeda Breakthrough*, shown a year later, Fleming, Dawnay and Andromeda are kidnapped and imprisoned in the Middle Eastern country of Azaran, where Intel has set up its own super-computer. Weather systems have been disrupted, violent storms are raging across the globe and the Earth's atmosphere is being eaten away. In this follow-up, the part of Andromeda was taken over by Susan Hampshire.

Now recognized as classic TV science fiction, *A for Andromeda* and *The Andromeda Breakthrough* were created by BBC producer John Elliot from a storyline by Cambridge astronomer and novelist Fred Hoyle. *A for Andromeda* was the BBC's first attempt at adult science fiction since the QUATERMASS serials and is well remembered for giving young drama school student Julie Christie her first starring role. The story was remade as a single-episode drama for BBC 4 in 2006, starring Kelly Reilly as Christine/Andromeda, Tom Hardy as Fleming, Jane Asher as Dawnay and David Haig as Vandenberg.

A&E

See *Always and Everyone.*

Abbot, Russ

(Russ Roberts; 1947–)

Tall, twinkly-eyed, Chester-born comedian and impressionist who entered showbiz as a member of the Black Abbots cabaret group (an OPPORTUNITY KNOCKS discovery). His TV breaks came from appearances in WHO DO YOU DO?, THE COMEDIANS and *Bruce Forsyth's Big Night* and led to a series he shared with its named star, *Freddie Starr's Variety Madhouse*. With Starr's departure, the show became *Russ Abbot's Madhouse* in 1980 (sometimes *Saturday Madhouse*) and allowed Abbot to begin introducing the farcical creations for which he became famous, such as inept superhero Cooperman (an exaggerated impersonation of Tommy Cooper), detective Barratt Holmes, air ace Boggles, Irish crooner Val Hooligan, rock'n'roller Vince Prince, secret agent Basildon Bond, and C. U. Jimmy, the indecipherable, kilted Scotsman. The same format was applied when the show switched to BBC 1 in 1986 and became *The Russ Abbot Show*. Back on ITV in 1994, Abbot pioneered some new creations, including the Noisy Family, Clueless Cleric and the good folk of Pimpletown, such as Percy Pervert and Mrs Verruca. In his sketch work he has been well supported by the likes of Bella Emberg, Les Dennis, Dustin Gee, Michael Barrymore and Jeffrey Holland, but Abbot has also featured in serious and sitcom roles, most notably as retired teacher Ted Fenwick in SEPTEMBER SONG, and as shoe salesman Ted Butler in MARRIED FOR LIFE, as well as in CASUALTY, HEARTBEAT, DOCTORS and AGATHA CHRISTIE'S MARPLE. He returned to sketches in 2002 with a role in *TV to Go*.

Abbott, Paul

(1960–)

Award-winning, Burnley-raised scriptwriter/producer, who worked on series like *Dramarama*, CORONATION STREET, CHILDREN'S WARD (which he developed with writing partner Kay Mellor) and CRACKER before penning acclaimed dramas like TOUCHING EVIL, RECKLESS, *Best of Both Worlds*, *Butterfly Collectors*, *The Secret World of Michael Fry*, CLOCKING OFF, LINDA GREEN, STATE OF PLAY, *Alibi* and SHAMELESS.

ABC [1]

(American Broadcasting Company)

American television network, for years the least successful of the three national networks. It was founded in 1943 by Edward J. Noble, the maker of Life Savers confectionery, when he purchased a radio network from NBC. In 1953 the company merged with United Paramount Theaters. Despite struggling against its competitors, CBS and NBC, from its earliest days (largely because it owned fewer affiliate stations), ABC has nevertheless made its mark on US television history. It was the first company to bring Hollywood studios into TV production, thereby accelerating the move from live to filmed broadcasts. It notched numerous sports firsts in the USA (its most-watched programme is still *Monday Night Football*), and among its other programming successes have been BATMAN, HAPPY DAYS, THE SIX MILLION DOLLAR MAN, ROSEANNE, HOME IMPROVEMENT, NYPD BLUE, DESPERATE HOUSEWIVES and three of the biggest mini-series ever: ROOTS, THE THORN BIRDS and THE WINDS OF WAR. By the end of the 1970s, ABC had elevated itself into the top bracket of US TV, becoming a very serious competitor to the two big networks. The company was bought by Capital Cities Communications in 1986 and was then acquired by the Walt Disney Corporation in 1995.

ABC [2]

(Associated Broadcasting Company)

Early ITV franchise-holder covering the Midlands and the North of England at weekends only. An offshoot of the ABC (Associated British Cinemas) theatre chain, the company was owned mainly by ABPC (Associated British Picture Corporation), although Warners also held shares in the 1950s. ABC went on air on 18 February 1956 in the Midlands and on 5 May 1956 in the North. Its network programming successes included ARMCHAIR THEATRE, OPPORTUNITY KNOCKS and THE AVENGERS. At the behest of the ITA, during the 1968 franchise reassessments the company merged with Associated-Rediffusion to create Thames Television. ABC then gave up its Midlands and North of England franchises but, as Thames, took over London's Monday to Friday coverage.

Abigail's Party ★★★★

UK (BBC) Drama. BBC 1 1977
DVD: BBC

Beverly	**Alison Steadman**
Sue	**Harriet Reynolds**
Laurence	**Tim Stern**
Angela	**Janine Duvitski**
Tony	**John Salthouse**

Writer **Mike Leigh**
Producer **Margaret Matheson**

● ***Marital friction ruins a pretentious evening in suburbia.***

Abigail, the eponymous entertainer of this exalted PLAY FOR TODAY, is never actually seen. She is in the house next door, throwing a party for her teenage friends. It might, therefore, have been more appropriate to call the drama 'Beverly's Party', for that is where the action takes place. To coincide with the teenage bash, neurotic neighbour Beverly has organized her own little gathering for the grown-ups. Along with Abigail's anxious mother, Sue, local residents Angela and Tony are invited, and making up the select group is Beverly's stressed-out husband, Laurence. As the evening drags by, the drink flows freely, the grating Beverly forces everyone to endure the 'fantastic' Demis Roussos on the stereo, and marital tensions reach fever pitch as she obliviously sails through a series of social blunders.

Abigail's Party was the play that confirmed the talents of writer/director Mike Leigh and his then wife, actress Alison Steadman, who had previously collaborated on an earlier *Play for Today*, NUTS IN MAY. It had first been performed on stage at the Hampstead Theatre and some of the dialogue, even in the televised version, was improvised. The play has become a cult and, in 1997, BBC 2 presented an *Abigail's Party* night to commemorate the 20th anniversary of its first transmission.

About the Home ★

UK (BBC) Magazine. BBC 1951–8

Presenter **Joan Gilbert**

Producer **S. E. Reynolds**

● ***Practical tips for housewives.***

This long-running afternoon programme was designed to help housewives improve domestic skills such as cookery and needlework, although other items covered included shopping, deportment and even puppy training. Home-improvement tips from Barry Bucknell proved so popular that he gained his own series, *Do It Yourself*, in 1957.

Absolutely ★★★

UK (Absolutely) Comedy. Channel 4 1989–91; 1993

Gordon Kennedy, Jack Docherty, Moray Hunter, Morwenna Banks, Peter Baikie, John Sparkes

Producers **Alan Nixon, David Tyler**

● ***Eccentric sketch show with a Scottish accent.***

Absolutely drew together some of Scotland's new breed of comics and gave them a licence for creativity. The result was a collection of surreal and silly sketches and some novel characters. Morwenna Banks perfected the 'Yes, it's twue', worldly wise junior schoolgirl, Moray Hunter became the anoraky Calum Gilhooley and the Welsh member of the team, John Sparkes, created accident-prone DIY expert Denzil and the lavatorial Frank Hovis. The parish council of the fictitious village of Stoneybridge was also featured on a regular basis, and Jack Docherty portrayed rabid nationalist McGlashen. Docherty and Hunter (both formerly of FRIDAY NIGHT LIVE) took their creations, Donald McDiarmid and George McDiarmid – 'two friends with but a single surname' – into a spin-off series, *Mr Don and Mr George*, in 1993.

Absolutely Fabulous ★★★

UK (Saunders & French/BBC) Situation Comedy. BBC 2 1992/ BBC 1 1994–6; 2001–4
DVD: BBC

Edina Monsoon	**Jennifer Saunders**
Patsy Stone	**Joanna Lumley**
Saffron Monsoon	**Julia Sawalha**
Bubble	**Jane Horrocks**

Mother .... **June Whitfield**
Katy Grin .... **Jane Horrocks**
John .... **Felix Dexter**

Creators **Jennifer Saunders, Dawn French**
Writer **Jennifer Saunders**
Producers **Jon Plowman, Jonathan P. Llewellyn, Jo Sargent**

A neurotic PR agent and her fashion editor friend live in a world fuelled by drink and drugs.

Edina Monsoon, a single mother of two children, by different fathers, is head of her own public relations agency. Her long-time friend, Patsy Stone, is editor of a fashion magazine. Work for both of them, however, is one long lunchbreak at a trendy restaurant, a spell of shopping at Harvey Nicks or an evening's clubbing. Striving to be seen in all the right places, rubbing shoulders with every celebrity they can find, they ladle out 'darlings' and 'sweeties' as – like overdressed pantomime dames – they struggle to reclaim their late-1960s youth.

Edina shares her three-storey, expensively appointed home in Holland Park with teenage daughter Saffron (her son, Serge, is initially away at university). However, theirs is not the usual mother–teenager relationship, but quite the reverse. Edina is the disruptive influence, staying out late, getting drunk, throwing tantrums and selfishly spoiling all her daughter's fun. Saffy is simply too sensible to be corrupted by her mother; she is a plain Jane who prefers science to sex and books to booze. Their incompatibility is highlighted whenever Patsy arrives to drag Edina off to a fashion shoot or wild party, much to the disapproval of both Saffron and Edina's mother. The archetypal society slag, Patsy lives on a diet of cigarettes, drink, drugs and younger men. She's not happy unless she is smoking, slurping, sniffing or sleeping with someone. Also seen is Bubble, Edina's chirpy but brainless northern secretary.

Derived from a sketch in *French and Saunders*, in which Dawn French played the swotty daughter, *Absolutely Fabulous* emerged from its first season clutching a handful of awards, with Joanna Lumley singled out for her successful first stab at comedy and the way in which she gleefully debunked her customary aristocratic roles. From the second season, it earned itself a BBC 1 time slot, but the series appeared to wind up in 1996. However, in 2000, Saunders, Lumley, Sawalha, Horrocks and Whitfield worked together on a one-off comedy penned by Saunders called *Mirrorball*, which inspired them to reunite for another series of *Absolutely Fabulous* in 2001 and a Christmas special in 2002. A new character introduced at this time was buoyant TV presenter Katy Grin (played, like Bubble, by Jane Horrocks). More episodes followed in 2003 in which Saffy has a partner, John, and gives birth to a daughter, Jane; there was a Christmas special in 2004.

Saunders and Lumley, in the guise of Edina and Patsy, also turned up in one episode of ROSEANNE, although plans for a US version of the series proved shortlived. A similarly themed, but typically toned-down, comedy entitled *High Society* starred Jean Smart and Mary McDonnell and was screened in the States in 1995–6 but it was not well received. *Absolutely Fabulous*'s theme song, Bob Dylan's 'This Wheel's on Fire', was sung by Jennifer Saunders's husband, Adrian Edmondson, with Julie Driscoll (now Julie Tippetts), vocalist on the original, 1968, hit version by the Brian Auger Trinity.

Access Television

Programmes produced by members of the public or by pressure groups, who are given editorial control of the project but are also offered the assistance of a professional crew. It is otherwise known as public access. The BBC's *Open Door*, beginning in 1973, was one of the most famous British examples, while the wacky *Manhattan Cable* compilations revealed just how much further public access is taken in the USA's cable industry.

Ace of Wands ✶✶

UK (Thames) Children's Adventure. ITV 1970–2

Tarot .... **Michael Mackenzie**
Sam Maxsted .... **Tony Selby**
Lillian ('Lulli') Palmer .... **Judy Loe**
Mr Sweet .... **Donald Layne-Smith**
Mikki .... **Petra Markham**
Chas .... **Roy Holder**

Creator **Trevor Preston**
Producers **Pamela Lonsdale, John Russell**

A young stage magician tackles crime and evil in his spare time.

Tarot is a magical entertainer, a combination of conjurer and escapologist, whose youthful appearance conceals a mysterious background and a resourceful mind. Billed as 'a 20th-century Robin Hood, with a pinch of Merlin and a dash of Houdini', he is assisted in his adventures by Sam and Lulli. Sam, a reformed ex-convict, shares Tarot's luxury apartment and builds many of his stage props, while Lulli, an orphan and fellow telepath, is Tarot's stage partner. Mr Sweet, an eccentric, tweed-suited man who runs an antiquarian bookshop and rides a motorbike, also lends a hand, chipping in with his expert knowledge of the insect world. In the background perches Ozymandias, a Malayan fishing owl.

The so-called 'Ace of Wands' and his companions run into a host of weird and wonderful, Batman-esque supercriminals, with names like Madame Midnight, Mr Stabs and Ceribraun. But perhaps the most sinister is Mama Doc, who turns people into dolls which bleed when broken. In the final season, Sam – who has moved into road haulage – and the recently wed Lulli are replaced by Mikki and Chas. Mikki, another telepath, works as a reporter, and Chas is her photographer brother: together they run their own 'Chasem' investigation agency. Mr Sweet, now based at a university, is also seen again. Andrew Bown provides the music.

Ackland, Joss

CBE (1928–)

London-born actor regularly seen in guest star roles. He supported Alec Guinness in TINKER, TAILOR, SOLDIER, SPY and also appeared in the ITV George Smiley dramatization, *A Murder of Quality*, as well as playing the spymaster Cumming in Somerset Maugham's ASHENDEN. Earlier, he was newspaper editor William Stevens in *Kipling*, D'Artagnan in *The Further Adventures of the Musketeers*, widower Joseph Lockwood in the sitcom *Thicker Than Water*, Charles Bronte in THE CREZZ, and for a while took the part of Inspector Todd in Z CARS. Other credits have included THE GOLD ROBBERS, COUNTRY MATTERS, ENEMY AT THE DOOR, MISS MARPLE, HENRY VIII (Henry VII) and MIDSOMER MURDERS, plus numerous single dramas, including SHADOWLANDS and *Daisies in December*.

Actor's Life for Me, An ✶✶

UK (BBC) Situation Comedy. BBC 1 1991

Robert Neilson .... **John Gordon-Sinclair**
Sue Bishop .... **Gina McKee**
Desmond Shaw .... **Victor Spinetti**

Writer **Paul Mayhew-Archer**
Producer **Bryan Izzard**

● ***The farcical exploits of a struggling actor with ideas above his station.***

Robert Neilson is an actor – not a Hollywood star or a household name, however. In fact, he has only ever secured one important job, as the face of 'Dobermann' aftershave. Nevertheless, the optimistic Neilson sets his sights high and longs to tread the boards as Hamlet or Lear, even fantasizing about sharing the limelight with such names as Kim Basinger. The reality, however, lies in bit parts and character roles, which is the best his unreliable agent, Desmond, can get for him. Sue is the girlfriend who tries, vainly, to ensure that Robert doesn't get too carried away with his own hype. The six-episode series was developed for television from writer Paul Mayhew-Archer's own Radio 2 series of the same name, which also starred John Gordon-Sinclair (but as Robert Wilson). On radio, Sue was initially played by Caroline Quentin, before Gina McKee assumed both TV and radio roles, and Gary Waldhorn played Desmond.

Adam Adamant Lives! ✶

UK (BBC) Science Fiction. BBC 1 1966–7
DVD: Meridian Entertainment

Adam Adamant .... **Gerald Harper**
Georgina Jones .... **Juliet Harmer**
William E. Simms .... **Jack May**
The Face .... **Peter Ducrow**

Creators **Donald Cotton, Richard Harris**
Producer **Verity Lambert**

● ***An Edwardian adventurer, trapped in ice, thaws out in the Swinging Sixties.***

Adam Llewellyn De Vere Adamant is a legend in his own lifetime: a smooth, dashing man of action who counters crooks and defends the weak in turn-of-the-century England. However, in 1902, he is ensnared by his arch-enemy, a megalomaniac in a leather mask known only as 'The Face'. Injected with a preservative drug, Adamant is encased in a block of ice and left to posterity. In 1966 a group of London workmen discover his body and thaw it out. Adam Adamant, now aged 99, but still with the body of a 36-year-old, is back in action.

However, swinging London, buzzing with loud noise, bright lights and the permissive society, confuses the revitalized adventurer. To his rescue rides Georgina Jones, a trendy young nightclub DJ and an Adam Adamant fan (who has learned about the great man's exploits from her grandfather). Together with Georgie and William E. Simms, a former music hall artist who becomes his manservant, our hero (still sporting Edwardian clothing) again turns his attentions to the criminal fraternity. They embark on a series of AVENGERS-style, off-beat adventures in which Adamant's keen intellect (he has an amazing memory and degrees from several universities), athletic abilities (he is a keen boxer) and adroitness with weapons (especially his sword) are put to excellent use. In the second series, his old enemy, The Face, returns to instigate yet more trouble.

Alive with the colour of Carnaby Street (despite being taped in black and white), *Adam Adamant Lives!* is firmly set in the era of mini-skirts, mods and early psychedelia, with much interest derived from the jarring juxtaposition of Edwardian morals with the liberal society of the 1960s. The series provided Gerald Harper with a chance to develop his suave toff image which reached its pinnacle in HADLEIGH three years later. It also opened doors for behind-the-scenes crew-members such as Ridley Scott, who went on to direct films like *Alien* and *Blade Runner*. The James Bond-like theme music was sung by Kathy Kirby.

Adam Dalgliesh

See *P. D. James*.

Adams, Tom

(1938–)

London-born actor making his TV debut as a crook in DIXON OF DOCK GREEN and moving on to other supporting, as well as leading, roles, which have generally been of a stern and serious nature. He was Guy Marshall in EMERGENCY – WARD 10, Major Sullivan in *Spy Trap*, Daniel Fogarty in THE ONEDIN LINE, Dr Guy Wallman in GENERAL HOSPITAL, DCI Nick Lewis in *The Enigma Files*, and Malcolm Bates in EMMERDALE FARM. In contrast, he also played news anchor Tom Whitelamb in the news spoof *Focus North*. Other credits have included THE AVENGERS, JOURNEY TO THE UNKNOWN, *Villains, West Country Tales, Strike it Rich*, DOCTOR WHO, REMINGTON STEELE and CASUALTY.

Adamson, Peter

(1930–2002)

Burly, gruffly spoken, Liverpool-born actor who is remembered by all as Len Fairclough, CORONATION STREET's 1960s/70s he-man. In the 1950s Adamson enjoyed small parts in Granada series like KNIGHT ERRANT and *Skyport*, before joining the *Street* in 1961. He filled the role of heavy-drinking, womanizing builder Fairclough for 22 years, until alleged off-screen indiscretions led to his dismissal by Granada. The writers had the two-timing Fairclough killed in a car crash on the way home from visiting a mistress.

Addams Family, The ✶✶✶

US (Filmways) Situation Comedy. ITV 1965–6 (US: ABC 1964–6)

Morticia Addams .... **Carolyn Jones**
Gomez Addams .... **John Astin**
Uncle Fester Frump .... **Jackie Coogan**
Lurch .... **Ted Cassidy**
Grandmama Addams .... **Blossom Rock**
Pugsley Addams .... **Ken Weatherwax**
Wednesday Thursday
Addams .... **Lisa Loring**
Cousin Itt .... **Felix Silla**
Thing .... **Ted Cassidy**

Creator **David Levy**

● ***The misadventures of a macabre family, based on the cartoon strip by Charles Addams.***

Introduced by an annoyingly catchy, finger-clicking theme song, the weird and wonderful Addams Family is headed by Gomez, a lawyer and man of independent wealth, with his sultry, slinky wife, Morticia. They live in a musty, spooky Victorian mansion, in a street appropriately called Cemetery Ridge, with Morticia's bald, habit-wearing Uncle Fester; Gomez's mother, Grandmama (a witch); their son, Pugsley; daughter, Wednesday; and a high-pitched, gobbledegook-speaking mass of hair called Cousin Itt. Their servants are a disembodied hand in a box known as Thing and a 6 foot 9 inch butler named Lurch, who groans the question, 'You rang?', when summoned by a gong which shakes the whole house.

In line with their strange but pleasure-filled lifestyle, the family keeps unusual pets. Gomez takes delight in his octopus, Aristotle; Morticia is comforted by her man-eating African Strangler called Cleopatra; and Homer, Wednesday's pet, is a Black Widow spider. For toys, Pugsley has an electric chair and a gallows, while Wednesday plays with a headless doll. Gomez, on the other hand, indulges his violent instincts by blowing up toy trains or sword swallowing, if he isn't fencing his wife or devouring her with kisses at the slightest hint of a French word. Fester lights electric bulbs in his mouth, Grandmama practises knife-throwing and Lurch is often called upon to play the harpsichord. Cousin Itt is easily pleased: it hangs upside down in the chimney. And yet, for all their eccentricities, the Addams Family believe that they are normal and that it is the world around them that is bizarre. As a result, whenever contact is made with neighbours, or other 'ordinary' folk, misunderstanding is rife. The same premise was used in THE MUNSTERS, which reached TV screens at about the same time.

The cast had a good pedigree. Carolyn Jones was already a Hollywood name; Astin had previously starred in *I'm Dickens, He's Fenster*; Jackie Coogan, at the age of four, had appeared with Chaplin in *The Kid*; and Blossom Rock was the sister of singer Jeanette McDonald. A trio of Addams Family movies followed in the 1990s, initially with Anjelica Huston as Morticia and Raul Julia as Gomez.

Adie, Kate

OBE (Kathryn Adie; 1945–)

Kate Adie was born in Sunderland, and joined the BBC in 1968 as a technician in local radio in Durham, having spent three years with the National Youth Theatre. She became a producer at Radio Bristol in 1970 and moved to BBC South as a reporter in 1977, before joining the BBC national news set-up in 1979. In 1980 she covered the siege of the Iranian Embassy in London and went on to make her name as an on-the-spot reporter in the most hazardous situations, in places as diverse as Libya, Tiananmen Square, the Gulf and Kosovo. She was appointed the BBC's Chief News Correspondent in 1989.

Admags

Short for advertising magazines, admags are programmes that are used to promote commercial products, generally employing less than subtle techniques. The practice was commonplace in Britain following the advent of ITV in 1955 but was outlawed by Parliament in 1963. Probably the best-remembered admag is *Jim's Inn*, a pub-orientated programme set in the fictitious village of Wembleham, hosted by 'landlords' Jimmy and Maggie Hanley. Customers used to wander in and discuss their latest bargains over a pint or two. Other notable admags in the UK were Noele Gordon's *Homes and Gardens* (1956), Peter Butterworth and Janet Brown's *Where Shall We Go?* (also 1956) and John Slater's *Slater's Bazaar* (from 1957).

Adrian Mole: The Cappuccino Years

See *Secret Diary of Adrian Mole, Aged 13 ¾, The.*

Adventure Game, The ✳

UK (BBC) Game Show. BBC 1 1980; BBC 2 1981; 1984–6

Gnoard	**Charmian Gradwell**
Gandor	**Christopher Leaver**
Argond	**Ian Messiter**
Argond	**Moira Stuart**
His Highness The Rangdo	**Kenny Baker**
Dagnor	**Bill Homewood**
Dorgan	**Sarah Lam**

Creator **Patrick Dowling**
Producers **Patrick Dowling, Ian Oliver, Christopher Tandy**

● ***The* CRYSTAL MAZE *meets* DOCTOR WHO *in a mind-bending kids' game show.***

Millions of light years away, on the far edge of the galaxy, lies a little red planet called Arg. It is home to a race of shape-changing dragons and unfortunately three humans are marooned here in each episode of *The Adventure Game*. The human contestants must find a vital crystal that can power their spaceship home, and to do this they have to solve a series of physical and mental problems devised by the native Argonds (who usually appear in human form). Working as a team, the Earthlings may just have a chance. Following an initial Saturday morning run on BBC 1, *The Adventure Game* was switched to weekday evenings on BBC 2, to capture a more adult audience. First-season regular (but unnamed) Argonds Moira Stuart and Ian Messiter had left, and their colleagues Charmian Gradwell and Christopher Leaver were now given the titles Gnoard and Gandor (said to be niece and nephew of the grumpy, 2,000-year-old ruler of the planet, The Rangdo, who mostly disguised himself as an aspidistra). The format was tweaked so that the three contestants needed to rescue former BLUE PETER host Lesley Judd, knowing that one of their party was in fact in league with the Argonds (it turned out to be Judd throughout the series). For series three, Judd had disappeared but the assorted puzzles remained, including the 'traditional' Arg game of Drogna (involving a grid of assorted colours and shapes) and confrontations with the Red Salamander of Arg. The winner of the game claimed the Great Crystal of Arg. A new Argond introduced at this time was Dagnor, and joining in the fourth and final series was Dorgan, a replacement for Gnoard (all names, in case it has somehow not been spotted, being anagrams of the word 'dragon'). Creator Patrick Dowling cited the influences of psychologist Edward de Bono, the game of Dungeons and Dragons and even Lewis Carroll's absurdist reasoning in devising the game.

Adventure Weekly ✳

UK (BBC) Children's Drama. BBC 1 1968–9

Peter Perkins	**Brent Oldfield**
'Tubby' Taylor	**Ian Ellis**
'Swot' English	**Frank Barry**
Andy Rogers	**Len Jones**
Frederica 'Fred' Somers	**Elizabeth Dear**

Mr Filling .... **Bartlett Mullins**

Writers **Shaun Sutton, Peter J. Hammond, Victor Pemberton, Ian Shurey**
Producer **John McRae**

● ***Four boys and a girl run their own newspaper.***
Adventure Weekly is the name of the newspaper published by a group of schoolkids in the fictitious town of Cliffsea on the south coast. Twelve-year-old Peter Perkins is the editor. He's often too imaginative and daring for his own good, but his dad owns the local rag, the *Cliffsea Recorder*, where *Adventure Weekly* is printed, so he inevitably calls the shots. Sports editor is armchair fan 'Tubby' Taylor, an ardent supporter of Cliffsea United, while the paper's newshound is 'Swot' English, a bright bespectacled lad who likes digging out dirt on the teachers at school. Last of the founder members is Andy Rogers, a techno-fiend who owns a camera and is therefore, by default, the photographer. However, this all-male team is soon joined by 'Fred' Somers, a pigtailed girl who – much to their annoyance – outshines them in everything they do and quickly proves her worth to the paper. From a shaky start, *Adventure Weekly* wins its spurs, as the snoopy kids expose crooks, deal with an unexploded bomb and generally prove themselves to be a boon to the neighbourhood.

Adventurer

See *Smuggler*.

Adventurer, The ✶

UK (Scoton/ITC) Secret Agent Drama. ITV 1972–3
DVD: Network (part of *ITC 50* compilation)

Gene Bradley .... **Gene Barry**
Mr Parminter .... **Barry Morse**
Diane Marsh .... **Catherine Schell**
Gavin Jones .... **Garrick Hagon**
Vince .... **Stuart Damon**

Producer **Monty Berman**

● ***A US secret agent operates under the cover of an international film star.***
Gene Bradley is a wealthy, jet-setting movie celebrity who indulges himself in business ventures of all kinds, but whose real job involves secret assignments for US intelligence. Employing his acting skills to the full and taking on various disguises, Bradley is an international knight who rides to the rescue of threatened women, defecting scientists and others in need. His assignments are provided by his 'manager', Mr Parminter, and he is accompanied by fellow agents Gavin Jones and Diane Marsh. John Barry provides the theme music.

Adventures of Aggie, The ✶

UK (Mid Ocean) Situation Comedy. ITV 1956–7

Aasgard Agnette ('Aggie') Anderson .... **Joan Shawlee**

Writers **Ernest Borneman, Martin Stern**
Producer **Michael Sadlier**

● ***A fashion saleswoman travels the world and finds danger in every city.***
High-spirited American Aasgard Agnette Anderson – Aggie to her friends – works as a scout for a top London fashion house but her business assignments, in glamorous locations (Venice, Egypt, Paris and more), lead our hapless heroine unfailingly into murder, espionage, smuggling and other crime. This early series featured many up-and-coming stars, including Christopher Lee, Dick Emery, Patrick McGoohan and Anthony Valentine.

Adventures of Black Beauty, The ✶

UK (LWT/Talbot/Freemantle) Children's Adventure. ITV 1972–4
DVD: Network

Dr James Gordon .... **William Lucas**
Victoria Gordon .... **Judi Bowker**
Kevin Gordon .... **Roderick Shaw**
Amy Winthrop .... **Charlotte Mitchell**
Albert .... **Tom Maiden**
Jenny Gordon .... **Stacy Dorning**
Ned Lewis .... **Stephen Garlick**
Squire Armstrong .... **Michael Culver**

Executive Producer **Paul Knight**
Producer **Sidney Cole**

● ***A black stallion is the pride and joy of a young Victorian girl.***
This series, based on Anna Sewell's classic children's novel and fondly remembered for its 'Galloping Home' theme tune by Denis King, is set in 1877 on a spacious English country estate in the fictitious village of Five Oaks. Vicky Gordon is the young, impulsive owner of a thoroughbred, Black Beauty, which was badly treated by a succession of cruel owners before Vicky and her family took him in and nursed him back to health. Brother Kevin lends a hand and their dad, a doctor, and Amy, his housekeeper, are also drawn into the horsey goings-on. Most stories have little to do with the original book and revolve around escaped criminals, burning barns and such like. When star Judi Bowker left after the first series, Stacy Dorning was cast as Jenny, Vicky's sister who had apparently, till now, been away at school. Ned, Amy's scruffy nephew, was also introduced, and the adventures continued. Dorning later appeared in the 1990 reworking of the series, entitled *The New Adventures of Black Beauty*, playing the now married Jenny Denning (events had moved on to 1902 and the action now took place in New Zealand). William Lucas also reprised his role as Dr Gordon.

Adventures of Champion, The

See *Champion the Wonder Horse*.

Adventures of Don Quick, The ✶

UK (LWT) Science Fiction. ITV 1970

Capt. Don Quick .... **Ian Hendry**
Sgt Sam Czopanser .... **Ronald Lacey**

Writers **Peter Wildeblood, Kenneth Hill, Keith Miles, Charlotte Plimmer, Dennis Plimmer**
Executive Producer **Peter Wildeblood**

● ***A space engineer tilts at windmills across the cosmos.***
Cervantes in the space age is the theme of this science-fiction satire in six parts. Don Quick is a modest engineer, working for the Intergalactic Maintenance Squad. The job takes him all across the universe but he suffers from delusions of grandeur,

believing himself to be an itinerant ambassador for the Earth with a duty to right wrongs. Along with his sidekick, Sam Czopanser, the interfering mechanic travels to an assortment of planets, all inhabited by strange races – such as a planet of women who shrink men to a mere six inches in height. His efforts to adjust imbalances in the societies he encounters inevitably end in failure.

Adventures of Hiram Holliday, The ✶✶

US (NBC/California) Situation Comedy. BBC 1960–1 (US: NBC 1956–7)

Hiram Holliday .... **Wally Cox**
Joel Smith .... **Ainslie Pryor**

Producer **Philip Rapp**

● ***A mild-mannered newspaper employee stumbles into intrigue around the world.***

Having saved his New York newspaper from libellous embarrassment with his proofreading talents (he inserted a vital comma), meek and gangly Hiram Holliday is rewarded with $8,000 and a month's salary-paid vacation. He adds the money to his savings, and the time to the holiday he is already due, and decides on the trip of a lifetime around the world, setting sail on the good ship *Britannique*. In addition to proofreading, the inoffensive, bespectacled Holliday possesses many other remarkable skills, which range from plane piloting to fencing and scuba diving. His publisher recognizes these and hopes they will make good reading when brought into play as Hiram tours the world. To bring back the stories, reporter Joel Smith is dispatched alongside Holliday and he witnesses no end of precarious situations, from which our hero extracts himself with improbable ease.

The half-hour series was the first comedy to be 'stripped' in the UK, i.e. played at the same time (7 p.m., in this case) on consecutive nights of the week (as a seasonal replacement for TONIGHT). The Holliday character was based on short stories published in 1939 by Paul Gallico (author of *The Poseidon Adventure*) and the series ran for 26 episodes.

Adventures of Long John Silver, The ✶

Australia (Treasure Island) Adventure. ITV 1957
DVD: Cascadia Entertainment (part of *Golden Years of TV: The Swashbucklers* compilation) or **Platinum Disc** (Region 1 only)

Long John Silver .... **Robert Newton**
Jim Hawkins .... **Kit Taylor**
Purity Pinker .... **Connie Gilchrist**
Patch .... **Grant Taylor**
Governor Strong .... **John Sherwood**

Producers **Mark Evans, Joseph Kaufman**

● ***The further adventures of Treasure Island's scurrilous, one-legged ship's cook.***

In this TV follow-up to successful cinema films, the era is the 1700s and Silver and his cabin-boy friend, Jim Hawkins, are based on Porto Bello, an island in the Spanish Main. Here they work on behalf of Governor Strong, thwarting the advances of the Spanish fleet and preserving the island for the British Crown, with a dash of treasure-hunting thrown in for good measure. Off-duty, the rolling-eyed, grog-swiller can be found in Purity Pinker's pub, the Cask and Anchor. Sadly, Robert Newton died not long after this series was made.

Adventures of Parsley, The

See *Herbs, The*.

Adventures of Rin-Tin-Tin, The ✶

US (Herbert B. Leonard/Screen Gems) Children's Adventure. ITV 1956–61 (US: ABC 1954–9)

Cpl Rusty 'B' Company .... **Lee Aaker**
Lt. Ripley 'Rip' Masters .... **James L. Brown**
Sgt Aloysius 'Biff' O'Hara .... **Joe Sawyer**
Cpl Randy Boone .... **Rand Brooks**
Col. Barker .... **John Hoyt**

Producer **Herbert B. Leonard**

● ***An orphan and his talented Alsatian become members of a US Cavalry troop.***

Two survivors of a wagon train raid, 11-year-old Rusty and his pet German Shepherd dog, Rin-Tin-Tin, are rescued by the US Cavalry sometime in the 1880s. 'B' Company of the 101st unit ('The Fighting Blue Devils') take them back to their camp, near the fictional town of Mesa Grande in Arizona, where they are adopted by Lt. Rip Masters and Sgt Biff O'Hara and become members of the troop. Hiding themselves away when big-wig Colonel Barker comes to inspect the camp, Rusty and 'Rinty' unearth a plot against the officer's life. They save the day and Rusty is awarded corporal's stripes and invited to live on the base with 'Private' Rinty for as long as he wishes.

The action dog, at one time a great movie rival of the collie Lassie, is quickly at the forefront of Cavalry activity, leading charges against Apache Indians (spurred on by a 'Yo ho, Rinty'), sniffing out danger and wresting weapons from enemy hands. Two of the dogs that played the lead were actually descendants of the former German army dog whose film debut came in the 1922 offering *The Man from Hell's River*. He was such a box-office hit in those silent days that he saved Warner Brothers from bankruptcy. In this 1950s series, he generated a new legion of young fans.

Adventures of Robin Hood, The ✶✶

UK (ITC/Sapphire/Weinstein) Adventure. ITV 1955–60
DVD: Network

Robin Hood .... **Richard Greene**
Maid Marian .... **Bernadette O'Farrell**
Patricia Driscoll
Friar Tuck .... **Alexander Gauge**
Little John .... **Archie Duncan**
Rufus Cruikshank
Sheriff of Nottingham .... **Alan Wheatley**
Prince John .... **Hubert Gregg**
Brian Haines
Donald Pleasence
Will Scarlett .... **Ronald Howard**
Paul Eddington
Alan-a-Dale .... **Richard Coleman**
Derwent .... **Victor Woolf**
Deputy Sheriff .... **John Arnatt**
Joan .... **Simone Lovell**

Prince Arthur .... **Peter Asher**
Richard O'Sullivan
Jonathan Bailey

Executive Producer **Hannah Weinstein**
Producer **Sidney Cole**

● ***Dashing tales of the 12th-century hero.***

Robbing the rich and saving the poor in this early costume drama was Richard Greene, an actor forever identified thereafter with the man in Lincoln green from Sherwood Forest. The series was broadly based on the Robin Hood legend, with Robin of Locksley, the Earl of Huntingdon, forced to rebel against the cruel Regent, Prince John, and his local henchman, the Sheriff of Nottingham. All the traditional clan are here, from Friar Tuck to Little John, plus Lady Marian Fitzwalter, known to the Merrie Men as Maid Marian.

The Adventures of Robin Hood was one of the pioneers of British television in America. Thoroughly popular with younger viewers, it inspired a host of other rousing costume dramas, such as WILLIAM TELL, THE BUCCANEERS and THE ADVENTURES OF SIR LANCELOT. The theme song, sung by Dick James, was a hit single in 1956. Note the famous names in the cast list, especially Paul Eddington, Richard O'Sullivan and PICTURE BOOK presenter Patricia Driscoll.

Adventures of Robinson Crusoe, The ✶✶

France (Franco London Film) Children's Drama. BBC 1 1965

Robinson Crusoe .... **Robert Hoffman**
Narrator .... **Lee Payant**

Writers **Jean-Paul Carrière, Pierre Reynal, Jacques Somet**
Producer **Henry Deutschmeister**

● ***A shipwrecked sailor builds a new life on a tropical island.***

This adaptation of Daniel Defoe's classic novel was a familiar sight on children's television in the 1960s, being repeated a number of times after its 1965 debut. Made in France and dubbed into English, it tells Crusoe's story in full, even exploring his pre-shipwreck life through flashbacks which feature his childhood in York, his apprenticeship as a lawyer, his running away to sea and his earlier maritime adventures. Now stranded on the island, he sets about building himself a new existence. The 12-part series – which featured one of TV's most memorable theme tunes – was filmed in the Canary Islands.

Adventures of Sherlock Holmes, The/ The Return of Sherlock Holmes/ The Casebook of Sherlock Holmes/ The Memoirs of Sherlock Holmes ✶✶✶

UK (Granada) Detective Drama. ITV 1984–5 (*Adventures*)/1986; 1988 (*Return*)/1991 (*Casebook*)/1994 (*Memoirs*)
DVD: Granada Ventures

Sherlock Holmes .... **Jeremy Brett**
Dr John Watson .... **David Burke** *(Adventures)*
Edward Hardwicke
Mrs Hudson .... **Rosalie Williams**
Insp. Lestrade .... **Colin Jeavons**
Mycroft Holmes .... **Charles Gray**

Executive Producer **Michael Cox**
Producers **Michael Cox, June Wyndham Davies**

● ***Conan Doyle's celebrated sleuth, depicted in all his original colour.***

After 90 years of trying, and with some 70 actors attempting the title role on film and TV, it wasn't until 1984 that fans found the celluloid Sherlock Holmes they really liked. Generally accepted as being the closest in detail, style and mood to the author's original tales (published in the Victorian *Strand Magazine*), Granada's treatment pitched Jeremy Brett into the famous role, a part with which he became indelibly linked. Quite different from the stereotyped Basil Rathbone version, Brett's Holmes is a man of intelligence and courage, but also a reflective, tactful man with a dark side; a man seen wide-eyed and moody under the influence of cocaine; and a man with respect, not just tolerance, for his trusty (and surprisingly spritely) companion, Watson. The settings are realistic, too, and well researched, re-creating Sidney Paget's original *Strand* illustrations.

Two series of Holmes tales were initially revived, culminating in *The Final Problem*, in which our hero is seen to meet his end in a confrontation with the evil Moriarty at Reichenbach Falls. But the pipe-smoking, violin-playing detective resurfaced in two further series, entitled *The Return of Sherlock Holmes*, in which Watson was played by Edward Hardwicke. Hardwicke also kept the role for the two-hour versions of *The Sign of Four* and *The Hound of the Baskervilles*, as well as all subsequent adventures, which went out under the titles of *The Casebook of Sherlock Holmes* and *The Memoirs of Sherlock Holmes*. Three interim films, in 1993, were billed simply as *Sherlock Holmes*.

Adventures of Sir Lancelot, The ✶

UK (Weinstein/Sapphire/ITC) Adventure. ITV 1956–7
DVD: Network

Sir Lancelot du Lac .... **William Russell**
Queen Guinevere .... **Jane Hylton**
King Arthur .... **Bruce Seton**
Ronald Leigh-Hunt
Merlin .... **Cyril Smith**
Sir Kay .... **David Morrell**
Brian .... **Robert Scroggins**

Executive Producer **Hannah Weinstein**
Producers **Sidney Cole, Dallas Bower, Bernard Knowles**

● ***Stories of the celebrated Knight of the Round Table, arguably misplaced in the 14th century.***

Sir Lancelot du Lac is the Queen's Champion – 'the bravest knight the world has ever seen', according to the theme song – and the man who wards off all threats to her court at Camelot. In the background is King Arthur, his famous sword Excalibur, the revered sorcerer Merlin, plus Lancelot's squire, former kitchen-boy Brian. The authenticity of the settings for the series was researched at Oxford University, but the era was moved from Sir Lancelot's alleged time of the sixth century up to the 1300s. No mention was made of his dalliance with Queen Guinevere or the conception of Sir Galahad behind the King's back.

William Russell became one of TV's first heart-throbs through this role. He later played Ian Chesterton, a DOCTOR WHO assistant, before arousing fond memories in middle-aged female viewers when he returned as Ted Sullivan in CORONATION STREET in the early 1990s.

Adventures of Superman, The

See *Superman*.

Adventures of the Scarlet Pimpernel, The ★★

UK (Towers of London/ITP) Adventure. ITV 1955–6

Sir Percy Blakeney/The Scarlet Pimpernel .... **Marius Goring**
Chauvelin .... **Stanley Van Beers**
Sir Andrew Ffoulkes .... **Patrick Troughton**
The Countess .... **Lucie Mannheim**
Prince Regent .... **Alexander Gauge**
Lord Richard Hastings .... **Anthony Newlands**

Producers **Anthony Gilkison, Dennis Vance, Marius Goring, David MacDonald**

The daring escapades of a mysterious hero in Georgian England and Revolutionary France.

Although ruthlessly persecuted by the cruel Chauvelin and his followers, the aristocrats of France know they have an ally to count on: the elusive and intriguing Scarlet Pimpernel, alias English nobleman Sir Percy Blakeney. In contrast to his dashing *alter ego*, Blakeney is weak and foppish, always cleverly deflecting suspicion of his true identity. He is also a master of disguise, and elaborate costume and make-up changes contrive to preserve our hero from a violent death at the guillotine. The series was based on the book by Baroness Orczy.

The character returned to the screen in *The Elusive Pimpernel* (BBC 1 1969), with Anton Rodgers as star. In 1999 Richard E. Grant became Blakeney in another rendering, simply called THE SCARLET PIMPERNEL.

Adventures of the Seaspray ★

Australia (Pacific/Screen Gems) Children's Adventure. ITV 1966–7

Capt. Dan Wells .... **Walter Brown**
Mike Wells .... **Gary Gray**
Sue Wells .... **Susanne Haworth**
Noah Wells .... **Rodney Pearlman**
Willyum Lesi .... **Leone Lesianawai**

Producer **Roger Mirams**

A freelance writer and his family find excitement in the South Pacific.

Widowed Australian Dan Wells is a writer in search of ideas, travelling the southern seas in his schooner, the *Seaspray*, in pursuit of a good story. Accompanying him are his two sons, Mike and Noah, and his daughter, Sue, with Willyum their Fijian deckhand. Confronting smugglers, castaways and hunted criminals, the Wells family traverse the South Pacific, visiting most ports of call along the way, from New Zealand to New Guinea and Fiji, introducing younger viewers to the colourful culture of Oceania.

Adventures of Tugboat Annie, The ★

Canada (Normandie) Situation Comedy. ITV 1957–8

'Tugboat' Annie Brennan .... **Minerva Urecal**
Capt. Horatio Bullwinkle .... **Walter Sande**
Whitey .... **Don Baker**
Pinto .... **Don Orlando**
Jake .... **James Barron**

Rivalry and excitement at sea with two tugboat captains.

Widow Annie Brennan is the stocky, booming-voiced skipper of the *Narcissus*, a tug based in a harbour on the north-west coast of America. Her main aim in life is to get the better of fellow skipper Horatio Bullwinkle, but, though the pair fight like cat and dog for the best jobs and trade generously in insults, they also share many an ocean adventure. Whitey and Pinto are Annie's deckhands, and Jake is Bullwinkle's crewman. The series was based on a cartoon strip by Norman Reilly Raine and followed a 1933 film starring Marie Dressler and Wallace Beery.

Adventures of Twizzle, The ★

UK (AP Films/Associated-Rediffusion) Children's Entertainment. ITV 1957–9

Twizzle .... **Denise Bryer** *(voice)*

Creator/Writer **Roberta Leigh**

Puppet tales of a toy with elastic arms and legs.

Notable for being Gerry Anderson's first contribution (as director) to British television, *The Adventures of Twizzle* concerns a toy with a Wee Willy Winkie hat and stretchable arms and legs. Twizzle runs away from a toy shop and ends up in all sorts of scrapes but at his side is a large cat named Footso (after his enormous paws). Twizzle and Footso build a haven for stray toys, a sort of refuge from naughty children. They call it Stray Town, and that is where most of the adventures take place. Among the mistreated and neglected toys are Chawky (a white-faced golliwog), Jiffy the Broomstick Man, Polly Moppet, Candy Floss (a 'Mamma doll' which can't say 'Mamma') and Bouncy (a ball which has lost its bounce).

The brains behind *Twizzle* was Roberta Leigh, later noted for TORCHY and SPACE PATROL. However, it is largely for Anderson's direction that the series is remembered today, even though he contributed to only the first 26 episodes.

Affiliate Station

An independent TV station that links up with one of the large networks to take a proportion of the latter's programming in exchange for a fee, but still leaving gaps in its schedule for its own local output. Affiliate stations are commonplace in the USA and are used by the major networks to extend their audiences. The smaller stations gain from being able to offer first-run, highly rated programmes at no expense to themselves.

African Patrol ✳

UK (Gross-Krasne/Kenya) Adventure. ITV 1958–9

Chief Insp. Paul Derek .... **John Bentley**

Producer **George Breakston**

● ***Law and order with a jungle policeman.***

British Patrol Inspector Paul Derek works in the African bush, using his expert knowledge of East African safari country to keep the peace. It is his duty to thwart poachers and other criminals who disturb the natural balance of the environment. The series was filmed entirely on location in Africa. Star John Bentley re-emerged in the 1960s and 1970s as Hugh Mortimer in CROSSROADS.

After Henry ✳✳✳

UK (Thames) Situation Comedy. ITV 1988–90; 1992

Sarah France .... **Prunella Scales**
Eleanor Prescott .... **Joan Sanderson**
Clare France .... **Janine Wood**
Russell Bryant .... **Jonathan Newth**
Vera Poling .... **Peggy Ann Wood**

Writer **Simon Brett**
Producers **Peter Frazer-Jones, Bill Shepherd**

● ***A widow shares her home with her demanding mother and her obstinate daughter.***

This gentle comedy, contrasting the lives of three generations of women, focuses chiefly on the one in the middle. Sarah France is the fortysomething widow of the late Dr Henry France, a man who was much loved and is now greatly missed. She shares her home in Stipton with her young, headstrong daughter, Clare, and suffers intrusions from her domineering mother, Eleanor, who lives in an adjoining granny flat. Much of the humour arises from Sarah's attempts to reconcile the various generations, which are not without pain and anguish. Sarah's confidant is Russell, her boss at Bygone Books, an antiquarian bookshop. Vera Poling is Eleanor's geriatric rival.

After Henry transferred to television after three successful years on BBC Radio. Prunella Scales reprised her radio role, as did Joan Sanderson, although Russell was played by Benjamin Whitrow and Clare by Gerry Cowper in the sound version.

Agatha Christie Hour, The ✳

UK (Thames) Thriller. ITV 1982

Executive Producer **John Frankau**
Producer **Pat Sandys**

● ***An anthology of the Mistress of Crime's lesser-known tales.***

This series does not feature the mighty Hercule Poirot, nor does Miss Marple steal the limelight. For once, Agatha Christie's earlier characters are introduced to television in these ten 1920s dramas, which are generally lighthearted, unassuming period adventures, with the cast changing for each episode.

Agatha Christie's Marple

See *Miss Marple*.

Agatha Christie's Partners in Crime ✳✳

UK (LWT) Detective Drama. ITV 1983–4
DVD: Cinema Club

Tommy Beresford .... **James Warwick**
Tuppence Cowley/Beresford .. **Francesca Annis**
Albert .... **Reece Dinsdale**
Insp. Marriott .... **Arthur Cox**

Writers **Pat Sandys, David Butler, Jonathan Hales, Paul Annett, Gerald Savory**
Producer **Jack Williams**

● ***A society husband and wife catch crooks in the 1920s.***

Fun-loving Tommy Beresford and Tuppence Cowley meet up after World War I (she has nursed him back to health from wartime wounds) and join forces as amateur detectives. They soon turn their hobby into a full-time business, forming a detective agency. Getting married, they swan around the high society of the 1920s, tackling crime wherever it raises its ugly head, assisted by Albert, a film-crazy former lift attendant whom they employ as an office boy. Tommy and Tuppence's lively, husband-and-wife posturing and teasing become a feature of this ten-part series, which was based on two of Agatha Christie's lesser-known characters. Joseph Horovitz supplied the music. The first episode, *Agatha Christie's The Secret Adversary*, was a feature-length special.

Agatha Christie's Poirot ✳✳

UK (LWT/Carnival/Granada/Chorion) Detective Drama. ITV 1989–93; 1995; 2000; 2002–4; 2006–
DVD: Granada Ventures

Hercule Poirot .... **David Suchet**
Capt. Arthur Hastings .... **Hugh Fraser**
Insp./Chief Insp. Japp .... **Philip Jackson**
Miss Lemon .... **Pauline Moran**

Executive Producers **Nick Elliott, Linda Agran**
Producers **Brian Eastman, Margaret Mitchell, Trevor Hopkins**

● ***The cases of the famous Belgian detective.***

Along with beer and Tin Tin, Hercule Poirot is one of Belgium's greatest exports, even if he was only a figment of Agatha Christie's fertile imagination. Having already been characterized by the likes of Albert Finney and Peter Ustinov on film, Poirot came to TV in the capable hands of British actor David Suchet, brother of ITN newscaster John. The series pitches him into the *art deco* London of the 1930s, giving him a small flat in the luxurious Whitehaven Mansions and allowing crime to follow him wherever he goes.

Joining the fastidious sleuth with the curly moustache, fancy cane and 'little grey cells' are his loyal companion, Captain Hastings, a sporty, well-heeled ladies' man who drives a green Lagonda, and secretary Miss Lemon. Also on the scene is the inept Inspector Japp, a Scotland Yard officer who never fails to point the finger at the wrong suspect. Putting matters right, Poirot, with his pronounced continental accent, calmly gathers together all the likely candidates and, after a meticulous explanation of the facts, quietly and efficiently nails the guilty party.

Two feature-length *Poirot* episodes were shown in 1996 and 1997, after the series as such ended; these were followed after a three-year gap by a two-part dramatization of *The Murder of Roger Ackroyd* in 2000 and then two further single adventures, *Murder in Mesopotamia* and *Evil under the Sun*, in 2002. Four new stories were aired in each of the years 2003, 2004 and 2006.

Age of Kings, An ★★★

UK (BBC) Drama Anthology. BBC 1960

Producer **Peter Dews**

● ***The ambitious dramatization of five Shakespearean plays as an historical project.***

In *An Age of Kings*, the kings in question are Richard II, Henry IV, Henry V, Henry VI and Richard III, as portrayed by William Shakespeare in his plays of the same titles. Spread over 15 episodes, initially screened a fortnight apart, the plays were dramatized in sequence to give the overall effect of depicting a continuous stretch (86 years) of British history. Always as a backdrop were the lust for the throne and the burdens of wearing the crown. Michael Hayes directed the plays and the theme music was composed by Sir Arthur Bliss. Featured actors included Robert Hardy, Paul Daneman, David William, Sean Connery and Eileen Atkins.

Agony ★★/Agony Again ★

UK (LWT/BBC/Humphrey Barclay) Situation Comedy. ITV 1979–81 (*Agony*); BBC 1 1995 (*Agony Again*)

Jane Lucas .... **Maureen Lipman**
Bea .... **Maria Charles**
Laurence Lucas .... **Simon Williams**
Andy Evol .... **Peter Blake** (*Agony*)
Val .... **Diana Weston** (*Agony*)
Diana .... **Jan Holden** (*Agony*)
Rob .... **Jeremy Bulloch** (*Agony*)
Michael .... **Peter Denyer** (*Agony*)
Mr Mince .... **Robert Gillespie** (*Agony*)
Vincent Fish .... **Bill Nighy** (*Agony*)
Junior Truscombe .... **Robert Austin** (*Agony*)
Richard .... **Niall Buggy** (*Again*)
Michael Lucas .... **Sacha Grunpeter** (*Again*)
Daniel .... **David Harewood** (*Again*)
Debra .... **Doon Mackichan** (*Again*)
Catherine .... **Valerie Edmond** (*Again*)

Creators **Anna Raeburn, Len Richmond**
Producers **John Reardon** (*Agony*); **Humphrey Barclay, Christopher Skala** (*Again*)

● ***A successful agony aunt's own life is a mess.***

Jane Lucas is the popular problem-page editor for *Person* magazine and also runs her own radio phone-in. However, for all the sound advice she gives to distressed readers and listeners, her personal life is far from straightforward and she is surrounded by people liable to make things worse. These are her psychiatrist husband, Laurence, who doesn't understand people (and from whom she eventually parts); her typically Jewish mother, Bea, who dispenses advice and worries over her; and a couple of gay friends (Rob and Michael) who are always quarrelling – all this on top of 'friends' at work who seek her professional advice for their own little worries. These include her dragon-like editor, Diana, her virtuous secretary, Val, and radio DJ Andy Evol.

The series was created by (and based on the real life of) agony aunt Anna Raeburn. A sanitized American version, *The Lucie Arnaz Show* (CBS 1985), starred Lucille Ball's daughter in the lead role. In 1995 the series was revived by the BBC under the title of *Agony Again*. This time Jane is the host of the TV talk show *Lucas Live*. However, she is still pestered by her mother and those around her, who include her gay son, Michael, her new man, Daniel, and her ex-husband, Laurence, whom she can never quite let go.

Agutter, Jenny

(1952–)

English actress first seen on TV as a teenager, playing roles like Kirsty Kerr in THE NEWCOMERS, Bobbie in THE RAILWAY CHILDREN and Fritha in THE SNOW GOOSE. Her later credits have included single dramas like SHELLEY, plus SILAS MARNER (Nancy Lammeter), THE BUCCANEERS (Idina Hatton), AND THE BEAT GOES ON (Connie Spencer), *A Respectable Trade* (Lady Scott), a new version of *The Railway Children* (this time playing Mother), *The Alan Clark Diaries* (Jane Clark) and SPOOKS (Tessa Phillips). Guest appearances have come in series such as *Shadows*, THE SIX MILLION DOLLAR MAN, *The All New Alexei Sayle Show*, BRAMWELL, MAGNUM, PI, BOON, LOVE HURTS, HEARTBEAT, THE INSPECTOR LYNLEY MYSTERIES, AGATHA CHRISTIE'S MARPLE, NEW TRICKS and AGATHA CHRISTIE'S POIROT.

Aherne, Caroline

(1963–)

Manchester-born, former BBC secretary and local radio presenter, acclaimed as one of the brightest comic talents of the 1990s, thanks to her creation of geriatric chat show host MRS MERTON. The character was later spun off into a sitcom, MRS MERTON AND MALCOLM, before being set aside by Aherne as she concentrated more on developing THE ROYLE FAMILY (and playing Denise Royle) with her long-time writing and performing partner, Craig Cash. Aherne has also been a member of THE FAST SHOW team and, again with Cash, compiled the documentary *Back Passage to India*. She briefly moved to Australia, where she co-wrote and co-produced (with Peter Herbert), and directed the comedy DOSSA AND JOE. Initially billed as Caroline Hook for her early TV appearances, she reverted to her maiden name in 1996 after the break-up of her marriage to former New Order bass player Peter Hook.

Ain't Misbehavin'[1] ★

UK (BBC) Situation Comedy. BBC 1 1994–5

Clive Quigley .... **Peter Davison**
Sonia Drysdale .... **Nicola Pagett**
Melissa Quigley .... **Lesley Manville**
Karen Drury
Dave Drysdale .... **John Duttine**
Mrs Ramona Whales .... **Polly Hemingway**
Chuck Purvis .... **Ian McNeice**
Paul Brooke
Lester Whales .... **Barry Stanton**

Writer **Roy Clarke**
Executive Producer **James Gilbert**
Producer **Tony Dow**

● ***A cuckolded couple join forces to ruin their partners' secret lives.***

The discovery that their respective spouses are having an

affair draws together wimpy small businessman Clive Quigley and calculating hairdresser Sonia Drysdale. Their interest isn't romantic: the mutual attraction lies in secretly scuppering the relationship between Clive's adulterous wife, Melissa, and Sonia's philandering husband, Dave. With a private detective named Purvis snooping around, and the jealous husband of Clive's secretary, Mrs Whales, suspecting Clive of being up to no good, it is a tangled knot indeed. A comedy of misunderstanding, mistrust and mismatches, *Ain't Misbehavin'*, set in Yorkshire, ran for two series (12 episodes). Paul Jones sang the theme song, a version of the Fats Waller classic that shares its title with the programme.

Ain't Misbehavin' [2] ✶

UK (Clapp Trapp) Comedy Drama. ITV 1997

Eric Trapp .... **Robson Green**
Eddie Wallis .... **Jerome Flynn**
Dolly Nightingale .... **Julia Sawalha**
Ray Smiles .... **Warren Mitchell**
Clara Van Trapp .... **Jane Lapotaire**
Maxie Morrell .... **Jim Carter**
Malky Fraser .... **James Cosmo**
Mrs Jilkes .... **June Brown**
Bing Williams .... **George Melly**
Spadger .... **Graham Stark**

Writer **Bob Larbey**
Producer **George Gallaccio**

● ***The misadventures of a pair of 1940s big band musicians.***

Eddie Wallis would have loved to have had the chance to fight for his country in World War II. Unfortunately, a plane crash has left him suffering from the wrong sort of blackouts you need in wartime, and he has been retired to civvy street. Falling back on his musical skills, he joins the Ray Smiles Orchestra, a swing band, where he strikes up a friendship with wide-boy and ladies' man Eric Trapp, who, unlike Eddie, has no intention whatsoever of aiding the war effort. The pair find themselves out of their depth in inter-gang rivalries and other scrapes as the Nazi bombs fall all around and Eddie hankers for the attentions of Berkeley Square beauty Dolly Nightingale, a lady way beyond his social station. Also seen are band singer Bing Williams and band leader Ray Smiles, who fancies his chances with Eric's Jewish mum, Clara.

This three-part comedy drama was produced by Robson Green's and Jerome Flynn's own company, Clapp Trapp Productions. It allowed them to continue their successful screen partnership – echoing their earlier roles in SOLDIER, SOLDIER – as well as advance their singing careers by belting out nostalgic 1940s songs.

Aird, Holly

(1969–)

British actress coming to the fore young in *The History of Mr Polly* in 1980 and THE FLAME TREES OF THIKA (Elspeth Grant), before moving on to the sitcoms *Affairs of the Heart* (Rosemary) and DOUBLE FIRST (Ellen), and the drama MOTHER LOVE. She then secured prominent roles in the seaside comedy HOPE IT RAINS (Jace), SOLDIER, SOLDIER (Nancy Thorpe/Garvey), DRESSING FOR BREAKFAST (Carla), *Have Your Cake and Eat It* (Allie Gray) and WAKING THE DEAD (Dr Frankie Wharton). Other credits include *Seal Morning* (Rowena Farre), *Sea Dragon* (Ffion), MISS MARPLE, INSPECTOR MORSE, KAVANAGH QC and *Circles of Deceit* (Sarah Ellis).

Airline [1] ✶

UK (Yorkshire) Drama. ITV 1982

Jack Ruskin .... **Roy Marsden**
Peter Witney .... **Richard Heffer**
McEvoy .... **Sean Scanlan**
Jennie Shaw .... **Polly Hemingway**
Ernie Cade .... **Terence Rigby**

Creator **Wilfred Greatorex**
Executive Producer **David Cunliffe**
Producer **Michael Ferguson**

● ***An RAF pilot starts his own airline in the immediate post-war years.***

In 1946 Jack Ruskin, demobbed after World War II but with flying still in his blood, struggles to find work with civilian airlines and so chances his arm by founding his own. His partner in the new Ruskin Air Services is forces colleague Peter Witney. Operating with an old Dakota aircraft Ruskin has bought, they aim to cut themselves a slice of the world cargo market. However, the business has difficulty getting off the ground, in more ways than one.

Ensnared by shady business deals and hampered by bad weather, Ruskin Air Services offers its staff and management an uncomfortable ride, as Jack lurches from one financial crisis to another. But his entrepreneurial spirit is not to be denied. He raises his sights, takes on passenger transport and later becomes involved in the Berlin Airlift. Ernie Cade is the company's dodgy backer, McEvoy is the company engineer and Jennie Shaw is Jack's girlfriend. Tony Hatch provided the music.

Roy Marsden, Polly Hemingway (Marsden's then real-life wife) and the whole *Airline* ethos was borrowed for a British Airports Authority commercial several years later, a move which, it was reported, brought an unsuccessful lawsuit from the show's creator, Wilfred Greatorex.

Airline [2]

See *Airport*.

Airport ✶✶

UK (BBC) Documentary. BBC 1 1996–2003; 2005

Narrators **John Nettles, Liza Tarbuck**

Executive Producers **Jeremy Mills, Clare Paterson, Edwina Vardey**

● ***A look at the complicated working lives of staff at Heathrow Airport.***

One of the first of the 1990s influx of 'docu-soaps', *Airport* focuses on life at the UK's busiest airport, Heathrow. Many facets of the running of the airport are explored, from the inevitable lost luggage and suspect packages to delayed flights, travelling superstars and attempted drug smuggling, although attention occasionally wavers from the original focus on the logistics of airport life to more trivial side-issues concerning some of the airport's increasingly famous employees. These have included photographer Dennis Stone; British Midland dispatcher Viv Eggins; VIP liaisons Anita Newcourt and Sara Collins; PC Dave Kidd; terminal duty officers Jean Marie Lavillard and Michèle Harris; customs officers Cath Hall and Garth Powell; journalist Steve Meller; photographer

Russell Clisby; Air Jamaica co-ordinator Merla Celestine; traffic warden Jean Dibble; animal welfare man Stuart King; Aer Lingus supervisor Siobhan Feeney; immigration officers Rob Scott, Jo Salmon, Eric Day and Caroline Acheson; air traffic controller Phil Hartwick; Canadian Airlines officer Kelvin Ogunjimi; dispatcher Elaine Pringle; WPC Annabel Davis; paramedics Eric McGill and Jane Heppolette; and Maria Demetrious from Cyprus Airways. However, the undoubted discovery of the series has been Aeroflot supervisor-turned-TV-presenter, Jeremy Spake.

Some Christmas specials have also been produced, including one showing the main characters in a one-off job swap. In 2001 a spin-off series placed events at *Miami Airport* under the spotlight. The success of *Airport* prompted ITV to launch their own equivalent series, *Airline* (1998–), featuring initially staff of Britannia Airways and later easyJet (showcasing in particular Luton Airport check-in girl Katrina Leeder; other airports featured later).

Airwolf ✶

US (Bellisarius/Universal) Adventure. ITV 1984–6 (US: CBS 1984–6; USA Cable 1986–8)
DVD: Universal

Stringfellow Hawke	**Jan-Michael Vincent**
Dominic Santini	**Ernest Borgnine**
Michael Archangel	**Alex Cord**
Marella	**Deborah Pratt**
Caitlin O'Shannessy	**Jean Bruce Scott**

Creator **Donald P. Bellisario**
Executive Producers **Bernard Kowalski, Donald P. Bellisario**

● ***Thrills and spills with a high-tech helicopter.***

When *Airwolf*, a new breed of super helicopter, is spirited away to Libya by its designer, the US government calls on the services of ace pilot Stringfellow Hawke to retrieve it for Uncle Sam. Hawke, a cello-playing mountain recluse, fulfils his mission but refuses to hand the aircraft back until the US finds his brother, St John, who is still missing in Vietnam. In the meantime, Hawke flies secret and spectacular assignments with the super chopper for a government agency known as The Firm. His contact there is Archangel, who dons white clothing, wears an eye patch and carries a stick. Hawke's accomplice on his missions is middle-aged co-pilot Dominic Santini, and he is also joined by female pilot Caitlin O'Shannessy in later episodes. Marella, Archangel's attractive brunette assistant, sometimes represents The Firm.

Airwolf itself is a pretty impressive piece of machinery. An attack helicopter, it has a massive array of weapons and is capable of supersonic flight. It is not unique, however. At the same time, another high-tech chopper, BLUE THUNDER, also began its own series.

A. J. Wentworth, BA ✶

UK (Thames) Situation Comedy. ITV 1982

A. J. Wentworth	**Arthur Lowe**
Matron	**Marion Mathie**
Revd R. G. Saunders ('Headmaster')	**Harry Andrews**
Rawlinson	**Ronnie Stevens**
Gilbert	**Michael Bevis**
Miss Coombes	**Debbie Davies**

Writer **Basil Boothroyd**
Producer **Michael Mills**

● ***The exploits of an absent-minded schoolteacher.***

In his last TV series, recorded just weeks before he died, Arthur Lowe plays a maths teacher, based in a 1940s prep school, who is obsessed with old-fashioned school virtues. Fighting internal battles with his arch-enemy, Matron, the disaster-prone but dignified teacher is mostly preoccupied by such trivial matters as the high cost of pen nibs. The snooty cleric, the Reverend R. G. Saunders, is the school's headmaster. The series was based on stories by H. F. Ellis, although just six episodes were made.

Alagiah, George

(1955–)

Born in Sri Lanka and brought up in Ghana, George Alagiah moved to Britain as a schoolboy aged 12. After working for an international news magazine, he joined BBC news as foreign correspondent in 1989, moving to the post of South Africa correspondent in 1994. In 1999, Alagiah took over as host of the BBC's *One O'Clock News* and other bulletins, and then raised Establishment eyebrows by being the first male newsreader to dispense with a tie when presenting the news on the digital channel BBC 4. Since January 2003 he has fronted the BBC's main early evening news programme. Alagiah has also presented episodes of the *Assignment* series.

Alan, Ray

(1930–)

London-born ventriloquist/comedian ubiquitous in the 1950s and 1960s with his Mikki the Martian, Lord Charles, Tich and Quackers and Ali Cat dummies. In the 1970s and 1980s, Alan branched out into panel games, compering shows like *Three Little Words* and *Where in the World?* for HTV, and devising *Give Me Your Word* for the BBC. He also appeared regularly on THE GOOD OLD DAYS, calling on the experience he gained in variety theatre before TV beckoned (as a teenager, he worked as a call boy at Lewisham Hippodrome). In the 1980s, he guested alongside comedians Bobby Davro and Mike Reid in their own showcases. As a writer (often under the pseudonym of Ray Whyberd), Alan contributed scripts for HANCOCK, BOOTSIE AND SNUDGE, THE TWO RONNIES, Dave Allen and the Jimmy Cricket series *And There's More*.

Alas Smith and Jones ✶✶*/Smith and Jones* ✶

UK (BBC/Talkback) Comedy. BBC 2 1984–7; BBC 1 1989; 1991–2; 1995; 1997–8
DVD: BBC

Mel Smith, Griff Rhys-Jones

Producers **Martin Shardlow, Jimmy Mulville, John Kilby, Jamie Rix, Jon Plowman, Jon Magnusson**

● ***Comedy sketches with two members of the*** NOT THE NINE O'CLOCK NEWS ***team.***

Mimicking the title of the 1970s Western series starring Pete Duel and Ben Murphy, this vehicle for Mel and Griff's talents is best remembered for the 'head-to-head' scenes, where the idiotic Smith attempts to explain something straightforward to the even dimmer Jones. Another notable feature was the spoof home-video slot, years before Jeremy Beadle picked up a camcorder. After several seasons, the first word of the title was dropped and the show, taken into independent production, became simply *Smith and Jones*, switching to BBC 1 at the same time.

Albert

See *Dear Mother . . . Love Albert.*

Albion Market ✶

UK (Granada) Drama. ITV 1985–6

Derek Owen	**David Hargreaves**
Tony Fraser	**John Michie**
Lynne Harrison	**Noreen Kershaw**
Roy Harrison	**Jonathan Barlow**
Lisa O'Shea	**Sally Baxter**
Morris Ransome	**Bernard Spear**
Miriam Ransome	**Carol Kaye**
Duane Rigg	**Alistair Walker**
Larry Rigg	**Peter Benson**
Brenda Rigg	**Valerie Lilley**
Phil Smith	**Burt Caesar**
Raju Sharma	**Dev Sagoo**
Jaz Sharma	**Paul Bhattacharjee**
Lam Quoc Hoa	**Philip Tan**
Ly Nhu Chan	**Pik-Sen Lim**
Ted Pilkington	**Anthony Booth**
Viv Harker	**Helen Shapiro**
Geoff Travis	**Geoffrey Leesley**
Keith Naylor	**Derek Hicks**

Executive Producer **Bill Podmore**

Day-to-day ups and downs in a Manchester market.

Contrived as a sister programme to CORONATION STREET, with the aim of lifting ITV's weekend schedules (it went out on Fridays and Sundays), *Albion Market* arrived with a bang and left with a whimper. Much was made of the launch of this ambitious new series, but its poor audience ratings (beaten by *Wogan* and OPEN ALL HOURS) resulted in some ITV regions moving it to even less advantageous time-slots and *Albion Market* eventually shut up shop a year after it began, after exactly 100 half-hour episodes.

Set in a covered Manchester market (actually a converted Salford warehouse), the series monitored the complex lives of an ethnically mixed group of stall holders. At the forefront of the action were the likes of hunky, cake-selling wide-boy Tony Fraser, his 19-year-old girlfriend, Lisa O'Shea, her mum, Lynne Harrison, who ran a domestic goods stall, and Lynne's two-timing, no-good husband, Roy. Lam Quoc Hoa and Ly Nhu Chan were Vietnamese refugee cousins, Raju and Jaz Sharma were expelled Ugandan denim merchants, and Morris and Miriam Ransome were the Jewish couple who ran the pottery stall. Derek Owen was the harassed market supervisor, Phil, the West Indian, worked in the café and Duane Rigg was the market's teenage delinquent. Towards the end of its run, two new personalities were introduced in an attempt to give the show a lift. Sixties pop singer Helen Shapiro played Viv, a hairdresser, and former TILL DEATH US DO PART 'Scouse git' Tony Booth was seen as Ted Pilkington, licensee of the market's local, The Waterman's Arms.

Alda, Alan

(Alphonso d'Abruzzo; 1936–)

New York City-born actor/comedian/writer/director who shot to fame as Hawkeye Pierce in M*A*S*H. An ever-present in the series' 11-year run (though he did not appear in the original film), he gradually became one of the programme's creative controllers and picked up Emmys for acting, writing and directing on the show. Earlier, Alda had filled a satirist's chair on the US version of THAT WAS THE WEEK THAT WAS and made guest appearances in THE PHIL SILVERS SHOW, and the 1960s American dramas *The Nurses, The Trials of O'Brien* and *Coronet Blue*. Thanks to his extensive cinema work, his TV appearances have been thin since *M*A*S*H* ended, but he did create the sitcom *We'll Get By* and play Jack Burroughs in another sitcom he devised, *The Four Seasons*, based on his film of the same title. In 1999, he returned to the small screen as Dr Gabriel Lawrence in ER, and from 2004 he played Republican presidential candidate Arnold Vinick in THE WEST WING. He is the son of actor Robert Alda.

Alderton, John

(1940–)

Lincolnshire-born British comedy actor first seen in EMERGENCY – WARD 10 as Dr Richard Moone (alongside his first wife, Jill Browne) but best remembered as the hapless, naïve schoolteacher, Bernard Hedges, in PLEASE SIR! and *The Fenn Street Gang*. It was these series that launched Alderton into a succession of other sitcoms, most notably MY WIFE NEXT DOOR, THE UPCHAT LINE, WODEHOUSE PLAYHOUSE and *Father's Day*. Straight parts have still been welcomed, however. Alderton played chauffeur Thomas Watkins in UPSTAIRS, DOWNSTAIRS (opposite his second wife, Pauline Collins), and this led to a spin-off series, *Thomas and Sarah*. The duo have also starred together in the comedy NO HONESTLY and the rustic drama FOREVER GREEN, and provided voices for THE MR MEN follow-up, *Little Misses*. Alderton was also the narrator of the animation FIREMAN SAM and has made guest appearances in series like TALES OF THE UNEXPECTED, THE MRS BRADLEY MYSTERIES, HEARTBEAT, PEAK PRACTICE, DALZIEL AND PASCOE, DOWN TO EARTH and DOC MARTIN. In 2004 he was Mr Outhouse in HE KNEW HE WAS RIGHT.

Aldridge, Michael

(1920–94)

Distinguished, Somerset-born actor, a 1960s star as Dimmock in THE MAN IN ROOM 17, who resurfaced in 1985 as Seymour Utterthwaite, Foggy Dewhurst's replacement in LAST OF THE SUMMER WINE, and the inquisitive old buffer Caldicott, in CHARTERS AND CALDICOTT. He was also seen in *Love for Lydia, Love in a Cold Climate, Raven* (Prof. Young), TINKER, TAILOR, SOLDIER, SPY (Percy Alleline), MALICE AFORETHOUGHT (Sir Bernard Deverell), SPYSHIP (Sir Peter Hillmore), GAME, SET AND MATCH (Silas Gaunt), *The December Rose* (Lord Stirling), THE CHRONICLES OF NARNIA (the Professor) and *Stanley and the Women* (Dr Alfred Nash), with guest spots in series such as TALES OF THE UNEXPECTED and INSPECTOR MORSE.

Alexander, Jean

(1926–)

Liverpool-born actress for ever known to viewers as CORONATION STREET's Hilda Ogden. After appearances in DEADLINE MIDNIGHT, *Jacks and Knaves*, TOP SECRET, *Badger's Bend* and Z CARS, Jean Alexander joined the regulars on the *Street* in 1964 (having been seen briefly as a landlady in 1962), donning Hilda's curlers and pinny and moving into number 13 with Bernard Youens as her layabout husband, Stan. When she decided to retire, 23 years later, she had made Hilda a national institution. Her finest hour came in 1984 with the death of Youens and the passing of Stan, when she turned in one of the most acclaimed and moving pieces of acting in TV history. In the 1970s, while working on the *Street*, she appeared in the kids' drama series THE INTRUDER (Miss Binns), but in her post-Hilda days, Alexander has appeared as Granny Trellis in the sitcom RICH TEA AND SYMPATHY, Lily in THE PHOENIX AND THE CARPET and Kathleen Beresford in WHERE THE HEART IS, and enjoyed cameo performances in *Adam's Family Tree*, HEARTBEAT, BARBARA, *The Afternoon Play* and as Auntie Wainwright in LAST OF THE SUMMER WINE. She also provided voices for the Robbie the Reindeer cartoon *Hooves of Fire*.

Alexander, Sarah

(1971–)

Blonde English actress, daughter of a Panorama producer, whose major roles have included Susan in COUPLING, Mel in THE WORST WEEK OF MY LIFE and Dr Angela Hunter in GREEN WING. Sarah has also hosted THE 11 O'CLOCK SHOW and appeared in SMACK THE PONY, *Armstrong and Miller* and *Kappatoo* (Melanie). Guest parts have come in the likes of LOVEJOY, ANNA LEE, THE BILL, CATHERINE COOKSON, DROP THE DEAD DONKEY, RED DWARF, MIDSOMER MURDERS, DR TERRIBLE'S HOUSE OF HORRIBLE and *Look around You*.

Alexander, Terence

(1923–)

London-born actor who achieved semi-star status as Charlie Hungerford in BERGERAC. His earlier credits ranged from the 1950s aviation adventure series GARRY HALLIDAY (Bill Dodds), THE FORSYTE SAGA (Montague Dartie) and THE PALLISERS (Lord George), to the comedies *All Aboard, My Pal Bob*, HANCOCK'S HALF-HOUR, *The Dick Emery Show*, TERRY AND JUNE (Malcolm), THE FALL AND RISE OF REGINALD PERRIN, *Just Liz, Devenish*, and *Ben Travers Farces*. He has also been seen in THE NEW STATESMAN (Sir Greville McDonald), THE DETECTIVES (Charlie Hungerford again) and CASUALTY, plus single dramas and as comedy support for the likes of Eric Barker, Les Dawson, Jim Davidson and Allan Stewart. Among his many guest appearances are roles in 1960s classics like THE AVENGERS, THE BARON and GHOST SQUAD, plus THE PERSUADERS! and DOCTOR WHO.

ALF ★★

US (Lorimar) Situation Comedy. ITV 1987–9 (US: NBC 1986–90)
DVD: Lions Gate (Region 1 only)

ALF .... **Paul Fusco** *(voice only)*
Willie Tanner .... **Max Wright**
Kate Tanner .... **Anne Schedeen**
Lynn Tanner .... **Andrea Elson**
Brian Tanner .... **Benji Gregory**
Raquel Ochmonek .... **Liz Sheridan**
Trevor Ochmonek .... **John LaMotta**

Creators **Paul Fusco, Tom Patchett**
Executive Producers **Bernie Brillstein, Tom Patchett**

● ***An Alien Life Form (ALF) is looked after by a suburban American family.***

When ALF crash-lands his spacecraft on the Tanner family's garage roof, they take him into their kitchen and into their care. Just like ET, ALF instantly wins over his adoptive family. Unable to return home, as his planet (Melmac) has blown up and his spacecraft is beyond repair, he settles into a domestic lifestyle, to the bemusement of the Tanners' slow-witted neighbours, the Ochmoneks. Although warm-hearted, this furry, wisecracking alien is also somewhat mischievous, with a penchant for watching TV and over-eating. His favourite food is cat, sadly for the Tanners' own pet, Lucky. He is said to be 229 years old and, on his own planet, went by the name of Gordon Shumway. Like Mork in MORK AND MINDY, he presents viewers with a cynical view of the way of life on Earth. ALF's gravelly voice belonged to Paul Fusco, one of the show's creators.

Alfred Hitchcock Presents ★★

US (Universal/Shamley) Suspense Anthology. ITV 1957–66
(US: CBS 1955–60; NBC 1960–2; CBS 1962–4; NBC 1964–5)
DVD: Universal (Region 1 only)

Host **Alfred Hitchcock**

Executive Producer **Joan Harrison**
Producer **Norman Lloyd**

● ***An anthology of murder mysteries with a sting in the tale, introduced by the 'Master of Suspense'.***

Alfred Hitchcock himself directed only about 20 of the 300-plus episodes in this series, but he was very involved in selecting stories and plots (often from the work of authors such as Roald Dahl, Ray Bradbury and H. G. Wells). Other directors who worked on the programmes included Robert Altman, Sydney Pollack and William Friedkin, while famous actors such as Robert Redford, Burt Reynolds, Walter Matthau, Charles Bronson, Steve McQueen and William Shatner occasionally starred.

Each programme is introduced by Hitchcock with a creaky 'Good evening' and wraps up with his postscript, glibly explaining how the perpetrator of what seemed a perfect crime had been found out. Very often these deadpan intros and tailpieces have nothing at all to do with the actual tale being told, but are just a device allowing Hitchcock to appear in a bizarre and macabre setting – sitting in an electric chair or impaled on a pole like a scarecrow, for instance – highlighting his renowned black humour. No allusion is ever made to these weird props, and he delivers his piece to camera as if all is perfectly normal. The stories themselves are cleverly crafted, centring on crimes such as murder and blackmail, but each has a surprising twist in the tail. The series primarily consisted of 30-minute dramas, but over 90 stories were made in a 60-minute format and went out as *The Alfred Hitchcock Hour*. The doodled caricature used as the show's logo was drawn by the man himself, while the jaunty but sinister theme music was based on Gounod's 'Funeral March of a Marionette'.

The concept was intriguingly revived in the 1980s, using new stories or reworkings of old tales, but with the original

Hitchcock segments repainted in colour by computer technology. The producer of the original series was Norman Lloyd, who also acted and went on to become Dr Daniel Auschlander in ST ELSEWHERE.

Alfresco ✶

UK (Granada) Comedy. ITV 1983–4

Stephen Fry, Hugh Laurie, Emma Thompson, Ben Elton, Siobhan Redmond, Robbie Coltrane

Producers **Sandy Ross, John G. Temple**

● ***Comedy sketch vehicle for future big names.***

If asked to name Britain's biggest comedy and drama names at the end of the 20th century, many viewers would have included most of the stars in the above list. Back in 1983, however, Fry, Laurie, Thompson, Elton, Redmond and Coltrane were virtual unknowns, fledgling talents given their wings by Granada, which plucked them from training schools like the Cambridge Footlights and the Edinburgh Fringe in the hope of providing a response to the BBC's NOT THE NINE O'CLOCK NEWS. Here they fooled around in a late-night mélange of skits, most written by Ben Elton and some, experimentally, shot outdoors with hand-held video cameras. Two series were produced.

Alias Smith and Jones ✶✶

US (Universal) Western. BBC 2 1971–4 (US: ABC 1971–3)

Hannibal Heyes (Joshua Smith) ..... **Pete Duel**
Roger Davis
Jed 'Kid' Curry (Thaddeus Jones) ..... **Ben Murphy**
Clementine Hale ..... **Sally Field**
Harry Briscoe ..... **J. D. Cannon**
Narrator ..... **Roger Davis**
Ralph Story

Creator/Producer **Glen A. Larson**
Executive Producer **Roy Huggins**

● ***Jaunty exploits of a pair of likeable ex-bank robbers on the run in the Wild West.***

Hannibal Heyes and Kid Curry are two members of the Devil Hole Gang, wanted for a series of bank robberies. However, giving themselves up, they strike a deal with the Governor of Kansas so that if they stay out of trouble for a year they will be granted a pardon. The only snag is that virtually every lawman thinks the pair are still on the run, and plenty of other outlaws still hold a grudge against them or are keen to tempt them off the straight and narrow. Under their new identities of Joshua Smith and Thaddeus Jones, they roam the West, trying desperately to keep their heads down. But by the time the series closes they still haven't received their pardon. Clementine Hale, a friend of Curry's, is introduced in later episodes.

The series was devised as a TV cash-in on the huge success of the film *Butch Cassidy and the Sundance Kid*, but it was rocked at the end of 1971 by the suicide of Pete Duel. Roger Davis, the narrator of the series, was recast as Hannibal Heyes, and Ralph Story was brought in to do the voice-overs. Two TV movies were put together from various episodes of the series: *The Gun and the Nun* and *The Long Chase*.

Alice in Wonderland ✶✶✶

UK (BBC) Drama. BBC 1 1966
DVD: BFI Video Publishing

Alice ..... **Anne-Marie Mallik**
Mouse ..... **Alan Bennett**
Mad Hatter ..... **Peter Cook**
Frog Footman ..... **John Bird**
White Rabbit ..... **Wilfrid Brambell**
Dodo ..... **Finlay Currie**
Mock Turtle ..... **John Gielgud**
March Hare ..... **Michael Gough**
Dormouse ..... **Wilfrid Lawson**
Queen of Hearts ..... **Alison Leggatt**
Duchess ..... **Leo McKern**
Caterpillar ..... **Michael Redgrave**
Gryphon ..... **Malcolm Muggeridge**
King of Hearts ..... **Peter Sellers**

Writer/Producer **Jonathan Miller**

● ***Imaginative and controversial take on the classic children's novel.***

Jonathan Miller's star-studded interpretation of Lewis Carroll's famous children's tale set out to re-create, through exquisite period detail, the original 19th-century, middle-class atmosphere that surrounded its writing. Miller's aim was to look beyond the now-definitive Tenniel illustrations of the characters to take the book right back to its roots and gain an understanding of the Victorian views on children. Part of the plan was finding the right Alice. He discovered her in Anne-Marie Mallik, a 13-year-old with no ambitions to become an actress. To his pleasure, she gave a down-to-earth portrayal, with none of the sweetness child actors often bring to the role, as Alice – exemplifying Victorian childhood – encounters the mystifying, illogical world of adults through her adventures. The 80-minute film, aimed at adults rather than children, was also directed by Miller and complemented by a haunting soundtrack by Indian musician Ravi Shankar. It was broadcast just after Christmas 1966.

All About Me ✶

UK (Celador) Situation Comedy. BBC 1 2002–3

Colin Craddock ..... **Jasper Carrott**
Rupinder Craddock ..... **Meera Syal**
Nina Wadia
Raj ..... **Jamil Dhillon**
Luke Allder *(voice)*
Peter Craddock ..... **Ryan Cartwright**
Sima ..... **Natalia Keery-Fisher**
Leo Craddock ..... **Robert Cartin**
Kavita ..... **Alina Iqbal**
Billy ..... **Jonty Stephens**
Miriam ..... **Ann Bryson**

Writers **Steven Knight, Tanika Gupta, Geoff Rowley, John Phelps, Paul Alexander**
Producers **Mike Whitehill, Richard Boden**

● ***A child with disabilities observes life in his mixed-race family.***

In many respects, *All About Me* is a traditional family sitcom, albeit based around a family that in itself is far from traditional. Colin Craddock is a Birmingham builder now married to his second wife, Rupinder, herself also previously divorced.

They each have two children (Colin's Peter and Leo, and Rupinder's Raj and Kavita), and Rupinder also looks after her younger sister, Sima. Tradition plays its hand in the humour, which is generated largely from parent and children conflicts and minor domestic crises. For instance, when the family gains a new baby (Jay) at the end of series one, this leads both Colin and some of the other children to feel a little neglected. However, what marks this series out from the crowd is its central inclusion of a child with cerebral palsy. Very often the goings-on in the Craddock household are seen through the eyes of 12-year-old Raj (the 'Me' of the title), who is confined to a wheelchair. To further this idea, the character was provided with a synthesized voicebox from series two, enabling Raj to speak aloud his comments and interact more with the family (previously only a voice-over of his thoughts was provided). Also in series two, Meera Syal was replaced by her GOODNESS GRACIOUS ME colleague, Nina Wadia, in the role of Rupinder.

All along the Watchtower ✶

UK (BBC) Situation Comedy. BBC 1 1999

Flt Lt. Simon Harrison	**Chris Lang**
Wing Commander Campbell-Stokes	**Roger Blake**
Airman Tench	**Felix Bell**
Iain Guthrie	**Tony Roper**
Eilidh Guthrie	**Zoë Eeles**
Douggie Maclaggan	**Tom Watson**
Mrs Mulvey	**Georgie Glen**
Callum	**Michael Blair**

Writers **Pete Sinclair, Trevelyan Evans**
Producer **Peter Thornton**

Three RAF men are the only inhabitants of a deserted Scottish air base.

It may be the late 1990s, and the Cold War long thawed out, but no one has told the staff of the early-warning station at RAF Auchnacluchnie. Up here in the bleak Scottish Highlands, eccentric Wing Commander Campbell-Stokes and his young aide, Airman Tench, are still on high alert in case of Soviet attacks. Then in comes Flt Lt. Simon Harrison to evaluate their work and efficiency. When he discovers that, owing to an administrative error, there are only two men living on a base that still receives supplies for 300, he decides that their cushy little number is up and plans to recommend its closure. However, the base is part of an isolated, close-knit community headed up by Iain Guthrie, the local hotelier, and his attractive teacher daughter, Eilidh. And when he realizes how important the base is to the village, and its under-subscribed school, Harrison changes his report, only to find that he is given a permanent posting to Auchnacluchnie as a result. Just six episodes of this Sunday teatime, BBC Scotland comedy were produced.

All at No. 20 ✶

UK (Thames) Situation Comedy. ITV 1986–7

Sheila Haddon	**Maureen Lipman**
Monica Haddon	**Lisa Jacobs**
Richard Beamish	**Gary Waldhorn**
Carol	**Gabrielle Glaister**
Chris	**Gregory Doran**
Hamish	**David Bannerman**
Henry	**Martin Clunes**
Candy	**Carol Hawkins**

Creator **Richard Ommanney**
Writers **Richard Ommanney, Ian Davidson, Peter Vincent, Alex Shearer**
Producers **Peter Frazer-Jones, Mark Stuart**

A widow takes in lodgers to make ends meet.

Eighteen months after being left widowed and broke by a husband who possessed no life insurance, Londoner Sheila Haddon is faced with a predicament. She has a student daughter, Monica, to bring up and cannot simply rely on support from old friend (and would-be suitor) Richard Beamish, so she takes on part-time typing and other secretarial work and opens up her heavily mortgaged house to young lodgers. Understandably, the natural balance of her life is altered for ever as a succession of oddballs invade her home. First to arrive, and upset the tranquillity of No. 20, are Chris – new in London and looking for excitement, as well as a fast buck – Scotsman Hamish and medical man Henry. Also on board is Monica's friend, Carol, with Candy, a new lodger, joining in the second series.

All Creatures Great and Small ✶✶✶

UK (BBC) Drama. BBC 1 1978–80; 1983; 1985; 1988–90
DVD: BBC

James Herriot	**Christopher Timothy**
Siegfried Farnon	**Robert Hardy**
Tristan Farnon	**Peter Davison**
Helen Alderson/Herriot	**Carol Drinkwater**
	Lynda Bellingham
Mrs Hall	**Mary Hignett**
Mrs Pumphrey	**Margaretta Scott**
Calum Buchanan	**John McGlynn**
Deirdre McEwan	**Andrea Gibb**
Mrs Greenlaw	**Judy Wilson**
Jimmy Herriot	**Oliver Watson**
Rosie Herriot	**Rebecca Smith**
Mrs Alton	**Jean Heywood**

Producer **Bill Sellars**

Tales from a vet's life in the Yorkshire Dales.

Based on the celebrated autobiographical novels of James Herriot, *All Creatures Great and Small* proved to be an enormous success as a TV series, inspired by a 1974 cinema version featuring Simon Ward, and its 1976 sequel, *It Shouldn't Happen to a Vet*, starring John Alderton. With Christopher Timothy now pulling on the vet's wellies, the TV adaptation (with its echoes of DR FINLAY'S CASEBOOK) took viewers back to the 1930s as Herriot arrives at Skeldale House, home of the veterinary practice in the North Riding town of Darrowby (the real-life Askrigg). There he joins senior partner Siegfried Farnon, his easy-going brother, Tristan, and housekeeper Mrs Hall, helps to build up the practice and deals with all manner of agricultural and domestic animal ailments. If James is not preventing foot and mouth or groping around up a cow's posterior, he is treating the likes of Tricki-Woo, the pampered Pekinese owned by villager Mrs Pumphrey.

James meets and marries Helen Alderson (later to bear him a son, Jimmy, and a daughter, Rosie), before the series 'ends' after three years when James and Tristan head off to join the war effort (Herriot's original novels had run out). A couple of Christmas specials kept the concept alive during the early

1980s, before public clamour was answered with a new series in 1988.

With Peter Davison largely tied up elsewhere and his appearances restricted to a minimum, a new vet is added to the cast: the naïve, badger-keeping idealist, Calum Buchanan, joins the practice. The part of Helen is taken over by 'Oxo mum' Lynda Bellingham, and the time has moved on to the post-war years. The writers invented new stories and situations for the team, but the cosy, country air, the slow pace of village life and the warm, gentle humour are maintained. The series ran for three more seasons, plus another Christmas special. The programme's sweeping theme music was composed by Johnny Pearson.

All for Love ✶✶

UK (Granada) Drama Anthology. ITV 1982–3

Producer **Roy Roberts**

● ***An anthology of modest love tales.***

Adapting the works of some less-familiar writers, including William Trevor, Francis King, Rumer Godden and Elizabeth Taylor (not the actress!), *All for Love* pieces together a collection of self-contained dramas, with romance as the central theme. Among the stars signed up for leading roles were Joan Plowright, Frank Finlay, Geraldine McEwan, Nigel Havers, Lionel Jeffries, Jean Simmons and Maggie Smith. Bob Larbey was among the various scriptwriters.

All Gas and Gaiters ✶✶

UK (BBC) Situation Comedy. BBC 1 1967; 1969–71

DVD: BBC

Revd Mervyn Noote .... **Derek Nimmo**
Bishop .... **William Mervyn**
Archdeacon .... **Robertson Hare**
Dean .... **John Barron**
Ernest Clark

Writers **Edwin Apps, Pauline Devaney**
Producers **Stuart Allen, John Howard Davies**

● ***Fun and games in the cloisters of a cathedral.***

Gently poking fun at the clergy (one of the first comedies to do so), *All Gas and Gaiters* centres on the farcical team at St Ogg's Cathedral, namely its bishop, archdeacon and, particularly, its bumbling, ultra-sincere, plummy chaplain, the Revd Mervyn Noote. Their adversary is the rather sober Dean. Nimmo later took his dithery clerical creation on to OH BROTHER and its sequel, *Oh Father*, playing Brother/Father Dominic. *All Gas and Gaiters* began life as a COMEDY PLAYHOUSE presentation in 1966, with the subsequent five series scripted by husband and wife writers Edwin Apps and Pauline Devaney.

All in Good Faith ✶

UK (Thames) Situation Comedy. ITV 1985–8

Revd Philip Lambe .... **Richard Briers**
Emma Lambe .... **Barbara Ferris**
Susan Jameson
Peter Lambe .... **James Campbell**
Miranda Lambe .... **Lydia Smith**
Major Andrews .... **James Cossins**
Oscar Randolph .... **T. P. McKenna**
John Woodvine
Desmond .... **Frank Middlemiss**

Writer **John Kane**
Producers **John Howard Davies, Peter Frazer-Jones**

● ***A middle-aged vicar leaves his cosy country parish for an inner-city post.***

Stricken by a mid-life crisis of conscience, the Revd Philip Lambe decides to give up his homely, rural church and its friendly, wealthy parishioners to seek pastures new in the heart of a modern Midlands city (ironically named Edendale) – much to the shock and dismay of his wife, Emma, son, Peter, and daughter, Miranda. The series explores the Lambes' problems in their new, troubled environment, with typical sitcom stress resulting from dealings with a poltergeist and a double-booked parish hall. Major Andrews is Lambe's churchwarden in series one; Oscar Randolph is a local supermarket tycoon dragged into fundraising affairs in later series.

All in the Family/Archie Bunker's Place ✶✶✶

US (Yorkin-Lear) Situation Comedy. BBC1/BBC2 1971–5 (US: CBS 1971–83)

DVD: Sony (Region 1 only)

Archie Bunker .... **Carroll O'Connor**
Edith Bunker .... **Jean Stapleton**
Gloria Stivic .... **Sally Struthers**
Mike Stivic .... **Rob Reiner**
Lionel Jefferson .... **Mike Evans**
Louise Jefferson .... **Isabel Sanford**
Henry Jefferson .... **Mel Stewart**
George Jefferson .... **Sherman Hemsley**
Irene Lorenzo .... **Betty Garrett**
Frank Lorenzo .... **Vincent Gardenia**

Creators **Norman Lear, Bud Yorkin**
Writer/Producer **Norman Lear**

● ***Innovative American sitcom featuring an arrogant, bigoted labourer and his many prejudices.***

Archie Bunker is America's Alf Garnett and his family, too, bears a strong resemblance to members of the Garnett household. Archie's wife, Edith, affectionately known as 'Dingbat', is somewhat dim, and his sales assistant daughter, Gloria, has disappointed her father by marrying Mike, an antagonizingly liberal sociology student of Polish extraction, whom Archie calls 'Meathead'. They live with the Bunkers and add to the domestic friction.

Victims of Archie's pigheadedness are his mixed-race colleagues at the Prendergast Tool and Die Company, and the Bunkers' ethnic neighbours in Queens, NYC, the Jeffersons (black) and the Lorenzos (Italian). The Jeffersons were eventually given their own series, and another spin-off was *Maude*, based around Edith's cousin, Maude Findlay (played by Bea Arthur).

The series ran until 1983 in the USA, but towards the end of the 1970s the programme format was drastically restructured. Archie buys shares in a bar and Gloria, Mike and their son, Joey, move to California. A little niece, Stephanie Mills (played by Danielle Brisebois), fills the gap by moving in with Archie and Edith, but actress Jean Stapleton eventually tired of the series and was written out. Edith, it is revealed, has died of a stroke. During these changes, the series was renamed *Archie Bunker's Place*.

Unashamedly based on Johnny Speight's TILL DEATH US DO PART, *All in the Family* became a landmark in US television comedy and was the top show for five years. This was a programme that dared to raise such issues as race, politics and sex. No one had dared to speak like that on American TV before and, after Archie Bunker, the twee, 'Honey I'm home' domestic sitcom was dead. Like Alf Garnett in the UK, he became part of American society.

All Night Long ✱

UK (BBC) Situation Comedy. BBC 1 1994

Bill Chivers	**Keith Barron**
Vanda	**Maureen Beattie**
Clare	**Dinah Sheridan**
Tom	**Angus Lennie**
Terry	**Jacqueline Reddin**
WPC Jackson	**Jan Winters**
PC Digby	**John Phythian**
Wally	**Paul Grunert**
Courtney	**Robert McKewley**

Writers **Dick Fiddy, Mark Wallington**
Producer **Harold Snoad**

An all-night bakery is the rendezvous for a gang of nocturnal workers.

This short-lived (six-episode) comedy was set in Chivers Bakery somewhere in London. Owner Bill Chivers has a chequered past. He used to be a burglar but now makes dough honestly and his cakes no longer contain files. However, his life is complicated by the small group of people who like to use his premises as an all-night community centre – people like wheelchair-bound Clare, who drops in for inspiration for her latest thriller novel; stripper Terry; Wally, a mini-cab driver; and comedy coppers Jackson and Digby. Helping and hindering Bill are Scots sweeper-up Tom, possibly illegal Romanian immigrant Vanda, and Courtney, another crook on the road to reform.

All Our Yesterdays ✱✱

UK (Granada) Documentary. ITV 1960–73; 1987–9

Presenters **James Cameron, Brian Inglis, Bernard Braden**

Producers **Tim Hewat, Douglas Terry, Jeremy Isaacs, David Plowright, Bill Grundy, Mike Murphy**

Nostalgic documentary series looking back 25 years in time.

Using old cinema newsreels, *All Our Yesterdays* reflected on events taking place in the world in the same week 25 years earlier. Consequently, the first programme looked back to a week in the year 1935. Foreign correspondent James Cameron added footnotes to the film coverage until he was replaced as frontman by Brian Inglis after one year. When the series was resurrected in 1987, Bernard Braden was the new host and television archives were raided for footage. Over 600 editions were produced.

All Quiet on the Preston Front

See *Preston Front*.

All Square

See *It's a Square World*

All Star Comedy Carnival

See *Christmas Night with the Stars*.

All the King's Men ✱✱✱

UK (BBC/WGBH Boston) Historical Drama. BBC 1 1999
DVD: BBC

Capt. Frank Beck	**David Jason**
Queen Alexandra	**Maggie Smith**
Sgt Ted Grimes	**William Ash**
Lady Frances	**Sonya Walger**
2nd Lt. Hon. Frederick Radley	**Stuart Bunce**
King George V	**David Troughton**
Cpl Herbert Batterbee	**Ed Waters**
Pte Chad Batterbee	**Tom Burke**
Pte Will Needham	**James Murray**
Pte Davy Croft	**Ben Crompton**
Pte George Dacre	**Danny Worters**
Arthur Beck	**Eamon Boland**
Lt. Alec Beck	**Jo Stone-Fewings**
2nd Lt. Evelyn Beck	**James Hillier**
Mary Beck	**Phyllis Logan**
Capt. Claude Howlett	**Patrick Malahide**
Peggy Batterbee	**Emma Cunniffe**
Oswald Yeoman	**Adam Kotz**
Queen Mary	**Gaye Brown**
Revd Pierrepoint Edwards	**Ian McDiarmid**

Writer **Alma Cullen**
Executive Producers **Hilary Salmon, Jane Tranter, Rebecca Eaton**
Producer **Gareth Neame**

A battalion of royal-estate workers mysteriously vanishes during a World War I battle.

On 12 August 1915 a company of men, known as the 5th Battalion Norfolk Regiment and formed from workers on the royal Sandringham estate, was sent to break through Turkish defences on the Sulva Plain at Gallipoli. A strange mist was said to have enveloped them and they were not heard of again. Word was spread that they might have been taken, providentially, to Heaven. In 1991, Prince Edward narrated a documentary film that suggested that the men had in fact been captured by the Turks and shot. A mass grave had been discovered. It was the incompetence and arrogance of its commanding generals that took care of the men, not some divine chaperone. Through miscalculation and bad communications, the officers had sent these brave and loyal Norfolk men to their deaths and, despite personal interest from Queen Alexandra, whose estate workers they were, they declined to get to the bottom of the story.

Prince Edward was also allied to this film dramatization of those tragic events, which was based on the book *The Vanished Battalion*, by Nigel McCrery, and royal sanction was given for the use of the Sandringham estate for filming. The story leads with Frank Beck, a land agent who was asked by King Edward VII in 1909 to put together a territorial army out of the estate employees. At 53, Beck was officially too old to go himself when World War I broke out, but, seeing himself as the father figure, he defied orders and went anyway. Among his men – drawn from all parts of society, from stable boys to toffs – were his brother, Arthur, and medical officer Claude

Howlett. The Revd Pierrepoint Edwards is the man charged by royalty to discover the truth. With torrid battle scenes filmed on the Andalusian coast of Spain, this feature-length drama was directed by Julian Jarrold and won much acclaim.

All You Need is Love ✶✶

UK (LWT/Theatre Projects) Documentary. ITV 1977

Producers **Richard Pilbrow, Neville C. Thompson**

● ***A history of 20th-century popular music.***
Researched in depth, this 17-part documentary traces the development of popular music in all its strands, from jazz and blues to 1970s chart pop and progressive rock. Much obscure footage is retrieved and interviews with music legends are wrapped around the narrative. The brains behind the project was Tony Palmer, one of the first heavyweight rock critics and producer of the controversial 1968 OMNIBUS film *All My Loving*, which interwove music and musicians with horrifying scenes of war and war crimes. Palmer also penned the accompanying book, published by Futura.

All Your Own ✶

UK (BBC) Children's Entertainment. BBC 1952–61

Presenters **Huw Wheldon, Jimmy Logan, Brian Johnston, Cliff Morgan**

Editors **Cliff Michelmore, Joanne Symons**
Producers **Michael Westmore, Tony Arnold, Barbara Hammond**

● ***Showcase for young talents and children's hobbies.***
Hosted for the most part by future BBC Television Managing Director Huw Wheldon, and edited by a young Cliff Michelmore from 1952, *All Your Own* invited youngsters from all over the UK to show off their skills and talents or discuss their hobbies and pastimes. Guitarist John Williams was featured on one programme and used it as a stepping stone to greater things. Led Zeppelin's Jimmy Page was, it has been reported, another youthful guest.

Allen, Dave

(David Tynan O'Mahony; 1936–2005)

Suave Irish comedian, a former journalist and Red Coat, famed for monologues casually delivered from a high stool with a drink and cigarette to hand. His favourite hunting grounds were sex and religion (also parodied in short sketches and echoed in his closing catchphrase, 'May your god go with you'). After he initially appeared on *The Val Doonican Show* in 1965 and compered SUNDAY NIGHT AT THE LONDON PALLADIUM, Allen's first solo series was *Tonight with Dave Allen*, for ITV in 1967, which was followed by *The Dave Allen Show* for BBC 2. However, it was through numerous series of *Dave Allen at Large* for the BBC in the 1970s that he became a household name. Later 1970s contributions included *Dave Allen and Friends, Dave Allen* and the documentary *Dave Allen in Search of the Great English Eccentric*. He returned to television (and ITV) in the 1990s with a new (and somewhat controversial) series of frank monologues.

Allen, Gracie

(1902–64)

The scatterbrained TV and real-life wife of George Burns. Together they worked their way from vaudeville, through radio to TV, where, in 1950, they created one of America's earliest comedy hits, THE BURNS AND ALLEN SHOW, in which they played themselves in a sitcom environment. Gracie's trademarks were a confused logic and a flair for malapropisms. After eight years, Gracie retired, leaving George to continue alone. She died in 1964 after a long illness. Note: although her year of birth is given here as 1902, it may easily be 1895 or even 1906 – the truth remains a mystery.

Allen, Irwin

(1916–91)

American producer/director responsible for some of the most extravagant science-fiction series of the 1960s, all created on the tightest of budgets. Much use was made of stock film footage and cinema cast-offs to add depth to his studio-bound dramas. His first major TV offering was VOYAGE TO THE BOTTOM OF THE SEA in 1964, inspired by his 1962 film release with the same title (and most of the same props). Then came LOST IN SPACE, THE TIME TUNNEL and LAND OF THE GIANTS, as well as the less memorable *The Swiss Family Robinson*. Irwin later co-directed the Oscar-winning movie *The Towering Inferno*.

Allen, Jim

(1926–99)

Manchester-born former miner and socialist-minded playwright, often in collaboration with director Ken Loach, who moved on from scripting for CORONATION STREET to creating some particularly poignant – and controversial – dramas for the BBC, most notably *The Lump* (1967), *The Big Flame* (1969), *The Rank and File* (1971) and the series DAYS OF HOPE. The last enraged pillars of the Establishment, who claimed it crossed the boundary between fiction and propaganda in its story of two young pacifist lovers in the era of the Great War and General Strike. Later works included *The Spongers* (1978), UNITED KINGDOM (1981) and *The Gathering Seed* (1983).

Allen, Keith

(1953–)

Llanelli-born comedian/actor often associated with 'bad boy' parts, but with a range of roles to his name. These include Rex in MAKING OUT, Thompson in A VERY BRITISH COUP, Jackson Pace in *Jackson Pace: The Great Years*, Jonas Chuzzlewit in MARTIN CHUZZLEWIT, Shelley in *The Bite*, Byron Flitch in *Born to Run*, Dexter in ROGER ROGER, Jack in *Jack of Hearts*, Vinnie in BOB MARTIN, Peter Savage in ADRIAN MOLE: THE CAPPUCCINO YEARS, Major Gen. Colin Gubbins in *Killing Hitler* and Tony Whitman in *Bodies*. Previously, he was one of the COMIC STRIP team, featuring in most of their satires. He also presented and directed *You're Fayed*, a documentary about Mohamed Al Fayed. Guest appearances have been in series like THE YOUNG ONES, *Sharman*, DANGERFIELD, INSPECTOR MORSE, MURDER IN MIND, SPACED, BLACK BOOKS, NEW TRICKS and AGATHA CHRISTIE'S MARPLE. Allen has also dabbled in songwriting and he co-wrote the 1990 England World Cup Squad/New Order hit,

'World in Motion', as well as the later football anthem 'Vindaloo' (performed by Allen as Fat Les).

Allen, Patrick

(1927–)

Square-jawed, bass-voiced actor and voice-over specialist, born in Malawi and perhaps best remembered as the man in the helicopter in the Barratt homes commercial, though also star of several dramas, including CRANE, BRETT and *Hard Times*. His other TV credits have included *Glencannon* (as Bosun Hughes), *The Dick Emery Show*, THE WINDS OF WAR, THE BLACK ADDER, THE BRACK REPORT (Barry Madoc), *Body and Soul* (Walter Street), numerous single plays, plus guest roles in assorted action series like THE AVENGERS, THE ADVENTURES OF AGGIE, MAN IN A SUITCASE, OUT OF THIS WORLD, THE CHAMPIONS, UFO, THE PROTECTORS, VAN DER VALK and THE RETURN OF SHERLOCK HOLMES. In the 1990s, he provided voice-overs for THE SMELL OF REEVES AND MORTIMER. Allen married actress Sarah Lawson (the third governor in WITHIN THESE WALLS).

Allen, Ronald

(1930–91)

Although Ronald Allen is best recalled as lugubrious David Hunter in CROSSROADS, his career began well before that famous motel opened its doors. His matinee-idol looks could well have seen him in Hollywood in the 1950s, but the several small film roles he gained failed to take him to the top. However, his TV break came in 1962, when he was cast as editor Ian Harman in the woman's magazine drama COMPACT, a part which he followed in 1966 with that of Mark Wilson, one of Brentwich United's managers, in the soccer drama UNITED! Otherwise, he guested in THE AVENGERS, DANGER MAN and DOCTOR WHO and joined *Crossroads* in 1969, remaining with the programme for 16 years, until he was surprisingly axed by a new regime in 1985, together with his screen (and future real-life) wife, Sue Lloyd. Later, the suave but rather starchy Allen was seen to 'loosen up', taking a cameo role as the gay Uncle Quentin in the COMIC STRIP's *Five Go Mad in Dorset*.

'Allo 'Allo ★★★

UK (BBC) Situation Comedy. BBC 1 1984–9; 1991–2
DVD: Universal

René Artois	**Gorden Kaye**
Edith Artois	**Carmen Silvera**
Yvette Carte-Blanche	**Vicki Michelle**
Maria Recamier	**Francesca Gonshaw**
Michelle Dubois	**Kirsten Cooke**
Col. Kurt Von Strohm	**Richard Marner**
Capt. Hans Geering	**Sam Kelly**
Lt. Gruber	**Guy Siner**
Helga Geerhart	**Kim Hartman**
Herr Otto Flick	**Richard Gibson**
	David Janson
Englebert Von Smallhausen	**John Louis Mansi**
Officer Crabtree	**Arthur Bostrom**
Gen. Erich Von Klinkerhoffen	**Hilary Minster**
Mimi La Bonq	**Sue Hodge**
Monsieur Roger Leclerc	**Jack Haig**
	Derek Royle
	Robin Parkinson
Monsieur Alphonse	**Kenneth Connor**
Fanny La Fan/Leclerc	**Rose Hill**
Flying Officer Fairfax	**John D. Collins**
Flying Officer Carstairs	**Nicholas Frankau**
Capt. Alberto Bertorelli	**Gavin Richards**
	Roger Kitter

Creators **Jeremy Lloyd, David Croft**
Producers **David Croft, John B. Hobbs**

A wartime French café-owner is in demand with both the Germans and the Resistance.

René Artois is the proprietor of a café (Café René) in the northern French town of Nouvion. He runs the bar with his wife, Edith, and a couple of shapely waitresses, Yvette and Maria. At least, that is until the Germans occupy the town. He then finds himself having to pander to the local Nazis, headed by Colonel Von Strohm, the clumsy Captain Geering and the gay Lt. Gruber. At the same time, his bar is taken over as a French Resistance safehouse, primarily to house two gormless British airmen, Fairfax and Carstairs (Adamson in the pilot episode, shown in 1982). In this way, this man's war becomes rather more trying than others'.

Introducing each episode by speaking to camera, René updates viewers on earlier happenings (the show is run as a serial farce). Usually, the highly exaggerated plots centre on René's reluctant attempts to help the airmen escape, or to sabotage the Germans' efforts to steal a priceless painting, the so-called *Fallen Madonna with the Big Boobies* by Van Clomp. Instigator of most of the action is the local Resistance leader, Michelle, commandeerer of René's bar and supplier of the show's prime catchphrase, 'Leesten very carefully. I shall say this only wance.' Michelle is aided by Officer Crabtree, an inept British agent disguised as a gendarme, spouting appalling French which translates into warped English phrases like 'Good moaning'. (The use of stereotypical accents to convey different languages was one of *'Allo 'Allo*'s successes.) Also influencing affairs is the cruel Herr Flick, the limping local Gestapo chief who demands kinky affection from his adjutant, Helga, and abuses his incompetent sidekick, Von Smallhausen.

Around the central action there are plenty of subplots: René's steamy affairs with both Yvette and Maria (later replaced by Mimi), the marriage of Edith's partly deaf, bedridden mother, Fanny, to ageing Resistance forger Leclerc, and René's alleged death, which allows Edith to court Monsieur Alphonse, the local vintner and undertaker with a 'dicky ticker' and a 'small 'earse with a small 'orse'. But the programme also has well-rehearsed running jokes: Edith's excruciating singing, for instance, which forces the bar's customers to stuff their ears with cheese; Lt. Gruber's advances to René; and René's (codename Nighthawk) laboured attempts to get the wireless to work from its secret hiding place beneath Fanny's chamber pot (the series took its name from his opening words to London).

Rich in innuendo and slapstick, *'Allo 'Allo* was much criticized for its 'bad taste', though it always claimed to be poking fun at over-the-top wartime dramas and not at the cruelty of war itself. SECRET ARMY was its main target. When it ended, after nearly nine years, the war had finished and Nouvion was liberated. Viewers were treated to a 'flashforward' to the present day and introduced to René's son (also played by Gorden Kaye), who explained what had happened to the locals in the post-war years to a visiting Gruber, who had, surprisingly, married Helga. A West End stage version, with original cast members, was also produced.

Ally McBeal ★★★

US (20th Century Fox/David E. Kelley) Comedy Drama. Channel 4 1998–2002 (US: Fox 1997–2002)
DVD: Fox

Ally McBeal .... **Calista Flockhart**
Billy Thomas .... **Gil Bellows**
Georgia Thomas .... **Courtney Thorne-Smith**
Richard Fish .... **Greg Germann**
Renée Radick .... **Lisa Nicole Carson**
Elaine Vassal .... **Jane Krakowski**
John 'The Biscuit' Cage .... **Peter MacNicol**
Jennifer 'Whipper' Cone .... **Dyan Cannon**
Dr Tracey Clark .... **Tracey Ullman**
Ling Woo .... **Lucy Liu**
Nelle Porter .... **Portia de Rossi**
Mark Albert .... **James LeGros**
Larry Paul .... **Robert Downey Jr**
Corretta Lipp .... **Regina Hall**
Glenn Foy .... **James Marsden**
Jenny Shaw .... **Julianne Nicholson**
Raymond Milbury .... **Josh Hopkins**
Maddie Harrington .... **Hayden Panettiere**

Creator/Executive Producer **David E. Kelley**
Producers **Mike Listo, Jonathan Pontell**

● ***An ambitious but neurotic girl works in a quirky law firm.***

Described by some critics as a 'love it or loathe it' series, *Ally McBeal* was the US hit of 1997–8, setting a new agenda with its off-beat format, focus on moral dilemmas and exploration of the emotional outpourings of the title character. In the opening episode, the 27-year-old Ms McBeal walks out of her job in a large Boston law practice after being sexually harassed by her boss. She bumps into Richard Fish, a money-mad old college friend, and accepts an offer of a job at his new law firm instead. Unfortunately, Fish has also taken on Ally's ex-lover, Billy Thomas, the man she has been longing for since their Harvard days and before. The fact that he is now married to a beautiful and successful fellow lawyer (later colleague), Georgia, makes the situation even less comfortable. (This emotional triangle features prominently in the stories to follow.)

Fish is an appropriate head of this wacky law firm, which also features his wily, oddball partner, John Cage – nicknamed 'The Biscuit' – and gossipy, singing secretary Elaine. Many of the team's deeper conversations take place in the unisex loo at Cage/Fish & Associates. External support for the neurotic Ally comes from her down-to-earth roommate, district attorney Renée Radick. Also seen at times are Fish's older lover, judge 'Whipper' Cone, and Ally's straight-talking but crazy analyst, Dr Tracey Clark. Icy Nelle Porter and single-minded Ling Woo are later additions to the legal team, and also prominent is Robert Downey Jr as lawyer Larry Page, a man who steal's Ally's heart (albeit briefly as Downey was arrested mid-series for violating his parole conditions and had to be written out). In the final season, an intriguing addition is Maddie Harrington, Ally's long-lost daughter.

To highlight the heroine's mental turmoil, the producers introduced fantasy cartoon elements, like Ally's foot forcing its way into her mouth whenever she dropped a clanger, or arrows pounding into her heart when she was rejected in love. Her vibrant imagination comes to life, too, such as in scenes where she romps naked with Billy in a mug of cappuccino. There is also a computer-generated dancing baby named Mr Huggy that bops to the song 'Hooked on a Feeling' and personifies Ally's subconscious desire to have a child of her own. The baby gained a cult following and a catalogue of successful spin-off merchandise.

Ally McBeal turned unknown actress Calista Flockhart into a superstar and thrust her into the limelight as a style guru. Her character's comfy pyjamas became the rage at American department stores, her hemlines were attacked by puritans for being much too short, and her ultra-slim figure brought concern for the way it 'promoted' the thin look among impressionable girls. However, plenty of female viewers identified with McBeal's frank expression of a modern woman's mind. A CD of *Ally McBeal* music featured tracks by singer Vonda Shepard, who performed in most episodes. Other musical stars to make cameo appearances were Barry White, Tina Turner, Sting, Jon Bon Jovi and Elton John.

Always and Everyone/A&E ★★

UK (Granada) Medical Drama. ITV 1999–2002

Robert Kingsford .... **Martin Shaw**
Dr Christine Fletcher .... **Niamh Cusack**
Mike Gregson .... **David Harewood**
Louise Macken .... **Esther Hall**
Stuart Phelan .... **Paul Warriner**
Dr David Scobie .... **David Partridge**
Cathy Jordan .... **Jane Slavin**
Yvonne .... **Kim Vithana**
Terry Harker .... **Connor McIntyre**
Judy Enshaw .... **Katie McEwen**
Issy .... **Catherine Russell**
Freddie .... **Bill Rodgers**
Alan .... **Dean Williamson**
Andrew Argyle .... **Dominic Mafham**
Stella .... **Cathy Tyson**
Kate Brady .... **Tamzin Malleson**
Jack Turner .... **Michael Kitchen**
Sam Docherty .... **Jane Danson**
Raz Amin .... **Silas Carson**
Danny Barton .... **James Murray**
Ruth Cole .... **Jaye Griffiths**
James Da Costa .... **Ben Taylor**
Poppy Jonston .... **Michele Austin**
Sunita Verma .... **Parminder Nagra**
Raj Verma .... **Bhasker Patel**
Jean Kenning .... **Judy Holt**
Jeffrey Drummond .... **Don Gallagher**

Producers **Francis Hopkinson, Pamela Wilson, David Boulter, Richard Broke**

● ***Every day brings a new challenge for the staff of a modern casualty unit.***

There's rarely a quiet moment in the accident and emergency ward of St Victor's Hospital NHS Trust in Manchester, as the dedicated staff can confirm. Heading up the pressurized unit are consultant surgeon Robert Kingsford and head registrar Christine Fletcher – work rivals inevitably doomed to fall into an intimate relationship following early personal tragedy for Kingsford. They cope calmly and for the most part rationally with a steady influx of road accident victims, would-be suicides and drunks who decide to extend their night out into these modern, well-maintained hospital wards. Kingsford and Fletcher are assisted by a capable bunch of medics including Mike Gregson, Stuart Phelan, Louise Macken, Cathy Jordan and David Scobie, who, like their superiors, are not short of the odd personal or family problem, plus ancillary staff such as the security guards, who supply light relief as they monitor the closed-circuit video images. New internal stresses are introduced later with the arrival of egocentric trauma surgeon Jack Turner and feisty nurse Sam Docherty among others.

Despite being mocked as a British ER on its arrival, *A&E* (as it became from series three in 2001, dispensing with the contrived original title, *Always and Everyone*) instantly delivered the goods as far as both critics and viewers were concerned. By shunning the 'how the accident happened' preamble, trimming back the hysteria and concentrating mainly on the workings of a skilled team, it proved there *was* room in the schedules for yet another medical drama.

Amazing Spider-Man, The ✳

US (Charles Fries) Science Fiction. ITV 1981 (US: CBS 1978)

Peter Parker/Spider-man .... **Nicholas Hammond**
Rita Conway .... **Chip Fields**
J. Jonah Jameson .... **Robert F. Simon**
Capt. Barbera .... **Michael Pataki**
Julie Masters .... **Ellen Bry**

Executive Producers **Charles Fries, Daniel R. Goodman**

A young scientist acquires superhuman powers after a bite from a contaminated spider.

Peter Parker is a student scientist at Empire State University in New York and works part-time as a photographer at the *Daily Bugle*. One day, he is bitten on the hand by a radioactive spider and as a result is endowed with weird spider-like skills and instincts. He gains a strange sixth sense (which allows him to anticipate danger), incredible strength and the power to climb sheer walls and walk on ceilings. Using his scientific knowledge, Parker then develops a special liquid which, when shot from his wrist, soldifies in the air to act as a tough cable, like a spider's web. Anonymously he begins to use his abilities for the benefit of mankind, donning a blue and red costume to track down criminals. Sadly, Parker is never at ease with his dual identity, being a rather gentle, restrained person who abhors violence. J. Jonah Jameson is his superior at the paper and Rita, his secretary, is Parker's best friend. Girlfriend photographer Julie Masters is added later in the run. This short-lived series was based on the *Marvel* comic strip created by Stan Lee and illustrator Steve Ditko. A cartoon version had already been seen in the late 1960s, with the hero's voice provided by Bernard Cowan and Paul Sols.

Amazing Stories

See *Steven Spielberg's Amazing Stories*.

Ambassador ✳✳

UK (Ecosse Films/BBC) Drama. BBC 1 1998–9

Harriet Smith .... **Pauline Collins**
John Stone .... **Denis Lawson**
Stephen Tyler .... **William Chubb**
Kevin Flaherty .... **Owen Roe**
Julian Wadham .... **Dominic Mafham**
Jennifer .... **Alison McKenna**
Becky .... **Sarah Markland**
Nate Smith .... **Tim Matthews**
Sam Smith .... **Tom Connolly**
Catherine Grieve .... **Eve Matheson**
Michael Cochrane .... **Peter Egan**
Eileen .... **Gina Moxley**
Susan .... **Sinead Clarkin**

Producers **Stephen Smallwood, Louise Berridge**

Problems for a female British ambassador.

Harriet Smith is the new British Ambassador to the Republic of Ireland. The sensitive Anglo-Irish relationship notwithstanding, it is a tricky appointment, made even trickier by Harriet's emotional response to situations, her straight talking and her grammar school upbringing that sets her at odds with surrounding Establishment figures. Problems range from Irish accusations that the British have sunk one of their trawlers to hostage-taking, drug-smuggling and attempted assassination. It is not the first time that Harriet's life has been placed in threat: previously, in Beirut, her own husband was killed by a bomb that was intended for her. This has left her struggling to manage the upbringing of her two sons, Nate, a hard-to-handle student also living in Dublin, and the young Sam, who still lives with his mother. Supporting Harriet professionally is secret service agent John Stone.

The second series introduces a love interest for Harriet in the form of dodgy construction magnate Michael Cochrane, and Harriet's personal life is placed more under the spotlight than in early episodes. She also gains a new assistant in Catherine Grieve.

America ✳✳✳✳

UK (BBC) Documentary. BBC 2 1972–3
DVD: BBC

Presenter **Alistair Cooke**

Writer **Alistair Cooke**
Producer **Michael Gill**

Thoughtful retrospective on the growth of the USA.

'A personal history of the United States' is the subtitle to this well-considered account of the birth and development of a nation, presented from the viewpoint of Alistair Cooke, a top British correspondent and an American citizen. Cooke's dual nationality allows him to portray the USA from both internal and external viewpoints, fashioning a TV history designed for consumption on both sides of the Atlantic. In 13 episodes he charts the hopes, experiences and achievements of the men who shaped the most powerful country in the world, tracing developments from before Columbus right up to the Nixon era.

His compassionate, gentle narration and poignant anecdotes allow Cooke to convey the enormousness of the problems facing the earliest settlers, and he incisively analyses the political movements and the agricultural and industrial changes that moulded the country over the centuries, winning wide acclaim for his understanding and perception. His conclusion centres on the fact that America at the turn of the 1970s falls a long way short of the dreams of its founding fathers.

Alistair Cooke was for many years the *Guardian*'s Chief America Correspondent. His *Letter From America* was the longest-running single radio programme (from 1940 to 2004) and could be heard weekly on Radio 4.

American Broadcasting Company

See *ABC*.

Amos Burke – Secret Agent

See *Burke's Law*.

Amos 'n' Andy ★★

US (CBS) Situation Comedy. BBC 1954–7 (US: CBS 1951–3)
DVD: Education 2000 (Region 1 only)

Amos Jones	**Alvin Childress**
Andy Brown	**Spencer Williams Jr**
George 'The Kingfish' Stevens	**Tim Moore**
Algonquin J. Calhoun	**Johnny Lee**
Sapphire Stevens	**Ernestine Wade**
Mama	**Amanda Randolph**
Lightnin'	**Nick O'Demus**

Producers **Freeman Gosden, Charles Correll**

Controversial comedy set in a black neighbourhood.

Persona non grata among TV shows these days, *Amos 'n' Andy* was nevertheless a huge hit in its heyday. Based on a long-running US radio series starring Freeman Gosden and Charles Correll, which began in 1928 (and was spun off into a movie called *Check and Double Check* in 1930), it features a cast of black characters nominally headed by Amos Jones and Andy Brown (Gosden and Correll were white, so they needed to recruit black replacements when the show transferred to TV). However the real lead is George Stevens, the Bilko-esque leader of the Mystic Knights of the Sea fraternity, from which he derives his nickname, The Kingfish. It is The Kingfish's half-baked plans for betterment and petty swindles that form the core of the action, with Andy seen as a rather dim member of the main man's brotherhood and Amos as the savvy taxi driver (for his own Fresh Air Company) who relates the background to stories. Sapphire is The Kingfish's wife, sharing the sceptical female role with her redoubtable Mama.

Set in Harlem, *Amos 'n' Andy* was a televisual pioneer: this was the first show to feature an all-black cast. It drew on every black stereotype so far conceived but supporters defiantly point to the positives: that this was a show which portrayed blacks of all walks of life and not just the down-trodden – exemplified by lesser characters Algonquin J. Calhoun and Lightnin', a lawyer and a broom-pushing janitor, respectively. However, in time, the show became labelled racist; by the mid-1960s reruns were off the air completely and its screenings remain extremely few and very far between today.

Amy Prentiss ★

US (Universal) Police Drama. ITV 1976 (US: NBC 1974–5)

Amy Prentiss	**Jessica Walter**
Det. Tony Russell	**Steve Sandor**
Det. Rod Pena	**Arthur Metrano**
Det. Contreras	**Johnny Seven**
Jill Prentiss	**Helen Hunt**
Joan Carter	**Gwenn Mitchell**

Executive Producer **Cy Chermak**

A 35-year-old widow becomes San Francisco's first female Chief of Detectives.

When her boss dies suddenly, 35-year-old Amy Prentiss is chosen to succeed him. However, there has never been a female Chief of Detectives in the SFPD before and, for her colleagues, that takes a bit of getting used to. All the same, fighting prejudice, this is one lady cop who is determined to make the grade. She also has the challenge of bringing up her young daughter, Jill. *Amy Prentiss* aired as part of the MYSTERY MOVIE sequence, but didn't last more than three outings. The pilot had been an episode of A MAN CALLED IRONSIDE.

Anchor/Anchorman

The person who presents a news, current affairs, sports or magazine programme, linking contributions from other reporters or cueing in prerecorded inserts. In some instances, the anchor is instrumental in setting the tone or style of the programme. The term has also been employed for the question master in a quiz or game show. It was reportedly first used in 1952 by Sig Mickelson, President of CBS News, when describing the fundamental role played by celebrated news frontman Walter Cronkite in CBS bulletins.

And Mother Makes Three/And Mother Makes Five ★

UK (Thames) Situation Comedy. ITV 1971–3/1974–6

Sally Harrison/Redway	**Wendy Craig**
Simon Harrison	**Robin Davies**
Peter Harrison	**David Parfitt**
Auntie Flo	**Valerie Lush**
Mr Campbell	**George Selway**
David Redway	**Richard Coleman**
Jane Redway	**Miriam Mann** *(Makes Three)*
	Maxine Gordon *(Makes Five)*
Joss Spencer	**Tony Britton** *(Makes Five)*
Monica Spencer	**Charlotte Mitchell** *(Makes Five)*

Creator/Writer **Richard Waring**
Producer **Peter Frazer-Jones**

A young widow struggles to cope with her two trying sons.

Left with two young boys, Simon and Peter, when her husband dies, scatty housewife Sally Harrison takes a job at a vet's surgery. Working for Mr Campbell, she struggles along through daily mishaps in traditional sitcom fashion, calling on the help of her Auntie Flo, whom she persuades to join the household. Further assistance comes eventually from the new man in her life, David Redway, a widower with a young daughter named Jane. Sally later works in David's antiquarian bookshop, a marriage ensues and the series turned into *And Mother Makes Five*, in 1974, when they all move in together. Auntie is rehoused in the flat above the shop and the Spencers become their next-door neighbours.

And the Beat Goes On ★★

UK (Mersey) Drama. Channel 4 1996

Ritchie O'Rourke	**Danny McCall**
Connie Spencer	**Jenny Agutter**
Pop	**Norman Rossington**
Charlie Woods	**John McArdle**
Christine Spencer	**Lisa Faulkner**
Nicholas Spencer	**Stephen Moore**
Kenneth Fairbrother	**Dominic Jephcott**
Cathy Williams	**Katy Carmichael**
Mickey O'Rourke	**Roy Brandon**
Mary-Ann O'Rourke	**Eileen O'Brien**
Gloria O'Rourke	**Lynda Thornhill**
Sean Daley	**John Elmes**
Howard Clegg	**Philip McGough**
Danny McVey	**Martin O'Brien**

Francis .... **Peter Firth**
Alec Smart .... **Karl Lornie**

Writer **Joe Ainsworth**
Executive Producer **Phil Redmond**
Producer **Mal Young**

Two Merseyside families come to terms with the challenges of a new decade.

In an attempt to escape the sentimental, 'golden age' depiction of life in the 1960s, *And the Beat Goes On* majors on social injustices and pre-permissive mores. It is 1960: the hardships of the post-war years are coming to an end and a new consumer society is well on its way, but for some the comforts of life remain out of reach. Finding drama in crime, addiction, illicit romance and the dreaded sins of homosexuality and unplanned pregnancy, this eight-part series centres on two Liverpool families, the O'Rourkes and the Spencers, who find their lives intertwined. The former is working class, the latter middle class and they are epitomized by their troubled teenage offspring, Ritchie and Christine, who are liberated by the new freedoms allowed to youth but hamstrung by the setting in which they have to grow up. It's all a long way from the *Summer of Love*.

Anderson, Clive

(1952–)

Stanmore-born presenter and humorist, coming to the fore as chairman of the improvisation show WHOSE LINE IS IT ANYWAY? Anderson, a barrister by first profession, was President of the Cambridge Footlights club in the early 1970s and performed stand-up routines at The Comedy Store and other clubs before breaking into television as a writer on programmes such as NOT THE NINE O'CLOCK NEWS and ALAS SMITH AND JONES. After *Whose Line Is It Anyway?*, he graduated to his own Channel 4 chat show, *Clive Anderson Talks Back*, and also stood in on *Wogan* and POINTS OF VIEW. Then came the BBC 2 information programme NOTES AND QUERIES WITH CLIVE ANDERSON. From 1995 Anderson appeared in *Our Man in . . .*, a series of light-hearted documentaries from exotic locations around the world. His chat show moved to BBC 1 in 1996 under the title *Clive Anderson All Talk*. Other credits have included hosting WHAT THE PAPERS SAY, *Just for Laughs* and *God Almighty*, presenting a documentary on the Bayeux Tapestry called *Every Picture Tells a Story*, chairing the political comedy quiz *If I Ruled the World*, asking the questions on the Discovery Channel's revival of MASTERMIND, taking one of the GREAT RAILWAY JOURNEYS OF THE WORLD, and fronting *The Big Read*, the quiz *Back in the Day* and *The Sport Show*.

Anderson, Gerry

MBE (1929–)

British television's puppet-master, Gerry Anderson, began his TV career working as director for Roberta Leigh, creator of THE ADVENTURES OF TWIZZLE and TORCHY THE BATTERY BOY. However, Anderson had already set up his own film company with colleague Arthur Provis (Anderson/Provis Films – APF) and, seeing the potential of such animation, launched his own series, FOUR FEATHER FALLS, in 1960. This story of a courageous, crooning Western lawman with magic feathers to protect him was sold to Granada, and Anderson was up and running.

It wasn't until 1962, when he created SUPERCAR, that Anderson embarked on science fiction. These dashing tales of a vehicle that could go anywhere and do anything heralded a new era for TV sci-fi, although it also proved a little too expensive for Granada. Thankfully, Lew Grade stepped in and ITC became Anderson's new backers. *Supercar*'s more adventurous follow-up, FIREBALL XL5, concerning the exploits of Steve Zodiac and his crew, proved very popular, so popular in fact that Anderson decided to go for colour on his next project. This was STINGRAY, the adventures of a supersub and its fearless commander, Troy Tempest. All the while, Anderson's new 'Supermarionation' was reaching maturity, the puppets' strings becoming ever finer and their mouths synchronized with the dialogue for added realism. Working closely with Anderson were Barry Gray (who supplied all the rousing theme tracks), special effects expert Derek Meddings, and co-producer Reg Hill. Involved in the scripting, and supplying some of the female voices, was Gerry's then wife, Sylvia Anderson.

Their next opus proved to be their masterpiece. THUNDERBIRDS, filmed in 50-minute episodes, focused on the agents of International Rescue, an anonymous world-protection force with a fleet of super aircraft. After *Thunderbirds*, Anderson's puppetry was perfected in CAPTAIN SCARLET AND THE MYSTERONS, produced by Century 21 Productions (as APF had now become). Gone were awkward, bulbous-headed puppets, in came perfectly proportioned, beautifully characterized human models, as the indestructible Spectrum agent and his colleagues fought off the vengeful raiders from Mars. Following these last two successes was always going to be difficult, and the Anderson team disappointed fans with two tamer offerings, namely JOE 90 and THE SECRET SERVICE. This led Anderson to look more seriously at live action as the way forward, spawning UFO as the next project. Sci-fi was subsequently abandoned when he turned his attention to THE PROTECTORS, starring Robert Vaughn, Nyree Dawn Porter and Tony Anholt as a trio of international crime-fighters; but it was back on the table when SPACE: 1999, with Martin Landau and Barbara Bain, arrived in 1975. The major 1980s offering was TERRAHAWKS, a return to puppetry featuring the grizzly alien Zelda, although there was also a collection of short detective spoofs, *Dick Spanner PI*, shown on Channel 4 in 1985. Ten years later, Anderson was back in orbit, combining live and model action in the expensively produced SPACE PRECINCT, featuring the exploits of a trans-universal police force. He followed this with more animation in *Lavender Castle*, a children's space saga featuring Captain Thrice and his crew aboard the spaceship *Paradox*, in 1999. Anderson resurrected one of his greatest successes in 2005, when *Captain Scarlet* was remade using computer-generated graphics.

Anderson, Gillian

(1968–)

Chicago-born, London-raised actress who became an international star as Dana Scully in THE X-FILES. In 1996 she recrossed the Atlantic to present the BBC's science series, *Future Fantastic*, returning in 2005 to play Lady Dedlock in BLEAK HOUSE.

Anderson, Jean

(1907–2001)

Sussex-born actress specializing in crusty, upper-class roles and most familiar as the scheming Mary Hammond in THE BROTHERS. Her other lead credits included the mother in two separate productions of THE RAILWAY CHILDREN, plus TENKO (Joss Holbrook), and there were plenty of supporting roles, from DR FINLAY'S CASEBOOK, THE GOOD GUYS, HEARTBEAT and THE HOUSE OF ELIOTT to INSPECTOR MORSE, CAMPION, CATHERINE COOKSON's *The Black Velvet Gown* (Madam Gullmington), GBH (Dr Goldup), TRAINER, KEEPING UP APPEARANCES and *Endgame*.

Andrews, Anthony

(1948–)

Suave English leading man, coming to the fore as the Earl of Silverbridge in THE PALLISERS and as Lt. Brian Ash in Thames TV's DANGER UXB. BRIDESHEAD REVISITED followed (playing Sebastian Flyte), for which he picked up a BAFTA award as Best Actor on TV. Other notable credits have included UPSTAIRS, DOWNSTAIRS, THE DUCHESS OF DUKE STREET, *Ivanhoe, Z for Zachariah, Suspicion, The Woman He Loved* (Duke of Windsor) and the elaborate mini-series *AD (Anno Domini)*, in which he played Nero. Guest appearances have been in offerings like THE LOVE BOAT, THE RUTH RENDELL MYSTERIES, ROSEMARY AND THYME and AGATHA CHRISTIE'S MARPLE. More recently he was seen in *Love in a Cold Climate* (Boy Dougdale) and CAMBRIDGE SPIES (King George VI). Trivia buffs will know that Andrews was originally cast as Bodie in THE PROFESSIONALS but lost the part because he and Martin Shaw looked too similar in screen tests.

Andrews, Eamonn

CBE (1922–87)

Former boxer (the All Ireland Juvenile Champion) and sports commentator who became one of TV's most durable comperes. Having built a successful career in radio, in both Ireland and Britain, Andrews's first TV break came in 1951 when he was selected as host of WHAT'S MY LINE?, the BBC's new panel game. In 1955, he became presenter of THIS IS YOUR LIFE, a light-hearted, biographical tribute show imported from the USA. Ironically, Andrews was surprised in the first show by American compere Ralph Edwards and became the programme's first victim. *What's My Line?* and *This is Your Life* were to become stalwarts of Andrews's TV career, although he also dabbled in children's television through *Playbox* and, most notably, CRACKERJACK. When his BBC contract lapsed in 1964 (*This is Your Life* was cancelled), he moved to ITV to host WORLD OF SPORT and his own late-night celebrity series, *The Eamonn Andrews Show* (echoing the title of a 1956 BBC comedy show Eamonn had presented). *This Is Your Life* was revived by Thames in 1969 and *What's My Line?* returned in 1984 (again courtesy of Thames, for whom Andrews presented the nightly news magazine, *Today*, for ten years). His other credits included *Time for Business* and the ambitious satellite quiz TOP OF THE WORLD. Eamonn Andrews died in 1987 from heart disease. In his career, he had been voted Television Personality of the Year four times and had helped to set up RTE, the Irish television corporation.

Andromeda Breakthrough, The

See *A for Andromeda*.

Andy Capp ✳

UK (Thames) Situation Comedy. ITV 1988

Andy Capp .... **James Bolam**
Flo Capp .... **Paula Tilbrook**
Percy .... **Keith Marsh**
Ruby .... **Susan Brown**
Milkie .... **Ian Bleasdale**
Bookie .... **Mike Savage**
Clifford .... **George Waring**
Meredith .... **Andy Mulligan**
Shirley .... **Colette Stevenson**
Chalkie .... **Keith Smith**
Walter .... **Kevin Lloyd**
Mother-in-law .... **Shirley Dixon**
Jack .... **John Arthur**
Pawnbroker .... **Richard Tate**
Mr Watson .... **Philip Lowrie**
Vicar .... **Ian Thompson**

Writer **Keith Waterhouse**
Producer **John Howard Davies**

● ***A workshy Geordie seeks only a lazy, trouble-free life.***

Created in 1957 for the northern edition of the *Daily Mirror* (later going national and even international), Andy Capp was the invention of Hartlepool-born cartoonist Reg Smythe. In his new character he instilled all the virtues of a bone-idle, philandering chauvinist whose days were spent boozing, gambling, smoking, playing football or curled up on the sofa fast asleep. Although Capp is clearly from the north-east, he is easily identified as the everyman waster. He lives life constantly on the run from debt collectors and his aggressive, rolling-pin-wielding wife of some 25 years. Beneath the ever-present headscarf and curlers, Flo barely conceals her contempt for her flat-capped layabout husband and is egged on in her domestic battles by her vociferous, disapproving mother.

The same characteristics feature in this television incarnation portrayed by James Bolam. All the leading lights of the newspaper strip make an appearance, deliberately painted larger than life and bringing a cartoon-like element into the production. Strangely, despite the hero's pedigree, scripts from Keith Waterhouse and direction from producer John Howard Davies, *Andy Capp* failed to click and lasted only one short run of six episodes.

Andy Pandy ✳✳

UK (BBC) Children's Entertainment. BBC 1950–5; 1957; BBC 1 1970; BBC 2 2002–3

Creators **Freda Lingstrom, Maria Bird**
Narrators **Maria Bird, Vera McKechnie, Tom Conti**
Producers **Peter Thompson, David Boisseau, Freda Lingstrom, Jean Flynn**

● ***The domestic adventures of a puppet toddler and his toy friends.***

Dressed in a blue-and-white-striped suit, with a matching floppy hat, Andy Pandy was one of the pioneers of children's TV in the early 1950s. In fact, thanks to endless repeats, he remained a source of fun for infants right through the 1960s, too. Taking up the King of the Kids' Show baton from Muffin the Mule, Andy was a cherub-faced toddler who lived in a picnic basket. He first appeared solo, but then was joined by the moth-eaten Teddy and, later, a rag doll named Looby Loo.

In these early episodes, Andy and Teddy's adventures involve simple pleasures, stretching no further than a ride on a swing or a turn on the see-saw, accompanied by a rather patronizing commentary from co-creator/writer/narrator Maria Bird and shrill, jingly songs, voiced by Gladys Whitred and Julia Williams. The greatest excitement comes when their backs are turned and Looby Loo springs to life. With her plain features, yellow plaits and polka-dot dress, Looby plays, dances and then skips to 'Here We Go Looby Loo'. At the end of each show, Andy and Teddy pop back in the basket to the strains of the closing song, which declares it is 'Time to go home' (later 'Time to stop play').

Andy Pandy was jointly the brainchild of Maria Bird and Freda Lingstrom, later Head of the BBC's Children's Department, and first aired in 1950, marking an expansion in programmes for younger viewers. Its first slot was Tuesday at 3.45 p.m., and it was soon joined by similar programmes on other days, making up the WATCH WITH MOTHER strand. Only 26 original programmes were made, but they were repeated constantly until 1969. Thirteen new, colour episodes were written and produced by Freda Lingstrom in 1970, to replace the fading black-and-white films, with former PICTURE BOOK presenter Vera McKechnie relating events and Valerie Cardnell providing the songs. The puppets' chunky strings (a world away from the micro-wires used by Gerry Anderson) were initially pulled by Audrey Atterbury and Molly Gibson (Cecil and Madge Stavordale and Christopher Leith in 1970). An all-new, string-free *Andy Pandy* resurfaced in 2002, produced by Cosgrove Hall for Ben Productions and the BBC. The new stop-frame-animated puppet now lived in his own house, close to similar homes for Teddy and Looby Loo. New friends – Hissy Missy (a snake/draught excluder), Bilbo (a sailor), Tiffo (a dog) and Orbie (a bouncing ball) – were added and Tom Conti took over as narrator. This series first aired on BBC Choice.

Angelis, Michael

(1952–)

Liverpudlian actor, often in comic roles like that of Lucien, the rabbit-loving brother of Carol Boswell in THE LIVER BIRDS. He also starred as Chrissie in BOYS FROM THE BLACKSTUFF and Max in I WOKE UP ONE MORNING. Angelis appeared as Danny in WORLD'S END, Martin Niarchos in GBH and Harold Craven in LUV, as well as playing gay bartender Arnie in SEPTEMBER SONG, DI Kilshaw in *Melissa*, Will Shaker in the comedy *Giving Tongue*, Donald Lewis in *The Jump* and Chris in PLAYING THE FIELD, and taking over as narrator of THOMAS THE TANK ENGINE AND FRIENDS from Ringo Starr. Other credits have included ROCK FOLLIES, REILLY – ACE OF SPIES, BREAD, BOON, BETWEEN THE LINES, *Wail of the Banshee* (Merlin), LOVEJOY, CASUALTY, HOLBY CITY, HEARTBEAT, A&E, AUF WIEDERSEHEN, PET (Mickey Startup), *Sweet Medicine*, A TOUCH OF FROST and MERSEYBEAT. He married Coronation Street actress Helen Worth.

Angels ✶

UK (BBC) Medical Drama. BBC 1 1975–6; 1978–83

Patricia Rutherford .... **Fiona Fullerton**
Jo Longhurst .... **Julie Dawn Cole**
Sita Patel .... **Karan David**
Ruth Fullman .... **Lesley Dunlop**
Shirley Brent .... **Clare Clifford**
Maureen Morahan .... **Erin Geraghty**
Miss Heather Windrup .... **Faith Brooks**
Stewart Farrar .... **Jeremy Wilkin**
Linda Hollis .... **Janina Faye**
Elaine Fitzgerald .... **Taiwo Ajai**
Sarah Regan .... **Debbie Ash**
Jennifer Sorrell .... **Marsha Millar**
Sister Easby .... **June Watson**
Pauline Smart .... **Christine Akehurst**
Anna Newcross .... **Joanna Munro**
Jean MacEwen .... **Carol Holmes**
Jay Harper .... **Shelley King**
Brenda Cotteral .... **Kate Saunders**
Sarah Lloyd-Smith .... **Claire Walker**
Kate Lock
Katy Betts/Smart .... **Shirley Cheriton**
Sandra Ling .... **Angela Bruce**
Fleur Barrett/Frost .... **Sharon Rosita**
Adrienne O'Shea .... **Fay Howard**
Elizabeth Fitt .... **Susan Gilmore**
Rose Butchins .... **Kathryn Apanowicz**
Beverley Slater .... **Judith Jacob**
Ron Frost .... **Martin Barrass**
Den Booth .... **Ken Sharrock**
Roger Smart .... **Gary Whelan**
Tracey Willoughby/Carr .... **Julia Williams**
Valerie Price .... **Deborah Manship**
Linda Mo .... **Sarah Larn**
Vicky Smith .... **Pauline Quirke**
Alison Streeter/Clarke .... **Juliet Waley**
Dave Nowell .... **Neil West**
Janet Dickens .... **Michelle Martin**
Nargis Khan .... **Mamta Kash**
Josh Jones .... **Tony Armatrading**
Chris Carr .... **Martin Rutledge**
Ayo Lapido .... **Joy Lemoine**

Creator **Paula Milne**
Producers **Ron Craddock, Julia Smith, Ben Rea**

● ***Student nurses struggle with their lives and careers.***

Beginning as a 50-minute drama series, then in 1979 switching to two half-hour episodes a week, *Angels* tells tales of student nurses of St Angela's Hospital, Battersea, and, later, the brand-new Heath Green Hospital in Birmingham. It shows them at work and at play and, shot in semi-documentary style, it exposes their long hours and thankless chores. Although they are angels, these nurses are no saints, which came as a shock to some viewers expecting another dose of EMERGENCY – WARD 10's soppy romance. In many ways, *Angels*, with its grittiness, can be seen as a forerunner of EASTENDERS. Producer Julia Smith went on to create the latter and perhaps used *Angels* as a dress-rehearsal for the East End drama (even though *Angels* was seen only in 13-week blocks and not all year round). Some of the stars, too – Shirley Cheriton, Kathryn Apanowicz and Judith Jacobs – moved to Albert Square, while others, like Pauline Quirke, Fiona Fullerton and Lesley Dunlop, found different avenues to success.

Angels was partly filmed at St James's Hospital, Balham.

Anglia Television

The independent television company serving East Anglia since 27 October 1959 from a headquarters in Norwich and a handful of smaller studios around the region. Inheriting a predominantly agricultural and rural area, the company at first pitched its regional programmes accordingly, although, with gradual expansion into the industrial centres of the East Midlands, its style became more cosmopolitan. In the early 1970s it relinquished coverage of Lincolnshire and Humberside to Yorkshire Television (a transmitter swap contrived by the IBA) and nearly joined Yorkshire and Tyne Tees in a joint holding company, Trident Television. Although the other two companies went ahead, the IBA refused Anglia permission to become Trident's 'third prong'. Nationally, Anglia did very well in the quiz show line in the 1970s, thanks to SALE OF THE CENTURY and *Gambit* in particular. The company also built up a reputation for talk shows like *Vanessa* and *Trisha* and competent drama, with the likes of P. D. JAMES's Adam Dalgliesh mysteries, THE CHIEF and JILLY COOPER'S RIDERS all contributions to the network. Probably its best-known series, however, was TALES OF THE UNEXPECTED, which notched up huge international sales. Yet Anglia's name for drama has been dwarfed by its worldwide status as a maker of natural history films, thanks to the acclaim showered on SURVIVAL since it began in 1961. Having been taken over by United News and Media in the 1990s, Anglia became part of the Granada Media group in 2000, eventually disappearing when ITV plc was created from the merger of Granada and Carlton in 2004. The region is now covered by ITV Anglia.

Anholt, Tony

(1941–2002)

One of TV's great smoothies, Singapore-born Tony Anholt's first starring role was as Paul Buchet in THE PROTECTORS, alongside Robert Vaughn and Nyree Dawn Porter. In 1975 he popped up in CORONATION STREET playing David Law, the crooked boss of a model agency, but it was not until the 1980s that his career really revived, when he was cast as tycoon Charles Frere in HOWARDS' WAY. His other TV credits included THE STRAUSS FAMILY (Eduard), SPACE: 1999 (First Officer Tony Verdeschi), A FAMILY AT WAR, TRIANGLE (Nick Stevens), plus numerous guest spots in the likes of MINDER, BULMAN and ONLY FOOLS AND HORSES. He was the father of actor Christien Anholt.

Animal Hospital ✶✶

UK (BBC) Factual. BBC 1 1994–2003

Presenters **Rolf Harris, Lynda Bryans, Steve Knight, Mairi McHaffie, Shauna Lowry, Rhodri Williams, Christa Hart, Edwina Silver, Jamie Darling**

Executive Producers **Lorraine Heggessey, Sarah Hargreaves, Jane Aldous, Clare Sillery**

● ***Tears and joy at an RSPCA-run centre for sick animals.***

Animal Hospital began as *Animal Hospital Live*, a twice-daily report on events at Harmsworth Memorial Hospital in Holloway, London, in August 1994. The reports ran for five days only, but viewer response to the heart-warming (but also sometimes heart-rending) tales of pet woes was so great that a Christmas Day special followed, then a full series in January 1995. Entitled *Animal Hospital Week*, it highlighted happenings over seven days at the hospital.

Harmsworth, named after Sir Harold Harmsworth and funded by the RSPCA, takes care of animals whose owners are on benefit and cannot meet veterinary charges, and it also looks after wild animals brought in by caring members of the public. The series proved to be a mixed blessing for the hospital: on the one hand it sent out a clear message about animal welfare, but on the other it caused the hospital to be inundated with injured pets whose owners could and should have paid for treatment elsewhere. Chief vet David Grant was the human star, while celebrity patients included Snowy the poodle and Dolly the bull terrier.

In 1995 the title was simplified to *Animal Hospital* and a ten-minute bulletin for younger viewers was added to the Children's BBC schedules. At Christmas that year a special *Animal Hospital Down Under* saw host Rolf Harris return to his homeland to visit the Currumbin Wildlife Sanctuary in Queensland. (Rolf popped back to Australia in the run-up to the Sydney Olympics for the two-part *Animal Hospital in Oz*.)

From 1996, the programme ran twice a year, with the autumn series mostly remaining at Harmsworth and the spring series moving to new locations. With the subtitle 'On the Hoof', spring 1996 followed developments at Bedfordshire's Whipsnade Wild Animal Park. In spring 1997, the series headed out to the Hampden Veterinary Hospital in Aylesbury, to reflect on animal stories from the country, while in 1998 the spring programmes focused on Harmsworth's sister RSPCA hospital in Putney, London, featuring vet Tessa Bailey and her team. Putney became the year-round venue in 1999, and in 2000 the team moved north to cover events in Salford and at Stapeley Grange, near Nantwich, before returning to Putney. After 2001, series mostly alternated between Salford and Harmsworth. Highlight packages aired under the title *Animal Hospital Revisited*; in summer 1998 the *Animal Hospital Roadshow* toured animal centres around Britain for six weeks; and at Christmas 1998 *Animal Hospital: Fleas and All* offered a behind-the-scenes look at the making of the series. In 2004, a ten-year retrospective aired under the title *Animal Hospital – the Big Story*.

Animal Magic ✶✶✶

UK (BBC) Natural History. BBC 1 1962–83

Presenters **Johnny Morris, Terry Nutkins**

Producers **Winwood Reade, Jeffrey Boswell, Douglas Thomas, George Inger**

● ***A whimsical look at the world of animals for younger viewers.***

Hosted by the inimitable Johnny Morris, the man who talked *for* animals, *Animal Magic* was a stalwart of the BBC's children's output for 21 years. As well as welcoming guest animals into the studio (always a hazardous practice), Morris went out and about (including overseas to places like the Sudan and Japan) to see creatures at work and play. A favourite stamping ground was Bristol Zoo, and 'Keeper Morris' later over-dubbed the films he made, putting humorous words in the animals' mouths. Camels were his favourite beasts because they always looked as if they were talking. Also seen at times were reports from Tony Soper. Terry Nutkins joined Morris in the 1980s.

Animal, Vegetable, Mineral? ✶

UK (BBC) Panel Game. BBC 1952–9

Chairmen **Lionel Hale, Glyn Daniel**

Creator **Nora Wood**
Producers **Paul Johnstone, David Attenborough**

● ***Erudite, name-the-item quiz.***

Unusually popular, considering its learned tone, *Animal, Vegetable, Mineral?* was one of the BBC's first major panel games. Once a fortnight a team of three experts tried to identify a succession of objects taken from Britain's museums, giving the UK's great 'national inheritance' a plug in the process. The first chairman was Lionel Hale, but a Cambridge University Fellow, Glyn Daniel, soon took over proceedings. Among the numerous experts taking part were archaeologist

Sir Mortimer Wheeler, Adrian Digby, Norman Cook, Dr W. E. Swinton, Dr Julian Huxley, Jacquetta Hawkes, Professor Thomas Bodkin and other cerebral folk. David Attenborough was the programme's chief producer. A short-lived revival followed in 1971.

Animals of Farthing Wood, The ✶✶

Europe (Telemagination/La Fabrique/Praxinos) Cartoon. BBC 1 1993–5

Voices:

Badger/Toad/Bully/Spike/White Stag	**Ron Moody**
Owl/Weasel	**Sally Grace**
Adder/Cleo/Dash/Lady Blue	**Pamela Keevil-Kral**
Fox/Plucky/Hare/Trey	**Rupert Farley**
Mole/Whistler	**Jeremy Barrett**
Vixen/Charmer	**Stacey Jefferson**
Scarface/Ranger	**Jon Glover**

Writers **Valerie Georgeson, Steve Walker**
Executive Producer **Theresa Plummer-Andrews**
Producer **John M. Mills**

A motley band of wild animals seeks a new home.

Disaster strikes the creatures of Farthing Wood when humans encroach on their territory. New houses are planned for the site and man, in his usual ruthless fashion, literally bulldozes the animals out of their habitat. When their main water supply is filled in, the animals realize it's time to go – but where? Thankfully they have a true leader in Fox, who rallies his troops, makes them all sign up to live in harmony with each other, banning internal feuding – and feeding. He sets out to lead them to a better place named White Deer Park, a wildlife sanctuary once spotted by Toad. By the end of series one, the creatures have reached their new home, but in series two have to face the hardships of winter and resentment of their presence by the blue foxes, led by the vicious Scarface and Lady Blue. In the final series, the park is overrun by evil rats. Over the three series the animals have fun and games but also face many daily dangers, and, unlike in most children's cartoons, there's not always a joyful ending, with heart-tugging deaths underlining that a wild animal's lot is not necessarily a happy one. Other major characters include Fox's intelligent mate, Vixen; their appropriately named sons, Bold and Plucky; Bold's own mate, Whisper; the venerable Badger; the excitable Mole; Crow; pompous Owl; tittle-tattling Adder; Whistler, the heron; Mr Pheasant; Kestrel; naive Weasel; and the White Stag, lord of their new reserve. With echoes of *Watership Down* and THE WIND IN THE WILLOWS, *The Animals of Farthing Wood* – based on novels by Colin Dann – was commissioned by the European Broadcasting Union (19 different broadcasting organizations, including the BBC). It ran to 39 episodes and was screened throughout the continent in various languages.

Anna and the King ✶

US (20th Century-Fox) Situation Comedy. ITV 1973 (US: CBS 1972)

King Mongkut	**Yul Brynner**
Anna Owens	**Samantha Eggar**
Kralahome	**Keye Luke**
Louis Owens	**Eric Shea**
Crown Prince Chulalongkorn	**Brian Tochi**
Lady Thiang	**Lisa Lu**
Princess Serena	**Rosalind Chao**

Executive Producer **Gene Reynolds**

An attractive American widow charms the King of Siam while teaching his children.

A spin-off from the successful stage and film musical *The King and I* (based on the book by Margaret Landon, itself a version of a true story), *Anna and the King* brings back Yul Brynner as the shaven-headed King of Siam. It also pitches Samantha Eggar into the Deborah Kerr role of the English governess who teaches the King's children back in the 1860s. Here, however, Anna is Americanized and her surname shortened from the real-life Leonowens to a simple Owens. What's more, with the musical numbers cut, the concept becomes a gentle comedy. Kralahome (played by future KUNG FU actor Keye Luke) is the King's officious right-hand man, Lady Thiang is one of the King's numerous wives, and Louis is Anna's own 12-year-old son. Just 13 episodes were produced.

Anna Karenina ✶✶✶

UK (Company/Channel 4/WGBH Boston) Drama. Channel 4 2000
DVD: Cinema Club

Anna Karenina	**Helen McCrory**
Karenin	**Stephen Dillane**
Oblonsky	**Mark Strong**
Dolly	**Amanda Root**
Count Vronsky	**Kevin McKidd**
Levin	**Douglas Henshall**
Kitty	**Paloma Baeza**
Nikolai	**Paul Rhys**
Betsy	**Abigail Cruttenden**
Countess Vronskaya	**Sara Kestelman**
Princess Shcherbatskya	**Gillian Barge**
Prince Shcherbatsky	**Malcolm Sinclair**
Annushka	**Victoria Carling**
Seriozha	**Jackson Leach**
Yashvin	**Tom Ward**

Writer **Allan Cubitt**
Executive Producers **George Faber, Suzan Harrison, Charles Pattinson**
Producer **Matthew Bird**

The wife of a Russian politician is shunned by society after her affair with another man.

David Blair directs this four-part adaptation of Tolstoy's novel from the 1870s. Anna is the wife of prominent Russian government minister Karenin and enjoys all the trappings of society as a result. However, her life changes and her marriage is rocked when she temporarily leaves St Petersburg to help her brother, whose own marriage is falling apart. At Moscow station, Anna meets and falls in love with dashing military man Count Vronsky. They begin a relationship and she falls pregnant with the Count's child. Her disgrace sees her sidelined by society but compelled to live in a marriage prison with a husband who refuses a divorce. The consequences are increasingly tragic. The parallel relationship of social comrades Levin and Kitty is used to contrast Anna's unfortunate circumstances and to underline the social mores prevalent in 19th-century Russia. The drama was filmed on location in Poland.

Anna Karenina had previously been dramatized twice for television by the BBC (BBC 1961: with Claire Bloom as Anna, Marius Goring as Karenin and Sean Connery as Vronsky in a single drama directed by Rudolph Cartier; BBC 2 1977: Nicola Pagett as Anna, Eric Porter as Karenin and Stuart Wilson as Vronsky, in ten episodes written and produced by Donald Wilson). Jacqueline Bisset, Christopher Reeve (Vronsky) and Paul Scofield (Karenin) also starred in a US TV movie version in 1985.

Anna Lee ✶

UK (LWT/Carnival) Detective Drama. ITV 1994

Anna Lee	**Imogen Stubbs**
Selwyn Price	**Brian Glover**
Commander Martin Brierly	**John Rowe**
Bernie Schiller	**Peter Wight**
Beryl Doyle	**Sonia Graham**
Stevie Johnson	**Wilbert Johnson**

Producer **Brian Eastman**

● ***The cases of a feisty, blonde private eye.***

Anna Lee has just left the police force and joined the Brierly Detective Agency, based in Kensington High Street, as a private investigator. She is headstrong, impulsive and prone to emotional influence, but also has the useful knack of acquiring the trust of others. However, dashing around the streets of the capital in a beaten-up Sunbeam Alpine soft-top, a jazzy music score urging her on, she regularly finds herself in deeper water than anticipated. Back at her home in Coalville Square, her neighbour is Selwyn Price, a wrestler turned antiques dealer. Despite employing some of the best scripting talent (Andrew Davies wrote the pilot, screened in 1993, and Anthony Horowitz penned some of the other stories), the series, based on the original novel by Liza Cody, proved short-lived (only six feature-length films, including the pilot). In the pilot (produced by Sue Birtwistle), Lee's boss, Commander Brierly, was played by Michael Bryant, his uppity secretary, Beryl, by Barbara Leigh-Hunt and Bernie, a friendly colleague, by Ken Stott. When the series arrived, there was also a fashion change to shore up Lee's detective credentials at the expense of her racy looks: out went the short skirts that had seriously distracted male viewers and in came tomboyish jeans and waistcoats.

Anne of Avonlea

See *Anne of Green Gables*.

Anne of Green Gables/Anne of Avonlea ✶✶

UK (BBC) Drama. BBC 1 1972/1975

Anne Shirley	**Kim Braden**
Matthew Cuthbert	**Elliott Sullivan**
Marilla Cuthbert	**Barbara Hamilton**
Thomas Lynde	**Edmond Bennett**
	Gordon Sterne *(Avonlea)*
Rachel Lynde	**Avis Bunnage**
	Madge Ryan *(Avonlea)*
Diana Barry	**Jan Francis**
Gilbert Blythe	**Robin Halstead**
	Christopher Blake *(Avonlea)*
Josie Pye	**Angela Walker**
Ruby Gillis	**Kim Hardy**
Jane Andrews	**Zuleika Robson**
Miss Stacey	**Kate Beswick**
Mr Harrison	**David Garfield** *(Avonlea)*
Anthony Pye	**Ian Allis** *(Avonlea)*
Davy Keith	**Nicholas Lyndhurst** *(Avonlea)*
Dora Keith	**Annabelle Lanyon** *(Avonlea)*
Judson Parker	**Ed Bishop** *(Avonlea)*
Fred Wright	**Martin Neil** *(Avonlea)*
Paul Irving	**Keith Steven** *(Avonlea)*
Charlie Sloan	**Peter Settelen** *(Avonlea)*
Philippa Gordon	**Sabina Franklyn** *(Avonlea)*
Jonas Blake	**David Troughton** *(Avonlea)*
Roy Gardner	**Anthony Forrest** *(Avonlea)*

Writers **Julia Jones** *(Green Gables)* **Elaine Morgan** *(Avonlea)*
Producer **John McRae**

● ***An orphan girl makes a big impression on a quiet country community.***

Prince Edward Island, Canada, at the turn of the 20th century: young orphan Anne Shirley is sent, by mistake, to be fostered by elderly farmers Marilla and Matthew Cuthbert. They really want a boy, who can help out around their smallholding (Green Gables), but they decide to keep Anne, who becomes their pride and joy. Endlessly romantic and dreamy, annoyingly talkative, but very bright and approachable, Anne blossoms at Green Gables, eventually passing to go to college. Her best friend is Diana Barry; arch-enemy is Gilbert Blythe, the boy who rudely insults Anne's red hair. Three years after this five-part adaptation of L. M. Montgomery's classic novel, the BBC dramatized her sequel, *Anne of Avonlea*, in six episodes. Marilla is now sadly a widow and glad to have Anne back at home and teaching at the local school in Avonlea. Anne, aged 17 and typically headstrong, has many fallings out with colleagues, parents and pupils, but becomes surprisingly close to the once-hateful Gilbert, with whom she later enrols as a student at Redmond College. Joan Craft directed both serials (heartwarming Sunday teatime fodder), which starred Kim Braden (daughter of Bernard Braden and Barbara Kelly) as the irrepressible Anne.

Canada produced another well-received adaptation of *Anne of Green Gables* in 1985 (written and produced by Kevin Sullivan and starring Megan Follows as Anne, Colleen Dewhurst as Marilla and Richard Farnsworth as Matthew), following up with *Anne of Avonlea* in 1987. A third instalment, *Anne of Green Gables: The Continuing Story*, was released in 2000. There was also a series, *Road to Avonlea* (1989–96), with Dewhurst again as Marilla but this time no Anne.

Annie's Bar ✶✶

UK (Ardent) Comedy Drama. Channel 4 1996

David Dashwood	**Dominic Taylor**
Terry Dunning	**Larry Lamb**
Stiggy Bedford-Bounds	**Geoff McGivern**
Vernon Du Chine	**Paul Brooke**
Nick Buckley	**Gavin Richards**
Gilly Jones	**Sarah Neville**
Graham Keegan	**Eamon Boland**
Brian Lightfoot	**Christopher Ashley**
Antonia Courtney	**Elizabeth Bennett**
Philip Salisbury	**Jonathan Coy**
Jimmy McKenzie	**Tom Watson**
Gwyneth Holmes	**Rosemary Martin**
Candy Aloha	**Sarah Lee Jones**
Fleur Mortimer	**Steffanie Pitt**
Laura Dashwood	**Kate Maravan**
Reg	**Tim Wylton**
Darren Watling	**Thomas Russell**

Joan Fairlie .... **Marjorie Yates**

Writer **Andy Armitage**
Producer **Richard Handford**

A new MP gets to grips with life in the Commons.

David Dashwood is a newly elected Conservative Member of Parliament. As he quickly realizes, however, getting elected is merely the first of the challenges facing him as he tries to cope with the protocol, pressures and peccadilloes that pervade the House of Commons. Making each day more difficult are menacing Tory whip Terry Dunning; Dunning's Labour counterpart, Graham Keegan; flirty Antonia Courtney; and Dashwood's own wife, Laura. Despite all this, Dashwood begins to find his feet and the series reaches a climax as, rebelling against the party line, he threatens to bring down the Government. As the title signposts, much of the gossip, scheming and skullduggery is exposed in Annie's Bar, a real-life watering hole shared by MPs and the media within the Parliament complex. Episodes were shot only just before transmission to ensure that breaking political stories could be accommodated and production was handled by Prince Edward's company, Ardent Productions. Just one series of ten half-hour programmes was made.

Annis, Francesca

(1944–)

British actress, best remembered on TV for her acclaimed portrayal of Lillie Langtry in LILLIE, reprising a role she had played in some episodes of EDWARD THE SEVENTH. Earlier she had appeared in *Great Expectations* (Estella) and *Madame Bovary* (title role) for the BBC, and later starred in the Agatha Christie dramas *Why Didn't They Ask Evans?*, *The Secret Adversary* and AGATHA CHRISTIE'S PARTNERS IN CRIME (Tuppence Beresford). In the 1990s she appeared as Kitty O'Shea in *Parnell and the Englishwoman*, Katya Princip in THE GRAVY TRAIN GOES EAST, Celia Hardcourt in *Deadly Summer*, Angela Berridge in BETWEEN THE LINES, Anna Fairley in RECKLESS, Mrs Kirkpatrick in WIVES AND DAUGHTERS and Margrethe Bohr in *Copenhagen*. In 2000 she starred as Ellen Richmond in the thriller *Deceit*. Some of her first TV appearances came in episodes of DANGER MAN and DR FINLAY'S CASEBOOK. Other guest spots have included DALZIEL AND PASCOE, and JERICHO.

Announcer

The person who, either in vision or simply by voice-over, links programmes, reads trails and provides important additional information to viewers. He/she is also known as a continuity announcer. The BBC has long abandoned on-screen announcers, though its early broadcasts were characterized by the presence on camera of personalities such as Jasmine Bligh, Elizabeth Cowell, Leslie Mitchell, Mary Malcolm, McDonald Hobley and Sylvia Peters. ITV held on to in-vision announcers longer, but now also relies on off-screen links.

Ant and Dec

See *McPartlin, Anthony*.

Anthology

A collection of dramatic works, generally by various authors, with no continuous characters or plots, even though the stories may share a common theme or style. Examples include OUT OF THE UNKNOWN, THRILLER and COUNTRY MATTERS. Sometimes one character or actor is employed as the host of each programme, to hold the concept together, as exemplified by Alfred Hitchcock in ALFRED HITCHCOCK PRESENTS or Rod Serling in THE TWILIGHT ZONE.

Antiques Roadshow ✶✶

UK (BBC) Antiques. BBC 1 1979–

Presenters **Bruce Parker, Angela Rippon, Arthur Negus, Hugh Scully, Michael Aspel**

Producers **Robin Drake, Christopher Lewis, Michele Burgess, Stephen Potter, Simon Shaw**

A team of experts values the treasured possessions of members of the public.

A Sunday afternoon favourite, *Antiques Roadshow* has travelled the length and breadth of the United Kingdom, inviting viewers to drop in and have their family heirlooms valued. Since the first broadcast in 1979, there has been much raiding of attics and basements across the land, in the hope of discovering something of value. Punters have queued up, cherished items in hand, awaiting the verdict of one of the experts, who have all been drawn from leading auction houses and dealerships.

Participants have explained how the items came into their family's possession, and the specialists have then provided more background information, explaining where, when and by whom it was probably made, and winding up with a financial valuation. One piece a week has usually proved to be a real find – a magnificent specimen of furniture, a long lost work by a distinguished artist, etc. – much to the delight of both the excited connoisseur and the gasping proprietor. Among the longest-serving experts are David Battie and Hugh Morley-Fletcher (both porcelain), Simon Bull (timepieces), Roy Butler (militaria), and David Collins and Philip Hook (both paintings). Some have become celebrities in their own right – 'potaholic' Henry Sandon, his son, John Sandon, furniture specialist John Bly, and ceramics man Eric Knowles, for instance. Hugh Scully hosted proceedings for many years until his departure in 2000.

A young persons' special, entitled *Antiques Roadshow – the Next Generation*, has been screened occasionally.

Appleyards, The ✶

UK (BBC) Children's Drama. BBC 1952–7

Mr Appleyard .... **Frederick Piper**
Douglas Muir
Mrs Appleyard .... **Constance Fraser**
John Appleyard .... **David Edwards**
Janet Appleyard .... **Maureen Davis**
Tessa Clarke
Sylvia Bidmead
Tommy Appleyard .... **Derek Rowe**
Margaret Appleyard .... **Patricia Wilson**
Patricia Fryer
Carole Olver
Joe .... **John Garley**
Ronnie Grant .... **Robert Dickens**
Mr Wheeler .... **Douglas Hurn**
Sally Wheeler .... **Julie Webb**

	Erica Houen
Hazel	**Barbara Brown**
Mr Spiller	**C. B. Poultney**

Producers **Naomi Capon, Kevin Sheldon**

Major moments in the life of a suburban, middle-class family.

The Appleyards was an early children's soap opera, transmitted once a fortnight as part of the *Children's Television* slot (around 5 p.m.). It featured the Appleyard family – mum, dad, teenagers John and Janet, and younger siblings Tommy and Margaret – and picked up a number of awards during its five-year run, which saw the children grow older and start to leave the nest. John joined the RAF and then became an air steward, for instance, and Tommy took a job as a grocer's assistant. Among those also seen were Joe, the friendly milkman; Ronnie Grant, the boy next door who joined the army; annoying neighbour Mr Spiller; and Hazel, Margaret's best friend. A reunion special, entitled *Christmas with the Appleyards*, was shown in 1960.

Apprentice, The ★★★

UK (Talkback Thames) Reality. BBC 2 2005–

Creator **Mark Burnett**
Editors **Peter Moore, Daniel Adamson**

Aspiring entrepreneurs compete for a guarantee of a big-salary job.

Fourteen candidates enter the bear pit of this TV reality contest, their goal being to secure the top prize of a six-figure-salaried, one-year job with one of Sir Alan Sugar's companies. Over 12 weeks they battle it out through a series of tests and projects to see who gets the multimillionaire businessman's final nod. Each week one contestant is fired: the meek and guileless are weeded out as only the tough and focused find favour. Margaret Mountford and Nick Hewer are Sugar's colleagues on 'The Board'. The winner of the first series was former London Underground transport manager Tim Campbell, with Saira Khan the runner-up. Series two was won by Michelle Dewberry, a one-time supermarket check-out girl, who narrowly defeated Ruth Badger. This strangely gripping UK series was based on a US original of the same title (BBC 2 2004), in which famed entrepreneur Donald Trump was responsible for the ruthless hiring and firing.

Aquarius ★

UK (LWT) Arts. ITV 1970–7

Presenters **Humphrey Burton, Russell Harty, Peter Hall**

Editor **Humphrey Burton**

Late-night arts magazine.

Produced fortnightly, on Saturday or Sunday nights, *Aquarius* was originally hosted by its editor, Humphrey Burton, though Russell Harty and Peter Hall took over in later years, when the programme was screened weekly. A rival to the BBC's OMNIBUS, *Aquarius* incorporated reports on all aspects of the artistic and cultural world. During its seven years, the series included items on the likes of Salvador Dali, Artur Rubinstein, Pablo Casals and Stanley Spencer. When it ended in 1977, it was succeeded by THE SOUTH BANK SHOW.

Archie Bunker's Place

See *All in the Family.*

Are You Being Served? ★★

UK (BBC) Situation Comedy. BBC 1 1973–9; 1981; 1983; 1985
DVD: BBC

Mrs Betty Slocombe	**Mollie Sugden**
Mr Wilberforce Humphries	**John Inman**
Capt. Stephen Peacock	**Frank Thornton**
Mr Cuthbert Rumbold	**Nicholas Smith**
Miss Shirley Brahms	**Wendy Richard**
Mr Ernest Grainger	**Arthur Brough**
Mr Dick Lucas	**Trevor Bannister**
Mr Mash	**Larry Martyn**
Mr Harman	**Arthur English**
Mr Percival Tebbs	**James Hayter**
Mr Spooner	**Mike Berry**
Young Mr Grace	**Harold Bennett**
Mr Harry Goldberg	**Alfie Bass**
Old Mr Grace	**Kenneth Waller**

Creators/Writers **Jeremy Lloyd, David Croft**
Executive Producer **David Croft**
Producers **David Croft, Bob Spiers, Michael Shardlow**

Fun and games at a traditional department store.

Chock-full of nudge-nudge, wink-wink innuendo, this long-running farce centres on the members of staff in the clothing department on the first floor of Grace Brothers. Clearly divided into male and female sections, supervised by department manager Mr Rumbold and floor walker Captain Peacock, the clothing section employs some well-defined comedy stereotypes. On the men's side there is swishy homosexual Mr Humphries, declaring 'I'm free' whenever a customer needs attention and always poised to take that inside leg measurement. He works alongside grouchy old Mr Grainger (in later episodes Mr Tebbs) and the department junior, Mr Lucas, who is later replaced by Mr Spooner. In charge of the ladies' cash desks, amid the intimate apparel, is billowing Mrs Slocombe, a superficially dignified mistress of the unfortunate phrase, who brings howls of laughter from the studio audience with her fluorescent rinses and her constant worries about her pussy. She is ably supported in the battle of the sexes by buxom young Miss Brahms. Overseeing the whole operation, and telling everyone that they've 'all done very well', is the store's owner, doddery Young Mr Grace, a failing geriatric with a dolly bird on each arm (superseded eventually by the equally senile Old Mr Grace). Mr Harman is the cantankerous caretaker who takes over from militant trade unionist Mr Mash.

Though plots were thin and obvious, the in-jokes kept coming – for 12 years. Even then the characters refused to die, with Messrs Peacock, Humphries and Rumbold, Mrs Slocombe and Miss Brahms resurfacing in a revival, set at a country hotel. Now under the banner of *Grace and Favour* (BBC 1 1992–3), the team has been made redundant at Grace Brothers, following the death of Young Mr Grace, and discovers that the firm's pension fund has been invested in the run-down Millstone Manor, where Mr Rumbold is the struggling manager. With nothing to lose, the others decide to join him in an attempt to turn the business around, hoping the country air might do them good. Two series were made.

The pilot for *Are You Being Served?* was an episode of COMEDY PLAYHOUSE seen in 1972, and the series was based on writer Jeremy Lloyd's personal experience of working at Simpson's of

Piccadilly. John Inman had a minor hit with a novelty spin-off record, 'Are You Being Served Sir', in 1975, and a feature film version was released in 1977.

Arena ✱✱

UK (BBC) Arts. BBC 2 1975–

Editors **Alan Yentob, Nigel Finch, Anthony Wall**

● ***All-embracing, popular arts series.***

The umbrella title of *Arena* has encompassed documentary features on many subjects. Indeed, in its early days each edition was categorized by a subtitle – *Arena: Theatre, Arena: Art and Design* and *Arena: Cinema*, for instance. The categories alternated weekly. Some contributions have been seriously arty, others more trivial and populist. One highlight in 2005 was Martin Scorsese's biographical film *No Direction Home – Bob Dylan*.

Aristocrats ✱✱

UK (BBC/Irish Screen/WGBH Boston) Drama. BBC 1 1999

Lady Emily .... **Geraldine Somerville**
Siân Phillips *(older)*
Hayley Griffiths *(younger)*
Lady Sarah .... **Jodhi May**
Sheila Ruskin *(older)*
Lady Louisa .... **Anne-Marie Duff**
Diana Quick *(older)*
Lady Caroline .... **Serena Gordon**
Henry Fox .... **Alun Armstrong**
Duke of Richmond .... **Julian Fellowes**
Duchess of Richmond .... **Diane Fletcher**
Lord Kildare .... **Ben Daniels**
King George II .... **Clive Swift**
Charles, 3rd Duke of Richmond .... **Tom Beard**
Geoffrey Beevers *(older)*
Mary, 3rd Duchess .... **Katherine Wogan**
Carmen du Sautoy *(older)*
Bunbury .... **Andrew Havill**
Lord William Gordon .... **Gary Cady**
Prince of Wales .... **Luke de Lacey**
Charles James Fox .... **Hugh Sachs**
Trevor Ray *(older)*
Ste Fox .... **Toby Jones**
Tom Conolly .... **Tom Mullion**
Paul Ridley *(older)*
Susan Fox-Strangeways .... **Pauline McLynn**
William Ogilvie .... **George Anton**
David Grant *(older)*
George Napier .... **Martin Glyn Murray**
Jeremy Bulloch *(older)*
Lord Edward Fitzgerald .... **John Light**

Writer **Harriet O'Carroll**
Producers **Christopher Hall, David Snodin**

● ***Four great-granddaughters of King Charles II are launched into society from their home in Ireland.***

Based on Stella Tillyard's account of the real-life Lennox sisters, this six-part costume drama, set in the 18th century, provided lavish Sunday evening viewing. The sisters are the daughters of the second Duke of Richmond. The eldest, Caroline, is headstrong and elopes with a commoner politician, Henry Fox, more than 20 years her senior. The next daughter, the extravagant Emily, patiently woos and marries Lord Kildare, a less than satisfactory choice for her father, as Kildare is rich but of dubious lineage. The charitable Louisa comes next, marrying Ireland's wealthiest man and giving up much of her time to worthwhile causes. Finally there is the unpredictable, flirtatious Sarah, who brings the family name into disrepute through her unbecoming behaviour, especially with the Prince of Wales. Unlike the one-dimensional women often portrayed in this age of powerful men, these sisters show themselves to be manipulative, liberated and far from submissive.

The serial – reputedly costing over £6 million to create – begins in 1742 and continues through to the early 19th century, when the surviving sisters are depicted in their latter years. Although two of the sisters move to England, the series was shot entirely in Ireland, using some of the houses in which the real Lennox sisters once lived. Siân Phillips, who played the older Emily, also acted as narrator.

Arlott, John

(1914–91)

Revered cricket commentator and wine expert whose rich Hampshire burr is badly missed in cricketing circles. He joined the BBC in 1945 as a poetry specialist, after 11 years in the police force, and, though he did plenty of TV work in the 1960s, his later contracts were once again with BBC Radio. He pulled stumps on a 33-year commentating career at the Centenary Test in 1980, taking retirement in the Channel Islands.

Armchair Theatre ✱✱✱

UK (ABC/Thames) Drama Anthology. ITV 1956–74

Producers **Dennis Vance, Sydney Newman, Leonard White, Lloyd Shirley**

● ***Influential, long-running series of single dramas.***

Although initiated in 1956 (with the play *The Outsider*, starring David Kossoff and Adrienne Corri), and successful under first producer Dennis Vance, *Armchair Theatre* really began to gain authority in 1958, with the arrival of Canadian producer Sydney Newman. In his five years in charge (before leaving for the BBC, where he created DOCTOR WHO among other offerings), Newman focused on contemporary themes and 'real' issues, and such grubby realism earned the series the unfortunate nickname of 'Armpit Theatre'.

Newman assembled around him some of the top dramatic talents of the day, including such directors as Philip Saville, George More O'Ferrall and William T. Kotcheff, story editors Irene Shubik and Peter Luke, and young playwrights such as Harold Pinter, Alun Owen, Robert Muller and Ray Rigby. Pinter's first TV play, *A Night Out*, was a 1960 *Armchair Theatre* production and Owen's *Lena, O My Lena* was another of that year's contributions. There were quality performers in front of the camera, too; they included Tyrone Power, Flora Robson, Gracie Fields, Joan Greenwood, Billie Whitelaw, Donald Pleasence, Tom Courtenay and a young Diana Rigg. Some early plays were transmitted live, and the perils of such practice were cruelly highlighted in 1958, when actor Gareth Jones collapsed and died during a rendition of a play entitled *Underground*.

The series produced some notable spin-offs. A 1962 version of John Wyndham's *Dumb Martian* was used as a taster for the new OUT OF THIS WORLD science-fiction anthology which began the following week, while James Mitchell's *A Magnum for Schneider*, in 1967, resulted in the hugely popular CALLAN series. *Armchair Theatre* survived the ITV franchise swap of 1968, with production switching from ABC to the newly formed Thames Television. Thames later tinkered with the format, introducing *Armchair Cinema*, a film-based equivalent, which included *Regan*, the pilot for THE SWEENEY, among its successes.

Armchair Theatre became compulsive Sunday night entertainment for many viewers, particularly during its heyday at the turn of the 1960s. The alternative title of *Armchair Summer Theatre* was occasionally used for seasonal episodes, while *Armchair Mystery Theatre* (1960–5) was a variation on the theme by the same production team.

Armistead Maupin's Tales of the City/More Tales of the City ✶✶

UK (Channel 4/Working Title) Drama. Channel 4 1993; 1998
DVD: Channel 4

Anna Madrigal	**Olympia Dukakis**
Mona Ramsey	**Chloe Webb**
	Nina Siemaszko *(More Tales)*
Michael Tolliver	**Marcus D'Amico**
	Paul Hopkins *(More Tales)*
Brian Hawkins	**Paul Gross**
	Whip Hubley *(More Tales)*
Mary Ann Singleton	**Laura Linney**
Edgar Halcyon	**Donald Moffat**
Jon Fielding	**William Campbell**
Beauchamp Day	**Thomas Gibson**
DeDe Halcyon Day	**Barbara Garrick**
Frannie Halcyon	**Nina Foch**
	Diane Leblanc *(More Tales)*
D'orothea Wilson	**Cynda Williams**
	Françoise Robertson *(More Tales)*
Norman Neal Williams	**Stanley Desantis**
Archibald Gidde	**Ian McKellen**
Mother Mucca	**Jackie Burroughs** *(More Tales)*
Burke Andrew	**Colin Ferguson** *(More Tales)*
Betty Ramsey	**Swoosie Kurtz** *(More Tales)*

Writer **Richard Kramer**
Producers **Alan Poul, Anthony Root**

Bohemian life in a San Francisco boarding house during the 1970s.

RISING DAMP this is not. *Tales of the City* focuses on the goings-on at 28 Barbary Place, a San Francisco boarding house run by a marijuana-growing transsexual, Anna Madrigal (her name is an anagram of 'a man and a girl'). It opens with the arrival of the naïve, 25-year-old Mary Ann Singleton, fresh from Cleveland, Ohio, and out to enjoy everything San Francisco has to offer. She joins a liberated household that exemplifies the *laissez-faire* atmosphere that pervaded the Californian city during the 1970s. Sharing the spotlight are gay Michael 'Mouse' Tolliver; his boyfriend, gynaecologist Jon Fielding; emotionally strained advertising copywriter Mona Ramsey; lawyer-turned-waiter Brian Hawkins; and Mrs Madrigal's true love, Edgar Halcyon.

The series was based on the first of six books by local writer Armistead Maupin, which first appeared in serial form in the *San Francisco Chronicle* in 1976. THIRTYSOMETHING writer Richard Kramer was brought in to handle the TV adaptation, which caused a flutter with its gay love scenes, nudity and open treatment of the drugs issue. Rod Steiger made a cameo appearance as a bookstore owner.

Five years after Channel 4 screened the five-part series, it broadcast a six-part sequel, entitled *More Tales of the City* (following Maupin's second novel). Still set in Barbary Place, it features largely the same cast of characters, although there are several actor changes, including the replacement of DUE SOUTH star Paul Gross. New in town is Mother Mucca, a retired madame from Winnemucca, Nevada, who becomes a guardian figure for the frustrated Mona.

Armstrong, Alun

(1946–)

Northern English actor seen in both comedy and drama, in such programmes as *Villains*, THE STARS LOOK DOWN (Joe Gowlan), DAYS OF HOPE, A SHARP INTAKE OF BREATH, PORRIDGE, INSPECTOR MORSE, BULMAN and *Stanley and the Women*. He was also Squeers in *The Life and Adventures of Nicholas Nickleby* and played Roy Grade in *Goodbye Cruel World*, as well as hated stepfather Gerald in *Goggle Eyes*, Uncle Teddy in *The Life and Times of Henry Pratt*, and corrupt politician Austin Donohue in OUR FRIENDS IN THE NORTH. Later Armstrong starred as Henry Fox in ARISTOCRATS, gardening gangster Teddy Middlemass in *Underworld*, DCI Frank Jefferson in *In the Red*, Mr Flemyng in OLIVER TWIST, Dan Peggotty in DAVID COPPERFIELD, ACC George Oldfield in *This Is Personal – the Hunt for the Yorkshire Ripper*, George Mole in ADRIAN MOLE: THE CAPPUCCINO YEARS, Neil in BEDTIME, Richard Bolton in *Sparkhouse*, Martin in *Inquisition*, DCI Charlie Macintyre in MESSIAH 2, Brian Lane in NEW TRICKS, Peter Delaney in *Between the Sheets*, Mr Evans in CARRIE'S WAR and Bucket in BLEAK HOUSE. He has featured in numerous single dramas, including *Brazen Hussies*, *When I'm Sixty-Four* and Alan Plater's *Get Lost!*, an early version of THE BEIDERBECKE AFFAIR.

Army Game, The ✶

UK (Granada) Situation Comedy. (ITV) 1957–61
DVD: Network

Major Upshot-Bagley	**Geoffrey Sumner**
	Jack Allen
CSM Percy Bullimore	**William Hartnell**
CSM Claude Snudge	**Bill Fraser**
Cpl Springer	**Michael Medwin**
Pte 'Excused Boots' Bisley	**Alfie Bass**
Pte 'Cupcake' Cook	**Norman Rossington**
	Keith Banks
Pte 'Popeye' Popplewell	**Bernard Bresslaw**
Pte 'Prof' Hatchett	**Charles Hawtrey**
	Keith Smith
Capt. Pilsworthy	**Bernard Hunter**
Major Geoffrey Gervaise Duckworth	**C. B. Poultney**
Pte Leonard Bone	**Ted Lune**
Cpl 'Flogger' Hoskins	**Harry Fowler**
Capt. Pocket	**Frank Williams**
Pte Dooley	**Harry Towb**
Lance-Corporal Ernest 'Moosh' Merryweather	**Mario Fabrizi**
Pte Billy Baker	**Robert Desmond**
Pte 'Chubby' Catchpole	**Dick Emery**

Creator **Sid Colin**

Producers **Milo Lewis, Max Morgan-Witts, Peter Eton, Eric Fawcett**

The schemes and scams of a gang of National Service soldiers.

This extremely popular early comedy was set in Hut 29 of the Surplus Ordnance Depot at Nether Hopping, somewhere near Itchwick in remotest Staffordshire, and featured the exploits of a mixed bag of army conscripts. At the forefront are Private 'Bootsie' Bisley, so named because he is allowed to wear plimsolls instead of boots; private Hatchett, who knits to pass the time and is known as 'The Professor'; Liverpudlian Private 'Cupcake' Cook, taking his name from the many food parcels his mother sends him; gormless Private 'Popeye' Popplewell; and their Cockney spiv ringleader, Corporal Springer. Trying to knock them into shape are bellowing Sgt-Major Bullimore and then (when future DOCTOR WHO Bill Hartnell left to star in the very similar *Carry On Sergeant*) pompous Sgt-Major Claude Snudge. Toffee-nosed, pig-breeding Major Upshot-Bagley is nominal head of the camp, with Captain Pocket his adjutant.

There were many personnel changes in the series' four-year run. Upshot-Bagley was replaced by other commandants (Pilsworthy and Duckworth) and new conscripts were brought in. Popeye was succeeded by the equally dense (and toothless) Private Bone, Springer by another chirpy Londoner, 'Flogger' Hoskins, and other new arrivals included 'Chubby' Catchpole, Lance-Corporal Ernie Merryweather and Privates Dooley and Baker. Of the characters that remained, some changed actors. Barry Took and Marty Feldman were among the numerous writers involved.

The Army Game was originally transmitted live once a fortnight, though when its popularity increased it switched to once a week. In 1958, the series engendered a spin-off film, *I Only Arsked* (based on Popeye's catchphrase). In the same year 'The Signature Tune of "The Army Game"' was a top five hit for Michael Medwin, Bernard Bresslaw, Alfie Bass and Leslie Fyson, and in 1960 a sequel series, BOOTSIE AND SNUDGE, was produced.

Arnaz, Desi

(Desiderio Alberto Arnaz y de Acha; 1917–86)

Cuban-born musician and band leader who, as Lucille Ball's real and on-screen husband, became one of TV's earliest superstars. Arnaz grew up in a wealthy Cuban family, but in 1933, with the installation of the Batista regime, he fled, penniless, to Miami with his mother. His Latin looks and musical abilities secured him work with bands like Xavier Cugat's and saw him arrive in Hollywood. There he met the up-and-coming Lucille Ball and they married in 1940. Ten years later, to save their turbulent marriage, they agreed to work together on a new TV comedy, I LOVE LUCY – the mother of all sitcoms – playing husband and wife duo, Lucy and Ricky Ricardo. To produce the show, Arnaz founded their own production company, Desilu (later responsible for shows such as THE UNTOUCHABLES and MANNIX). However, their marriage was not to last and they divorced in 1960. Lucy persevered with her scatterbrained TV characterizations, while Desi turned more to production. In later years he was seen only rarely on screen.

Arness, James

(James Aurness; 1923–)

The brother of MISSION: IMPOSSIBLE's Peter Graves, a strapping giant of an actor who became synonymous with the Western lawman, thanks to his long-running portrayal of Marshal Matt Dillon in GUNSMOKE. Arness, a veteran of the Anzio campaign in World War II, entered the movie business in the 1940s, winning parts in assorted B-movies, most memorably *The Thing* and *Them!*. In 1955 he was recommended for the *Gunsmoke* role by his friend John Wayne, and reluctantly accepted, fearing that a flopped TV series would jeopardize his cinema career. To help things along and guarantee a big audience, Wayne offered to introduce the very first *Gunsmoke* episode. Arness need not have worried. The series ran for 20 years on US TV and during that time he had no cause to look for other TV work. Indeed, by the close, he was also part-owner of the production. Following the cancellation of *Gunsmoke* in 1975, Arness returned to the screen as Zeb Macahan in *How the West was Won* and then took on the role of veteran cop Jim McClain in MCCLAIN'S LAW.

Arnold, Roseanne

See *Roseanne*.

Around the World in 80 Days ★★★★/Pole to Pole ★★★/ Full Circle ★★/ Sahara with Michael Palin ★/ Himalaya with Michael Palin ★★

UK (BBC) Documentary. BBC 1 1989/1992/1997/2002/2004
DVD: BBC

Presenter **Michael Palin**

Producers **Clem Vallence, Roger Mills** *(Sahara/Himalaya)*

Bold but light-hearted expeditions into unlikely quarters of the world.

Michael Palin's hugely successful series of travelogues began with *Around the World in 80 Days* in 1989. Initially earmarked as a vehicle for Alan Whicker, it pitched the ex-*Python* into the role of a modern-day Phileas Fogg. The aim of the venture was to follow closely the path set by Jules Verne's hero, travelling around the world in 80 days and using just land and sea transport (the only methods available 115 years earlier, when Fogg's fictitious journey took place). However, Palin discovered that Fogg's network of passenger liners had long disappeared, and he was forced to rely on unpredictable merchant vessels for large sections of his journey. Delays at customs points, narrowly missed departures and uncooperative locals added to the tension as Palin sought to return to London's Reform Club within the imposed time limit. His voyage took him on the Orient Express, on numerous ferries and by land across Saudi Arabia and the United Arab Emirates. Most dramatically, he boarded a primitive dhow for the crossing of the Arabian Sea. He then crossed India, China and the USA by train, before steaming into Felixstowe for the last leg into London. The circumnavigation took place in 1988.

Supporting Palin on his travels were his 'Passepartout', an openly acknowledged production team of producer/director Clem Vallence, co-director Roger Mills and a film crew. Half the team followed Palin as far as Hong Kong and the others completed the trip home. They shot film on 77 of the 80 days and their recordings were edited into seven intriguing episodes. An accompanying book, written by Michael Palin, was a massive success, selling over half a million copies.

A second adventure followed in 1991. In *Pole to Pole*, Palin and his team (including several *80 Days* veterans) attempted to travel from the North to the South Pole, using only public transport where available and sticking as closely as possible to the 30° East meridian. The exhausting 141-day voyage took them through the Soviet Union just days before its collapse and then down through civil-war-ravaged Africa. Again, a book accompanied the eight-part series, which was screened in 1992.

An even more ambitious venture took place in 1996 (aired in 1997). In the ten-part *Full Circle*, Palin and his pals attempted to follow the line of the Pacific Rim, beginning and ending at Little Diomede Island in the Bering Strait, but taking in stops in Russia, China, Australasia, and South, Central and North America *en route* – a distance of nearly 50,000 miles completed within the set deadline of one calendar year, with just one short stop in the middle, when Palin flew home to visit his wife, who had been receiving treatment for a brain tumour. Another best-selling book followed, as it did for *Michael Palin's Hemingway Adventure* in 1999, a similar but less structured four-part series in which Palin visited the haunts of one of his favourite authors, Ernest Hemingway.

In 2002, the BBC aired *Sahara with Michael Palin*, a four-part account of a journey made the year before across the inhospitable Sahara desert, beginning and ending at Gibraltar but visiting Morocco, Algeria, Western Sahara, Mauritania, Senegal, Mali, Niger, Libya and Tunisia, all the while flirting with unforgiving heat, terrorism and dodgy breakfasts of rank camel liver. The six-part *Himalaya with Michael Palin* followed in 2004, taking TV's most genial travel presenter from the Afghan border of Pakistan, across the great mountain range to the Bay of Bengal, via India, Nepal, Tibet, China, Butan and Bangladesh.

Arrest and Trial ★★

US (Revue/Universal) Police/Legal Drama. BBC 1 1964 (US: ABC 1963–4)

DS Nick Anderson .... **Ben Gazzara**
Attorney John Egan .... **Chuck Connors**
Deputy DA Jerry Miller .... **John Larch**
Assistant Deputy DA Barry Pine .... **John Kerr**
DS Dan Kirby .... **Roger Perry**
Det. Lt. Bone .... **Noah Keen**
Jake Shakespeare .... **Joe Higgins**
Mitchell Harris .... **Don Galloway**
Janet Okada .... **Jo Anne Miya**

Producer **Frank P. Rosenberg**

● ***Innovative drama series, comprising programmes of two separate halves: the first showing a criminal investigation, the second the subsequent trial.***

Setting the pattern for a host of crime movies many years later, *Arrest and Trial* depicts the exploits of Detective Sergeant Nick Anderson of the LAPD and local defence lawyer John Egan. The first 45-minute segment of each programme concerns itself with the execution of a crime and the efforts of Anderson and his colleagues to find the culprit. The second 45 minutes are then devoted to the trial, giving Egan and his legal eagles the chance to negate Anderson's good work by getting the defendant off the hook.

Art Attack ★★

UK (TVS/Media Merchants/Scottish) Children's Entertainment. ITV 1990–

Presenter **Neil Buchanan**

Producer **Tim Edmunds**

● ***Lively arts and crafts workshop.***

Art with attitude is the theme of this inspirational series that encourages kids (aged 4–16) to give painting, drawing and other forms of arts and crafts a go. Red-sweatered, energetic host Neil Buchanan (formerly of Saturday morning's NO. 73 and MOTORMOUTH, and rock bands Marseille and Nazareth) conducts proceedings (and comes up with all the ideas), experimenting with larger-than-life pictures, creating offbeat sculptures, making giant portraits out of bin bags and painting up old T-shirts to good effect. One of the best-remembered stunts saw him fashion a portrait of the Queen out of £10 notes (£200,000 in total) for her 40th year on the throne. Buchanan's confessed aim is to help youngsters break through the 'I can't do that' barrier. From the start, the series threatened to 'give your eyeballs a shock' and it easily survived the demise of its original production company, TVS. The series has now been screened around the world. Some 'Christmas Cracker' specials, offering advice on festive creations, have also been produced.

Artemis 81 ★

UK (BBC) Drama. BBC 1 1981

Gideon Harlax .... **Hywel Bennett**
Gwen Meredith .... **Dinah Stabb**
Von Drachenfels .... **Dan O'Herlihy**
Jed Thaxter .... **Ian Redford**
Laura Guise .... **Margaret Whiting**
Magog .... **Sevilla Delofski**
Asrael .... **Roland Curram**
Helith .... **Sting**
Tristram Guise .... **Anthony Steel**
Sonia .... **Mary Ellen Ray**
Pastor .... **Cornelius Garrett**
Pastor's wife .... **Siv Borg**
Gorgon scholar .... **Sylvia Coleridge**
Exhibitioner .... **Daniel Day Lewis**
Hitchcock blonde .... **Ingrid Pitt**

Writer **David Rudkin**
Producer **David Rose**

● ***An author of paranormal books becomes tangled up in the fate of humanity.***

In this three-hour film, shown the Tuesday after Christmas 1981, Gideon Harlax is a writer of successful novels. His works are based on enigmatic, unexplained events, and are filled with allusions to the paranormal. When he discovers a strange series of events – the shattering of an exhibits case belonging to a Danish museum; bits of a pagan statue hidden in cars on a North Sea ferry; and the later deaths of ferry passengers – and encounters an old musician named Von Drachenfels, who fears that a curse he has been subjected to will result in the end of the planet, Gideon thinks he has exciting material for his next project. But he quickly finds that forces from the past are less than pleased with his efforts to exploit human tragedy in this way. Supernatural creatures Asrael (the Angel of Death) and Helith (the Angel of Life) are seen fighting for control of man's destiny. Back on Earth, Gwen Meredith is the girl who loves Gideon but who finds that he is what the Greeks describe as being 'in the thrall of Artemis' (introverted and beyond her reach).

This puzzling, futuristic tale – set in locations as varied as Denmark, East Anglia and north Wales – has notable Hitchcockian influences, a fact conceded by writer David Rudkin, a huge fan of the Master of Suspense. The drama is also notable for early appearances by Sting and Daniel Day Lewis. Dave Greenslade provides the music; Alastair Reid directs.

Arthur, Beatrice

(Bernice Frankel; 1923–)

Tall, forceful stalwart of American sitcoms, who gained international recognition late in her career as Dorothy in THE GOLDEN GIRLS. Earlier, Arthur had played Archie Bunker's cousin, Maude Findlay, in ALL IN THE FAMILY and in her own spin-off, *Maude*. She also starred in *Amanda's*, the US version of FAWLTY TOWERS. More recent guest appearances have come in ELLEN, MALCOLM IN THE MIDDLE and CURB YOUR ENTHUSIASM.

Arthur C. Clarke's Mysterious World ✶

UK (Yorkshire) Documentary. ITV 1980

Host **Arthur C. Clarke**
Narrator **Gordon Honeycombe**

Executive Producer **John Fairley**
Producer **Simon Welfare**

● ***The Earth's strange phenomena investigated by the celebrated science-fiction writer.***

Hosting this documentary series from his Sri Lankan home, novelist Arthur C. Clarke turns his attention away from fiction and towards the weird and wonderful, unexplained real-life phenomena to be witnessed around the world. Looking at the strange moving rocks of America's Death Valley, investigating ancient stone circles, and discussing how it can rain frogs are just some of the topics covered as Clarke focuses on mysteries of the world that challenge modern-day thinking. Former ITN newscaster Gordon Honeycombe handled the narration of this half-hour series.

Arthur of the Britons ✶

UK (HTV) Adventure. ITV 1972–3

Arthur	**Oliver Tobias**
Llud	**Jack Watson**
Kai	**Michael Gothard**
Mark of Cornwall	**Brian Blessed**
Cerdig	**Rupert Davies**

Executive Producer **Patrick Dromgoole**
Producer **Peter Miller**

● ***A dashing young Celtic leader takes on the Saxon invaders.***

With no Camelot, no Guinevere and no Merlin, this series dispels the myth of round tables, chivalrous knights and mystic sorcery, bringing Arthur back down to earth with a bump. Here, young and ruggedly good-looking, the legendary king is depicted as a sixth-century Welsh ruler who fronts a tough, swashbuckling army of Celts against intruders from the East led by Cerdig. Supported by the pagan Llud the Silver Hand and Kai, a Saxon orphan, Arthur's aim is to unite the native tribes of Britain against the invading Saxon forces. Tough battles ensue and there are woodland skirmishes aplenty. The Saxons apart, Arthur's other great rival is the powerful Mark of Cornwall. Many guest artists featured in the series, including Michael Gambon, Tom Baker and Catherine Schell.

As Time Goes By ✶✶✶

UK (Theatre of Comedy) Situation Comedy. BBC 1 1992–8; 2000; 2002; 2005
DVD: Universal

Jean Pargetter/Hardcastle	**Judi Dench**
Lionel Hardcastle	**Geoffrey Palmer**
Judith Pargetter/Deacon	**Moira Brooker**
Alistair Deacon	**Philip Bretherton**
Sandy	**Jenny Funnell**
Rocky Hardcastle	**Frank Middlemass**
Madge Hardcastle	**Joan Sims**
Penny	**Moyra Fraser**
Stephen	**Paul Chapman**
Mrs Bale	**Janet Henfrey**
Harry	**David Michaels**
	Daniel Ryan

Creator/Writer **Bob Larbey**
Executive Producers **Philip Jones, John Reynolds**
Producer **Sydney Lotterby**

● ***Two middle-aged former lovers rekindle their romance.***

Taking its inspiration from the 1931 song, voiced by Joe Fagin over the credits, *As Time Goes By* is a will-they, won't-they, gentle comedy about two young lovers who have gone their separate ways, only to rediscover each other in middle age. Jean Pargetter and Lionel Hardcastle had each mistakenly believed the other had broken off their youthful romance and both drifted off to marry someone else. Jean, a nurse, and Lionel, a second lieutenant in the Middlesex Regiment, had met in Hyde Park, but when Lionel was posted to Korea a vital letter from Jean never reached him. After 38 years, fate brings them together again when Lionel, now divorced, employs Jean's secretarial agency (Type For You) to type up his book, *My Life in Kenya*, which describes his career as a coffee planter in East Africa. Jean's husband, David, has died and she lives with her twice-married daughter, Judith, who one evening brings Lionel home after dinner, with obvious consequences. Jean and Lionel are wed in the 1995 series. Also seen are Jean's efficient secretary, Sandy, and Lionel's pushy publisher, Alistair (Judith's boyfriend). After officially ending in 2002, *As Time Goes By* returned for two special episodes at Christmas 2005. The series was created by Bob Larbey from an original idea by Colin Bostock Smith. In 1997, it was reworked into a comedy series for Radio 2.

Ascent of Man, The ✶✶✶

UK (BBC/Time-Life) Documentary. BBC 2 1973
DVD: BBC

Writer/Presenter: **Dr Jacob Bronowski**

Producer **Adrian Malone**

● ***An inspirational account of man's scientific and philosophical progress.***

Through the eyes of Polish-born, California-based historian and philosopher Dr Jacob Bronowski, this 13-part series reflects on the development of man through his technological achievements. It considers how new inventions and discoveries have changed social and moral patterns, thus revealing how man has become the shaper of his own environment. From the use of primitive tools to the effects of the Industrial Revolution and beyond, vivid examples and illustrations sugar the pill for less scientifically minded viewers, as do the charisma and enthusiasm of the curious, hunched presenter. Bronowski travelled the world for the series – which was described as a 'personal view' – and worked so hard in the four years of production that he collapsed from exhaustion at its completion and died the following year. He was an unlikely TV star, but his series was widely acclaimed.

Ash, Leslie

(1960–)

British actress, formerly a teenage model and star of a Fairy Liquid advert when aged four. One of her first leading roles was as Nancy Gray in the sitcom THE HAPPY APPLE. She then starred as computer whiz-kid Fred Smith in C.A.T.S. EYES, although there had been plenty of minor parts in series like WORLD'S END, SECONDS OUT, SHELLEY and THE TWO RONNIES. Ash was also a dancer with the Black and White Minstrels and co-presenter of Channel 4's rock show THE TUBE for a while. Later, as well as appearances in PERFECT SCOUNDRELS, LOVE HURTS, HAGGARD and JUDGE JOHN DEED, she starred as Deborah in MEN BEHAVING BADLY, Jo in STAY LUCKY, Karen Buckley in WHERE THE HEART IS and Inspector Charlie Eden in MERSEYBEAT. Ash was also a panellist in the revival of GOING FOR A SONG. She is married to ex-footballer Lee Chapman, with whom she hosted the series *Dinner Dates*, and is sister of actress/dancer Debbie Ash.

Ashcroft, Dame Peggy

(Edith Margaret Emily Ashcroft; 1907–91)

Notable British stage and, occasionally, film actress who added television credits to her name in her later years. Most memorably, Dame Peggy appeared as Queen Mary in EDWARD AND MRS SIMPSON and Barbie, the missionary, in Granada's lavish THE JEWEL IN THE CROWN. She also starred in Stephen Poliakoff's single drama CAUGHT ON A TRAIN (Frau Messner) and played seaside landlady Miss Dubber in A PERFECT SPY.

Ashenden ✳✳✳

UK (Kelso Films) Drama. BBC 1 1991

John Ashenden	**Alex Jennings**
Cumming	**Joss Ackland**
R	**Ian Bannen**
Giulia Lazzari	**Harriet Walter**
Grantly Caypor	**Alan Bennett**
Anna Caypor	**Anna Carteret**
John Quincy Harrington	**René Auberjonois**
Gen. Carmona	**Alfred Molina**
Aileen Somerville	**Elizabeth McGovern**

Writer **David Pirie**

Producer **Joe Knatchbull**

● ***A writer poses as a spy during World War I.***

This four-part series, based on spy stories by Somerset Maugham, recounts the adventures of West End playwright-turned-secret-agent John Ashenden. The suave, but aloof and enigmatic, Ashenden uses his profession as a cover to do his bit for his country after being recruited to the fledgling secret service during World War I. His boss and recruiter is an army man known simply as R who shares control of the agency with the rebellious Cumming, who invented it all. Ashenden's cases include persuading music hall dancer Giulia Lazzari to betray her Indian terrorist lover, and a mysterious encounter with Englishman Grantly Caypor and his German wife, Anna, in a Swiss alpine hotel. Ashenden also deals with a disastrously brash American businessman, John Quincy Harrington, in Russia on the eve of the Revolution, and finally leads Mexican hitman General Carmona to Italy to murder a courier carrying important documents, falling at the same time for young American Aileen Somerville. All this is a voyage of discovery for the cerebral Ashenden, who soon recognizes his own capacity for double dealing.

Maugham's stories were based on his own personal experiences as a spy during World War I. This dramatization was directed by Christopher Morahan.

Ask Aspel ✳

UK (BBC) Children's Entertainment. BBC 1 1970–3; 1976–81

Presenter **Michael Aspel**

Producers **Iain Johnstone, Will Wyatt, Frances Whitaker, Granville Jenkins**

● ***Long-running children's request show.***

Taking over from *Junior Points of View* as the kiddies' feedback series, *Ask Aspel* encouraged youngsters to write in with their views on the BBC's latest offerings. Host Michael Aspel also played requested snippets, and interviews with star guests filled out the programme.

Ask the Family ✳

UK (BBC) Quiz. BBC 1 1967–84; 1999; BBC 2 2005

Presenters **Robert Robinson, Alan Titchmarsh, Richard McCourt, Dominic Wood**

Producers **Cecil Korer, Linda McCarthy, Mark Patterson, Mirella Breda**

● ***Mind-bending quiz for cerebral families.***

Open to families of four (often teachers and their egg-headed offspring), *Ask the Family* was a surprisingly durable, early-evening intellectual quiz. Host Robert Robinson fired off a succession of riddles, mental posers and general knowledge questions, some directed to 'children only', 'mother and younger child', 'father and elder child' or other combinations of contestants. The winning family then progressed through the annual knock-out tournament.

Ask the Family was revived on UKGold in spring 1999, with the series screened later in the year on BBC 1. Alan Titchmarsh was the new host. The series was resurrected one more time as *Dick & Dom's Ask the Family* in 2005, introducing an air of surrealism and controlled chaos in the presenters' established style, and allowing any family members – not just parents and their children – to take part.

Askey, Arthur
CBE (1900–1982)

Indefatigable, Liverpool-born, diminutive music hall veteran who became one of post-war TV's biggest names, appearing in assorted variety spectaculars and, from 1952, his own series, BEFORE YOUR VERY EYES. The series moved to ITV in 1956, a year after the new network had recorded Askey's Blackpool summer show and screened it in five parts under the title *Love and Kisses*. In 1957, Askey appeared with his former partner, Richard Murdoch, in *Living It Up*, a re-creation of their popular 1930s radio show, *Band Waggon*, and then, in 1961, he starred in a sitcom, *The Arthur Askey Show*. The following year, back with the BBC, he shared the limelight with Alan Melville in *Raise Your Glasses*. Always popular, Askey was on our screens till the end. In the 1970s he was a familiar panellist on the gag game show *Jokers Wild* and one of the regular (and kindest) judges on the talent show NEW FACES, never failing to shower the contestants with praise, however dire their act.

Asner, Ed
(1929–)

American actor famous as grouchy news editor LOU GRANT in THE MARY TYLER MOORE SHOW (a performance which won him three Emmys). When the sitcom ended, he made an unusual move, staying in the same role when Grant was shipped to the West Coast to become editor of the *Los Angeles Tribune* in a straight drama sequel. Another Emmy followed. After several successful seasons, Lou Grant was cancelled amid rumours of a rift between the producers and the star, revolving around his outspoken political views. Asner's earliest TV credits included guest spots in programmes like THE FBI, THE DEFENDERS, A MAN CALLED IRONSIDE and THE FUGITIVE, as well as a continuous role in a series called *Slattery's People*. He also starred as Axel Jordache in RICH MAN, POOR MAN and the slave ship's Captain Davies in ROOTS (earning two more Emmys), as well as in the high school drama *The Bronx Zoo*, *Thunder Alley* (about a retired racing driver), and *The Trials of Rosie O'Neill* (Walter Kovatch). More recent guest spots have been in MORE TALES OF THE CITY, *Dharma & Greg* and THE X-FILES. In 2004 he featured in a new US sitcom called *Center of the Universe* (Art Barnett).

Aspel, Michael
OBE (1933–)

London-born presenter and chat show host, initially seen on BBC TV news programmes in the 1950s, after working as an actor on BBC Wales radio and as a TV announcer. Since then he has presented CRACKERJACK, COME DANCING, MISS WORLD, *Ace of Clubs*, ASK ASPEL, CHILD'S PLAY, *Ultra Quiz*, *Star Games*, GIVE US A CLUE, *The Six O'Clock Show* (London), *Aspel and Company*, a revival of BLOCKBUSTERS and the paranormal series *Strange But True*, as well as taking over from Eamonn Andrews as holder of the big red book in THIS IS YOUR LIFE. In 2000 he succeeded Hugh Scully as anchor of ANTIQUES ROADSHOW and in 2001 he replaced Michael Parkinson in the chair of GOING FOR A SONG. He is married to, though separated from, actress Elizabeth Power (Mrs Hewitt in EastEnders).

Assignment Foreign Legion ✱

UK (Anthony Bartley) Drama Anthology. ITV 1956

Host **Merle Oberon**

Executive Producer **Anthony C. Bartley**

A female correspondent unearths true stories of the French Foreign Legion.

Former Hollywood starlet Merle Oberon travelled to Algeria and Morocco to film this series, working closely with the French Foreign Legion. When nationalist activists in those countries began to rebel, filming was completed in England. Each episode dramatizes a real-life tale of Legionnaires (motto: 'Honour, Valour, Fidelity and Discipline') during World War II and is introduced by Oberon, who plays a roving reporter, among other roles.

Associate Producer

The close assistant to the producer, usually on set dealing with everyday logistics of production, leaving the producer free to handle the overall project. Also sometimes called Line Producer.

Associated-Rediffusion

Company formed by Broadcast Relay Services and Associated Newspapers to operate the very first ITV franchise. A-R (as it became known) went on air on 22 September 1955 and covered London on weekdays. The company shortened its name to Rediffusion in the mid-1960s and was forced by the ITA to merge with ABC in 1968. The resulting company, Thames Television, retained the London weekday franchise. Among A-R's successes were TAKE YOUR PICK, DOUBLE YOUR MONEY, DO NOT ADJUST YOUR SET and READY, STEADY, GO!. The name Associated-Rediffusion was bought by TV critic Victor Lewis-Smith in the 1990s and is now used for his own independent production company.

Associated Television
See *ATV*.

Astin, John
(1930–)

American comic actor chiefly remembered as Gomez in THE ADDAMS FAMILY. Previously, he had scored a success as Harry Dickens in the sitcom I'M DICKENS, HE'S FENSTER, and was later one of the actors to play The Riddler in BATMAN, as well as appearing in *The Pruitts of Southampton*. His attention then switched to directing, working on programmes like CHIPS and HOLMES AND YOYO, although he continued on screen in series like *Mary*, WELCOME BACK, KOTTER, *Operation Petticoat*, *Night Court*, EERIE, INDIANA (Mr Radford) and *The Adventures of Brisco County, Jr*. In the late 1990s, Astin made a guest appearance in the remake of his greatest triumph, playing Grandpapa Addams in *The New Addams Family*. He was at one time married to former child actress Patty Duke (Astin).

Astronut Show, The ✶

US (CBS Terrytoons) Cartoon. BBC 1 1968 (US: Syndicated 1965)

Voices:
Astronut .... **Dayton Allen**
Oscar Mild .... **Bob McFadden**

Executive Producer **Bill Weiss**

● ***The adventures of an amiable little extraterrestrial.***

Astronut, a friendly but odd-looking space traveller with a giant head, two antennae, but no body (save tiny feet), arrives on Earth in a small bubble-like spacecraft and quickly makes friends with Oscar Mild, a timid, very ordinary Earthling. Like Mork ten years later, this superhuman always means well, even if his behaviour is rather eccentric, and he never fails to bring new excitement to Oscar's mundane little life. Astronut, who is capable of changing his shape to avoid detection, first appeared in an episode of DEPUTY DAWG. Other parts of *The Astronut Show* were devoted to the exploits of Sidney (a baby elephant), Hashimoto (a Japanese mouse with judo skills) and Luno (a flying horse).

At Home with the Braithwaites ✶✶

UK (Yorkshire) Drama. ITV 2000–3
DVD: Acorn Media

Alison Braithwaite .... **Amanda Redman**
David Braithwaite .... **Peter Davison**
Pauline Farnell .... **Lynda Bellingham**
Marion Riley .... **Sylvia Syms**
Megan Hartnoll .... **Julie Graham**
Mike Hartnoll .... **Kevin Doyle**
Virginia Braithwaite .... **Sarah Smart**
Charlotte Braithwaite .... **Keeley Fawcett**
Sarah Braithwaite .... **Sarah Churm**
Elaine Fishwick .... **Judy Holt**
Denise Skidmore .... **Ishia Bennison**
Colin Skidmore .... **Garry Cooper**
Phil Skidmore .... **Damian Zuk**
Audrey Crowther .... **Hazel Douglas**
Kieran .... **Jonathan Le Billon**
Tamsin .... **Lucy Whelan**
Graham Braithwaite .... **Ray Stevenson**
Helen Braithwaite .... **Elizabeth Rider**
Daniel Wolfenden .... **Alun Raglan**
Beth Wolfenden .... **Amelia Curtis**
Jordan Fishwick .... **Ben Douglas**
Corrie Greenop
Scott Cooper
Nick Bottomley .... **Adam Rayner**
Ciara Pickering .... **Rachel Leskovac**

Creator **Sally Wainwright**
Writers **Sally Wainwright, Jonathan Harvey, Katie Baxendale**
Producers **Hugh Warren, Jacky Stoller, Giles Pilbrow, Kieran Roberts, Morag Fullarton, Sue Pritchard**

● ***A middle-class family's life is turned upside down by a lottery win.***

A suburban family in Yorkshire: husband, wife and three daughters – nothing unusual there perhaps, except that this is a household cluttered with secrets. Dad David is carrying on with mistress Elaine, snatching moments of passion in car parks, and the self-centred kids all have their own little vices, too. Virginia is in love with Megan, the woman next door; her sister, Sarah, is sure to end up in trouble with her clandestine boyfriend, Phil; and third sibling Charlotte is no angel at school. But there is no bigger secret than the fact that 40-year-old mum, Alison, has just won £38 million on the Euro-Lottery and decides not to tell the others. Knowing the effect it would have on her dysfunctional, greedy family, she decides to put the money into good causes, setting up a charitable trust assisted by friends Pauline Farnell and Marion Riley. Despite her best efforts, however, the press gets hold of her story and by the end of the first series, the family is aware of her fortune – and the other secrets have also begun to unfold. When they return in series two, set seven months later, the Braithwaites have decided to cash in some of their new-found wealth and have moved to a mansion, but money does not solve their deep family rifts. A second honeymoon fails to ignite the flame of happiness, especially when David's brother, an ex-boyfriend of Alison's, makes an appearance. With series three, the sweetness of a DBE for charity work is soured for Alison by an unwanted pregnancy and a court case over her right to claim the lottery prize in the first place. By the fourth and final series, divorce is on the cards for Alison and David. This family's roller-coaster ride is far from over.

At Last the 1948 Show ✶✶

UK (Rediffusion) Comedy. ITV 1967
DVD: Boulevard Entertainment

John Cleese, Tim Brooke-Taylor, Graham Chapman, Marty Feldman, Aimi Macdonald

Writers **John Cleese, Tim Brooke-Taylor, Graham Chapman, Marty Feldman**
Executive Producer **David Frost**

● ***Manic comedy sketch series.***

Emerging from the funny side of THE FROST REPORT and masterminded by David Frost himself, *At Last the 1948 Show* was one of the stepping-stone programmes which led to MONTY PYTHON'S FLYING CIRCUS and a whole new generation of British comedy. Although essentially a sketch show, its skits were unrelated, in the manner perfected later by *Python*. The humour was visual, wacky and verging on the surreal, and there was also a heavy dose of slapstick (foreshadowing Tim Brooke-Taylor's days in THE GOODIES). Aimi Macdonald supported the show's writer-performers, linking events in her trademark whiny voice.

A-Team, The ✶

US (Universal/Stephen J. Cannell) Adventure. ITV 1983–8 (US: NBC 1983–7)
DVD: Universal

Col. John 'Hannibal' Smith ..... **George Peppard**
Sgt Bosco 'BA' Baracus .... **Mr T (Lawrence Tureaud)**
Lt. Templeton Peck ('Faceman') .... **Dirk Benedict**
Capt. H. M. 'Howling Mad' Murdock .... **Dwight Schultz**
Amy Amanda Allen ('Triple A') .... **Melinda Culea**
Col. Lynch .... **William Lucking**
Col. Roderick Decker .... **Lance LeGault**
Tawnia Baker .... **Maria Heasley**

Gen. Hunt Stockwell .... **Robert Vaughn**
'Dishpan' Frankie Sanchez ...... **Eddie Velez**
Carla .... **Judy Ledford**

Creators/Executive Producers **Stephen J. Cannell, Frank Lupo**

● ***Four soldiers of fortune use their diverse skills to help citizens in trouble.***

The A-Team, an unlikely group of heroic renegades, had worked together as commandos in the Vietnam War, only to be captured behind enemy lines and accused of raiding the Bank of Hanoi four days after the war ended in 1972. They maintain they were under orders to do so, but, with no proof, the gang is imprisoned by their own country. Following their escape to LA, the series tells how they evade attempts to recapture them – first by Colonel Lynch, then by Colonel Decker – and their mercenary-style righting of wrongs along the way.

Each member of the Team is a specialist. The cigar-chewing leader, Hannibal Smith, is a master of disguise; Howling Mad Murdock is a brilliant but crazy pilot who has to be sprung from a psychiatric hospital to join the Team on their missions; the gold-swathed BA ('Bad Attitude') is the inventive mechanic, a Mohican-haired giant of a man who dreads flying with Murdock; while Faceman (played by Tim Dunigan in the pilot episode) is the smooth talker and procurer of their material needs. Together they travel the world in a heavily armed transit van, initially accompanied by attractive journalist Amy Allen.

Although their escapades are often violent, they are never gory. This is comic-book action, with plenty of crashes and explosions but little blood. A few years into the programme's run, the guys are eventually caught by General Stockwell, but they avoid the firing squad by becoming undercover Government agents. At this time, a new member, Dishpan, joins the squad. Music for *The A-Team* was composed by Mike Post and Pete Carpenter.

Atkinson, Rowan

(1955–)

Newcastle-born, rubber-faced comedian and comic actor who began performing while a postgraduate at Oxford. His first TV showcase came in 1979 in a one-off called *Rowan Atkinson Presents . . . Canned Laughter*, but he quickly moved on to NOT THE NINE O'CLOCK NEWS. His major roles since that groundbreaking sketch show have been the weaselly historical blackguard Edmund BLACKADDER, the gormless near-mute MR BEAN (also voicing the animated version), and the pedantic Inspector Raymond Fowler in THE THIN BLUE LINE. Atkinson also devised and narrated the documentary series *Funny Business*.

Atletico Partick ✶

UK (BBC) Situation Comedy. BBC 1 1996

Jack Roan .... **Gordon Kennedy**
Ally .... **Tom McGovern**
Pettigrew .... **Iain McColl**
Bonner .... **Clive Russell**
Gazza .... **Ronnie Letham**
Lachie .... **Steven McNicoll**
McStick .... **Gavin Mitchell**
Karen Roan .... **Aline Mowat**
Marie .... **Anne Marie Timoney**
Sean .... **Jonathan Watson**
Sally .... **Nicola Park**
Dr Maitland .... **Tony Curran**

Writer **Ian Pattison**
Producer **Colin Gilbert**

● ***Trials on and off the field for a Sunday football team.***

Atletico Partick is an unfortunately named amateur soccer team in Scotland. Despite the best attentions of ambitious coach Bonner, the side consists mostly of no-hopers – on the field and off. With the exception of leading striker Ally, who also hits the net with all the women he approaches, the definitely unathletic team is a shambles. Take Jack Roan, for instance, a midfielder whose wife's indiscretions are causing him plenty of headaches. Or Pettigrew, the goalkeeper whose wife takes up witchcraft. Over six episodes, the team struggles to make an impact in the local Sunday league and the prestigious Streaky Bacon Cup. The series followed a pilot episode in 1995, entitled *Atletico Partick AFC*, in which the coach/manager was called Jinky Baird (but still played by Clive Russell).

Attachments ✶✶✶

UK (World) Drama. BBC 2 2000–2

Lucy 'Luce' Jennings .... **Claudia Harrison**
Mike Fisher .... **Justin Pierre**
Sophie Moore .... **Amanda Ryan**
Jake Plaskow .... **David Walliams**
Brandon Dyer .... **Iddo Goldberg**
Reece Wilson .... **William Beck**
Yvonne Harper .... **Sally Rodgers**
Fran Chapel .... **Poppy Miller**
Will Newman .... **William Gaminara**
Katherine McGuire .... **Elizabeth Marmur**
Murray .... **Andrew Sachs**
Zoe Atkins .... **Romola Garai**
Sawyer .... **Sandy Welch**
Olly .... **Razaaq Adoti**
Kerry .... **Julie Smith**
Patrick Deely .... **Karl Shiels**
Ren Spencer .... **Christine Entwistle**
Tyler Clarkson .... **Indra Ove**
Kumari Dalta .... **Anjali Mya Chadha**
Maxine .... **Sally Edwards**
David .... **Tim Preece**

Creator/Executive Producer **Tony Garnett**
Producer **Simon Heath**

● ***Business woes and personal frictions with the young team at a fledgling Internet site.***

Husband and wife Mike Fisher and Luce Jennings have plans to launch their own commercial website, based on the world of showbiz. Failed musician Mike has planned it all out in a bedroom at home and has been running the site as a hobby, and now level-headed Luce's professional publishing skills are being harnessed to make seethru.co.uk work. They assemble a team of variously talented twentysomethings and set about acquiring finance to get the site up and running. Two series then follow their ups and downs in the world of dotcom start-ups and the evolving personal relationships among the gang: the financial stresses, the secret liaisons, the constant bitching, the boozy nights, the strong language and the drug abuse. The team includes plain-speaking lesbian Sophie, who takes charge of site content and writes an irreverent column;

geeky, skateboarding programmer Brandon; talented site designer Jake; Reece, the site's obnoxious coder; Yvonne, the duplicitous marketing manager; Zoe, the teenage editorial assistant; and, later, Pat Deely, the music editor. Will is the devious venture capitalist from Proctor Investments who, with unfavourable terms, eventually stumps up the cash for the site to stay online. Fran is Mike and Luce's lodger, with problems of her own.

A total of 26 episodes were produced, the first series of ten lasting 50 minutes each, the second trimmed to 30-minute helpings. To accompany the series a dedicated website, also called seethru.co.uk, was set up, mirroring the one in the series in its sensational news, gossip and humour content.

Attenborough, Sir David

CBE (1926–)

Television's leading naturalist, London-born David Attenborough, younger brother of (Lord) Richard, studied natural science at Cambridge. Joining the BBC as a trainee in 1952, he went on to produce ANIMAL, VEGETABLE, MINERAL? and to host and produce the long-running ZOO QUEST, before being made Controller of BBC 2 in 1965 (overseeing among other things the commissioning of THE WORLD ABOUT US and the launch of colour television), and the BBC's Director of Programmes in 1969. Although he never totally abandoned wildlife to concentrate on administration (making THE TRIBAL EYE in 1975, for instance), it was not until 1979 that he returned to television in a big way, when he launched his mammoth production LIFE ON EARTH. This seminal work was followed by THE LIVING PLANET in 1984, TRIALS OF LIFE in 1990, *The Private Life of Plants* in 1995, THE LIFE OF BIRDS in 1998, THE BLUE PLANET in 2001, *The Life of Mammals* in 2002 and *Life in the Undergrowth* in 2005. He has also contributed to *Wildlife on One, The Natural World, Life in the Freezer* and countless other nature programmes, produced the Queen's Christmas broadcast, and presented documentaries like *Lost Gods of Easter Island, State of the Planet* and *Great Natural Wonders of the World*. His whispering, authoritative delivery has been much mimicked by impressionists.

ATV

(Associated Television)

The ITV franchise-holder for London at weekends and the Midlands on weekdays from 1956 to 1968, and then the seven-day contractor for the Midlands from 1968 to 1981. ATV began life as ABC (Associated Broadcasting Company) but was forced to change its name to avoid confusion with Associated British Cinemas, which ran the early franchises for the Midlands and the North at weekends. The company was a merger of interests between Lew Grade and Prince Littler's ITC (which initially owned 50 per cent) and a consortium headed by Norman Collins and Sir Robert Renwick, which had originally been awarded the franchise but which seemed to be having difficulties starting up. ATV went on air on 24 September 1955 in London and on 17 February 1956 in the Midlands. ITC was swallowed up by ATV in 1957, and ATV was itself reconstituted as Central Independent Television to meet the requirements of the IBA's 1981 franchise changes. Central subsequently took over ATV's Midlands area. Among ATV's many programming successes were SUNDAY NIGHT AT THE LONDON PALLADIUM, DANGER MAN, THE SAINT, CROSSROADS and THE MUPPET SHOW, plus the Gerry Anderson futuristic puppet dramas.

Audience with . . . , An ✶

UK (LWT/Channel 4) Variety. ITV 1980–1; Channel 4 1983–5; ITV/Channel 4 1988; Channel 4 1990; ITV 1994–9; 2001–2; 2004–
DVD: Granada Ventures

One-hour showcase for light entertainment stars.

Beginning on Boxing Day 1980 and continuing, sporadically (over two channels), ever since, *An Audience with . . .* has featured some of the biggest names in British variety, plus top stars from overseas. The format has been simple: the star has performed highlights from his or her act, sung a few songs, cracked a few gags and taken well-rehearsed 'prompt' questions from the prominent celebrity audience. One 45-minute programme, *An Audience with Sooty*, to celebrate the glove puppet's 40th birthday, was shown during Children's ITV.

The performers featured to date have been: Dame Edna Everage (three times); Dudley Moore; Kenneth Williams; Mel Brooks; Joan Rivers (twice); Billy Connolly; Peter Ustinov; Victoria Wood; Jackie Mason; Bob Monkhouse; Jimmy Tarbuck; Ken Dodd (twice); Shirley Bassey; Freddie Starr (twice); Sooty; Bruce Forsyth; Alf Garnett (Warren Mitchell); Elton John; Ronnie Corbett; The Spice Girls; Rod Stewart; The Bee Gees; Tom Jones; Cliff Richard; Diana Ross; Kylie Minogue; Des O'Connor; Ricky Martin; Lulu; Brian Conley; Donny Osmond; Harry Hill; Joe Pasquale and Al Murray.

Auf Wiedersehen, Pet ✶✶✶✶

UK (Witzend/Central/BBC/Ziji) Comedy Drama. ITV 1983; 1986
BBC 1 2002; 2004
DVD: Carlton/VCI

Dennis Patterson	**Tim Healy**
Leonard 'Oz' Osborne	**Jimmy Nail**
Neville Hope	**Kevin Whately**
Wayne Norris	**Gary Holton**
Brian 'Bomber' Busbridge	**Pat Roach**
Barry Taylor	**Timothy Spall**
Albert Moxey	**Christopher Fairbank**
Brenda Hope	**Julia Tobin**
Ally Fraser	**Bill Paterson**
Wyman Norris	**Noel Clarke**
Jeffrey Grainger	**Bill Nighy**
Mickey Startup	**Michael Angelis**
Joe Saugus	**Gordon Tootoosis**
Tatiana	**Branka Katic**
Gary Turnbull	**Clive Russell**
Pru Scott-Johns	**Caroline Harker**
Tarquin	**Alexander Hanson**
Ofelia Ortiz	**Josefina Gabrielle**
Chrissie	**Sandra James-Young**

Creators **Dick Clement, Ian La Frenais, Franc Roddam**
Executive Producers **Allan McKeown, Laura Mackie, Franc Roddam**
Producers **Martin McKeand, Joy Spink, Chrissy Skins**

The misadventures of a gang of building workers on secondment overseas.

With jobs scarce in the recession-ridden UK of the early 1980s, the Geordie trio of Dennis, Neville and Oz decide to leave their wives and girlfriends in search of employment overseas. Dennis is the most mature of the three, philosophical and reasonably sensible. Neville is the drippy one, emotionally strained at having to leave his new wife, Brenda, while Oz is the archetypal slob: big, fat, bigoted and dense. They are taken on as labourers on a Düsseldorf building site, where they share a hut with four other expatriates – boring Brummie electrician Barry, Cockney carpenter Wayne, level-headed Bristolian wrestler Bomber and Scouse petty crook Moxey. The seven make quite a team. Sharing each other's joys, despairs, hopes and worries, they drink and womanize through their tour of duty, edging from scrape to scrape and from scam to scam.

In the second season, shown two years later, the boys are reunited to renovate the Derbyshire mansion of Newcastle gangster Ally Fraser, for whom Dennis has been forced to work after amassing gambling debts. When that ends, the lads head off for a few episodes' labour under the Spanish sun, building a swimming pool at Ally's villa. One sad aspect of this last series was the death of actor Gary Holton, who was, nevertheless, still seen in all episodes, thanks to early location filming and the subtle use of a double. The show's original closing theme song, 'That's Living Alright' by Joe Fagin, was a top three hit in 1984.

It was a brave move to bring back such a successful and fondly remembered series, but writers Dick Clement and Ian La Frenais and the cast reunited for a new batch of episodes in 2002, which were well received. By this time, Oz has decided to take life seriously, largely kicking the drink habit and looking to make business work for him. A spell in jail alongside disgraced politician/wheeler-dealer Jeffrey Grainger has set him up with an idea for dismantling and selling the transporter bridge at Middlesbrough. He needs help, however, and recalls his old buddies so that the magnificent seven can ride again, this time into the desert sun of Arizona. There the bridge is used to span a canyon, rendering a casino, owned by native Chocanaw Americans, more profitable, and so saving their community. To replace the late Gary Holton, Noel Clarke was cast as his son, Wyman. A new theme song, 'Why Aye Man', was supplied by Mark Knopfler. In 2004 the lads returned for a tour of duty in Cuba, renovating the British Embassy, before a two-part Christmas special concluded matters once and for all, with the team working in Laos and Thailand (sadly without Bomber: actor Pat Roach was ill and died while the others were already filming).

Auntie's Bloomers/Auntie's Sporting Bloomers

See *It'll Be Alright on the Night.*

Autocue

Trade name for a means of projecting a script on to a screen in front of a camera lens to allow presenters to read their lines; the words remain unseen by viewers. The system is universally used for news bulletins and other programmes using set scripts. Other trade names include Teleprompt.

Automan ✶

US (Kushner-Locke/Glen Larson/Twentieth) Science Fiction. BBC 1 1984 (US: ABC 1983–4)

Walter Nebicher	**Desi Arnaz Jr**
Automan	**Chuck Wagner**
Lt. Jack Curtis	**Robert Lansing**
Roxanne Caldwell	**Heather McNair**
Capt. E. G. Boyd	**Gerald S. O'Loughlin**

Creator/Executive Producer **Glen A. Larson**

A bored police computer operator invents a hologram detective.

Walter Nebicher works in the computer department of the Los Angeles Police Department, but longs to be out on the streets chasing the bad guys. Unfortunately, his grouchy boss, Capt. Boyd, confines Walter to base, where he whiles away his time inventing computer games. One day, however, he creates Automan, a three-dimensional hologram that springs from the screen and gives Walter the chance to make the grade as a real policeman. Programmed with all Walter's knowledge, Automan is an extremely useful ally. He can pass through walls and gain access to information human cops cannot reach. He is also programmed with the detective skills of all the top fictional sleuths, like Sherlock Holmes. However, because only he knows of Automan's existence, Walter is able to take all the credit for the squad's amazing success rate. Out on assignment, the ever-smiling Automan is able to call on the help of his brother computers and other electronic devices, and, whenever danger looms for his human colleague, he allows Walter to merge into the hologram and hide. But Automan does have his shortcomings, too. These mainly concern the amount of power he uses up, which causes surrounding lights to fade. At times when power stations are struggling to cope with demand (day time), he is likely to disappear altogether, leaving Walter firmly in the lurch. Working with Walter and Automan is Cursor, the flashing marker on a computer screen that comes to life as a hexagonal blob. Cursor follows the duo around, chases women and is generally called upon to draw up a fast car or some other useful equipment. Also seen are Roxanne Caldwell, Walter's police officer girlfriend, and Walter's supervisor, Lt. Curtis.

Autry, Gene

(1907–98)

Texan singing cowboy of the 1930s and 1940s who quickly clambered aboard the TV bandwagon when it began rolling in the 1950s. His *Gene Autry Show*, popular with American kiddies, was a small-screen version of his cinema antics and radio series, with bumbling sidekick Pat Buttram still in tow. 'Back in the Saddle Again' became his theme song. He later developed his own business empire. Apart from owning the Challenge record label, a baseball team, a host of radio and TV stations across the States and assorted hotels, he also founded Flying A Productions. This was the company responsible for such hits as THE RANGE RIDER and CHAMPION THE WONDER HORSE (Champion was Autry's own trusty steed).

Avengers, The ✶✶✶✶

UK (ABC) Secret Agent Drama. ITV 1961–9
DVD: Contender Entertainment

John Steed	**Patrick Macnee**
Dr David Keel	**Ian Hendry**
Carol Wilson	**Ingrid Hafner**
Catherine Gale	**Honor Blackman**
Venus Smith	**Julie Stevens**
Dr Martin King	**Jon Rollason**
One-Ten	**Douglas Muir**
One-Twelve	**Arthur Hewlett**
Emma Peel	**Diana Rigg**
Tara King	**Linda Thorson**
'Mother'	**Patrick Newell**

Rhonda .... **Rhonda Parker**

Creators **Sydney Newman, Leonard White**
Executive Producers **Albert Fennell, Julian Wintle, Gordon L. T. Scott**
Producers **Leonard White, John Bryce, Julian Wintle, Albert Fennell, Brian Clemens**

Very British adventure series featuring a suave, gentleman agent and his athletic female partners.

The Avengers began life as a spin-off from a programme called POLICE SURGEON, which starred Ian Hendry as Dr Geoffrey Brent. In *The Avengers* Hendry plays Dr David Keel, who, when his girlfriend is murdered by a drugs gang, goes to British Intelligence and an agent called John Steed for help in 'avenging' her death – hence the title. The early episodes, with Steed acting as a foil for the amateur sleuth, are essentially cops-and-robbers fare; also seen at this time are Carol Wilson, Keel's secretary, and Steed's bosses, One-Ten and One-Twelve. Following Hendry's departure during a technicians' strike, Steed is temporarily partnered by Dr Martin King, nightclub singer Venus Smith and then by one Avenger who stays, Cathy Gale.

Immaculately turned out in a three-piece suit, Steed oozes class. He lives in a select London district, drives a vintage Bentley and, among other idiosyncrasies, insists on his coffee being stirred anticlockwise. His manners are impeccable at all times. He can defend himself from attack (often with a sword drawn from his umbrella) and still exhibit the utmost courtesy to his adversary. (This versatile umbrella – which also performs other remarkable functions – together with Steed's protective bowler hat, was adopted as the show's trademark.) With Cathy Gale, a widowed anthropologist and judo expert, Steed's career moves from mundane detection and basic counter-intelligence into the world of futuristic international intrigue. Dressed in tight-fitting leather and 'kinky' boots, Gale brings a new raciness to the programme. However, after two series, Honor Blackman left to play Pussy Galore in *Goldfinger* and was replaced by Patrick Macnee's most celebrated colleague, Diana Rigg.

The karate-chopping, kung fu kicking, ultra-fashionable Mrs Peel (widow of test pilot Peter Peel) lives in the fast lane, speeding around in a Lotus Elan. Her name, it is said, was taken from the British film industry expression 'M-Appeal', meaning 'man appeal'. With her arrival *The Avengers* aimed more at the US market and played up the picture postcard, English village stereotype in its settings. Viewed today, these episodes appear very British and redolent of the Swinging Sixties. It was also during this period that arty programme titles were introduced and Johnny Dankworth's original theme track was replaced by new dramatic music by Laurie Johnson.

When Rigg left after three seasons to return to the stage (Peter Peel was, it seemed, found alive), another accomplice was required. Unknown actress Linda Thorson was introduced as farm girl Tara King and, for the first time, a romantic liaison for Steed was suggested. Unlike her predecessors, King is not a martial arts expert, but she is just as aggressive when necessary, laying out opponents with a swipe of her brick-laden handbag or simply with a bunch of fives.

In the 1970s the programme was revived under the title THE NEW AVENGERS, with Steed (now in his 50s) having the benefit of two rather more active assistants, weapons expert Mike Gambit and Purdey, a high-kicking ex-ballet dancer.

The plots of *The Avengers* are always far-fetched but highly inventive, usually focusing on zany attempts to take over the world. They echo the exploits of James Bond, in a less extravagant way, but still with gadgets and gimmicks galore. Steed and Tara are even given their own version of Bond's boss, 'M', in the form of the wheelchair-bound 'Mother', with his Amazonian secretary, Rhonda. Best remembered among the baddies are the cybernauts (not to be confused with DOCTOR WHO's cybermen).

Aweful Mr Goodall, The ★★

UK (LWT) Spy Drama. ITV 1974

Mr Jack Goodall .... **Robert Urquhart**
Millbrook .... **Donald Burton**
Alexandra Winfield .... **Isabel Dean**

Producer **Richard Bates**

A retired civil servant still works for the intelligence services.

After more than 15 years as a lieutenant-colonel in MI 5 and DI 5, 55-year-old widower Jack Goodall has hung up his spy-catching equipment and happily retired to Eastbourne. However, he finds the intelligence game hard to give up, especially as he is endowed with a kind of sixth sense, a nose for intrigue which makes him invaluable to his former employers. These are fronted by Millbrook, Head of Section at a British security department. Six episodes were produced.

Ayckbourn, Sir Alan

(1939–)

London-born playwright responsible for light dramas often concerning the middle classes. His TV credits have included *Bedroom Farce*, the children's single comedy *Ernie's Incredible Illucinations*, episodes of HARK AT BARKER (under the pseudonym of Peter Caulfield), and the trilogy *The Norman Conquests* (consisting of *Table Manners*, *Living Together* and *Round and Round the Garden*), which viewed the relationship between three couples from three individual vantage points.

Ayres, Pam

MBE (1947–)

British colloquial poet with a yokel accent who came to fame after winning appearances on OPPORTUNITY KNOCKS in 1975. There followed several TV series, such as *What's On Next?* and *The Main Attraction*, and assorted guest appearances on the likes of THE BLACK AND WHITE MINSTREL SHOW. More recently, she helped voice the animation series *Rex the Runt*.

Babar ✳

France (Télé-Hachette) Children's Entertainment. BBC 1 1969

Narrator **Eric Thompson**

Writer **Peggy Miller**

● ***A baby elephant learns to live in a town.***

Another of the BBC's fondly remembered teatime fillers, *Babar* was brought from France by Peggy Miller, who also wrote the English scripts for the five-minute films. The character first appeared in a book, *The Story of Babar*, in 1931, written and illustrated by Jean de Brunhoff. De Brunhoff followed up with five more books before he died in 1937, leaving creative control in the hands of his young son, Laurent. For this television version, Laurent favoured actors in masks and costumes rather than animation, as the tale unfolds of a very young orphan elephant who leaves the Great Forest and ends up in a small French town. There he is befriended by the Old Lady, who teaches him the best social manners. Twenty-six episodes were shown. A cartoon version, made by the Nelvana company, was later produced, taking the Babar story back to the jungle.

Babes in the Wood ✳

UK (Lucky Dog/Carlton) Situation Comedy. ITV 1998–9

Charlie	**Karl Howman**
Ruth	**Samantha Janus**
Leigh	**Denise Van Outen**
Caralyn	**Natalie Walter**
Benito	**Mark Hayford**
Frankie	**Madeleine Curtis**

Creator **Geoff Deane**
Writers **Geoff Deane, Paul Alexander, Simon Braithwaite, Fleur Costello**
Producers **Kenton Allen, Pete Ward**

● ***The sex-dominated lives of three girls and their Cockney neighbour.***

The 'Wood' being St John's Wood, this punchy, in-your-face comedy focuses on a trio of single blonde flatmates, who don't always see eye to eye. The girls are neurotic Ruth, 'ladette' waitress Leigh and dippy Caralyn, and they share a swish apartment across the hall from ladies' man divorcé Charlie, a local wideboy. Coarse humour is derived from their petty domestic squabbles but more so from the various one-night stands the plain-talking foursome indulge in. Charlie, being the older man, struggles to find his true role with the girls: is he a father figure, or in with a chance?

Radio Times reported that the series followed an unscreened pilot episode in which Dani Behr was cast alongside Samantha Janus and Denise Van Outen. For series two, in 1999, Janus – her character married off – was replaced by Madeleine Curtis as new brunette flatmate Frankie. The series was created by Geoff Deane, former vocalist with 1980s pop band Modern Romance.

Babylon 5 ✳✳✳

US (Babylonian) Science Fiction. Channel 4 1994–9
(US: Syndicated 1993–7; TNT 1998)
DVD: Warner Home Video

Commander/Ambassador Jeffrey Sinclair	**Michael O'Hare**
Security Chief Michael Garibaldi	**Jerry Doyle**
Lt. Commander/Commander Susan Ivanova	**Claudia Christian**
Dr Stephen Franklin	**Richard Biggs**
Ambassador Londo Mollari	**Peter Jurasik**
Ambassador Delenn	**Mira Furlan**
Lennier	**Billy Mumy**
Ambassador G'Kar	**Andreas Katsulas**
Vir Cotto	**Stephen Furst**
PSI Corps Telepath Talia Winters	**Andrea Thompson**
Na'Toth	**Caitlin Brown**
	Mary Kay Adams
Ambassador Kosh	**Ardwight Chamberlain**
Capt. John Sheridan	**Bruce Boxleitner**
Mr Morden	**Ed Wasser**
Lt. Warren Keffer	**Robert Rusler**
Sgt Zack Allen	**Jeff Conaway**
Al Bester	**Walter Koenig**
Ranger Marcus Cole	**Jason Carter**
PSI Corps Telepath Lyta Alexander	**Patricia Tallman**
Lorien	**Wayne Alexander**
Cartagia	**Wortham Krimmer**
Capt. Elizabeth Lochley	**Tracy Scoggins**

Creator/Executive Producer **J. Michael Straczynski**

● ***Hopes for peace in the universe rest in a neutral space station.***

Babylon 5 is a five-mile-long space station (the last of the *Babylon* fleet), a neutral-space base/home/playground for 250,000 creatures from all across the galaxy also used as a centre for peace talks among the five major solar systems. The year is AD 2257, in the aftermath of a bitter inter-galactic conflict. On board is an ambassador from each of the powers controlling the solar systems: the Earth Alliance, the Centauri Republic (now in decline), the Narn Regime, the Minbari Federation and the Vorlon Empire. Londo Mollari is the bullish Centauri ambassador, a creature of many vices, from gambling to womanizing; the hairless Delenn is from Minbari (but becomes more of an Earth-hybrid as the series progresses); the snake-like G'Kar is from Narn; and the enigmatic Kosh, encased in a survival suit, comes from Vorlon. Station commander Jeffrey Sinclair also acts as the Earth's representative. But keeping order among the mutually suspicious, squabbling aliens is not easy, as their respective worlds continued to wage battle outside, nor is protecting the station from outside attack from adversaries like the Shadows (with their ally Morden) or infiltrators – smugglers, hustlers, etc. – who use the station as a staging post. Under Sinclair, eager Lt. Commander Susan Ivanova mostly runs the station, supported by security chief Jim Doyle, doctor Stephen Franklin and telepath Talia

Winters (later replaced as peace talks telepath by Lyta Alexander). Sinclair gives way after one season to decorated war hero Captain John Sheridan, who develops a romantic relationship with Delenn. Also seen are alien associates: Vir, Londo Mollari's henchman; Na'Toth, G'Kar's sidekick; and Lennier, a Minbari aide (played by grown-up *Lost in Space* child Billy Mumy). Elizabeth Lochley is introduced as new station commander in the final episodes.

Creator J. Michael Straczynski (who, unusually for a US series, was the sole writer of many episodes) marked out a five-year plan for *Babylon 5*, encompassing 110 episodes. With each new season, the time moved on: series two was set in 2259, series three in 2260. Halfway through the five-year run, the station declared independence from Earth. The five seasons were duly completed, although fears over whether the last series would be commissioned led to the final episode (set in 2281) being shot early in case it was needed to climax season four. Guest stars included David McCallum, June Lockhart and Michael York. A spin-off series, *Crusade*, starring Gary Cole, was shown on Sky 1 from 1999.

Bachelor Father ✶

UK (BBC) Situation Comedy. BBC 1 1970–1

Peter Lamb	**Ian Carmichael**
Harry	**Gerald Flood**
Mr Gibson	**Colin Gordon**
Mary	**Rona Anderson**
Mrs Rathbone	**Sonia Graham**
Mrs Pugsley	**Joan Hickson**
Anna	**Briony McRoberts**
Ben	**Ian Johnson**
Donald	**Roland Pickering**
	Andrew Bowen
Jane	**Beverley Simons**
Freddie	**Michael Douglas**
Norah	**Diana King**
Ginny	**Jacqueline Cowper**
Jo	**Geraldine Cowper**
Christopher	**Kevin Moran**

Writer **Richard Waring**
Producer **Graeme Muir**

● ***A wealthy bachelor decides he still wants a family, despite not having a wife.***

Peter Lamb loves children, but his romantic liaisons have never amounted to much and he still hasn't married. Undaunted, he makes himself available as a foster parent, taking in assorted foster children, who cause him plenty of concern. Also in the fray are social workers, teachers, Peter's extended family and next-door neighbour Harry. The series was based on the real-life story of Peter Lloyd Jeffcock, bachelor foster parent of 12 children.

Back to the Floor ✶✶

UK (BBC) Documentary. BBC 2 1997–2002

Narrator **Neil Pearson**

Executive Producers **Robert Thirkell, Bill Grist**
Producers **Hugh Dehn, Joanna Ball**

● ***Senior executives experience for themselves the problems facing their workforce.***

From the first episode, where Terry Brown, commercial director of Unijet, dons a blue polyester blazer to become a holiday rep with his own company, *Back to the Floor* offers an intriguing glimpse into the yawning gulf that exists between the boardroom and the shop floor. What the likes of Brown discover is usually not to their liking, exposing the consequences for the coal-face worker of decisions made at top level. Improvements must be made, seems to be the resigned mantra of the humbled director at the end of a trying week.

Following Brown in bravely facing up to challenges away from the executive suite are the likes of Lt. General Sir Hew Pike, a Falklands veteran returning to the ranks; Tony Marshall, MD of Butlin's, hoping to cut the mustard as a Red Coat; RSPCA director general Peter Davies, who goes back to work as an animal inspector; Paul Whitehouse, chief constable of Sussex, heading back on the beat; and director general of the Prison Service Martin Narey taking a turn at being a warder. Overall, their experiences reveal just how little employees are valued and, very often, how inadequately they are resourced and supported.

Some revised repeats, showing bosses returning to the floor once again to see if progress had been made, were screened under the title *Back to the Floor . . . Again*.

Backup ✶

UK (BBC) Police Drama. BBC 1 1995; 1997

Sgt Bill Parkin	**Martin Troakes**
PC Eric 'Token' Warren	**Christopher John Hall**
PC Gill 'Dippy' Copson	**Katrina Levon**
PC John 'Thug' Barrett	**Nick Miles**
PC Ian 'Jock' Macrae	**Alex Norton**
PC Lionel 'Oz' Adams	**William Tapley**
PC Roger 'Flub' Tennant	**Calum Macpherson**
PC Susan 'Bruce' Li	**Colette Koo**
PC Wayne 'Bog' Cheetham	**Oliver Milburn**
Insp. 'Jean' Harlow	**Wayne Morris**
DI Overton	**Peter Sullivan**
Supt Hallsworth	**Sam Cox**
DCI Chivers	**Suzan Crowley**
PC Goole	**Christopher Quinn**
Kate Warren	**Beverley Hills**
Brenda Parkin	**Amelda Brown**
Sgt Jim Reaper	**James Gaddas**
PC Steve 'Hiccup' Higson	**Matthew Rhys**
DS Kath Reaper	**Kate Gartside**

Creator **Nigel McCrery**
Producer **Hilary Salmon**

● ***Every day is a challenge for a police support team.***

Moving behind the front line of police work, this series focuses on the crew of officers who answer the often-heard call for 'Backup'. At the centre of the action is Charlie Serial, one of the Transit van-loads of police officers who form the Operational Support Unit. Their job is to respond to any situation, from crowd and riot control or drugs raids to tragic rail accidents or painstaking fingertip searches for vital evidence. Teamwork is essential, but so is a sense of humour, because these nine officers work together in a claustrophobic environment, often under extreme pressure and in the face of trauma – a situation that can lead to the development of strong personal relationships. Created by Nigel McCrery, himself a veteran of police 'Backup' work, the series aimed to reveal the human faces that are so often rendered anonymous by plastic shields and riot gear.

Bad Girls ✶✶

UK (Shed/Granada) Drama. ITV 1999–
DVD: VCI

Julie Saunders	**Victoria Alcock**
Julie Johnston	**Kika Mirylees**
Carol Byatt	**Ashley Miller**
Denny Blood	**Alicia Eyo**
Michelle 'Shell' Dockley	**Debra Stephenson**
Lorna Rose	**Luisa Bradshaw-White**
Sylvia 'Bodybag' Hollamby	**Helen Fraser**
Jim Fenner	**Jack Ellis**
Rachel Hicks	**Joanne Froggatt**
Nikki Wade	**Mandana Jones**
Helen Stewart	**Simone Lahbib**
Dominic McAllister	**Joe Shaw**
Zandra Plackett	**Lara Cazalet**
Monica Lindsay	**Jane Lowe**
Crystal Gordon	**Sharon Duncan-Brewster**
Robin Dunstan	**Gideon Turner**
Officer Blakeson	**Eugene Walker**
Sean Parr	**Oliver Fox**
Simon Stubberfield	**Roland Oliver**
Yvonne Atkins	**Linda Henry**
Dr Nicholson	**Philip McGough**
Karen Betts	**Claire King**
Marilyn Fenner	**Kim Taylforth**
Jessie Devlin	**Denise Black**
Di Barker	**Tracey Wilkinson**
Josh Mitchell	**Nathan Constance**
Barbara Hunt	**Isabelle Amyes**
Shaz Wiley	**Lindsey Fawcett**
'Mad' Tessa Spall	**Helen Schlesinger**
Dr Thomas Waugh	**Michael Higgs**
Gina Rossi	**Lisa Turner**
Buki Lester	**Kim Oliver**
Charlotte Myddleton	**Kate Steavenson-Payne**
Mark Waddle	**Paul Opacic**
Maxine 'Maxi' Purvis	**Kerry Norton**
Tina Purvis/Julie O'Kane	**Victoria Bush**
Al Mackenzie	**Pauline Campbell**
Femi Bada	**Anthonia Lanre Ajose**
Virginia O'Kane	**Kate O'Mara**
Neil Grayling	**James Gaddas**
Cassie Tyler	**Kellie Bright**
Roisin Connor	**Siobhan McCarthy**
Rhiannon Dawson	**Jade Williams**
Snowball Merriman	**Nicole Faraday**
Phyllida 'Phyl' Oswyn	**Stephanie Beacham**
Beverley 'Bev' Tull	**Amanda Barrie**
Dr Malcolm Nicholson	**Philip McGough**
Colin Hedges	**Tristan Sturrock**
Revd Henry Mills	**Michael Elwyn**
Buki Lester	**Kim Oliver**
Selena Gleeson	**Charlotte Lucas**
Kris Yates	**Jennifer Ness**
Frances Myers	**Eva Pope**
Natalie Buxton	**Dannielle Brent**
Darlene Cake	**Antonia Okonma**
Janine Nebeski	**Nicola Stapleton**
Arun Parmar	**Rebecca Hazlewood**
Pat Kerrigan	**Liz May Brice**
Sister Thomas More	**Colette O'Neil**
Kevin Spiers	**Andrew Scarborough**
Vicky Floyd	**Orlessa Atlas**
Sheena Williams	**Laura Rogers**
Joy Masterton	**Ellie Haddington**
Louise 'Lou' Stoke	**Amanda Donohoe**
Dr Raven Dunlop	**Colin Salmon**
Donny Kimber	**Sid Owen**
Mandy Goodhue	**Angela Bruce**

Producers **Brian Park, Claire Phillips, David Crean, Cameron Roach, Rachel Snell, Sharon Houlihan**

● ***The seedy world of a women's jail.***

Brutal, nasty, violent, grimy, sleazy, tawdry and over the top: just some of the descriptions pinned to this sparky drama, which nevertheless attracts massive audiences. Larkhall women's prison is the setting and the main characters are a mixed bag of convicts who live on G Wing. Governor of the wing is over-liberal Helen Stewart, who immediately causes friction – among both inmates and staff – with a new regime she tries to impose, while other dramas brew in the petty squabbles, traumatic personal lives and sheer criminal nature of those confined. Among the leading characters is Shell Dockley, a psychotic bisexual doing life for murder, who rules the roost and bullies the other prisoners; Shell's henchwoman, the macho Denny Blood; resident intellectual Nikki Wade, a lesbian, who draws governor Stewart into an affair; vulnerable drug offender Rachel Hicks; the 'Two Julies', a pair of prostitute cellmates; middle-class Monica Lindsay, in for fraud; heroin addict Zandra Plackett; unscrupulous warder Jim Fenner and similarly unreliable fellow officer Sylvia Hollamby. Later arrivals include gangster's widow Yvonne Atkins; punky Shaz Wiley; drippy Di Barker; glamorous new warder, and later wing governor, Karen Betts; wheelchair-bound Virginia O'Kane; new (gay) prison governor Neil Grayling; porn star Snowball Merriman; compulsive liar Buki Lester; 'Costa Cons' Phyl Oswyn and Bev Tull; heroin junkie warder Colin Hedges; prostitute Frances Myers (who turns out to be the new wing governor); sophisticated Natalie Buxton; acid-tongued Darlene Cake; credit card crooks Janine and Arun; steely-eyed Pat Kerrigan; and elderly nun Sister Thomas. In one story in series six, Tanya Turner (Zoë Lucker), a character from FOOTBALLERS' WIVES, spends time in Larkhall. Although never easy viewing, *Bad Girls* remains compelling for many.

Badger ✶

UK (Feelgood Fiction/BBC) Drama. BBC 1 1999–2000

DCTom McCabe	**Jerome Flynn**
Jim Cassidy	**Adrian Bower**
Steph Allen	**Phillippa Wilson**
Claire Armitage	**Rebecca Lacey**
David Armitage	**Kevin Doyle**
Wilf McCabe	**Alison Mac**
Julia	**Jayne Charlton McKenzie**
Liam Allen	**Scott Karalius**
Ralph Allen	**Conor Mullen**
Ray	**Brendan Healey**

Creator **Kieran Prendiville**
Executive Producers **Laurence Bowen, Philip Clarke**
Producers **Murray Ferguson, Ann Tricklebank**

● ***The cases of a Geordie police wildlife officer.***

DC Tom McCabe works for the Northumbria and City police force. Based in Newcastle, he runs through the usual police chores – catching burglars, keeping the peace, etc. – but also has a remit to investigate cruelty to wildlife. This being the gloriously unspoilt north-east, there is plenty of wildlife to protect and helping the caring copper in his task is local RSPB investigator Claire Armitage (who happens to be the wife of McCabe's boss, David) and young bag carrier Jim Cassidy. A typical day's work might involve tracking down poachers, rounding up illegal taxidermists or mounting a guard on a threatened badger sett. Wilf is Tom's troublesome teenage daughter, who takes a shine to Cassidy; divorcée Steph Allen, a vet in charge of an animal sanctuary, is McCabe's own love interest; and Liam is Steph's schoolboy son. Steph's estranged husband, Ralph, is seen in series two.

Badger was based on real-life police wildlife liaison officer Paul Henery, who joined the crew as consultant in a bid to raise public awareness of the fact that police will certainly act in cases of animal cruelty.

BAFTA

The British Academy of Film and Television Arts was formed in 1959 as the Society of Film and Television Arts by the amalgamation of the British Film Academy and the Guild of Television Producers and Directors. It was reorganized and given its current name in 1975. Membership is comprised of senior creative workers in the film and television industries, and the aim of the Academy is to raise production standards in both media. The BAFTA Awards, announced annually since 1975, with trophies modelled on classical drama masks, have become a highlight of the TV calendar. These began as The British Film Academy Awards in 1947, developing into The Society of Film and Television Arts Awards in 1969.

Bagdad Cafe ✶

US (Zev Braun/New World) Situation Comedy. Channel 4 1991 (US: CBS 1990–1)

Brenda	**Whoopi Goldberg**
Jasmine Zweibel	**Jean Stapleton**
Juney	**Scott Lawrence**
Debbie	**Monica Calhoun**
Rudy	**James Gammon**
Dewey Kunkle	**Sam Whipple**
Sal	**Cleavon Little**

Two unlikely friends run an out-of-the-way truck stop.

Based on the 1987 German film of the same name, directed by Percy Adlon, *Bagdad Cafe* is a comedy constructed around an isolated motel/diner in the Mojave Desert, California. Its disorganized proprietor is Brenda, who runs the show with the great help of the methodical Jasmine, a woman who walked to the Cafe after a bust-up with her husband. A seemingly incompatible coupling (depicted not least in their different-coloured skins), the smart-tongued, cynical Brenda and the thoughtful, generous Jasmine become good pals and colleagues. Also seen are Juney, Brenda's piano-playing son and cook (a single parent), Debbie, her teenage daughter, and Rudy, one of the precious few regular customers. Rudy's nephew, Dewey, arrives later to take over as cook. From time to time, Sal, Brenda's womanizing husband, shows his face. The series died with the abrupt departure of star Whoopi Goldberg and only 15 episodes were produced. Only Monica Calhoun, who played Debbie, featured in the original film.

Bagpuss ✶✶✶

UK (Smallfilms) Children's Entertainment. BBC 1 1974
DVD: 4 Front Video

Narrator **Oliver Postgate**
Creators **Peter Firmin, Oliver Postgate**
Writer **Oliver Postgate**

A fat, baggy, cloth cat lives on a cushion in a shop window.

Bagpuss is the story of a magic lost-and-found shop (Bagpuss & Co.), owned by a Victorian girl named Emily. Emily brings to the shop interesting items she has discovered, with the aim of repairing them and returning them to the owner. To do so, she relies on the help of her fat, pink-and-white-striped cloth cat, Bagpuss, and his industrious little friends. Reciting her magical spell, Emily awakens Bagpuss from sleep (the picture turns from sepia into colour) and he and the other inhabitants of the shop then set about repairing whatever Emily has found. Down from a shelf comes Professor Yaffle, a wooden woodpecker bookend with a German accent. He provides the brains for the task ahead and leads the investigation into the identity and usefulness of the object. Up pops Madeleine the maternal rag doll, Gabriel the toad begins to strum his banjo and the mice fire up their Marvellous Mechanical Mouse Organ with bellows. Head mouse Charlie keeps his crew ahead of the game, and the whole team chant and sing their way through their chores. Once the item has been mended, it is placed in the window in the hope that its owner will call and, at this point, Bagpuss crawls gratefully back to sleep.

Only 13 episodes of *Bagpuss* were ever produced, but reruns abounded. The girl seen as Emily in the sepia sequences at the start of the programme was Emily Firmin, daughter of co-creator Peter Firmin. The music was supplied by folk musicians Sandra Kerr and John Faulkner.

Bailey, Bill

(1964–)

Bath-born comic who trained as a classical musician before turning to stage comedy. An early sitcom role came in *Tygo Road* (Spinnij). Later, after guest appearances on HAVE I GOT NEWS FOR YOU and regular slots as a team captain in the sci-fi quiz *Space Cadets* and the comic debate series *Head on Comedy* with Jo Brand, Bailey – noted for his wispy, flyaway hair – featured in the sitcom SPACED (Bilbo). He then starred alongside Dylan Moran in the award-winning BLACK BOOKS (Manny Bianco). In 2002 he replaced Sean Hughes as a team captain in the pop-comedy quiz NEVER MIND THE BUZZCOCKS and appeared in the sitcom WILD WEST (Doug). Bailey has also been seen in his own stand-up showcases such as *Is It Bill Bailey?*. Other credits include *15 Storeys High* (Coggers) and countless panel games.

Bailey, Robin

(1919–99)

Nottinghamshire-born actor fond of crusty codger parts, perhaps best remembered as the cynical Uncle Mort in the Brandon saga, I DIDN'T KNOW YOU CARED. Previously, however, he had compered *The 64,000 Dollar Question* in the 1950s and appeared in a host of major series, including *Dimension of Fear* (Col. Alan Renton), THE PALLISERS (Mr Gresham), THE NEWCOMERS (Andrew Kerr) and UPSTAIRS, DOWNSTAIRS. In 1983 he took over the role of Redvers POTTER from the late Arthur Lowe and, two years later, he was cast as Charters alongside Michael Aldridge's Caldicott in the BBC's revival of the two snoopy old public school duffers, CHARTERS AND CALDICOTT. In the same year he played Sir Leicester Dedlock in BLEAK HOUSE. Among his other credits were *The Punch Review*, *Sorry I'm A Stranger Here Myself* (as hen-pecked librarian Henry Nunn), JANE (The Colonel), *Tales from a Long Room* (The Brigadier), RUMPOLE OF THE BAILEY (Judge Graves), *Took and Co.*, A DANCE TO THE MUSIC OF TIME (Uncle Alfred) and *Tinniswood Country* (Uncle Mort again), with guest appearances in the likes of KAVANAGH QC, DALZIEL AND PASCOE, and *Albert and Victoria*. Bailey was married to actress Patricia Weekes.

Bain, Barbara
(1931–)

American actress, once the wife and co-star of Martin Landau (in MISSION: IMPOSSIBLE and SPACE: 1999). Earlier appearances came in *Richard Diamond, Private Detective* (as Karen Wells, opposite David Janssen) and series such as HAWAIIAN EYE, PERRY MASON, THE DICK VAN DYKE SHOW, WAGON TRAIN and BEN CASEY. More recently, she has made guest appearances in series such as MURDER, SHE WROTE and DIAGNOSIS MURDER.

Baird, John Logie
(1888–1946)

Scottish inventor, widely acknowledged as the father of television, although not the first to experiment in the field. In 1925 Baird demonstrated a mechanical scanning television system which produced a rudimentary picture. A year later, he had improved its efficiency so that human faces became recognizable. After much badgering, the BBC picked up Baird's invention and placed it central to their television experiments in 1929. However, rival systems, using electronic rather than mechanical scanning, quickly proved more effective and the Corporation switched to EMI-Marconi's cathode-ray tube version a year after regular broadcasts began in 1936. Undaunted, Baird continued to progress his brainchild, experimenting with colour images. Earlier he had also devised a primitive form of video disc, using wax records, and even managed to transmit a TV signal across the Atlantic in 1928, years before satellite relays became a possibility. Just before his death, he had successfully worked on stereoscopic television images.

Baker, Bob
(1939–)

British scriptwriter, usually in collaboration with Dave Martin, who specializes in children's science fiction. Their biggest successes have been for HTV, with series such as SKY, *King of the Castle* and *Into the Labyrinth*. Other credits include the TV movie *Thick As Thieves*, *Pretenders*, ARTHUR OF THE BRITONS, *Follow Me*, *Jangles*, *Murder at the Wedding* and episodes of Z CARS, DOCTOR WHO, HUNTER'S WALK, TARGET, SHOESTRING and BERGERAC. Baker has also co-scripted some of the WALLACE & GROMIT films.

Baker, Colin
(1943–)

British actor favoured in pompous, confident roles. He first came to light in THE BROTHERS, playing the unscrupulous whiz-kid, Paul Merroney, although his most prominent role was as the sixth DOCTOR WHO. He has also been seen in episodes of THE EDWARDIANS, BLAKE'S 7, CASUALTY, JONATHAN CREEK, THE BILL, DANGERFIELD, HOLLYOAKS, the children's series *Harry's Mad* and the dramas A DANCE TO THE MUSIC OF TIME (Canon Fenneau), *The Waiting Time* (Giles Fleming), *The Young Indiana Jones Chronicles* and *The Afternoon Play*. His first wife was Liza Goddard.

Baker, Danny
(1957–)

Garrulous Londoner who specializes in pop culture nostalgia. Formerly a *New Musical Express* journalist, he joined LWT's *Six O'Clock Show* and then moved on to the daytime cartoon quiz *Win Lose or Draw* and the series *Bazaar*. However, greater prominence came after he took over the Radio 5 breakfast show, *Morning Edition*, which led to his hosting assorted game shows, ranging from *Bygones* to *Pets Win Prizes*, as well as his own Saturday night chat shows, guesting as host of THE BIG BREAKFAST and fronting retro football in *Match of the Eighties*. He is also much seen in TV commercials, has provided scripts for award ceremonies and other shows like *Before They were Famous* and TFI FRIDAY, and presented the series of humorous/nostalgic shorts, *TV Heroes*. He was also a regular contributor to *The Terry and Gaby Show*.

Baker, George
(1931–)

Versatile TV actor/writer most closely associated with the rural detective Inspector Wexford, in THE RUTH RENDELL MYSTERIES (for which he also scripted some episodes). His other major credits have included Tiberius in I, CLAUDIUS, Stanley Bowler in *Bowler* (a spin-off from *The Fenn Street Gang*), the smarmy Tory, Godfrey Eagan, in NO JOB FOR A LADY and Lord Dorincourt in *Little Lord Fauntleroy*. Over the years there have been plenty of other notable appearances, in the likes of *Undermind*, THE MASTER (Squadron Leader Frinton), THE PRISONER (as one of the Number 2s), DOCTOR WHO, UP POMPEII (Jamesus Bondus), TRIANGLE (David West), ROBIN OF SHERWOOD (Sir Richard of Leaford), GOODBYE MR CHIPS (Meldrum), *Room at the Bottom*, HART TO HART, MISS MARPLE, BERGERAC, A WOMAN OF SUBSTANCE (Bruce McGill), DEAD HEAD (Eldridge), CORONATION STREET (Cecil Newton), MIDSOMER MURDERS, SPOOKS and single dramas such as Dennis Potter's *Alice* (playing Lewis Carroll). His third wife is Wexford co-star Louie Ramsay.

Baker, Hylda
(1905–86)

Lancashire-born comedienne, for ever identified as Nellie Pledge, one of the squabbling siblings (with Jimmy Jewel) who ran the pickle factory in NEAREST AND DEAREST. However, Hylda Baker's career began in music hall and she toured with many of the big names in the 1940s. In the 1950s, she branched out on her own, hitting the limelight in an episode of THE GOOD OLD DAYS in 1955. In those days it was her act with

Cynthia (a man in drag) which brought most laughs. 'She knows you know' became her catchphrase. TV series followed: *Be Soon*, OUR HOUSE (Henrietta), *Best of Friends* and subsequently *Nearest and Dearest* in 1968. Baker also starred as pub landlady Nellie Pickersgill in another sitcom, *Not on Your Nellie*. Although she was equally adept at straight drama (for instance in David Mercer's 1961 play, *Where the Difference Begins*, and in a couple of episodes of Z CARS), her comic timing, jerky mannerisms and flair for the double entendre and malapropism made her one of TV's most distinctive comic stars in the 1960s and 1970s.

Baker, Richard

OBE (1925–)

Willesden-born Cambridge Footlights and repertory actor who, in 1954, became BBC Television's first newsreader, having joined the BBC as an announcer on the Third Programme in 1950. Although initially supplying just the voice behind the pictures in BBC TELEVISION NEWSREEL, Baker was later chosen as one of the main three 'in-vision' newsreaders, along with Kenneth Kendall and Robert Dougall. He presented the news until 1982 and has subsequently concentrated on his first love, classical music, appearing on such programmes as OMNIBUS, *The Proms* and FACE THE MUSIC. In contrast, he also provided the narration for the WATCH WITH MOTHER animation, MARY, MUNGO AND MIDGE.

Baker, Robert S.

(1916–)

British producer heavily involved with ITC adventure series of the 1960s, often in collaboration with Monty Berman. Among his efforts were THE SAINT (and, in the 1970s, THE RETURN OF THE SAINT), THE BARON, GIDEON'S WAY and THE PERSUADERS!.

Baker, Tom

(1934–)

Liverpool-born actor, known for eccentric characters and famous as the fourth DOCTOR WHO. In the 1980s he was the decadent priest, Father Ferguson, in THE LIFE AND LOVES OF A SHE DEVIL, donned the deerstalker of Sherlock Holmes in THE HOUND OF THE BASKERVILLES, played Professor Plum in CLUEDO and Puddleglum in THE CHRONICLES OF NARNIA, and guest-starred in BLACKADDER. In more recent years, he has filled the role of Manfred Fischer in SELLING HITLER, Professor Geoffrey Hoyt in MEDICS, the ghostly Wyvern in RANDALL AND HOPKIRK (DECEASED) and Donald MacDonald in MONARCH OF THE GLEN, as well as providing voice-overs for LITTLE BRITAIN and *Trouble at the Top*, and playing Captain Baker in *Fort Boyard*. He hosted the kids' literature programme, THE BOOK TOWER, in the 1970s, and even earlier roles came in series like DIXON OF DOCK GREEN and ARTHUR OF THE BRITONS. His second wife was *Doctor Who* co-star Lalla Ward.

Bakewell, Joan

CBE (1933–)

Stockport-born intellectual presenter, joining the BBC as a studio manager and becoming one of the early stars of BBC 2 as an interviewer on LATE NIGHT LINE-UP after a time as an advertising copywriter. In subsequent years she struggled to shake off the tag of 'the thinking man's crumpet', bestowed on her by Frank Muir. Other TV credits have included FILM 72, *Reports Action*, *On the Town*, HOLIDAY and many years as presenter of the Sunday late-night morality programme *Heart of the Matter*. She also fronted the series *My Generation* and *Taboo*, and was the BBC's Arts Correspondent in the 1980s.

Bakula, Scott

(1954–)

American actor star of *Eisenhower & Lutz* (Bud Lutz Jr), QUANTUM LEAP (Sam Beckett) and STAR TREK: ENTERPRISE (Capt. Jonathan Archer). He also starred in US series called *Gung Ho* (Hunt Stevenson), *Mr & Mrs Smith* (Mr Smith) and *A Girl Thing* (Paul Morgan), and made several guest appearances in MURPHY BROWN (Peter Hunt). Other appearances have been made in *Designing Women*, MATLOCK and DREAM ON.

Balamory ✱✱

UK (BBC) Children's Entertainment. BBC1/2 2003–5
DVD: BBC

Miss Hoolie	**Julie Wilson Nimmo**
Archie	**Miles Jupp**
Suzie Sweet	**Mary Riggans**
Penny Pocket	**Kim Tserkezie**
PC Plum	**Andrew Agnew**
Spencer	**Rodd Christiensen**
Edie McCredie	**Juliet Cadzow**
Josie Jump	**Buki Abib**

Creator/Producer **Brian Jameson**
Executive Producer **Lucille McLaughlin**

A toddler's eye view of life on a colourful Scottish island.

Described as TV's first pre-school soap, *Balamory* was created for the digital channel CBeebies in autumn 2002 but proved so popular that wider exposure via BBCs 1 and 2 was inevitable. Action takes place in the homely Scottish island community of Balamory and is introduced by the local schoolteacher, Miss Hoolie, who like her neighbours lives in a brightly coloured house (hers is green). Elsewhere in town reside Archie, the kilt-wearing local inventor, who lives in a pink castle; Suzie Sweet and Penny Pocket, who run the shop and café (coloured red); genial law enforcer PC Plum (white house); Spencer, a painter and decorator with a musical ladder (orange house); Edie McCredie, the minibus driver (blue house); and lively Josie Jump, the fitness teacher (yellow house). Together, blending live action and recorded documentary, they negotiate daily dramas that vary from coughs and colds to the death of a pet cat, jauntily charming 3–6-year-olds along the way. Adding to the fun are songs, dances and a story of the day, with Miss Hoolie's young pupils sharing the limelight with the older stars.

External filming took place in the Mull port of Tobermory, where the houses are already multi-coloured, while indoor shots were taken on a college campus in Glasgow. Production was efficient and rapid, with up to 16 episodes of 20 minutes each recorded within a fortnight.

Baldy Man, The ✶

UK (Working Title/Carlton/Yorkshire) Situation Comedy. ITV 1995; 1997–8

The Baldy Man .... **Gregor Fisher**

Executive Producer **Simon Wright**
Producer **Colin Gilbert**

● ***Daily disaster with a vain, follically challenged loser.***

Out of NAKED VIDEO, via commercials for Hamlet cigars (remember the photo booth?), The Baldy Man gains his own slapstick series – albeit a collection of occasional films. With each 30-minute episode divided into two stories, our hero blunders his way through a succession of mishaps, all the while admiring his own looks and patching up his shiny pate with the few strands of hair he can still call his own. In the manner of Mr Bean, and similarly silent except for the regular grunts and groans, Gregor Fisher's creation is a sad creature with high hopes in life that are doomed to failure.

Ball, Bobby

(Robert Harper; 1944–)
See *Cannon, Tommy.*

Ball, Johnny

(1938–)

Quirky presenter of intelligent programmes for children. Born in Bristol, he went on to become a Red Coat and clubland comedian, his TV break arriving with PLAY SCHOOL, on which he was a regular for a number of years. He then progressed to the likes of PLAY AWAY, *Star Turn*, *Secret's Out* and *Cabbages and Kings*, before his biggest success, *Think of a Number*, and follow-ups *Think Again* and *Johnny Ball Reveals All*. The father of radio and TV presenter Zoë Ball, he has also written for programmes like DON'T ASK ME and CRACKERJACK.

Ball, Lucille

(1911–89)

The doyenne of TV comediennes, Lucille Ball came to television after 20 years' experience on stage and screen. Although considered to be 'the new Harlow' by some, Ball never quite made it to the top in pre-war Hollywood and switched her attention instead to radio in 1948. When she took on the role of a scatterbrained housewife in the series *My Favorite Husband*, her card was marked for the rest of her career. This series was soon translated to television as I LOVE LUCY, co-starring her real-life husband, Desi Arnaz, and produced by their own company, Desilu. The show went on to set standards for other sitcoms to follow. As Lucy Ricardo, Ball became one of TV's earliest superstars and, when her marriage to Arnaz irretrievably broke down, she persevered alone, still as the hapless housewife (albeit in various guises) in the follow-up series, THE LUCY SHOW and HERE'S LUCY. Although a late attempt to return to television in the 1980s with *Life With Lucy* was not a success, viewers have always had plenty of opportunity to enjoy her pioneering comic talents, as reruns of *I Love Lucy* are never far from the screen.

Ball, Nicholas

(1946–)

Actor born in Leamington Spa, who came to light as Colin Pitman in THE CREZZ and progressed to his own series, HAZELL, playing a cynical London private eye. Among his later credits have been the parts of film director Alan Hunter in COLIN'S SANDWICH, Larry Lockton in *The Man Who Made Husbands Jealous*, DCI Nick Hall in THIEF TAKERS, John Dawson in THE COMMANDER and Garry Ryan in FOOTBALLERS' WIVES, plus smaller roles in the likes of ROGUE MALE, HAMMER HOUSE OF HORROR, BERGERAC, *Dramarama*, HEARTBEAT, HARBOUR LIGHTS, JONATHAN CREEK, DOCTORS, COLD FEET, *The Courtroom* and NEW TRICKS. He was the first husband of Pamela Stephenson.

Ball, Zoë

(1970–)

Lancashire-born, energetic presenter/DJ, the daughter of children's presenter Johnny Ball. Her TV career began as a runner with Granada, from which she progressed to the position of researcher on THE BIG BREAKFAST and then on to fronting Children's BBC and various kids' series, including *Playdays*, *Short Change*, *Fully Booked*, *The O Zone* and the art show *Smart*. In 1996 she returned to *The Big Breakfast* to replace Gaby Roslin as host, although she soon moved on to front LIVE AND KICKING and editions of TOP OF THE POPS. She has also presented *The Priory*, *The Real Birth Show*, *Class of . . .*, and THE BRIT AWARDS, and is married to DJ Fat Boy Slim.

Ballykissangel ✶✶

UK (BBC/Ballykea/World) Drama. BBC 1 1996–9; 2001
DVD: BBC

Father Peter Clifford .... **Stephen Tompkinson**
Assumpta Fitzgerald .... **Dervla Kirwan**
Brian Quigley .... **Tony Doyle**
Father MacAnally .... **Niall Toibin**
Niamh Quigley/Egan/Dillon ... **Tina Kellegher**
Ambrose Egan .... **Peter Hanly**
Brendan Kearney .... **Gary Whelan**
Padraig O'Kelly .... **Peter Caffrey**
Siobhan Mehigan/Kearney ..... **Deirdre Donnelly**
Liam .... **Joe Savino**
Kathleen .... **Áine Ní Mhúirí**
Donal .... **Frankie McCafferty**
Eamon .... **Birdy Sweeney**
Dr Michael Ryan .... **Bosco Hogan**
Timmy Joe Galvin .... **Stephen Kennedy**
Enda Sullivan .... **Stephen Brennan**
Imelda Egan .... **Doreen Keogh**
Kevin .... **John Cleere**
Mrs Bella Mooney .... **Pauline McLynn**
Sean Dillon .... **Lorcan Cranitch**
Orla O'Connell .... **Victoria Smurfit**
Father Aidan O'Connell .... **Don Wycherley**
Emma Dillon .... **Kate McEnery**
Danny Byrne .... **Colin Farrell**
Leo .... **Jimmy Nesbitt**
Conor Devlin .... **Owen Teale**
Kieran Egan .... **Sam Farrar**
Uncle Minto .... **James Ellis**
Supt/Insp. Foley .... **Alan Barry**

Paul Dooley	**Owen Roe**
Oonagh Dooley	**Marion O'Dwyer**
Dermot Dooley	**Ciaran Owens**
Grainne Dooley	**Katie Cullen**
Frankie Sullivan	**Catherine Cusack**
Father Vincent Sheahan	**Robert Taylor**
Avril Burke	**Susannah Doyle**
Louis Dwyer	**Mick Lally**
Edso Dowling	**Paul Ronan**

Creator **Kieran Prendiville**
Producers **Joy Lale, Chris Griffin, Chris Clough, David Shanks**
Executive Producers **Tony Garnett, Jeremy Gwilt, Robert Cooper**

An English priest takes up a new post in a small Irish town.

Father Peter Clifford, an enthusiastic but naïve Catholic priest, knows that his new posting to St Joseph's church in the town of Ballykissangel will be a trying experience from the moment he set eyes on the community. His superior, Father MacAnally, like the rest of the neighbourhood, is a traditionalist and has simply not moved with the times, and the people are God-fearing, yet loathe the clergy. The archetypal fish out of water, this modern-thinking priest quickly needs to grasp the off-beat logic of the colourful townsfolk and learn all about their different way of life. To do so, he leans heavily on the town's feisty publican, Assumpta Fitzgerald, landlady of Fitzgerald's bar. Their relationship is stormy but always threatens to break into romance, with all the complications that an affair between a priest and a publican can bring. Even Assumpta's marriage to journalist Leo fails to break the undeclared bond that exists between her and the priest. Clifford must also come to terms with the town's Mr Big, the conniving Brian Quigley, the only man (apart from Clifford) with an eye to the future – not to mention a fast punt.

After three hugely successful seasons, stars Stephen Tompkinson and Dervla Kirwan decided to leave *Ballykissangel*. Following a traumatic finale in which Peter expresses his feelings for Assumpta, only to see her die in his arms after electrocution, the priest decides to seek pastures new. His position at the church is filled by former monk Father Aidan O'Connell, but more attention is given to other new arrivals: unpopular widower Sean Dillon, a self-made man returning home after 20 years; his 17-year-old daughter Emma; and Orla, the new priest's attractive, but worldly wise, sister. Fitzgerald's is bought by Quigley. The final series, in 2001, saw further changes. The death of actor Tony Doyle meant that Quigley needed to be written out in a Reggie Perrin-esque 'clothes-on-a-beach' fashion, and another new priest, rugged Australian Vincent Sheahan, hits town and buys up Fitzgerald's. At the same time, Tony Doyle's real daughter, Susannah Doyle, is introduced as racing stable manager Avril Burke.

The series was the brainchild of former TOMORROW'S WORLD presenter Kieran Prendiville, who also scripted many episodes. It drew comparisons with the US series NORTHERN EXPOSURE, so similar was its premise of a stranded man struggling to cope in a totally alien, and rather kooky, environment. Although loosely based on clerical goings-on in the village of Ballykissanne, County Kerry, where Prendiville spent holidays as a child, *Ballykissangel* was filmed in Avoca, a sleepy County Wicklow town that soon became a major tourist attraction.

Bamber, David

(1954–)

English actor, in comic as well as straight parts. His TV highlights have included the roles of Mr Collins in PRIDE AND PREJUDICE and Eric Slatt in CHALK. Other credits have included THE BUDDHA OF SUBURBIA (Shadwell), *Stalag Luft* ('The Prof'), *My Night with Reg, My Dad's a Boring Nerd, Neville's Island* (Angus), MURDER MOST HORRID, WYCLIFFE, THE RAILWAY CHILDREN (Dr Forrest), DANIEL DERONDA (Lush), *Pollyanna* (Revd Ford), *Beethoven* (Prince Lichnowsky), MIDSOMER MURDERS and ROME (Marcus Tullius Cicero). He is married to actress Julia Swift (daughter of David Swift).

Banacek ★★

US (Universal) Detective Drama. ITV 1975–7 (US: NBC 1972–4)

Thomas Banacek	**George Peppard**
Jay Drury	**Ralph Manza**
Felix Mulholland	**Murray Matheson**
Carlie Kirkland	**Christine Belford**

Creator **Anthony Wilson**
Executive Producer **George Eckstein**
Producer **Howie Horowitz**

Tales of a modern-day bounty hunter.

Cool, calm and sophisticated Thomas Banacek is a wealthy man. He lives in a mansion in Boston's prosperous Beacon Hill area and is driven around by a chauffeur, Jay Drury. The reason for his wealth? He is good at collecting rewards from insurance companies. He specializes in retrieving stolen valuables and, on a 10 per cent rake-off, the greater the prize, the richer he becomes. The loot may be gold bullion, or perhaps a prize racehorse. On one occasion it is even a professional footballer. Felix Mulholland, proprietor of Mulholland's Rare Book and Print Shop, is Banacek's best friend, and Carlie Kirkland, another insurance agent, becomes his rival and romantic interest.

Banacek made George Peppard popular with Polish-Americans. These people had long been the butt of everyday humour, and at last here was a TV hero to show the world that they really could be clever. Plenty of Polish sayings found their way into the script. The series was shown as part of the MYSTERY MOVIE anthology.

Banana Splits, The ★★★

US (Hanna-Barbera) Children's Comedy. BBC 1 1970 (US: NBC 1968–70)

Voices:

Fleegle	**Paul Winchell**
Bingo	**Daws Butler**
Drooper	**Alan Melvin**
Snorky	**Don Messick**

Executive Producers **William Hanna, Joseph Barbera**

Zany comedy featuring four animal pop stars.

The Banana Splits are an animal pop group, a sort of zoological Monkees, miming to prerecorded tracks and dashing around their home and neighbourhood in a series of fast-action sequences. Played by men in outsize costumes, the four are Fleegle, a dog guitarist; Bingo, a bongo-playing gorilla; Drooper, a lion; and Snorky, an elephant. At ROWAN AND

MARTIN'S LAUGH-IN pace, these wacky creatures link cartoon inserts such as *The Arabian Knights, The Micro Ventures, The Hillbilly Bears* and *The Three Musketeers*. There is also a live-action adventure entitled *Danger Island* (starring Frank Aletter as Professor Irwin Haydn). Wisecracks and slapstick scenes are the order of the day. Drooper unsuccessfully tries to take out the trash (the bin refuses to accept rubbish), Fleegle wrestles with the mailbox for the mail, and a stroppy cuckoo clock makes time-telling less than easy. Seldom does an episode pass without someone yelling 'Hold the bus!'. Regular features are Banana Buggie races, song and dance from the rival Sour Grape Girls gang, and an 'information' spot called 'Dear Drooper', where the know-all lion attempts to answer viewers' queries. All the same, the show is probably best remembered for its catchy 'One banana, two banana' theme song. Episodes were shown again as part of THE BIG BREAKFAST on Channel 4.

Bananaman ★★

UK (101) Cartoon. BBC 1 1983–4; 1986; 1988
DVD: Delta Music

Narrator **Tim Brooke-Taylor**
Other voices **Tim Brooke-Taylor, Graeme Garden, Bill Oddie, Jill Shilling**

Writer **Bernie Kaye**
Producer **Trevor Bond**

● ***A schoolboy saves the world by eating bananas.***

In 1983, it was good to be a cartoon superhero. Not only did SUPERTED become a TV star, so did Bananaman. In five-minute helpings directed by Terry Ward and voiced by THE GOODIES (plus Jill Shilling), young viewers were introduced to Eric Twinge, a puny schoolboy from 29 Acacia Road. Eric scoffs a few bananas and lo and behold becomes the mighty (if a bit dense) Bananaman, ready to confront whatever danger is lurking around the corner, in a striking blue and yellow costume. Although he is usually helped out by police chief O'Reilly, and chums Crow and Appleman, Bananaman also has a bunch of familiar enemies, including General Blight, The Weatherman and Dr Gloom. The series was based on the strip first seen in *Nutty* comic, which later merged with the *Dandy*. David Cooke provided the music.

Band of Brothers ★★★

US (Play Tone/Dreamworks/HBO) War Drama. BBC 2 2001
DVD: Universal

Lt./Capt./Major Richard D. Winters	**Damian Lewis**
Lt. Herbert Sobel	**David Schwimmer**
Sgt Joseph Toye	**Kirk Acevedo**
Sgt Denver 'Bull' Randleman	**Michael Cudlitz**
Col. Robert F. Sink	**Dale Dye**
George Luz	**Rick Gomez**
Sgt Donald G. Malarkey	**Scott Grimes**
Sgt William 'Wild Bill' Guarnere	**Frank John Hughes**
Capt. Lewis Nixon	**Ron Livingston**
Frank J. Perconte	**James Madio**
Robert 'Popeye' Wynn	**Nicholas Aaron**
Sgt Carwood Lipton	**Donnie Wahlberg**
Lester 'Leo' Hashey	**Mark Huberman**
Pte Albert Blithe	**Marc Warren**
Lt. Harry F. Welsh	**Rick Warden**
John W. Martin	**Dexter Fletcher**
Joseph Ramirez	**Rene L. Moreno**
Lt. Lynn 'Buck' Compton	**Neal McDonough**
Eugene Roe	**Shane Taylor**
Donald Hoobler	**Peter McCabe**
Pte John Hall	**Andrew Scott**
Lt./Capt. Ronald Spiers	**Matthew Settle**
Joseph Liebgott	**Ross McCall**
Floyd Talbert	**Matthew Leitch**
Lt. Fred 'Moose' Heyliger	**Stephen McCole**
Warren Muck	**Richard Speight Jr**
Robert Strayer	**Phil McKee**
Alex Penkala	**Tim Matthews**
Edward 'Babe' Heffron	**Robin Laing**
Lt. Norman Dike Jr	**Peter O'Meara**
Pte David Kenyon Webster	**Eion Bailey**
Lt. Hank Jones	**Colin Hanks**
Alton M. More	**Doug Allen**
Darrell 'Shifty' Powers	**Peter Youngblood-Hills**

Executive Producers **Steven Spielberg, Tom Hanks**

● ***Graphic account of a paratroop company's horrific wartime experiences.***

Based on the factual book of the same title by Stephen E. Ambrose, *Band of Brothers* looks at World War II through the eyes of one American paratroop company. Easy Company, part of the 506th Regiment of the US Army's 101st Airborne Division, enters the fray on D-Day. Previously, the company is shown undertaking harsh training in Georgia from 1942, then getting acclimatized to Europe in the Wiltshire village of Aldbourne. In the early hours of 6 June 1944, the men are dropped amid heavy fire behind German lines to support forces arriving by sea. Over ten episodes, the drama follows Easy Company across Europe as the war draws to a climax, through France, Holland, Belgium and Germany to their attack on Hitler's own fortress at Berchtesgaden in Bavaria. New recruits are brought in to replace men who have, literally, given everything. Despite its $120 million budget and its star-name producers, *Band of Brothers* is certainly not another Hollywood tale of Americans winning the war. Steven Spielberg and Tom Hanks set out to pay genuine tribute to the real members of Easy Company, many of whom perished during the conflict, with others still bearing the mental and physical scars of their experiences. Some of the veterans provided their own thoughts and memories as a preface to each episode. They were also brought together in a special programme, *We Stand Alone Together – the Men of Easy Company*, screened the week after the drama concluded. To convey the bloody brutality of events, the script is largely dehumanized, with very few characters standing out above the complexities of the action. Filming in washed-out colour adds to the period feel and also removes more of the Hollywood gloss. The battle scenes pull no punches: men shockingly killed in mid-conversation; limbs graphically blown away; relentless noise, nausea and utter confusion everywhere – this is not comfortable viewing. Of the characters that do come to the fore, most prominent is Easy Company leader Major Dick Winters, a silent, but resourceful and tough man who commands instant respect.

The series was shot in Britain, using a disused airfield near Hatfield (formerly employed for Spielberg's movie *Saving Private Ryan*), where various European settings, plus forests, rivers and dykes were authentically reconstructed. The mammoth crew included some 500 actors with speaking parts. All the actors in Easy Company attended a military boot camp to toughen them up into their roles, which were based on real people. Tom Hanks also directed one episode; other directors included David Leland and Richard Loncraine. Hanks's son, Colin, was cast as enthusiastic young Lt. Hank Jones.

Band of Gold/Gold ✶✶

UK (Granada) Drama. ITV 1995–7
DVD: Network

Carol Johnson	**Cathy Tyson**
Rose Garrity	**Geraldine James**
Anita Braithwaite	**Barbara Dickson**
Tracy Richards	**Samantha Morton**
George Ferguson	**Tony Doyle**
Curly	**Richard Moore**
Bob	**Anthony Milner**
Steve Dixon	**Ray Stevenson**
Insp./DCI Newall	**David Schofield**
Dez	**Ahsen Bhatti**
Mr Moore	**Philip Martin Brown**
Colette	**Lena Headley**
Joyce Webster	**Rachel Davies**
Smiley	**Darren Tighe**
Vinnie Marshall	**Adam Kotz**
Brian Roberts	**Peter Firth**
Rabbit	**Justin Chadwick**
Brenda Taylor	**Margo Gunn**
Mrs Minkin	**Anita Carey**
Emma Johnson	**Laura Kilgallon**
Alf Black	**David Bradley**
Paula Graham	**Janet Dibley** *(Gold)*
DI Cooper	**Fiona Allen** *(Gold)*
Chubbs	**David Ross** *(Gold)*
Lloyd	**Darren Warner** *(Gold)*
Lisa	**Jayne Ashbourne** *(Gold)*
Insp. Henryson	**Kern Falconer** *(Gold)*
Mr Smithson	**Mark Strong** *(Gold)*

Creator **Kay Mellor**
Writers **Kay Mellor, Mark Davies Markham** *(Gold)*, **Catherine Johnson** *(Gold)*
Producers **Tony Dennis, Elizabeth Bradley, Gillian McNeill** *(Gold)*

Bleak portrayal of the lives of a group of prostitutes.
Set in Bradford, *Band of Gold* introduces viewers to the miserable world of life on the game. It features four women who have taken up prostitution for differing reasons and wraps their stories around the hunt for the murderer of young mother Gina Dixon, who had turned to the game to pay off a loan shark. Carol is the matter-of-fact, hygiene-obsessed hooker, happy to be shocking the neighbours; Rose is the experienced, matriarchal figure who continually fails to start a new life; Anita is selfish and scheming; and misguided teenage blonde Tracy is a drug abuser. George Ferguson is Anita's married boyfriend and the villain who makes the girls' life even more difficult. By the end of the six-part drama, the foursome have decided to leave the grime of the streets and set up their own cleaning co-operative, Scrubbit.

When the series returned for another six episodes a year later, the girls found it difficult to shake off their past on the 'Lane'. A new arrival, a sado-masochism specialist named Colette, joins the throng and more murders ensue, underlining again the programme's core message, that prostitution is not a glamorous industry (although, contrarily, Bradford police claimed that the series had been responsible for an upsurge in activity in the city's red light area). A third series, of three two-part stories, arrived in 1997. Re-titled *Gold*, this time only Rose and Carol remain of the original four girls. Now both past the age of 40, they once again attempt to go straight, Rose with a new job as a liaison officer between the social services and local prostitutes, and Carol with the help of a generous inheritance from a former punter. However, they are constantly hindered by their troubled past and yet more mysterious killings. *Band of Gold*'s theme song, a version of 'Love Hurts', was performed by star Barbara Dickson.

Bannister, Trevor

(1936–)

Familiar character and comic actor, starring in the 1960s dramas *Object Z* (Peter Barry) and *The War of Darkie Pilbeam*, and the sitcoms THE DUSTBINMEN (Heavy Breathing) and ARE YOU BEING SERVED? (Mr Lucas). Among other series, Bannister was also seen in *Wyatt's Watchdogs* (Peter Pitt) and made guest appearances in the likes of STEPTOE AND SON, THE TOMORROW PEOPLE and LAST OF THE SUMMER WINE.

Bar Mitzvah Boy ✶✶✶

UK (BBC) Drama. BBC 1 1976

Victor Green	**Bernard Spear**
Rita Green	**Maria Charles**
Eliot Green	**Jeremy Steyn**
Lesley Green	**Adrienne Posta**
Harold	**Jonathan Lynn**
Grandad Wax	**Cyril Shaps**
Rabbi Sherman	**Jack Lynn**

Writer **Jack Rosenthal**
Producer **Graeme McDonald**

A young Jewish boy bottles out of his bar mitzvah.
Adrenaline is rushing through the Green household in London as the family prepares for 13-year-old son Eliot's ritual passage from boy to man. There is heightened tension between taxi driver dad Victor and Valium-soothed mum Rita, and suddenly Eliot is not sure if he wants his bar mitzvah ceremony to go ahead. On the day, he runs away from the synagogue in the middle of proceedings, eventually confiding that if the men in his family (including sister Lesley's soppy, domesticated boyfriend, Harold) are supposed to be his role models, then he doesn't want to be a man after all. Seeking solace in a playground, Eliot proves he has not forgotten his ceremonial lines, which the rabbi declares to be good enough for him – so the boy is bar mitzvahed after all. Directed by Michael Tuchner, this comedic insight into Jewish life is one of the best-remembered offerings from the PLAY FOR TODAY series.

Barbapapa ✶

Netherlands (Polyscope) Animation. BBC 1 1975

Narrator **Michael Flanders**

Creators **Annette Tison, Talus Taylor**

Gentle humour from a family of metamorphic blobs.
The brainchild of 38-year-old American maths and science teacher Talus Taylor and French architect Annette Tison, nine years his junior, Barbapapa is a pink, soft, smiley creature who can change his shape 'like magic'. He's the head of a family of similarly odd cellular beings that includes Barbamama

(coloured black) and seven Barbababies, among them Barbabeau (a black hairy artist), Barbalib (an orange, typical 1970s feminist) and the appropriately titled Barbabright (the clever blue one). The other offspring are Barbabravo (red with Sherlock Holmes deerstalker hat), Barbazoo (yellow and animal-friendly), Barbalala (musical and green) and Barbabelle (vain and purple). The creators (later husband and wife) devised the weird characters while passing romantic doodles across Parisian café tables. Appearing in books in France from 1970, Barbapapa arrived on UK TV as a pre-early evening news cartoon in 1975. A series of new films was produced by Kodansha (the characters' Japanese publisher) in the late 1990s.

Barbara ✱✱

UK (Carlton/Central) Situation Comedy. ITV 1999–2003

Barbara Liversidge	**Gwen Taylor**
Ted Liversidge	**Sam Kelly**
Neil Liversidge	**Benedict Sandiford**
Jean	**Sherrie Hewson**
Linda Pond	**Elizabeth Carling**
Martin Pond	**Mark Benton**
Doreen	**Madge Hindle**
Phil	**John Arthur**
Bob	**Rob Brydon**
Queenie	**Jean Alexander**

Writers **Mark Bussell, Rob Clark, Ramsay Gilderdale, Graham Mark Walker, Justin Sbresni**
Producers **Mark Bussell, Justin Sbresni**

● ***An opinionated Yorkshirewoman can't resist interfering in other people's affairs.***

Barbara Liversidge, fiftysomething mother of two, lives in Yorkshire with Ted, her dopey, long-suffering, brow-beaten, cab-driver husband of 30-odd years. Their grown-up children are Linda (now married to Geordie TV reporter Martin Pond and hoping to start a family) and still-in-the-nest, accident-prone Neil. During the day, Barbara patrols the reception desk at the local surgery, where, with accomplice Doreen, she strikes fear into the hearts of anyone who wishes to see a doctor. But, although Barbara seems a hard nut to crack, her kernel is definitely golden. Also central to Barbara's life is Jean, her promiscuous sister, and occasionally seen is Ted's troublesome geriatric mother, Queenie.

From an unpromising pilot episode (part of the *Comedy Firsts* anthology) in 1995, Barbara eventually blossomed into a durable ITV sitcom, despite unsympathetic scheduling and puzzlingly truncated series. The series actually featured several cast changes from the pilot, which saw Shirley Anne Field in the role of Jean, Caroline Milmoe as Linda and Glen Davies as Martin.

Barber, Glynis

(Glynis van der Reit; 1955–)

South African actress who arrived on TV as Soolin, the blonde gunslinger in BLAKE'S 7, before stripping down to her underwear in the title role of JANE, BBC 2's revival of the *Daily Mirror*'s wartime cartoon heroine. From there, Barber moved on to THE FURTHER ADVENTURES OF LUCKY JIM, then switched to detective work when cast as the plummy Harriet Makepeace in DEMPSEY AND MAKEPEACE, opposite her future husband, Michael Brandon. Her other credits have included THE SANDBAGGERS, TALES OF THE UNEXPECTED, *Night and Day* (Fiona Brake) and *Family Affairs* (Belinda Heath), plus guest appearances in such programmes as DOCTORS, THE BILL and MURPHY'S LAW.

Barbera, Joseph

(1911–)

See *Hanna, William.*

Barchester Chronicles, The ✱✱✱

UK (BBC) Drama. BBC 2 1982
DVD: BBC

Revd Septimus Harding	**Donald Pleasence**
Dr Grantly	**Nigel Hawthorne**
Susan Grantly	**Angela Pleasence**
Bishop Grantly	**Cyril Luckham**
John Bold	**David Gwillim**
Eleanor Harding/Bold	**Janet Maw**
Finney	**John Ringham**
Bunce	**Joseph O'Connor**
Mary Bold	**Barbara Flynn**
Tom Towers	**George Costigan**
Samuel Grantley	**William Redgrave**
Dr Proudie	**Clive Swift**
Mrs Proudie	**Geraldine McEwan**
Revd Obadiah Slope	**Alan Rickman**
Signora Madeline Neroni	**Susan Hampshire**
Quiverful	**Jonathan Adams**
Mrs Quiverful	**Maggie Jones**
Bertie Stanhope	**Peter Blythe**
Charlotte Stanhope	**Susan Edmonstone**
Dr Vesey Stanhope	**Richard Bebb**
Dr Francis Arabin	**Derek New**
Wilfred Thorne	**Richard Leech**
Miss Thorne	**Ursula Howells**

Writer **Alan Plater**
Producer **Jonathan Powell**

● ***Social skulduggery in a quiet Victorian cathedral city.***

Anthony Trollope's first two tales of fictional Barsetshire, and its county town of Barchester, are brought to life in this seven-part dramatization by Alan Plater, directed by David Giles, with music by Derek Bourgeois. Drawing initially from Trollope's 1855 novel *The Warden*, it introduces the Revd Septimus Harding, a mild-mannered, close friend of the local bishop, who has a very nice little life, thanks to money generated by Hiram's Hospital, a charitable concern in his care. While its inmates have not benefited to any great degree from the steady increase in income, Harding certainly has, although his secret is about to be betrayed to the world. Assiduous local medic John Bold leaks details of Harding's sinecure to the national press and although Harding is encouraged to fight the accusations by the conceited Archdeacon Grantly (son of the bishop, and husband of Harding's own daughter, Susan), the meek cleric is happy to concede. Eventually Bold marries Harding's other daughter, Eleanor.

The story takes a new turn with the death of the bishop and the race to succeed him (following Trollope's next novel, *Barchester Towers*, published in 1857). When timid Dr Proudie arrives to take up the post, he is accompanied by a manipulative wife who brings further unrest to once tranquil Barsetshire by installing a parson, Mr Quiverful, as the new warden of the hospital. Further aggravating the social situation (and Mrs Proudie, his one-time promoter) is the new chaplain, oily Obadiah Slope, who has ambitions of his own. However, Slope's plans to marry the now widowed Eleanor Bold are scuppered by his dalliance with impoverished Italian beauty Signora Vesey-Neroni and Eleanor eventually weds the new dean, Dr Arabin.

Arthur Lowe was the original choice to play the gentle Revd Harding but he died before the series went into production and was replaced by Donald Pleasence. This allowed a genuine father–daughter relationship to be introduced, with Pleasence's own daughter, Angela, playing Harding's daughter, Susan.

Barclay, Humphrey

(1941–)

Former Cambridge Footlights graduate and mastermind of the 1963 revue *Cambridge Circus*, which featured such up-and-coming performers as John Cleese, Tim Brooke-Taylor, Bill Oddie, Graham Chapman, Jonathan Lynn and Graeme Garden. Barclay then moved into television, working as a comedy producer with Rediffusion and then LWT. His many credits have included DO NOT ADJUST YOUR SET (for which he discovered David Jason), THE COMPLETE AND UTTER HISTORY OF BRITAIN, HARK AT BARKER, DOCTOR IN THE HOUSE (and its sequels), NO – HONESTLY, THE TOP SECRET LIFE OF EDGAR BRIGGS, *Lucky Feller, Blind Men*, TWO'S COMPANY, NOBODY'S PERFECT, *End of Part One*, ME & MY GIRL, A FINE ROMANCE, WHOOPS APOCALYPSE, HOT METAL and THAT'S LOVE, plus shows starring Cannon and Ball, Stanley Baxter, Hale and Pace, and Emma Thompson. In the 1980s Barclay set up his own production company, Humphrey Barclay Productions, which contributed series such as *Dream Stuffing, Relative Strangers*, DESMOND'S, SURGICAL SPIRIT, UP THE GARDEN PATH, BRIGHTON BELLES, *Conjugal Rites* and AGONY AGAIN. More recent credits have been for the sitcoms DUCK PATROL, SPACED, ALL ABOUT ME, the single comedy *Bostock's Cup* and television pantomimes.

Baretta ✶

US (Public Arts/Roy Huggins/Universal) Police Drama.
ITV 1978–9 (US: ABC 1975–8)
DVD: MCA Home Video (Region 1 only)

Det. Tony Baretta	**Robert Blake**
Insp. Shiller	**Dana Elcar**
Lt. Hal Brubaker	**Edward Grover**
Billy Truman	**Tom Ewell**
Rooster	**Michael D. Roberts**
Fats	**Chino Williams**

Creator **Stephen J. Cannell**
Executive Producers **Roy Huggins, Bernard L. Kowalski, Anthony Spinner**
Producer **Jo Swerling Jr**

The cases of an unconventional, scruffy cop of Italian origin.

Son of hard-up Italian immigrants, Tony Baretta was another of those unorthodox, 1970s American policemen. Preferring the T-shirt, jeans and cap mode of dress to smart shirts, ties and pressed trousers, he uses his earthy background, streetwise appearance and local knowledge to great effect in infiltrating local gangs and crime syndicates, with his skill at disguise also coming to the fore. Baretta is a lone operator, driving a car known as *The Blue Ghost* and taking assignments from the crabby Insp. Shiller, who is later replaced by Lt. Brubaker. Billy Truman is the house detective at the seedy King Edward Hotel where Tony lives, Rooster and Fats are Baretta's informants, and Fred is his pet cockatoo and confidant. Though rather violent, *Baretta* also offers moments of comic relief and became a big hit in the USA, knocking CANNON out of the ratings. It was the direct replacement for another cop show, *Toma*, which had starred Tony Musante (when Musante left, Robert Blake was offered the role of Toma, but, with ratings slipping, it was agreed to start again from scratch, switching locations from New Jersey to a big Western city – to all intents and purposes Los Angeles – and installing a new lead character at the same time). Sammy Davis Jr performed the theme song, 'Keep Your Eye on the Sparrow'.

Barker, Ronnie

OBE (1929–2005)

Comedian and comic actor born in Bedford, universally recognized as one of television's finest. From his earliest appearances in IT'S A SQUARE WORLD (with Michael Bentine), THE SEVEN FACES OF JIM (with Jimmy Edwards) and THE FROST REPORT (alongside John Cleese and Ronnie Corbett), Barker enjoyed a reputation second to none for comic timing and verbal dexterity. He was given a showcase series in 1968, *The Ronnie Barker Playhouse*, in one episode of which he introduced the character of Lord Rustless, who was then spun off into two series of his own, HARK AT BARKER, and *His Lordship Entertains*. In 1971 Barker was paired again with Ronnie Corbett for THE TWO RONNIES, a mixture of monologues, soliloquies and humorous sketches which ran for 15 years, with some material written by Barker himself under the pen-name of Gerald Wiley. *Six Dates with Barker*, aired in 1971, and another anthology series, *Seven of One* in 1973, yielded two major sitcoms and two of TV's brightest creations. The first, PORRIDGE, saw Barker's classic portrayal of the old lag Fletcher (later set free in *Going Straight*). The second, OPEN ALL HOURS, featured the stuttering, penny-pinching grocer Arkwright. Some of his other efforts were understandably less memorable, namely the short-sighted removal man CLARENCE (written by Barker under the name of Bob Ferris) and the flamboyant, lecherous Welsh photographer THE MAGNIFICENT EVANS. Barker's other credits over the years included parts in lesser comedies like *The TV Lark, Bold as Brass* and *Foreign Affairs*. He retired from showbiz in 1988 but was tempted back with the role of Churchill's butler, David Inches, in the single drama THE GATHERING STORM in 2002, illustrating again the quality straight acting skills seen in earlier productions like *When We are Married*, in which he played Henry Ormonroyd. Barker's final TV role was to resume his partnership with Ronnie Corbett for *The Two Ronnies Sketchbook*, a series of highlights from the golden era.

Barker, Sue

(1956–)

Devon-born former tennis professional (one-time French Open champion) who turned to sports presenting after hanging up her racket in 1985. Following commentating work for Channel 7 in Australia, she joined Sky Sports and then moved to the BBC as presenter of *Sunday Grandstand*, GRANDSTAND and various sporting events, including Wimbledon and the Olympic Games. In 1997 she succeeded David Coleman as chair of A QUESTION OF SPORT.

Barkworth, Peter

(1929–)

Kent-born actor, generally in upper-middle-class parts, probably best recalled as the retiring bank manager Mark Telford in TELFORD'S CHANGE. Previously, Barkworth had appeared as Kenneth Bligh in THE POWER GAME, starred as Vincent in the wartime drama MANHUNT, played detective Arthur Hewitt in THE RIVALS OF SHERLOCK HOLMES and added a run of smaller roles in series like THE AVENGERS, OUT OF THE UNKNOWN, DOCTOR WHO and COLDITZ. He also took on the roles of Eustace Morrow in GOOD GIRL, Stanley Baldwin in WINSTON CHURCHILL – THE WILDERNESS YEARS, and that of computer executive Geoffrey Carr in *The Price*, and was also seen in LATE STARTER and SECRET ARMY. In 1977 Barkworth picked up a BAFTA award for his performance in Tom Stoppard's *Play of the Week, Professional Foul*. More recently, he has been seen in HEARTBEAT.

Barlow, Thelma

(1937–)

Middlesbrough-born actress who spent 26 years as the dithering Mavis Riley/Wilton in CORONATION STREET but has since starred in DINNERLADIES (Dolly) and DAVID COPPERFIELD (Mrs Heep). Other appearances over her career have come in *A Stranger on the Hills*, VANITY FAIR, MURDER MOST HORRID, STIG OF THE DUMP, FAT FRIENDS, THE ROYAL, WHERE THE HEART IS and AGATHA CHRISTIE'S MARPLE.

Barlow at Large/Barlow ✶

UK (BBC) Police Drama. BBC 1 1971; 1973/1974–5

Det. Chief Supt Charlie Barlow ..... **Stratford Johns**
DS David Rees ..... **Norman Corner**
A. G. Fenton ..... **Neil Stacy**
DI Tucker ..... **Derek Newark** *(Barlow)*

Creator **Elwyn Jones**
Producers **Leonard Lewis, Keith Williams**

An aggressive police detective is assigned to the Home Office.

In this, the third part of the Charlie Barlow story, the former Z CARS and SOFTLY, SOFTLY bully boy is somewhat uncomfortably installed in Whitehall, working with a rather smarmy superior, A. G. Fenton, with whom he doesn't always see eye to eye. As part of the Police Research Services Branch, his job is to help regional police forces with any difficult cases they encounter. Although he is accompanied by Detective Sgt Rees, he always seems a little lost without his old mucker, John Watt. The series evolved into another sequel, simply entitled *Barlow*, in which he was joined by DI Tucker.

Barnaby ✶

France (Q3) Children's Entertainment. BBC 1 1973

Voices **Colin Jeavons, Charles Collingwood, Gwenllian Owen, Percy Edwards**

Creator **Albert Barillé**
Producer (UK) **Michael Grafton-Robinson**

A bear with hidden talents makes his way in the world.

Colargol: sounds like a mouthwash but in fact it's a bear – a bear we know as Barnaby. The character was created in books by Olga Puchine and everywhere apart from the UK (and Canada, where he is known as Jeremy), he answers to that gargling name. This is odd as the theme song makes it perfectly clear: 'Barnaby the bear is my name. Never call me Jack or James', he declares. His story, though, is the same the world over. Barnaby is a little woolly bear living in a forest. One day he asks the birds to teach him to sing and, with his new-found talent, joins Mr Pimoulu's Circus. There he shares the limelight with musical monkeys Ricky and Dicky, some cats who ride the high trapeze, Sara the seal and Pimoulu's own wife, who performs a high-wire act after selling the tickets. But Barnaby is not happy here and his woodland friends help him escape. He then learns to swim but has to be rescued at sea by some sailors, who unfortunately make sure he works hard on their ship in return. He flees, along with his friends Crow and Rat, and takes a holiday at the seaside before attending Crow's wedding party. Dubbed into English from the original French, Barnaby was introduced as part of the WATCH WITH MOTHER strand. The featured singing group was The Cooperation.

Barnaby Jones ✶

US (Quinn Martin) Detective Drama. ITV 1974–80 (US: CBS 1973–80)

Barnaby Jones ..... **Buddy Ebsen**
Betty Jones ..... **Lee Meriwether**
Jedediah Romano (J. R.) Jones **Mark Shera**
Lt. Joe Taylor ..... **Vince Howard**
Lt. John Biddle ..... **John Carter**

Executive Producer **Quinn Martin**
Producers **Gene Levitt, Philip Salzman, Robert Sherman**

A Los Angeles private eye comes out of retirement to find the killer of his son.

Barnaby Jones, after an impressive career as a private eye, has relaxed into a horse-breeding retirement. But when his son, Hal, the new proprietor of the Jones Detective Agency, is murdered on a case, he sets about tracking down the killer. After nailing his man, Barnaby turns his back on retirement and takes over control of the firm once more, assisted by his widowed daughter-in-law, Betty (played by Lee Meriwether, Miss America 1955). Barnaby's young cousin, law student J. R. Jones, is recruited to the team in the fifth series, following the murder of his father.

Like most TV private eyes in the 1970s, Barnaby is unconventional. The softly spoken, milk-drinking gum-shoe uses his vague, totally unassuming appearance to trick criminals into a false sense of security and then pounces when they least expect it. He backs this up by being thoroughly methodical, working on cases in a special crime lab he has constructed at home.

Through this role, star Buddy Ebsen quickly dispelled any fears of typecasting that may have existed following his years as millionaire bumpkin Jed Clampett in THE BEVERLY HILLBILLIES.

Barnett, Lady Isobel
(1918–80)

Born in Scotland, Isobel Barnett worked as a GP for a number of years before becoming a Justice of the Peace. In 1953 she joined the new game show WHAT'S MY LINE? as a resident panellist, and her graceful manner and shrewd questioning quickly endeared her to viewers. She later appeared in various other panel games, on radio as well as TV, but her life ended on a sad note when she committed suicide in 1980, a week after being found guilty of petty shoplifting. She was the wife of a former Lord Mayor of Leicester, Sir Geoffrey Barnett.

Barney Miller ***

US (Four D) Situation Comedy. ITV 1979–83 (US: ABC 1975–82)
DVD: Columbia Tristar (Region 1 only)

Capt. Barney Miller .... **Hal Linden**
Det. Phil Fish .... **Abe Vigoda**
DS Chano Amenguale .... **Gregory Sierra**
Det. Stanley Wojohowicz ('Wojo') .... **Maxwell Gail**
Det. Nick Yemana .... **Jack Soo**
Det. Ron Harris .... **Ron Glass**
Elizabeth Miller .... **Barbara Barrie**
Rachael Miller .... **Anne Wyndham**
David Miller .... **Michael Tessier**
Bernice Fish .... **Florence Stanley**
Det. Janice Wentworth .... **Linda Lavin**
Insp. Frank Luger .... **James Gregory**
Officer Carl Levitt .... **Ron Carey**
Det. Baptista .... **June Gable**
Det. Arthur Dietrich .... **Steve Landesberg**
Lt. Scanlon .... **George Murdock**

Creators **Danny Arnold, Theodore J. Flicker**
Executive Producer **Danny Arnold**
Producers **Chris Hayward, Arne Sultan**

Life in a Greenwich Village police station under its genial Jewish captain.

Barney Miller is set in New York's 12th Precinct police station. Although the eponymous character's family life features prominently in early episodes, it is quickly pushed into the background and all subsequent action takes place in the old precinct house. This soon becomes home to all kinds of weird and wonderful callers, as well as a motley crew of police officers.

Barney is very much the father figure of the station, a compassionate and good listener. His office even has a leather couch for those who need to pour their hearts out. His colleagues include the decrepit Fish, grumbling his way through his last years on the force and always in need of a bathroom. On retirement, he is given his own spin-off series, *Fish*. There are also the naïve, people-loving Wojo, the philosophical Yemana (who makes dreadful coffee and follows horse racing) and fast-talking Puerto Rican Amenguale, who is later replaced by Dietrich, a walking encyclopedia. Black prankster Ron Harris eventually has a book published (*Blood on the Badge*); Levitt is the 5 foot 3 inch officer who longs to be a detective but is 'too short'; and Inspector Luger is Barney's boss.

Barney Miller is a police show that relies on talk, not action. There are no car chases, no explosions and none of the fast talk seen in TV's cop dramas. Instead, the humane side of policing is revealed through the inter-personal relationships of the multi-ethnic officers and the social misfits they bring in. As a result, the programme was much appreciated by real-life police officers for its authenticity, and the stars were made honorary members of the New York Police Department. The series ends when the police station is declared a historic site, after the discovery that it was once used by Teddy Roosevelt when he was President of the New York Police Board in the 1890s. Barney and Levitt are promoted, but the gang is dispersed across the city. The pilot for the show was a segment in a comedy anthology, *Just for Laughs*, called *The Life and Times of Captain Barney Miller*.

Baron, The *

UK (ITC) Secret Agent Drama. ITV 1966–7
DVD: Network

John Mannering ('The Baron') .... **Steve Forrest**
Cordelia Winfield .... **Sue Lloyd**
John Alexander Templeton-Green .... **Colin Gordon**
David Marlowe .... **Paul Ferris**

Producer **Monty Berman**

An international art dealer works as an undercover agent in his spare time.

In this series, very loosely based on the British Intelligence agent created by John Creasey, Steve Forrest starred as John Mannering, a suave American antiques expert who helps the Secret Service whenever a crime involves the theft of valuable pieces, or whenever art is involved in subterfuge in some way. His nickname, the title of the programme, is taken from his family's ranch in Texas (although in Creasey's stories Mannering was British, not American).

Millionaire Mannering drives a Jensen (registration BAR 1) and owns exclusive antiques shops in London, Washington and Paris, from which he plans his secret missions. In his assignments for John Templeton-Green of British Intelligence, he is joined by attractive Cordelia Winfield of the Special Branch Diplomatic Service. David Marlowe is sometimes seen as Mannering's business associate. Edwin Astley provided the music.

Barr, Robert
(1909–99)

Glasgow-born writer and producer with many successes for the BBC, which he joined in 1946, bringing with him a distinguished record as war correspondent. His work included episodes of MAIGRET, Z CARS, SOFTLY, SOFTLY, THE VIEW FROM DANIEL PIKE, *Parkin's Patch*, SECRET ARMY and ENEMY AT THE DOOR, although even earlier credits were the documentary *Germany Under Control* in 1946, *Saturday Night Stories* (as producer) in 1948, a 1949 adaptation of H. G. Wells's *The Time Machine* and the police drama *Pilgrim Street* (again as producer) in 1952. The 1959 series SPY-CATCHER and the 1963 series *Moonstrike* were the peaks of his writing career, but he also created *Gazette*, from which HADLEIGH was derived.

Barr, Roseanne
See *Roseanne*.

Barraclough, Roy

MBE (1935–)

Lancashire-born actor and comedian, partner to Les Dawson on numerous occasions (particularly as Cissie and Ada, the two gossipy women), but better known as Alec Gilroy, landlord of the Rovers Return in CORONATION STREET, a character he has played on and off since 1972 (in addition to four other *Street* visitors). Earlier appearances included contributions to various dramas and sitcoms from *The War of Darkie Pilbeam*, *Castle Haven* and NEAREST AND DEAREST to NEVER MIND THE QUALITY, FEEL THE WIDTH and LOVE THY NEIGHBOUR. He was also one of the leads in the comedy *The More We are Together* (Frank Wilgoose), played major parts in the children's comedies PARDON MY GENIE (Mr Cobbledick) and *T-Bag Strikes Again*, and starred as Leslie Flitcroft in MOTHER'S RUIN. Barraclough was also part of the *Revolver* sketch show team and played Arthur Swarbrick in the single comedy *Bostock's Cup*. More recently, he was Harold Waterman in *A Thing Called Love*, Sean in HEARTLESS and the Revd Onan van Kneck in *Funland*. Scores of guest appearances – in the likes of PEAK PRACTICE, CADFAEL, THE MRS BRADLEY MYSTERIES, BARBARA, HOLBY CITY and HEARTBEAT – add to his portfolio.

Barrett, Ray

(1927–)

Australian-born, rugged-looking actor whose first starring role was as Dr Don Nolan in EMERGENCY – WARD 10. As well as making appearances in series like *Educating Archie*, Z CARS and DOCTOR WHO, he starred as Peter Clarke in the GHOST SQUAD sequel, *GS5*, before taking his best-remembered part, that of oil executive Peter Thornton in MOGUL and THE TROUBLESHOOTERS. From then on, Barrett was a regular face in British TV drama, and his voice was familiar, too. Among other voice-overs, he provided the dialogue for STINGRAY's Commander Shore and THUNDERBIRDS' John Tracy in Gerry Anderson's puppet classics. In 1976 he returned to Australia and continued to win plaudits for his performances in film and television Down Under.

Barrie, Amanda

(Shirley Ann Broadbent; 1935–)

Although known today as the late Alma Sedgewick/Baldwin/Halliwell in CORONATION STREET, Lancashire-born Amanda Barrie's TV credits have been numerous and varied, ranging from hostessing on DOUBLE YOUR MONEY and presenting the kids' show, *Hickory House*, to supporting Morecambe and Wise in their first TV outing, *Running Wild* (1954), and playing the Queen of Tonga in the pantomime *Dick Whittington*. She was also seen in the likes of THE SEVEN FACES OF JIM, *Bulldog Breed* (Sandra Prentiss), *The Reluctant Romeo* (Geraldine Woods), *Time of My Life* (Joan Archer) and L FOR LESTER (Sally Small), plus series such as ARE YOU BEING SERVED? and SPOONER'S PATCH. She joined the *Street* briefly in 1981 and became a member of the regular cast in 1988. Recent credits include a guest role in DOCTORS and the part of Bev Tull in BAD GIRLS.

Barrie, Chris

(1960–)

British comedian, impressionist and comic actor, whose most memorable roles have been as the obnoxious Arnold Rimmer in RED DWARF and the incompetent Gordon Brittas in THE BRITTAS EMPIRE. Barrie has also contributed to shows like *Carrott's Lib*, SATURDAY LIVE, *Pushing Up Daisies*, *Coming Next . . .*, BLACKADDER and SPITTING IMAGE, where his impressionist talents were put to good use. Barrie also starred in a third, less successful sitcom, *A Prince Among Men* (ex-footballer Gary Prince). Other credits have included *The Entertainers*, THE YOUNG ONES, FILTHY RICH AND CATFLAP, *Lenny Henry Tonite* and *Massive Machines* (presenter). He has also been a team captain in the quiz *Petrolheads*.

Barron, John

(1920–2004)

Tall, booming, London-born actor generally cast in eccentric roles. He is best known for his C. J. in THE FALL AND RISE OF REGINALD PERRIN ('I didn't get where I am today . . .'), but he first came to viewers' attention in EMERGENCY – WARD 10 (Harold de la Roux), *Glencannon* and ALL GAS AND GAITERS (the Dean), before playing the warped scientist Morgan Devereaux in the sci-fi serial TIMESLIP, the Minister in DOOMWATCH, the Vicar in POTTER, US security adviser The Deacon in WHOOPS APOCALYPSE and assorted supporting roles in comedy and drama series, including CROWN COURT.

Barron, Keith

(1936–)

Yorkshire-born actor whose TV work has swung between drama and comedy. In the 1960s he made his name as an angry young man in the title role of Dennis Potter's STAND UP, NIGEL BARTON and its sequel, *Vote, Vote, Vote for Nigel Barton*. In the 1980s he starred as David Pearce in DUTY FREE and, in contrast, the love-lorn taxi-driver Tom in the drama TAKE ME HOME. He played Guy Lofthouse in THE GOOD GUYS and other credits have included THE ODD MAN and IT'S DARK OUTSIDE (Sgt Swift), THE FURTHER ADVENTURES OF LUCKY JIM (the 1967 version; Jim Dixon), MY GOOD WOMAN (Philip Broadmore), *No Strings* (Derek), PRINCE REGENT (Charles James Fox), TELFORD'S CHANGE (Tim Hart), LATE EXPECTATIONS (Ted Jackson), LEAVING (Daniel Ford), *Room at the Bottom* (TV boss Kevin Hughes), HAGGARD (title role), ALL NIGHT LONG (Bill Chivers), CATHERINE COOKSON'S *The Round Tower* (Jonathan Ratcliffe), *Close Relations* (Gordon Hammond), *In the Red* (BBC 1 Controller), *Madame Bovary* (L'Heureux), NCS MANHUNT (Supt. Bob Beausoleil), *Take Me* (Don Chambers), WHERE THE HEART IS (Alan Boothe), DEAD MAN WEDS (Sandy Ball), *Johnny and the Bomb* (Sir Walter), and the single dramas *This Could be the Last Time* (Glyn), *Plain Jane* (Thomas Reynolds) and ENGLAND EXPECTS (Larry). He was also seen in A FAMILY AT WAR, UPSTAIRS, DOWNSTAIRS, *About Face*, HOLDING THE FORT, *Stay with Me 'til Morning*, THE RUTH RENDELL MYSTERIES, DROVERS' GOLD, *Screen One*'s *Gobble*, DALZIEL AND PASCOE, MIDSOMER MURDERS, CLOCKING OFF, NEW TRICKS, *Brief Encounters*, FOYLE'S WAR and JUDGE JOHN DEED. Additionally, he narrated the series *It's Grim up North*. Keith is the father of actor James Barron.

Barry, Gene

(Eugene Klass; 1921–)

American supporting actor of the 1950s who flourished in the 1960s, winning glamorous title roles in BAT MASTERSON, BURKE'S LAW, *The Name of the Game* and THE ADVENTURER (Steve Bradley). In the 1970s and 1980s he concentrated on more lavish productions, particularly TV movies, but in 1994 he returned to our screens as Amos Burke, the millionaire head of Los Angeles Police's homicide department. Guest appearances include a role in CHARLIE'S ANGELS.

Barry, Michael
(1910–)

Head of BBC Drama in the pioneering days of the 1950s, responsible for commissioning such classics as QUATERMASS and 1984. Previously, as producer, Barry had introduced the BBC's limited audience to such dramas as Edgar Wallace's *The Case of the Frightened Lady* and *Smoky Cell* (both 1938), *Toad of Toad Hall* (1946) and *Boys in Brown* (1947). In 1965 he produced a Royal Shakespeare Company trilogy of plays under the banner of *The Wars of the Roses*.

Barrymore, Michael
(Michael Parker; 1952–)

Tall, energetic, London-born comedian and quiz show host. After appearing on NEW FACES and WHO DO YOU DO? and in support of Russ Abbot, Michael Barrymore found a niche of his own in the 1980s and 1990s in such shows as *Get Set, Go!, Michael Barrymore's Saturday Night Out, Live from Her Majesty's, Barrymore* (a chance for the public to show off their party pieces), the 'strike the screen' quiz STRIKE IT LUCKY, *Michael Barrymore's My Kind of People, Michael Barrymore's My Kind of Music, Kids Say the Funniest Things*, and the children's series *Mick and Mac*. His humour is based on physically exhausting, almost acrobatic routines and gentle mimicry of his programme participants, with his catchphrase 'Awight!' well to the fore. In 2000 he accepted his first drama role, playing game show host BOB MARTIN and also presented *Barrymore on Broadway*. However, major problems in his personal life in 2002 undermined his TV career, which has yet to bounce back, despite an appearance on *Celebrity* BIG BROTHER.

Basehart, Richard
(1914–84)

American actor chiefly remembered by TV viewers as Admiral Harriman Nelson in VOYAGE TO THE BOTTOM OF THE SEA. Other credits (as guest star) included BEN CASEY, THE TWILIGHT ZONE, GUNSMOKE, MARCUS WELBY, MD and THE LOVE BOAT, plus a catalogue of TV movies. Basehart also provided narration for KNIGHT RIDER.

Bass, Alfie
(1921–87)

Cockney comedian who enjoyed a long film and TV career. One of his earliest small-screen appearances was in the drama *The Bespoke Overcoat* in 1954, although it was as the pessimistic Private 'Excused Boots' Bisley – 'Bootsie' for short – in THE ARMY GAME that he shot to fame in 1957. This led to a sequel, BOOTSIE AND SNUDGE, and then a third sitcom for the character, *Foreign Affairs*. Bass and his co-star Bill Fraser then explored new ground in *Vacant Lot* (with Bass as Alf Grimble). His later TV work included the sitcoms TILL DEATH US DO PART (Bert), ARE YOU BEING SERVED? (Mr Goldberg) and *A Roof over My Head* (Flamewell), the adventure series DICK TURPIN (Isaac Rag) and a 1974 revival of *Bootsie and Snudge*.

Bat Masterson ✶

US (Ziv-United Artists) Western. ITV 1959–62 (US: NBC 1958–61)
DVD: Brentwood Home Video (Region 1 only: part of *Great Western TV Shows* compilation)

Bat Masterson .... **Gene Barry**

Producers **Andy White, Frank Pittman**

● ***A refined gambler is the people's champion in the Wild West.***

Based on the real-life William Barclay ('Bat') Masterson, one-time lawman in Dodge City, this early Western depicts our hero as a debonair, well-groomed, professional gambler, at odds with the grimy frontier world he inhabits. Noted for his fine clothes, bowler hat and golden-crowned walking stick, Masterson is, all the same, no pushover for the foul-breathed, stubble-chinned baddies he encounters on his travels, but he always prefers to use his brain rather than brawn to get the desired result. Actor and character came together again nearly 30 years after they went their separate ways, when Gene Barry stepped once more into Masterson's hand-made boots in an episode of the 1980s Western series *Paradise*.

Bates, Sir Alan
CBE (1934–2003)

Derbyshire-born leading man, mostly working in the cinema but with some notable TV roles to his name. These included Michael Henchard in THE MAYOR OF CASTERBRIDGE, John Mortimer in *A Voyage around My Father*, Guy Burgess in AN ENGLISHMAN ABROAD, Alfred Jones in DOCTOR FISCHER OF GENEVA, Marcel Proust in *102 Boulevard Haussman*, Oliver in *Oliver's Travels*, Uncle Matthew in *Love in a Cold Climate* and King George V in *Bertie and Elizabeth*.

Bates, Michael
(1920–78)

Versatile actor who was part of the original trio of childish old men in LAST OF THE SUMMER WINE (playing Blamire) and starred (blacked up) as the lead wallah, Rangi Ram, in IT AIN'T HALF HOT MUM. His earlier credits included several one-off dramas, such as a 1965 version of *A Passage to India* (again blacked up) and THE STONE TAPE, the police series CLUFF (Insp. Mole), and the sitcoms *Mr John Jorrocks* (Duke of Donkeyton), MR DIGBY DARLING (Norman Stanhope) and *Turnbull's Finest Half-Hour* (Major Clifford Turnbull). The Indian connections should not have been surprising: Bates was born in the subcontinent and spoke Urdu.

Bates, Ralph
(1940–91)

Hammer horror actor who showed his versatility in two diverse TV roles, namely the mean, moody George Warleggan in POLDARK and the wimpish lonely heart, John Lacey, in DEAR JOHN. Other TV credits included the 1960s satire series *Broad and Narrow*, the parts of Caligula in THE CAESARS, Michel Lebrun in MOONBASE 3 and Paul Vercors in SECRET ARMY, and appearances in THE SIX WIVES OF HENRY VIII, CRIME OF PASSION and TALES OF THE UNEXPECTED. Bates, a descendant of French scientist Louis Pasteur, died of cancer in 1991. His two wives were both actresses, Joanna Van Gyseghem and Virginia

Wetherall, and he has left two acting children. His daughter Daisy was seen in FOREVER GREEN, among other series, and his son William appeared as his son in *Dear John*.

Batman ✳✳✳

US (20th Century-Fox/Greenway) Science Fiction. ITV 1966–8 (US: ABC 1966–8)

Bruce Wayne (Batman) .... **Adam West**
Dick Grayson (Robin) .... **Burt Ward**
Alfred Pennyworth .... **Alan Napier**
Aunt Harriet Cooper .... **Madge Blake**
Police Commissioner Gordon . **Neil Hamilton**
Chief O'Hara .... **Stafford Repp**
Barbara Gordon (Batgirl) .... **Yvonne Craig**
The Joker .... **Cesar Romero**
The Riddler .... **Frank Gorshin**
John Astin
The Penguin .... **Burgess Meredith**
Catwoman .... **Julie Newmar**
Eartha Kitt
Lee Ann Meriwether
Narrator .... **William Dozier**

Executive Producer **William Dozier**
Producer **Howie Horowitz**

Camp TV version of the popular comic strip created by Bob Kane in 1939.

Batman was renowned for its purposeful overacting, corny quips and far-fetched storylines. It made a star out of Adam West, albeit a very typecast star, and featured a host of celebrities anxious to grab a piece of what was a very successful series. The series plays the story very close to the comic book in style and substance, with the addition of Aunt Harriet to detract from the suspicious nature of three men sharing a house. The three are millionaire playboy Bruce Wayne, his 15-year-old ward, Dick Grayson, and their gaunt English butler, Alfred. Only Alfred knows that the other two are really the famous Batman and Robin, crime fighters extraordinaire.

The 'Dynamic Duo' live 14 miles outside Gotham City, at Wayne Manor, beneath which is concealed Batman's headquarters, the Batcave. A flick of the switch hidden in a bust of Shakespeare reveals firemen's poles (the 'Batpoles') behind a bookcase that allow them to descend to the cave. Remarkably, on reaching the bottom, they are already clothed in their famous crime-fighting gear and masks. In this high-tech den they puzzle and ponder over the amazing crimes which time and again afflict the city, before setting out to wreak vengeance on the underworld, a vengeance promised by Wayne when he was criminally orphaned in his teens.

Their enemies (or 'arch-enemies') are most frequently the Joker, adorned with a sick painted smile, the Riddler, in his question-marked catsuit, the waddling Penguin, with his cigarette holder, and the leather clad Catwoman, although the series also introduces some baddies not known in the comic strip. These include Egghead (Vincent Price), King Tut (Victor Buono), Mr Freeze (Otto Preminger) and the Bookworm (Roddy McDowall).

Batman and Robin rocket into action in the Batmobile, a converted 17-foot-long Lincoln Continental, but this is just one of their many gadgets and ingenious devices. Adam West plays the lead very drily, while Burt Ward's Robin is dramatically excitable and prone to 'Holy' expressions of farcical topicality, like 'Holy sewer pipe!' as the Riddler emerges from a manhole, and 'Holy fork in the road!'. The villains are ridiculously twisted: the Joker loves to play nasty tricks, while the Riddler always gives our heroes a seemingly unfathomable clue. The action is laughably violent and partially obscured by exclamations like 'Pow!', 'Zap!' and 'Thud' writ large on the screen. Each episode closes with a cliffhanger in the style of the old movie serials.

Our heroes are usually summoned into action by the desperate Commissioner Gordon over the Batphone, or by the Batsignal in the sky. However, if Commissioner Gordon is himself usually helpless, his librarian daughter certainly is not. She joins the series late in its run as Batgirl, aboard the Batcycle, with her true identity unknown even to her crime-busting colleagues.

Battle of the Planets ✳✳

Japan (Gallerie International/Tatsunoko/Sandy Frank) Cartoon. BBC 1 1979–84
DVD: Universal

Voices:
7-Zark-7 .... **Alan Young**
Mark Venture .... **Casey Kasem**
Princess .... **Janet Waldo**
Jason .... **Ronnie Schell**
Keyop .... **Alan Young**
Tiny Harper .... **Alan Dinehart**
Zoltar .... **Keye Luke**
Security Chief Anderson .... **Alan Dinehart**

Executive Producer **Jameson Brewer**
Producer **David E. Hanson**

The adventures of G-Force, five heroic defenders of the Earth.

Bravely protecting our planet and its galaxy from invasion by the alien Zoltar, ruler of the barren planet of Spectra, G-Force consists of five superhuman teenage orphans commanded by the courageous Mark Venture. His colleagues are the lovely Princess (who adores Mark), the impetuous Jason, the beeping and whirring Keyop, and chubby Tiny, the pilot of their spacecraft, the *Phoenix* (which transforms itself into a fiery bird whenever in danger – usually every episode). All enjoy amazing powers that, when combined, let loose a destructive whirlwind. Their assignments are masterminded by 7-Zark-7, a robot based in their Center Neptune HQ, deep beneath the Pacific Ocean. For company, the robot has a dog, 1-Rover-1. Also at Center Neptune is Anderson, the security chief. The series was an edited version of the Japanese hit *Gatchaman*, later also repackaged as *G-Force*, and *Eagle Riders*.

Battlestar Galactica/Galactica 1980 ✳

US (Universal/Glen A. Larson) Science Fiction. ITV 1980–1/1984 (US: ABC 1978–9/1980)
DVD: Universal

Commander Adama .... **Lorne Greene**
Capt. Apollo .... **Richard Hatch**
Lt. Starbuck .... **Dirk Benedict**
Lt. Boomer .... **Herb Jefferson Jr**
Athena .... **Maren Jensen**
Flt Sgt Jolly .... **Tony Swartz**
Boxey .... **Noah Hathaway**
Col. Tigh .... **Terry Carter**
Cassiopeia .... **Laurette Spang**
Count Baltar .... **John Colicos**

Sheba	**Anne Lockhart** *(Galactica 1980)*
Capt. Troy	**Kent McCord** *(Galactica 1980)*
Lt. Dillon	**Barry Van Dyke** *(Galactica 1980)*
Jamie Hamilton	**Robyn Douglass** *(Galactica 1980)*
Dr Zee	**Robbie Risk** *(Galactica 1980)*
	Patrick Stuart *(Galactica 1980)*
Col. Sydell	**Allan Miller** *(Galactica 1980)*
Xavier	**Richard Lynch** *(Galactica 1980)*

Executive Producer **Glen A. Larson**
Producers **John Dykstra, Leslie Stevens**

● ***Much-hyped cross between the* Book of Exodus *and* WAGON TRAIN.**

In the seventh millennium, 12 of the 13 humanoid civilizations have been wiped out by the treacherous Cylons, enemies of humanoids for a thousand years. A motley convoy of 220 small ships joins the battlestar spaceship *Galactica* in making a break for the last remaining refuge, the mythical 'Golden Planet' (Earth). However, as it meanders through the universe, it is stalked by the Cylons and subject to regular attacks.

Adama is the commander of the ship, a Moses figure aided by his son, Apollo, head of the Viper fighter squadron. Starbuck is the impetuous top-gun pilot, roguishly appealing, especially to Adama's daughter, Athena, the communications officer. Other members of the crew include second-in-command Colonel Tigh, Cassiopeia, the medic, and Boomer, another pilot. Villain of the piece is Count Baltar, who has betrayed the humanoids to the Cylons. The players are not clothed in futuristic garments, but in gowns and tunics reminiscent of Earth's early civilizations. The evil, robotic Cylons, on the other hand, have a chrome appearance and peer in sinister fashion through two red light-beam 'eyes'. The malign nature of the enemy is further emphasized by the batlike wings of its spacecraft, whereas *Galactica* is more of a comfortable city in space, one mile wide.

The special effects, with lasers and colourful explosions aplenty, are spectacular and were handled by producer John Dykstra, who had previously worked on *Star Wars*, but the storylines found plenty of critics. As a result the programme was halted, and revamped in a new form known as *Galactica 1980*. This moves the time on 30 years and sees the ship arriving on Earth, only to find the Cylons plotting its destruction. Lorne Greene as Adama is the sole survivor of the original cast. He is now assisted by Captain Troy, a grown-up version of Adama's adopted son, Boxey, who was seen in the original series.

The pilot episode of *Battlestar Galactica* received a cinema release in the UK, in an attempt to recoup money lost after the series flopped in the USA. In 2004, the series was exhumed – or 're-imagined' – and brought back to TV in some style. Abandoning the campness and kitsch of the original, this *Battlestar Galactica* was described as sci-fi in the post-9/11 world, with graphic violence and flawed heroes. Edward James Olmos starred as Commander William 'Husker' Adama, Jamie Bamber played his son, Captain Lee Adama/Apollo and also appearing were Katee Sackhoff (pilot Kara Thrace/Starbuck), Grace Park (Lt. Sharon Valerii/Boomer – like Starbuck now female!), Tricia Helfer (Number Six), James Callis (Dr Gaius Baltar) and Mary McDonnell (Laura Roslin, President of the 12 Colonies of Kobol.) The new series was screened on Sky One in the UK, strangely in advance of its first showing on US TV.

Baverstock, Donald

(1924–95)

Influential BBC current affairs producer of the 1950s and 1960s, responsible to no small degree for such programmes as *Highlight*, TONIGHT, SONGS OF PRAISE and THAT WAS THE WEEK THAT WAS. He later became head of BBC 1 before moving on to the fledgling Yorkshire Television, where he was programme director from 1968 to 1973.

Baxendale, Helen

(1969 –)

Yorkshire-born, Staffordshire-raised actress seen as Dr Claire Maitland in CARDIAC ARREST before starring as Cordelia Gray in AN UNSUITABLE JOB FOR A WOMAN, Rachel Bradley in COLD FEET and Pandora Braithwaite in ADRIAN MOLE: THE CAPPUCCINO YEARS. She also appeared in *Screen One*'s *Truth or Dare* (lawyer Lorna Johnston), *Screen Two*'s *Crossing the Floor* (politician's mistress Ruth Clarke) and *The Investigator* (lesbian military policewoman Caroline Meagher). Additionally, Baxendale has made guest appearances in DANGERFIELD, MURDER IN MIND and FRIENDS (Ross's girlfriend, Emily).

Baxter, Raymond

(1922–2006)

Distinguished BBC presenter, born in Ilford. He was heard to best effect in coverage of air shows (he was a World War II RAF pilot, which led him to join BFBS and then the BBC), royal occasions and motor sports events. He presented the weekly science programme TOMORROW'S WORLD for 12 years and returned for the retrospective *Tomorrow's World Time Machine* in the 1990s. His other credits included *Eye on Research* and *The Energy File*, and a guest appearance in THE GOODIES.

Baxter, Stanley

(1926–)

Scottish comedian and impersonator, fond of mimicking TV's *grandes dames* and Hollywood idols. Following his breakthrough in 1950s series like CHELSEA AT NINE and *On the Bright Side*, Baxter launched his long-running sketch series, *The Stanley Baxter Show*, in 1963, and appeared in his own fortnightly comedy, *Baxter on . . .*, which included programmes on travel, television, law, and theatre, a year later. He switched channels in 1972 to present *The Stanley Baxter Picture Show*, the first in a series of specials. *The Stanley Baxter Series* in 1981 took him back to weekly productions, but since then he has been seen only in one-offs once more. He did, however, take the lead role in the children's comedy MR MAJEIKA.

Bayldon, Geoffrey

(1924–)

Leeds-born actor fondly remembered as CATWEAZLE, the 11th-century sorcerer trapped in the 20th century. Among his other TV credits have been Z CARS, THE AVENGERS, THE SAINT, *The Victorians*, THE WOMAN IN WHITE (Mr Fairlie), THE TOMORROW PEOPLE, EDWARD THE SEVENTH (Sir Henry Campbell-Bannerman), *Devenish* (Neville Liversedge), ALL CREATURES GREAT AND SMALL, BERGERAC, BLOTT ON THE LANDSCAPE (Ganglion), WORZEL GUMMIDGE (The Crowman), STAR COPS, CASUALTY, MIDSOMER MURDERS, WHERE THE HEART IS, WAKING THE DEAD and HEARTBEAT, plus numerous single dramas, as well as taking the role of The Professor in *Fort Boyard*.

Baywatch ✱✱

US (Tower 12/All American) Drama. ITV 1990–7 (US: NBC 1989–90; Syndicated 1991–2001)

Lt. Mitch Buchannon .... **David Hasselhoff**
Jill Riley .... **Shawn Weatherly**
Craig Pomeroy .... **Parker Stevenson**
Eddie Kramer .... **Billy Warlock**
Shauni McLain .... **Erika Eleniak**
Trevor Cole .... **Peter Phelps**
Gina Pomeroy .... **Holly Gagnier**
Hobie Buchannon .... **Brandon Call**
Jeremy Jackson
Gayle Buchannon .... **Wendie Malick**
John D. Cort .... **John Allen Nelson**
Lt. Garner Ellerbee .... **Gregory Alan-Williams**
Capt. Don Thorpe .... **Monte Markham**
Harvey Miller .... **Tom McTigue**
Lt. Ben Edwards .... **Richard Jaeckel**
Matt Brody .... **David Charvet**
C. J. Parker .... **Pamela Anderson/Lee**
Lt. Stephanie Holden .... **Alexandra Paul**
Summer Quinn .... **Nicole Eggert**
Jimmy Slade .... **Kelly Slater**
Jackie Quinn .... **Susan Anton**
Caroline Holden .... **Yasmine Bleeth**
Logan Fowler .... **Jaason Simmons**
Cody Madison .... **David Chokachi**
Donna .... **Donna D'Errico**
Neely Capshaw .... **Gina Lee Nolin**
Samantha .... **Nancy Valen**

Creators **Michael Berk, Douglas Schwartz, Gregory J. Bonann**
Executive Producers **Michael Berk, Douglas Schwartz, Gregory J. Bonann, David Hasselhoff**

● ***Thrills and spills with scantily clad LA lifeguards.***

The Los Angeles County lifeguards are the stars of this all-action seaside romp, known variously as 'Barewatch' and 'Boobwatch' because of its acres of tanned flesh. Chief hunk and programme mastermind was David Hasselhoff in the guise of Mitch Buchannon, at the outset a newly installed lieutenant in the seaside patrol force. Working alongside Mitch in the early days are his lawyer friend, Parker Stevenson, and Jill Riley, sadly killed by a shark during the first season. Thorpe is Buchannon's officious captain, and assorted rookie lifeguards mill around the team's Malibu Beach headquarters. These include Shauni McLain, Trevor Cole and Eddie Kramer. Part of the fabric is Mitch's son, Hobie, who lives with his dad following Mitch's marriage break-up; and officers from the LAPD beach patrol squad, particularly Garner Ellerbee, are also seen. John D. Cort runs the local beach shop, Sam's Surf and Dive.

Despite success outside the USA, *Baywatch* was cancelled after just one season. Hasselhoff and a consortium of three others pooled resources to finance the production of more episodes, which they sold into syndication and to networks overseas. The almost cult following the series enjoyed in the UK no doubt swayed their decision. With the fresh set-up, new characters appear, including Ben Edwards, a weather-beaten but good-natured lifeguard, and young joker Harvey Miller. Matt Brody, C. J. Parker and Stephanie Holden are among the later recruits. From 1995, in the UK the series was billed as *New Baywatch*. A spin-off series, *Baywatch Nights*, in which Mitch becomes a detective, was screened in 1996. *Baywatch* was itself revamped in 2000 with a switch of location to *Baywatch Hawaii*.

Bazalgette, Peter

(1953–)

British independent TV producer and pioneer of lifestyle and reality television, whose early television work was with BBC News and then as a researcher for THAT'S LIFE. Through his company Bazal (now part of Endemol UK, of which Bazalgette is chairman), he has been responsible for such hits as FOOD AND DRINK, *Ready, Steady, Cook*, CHANGING ROOMS, *Can't Cook, Won't Cook*, GROUND FORCE and BIG BROTHER. Bazalgette has also been a member of the board of Channel 4.

BBC

(British Broadcasting Corporation)

Britain's major broadcasting organization was founded as the British Broadcasting Company in 1922, with executives drawn from the ranks of radio receiver manufacturers who had been invited to provide a broadcasting service by the Postmaster General. Then, as today, funding was provided by a licence fee, payable by all users of radio (now TV) sets, at a rate set by Parliament. To this day, neither the BBC's radio nor television service has accepted paid advertising. The company was reconstituted as the British Broadcasting Corporation (a public corporation, working 'as a trustee for the national interest') on 1 January 1927, and since that time has derived its authority from a Royal Charter. The Charter has been considered for renewal every ten years or so, each time instigating a heated debate about the role of the BBC and its funding.

Organizationally, the BBC is headed by a board of Governors, all appointed by the Queen on the advice of the Government, for a five-year term. Day-to-day control is assumed by the Director-General and his executives. The BBC's first Director-General, and effectively the father of public service broadcasting in the UK, was John (later Lord) Reith, who instilled in programme-makers his belief in the need to 'Educate, Inform, Entertain'.

The BBC began television experiments in 1932, from a studio in Broadcasting House, Portland Place, London. On 2 November 1936 the Corporation inaugurated the world's first regular high-definition television service, but this was suspended on 1 September 1939 for defence reasons, with war imminent. It resumed on 7 June 1946, with the same Mickey Mouse cartoon (*Mickey's Gala Premiere*) that had closed the station down seven years earlier. A major milestone in the development of the television service was the Coronation of Queen Elizabeth II in 1953. The BBC covered the proceedings live, and sales of television sets rocketed. However, its monopoly position as the UK's only television broadcaster was broken with the launch of ITV in 1955.

On 29 June 1960 the BBC opened its new Television Centre in Shepherd's Bush, West London, having previously broadcast from Alexandra Palace and the old film studios at Lime Grove. On 20 April 1964 the Corporation's second channel, BBC 2, was launched (although a power cut curtailed its opening night). Broadcasting in the UHF, 625-line format, and promoted initially with cartoon kangaroos Hullabaloo and Custard, the new channel's focus was on minority-interest programmes, innovation and education. It has since made a name for itself in pioneering cutting-edge comedy, as well as arts and culture. More than 40 years on, the channel's heritage is impressive, with programme highlights including PLAY SCHOOL, CIVILISATION, THE GREAT WAR, NOT THE NINE O'CLOCK NEWS, BOYS FROM THE BLACKSTUFF, THE OLD GREY WHISTLE TEST, THE FORSYTE SAGA, I, CLAUDIUS and THE OFFICE.

Colour broadcasts began on BBC 2 on 1 July 1967 (initially only five hours a week). The colour service was officially inaugurated on 2 December of the same year and spread to BBC 1 (and ITV) on 15 November 1969. Both BBC channels have allowed for regional opt-out programmes, to cover local news, current affairs, sports and entertainments. These are prepared by a network of BBC studios around the country. In 1991, BBC World Service Television was launched. This largely satellite channel beams BBC news and entertainment programmes around much of the world, 24 hours a day. Also in the 1990s, NICAM stereo sound was introduced and, with the arrival of digital broadcasting, the BBC launched a tranche of new channels: BBC News 24 (9 November 1997), BBC Choice (general interest, 23 September 1998), BBC Parliament (formerly the Parliamentary Channel, taken over and repackaged 23 September 1998) and BBC Knowledge (education, 1 June 1999). Two new digital channels for children, CBBC (for ages 6–13) and CBeebies (for the under-6s), were introduced, on 11 February 2002. BBC Knowledge was superseded by BBC 4 on 2 March 2002, using the slogan 'Everybody needs a place to think'. Its output is directed at the brain that receives only meagre rations from other channels, boosting the BBC's cultural output and offering viewers another chance to see landmark documentaries, comedies and dramas from television's past. BBC Choice gave way to BBC 3 on 9 February 2003. Johnny Vaughan hosted the opening show, setting the tone for its diet of young people's comedy, music and other entertainment. In 2002, the BBC was part of a consortium that rescued the terrestrial digital service formerly run by ITV Digital, launching it as Freeview.

In technical terms and also programme-wise, the BBC has a reputation second to none in world broadcasting. Its news coverage has been viewed as authoritative, and its drama output – particularly its period classics – is legendary. However, the 1990s witnessed a degree of turmoil within the organization. Under the 1989 Broadcasting Bill, 25 per cent of all programmes now have to be supplied by independent contractors. This inevitably led to an immediate loss of BBC jobs. Another consequence was 'Producer Choice'. This system of allocating cash to BBC programme-makers to buy technical and other services, from either within the BBC or without, was introduced by Director-General John Birt, the man charged with leading the Corporation through its next Royal Charter renewal, in 1996. It did not prove popular with BBC employees. However, the BBC duly gained its eighth Royal Charter and Birt was eventually succeeded as Director-General in January 2000 by Greg Dyke, who immediately aimed to slash bureaucracy and declared his support for programme-makers. Regrettably to many insiders, in 2004 Dyke (along with BBC Chairman Gavyn Davies) became a victim of the Hutton Inquiry into the death of Government scientist Dr David Kelly, his backing of the editorial team at the core of the dispute making his position untenable. He was replaced by Channel 4 Chief Executive Mark Thompson.

Directors-General of the BBC

1927–38 .... **John Reith**
1938–42 .... **Frederick Ogilvie**
1942–3 .... **Cecil Graves/Robert Foot**
1943–4 .... **Robert Foot**
1944–52 .... **William Haley**
1952–9 .... **Ian Jacob**
1960–9 .... **Hugh Carleton Greene**
1969–77 .... **Charles Curran**
1977–82 .... **Ian Trethowan**
1982–7 .... **Alasdair Milne**
1987–93 .... **Michael Checkland**
1993–2000 .... **John Birt**
2000–4 .... **Greg Dyke**
2004– .... **Mark Thompson**

BBC Sports Personality of the Year

See *Sports Review of the Year*.

BBC Television Newsreel, The ✳

UK (BBC) News. BBC 1948–54

Editor **D. A. Smith**
Producer **Harold Cox**

News events from around the world.

Hardly topical, and consisting largely of fading news items, *The BBC Television Newsreel* was BBC TV's first attempt at presenting news footage. Previously, the news had been conveyed in sound only, radio fashion, and up-to-date, in-vision news bulletins were still six years away (they began in 1954). This programme filled the gap, using the style of cinema newsreels, but running for 15 minutes instead of ten and including fewer stories. International items were incorporated, thanks to an exchange deal with America's NBC network. The same programme was initially transmitted four times a week, on Mondays, Wednesdays and twice on Saturdays.

BBC Television Shakespeare, The ✳✳

UK (BBC) Drama Anthology. BBC 2 1978–85
DVD: BBC

Producers **Cedric Messina, Jonathan Miller, Shaun Sutton**

Ambitious staging of all 37 Shakespeare plays.

Creating the definitive television version of Shakespeare's *oeuvre* proved even more difficult than imagined when the BBC launched the project in 1978. Some productions ran into 'technical' troubles and the numerous styles applied by directors resulted in a rather piecemeal effect for the series as a whole. Some plays, for instance, were totally studio-bound, while others were shot on location. Cedric Messina was the brains behind the concept and took charge of production for the first two years. Jonathan Miller was drafted in to continue the project and Shaun Sutton completed affairs.

Among the stars appearing over the seven years were Anthony Hopkins, Helen Mirren, Derek Jacobi, John Gielgud, Wendy Hiller, James Bolam, Virginia McKenna, Timothy West and Anthony Quayle. Perhaps the most unusual casting was of John Cleese as *The Taming of the Shrew*'s Petruchio. Desmond Davis, Herbert Wise, Basil Coleman and David Giles were among the directors employed.

BBC-3 ✳✳

UK (BBC) Comedy. BBC 1 1965–6

John Bird, Robert Robinson, Lynda Baron, David Battley, John Fortune, Bill Oddie, Alan Bennett, Leonard Rossiter, Roy Dotrice

Producer **Ned Sherrin**

● ***Controversial programme of topical humour and debate.***

Son of THAT WAS THE WEEK THAT WAS, by way of NOT SO MUCH A PROGRAMME, MORE A WAY OF LIFE, this late-night satire show is chiefly remembered today for allowing the first known use of the 'F' word on national television. It came in 1965 during an interview with Kenneth Tynan about theatre censorship. Such frank discussions mingled with sketches, filmed inserts and music in the programme plan, but the show never achieved the heights of *TW3*, despite employing writers like David Frost, Christopher Booker, John Mortimer and Keith Waterhouse. Supporting the principals on screen were the likes of Malcolm Muggeridge, Patrick Campbell, Harvey Orkin, Denis Norden and Norman St John Stevas.

Beacham, Stephanie

(1947–)

Casablanca-born actress often seen in the determined female role. Her most prominent part has been as Sable Colby in DYNASTY and THE COLBYS, transatlantic success arriving after several notable performances on British television. Among these were the parts of Rose Millar in TENKO and CONNIE in the series of the same name. Her earlier credits included guest appearances in THE SAINT, ARMCHAIR THEATRE, CALLAN, JASON KING, UFO, THE PROTECTORS, *Marked Personal* and HADLEIGH. More recently, she has been seen in the US sitcom *Sister Kate*, and as Mrs Peacock in CLUEDO, Iris McKay in BEVERLY HILLS 90210, Molly Carter in JILLY COOPER'S RIDERS, Dr Kristin Westphalen in SEAQUEST DSV, Dorothea Grant in NO BANANAS, Vernice Green in *Having It Off* and Phyl Oswyn in BAD GIRLS.

Beadle, Jeremy

MBE (1948–)

British presenter of audience participation shows, especially those involving pranks, stunts and hidden cameras. Breaking into television as one of the four original presenters of GAME FOR A LAUGH, Beadle has since hosted *Eureka!, Beadle's About, Beadle's Box of Tricks, People Do the Funniest Things*, YOU'VE BEEN FRAMED, *Win Beadle's Money, Banged up with Beadle* and the crossword game show *Definition*. He has also worked as a writer and consultant on other programmes, was one of the earliest presenters on GMTV and fronted the *Banged up with Beadle* segment of *Ant and Dec's Saturday Night Takeaway*.

Bean, Sean

(1959–)

Sheffield-born actor with a Shakespearean stage background. On television he starred as Lovelace in *Clarissa*, Mellors in LADY CHATTERLEY, Paul in *A Woman's Guide to Adultery*, Dominic O'Brien in CATHERINE COOKSON'S *The Fifteen Streets* and Richard Sharpe in SHARPE. Other credits include INSPECTOR MORSE, Andy McNab in *Bravo Two Zero* and Robert Aske in HENRY VIII. He also provided the voice of Dark in *Pride*, more voices for the animated version of *The Canterbury Tales*, and narrated the documentary *D-Day to Berlin*. Bean's second wife was actress Melanie Hill and his third wife was *Sharpe* co-star Abigail Cruttenden.

Beast ★★

UK (Little Pond) Situation Comedy. BBC 1 2000–1

Nick	**Alexander Armstrong**
Kirsten	**Doon Mackichan**
Briony	**Sylvestra Le Touzel**
Andrew	**Steven Alvey**
Jade	**Emma Pierson**

Creator/Writer **Simon Nye**
Producers **Julian Meers, Paul Schlesinger, Margot Gavan Duffy**

● ***An incompetent vet hates his job.***

Nick is a veterinary surgeon who has inherited a rural practice somewhere in Gloucestershire. The trouble is, he's not very good at his job and doesn't really like animals: he's rather more interested in their female owners, or in ways of swindling gullible clients. Kirsten is the practice manager who often bails Nick out of his daily disasters, boring Andrew and starchy Briony are vet colleagues, and Jade is their dopey trainee. Humour comes from unsuccessful womanizing, practice friction and, yes, even botched operations and diagnoses. Two series of six episodes each were produced.

Beaton, Norman

(1934–94)

Guyanese actor, star of the barber shop series DESMOND'S (Desmond Ambrose). His earlier work took in leading roles in EMPIRE ROAD (Everton Bennett) and THE FOSTERS (Samuel Foster), and he was also seen in DEAD HEAD (Caractacus) and HAMMER HOUSE OF HORROR, among other dramas.

Beau Geste ★★

UK (BBC) Drama. BBC 1 1982
DVD: BBC

Beau Geste	**Paul Hawkins** *(young)*
	Benedict Taylor
John Geste	**Paul Critchley** *(young)*
	Jonathon Morris
Digby Geste	**Robin Crane** *(young)*
	Anthony Calf
Sgt Major Lejaune	**John Forgeham**
Lady Brandon	**Wendy Williams**
Major de Beaujolais	**David Sumner**
Buddy	**Barry Dennen**
Hank	**Christopher Malcolm**
Isobel	**Sian Pattenden** *(young)*
	Sally Baxter
Claudia	**Lucy Baker** *(young)*
	Julia Chambers
Augustus Brandon	**Christopher Reilly** *(young)*
	Philip Shelley
Boldini	**Stefan Gryff**
Capt. Renouf	**Damien Thomas**
Cpl Dupré	**John Challis**

Writer **Alistair Bell**
Producer **Barry Letts**

● ***Three brothers stick together against all odds in the French Foreign Legion.***

P. C. Wren's dashingly romantic tale (1924) of three brothers who endure the brutalities of life in the French Foreign Legion was dramatized by the BBC in eight episodes for Sunday teatime viewing. The story begins with a relief column under Major de Beaujolais arriving at the Legion's Fort Zinderneuf, which has been under siege by Tuareg tribesmen. What the Major finds there is not only distressing but quite baffling, and serves as a prelude to take us back through the life stories of the Geste brothers. Michael (called Beau because of his good looks), John and Digby Geste have been raised by their aunt, Lady Brandon. Their 19th-century upbringing (Eton) instils in them a burning sense of duty and loyalty, not least to each other. When the family's precious Blue Water sapphire goes missing, the brothers close ranks to shield one another from suspicion then break out to find their way in the world. They end up in the French Foreign Legion, where their friends are Americans Hank and Buddy, but where life is dour and punishing. Blistering heat, hand-to-hand warfare against local insurgents and desert madness are just some of the hardships they encounter, but beyond all these there is a further trial, in the shape of Sgt Major Lejaune, who is both sadistic and vindictive. When the soldiers are posted to Fort Zinderneuf, and his alcoholic superior Capt. Renouf commits suicide, Lejaune has the Geste brothers at his mercy. He believes the gemstone is in their possession and makes every effort to obtain it. The ranks rise up and plan mutiny, but they are thwarted by the timing of the Tuareg attack. The men fight bravely but the end is nigh. Stephen Deutsch composed the theme music to this faithful but rather lacklustre, low-budget adaptation.

Beauty and the Beast ✶✶

US (Republic Pictures) Adventure. ITV 1988–91
(US: CBS 1987–90)

Assistant DA Catherine Chandler	**Linda Hamilton**
Vincent	**Ron Perlman**
Father	**Roy Dotrice**
Deputy DA Joe Maxwell	**Jay Acavone**
Edie	**Ren Woods**
Kipper	**Cory Danziger**
Mouse	**David Greenlee**
Diana Bennett	**Jo Anderson**
Gabriel	**Stephen McHattie**
Elliott Burch	**Edward Albert**

Creator **Ron Koslow**
Executive Producers **Ron Koslow, Paul Junger Witt, Tony Thomas, Stephen Kurzfeld**

A beautiful girl's life is saved by a deformed man, who then protects her in her fight against crime.

This adventure series has links with both the fairytale world and *The Phantom of the Opera*. When attractive attorney Catherine Chandler is attacked and left for dead in Central Park, New York, her life is saved by the strangely deformed Vincent (his face is marked like a lion), who takes her to his underground refuge and nurses her back to health. When she returns to civilization, the love and the strong telepathic bond which have grown between them allow Vincent to spring to her assistance whenever she falls into danger.

Vincent, for all his grotesque looks, is a compassionate, gentle soul and a lover of poetry. But he lives among the shadows, hitching rides on top of tube trains. Abandoned as a child, he was taken in by the people who lived in the catacombs beneath Manhattan ('Tunnel World'), where he was raised by a reclusive genius known as Father. Kipper and Mouse are Father's helpers.

After an initially platonic relationship, Catherine and Vincent fall in love and the fairytale continues until Catherine is kidnapped and murdered by Gabriel, head of a criminal organization (but not before she has given birth to Vincent's son). Diana Bennett is brought in by Catherine's boss to investigate the case, and she becomes Vincent's new friend. Assisted by businessman Elliott Burch, they track down and kill Gabriel, leaving Vincent and his son to retreat to their peaceful underworld home.

Beckinsale, Richard

(1947–79)

Affable comedy actor whose tragic early death cut short a TV career that had already produced some classic roles. He is probably best recalled as Ronnie Barker's cellmate, Godber, in PORRIDGE and *Going Straight*, although he was just as popular as the sex-starved Geoffrey opposite Paula Wilcox in THE LOVERS and Rigsby's medical student tenant, Alan Moore, in RISING DAMP. Among his early work was the kids' sketch show *Elephant's Eggs in a Rhubarb Tree* and he also appeared in *Couples*. His last series was *Bloomers*, in which he played Stan, a resting actor who became a partner in a florist's. His two daughters, Samantha, from his first marriage, and Kate, from his second marriage to actress Judy Loe, are both actresses.

Bed-Sit Girl, The ✶

UK (BBC) Situation Comedy. BBC 1 1965–6

Sheila Ross	**Sheila Hancock**
Dilys	**Dilys Laye**
David	**Derek Nimmo**
Liz	**Hy Hazell**

Writers **Ronald Chesney, Ronald Wolfe**
Producers **Duncan Wood, Graeme Muir**

A single girl dreams of a more glamorous life.

Living in a bed-sit and working as a typist doesn't amount to much for dreamy, disorganized Sheila Ross. She envies the exotic lifestyle of her air stewardess neighbour, Dilys, with whom she fights for eligible bachelors with little success. When Dilys moves on after the first season, Sheila gains a boyfriend in the form of David, her next-door neighbour, but her girly chats continue with the worldly wise Liz, who also lives in the house.

Bedtime ✶✶

UK (Hat Trick) Situation Comedy. BBC 1 2001–3
DVD: VCI

Andrew Oldfield	**Timothy West**
Alice Oldfield	**Sheila Hancock**
Paul Newcombe	**Stephen Tompkinson**
Sarah Newcombe	**Claire Skinner**
Sapphire	**Emma Pierson**
Gulliver	**David Gillespie**
Ruby	**Meera Syal**
Jools	**Victoria Carling**
Neil Henshaw	**Alun Armstrong**
Ralph Henshaw	**Adam Paul Harvey**
Simon	**Kevin McNally**

Faith	**Doon MacKichan**
Stacey	**Sienna Miller**
Ronnie	**James Bolam**
Jill	**Fay Ripley**
John	**Neil Stuke**
Mohammad	**Vincent Ebrahim**
Ray	**Nicholas Farrell**
Mumtaz	**Preeya Kalidas**
Nigel	**Paul Clarkson**

Creator/Writer **Andy Hamilton**
Executive Producers **Denise O'Donoghue, Jimmy Mulville**
Producer **Sue Howells**

Three couples have trouble sleeping, thanks to problems in their personal lives.

Andrew and Alice, Paul and Sarah, Sapphire and Gulliver – three sets of adjoining neighbours in the London suburbs with one thing in common: getting to sleep at night is not easy when there's so much on your mind. Andy Hamilton's unusual offering – a quietly successful amalgam of comedy and soap – explores each of the three relationships, hinting at something dark and unexpected within each one. For retired couple Andrew and Alice, among other things, it is the transatlantic phone calls from their daughter, Jools, that inspires restlessness. Could it be that she's being abused by her husband? For Paul and Sarah, it's not only exhaustion caused by their fractious baby that is driving a rift between them. There's also Sarah's suspicion that he's having an affair. For Sapphire and Gulliver (a famous TV gardener), there's an equally unsavoury dish on the menu – betrayal. Should New Zealander Sapphire reveal all about her relationship with him? If tabloid journalist Ruby has anything to do with it she will.

Bedtime was screened three nights a week for two weeks by BBC 1 in 2001 and returned in the same format a year later for a second series. This time either side of frustrated Alice and grouchy Andrew live Neil and Ralph, and Simon and Faith, the former a recently bereaved father and son, the latter a writer and a Government spin doctor. The twilight torment continues as yet again worry and suspicion raise their heads.

A third helping – this time of only three episodes – was delivered in the run-up to Christmas 2003. The Oldfields decide to spend the festive season with their daughter and her husband, Nigel, whose neighbours also have trouble getting some rest. On one side is Jill, a mother of two and wife of John, who complains down the phone of feeling suicidal; on the other is local grocer Mohammad, whose Christmas gift from the community is a brick through his shop window.

Hamilton also directs all the three series.

Beeny, Christopher

(1941–)

British actor whose first TV outing was as Lenny (aged 12) in THE GROVE FAMILY, the grandmother of all UK soaps, way back in 1954. However, most viewers remember him as Edward, the footman, in UPSTAIRS, DOWNSTAIRS, or as Thora Hird's hapless nephew, Billy, in the funereal sitcom IN LOVING MEMORY. He briefly played Geoffrey, Paula Wilcox's neighbour, in MISS JONES AND SON, and was also seen as Tony in the 1970s revival of THE RAG TRADE, taking on the foreman role vacated by Reg Varney. Other appearances have included DIXON OF DOCK GREEN, EMERGENCY – WARD 10, ARMCHAIR THEATRE, Z CARS, THE PLANE MAKERS, LAST OF THE SUMMER WINE (Teasdale) and the kids' programme PLAY AWAY.

Before Your Very Eyes ✶

UK (BBC/Associated Rediffusion/Jack Hylton) Comedy. BBC 1952–5; ITV 1956–8

Arthur Askey, Diana Decker, Dickie Henderson, Wallas Eaton, Sabrina

Writers **Sid Colin, Talbot Rothwell, David Climie, Kavanagh Productions**
Producers **Kenneth Carter, Bill Ward**

Gag fest for an established music hall star.

This popular fortnightly vehicle for Arthur Askey was expanded after the first series to include two regular foils for the diminutive Liverpudlian comic. Dickie Henderson (first billed as Dick Henderson Jnr) and Diana Decker joined Eric Robinson's orchestra to support Askey with his gags and sketches. To these were added Wallas Eaton and the famously busty Sabrina (real name Norma Sykes) in 1955. In addition to the scripted humour, each show featured a surprise for its star. In one programme Askey had thrown an empty bucket offstage only for a stagehand to fill it with water and throw it back. Askey's rapid response encouraged the production team to continue with such pranks to test his impromptu wit. This was just one example of how Askey refused to conform to the strictures of television production (he would also talk directly to the audience, commenting on the show, in the style of THE BURNS AND ALLEN SHOW). In 1956, Askey signed up with the fledgling ITV, taking *Before Your Very Eyes* (named after one of his catchphrases) and Sabrina with him, the show running (live) for a further two years.

Beggar My Neighbour ✶

UK (BBC) Situation Comedy. BBC 1 1967–8

Gerald Garvey	**Peter Jones**
	Desmond Walter-Ellis
Rose Garvey	**June Whitfield**
Harry Butt	**Reg Varney**
Lana Butt	**Pat Coombs**

Writers **Ken Hoare, Mike Sharland**
Producers **David Croft, Eric Fawcett**

Neighbour and family conflict in the London suburbs.

Gerald Garvey lives with his wife, Rose, in Muswell Hill. Rose's sister, Lana Butt, and her husband, Harry, live next door, but things are far from cosy because of their unequal prosperity. Harry is an overpaid fitter, while Gerald is an underpaid junior executive, which makes the flashy Butts the haves and the impoverished Garveys the have-nots. The Garveys' attempts to keep up with the Joneses (or Butts) provide most of the humour. The programme stemmed from a 1966 COMEDY PLAYHOUSE pilot and ran for three series.

Beggarman, Thief

See *Rich Man, Poor Man*.

Behind the Bike Sheds ✶✶

UK (Yorkshire) Children's Comedy. ITV 1983–5

Pericles Braithwaite	**Cal McCrystal**

Poskitt .... **Kjartan Poskitt**
Miss Megan Bigge
('Megapig') .... **Val McLane**
Whistle Willie .... **Ken Jones**
Joe .... **Tony Slattery**
Trolly Molly .... **Sara Mair-Thomas**

Writers **Rick Vanes, John Yeoman, Jan Needle, Tony Slattery**
Producers **Alister Hallum, Peter Tabern**

Lively, colourful take on the mayhem of school days.

A light-hearted mix of comedy and music, with sketches and monologues, *Behind the Bike Sheds* reflects anarchically on school life, with wacky teachers and rebellious kids tackling subjects like school meals, parents' day and sports in each episode. In the first series, Pericles Braithwaite is the devious headmaster of Fully Comprehensive, a terrible school in a terrible district (with something dark and mysterious hidden in its boiler room). Poskitt is his dogsbody caretaker. In series two (seen in 1985), these characters have left to be replaced by new principal Megan Bigg (or Megapig, as the kids christen her) and her sidekick, Whistle Willy. Also seen are Trolly Molly and Joe (played by co-writer, for this series, Tony Slattery). The pupils are played by Paul Charles, Marion Conroy, Joanne Dukes, Jenny Jay, Alix McAlister, Nikki Stoter, Adam Sunderland, Lee Whitlock, Andrew Jones, Julie Macauley, Martha Parsey, Lee Sparke and Linus Staples. Resident dance troupe for series one is the BTBS Dancers and for series two The Harehills Dance Group. Richie Close is the original composer, succeeded by Mike Moran and Richard Cottle for the second run of programmes.

Beiderbecke Affair, The/ The Beiderbecke Tapes/ The Beiderbecke Connection ★★

UK (Yorkshire) Drama. ITV 1985/1987/1988
DVD: Cinema Club

Trevor Chaplin .... **James Bolam**
Jill Swinburne .... **Barbara Flynn**
DS/DI Hobson .... **Dominic Jephcott** *(Affair/ Connection)*
Mr Carter .... **Dudley Sutton**
Mr Wheeler .... **Keith Smith**
Big Al .... **Terence Rigby** *(Affair/ Connection)*
Little Norm .... **Danny Schiller** *(Affair/ Connection)*
Chief Supt Forrest .... **Colin Blakely** *(Affair)*
Sylvia .... **Beryl Reid** *(Tapes)*
Peterson .... **Malcolm Storry** *(Tapes)*
John .... **David Battley** *(Tapes)*
Bella Atkinson .... **Maggie Jones** *(Tapes)*
Ivan .... **Patrick Drury** *(Connection)*

Writer **Alan Plater**
Executive Producers **David Cunliffe** *(Affair/Tapes)*, **Keith Richardson** *(Connection)*
Producers **Anne W. Gibbons** *(Affair)*, **Michael Glynn** *(Tapes/ Connection)*

Two schoolteachers unravel a web of corruption, against a background of classic jazz.

In *The Beiderbecke Affair*, Leeds comprehensive woodwork master Trevor Chaplin and his English teacher girlfriend Jill Swinburne have really rather modest ambitions. He's looking for a set of Bix Beiderbecke records, following a mix-up in his mail order, and she is seeking election to the local council on a conservation ticket. However, fate takes a hand to lead them into a murky world of underhand dealing, bureaucracy and corruption, bringing their relationship into crisis and themselves into conflict with the police.

Such was the success of this quirky, light-hearted six-parter that a sequel, *The Beiderbecke Tapes*, appeared two years later. In this two-part tale, Trevor buys some jazz tapes from the barman of an empty pub, only to find that one contains a recording of plans to dump nuclear waste in the Yorkshire Dales. Having survived that escapade, he and Jill resurface for a third and final time in the four-part *The Beiderbecke Connection*, which brings them into contact with a Russian refugee and sees them attract suspicion from the authorities.

Music plays a sizeable part in these genial tales of intrigue in which the hero and heroine travel around in a beaten-up old motor, reluctantly playing detective and running into all kinds of odd characters. They are accompanied by the sounds of jazz-great Bix Beiderbecke, re-created for the series by Kenny Baker, with new music by Frank Ricotti. Writer Alan Plater had earlier contributed a similar series under the title of *Get Lost!*. Screened in 1981, this four-parter saw two teachers, played by Alun Armstrong and Bridget Turner, investigating missing persons.

Believe Nothing ★★

UK (Alomo) Situation Comedy. ITV 1 2002
DVD: Fremantle Home Entertainment

Prof. Adonis Cnut .... **Rik Mayall**
Brian Albumen .... **Michael Maloney**
Dr Hannah Awkward .... **Emily Bruni**
Chairman .... **Don Warrington**

Creators/Writers **Laurence Marks, Maurice Gran**
Producer **Charlie Hanson**

A brilliant but bored academic joins an international agency that secretly controls the world.

Adonis Cnut is a quadruple professor at Queen Edward's College, Oxford, but his talents are clearly wasted in academia. When the call comes for him to join an undercover body called the Council for International Progress, the egocentric brainiac accepts the challenge. His job: to help put into practice fiendish plans that will maintain the world's political order. Thus, assisted by Brian Albumen, his oily butler, and a fellow academic, Dr Hannah Awkward (a pedantics specialist with a chronic self-esteem problem, despite Cnut's lust and advances), Cnut becomes a modern-day Machiavelli. Through a generous helping of scatological humour and innuendo (loud echoes of Rik Mayall's earlier successes in THE YOUNG ONES and THE NEW STATESMAN), our hero whispers in the ear of the powerful to achieve his organization's shady goals. Typical of his subterfuge is his encouragement of the Prime Minister to declare war on Cuba as a means to winning a referendum on the Euro. Cloning and GM crops are other hot issues.

Despite reasonable reviews and appearances from guest stars like Rory Bremner and Melvyn Bragg, *Believe Nothing* flopped with audiences and only one series of six programmes was produced.

Bell, Ann

(1940–)

Cheshire-born actress, best known as Marion Jefferson, the British group leader, in TENKO and seen later as Gracie Ellis, the finishing school headmistress, in the rock 'n' roll retrospective, HEAD OVER HEELS, with plenty of other credits before and after. These have included the parts of Jane Eyre in the 1963 adaptation, Maria in the 1965 version of *For Whom the Bell Tolls* and Mary Webster in the 1988 sitcom DOUBLE FIRST, as well as appearances in THE SAINT, MR ROSE, CALLAN, DANGER MAN, THE BARON, WAR AND PEACE, TUMBLEDOWN, CHRISTABEL (Mrs Burton), INSPECTOR MORSE, MEDICS, AGATHA CHRISTIE'S POIROT, DOCTOR FINLAY, CASUALTY, *The Ice House*, THE WOMAN IN WHITE (Mrs Rideout), HEARTBEAT and MIDSOMER MURDERS. She was married to the late Robert Lang, with whom she appeared in THE FORSYTE SAGA (Aunt Hester).

Bell, Martin

OBE (1938–)

Experienced BBC reporter, its diplomatic correspondent, chief North American correspondent and foreign affairs correspondent, among other posts, during his 35 years with the Corporation. He is best known, however, for his work as a war reporter, covering 11 major conflicts from Vietnam to Bosnia, in which he was hit by shrapnel and wounded in 1992. After recovery, Bell decided to leave the BBC and stand as independent, 'anti-sleaze' Parliamentary candidate for Neil Hamilton's Tatton constituency in 1997, which he won with the support of the Labour and Liberal Democrat parties. His distinctive attire has earned him the nickname 'the man in the white suit'.

Bell, Tom

(1932–)

Liverpool-born actor, often seen in dry, unsmiling roles. His credits have included HOLOCAUST (Adolf Eichmann), REILLY – ACE OF SPIES (Dzerzhinsky), *The Rainbow*, CHANCER (John Love), KING'S ROYAL (Sir Fergus King), CATHERINE COOKSON'S *The Cinder Path* (Edward MacFell), PRIME SUSPECT (DS Bill Otley), *Four Feathers* (Frank Yallop) and *Pollyanna* (Old Tom). His other major parts have varied from menacing hero/villain Frank Ross in OUT and Walter Morel in *Sons and Lovers* to waxworks owner Harry Nash in the sitcom HOPE IT RAINS and the patriotic Thomas Slater in NO BANANAS. Guest appearances have come in series as diverse as ARMCHAIR THEATRE, PLAY FOR TODAY, ANGELS, SPENDER, *The Young Indiana Jones Chronicles*, DALZIEL AND PASCOE, DR TERRIBLE'S HOUSE OF HORRIBLE and WAKING THE DEAD.

Bellamy, David

OBE (1933–)

Enthusiastic, bearded, London-born naturalist, much mimicked by TV impressionists in the 1970s and 1980s. After a few early programmes like *Bellamy on Botany* and *Bellamy's Britain* for the BBC, and then prime-time exposure on ITV's DON'T ASK ME, he launched into a run of successful, light-hearted documentary series, which included *Bellamy's Europe*, the award-winning *Botanic Man, Up a Gumtree, Bellamy's Backyard Safari* (in which he was shrunk by special effects to explore the wilderness of a typical garden), *Bellamy's New World, Bellamy's Bugle, Bellamy on Top of the World, Bellamy's Bird's Eye View* and *Bellamy Rides Again*.

Belle and Sebastian/Belle, Sebastian and the Horses ✱✱

France (RTF/Gaumont Television Paris) Children's Drama. BBC 1 1967–8

DVD: Network

Sebastian	**Mehdi**
César	**Edmond Beauchamp**
Guillaume	**Jean Michel Audin**
Jean	**Dominique Blondeau**
Angélina	**Paloma Matta**
Céléstine	**Hélène Dieudonné**
Norbert	**Morice Poli**
Pierre Maréchal	**Claude Giraud** *(Horses)*
Sylvia	**Louise Marleau** *(Horses)*

Writer **Cécile Aubry**
Executive Producer **Ettienne Laroche**
Producer **Hélène Gagarine**

A French gypsy boy befriends a Pyrenean mountain dog. Eight-year-old Sebastian, an abandoned gypsy boy, was found by old César and brought up on his farm, alongside his own grandchildren, Jean and Angélina. One day, tales begin to arrive in their French Alpine village, Saint-Martin, close to the Italian border, of a big, wild, white dog which is on the loose in the mountains. Villagers are suspicious of the beast but little Sebastian, using his gypsy know-how, brings the dog under control, names it Belle and proceeds to wander the hills with his new friend, tumbling into adventure, rooting out smugglers and averting avalanches.

Made in France and dubbed into English, the 13-part serial was a heart-warming element in the BBC's children's output in 1967. A second series of the same length, entitled *Belle, Sebastian and the Horses*, followed a year later. The young star of both series, known simply as Mehdi, was the son of French film star Cécile Aubry, who provided the scripts.

Bellingham, Lynda

(1948–)

Canadian-born actress, the mum in a collection of Oxo commercials, but already familiar to TV viewers from series such as GENERAL HOSPITAL (Nurse Hilda Price), Z CARS, *The Pink Medicine Show, Tell Tarby, The Fuzz* (WPC Purvis), MACKENZIE (Ruth Isaacs) and *Murphy's Mob* (Elaine Murphy). She was also a guest in DOCTOR WHO, ANGELS, DON'T FORGET TO WRITE, THE SWEENEY and SHOESTRING, and replaced Carol Drinkwater as Helen Herriot in ALL CREATURES GREAT AND SMALL, before becoming Faith Grayshot in the comedy SECOND THOUGHTS and its sequel, *Faith in the Future*. More recently, Bellingham was seen in AT HOME WITH THE BRAITHWAITES (Pauline Farnell). Other roles have come in MARTIN CHUZZLEWIT (Mrs Lupin), *Happy Together* (Teresa), *Reach for the Moon* (Penny Martin), *My Uncle Silas*, MIDSOMER MURDERS, DALZIEL AND PASCOE, THE LAST DETECTIVE, THE BILL, MURDER IN SUBURBIA, *The All Star Comedy Show* and HOLBY CITY. She also narrated the series *My Life in the Real World*.

Bellisario, Donald P.

(1935–)

The creator and executive producer of MAGNUM PI, *Tales of the Gold Monkey* and AIRWOLF and later founder of his own production company, Bellisarius, responsible for such hits as QUANTUM LEAP, *JAG*, *Tequila and Bonetti* and *Navy NCIS* (a *JAG* spin-off). His earlier work took in KOJAK (as writer) and BATTLESTAR GALACTICA (as writer/producer).

Ben Casey ✱✱

US (Bing Crosby) Medical Drama. ITV 1961–7 (US: ABC 1961–6)

Dr Ben Casey .... **Vince Edwards**
Dr David Zorba .... **Sam Jaffe**
Dr Maggie Graham .... **Bettye Ackerman**
Dr Ted Hoffman .... **Harry Landers**
Nick Kanavaras .... **Nick Dennis**
Nurse Wills .... **Jeanne Bates**
Jane Hancock .... **Stella Stevens**
Dr Mike Rogers .... **Ben Piazza**
Dr Daniel Niles Freeland .... **Franchot Tone**
Dr Terry McDaniel .... **Jim McMullan**
Sally Welden .... **Marlyn Mason**

Creator **James E. Moser**
Producer **Matthew Rapf**

A gifted but brooding young surgeon works at a large hospital.

Unlike baby-faced Dr Kildare, his screen rival in the early 1960s, Ben Casey is surly, tough and determined. He works as a neurosurgeon at the County General Hospital and is very much a rebel who will happily flout the rules if it is in his patient's interest. His stabilizing influence, however, is the venerable Dr Zorba, a white-haired, mad scientist type, whom Casey respects enormously. It is Zorba who speaks the dramatic words which open each programme and sum up the extremes of hospital life: 'Man; Woman; Birth; Death; Infinity'. When Zorba leaves, the Chief of Surgery role is assumed by Dr Freeland. Other familiar faces are Nick Kanavaras, the hospital orderly, Dr Ted Hoffman and Nurse Wills.

Ben Casey was a bold series which was never afraid to tackle difficult subjects like abortion. It was also shot in such a way (extreme close-ups, etc.) that the true tension of critical medicine was effectively conveyed. Romance was kept to the sidelines and, for all his macho appeal, Casey was only rarely linked with a woman. His relationship with anaesthetist Maggie Graham is softly alluded to, but his most dramatic entanglement comes with beautiful Jane Hancock, a coma victim, for whose attentions he fights with Dr Mike Rogers.

Ben Casey became less convincing and 'soapier' towards the end of its run and finally drew to a close in the USA in 1966, five months before DR KILDARE. During its five years on air it had made a sex symbol out of the profusely hairy Vince Edwards, a handsome young actor discovered by Bing Crosby, whose company produced the series.

Ben Hall ✱✱

UK/Australia (BBC/ABC) Drama. BBC 1 1975

Ben Hall .... **Jon Finch**
Biddy Walsh/Hall .... **Evin Crowley**
Frank Gardiner .... **John Castle**
Sgt/Chief Insp. Garland .... **Vincent Ball**
Trooper/Chief Insp. Sir Frederick Pottinger .... **Brian Blain**
Kate Owen .... **Sandra Lee Patterson**
Billy Dargin .... **Jack Charles**
John Piesley .... **Hugh Keays-Byrne**
Pa Walsh .... **Tom Farley**
Ma Walsh .... **Ruth Cracknell**
Jack McGuire .... **Alfred Bell**
Helen McGuire .... **Diana McLean**
Warrigal Walsh .... **Chris King**
Troy .... **Michael Aitkens**
George Owen .... **Ian Dyson**
Flash Johnny Gilbert .... **John Orscik**
Jack Taylor .... **Alister Smart**
'Goobang' Mick Connolly .... **Frank Gallacher**
Mary Delaney/Connolly .... **Alexandra Hynes**
Bacon .... **John Cousins**
Long Tom Coffin .... **Tom Oliver**
Mr Daley .... **Ed Thompson**
Mrs Daley .... **Melissa Jaffer**
Jock .... **Kevin Healy**
Johnny Vane .... **Harold Hopkins**
Capt. Adams .... **Ken Goodlet**
Morrison .... **Brian James**
Cowper .... **Ric Hutton**
Angela .... **Elizabeth Alexander**
O'Meally .... **Barry Hill**

Producer **Neil McCallum**

A frustrated and desperate cattle rancher becomes Australia's most wanted criminal.

Based on the life story of the real Ben Hall, Australia's most famous outlaw until the arrival of Ned Kelly some 15 years later, this 13-part production, with music provided by Bruce Smeaton, was filmed Down Under. History has it that Hall was a bandit with a difference. His gang was noted for its chivalry and fairness. They mostly took only what they needed and even respected their victims. Their deeds are celebrated in songs and folk lore. Hall's nemesis was Trooper Pottinger, an aristocrat who was quickly promoted way above his ability. It was, in many ways, Pottinger's relentless hounding that eventually turned Hall into a hardened criminal.

The series is set in the late 1850s and depicts Hall as a reluctant law-breaker, forced into banditry when his life is turned upside down by misfortune and malice. A cattle farmer by trade, Hall lives in the Wheogo district of New South Wales. He takes a shine to Biddy Walsh, the daughter of two old stagers, and they marry. But tragedy lies around the corner. A drought wipes out their livestock, Ben is mistakenly arrested for murder, and Biddy wants to sell their dry, fly-blown ranch and move to a more prosperous area, a move which Hall resists. In order to re-equip his farmstead, Hall joins the gold rush, leaving a pregnant Biddy at home. Estrangement follows and, when Hall feels he has nothing left to lose, he joins the gang of notorious outlaw Frank 'Darkie' Gardiner. Thus begins his life as a bushranger, hiding out in the Weddin' Mountains and relying on the support of friendly locals. Pottinger and his lawmen use every device to entice Hall out of hiding, including jailing innocent settlers and kidnapping Biddy. Eventually, when the law is changed to make it illegal for anyone to harbour outlaws, Hall is forced on to the run, a £1,000 dead-or-alive bounty on his head.

Benaud, Richie

(1930–)

Australian former leg-spin bowler, batsman and Test captain who has become one of the most respected commentators on the game of cricket, working for Channel Nine in Australia and for the BBC (1963–99) and, latterly, Channel 4 in the UK (retiring from UK broadcasts in summer 2005). His first career (alongside cricket) was as a crime reporter.

Bennett, Alan

(1934–)

Bespectacled, gently spoken, Leeds-born playwright, actor and narrator, a former *Beyond the Fringe* star, also seen in the satire show BBC-3 and Jonathan Miller's TV version of ALICE IN WONDERLAND when starting out in television. In the 1980s he was Lord Pinkrose in FORTUNES OF WAR, and in the 1990s he played Grantly Caypor in ASHENDEN and historian Hugh Trevor-Roper in the drama SELLING HITLER, provided the voice of Mole in an ITV animation of *The Wind in the Willows*, hosted *The Abbey*, a three-part documentary about Westminster Abbey for BBC 2, took the role of Sillery in A DANCE TO THE MUSIC OF TIME, and narrated the drama *The Young Visiters*. However, it has been for his collection of TV dramas that he has won most praise. The highlights have included *A Day Out* (1972), *Sunset across the Bay* (1975), *A Little Outing* (1977), *One Fine Day* (1979), *Objects of Affection* (1982), *The Insurance Man* (1986), *A Question of Attribution* (1991) and AN ENGLISHMAN ABROAD (1983). He has also written a series of comedy sketches, *On the Margin*, an anthology series called *By Alan Bennett – Six Plays*, and received acclaim for TALKING HEADS and its follow-up, *Talking Heads 2*. These seasons of monologues epitomized Bennett's flair for character observation and realistic dialogue, as well as offering performers like Thora Hird and Bennett himself the chance to shine. More monologues followed in *Telling Tales* in 2000, in which his own early life in Leeds came under the spotlight.

Bennett, Harve

(Harve Fischman; 1930–)

US producer of action series like THE SIX MILLION DOLLAR MAN, THE BIONIC WOMAN, GEMINI MAN and THE INVISIBLE MAN, as well as the mini-series, RICH MAN, POOR MAN.

Bennett, Hywel

(1944–)

Welsh actor, very popular in British films of the 1960s, whose most durable television role was as the unemployed graduate James SHELLEY. One of his earliest TV appearances was in a 1960s DOCTOR WHO story and he has also played memorable parts in MALICE AFORETHOUGHT (Dr Bickleigh), PENNIES FROM HEAVEN (Tom), TINKER, TAILOR, SOLDIER, SPY (Ricki Tarr), KARAOKE (Arthur 'Pig' Mailion), *Harpur and Iles* (Desmond Iles), NEVERWHERE (Mr Croup), *Lloyd and Hill*, *The Quest* (Ronno), EASTENDERS (Jack Dalton), THE BILL (Peter Baxter), plus various plays and films, including the sci-fi fantasy, ARTEMIS 81. He was once married to READY, STEADY, GO! presenter Cathy McGowan and is the brother of actor Alun Lewis.

Bennett, Lennie

(Michael Berry; 1938–)

Northern comedian and game show host, formerly one half of Lennie and Jerry (with Jerry Stevens). He first appeared on THE GOOD OLD DAYS in 1966 after working for a while as a journalist, and his later credits have included *Lennie and Jerry*, THE COMEDIANS, *London Night Out*, *Starburst*, *Bennett Bites Back* and *All Star Secrets*. He also hosted *Punchlines* and *Lucky Ladders*.

Benny, Jack

(Benjamin Kubelsky; 1894–1974)

One of TV's earliest celebrities. Jack Benny's career began in music in the 1920s. As a vaudeville violinist, he billed himself as Ben K. Benny, soon adding humour to his routine and becoming Jack Benny. Although he made a number of films, his greatest success pre-TV came on American radio, where he finely tuned the character traits that were to become so popular later. Playing himself in the long-running *Jack Benny Show* (with announcer Don Wilson and Eddie 'Rochester' Anderson, his valet, in support), he quickly gained a reputation for his stinginess, his lied-about age (always 39) and his appalling violin playing. He was married to his sometime co-star, Mary Livingstone.

Benson ★★

US (Witt–Thomas–Harris) Situation Comedy. ITV 1980–9 (US: ABC 1979–86)

Benson Dubois	**Robert Guillaume**
Governor Gene Gatling	**James Noble**
Katie Gatling	**Missy Gold**
Gretchen Kraus	**Inga Swenson**
Marcie Hill/Slater	**Caroline McWilliams**
John Taylor	**Lewis J. Stadlen**
Clayton Endicott III	**René Auberjonois**
Pete Downey	**Ethan Phillips**
Frankie	**Jerry Seinfeld**
Denise Stevens/Downey	**Didi Conn**
Mrs Rose Cassidy	**Billie Bird**
Senator Diane Hartford	**Donna LaBrie**

Creator **Susan Harris**
Executive Producers **Paul Junger Witt, Tony Thomas, John Rich**

A wisecracking butler rises through the ranks of the political establishment.

Acerbic butler Benson Dubois discovered a new career on leaving the Tate household in the sitcom SOAP. In this spin-off, he takes up an appointment as valet to Governor Gene Gatling (Jessica Tate's cousin), running the house and taking every opportunity to keep the naïve widower in check. Also under the mansion roof are precocious daughter Katie, whom Benson effectively raises, and redoubtable German housekeeper Gretchen. Marcie is Gatling's secretary. Benson's influence usually surpasses that of the Governor's official political aides – John Taylor and, later, Clayton Endicott – and that of his press officer, Pete Downey, so much so that the butler's talents are soon rewarded with a move into the political hierarchy. Indeed, when the series ends, he is challenging Gatling for the Governor's office itself. At this time, Denise is Benson's own secretary and Senator Diane Hartford his fiancée. The series, which ran longer than *Soap*, also provided an early opportunity for Jerry Seinfeld, who played gag writer Frankie.

Bentine, Michael

CBE (1922–96)

Watford-born, part-Peruvian comedian and one-time Goon, the deviser and presenter of some of TV's most bizarre comedy shows. These included *The Bumblies* (a 1954 puppet animation for kids, featuring creatures from the planet Bumble), *Yes, It's the Cathode-Ray Tube Show!* (1957, with Peter Sellers), *After Hours* (1958–9), the influential IT'S A SQUARE WORLD (1960), *All Square* (1966) and *Michael Bentine's Potty Time* (with more puppets in 1973, spun off from *Michael Bentine Time* the previous year). He also hosted the hobbies programme *Madabout* and one of his last credits was providing voices for another puppet series, *The Great Bong*.

Bentley, John

(1916–)

British film actor who re-emerged in the 1970s as Hugh Mortimer, Meg Richardson's ill-fated new husband in CROSSROADS. Playing the millionaire businessman, he had attempted to win Meg's hand as far back as 1965, but received the brush-off. Reconciled, their 1975 wedding was one of the TV events of the year. Previously, Bentley had starred as Chief Inspector Paul Derek in the 1950s jungle adventure series AFRICAN PATROL. His TV portfolio also includes *Strictly Personal* and ARMCHAIR THEATRE.

Benton, Mark

(1965–)

Prolific, Middlesbrough-born, former Shakespearean actor, mostly cast in comic roles such as Eddie in EARLY DOORS and Howie in *Northern Lights*. Benton has also been seen in CATHERINE COOKSON*'s The Girl* (butcher Fred Loam), *Eureka Street* (Chuckie Lurgan), SEE YOU FRIDAY (Bernie), BARBARA (Martin Pond), *The Booze Cruise* (Dave Bolton), *Planespotting* (Paul Coppin), *Catterick* (Mark), *Nature Boy* (Fred), *The Second Coming* (Johnny Tyler), CLOCKING OFF (Colin Wilkes), *Quite Ugly One Morning* (Darren Mortlake), *Monkey Trousers, King of Fridges* (Alan), and *I'm With Stupid* (Sheldon). Guest appearances have come in series as varied as BABES IN THE WOOD, KAVANAGH QC, *Moving Story*, BOON, PRESTON FRONT, THE GOVERNOR, KISS ME KATE, A SMALL SUMMER PARTY, DR TERRIBLE'S HOUSE OF HORRIBLE, HUMAN REMAINS, BORN AND BRED, MURPHY'S LAW, DOCTOR WHO, THE INSPECTOR LYNLEY MYSTERIES and *Afterlife*.

Bergerac ✳✳

UK/Australia (BBC/The Seven Network) Police Drama. BBC 1 1981; 1983–91
DVD: Cinema Club

DS Jim Bergerac	**John Nettles**
Charlie Hungerford	**Terence Alexander**
Chief Insp. Barney Crozier	**Sean Arnold**
Francine Leland	**Cecile Paoli**
Deborah Bergerac	**Deborah Grant**
Marianne Bellshade	**Celia Imrie**
Susan Young	**Louise Jameson**
Philippa Vale	**Liza Goddard**
DC Terry Wilson	**Geoffrey Leesley**
Danielle Aubry	**Thérèse Liotard**
Insp. Victor Deffand	**Roger Sloman**
DC Willy Pettit	**John Telfer**
DC Ben Lomas	**David Kershaw**
Diamante Lil	**Mela White**
Charlotte	**Annette Badland**
Peggy Masters	**Nancy Mansfield**
Dr Lejeune	**Jonathan Adams**

Creator **Robert Banks Stewart**
Producers **Robert Banks Stewart, Jonathan Alwyn, George Gallaccio, Juliet Grimm**

A single-minded copper roots out smugglers and swindlers in Jersey.

Jim Bergerac does not have the best credentials to be a policeman, physically or mentally – a gammy leg causes him to limp, and he was once a drunk. His life has been in ruins, with his wife, Deborah, leaving him and his career in the balance. Turning over a new leaf, he becomes the Channel Islands' most successful detective, displaying genuine determination to get to the bottom of cases.

Working for the Bureau des Etrangers (which deals with crimes involving non-island folk) and tearing around in a 1947 Triumph sports car, his gaze falls upon visitors and tourists up to no good, and he is never afraid of getting physical in the search for justice. His superiors and colleagues (like Barney Crozier) regularly question his methods, but always supportive is his amiable ex-father-in-law, Charlie Hungerford, a businessman constantly on the fringe of dodgy deals.

Despite his new dedication to the job, Bergerac is never far from the temptation of the bottle, especially when there is trouble in his personal life, as the girls come and go. First there is tourist officer Francine Leland, and then lawyer Marianne Bellshade, before estate agent Susan Young provides some stability for a while. Their relationship ends with her murder. There is even more spark in his occasional encounters with Philippa Vale, a glamorous jewel-thief. It is Bergerac's obsession with a woman which eventually brings the series to a close. Jim's relationship with French girl Danielle Aubry sees him leaving Jersey to work as a private investigator in Provence. Though the final series featured Jim returning to the island on several assignments, it was only a matter of time before the programme finally called it a day.

Bergerac employed a number of semi-regulars who ensured continuity during the programme's 10-year run. These included Diamante Lil, proprietress of the bar Lil's Place, and pathologist Dr Lejeune. Such longevity was not anticipated when the series began. It was intended as a short filler and was developed only because Trevor Eve had refused to continue with SHOESTRING. *Bergerac* was also good for Jersey. It gave the island's tourist trade an enormous lift. John Nettles, who had become to Jersey what Steve McGarrett had been to Hawaii and Inspector Morse was to become to Oxford, also made it his home.

Berkeley Square ✳✳

UK (BBC) Drama. BBC 1 1998
DVD: BFS Entertainment (Region 1 only)

Matty Wickham	**Clare Wilkie**
Hannah Randall	**Victoria Smurfit**
Lydia Weston	**Tabitha Wady**
Arnold St John	**Sean Murray**

Victoria St John	**Hermione Norris**
Tom St John	**Laurence Owen**
Harriet St John	**Emily Canfor-Dumas**
Mrs McClusky	**Kate Williams**
Ned Jones	**Jason O'Mara**
Lady Constance Lamson-Scribener	**Briony Glassco**
Lord George Lamson-Scribener	**Rupert Frazer**
Nanny Collins	**Rosemary Leach**
Nanny Simmons	**Ruth Sheen**
Cook	**Maggie McCarthy**
Pringle	**Amy Hodge**
Fowler	**Peter Forbes**
Gibbons	**Maurice Yeoman**
Capt. Mason	**William Scott-Masson**
Mrs Bronowski	**Etela Pardo**
Jack Wickham	**Stuart Laing**
Lord Hugh Lamson-Scribener	**Nicholas Irons**
Elspeth Hutchinson	**Phyllida Hancock**
Nathaniel Hutchinson	**Mark Saban**
Bertie Hutchinson	**Adam Hayes**
Great Aunt Effie	**Rosalind Knight**
Isabel Hutchinson	**Sophie Walker**

Creator **Deborah Cook**
Writers **Deborah Cook, Amanda Coe, Simon Ashdown, Lilie Ferrari**
Producer **Alison Davis**

Three young nannies battle against oppressive society in early 20th-century London.

Beginning in 1902, this ten-part drama relates events in the lives of three young girls who arrive in London, at more or less the same time, to take up positions as nannies to prosperous families in Berkeley Square. Irish girl Hannah Randall has fallen on hard times. Her love affair with an aristocratic Yorkshire youth has ended in tragedy: he has died and she is left, literally, holding the baby. She comes to London and has to forge a reference to find work, tearfully farming out care of her own child (Billy) to immigrant Mrs Bronowski in Limehouse, where his presence can remain a secret. Hannah secures nanny work with the Hutchinson household, bringing love for seven-year-old Bertie and his three-month-old sibling where the largely absent parents and her boss, Nanny Simmons, have failed. When the family's Great Aunt Effie moves in to hold the fort, she brings her reckless niece Isabel, who toys with Hannah as a friend.

Eastender Matty Wickham has been in service since she was 12 and has now risen to the respectable position of nanny to the St John family. Caring for seven-year-old Tom, Harriet aged five and 18-month-old Imogen, she works for Arnold St John and his troublesome wife, Victoria, although it is Mrs McClusky, the housekeeper, who barks out the orders. McClusky's secret son, Ned, is the footman who steals Matty's heart.

Naïve, poorly educated Lydia Weston has escaped to London from the strains of caring for her ten brothers and sisters. She has taken a position with the family who own the land her Devon family inhabit. In her new role as nursemaid, she has to cope with the hostility being shown to her by Nanny Collins, whose best days as a child carer are sadly behind her and who is no longer wholly trusted to look after baby Ivo. Lydia's employers are Lord Lamson-Scribener and his American second wife, Constance. Hugh is the son who spells trouble.

The new jobs inflict a steep learning curve on each of the girls and the series follows the ups and downs in their (limited) private lives as well as in work, offering a detailed picture of early Edwardian society and its domineering class system.

Berle, Milton

(Mendel Berlinger; 1908–2002)

Although his name means little to younger British viewers, New York-born Milton Berle was 'Mr Television' to US audiences in the 1950s. A former child silent-movie star and later an established vaudevillian, he broke into television in 1948 as host of the variety show *The Texaco Star Theater* (later *The Milton Berle Show*). So popular were his brash comic sketches, buffoonery, outrageous costumes and awful puns that NBC quickly signed him up on a 30-year contract. His best years were in the early 1950s and his humour soon dated, but he continued to appear sporadically until the 1980s. British viewers may have caught 'Uncle Miltie' as guest star in THE DEFENDERS, F TROOP (Wise Owl), BATMAN (Louie the Lilac), in some episodes of THE LOVE BOAT, the comedy compilation *Just for Laughs*, or in one of his TV movies.

Berlusconi, Silvio

(1936–)

Italian media magnate and owner of the AC Milan football club who became his country's Prime Minister (1994–6 and 2001–6). Berlusconi's television interests began almost by chance when he established a small closed-circuit station in the Milan suburb that he was developing as part of his real-estate business. This grew into TeleMilano, which evolved into the national network Canale 5, following the deregulation of television in Italy. He subsequently added two more commercial channels to his empire, Retequattro and Italia 1 (giving himself three national networks to match the three controlled by the state-owned RAI corporation), as well as pioneering pay TV in Italy via his shareholding in Telepiù. Berlusconi has also had interests in French television, through La Cinq, Spain, via Tele 5, and Germany, via Telefünf.

Berman, Monty

(1912–2006)

British TV producer of action series for ITC, working closely with Robert S. Baker in developing programmes like THE SAINT, THE BARON and GIDEON'S WAY, and with Dennis Spooner on RANDALL AND HOPKIRK (DECEASED), DEPARTMENT S and THE CHAMPIONS. He also produced THE ADVENTURER.

Bernstein, Lord Sidney

(1899–1993)

British film and television executive who, after building up his father's cinema chain (and introducing the idea of a Saturday matinee for kids), worked as a consultant for the Ministry of Information in World War II. Later he produced three films for Alfred Hitchcock and went on to found Granada Television (and the whole Granada group) with his brother, Cecil. Granada (the name was inspired by a walking holiday in Spain) introduced commercial television to the North of England in 1956, and Bernstein succeeded in running it almost as a family business for many years. He was made a life peer in 1969.

Berry, Nick

(1963–)

Former child actor whose best-known television work has been as Simon 'Wicksy' Wicks in EASTENDERS, PC Nick Rowan in HEARTBEAT, harbour master Mike Nicholls in HARBOUR LIGHTS and undercover cop Liam Ketman in IN DEEP. Other credits have included *Dramarama*, THE GENTLE TOUCH, BOX OF DELIGHTS, CLUEDO, and the single dramas *Paparazzo* (photographer Rick Caulker), *Respect* (ex-boxer Bobby Carr), *Black Velvet Band* (Martin Tusco) and *The Mystery of Men* (Colin Dunbar). He also runs his own production company, Valentine Productions. Berry's wife is actress Rachel Robertson.

Beryl's Lot ✳✳

UK (Yorkshire) Comedy Drama. ITV 1973–7

Beryl Humphries	**Carmel McSharry**
Tom Humphries	**Mark Kingston**
	George Selway
Rosie Humphries	**Verna Harvey**
Jack Humphries	**Brian Capron**
Babs Humphries	**Anita Carey**
Trevor Tonks	**Tony Caunter**
Vi Tonks	**Barbara Mitchell**
Horace Harris	**Robert Keegan**
Wully Harris	**Annie Leake**
Charlie Mills	**Norman Mitchell**
Wacky Waters	**Johnny Shannon**
Fred Pickering	**Robin Askwith**
Freda	**Queenie Watts**

Writers **Kevin Laffan, Bill MacIlwraith, Charles Humphreys**
Executive Producers **Peter Willes, David Cunliffe**
Producers **John Frankau, Jacky Stoller, Derek Bennett**

A milkman's wife tries to better herself in middle age.

One morning, at the age of 40, charlady Beryl Humphries wakes up and decides she hasn't done enough with her life. Married to Tom, a milkman, she realizes she wants to be more than a cleaner and, to the surprise of her children, Rosie, Jack and Babs, and that of her many friends and neighbours, she sets about improving her lot, signing up for evening classes.

The series was based on the life of cook Margaret Powell, also a milkman's wife, who passed 'O' and 'A' levels while in her 50s and at the age of 61 had her first book published.

Best of the West ✳✳

US (Weinberger-Daniels/Paramount) Situation Comedy. BBC 1 1982–3 (US: ABC 1981–2)

Marshal Sam Best	**Joel Higgins**
Elvira Best	**Carlene Watkins**
Daniel Best	**Meeno Peluce**
Parker Tillman	**Leonard Frey**
Doc Jerome Kullens	**Tom Ewell**
Frog	**Tracey Walter**
Laney Gibbs	**Valri Bromfield**

Creator **Earl Pomerantz**

An inexperienced storekeeper is the unlikely hero of a rough frontier town.

Philadelphian Sam Best is a Civil War veteran who, in the 1860s, leaves civilization behind to run a general store in the frontier town of Copper Creek, Montana. There he accidentally becomes the new marshal. Thus he is charged with keeping law and order among the locals, something he struggles to do in his own home, where his confused Southern belle wife, Elvira, and his ten-year-old city-kid son, Daniel, won't settle. All around the Bests are some hoary old Western characters – deliberate clichés, in fact, as this is the spoof Wild West, not the real thing. There's the drunken doctor (Jerome Kullens), the nasty businessman (Parker Tillman, who runs the Square Deal Saloon and all the rackets in town), his dopey sidekick (Frog) and the tough backwoodswoman (Laney Gibbs).

Betamax

See *VHS*.

Between the Lines ✳✳✳

UK (BBC/Island World) Police Drama. BBC 1 1992–4
DVD: BBC

Det. Supt. Tony Clark	**Neil Pearson**
DI Harry Naylor	**Tom Georgeson**
DS Maureen Connell	**Siobhan Redmond**
Chief Supt. John Deakin	**Tony Doyle**
Commander Brian Huxtable	**David Lyon**
Sue Clark	**Lynda Steadman**
Jenny Dean	**Lesley Vickerage**
Chief Supt. Graves	**Robin Lermite**
Commander Sullivan	**Hugh Ross**
Angela Berridge	**Francesca Annis**
Joyce Naylor	**Elaine Donnelly**
Kate Roberts	**Barbara Wilshere**
Sarah Teale	**Sylvestra le Touzel**

Creator **J. C. Wilsher**
Executive Producer **Tony Garnett**
Producers **Peter Norris, Joy Lale**

The professional and private lives of a police internal investigator.

Between the Lines revolves around the somewhat complex life of Detective Supt. Tony Clark, an ambitious but headstrong member of the Complaints Investigation Bureau (CIB), a division of the Metropolitan Police. As the head of a team of two detectives, it is Clark's job to root out bent coppers – at all levels in the force. Unfortunately, the hard-drinking, emotionally immature Clark is also a pawn in political games played by his superiors, and his job is further complicated by his own turbulent private life. His biggest problem, it seems, is keeping his trousers on. (Indeed, the series was cruelly nicknamed 'Between the Sheets' and even 'Between the Loins'.) His marriage breaks up because of an affair with WPC Jenny Dean, and other women, such as Home Office official Angela Berridge and TV producer Sarah Teale, also drift into his bed during the programme's three-series run.

Clark's sidekicks are Harry Naylor and Mo Connell. Harry, the chain-smoking dependable-copper type, becomes increasingly more reckless and violent in his work as his wife's terminal illness develops, while Mo's own personal affairs (of the gay variety) begin to infiltrate her working world, too. Above Clark initially are Commander Huxtable and Chief Supt. John Deakin. Clark manages to nail the menacing Deakin for corruption at the end of the first series, but Deakin wriggles off the hook and remains a powerful influence in Clark's life, particularly in the third series when Clark, Naylor and Connell find themselves outside the force and Deakin controls their work as security advisers.

Between the Lines was an unexpected hit, picking up many awards and opening new doors for its star, Neil Pearson, previously seen as randy Dave Charnley in the Channel 4 comedy DROP THE DEAD DONKEY.

Beverly Hillbillies, The ✳✳✳

US (Filmways) Situation Comedy. ITV 1963–71 (US: CBS 1962–71)
DVD: Classic Entertainment

Jed Clampett	**Buddy Ebsen**
Daisy Moses (Granny)	**Irene Ryan**
Elly May Clampett	**Donna Douglas**
Jethro Bodine	**Max Baer Jr**
Milburn Drysdale	**Raymond Bailey**
Jane Hathaway	**Nancy Kulp**
Cousin Pearl Bodine	**Bea Benaderet**
Mrs Margaret Drysdale	**Harriet MacGibbon**
Jethrene Bodine	**Max Baer Jr**
John Brewster	**Frank Wilcox**
Ravenswood	**Arthur Gould Porter**
Janet Trego	**Sharon Tate**
Lawrence Chapman	**Milton Frome**
John Cushing	**Roy Roberts**
Dash Riprock	**Larry Pennell**
Homer Cratchit	**Percy Helton**
Shorty Kellems	**George 'Shug' Fisher**
Shifty Shafer	**Phil Silvers**
Flo Shafer	**Kathleen Freeman**
Mark Templeton	**Roger Torrey**

Creator/Producer **Paul Henning**
Executive Producer **Al Simon**

A family of country bumpkins strikes oil, becomes rich and moves to a wealthy neighbourhood.

When Jed Clampett goes out hunting on his land, he discovers more than he bargains for. Stumbling across a bubbling oil-reservoir means that life in Bug Tussle in the Ozark Mountains is about to end for Jed and his family. They sell the drilling rights to John Brewster of the OK Oil Company and, with their new-found wealth, pack their bags on to their rickety old boneshaker and head for the city, taking up residence among the rich and famous of Beverly Hills. And that's where the comedy begins, for this family is not designed to live in an urban mansion. They are used to the rough and ready wild outdoors and think smog is a small hog. It is their inability to adapt to modern conveniences and day-to-day life in a prosperous neighbourhood that provides the laughs.

Although Jed himself is fairly level-headed, the same can't be said for the other members of the Clampett family. Granny, his wrinkly, irritable mother-in-law, fights manfully against modern-day comforts and still tries to buy such items as possum innards for her many potions and recipes. Elly May supplies the glamour as Jed's animal-loving daughter whom Granny is always trying to marry off, while brawny Cousin Jethro (played by the son of former world boxing champion Max Baer) is a dim, clumsy womanizer.

The Clampetts are chaperoned by Milburn Drysdale, President of the Commerce Bank, which holds their money. Assisted by the starchy Jane Hathaway, Drysdale moves the family into the house next to his own, in order to keep an eye on them and to keep out poachers, including his rival, John Cushing, of the Merchant's Bank. Snooty Mrs Drysdale, however, is not so pleased to have the Clampetts as neighbours: they hardly allow her to keep up appearances, and she hates her husband's grovelling.

Max Baer Jr also takes the part of Jethro's sister, Jethrene, in the early episodes, and another original character is Cousin Pearl Bodine, mother of Jethro and Jethrene. But as the series develops, so the storyline moves along. Jethro finally graduates from school and, in his quest for true playboy status, begins investing in flawed business ventures. The Clampetts purchase a majority holding in Mammoth Studios, run by Lawrence Chapman, which leads to Elly May's romance with film star Dash Riprock (né Homer Noodleman). Before the series closes (after nine years on US TV), she at last finds her Mr Right, in the shape of navy frogman Mark Templeton. By this time the Clampetts' fortune has risen from a comfortable $25 million to a mighty $95 million.

Occasional visitors to the show throughout its run were musicians Lester Flatt and Earl Scruggs, banjo-picking performers of the memorable theme song, 'The Ballad of Jed Clampett'.

Beverly Hills 90210 ✳

US (Twentieth Century-Fox/Torand/Spelling Entertainment) Drama. ITV 1991–2 (US: Fox 1990–2000)

Brenda Walsh	**Shannen Doherty**
Brandon Walsh	**Jason Priestley**
Jim Walsh	**James Eckhouse**
Cindy Walsh	**Carol Potter**
Kelly Taylor	**Jennie Garth**
Steve Sanders	**Ian Ziering**
Dylan McKay	**Luke Perry**
David Silver	**Brian Austin Green**
Andrea Zuckerman	**Gabrielle Carteris**
Donna Martin	**Tori Spelling**
Scott Scanlon	**Douglas Emerson**
Chris Suiter	**Michael St Gerard**
Nat	**Joe E. Tata**
Henry Thomas	**James Pickens Jr**
Emily Valentine	**Christine Elise**

Creator **Darren Star**
Executive Producer **Charles Rosin**
Producers **Aaron Spelling, Darren Star, Sigurjon Sighvatsson**

Teenage years in America's most select residential neighbourhood.

Beverly Hills 90210 is a zip code to die for, the zip code of the most fashionable residential area on the West Coast, a place where film stars and hugely successful business folk mingle in an atmosphere of gaudy prosperity. Into this glamorous setting step the Walshes, an altogether unassuming new family in town. Arriving from Minnesota, accountant dad Jim, wife Cindy and 16-year-old twins Brenda and Brandon are comfortably well off but strangely content with their lot, unlike their showy, ambitious neighbours. As they settle into their new environment, the kids, with their friends at West Beverly Hills High, provide the real focus of the series.

Dealing with realistic 1990s teen troubles like safe sex and drugs, as well as traditional adolescent woes such as peer pressure and school grades, *Beverly Hills 90210* quickly gathered a cult following among younger viewers. Apart from the Walsh family, the main characters are Brenda's snooty friend, Kelly; Steve, Kelly's ex-boyfriend and adopted son of TV star Samantha Sanders; Brandon's surfing buddy, Dylan (Brenda's boyfriend); Andrea, the editor of the school newspaper; insecure David Silver; David's pal, Scott; and Donna, another of Brenda's friends (played by the daughter of TV executive Aaron Spelling).

So much did the series involve itself in teenage troubles that, in the USA, *Beverly Hills 90210* was followed each week by a list of special help lines, encouraging kids to call if they had experienced the problems highlighted in that particular episode. Later series were run on Sky One, as was a spin-off series, *Melrose Place*.

Bewes, Rodney

(1938–)

Bingley-born comedy actor, one of TV's LIKELY LADS (Bob Ferris) in the 1960s and 1970s. He first appeared as a teenager on children's TV and later starred as Albert Courtnay in DEAR MOTHER . . . LOVE ALBERT (which he co-wrote and co-produced) and its follow-up, *Albert*, as well as playing Reg Last in *Just Liz*, and the straight man to BASIL BRUSH. Numerous guest appearances have included parts in DOCTOR WHO and Z CARS. In 2002 he took a cameo role as a news vendor in *Ant and Dec's Tribute to the Likely Lads*.

Bewitched ✳✳✳

US (Screen Gems) Situation Comedy. BBC 1 1964–76 (US: ABC 1964–72)
DVD: Sony

Samantha Stephens	**Elizabeth Montgomery**
Darrin Stephens	**Dick York**
	Dick Sargent
Endora	**Agnes Moorehead**
Maurice	**Maurice Evans**
Larry Tate	**David White**
Louise Tate	**Irene Vernon**
	Kasey Rogers
Tabitha Stephens	**Erin and Diane Murphy**
Adam Stephens	**David and Greg Lawrence**
Abner Kravitz	**George Tobias**
Gladys Kravitz	**Alice Pearce**
	Sandra Gould
Aunt Clara	**Marion Lorne**
Uncle Arthur	**Paul Lynde**
Esmerelda	**Alice Ghostley**
Dr Bombay	**Bernard Fox**

Creator **Sol Saks**
Executive Producer **Harry Ackerman**
Producers **William Asher, Danny Arnold**

● ***An attractive young witch marries a human and tries to settle down.***

Darrin Stephens is given a big surprise on his wedding day: he learns that his beautiful blonde bride, Samantha, is actually a witch who has been around for hundreds if not thousands of years. She is, however, tired of the supernatural life and wants to become part of normal society. She promises Darrin that she will rein back her magic, and the newlyweds set up home deep in Connecticut suburbia.

However, all does not go to plan, largely because of Endora, Samantha's mother, who fiercely opposes this 'mixed' marriage and uses every opportunity to cast spells on her unfortunate son-in-law, changing him into chimps and frogs at will. She makes no effort to learn his name, calling him variously Darwin, Donald, Durwood or something equally wrong. All of this is rather irritating for the hapless Darrin, an ambitious advertising executive with McMann and Tate. Whenever he manages to worm his way into boss Larry Tate's good books, there is Endora to foul things up. Fortunately, Samantha is always on hand to put things straight.

Samantha herself is very content in her domesticated life. She and Darrin are happy in their marriage, but she can never quite resist the temptation to twiddle her nose and let magic do the housework. Occasional visitors to the bizarre Stephens home are Samantha's confused Aunt Clara, a clumsy witch who forgets how to undo her spells, Maurice, Samantha's father, and practical joker Uncle Arthur. And then there are Abner and Gladys Kravitz, the neighbours. Witnessing the amazing events in the house next door from behind her twitching curtains, Gladys always fails to attract her husband's attention in time. Not surprisingly, he thinks she is barmy.

The Stephenses soon begin a family, with Tabitha the first-born. She inherits her mother's special powers, and the gift is also passed on to her brother, Adam, born a few years later. Later additions to the cast are Esmerelda, a bungling, failing sorceress who is taken on as housekeeper, and the ineffective Dr Bombay.

Bewitched saw many personnel changes in its run and caused much confusion when, unannounced, star Dick York was suddenly replaced by Dick Sargent (York suffered continually from back trouble and eventually could not go on). Alice Pearce, who originally played Gladys Kravitz, died in 1966, and the part of Louise Tate, Larry's wife, was also played by two actresses. A convention in American TV production was to use twins to play young children, to circumvent the limited hours minors were allowed to work. As a result, both Tabitha and Adam were played by twins, Tabitha by three sets before one of the last pair, Erin Murphy, took on the role full-time. When Tabitha grew up, she was given her own spin-off series, *Tabitha*, in which, played by Lisa Hartman, she worked for a Los Angeles TV station.

Bewitched was based on the 1942 film *I Married a Witch*, which, in turn, was taken from Thorne Smith's 1941 novel, *The Passionate Witch*.

Bhaskar, Sanjeev

OBE (1964–)

Actor/comedian/writer/musician born in Ealing of Punjabi parentage. Abandoning his first career in arts marketing, Bhaskar broke into broadcasting through radio shows like GOODNESS GRACIOUS ME, which he and his colleagues then took to television. Other early TV appearances came in THE REAL MCCOY. For 2001, he devised and presented *Position Impossible: in Search of the Kama Sutra* and then starred in THE KUMARS AT NO. 42, playing spoof chat show host Sanjeev Kumar. Other credits have been for the comedy shows *We Know Where You Live* and *Small Potatoes*, the sitcoms CAPTAIN BUTLER (Adeel), *Pork Pie*, KEEPING MUM and THE GRIMLEYS, dramas like DALZIEL AND PASCOE and *Life isn't All Ha Ha Hee Hee* (Akaash), and the pantomime *Dick Whittington* (The Mayor). Bhaskar has also hosted the UK Food series *Delhi Belly* and in 2005 starred as detective Vik Chopra in *Chopratown*. Bhaskar married his regular co-star Meera Syal the same year.

Big Breadwinner Hog ✳

UK (Granada) Crime Drama. ITV 1969

Hog	**Peter Egan**
Ackerman	**Donald Burton**
Edgeworth	**Rosemary McHale**
Grange	**David Leland**
Lennox	**Timothy West**
Raspery	**Peter Thomas**
Izzard	**Alan Browning**

Singleton .... **Tony Steedman**
Ryan .... **Godfrey Quigley**

Producer **Robin Chapman**

● ***A vicious underworld mobster strives to be Mr Big.***
Young, handsome Hog is a villain. A nasty villain. The sort of villain you really don't want to cross. He is also ambitious, aiming to be London's gangland king, and he will stop at nothing to achieve that goal. But, with the established city mobsters resisting his rise to power, the scene is set for some particularly violent action. In one episode, acid is thrown in someone's face; in others, beatings are commonplace. (Indeed the violence was so heavy that an apology had to be made to viewers. It seems the public of 1969 were not yet ready for the criminal fraternity to be shown in all their gory colours.)

Big Break ✳

UK (BBC) Game Show. BBC 1 1991–2002

Presenters **Jim Davidson, John Virgo**

Producers **John Burrowes, Geoff Miles, David Taylor**

● ***Pots mean prizes in a snooker-based quiz.***
In 1984, the BBC conjured up a quiz show that combined general knowledge with the game of snooker. Called *Pot the Question*, it was chaired by Stuart Hall and celebrity team captains were Patrick Mower and Denis Law. It didn't last long. The Corporation returned to the concept seven years later and landed themselves with a major hit that ran for 11 years. *Big Break* doesn't follow the same rules as *Pot the Question* (nor for that matter Radio 1's 'snooker on the radio' quiz, *Give Us a Break*, hosted by Dave Lee Travis on his weekend programme), but maintains the unorthodox mix of quiz knowledge and snooker skill. The quiz this time is handed to members of the public who answer questions to gain time for their professional snooker playing partners to pot balls on the table. Three teams of two (one contestant and one professional) are whittled down to one winner over the course of the programme. John Virgo referees and encourages participants to attempt elaborate trick shots; Jim Davidson (in family mode) is the wisecracking host. The theme song, composed by Mike Batt, is sung by Captain Sensible. A junior version, *Big Break: Stars of the Future*, was also produced.

Big Breakfast, The ✳✳✳

UK (Planet 24) Entertainment. Channel 4 1992–2002

Presenters **Chris Evans, Gaby Roslin, Paula Yates, Bob Geldof, Mark Lamarr, Keith Chegwin, Mark Little, Paul Ross, Richard Orford, Lily Savage, Zoë Ball, Danni Minogue, Sharron Davies, Rick Adams, Vanessa Feltz, Denise Van Outen, Johnny Vaughan, Melanie Sykes, Kelly Brook, Sara Cox, Liza Tarbuck, Richard Bacon, Gail Porter, Paul Tonkinson, Donna Air, Amanda Byram**

Editor **Sebastian Scott**
Executive Producers **Charlie Parsons, Bob Massie, Lisa Clark, Duncan Gray, Ed Forsdick**

● ***Fast-moving, weekday morning (7–9 a.m.) entertainment mix.***
Departing from the established news- and magazine-based format of other breakfast TV shows, *The Big Breakfast* placed the emphasis on fun from the start. Its all-action combination of competitions, interviews, film reviews and music videos was designed to appeal to the younger end of the audience spectrum, with news items restrained to brief headlines every 20 minutes (supplied by ITN and read by Peter Smith, Angela Rippon or Phil Gayle). A real house (three converted lock-keepers' cottages) in East London – and not a typical TV studio – was used for production, adding a cramped, chaotic atmosphere.

In the early programmes, Bob Geldof (director of the production company, Planet 24) conducted a series of prerecorded interviews with major figures on the world stage, although these were soon abandoned in favour of more trivial items. His then wife, Paula Yates, was also involved, welcoming celebrities into her boudoir and discussing fashion and other issues on her bed (her role was later assumed by Lily Savage and Vanessa Feltz, among others). A real family joined the programme each week, and Keith Chegwin or Richard Orford spent many mornings interviewing motorists in traffic jams and knocking up families in 'Down Your Doorstep'. Other features included 'Cupid's Arrow' (real-life tales of romance), American imports like THE BANANA SPLITS, sketches with puppets Zig and Zag (later stars of their own series), and 'Snap, Cackle and Pop' (entertainment news). However, the first real success story of the programme was host Chris Evans, who became TV's hottest property in the mid-1990s. The last ever edition was broadcast on Good Friday 2002.

Big Brother ✳✳✳

UK (Bazal/Endemol) Reality. Channel 4 2000–
DVD: VCI

Presenter **Davina McCall**

Creator **John De Mol**
Executive Producers **Ruth Wrigley, Conrad Green, Phil Edgar Jones, Gigi Eligoloff, Marion Farrelly, Shirley Jones, Sharon Powers, Claire O'Donohoe, Paul Osbourne**

● ***Voyeuristic 'reality soap' featuring the inhabitants of a TV show-house.***
The most talked-about programme of summer 2000 was *Big Brother*. This controversial concept was imported from the Netherlands, where it had taken the country by storm, generating entertainment out of the spectacle of young people living together in a specially adapted house, sealed off from the rest of the world. In the UK, the house was constructed behind barbed-wire fences in Bow, East London, and became home to ten willing participants for seven weeks. Strategically positioned cameras, two-way mirrors and compulsory radio microphones allowed viewers, through edited highlights (and Internet junkies for 24 hours a day), to spy on their every move – even the bathroom was bugged. The overall intention was, as the programme's publicity candidly put it, to provide 'pore-close TV', studying personal interaction and human behaviour. Critics saw it instead as a descent into voyeurism.

The contestants, chosen from an application-list of some 40,000, were vetted for psychological and social strengths and then thrown together for better or for worse. Each week they were assigned a group task and were also responsible for things like compiling their own shopping lists on a tight budget. Also each week, they nominated two of their number to face eviction, with one losing his or her place at the hands of the voting viewing public. In this way their total dwindled down to a final three, the highest-polling of these walking away with a cheque for £70,000. Along the way, one contestant, Nick Bateman, was expelled for breaking the rules and was substituted by Claire Strutton. The other participants were Melanie Hill, Anna Nolan, Darren Ramsey, Andrew Davidson, Thomas McDermott, Nichola Holt, Caroline O'Shea, Sada Walkington and Liverpudlian builder Craig Phillips, who ran out the eventual winner, generously donating his prize to a young friend with Down's syndrome who needed a vital operation in the USA.

From nothing *Big Brother* quickly gained a big following. Contestants enjoyed celebrity status and crowds of fans gathered at the gates of the house's compound to catch sight of the next evictee. Davina McCall summarized proceedings and interviewed the contestants as they left the TV equivalent of a goldfish bowl. The series was reproduced all over the world and led to a plethora of copycat programmes. A second UK series was produced in 2001, with additional coverage provided by the digital channel E4. It was won by Brian Dowling, who went on to host SM:TV LIVE. Earlier that year, Channel 4 teamed up with the BBC to present *Celebrity Big Brother* for Comic Relief. Six stars – Anthea Turner, Chris Eubank, Vanessa Feltz, Keith Duffy, Claire Sweeney and Jack Dee – braved the house for one week, with Dee taking the honours. Big Brother 3 in 2002 saw a move to a new house constructed at Elstree, and Kate Lawler the victorious inmate. The winners of the series 2003–5 were Cameron Stout, Nadia Almada and Anthony Hutton, respectively. *Celebrity Big Brother* returned (on Channel 4 only) in autumn 2002, the winner being former Take That performer Mark Owen, outlasting Anne Diamond, Goldie, Melinda Messenger, Sue Perkins and Les Dennis. More celebrities put themselves in the spotlight in 2005, with Bez (Mark Berry) from the band Happy Mondays seeing off Brigitte Nielsen, Caprice, Germaine Greer, Lisa I'Anson, Jeremy Edwards, John McCririck, Jackie Stallone and Kenzie (James McKenzie) from boy rappers Blazin' Squad. Yet more *Celebrity Big Brother* arrived in 2006, confining together MP George Galloway, Rula Lenska, Michael Barrymore, Maggot from Goldie Looking Chain, model Jodie Marsh, ex-Football Association secretary Faria Alam, basketball player Dennis Rodman, Dead or Alive singer Pete Burns, Preston from Ordinary Boys, actress Traci Bingham and non-celebrity 'plant' Chantelle, the surprising winner. The Geordie voice announcing the show belongs to actor Marcus Bentley.

In summer 2003, a group of 18-year-olds was invited to the house and their inter-relationship was recorded over two weeks. The declared intention was to broadcast it in the morning as an educational show but when *Teen Big Brother: the Experiment* was finally edited and made it to air, it had earned itself a late-night slot, thanks to the language of the inmates and the fact that two of them were shown having sex beneath a duvet.

Big Deal ★★

UK (BBC) Drama. BBC 1 1984–6

Robby Box .... **Ray Brooks**
Jan Oliver .... **Sharon Duce**
Debby Oliver .... **Lisa Geoghan**
Tommy .... **James Ottaway**
Henry Diamond .... **Tony Caunter**
Joan .... **Deirdre Costello**
Geordie .... **Andy Mulligan**
Irish .... **Alan Mason**
Vi Box .... **Pamela Cundell**
Ferret .... **Kenneth Waller**
Dick Mayer .... **Stephen Tate**
Kipper .... **Roger Walker**
Black George .... **Alex Tetteh-Lartey**
Alison Diamond .... **Marion Bailey**

Creator/Writer **Geoff McQueen**
Producer **Terence Williams**

A middle-aged gambler attempts to kick the habit.

At the age of 40 Londoner Robby Box has not done a day's work since leaving school. Instead, he makes a living playing poker and betting on horses and dogs. The sudden realization, however, that his life is passing him by and that he has nothing to show for his misspent youth encourages Box to 'go straight', calling on the help of his girlfriend, Jan, and her teenage daughter, Debby. Things don't entirely go to plan, though, especially with the taxman on Robby's tail and Jan always likely to walk out on him. For Jan, too, has her problems. She wants Robby to change but, paradoxically, loves him just the way he is. In the second season Robby's efforts to become respectable lead to his taking over The Dragon Club, but life doesn't get any easier.

Big Jim and the Figaro Club ★★

UK (BBC) Situation Comedy. BBC 2 1981

Jim .... **Norman Rossington**
Nimrod .... **David John**
Turps .... **Sylvester McCoy**
Chick .... **David Beckett**
Ned .... **Gordon Rollings**
Harold Perkins .... **Roland Curram**
Narrator .... **Bob Hoskins**

Creator/Writer **Ted Walker**
Producer **Colin Rose**

A group of builders stick together in the evolving post-war years.

The era is the early 1950s, a time when young men had returned from military service to an England that no longer seemed full of promise. Where, at one time, anything had seemed possible, life was now turning just a little sour. Determined not to let this get the better of them is this anarchic group of labourers working for a seaside town council. Head of the gang is Big Jim, a carpenter by trade and as honest and reliable a man as you could want in a group leader. Jim is thoroughly loyal to his comrades and his quiet approach to life and inscrutable appearance belie a sharp brain and a quick sense of humour (the character was modelled by star Norman Rossington – himself a qualified carpenter prior to taking up acting – on his own grandfather, a personal hero). The other members of the so-called Figaro Club, who work and play together, and speak their own kind of language, include Turps, the reckless painter, old Ned and young Nimrod, seen as something of a surrogate son to Big Jim. In the face of hassle and grief from their nasty nemesis, clerk of works Perkins, a social climber, they look out for each other, take care of the vulnerable and nonchalantly redefine the important values of friendship and loyalty in changing times.

The series, filmed in Exmouth, was spun off an episode of BBC 2's anthology series *Turning Year Tales* in 1979, in which we are introduced to the Figaro Club by the return of student College (played by Patrick Murray), who has come down from Cambridge to see his old mates and work for the summer. A postscript was provided to this short-lived series by a Radio 4 version that aired in 1987. The cast resumed the same roles, with the exception of Harold Goodwin taking over as Ned from the late Gordon Rollings, and Bernard Cribbins replacing Bob Hoskins as narrator. Most of these radio episodes were co-written by creator Ted Walker and the TV series producer Colin Rose.

Big One, The ✶

UK (Hat Trick) Situation Comedy. Channel 4 1992

Deddie Tobert .... **Sandi Toksvig**
James Howard .... **Mike McShane**

Writers **Sandi Toksvig, Elly Brewer**
Producers **Mary Bell, Jimmy Mulville**

● ***Two incompatible flat-sharers fall in love.***

To prove once again that love is a many-splendoured thing, this seven-part comedy builds a romance around the giant James Howard, an American novelist, and his diminutive English flatmate, Deddie Tobert, an advertising writer. In the fashion of THE ODD COUPLE, Tobert and Howard rub each other up the wrong way (he's fastidiously tidy, she's a slob), and their backgrounds are totally different, but love blossoms all the same – even if neither party can summon up the courage to say so.

Big Time, The ✶✶

UK (BBC) Documentary. BBC 1 1976–7; 1980

Presenter/Producer **Esther Rantzen**

● ***Amateurs become professionals for a day.***

Esther Rantzen was responsible for this series, which enabled ordinary viewers to achieve lifelong ambitions. Among those featured was a housewife who was given the chance to prepare a banquet at a swish hotel, falling foul along the way of an unsympathetic Fanny Cradock, whose bitter critique of the poor lady's best efforts was credited with ending her own TV career. There was also a vicar who wrote a newspaper gossip column and a sales assistant who joined a circus. However, the real success story concerned Scottish teacher Sheena Easton, who, from singing part-time in clubs, not only cut a record but went on to become an international star in her own right. Two series were produced, with a three-year gap in between.

Big Train ✶✶

UK (Talkback) Comedy. BBC 2 1998; 2002
DVD: BBC

Amelia Bulmore, Julia Davis, Kevin Eldon, Mark Heap, Simon Pegg, Rebecca Front, Tracy-Ann Oberman, Catherine Tate

Creators/Writers **Graham Linehan, Arthur Mathews**
Producers **Sioned Wiliam, Phil Clarke**

● ***Silly, sometimes dark, surreal sketch show from the creators of* FATHER TED.**

Echoes of Father Dougal's off-beat logic resound through this two-series collection of filmed sketches and sight gags, along with other moments of madness that could equally have been witnessed on Craggy Island. Highlights include the fan-adoration of Hitler in his dressing room after a Nazi rally; an international staring contest; nuns penned up as exhibits in a zoo; a Francophone tortoise; a group of show-jumpers who long to be firemen; and a Florence Nightingale who speaks the sort of language hardly fitting for the hospital bedside. Amelia Bulmore and Julia Davis, who appeared in the first series, were replaced by Rebecca Front, Tracy-Ann Oberman and Catherine Tate for series two, screened just over three years later. These later programmes were penned solely by Arthur Mathews.

Big Valley, The ✶

US (Four Star) Western. ITV 1965–70 (US: ABC 1965–9)

Victoria Barkley .... **Barbara Stanwyck**
Jarrod Barkley .... **Richard Long**
Nick Barkley .... **Peter Breck**
Heath Barkley .... **Lee Majors**
Audra Barkley .... **Linda Evans**
Eugene Barkley .... **Charles Briles**
Silas .... **Napoleon Whiting**

Producers **Jules Levy, Arthur Gardner, Arnold Laven**

● ***Life with a cattle-ranching family in California's San Joaquin Valley.***

The Big Valley tells the story of hard-headed widow Victoria Barkley and her ranching family in the 1870s Old West. Her sons range from refined lawyer Jarrod to brawny Nick, the foreman on the 30,000-acre holding. Heath is the good-looking one, although he is not Victoria's own (being the illegitimate son of her late husband, Tom, and an Indian squaw), and the youngest son is Eugene, a bashful youth seen only in the earliest episodes. Victoria also has a beautiful but impetuous daughter named Audra. Silas is the family's black servant. Storylines follow the usual Western pattern, revolving around constant battles with rustlers, criminals and con men.

Future SIX MILLION DOLLAR MAN Lee Majors made his TV debut in this series, and Linda Evans also went on to bigger and better things (as Krystle in DYNASTY).

Biggins, Christopher

(1948–)

Bespectacled actor/comedian/presenter, initially finding favour as the effeminate Lukewarm in PORRIDGE, the Revd Ossie Whitworth in POLDARK and Nero in I, CLAUDIUS. He was also Adam Painting in RENTAGHOST, the Revd Whiting in *Brendon Chase*, Mr Tonks in THE PHOENIX AND THE CARPET, and co-host of SURPRISE, SURPRISE with Cilla Black. His other TV credits have included *Watch This Space*, THE LIKELY LADS, PAUL TEMPLE, UPSTAIRS, DOWNSTAIRS, SHOESTRING, MASADA, *Dramarama*, CLUEDO (Revd Green) and *On Safari*.

Biggles ✶

UK (Granada) Children's Adventure. ITV 1960

Insp. 'Biggles' Bigglesworth .... **Neville Whiting**
Ginger .... **John Leyton**
Bertie .... **David Drummond**
Von Stalheim .... **Carl Duering**

Producers **Harry Elton, Kitty Black**

● ***The adventures of a celebrated flying ace.***

In this action-packed series, Biggles, Captain W. E. Johns's daredevil pilot, has left the Air Force with his chums Ginger and Bertie and is attached to Scotland Yard. Now a Detective Air Inspector, the intrepid air ace turns his sights away from enemy aircraft and on to airborne villains, ensuring each episode has a thrilling flying sequence and a cliffhanger ending. Among the show's writers was a young man called Tony Warren, who went on to devise CORONATION STREET, while John Leyton, who played Ginger, became more famous as a pop singer, topping the charts with 'Johnny Remember Me' a year after *Biggles* was screened.

Bill, The ✳✳

UK (Thames) Police Drama. ITV 1984–
DVD: Network

DI Roy Galloway .... **John Salthouse**
Sgt Bob Cryer .... **Eric Richard**
PC Francis 'Taffy' Edwards .... **Colin Blumenau**
PC Dave Litten .... **Gary Olsen**
PC/DC Jim Carver .... **Mark Wingett**
WPC/Sgt June Ackland/Carver .... **Trudie Goodwin**
WPC/WDC Viv Martella .... **Nula Conwell**
PC Timothy Able .... **Mark Haddigan**
DS Ted Roach .... **Tony Scannell**
WPC Claire Brind .... **Kelly Lawrence**
PC Reg Hollis .... **Jeff Stewart**
PC Tony 'Yorkie' Smith .... **Robert Hudson**
PC Robin Frank .... **Ashley Gunstock**
Chief Supt. Charles Brownlow **Peter Ellis**
PC Abe Lyttleton .... **Ronnie Cush**
PC Richard Turnham .... **Chris Humphreys**
PC Pete Muswell .... **Ralph Brown**
Insp. Brian Kite .... **Simon Slater**
Sgt Tom Penny .... **Roger Leach**
Sgt Alec Peters .... **Larry Dann**
PC Nick Shaw .... **Chris Walker**
PC Ken Melvin .... **Mark Powley**
PC Danesh Patel .... **Sonesh Sira**
Insp. Christine Frazer .... **Barbara Thorn**
PC Pete Ramsey .... **Nick Reding**
DCI Gordon Wray .... **Clive Wood**
PC Malcolm Haynes .... **Eamonn Walker**
PC Phil Young .... **Colin Aldridge**
Chief Insp. Derek Conway .... **Ben Roberts**
Insp. Andrew Monroe .... **Colin Tarrant**
DCI Kim Reid .... **Carolyn Pickles**
DI Frank Burnside .... **Christopher Ellison**
DS Alistair Greig .... **Andrew Mackintosh**
DC Alfred 'Tosh' Lines .... **Kevin Lloyd**
DC Mike Dashwood .... **Jon Iles**
Sgt John Maitland .... **Sam Miller**
PC Tony Stamp .... **Graham Cole**
PC Dave Quinnan .... **Andrew Paul**
WPC Cathy Marshall .... **Lynne Miller**
PC Steven Loxton .... **Tom Butcher**
WPC Norika Datta .... **Seeta Indrani**
WPC Delia French .... **Natasha Williams**
WPC Suzanne Ford .... **Vikki Gee-Dare**
PC George Garfield .... **Huw Higginson**
PC Ron Smollett .... **Nick Stringer**
Sgt Matthew Boyden .... **Tony O'Callaghan**
DI/DCI Jack Meadows .... **Simon Rouse**
PC Barry Stringer .... **Jonathan Dow**
DC Alan Woods .... **Tom Cotcher**
DS/Det. Insp. Harry Haines .... **Gary Whelan**
DS/DI Chris Deakin .... **Shaun Scott**
WPC/WDC Suzi Croft .... **Kerry Peers**
DS Danny Pearce .... **Martin Marquez**
PC Mike Jarvis .... **Stephen Beckett**
Sgt Ray Steele .... **Robert Perkins**
DI Sally Johnson .... **Jaye Griffiths**
WPC Donna Harris .... **Louise Harrison**
DC Rod Skase .... **Iain Fletcher**
PC Gary McCann .... **Clive Wedderburn**
Chief Insp. Philip Cato .... **Philip Whitchurch**
WDS Jo Morgan .... **Mary Jo Randle**
WPC Polly Page .... **Lisa Geoghan**
DS Don Beech .... **Billy Murray**
PC Nick Slater .... **Alan Westaway**
WPC Debbie Keane .... **Andrea Mason**
Chief Insp. Paul Stritch .... **Mark Spalding**
DS John Boulton .... **Russell Boulter**
DI Scales .... **Oliver Haden**
WDC Liz Rawton .... **Libby Davison**
WPC Jamilla Blake .... **Lolita Chakrabarti**
DS Geoff Daly .... **Ray Ashcroft**
DS Dave Merrick .... **Tom Mannion**
Sgt Stuart Lamont .... **Steve Morley**
DC Tom Proctor .... **Gregory Donaldson**
PC Luke Ashton .... **Scott Neal**
PC Sam Harker .... **Matthew Crompton**
WPC Vicky Hagen .... **Samantha Robson**
PC Eddie Santini .... **Michael Higgs**
WPC DaSilva .... **Melissa Lloyd**
WDC Kerry Holmes .... **Joy Brook**
DC Duncan Lennox .... **George Rossi**
WPC Di Worrell .... **Jane Wall**
DC Danny Glaze .... **Karl Collins**
PC/Sgt Dale Smith .... **Alex Walkinshaw**
WPC Cass Rickman .... **Suzanne Maddock**
DS Claire Stanton .... **Clara Salaman**
DC Mickey Webb .... **Chris Simmons**
Supt. Tom Chandler .... **Steve Hartley**
DC Paul Riley .... **Gary Grant**
DC Kate Spears .... **Tania Emery**
PC Nick Klein .... **René Zagger**
DI Alex Cullen .... **Ged Simmons**
DS Debbie McAllister .... **Natalie Roles**
DS Vik Singh .... **Raji James**
PC Ben Hayward .... **Ben Peyton**
PC Roz Clarke .... **Holly Davidson**
Sgt Craig Gilmore .... **Hywel Simons**
PC Des Taviner .... **Paul Usher**
DC Eva Sharpe .... **Diane Parish**
PC Cathy Bradford .... **Connie Hyde**
Det. Supt. Susan Devlin .... **Jane Slavin**
Insp. Gina Gold .... **Roberta Taylor**
DC Ken Drummond .... **Russell Floyd**
PC/Acting DC Gary Best .... **Ciaran Griffiths**
PC Kerry Young/Ashton .... **Beth Cordingly**
TDC/DC Brandon Kane .... **Pal Aron**
DS Phil Hunter .... **Scott Maslen**
FDO Roberta 'Robbie' Cryer .... **Moya Brady**
Acting DI/DS Samantha Nixon .... **Lisa Maxwell**
Supt. Adam Okaro .... **Cyril Nri**
PC Gemma Osbourne .... **Jane Danson**
PC Ruby Buxton .... **Nicola Alexis**
PC Honey Harman .... **Kim Tiddy**
Sgt/PC Sheelagh Murphy .... **Bernie Nolan**

PC Cameron Tait .... **Daniel Macpherson**
DC Juliet Becker .... **Rae Baker**
DC/DS Ramani De Costa .... **Thusitha Jayasundera**
DC Terry Perkins .... **Bruce Byron**
DCI Andrew Ross .... **Don Donachie**
PC Gabriel/David Kent .... **Todd Carty**
PC/Acting Sgt Yvonne Hemmingway .... **Michele Austin**
DC Rob Thatcher .... **Brian Bovell**
SRO Marilyn Chambers .... **Vickie Gates**
DI Neil Manson .... **Andrew Lancel**
DI Stephen Madden .... **Crispin Letts**
Dr Hugh Wallis .... **Robert Gwilym**
Dean McVerry .... **Luke Hamill**
PC Andrea Dunbar .... **Natalie J. Robb**
PC Lance Powell .... **Ofo Uhiara**
DC Suzie Sim .... **Wendy Kweh**
PC Steve Hunter .... **James Lloyd**
Sgt Mark Rollins .... **Stefan Booth**
DI Morell .... **Tanya Franks**
PC Leela Kapoor .... **Seema Bowri**
PC Roger Valentine .... **John Bowler**
DC Jo Masters .... **Sally Rogers**
PC Amber Johannsen .... **Myfanwy Waring**
PC Dan Casper .... **Chris Jarvis**
SRO Julian 'JT' Tavell .... **Nick Patrick**
Kate Maltby .... **Tamsin Skan**
PSCO/PC Laura Bryant .... **Melanie Kilburn**
DC Zain Nadir .... **TJ Ramini**
Supt. Amanda Prosser .... **Serena Gordon**
Chief Supt Ian Barratt .... **John McArdle**
Sgt Rochelle Barratt .... **Anna Acton**
PC Will Fletcher .... **Gary Lucy**
PC Lewis Hardy .... **Aml Ameen**
PC Emma Keane .... **Melanie Gutteridge**
DC/DS Stuart Turner .... **Doug Rao**

Creator **Geoff McQueen**
Executive Producers **Lloyd Shirley, Peter Cregeen, Michael Chapman, Paul Marquess**
Producers **Michael Chapman, Peter Cregeen, Richard Bramall, Brenda Ennis, Michael Ferguson, Geraint Morris, Pat Sandys, Michael Simpson, Tony Virgo, Peter Wolfes, Richard Handford, Mike Dormer, Chris Clough, Jamie Nuttgens, Chris Lovett, Tom Cotter, Carol Wilks, Pippa Brill, Baz Taylor, Jeannine Jones, Caroline Levy, Susan Mather, Lachlan Mackinnon, Lis Steele, Tim Key, Rachel Wright, Susan Breen, Donna Wiffen, Andrea Sapsford**

The rigours of day-to-day inner-city policing.

The Bill focuses on life at the Sun Hill police station, somewhere in London's East End, showing local law-enforcers in their everyday work, catching crooks, keeping the peace and dealing with the general public. Criticized by some real policemen for its portrayal of policing methods (but loved by other members of the force), *The Bill* was once attacked for suggesting – years ahead of the Stephen Lawrence tragedy and subsequent inquiry – that racism was a facet of today's force. Nevertheless, the series built its reputation on showing just how policemen cope with the realities of the modern world, showing officers of the law as people with a job to do, however unpleasant that job may be.

Head of the station initially was Chief Supt. Charles Brownlow, a man mainly concerned with the image of his force, but an ever-changing squad of inspectors, sergeants, detectives and constables has carried out the donkey work. Most notable have been Bob Cryer, the paternal station officer, the hot-headed DCI Galloway (who was never afraid to bend the rules) and his devious successor, DCI Burnside (given his own spin-off series, *Burnside*, in 2000; a further spin-off from the series, *MIT/Murder Investigation Team*, arrived in 2003). Young PCs 'Taffy' Edwards and Jim Carver, hypochondriac Reg Hollis, ambitious Dave Litton, impetuous Ted Roach, well-groomed Mike Dashwood, scruffy 'Tosh' Lines and dependable WPCs Ackland and Martella have also been prominent, as has DS Don Beech, a bent copper whose escape to Australia was covered in a 90-minute special in 2001.

The Bill began in 1983 as an episode of Thames TV's STORYBOARD series, entitled *Woodentop* (a CID nickname for uniformed officers). After four years as an hour-long drama, it 'turned tabloid', splitting into two self-contained, half-hour episodes each week. A new rule was added: there had to be a police person in every scene. Hand-held camerawork was introduced to provide a touch of on-the-streets realism and it certainly helped with the pace of the programme, although characterization and plot development were victims of the truncated format. In 1998, the famous 'plodding feet' title-sequence was dropped and later that year, with ratings falling, *The Bill* reverted to a one-hour format. Since then a variety of formats have been employed, with storylines stretched over a number of episodes, or packed into a feature-length edition, although in recent years the series has settled down into two one-hour packages a week. In 2002 new executive producer Paul Marquess oversaw a cull of some of the programme's stars, written out after a race riot led to the torching of Sun Hill. A raft of new characters took their places, including murdering WPC Cathy Bradford and PC Gabriel Kent, who is not everything he claims to be. Increased interest in the main characters' personal lives followed and the true story of policing that the series set out to tell at its outset has become lost more than ever beneath soap-style storylines.

To celebrate the programme's 20th birthday, a live episode was transmitted in October 2003 – an exercise repeated as part of ITV's 50th anniversary commemorations in September 2005.

Bill Brand ✶✶

UK (Thames) Drama. ITV 1976

Bill Brand .... **Jack Shepherd**
Miriam 'Mim' Brand .... **Lynne Farleigh**
Alf Jowett .... **Allan Surtees**
Frank Hilton .... **Clifford Kershaw**
Albert Stead .... **John Barrett**
Alex Ferguson .... **Cherie Lunghi**
Eddie Brand .... **Dave Hill**
Bernard Shaw .... **Colin Jeavons**
Angie Shaw .... **Carole Hayman**
Mr Brand .... **Harry Markham**
Mrs Brand .... **Anne Dyson**
David Last .... **Alan Badel**
Hughie Marsden .... **James Garbutt**
Reg Starr .... **Douglas Campbell**
Winnie Scoular .... **Rosemary Martin**
Mapson .... **Richard Butler**
June Brand .... **Karen Silver**
Michael Brand .... **Philip Cox**

Creator/Writer **Trevor Griffiths**
Executive Producer **Stella Richman**
Producer **Stuart Burge**

Problems in the life of a left-wing MP.

Somewhat autobiographical in tone, Trevor Griffiths's *Bill Brand* focuses on a young, idealistic lecturer who climbs his way up the socialist ladder to become a Member of Parliament. Bill Brand teaches Liberal Studies at Leighley Tech, until the chance to stand in a by-election in the Leighley constituency arises. Representing the Labour Party, he wins with a majority of 2,800 and heads south to Westminster. Once elected, however, Brand finds himself torn between party loyalties and personal conviction. He's a fundamental socialist and believes in nationalization. He'd rather be on the knocker than on TV. So, he refuses to toe the line, flouting whips and supporting striking textile workers. All the while, Brand's private life remains tangled, especially as his marriage to Mim, a medical social worker, is a sham on account of his long-running affair with solicitor Alex Ferguson. Jane and Michael are the Brands' two young children. Eleven episodes were made (divided into 'acts' rather than 'parts'), with music composed by Jack Trombey.

Billy Bunter of Greyfriars School ✳

UK (BBC) Situation Comedy. BBC 1952–7; 1959–61

Billy Bunter .... **Gerald Campion**

Creator/Writer **Frank Richards**
Producers **Joy Harington, David Goddard, Pharic Maclaren, Shaun Sutton, Clive Parkhurst**

● ***Jolly japes and wizard wheezes with a plump boarding school pupil.***

At times performed live twice on a Friday night (at teatime for children and at 8 p.m. for grown-ups) in the days before videotape, *Billy Bunter of Greyfriars School* was one of the BBC's earliest long-running comedies. Scripted by Frank Richards and based on his *Magnet* comic stories, it told tales of the ever-hungry William George Bunter, the Fat Owl of the Remove. Twenty-nine-year-old Gerald Campion filled out for the part and let loose a barrage of 'Crikey!'s and 'Yaroo!'s in raiding tuck shops, avoiding canings and waiting for postal orders from Bunter Court. Mocking Bunter was the beastly schoolboy posse of Harry Wharton, Frank Nugent, Bob Cherry, Hurree Jamset Ram Singh and Johnny Bull (played by a host of young performers), all avoiding the clutches of arch-enemy form-master Mr Quelch (played initially by Kynaston Reeves). Guesting among the boys were aspiring actors like Anthony Valentine, Michael Crawford, Melyvn Hayes and David Hemmings.

Billy Liar ✳✳

UK(LWT) Situation Comedy. ITV 1973–4

Billy Fisher .... **Jeff Rawle**
Geoffrey Fisher .... **George A. Cooper**
Alice Fisher .... **Pamela Vezey**
Grandma .... **May Warden**
Mr Shadrack .... **Colin Jeavons**
Barbara .... **Sally Watts**

Writers **Keith Waterhouse, Willis Hall**
Producer **Stuart Allen**

● ***A teenager wallows in a world of make believe.***

Billy Fisher lives in a suburban house in the North, with his mum, dad and 79-year-old gran. For a job, he is employed by Mr Shadrack as an undertaker's assistant, but this boring life is quickly forgotten once drippy Billy drifts off into another of his daydreams. In his own little world, Billy is top dog, a magnet for women and easily the match for his angry 'bloody' father, Geoffrey, a TV repair man. Sadly, all these little dreams (seen as fantasy sequences) must come to an end, usually with the long-haired Billy suffering the consequences of his Walter Mitty-like existence. Light humour also comes from Grandma's offbeat reminiscences of the old days and her shrieking laugh. Barbara is Billy's long-suffering girlfriend. The 26 episodes were scripted by Keith Waterhouse and Willis Hall and based on Waterhouse's own novel of the same name (and film of 1963, starring Tom Courtenay). Peter Skellern sang the theme song, which was composed by John Worth. A US version, just called *Billy*, with Steve Guttenberg in the title role, was made in 1979.

Bingham, Charlotte

(1942–)

See *Brady, Terence.*

Bionic Woman, The ✳

US (Universal/Harve Bennett) Science Fiction. ITV 1976–9
(US: ABC 1976–7; NBC 1977–8)
DVD: Universal

Jaime Sommers .... **Lindsay Wagner**
Oscar Goldman .... **Richard Anderson**
Dr Rudy Wells .... **Martin E. Brooks**
Jim Elgin .... **Ford Rainey**
Helen Elgin .... **Martha Scott**
Peggy Callahan .... **Jennifer Darling**

Creator **Kenneth Johnson**
Executive Producer **Harve Bennett**

● ***A girl with superhuman abilities works for a counter-espionage agency.***

In this spin-off from THE SIX MILLION DOLLAR MAN, Steve Austin's one-time girlfriend, Jaime Sommers, takes centre stage. In the original series, Jaime broke up with Steve when he became an astronaut, but they were temporarily reunited after she was crippled in a sky-diving accident. Jaime was then given the same bionic treatment as her boyfriend, endowing her with special abilities.

She now has bionic legs which allow her to run fast, a bionic ear for long-distance hearing and the strength of a bionic right arm. With these new skills, and in her own series, she settles down to life as a schoolteacher at the Ventura Air Force base in Ojai, California, although, in repayment for her futuristic medical treatment, she also works for the anti-espionage agency OSI (Office of Scientific Information). Steve, too, undertakes secret missions for OSI and, inevitably, the two are drawn together yet again. Sadly, the damage to Jaime's memory has wiped out her love for him, but this doesn't affect their working relationship. Jaime even takes up residence in an apartment at the farm owned by Steve's mother and stepfather (Helen and Jim Elgin).

The series also introduces Max, the bionic Alsatian dog, as a companion for Jaime, and the Bionic Boy (played by Vincent Van Patten). But more often seen are OSI executive Oscar Goldman and Dr Rudy Wells, the pioneer of bionic medicine. These characters, and that of Peggy Callahan, Oscar's secretary, also appear in *The Six Million Dollar Man*.

Bird, John
(1936–)

Nottingham-born comedian, actor, writer and director, a graduate of the Cambridge Footlights troupe. His earliest TV credits included THAT WAS THE WEEK THAT WAS, NOT SO MUCH A PROGRAMME, MORE A WAY OF LIFE, BBC-3, and Jonathan Miller's ALICE IN WONDERLAND, although he has more recently enjoyed success as support to Rory Bremner (in *Bremner, Bird and Fortune*, with long-time performing partner John Fortune) and as Douglas Bromley in EL C.I.D.. As well as notable appearances in BLUE REMEMBERED HILLS (Raymond), OXBRIDGE BLUES and A VERY PECULIAR PRACTICE (Ernest Hemmingway), he has starred in a couple of comedies of his own, namely *A Series of Bird's* and *With Bird Will Travel*, plus *Well Anyway, The Long Johns* (the last two shared ventures with Fortune), and the sketch shows *The Late Show, World in Ferment, After That, This, Beyond a Joke* and *Grubstreet* (often with Eleanor Bron). Bird has also featured prominently in the sitcoms THE GROWING PAINS OF ADRIAN MOLE, *If It Moves, File It* (civil servant Quick), JOINT ACCOUNT (Ned Race), EDUCATING MARMALADE (Mr Atkins), CHAMBERS (pompous barrister John Fuller-Carp) and *Absolute Power* (Martin McCabe), plus the game show CLUEDO (Professor Plum) and the dramas TO PLAY THE KING (Bryan Brynford-Jones), *Giving Tongue* (Lord Jessop), *In the Red* (Radio 4 Controller) and *Winter Solstice* (Barry). Guest appearances have come in JANE, TRAVELLING MAN, INSPECTOR MORSE, JONATHAN CREEK, ONE FOOT IN THE GRAVE and other major series.

Bird, Michael J.
(1928–2001)

Busy British screenwriter, contributing to scores of series in the 1970s and 1980s in particular, from THE INFORMER, MR ROSE, JOURNEY TO THE UNKNOWN, HADLEIGH, PAUL TEMPLE, SPECIAL BRANCH, BRETT and THE ONEDIN LINE to THE EXPERT, GENERAL HOSPITAL, QUILLER, WARSHIP, SECRET ARMY, THE FOURTH ARM and ARTHUR OF THE BRITONS. However, he is better known for his own mystery serials, some set in the Greek islands. These included THE LOTUS EATERS, WHO PAYS THE FERRYMAN?, *The Aphrodite Inheritance*, THE DARK SIDE OF THE SUN, THE OUTSIDER and MAELSTROM. He also penned the single drama *West of Paradise*, among other work.

Bird of Prey ★★★

UK (BBC) Drama. BBC 1 1982

Henry Jay	**Richard Griffiths**
Anne Jay	**Carole Nimmons**
Tony Hendersly	**Jeremy Child**
Charles Bridgnorth	**Nigel Davenport**
Harry Tompkins	**Roger Sloman**
Rochelle Halliday	**Ann Pennington**
Mario	**Guido Adorni**
Dino	**Eddie Mineo**
Hugo Jardine	**Christopher Logue**

Writer **Ron Hutchinson**
Producer **Michael Wearing**

● ***A Government employee stumbles into international intrigue.***

Henry Jay, a civil servant in his mid-30s, is working on a case of computer fraud when by chance he unearths a massive financial conspiracy. He decides to investigate further and, despite the close attentions of a shadowy agency known as Le Pouvoir and various bureaucratic attempts to silence him, Jay proves to be a determined detective, discovering clues that point to the involvement of a Euro MP by the name of Hugo Jardine.

Following the success of this four-part drama, dubbed 'a thriller for the electronic age', a sequel, entitled *Bird of Prey 2*, was made in 1984. In this, Henry, on the run with his wife, Anne, continues to expose the murky activities of Le Pouvoir.

Birds of a Feather ★★

UK (Alomo) Situation Comedy. BBC 1 1989–94; 1997–8
DVD: Prism Leisure

Sharon Theodopolopoudos	**Pauline Quirke**
Tracey Stubbs	**Linda Robson**
Dorien Green	**Lesley Joseph**
Chris Theodopolopoudos	**David Cardy**
	Peter Polycarpou
Darryl Stubbs	**Alun Lewis**
	Doug McFerran
Garth Stubbs	**Simon Nash**
	Matthew Savage
Marcus Green	**Nickolas Grace**
	Stephen Greif
Melanie Fishman	**Jan Goodman**

Creators **Laurence Marks, Maurice Gran**
Executive Producer **Allan McKeown**
Producers **Esta Charkham, Nic Phillips, Candida Julian-Jones, Charlie Hanson, Tony Charles**

● ***Two sisters live together after their husbands are sent to jail.***

Tracey and Sharon are two adopted sisters from North London. Of the two, Tracey has patently done better for herself. She has a £¾-million neo-Georgian home called 'Dalentrace' in Bryan Close in the Essex suburb of Chigwell, whereas Sharon still lives in Camelot House, a seedy council tower block in Edmonton. Furthermore, Tracey's son, Garth, now attends a public school. What she doesn't realize is that her childhood-sweetheart husband, Darryl, is paying for all this on the proceeds of crime. All is revealed when he and Sharon's dim Greek husband, Chris, are arrested for armed robbery and earn themselves 12-year prison sentences. At this point Sharon moves in with Tracey and sets about finding a new man in her life. Indeed, sex – or at least talk of it – becomes their main obsession, even though they still visit their partners in Maidstone prison. Money problems form their other preoccupation as Darryl's ill-gotten cash begins to run out, and Sharon opens up a café to earn a living.

The girls' lives are regularly spiced up by Dorien Green, their snooty, man-eating, Jewish next-door neighbour, who enjoys a succession of toy boys in the absence of her accountant husband, Marcus (who has been impotent since the 1987 stock market crash). Dorien's great rival on the local social scene is Melanie Fishman.

After a two-and-a-half-year hiatus, *Birds of a Feather* returned to the screen in 1997, picking up the story at the point where the two husbands are (temporarily) released from prison. The house in Chigwell has to go to make ends meet and the girls are forced to move to humbler accommodation in Hainault. Dorien, too, faces a new future: Marcus, it seems, has been sharing his life with another wife and a son, and Dorien, too, has to move downmarket to Hainault. In yet later episodes, the girls found their own cleaning company, Maids of Ongar.

An American version, made in 1992, called *Stand by Your Man* and featuring characters named Rochelle, Lorraine and Adrienne, was not a great success.

Birt, Lord John

(1944–)

Director-General of the BBC whose internal reforms caused much unease in the early 1990s. The streamlining of staff and the introduction of the 'Producer Choice' internal market system proved the most inflammatory, as Birt was charged with leading the BBC through a particularly difficult period in a new multi-channel environment and with the BBC's Charter due for renewal in 1996. Birt's career took off at Granada, where, as producer, he was responsible in 1968 for NICE TIME, the innovative comedy show starring Jonathan Routh, Kenny Everett and Germaine Greer, and worked on WORLD IN ACTION. He later moved to LWT, where his input into current affairs television proved equally influential (among other projects he was executive producer of WEEKEND WORLD). He eventually took over as Head of Features and Current Affairs before rising to Programme Controller in 1981. He joined the BBC as Deputy Director-General in 1987, brought in by the then Director-General, Michael Checkland, to reappraise the BBC's journalistic operations. He was named, somewhat controversially, as the next Director-General in 1991, while Checkland still had two years of his contract to run. As he bowed out of the BBC hot seat, he was given a life peerage in December 1999.

Births, Marriages and Deaths ★★★

UK (Tiger Aspect) Drama. BBC 2 1999
DVD: Prism Leisure

Alan	**Ray Winstone**
Terry	**Mark Strong**
Graham	**Phil Davis**
Alex	**Maggie O'Neill**
Pat	**Michelle Fairley**
Molly	**Tessa Peake-Jones**

Writer **Tony Grounds**
Producer **Greg Brenman**

● ***An eve-of-wedding tragedy jeopardizes a lifelong friendship.***

When three old schoolmates get together for a day out, the consequences prove to be far greater than they would ever have imagined. It's Terry's stag do. He's about to get married to the pregnant Pat, mother of two young sons, and his mate Alan wants to do him proud. Alan has worked his way to a position of affluence and now wears flash suits and lives with wife, Alex, and kids in a big house with a swimming pool. He wants to do well by his friends, but tends to be manipulative and overbearing rather than helpful. The third mate is worried, easily burdened Graham, who has a happy marriage to Molly and lives in a council flat. The lads have a hectic day out, reflecting on 40 years of friendship and their old schooldays. The memory of their cruel headmaster stirs them to pay him a visit, to frighten him in return for past miseries. Sadly, it all goes wrong: the teacher dies and when his house is searched some deadly secrets are unearthed that shatter the boys' relationship for good. With lots of drunken behaviour, reels of East End banter and always a surprise up its sleeve, *Births, Marriages and Death* (the title reflecting three key events in life that challenge friendship) was unusual, colourful and very successful. The four parts were directed by Adrian Shergold.

Bit of a Do, A ★★

UK (Yorkshire) Comedy Drama. ITV 1989
DVD: Cinema Club

Ted Simcock	**David Jason**
Rita Simcock	**Gwen Taylor**
Elvis Simcock	**Wayne Foskett**
Paul Simcock	**David Thewlis**
Laurence Rodenhurst	**Paul Chapman**
Liz Rodenhurst/Badger	**Nicola Pagett**
Simon Rodenhurst	**Nigel Hastings**
Jenny Rodenhurst/Simcock	**Sarah-Jane Holm**
Neville Badger	**Michael Jayston**
Rodney Sillitoe	**Tim Wylton**
Betty Sillitoe	**Stephanie Cole**
Carol Fordingbridge	**Karen Drury**
Gerry Lansdown	**David Yelland**
Corinna Price-Rodgerson	**Diana Weston**
Geoffrey Ellsworth-Smythe	**Malcolm Tierney**
Lucinda Snellmarsh	**Amanda Wenban**
Eric	**Malcolm Hebden**
Sandra	**Tracy Brabin**

Creator/Writer **David Nobbs**
Executive Producer **Vernon Lawrence**
Producer **David Reynolds**

● ***Social rivalry between two families who meet at local functions.***

Set in a small Yorkshire town, where everyone knows everyone else's business, *A Bit of a Do* focuses on the relationships between members of the Rodenhurst and Simcock families. Laurence Rodenhurst is a dentist, while the socially inferior Ted Simcock runs an iron foundry. The first 'do' that brings them together is the marriage of Laurence's daughter, Jenny, to scruffy Paul, Ted's son. During the reception, Ted enjoys some extra-marital exercise with Laurence's wife, Liz, which results in an unplanned offspring and the break-up of Ted's marriage to Rita.

Other 'dos' the families attend included the Angling Club Christmas party, the Dentists' Dance and the crowning of Miss Frozen Chicken UK at the Cock-a-Doodle Chickens event. As the series progresses, Laurence dies, Liz picks up with widower Neville Badger, Ted's business hits hard times and Jenny marries her brother-in-law, Elvis. Rodney and Betty Sillitoe are boozy regulars at every function, and also seen are barman Eric and waitress Sandra. The episodes were dramatized by David Nobbs from his own novels.

Bixby, Bill

(1934–93)

American actor famous as the mild-mannered Dr David Banner in THE INCREDIBLE HULK, with earlier starring roles as Anthony Blake in THE MAGICIAN (a part for which he learned conjuring tricks) and Tim O'Hara in MY FAVORITE MARTIAN. His other major TV credit was in a comedy series not seen in the UK, *The Courtship of Eddie's Father*. Bixby also turned his hand to directing, calling the shots for TV movies and on some episodes of RICH MAN, POOR MAN, as well as appearing in front of the camera as Willie Abbott in that mini-series.

Bizzy Lizzy ✶

UK (Westerham Art Films) Children's Entertainment. BBC 1 1967

Narrator **Julie Stevens**

Writers **Maria Bird, Freda Lingstrom**

● ***Adventures with a girl who is granted four wishes a day.***
Bizzy Lizzy is a wispy-haired little girl puppet with a magic wishing flower on her dress. She is allowed four wishes by touching the flower, but if she wishes a fifth time all her wishes fly away (an inevitable consequence, because she never learns). Little Mo is Bizzy Lizzy's friend. After appearing as a segment of PICTURE BOOK in the 1950s, Bizzy Lizzy was given her own series in 1967, under the WATCH WITH MOTHER banner. Gillian Norton provided the singing voice and Audrey Atterbury, Molly Gibson and Christopher Leith pulled the strings.

Black, Cilla
OBE (Priscilla White; 1943–)

Liverpudlian singer turned presenter whose career break came while working as a cloakroom attendant and occasional vocalist at The Cavern club, famous for The Beatles' early performances. Spotted by Brian Epstein, Black secured a recording contract and notched up two number ones with 'Anyone Who Had a Heart' and 'You're My World'. She ventured into television in 1968, gaining her own Saturday night series, *Cilla*, on BBC 1, which ran for several years. In these live programmes she sent an outside broadcast team to surprise unsuspecting residents somewhere in the UK. She also gave viewers the chance to choose the Song for Europe. Black later tried her hand at sitcom in *Cilla's Comedy Six* and *Cilla's World of Comedy*, and after a quiet period during the 1970s she resurfaced as host of SURPRISE, SURPRISE (in 1984) and BLIND DATE (in 1985). In 1998, she launched another Saturday evening show, *Cilla's Moment of Truth*. Five years later, she dropped a TV bombshell by announcing in a special live episode that she was quitting *Blind Date* after 18 years.

Black and White Minstrel Show, The ✶

UK (BBC) Variety. BBC 1 1958–78

Creator **George Inns**
Producers **George Inns, Ernest Maxin, Brian Whitehouse**

● ***Sing-along variety show featuring the Mitchell Minstrels and guests.***
Stemming from a one-off special entitled *The 1957 Television Minstrels*, this old-fashioned, fast-moving series was a showcase for conductor George Mitchell's Mitchell Minstrels and especially lead vocalists Dai Francis, John Boulter and Tony Mercer. Other long-serving Al Jolson lookalikes were Benny Garcia, Les Rawlings, Andy Cole and Les Want, and female contributions came from Margo Henderson, Margaret Savage, Penny Jewkes, Delia Wicks and others. In the background the Television Toppers dancers (previously stars of *Toppers About Town*) provided the glamour. Adding light relief were comedians like Leslie Crowther, George Chisholm and Stan Stennet.

The Minstrels specialized in schmaltzy medleys in the sing-along vein, some originating from America's deep South (like the 19th-century minstrel concept itself). Other tunes were of country and western origin, or were derived from foreign folk cultures. The programme was a Saturday night favourite, but, by the end of the 1970s, the political incorrectness of men with blacked-up faces and broad white smiles resulted in its cancellation after over 20 years on air.

Black Beauty
See *Adventures of Black Beauty, The*.

Black Books ✶✶✶

UK (Assembly/Chrysalis) Situation Comedy. Channel 4 2000; 2002; 2004
DVD: VCI

Bernard Black .... **Dylan Moran**
Manny Bianco .... **Bill Bailey**
Fran Katzenjammer .... **Tamsin Greig**

Writers **Graham Linehan, Dylan Moran, Arthur Mathews, Andy Riley, Kevin Cecil**
Executive Producer **William Burdett-Coutts**
Producers **Julian Meers, Nira Park**

● ***The crazy world of a manic bookshop proprietor and his put-upon assistant.***
Irishman Bernard Black runs Black Books, a small London bookshop. Unfortunately, he hates his customers with a passion and therefore fails to sell many books. One book he does manage to shift is *The Little Book of Calm*, to over-stressed accountant Manny Bianco. Later, in a drunken stupor, Bernard offers Manny a job and the two consequently run the shop together. In a comedy of contrasts (even their names imply opposites), the fastidious, neurotic Manny tries vainly to keep the dishevelled, chain-smoking, red-wine-swilling Bernard in order, rearranging the shelves and cleaning up the private quarters above and behind the shop. The angry, ranting Bernard bites back by frequently sacking or abusing Manny, which leads to the intervention of Fran, the insecure oddball who runs the trendy furniture shop next door. With lunatic, super-surreal moments, and a chain of eccentric customers added to the pot, *Black Books* made an immediate impact on fans missing the dear departed FATHER TED (largely from the same stable).

Black Silk ✶✶

UK (BBC) Legal Drama. BBC 2 1985

Larry Scott .... **Rudolph Walker**
Julie Smythe .... **Kika Markham**
Marjorie Scott .... **Mona Hammond**
Jasmine Scott .... **Suzette Llewellyn**
Josie Patten .... **Annie Bruce**

Creators **Mustapha Matura, Rudy Narayan**
Producer **Ruth Boswell**

● ***A talented black lawyer is a hero for the underclasses.***
Larry Scott is a gifted, dynamic barrister based in an otherwise all-white chambers in London. His mission in life is to help the underprivileged, especially in the black community, where he enjoys massive respect. Thus Scott takes on cases that other briefs won't handle, such as fighting for an alleged Irish terrorist; assisting a Pakistani lady who is illegally detained in immigration; defending a member of a reggae band (played

by Brinsley Forde of Aswad) who has been accused of attacking a right-wing activist. His colleague, Julia Smythe, a white woman with left-leaning sympathies, is his girlfriend, although he still sees his Jamaican ex-wife every week for a traditional Caribbean Sunday. Jasmine is Larry's 16-year-old daughter.

The eight-part series was based on an idea passed to star Rudolph Walker by a friend, Guyanese barrister Rudy Narayan.

Blackadder ★★★★

UK (BBC) Situation Comedy. BBC 1 1983; 1986–7; 1989
DVD: BBC

The Black Adder (1983)

Edmund, Duke of Edinburgh ('The Black Adder')	**Rowan Atkinson**
Baldrick	**Tony Robinson**
Percy	**Tim McInnerny**
Richard IV	**Brian Blessed**
Queen	**Elspet Gray**
Prince Harry	**Robert East**

Blackadder II (1986)

Lord Edmund Blackadder	**Rowan Atkinson**
Baldrick	**Tony Robinson**
Queen Elizabeth I	**Miranda Richardson**
Lord Melchett	**Stephen Fry**
Lord Percy	**Tim McInnerny**
Nursie	**Patsy Byrne**

Blackadder the Third (1987)

Edmund Blackadder	**Rowan Atkinson**
Baldrick	**Tony Robinson**
George, Prince of Wales	**Hugh Laurie**
Mrs Miggins	**Helen Atkinson-Wood**

Blackadder Goes Forth (1989)

Capt. Edmund Blackadder	**Rowan Atkinson**
Pte S. Baldrick	**Tony Robinson**
Lt. The Honourable George Colthurst St Barleigh	**Hugh Laurie**
Gen. Sir Anthony Cecil Hogmanay Melchett	**Stephen Fry**
Capt. Kevin Darling	**Tim McInnerny**

Semi-regulars:

Lord Flashheart (*II/Goes Forth*)	**Rik Mayall**
Kate/Bob (*II*)/Driver Parkhurst (*Goes Forth*)	**Gabrielle Glaister**
Princess Maria (*The Black Adder*)/Lady Whiteadder (*II*)	**Miriam Margolyes**
Amy Hardwood (*The Third*)/ Nurse Mary (*Goes Forth*)	**Miranda Richardson**

Creators **Rowan Atkinson, Richard Curtis**
Writers **Rowan Atkinson, Richard Curtis, Ben Elton**
Producer **John Lloyd**

● ***Historical double-dealing with various generations of a cowardly family.***

Blackadder was a collection of comedies which, although running into four eras, splits neatly into two clear parts: the first series and the rest. Viewers who later came to love the devious, treacherous, selfish rogue of *Blackadder II, Blackadder the Third* and *Blackadder Goes Forth* were not over-enamoured of the character portrayed in the first series, which was simply entitled *The Black Adder*. This series was written by Rowan Atkinson and Richard Curtis. By the second generation, Ben Elton had replaced Atkinson as co-writer and the scripts were graced with more rounded plots and filled with choice one-liners.

The Blackadder saga begins with Edmund, Duke of Edinburgh. Crudely based on supposedly true historical accounts, the comedy comes from the feeble-mindedness of the cringing duke and his sly, cowardly ways. Filmed around Alnwick Castle in Northumberland, at great expense, it is set during the Wars of the Roses, as the houses of Lancaster and York battle for the English throne, with Edmund allegedly the son of Richard IV, one of the Princes in the Tower.

By the second series (the concept having just survived cancellation) Edmund Blackadder, great-great-grandson of the original Black Adder and a courtier of Queen Elizabeth I, has added buoyant confidence to his ancestor's repertoire of deceit and cruelty. He is admirably complemented in his Tudor treachery by an overgrown-schoolgirl version of the Virgin Queen, as well as a pompous rival, Lord Melchett, and a foppish hanger-on, Lord Percy. But the best support comes from rodent-like manservant Baldrick, like Lord Percy an even stupider descendant of a character first seen in *The Black Adder*.

For *Blackadder the Third*, time has moved on two centuries to the Georgian age, and the Blackadder in question is butler to the idiotic George, Prince of Wales. In between frequenting Mrs Miggins's coffee shop and cuffing Baldrick about the ear, Blackadder schemes his way in and out of the society groups who surround the Prince, meeting the likes of Dr Johnson (Robbie Coltrane) and the Duke of Wellington (Stephen Fry).

The last incarnation comes in the World War I trenches of *Blackadder Goes Forth*. Here the weaselly Captain Edmund Blackadder works every ruse in the book to try to flee the impending carnage, but is inhibited by his imbecile lieutenant, George, and, of course, Private Baldrick. Then there is the arrogant, insensitive General Melchett, booming out orders to his subservient adjutant, Captain Darling, yet another object of contempt for our hero. The tragedy and futility of the Great War are never ridiculed and the series concludes in rich pathos. As all the 'ordinary men' (not the General, of course) are forced 'over the top' to certain death, the slow-motion action fades silently into a field of swaying poppies.

Series two to four were essentially performed by what amounted to a high-class repertory company. Joining Atkinson and Tony Robinson in their roles as Blackadder and Baldrick were Stephen Fry, Hugh Laurie, Miranda Richardson, Tim McInnerny and Rik Mayall, each reprising parts played in earlier series. There was also a Christmas special in 1988 set in various time zones, including the future, and depicting Blackadder as Ebenezer Scrooge in reverse – he begins the story a kind and generous patrician, winding up as the Blackadder we have all grown to know, love and hate. A short insert (*Blackadder: The Cavalier Years*) was produced for Comic Relief in 1988, placing the troupe in the Civil War era, with Stephen Fry as King Charles I, while a special time-travelling film made for screening at the Millennium Dome, entitled *Blackadder Back and Forth*, was eventually given its TV première by Sky One in October 2000 and later screened by the BBC.

Blackeyes ★★

UK (BBC/Australian Broadcasting Corporation/Television New Zealand) Drama. BBC 2 1989

Maurice James Kingsley	**Michael Gough**
Jessica	**Carol Royle**
Jeff	**Nigel Planer**
Blackeyes	**Gina Bellman**
Jamieson	**Colin Jeavons**

Andrew Stilk	**Nicholas Woodeson**
Det. Blake	**John Shrapnel**
Mark Wilsher	**David Westhead**
Colin	**Gary Love**
Little Jessica	**Hannah Morris**
Narrator	**Dennis Potter**

Writer **Dennis Potter**
Producer **Rick McCallum**

● ***A model finds her life story is distorted in a novel.***

Controversial, even by Dennis Potter's standards, and predictably slated by the Establishment for its nudity, *Blackeyes* is the story of Jessica, a former model. Angrily discovering that her 77-year-old Uncle Maurice has written a successful sexy novel called *Blackeyes*, which is based on her own real-life modelling experiences, she desperately wants to rewrite the tale more truthfully, but lacks the required skill. Blackeyes was her professional name.

Immersed in a typically Potter-esque amalgam of reality and fiction, slimy advertising men like Stilk and Jamieson and the seemingly decent copywriter Jeff play their parts in showing how young girls can be abused in the glamour industry. Potter also directed and narrated the four episodes. Max Harris composed the music.

Blackman, Honor

(1927–)

British leading lady, a graduate of the Rank charm school who sprang to fame as the athletic Cathy Gale in THE AVENGERS, having already appeared in the series THE FOUR JUST MEN (Nicole) and PROBATION OFFICER (Iris Cope). After two years as Gale, Blackman headed for Hollywood, winning the part of Pussy Galore in *Goldfinger*. In recent times, her most prominent role has been as Laura West in THE UPPER HAND, although she has also been seen in other comedy series like ROBIN'S NEST (Marion Nicholls) and NEVER THE TWAIN (Veronica Barton). Additional credits over the years have ranged from THE INVISIBLE MAN, GHOST SQUAD and COLUMBO to TOP SECRET, the mini-series LACE, DOCTOR WHO, DR TERRIBLE'S HOUSE OF HORRIBLE, MIDSOMER MURDERS, THE ROYAL, *Revolver*, NEW TRICKS and CORONATION STREET (Rula Romanoff). Her second husband was actor Maurice Kaufmann.

Blackpool ★★★

UK (BBC) Drama. BBC 1 2004
DVD: BBC

Ripley Holden	**David Morrissey**
Natalie Holden	**Sarah Parish**
DI Peter Carlisle	**David Tennant**
Shyanne Holden	**Georgia Taylor**
Danny Holden	**Thomas Morrison**
Terry Corlette	**John Thomson**
Adrian Marr	**Steve Pemberton**
Jim Allbright	**David Hounslow**
Hallworth	**David Bradley**
DC Blythe	**Bryan Dick**
Steve	**Kevin Doyle**
Hailey	**Lisa Millet**

Writer **Peter Bowker**
Executive Producers **Sally Haynes, Laura Mackie**
Producer **Kate Lewis**

● ***A ruthlessly ambitious arcade owner is prime suspect for a murder.***

Julie Anne Robinson and Coky Giedroyc direct this vibrant musical thriller set amid the bright lights of northern England's most famous seaside town. Ripley Holden feels he is on the verge of the big time. The unscrupulous local entrepreneur has just taken possession of his first amusement arcade and has plans to turn Blackpool into the Vegas of Lancashire. Unfortunately, following the glitz and glamour of the big opening night, Ripley's world begins to turn sour when the body of a young man is found on the arcade's premises. Enter DI Carlisle, a doggedly determined young Scottish detective who takes an instant dislike to the swaggering Holden and resolves to pin the murder on him. To complicate matters, however, Carlisle's emotions run in the opposite direction when he meets Holden's long-suffering, cheated-on wife, Natalie, and an affair is born. As the police investigation takes a hold, Ripley's finances take a nose dive, driving a deeper rift between the brassy businessman and his enigmatic accuser. Wrapped up in the mystery are also Danny, Holden's mixed-up, drug-pedalling son, and Shyanne, Holden's feisty daughter, whose new boyfriend, Steve, was at school with her dad – much to Ripley's disgust. Terry, Adrian and Jim are Holden's unreliable mates and nervous fellow investors.

Resurrecting the Dennis Potter formula of breaking up the action with song and dance, *Blackpool* sees its stars lip-synch to a string of established pop hits in each of its six episodes – a device that, along with some sharp dialogue, colourfully lightens the tone.

In 2006 David Morrissey returned as Holden in a one-off feature-length sequel called *Viva Blackpool*. This time Ripley is seen running a Vegas-style wedding chapel with Shyanne.

Blair, Isla

(1944–)

RADA-trained actress born in India, married to actor Julian Glover and mother of actor Jamie Blair. Among her many credits have been roles in *The Liars*, THE DOCTORS (Linda Carpenter), THE CREZZ (Emma Antrobus), AN ENGLISHMAN'S CASTLE, THE HISTORY MAN (Flora Beniform), WHEN THE BOAT COMES IN (Lady Caroline), THE BOUNDER (Laura), *The Dickie Henderson Show*, TAGGART, MOTHER LOVE (Ruth), *The Advocates* (Katherine Dunbar), THE FINAL CUT (Claire Carlsen), INSPECTOR MORSE, A TOUCH OF FROST (Rosalie Martin), *True Tilda* (Mrs Mortimer), *Heaven on Earth* (Mary Weston), MIDSOMER MURDERS and NEW TRICKS. In 2005 she played Home Minister Blaker in BBC 4's live revival of THE QUATERMASS EXPERIMENT.

Blair, Lionel

(Henry Lionel Ogus; 1931–)

Canadian-born dancer and TV personality, choreographer for SUNDAY NIGHT AT THE LONDON PALLADIUM and later one of the team captains on GIVE US A CLUE and host of NAME THAT TUNE. He was one of the veterans forming the company of the sketch show *Revolver* and in 2003 he joined the cast of CROSSROADS (dance teacher Valentine Starwood). Guest appearances over the years have taken in series like THE PERSUADERS!.

Blakely, Colin
(1930–87)

Northern Irish classical actor whose TV roles were usually in the quietly determined vein. His most prominent part was Jesus Christ in Dennis Potter's controversial play *Son of Man*, in 1969, although he also starred as Lew Burnett in THE HANGED MAN and was very nearly cast as the lead in TARGET, the BBC's answer to THE SWEENEY. Other TV credits included the Alun Owen plays *Lena, O My Lena* and *Shelter*, and the dramas *The Breaking of Colonel Keyser, Peer Gynt, The Birthday Party, Drums along Balmoral Drive, Operation Julie* (DI Richard Lee), *Cousin Bette* (Steinbock), THE BEIDERBECKE AFFAIR (Chief Supt. Forrest) and PARADISE POSTPONED (Dr Salter).

Blake's 7 ✶✶

UK (BBC) Science Fiction. BBC 1 1978–81
DVD: BBC

Roj Blake .... **Gareth Thomas**
Kerr Avon .... **Paul Darrow**
Jenna Stannis .... **Sally Knyvette**
Vila Restal .... **Michael Keating**
Cally .... **Jan Chappell**
Zen .... **Peter Tuddenham** *(voice only)*
Gan Olag .... **David Jackson**
Orac .... **Peter Tuddenham** *(voice only)*
Dayna Mellanby .... **Josette Simon**
Capt. Del Tarrant .... **Steven Pacey**
Soolin .... **Glynis Barber**
Supreme Commander Servalan .... **Jacqueline Pearce**
Commander Travis .... **Stephen Greif**
Brian Croucher
Slave .... **Peter Tuddenham** *(voice only)*

Creator **Terry Nation**
Producers **David Maloney, Vere Lorrimer**

In the distant future, a band of escaped criminals fights back against an oppressive government.

At some time in the third century of the second calendar, the populated worlds of our galaxy find themselves at the mercy of a cruel, remorseless dictatorship known as The Federation. This ruthless regime tolerates no opposition. Petty criminals, by way of pay-offs, are allowed to exist and make life a misery for the population, but no political dissent is tolerated. There are, however, small bands of resistance. One such band is comprised of escaped prisoners, led by the falsely convicted Roj Blake. On their way to exile on the penal colony of Cygnus Alpha, they have made their burst for freedom in an abandoned spacecraft renamed *Liberator*, and now they wander the galaxy avoiding recapture, hell bent on sabotaging the activities of The Federation.

Blake, a natural-born leader, becomes a genuine freedom fighter, a hero in a corrupt universe. But even if he himself is a Robin Hood figure, his followers are far from merry men. His number two, computer genius Kerr Avon, is an ambitious, arrogant man, given only to preserving his own skin, while the safe-cracker, Vila, suffers from a broad yellow streak. There are also smuggler/pilot Jenna Stannis, Cally, a combative, telepathic native of the planet Auron, and the brawny Gan, who has an electronic limiter fitted to his brain to prevent him killing others. Although their well-being depends on mutual assistance, this is never a team, rather a collection of squabbling, selfish renegades thrown together by outside pressures.

The seventh member of the group is the *Liberator*'s master computer, Zen, but characters come and go during the programme's run and the composition of the Seven changes. Gone are Gan and Jenna when mercenary Del Tarrant and weapons expert Dayna Mellanby are added to the cast, with the beautiful blonde Soolin, a crack shot, joining later. Not even Blake is a fixture. He disappears at the end of the second series, to be replaced as leader by the stony-faced Avon. There are also new computers, Orac and, in *Scorpio* (a new spacecraft which replaces the destroyed *Liberator*), Slave. In pursuit of the rebels are Supreme Commander Servalan, icy and calculating, and her vicious henchman, Travis, whom Blake once blinded in one eye. Blake returns briefly, just long enough to be killed by Avon in the very last episode.

For all their efforts, the Seven only ever succeed in causing minor problems for The Federation. Their cause is a hopeless one, and a sense of futility pervades the series. Despite a lacklustre final season, when the budget had clearly been slashed, *Blake's 7* achieved cult status, not just in the UK but in America, too. Most of the regulars were reunited for a one-off Radio 4 special in 1998, but with Paula Wilcox providing the voice for Soolin and Angela Bruce playing Dayna.

Blanc, Mel
(1908–89)

Hollywood's most celebrated cartoon voicer, famous for the likes of Bugs Bunny, Daffy Duck, Sylvester, Tweety Pie, Woody Woodpecker, Porky Pig and Speedy Gonzales. His television voices included Barney Rubble and Dino in THE FLINTSTONES, Cosmo C. Spacely in THE JETSONS and Twiki the robot in BUCK ROGERS IN THE 25TH CENTURY. He actually appeared in vision with Jack Benny in the 1950s, playing Benny's violin teacher, Professor LeBlanc.

Bland, Sir Christopher
(1938–)

Successful businessman, one-time Conservative councillor and TV executive (Deputy Chairman of the IBA, Director of ITN and Chairman of LWT), who became the BBC's Chairman in 1996, on a five-year contract. He was replaced by his deputy, Gavyn Davies, in 2002. Bland represented Ireland at fencing in the 1960 Olympics.

Blankety Blank ✶

UK (BBC/Grundy) Game Show. BBC 1 1979–90; 1997–9; ITV 2001–2

Presenters **Terry Wogan, Les Dawson, Lily Savage**
Producers **Alan Boyd, Marcus Plantin, Stanley Appel, Dean Jones**

Contrived comic guessing game.

Considering its dire prizes and contrived format, *Blankety Blank* proved remarkably durable. It was undoubtedly established by the appeal of first host Terry Wogan (with his unusual, magic wand-like microphone), but it remained popular when Les Dawson took charge in 1984. What the four contestants (two sets of two) had to do was guess the missing word in a somewhat risqué statement read out by the host. To edge towards the prizes, their word had to match guesses made by a panel of six celebrities. The more matches made, the more points (circles or triangles) were accrued. With celebrity help (or hindrance), the winning contestant then had to complete a short, final phrase, hopefully matching it to a word selected in a public survey to win one of the prizes, which were staggeringly modest (Dawson once quipped, 'Some prizes are so bad, they're left in the foyer'). Losing contestants walked away with a *Blankety Blank* chequebook and pen. Of more interest to the viewer were the exchanges between the host and the celebrity panel, which deliberately overshadowed the main contest.

The show was revived for a Christmas special in 1997, with Lily Savage (Paul O'Grady) at the helm. A series followed in 1998, and a year later the title was changed to *Lily Savage's Blankety Blank*. The programme moved to ITV in 2001.

Bleak House [1] ★★★

UK (BBC) Drama. BBC 2 1985
DVD: BBC (Region 1 only)

Lady Honoria Dedlock	**Diana Rigg**
John Jarndyce	**Denholm Elliott**
Esther Summerson	**Rebecca Sebborn** *(young)*
	Suzanne Burden
Sir Leicester Dedlock	**Robin Bailey**
Richard Carstone	**Philip Franks**
Ada Clare	**Lucy Hornak**
Mr Tulkinghorn	**Peter Vaughan**
Grandfather Smallweed	**Charlie Drake**
Miss Flite	**Sylvia Coleridge**
Harold Skimpole	**T. P. McKenna**
Lord Chancellor	**Graham Crowden**
Krook	**Bernard Hepton**
Sgt George	**Dave King**
Jo	**Chris Pitt**
William Guppy	**Jonathan Moore**

Writer **Arthur Hopcraft**
Executive Producer **Jonathan Powell**
Producers **John Harris, Betty Willingale**

A young orphan witnesses legal and social corruption in 19th-century London.

Dickens's withering attack on the Victorian legal system was dramatized by Arthur Hopcraft in eight parts, with Ross Devenish directing and Geoffrey Burgon adding the soundtrack. The story concerns Esther Summerson, an orphan who is called to London to meet her guardian, John Jarndyce, for the first time. Also in the bachelor's care are young Richard Carstone and his cousin (later his wife) Ada Clare, wards of court in the notorious Jarndyce and Jarndyce legal case – a costly dispute that has been running for so long that it has become a laughing stock. They are awaiting their share of an estate that shows no signs of being settled, much to the benefit of profligate lawyers. Around this initial theme are constructed numerous eccentric characters and subplots, in typical Dickens fashion, not least the story of Lady Dedlock, who turns out to be Esther's real mother, and the efforts of the devious lawyer Tulkinghorn to expose her scandal. *Bleak House* had been previously dramatized in 1959 (BBC: Diana Fairfax as Esther, Colin Jeavons as Richard, Elizabeth Shepherd as Ada, Andrew Cruickshank as John Jarndyce, Iris Russell as Lady Dedlock, David Horne as Sir Leicester and John Phillips as Tulkinghorn). It was revived for television yet again in 2005, this time as a prime-time soap opera (see below).

Bleak House [2] ★★★★

UK (BBC) Drama. BBC 1 2005
DVD: BBC

Lady Honoria Dedlock	**Gillian Anderson**
Mr Tulkinghorn	**Charles Dance**
John Jarndyce	**Denis Lawson**
Esther Summerson	**Anna Maxwell Martin**
Chancellor	**Ian Richardson**
Sir Leicester Dedlock	**Timothy West**
Miss Flite	**Pauline Collins**
Mrs Rouncewell	**Anne Reid**
Snagsby	**Sean McGinley**
Clamb	**Tom Georgeson**
Mrs Jellyby	**Liza Tarbuck**
Caddy Jellyby	**Nathalie Press**
Harold Skimpole	**Nathaniel Parker**
Mrs Pardiggle	**Roberta Taylor**
Jenny	**Charlie Brooks**
Krook	**Johnny Vegas**
Mr Kenge	**Alistair McGowan**
Gridley	**Tony Haygarth**
Richard Carstone	**Patrick Kennedy**
Ada Clare	**Carey Mulligan**
William Guppy	**Burn Gorman**
Lawrence Boythorn	**Warren Clarke**
Nemo	**John Lynch**
Mr Bayham Badger	**Richard Griffiths**
Mrs Badger	**Joanna David**
Phil Squod	**Michael Smiley**
Smallweed	**Phil Davis**
Old Mr Turveydrop	**Matthew Kelly**
Prince Turveydrop	**Bryan Dick**
Hortense	**Lilo Baur**
Jo	**Harry Eden**
Allan Woodcote	**Richard Harrington**
Rose	**Emma Williams**
Bucket	**Alun Armstrong**
Sgt George	**Hugo Speer**
Mr Chadband	**Robert Pugh**
Mrs Chadband	**Catherine Tate**

Writer **Andrew Davies**
Producer **Nigel Stafford-Clark**

Contemporary treatment of the Dickens classic.

Dickens's brutal critique of the Victorian legal system (as described in the entry for the 1985 version above) found a new audience when the BBC decided to split it up into 15 half-hour episodes and run it twice weekly in prime time as a soap opera. A star-studded cast and the distinguished pen of Andrew Davies ensured the ambitious project was a triumph from start to finish.

Bleasdale, Alan

(1946–)

Liverpudlian playwright whose work has reflected social injustice through wry humour and sharp characterizations. His first TV play was *Early to Bed* in 1975, but it was his drama *The Black Stuff*, screened in 1980, which attracted more interest. With unemployment poised to soar in Britain, Bleasdale's skilful observation of a band of Scouse tarmac-layers, working away from home and hovering on the brink of the dole, gave more than a hint of his work to come. It ultimately led to a complete series, BOYS FROM THE BLACKSTUFF, a 1982 five-part sequel which explored the stresses life on the dole brought to its main characters, including the celebrated Yosser ('Gissa job') Hughes. Earlier, Bleasdale had rewritten the intended first episode of the series as the one-off play *The Muscle Market*. In 1984 he developed his own SCULLY novels (as first seen in a 1978 PLAY FOR TODAY) for Channel 4, creating a 'real world' teenage drama, before embarking on another controversial series for the BBC. This time it was THE MONOCLED MUTINEER, the four-part story of Percy Toplis, a World War I army rebel who was executed by the Secret Service. The Tory press was outraged. In 1991, back on Channel 4, Bleasdale turned his attention once more to Liverpool and the contrasting lifestyles of rising political star Michael Murray (Robert Lindsay) and gentle schoolteacher Jim Nelson (Michael Palin) in the much-acclaimed GBH. For the same channel he switched to production, offering a helping hand to aspiring writers in the four-part anthology *Alan Bleasdale Presents*, in 1994, and then wrote and produced *Jake's Progress* in 1995, a drama about family tensions starring Robert Lindsay again and Julie Walters (for whom Bleasdale had contributed material for a one-off showcase in 1991). *Melissa*, a murder-mystery inspired by the writings of Francis Durbridge, followed in 1997. In 1999, his adaptation of OLIVER TWIST was screened by ITV.

Bless Me, Father ✱✱

UK (LWT) Situation Comedy. ITV 1978–81
DVD: Acorn Media (Region 1 only)

Father Charles Duddleswell .... **Arthur Lowe**
Father Neil Boyd .... **Daniel Abineri**
Mrs Pring .... **Gabrielle Daye**
Bishop O'Reilly .... **Derek Francis**

Creator/Writer **Peter de Rosa**
Producer **David Askey**

● ***The misadventures of a hapless Catholic priest.***
Father Duddleswell is the Irish priest of St Jude's, a parish in the London suburb of Fairwater, some time in the early 1950s. Together with his newly ordained, bashful young colleague, Father Neil, he aims to bring hope, peace and order to the community, though even his best-laid plans are prone to failure. Storylines centre on the disasters that befall St Jude's (St Jude, not coincidentally, is the patron saint of lost causes), such as the time when crossed wires link the confession box to the church Tannoy system. Mrs Pring is the priest's housekeeper. The stories came from the pen of Peter de Rosa, himself a former priest who had previously written books under the name of Neil Boyd.

Bless This House ✱✱

UK (Thames) Situation Comedy. ITV 1971–4; 1976
DVD: Network

Sid Abbott .... **Sidney James**
Jean Abbott .... **Diana Coupland**
Mike Abbott .... **Robin Stewart**
Sally Abbott .... **Sally Geeson**
Trevor .... **Anthony Jackson**
Betty .... **Patsy Rowlands**

Creators **Vince Powell, Harry Driver**
Producer **William G. Stewart**

● ***Generation-gap comedy with a suburban family.***
Cheery, pipe-chewing Londoner Sid Abbott, a middle-aged stationery salesman, is fond of booze, women and football. He still considers himself one of the lads, but has little chance to prove it, as his long-suffering wife, Jean, is always around to keep him in check. They live in Birch Avenue, Putney, with their two teenage children, and this is where their real problems begin. Mike (trendily garbed in beads and Afghan coat) has just left art college and is far too busy protesting about this and that to find himself a job; with-it Sally, apple of her dad's eye, is in the final year of grammar school. Sadly their 1970s morals and vices are a touch too daring for their rather staid parents, who are constantly bemused at the permissive society and seldom fail to jump to the wrong conclusion. Trevor is Sid's next-door neighbour and drinking pal at the Hare and Hounds, with Betty his nagging wife.

A big ratings success, *Bless This House* numbered among its writers Carla Lane and its creators, Vince Powell and Harry Driver. Produced by future FIFTEEN TO ONE host William G. Stewart, it was Sid James's last major television series. Geoff Love wrote the theme music. A feature film version was issued in 1972.

Blessed, Brian

(1937–)

Large, Yorkshire-born actor, whose full-blooded performances have earned gentle mimicry. He first came to light in Z CARS, in which, as PC Fancy Smith, he was one of the original stars. Then, in 1966, he played Porthos in the BBC's adaptation of *The Three Musketeers*. In the 1970s and 1980s he was Augustus in I, CLAUDIUS, Mark of Cornwall in ARTHUR OF THE BRITONS and another 'historical' character, King Richard IV, in the first series of BLACKADDER. Blessed also played Basileos in *The Aphrodite Inheritance*, then proved to be a well-cast successor to Robert Newton in JOHN SILVER'S RETURN TO TREASURE ISLAND. Among his many other TV credits have been episodes of JUSTICE, HADLEIGH, PUBLIC EYE, *Churchill's People*, SPACE: 1999, THE SWEENEY, *Boy Dominic* (William Woodcock), TALES OF THE UNEXPECTED, MINDER, WAR AND REMEMBRANCE, *Kidnapped* (Cluny McPherson), *Enid Blyton's Castle of Adventure* (Sam), LADY CHATTERLEY, TOM JONES (Squire Western) and *Winter Solstice* (Max). He also provided the voice of the wild boar in *The Legend of the Tamworth Two*. In the footsteps of Hillary and Tensing, he fulfilled a long-held ambition by climbing Mount Everest in the early 1990s. He is married to actress Hildegard Neil.

Blethyn, Brenda

OBE (1946–)

Kent-born, Oscar-nominated actress seen in dramatic and comedy roles. She starred as Alison Little and Erica Parsons in the sitcoms CHANCE IN A MILLION and THE LABOURS OF ERICA, respectively; Shirley Frame in the comedy drama *All Good Things*; Margaret Amir in THE BUDDHA OF SUBURBIA; Miriam 'Mim' Dervish in OUTSIDE EDGE; Hazel Delany in *Between the Sheets*; and Jess Copplestone in *Belonging*. Other credits have included P. D. JAMES's *Death of an Expert Witness*, ALAS SMITH AND JONES, *That Uncertain Feeling* and *Screen One's The Bullion Boys*.

Bligh, Jasmine

(1913–91)

One of television's first personalities, Jasmine Bligh joined the BBC in 1935, becoming, together with Elizabeth Cowell and Leslie Mitchell, one of the three host-announcers for the Corporation's TV test transmissions. Her earlier experience as an actress stood her in good stead in those days before autocues, as she had to learn all her announcements word for word. Although television was suspended during World War II, Bligh returned to our screens to open up the new post-war service in 1946. After abandoning television work for a while, she returned to the BBC to narrate the *Noddy* series and she resurfaced yet again in the 1970s as presenter of Thames TV's daytime magazine, *Good Afternoon*. Jasmine Bligh was a descendant of Captain Bligh, of *Bounty* fame.

Blind Date ✳✳

UK (LWT) Game Show. ITV 1985–2003

Presenter **Cilla Black**

Producers **Gill Stribling-Wright, Kevin Roast, Michael Longmire, Thelma McGough, Chris O'Dell, Isobel Hatton, Martin Redman, Lee Connolly**

● ***Girls and guys select unseen partners for a prize trip.***

In this dating service of the air, young men and women selected a member of the opposite sex to join them on a 'blind date' excursion. Three unseen contestants delivered rehearsed answers to three scripted questions posed by a boy or girl looking for a date. On the strength of their answers, one was chosen to accompany the questioner on a special trip. This may have involved anything from a week on the Mediterranean to a day at a safari park, depending on their luck in drawing envelopes. The following week the blind daters returned to tell all about their experience and to give honest opinions about their unfortunate partners. Cilla Black egged them on. In 2002, despite a major revamp of the show in response to collapsing ratings, Cilla dropped a bombshell by announcing on a live edition that she intended to leave, an announcement that sounded the death knell for the series after 18 years.

The first couple to marry as a result of meeting on the programme were Sue Middleton and Alex Tatham. Their 1991 wedding was captured in a special programme entitled *Blind Date Wedding of the Year*. Actress Amanda Holden was once one of the show's contestants.

Blockbusters ✳✳

UK (Central) Quiz. ITV 1983–94; BBC 2 1997

Presenters **Bob Holness, Michael Aspel**

Producers **Graham C. Williams, Tony Wolfe, Terry Steel, Bob Cousins**

● ***Daily general-knowledge quiz for sixth-formers.***

In this easy-going contest, Bob Holness asked the questions and three 16- to 18-year-old students (two versus one) provided answers to light up hexagonal blocks on an electronic board. The team of two had to score a line of five blocks across a board to win a game, while the single contestant needed four in a row down the board. Each block selected bore the initial letter of the answer and much fun was had when contestants asked, 'Can I have a P please, Bob?' Money was awarded for every correct answer and matches consisted of the best of three games. The winning pupil (or one of the twosome) was then put on the 'hot spot'. He or she, by answering more questions, had to light up a path across the board in 60 seconds to win a prize. The hot-spot prizes increased in value with the more wins that were achieved, but five wins were the maximum for any contestant(s).

Blockbusters gained a cult following among schoolkids and adults alike, and the studio audience enthusiastically showed their support by hand-jiving to the rousing theme music. *Blockbusters* briefly returned to the screen in 1997 on BBC 2, with Michael Aspel in the chair aiming for a more mature audience. The series was exhumed once more in 2000 by Sky One, with Liza Tarbuck as host.

Blocker, Dan

(1928–72)

Massive American actor, fondly remembered as the gentle giant, Hoss Cartwright, in BONANZA, although he appeared in other earlier TV Westerns, including GUNSMOKE and *Cimarron City*. *Bonanza* lasted only one series after Blocker's untimely death.

Blood Money ✳✳

UK (BBC) Detective Drama. BBC 1 1981

Chief Supt. Meadows	**Bernard Hepton**
Capt. Percival	**Michael Denison**
Irene Kohl	**Juliet Hammond-Hill**
Rupert Fitzcharles	**Grant Ashley Warnock**
James Drew	**Stephen Yardley**
Danny Connors	**Gary Whelan**
Charles Vivian	**Cavan Kendall**
DI Perry	**Jack McKenzie**
Insp. Clark	**Daniel Hill**
WPSgt Barratt	**Anna Mottram**

Writer **Arden Winch**
Producer **Gerard Glaister**

● ***The son of a UN official is held to ransom.***

Shock waves ripple through diplomatic ranks when the young son of the Administrator General of the United Nations is kidnapped by a gang of German terrorists, headed by Irene Kohl. On their trail is Captain Percival of Special Intelligence, who has been called in to assist policeman Meadows in the search for the boy. Their painstaking efforts to retrieve him safe and well run through six episodes. Percival later resurfaces in the dramas SKORPION and COLD WARRIOR.

Bloody Sunday ✳✳✳

UK (January Films) Drama. ITV 1 2002
DVD: Cinema Club

Ivan Cooper	**James Nesbitt**
Kevin McCorry	**Allan Gildea**
Eamonn McCann	**Gerard Crossan**
Bernadette Devlin	**Mary Moulds**
Bridget Bond	**Carmel McCallion**
Major Gen. Ford	**Tim Pigott-Smith**

Brigadier MacLellan .... **Nicholas Farrell**
Major Steele .... **Chris Villiers**
Col. Tugwell .... **James Hewitt**
Gerry Donaghy .... **Declan Duddy**
Mary Donaghy .... **Joanne Lindsay**

Writer **Paul Greengrass**
Producer **Mark Redhead**

● ***A lawful protest march leads to one of the blackest days in Northern Irish history.***

'A love letter to the civil rights movement' was how producer Mark Redhead described this feature-length drama in the face of accusations of pro-IRA bias from critics who had never even seen the production. What *Bloody Sunday* set out to do, he said, was to be a vehicle for peace.

Writer/director Paul Greengrass's film tensely dramatizes the events of 30 January 1972, so-called Bloody Sunday, when 13 civil rights marchers were gunned down and 15 more wounded on the streets of Derry. Taking evidence from the Saville Inquiry into the tragedy, among other sources, it powerfully explores, using documentary techniques (hand-held cameras), how a planned protest against the Government's internment without trial policy in Northern Ireland spiralled out of control. It examines the day from both sides – from within the assembled ranks of marchers and from within the corps of paratroopers monitoring the event. Re-creating newsreel footage of the time, it sickeningly shows the chaos and gore following the shots that ring out from the army lines, leaving the viewer to judge where blame for the carnage should lie. Central to the day's events are local MP Ivan Cooper, one organizer of the march, Brigadier MacLellan, officer in charge of the Parachute Regiment, and General Ford, his superior.

Bloody Sunday was one of two dramas to recall the trauma of this bleak day. Eight days after its transmission on ITV 1 in January 2002, Channel 4 broadcast SUNDAY, scripted by Jimmy McGovern, directed by Charles McDougall and starring Christopher Eccleston as General Ford. While similarly acclaimed, this version of events focuses more on events before and after the tragedy, running from 1968 through to the Widgery Report into the tragedy that was published three months later, highlighting just what a recruitment bonus Bloody Sunday proved to be for the IRA.

Bloomin' Marvellous ✶

UK (DLT/Theatre of Comedy) Situation Comedy. BBC 1 1997–8

Jack Deakin .... **Clive Mantle**
Liz Deakin .... **Sarah Lancashire**
Shaz .... **Kathryn Hunt**
Jeff .... **Iain Rogerson**
Dad .... **David Hargreaves**
Mam .... **Judith Barker**
Doug .... **Tim Preece**

Creators/Writers **John Godber, Jane Thornton**
Producer **Sydney Lotterby**

● ***Mid-life crisis spurs a couple into starting a family.***

For successful York couple Jack and Liz Deakin things are progressing very nicely indeed, thank you – until 39-year-old Jack, a writer-in-residence at a university, suffers a brush with death and the couple's outlook on life dramatically changes. Suddenly they realize that Old Father Time is marching relentlessly forward and, if they want to have children, they'd better get a move on. Through this eight-part series, we share the joys of a drawn-out pregnancy, as the self-obsessed Jack worries where his life has gone and Liz, as practical as ever, tries to get on with the business of preparing for motherhood, leaving behind her career as a reporter with a local radio station. Shaz and Jeff are the friends they confide in, but their own marriage is on the rocks. The series was based on the real-life experience of husband and wife writers John Godber and Jane Thornton, who scripted episodes individually.

Blossom ✶

US (Impact Zone/Witt-Thomas/Touchstone) Situation Comedy. Channel 4 1992–5 (US: NBC 1991–5)

Blossom Russo .... **Mayim Bialik**
Nick Russo .... **Ted Wass**
Anthony Russo .... **Michael Stoyanov**
Joey Russo .... **Joey Lawrence**
Six Le Meure .... **Jenna Von Oÿ**
Buzz Richman .... **Barnard Hughes**
Vinnie Bonitardi .... **David Lascher**
Rhonda Jo Applegate .... **Portia Dawson**
Shelly Russo .... **Samaria Graham**
Carol .... **Finola Hughes**
Kennedy .... **Courtney Chase**

Creator **Don Reo**
Executive Producers **Gene Reynolds, Paul Junger Witt, Tony Thomas, Don Reo**

● ***A teenage girl tries to make sense of life in a dysfunctional family.***

Thirteen-year-old Blossom is the only female in a house full of men. She lives in Los Angeles with her divorced dad, Nick, a studio musician, and her two older brothers, the reformed substance-abuser Anthony and the dopey girl-fiend Joey. Though mature beyond her years, nevertheless Blossom has to deal with the usual teenage traumas of becoming a woman, dating, school, drugs, etc. She does so with the help of her video diary and her best friend, Six (so-named because she is the sixth child of her family). Vinnie is her rough and ready boyfriend. Also in the picture is lively grandad Buzz, trying to come to terms with his advancing years, plus assorted girlfriends for the boys, most notably Rhonda, who dates Anthony, and then Shelly, who becomes Anthony's wife. Dad Nick also finds romance when he weds single mother Carol, bringing six-year-old daughter Kennedy into the fold. Popular with teenage girls, who associated with the feisty lead character, *Blossom* was noted for its fantasy sequences, particularly in the earliest episodes. Stars like Sonny Bono, Estelle Getty and Rhea Perlman guested in some of Blossom's dreams.

Blott on the Landscape ✶✶

UK (BBC) Comedy Drama. BBC 2 1985
DVD: BBC

Sir Giles Lynchwood, MP .... **George Cole**
Lady Maud Lynchwood .... **Geraldine James**
Blott .... **David Suchet**
Mrs Forthby .... **Julia McKenzie**
Dundridge .... **Simon Cadell**
Ganglion .... **Geoffrey Bayldon**
Hoskins .... **Paul Brooke**
Densher .... **Jeremy Clyde**

Writer **Malcolm Bradbury**
Producer **Evgeny Gridneff**

● *An unscrupulous MP plans to build a motorway through his wife's ancestral home.*

Sir Giles Lynchwood is the Member of Parliament for South Worfordshire, a man with weird fetishes (which are indulged in extrovert sex sessions down in London) and a greedy desire to make more money. One of his plans is to direct a new motorway through the grounds of his wife's stately home, Handyman Hall, which is picturesquely set in Cleene Gorge. Rallying to its defence, the eccentric Lady Maud (a devotee of country sports) fights tooth and nail to preserve her home, assisted by her surreptitious gardener, Blott. Mrs Forthby is the housekeeper and Dundridge the hapless man from the ministry who ends up immersed in the murky goings-on.

This six-part series was an adaptation by Malcolm Bradbury of Tom Sharpe's black comic novel of the same name. Filming took place at Stanage Park, near Ludlow.

Blue Heaven ✶

UK (Fine Time) Situation Comedy. Channel 4 1994

Frank Sandford .... **Frank Skinner**
Roache .... **Conleth Hill**
Ivy Sandford .... **Paula Wilcox**
Jim Sandford .... **John Forgeham**

Writer **Frank Skinner**
Producer **Jo Sargent**

● *The frustrations of an aspiring musician in the West Midlands.*

Unemployed Brummie Frank is the singer in Blue Heaven, a musical duo he has formed with his mate, Roache, who plays keyboards. This six-part comedy follows their attempts to get a break in whichever way they can, which includes writing a song for Frank's beloved West Bromwich Albion FC. Hindering their progress are the likes of the DSS, rival musicians and Frank's own mum and dad, she an alcoholic, he a raging homophobe. This partly autobiographical series by stand-up comic Frank Skinner followed a pilot shown in 1992 as part of the *Bunch of Five* showcase for new comedies.

Blue Murder ✶✶

UK (Granada) Police Drama. ITV 1 2003–4
DVD: Granada

DCI Janine Lewis .... **Caroline Quentin**
DI Richard Mayne .... **Ian Kelsey**
DCS Hackett .... **David Schofield**
DS Butchers .... **Paul Loughran**
DS Shap .... **Nicholas Murchie**
Tom Lewis .... **Ceallach Spellman**
Pete Lewis .... **Joe Tucker**
Michael Lewis .... **Geoff Breton**
Eleanor Lewis .... **Catherine Jenkins**
Connie .... **Nina Fog**
Shaz Chowdhary .... **Sushil Chudasama**

Creator **Cath Staincliffe**
Writers **Cath Staincliffe, John Fay, Matthew Hall, Jeff Povey**
Executive Producer **Carolyn Reynolds**
Producer **Hugh Warren**

● *A single mum is also an ambitious high-ranking CID officer.*

Janine Lewis is a harassed mother who also happens to be an effective police officer. Despite battling to meet the domestic needs of kids Michael, Tom and Eleanor, she still finds time to chirpily rally her loyal troops and solve Manchester's most enigmatic crimes, even if her cynical, sexist boss, DCS Hackett, never seems totally happy with her performance. Richard Mayne is Janine's ambitious right-hand man, with whom she almost had a fling during their training days, and Shap and Butchers are the Plods, the former never afraid to bend the rules, the latter a by-the-book copper. At home, husband Pete is never the rock of support she needs, and, it turns out, has a wandering eye. This is Janine's life in the first outing of *Blue Murder*, a two-parter screened in 2003. By the time of the first four-episode series (aired a year later), Janine also has a new baby on her hands, and, although duplicitous Pete is still on the scene, he now wants a divorce.

This *Blue Murder* is unconnected with another ITV drama of the same title broadcast in February 2000, a feature-length thriller featuring a detective (Gary Mavers) encouraged by a scheming wife (Jemma Redgrave) to murder her obnoxious millionaire husband.

Blue Peter ✶✶✶

UK (BBC) Children's Magazine. BBC 1 1958–

Presenters **Leila Williams, Christopher Trace, Anita West, Valerie Singleton, John Noakes, Peter Purves, Lesley Judd, Simon Groom, Christopher Wenner, Tina Heath, Sarah Greene, Peter Duncan, Janet Ellis, Michael Sundin, Mark Curry, Caron Keating, Yvette Fielding, John Leslie, Diane-Louise Jordan, Anthea Turner, Tim Vincent, Stuart Miles, Katy Hill, Romana D'Annunzio, Richard Bacon, Konnie Huq, Simon Thomas, Matt Baker, Liz Barker, Zöe Salmon, Gethin Jones, Andy Akinwolere**

Creator **John Hunter Blair**
Producers/Editors **John Hunter Blair, Rosamund Davies, Clive Parkhurst, Biddy Baxter, Lewis Bronze, Oliver MacFarlane, Steve Hocking, Bridget Caldwell, Richard Marson**

● *Long-running children's magazine.*

Blue Peter is one programme most of Britain's thirty- and fortysomethings grew up with. It began as an idea of BBC producer John Hunter Blair in 1958 and was scheduled for a mere seven-week run, with each programme lasting just 15 minutes. Actor Christopher Trace and former Miss Great Britain Leila Williams were the first hosts and helped set the safe, middle-class tone which was to characterize the programme for years to come. From the outset the emphasis was on 'toys, model railways, games, stories, cartoons'. However, the golden age of *Blue Peter* was undoubtedly the mid-1960s, when, with the programme extended to a half-hour in length, and well entrenched in its Monday and Thursday teatime slots, its best-known trio of presenters were Valerie Singleton, John Noakes and Peter Purves.

Over the years, the programme's trademarks have been its unwhistlable hornpipe theme tune (entitled 'Barnacle Bill'), and its *Blue Peter* badges (bearing the ship logo devised by Tony Hart) for contributors. (There are five badges to be won: white with a blue ship for correspondents and participants in the programme; blue with a silver ship for contributing recipes or other new creations – if you've already won the first badge; green with a white ship for ecologically related letters; competition-winner badges; and the rare, much-coveted gold badge for extraordinary acts and achievements.) The running order has mixed together interviews with guests, chats to precocious kids with unusual hobbies, assorted competitions (design the UK's Christmas stamps was one), the daredevil exploits of the intrepid John Noakes and later Peter Duncan (both went on to star in their own spin-offs, *Go with Noakes* and *Duncan Dares*), and educational and historical inserts. In the early days, the illustrated tales of *Packi* (an elephant drawn, again, by Tony Hart), *Bengo*, a puppy, and space travellers *Bleep and Booster* (the last two sketched by William Timyn) were occasional features, and, for years, Percy Thrower looked after the *Blue Peter* garden. Chris Trace diligently cared for the elaborate *Blue Peter* train set, and rides on the programme's namesake steam engine, the 532 *Blue Peter*, have also been scheduled. A new-born baby became a regular visitor to the show in 1968. Daniel Scott became the *Blue Peter* Baby, allowing Noakes and Purves to make a complete hash of changing his nappy.

The programme's animals have shared equal billing with its human hosts. Among the most famous *Blue Peter* pets have been dogs Petra (who actually died after just one programme and was replaced by a lookalike for the rest of her days), Patch, Shep, Goldie, Bonnie and Mabel; Jason, the Siamese cat, and fellow felines Jack, Jill and Willow; Joey, the parrot; Honey, the guide dog, and Fred (later discovered to be Freda), the tortoise. Guest animals have proved particularly troublesome (especially as the show has always gone out live), with the chaos caused by Lulu, the defecating elephant, almost matched by a troupe of feuding St Bernards some years later.

Each year the pets have been packed off to the country for the summer while their masters have headed for exotic climes in the annual *Blue Peter* expedition. Places visited have included Ceylon (now Sri Lanka) and the USA. Each Christmas has been heralded by the lighting of the advent crown (made from two tinsel-lagged coat-hangers) and a blast from the Chalk Farm Salvation Army Band. Indeed, *Blue Peter*'s Heath Robinson creations like the advent crown have gone into folklore, primarily because of the imaginative use of egg cartons, used toilet-rolls, detergent bottles (Squeezy was never mentioned) and sticky-backed plastic (nor was Fablon). For many years, these were largely the ideas of Margaret Parnell. 'Here's one I made earlier' became a catchphrase.

Another annual feature has been the *Blue Peter* Appeal, raising funds for worthy causes, although not often by asking for money. Instead, used stamps, milk-bottle tops, paperback books, old wool, aluminium cans and other such recyclables have been collected and sold in bulk to bring in cash. Among the best-remembered appeals have been those for Guide Dogs for the Blind, inshore lifeboats (seven supplied to date), Biafran war victims, horse-riding centres for children with disabilities and equipment for children's hospitals and Romanian orphanages.

As well as the spin-off series mentioned above, another extra was the *Blue Peter Royal Safari to Africa* in 1971, in which Val accompanied HRH Princess Anne (the Princess Royal) into the Kenyan outback. It led to other *Blue Peter Special Assignments* for Val and allowed her to retire from the twice-weekly programme with grace. In 2000, the programme introduced the annual Blue Peter Book Awards, for children's literature. The Blue Peter Prom has offered a further cultural offshoot, aiming to introduce youngsters to classical music in the summer.

Nearly 50 years after making its debut, *Blue Peter* is still going strong. It survived a rumpus over presenter Janet Ellis's unmarried pregnancy (another of her children is singer Sophie Ellis-Bextor), the retirement of long-serving programme editor Biddy Baxter in 1988, and even the sacking of presenter Richard Bacon in 1998 for admitting cocaine abuse. A third weekly programme was added in 1995, with the schedule changed to Monday, Wednesday and Friday.

Blue Planet, The ★★★

UK (BBC/Discovery) Natural History. BBC 1 2001
DVD: BBC

Narrator **David Attenborough**

Producers **Alastair Fothergill, Andy Byatt, Martha Holmes**

● ***Stunningly photographed, ground-breaking survey of the sea and the creatures that call it home.***

While many films had been made about life beneath the waves, never had such a comprehensive study of marine creatures in their own habitat been produced before *The Blue Planet*. Costing £7 million, the eight-film project was the brainchild of producer Alastair Fothergill, who relinquished his role as head of the BBC's Natural History Unit to make the series. By exploring all types of ocean environment, from frozen wastes to tropical waters, numerous dramatic moments were captured: a killer whale pursuing a grey whale and cub, for instance; a polar bear capturing a beluga whale trapped beneath the ice; and turtles beaching in droves to lay their eggs. There was also a re-creation of a famous scene from THE TRIALS OF LIFE, in which a killer whale pounced on seal pups on a Patagonia beach. Cameramen bravely descended more than a mile below the waves to photograph creatures never or seldom seen before, like the angler fish or the fangtooth, yet, danger apart, *The Blue Planet* was also a trial of patience. Filming animals on land is difficult enough, even though you generally know where they can be found; filming creatures of the sea can be like seeking a needle in a haystack. David Attenborough voiced (and wrote some of) the commentary. Episodes were followed by a segment called *Making Waves*, in which the crew explained how certain sequences were shot. In 2004, highlights of the series were edited into a feature-length film called *Deep Blue*.

Blue Remembered Hills ★★★

UK (BBC) Drama. BBC 1 1979
DVD: BBC

Willie .... **Colin Welland**
Peter .... **Michael Elphick**
John Harris .... **Robin Ellis**
Raymond .... **John Bird**
Angela .... **Helen Mirren**
Audrey .... **Janine Duvitski**
Donald Duck .... **Colin Jeavons**

Writer **Dennis Potter**
Producer **Kenith Trodd**

● ***A group of children while away a wartime summer but tragedy lurks around the corner.***

This typically inventive Dennis Potter PLAY FOR TODAY cast adult actors in the roles of schoolchildren enjoying the summer holidays during World War II. The not-so-innocent kids (between Standards 1 and 2 – now known as Years 3 and 4) are podgy Willie, Peter (a bully), the hard but fair John, the stuttering Raymond (wearing a cowboy suit) and pram-pushing girls Angela and Audrey. Their long summer's day sees them looking for adventure, which they find in the killing of a squirrel, a move they immediately regret. They fool around in the woods, scrapping, telling fibs and tall stories, and hiding from a supposed Italian POW escapee. However, tragedy awaits petty arsonist Donald Duck, a boy whose own father is a prisoner in Japan and who is, for the other children, an object of derision. Brian Gibson directed the play which, from the accents, was apparently set in Dennis Potter's homeland of the Forest of Dean.

Blue Thunder ✶

US (Rastar/Columbia) Police Drama. BBC 1 1984 (US: ABC 1984)

Frank Chaney .... **James Farentino**
Clinton 'Jafo' Wonderlove .... **Dana Carvey**
Lyman 'Bubba' Kelsey .... **Bubba Smith**
Richard 'Ski' Butowski .... **Dick Butkus**
Capt. Ed Braddock .... **Sandy McPeak**
J. J. Douglas .... **Ann Cooper**

Executive Producer **Roy Huggins**
Producers **David Moessinger, Jeri Taylor, Donald A. Baer**

Thrills and spills with a powerful super-helicopter.
Blue Thunder is the secret weapon of the Astro Division of the Los Angeles police. Piloted by the headstrong, opinionated Frank Chaney, a Vietnam veteran, this high-tech chopper is capable of incredible speeds and is practically invulnerable. Deflecting machine-gun fire or slinking quietly across the sky in 'whisper mode', the black supercopter is also equipped with powerful weaponry of its own, plus night sensors and laser tracking facilities. It is able to listen in to conversations from 10,000 feet. Assisting Chaney is young computer genius Clinton Wonderlove, or 'Jafo' ('Just Another Frustrated Observer') as he hates being known (played by a pre-*Wayne's World* Dana Carvey), as well as two former gridiron footballers, Ski Butowski and Bubba Kelsey, who track *Blue Thunder* in a mobile support truck. Boss of the Blue Thunder Unit (assembled by APEX, a US government agency) is Captain Braddock. The series – which ran to only 11 episodes – was based on the 1983 cinema film of the same title and aired more or less at the same time as AIRWOLF, which was also inspired by the movie.

Bluebell ✶✶

UK (BBC) Drama. BBC 1 1986

Margaret Kelly/Leibovici
('Bluebell') .... **Carolyn Pickles**
Aunt Mary .... **Carmel McSharry**
Alfred Jackson .... **Ian Thompson**
Helen .... **Annie Lambert**
Marcel Leibovici .... **Philip Sayer**
Paul Derval .... **Michael N. Harbour**
Maurice Chevalier .... **Peter Reeves**
Tess .... **Gillian Winn**
Pierre .... **John Arnatt**
Mistinguett .... **Thelma Ruby**
Lucy .... **Miranda Coe**
Sister Mary .... **Margaret D'Arcy**
Kurt Burnitz .... **Peter Machin**
Guy .... **Anthony Herrick**
Lefebre .... **Alan Downer**
Mme Reynard .... **Ann Heffernan**

Writer **Paul Wheeler**
Executive Producer **Richard Bates**
Producer **Brian Spiby**

An Irish orphan forms the world's leading dance troupe.
A biopic in eight parts, directed by Moira Armstrong, *Bluebell* tells the rags to riches story of Margaret Kelly, a Dublin-born orphan who became one of the most famous dancers in the world. Raised by her Aunt Mary in Liverpool during the depressed 1920s, the sickly Kelly is encouraged to dance by a doctor, to strengthen her feeble limbs. She becomes so proficient that, by the age of 14, she is part of a Scottish dance troupe, the Hot Jocks. A year later, she is touring Europe and then becomes captain of the Alfred Jackson Girls, a dance company performing at Paris's famous Folies Bergère. When the troupe is sacked, Kelly ('Miss Bluebell') forms her own unit, calling them the Bluebell Girls after her own childhood nickname. They take Europe by storm but their success is curtailed by the outbreak of World War II. Kelly is interned in France as an alien. Her Jewish husband, Marcel Leibovici, is taken to a concentration camp, but escapes. Margaret then keeps him in hiding for two years. She is convinced that the Germans will never win the war, but their lives are constantly in danger. Music was provided by Ilona Sekacz.

Bo' Selecta! ✶✶

UK (Talkback) Comedy. Channel 4 2002–3
DVD: Channel 4

Avid Merrion .... **Leigh Francis**

Executive Producer **Phil Clarke**
Producer **Spencer Millman**

An obsessive superfan reports from the world of celebrity.
Each week, from his grubby bedroom, Avid Merrion brings the world up to date with all the latest news and gossip from the showbiz world. But Merrion, a sad, quirky guy with a Scandinavian accent and a crude line in humour, is not merely content to talk about his heroes. He also sets out to stalk the big names. The celebrities themselves – Britney Spears, the Osbournes, Michael Jackson and others – he portrays as grotesque caricatures, complete with funny wigs, glasses and rubber chins. Supporting Merrion is a puppet bear interviewer whose excitement in the presence of greatness tends to show rather too obviously at times. The creation of Yorkshireman Leigh Francis, Merrion first came to light in *Big Brother's Little Brother*, an E4 support show to the Channel 4 reality show (winning BIG BROTHER contestant Craig Phillips was later seen locked up in Merrion's cupboard in *Bo' Selecta!*). The programme's title is taken from the title of the first hit for Craig David (another victim), 'Re-Rewind The Crowd Say Bo Selecta'. Highlights of the first series were shown under the title of *Proper Bo' Selecta* and a Christmas special was produced in 2003 called *Ho Ho Ho Selecta!*. The same Christmas, a spin-off single called 'Proper Crimbo' reached the UK Top Five.

Boat, The ✶✶✶

Germany (Bavaria Atelier) War Drama. BBC 2 1984
DVD: Columbia Tristar

Captain .... **Jürgen Prochnow**
Lt. Werner .... **Herbert Grönemeyer**
Chief Engineer .... **Klaus Wenneman**
1st Lieutenant .... **Hubertus Bengsch**
2nd Lieutenant .... **Martin Semmelrogge**
Bridge Officer .... **Bernd Tauber**
Ullman .... **Martin May**
Johann .... **Erwin Leder**

Writer **Wolfgang Petersen**
Producer **Günter Rohrbach**

A German U-boat crew fight for survival during World War II.

Subtitled in English, writer/director Wolfgang Petersen's German film (*Das Boot*) about a Nazi submarine patrol won many plaudits for its uncompromising grimness and the way in which it portrayed the nightmare of war below the sea. The drama unfolds over six episodes, starting in autumn 1941 with the noisy last night of shore leave for the crew of U-boat U-96, which is about to join the 'wolf packs' attacking Allied supply ships in the North Atlantic. It turns out to be a mission from hell as the submariners face attacks themselves from destroyers and end up claustrophobically stranded on the seabed with their air supplies running out. Monitoring the trauma is war reporter Lt. Werner, assigned to report on life with a U-boat crew, and quickly growing to realize that it is anything but romantic. The series – noted for humanizing Germans in ways not often seen in wartime dramas – was expanded from Petersen's Oscar-nominated 1981 film of the same name, which, in turn, was based on the novel *Das Boot* by Lothar-Günther Buchheim. Music was by Klaus Doldinger.

Bob and Rose ✶✶

UK (Red) Comedy Drama. ITV 1 2001
DVD: Carlton

Bob Gossage	**Alan Davies**
Rose Cooper	**Lesley Sharp**
Andy Lewis	**Daniel Ryan**
Holly Vance	**Jessica Stevenson**
Carol Cooper	**Barbara Marten**
Trevor Gadds	**Dave Hill**
Dean Gadds	**Christopher Fountain**
Janet Blane	**Carla Henry**
Anita Kendrick	**Katy Cavanagh**
Carl Smith	**Michael Begley**
Monica Gossage	**Penelope Wilton**
William Gossage	**John Woodvine**
Marina Marquess	**Siobhan Finneran**

Creator/Writer **Russell T. Davies**
Executive Producer **Nicola Shindler**
Producer **Ann Harrison-Baxter**

A gay man falls in love with a woman, much to his great surprise.

Rose Cooper lives at home with her mum, Carol. However, with Carol's oily boyfriend, Trevor, looking to move in, the pressure is on for her to move out. If only her boyfriend, Andy, could summon up the courage to propose, it would be the perfect solution for them all. However, things take an unexpected turn when Rose bumps into single teacher Bob Gossage in the street one night. They strike up an immediate friendship, which grows into a relationship that shocks Bob, who is an out-of-the-closet homosexual. What follows is a humorous six-part drama that explores the stresses and strains of their relationship, and the stresses and strains within Bob's own sexuality. At first, Bob and Rose attempt to keep their affair under wraps, but they are eventually forced to reveal all to the world. This inspires jealous attempts to break them up by friend Holly Vance, who tries to involve the confused Andy, as well as Bob's ex, Carl Smith. The series, shot in Manchester, was a much softer option than writer Russell T. Davies's earlier TV hit: Channel 4's QUEER AS FOLK. Davies revealed the story was based on real-life events concerning friends of his own.

Bob Martin ✶✶

UK (Granada) Situation Comedy. ITV 2000–1

Bob Martin	**Michael Barrymore**
Greg	**Denis Lawson**
Vinnie	**Keith Allen**
Timmy	**Marshall Lancaster**
Beverley Jordan	**Tracy-Ann Oberman**
Paula	**Deborah Grant**
Jean	**Valerie Holliman**

Writers/Producers **Bob Mills, Jeff Pope**
Executive Producer **Andy Harries**

A game show host is desperate to make the big time.

Bob Martin is a TV presenter hovering unhappily on the fringe of the celebrity B-list. His misplaced ambition is to make that vital breakthrough into stardom, by hatching unrealistic schemes to take over the Eurovision Song Contest from Terry Wogan or winning a major award for his quiz series, *Quickfire*. Sadly, the self-doubts and social inadequacies that plague the man, as well as his obvious lack of star quality, tend to inhibit his success. Coiffured and camp Greg is Bob's smooth-talking Scottish producer and unscrupulous womanizer Vinnie is the show's equally ambitious warm-up comedian and gag writer. Other members of the *Quickfire* team include geeky researcher Timmy and celebrity booker Beverley. Paula is Bob's man-eating agent. Guest stars who feature, playing exaggerated versions of themselves, include Anthea Turner, Paul Ross, Amanda Donohoe, Clive Anderson, Dani Behr, Lynda Bellingham, Michael Aspel, Stephen Fry and Jimmy Savile.

With an echo of THE LARRY SANDERS SHOW in its exposé of two faces of showbiz (smarmy on-screen and ruthless off it), the critically acclaimed *Bob Martin* ran for two series of six programmes, shortly before star Michael Barrymore's personal life became the subject of countless tabloid headlines and his career's consequent nose dive.

Bob the Builder ✶✶

UK (HIT) Children's Entertainment. BBC 1 1999–2005
DVD: HIT Entertainment

Voices:

Bob	**Neil Morrissey**
Wendy	**Kate Harbour**

Creator **Keith Chapman**
Executive Producers **Theresa Plummer-Andrews, Kate Fawkes**
Producer **Jackie Cockle**

The adventures of a versatile builder and his machine team.

'Can we fix it?' 'Yes we can.' The wholesome stories of builder Bob and his team proved an instant hit with younger viewers, the punchy theme song climbing to the top of the UK record charts at Christmas 2000 (soon followed by another number one for Bob with a version of 'Mambo No. 5'). Sales of the programme quickly followed all over the world (to more than 100 countries). Bob, dressed in checked shirt, practical dungarees, tool belt and yellow hard hat, is assisted in his many jobs in and around Bobsville by pony-tailed, blue-hatted business partner Wendy and a crew of talking vehicles and machinery. Scoop is the yellow digger and chief piece of kit, Muck the red dumper truck, Dizzy the orange cement mixer, Lofty the blue nervous crane and Roley the green steamroller. Much work is done for locals like Mr Bentley (the local council official), Mr

Beasley, Mrs Broadbent, Mrs Potts or Farmer Pickles, whose tractor, Travis, also lends a hand and whose mischievous scarecrow, Spud, delights in causing havoc where possible. Pilchard is Bob's cat and there's also Bird, who whistles to communicate with the machines. J. J., Molly, Skip and Trix are later additions to Bob's world. The emphasis throughout is on getting jobs done through co-operation (the series was devised with a positive pro-social message). The models are animated by HOT Animation, and in addition to Neil Morrissey and Kate Harbour, other voices are provided by Rob Rackstraw. One famous guest voicer was Chris Evans, who provided vocals for a bespectacled, ginger-haired rock star named Lenny Lazenby. He returned in a 2001 Christmas special, which also featured Elton John and Noddy Holder. An Easter special in 2004, *The Knights of Can-a-Lot*, featured the guest voices of June Whitfield and Richard Briers as Bob's mum and dad. In 2005, the series was retitled *Bob the Builder: Project: Built It!* and saw Bob and his gang building an eco-friendly town in Sunflower Valley, the countryside area in which he grew up.

Bochco, Steven

(1943–)

After a chequered career writing and producing shows like COLUMBO, MCMILLAN AND WIFE, THE SIX MILLION DOLLAR MAN, *Griff* and *Delvecchio*, Steven Bochco's career took a sharp upturn when he created HILL STREET BLUES. Although his next series, *Bay City Blues*, was a flop, he then bounced back with LA LAW. Setting a new style for TV drama in these series (ensemble casts, continuing storylines, awkward topics, etc.), he earned himself a prestigious contract with ABC, for whom he went on to develop HOOPERMAN, the less successful DOOGIE HOWSER, MD and COP ROCK, which attempted to combine pop songs with police action. Enjoying far greater acclaim was his next offering, NYPD BLUE, topped yet again by the groundbreaking MURDER ONE. Later productions like *Public Morals, Brooklyn South, Total Security, City of Angels, Philly, Commander in Chief, Blind Justice* and *Over There* proved less successful. Bochco's wife, Barbara Bosson, has been seen in many of his productions.

Bod ✶

UK (Bodfilms) Animation. BBC 1 1975–6
DVD: Contender

Narrators **John Le Mesurier, Maggie Henderson**

Writer/Producer **Michael Cole**

The simple world of a simple cartoon creation.

'Here comes Bod,' declares John Le Mesurier – and that is effectively it, for nothing particularly eventful happens in the life of this serene, hairless cartoon character in a yellow dress. There are only four other people in Bod's world: Aunt Flo, PC Copper, Frank the Postman and Farmer Barleymow, and they add little to the excitement. The odd moment of surrealism lifts affairs, but this is minimalist TV in both subject and execution, yet no less fondly remembered for that. Derek Griffiths provides the jazzy music. Bod's five-minute adventures were packaged up with those of Alberto Frog and his Amazing Animal Band (whose main concerns were music and milkshakes) for WATCH WITH MOTHER presentations.

Bodyguards ✶✶

UK (Zenith/Carlton) Drama. ITV 1997

DI Liz Shaw .... **Louise Lombard**
DI Ian Worrell .... **Sean Pertwee**
Commander Alan Macintyre .. **John Shrapnel**
Robert Ferguson .... **Pip Torrens**

Creator **Jeffrey Caine**
Writers **Jeffrey Caine, Julian Jones, Steve Griffiths**
Producer **Nigel Stafford-Clark**

A crack police squad put their lives on the line to protect VIPs.

After a spate of security lapses, the Government decides it needs to establish a specialist police squad to protect prominent figures, be they from the world of politics, business, royalty or celebrity. Step forward the Close Protection Group (CPG). In the pilot episode, screened at Easter 1996, former Special Branch agent Liz Shaw, ex-fighter pilot Ian Worrell and their chief, Alan Macintyre, are charged with the security of two competing candidates for the presidency of an African republic during an international governmental conference. In the six-episode series proper (starting a year later), the trio take on clients as varied as threatened witnesses and an author in danger of assassination from Islamic militants. This all-action, stunt-filled adventure series was created by Jeffrey Caine, who co-scripted the Bond film *Goldeneye* and had previously created THE CHIEF.

Bognor ✶

UK (Thames) Adventure. ITV 1981

Simon Bognor .... **David Horovitch**
Monica .... **Joanna McCallum**
Parkinson .... **Ewan Roberts**
Lingard .... **Tim Meats**

Executive Producer **John Frankau**
Producer **Bernard Krichefski**

The low-key investigations of a Department of Trade agent.

This short-lived, twice-weekly series centred on the Special Investigations Department of the Board of Trade (SIDBOT) and, in particular, its rather hapless functionary, Bognor. Under orders from his superior, Parkinson, and with the help of his assistant, Monica, the amiable hero delves into such crimes as the theft by Communists of a secret formula for honey, the death of the gossip columnist (Samuel Pepys) of the *Daily Globe* and some shady goings-on at a dog show. Played light-heartedly, it was based on the books by Tim Heald. A year later, Bognor resurfaced in a three-part mini-series entitled *Just Desserts*, in which he suffers a dining out allergy while investigating corruption in the restaurant trade. The theme music was written by Mike Steer.

Boht, Jean

(1936–)

Although synonymous now with the long-suffering Nellie Boswell in the dole sitcom BREAD, Jean Boht's television career has stretched over programmes like MR ROSE, THE SWEENEY, JULIET BRAVO, SPYSHIP and the Alan Bleasdale dramas BOYS FROM THE BLACKSTUFF and SCULLY (Gran). She also appeared in I WOKE UP ONE MORNING, *The Cloning of Joanna May* and the unsuccessful BRIGHTON BELLES, the UK translation of THE GOLDEN GIRLS (Josephine). More recent credits have come in small parts in DOCTORS, HOLBY CITY and THE BILL. She is married to composer Carl Davis.

Bolam, James

(1938–)

Sunderland-born actor/comedian, one of TV's LIKELY LADS (Terry Collier) in the 1960s and 1970s, but enjoying a varied TV career since those days. He gained a new following as Jack Ford in WHEN THE BOAT COMES IN, appeared in the BBC TELEVISION SHAKESPEARE production of *As You Like It* and played nosy schoolteacher Trevor Chaplin in THE BEIDERBECKE AFFAIR and its sequels. Not abandoning comedy, he has taken the roles of Roy Figgis in ONLY WHEN I LAUGH, Nesbitt Gunn in *Room at the Bottom*, Father Matthew in *Father Matthew's Daughter*, Bill MacGregor in SECOND THOUGHTS and Ted Whitehead in the one-off *Eleven Men against Eleven*. He also played the lead in ANDY CAPP and over the years has been seen in programmes like TAKE THREE GIRLS, THE PROTECTORS, EXECUTIVE STRESS, *Sticky Wickets, Have Your Cake and Eat It* (Nat Oliver), *The Missing Postman* (Clive Peacock), *The Stalker's Apprentice* (serial killer Helmut Kranze), MIDSOMER MURDERS, *Dirty Tricks* (Insp. Moss), CLOSE AND TRUE (Graham True), *Pay and Display* (Sydney), *Shipman* (Harold Shipman), DALZIEL AND PASCOE, BORN AND BRED (Arthur Gilder), NEW TRICKS (Jack Halford), HE KNEW HE WAS RIGHT (Mr Crump) and *The Afternoon Play*. He is married to actress Susan Jameson.

Bomber Harris ✶✶

UK (BBC) Historical Drama. BBC 2 1989
DVD: DD Home Entertainment

Sir Arthur Harris .... **John Thaw**
Winston Churchill .... **Robert Hardy**
Sir Charles Portal .... **Frederick Treves**
Air Marshal Sir Robert Saundby .... **Bernard Kay**
Wing Commander Harry Weldon .... **John Nettleton**
Jillie Harris .... **Sophie Thompson**
Magnus Spence .... **Roy Spencer**

Writer **Don Shaw**
Producer **Innes Lloyd**

● ***Biopic of the senior RAF officer who advocated area bombing of Nazi Germany.***

Five years after the death of Sir Arthur 'Bomber' Harris, BBC 2 screened this feature-length drama highlighting his role during World War II. As commander-in-chief of Bomber Command 1942–5, Harris was a controversial figure, the architect of the mass bombing of industrial areas, which he considered an effective means to end the conflict. Whereas precision bombing of specific targets had been the RAF's previous strategy, now whole cities entered the equation, as a way of lowering German morale and wiping out the economic base. With innocent people suffering as a result, the policy drew much criticism. Nevertheless, Harris maintained the support of premier Winston Churchill and the respect of those who served under his command. The play was directed by Michael Darlow.

Bonanza ✶✶✶

US (NBC) Western. ITV 1960–73 (US: NBC 1959–73)
DVD: Classic Entertainment

Ben Cartwright .... **Lorne Greene**
Little Joe Cartwright .... **Michael Landon**
Eric 'Hoss' Cartwright .... **Dan Blocker**
Adam Cartwright .... **Pernell Roberts**
Hop Sing .... **Victor Sen Yung**
Sheriff Roy Coffee .... **Ray Teal**
Mr Canaday ('Candy') .... **David Canary**
Dusty Rhoades .... **Lou Frizzel**
Jamie Hunter .... **Mitch Vogel**
Griff King .... **Tim Matheson**

Creator/Producer **David Dortort**

● ***The adventures of an all-male ranching family in the 1860s.***

This hugely successful Western opens with a pounding theme song and a map which bursts into flames. It is the story of the Cartwright family, owners of the 1,000-square-mile Ponderosa ranch, set on the edge of Virginia City, Nevada. Head of the family is father Ben, and he is ably supported by his three sons, all from different, deceased mothers. The pensive (and eldest) one is Adam, then comes slow-witted, 21-stone Hoss who, for all his bulk, can be as meek as a kitten. (The name 'Hoss' means 'good luck' in Norwegian and is a tribute to his Scandinavian mother, who was killed by Indians.) The third son is Little Joe, an impetuous lad with an eye for the girls. The Cartwrights' kitchen is looked after by Chinese cook Hop Sing.

The series revolves around the family's encounters with the dregs of society, their own self-preservation and the help they give to others. There are many guest stars throughout its run, but also a few cast changes. Pernell Roberts left the show after six years and was not replaced for a couple of seasons. Then along comes Candy, to work as a ranch hand. One of Ben's friends, Dusty Rhoades, is taken on when Candy temporarily moves away, and also seen is orphaned teenager Jamie Hunter. But the series was dealt a mortal blow by the sudden death of actor Dan Blocker in 1972 and, when Lorne Greene suffered a mild heart attack a few months later, the end of the series was in sight. By then *Bonanza* had been a Sunday night favourite in the USA for 14 years. Some time later, three sequel movies were produced, featuring descendants of the Cartwright clan: *Bonanza: the Next Generation* (1988), *Bonanza: the Return* (1993) and *Bonanza: Under Attack* (1995).

Bond, Jennie

(1950–)

Hertfordshire-born BBC journalist and newsreader who became the Corporation's royal correspondent in 1989, covering such major stories as the deaths of Princess Diana and the Queen Mother, and the Queen's Golden Jubilee. Previously, Bond was a local newspaper reporter and then a producer and news correspondent for the BBC. Since leaving BBC News in 2003, Bond has presented *Jennie Bond's Royals* for five and introduced the game show *Cash in the Attic*. She is married to journalist/broadcaster Jim Keltz.

Bond, Julian
(1930–)

British dramatist and producer, contributor to THE SAINT and UPSTAIRS, DOWNSTAIRS, and creator of POLICE SURGEON (the series that led to THE AVENGERS). His later TV successes included *A Man of Our Times, The Ferryman* (for the *Haunted* anthology), DICK BARTON – SPECIAL AGENT (with Clive Exton), *Love for Lydia, Fair Stood the Wind for France*, STRANGERS AND BROTHERS, episodes of OUT OF THIS WORLD, TALES OF THE UNEXPECTED, THE DUCHESS OF DUKE STREET, WINGS, and THE RUTH RENDELL MYSTERIES, and the Channel 4 adaptation of THE FAR PAVILIONS.

Bond, Samantha
(1962–)

British actress (James Bond's Miss Moneypenny in the cinema) noted for TV roles such as Mary Mackenzie in THE GINGER TREE, Liz Probert in RUMPOLE OF THE BAILEY, Bridget Mordaunt in CATHERINE COOKSON'S *The Black Candle*, Sarah Baylis in *Tears before Bedtime*, Isabel in *Family Money*, Patricia Whitton in *The Hunt*, DS Maureen Picasso in NCS MANHUNT, Lisa Shore in *Distant Shores* and Kate Donovan in DONOVAN. She has been seen also in *Mansfield Park*, AGATHA CHRISTIE'S POIROT, INSPECTOR MORSE, THE BILL, KAVANAGH QC, MIDSOMER MURDERS, CANTERBURY TALES and P. D. JAMES. Her father is actor Philip Bond, her sister is actress Abigail Bond and her late mother was THE BILL producer Pat Sandys.

Bonehead ✱

UK (BBC) Children's Comedy. BBC 1960–2

Bonehead .... **Colin Douglas**
Boss .... **Paul Whitsun-Jones**
Happy .... **Douglas Blackwell**

Creator/Writer/Producer **Shaun Sutton**

● ***Three inept crooks prove that crime doesn't pay.***

Bonehead introduced kids to three of the most incompetent villains ever seen on television. Head of the trio is bulky, gangster-like Boss, deviser of great plans which always end in failure; also in the team is the ironically named Happy. However, it is the dim-witted Bonehead, a lovable imbecile, who is the show's nominal star. Two seasons were made, before actor Colin Douglas moved on to more sensible dramas, like A FAMILY AT WAR.

Boney ✱

Australia (Norfolk International) Police Drama. ITV 1975

DI Napoleon Bonaparte
('Boney') .... **James Laurenson**

Executive Producers **Bob Austin, Lee Robinson**
Producer **John McCallum**

● ***The cases of an Aborigine detective.***

Although a white man 'coloured up', New Zealander James Laurenson took the lead in this popular series about an Aborigine police detective whose beat is the Australian bush. It shouldn't be the busiest patch for crime, but Boney finds plenty to keep him occupied among the farmers, prospectors and drifters of the outback. The series was based on the novels by Arthur Upfield.

Bonjour La Classe ✱

UK (Talkback) Situation Comedy. BBC 1 1993

Laurence Didcott .... **Nigel Planer**
Donald Halifax .... **Peter Woodthorpe**
Jean Halifax .... **Polly Adams**
Leslie Piper .... **Nicholas Woodeson**
Eric Sweety .... **David Troughton**
Harriet Humphrey .... **Victoria Carling**
Gilbert Herring .... **Robert Gillespie**
Mr Leonard Wigley .... **Timothy Bateson**
Adam Huntley .... **Bryan Dick**
Lucy Cornwell .... **Rebecca Callard**
Clive Crotty .... **David Larkin**
Hugo Botney .... **Daniel Newman**
Anthony Zalacosta .... **Simeon Pearl**
Pamela .... **Camilla Power**

Writers **Paul Smith, Terry Kyan**
Producer **Jamie Rix**

● ***An idealistic and over-enthusiastic teacher brings chaos to his new school.***

Hapless Laurence Didcott joins the French department of the fee-paying Mansion School where his acute keenness to improve and impress are quite unreciprocated. However, oblivious to the apathy and cynicism that grip the staffroom, he presses on with boundless energy in imaginative classroom and extracurricular activities, usually with disastrous consequences. The ingenuous Didcott ploughs a lone furrow, teased and tricked by his unruly pupils and viewed as a crank by his fellow teachers, including his boss, Donald Halifax, the grouchy Head of Modern Languages, whose wife, Jean, is school secretary. Eric Sweety is the sports and science master, resigned to the impossibilities of school life; vain, effeminate Gilbert Herring is the Head of Music; and Harriet Humphrey is the drama mistress. The ambitious but ineffectual headmaster, Leslie Piper, concerns himself more with perpetuating his own name through projects like the Piper Arts Centre than with improving teaching standards, leaving real control of the 235-year-old public school in the hands of the tyrannical bursar, Mr Wigley.

Bonneville, Hugh
(1963–)

British actor, often cast in upper-class roles and prominent in such dramas as *Breakout* (Peter Schneider), *The Man Who Made Husbands Jealous* (Ferdinand Fitzgerald), TAKE A GIRL LIKE YOU (Julian Ormerod), THE CAZALETS (Hugh Cazalet), *Madame Bovary* (Charles Bovary), MOSLEY (Robert Boothby), *Armadillo* (Torquil Helvoir-Jayne), THE GATHERING STORM (Ivo Pettifer), TIPPING THE VELVET (Ralph Banner), DANIEL DERONDA (Henleigh Grandcourt), DOCTOR ZHIVAGO (Andrey Zhivago), *Hear the Silence* (Dr Andrew Wakefield) and *The Robinsons* (George Robinson). Bonneville played Wren in *Wren – the Man Who Built Britain* and provided the voice of the adult Ben Trotter in *The Rotters Club*. Other appearances have come in programmes like BETWEEN THE LINES, CHANCER, *Stalag Luft, The Scold's Bridle, Heat of the Sun*, BUGS, CADFAEL, THE MEMOIRS OF SHERLOCK HOLMES, MIDSOMER MURDERS and THE COMMANDER, as well as comedies such as HOLDING THE BABY (Gordon Muir), GET WELL SOON (Norman Tucker), MARRIED

FOR LIFE (Steve Hollingsworth), SEE YOU FRIDAY (Daniel) and MURDER MOST HORRID.

Boom

An extendible, manoeuvrable arm holding a microphone which may be positioned, out of shot, over actors' and presenters' heads to pick up voices.

Boon ✳✳

UK (Central) Comedy Drama. ITV 1986–92
DVD: Network

Ken Boon .... **Michael Elphick**
Harry Crawford .... **David Daker**
Doreen Evans .... **Rachel Davies**
Ethel Allard .... **Joan Scott**
Rocky Cassidy .... **Neil Morrissey**
Debbie Yates .... **Lesley-Anne Sharpe**
Laura Marsh .... **Elizabeth Carling**
Alex Wilton .... **Saskia Wickham**

Creators **Jim Hill, Bill Stair**
Executive Producers **Ted Childs, William Smethurst**
Producers **Kenny McBain, Esta Charkham, Michele Buck, Simon Lewis**

● ***A kind-hearted fireman becomes a freelance troubleshooter.***

When Ken Boon is forced to leave the fire service on grounds of ill-health (he has damaged his lungs in a heroic rescue), he struggles to make ends meet. After a succession of failed money-making schemes, including a disastrous market-gardening venture, he places an ad in the local press. It reads: 'Ex-fireman seeks interesting work – anything legal considered.' In response he is offered a variety of strange jobs, from child-minding to private detective work, not all of them, as he hopes, strictly legal. But the stocky, lugubrious Boon, with his heart of gold, is a soft touch, committed to his work and unhappy about letting down employers. His early associates are Doreen Evans and Ethel Allard.

Boon considers himself an urban cowboy, cruising the streets of the Midlands on his silver charger, a 650-c.c. BSA Norton motorbike, which he calls 'White Lightning'. He soon makes his hobby his business by opening a courier agency, The Texas Rangers, and employing a dopey biker by the name of Rocky Cassidy as his sidekick, and teenager Debbie Yates as his secretary. Ken's best friend is fireman-turned-hotelier Harry Crawford, a businessman of little brain who moves from premises to premises, trading up, until he finally goes bust as owner of a country house hotel. Ken, who is by this time working as a private eye with Rocky and a new secretary, Laura Marsh, agrees to join Harry in a new venture, Crawford Boon Security. Laura is later replaced by the resourceful Alex Wilton.

Although the series ended in 1992, one episode remained untransmitted until 1995. The show's theme song, 'Hi Ho Silver', by Jim Diamond, was a UK top five hit in 1986.

Boone, Richard

(1917–81)

American actor, a hit in the roles of hired gun Paladin in HAVE GUN WILL TRAVEL and Wild West detective HEC RAMSEY. His lesser successes included *Medic* and an anthology, *The Richard Boone Show*, both largely confined to US TV. Like singer Pat Boone, Richard Boone was a descendant of frontiersman Daniel Boone.

Boots and Saddles ✳

US (California National) Western. BBC 1958–60 (US: Syndicated 1957–9)

Capt. Shank Adams .... **Jack Pickard**
Lt. Col. Hayes .... **Patrick McVey**
Lt. Kelly .... **Gardner McKay**
Lt. Binning .... **David Willock**
Sgt Bullock .... **John Alderson**
Luke Cummings .... **Michael Hinn**

Creators **Robert A. Cinader**
Producers **George M. Cahan, Robert Stillman**

● ***Cavalry patrols in the Wild West.***

Subtitled *The Story of the Fifth Cavalry*, *Boots and Saddles* tells of brave uniformed men tackling Indians and other 'baddies' in the American West of the 1870s. Shank Adams is the Captain in charge of the troop, supported by Lt. Colonel Hayes and Lieutenants Kelly and Binning. Luke Cummings is their scout. Thirty-nine half-hour episodes were made, and they appeared to be more popular in the UK than in their native USA.

Bootsie and Snudge ✳

UK (Granada) Situation Comedy. ITV 1960–3; 1974

Bootsie Bisley .... **Alfie Bass**
Claude Snudge .... **Bill Fraser**
Hesketh Pendleton .... **Robert Dorning**
Henry Beerbohm 'Old' Johnson .... **Clive Dunn**

Producers **Peter Eton, Milo Lewis, Eric Fawcett, Bill Podmore**

● ***Two National Service veterans are back in Civvy Street.***

This spin-off from THE ARMY GAME focuses on two of its most popular characters, Pte 'Excused Boots' Bisley and the bullying Sgt-Major Claude Snudge. It relates how the old sparring partners take up positions in a seedy gentlemen's club called The Imperial. Bootsie appropriately becomes boot boy, while Snudge is the new major-domo. The club is run by its Right Honourable Secretary, Hesketh Pendleton, and Clive Dunn gives one of his first 'old man' performances as the decrepit 83-year-old barman, Old Johnson. Most of the scripts were penned by Marty Feldman and Barry Took.

In 1964 Bootsie and Snudge were seen in diplomatic circles in the series *Foreign Affairs* (they are given jobs at the British Embassy in the city of Bosnik), and Alfie Bass and Bill Fraser went on to play similar characters (this time known as Alf Grimble and William Bendlove, respectively) in the 1967 series *Vacant Lot*. *Bootsie and Snudge* was resurrected in 1974, but the characters' relationship was reversed, with Bootsie now the powerful force, having won the football pools, and Snudge the lowly man from the pools company. The revival was short-lived.

Border Cafe ✶✶✶

UK (Hartswood) Comedy Drama. BBC 1 2000

Charlotte Smith	**Elizabeth Carling**
David Doyle	**Sean Gallagher**
Ronnie	**Georgia Mackenzie**
Kidder Doyle	**Antony Strachan**
Edwardian Clive	**Michael Attwell**
Doug Roscoe	**Michael Elwyn**
Max	**Tom Goodman-Hill**
Danesy	**Dean Lennox-Kelly**
Beejay	**Richard Mylan**
Naomi	**Nia Roberts**
Beth	**Catrin Powell**
Chris Caine	**Mark Bazeley**

Writer **Tim Firth**
Executive Producer **Beryl Virtue**
Producers **Elaine Cameron, Chris Griffin**

● ***An isolated diner becomes a hub for the local eccentrics.***

The Border Café is an American-style diner (a converted garage) on the edge of fictional Hayle Point, somewhere along the Wales–England border (hence its name). The new owner is Charlotte Smith, a rock chick who has turned her back on her band, True North, and the entire showbiz world just to shack up with boyfriend David Doyle. Helping them run the café are waitress Ronnie, a former Charlotte clone in a tribute band, and David's dim brother, Kidder, who is the rather inept chef. Throw in a selection of offbeat regulars – including bus driver Clive and mad Welsh sisters Naomi and Beth – and the scene is set for some bizarre goings-on and some intriguing insights into the lives of the main characters. Penned by PRESTON FRONT creator Tim Firth, each of the eight episodes is named after a rock track: *Rock 'n' Roll Suicide, More Than This, Different for Girls, Rock the Casbah, Under Cover of the Night, Shot by Both Sides, Please Please Please Let Me Get What I Want* and *It's All Over Now Baby Blue*.

Border Television

Based in Carlisle, Border was the ITV contractor for the extreme north-west of England, the Scottish borders and the Isle of Man, taking to the air on 1 September 1961 (Isle of Man from 26 March 1965). One of the UK's smallest broadcasters, Border successfully retained its franchise on every occasion but did not contribute significantly to the national ITV network. Perhaps the best-known offering was the married couples' quiz, MR AND MRS, hosted by Derek Batey (who, along with arts critic Melvyn Bragg, was a Border director). Having expanded into radio through its Century Radio brand, Border was taken over by the Capital Radio group in 2000 and was then sold to Granada in 2001, ultimately becoming part of ITV plc.

Borgias, The ✶

UK (BBC) Historical Drama. BBC 2 1981

Rodrigo Borgia	**Adolfo Celi**
Cesare Borgia	**Oliver Cotton**
Giuliano della Rovere	**Alfred Burke**
Lucrezia Borgia	**Anne Louise Lambert**
Juan Borgia	**George Camiller**

Creator/Producer **Mark Shivas**
Writers **John Prebble, Ken Taylor**

● ***Much-ridiculed dramatization of the tyranny of an infamous Italian family.***

Set in the 15th century, *The Borgias* aims to expose the excesses and vices of late-Renaissance Italy. At the heart of the action is the hideous Rodrigo Borgia, a man who has bribed his way to the title of Pope Alexander VI. A wonderfully impious man, Rodrigo's cruelty and greed are surpassed only by the barbarity of his son, Cesare, and his treacherous daughter, Lucrezia, mistress of poison. They murder, debase, plunder, rape and violate their way to power, becoming the most hated, but most potent, family in Italy.

Regrettably, because of star Adolfo Celi's fractured English, the series became rather difficult to follow and collapsed into an unintentional parody of historical drama. Pitched in the same vein as I, CLAUDIUS and other BBC epics, *The Borgias* failed magnificently to reach the same heights. What should have been the most shocking moments were rendered laughable by over-the-top performances and weak scripting. Critics were not impressed, nor was the Vatican, which issued a note of censure.

Born and Bred ✶✶

UK (BBC) Drama. BBC 1 2002–5
DVD: Acorn Video

Arthur Gilder	**James Bolam**
Tom Gilder	**Michael French**
Deborah Gilder	**Jenna Russell**
Phyllis Woolfe	**Maggie Steed**
Revd Brewer	**Clive Swift**
Wilf Bradshaw	**John Henshaw**
Linda Cosgrove	**Tracey Childs**
Len Cosgrove	**Peter Gunn**
Jean Bradshaw/Mills	**Naomi Radcliffe**
Eddie Mills	**Samuel James Hudson**
Helen Gilder	**Charlotte Salt**
Mr Boynton	**Donald Gee**
Michael Gilder	**Ross Little**
Catherine Gilder	**Polly Thompson**
Miss Matthews	**Joan Worswick**
	Shirley White
Dr Donald Newman	**Richard Wilson**
Dr Nick Logan	**Oliver Milburn**
Henry Williamson	**Nigel Havers**
Pip Gilder	**Evan Fortescue**
Nancy Brisley	**Kelly Harrison**
Laura Benhams	**Michaela Megran-Handley**

Creators **Chris Chibnall, Nigel McCery**
Executive Producers **Simon Lewis, Susan Hogg**
Producers **Phil Collinson, Chris Clough, Chris Griffin**

● ***A father and son are the dedicated GPs in a Lancashire village.***

'*Heartbeat* meets *All Creatures Great and Small*, with a brief stop at *Last of the Summer Wine*' – that was *Radio Times*'s opening summary of this soft, fluffy, peak-time drama. Set in the 1950s, *Born and Bred* takes a warmly nostalgic look at life in the fictional Lancashire town of Ormston. Central to the action are father and son doctors Arthur and Tom Gilder, the first a widower on the point of retirement unless he can persuade his son to relocate to the village from Manchester to share his workload. Somewhat against his instincts, Tom duly obliges and returns home along with his wife, Deborah, and four children, Helen (aged 17), Michael (11), Catherine (7) and 18-month-old Philip ('Pip'), as well as a head full of new-fangled medical ideas that sit uncomfortably with his dyed-in-the-wool dad. Tom's efforts to modernize the surgery and establish a 'for the people' cottage hospital (Ormston Memorial) lead the plot in the early episodes. However, in this close-knit community there are plenty of colourful characters with stories of their own to contribute.

Linda is one of Tom's old flames, now married to his old mate, dopey copper Len Cosgrove. Mr Boynton is the local grocer. Comical Eddie runs the garage. Revd Brewer is the unorthodox, Morris Minor-driving vicar, kindly in his ways but always prone to a little drinking, smoking and gambling. Wilf is the stationmaster with only a handful of trains a day to distract him from all kinds of ruses and scrapes, and Jean is Wilf's daughter. She runs a scrapyard and fancies Eddie. Meanwhile, Phyllis is the brassy publican at The Signalman's Arms with an ear for everyone's gossip.

Major changes to the series were required when James Bolam left midway through series three (Arthur moves to New Zealand), with Richard Wilson taking over as his character's replacement, Dr Donald Newman. Yet more cast changes took place for series four, with tragedy befalling Tom and substitute doctor Nick Logan riding dashingly into the village on his motorcycle. Rattenbury Hospital surgeon Henry Williamson, who's covering for Newman, finds it difficult to work with Logan, who once tried to steal his wife, and Deborah's flighty sister, Nancy, arrives to turn the heads of the local menfolk. Sadly for its fans, the series was denied a cosy finish, being cancelled without happily resolving on-going story lines.

Born and Bred is never short of a classy guest star. Roger Lloyd Pack, Denise Welch, David Troughton, Gwen Taylor and Frances de la Tour all feature at some point and Stephanie Cole and Una Stubbs make appearances in a Christmas special first screened in 2003. One of the lesser-known cast members is young Ross Little, brother of THE ROYLE FAMILY's Ralf. The series was filmed in the Ribble Valley village of Downham.

Borrowers, The ✶✶

UK (Working Title) Drama. BBC 1 1992–3
DVD: BBC

Pod Clock	**Ian Holm**
Homily Clock	**Penelope Wilton**
Arrietty Clock	**Rebecca Callard**
George	**Paul Cross**
Mrs Driver	**Siân Phillips**
Crampfurl	**David Ryall**
Spiller	**Daniel Newman**
Mildeye	**Tony Haygarth**
Uncle Hendreary	**Stanley Lebor**
Aunt Lupy	**Pamela Cundell**
Eggletina	**Victoria Donovan**
Ditchly	**Ben Chaplin**
Ilrick	**Ross McCall**
Mr Pott	**Richard Vernon**
Miss Menzies	**Gemma Jones**
Mr Platter	**Robert Lang**
Mrs Platter	**Judy Parfitt**

Writer **Richard Carpenter**
Producer **Grainne Marmion**

Every day is a battle for survival for a family of little people.

Life's a struggle when you're only 15 cm tall. You can live behind skirting boards or beneath the floors in the houses of 'human beans' but you have to venture out every now and then to get domestic supplies. That's the danger faced by Pod, who fends for his fearful wife, Homily, and inquisitive 14-year-old daughter, Arrietty, by 'borrowing' from their oblivious giant neighbours. One day, however, Pod takes Arrietty on one of his excursions into the wider world and sets in train events that are to make life for the Borrowers much harder than before, as big folk like Mrs Driver start to close in (not to mention their cats and dogs). This six-part adaptation of Mary Norton's 1950s novels *The Borrowers* and *The Borrowers Afield* was followed a year later with six more episodes derived from Norton's *The Borrowers Afloat* and *The Borrowers Aloft*. This time the family has sought refuge in the village of Little Fordham, a model village created by retired railwayman Mr Potts.

Bosanquet, Reginald

(1932–84)

Popular ITN newsreader of the 1960s and 1970s, whose lively private life became regular tabloid fare. Bosanquet, the son of Middlesex and England cricketer B. J. T. Bosanquet (the man who invented the delivery called the 'googly', still known as the 'Bosie' Down Under), joined ITN at its inception in 1955 as a trainee. From there he developed into one of its leading reporters, eventually becoming diplomatic correspondent and presenting programmes like ROVING REPORT and *Dateline*. In 1967 he was chosen as one of the newscasters to launch the revolutionary *News at Ten*, and his on-air partnerships with Andrew Gardner and Anna Ford proved particularly popular with viewers, who enjoyed the sense of unpredictability he brought to newsreading. However, his rather stilted delivery and lop-sided smirk were the result of a medical condition and nothing more sinister, like drink, as some columnists had it. Bosanquet resigned from ITN in a blaze of publicity in 1979, during a lengthy technicians' strike and presented a few reports for NATIONWIDE before his death in 1984.

Bosley, Tom

(1927–)

American actor, familiar as the sympathetic father, Howard Cunningham, in the nostalgic sitcom HAPPY DAYS. His 'pop' roles had begun earlier, when he provided the voice for harassed Harry Boyle in WAIT TILL YOUR FATHER GETS HOME, although later Bosley switched from dad to detective, playing Sheriff Amos Tupper in MURDER, SHE WROTE and the title role in FATHER DOWLING INVESTIGATES. His TV career began in 1964 in the US version of THAT WAS THE WEEK THAT WAS and continued through the likes of *The Debbie Reynolds Show*, in which he played Debbie's brother-in-law, Bob Landers, and *The Dean Martin Show*. He was also narrator for the showbiz retrospective *That's Hollywood*, and has appeared as guest star in many other series. In recent years he has been seen in a US soap opera called *Port Charles* and made a guest appearance in ER.

Bosom Buddies ✶✶

US (Miller-Milkis-Boyett/Paramount) Situation Comedy.
ITV 1982–4 (US: ABC 1980–2)

Kip Wilson ('Buffy')	**Tom Hanks**
Henry Desmond ('Hildegarde')	**Peter Scolari**
Amy Cassidy	**Wendie Jo Sperber**

Sonny Lumet .... **Donna Dixon**
Isabelle Hammond .... **Telma Hopkins**
Lilly Sinclair .... **Lucille Benson**
Ruth Dunbar .... **Holland Taylor**

Executive Producers **Thomas L. Miller, Edward K. Milkis, Robert L. Boyett, Chris Thompson**

Two lusty young men pretend to be girls to stay at a females' residence.
Some Like It Hot for the 1980s. Kip Wilson (an early TV role for Tom Hanks) and Henry Desmond are two junior advertising executives who, one day, discover that their apartment house in New York is being razed to the ground. Desperate for somewhere to stay, they pick up on a suggestion from colleague Amy Cassidy that they move into her own residence. Unfortunately, the Susan B. Anthony hotel is for women only. Undeterred, the boys decide to don drag and step over the threshold. Pretending to be their own sisters, Buffy and Hildegarde, they take up accommodation, appreciating the low rent and titillated by the gorgeous girls that surround them, especially blonde Sonny. Only Amy is aware of their true identity at first, but soon all the girls are in the know as the boys try to keep their secret from hotel manager Lilly Sinclair. Ruth Dunbar is the boss at the advertising agency where Kip is an illustrator and Henry a copywriter. She and Amy later move with the lads when they set up their own production company, 60 Seconds Street. Billy Joel's 'My Life' was used as the programme theme song.

Boss Cat ***

US (Hanna-Barbera) Cartoon. BBC 1962–3 (ABC 1961–2)
DVD: Warner Home Video (Region 1 only)

Voices:
Top Cat ('TC') .... **Arnold Stang**
Benny the Ball .... **Maurice Gosfield**
Choo Choo .... **Marvin Kaplan**
Spook .... **Leo De Lyon**
The Brain .... **Leo De Lyon**
Fancy-Fancy .... **John Stephenson**
Officer Dibble .... **Allen Jenkins**
Pierre .... **John Stephenson**
Goldie .... **Jean Vander Pyl**
Honey Dew .... **Sallie Jones**

Creator **Joseph Barbera**
Executive Producers **William Hanna, Joseph Barbera**

A scheming tom leads a scrounging squad of alley cats.
Boss Cat, or *Top Cat* as it was known outside Britain (the UK already had a cat food of that name), is a feline version of *Sgt Bilko*. Fort Baxter gives way to a Manhattan alleyway and uniforms are swapped for fur coats, but otherwise the guys are all there, from the sweet-talking con cat leader to the dimmest-of-the-dim fall guy. The gang is headed by Top Cat, commonly known as TC, who lives in a luxurious dustbin, eats scraps from the local deli, drinks milk from nearby doorsteps and uses the local police phone to make calls, much to the consternation of the neighbourhood copper, Officer Dibble. Like Bilko, TC always has an eye for a fast buck, or the equivalent in cat terms. His dense henchmen, the equivalent of Bilko's platoon, are Brain, Fancy-Fancy, Spook, Choo Choo and Benny the Ball, the last voiced by Maurice Gosfield, Pte Doberman in THE PHIL SILVERS SHOW. Pierre, Goldie and Honey Dew are other moggies seen.

Bottle Boys *

UK (LWT) Situation Comedy. ITV 1984–5

Dave Deacon .... **Robin Askwith**
Stan Evans .... **Richard Davies**
Jock Collins .... **Phil McCall**
Billy Watson .... **Dave Auker**
Joe Phillips .... **Oscar James**
Sharon Armstrong .... **Eve Ferret**
Wilf Foley .... **Leo Dolan**

Creator/Writer **Vince Powell**
Producer **Stuart Allen**

An inept milkman and his colleagues fail to deliver.
Set in the financially rocky Dawson's Dairy, *Bottle Boys* relates the daily disasters that afflict football-crazy Cockney milkman Dave Deacon. His exasperated boss is Welshman Stan Evans and his unreliable colleagues include boozy Scotsman Jock Collins and randy West Indian Joe Phillips. Hopeless secretary Sharon Armstrong provides the blue-uniformed lads with some female company and an excuse to air their non-PC jokes. Star Robin Askwith had previously made a name for himself in the raunchy *Confessions of a . . .* film comedies, with which this series shared numerous characteristics. Two series were made.

Bottom **

UK (BBC) Situation Comedy. BBC 2 1991–2; 1995
DVD: BBC

Richie Richard .... **Rik Mayall**
Eddie Hitler .... **Adrian Edmondson**

Creators/Writers **Rik Mayall, Adrian Edmondson**
Producer **Ed Bye**

Two no-hopers share a derelict flat.
Bottom – or *Your Bottom*, as its stars had considered calling it (hoping viewers would declare, 'I saw *Your Bottom* on the telly last night') – focuses on the directionless lives of a pair of obnoxious flatmates. Richie and Eddie are characters straight out of the Mayall and Edmondson stock repertoire and bear more than a passing resemblance to their roles in THE YOUNG ONES. Richie, cringingly self-centred, dreams of having sex – with anyone; Eddie, graphically violent and purposefully direct, fouls up his flatmate's best-laid plans. Constantly bickering and endlessly battering each other, they live in squalor above a Hammersmith shop but virtually destroy their putrid flat in every episode, amid an avalanche of jokes about smells, vomiting and other disgusting habits. They really are at the *Bottom* of life's pile.

Boudica **

UK (Box/WGBH) Drama. ITV 1 2003

Boudica .... **Alex Kingston**
Prasutagus .... **Steven Waddington**
Isolda .... **Emily Blunt**
Siora .... **Leanne Rowe**
Connach .... **Ben Faulks**
Dervalloc .... **Hugo Speer**
Severus .... **Angus Wright**
Magior .... **Gary Lewis**

Catus Decianus .... **Steve John Shepherd**
Claudius .... **Jack Shepherd**
Didius .... **Gideon Turner**
Nero .... **Andrew Lee Potts**
Agrippina .... **Frances Barber**
Suetonius .... **Michael Feast**

Writer **Andrew Davies**
Executive Producers **Gub Neal, Patrick Irwin, Justin Thomson-Glover, Rebecca Eaton**
Producer **Matthew Bird**

Warrior queen Boudica leads her Celtic tribe against the empirical Romans.

On the death of her husband, Prasutagus, Boudica, first-century queen of the Iceni, finds that the loose pact he had negotiated with the invading Romans counts for nothing. Her attempts at renegotiating the deal prove futile and, unprovoked, crazed emperor Nero decides to crush local rebellion, invading the Iceni territory of eastern England. Boudica is captured and flogged, while her daughters, Isolda and Siora, are violated in front of their mother. She vows revenge, gathers assistance from neighbouring tribes and finds both moral and intimate support in the shape of heroic young warrior Dervalloc. Stepping aboard her chariot, she leads her people to a temporary victory, taking Colchester from the brutal occupation force. But the Romans are not through. With feared general Suetonius at the helm, the enemy fights back, hunting down the Iceni amid scenes of great bloodshed.

This ambitious, feature-length drama cost an estimated £3 million to make and was shot on location in Romania.

Bough, Frank

(1933–)

Avuncular presenter who, as host of regional news magazine *Look North* and then GRANDSTAND from 1968, followed by NATIONWIDE, HOLIDAY and BREAKFAST TIME, became a household name, although things took a turn for the worse in the late 1980s when indiscretions in his private life hit the headlines. He has since returned to the screen on lower-key programmes for Sky and regional companies, and has occasionally presented sport on ITV (including the 1991 Rugby World Cup).

Bounder, The ✶

UK (Yorkshire) Situation Comedy. ITV 1982–3
DVD: BFS (Region 1 only)

Howard .... **Peter Bowles**
Trevor Mountjoy .... **George Cole**
Mary Mountjoy .... **Rosalind Ayres**
Laura .... **Isla Blair**

Creator/Writer **Eric Chappell**
Producer **Vernon Lawrence**

A conman is a cuckoo in his sister and brother-in-law's nest.

Fresh out of jail after serving time for embezzlement, the suave and untrustworthy Howard finds a roof over his head, courtesy of his sister, Mary, but much to the dismay of her dependable estate agent husband, Trevor. They hope he will turn over a new leaf, but then Howard meets Laura, the young, attractive and *rich* widow living next door – just one temptation for him to return to his wicked ways.

Bouquet of Barbed Wire ✶✶

UK (LWT) Drama. ITV 1976
DVD: Cinema Club

Peter Manson .... **Frank Finlay**
Prue Manson/Sorenson .... **Susan Penhaligon**
Gavin Sorenson .... **James Aubrey**
Cassie Manson .... **Sheila Allen**
Sarah Francis .... **Deborah Grant**

Writer **Andrea Newman**
Executive Producer **Rex Firkin**
Producer **Tony Wharmby**

A father's incestuous love for his daughter wrecks his family.

Publisher Peter Manson, his wife, Cassie, and daughter, Prue, live in middle-class harmony in Surrey. Then in steps American Gavin Sorenson and their lives begin to crumble. Gavin marries Prue, and a wave of lust, infidelity and incest sweeps over the family to the point where Peter's obsession with his pouting daughter finally tears the family apart. *Bouquet of Barbed Wire*, written by Andrea Newman from her own novel, graphically reveals the turmoil such steamy, forbidden passions can provoke and the drama fully enjoyed the attentions of the tabloid press. Although Prue dies after childbirth at the end of the serial, a sequel, *Another Bouquet*, followed a year later. It sees Cassie resuming a relationship with Gavin, and Peter falling for Gavin's new girlfriend. Clearly, lessons have not been learned!

Bourbon Street Beat ✶

US (Warner Brothers) Detective Drama. ITV 1963 (US ABC 1959–60)

Cal Calhoun .... **Andrew Duggan**
Rex Randolph .... **Richard Long**
Melody Lee Mercer .... **Arlene Howell**
Kenny Madison .... **Van Williams**
The Baron .... **Eddie Cole**

Producers **William T. Orr, Charles Hoffman**

The investigations of a New Orleans detective agency.

Cal Calhoun and Rex Randolph are the founding partners of Randolph and Calhoun, Special Services, based next to the Old Absinthe House in the French Quarter of New Orleans, in this 77 SUNSET STRIP clone from Warner Brothers. Fellow members of the team are rookie Kenny Madison and attractive secretary Melody Lee Mercer, played by former Miss America Arlene Howell. The Baron, a jazz pianist, is one of their contacts. As a gimmick, the two leads always greet each other by rubbing the soles of their shoes together! The series only lasted one year, before the partnership broke up. Randolph left Louisiana to join the team on *Sunset Strip* and Madison moved east to *Surfside 6*. Jerry Livingston and Mack David scored the theme tune.

Bowen, Jeremy

(1960–)

Cardiff-born journalist and newsreader who joined the BBC as a news trainee in 1984 and later covered conflicts in the Gulf, Afghanistan, the Balkans, Chechnya and the Middle East (he was the BBC's Middle East correspondent for five years).

In 2000, Bowen moved indoors, to host a revamp of *Breakfast* with Sophie Raworth, eventually leaving two years later. He has also presented the documentaries *Son of God*, *Booze*, *Moses* and *Noah's Ark*.

Bowen, Jim

(James Whittaker; 1937–)

Cheshire-born comic and game show presenter, a former schoolteacher and nightclub comedian, unearthed by THE COMEDIANS and then seen as the sole adult in the YOU MUST BE JOKING! team. As host of the darts quiz BULLSEYE he gained a reputation for his forthright, down-to-earth treatment of contestants and his fumbling presentation. 'Great', 'smashing' and 'super' became his catchphrases. He also made guest appearances in MUCK AND BRASS and EL C.I.D. (playing himself), in JONATHAN CREEK and in PETER KAY'S PHOENIX NIGHTS.

Bowler, Norman

(1932–)

London-born actor who has meandered from one successful series to another. Among his best-known roles are David Martin in *Park Ranger*, DI Harry Hawkins in SOFTLY, SOFTLY, Sam Benson in CROSSROADS and, most recently, Frank Tate in EMMERDALE. His other appearances range from DEADLINE MIDNIGHT, HARPERS WEST ONE and THE RATCATCHERS to JESUS OF NAZARETH, *Into the Labyrinth* and KING AND CASTLE.

Bowles, Peter

(1936–)

Suave, London-born actor, star of numerous series, often in a slightly untrustworthy role. His major credits include Toby Meres in the pilot for CALLAN (ARMCHAIR THEATRE'S *A Magnum for Schneider*), Guthrie Featherstone in RUMPOLE OF THE BAILEY, Richard DeVere in TO THE MANOR BORN, Archie Glover in ONLY WHEN I LAUGH, Howard in THE BOUNDER, Neville Lytton in LYTTON'S DIARY (which he also created), Major Sinclair Yeates in THE IRISH RM and conman Guy Buchanan in PERFECT SCOUNDRELS. Other appearances have been in *Doctor Knock*, THE SAINT, THE AVENGERS, CRANE, THE BARON, THE PRISONER, SURVIVORS, *Good Girl* (Colin Peale), *Churchill's People*, SPACE: 1999, I, CLAUDIUS (Caractacus), THE CREZZ (Ken Green), RISING DAMP, PENNIES FROM HEAVEN, EXECUTIVE STRESS (Donald Fairchild), RANDALL AND HOPKIRK (DECEASED), HOLBY CITY and JERICHO, as well as Ken Russell's 1966 film, *Isadora*, and the mini-series *A Shadow on the Sun* and *Little White Lies* (Oliver).

Box of Delights, The ★★★

UK (BBC) Children's Drama. BBC 1 1984
DVD: BBC

Kay Harker .... **Devin Stanfield**
Abner Brown .... **Robert Stephens**
Cole Hawlings .... **Patrick Troughton**
Peter .... **Crispin Mair**
Maria Jones .... **Joanna Dukes**
Foxy Faced Charles .... **Geoffrey Larder**
Herne the Hunter .... **Glyn Baker**
Chubby Joe .... **Jonathan Stephens**
Bishop of Tatchester .... **John Horsley**
Mouse .... **Simon Barry**
Rat .... **Bill Wallis**
Caroline Louisa .... **Carol Frazer**
Inspector .... **James Grout**
Sylvia Daisy Pouncer .... **Patricia Quinn**

Writer **Alan Seymour**
Producer **Paul Stone**

● ***A schoolboy takes possession of a magic box.***

Young Kay Harker is travelling home by train for the Christmas holidays sometime in the 1930s. The weather has turned icy and wolves can be heard in the countryside. The atmosphere is strange and Kay thinks something weird is about to take place. He is not wrong. Alighting at Musborough Junction, he meets a Punch and Judy showman named Cole Hawlings. But this is no ordinary travelling entertainer. Hawlings is the keeper of the elixir of life as well as a scruffy old box that, it turns out, has magical powers. The showman is perpetually on the run – has been for some 600 years – and sometimes needs a human helping hand to keep his magical properties safe. Kay agrees to take the box home to his house, Seekings, near Tatchester, and thus begins a dramatic adventure in which ancient heroes return and Kay must confront a spooky clergyman named Abner, who is nothing but a sorcerer and a crook. Also part of the action is Maria, an especially troublesome schoolgirl. A budget of £1 million (the highest ever at the time for a BBC children's programme) and the latest TV special effects were employed to bring John Masefield's 1935 classic novel to life, allowing our hero to fly through the air and sail in a toy boat, among other feats. Renny Rye directed the six parts.

Boyd, William

(1895–1972)

Silver-haired American actor for ever remembered as HOPALONG CASSIDY, a role he literally made his own, buying the TV rights to the character. However, Cassidy had only hopped along when Boyd's career seemed just about over, in 1934, with his days as a leading man in dramatic films of the 1920s fading fast. Boyd, despite his dislike of horses, learned to ride and never looked back. The character made him a millionaire.

Boyd QC ★★

UK (Associated-Rediffusion) Legal Drama. ITV 1956–61; 1963–4

Richard Boyd QC .... **Michael Denison**
Jack .... **Charles Leno**

Writer **Jack Roffey**
Executive Producer **Caryl Doncaster**

● ***The ups and downs of a barrister's life.***

Suave, elegant Richard Boyd, QC, is the gentle hero of this series of courtroom dramas. Ably supported by his clerk, Jack (who also acts as narrator), he prosecutes at times, but usually defends, generally turning up the right result. Filmed in semi-documentary style, the series was one of the first programmes to explore the world of the British judiciary, becoming a major hit, particularly towards the end of its long run.

Boyle, Katie

(Caterina Irene Elena Maria Imperiali di Francavilla; 1926–)

International presenter who graced several EUROVISION SONG CONTESTS and some editions of IT'S A KNOCKOUT, putting her multilingual skills to full use. Born into an aristocratic Italian family, Boyle nevertheless has always seemed eminently English. A former *Vogue* fashion model, she was a familiar face on 1950s and 1960s panel games and variety shows (like *Quite Contrary* and JUKE BOX JURY) and has written an agony aunt column for the *TV Times*.

Boys from the Blackstuff ✳✳✳✳

UK (BBC) Drama. BBC 2 1982
DVD: BBC

Chrissie Todd .... **Michael Angelis**
Yosser Hughes .... **Bernard Hill**
Thomas Ralph 'Dixie' Dean .... **Tom Georgeson**
George Malone .... **Peter Kerrigan**
Loggo Logmond .... **Alan Igbon**
Kevin Dean .... **Gary Bleasdale**
Angie Todd .... **Julie Walters**
Frankie Malloy .... **Shay Gorman**
Miss Sutcliffe .... **Jean Boht**
Jean .... **Gilly Coman**
The Wino .... **James Ellis**

Writer **Alan Bleasdale**
Producer **Michael Wearing**

A gang of tarmac layers face life on the dole.

In 1980, Alan Bleasdale's single drama *The Black Stuff* was shown. It focused on a tarmac gang working away from their home city of Liverpool. It proved so magnetic that the BBC asked Bleasdale to write a series of connected plays, one for each of the main characters. The first of the follow-ups was reworked into a drama called *The Muscle Market*, but the remaining five scripts were put together as a black comedy-drama called *Boys from the Blackstuff*.

In the series the lads are back home. Out of work and signing on in a desolate city riddled with unemployment, their future looks bleak (reflecting the prospects of millions like them around the country at the time). At the forefront of the gang is Yosser Hughes, a man so desperate for work to keep his family afloat that he begs people to 'Gissa job', claiming 'I can do dat.'

In these poignant episodes Yosser and his contemporaries become standard-bearers for men who are willing to work but who are having to suffer the indignities of life on the 1980s scrapheap.

Boys from the Bush, The ✳

UK (Cinema Verity/Entertainment Media/BBC) Comedy Drama. BBC 1 1991–2

Reg Toomer .... **Tim Healy**
Dennis Tontine .... **Chris Haywood**
Leslie .... **Mark Haddigan**
Arlene Toomer .... **Nadine Garner**
Doris Toomer .... **Pat Thomson**
Delilah .... **Kris McQuade**
Corrie .... **Kirsty Child**
Stuart Stranks .... **Rob Steele**
Stevie Stranks .... **Russell Fletcher**

Creator **Douglas Livingstone**
Producers **Verity Lambert, David Shanks**

Life with an expat detective and his Australian partner.

Although Reg Toomer has lived in Australia for over 20 years, there is only one Bush for him and that is Shepherd's Bush. However, while pining for his long-lost football team, Queens Park Rangers, he still has a business to look after in Melbourne. Melbourne Confidential is part-marriage consultancy and part-detective agency, but, as long as it pays, any job is considered. Reg's unlikely partner is Aussie Dennis Tontine, a man obsessed with women, but who is on the run from both middle age and his former wife. Also involved are Reg's daydreaming missus, Doris, and their man-hungry, starry-eyed daughter, Arlene. Les is Reg's second cousin and Arlene's on-off lover, who becomes one of the company's private eyes. Dodgy tycoon Stuart Stranks and his amorous son, Stevie, are added to the cast in the second series.

Brack Report, The ✳✳

UK (Thames) Drama. ITV 1982

Paul Brack .... **Donald Sumpter**
Pat Brack .... **Patricia Garwood**
Angela Brack .... **Jenny Seagrove**
Oliver Brack .... **Neil Nisbet**
Sarah Challen .... **Sue Robinson**
Harold Harlan .... **Robert Lang**
Sophie Ferris .... **Toria Fuller**
Liz Martin .... **Susan Maudslay**
Jennie Strong .... **Colette O'Neil**
Kate Randall .... **Wanda Ventham**
Barry Madoc .... **Patrick Allen**
Brian Fletcher .... **Tom Chadbon**
Norman Phillips .... **Antony Carrick**

Creator **Christopher Penfold**
Writers **Christopher Penfold, John Elliot, Bruce Stewart, David Pinner**
Executive Producer **John Frankau**
Producer **Richard Bates**

A principled scientist speaks out against the Establishment's infatuation with nuclear power.

When an earthquake inflicts damage on a nuclear power station, the impact is hushed up by the powers that be – something that alarms scientist Paul Brack, who works there. So disturbed is he at this flagrant disregard for public safety that he is torn between throwing in his job and staying on for the financial well-being of his family, but his principles eventually win through. He quits to work for energy consultant Harold Harlan of Harlan International, a man, Brack believes, who can persuade the authorities to look again at the safety of nuclear power. Harlan, however, has other ideas and intends to use Brack for his own ends. Brack subsequently turns his attention to the potential benefits of alternative energy providers, wind, wave and solar, only to find that political will is stacked against them. In the meantime, his family problems increase when he begins a relationship with colleague Sarah Challen. *The Brack Report* a ten-part drama, encapsulated the concerns held by many in the early 1980s over the dangers of nuclear power. Music was provided by Christopher Gunning.

Bradbury, Sir Malcolm

CBE (1932–2000)

Sheffield-born novelist and one-time Professor of American Studies at the University of East Anglia who often reflected his academic background in his writing and became one of TV's most controversial playwrights. Some of his earliest work was for THAT WAS THE WEEK THAT WAS, leading to plays like *The After Dinner Game* in 1975 and *Standing in for Henry* in 1980, although his greatest successes were in adapting Tom Sharpe's BLOTT ON THE LANDSCAPE and PORTERHOUSE BLUE for television in 1985 and 1987. His own novel THE HISTORY MAN had itself been adapted (by Christopher Hamilton) in 1981 and drew criticism for its raunchy sexual content. Bradbury's later work included *Anything More Would be Greedy* (1989), THE GRAVY TRAIN and *The Gravy Train Goes East*, versions of Kingsley Amis's THE GREEN MAN and Stella Gibbons's COLD COMFORT FARM, an adaptation of Mark Tavener's *In the Red*, and episodes of INSPECTOR MORSE, KAVANAGH QC, DALZIEL AND PASCOE and A TOUCH OF FROST.

Braden, Bernard

(1916–93)

Canadian actor and presenter, one of TV's first consumers' champions. He moved to the UK in 1949 after working in Canadian radio and embarked on a theatre and radio career. On television, he began by presenting schools' programmes, was one of the BBC's team covering THE CORONATION and was then chairman of THE BRAINS TRUST (1957) and host of the sports magazine *Let's Go* (1959). Very often he was seen in tandem with his wife, Barbara Kelly, in programmes like *Kaleidoscope* and the sitcom *B and B*, and with other partners in comedies such as *Bath-Night with Braden* and *Early to Braden*. ON THE BRADEN BEAT and BRADEN'S WEEK were other contributions, the last (beginning in 1968) introducing a young researcher by the name of Esther Rantzen. *Braden's Week*, with its consumer content, proved to be the inspiration for Esther's THAT'S LIFE. Sacked by the BBC for promoting Stork margarine on ITV, Braden returned to Canadian television before resurfacing on programmes such as *After Noon Plus* and a revamped ALL OUR YESTERDAYS in 1987. Among his three children was actress Kim Braden (star of the BBC's version of ANNE OF GREEN GABLES).

Braden's Week ✶✶

UK (BBC) Entertainment. BBC 1 1968–72

Presenter **Bernard Braden**
Editors **Desmond Wilcox, Bill Morton**
Producers **John Lloyd, Adam Clapham, Tom Conway**

Saturday evening slice of light entertainment and consumer affairs.

The clear ancestor of THAT'S LIFE, *Braden's Week* not only humorously reviewed the week's events but was also an early consumers' champion, tackling thorny subjects with a light touch. Bernard Braden fronted affairs, supported by a team of reporter/researchers who included John Pitman, Esther Rantzen and Harold Williamson. Williamson specialized in interviewing children. Rantzen and producer John Lloyd headed off to *That's Life* once *Braden's Week* came to a controversial end in 1972. The BBC were unhappy that Braden had decided to advertise Stork margarine on ITV and dismissed him, claiming it was not viable for the host of a consumer programme to be seen endorsing goods commercially.

Bradley, David

(1942–)

Yorkshire-born Shakespearean actor (Argus Filch in the *Harry Potter* films). On TV he has been most prominent as David Crimple in MARTIN CHUZZLEWIT, Alf Black in BAND OF GOLD, Eddie Wells in OUR FRIENDS IN THE NORTH, Arnold Springer in RECKLESS, Dave Waters in CATHERINE COOKSON'S *The Moth*, Supt. Hines in *Kiss and Tell*, Rogue Riderhood in OUR MUTUAL FRIEND, Sir Pitt Crawley in VANITY FAIR, Ray Wilson in *The Wilsons*, Mr Broune in THE WAY WE LIVE NOW, Jake in WILD WEST, Councillor Vall in THE MAYOR OF CASTERBRIDGE, Elliot in *Station Jim*, Sir Edmund Berry Godfrey in CHARLES II – THE POWER AND THE PASSION, Hallworth in BLACKPOOL and Archie in *Mr Harvey Lights a Candle*. Guest appearances have come in THE PROFESSIONALS, BETWEEN THE LINES, *Full Stretch*, A TOUCH OF FROST, WYCLIFFE, CRACKER, MIDSOMER MURDERS and other series.

Brady, Terence

(1939–)

British writer and actor, the husband of writing partner Charlotte Bingham. Together they have penned a number of successful sitcoms, including NO – HONESTLY, YES – HONESTLY, *Father Matthew's Daughter* and TAKE THREE GIRLS. They also wrote PIG IN THE MIDDLE (in which Brady also starred) and its American clone, *Oh Madeline*, as well as episodes of ROBIN'S NEST and dramas like UPSTAIRS, DOWNSTAIRS, *Thomas and Sarah*, NANNY, FOREVER GREEN and JILLY COOPER'S RIDERS, plus sketches for *Marti Caine*. On screen, Brady has been seen in comedies such as *Broad and Narrow*, *Dig This Rhubarb* and *Cribbins*. Bingham is now a successful novelist.

Brady Bunch, The ✶

US (Paramount) Situation Comedy. ITV 1975–82
(US: ABC 1969–74)
DVD: Paramount (Region 1 only)

Mike Brady	**Robert Reed**
Carol Brady	**Florence Henderson**
Alice Nelson	**Ann B. Davis**
Marcia Brady	**Maureen McCormick**
Greg Brady	**Barry Williams**
Jan Brady	**Eve Plumb**
Peter Brady	**Christopher Knight**
Cindy Brady	**Susan Olsen**
Bobby Brady	**Michael Lookinland**

Creator/Executive Producer **Sherwood Schwartz**

A widow with three daughters sets up home with a widower and his three sons.

The petty domestic squabbles of two families joined together by second marriage provide the laughs in this saccharine-sweet, middle-class comedy. Following the death of his wife, architect Mike Brady has been left with the care of his three sons, Greg, Peter and Bobby. He meets equally lonesome widow Carol Martin, mother of three girls, Marcia, Jan and Cindy. Romance quickly ensues and the two families set up home together in suburban LA, assisted by Mike's long-serving housekeeper, Alice Nelson, and shaggy dog, Tiger. Dramatic highspots concern the battle for the bathroom, the dating game and various boy v. girl prejudices. Spin-offs included the cartoon series *The Brady Kids* in 1972 and the live-action *The Brady Bunch Hour* in 1977, which took the family into their own TV variety show. There was a further follow-up in 1981, *The Brady Brides*, which picked up the story of the two elder girls, Marcia and Jan, in married life, sharing a house with their respective husbands. Mum was still at hand and Alice never far away when help was required. In 1990, the concept was reheated again, when most of the original cast reconvened for *The Bradys*. This time grandchildren had pervaded the already bulging Brady residence but the mood was considerably more downbeat, as 1970s optimism and the freedom of youth caved into the harsher realities of the 1990s and the responsibilities of adulthood. There have also been various TV movies featuring the family, plus a satirical feature film, *The Brady Bunch Movie*, starring Shelley Long and Gary Cole, in 1995, cheekily portraying the family dealing with the 1990s while stuck in a 1970s time warp. This was followed by the even more subversive *A Very Brady Sequel* (1996).

Bragg, Lord Melvyn

(1939–)

Cumbrian presenter, novelist and playwright, widely acknowledged as TV's Mr Arts after his work as editor and host of THE SOUTH BANK SHOW and the paperback review *Read All About It*, and appearances on *The Late Show*. Earlier he worked as a producer and writer on the influential MONITOR series, for which he collaborated closely with Ken Russell. He joined Russell again in 1978 to script *Clouds of Glory*, two films about the Lakeland poets. Bragg has also edited various other arts programmes, and has been Head of Arts at LWT, as well as Chairman of Border Television. His 1992 drama *A Time to Dance*, adapted from his own novel, drew criticism for its bold sex scenes. He chaired the series *The Big Idea*, presented the documentary *Bragg on America*, and in 1999 looked at the history of Christianity in *Two Thousand Years*. In 2001 he studied *The Apostles* and in 2002 produced and presented a linguistic documentary series called *The Adventure of English*. More recently, he has chaired the debate programme *Not Just on Sunday* and fronted *The Story of ITV: the People's Channel*. Bragg also made a guest appearance as an interviewer in the Harry Enfield spoof, *Norbert Smith – a Life*. He is married to writer/producer Cate Haste.

Brains Trust, The ✶

UK (BBC) Discussion Programme. BBC 1955–61; BBC 2 1996

Chairmen **Hugh Ross Williamson, Michael Flanders, Norman Fisher, Alan Melville, Hubert Gregg, Malcolm Muggeridge, Bernard Braden, Robert Kee, Mary Ann Sieghart**

Creator **Howard Thomas**
Producers **John Furness, Peter Brook, Michael Roberts, Jack Ashley**

● ***A panel of unprimed intellectuals answer questions from listeners.***

This completely unscripted discussion programme began on BBC Radio in 1941, at the height of the Blitz, and became a valuable morale-lifter during the hostilities. Its popularity stemmed as much from the badinage among its three main participants (Professor C. E. M. Joad, Commander A. B. Campbell and Dr Julian Huxley) as from the knowledge it imparted. When this television version began, 14 years later, a more sober tone prevailed, with the intimacy of the cramped radio studio replaced by a TV set filled with armchairs and coffee tables. The first host was Hugh Ross Williamson and the panel changed on a regular basis. Guests included such diverse personalities as Julian Huxley, Bertrand Russell, Egon Ronay and the Archbishop of Cape Town, but one of the stalwarts was Dr Jacob Bronowski (later to compile THE ASCENT OF MAN). Viewers' contributions varied from the sublime to the ridiculous, taking in factual queries, philosophical posers and, at times, almost rhetorical questions, and the panellists (unaware of what was going to be asked) made every effort to provide a coherent and accurate response.

The Brains Trust was exhumed for a six-programme late-night series in 1996, with the Assistant Editor of *The Times*, Mary Ann Sieghart, in the chair and panellists including Jonathan Miller, philosopher Edward de Bono and novelist Ben Okri.

Brake, Patricia

(1942–)

British actress headlining in a number of major series, particularly ELDORADO (Gwen Lockhead). Among her other credits have been PORRIDGE and *Going Straight* (Ingrid Fletcher), *The Glums* (Eth), *Second Time Around* (Vicki), *Troubles and Strife* (Cherry), 2 POINT 4 CHILDREN (Tina) and *Looking After Jo Jo* (Doro), plus scores of guest appearances in series like MIDSOMER MURDERS, MCCREADY AND DAUGHTER, HOLBY CITY and CORONATION STREET (Viv Baldwin). She also played Julie Renfield in the US sitcom *The Ugliest Girl in Town*.

Brambell, Wilfrid

(1912–85)

Diminutive Dublin-born actor for ever cherished by viewers as grubby old Albert Steptoe in STEPTOE AND SON, a role he played, off and on, for 12 years from 1962. Brambell's first television appearances were a mixture of comedy parts (in shows that included LIFE WITH THE LYONS) and serious drama. He appeared as a drunk in the science-fiction milestone THE QUATERMASS EXPERIMENT and also popped up in 1984, as an old tortured prisoner, as well as in programmes like THE ADVENTURES OF AGGIE. Typecast as old man Steptoe, Brambell's subsequent TV work was thin on the ground, although he did take up a few film roles, playing Paul's grandfather, for instance, in The Beatles' *A Hard Day's Night*, and was also seen in Jonathan Miller's ALICE IN WONDERLAND, plus a couple of COMEDY PLAYHOUSE pilots. He was another Albert, one of the patients, in Peter Tinniswood's 1970 sitcom *Never Say Die*, and also appeared in *Dramarama*. One of Brambell's last television appearances was as a guest in an episode of CITIZEN SMITH.

Bramwell ✶✶

UK (Whitby Davison/Carlton) Drama. ITV 1995–8
DVD: Shanachie (Region 1 only)

Eleanor Bramwell .... **Jemma Redgrave**
Robert Bramwell .... **David Calder**
Sir Herbert Hamilton .... **Robert Hardy**
Lady Cora Peters .... **Michele Dotrice**
Nurse Ethel Carr .... **Ruth Sheen**
Kate .... **Keeley Gainey**

Daniel Bentley	**Cliff Parisi**
Dr Joe Marsham	**Kevin McMonagle**
Dr Finn O'Neill	**Andrew Connolly**
Sidney Bentley	**Ben Brazier**
Alice Costigan	**Maureen Beattie**

Creators/Producers **Lucy Gannon, Tim Whitby, Harriet Davison**

A female doctor battles against prejudice to care for the urban poor.

Set at the outset in 1895, this Victorian medical drama tells the story of ambitious doctor Eleanor Bramwell, who lives in Islington with her physician father, Robert. It relates how she launches a crusade to provide medical care for the poor in the East End of London and how she vainly tries to gain the respect of her chauvinistic male peers, such as blustering Sir Herbert Hamilton. The contrast between the health care available to Eleanor's wealthy private clients in Mayfair and the squalor and degradation endured by her most impoverished patients is the driving force that leads her to found the Thrift Infirmary. There she is assisted by the understanding Dr Joe Marsham.

Recalling an age of medical discovery, *Bramwell* reflects on the introduction of such advances as antisepsis and anaesthesia, as well as less successful, often stomach-turning, new treatments. Romantic interest is added for Eleanor in the form of Irish doctor Finn O'Neill (who then jilts her), and later for her father by brewery owner and Thrift benefactor Alice Costigan (whom he marries). After three series up to 1997, *Bramwell* returned briefly in 1998 as two feature-length episodes which take the story on to the year 1899 and the Boer War. Stephen Warbeck composed the music.

Branagh, Kenneth
(1960–)

Belfast-born actor and director, famously once married to Emma Thompson, with whom he starred in the wartime drama FORTUNES OF WAR, playing Guy Pringle. Branagh also supported Emma in her own comedy series, *Thompson*, but decided to further his career in the film world rather than build a television portfolio. However, he returned to the small screen in the new millennium with acclaimed performances as Gen. Reinhard Heydrich in CONSPIRACY and as the polar explorer SHACKLETON, which followed documentary narration on series like *Anne Frank Remembered, The Cold War, Cinema Europe: the Other Hollywood, Great Composers*, WALKING WITH DINOSAURS (and its sequels) and *World War I in Colour*. An early TV role came as Billy Martin in the PLAY FOR TODAY *Too Late to Talk to Billy* (while still a student at RADA), which was followed by two further plays about the same Northern Irish youth, *A Matter of Choice for Billy* and *A Coming to Terms for Billy*. Branagh also appeared in MAYBURY and the dramas *Easter 2016, To the Lighthouse* (Charles Tansley), *Boy in the Bush* (Jack Grant), *Ghosts* (Oswald), *The Lady's Not for Burning* (Thomas Mendip), *Strange Interlude* (Gordon Evans), *Look Back in Anger* (Jimmy Porter) and *The Shadow of a Gunman* (Donal Davoren).

Brand, Jo
(1957–)

Dry, self-deprecating, English comic, seen in series like SATURDAY LIVE and eventually her own showcases, *Jo Brand Through the Cakehole* and *Jo Brand: Like It or Lump It*. Brand is a former psychiatric nurse. Her forthright material has focused on her own appearance (she has referred to herself as the 'Sea Monster') and the inadequacies of the male sex. Other credits have included a comic trawl through the TV archives in *Bad Sports*, the mock debate series, *Head on Comedy with Jo Brand, Jo Brand's Commercial Breakdown, Jo Brand's Hot Potatoes* and the occasional series *The Horror of*... She hosted *Rudest Home Videos* and was a team captain in the panel game 29 MINUTES OF FAME.

Brand, Joshua
(1951–)

Writer/producer whose highly successful work with partner John Falsey has included STEVEN SPIELBERG'S AMAZING STORIES, ST ELSEWHERE, *A Year in the Life*, NORTHERN EXPOSURE and *I'll Fly Away*. Together they run Falahey-Austin Street Productions.

Branded ✶

US (Goodson-Todman) Western. ITV 1965–6 (US: NBC 1965–6)

Jason McCord	**Chuck Connors**

The wanderings of an ex-soldier, dismissed from the army for cowardice.

It is the 1880s and Jason McCord, once a star pupil at West Point, has been dishonourably discharged from the rank of captain in the US Army, accused of cowardice. The only survivor of an Indian massacre at the Battle of Bitter Creek in Wyoming, he had lost consciousness and somehow had been spared. However, the top brass believe he had run away and kick him out of the army.

In an effort to clear his name, McCord meanders across the Wild West, using his skills as an engineer and a mapmaker in a variety of jobs but predominantly aiming to prove to the world that he is no chicken. He also hopes to gather some clues as to what really happened on that fateful day. But, by the end of the series' short run, despite unearthing occasional evidence in his favour, viewers are no nearer to knowing the truth about poor McCord.

Brandreth, Gyles
(1948–)

Professional game show panellist and TV trivialist, wearer of bold sweaters and deviser of various quizzes and puzzles. His work has included CALL MY BLUFF, *Tell the Truth, Puzzle Party, Catchword, Babble, The Railway Carriage Game*, COUNTDOWN (holds the record for appearances in Dictionary Corner), DEAR LADIES (as co-writer), *Public Opinion*, an adaptation of *Alice through the Looking Glass*, and various pieces for breakfast television. A prolific author and Scrabbler, he was Conservative MP for Chester 1992–7.

Brass ✶✶

UK (Granada) Situation Comedy. ITV/Channel 4 1983–4/1990
DVD: Cinema Club

Bradley Hardacre	**Timothy West**
Patience Hardacre	**Caroline Blakiston**
George Fairchild	**Geoffrey Hinsliff**
	Geoffrey Hutchings
Agnes Fairchild	**Barbara Ewing**
Austin Hardacre	**Robert Reynolds**
	Patrick Pearson
Morris Hardacre	**James Saxon**
Charlotte Hardacre	**Emily Morgan**
Isobel Hardacre	**Gail Harrison**
Dr Macduff	**David Ashton**
Lord Mountfast	**John Nettleton**
Jack Fairchild	**Shaun Scott**
Matthew Fairchild	**Gary Cady**

Creators/Writers **John Stevenson, Julian Roach**
Producers **Bill Podmore, Gareth Jones, Mark Robson**

Social injustice, family rivalries and red-hot passion in the 1930s industrial North.

Set in the fictitious town of Utterley, *Brass* exposes the open animosity between two rival families, one rich and powerful, the other poor and subservient, which results in much 'trouble at mill'. At the heart of the action is cruel, power-crazed Bradley Hardacre, a self-made man with interests in mining, munitions and especially cotton milling. His loopy, bitter wife, Patience, though confined to a wheelchair, is a chronic alcoholic; and his children, too, all have their quirks: Austin is ambitious and wants to take over the Empire; Morris is intelligent but immoral; Charlotte is the innocent do-gooder with feminist tendencies; and Isobel is a temptress who later marries into nobility. Working for the Hardacres are the Fairchilds, headed by 'Red' Agnes, who, as well as stoking conflict in the workplace, is also Bradley's mistress. Her sons, Jack and Matthew, are openly hostile to their betters, but her husband, George, is just happy to be in their employ.

This tongue-in-cheek parody of TV's gritty, northern industrial dramas was briefly revived by Channel 4 in 1990, with many of the actors resuming their original roles. For the new series the action was set in 1939 at the outset of war.

Brass Eye ✶✶

UK (Talkback) Comedy. Channel 4 1997; 2001
DVD: VCI

Presenter **Chris Morris**

Producers **Chris Morris, Caroline Leddy, Phil Clarke**

Spoof investigations into social issues.

THE DAY TODAY presenter Chris Morris returned to television with this even spikier combination of satire and send-up, but not before Channel 4 had had second thoughts about letting him loose at all with *Brass Eye*. The series was intended for transmission in November 1996 but was held back for two months for 'review'. When eventually aired, the six episodes – themed around animals, drugs, science, sex, crime and moral decline – certainly kicked up some dust with their edgy mix of current affairs and comedy. Graphic-led tabloid TV news and sensationalist documentaries were the main targets but most striking was the way in which Morris skilfully manoeuvred celebrities into endorsing fictitious campaigns (a politician speaking out on the dangers of the new drug 'cake', for instance). Morris returned to the screens four years later with an even more controversial one-off programme on paedophilia, which drew widespread condemnation for its subject matter but was nevertheless nominated for a BAFTA award.

Bravo

Launched in 1980 as an American cable station specializing in foreign films and the performing arts, Bravo has since undergone two major conversions. Now available on cable and digital television in Europe, the channel moved on to focus on cult (mostly American) TV programmes from bygone days (under the umbrella title of *Timewarp Television*), weepy old movies and weird science-fiction films. However, now owned by Flextech, it has since changed direction yet again and targets its appeal on young males with action flicks, sport and laddish programmes revolving around sex, drink and crime.

Bread ✶✶

UK (BBC) Situation Comedy. BBC 1 1986–91
DVD: Universal

Nellie Boswell	**Jean Boht**
Freddie Boswell	**Ronald Forfar**
Joey Boswell	**Peter Howitt**
	Graham Bickley
Jack Boswell	**Victor McGuire**
Aveline Boswell	**Gilly Coman**
	Melanie Hill
Adrian Boswell	**Jonathon Morris**
Billy Boswell	**Nick Conway**
Grandad	**Kenneth Waller**
Lilo Lil	**Eileen Pollock**
Shifty	**Bryan Murray**
Martina	**Pamela Power**
Julie	**Caroline Milmoe**
	Hilary Crowson
Oswald	**Giles Watling**
Derek	**Peter Byrne**
Celia Higgins	**Rita Tushingham**
Leonora Campbell	**Deborah Grant**

Creator/Writer **Carla Lane**
Producers **Robin Nash, John B. Hobbs**

The trials of a Liverpool family confidently living life on the dole.

The Boswells are the scourge of the DHSS. Although they attempt to make their own way in the world, like many families in the 1980s they are forced to rely on state handouts. But they do so with pride and dignity. They know their entitlements and exploit all the loopholes. Head of their claustrophobic terraced household at 30 Kelsall Street is Nellie Boswell, a devout Catholic housewife who demands the presence of her loyal family at mealtimes, which is when most of the squabbling takes place. Her husband, Freddie, is a waster who spends most of his time in an allotment shed with local strumpet Lilo Lil, so Nellie relies more on her eldest son, the leather-clad Joey, to bring his siblings into line. Squeaky-voiced daughter Aveline is a tasteless dresser who longs to be a model but ends up marrying a vicar named Oswald. Dry, philosophical Jack is the soft-hearted son, Adrian is a poetic, gentle soul, who changes his name from Jimmy to something more appropriate, and the youngest son, Billy, is his antithesis – tactless, big-mouthed and impulsive. Replacing Jack (who has disappeared to America) in some episodes is their cousin Shifty, an appropriately named Irish jailbird. Completing the line-up are the Boswells' impatient and intolerant Grandad, who lives next door and constantly yells for his dinner, their dog Mongy and the exasperated DHSS counter-clerk, Martina. Also in the action are assorted friends, lovers, wives and neighbours.

Breakfast News

See *Breakfast Time*.

Breakfast Time ✶

UK (BBC) News Magazine. BBC 1 1983–9

Presenters **Frank Bough, Selina Scott, Nick Ross, Mike Smith, Debbie Greenwood, John Mountford, Sue Cook, Sally Magnusson, Jeremy Paxman**

Editor **Ron Neil**

Britain's first national breakfast television programme.

Airing at 6.30 a.m. on 17 January 1983, *Breakfast Time* raced past its commercial rival, TV-am's *Good Morning Britain*, to be the first breakfast television programme seen nationally across the UK. Its bright 'sun' logo and cosy studio set reflected the programme's intention to offer a relaxed and informal introduction to the day. Avuncular Frank Bough and Selina Scott were the main hosts, supported by specialist presenters like Francis Wilson (weather), Diana Moran – the 'Green Goddess' (fitness), Russell Grant (horoscopes), Glynn Christian (cookery) and Chris Wilson (gossip column). The news was read by Debbie Rix and, later, by Fern Britton and Sue Carpenter, while sport was handled by David Icke and then by Bob Wilson. Nick Ross, Mike Smith, Debbie Greenwood, John Mountford, Sue Cook, Sally Magnusson and Jeremy Paxman also took their places on the red leather sofa at various times.

In 1989 the magazine element of the programme was dropped in favour of in-depth news coverage. The programme title was changed to *Breakfast News* and newsreaders such as Nicholas Witchell and Jill Dando replaced the jovial, casual presenters. In 2000, the programme became known simply as *Breakfast*.

Breaking the Code ✶✶✶

UK (The Drama House/BBC/WGBH Boston) Drama. BBC 1 1997

Alan Turing	**Derek Jacobi**
	William Mannering *(young)*
Sara Turing	**Prunella Scales**
Dilwyn Knox	**Richard Johnson**
Mick Ross	**Alun Armstrong**
Pat Green	**Amanda Root**
John Smith	**Harold Pinter**
Ron Miller	**Julian Kerridge**
Christopher Morcom	**Blake Ritson**

Writer **Hugh Whitemore**
Producer **Jack Emery**

The personal and professional troubles of a mathematical genius.

Hugh Whitemore's triumphant stage dramatization of the life of Alan Turing proved just as successful when it transferred to television in this one-off drama. Turing is a brilliant mathematician, working for the Government at Bletchley Park in Buckinghamshire during World War II. His mission is to crack the Enigma code being used by the Germans. In so doing, he is pivotal, in many observers' view, for the Allies gaining the upper hand in the conflict. With direction from Herbert Wise, Whitemore tells Turing's story from his schoolboy days through to life after the war, when – equally unwilling to compromise in his private life or in his work – he falls foul of the prevailing laws against homosexuality. He becomes a victim of the state he helped preserve. Sara Turing is his haughty mother; Dilwyn Knox is Turing's boss; Pat Green is the girl who wants to marry him; and John Smith is the security services man who instructs Turing to bury his homosexuality.

Whitemore's original play was itself influenced by a book, *Alan Turing: the Enigma*, by Andrew Hodges.

Bremner, Rory

(1961–)

Edinburgh-born impressionist, majoring in topical satire. As well as having his own series for the BBC (*Now – Something Else* and *Rory Bremner*, particularly) and various offerings on Channel 4 (*Rory Bremner ... Who Else?* and *Bremner, Bird and Fortune*, most notably), Bremner has also contributed to SPITTING IMAGE and *Breakfast With Frost*. In contrast, he took the role of Kevin Beesely in the drama *You, Me and It*. More recently, he was team captain in the panel game *Mock the Week*. His speciality take-offs include Richie Benaud, Desmond Lynam, Barry Norman, Denis Norden and Tony Blair.

Brett ✶✶

UK (BBC) Drama. BBC 1 1971

H. Thomas Brett	**Patrick Allen**
Nick Brunel	**Robin Bailey**
Françoise Leroy	**Hannah Gordon**
William Saxby	**Peter Bowles**
Lois	**Jean Macfarlane**
Treville	**Noel Willman**
Alderman/Sir Goronwy Griffiths	**Windsor Davies**
Huw Morgan	**Aubrey Richards**
Spencer Griffiths	**Michael Hawkins**
Gwyneth	**Beth Owen**
	Jennifer Lee
Morris	**Glyn Houston**
Sam	**Raymond Brody**
Caroline Fleming	**Judith Arthy**
Howard K. Fleming	**Clive Revill**
Louise Fleming	**Helen Horton**
Gerald Delamore	**Anthony Ainley**
Duffy	**Rio Fanning**

Creators **Compton Bennett, Derek Glynne**
Producer **Royston Morley**

A ruthless entrepreneur has a shady past.

Brett is a businessman who gets his kicks from risky deals. He's ambitious, powerful and wealthy but one day he receives a shock that causes him to reflect on his turbulent life to date. Told in flashback over 19 episodes (with writers including Michael J. Bird, Elwyn Jones and Donald Bull), Brett's past is revealed in all its controversial colour. He is brought up in Wales and starts out as a reporter on a Valleys newspaper, the *Aberyswen Gazette*. However, his investigative work brings him into conflict with the police – a foreshadow of what is to follow. Brett then writes a novel called *The Ruined Valley*, which looks like making his fortune when it is acquired for Hollywood treatment, with Brett himself engaged as writer. He starts working on the script but realizes that his involvement is but a placebo: other writers are working on a version that the studio really wants. His views of Hollywood are further jaundiced by the Establishment witchhunts of the 1950s that are driving good writers and actors out of the business because they are suspected of 'un-American' views. Brett later journeys through Central America and on his return meets and marries wealthy American Caroline Fleming. Howard, his new father-in-law, is head of the powerful Fleming Corporation, which Brett could take over – but only if he plays Howard's little game. Instead he returns to Britain and begins amassing a fortune by investing in marinas. But pride comes before a fall and, with his past catching up with him, Brett is destined to spend time in prison – a far cry from his luxury home in London's Fitzroy Place.

Brett, Jeremy

(Jeremy Huggins; 1933–95)

English Shakespearean and character actor now associated with Conan Doyle's Sherlock Holmes, having given his moody portrayal of the celebrated detective for over ten years. He played D'Artagnan in the BBC's 1966 version of *The Three Musketeers*, Count Kinsky in JENNIE, LADY RANDOLPH CHURCHILL and Maxim de Winter in its 1979 adaptation of REBECCA. He was William Pitt the Younger in *No. 10* and took parts in many series, such as THE CHAMPIONS, COUNTRY MATTERS, *Affairs of the Heart*, SUPERNATURAL, *Haunted* and MOTHER LOVE. Brett's first wife was actress Anna Massey.

Bretts, The ✶

UK (Central) Drama. ITV 1987
DVD: BFS Entertainment (Region 1 only)

Charles Brett .... **Norman Rodway**
Lydia Brett .... **Barbara Murray**
Edwin Brett .... **David Yelland**
Martha Brett .... **Belinda Lang**
Thomas Brett .... **George Winter**
Alfred Sutton .... **Tim Wylton**
Nell Caldwell .... **Victoria Burton**
John Caldwell .... **Charles Collingwood**
Perdita Brett .... **Sally Cookson**
George Brett .... **Frank Middlemass**
Maeve Brett .... **Helen McCarthy**
Emily .... **Rebecca Lacey**
Flora Evans .... **Rhoda Lewis**
Patrick Hegarty .... **Billy Boyle**
Jean Lacy .... **Janet Maw**

Creator **Rosemary Anne Sisson**
Executive Producers **Ted Childs, Colin Callender, Frank Marshall**
Producer **Tony Charles**

● ***The lives and loves of a theatrical family.***

Charles Brett is an actor, a West End star of the 1920s whose hyper-dramatic nature lands him in as much melodrama off stage as on. A terrible womanizer, he is constantly at odds with his wife, Lydia, another prize flouncer who stars in musical comedies under the stage name of Lydia Wheatley. These are the highly strung heads of the household (Nightingale Grove in Hampstead) who look down on their various troubled offspring, including Edwin, who only becomes a star once the movies arrive, and his twin sister, Martha. A World War I widow (her husband had been Edwin's best friend), Martha lives life to the full and, like her parents, is no stranger to outrageous behaviour – and its consequences. Third and fourth siblings are Thomas, a quieter child who finds his niche in writing plays, and Nell, who shunned the stage altogether, married stockbroker John Caldwell and now has two children of her own. Baby of the family is Perdita who, despite having been banished to a convent to deny her access to the stage, will not be thwarted in her relentless quest for fame. In UPSTAIRS, DOWNSTAIRS fashion, members of the servant class also have their say. Jean Lacy is the secretary, butler Alfred Sutton is a failed actor who would have loved to reach the heights of his employers, and Patrick Hegarty is the chauffeur who attracts the ladies (across the classes). Flora is a film fanatic who was nanny to the children but has been maintained as the (not terribly good) cook, and then there is Emily, a parlour maid whose inquisitive nature regularly gets her into trouble. With Charles's parents, George and Maeve – itinerant actors who can't give up the limelight – also dropping by, *The Bretts* is a story of four generations of an acting family coming to terms with a rapidly developing industry and a time of social change. One major story line concerns the unexpected purchase by Charles of the Princess Theatre and the subsequent trauma when it burns down. However, the trials of this particular family failed to charm the viewers. Their shallow tantrums, posing and posturing instilled little warmth. Director of the 11-part serial was Ronald Wilson.

Brides in the Bath, The ✶✶

UK (Yorkshire) Drama. ITV 1 2003

George Joseph Smith .... **Martin Kemp**
Sir Edward Marshall-Hall .... **Richard Griffiths**
Bessie Mundy .... **Charlotte Randle**
Alice Burnham .... **Emma Ferguson**
Caroline Thornhill .... **Jennifer Calvert**
Mrs Crossley .... **Susan Brown**
Elizabeth Burnham .... **Joanna David**
Charles Burnham .... **Peter Wight**
Margaret Lofty .... **Carolyn Backhouse**
Edith May Smith .... **Tracey Wilkinson**
Howard Mundy .... **Anthony Calf**

Writer **Glenn Chandler**
Executive Producer **David Reynolds**
Producer **Alan Dossor**

● ***A charming but deadly villain murders his wealthy wives.***

This two-hour reconstruction of the true events surrounding the 'Brides in the Bath' murders perpetrated by George Joseph Smith between 1912 and 1914 was ITV 1's big New Year's Eve presentation in 2003. The story reveals how the silver-tongued, duplicitous Londoner adopted various false identities to ensnare into marriage three prosperous women – Bessie Mundy, Alice Burnham and Margaret Lofty – then drown them in the bath. Smith was finally arrested in 1915 and Sir Edward Marshall-Hall was the barrister charged with saving him from the gallows. He was unsuccessful. The screenplay was penned by TAGGART creator Glenn Chandler and filming took place in a number of Yorkshire towns and cities.

Brideshead Revisited ★★★★

UK (Granada) Drama. ITV 1981
DVD: Granada Ventures

Charles Ryder	**Jeremy Irons**
Lord Sebastian Flyte	**Anthony Andrews**
Lord Alex Marchmain	**Laurence Olivier**
Edward Ryder	**John Gielgud**
Lady Julia Flyte	**Diana Quick**
Lady Marchmain	**Claire Bloom**
Lady Cordelia Flyte	**Phoebe Nicholls**
Lord Brideshead	**Simon Jones**
Anthony Blanche	**Nickolas Grace**
Jasper	**Stephen Moore**
Collins	**Christopher Good**
Lunt	**Bill Owen**
Viscount 'Boy' Mulcaster	**Jeremy Sinden**
Nanny Hawkins	**Mona Washbourne**
Sgt Block	**Kenneth Cranham**
Lt Hooper	**Richard Hope**
Mr Samgrass	**John Grillo**
Rex Mottram	**Charles Keating**
Celia Mulcaster/Ryder	**Jane Asher**
Kurt	**Jonathan Coy**
Cara	**Stéphane Audran**

Writer **John Mortimer**
Producer **Derek Granger**

Aristocratic decadence in the inter-war years.

Brideshead Revisited is the story of Army Captain Charles Ryder, whose unit is stationed in the grounds of Brideshead Castle in Wiltshire during the closing days of World War II (1944). But Ryder himself has been here before, and during this 11-part drama he recounts events in his earlier life, reflecting on the passing of an era.

Charles's connections with Brideshead begin with Sebastian Flyte, the teddy-bear ('Aloysius') carrying son of Lord Marchmain, proprietor of the estate. They meet at Oxford in the 1920s and Charles tumbles in with Sebastian's drunkenly decadent troupe of gay young blades. He becomes a house guest at Brideshead and later falls for Julia, Sebastian's sister. With the family, Charles (a painter) travels extensively, and life in this aristocratic household opens his eyes to many things. He is fascinated by their behaviour, their mannerisms, their conversations. The beautiful Marchmain estate, with its gardens, fountains and private chapel, hold him in awe. Indeed, he is absorbed by their closed, extravagant world and a style of living that belongs to an age rapidly drawing to a close. But it is the overwhelming power that Catholicism exerts over the family which proves most intriguing.

Brideshead Revisited, closely adapted by John Mortimer from Evelyn Waugh's passionate novel, very nearly became one of television's great disaster stories. Soon after production had begun (using Castle Howard in Yorkshire as the fictitious Brideshead, with other scenes shot at Tatton Park, Cheshire) filming was halted by an ITV technicians' dispute. By the time the strike ended, many of the cast and crew had other commitments, contracts had run out and it seemed that the work would never be finished. But to scrap the project would have been almost as costly as continuing, so the decision was made by Granada to press on. Director Michael Lindsay-Hogg had to be replaced by young Charles Sturridge, and Jeremy Irons was dragged away for three months to make *The French Lieutenant's Woman*. But, at more than twice the original cost, *Brideshead Revisited* did eventually reach the TV screen. For many viewers, it was well worth the wait. The beauty of the photography and easy pace of the rich narrative won many fans. Awards were showered on the production and sales around the world were enormous. The theme music was written by Geoffrey Burgon.

Briers, Richard

CBE (1934–)

Popular, London-born actor, often in whimsical, slightly eccentric roles. Richard Briers first found TV fame in the early 1960s, as Roger Thursby in BROTHERS IN LAW and George Starling in THE MARRIAGE LINES. However, it was more than ten years later, after other comedy roles in series like *Ben Travers Farces, Tall Stories* and the sitcom *Birds on the Wing* (Charles Jackson), that he became a household name. His portrayal of Tom Good, with Felicity Kendal as his spirited wife, in THE GOOD LIFE, inspired some viewers to leave the rat race and give self-sufficiency a go. After an appearance in *The Norman Conquests*, and a lead role in the sketch show *One-Upmanship*, plus lesser success in the sitcoms THE OTHER ONE (Ralph) and GOODBYE MR KENT (Travis Kent), Briers bounced back in EVER DECREASING CIRCLES, as the pedantic Martin Bryce opposite an exasperated Penelope Wilton. In 1985 he took on the role of vicar Philip Lambe in ALL IN GOOD FAITH. After time on the stage, he returned to the small screen in 1993 in IF YOU SEE GOD, TELL HIM, playing Godfrey Spry, a man with an attention span of only 30 seconds, and followed this with the part of George in *Screen Two*'s *Skallagrigg*. In 1995 he starred as ex-diplomat Tony Fairfax in another sitcom, DOWN TO EARTH, and appeared in the one-off *P. G. Wodehouse's Heavy Weather* (Threepwood). Later he was seen as Sir Charles Fairley in the slave drama *A Respectable Trade*, as Hector Macdonald in MONARCH OF THE GLEN, as Joseph Paxton in *Victoria and Albert* and as Larry James in *Dad*, as well as in numerous guest roles (INSPECTOR MORSE, MIDSOMER MURDERS, etc.). Briers is also a voice-over specialist – he narrated the cartoon series ROOBARB and NOAH AND NELLY, and has contributed to BOB THE BUILDER – and has also won plaudits for his classical roles, which have included Malvolio in *Twelfth Night*. He is married to actress Ann Davies and is the father of actress Lucy Briers.

Briggs, Johnny

(1935–)

London-born actor, earlier in his career often seen on the wrong side of the law. His television break came when he switched sides to become DS Russell in NO HIDING PLACE, progressing into soap opera in 1973 with CROSSROADS (Clifford Leyton) and ultimately assuming his most famous *alter ego*, that of devious businessman Mike Baldwin in CORONATION STREET, in 1976. In the 1960s and 1970s Briggs also appeared in programmes as diverse as THE PLANE MAKERS, THE SAINT, Z CARS, MOGUL, THE AVENGERS, LOVE THY NEIGHBOUR, MY WIFE NEXT DOOR, BRIGHT'S BOFFINS (Tippy the Tipster), NO – HONESTLY, YUS MY DEAR and THICK AS THIEVES.

Bright's Boffins ★

UK (Southern) Children's Situation Comedy. ITV 1970–2

Group Capt. Bertram Bright	**Alexander Doré**
Molly McCrandle	**Avril Angers**
Sgt Thumper	**Denis Shaw**
Berk	**George Moon**

Prof. Farthing .... **Bartlett Mullins**
Julie Farthing .... **Belinda Sinclair**
Peter Vincent .... **Anthony Verner**
'Dogsears' Dawson .... **Gordon Rollings**
'Catseyes' Kavanagh .... **Dominic Roche**
Oswald .... **Sadie Corre**
Marmaduke .... **Eddie Reindeer**
Tippy the Tipster .... **Johnny Briggs**

Writers **Keith Miles, Dennis Goodwin, Dominic Roche**
Producer **Peter Croft**

● ***The misadventures of a team of inept government scientists.***

Group Captain Bertram Bright is the idiotic leader of a band of RAF buffoons who work at an obscure Government research centre. Appropriately named Halfwitt House (real-life Rhinefield House in the New Forest), the building is home to assorted nuts and fruitcakes, including head of security Sgt Thumper and an extraterrestrial named Oswald. Most of the crew's time seems to be devoted to testing out the wacky inventions of resident scientist Prof. Farthing. What time remains is allocated to helping Bright deceive and cheat the authorities so that they can cling on to their minuscule budget, keeping the establishment open as the Government axe is sharpened. At the start of the second series Halfwitt House has burned to the ground and Bright and his boffins are forced to take up residence in the disused Great Wiffington railway station (renamed 'Larst Halt'; filmed at Liss, Hampshire). The team move on to yet another new base – a country farmhouse – in the third and final series. Dominic Roche, who wrote most of the episodes, also appeared regularly in the programme, taking a number of small roles.

Brighton Belles ✶

UK (Carlton) Situation Comedy. ITV 1993–4

Frances .... **Sheila Hancock**
Annie .... **Wendy Craig**
Bridget .... **Sheila Gish**
Josephine .... **Jean Boht**

Creator **Susan Harris**
Writer **Christopher Skala**
Producer **Humphrey Barclay**

● ***British adaptation of* THE GOLDEN GIRLS.**

Christopher Skala took SUSAN HARRIS's early scripts for the hit US sitcom THE GOLDEN GIRLS and shaped them into a British comedy. Transferring the action from Miami to Brighton, Skala re-created the 'life begins at 60' atmosphere of the American original, sticking closely to the established character profiles but renaming and repositioning them for UK consumption. Thus we have Frances (the Dorothy character), a former headmistress now in her early 60s and divorced from husband Gilbert. Sarcasm is her trademark. Annie (Rose) grew up on a farm in Wiltshire and is therefore out of touch with the wider world, while Bridget (Blanche), whose house they live in, is a man-hungry vamp who works as a curator in a museum. These three are joined (in the pilot episode) by Frances's homeless mother, Josephine (Sophia). A plain-speaking Scotswoman in her 80s, she was once married to a Glaswegian gangster and knows a thing or two about life as a result.

The pilot for *Brighton Belles* was shown as part of ITV's 1993 COMEDY PLAYHOUSE anthology. That the subsequent series didn't fare well must have had something to do with the fact that UK viewers were already very familiar with the highly polished American original.

Brit Awards, The

See *Brits, The.*

British Academy of Film and Television Arts

See *Bafta.*

British Broadcasting Corporation

See *BBC.*

British Comedy Awards, The ✶✶

UK (LWT) Comedy/Awards. ITV 1990–

Presenters **Michael Parkinson, Jonathan Ross**

Producers **Michael Hurll, Susie Dark, Alasdair MacMillan, Alex Hardcastle, Helen Kristic**

● ***Annual awards bash dedicated to the art of mirth-making.***

The British Comedy Awards has grown from a nervous start in 1990, when Michael Parkinson formally dealt out the honours to the assembled giants of humour at the London Palladium. A year later, the venue was moved to LWT's studios, Jonathan Ross took over as host, a lighter, more risqué tone was adopted and the ceremony was well on its way to establishing itself as one of the focal points of the comedy calendar. Not that everyone has given the proceedings due respect. Chris Evans, having taken his fill of the 'Jester' plaques, promptly announced that he didn't want any more and reportedly gave one of his trophies to a waitress. Among the 'highlights' has been Spike Milligan's uproarious 'grovelling bastard' riposte to the Prince of Wales, who had sent his comedy hero a written tribute to coincide with Spike's receipt of a lifetime achievement award. Equally infamous was Julian Clary's crude remark about Norman Lamont. Such are the risks of broadcasting live.

British Record Industry Awards, The

See *Brits, The.*

British Satellite Broadcasting

See *BSkyB.*

British Sky Broadcasting

See *BSkyB.*

Brits, The/The Brit Awards ✶

UK (BBC/Carlton). BBC 1 1985–92; ITV 1993–

Presenters **Noel Edmonds, Jonathan King, Samantha Fox, Mick Fleetwood, Cathy McGowan, Richard O'Brien, Elton John, RuPaul, Chris Evans, Ben Elton, Johnny Vaughan, Davina McCall, Ant and Dec, Zoë Ball, Frank Skinner, Cat Deeley**

Producers **Michael Hurll, Michael Appleton, Jonathan King, Chris Cowie, Malcolm Gerrie, Andy Ward, Rocky Oldham, Guy Freeman, Helen Terry**

Often controversial annual awards bash for the British recording industry.

The British Record Industry Awards began life as a black-tie occasion for record company executives in 1977 to celebrate 100 years of recorded music. The idea was resurrected in 1982 and became an annual affair, but the event has only been televised since 1985. The 150 or so companies that form the British Phonographic Industry all have votes in determining each year's winners in a range of categories, from Best Male and Female Artists to Best Album. However, after criticism that only headline artists were picking up accolades, the voting system was revamped in 1994 to reflect the broader church of British pop music. Some viewer voting was also added. Noel Edmonds hosted the first televised gong show (still a dinner-jacket affair at the Grosvenor House Hotel), with Mike Smith adding commentary. A major revamp in 1989 saw the name change to 'The Brits' and resulted in one of TV's all-time great disaster shows, when the 'little and large' combination of page 3 model Samantha Fox and Fleetwood Mac drummer Mick Fleetwood fumbled their way through a series of calamities (failing autocues, fluffed lines, wrong guests being announced, etc.). ITV took over broadcast coverage in 1993. The ceremony has long departed from its formal roots and has now become notorious for the posturing and political views of a handful of publicity-conscious guests. In 1991 Sinead O'Connor boycotted the event because of the Gulf War; in 1996 Pulp's Jarvis Cocker gatecrashed Michael Jackson's stage routine and waggled his bottom in protest at the American star's messianic act; and in 1998 Danbert Nobacon of Chumbawamba threw a bucket of water over Deputy Prime Minister John Prescott. A rather more sedate companion ceremony, *The Classical Brits*, was launched in 2000 (ITV) with Trevor McDonald hosting affairs at the Royal Albert Hall. Classical awards had previously been discretionary add-ons to the main rock and pop event.

Brittas Empire, The ✱✱

UK (BBC) Situation Comedy. BBC 1 1991–4; 1996–7
DVD: Eureka Video

Gordon Brittas	**Chris Barrie**
Helen Brittas	**Pippa Haywood**
Laura Lancing	**Julia St John**
Carole	**Harriet Thorpe**
Colin Wetherby	**Michael Burns**
Tim Whistler	**Russell Porter**
Gavin Featherly	**Tim Marriott**
Angie	**Andrée Bernard**
Julie	**Judy Flynn**
Linda	**Jill Greenacre**
Penny Bidmead	**Anouschka Menzies**
Councillor Druggett	**Stephen Churchett**

Creators **Richard Fegen, Andrew Norriss**
Producer **Mike Stephens**

An over-zealous manager brings chaos to a modern sports centre.

Insufferable, pedantic, patronizing, incompetent and accident-prone are all inadequate ways of describing Gordon Brittas, manager of the Whitbury Newtown leisure centre. Whatever he attempts inevitably ends in failure and near loss of life. Brittas runs his little kingdom with a firm hand, planning events meticulously and laying down the law to his unfortunate staff. With disaster always lurking around the corner, it is left to his level-headed number two, Laura, to pick up the pieces and restore calm. Julie, his secretary, simply despairs, and the only member of staff who looks up to Brittas is loyal Colin, the dim, Geordie maintenance man. Other team members are tearful, often homeless receptionist Carol (who keeps her children in a cupboard behind her desk), ambitious coaches Tim and Gavin, and sports assistant Linda. Gordon's wife, Helen, looks after his children, including twins Matthew and Mark, and pops tranquillizers to keep herself sane.

The series appeared to have ended in 1994, when the sanctimonious menace was appointed a European Commissioner, but the indestructible Brittas survived this, and being flattened by a water tank, only to resurface, to everyone's dismay – especially his wife's – in 1996. A new arrival at the centre at this time is Penny, boss of the privatized sauna/solarium. Even when the end did finally arrive for the series, the grotesque Gordon was not through. He (with wife Helen) resurfaced as a fitness counsellor on BBC 1's short course *Get Fit with Brittas*, in summer 1997.

Creators Richard Fegen and Andrew Norriss penned all episodes up to the final two series, when various other writers were introduced.

Britton, Fern

(1958–)

British presenter of news and lifestyle programmes, the daughter of actor Tony Britton. Among her many credits have been BREAKFAST TIME, *The Television Show, The Brian Conley Show*, GMTV, *Ready Steady Cook, DIY Disaster, This Morning, Loose Women, Soapstar Superstar*, and regional news magazines like *Coast to Coast*. She married TV chef Phil Vickery in 2000.

Britton, Tony

(1924–)

British actor, familiar in snooty, upper-class parts. His most successful TV roles have been as Chris Collinson in *The Nearly Man*, James Nicholls in ROBIN'S NEST, Dr Toby Latimer in DON'T WAIT UP and Vivian Bancroft in DON'T TELL FATHER, although other credits have included FATHER, DEAR FATHER (Bill Mossman), AND MOTHER MAKES FIVE (Joss Spencer), STRANGERS AND BROTHERS and THE WAY WE LIVE NOW (Lord Alfred Grendall), plus ARMCHAIR THEATRE presentations and plays like *The Dame of Sark* (1976). A recent guest appearance came in MY DAD'S THE PRIME MINISTER. He is the father of presenter Fern Britton.

Broadbent, Jim

(1949–)

Oscar-winning English actor, in comic and dramatic roles. His major credits have come in SILAS MARNER (Jem Rodney), GONE TO THE DOGS (Jim Morley), GONE TO SEED (Monty Plant), *Heroes and Villains* (Col. A. D. Wintle: *The Last Englishman*), *Screen One*'s *Wide-Eyed and Legless* (Deric Longden), THE PETER PRINCIPLE (Peter Duffley), THE GATHERING STORM (Desmond Morton) and *The Young Visiters* (Alfred Salteena), with other parts in series like *Birth of a Nation, Dramarama*, BIRD OF PREY, THE COMIC STRIP PRESENTS, HAPPY FAMILIES, INSPECTOR MORSE, BLACKADDER, *Victoria Wood*, MURDER MOST HORRID, and a few appearances as the slimy Roy Slater in ONLY FOOLS

AND HORSES (Broadbent, in fact, turned down the role of Del Boy before it was offered to David Jason). His voice has also been heard in THE STAGGERING STORIES OF FERDINAND DE BARGOS, *Pride* (Eddie) and in the *Percy the Park Keeper* animations.

Broadcasting

The transmission of radio or TV signals to be received by the general public, as opposed to narrowcasting, cable or closed-circuit systems that supply signals to only a limited audience.

Broker's Man, The ✶

UK (Bentley) Drama. BBC 1 1997–8

Jimmy Griffin	**Kevin Whately**
Vinny Stanley	**Al Hunter Ashton**
Harriet Potter	**Sarah Jane Potts**
	Charlotte Bellamy
Sally Griffin	**Annette Ekblom**
Jodie Griffin	**Holly Davidson**
Dominic Griffin	**Danny Worters**
Gabby Rodwell	**Michelle Fairley**
Alex 'Godzilla' Turnbull	**Peter Firth**
	John McEnery
Claudette Monro-Foster	**Jill Baker**
Frank Mortimer	**Trevor Byfield**

Creators **Al Hunter Ashton, Tim O'Mara**
Producers **Adrian Bate, Carol Wilks**

● ***The perilous world of an insurance claims investigator.***

Jimmy Griffin, once a policeman, now runs his own business, working as an insurance investigator. This means he snoops around trying to discover if claims received by insurance companies are legitimate. But forget water-damaged carpets and broken windows: Griffin's workload usually involves serious fraudsters. Assisted by sidekicks Harriet Potter (keen and young) and Vinny Stanley (a copper thrown out of the force for drunk-driving – played by co-creator Al Hunter Ashton), he may be tracking the thieves of a shipping container in Amsterdam or looking for the true cause of a nightclub fire. It's a dangerous world, inhabited by some unsavoury characters who will stop at nothing to protect their interests. Making life even more difficult is 'Godzilla' Turnbull, the broker who employs him and who hates paying out on claims, plus the two women in his world, ex-wife Sally and secret girlfriend Gabby, another insurance broker. Little wonder he's always in a bad mood. Jodie and Dominic are his two kids.

Bronco ✶

US (Warner Brothers) Western. BBC 1959–64 (US: ABC 1958–62)

Bronco Layne	**Ty Hardin**

● ***A former Confederate Army captain drifts across the Wild West.***

Bronco was a series that evolved out of CHEYENNE and a star-versus-studio squabble; the star was Clint Walker, of *Cheyenne*, and the studio was Warner Brothers. Failing to resolve the dispute, Warners recast *Cheyenne* with a new lead character, pitching Ty Hardin into the role of Bronco Layne. Eventually Walker returned to the fold, but Bronco continued in his own series. To add to the confusion, some *Bronco* episodes were then screened in the USA under the umbrella title of *Cheyenne*, as part of a rotating trilogy which also included *Sugarfoot*, starring Will Hutchins (shown in the UK as *Tenderfoot*).

The character of Bronco is very much a loner. With the end of the Civil War, he heads west, where he meets up with the likes of Billy the Kid and Jesse James, but he is never given a regular supporting cast.

Bronowski, Jacob

(1902–74)

Polish-born scientist Jacob Bronowski became an unlikely TV hero in 1973 when his ambitious TV series THE ASCENT OF MAN was screened on BBC 2. His raw enthusiasm, curious hunched poses and evident erudition produced a winning combination for viewers, many of whom would never have watched such an academic series without him. Sadly, he had little time to enjoy his new fame, dying a year later at the age of 72, exhausted by his efforts on the series. Bronowski had been educated at Cambridge and settled with his family in Britain. As well as writing various scientific tomes he had also presented several programmes in the same vein on television and was a member of THE BRAINS TRUST.

Brooke-Taylor, Tim

(1940–)

British comic actor and writer, a product of the Cambridge Footlights. Emerging from innovative 1960s comedy shows like ON THE BRADEN BEAT, THE FROST REPORT (writing with Eric Idle), AT LAST THE 1948 SHOW, *Twice a Fortnight* (largely as writer), *Broaden Your Mind* and *Marty* (straight man to Marty Feldman), he hit the big time as one of THE GOODIES. From there he moved into sitcom with less success, in *His and Hers* (Toby Burgess), *The Rough with the Smooth* (Richard Woodville, also as co-writer), ME AND MY GIRL (Derek Yates) and *You Must be the Husband* (Tom Hammond). He was also seen in the sketch shows *Hello Cheeky* and *Assaulted Nuts*, as Victor Meldrew's next-door neighbour in ONE FOOT IN THE GRAVE, and as the Chaplain in *TLC*. With the other Goodies, he supplied voices for the cartoon series BANANAMAN. In recent years he has made guest appearances in CROSSROADS, *Absolute Power* and HEARTBEAT, hosted the daytime quiz *Beat the Nation* with fellow Goodie Graeme Garden, and presented *Golf Clubs with Tim Brooke-Taylor* for digital TV.

Brooks, James L.

(1940–)

American writer/producer whose first success came with THE MARY TYLER MOORE SHOW, followed by one of its spin-offs, RHODA (both with his partner, Allen Burns). Brooks moved on to TAXI, *The Associates* and LOU GRANT, before branching out into movies (*Terms of Endearment, Broadcast News, Big*, etc.), then returning to TV with *The Tracey Ullman Show* and THE SIMPSONS (as executive producer). Other credits include *The Days and Nights of Molly Dodd, Eisenhower and Lutz* (as writer), *Phenom, The Critic* and *What About Joan?*

Brooks, Ray

(1939–)

Sussex-born actor whose big TV break came in the harrowing 1966 play, CATHY COME HOME. After appearances in programmes such as GIDEON'S WAY, CORONATION STREET, RANDALL AND HOPKIRK (DECEASED) and TAXI (the UK version), Brooks narrated the animations MR BENN and KING ROLLO, and then starred as Robbie Box in BIG DEAL in 1984. Subsequently, he has appeared in *Running Wild* (retro teddy boy Max Wild), *The World of Eddie Weary* (title role), P. D. JAMES's *Death of an Expert Witness*, GROWING PAINS (Tom Hollingsworth), TWO THOUSAND ACRES OF SKY (Terry Marsh) and EASTENDERS (Joe Macer).

Brookside ★★

UK (Mersey) Drama. Channel 4 1982–2003
DVD: Fremantle Home Entertainment

Roger Huntington .... **Rob Spendlove**
Heather Huntington/Haversham/Black .... **Amanda Burton**
Sheila Grant/Corkhill .... **Sue Johnston**
Bobby Grant .... **Ricky Tomlinson**
Barry Grant .... **Paul Usher**
Damon Grant .... **Simon O'Brien**
Karen Grant .... **Shelagh O'Hara**
Paul Collins .... **Jim Wiggins**
Annabelle Collins .... **Doreen Sloane**
Lucy Collins .... **Katrin Cartlidge**
Maggie Saunders
Gordon Collins .... **Nigel Crowley**
Mark Burgess
Gavin Taylor .... **Daniel Webb**
Petra Taylor .... **Alexandra Pigg**
Matty Nolan .... **Tony Scoggo**
Terry Sullivan .... **Brian Regan**
Gizzmo Hawkins .... **Robert Smith**
Ducksie Brown .... **Mark Birch**
George Williams .... **Doc O'Brien**
Alan Partridge .... **Dicken Ashworth**
Samantha Partridge .... **Dinah May**
Harry Cross .... **Bill Dean**
Edna Cross .... **Betty Alberge**
Michelle Jones .... **Tracey Jay**
George Jackson .... **Cliff Howells**
Marie Jackson .... **Anna Keaveney**
Gary Jackson .... **Allan Patterson**
George Jackson Jr .... **Steven Patterson**
Teresa Nolan .... **Ann Haydn Edwards**
Pat Hancock .... **David Easter**
Kate Moses .... **Sharon Rosita**
Sandra Maghie .... **Sheila Grier**
Tommy McArdle .... **Malcolm Tierney**
Kevin Cross .... **Stuart Organ**
Sally Haynes .... **Roberta Kerr**
Ralph Hardwick .... **Ray Dunbobbin**
Thomas 'Sinbad' Sweeney .... **Michael Starke**
Jack Sullivan .... **William Maxwell**
Vicki Cleary .... **Cheryl Leigh**
Billy Corkhill .... **John McArdle**
Doreen Corkhill .... **Kate Fitzgerald**
Rod Corkhill .... **Jason Hope**
Tracy Corkhill .... **Justine Kerrigan**
Jimmy Corkhill .... **Dean Sullivan**
Nicholas Black .... **Alan Rothwell**
Julia Brogan .... **Gladys Ambrose**
Kirsty Brown .... **Joanne Black**
Madge Richmond .... **Shirley Stelfox**
Christopher Duncan .... **Stifyn Parri**
Debbie McGrath .... **Gillian Kearney**
Sizzler .... **Renny Krupinski**
Mona Harvey/Fallon .... **Margaret Clifton**
Jonathan Gordon-Davies .... **Steven Pinner**
Laura Wright/Gordon-Davies . **Jane Cunliffe**
Jamie Henderson .... **Sean McKee**
Sue Harper/Sullivan .... **Annie Miles**
Frank Rogers .... **Peter Christian**
Chrissy Rogers .... **Eithne Browne**
Sammy Rogers/Daniels/Deveraux .... **Rachael Lindsay**
Geoff Rogers .... **Kevin Carson**
Stephen Walters
Katie Rogers .... **Debbie Reynolds**
Diane Burke
Cheryl Boyanowsky .... **Jennifer Calvert**
Nisha Batra .... **Sunetra Sarker**
Kathy Roach .... **Noreen Kershaw**
'Tommo' Thompson .... **John O'Gorman**
Nikki White .... **Michelle Byatt**
'Bumper' Humphries .... **James Mawdsley**
Michael Choi .... **David Yip**
Caroline Choi .... **Sarah Lam**
Sean Roach .... **Derek Hicks**
Mick Johnson .... **Louis Emerick**
Owen Daniels .... **Danny McCall**
Marcia Barrett .... **Cheryl Maiker**
Josie Johnson .... **Suzanne Packer**
Gemma Johnson .... **Naomi Kamanga**
Carla Jarrett
Leo Johnson .... **Leeon Sawyer**
Steven Cole
Diana Spence/Corkhill .... **Paula Frances**
Margaret Clemence .... **Nicola Stephenson**
Derek O'Farrell .... **Clive Moore**
D-D Dixon .... **Irene Marot**
Ron Dixon .... **Vince Earl**
Cyril Dixon .... **Allan Surtees**
Jacqui Dixon/Farnham .... **Alexandra Fletcher**
Mike Dixon .... **Paul Byatt**
Tony Dixon .... **Gerard Bostock**
Mark Lennock
Max Farnham .... **Steven Pinder**
Patricia Farnham .... **Gabrielle Glaister**
Jackie Corkhill .... **Sue Jenkins**
Jimmy Corkhill Jr .... **George Christopher**
Graeme Curtis .... **David Banks**
Fran Pearson .... **Julie Peasgood**
Ellis Johnson .... **Francis Johnson**
John Harrison .... **Geoffrey Leesley**
Barbara Harrison .... **Angela Morant**
Keith Rooney .... **Kirk Smith**
Lindsey Corkhill/Stanlow/Phelan .... **Claire Sweeney**
Susannah Farnham/Morrisey **Karen Drury**
Angela Lambert .... **Hilary Welles**
Leanne Powell .... **Vickie Gates**
Peter Harrison .... **Robert Beck**
David 'Bing' Crosbie .... **John Burgess**
Jean Crosbie .... **Marcia Ashton**
Karyn Clark .... **Joanna Phillips-Lane**
Ruth Sweeney .... **Mary Healey**
Anna Wolska .... **Kazia Pelka**
Lyn Matthews/Rogers .... **Sharon Power**
Marianne Dwyer .... **Jodie Hanson**
Joe Halsall .... **Susie Ann Watkins**
Brian Kennedy .... **Jonathan Caplan**
Penny Crosbie .... **Mary Tamm**
Bev McLoughlin/Gonzales .... **Sarah White**

Carol Salter	**Angela Walsh**
Garry Salter	**Stephen Dwyer**
Mandy Jordache/Dutton	**Sandra Maitland**
Trevor Jordache	**Bryan Murray**
Beth Jordache	**Anna Friel**
Rachel Jordache/Wright/ Dixon	**Tiffany Chapman**
Brenna Jordache	**Gillian Hanna**
Simon Howe	**Lee Hartney**
Mo McGee	**Tina Malone**
Audrey Manners	**Judith Barker**
Emma Piper	**Paula Bell**
Eddie Banks	**Paul Broughton**
Rosie Banks	**Susan Twist**
Carl Banks	**Stephen Donald**
Sarah Banks	**Andrea Marshall**
Lee Banks	**Matthew Lewney**
Jenny Swift	**Kate Beckett**
George Manners	**Brian Murphy**
Gary Stanlow	**Andrew Fillis**
Christian Wright	**Philip Dowd**
Peter Phelan	**Samuel Kane**
Shane Cochran	**Richard Norton**
Kenny Maguire	**Tommy Boyle**
Bel Simpson	**Lesley Nightingale**
Ollie Simpson	**Michael J. Jackson**
Georgia Simpson	**Helen Grace**
Nat Simpson	**John Sandford**
Danny Simpson	**Andrew Butler**
Val Walker	**Pauline Fleming**
Jules Bradley/Simpson	**Sarah Withe**
J. C. Bradley	**Ken Sharrock**
Anne Bradley	**Faith Brown**
Elaine Davies/Johnson	**Beverley Hills**
Cassie Charlton	**Ebony Gray**
Gladys Charlton	**Eileen O'Brien**
Timothy 'Tinhead' O'Leary	**Philip Olivier**
Tanya Davies	**Heather Tomlinson**
Carmel O'Leary	**Carol Connor**
Ben O'Leary	**Simon Paul**
Melanie O'Leary	**Elizabeth Lovelady**
Eleanor Kitson	**Georgia Reece**
Mollie Marchbank	**Diane Keen**
Lisa Morrisey	**Amanda Nolan**
Louise Hope	**Lisa Faulkner**
Greg Shadwick	**Mark Moraghan**
Margi Shadwick	**Bernadette Foley**
Nikki Shadwick	**Suzanne Collins**
Emily Shadwick/O'Leary	**Jennifer Ellison**
Jason Shadwick	**Vincent Price**
Jessie Shadwick/Hilton	**Marji Campi**
Marcus Seddon	**Matthew Brenher**
Katrina Evans	**Ann-Marie Davies**
Pauline Robson	**Kim Taylforth**
Andrea Robson	**Juanne Fuller**
Alec O'Brien	**Al T. Kossy**
Niamh Musgrove	**Barbara Drennan**
Joey Musgrove	**Dan Mullane**
Luke Musgrove	**Jason Kavanagh**
Matt Musgrove	**Kristian Ealey**
Kelly Musgrove	**Natalie Earl**
Ryan Musgrove	**Samuel James Hudson**
Franki	**Linda Lusardi**
Anthea Russel/Brindley/ Dixon	**Barbara Hatwell**
Megan Brindley	**Cheryl Mackie**
Callum Finnegan	**Gerard Kelly**
Rose Finnegan	**Amanda Noar**
Dr Darren Roebuck	**Timothy Deenihan**
Victoria Seagram/Wilcox/ Shadwick	**Patricia Potter**
Nathan Cuddington	**Marcus Hutton**
Jerome Johnson	**Leon Lopez**
Dave Burns	**Simon Chadwick**
Shelley Bowers	**Alexandra Wescourt**
Ray Hilton	**Kenneth Cope**
Diane Murray	**Bernie Nolan**
Marty Murray	**Neil Caple**
Steve Murray	**Steven Fletcher**
Adele Murray	**Katy Lamont**
Anthony Murray	**Raymond Quinn**
Lance Powell	**Mickey Poppins**
Andrew Taylor	**Sean Harrison**
Brigid McKenna	**Meg Johnson**
Clint Moffat	**Greg Pateras**
Robbie Moffat	**Neil Davies**
Kitty Hilton	**Jean Heywood**
Carl Beacham	**David Groves**
Leanne Powell	**Vickie Gates**
Josh McLoughlan	**Adam McCoy**
Nisha Batra	**Sunetra Sarker**
Fred Gonzales	**Richard Calkin**
Yvonne Johnson	**Suzette Llewellyn**
Christy Murray	**Glyn Pritchard**
Michelle Tan	**Stacy Liu**
Jeff Evans	**Les Dennis**
Paige Kelly/Howard	**Chelsea Farrell**
Neil Kelly	**Guy Parry**
Imelda Clough	**Billie Clements**
Helen Carey	**Kerry Peers**
Dr Gary Parr	**Ben Hull**
Gabby Parr	**Stephanie Chambers**
Debbie Gordon	**Annette Ekblom**
Alan Gordon	**John Burton**
Stuart Gordon	**David Lyon**
Kirsty Gordon	**Jessica Noon**
Ali Gordon	**Kristopher Mochrie**
Dan Morrisey	**Matthew Crompton**
Ruth Smith/Gordon	**Lynsey McCaffrey**
Luke Smith	**Callum Giblin**
Sean Smith	**Barry Sloane**
Nic Howard	**James Sarsfield**
Jan Murray	**Helen Sheals**
Josh Dixon	**Jack McMullen**
Jack Michaelson	**Paul Duckworth**

Creator/Executive Producer **Phil Redmond**
Producers **Nicholas Prosser, Mal Young, Ric Mellis, Sue Sutton Mayo, Paul Marquess, Nicky Higgins, David Hanson**

Innovative Channel 4 soap opera.

Brookside was the series that changed the concept of soap opera in Britain. Taking to the air on Channel 4's opening night, it aimed to make realism the key to its success. Creator Phil Redmond (formerly of GRANGE HILL) went out and bought a new housing estate in Liverpool, using the various homes as permanent, 'live-in' sets and shunning the wobbly walls of studio mock-ups. Lightweight, hand-held cameras provided a newsy, ever-moving image of life in Brookside Close. Redmond also went for realism in his characters. They spoke dialectically in heavy, guttural, Merseyside accents, the kids in particular using real swear-words, not transparent euphemisms. Their lives were purposefully down to earth and unromantic, and storylines revolved around the bleakness of life on the dole and the salvation provided by the black economy. Subsequently, other normally 'taboo' subjects such as homosexuality, suicide, AIDS, religious fanaticism, rape and drug abuse all had an airing in *Brookside*.

The first residents of the Close included the working-class Grants, the snooty Collinses and young couples Roger and Heather Huntington and Gavin and Petra Taylor. Some characters like Barry Grant remained with the series for years, but plenty of new faces moved in and out of the cul-de-sac. Major contributors included crotchety old Harry Cross, the Corkhills, the Rogers, the Dixons, the Johnsons, the Farnhams, the Crosbies, the Jordaches and window cleaner Sinbad.

Redmond's initial frankness went unrewarded. Audiences dwindled and a change of tack was required. Out went some of the grimmer characters and in came one or two comic creations, to bring some levity. Bad language was toned down and a few more sensationalist elements were introduced. Storylines like the 'Free George Jackson' campaign (revolving around a jailed, innocent fireman) garnered media attention, and a drawn-out siege, ending in a double death, also brought in the viewers. Other audience-grabbing plots included the death of Terry Sullivan's wife and son; the lesbian kiss between Beth Jordache and Margaret Clemence; the discovery of wife-batterer Trevor Jordache's body beneath a patio and the subsequent murder trial; and the incestuous relationship between brother and sister Nat and Georgia Simpson.

Brookside (the working title was *Meadowcroft* until Redmond stumbled across the real Brookside Close) was originally screened twice a week, with a Saturday omnibus, but was expanded to three weekly episodes in 1990. In October 2002, however, the programme was cut back to only the Saturday edition. The demise of *Brookside* seemed imminent with the loss of its weekday evening slots, although a year's grace was promised. The programme finally ended with a feature-length episode, screened late on a Tuesday night in November 2003.

Spin-offs from *Brookside* included the three-part *Damon and Debbie* (1987, focusing on the dispirited son of the Grant family and his schoolgirl girlfriend as they went on the run from the police in York), and a two-part schools programme, *South* (part of Channel 4's *The English Programme* in 1988, featuring Tracy Corkhill and her boyfriend, Jamie).

Brosnan, Pierce

(1953–)

Irish actor, TV's REMINGTON STEELE but later cast as James Bond, a role earmarked for him for a number of years. Contractual obligations to *Steele* meant that he missed out on the Bond role when Timothy Dalton took over and it seemed his chance had gone. However, when Dalton stepped aside in 1993, Brosnan was once again first choice to play the suave secret agent. His other TV credits have included NANCY ASTOR, *The Manions of America*, THE PROFESSIONALS (guest) and *Noble House*. His first wife was actress Cassandra Harris, who died in 1991. In 2001 he married former model/journalist Keely Shaye Smith.

Brothers, The ✳✳✳

UK (BBC) Drama. BBC 1 1972–6

Mary Hammond	**Jean Anderson**
Edward Hammond	**Glyn Owen**
	Patrick O'Connell
Brian Hammond	**Richard Easton**
David Hammond	**Robin Chadwick**
Jennifer Kingsley/Hammond	**Jennifer Wilson**
Ann Hammond	**Hilary Tindall**
Carol Hammond	**Nicola Moloney**
	Annabelle Lanyon
	Debbie Farrington
Jill Hammond	**Gabrielle Drake**
Barbara Kingsley/Trent	**Julia Goodman**
Bill Riley	**Derek Benfield**
Harry Carter	**Mark McManus**
Pamela Graham	**Anna Fox**
Nicholas Fox	**Jonathan Newth**
Julie Lane	**Gillian McCutcheon**
Martin Farrell	**Murray Hayne**
Sir Neville Henniswode	**Carleton Hobbs**
Paul Merroney	**Colin Baker**
Clare Miller	**Carole Mowlam**
Gwen Riley	**Margaret Ashcroft**
April Winter/Merroney	**Liza Goddard**
Jane Maxwell	**Kate O'Mara**
Don Stacey	**Mike Pratt**

Creators **Gerard Glaister, N. J. Crisp**
Producers **Gerard Glaister, Ken Riddington, Bill Sellars**

● ***Three brothers fight for control of the family haulage business.***

When 70-year-old Robert Hammond dies, his eldest son, Edward ('Ted'), braces himself to take over the family's long-distance-lorry business, Hammond Transport Services. After all, he has helped to build up the company. However, with the reading of the will, he learns that his two younger brothers have inherited equal shares, and his hard-nosed mother, Mary, who suffers from a heart condition, is just as reluctant to give up her influence. To make matters worse, Robert's mistress, Jennifer Kingsley, has also been handed a slice of the cake.

For over four years *The Brothers* played out the boardroom and bedroom battles of this squabbling family and became a firm Friday, then Sunday, night favourite. Keeping the trucks conveniently in the background, the series follows Edward's attempts to assert his authority over his brothers (David, a restless young graduate, and Brian, a boring accountant), and the whole family's concern over the involvement of the prim Jennifer, who eventually marries Edward. The truckers are represented by the working-class Bill Riley and his wife, Gwen.

Later additions to the cast are future DOCTOR WHO Colin Baker as obnoxious financial whiz-kid Paul Merroney (an early J. R. Ewing), his disillusioned wife, April, and Kate O'Mara as air-freight baroness Jane Maxwell, and storylines focus on the company's attempts to go public and expand into a global market.

Brothers in Law ✳✳

UK (BBC) Situation Comedy. BBC 1962

Roger Thursby	**Richard Briers**
Henry Blagrove	**Richard Waring**
Kendall Grimes	**John Glyn-Jones**
Sally Mannering	**June Barry**

Writers **Denis Norden, Frank Muir**
Producer **Graeme Muir**

● ***A trainee barrister fumbles his way through his early cases.***

Roger Thursby is an enthusiastic pupil barrister undertaking his first year in chambers. Although he is chaperoned by the more experienced Henry Blagrove and veteran Kendall Grimes, his courtroom experiences descend into farce as he struggles with the vagaries of legal life. Sally Mannering is his supportive girlfriend.

Brothers in Law was based on a novel of the same name by Henry Cecil which had been filmed by the Boulting Brothers in 1956. Cecil also contributed to Denis Norden and Frank Muir's TV scripts for the series, which gave Richard Briers his first leading role and led to THE MARRIAGE LINES and greater things. A judge who appeared in the final episode was given his own spin-off series in 1963. Named *Mr Justice Duncannon*, it pitched DR FINLAY'S CASEBOOK star Andrew Cruickshank into the title role.

Brothers McGregor, The *

UK (Granada) Situation Comedy. ITV 1985–8

Wesley McGregor .... **Paul Barber**
Cyril McGregor .... **Philip Whitchurch**
Dolly McGregor .... **Jean Heywood**
Glenys Pike .... **Jackie Downey**
Colwyn Stanley .... **Allan Surtees**

Creators/Writers **John Stevenson, Julian Roach**
Executive Producer **Bill Podmore**
Producer **Bernard Thompson**

Two half-brothers – one black, one white – run a used-car business in Liverpool but hope for better things.

Half-brothers Cyril and Wesley McGregor share the same mother (Dolly) but different fathers. Cyril's dad has died and Wesley's, a black West African missionary, abandoned Dolly at the registry office. Now, still sharing their mum's Merseyside tower block flat, the boys work together, running the family's ropey second-hand car firm, Rathbone Motors. However, both strive for more from life. Wesley dreams of being a business tycoon, or a politician. He is President of the CBI (Confederation of Black Industrialists). The older Cyril, a part-time club singer and bouncer at the Blue Cockatoo Club, thinks he is the new Frank Sinatra. The club is owned by Colwyn Stanley, another old flame of Dolly's. Also seen is Glenys, Cyril's dopey fiancée of some six years' engagement, ever hopeful of a marriage that is never likely to take place. Cheeky Scouse humour and a relentless, misplaced confidence are the hallmarks of the series, which was a spin-off from CORONATION STREET, following the brothers' appearance (with different actors in the roles) in the Rovers Return on the occasion of Eddie Yeats's engagement party.

Brown, Derren

(1971–)

Croydon-born psychological illusionist whose well-publicized Russian roulette stunt in 2003 proved particularly controversial. Brown successfully predicted which chamber of a revolver housed a live bullet while holding the gun to his head, although there were later claims by supervising authorities that live ammunition had not been used. This has been one troublesome aspect of an otherwise startling TV career. In series like *Derren Brown: Mind Control*, the star has bemused and astonished both studio and viewing audiences with his breathtaking 'mind reading' skills, hypnotism and other routines, all carried off with a disarming hint of nervousness as if they're all going to fail. Other offerings have included *Derren Brown: Séance* (challenging spiritualism), *Derren Brown: Messiah* (debunking the paranormal and those who seek to profit from it), *Derren Brown: Trick of the Mind* (mischief making with the public and celebrities), *Derren Brown: the Gathering* (celebrity audience) and *Derren Brown: the Heist* (persuading middle managers attending a motivational seminar to attempt an armed robbery).

Brown, June

(1927–)

Suffolk-born Shakespearean and character actress much seen in films and television before achieving star status as gossipy hypochondriac Dot Cotton in EASTENDERS. Viewers may also recall her as Aunt Sally in the sitcom *Now and Then*, and in the children's comedy *Pirates*, as well as in CORONATION STREET, THE DUCHESS OF DUKE STREET (Louisa's mother), THE SWEENEY, *Churchill's People*, SOUTH RIDING, *The Prince and the Pauper, Shadows, God's Wonderful Railway*, THE BILL, OLIVER TWIST (Mrs Mann), LACE, MINDER, AIN'T MISBEHAVIN' (Mrs Jilkes), GORMENGHAST (Nannie Slagg) and *Marjorie and Gladys* (Gladys Gladwell). Her first husband was the late actor John Garley while her second husband, Robert Arnold, who died in 2003, played PC Swain in DIXON OF DOCK GREEN, in which June herself took small roles.

Browne, Jill

(1937–91)

One of TV's earliest sweethearts, playing trainee nurse (later Sister) Carole Young in EMERGENCY – WARD 10, Jill Browne found herself inundated with fan mail from male viewers. In 1964, having just been dropped from the hospital soap, she married former co-star John Alderton, although the marriage ended in 1970. Her other major TV role – in the pub variety show *The New Stars and Garters* – was not a success and she eventually left the business, marrying theatre producer Brian Wolfe in 1971.

Bruce, Fiona

(1964–)

Singapore-born presenter of such programmes as CRIMEWATCH UK, *The Antiques Show*, *The Search* and *Real Story with Fiona Bruce*, as well as BBC news bulletins, beginning as a reporter with BREAKFAST NEWS after researching for PANORAMA. She has also reported for programmes like NEWSNIGHT, *Public Eye* and *Your NHS*, narrated the documentary series *Food Police*, and chaired the panel game CALL MY BLUFF.

Brunson, Michael

OBE (1940–)

ITN's Political Editor until his retirement in 2000, Norwich-born Michael Brunson began his broadcasting career with BBC External Services in 1964 as a writer/producer. He moved to BBC Radio South-East the same year, before becoming an assistant producer on 24 HOURS in 1966. He joined ITN in 1968, was its US correspondent, 1972–7, and then European correspondent, 1979–80. Brunson was also seen as a newscaster between 1977 and 1981. In 1980 he took over as Diplomatic Editor, a post he held until becoming Political Editor in 1986. He now works as a freelance contributor to political programmes.

Brush, Basil

Puppet fox created and voiced by Ivan Owen (formerly the operator of Yoo-Hoo the Cuckoo in the 1950s *Billy Bean and His Funny Machine* and dog Fred Barker in *Tuesday Rendezvous*, FIVE O'CLOCK CLUB, etc.). Basil's gap-toothed grin, effervescent character and posh voice (more than reminiscent of Terry-Thomas), not to mention his trademark 'Boom boom' and roaring laugh, made him a favourite of both children and adults. The puppet was made for Owen by Peter Firmin, half of the Smallfilms team who devised IVOR THE ENGINE, NOGGIN THE NOG, *et al.* He first appeared in *The Three Scampis* in 1962 (alongside Howard Williams and a Scottish hedgehog called Spike McPike voiced by Wally Whyton), and then guest-starred with David Nixon, before hiring a succession of straight men to read stories to him and act with him in little pantomimes on his own Saturday teatime series from 1968 to 1980. Rodney Bewes was first into the role, then came Derek Fowlds, Roy North, Billy Boyle and Howard Williams (again). Each week, viewers were greeted with a cheery 'Hello, hello, hello, and to the show, wel-el-el-come!'. The wily fox was later a regular guest on CRACKERJACK and then resurfaced alongside Doug Ridley in a Border TV series called *Basil's Joke Machine* (ITV 1986). He was a team captain on *Fantasy Football League* in the 1990s. The character was sold to businessman Bill Haslam in 1997 and resurfaced in his own sitcom, *The Basil Brush Show*, in 2002, accompanied by new straight man Stephen (played by Christopher Pizzey), but sadly without the voice of Ivan Owen, who died in 2000.

Brush Strokes ★★

UK (BBC) Situation Comedy. BBC 1 1986–91
DVD: Universal

Jacko	**Karl Howman**
Jean	**Nicky Croydon**
Sandra	**Jackie Lye**
Elmo Putney	**Howard Lew Lewis**
Lionel Bainbridge	**Gary Waldhorn**
Veronica Bainbridge	**Elizabeth Counsell**
Lesley Bainbridge	**Kim Thomson**
	Erika Hoffman
Eric	**Mike Walling**

Creators/Writers **John Esmonde, Bob Larbey**
Producers **Sydney Lotterby, Mandie Fletcher, Harold Snoad, John B. Hobbs**

A chirpy London decorator has an eye for the ladies, but also a heart of gold.

This gentle comedy focuses on the life of Jacko, an appropriately named Cockney Jack the Lad who lives in Motspur Park and works for Bainbridge's, a small family painting and decorating company. His work colleague (and landlord) is his down-to-earth brother-in-law, Eric (noted for his NHS specs), and his boss is the intolerant Lionel. Lionel's wife, Veronica, takes over when Lionel dies and one of the girls Jacko dates is Lionel's snooty daughter, Lesley. However, Jacko's soft spot is really reserved for Sandra, Bainbridge's Geordie secretary. Also seen are Jean, Eric's wife and Jacko's sensible sister, and bulky Elmo Putney, gormless landlord of the local boozer, The White Hart. Elmo briefly emigrates to Australia, discovers opals with the aid of his pet dingo and returns in style to London to open a ghastly pink wine-bar (imaginatively dubbed Elmo Putney's Wine Bar), where Lesley takes a job waitressing.

The programme's credits show Jacko working his way along a wall with a paint roller and feature a theme song by Dexy's Midnight Runners. Entitled 'Because of You', it entered the Top Twenty in 1986.

Bryan, Dora

OBE (Dora Broadbent; 1924–)

Lancashire-born, former child performer who became one of the UK's favourite comediennes in the 1950s–70s, starring in shows like *Our Dora* (Dora), *Happily Ever After* (Dora Morgan), *According to Dora*, *Before the Fringe* and *Both Ends Meet/Dora* (Dora Page). In recent years she has played Mrs Carpenter in ON THE UP, Kitty Flitcroft in MOTHER'S RUIN, Mrs Mim in *Virtual Murder* and Ms Trethrewick in *Vic and Bob in Catterick*, as well as enjoying a run of high-profile guest appearances in series like LAST OF THE SUMMER WINE (Roz), HEARTBEAT, HOLBY CITY and ABSOLUTELY FABULOUS.

Brydon, Rob

(Robert Brydon Jones; 1965–)

Welsh comedian, writer and actor whose rise to fame was sparked by his solo performance as the relentlessly cheerful divorcé, Keith Barret, in MARION AND GEOFF. He has since starred in the Marion and Geoff spin-offs, *A Small Summer Party* and *The Keith Barret Show*, and alongside Julia Davis in HUMAN REMAINS. He played Mr Alf in THE WAY WE LIVE NOW, headlined in an episode of MURDER IN MIND, appeared as faded cult TV star Andy Van Allen in *Cruise of the Gods*, and starred as Dr Paul Hamilton in *Supernova*. He wrote, and voiced the part of Peter De Lane, in the movies spoof *The Director's Commentary*, and took the title role in *Kenneth Tynan: In Praise of Hardcore*. Other appearances have been in the dramas *The Healer*, *Cold Lazarus* (see KARAOKE) and AGATHA CHRISTIE'S MARPLE, and the comedies *Paul Merton in Galton & Simpson's . . .*, MARRIED FOR LIFE, BARBARA and I'M ALAN PARTRIDGE, as well as the TV film *The Lord of Misrule* and TOTP2. He is script editor of LITTLE BRITAIN, also making guest appearances in the show. Brydon's first broadcasting experience came on radio and television in Wales in the 1980s as an early morning DJ and programme announcer, using his real name of Rob Jones.

BSB

See *BSkyB*.

BSkyB

(British Sky Broadcasting)

The major DBS (Direct Broadcasting by Satellites) station in the UK, formed by a merger of Sky Television and British Satellite Broadcasting (BSB) in 1990. The two companies had previously been rivals.

BSB was the company selected by the IBA to provide satellite television to the UK. In accordance with IBA advice, it opted for a technically advanced system using novel 'squarial' dishes, which were designed to receive signals from the specially constructed Marco Polo satellite. However, development problems ensued and BSB was beaten into the marketplace by Sky, an 'unofficial' company, which used larger, round dishes and transmitted from the Astra satellite. Being independently owned, and operating out of Luxembourg, Astra was beyond the control of UK broadcasting regulators. Sky had developed from a primitive satellite channel known as

Satellite TV, which broadcast to cable stations (for onward transmission) around Europe from 1982, using existing telecom satellites. Satellite TV was bought by Rupert Murdoch's News International and, with a change of name to Sky, began satellite/cable experiments in the UK, using Swindon as its testing ground. By the time the Astra satellite went into orbit in December 1988, Sky was well established and able to launch four satellite channels direct to homes in February of the following year.

The Marco Polo and Astra systems, however, were incompatible and this meant that viewers had to gamble on which to purchase (in much the same way as the incompatible VHS and Betamax home video systems clashed head to head, with the result that Betamax soon became obsolete). Although Sky continued to lose money, the fact that it was already up and running by the time BSB finally went on air in 1990 proved terminal for BSB, and the latter company was forced into a merger (resembling more of a takeover) with its rival later that year. Only the Astra system is now in use. BSkyB is now the official company name, but just the name Sky is used for the various channels operated by the company.

On 1 October 1998 the company launched Sky Digital and is now a digital-only service, offering a raft of channels, including Sky One (a general entertainments channel); Sky News; various Sky Sports channels; and countless film and pay-per-view movie channels. The company also markets a wide range of other channels in subscriber packages. These include UKTV Gold, UKTV Style, UKTV Food, UKTV Documentary and UKTV Drama; Bravo; Living; Disney Channel; National Geographic; Hallmark; History; Biography; Men and Motors; Challenge TV; Paramount; Sci-Fi; The Discovery Channel; Home and Leisure; MUTV; Performance; Animal Planet; British Eurosport; MTV; VH 1; Nickelodeon; Nick Jnr; Boomerang; and Cartoon Network. BSkyB also supplies some of its own channels for cable networks.

Buccaneer ✶✶

UK (BBC) Drama. BBC 1 1980

Tony Blair	**Bryan Marshall**
Charles Burton	**Clifford Rose**
Monica Burton	**Pamela Salem**
Ray Mason	**Mark Jones**
Kim Hayward	**Carolyn Courage**
Pete	**Brian Hall**
Paul Blair	**Cecil Humphreys**
Janet Blair	**Shirley Anne Field**
Audrey Mason	**Sally Sanders**
Admiral Harkness	**Noel Johnson**
David Cohn	**Geoffrey Davion**
Lord Champlieu	**Julian Curry**
Hassan Hilmy	**James Brockington**
Monty Bateman	**Allan Corduner**

Creators **Eric Paice, N. J. Crisp**
Writers **J. B. Flack, N. J. Crisp, John Brason, David Crane, Ben Steed**
Producer **Gerard Glaister**

A dangerously ambitious pilot wants his own airline to succeed at all costs.

He may be clever and well spoken, but Tony Blair is a devious and roguishly ambitious man. At least in this series he is. In what was another of N. J. Crisp and Gerard Glaister's Sunday evening family drama series, *Buccaneer* relates the adventures of the said Mr Blair, an airline pilot who will stop at nothing to be successful. The story begins when a Britannia aircraft owned by the ailing Red-Air freight company is grounded during a political coup in central Africa. The company is near bankruptcy and Blair sees this as his opportunity to take whatever he can get. With the help of financial associate Charles Burton and his wife, Monica, he acquires the one (ageing)-plane airline from owner Ray Mason, but then struggles to make it viable in the face of revenge attacks from the bitter Mason and dodgy business deals of his own making. His hazardous (in more ways than one) shipments include weapons, animals for safari park owner Lord Champlieu, and oil for Anglo Oil. At any moment, Blair's short fuse is likely to burn away as he becomes the buccaneer of the programme's title. Just one series of 13 episodes was made.

Buccaneers, The ✶

UK (ITP/Sapphire) Adventure. ITV 1956–7
DVD: Network

Dan Tempest	**Robert Shaw**
Lt. Beamish	**Peter Hammond**
Governor Woodes Rogers	**Alec Clunes**
Blackbeard	**George Margo**
	Terence Cooper
Armando	**Edwin Richfield**
Taffy	**Paul Hansard**
Dickon	**Wilfrid Downing**
Gaff Guernsey	**Brian Rawlinson**
Van Brugh	**Alec Mango**
Bassett	**Neil Hallett**
Pop	**Willoughby Gray**
Estaban	**Roger Delgado**

Executive Producer **Hannah Weinstein**
Producers **Sidney Cole, Ralph Smart, Pennington Richards**

A pirate swears loyalty to the king, receives a pardon and defends the colonies from the Spanish.

In 1718 pirate Dan Tempest is the leader of a band of freebooters in the British Caribbean province of New Providence. However, he is persuaded by Lt. Beamish, the new deputy governor, to switch sides and fight on behalf of the Crown against the advancing Spanish, and to help counter the disruptive influence of other pirates, such as the famous Blackbeard. Armando, Taffy and Gaff are all loyal members of Tempest's swashbuckling crew on the brig *Sultana*, with Dickon, a stowaway-turned-cabin-boy, and Captain Morgan, Tempest's pet monkey, also seen. Van Brugh is an untrustworthy local businessman in Nassau, where the action mainly takes place. Estaban (played by Roger Delgado, the future Master in DOCTOR WHO) is one of the Spanish principals.

With its 'a-roving' theme song, *The Buccaneers* was reputedly TV's first pirate series and was also unusual in that its lead character did not appear until the third episode, the first two being devoted to setting the scene. The sea sequences were filmed off Falmouth and the ship featured was a showbusiness veteran, having already played the part of the *Hispaniola* in Disney's *Treasure Island* and the *Peaquod* in John Huston's *Moby Dick*.

Buchanan, Colin

(1967–)

Scottish actor, familiar as detective Peter Pascoe in DALZIEL AND PASCOE and previously as TA man Hodge in PRESTON FRONT. Buchanan has also starred in *Agatha Christie's The Pale Horse* (sculptor Mark Easterbrook), *Witness Against Hitler*

(Peter Yorck), MOLL FLANDERS (Rowland) and CATHERINE COOKSON's *The Secret* (Freddie Musgrave).

Buck Rogers in the 25th Century ✶✶

US (Universal/Glen A. Larson) Science Fiction. ITV 1980–2
(US: NBC 1979–81)
DVD: Universal

Capt. William 'Buck' Rogers	**Gil Gerard**
Col. Wilma Deering	**Erin Gray**
Dr Elias Huer	**Tim O'Connor**
Twiki	**Felix Silla**
	Mel Blanc *(voice)*
	Bob Elyea *(voice)*
Dr Theopolis	**Eric Server** *(voice only)*
Princess Ardala	**Pamela Hensley**
Kane	**Henry Silva**
	Michael Ansara
Hawk	**Thom Christopher**
Dr Goodfellow	**Wilfred Hyde-White**
Admiral Asimov	**Jay Garner**
Crichton	**Jeff David** *(voice only)*
Lt. Devlin	**Paul Carr**
Narrator	**William Conrad**

Executive Producers **Glen A. Larson, John Mantley**
Producers **Richard Caffey, John Gaynor, David J. O'Connell, Leslie Stevens, Bruce Lansbury, John G. Stevens, Calvin Clements**

An astronaut is rocketed 500 years into the future.

The comic-strip character Buck Rogers was given a second bite of the TV cherry in this series, following an earlier dramatization seen in the USA in 1950. On this occasion, the space hero finds himself in the 25th century, in the year 2491 to be precise. His space capsule (*Ranger 3*), launched in 1987, goes missing for 504 years, but, being in suspended animation, Rogers survives the experience, awaking aboard a Draconian spaceship on its way to a peace conference on Earth. The planet, devastated by nuclear war, has forged a new civilization based in a futuristic city (New Chicago) in the Midwest. Outside the city is Anarchia, a wilderness housing the dregs of a mutilated society. The Draconians aim to take control. Rogers, although initially viewed with suspicion by the Earth Defense Directorate, becomes the planet's ally in fighting off the aliens, who are led by the glamorous Princess Ardala and her sidekick, Kane. Rogers discovers romance with attractive defence commander Wilma Deering, and teams up with top scientist Dr Huer, who supplies a new robot chum, Twiki, and also the computer Dr Theopolis, usually seen as a disc around Twiki's neck.

In its second season the series changed considerably. Buck and Twiki are no longer on Earth but on the spaceship *The Searcher*, seeking out Earthlings who have fled the holocaust. They are now supported by Admiral Asimov (supposedly a descendant of the science-fiction writer, Isaac Asimov), Lt. Devlin and old, inquisitive scientist Dr Goodfellow. Also aboard are Hawk (a half-man, half-bird from the planet Throm) and a pompous robot named Crichton.

While the series was not without its critics, its tongue-in-cheek presentation and elaborate special effects proved to be its saving graces. The pilot, explaining Rogers's arrival in the future, was initially released in cinemas.

Bucknell, Barry

(1912–2003)

TV 'home improvement' expert whose programmes in the 1950s and early 1960s included *Do It Yourself* and *Bucknell's House*, in which he refitted a derelict Victorian house in Ealing. A former motor engineer, he first appeared in part of the magazine ABOUT THE HOME.

Buddha of Suburbia, The ✶✶

UK (BBC) Drama. BBC 2 1993

Karim Amir	**Naveen Andrews**
Haroon Amir	**Roshan Seth**
Margaret Amir	**Brenda Blethyn**
Eva Kay	**Susan Fleetwood**
Charlie Kay	**Steven Mackintosh**
Jamila	**Nisha Nayar**
Changez	**Harish Patel**
Uncle Ted	**John McEnery**
Auntie Jean	**Janet Dale**
Anwar	**Badi Uzzaman**
Jeeta	**Surendra Kochar**
Shadwell	**David Bamber**
Helen	**Vicky Murdock**
Eleanor	**Jemma Redgrave**
Matthew Pyke	**Donald Sumpter**
Marlene Pyke	**Sarah Neville**

Writers **Hanif Kureishi, Roger Michell**
Producer **Kevin Loader**

An Asian youth's voyage of personal discovery in the turbulent 1970s.

Bromley, south London in the early 1970s. Seventeen-year-old Karim lives with his Indian dad and his English mum but it is a troubled home. Dad Haroon is a bit of a local celebrity, spending his evenings, on the face of it, giving lessons in meditation and spiritual awareness to the chattering classes, but mostly carrying on an affair with the socially ambitious Eva Kay. Karim is also engaged in early sexual fumblings – with his long-time Indian friend, Jamila, and Eva's pretentious son, Charlie. As the decade progresses, Karim's attitude to life changes with the times and his own experiences. He becomes an actor, working for devious director Matthew Pyke and falling in love with troubled actress Eleanor. The spoilt Charlie, meanwhile, becomes a punk rock star, and Jamila is landed with an arranged husband, Changez, who is not only disabled but a complete jerk to boot. Alongside these personal tales, tensions between orthodox Asian culture and Western promiscuity also play a role, but the real stars here are the 1970s themselves, lurching from post-hippy oriental mysticism to brutal skinhead thuggery, via glam rock, flares and the three-day week. The controversial four-part drama was based on Hanif Kureishi's 1991 Whitbread Prize-winning novel of the same name, adapted for television by Kureishi (scriptwriter for Channel 4's acclaimed 1985 movie *My Beautiful Laundrette*) and director Roger Michell. David Bowie provided the theme song (which was a minor UK hit in 1993) and the incidental music.

Budgie ✳✳

UK (LWT) Comedy Drama. ITV 1971–2

Budgie Bird .... **Adam Faith**
Charlie Endell .... **Iain Cuthbertson**
Hazel .... **Lynn Dalby**
Jean .... **Georgina Hale**
Mrs Endell .... **June Lewis**
Jack Bird .... **George Tovey**
Laughing Spam Fritter .... **John Rhys-Davies**
Grogan .... **Rio Fanning**

Writers **Keith Waterhouse, Willis Hall**
Executive Producer **Rex Firkin**
Producer **Verity Lambert**

A chirpy London spiv keeps hoping things will turn up.

Budgie Bird is a born loser. Always down on his luck, he nevertheless believes that life is about to change. For him Easy Street is just around the corner, but everyone knows that the yellow brick road is leading only to one place – jail. Shunning regular employment, he clings to the fringes of the Soho underworld, filled with ambitious plans and ideas for his personal betterment, all doomed to instant failure. The best he can manage is a job as a runner for Glaswegian gangster Charlie Endell, proprietor of a dodgy book shop. Endell is a local 'Mr Big' who is always happy to let Budgie take the rap for his illegal activities. But, despite being used and pushed around, the long-haired delinquent remains an eternal optimist, meandering through life, dreaming up worthless ways of making his fortune, ducking and diving and incurring the wrath of the local heavies. Jean is his estranged wife and Hazel his long-suffering girlfriend. Laughing Spam Fritter and Grogan are two other members of the Soho low-life.

The series brought a new direction to the career of 1960s pop star Adam Faith, who returned to TV 20 years later in LOVE HURTS after remarkable interim success as a City wheeler-dealer. A short-lived *Budgie* spin-off, *Charles Endell Esquire*, set in Glasgow and featuring Iain Cuthbertson but not Adam Faith, was seen in 1979.

Buerk, Michael

(1946–)

Solihull-born TV journalist and newsreader whose reports on the Ethiopian famine of 1984 were instrumental in alerting the world to the scale of the human tragedy unfolding in Africa. He returned to the scene of the suffering in 2004 for a *This World* reassessment of the progress being made. After starting out in newspapers, Buerk joined BBC Radio Bristol and then moved into television with HTV. He joined BBC TV news in 1973. Among his postings was a four-year stint in South Africa. He has since anchored the BBC's main news bulletins and presented programmes like *Nature, 999, The Soul of Britain*, SONGS OF PRAISE, *The Hand of God, Wren – the Man Who Built Britain* and a short-lived version of his Radio 4 programme, *The Moral Maze*.

Buffy the Vampire Slayer ✳✳✳

US (Mutant Enemy/Kuzui/Sandollar/Twentieth Century-Fox) Comedy Drama. BBC 2 1998–2003 (US: WB 1997–2003)
DVD: Fox

Buffy Anne Summers .... **Sarah Michelle Gellar**
Alexander 'Xander' Harris ...... **Nicholas Brendon**
Willow Rosenberg .... **Alyson Hannigan**
Rupert Giles .... **Anthony Stewart Head**
Cordelia Chase .... **Charisma Carpenter**
Joyce Summers .... **Kristine Sutherland**
The Master .... **Mark Metcalf**
Angel .... **David Boreanaz**
Oz .... **Seth Green**
Spike .... **James Marsters**
Jenny Kalender .... **Robia LaMorte**
Drusilla .... **Juliet Landau**
Mayor Richard Wilkens III ...... **Harry Groener**
Mr Trick .... **K. Todd Freeman**
Anya Emerson .... **Emma Caulfield**
Riley Finn .... **Marc Blucas**
Maggie Walsh .... **Lindsay Crouse**
Tara Maclay .... **Amber Benson**
Dawn Summers .... **Michelle Trachtenberg**
Kennedy .... **Iyari Limon**
Principal Robin Wood .... **D. B. Woodside**

Creator **Joss Whedon**
Executive Producers **Joss Whedon, Gail Berman, Sandy Gallin, David Greenwalt, Fran Rubel Kuzui, Kaz Kuzui, Marti Noxon**

A teenage schoolgirl saves her town from the creatures of Hell.

A 1992 teen movie, starring Kristy Swanson and Donald Sutherland, was responsible for one of TV's biggest cult hits of the turn of the millennium. Adopting the same name, television's *Buffy* pitches Sarah Michelle Gellar into the title role of a high school girl fresh in town but soon to be its saviour.

Buffy Summers has previously been expelled from a school in LA for starting a fire (actually burning out some demons) and now arrives with her divorcée mother, Joyce, in the town of Sunnydale, California, as a second-year student at Sunnydale High School. It turns out that the settlement sits right on top of a gateway to Hell, and it is up to Buffy to don her mantle of vampire-slayer (in every generation there is 'a chosen one') to preserve its residents from the creatures of the deep. Bloodsuckers, witches and monsters of all persuasions are seen off by the plucky little blonde. Assigned as Buffy's mentor ('Watcher') is school librarian Giles (British actor Anthony Head, late of Nescafé commercials and JONATHAN CREEK). Buffy's friends and sometime rivals in the teen market are Willow, Cordelia, and Xander, and outside of school they – and assorted young vampires – frequent The Bronze club. Other notable characters are the menacing Master, punky Spike, Oz, a werewolf who is later Willow's boyfriend, demon Anya who nearly marries Xander, and Dawn, Buffy's mysterious younger sister. One important ally is decent vampire Angel, who becomes Buffy's beau but whom she is once forced to knife when he turns bad again. He is given his own series, *Angel* (in which he relocates to LA), and Buffy moves on to Sunnydale's branch of the University of California. Later Buffy is actually killed, but is of course brought back to life to continue the series. The series concluded in 2003 with an almighty battle against the forces of evil.

Camped up to the full, with plenty of butt-kicking, *Buffy*, a veritable death fest wrapped in humorous clothes, was first screened on Sky One in the UK. To add to its quirkiness, one episode was shot as a musical extravaganza with full orchestration and big dance numbers.

Bugs ✱

UK (BBC/Carnival Films) Science Fiction. BBC 1 1995–9
DVD: Revelation

Ed .... **Craig McLachlan**
Steven Houghton
Ros Henderson .... **Jaye Griffiths**
Nick Beckett .... **Jesse Birdsall**
Jan .... **Jan Harvey**
Alex .... **Paula Hunt**
Channing .... **Michael Grandage**
Adam .... **Joseph May**
Christa .... **Sandra Reinton**

Producer **Brian Eastman**

A trio of agents armed with high-tech gizmos save the world from subversive forces.

Bugs brought a return to British television of the gadget. What James Bond had been doing in the cinema for decades, and what programmes like THE AVENGERS had once revelled in, was now back in prime time. This Saturday evening escapist fantasy featured three very fit, intelligent, braver-than-brave heroes. Former services man and Government agent Beckett joins forces with daredevil Ed and computer/electronics genius Ros to provide answers to the world's many problems. In each episode the threesome are tested to the extreme by fiendish villains armed with devices as varied as poisonous electronic mosquitoes, agricultural viruses and voice-activated bombs. To save the day, they are called upon to use their martial arts skills, climb through air-ducts, dive underwater or even walk in space, usually with a clock counting down in the background. The setting for the series is London, although the location is never officially declared, the producers preferring anonymity with an eye on international sales.

If the futuristic tone of *Bugs* seems familiar, this is not surprising. The series consultant was Brian Clemens, the man behind most of *The Avengers*' most fondly remembered tales. After three series, *Bugs* gains a more human face. The gadgetry and loud explosions remain, but now personal matters begin to intrude on the plot. Romance rears its ugly head, with Beckett chasing Ros and Ros dating businessman Channing. At the same time, the three principals start work for Jan, head of a secret Government department called the Bureau, and her business-like assistant, Alex. A year later, former NEIGHBOURS star Craig McLachlan left and was replaced in the role of Ed by Steven Houghton. The series concluded with three episodes in August 1999.

Bullen, Mike

British writer/executive producer of popular TV drama series, creating COLD FEET, SUNBURN, LIFE BEGINS and *All About George*. Bullen is also an award-winning radio producer and presenter.

Bullseye ✱✱

UK (ATV/Central) Game Show. ITV 1981–95

Presenter **Jim Bowen**

Creators **Andrew Wood, Norman Vaughan**
Producers **Peter Holmans, Bob Cousins**

Quiz based around the game of darts.

A good throwing action and a fair level of general knowledge were what was required in this long-running game show in which comic Jim Bowen welcomed three pairs of contestants to throw darts and answer questions to win cash and prizes. The first segment of the game involved a standard dartboard. One team member aimed three darts and the other collected cash to the value of the score achieved by answering a question correctly. After three rounds of darts the team with the lowest aggregate score was eliminated. The consolation prize was a 'bendy Bully' (a rubber dummy of the show's bull mascot). The two remaining pairs then moved on to the category dartboard, where the thrower aimed for a specialist subject and the partner, again, answered to win cash. Once more the lower scorers were eliminated. The final game saw both partners in the remaining team throwing darts at a prize dartboard (six for the main thrower, three for the non-darter), hoping to hit numbers which corresponded to washing machines, colour TVs, etc. When all the prizes won by the top duo had been totalled up, they were offered the chance to gamble them for a star prize, hidden behind screens. With three darts each, if they scored a total of 101 or more the star prize was theirs. Any less and the prizes were forfeited. Cruelly, Bowen always invited losing contestants to 'Look what you would have won', whipping back the screen to reveal a speedboat, a new car or a foreign holiday for four people. An additional element of the programme involved a guest professional player throwing nine darts for charity. Darts commentator Tony Green kept score throughout.

It is fair to say that *Bullseye* (co-devised by comic Norman Vaughan) was one of the most unlikely TV successes produced by Central Television. Host Jim Bowen became notorious for his insensitive handling of contestants ('What do you do for a living?' 'I'm unemployed, Jim.' 'Super.') and his various gaffes. Some recorded programmes were allegedly binned, being judged too poor to transmit, but the series quickly built up a cult following, particularly among students.

Bullseye was briefly revived as one instalment of *Ant & Dec's Game Show Marathon* in 2005, a series that celebrated the best-loved game shows in ITV's 50-year history. In 2006, *Bullseye* was brought back by Challenge TV, with comedian Dave Spikey the new host.

Bulman ✱✱

UK (Granada) Detective Drama. ITV 1985; 1987

George Bulman .... **Don Henderson**
Lucy McGinty .... **Siobhan Redmond**
William Dugdale .... **Thorley Walters**

Creator **Kenneth Royce**
Writer **Murray Smith**
Executive Producer **Richard Everitt**
Producers **Steve Hawes, Sita Williams**

An ex-policeman retires to the world of antiques but is coaxed back into private detection.

Sgt George Bulman first appears in THE XYY MAN, pursuing the aggressive chromosome freak, Spider Scott. The character then re-emerges in the series STRANGERS, but his personality and character traits have changed dramatically. Although still uncompromising, he has become rather eccentric and less conventional, wearing fingerless grey gloves on duty and sporting gold-rimmed reading spectacles. In this follow-up series of his own, the character becomes quirkier still.

Bulman has retired from the force to open an antiques shop

and repair clocks in the Shanghai Road, south-west London. But his knowledge of the criminal world and his powers of detection are too great to lay to waste and he finds himself dragged back into action. Egging him on is Lucy McGinty, the daughter of a former colleague. A Medieval Studies student, she has thrown it all in to work with George and learn his criminology skills. An academic secret serviceman named William Dugdale, a throwback to *Strangers* days, is also seen.

The softly spoken Bulman's trademarks include his 2CV car, a knowledge of the classics and the use of a nasal inhaler. He always carries a plastic bag, too. Several of these gimmicks were introduced by accident. For instance, actor Don Henderson first used an inhaler because he really did have a cold, and the gloves were employed to cover up a stubborn wedding ring which couldn't be removed (Bulman was divorced). A scarf covered Henderson's throat cancer surgery scars, and the fact that he sometimes talked in a whisper was also connected to this ailment.

Burke, Alfred

(1918–)

British actor and writer, remembered for his long-running portrayal of the down-at-heel private detective Frank Marker, in PUBLIC EYE. Among his later roles were the Revd Patrick Brontë in *The Brontës of Haworth*, the Nazi Major Richter in ENEMY AT THE DOOR, Long John Silver in *Treasure Island*, Giuliano della Rovere in THE BORGIAS, an admiral in LONGITUDE and guest spots in BERGERAC and HOLBY CITY.

Burke, James

(1936–)

Excitable, bespectacled presenter, particularly adept at explaining complex scientific issues in layman's terms on programmes like TOMORROW'S WORLD and his own series, *The Burke Special*, CONNECTIONS, *The Real Thing* and *The Day the Universe Changed*, in the 1970s and 1980s. He was also part of the BBC's team covering the *Apollo* moon missions and was scientific adviser on the drama series MOONBASE 3.

Burke, Kathy

(1964–)

Award-winning English actress seen in both comic and straight drama roles. She first gained attention when providing strong support to Harry Enfield in his various series (playing, among other characters, Waynetta Slob and Perry the teenager). She was Martha in the drama MR WROE'S VIRGINS, Sharon in COMMON AS MUCK, Honour the maid in TOM JONES and starred as Linda La Hughes in the comedy GIMME GIMME GIMME. Other credits have included A VERY PECULIAR PRACTICE, ABSOLUTELY FABULOUS (Magda), MURDER MOST HORRID, *Ted and Ralph, Twenty Thousand Streets under the Sky* and Channel 4's short-film showcase *Shooting Gallery*. She also narrated the docusoap *Pleasure Island*.

Burke's Law/Amos Burke – Secret Agent ✳

US (Four Star) Detective Drama. ITV 1963–6 (US: ABC 1963–5/1965–6; CBS 1994–5)

Capt. Amos Burke .... **Gene Barry**
Det. Tim Tilson .... **Gary Conway**
DS Lester Hart .... **Regis Toomey**
Henry .... **Leon Lontoc**
Sgt Ames .... **Eileen O'Neill**
'The Man' .... **Carl Benton Reid** *(Secret Agent)*

Creators **Ivan Goff, Ben Roberts**
Producer **Aaron Spelling**

The cases of the head of the Los Angeles homicide squad, a multi-millionaire.

This glossy series focuses on Captain Amos Burke, the obscenely wealthy boss of the LAPD's murder squad, who is dragged away from society functions and expensive wining and dining to head up all manner of homicide investigations. Burke cruises to the scene of crime in the back of a Rolls-Royce, driven by his chauffeur, Henry. There he is assisted by young detective Tim Tilson and wise veteran sergeant Lester Hart. Policewoman Ames is added to Burke's staff later. As unlikely as it seems, the debonair bachelor is evidently the right man for this particular job, as most of the victims appear to come from the élite end of society. Each episode is subtitled *Who killed . . .* ?, with the name of that week's unfortunate victim filling the gap.

Burke eventually quits the police force to become an undercover agent, and sets out on the trail of criminals all over the world. His contact is known only as 'The Man' and is the sole supporting actor in the new-look series. With this change of tack (a response to the success of THE MAN FROM U.N.C.L.E.), the programme was renamed *Amos Burke – Secret Agent*.

Burke's Law, nicely sprinkled with humour and littered with famous guest stars (sometimes more than half a dozen in one episode), was originally planned as a vehicle for Dick Powell, who had played the character in an American anthology series a year or two earlier. It was revived in 1994, with Gene Barry again in the title role. Taking things somewhat easier, in accordance with his age, he now relies on the help of his son, Peter (played by Peter Barton). The role of Henry is taken over by Danny Kamekona.

Burnet, Sir Alastair

(James Burnet; 1928–)

British news and current affairs presenter who joined ITN as political editor in 1963. Despite taking over as editor of *The Economist*, Burnet preserved his ITN career and became one of the first two newscasters on *News at Ten* in 1967 (with Andrew Gardner). Although he left for the BBC and PANORAMA in 1972, and went on to edit the *Daily Express*, he later returned to ITN to launch *News at 5.45*. Subsequently he anchored *News at Ten* for many years. His other television work included THIS WEEK, as well as numerous election programmes, Budgets, royal interviews and commentaries on State occasions. He was knighted in 1984 and retired in 1990.

Burns, George

(Nathan Birnbaum; 1896–1996)

New York-born, cigar-puffing vaudeville comic whose partnership with his scatterbrained wife, Gracie Allen, proved successful on stage, radio and ultimately television. THE BURNS AND ALLEN SHOW revolutionized TV comedy in the 1950s (with its debunking of television conventions) and was a hit on both sides of the Atlantic. With Gracie's retirement and subsequent death, George's career seemed to fade out, but he bounced back in the mid-1970s with a run of cinema successes (such as *The Sunshine Boys* and *Oh God!*) and even began a new US TV series, *The George Burns Comedy Week*, in 1985. He performed right up to his 100th birthday, passing away just a few weeks later.

Burns, Gordon

(1942–)

Presenter, narrator and quiz show host, from 1977 questionmaster on THE KRYPTON FACTOR. Born in Belfast, Burns began his career with Ulster Television (as sports editor and news presenter). From there he moved to Granada, working on WORLD IN ACTION and *Granada Reports*. He has also presented *Password*, SURPRISE, SURPRISE with Cilla Black, and various regional programmes, and devised and hosted the game show *A Word in Your Ear*.

Burns and Allen Show, The ***

US (CBS) Situation Comedy. BBC 1955–61 (US: CBS 1950–8)

George Burns	**Himself**
Gracie Allen	**Herself**
Blanche Morton	**Bea Benaderet**
Harry Morton	**Fred Clark**
	Larry Keating
Harry Von Zell	**Himself**
Ronnie Burns	**Himself**

Producer **Ralph Levy**

Television vehicle for a vaudeville act that had been running for 30 years.

Real-life husband and wife George Burns and Gracie Allen had long been stage and radio partners. As television began to take off, they moved into this unexplored medium and, in doing so, laid down benchmarks for other comedians to follow. Their series is essentially a sitcom, although extended dialogues between the two stars offer more than an echo of their variety days. In the style of I LOVE LUCY and other contemporary US comedies, this one is domestic-based, with the pair playing a husband and wife living in Beverly Hills. Like Lucy, Gracie's confidante is her next-door neighbour, in this case Blanche Morton. The latter's husband, Harry, has a short fuse, which contrasts sharply with the relaxed approach of the philosophical Burns. However, Burns does have an advantage. It is his show and he is able to step out of the action and talk to the audience, pondering what to do next or how the plot should develop. He even has a TV set to watch scenes involving the others and can drag the show's announcer, Harry Von Zell, into the action. It's easy to see where Garry Shandling's inspiration came from. (See IT'S GARRY SHANDLING'S SHOW.)

Gracie's character is a real scatterbrain, but what drives many guest stars to despair are her alternative logic and strange reasoning with which they just can't argue. Thankfully, tolerant George understands her. Why else would he fall for the same ending each week: 'Say "Goodnight", Gracie'; 'Goodnight Gracie'? (An ending copied by Rowan and Martin in LAUGH-IN). The Burns's son, Ronnie, also appeared, but the show ended in America in 1958, when Gracie announced her retirement from the business. Co-star Bea Benaderet went on to provide the voice for Betty Rubble in THE FLINTSTONES and the irrepressible George soldiered on alone.

Burr, Raymond

(1917–93)

Canadian actor, star of two of the best-loved series of the 1950s and 1960s, PERRY MASON and A MAN CALLED IRONSIDE. Between them, these series notched up 18 years of continuous success for their star, leaving him little time to play other roles. Burr did take up the offer of a few TV movies and mini-series (including *79 Park Avenue*), but it wasn't until he revived the old legal-eagle Mason in 1986 that he was prominent on our screens again. Earlier in his career Burr had appeared in around 90 movies.

Burton, Amanda

(1956–)

Northern Irish actress, best known for her roles as Heather Haversham in BROOKSIDE, Dr Beth Glover in PEAK PRACTICE and Dr Sam Ryan in SILENT WITNESS. To add to parts in BOON (Margaret Daly) and INSPECTOR MORSE, other credits have included the dramas *The Gift* (dying young mother Lynn Ransom), *Precious Blood* (Rosie Willis), *Forgotten* (Rachel Monroe), *Little Bird* (Rachel Lewis) and *The Whistle Blower* (Laura Tracey), plus a *Born to Be Wild* nature programme about bears. More recent productions have included *Helen West* (title role), *Pollyanna* (Aunt Polly) and THE COMMANDER (Commander Clare Blake).

Burton, Humphrey

CBE (1931–)

British arts presenter, producer and director, associated with such programmes as MONITOR, OMNIBUS and AQUARIUS. He joined the BBC as a studio manager in 1955, moving on to *Monitor* three years later and becoming the Corporation's first Head of Music and Arts Programmes, 1965–7, a position he reclaimed in 1975 and held until 1981, after being one of the founders of London Weekend Television in the interim period.

Busman's Holiday *

UK (Granada/Action Time) Quiz. ITV 1985–93

Presenters **Julian Pettifer, Sarah Kennedy, Elton Welsby**

Executive Producers **Stephen Leahy, Dianne Nelmes**
Producers **Stephen Leahy, Patricia Pearson, Richard Bradley, Jenny Dodd, Kieran Roberts**

Teams compete for a chance to see how their own jobs are done in other corners of the world.

In this occupational quiz, three teams of workers from various professions were cross-examined about each other's jobs and answered questions about their own specialities. A general knowledge element was also thrown in. The three teams were whittled down to one, which then collected a European or worldwide 'Busman's Holiday'. This saw the three members whisked away to an exotic location to see how their jobs were carried out in that part of the world. A film was made of their experience and shown as an insert in the next programme. Contestants included the likes of seaside landladies, hovercraft pilots, antiques dealers, osteopaths and wardens of stately homes. Julian Pettifer was the original host, succeeded by Sarah Kennedy and then Elton Welsby.

Butler, Daws
(1916–88)

American cartoon voicer, the voice of Yogi Bear, Huckleberry Hound and scores of Hanna-Barbera characters, including Elroy Jetson, Lambsy in *It's the Wolf* and Peter Perfect and others in WACKY RACES.

Butterflies ✶✶
UK (BBC) Situation Comedy. BBC 2 1978–80; 1983
DVD: Acorn Media

Ria Parkinson	**Wendy Craig**
Ben Parkinson	**Geoffrey Palmer**
Russell Parkinson	**Andrew Hall**
Adam Parkinson	**Nicholas Lyndhurst**
Leonard Dunn	**Bruce Montague**
Ruby	**Joyce Windsor**
Thomas	**Michael Ripper**

Creator/Writer **Carla Lane**
Producers **Gareth Gwenlan, Sydney Lotterby**

● ***The frustrations of an overlooked suburban housewife.***
Ria Parkinson's role in life is already over, it seems, after 19 years of marriage. Her two slightly wayward sons, Russell and Adam, have grown up and now have lives of their own, and her dentist husband, Ben, a manic depressive, is too wrapped up in his work and his hobby (butterfly collecting) to find time for her, so Ria tumbles into a mini midlife crisis. Making matters worse is the lack of respect she gets at home – a situation partly fuelled, it must be said, by her poor housekeeping skills and particularly her cooking, which renders anything more complicated than corn flakes a game of chance. To ease the pain, she contemplates an extra-marital affair with recently divorced Leonard Dunn, a smooth, wealthy businessman she meets in a restaurant, although it barely amounts to more than words. Ruby is the Parkinsons' rough-and-ready daily, often bemused at the strange goings-on in the household, and Thomas is Leonard's chauffeur. Creator Carla Lane conceded later that the character of Ria was largely based on herself. The series proved to be a useful stepping-stone for actor Nicholas Lyndhurst, taking him out of the realm of child stars and into adult performances. Before *Butterflies* had ended, ONLY FOOLS AND HORSES had begun. A version of Dolly Parton's 'Love Is Like a Butterfly' was used for the theme tune. The cast was reunited for a special CHILDREN IN NEED sketch in 2000.

Butterworth, Peter
(1919–79)

Carry On actor whose television work stretched from the 1940s through to his death in 1979. Credits included his own series, *Butterworth Time*; the children's programmes *Kept In*, *Those Kids* (Mr Oddy), *Saturday Special* and CATWEAZLE (Groome); the early sketch shows *How Do You View?* and *Two's Company*; the sitcoms *Friends and Neighbours*, *Meet the Champ* (a boxing trainer), *Bulldog Breed* (Henry Broadbent), *Kindly Leave the Kerb* (busker Ernest Tanner), *A Class by Himself* (the valet Clutton) and *Odd Man Out* (Wilf); plus straight drama roles in DOCTOR WHO (the Time Meddler), EMERGENCY – WARD 10, DANGER MAN, THE ODD MAN and PUBLIC EYE. He was married to impressionist Janet Brown and father of actor Tyler Butterworth, appearing with Janet many times in the 1950s, including on the admag *Where Shall We Go?*.

Button Moon ✶
UK (Thames) Children's Entertainment. ITV 1980–3; 1985–8
DVD: Fremantle Home Entertainment

Narrator **Robin Parkinson**

Writer **Ian Allen**
Executive Producer **Charles Warren**

● ***Puppet adventures on a friendly satellite with a kitchen-sink family.***
Button Moon shines in Blanket Sky and casts its light over Junk Planet, where the Spoon family (who have wooden spoons for arms) live. This fondly remembered series follows the adventures of Mr Spoon as he packs up his telescope, jumps in his spaceship (a baked-bean can with a funnel on top) and sails to Button Moon to see what he can see. Joined by Mrs Spoon, daughter Tina and sometimes family friend Eggbert, he enjoys adventures with intriguing characters like Rag Doll, and Elsie and Charlie Tap. Peter Davison performed the theme song with his then wife, Sandra Dickinson.

By the Sword Divided ✶✶
UK (BBC) Drama. BBC 1 1983; 1985
DVD: Acorn Media

Anne Lacey/Fletcher	**Sharon Mughan**
Sir Thomas Lacey	**Timothy Bentinck**
John Fletcher	**Rob Edwards**
Lucinda Lacey/Ferrar	**Lucy Aston**
Sir Martin Lacey	**Julian Glover**
Major Gen. Horton	**Gareth Thomas**
Susan Protheroe	**Judy Buxton**
Capt. Hannibal Marsh	**Malcolm Stoddard**
King Charles I	**Jeremy Clyde**
Sir Henry Parkin	**Charles Kay**
Nathaniel Cropper	**Andrew Maclauchlan**
Goodwife Margaret	**Rosalie Crutchley**
Will Saltmarsh	**Simon Dutton**
Walter Jackman	**Edward Peel**
Capt. Charles Pike	**Mark Burns**
Rachel	**Debbie Goodman**
Emma Bowen/Skinner	**Janet Lees Price**
Hannah Jackman	**Joanna Myers**
Dick Skinner	**Peter Guinness**
Hugh Brandon	**Simon Butteriss**
Mrs Dumfry	**Claire Davenport**
Sir Ralph Winter	**Robert Stephens**
Sir Austin Fletcher	**Bert Parnaby**
Oliver Cromwell	**Peter Jeffrey**
Frances Neville/Lacey	**Joanna McCallum**
King Charles II/Will Jones	**Simon Treves**
Minty	**Eileen Way**
John Thurloe	**David Collings**

Creator **John Hawkesworth**
Producers **Brian Spiby, Jonathan Alwyn**

● ***A family is torn apart by the English Civil War.***
Beginning in May 1640, *By the Sword Divided* tells the story of a noble English family as Civil War looms. Head of the family is Sir Martin Lacey, a staunch Royalist who finds his

relatives siding with his Parliamentarian opponents and his own daughters marrying into 'the other side'. In the course of the first series, Sir Martin fights at Edgehill, the Laceys' home at Arnescote Castle falls under siege from Cromwell's troops and the family silver is smuggled to the King at Oxford, all this taking events up to summer 1647. The second series, which aired in 1985, covers the period 1648–60 and picks up with Arnescote Castle firmly in the hands of Sir Martin's daughter, Anne, and her Parliamentarian husband, John Fletcher. It continues through the execution of Charles I, a visit from Cromwell, assorted witch hunts, the arrival of Charles II, Royalist attempts to regain Arnescote and the eventual restoration of the monarchy, with family turmoil, as always, competing fiercely with external hostilities.

Bygraves, Max

(Walter Bygraves; 1922–)

London-born entertainer who earned the nickname 'Max' after an impression he performed of Max Miller while in the RAF. Although training as a carpenter, Bygraves was able to turn professional as a singer and comedian soon after the war, working on stage, radio, records and film, eventually arriving on television with his *Singalongamax* nostalgic music shows, numerous Royal Variety Performances and one-off specials. His hosting of FAMILY FORTUNES proved less successful and the series was cancelled, only to be brought back a few years later with Les Dennis in charge. In 2001, he hosted a series of Christmas shorts called *Max's Crackers* for Channel 4. 'I wanna tell you a story' became his catchphrase over the years.

Byker Grove ✶✶

UK (Zenith North) Children's Drama. BBC 1 1989–2006

Michael .... **Gordon Griffin**
Julie Warner .... **Lucy Walsh**
Donna Bell .... **Sally McQuillan**
Nicola Dobson .... **Jill Halfpenny**
Spuggie Campbell .... **Lyndyann Barrass**
Martin 'Gill' Gillespie .... **Caspar Berry**
Winston .... **Craig Reilly**
Mary O'Malley .... **Lyn Douglas**
Rajeev .... **Daniel Larson**
Clare Warner .... **Jenny Twigge**
Andrew 'Cas' Pearson .... **Niall Shearer**
Geoff Keegan .... **Billy Fane**
Hayley .... **Amanda Webster**
Alison .... **Victoria Murray**
Jim Bell .... **Colin MacLachlan**
Duncan .... **Declan Donnelly**
Ian Webster .... **Craig Grieveson**
Lisa .... **Jayne Mackenzie**
Fraser Campell .... **John Jefferson**
Carl .... **Peter Eke**
Polly .... **Denise Welch**
Brad .... **Michael Nicholson**
Jan .... **Morten Lind**
Marilyn 'Charley' Charlton .... **Michelle Charles**
Peter Jenkins ('PJ') .... **Anthony McPartlin**
Dexter .... **Gavin Kitchen**
Robert .... **Christopher Hardy**
Jemma Dobson .... **Nicola Ewart**
Gwen .... **Linda Huntley**
Kelly .... **Louise Towers**
Beckett .... **Roger Lloyd Pack**
Speedy .... **Stephen Bradley**
Leah Carmichael .... **Jayni Hoy**
Noddy .... **Brett Adams**
Angel O'Hagan .... **Vicky Taylor**
Debbie Dobson .... **Nicola Bell**
Morph .... **Tracy Dempster**
Paul .... **Joe Caffrey**
Marcus Bewick .... **David Oliver**
Oliver Stone
Amanda Bewick .... **Gemma Graham**
Patsy .... **Justine McKenzie**
Frew .... **Luke Dale**
Kath .... **Lesley Saint John**
Charlie Charlton .... **Donna Air**
Lou Gallagher .... **Annie Orwin**
Barney Hardy .... **Stephen Carr**
Lee Ratcliffe .... **Rory Gibson**
Greg Watson .... **Dale Meeks**
Gary Crawford
Gary Hendrix .... **George Trotter**
Marie .... **Louise Mostyn**
Anna Turnbull .... **Claire Graham**
Alfie Turnbull .... **Andrew Smith**
Flora .... **Kerryann Christiansen**
Arran .... **Neil Blackstone**
Dace .... **Leslie Baines**
Ed .... **Grant Adams**
Laura Dobson .... **Emma Brierley**
Karen .... **Kimberly Dunbar**
Brigid O'Hagan .... **Joanne McIntosh**
Ashley .... **Shaun Mechen**
Terry .... **Chris Woodger**
Sita .... **Gauri Vedhara**
Philip .... **Philip Miller**
Leanne Henderson .... **Vikki Spensley**
Jake .... **Nick Figgis**
Cher .... **Jody Baldwin**
Rob .... **Gavin Makel**
Teraise O'Hagan .... **Adele Taylor**
Jack .... **Edward Scott**
Sian .... **Charlie Hardwick**
Harry .... **Leah Jones**
Ben Carter .... **Andrew Hayden Smith**
Nikki Watson .... **Siobhan Hanratty**
Ollie .... **Louis Watson**
Regina O'Hagan .... **Jade Turnbull**
Laura .... **Louise Henderson**
Barry .... **Stephen Douglass**
Nat .... **Alexa Gibb**
Emma Miller .... **Holly Wilkinson/Matthews**
Tom .... **Ronan Patterson**
Matt Tyler .... **Adam Henderson Scott**
Claire Rivers .... **Victoria Hawkins**
Liam .... **Pete Hepple**
Stumpy McLoughlin .... **Paul Meynell**
Maggie .... **Janine Birkett**
Tina Meredith .... **Lynne Wilmot**
Akili Johnson .... **Patrick Miller**
Juliet .... **Beverley Hills**
Peter .... **Bill Fellows**
Joe Dakin .... **Chris Beattie**
Bill Dakin .... **Adam John Ironside**
Bradley Clayton .... **Nicholas Nancarrow**
Paul Johnson .... **Patrice Etienne**
Eve Johnson .... **Rory Lewis**
Adam Brett .... **Alex Beebe**
Luke Brett .... **Dominic Beebe**
Stella Reece .... **Emma Littlewood**

Steve	**Andrew Landsbury**
Sarah Young	**Sammy Dobson**
Jodie Reece	**Sophie Blench**
Beth McGregor	**Jennifer Wilson**
Jamie Parker/Harper	**Matthew Edgar**
Robert Hunter	**Thomas Graham**
Craig	**Robert Price**
Hayley Robinson	**Heather Garrett**
Alan	**Duncan Ford**
Anjali	**Nisha Joshi**
Mukasa	**Simon Yugire**
Fraser	**Neil Armstrong**
Dom Meredith	**Daymon Britton**
Lesley	**Grace Stilgrove**
Helen	**Phillipa Wilson**
Sadie Fox	**Bridie Hales**
Leanne	**Rachael Lee**
Mickey Murray	**Daniel Waterston**
Kate Best	**Alex Gardner**
Spencer	**Leon Scott**
Andrew 'Spud' Tate	**Jamie Tulip**
Keith Henderson	**Tony Neilson**
Jeanette Wilson	**Tracy Gillman**
Norm	**Chris Larner**
Binnie	**Jonathan Ferguson**
Lucy Summerbee	**Chelsea Halfpenny**
Zoe McCormack	**Hannah Clementson**
Sam	**Laura Norton**
Scott Jackson	**Matthew Forster**
Chrissie Harrison	**Sarah Lawton**
Kylie Wylie	**Gayna Millican**
Vicky Murray	**Jo McGarry**
Kevin McLaughlin	**Joseph Mc-Cabe**
Candice-Marie Harper	**Kate Heslop**
Jessica Jones	**Julianne Johnson**
Danielle Blake	**Chloe Stanley**
Charlotte Murray	**Altea Claveras**
Peter 'Gadget'	**Daniel Watson**

Creator **Adele Rose**
Executive Producers **Andrea Wonfor, Peter Murphy**
Producers **Matthew Robinson, Morag Bain, Stephen McAteer**

Popular teenage soap, set in a Newcastle youth centre.
When teenager Julie Warner moves with her family to Newcastle, she immediately hates her new home, until she meets new friends at Byker Grove youth centre. This is the device used to introduce viewers to a gang of north-eastern youths who dabble in all the usual vices but enjoy lasting friendships along the way. Touchy subjects, including death, homosexuality, racism, teenage marriage, divorce, joy-riding and homelessness, were tackled during the series' long run which was due to end in autumn 2006. The programme was recorded at Benwell Towers, a 19th-century house on Tyneside.

Byker Grove, predictably, also had its pop successes. Characters PJ and Duncan (launch-pad characters for children's TV presenters Ant and Dec) enjoyed an extended run of hit singles, and 'Love Your Sexy . . . !!' was a minor hit in 1994 for Byker Grooove! (Vicky Taylor, Jayni Hoy and Donna Air – the last going on to host THE BIG BREAKFAST, among other programmes). The theme music for the programme itself was by the Kane Gang. Another *Grove* prodigy was soap star and STRICTLY COME DANCING winner Jill Halfpenny, whose niece, Chelsea, joined the series in 2004.

Byrne, John
MBE (1940–)

Scottish painter and playwright whose TUTTI FRUTTI was one of the most highly acclaimed drama serials of the late 1980s. He followed it up with YOUR CHEATIN' HEART and the *Screenplay* production *Boswell and Johnson's Tour of the Western Isles*. Byrne also contributed to the sketch series *Scotch and Wry*.

Byrne, Peter
(1928–)

For years Jack Warner's son-in-law, Andy Crawford, in DIXON OF DOCK GREEN, Peter Byrne pleased his female admirers by turning out again in the 1980s, playing the part of Nellie Boswell's fancy man in BREAD. Over the years his other appearances have included parts in *The New Canadians*, BLAKE'S 7 and his earliest programme, *The Pattern of Marriage*, in 1953.

Byrnes, Edd
(Edward Breitenberger; 1933–)

Short-lived cult figure of the late 1950s and early 1960s, otherwise known as Kookie, the jive-talking car-park attendant in 77 SUNSET STRIP. After that role ended in 1963 the blond-haired Byrnes found work difficult to come by, meandering in and out of minor series and spaghetti Westerns, and then taking guest spots in programmes like MURDER, SHE WROTE. He had a hit single (with Connie Stevens) in 1960, entitled 'Kookie, Kookie (Lend Me Your Comb)', based on his excessive grooming in the series.

Cable

A system involving the relay of television programmes via a network of cables, using one central reception/transmission centre. Initially cable was introduced to provide TV pictures to parts of the country where aerial reception was poor or non-existent. Rediffusion was one such supplier in the UK. However, with the new generation of cabling, and the introduction of optical fibre (allowing many more channels to be carried), a host of new cable companies has sprung up across the UK, the most prominent being NTL. These now use digital technology and provide dedicated cable channels, alongside satellite channels and locally made community programmes.

Cable News Network

See *CNN*.

Cadell, Simon

(1950–96)

British dramatic and comedy actor accomplished in strait-laced, nervous roles such as entertainments manager Jeffrey Fairbrother in HI-DE-HI!, the hapless civil servant Dundridge in BLOTT ON THE LANDSCAPE, estate agent Larry Wade in LIFE WITHOUT GEORGE and actor Dennis Duval in SINGLES. His other TV credits included HADLEIGH, HINE, THE GLITTERING PRIZES, WINGS, SPACE: 1999, *About Face*, the 1976 play *The Dame of Sark*, the similar in content ENEMY AT THE DOOR (Hauptmann Reinicke), and EDWARD AND MRS SIMPSON. Cadell also voiced the *Bump* elephant cartoons and his last TV appearance was in *Circles of Deceit* (Brendan Rylans) in 1996. He was the brother of actress Selina Cadell and son-in-law of writer/producer David Croft.

Cade's County ★★

US (Twentieth Century-Fox) Police Drama. ITV 1972 (US: CBS 1971–2)

Sam Cade .... **Glenn Ford**
J. J. Jackson .... **Edgar Buchanan**
Arlo Pritchard .... **Taylor Lacher**
Rudy Davillo .... **Victor Campos**
Pete .... **Peter Ford**
Joannie Little Bird .... **Sandra Ego**
Betty Ann Sundown .... **Betty Ann Carr**

Executive Producer **David Gerber**
Producer **Charles Larson**

Exciting moments in the life of a chief lawman.

This modern Western focuses on Sheriff Sam Cade, leading crimebuster of Madrid County, California. Cade himself is mainly rooted to his Madrid town base, but his deputies out and about, keeping the peace around the large desert county, are J. J. Jackson, an experienced veteran, and younger colleagues Arlo, Rudy and Pete (played by Glenn Ford's son). Two real-life Native American girls, Sandra Ego and Betty Ann Carr, play police dispatchers Joannie Little Bird and Betty Ann Sundown.

Cadfael ★★

UK (Central/Carlton) Detective Drama. ITV 1994–8
DVD: Carlton

Brother Cadfael .... **Derek Jacobi**
Hugh Beringar .... **Sean Pertwee**
Eoin McCarthy
Anthony Green
Prior Robert .... **Michael Culver**
Abbot Heribert .... **Peter Copley**
Abbot Radulfus .... **Terrence Hardiman**
Brother Jerome .... **Julian Firth**
Brother Oswin .... **Mark Charnock**

Executive Producer **Ted Childs**
Producer **Stephen Smallwood**

The investigations of a medieval monk detective.

Adapted from, or based on, the novels by Ellis Peters (pseudonym of the late Edith Pargeter), this series of sporadic adventures features Brother Cadfael, a Welsh Benedictine monk living in Shrewsbury's St Peter and St Paul abbey during the reign of King Stephen. His first television outing came in an adaptation of Ms Peters's second novel, *One Corpse Too Many*, set during a siege of the Shropshire market town in the year 1138.

The fiftysomething Cadfael has turned to the cloisters late in life, having been a crusader and even fathered a son. However, his inquiring mind will not confine itself to reflections on the Good Book or tending the monastery herb gardens, and the merest sniff of intrigue sets the self-effacing sleuth's investigative juices flowing. His success rate is phenomenal, considering he can call on none of today's technology or advances in forensic science. To ensure the correct setting and atmosphere, the producers took filming over to the Fot studios, near Budapest, where they reconstructed medieval Shrewsbury, complete with a mini River Severn. Experts were employed as consultants on historical, religious and musical matters. Each of the 12 episodes ran to 90 minutes and guest stars included soap actors Roy Barraclough, Anna Friel and Peter Baldwin.

Caesars, The ★★

UK (Granada) Historical Drama. ITV 1968

Augustus .... **Roland Culver**
Germanicus .... **Eric Flynn**
Tiberius .... **André Morell**
Sejanus .... **Barrie Ingham**
Caligula .... **Ralph Bates**
Claudius .... **Freddie Jones**
Livia .... **Sonia Dresdel**

Writer/Producer **Philip Mackie**

Power and corruption in ancient Rome.

Pre-dating the celebrated I, CLAUDIUS by eight years, *The*

Caesars tackles the same subject, namely the political dog-fighting of Imperial Rome and the craven pastimes of its foremost citizens. Written and produced by Granada's Head of Drama, Philip Mackie, and directed by Derek Bennett, it was, in critics' eyes, no less successful. The six episodes focus chiefly on the six emperors and generals Augustus, Germanicus, Tiberius, Sejanus, Caligula and Claudius, with the scheming matriarch, Livia, also immersed in the action. Overall, a compact study of Rome's decline and fall is compiled.

Café Continental ✶

UK (BBC) Variety. BBC 1947–53

Creator/Producer **Henry Caldwell**

● ***International cabaret presented from a fake nightclub.***

This initially 45-minute, later one-hour, variety show took the form of a Saturday night visit to a sophisticated international cabaret and dining club, complete with presiding *maître d'hôtel* and master/mistress of ceremonies. Claude Frédéric and Pier Auguste were two of the artists to take the roles of the former; Al Burnett and Hélène Cordet two to take the latter. Sydney Jerome was the orchestra leader. Probably the biggest name to appear behind the Café's smart swing doors was Folies Bergère star Josephine Baker (in 1948).

Cagney and Lacey ✶✶

US (Orion) Police Drama. BBC 1 1982–8 (US: CBS 1982–8)
DVD: Universal

Det. Mary Beth Lacey .... **Tyne Daly**
Det. Christine Cagney .... **Meg Foster**
Sharon Gless
Lt. Bert Samuels .... **Al Waxman**
Det. Mark Petrie .... **Carl Lumbly**
Det. Victor Isbecki .... **Martin Kove**
Det. Paul La Guardia .... **Sidney Clute**
Deputy Insp. Marquette .... **Jason Bernard**
Desk Sgt Ronald Coleman .... **Harvey Atkin**
Harvey Lacey .... **John Karlen**
Harvey Lacey Jr .... **Tony La Torre**
Michael Lacey .... **Troy Slaten**
Alice Lacey .... **Dana and Paige Bardolph**
Michelle Sepe
Sgt Dory McKenna .... **Barry Primus**
Insp. Knelman .... **Michael Fairman**
Det. Jonah Newman .... **Dan Shor**
David Keeler .... **Stephen Macht**
Det. Manny Esposito .... **Robert Hegyes**
Det. Al Corassa .... **Paul Mantee**
Josie .... **Jo Corday**
Tom Basil .... **Barry Laws**
Charlie Cagney .... **Dick O'Neill**
Det. Verna Dee Jordan .... **Merry Clayton**
Nick Amatucci .... **Carl Weintraub**

Creators **Barney Rosenzweig, Barbara Avedon, Barbara Corday**
Executive Producer **Barney Rosenzweig**
Producer **Richard A. Rosenbloom**

● ***Two female cops win through in a man's world, despite the pressures of their personal lives.***

Cagney and Lacey was a pioneer among TV cop series. It broke new ground in that it allowed women to be seen in the buddy-buddy context epitomized by series like STARSKY AND HUTCH. Based on two women, Mary Beth Lacey and Chris Cagney, cops paired together as a team on the New York streets, it struck a firm feminist stance in rejecting all the established preconceptions of women on television. The two heroines are seen holding their own in a tough, tough world, where the conflict and male prejudice they meet within the police force is sometimes as great as the violence outside.

Cagney and Lacey is not the usual cops-and-robbers fare. It shows the grimier side of police work, the ups *and* the downs, and the girls are more than partners. In the sanctuary of the ladies' room at the police station, they pour their hearts out to each other, discussing the strains of work and their personal worries. Mary Beth is married (to construction worker Harvey Lacey) with young sons (Harvey Jr and Michael) and later a daughter (Alice). She has come from a broken home, went through an abortion at 19 and has battled her way through a breast cancer scare. Chris is ambitious and single, but, dreading being alone all her life, she is continually drawn into unsuccessful relationships, such as with attorney David Keeler.

The programme never shirks heavy issues, such as Chris's occasional alcohol-dependency and the drug addiction of her one-time boyfriend, fellow cop Dory McKenna. In one episode she is even raped. Her alcoholic father, Charlie, also once on the force, appears from time to time until he dies, ironically just before she wins promotion to sergeant.

The series was not an instant hit in the States. After a pilot starring Loretta Swit of M*A*S*H in the part of Cagney, a short first series was produced, with Meg Foster cast alongside Tyne Daly. However, it was criticized for being too hard and too unfeminine, and so, when the next episodes were made, the producers softened it up, replacing Foster with Sharon Gless. Even then the studio was not impressed with the ratings and they cancelled the show, only for it to be brought back by huge public demand. A handful of TV movies featuring the characters were made in the 1990s.

Caine, Marti

(Lynne Shepherd; 1945–95)

Sheffield-born comedienne and singer, a former model who came to fame via the NEW FACES talent-spotting show (she won the 1975 series), a programme she hosted for three series on its revival in 1986. In between, she starred in her own comedy/variety shows (*Nobody Does It Like Marti*, *Marti* and *The Marti Caine Show*) and attempted sitcom with HILARY, in which she played an accident-prone TV researcher. Her last series was *Joker in the Pack*. Marti's stage name was, she claimed, taken from gardening terminology – 'tomato canes'.

Call My Bluff ✶✶

UK (BBC) Panel Game. BBC 2 1965–88; BBC 1 1996–2003; 2005

Presenters **Robin Ray, Joe Melia, Peter Wheeler, Robert Robinson, Bob Holness, Fiona Bruce**

Creators **Mark Goodson, Bill Todman**
Producers **T. Leslie Jackson, Bryan Sears, Johnny Downes**

● ***Panel game based on the true meaning of obscure words.***

Despite lasting just six months in its native USA, *Call My Bluff* was a stalwart of the BBC 2 schedule almost from the channel's inception until 1988. In keeping with the more erudite nature of the BBC's second channel, this programme looks at strange words, with two teams of three celebrities attempting to mislead each other as to the true meaning of arcane dictionary entries. Each panellist gives a lengthy, humorous definition of the word offered up by the chairman and the other team has to decide which description is genuine. Success or failure is denoted by the turning over of the description cards to reveal, in big letters, TRUE or BLUFF.

The programme's first chairman was Robin Ray, although the longest serving and best known was Robert Robinson (from 1967). Joe Melia and Peter Wheeler also hosted proceedings in the early days. Frank Muir and Robert Morley were the first team captains, Patrick Campbell later replaced Morley and Arthur Marshall took over from the late Campbell in the 1980s. However, numerous other celebrities also stood in as team captains. They included Kenneth Horne, Alan Melville and Kenneth Williams.

A one-off revival was shown in 1994 with Joanna Lumley opposing Frank Muir and with Robert Robinson in the chair, before the series returned at lunchtimes on BBC 1 in 1996. New chairman was Bob Holness, with Alan Coren and Sandi Toksvig acting as captains. Fiona Bruce took over the chair in 2003, assisted by team captains Coren and Rod Liddle.

Callan ★★★

UK (ABC/Thames) Secret Agent Drama. ITV 1967–72
DVD: Clear Vision Video

David Callan	**Edward Woodward**
Lonely	**Russell Hunter**
Hunter	**Ronald Radd**
	Michael Goodliffe
	Derek Bond
	William Squire
Toby Meres	**Anthony Valentine**
Cross	**Patrick Mower**
Hunter's secretary	**Lisa Langdon**

Creator **James Mitchell**
Executive Producer **Lloyd Shirley**
Producer **Reginald Collin**

The assignments of a brutal British Intelligence agent.

Although similarly based in the secret world of international subterfuge, *Callan* is a far cry from the glamour of James Bond. The hero is a hard man, edgy and friendless. He works for the intelligence service, bluntly snuffing out enemies and others who represent a danger to British security. But he is also a rebel and a thinker who brings his own version of justice into play, rather than just killing willy-nilly as instructed. Callan, as a consequence, is constantly in trouble with his superiors.

In his first appearance, in a 1967 episode of ABC's ARMCHAIR THEATRE called *A Magnum for Schneider*, Callan himself was the target. He had been given the chance to retrieve his dodgy reputation within British Intelligence by bumping off an enemy agent, but this was merely a ruse to nail him for murder and so dispose of him. Turning the tables, Callan won through and public interest in the character led to a fully fledged series later the same year.

In the series the star is assisted by a dirty, smelly petty crook called Lonely, who supplies him with under-the-counter firearms and useful information. Callan treats Lonely, one of life's perpetual losers, with complete disdain. At the same time, though, he protects his little accomplice, finding him a job as driver of the communications car, a taxi filled with high-tech listening devices. Within the intelligence service, Callan's immediate boss is Hunter, not a specific person but a codename for the various heads of department supervising him. Then there is Meres (played by Peter Bowles in the *Armchair Theatre* play), a fellow agent who resents Callan's position and contrives to dislodge him. Another agent seen later, the trigger-happy Cross, shares the same sentiments.

Nine years after the series ended, Callan was brought back in a one-off 90-minute play for ATV entitled *Wet Job*. Now retired and running a militaria shop under the alias of David Tucker, he is re-enlisted by the security services for one last mission. Hunter is played by Hugh Walters and Lonely resurfaces, too, in the unlikely role of a bathroom store proprietor.

Callan, with its swinging naked light-bulb opening sequence, was created by writer James Mitchell, who was later responsible for WHEN THE BOAT COMES IN. A cinema version was released in 1974.

Callard, Beverley

(1958–)

Leeds-born actress, who joined CORONATION STREET as Liz McDonald in 1989, having briefly played another character (June Dewhurst) five years earlier. She left in 1998 but has since returned temporarily. Callard has also been seen in the comedies THE PETER PRINCIPLE (Barbara) and TWO PINTS OF LAGER AND A PACKET OF CRISPS (Flo Henshaw), as well as in EMMERDALE (Angie Richards), DEAR LADIES, *Hell's Bells*, THE PRACTICE, THE BILL, and the *Screen Two* film *Will You Love Me Tomorrow?*, sometimes billed as Beverley Sowden. Actress Rebecca Callard is her daughter.

Callard, Rebecca

(1976–)

Actress daughter of Beverley Callard who, like her mum, once acted under the surname of Sowden. Rebecca appeared alongside Beverley in the *Screen Two* film *Will You Love Me Tomorrow?* but has a host of other credits to her name, most notably as Arrietty in THE BORROWERS, Kate Morris in THE GRAND, Harriet Marsh in *Plotlands* and Laura Hutchings in SUNBURN. Other appearances have been in BONJOUR LA CLASSE (Lucy Cornwell), CHILDREN'S WARD (Fiona Brett), BAND OF GOLD, CASUALTY, *Life Support*, PEAK PRACTICE, SEPTEMBER SONG (Vicky), *Chiller*, HETTY WAINTHROPP INVESTIGATES, THE MRS BRADLEY MYSTERIES, the animation *The Miracle Maker* (voice of Tamar), BORN AND BRED, DOC MARTIN and *Lorna Doone* (Ruth Huckaback).

Callow, Simon

CBE (1949–)

London-born stage and screen actor, on television in roles as diverse as Tom Chance in the comedy CHANCE IN A MILLION and Count Fosco in THE WOMAN IN WHITE. Other major parts have included Mr Micawber in DAVID COPPERFIELD, Hugo in DEAD HEAD, John Mortimer in *The Trials of Oz*, Edward Feathers in *Little Napoleons*, Vicar Ronnie in *Screen Two*'s *Femme Fatale*, Rupert Halliday QC in TRIAL AND RETRIBUTION and Galileo in *Galileo's Daughter*. Callow was also seen in *Angels in America* and provided voices for the animation *Shoebox Zoo*. Among the numerous series in which he has made guest appearances are INSPECTOR MORSE, AGATHA CHRISTIE'S MARPLE, MIDSOMER MURDERS and DOCTOR WHO (playing Charles Dickens).

Camberwick Green/Trumpton/Chigley ★★★★

UK (Gordon Murray) Children's Entertainment. BBC 1 1966/1967/1969
DVD: Firefly

Narrator **Brian Cant**

Creator/Producer **Gordon Murray**
Writers **Gordon Murray, Alison Prince** *(Trumpton)*

● ***Rural puppet soap operas for kids.***

Animated by Bob Bura and John Hardwick, Gordon Murray's rustic puppet trilogy began in 1966, when *Camberwick Green* took over the Monday WATCH WITH MOTHER slot. It gave children an insight into the lives of the folk of Camberwick Green, a small village deep in the English countryside. Each episode opens and ends with a shot of a musical box, 'wound up and ready to play', from which one of the villagers slowly emerges, allowing viewers to follow them as they go about their typical day. Sadly, a minor tragedy always strikes at some point and the gallant lads at Pippin Fort (Armitage, Featherby, Higgins, Hopwood, Lumley and Meek), under the command of Captain Snort and Sgt Major Grout, are usually called in to restore order. The good people of Camberwick Green are: Windy Miller of Colley's Mill; Roger Varley, the chimney sweep; Mr Carraway, the fishmonger; gossipy Mrs Honeyman, the chemist's wife (and her baby boy); Dr Mopp with his bone-shaker car; farmer Jonathan Bell; Mr Crockett, the garage owner; Mickey Murphy, the baker (with children Paddy and Mary); salesman Mr Dagenham; Thomas Tripp, the milkman; Peter Hazel, the postman; Mrs Dingle, the postmistress (and Packet, the Post Office puppy), and, of course, PC McGarry (number 452). A pierrot puppet turns over the opening and closing titles.

A few *Camberwick Green* characters appeared in the spin-off series *Trumpton*, a year later, dropping in on an occasional basis. This time the action has moved to the larger town of Trumpton, where the role played earlier by the soldiers of Pippin Fort is assumed by Capt. Flack's courageous local firemen: Pugh, Pugh, Barney McGrew, Cuthbert, Dibble and Grubb. Mrs Honeyman gives way to the blethering hat maker Miss Lovelace and her yapping Pekinese dogs (Mitzi, Daphne and Lulu), and also featured are the Mayor; his driver, Philby; the Town Clerk, Mr Troop; florist Mrs Cobbit; carpenter Chippy Minton, his wife, Dora, and his son, Nibbs; clock maker Mr Platt; Mr Clamp, the greengrocer; park-keeper Mr Craddock; rag and bone man Raggy Dan; window cleaner Mr Robinson; decorator Walter Harking; ice cream man Mr Antonio; printer Mr Munnings; telephone engineer Mr Wantage and his assistant, Fred; plumber Mr Wilkins; borough engineer Mr Bolt; bill sticker Nick Fisher; and Policeman Potter. The start of each episode focuses on the Trumpton clock, 'telling the time for Trumpton', and all programmes end with a fire brigade band concert in the park.

The third instalment of this puppet melodrama came from Chigley, a hamlet described as being 'near Camberwick Green, Trumptonshire'. This is an altogether more modest little settlement, chiefly consisting of a biscuit factory, a canalside wharf, a pottery and a stately home, Winkstead Hall. The last belongs to Lord Belborough, a charitable aristocrat who, with his loyal butler, Mr Brackett, runs a steam train known as *Bessie* for the benefit of the local people. Goods are ferried in and out at Treddles Wharf, where the bargees like Mr Rumpling and dockers are supervised by Mr Swallow. Cresswells Chigley Biscuits, meanwhile, is in the hands of Mr Cresswell, and his employees (including biscuit stamper Willie Munn) hold a dance to the music of a barrel organ after the six o'clock whistle at the end of each episode. Also seen are Harry Farthing, the potter-cum-sculptor, and his daughter, Winnie; Mr Clutterbuck, the builder; Mr Bilton, Belborough's gardener; and assorted cross-over characters from both *Camberwick Green* and *Trumpton*.

Despite only 13 episodes being made of each series, repeat showings continued for many years. While the storylines were always very limited and the songs (by Freddie Phillips) crushingly repetitive, Brian Cant's whimsical delivery and the quality of the animation and characterization have made this little trilogy into children's television classics.

Cambridge Spies ★★★

UK (BBC/Perpetual Motion) Drama. BBC 2 2003
DVD: BBC

Kim Philby	**Toby Stephens**
Guy Burgess	**Tom Hollander**
Anthony Blunt	**Samuel West**
Donald Maclean	**Rupert Penry-Jones**
Otto	**Marcel Iures**
Jack Hewit	**Stuart Laing**
Queen Elizabeth	**Imelda Staunton**
King George VI	**Anthony Andrews**
Col. Winters	**Ronald Pickup**
James Jesus Angleton	**John Light**
Melinda Maclean	**Anna-Louise Plowman**
Guy Liddell	**Angus Wright**

Writer **Peter Moffat**
Executive Producers **Laura Mackie, Gareth Neame, Sally Woodward**
Producer **Mark Shivas**

● ***Four student friends form the most notorious spy ring in British 20th-century history.***

Against the idyllic backdrop of Cambridge in 1934, Kim Philby, Guy Burgess, Donald Maclean and Anthony Blunt are four restless, idealistic souls, repelled by the rise of fascism in continental Europe. Their response is to throw in their lot with the communists of the Soviet Union, passing on Western secrets from the positions they take up within the British Establishment. The arrogant Blunt is the mastermind of the quartet, the chief recruiter for the cause, a man who becomes Surveyor of the King's Pictures. Dashing Philby is a womanizer, and the most effective spy of the bunch, working out of MI6 during the war. Nervy, troubled Maclean joins the Foreign Office, while Burgess is the weakest link, a boozy, homosexual, eccentric troublemaker who becomes a BBC producer. Otto is their Soviet minder. Their tale is one of close bonding, a passion for social justice and the recognition that, in their precarious position, it is very much a case of all for one and one for all. Over 17 years, their activities for the KGB – betrayals that led to the deaths of many British agents – take them to such locations as Vienna, Paris, New York, Washington and Moscow. Tim Fywell directs the four-part drama.

Cameron, James

OBE (1911–85)

British current affairs reporter of the 1960s and 1970s. He was the first commentator on the retrospective series, ALL OUR YESTERDAYS, and later turned to drama writing. The 1979

Screenplay presentation, *The Sound of the Guns*, was his first offering.

Camomile Lawn, The ✳✳✳

UK (Zed) Drama. Channel 4 1992
DVD: Cinema Club

Helena Cuthbertson .... **Felicity Kendal**
Richard Cuthbertson .... **Paul Eddington**
Max Erstweiler .... **Oliver Cotton**
Calypso .... **Jennifer Ehle**
Rosemary Harris *(older)*
Polly .... **Tara Fitzgerald**
Virginia McKenna *(older)*
Sophy .... **Rebecca Hall**
Claire Bloom *(older)*
Oliver .... **Toby Stephens**
Richard Johnson *(older)*
Hector/Hamish .... **Nicholas Le Prevost**
Monika .... **Trudy Weiss**
Paul Floyer .... **Jeremy Brook**
David Floyer .... **Joss Brook**
Walter .... **Ben Walden**
Tony .... **James Gaddas**
Elizabeth .... **Maria Miles**
Sarah .... **Polly Adams**
George .... **Donald Pickering**
Iris .... **Vivienne Ritchie**

Writer **Ken Taylor**
Producers **Sophie Balhetchet, Glenn Wilhide**

Cousins gather at a funeral and family secrets are finally disclosed.

It is 1939 and five young cousins and family friends meet up at the seaside home of their Uncle Richard and Aunt Helena for one last frivolous summer before the clouds of war begin to darken the sky. On the fragrant camomile lawn of the Cornish house the last joys of childhood are played out. With the onset of hostilities, there is soon growing up to be done all round. Among the cousins is beautiful Calypso, pursued by the lusty Oliver. Then there is Walter, the resilient Polly and little Sophy. Joining them are twins David and Paul. Alongside Richard and Helen live Max and Monika, a virtuoso Jewish-German violinist and his wife who decide to weather the storm of war in Britain. Action switches between Cornwall and London as the story progresses. Calypso marries the wealthy Hector, Polly falls pregnant, and Helena lives secretly with Max as Richard's disabilities confine him to Cornwall. Walter joins the Navy and the twins become RAF officers. Throughout, there are 'flashforwards' to 1984 when older versions of Calypso, Polly, Sophy, Oliver and other survivors gather on the camomile lawn for Max's funeral and look back with affection on the heady days of their youth. Inevitably, secrets, long preserved, begin to leak out. The four-part drama, the first TV serial to be directed by Sir Peter Hall, was based on the novel of the same name by Mary Wesley. Hall's own daughter, Rebecca, played Sophy and another interesting piece of casting saw the older Calypso played by Jennifer Ehle's own mother, Rosemary Harris.

Campaign ✳

UK (BBC) Drama. BBC 2 1988

Sarah Copeland .... **Penny Downie**
Gordon Lochhead .... **Gary Waldhorn**
Warren Greenbank .... **John Fortune**
David Postgate .... **Jeremy Clyde**
Rose Thompson .... **Rosalind Bennett**
Paul Copeland .... **Miles Anderson**
Daniel Copeland .... **Robbie Engels**
Linda Prentice .... **Josie Lawrence**
Stephen Hallam .... **David Cardy**
Helen Marriott .... **Kate Lynn-Evans**
Nick Faulds .... **Stephen Mann**
Dee Vincent .... **Caroline Lee Johnson**
Carol Braithwaite .... **Camille Coduri**
Jane Malcolm .... **Diana Blackburn**
Mike Sutherland .... **Fraser Downie**
Clayton Yock .... **Peter-Hugo Daly**
Francis Salk .... **Thomas Wheatley**
Sally Byfleet .... **Rebecca Pidgeon**
Kim Greenbank .... **Charlotte Coleman**
Geoffrey Talbot .... **Tony Matthews**

Writer **Gerard MacDonald**
Producer **Ruth Boswell**

Love and war in the cut-throat world of advertising.

There's a power struggle at the heart of the Hamilton Forbes & Kent advertising agency, with colleagues seeking to undermine each other. It could hardly come at a worse time. There's a general election looming and the agency holds the government account. Most attention is devoted to Sarah Copeland, the acting creative director who is torn between her career and parenthood. With husband Paul deserting her, she leaves her little boy in the care of 'mother's helper' Rose Thompson. Back at work her colleagues include art director Warren Greenbank, an alcoholic cricket fan, who has a teenage daughter, Kim; managing director David Postgate; his deputy Gordon Lochhead; and secretary Sally Byfleet. Ambitious Stephen Hallam wants to break out and set up his own firm, and womanizes extravagantly in the meantime. Brought in to make presentations is lesbian film-maker Linda Prentice. The six-part series charts the numerous personal affairs, fierce business rivalries and the ups and downs (mostly downs) of a problematic election campaign. Brian Farnham directs.

Campbell, Cheryl

(1949–)

British actress with a number of high-profile TV roles to her name, most notably the parts of Eileen in PENNIES FROM HEAVEN and Vera Brittain in TESTAMENT OF YOUTH. Her TV debut came in an episode of Z CARS and other major credits have been in dramas like LILLIE (Sarah Bernhardt), *Agatha Christie's The Seven Dials Mystery*, MISS MARPLE, MALICE AFORETHOUGHT (Madeleine Cranmere), BOON, THE RUTH RENDELL MYSTERIES, BRAMWELL, INSPECTOR MORSE, THE CASEBOOK OF SHERLOCK HOLMES, *The Mill on the Floss* (Bessy Tulliver), MONSIGNOR RENARD (Madeleine Claveau), A TOUCH OF FROST, MIDSOMER MURDERS, THE WAY WE LIVE NOW (Lady Carbury), FOYLE'S WAR, WILLIAM AND MARY (Molly Gilcrest/Straud), WAKING THE DEAD and *To the Ends of the Earth* (Lady Somerset).

Campbell, Nicky

(1961–)

Edinburgh-born former Radio 1 DJ, now a presenter with Radio 5 Live, whose TV credits have been varied, to say the least. They include hosting TOP OF THE POPS, WHEEL OF FORTUNE, NEWSNIGHT, PANORAMA, WATCHDOG and *Your NHS*, plus topical debates like *Now You're Talking* and the quiz *Come and Have a Go . . . if You Think You're Smart Enough*.

Campbells, The ✶✶

UK (Scottish) Adventure. ITV 1986; 1988–90

Dr James Campbell	**Malcolm Stoddard**
Emma Campbell	**Amber Lea Weston**
Neil Campbell	**John Wildman**
John Campbell	**Eric Richards**
Capt. Thomas Sims	**Cedric Smith**
Rebecca Sims	**Wendy Lyon**
Harriet Sims	**Brigit Wilson**
Gabriel Leger	**Julien Poulin**
Mary MacTavish	**Rosemary Dunsmore**

Producers **John Delmage, Leonard White, Robert Love, Jim McCann**

● ***Trials of life for a Scottish family in a new land.***

The Campbells, like many of their 19th-century contemporaries, have left their native country in search of a better life. Head of the household is widower James Campbell, whose honest attempts to improve medicine and justice for his poor neighbours have seen him sadly fall foul of both the law and the local laird in Scotland, prompting the family's departure. Emigrating to an unknown territory of Canada, he soon discovers this is no easy option. Joining James on his adventure are daughter Emma and sons Neil and John. The series tracks their day-to-day struggles in a hard and forbidding land, facing trouble from Iroquois indians, encountering new diseases, engaging in vibrant politics and dealing with the many outsiders who find their way into their community. Mary MacTavish is taken on as the Campbell's housekeeper; the Sims family are their neighbours. Despite the hostile conditions, James sticks at his task, only returning to Scotland twice: once to claim a possible inheritance, the second time to lecture in Edinburgh while Emma attends finishing school. Long runs of this 30-minute family adventure series were screened on Sunday afternoons or mornings.

Campion ✶✶

UK (BBC/Consolidated/WGBH Boston) Detective Drama. BBC 1 1989–90

DVD: Acorn Video

Albert Campion	**Peter Davison**
Magersfontein Lugg	**Brian Glover**
Chief Insp. Stanislaus Oates	**Andrew Burt**

Producers **Ken Riddington, Jonathan Alwyn**

● ***Murder investigations in the 1930s with an unassuming genteel detective.***

Albert Campion, the creation of novelist Margery Allingham and star of 26 books, first reached the TV screen in 1959 in the BBC serial *Dancers in Mourning*. In this and the follow-up, *Death of a Ghost*, a year later, he was played by Bernard Horsfall. Campion reappeared later in the 1960s in the anthology series DETECTIVE. On that occasion he was played by Brian Smith. However, it was the 1989–90 series, starring Peter Davison, which really brought him to the attention of the viewing public.

Practising his skills in the 1930s, in the same prosperous circles as Lord Peter Wimsey and Hercule Poirot, the aristocratic Campion is a determined and shrewd amateur sleuth, with strong moral principles – even if his mild-mannered appearance conveys quite the opposite. Sporting large, horn-rimmed glasses and with his amiable and unassuming personality pushed well to the fore, villains think it easy to shrug off Campion and his inquiries. They soon learn better, as our hero doggedly pieces together the relevant clues. Also at hand is Campion's brawny, down-to-earth manservant, a reformed burglar named Lugg, whose duties range from taking care of the baggage to obtaining information his master cannot reach by mixing with the lower classes. The duo ride around the East Anglia countryside in a splendid vintage Lagonda, wrapping up crimes before their Scotland Yard associate, Stanislaus Oates, can move in. Star Peter Davison also sings the theme song.

Campion, Gerald

(1921–2002)

British actor, TV's BILLY BUNTER OF GREY FRIARS SCHOOL in the 1950s (even though in his 30s at the time). No other starring roles followed and Campion turned instead (somewhat fittingly) to the restaurant business, although he still took small parts in TV comedies and dramas, such as *The World of Beachcomber* and THE RETURN OF SHERLOCK HOLMES.

Candid Camera ✶✶✶

UK (ABC) Comedy. ITV 1960–7

Presenters **Bob Monkhouse, Jonathan Routh**

Creator **Allen Funt**

● ***Hidden-camera stunts at the expense of the general public.***

Candid Camera was imported into the UK from the USA, where it had been devised by arch-prankster Allen Funt. Funt began gauging the public's reaction to unusual, not to say bizarre, situations in his radio show, *Candid Microphone*. It transferred to television in 1949 with the same title, before becoming *Candid Camera* in 1953. ABC produced the UK version, installing Bob Monkhouse as its host and sending Jonathan Routh out and about in search of gullible citizens. Hidden cameras surreptitiously witnessed their reactions to impossible situations – a man selling £5 notes for £4 10s, garage mechanics asked to discover why a car wouldn't start and finding it had no engine, etc. Eventually, the poor punters were put out of their misery with the words 'Smile, you're on *Candid Camera*.' The series was revived by LWT in 1974, when it was produced and presented by Peter Dulay.

Cannell, Stephen J.

(1941–)

American producer and writer of all-action series in the 1970s and 1980s, whose first major success was THE ROCKFORD FILES. His production company was also responsible for THE A-TEAM, HARDCASTLE AND MCCORMICK, HUNTER, *Riptide* and *Tenspeed and Brown Shoe*, among other series.

Cannon ✶✶

US (Quinn Martin) Detective Drama. BBC 1 1972–8 (US: CBS 1971–6)

Frank Cannon .... **William Conrad**

Executive Producer **Quinn Martin**
Producer **Anthony Spinner**

● ***An overweight, middle-aged private detective puffs and pants after crooks in Los Angeles.***

William Conrad was the only star of this successful series, which had been tailor-made for him. After 11 years of providing the voice of Matt Dillon in the American radio version of GUNSMOKE, he was denied the role when it switched to TV because of his physical appearance (James Arness got the job). *Cannon*, at last, was his overdue reward.

Frank Cannon is an unlikely detective. He loves the good life and his body bears the scars. His hefty frame means that every case is a real effort, particularly when it comes to a sweaty chase after a fleeing murderer, because, having no sidekick, Cannon has to do all the legwork himself. Still, he is well reimbursed for his work, charging enough to keep up his *bon viveur* lifestyle and to repair the big Lincoln Continental he prangs around the LA streets.

Cannon was one of the first gimmicky cops. After him came KOJAK, MCCLOUD and COLUMBO. The series first aired in the UK under the umbrella title of *The Detectives*, in sequence with THE ROCKFORD FILES, HARRY O and A MAN CALLED IRONSIDE.

Cannon, Tommy

(Thomas Derbyshire; 1938–)

The stage partner of diminutive northern comic Bobby Ball. After a long apprenticeship as the Shirell Brothers and then the Harper Brothers, former welders Cannon and Ball arrived on television courtesy of a not so promising debut on OPPORTUNITY KNOCKS in 1968 and did not secure their own show until 1979 (following guest appearances with Bruce Forsyth). As well as their own peak-time variety shows (mostly scripted by Sid Green), the duo have also attempted a quiz, *Cannon and Ball's Casino*, and a sitcom, PLAZA PATROL, playing shopping-centre security men Bernard Cooney (Cannon) and Trevor Purvis (Ball). More recently, they were seen in the sketch show *Revolver*. Bobby Ball has also made appearances as Lenny in LAST OF THE SUMMER WINE and was a guest star in HEARTBEAT.

Cant, Brian

(1933–)

Whimsical children's TV presenter, popular in the 1960s and 1970s in PLAY SCHOOL, PLAY AWAY and as the voice behind CAMBERWICK GREEN, TRUMPTON and CHIGLEY. More recently, he has hosted the series *Bric-a-Brac* and *Dappledown Farm*. As an actor, Cant has made guest appearances in various series, including DOCTOR WHO, *Dramarama*, DOCTORS, CASUALTY and THE BILL. As a writer, he has co-scripted *Softies* and *MechaNick* with his wife, Cherry Britton, sister of Fern and daughter of Tony.

Canterbury Tales ✶✶

UK (BBC) Drama. BBC 1 2003
DVD: IMC Vision

Nick Zakian .... **James Nesbitt** *(Miller's Tale)*
John Crosby .... **Dennis Waterman** *(Miller's Tale)*
Alison Crosby .... **Billie Piper** *(Miller's Tale)*
Danny Absolon .... **Kenny Doughty** *(Miller's Tale)*
Beth Craddock .... **Julie Walters** *(Wife of Bath's Tale)*
Jerome .... **Paul Nicholls** *(Wife of Bath's Tale)*
James .... **Bill Nighy** *(Wife of Bath's Tale)*
Ace .... **John Simm** *(Knight's Tale)*
Paul .... **Chiwetel Ejiofor** *(Knight's Tale)*
Emily .... **Keeley Hawes** *(Knight's Tale)*
Theo .... **Bill Paterson** *(Knight's Tale)*
Jetender .... **Om Puri** *(Sea Captain's Tale)*
Meena .... **Indira Varma** *(Sea Captain's Tale)*
Pushpinder .... **Nitin Ganatra** *(Sea Captain's Tale)*
Arty .... **Jonny Lee Miller** *(Pardoner's Tale)*
Colin .... **William Beck** *(Pardoner's Tale)*
Baz .... **Ben Bennett** *(Pardoner's Tale)*
Kitty Norman .... **Samantha Whittaker** *(Pardoner's Tale)*
Alan King .... **Andrew Lincoln** *(Man of Law's Tale)*
Constance Musa .... **Nikki Amuka-Bird** *(Man of Law's Tale)*
Leila King .... **Kika Markham** *(Man of Law's Tale)*
Mark Constable .... **Adam Kotz** *(Man of Law's Tale)*
Nicky Constable .... **Rakie Ayola** *(Man of Law's Tale)*

Writers **Peter Bowker** *(Miller's Tale)*, **Sally Wainwright** *(Wife of Bath's Tale)*, **Tony Marchant** *(Knight's Tale)*, **Avie Luthra** *(Sea Captain's Tale)*, **Tony Grounds** *(Pardoner's Tale)*, **Olivia Hetreed** *(Man of Law's Tale)*
Executive Producer **Franc Roddam**
Producer **Kate Bartlett**

● ***Selection of Chaucerian stories retold for the 21st century.***

Alarming purists but offering easy access to the thrust of Chaucer's classic work, this series of six stories redresses the mannekin of the poet's bawdy, 14th-century masterpiece in modern-day clothes. *The Miller's Tale* is transposed to a karaoke pub in Kent, *The Wife of Bath's Tale* moves to the world of TV production, and *The Knight's Tale* has a new home in a prison. *The Sea Captain's Tale* is adapted to shopping addiction and debt in a wealthy Asian community, *The Pardoner's Tale* focuses on three layabouts trying to cash in on the disappearance of a teenager in Rochester, and *The Man of Law's Tale* involves a Nigerian refugee washed up in Chatham docks. With major actors in roles penned by top TV dramatists, the project underlines how human emotions can run riot with our lives, just as they did in Chaucer's time.

The Canterbury Tales was no stranger to television by the time this series appeared. BBC 2 had dramatized 14 tales (including *The Prologue*) over seven episodes in 1969, with a cast that included Joss Ackland, Geoffrey Bayldon and Ian Richardson. An animated version, voiced by Bob Peck, Sean Bean, Billie Whitelaw, Richard Griffiths, Tim McInnerny, Imelda Staunton, Bill Nighy and John Wood, covered six tales over two episodes on BBC 2 in 1998. While this was performed in modern English, a Middle English repeat was shown a day later.

See also TRINITY TALES for television work inspired by Chaucer.

Capital City ***

UK (Thames/Euston Films) Drama. ITV 1989–90

Max Lubin .... **William Armstrong**
Leonard Ansen .... **John Bowe**
James Farrell .... **Denys Hawthorne**
Jimmy Destry .... **Dorian Healy**
Declan McConnochie .... **Douglas Hodge**
Chas Ewell .... **Jason Isaacs**
Sirkka Nieminen .... **Joanna Kanska**
Lee Wolf .... **Richard Le Parmentier**
Michelle Hauptmann .... **Trevyn McDowell**
Hannah Burgess .... **Anna Nygh**
Wendy Foley .... **Joanna Phillips-Lane**
Hudson Talbot .... **Rolf Saxon**

Creator **Andrew MacLear**
Producer **Irving Teitelbaum**
Executive Producers **Andrew Brown, John Hambly**

● ***Hectic wheeling and dealing in the offices of a City bank.***
Capital City is set in the dealing rooms of the fictious Shane Longman bank, taking a long look at the perils of currency and Stock Market trading and the pressures these bring to personal lives. Among the prominent characters are eccentric new ideas-man Max Lubin; outrageous womanizer Declan McConnochie and the German girl he chases after, Michelle Hauptmann; Declan's former live-in lover, Sirkka Nieminen; computer manager Hannah Burgess; Hudson Talbot, an American whose wife has abandoned him with their baby; dealing room manager Wendy Foley, who has worked her way up in the bank; obnoxious junior dealer Jimmy Destry; Jimmy's house sharer, Chas Ewell; and the man who has built the bank's fortune, Head of Banking Activities Leonard Ansen. Flashing computer screens, phones strapped to ears and cries of 'Buy!' and 'Sell!' help convey the frenetic pace of life in the City. Away from work, the obscene amounts of money being made – and sometimes lost – by the yuppie workers are reflected in their extravagant lifestyles.

Captain Butler *

UK (Essential) Situation Comedy. Channel 4 1997
DVD: HIT Entertainment

Capt. Butler .... **Craig Charles**
Bosun .... **Shaun Curry**
Cliff .... **Roger Griffiths**
Adeel .... **Sanjeev Bhaskar**
Lord Roger .... **Lewis Rae**

Writers **John Smith, Rob Sprackling**
Producer **Christopher Skala**

● ***Yellow-bellied, clumsy pirates go in search of plunder.***
In a six-part tale of cowardice and ineptitude on the high seas (a deliberately obvious studio set), Captain Butler and his cronies, Bosun, Cliff, Adeel and Lord Roger, set out to pirate their way to a fortune but end up being tried for their crimes. Along the way they do their best to avoid trouble but nevertheless encounter some larger-than-life figures, including Lord Nelson (played by Robert Llewellyn). Meanwhile their reluctant leader falls hopelessly in love with a mermaid and then faces mutiny from his hapless crew as their money-grabbing plans constantly fall flat.

Captain Pugwash **

UK (John Ryan) Children's Entertainment. BBC 1 1957–66; 1974–5; ITV 1998

Narrator **Peter Hawkins**

Creator/Writer **John Ryan**
Producers **Gordon Murray, John Ryan**

● ***The maritime adventures of a blustery pirate and his crew.***
Animated by John Ryan in the most basic fashion, with crudely drawn characters making the simplest of movements against a static background, *Captain Pugwash* was a remarkably cheap series to produce. All the same, it became a perennial favourite and a great filler programme for the BBC. First appearing in 1957, and updated in colour in the 1970s, it relates tales of pirate Captain Horatio Pugwash, podgy skipper of the *Black Pig*. His hapless crew are work-shy and rather dense: Master Mate, able seamen Barnabas and Willy, and loyal cabin boy Tom. Most of the time they seek to avoid the clutches of the barbarous Cut Throat Jake, a black-bearded pirate of the worst order, and the five-minute episodes run in serial form, each ending with a cliffhanger finish. The distinctive accordion sea-shanty theme music, 'The Hornblower', was performed by Tommy Edmondson and the many voices belonged to the Bill and Ben vocalist, Peter Hawkins.

The jaunty pirate returned to the screen in 13 new stories entitled *The Adventures of Captain Pugwash*, in 1998. Luscious Lill is one of the new characters complementing the old favourites as they ply the seas around the island of Mucho-Buffo.

Such was the success of *Captain Pugwash* that it spawned a *Radio Times* cartoon strip and a successor series in 1972, THE ADVENTURES OF SIR PRANCELOT.

Captain Scarlet and the Mysterons ***

UK (Century 21/ITC) Children's Science Fiction. ITV 1967–8
DVD: Carlton

Voices:
Capt. Scarlet (Paul Metcalfe) .. **Francis Matthews**
Col. White (Charles Gray) .... **Donald Gray**
Capt. Blue (Adam Svenson) .... **Ed Bishop**
Capt. Grey (Bradley Holden) ... **Paul Maxwell**
Capt. Magenta (Patrick Donaghue) .... **Gary Files**
Capt. Ochre (Richard Fraser) ... **Jeremy Wilkin**
Lt. Green (Seymour Griffiths) .... **Cy Grant**
Dr Fawn (Edward Wilkie) .... **Charles Tingwell**
Melody Angel (Magnolia Jones) .... **Sylvia Anderson**
Harmony Angel (Chan Kwan) **Lian-Shin**
Symphony Angel (Karen Wainwright) .... **Janna Hill**
Rhapsody Angel (Dianne Sims) .... **Liz Morgan**

Destiny Angel (Juliette Pontoin)	**Liz Morgan**
Capt. Black (Conrad Turner)	**Donald Gray**
The Voice of the Mysterons	**Donald Gray**
World President	**Paul Maxwell**

Creators **Gerry Anderson, Sylvia Anderson**
Producer **Reg Hill**

An indestructible puppet super-agent takes on a vengeful alien force.

In the year 2068, Spectrum, the world's security command, undertakes a mission to Mars, a mission which turns to disaster. When the native Mysterons lock their antennae on to the landing party, they are mistaken for guns and the order is given for a Mysteron city to be destroyed. In response, the Mysterons slaughter the Spectrum envoys, including their leader, Captain Black, vowing to wreak vengeance on the people of Earth.

The Mysterons possess the remarkable power of retro-metabolism – the re-creation of destroyed matter, which renders it indestructible at the same time. The first thing they do is to reconstruct their destroyed city and piece together Captain Black, formerly Spectrum's top agent, for use against his former allies. The Mysterons also try to destroy and re-create another Spectrum officer, Captain Scarlet, but this time their plan fails and, although Scarlet becomes indestructible, he nevertheless remains loyal to Spectrum and proves time and again crucial in the defence of the Earth.

Spectrum, operating from a floating control-centre called Cloudbase, is run by Colonel White. The other agents and officers are also codenamed after colours, with uniforms to reflect their identities, and they are ably supported by the five female pilots of Angel Interceptor aircraft: Melody, Harmony, Symphony, Destiny and Rhapsody. All operatives race into action on the command 'SIG' ('Spectrum Is Green').

In each episode the Mysterons threaten the Earth's security by attacking key command centres or personnel, sabotaging world conferences or simply gunning for Spectrum. The aliens themselves are never seen, but the introduction to each programme features the gravelly 'Voice of the Mysterons', reiterating their avowed intention to gain revenge. As the voice booms out, two rings of light play over a dead body or wrecked aircraft, indicating that the regeneration process is under way. Spectrum needs to be well equipped to handle the Mysteron threat but, despite its Spectrum Pursuit Vehicles (SPVs), Maximum Security Vehicles (MSVs) and other high-tech wizardry, it still relies heavily on one man – the indestructible (if rather humourless) Captain Scarlet.

The producers' attention to detail in this series was remarkable. For the first time Gerry Anderson puppets were perfect in proportion, with the electronic circuitry that made his earlier marionettes 'big-headed' transferred into the puppets' bodies. The puppets were also made to look like the actors who supplied their voices. Scarlet, for instance, was a model of Francis Matthews (who adopted his best 'Cary Grant' voice for the role). The characterization, too, was more detailed than in previous efforts. The agents were given private lives and real identities (Scarlet was really Paul Metcalfe), and were furnished with other biographical data. It was revealed, for instance, that the Trinidadian communications specialist, Lt. Green, and the American Captain Grey had both previously been assigned to WASP on the STINGRAY project, and that Diane Sims (Rhapsody Angel) had once worked with Lady Penelope of THUNDERBIRDS fame. The closing theme song was performed by 'The Spectrum'.

In 2005, ITV 1 premiered *Gerry Anderson's New Captain Scarlet* in its Saturday morning kids' show *Ministry of Mayhem*. Now computer-generated rather than hung on strings (allowing far more flexibility and livelier action sequences), and costing nearly £1 million an episode as opposed to the original's £25,000, the new series coined the term 'hypermarionation' and included some notable character changes: Lt. Green and Captain Ochre, for instance, are now both female.

Captain Zep – Space Detective ✳

UK (BBC) Children's Science Fiction. BBC 1 1983–4

Capt. Zep	**Paul Greenwood**
	Richard Morant
Jason Brown	**Ben Ellison**
Prof. Spiro	**Harriet Keevil**
Prof. Vana	**Tracey Childs**

Writers **Dick Hills, Colin Bennett**
Executive Producer **Molly Cox**
Producer **Christopher Pilkington**

Space whodunnits for kids.

This innovative series played the age-old game of whodunnit but set the action in outer space, in the year 2095. Hosting proceedings was Captain Zep, allegedly the most famous space detective of all time. Each week, he revealed how he and his support crew – navigator Jason Brown and scientific adviser Professor Spiro, later replaced by Professor Vana – had visited new planets in a ship called *Zep One* and investigated a variety of space crimes. They then asked a studio panel – supposedly students at the SOLVE (Space Office of Law Verification and Enquiry) academy of space detectives – a series of questions, giving them the chance to spot the culprit themselves. Viewers were also given the chance to win a SOLVE badge by answering two supplementary questions. The rudimentary special effects included background illustrations and colour separation overlay (see CHROMA KEY).

Caption Roller

Mechanical system of running continuous captions that can be superimposed over another shot or filmed independently. It has traditionally been used for a programme's closing credits, although computer-generated graphics have now taken over.

Car 54, Where are You? ✳✳

US (Euopolis) Situation Comedy. ITV 1964–5 (US: NBC 1961–3)
DVD: MGM (Region 1 only)

Officer Gunther Toody	**Joe E. Ross**
Officer Francis Muldoon	**Fred Gwynne**
Lucille Toody	**Bea Pons**
Capt. Martin Block	**Paul Reed**
Officer O'Hara	**Albert Henderson**
Officer Anderson	**Nipsey Russell**
Officer Antonnucci	**Jerome Guardino**
Officer Steinmetz	**Joe Warren**
Officer Riley	**Duke Farley**
Officer Murdock	**Shelley Burton**
Officer Leo Schnauser	**Al Lewis**
Sylvia Schnauser	**Charlotte Rae**
Officer Kissel	**Bruce Kirby**
Officer Ed Nicholson	**Hank Garrett**

Creator/Producer **Nat Hiken**

● ***The slapstick exploits of an inept team of New York City cops.***

Hot on the heels of his success with THE PHIL SILVERS SHOW, producer Nat Hiken introduced viewers to *Car 54, Where are You?* and the ropiest bunch of cops yet seen on TV. At the forefront are Toody and Muldoon, the former short, podgy and amiable, the latter tall and sullen. Not only do they look odd together, they are also pretty hopeless in action. Their beat is in the 53rd Precinct, the troubled Bronx, although you really wouldn't know it as the series plays only on the lighter side of police work. Much of the fun comes from within the police station itself.

In casting the series, Hiken brought Joe E. Ross with him from *Bilko* (he had played Sgt Rupert Ritzik and Bea Pons played his nagging wife, as here). His co-star, Fred Gwynne, was to go on to greater fame as Herman in THE MUNSTERS. Al Lewis joined him as Grandpa in that series. *Car 54, Where are You?* was rerun on Channel 4 in 1983.

Cardiac Arrest ✶✶

UK (Island World/World/BBC) Medical Drama. BBC 1 1994–6

Dr Andrew Collin .... **Andrew Lancel**
Dr Claire Maitland .... **Helen Baxendale**
Dr Monica Broome .... **Pooky Quesnel**
Dr Rajesh Rajah .... **Ahsen Bhatti**
Sister Pamela Lockley .... **Melanie Hill**
Dr James Mortimer .... **Jo Dow**
Staff Nurse Caroline Richards **Jayne Mackenzie**
Mr Simon Betancourt .... **Danny Webb**
Mr Ernest Docherty .... **Tom Watson**
Dr Graham Turner .... **Michael Mackenzie**
Mr Cyril 'Scissors' Smedley ..... **Peter O'Brien**
Dr Barry Yates .... **Fred Pearson**
Mr Adrian Devries .... **Jack Fortune**
Sister Julie Novac .... **Jacquetta May**
Sister Debbie Pereira .... **Gabrielle Cowburn**
Mrs Isobel Trimble .... **Angela Douglas**
Dr Phil Kirkby .... **Andrew Clover**
Staff Nurse Pam Charnley ...... **Mandy Matthews**
Dr Liz Reid .... **Caroline Trowbridge**
Dr Sarah Hudson .... **Selina Cadell**
Student Nurse Kirsty Thomas **Lisa Harkus**
Dr Horton .... **Clare Clifford**
Mr Paul Tennant .... **Nicholas Palliser**
CN Patrick Garden .... **Peter Biddle**
Sister Jackie Landers .... **Ellen Thomas**
Staff Nurse Susan Betts .... **Katy Hale**
Staff Nurse Luke Terry .... **Sue Patt**

Creator/Writer **John MacUre**
Executive Producer **Tony Garnett**
Producers **Margaret Matheson, Paddy Higson**

● ***Bleak drama series painting a depressing picture of British hospital life.***

Shot in pseudo-documentary style, with the aim of minimizing sentimentality, jargon-heavy *Cardiac Arrest* sets out to depict the life of a junior doctor and his colleagues in a hectic big-city hospital. The doctor in question is Andrew Collin, newly qualified and stepping onto Crippen Ward full of idealism and hope for a rewarding career. However, he is soon brought down to earth by the chaos around him and the exhausting, sleepless shifts he is expected to work. His peers include cynical Claire Maitland and incident-prone Rajesh Rajah. James Mortimer is the good-looking, bisexual anaesthetist who discovers he is HIV positive and Paul Tennant is the hospital manager. By the second series, Collin and his housemen friends have been promoted to senior house officers, following the influx of new graduates like public schoolboy Phil Kirkby. Also new is rollerblading Australian surgeon Cyril Smedley. In series three, Liz Reid is the inept novice houseman and Sarah Hudson the new consultant.

Although the writer, John MacUre, was himself a practising junior doctor, who had answered an advert for (comedy) scriptwriters in the *British Medical Journal*, the series was panned by the Royal College of Nursing for being 'insulting' to real-life hospital staff. The black-humoured characters were shown getting things wrong, covering up mistakes and occasionally working a ruse. Some critics said that the good side of hospital care was never revealed. But MacUre declared himself ready to shock from the outset, claiming that people would be amazed if they saw what really happened in our hospitals. By the third series, however, the embittered tone had mellowed somewhat, with greater emphasis placed on characters' personal lives. With episodes 30 minutes in length, *Cardiac Arrest* was filmed at Drumchapel Hospital in Glasgow.

Cargill, Patrick

(1918–96)

Although gaining a reputation as Britain's leading farceur in the 1970s, thanks to series like FATHER, DEAR FATHER (novelist Patrick Glover), THE MANY WIVES OF PATRICK (antiques dealer Patrick Woodford) and the anthology *Ooh La La*, London-born Patrick Cargill's earlier television roles had been in quite a different vein. After appearing as a baddie in THE ADVENTURES OF ROBIN HOOD, Cargill was cast as mysterious agent Miguel Garetta (who worked under the identity of an Argentinian businessman) in TOP SECRET, and later played one of the Number 2s in THE PRISONER. He also guest-starred in action series like THE AVENGERS and MAN IN A SUITCASE. However, his flair for comedy was already apparent. He played the doctor in the famous HANCOCK'S HALF HOUR sketch 'The Blood Donor', for instance, and also appeared in the follow-up series, *Hancock*, and then supported Brian Rix in *Dial RIX*. After his television heyday, Cargill returned to the stage. He died after being knocked down by a hit-and-run driver in Sydney, Australia.

Carling, Liz

(1967–)

Middlesbrough-born actress, seen in dramas and comedies like BOON (Laura Marsh), BARBARA (Linda), CROCODILE SHOES (Wendy), GOODNIGHT SWEETHEART (Phoebe), CATHERINE COOKSON'S *The Secret* (Connie), BORDER CAFÉ (Charlotte) and CASUALTY (Selena Donovan/Manning), as well as taking smaller roles in series like MEN BEHAVING BADLY.

Carlton Television

The contractor for the London weekday ITV franchise, Carlton was part of Carlton Communications, which also later acquired Central Television (renamed Carlton Central), Westcountry (Carlton Westcountry) and HTV. The company also held 50 per cent of ONdigital, the failed terrestrial digital provider. Additionally, Carlton owned game show specialists Action Time and production company Planet 24. In 2004 Carlton merged with Granada to create ITV plc. Carlton's television history begins with its surprising defeat of Thames Television in the bid for the London ITV area in the 1991 franchise auctions. The company took to the air on 1 January 1993 and among the group's best-known contributions to the ITV network were KAVANAGH QC and PEAK PRACTICE.

Carlyle, Robert

OBE (1961–)

Glasgow-born, noted method actor who made a huge impression with his portrayal of psychotic killer Albie in CRACKER and went on to enjoy a more relaxed encounter with crime as Highland copper HAMISH MACBETH. His other major TV roles have been as Nosty in *Screenplay's Safe*, Graham in *Screen Two's Priest*, petty criminal John Joe 'Jo Jo' McCann in *Looking After Jo Jo*, Ray in *Face*, Hitler in *Hitler: the Rise of Evil*, King James I in *Gunpowder, Treason and Plot*, and DI Tom Monroe in *The Class of '76*. He has also been seen in series like *The Advocates*, *99–1* and THE BILL.

Carmichael, Ian

(1920–)

RADA-trained, Yorkshire-born actor whose TV high spot was as Lord Peter Wimsey, the toff detective created by Dorothy L. Sayers. In similar style, he had earlier perfected the silly-ass comic character, playing Bertie in THE WORLD OF WOOSTER, before becoming the harassed foster dad, Peter Lamb, in BACHELOR FATHER. His other TV credits have included ALL FOR LOVE, *Just A Nimmo*, BRAMWELL, SURVIVAL (narrator), the voice of Rat in THE WIND IN THE WILLOWS, and the parts of Sir James Menzies in STRATHBLAIR, Lord Cumnor in WIVES AND DAUGHTERS and T. J. Middleditch in THE ROYAL, although he first appeared on television way back in the 1940s and 1950s, in variety and sketch shows.

Caroline in the City ★★

US (Barron Pennette/Three Sisters/CBS) Situation Comedy.
Channel 4 1996–8 (US: NBC 1995–9)
DVD: Revelation

Caroline Duffy	**Lea Thompson**
Del Cassidy	**Eric Lutes**
Richard Karinsky	**Malcolm Gets**
Annie Spadaro	**Amy Pietz**
Charlie	**Andy Lauer**
Remo	**Tom La Grua**
Julia Mazzone/Karinsky	**Sofia Milos**

Creators **Dottie Dartland, Fred Barron, Marco Pennette**
Executive Producers **Fred Barron, David Nicholls, Marco Pennette**

● ***The life and loves of a successful, if rather naive, single girl in Manhattan.***

Caroline Duffy is an accomplished cartoonist, living in the Tribeca district of New York City. She draws the popular *Caroline in the City* strip, loosely based on her own experiences as a single girl in the Big Apple, and this has also been exploited for a series of greetings cards and calendars. Del Cassidy is the guy with the lush locks that she keeps getting involved with (he also runs the Cassidy Greeting Cards company), although her heart really belongs to Richard Karinsky, the sardonic, hard-up artist she has employed to help in her apartment-cum-studio. The old will-they/won't-they idea is a running theme, despite the fact that Richard is briefly married to waitress Julia Mazzone. Charlie is the wacky guy who runs errands for the card company (to which Caroline relocates after it is taken over by a big firm), Annie is Caroline's smart mouthed neighbour (a dancer), and Remo runs the Italian restaurant that hosts most of the intimate dinners. Salty is Caroline's pet cat.

Caroline in the City arrived with a splash in the US, knocking FRIENDS off the top of the ratings, but ended after just four seasons. Cartoons used throughout this romantic comedy were drawn by Bonnie Timmons.

Carpenter, Harry

OBE (1925–)

Durable BBC sports presenter and boxing commentator (over four decades), who retired from GRANDSTAND, SPORTSNIGHT, Wimbledon, the Olympics, the Boat Race and Open Golf coverage in the early 1990s, before finally counting himself out of the boxing game at the 1994 Commonwealth Games. His friendship with heavyweight Frank Bruno marked the latter years of his career – 'Know what I mean, 'Arry?'

Carpenter, Richard

OBE (1933–)

Former actor (Peter Parker in KNIGHT ERRANT and Mr Victor in EMERGENCY – WARD 10) turned writer of mostly juvenile adventures whose major contributions have been CATWEAZLE, THE GHOSTS OF MOTLEY HALL, DICK TURPIN, SMUGGLER, ROBIN OF SHERWOOD, THE BORROWERS, *The Winjin' Pom*, *True Tilda* and *I was a Rat*. He has also contributed to series like *Look and Read*, THE ADVENTURES OF BLACK BEAUTY, *The Famous Five*, *The Baker Street Boys*, HANNAY and THE SCARLET PIMPERNEL.

Carr, Jimmy

(1972–)

English comedian, a Cambridge graduate, finding his forte as host of Channel 4's many nostalgic *100 Greatest . . .* shows. Carr has also hosted the game shows *Your Face or Mine?*, *Distraction* and *8 out of 10 Cats*, and been seen in various other panel games.

Carradine, David

(John Arthur Carradine; 1936–)

American actor whose TV fame is owed chiefly to the part of Kwai Chang Caine in the 1970s martial arts Western, KUNG FU, a series he revived in the 1990s. If he appeared at home in the character, it was because Caine's philosophical approach to life was not, it has been reported, that far removed from Carradine's own thoughtful disposition. His sad, gaunt features were also put to good use in the 1960s cowboy series *Shane*, in which he played the title role, and shows like ALFRED HITCHCOCK PRESENTS and A MAN CALLED IRONSIDE. In the 1980s he resurfaced in the mini-series NORTH AND SOUTH and later made guest appearances in programmes like MATLOCK and *Alias*. David is a member of the famous Hollywood acting family, son of John Carradine and half-brother to Keith and Robert.

Carrie and Barry ★★

UK (Hartswood) Situation Comedy. BBC 1 2004–5
DVD: BBC

Barry	**Neil Morrissey**
Carrie	**Claire Rushbrook**
Kirk	**Mark Williams**
Michelle	**Michelle Gomez**
Sinead	**Sarah Quintrell**
Adrian	**Mathew Horne**

Writer **Simon Nye**
Executive Producers **Beryl Vertue, Mark Freeland**
Producer **Sue Vertue**

● ***Ups and downs in the life of a frisky couple.***

Fortysomething couple Carrie and Barry are always keen to keep the spice in their love life. That's one reason why they've installed a hot tub in their garden in West London, or enjoy dressing-up games. Sadly, in true sitcom fashion, things never work out as planned. In their professional lives, Carrie is a beautician and Barry drives a taxi – a job he shares with his dopey mate, Kirk. Glum barmaid Sinead is Barry's teenage daughter from an earlier marriage, while Michelle is Carrie's acid-tongued workmate. This post-watershed offering from the MEN BEHAVING BADLY team ran for six episodes in 2004 and returned for six more a year later. This time around there's even more hassle in the Carrie and Barry house as Barry has lost his driving licence and is therefore out of work, while Sinead has acquired a boyfriend.

Carrie's War ★★

UK (BBC) Children's Drama. BBC 1 1974
DVD: Acorn Media (2004 version)

Carrie Willow	**Juliet Waley**
	Shirley Dixon *(adult)*
Nick Willow	**Andrew Tinney**
Mr Evans	**Aubrey Richards**
Miss Lou Evans	**Avril Elgar**
Hepzibah Green	**Rosalie Crutchley**
Albert Sandwich	**Tim Coward**
Mr Johnny	**Matthew Guinness**
Mrs Gotobed	**Patsy Smart**
Miss Fasackerly	**Valerie Georgeson**

Writer **Marilyn Fox**
Executive Producer **Anna Home**

● ***Two young Londoners find life difficult as evacuees in Wales.***

Young Carrie Willow and her even younger brother Nick are evacuees, shipped out of London in the early years of World War II into the completely foreign environment of the Welsh valleys. The siblings are billeted above a grocer's shop with stern local councillor Mr Evans and his timid but loving sister, Lou. Their host's more prosperous other sister, Mrs Gotobed, lives in a farmhouse called Druid's Bottom with her mysterious housekeeper, Hepzibah and the simple-minded Mr Johnny, but the family is estranged and only Carrie and Nick are able to provide a link between the two households. As the children struggle to come to terms with the hardships of life in a mining community, and its strict Baptist tradition, they uncover personal secrets that make their stay in Wales intriguing, if not entirely comfortable. Paul Stone directs this atmospheric five-part drama, which was based on the novel by Nina Bawden, published in 1973.

On New Year's Day 2004, BBC 1 offered a single drama adaptation of Bawden's book. This time Keeley Fawcett plays Carrie and Jack Stanley takes the role of Nick, with Alun Armstrong as Mr Evans, Lesley Sharp as Lou, Geraldine McEwan as Mrs Gotobed and Pauline Quirke as Hepzibah.

Carroll, Leo G.

(1892–1972)

Distinguished British actor, a star in his seventies as the sober Mr Waverly in THE MAN (and *The Girl*) FROM U.N.C.L.E. Earlier, playing men of authority, Carroll featured in numerous Hollywood movies, including several Hitchcock classics. He arrived on TV in the ghostly 1950s sitcom, TOPPER, playing the title role, Cosmo Topper, and also starred in a short-lived version of Bing Crosby's film *Going My Way*, in 1962. Other television credits included A MAN CALLED IRONSIDE. However, it is as the boss of Napoleon Solo, Illya Kuryakin and April Dancer in the mid-1960s that he is best remembered.

Carrott, Jasper

OBE (Robert Davis; 1945–)

Broad Brummie comic, a sharp observer of public failings who hosted his own series on BBC 1 throughout most of the 1980s. His earlier work came on BBC regional television, where he gained a cult following which took him into the record charts in 1975 with 'Funky Moped'/'Magic Roundabout'. He contributed material for TISWAS and there followed a series of *The Jasper Carrott Show* for LWT, along with a few one-off shows and spoof documentaries, such as *Carrott Del Sol*. However, it was in *Carrott's Lib*, *Carrott Confidential* and *Canned Carrott* that he established himself in the mainstream of British comedy, combining long, satirical, often ranting monologues (about Reliant Robins, Birmingham City FC, *Sun* readers, etc.) with assorted sketches (assisted at various times by the likes of Emma Thompson, Chris Barrie, Steve Punt and Hugh Dennis). One segment of *Canned Carrott*, THE DETECTIVES, a send-up of ITV cop shows like SPECIAL BRANCH and THE SWEENEY, and co-starring Robert Powell, was spun off into its own half-hour series. *The Jasper Carrott Trial*, in 1997, was a retrospective of his best sketches pieced together as part of a mock court case. In 1999 he returned to stand-up in *Jasper Carrott – Back to the Front*, and in 2002 he starred in a sitcom, ALL ABOUT ME (Colin). He has also been seen in *24 Carrott Gold*, a highlights package of his live shows. Carrott is also a shareholder in the production company Celador, makers of WHO WANTS TO BE A MILLIONAIRE? Actress Lucy Davis (Dawn in THE OFFICE) is his daughter.

Carson, Frank

(1926–)

Irrepressible, Ulster-born, bespectacled stand-up comedian, fond of laughing at his own jokes because 'It's the way I tell 'em.' After coming to light on OPPORTUNITY KNOCKS and as one of THE COMEDIANS, he popped up to spout his juvenile gags on the raucous TISWAS programme. He also contributed to THE GOOD OLD DAYS and, in 1981, starred in his own variety-show-cum-sitcom, as Frank O'Grady, manager of *Ballyskillen Opera House*.

Carson, Johnny

(1925–2005)

An American institution, Johnny Carson hosted *The Tonight Show* for 30 years, garnering huge audiences with his boyish looks, cheeky grin and quick wit. Carson did little else on TV after his run as host of the show began in 1962, save a few guest appearances and the occasional piece of emceeing. In 1981 he attempted to bring his show to Britain but it didn't catch on. On his retirement in 1992, NBC named comedian Jay Leno as Carson's *Tonight* successor.

Carson, Violet

OBE (1898–1983)

In the shape of CORONATION STREET battleaxe Ena Sharples, Violet Carson brought us one of television's unforgettable characterizations. An original member of the cast in 1960 (at the age of 62), she stayed with the show until 1980, enjoying some glorious spats with the Street's vixen, Elsie Tanner, and some classic moments in the snug of the Rovers with Minnie Caldwell and Martha Longhurst. But beneath Ena's hairnet, Violet Carson's natural talent lay in music. She played piano for Wilfrid Pickles in the radio quiz *Have a Go*, and in her later years was a regular guest on STARS ON SUNDAY, singing and playing the organ. Once *Coronation Street* had taken off, Carson had few other opportunities to show off her acting skills, however, although some viewers still recalled her as Auntie Vi on radio's *Children's Hour* and as an early contributor to *Woman's Hour*.

Carter, Jim

(1951–)

Established British actor with scores of TV credits. Most recently these have included THE WAY WE LIVE NOW (Mr Brehgert), *Pompeii – the Last Day* (Polybius), *Oliver Cromwell: Warts and All* (Cromwell), *London* (Henry Fielding), *Von Trapped* (Larry Lavelle) and *Dinotopia* (Mayor Waldo). Previously Carter had been seen in THE SINGING DETECTIVE (Mr Marlow), A VERY BRITISH COUP (Newsome), *Harpur and Iles* (Tenderness Mellick), *The Missing Postman* (Lawrence Pitman) and AIN'T MISBEHAVIN' (Maxie Morrell). Guest appearances have come in series like WIDOWS, THE MONOCLED MUTINEER, *Lost Empires*, A YEAR IN PROVENCE, SOLDIER, SOLDIER, MINDER, COOGAN'S RUN, CRACKER, THE SCARLET PIMPERNEL, MURDER MOST HORRID, HORNBLOWER, *Strange*, MIDSOMER MURDERS, DALZIEL AND PASCOE and BLUE MURDER. He is married to Imelda Staunton.

Carter, Lynda

(1951–)

Statuesque former Miss USA (1973), understandably cast as TV's WONDER WOMAN, given her Amazonian figure. She has since appeared in assorted TV movies, as well as an unsuccessful detective series with Loni Anderson, *Partners in Crime*, and *Hawkeye*, a series based on *Last of the Mohicans*. Recent guest appearances came in LAW AND ORDER.

Cartier, Rudolph

(1904–94)

Viennese director/producer who arrived in the UK in the late 1930s, joining the BBC in 1952. He stayed with the Corporation for 25 years, bringing with him the influences of continental cinema and directing some of its most influential plays and serials. His treatment of Nigel Kneale's *The* QUATERMASS *Experiment* (and its sequels) shocked the country, his 1984 was a milestone, and both helped to establish him as a seminal figure in TV drama. His work also covered TV opera (*Otello* in 1959 and *Carmen* in 1962, for instance) as he demonstrated his love of the spectacular and his adventurous, extravagant approach to studio drama. Among his other major contributions were *Sunday-Night Theatre* offerings like *The White Falcon* (1956), plus *Arrow to the Heart* (1952), *Wuthering Heights* (1953), *Thunder Rock* (1955), *Captain of Koepenick* (1958), *Mother Courage and Her Children* (1959), ANNA KARENINA, *Rashomon* (both 1961), *Dr Korczak and the Children* (1962), *Stalingrad* (1963, for the *Festival* anthology), *The July Plot* (a 1964 WEDNESDAY PLAY) and *Lee Oswald – Assassin* (a 1966 PLAY OF THE MONTH). He also directed more mundane BBC efforts like episodes of MAIGRET, OUT OF THE UNKNOWN and Z CARS.

Cartoon Network

The world's first 24-hour all-cartoon channel was launched by Turner Broadcasting (now owned by Time Warner) on cable in the USA in 1992. The channel has been available courtesy of the Astra satellite system in Europe since 1993, and more recently via digital services. It provides a showcase for Hanna-Barbera, Warner Brothers and MGM animations – including classics like SCOOBY DOO, THE FLINTSTONES and TOM AND JERRY.

Carty, Todd

(1963–)

Irish-born actor whose earliest TV appearance came in Z CARS, OUR MUTUAL FRIEND and assorted juvenile parts, although it was as Tucker Jenkins in the school drama GRANGE HILL that he gained his first major role. Out of this came his own spin-off, *Tucker's Luck*, which followed Jenkins as he left school. When actor David Scarboro, who played Mark Fowler in EASTENDERS, died in 1988, Carty was drafted in (two years later) to join numerous other former *Grange Hill* stars in Albert Square. Later he gained infamy as the villainous PC Gabriel Kent in THE BILL. Other credits include Pentecost in the single drama *Black Velvet Band*, narration for the docusoap *Paddington Green*, and a guest appearance in HEARTBEAT.

Casanova [1] ★★

UK (BBC) Drama. BBC 2 1971

DVD: BBC

Giovanni Casanova	**Frank Finlay**
Lorenzo	**Norman Rossington**
Cristina	**Zienia Merton**
Barberina	**Christine Noonan**
Schalon	**Patrick Newell**
Senator Bragadin	**Geoffrey Wincott**
Senior Inquisitor	**Ronald Adam**
Valenglart	**David Swift**

Genoveffa .... **Lyn Yeldham**
Anne Roman-Coupier .... **Ania Merson**

Writer **Dennis Potter**
Producer **Mark Shivas**

● ***The famed 18th-century Italian poet and lover reflects on his life.***

In this six-part, hour-long drama, Giovanni Casanova from his prison cell casts his mind back over the events of his life, evaluating whether his actions have been just and his deeds honourable. He questions the dogmas of the time and attempts to find escape, physical and mental, from his incarceration at the hands of the Spanish Inquisition. The flashback sequences, taking the romantic writer from the age of 30 to his death at 73, when he was 'imprisoned' as a librarian in the court of a Czech count, major on bold language, nudity and sexual antics (leading Mrs Whitehouse to accuse the series of gross indecency: writer Dennis Potter hit back, claiming his work was, on the contrary, very moral).

Casanova ² ✳✳✳✳

UK (Red/Power/BBC/Granada) Drama. BBC 1 2005
DVD: Warner Music Vision

Giacomo Casanova .... **David Tennant** *(young)*
Peter O'Toole *(old)*
Edith .... **Rose Byrne**
Henriette .... **Laura Fraser**
Rocco Scappino .... **Shaun Parkes**
Duke of Grimani .... **Rupert Penry-Jones**
Villars .... **Matt Lucas**
Bellino .... **Nina Sosanya**
Casanova's mother .... **Dervla Kirwan**
Argenti .... **Simon Day**
Dr Gozzi .... **Mark Heap**
Bragadin .... **Freddie Jones**
Jack .... **James Holly** *(young)*
Brock Everitt-Elwick *(older)*
Tom Burke *(adult)*

Writer **Russell T. Davies**
Producer **Gillian McNeill**

● ***The raunchy, eventful life of Venice's celebrated lothario.***

The year is 1793. Legendary lover Casanova is an ageing and isolated man, working as a librarian at the Castle Dux. He is derided by the rest of the staff but finds an ally and confidante in the form of new maid Edith, who is fascinated by the legends that surround him. She coaxes him into revealing all about his remarkable life and so, via flashbacks, we return to the Venice of Casanova's birth and his abandonment a few years later by an actress mother more concerned with building her own international reputation. We follow the initially timid young lad as he learns how sex can boost confidence and aid learning abilities. He becomes both a rake and a scholar. However, despite all the women he manages to conquer, there remains one girl he cannot call his own. She is Henriette, a kindred spirit who is sadly betrothed to the spiteful Grimani, a man destined to be Casanova's rival throughout most of his life. Even when Casanova finds unexpected wealth and Henriette agrees to go with him, their plans are ruined when he is convicted for treason on spurious grounds engineered by Grimani himself. Never a man to be confined, Casanova breaks out of prison and flees to France, England, Germany and other parts of Europe seeking a pardon that will allow him to return to Venice, amassing and losing large fortunes by turn. His constant chaperone is Rocco, an equally roguish manservant, who also brings along little Jack, just one, it seems, of Casanova's unfortunate offspring. Another figure who looms large in Casanova's story is Bellino, an internationally renowned singer, who initially masquerades as a castrato but again becomes one of the loves of Casanova's life. The three episodes conclude with the sick old man dying in the care of Edith, believing – erroneously – that Henriette is finally on her way to see him.

Russell T. Davies's new take on the Casanova legend, directed by Sheree Folkson, is colourful and sparky, using modern vernacular and inventive scene planning to create a funny, bawdy, sometimes magical production. Filmed on location in Dubrovnik as well as Venice, it was shown first on BBC 3 before transferring to BBC 1 a few weeks later.

Case Histories of Scotland Yard ✳

UK (Anglo Amalgamated Films) Police Drama Anthology. ITV 1955

Insp. Duggan .... **Russell Napier**
Insp. Ross .... **Kenneth Henry**
Sgt Mason .... **Arthur Gomez**

Host **Edgar Lustgarten**

Producers **Jack Greenwood, Alec C. Snowden**

● ***Drama series based on actual Scotland Yard case files.***

Introduced by noted journalist and criminologist Edgar Lustgarten, this early half-hour film series was particularly popular in the USA (where it was known simply as *Scotland Yard*). It offers dramatized accounts of real-life crimes which have been investigated by the men of the Metropolitan Police. Although casts change every episode, a few characters like Inspector Duggan appear on a semi-regular basis.

Casebook of Sherlock Holmes, The

See *Adventures of Sherlock Holmes, The.*

Casey, Daniel

(1972–)

Actor born in Stockton-on-Tees, son of former NATIONWIDE and *The Money Programme* presenter Luke Casey. Daniel Casey is undoubtedly still best known as Sgt Troy in MIDSOMER MURDERS, although since leaving the series he has also starred in STEEL RIVER BLUES (Tony Barnes) and appeared in SILENT WITNESS, MURDER IN SUBURBIA and *Hex*. Earlier credits include OUR FRIENDS IN THE NORTH (Anthony Cox), PEAK PRACTICE, A TOUCH OF FROST, CATHERINE COOKSON*'s The Wingless Bird* (Robbie Felton) and THE GRAND.

Casey Jones ✳✳

US (Columbia/Briskin) Children's Western. BBC 1958 (US: Syndicated 1958)

John Luther 'Casey' Jones .... **Alan Hale Jr**
Casey Jones Jr .... **Bobby Clark**
Alice Jones .... **Mary Lawrence**
Wallie Simms .... **Dub Taylor**
Red Rock .... **Eddy Waller**
Sam Peachpit .... **Pat Hogan**

● *Excitement on a Midwestern railroad in the 1890s.*

Based on the mournful ballad in which the hero is tragically killed, this series for youngsters is much more perky. Casey Jones (steamin' and a-rollin') is an engineer for the Illinois Central Railroad, the man behind the throttle of the celebrated *Cannonball Express*. Living with his wife, Alice, his young son, Casey Jr, and dog, Cinders, in Jackson, Tennessee, and loyally supported by his railroad colleagues, Wallie Simms, the fireman, and Red Rock, the conductor, Casey somehow always manages to fulfil his missions, in the face of the greatest adversity. This is one Casey Jones who will not die.

Cash, Craig

(1960–)

Manchester-born comic actor and writer, jointly responsible with Caroline Aherne for THE ROYLE FAMILY, in which he played gormless boyfriend Dave. With Aherne he also appeared as Malcolm in MRS MERTON AND MALCOLM, and made a documentary entitled *Back Passage to India*. More recently, Cash has co-written (with Phil Mealey) and directed EARLY DOORS, also playing pub regular Joe.

Cassidy, David

(1950–)

Actor/singer heart-throb of the 1970s, soaring to international fame as Keith Partridge in THE PARTRIDGE FAMILY, in which he starred with his own stepmother, Shirley Jones. On the back of the series he topped the record charts on both sides of the Atlantic with songs like 'How Can I Be Sure' and 'Daydreamer', as well as having Partridge Family hits. Since those heady days TV work has been thin, except for an unusual detective series created specifically for him in 1978, *David Cassidy – Man Undercover*, in which he played Officer Dan Shay. His earliest work consisted of minor parts in series like BONANZA, while recent guest appearances include a role in MALCOLM IN THE MIDDLE. Cassidy's first wife was actress Kay Lenz. His father was actor Jack Cassidy and his brother, Shaun, has also made showbiz his career.

Cassidy, Ted

(1932–79)

Giant American actor, chiefly remembered in his guise of Lurch, the groaning butler in THE ADDAMS FAMILY. (He also played the hand, Thing, unless Lurch was also in shot.) Later Cassidy appeared as Injun Joe in *The New Adventures of Huck Finn* and provided the voice for numerous Hanna-Barbera characters, including Frankenstein Jr. He died following heart surgery in 1979.

Castaway 2000 ★★

UK (BBC/Lion) Documentary. BBC 1 2000–1

Executive Producers **Jeremy Mills, Colin Cameron**
Producer **Chris Kelly**

● *Year-long social experiment on a barren Scottish island.*

Castaway 2000 took 36 men, women and children out of their day-to-day existence and asked them to live together for one year in basic conditions. The setting was the island of Taransay, a short sea crossing from Harris in the Outer Hebrides. Measuring just two miles by three, the isle was so bleak and weather-ravaged that the last two crofters had abandoned it decades earlier. Now people used to the comforts of modern life were asked to return to nature, to survive and care for themselves like latter-day Robinson Crusoes.

The castaways were given only the most basic amenities: primitive shelters, communal showers, compost toilets, some livestock and an annual shopping budget of £50,000 to buy essential goods, which were delivered fortnightly by mail boat. The island's one house was turned into a home for the two families who signed up, and a schoolhouse was brought up to scratch to house the pupils for three hours a day. A cowshed was converted to a kitchen/dining room but, in order to eat, the residents had to grow their own vegetables and slaughter their own meat. Water was filtered from one of the island's lochs; electricity came from a wind turbine and a hydro-power unit. Emergencies were covered by a back-up generator, coastguard VHF radio and a satellite phone. For entertainment, a music system and a piano were provided. A confessional box, complete with a surveillance video camera, allowed inhabitants to get grumbles off their chest (there were many).

Around 4,500 people applied for this unusual career break. These were whittled down by a psychologist and a survival expert, through assault courses and trials of character and resourcefulness, into the final selection, a mix of people from all walks of life, with ages stretching from three to 58. Arrivals began on New Year's Day 2000. A film crew then returned fortnightly to see how life was progressing, adding an outsider's view to the video shot by the islanders themselves on a daily basis. The initial idea was to broadcast the set-up and the arrival of the islanders and then wait until the year was complete before televising more episodes. However, media interest in the project proved so great that updates were shown at intervals through the year (some airing as *Castaway Diaries*). Family visitors were allowed onto the island for a week in the summer; journalists were given similar access later in the year.

The project did not get off to the smoothest start. Two families immediately returned to the mainland, claiming that promised facilities were not in place. They and other castaways eventually joined the throng a few weeks late. The first to quit was builder Ray Bowyer, who fell out with most of the other residents, criticizing the work ethic of the younger men in particular. Other premature departees were gay psychotherapist Ron Copsey, the Seventh Day Adventist Carey family, and lonely mum Hilary Freeman. Prominent survivors were Roger Stephenson, the island's doctor, and his family (his wife, Rosemary, becoming pregnant on Taransay), and Ben Fogle (with black labrador, Inca). A former *Tatler* picture editor and son of actress Julia Foster and vet Bruce Fogle, Ben became the programme's heart-throb and set himself up for a new career as a TV presenter.

As the end approached, viewers were treated to regular live instalments on the castaways' final day on the island, showing them packing up, pondering the year behind them, reflecting on relationships forged and broken, and wondering what lay ahead after this life-changing experience.

Castle, Roy

OBE (1932–94)

Popular, extremely versatile entertainer whose talents stretched from singing and dancing to playing obscure musical instruments. Early in his career he acted as straight man to Jimmy James, coming to the fore as a star in his own right in the 1950s sketch show *New Look*. He then appeared in numerous films, ranging from *Dr Who and the Daleks* to *Carry On up the Khyber*. From 1972 he hosted the superlatives show, RECORD BREAKERS (holding some world records himself), and his other TV offerings included *Castle Beats Time, The Roy Castle Show*, Ronnie Barker's *Seven of One* and the religious travelogue, *Castle's Abroad*. The last years of his life were dedicated to fighting (and raising the profile of) lung cancer, a disease he claimed he had contracted from passive smoking, having spent years playing the trumpet in smoky clubrooms.

Casualty ★★

UK (BBC) Medical Drama. BBC 1 1986–

Charlie Fairhead .... **Derek Thompson**
Lisa 'Duffy' Duffin .... **Catherine Shipton**
Megan Roach .... **Brenda Fricker**
Dr Ewart Plimmer .... **Bernard Gallagher**
Clive King .... **George Harris**
Kuba Trzcinski .... **Christopher Rozycki**
Susie Mercier .... **Debbie Roza**
Dr Barbara 'Baz' Samuels/ Hayes/Fairhead/Wilder .... **Julia Watson**
Andrew Ponting .... **Robert Pugh**
Sandra Mute .... **Lisa Bowerman**
Elizabeth Straker .... **Maureen O'Brien**
Karen O'Malley .... **Katie Hardie**
Dr Mary Tomlinson .... **Helena Little**
Cyril James .... **Eddie Nestor**
Dr David Rowe .... **Paul Lacoux**
Valerie Sinclair .... **Susan Franklyn**
Shirley Franklin .... **Ella Wilder**
Kiran Joghill .... **Shaheen Khan**
Alison McGrellis .... **Julie Graham**
Julie Stevens .... **Vivienne McKone**
Keith Cotterill .... **Geoffrey Leesley**
Sadie Tomkins .... **Carol Leader**
Dr Lucy Perry .... **Tam Hoskyns**
Alex Spencer .... **Belinda Davison**
Dr Andrew Bower .... **William Gaminara**
Philip Bretherton
Dr Beth Ramanee .... **Mamta Kaash**
Dr Julian Chapman .... **Nigel Le Vaillant**
Jimmy Powell .... **Robson Green**
Tony Walker .... **Eamon Boland**
Martin 'Ash' Ashford .... **Patrick Robinson**
Helen Green .... **Maggie McCarthy**
Norma Sullivan .... **Anne Kristen**
Josh Griffiths .... **Ian Bleasdale**
Jane Scott .... **Caroline Webster**
Kelly Liddle .... **Adie Allen**
Patricia Baynes .... **Maria Friedman**
Dr Rob Khalefa .... **Jason Riddington**
Kate Miller .... **Joanna Foster**
Sandra Nicholl .... **Maureen Beattie**
Maxine Price .... **Emma Bird**
Simon Eastman .... **Robert Daws**
Dr Mike Barratt .... **Clive Mantle**
Brian Crawford .... **Brendan O'Hea**
Mark Calder .... **Oliver Parker**
Mie Nishi-Kawa .... **Naoko Mori**
Frankie Drummer .... **Steven O'Donnell**
Dave Masters .... **Martin Ball**
Rachel Longworth .... **Jane Gurnett**
Dr Karen Goodliffe .... **Suzanna Hamilton**
Adele Beckford .... **Doña Croll**
Kenneth Hodges .... **Christopher Guard**
Helen Chatsworth .... **Samantha Edmonds**
Mary Skillett .... **Tara Moran**
Lucy Cooper .... **Jo Unwin**
Kate Wilson .... **Sorcha Cusack**
Eddie Gordon .... **Joan Oliver**
Matt Hawley .... **Jason Merrells**
Adam Cooke .... **Steven Brand**
Jude Kocarnik .... **Lisa Coleman**
Liz Harker .... **Sue Devaney**
Dr Daniel Perryman .... **Craig Kelly**
Laura Milburn/Ashford .... **Lizzy McInnerny**
Peter Hayes .... **Robert Duncan**
Trevor Wilson .... **Michael N. Harbour**
Richard McCabe .... **Gray O'Brien**
Gloria Hammond .... **Ganiat Kasumu**
Sam Colloby .... **Jonathan Kerrigan**
Jack Hathaway .... **Peter Birch**
David Sinclair .... **Vas Blackwood**
Monica .... **Soo Drouet**
Mark Grace .... **Paterson Joseph**
Dr Georgina 'George' Woodman .... **Rebecca Lacey**
Tina Seabrook .... **Claire Goose**
Amy Howard .... **Rebecca Wheatley**
Elliot Matthews .... **Peter Guinness**
Derek 'Sunny' Sunderland .... **Vincenzo Pellegrino**
Penny Hutchens .... **Donna Alexander**
Eve Montgomery .... **Barbara Marten**
Adam Osman .... **Pal Aron**
Chloe Hill .... **Jan Anderson**
Max Gallagher .... **Robert Gwilym**
Sean Maddox .... **Gerald Kyd**
PC Pat Garratt .... **Ian Kershaw**
Marius Lupescu .... **Patrick Romer**
Holly Miles .... **Sandra Huggett**
Finlay Newton .... **Kwame Kwei-Armah**
Barney Woolfe .... **Ronnie McCann**
Mel Dyson .... **Michelle Butterly**
Dr Patrick Spiller .... **Ian Kelsey**
Spencer .... **Ben Keaton**
Dan Robinson .... **Grant Masters**
Colette Kierney/Griffiths .... **Adjoa Andoh**
Tom Harvey .... **Kieron Forsyth**
Anna Paul .... **Zita Sattar**
Nikki Marshall .... **Kelly Harrison**
Dillon Cahill .... **Dan Rymer**
Sgt Rachel James .... **Amy Robbins**
Comfort Jones .... **Martina Laird**
Jack Vincent .... **Will Mellor**
Jeff McGuire .... **Bob Mason**
Dr Lara Stone .... **Christine Stephen-Daly**
Tony Vincent .... **Lee Warburton**
Dr Simon Kaminski .... **Christopher Colquhoun**
Harry Harper .... **Simon MacCorkindale**
Roxanne Bird .... **Loo Brealey**
Ryan Johnson .... **Russell Boulter**
Eddie Vincent .... **Philip Martin Brown**
Merlin Jameson .... **Orlando Seale**
Jane Winter .... **N'Deaye Baa-Clements**
Bex Reynolds .... **Sarah Manners**
Luke Warren .... **Matthew Wait**
Tess Beteman .... **Suzanne Packer**
Jim Brodie .... **Maxwell Caulfield**
Claire Guildford .... **Leanne Wilson**
John 'Abs' Denham .... **James Redmond**
Tally Harper .... **Holly Davidson**
Dr Selena Donovan/Manning **Elizabeth Carling**
DI Will Manning .... **Gary Mavers**

Nina Farr	**Rebekah Gibbs**
Ellen Zitek/Denham	**Georgina Bouzova**
Sam Bateman	**Luke Bailey**
Guppy Sandhu	**Elyes Gabel**
Paul 'Woody' Joyner	**Will Thorp**
Pete Guildford	**Adam James**
Maggie Coldwell	**Susan Cookson**
Stan Powell	**Jack Smethurst**
Bruno Jenkins	**Mark Bonnar**
Kelsey Philips	**Janine Mellor**
Fleur Butler	**Laura Donnelly**
Jas Sandhu	**Madhav Sharma**
Nathan Spencer	**Ben Price**
Alice Chantry	**Sam Grey**

Creators **Jeremy Brock, Paul Unwin**
Producers **Geraint Morris, Peter Norris, Michael Ferguson, Corinne Hollingworth, Rosalind Anderson, Sally Haynes, Johnathan Young, Alexei de Keyser, Tim Bradley, Rachel Wright, Mervyn Watson, Amanda Silvester, David Crean, Tim Holloway, Foz Allan, Pippa Brill, Richard Handford, Steve Lightfoot, Lowri Glain, Sue Howells, Alex Perrin, Sophie Fante, Jane Hudson, Jane Steventon, Margaret Boden**

A hectic night's work in a city's accident and emergency unit.

Set at night-time in the casualty department of Holby (a thinly disguised Bristol) City Hospital, this extremely popular series has echoed American imports like HILL STREET BLUES and ST ELSEWHERE in its construction, with one disturbing lead story merged with one or two more light-hearted sub-plots to ease tension and add contrast. While the 'stars' of each show have been the various patients, of the regular cast the main man for many series was Charlie Fairhead, the avuncular charge nurse. In the early years he shared the limelight with maternal Megan Roach and the outspoken, single-mother senior nurse, Lisa 'Duffy' Duffin. Among the other notable cast members have been 'Baz' Hayes, Charlie's ideal woman who left her husband, Peter, to have Charlie's baby (Louis); ex-surgeon Ewart Plimmer; heart-throb Dr Julian Chapman; Geordie porter Jimmy Powell; and dependable Martin 'Ash' Ashford, who eventually married hospital PR manager Laura Milburn. There were also nose-stud-wearing union rep Jude Kocarnik, who was almost stabbed to death; her boyfriend, receptionist Matt Hawley; shopping addict Kate Wilson; and single parent George Woodman. However, new supporting casts have arrived with each season, and only a few characters have lasted any great length of time. This is possibly because the action in *Casualty* has traditionally come more from events in the wards than from the personal lives of its characters, although the characters have increasingly come through over the years. Charlie, for example, has suffered from alcohol addiction, a nervous breakdown and numerous romantic upheavals. Indeed, as the series has progressed to being on air virtually all year, increasingly far-fetched plots and a climbing mortality rate among Holby staff members have chipped away at its plausibility.

The series has never been afraid to court controversy. The status of the NHS has always been an issue, much to the dismay of some politicians, and touchy medical matters have bravely been covered, including AIDS and anorexia. Other social menaces like terrorism, rioting, rape, arson and plane crashes have been given equal prominence and drawn similar venom from sensitive critics. Production-wise, too, *Casualty* has been daring. The 1994–5 season was initially shot on film to add greater depth and slickness. However, viewers preferred the tamer atmosphere of videotape, and later episodes were electronically recorded as before.

Among the numerous guest stars playing the walking wounded have been Kate Winslet, Robert Carlyle, Alfred Molina, Dorothy Tutin, Norman Wisdom, Minnie Driver, Hywel Bennett, Patsy Kensit, Phill Jupitus and Prunella Scales.

An episode in November 1998 introduced guest characters as a preamble to a spin-off series, HOLBY CITY. Some special *Casualty@Holby City* cross-over episodes have been screened since, including an interactive story in 2005 that gave viewers the chance to vote for the patient they felt should receive a vital transplant.

Catchphrase ✶✶

UK (TVS/Meridian/Action Time/Carlton) Game Show.
ITV 1986–2002

Presenters **Roy Walker, Nick Weir, Mark Curry**

Executive Producers **John Kaye Cooper, Stephen Leahy**
Producers **Graham C. Williams, Frank Hayes, Liddy Oldroyd, Patricia Mordecai, Royston Mayoh, Patricia Pearson**

Spot-the-saying quiz involving complex computer graphics.

'See what you say and say what you see' was the *Catchphrase* catchphrase. This undemanding game show asked two contestants to solve a series of computer-generated visual puzzles representing well-known phrases or sayings. Wrong guesses were initially generously rejected by host Roy Walker with his own trademark quips like 'It's good, but it's not right', until Walker was succeeded by new host Nick Weir in 2000. In 2002 Mark Curry became front man and the show switched to a daily slot for a final hurrah. Cash and travel prizes were awarded to successful contestants.

Catherine Cookson ✶✶

UK (Tyne Tees/Worldwide/Festival Films) Drama. ITV 1989; 1991; 1993–2000
DVD: Cinema Club

The Fifteen Streets (1989)

John O'Brien	**Owen Teale**
Mary Llewellyn	**Clare Holman**
Dominic O'Brien	**Sean Bean**
Peter Bracken	**Ian Bannen**
Christine Bracken	**Jane Horrocks**
Beatrice Llewellyn	**Billie Whitelaw**
James Llewellyn	**Frank Windsor**

Writer **Gordon Hann**

The Black Candle (1991)

Bridget Mordaunt	**Samantha Bond**
William Filmore	**Denholm Elliott**
Lionel Filmore	**Nathaniel Parker**
Douglas Filmore	**Robert Hines**
Victoria Mordaunt	**Tara Fitzgerald**
Daisy Bennett	**Siân Phillips**

Writer **Gordon Hann**

The Black Velvet Gown (1991)

Riah Millican	**Janet McTeer**
Percival Miller	**Bob Peck**
Bridget Millican	**Geraldine Somerville**
Madam Gullmington	**Jean Anderson**

Writer **Gordon Hann**

The Man Who Cried (1993)

Abel Mason .... **Ciaran Hinds**
Florrie Donelly .... **Kate Buffery**
Hilda Maxwell .... **Amanda Root**
Lena Mason .... **Angela Walsh**
Dick Mason .... **James Tomlinson**
Ben Walden

Writer **Stan Barstow**

The Cinder Path (1994)

Victoria Chapman .... **Catherine Zeta Jones**
Charlie MacFell .... **Lloyd Owen**
Edward MacFell .... **Tom Bell**
Nellie Chapman .... **Maria Miles**
Mary MacFell .... **Rosalind Ayres**
Ginger Slater .... **Antony Byrne**

Writer **Alan Seymour**

The Dwelling Place (1994)

Cissie Brodie .... **Tracey Whitewell**
Lord Fischel .... **James Fox**
Clive Fischel .... **Edward Rawle-Hicks**
Matthew Turnbull .... **Ray Stevenson**
Cunningham .... **Philip Voss**
Rose Turnbull .... **Julie Hesmondhalgh**
Isabelle Fischel .... **Lucy Cohu**

Writer **Gordon Hann**

The Glass Virgin (1995)

Annabella Lagrange .... **Emily Mortimer**
Edmund Lagrange .... **Nigel Havers**
Manuel Mendoza .... **Brendan Coyle**
Rosina .... **Christine Kavanagh**
Betty Watford .... **Jan Graveson**
Lady Constance .... **Sylvia Syms**

Writer **Alan Seymour**

The Gambling Man (1995)

Rory Connor .... **Robson Green**
Charlotte Kean .... **Sylvestra Le Touzel**
Frank Nickle .... **Bernard Hill**
Janie Waggett .... **Stephanie Putson**
Lizzie O'Dowd .... **Anne Kent**
Jimmy Connor .... **Dave Nellist**

Writer **T. R. Bowen**

The Tide of Life (1996)

Emily Kennedy .... **Gillian Kearney**
Sep McGilby .... **John Bowler**
Larry Birch .... **Ray Stevenson**
Lucy Kennedy .... **Susie Burton**
John Kennedy .... **Berwick Kaler**
Con Fulwell .... **Justin Chadwick**
Rona Birch .... **Diana Hardcastle**
Nick Stuart .... **James Purefoy**

Writer **Gordon Hann**

The Girl (1996)

Hannah Boyle .... **Siobhan Flynn**
Ned Ridley .... **Jonathan Cake**
Anne Thornton .... **Jill Baker**
Matthew Thornton .... **Malcolm Stoddard**
Fred Loam .... **Mark Benton**
Mrs Loam .... **Susan Jameson**

Writer **Gordon Hann**

The Wingless Bird (1997)

Agnes Conway .... **Claire Skinner**
Charles Farrier .... **Edward Atterton**
Reg Farrier .... **Julian Wadham**
Alice Conway .... **Anne Reid**
Arthur Conway .... **Frank Grimes**
Jessie Conway .... **Michelle Charles**
Robbie Felton .... **Daniel Casey**
Col. Farrier .... **Dinsdale Landen**
Grace Farrier .... **Elspet Gray**

Writer **Alan Seymour**

The Moth (1997)

Robert Bradley .... **Jack Davenport**
Sarah Thorman .... **Juliet Aubrey**
Dave Waters .... **David Bradley**
Millie Thorman .... **Justine Waddell**
Alice Bradley .... **Janet Dale**
Reginald Thorman .... **Jeremy Clyde**
Kate Thorman .... **Judy Loe**

Writer **Gordon Hann**

The Rag Nymph (1997)

Aggie Winkowski .... **Val McLane**
Millie Forester .... **Perdita Weeks**
Honeysuckle Weeks
Ben .... **Alec Newman**
Bernard Thompson .... **Crispin Bonham-Carter**
Raymond Crane-Boulder .... **Patrick Ryecart**

Writer **T. R. Bowen**

The Round Tower (1998)

Vanessa Ratcliffe .... **Emilia Fox**
Angus Cotton .... **Ben Miles**
Jane Ratcliffe .... **Jan Harvey**
Jonathan Ratcliffe .... **Keith Barron**
Arthur Brett .... **Denis Lawson**

Writer **T. R. Bowen**

Colour Blind (1998)

Bridget Paterson .... **Niamh Cusack**
Rose Angela Paterson .... **Carmen Ejogo**
Jimmy Paterson .... **Tony Armatrading**
Kathie McQueen .... **Dearbhla Molloy**
Cavan McQueen .... **Walter McMonagle**
Matt McQueen .... **Ian Embleton**

Writer **Gordon Hann**

Tilly Trotter (1999)

Tilly Trotter .... **Carli Norris**
Mark Sopwith .... **Simon Shepherd**
Simon Bentwood .... **Gavin Abbott**
Ellen Ross .... **Beth Goddard**
Biddy Drew .... **Madelaine Newton**
Katie Drew .... **Sarah Jane Foster**
Mrs Forefoot Meadows .... **Rosemary Leach**

Writer **Ray Marshall**

The Secret (2000)

Freddie Musgrave .... **Colin Buchanan**
Maggie Hewitt .... **Clare Higgins**
Belle .... **Hannah Yelland**
Marcel Birkstead .... **Stephen Moyer**
Connie .... **Liz Carling**
Mrs Birkstead .... **June Whitfield**
Freeman .... **Terence Hillyer**

Writer **T. R. Bowen**

A Dinner of Herbs (2000)

Kate Makepeace	**Billie Whitelaw**
Roddy Greenbank	**Jonathan Kerrigan**
	Rupert Frazer
Hal Roystan	**Tom Goodman Hill**
	David Threlfall
Mary Ellen Lee/Roystan	**Melanie Clark Pullen**
	Jane Arden
Kate Roystan	**Debra Stephenson**
Mr Mulcaster	**Tim Healy**

Writers **Christopher Green, Ray Marshall**
Producer (all series) **Ray Marshall**

Adaptations of the historical novels by one of Britain's best-selling authors.

Worldwide International Television producer Ray Marshall could hardly believe that such a prolific and popular novelist as Dame Catherine Cookson had never seen her works dramatized for television, with the exception of her stories about THE MALLENS in the 1970s. Consequently, he took the opportunity to bring her book *The Fifteen Streets* to the screen in 1989 and didn't look back. He followed it up with *The Black Candle* and *The Black Velvet Gown* and then set up his own production company, Festival Films, to work on the rest of Dame Catherine's extensive output (initially in conjunction with Worldwide).

Cookson's tales major on the downtrodden heroine who hopefully wins through. Set in the north-east of England, and usually in the early years of the 20th century (although *The Round Tower* was set in the 1950s and 1960s, and *Tilly Trotter* in the mid-1800s), they have proved as popular on television as in print. Her intricate plots, matter-of-fact social commentaries and three-dimensional characters provided the TV dramatists with more than enough to work on. Most of the stories (billed as *Catherine Cookson's The Glass Virgin*, etc.) were dramatized in three parts.

Cathode Ray Tube

The electron tube invented by Karl Ferdinand Braun in 1897 that was modified by Philo T. Farnsworth and Vladimir Zworykin in the 1920s to display television pictures. The device includes a gun that fires a stream of electrons at a phosphor-coated screen, causing it to glow and so display the TV image. Familiarly known as the 'tube', early versions were expensive and not known for their longevity. A common gripe with viewers in the 1950s and 1960s was that their 'tube had gone'.

Cathy Come Home ✳✳✳✳

UK (BBC) Drama. BBC 1 1966
DVD: BFI Video Publishing

Cathy Ward	**Carol White**
Reg Ward	**Ray Brooks**
Mrs Ward	**Winnifred Dennis**

Writer **Jeremy Sandford**
Producer **Tony Garnett**

Documentary-style drama focusing on the plight of a homeless mother and her children.

Cathy Come Home was possibly the most important contribution made by THE WEDNESDAY PLAY. This grim offering tells of Cathy, a young northern lass who makes her way to the bright lights of London, meets and marries a local van-driver (Reg) and soon finds herself mother of three young children (Sean, Stephen and Marlene). It reveals how the family is torn apart by the fact that they soon have no permanent roof over their heads, following Reg's accident at work and his subsequent struggle for employment. It shows how they lurch steadily downmarket, from a comfortable maisonette to Reg's mum's overcrowded, squalid tenement, to run-down lodgings, to a pokey caravan on an unhealthy site, to a derelict house, and finally to a hostel for the homeless, where the father is separated from his wife and children. Physically torn apart, Cathy and Reg grow increasingly distant emotionally until he stops paying for the family's keep and they are thrown on to the streets. The despair and helplessness experienced by Cathy as her kids are taken into care touched the hearts of viewers and led to angry calls for action to prevent such tragic circumstances. Shelter, the homeless charity, was able to capitalize on the furore and become an important voice in housing matters.

The play was directed by Ken Loach, who used documentary, news-style camera angles and hand-held cameras in the search for realism. The soundtrack was punctuated with urban noise, and scenes were kept short and snappy to avoid over-dramatization. Housing facts and figures were quoted throughout the play, adding a political commentary to the events in view.

C.A.T.S. Eyes ✳

UK (TVS) Detective Drama. ITV 1985–7

Maggie Forbes	**Jill Gascoine**
Pru Standfast	**Rosalyn Landor**
Frederica 'Fred' Smith	**Leslie Ash**
Nigel Beaumont	**Don Warrington**
Tessa Robinson	**Tracy-Louise Ward**

Creator **Terence Feely**
Executive Producer **Rex Firkin**
Producers **Dickie Bamber, Frank Cox, Raymond Menmuir**

A female detective agency is really a front for a Home Office security team.

C.A.T.S. Eyes is a yarn about three intrepid girl agents – a sort of British CHARLIE'S ANGELS. Head of the team is Pru Standfast, a tall Oxford graduate once with the War Office, renowned for her organizational abilities. Her colleagues are ex-policewoman Maggie Forbes and young computer buff, Fred Smith. Forbes has 18 years of police experience behind her (see THE GENTLE TOUCH) and brings formal detection skills to the team. Smith, in addition to her computer wizardry, is an ace driver. Together they operate as the Eyes Enquiry Agency, a front for a Home Office investigation team known as Covert Activities Thames Section (C.A.T.S.). Their missions take them into the areas of international espionage, corruption, terrorism and organized crime, and supporting their efforts and keeping an eye on their work is Ministry man Nigel Beaumont. When the show returned for a second season, changes had been made. Most notably, Pru Standfast had gone, Forbes had taken over as leader and a new recruit, Tessa Robinson, had been added.

Catweazle ✳✳

UK (LWT) Children's Science Fiction. ITV 1970–1
DVD: Network

Catweazle	**Geoffrey Bayldon**
Edward 'Carrot' Bennet	**Robin Davis**

Mr Bennet .... **Charles Tingwell**
Sam Woodyard .... **Neil McCarthy**
Cedric Collingford .... **Gary Warren**
Lord Collingford .... **Moray Watson**
Lady Collingford .... **Elspet Gray**
Groome .... **Peter Butterworth**

Creator/Writer **Richard Carpenter**
Executive Producer **Joy Whitby**
Producers **Quentin Lawrence, Carl Mannin**

An 11th-century wizard is stranded in the 20th century.

Catweazle, an alchemist in Norman times, is attempting to harness the power of flight when, with knights on horseback in pursuit, his magic fails him. He leaps into a pond and resurfaces (along with pet toad Touchwood) 900 years into the future. In an age when man really can fly, this scrawny rag-bag of a wizard is astounded and absorbed by simple, everyday objects. Items like the light bulb ('electrickery', as he calls it) or the telephone ('telling bone') are simply beyond his comprehension. As he strives to find a way back to his own time, Catweazle is befriended by teenager Carrot, a farmer's son, who soon discovers that life isn't easy with an ancient magician in tow.

Despite at last finding a way home at the end of the first series, Catweazle promptly returns to our time for a second run, on this occasion arriving in the village of King's Farthing and finding a new ally in Cedric, son of Lord and Lady Collingford. Still struggling to master the art of flight, he now also seeks the mystic 13th sign of the zodiac, which will enable him to return to his own age. Finally achieving his objective, Catweazle disappears back into the past for good.

The title of the series was allegedly drawn from a word creator Richard Carpenter had seen scratched onto a gate.

Caught on a Train ★★★

UK (BBC) Drama. BBC 2 1980
DVD: BBC

Frau Messner .... **Peggy Ashcroft**
Peter .... **Michael Kitchen**
Lorraine .... **Wendy Raebeck**
Preston .... **Michael Sheard**
Kellner .... **Ingo Mogendorf**
Dietrich .... **Louis Sheldon**
Hans .... **Michael Kingsbury**

Writer **Stephen Poliakoff**
Producer **Kenith Trodd**

A long rail journey proves eventful but uncomfortable for a young English traveller.

Peter Duffell directed this single drama, part of BBC 2's *Playhouse* showcase. As the title suggests, the action takes place on a very busy Ostend to Vienna night express train. A young Englishman, a prickly book publicist named Peter, finds himself confined to a carriage with an attractive American girl, Lorraine, and a snooty Viennese lady, Frau Messner. Messner treats Peter with disdain, arrogantly giving him orders and embarrassing him in front of the others. The journey and its unfortunate events thus turn into a tense, uncomfortable experience for all concerned and not at all what Peter had in mind when he boarded the train, as both young and old become quite intolerant of each other. The drama was shot partly on location and partly in a disused railway car near Peterborough. Author Stephen Poliakoff based the story on real-life experiences of his own. Mike Westbrook supplied the music.

Cazalets, The ★★★

UK (BBC/WGBH/Cinema Verity) Drama. BBC 1 2001
DVD: WGBH Boston (Region 1 only)

Hugh Cazalet .... **Hugh Bonneville**
Edward Cazalet .... **Stephen Dillane**
Rupert Cazalet .... **Paul Rhys**
Viola 'Villy' Cazalet .... **Lesley Manville**
Sybil Cazalet .... **Anastasia Hille**
Zoe Cazalet .... **Joanna Page**
Rachel Cazalet .... **Catherine Russell**
Kitty 'The Duchy' Cazalet .... **Ursula Howells**
William 'The Brig' Cazalet .... **Frederick Treves**
Clarissa 'Clary' Cazalet .... **Florence Hoath**
Louise Cazalet .... **Emma Griffiths Malin**
Polly Cazalet .... **Claudia Renton**
Diana Macintosh .... **Anna Chancellor**
Sid .... **Penny Downie**
Frank Tonbridge .... **John McArdle**
Miss Millament .... **Patsy Rowlands**
Mrs Mabel Cripps .... **Jacqueline Tong**
Teddy Cazalet .... **Ben Simpson**
Neville Cazalet .... **Alex Pownall**
Lydia Cazalet .... **Francesca Wicks**
Michael Hadleigh .... **Mark Bazeley**
Christopher Castle .... **Nicholas Audsley**

Writer **Douglas Livingstone**
Executive Producers **Pippa Harris, Jane Tranter**
Producers **Verity Lambert, Joanna Lumley**

War turns a prosperous family's life upside down.

Based on the novels *The Light Years* and *Marking Time*, by Elizabeth Jane Howard, this six-part serial, directed by Suri Krishnamma, centres on the well-heeled Cazalet family as they make the journey from the sunshine summer of 1937 into the dark days of World War II. The family has earned its fortune through timber and is very comfortably off, not to say spoilt, self-centred and somewhat prejudiced. Head of the clan, visually impaired William Cazalet, known to all as 'The Brig', and his organized wife Kitty ('The Duchy') now look down on an extended family of sons, daughters, in-laws and close friends who seek out the Cazalet country retreat in Sussex as a home from home and handy refuge from the air raids of London. Their three sons are Edward (a racist ladies' man, who, with Diana Macintosh, cheats on his ex-ballerina wife, Villy, and then tries to seduce his nubile daughter, Louise), troubled Hugh (in contrast, a rock of support for his terminally ill wife, Sybil) and artistic socialist Rupert (a widower who has married again – the materialistic Zoe – joins the Navy and goes missing at Dunkirk). Their sister, Rachel, stays close to her parents but is enticed towards lesbian leanings by her long-time friend, Sid, a music teacher. Also prominent is the next generation, especially Louise, who becomes an actress and falls in love with portrait artist Michael Hadleigh; Polly, who suffers along with her parents Hugh and Sybil; Clary, Rupert's distraught daughter, and the girls' pacifist cousin, Christopher Castle. The 'downstairs' element also features, largely in the form of chauffeur Tonbridge and cook Mrs Cripps, who discover an 'understanding'.

The series was also notable for the involvement of actress Joanna Lumley on the other side of the camera. Admitting she'd always loved Howard's novels, she was invited to co-produce by Verity Lambert. Regrettably, *The Cazalets* suffered the same fate as series like THE TRIPODS and THE HOUSE OF ELIOTT, in being cancelled before its story was fully told (it closed at the end of 1941, shortly after the Japanese attack on Pearl Harbor). Despite acclaim, a second series, perhaps following Howard's two further novels, which took the story up to 1947, was not commissioned.

Cazenove, Christopher

(1945–)

Aristocratic British actor who, after success as Richard Gaunt in THE REGIMENT, George Cornwallis-West in JENNIE, LADY RANDOLPH CHURCHILL and as the Honourable Charles Tyrrell in THE DUCHESS OF DUKE STREET, flew to the USA to star as Ben Carrington in DYNASTY. Among his other credits have been the US comedy *A Fine Romance*, THE RIVALS OF SHERLOCK HOLMES, *Affairs of the Heart*, LADY KILLERS, *Jenny's War*, LOU GRANT, *Kane and Abel* and, more recently, JUDGE JOHN DEED (Row Colemore), TIMEWATCH: ZULU: THE TRUE STORY and guest appearances in *Charmed*, DALZIEL AND PASCOE and *Fun at the Funeral Parlour*. Cazenove was once married to actress Angharad Rees.

CBBC

Free-to-view digital channel for the 6–13 age group, launched on 11 February 2002, with programmes like *The Saturday Show Extra*, *Cave Girl*, *Xchange*, plus regular NEWSROUND updates, among the early offerings.

CBeebies

Digital channel for pre-school children, launched on 11 February 2002, with an emphasis on learning through play. Featured programmes initially included *The Story Makers*, *Smarteenies*, *The Shiny Show*, BOB THE BUILDER, TWEENIES, *Brum* and a revival of ANDY PANDY.

CBS

CBS was, for many years, America's number one network. Founded in 1927 as United Independent Broadcasters by Arthur Judson, the company quickly took on a partner, the Columbia Phonograph and Records Company, at the same time renaming itself Columbia Phonograph Broadcasting System. When the phonograph company pulled out because of increasing losses, the name was shortened to Columbia Broadcasting System (CBS). In 1929 William S. Paley bought control of the company and became its most influential executive. He remained on the board until 1983, leading CBS into television, aggressively signing up affiliate stations and making the network America's first choice. In 1974 the company name was changed from Columbia Broadcasting System to CBS Inc., and various internal power struggles in the 1970s and 1980s ensued, reflecting CBS's fall from the top spot. The company temporarily diversified into publishing, toys and other interests and was taken over by the Tisch family, owners of the Loews Corporation. In 1995 CBS was bought by Westinghouse Electric Corporation. In its heyday CBS boasted the biggest stars and the top shows: I LOVE LUCY, THE HONEYMOONERS, THE DICK VAN DYKE SHOW, ALL IN THE FAMILY and M*A*S*H* all aired on CBS, and the station was also home to revered news journalists Ed Murrow and Walter Cronkite. In recent years the biggest hits have been modest in comparison, namely MURDER, SHE WROTE, MURPHY BROWN, *Everybody Loves Raymond* and CSI: CRIME SCENE INVESTIGATION. The business became part of the Viacom group in 2000, but was de-merged as CBS Corporation at the end of 2005.

CD:UK

See *SM:TV Live*.

Celeb ✳

UK (Tiger Aspect) Situation Comedy. BBC 1 2002

Gary Bloke .... **Harry Enfield**
Debs Bloke .... **Amanda Holden**
Troy Bloke .... **Leo Bill**
Johnson .... **Rupert Vansittart**
Grandma .... **Alison Steadman**

Writers **Charles Peattie, Mark Warren**
Producer **Ed Bye**

A wrinkly rocker has more money than sense.

A lifetime of rock'n' roll excess has taken its toll on fiftysomething metal musician Gary Bloke, whose music is out of vogue but whose celebrity and wealth keep him in the public eye. To fill his time, he struts and swaggers around his country mansion holding parties, trying to network with fellow rock stars and keeping groupies, stalkers and love children at bay. Semi-stoned and stubble-chinned, dopey Gary has a stack of money but is never sure how to spend it. Thankfully, he is chaperoned by his bimbette wife, Debs, a former model, and his resourceful butler, Johnson, who tends to bail him out of his latest woes. Troy is Gary's equally thick son by a previous marriage. Musical guests include Roy Wood.

The six-episode series was based on a cartoon strip in *Private Eye* but, for critics and audiences alike, it failed to translate to TV. Maybe the fact that a real life tale of an ageing rock star in a mansion (THE OSBOURNES) beat it to air had something to do with it.

Celebrity Squares ✳

UK (ATV/Central) Quiz. ITV 1975–9/1993–5

Presenter **Bob Monkhouse**

Producers **Paul Stewart Laing, Glyn Edwards, Peter Harris, Gill Stribling-Wright, Danny Greenstone**

Noughts and crosses quiz featuring showbusiness personalities.

In this light-hearted game show nine celebrities inhabited the squares of a giant (18-foot) noughts and crosses board. Two contestants took turns to nominate celebrities to answer general knowledge questions and then tried to work out if the celebrity's answer was right or wrong. If they guessed correctly, they won an X or an O for that space on the board and a line of three noughts or three crosses earned cash and prizes. Quick-fire gags and contrived answers abounded as the quiz element played second fiddle to comedy. Kenny Everett provided the wacky voice-overs. The celebrities taking part in the first show were Diana Dors, Leslie Crowther, Aimi McDonald, Alfred Marks, Vincent Price, Hermione Gingold, Terry Wogan, Arthur Mullard and William Rushton.

One segment of the programme saw the tables turned on host Bob Monkhouse. Each celebrity fired a question at him and his correct answers collected money for charity. *Celebrity Squares*, which was revived in 1993 after a 14-year absence, was a copy of the popular American game show *Hollywood Squares*.

Central

The ITV contractor for the Midlands, Central Independent Television came into being as a restructured version of ATV, which previously held the Midlands franchise. It went on air on 1 January 1982 and retained its franchise in 1991 with a bid of just £2,000 (there were no challengers). Central was later taken over by Carlton Communications, the franchise-holder for London weekdays, becoming known as Carlton Central, before being subsumed into ITV plc. Among the company's many programming successes were AUF WIEDERSEHEN, PET, CROSSROADS, BLOCKBUSTERS, THE PRICE IS RIGHT and SPITTING IMAGE.

Chair, The ✶✶

UK (Touchdown/BBC) Quiz. BBC 1 2002

Presenter **John McEnroe**

Creators **Julie Christie, Daryll McEwen, Brian Bigg**
Producer **Suzy Lamb**

Contestants' heart rates help determine quiz show success.

How well a contestant can cope under pressure is the hook of this quiz hosted by former tennis champ John McEnroe. Each entrant is wired to a monitor and, using his/her resting heart rate as a guide, is given a red-line heart rate threshold (70 per cent above resting rate) within which to work to win money. As pressure increases, the heart rate tends to increase. Additionally, to add to the discomfort, the threshold is lowered when questions are answered correctly. Any time spent above the red line results in prize money ebbing away. The key to success, therefore, is regulating the heart rate to keep below the red line. The series was based on a format from New Zealand that had already found success in the USA, although some of the excesses (using wild animals to scare contestants during questioning, for instance) were omitted.

Chalk ✶✶

UK (Pola Jones) Situation Comedy. BBC 1 1997

Eric Slatt .... **David Bamber**
Mr Richard Nixon .... **John Wells**
Dan McGill .... **Martin Ball**
Amanda Trippley .... **Amanda Boxer**
Suzy Travis .... **Nicola Walker**
Janet Slatt .... **Geraldine Fitzgerald**
Mr Carkdale .... **John Grillo**
Mr Humboldt .... **Andrew Livingston**
Mr Kennedy .... **Duncan Preston**
Jason Cockfoster .... **Damien Matthews**

Writer **Steven Moffat**
Producer **Andre Ptaszynski**

An incompetent deputy head's school is gripped by anarchy.

Mr Nixon is the good-hearted headmaster of Galfast High School – headmaster, that is, in name only, for he shows precious little leadership and has been known to hide himself away in cupboards. But when a school is as chaotic as this one, it's hardly a wonder. In his absence, the day-to-day organization falls to his hyperactive deputy, Eric Slatt, which only serves to deepen the many crises that face the school (most of Slatt's own making). Slatt is certainly keen, but regrettably he is also unbalanced, tactless, clumsy, snobby, sarcastic, at times pointlessly aggressive and always prone to appalling errors of judgement (an academic version of Basil Fawlty, it was widely noted). His long-suffering wife, Janet, works as the school secretary and other members of staff (resigned to days of misery) include blasphemous head of English Mr Carkdale, dopey Dan McGill, neurotic music teacher Amanda Trippley and new girl Suzi Travis – at last someone sane – for whom the experience is a real eye-opener. Two series of this typically farcical Steven Moffat comedy were produced, both shown in 1997. In the second series, Nixon was replaced by new, equally barking headmaster Mr Kennedy.

Chalk and Cheese ✶✶

UK (Thames) Situation Comedy. ITV 1979

David Finn .... **Michael Crawford**
Rose Finn .... **Gillian Martell**
Roger Scott .... **Robin Hawdon**
Amanda Scott .... **Julia Goodman**

Writer **Alex Shearer**
Producer **Michael Mills**

A working-class Londoner alienates his socially ambitious neighbour.

Still hot from the euphoria of SOME MOTHERS DO 'AVE 'EM, Michael Crawford starred in this much less successful sitcom for ITV. Crawford plays David Finn, a Hackney man who proudly lives down to his roots, despite now residing in a middle-class street. Finn is as irritating as Crawford's earlier Frank Spencer, especially to upwardly mobile marketing executive Roger Scott (cheese to Finn's chalk). The two meet in a maternity ward when their wives, Rose and Amanda, are giving birth. Unfortunately, Scott then moves next door to the Finns and can't escape his opinionated, annoying neighbour. Just one series was produced, based on a pilot episode called *Spasms* which starred Jonathan Pryce as Finn, Miriam Margolyes as his wife and Jenny Cox as Scott's wife (only Robin Hawdon continued into the series), and was shown in 1977.

Challenge Anneka ✶✶

UK (Mentorn). BBC 1 1989–95

Presenter **Anneka Rice**

Creator **Anneka Rice**
Producer **Tom Gutteridge**

Anneka Rice works against the clock to complete an ambitious project.

Piloted as part of CHILDREN IN NEED in 1988, when star Anneka Rice battled against the odds to arrange for an orchestra to perform the '1812 Overture' on the Thames, freeze part of the river for a skating ballet and organize a firework display, all within a few days, *Challenge Anneka* was soon launched as a series of 40-minute programmes. Each week, a new challenge was set by a member of the public – seemingly impossible tasks like staging a West End farce, or converting an old church into a circus training school, within 24 hours. Rice – unaware of what was involved until the start of the programme – then donned her bright overalls, boarded her 'Challenger' jeep and set about coercing people into helping her meet the challenge on time. All challenges were aimed at providing lasting benefit and those that gained included charities and other worthy causes. In her *Challenge* role, Rice once made a guest appearance in 2 POINT 4 CHILDREN.

Challenge TV

Satellite and cable channel that specializes in reruns of game shows and quizzes. Its daily fare is a diet of CATCHPHRASE, FAMILY FORTUNES, 3-2-1, THE KRYPTON FACTOR, 100% and the like, most seen long ago on terrestrial TV. Some new versions of favourites like SALE OF THE CENTURY and one or two first-run series such as *Splitsecond* and *Defectors* have brought the channel more up to date. Live viewer phone-in competitions, and the inclusion of non-quizzes like CANDID CAMERA from the USA, have broadened its appeal.

Challenge TV is part of the Flextech group but it evolved from a broadcaster called The Family Channel. That had been established in the USA in 1977 as CBN Satellite Service, providing religious programmes for the non-profit-making Christian Broadcasting Network, later developing into CBN Cable Network and focusing instead on 'wholesome', morally sound entertainment. The channel's Christian roots were further distanced by the change of the name to The Family Channel in 1988. It was launched under that name in the UK in September 1993, the same year that its then parent company, International Family Entertainment (IFE), bought the disenfranchised TVS and its Maidstone studios for £58 million. The Family Channel's UK broadcasts were based around material suitable for viewing by the entire family, mixing heart-warming drama series like *Road to Avonlea* and THE DARLING BUDS OF MAY with comedy and quiz shows, leading ultimately to the current quiz-show-led format and the change of name to Challenge TV.

Chalmers, Judith

OBE (1936–)

Manchester-born presenter and announcer, for many years host of ITV's travelogue, WISH YOU WERE HERE . . . ? Chalmers began her career as a child actor at the age of 13, working on BBC Radio's *Children's Hour*, and her later radio credits have included *Family Favourites, Woman's Hour* and her own Radio 2 morning show. On TV she has been seen on COME DANCING, *Afternoon Plus, Castle in the Country* and various beauty contests, including MISS WORLD. She has also been heard providing voices for the *Rex the Runt* animation. Married to former broadcaster Neil Durden-Smith, Chalmers is the mother of presenter Mark Durden-Smith and sister of actress/radio presenter Sandy Chalmers.

Chamberlain, Richard

(1935–)

A 1960s heart-throb actor with boyish looks, gaining international fame as the dedicated young Dr Kildare. Although initially typecast after playing Kildare for five years, Chamberlain has since managed to break into other starring roles in film and on TV, often in mini-series and most notably in *The Count of Monte Cristo* and *The Man in the Iron Mask*, and as Alexander McKeag in *Centennial*, as the English captain John Blackthorne (or Anjin) in SHOGUN and as the troubled Australian priest Ralph de Bricassart in THE THORN BIRDS. A recent guest appearance came in WILL AND GRACE.

Chambers ✶✶

UK (BBC) Situation Comedy. BBC 1 2000–1

John Fuller-Carp .... **John Bird**
Ruth Quirke .... **Sarah Lancashire**
Hilary Tripping .... **James Fleet**
Vince Griffin .... **Jonathan Kydd**
Alex Kahn .... **Nina Wadia**

Creator/Writer **Clive Coleman**
Producer **Paul Schlesinger**

● ***A team of legal eagles aspires to greatness but falls well short.***

Chambers (penned by barrister Clive Coleman) is set in Forecourt Buildings, a London legal practice, where greed, ambition and office politics are the dominant tendencies. John Fuller-Carp is the main man, an arrogant, mendacious, right-wing buffoon who, by hook or by crook, believes he can rise to the top of his trade and become a QC but clearly is always doomed to fail. His partners are inept and naive Hilary Tripping, an archetypal simple toff, and Ruth Quirke, who is rather better at her job than the others but whose disastrous personal life proves to be a real impediment to success. (Ruth is replaced in series two by new junior partner Alex Kahn.) Vince is their clerk of chambers.

After initial success on Radio 4 (from 1996), the same cast was reunited for this televisual outing, although Sarah Lancashire was in fact the second actress to play Ruth on radio, having taken over the role from Lesley Sharp.

Champion the Wonder Horse ✶✶

US (Flying A) Children's Adventure. BBC 1956–7 (US: CBS 1955–6)
DVD: Elstree Hill Entertainment

Ricky North .... **Barry Curtis**
Sandy North .... **Jim Bannon**
Will Calhoun .... **Francis McDonald**
Sheriff Powers .... **Ewing Mitchell**

Executive Producer **Armand Schaefer**
Producer **Louis Gray**

● ***A boy and his horse find adventure in the Wild West.***

Ricky North lives on his Uncle Sandy's North Ranch, somewhere in Texas, in the 1880s. His pride and joy is Champion, once leader of a herd of wild horses and now domesticated to the point where Ricky (but no one else) can safely ride him. From the very first episode, when Champion hauls Ricky to safety with a rope looped around his neck, it is clear that this is no ordinary nag. Indeed, the haughty stallion continues to earn his keep, constantly foiling criminals, alerting his owner to freak natural disasters and generally keeping the young boy out of trouble. Rebel, Ricky's German Shepherd dog, also lends a paw from time to time.

The series (known in America, and sometimes billed in the UK, as *The Adventures of Champion*) was created by Gene Autry in celebration of Champion, who was his own horse. Only 26 episodes were ever made.

Champions, The ✶✶

UK (Scoton/ITC) Science Fiction. ITV 1968–9
DVD: Granada Ventures

Craig Stirling .... **Stuart Damon**
Sharon McCready .... **Alexandra Bastedo**
Richard Barrett .... **William Gaunt**
Commander W. L. Tremayne .. **Anthony Nicholls**

Creators **Monty Berman, Dennis Spooner**
Producer **Monty Berman**

● ***Three superhumans help maintain peace in the world.***

In this 'Six Million Dollar Man meets *Lost Horizon*' caper, American Craig Stirling and Britons Sharon McCready and Richard Barrett work for the international peace agency Nemesis. But these are no run-of-the-mill secret agents. Having suffered a plane crash in the Himalayas on a mission to China, they were saved and healed by an old man from a reclusive Tibetan civilization. Thus endowed with superhuman powers, they now have senses so finely tuned that they can hear, see and smell acutely. They also have enhanced strength and stamina, and special mental powers like telepathy.

Promising to preserve the lost city's anonymity, the trio return to the West and begin to use their remarkable talents on behalf of Nemesis. Their boss, Tremayne (based in Geneva), issues them with assignments aimed at defusing international flashpoints and potential sources of world tension. The policy is to maintain the existing balance of power between nations. The agents' special attributes, however, always remain a secret, and they are certainly not infallible or invincible, needing to work very much as a team. Although they are as mortal as any other human, they become 'Champions of law, order and justice'.

Chance in a Million ✶✶

UK (Thames) Situation Comedy. Channel 4 1984; 1986

Tom Chance .... **Simon Callow**
Alison Little .... **Brenda Blethyn**
Mr Little .... **Ronnie Stevens**
Hugh Walters
Mrs Little .... **Deddie Davies**

Writers **Andrew Norriss, Richard Fegen**
Producer **Michael Mills**

● ***Muddle and misfortune beset a man with an unusual speech impediment.***

Tom Chance is a man for whom luck is never in. Nothing, for him, ever pans out as it should. Coincidences work against the chivalrous, emotionally immature bachelor, such as when he goes on a blind date and meets the wrong woman. However, the girl he does meet, Alison Little, a timid librarian, eventually becomes his wife, much against the advice of her mum and dad. Chance also has the strange habit of speaking in truncated sentences, rather like a telegram is written, omitting definite and indefinite articles. Little wonder confusion reigns.

Chancer ✶✶

UK (Central) Drama. ITV 1990–1
DVD: Network

Stephen Crane/Derek 'Dex' Love .... **Clive Owen**
James Blake .... **Leslie Phillips**
Joanna 'Jo' Franklyn .... **Susannah Harker**
Jamie Douglas .... **Sean Pertwee**
Penny Nichols .... **Caroline Langrishe**
Victoria Douglas .... **Lynsey Baxter**
Robert Douglas .... **Benjamin Whitrow**
Gavin Nichols .... **Matthew Marsh**
Thomas Franklyn .... **Peter Vaughan**
Marcus Worton .... **Stephen Tompkinson**
Piers Garfield-Ward .... **Simon Shepherd**
Richard Nichols .... **Nicholas Shelton**
Tom Nichols .... **Sam London**
Colin Morris .... **Robert Glenister**
Mary Douglas .... **Caroline Blakiston**
Willy Stebbings .... **Ralph Riach**
John Love .... **Tom Bell**
Tommy Love .... **Wayne Foskett**
Anna .... **Louise Lombard**

Writers **Guy Andrews, Simon Bruce, Tony Grounds**
Executive Producer **Ted Childs**
Producer **Sarah D. Wilson**

● ***A slick, young wheeler-dealer comes to the rescue of an ailing motor company.***

Banker Stephen Crane represents new money. An arrogant yuppie type with a penchant for living on the edge, he knows all about computer fiddles, insider dealing and other City scams. Called in to save struggling Manchester sports-car firm Douglas Motors from ruin, Crane turns the company around but finds his past closing in on him. He is eventually cornered by the police, who want him for a fraud he perpetrated while still a teenager. Also seen are corrupt financier Jimmy Blake (Crane's former boss at the bank), sisters Penny Nichols and Victoria Douglas, and the girl in Crane's life, Jo Franklyn. In the second series, after six months behind bars, Crane emerges into the outside world with a change of identity. Now using his real name of Derek Love, and familiarly known as Dex, he leaves the flashy suits of City life behind him, in favour of new delvings into the world of fraud. Dutch art treasures and counterfeit casino chips are his adopted devices and he becomes involved in a bid to save an ancestral home. He still holds a torch for Jo, though mysterious secretary Anna also has her attractions. Blake is also on the scene again, this time as the co-owner of the casino. Jan Hammer composed the theme music.

Chandler and Co. ✶✶

UK (Skreba/BBC) Drama. BBC 1 1994–5

Elly Chandler .... **Catherine Russell**
Dee Tate .... **Barbara Flynn**
Larry Blakeston .... **Peter Capaldi**
David Tate .... **Struan Rodger**
Kate Phillips .... **Susan Fleetwood**
Benji Phillips .... **Graham McGrath**
Simon Wood .... **Bill Britten**
Dr Mark Judd .... **Adrian Lukis**

Creator **Paula Milne**

Producer **Anne Skinner**
Executive Producer **Michael Wearing**

Sisters-in-law set up their own private detection agency.
Elly Chandler has recently divorced her philandering husband, Max, and needs a new challenge in life. Inspired by Larry Blakeston, the private eye she hired to expose her husband's infidelity, she decides to set up her own investigation firm, roping in Max's sister, Dee, and turning to the now-retired Blakeston for advice and surveillance equipment. Dee is a reluctant partner and has told her husband, David, that she is going to be involved only until Elly has found her feet. However, it is hard for Dee to detach herself from the business, even though detective work turns out to be a lot less fun than the girls have imagined, bringing danger to themselves and their families.

In the second series, set a couple of years on, Dee has finally left the agency and Larry has also departed. A more confident Elly gains a new partner, Kate Phillips, and a new boyfriend, Dr Mark Judd.

Changing Rooms ✳✳

UK (Bazal/BBC) Lifestyle. BBC 2 1996–7; BBC 1 1998–2004
DVD: Warner Vision International

Presenters **Carol Smillie, Laurence Llewelyn-Bowen**

Executive Producer **Linda Clifford**
Producers **Ann Hill, Pauline Doidge, Caspar Peacock, Ann Booth-Clibborn, Mary Ramsay, Susannah Walker, Suzy Carter, Nigel Mercer, Claire Richmond, Joanne Haddock**

Neighbours simultaneously redecorate each other's home.
With a time-limit of two days and a budget of just £500, two sets of neighbour friends attempted to improve a room in each other's home in this surprisingly successful series. Given the help of a professional designer (Graham Wynne, Michael Jewitt, Laura McCree, Oliver Heath, Gordon Williams, Rowena Johnson and, more notably, Linda Barker, Laurence Llewelyn-Bowen and Anna Ryder Richardson), plus the assistance of crafty carpenter 'Handy Andy' Kane, they set about transforming the look of one of their friends' rooms. The series inspired viewing DIYers, but has also been panned for some of its over-the-top designs, quick fixes and cheapo decorations. At the end of each show, the neighbours were taken back to their own home and shown the results – often to delight, but occasionally to heartbreak. Carol Smillie introduced the programme, and reported on progress throughout, until 2003, when Llewelyn-Bowen moved to front of house.

Changing Rooms, beginning modestly on BBC 2 but transferring to BBC 1 after two years, was one of the first of a new tranche of lifestyle/DIY programmes – *Home Front, All Mod Cons, Change That*, etc. – that had viewers queuing outside B&Q on a Sunday morning. The series merged with a sister programme for a special in 2000 entitled *When Changing Rooms Met Ground Force*, in which interior decorating and gardening specialists switched jobs.

Channel

The frequency allocated to a TV service.

Channel 3

See *ITV*.

Channel 4

Britain finally received its fourth channel in 1982, after years of debate. Channel 4 was set up as a wholly owned subsidiary of the IBA, with the brief to serve minority interests and encourage innovation through programming supplied by outside independent producers. Its first chief executive was Jeremy Isaacs and he 'sugared the pill' of minority programming by buying in popular overseas series like CHEERS and *The Paul Hogan Show*. The channel – first airing on 2 November 1982 – proved more successful than doubters had predicted. Some felt that its narrow target audience would not generate sufficient advertising revenue. However, it did so well that the basis of its advertising sales was changed in 1993. Whereas sales were originally the responsibility of the other ITV companies, who then paid for the upkeep of Channel 4 through a levy on their incomes, since 1993 Channel 4 has sold its own advertising. At the same time, its corporate structure was changed so that it became a non-profit-making organization licensed and regulated by the ITC.

Channel 4 has always courted controversy and provided a valuable mouthpiece for minority groups, but it has also excelled at commissioning award-winning films. *Room with a View, the Madness of King George* and *Four Weddings and a Funeral* are just three examples. In recent years, the channel's innovative coverage of cricket also reaped acclaim. The first programme seen on Channel 4 was COUNTDOWN, which is still being screened today. Almost as durable was the revolutionary soap BROOKSIDE, and other Channel 4 successes have included THE TUBE, GBH, THE FAR PAVILIONS, FATHER TED, BIG BROTHER and *Channel 4 News*. Michael Grade became chief executive (1989–97), following Jeremy Isaacs's departure, and was himself succeeded in the post by Michael Jackson. Jackson resigned in 2001 and was replaced by Mark Thompson, who left to become BBC Director General in 2004 and was replaced by Andy Duncan. In 1998 Channel 4 launched Film Four, a subscription-based satellite/digital channel dedicated to movies. In 2001 a sister digital channel called E4, majoring on youth entertainment, arrived followed by a more adult digital channel, More 4, in 2005, focusing on films, documentaries, current affairs and drama.

Channel 4 does not cover Wales, which is served by a bilingual channel, S4C.

Channel 5

See *five*.

Channel Television

The smallest of the ITV contractors, Channel Television went on air on 1 September 1962 to serve the various Channel Islands (which were represented in the company's first logo of six linked hexagons). Early on there were serious doubts as to whether such a small audience would generate enough advertising income to keep an independent television service alive, but Channel is still afloat – and independent – after more than 40 years. (A reflection of the size of the area was the fact that the company retained its franchise in the 1991 auctions with a bid of just £1,000.) To make ends meet, at various times Channel has been forced to link up with WESTWARD, TSW, TVS and MERIDIAN for advertising sales and administration. These companies have also been the suppliers of ITV national output to Channel, beaming programmes over the English Channel for relay by local transmitters.

Another consequence of low advertising turnover has been the almost negligible contribution Channel has been able to make to network programming (the most prominent examples have been editions of *About Britain* and HIGHWAY), although Channel – or CTV – has won many fans for its local news and regional documentary service, including some programmes in French and Portuguese. The station mascot, Oscar Puffin, has enjoyed his own children's series, *Puffin's Pla(i)ce*, for many years. Channel operates main studios in Jersey, with smaller studios in Guernsey, and remains independent of the newly formed ITV plc.

Chapman, Graham

(1941–89)

Tall, satirical comedian, a qualified doctor and stalwart of the MONTY PYTHON team. Previously Chapman had been seen with John Cleese and others in AT LAST THE 1948 SHOW and he was also a prolific writer for other series (usually in conjunction with Cleese). His script credits included THE FROST REPORT, *Marty, Broaden Your Mind*, THE TWO RONNIES and the DOCTOR IN THE HOUSE sequence of sitcoms, as well as the Ronnie Corbett series NO – THAT'S ME OVER HERE, NOW LOOK HERE . . . and *The Prince of Denmark* (the last two with Barry Cryer).

Chappell, Eric

(1933–)

British comedy writer, responsible for some of ITV's most popular sitcoms, namely RISING DAMP, THE SQUIRRELS, THE BOUNDER, ONLY WHEN I LAUGH, *Misfits*, FIDDLERS THREE, HAGGARD, HOME TO ROOST, SINGLES and DUTY FREE (the last two in collaboration with Jean Warr).

Character Generator

A device for superimposing text (captions, names, etc.) on to the TV picture. Also known as a caption generator, or by tradenames like Anchor and Aston.

Charles, Craig

(1964–)

Liverpudlian poet, comedian and actor, best known for starring as space slob Dave Lister in RED DWARF. Charles has also starred as CAPTAIN BUTLER, presented *Them and Us, Night Network*, THE BIG BREAKFAST, *Craig Goes Mad in Melbourne* and ROBOT WARS, narrated *Takeshi's Castle* for Challenge TV, and appeared in *The Marksman*, THE GOVERNOR (Eugene Buffy), EASTENDERS, HOLBY CITY, DOCTORS and CORONATION STREET (Lloyd Mullaney).

Charles II – The Power and the Passion ★★

UK (BBC/A&E) Historical Drama. BBC 1 2003
DVD: BBC

Charles II	**Rufus Sewell**
George Villiers, Duke of Buckingham	**Rupert Graves**
Barbara Villiers, Lady Castlemaine	**Helen McCrory**
Sir Edward Hyde	**Ian McDiarmid**
Queen Henrietta Maria	**Diana Rigg**
James, Duke of York	**Charlie Creed-Mills**
Queen Catharine of Braganza	**Shirley Henderson**
Lord Shaftesbury	**Martin Freeman**
Monmouth	**Christian Coulson**
Gen. Monck	**Garry Cooper**
Charles I	**Martin Turner**
Anne Hyde	**Tabitha Wady**
Hopkins	**Nick Bagnall**
Ormonde	**Peter Wight**
Arlington	**Robert East**
Clifford	**Dorian Lough**
Lady Frances Stewart	**Alice Patten**
Sir Edmund Berry Godfrey	**David Bradley**
Minette	**Anne-Marie Duff**
Louise de Kéroualle	**Mélanie Thierry**
Louis XIV	**Perkins Lyautey**
Monsieur	**Cyrille Thouvenin**
Nell Gwynn	**Emma Pierson**
Earl of Danby	**Shaun Dingwall**
William of Orange	**Jochum Ten Haaf**
Titus Oates	**Eddie Marsan**

Writer **Adrian Hodges**
Executive Producers **Laura Mackie, Delia Fine**
Producer **Kate Harwood**

● ***Bold reconstruction of the reign of the Merry Monarch.*** Beginning with his impoverished life in exile in the 1640s–1650s, and ending with his death in 1685, this raunchy four-part dramatization of the life of King Charles II explores his return to the throne after the death of Oliver Cromwell, and his gory persecution of the murderers of his father, Charles I. It delves into his religious ambivalence at a time of Protestant/Catholic conflict, and follows his reaction to the major events of his reign, the Great Plague and the Great Fire of London. While reflecting his power, it also wallows in his passion, revealing (in more ways than one) the many women in his life, from his long-suffering yet loyal Portuguese wife, Catharine of Braganza, to orange-seller Nell Gwynn, via villainous long-term mistress (and mother of at least five of his illegitimate children) Barbara Villiers, the hard-to-get Lady Frances Stewart and duplicitous French aristocrat Louise de Kéroualle. Buckingham is the king's oldest friend. Partly filmed in the Czech Republic, the serial – directed by Joe Wright – was renamed *The Last King* for transmission in the US.

Charlie Chan

See *New Adventures of Charlie Chan, The.*

Charlie's Angels ✱✱

US (Spelling-Goldberg) Detective Drama. ITV 1977–82
(US: ABC 1976–81)
DVD: Sony

Sabrina Duncan .... **Kate Jackson**
Jill Munroe .... **Farrah Fawcett-Majors**
Kelly Garrett .... **Jaclyn Smith**
Kris Munroe .... **Cheryl Ladd**
Tiffany Welles .... **Shelley Hack**
Julie Rogers .... **Tanya Roberts**
John Bosley .... **David Doyle**
Charlie Townsend .... **John Forsythe** *(voice only)*

Executive Producers **Aaron Spelling, Leonard Goldberg**
Producers **Rick Husky, David Levinson, Barney Rosenzweig**

Three beautiful ex-policewomen work undercover for a mysterious detective agency boss.

In this glitzy romp, Sabrina Duncan, Kelly Garrett and Jill Munroe are the original team of Angels – former police academy girls 'rescued' by Charlie Townsend to work for his Los Angeles detective agency, Townsend Investigations. Sabrina, nominal leader of the trio, is a multilinguist, Kelly is a former showgirl, while Jill is an athletic blonde. Charlie himself is never seen, only heard on the telephone (and in the intro), leaving the avuncular John Bosley to act as the girls' personal contact.

The Angels are able to take on missions that are out of bounds for most other investigators. Their stunning looks allow them to work undercover (often with little cover), as nightclub singers, models, strippers and even army recruits. Although their assignments are rough and dangerous, the girls' appearance is never less than immaculate (their skimpy outfits – often without bras – led to *Charlie's Angels* being labelled as 'jiggly' TV).

The first changes in the series came with the departure of Farrah Fawcett-Majors (later just Fawcett after her divorce from Lee Majors) to pursue a film career. She did agree to make occasional guest appearances, but her permanent replacement was Alan Ladd's daughter-in-law, Cheryl, as Jill's younger sister, Kris. Two more Angels are also brought in later. Tiffany Welles, daughter of a Connecticut police chief, takes over from Sabrina, then she, in turn, is replaced by Julie Rogers. The voice of the enigmatic Charlie was provided by John Forsythe, later Blake Carrington in DYNASTY.

A film version starring Drew Barrymore, Cameron Diaz and Lucy Liu was released in 2000, with a sequel, *Charlie's Angels: Full Throttle*, following in 2003.

Charmer, The ✱✱

UK (LWT) Drama. ITV 1987
DVD: Cinema Club

Ralph Ernest Gorse .... **Nigel Havers**
Donald Stimpson .... **Bernard Hepton**
Joan Plumleigh-Bruce .... **Rosemary Leach**
Clarice Mannors .... **Fiona Fullerton**
Pamela Bennett .... **Abigail McKern**
Alison Warren .... **Judy Parfitt**

Writer **Allan Prior**
Executive Producer **Nick Elliott**
Producer **Philip Hinchcliffe**

A suave young con-merchant wins the hearts of wealthy ladies.

Ralph Gorse is a cad. Exercising his skill at smooth talk, he works his way around the seaside resorts and towns of 1930s Britain preying on rich, gullible ladies who just cannot resist his good looks and gentle manner. No sooner have they taken him to their hearts than he is away with the family silver or at least a wallet full of 'borrowed' notes. It all works very well until he meets the delightfully tweedy Joan Plumleigh-Bruce in Reading and dupes her out of £1,000. Gorse is himself infatuated with the lovely Clarice Mannors and – despite driving a flashy blue MG Magna – needs every penny of Joan's money to support his claims to Clarice's attentions. Regrettably, he has not taken into account Joan's estate agent friend, Donald Stimpson, who is intent on revenge. The series, which begins in September 1938, was based on books by Patrick Hamilton.

Charters and Caldicott ✱✱

UK (BBC/Network Seven) Detective Drama. BBC 1 1985

Charters .... **Robin Bailey**
Caldicott .... **Michael Aldridge**

Writer **Keith Waterhouse**
Producer **Ron Craddock**

Two retired old buffers immerse themselves in murder.

Appearing initially as bit characters in Hitchcock's *The Lady Vanishes* in 1938, Charters and Caldicott were portrayed by actors Basil Radford and Naunton Wayne as a couple of well-meaning, upper class twits with no grasp of reality. Their eccentric Englishmen abroad roles simply brought a touch of comic relief to an otherwise spooky and melodramatic tale. Soon afterwards, however, they resurfaced in another cameo role in *Night Train to Munich*, before gaining top billing in their own vehicle, *Crooks' Tour*, in 1940. Over 40 years later they became stars of their own BBC series.

Now in retirement, the two perpetual schoolboys were played by Robin Bailey and Michael Aldridge. They enjoy regular monthly lunches at their Pall Mall club, where they discuss the inadequacies of women, the wonders of cricket and how things simply aren't as they used to be. Strictly public school, they pity people who do not share their backgrounds and interests, and voice prejudiced concerns about the state of the world. Charters, a widower, lives in a country cottage near Reigate and religiously hails a Green Line bus on the first Friday of every month to meet his chum, Caldicott, at his residence in Viceroy Court, Kensington. However, when a girl's body is discovered at Caldicott's flats, the old buffers find themselves embarking on the trail of a murderer.

Chat Show

See *Talk show*.

Chataway, Sir Christopher

(1931–)

London-born middle-distance athlete turned broadcaster who read the news for ITN in its early days. He later joined the BBC's PANORAMA, before switching to politics, becoming a Conservative MP and subsequently Postmaster-General. He was the BBC's first *Sports Personality of the Year*, in 1954.

Cheaters, The ✶

UK (Danziger) Detective Drama. ITV 1961–2

John Hunter .... **John Ireland**
Walter Allen .... **Robert Ayres**

Producers **Edward J. Danziger, Harry Lee Danziger**

● ***The investigations of an insurance inspector.***

The door-to-door inquiries of claims inspector John Hunter form the basis of this series. Diligent and honest, Hunter and his assistant, Walter Allen, are relentless in their pursuit of nasty people who try to swindle his company, the Eastern Insurance Company, at the ultimate expense of decent policy-holders. Those who attempt crafty frauds and fiddles are quickly sussed out. Star John Ireland went on to play Jed Colby in RAWHIDE.

Checkland, Sir Michael

(1936–)

BBC Director-General from 1987 to 1993, when he was succeeded in rather controversial circumstances by his former deputy, John Birt. Checkland had previously been Deputy Director-General himself (from 1985) and was an expert in the financial affairs of the Corporation, joining the BBC in 1964 as an accountant and working his way up to chief accountant status. In 1977 he became controller of planning and resource management for the television division. The announcement (surprisingly well in advance) of John Birt's promotion to the Director-General position made Checkland's last two years in the position somewhat uncomfortable and led some commentators to label him a lame duck controller. Checkland became a member of the Independent Television Commission in 1997.

Cheers ✶✶✶✶

US (Paramount) Situation Comedy. Channel 4 1982–93 (US: NBC 1982–93)
DVD: Paramount

Sam Malone .... **Ted Danson**
Diane Chambers .... **Shelley Long**
Carla Tortelli/LeBec .... **Rhea Perlman**
Ernie Pantusso ('Coach') .... **Nicholas Colasanto**
Norm Peterson .... **George Wendt**
Cliff Clavin .... **John Ratzenberger**
Dr Frasier Crane .... **Kelsey Grammer**
Woody Boyd .... **Woody Harrelson**
Rebecca Howe .... **Kirstie Alley**
Dr Lilith Sternin/Crane .... **Bebe Neuwirth**
Janet Eldridge .... **Kate Mulgrew**
Evan Drake .... **Tom Skerritt**
Eddie LeBec .... **Jay Thomas**
Robin Colcord .... **Roger Rees**
Kelly Gaines/Boyd .... **Jackie Swanson**
John Hill .... **Keene Curtis**
Paul .... **Paul Willson**

Creators/Producers **Glen Charles, Les Charles, James Burrows**

● ***Laughs with the staff and regulars at a Boston bar.***

Cheers bar (established 1895) is owned by former Boston Red Sox pitcher Sam 'Mayday' Malone, a reformed alcoholic and a successful womanizer. But he meets his match in the first episode of this cult comedy with the arrival of Diane Chambers, an over-educated academic researcher. Ditched by her husband-to-be, she accepts Sam's offer of a job as a waitress, a move which leads to years of good-natured sparring and on-off relationships with her boss.

Revolving around Sam and Diane's intermittent romance are the lives of the other staff and bar regulars. Carla Tortelli, a sharp-tongued, streetwise mother of countless kids, is the perfect antidote to the sophisticated Diane, and Ernie Pantusso, the mild-mannered ex-Red Sox coach, is another leading character in the show's early years. His naïvety and absent-mindedness were much missed when actor Nicholas Colasanto died in 1985, but the gap is soon filled with the arrival of Woody Boyd, a young farmboy from the backwaters of Hanover, Indiana. He comes to Boston to meet Coach, his pen-pal, takes a job behind the bar and eventually marries the extremely wealthy but rather dizzy Kelly Gaines.

Woody's innocence and gullibility are genially abused by regulars Norm, Cliff and Frasier. Norm, an accountant, spends most of his waking life in Cheers savouring freedom from his wife, Vera, while know-all Cliff, the mailman, is the butt of all the jokes. The third regular is Frasier Crane, an insecure psychiatrist who is introduced as Diane's new fiancé. However, their relationship breaks up and the pompous, emotional shrink joins Cliff and Norm as one of the losers hugging the bar. He eventually finds his perfect partner in a severe, intellectual colleague, Dr Lilith Sternin, and they have a son, Frederick.

Four years into its run, *Cheers* was forced into a major recast. Not only does Coach die but Diane, too, says goodbye to the bar – and to Sam – taking herself away for six months to write a book. Sam knows that she will not return, so he sells the bar to a leisure conglomerate, buys a boat and plans to sail around the world. When the next series opens, Sam's boat has sunk and he has returned to Cheers to talk his way into a job. Only this time he is just a member of staff, responsible to sultry new manageress Rebecca Howe. Another love-hate relationship begins.

Frigid and sycophantic, Rebecca is a real career-chaser. For a while she pursues company bigwig Evan Drake, then her attention turns to smarmy English businessman Robin Colcord. When Colcord uses her to gain inside knowledge of her company in order to launch a take-over bid, Sam shops him and is given back his bar for only $1 as a reward. Rebecca stays on as manageress and later as a partner.

In the extended final episode of *Cheers*, Diane walks back into Sammy's life. Her book has been published and has picked up a major award, but she and Sam still cannot make their relationship work, and she leaves once more. This time, it is clearly for good.

Although the inside shots of the bar were studio-produced, the exterior of Cheers was a real Boston bar, The Bull and Finch, which now does a roaring tourist trade. After 11 years one element of *Cheers* was allowed to live on as Frasier, now separated from Lilith, was given his own spin-off series, FRASIER.

Chef! ✶✶

UK (APC/Crucial) Situation Comedy. BBC 1 1993–4; 1996
DVD: BBC

Gareth Blackstock .... **Lenny Henry**
Janice Blackstock .... **Caroline Lee Johnson**
Everton .... **Roger Griffiths**
Lucinda .... **Claire Skinner**
Piers .... **Gary Parker**

Otto .... **Erkan Mustafa**
Lola .... **Elizabeth Bennett**
Gustave .... **Ian McNeice**
Jeff Nuttall
Donald .... **Gary Bakewell**
Crispin .... **Tim Matthews**
Alice .... **Hilary Lyon**
Debra .... **Pui Fan Lee**
Alphonse .... **Jean Luc Rebaliati**
Cyril Bryson .... **Dave Hill**
Savanna .... **Lorelei King**
Renee Bryson .... **Sophie Walker**
Vincenzo .... **Vincent Walsh**

Creator **Lenny Henry**
Writer **Peter Tilbury**
Executive Producer **Polly McDonald**
Producer **Charlie Hanson**

An egocentric chef strives to succeed in his own restaurant.

Gareth Blackstock is the gifted *chef de cuisine* at Le Château Anglais, a stately French restaurant deep in the Oxfordshire Cotswolds. When the Château runs into financial difficulties, he and his wife, Janice, sell Linden Cottage, their picture-postcard home, and buy control themselves. Keen to build on his Michelin two-star status, Blackstock finds his ambitions hindered by his inept kitchen hands, especially the accident-prone soul food specialist, Everton. No one escapes the chef's fits of pique, as he lambasts staff and customers alike with pearls of sarcastic abuse. But, although he rules with a rod of iron, Gareth deep down nurses a fragile ego. This is tested particularly in the third and final series (two years after the second), when his marriage breaks down and the restaurant is bought by the rather down-market Cyril Bryson, whose spoilt daughter, Renee, comes to work in the kitchen.

Well supported by a team of top chef advisers, particularly John Burton-Race, Lenny Henry and writer Peter Tilbury – who scripted the first two series – gave viewers a revealing insight into the world of a top kitchen, with its exacting standards and finest attention to detail, gently parodying the celebrity status of Britain's leading chefs.

Chegwin, Keith

(1957–)

Exuberant Liverpudlian actor, presenter and musician (in the band Kenny), whose earliest appearances were in programmes like JUNIOR SHOWTIME, THE LIVER BIRDS, THE TOMORROW PEOPLE, *My Old Man, The Wackers* (Raymond Clarkson) and OPEN ALL HOURS. In 1976 his big break came with MULTI-COLOURED SWAP SHOP, for which he was roving reporter/entertainer. He stayed with the Saturday morning show when it evolved into *Saturday Superstore*, and was married for some time to one of his co-presenters, Maggie Philbin. His own kids' music show, *Cheggers Plays Pop*, followed, as well as a couple of investigative series, *Cheggers' Action Reports* and *Cheggers Checks It Out*. In the 1990s he appeared regularly on satellite television, hosted THE BIG BREAKFAST, featured on GMTV and presented the revival of IT'S A KNOCKOUT. In 2000 he controversially appeared nude in the Channel 5 naturists' game show, *Naked Jungle*. Other credits include *Cheggers's Challenge* and *Fear Factor* (for Sky One). Chegwin is the brother of radio broadcaster Janice Long.

Chelmsford 123 ★★

UK (Hat Trick) Situation Comedy. Channel 4 1988; 1990

Aulus Paulinus .... **Jimmy Mulville**
Badvoc .... **Rory McGrath**
Grasientus .... **Philip Pope**
Functio .... **Robert Austin**
Mungo .... **Neil Pearson**
Blag .... **Howard Lew Lewis**
Gargamadua .... **Erika Hoffman**
Wolfbane .... **Geoffrey McGivern**

Writers **Rory McGrath, Jimmy Mulville**
Producers **Denise O'Donoghue, Adrian Bate**

A refined Roman is exiled to the hardships of chilly Britain.

The year is AD 123. In Rome, Aulus Paulinus makes a grave error. He accidentally insults the girlfriend of the emperor and for his sins is assigned to the worst job in the empire – governor of Britain. Reluctantly taking up his new position in Chelmsford, the pampered Paulinus suffers immediately from the miserable climate and atrocious food. Worse still, he comes face to face with his new sparring partner, the hairy Badvoc, leader of the beer-swilling Celts. Badvoc is an uncouth, cunning man who can't decide whether to fight the Romans or merely swindle them of all their wealth. Opening scenes in Latin, with English subtitles, marked a first for British sitcoms.

Chelsea at Nine ★

UK (Granada) Variety. ITV 1957–60

Producer **Denis Forman**

International cabaret direct from a London theatre.

Chelsea at Nine was Monday night's big variety offering, presented by Granada Television from its Chelsea Palace theatre. It showcased top transatlantic stars (the likes of Billie Holiday, Alan Young and Ferrante and Teicher appeared), with American directors employed to give the show an international sheen. As well as major entertainment names of the day, the programme included regular comedy skits from the team of Mai Zetterling, Dennis Price and Irene Handl, and excerpts from contemporary theatre shows, while The Granadiers were the house song-and-dance troupe, directed by Cliff Adams. With a timing change, the series became *Chelsea at Eight* in 1958 and, in the same year, adopted the title of *Chelsea Summertime* for its seasonal programmes. The first compere was David Hutcheson; Bernard Braden also hosted.

Chesney, Ronald

(1920–)

British comedy writer, usually in tandem with Ronald Wolfe. Together they penned THE RAG TRADE, MEET THE WIFE, THE BED-SIT GIRL, *Sorry I'm Single, Wild, Wild Women*, ON THE BUSES, *Don't Drink the Water*, ROMANY JONES, *Yus My Dear, Watch This Space, Take a Letter, Mr Jones . . .*, an episode of 'ALLO 'ALLO and sketches for Dora Bryan in *According to Dora*. Chesney also collaborated with Marty Feldman (and Wolfe) on the 1950s series *Educating Archie*. Chesney is also noted as a professional harmonica player.

Chessgame ✶✶

UK (Granada) Secret Agent Drama. ITV 1983

David Audley	**Terence Stamp**
Nick Hannah	**Michael Culver**
Faith Steerforth/Audley	**Carmen Du Sautoy**
Hugh Roskill	**Robin Sachs**
Sir Alec Russell	**John Horsley**
Guy Llewellyn	**John Rowe**
Igon Panin	**George Pravda**
Curieff	**Christopher Rozycki**
Jake Shapiro	**John Grillo**
Grace Appleby	**Carolyn Colquhoun**
Dan McLachlan	**Anthony Calf**
Polly Epton	**Caroline Bliss**
Sir Geoffrey Hobson	**Willoughby Gray**
Handforth-Jones	**Richard Pearson**
Charles Epton	**Seymour Green**
Jean Sherman	**Matyelok Gibbs**

Writers **Murray Smith, John Brason**
Producer **Richard Everitt**

● ***The cases of an academic-turned-intelligence officer.***
When a lake is drained in order to build a new motorway, the wreckage of a plane that crashed 27 years before is discovered. Its cargo is missing and this intrigues both British intelligence and their Russian counterparts. Oxford don David Audley is drafted in to investigate this and other mysteries during this drama's six-episode run. At one point a member of Audley's team is killed when attention turns to Middle Eastern terrorists; at another, the strange death of an Oxford student leads to yet more subterfuge. *Chessgame* was based on novels by Anthony Price and gave movie favourite Terence Stamp his first major television role.

Cheyenne ✶✶

US (Warner Brothers) Western. ITV 1958–64 (US: ABC 1955–63)
DVD: Warner Home Video (Region 1 only)

Cheyenne Bodie	**Clint Walker**
Bronco Layne	**Ty Hardin**
Smitty	**L. Q. Jones**

● ***A wanderer works his way across the American West.***
Based on the 1947 film of the same name starring Dennis Morgan, *Cheyenne* relates the adventures of Cheyenne Bodie, a drifter who travels the Wild West in the years following the Civil War. The hero is a frontier scout, a strapping giant of a man who has learnt Indian skills and now strays from town to town, from job to job and from girl to girl. Constantly falling foul of outlaws and villains, Bodie is often on the receiving end of a severe beating. He does, however, enjoy some friendly company during the first series in the shape of Smitty, a mapmaker.

Of as much interest as the programme itself were the behind-the-scenes wrangles. When Clint Walker walked out after a legal dispute with Warner Brothers, he was temporarily replaced in the lead by Ty Hardin as Bronco Layne. When Walker was reinstated, Hardin was not dropped but given his own spin-off series, BRONCO.

Chicago Hope ✶✶

US (David E. Kelley/Twentieth Century-Fox) Medical Drama. BBC 1 1995–2000 (US: CBS 1994–2000)

Dr Jeffrey Geiger	**Mandy Patinkin**
Dr Aaron Shutt	**Adam Arkin**
Nurse Camille Shutt	**Roxanne Hart**
Dr Phillip Watters	**Hector Elizondo**
Dr Arthur Thurmond	**E. G. Marshall**
Alan Birch	**Peter MacNicol**
Angela Giandamenico	**Roma Maffia**
Dr Karen Antonovich	**Margaret Colin**
Dr Daniel Nyland	**Thomas Gibson**
Dr Geri Infante	**Diane Venora**
Dr Billy Kronk	**Peter Berg**
Dr Dennis Hancock	**Vondie Curtis-Hall**
Laurie Geiger	**Kim Greist**
Dr Kate Austin	**Christine Lahti**
Dr Diane Grad	**Jayne Brook**
Maggie Atkisson	**Robyn Lively**
Dr John Sutton	**Jamey Sheridan**
Judge Harold Aldrich	**Stephen Elliott**

Creator **David E. Kelley**
Executive Producers **John Tinker, Bill D'Elia**

● ***Earnest medical drama set in a busy city hospital.***
Chicago Hope Hospital, in the city of the same name, has more than its fair share of medical and personal crises, but in a much more restrained, soapy way than in its US rival ER, which is also set in the Windy City (and strangely was its cross-channel rival on Thursday evenings in the US: *ER* won that battle, but *Chicago Hope* prospered in another time-slot for several more years).

The state-of-the-art hospital specializes in medical innovation, and chief among the healers are estranged surgeon and wife Aaron and Camille Shutt, along with level-headed chief surgeon Phillip Watters, fading doctor Arthur Thurmond and the gifted but unnecessarily rude and explosive Dr Jeffrey Geiger. Also prominent is legal adviser Alan 'The Eel' Birch. Viewers of a fragile constitution quailed at the sight of so many organ close-ups and pumping blood, and UK transmission was gradually switched from Saturday peak hours to late Tuesday nights, as the series began to fade out on this side of the Atlantic.

Chico and the Man ✶✶

US (Komack/Wolper) Situation Comedy. BBC 1 1974–5 (US: NBC 1974–8)
DVD: Warner Home Video (Region 1 only)

Ed Brown ('The Man')	**Jack Albertson**
Chico Rodriguez	**Freddie Prinze**
Louie Wilson	**Scatman Crothers**
Mabel	**Bonnie Boland**
Mando	**Isaac Ruiz**
Raul Garcia	**Gabriel Melgar**

Creator/Executive Producer **James Komack**

● ***A smart-talking young Mexican and a cantankerous all-American run a backstreet garage.***
Grouchy old widower Ed Brown owns a run-down garage in the suburbs of Los Angeles. One day he gains a new business partner with the arrival of young Mexican-American ('Chicano') Chico Rodriguez. Chico flatters 'The Man' with his

interest in the operation but Brown is also more than a bit wary of why Chico should want to get involved. His fears are soon laid to rest, however, when the young man cleans up the joint, touts for new business and sets up home in an old truck inside the garage. The chalk and cheese relationship between Chico and The Man is thus established, with lots of gentle sparring and soft fallings-out as interracial differences are explored. Other characters dropping by the garage are dustman Louie, postwoman Mabel and Mando, a friend of Chico's. In later episodes, not screened as part of the original BBC 1 run, The Man acquired a new 'Chico', after the tragic death of star Freddie Prinze in 1977. Rodriguez was written out and Gabriel Melgar was added to the cast as 12-year-old illegal immigrant Raul Garcia. Jose Feliciano provided the theme song.

Chief, The ✶✶

UK (Anglia Films) Police Drama. ITV 1990–1; 1993–5

Chief Constable John Stafford	**Tim Pigott-Smith**
ACC Anne Stewart	**Karen Archer**
Dr Elizabeth Stafford	**Judy Loe**
Det. Chief Supt. Jim Gray	**Eamon Boland**
Emma Stafford	**Sara Griffiths**
Tim Stafford	**Ross Livingstone**
Martin Stewart	**David Cardy**
ACC/Chief Constable Alan Cade	**Martin Shaw**
Det. Chief Supt. Sean McCloud	**Stuart McGugan**
Nigel Crimmond	**Michael Cochrane**
Colin Fowler	**T. P. McKenna**
Alison Dell	**Ingrid Lacey**
Andrew Blake	**Julian Glover**
DOC Wes Morton	**Bosco Hogan**
Det. Supt. Rose Penfold	**Gillian Bevan**
Sam Lester	**Davyd Harries**
PC Charlie Webb	**Brian Bovell**

Creator **Jeffrey Caine**
Executive Producer **Brenda Reid**
Producers **Ruth Boswell, John Davies**

The problems facing the Chief Constable of a regional police force.

When John Stafford gains promotion to the rank of Chief Constable of Eastland, an East Anglian police force, he quickly makes himself a number of enemies. Bringing with him Anne Stewart, his CID supremo from Nottinghamshire, and promoting her to Head of Crime and Operations is not a good start and immediately triggers resentment among Eastland's long-serving officers. But when the outspoken Chief begins to lay down the law on police drinking and aggressive police driving, and then refuses to ban a student protest against a visiting Government minister, he is made very aware of the disillusionment all around him, including from those who have appointed him. However, *The Chief* is also a personal drama, revealing how Stafford copes with the pressures of office, how he and his doctor wife, Elizabeth, struggle to keep their teenage kids in check, and how Anne's marriage founders when her husband, Martin, starts to resent her devotion to work.

After two seasons a major cast change was enforced. Stafford moves to a job with Europol in Brussels and the race to replace him is won by smart, ambitious Metropolitan Police officer Alan Cade, another man set to ruffle feathers in Eastland. First to take umbrage is Anne, who has been overlooked for the job. But some biting home truths from Alison Dell, Cade's PR consultant, help him sharpen up his act.

The Chief is not a standard cops-and-robbers series. Instead of dwelling on day-to-day routine police work, it focuses on the principles and policies of crime prevention, homing in on the crucial decisions that an officer at the top of the ladder has to make. For authenticity, John Alderson, former Chief Constable of Devon and Cornwall, acted as adviser.

Chigley

See *Camberwick Green*.

Children in Need ✶✶✶

UK (BBC) Telethon. BBC 1 1980–

Presenters **Terry Wogan, Esther Rantzen, Sue Cook, Gaby Roslin, Natasha Kaplinsky, Fearne Cotton**

Star-studded annual appeal marathon.

From humble origins on radio on Christmas Day 1927, *Children in Need* has progressed to become one of the highlights of the British TV year, taking over BBC 1's entire evening schedule (apart from the news) on the second or third Friday in November. The first major TV appeal was held in 1980, when the now established format was launched, involving seven hours of live television. Terry Wogan and Esther Rantzen were the first hosts, with the assistance at times of Andi Peters and numerous celebrity guests. Esther Rantzen also used to welcome the year's Children of Courage. BBC regional presenters have taken charge of the numerous opt-out segments, which have covered fund-raising events locally.

Throughout the evening, appeals for cash donations to help deprived children have been made, with running totals announced on a regular basis. Family-orientated features have filled the early part of the programme – singing chefs, dancing weathermen, soap stars out of character, etc. – with a more mellow atmosphere prevailing towards the closedown at around 2 a.m. After midnight, stars of West End shows have tended to drop in with buckets of cash collected from their own audiences. To generate further interest, novel stunts such as 3-D (a complex DOCTOR WHO meets EASTENDERS story in 1993) and 'scratch and sniff' Smell-o-Vision (1995) experiments have been attempted.

The 1980 appeal raised £1.2 million, but some years have seen in excess of £20 million filling the coffers. Reports on how the money has been spent have been shown in the following year's programme. The appeal's mascot has been Pudsey, a forlorn-looking, bandaged teddy bear.

Children of the Stones ✶✶

UK (HTV) Children's Science Fiction. ITV 1977
DVD: Second Sight

Hendrick	**Iain Cuthbertson**
Adam Brake	**Gareth Thomas**
Matthew Brake	**Peter Demin**
Dai	**Freddie Jones**
Margaret	**Veronica Strong**
Sandra	**Katharine Levy**
Mrs Crabtree	**Ruth Dunning**
Miss Clegg	**June Barrie**
Bob	**Ian Donnolly**
Jimmo	**Gary Lock**

Kevin	**Darren Hatch**
Mrs Warner	**Peggy Ann Wood**
Dr Lyle	**Richard Matthews**
Link	**John Woodnutt**

Writers **Jeremy Burnham, Trevor Ray**
Executive Producer **Patrick Dromgoole**
Producer **Peter Graham Scott**

● ***A village is held spellbound by its ancient stone circle.*** When scientist Adam Brake and his son, Matthew, turn up in the village of Milbury, renowned for its Neolithic stone circle, they find all the locals in a curious, lethargic trance. Only themselves and other newcomers to the village seem unaffected. They investigate and discover that the squire, Hendrick, a local astronomer who has discovered a black hole, is responsible for the weird state of affairs. They also calculate that it is the alignment of his black hole with the stone circle that provides the power for his psychic domination of the local people and they set out to wreck his energy source. *Children of the Stones* was another of HTV West's imaginative sci-fi series for kids, thoughtfully combining ancient mythology with futuristic fantasy.

Children's Ward/The Ward ★★

UK (Granada) Children's Drama. ITV 1989–2000

Dr Charlotte Woods	**Carol Harvey**
Dave Spencer	**Andrew Hall**
Dr McKeown	**Ian McCulloch**
Nurse Gary Miller	**Tim Stanley**
Jan Stevens	**Nina Baden-Semper**
Fiona Brett	**Rebecca Sowden**
Nurse/Sister Diane Meadows/ Gallagher	**Janette Beverley**
Alex Walker-Green	**Robert Fenton**
Billy Ryan	**Tim Vincent**
Tiffany Kendall	**Kate Emma-Davies**
Ben Croft	**Kim Burton**
George	**Laurence Porter**
Darren Walsh	**William Ash**
Keely Johnson	**Jenny Luckcraft**
Dawn Khatir	**Leyla Nejad**
Jack Crossley	**Ken Parry**
Mags	**Rita May**
Mathew McCann	**Dean Gatiss**
Dr Kieran Gallagher	**Tom Higgins**
'JJ'	**Chris Bisson**
Amanda	**Nicola Stephenson**
Nurse/Sister Mitchell	**Judy Holt**
Baby Ben	**Joseph Kennedy**
Lisa	**Rachel Egan**
Sean	**Adam Sutherland**
Lob	**Darren Brennan**
Spida	**Mark Hamer**
Thea Bartlett	**Chloe Newsome**
Melanie	**Abbie Choyce**
Steve Bailey	**Michael Bray**
Linda	**Christine Anderson**
James Boyce	**Carl Rice**
Dr Tanya Davies	**Kiran Hocking**
	Emma Longbottom
Lee Jones	**Kieran O'Brien**
Cal Spicer	**Mark Dixon**
	Elliott Tiney
Bryony Shaeffer	**Sarah Cooper**
Katy Grahams	**Margery Bone**
Lucy Clarkson	**Emily Oldfield**
Danny Phillips	**Michael Friel**
Jay Langdon	**Nirjay Mahindru**
Rowena Easson	**Catherine Grimes**
Gail Bevan	**Gillian Waugh**
Baby Jack	**Nyle Rogers**
Dr Brian Stoker	**Matthew Marsh**
Adam Bellingham	**Richard Hanson**
Thomas	**Ben Sowden**
Deva	**Paul Walton**
Lenny	**Adam Durham**
Rob	**Clinton Blake**
Donna	**Zoë Owen**
Liam	**Lewis Marsh**
Sarah/Shona	**Hayley Fairclough**
Paula James	**Emma Belton**
	Jane Danson
Maddie	**Emma Johnston**
Gary	**Ronnie McCann**
Sharna/Yasmin	**Venna Tulsiani**
Fran	**Fiona Richards**
Gillian	**Kelly Foster**
Kimberley	**Jenny Mobey**
Anne Morris	**Josephine Welcome**
Swifty	**Patrick Connolly**
Joe Lloyd	**Steven Arnold**
Hannah	**Stacey Heywood**
Zed	**Julian Kerridge**
Kirsty	**Sarahjane Potts**
Jamie	**Adam Rowbottom**
Richard	**Garry Crystal**
Martin	**Ben Hull**
Dan	**Kevin Knapman**
Dr Julie Barrow	**Jemma Brown**
	Victoria Finney
Peanut	**Adam Musson**
Geraldine	**Maxine Peake**
Gareth	**Jamie Harrison**
Fiona	**Jessica Manley**
	Sharon Muircroft
Lenny/Tony	**Kirk Smith**
Tamsin	**Carolyn Bazely**
Dr Adam Sullivan	**David Elliot**
Nurse Nick Williams	**Phillip King**
Stephanie	**Leanne Molloy**
Chas	**Chris Cooke**
Martin	**Steven Nuttall**
Rachel	**Alison Darling**
Josie	**Samantha Smith**
Ritchie	**Frank Lauder**
David	**Oliver Furness**
Tim O'Halloran	**Paul Fox**
Katie	**Lucy Bradburn**
Scott Morris	**Anthony Lewis**
Greg Casson	**Gregg Baines**
Claire	**Tina O'Brien**
Lisa	**Micaiah Dring**
Geri Stevens	**Kelly Greenwood**
Phoenix	**Gus Gallagher**
Sylvia Dickinson	**Brigit Forsyth**
Robbie	**Ralf Little**
Tash Naylor	**Vicky Binns**
Sophie	**Kirsty Elsby**
Louie	**Heston Aniteye**
Si	**Jonathan Taylor**
Davey Pearson	**John Catterall**
Sam	**Ben Stapleton**

Richard	**Ben Sherriff**
Vicky	**Kate West**
Kate	**Louise Bromilow**
Becky	**Holly Scourfield**
Lizzie	**Tara Pendergast**
Ewan	**Tim Robbins**
Marcus Oliver	**Danny Edwards**
Nurse Joe Ellis	**Matthew Booth**
Auni	**Josh Maguire**
Delli	**Miranda Hutcheon**
Sarah	**Sadie Pickering**
Tommy	**Charlie Ryan**
Rick	**Richard Cadman**
Zoe	**Rebecca Norris**
Big Bob	**Claude Close**
Adam	**Oliver Hamilton**
Alex	**Hannah King**

Executive Producers **Nick Wilson, David Liddiment**
Producers **Rod Natkiel, Gareth Morgan, Russell Davies**

Life is never dull on a juvenile ward.

Recuperation in hospital is anything but boring if you're one of the kids on Ward B1 of South Park General Hospital. This long-running drama sees its regularly changing core of inmates (and those returning for treatment) involved in all sorts of controversies, from sexual abuse, alcoholism and HIV to racism, anorexia and teenage pregnancy. The pains of growing up are experienced alongside the pains that have hospitalized them, but there is always something going on to help take their minds off their ailments, even though sadness is often just around the corner. The kids set up a hospital radio service and get even more involved in the running of the hospital when they start a fight to keep the threatened ward open in the face of cutbacks. Among the rising talents to be nurtured by the series are Rebecca Callard (billed as Sowden), Ralf Little, Tim Vincent, Chris Bisson, Nicola Stephenson, Kieran O'Brien and Tina O'Brien. The programme's many writers included Paul Abbott, Kay Mellor and Russell T. Davies. The series was retitled *The Ward* between 1995 and 1999. A special Christmas Day episode aired in 1991.

Child's Play ✱✱

UK (Talbot/LWT) Game Show. ITV 1984–8

Presenter **Michael Aspel**

Producers **Keith Stewart, Richard Hearsey**

Guess-the-word panel game with children describing.

'Out of the mouths of babes and sucklings . . .' Based on an American format, *Child's Play* gave a group of primary schoolkids a series of words – 'Brain', 'Paradise', 'Terry Wogan', etc. – and asked them to explain their meaning, but without actually using the words themselves (if they did, a cartoon 'oops' bubble was pasted over the mouth and a bleep masked the sound). Much hilarity followed as the kids struggled with words they barely understood or, more likely, did not understand at all, pulling expressive faces and conjuring up all kinds of bizarre images. Studio-based celebrity panellists watched the films and scored points by identifying the words in question.

Chiles, Adrian

(1967–)

Birmingham-born radio and TV journalist, presenter of series as varied as *Working Lunch*, MATCH OF THE DAY 2 and *So What Do You Do All Day?* A former newspaper sports reporter, he is married to radio presenter Jane Garvey.

Chinese Detective, The ✱✱

UK (BBC) Police Drama. BBC 1 1981–2

DS Johnny Ho	**David Yip**
DCI Berwick	**Derek Martin**
DS Donald Chegwyn	**Arthur Kelly**
Joe Ho	**Robert Lee**

Creator **Ian Kennedy Martin**
Producer **Terence Williams**

Life on the beat with an ethnic copper.

Britain's first Chinese police hero was Detective Sgt Johnny Ho. Ho has joined the police partly as a means of clearing his father's name, but has been refused entry to the Metropolitan Police on grounds of height. Finding a way in elsewhere, Ho manages to work his way back to London's Limehouse district, where he finds the going tough and his colleagues unsupportive. A natural loner, he encounters plenty of harassment, not least from his rigid boss, DCI Berwick, who hates his scruffy appearance and sloppy behaviour. To bring Ho back into line, he pairs him with experienced sergeant, Donald Chegwyn.

The Chinese Detective came from the pen of THE SWEENEY creator, Ian Kennedy Martin. Not surprisingly, the real police did not appreciate the suggestion that racism existed in the ranks, whether intentional or not.

Chips ✱

US (MGM) Police Drama. ITV 1979–87 (US: NBC 1977–83)

Officer Francis 'Ponch' Poncherello	**Erik Estrada**
Officer Jonathan Baker	**Larry Wilcox**
Sgt Joe Getraer	**Robert Pine**
Officer Gene Fritz	**Lew Saunders**
Officer Baricza	**Brodie Greer**
Officer Sindy Cahill	**Brianne Leary**
Harlan	**Lou Wagner**
Officer Grossman	**Paul Linke**
Officer Bonnie Clark	**Randi Oakes**
Officer Turner	**Michael Dorn**
Officer Steve McLeish	**Bruce Jenner**
Officer Bobby 'Hot Dog' Nelson	**Tom Reilly**
Officer Kathy Linahan	**Tina Gayle**
Cadet Bruce Nelson	**Bruce Penhall**
Officer Webster	**Clarence Gilyard Jr**

Creator **Rick Rosner**
Producers **Rick Rosner, Cy Chermak, Ric Randall**

The adventures of two hunky police motorcyclists in and around Los Angeles.

Baker and Ponch work as a team for the California Highway Patrol (CHiPS): fair-haired Baker is the sensible, serious one; swarthy Ponch is his devil-may-care partner, often falling foul of their boss, Sgt Getraer. The lads are both single and their private lives mingle with crime-fighting in every action-packed episode. The supporting cast includes a mechanic, Harlan, and a sequence of female cops, beginning with Sindy Cahill (later replaced by Bonnie Clark and then Kathy Linahan).

At one point Erik Estrada was in dispute with the programme's makers and was replaced by Olympic decathlon champion Bruce Jenner, who duly made way for Estrada when the matter was resolved. Larry Wilcox was the first to make a permanent break and Baker is written out before the final season. Ponch then gains a new partner, Bobby Nelson, and Nelson's brother, Bruce, is also seen, played by another sports star, speedway rider Bruce Penhall.

Chocky ✶✶

UK (Thames) Children's Science Fiction. ITV 1984–6
DVD: Second Sight

Matthew Gore	**Andrew Ellams**
Chocky	**Glynis Brooks** *(voice only)*
Mary Gore	**Carol Drinkwater**
David Gore	**James Hazeldine**
Polly Gore	**Zoe Hart**
Aunt Cissie	**Angela Galbraith**
Albertine Meyer	**Anabel Worrell**
Arnold Meyer	**Prentis Hancock**
Dr Deacon	**Ed Bishop**
Mrs Gibson	**Joan Blackham**
Prof. Ferris	**Richard Wordsworth**
Prof. Wade	**Kristine Howarth**
Dr Liddle	**Illona Linthwaite**

Creator **John Wyndham**
Writer **Anthony Read**
Executive Producers **Pamela Lonsdale, Brian Walcroft** *(Challenge)*
Producers **Vic Hughes, Richard Bates** *(Challenge)*

● ***A schoolboy forms a friendship with an alien lifeform.***
When 12-year-old Matthew Gore starts talking to himself, his parents are understandably concerned. However, his schoolwork inexplicably improves, and he begins to produce unusual paintings and drawings. Behind this strange turn of events is Chocky, a being from a distant galaxy who has arrived on Earth to bring us a new, inexhaustible source of energy. Chocky remains unseen to all, except, on occasions, to Matthew, when she appears as a swirling ball of green mist. After an initial adventure, Chocky returned a year later in a series entitled *Chocky's Children*. Matthew, on holiday at his aunt's, meets up with a young girl named Albertine and discovers that Chocky is back and in need of help. With the menacing Dr Deacon in pursuit, 'Chocky's Children' – her friends around the globe – are called upon to help out. Chocky returned for a third and final time in *Chocky's Challenge*, in which she guides Albertine, now studying maths at Cambridge University, in the construction of a cosmic energy collector, a device that will, at last, provide the answer to the Earth's power problems. But their secret leaks out and, once again, they find themselves in danger, especially from the treacherous Mrs Gibson. The series were based on the novels of John Wyndham (*Chocky* was his last published work, in 1968).

Chorlton and the Wheelies ✶✶

UK (Cosgrove Hall/Thames) Children's Entertainment.
ITV 1976–7; 1979
DVD: Fremantle

Narrator **Joe Lynch**

Writer **Brian Trueman**
Executive Producer **John Hambley**
Producers **Brian Cosgrove, Mark Hall**

● ***A cheerful dragon brings colour and joy to an oppressed people.***
Wheelie World is not a happy place. Ensnared in the power of a wicked witch named Fenella, who lives in a kettle called Spout Hall on the fringes of Wheelie Kingdom, the land desperately needs an injection of cheer. Cue Chorlton, the Happiness Dragon, who hatches out of a gaily-coloured egg and becomes a hero for all the Wheelies as he thwarts Fenella's every attempt to regain control. His down-to-earth Northern tones contrast evocatively with Fenella's strident Welsh accent ('Ffestiniog!'). Three series (39 episodes) were made.

Christabel ✶✶

UK (BBC) Drama. BBC 2 1988

Christabel Burton/Bielenberg	**Elizabeth Hurley**
Mr Burton	**Geoffrey Palmer**
Mrs Burton	**Ann Bell**
Peter Bielenberg	**Stephen Dillon**
Adam Von Trott	**Nigel Le Vaillant**
Nicky Bielenberg	**Sam Preston** *(young)*
	Toby Lawson *(older)*
	Alastair Haley *(older again)*
John Bielenberg	**Ryan Le Neveu** *(young)*
	Andrey Justice *(older)*
	James Exell *(older again)*
Lexi	**Suzan Crowley**

Writer **Dennis Potter**
Producer **Kenith Trodd**

● ***A young English mother protects her family behind enemy lines during World War II.***
In September 1934, Christabel Burton, an English girl with aristocratic connections, marries Peter Bielenberg, a German law student, much against the wishes of her family. They move to Germany and, when war breaks out, she becomes trapped, a fish out of water thanks to her intrinsically English outlook and upbringing. As the bombs begin to fall, she seeks refuge for herself and her two sons, Nicky and John, in the Black Forest, but Peter is involved in secret work against the Nazi state and, as the war nears its end, he is imprisoned in a concentration camp for high treason.

Dennis Potter's four-part adaptation of Christabel Bielenberg's remarkable, true life story, *The Past is Myself*, is directed by Adrian Shergold, with music provided by Stanley Myers.

Christmas Carol, A ✶✶

UK (LWT). ITV 2000

Eddie Scrooge	**Ross Kemp**
Eddie's dad	**Warren Mitchell**

Joyce .... **Liz Smith**
Eric .... **Charles Simon**
Bella .... **Angeline Ball**
Marley .... **Ben Fearon**
Bob Cratchett .... **Michael Maloney**
Sue Cratchett .... **Lorraine Ashbourne**
Tim Cratchett .... **Ben Tibber**
Julie .... **Mina Anwar**

Writer **Peter Bowker**
Executive Producers **Laura Mackie, Jo Wright**
Producer **Joshua St Johnston**

A mean-minded thug finds redemption over Christmas.

This gritty, modern take on Dickens's festive tale moves the action to a rundown council estate and gives centre stage to one Eddie Scrooge, a thoroughly unpleasant loan shark who looks forward to Christmas Day because most people are at home and he can call in more debts. This means no time with the family for Scrooge's clerk, Bob Cratchett, whose son Tim is in hospital suffering from cystic fibrosis. Fortunately, a succession of ghosts helps change Scrooge's character for the better, beginning with that of his alcoholic father, then that of his late partner, Marley. Bella is Eddie's nurse girlfriend, with whom he is finally reconciled. This one-off, 90-minute drama was penned by Peter Bowker from an idea suggested by star Ross Kemp himself. It was directed by Catherine Morshead.

Christmas Night with the Stars ★★★

UK (BBC) Variety. BBC 1 1958–60; 1962–4; 1967–72; BBC 2 1994

Hosts **David Nixon, Eamonn Andrews, Jack Warner, Rolf Harris, Morecambe and Wise, Val Doonican, Cilla Black, The Two Ronnies**

Producers **Graeme Muir, Stuart Morris and others**

Festive light entertainment showcase.

The highlight of Christmas Day viewing for many years, *Christmas Night with the Stars* was the BBC's way of showing off the talent it housed in its stable. The package, hosted by one of the top entertainment names of the day, consisted of music, dancing and specially recorded sketches based on contemporary sitcoms. THE RAG TRADE, SYKES, TILL DEATH US DO PART, STEPTOE AND SON, NOT IN FRONT OF THE CHILDREN, DAD'S ARMY and HARRY WORTH, were among the comedies contributing over the years. Among the other guests were the Black and White Minstrels, Stanley Baxter, Kenneth McKellar, Russ Conway, Billy Cotton, Dick Emery, Lulu and the MONTY PYTHON team. The concept was revived as a one-off in 1994, entitled *Fry and Laurie Host a Christmas Night with the Stars*, featuring comedy clips from THE FAST SHOW and RAB C. NESBITT, plus pieces from, among others, Reeves and Mortimer, Alexei Sayle and Steve Coogan in his guise of Alan Partridge. There was also archive footage of earlier *Christmas Nights*.

In response, ITV launched its own festive package, entitled *All Star Comedy Carnival* (1969–73), with short pieces from programmes like DOCTOR IN THE HOUSE, ON THE BUSES, PLEASE SIR!, FATHER, DEAR FATHER, THE DUSTBINMEN, THE LOVERS, FOR THE LOVE OF ADA, LOVE THY NEIGHBOUR and MAN ABOUT THE HOUSE. Des O'Connor, Max Bygraves, Mike and Bernie Winters and Jimmy Tarbuck hosted proceedings in turn. In 1996, ITV offered a one-off *Des O'Connor's Christmas Night with the Stars*, an extension of his regular chat show.

Chroma Key

Another term for colour separation overlay, i.e. the electronic technique that allows one colour in the picture (usually blue or green) to be filled with another image. It has been used over the years for studio backdrops and also for crude special effects. Blue and green are the most popular choices as they are not common in human skin colourings.

Chronicle ★★

UK (BBC) Historical Documentary. BBC 2 1966–91

Presenters **Glyn Daniel, Magnus Magnusson**

Producers **Paul Johnstone, Bruce Norman, Roy Davies**

New developments in the world of history and archaeology.

This monthly educational series looked at the latest findings of the world's leading archaeologists and historians. Cambridge archaeologist (and former ANIMAL, VEGETABLE, MINERAL? chairman) Glyn Daniel was the first host, with a pre-MASTERMIND Magnus Magnusson taking over later. One of the best-remembered stories was the excavation into mysterious Silbury Hill in Wiltshire.

Chronicles of Narnia, The ★★

UK (BBC) Children's Drama. BBC 1 1988–90
DVD: BBC

Peter Pevensie .... **Richard Dempsey**
Susan Pevensie .... **Sophie Cook**
Edmund Pevensie .... **Jonathan R. Scott**
Lucy Pevensie .... **Sophie Wilcox**
The White Witch .... **Barbara Kellerman**
Prince/King Caspian .... **Jean-Marc Perret**
Samuel West
Geoffrey Russell
King Miraz .... **Robert Lang**
Dr Cornelius .... **Henry Woolf**
Reepicheep .... **Warwick Davis**
Trumpkin .... **Big Mick**
Eustace Scrubb .... **David Thwaites**
Jill Pole .... **Camilla Power**
Puddleglum .... **Tom Baker**
Aslan .... **Ronald Pickup** *(voice only)*

Writer **Alan Seymour**
Producer **Paul Stone**

Adaptations of the classic children's fantasies by C. S. Lewis.

Employing a plethora of animal costumes and extensive special effects, the BBC set out to dramatize C. S. Lewis's epic stories of the fictitious world of Narnia. In the end, four of his seven books were covered, beginning with the first, *The Lion, the Witch and the Wardrobe. Prince Caspian, Voyage of the Dawn Treader* and *The Silver Chair* followed. A particular feature was the complicated human and mechanical operation of the giant lion which represented Aslan, the awesome Narnia deity. *The Lion, the Witch and the Wardrobe* had previously been dramatized by Trevor Preston for ABC (ITV 1967), with Bernard Kay as Aslan.

Chuckle Brothers

(Paul Elliot; and Barry Elliot; 1944–)

Rotherham-born slapstick kids' comedians with their own long-running show, *Chucklevision*, on children's BBC. Previously they had been seen in *The Chucklehounds* (dressed as dogs) and they later starred in *To Me . . . To You* (a game show named after one of their catchphrases). Before claiming star status, the real-life brothers had won NEW FACES and appeared in TV variety shows like THE GOOD OLD DAYS, *Summertime Special* and 3-2-1. Their dad was variety comedian Gene Patton.

Churchill, Donald

(1930–91)

British actor and playwright whose writing credits included *Never a Cross Word, Moody and Pegg* (with Julia Jones), Charlie Drake's comedy *Who is Sylvia?* (co-written with Drake), and an adaptation of Dickens's *Our Mutual Friend*. He also wrote for series like ARMCHAIR THEATRE and THE SWEENEY. On screen, he starred in the 1958 sitcom *Trouble for Two* (a cleaner), *Ask for King Billy, Bulldog Breed* (the hapless Tom Bowler), SPOONER'S PATCH (as Inspector Spooner, succeeding Ronald Fraser), *It's Not Me – It's Them* (the constantly unemployed Albert Curfew), *The Sun Trap* (expat Peter Halliday) and *Good Night and God Bless* (as Ronnie Kemp, a game show host; also as co-writer). Among his other appearances were parts in EL C.I.D. (Metcalf), C.A.T.S. EYES, DON'T WAIT UP, BERGERAC and *Stanley and the Women*. Churchill was married to actress Pauline Yates.

Cinema ✶✶

UK (Granada) Film Review. ITV 1964–75

Presenters **Bamber Gascoigne, Derek Granger, Michael Scott, Mark Shivas, Michael Parkinson, Clive James, Brian Trueman**

Producers **Derek Granger, John Hamp, Peter Wildeblood, Mark Shivas**

● ***Long-running weekly film magazine.***

Eight years before Barry Norman began reviewing films in FILM 72, Granada launched its own half-hour series about the world of the silver screen. *Cinema* ran for 11 years and over 500 episodes, mixing critiques of the latest releases, interviews with film celebrities and some retrospective material. A common theme or a personality linked most items. Its first host, Bamber Gascoigne, occupied the presenter's chair for just three months, and the best-remembered frontmen were later incumbents Mike Scott and Michael Parkinson. The programme's natural 'successor' was the junior film magazine *Clapperboard* (also from Granada), hosted by Chris Kelly, which began in 1972 and ran for ten years.

Circus Boy ✶✶

US (Herbert B. Leonard/Screen Gems) Children's Adventure. BBC 1957–8 (US: NBC 1956–7; ABC 1957–8)

Corky	**Mickey Braddock**
Joey	**Noah Beery Jr**
Big Tim Champion	**Robert Lowery**
Hank Miller	**Leo Gordon**
Little Tom	**Billy Barty**
Swifty	**Olin Howlin**
Barker	**Eddie Marr**
Pete	**Guinn Williams**
Col. Jack	**Andy Clyde**
Elmer Purdy	**Sterling Holloway**

Producers **Herbert B. Leonard, Norman Blackburn**

● ***An orphan's adventures in a travelling circus.***

When little Corky's parents were killed in a wire-walking act, he was adopted by Big Tim Champion, proprietor of the Champion Circus. Earning his keep by caring for Bimbo, the baby elephant, Corky is surrounded by a giant, colourful family, including Little Tom the midget, Joey the clown, and animals like Sultan the tiger and Nuba the lion. As the circus moves from town to town, so each story unfolds.

Star Mickey Braddock later achieved considerably more fame, under his real name of Dolenz, as drummer in The Monkees pop group.

Cisco Kid, The ✶

US (The Cisco Company/Ziv) Children's Western. BBC 1954 (US: Syndicated 1950–5)

The Cisco Kid	**Duncan Renaldo**
Pancho	**Leo Carrillo**

Producer **Philip N. Krasne**

● ***The exploits of a Mexican Robin Hood and his fat, smiling sidekick.***

In the late 19th century, the Cisco Kid and his partner, Pancho, travel around the south-western United States, helping the oppressed, thwarting bandits and steering clear of sheriffs and deputies who think they are outlaws. They keep violence to a minimum, with Cisco confining himself to shooting guns from his opponents' hands, sometimes aided by the totally unathletic Pancho, who is an expert with the whip.

Cisco is a ladies' man, a bit of a dandy, dressed up in finely embroidered shirts and silver spurs. He sports a giant sombrero and is quite a charmer. Pancho's only affair, however, is with his food. Cisco's horse is Diablo (with whom star Duncan Renaldo continued to make personal appearances long after the show had ended), while Pancho rides Loco, but these are two very unlikely cowboys. Their adventures are played largely for laughs and Pancho's abysmal grip of the English language is milked to the full.

The Cisco Kid was created by writer O. Henry and the character appeared in the cinema as early as the 1920s. Duncan Renaldo had already played the part in the movies before the TV series was conceived and was in his 50s by the time it was made. Leo Carrillo was even older, in his 70s. Unusually for TV series of this period, it was filmed in colour.

Citadel, The ✶✶

UK (BBC) Drama. BBC 1 1983

Dr Andrew Manson	**Ben Cross**
Christine Barlow/Manson	**Clare Higgins**
Dr Page	**Tenniel Evans**
Blodwen Page	**Cynthia Grenville**
Annie Hughes	**Beryl Nesbitt**

Philip Denny	**Gareth Thomas**
Joe Morgan	**David Pugh**
Dr Llewellyn	**Raymond Bowers**
David Hope	**David Gwillim**
Charles Ivory	**John Nettleton**
Robert Stillman	**Don Fellows**
Con Boland	**Niall Buggy**
Freddie Hamson	**Michael Cochrane**
Nurse Sharp	**Avril Elgar**

Writer **Don Shaw**
Producer **Ken Riddington**

An idealistic young doctor fights injustice in pre-NHS days.

Newly qualified doctor Andrew Manson arrives in the Welsh mining town of Drineffy to take up a position in the practice of Dr Page. His enthusiasm is very evident, but sadly his dreams are shattered once he realizes just how corrupt and unfair society can be (the 'citadel' being medical bureaucracy). Manson, however, fights back and soon begins his career progression, moving to another mining village, Aberalaw, as an employee of the local Medical Aid Society, dealing with all the filthy illnesses and disabilities caused by coal mining. He becomes an adviser to a Government quango, then moves to London, where he scrapes a living as a GP before climbing to the heights of Harley Street. Christine Barlow is the girl who becomes Manson's wife. The series was an adaptation in ten parts of the largely autobiographical 1937 novel of the same name by A. J. Cronin (the actual house where Cronin had lived in Tredegar – doubling here as Aberalaw – was used for filming). Associated Rediffusion had previously dramatized the book in 1960, casting NO HIDING PLACE star Eric Lander as Manson.

Citizen James ✳✳

UK (BBC) Situation Comedy. BBC 1960–2

Sidney Balmoral James	**Sid James**
William 'Bill' Kerr	**Bill Kerr**
Liz Fraser	**Liz Fraser**
Charlie	**Sydney Tafler**

Writers **Ray Galton, Alan Simpson, Sid Green, Dick Hills**
Producers **Duncan Wood, John Street, Ronald Marsh**

A London sponger takes on society and usually gets beaten.

Resuming his role as a Cockney layabout with contempt for authority, Sid James branched out from HANCOCK'S HALF HOUR and into this series of his own. His new sparring partners are Australian Bill Kerr and girlfriend Liz Fraser, the owner of a club. Charlie, a bookie's sidekick, is added later in the series when James sets himself up as a champion of the underdog and fighter for lost causes (usually with the wrong result).

Citizen Smith ✳✳

UK (BBC) Situation Comedy. BBC 1 1977–80

Walter Henry 'Wolfie' Smith	**Robert Lindsay**
Ken Mills	**Mike Grady**
Tucker	**Tony Millan**
Anthony 'Speed' King	**George Sweeney**
Shirley Johnson	**Cheryl Hall**
Charlie Johnson	**Peter Vaughan**
	Tony Steedman
Florence Johnson	**Hilda Braid**
Harry Fenning	**Stephen Greif**
Ronnie Lynch	**David Garfield**

Creator/Writer **John Sullivan**
Producers **Dennis Main Wilson, Ray Butt**

The failed missions of a work-shy revolutionary in Tooting.

'Power to the People!' Wolfie Smith is the Che Guevara of south-west London – or so he believes. Sporting an Afghan coat and a commando beret, he is the guitar-strumming figurehead of the Tooting Popular Front (TPF), a team of hapless Marxist freedom fighters whose members total six in number. His right-hand man is Ken, a weedy, vegetarian pacifist-cum-Buddhist with whom he shares a flat above the home of Charlie and Florence Johnson, the parents of Wolfie's girlfriend, Shirley. (Played by Robert Lindsay's real wife at the time, Cheryl Hall, Shirley appeared in only the first three seasons, when she worked in the Sounds Cool record shop.) Shirley's dad, a security guard at Haydon Electronics, is an irascible social-climbing Yorkshireman who has no time for 'that bloody yeti', as he brands Wolfie. (Peter Vaughan also left the series after three years, handing the role to Tony Steedman.) His dopey wife, on the other hand, is genuinely fond of the lodger she mistakenly knows as 'Foxy'.

The other main characters in the TPF are Tucker and Speed. Tucker, a nervous family man with a formidable wife (June) and nine kids, owns the van the gang use for their 'manoeuvres'. Speed is the team's hard man, a brainless, violent thug who drifts in and out of jail. Lurking in the background is the manor's Mr Big, Harry Fenning, owner of Wolfie's local, The Vigilante. Fenning is replaced in the last series by the just as nasty, but cruelly hen-pecked, Welsh gangster, Ronnie Lynch.

Wolfie's cack-handed attempts at liberating the proletariat, in between shirking jobs and cadging pints, provide the focus for the series. 'Come the glorious day,' he threatens, his enemies will be lined up against the wall for a 'last fag', then 'bop, bop, bop', the struggle will be over. But with such inept ideas and such gormless allies, capitalism is never in any danger. After all, who takes notice of a revolutionary who rides a scooter?

Citizen Smith was John Sullivan's big break. The writer of ONLY FOOLS AND HORSES, JUST GOOD FRIENDS, DEAR JOHN, etc., was working as a scene shifter at the BBC at the time. Convinced he could produce something better than the humourless sitcoms he was watching, he created the character of an ageing hippie turned working-class hero, whose support for Fulham FC was yet another lost cause. The script was taken up for an episode of COMEDY PLAYHOUSE in 1977 (in which Artro Morris played Shirley's dad) and a full series was commissioned the same year.

City Central ✳✳

UK (BBC) Police Drama. BBC 1 1998–2000

PC Terry Sydenham	**Paul Nicholls**
PC Colin Jitlada	**Ian Aspinall**
PC Steve Jackson	**Stephen Lord**
DI Tony Baynham	**Ray Stevenson**
DS Ray Pickering	**Ian Burfield**
Sgt Yvonne Mackey	**Lorraine Ashbourne**
PC Pete Redfern	**Dave Hill**

PC Sue Chappel	**Ashley Jensen**
PC/DC Mary Sutcliffe	**Sarah Kirkman**
DS Jane McCormack	**Kate Gartside**
Chief Insp. George Barnard	**Terence Harvey**
Insp. Mike Willis	**Andrew Readman**
PC Richard Law	**Michael Begley**
PC Nick Green	**Sean McKenzie**
DC Danny Abbott	**John Brobbey**
Sgt Paul Dobson	**Philip Martin Brown**
Lucy Barnard	**Emily Hamilton**
Nikki Reed	**Christine Tremarco**
Alison Beasely	**Caroline Carver**
PC Kate Foster	**Jennifer Luckraft**
	Jayne Dowell
Maggie Baynham	**Jayne Charlton McKenzie**
PC Judy Byrd	**Katie Blake**
DCI Jack Carter	**George Costigan**
PC Clive Gardner	**Martin Walsh**
DC Janet Miller	**Connie Hyde**

Creator **Tony Jordan**
Producers **John Yorke, Ken Horn**

● ***Work at an inner-city police station means humour as well as horror.***

City Central was the BBC's attempt to create a Saturday-night, mainstream police series in the Z CARS mould, but bringing the format up to date. Set in the crumbling Christmas Street nick in a northern city (Manchester), it featured a team of PCs, detectives and the odd superior officer who combined moments of genuine heroism with day-to-day petty rule-bending, the aim being a realistic, but at times amusing, portrayal of policing in the 1990s. Episode one sees new probationer Terry Sydenham arriving for work with the South-East Lancashire Constabulary, wide-eyed, nervous but keen to impress. He is teamed with seen-it-all-before community copper Pete Redfern, a man 20 years on the beat, and, despite being thrown in at the deep end by getting blown up during a domestic incident, Terry resiliently turns up for work again the next day. Terry's other colleagues include the hot-headed Steve Jackson, Steve's flirtatious patrol partner Sue Chappel, fastidious Colin Jitlada (from a poor Asian background) and his mumsy partner Mary Sutcliffe – all supervised by the even more maternal station sergeant, Yvonne Mackey. Then there's the CID trio of Ray Pickering (a womanizing Londoner up from the Met), his equally philanderous boss, Tony Baynham, and blonde Jane McCormack, a rural officer gaining urban experience. Series two appeared even lighter in tone (but not without its dark moments) and new recruits to the team included head-turner PC Judy Byrd. The third series introduced abrasive DI Jack Carter, young PC Clive Gardner and new DC Janet Miller.

Civilisation ✱✱✱

UK (BBC) Documentary. BBC 2 1969

Presenter **Kenneth Clark**

Producers **Michael Gill, Peter Montagnon**

● ***Chronicle of human cultural development and the benefits it has brought to the world.***

This documentary looks at history not from a perspective of dates and battles but through the ideas and values that have shaped humankind over the centuries. Charting developments since the Dark Ages, Kenneth Clark's aim is to show viewers, through examples of art and architecture, how man has risen above the common beast, how he has discovered 'Civilisation'. The work – inspired by a fear that man was slipping back into moral chaos – profiles men of genius (painters, thinkers, poets and musicians, people who have brought order to our lives) in an attempt to prove that we really are above all the hassles of the modern-day industrial society. Presented in an old-fashioned, simple style, shunning clever TV gimmickry and relying on good prose over well-framed images, the series was a remarkable success, especially considering the contemporary climate in which Andy Warhol, Jackson Pollock, The Beatles and Flower Power had asserted their heavy influence. Clark, a highbrow, learned art historian and former Chairman of the Independent Television Authority, became an unlikely TV hero, a status he did not in the least relish.

Claire ✱✱

UK (BBC) Drama. BBC 1 1982

Pam Hunter	**Lynn Farleigh**
Tony Hunter	**William Gaunt**
Claire Terson	**Caroline Embling**
Robert Hunter	**Neil Nisbet**
Emma Williamson	**Jane Downs**
Sophie Stevens	**Carole Nimmons**
Susan Adams	**Elizabeth Bennett**

Writer **Alick Rowe**
Producer **Ron Craddock**

● ***A troubled orphan creates rifts in a once happy household.***

Teenager Claire has lived in a children's home for nearly eight years but now has the opportunity to build a new life with Pam and Tony Hunter. The Hunters, middle-class parents of adolescent son Robert, feel that they would now like to foster, and then possibly adopt, a child, and Claire seems like the right person. However, things don't entirely go to plan. Claire has misgivings about leaving the environment in which she has spent most of her life, and Robert is uncertain about the effect another child will have on his happy home. When Claire stakes her claims for independence and respect through bad behaviour, Pat and Tony, too, are no longer convinced that they have made the right move. Their marriage begins to suffer, and Tony embarks on an affair. Unwise sexual fumblings between Claire and Robert only make matters worse, as the Hunters' family life is shattered. With music by Joseph Horovitz, John Gorrie directs the six episodes.

Clangers ✱✱✱

UK (Smallfilms) Children's Entertainment. BBC 1 1969–72; 1974

Creators/Writers/Producers **Oliver Postgate, Peter Firmin**

● ***The moral adventures of the mousey inhabitants of a blue planet.***

Strange, pink and woolly, the Clangers are mouse-like creatures with pronounced noses and perky ears who live inside a small blue planet. They wear personal suits of armour for protection from the many meteorites that break through the thin atmosphere, and they take their name from the sound made when they batten down their dustbin-lid hatches and retreat underground. The Clangers speak only in musical whistles – to each other and to the other inhabitants of their planet, the Soup Dragon and the Froglets. The Soup Dragon lives in the soup wells, where the Clangers' staple diet is obtained (they also eat Blue String Pudding), while the Froglets are small orange amphibians who live in a deep pond and travel around in a top hat. Also seen is the Iron Chicken (and its chick), a metal bird that nests a little way out in space. The Clangers themselves are Major and Mother Clanger, Granny, Aunty, Small and Tiny.

The Clangers' world is a little haven of peace and happiness. Apart from minor concerns like how to pick notes from music trees to propel Major Clanger's boat, their only worries are occasional disturbances from aliens or stray alien inventions. These instances are used to moral effect, revealing just how happy uncluttered, modest lives could be and how beneficial it is to live in peace with one's neighbours.

This five-minute, pre-evening-news animation came from the Smallfilms duo of Oliver Postgate and Peter Firmin, who were also responsible for NOGGIN THE NOG, POGLES' WOOD, BAGPUSS and IVOR THE ENGINE.

Clapperboard [1]

See *Cinema*.

Clapperboard [2]

A hinged marker board used during filming to indicate the title of the programme, the scene and the take. The board is hinged to allow its two parts to be 'clapped' together at the start of the take, the noise of the clap then being used to synchronize sound and vision tracks in editing. New electronic systems have gradually undermined the clapperboard's usefulness.

Clarence ✱✱✱

UK (BBC) Situation Comedy. BBC 1 1988

Clarence Sale .... **Ronnie Barker**
Jane Travers .... **Josephine Tewson**

Writer **Bob Ferris**
Producer **Mike Stephens**

A short-sighted removals man sets up home in the country with an out-of-work parlourmaid.

Londoner Clarence Sale, a middle-aged, self-employed removals man with his own company (Get A Move On), is clumsy and short-sighted. Not that this does anything to dampen his confidence. Meeting up with Jane Travers, an unemployed parlourmaid to the rich, on Coronation Day 1937, he takes her back to his Peckham flat for some fish and chips. There they begin a gentle romance that develops when they move out to the Oxfordshire countryside, taking up residence in a run-down cottage Travers has inherited from her aunt. The ensuing episodes revolve around Clarence's attempts to bed Travers, their acclimatization in the country and Clarence's abysmal eyesight.

The series was written by Ronnie Barker under the pseudonym of Bob Ferris.

Clark, Lord Kenneth

(1903–83)

London-born art historian whose 13-part CIVILISATION in 1969 was fêted as a television masterpiece. The spin-off book proved equally profitable for the BBC and was one of the first successful 'TV tie-ins'. Earlier in his life Clark had been Director of the National Gallery, worked for the Ministry of Information in World War II, assumed the chairmanship of the Arts Council and then became first Chairman of the Independent Television Authority (1954–7). In 1964 he presented the series *Great Temples of the World*, and among his other contributions were talks on Rembrandt and series like *Landscape Into Art, Discovering Japanese Art, Pioneers of Modern Painting* and *Romantic v. Classic Art*. He was made a life peer in 1969 and one of his sons was the late Conservative MP Alan Clark.

Clarke, Margi

(1954–)

Liverpudlian actress, a former Granada presenter (*What's On*), mostly seen in coarse, down-to-earth roles such as Queenie in MAKING OUT, CORONATION STREET's Jackie Dobbs and Joan Short in *Family Affairs*. Her GOOD SEX GUIDE in 1993 caused quite a stir, and she also appeared in the two-part drama *Soul Survivors* (Connie). Clarke is the sister of actress/writer Angela Clarke and writer/director Frank Clarke (who wrote the film drama *Letter to Brezhnev* that gave Margi her break).

Clarke, Roy

OBE (1930–)

British comedy writer responsible for such series as THE MISFIT, LAST (and *First*) OF THE SUMMER WINE, OPEN ALL HOURS, ROSIE, THE MAGNIFICENT EVANS, *Mann's Best Friends, Flickers*, PULASKI, POTTER, *The Clairvoyant*, KEEPING UP APPEARANCES, DON'T TELL FATHER, THE SHARP END, AIN'T MISBEHAVIN' and SPARK. His humour is of the gentle nature, relying on shrewd observation of character, and most of his work has been set in his native Yorkshire. Clarke has also contributed to drama series like MR ROSE, THE TROUBLESHOOTERS and MENACE, and he wrote the *Screen One* drama *A Foreign Field*.

Clarke, Warren

(Alan Clarke; 1947–)

Lancashire-born actor, best known as cop Andy Dalziel in DALZIEL AND PASCOE but seen in a variety of roles (including comic) and most notably in SOFTLY, SOFTLY (DS Stirling), SHELLEY (Paul), *The Home Front*, THE ONEDIN LINE (Josiah Beaumont), JENNIE, LADY RANDOLPH CHURCHILL (Winston Churchill), OUR MUTUAL FRIEND (Bradley Headstone), THE JEWEL IN THE CROWN ('Sophie' Dixon), THE MANAGERESS (Martin Fisher), NICE WORK (Vic Wilcox), *Sleepers* (Albert Robinson), *All Good Things* (Phil Frame), GONE TO THE DOGS (Larry Patterson), GONE TO SEED (Winston), *All in the Game* (Kenny Dawes), *Conjugal Rites* (voice of Toby the dog), THE HOUSE OF WINDSOR (Max Kelvin), *Moving Story* (Bamber), *A Respectable Trade* (Josiah Cole), *The Locksmith* (Roland Pierce), *Giving Tongue* (Pollin), *In the Red* (George Cragge), *The Mystery of Men* (Vernon), DOWN TO EARTH (Brian Addis), *The Debt* (Geoff Dresner), *The Deputy* (Deputy Prime Minister Bob Galway), and BLEAK HOUSE (Lawrence Boythorn). His guest appearances have been many (including as Elsie Tanner's nephew, Gary, in CORONATION STREET).

Clarkson, Jeremy

(1960–)

Forthright, Doncaster-born motoring presenter who made his name in TOP GEAR and has moved on to front his own series, like *Jeremy Clarkson's Motorworld, Jeremy Clarkson's Extreme Machines, Clarkson's Car Years, Jeremy Clarkson Meets the Neighbours, Speed, Inventions That Changed the World*, and the chat show *Clarkson*, as well as the mechanical combat contest ROBOT WARS. In the BBC's *Great Britons* series, he presented a compelling case for Isambard Kingdom Brunel. He returned to *Top Gear* in 2002.

Clary, Julian

(1959–)

Surbiton-born camp comedian specializing in double entendres and innuendo. After appearances on SATURDAY LIVE, his TV break came in the game show *Trick or Treat*, in which he was billed as The Joan Collins Fan Club and was accompanied by his pet, Fanny the Wonderdog. He has since advanced to his own series, such as *Sticky Moments with Julian Clary*, the sitcom *Terry and Julian, All Rise for Julian Clary, Mr and Mrs with Julian Clary* and *Prickly Heat* (the last for Sky), and has also been a team captain in the comedy quiz IT'S ONLY TV BUT I LIKE IT. Another game show he piloted in both the UK and US, called *In the Dark*, never made it to a series. Clary also appeared in the feature-length comedy *Brazen Hussies* ('Man in the Moon'), played coffin maker William Clarke in *Virtual Murder* and starred as the cat in *Dick Whittington*, among other TV pantomime roles.

Classical Brits, The

See *Brits, The*.

Clayhanger **

UK (ATV) Drama. ITV 1976

Edwin Clayhanger	**William Relton**
	Peter McEnery
Darius Clayhanger	**Harry Andrews**
Clara Clayhanger	**Rosemary Blake**
Maggie Clayhanger	**Thelma Whiteley**
Auntie Hamps	**Joyce Redman**
Miss Ingamells	**Diana Rayworth**
Stifford	**Hugh Walters**
Osmond Orgreave	**John Horsley**
Janet Orgreave	**Louise Purnell**
Mrs Orgreave	**Connie Merrigold**
Hilda Lessways/Clayhanger	**Janet Suzman**
George Cannon	**Denis Quilley**
Arthur Dayson	**Geoffrey Hutchings**
Florrie	**Erin Geraghty**
Big James	**Bruce Purchase**
Tom Orgreave	**Geoffrey Drew**
Miss Gailey	**Renee Asherson**
Mr Boutwood	**John Stratton**
Albert Benbow	**Clive Swift**
Clara Benbow	**Anne Carroll**
Tom Swetnam	**Paul Jesson**
George Cannon Jr	**Timothy Woolgar**
Ada	**Julie Peasgood**
Tertius Ingpen	**Denholm Elliott**

Writer **Douglas Livingstone**
Executive Producer **Stella Richman**
Producers **David Reid, Douglas Livingstone**

Provincial life with two generations of a Victorian family.

Based on Arnold Bennett's novels *Clayhanger, Hilda Lessways, These Twain* and *Roll Call*, this mammoth, 26-part series was perhaps ITV's answer to THE FORSYTE SAGA, if somewhat less compelling. The setting is the 'Five Towns', Bennett's vision of the Potteries area (today's Stoke-on-Trent), with Bursley the main centre. Here, the Clayhanger family is headed by industrious Darius Clayhanger, a self-made printer who wants his son, Edwin, to follow in his footsteps. Edwin, however, has other plans, and sees himself as an architect instead. Entwined in Edwin's life is the wilful Hilda Lessways, who marries her boss, newspaper proprietor George Cannon, only to find the marriage is bigamous. Edwin and Hilda eventually wed but their lives do not run smoothly as the decades pass. Charting an age of industrial, social and religious change, the drama also moves to Brighton, where Cannon runs a boarding house, and Dartmoor, where he is imprisoned following his bigamy. The BBC dramatized two of Bennett's novels, *Clayhanger* and *Hilda Lessways*, under the single title of *Hilda Lessways* in 1959 (Judi Dench as Hilda, Brian Smith as Edwin, William Squire as Cannon and Violet Carson as Auntie Hamps).

Cleese, John

(1939–)

Tall, Somerset-born actor/comedian/writer, a Cambridge Footlights graduate who was already a TV legend thanks to MONTY PYTHON'S FLYING CIRCUS when achieving even greater acclaim for his manic FAWLTY TOWERS (star and co-writer with then wife, Connie Booth). Pre-*Python*, Cleese had appeared with Ronnies Barker and Corbett in THE FROST REPORT, and with Graham Chapman *et al.* in AT LAST THE 1948 SHOW. He later supported Les Dawson in SEZ LES and played Petruchio in the BBC's 1980 presentation of *The Taming of the Shrew*. Cleese also wrote (mostly in collaboration with Chapman) for David Frost, THAT WAS THE WEEK THAT WAS, *Broaden Your Mind, Marty* and the DOCTOR IN THE HOUSE series. His numerous guest appearances have taken in shows as diverse as WHOOPS APOCALYPSE, CHEERS, THE AVENGERS, THE GOODIES, DOCTOR WHO, THE MUPPET SHOW, THIRD ROCK FROM THE SUN and WILL AND GRACE, although in recent years film work has taken over. He did, however, indulge his fascination with lemurs in a *Born to be Wild* expedition to Madagascar in 1998 and fronted the factual series *The Human Face* in 2001.

Clemens, Brian

(1931–)

British producer and scriptwriter, whose work for ITC in the 1960s earned him a following among fans of TV adventure. By far his greatest impact was in THE AVENGERS, although he also contributed to THE MAN FROM INTERPOL, THE INVISIBLE MAN, DANGER MAN, ADAM ADAMANT LIVES!, THE CHAMPIONS, THE PERSUADERS!, THE PROTECTORS and QUILLER, as well as creating THE PROFESSIONALS and the suspense anthology THRILLER, and co-creating the sitcom MY WIFE NEXT DOOR (with Richard Waring). In the 1980s and 1990s, Clemens worked on series like BERGERAC, REMINGTON STEELE, FATHER DOWLING INVESTIGATES, the revival of PERRY MASON and *Highlander*. He was heavily involved with *C15: The New Professionals* and was also series consultant on the high-tech action drama BUGS.

Clement, Dick

(1937–)

British writer and producer, partner of Ian La Frenais and creator of some of British television's classic comedies. Essex-born Clement teamed up with Geordie insurance salesman La Frenais in the early 1960s and scripted a series about two young pals from Newcastle, THE LIKELY LADS, which became one of BBC 2's first hits and was successfully revived in the 1970s as WHATEVER HAPPENED TO THE LIKELY LADS? The duo went on to create PORRIDGE, and their success continued into the 1980s with AUF WIEDERSEHEN, PET. Among their other offerings over the years have been THE FURTHER ADVENTURES OF LUCKY JIM (two versions), *Mr Aitch*, THICK AS THIEVES, *Mog*, the *Porridge* sequel *Going Straight* and an episode of *Lenny Henry Tonite*. In the 1990s they penned the limousine-for-hire drama *Full Stretch*, and the sitcoms *Freddie and Max, Old Boy Network* and OVER THE RAINBOW, the last inspired by their own screenplay for the film *The Commitments*. They also contributed episodes to SHINE ON HARVEY MOON and Billy Connolly's US series *Billy*, as well as material for Tracey Ullman. Recent work has included a revival of *Auf Wiedersehen, Pet*, plus the dramas *Archangel* and *The Rotters' Club*. One of Clement's early credits was as a writer and producer for NOT ONLY . . . BUT ALSO . . ., while La Frenais (without Clement) has adapted Jonathan Gash's LOVEJOY novels for television, co-created SPENDER with Jimmy Nail and contributed to the 1972 sitcom THE TRAIN NOW STANDING. Together and separately, they have worked as script editors on several other programmes.

Cleopatras, The ✶

UK (BBC) Drama. BBC 2 1983

Cleopatra	**Michelle Newell**
Pot Belly	**Richard Griffiths**
Cleopatra II	**Elizabeth Shepherd**
Cleopatra Thea	**Caroline Mortimer**
Cleopatra IV	**Sue Holderness**
Cleopatra Tryphaena	**Amanda Boxer**
Cleopatra Selene	**Prue Clarke**
Cleopatra Berenike	**Pauline Moran**
Chickpea	**David Horovitch**
Alexander	**Ian McNeice**
Theodotus	**Graham Crowden**
Fluter	**Adam Bareham**
Mark Antony	**Christopher Neame**
Julius Caesar	**Robert Hardy**
Charmian	**Shirin Taylor**
Arsinoe	**Francesca Gonshaw**
Iras	**Carole Harrison**

Writer **Philip Mackie**
Producer **Guy Slater**

● ***The history of Greek rule in ancient Egypt.***

This wry, 'horror-comic' look at the unscrupulous, incestuous dynasty of Greek women who ruled Egypt from 145 BC to 35 BC was played rather deadpan. The aim was to avoid flippancy but also to skip over the more grotesque incidents. In eight parts, the story of the Cleopatras is told by the last Cleo (played by Michelle Newell, who also plays her great-grandmother), and flashes back to her six ruthless ancestors of the same name. Also involved in the sordid goings-on is the flabby Pot Belly. Dozens of brave girls with little hair and even less clothing wobble around in the background. Actress Amanda Boxer even shaved her head for her role. Sadly, the series failed to achieve respect and suffered the ridicule of both critics and viewers.

Climber, The ✶

UK (BBC) Situation Comedy. BBC 1 1983

Harry Lumsdon	**Robin Nedwell**
Ted	**David Battley**
Shirley	**Jacqueline Tong**
Reg	**David Williams**
Mr Thomas	**Jack Watson**

Writer **Alex Shearer**
Producer **Alan J. W. Bell**

● ***A manual worker thinks he can improve his social standing, but reality is rather different.***

Having worked in a bakery for 16 years, Harry Lumsdon feels he can do no more with his life. One day, however, he fills in an IQ test and discovers, to his amazement, that he has a rating of 166 and is possibly a genius (the truth being that he has added up the scores incorrectly). Instilled with new inner-belief, Harry decides to change his life and improve his position within the company, but his misplaced over-confidence only leads to disaster – time and again. This six-episode series included guest appearances from Spike Milligan and 'Dr Finlay' Bill Simpson.

Clive James – Fame in the Twentieth Century ✶✶

UK (BBC) Documentary. BBC 1 1993

Writer/Presenter **Clive James**
Producer **Beatrice Ballard**

● ***Decade-by-decade look at the famous and infamous in the 20th century.***

In this nostalgic, eight-part series, Clive James, with his usual wry observation, looked back over the 20th century, the first century to experience the power of mass media and all its fame-creating potential. He scrutinized the people who had made the news and gained celebrity status in each decade, examining how and why they came to the fore. He then scratched away the veneer to reveal the truth behind the headlines. Archive footage traced the lives of leading politicians, film stars, criminals and pioneers, from Charlie Chaplin and Mahatma Gandhi to Madonna and Norman Schwarzkopf.

Clochemerle ✶✶✶

UK (BBC/Bavaria Atelier) Comedy. BBC 2 1972

Mayor Barthélemy Piechut	**Cyril Cusack**
Curé Ponosse	**Roy Dotrice**
Ernest Tafardel	**Kenneth Griffith**
Justine Putet	**Wendy Hiller**
Adèle Torbayon	**Cyd Hayman**
The Baroness Courtebiche	**Micheline Presle**
Alexandre Bourdillat	**Hugh Griffith**
Nicholas the Beadle	**Bernard Bresslaw**
Hortense Girodot	**Madeline Smith**
Monsieur Girodot	**Wolfe Morris**

Rose Bivaque .... **Georgina Moon**
Narrator .... **Peter Ustinov**

Writers **Ray Galton, Alan Simpson**
Producer **Michael Mills**

● ***Plans to install a new pissoir in a French village result in civil unrest.***

Gabriel Chevallier's 1934 comedy was adapted by Ray Galton and Alan Simpson in nine parts to create this gentle farce. It concerns the good people of Clochemerle, who are divided over plans to open a new urinal in the centre of the small French village. Reaction from the snootier members of society, and especially the prim ladyfolk, reaches such a peak that the army is called in to quell the unrest. Filmed in France, in the village of Marchampt in Beaujolais, the series attracted a celebrated cast of both British and French performers.

Clocking Off ★★★

UK (Red) Drama. BBC 1 2000–3
DVD: inD DVD

James 'Mack' Mackintosh .... **Philip Glenister**
Trudy Graham .... **Lesley Sharp**
Yvonne Kalakowski .... **Sarah Lancashire**
Julie O'Neill .... **Siobhan Finneran**
Katherine Mackintosh .... **Christine Tremarco**
Martin Leach .... **Jason Merrells**
Kev Leach .... **Jack Deam**
Steve Robinson .... **Wil Johnson**
Sylvia Robinson .... **Diane Parish**
Jake Robinson .... **Jake Sampson**
Freda Wilson .... **Joan Kempson**
Brian Pringle .... **Paul Oldham**
Ade Cameron .... **Tony Mooney**
Barry Sleight .... **Steve Jackson**
Bev Ratcliffe/Aindow .... **Lindsey Coulson**
Barney Watson .... **Ben Crompton**
Ronnie Anderson .... **Ricky Tomlinson**
Nick Anderson .... **William Ash**
Babs Fisher/Leach .... **Ashley Jensen**
Grace Eastwood .... **Lisa Millet**
Suzie Davidson .... **Nicola Stephenson**
Hannah Phillips .... **Katisha Kenyon**
Jenny Wood .... **Sophie Okonedo**
Peggy Hargreaves .... **Alice Barry**
Kim Anderson .... **Emma Cunniffe**
Alan Preston .... **Robert Pugh**
Gary Dugdale .... **Marshall Lancaster**
Pat Fletcher .... **Pam Ferris**
Jamie Campbell .... **Derek Riddell**
Colin Wilkes .... **Mark Benton**

Creator **Paul Abbott**
Executive Producer **Nicola Shindler**
Producers **Ann Harrison-Baxter, Juliet Charlesworth**

● ***Workers at a northern textiles factory each have a tale to tell.***

Though the setting for this acclaimed series is Mackintosh Textiles, a fabric factory in the north-west of England, nearly all the action revolves around the private lives of its machinists, supervisors, warehousemen, drivers, security guards and other employees. For much of the time the regular cast plays a background role, providing little more than a context for the major storyline of the week. However, most of the team then get to enjoy their day in the sun, with an episode devoted to their own tangled personal lives. Initial boss of the company is 'Mack' Mackintosh, a man with wife problems. His equally troubled PA is Trudy Graham. The series' powerful writing, by creator Paul Abbott and others, was widely praised, as were strong performances by the leading men and women and notable guest appearances from the likes of John Simm, Christopher Eccleston and David Morrissey.

Clooney, George

(1961–)

American actor attaining star status thanks largely to his role as Dr Doug Ross in ER. Previously, Clooney had been seen as Booker Brooks in ROSEANNE, as well as in several other US sitcoms (including one called, strangely, *E/R*), the soap, *Sisters*, and the police dramas *Bodies of Evidence* and *Sunset Beat*, most of which never aired in the UK. Clooney also made a guest appearance in MURDER, SHE WROTE, among other series. Late singer Rosemary Clooney was his aunt, and he is the son of Nick Clooney, a TV presenter and variety host. Clooney was once married to actress Talia Balsam.

Close and True ★★★

UK (Coastal/United) Drama. ITV 2000

John Close .... **Robson Green**
Graham True .... **James Bolam**
Stephen Sheedy .... **Mark Moraghan**
Paula Farrent .... **Kerry Rolfe**
Mark Sheedy .... **Jamie Bell**
Mary Close .... **Pamela Ruddock**
Sally Ann Mae .... **Susan Jameson**
Kim Cotton .... **Kerryann Christiansen**
Ibi Badgioni .... **Nicola Grier**
Jessica Laing .... **Louise Delamere**
Gordon .... **Richard Sands**

Creators **Tony Etchells, Rebecca Keane**
Writers **Tony Etchells, Andrea Earl**
Executive Producers **Michele Buck, Sandra Jobling, Damien Timmer**
Producer **Rebecca Keane**

● ***A Geordie boy returns home to take over an ailing legal practice.***

Responding to a desperate cry for help from boyhood friend Steve Sheedy, London commercial lawyer John Close returns to his home town of Newcastle upon Tyne. It seems Sheedy is in a spot of trouble and needs his old mate to get him off a charge of attempted murder. Close not only has to plan the defence but also learn the ropes of criminal law while so doing. He also needs to get used to the idea of being back in a city that fills him with mixed memories. As a shy, polite man with a strange phobia about water, Close soon begins to feel out of his depth. He sticks at the task, however, and his efforts bring him into contact with Simons and True, a solicitors' firm run by the eccentric but brilliant Graham True, a man being treated in Ridgeway House hospital for psychiatric illness. Before he knows it, Close has joined True as partner in the struggling legal aid practice, taking over from junior partner Colin Simons, who skips the country, leaving behind a pile of unpaid bills. John's new professional colleagues are Sally Ann, the dry, frosty secretary who keeps the firm shipshape and Newcastle fashion; Kim, Sally Ann's less than efficient assistant; and Ibi Badgioni, a hard-headed Glaswegian barrister that Close employs. On the personal side, Mary is Close's widowed mother, who works in a chip shop; Jessica, a bank manager, is an old flame; Paula is Steve's ex-wife with whom John has an affair, and Mark is Steve and Paula's teenage son (played by Billy Elliot star Jamie Bell).

Close and True was well received by critics, praised for being warm, funny, inventive and not too cloying, but still only six episodes were produced.

Close Down

In the days before 24-hour television, the final announcement of the TV day, often involving a look at the clock, a preview of the next day's fare and a rendition of the national anthem and the station signature tune.

Closed Circuit

A television system that is not broadcast but transmitted via a sequence of cables or by microwaves to a restricted number of receivers. It is generally in use in educational establishments, but has been used for showing major sporting or entertainment events to a limited audience in theatres or stadia.

Close-up

A detailed shot of an object or, more commonly, a head-and-shoulders shot of the presenter or actor.

Closing Titles

The roll-call of performers' and technicians' credits seen at the end of a television programme or film.

Clothes Show, The ✶

UK (BBC) Fashion. BBC 1 1986–98

Presenters **Selina Scott, Jeff Banks, Jane Lomas, Jasmine Fadhli, Caryn Franklin, Siobhan Maher, Lucy Pilkington, Raj Dhanda, Sheryl Simms, Brenda Emmanus, Vanessa Scott, Ann-Marie Gwatkin, Ged Gray, Tim Vincent**

Producers **Roger Casstles, Clare Stride, Colette Byrne, Karen Hughes**

● ***Off-the-peg collection of fashion news and features.***

Covering all aspects of the rag trade, and fashions for all shapes, sizes, ages, genders and pockets, *The Clothes Show* was launched as a midweek afternoon programme with an evening repeat, before lodging itself in a Sunday afternoon slot for ten years. As well as previewing and reviewing the latest collections, the series offered interviews with top designers, profiles of chain stores and other magazine-type items, plus a number of regular competitions. These included contests for schoolkid designers, new models, a Bride of the Year, and the Needlematch competition for talented sewers, knitters and embroiderers. Such was the popularity of the show at its peak that a BBC magazine was issued as a complement and *The Clothes Show Live* played to big audiences at Olympia. Host Jeff Banks admitted he had been striving to get such a show on air for a number of years before BBC Pebble Mill finally came up with the goods.

Cluedo ✶

UK (Granada/Action Time) Game Show. ITV 1990–3

Season One

Host .... **James Bellini**
Mrs Peacock .... **Stephanie Beacham**
Mrs White .... **June Whitfield**
Col. Mustard .... **Robin Ellis**
Miss Scarlett .... **Tracy-Louise Ward**
Revd Green .... **Robin Nedwell**
Prof. Plum .... **Kristoffer Tabori**

Season Two

Host .... **Chris Tarrant**
Mrs Peacock .... **Rula Lenska**
Mrs White .... **Mollie Sugden**
Col. Mustard .... **Michael Jayston**
Miss Scarlett .... **Koo Stark**
Revd Green .... **Richard Wilson**
Prof. Plum .... **David McCallum**

Season Three

Host .... **Richard Madeley**
Mrs Peacock .... **Susan George**
Mrs White .... **Pam Ferris**
Col. Mustard .... **Lewis Collins**
Miss Scarlett .... **Lysette Anthony**
Revd Green .... **Christopher Biggins**
Prof. Plum .... **Tom Baker**

Season Four

Host .... **Richard Madeley**
Mrs Peacock .... **Joanna Lumley**
Mrs White .... **Liz Smith**
Col. Mustard .... **Leslie Grantham**
Ms Scarlett .... **Jerry Hall**
Revd Green .... **Nicholas Parsons**
Prof. Plum .... **John Bird**

Executive Producer **Dianne Nelmes**
Producers **Stephen Leahy, Brian Park, Kieran Roberts, Mark Gorton**

● ***Celebrity whodunnit, based on the enormously successful board game invented by Anthony Pratt in 1944.***

In this light-hearted, studio-bound mystery, a murder was committed each week at Arlington Grange (not at Tudor Close, as in the board game), a house owned by society widow Mrs Peacock. What the two teams of two celebrities had to do was work out whodunnit, where in the house and with what weapon, having viewed the video evidence and closely questioned the suspects. Apart from Mrs Peacock, there were also the flighty Miss Scarlett, housekeeper Mrs White, retired military man Colonel Mustard, decidedly dodgy vicar Reverend Green and eccentric Professor Plum. The cast changed every season, including for a 1990 Christmas special, which saw Kate O'Mara as Mrs Peacock, Joan Sims as Mrs White, Toyah Wilcox as Miss Scarlett, David Robb as Colonel Mustard, Derek Nimmo as Reverend Green and Ian Lavender in the role of Professor Plum. James Bellini hosted this one-off. The series was not entirely dissimilar to the earlier WHODUNNIT?

Cluff ✶✶

UK (BBC) Police Drama. BBC 1 1964–5

DS Caleb Cluff .... **Leslie Sands**

Insp. Mole	**Eric Barker**
	Michael Bates
DC Barker	**John Rolfe**
PC Harry Bullock	**John McKelvey**
Annie Croft	**Olive Milbourne**

Creator **Gil North**
Producer **Terence Dudley**

Easy-paced policing with an old-fashioned Yorkshire detective.

Caleb Cluff is a traditional sort of copper. Not for him the exhausting business of tearing around after criminals, largely because there aren't that many where he lives (fictional Gunnershaw) at that time (the early 1960s). No, this detective is painfully slow about his business, much to the annoyance of his superior, Inspector Mole, but he is also good at his job, probably because he is so thorough and takes time to get to know everyone. His young sidekick, DC Barker, certainly benefits from his methodical approach.

The tweed-suited Cluff's idea of fun is a good walk, with a pipe in his mouth, chestnut walking stick in his hand and Clive, his loyal black-and-tan dog, at his side. He lives alone, and is looked after by a daily housekeeper, Annie Croft. Created by Gil North, the character had first appeared as part of the DETECTIVE anthology series.

Clunes, Martin

(1962–)

London-born actor-director, the son of the late classical actor Alec Clunes. His first major TV part came in DOCTOR WHO and Clunes then moved on to specialize in upper-class roles, although his greatest success has been in quite a different vein, as 1990s lad Gary Strang in MEN BEHAVING BADLY. His other major roles have been in ALL AT NUMBER 20 (lodger Henry), NO PLACE LIKE HOME (son Nigel Crabtree), JEEVES AND WOOSTER (Barmy Fotheringay Phipps), DEMOB (ex-army entertainer Dick Dobson), *An Evening with Gary Lineker* (Dan), *Touch and Go* (wifeswapper Nick Wood), *Over Here* (Group Captain Barker), *Hunting Venus* (New Romantic has-been Simon Delancey, also as director), *Sex 'n' Death* (TV show host Ben Black), GORMENGHAST (Professor Flower), *Dirty Tricks* (Edward), *Lorna Doone* (Jeremy Stickles) and the pantomime *Aladdin* (Abanazer), with smaller/guest parts in series like *About Face*, HANNAY, BOON, INSPECTOR MORSE, LOVEJOY, GONE TO THE DOGS (Pilbeam), *Rik Mayall Presents*, RIDES, BONJOUR LA CLASSE, *Moving Story* and *The Lord of Misrule* (Minister for Defence). In 2000 he presented the documentary series *Men Down Under* with Neil Morrissey and he has also fronted a *Born to be Wild* special. More recent credits have come in the dramas *A is for Acid* (John George Haigh), GOODBYE MR CHIPS (Mr Chipping), WILLIAM AND MARY (William Shawcross), *The Booze Cruise* (Clive Rainer), DOC MARTIN (Dr Martin Ellingham), *Beauty* (Tom Fitzhenry) and *Fungus the Bogeyman* (George White). Clunes also provides the voice for cartoon dog *Kipper*. He is married to TV producer Philippa Braithwaite.

CNN

(Cable News Network)

CNN was founded in Atlanta by Ted Turner in 1980, against the advice of experts of the day who believed that a dedicated, round-the-clock news channel could not survive in the limited world of cable. Indeed, the first few years in the company's history were unremarkable and it was not until 1985 that it enjoyed its first year in profit. In 1982 a second channel, majoring on continuous 30-minute news summaries and known initially as CNN-2, was launched; it is now called CNN Headline News. In 1985 a third channel, with a global rather than American bias, was opened up. Called CNN International, it is this channel that can be seen all around the planet and that has led the field in gathering and disseminating international news. Its uniqueness was underscored by the outbreak of the Gulf War in 1991, when CNN became the channel to watch for 'as it happens' reports on air raids and other unfolding events. CNN International has been supplied to hotels and other broadcasting stations since its earliest days and became available to European homes via the Astra satellite system in 1992 and later via digital services. CNN is now part of Time Warner.

Cockles ★★

UK (BBC) Situation Comedy. BBC 1 1984

Arthur Dumpton	**James Grout**
Gloria du Bois	**Joan Sims**
Jacques du Bois	**Norman Rodway**
George	**Tim Wylton**
Emma	**Elizabeth Edmonds**
Madame Rosa	**Fanny Carby**
Mabel Gutteridge	**Jane Lowe**
Graham	**David Bamber**

Writer **Douglas Livingstone**
Producer **Ruth Boswell**

A lonely Londoner looks for happiness in the seaside resort he loved as a child.

When Arthur Dumpton is made redundant he chooses to leave London and return to Cocklesea, the seaside resort he frequented as a schoolboy. Already deserted by his wife (she ran off with his best friend), he hopes to re-create the glorious days of his youth. With lay-off cheque in hand, he seeks out boyhood friend Jacques du Bois, who, it turns out, is a failed landscape painter, and, unfortunately for Arthur, also a con man. Jacques is married to the long-suffering, somewhat overdressed Gloria (Arthur's one-time sweetheart). Gloria is proprietress of the Sunnysides Guest House but business is not great because Cocklesea is fading fast. Its pleasures appear to be all in the past and tourists are shunning its advances. With bigoted Jacques's bogus advice, the optimistic, easily hoodwinked Arthur ploughs his wealth into schemes to rejuvenate the resort. Six 55-minute episodes were produced.

Codename ★★

UK (BBC) Drama. BBC 2 1970

Sir Iain Dalzell	**Clifford Evans**
Philip West	**Anthony Valentine**
Diana Dalzell	**Alexandra Bastedo**
Culliford	**Brian Peck**

Creators **David Proudfoot, Bill Hays**
Producer **Gerard Glaister**

A university is the secret base of a government spy agency.

In this international espionage caper, the top man is Sir Ian Dalzell, on the face of it Master of Cambridge College but, in truth, also the head of MI 17, a British government spy ring. His agents all work undercover at the college as teachers, or masquerade as students. They include Philip West and Dalzell's own daughter, Diana. Thirteen episodes in all were produced, penned by writers like N. J. Crisp, Robert Barr and Tony Williamson, and featuring guest stars such as Patrick Allen, Maureen Lipman, Andrew Sachs and Terence Alexander.

Cohen, Sacha Baron

(1972–)

Cambridge history graduate (and Footlights member) Sacha Baron Cohen shot to fame in 1998 in Channel 4's late night comedy offering THE 11 O'CLOCK SHOW, with his wickedly satirical creation Ali G. Allegedly a black youth (though clearly white) from Staines, Ali G adopted black American slang and teased politicians and other authoritarian figures with patently stupid questions that they could not afford to dismiss. But the 'hipness' of British youth culture was as much ridiculed as the pomp of celebrity and power. The fact that 'Ali G' was an abbreviation of the name Alistair Graham underlined how tongue-in-cheek the characterization was. Highlights of Cohen's performances were edited together in *Da Best of Ali G* and then in 2000 he gained his own series, *Da Ali G Show*. He has also progressed to other comic creations, including Kazakhstani TV reporter Borat Karabzhanov, seen exploring English culture in the one-off *The Best of Borat* and *Borat's Television Programme*. An early TV appearance for Cohen came in *Jack and Jeremy's Police 4* in 1995, a sketch show in which he supported Jack Dee and Jeremy Hardy. Recently, he has made a guest appearance in CURB YOUR ENTHUSIASM.

Colbourne, Maurice

(Roger Middleton; 1939–89)

Determined-looking British actor whose big TV break came as John Kline in the violent GANGSTERS series. However, it is as Tom Howard in the maritime soap HOWARDS' WAY that he is best remembered, and it was while working on the fifth series of the show that he died of a heart attack. Among his other credits were THE DAY OF THE TRIFFIDS (Jack Coker), JOHNNY JARVIS (Jake), the part of Charles Marston in THE ONEDIN LINE and guest spots in SHOESTRING, DOCTOR WHO, VAN DER VALK and THE RETURN OF THE SAINT.

Colbys, The ✶

US (Aaron Spelling) Drama. BBC 1 1986–7 (US: ABC 1985–7)

Jason Colby .... **Charlton Heston**
Sable Scott Colby .... **Stephanie Beacham**
Francesca Scott Colby/ Langdon .... **Katherine Ross**
Jeff Colby .... **John James**
Fallon Carrington/Colby .... **Emma Samms**
Monica Colby .... **Tracy Scoggins**
Miles Colby .... **Maxwell Caulfield**
Bliss Colby .... **Claire Yarlett**
Zachary Powers .... **Ricardo Montalban**
Constance Colby .... **Barbara Stanwyck**
Lord Roger Langdon .... **David Hedison**
Garrett Boydston .... **Ken Howard**
Hutch Corrigan .... **Joseph Campanella**
Sean McAllister .... **Charles Van Eman**
Channing Carter/Colby .... **Kim Morgan Greene**
Senator Cash Cassidy .... **James Houghton**
Adrienne Cassidy .... **Shanna Reed**
Hoyt Parker/Phillip Colby .... **Michael Parks**

Creator **Aaron Spelling**
Writers **Robert Pollock, Eileen Pollock**
Producers **Richard Shapiro, Esther Shapiro**

● ***Glamorous spin-off from DYNASTY, initially entitled* Dynasty II – The Colbys.**

This soap is set in Los Angeles, around the wealthy Colby family, who had been introduced in a few episodes of *Dynasty* before being left to their own devices. The central character is Jason Colby, head of Colby Enterprises, a company with a finger in more than one pie. Oil, real estate, aeronautics and shipping all contribute to its success. Similar to *Dynasty*'s Blake Carrington in many respects, Jason is proud, ruthless and exceptionally rich, not that that makes him or his family particularly happy. His wife, Sable, is usually in the thick of the action, fighting with her sister, Frankie, and attempting to murder Constance, Jason's sister, the matriarch of Belvedere, the family's estate. The younger generation are represented by Miles (Jason and Sable's son), Monica (their elder daughter), and Bliss (their younger daughter). The link with *Dynasty* comes through the character of Jeff Colby, who is Frankie's son and Jason's nephew (though later revealed to be his son, too).

The Colbys runs the gamut of the usual soap stories – illicit affairs, divorce, terminal illness, inheritance disputes, acts of vengeance and commercial wrangles – and introduces a host of temporary characters. But it also takes the genre to higher planes (or lower depths, depending on the point of view) when Fallon, Jeff's love from *Dynasty* (who has already been resurrected from a fatal plane crash and has married Miles in a fit of amnesia), witnesses the landing of a UFO and is whisked away to galaxies new. This was meant to be an end-of-season cliffhanger, but *The Colbys* never came back. Despite the enormous sums of money spent on performers, clothes and sets, the ratings were disastrous. It was left to *Dynasty* to bring Fallon back down to Earth.

Cold Comfort Farm ✶✶✶

UK (BBC/Thames) Drama. BBC 1 1995
DVD: Acron Media

Judith Starkadder .... **Eileen Atkins**
Flora Poste .... **Kate Beckinsale**
Aunt Ada Doom .... **Sheila Burrell**
Mr Mybug .... **Stephen Fry**
Adam Lambsbreath .... **Freddie Jones**
Mrs Smiling .... **Joanna Lumley**
Amos Starkadder .... **Ian McKellen**
Mrs Beetle .... **Miriam Margolyes**
Seth Starkadder .... **Rufus Sewell**
Reuben Starkadder .... **Ivan Kaye**
Elfine Starkadder .... **Maria Miles**
Charles Fairford .... **Christopher Bowen**
Mrs Hawk-Monitor .... **Angela Thorne**
Dick Hawk-Monitor .... **Rupert Penry-Jones**

Writer **Malcolm Bradbury**
Producer **Alison Gilby**

● ***A city girl tries to better her rustic relatives.***

New Year's Day 1995 saw the premier of *Cold Comfort Farm*, directed by movie giant John Schlesinger. Malcolm Bradbury takes Stella Gibbons's 1932 satire on novels about nature and rural life and brings it colourfully to the small screen, peopled with a cast of great character actors. Flora Poste is heroine of the piece, a spirited, interfering girl aged around 20, an aspiring Jane Austen who is doomed to rely on the goodwill of her distant relatives, the Starkadders, after the sudden death of her parents. She arrives at Cold Comfort Farm – a rundown holding in Sussex, where the cows are skinny and the crops blighted – and sets about reforming the lives of her country cousins. Cousin Judith Starkadder is the dried-up mother of two sons – Seth, a womanizing movie lover, and Reuben, an industrious farm labourer – and a daughter, Elfine, whom Flora hopes to marry off in better circumstances outside the clan. Amos is Judith's fire-and-brimstone preacher husband, while up in the attic lives family matriarch Aunt Ada Doom, dedicated to keeping the anarchic family united. Ada was traumatized as a child when she witnessed 'something nasty in the woodshed', a mystery that has never been revealed. Other characters central to the action are veteran cowhand Adam Lambsbreath and snappy domestic help Mrs Beetle. Mybug is the local author, a D. H. Lawrence parody intent on warming up frigid Englishwomen through his work, while Mrs Smiling, a London society hostess, and Charles Fairford, a trainee preacher, are Flora's two supporters.

Cold Comfort Farm had previously been dramatized for television in three parts by David Turner (BBC 2 1968), starring Sarah Badel as Flora, Alastair Sim as Amos, Brian Blessed as Reuben, Peter Egan as Seth, Fay Compton as Aunt Ada, and Rosalie Crutchley as Judith.

Cold Enough for Snow

See *Eskimo Day*.

Cold Feet ★★★

UK (Granada) Comedy Drama. ITV 1998–2003
DVD: Granada

Adam Williams	**James Nesbitt**
Rachel Bradley	**Helen Baxendale**
Pete Gifford	**John Thomson**
Jenny Gifford	**Fay Ripley**
David Marsden	**Robert Bathurst**
Karen Marsden	**Hermione Norris**
Ramona Ramirez	**Jacey Salles**
Jo Ellison	**Kimberley Joseph**

Creator **Mike Bullen**
Writers **Mike Bullen, David Nicholls, Matt Greenhalgh**
Executive Producers **Andy Harries, Christine Langan, Mike Bullen**
Producers **Christine Langan, Spencer Campbell**

● ***Ups and downs in the lives of three middle-class couples.***

Variously described as 'FRIENDS with children' and 'THIS LIFE with laughs', *Cold Feet* focuses on three comfortably off couples in their 30s, drawing humour from their day-to-day travails and the efforts they make (or don't) to work at their relationships. Couple number one are Adam, a systems analyst, and Rachel, an advertising executive, who met in the pilot episode, shown at Easter 1997 – 'Cold Feet' referring to his continual fear of commitment. Their friends are insurance clerk Pete and stay-at-home Jenny, trying to conceive in the pilot but giving birth at the start of the first series. Sleepless nights and other baby matters fill their life. Completing the sextet are David and Karen, he a well-heeled, career-dominated management consultant, she a book editor who has given up work to care for their baby son, Joshua, and who now finds home life boring. The setting, refreshingly, is Manchester, not London, and there are technical innovations, too, with overlapping scenes and the use of flashbacks providing a novel twist.

Despite winning Montreux's celebrated Golden Rose for the pilot programme, *Cold Feet* almost didn't make it into a series, having performed poorly audience-wise in a late time-slot. However, when it eventually returned, it proved to be one of ITV's major hits of the late 1990s. Four further series continued to explore the deterioration in each relationship, dealing with adultery, depression, sickness and alcoholism, among other 'difficult' subjects.

A US version of the series, with the same title and set in Seattle, aired briefly on NBC in 1999, starring David Sutcliffe and Jean Louisa Kelly, among others.

Cold Warrior ★★

UK (BBC) Spy Drama. BBC 1 1984

Capt. Percival	**Michael Denison**
Danny	**Dean Harris**
Jo	**Lucy Fleming**
Sir William Logie	**David Swift**

Creator **Arden Winch**
Producer **Gerard Glaister**

● ***The cases of a toff spymaster.***

After previous TV outings in BLOOD MONEY and SKORPION, the ultra-civilized Captain Percival takes centre stage in this eight-part series. The former public schoolboy, kitted out with bowler hat and brolly, employs his considerable intellect and impeccable manners to bring to heel all who threaten Britain's national security.

Colditz ★★★

UK (BBC/Universal) Drama. BBC 1 1972–4

Lt. Col. John Preston	**Jack Hedley**
Capt. Pat Grant	**Edward Hardwicke**
Flt Lt./Major Phil Carrington	**Robert Wagner**
Flt Lt. Simon Carter	**David McCallum**
Kommandant	**Bernard Hepton**
Lt. Dick Player	**Christopher Neame**
Capt. George Brent	**Paul Chapman**
Hauptmann Ulmann	**Hans Meyer**
Capt. Tim Downing	**Richard Heffer**
Pilot Officer Muir	**Peter Penry-Jones**
Major Horst Mohn	**Anthony Valentine**
Squadron Leader Tony Shaw	**Jeremy Kemp**
Lt. Col. Max Dodd	**Dan O'Herlihy**

Creators **Brian Degas, Gerard Glaister**
Producer **Gerard Glaister**

● ***Prisoners of war attempt to flee an escape-proof German castle.***

Based on the book by Major Pat Reid, a genuine survivor of Colditz who acted as technical adviser, this series follows the adventurous bids for freedom of a group of high-level Allied POWs, most of whom have already succeeded in escaping from other prison camps. After an initial three episodes which show how all the main characters arrive at Castle Colditz (a supposedly impregnable fortress, known as Oflag IV C, perched high on sheer cliffs in eastern Germany), the series settles down into a portrayal of the rivalry and suspicions that exist among the various Allied nationalities. Their relationship with their German captors is also in focus. Although a mutual respect develops between the POWs, led by the British Lt. Col. Preston, and the camp's tolerant Kommandant, friction increases when the SS threatens to take over the castle and when, in the second series, the sadistic Major Mohn is introduced.

The desperate escape plans include launching home-made gliders off the castle roof, as well as the more conventional guard impersonations and wall scalings. One inmate, Wing Commander Marsh, works on insanity as a means of getting out. He succeeds but, when finally freed, the stress of acting mad has actually warped his mind. Guest stars come and go, and the progress of the war outside the castle walls is used as a backdrop to events in the closed world of Colditz itself. The series concludes with liberation in 1945.

Colditz revived the flagging career of Robert Wagner, who played Canadian airman Phil Carrington. The series also led to a variety of spin-off ventures, ranging from bizarre holidays at the real castle to a children's board game. The inspiration had been the 1955 film *The Colditz Story*, starring John Mills and Eric Portman.

In 2005, ITV 1 screened a new two-part drama with the same title and based loosely on events at Colditz Castle. It starred Damien Lewis as Nicholas McGrade, who escapes and begins a relationship with Lizzie Carter (Sophie Myles), the girlfriend of his buddy, Jack Rose (Tom Hardy), sadly still behind the bars of the German fortress. Timothy West and James Fox also appeared.

Cole, George

OBE (1925–)

For most viewers, London-born George Cole is, and always will be, Arthur Daley. Though his TV work has been prolific and varied, his portrayal of MINDER's Cockney spiv with a lock-up full of dodgy goods and a fine line in persuasive banter has dwarfed all his other contributions to the small screen. Cole came to television after a successful stage, radio and film career in which he worked closely with Alastair Sim, and his profile as a rather unreliable, Jack-the-lad figure was established by the St Trinian's films, in which he played Flash Harry. In 1960, his radio role of David Bliss, in the comedy A LIFE OF BLISS, moved to television, and Cole never looked back. He went on to star in *A Man of Our Times* (Max Osborne), DON'T FORGET TO WRITE (Gordon Maple), THE BOUNDER (Trevor), BLOTT ON THE LANDSCAPE (Sir Giles Lynchwood), COMRADE DAD (Reg Dudgeon), ROOT INTO EUROPE (Henry Root), MY GOOD FRIEND (Peter Banks), DAD (Brian Hook) and *An Independent Man* (Freddie Patterson), as well as appearing in offerings as diverse as The GOLD ROBBERS, UFO, *The Voyage of Charles Darwin, Natural Causes, Heggerty Haggerty, The Sleeper* (George Gleeson), *Bodily Harm* (Sidney Greenfield), *Family Business* and HEARTBEAT, plus numerous single dramas like *Station Jim* (Stationmaster Pope).

Cole, John

(1927–)

Northern Ireland-born BBC political editor 1981–92. Cole began his journalistic career with the *Belfast Telegraph*, before joining the *Guardian* in 1956 and moving on to the *Observer* in 1975. In the 1980s he was one of the most familiar faces (and voices) on British television, earning great respect from both viewers and politicians. Cole has also been seen on WHAT THE PAPERS SAY and has compiled some reports for HOLIDAY. His TV memoirs, *A Progress through Politics*, were shown in 1995.

Cole, Stephanie

OBE (1941–)

Warwickshire-born actress, usually seen as a hard-headed female, as exemplified by the roles of Dr Beatrice Mason in TENKO and Diana Trent in WAITING FOR GOD. She was also Mrs Featherstone, a grouchy customer in OPEN ALL HOURS, Agnes Langtry in LILLIE, Sarah Mincing in the children's series *Return of the Antelope*, Betty Sillitoe in A BIT OF A DO, the senile Peggy in KEEPING MUM, retired headmistress Lizzie Cameron in *Life as We Know It* and Joan Norton in DOC MARTIN. Cole has also appeared in *Tropic, About Face*, AGATHA CHRISTIE'S POIROT, *Screen Two's Memento Mori* (Dame Lettie Colston), and the single drama *Back Home* (Beattie Langley), and performed one of Alan Bennett's TALKING HEADS monologues. Her second husband was the late actor/writer Peter Birrel, once a member of the Manchester band Freddie and the Dreamers.

Coleman, Charlotte

(1968–2001)

British actress, the daughter of actress Ann Beach and sister of actress Lisa Coleman. Charlotte began acting at the age of eight and moved on to star in WORZEL GUMMIDGE (Sue Peters), EDUCATING MARMALADE and *Danger – Marmalade at Work* (Marmalade Atkins), ORANGES ARE NOT THE ONLY FRUIT (Jess), *Freddie and Max* (Freddie), *Olly's Prison* (Shiela), *Giving Tongue* (Barb Gale) and HOW DO YOU WANT ME? (Lisa Lyons), with smaller roles in dramas and comedies like INSPECTOR MORSE, CAMPAIGN (Kim Greenbank), *Oliver's Travels* (Cathy), *The Vacillations of Poppy Carew* and *Gayle's World*. One of her last TV appearances was alongside her sister, Lisa, in an episode of MCCREADY AND DAUGHTER.

Coleman, David

OBE (1926–)

Former journalist and Cheshire mile athletics champion who was one of the BBC's most prominent sports commentators and presenters from the 1950s. Previously editor of the *Cheshire County Express* and a radio presenter, Coleman established himself as a BBC political reporter, then as contributor to *Sports Special*, before becoming main host of GRANDSTAND and one of MATCH OF THE DAY's commentary team. He then took on his own midweek sports magazine, *Sportsnight With Coleman* (later SPORTSNIGHT), as well as fronting the viewer-feedback programme *Biteback*. Over the years he became known for his detailed background research (put to good use when ad-libbing on *Grandstand* during the teleprinter results spot, for instance) and for the rather unfortunate turn of phrase which gave rise to the neologism 'Colemanballs' (thanks to *Private Eye*). He latterly specialized in athletics commentary and retired after the Sydney Olympics in 2000. Coleman was also chairman of A QUESTION OF SPORT, 1979–97.

Colin's Sandwich ★★★

UK (BBC) Situation Comedy. BBC 2 1988; 1990

Colin Watkins .... **Mel Smith**
Jenny Anderson .... **Louisa Rix**
Des .... **Mike Grady**
Mr Travers .... **Andrew Robertson**
Trevor Blacklock .... **Tony Haase**

Graham .... **Lee Cornes**
Sarah .... **Jane Booker**
John Langley .... **Michael Medwin**
Alan Hunter .... **Nicholas Ball**

Writers **Paul Smith, Terry Kyan**
Producer **John Kilby**

● ***An under-achieving British Rail clerk lacks the conviction to become a writer.***

Described by some as 'Hancock for the 1980s', *Colin's Sandwich* revolves around the efforts of terminal worryguts Colin Watkins to balance his daytime job in the British Rail complaints department with a fledgling career as a writer of thriller stories. The acceptance of one of his tales for the *Langley Book of Horror* does nothing to ease the pressure as Colin toys with the idea of becoming a professional scribe. Later episodes see Colin still holding down his BR position while struggling to pen a screenplay for pig-ignorant, cult film director Alan Hunter. Colin's girlfriend, Jenny, bears the brunt of his neurotic, self-questioning rants, while his anoraky pal, Des, and other yuppie acquaintances, like the love-lorn Sarah, just get in the way. At work, his moronic colleagues Trevor and Graham and his delegating boss, Mr Travers, help drive Watkins further round the bend.

Collins, Joan

OBE (1933–)

London-born movie actress of the 1950s and 1960s who hit the big time through raunchy films and glossy television in the 1970s. Her most prominent role has been as the vicious Alexis Carrington/Colby in DYNASTY, making her queen of the soap bitches. Among her other TV credits (most as a guest) have been THE HUMAN JUNGLE, THE VIRGINIAN, THE MAN FROM U.N.C.L.E., BATMAN, STAR TREK, MISSION: IMPOSSIBLE, *Orson Welles Great Mysteries*, SPACE: 1999, THE PERSUADERS!, STARSKY AND HUTCH, FANTASY ISLAND, TALES OF THE UNEXPECTED, *Monte Carlo*, *Hotel Babylon* and *Sins* (a mini-series produced by her own company). In 2002 she joined the cast of the long-running American daytime soap *Guiding Light*. She is sister to novelist Jackie Collins and was once married to entertainer Anthony Newley (one of five husbands).

Collins, Lewis

(1946–)

British actor whose television break came alongside Diane Keen and David Roper in THE CUCKOO WALTZ, playing unwanted lodger Gavin Rumsey. After this came THE PROFESSIONALS, in which as Bodie he was teamed up with Martin Shaw's Doyle. His other appearances have included parts in WARSHIP, THE NEW AVENGERS, ROBIN OF SHERWOOD, *Jack the Ripper*, CLUEDO (Colonel Mustard) and THE GRIMLEYS. In 2002 he made a guest appearance in THE BILL.

Collins, Michelle

(1963–)

London-born actress, once a singer with Mari Wilson and the Wilsations, whose major roles have included Stephanie Wild in the sitcom *Running Wild*, Cindy Beale in EASTENDERS, Susie in REAL WOMEN, holiday rep Nicki Matthews in SUNBURN (also singing the theme song), Maxine Gaines in *Up Rising* and Diana Wakeham in *The Sleeper*. Collins has also starred as Kathy Lawrence in *Daylight Robbery*, DI Judy Hill in *Lloyd and Hill*, Abby Wallace in TWO THOUSAND ACRES OF SKY, Julie in *Perfect*, Gina in *Ella and the Mothers*, Sarah Barton in *Single*, Marigold Westward in *The Illustrated Mum* and Donna Harris in *Can't Buy Me Love*. Guest appearances take in series like SEA OF SOULS and THE LAST DETECTIVE. In addition, she once hosted THE WORD and in 2000 presented *Michelle in Brazil*, a documentary about the plight of street children.

Collins, Pauline

OBE (1940–)

British actress who shot to fame as Sarah, the parlourmaid in UPSTAIRS, DOWNSTAIRS. So popular was her character that a spin-off, *Thomas and Sarah*, was produced for her and her real-life husband, John Alderton. Collins's TV break had come with EMERGENCY – WARD 10 and was followed by her first starring role as Dawn in THE LIVER BIRDS, alongside Polly James. However, after a short first series, Nerys Hughes joined as James's new flatmate and Collins left. Post-*Upstairs, Downstairs*, she has starred with hubby Alderton on three further occasions – as Clara Danby in the sitcom NO – HONESTLY, as various characters in WODEHOUSE PLAYHOUSE and as Harriet Boult in FOREVER GREEN. Collins also made guest appearances, in P. D. JAMES's *The Black Tower* and DOCTOR WHO. Her most recent starring roles have been as Aileen Matthews in the *Screen Two* drama *Flowers of the Forest*, as Harriet Smith in AMBASSADOR, as Betty Silver in *Man and Boy*, as Dr Catherine Kendall in *Sparkling Cyanide*, and as Miss Flite in BLEAK HOUSE.

Colonel March of Scotland Yard ✳

UK (Criterion/Panda) Police Drama. ITV 1956

Col. Perceval March .... **Boris Karloff**
Insp. Ames .... **Ewan Roberts**

Producer **Hannah Weinstein**

● ***The strange cases of a specialist detective.***

One-eyed Colonel March works for D-3, the Department of Queer Complaints at Scotland Yard, a position that leads to his involvement in seemingly unsolvable cases. Sometimes it appears the supernatural has played a hand in murder. On other occasions, supposedly impossible crimes land on his desk (including a murder in a sealed compression chamber where no one can have reached the victim). March even confronts the Abominable Snowman in one episode. Nevertheless, the dogged detective, who sports a black patch over his left eye, always finds the answer. The tales were based on stories by Carter Dickson (John Dickson Carr).

Colour Television

Although initially earmarked for 1956–7, colour television did not officially begin in the UK until 2 December 1967, some 13 years after the USA had begun regular colour broadcasts (although, it is true to say, significant colour viewing figures in the USA were not established until around 1965). The factors that inhibited the development of colour in the UK were varied. They included the need for the Government to approve a suitable system, preferably in conjunction with its European neighbours so that standard technology was achieved. The American NTSC system was initially employed by the BBC for test transmissions, which began in 1962, but was quickly dropped in favour of the French SECAM technology.

Eventually it was the German-originated PAL system, a 625-line variant of the 525-line NTSC system, that was adopted in the UK.

Coltrane, Robbie

OBE (Anthony McMillan; 1950–)

Scottish actor (Hagrid in the *Harry Potter* films) whose early television work took in A KICK UP THE EIGHTIES, LAUGH??? I NEARLY PAID MY LICENCE FEE, ALFRESCO and various COMIC STRIP plays. He also appeared in THE YOUNG ONES, METAL MICKEY, GIRLS ON TOP, BLACKADDER and SATURDAY LIVE before starring as Danny McGlone in John Byrne's rock 'n' roll comedy drama TUTTI FRUTTI. He has since had his own show, appeared with Emma Thompson, featured in Dario Fo's *Mistero Buffo*, starred as Liam Kane in *Screen One's Alive and Kicking* and Captain Chisholm in *The Ebb-Tide*, and played Dr Samuel Johnson in *Boswell & Johnson's Tour of the Western Islands* and Tweedledum in *Alice in Wonderland*. However, his best-known role has been that of Fitz in the acclaimed crime drama CRACKER. In 1993 he made a light-hearted American road film documentary, *Coltrane in a Cadillac*, which he followed up with *Coltrane's Planes and Automobiles*, and in 1995 narrated *The Limit*, a series about structural engineering. In 2003 Coltrane starred as Jack Lennox QC in *The Planman*. He has since provided the voice of James for the animation *Pride* and made a guest appearance in *Still Game*.

Columbo ✳✳

US (Universal) Detective Drama. ITV 1972–9; 1991–4
(US: NBC 1971–8)
DVD: Universal

Lt. Columbo .... **Peter Falk**

Creators **Richard Levinson, William Link**
Executive Producers **Roland Kibbee, Dean Hargrove, Richard Alan Simmons**
Producers **Edward K. Dodds, Everett Chambers, Richard Alan Simmons, Stanley Kallis**

● ***The clever investigations of a seemingly harmless detective.***

Each episode of *Columbo* opens in the thick of the action. A murder is committed and the culprits quickly cover their tracks, pulling off an apparently perfect crime. However, soon on the scene is America's most unlikely policeman, Lt. Columbo, and, by piecing together even the most minute fragments of evidence, the LA-based detective always gets his man. Of course, viewers come to expect Columbo to be successful, but the same can't be said for the murderers. Lulled into a false sense of security by his tramp's raincoat, battered old car, well-chewed cigar and polite manner, they just can't believe that this scruffy old cop can nail them. But, by throwing his suspects off guard, Columbo knows he can catch them unawares. From the outset he seems to know who the murderer is, and viewers are able to watch the battle of wills that develops between the culprit manoeuvring to allay suspicion and the detective homing in on his prey. Much mentioned, but never seen, is his wife, although she does appear in her own spin-off series, *Mrs Columbo*, played by Kate Mulgrew. Columbo's lone companion seems to be his bassett hound, Fang.

The character of Columbo was allegedly modelled on Petrovich, an inspector in Dostoevsky's *Crime and Punishment*, and first reached the screen in a segment of USA's *Sunday Mystery Hour*, way back in 1961. Then the character was played by Bert Freed. When Columbo was looked at again in the late 1960s, Bing Crosby and Lee J. Cobb were two names touted for the role. Both were unavailable, so in stepped Peter Falk to appear in two TV movies, *Prescription: Murder* in 1968 and *Ransom for a Dead Man* in 1971. When in full production, with feature-length episodes, the show aired as part of the MYSTERY MOVIE anthology, although it has also been billed simply under its own title. Guest stars abound, from Dick Van Dyke and William Shatner to Patrick McGoohan and Donald Pleasence. The detective returned in the 1990s in a new series of two-hour adventures.

Combat ✳✳

UK (Selmur) War Drama. ITV 1963–8 (US: ABC 1962–7)
DVD: Image Entertainment (Region 1 only)

Lt. Gil Hanley .... **Rick Jason**
Sgt Chip Saunders .... **Vic Morrow**
PFC Paul 'Caje' Lemay .... **Pierre Jalbert**
Pte William G. 'Wildman' Kirby .... **Jack Hogan**
Littlejohn .... **Dick Peabody**
Doc Walton .... **Steven Rogers**
Doc .... **Conlan Carter**
Pte Braddock .... **Shecky Greene**
Pte Billy Nelson .... **Tom Lowell**

Producer **Gene Levitt**

● ***A US Army platoon fights its way across Europe in the wake of D-Day.***

Filmed for most of its run in black and white, and interspersed with some actual war footage, *Combat* was the most successful of the new breed of 1960s war sagas. It features K Company, Second Platoon, of the US Army, which is headed by Lt. Gil Hanley. With Hanley are Sgt Chip Saunders and a varied company of men, most notably the wisecracking Braddock, a Cajun known simply as 'Caje' and an impressionable young medic, Doc Walton. While the war is hard to avoid, other aspects of platoon life are also handled, and realism is the bedrock of the series. Robert Altman directed many of the episodes, which aired on US TV from 1962 and which were seen sporadically around the ITV network.

Come Back Mrs Noah ✳

UK (BBC) Situation Comedy. BBC 1 1978

Mrs Noah .... **Mollie Sugden**
Clive Cunliffe .... **Ian Lavender**
Carstairs .... **Donald Hewlett**
Fanshaw .... **Michael Knowles**
Garfield Hawk .... **Tim Barrett**
Scarth Dare .... **Ann Michelle**
TVpresenter .... **Gorden Kaye**
Technician .... **Jennifer Lonsdale**

Writers **Jeremy Lloyd, David Croft**
Producer **David Croft**

● ***A housewife is lost in space.***

When, in the 21st century, housewife Mrs Noah wins herself a trip round *Britannia Seven*, Britain's newest spaceship, little does she know that her excursion will be so adventurous. Accidentally blasted into orbit, she and a hotchpotch crew find themselves floating round the world at 56,325 kmh

(35,000 mph), as Mission Control fights desperately to retrieve their craft. Among those alongside Mrs Noah is roving TV reporter Clive Cunliffe.

Despite coming from the pen of the creators of 'ALLO 'ALLO and featuring the usual Croft/Perry/Lloyd repertory company actors, with Mollie Sugden in full sail, this sitcom failed to take off and survived only one short season (plus a pilot at the end of 1977).

Come Dancing ✶

UK (BBC) Entertainment. BBC 1 1950–95

Creator **Eric Morley**
Producers **Aubrey Singer, Barrie Edgar, Ray Lakeland, Philip Lewis, Simon Betts**

● ***Enduring ballroom dancing contest.***

One of television's longest-running programmes, *Come Dancing* proved remarkably durable. Initially conceived as a showcase for events from regional ballrooms, with professionals Syd Perkins and Edna Duffield offering instruction for viewers at home, it assumed the more familiar dance-contest format in 1953. The competition later took the form of an inter-regional knock-out, pitting teams from areas such as Home Counties North against the South-West, or some other part of the UK. The last series, in 1995, featured contestants from various European countries. Swathed in a sea of sequins, the athletic, mostly amateur, enthusiasts competed in various formal dance categories, from the tango to the paso doble. There was also a section for formation dancing, and newer crazes like rock 'n' roll were incorporated over the years. The deviser of the programme, Mecca's Eric Morley, also emceed proceedings, although the programme's presenters and on-the-floor comperes were many. The most notable included Leslie Mitchell, Peter Dimmock, McDonald Hobley, Sylvia Peters, Peter West, Brian Johnston, Pete Murray, Don Moss, Keith Fordyce, Michael Aspel, Judith Chalmers, Terry Wogan, Noel Edmonds, Peter Marshall, Angela Rippon, David Jacobs and Rosemarie Ford. The first ever episode was broadcast from London's Lyceum Ballroom and featured Harry Roy and his Band.

See also STRICTLY COME DANCING.

Comedians, The ✶✶

UK (Granada) Comedy. ITV 1971–4; 1979; 1984–5; 1992

1971–4
Frank Carson, Bernard Manning, Colin Crompton, Ken Goodwin, Mike Reid, Jim Bowen, Charlie Williams, Duggie Brown, Mike Burton, George Roper, Tom O'Connor, Russ Abbot, Lennie Bennett, Jos White, Dave Butler, Steve Faye, Alan Brady, Eddie Flanagan, Pat Mooney, Jimmy Marshall

1979
Stan Boardman, Roy Walker, Johnny Carroll, Vince Earl, Charlie Daze, George King, Harry Scott, Lee Wilson, Mick Miller, Ivor Davis, Hal Nolan, Pat Tansey, Mike Kelly, Bobby Kaye

1984–5
Bernard Manning, Frank Carson, George Roper, Greg Rogers, Stan Boardman, Eddie Flanagan, Tony Jo, Pauline Daniels, Ollie Spencer, Harry Black, Duggie Brown

1992
Tom Pepper, Pauline Daniels, Jimmy Bright, Tony Gerrard and others

Producers **John Hamp, Ian Hamilton**

● ***Wall-to-wall gags from leading club comics.***

With musical interludes from Shep's Banjo Boys, *The Comedians* was a showcase for the top talent from the northern clubs. Producer John Hamp brought the country's fastest wise-crackers into the studio, recorded their (somewhat cleaned-up) routines before a live audience, then inter-cut their gags to create a non-stop barrage of quick-fire jokes. Snappy editing ensured a lively pace, and a joke a minute, at the very least, was guaranteed.

The Comedians launched the television careers of a number of funny men (and future game show hosts), the best-remembered being listed above. These included abrasive Bernard Manning, weedy Colin Crompton (the pair came together again later in WHEELTAPPERS' AND SHUNTERS' SOCIAL CLUB), Ken 'Settle down now' Goodwin, Mike 'Terr-i-fic' Reid, Frank 'It's the way I tell 'em' Carson and Jim 'Smashing, super' Bowen. Lennie Bennett, Tom O'Connor and Russ Abbot were three other performers who carved out new careers after appearances on the show, Duggie Brown (brother of CORONATION STREET's Lynne Perrie) has since turned to acting (with appearances in BROOKSIDE), but Charlie Williams, a black comic with a thick Yorkshire accent, unfortunately failed to make the grade when given charge of THE GOLDEN SHOT and has seldom been seen since.

The Comedians was revived in 1979, with a new intake of stand-up comics that included Roy Walker and Stan Boardman. A third revival in 1984, with many old hands plus more new talent, proved less memorable, as did a fourth in 1992. *The Comedians Christmas Cracker*, a one-off in December 1993, celebrated the programme's 21st birthday in the company of old stalwarts like Manning, Carson, Bowen, Brown, Boardman, Williams and Goodwin.

Comedy Playhouse ✶✶

UK (BBC/Carlton) Situation Comedy Anthology. BBC 1 1961–74; ITV 1993

Creator **Tom Sloan**

● ***Sporadic collections of sitcom pilots.***

Comedy Playhouse was an umbrella title given to occasional series of single comedies. Each comedy acted as a pilot and, if successful, stood a fair chance of being extended into a series of its own. Ray Galton and Alan Simpson wrote the first collection, but many other writers (including Johnny Speight, Roy Clarke and Richard Waring) made contributions later. The most famous of *Comedy Playhouse*'s protégés were STEPTOE AND SON (piloted as *The Offer* in 1962), TILL DEATH US DO PART and THE LIVER BIRDS. Others included ALL GAS AND GAITERS, NOT IN FRONT OF THE CHILDREN, ME MAMMY, LAST OF THE SUMMER WINE and HAPPY EVER AFTER.

Similar in concept was *Comedy Special* in 1977, which introduced CITIZEN SMITH, and the 1973 Ronnie Barker showcase *Seven of One*, which included OPEN ALL HOURS and *Prisoner and Escort*, the pilot for PORRIDGE. Carlton resurrected *Comedy Playhouse* in 1993, giving birth to two series, BRIGHTON BELLES (the UK version of THE GOLDEN GIRLS) and THE 10%ERS.

Comic Relief ★★★

UK (BBC) Telethon. BBC 1 1988–9; 1991; 1993; 1995; 1997; 1999; 2001; 2003; 2005

● ***Comedy charity marathon.***

Exploiting the talents of comedians and comic actors from various generations and backgrounds, *Comic Relief* is a sort of CHILDREN IN NEED with gags. It sprang from a 1986 OMNIBUS compilation programme of the highlights of three live Comic Relief concerts staged at the Shaftesbury Theatre, London, in the same year, as an extension to the Live Aid music projects. The first fully fledged *Comic Relief* extravaganza – largely the brainchild of writer Richard Curtis – was hosted by Griff Rhys Jones and Lenny Henry in 1988. Proceeds (over £15 million initially, rising through the years to over £26 million per event) went then (as later) to help famine victims in Africa, and the needy closer to home. The second *Comic Relief* came a year later, in 1989, but the appeal has since settled into a biennial routine, taking place on a date in February/March which has been dubbed 'Red Nose Day' (clowns' red noses of assorted designs being sold to raise money).

Appeals for cash have been made throughout the evening's live programming, with running totals announced at regular intervals. Reports on how funds have been spent have punctuated each appeal. Viewers have been invited to bid for their favourite clips from old comedy series, and special segments of contemporary comedies have been produced. Among the many comedians giving their time to the show have been Jasper Carrott, Rowan Atkinson, Tony Robinson, Ken Dodd, Jonathan Ross, Stephen Fry, Ben Elton, Frank Carson, Jo Brand, Julian Clary, French and Saunders, Harry Enfield, Ernie Wise, Paul Merton, Ian Hislop, Hale and Pace, Rory Bremner, Victoria Wood, Reeves and Mortimer, Graham Norton, Steve Coogan, Sacha Baron Cohen, Frank Skinner, David Baddiel, Harry Hill, Ricky Gervais, Rob Brydon and the SPITTING IMAGE and LITTLE BRITAIN teams, as well as other stars like Hugh Grant, Richard Wilson, Joanna Lumley, Cilla Black, Chris Tarrant, Bill Wyman, Barry Norman, Tom Jones, Chris Evans and Ant and Dec.

In 1999, *Comic Relief's Great Big Excellent African Adventure*, shown in the weeks leading up to the main broadcast, sent celebrities like Stephen Fry, Geri Halliwell, Ruby Wax, Michael Palin and Paul Bradley to the strife-ridden continent to report on the appalling hardships faced by the local people. *Radio Times* for the week beginning 6 March 1999 was devoted to *Comic Relief* and spoof-edited by Victoria Wood. In June 1999, BBC 1 screened *Comic Relief: The Debt Wish Show*, a recording of two concerts at the Brixton Academy, London, organized to campaign for the cancellation of Third World debt. As part of 2001's *Comic Relief* (slogan: 'Say Pants to Poverty'), a special celebrity edition of BIG BROTHER was produced. In 2003 and 2005 *Comic Relief Does Fame Academy* saw a host of brave celebrities facing up to vocal training, live performances and withering critiques from the FAME ACADEMY judges. Also in 2005, Peter Kay's video for Tony Christie's '(Is This the Way to) Amarillo' bounced off the programme and into the charts, where it remained at number 1 for seven weeks.

Comic Strip Presents, The ★★★

UK (Filmworks/Comic Strip) Comedy. Channel 4 1982–4; 1986; 1988; BBC 2 1990; 1992–3; Channel 4 1998; 2000
DVD: VCI

Peter Richardson, Dawn French, Jennifer Saunders, Adrian Edmondson, Rik Mayall, Daniel Peacock, Robbie Coltrane, Nigel Planer, Alexei Sayle, Keith Allen

Producers **Michael White, Ben Swaffer** (Channel 4), **Lolli Kimpton** (BBC 2)

● ***Spoof and satire with a new generation of comedians.***

The Comic Strip, a Soho comedy club opened by writer Peter Richardson in 1980, was the venue that gave early opportunities to many of the 1980s' most successful young comedians. Its compere was Alexei Sayle and prominent among its performers were French and Saunders, Nigel Planer, Rik Mayall and Adrian Edmondson. *The Comic Strip Presents* was its television manifestation, but, instead of focusing on stand-up routines, it centred on satire and send-up. The premiere was an Enid Blyton spoof, *Five Go Mad in Dorset*, which rounded off Channel 4's first night in 1982. A half-hour parody of the snooty, class themes of Blyton's books, it cast French and Saunders as George and Anne, with Adrian Edmondson as Dick and Peter Richardson as Julian. Memorably, it also featured serious-looking CROSSROADS star Ronald Allen as Uncle Quentin, proudly declaring himself to be a homosexual.

Five Go Mad in Dorset led to five series of Comic Strip productions, plus occasional specials, all drawing their humour more from atmosphere and characterization than from jokes and one-liners. Titles were as varied as *War, The Beat Generation, A Fistful of Travellers' Cheques* and *Bad News Tour* (featuring an inept heavy metal band). One notable episode, entitled *The Strike*, explored the miners' dispute through the eyes of Hollywood, with Peter Richardson playing Al Pacino in the role of Arthur Scargill, and Jennifer Saunders as Meryl Streep, playing Scargill's wife. The same theme was extended to a later production, *GLC*, in which Robbie Coltrane was Charles Bronson playing Ken Livingstone. *The Bullshitters* (a parody of THE PROFESSIONALS) was not officially a Comic Strip production, but did feature a few members of the team. With its stars now name performers, *The Comic Strip Presents* moved to BBC 2 in the 1990s, before resurfacing on Channel 4 on Easter Sunday 1998 for a one-off production, *Four Men in a Car*, which was followed by *Four Men in a Plane* in January 2000 and *Sex Actually* in December 2005.

Coming Home/Nancherrow ★★

UK (Portman) Drama. ITV 1998/1999
DVD: Acorn Video

Judith Dunbar	**Emily Mortimer**
	Keira Knightly *(young)*
	Lara Joy Körner *(Nancherrow)*
Loveday Carey-Lewis	**Katie Ryder Richardson**
	Poppy Gaye *(young)*
Diana Carey-Lewis	**Joanna Lumley**
Colonel Edgar Carey-Lewis	**Peter O'Toole**
Jeremy Wells	**George Asprey**
Edward Carey-Lewis	**Paul Bettany**
Athena Carey-Lewis	**Gruschenka Stevens**
Tommy Mortimer	**Patrick Ryecart**
Jess	**Brooke Kinsella**
	Emily Hamilton *(Nancherrow)*
Gus	**Heikko Deutschmann**
	Philipp Mogg *(Nancherrow)*
Walter	**Quentin Jones**
	Tristan Gemmill *(Nancherrow)*
Aunt Louise	**Penelope Keith**
Billy Fawcett	**David McCallum**

Miss Catto	**Susan Hampshire**
Viscount Berryann	**Robert Hardy** *(Nancherrow)*
Robin Jarvis	**Donald Sinden** *(Nancherrow*
Dashka	**Lynda Baron** *(Nancherrow)*
Nesta Carew	**Samantha Beckinsale** *(Nancherrow)*
Lord Peter Awliscombe	**Patrick Macnee** *(Nancherrow)*

Writer **John Goldsmith**
Producer **David Cunliffe**

Two tales of an aristocratic family set in the years around World War II.

Cornwall in the late 1930s: a happy time, with little thought of the impending war. It is here that a friendship develops between Judith Dunbar and the wealthy, but headstrong Loveday Carey-Lewis, a friendship that sees Judith being taken into the family fold at their glorious country estate, Nancherrow. Regrettably, the turmoil of war spells an end to these blissfully joyful days for Judith and to her budding romance with Loveday's brother, Edward. This two-part drama was based on the novel of the same name by Rosamunde Pilcher, and reputedly cost some £4 million to produce. Carl Davis provided the music. A year later, ITV returned to the story in another two-part adaptation, this time of Pilcher's sequel, *Nancherrow*. The action resumes in 1947, when Loveday inherits the now-decaying estate from her late father.

Commander, The ***

UK (La Plante) Police Drama. ITV 2005–
DVD: Contender

Commander Clare Blake	**Amanda Burton**
DCI Mike Hedges	**Matthew Marsh**
DI Carol Browning	**Poppy Miller**
DI Ken Miles	**Thomas Lockyer**
DCS Les Branton	**Pip Torrens**
George Hart	**Ron Donachie**
Eddie Myers	**Terence Hillyer**
Gina Moore	**Gillian Goodman**
DAC Edward Sumpter	**Anthony Valentine**
DS Brian Hall	**Paul Brightwell**
Sara Blake/Dawson	**Lizzie McInnerny**
John Dawson	**Nicholas Ball**
Dr Jane Wellesley	**Susan Wooldridge**
Sgt Phil Vos	**Stuart Graham**

Creator/Writer **Lynda La Plante**
Producers **Lynda La Plante, Peter McAleese**

A top policewoman's personal life has repercussions for her career.

Commander Clare Blake is a high-flying Metropolitan Police officer, charged with leading the Serious Crime Group. Her job is to oversee murder cases and clean up the act of the force itself. Inevitably, there is resentment among male colleagues that this attractive woman is in a position to give them orders, but she is tough, determined and generally makes a good fist of her job. Not that she is perfect, by any means. A fling with convicted murderer James Lampton (played by Hugh Bonneville) in the pilot episode underlines just that, and provides plenty of ammunition for her detractors as the rather edgier series develops. Dark and intense in typical Lynda La Plante fashion, *The Commander* reveals how a career woman wielding lots of power can't resist playing with fire, threatening not only her job but her life too.

Two two-part episodes, shown in 2005, herald the series proper, following the pilot episode in 2003 in which Blake's colleague, Branton, was played by Nicholas Jones, her old friend, former DCI George Hart, by David Calder, and DAC Sumpter by Christopher Robbie.

Commercial

A television advertisement that may vary in length from a few seconds to a few minutes. In the UK these are grouped together in commercial breaks lasting several minutes, which are screened between and also during programmes. In other countries and on some digital networks commercials are seen between programmes only. In the USA, breaks are more frequent and have traditionally been more rigidly enforced, causing much concern when programmes have been halted to accommodate a break. Commercial television (via ITV) arrived in the UK on 22 September 1955 and the first advert in the first 'natural break' (as it was then termed) was for Gibbs SR toothpaste. Then, as now, there were strict rules regarding advertising. Today the regulatory body Ofcom monitors commercials, with the main concerns being that they do not mislead, do not encourage or condone harmful behaviour and do not cause widespread or exceptional offence. Certain products, in line with Government legislation, are prohibited (tobacco, etc.), and controversial subjects like alcohol, financial services, children's goods, medical products and religious and charitable concerns are subject to more detailed regulation. An average of seven minutes per hour of advertising is now allowed on ITV, Channel 4 and Channel 5, with an average of eight minutes per hour during peak hours (7–9 a.m. and 6–11 p.m.) and a maximum of 12 minutes in any hour. Non-terrestrial (digital/satellite) stations can offer an average of nine minutes' worth per hour (maximum 12 minutes per hour), although shopping channels are not restricted in the same way. The timing of commercials is also controlled. No advertising is allowed during religious services, for example.

Common As Muck **

UK (BBC) Comedy Drama. BBC 1 1994; 1997

Nev	**Edward Woodward**
Foxy	**Tim Healy**
Ken	**Neil Dudgeon**
Bernard	**Richard Ridings**
Sunil	**Anthony Barclay**
Jonno	**Stephen Lord**
John Parry	**Roy Hudd**
Dulcie	**Freda Dowie**
George Ward	**Paul Kember**
Denice	**Nimmy March**
Guy Simmons	**Ian Mercer**
Mr Arnold	**George Raistrick**
Jean	**Shirley Stelfox**
Philip Edwards	**Thomas Craig**
Moira	**Tina Malone**
Sandra	**Candida Rundle**
Marie	**Michelle Holmes**
Ted	**Mike Kelly**
Brian Forget	**Douglas Henshall**
Sharon	**Kathy Burke**
Diane Parry	**June Watson**
Derek	**Frank Finlay**
Irene	**June Whitfield**
Mike Roberts	**Paul Shane**
Christine Stranks	**Lesley Sharp**

Nat Prabhaker .... **Saeed Jaffrey**
Dougie Hodd .... **Terence Rigby**
Reg Vickers .... **Alexei Sayle**
Vinny .... **William Ivory**

Writer **William Ivory**
Producers **John Chapman, Catherine Wearing**

A team of binmen fight to prevent their jobs being privatized.

Set in the fictional northern town of Hepworth, this comedy drama explores the lives of a team of unruly dustbinmen – the so-called 'Supercrew' – who discover that the local council is planning to put out their work to private tender because of their lousy attitude and poor performance. In a panic over likely job-losses, the lads pull out the stops to try to keep the contract for their DOG (Direct Operations Group) council subsidiary, in the face of glossy promises from Belgian outsiders, Propre UK. Among the numerous colourful characters are gloomy veteran Nev; mad driver Foxy; Foxy's son, Jonno; punchy Ken; simple-minded Bernard; student Sunil; and cleansing manager John Parry. Their families also play a part. Stripper/Miss Parks and Gardens Marie was played by Michelle Holmes, who (as Tina Fowler to his Eddie Ramsden) had once played writer William Ivory's girlfriend in CORONATION STREET.

When the lads return for a second series, a new threat hangs over their workplace: property tycoons want to redevelop their yard. Nev has retired after 45 years and is planning to marry gold-digging new flame Irene, while the other guys are involved in new ventures like interior decorating and owning a hairdressing salon. Corruption hangs heavy in the air and the crew do their best to expose it.

At times dark and moody, but always capable of breaking into mirth, *Common as Muck* was well received by both viewers and critics.

Como, Perry

(Pierino Como; 1913–2001)

Laid-back Italian-American crooner whose variety shows in the 1950s (and extravagant Christmas specials later) were hits on both sides of the Atlantic.

Compact ✳

UK (BBC) Drama. BBC 1 1962–5

Joanne Minster .... **Jean Harvey**
Jimmy Saunders .... **Nicholas Selby**
Richard Lowe .... **Moray Watson**
Mark Viccars .... **Gareth Davies**
Alison Gray/Morley .... **Betty Cooper**
Alec Gordon .... **Leo Maguire**
Sally Henderson/Harmon .... **Monica Evans**
Lily Todd/Kipling .... **Marcia Ashton**
Maggie Clifford/Brent .... **Sonia Graham**
Ruth Munday .... **Anna Castaldini**
Sir Charles Harmon .... **Newton Blick**
Arnold Babbage .... **Donald Morley**
Mary/Augusta 'Gussie' Brown/ Beatty .... **Frances Bennett**
Kay Livingstone/Babbage .... **Justine Lord**
Iris Alcott/Millet .... **Louise Dunn**
Ian Hart/Harmon .... **Ronald Allen**
Gillian Nesbitt .... **Dilys Watling**
Sylvia Grant .... **Vicky Harrington**
Eddie Goldsmith .... **Patrick Troughton**
Paul Constantine .... **Tony Wright**
Clancey .... **Ann Morrish**
Mr Kipling .... **Blake Butler**
Lois James/McClusky .... **Dawn Beret**
Mike McClusky .... **Clinton Greyn**
Lynn Bolton .... **Bridget McConnel**
Tim Gray .... **Scot Finch**
Kathy Sherwood .... **Penny Morrell**
Adrian Coombs .... **Robert Desmond**
Carol 'Copper' Beach .... **Mandy Miller**
Bryan Marchant .... **Keith Buckley**
Clare Farrell/Viccars .... **Janet Hargreaves**
Stan Millet .... **Johnny Wade**
Susan Caley .... **Sonia Fox**
Edmund Bruce .... **Robert Flemyng**
Tony Marchesi .... **Norman Florence**
Mrs Chater .... **Beryl Cooke**
Alan Drew .... **Basil Moss**
Anthea Keane .... **Julia Lockwood**
Camilla Hope .... **Carmen Silvera**
Celia Randall .... **Rachel Gurney**
David Rome .... **Vincent Ball**
Lorna Wills-Ede .... **Brenda Kaye**
Ken Hawkins/Geoffrey Gray ... **Edward Evans**
Doug Beatty .... **Lawrence James**
Michele 'Mitch' Donnelly .... **Diana Beevers**
Ben Bishop .... **Bill Kerr**
Cheryl Fine .... **Jan Miller**
Rosalind Garner .... **Jennifer Wood**
Tessa March .... **Bridget Armstrong**
Harry Cornell .... **Lionel Murton**
Elliot Morrow .... **Maurice Browning**
Anne Appleby .... **Jennifer Wilson**
Julia Preston .... **Polly Adams**

Creators **Hazel Adair, Peter Ling**
Producers **Alan Bromly, Douglas Allen, Morris Barry, Bernard Hepton, Joan Craft, Harold Clayton, William Sterling**

The lives and loves of the staff at a women's magazine.

This fondly remembered BBC soap was set in the high-rise, Victoria offices (Enterprise House) of *Compact*, a glossy magazine that majored in schmaltzy fiction and other matters of female interest. As the programme blurb declared, the aim was to focus on 'the talented and temperamental people who worked on a topical magazine for the busy woman'.

The magazine's first editor is Joanne Minster. Also part of the team are fiction editor Mark Viccars, photographer Alec Gordon, features editor Jimmy Saunders, art director Richard Lowe, accountant Mr Babbage and assorted writers and secretaries. The problem page editor is Alison Morley. (Her name was originally given as Alison Gray, until the producers realized there was already a contributor to *Reader's Digest* with that name.)

Action centres around the hassle of getting the magazine on to the presses each week, with staff squabbles promoted to the realms of high drama. Personal relationships bloom and die, and there is much sparring for position in the office. Ian Harmon, son of Sir Charles Harmon (the chairman of Harmon Enterprises Incorporated, the magazine's proprietor), arrives from America, using the undercover name of Ian Hart and bringing with him suave looks and gentlemanly behaviour. Before long he marries Sally, his secretary. Other major figures to work on the magazine include features editor Gussie Brown (who, embarrassed by her Christian name, at first pretends her name is Mary), American fashion editor Lois James, managing editor Edmund Bruce (brought in from rival magazine *Lady Fair*), novelist-turned-fiction-editor Camilla Hope, librarian Alan Drew and showbusiness editor David Rome.

Compact was screened twice a week. It was criticized for being too wholesome and goody-goody (despite touching on one or two controversial items, like unmarried mothers and drug abuse), but it was very successful in the ratings. All the same, the BBC bosses were less than satisfied. They pulled the plug on the series in July 1965, after just three years on air.

Complete and Utter History of Britain, The ★★

UK (LWT) Comedy. ITV 1969

Terry Jones, Michael Palin, Colin Gordon, Roddy Maude-Roxby, Wallas Eaton, Melinda May, Diana Quick, Ted Carson, Colin Cunningham, John Hughman, Johnny Vyvyan

Writers **Terry Jones, Michael Palin**
Producer **Humphrey Barclay**

● ***Spoof retelling of the major events in Britain's past.***

Marginally predating their massive success in MONTY PYTHON'S FLYING CIRCUS, Terry Jones and Michael Palin came up with this novel idea for Sunday nights on ITV. In a busy half-hour, an erudite studio host (played by Colin Gordon) offers an intriguing insight into British history by introducing TV flashbacks to major events. The first clip ever took viewers back to 2564 BC but then the action jumped forward to the 11th century and the Norman invasion. Later instalments tell the inside story of other key moments – all, of course, gloriously spoofed in the Pythonesque manner we now take for granted. There are 'Golden Year Awards' for an often-overlooked year, such as 1065; NEWS AT TEN-style headlines announcing historic feats; and interviews with kings and other famous people, who are quizzed like sports stars after a big match. Roddy Maude-Roxby appears as the clumsy Professor Weaver to add his own incisive analysis of events or items dragged out of the mists of time. Music is provided by Barry Booth. Six episodes were shown.

Comrade Dad ★★

UK (BBC) Situation Comedy. BBC 2 1986

Reg Dudgeon .... **George Cole**
Treen Dudgeon .... **Barbara Ewing**
Bob Dudgeon .... **David Garlick**
Gran .... **Doris Hare**
Zo Dudgeon .... **Claire Toeman**
Scaff .... **Nicholas Bond Owen**
Cliff .... **David Battley**

Writers **Ian Davidson, Peter Vincent**
Producer **John Kilby**

● ***Life in Soviet Britain with a London family.***

In this futuristic comedy set in 1999, London is now known as Londongrad, following a bloodless coup by the Soviet Union on 27 June 1989. Under the totalitarian regime, citizens are monitored by satellites and food shortages are commonplace. In this new country called USSR/GB live the Dudgeons, a working-class family headed by the canny Reg, a proud Party man, who loyally and optimistically follows the system to bring whatever little pleasures are out there into the family fold. The seven-episode series followed a pilot shown in 1984, in which Reg's wife, Treen, was played by Colette O'Neil, son Bob by Lee Whitlock, and Gran by Anna Wing.

Confessions ★★

UK (Hat Trick) Entertainment. BBC 1 1995–8

Presenter **Simon Mayo**

Producers **Mark Linsey, Barbara Lee**

● ***Shocking but funny revelations from the public.***

Bringing to television a feature of his Radio 1 show, DJ Simon Mayo introduced celebrities and members of the public who had long-held, humorous secrets that they wished to confess. Unwitting studio audience members were pulled in front of the cameras and quizzed over a shameful incident in their past, with an exotic holiday awarded to the week's 'star confessor'. A 'Forgive Me Booth' was used to help other miscreants get things off their chest by owning up to practical jokes played, lies told, or the truth behind certain stories. Later series saw cameras patrolling the country for more confessions from the public, plus a new game in which the genuine 'confessor' out of a trio of storytellers had to be identified to gain a prize.

Conley, Brian

(1961–)

London-born entertainer, hosting his own comedy-variety shows – including *Brian Conley – This Way Up* and *The Brian Conley Show* – plus *The National Lottery – We've Got Your Number*, and also starring as petty crook Kenny Conway in TIME AFTER TIME and sadistic gym teacher Doug Digby in THE GRIMLEYS. *Five Alive* and *Summertime Special* featured among his earlier credits. He has also made a guest appearance in AGATHA CHRISTIE'S MARPLE.

Connections ★★

UK (BBC/Time-Life) Documentary. BBC 1 1978

Presenter **James Burke**

● ***How scientific progress has changed the world.***

This ambitious series attempts to explain the relationship between technological achievement and the course of world history. The case is argued in a lively but highly informative manner by ex-TOMORROW'S WORLD presenter James Burke.

Connie ★★

UK (Central) Drama. ITV 1985

Connie .... **Stephanie Beacham**
Bea .... **Brenda Bruce**
Hector .... **Paul Rogers**
Nesta .... **Pam Ferris**
Jamieson .... **Richard Morant**
Arnie .... **George Costigan**
Babs .... **Claire Parker**

Dev	**Peter Straker**
Leroy	**Roy Lee**
Lisa	**Georgia Allen**

Writer **Ron Hutchinson**
Producer **Nicholas Palmer**

A cheated entrepreneur fights to regain her business.
Connie works in the rag trade. At least she did until she was swindled out of her chain of boutiques. Now, however, after eight years' exile in Greece, and despite being penniless, she has decided to return to the Midlands to reclaim what is rightfully hers. She takes a job with House of Bea, run by Bea and her husband, Hector, and from this position of influence starts to worm her way once again into the fabric of the local fashion scene. One person who has to look out is stepsister Nesta, who snapped up Connie's old shops, but there are plenty of other local business folk who must beware now that the feisty, determined Connie is back in town. Jamieson, Connie's boyfriend, also needs to be on his toes.

For star Stephanie Beacham, the series proved to be a useful springboard to the more elaborate soaps of America and shortly after production on *Connie* ended she jetted off to feature as Sable in THE COLBYS and DYNASTY. The theme song was by Willy Russell.

Connolly, Billy

CBE (1942–)

Partick-born comedian and actor, familiarly known as 'The Big Yin'. Connolly, a former shipyard welder, was once a member of the Humblebums folk duo with Gerry Rafferty, before turning to stand-up comedy. His TV successes have come on both sides of the Atlantic. He starred in the US series *Head of the Class* and *Billy* (in both as teacher Billy MacGregor), and in the UK has made appearances on NOT THE NINE O'CLOCK NEWS, THE COMIC STRIP PRESENTS, *The Kenny Everett Video Show* and MINDER. He has starred in his own comedy specials and in 1994 began a series of documentaries with *Billy Connolly's World Tour of Scotland*, followed two years later by *Billy Connolly's World Tour of Australia, Billy Connolly's World Tour of Ireland, Wales and England* in 2001, and *Billy Connolly's World Tour of New Zealand* in 2004. The BBC also packed him off to the North Pole for a survival course in *Billy Connolly: a Scot in the Arctic*, and then rewarded him with *An Evening in with Billy Connolly* (four hours on BBC 2) in 1996. A year later, he took the lead in the *Screen One* drama *Deacon Brodie*. This followed the 1993 *Screen One* offering *Down among the Big Boys*, in which Connolly starred as criminal JoJo Donnelly. He also played photographer Kingdom Swann in the single drama *Gentlemen's Relish* in 2001. In the 1980s, he co-wrote and performed the theme song for the children's series SUPERGRAN. Connolly is married to former comic actress Pamela Stephenson.

Connors, Chuck

(Kevin Connors; 1921–92)

Athletic American actor, a former professional baseball player who turned to film and television and starred in various action series, particularly as Lucas McCain in THE RIFLEMAN, Jason McCord in BRANDED and Jim Sinclair in *Cowboy in Africa*. He also played defence attorney John Egan in ARREST AND TRIAL and, in the 1970s, resurfaced in ROOTS, taking the part of Tom Moore. Other TV credits included episodes of FANTASY ISLAND, THE SIX MILLION DOLLAR MAN and MURDER, SHE WROTE.

Conrad, William

(William Cann; 1920–94)

Gravel-voiced American actor, a fighter pilot in World War II but for ever remembered by viewers as the huffing and puffing, overweight private eye, Frank Cannon. It was a starring role at last for Conrad, who had missed out on several previous occasions. His resonant voice had made him a prolific radio actor and announcer, and he had been seen in numerous films in the 1940s and 1950s, but his portly frame always spoiled his chances of on-screen TV success. GUNSMOKE was a point in question. Although he had voiced the part of Matt Dillon for years on US radio, there was no way the producers could cast Conrad as the strapping marshal of Dodge City, and the role went instead to James Arness. Conrad, consequently, concentrated on work behind the camera. He produced/directed episodes of series like NAKED CITY, 77 SUNSET STRIP and, ironically, *Gunsmoke*. He also provided narration for such programmes as THE FUGITIVE, THE INVADERS and BUCK ROGERS IN THE 25TH CENTURY, but it wasn't until Frank Cannon was born that his screen success was assured. He followed it with two more detective romps, NERO WOLFE and JAKE AND THE FATMAN but he still continued to dabble in voice-overs, speaking the lines of the LONE RANGER in the 1980s cartoon revival, for instance.

Conspiracy ★★★

UK/US (BBC/HBO) Historical Drama. BBC 2 2002
DVD: Warner Home Video

Gen. Reinhard Heydrich	**Kenneth Branagh**
Lt. Col. Adolf Eichmann	**Stanley Tucci**
Dr Friedrich Kritzinger	**David Threlfall**
Dr Gerhard Klopfer	**Ian McNeice**
Dr Wilhelm Stuckart	**Colin Firth**
Dr Josef Buhler	**Ben Daniels**
Major Rudolf Lange	**Barnaby Kay**
Martin Luther	**Kevin McNally**
Dr Georg Leibbrandt	**Ewan Stewart**
Erich Neumann	**Jonathan Coy**
Gen. Heinrich Muller	**Brendan Coyle**
Dr Roland Freisler	**Owen Teale**
Lt. Gen. Otto Hoffmann	**Nicholas Woodeson**
Dr Alfred Meyer	**Brian Pettifer**
Col. Karl Schöngarth	**Peter Sullivan**

Writer **Loring Mandel**
Executive Producers **Frank Pierson, Frank Doelger, David M. Thompson, Peter Zinner**
Producer **Nick Gillott**

Genocide is on the agenda at a conference of Nazi leaders.
Based on the sole surviving copy of the minutes, this feature-length drama re-created a chilling meeting that took place in a mansion at Wannsee, on the outskirts of Berlin, on 20 January 1942. At a specially convened conference of 15 leading Nazi Party and military personnel, General Reinhard Heydrich, deputy chief of the Gestapo, calmly but determinedly led his guests in a discussion of the 'Final Solution' – a nauseatingly euphemistic term for the extermination of the European Jews. This award-winning drama reveals how the cool and calculating Heydrich bent the will of his colleagues into supporting plans drawn up by the Nazi hierarchy inside just 90 minutes. It is a harrowing, momentous decision that is being taken, but the language around the table is weasely and evasive and the atmosphere shockingly casual. Heydrich

charmingly manipulates affairs, halting so that guests can partake of a sumptuous buffet and fine wines, showing deference for other peoples' views at times, but exposing his cruel inner steel when necessary to put down any dissent that arises. Viewers are left wondering how such apparently bright, cultured men could even contemplate the brutality that was to follow. Frank Pierson directed.

Constant Hot Water ✳

UK (Central) Situation Comedy. ITV 1986

Phyllis Nugent .... **Patricia Phoenix**
Miranda Thorpe .... **Prunella Gee**
Frank Osborne .... **Steve Alder**
Norman Nugent .... **Roger Kemp**
Trevor .... **Mohammed Ashiq**
Jeff .... **Kevin Lloyd**
Brian .... **Al Ashton**
Paddy .... **Joe McPartland**

Writer **Colin Pearson**
Producer **Paula Burdon**

● ***A fiery seaside landlady is determined to preserve the tone of the neighbourhood.***

A chance for Pat Phoenix to prove she could play other roles than Elsie Tanner, *Constant Hot Water* cast the former CORONATION STREET star in the part of Phyllis Nugent, a boarding house proprietor in seaside Bridlington. With more than a foreshadowing of KEEPING UP APPEARANCE's Hyacinth Bucket in her character, Phyllis is an interfering, gossipy busybody who dislikes soiling her hands, is not averse to a spot of social climbing (she only accepts professional guests) and frowns on anyone who might bring the neighbourhood into disrepute. Her fears reach fever point when young Miranda Thorpe takes over the next door B&B and starts to attract the attentions of the local menfolk – even her removals man, Frank Osborne. Phyllis muscles in to ensure Miranda knows where she stands. Norman is Phyllis's long-suffering husband. Bernard Thompson directs and Instant Sunshine provide the music for the six episodes. Pat Phoenix died seven months after the series aired.

Conti, Tom

(1941–)

Scottish actor of Italian descent, popular on stage and film but also prominent on TV thanks to dramas like *The Flight of the Heron, Madame Bovary* (Charles Bovary), THE GLITTERING PRIZES (Adam Morris), *The Norman Conquests, Voices Within* and Dennis Potter's *Blade on the Feather*, as well as comedies like OLD BOY NETWORK (Lucas Frye). More recently, Conti made guest appearances in FRIENDS, played Bob Jones in *I was a Rat* and starred in the forensic investigation series DONOVAN (Joe Donovan). He has also narrated series such as the music documentary *Sound Stories* and the revamp of Andy Pandy.

Continuity Announcer

See *Announcer*.

Contrast

The relationship between the lightest and darkest elements of a TV picture.

Control Desk

Found in the control room or gallery, the control desk houses the vision mixer and other technical apparatus used by the director, his production assistant and other technicians as they monitor recordings or live transmissions.

Conviction ✳✳✳

UK (Red) Police Drama. BBC 2 2005
DVD: Ind DVD

Ray Fairburn .... **Nicholas Gleaves**
Joe Payne .... **Ian Puleston-Davies**
Lucy Romanis .... **Laura Fraser**
Chrissie Fairburn .... **William Ash**
Lenny Fairburn .... **David Warner**
Robert Seymour .... **Reece Dinsdale**
Sol Draper .... **Jason Done**
Jason Buliegh .... **Jason Watkins**
Sandra Buliegh .... **Sharon Duce**
Miriam Payne .... **Linzey Cocker**
Lily Payne .... **Sarah Kirkman**
Angela Fairley .... **Georgia May Foote**
Tom Tiernan .... **Steve Evets**
Beth Caffrey .... **Zoe Henry**
Polly Caffrey .... **Dominique Jackson**
Jemma Ryan .... **Angel Coulby**

Writer **Bill Gallagher**
Executive Producers **Nicola Shindler, Gareth Neame**
Producer **Ann Harrison-Baxter**

● ***Gripping exploration of the psychological torment that can be inflicted by murder.***

A police drama with a difference, *Conviction* explores the problems a guilty conscience can bring, especially when there's a danger that something dreadful you've committed will soon come to light. The story features a small core of hard-nosed, hard-drinking police officers who think they've found the killer of a 12-year-old girl. Paedophile Jason Buliegh is the suspect but, it seems, he is in the clear. Two of the officers, abrasive Joe Payne and easily led Chrissie Fairburn, while returning home from a drunken party, are determined to make him pay all the same. Buliegh is abducted, taken to woodland and beaten to death. They bury the body but now the real trouble begins. Chrissie is badly disturbed at what has happened and Joe, while tortured himself at what he's done, rightly thinks Chrissie is becoming a loose cannon, especially when he starts befriending Buliegh's distressed mother. There is more danger promised from Chrissie's dad, Lenny, an ex-copper himself but now suffering from Alzheimer's. He was in the car that fateful night, and, alarmingly, shows signs of remembering what happened. To complicate matters, Chrissie's elder brother, Ray, is the officer in charge of the case and his sister, Beth, is Buliegh's lawyer. Robert Seymour is the thoughtful, unusually quiet CID officer whose incisive mind threatens to unravel the whole sorry situation.

Using flashbacks and flashforwards, fantasy sequences, snappy editing and a stylized tone from directors Marc Munden and David Richards, *Conviction* delves into the darker side of the conscience and investigates the pressures that being involved in a notorious murder case can bring both at work and within the family at the end of the day. The six episodes were shown first on BBC 3 in 2004.

Conway, Russ

(Trevor Stanford, DSM; 1925–2000)

British piano-playing celebrity of the late 1950s and early 1960s, a stalwart of variety spectaculars and series like *The Billy Cotton Band Show*. Self-taught, he sold millions of copies of records like 'Sidesaddle' and 'Roulette' before he faded off UK TV screens.

Coogan, Steve

(1965–)

Manchester-born comedian and actor, acclaimed for a series of character creations, most notably self-important sports-presenter-turned-chat-show-host Alan Partridge. Partridge was first seen in THE DAY TODAY (based on earlier success in Radio 4's *On the Hour*) and later in his own series, KNOWING ME, KNOWING YOU WITH ALAN PARTRIDGE (another follow-up from radio) and I'M ALAN PARTRIDGE. Almost as popular has been the foul-mouthed brother-and-sister combination of boozy Paul and slutty Pauline Calf, who first appeared in comedy revues like *Saturday Zoo* and went on to feature in their own one-off programmes *The Paul Calf Video Diary* and *Three Fights, Two Weddings and a Funeral*. The squabbling siblings also appeared in a series of comedy playlets called *Coogan's Run* (BBC 2 1995), along with new characters such as obnoxious salesman Gareth Cheeseman, quiz machine freaks Guy and Stuart Crump, museum creator Tim Fleck, club singer Mike Crystal and handyman Ernest Moss. Another Coogan creation was Portuguese crooner Tony Ferrino. In 2001 Coogan co-wrote and starred in a series of Hammer horror spoofs, DR TERRIBLE'S HOUSE OF HORRIBLE, and, through his own company, Baby Cow, produced among other offerings *The Sketch Show*, plus Rob Brydon's HUMAN REMAINS and MARION AND GEOFF, Coogan himself playing Geoff in the special *A Small Summer Party*. Coogan and Brydon also teamed up in the single drama *Cruise of the Gods* (with Coogan as Nick Lee). He has also provided voices for SPITTING IMAGE, the *Robbie the Reindeer* cartoons, *Combat Sheep* (Harris) and *I am Not an Animal*, featured in the sketch show *Monkey Trousers*, and once featured regularly in THE KRYPTON FACTOR inserts. In 1997 he made his straight acting debut as journalist Mike Gabbart in soccer scandal drama *The Fix*, and in 2003 was seen in the title role in *The Private Life of Samuel Pepys*. In 2006 Coogan launched another new creation, pest-controller and former roadie Tommy Saxondale in *Saxondale*.

Cook, Peter

(1937–95)

Dry, satirical, Torquay-born comedian, a Cambridge Footlights graduate whose celebrated two-year partnership with Dudley Moore in NOT ONLY . . . BUT ALSO . . . in the mid-1960s followed a couple of years of success with the *Beyond the Fringe* revue. Cook's collaborators in those early days included Moore, Jonathan Miller and Alan Bennett, and it was during that time that he developed his philosophical E. L. Wisty character, complete with grubby mac and flat cap, which he brought to TV in ON THE BRADEN BEAT in 1964. In 1966 he played the Mad Hatter in Miller's adaptation of ALICE IN WONDERLAND. After moving into film, Cook returned to television in the late 1970s, appearing as a seedy dance-hall manager in the late-night rock show *Revolver*, and in 1981 he switched to sitcom, starring with Mimi Kennedy in *The Two of Us*, the American version of TWO'S COMPANY (as butler Robert Brentwood). Among his other credits were GONE TO SEED (unscrupulous property developer Wesley Willis), King Richard III in *The Black Adder* (BLACKADDER series one), the series of spoof shorts *A Life in Pieces* (his long-established creation Sir Arthur Streeb-Greebling being interviewed by Ludovic Kennedy), the voice of the *Viz* cartoon character Roger Mellie, and assorted cameo performances. Cook was co-founder of London's Establishment Club in 1960 and became a major shareholder in the fledgling *Private Eye* magazine in the same year.

Cook, Roger

(1943–)

New Zealand-born, Australia-raised investigative reporter, first on radio in the UK (*The World at One* and *Checkpoint*), after working for Australian TV. Through his ITV series *The Cook Report*, Cook exposed any number of fraudsters and con men, as well as upbraiding the authorities on behalf of the consumer. Cook bravely tackled the most risqué of subjects and the most violent of characters, from child pornographers and badger-baiters to terrorists and racketeers. His camera-in-the-face method of confronting his targets has been much mimicked.

Cook, Sue

(1949–)

Middlesex-born, former radio broadcaster and TV news and current affairs presenter (NATIONWIDE) who for many years was co-host of the annual CHILDREN IN NEED appeals. She has also presented BREAKFAST TIME, *Out of Court*, *Collector's Lot*, *Hampton Court Palace* and *Maternity Hospital*, worked on various magazine programmes, and fronted CRIMEWATCH UK for 11 years. She was once married to classical guitarist John Williams.

Cooke, Alistair

KBE (Hon.) (1908–2004)

Manchester-born journalist, later an American citizen, who presented Radio 4's *Letter from America* from 1940 until just weeks before his death in 2004. A one-time BBC film critic, for many years Cooke was the *Guardian*'s chief US correspondent and he also worked for American radio stations as a specialist in British affairs. He first appeared on British television in the 1930s, presenting a short programme, *Accent in America*, although his TV masterpiece was undoubtedly AMERICA, a 13-week personal analysis of the birth and development of a nation, delivered in his customarily modest but incisively knowledgeable style and filled with feeling and affection for his adopted homeland. In the USA he was host of *Masterpiece Theater*, an anthology series of top British drama programmes like UPSTAIRS, DOWNSTAIRS, THE SIX WIVES OF HENRY VIII and POLDARK. *Alistair Cooke – Postcards from America* was a collection of his radio commentaries brought to television as a posthumous tribute.

Cooke, Brian

Liverpool-born comedy scriptwriter, often in collaboration with Johnnie Mortimer (see Mortimer's entry for joint credits). Individually, Cooke has also contributed TRIPPER'S/SLINGER'S DAY plus *Close to Home* and KEEP IT IN THE FAMILY, both of which went on to have US versions scripted by Cooke himself (*Starting from Scratch* and *Too Close for Comfort*, respectively).

Cool for Cats ✳

UK (Associated-Rediffusion) Pop Music. ITV 1956–61

Hosts **Ker Robertson, Kent Walton**

Creator **Joan Kemp-Welch**

Britain's first pop music show.

Billed variously as 'A disc programme for Squares', and 'A square disc programme', *Cool for Cats* was British TV's first pop music showcase, airing the latest single releases. Given its minuscule budget, the programme was forced to rely on artists miming and the talents of a resident dance group (led by Douglas Squires) which, to ring the changes, used the stairs and passageways of Associated-Rediffusion's offices as well as its studios. All the same, the 15-minute programme proved particularly popular and was screened more than once a week. Journalist Ker Robertson, the first host, was succeeded after a few weeks by Kent Walton, later better known for his ITV wrestling commentaries. Robertson went on to become the show's record arranger.

Coombs, Pat

(1926–2002)

Wiry Cockney comedy actress, typically in dithery or distressed parts, or as a timid soul dominated by a female dragon. She appeared in just such a role with Peggy Mount in the retirement home comedy YOU'RE ONLY YOUNG TWICE, playing Cissie Lupin, having previously played Violet, Mount's sister-in-law, in LOLLIPOP LOVES MR MOLE. Her comedy career began with Arthur Askey (she was Nola in the radio show *Hello Playmates*) and some of her earliest TV appearances were with Bill Maynard, Terry Scott, Tony Hancock, Cyril Fletcher and Jimmy Edwards. Coombs then appeared in *Barney is My Darling* (Miss Hobbitt) and starred in the sitcom BEGGAR MY NEIGHBOUR, as Reg Varney's wife, Lana Butt. She later joined Stephen Lewis (playing his sister, Dorothy) in the ON THE BUSES spin-off, *Don't Drink the Water*, and over the years was also seen in programmes like *Marty*, *The Dick Emery Show*, TILL DEATH US DO PART, *Wild, Wild Women* (Daisy), THE LADY IS A TRAMP (Lanky Pat) and the kids' series HOGG'S BACK (Mrs Mac), ROY'S RAIDERS, *Ragdolly Anna* and MR MAJEIKA. Coombs also spent some time in EASTENDERS, as Girl Guide leader Marge Green.

Cooper, Tommy

(1922–84)

Tall, Caerphilly-born comedian, notorious as the fez-wearing magician with the bad gags and bemused look whose tricks always failed. Tommy Cooper's hugely successful career began in the army and continued after the war on the London variety circuit. In the 1950s he branched out into television, appearing in series like *It's Magic* and winning a run of his own series, including *Cooper – Life with Tommy*, *Cooper's Capers*, *Cooperama*, *Life With Cooper*, *Cooper at Large*, *The Tommy Cooper Hour*, *Cooper King-Size* and *Cooper – Just Like That!* (after his catchphrase). He became a cult comedian and enjoyed great respect among his fellow artistes. It was actually on television that he died, suffering a heart attack while appearing on *Live from Her Majesty's*.

Cop Rock ✳

US (Steven Bochco/Twentieth Century-Fox) Musical Drama. BBC 1 1991 (US: ABC 1990)

Chief Roger Kendrick	**Ronny Cox**
Major Louise Plank	**Barbara Bosson**
Capt. John Hollander	**Larry Joshua**
Officer Andy Campo	**David Gianopoulos**
Det. Vincent LaRusso	**Peter Onorati**
Det. Joseph Gaines	**Mick Murray**
Det. Ralph Ruskin	**Ron McLarty**
Officer Vicki Quinn	**Anne Bobby**
Officer Franklin Rose	**James McDaniel**

Creators **Steven Bochco, William M. Finkelstein**
Executive Producer **Steven Bochco**

Innovative mix of police drama and contemporary music.

Noted for being one of Steven Bochco's less successful creations, *Cop Rock* – somewhat bizarrely – took straight, often grimy, crime drama stories and cut into them bursts of rock, pop, soul, gospel, rap and other kinds of music. Police, crooks, judges, juries, drug dealers *et al.* were prone to breaking into song as a means of pouring out their inner feelings. The tunes for the pilot show were written by Randy Newman (he also penned the theme song, 'Under the Gun'); later shows had tracks (up to five per episode) from other writers supervised by Mike Post. The setting was Los Angeles, whose fictitious corrupt mayor, Louise Plank, was played by Bochco's wife, Barbara Bosson. Among the regular cops was Wild West buff Kendrick, his level-headed team leader Hollander, keen young Gaines, married (but mismatched in age) detectives Ruskin and Quinn, Quinn's patrol partner Campo, and the violent LaRusso. Clearly influenced by Dennis Potter's THE SINGING DETECTIVE, it was not cheap to produce, but viewers found it weird rather than gripping, resulting in an early cancellation.

Cope, Kenneth

(1934–)

British actor/scriptwriter who came to the fore in the early 1960s as one of the presenters of THAT WAS THE WEEK THAT WAS and as a semi-regular in CORONATION STREET, turning up from time to time as Scouser Jed Stone, the petty crook Minnie Caldwell adored and knew as Sonny Jim. However, it was as the deceased part of RANDALL AND HOPKIRK (DECEASED) that he is best remembered, playing the ghost detective Marty Hopkirk. Other credits have included WHACK-O! (schoolmaster Price Whittaker), DIXON OF DOCK GREEN, Z CARS, THE AVENGERS, *We Have Ways of Making You Laugh*, BERGERAC, SHELLEY (DHSS clerk Forsyth), MINDER, STRANGERS, *Bootle Saddles*, DOCTOR WHO, BROOKSIDE (Ray Hilton), CASUALTY, A TOUCH OF FROST, MISS MARPLE, DOCTORS, WAKING THE DEAD and THE BILL. Among his writing successes have been the kids' soccer series *Striker*, the sitcom *Thingumybob* and episodes of THE DUSTBINMEN, THE SQUIRRELS and A SHARP INTAKE OF BREATH.

Copper's End ✶

UK (ATV) Situation Comedy. ITV 1971

Sgt Sam Short	**Bill Owen**
PC Eddie Edwards	**Richard Wattis**
Sgt Penny Pringle	**Josephine Tewson**
PC Chipper Collins	**George Moon**
PC Dinkie Dinkworth	**Royce Mills**
Chief Supt. Ripper	**Kevin Brennan**

Creator **Ted Willis**
Writers **David Cumming, Derek Collyer, Paul Wheeler**
Producer **Shaun O'Riordan**

● ***One-series sitcom set in England's most slovenly police station.***

Though dreamt up by Ted Willis, this bunch of coppers in the fictional town of Copper's End were a world away from reliable old George Dixon, Willis's greatest creation. How he would have coped with an inept sergeant who hired out the panda car for social functions and driving lessons, or a shiftless team of PCs more interested in playing cards than plodding the beat, is anyone's guess. At least the newly arrived Sgt Penny Pringle may have earned some respect, keen, as she was, on bringing the station to heel.

Co-production

A programme made jointly by two or more companies, sometimes from more than one country, in an effort to spread the financial risk.

Cops, The ✶✶✶

UK (World/BBC) Police Drama. BBC 2 1998–2001

WPC Mel Draper	**Katy Cavanagh**
Sgt Edward Giffen	**Rob Dixon**
PC Roy Bramell	**John Henshaw**
PC Mike Thompson	**Steve Jackson**
PC Danny Rylands	**Jack Marsden**
WPC/Sgt Natalie Metcalf	**Clare McGlinn**
PC Jaz Shundara	**Parvez Qadir**
DS/Insp. Alan Wakefield	**David Crellin**
PC Colin Jellicoe	**Steve Garti**
PC Dean Wishaw	**Danny Seward**
Cindy	**Margaret Blakemore**
Standish	**Sue Cleaver**
Chief Insp. Newland	**Mark Chatterton**
Stowe	**Ken Kitson**
Maggie Hayes	**Jan Pearson**
WPC Amanda Kennett	**Paulette Williams**
Darril Stone	**Stuart Goodwin**
Ellen	**Deirdre Costello**
WPC Karen MacGuire	**Kitty Simpson**
John Martins	**Michael McNally**

Creators **Jimmy Gardner, Robert Jones, Anita J. Pandolfo**
Executive Producer **Tony Garnett**
Producers **Eric Coulter, Ann Harrison-Baxter**

● ***Innovative police drama with the feel of a documentary.***

Thanks to the use of documentary-style camerawork and a cast of largely unknown actors, *The Cops* left viewers wondering whether this televised police work was actually real or fictitious. Set in the northern town of Stanton (real life Bury), and particularly on the streets of the troublesome Skeetsmore estate, its stories major on the stresses of being a part of the force, rather than traditional cops-and-robbers fare; violence features prominently and strong language ensures the series is light years away from the days of Dixon of Dock Green.

These boys and girls in blue are hardly a perfect bunch. The leading characters include probationary WPC Mel Draper, whose drug use helps her through the shifts; modernizing new sergeant Edward Giffen; Hindu probationer Jaz Shundara; his wily partner, Colin Jellicoe; old-fashioned, non-PC PC Roy Bramell; level-headed Danny Rylands; socially aware, ambitious WPC Natalie Metcalf; and the mostly sensible, but always volatile, Dean Wishaw. Experienced producer Tony Garnett works on getting the right balance, with the odd flash of humour lightening the load and occasional heart-rending moments adding sentiment.

Though quite different in tone, *The Cops* was not unlike Z CARS in that it moved police drama on to a new level and drew immediate criticism from the police force itself – which had co-operated in the filming – for the unfavourable image it portrayed of today's law-enforcers. Unsurprisingly, similar assistance was not forthcoming for series two and three.

Corbett, Harry

OBE (1918–89)

'Bye bye, everybody, bye, bye.' These weary, resigned closing words of each show became the catchphrase of Harry Corbett, a genial northern entertainer, the man who gave the world SOOTY and Sweep. Beginning his working life as an electrical engineer, Corbett, an amateur pianist and magician, transformed his life in 1948 when he purchased a bear glove-puppet on Blackpool's North Pier for 7/6d (38p). He built the bear into his magic act, which led to an appearance on the BBC's *Talent Night* in 1952. The bear was simply known as Teddy at the time, but after applying some chimney soot to his ears and nose, in order to add more character, he was rechristened Sooty. In 1955, Harry and Sooty were given their own series, *The Sooty Show*. A couple of years later, Sweep, a squeaky, rather dim dog with a lust for sausages, joined Sooty, making Corbett's life a misery as they spoiled his magic tricks, sprayed him with water and hit him around the head with a balsa-wood hammer. Corbett then introduced other characters to the show, including Kipper the cat, Butch the dog and Ramsbottom the snake, but most controversial was its first female star, Soo, a cute panda who did all the housework. In 1968 Corbett switched channels, taking his puppets to ITV, where he stayed until he suffered a heart attack in 1975. His son, Matthew, then took over as Sooty and Sweep's harassed straight man, eventually selling the rights to the puppets for £1.4 million in 1996, but keeping a hand in the business, so to speak, for another two years. Sooty has since been accompanied on TV by Richard Cadell.

Corbett, Harry H.

OBE (1925–82)

Although he subsequently appeared in a range of TV shows, Harry H. Corbett will for ever be remembered as Harold Steptoe, the seedy rag-and-bone man with artistic pretensions whose dreams were constantly shattered by his vulgar old dad. Corbett came to television via film and the Shakespearean and classical stage, having served in the Marines in the war and then training as a radiographer. STEPTOE AND SON arrived in 1962 and ran – off and on – for 12 years, leaving Corbett heavily typecast, despite numerous appearances in programmes like THE GOODIES, TALES OF THE UNEXPECTED and SHOESTRING, his own three sitcoms – as the status-seeking *Mr Aitch* in 1967, the determined bachelor Alfred Wilcox in *The Best Things in Life* in 1969, and newsagent *Grundy* in 1980 – and a prominent role in the comedy POTTER, as local gangster Harry Tooms. Corbett, whose first wife had been comedienne Sheila Steafel, died of a heart attack in 1982, ironically three years before his TV father, Wilfrid Brambell. The 'H' in his name stood, allegedly, for 'Hanything' and was included to avoid confusion with Harry Corbett of SOOTY fame. His daughter is actress Susannah Corbett.

Corbett, Ronnie

OBE (1930–)

Tiny, bespectacled, Edinburgh-born comedian and comic actor, one half of the celebrated TWO RONNIES partnership. Ronnie Corbett's TV career actually began on CRACKERJACK in the 1950s and progressed via series like *The Dickie Henderson Show* and *It's Tarbuck* to THE FROST REPORT (on which he worked for the first time with Barker). His own sitcom, NO – THAT'S ME OVER HERE, and a comedy/variety series, *The Corbett Follies*, followed. Then, in 1971, he was teamed once again with Barker for *The Two Ronnies*. One of the show's highlights was Corbett's drawn-out monologue, delivered from an outsize armchair. During the programme's lengthy run, Corbett moved back into situation comedy with the series, NOW LOOK HERE . . ., *The Prince of Denmark* and SORRY!, the last providing the final outing for his various 'mummy's boy' comedy roles. His own sit-down/sketch series, *The Ronnie Corbett Show*, was shown in 1987. In the 1990s he hosted *Small Talk*, a humorous quiz game based on children's views of the world, and was a regular on *The Ben Elton Show*. Corbett also has plenty of guest appearances to his name and was part of the *All Star Comedy Show* team. In 2005, he once again teamed up with Ronnie Barker for *The Two Ronnies Sketchbook*, a compilation of their greatest bits, with some new material, that proved to be Barker's TV swan song.

Coronation, The ✶

UK (BBC) Documentary. BBC 1953

Commentators **Richard Dimbleby, Berkeley Smith, Chester Wilmot, Max Robertson, Michael Henderson, Mary Hill, Brian Johnston, Bernard Braden**

Live coverage of the Queen's coronation.

Widely recognized as the catalyst that made television a must for most British citizens, *The Coronation of Queen Elizabeth II* on 2 June 1953 was a mammoth undertaking for the BBC. Coverage ran from 10.15 a.m. (after an hour's worth of test signal, so viewers could tune in their primitive sets) and ran to 5.20 p.m., ending with an RAF salute. Cameras covered the Queen's procession to Westminster Abbey, the coronation service, the state procession through London, and the Queen's appearance on the balcony of Buckingham Palace. Events within the Abbey were described by Richard Dimbleby. Other commentators were Berkeley Smith and Chester Wilmot outside Buckingham Palace; Max Robertson on Victoria Embankment; Michael Henderson and Mary Hill outside Westminster Abbey; and Brian Johnston and Bernard Braden at Grosvenor Gate (Hyde Park). To catch the occasion, citizens without sets squeezed into wealthier neighbours' front rooms and it is estimated that some 20 million people watched the broadcast, even though there were only around 2 million sets in Britain at the time (many of which had been purchased specifically for the occasion). Two separate telerecordings were made of the day's momentous events. The first set of equipment produced an edited version for broadcast at 8 p.m. the same evening and recordings that were sent to certain European TV companies and also to the USA and Canada by waiting RAF Canberra aircraft; the second recorded the day for the archives. On a much more modest scale, the BBC had also covered the coronation of the Queen's father, King George VI, on 12 May 1937. This was an adventurous and major undertaking for the BBC but cameras were not allowed inside Westminster Abbey and, with television sets so few and far between, it had nothing of the impact of the 1953 occasion.

Coronation Street ✶✶✶✶

UK (Granada) Drama. ITV 1960–
DVD: Network

Ena Sharples	**Violet Carson**
Annie Walker	**Doris Speed**
Jack Walker	**Arthur Leslie**
Elsie Tanner/Howard	**Pat Phoenix**
Dennis Tanner	**Philip Lowrie**
Frank Barlow	**Frank Pemberton**
Ida Barlow	**Noel Dyson**
Ken Barlow	**William Roache**
David Barlow	**Alan Rothwell**
Martha Longhurst	**Lynne Carol**
Minnie Caldwell	**Margot Bryant**
Elsie Lappin	**Maudie Edwards**
Ivan Cheveski	**Ernst Walder**
Linda Cheveski	**Anne Cunningham**
Harry Hewitt	**Ivan Beavis**
Christine Hardman/Appleby	**Christine Hargreaves**
May Hardman	**Joan Heath**
Susan Cunningham	**Patricia Shakesby**
Albert Tatlock	**Jack Howarth**
Florrie Lindley	**Betty Alberge**
Esther Hayes	**Daphne Oxenford**
Leonard Swindley	**Arthur Lowe**
Concepta Riley/Hewitt/Regan	**Doreen Keogh**
Lucille Hewitt	**Jennifer Moss**
Valerie Tatlock/Barlow	**Anne Reid**
Emily Nugent/Bishop	**Eileen Derbyshire**
Billy Walker	**Kenneth Farrington**
Joan Walker/Davies	**June Barry** **Dorothy White**
Len Fairclough	**Peter Adamson**
Alf Roberts OBE	**Bryan Mosley**
Bill Gregory	**Jack Watson**
Jed Stone	**Kenneth Cope**
Sheila Birtles/Crossley	**Eileen Mayers**
Doreen Lostock	**Angela Crow**
Dot Greenhalgh	**Joan Francis**
Nancy Leathers	**Norah Hammond**
Joe Makinson	**Brian Rawlinson**
Arnold Tanner	**Frank Crawshaw**
Jerry Booth	**Graham Haberfield**
Dave Smith	**Reginald Marsh**
Myra Dickenson/Booth	**Susan Jameson**
Neil Crossley	**Geoffrey Matthews**
David Robbins	**Jon Rollason**
Charlie Moffitt	**Gordon Rollings**
Hilda Ogden	**Jean Alexander**
Stan Ogden	**Bernard Youens**

Character	Actor
Irma Ogden/Barlow	**Sandra Gough**
Trevor Ogden	**Jonathan Collins**
	Don Hawkins
Rita Bates/Littlewood/Fairclough/Sullivan	**Barbara Mullaney/Knox**
William Piggott	**George A. Cooper**
Sandra Petty	**Heather Moore**
Lionel Petty	**Edward Evans**
Jim Mount	**Barry Keagan**
Susan Barlow/Baldwin	**Katie Heanneau**
	Susi Patterson
	Wendy Jane Walker
	Joanna Foster
Peter Barlow	**John Heanneau**
	Mark Duncan
	Christopher Dormerr
	Linus Roache
	Joseph McKenna
	David Lonsdale
	Chris Gascoyne
Ruth Winter	**Colette O'Neil**
Nellie Harvey	**Mollie Sugden**
Ray Langton	**Neville Buswell**
Bet Lynch/Gilroy	**Julie Goodyear**
Ernest Bishop	**Stephen Hancock**
Steve Tanner	**Paul Maxwell**
Joe Donnelli	**Shane Rimmer**
Audrey Bright/Flemming	**Gillian McCann**
Dickie Flemming	**Nigel Humphreys**
Maggie Clegg/Cooke	**Irene Sutcliffe**
Les Clegg	**John Sharp**
Gordon Clegg	**Bill Kenwright**
George Greenwood	**Arthur Pentelow**
Tommy Deakin	**Paddy Joyce**
Betty Turpin/Williams	**Betty Driver**
Cyril Turpin	**William Moore**
Alice Pickens	**Doris Hare**
Janet Reid/Barlow	**Judith Barker**
Bernard Butler	**Gorden Kaye**
Sandra Butler	**Patricia Fuller**
Ted Loftus	**Ted Morris**
Alan Howard	**Alan Browning**
Mavis Riley/Wilton	**Thelma Barlow**
Frank Bradley	**Tommy Boyle**
Ivy Tilsley/Brennan	**Lynne Perrie**
Edna Gee	**Mavis Rogerson**
Norma Ford	**Diana Davies**
Jacko Ford	**Robert Keegan**
Ron Cooke	**Eric Lander**
Alec Gilroy	**Roy Barraclough**
Deirdre Hunt/Langton/Barlow/Rachid	**Anne Kirkbride**
Vera Hopkins	**Kathy Staff**
Tricia Hopkins	**Kathy Jones**
Idris Hopkins	**Richard Davies**
Granny Megan Hopkins	**Jesse Evans**
Blanche Hunt	**Maggie Jones**
Eddie Yeats	**Geoffrey Hughes**
Vera Duckworth	**Elizabeth Dawn**
Gail Potter/Tilsley/Platt/Hillman	**Helen Worth**
Ralph Lancaster	**Kenneth Watson**
Fred Gee	**Fred Feast**
Terry Bradshaw	**Bob Mason**
Derek Wilton	**Peter Baldwin**
Mike Baldwin	**Johnny Briggs**
Suzie Birchall	**Cheryl Murray**
Renee Bradshaw/Roberts	**Madge Hindle**

Character	Actor
Tracy Langton/Barlow/Preston	**Christabel Finch**
	Holly Chamarette
	Dawn Acton
	Kate Ford
Steve Fisher	**Lawrence Mullin**
Ida Clough	**Helene Palmer**
Brian Tilsley	**Christopher Quinten**
Bert Tilsley	**Peter Dudley**
Audrey Potter/Roberts	**Sue Nicholls**
Arnold Swain	**George Waring**
Martin Cheveski	**Jonathon Caplan**
Ron Sykes	**Bobby Knutt**
Johnny Webb	**Jack Smethurst**
Nicky/Nick Tilsley/Platt	**Warren Jackson**
	Adam Rickitt
Alma Sedgewick/Baldwin/Halliwell	**Amanda Barrie**
Eunice Nuttall/Gee	**Meg Johnson**
Gordon Lewis	**David Daker**
Marion Willis/Yeats	**Veronica Doran**
Sharon Gaskell/Bentley	**Tracie Bennett**
Maggie Dunlop/Redman	**Jill Kerman**
Tom 'Chalkie' Whitely	**Teddy Turner**
Craig Whitely	**Mark Price**
Phyllis Pearce	**Jill Summers**
Victor Pendlebury	**Christopher Coll**
Dr Lowther	**Robert Scase**
Percy Sugden	**Bill Waddington**
Jack Duckworth	**William Tarmey**
Terry Duckworth	**Nigel Pivaro**
Norman 'Curly' Watts	**Kevin Kennedy**
Shirley Armitage	**Lisa Lewis**
Kevin Webster	**Michael Le Vell**
Sally Waterman	**Vicki Chambers**
Mark Redman	**Thomas Hawkeswood**
	Christopher Oakes
	Chris Cook
	Paul Fox
Bill Webster	**Peter Armitage**
Debbie Webster	**Sue Devaney**
Elaine Prior/Webster	**Judy Gridley**
George Wardle	**Ron Davies**
Gloria Todd	**Sue Jenkins**
Martin Platt	**Sean Wilson**
Harry Clayton	**Johnny Leeze**
Connie Clayton	**Susan Brown**
Andrea Clayton	**Caroline O'Neill**
Sue Clayton	**Jane Hazelgrove**
Sam Tindall	**Tom Mennard**
Frank Mills	**Nigel Gregory**
Stella Rigby	**Vivienne Ross**
Jenny Bradley	**Sally Ann Matthews**
Alan Bradley	**Mark Eden**
Sally Seddon/Webster	**Sally Whittaker**
Ian Latimer	**Michael Looney**
Sarah Louise Tilsley/Platt	**Lynsay King**
	Tina O'Brien
Don Brennan	**Geoff Hinsliff**
Sandra Stubbs	**Sally Watts**
Tina Fowler	**Michelle Holmes**
Dawn Prescott	**Louise Harrison**
Liz McDonald	**Beverley Callard**
Jim McDonald	**Charles Lawson**
Andy McDonald	**Nicholas Cochrane**
Steve McDonald	**Simon Gregory**
Wendy Crozier	**Roberta Kerr**
Mark Casey	**Stuart Wolfenden**

Character	Actor
Reg Holdsworth	**Ken Morley**
Kimberley Taylors	**Suzanne Hall**
Eddie Ramsden	**William Ivory**
Nigel Ridley	**John Basham**
Maurice Jones	**Alan Moore**
Des Barnes	**Philip Middlemiss**
Steph Barnes	**Amelia Bullmore**
Vicky Arden/McDonald	**Helen Warburton**
	Chloë Newsome
Felicity 'Flick' Khan	**Rita Wolf**
Angie Freeman	**Deborah McAndrew**
Phil Jennings	**Tommy Boyle**
Rosie Webster	**Emma Collinge**
	Helen Flanagan
Marie Lancaster/Ramsden	**Joy Blakeman**
Peter Ingram	**Tony Osoba**
Jackie Ingram/Baldwin	**Shirin Taylor**
Raquel Wolstenhulme/Watts	**Sarah Lancashire**
Brendan Scott	**Milton Johns**
Lisa Horten/Duckworth	**Caroline Milmoe**
Ted Sullivan	**William Russell**
Denise Osbourne	**Denise Black**
Neil Mitchell	**John Lloyd Fillingham**
Carmel Finnan	**Catherine Cusack**
Doug Murray	**Brian Hibbard**
Paula Maxwell	**Judy Brooke**
Maureen Naylor/Holdsworth/Elliott	**Sherrie Hewson**
Maud Grimes	**Elizabeth Bradley**
Fiona Middleton	**Angela Griffin**
Tanya Pooley	**Eva Pope**
Charlie Whelan	**John St Ryan**
Norris Cole	**Malcolm Hebden**
Tricia Armstrong	**Tracy Brabin**
Jamie Armstrong	**Joseph Gilgun**
Revd Bernard Morten	**Roland MacLeod**
Samir Rachid	**Al Nedjari**
Maxine Heavey/Peacock	**Tracy Shaw**
Rodney Bostock	**Colin Proctor**
Billy Williams	**Frank Mills**
Josie Clarke	**Ellie Haddington**
Anne Malone	**Eve Steele**
Daniel Osbourne	**Lewis Harney**
Eric Firman	**Malcolm Terris**
Tony Horrocks	**Lee Warburton**
Judy Mallett	**Gaynor Faye**
Gary Mallett	**Ian Mercer**
Stephen Reid	**Todd Boyce**
Fred Elliott	**John Savident**
Ashley Peacock	**Stephen Arnold**
Joyce Smedley	**Anita Carey**
Kelly Thomson	**Sarah Moffett**
Sophie Webster	**Ashleigh Middleton**
	Emma Woodward
Claire Palmer	**Maggie Norris**
Becky Palmer	**Emily Aston**
Sean Skinner	**Terence Hillyer**
Samantha Failsworth	**Tina Hobley**
Roy Cropper	**David Neilson**
Alan McKenna	**Glenn Hugill**
Chris Collins	**Matthew Marsden**
Natalie Horrocks/Barnes	**Denise Welch**
Zoe Tattersall	**Joanne Froggatt**
Les Battersby/Battersby-Brown	**Bruce Jones**
Janice Battersby	**Vicky Entwistle**
Leanne Battersby/Tilsley	**Jane Danson**
Toyah Battersby	**Georgia Taylor**
Jon Lindsay	**Owen Aaronovitch**
Pam Middleton	**Elizabeth Estensen**
Geoffrey 'Spider' Nugent	**Martin Hancock**
Hayley Patterson/Cropper	**Julie Hesmondhalgh**
David Platt	**Thomas Ormson**
	Jack P. Shepherd
Greg Kelly	**Stephen Billington**
Jackie Dobbs	**Margi Clarke**
Charlie West	**Keith Clifford**
Michael Wall	**Dominic Rickhards**
Lorraine Brownlow	**Holly Newman**
Linda Sykes/Baldwin	**Jacqueline Pirie**
Alison Wakefield/Webster	**Naomi Radcliffe**
Aiden O'Donnall	**Kieran Flynn**
Ian Bentley	**Jonathan Guy Lewis**
Ravi Desai	**Saeed Jaffrey**
Nita Desai	**Rebecca Sarker**
Vikram Desai	**Chris Bisson**
Julia Stone	**Fiona Allen**
Ted Cooper	**David Peart**
Tyrone Dobbs	**Alan Halsall**
Danny Hargreaves	**Richard Standing**
Vinny Sorrell	**James Gaddas**
Melanie Tindell	**Nicola Wheeler**
Tom Ferguson	**Tom Wisdom**
Doreen Heavey	**Prunella Gee**
Beryl Peacock	**Anny Tobin**
Rebecca Hopkins	**Jill Halfpenny**
Gwen Loveday/Davies	**Annie Hulley**
Debs Brownlow	**Gabrielle Glaister**
Duggie Ferguson	**John Bowe**
Dev Alahan	**Jimmi Harkishin**
Maria Sutherland	**Samia Ghadie/Smith**
Bethany Platt	**Amy Walton**
	Emily Walton
	Mia Louise Cookson
Jez Quigley	**Lee Boardman**
Dennis Stringer	**Charles Dale**
Eileen Grimshaw	**Sue Cleaver**
Geena Gregory	**Jennifer James**
Anthony Stephens	**John Quayle**
Edna Miller	**Joan Kempson**
Emma Taylor/Watts	**Angela Lonsdale**
Charlie Ramsden	**Clare McGlinn**
Dr Matt Ramsden	**Stephen Beckett**
Candice Stowe	**Nikki Sanderson**
Karen Phillips/McDonald	**Suranne Jones**
Bobbi Lewis	**Naomi Russell**
Sam Kingston	**Scott Wright**
Molly Hardcastle	**Jacqueline Kington**
Kirk Sutherland	**Andrew Whyment**
Amanda Stephens	**Martine Brown**
Adam Barlow	**Iain de Caestecker**
	Sam Robertson
Peter Hartnell	**Eamonn Riley**
Jason Grimshaw	**Ryan Thomas**
Todd Grimshaw	**Bruno Langley**
Darren Grimshaw	**Nicholas Zabel**
Evelyn Sykes/Elliott	**Melanie Kilburn**
Ryan Sykes	**Matthew Dunster**
Boris Weaver	**Mark Hallett**
Sunita Parekh/Alahan	**Shobna Gulati**
Fiz Brown	**Jennie McAlpine**
Alex Swinton	**Joe Simpson**
Sheila Hayes	**Jenni Williams**
Wayne Hayes	**Gary Damer**
Shelley Unwin/Barlow	**Sally Lindsay**
Richard Hillman	**Brian Capron**

Stan Wagstaff .... **Jack Smethurst**
Ernie Wagstaff .... **Stuart Golland**
Karl Harper .... **Anthony Barclay**
Sandra Milligan .... **Francesca Manning**
Hazel Wilding .... **Kazia Pelka**
Aidan Critchley .... **Dean Ashton**
Archie Shuttleworth .... **Roy Hudd**
Joe Carter .... **Jonathan Wrather**
Lillian Spencer .... **Maureen Lipman**
Danielle Spencer .... **Kelly Wenham**
Timothy Spencer .... **Jonathan Wright**
Sandy George .... **Sandra Hunt**
Ciaran McCarthy .... **Keith Duffy**
Naveen Alahan .... **Parvez Qadir**
Harry Flagg .... **Iain Rogerson**
Angela Nelson/Harris .... **Kathryn Hunt**
Katy Nelson/Harris .... **Lucy-Jo Hudson**
Craig Nelson/Harris .... **Richard Fleeshman**
Tommy Nelson/Harris .... **Thomas Craig**
Lucy Richards/Barlow .... **Katy Carmichael**
Mick Hopwood .... **Ian Gain**
Claire Casey/Peacock .... **Julia Haworth**
Maz O'Loughlin .... **Emma Rydal**
Tony Stewart .... **Alan Igbon**
Brenda Fearns .... **Julia Deakin**
Maya Sharma .... **Sasha Behar**
Charlie Stubbs .... **Bill Ward**
Cilla Brown/Battersby-Brown **Wendi Peters**
Fiz Brown .... **Jennie McAlpine**
Tim Marsden .... **Daniel Pape**
Karl Foster .... **Chris Finch**
Frankie Baldwin .... **Debra Stephenson**
Danny Baldwin .... **Bradley Walsh**
Sonia Marshall .... **Tina Gambe**
Patrick Tussel .... **Trevor Dwyer-Lynch**
Bev Unwin .... **Susie Blake**
Chesney Brown/
Battersby-Brown .... **Sam Aston**
Jamie Baldwin .... **Rupert Hill**
Sean Tully .... **Antony Cotton**
Violet Wilson .... **Jenny Platt**
Kelly Crabtree .... **Tupele Dorgu**
Warren Baldwin .... **Danny Young**
Amy Barlow .... **Rebecca Pike**
Joshua Peacock .... **Benjamin Beresford**
Ian Davenport .... **Philip Bretherton**
Penny King .... **Pauline Fleming**
Carol Baldwin .... **Lynne Pearson**
Lloyd Mullaney .... **Craig Charles**
Phil Nail .... **Clive Russell**
Keith Appleyard .... **Ian Redford**
Diggory Compton .... **Eric Potts**
Nathan Harding .... **Ray Fearon**

Creator **Tony Warren**
Producers **Stuart Latham, Derek Granger, H. V. Kershaw, Margaret Morris, Tim Aspinall, Howard Baker, Peter Eckersley, Jack Rosenthal, Michael Cox, Richard Everitt, Richard Doubleday, John Finch, June Howson, Brian Armstrong, Eric Prytherch, Susie Hush, Bill Podmore, Leslie Duxbury, Pauline Shaw, Mervyn Watson, John G. Temple, David Liddiment, Carolyn Reynolds, Tony Wood, Sue Pritchard, Brian Park, David Hanson, Jane Macnaught, Kieran Roberts, Steve Frost**

● ***Working-class life in a northern back-street.***

Coronation Street is a British institution. However, after the first episode went out at 7 p.m. on 9 December 1960 one critic famously declared that it had no future, being all doom and gloom. Like the Decca records executive who turned down The Beatles, he couldn't have been more wrong. The '*Street*' is now well over 40 years old and still at the top of the ratings. That said, anyone viewing early recordings will immediately recognize how the series has changed over the years. It began in an age of industrial grime and sweat but has progressed to reflect the many changes that have taken place in British life. The smoking chimney pots and leaden skies of the early programme credits echoed a dour but vibrant society, and creator Tony Warren (a 23-year-old Granada staff-writer, tired of adapting Biggles stories) initially produced scripts similar to the kitchen-sink dramas seen on ARMCHAIR THEATRE. But the programme quickly mellowed, introducing more humour and occasional farcical elements. Indeed, the programme wandered so far from Warren's original goals that at one time he disowned it. These days, *Coronation Street* plays almost like a situation comedy, although shocks, tragedy and moments of high drama are liberally dispersed throughout its episodes. Warren himself later conceded that with society growing 'softer', *Coronation Street* has had to follow suit.

The programme is set in the fictional Manchester suburb of Weatherfield, Coronation Street (the working name was *Florizel Street* but, allegedly, sounded too much like a lavatory cleaner) being a typical northern back-street terrace with a pub on one corner and a shop on the other. The first ever scene took place in the shop on the day that Florrie Lindley arrived to take over the business from the retiring Elsie Lappin. Also in that historic original cast were Annie and Jack Walker, landlords of the pub, the Rovers Return. The genial Jack (and actor Arthur Leslie) died in 1970, but Annie, the *Street*'s duchess and mistress of the withering look, held the licence until 1983, when she retired and left the series. Ena Sharples was the local hair-netted battleaxe, caretaker of the Glad Tidings Mission. Her OAP friends in the pub's snug were meek-and-mild Minnie Caldwell and Martha Longhurst, who was sensationally killed off in 1964, slumping dead over her milk stout. Another veteran was pensioner Albert Tatlock, proud of his war medals but never too proud to cadge a free rum if one was offered. Elsie Tanner was the fiery brunette whose promiscuity nettled the local puritans (especially Ena), and Dennis was her layabout son. And then there were the Barlows, hard-working, salt of the earth dad, Frank, his loyal wife, Ida (soon to be crushed by a bus), and two sons, Ken and David. David, a one-time professional footballer, was subsequently killed in a car accident in Australia, while Ken, always the *Street*'s intellectual (thrice-married: to Albert Tatlock's niece Valerie, to suicide victim Janet Reid and to Deirdre Langton – the last on two occasions), is today the only remaining original cast member.

Over the years the series has introduced plenty of other memorable characters. Leonard Swindley, the teetotal, lay-preaching draper at Gamma Garments, was jilted at the altar by the mousey Emily Nugent. Swindley later starred in the spin-off series PARDON THE EXPRESSION. Nugent, another long-serving member of the cast, went on to marry photographer Ernie Bishop and, after he was shot dead in a wages snatch, wed bigamist Arnold Swain. Lucille Hewitt was the troublesome teenager who lived with the Walkers after her father, Harry, and barmaid step-mother, Concepta, left for Ireland, while Len Fairclough was the *Street*'s he-man, a hard-drinking, roughly hewn builder who eventually signed away his bachelorhood (after years of flirtation with Elsie Tanner) in a marriage to red-headed singer Rita Littlewood. After 23 years in the series, he was killed off in a car crash in 1983, following a visit to his mistress. Lovable Jerry Booth was Len's stuttering assistant at the builder's yard. His place was taken later by the untrustworthy Ray Langton.

Stan and Hilda Ogden moved into number 13 in 1964 and forged one of TV's great double acts, a partnership that was broken only by actor Bernard Youens's illness and subsequent death in 1984. A combination of a work-shy boozer and a tittle-tattling skivvy, the Ogdens were the unluckiest couple on television, although their misfortune was usually self-inflicted. For many, Hilda's grief when Stan died provided moments of unsurpassable drama, and actress Jean Alexander's performance won universal acclaim. The Ogdens' wayward daughter, Irma, became David Barlow's wife, while their lodger, chortling jailbird dustman Eddie Yeats, was one of the show's most popular stars of the 1970s.

With the retirement of Annie Walker, the Rovers Return eventually passed into the hands of brassy, buxom Bet Lynch, the tarty, blonde barmaid who first arrived in the series in 1966 and became a fixture in 1970. Bet took over as the *Street*'s mother confessor, although her own problems (notably with men – including her failed marriage to entertainments agent Alec Gilroy) were far from trivial. One of her liaisons was with rag-trade wide boy, Mike Baldwin, arch-enemy of Ken Barlow (having tried to steal Ken's wife, Deirdre, and then marrying his daughter, Susan). Rita Fairclough's harrowing ordeal at the hands of vicious Alan Bradley was another *Coronation Street* highlight, ending with Bradley's death beneath the wheels of a Blackpool tram. Twittering away behind Rita was Mavis, her dithery colleague in The Kabin newsagent's shop, and regular interruptions came from Mavis's wimpy suitors, Derek Wilton and Victor Pendlebury.

The younger element has also been well represented. In the 1970s action focused around flighty shop assistant Suzie Birchall, corner shop girl Tricia Hopkins and insecure Gail Potter. Gail has since matured into a mother of three, and wed three times. Her first husband was the brawny Brian Tilsley (son of Ivy, arch-nagger, devout Catholic and one-time factory shop steward), while her second husband was trainee nurse Martin Platt, one of the 1980s' intake of teenagers. In 2002, she married murderous Richard Hillman. Along with Martin, the 1980s brought in star-gazing binman (later supermarket manager) Curly Watts, bookie Des Barnes and mechanic Kevin Webster and his blonde wife, Sally. Occasionally on the scene was sneering Terry Duckworth, the ne'er-do-well son of shiftless Jack and loud-mouthed Vera, who assumed the Ogden's crown as the *Street*'s perpetual losers.

Shopkeeper Alf Roberts was one of the series' senior figures after becoming a permanent cast member in 1968, no doubt helped by the fact that he was Weatherfield's mayor on two occasions. His second wife, Renee, was killed in a car accident, and Alf later suffered at the hands of his spendthrift third wife, Audrey, Gail's unreliable mother. Among the other senior characters have been policeman's widow Betty Turpin (the pub's homely barmaid and ace hot-pot cook); gravel-voiced, blue-rinsed Phyllis Pearce and the apple of her eye, war cook Percy Sugden, Emily's insensitive lodger; and the endlessly bickering McDonald family. Another cult character was Reg Holdsworth, the pompous retail executive.

In recent years, the most notable newcomers have included the 'neighbours from hell', the Battersbys; black-pudding-maker-turned-corner-shop-keeper Fred Elliott, and transsexual Hayley Patterson. Dramatic high spots have continued to keep the series at the top of the ratings. The exits (in various styles) of Bet, Derek and Mavis brought a tear to many a viewer's eye, as did the short-lived marriage of Curly to former check-out girl Raquel. The wrongful conviction of Deirdre for financial fraud ignited the nation and campaigns were organized to 'free the Weatherfield one'.

Coronation Street's writers have been many, with the most notable including John Finch, Jack Rosenthal, Harry Driver, Harry (H. V.) Kershaw, Adele Rose, Jim Allen, John Stevenson, Kay Mellor, Paula Milne and Paul Abbott. The series' melancholic solo-cornet theme tune was written by Eric Spear. In addition to the cast list above, the roll-call of 'guesting' actors and actresses is impressive to say the least. Among those cutting their teeth in the series have been singers Peter Noone of Herman's Hermits (Len Fairclough's son, Stanley), Monkee Davy Jones (Ena Sharples's grandson, Colin Lomax) and Michael Ball (Malcolm Nuttall, Kevin Webster's one-time rival in love), as well as the likes of Joanna Lumley (Ken Barlow's girlfriend, Elaine Perkins), Prunella Scales (bus conductress Eileen Hughes), Martin Shaw (hippie Robert Croft), Ray Brooks (Norman Phillips), Michael Elphick (Douglas Wormald, who wanted to buy The Kabin), Paula Wilcox (Ray Langton's sister, Janice), Peter Dean (lorry driver Fangio Bateman), Stan Stennett (Norman Crabtree, Hilda Ogden's chip-shop-owning brother), Richard Beckinsale (a policeman), THE GOOD OLD DAYS compere Leonard Sachs (Sir Julius Berlin), Paul Shane (Post Office worker Frank Draper), Bill Maynard (music agent Mickey Malone), Ben Kingsley (a Jack-the-lad who chatted up Irma Ogden and Valerie Barlow), Max Wall (Elsie Tanner's friend, Harry Payne) and a very young Joanne Whalley-Kilmer (Pamela Graham). Singer Chris Sandford appeared as binman Walter Potts, aka pop hopeful Brett Falcon, who recorded the song 'Not Too Little Not Too Much', a real-life Top Twenty hit in 1963. Recent guests have included Bernard Cribbins, Honor Blackman, Ian McKellen and rock band Status Quo.

Originally screened live on Fridays, with a recorded episode shown on Mondays, *Coronation Street* switched to Monday and Wednesday evenings in 1961 and was, for the first time, fully networked (the earliest episodes were not seen in the Midlands or in the Tyne-Tees area). From 1989, a third helping was served up on Fridays in a bid to win the soap war with BBC rival EASTENDERS. A fourth weekly episode – on Sunday – was added in 1996, and a fifth – a second Monday instalment – began in 2002. *Coronation Street* has also been viewed with much pleasure all around the world, although one of the few places it has yet to catch on is the USA. America did produce its own copycat soap, however, in the shape of PEYTON PLACE. Outliving its glamorous American clone by many years, *Coronation Street* is now the world's longest-running fictitious television series.

Corridor People, The ✶

UK (Granada) Detective Drama. ITV 1966

Kronk	**John Sharp**
Syrie Van Epp	**Elizabeth Shepherd**
Phil Scrotty	**Gary Cockrell**
Insp. Blood	**Alan Curtis**
Sgt Hound	**William Maxwell**

Creator/Writer **Eddie Boyd**
Producer **Richard Everitt**

A CID man and a private detective hunt down an international crime queen.

Victim as Birdwatcher, Victim as Whitebait, Victim as Red and *Victim as Black* were the off-beat titles of the four episodes which made up this short-lived, stylish but quirky thriller series. Featuring prominently in the surreal action are Kronk, a chubby and paternal CID figure, and Phil Scrotty, an American private eye. Their target is Syrie Van Epp, a clever, glamorous Persian whose true love is money and who will do anything to get it. Kronk's unwilling sidekicks are named – tongue residing comfortably in cheek – Blood and Hound. Derek Hilton provided the music.

Cosby, Bill

(1937–)

Hugely successful American comedian/actor/producer, a former nightclub comic whose TV career began with I SPY in 1965. In playing the part of Alexander Scott, Cosby became the first black actor to co-star in a US prime-time drama series. He followed *I Spy* with a succession of comedy, variety and children's programmes, most of which were not aired in the UK, including the cartoon series *Fat Albert and the Cosby Kids*. After spending eight years out of television, during which he gained a doctorate in education, he was tempted back by the offer of a sitcom over which he had complete creative control. The result was THE COSBY SHOW, and his portrayal of caring dad Cliff Huxtable enabled Cosby to give vent to his own philosophies of how to raise and educate children. The show picked up numerous awards and was a massive ratings success. More recently Cosby has filled Groucho Marx's shoes in the revival of the 1950s US quiz show *You Bet Your Life*, played criminologist Guy Hanks in *The Cosby Mysteries*, and starred in the US version of ONE FOOT IN THE GRAVE, known simply as *Cosby* (Hilton Lucas). He has also produced the animation *Little Bill* and written the theme music for several of his own programmes.

Cosby Show, The ★★★★

US (Carsey-Werner) Situation Comedy. Channel 4 1985–94
(US: NBC 1984–92)
DVD: Urban Works

Dr Heathcliff (Cliff) Huxtable	**Bill Cosby**
Clair Huxtable	**Phylicia Ayres Allen/Rashad**
Denise Huxtable Kendall	**Lisa Bonet**
Theodore Huxtable	**Malcolm-Jamal Warner**
Vanessa Huxtable	**Tempestt Bledsoe**
Rudy Huxtable	**Keshia Knight Pulliam**
Sondra Huxtable/Tibideaux	**Sabrina Le Beauf**
Peter Chiara	**Peter Costa**
Anna Huxtable	**Clarice Taylor**
Russell Huxtable	**Earle Hyman**
Elvin Tibideaux	**Geoffrey Owens**
Kenny ('Bud')	**Deon Richmond**
Cockroach	**Carl Anthony Payne**
Denny	**Troy Winbush**
Lt. Martin Kendall	**Joseph C. Phillips**
Olivia Kendall	**Raven Symone**
Pam Turner	**Erika Alexander**

Creators **Bill Cosby, Ed Weinberger, Michael Leeson**
Producer **Bill Cosby**

Family life in a caring New York household.

After a chequered TV past, Bill Cosby created this gentle sitcom and turned it into one of US TV's biggest-ever moneyspinners. *The Cosby Show* follows developments in the life of a black middle-class family, showing the children growing up, leaving school and college, eventually getting married and having children of their own. The parents are the charming Cliff Huxtable, an obstetrician, and his confident lawyer wife, Clair. Their children range in age at the outset from Sondra, a Princeton student, to five-year-old Rudy with, in between, teenagers Denise – later spun off into her own sitcom, *A Different World* (Channel 4 1988–94) – and Theo, plus eight-year-old Vanessa. The children's friends are also included. Cockroach is a pal of Theo's, while Peter and Bud are two of Rudy's classmates. Anna and Russell, Cliff's parents, make occasional appearances and, later, the Huxtables take in Pam Turner, the teenage daughter of a distant cousin from the Brooklyn slums. The family live in a New York terraced house, from where Cliff also practises his medicine.

Bill Cosby wasn't just the show's creator; his control was evident throughout. He was involved in many aspects of the production and the series became a personal statement about how he felt children should be brought up, i.e. with firmness and love, a philosophy he had developed while taking an education degree in the 1970s.

Cotton, Bill

CBE (1928–)

The son of bandleader Billy Cotton, Bill Cotton's showbusiness career began in Tin Pan Alley as a record plugger. He was joint MD of Michael Reine Music Co., 1952–6, before joining the BBC as a light entertainment producer. He became Assistant Head of Light Entertainment in 1962, moving up to Head of Variety in 1967. From 1970 he was Head of Light Entertainment and progressed to Controller of BBC 1 in 1977, and then Deputy Managing Director of BBC Television in 1981. After time spent chairing BBC Enterprises, Cotton was installed as Managing Director of BBC Television in 1984. In 1988 he left to join the Noel Gay Organization. He became Deputy Chairman of Meridian in 1991, and Chairman from 1996.

Cotton, Billy

(1899–1969)

'Wakey, wakey!' With a yell like this, and a rousing rendition of his theme tune, 'Somebody Stole My Gal', jovial bandleader Billy Cotton ensured viewers never missed the start of his weekly variety revue. With its emphasis on comedy and music, *The Billy Cotton Band Show* was a stalwart of the BBC's programming for 12 years from 1956, and Cotton also had success with *Wakey Wakey Tavern* and *Billy Cotton's Music Hall*, as well as being seen in variety programmes like *Saturday Showtime* and *The Tin Pan Alley Show*. Cotton arrived on television via BBC radio. He first broadcast in 1924, and his *Band Show* was a Sunday lunchtime favourite for 19 years from 1949. He was also a keen sportsman (top level motor racing, particularly), despite his 17-stone frame. His son, Bill Cotton Jr (who also produced some of his dad's programmes), later became Managing Director of BBC Television.

Coulson, Lindsey

(1960–)

Since leaving her role as Carol Jackson in EASTENDERS, London-born Lindsey Coulson has never looked back. Her major roles since have included Dr Cathy Harding in *Out of Hours*, Bev Ratcliffe in CLOCKING OFF, Cheryl in *Manchild*, Claire Eustace in PARADISE HEIGHTS, Lynda in *The Stretford Wives*, Annie Nobel in *Feather Boy*, Joanna Sands in *She's Gone*, Maggie Shields in *The Stepfather*, Kath in *Every Time You Look at Me* and DS Rosie MacManus in MURDER INVESTIGATION TEAM. Lindsey's TV debut came in a children's series called *A Bear Behind* and she joined *EastEnders* in 1993. She has also been seen in series like DALZIEL AND PASCOE, THE LAST DETECTIVE and WHERE THE HEART IS.

Count Dracula ✶✶

UK (BBC) Drama. BBC 2 1977

Count Dracula .... **Louis Jourdan**
Prof. Van Helsing .... **Frank Finlay**
Lucy Westenra .... **Susan Penhaligon**
Wilhelmina 'Mina' Westenra . **Judi Bowker**
Renfield .... **Jack Shepherd**
Dr John Seward .... **Mark Burns**
Jonathan Harker .... **Bosco Hogan**
Mrs Westenra .... **Ann Queensberry**

Writer **Gerald Savory**
Producer **Morris Barry**

● ***Largely faithful rendering of the classic vampire story.***

Described as 'A Gothic Romance', Gerald Savory's adaptation of Bram Stoker's majestic horror tale was one of the highlights of the 1977 Christmas season, hogging two and a half hours of one evening (it was split into three parts for broadcast in the USA). Anyone anticipating another Hammer-style gore-fest was disappointed as this version picks up on the psychology of the original novel rather than simply working over its bloody nature. That said there are enough nightmarish sequences to keep the spine nice and cold. The tale is the same, of young solicitor Jonathan Harker, who meets Dracula at his Transylvanian castle; of Dracula's visit to Whitby; and of Jonathan's girlfriend, Mina, and her flighty sister, Lucy (only friends in the book), who fall prey to the suave nocturnal count's thirsty advances in spite of the attentions of the eccentric Professor Van Helsing. Philip Saville directs and Kenyon Emrys-Roberts provides the haunting music.

Count of Monte Cristo, The ✶

UK (ITP/TPA) Adventure. ITV 1956

Edmund Dantès .... **George Dolenz**
Jacopo .... **Nick Cravat**
Rico .... **Robert Cawdron**

Producers **Sidney Marshall, Dennis Vance**

● ***A falsely imprisoned man learns of lost treasure from a fellow inmate and escapes to claim it.***

In 18th-century France, Edmund Dantès has been wrongly convicted of crimes against the state and incarcerated in the infamous Château d'If. There, a dying prisoner tells of the treasure to be found on the island of Monte Cristo and Dantès breaks free to take it for his own, setting himself up as a nobleman on the proceeds. The original story comes from the novel of the same name by Alexandre Dumas, although the TV series expands on Dantès's swashbuckling adventures, making the Frenchman a kind of Robin Hood battling for fairness and justice for all, and travelling all around Europe. Star George Dolenz was the father of a future Monkee, Mickey.

Countdown ✶✶

UK (Yorkshire) Game Show. Channel 4 1982–

Presenters **Richard Whiteley, Carol Vorderman, Desmond Lynam**

Creator **Armand Jammot**
Executive Producers **Frank Smith, John Meade**

● ***Daily afternoon words-and-numbers game.***

The aim for the two *Countdown* contestants is to construct, in 30 seconds, the longest word they can from nine letters chosen at random. Whoever uses up the most letters in forming a word earns the same number of points as letters used. Between word rounds a couple of numbers games are introduced. For these, the contestants need to add, subtract, multiply and divide randomly selected numbers to arrive at a given total (or as close to it as possible). The contestant with the sum nearest the total gains up to ten more points. The final round is the *Countdown* conundrum, an anagram worth ten points for first correct solution. The higher-scoring contestant then meets a new challenger in the next programme, and the series' best participants take part in an end-of-term knockout to find the overall champion.

Richard Whiteley – master of the excruciating pun – hosted proceedings from day one until his untimely death in 2005, whereupon Des Lynam assumed control. Carol Vorderman has been the numbers and letters girl and Beverley Isherwood and Kathy Hytner acted as hostesses in the early programmes. Although there is a resident lexicographer (Susie Dent, the most familiar face), a guest celebrity helps verify the words, and those gleefully undertaking this chore have included Ted Moult, Kenneth Williams, Sylvia Syms, Nigel Rees, Philip Franks, Geoffrey Durham, Richard Stilgoe and Gyles Brandreth. *Countdown* was the first programme to be seen on Channel 4 and was based on a French concept. It had previously been trialled on Yorkshire ITV during summer 1982, under the title *Calendar Countdown*.

Counterstrike ✶✶

UK (BBC) Science Fiction. BBC 1 1969

Simon King .... **Jon Finch**
Mary .... **Sarah Brackett**

Creator **Tony Williamson**
Producer **Patrick Alexander**

● ***An alien agent thwarts an extraterrestrial takeover of the Earth.***

Strange events are taking place all over the world, as Simon King discovers. Posing initially as a journalist, he unmasks two 'respectable' businessmen, witnesses adults acting as children and uncovers a plot against the richest man in the world. All these events, and more, are linked to a planned invasion of Earth by a race of aliens called Centaurans. It is up to Simon – himself an alien sent to intervene by the space equivalent of the United Nations – and his doctor friend, Mary, to save the planet.

Country Diary of an Edwardian Lady, The ✶✶

UK (Central) Drama. ITV 1984
DVD: Bfs Entertainment (Region 1 only)

Edith Holden .... **Pippa Guard**
Emma Holden .... **Elisabeth Choice**
Arthur Holden .... **Brian Rawlinson**
Effie Holden .... **Lill Roughley**
Winnie Holden .... **Isabelle Amyes**
Bernard Holden .... **Tim Munro**
Violet Holden .... **Jill Benedict**
Kenneth Holden .... **Anthony Daniels**

Evelyn Holden/Matthews .... **Allyson Rees**
Denovan Adam .... **Rikki Fulton**
Ernest Smith .... **James Coombes**
Frank Matthews .... **Graham Padden**
Mrs Denovan Adam .... **Denyse Alexander**

Writers **Elaine Feinstein, Dirk Campbell**
Executive Producer **Brian Lewis**
Producer **Patrick Gamble**

A schoolteacher takes delight in the wonders of nature.

The Country Diary of an Edwardian Lady is a lovingly composed portrait of rural life. Written by schoolteacher Edith Holden in 1906, and filled with illustrations of birds, plants and other wildlife, its original title was *Nature Notes for 1906* and its uncommercial purpose was to inspire her pupils to take an interest in nature. Edith died aged 48 but her great-niece, Rowena Stott, took it to a publisher in 1976. It sold more than 5 million copies, also generating a range of merchandise featuring Edith's artwork, from tea towels to oven mitts.

This series builds on the success of the book by exploring the life of Edith Holden. It begins at New Year 1906 and ends in 1920, when Edith tragically dies, drowning in a pool at Kew Gardens. Each of the 12 episodes is based around a month of the year, showing Edith growing up as one of seven children, studying art and eventually marrying Ernest Smith, all the while taking an interest in the wildlife that surrounds her Warwickshire home and that she witnesses on visits to Scotland and Devon. The exact truth of Edith's life is still unknown, so writers Elaine Feinstein and Dirk Campbell piece together what they can and make assumptions for the rest. To ensure Edith's vision of the joys of nature was properly highlighted, a natural history film unit shot special scenes of the countryside to bolster the drama.

Country Matters ***

UK (Granada) Drama Anthology. ITV 1972–3

Producer **Derek Granger**

Dramatization of assorted rustic stories.

This anthology of 13 attractively framed country tales was adapted from the works of H. E. Bates and A. E. Coppard. Featuring stars like Ian McKellen, Joss Ackland, Pauline Collins, Jane Lapotaire, Michael Elphick, Jeremy Brett and Gareth Thomas, the plays revolve around love, rivalry and times of adversity in beautiful rural locations.

Coupling ***

UK (Hartswood) Situation Comedy. BBC 2 2000–4
DVD: BBC

Steve Taylor .... **Jack Davenport**
Jane Christie .... **Gina Bellman**
Susan Walker .... **Sarah Alexander**
Sally Harper .... **Kate Isitt**
Patrick Maitland .... **Ben Miles**
Jeff Murdock .... **Richard Coyle**
Oliver Morris .... **Richard Mylan**
Tamsin .... **Olivia Caffrey**

Creator/Writer **Steven Moffat**
Executive Producer **Beryl Vertue**
Producer **Sue Vertue**

Six friends struggle to put the sex in 'sextet'.

Sex has never been so complicated as it is for this group of young friends. For a start, Steve used to go out with Jane, and Susan used to date Patrick, but things have changed around a bit. That's even before you begin to pick your way through each person's complicated mindset. Steve, for instance, is always edgy and wants to be sure he's doing the right thing. Jane – a radio traffic reporter – is completely psychotic, and when in the first episode, for example, Steve tries to dump her for Susan, she just can't get the message. Susan is the uninhibited blonde, vain beautician Sally is always worrying about her ageing body, and Patrick is the quietly arrogant, stout-sipping right-winger who never fails to pull a girl. And then there's geeky Jeff, the paranoid Welsh accountant who works in the same office as Susan. He's the resident sexual psychologist, with a bizarre, perverted slant on the world of women and an unfortunate habit of lying under pressure. Usually dividing themselves into male and female trios in a psychological battle of the sexes, the gang hangs out in a trendy basement bar where most of the farcical situations are hatched. For the final series, in 2004, Jeff is replaced by Oliver, a porn addict who runs the Hellmouths sci-fi memorabilia shop, and the centre of attention is Susan's pregnancy and the troubles it causes Steve.

Inevitably drawing comparisons with America's FRIENDS, *Coupling* was, however, much quirkier and far more sexually graphic, with episodes bound together by the gaffes, misunderstandings, flashbacks and parallel storylines that typically feature in writer Steven Moffat's work. Mari Wilson sang the theme song, 'Perhaps, Perhaps, Perhaps'.

Court Martial **

UK/US (MCA/ITC/Roncom) Legal Drama. ITV 1965–6

Capt. David Young .... **Bradford Dillman**
Major Frank Whittaker .... **Peter Graves**
Sgt John MacCaskey .... **Kenneth J. Warren**
Sgt Yolanda Perkins .... **Angela Browne**
Sgt Wendy .... **Diane Clare**

Producers **Robert Douglas, Bill Hill**

A team of military lawyers investigates crimes committed during the war.

Based in England during World War II, the industrious legal eagles of the US Army Judge Advocate General's Office are assigned to the continent of Europe. Their mission: to track down perpetrators of war crimes and bring them to justice. Each episode devotes much time to their excursions into war-torn Europe, winding up with the court martial proceedings themselves. Major Frank Whittaker is senior officer and chief prosecutor, Captain David Young the defending barrister. Sgt John MacCaskey is their aide. The series was spun off a two-part drama entitled *The Case against Paul Ryker*, which aired as part of the *Kraft Suspense Theater* anthology in the USA.

Courtroom, The

See *Crown Court*.

Cousins **

UK (BBC) Natural History. BBC 1 2000

Presenter **Charlotte Uhlenbroek**

Producer **Bernard Walton**

Revealed: the animals that most resemble human beings.
In this three-part series, zoology and psychology graduate Dr Charlotte Uhlenbroek (her doctorate is in animal communication) takes viewers around the world to explore the lives and habits of our closest animal relations. Stars of the show are the collection of lemurs, baboons, monkeys, orang-utans, gorillas and chimpanzees of Africa and Asia that colourfully illustrate the great similarities – in behaviour and dexterity – that exist between humans and other primates.

Cousteau, Jacques

(1910–97)

French marine expert and former Navy officer who was largely responsible for the development of the aqualung (and the new freedom it gave divers) during World War II. He also won his country's prestigious *Légion d'honneur* medal. In the post-war years he branched out into cinematic documentaries that charted his scientific explorations beneath the waves. Working from his converted minesweeper, *Calypso*, Cousteau later revealed the mysteries of the deep to TV viewers, in series like *Under the Sea*, THE WORLD ABOUT US, the internationally successful *Undersea World of Jacques Cousteau* (which ran for eight years) and *The Cousteau Odyssey*. His entertaining, authoritative, rather nasal delivery opened up the complexities of marine biology to an enthralled general public and earned him numerous awards. In his later years he was a vociferous environmental campaigner.

Cowell, Simon

(1959–)

Former head of A&R at RCA records, who shot to fame as an outspoken, controversial judge for POP IDOL, its US equivalent, *American Idol*, and THE X FACTOR (the last produced by his own company, Syco).

Cracker ★★★★

UK (Granada) Police Drama. ITV 1993–6
DVD: Cinema Club

Eddie 'Fitz' Fitzgerald	**Robbie Coltrane**
Judith Fitzgerald	**Barbara Flynn**
DS Jane Penhaligon	**Geraldine Somerville**
DCI David Bilborough	**Christopher Eccleston**
DS Jimmy Beck	**Lorcan Cranitch**
Mark Fitzgerald	**Kieran O'Brien**
DCI Wise	**Ricky Tomlinson**
DC Harriman	**Colin Tierney**
Temple	**Robert Cavanah**
Skelton	**Wilbert Johnson**

Creator **Jimmy McGovern**
Producers **Gub Neal, Paul Abbott, Hilary Bevan Jones**

A larger-than-life police psychologist cracks crimes but fails to keep his own life in order.
'Fitz' Fitzgerald is an outstanding but totally unconventional criminal psychologist, working freelance for the Greater Manchester Police. His speciality is reading a criminal's mind, drawing up character profiles and helping the police break down a suspect's outer shell, although his approach is often crude, insensitive and far from gentle. Bilborough (and later Wise) is the DCI at the Anson Road station who calls on Fitz's services, and 'Panhandle' Penhaligon is the sergeant usually dispatched as his chaperone. As brilliant as Fitz is at his job, his own personal life is a mess. Grossly overweight, a heavy drinker, a compulsive gambler and a chain-smoker, Fitz can 'spot a guilty cough in a football crowd but not know if World War III was breaking out in his living room', according to Panhandle. And when Fitz's long-suffering wife, Judith, walks out on him, he only makes matters worse by embarking on a stormy affair with his attractive police associate.

Intense, shocking and riddled with unexpected twists and turns, *Cracker* won universal acclaim, with Robbie Coltrane collecting the BAFTA Best Actor award for his efforts. It was also graphically and realistically violent, although such excesses were presented in a defiantly unglorified manner. The programme ended after three series in 1995, but a two-hour special, set in Hong Kong, followed in October 1996. An American version, entitled *Fitz* and starring Robert Pastorelli, was shown on ITV in 1998.

Crackerjack ★★

UK (BBC) Children's Entertainment. BBC 1955–84

Presenters **Eamonn Andrews, Leslie Crowther, Michael Aspel, Ed Stewart, Stu Francis**
Other regulars **Joe Baker, Jack Douglas, Ronnie Corbett, Michael Darbyshire, Eddie Leslie, Pearl Carr, Teddy Johnson, Raymond Rollett, Vivienne Martin, Peter Glaze, Jillian Comber, Pip Hinton, Valerie Walsh, Christine Holmes, Rod McLennan, Frances Barlow, Don Maclean, Little and Large, Stuart Sherwin, Heather Barbour, Elaine Paige, Jacqueline Clarke, Jan Hunt, Bernie Clifton, Val Mitchell, The Krankies, Jan Michelle, Leigh Miles, Sally Ann Triplett, Julie Dorne Brown, Sara Hollamby, Ling Tai**

Producers **Johnny Downes, Peter Whitmore, Brian S. Jones, Robin Nash, Brian Whitehouse, Paul Ciani**

Live music and comedy show for kids.
In the USA, *Crackerjack* is a brand of popcorn – an appropriate name for this variety show, which leaned heavily on top pop stars and corny jokes to carry the day. But carry the day it did – on Wednesdays, Thursdays or Fridays, at five to five (or thereabouts), for no less than 29 years. With its trademark '*Crackerjack*' echo from the studio audience every time the programme's name was mentioned, it offered speeded-up slapstick sketches (most memorably featuring a young Leslie Crowther and former Crazy Gang extra Peter Glaze), the latest pop hits (big names appearing included Roy Orbison, Tom Jones and Cliff Richard) and a sing-along, grand finale, usually comprising a medley of chart records with 'funny' new words added. Music was provided initially by The Harry Parry Sextet, then Eddie Mendoza and His Band and also, for many years, by the Bert Hayes Sextet/Octet. In between, competitions held sway. These were strictly divided into boys' and girls' games in the show's formative years, and best remembered is *Double or Drop* (which was devised by the programme's first host, Eamonn Andrews, and ran until 1964). In *Double or Drop*, kids answered questions and were then loaded up with prizes which, if dropped, were confiscated. Wrong answers led to armfuls of booby-prize cabbages. Another popular game was *Jig-Jak*, introduced in 1964. This involved answering questions to gain a piece of a jigsaw featuring a famous person's face. The first competitor to spot the celebrity gained the prize, but all contestants, win or lose, walked away with a coveted *Crackerjack* pencil. *Take a Letter* featured prominently in later series.

Ronnie Corbett and Jack Douglas cut their TV teeth on *Crackerjack* and Leslie Crowther's career was done no harm by an eight-year stretch as comic and then compere. Richard Hearne's Mr Pastry was also a regular guest in the 1950s. Eamonn Andrews and Michael Aspel moved on to bigger and better things, while later hosts Ed 'Stewpot' Stewart and Stu 'I could crush a grape' Francis were established children's entertainers who found their niche with the programme. Reassuring female hostesses like Jillian Comber, Pip Hinton and Christine Holmes became almost as popular as the male stars. The audience was made up of schoolkids from the Home Counties (they were only invited if they could get to the BBC Television Theatre by 5pm without missing school).

Cradock, Fanny

(Phyllis Cradock; 1909–94)

Fanny Cradock was one of the small screen's first cooks and an unlikely star of TV's golden age. Shunning the apron in favour of impractical evening gowns and pearls, she epitomized the rather starchy attitude prevalent in the BBC in the 1950s. She and her third husband, Major John Cradock, were published gourmets, writing the *Bon Viveur* column in the *Daily Telegraph*. They joined the BBC in 1955 to present *Kitchen Magic* but were soon snapped up by the new, less pompous ITV, where, instead of being Phyllis and John, they became Fanny and Johnny and hosted *Fanny's Kitchen, Chez Bon Viveur* and *The Cradocks*. They also chipped in with the *Happy Cooking* sequence in the kids' series *Lucky Dip*. Although they were generally billed as a twosome, it was Fanny who was clearly in charge, leaving the monocled Johnny hovering in the background as she thrashed a few eggs around or whipped up a pudding. Her rather brusque, demanding style made her and Johnny (often jokingly portrayed as a kitchen boozer) easy targets for comedians like Benny Hill. They rejoined the BBC in the 1960s, presenting programmes like *Giving a Dinner Party, Fanny Cradock Invites* and *Fanny Cradock Cooks for Christmas*, carrying on until retirement in the 1970s. Johnny died in 1987.

Craig, Daniel

(1968–)

British actor – unveiled in 2005 as the new James Bond – whose acclaimed performance as the sad Geordie in OUR FRIENDS IN THE NORTH ensured plenty of follow-up work, in dramas such as *Kiss and Tell* (Matt Kearney), *The Ice House* (DS Andy McLoughlin), MOLL FLANDERS (Jemmy), SWORD OF HONOUR (Guy Crouchback), *Shockers: the Visitor* ('Richard'), *Copenhagen* (Werner Heisenberg) and *Archangel* (Fluke Kelso). Previously, Craig had been seen in BOON, HEARTBEAT and *Screen Two*'s *Genghis Cohn* (Lt. Guth), among other productions.

Craig, Michael

(Michael Gregson; 1928–)

Silver-haired British actor, born in India. A Rank movie star of the 1950s and 1960s, his starring TV roles have included Johann in the steamy *Husbands and Lovers*; 50-year-old Harry who fell in love with a girl half his age in the sitcom *Second Time Around*; William Parker, the dad of the Australia-bound family in *The Emigrants*; and ship's officer John Anderson in TRIANGLE. Other credits have included DOCTOR WHO.

Craig, Wendy

(1934–)

Durham-born actress/writer strongly associated with daffy, harassed-mother roles, evidenced in such series as NOT IN FRONT OF THE CHILDREN (Jennifer Corner), AND MOTHER MAKES THREE/FIVE (Sally Harrison/Redway, also some episodes as writer) and BUTTERFLIES (Ria Parkinson). She branched out into serious drama in her own creation NANNY (playing 1930s nanny Barbara Gray), but returned to sitcom with the short-lived LAURA AND DISORDER, a series that she co-wrote (under her pen-name of Jonathan Marr) and in which she played accident-prone divorcée Laura Kingsley arriving back in the UK after ten years in America. In the 1990s, Craig was seen in the GOLDEN GIRLS clone BRIGHTON BELLES (Annie), while her earliest credits included the 1964 comedy *Room at the Bottom*, episodes of DANGER MAN and various single dramas. In recent years, she has played Aunt Juley in THE FORSYTE SAGA and Matron in THE ROYAL and made a guest appearance in MIDSOMER MURDERS.

Crane ✱

UK (Associated-Rediffusion) Adventure. ITV 1963–5

Richard Crane	**Patrick Allen**
Col. Mahmoud	**Gerald Flood**
Halima	**Laya Raki**
Orlando O'Connor	**Sam Kydd**

Creators **Patrick Alexander, Jordan Lawrence**
Producer **Jordan Lawrence**

● ***The adventures of a city businessman turned contrabrand dealer in North Africa.***

Bored by the routine of city life, Richard Crane takes himself off to sunny Morocco, buys a boat and opens a beachfront bar near Casablanca. To pass the time, he indulges himself in petty smuggling: minor items like tobacco and booze. Keeping an eye on his activities is elegant local police chief Colonel Mahmoud, although he and Crane sometimes work together against 'serious' criminals. Crane's well-worn friend and accomplice is Orlando O'Connor, a former member of the French Foreign Legion. (O'Connor later appeared in his own spin-off series for children, ORLANDO.) Halima is the café's sultry young bartender. Star Patrick Allen, an actor with a booming, authoritative voice, went on to further success off-camera, cornering the market in advert voice-overs.

Cranham, Kenneth

(1944–)

Dunfermline-born actor, well versed in rough-diamond roles and with a host of one-off dramas and guest appearances to his name. Among his starring roles have been Harvey Moon, the demobbed RAF corporal in SHINE ON HARVEY MOON, the over-zealous Pastor Finch in ORANGES ARE NOT THE ONLY FRUIT and villain Gus Mercer in EL C.I.D. Other credits have included *A Sort of Innocence*, CORONATION STREET, DANGER UXB (Jack Salt), THÉRÈSE RAQUIN (Camille Raquin), REILLY – ACE OF SPIES (Lenin), BRIDESHEAD REVISITED (Sgt Block), *Chimera* (Hennessey), INSPECTOR MORSE, BOON, *Rules of Engagement*, VAN DER VALK, BERGERAC, MURDER MOST HORRID, THE TENANT OF WILDFELL HALL (Revd Millward), OUR MUTUAL FRIEND (Silas Wegg), *Without Motive* (DC Supt. Derek Henderson), DALZIEL AND PASCOE, HEARTBEAT, NCS MANHUNT, *The Sins, Night Flight* (Ted

Atwell), *Dickens* (John Forster), *Pollyanna* (Mr Pendleton), *Sparking Cyanide* (George Barton), *Killing Hitler* (Brigadier Sir Stewart Menzies), *The Genius of Mozart* (Leopold Mozart), *Genghis Khan* (voice of Genghis), MURDER INVESTIGATION TEAM and ROME (Pompey Magnus). He has also re-created real-life barristers, playing Michael Mansfield QC in *The Murder of Stephen Lawrence* and George Carmen QC in *Justice in Wonderland* (the Hamilton/Al Fayed case). Cranham's first wife was actress Diana Quick and second wife actress Fiona Victory.

Cranitch, Lorcan

(1959–)

Dublin-born actor coming to light as the devious DS Jimmy Beck in CRACKER and moving on to star as GEORGE SMITH in *Screen One's Deacon Brodie*, Larry Duggan in *The Heart Surgeon*, Stephen in *Close Relations*, Sean Dillon in BALLYKISSANGEL, Michael McCready in MCCREADY AND DAUGHTER and Bernard Cleve in *My Fragile Heart*. He has also appeared in SHACKLETON (Wild), HORNBLOWER (Wolfe), *Omagh* (Chief Constable Flanagan) and ROME (Erastes), and made guest appearances in series like SPOOKS and THE BILL.

Crapston Villas ✶✶

UK (Spitting Image) Animation. Channel 4 1995; 1997–8
DVD: Troma (Region 1 only)

Voices:
Flossie Gluck .... **Jane Horrocks**
Marge Stenson .... **Alison Steadman**
Delia .... **Liz Smith**

Other voices **Morwenna Banks, Felix Dexter, Alistair McGowan, Lesley-Anne Sharpe, Steve Steen, John Thomson**

Writer/Executive Producer **Sarah Ann Kennedy**
Producer **Richard Bennett**

● ***Scatological humour with the claymation residents of a crummy London house.***

This startling, animated series of comedy shorts (each ten minutes long) focuses on life in a run-down Victorian house in Slumington, London SE69. Crapston Villas – divided into flats – is home to a bizarre and mostly unpleasant bunch of characters. In Flat B live failed film director Jonathan Jolly, his girlfriend, Sophie Cross, and their puking, farting cat, Fatso. They take in a lodger, struggling actress Flossie, who becomes friends with the gay couple upstairs in Flat D, Robbie Starr and Larry Palmer. Robbie's religious fanatic mother, Delia, is also seen. Single mum Marge Stenson and her two delinquent kids, Samantha (9) and Woody (16), together with Enid, the kleptomaniac granny, live in Flat C. Debauchery and bad language abound, with every vice explored, in this soap opera spoof that sends up all shades of London life, targeting anyone from yuppy to policeman, student to feminist. Two series were produced.

Craven, John

CBE (1940–)

Leeds-born presenter whose first TV appearances came at the age of 16 on *Sunday Break*. Later he was seen on regional news magazines, including *Look North* and *Points West*, and the kids' show *Search*, before he secured the job of children's news presenter on his own *John Craven's* NEWSROUND. From this came MULTI-COLOURED SWAP SHOP (encouraging a 'News Swap'), its successor, *Saturday Superstore*, and programmes like *Brainchild* and *The Show Me Show*. More recently he has been host of *Countryfile* and programmes such as *Animal Sanctuary* and *Castle in the Country*.

Crawford, Broderick

(William Broderick Crawford; 1911–86)

The man who gave the world the catchphrase 'Ten-Four'. Brawny Broderick Crawford's career began in 1930s gangster movies, in the sort of shady role he was initially to take into television. However, it was on the other side of the law that he made his name, playing Chief Dan Matthews in the hugely successful HIGHWAY PATROL. His bulky frame leaning against a car window, hollering 'Ten-Four' down the radio, is fondly remembered by viewers. Although he did secure lead roles in a couple of other American series (*King of Diamonds* and *The Interns*) after *Highway Patrol* ended in 1959, he was mostly seen by British viewers in guest appearances in TV movies and shows such as GET SMART, BURKE'S LAW and RAWHIDE. The son of comedienne Helen Broderick, he won the Oscar for Best Actor in 1949 for his performance in *All the King's Men*.

Crawford, Michael

OBE (Michael Dumble Smith; 1942–)

Salisbury-born actor whose starring role in SOME MOTHERS DO 'AVE 'EM came after years of supporting parts in early ITC adventures like SIR FRANCIS DRAKE (playing Drake's nephew, John), comedies such as BILLY BUNTER OF GREYFRIARS SCHOOL and NOT SO MUCH A PROGRAMME, MORE A WAY OF LIFE, and such dramas as POLICE SURGEON, PROBATION OFFICER and EMERGENCY – WARD 10. However, it was as the accident-prone Frank Spencer that he made his name, winning huge acclaim for his comic performances and exhausting stunt routines. From this base, Crawford moved on to the less successful CHALK AND CHEESE (Dave Finn, a Cockney among posher neighbours), and then more into theatre, although still finding time to pop up as a guest star and singer on variety shows.

Crazy Like a Fox ✶✶

US (Columbia) Detective Drama. ITV 1986 (US: CBS 1984–6)

Harry Fox .... **Jack Warden**
Harrison K. Fox .... **John Rubinstein**
Cindy Fox .... **Penny Peyser**
Josh Fox .... **Robby Kiger**
Allison Ling .... **Lydia Lei**
Patricia Ayame Thomson
Lt. Walker .... **Robert Hanley**

Executive Producers **George Schenck, Frank Cardea**

● ***A respectable lawyer's world is drawn into his father's detective investigations.***

Harry Fox, a 55-year-old San Francisco private eye, is a lovable, streetwise rogue who expects his son, Harrison, to help him in his work. The only trouble is that Harrison is a conventional type of guy, an attorney who would rather be in his office than out on a car chase. But his dad is not the kind to take no for an answer, especially if, after all, he is only trying to dig up evidence for one of his boy's court cases, so poor Harrison finds himself constantly in the fast lane. Harrison's family consists of his wife, Cindy, and son, Josh, and they, too, help out from time to time. Allison is Harrison's secretary. The co-star of this series, John Rubinstein, was the son of classical pianist Artur Rubinstein. The cast reunited in 1987 for a one-off TV movie, *Still Crazy Like a Fox*, which was set in London.

Credits

The roll-call of programme participants (both in front of and behind the cameras), usually seen at the end of the programme. Occasionally credits are given during the opening titles, but usually these are confined to the major stars and the writers.

Crew

The technical team working on a programme, essentially the operators of sound, lighting and camera equipment, but, in wider terms, associated staff involved in make-up, wardrobe, set construction, etc.

Crezz, The ✱✱

UK (Thames) Drama. ITV 1976

Charles Bronte .... **Joss Ackland**
Jackie Bronte .... **Elspet Gray**
Esther Bronte .... **Briony McRoberts**
Emily Bronte .... **Joan Hickson**
Cyril Antrobus .... **Anthony Nicholls**
Emma Antrobus .... **Isla Blair**
Ken Green .... **Peter Bowles**
Sue Green .... **Carol Nimmons**
Dr Balfour Harvey .... **Hugh Burden**
Colin Pitman .... **Nicholas Ball**
Brenda Pitman .... **Janet Key**
Giles Pitman .... **Grant Bardsley**
Tracy Pitman .... **Charlotte Fitzgerald**
Consuela .... **Jiggy Bhore**
Major Rice .... **Gerald James**
Lady Clarke .... **Aimee Delamain**
Miss Hart .... **Gillian Raine**
Clarence Henderson .... **Anton Phillips**
Hafez Aziz .... **Tariq Yun**
Joe Macarthy .... **Alan Devlin**
Bridget Macarthy .... **Eileen O'Brien**
George Smith .... **Frank Mills**
Molly Smith .... **Hilda Braid**
Bing Smith .... **Lee Walker**
Jane Smith .... **Linda Robson**
Denny .... **Paul Greenhalgh**
Terry .... **Roland Curram**

Creator **Clive Exton**
Producer **Paul Knight**

● ***Tales of the residents of a London crescent.***

Set in fictious Carlisle Crescent, a Victorian street in West London, this series delivers 12 soapy, hour-long plays about the people who live in The Crezz. Personal crises and the relationships between the various elements of the wide social mix take centre stage.

Prominent are the Brontes. Charles is a lecturer in Middle English and he takes a keen interest in raising standards in the Crescent. His wife is Jackie and his daughter is Esther, with his mother, Emily, also showing her face at times. Ken Green is a rather neurotic sci-fi writer, married to Sue but conducting an affair with neighbour Emma Antrobus, the considerably younger wife of barrister Cyril Antrobus. Colin Pitman runs his own advertising agency, but is not doing as well as his wife, Brenda, who also works in advertising. Giles and Tracy are their young children and Consuela is their au pair. Living elsewhere in The Crezz are deeply dull know-all Major Rice; eccentric Lady Clarke; Victoria and Albert Museum worker Miss Hart; West Indian travel agent Clarence Henderson; snooty Dr Balfour-Harvey, whose practice is based at one end of the street; Hafez Aziz, the manager of the local Landseer Hotel; gay antiques dealers Denny and Terry; and van driver Joe Macarthy, a working-class man of Irish stock who lives in a scruffy, rented flat with his wife, Bridget, and their four kids. Completing the residents list are George Smith, a ticket collector for London Underground, and his supermarket assistant wife, Molly, unemployed biker son, Bing, and teenage daughter, Jane.

After beginning in a prime-time slot, *The Crezz* sadly failed to bring in the business and was shunted by ITV to the post-NEWS AT TEN graveyard half-way through its run.

Cribb ✱✱

UK (Granada) Police Drama. ITV 1980–1
DVD: Acorn Media

DS Cribb .... **Alan Dobie**
Constable Thackeray .... **William Simons**
Chief Insp. Jowett .... **David Waller**

Executive Producer **Peter Eckersley**
Producer **June Wyndham Davies**

● ***Victorian crime detection with a persistent CID officer.***

Sgt Cribb, a dry, stubborn detective, works for the newly formed Criminal Investigation Department, inaugurated to clean up the grimy streets of London in the time of Jack the Ripper. Cribb, a tough and determined officer with an eye for the ladies, outwits the city's cleverest crooks (and his smartest colleagues) to bring to book all who cross his path. He is assisted in his investigations by loyal Constable Thackeray, with Chief Inspector Jowett, the commanding officer, often getting in the way.

The series, based on the novels of Peter Lovesey, involves its hero in all manner of crimes, from blackmail to murder, usually set against the backdrop of the Victorians at leisure, with prize-fighting, the music hall and a six-day walking marathon among the featured activities. The detail is well researched and genuine events like the publication of Jerome K. Jerome's *Three Men in a Boat* and the purchase of London Zoo's elephant, Jumbo, by Barnum & Bailey's Circus, are woven into the plots. The series was spun off a 90-minute pilot episode, seen as part of Granada's *Screenplay* anthology in 1979.

Cribbins, Bernard

(1928–)

Whimsical, Oldham-born actor/comedian, a familiar voice as well as face on television. The milestones of his long TV career have been his own show, *Cribbins*, the sketch show *Get the Drift*, THE WOMBLES (for which he provided the narration), *Cuffy* (as the eponymous tinker, spun off from SHILLINGBURY TALES), *High and Dry* (Ron Archer, owner of a seaside pier) and *Langley Bottom* (Seth Raven). These accompany numerous contributions to THE GOOD OLD DAYS and JACKANORY, guest spots in series as varied as THE AVENGERS, FAWLTY TOWERS, DALZIEL AND PASCOE, LAST OF THE SUMMER WINE, BARBARA, DOWN TO EARTH and CORONATION STREET (Wally Bannister), and assorted panel-game appearances, including as host of *Star Turn*. Cribbins was also the voice of Buzby, the chatty bird in the BT commercials.

Crime and Punishment ***

UK (BBC) Drama. BBC 2 2002

Rodyon Raskolnikov .... **John Simm**
Porfiry .... **Ian McDiarmid**
Razumikhin .... **Shaun Dingwall**
Pulcheria .... **Geraldine James**
Dunya .... **Kate Ashfield**
Sonia .... **Lara Belmont**
Marmeladov .... **Philip Jackson**
Luzhin .... **David Haig**
Katerina .... **Katrin Cartlidge**
Svidrigailov .... **Nigel Terry**
Zosimov .... **Mark Benton**
Lizaveta .... **Heather Tobias**
Zamyotov .... **Darren Tighe**
Semyonovich .... **Sean McKenzie**

Writer **Tony Marchant**
Producer **David Snodin**

A young malcontent is tortured by his own crimes.

In 19th-century St Petersburg, Raskolnikov is an impoverished young student, angry at the injustices he sees in society. Thinking himself morally superior to those around him and determined to make a change, he burgles and murders Alyona, a greedy old pawnbroker, but things spiral out of control and Raskolnikov kills her elderly, innocent sister, too. Soon he is pursued from two quarters – by wily magistrate Porfiry and by his own nagging conscience. Solace is provided by prostitute Sonia, but Raskolnikov needs to find personal redemption if his life is to mean anything any more.

Julian Jarrold directs this arty, in-your-face two-parter based on the novel from 1866 by Fyodor Dostoyevksy. For authenticity, filming took place in St Petersburg itself during its disorientating summer period of 'white nights', when the sun never fully sets. The book had been previously dramatized by Jack Pulman, with John Hurt in the lead role and Timothy West as Porfiry (BBC 2 1979).

Crime of Passion **

UK (ATV) Legal Drama Anthology. ITV 1970–3

President of the Court .... **Anthony Newlands**
Maître Savel .... **Daniel Moynihan**
Maître Lacan .... **John Phillips**
Maître Dubois .... **Bernard Archer**

Creator **Ted Willis**
Producers **Cecil Clarke, Robert D. Cardona, Ian Fordyce**

French barristers do battle over crimes of the heart.

Created by Ted Willis, using authentic French court cases ('Crime of Passion' is a legitimate defence in France), this series features Maître Lacan for the prosecution and Maître Savel for the defence. Another lawyer, Maître Dubois, is seen in the last series. Each episode, poignantly given the name of its lead character – 'Catherine', 'Danielle', 'Gerard', etc. – opens showing the crime in question, before moving on to the trial and finally the verdict of the Judge, the President of the Court. Among the guest stars are Felicity Kendal, Johnny Briggs, Ralph Bates and Tessa Wyatt.

Crime Sheet *

UK (Associated-Rediffusion) Police Drama. ITV 1959

Det. Chief Supt. Tom Lockhart **Raymond Francis**

Creator **Glyn Davies**
Producer **Barry Baker**

The second part of the Supt. Lockhart trilogy.

In this series, the sharp-witted, snuff-taking Supt. Lockhart of MURDER BAG has been promoted to detective chief superintendent and now casts his net farther afield than mere murder investigations. His talents are employed on crime of all sorts, but he remains so diligent and infallible in his pursuit of villains that he is quickly transferred to Scotland Yard and NO HIDING PLACE. Two years later, Associated-Rediffusion revived the title *Crime Sheet* for a play starring Gerald Case as Chief Supt. Carr.

Crime Story **

US (New World) Police Drama. ITV 1989 (US: NBC 1986–8)
DVD: Anchor Bay Entertainment

Lt. Mike Torello .... **Dennis Farina**
Ray Luca .... **Anthony Denison**
Pauli Taglia .... **John Santucci**
David Abrams .... **Stephen Lang**
Sgt Danny Krychek .... **Bill Smitrovich**
Det. Joey Indelli .... **William Campbell**
Det. Walter Clemmons .... **Paul Butler**
Det. Nate Grossman .... **Steve Ryan**
Manny Weisbord .... **Joseph Wiseman**

Creators **Chuck Adamson, Gustave Reininger**
Executive Producer **Michael Mann**

A no-nonsense detective doggedly pursues an ambitious gangster.

Chicago in the early 1960s is the initial setting for this big-budget gangster serial. At the heart of the action is Lt. Mike Torello, a plain-speaking cop who heads up the city's MCU (Major Crime Unit). His eyes are firmly fixed on an up-and-coming mobster named Ray Luca, a man who will stop at nothing in the pursuit of power. With his team of detectives, and attorney David Abrams in tow, Torello stalks the Teflon-coated Luca and his cack-handed sidekick, Pauli Taglia, until they finally leave the Windy City for a new, more lucrative home among the legalized gambling dens of Las Vegas. Even then the game is not up, as the MCU is turned into a national response unit, allowing Torello to move in once more on his quarry, who is now rapidly becoming an international Mr Big. With washed-out colour images, and Del Shannon's 'Runaway' as its theme track, there's no mistaking the era in which *Crime Story* is staged. If the stylish production seems familiar, blame executive producer Michael Mann, who had already achieved similar results with MIAMI VICE. To underline the serial's authenticity, it was revealed that star Dennis Farina had himself trodden the gangster beat as a police officer in Chicago in the 1960s.

Crime Traveller ✶

UK (Carnival Films) Science Fiction. BBC 1 1997
DVD: Revelation

Jeff Slade .... **Michael French**
Holly Turner .... **Chloë Annett**
Chief Insp. Kate Grisham .... **Sue Johnston**
Morris .... **Paul Trussell**
Nicky Robson .... **Richard Dempsey**
Danny .... **Bob Goodey**

Creator/Writer **Anthony Horowitz**
Producer **Brian Eastman**
Executive Producer **Caroline Oulton**

● ***A policeman discovers he can crack crime by nipping back in time.***

Unconventional copper Jeff Slade has just made one mistake too many. Blowing an undercover operation by chasing the main suspect, against the orders of his no-nonsense boss, Grisham, he has put his job on the line. He is saved, however, by police science officer Holly Turner, who decides to use the time machine developed by her late dad to unearth vital evidence that will help out Slade. Realizing something funny has occurred, Slade confronts Holly, who reveals the time machine built into her flat. The temptation proving too great, Slade uses the machine for his own ends to trap a killer, and, much against Holly's wishes, the duo continue to dart back in time to solve some baffling crimes. The usual time-travelling caveats – making sure you don't bump into yourself, getting back within a set time-limit, etc. – add to the tension. Also seen are new-graduate policeman Nicky Robson, somewhat dim copper Morris, and Danny, the constantly bemused janitor at Holly's apartment block.

Despite good pre-publicity and the fact that this was Michael French's first starring role after EASTENDERS, *Crime Traveller* failed to hit the spot with the viewing public and only one series of eight 50-minute episodes was made.

Crimewatch UK ✶✶

UK (BBC) Factual. BBC 1 1984–

Presenters **Nick Ross, Sue Cook, Jill Dando, Fiona Bruce**

Editors/Producers **Peter Chafer, Nikki Cheetham, Gerry McClellend, Liz Mills, Seetha Kumar, Katie Thomson, Gaby Koppel, Sarah-Jane Cohen, Karen Benveniste, Sally Dixon, Doug Carnegie**

● ***Crime recontruction series inviting viewer assistance in catching villains.***

Based on the German series *File XY Unsolved*, and originally scheduled for just three editions, *Crimewatch UK* combines dramatic re-enactments of unsolved crimes with a plea to the general public to ring in with further information. Tips on crime prevention are also included and 'treasure trove' spots allow burgled viewers to reclaim stolen property. Two resident police officers, David Hatcher and Helen Phelps, plus visiting detectives, initially helped give the police side of each story. Phelps later left the force and joined the programme's production team. Her place alongside Hatcher was taken by Jacqui Hames. Original co-presenter Sue Cook left in 1995 and was succeeded by Jill Dando, who fronted the programme with Nick Ross until her tragic death in 1999, when she was replaced by Fiona Bruce. The programme airs monthly, and occasional review programmes (entitled *Crimewatch File*) have also been made, bringing viewers up to date with past stories. The series' clear-up rate has been impressive, with more than 400 arrests made as a result of new information given by viewers. To allay viewers' fears, Ross has nearly always signed off with the words: 'Don't have nightmares. Do sleep well.'

Criss Cross Quiz ✶

UK (Granada) Quiz. ITV 1957–67

Presenter **Jeremy Hawk**

● ***Long-running noughts-and-crosses quiz.***

This popular game show took the form of noughts and crosses with questions. One contestant scored crosses, the other scored noughts and, by giving correct answers, both sought to make a line of three, either vertically, diagonally or horizontally. For each correct answer cash was forthcoming, and large totals were possible. Jeremy Hawk (father of actress Belinda Lang) was the original questionmaster of this thrice-weekly show, and he also hosted a children's version, *Junior Criss Cross Quiz*, which ran for the same number of years. Chris Kelly was another presenter of the youth version, as were (at various times) Bob Holness, Mike Sarne, Chris Howland, Gordon Luck, Peter Wheeler, Mark Kelly, Bill Grundy and soccer star Danny Blanchflower. *Criss Cross Quiz* was derived from the American game show *Tic Tac Dough*.

Crocodile Shoes ✶✶

UK (Big Boy) Drama. BBC 1 1994; 1996

Jed Shepperd .... **Jimmy Nail**
Ade Lynn .... **James Wilby**
Emma Shepperd .... **Melanie Hill**
Pep .... **John Bowler**
Caroline Carrlson .... **Alex Kingston**
Alan Clarke .... **Christopher Fairbank**
Snotter .... **Vince Pellegrino**
Ox .... **Oliver Haden**
Carmel Cantrell .... **Amy Madigan**
Lou Benedetti .... **Burt Young**
Archie Tate .... **Sammy Johnson**
Wendy .... **Elizabeth Carling**
Lucy .... **Sara Stewart**
Roxanne Pallenberg .... **Nadeshda Richter Brennicke**
Omo .... **Jeffrey Knox**
Big Chrissie .... **Paul Palance**
Warren Bowles .... **Robert Morgan**

Creator/Writer **Jimmy Nail**
Executive Producers **Linda James, Jimmy Nail, Jen Samson**
Producer **Peter Richardson**

● ***A Geordie manual worker becomes an international country and western star.***

Jed Shepperd works as a lathe-operator in a Newcastle factory but harbours hopes of becoming a country singer. His dreams turn to reality when his sister, Emma, secretly sends a tape of Jed's songs off to Ade Lynn, a struggling A&R man for a London-based record company. Lynn recognizes the talent and signs up Shepperd for himself, refashioning his image, propelling him to fame and using his cut of the proceedings to fuel his drugs habit. The ingenuous Shepperd is whisked to Nashville, where he attracts the romantic attentions of top country star Carmel Cantrell. In the second series, shown two years later, the drugs dealers have caught up with Lynn, and Shepperd is suspected of his murder. His record company is keen to recover a £500,000 advance on his second album (not yet recorded), a tabloid journalist is on his tail, and he finds himself framed for drug peddling. Right back on his uppers, the former star sets about clearing his name and finding the real killers.

Allowing creator Jimmy Nail to indulge his own passion for singing, *Crocodile Shoes* spawned a handful of hit singles.

Croft, David

OBE (David Sharland; 1922–)

British child actor turned comedy writer and producer, particularly in collaboration with Jimmy Perry and Jeremy Lloyd. With Perry, Croft created the doyen of British sitcoms, DAD'S ARMY, and went on to script (and produce) comedy favourites IT AIN'T HALF HOT, MUM and HI-DE-HI! These reflected Croft's experiences as an ARP warden, a military entertainments officer in India and a producer of stage shows at Butlins. Croft and Perry also contributed to YOU RANG, M'LORD? With Lloyd, Croft wrote OH HAPPY BAND!, ARE YOU BEING SERVED?, COME BACK MRS NOAH, 'ALLO 'ALLO and *Grace and Favour*. With Richard Spendlove, he created OH DOCTOR BEECHING! Croft's production credits have also included the sitcoms *The Eggheads* (also as co-writer with Richard Waring), *A World of His Own*, HUGH AND I, BEGGAR MY NEIGHBOUR and UP POMPEII!, as well as *The Benny Hill Show* and *The Dick Emery Show*. His daughter, Penny, co-wrote the sitcom LIFE WITHOUT GEORGE, which starred his son-in-law, the late Simon Cadell.

Cronkite, Walter

(1916–)

An American institution, Walter Cronkite was the USA's foremost newsreader and commentator for some 20 years. Joining CBS as a reporter in 1950, he moved up to newsreader and news editor on the network's *Evening News* in 1962, quickly establishing himself as the country's most trusted anchorman. His avuncular, cosy, sometimes emotional style and his 'That's the way it is' sign-off became his trademarks.

Crosbie, Annette

OBE (1934–)

Scottish actress best known as Margaret, the long-suffering wife of Victor Meldrew, in ONE FOOT IN THE GRAVE. Her television career, however, has spanned over three decades and has included the role of Catherine of Aragon in THE SIX WIVES OF HENRY VIII, and a BAFTA award-winning portrayal of Queen Victoria in EDWARD THE SEVENTH. In addition to assorted one-off plays, Crosbie's other notable performances have included a Resistance worker in THE WHITE RABBIT; Henrietta Labouchere in LILLIE; Helen Langrishe in *Langrishe, Go Down*; Liz, Keith Barron's frumpy wife, in TAKE ME HOME; and Joyce, Mel Smith's mother, in COLIN'S SANDWICH. She was also seen in John Mortimer's PARADISE POSTPONED and played Janet in the 1993 revival of DOCTOR FINLAY, Edith Sparshott in AN UNSUITABLE JOB FOR A WOMAN, Aunt Doreen in *Underworld* and Hattie in *Anchor Me*, as well as supporting Rory Bremner. Other recent credits have included MURDER ROOMS: THE DARK BEGINNINGS OF SHERLOCK HOLMES, OLIVER TWIST (Mrs Bedwin), HEARTBEAT, WAKING THE DEAD, MURDER IN MIND, *Bodily Harm* (Sheila Greenfield), BLACK BOOKS (Manny's mum), *Quite Ugly One Morning* (Mrs Kinross), *Footprints in the Snow* (Julie's mum), MIDSOMER MURDERS and WILLIAM AND MARY.

Crosby, Bing

(Harry Lillis Crosby; 1903–77)

Internationally renowned crooner and light actor whose television work was largely confined to guest appearances and variety shows, with an attempt at sitcom in *The Bing Crosby Show* (as structural designer Bing Collins) proving less rewarding. However, his behind-the-scenes credits were important and his film company, Bing Crosby Productions, was responsible for several US hit series, including BEN CASEY. Trivia buffs will note that Crosby was the first choice for the role of COLUMBO but turned it down, allegedly because it would have interfered with his golf.

Crossroads ★★

UK (ATV/Central/Carlton) Drama. ITV 1964–88; ITV 1 2001–3
DVD: Network

Meg Richardson/Ryder/Mortimer	**Noele Gordon**
Jill Richardson/Crayne/Harvey/Chance	**Jane Rossington**
Sandy Richardson	**Roger Tonge**
Kitty Jarvis	**Beryl Johnstone**
Dick Jarvis	**Brian Kent**
Brian Jarvis	**David Fennell**
Janice Gifford/Jarvis	**Carolyn Lyster**
Carlos Rafael	**Anthony Morton**
Marilyn Gates/Hope	**Sue Nicholls**
	Nadine Hanwell
Christine Fuller/Palmer	**Alex Marshall**
Mrs Blundell	**Peggy Aitchison**
Owen Webb	**George Skillan**
Benny Willmot	**Deke Arlon**
Amy Turtle	**Ann George**
Hugh Mortimer	**John Bentley**
Philip Carroll	**Malcolm Young**
Josefina Rafael	**Gillian Betts**
Ralph Palmer	**Norman Jones**
Ruth Bailey/Fraser	**Pamela Greenall**
Sam Redway	**John Porter Davison**
Stephanie 'Stevie' Harris	**Wendy Padbury**
Penny Richardson	**Diane Grayson**
Diane Lawton/Parker/Hunter	**Susan Hanson**
Andy Fraser	**Ian Paterson**
Derek Maynard	**Brian Hankins**
Dave Cartwright	**John Hamill**
Barry Hughes	**Patrick Marley**
Kevin McArthur	**Vincent Ball**
Geoffrey Steele	**Lew Luton**
Shirley Perkins	**Jacqueline Holborough**
Enoch Jarvis	**Jack Hayes**
Eleanor Chase	**Gillian Wray**
Marie Massinet	**Colette Gleeson**
Pepe Costa	**Stephen Rea**
Miss Edith Tatum	**Elisabeth Croft**
Vince Parker	**Peter Brookes**
Malcolm Ryder	**David Davenport**
Ted Hope	**Charles Stapley**
Tish Hope	**Joy Andrews**
Peter Hope	**Neville Hughes**
Lynn Hope	**Patsy Blower**

Mrs Witten .... **Jo Richardson**
Joyce Wood .... **Penelope Goddard**
Myrtle Cavendish .... **Gretchen Franklin**
Nick Van Doren .... **Peter Doyes**
David Hunter .... **Ronald Allen**
Rosemary Hunter .... **Janet Hargreaves**
Chris Hunter .... **Freddie Foot**
Stephen Hoye
Tessa Wyvern .... **Eva Wishaw**
John Crayne .... **Mark Rivers**
Sandra Gould .... **Diane Keen**
Paul Stevens .... **Paul Greenwood**
Don Rogers .... **Albert Shepherd**
Melanie Harper .... **Cleo Sylvestre**
Mrs Ash .... **Kathleen St John**
Archie Gibbs .... **Jack Haig**
Mr Lovejoy .... **William Avenell**
Wilf Harvey .... **Morris Parsons**
Stan Harvey .... **Edward Clayton**
Sheila Harvey/Mollison .... **Sonia Fox**
Vera Downend .... **Zeph Gladstone**
Sarah-Jane Harvey .... **Sorrel Dunger**
Sophie Cook
Holly Newman
Jane Smith .... **Sally Adcock**
Clifford Leyton .... **Johnny Briggs**
Sharon Metcalfe .... **Carolyn Jones**
Mr Booth .... **David Lawton**
Shughie McFee .... **Angus Lennie**
Dr Butterworth .... **Tony Steedman**
Kate Hamilton .... **Frances White**
Anthony Mortimer .... **Jeremy Sinden**
Paul Ross .... **Sandor Elès**
Carney .... **Jack Woolgar**
Jim Baines .... **John Forgeham**
Benny Hawkins .... **Paul Henry**
Ed Lawton .... **Thomas Heathcote**
Doris Luke .... **Kathy Staff**
Marian Owen .... **Margaret John**
Iris Scott .... **Angela Webb**
Kath Brownlow/Fellowes .... **Pamela Vezey**
Arthur Brownlow .... **Peter Hill**
Glenda Brownlow/Banks .... **Lynette McMorrough**
Ron Brownlow .... **Ian Liston**
Dr Farnham .... **Allan Lander**
Kevin Banks .... **David Moran**
Joe MacDonald .... **Carl Andrews**
Adam Chance .... **Tony Adams**
Lloyd Munro .... **Alan Gifford**
Barbara Brady/Hunter .... **Sue Lloyd**
Reg Cotterill .... **Ivor Salter**
Alison Cotterill .... **Carina Wyeth**
J. Henry Pollard .... **Michael Turner**
Miranda Pollard .... **Claire Faulconbridge**
Valerie Pollard .... **Heather Chasen**
Oliver Banks .... **Kenneth Gilbert**
Sally Banks .... **Wendy Williams**
Eddie Lee .... **Roy Boyd**
Victor Lee .... **Victor Winding**
Tom Peterson .... **Graham Rees**
Rita Hughes .... **Lynn Dalby**
Becky Foster .... **Maxine Gordon**
Gilbert Latham .... **Royce Mills**
Carole Sands .... **Jo-Anne Good**
Sid Hooper .... **Stan Stennett**
Mavis Hooper .... **Charmian Eyre**
Roy Lambert .... **Steven Pinder**
Anne-Marie Wade .... **Dee Hepburn**
Reg Lamont .... **Reginald Marsh**
Jennifer Lamont .... **Jean Kent**
Ashley Lamont .... **Martyn Whitby**
Rose Scott .... **Val Doothman**
Richard Lord .... **Jeremy Mason**
Walter Soper .... **Max Wall**
Colin Sands .... **Paul Blake**
Ken Sands .... **John Malcolm**
Lisa Walters .... **Francesca Gonshaw**
John Latchford .... **Arthur White**
Dr James Wilcox .... **Robert Grange**
Douglas Brady .... **Nigel Williams**
Larry Wilcox .... **Paul Ashe**
Stephen Fellowes .... **John Line**
Pat Reddington .... **Rosemary Smith**
Nicola Freeman .... **Gabrielle Drake**
Daniel Freeman .... **Philip Goodhew**
Barry Hart .... **Harry Nurmi**
Clifford Wayne .... **Michael Drew**
Sam Benson .... **Norman Bowler**
Mickey Doyle .... **Martin Smith**
Mr Darby .... **Patrick Jordan**
Lorraine Baker .... **Dorothy Brown**
Mrs Meacher .... **Stella Moray**
Georges-André Arnaud .... **Jean Badin**
Tracey Hobbs .... **Colette Barker**
Mrs Tardebigge .... **Elsie Kelly**
Charlie Mycroft .... **Graham Seed**
Tommy Lancaster .... **Terence Rigby**
Mary Lancaster .... **Francis Cuka**
Debbie Lancaster .... **Kathryn Hurlbutt**
Lisa Lancaster .... **Alison Dowling**
Mrs Babbitt .... **Margaret Stallard**
Beverley Grice .... **Karen Murden**
Margaret Grice .... **Meryl Hampton**
Ray Grice .... **Al Ashton**
Ranjit Rampul .... **Ashok Kumar**
John Maddingham .... **Jeremy Nicholas**
Jamie Maddingham .... **Christopher Duffy**
Kate Russell .... **Jane Gurnett**
Patrick Russell .... **Neil McCaul**
Nicola Russell .... **Julia Burchell**
Tracey Booth .... **Cindy Marshall-Day**
Jake Booth .... **Colin Wells**
Virginia Raven .... **Sherrie Hewson**
Chloe Simms .... **Rhea Bailey**
Bradley Clarke .... **Luke Walker**
Daniel Curtis .... **Jack Curtis**
Beena Shah .... **Rebecca Hazlewood**
Minty Sutton .... **Peter Dalton**
Billy Taylor .... **Gilly Gilchrist**
Phil Berry .... **Neil Grainger**
Scott Booth .... **Keiran Hardcastle**
Rocky Wesson .... **Roger Sloman**
Ray Dobbs .... **James McKenzie Robinson**
Des White .... **Marc Jordan**
Kully Gill .... **Sarah Nerwal**
Joanne Gibson .... **Rebecca Clarke**
Sarah-Jane Harvey/Louise Dixon .... **Joanne Farrell**
Oona Stocks .... **Di Sherlock**
Mandy Stocks .... **Natasha Marquiss**
Mark Russell .... **Max Brown**
Richard .... **Gary Webster**
Diane .... **Carol Royle**
Arthur .... **John Cater**
Dave Stocks .... **Jim Dunk**
Julie Noakes .... **Sheila Tait**

Brian Noakes	**Colin MacLauchlan**
Mike Kitson	**Jonathan Guy Lewis**
Vic Barnes	**Ray Lonnen**
Stephen	**Noel White**
Eddie Weaver	**Ramon Tikaram**
Jazz Williams	**Belinda Everett**
Sam Delaney	**Jonathan Wrather**
Abbie Baker	**Raine Davison**
Helen Raven	**Lucy Pargeter**
Angel Samson	**Jane Asher**
Max Samson	**Stuart Milligan**
Jimmy Samson	**Graham McGrath**
Suzie Samson	**Emma Noble**
Betty Waddell	**Anne Charleston**
Lola Wise	**Freema Agyeman**
Belle Wise	**Jessica Fox**
Philomena Wise	**Shauna Shim**
Joe Lacey	**Richard Burke**
Ethan Black	**John Bowler**

Creators **Hazel Adair, Peter Ling**
Producers **Reg Watson, Pieter Rogers, Jack Barton, Phillip Bowman, Marian Nelson, William Smethurst, Michele Buck, Kay Patrick, Yvon Grace, Peter Rose**

The day-to-day events at a Midlands motel.

Few programmes have endured as much ridicule as *Crossroads*. At the same time, few programmes have won the hearts of so many viewers. From its earliest days, *Crossroads* was taunted with criticisms of its wobbly sets and often wobblier performers. Lines were fluffed or simply forgotten, scripts were wooden and plots transparent, but much of this could be put down to the demands of a hectic recording schedule, given that *Crossroads* began as a five-times-a-week early-evening serial. Despite this and the constraints of a small budget, its popularity was such that it ran and ran – for 24 years in all.

The programme's queen bee was Meg Richardson, widowed owner of the Crossroads Motel, set in the fictitious village of King's Oak, somewhere in the West Midlands. Around her buzzed her next-of-kin: daughter Jill, son Sandy and sister Kitty, with Kitty's husband, Dick, and architect son Brian. Meg's extended family were the motel staff, most of them dyed-in-the-wool Brummies, with the notable exception of Spanish chef Carlos Rafael. The most popular employees over the years included Diane Lawton, the blonde waitress who steadily worked her way up the motel ladder, singing waitress Marilyn Gates, gossipy little Amy Turtle, pompous chef Mr Lovejoy, hairstylist Vera Downend (who lived on a houseboat), coffee bar worker Benny Willmot, gardener Archie Gibbs, gruff nightwatchman Carney, spinster Doris Luke, oily restaurant manager Paul Ross, Scots chef Shughie McFee and receptionist Anne-Marie Wade. At the Crossroads garage worked Jim Baines, Sid Hooper and Joe McDonald, and the good folk of King's Oak also had a look-in, especially miserable old Wilf Harvey (whose electrician son, Stan, married Jill), postmistress Miss Tatum, antiques dealers Tish and Ted Hope and shopkeeper Roy Lambert. Probably the best loved of all *Crossroads* characters, however, was the slow-witted, woolly-hatted Benny Hawkins, first seen as a labourer at Diane's uncle's farm. He followed 'Miss Diane' back to King's Oak, but continued to suffer more than his fair share of misfortune, including the death of his gypsy girlfriend, Maureen Flynn, on their wedding day.

But tragedy and romance were the name of the game at Crossroads. Young Sandy was crippled in a car accident and spent most of his time afterwards in a wheelchair (actor Roger Tonge was later confined to a wheelchair himself, before dying prematurely in 1981). Jill married three times (once bigamously) and Meg herself married twice. Her first new husband, Malcolm Ryder, tried to poison her, and she later fell for old flame Hugh Mortimer, a millionaire businessman who then died of a heart attack while being held as a terrorists' hostage. This may sound rather far-fetched, but such extravagant storylines were always possible. In 1967, a rediscovered wartime bomb blew up the motel. In 1981 it was destroyed by fire but rose again, phoenix-like, from the ashes. However, *Crossroads* was also a brave serial and could be stonily earnest at times. It tackled issues other soaps happily shirked, these ranging from teenage runaways, abortion and test-tube babies to racism, rape and physical handicaps.

Power struggles contributed to much of the action, too. Suave David Hunter was brought in as partner in 1969 and he shared Meg's limelight until she was written out in 1981 (she sailed away on the *QE II* to a new life). Four years later, David and his novelist wife Barbara were also dispatched to pastures new. In their place, fighting for control of the motel, were Jill, Adam Chance (her smoothie husband), tycoon J. Henry Pollard, new leading lady Nicola Freeman and businessman Tommy Lancaster. It was when Daniel Freeman, Nicola's stepson, assumed control in 1988 that the series finally ended. By this time, the motel had changed its name to King's Oak Country Hotel. Jill, who had spoken the first ever words on the series – 'Crossroads Motel. Can I help you?' – also spoke the last, as she drove away with the new man in her life, John Maddingham, to open up a small hotel in the west.

Crossroads also focused on the motel guests, some of whom were celebrities indulging a fancy to appear in the show. These included Bob Monkhouse, Ken Dodd and Larry Grayson, who in one of his appearances acted as chauffeur to Meg and Hugh Mortimer on their wedding day. Some big names were given their break on the series. Malcolm McDowell played PR man Crispin Ryder, Diane Keen was waitress Sandra Gould and Elaine Paige was seen in the guise of Caroline Winthrop. Another guest was singer Harriet Blair, played by Stephanie de Sykes, who then took her song in the programme, 'Born with a Smile on My Face', to number two in the 1974 charts. It wasn't the first *Crossroads* hit: Sue Nicholls (later Audrey Roberts in CORONATION STREET) made the Top Twenty with 'Where Will You Be' in 1968. Nor was it the last: Simon May recorded a vocal version of his 'Summer of My Life' tune in 1976, Paul Henry spoke the words of 'Benny's Theme' (played by the Mason Glen Orchestra) in 1978 and Kate Robbins (in the series as Kate Loring) succeeded with 'More Than in Love' in 1982. Paul McCartney and Wings' reworking of Tony Hatch's thumpingly catchy theme tune was used on some episodes (particularly those with sad or soppy endings) but, under producer William Smethurst in 1987, a new theme tune by Max Early and Raf Ravenscroft was introduced.

Devised by former COMPACT writers Hazel Adair and Peter Ling, from an idea by producer Reg Watson (later of PRISONER: CELL BLOCK H and NEIGHBOURS fame), *Crossroads*' working title was *The Midland Road*. Adopting the snappier name, the series began in 1964 but, despite gaining a cult following, was not fully networked by ITV until 1972. Its heavy workload was cut to four episodes a week in 1967, and then, on the instructions of the IBA, which was concerned about its quality, to three episodes a week in 1980. When the plug was pulled altogether in 1988, after over 4,500 programmes, there was a huge outcry, but the bosses at Central Television were adamant that *Crossroads*' day was done and refused to reconsider. In its place, fans had to make do with Victoria Wood's cheeky send-up, *Acorn Antiques*.

However, *Crossroads* is not the sort of serial that gives in easily. It was revived as a daily serial by ITV in 2001, bringing back Jill, Adam Chance, Doris Luke and Jill's (now grown up) daughter, Sarah-Jane, alongside a host of new characters in a plush hotel setting. It didn't work and wound up in summer 2002. When *Crossroads* returned yet again in early 2003 there had been another clear-out. Jane Asher arrived as new owner Angel Samson and big name guest stars like Kate O'Mara, Lionel Blair, Linda Robson and Les Dennis were lined up as the series, under new producer Yvon Grace, went camp in a purposeful bid for the gay audience. The ploy – perhaps unsurprisingly – didn't succeed and *Crossroads* closed its doors once again later in the year, the events of the previous months simply dismissed as a reverie enjoyed by a supermarket check-out assistant named Angela, who dreamed of herself as demanding motel boss Angel Samson, and her colleagues and customers as other Crossroads regulars!

Crow Road, The ★★★

UK (Union Pictures/BBC) Drama. BBC 2 1996
DVD: Second Sight

Prentice McHoan .... **Joseph McFadden**
Kenneth McHoan .... **Bill Paterson**
Rory McHoan .... **Peter Capaldi**
Ashley Watt .... **Valerie Edmond**
Fiona Urvill .... **Stella Gonet**
Fergus Urvill .... **David Robb**
Lewis McHoan .... **Dougray Scott**
Janice .... **Patricia Kerrigan**
Hamish McHoan .... **Paul Young**
Lachlan Watt .... **Alex Norton**
Mary McHoan .... **Elizabeth Sinclair**
Verity .... **Simone Bendix**
Aunt Antonia .... **Claire Nielsen**
Margot McHoan .... **Gudrun Ure**

Writer **Bryan Elsley**
Executive Producers **Andrea Calderwood, Kevin Loader, Franc Roddam**
Producer **Bradley Adams**

● ***A Scots lad tries to unearth the truth about his uncle's disappearance.***
Student Prentice McHoan has always been puzzled by the fact that his Uncle Rory disappeared in strange circumstances several years ago, after setting out to visit the family home. He finally decides to find out more and, armed with extracts from Rory's written work, follows his trail back to the Highlands. Several other family mysteries and personal animosities within the clan contrive to make the discovery of the truth only more difficult. Verity is the cousin Prentice sets his heart on, but she is stolen by his brother, Lewis, a stand-up comedian; but at least he is comforted by Rory's former girlfriend, Janice, and his own life-long friend, Ashley Watt, as he gradually learns the truth about his family and himself.

This intriguing serial, based on the novel by Iain Banks, was made in four one-hour episodes, with flashbacks revealing important evidence from years gone by and the lost Uncle Rory reappearing as a figment of Prentice's imagination. Plenty of sharp humour provided balance, and *The Crow Road* earned itself a host of commendations.

Crown Court ★★

UK (Granada) Drama. ITV 5 1972–84

● ***Long-running afternoon courtroom drama.***
Presenting a different case each week, over three half-hour episodes, *Crown Court* was a stalwart of ITV's first afternoon schedules. Viewers were treated to hearings on a variety of subjects, from drug-pushing to murder, and then awaited the deliberations of the jury (a panel of viewers), which were revealed at the close of the last episode. Many distinguished actors graced this popular series, including the likes of John Le Mesurier, Bob Hoskins, Ben Kingsley, Juliet Stevenson, Pauline Quirke, Michael Elphick, Liz Fraser, Michael Gough, Jack Shepherd and Connie Booth. Richard Wilson was a regular, playing barrister Jeremy Parsons QC. The setting was the fictitious Fulchester Crown Court. A similarly styled series, *Verdict*, was screened on ITV in 1998, and in 2004 Channel 4 launched a daytime series called *The Courtroom*, another take on the same idea.

Crowther, Leslie

CBE (1933–96)

Nottingham-born funny man – the son of stage actor Leslie Crowther Sr – who sprang to fame as resident clown on the kids' show CRACKERJACK in 1960 and stayed with the series for eight years, finally acting as compere. As well as regular appearances in variety programmes like THE BLACK AND WHITE MINSTREL SHOW, *Hi Summer*, *The Saturday Crowd* and *Starburst*, Crowther also dabbled in sitcom. He starred as bachelor Thomas Jones in *The Reluctant Romeo*, Clive Gibbons, a husband beholden to a charity-obsessed wife, in MY GOOD WOMAN, and mummy's boy Tony Marchant in *Big Boy Now*. He ventured as well into game shows, hosting RUNAROUND and the 'Come on down' shopping quiz THE PRICE IS RIGHT, also presenting *Whose Baby?* and the look-alike talent show STARS IN THEIR EYES. Over the years he had various showcases of his own, including *Crowther's in Town*, *The Crowther Collection* and *Leslie Crowther's Scrapbook*, but his career was abruptly halted by a serious car accident in 1992. Leslie was the father of actress Liz Crowther.

Cruickshank, Andrew

MBE (1907–88)

Distinguished Scottish stage and screen actor who arrived on television in the 1930s . He starred in a 1959 version of *Bleak House* and in 1962 he was cast as the grouchy Dr Cameron in DR FINLAY'S CASEBOOK, a role he filled until the series ended in 1971. His other TV work included *Mr Justice Duncannon*, the satire THE OLD MEN AT THE ZOO (Mr Sanderson) and the part of eccentric old Mr Hodinett in KING AND CASTLE.

Cruise, The ★

UK (BBC) Documentary. BBC 1 1998

Executive Producer **Olivia Lichtenstein**
Producer **Christopher Terrill**

● ***Fly-on-the-wall tales from a luxury liner.***
This twice-weekly docu-soap whisked winter-weary viewers

away to the exotic world of the cruise ship *Galaxy* as it toured the sun-kissed Caribbean. On its voyage (recorded by producer/director Christopher Terrill over seven weeks), the series explored the lives of many of the 1,000 crew members – from captain Iakovos Korres to DJ Scotty, husband and wife casino workers Dale and Mary, singer Michelle, dancer Jack and juggler-comedian Sean. The 2,000 fare-paying passengers (some happy, some not so happy) that joined the ship every week also featured. However, from the start the star of the series was obvious. The ship's headline singer, Jane McDonald, from Wakefield, a veteran of the northern clubs, touched viewers with her openness before the camera. Allowing the team to witness not just her stage show but her pre-performance nerves and post-performance anxieties brought her instant fame. McDonald later became a BBC presenter (THE NATIONAL LOTTERY LIVE, *Star for a Night*) and was featured in a 1998 New Year's Eve special, *Jane's Cruise to the Stars*, which charted her rocket-fuelled rise to celebrity. A one-off *Cruise* special in July 1998 celebrated Jane's marriage to Danish engineer Henrik Brixen back in the Caribbean.

Cryer, Barry

OBE (1935–)

Leeds-born comedian and sketch-writer, at times providing scripts for some of the world's finest, including Bob Hope and George Burns. As well as behind-the-scenes work on the comedies NO – THAT'S ME OVER HERE!, DOCTOR IN THE HOUSE, NOW LOOK HERE . . ., *The Prince of Denmark* and *Langley Bottom* (in collaboration with such writers as Graham Chapman and John Junkin), Cryer has also been a familiar face in front of the camera, particularly on panel games and sketch shows like AT LAST THE 1948 SHOW and *Hello Cheeky*. He hosted the quick-fire gag show *Jokers Wild* in the 1970s and *The Stand Up Show* in the 1990s, and was one of the team on *What's On Next?*, a regular in *The Steam Video Company*, and part of the *Assaulted Nuts* sketch show gang, and took the part of Lance Boyle in *Believe Me*. The roll-call of artists he has supplied gags for reads like a *Who's Who* of TV comedy: THE TWO RONNIES, Morecambe and Wise, Bruce Forsyth, Max Bygraves, Bob Monkhouse, Marty Feldman, Dick Emery, Frankie Howerd, Mike Yarwood, Bernie Winters, Stanley Baxter, Des O'Connor, Kenny Everett, Jasper Carrott, Tommy Cooper, Leslie Crowther, Bobby Davro, Jim Davidson, Les Dennis, Little and Large, Les Dawson, Russ Abbot and Rory Bremner.

Crystal Maze, The ★★

UK (Chatsworth) Game Show. Channel 4 1990–5

Presenters **Richard O'Brien, Edward Tudor-Pole**
Producers **Malcolm Heyworth, David G. Croft**

Prizes await contestants skilled at physical and mental puzzles.

In this cross between THE KRYPTON FACTOR and Indiana Jones, impish Mazemaster Richard O'Brien invited a team of contestants (all aged strictly under 40) to tackle a series of mental and physical games with the aim of winning time-crystals. The more crystals collected, the longer the team were given in the finale to gather floating strips of gold foil which then translated into prizes. If a contestant ran out of time in any of the games, he or she was sealed into the room housing the game and a crystal was forfeited to extricate him or her if necessary. All the games were thematically linked to four fantasy zones (Aztec, Futuristic, Medieval and Industrial, the last replaced by Ocean later) similar to those seen in computer games, and the quality of the imaginative sets ensured a good 'Dungeons and Dragons' atmosphere. The programme quickly earned itself a cult following, and a children's edition was shown at Christmas 1991. In 1994 O'Brien left and was replaced by Ed Tudor-Pole.

Crystal Tipps and Alistair ★★

UK (BBC/Q3) Animation. BBC 1 1972–4
DVD: Contender

Creator **Hilary Hayton**
Writers **Hilary Hayton, Graham McCallum**
Producer **Michael Grafton-Robinson**

Quirky, psychedelic animation about a girl and her dog.

Crystal Tipps and Alistair was a product of the BBC's animation department, a unit that barely got off the ground in the early 1970s. Employing just one illustrator and one animator, it was soon disbanded and this series – employing cut-out animated figures and loud colours – was subsequently made by outside contractors. It featured the simplistic but surreal adventures of a girl with a very bushy, violet-coloured hair-do (Crystal Tipps) and her large, square-headed dog (Alistair). The five-minute programmes were screened in the 'MAGIC ROUNDABOUT slot' just before the early evening news. A pilot episode was broadcast in 1971.

CSI: Crime Scene Investigation ★★★

US (Alliance Atlantis/Jerry Bruckheimer/CBS) Police Drama. Channel 5 2001– (US: CBS 2000–)
DVD: Momentum Pictures

Gil Grissom	**William Petersen**
Catherine Willows	**Marg Helgenberger**
Warrick Brown	**Gary Dourdan**
Sara Sidle	**Jorja Fox**
Nick Stokes	**George Eads**
Capt. Jim Brass	**Paul Guilfoyle**
Greg Sanders	**Eric Szmanda**
Dr Albert Robbins	**Robert David Hall**

Creator **Anthony E. Zuiker**
Executive Producers **Jerry Bruckheimer, Jonathan Littman, Sam Strangis, Carol Mendelsohn, Ann Donohue, Anthony E. Zuiker, James C. Hart**

A crack team of pathologists solve murders in America's gambling capital.

Gil Grissom is the leader of a team of forensic pathologists combing their way through the corpses of Las Vegas and the surrounding desert. Shrewd, pensive and respected, Grissom heads up a fivesome which also includes Catherine Willows (one-time lap dancer now single mother of a young daughter), Warrick Brown (clever, frustrated by authority and addicted to gambling), no-nonsense, smoky-voiced brunette Sara Sidle and the newly promoted Nick Stokes (Brown's rival). Supported by medical examiner Al Robbins, lab technician Greg Sanders and police officer Jim Brass, the team deals in physical evidence alone. Ignoring verbal accounts and devoting themselves to the purely scientific, Grissom and his gang dig deep into the heart of murder investigations, often from the starting point of a particularly gruesome, decomposing body.

With its relentless pace, thumping rock soundtrack, crisp

jargon-filled dialogue, snappy camerawork, innovative effects and lots of aerial shots of colourful Vegas, the series was an instant hit in the USA and was one of the first big drama purchases by Channel 5. One episode from series two showed Willows and Brown being temporarily dispatched to Florida – a tried and tested way of introducing a spin-off series. The resultant *CSI: Miami*, starring David Caruso as Horatio Caine, was launched in the USA in autumn 2002 (UK: five 2003–), with a further spin-off, *CSI: NY*, set in New York, arriving in 2004 and starring Gary Sinise as Det. Mac Taylor (five 2005–). Symptomatic of the class oozed by the series was the fact that Quentin Tarantino directed one episode shown in 2005 in the UK.

CTV

See *Channel Television*.

Cuckoo Waltz, The ✶✶

UK (Granada) Situation Comedy. ITV 1975–7; 1980

Chris Hawthorne .... **David Roper**
Felicity 'Fliss' Hawthorne .... **Diane Keen**
Gavin Rumsey .... **Lewis Collins**
Connie Wagstaffe .... **Clare Kelly**
Austen Tweedale .... **John McKelvey**
Adrian Lockett .... **Ian Saynor**

Writers **Geoffrey Lancashire, John G. Temple**
Producers **Bill Gilmour, Brian Armstrong, John G. Temple**

● ***Two hard-up newlyweds take in a lodger and live to regret it.***

Chris and Fliss Hawthorne are young, recently married and in love. However, their cash flow is virtually non-existent and they are as poor as the proverbial church mice. Their living-room furniture consists of a deckchair marked 'Property of Prestatyn UDC' and they have no room for the luxuries of life, a fact that makes Chris rather doleful. Fliss generally cheers him up with a murmur of 'Chris-Fliss-Kiss', followed by a quick snog. To ease their financial problems, the Hawthornes take in Chris's friend, Gavin Rumsey, a refugee from a broken marriage, as their lodger. Unlike his hosts, sporty Gavin always has cash to burn. He brings with him a vanload of expensive furniture and a flashy car. He also tends to flirt with his pretty landlady, who always remains loyal to her lacklustre journalist husband. When Fliss gives birth to twins, further demands are placed on the Hawthornes' meagre resources and, as a result, Gavin remains the 'cuckoo' for three seasons. However, when the series returned after a three-year hiatus, he had given way to another lodger, Adrian Lockett, who, to complicate matters, also quickly became besotted with Fliss.

Cue

The signal (usually visual) given to a presenter or actor to start speaking or moving. Camera operators and other technicians also have to be 'cued', although their cues are usually vocal and given via their headphones.

Cue Card

See *Idiot board*.

Culloden ✶✶✶✶

UK (BBC) Drama. BBC 1 1964
DVD: BFI Video Publishing

Writer/Producer **Peter Watkins**

● ***Influential re-creation of the defeat of Bonnie Prince Charlie.***

Describing itself as an account of 'one of the most mishandled and bloody battles ever fought in Britain', this landmark drama-documentary relates events at the Battle of Culloden. Using descendants of the original warriors, it re-enacts the bloody conflict of 16 April 1746, near Inverness, in which the English under the Duke of Cumberland crushed the second Jacobite rebellion. Demythologizing the romance of Charles Edward Stuart ('Bonnie Prince Charlie') and his followers, the film also considers the impact of the battle on the subsequent history of Britain.

Producer Peter Watkins (THE WAR GAME) also directs, on a low budget, using newsreel cameras to give the impression that television is covering the action as it happens. A documentary-style narrative overlays proceedings, and participants in the battle – their faces weathered and tense – are interviewed before, during and after the conflict. Key characters on both sides are introduced, highlighting their social positions and weaponry. Many are unwilling men coerced into battle through the iniquitously feudal clan structure. 'Expert analysis' is provided of the battlefield prior to the start of the fighting, and later of the various tactics employed, and cameras are positioned in the midst of the mayhem. The upshot is that Charles Edward Stuart is exposed as a vain man, a foreigner with no battle plan and little consideration for his followers, whom he led into battle unprepared, hungry and over-tired against the latest artillery, muskets and an organized cavalry. Some 1,200 men are left dead or dying after just 68 minutes of fighting. The followers of the Duke of Cumberland show no magnanimity in victory, persecuting and killing the injured and the innocent folk of the region, laying bare the Highlands for centuries to come.

Culshaw, Jon

(1968–)

Popular English impressionist, star of *Alter Ego*, DEAD RINGERS, *The Impressionable Jon Culshaw* and *Jon Culshaw's Commercial Breakdown*. His specialist take-offs include George W. Bush, Tony Blair, Dale Winton, William Hague, Tom Baker and Ozzie Osbourne. A one-time radio presenter (once, on Capital Radio, getting through to Tony Blair in Downing Street by pretending to be William Hague), he has also provided voices for SPITTING IMAGE and *2DTV*.

Cunliffe, David

(1935–)

British TV executive, for a number of years Controller of Drama at Yorkshire Television, although previously working as producer/director for Granada, LWT and the BBC. Among his credits have been *Saturday Night Theatre*, THE ONEDIN LINE, HADLEIGH, THE MAIN CHANCE, EMMERDALE FARM, WILDE ALLIANCE, BERYL'S LOT, RAFFLES, FLAMBARDS, AIRLINE, THE BEIDERBECKE AFFAIR, HARRY'S GAME, HORACE, OLIVER'S TRAVELS, COMING HOME/NANCHERROW, *Victoria and Albert*, and *Winter Solstice*.

Curb Your Enthusiasm ★★★

US (HBO Situation Comedy. BBC 2 2003 (US: HBO 2000–)
DVD: HBO Video

Larry David .... **Larry David**
Cheryl David .... **Cheryl Hines**
Jeff Greene .... **Jeff Garlin**
Susie Greene .... **Susie Essman**
Richard Lewis .... **Richard Lewis**
Wanda .... **Wanda Sykes**

Creator **Larry David**
Executive Producers **Larry David, Jeff Garlin, Gavin Polone, Robert B. Weide, Larry Charles**

Trying days in the life of a hapless Hollywood scriptwriter.
Former stand-up comedian Larry David plays himself in this mock fly-on-the-wall documentary series that breaks away from American comedy tradition by abandoning the laugh track and falling back on its stars' improvisational skills (the plots are preplanned but the dialogue is largely made up on the hoof). David is an opinionated, obsessive, very competitive Santa Monica-based actor and writer (the real David was co-creator of SEINFELD) whose life is plagued by unfortunate circumstance. Anything can trigger a sequence of painfully embarrassing incidents – it could be an unfortunately tasteless remark, a spelling mistake in a newspaper obituary, or even just a badly cut pair of trousers that, regrettably, protrudes in the groin area. It is then left to the not surprisingly neurotic David, his wife Cheryl or manager Jeff to extricate him from the ensuing, cringe-inducing mess. Joining David in the mêlée of misfortune are real-life Hollywood personalities such as Ted Danson, Joan Rivers, Martin Scorsese, Michael York, Mel Brooks, David Schwimmer and former Seinfeld colleagues Jason Alexander and Julia Louis-Dreyfus. The series, which evolved from an HBO special entitled *Larry David: Curb Your Enthusiasm*, aired first on BBC 4 in the UK, before transferring to BBC 2. Digital channel E4 then snapped up series three.

Curran, Sir Charles

(1921–80)

BBC Director-General, 1969–77, Dublin-born Charles Curran joined the BBC as a radio producer in 1947, before leaving for a career in newspapers. He rejoined the Corporation in 1951 and worked his way up the administrative ladder, eventually succeeding Hugh Greene as Director-General. Curran was also President of the European Broadcasting Union and Chief Executive of the Visnews news agency.

Curry and Chips ★

UK (LWT) Situation Comedy. ITV 1969

The Foreman .... **Eric Sykes**
Kevin O'Grady ('Paki-Paddy') .. **Spike Milligan**

Creator/Writer **Johnny Speight**
Producer **Keith Beckett**

An Irish-Pakistani starts work at a factory and suffers abuse.
There have been few comedy series more controversial than *Curry and Chips*. Penned by TILL DEATH US DO PART creator Johnny Speight, it looks at life in the factory of Lillicrap Ltd, a factory making cheap souvenirs. Newly arrived is Kevin O'Grady, an Asian with an Irish father, a genetic combination that results in his nickname of Paki-Paddy. Played by a blacked-up Spike Milligan, Paki-Paddy suffers racist taunts from his workmates, even though Eric Sykes's foreman is rather more liberal in his outlook. Speight's intention was to turn such bigotry and narrow-mindedness into ridiculous caricatures, but viewers and critics found the crude 'factory' language too much to swallow, and only one series was made. Actors like Kenny Lynch, Sam Kydd, Geoffrey Hughes and Norman Rossington provided support for the principals.

Curtis, Richard

CBE (1956–)

British comedy writer, best known for his screenplays for the award-winning films *Four Weddings and a Funeral* and *Notting Hill*. His earlier writing was in collaboration with former Oxford colleague Rowan Atkinson and then with Ben Elton, and his major credits are NOT THE NINE O'CLOCK NEWS, SPITTING IMAGE, BLACKADDER, MR BEAN, THE VICAR OF DIBLEY, the *Robbie the Reindeer* cartoons (writer/producer) and *The Girl in the Café*. Curtis has also been the brains behind COMIC RELIEF.

Curtis, Tony

(Bernard Schwartz; 1925–)

Hollywood film name whose television experience has been confined to action adventures such as THE PERSUADERS! (playing millionaire Danny Wilde), *McCoy* (a confidence trickster) and VEGA$ (casino boss Phil Roth). In 2005 he made a guest appearance in CSI: CRIME SCENE INVESTIGATION.

Cusack:

SINÉAD (1948–), SORCHA (1949–), NIAMH (1959–), CATHERINE (1969–)

Four Irish actress sisters, the daughters of actor Cyril Cusack (1910–93).

Sinéad is married to Jeremy Irons and has been seen in dramas like *Scoop*, QUILLER, *Tales from Hollywood* (Nelly Mann), *Have Your Cake and Eat It* (Charlotte Dawson), *Oliver's Travels* (WPC Diane Priest), *North and South* (Hannah), *Winter Solstice* (Elfrida Phipps), *Dad* (Sandy James), and *The Strange Case of Sherlock Holmes and Arthur Conan Doyle* (Mary Doyle).

Sorcha is probably best known as Kate Wilson in CASUALTY but also starred in *Plastic Man* (Erin MacConnell) and *Eureka Street* (Caroline), and has featured in BROOKSIDE, INSPECTOR MORSE, MAIGRET, AGATHA CHRISTIE'S POIROT, SILENT WITNESS, THE INSPECTOR LYNLEY MYSTERIES, JUDGE JOHN DEED and the kids' series *The Square Leopard*.

Niamh's biggest roles have been as Kate Rowan in HEARTBEAT and Christine Fletcher in A&E, and she has also appeared in JEEVES AND WOOSTER, CATHERINE COOKSON*'s Colour Blind* (Bridget Paterson), *The World of Peter Rabbit* (Beatrix Potter), QED's dramatizations, *Cause of Death* (solicitor Mary McGuire), *Too Good to be True* (Tina Lewis), and the single dramas *Rhinoceros* (Julie Flynn) and *Little Bird* (Ellen Hall), as well as providing voices for *The World of Peter Rabbit and Friends*. She has also made guest appearances in THE LAST DETECTIVE and AGATHA CHRISTIE'S MARPLE.

Half-sister Catherine's most prominent appearances have been as psychotic student nurse Carmel Finnan in CORONATION STREET and as Frankie Sullivan in BALLYKISSANGEL, with other parts in DOCTOR WHO, THE CHIEF, THE BILL, CADFAEL and JONATHAN CREEK.

Cushing, Peter

OBE (1913–94)

Hammer horror master Peter Cushing was also a prolific TV performer, even if you just take into account the number of times he appeared on *The Morecambe and Wise Show* requesting a cheque. He played Winston Smith in the controversial 1954 adaptation of George Orwell's 1984 and SHERLOCK HOLMES for the BBC in 1968, and cropped up in many other single dramas and series as a guest performer, from THE AVENGERS to SPACE: 1999 and, of course, HAMMER HOUSE OF HORROR.

Cuthbertson, Iain

(1930–)

Glaswegian actor, chiefly remembered as seedy spiv Charlie Endell in BUDGIE and its sequel, *Charles Endell Esquire*, and the Scottish lawyer John Sutherland in SUTHERLAND'S LAW. His other major performances have included roles in *The Borderers, Diamond Crack Diamond* (lawyer Mark Terson), *Scotch on the Rocks*, THE STONE TAPE (Collinson), TOM BROWN'S SCHOOLDAYS (Dr Arnold), CHILDREN OF THE STONES (psychic megalomaniac Hendrick), *The Voyage of Charles Darwin, Rep* (theatre troupe manager J. C. Benton), SUPERGRAN (the nasty Scunner Campbell), A PERFECT SPY (Makepeace Watermaster), *The Guilty* (Lord Chancellor), *Headhunters* (Malcolm Standish), *Oliver's Travels* (Davidson) and *Painted Lady* (Sir Charles Stafford). Cuthbertson has also enjoyed many guest appearances in series as varied as Z CARS, THE DUCHESS OF DUKE STREET, SURVIVORS, RIPPING YARNS, DANGER UXB, THE RACING GAME, DOCTOR WHO, *Return of the Antelope*, RAB C. NESBITT, MINDER and INSPECTOR MORSE. He is married to actress Anne Kirsten.

Cutting It ✳✳

UK (BBC) Drama. BBC 1 2002–5

DVD: Contender

Mia Bevan	**Amanda Holden**
Allie Henshall	**Sarah Parish**
Gavin Ferraday	**Jason Merrells**
Finn Bevan	**Ben Daniels**
Darcey Henshall	**Angela Griffin**
Sydney Henshall	**Siân Reeves**
Ruby Ferris	**Lucy Gaskell**
Shane Ince	**James Midgley**
Eugene Eubank	**Pearce Quigley**
Brawdie Henshall	**Annette Badland**
Tom Henshall	**Bill Thomas**
Calypso Henshall	**Rebecca Bellamy**
Smedley Butt	**Philip Martin Brown**
Mrs Pargetter	**Enid Dunn**
Charlie Wolfe	**Vincent McGuire**
Mrs Goldwag	**Patsy Ghadie**
Zinnia Raggitt	**Cherie Lunghi**
Ross Peagrum	**Terry Christian**
Liam Carney	**James Murray**
Melissa Devereux	**Christine Stephen-Daly**
Troy Gillespie	**David Leon**
Craig Gutteridge	**Andrew Moss**
Dido Gutteridge	**Keri Arnold**
Fuchsia Gutteridge	**Samantha Siddall**
Elayne Quigley	**Rachel Davies**
Mildred Flaherty	**Doreen Keogh**

Writer/Executive Producer **Debbie Horsfield**
Producers **Diederick Santer, Kate Crow**

Rival hair stylists have more to fight over than customers.

Allie Henshaw runs the successful Henshaw–Ferraday hairdressing salon in Manchester with her other half, Gavin Ferraday. Things seem to be flowing very nicely but there's conflict within the partnership, because Gavin now wants to have children and Allie is firmly set against the idea. On the business front, after ten prosperous years, expansion is on the cards and they are about to sign the lease on a second premises across the road when they are mysteriously gazumped. The rival bidders turn out to be Mia Bevan and her wealthy husband, Finn. They open up their own salon (Blade Runner) in competition and immediately begin to steal Allie's best customers, much to the dismay of Allie's team of stylists and beauticians, which includes her sisters Darcey (a beautician) and Sydney (a manicurist), plus loud-mouthed junior Ruby. It is soon obvious that Mia's saccharine smile conceals a bitchy interior. A less predictable discovery is that smoothy Finn is actually an old flame of Allie's and his arrival has set in train a sequence of events that turns her world upside down. Three further series then explore the convoluted relationships that prove to be more tangled than a 1970s perm, with new cast additions including Zinnia Raggitt, Mia's ex-porn star mother, Ross Peagrum, a local TV presenter, Liam Carney, a former member of a boy band who invests in the business, and Aussie crimper Melissa Devereux.

Cybill ✳✳

UK (River Siren/Carsey-Werner) Situation Comedy. Channel 4 1996–9 (US: CBS 1995–8)

Cybill Sheridan	**Cybill Shepherd**
Maryann Thorpe	**Christine Baranski**
Jeff Robbins	**Tom Wopat**
Ira Woodbine	**Alan Rosenberg**
Rachel Blanders	**Dedee Pfeifer**
Kevin Blanders	**Peter Krause**
Zoey Woodbine	**Alicia Witt**
Sean	**Jay Paulson**
Justin Thorpe	**Danny Masterson**
Richard Thorpe	**Ray Baker**

Creator **Chuck Lorre**
Executive Producers **Marcey Carsey, Tom Werner, Caryn Manderbach, Cybill Shepherd, Harold M. Gould**

Life goes on at 40 for a fading Hollywood actress.

Cybill Sheridan is an ageing actress struggling to regain the major roles that used to come her way when she was young. Now all she is fed are bit parts in commercials and second-rate films that rather demean her talents. Feeling her age, she is surrounded by her two daughters Rachel (22, married to Kevin and a mother) and Zoey (16, moody and independent-minded), plus ex-husbands Jeff, a dopey stuntman, and Ira, a neurotic Jewish writer. Solace and encouragement to wild living come from her wisecracking, boozy pal Maryann Thorpe, another divorcée. Richard ('Dr Dick') is the estranged husband with whom Maryann longs to get even – but he is not to be confused with a new Dr Dick, a vet, whom she dates later. Maryann's son, Justin, is also seen. As the series progresses, Cybill does edge back into the big(ger) time, with a prominent role in a science-fiction series called *Lifeforms* that is all too quickly cancelled, and a part in a movie called *Punchout*, that, disappointingly, goes straight into video. Maryann's desire for vengeance on her duplicitous ex-husband ultimately results in her and Cybill's arrest for the murder of Dr Dick in the final episode. Although the credits declare the story 'To be continued', the show was cancelled after four seasons.

Dad ✱✱

UK (BBC) Situation Comedy. BBC 1 1997; 1999

Brian Hook .... **George Cole**
Alan Hook .... **Kevin McNally**
Beryl Hook .... **Julia Hills**
Vincent Hook .... **Toby Ross-Bryant**

Creator/Writer/Executive Producer **Andrew Marshall**
Producer **Marcus Mortimer**

● ***Being a son, as well as a father, spells double trouble.***

Having a teenage son is only half of Alan Hook's worries: the other half come from the fact that his equally exasperating father lives nearby. For Alan, well-meaning dad Brian has perfected the art of annoying interference, while always remaining defiantly cheerful and set in his ways. This problem is basically not Brian's, but is of neurotic Alan's making. He sees himself stuck between two generations, trying to appear cool and liberated to 18-year-old Vincent but unwittingly picking up irritating habits and old-fashioned values from his own father. Combined with blanching memories of Brian's various faux pas during his own adolescent years, and genuine concerns over his dad's health, it all makes life for Alan and wife Beryl more complicated than it really should be.

Dad's Army ✱✱✱✱

UK (BBC) Situation Comedy. BBC 1 1968–77
DVD: BBC

Capt. George Mainwaring ...... **Arthur Lowe**
Sgt Arthur Wilson .... **John Le Mesurier**
L/Cpl Jack Jones .... **Clive Dunn**
Pte James Fraser .... **John Laurie**
Pte Joe Walker .... **James Beck**
Pte Frank Pike .... **Ian Lavender**
Pte Charles Godfrey .... **Arnold Ridley**
Chief ARP Warden William Hodges .... **Bill Pertwee**
The Vicar (Revd Timothy Farthing) .... **Frank Williams**
The Verger (Mr Maurice Yeatman) .... **Edward Sinclair**
Mrs Mavis Pike .... **Janet Davies**
Mr/Pte Cheeseman .... **Talfryn Thomas**
Mrs Marcia Fox .... **Pamela Cundell**
Mrs Anthea Yeatman .... **Olive Mercer**
Pte Sponge .... **Colin Bean**

Creators/Writers **Jimmy Perry, David Croft**
Producer **David Croft**

● ***The bumbling exploits of a World War II Home Guard platoon in an English coastal town.***

Drawing nostalgically on 1940s Britain, this long-running farce has been described as *the* classic British sitcom. It focuses on the misadventures of the Local Defence Volunteers of fictional Walmington-on-Sea (supposedly Bexhill). In true Home Guard tradition, the platoon is comprised of men too old, too young or too weak to take their place on the front line (hence, 'Dad's Army').

Self-appointed head of the unit is Captain George Mainwaring, the town's pompous, incompetent bank manager with a tragically misplaced sense of his own importance. His much-maligned second in command, in the bank as well as in uniform, is Arthur Wilson. Public-school-educated and polite to the point of asking the platoon if they 'would mind awfully falling in', he is far more level-headed than Mainwaring and never fails unwittingly to undermine his CO. Next in line is the town's butcher, Jack Jones, a fading veteran of Kitchener's army and master of the long-winded, far from pertinent tale, but a man with the heart of a lion and always the first to volunteer for the most dangerous tasks.

The other key members of the platoon are just as distinctive. Private Fraser is a rolling-eyed, penny-pinching Scottish undertaker, and Godfrey is the company's doddery, weak-bladdered first-aider, who lives in a picture-postcard cottage with his sisters, Dolly and Cissy. Private Walker and movie-mad teenager Frank Pike are the other two principals, Walker a black market spiv (a role originally earmarked for writer Jimmy Perry himself) and Pike a bank clerk and mummy's boy whose mother conducts a semi-covert affair with Sgt Wilson – his 'Uncle Arthur'.

Valiantly failing to patrol the resort or to fulfil demanding military exercises, the platoon are constantly nettled by the local ARP warden, Mr Hodges, the greengrocer. He and 'Napoleon' (as he labelled Mainwaring) jostle for military command in the town, and disputes over the use of the church hall for parade nights lead to the interference of the whingeing Vicar and his loyal verger, Mr Maurice (although also called Henry on one occasion) Yeatman. Other characters who pop up from time to time included toothy Welsh reporter Mr Cheeseman and Jones's rotund lady friend, Mrs Fox (like Mr Yeatman subject to more than one first name: generally Marcia but also Mildred).

Bound together with 1940s tunes vocalized by Bud Flanagan, the series conjured up some of the most memorable lines in TV comedy. Mainwaring's 'Stupid boy' (to Pike), Wilson's ominous 'Do you think that's wise, sir', Jones's 'Permission to speak, sir' and 'Don't panic', and Fraser's 'We're doomed' all became catchphrases. With the exception of young Ian Lavender, the cast had all done their time on stage and screen, and Arnold Ridley was also the author of *The Ghost Train*, a much-adapted stage play. The death of James Beck in 1973 (ironically one of the youngest cast members) was not allowed to stop the series. The cast was full and talented enough to continue, and lesser characters like Private Sponge were given more prominence in support. A film version of *Dad's Army* was released in 1971.

Daktari ✱✱

US (MGM/Ivan Tors) Adventure. BBC 1 1966–9 (US: CBS 1966–9)

Dr Marsh Tracy .... **Marshall Thomspon**
Paula Tracy .... **Cheryl Miller**
Jack Dane .... **Yale Summers**
District Officer Hedley .... **Hedley Mattingly**
Mike .... **Hari Rhodes**
Bart Jason .... **Ross Hagen**

Jenny Jones	**Erin Moran**

Creators **Ivan Tors, Art Arthur**
Executive Producer **Ivan Tors**
Producer **Leonard Kaufman**

The adventures of an American vet based at an African wildlife compound.

'Daktari' means 'doctor' in an African language, and this series revolves around Marsh Tracy, respected animal doctor and head of the Wameru Study Centre for Animal Behaviour. He is assisted by his daughter, Paula, American conservationist Jack Dane, and Mike, a native African. Hedley, a British game-warden, calls upon Tracy for advice and help from time to time. Later arrivals are hunter-turned-guide Bart Jason and a seven-year-old orphan, Jenny Jones, whom the Tracys adopt. Together they deal with conservation issues, tackling the iniquitous hunting trade and riding to the rescue of stranded cubs and badly injured beasts.

The animals were the real stars of *Daktari*, especially Judy, the mischievous chimpanzee, and Clarence, who had already appeared in his own film, *Clarence the Cross-Eyed Lion* (also featuring Marshall Thompson and Cheryl Miller). It was this cinema release that inspired the TV series, which was filmed at producer Ivan Tors's Africa, USA wildlife park near Los Angeles. Child actress Erin Moran went on to greater success as Joanie in HAPPY DAYS.

Dallas ★★★

US (Lorimar) Drama. BBC 1 1978–91 (US: CBS 1978–91)
DVD: Warner Home Video

John Ross ('JR') Ewing Jr	**Larry Hagman**
Eleanor Southworth (Miss Ellie) Ewing/Farlow	**Barbara Bel Geddes**
	Donna Reed
John Ross ('Jock') Ewing	**Jim Davis**
Bobby Ewing	**Patrick Duffy**
Pamela Barnes/Ewing	**Victoria Principal**
Lucy Ewing/Cooper	**Charlene Tilton**
Sue Ellen Ewing	**Linda Gray**
Ray Krebbs	**Steve Kanaly**
Cliff Barnes	**Ken Kercheval**
Willard 'Digger' Barnes	**David Wayne**
	Keenan Wynn
Gary Ewing	**David Ackroyd**
	Ted Shackelford
Valene Ewing	**Joan Van Ark**
Liz Craig	**Barbara Babcock**
Jenna Wade	**Morgan Fairchild**
	Francine Tacker
	Priscilla Presley
Kristin Shepard	**Colleen Camp**
	Mary Crosby
'Dusty Farlow'	**Jared Martin**
Dr Ellby	**Jeff Cooper**
Donna Culver/Krebbs	**Susan Howard**
Dave Culver	**Tom Fuccello**
Harve Smithfield	**George O. Petrie**
Vaughn Leland	**Dennis Patrick**
Connie	**Jeanna Michaels**
Louella	**Meg Gallagher**
Jordan Lee	**Don Starr**
Mitch Cooper	**Leigh McCloskey**
John Ross Ewing III	**Tyler Banks**
	Omri Katz
Punk Anderson	**Morgan Woodward**
Mavis Anderson	**Alice Hirson**
Marilee Stone	**Fern Fitzgerald**
Afton Cooper	**Audrey Landers**
Rebecca Wentworth	**Priscilla Pointer**
Jeremy Wendell	**William Smithers**
Clayton Farlow	**Howard Keel**
Katherine Wentworth	**Morgan Brittany**
Mickey Trotter	**Timothy Patrick Murphy**
Holly Harwood	**Lois Chiles**
Mark Graison	**John Beck**
Peter Richards	**Christopher Atkins**
Serena Wald	**Stephanie Blackmore**
Paul Morgan	**Glenn Corbett**
Charlie Wade	**Shalane McCall**
Sly	**Deborah Rennard**
Phyllis	**Deborah Tranelli**
Jessica Montford	**Alexis Smith**
Mandy Winger	**Deborah Shelton**
Jamie Ewing/Barnes	**Jenilee Harrison**
Christopher Ewing	**Joshua Harris**
Jack Ewing	**Dack Rambo**
Angelica Nero	**Barbara Carrera**
April Stevens	**Sheree J. Wilson**
Ben Stivers/Wes Parmalee	**Steve Forrest**
Bruce Harvey	**Jonathan Goldsmith**
Casey Denault	**Andrew Stevens**
Carter McKay	**George Kennedy**
Rose McKay	**Jeri Gaile**
Don Lockwood	**Ian McShane**
Cally Harper/Ewing	**Cathy Podewell**
Tracy Lawton	**Beth Toussaint**
James Richard Beaumont	**Sasha Mitchell**
Michelle Stevens	**Kimberly Foster**
Jackie Dugan	**Sherril Lynn Rettino**
Kendall	**Danone Simpson**
Vanessa Beaumont	**Gayle Hunnicutt**
Stephanie Rogers	**Lesley-Anne Down**
Liz Adams	**Barbara Stock**
Sheila Foley/Hillary Taylor	**Susan Lucci**
Breslin	**Peter White**
LeeAnn De La Vega	**Barbara Eden**

Creator **David Jacobs**
Producer **Leonard Katzman**

A wealthy Texan oil family indulge in sexual and commercial intrigue, in a bid to unsettle their rivals and each other.

This prime-time American soap is based around the life and affairs (business and personal) of the Texan Ewing family and their associates and introduces one of television's all-time great bad guys, the legendary J. R. Ewing. The Ewings' wealth flows from the oil industry, thanks to the manoeuvring of John Ross ('Jock') Ewing, the head of the clan, who cheated his great rival, Digger Barnes, out of the proceeds of a giant oil-strike some 40 years ago. Jock also stole Digger's girl, Eleanor Southworth ('Miss Ellie'), leaving the two families the bitterest enemies since the Capulets and Montagues.

Jock and Ellie's three sons are John Ross Jr ('JR'), the rarely seen Gary, and Bobby. They live on the Southfork ranch in Braddock County, just outside Dallas. Gary moves away and into his own spin-off series, KNOTS LANDING, leaving JR and Bobby prime heirs to the Ewing fortune. Whereas JR is ruthless and bad and never happy unless he is hurting someone, Bobby is honest and good, almost his brother's missing conscience. Their relationship is always uneasy, and JR resents Bobby's involvement in Ewing Oil. Another leading character is ranch foreman Ray Krebbs, who turns out to be Jock's illegitimate son, and therefore also a Ewing.

The Ewing–Barnes rivalry has passed down a generation from Jock and Digger to JR and Cliff Barnes, who, as an Assistant District Attorney, explores every avenue for exposing Ewing corruption, in the hope of gaining revenge for his father's humiliation. Cliff eventually becomes head of his own family's oil enterprise, Barnes–Wentworth. The Ewings and the Barneses are forced together in the first episode of *Dallas* when Bobby controversially marries Cliff's sister, Pam. It is a sign of things to come, with marriage and divorce commonplace among these excessively wealthy, beautiful people. JR is married (twice) to Sue Ellen, a former Miss Texas but a helpless drunk, whom he cheats on unmercifully. Bobby has his girlfriends, too. Jenna is one, April another. And when Jock is killed in a helicopter accident in South America, Miss Ellie is remarried, to Clayton Farlow.

Amid all the marriages, extra-marital alliances and underhand wheeling and dealing, the series is punctuated by two key storylines. In the first, JR receives his come-uppance when he is victim of an attempted assassination. (The whole world spent months between series agonizing over 'Who shot JR?', and it wasn't an easy question to answer, so many were his enemies. In order to hold the suspense, the studio filmed several possible conclusions, so that not even the cast knew who had pulled the trigger. It turned out to be Kristin, Sue Ellen's pregnant – by JR – sister. JR recovers, Kristin leaves town and the baby, Christopher, is adopted by Bobby and Pam.)

The other storyline on which the series turns is the death and resurrection of Bobby. In one of TV's greatest comebacks, he is first murdered in a hit-and-run accident after saving Pam's life, and then (when the series began slipping in the ratings) he is miraculously reintroduced. This is achieved, quite unashamedly, by waking Pam from a dream to find Bobby lathering himself in the shower, turning all that has happened in the previous season into just a nightmare. (During the 'dream sequence' Pam marries Mark Graison.)

Other highlights in the series' long run are JR's loss of control of Ewing Oil to Bobby when his criminal dealings are discovered; his fight to regain power; his attempts to get Sue Ellen institutionalized for her alcoholism; Bobby being shot by his wife's half-sister, Katherine Wentworth; and the arrival of the suspicious Wes Parmalee, who claims to be Jock back from the dead and very nearly convinces Miss Ellie in the process. JR floats in and out of prisons and mental asylums, as his manoeuvring is matched by those around him. The marriages, divorces, illicit affairs, sneaky business-deals and overwhelming duplicity continue throughout the show's run.

By the series' close, JR's world has collapsed around him. His various ex-wives and children have all left home, Bobby has been given Southfork by Miss Ellie, who has gone to Europe with Clayton, and, worst of all, Cliff Barnes now owns Ewing Oil. In the final episode, inspired by the film *It's a Wonderful Life*, JR sits, drinks and reflects on his life. An angel/devil pops up to show him just how others might have lived had JR never been born. Some have a much happier life, others are less fortunate; but it all seems a bit much for JR to take. As he pulls out a revolver, viewers hear a shot. Only Bobby, who dashes into the room, sees exactly what has occurred. This was not quite the end for Dallas, however, as a couple of sequel TV movies – *Dallas: JR Returns* (1996) and *Dallas: the War of the Ewings* (1998) – followed.

As evidenced by its cast list, *Dallas* was never afraid to introduce new characters and situations. Nor did it ever shy from switching actors and actresses when pressed into it. When Barbara Bel Geddes became ill, a far from convincing replacement was found in Donna Reed. There were two Garys, two John Rosses (JR and Sue Ellen's son), two Diggers and two Kristins, including Mary Crosby (Bing's daughter). There were actually three Jennas, with Morgan Fairchild and Francine Tacker both making the odd appearance before Priscilla Presley (wife of Elvis) made the part her own.

Daly, Tyne

(1946–)

Tyne Daly was born to an acting family, and her first TV appearance came in an episode of THE VIRGINIAN, which she followed up with a stint in the US daytime soap *General Hospital*. After numerous TV and cinema movies, she finally gained stardom as Mary Beth Lacey in the detective series CAGNEY AND LACEY. She followed this in the 1990s with parts in the US drama series *Christy* and *Judging Amy*.

Dalziel and Pascoe ★★

UK (BBC) Police Drama. BBC 1 1996–2002; 2004–

Det. Supt. Andy Dalziel	**Warren Clarke**
DS/DI Peter Pascoe	**Colin Buchanan**
Ellie Soper/Pascoe	**Susannah Corbett**
DS Edgar Wield	**David Royle**
Cadet Sanjay Singh	**Navin Chowdhry**
Edward Soper	**Peter Halliday**
Mary Soper	**Sylvia Kay**
Dr Vickery	**Fred Pearson**
Deputy Chief Constable Raymond	**Malcolm Tierney**
WDC Shirley Novello	**Jo-Anne Stockham**
ACC Rebecca Fenning	**Pippa Haywood**
DC Carrie Harris	**Keeley Forsyth**
Dr Paul Ashurst	**James Puddephatt**
DS Dawn 'Spike' Milligan	**Katy Cavanagh**
Dr Frank Mason	**Joe Savino**
WPC 'Janet' Jackson	**Naomi Bentley**
DC Parvez Lateef	**Wayne Perrey**
WPC Kim Spicer	**Jennifer James**

Producers **Eric Abraham, Chris Parr, Paddy Higson, Lars MacFarlane, Nick Pitt, Andrew Rowley, Ann Tricklebank**

Two seemingly incompatible coppers crack crime in the north.

Detective Superintendent Andy Dalziel (pronounced 'De-yell') is a traditional Yorkshire copper, an abrasive, not surprisingly divorced, man with plenty of bark and the social deportment of a monkey. His new partner, sociology graduate DS (later DI) Peter Pascoe, is not only much younger, but gently spoken, more sensitive to civil liberties and considerably better mannered. Together, they make an unlikely but effective team, rooting out plenty of villains – mostly in Yorkshire's more industrial centres (in and around the fictional town of Wetherton). In the background (and sometimes more prominent) is Ellie, Pascoe's liberal-minded girlfriend/wife, a teacher of creative writing. The characters were created by novelist Reginald Hill and were first seen on television in the three-part ITV drama *A Pinch of Snuff*, which starred comedians Hale and Pace in straight dramatic roles. Writers on the BBC series included Alan Plater, Malcolm Bradbury and Stan Hey.

Dan August ★★

US (Quinn Martin) Police Drama. ITV 1976–8 (US: ABC 1970–1)

Det. Lt. Dan August .... **Burt Reynolds**
Sgt Charles Wilentz .... **Norman Fell**
Sgt Joe Rivera .... **Ned Romero**
Chief George Untermeyer .... **Richard Anderson**
Katy Grant .... **Ena Hartmann**

Executive Producer **Quinn Martin**
Producer **Adrian Samish**

● ***A home-town cop uses his local knowledge to track down criminals.***

In this short-lived series, Detective Lt. Dan August patrols his home-town beat in Santa Luisa, California. Having grown up with many of the area's offenders and their victims, the tough young cop takes a deep personal interest in his investigations, an interest which earns him respect and brings results. Made before Burt Reynolds hit the box office big time, the series lasted only one year but, capitalizing on the star's success, it fared much better on its reruns.

Dance, Charles

OBE (1946–)

West Midlands-born actor seen to best light in dramas like THE JEWEL IN THE CROWN, in which he played Guy Perron, the thriller series *The Secret Servant* (Harry Maxim), the sci-fi drama FIRST BORN (Edward Forester) and BLEAK HOUSE (Mr Tulkinghorn). He also played the title role in the mini-series version of *Phantom of the Opera*, with other credits including EDWARD THE SEVENTH (Prince Eddy), NANCY ASTOR, the *Screen Two* presentation *Century, Rebecca* (Maxim de Winter), *Justice in Wonderland* (Neil Hamilton), *Henry VIII* (Duke of Buckingham), *Looking for Victoria, Last Rights* (Richard Wheeler), *Fingersmith* (Mr Lilly) and *To the Ends of the Earth* (Sir Henry Somerset). Guest appearances take in dramas such as MURDER ROOMS: THE DARK BEGINNINGS OF SHERLOCK HOLMES, RANDALL AND HOPKIRK (DECEASED), FOYLE'S WAR and AGATHA CHRISTIE'S MARPLE.

Dance to the Music of Time, A ★★★

UK (Dancetime) Drama. Channel 4 1997
DVD: Cinema Club

Nicholas Jenkins .... **James Purefoy**
John Standing
Kenneth Widmerpool .... **Simon Russell Beale**
Charles Stringham .... **Paul Rhys**
Peter Templer .... **Jonathan Cake**
Jean Duport .... **Claire Skinner**
Lucy Fleming
Prof. Sillery .... **Alan Bennett**
Uncle Giles .... **Edward Fox**
Le Bas .... **Oliver Ford Davies**
J. C. Quiggin .... **Adrian Scarborough**
St John Clarke .... **John Gielgud**
Mrs Erdleigh .... **Gillian Barge**
Uncle Alfred .... **Robin Bailey**
Bob Duport .... **Nicholas Jones**
Audrey Maclintick .... **Zoë Wanamaker**
Maclintick .... **Paul Brooke**
Ted Jeavons .... **Michael Williams**
Moreland .... **James Fleet**
Priscilla .... **Caroline Harker**
Lady Isobel Tolland .... **Emma Fielding**
Joanna David
Pamela Flitton .... **Miranda Richardson**
Brightman .... **Eileen Atkins**

Writer **Hugh Whitemore**
Producer **Alvin Rakoff**

● ***The decline of the upper classes seen through the eyes of an observant writer.***

Nicholas Jenkins is the narrator of *A Dance to the Music of Time*, a four-part serial which studies the social changes that deflate the English upper classes over 50 turbulent years. Beginning in the 1920s, when Jenkins is an Eton schoolboy – a middle-class boy among wealthier peers – he introduces us to his contemporaries, most notably resident clown Widmerpool, a man destined to cross Jenkins's path on many an occasion in the decades to follow. The oafish Widmerpool always remains insensitive and foolish, but rises over the course of time to positions of influence, firstly in the army and then as a Labour MP. Other people to figure large in Jenkins's life are his scrounging Uncle Giles, Oxford associates Charles Stringham, Professor Sillery and novelist St John Clarke, and lovers Jean Duport and Isobel Tolland (later his wife). Also seen are mismarried Audrey Maclintock and man-eater Pamela Flitton, who marries Widmerpool. Crammed with star names, and merging comedy, tragedy, success and failure, the ambitious series winds up in the hippyish 1960s. It was dramatized by Hugh Whitemore from the mammoth, 12-volume series of novels by Anthony Powell, written over 24 years up to 1975.

Dancing in the Street: A Rock and Roll History ★★

US (BBC/WGBH) Documentary. BBC 2 1996 (US: PBS 1995)

Producer **Hugh Thomson**

● ***The story of rock and roll in ten parts.***

Costing some £5 million, and taking five years to reach fruition, the acclaimed *Dancing in the Street* turns back the clock to rediscover the roots of rock and roll music. With archive footage and revelatory interviews with some of the biggest artists, the series begins by tackling the mid-1950s, the introduction of black music to a white audience and the arrival of pioneers like Elvis Presley, Chuck Berry and Little Richard. In the final part, rap is showcased. In between, episodes major on the work of such giants as the Beach Boys, Phil Spector, The Beatles, Bob Dylan, Otis Redding, The Rolling Stones, Jimi Hendrix, The Grateful Dead, David Bowie, Bob Marley, The Clash, James Brown, Marvin Gaye and Stevie Wonder, as their particular slice of the rock and roll cake is examined. The series was titled simply *Rock & Roll* in the USA.

Dando, Jill

(1961–99)

Weston-super-Mare-born news and travel presenter whose brutal murder in 1999 shocked the nation. Jill had become a favourite with viewers, thanks to her homely, genuine presentation style. Her career began in local newspapers and BBC local radio before she joined ITV in the south-west and then the BBC in the same region. In 1998 she moved to BREAKFAST

TIME, and her national TV credits went on to include *Safari UK*, SONGS OF PRAISE, HOLIDAY (host from 1993, plus its spin-offs), CRIMEWATCH UK (from 1995) and the *Six O'Clock News*. Her last series, *Antiques Inspectors*, was first aired the day before she died.

Danger Man ★★★

UK (ATV/Pimlico Films) Secret Agent Drama. ITV 1960–2; 1964–6; 1968
DVD: Carlton

John Drake .... **Patrick McGoohan**
Hobbs .... **Peter Madden**

Creator **Ralph Smart**
Executive Producer **Ralph Smart**
Producers **Sidney Cole, Aida Young**

The adventures of a sophisticated, globe-trotting intelligence agent.

John Drake works for NATO, covertly assisting governments wherever security breaches are suspected. His aim is to preserve world peace and he risks life and limb to achieve it. He is highly competent, athletic, cool and sharp-witted. He is a man of few words who intensely dislikes violence but often needs to tackle his enemies head on. He drinks only little, and womanizes to the same modest extent. His missions take him to all parts of the world.

Two years after the initial half-hour episodes ended in 1962, the producers were spurred back into action by the success of the first James Bond movies. Drake was recast in a new, hour-long series, as a member of the British Secret Service, a Special Security Agent working for M19. This time he also had an immediate boss, Hobbs, and, inspired by Bond, his array of electronic gadgetry had increased. This series was screened under the title of *Secret Agent* in the USA. Patrick McGoohan directed some episodes himself.

Danger – Marmalade at Work

See *Educating Marmalade*.

Danger UXB ★★★

UK (Thames/Euston Films) Drama. ITV 1979
DVD: Anchor Bay Entertainment

Lt. Brian Ash .... **Anthony Andrews**
Sgt James .... **Maurice Roëves**
Susan Mount .... **Judy Geeson**
Cpl Mould .... **Norman Chappell**
Sapper Jim Wilkins .... **George Innes**
Norma Baker .... **Deborah Watling**
Mrs Baker .... **Marjie Lawrence**
Cpl Samuel Horrocks .... **Ken Kitson**
Sapper/L/Cpl Jack Salt .... **Kenneth Cranham**
Dr David Gillespie .... **Iain Cuthbertson**
Capt./Major Francis .... **Ken Farrington**
Lt. Ivor Rogers .... **Jeremy Sinden**

Creators **John Hawkesworth, John Whitney**
Producer **John Hawkesworth**
Executive Producer **Johnny Goodman**

High-drama series charting the bravery of a World War II bomb disposal squad.

These stories are drawn from the memoirs of real-life sapper Major A. P. Hartley and follow the progress of a bomb disposal company (UXB standing for unexploded bomb) from the Blitz to D-Day. Hero of the piece is young Lt. Brian Ash, like many of his colleagues learning the ropes as he goes along. Newly commissioned, he joins the 97 Tunnelling Company of the Royal Engineers, only to discover, to his horror, that the regiment is now involved in bomb disposal. The bare minimum of training is provided and the life-expectancy of a sapper is a mere seven weeks. Ash is thrown immediately in at the deep end as commander of 347 Section, taking the position (and the lodgings) of a recently killed officer. Susan Mount, married daughter of explosives boffin Dr Gillespie, provides Ash's romantic interest, although he also needs to fend off the attentions of Norma, the flighty daughter of his landlady, Mrs Baker.

In his work, there is no room for trial and error, and Ash relies heavily on the knowledgeable Sgt James. Each mission places the sappers in impossible positions, a hair's breadth away from oblivion. Some do not make it, dragging emotion into the plots; others, like Brian Ash, survive to dispose of other bombs.

Dangerfield ★★

UK (BBC) Drama. BBC 1 1995–9

Dr Paul Dangerfield .... **Nigel Le Vaillant**
Dr Joanna Stevens .... **Amanda Redman**
DI Ken Jackson .... **George Irving**
Marty Dangerfield .... **Sean Maguire**
Tim Vincent
Al Dangerfield .... **Lisa Faulkner**
Tamzin Malleson
Terri Morgan .... **Katy Murphy**
Dr Nick McKenzie .... **Bill Wallis**
Dr Shaaban Hamada .... **Nadim Sawalha**
Kate Durrani .... **Kim Vithana**
DC Nicky Green .... **Tracy Gillman**
Julia Caxton .... **Catherine Terris**
PC Nigel Spenser .... **Mo Sesay**
PC Georgie Cudworth .... **Eleanor Martin**
Sgt Keith Lardner .... **Roderick Smith**
Liz Moss .... **Jacquetta May**
Dr Annie Robbins .... **Fiona Victory**
DS Helen Diamond .... **Nicola Cowper**
DI Frank Dagley .... **Michael Melia**
Angela Wakefield .... **Marcia Warren**
Dr Jonathan Paige .... **Nigel Havers**
PC Liam Walsh .... **Linford Brown**
Jojo .... **Sam Loggin**
Dr Ross Freeman .... **Adrian Bower**
DI Gillian Cramer .... **Jane Gurnett**
DC Gary Monk .... **Ian Gain**
PC Tom Allen .... **Julian Kay**
Beth Saunders .... **Lynsey Baxter**
Matt Gregory .... **Idris Elba**
Molly Cramer .... **Frances White**

Creator **Don Shaw**
Executive Producer **Chris Parr**
Producers **Adrian Bate, Peter Wolfes, Beverley Dartnall**

A GP solves murder cases in rural Warwickshire.

Doctor Paul Dangerfield has been through an emotional time. Scarred by the car-crash death of his wife, he has been left with the care of their two teenage children, Alison and Marty. He throws himself into his work, charging around in a Land Rover Discovery with a mobile phone pressed to his ear (much to the concern of viewers, who complained so much that a hands-free version was fitted for later series). His day job is that of a country GP, but Dangerfield also helps out the local constabulary as a police surgeon – a mix of roles that ensures he has feet in both medicine and crime camps, but often to the satisfaction of neither. Family troubles add yet another dimension.

Dangerfield's colleagues include fellow doctor Joanna Stevens and solicitor Kate Durrani, both of whom have designs on the handsome hero. DI Ken Jackson is his accomplice on the force. In the second series, a new arrival, forensics expert – and falconry addict – Terri Morgan has been introduced to allow Dangerfield to delve that much more deeply into his criminal investigations. A series later, this is toned down with the departure of Terri. Dangerfield moves out of his country home into a more modest house in Warwick, and his children are now played by different actors. There are new colleagues in the surgery (Dr Annie Robbins) and at the station (DI Frank Dagley and DS Helen Diamond) and, as his tragic past finally catches up with him, Dangerfield seeks help from bereavement counsellor Liz Moss. In the next series, Dr Jonathan Paige, an old friend of Dangerfield's played by Nigel Havers, is introduced in preparation for the exit of star Nigel Le Vaillant. Havers takes over the lead from the next season, the series keeping the same title as Paige is installed in the Dangerfield Health Centre. He is joined on the police side by DI Gillian Cramer, with added romantic interest coming from art critic Beth Saunders. Soon Paige has succumbed to the inevitable and abandoned his general practice in favour of full-time police work.

Dangermouse ★★★

UK (Cosgrove Hall/Thames) Carlton. ITV 1981–7; 1991–2
DVD: Fremantle

Voices:

Dangermouse	**David Jason**
Penfold	**Terry Scott**
Baron Greenback	**Edward Kelsey**
Nero	**David Jason**
Col. K	**David Jason**
Stiletto Mafioso	**Brian Trueman**
Narrator	**David Jason**

Creators **Mike Harding, Brian Trueman**
Writers **Brian Trueman, Angus Allen**
Executive Producer **John Hambley**
Producers **Brian Cosgrove, Mark Hall**

The all-action adventures of a mouse secret agent and his nervous sidekick.

Working for the British Secret Service from a base in a Baker Street postbox, Dangermouse – 'the greatest secret agent in the world' – is the saviour of civilization on more than one occasion. This eye-patch-wearing, white-suited, daring hero is usually called into action by his whiskery boss, Colonel K, to deal with the fiendishly inventive plans of megalomaniac toad Baron Greenback. At the cool-headed Dangermouse's side is the timid, bespectacled Penfold (prone to fretful exclamations like 'Crikey'), while Greenback's chief henchman is the caterpillar Nero, supported by a group of gangster crows headed by Stiletto Mafioso. Another adversary is Count Duckula, a vegetarian vampire (also voiced by David Jason and later spun off into his own series).

Pacily narrated, with parodies on James Bond and other dashing heroes (not to mention plays on adult literature), the *Dangermouse* stories were often episodic (five parts to each tale) and proved a hit with all ages. Co-creator Mike Harding supplied the musical content.

Daniel, Glyn

(1914–86)

British archaeologist who became a prominent TV personality in the 1950s and 1960s, thanks to his appearances as host of ANIMAL, VEGETABLE, MINERAL? and CHRONICLE. He was a don at Cambridge.

Daniel Boone ★★

US (Arcola-Fesspar/Twentieth Century-Fox) Western. ITV 1965–71 (US: NBC 1964–70)

Daniel Boone	**Fess Parker**
Yadkin	**Albert Salmi**
Mingo	**Ed Ames**
Rebecca Boone	**Patricia Blair**
Jemima Boone	**Veronica Cartwright**
Israel Boone	**Darby Hinton**
Cincinnatus	**Dal McKennon**
Jericho Jones	**Robert Logan**
Gideon	**Don Pedro Colley**
Gabe Cooper	**Roosevelt Grier**
Josh Clements	**Jimmy Dean**

Executive Producers **Aaron Rosenberg, Aaron Spelling**
Producers **George Sherman, Barney Rosenzweig, Joseph Silver**

Tales of one of America's great folk heroes.

In this series, created to capitalize on Fess Parker's earlier success as Davy Crockett, the actor plays the lead in much the same way, even to the point of wearing the same racoon-skin cap. It is, of course, something of an exaggeration of the life of the real Daniel Boone, who was one of America's great frontiersmen.

Boone lived during the American Wars of Independence, in the area bordering North Carolina, Kentucky and Tennessee. As played by Parker, he is one of the pioneers: a calm, peaceful, strong hero who carves new paths into the vast unknown continent, surveying and mapping the landscape, hunting wild animals, and befriending or fighting off Indians. Larger than life, he is seen in the title sequence splitting a tree with a single throw of an axe.

With his wife, Rebecca, and children, Jemima and Israel, Boone is based in the town of Boonesborough, where among his associates are the town barkeeper, Cincinnatus, and an Oxford-educated Cherokee Indian named Mingo. Yadkin, a friend from the backwoods, travels with him on his early forays, and another pioneer, Jericho Jones, joins Boone later in the series. Also seen are Josh Clements, a trapper, Gideon, an Indian, and an escaped slave, Gabe Cooper.

The series was first screened in its native USA in 1964 and received sporadic showings around the ITV network.

Daniel Deronda ★★★

UK (BBC) Drama. BBC 1 2003
DVD: BBC Warner (Region 1 only)

Daniel Deronda	**Hugh Dancy**
Mr Henleigh Grandcourt	**Hugh Bonneville**
	Joe Starrs *(young)*

Gwendolen Harleth	**Romola Garai**
Mirah Lapidoth	**Jodhi May**
Sir Hugo Mallinger	**Edward Fox**
Lydia Glasher	**Greta Scacchi**
Lush	**David Bamber**
Mrs Davilow	**Amanda Root**
Herr Klesmer	**Allan Corduner**
Mrs Meyrick	**Celia Imrie**
Hans Meyrick	**Jamie Bamber**
Revd Gascoigne	**Michael Attwell**
Rex Gascoigne	**Jordan Frieda**
Catherine Arrowpoint/ Klesmer	**Anna Steel**
Mr Arrowpoint	**Michael Elwyn**
Mrs Arrowpoint	**Delia Lindsay**
Lord Brackenshaw	**Nicholas Day**
Vandernoodt	**Nikolas Grace**
Kate Meyrick	**Kate Maberly**
Mab Meyrick	**Lisa Jackson**
Phoebe Meyrick	**Serena Martin**
Bertha Davilow	**Gillian Maguire**
Fanny Davilow	**Anna Popplewell**
Isobel Davilow	**Anna Maguire**
Mordecai	**Daniel Evans**
Ezra Cohen	**Simon Schatzberger**
Mrs Cohen	**Diana Brooks**
Adelaide Cohen	**Lesley Stratton**
Rebecca Cohen	**Sarah Marks**
Jacob Cohen	**Daniel Marks**
Lady Mallinger	**Georgie Glen**
Contessa	**Barbara Hershey**

Writer **Andrew Davies**
Producer **Louis Marks**

An impoverished aristocrat chooses the wrong husband.
Gwendolen Harleth is a flirty society girl who hopes to make her fortune through marriage when her private income collapses along with the family business. She chooses, rather unwisely, the pompous and sinister Henleigh Grandcourt, although her real attraction is towards orphan Daniel Deronda. Deronda, equally smitten with Gwendolen, is an altogether different being to Grandcourt, gentle and sincere. He believes his father to be Sir Hugo Mallinger and himself therefore related to Grandcourt. He would be a far better choice for Gwendolen, but she is a woman who knows her own mind and has to suffer the consequences when her overly optimistic marriage to Grandcourt becomes a nightmare and their home at Reylands a prison. Meanwhile, Deronda's quest to find his roots draws him into London's Jewish community when he forms a bond with suicidal singer Mirah Lapidoth, after rescuing her from drowning. Other leading characters include Lush, Grandcourt's oily sidekick; Lydia Glasher, the woman who bore Grandcourt's children but finds herself rejected; the Davilows, Gwendolen's family; Mordecai, Mirah's intellectual brother; and the Contessa, Deronda's real mother, an international singing star who gave up her son to save her career but now, on her deathbed, seeks reconciliation. Andrew Davies adapted George Eliot's final novel (published 1876) in three one-hour episodes. Tom Hooper directs. Daniel Deronda had previously been dramatized in six episodes (BBC 2: 1970), with Robert Hardy as Grandcourt, Martha Henry as Gwendolen and John Nolan as Deronda.

Daniels, Paul

(Newton Edward Daniels; 1938–)

Middlesbrough-born comedian and illusionist, also a host of quiz shows and panel games. Before gaining his own BBC magic show, Daniels took his nightclub act in and out of TV variety programmes, appearing on OPPORTUNITY KNOCKS and WHEELTAPPERS' AND SHUNTERS' SOCIAL CLUB among other series, and briefly presenting his own variety showcase for Granada, *Paul Daniels' Blackpool Bonanza*. In the 1980s he became TV's most popular magician and used his success to branch out into kids' television with *Wizbit* and game shows, hosting *Odd One Out*, EVERY SECOND COUNTS and *Wipeout*, before continuing with stage trickery in *Paul Daniels' Secrets*. Daniels was also seen in a documentary, *Paul Daniels in a Black Hole*. He is married to his glamorous assistant, Debbie McGee, and his son (and former assistant) Martin is now an entertainer in his own right, a one-time presenter of GAME FOR A LAUGH.

Danson, Jane

(Jane Dawson; 1978–)

British actress probably best-known as CORONATION STREET'S Leanne Battersby but already with a number of other high-profile roles on her CV. These include Eileen Critchley in GBH (billed under her real surname of Dawson), Paula James in CHILDREN'S WARD, Chas in the kids' comedy *Out of Tune*, Monica Jones in THE GRAND, Betty Seagrim in TOM JONES, Sam Docherty in A&E and WPC Gemma Osbourne in THE BILL. Guest appearances include a part in DOCTORS.

Danson, Ted

(1947–)

Square-jawed American actor whose huge success as romeo bartender Sam Malone in the sitcom CHEERS won him a run of Hollywood starring parts and the title role in the TV adaptation of GULLIVER'S TRAVELS. Danson's earlier work included a couple of years in the US daytime soap *Somerset*, and minor appearances in MAGNUM, PI and BENSON, with his most recent credits coming in the US series *Ink* and *Becker*, plus a guest slot in CURB YOUR ENTHUSIASM. He is married to actress Mary Steenburgen.

Dark Side of the Sun, The ✱✱

UK (BBC) Drama. BBC 1 1983

Raoul Lavalliere	**Peter Egan**
Don Tierney	**Patrick Mower**
Anne Tierney	**Emily Richard**
David Bascombe	**Christopher Scoular**
Ismini Christoyannis	**Betty Arvaniti**
Von Reitz	**Michael Sheard**

Writer **Michael J. Bird**
Producer **Vere Lorrimer**

Other-wordly terror in a sinister Greek fortress.
Photographer Don Tierney is intrigued by the so-called 'Kastello', a mysterious, heavily guarded castle on the island of Rhodes, owned by a certain Raoul Lavalliere. He sets out to find out more, but never returns. He has been killed. Don's wife, Anne, then visits the castle, unaware of its dark secrets,

but soon has the feeling that the place is haunted. This spooky, six-part tale of the supernatural was penned by 'Greek island' specialist Michael J. Bird, who also wrote THE LOTUS EATERS and WHO PAYS THE FERRYMAN?

Dark Skies ★★

US (Bryce Zabel/Columbia) Science Fiction. Channel 4 1997 (US: NBC 1996–7)

John Loengard .... **Eric Close**
Kimberly Sayers .... **Megan Ward**
Capt. Frank Bach .... **J. T. Walsh**
Phil Albano .... **Conor O'Farrell**
Jim Steele .... **Tim Kelleher**
Dr Charlie Halligan .... **Charley Lang**
Juliet .... **Jeri Lynn Ryan**

Creators **Bryce Zabel, Brent V. Friedman**
Executive Producers **Bryce Zabel, James D. Parriott, Joseph Stern**

● ***History is a lie: aliens have invaded the Earth.***
A conspiracy theorist's idea of heaven, *Dark Skies* is a mix of THE X-FILES and THE INVADERS, set nostalgically in the 1960s. John and Kimberly are two college graduates who find employment in Washington, DC, in 1961. Being close to the Kennedy administration, they uncover an awesome secret, that the Earth has been battling against extraterrestrials for more than a decade. It seems that it all began in Roswell in 1947, when the aliens who landed there were met by President Truman, who sued for peace. Regrettably, his words fell on deaf ears and now the aliens (dubbed the Hive) are everywhere, even assuming the form of prominent Washington officials. Facing up to the threat is a secret government agency known as Majestic-12, headed by naval man Frank Bach with his security chief, Phil Albano. Inevitably, however, it falls to John and Kimberly, and the resistance movement they found called Dark Skies, to fight the Earth's corner as they are pursued across the USA by enemies on both sides. Their travels bring them close to notable (real-life) happenings that are revealed to have had alien connections, including the Kennedy assassination, the Beatles' appearance on *The Ed Sullivan Show* and the Vietnam War. Numerous contemporary figures – senior politicians like Hubert Humphrey, Henry Kissinger, Bobby Kennedy and George Bush – are also depicted. The producers' intention was to continue the story, decade by decade, through to the present day in future seasons, but, despite winning lots of fans, *Dark Skies* did not survive beyond one series. Another alien conspiracy, perhaps?

Darling Buds of May, The ★★★

UK (Yorkshire/Excelsior Group) Comedy Drama. ITV 1991–3
DVD: Granada Ventures

Sidney Charles 'Pop' Larkin .... **David Jason**
Ma Larkin .... **Pam Ferris**
Mariette Larkin/Charlton .... **Catherine Zeta Jones**
Cedric 'Charley' Charlton .... **Philip Franks**
Primrose Larkin .... **Julie Davies**
Abigail Romison
Montgomery Larkin .... **Ian Tucker**
Petunia Larkin .... **Christina Giles**
Zinnia Larkin .... **Katherine Giles**
Victoria Larkin .... **Stephanie Ralph**
Edith Pilchester .... **Rachel Bell**
Ernest Bristow .... **Michael Jayston**
The Brigadier .... **Moray Watson**

Writers **Bob Larbey, Richard Harris, Paul Wheeler**
Executive Producers **Richard Bates, Vernon Lawrence**
Producers **Robert Banks Stewart, Peter Norris, Simon Lewis**

● ***Tales of a happy-go-lucky rural Kent family in the 1950s.***
Based on H. E. Bates's five Larkin books (which began with a novel entitled *The Darling Buds of May*), this hugely popular, wholesome series engendered a 'feel good' factor in viewers. Here was a family that chortled its way through life, enjoying the simple pleasures of the countryside and having little time for the stresses of the real world. Head of the clan is boisterous Pop Larkin, a man of independent means who runs a 22-acre smallholding and earns a bob or two wherever he can. Larkin by name and larking by nature, Pop is seldom flustered and usually has an answer for every problem. His irrepressible common-law wife (they have skipped the formality of marriage), known to all as Ma, is a roly-poly, laugh-a-minute character, always at work in the kitchen preparing gigantic feasts for breakfast, lunch and dinner (which Pop liberally douses with ketchup) and snacks for moments in between. Their six children begin with their beautiful eldest daughter, Mariette, and are generally named after assorted flowers. In the first episode, Cedric Charlton, a naïve, young, poetry-loving Inland Revenue official, calls to investigate Pop's affairs. Befuddled by Pop's anti-tax logic, 'Charley' stays for lunch, falls in love with Mariette and never leaves. They marry and Mariette gives birth to a son, John Blenheim. 'Perfick', as Pop would have put it.

Working as executive producer on the series was Richard Bates, son of the Larkins' creator, who had originally sold the rights of the novels to an American company, but bought them back when their adaptation was slow to get off the ground. He took the idea to Yorkshire Television and gave the company one of its greatest hits. Bob Larbey wrote the first series, with other writers employed for later episodes. A less subtle American film version of *Darling Buds*, entitled *The Mating Game*, starring Debbie Reynolds and Tony Randall, was released in 1959.

Darren, James

(James Ercolani; 1936–)

American leading man/director whose TV high spots have included THE TIME TUNNEL (lost scientist Dr Tony Newman) and T. J. HOOKER (Officer Jim Corrigan). He has also appeared as a guest star in FANTASY ISLAND, VEGA$, *Melrose Place* and STAR TREK: DEEP SPACE NINE, among many other series. Small-screen success came after movie fame in the 1950s, when he was cast as a teenage heart-throb figure. He even branched out into singing, hitting the UK charts in the early 1960s with 'Goodbye Cruel World' and three other discs.

Dastardly and Muttley in Their Flying Machines

See *Wacky Races*.

Davenport, Jack

(1973–)

English actor, the son of Maria Aitken and Nigel Davenport. His TV break came with the series THIS LIFE, in which he played Miles. This led to the lead roles of Robert Bradley in CATHERINE COOKSON'S *The Moth*, DS Michael Colefield in *Ultraviolet*, Harry Fairfield in *The Wyvern Mystery* and Steve in the comedy COUPLING. Other parts have come in *Dickens* (Charley Dickens), *The Real Jane Austen*, *Eroica* (Prince Lobkowitz) and AGATHA CHRISTIE'S MARPLE. Davenport also narrated the documentary series *The Showbiz Set*, among many voice-overs. His brother and sister, Hugo and Laura, are also both actors. Davenport is married to actress Michelle Gomez.

Davenport, Nigel

(1928–)

Cambridgeshire-born actor, much seen on television. He is particularly associated today with tetchy businessman roles, thanks to appearances as Sir Edward Frere in HOWARDS' WAY and James Brant in TRAINER. Among his career high spots have been the parts of Councillor Robert Carne in SOUTH RIDING, Arthur Conan Doyle in THE EDWARDIANS, Jack Hoxton in the sitcom DON'T ROCK THE BOAT, King George III in PRINCE REGENT, the South African police chief in *The Biko Inquest*, Blackstock in *The Treasure Seekers*, and Sir Charles Pelham in LONGITUDE. He also starred in OIL STRIKE NORTH (Jim Fraser) and has had credits in such series as TRAVELLING MAN, *Madame Bovary*, BIRD OF PREY and MIDSOMER MURDERS. His second wife was actress Maria Aitken and he is the father of actors Jack and Laura Davenport.

David, Joanna

(1947–)

Lancaster-born actress, wife of Edward Fox and mother of Emilia Fox. Joanna David has appeared on British television since the early 1970s and is noted for her roles in period dramas and literary adaptations. These include Alice Munro in LAST OF THE MOHICANS, Sonya in WAR AND PEACE, Hannah in TENDER IS THE NIGHT, Ann Artingstall in FAME IS THE SPUR, Mary Eleanor Pearcey in LADYKILLERS, Jeanne Marie in LILLIE and Mrs de Winter in REBECCA. Joanna also played Mrs Gardiner in PRIDE AND PREJUDICE, Sophie Deane in *The Mill on the Floss*, Lady Isobel Tolland in A DANCE TO THE MUSIC OF TIME, Caroline Harris in *The Dark Room*, Mrs Heron in THE FORSYTE SAGA, Mary Duggan in *The Glass*, Lady Pomona Longestaffe in THE WAY WE LIVE NOW, Mrs Stanbury in HE KNEW HE WAS RIGHT, Averil in *Belonging*, Elizabeth Burnham in BRIDES IN THE BATH and Mrs Badger in BLEAK HOUSE. Among her numerous guest appearances are roles in WITHIN THESE WALLS, THE AGATHA CHRISTIE HOUR, MAIGRET, INSPECTOR MORSE, RUMPOLE OF THE BAILEY, THE DARLING BUDS OF MAY, THE MEMOIRS OF SHERLOCK HOLMES, BRAMWELL, A TOUCH OF FROST, MIDSOMER MURDERS, DALZIEL AND PASCOE, HEARTBEAT, FOYLE'S WAR, MONARCH OF THE GLEN and ROSEMARY AND THYME.

David Copperfield ★★★

UK (BBC) Drama. BBC 1 1999
DVD: BBC

David Copperfield	**Ciarán McMenamin**
	Daniel Radcliffe *(young)*
Clara	**Emilia Fox**
Peggotty	**Pauline Quirke**
Barkis	**Michael Elphick**
Mr Murdstone	**Trevor Eve**
Miss Murdstone	**Zoë Wanamaker**
Creakle	**Ian McKellen**
Mr Micawber	**Bob Hoskins**
Mrs Micawber	**Imelda Staunton**
Betsey Trotwood	**Maggie Smith**
Mr Dick	**Ian McNeice**
Uriah Heep	**Nicholas Lyndhurst**
Mrs Heep	**Thelma Barlow**
Mrs Crupp	**Dawn French**
Dan Peggotty	**Alun Armstrong**
Spenlow	**James Grout**
Steerforth	**Oliver Milburn**
	Harry Lloyd *(young)*
Mrs Steerforth	**Cherie Lunghi**
Pawnbroker	**Paul Whitehouse**

Writer **Adrian Hodges**
Producer **Kate Harwood**

A young orphan defies cruelty, disadvantage and social barriers in Victorian England.

Studded with stars and as rich and colourful as Dickens's original work, this two-part version of *David Copperfield* graced British TV screens over Christmas 1999. Possibly the least-known names on the cast list were the two actors who played the title role: Ciarán McMenamin and young Daniel Radcliffe (the latter now firmly established as the movie world's Harry Potter). Highlights included Nicholas Lyndhurst's greasy Uriah Heep, Ian McKellen's whispering schoolmaster Creakle, Maggie Smith's fussing Betsey Trotwood, Trevor Eve's sinister Mr Murdstone, Pauline Quirke's homely Peggotty, Dawn French's spoonerizing Mrs Crupp and Bob Hoskins's typically buoyant Mr Micawber. The drama, shot largely in Wisbech, Cambridgeshire, sprang from an idea that was based around John Sullivan adapting the novel and David Jason playing Micawber, alongside his ONLY FOOLS AND HORSES co-star, Lyndhurst. When the project fell through, Sullivan took his ideas – and Jason – to ITV and an off-shoot series called simply MICAWBER.

Previous television adaptations of *David Copperfield* have been in 1956 (BBC: with Robert Hardy as the hero), 1966 (BBC 1: Christopher Guard, supported by Ian McKellen), 1974 (BBC 1: David Yelland with Arthur Lowe as Micawber, Patricia Routledge as Mrs Micawber and Martin Jarvis as Heep), and 1986 (BBC 1: Colin Hurley with Simon Callow as Micawber).

Davidson, Jim

OBE (1953–)

Chirpy, Cockney comedian, fond of dirty jokes but somewhat toned down for television. He came to light on the talent show NEW FACES and has subsequently appeared in assorted variety specials, the gag show *What's On Next?*, his own sitcoms UP THE ELEPHANT AND ROUND THE CASTLE and HOME JAMES (Jim London in both), and his own game shows BIG BREAK and JIM DAVIDSON'S GENERATION GAME. He also fronted *Jim Davidson's Commercial Breakdown*. His third wife was presenter Alison Holloway.

Davies, Alan

(1966–)

Mop-haired comedian and actor, most familiar as sleuth JONATHAN CREEK, but also starring as time-share salesman Simon Treat in the series *One for the Road*, as duplicitous Russel Boyd in *A Many Splintered Thing*, as confused gay man Bob Gossage in BOB AND ROSE and as barrister Henry Farmer in *The Brief*.

He was a team captain in the advert quiz *The Best Show in the World . . . Probably* and is a regular loser on QI, and has also featured in *Urban Trauma* and *Stand Up with Alan Davies* – profiles and recordings of his stage work. Davies is married to his *Jonathan Creek* co-star, Julia Sawalha.

Davies, Andrew
(1936–)

Former university lecturer and one of British TV's foremost screenwriters. Cardiff-born Davies began his scripting career with one-off adaptations and plays like *The Signalman* (starring Denholm Elliott) in 1976 and *Fearless Frank* (starring Leonard Rossiter) in 1978, moving on to greater success with *The Legend of King Arthur*, adaptations of R. F. Delderfield's TO SERVE THEM ALL MY DAYS and DIANA, and the kids' comedy EDUCATING MARMALADE and its sequel, *Danger – Marmalade At Work*. He then delivered the surreal A VERY PECULIAR PRACTICE, set in the quirky world of Lowlands University, scripted MOTHER LOVE and reworked Michael Dobbs's HOUSE OF CARDS, TO PLAY THE KING, and THE FINAL CUT with great success. The most recent acclaim has come from his scripts for MIDDLEMARCH, PRIDE AND PREJUDICE, THE FORTUNES AND MISFORTUNES OF MOLL FLANDERS, JANE AUSTEN'S EMMA, VANITY FAIR, TAKE A GIRL LIKE YOU, A RATHER ENGLISH MARRIAGE, OTHELLO, THE WAY WE LIVE NOW, TIPPING THE VELVET, DANIEL DERONDA, DOCTOR ZHIVAGO, BOUDICA, HE KNEW HE WAS RIGHT, *Falling* and BLEAK HOUSE. In quite a different vein, he co-wrote the flat-share sitcom GAME ON and the fantasy drama *Wilderness*, with Bernadette Davis, and the kids' comedy *The Boot Street Band*, with Steve Attridge. Over the years, there have also been other notable pieces, such as *The Old Devils* and *Anglo-Saxon Attitudes*, as well as numerous one-off dramas like *Harnessing Peacocks, Getting Hurt* (part of the *Obsessions* season) and *Screen One/Two* productions like *Bavarian Night, Ball-Trap on the Côte Sauvage* and *A Very Polish Practice* (picking up where the earlier series left off).

Davies, Barry
MBE (1940–)

Sports commentator, with the BBC since 1969, and previously with ITV. Davies has commentated on most events, from soccer, tennis and ice skating to various Olympic sports. He also hosted QUIZ BALL.

Davies, Diana
(1936–)

Manchester-born actress, first coming to light as Freda Ashton's friend, Doris, in A FAMILY AT WAR but familiar to soap fans as Norma Ford in CORONATION STREET in the 1970s and, more recently, Caroline Bates in EMMERDALE. She has also enjoyed many other smaller roles over the years, in series like *Send in the Girls* (Sheila), JOHNNY JARVIS (Mrs Lipton), THE GRAND, WHERE THE HEART IS and THE VICE.

Davies, Dickie
(1933–)

Sports presenter, initially with Southern Television but host of WORLD OF SPORT from 1968 (billed originally as Richard Davies). Davies – noted for a trademark 'badger' streak in his hair – has also hosted other sporting events, including boxing, snooker and the Olympic Games, as well as the quiz show *Sportsmasters* (which he produced for HTV). He suffered a stroke in 1995 but recuperated well and returned to presentation with Sky Sports.

Davies, Freddie
(1937–)

British comedian known for his 'Parrotface' routine and his spluttering pronunciation. He found his way into television via OPPORTUNITY KNOCKS and was a variety show regular in the 1960s and 1970s, becoming particularly popular with younger viewers. He went on to star in his own kids' sitcom, *The Small World of Samuel Tweet* (as Tweet), but, more recently, Davies has been seen in straight roles in series like ALL QUIET ON THE PRESTON FRONT (Heron Man), CATHERINE COOKSON, BAND OF GOLD, HEARTBEAT and HARBOUR LIGHTS (George Blade), as well as making guest appearances in MY FAMILY BORN AND BRED and SENSITIVE SKIN.

Davies, Gavyn
OBE (1950–)

Gavyn Davies, Chief Economist at Goldman Sachs, was appointed new Chairman of the BBC in 2002, replacing Sir Christopher Bland. Davies had previously been Deputy Chairman. He resigned his post in 2004 after criticism of the BBC in the Hutton Report into the death of Dr David Kelly.

Davies, John Howard
(1939–)

Former child actor, star of such film classics as *Oliver Twist* and *Tom Brown's Schooldays*, who, after joining the BBC as a production assistant in the mid-1960s, became a producer/director for the BBC and later Thames, working largely on comedy shows. Among his contributions have been STEPTOE AND SON, ALL GAS AND GAITERS, THE VERY MERRY WIDOW, *The World of Beachcomber*, MONTY PYTHON'S FLYING CIRCUS, *Misleading Cases*, THE GOODIES, *As Good Cooks Go, No Strings*, WHOOPS BAGHDAD!, THE FALL AND RISE OF REGINALD PERRIN, THE GOOD LIFE, FAWLTY TOWERS, THE OTHER ONE, ANDY CAPP, *We'll Think of Something*, EXECUTIVE STRESS, ALL IN GOOD FAITH, AFTER HENRY, NO JOB FOR A LADY, HOPE IT RAINS, MR BEAN, LAW AND DISORDER and THE VICAR OF DIBLEY. In 1978 he was appointed the BBC's Head of Comedy, moving in 1982 to Head of Light Entertainment and later holding the same position at Thames.

Davies, Richard
(1926–)

Overtly Welsh character and comic actor. Although remembered by many as the couldn't-give-a-damn sports teacher, Pricey, in PLEASE SIR!, Davies has popped up in all manner of programmes, especially those needing a strong Welsh presence, including the drama THE CITADEL (Mr Watkins), the sitcom *Rule Britannia* (Taffy Evans) and the short-lived HTV soap *Taff Acre* (Max Johnson). For a while in the mid-1970s, as Idris Hopkins (married to Kathy Staff's Vera), he ran the corner shop in CORONATION STREET. Davies has also been seen in AND THE BEAT GOES ON (Father Hopkins), the comedies OH NO! IT'S SELWYN FROGGITT (Clive), BOTTLE BOYS (Stan Evans) and WHOOPS APOCALYPSE (Chancellor of the

Exchequer), plus the children's series ROBERT'S ROBOTS (Gimble) and *The Boot Street Band* (caretaker Dai Cramp). Guest appearances include roles in YES, MINISTER, FRANK STUBBS PROMOTES, ONE FOOT IN THE GRAVE and 2 POINT 4 CHILDREN.

Davies, Rupert

(1916–76)

With the strike of a match and a puff on his pipe at the start of each episode, Rupert Davies instantly became the French detective MAIGRET, a character he played for three years from 1960 and which he remained heavily associated with for the rest of his life. As Maigret, Davies also introduced the BBC's DETECTIVE anthology series, although it wasn't his first TV detective role; that was as Inspector Duff in the late-1950s production of THE NEW ADVENTURES OF CHARLIE CHAN. Earlier, Davies had taken the part of Vincent Broadhead in QUATERMASS II and played Seamus in SAILOR OF FORTUNE (alongside Lorne Greene), after moving into TV and films from the stage and radio. He also made guest appearances in programmes like THE INVISIBLE MAN and THE ADVENTURES OF AGGIE. In 1968 he provided the voice for Professor McClaine in JOE 90, and a few years later was Cerdig in ARTHUR OF THE BRITONS and Count Rostov in WAR AND PEACE, but his subsequent work was thin on the ground, as the millstone of *Maigret* hung ever heavier.

Davies, Russell T.

(1963–)

Swansea-born, award-winning scriptwriter, a former director and producer whose early work included scripts for *Chucklevision* and his own children's science-fiction series *Dark Season* and *Century Falls*. He later wrote for CHILDREN'S WARD (which he also produced) and contributed to *Revelations*, THE HOUSE OF WINDSOR, *Springhill*, THE GRAND, TOUCHING EVIL and LINDA GREEN. However, it is through more of his own creations that he has received most acclaim, notably BOB AND ROSE, QUEER AS FOLK, *The Second Coming* and MINE ALL MINE, as well as the new dramatization of the life of CASANOVA and the hugely successful revival of DOCTOR WHO, for which he was also executive producer.

Davies, Windsor

(1930–)

London-born but predominantly Welsh comic actor, the bawling Sgt Major Williams in IT AIN'T HALF HOT MUM. Davies's other major TV role has been as Oliver Smallbridge in the antique trade sitcom NEVER THE TWAIN, although his TV appearances have been plentiful, regular and have also included the parts of Mr Welsh in *Smith*, George Vance in a 1985 sitcom called *The New Statesman*, Lloyd George in MOSLEY, Pugh in *Mortimer's Law*, General Tuffo in VANITY FAIR and Rottcodd in GORMENGHAST. Recent guest roles take in series like SUNBURN, CASUALTY and MY FAMILY. Where his face hasn't appeared, his voice has been heard, as in the Gerry Anderson puppet series TERRAHAWKS (speaking the lines of Sgt Major Zero). 'Whispering Grass', his recording with *It Ain't Half Hot Mum* co-star Don Estelle, topped the charts in 1975.

Davis, Julia

(1966–)

Bath-born actress and writer, noted particularly for her roles both in front of the camera and behind the scenes in HUMAN REMAINS and NIGHTY NIGHT (in which she played the monstrous Jill Tyrell). Other credits include BRASS EYE, BIG TRAIN, *Jam*, DR TERRIBLE'S HOUSE OF HORRIBLE, *The Alan Clark Diaries* (Jenny Easterbook) and voices for *I am Not an Animal*.

Davison, Peter

(Peter Moffet; 1951–)

London-born actor, Tristan Farnon in ALL CREATURES GREAT AND SMALL, Dr Stephen Daker in A VERY PECULIAR PRACTICE, the 1930s detective Albert CAMPION, TV's fifth DOCTOR WHO and, since 2003, DC 'Dangerous' Davies in THE LAST DETECTIVE. Added to this notable list of starring roles are a handful of sitcoms, of varying success – SINK OR SWIM (Brian Webber), HOLDING THE FORT (Russell Milburn), FIDDLERS THREE (Ralph) and AIN'T MISBEHAVIN' (Clive Quigley) – plus dramas like *Love for Lydia* (Tom Holland), *Harnessing Peacocks* (Jim), *The Stalker's Apprentice* (DI Maurice Birt), *Cuts* (Henry Babbacombe), WUTHERING HEIGHTS (Joseph Lockwood), AT HOME WITH THE BRAITHWAITES (David Braithwaite), THE MRS BRADLEY MYSTERIES (Inspector Christmas), *Too Good to Be True* (Robert Lewis) and *Distant Shores* (Bill Shore). Guest appearances in programmes such as THE TOMORROW PEOPLE, *Kinsey*, MISS MARPLE, THE HITCH-HIKER'S GUIDE TO THE GALAXY and JONATHAN CREEK, and theme-music credits for the sitcom MIXED BLESSINGS and toddlers' series BUTTON MOON, add yet more to his portfolio. He was once married to actress Sandra Dickinson.

Davro, Bobby

(Robert Nankeville; 1959–)

Middlesex-born comedian and impressionist, coming to the fore via *Copy Cats* and much seen on variety and game shows, from *Go For It* to *Punchlines*. He has hosted several series of his own, including *Bobby Davro's on the Box, Bobby Davro's TV Weekly, Bobby Davro – Public Enemy Number 1, Davro's Sketch Pad, Davro* and *Bobby Davro: Rock with Laughter*. He also took charge of the *Run the Risk* game segment of LIVE AND KICKING and presented a revival of WINNER TAKES ALL for Challenge TV. More recently, he made a guest appearance in FOOTBALLERS' WIVES *Extra Time*. His stage name was taken from the name of his dad's shop – Davro's, which was itself derived from the names of Bobby and his brother (David and Robert).

Davy Crockett ★★

US (Disney) Adventure. ITV 1956 (US: ABC 1954–5)
DVD: Buena Vista

Davy Crockett .... **Fess Parker**
Georgie Russell .... **Buddy Ebsen**

Executive Producer **Walt Disney**
Producer **Bill Walsh**

● ***Tales of the great American frontiersman.***

'Born on a mountain top in Tennessee', according to the enormously successful theme song, Davy Crockett in reality was a one-time militia scout and a US Congressman who died in the legendary siege of the Alamo. For this action series, Crockett is portrayed as an all-American hero, helping to tame the Wild West and thwarting the advances of the Mexicans with the aid of his trusty rifle, Old Betsy, and his loyal sidekick, Georgie Russell. His racoon-skin cap became his trademark and was adopted by addicted children on both sides of the Atlantic as the merchandising spin-offs took hold. The series originally aired in the USA as part of the anthology series *Disneyland*.

Fess Parker took on a similar part in the 1960s, when he again donned a furry hat for the role of another American hero, Daniel Boone. Buddy Ebsen, meanwhile, went on to play a different sort of backwoodsman, Jed Clampett, in THE BEVERLY HILLBILLIES.

Dawn, Elizabeth

MBE (Sylvia Butterfield; 1939–)

CORONATION STREET's formidable Vera Duckworth, who arrived in Weatherfield in 1976 as one of the girls in Mike Baldwin's sweat-shop. Leeds-born Elizabeth Dawn's working life had begun in a real factory, before progressing via a stint in Woolworth's to singing in nightclubs. *Street* stardom eventually came after TV commercials, waitressing on WHEELTAPPERS' AND SHUNTERS' SOCIAL CLUB, playing a warden in CROWN COURT, making guest appearances with Larry Grayson, and taking minor roles in series like Z CARS and COUNTRY MATTERS and notable one-off plays like *Kisses at Fifty*, *Leeds United* and *The Greenhill Pals*. Other credits include *One Foot in the Past*.

Daws, Robert

(1959–)

English actor often seen in lighter roles, such as Peter James in *There Comes a Time . . .*, Roger Dervish in OUTSIDE EDGE, Tuppy Glossop in JEEVES AND WOOSTER, Sam in ROGER ROGER and Oscar in the single comedy *The Mystery of Men*. Daws was also Simon Eastman in CASUALTY, Piggy Garstone in THE HOUSE OF ELIOTT and Rod in *Office Gossip*. Other credits have included ROBIN OF SHERWOOD (Giscard), *The Missing Postman* (Peter Robson), TAKE A GIRL LIKE YOU (Dick Thompson), SWORD OF HONOUR (Major Hound) and HEARTBEAT/THE ROYAL (Dr Gordon Ormerod), plus guest appearances in the likes of PIE IN THE SKY and MIDSOMER MURDERS. His first wife was actress Amanda Waring and he is now married to his *Royal* co-star Amy Robbins.

Dawson, Les

(1933–93)

Manchester-born comedian, a former jazz pianist who used his keyboard skills to great effect in his useless-pianist routine. Otherwise, Dawson was noted for his dry, pessimistic delivery and his rich catalogue of mother-in-law and wife jokes. Discovered on OPPORTUNITY KNOCKS, he quickly moved on to star in his own YTV series, *Sez Les*, in which he developed characters like the seedy Cosmo Smallpiece, and perfected a gossipy housewife double act (Cissie and Ada) with Roy Barraclough. Taking over BLANKETY BLANK from Terry Wogan, he maintained the show's high ratings and, still with the BBC, he also hosted *The Les Dawson Show*. His career came full circle in 1990, when he became compere of *Opportunity Knocks*, succeeding Bob Monkhouse. One of his most unusual roles was that of a 100-year-old woman in the straight drama *Nona*, but his last appearance came in the comedy-drama DEMOB, in which he took the role of comic Morton Stanley.

Dawson's Creek ★★

US (Columbia TriStar) Drama. Channel 4 1998–2003; five 2004 (US: WB 1998–2003)
DVD: Sony

Dawson Leery	**James Van Der Beek**
Josephine 'Joey' Potter	**Katie Holmes**
Jennifer Lindley	**Michelle Williams**
Pacey Witter	**Joshua Jackson**
Mr Mitchell Leery	**John Wesley Shipp**
Mrs Gail Leery	**Mary-Margaret Humes**
Miss Tamara Jacobs	**Leann Hunley**
Francis/Evelyn 'Grams' Ryan	**Mary Beth Peil**
Bessie Potter	**Nina Repeta**
Abby Morgan	**Monica Keena**
Andie McPhee	**Meredith Monroe**
Jack McPhee	**Kerr Smith**
Deputy Doug Witter	**Dylan Neal**
Gretchen Witter	**Sasha Alexander**
Audrey Lidell	**Busy Philipps**

Creator **Kevin Williamson**
Executive Producers **Kevin Williamson, Paul Stupin, Charles Rosin, Greg Prange, Tom Kapinos, Alex Gansa, Deborah Joy LeVine**

● ***The pains of adolescent life in a quiet Massachusetts town.***

Set in the picturesque coastal settlement of Capeside, *Dawson's Creek* is a story of boys becoming men and girls becoming women during the traumatic high school years. Nominal star is Dawson Leery, an intense, 15-year-old would-be film-maker obsessed with Steven Spielberg and the only child of immature, squabbling parents (his mum is a TV newsreader, his dad runs a restaurant). Dawson's best friend is the tomboyish girl next door, Joey Potter, daughter of a jailbird dad and a mother who has died of cancer. She has been raised by her sister, Bessie. Third buddy is Pacey Witter, the lusty son of a police family who has a relationship with his English teacher, Miss Jacobs, and whose eventual affair with Joey leads to friction between Joey and Dawson. Then there is Jen, a blonde, promiscuous New York escapee who, like all the principals, learns maturity at Capeside High as the series develops. New in town later are Andie McPhee, Pacey's one-time girlfriend who falls into drug dependency, and her brother, Jack, who struggles with his homosexuality. Another arrival is the troublesome Abby Morgan, who drowns after falling off a bridge. Later episodes see the gang studying and working in Boston. When the series finally ran its course, it concluded with a reunion episode that moved the story on five years and looked at how life had panned out for the kids from Capeside.

Dawson's Creek was created by film-maker Kevin Williamson (*Scream* and *I Know What You Did Last Summer*). Outdoor action was shot in Wilmington, North Carolina, with the University of North Carolina doubling up as Capeside High.

Day, Sir Robin
(1923–2000)

The doyen of British political interviewers, London-born Robin Day was a barrister who joined the BBC as a radio producer in 1955. With the start of ITV, he moved to ITN to become one of its first two newscasters (along with Chris Chataway), also presenting the company's ROVING REPORT and *Tell the People*. In 1959 he left in order to stand as Liberal parliamentary candidate for Hereford, but, failing to win the seat, he returned to television as a reporter/presenter on PANORAMA, staying with the programme until 1972. In later years he hosted *Newsday*, all the BBC's main political events (as well as Radio 4's *The World at One*) and initiated QUESTION TIME in 1979. One famous interview for NATIONWIDE during the Falklands conflict was rudely interrupted when his interviewee, Defence Secretary John Nott, stormed out after being dubbed a 'here today, gone tomorrow politician'. Retiring in 1989, Day later took his brusque, breathy, yet dogged interviewing style – and his famous spotted bow-tie – to satellite and regional television.

Day of the Triffids, The ✶✶

UK (BBC/RCTV/ABC) Science Fiction. BBC 1 1981
DVD: BBC

Bill Masen .... **John Duttine**
Jo .... **Emma Relph**
Jack Coker .... **Maurice Colbourne**
Dr Soames .... **Jonathan Newth**
Susan .... **Lorna Charles**
Emily Dean *(young)*
John .... **Stephen Yardley**
Michael Beadley .... **David Swift**

Writer **Douglas Livingstone**
Producer **David Maloney**

● ***Man-eating giant plants blind the human race and begin to take over.***

Adapted from John Wyndham's classic 1951 novel of the same title, this six-part series tells of the monstrous triffids, alien plants that employ their three-pronged roots to move around our planet. The plants are initially assumed to be harmless, indeed useful by some parties, but as farmer Bill Masen discovers, they have a malevolent identity. With most of the population blinded by a brilliant cosmic display of alien power, it is left to Masen – who, by chance, has retained his sight – and his new friend, Jo, to lead the defence of the Earth against the carnivorous green menace. Ken Hannam directed.

Day Today, The ✶✶✶

UK (Talkback/BBC) Comedy. BBC 2 1994
DVD: BBC

Christopher Morris, Steve Coogan, Rebecca Front, Doon MacKichan, Patrick Marber, David Schneider

Creators/Writers **Christopher Morris, Armando Iannucci**
Executive Producer **Peter Fincham**
Producer **Armando Iannucci**

● ***Award-winning spoof news and current affairs programme.***

A sort of MONTY PYTHON meets NEWSNIGHT, *The Day Today* was the television manifestation of Radio 4's *On the Hour*. It takes the form of a TV news magazine, anchored by Christopher Morris, an argumentative, disdainful, Jeremy Paxman-like interviewer and reader of sensational but obscure headlines. Doon MacKichan presents business news in the guise of Collaterlie Sisters and Steve Coogan plays cringingly awful sports correspondent Alan Partridge (later given his own chat show, KNOWING ME, KNOWING YOU ... WITH ALAN PARTRIDGE, and sitcom, I'M ALAN PARTRIDGE). Typically quirky reports from the USA are provided by CBN's Barbara Wintergreen; Sylvester Stuart is the body-less weatherman with innovative graphics; Rosy May offers 'Enviromation'; Peter O'Hanraha-hanrahan deals with economic issues; Valerie Sinatra warns of traffic chaos from her mile-high travel tower, and Speak Your Brains is the weekly *vox pop* spot. The voice of Michael Alexander St John is also heard.

Days of Hope ✶✶✶

UK (BBC) Drama. BBC 1 1975

Ben Matthews .... **Paul Copley**
Sarah Hargreaves .... **Pamela Brighton**
Philip Hargreaves .... **Nikolas Simmonds**

Writer **Jim Allen**
Producer **Tony Garnett**

● ***Young idealism during the turbulent days of World War I and the General Strike.***

Much acclaimed but highly controversial, *Days of Hope*, set in the years 1916 to 1926, is the four-part story of three young northern Christians: farmer Ben Matthews, his sister, Sarah, and her husband, Philip. As well as being pacifists they are also socialists, working towards the election of a Labour Government, their lives touched by the dramatic events of the time and the poverty and injustice which surround them. Applauded for its courageous stance and undeniably impressive production, the mini-series was viciously slated by Conservative-minded critics for its subversive tone, historical inaccuracy and socialist sentiments. Ken Loach directed all four parts: *1916: Joining Up, 1921: Black Friday, 1924: The First Labour Government* and *1926: The General Strike*.

DBS
(Direct Broadcasting by Satellites)

Direct Broadcasting by Satellites was first conceived in the 1970s as a means of relaying TV signals to homes without the need for terrestrial transmitters or masts. At an international conference in 1977, Britain was allocated five channels, and the BBC was charged with setting up the first two, with a proposed air date of 1986. Unfortunately, numerous difficulties (not least lack of Government financial support) resulted in the concept, as it stood, being scrapped. The IBA took over the idea instead, eventually issuing a licence to a consortium known as British Satellite Broadcasting (BSB). BSB, in turn, ran into problems of its own. Although its Marco Polo satellite was soon in position, delays resulted from technical difficulties (particularly with the revolutionary smaller reception dish, the 'squarial'). BSB eventually went on air in spring 1990, but Rupert Murdoch's company, Sky, had stolen a march and was already broadcasting from the Luxembourg-owned Astra satellite, enjoying over a million viewers. In November of the same year, with both companies operating at a loss, BSB was forced to merge with Sky, creating British Sky Broadcasting (BSkyB).

De La Tour, Frances

(1944–)

British Shakespearean actress finding a comedy niche as the plain Jane, Miss Jones, in RISING DAMP. Among her other credits have been the anthologies CRIME OF PASSION and *Cottage To Let, Flickers*, TOM JONES (Aunt Western), the *Screen Two* drama *Genghis Cohn* (Dr Helga Feuchtwanger), Emma Porlock in *Cold Lazarus* (see KARAOKE) and the sitcoms A KIND OF LIVING (Carol Beasley), EVERY SILVER LINING (Shirley Silver) and DOWNWARDLY MOBILE (Rosemary). Guest appearances include roles in STAY LUCKY, HEARTBEAT, BORN AND BRED, AGATHA CHRISTIE'S POIROT, WAKING THE DEAD, *Sensitive Skin* and AGATHA CHRISTIE'S MARPLE.

Dead Head ★★

UK (BBC) Drama. BBC 2 1986

Eddie Cass .... **Denis Lawson**
Dana Cass .... **Lindsay Duncan**
Eldridge .... **George Baker**
Hugo Silver .... **Simon Callow**
Caractacus .... **Norman Beaton**
DI Malcolm .... **Don Henderson**
Jill .... **Susannah Bunyan**
Stoker .... **Larrington Walker**
Clyde .... **Winston Crooke**
Sandra .... **Tacy Kneale**
Clive .... **James Warwick**
Angela .... **Leonie Mellinger**
The Man .... **Ernest Clark**

Writer **Howard Brenton**
Producer **Robin Midgley**

● ***A petty thief goes on the run from the secret services.***
Life turns upside down for Eddie Cass when he accepts an unusual courier job. There are no drugs involved, he is assured, and the money's decent (£100 up front, £400 on delivery), but when he is given a fancy hat box to deliver to an address in London's West End, he can't help but be curious. Stupidly he looks inside, only to discover a human head, which he promptly ditches in the Thames. Soon the small-time crook finds himself on the run around Britain, evading questions from the CID, especially about his former wife, Dana, who, it seems, knows something about the whole grisly event. Among the people Cass bumps into along the way are Hugo Silver, a secret service agent now being pursued by the Establishment, and yuppie Sandra, who ties Eddie to a bed and rapes him. Directed by Rob Walker, this surreal four-part thriller from BBC Pebble Mill has echoes of a 1940s B-movie in style – although more graphically violent in places – as it weaves a tale of deceit, corrupt coppers, a menacing State, crimes in high places and their impact on the lowest levels of UK society. Music is by Richard Hartley.

Dead Man Weds ★★

UK (Red) Situation Comedy. ITV 1 2005

Gordon Garden .... **Dave Spikey**
Lewis Donat .... **Johnny Vegas**
Carol Sykes .... **Janice Connolly**
Gerry Stringer .... **Alan Rothwell**
Duane Guffog .... **Iain McKee**
Sandy Ball .... **Keith Barron**
Cliff the Clutch .... **Angus Barnett**
Paul King .... **Tim Healy**
Mad Kenny .... **Richard Bremner**
Myrtle Turtle .... **Amy Shaw**
Harold Turtle .... **Mike Roberts**
Chuck Newman .... **Michael Brandon**
Red .... **Tony Pitts**
Donna Havercroft .... **Nicola Stephenson**

Writer **Dave Spikey**
Producer **Sarah Smith**

● ***A new editor looks for a scoop for his rundown local newspaper.***
'It's Good News Week', declares the Hedgehoppers Anonymous 1965 hit used as the theme song for this quirky comedy. Not that there ever seems to be good news for the *Fogburrow Advertiser and News* – the local rag in a dozy northern town – to report. It keeps missing the major stories and resorting to offbeat front page headlines like 'Drunk Man Falls Over', 'Some Trains May Be Late' and the one used for the title of the programme. Now its editor, Jack Johnson, has just been blown up and his desk is taken over by former Fleet Street man Gordon Garden, whose dalliances with drugs and drink have precipitated his slide down the journalistic ladder. Somewhat aggrieved by the new appointment is idle chief reporter Lewis Donat, who fancies the editor's chair for himself, and completing the staff line-up are Carol Sykes, an ad sales lady who doesn't seem in the slightest bothered by the obscene phone calls she keeps getting, young reporter Duane Guffog, a would-be actor, and technologically challenged old duffer Gerry Stringer. When the team are not in the office, they can usually be found in The Douglas Bader pub, where Gordon is billeted and where regulars include Mad Kenny, local cabbie Cliff the Clutch and tourist guide Donna. Here landlord Paul King drums up trade through inventive games like 'Who's in Next?' and 'Flap the Kipper'. Gordon, however, wants to shake up the organization and smells scandal in the dubious activities of cow food manufacturer GeneUS, who may just be responsible for turning the local canal water blue. Unfortunately, the *Advertiser*'s proprietor, Sandy Ball, a friend of GeneUS director Chuck Newman, is not so keen for Gordon to intrude. Just six episodes of this refreshing comedy were produced, filmed in Bradwell, Derbyshire.

Dead Ringers ★★

UK (BBC) Comedy. BBC 2 2003–
DVD: BBC

Jon Culshaw, Jan Ravens, Mark Perry, Phil Cornwell, Kevin Connelly

Creator **Bill Dare**
Producers **Bill Dare, Gareth Edwards, Victoria Payne, Caroline Norris**

● ***Sharp, satirical showcase for top impressionists.***
Pioneered with a pilot programme in February 2002 on BBC 1, *Dead Ringers* made its series bow in November that year on BBC 2. Like numerous other comedies, it came to television from radio, having attracted a large and loyal following on Radio 4. Fleshing out their mimickry for TV is the same crew

of talented impressionists that starred on radio, converting radio gags into their televisual equivalents (spoof phone calls into hidden camera stunts, etc.) and adding new material appropriate for the second medium, much penned by Tom Jamieson and Nev Fountain. For topicality, material is written right up to the last moment and recordings made close to transmission. Specialisms include Jon Culshaw as Tony Blair and George Bush; Jan Ravens as Anne Robinson and Nigella Lawson; Mark Perry as Graham Norton and David Dickinson; Phil Cornwell as Michael Caine and Jack Nicholson; and Kevin Connelly as Andrew Neil and Sven-Goran Erickson. Christmas specials were screened in 2003 and 2004, as well as a US election special in October 2004.

Deadline Midnight ✶

UK (ATV) Drama. ITV 1960–1

Joe Dunn .... **Peter Vaughan**
Neville Crane .... **Jeremy Young**
Matt Stewart .... **Bruce Beeby**
Tom Douglas .... **James Culliford**
Peggy Simpson .... **Mary Law**
Mike Grieves .... **Glyn Houston**
Mark Byron .... **Olaf Pooley**

Producers **Hugh Rennie, Rex Firkin**

● ***Action and adventure with the reporters of a daily paper.***

Focusing on the investigations of the journalists of the *Daily Globe, Deadline Midnight* took its inspiration from the intrepid reporters of Fleet Street. Former *Daily Express* editor Arthur Christiansen acted as programme consultant to ensure authenticity, although many Fleet Street hacks were not impressed with proceedings. Peter Vaughan starred as the *Globe*'s news editor, Joe Dunn (replaced later by Glyn Houston as Mike Grieves), and the ever-changing cast was filled with relatively unknown actors in a quest for a realistic atmosphere.

Deal or No Deal ✶✶

UK (Endemol West) Game Show. Channel 4 2005–

Presenter **Noel Edmonds**

Executive Producer **Richard Hague**
Producer **Glenn Hugill**

● ***Contestants gamble on the contents of sealed boxes to win big money.***

There's £250,000 up for grabs, and no questions to answer in this game show except one: 'Deal or no deal?' Noel Edmonds comforts and cajoles 22 studio contestants divided into East and West Wings. Each contestant has selected a numbered box. Each box has been sealed by an independent adjudicator and contains a sum of money known only to that adjudicator (the sums climb in 22 stages from 1p to £250,000). One contestant is chosen at random to play each day, the others returning for a chance to reach the spotlight on future occasions. The contestant then embarks on a process of eliminating boxes to try to win as high a prize as possible. Five boxes can be selected in round one. They are opened and the sum of money they contain is withdrawn from the prize board that displays all 22 cash sums. The host then takes a telephone call from 'The Banker', who makes the contestant a financial offer to quit, based on the value of prizes left on the board. The question is posed for the first time: 'Deal or no deal?' Assuming the contestant opts for no deal, the game continues with three more boxes selected and their prize values eliminated from the board. The Banker rings again with another offer, which may be higher or lower, or even the same as the first offer, depending on what is still winnable on the board. So the game progresses, with several more elimination rounds and several more offers from the Banker, until the contestant either accepts the deal, or the last two boxes remain, one of which is the contestant's own box. These are duly opened to see whether the contestant has been right not to deal all along.

This daytime series, devised in Australia, brought Noel Edmonds back into the TV limelight after an absence of five years and quickly gathered a cult following.

Dean, Letitia

(1967–)

English actress whose early TV work included the parts of Lucinda in GRANGE HILL and Dawn in BROOKSIDE. However, it was as Sharon in EASTENDERS that she made her mark, following this up by playing Barbara, one of Charles II's 39 mistresses, in the musical drama *England, My England*, and then with the parts of Chris Cross in THE HELLO GIRLS and Charlotte in *Lucy Sullivan is Getting Married*. Other credits have included THE BILL, CASUALTY and DROP THE DEAD DONKEY.

Dear John ✶✶✶

UK (BBC) Situation Comedy. BBC 1 1986–7

John Lacey .... **Ralph Bates**
Kate .... **Belinda Lang**
Kirk St Moritz .... **Peter Blake**
Ralph Dring .... **Peter Denyer**
Louise Williams .... **Rachel Bell**
Mrs Arnott .... **Jean Challis**
Mrs Lemenski .... **Irène Prador**
Sylvia Watkins .... **Lucinda Curtis**
Ricky Fortune .... **Kevin Lloyd**
Wendy .... **Wendy Allnutt**

Creator/Writer **John Sullivan**
Producer **Ray Butt**

● ***A wimpy divorcé finds solace in an encounter group.***

Language teacher John Lacey is in for a shock on returning home from work one day. He finds a note from his wife, Wendy, revealing that she has left him for his best friend, taking Toby, their eight-year-old son, with her. In the subsequent divorce proceedings, John loses his house and is forced to move into a crummy bedsit. Among his new neighbours is the elderly Mrs Lemenski, a foreign immigrant who, because of some early misunderstandings, is sure John is completely crazy.

His social life in tatters, John spots an advert in a newspaper for The 1–2–1 Club, a divorced persons' encounter group, and decides to give it a go. The class is run by officious beauty consultant Louise Williams, whose chief interest is in her members' sexual problems and fetishes. Joining John in the group is Ralph Dring, one of life's great bores and the proud driver of a motorcycle combination. His Polish wife married him to avoid extradition and left him during their wedding reception. Also seen is Kate, an attractive but uptight girl whose three marriages have broken down because of her frigidity. This also seems to prevent her warming to John.

While other minor characters hover in the background (including the virtually silent Mrs Arnott, Sylvia with the silly laugh and faded rock star Ricky Fortune – of Ricky Fortune and the Fortunates), the other main character is Kirk St Moritz, a John Travolta lookalike, who has not even been married, let alone divorced, and attends simply to pick up 'frustrated chicks'. This spinner of exotic yarns, who claims to be a spy, turns out to be a dowdy mummy's boy whose real name is Eric Morris.

Writer John Sullivan sold the idea to an American company and spent some time as a consultant and writer on their version of the series. This aired in the UK as *Dear John: USA* and starred Judd Hirsch.

Dear Ladies ✶✶

UK (BBC) Situation Comedy. BBC 2 1983–4

Dr Evadne Hinge .... **George Logan**
Dame Hilda Bracket .... **Patrick Fyffe**

Writers **George Logan, Patrick Fyffe, Gyles Brandreth**
Producers **Mike Stephens, Peter Ridsdale Scott, Mike Smith**

● ***Two old ladies are the heartbeat of a tranquil English village.***

Fictitious Stackton Tressel in Suffolk is the setting for this wander behind the scenes of English rural life. Our guides are the musically minded Dr Evadne Hinge and Dame Hilda Bracket, who throw themselves headlong into the day-to-day affairs of their small community. The village is quintessentially sleepy but these game old biddies ensure there's always a spark about the place through their involvement with events and institutions like fêtes, gala lunches, arts festivals, amateur dramatics, the local cubs pack, the meals-on-wheels service and Stackton Cottage Hospital. Their overt aim is to maintain high standards in public life, but there's an inherent streak of vulgarity and anarchy in their own deportment.

The George Logan and Patrick Fyffe drag act had previously enjoyed TV success in the stand-up series *Hinge and Bracket* (BBC 2 1978–81). In January 1984 they temporarily left Stackton Tressel to lecture students at the Royal Northern College of Music in a one-off special entitled DEAR LADIES' MASTERCLASS.

Dear Mother . . . Love Albert ✶✶

UK (Thames/Yorkshire) Situation Comedy. ITV 1969–72

Albert Courtnay .... **Rodney Bewes**
Mr A. C. Strain .... **Garfield Morgan**
Vivian McKewan .... **Sheila White**
Mrs McKewan .... **Geraldine Newman**
Frances Ross .... **Mary Land**
Leslie Willis .... **Luan Peters**
Doreen Bissel .... **Liz Gebhardt**
Cheryl Hall *(Albert)*
Mrs Ada Bissel .... **Amelia Bayntun**

Creators/Writers/Producers **Rodney Bewes, Derrick Goodwin**

● ***A young man's letters home to his mother exaggerate his success in the big city.***

When naïve North Country lad Albert Courtnay moves to the bright lights of London he has high hopes. Unfortunately, life turns out to be rather more mundane than anticipated, not that he tells his mother this in his weekly letters home. Albert works for Mr A. C. Strain as a sales and marketing consultant in the Tomlinsons toffee factory, where he's not terribly good at his job but is very well liked. He lives with a Scottish landlady, Mrs McKewan, whose daughter, Vivian, fancies her chances with Albert. Later Albert moves into a flat with two girls, Frances and Leslie, to the disapproval of his new fiancée, Doreen Bissel, and his prospective mother-in-law. After three seasons, the title was shortened to *Albert*. The catchy theme song was written by Mike Hugg, with words and vocals by star Rodney Bewes.

Death of a Princess ✶

UK (ATV) Drama Documentary. ITV 1980

Princess Misha'al .... **Suzanne Abou Taleb**
Ryder .... **Paul Freeman**

Writer **Antony Thomas**
Producers **Antony Thomas, Martin McKeand**

● ***Highly controversial simulated documentary about the execution of an Islamic princess.***

Death of a Princess, a two-hour special, sparked off one of the mightiest rows ever caused by a television programme. It reconstructed the investigations made by writer/co-producer Antony Thomas into the case of a 19-year-old Arab princess who had wavered from strict adherence to the Islamic religion and committed adultery. The price she paid for this capital crime was public execution. No country was named in evidence, but Saudi Arabia was so offended with the programme and its open criticism of Islamic culture that it cut diplomatic ties with the United Kingdom. Arguments raged over the accuracy of the information, although Thomas claimed to have travelled widely and talked to various witnesses in the course of his research. Normality was restored only once Foreign Secretary Lord Carrington had openly condemned the film.

Death of an Expert Witness

See *P. D. James*.

Deayton, Angus

(1956–)

British writer, comedian and comic actor, an Oxford graduate and one-time collaborator with Rowan Atkinson. However, Deayton is best known as Patrick, Victor Meldrew's frustrated neighbour in ONE FOOT IN THE GRAVE, and as the long-time chairman of the topical satire show HAVE I GOT NEWS FOR YOU, until his controversial personal life led to his sacking in 2002. His other major credits have included KYTV (Mike Channel), MR BEAN, CHELMSFORD 123, *Alexei Sayle's Stuff*, TISWAS, *Doctor at the Top (see* DOCTOR IN THE HOUSE*)*, *Bad Company* (Paul Foot), the *Screen One* presentation *Lord of Misrule* (MI5 man), NIGHTY NIGHT (Don), *Marigold* (Kenneth More) and *Heartless* (Harry Holland), plus quirky documentary and feature programmes such as *In Search of Happiness*, *The Temptation Game*, *The Lying Game*, *A History of Alternative Comedy*, *Before They were Famous* and *Help Your Self with Angus Deayton*. Deayton also hosted the game show *Bognor or Bust* and the celebrity reality show HELL'S KITCHEN. He has also written for Rory Bremner and *Aspel & Co.*, and is a popular choice for commercial voice-overs.

Dee, Jack
(1962–)

Kent-born comedian and actor, known for his dry, unsmiling delivery. He was launched on television in *The Jack Dee Show* for Channel 4, following this with a sketch show, *Jack and Jeremy's Real Lives*, which he shared with Jeremy Hardy, before moving over to ITV with the cabaret show, *Jack Dee's Saturday Night*, and then *Jack Dee's Sunday Service*. In 2000 he presented an eight-part feature on Canada's *Just for Laughs* festival in *Jack Dee's Full Mountie* for the BBC and then fronted the topical *Jack Dee's Happy Hour*. He was team captain for the first series of IT'S ONLY TV BUT I LIKE IT (developed, like his other shows, by his own production company, Open Mike) and has also presented TOP OF THE POPS. As an actor, Dee has appeared in *Screen One's Gobble*, SILENT WITNESS, AMBASSADOR, DALZIEL AND PASCOE, JONATHAN CREEK, *The Deputy* (Stephen Sharples) and *Tunnel of Love* (Roy), as well as playing Doug Digby in the pilot of THE GRIMLEYS. He was winner of the first *Celebrity* BIG BROTHER contest in 2001 and at Christmas 2002 featured in the survival documentary *Jack Dee Sent to Siberia*. He returned to stand-up for the BBC with *Jack Dee Live at the Apollo*.

Dee, Simon
(Nicholas Henty Dodd; 1935–)

Controversial DJ and talk show presenter, at one time all the rage but quickly fading out of view. His heyday came with the trendy teatime pop and chat show *Dee Time*, in 1967, the year in which he also compered MISS WORLD. Later, he switched to ITV to host *The Simon Dee Show*. Previously, he had been the first voice on the pirate radio station Radio Caroline when it opened in 1964 and remained on the high seas until the following year. He then joined the BBC, presenting programmes like *Housewives' Choice* and *Midday Spin*, as well as contributing to Radio Luxembourg. Dee returned to television with a one-off revival of *Dee Time* for Channel 4 at Christmas 2003.

Deeley, Cat
(Catherine Deeley; 1976–)

Midlands-born presenter of children's and light entertainment series, most notably SM:TV, CD:UK, *The Record of the Year*, THE BRIT AWARDS, FAME ACADEMY and STARS IN THEIR EYES, plus MTV music programmes.

DEF II ★★

UK (BBC) Youth Magazine. BBC 2 1988–94

Executive Producer **Janet Street-Porter**

● ***Early-evening youth programming strand.***

The *DEF II* slot (roughly between 6 and 7.30 p.m. on Mondays and Wednesdays) was aimed at the 16- to 25-year-old market and emulated Channel 4's *Network 7* (also once in the care of Janet Street-Porter). Among the programmes airing under the *DEF II* umbrella were the *Rough Guide* series with Magenta De Vine and Sankha Guha, *Rapido* with Antoine de Caunes, the US comedies *Wayne's World* and THE FRESH PRINCE OF BEL-AIR, *Dance Energy* (later *D Energy*) with Normski, *Job Bank* (career profiles), *Liquid Television* (animations), the football magazine *Standing Room Only*, *Cyberzone* (a virtual-reality game show), *Behind the Beat* (a black music show), *Reportage* (news and views from around the world) and *Open to Question*, in which youngsters interviewed celebrities.

Defenders, The ★★★

US (Plautus) Legal Drama. BBC 1962–7 (US: CBS 1961–5)

Lawrence Preston	**E. G. Marshall**
Kenneth Preston	**Robert Reed**
Helen Donaldson	**Polly Rowles**
Joan Miller	**Joan Hackett**

Creator **Reginald Rose**
Producers **Herbert Brodkin, Robert Markell**

● ***Father and son lawyers defend clients accused of socially 'difficult' crimes.***

In this very well-respected courtroom series, two generations of a legally minded family are brought together in the conscientious partnership of Preston and Preston. Lawrence Preston is the father and the old hand, educating his rookie son, Kenneth, who is fresh from law school and full of worthy ideas. Together they undertake a variety of cases, often dealing with subjects that prick the public's conscience, such as civil rights, abortion and mercy killing; but, unusually for TV advocates, they don't always win. In early episodes the pair are supported by secretary Helen Donaldson, and Kenneth's girlfriend, Joan Miller, a social worker, is also seen.

Ralph Bellamy and William Shatner were the stars of the pilot episode, which was shown in 1957, four years before *The Defenders* became a series in the USA. In that pilot, the pair acted on behalf of a client played by Steve McQueen. Many famous guest stars embellished the show over the years, from the likes of Gene Hackman and Jon Voight to Robert Redford and Dustin Hoffman.

Demob ★★

UK (Yorkshire) Comedy Drama. ITV 1993
DVD: Bfs Entertainment (Region 1 only)

Ian Deasey	**Griff Rhys Jones**
Dick Dobson	**Martin Clunes**
Janet Deasey	**Amanda Redman**
Hedda	**Samantha Janus**
Rudy Lorimer	**James Faulkner**
Dr Pollock	**Harry Burton**
Edith	**Liz Fraser**
Marshall Gould	**George Melly**
Alan Deasey	**Luke Marcel**

Writers **Dean Lemmon, Andrew Montgomery**
Producer **Adrian Bate**

● ***Two NAAFI entertainers struggle to make the grade in post-war showbiz.***

Captain Dick Dobson and Lance Corporal Ian Deasey may be from different classes but one thing unites them: the love of the stage. During World War II, they entertain the troops with their comedy double act but things are not quite so funny when they are demobbed, return home and discover that times are hard. Nevertheless they can't resist the lure of the limelight. The act is reunited and they find work in seedy nightclubs like The Blue Parrot (where glamorous Hedda becomes a close ally) and variety theatres while balancing day jobs, home life and other, less wholesome, demands on their time, such as from conman Rudy Lorimer. A break on a ventriloquist's show for BBC radio ends in disaster and Ian's marriage to Janet heads for the rocks, as the comedy gives way to moments of pathos in recognition of the dashed hopes and family troubles of many former army men. This six-part series was particularly notable for its third episode, which included the last TV appearance of Les Dawson, playing comic Morton Stanley ('The King of Variety').

Demon Headmaster, The ✶✶

UK (BBC) Children's Science Fiction. BBC 1 1996–8

Demon Headmaster	**Terrence Hardiman**
Mrs Hunter	**Tessa Peake-Jones**
Eddy Hair	**Danny John-Jules**
Dinah Glass/Hunter	**Frances Amey**
Lloyd Hunter	**Gunnar Cauthery**
Harvey Hunter	**Thomas Szekeres**
Miss Wilberforce	**Roli Okorodudu**
Ian	**Anthony Cumber**
Mandy	**Rachael Goodyer**
Ingrid	**Kristy Bruce**
Rose Carter	**Katey Crawford Kastin**
Simon James	**James Richard**
Prof. Tim Dexter	**Richard Hope**
Michael Dexter	**Jay Barrymore**

Writer **Helen Cresswell**
Producer **Roger Singleton-Turner**

● ***A group of pupils thwart their headteacher's megalomania.***
Everyone at some time has had a teacher they hate, but for Lloyd and Harvey Hunter and their friends the situation is much more serious. They have discovered that their school is run by the Demon Headmaster. Until his plans for world domination come to fruition, the green-eyed evil head takes care to hypnotize his pupils, so that they can't report back to their parents at night. However, the Hunter brothers are prepared to fight back, forming SPLAT, the Society for the Protection of our Lives Against Them. They are aided by their intelligent foster sister, Dinah, who proves to be a real thorn in the principal's side. In series two, the Demon Headmaster, now installed at the BRC research centre, tries to take his revenge on Dinah (formally adopted into the Hunter family), through the use of genetic engineering. In the third series, although SPLAT believes the headmaster's days are over, he returns as a clone to make their lives a misery once more, working from a base at the University of Wessex. The series was adapted from novels by Gillian Cross. A one-off pantomime special, *The Demon Headmaster Takes Over TV* (written by kids' presenter Chris Jarvis), was shown on Christmas Day 1997.

Dempsey and Makepeace ✶✶

UK (LWT/Golden Eagle) Police Drama. ITV 1985–6
DVD: Network

Lt. James Dempsey	**Michael Brandon**
DS Harriet ('Harry') Makepeace	**Glynis Barber**
Chief Supt. Gordon Spikings	**Ray Smith**
DS Charles ('Chas') Jarvis	**Tony Osoba**

Creator **Tony Wharmby**
Executive Producer **Nick Elliott**
Producers **Tony Wharmby, Ranald Graham**

● ***A streetwise Yank and a plummy British aristocrat form an unlikely police partnership.***
James Dempsey is a New York cop from Manhattan's Ninth Precinct who, having uncovered corruption in his own force and shot dead his own partner, has been transferred to Britain for safety. Here he is teamed with Lady Harriet Makepeace, a stunning blonde Cambridge science graduate with distant claims to the throne who, for some reason, has decided to pursue a police career. The two form an uneasy partnership, working for SI 10, a covert division of Scotland Yard.

Dempsey is the typical brash American, a Vietnam veteran, hasty in his actions and fast on the trigger. Makepeace is a crack shot, a former archery champion, who, rather more subtly, achieves results by using her contacts in high places. In charge of the pair is vociferous Liverpudlian Gordon Spikings, with Chas, another detective, occasionally joining them in their investigations.

In all, *Dempsey and Makepeace* is a rather violent series, offering car chases aplenty and dragging in all sorts of criminals, from terrorists to drug-pushers. Stars Michael Brandon and Glynis Barber took their partnership on to a new footing when they were later married in real life.

Dench, Dame Judi

CH (Judith Dench; 1934–)

Award-winning, York-born actress, in straight drama and classical roles as well as comedy. While the 1980s and 1990s saw her star in two cosy domestic sitcoms – as Laura in A FINE ROMANCE (opposite her real-life husband, Michael Williams) and Jean in AS TIME GOES BY – Dench's TV career began in the mid-1960s, with appearances in Z CARS, MOGUL and assorted Shakespearean adaptations. Other notable performances have come in HILDA LESSWAYS (Hilda), *Love in a Cold Climate* (again with Williams), *Saigon, Year of the Cat, Langrishe, Go Down* (Imogen Langrishe), GOING GENTLY (Sister Scarli), *The Torch* (Aba), *Behaving Badly, Absolute Hell* (part of BBC 2's *Performance* season), LAST OF THE BLONDE BOMBSHELLS (Elizabeth) and John Hopkins's *Theatre 625* quartet, *Talking to a Stranger*. She also read stories for JACKANORY and has provided voices for the animation *Angelina Ballerina*. She was made a Companion of Honour in the Queen's Birthday Honours in 2005. Actress Finty Williams is her daughter.

Denis:

ARMAND (1897–1971) and MICHAELA (1914–2003)

A cross between David Attenborough and Fanny and Johnny Cradock, Armand and Michaela Denis were UK TV's first wildlife specialists. Through his interest in photography, Armand, a Belgian-born but Oxford-educated chemist, branched out into filming wildlife and met London-born Michaela in New York and again while filming in South America. They married and also teamed up professionally to bring the great outdoors to BBC viewers. Their distinctive presentation – he with his Belgian accent and she with her blonde, pin-up looks – brought them instant fame. Their series *Filming Wild Animals* and *Filming in Africa* in 1954 and 1955 were followed by *Michaela and Armand Denis* for ITV, before they returned to the BBC in 1957 to present *On Safari*, a series that ran for many years. On leaving television they retired to their home in Kenya, where Armand died in 1971. After a tragically short second marriage to Sir William O'Brien Lindsay, the last English Chief

Justice of Sudan (he died weeks after the ceremony), Michaela turned to spritual healing, setting up a centre in Nairobi.

Denison, Michael

CBE (1915–98)

Distinguished, Doncaster-born, Harrow- and Oxford-educated actor, first seen on TV in the 1930s in plays like Eugene O'Neill's *Marco Millions*. For eight years Denison was the suave Richard Boyd in ITV's BOYD QC, Britain's answer to PERRY MASON, although his later television appearances were less prominent, but included CROWN COURT, PRIVATE SCHULTZ, THE AGATHA CHRISTIE HOUR, RUMPOLE OF THE BAILEY, HOWARDS' WAY (Admiral Redfern) and one-off plays, including Joe Orton's *Funeral Games*. He also played Captain Percival in the 1980s secret service dramas BLOOD MONEY, SKORPION and COLD WARRIOR. Denison was married to actress Dulcie Gray.

Dennis, Les

(Leslie Heseltine; 1954–)

Liverpudlian light comedian, impressionist and actor, for a few years stage and screen partner of the late Dustin Gee. His TV break came when winning NEW FACES, from which he progressed to WHO DO YOU DO?, THE COMEDIANS, *Russ Abbot's Madhouse, Go for It*, assorted variety shows and his own vehicle (originally with Gee), *The Laughter Show*. In 1987 he took over as host of the quiz game FAMILY FORTUNES, and he has also hosted the talent show *Give Your Mate a Break*. Dennis has been increasingly seen in acting cameos, too, and played Jeff Evans in BROOKSIDE. He also appeared in *Jo Brand's Hot Potatoes, The Second Quest* (Johnny), CROSSROADS (Dr Ferguson), CASUALTY, *Hotel Babylon* and EXTRAS (parodying himself), and took part in *Celebrity* BIG BROTHER. His second wife was actress Amanda Holden.

Department S ✶✶

UK (Scoton/ITC) Detective Drama. ITV 1969–70
DVD: Granada Ventures

Jason King	**Peter Wyngarde**
Stewart Sullivan	**Joel Fabiani**
Annabelle Hurst	**Rosemary Nicols**
Sir Curtis Seretse	**Dennis Alaba Peters**

Creators **Monty Berman, Dennis Spooner**
Producer **Monty Berman**

A trio of special agents solve impossible cases for a division of Interpol.

Department S is the Paris-based secret wing of Interpol, the international police force, undertaking assignments that baffle regular detectives and government agents alike. The team's figurehead is the rakish Jason King, a thriller novelist who grapples with the facts of each case by putting himself in the shoes of his detective creation, Mark Caine. He is joined by the equally perceptive American action man, Stewart Sullivan (who loves to shoot down King's extravagant theories), and Annabelle Hurst, an attractive computer buff with an eye for detail. Their head of section is Oxbridge-educated African Sir Curtis Seretse.

The trio's cases range from investigating what has happened to an airliner strangely lost for six days to discovering how a tailor's dummy manages to crash a car. The inquiries call more for lateral thinking than for pure detection, but the unorthodox team always achieve results, despite striving to outdo each other along the way. The undoubted star, the flamboyant, womanizing King – wearer of magnificently psychedelic shirts and kipper ties – was soon given his own spin-off series, JASON KING.

Deputy Dawg ✶✶

US (Terrytoons) Cartoon. BBC 1 1963–4 (US: Syndicated 1960)

Voices **Dayton Allen**

Creator **Larz Bourne**
Executive Producer **Bill Weiss**

The misadventures of an inept and accident-prone lawkeeper.

Hounded by pesky varmints like short-sighted Vince (Vincent Van Gopher), dicky-bowed racoon Ty Coon, Muskie the muskrat and Pig Newton, Deputy Dawg strives in vain to maintain law and order in sleepy Mississippi. With frustrated yells of 'Just a cotton-picking moment' and 'Dagnabit Muskie', the drawling canine in the wide black hat tries desperately to defend a hen-house from would-be invaders. He answers to the show's only human, The Sheriff, for the succession of disasters and mishaps that befall him and from which he is rescued only by a stroke of good luck. Dayton Allen voiced Deputy Dawg, plus most of his adversaries. Ralph Bakshi, one of the show's directors, later enjoyed success with the controversial adult cartoon film *Fritz the Cat*.

Desmond's ✶✶✶

UK (Humphrey Barclay) Situation Comedy. Channel 4 1989–90; 1992–4

Desmond Ambrose	**Norman Beaton**
Shirley Ambrose	**Carmen Munroe**
Matthew	**Gyearbuor Asante**
Porkpie Grant	**Ram John Holder**
Lee	**Robbie Gee**
Tony	**Dominic Keating**
Sean Ambrose	**Justin Pickett**
Michael Ambrose	**Geff Francis**
Gloria Ambrose	**Kim Walker**
Louise	**Lisa Geoghan**
Beverley	**Joan Ann Maynard**
Mandy	**Matilda Thorpe**

Creator **Trix Worrell**
Producers **Humphrey Barclay, Charlie Hanson, Paulette Randall**

A Peckham barber's shop is the hub of the local West Indian community.

Grumpy Desmond Ambrose is the proprietor of Desmond's barber's shop in south-east London. He runs it with his wife, Shirley, with whom he has three children, Michael, Sean and Gloria. He also has many friends and acquaintances who use the shop as a meeting place. There they chew the fat, enjoy Shirley's refreshments, indulge in various social events and occasionally have their hair cut as well. Mixing various generations of black Londoners, *Desmond's* draws its humour from London street life and West Indian generation-gap conflicts, contrasting the ways and attitudes of the older, immigrant members with those of the youngsters, who were born and bred locally. Creator Trix Worrell wrote the majority of the episodes, and then all the scripts for the spin-off, *Porkpie* (1995–6), focusing on lollipop man Porkpie Grant, one of Desmond's friends from the old country, who went on to win the Lottery.

Desperate Housewives ✳✳✳

US (Touchstone) Comedy Drama. Channel 4 2005–
(US: ABC 2004–)
DVD: Buena Vista Home Entertainment

Susan Mayer .... **Teri Hatcher**
Bree Van De Kamp .... **Marcia Cross**
Gabrielle Solis .... **Eva Longoria**
Edie Britt .... **Nicollete Sheridan**
Lynette Scavo .... **Felicity Huffman**
Mary Alice Young .... **Brenda Strong**
Mike Delfino .... **James Denton**
Rex Van De Kamp .... **Steven Culp**
Carlos Solis .... **Ricardo Antonio Chavira**
Paul Young .... **Mark Moses**
Tom Scavo .... **Doug Savant**
Juanita Solis .... **Lupe Ontiveros**
Zach Young .... **Cody Kasch**
Julie Mayer .... **Andrea Bowen**
Martha Huber .... **Christine Estabrook**
Dr Goldfine .... **Sam Lloyd**
Felicia Tilman .... **Harriet Sansom Harris**
Andrew Van De Kamp .... **Shawn Pyfrom**
Danielle Van De Kamp .... **Joy Lauren**
John Rowland .... **Jesse Metcalfe**
Maisy Gibbons .... **Sharon Lawrence**
George Williams .... **Roger Bart**
Preston Scavo .... **Brent Kinsman**
Porter Scavo .... **Shane Kinsman**
Parker Scavo .... **Zane Huett**
Betty Applewhite .... **Alfre Woodard**
Matthew Applewhite .... **Mehcad Brooks**

Creator/Writer **Marc Cherry**
Executive Producers **Marc Cherry, Michael Edelstein, Tom Spezialy**

Five suburban family women spice up their lives.

It doesn't take much to infuriate conservative America, and *Desperate Housewives* did just that. This story of five women, who seek new thrills in their unfulfilled lives, undermined the concept of family life, according to right-wing Americans. While their homes in Wisteria Lane are plush, these girls are a frustrated bunch, tottering from one neurosis or obsession to another, hiding behind cloaks of duplicity and urgently boarding up cupboards full of skeletons. Their salvation lies in a heady mix of extra-marital affairs, booze and drugs, and their story is told by a former neighbour, Mary Alice Young, who at the outset commits suicide and thereafter provides a celestial commentary on her erstwhile buddies. So who are these screwed-up ladies? First there's divorcée Susan Mayer, illustrator of children's books and mother of plain-speaking teenage daughter Julie. Susan has plumber Mike Delfino in her sights, but he has a different agenda, it seems. Then there's annoyingly perfect domestic goddess Bree Van De Kamp, whose life is thrown into turmoil when husband Rex asks for a divorce. Gabrielle Solis is a former model, a trophy wife for flauntily rich husband Carlos who gets her kicks from preying on John, her hunky teenage gardener; Edie Britt is a serial divorcée always looking for a new male diversion; and Lynette Scavo is a one-time high-flying businesswoman who was forced to give up her career in favour of bringing up four brats and now resents every moment of it. Mrs Huber is the interfering old bat who lives down the street. For series two, there are new arrivals on Wisteria Lane. Betty Applewhite and her teenage son, Matthew, seem the perfect neighbours, but, naturally, they have a secret that begs to be revealed.

The overall impression is of a PEYTON PLACE on acid, with a dark comedic streak running through it like a stick of rock. However, clearly not all America was outraged by the ladies' antics as *Desperate Housewives* was one of the biggest new shows in the States in 2004. Guest stars like Ryan O'Neal, Richard Rowntree and Lesley Ann Warren helped boost the audience figures.

Destination Downing Street ✳

UK (TV Scripts/Associated-Rediffusion) Spy Drama. ITV 1957

Mike Anson .... **John Stone**
Jacques .... **Donald Morley**
Sylva .... **Sylva Langova**
Colin .... **Graham Crowden**
Phoebe .... **Diana Lambert**

Creator/Writer **St John Curzon**
Producer **Eric Maschwitz**

The adventures of a select team of secret agents, responsible directly to the Prime Minister.

When Britain is threatened by ruthless foreign saboteurs, there is only one person to call: secret agent Major Mike Anson. Anson, a former commando, is ably assisted in his counter-espionage by two former resistance fighters, Frenchman Jacques and Sylva, a Czech girl. Colin, a university-don-cum-explosives-expert, and Phoebe, a WAAF officer who works as the team's organizer, complete the line-up.

The quintet are initially brought together when a trio of disasters all strike uncannily at one time – an atomic scientist goes missing, a ship sinks and an African village disappears – the work, it seems, of an evil spy syndicate called ARKAB. Other similarly bizarre encounters follow. Such is the prestige of this hand-picked squad that they are answerable only to the PM himself (hence the title).

Detective ✳✳

UK (BBC) Detective Drama Anthology. BBC 1 1964; 1968–9

Chief Insp. Maigret .... **Rupert Davies**

Producers **David Goddard, Verity Lambert, Jordan Lawrence**

Anthology series giving air time to some of literature's finest detectives, as well as some novel TV sleuths.

This intriguing collection of detective tales appears just as interesting in retrospect as when it first reached the screens, for among the selected sleuths were characters who would soon gain their own series, albeit sometimes in the hands of other actors. *Detective* introduced viewers to Margery Allingham's Albert Campion, for instance, played here by Brian Smith, as well as G. K. Chesterton's Father Brown, as portrayed by Mervyn Johns, and Ngaio Marsh's Inspector Roderick Alleyn, depicted by Geoffrey Keen and Michael Allinson. Cluff and Sherlock Holmes, with their stars Leslie Sands and Douglas Wilmer, were launched into full series virtually straight away.

The other characters (some of whom appeared more than once) were Carter Dickson's Sir Henry Merrivale (David Horne and Martin Wyldeck); E. C. Bentley's Philip Trent (Michael Gwynn); Edmund Crispin's Professor Gervase Fen (Richard Wordsworth); Nicholas Blake's Nigel Strangeways (Glyn Houston and Bernard Horsfall); John Trench's Martin Cotterell (Alan Dobie); and Roy Vickers's Inspector Rason (Michael Hordern and John Welsh). Jeffery Farnol's Jasper Shrig (Patrick Troughton and Colin Blakely) was another featured investigator, as were Douglas Sanderson's Bob Race (Frank Lieberman); Selwyn Jepson's Eve Gill (Jane Merrow and Penelope Horner); Austin Freeman's Dr Thorndyke (Peter Copley); Delano Ames's Jane and Dagobert Brown (Joan Reynolds and Leslie Randall); H. C. Bailey's Reggie Fortune (Denholm Elliott); Joyce Porter's Detective Chief Inspector Dover (Paul Dawkins); and Colin Morris's Detective Chief Inspector Dew (Glynn Edwards). Also featured were Ethel Lina White's Miss Pye (Angela Baddeley); Clifford Witting's DC Peter Bradfield (Mark Eden); Clark Smith's Nicky Mahoun (Frederick Jaeger); Michael Innes's Sir John Appleby (Dennis Price and Ian Ogilvy); Ursula Curtiss's Robert Carmichael (Dudley Sutton); Anthony Berkeley's Roger Sheringham (John Carson); Hillary Waugh's Police Chief Fellows (Lee Montague); William Haggard's Charles Russell (Roland Culver); MacDonald Hastings's Montague Cork (Colin Douglas); Josephine Tey's Alan Grant (John Carson); R. C. Woodthorpe's Sir Luke Frinsby (Cyril Luckham); Edgar Jepson and Robert Eustace's Ruth Kelstern (Hannah Gordon); H. R. F. Keating's Inspector Ghote (Zia Mohyeddin); and Ludovic Peters's Ian Firth (David Buck) and John Smith (Meredith Edwards). Completing the line-up were Francis Didelot's Commissaire Bignon (Derek Godfrey and Edward Woodward), Edgar Allan Poe's Auguste Dupin (Edward Woodward, again) and Bill Fraser as William Guppy (based on Dickens's *Bleak House*).

The series was introduced for the first season by Rupert Davies in his famous guise of MAIGRET, although no Maigret tales were actually included. A gap of four years lapsed before the series resumed in 1968, continuing through to 1969.

Detectives, The ★★★

UK (Celador) Situation Comedy. BBC 1 1993–7

DC Bob Louis .... **Jasper Carrott**
DC Dave Briggs .... **Robert Powell**
Supt. Frank Cottam .... **George Sewell**

Writers **Steve Knight, Mike Whitehill**
Producers **Ed Bye, Nic Phillips**

● ***Spin-off series from* Canned Carrott, *featuring two incompetent detectives.***

Bob Louis and Dave Briggs are two gormless plain-clothes detectives who achieve results despite their best efforts. Paired on undercover investigations by their no-nonsense boss, Supt. Cottam, their bumbling and bickering, petty rivalry and hare-brained schemes usually spell disaster for themselves but, somehow, success for the force. Star names from other BBC series crop up from time to time: Jim BERGERAC and Charlie Hungerford in an episode set on Jersey, and Danny Kane from THE PARADISE CLUB in an East London gang story. Jerry Hall, Jimmy Tarbuck, Tony Jacklin, Frank Windsor, Noel Edmonds, John Ratzenberger and Tony Head all make cameo appearances.

The characters were named after television executives known to creators Steve Knight and Mike Whitehill (who went on to co-devise WHO WANTS TO BE A MILLIONAIRE? with the real-life Dave Briggs).

Diagnosis Murder ★★

US (Dean Hargrove/Fred Silverman/Viacom) Detective Drama. BBC 1 1999–2001 (US: CBS 1993–2001)

Dr Mark Sloan .... **Dick Van Dyke**
Dr Jack Stewart .... **Scott Baio**
Amanda Bentley/Livingston ... **Victoria Rowell**
Norman Briggs .... **Michael Tucci**
Det. Steve Sloan .... **Barry Van Dyke**
Delores Mitchell .... **Delores Hall**
Dr Jesse Travis .... **Charlie Schlatter**
Susan Hilliard .... **Kim Little**
Dr Madison Wesley .... **Joanna Cassidy**
Det. Cheryl Banks .... **Charmin Lee**
Alex Smith .... **Shane Van Dyke**

Creator **Joyce Burditt**
Executive Producers **Dean Hargrove, Fred Silverman, Tom Chehak, Mark Masuoka, William Rabkin, Dick Van Dyke, Lee Goldberg**

● ***A Los Angeles doctor is a keen amateur sleuth.***

Spun-off from an episode of JAKE AND THE FATMAN, *Diagnosis Murder* features a hospital doctor with a nose for crime. Dr Mark Sloan is chief of internal medicine at the Community General Hospital, where Jack Stewart (later replaced by Jesse Travis) and Amanda Bentley are doctor colleagues, Norman Briggs is the administrator and Delores Mitchell a nurse. But Sloan's work is far from confined to the wards and, wherever something suspicious raises its head, the determined doc heads off to investigate. His role as medical consultant to the LAPD helps keep him busy in this respect. Bringing the law into each case is Sloan's detective son, Steve (played by star Dick Van Dyke's own son, Barry). The easy-watching series was well used by the BBC as an afternoon filler, sometimes running several times a week.

Dial 999 ★

UK (ABC/Towers of London/Ziv) Police Drama. ITV 1958–9

DI Mike Maguire .... **Robert Beatty**
DS West .... **John Witty**

Producer **Harry Alan Towers**

● ***A Canadian Mountie is seconded to the Metropolitan Police.***

Inspector Mike Maguire is sent to London by the Royal Canadian Mounted Police to study advanced crime-detection techniques. Operating on a sort of 'work experience' basis, he is given an acting rank of detective inspector and assisted in his investigations by Detective Sgt West. Like other mounties, the tough but fair Maguire always gets his man. The series was made 'with the Co-operation of the Metropolitan Police and the Citizens of London' and involved much location filming.

Diamond, Anne

(1954–)

Birmingham-born journalist and presenter, whose work on ATV and Central's regional news programmes and then Nationwide eventually led to her appointment as co-host of the TV-am breakfast show, *Good Morning Britain*, as the company sought to brighten up its act. Alongside Nick Owen, she helped reconstruct the ailing station's viewing figures. After leaving the breakfast sofa she moved into quiz shows (*The Birthday Show*, with Benny Green) and daytime TV, hosting *The Time, The Place, This Morning* and *TV Weekly*, before teaming up with Nick Owen again for the BBC's *Good Morning with Anne and Nick*. Diamond also once presented MISS WORLD, was a contestant in *Celebrity* BIG BROTHER, has been seen in *The Wright Stuff* and has hosted the Meridian regional programme *Let's Meet* . . .

Diamonds ✳

UK (ATV) Drama. ITV 1981

Frank Coleman .... **John Stride**
Margaret Coleman .... **Hildegard Neil**
Dora Coleman .... **Doris Hare**
Barry Coleman .... **Ian McCulloch**
Joseph Coleman .... **Norman Wooland**
Catherine Coleman .... **Shirley Cain**
Elaine Coleman .... **Briony McRoberts**
Terry Coleman .... **William Relton**
Bernard de Haan .... **Simon Ward**
Tom Fabricius .... **Mark Kingston**
Mordecai Kremer .... **John Barrard**
David Kremer (de Kroog) .... **Michael Culver**

Creator/Writer **John Brason**
Executive Producer **David Reid**
Producer **John Cooper**

● ***The drama of business in London's Hatton Garden.***

This 13-part series follows the day-to-day dealings of Coleman and Sons, a leading diamond house, in a glitzy world where money means power. Boardrooms and bedrooms feature strongly and the stakes are always high. Head of the family and the firm is Joseph Coleman, and among his offspring is the ambitious Frank, married to Margaret. The company's knowledgeable buyer is Bernard de Haan. Stories revolve around all aspects of the diamond trade, taking in important decisions about cutting large gemstones at the risk of thousands of pounds if the work does not go well. However, this glimpse at a diamond dynasty lacked the sparkle of the likes of DALLAS and proved short-lived. It was created by former COLDITZ and SECRET ARMY writer John Brason.

Diana ✳✳✳

UK (BBC) Drama. BBC 1 1984

Jan Leigh .... **Stephen J. Dean** *(young)*
Kevin McNally
Diana Gayelorde-Sutton .... **Patsy Kensit** *(young)*
Jenny Seagrove
Uncle Luke .... **Fred Bryant**
Uncle Mark .... **Jack Watson**
Uncle Reuben .... **Iain Anders**
Aunt Thirza .... **June Marlow**
Mr Gayelorde-Sutton .... **Harold Innocent**
Mrs Gayelorde-Sutton .... **Elizabeth Bennett**
Drip .... **Gillian Raine**
Yves de Royden .... **Yves Aubert**
Raoul de Royden .... **Yves Beneyton**
Lt. Starkey .... **Adam Norton**
Alison Hill .... **Lynne Miller**
Alistair .... **Christopher Good**

Writer **Andrew Davies**
Producer **Ken Riddington**

● ***Society provides a barrier between a working-class man and his aristocratic lover.***

Jan is 15 and an orphan. Farmed out to relatives in Devon, he meets and falls in love with local girl Diana Gayelorde-Sutton, who happens to be heiress to a fortune. Over ten episodes, the story of their turbulent love life unfolds, as social standing, their disparate careers and World War II all rear their interfering heads. Jan – who becomes a Fleet Street journalist and then accepts an assignment abroad – loses and temporarily regains Diana at various stages in his life, but it is the class divide that really blocks his road to happiness. Like the earlier TO SERVE THEM ALL MY DAYS, the series was adapted by Andrew Davies from the novel by R. F. Delderfield.

Dibnah, Fred

MBE (1938–2004)

Britain's most famous steeplejack. Bolton-born Fred Dibnah's first TV appearance came as part of a programme called *Earning a Bob or Two*. His enthusiastic, matter-of-fact approach to his precarious job and his distinctive Lancashire accent proved so appealing that he was soon made the star of his own documentary, *Fred Dibnah, Steeplejack*, in 1979. More programmes were then produced, following Dibnah's work, including *Fred* and *A Year with Fred*. Dibnah later progressed to presenting documentaries himself, about Britain's great architectural and engineering past. *Fred Dibnah's Industrial Age, Fred Dibnah's Magnificent Monuments, Fred Dibnah's Victorian Heroes, Fred Dibnah's Building of Britain, Fred Dibnah's Age of Steam, Dig With Dibnah* and *Fred Dibnah's Made in Britain* were among his credits.

Dick & Dom's Ask the Family

See *Ask the Family*.

Dick and the Duchess ✳

US (Sheldon Reynolds) Situation Comedy. ITV 1958–9
(US: CBS 1957–8)

Richard Starrett .... **Patrick O'Neal**
Jane Starrett .... **Hazel Court**
Peter Jamison .... **Richard Wattis**
Insp. Stark .... **Michael Shepley**
Mathilda .... **Beatrice Varley**
Rodney .... **Ronnie Stevens**

Executive Producer **Nicole Milinaire**

● ***The assignments of an insurance claims investigator and his dizzy, aristocratic wife.***

American Richard 'Dick' Starrett works for a multinational insurance agency in London and has recently married above himself, to the daughter of an earl (hence his nickname for her, 'The Duchess'). Her family doesn't like him, or the fact that he is a commoner. Despite this, and his wife's continual interference in his work, they remain happily married. Peter Jamison is Dick's business associate and Rodney is a young colleague. Stark is the Scotland Yard inspector with whom Dick often has to liaise. Although made at Elstree, the series was shown first (and was more successful) in the USA.

Dick Barton – Special Agent ✳

UK (Southern) Secret Agent Drama. ITV 1979

Dick Barton .... **Tony Vogel**
Snowey White .... **Anthony Heaton**
Jock Anderson .... **James Cosmo**
Sir Richard Marley .... **John Gantrel**
Melganik .... **John G. Heller**

Writers **Clive Exton, Julian Bond**
Executive Producers **Terence Baker, Lewis Rudd**
Producer **Jon Scoffield**

Light-hearted television revival of a legendary radio hero.

Fearless, dependable Dick Barton, demobbed after six years in the Army, finds civilian life a touch too mundane for his liking. So, when he receives a call from an old friend, Sir Richard Marley, asking him to find his missing son and daughter, he willingly dashes once more into the fray, in the company of his former colleagues, Snowey and Jock. The trio then stumble into other inquiries, and more than once confront their evil adversary, Melganik.

Unfortunately, this twice-weekly, 15-minute serial failed to capture the public's imagination in the same way as the original radio series, which went out between 1946 and 1951 and drew audiences of 15 million. Radio's Barton, Noel Johnson, reputedly received 2,000 letters a week. Perhaps it was his very clean-cut, wholesome portrayal of the dashing former commando who shunned hard drink and loose women which endeared him to listeners. On TV, Tony Vogel's Barton is considerably more earthy.

Dick Turpin ✳✳

UK (Gatetarn/Seacastle/LWT) Adventure. ITV 1979–82
DVD: Network

Dick Turpin .... **Richard O'Sullivan**
Nick Smith ('Swiftnick') .... **Michael Deeks**
Sir John Glutton .... **Christopher Benjamin**
Capt. Nathan Spiker .... **David Daker**

Creator/Writer **Richard Carpenter**
Producers **Paul Knight, Sidney Cole**

Tales of the famous 18th-century highwayman.

Dick Turpin, cheated out of his wealth while on war duty in Flanders, decides to flout the law to regain his prosperity. His chief adversaries are the corrupt (and appropriately named) Sir John Glutton and Glutton's sneering, ambitious steward, Spiker. Assisted by Swiftnick, a young tearaway who becomes his closest companion, Turpin is soon considered a folk hero, riding to the aid of many a troubled countryman. The swashbuckling adventures see the pair in and out of prison as they do their bit for the common good, all the while trying to avoid the caress of the hangman's noose.

Dick Van Dyke Show, The ✳✳✳

US (Calvada/T&L) Situation Comedy. BBC 1963–7 (CBS 1961–6)
DVD: Image Entertainment

Rob Petrie .... **Dick Van Dyke**
Laura Petrie .... **Mary Tyler Moore**
Sally Rogers .... **Rose Marie**
Maurice 'Buddy' Sorrell .... **Morey Amsterdam**
Ritchie Petrie .... **Larry Mathews**
Melvin Cooley .... **Richard Deacon**
Dr Jerry Helper .... **Jerry Paris**
Millie Helper .... **Ann Morgan Guilbert**
Alan Brady .... **Carl Reiner**

Creator **Carl Reiner**
Executive Producer **Sheldon Leonard**
Producers **Carl Reiner, Sam Denoff**

Gentle mishaps in the life of a TV scriptwriter.

Rob Petrie is head writer for *The Alan Brady Show*, a TV comedy programme. With his wife, Laura (a former dancer), and son, Ritchie, he lives in the suburbia of New Rochelle, where dentist Jerry Helper and his wife, Millie, are their next-door neighbours. Rob's life also extends to the TV studio in New York where he works. His 'family' there include man-hungry Sally Rogers and wisecracking, loud-mouthed Buddy Sorrell. As a trio, they are constantly harassed by the arrogant Mel Cooley, the show's bald producer, who is also brother-in-law to the star, Alan Brady. Carl Reiner, who played the neurotic Brady, was, in fact, the show's creator and was not seen, only heard, for the first few seasons, before eventually making a visual appearance. Reiner had developed the series with himself in mind for the Dick Van Dyke role, but the networks were not impressed.

Many of the stars went on to further success: Jerry Paris became a successful producer and director, working on HAPPY DAYS among other programmes, while Mary Tyler Moore became a TV superstar, having her own series, THE MARY TYLER MOORE SHOW, and setting up the MTM production company. In the 1970s, Van Dyke returned in THE NEW DICK VAN DYKE SHOW (CBS 1971–4), in which he played TV talk show host Dick Preston, with Hope Lange as his wife, Jenny.

Dickens of London ✳

UK (YTV) Drama. ITV 1976

Charles Dickens .... **Simon Bell** *(child)*
Roy Dotrice *(old man)*
Gene Foad *(young man)*
John Dickens .... **Roy Dotrice**
Catherine Dickens .... **Diana Coupland**
Catherine Hogarth/Dickens .... **Patsy Kensit** *(child)*
Adrienne Burgess *(woman)*
Georgiana Hogarth .... **Christine McKenna**
Fanny Dickens .... **Pheona McLellan** *(child)*
Henrietta Baynes *(woman)*
Maria Beadnell .... **Karen Dotrice**
Mr Hogarth .... **Richard Leech**

Writer **Wolf Mankowitz**
Executive Producer **David Cunliffe**
Producer **Marc Miller**

The great writer looks back on his formative years.

This biopic focuses on an ageing, failing Charles Dickens as he recalls scenes from his early life. It follows his development up to the age of 32 and offers ample opportunity for viewers to identify people and events that shaped his writings. Roy Dotrice played Dickens as an old man and also the young Dickens's father.

Dickinson, Angie

(Angeline Brown; 1931–)

TV fame came quite late to former beauty queen Angie Dickinson, who had appeared with John Wayne in the film *Rio Bravo* (among other movies) way back in the 1950s. Although she won herself a selection of interesting guest-spots in programmes like PERRY MASON, THE FUGITIVE, ALFRED HITCHCOCK PRESENTS and DR KILDARE, it wasn't until 1974 that she was cast in a lead role, that of Sgt Pepper Anderson in POLICE WOMAN. The programme ran for four years, and she followed it up with the mini-series *Hollywood Wives* and then a couple of other drama series in the USA, neither of which made inroads on the other side of the Atlantic. Dickinson does, however, have plenty of TV movies to her name. She was once married to composer Burt Bacharach.

Dickinson, David

(1941–)

Cheshire-born, flamboyant presenter of antiques programmes, notably *The Antiques Show, Antiques Hunter*, GOING FOR A SONG, *Bargain Hunt* and *Dealing With Dickinson*, in which he became noted for his chalk-stripe suits, silk ties and golden tan, as well as the catchphrase 'cheap as chips'. An early TV appearance came in the documentary series *Modern Times*, while in 2005 he was given a guest role in the drama series HEARTBEAT.

Dickinson, Sandra

(Sandra Searles; 1948–)

Squeaky-voiced, blonde-haired, mainly comedy actress, the former wife of actor Peter Davison. Although born in Washington, DC, Dickinson's television work has been concentrated in the UK, taking in series as varied as THE TOMORROW PEOPLE, *What's On Next?*, TRIANGLE and THE TWO RONNIES. She also appeared with Roy Kinnear in *The Clairvoyant* (Lily), THE HITCH-HIKER'S GUIDE TO THE GALAXY (Trillian) and 2 POINT 4 CHILDREN (Tina). More recent guest appearances have come in SUNBURN and CASUALTY. Sandra has also provided voices for TELETUBBIES.

Did You See . . . ? ✱✱

UK (BBC) TV Review. BBC 2 1980–7; 1991–3

Presenters **Ludovic Kennedy, Jeremy Paxman**

Producers/Editors **John Archer, Sue Mallinson, Chris Mohr, Anne Tyerman**

● ***Intellectual reviews of the week's television programming.***

Chaired initially by Ludovic Kennedy, but from 1991 by Jeremy Paxman, *Did You See . . . ?* invited guests (usually writers, producers and politicians, rather than professional critics) to examine three of the previous week's TV offerings. Each guest was assigned one programme for close study and gave a full appraisal, with the others chipping in with their views in due course. Before the debate began, a brief overview of the week's TV happenings was provided by the host.

Diff'rent Strokes ✱✱

US (Tandem) Situation Comedy. ITV 1980–7 (US: NBC 1978–85; ABC 1985–6)

DVD: Columbia Tristar (Region 1 only)

Philip Drummond .... **Conrad Bain**
Arnold Jackson .... **Gary Coleman**
Willis Jackson .... **Todd Bridges**
Kimberly Drummond .... **Dana Plato**
Mrs Edna Garrett .... **Charlotte Rae**
Adelaide Brubaker .... **Nedra Volz**
Aunt Sophia .... **Dody Goodman**
Pearl Gallagher .... **Mary Jo Catlett**
Dudley Ramsey .... **Shavar Ross**
Charlene DuPrey .... **Janet Jackson**
Lisa Hayes .... **Nikki Swasey**
Maggie McKinney .... **Dixie Carter**
Mary Ann Mobley
Sam McKinney .... **Danny Cooksey**

Creators **Jeff Harris, Bernie Kukoff**

● ***Two orphaned boys are adopted by a New York millionaire.***

Eight-year-old Arnold Jackson and his 12-year-old brother Willis are two black kids left homeless after the death of their mother. She has worked as a housekeeper to wealthy Philip Drummond and has persuaded the white corporation head to take her sons under his wing. Somewhat reluctantly, wise-cracking, manipulative Arnold and his more sensible sibling move from Harlem into Drummond's luxurious Park Avenue penthouse apartment, where gradually they adapt to their new downtown lifestyle. They are then adopted by the caring Drummond and become brothers to Drummond's natural 13-year-old daughter, Kimberly. Mrs Garrett is the dippy new housekeeper, later replaced by Adelaide Brubaker (when actress Charlotte Rae quit to star in a spin-off series, *The Facts of Life*), and eventually by Pearl Gallagher. Drummond's scatterbrained sister, Sophia, is also seen, as are the boys' school colleagues Dudley, Lisa and Charlene. By the end of the series, Arnold is aged 15 and Drummond has married TV fitness guru Maggie McKinney, whose son, Sam, has become part of the action. Comedy is derived from the boys' incompatibility with their new surroundings and the wealthy white businessman's attempts to introduce his two black sons to influential associates. Most laughs, however, come from Gary Coleman's sparkling delivery, the wicked glint in his eye and the fact that such a small, chubby-faced person could be so articulate and confident (the truth was that Coleman suffered from a kidney ailment that had stunted his growth, making him appear younger than he really was – ten at the start of the series). Indeed, the programme was created specifically for Coleman by Norman Lear's Tandem Productions, after Coleman had appeared in an earlier sitcom, *Good Times*. While there was criticism from some quarters that the black–white relationship was not more advantageously explored, some stories did tackle unpleasant subjects like child abuse and racial prejudice. First Lady Nancy Reagan was a guest in one episode that majored on the fight against drugs.

Digital

Digital television was launched in the UK in October 1998. The new technology squeezes more channels into the space normally used to carry old-fashioned analogue TV channels, not only allowing more programming choice but also freeing up frequencies for uses such as mobile communications. It works by transmitting signals as a stream of binary digits, which helps eliminate interference. The signals are also compressed to discard unnecessary information, hence taking up less space.

There are three ways of receiving digital television. The first is by Digital Terrestrial Television, which uses existing transmitters and existing domestic aerials. Because digital signals require less space, six channels can be crammed into the same frequency as the old broadcasting system. These collections of channels are known as multiplexes, and initially six multiplexes were set up. One was operated by the BBC, another by ITV, Channel 4 and Teletext. A third was awarded to S4C Digital Networks to supply Channel 5, S4C and Scottish Gaelic programming, with the last three given to ONdigital (later ITV Digital) for its 'satellite'-style content of films, sport and minority channels. The last three are now home to Freeview.

The second means of receiving digital (and the first on air) is by Digital Satellite Television. Operated by BSkyB, this system uses satellite technology to beam down signals to a domestic digital dish (smaller than the former analogue dishes). Just as for its terrestrial equivalent, the fact that digital signals use less space means that there is room for more channels. The third method of digital broadcasting is Digital Cable Television, where channels are piped through cable networks to the home. All three systems require the use of a decoder box that reconstitutes digital signals for television sets, although increasingly new televisions include built-in decoders. Programmes broadcast digitally by the BBC, ITV, Channel 4, Channel 5 and S4C are free to view, as are some other channels, though many are sold as part of a subscriber package.

Early publicity surrounding digital television suggested viewers would be treated to greatly enhanced pictures and CD-quality sound. However, once commercial realities began to bite, these were played down. In order to wring maximum value out of their packages, providers squeezed as many channels as possible into the space available, resulting in pictures and sound that were only marginally better than delivered by good analogue reception. However, other digital benefits do include widescreen images, on-screen programme listings, limited 'ghosting' and other interference, the opportunity to order pay-per-view films and sporting events, the chance to 'interact' with broadcasts (casting votes, selecting news items, choosing camera angles, etc.), and scope for the development of commercial activities, such as home shopping and banking. On the negative side, if for some reason the signal becomes poor, reception will not simply deteriorate but will disappear altogether. It is planned that analogue services will be phased out in the next few years as digital coverage becomes comprehensive and decoder ownership widespread.

Dimbleby, David
(1938–)

Son of Richard and brother of Jonathan, David Dimbleby joined the BBC as a reporter in 1960 and has long been one of the Corporation's foremost political commentators and interviewers, working on programmes like PANORAMA, NATIONWIDE, *This Week, Next Week, The Dimbleby Talk-in* and most election coverages. In 1971 he ran into controversy when his 24 HOURS programme *Yesterday's Men* provoked anger among Labour politicians for an unfair and biased (they claimed) interview with deposed premier Harold Wilson. Dimbleby has also presented TOP OF THE FORM and, more notably, such documentaries as the award-winning *The White Tribe of Africa*, the analytical series *An Ocean Apart*, which looked at how the UK and the USA had developed in different cultural directions, and *Rebellion!*, which told the story of Rhodesia's transition into Zimbabwe. He has also presented *David Dimbleby's India* and *A Picture of Britain*, the latter looking at the UK from an artist's and writer's viewpoint. He is the current chairman of QUESTION TIME and was once married to cookery writer Josceline Dimbleby.

Dimbleby, Jonathan
(1944–)

After he followed his father, Richard, and elder brother, David, into the current affairs side of television (and radio), Jonathan Dimbleby's progress came largely thanks to the independent sector. Beginning as a reporter with the BBC in Bristol, Dimbleby switched to ITV to present THIS WEEK, *TV Eye* and some prominent individual documentaries. Then came FIRST TUESDAY (also as associate editor), before he joined the BBC to host the lunchtime political analysis show *On the Record*. In 1994 his interview with the Prince of Wales hit the headlines, Prince Charles conceding, at Dimbleby's prompting, that he had been unfaithful to Princess Diana. In 1997 his series *The Last Governor* chronicled the closing months of British rule in Hong Kong. More recently, he has hosted *Jonathan Dimbleby*, a Sunday lunchtime political debate for ITV. Dimbleby is married to writer Bel Mooney.

Dimbleby, Richard
CBE (1913–65)

Dimbleby is celebrated as one of Britain's finest broadcasters, and his radio work veered between light-hearted items like *Down Your Way* and *Twenty Qeustions* and sombre, graphic reporting. Joining the Corporation's news department in 1936, he became its first war correspondent and was the reporter who brought British listeners on-the-spot coverage of events like El Alamein and D-Day, even commentating from an RAF bomber over Germany. In doing so, he revealed a remarkable flair for conveying the awesome nature and true horror of such campaigns. Moving into television, he became synonymous with state occasions (the 1953 CORONATION was one of the high spots of his career), technical innovations (such as presenting new Eurovision and satellite links) and political debates. Once he was installed as anchorman of PANORAMA in 1955, the programme quickly took off and Dimbleby earned himself a unique position of trust in the country, at the same time becoming recognized internationally as the voice of the BBC. He died in 1965, not long after presenting the BBC's coverage of the state funeral of Sir Winston Churchill. His two sons, David and Jonathan, have both followed him into current affairs broadcasting.

Dimmock, Charlie
(Charlotte Dimmock; 1966–)

Red-haired, Southampton-born gardening presenter whose job as manager of a Romsey garden centre proved to be the launch-pad for a new TV career. Through series such as *Grass Roots*, GROUND FORCE, *Charlie's Garden Army, Charlie's Wildlife Gardens* and *Charlie's Gardening Neighbours* she put glamour into gardening at the turn of the millennium, drawing new viewers into the garden not just with her horticultural skills but also with her famously relaxed approach to upper-body support. *Cheer for Charlie* saw her undertaking trapeze training at a circus, and, in *Girls on Top*, she and Anna Ryder-Richardson tried their hands at other people's jobs.

Dimmock, Peter

CVO, OBE (1920–)

Former RAF pilot who became one of BBC Television's first outside broadcast producers and sports commentators, joining the Corporation in 1946. He hosted COME DANCING and SPORTSVIEW, and was in the chair for the first edition of GRANDSTAND in 1958. Dimmock was sports adviser to the European Broadcasting Union 1959–72, as well as being the liaison executive between the BBC and the royal family, 1963–77. In the 1970s he was General Manager of BBC Enterprises and then became an executive with America's ABC network.

dinnerladies ★★★

UK (Good Fun/Pozzitive/BBC) Situation Comedy. BBC 1 1998–2000

DVD: Universal

Bren .... **Victoria Wood**
Dolly Bellfield .... **Thelma Barlow**
Tony Martin .... **Andrew Dunn**
Anita .... **Shobna Gulati**
Philippa Moorcroft .... **Celia Imrie**
Twinkle .... **Maxine Peake**
Stan Meadowcroft .... **Duncan Preston**
Jean .... **Anne Reid**
Petula Gardeno .... **Julie Walters**
Mr Michael .... **Christopher Greet**
Jane .... **Sue Devaney**

Producers **Geoff Posner, Victoria Wood**

● ***Day-to-day laughs with the staff of a factory canteen.***

Victoria Wood's first sitcom is a character-led affair in which events play second fiddle to the personalities and socially observant banter that fills her stage shows. The ensemble is headed by the down-to-earth Bren, the sort of person who keeps her head when all about her are losing theirs and who can butter rolls and wash lettuce with the best, even if she does have trouble remembering certain words. Bren copes admirably with boss Tony (a chemotherapy survivor, later her boyfriend); daffy *Daily Mail*-reader Dolly; laid-back, oversexed Jean; punctilious handyman Stan (his dander permanently up); and drippy young helpers Twinkle and Anita. Highly strung personnel manager Philippa flits in and out with news of happenings elsewhere in the Manchester factory (HWD Components), and Bren's wacky mum, Petula, occasionally leaves her grubby caravan home to reveal her latest sexual conquests. Although stories nominally revolve around the visit of royalty or a Japanese take-over of the company, of greater importance to Bren and her colleagues are whether the bread man has delivered the right baps or if the toaster will actually work. But even these concerns are over-shadowed by the human dramas that unfold. With its heavy word-count and complex and witty dialogue, each *dinnerladies* (deliberately billed with a small initial 'd') episode was actually recorded twice, to allow the cast to guarantee spot-on performances. Just two series were made.

Direct Broadcasting by Satellites

See *DBS*.

Director

The creative/artistic executive in a production team. The director is the one who takes charge of the performances of the actors and camera crew, and who also supervises the post-production stages.

Director-General

The title given to the chief executive of the BBC.

Disappearing World ★★★

UK (Granada) Natural History. ITV 1970–93

Creator/Editor **Brian Moser**

● ***Long-running documentary series looking at civilizations in the far corners of the world.***

Former WORLD IN ACTION producer Brian Moser was the brains behind this award-winning collection of films on 'lost' tribes hidden away in the remotest parts of the planet. His reports on the customs and ways of life of such peoples as the Cuiva in Colombia, the Meo in Laos, the Mursi in Ethiopia and the Mehinacu in Brazil brought anthropology into the living room and revealed how ancient lifestyles were being threatened by the advance of the modern world. No commentators were used. The subjects spoke for themselves, in their own languages, and subtitles provided an English translation.

Discovery Channel, The

Founded in 1985 by John S. Hendricks, The Discovery Channel (part of Discovery Communications Inc.) has broadcast in Europe via the Astra satellite system since 1993 and on digital networks since 1998, but has been available on cable in the UK since 1989. The service is available in several languages around Europe and is provided by Discovery Networks Europe, which is programmed separately from the original American channels to take account of European interests. Through documentaries and other factual programmes, Discovery covers a very wide range of subjects in five programme genres: adventure, travel, nature, history and technology. It does not feature current affairs or the arts. The channel commissions many programmes of its own, some in conjunction with other broadcasters, but also carries suitable material first seen on terrestrial channels. Its sister (spin-off) channels include Discovery Home and Health, Discovery Civilisation, Discovery Travel and Living, Discovery Science, Discovery Wings, Discovery Kids, Discovery Real Time and Animal Planet.

Dish

A round aerial for receiving satellite transmissions. Attempts by the ill-fated British Satellite Broadcasting (BSB) to introduce a smaller, more angular 'squarial' for domestic use met with initial technical difficulties, although some versions were made available.

Disney, Walt

(Walter Elias Disney; 1901–66)

Although Walt Disney's contributions to television are small beer when compared to his influence in the cinema, nevertheless the man and his organization were responsible for some notable achievements on the box. His *Disneyland* anthology, first shown to US audiences in 1954, was instrumental in bringing Hollywood studios into the mainstream of television production. The series continued right into the 1990s, under various names, including *Walt Disney's Wonderful World of Color* and *The Wonderful World of Disney*, and was given credit for raising the standards of children's TV entertainment and education. Out of *Disneyland* came DAVY CROCKETT, an adventure series based loosely around the legendary frontiersman, and, a year after *Disneyland* started, *The Mickey Mouse Club* was launched, proving a huge hit with young mousketeers (ears and all) all across the States. Also popular in the 1950s was another Disney series, ZORRO. Although Disney himself refused to release his movie classics for TV consumption, believing that there would always be a new market for his theatrical cartoons, his company did instigate The Disney Channel in 1983, allowing this cable station to benefit from the organization's treasure trove of films and past programmes.

Dissolve

The merging of one shot into another, by fading one out at the same time as fading another in. It is also known as a mix.

District Nurse, The ✳✳

UK (BBC) Drama. BBC 1 1984; 1987

Megan Roberts	**Nerys Hughes**
David Price	**John Ogwen**
Gwen Harries	**Margaret John**
Hugh Morris	**Philip Raymond**
Dr O'Casey	**Rio Fanning**
Nesta Mogg	**Deborah Manship**
Teg	**Ken Morgan**
Bryn Morris	**Gareth Potter**
Dylan Roderick	**Ian Saynor**
Sarah Hopkin	**Elen Roger Jones**
Wil Hopkin	**Ernest Evans**
Evelina Williams	**Beth Morris**
Mrs Prosser-Davies	**Elizabeth Morgan**
Nora	**Nathalie Price**
Dr Charles Barclay	**Philip Hurdwood**
Revd Geraint Rhys	**Ifan Huw Dafydd**
Dr Emlyn Isaacs	**Freddie Jones**
Dr James Isaacs	**Nicholas Jones**
'Captain' Mansel	**Jack Walters**
Dilys Humphries	**Christine Pollon**
Ruth Jones	**Janet Aethwy**
R. T. Williams	**Owen Garmon**
Marie Anderson	**Carol Holmes**

Creators **Julia Smith, Tony Holland**
Producers **Julia Smith, Peter Edwards**

● ***A nurse fights for respect in the poverty-ridden South Wales valleys of the 1920s.***

Megan Roberts is the new 'Queen's Nurse' in the mining village of Pencwm. Typically conservative (with a small 'c'), the local residents treat their new arrival with suspicion. Perhaps it is her sit-up-and-beg pushbike and hideous hat that frighten the miners. More probably it is because she comes from *North* Wales and, what's more, is a walking symbol of uniformed authority. The fact that she is a woman, taking control in a man's world, only makes matters worse. Battling prejudice and ignorance at every turn, the determined and bossy Megan finally wins acceptance and is able to improve medical practice in the village. For the third series, shown three years later and set in 1932, Megan has moved to the seaside town of Glanmôr, where she lives in the busy household of Dr Emlyn Isaacs.

Diving to Adventure

See *Hass, Hans and Lotte.*

Dixon of Dock Green ✳✳

UK (BBC) Police Drama. BBC 1 1955–76

PC/Sgt George Dixon	**Jack Warner**
PC/DC/DS/DI Andy Crawford	**Peter Byrne**
Mary Dixon/Crawford	**Billie Whitelaw**
	Jeanette Hutchinson
	Anna Dawson
Sgt Flint	**Arthur Rigby**
PC 'Tubb' Barrell	**Neil Wilson**
Sgt Grace Millard	**Moira Mannion**
PC Bob Penney	**Anthony Parker**
Insp. Gordon/Insp./DI Cherry	**Robert Cawdron**
Duffy Clayton	**Harold Scott**
PC/DC Tommy Hughes	**Graham Ashley**
PC Glyn Jenkins	**David Lyn**
PC/DC 'Laudy' Lauderdale	**Geoffrey Adams**
Cadet/PC Jamie MacPherson	**David Webster**
PC/Sgt Johnny Wills	**Nicholas Donnelly**
WPC Kay Shaw/Lauderdale	**Jocelyne Rhodes**
Jenny Wren	**Hilda Fenemore**
DC Jack Cotton	**Michael Nightingale**
WP Sgt 'Scotty' Scott	**Ruth Lodge**
PC Bush	**Max Latimer**
WP Sgt Christine Freeman	**Anne Ridler**
WPC 'Barney' Barnes	**Janet Morris**
PC Clyde	**Christopher Gilmore**
PC Jones	**John Hughes**
WPC Alex Johns	**Jan Miller**
Cadet Michael Bonnet	**Paul Elliott**
PC/Sgt Wills	**Nicholas Donnelly**
PC/DC Swain	**Robert Arnold**
WPC Liz Harris/Swain	**Zeph Gladstone**
WP Sgt Jean Bell	**Patricia Forde**
PC Roberts	**Geoffrey Kenion**
WPC Shirley Palmer	**Anne Carroll**
PC Burton	**Peter Thornton**
Sgt Cooper	**Duncan Lamont**
WPC Betty Williams	**Jean Dallas**
PC Ted Bryant	**Ronald Bridges**
Det. Supt. Harvey	**Geoffrey Keen**
DC Pearson	**Joe Dunlop**
WDC Ann Foster	**Pamela Buchner**
PC Brian Turner	**Andrew Bradford**
WPC Sally Reed	**Jenny Logan**

PC Newton .... **Michael Osborne**
PC Forbes .... **Scott Fredericks**
DC Webb .... **Derek Anders**
DI/DCI Scott .... **Kenneth Watson**
DS Brewer .... **Gregory De Polnay**
PC Harry Dunne .... **Stephen Marsh**
DC Len Clayton .... **Ben Howard**
DS Alan Bruton .... **Richard Heffer**

Creator **Ted Willis**
Producers **Douglas Moodie, Ronald Marsh, Eric Fawcett, Joe Waters**

The cases of a traditional London bobby.
George Dixon was a policeman of the old school, the sort of dependable copper who helped old ladies across the road and whose idea of justice for young tearaways was a clip around the ear. Perhaps that was not surprising, given that the series began in the mid-1950s. But when you consider that it was still on our screens 21 years later, at a time when Jack Regan (THE SWEENEY) was dishing out knuckle sandwiches on the same London streets, it is easy to see just how dated this series had become. Indeed, even by 1962, the series was beginning to show its age, with the all-action men of Z CARS vying for viewers' attentions. But *Dixon of Dock Green* soldiered on, plodding its own beat, unashamedly unspectacular in style and content, and almost turning a blind eye to the rapidly rising crime rate.

George Dixon first saw the light of day in the 1949 Rank film *The Blue Lamp*, in which the genial veteran was gunned down by armed robber Dirk Bogarde. His creator, Ted Willis, exhumed the character six years later when the BBC were looking for a replacement for FABIAN OF SCOTLAND YARD. He placed PC Dixon at London's Dock Green police station, where he becomes a source of inspiration and comfort not only to the community but also to his younger colleagues. One such colleague is PC Andy Crawford, who goes on to marry George's daughter, Mary, and provide him with twin grandchildren.

It is Crawford and his more sprightly pals who take over the running around as Dixon grows older and is promoted in 1964 to the rank of desk sergeant, replacing Sgt Flint. Other familiar faces at the Dock Green nick in the early days are PCs 'Laudy' Lauderdale and 'Tubb' Barrell, and Sgt Grace Millard; but many other officers come and go over the years, including the ill-fated Bob Penney, shot on duty. Also seen is bad-penny rogue Duffy Clayton. After his promotion, Dixon rarely strays beyond the station counter (as Warner's advancing years began to take their toll; by the time the series ended in 1976, he was aged 80, and the last two seasons had shown him coming to terms with retirement).

Although it became atypical of a London policeman's lot (despite Ted Willis's thorough initial research at Paddington Green nick and regular story feeds from active force members), cosy *Dixon of Dock Green* – billed initially as 'Some stories of a London policeman' – remains one of British TV's most fondly remembered series. George's opening and closing monologues beneath the famous blue lamp, whistling 'Maybe It's Because I'm a Londoner' as he drifted into shot from the murky night, are classic TV memories, as is the lilting theme music, 'An Ordinary Copper', that wafted into living rooms every Saturday teatime.

Jack Warner, brother of music hall stars Elsie and Doris Waters, died five years after the series ended and his funeral turned into a tribute from fans and policemen alike. At the ripe old age of 85, George had bidden viewers his final 'Evening all'.

Dixon of Dock Green was revived for Radio 4 in 2005, with David Calder in the role of George Dixon and David Tennant as PC Crawford.

Do Not Adjust Your Set ★★★

UK (Rediffusion/Thames) Children's Comedy. ITV 1967–8/1968–9
DVD: Boulevard Entertainment

Eric Idle, Michael Palin, Terry Jones, David Jason, Denise Coffey, Terry Gilliam, The Bonzo Dog Doo-Dah Band

Writers **Eric Idle, Michael Palin, Terry Jones**
Producers **Humphrey Barclay, Ian Davidson**

Silly sketches and goofy gags for younger viewers.
Although aimed at the children's hour audience, this wacky series – billed as 'The Fairly Pointless Show' – was a direct predecessor of MONTY PYTHON'S FLYING CIRCUS and all that programme was to achieve. Corralling together for the first time the talents of Eric Idle, Michael Palin, Terry Jones and animator Terry Gilliam, plus comic actress Denise Coffey and promising newcomer David Jason, producer Humphrey Barclay offered a madcap, 25-minute show of sketches and sight gags. One element featured the zany adventures of superhero Captain Fantastic (Jason), who was hounded by his nemesis, Mrs Black (Coffey). Fantastic was also seen in MAGPIE. The Bonzo Dog Doo-Dah Band provided musical relief.

Dobie, Alan
(1932–)

Yorkshire-born actor, most highly acclaimed for his performance as the Victorian Detective Sgt CRIBB in the 1980 series of the same name. He played David Corbett in THE PLANE MAKERS in the mid-1960s, John Diamond in *Diamond Crack Diamond* in 1970, Prince Dmitri in Tolstoy's *Resurrection* in 1971 and Prince Andrei Bolkonsky in his WAR AND PEACE in 1972–3. Other credits have included THE TROUBLESHOOTERS, *Hard Times, Kessler, Master of the Game* and numerous single dramas. His first wife was actress Rachel Roberts.

Dobson, Anita
(1949–)

London-born actress still best known as boozy pub landlady Angie Watts in EASTENDERS. She arrived in Albert Square at the programme's inception, taking advantage of the show's popularity to have a Top Five hit with a vocal version of its theme song, 'Anyone Can Fall in Love', in 1986. Her other TV has ranged across appearances in programmes as diverse as PLAY AWAY, NANNY, AGATHA CHRISTIE'S PARTNERS IN CRIME, UP THE ELEPHANT AND ROUND THE CASTLE (Lois Tight), the single drama *The World of Eddie Weary, Smokescreen* (Gertie), DANGERFIELD and NCS MANHUNT. She also played Cath in the short-lived hairdressers' sitcom *Split Ends*, Ivy Osborne in the comedy GET WELL SOON, Donna Slaney in the drama series HEARTS AND BONES, and Sam Greene in Sky One's *The Stretch*. Recent guest appearances have come in HOLBY CITY, THE LAST DETECTIVE, NEW TRICKS and THE BILL.

Doc Martin ★★

UK (Buffalo/Home Run) Comedy Drama. ITV 1 2004–
DVD: Momentum

Dr Martin Ellingham	**Martin Clunes**
Louisa Glasson	**Caroline Catz**
Elaine Denham	**Lucy Punch**
PC Mark Mylow	**Stewart Wright**
Bert Large	**Ian McNeice**
Al Large	**Joe Absolom**
Joan Norton	**Stephanie Cole**
Robert Fenn	**Jeff Rawle**
Lady Susan Brading	**Celia Imrie**
Sir Gilbert Johnson	**Richard Johnson**
Pauline Lamb	**Katherine Parkinson**
Danny Steel	**Tristan Sturrock**
Julie Mitchell	**Angeline Ball**

Writers **Dominic Minghella, Edana Minghella, Richard Stoneman, Jack Lothian**
Executive Producer **Mark Crowdy**
Producer **Philippa Braithwaite**

A high-flying surgeon packs it all in for a general practice in Cornwall.

Martin Ellingham has been a surgeon for 12 years but then decides to turn his back on specialist medicine to take over a ramshackle general practice in sleepy Portwenn, Cornwall. The reason? It transpires he has developed a phobia about blood, but his new patients are yet to twig this. Instead they struggle to deal with his city ways, short temper and churlish bedside manner as this grumpy fish out of water comes to terms with his new life. Doc Martin is not quite a complete stranger, however, as his forthright old Auntie Joan runs a small-holding just outside the fishing town, and he spent many a childhood holiday in the area. He has also met another local resident prior to taking up his post. Louisa Glasson is the town's schoolteacher and a lay member of the medical trust that appoints him. The doc also finds her rather attractive, but can't quite make his feelings known. Meanwhile, on a daily basis, Ellingham has to cope with the wacky ways of Elaine, the useless practice receptionist (replaced by feisty Pauline in series two). PC Mylow is the depressed local law-man, and the father and son duo of Bert and Al Large are the oddball local plumbers.

Doc Martin came to ITV 1 via a short movie career. Star Martin Clunes had earlier played a character of the same name – albeit a rather more likeable one – in the 2000 film *Saving Grace*, which, like this series, was filmed in the winding streets of Cornwall's Port Isaac. This was followed by two spin-off prequels (again with Clunes) called *Doc Martin* and *Doc Martin and the Legend of the Cloutie*. The character's full name then, however, was Martin Bamford; his new last name here – Ellingham – is an anagram of the surname of main writer Dominic Minghella, younger brother of Oscar-winning writer/director Anthony Minghella. Ben Bolt and Minkie Spiro direct. Series producer Philippa Braithwaite is Clunes's real-life wife. Together they are directors of the production company, Buffalo Pictures.

Dockers ★★★

UK (Parallax Pictures/Initiative Factory) Drama. Channel 4 1999
DVD: Prism Leisure

Tommy Walton	**Ken Stott**
'Macca' Macaulay	**Ricky Tomlinson**
Jean Walton	**Chrissy Rock**
Andy Walton	**Lee Ross**
Paula Walton	**Christine Tremarco**
Sarah Walton	**Katy Lamont**
Kenny Walton	**Kristopher Lundon**
Thomas Walton	**Michael Ryan**
Big John	**James Foy**
Mrs Macaulay	**Joan Kempson**
Pete Macaulay	**David Parkinson**

Producer **Sally Hibbin**

Experimental drama based on a real-life dockers' strike.

Life-long friends Tommy Walton and Macca Macaulay have worked together on the Liverpool docks since they were lads. Now, however, friendships are stretched to the limit as an industrial dispute breaks out. Tommy's son, Andy, is part of a group of dockers who are dismissed by the management, and other workers – Tommy and Macca among them – walk out in support. Despite finding international solidarity for their cause, there are accusations of betrayal on a local level when the workforce is summarily sacked. As the dispute shows no sign of ending, relationships between the workers on the front line, as well as within their families picking up the pieces at home, begin to break down, particularly when Macca becomes a 'scab' and returns to his job. This hard-hitting, feature-length drama, directed by Bill Anderson, was based on the Liverpool dockers' dispute with the Mersey Docks and Harbour Company that ran for three years from 1995. Telling the story from the ground up, it employed some of the real strikers and their wives as writers, chaperoned by the seasoned Jimmy McGovern and novelist Irvine Welsh. A documentary, entitled *Dockers: Writing the Wrongs*, was shown by Channel 4 shortly before the drama itself. This explained how the film came to be made and revealed how McGovern and Welsh helped the dockers put their personal experiences and emotions into dramatic form.

Doctor at Large/in Charge/at Sea/ on the Go/Down Under/at the Top

See *Doctor in the House*.

Doctor Finlay ★★

UK (Scottish) Medical Drama. ITV 1993–6
DVD: John Williams Productions

Dr John Finlay	**David Rintoul**
Dr Cameron	**Ian Bannen**
Dr Neil	**Jason Flemyng**
Janet MacPherson/ Livingstone	**Annette Crosbie**
Brenda Maitland	**Margo Gunn**
Dr Gilmore	**Ralph Riach**
Angus Livingstone	**Gordon Reid**
Rhona Swanson	**Jackie Morrison**
Dr Napier	**Jessica Turner**

Producers **Peter Wolfes, Bernard Krichefski**

● ***In 1946 John Finlay returns to Tannochbrae after wartime service and finds things have changed.***

Moving on two decades from the classic 1960s series (DR FINLAY'S CASEBOOK), this *Doctor Finlay* is set amid the struggles of post-war revival. The old Arden House practice is now run down. Dr Cameron has grown tired and is troubled by the changes being enforced by the new National Health Service. Janet is no longer the gentle, inconspicuous housekeeper of the 1920s but a woman of the 1940s, hardened to the stresses, crises and inadequacies of wartime life. Into this background ambles Dr John Finlay, fresh from service as a major in the Royal Army Medical Corps, and, with some uncertainty, now reaching a crossroads in his career. He is not overpleased to be joined as partner by the young, impulsive Dr Neil, who has been taken on to help with Dr Cameron's workload.

With the arrival of the third series, in 1995, the year has progressed to 1949. Janet has married Angus Livingstone, abdicating her place as housekeeper to young Rhona Swanson, but still keeping an eye on Arden House in her new role of practice receptionist. Dr Neil has moved on to pastures new and his replacement is, somewhat provocatively, a woman, Dr Napier.

Although the village of Callander had served admirably as a setting for the original series, a new location had to be sought for the Tannochbrae of the 1940s. It was discovered in the Fife town of Auchtermuchty.

Dr Finlay's Casebook ★★

UK (BBC) Medical Drama. BBC 1962–71

Dr Alan Finlay	**Bill Simpson**
Dr Angus Cameron	**Andrew Cruickshank**
Janet	**Barbara Mullen**
Dr Snoddie	**Eric Woodburn**
Mistress Niven	**Effie Morrison**

Producers **Campbell Logan, Andrew Osborn, Gerard Glaister, Douglas Allen, Royston Morley, John Henderson**

● ***Young and old doctors share a Scottish village practice.***

Set in and around the settlement of Tannochbrae (real-life Callander) and starting in 1928, *Dr Finlay's Casebook* relates the ups and downs in the life of young, ambitious Dr Alan Finlay and his crusty ex-surgeon partner, Dr Angus Cameron (who was only 65 when the series ended, despite seeming much older). In the best tradition of medical dramas, the whippersnapper with the new-fangled ideas does not always see eye to eye with the stick-in-the-mud old hand; but all the same Tannochbrae is well served by its two dedicated GPs, who mutually benefit from their working arrangement. Watching over proceedings at their base, Arden House, is their trusty housekeeper, Janet, and also seen from time to time are odious Dr Snoddie and gossipy midwife Mistress Niven.

The series, which ran for nine years, despite keen competition from the likes of DR KILDARE and BEN CASEY, was based on stories published as *The Adventures of a Black Bag* by doctor-novelist A. J. Cronin (dramatized for Radio 4 in 2001 with John Gordon-Sinclair in the lead). The series was revived by ITV in 1993 (see DOCTOR FINLAY).

Doctor Fischer of Geneva ★★★

UK (Consolidated Productions/BBC) Drama. BBC 2 1984

Doctor Fischer	**James Mason**
Alfred Jones	**Alan Bates**
Anna-Luise Fischer	**Greta Scacchi**
Steiner	**Cyril Cusack**
Mrs Montgomery	**Clarissa Kaye**
Richard Deane	**Barry Humphries**
Divisionaire Krueger	**Hugh Burden**
Belmont	**David De Keyser**
Mr Kips	**Jacques Herlin**
Albert	**Nicholas Le Prevost**

Writer/Producer **Richard Broke**

● ***An affluent doctor plays cynical games with his pandering entourage.***

This adaptation of Graham Greene's novel of the same name was the first film ever to be sanctioned by the novelist himself. Indeed, Greene was actively involved in planning the production. It tells the story of a man with wealth untold (acquired from developing a flower-scented toothpaste business) but very little happiness, a man whose chief pleasure in life is belittling the selfish and the greedy. His game is to stage dinner parties at which he will encourage a band of cronies ('the Toads') who desire his favours and patronage to debase themselves in all kinds of ways. After humiliating them, he rewards them with financial prizes. Epitomizing the sort of game Fischer plays is his lavish winter banquet, held outdoors in the snow. For this he has loaded Christmas crackers with Swiss francs. The twist is this: in one cracker, there is also a bomb. Will the Toads go as far as to play this particular game? Fischer, however, hits a buffer with one of his guests, an Englishman named Jones, who has no money and harbours a distaste of all possessions. This is one man Fischer's money fails to impress and without that the doctor has no hold over him.

Michael Lindsay-Hogg directs the 100-minute drama, which was filmed in Lausanne and offered James Mason one of his last screen performances. Music was by Trevor Jones.

Doctor in the House ★★

UK (LWT) Situation Comedy. ITV 1969–70

Michael Upton	**Barry Evans**
Duncan Waring	**Robin Nedwell**
Dick Stuart-Clark	**Geoffrey Davies**
Paul Collier	**George Layton**
Huw Evans	**Martin Shaw**
Dave Briddock	**Simon Cuff**
Prof. Geoffrey Loftus	**Ernest Clark**
The Dean	**Ralph Michael**
Danny Hooley	**Jonathan Lynn**

Producer **Humphrey Barclay**

● ***Medical students run riot at London's St Swithin's Teaching Hospital.***

Loosely based on the *Doctor* books by Richard Gordon, which had been filmed in the 1950s with Dirk Bogarde in the lead role, this TV comedy led to a run of spin-off series: *Doctor at Large* (1971), *Doctor in Charge* (1972–3), *Doctor at Sea* (1974) and *Doctor on the Go* (1975–7). There was also an Australian version, *Doctor Down Under* (1981). The central character was initially naïve young student Michael Upton, but when Barry

Evans left the show in 1972, Robin Nedwell as Duncan Waring, one of Upton's friends in the first series, returned to take over centre stage. Among the other hell-raisers were the upper-crust, work-shy Dick Stuart-Clark, Welshman Huw Evans, genial Paul Collier and crazy Irishman Danny Hooley. Prim spoilsport Laurence Bingham (Richard O'Sullivan) was seen in the *Doctor at Large* and *Doctor in Charge* series. Haughty Professor Loftus cast a disapproving eye on the goings-on as the red-blooded students chased nurses, played childish pranks and generally caused chaos. The characters were revived in 1991 in a new BBC series, *Doctor at the Top*, which viewed the lads 20 years on in their respective practices.

Doctor in the House was a decisive step forward in the careers of several actors who played a major part in British sitcoms of the 1970s and 1980s. Richard O'Sullivan went on to his own series MAN ABOUT THE HOUSE, Barry Evans to MIND YOUR LANGUAGE, and George Layton to IT AIN'T HALF HOT MUM and behind-the-scenes scriptwriting on a host of comedy shows, and Jonathan Lynn teamed up with Anthony Jay to create the hugely successful YES, MINISTER. Writers on the *Doctor* series themselves included the GOODIES duo of Bill Oddie and Graeme Garden, as well as *Pythons* Graham Chapman and John Cleese. Cleese allegedly based his FAWLTY TOWERS on a hotelkeeper he had created for one of the *Doctor* episodes.

Dr Kildare ✶✶

US (Arena/MGM) Medical Drama. BBC 1 1962–6
(US: NBC 1961–6)

Dr James Kildare .... **Richard Chamberlain**
Dr Leonard Gillespie .... **Raymond Massey**
Dr Simon Agurski .... **Eddie Ryder**
Dr Thomas Gerson .... **Jud Taylor**
Susan Deigh .... **Joan Patrick**
Nurse Zoe Lawton .... **Lee Kurty**
Dr Lowry .... **Steven Bell**
Nurse Fain .... **Jean Inness**

Executive Producer **Norman Felton**

● ***A sensitive young doctor learns the ropes from an experienced senior physician.***

Baby-faced James Kildare works at the Blair General Hospital under the watchful eye of wise old Leonard Gillespie. The series begins with Kildare and two other doctors, Agurski and Gerson, taking up new posts at the hospital. The others leave after one season but dedicated Kildare stays on, battling with medical matters, furthering his knowledge and education, and striving to meet standards set by his mentor, Gillespie.

The programme keeps fairly true to life, exposing the moral and ethical dilemmas experienced by the medical fraternity and the suffering endured by patients and their families, although the initial hour-long dramas later give way to a half-hour serial format.

Dr Kildare made Richard Chamberlain into a household name. He even hit the charts with a vocal version of the theme song, 'Three Stars Will Shine Tonight', in 1962, and found it difficult to shake off the persona of the heart-throb doctor he portrayed so effectively. The character, which was created by Max Brand, had already appeared in several films in the 1930s and 1940s, played mainly by Lew Ayres, with Lionel Barrymore in the role of Gillespie.

Dr Quinn: Medicine Woman ✶✶

US (The Sullivan Company/CBS) Drama. ITV 1993–7
(US: CBS 1993–8)
DVD: A&E Home Video (Region 1 only)

Dr Michaela 'Mike' Quinn .... **Jane Seymour**
Byron Sully .... **Joe Lando**
Loren Brey .... **Orson Bean**
Matthew Cooper .... **Chad Allen**
Colleen Cooper .... **Erika Flores**
Jessica Bowman
Brian Cooper .... **Shawn Toovey**
Jake Slicker .... **Jim Knobeloch**
Revd Timothy Johnson .... **Geoffrey Lower**
Horace Bing .... **Frank Collison**
Robert E .... **Henry Sanders**
Grace .... **Jonelle Allen**
Emily .... **Heidi Kozak**
Cloud Dancing .... **Larry Sellers**
Hank Claggerty/Lawson .... **William Shockley**
Myra .... **Helene Udy**
Ingrid .... **Jennifer Youngs**
Dorothy Jennings .... **Barbara Babcock**
Olive Davis .... **Gail Strickland**
Preston A. Lodge III .... **Jason Leland Adams**
Dr Andrew Cook .... **Brandon Douglas**
Teresa Morales .... **Alex Meneses**
Daniel Simon .... **John Schneider**

Creator **Beth Sullivan**
Executive Producers **Beth Sullivan, Carl Binder, Philip Gerson, Chris Abbott**

● ***A female doctor challenges tradition in the Wild West.***

Michaela 'Mike' Quinn is a revolutionary. She has defied prevailing logic and convention by qualifying as a surgeon in Boston (it is 1860) and working at her father's practice. When he dies, she decides to take a job in the frontier town of Colorado Springs, much against her mother's wishes. The townsfolk are equally aghast when they realize their new medical person is a woman. But Mike quickly gains their confidence, aided by support from the rugged, mysterious Byron Sully (a future husband) and his pet wolf. She also becomes a surrogate mother, being handed the care of three orphans (Matthew, Colleen and Brian) when their mother, boarding-house keeper Charlotte Cooper, an early friend in the town, dies from a snake bite. Among the initially sceptical townsfolk are storekeeper Loren Brey, barber Jake Slicker, saloon-keeper Hank Claggerty, saloon girl Myra, postmaster Horace Bing and newspaper editor Dorothy Jennings. Cloud Dancing is the local friendly Native American.

Dr Terrible's House of Horrible ✶

UK (Baby Cow) Comedy. BBC 2 2001
DVD: BBC

Dr Terrible .... **Steve Coogan**

Creator **Graham Duff**
Writers **Steve Coogan, Graham Duff, Henry Normal**
Producer **Alison MacPhail**

● ***Creepy, hammed-up tales of the supernatural.***

Steve Coogan narrates this series of spoof Hammer horror-type thriller stories in the guise of the disfigured, white-tuxedoed Dr Terrible. He also appears in each tale as the dashing hero who struggles to defeat the various forces of evil that manifest themselves in each 30-minute helping. With titles like *Lesbian Vampire Lovers of Lust, Frenzy of Tongs, Curse of the Blood of the Lizard of Doom, And Now the Fearing, Voodoo Feet of Death* and *Scream, Satan, Scream*, it is not hard to see where the inspiration comes from. Stories of witch-finders, newlyweds trapped in a sinister Gothic castle, a man whose newly grafted feet have a mind of their own, and more are heavily laced with cheesy horror film clichés and pieced together with stock-in-trade imagery and techniques (more a homage than a send-up, claimed creator Graham Duff). Guest stars include Tim Pigott-Smith, Honor Blackman, Tom Bell and Angela Pleasence. Regrettably, the concept proved less successful than Duff and Coogan had hoped and only one series resulted.

Doctor Who ✱✱✱✱

UK (BBC) Science Fiction. BBC 1 1963–89; (Universal/BBC Worldwide/MCA) 1996; 2005–
DVD: BBC

Doctor Who .... **William Hartnell**
Patrick Troughton
Jon Pertwee
Tom Baker
Peter Davison
Colin Baker
Sylvester McCoy
Paul McGann
Christopher Eccleston
David Tennant

The Doctor's Assistants
Susan Foreman (*Hartnell*) .... **Carole Ann Ford**
Ian Chesterton (*Hartnell*) .... **William Russell**
Barbara Wright (*Hartnell*) .... **Jacqueline Hill**
Vicki (*Hartnell*) .... **Maureen O'Brien**
Steven Taylor (*Hartnell*) .... **Peter Purves**
Katarina (*Hartnell*) .... **Adrienne Hill**
Dorothea 'Dodo' Chaplet (*Hartnell*) .... **Jackie Lane**
Polly (*Hartnell/Troughton*) .... **Anneke Wills**
Ben Jackson (*Hartnell/Troughton*) .... **Michael Craze**
Jamie McCrimmon (*Troughton*) .... **Frazer Hines**
Victoria Waterfield (*Troughton*) .... **Deborah Watling**
Zoe Herriot (*Troughton*) .... **Wendy Padbury**
Liz Shaw (*Pertwee*) .... **Caroline John**
Jo Grant (*Pertwee*) .... **Katy Manning**
Sarah Jane Smith (*Pertwee/Tom Baker/Tennant*) .... **Elisabeth Sladen**
Lt. Harry Sullivan (*Tom Baker*) **Ian Marter**
Leela (*Tom Baker*) .... **Louise Jameson**
K9 (*Tom Baker/Tennant*) .... **John Leeson** *(voice only)*
David Brierley *(voice only)*
Romana (*Tom Baker*) .... **Mary Tamm**
Lalla Ward
Adric (*Tom Baker/Davison*) .... **Matthew Waterhouse**
Nyssa (*Tom Baker/Davison*) .... **Sarah Sutton**
Tegan Jovanka (*Tom Baker/Davison*) .... **Janet Fielding**
Vizlor Turlough (*Davison*) .... **Mark Strickson**
Perpugillian ('Peri') Brown (*Davison/Colin Baker*) .... **Nicola Bryant**
Melanie Bush (*Colin Baker/McCoy*) .... **Bonnie Langford**
Dorothy 'Ace' (*McCoy*) .... **Sophie Aldred**
Dr Grace Holloway (*McGann*) . **Daphne Ashbrook**
Chang Lee (*McGann*) .... **Yee Jee Tso**
Rose Tyler (*Eccleston/Tennant*) **Billie Piper**
Capt. Jack Harkness (*Eccleston*) .... **John Barrowman**
Mickey Smith (*Eccleston/Tennant*) .... **Noel Clarke**
Martha Jones (*Tennant*) .... **Freema Agyeman**

Others
Col./Brigadier Alastair Gordon Lethbridge Stewart (*Troughton/Pertwee/Tom Baker/Davison/McCoy*) .... **Nicholas Courtney**
Sgt/RSM Benton (*Pertwee/Tom Baker*) .... **John Levene**
Capt. Mike Yates (*Pertwee*) .... **Richard Franklin**
The Master (*Pertwee/Tom Baker/Davison/Colin Baker/McCoy/McGann*) .... **Roger Delgado**
Anthony Ainley
Eric Roberts
Davros (*Tom Baker/Davison/Colin Baker/McCoy*) .... **Michael Wisher**
David Gooderson
Terry Molloy
The Black Guardian (*Tom Baker/Davison*) .... **Valentine Dyall**
The White Guardian (*Tom Baker/Davison*) .... **Cyril Luckham**
The Valeyard (*Colin Baker*) .... **Michael Jayston**
The Inquisitor (*Colin Baker*) .... **Lynda Bellingham**
The Rani (*Colin Baker/McCoy*) .... **Kate O'Mara**
Jackie Tyler (*Eccleston/Tennant*) .... **Camille Coduri**

Creator **Sydney Newman**
Producers **Verity Lambert, Innes Lloyd, Peter Bryant, Barry Letts, Philip Hinchcliffe, Graham Williams, John Nathan-Turner, Phil Collinson**
Executive Producers (1996 film) **Alex Beaton, Philip Segal, Jo Wright**

● ***Classic science-fiction series concerning an eccentric time traveller.***

Doctor Who first reached the TV screens on the day after President Kennedy was assassinated. It quickly lodged itself into the Saturday teatime slot and gained a wonderful reputation for frightening children and entertaining adults. From behind the sofa, kids of all ages wallowed in the concept of a galactic do-gooder with unusual habits working his way around the dimensions of time and space, protecting the innocent and thwarting the oppressive.

Initially, *Doctor Who* had an educational thrust, with creator Sydney Newman intending to involve The Doctor in real historical events, showing viewers just how things had actually happened. But, although there were instances when our hero found himself at the Gunfight at the OK Corral, among the Aztecs, alongside Marco Polo or at the start of the Great Fire of Rome, for example, the idea was quickly dropped in favour of more popular scary monsters and superbeasts.

The Doctor is first encountered in the then today of 1963 in the episode *An Unearthly Child*. The child in question is his alleged granddaughter, Susan, a hyper-intelligent pupil at a London school. Her snooping teachers, Ian Chesterton and Barbara Wright, discover her home is an old police box, parked in a junk yard, where she lives with her grandfather, a mysterious, white-haired, tetchy old man dressed in Edwardian clothing. They sneak into the police box, only to find it is larger inside than out and is, in fact, a kind of spaceship. Fearing his secret will be made public, The Doctor activates the ship, takes off (dematerializes) and lands (materializes) on a prehistoric Earth inhabited by primitive tribesmen. Thus the first *Doctor Who* adventure begins.

It is at this point that we learn more about The Doctor's spaceship. It is known as the TARDIS, standing for Time And Relative Dimensions In Space, and, as implied, it can travel through time as well as space. Sadly, The Doctor has little control over it, and, as one adventure ends, so another begins, with the TARDIS depositing its reluctant crew in yet another perilous situation. (The cliffhangers at the end of the programme were always worth waiting for.)

As the series progresses, The Doctor's companions change frequently. Susan leaves her grandfather to stay on Earth in the year 2167, and Ian and Barbara eventually return to their own time. In their places, The Doctor picks up Vicki (a stranded Earth girl), Steven Taylor (a space pilot, played by future Blue Peter presenter Peter Purves) and Dodo, from Wimbledon. Then comes Polly, a scientist's secretary, and Ben, a Cockney merchant seaman, before The Doctor himself changes. In an episode called *The Tenth Planet*, something happens that will prove vital to the longevity of the series: The Doctor regenerates. Viewers learn that he has the power to revitalize himself when close to death. On this occasion, the grey locks and craggy features of William Hartnell give way to the pudding-basin haircut and elfish grin of Patrick Troughton. Along with his appearance, The Doctor's character also changes. His dour snappiness is replaced by sprightly *joie de vivre*, as Troughton turns The Doctor into a kind of scientific clown, a cosmic hobo in baggy checked trousers who passes the time piping up tunes on a recorder. With Doctor No. 2 travel Polly, Ben and then Scots Highlander Jamie (a pre-EMMERDALE Frazer Hines), Victoria, the orphaned daughter of an antiques shop owner, and a superintelligent alien named Zoe.

When Troughton decided to bow out, it was easy to drop in a replacement, given that the regeneration idea had been comfortably established, and, with his departure, another of The Doctor's many secrets is revealed. Viewers learn that The Doctor is actually one of the Time Lords, a race that lives on the planet Gallifrey and acts as guardians of the time concept. In fact, he has been a bit of a rebel, a runaway who stole a TARDIS, albeit not a very good one. Not only is its navigation control hopelessly flawed, but its chameleon circuits are also defunct. Consequently, instead of being able to change appearance to blend in with the background (as it did in 1963), it is now stuck in its police box guise. All the same, the Time Lords are not forgiving. Finally catching up with The Doctor, they put him on trial and exile him to Earth.

Troughton's successor, Jon Pertwee, plays the role as a brilliant scientist with martial arts skills, a dandy in a frilly shirt and a velvet jacket who drives a yellow vintage car named Bessie (registration WHO 1). He works as a consultant at UNIT (United Nations Intelligence Taskforce), commanded by Brigadier Lethbridge Stewart, a by-the-book, traditional army man who first appears as a Colonel in the Troughton days. Earth is suddenly under threat from all quarters, as malevolent aliens cast their eyes on the planet, and it is during this period that The Doctor's arch-rival, The Master, a scheming, mesmeric, renegade Time Lord with a goatee beard and a sinister smirk, makes his debut. Working with The Doctor at UNIT to counter such adversaries are scientist Liz Shaw, headstrong agent Jo Grant and tomboyish journalist Sarah Jane Smith.

Sarah Jane continues with the next Doctor, a madcap, mop-haired adventurer played by Tom Baker. Sporting a floppy hat, a flowing scarf and an inane grin, chewing jelly babies in times of danger, Baker's Doctor is once again airborne, the Pertwee version regaining his freedom late in the day. Baker's reign as The Doctor proves to be the longest (seven years) and spans no fewer than eight assistants, most notably alien warrior girl Leela, Time Lady Romana (or Romanadvoratrelundar, who regenerates, like The Doctor, into a new body), artful Adric, aristocratic Nyssa and, briefly, Australian air stewardess Tegan. There is also a robot dog, K9.

Baker is succeeded by the gentler, conscientious, cricket-loving Peter Davison depiction, who is admirably supported by Nyssa, Tegan and the schoolboy/alien Turlough. On Davison's departure, a Baker returns, but this time Colin, not Tom. Adding a touch more whimsy and a hefty dose of arrogance to the part, this plumper, curly-headed Doctor's time is short-lived, and he is not generally liked (he even squabbles with his American companion, Peri). He is briefly joined by the red-haired Mel before Sylvester McCoy is drafted in for the seventh portrayal of The Doctor. On this occasion, our hero is a dashing but dotty man of action, carrying a question-mark-shaped umbrella that mirrors his studious but quirky temperament. Much of his travelling is done alongside aggressive Londoner Ace.

After a gap of seven years, The Doctor returned to the screen, played by Paul McGann in a one-off TV movie shown in 1996. Sylvester McCoy is briefly involved at the start but his Doctor 'dies' and is regenerated into a dashing new body. Set in San Francisco on New Year's Eve 1999, the story sees the Doctor fighting once again to save the Earth from destruction at the hands of The Master (played by Eric Roberts, brother of Julia), assisted only by Dr Grace Holloway and Chinese youth Chang Lee.

Finally, after years of denying fans what they wanted, the BBC relented (perhaps partly persuaded by the large audience for BBC 2's *Doctor Who Night* in November 1999) and a new series was produced by BBC Wales for 2005. Russell T. Davies was the brains behind the project, setting the new, vibrant, contemporary tone for the series and scripting some episodes. Christopher Eccleston was brought in as a Doctor with a northern accent, a leather jacket and a rather dismissive, flippant attitude. Billie Piper joined him as Rose Tyler, a London shop assistant who falls for his enigmatic smile and promises of travel in time and space, and more than ever the suggestion of a physical relationship is brought to the fore. A dramatically redesigned Tardis lies centrestage, although the police box exterior remains. The revival was generally accepted to be a triumph for all concerned, but it proved to be a fleeting regeneration as, after just one series of 13 episodes, Eccleston jumped Tardis, leaving the Time Lord's heritage in the hands of a new Doctor played by David Tennant who added more wit and eccentricity to the role, instantly making it his own. With the departure of Billie Piper in 2006, it was announced that Freema Agyema had been cast as the Doctor's new companion, Martha Jones.

Over the years, the Doctor's enemies have been easily as important as his assistants. Among the most menacing are the Cybermen, inhabitants of Earth's twin planet, Mondas, who have replaced their decaying organs with artificial ones and have gradually turned into aggressive silver robot men. The Yeti are furry little robots sent to conquer the Earth; and other memorable invaders include the Ice Warriors (from Mars), the Sea Devils (prehistoric creatures reclaiming their planet from beneath the waves), the Silurians (the Sea Devils' reptile cousins) and The Rani, another rebel Time Lord. Giant ants called Zarbi are some viewers' favourite aliens, but top of the list for most have to be the Daleks, a ruthless race of metal megalomaniacs.

The Daleks are first encountered in the second *Doctor Who*

story, *The Dead Planet*. Set on the planet Skaro, it reveals how the Daleks, a dying race, have developed special transporter machines, armed with deadly ray guns, and are seeking to overcome the Thals, their peace-loving rivals. These transporters (with the seldom-seen squidgy Dalek mutants inside) skate around on castors, with a long suction arm (or occasionally a claw) to operate controls, and a Cyclops-style eye stick out of which to view the world. The Daleks' grating electronic voices provide one of the show's most frightening catchphrases: 'Ex-ter-min-ate!' In later, retrospective episodes, it is revealed that the Daleks are the mutated remains of the Kaled race, saved by a power-crazed scientist, Davros. Sadly, he refused to program the Daleks with compassion and they turned on him, too, in their relentless quest for domination.

Although often mocked for its primitive special effects and soundtracks, few programmes have earned more respect than *Doctor Who*. Two feature film copies were made in the early days – *Doctor Who and the Daleks* and *Daleks: Invasion Earth 2150 AD*, both starring Peter Cushing in the title role. The various incarnations of The Doctor have actually appeared together on more than one occasion. The first was in 1972 in a story entitled *The Three Doctors*, in which the incumbent, Pertwee, was given the help of his two predecessors to combat a threat to the Time Lords. By the time of the next reunion, *The Five Doctors*, in 1983, William Hartnell had died and his portrayal was given by Richard Hurndall. Tom Baker declined to appear, and footage from a never-finished production, *Shada*, was used to bring him into the action. Troughton and Colin Baker met up in *The Two Doctors* in 1985, and all except Hartnell/Hurndall, the late Troughton and the yet-to-be-conceived Eccleston and Tennant resurfaced for a short and extremely confusing 3-D TV experiment for 1993's CHILDREN IN NEED, in which they fought a collection of old enemies (particularly The Rani) in and around EASTENDERS' Albert Square. In 1999, a spoof *Doctor Who* was produced for COMIC RELIEF, beginning with Rowan Atkinson as The Doctor and Julia Sawalha as his assistant. The Doctor then progressed through various regenerations and ended up as Joanna Lumley. Jonathan Pryce played The Master. A new radio version, starring Jon Pertwee, Elisabeth Sladen and Nicholas Courtney, was aired on Radio 2 in 1996.

Doctor Who trivia is available in abundance. Allegedly he is around 750 years old and, being a Time Lord, has two hearts and is allowed 13 regenerations. Among his favourite gadgets is the sonic screwdriver, used for anything from opening electronic doors to detonating unexploded bombs. He is seldom called 'Doctor Who', but simply 'The Doctor' (or, somewhat confusingly, 'The Professor' by Ace). The atmospheric original theme music (modernized by later producers) was composed by Ron Grainer of the BBC's Radiophonic Workshop.

Dr Willoughby ✶✶

UK (Witzend) Situation Comedy. ITV 1999

Donna Sinclair	**Joanna Lumley**
Ralph Whatman	**Brian Protheroe**
Emma Goodliffe	**Isobel Middleton**
Crystal Reynolds	**Paula Bacon**
Mrs Ajax	**Gillian Barge**
Geraldine	**Tanya Moodie**
Gill	**Ursula Holden Gill**
Andy	**Scott Hickman**
Kelly	**Michelle Joseph**
Steve Lipton	**Ian Puleston-Davies**

Writer **Laurie Rowley**
Producer **Tony Charles**

An actress schemes to keep ahead of her soapstar rivals.

Take this comedy at face value and you'll believe that behind every successful actress is a vindictive bitch waiting to burst loose. Donna Sinclair is a soapstar, playing the part of dedicated, warm-hearted surgeon Dr Willoughby in a popular medical series. Off-set, however, Sinclair practises a different kind of surgery, cutting her acting rivals to pieces with her scalpel-like scheming. Jealous of their popularity, fearful of her true age being revealed in the press, desperate to win an award – these are just some of the emotions that drive the egocentric thespian to conspire against her colleagues, who include fellow cast members Ralph and Crystal, and producer Emma. Mrs Ajax is the studio cleaner. Just one series of six episodes was made.

Doctor Zhivago ✶✶

UK (Granada) Drama. ITV 1 2003
DVD: Cinema Club

Dr Yuri Zhivago	**Hans Matheson**
Andrey Zhivago	**Hugh Bonneville**
Victor Komarovksy	**Sam Neill**
Lara Guishar/Antipova	**Keira Knightley**
Amalia Guishar	**Maryam D'Abo**
Olya Demina	**Anne-Marie Duff**
Alexander Gromeko	**Bill Paterson**
Anna Gromeko	**Celia Imrie**
Tonya Gromeko/Zhivago	**Alexandra Maria Lara**
Pasha Antipov/Stelnikov	**Kris Marshall**
Mischa Gordon	**Daniele Liotti**
Mikulytsin	**Rudolf Pellar**
Vassya	**Vojtech Rohlicek**

Writer **Andrew Davies**
Producer **Anne Pivcevic**

Forbidden romance against the backdrop of the Bolshevik Revolution.

Boris Pasternak's sprawling epic had seemingly received the ultimate cinematic treatment in David Lean's 1965 version of *Doctor Zhivago*. This Granada production therefore was a bold venture. To be different, it took the story right back to the 1957 book, consciously creating a new adaptation rather than a film remake. In three episodes, Andrew Davies's screenplay follows the moving story of Yuri Zhivago, a poetic, bourgeois youth who arrives in Moscow after the suicide of his father to stay with his aunt, uncle and cousin Tonya. Despite marrying Tonya, the young doctor falls in love with the beguiling Lara Guishar, whom he glimpses first through a bakery window. She also has a troubled life, first forced into an unhappy liaison with the suave Viktor Komarovsky, her mother's manipulative lover, and eventually marrying Pasha, a distrustful boy closer to her own age. But it is the love that builds between Yuri and Lara that is the running thread, through the outbreak of World War I, as doctor and nurse together on the front line, and on to the momentous events of the Russian Revolution, when they realize that, should they even be able to get together, their future is threatened by the social changes engulfing their homeland. With scenes shot in the snowy Czech Republic and Slovakia, among other venues, and extras numbering some 2,500, the serial cost £7 million to produce. Giacomo Campiotti directs.

Doctors ✳

UK (BBC) Medical Drama. BBC 1 2000

Dr Brendan 'Mac' McGuire	**Christopher Timothy**
Dr Steve Rawlings	**Mark Frost**
Dr Helen Thompson	**Corrinne Wicks**
Dr Rana Mistry	**Akbar Kurtha**
Dr Caroline Powers	**Jacqueline Leonard**
Kate McGuire	**Maggie Cronin**
Tasha Verma	**Shabhana Akhtar Bakhsh**
Dr Harry Fisher	**Sean Arnold**
Anoushka Flynn	**Carli Norris**
Ruth Harding	**Yvonne Brewster**
Joanna Helm	**Sarah Manners**
Phil Thompson	**Mark Adams**
Dr Benjamin Kwarme	**Ariyon Bakare**
Dr Jude Carlyle	**Natalie J. Robb**
Dr Marc Eliot	**Tom Butcher**
Dr Kali Hamada	**Nicole Arumugam**
Faith Walker	**Eva Fontaine**
Katrina Bullen	**Tabitha Wady**
Dr Oliver Berg	**Laurence Penry-Jones**
Jerry Walsh	**Guy Burgess**
Father David	**Richard Standing**
Father Tom	**Tom O'Connor**
Dr Georgina 'George' Woodson	**Stirling Gallacher**
Dr Greg Robinson	**Ben Jones**
Carolina Shaw	**Ela Kay**
Julia Parsons/McGuire	**Diane Keen**
Nathan Bailey	**Akemnji Ndifornyen**
Chloe Pearce	**Keely Mills**
Ronnie Woodson	**Sean Gleeson**
Dr Jack Ford	**Steven Hartley**
Sarah Finch	**Andrea Green**
DI Lucy Roth	**Jane Robbins**
Dr Jimmi Clay	**Adrian Lewis Morgan**
Dr Elizabeth Croft	**Jaye Griffiths**
Amanda Clay	**Emma Samms**
Dr Nick West	**Michael McKell**
Bracken Woodson	**Jessica Gallagher**

Executive Producer **Mal Young**
Producers **Carson Black, Will Trotter, Beverley Dartnall**

Life with the team at a family health clinic.

Offering a daily dose of doctors and nurses, this weekday lunchtime drama, from the unit behind CASUALTY and HOLBY CITY, is set in the Riverside practice in Letherbridge, Birmingham (later relocated to the Mill Health Centre after Riverside burns down and the team merges with Best Practice). There GP Dr 'Mac' McGuire and his team of fellow doctors work through a caseload of patients with ailments ranging from Alzheimer's to infertility. Personal drama involving the practitioners themselves heightens the tension, not least when Mac is tried for murder or when he struggles against his alcohol addiction. Also seen are Kate, the surgery manager with whom Mac set up the centre, and who later becomes his second wife, and Julia, Mac's first wife, whom he remarries when his relationship with Kate breaks down. Other staff members include uptight, ambitious Marc Eliot; Helen Thompson, whose husband, Phil, tragically dies in a road accident; disorganized George Woodson; charmer Greg Robinson; dedicated Ben Kwarme; hot-headed Jack Ford; wise-cracking Welshman Jimmi Clay; nurse Faith Walker, whose husband, Jerry, is killed in a siege at the practice; and bubbly receptionist Sarah Finch.

Doctors, The ✳✳

UK (BBC) Drama. BBC 1 1969–71

Dr John Somers	**John Barrie**
Dr Roger Hayman	**Richard Leech**
Dr Elizabeth McNeal	**Justine Lord**
Mrs Hayman	**Irene Hamilton**
Dr Bill Conrad	**Barry Justice**
Tom Durham	**Paul Massie**
Nella Somers	**Alexandra Dane**
Molly Dolan	**Lynda Marchal**
Louise Hayman	**Irene Hamilton**
Mrs Baynes	**Maureen O'Reilly**
Mrs Groom	**Pamela Duncan**
Mrs Parsons	**Elsie Wagstaff**
Dr Linda Carpenter	**Isla Blair**
Dr Thomas Owens/Owen	**Nigel Stock**
Meg Owens/Owen	**Joan Newell**
Dr David Owens/Owen	**Drewe Henley**
Jo Hayman	**Elaine Mileham**
Dr Cheryl Barnes	**Janet Hargreaves**

Creator **Donald Bull**
Producers **Colin Morris, Bill Sellars**

Visits to a fictitious NHS practice.

The first twice-weekly BBC serial to be recorded in colour, *The Doctors* was another attempt by the Corporation to crack the soap-opera market, having had only limited success with COMPACT, UNITED! and THE NEWCOMERS. This time the setting is a general practice in North London which is headed by serious, pipe-smoking Dr John Somers. He is ably supported by the likes of Drs Roger Hayman, Liz McNeal and Bill Conrad, as well as, towards the close, Linda Carpenter and Welsh veteran Dr Thomas Owens – his surname eventually simplified to Owen in readiness for the spin-off, *Owen, MD* (1971–3). With limited resources, they aim to care for 9,000 patients.

The idea was to portray events with due realism, avoiding the schmaltz of American doctors series and skipping the romantic liaisons that characterized EMERGENCY – WARD 10 and similar UK offerings. However, despite the efforts of writers like Elaine Morgan and Fay Weldon, the net result was considered to be a worthy BBC drama without the hoped-for grittiness seen in EASTENDERS, which was still 14 years away.

Documentary

A programme focusing on facts – factual people, objects, instances or circumstances – for the purpose of reporting truth or educating the viewer. Inevitably, the maker's viewpoint is incorporated into the programme (whether directly in the narration or through the camera techniques and editing) and comment is made (sometimes purposefully, at other times unintentionally) on the matter in hand. This led 1930s documentary supremo John Grierson to describe the medium as 'the creative treatment of reality'. Documentary techniques have sometimes been borrowed by drama producers to bring an extra degree of realism or objectivity to their work.

Docu-Soap

Documentaries that follow events in the everyday lives of ordinary citizens are not new. Paul Watson captured the viewers' attention with THE FAMILY in 1974, for instance. However, in the late 1990s, the docu-soap, as it became known, gained a new lease of life. The major catalysts were AIRPORT, *Vets' School* and DRIVING SCHOOL, all in theory showing the general public going about their daily business, but of course really focusing only on moments of high drama or comedy. Selective editing ensured that there were no mundane moments to bore the audience, and only the most charismatic of personalities found their way on to the screen. These series inspired a whole raft of look-alikes as producers desperately sought new locations and professions that might just be good for a series or two. Traffic wardens, hotel workers, shop assistants, doctors, zoo keepers, policemen, holiday reps and rat-catchers all found their 15 minutes of fame before the craze – which had started to dominate peak-time schedules – began to subside.

Dodd, Ken

OBE (1927–)

Merseyside comic, a stalwart of variety shows and his own comedy programmes during the 1960s and 1970s. As well as stand-up routines in the classic music hall style (complete with tickling stick), Dodd has been known to burst into sentimental song (he had a string of hits in the 1960s, including the chart-topping 'Tears'). He also introduced us to the Diddymen – Dicky Mint, Mick the Marmalizer, Evan, Hamish McDiddy, Nigel Ponsonby-Smallpiece, *et al.* – who worked the jam-butty mines of Knotty Ash. They were presented either as kids in costume or in animated puppet sketches, with Dodd providing the voices. His programme titles have included *The Ken Dodd Show, Doddy's Music Box, Funny You Should Say That, Ken Dodd's World of Laughter, The Ken Dodd Laughter Show* and *Ken Dodd's Showbiz*, and other appearances have come in THE GOOD OLD DAYS, STARS ON SUNDAY, *A Question of Entertainment* (team captain) and *Alice in Wonderland* (Mr Mouse), with more intriguing 'straight' guest spots in CROSSROADS and DOCTOR WHO.

Dogtanian and the Three Muskehounds ✶✶

Spain (BRB) Cartoon. BBC 1 1985
DVD: Revelation

Creator/Writer/Executive Producer **Claudio Biern Boyd**

● ***The adventures of a heroic puppy and his dashing colleagues.***

In this fast-moving canine version of the Alexandre Dumas classic *The Three Musketeers*, Dogtanian is a puppy from Gascony who, riding a horse called Sandy, becomes a French national hero after teaming up with a trio of dogfighters, Athos, Porthos and Aramis (the Three Muskehounds). Under their motto of 'one for all and all for one', they champion the underdog throughout the country. Our hero's love interest is Juliette, a Crufts winner if ever there was.

Dolly

A mounting for a camera, usually on wheels or rails to allow camera movement.

Donnelly, Declan

(1975–)
See *McPartlin, Anthony.*

Donovan ✶✶

UK (Granada) Detective Drama. ITV 1 2005–

Joe Donovan .... **Tom Conti**
Kate Donovan .... **Samantha Bond**
Seth Donovan .... **Ryan Cartwright**
Nick Pushko .... **Dan Fredenburgh**
Evie Strauss .... **Amelia Bullmore**
Myrna Rovic .... **Katie Blake**

Writer **Mike Cullen**
Producer **Spencer Campbell**

● ***An expert in forensics leads the pursuit of truth in a series of difficult crimes.***

Joe Donovan was once a forensic advisor to the police but had lost his job because of a medical condition that caused him to suffer blackouts and to behave irrationally. He turned to writing about crime instead. His complaint now diagnosed and rectified, the thoroughly dedicated, hard-working Donovan has been appointed Chief Forensic Officer for a Home Office department known as FIU (Forensic Investigation Unit). His team consists of Nick, Evie and Myrna and together they investigate suspicious murders and other serious crimes. Kate is Donovan's wife of 25 years, but their relationship is rocky and she has had affairs in the past. Their son, Seth, is a biochemistry graduate who takes a job working with dad as a trainee in FIU.

The series followed on from a two-part pilot story shown in 2004, in which Donovan's medical problems came under the spotlight when he, himself, was put in the frame for murder.

Donovan, Jason

(1968–)

Blond Australian actor who shot to fame as Scott Robinson in NEIGHBOURS, using the series to launch a successful singing career. He was the second actor to take the part (following Darius Perkins) and came to Erinsborough via shows like *The Henderson Kids*. Outside Ramsay Street, Donovan also starred in the dramas *The Heroes*, playing a nervous young sailor, *Shadows of the Heart* and *I Can Jump Puddles* (Freddy). In recent years, he was seen in the Australian series *MDA*. His father, Terence Donovan, a veteran of Australian TV, also joined the *Neighbours* cast as Doug Willis.

Don't Ask Me ✶✶

UK (Yorkshire) Science. ITV 1974–8

Presenters **Derek Griffiths, Miriam Stoppard, Magnus Pyke, David Bellamy, Robert Buckman, Austin Mitchell, Brian Glover**

Producer **Duncan Dallas**

● ***The hows, whys and wherefores of science explained in everyday terms.***

Prompted by questions from a studio audience, Dr Magnus Pyke, Dr Miriam Stoppard and David Bellamy took the wonders of science, medicine and technology into Britain's living rooms. 'Why do golf balls have dimples?' and 'Do crocodiles shed tears?' were two typical queries, with one question always coming from a celebrity guest. Derek Griffiths hosted proceedings in the early days, before he was succeeded (briefly) by Adrienne Posta and then by Brian Glover. Dr Rob Buckman and future Labour MP Austin Mitchell also became part of the team. A follow-up series, *Don't Just Sit There*, featured the same pundits.

Don't Drink the Water

See *On the Buses*.

Don't Forget to Write! ★★★

UK (BBC) Situation Comedy. BBC 1 1977; 1979

Gordon Maple .... **George Cole**
Mabel Maple .... **Gwen Watford**
Tom Lawrence .... **Francis Matthews**

Creator/Writer **Charles Wood**
Producer **Joe Waters**

● ***A dramatist encounters problems in his personal and professional life.***

Gordon Maple is a moody, struggling screenwriter, supplying scripts for feature films that are never actually made, dealing with awkward movie producers who make his life difficult with their niggling demands. Maple is also prone to bouts of writer's block and, to compound the agony, his writer friend Tom Lawrence is altogether more successful. Mabel is Gordon's long-suffering wife.

Don't Forget To Write! had its origins in two plays which, like this series, were written by Charles Wood and starred George Cole and Gwen Watford. The first, entitled *A Bit of a Holiday*, was screened by Yorkshire Television as part of its 1968 anthology *The Root of All Evil*. The second, *A Bit of a Family Feeling*, aired in 1971 as part of Yorkshire's *The Ten Commandments* season.

Don't Forget Your Toothbrush ★★★

UK (Ginger) Game Show. Channel 4 1994–5

Presenters **Chris Evans, Jadene Doran**

Producer **Lisa Clarke**

● ***Innovative comedy game show offering a chance of a dream holiday to anyone in the studio audience.***

Musically supported by Jools Holland and guest bands, Chris Evans broke new ground with this live Saturday night game show. The entire studio audience was told to bring their passports and toothbrushes along, with the possibility that any of them could be leaving immediately at the end of the show on the holiday of a lifetime.

By 'exploding seats' to choose contestants and putting them through a sequence of wacky games and quizzes, winners were chosen and ultimately given the chance to answer enough questions to ensure their holiday was in Rio, not Rhyl, or Barbados, not Bognor. One week the whole audience was packed on to buses and taken away to EuroDisney. Among the games featured were a quiz involving a pop star who had to answer more questions about him or herself than an ardent fan, and an outside broadcast which called on an unsuspecting household and demanded that its residents throw a number of domestic items out of the windows within a given time. Despite immense popularity, only two series were made, Evans preferring to move on to new projects.

Don't Rock the Boat ★★

UK (Thames) Situation Comedy. ITV 1982–3

Jack Hoxton .... **Nigel Davenport**
Dixie Hoxton .... **Sheila White**
Les Hoxton .... **John Price**
Billy Hoxton .... **David Janson**

Writers **John Esmonde, Bob Larbey**
Producer **Mark Stuart**

● ***A widower marries a much younger woman, much to his sons' distress.***

Having lost his wife, Jack Hoxton has a peaceful existence, running a boatyard on a river, but his life changes when he starts dating a girl half his age. Glamorous Dixie is a former chorus girl who has been recently working as a magician's assistant, and she is most definitely not the sort of second wife Jack's grown-up sons, Les and Billy, think he should have. Nevertheless Jack and Dixie marry and share the family home, leaving the boys to find ways of keeping their late mum's memory alive and to generally make life difficult for the cuckoo in the nest. Dixie, however, is resilient and gives as good as she gets, and there is no sign that Jack is regretting his new marriage. Two series were produced.

Don't Tell Father ★

UK (BBC) Situation Comedy. BBC 1 1992

Vivian Bancroft .... **Tony Britton**
Natasha Bancroft .... **Susan Hampshire**
Kate Bancroft .... **Caroline Quentin**
Marvin Whipple .... **Philip Fox**
Garth Bancroft .... **Richard Ashton**
Ron Whipple .... **Jack Smethurst**
Stella Whipple .... **Anna Dawson**

Writer **Roy Clarke**
Producer **Harold Snoad**

● ***A pretentious elderly actor is the centre of his own universe.***

Vivian Bancroft, esteemed thespian (in his eyes at least), is the patriarchal figure in his own little world. Married, for the fifth time, to Natasha (20 years his junior), he is insufferably egocentric, opinionated and frightfully sensitive. He believes himself to be a socialist, while espousing values that would make Mrs Thatcher blanch. Kate is one of his daughters and Marvin is her boyfriend. Marvin's parents Ron and Stella also show their faces, and to accept him into the family fold is one of the themes of the series. Just six episodes were produced.

Don't Wait Up ★★

UK (BBC) Situation Comedy. BBC 1 1983–8; 1990
DVD: Universal

Dr Tom Latimer .... **Nigel Havers**
Dr Toby Latimer .... **Tony Britton**
Helen Latimer .... **Jane How**
Angela Latimer .... **Dinah Sheridan**
Madeleine Forbes/Latimer ..... **Susan Skipper**
Dr Charles Cartwright .... **Richard Heffer**
Simon Williams
Susan Cartwright .... **Tricia George**

Felicity Spicer-Gibbs .... **Jane Booker**

Creator/Writer **George Layton**
Producer **Harold Snoad**

Father and son doctors are brought together by divorce.
Hard-working GP Tom Latimer, newly divorced from Helen, loses his home and his surgery in the ensuing settlement. He manages to rent back the surgery but is forced to share a flat with his pompous dad, Toby, a Harley Street dermatologist who has just seen the break-up of his own marriage to Tom's mother, Angela. Playing on the generation gap, and also on the conflict between NHS and private medicine, the series sees the two men at each other's throats as they try to rebuild their lives, with Tom working for a reconciliation between his parents. Madeleine is Toby's secretary and Tom's new girlfriend (later wife). Charles Cartwright is Tom's practice partner.

Doogie Howser, MD ✶✶

US (Steven Bochco/Twentieth Century-Fox) Comedy Drama. BBC 1 1990–3 (US: ABC 1989–93)
DVD: Anchor Bay Entertainment (Region 1 only)

Dr Douglas 'Doogie' Howser .. **Neil Patrick Harris**
Dr David Howser .... **James B. Sikking**
Katherine Howser .... **Belinda Montgomery**
Vinnie Delpino .... **Max Casella**
Dr Benjamin Canfield .... **Lawrence Pressman**
Dr Jack McGuire .... **Mitchell Anderson**
Nurse Curly Spaulding .... **Kathryn Layng**
Wanda Plenn .... **Lisa Dean Ryan**
Janine Stewart .... **Lucy Boryer**
Dr Ron Welch .... **Rif Hutton**
Raymond Alexander .... **Markus Redmond**
Nurse Michele Faber .... **Robyn Lively**

Creators **Steven Bochco, David Kelley**
Producer **Steven Bochco**

A precocious teenage boy is a qualified hospital doctor.
The star of this half-hour 'dramedy' makes even fresh-faced DR KILDARE seem ancient. Dr Doogie Howser is in fact just 16 years old. Having raced through high school and university by the age of 10, the boy genius passes his medical exams aged 14 and is already into his second year as a resident at LA's Eastman Medical Center when the series begins. But, while his brain is simply years ahead, astounding his medical peers and many a worried patient, the rest of his body is trapped in an adolescent tomb without the maturity his status demands. Advice for the wunderkind, who is stuck between the responsibilities of adult life and the carefree world of the teenager, comes from protective mom and dad, Katherine and Dr David, as well as senior physicians at work, not least head honcho Dr Canfield and colleague Dr McGuire. However, constant reminders of his true age are supplied by his best buddy, and later roommate, Vinnie Delpino. Wanda Plenn is Doogie's girl, replaced eventually by nurse Michele Faber. Also seen is Raymond Alexander, a former street gang member for whom Doogie finds an orderly's job at the hospital.

Doomwatch ✶✶

UK (BBC) Science Fiction. BBC 1 1970–2
DVD: Meridian Entertainment

Dr Spencer Quist .... **John Paul**
Dr John Ridge .... **Simon Oates**
Tobias 'Toby' Wren .... **Robert Powell**
Colin Bradley .... **Joby Blanshard**
Pat Hunisett .... **Wendy Hall**
Minister .... **John Barron**
Barbara Mason .... **Vivien Sherrard**
Geoff Hardcastle .... **John Nolan**
Dr Fay Chantry .... **Jean Trend**
Dr Anne Tarrant .... **Elizabeth Weaver**
Commander Neil Stafford ...... **John Brown**

Creators **Gerry Davis, Kit Pedler**
Producer **Terence Dudley**

A special government department monitors dangers to society from scientific 'progress'.
Standing for the Department for the Observation and Measurement of Science, Doomwatch is a governmental agency dedicated to preserving the world from the dangers of unprincipled scientific research. The Government's intention in setting up the agency was to stifle protest and secure votes, and it believed it was establishing a quango with little power. However, its principal activists, the incorruptible Dr Spencer Quist and the heroic pairing of Dr John Ridge and Toby Wren, soon give Doomwatch some real bite.

Quist once worked on the creation of the atomic bomb but has since seen his wife die of radiation poisoning. Ridge is an all-action, woman-chasing, secret agent type, and Wren is a conscientious researcher. Together they take ecology into viewers' living rooms, questioning the real value of certain scientific discoveries in a series of dramas which, in many respects, are years ahead of their time. Among the problems they tackled are embryo research, subliminal messages, so-called 'wonder drugs', the dumping of toxic waste, noise pollution, nuclear weaponry, man-made viruses, genetic manipulation and animal exploitation. Consequently, *Doomwatch* has since been described as the first 'green' TV drama series. It was novel in another TV sense, too, taking the drastic and risky step of killing off one of its lead characters at the end of the first season: Wren is blown up while defusing a bomb on a seaside pier. Among his replacements is Dr Fay Chantry, who is introduced to strengthen the female content.

Radical, unusual and controversial, *Doomwatch* was the brainchild of former Doctor Who collaborators Gerry Davis and Kit Pedler. However, they became increasingly disillusioned with the series as mundane drama elements took hold. By the third and final season, they had severed their link completely and were openly voicing criticisms of storylines. A feature film of the same title was released in 1972, starring Ian Bannen, but Ridge, Quist and their Yorkshireman lab assistant Colin Bradley made only fleeting appearances in it.

In 1999, Channel 5 presented a one-off, feature-length revival of the concept, starring Trevor Eve, with Philip Stone taking on the role of Spencer Quist.

Doonican, Val

(1929–)

Relaxed Irish singer whose Saturday night variety shows became a staple of the BBC (and, briefly, ITV) diet in the late

1960s and 1970s. Mixing sentimental ballads with novelty songs like 'O'Rafferty's Motor Car', 'Delaney's Donkey' and 'Paddy McGinty's Goat', Doonican was a firm favourite with both old and young viewers, and his distinctive sweaters and cosy rocking-chair established themselves as his trademarks. Comedian Dave Allen was 'discovered' thanks to the weekly slot Doonican gave him.

Dorothy L. Sayers Mystery, A

See *Lord Peter Wimsey*.

Dors, Diana

(Diana Fluck; 1931–84)

Bold, blonde Swindon-born leading lady, a product of the Rank Charm School whose film career never quite reached the heights it promised. Later in life she found herself more in demand on television. She starred as Queenie Shepherd in the 1970 sitcom QUEENIE'S CASTLE, as rugby league manageress Di Dorkins in the 1973 comedy *All Our Saturdays*, played the commandant in THE TWO RONNIES saga *The Worm That Turned*, and also appeared as Mrs Bott in JUST WILLIAM. Her numerous guest spots included HAMMER HOUSE OF HORROR, THRILLER and villainous roles in both SHOESTRING and THE SWEENEY. She also briefly presented an afternoon chat show for Southern TV. Never short of personal problems, Diana Dors died in 1984 after major surgery. One of her last TV roles was as slimming presenter on TV-am's *Good Morning Britain*. In 1999 ITV dramatized her life story in *The Blonde Bombshell*, starring Keeley Hawes and Amanda Redman as Dors.

Dossa and Joe ✶✶✶

Australia/UK (Granada) Situation Comedy. BBC 2 2002

Dossa Bailey	**Anne Charleston**
Joe Bailey	**Michael Caton**
Vanessa	**Jeanie Drynan**
Bobby Bailey	**Ryan Johnson**
Big Sean	**Robert Bruning**
Chook	**Donal Forde**
Wayne	**Darren Gilshenan**
Robbo	**Joel Edgerton**
Charlie	**Roy Billing**

Creators/Writers/Producers **Caroline Aherne, Peter Herbert**

● ***Retirement threatens the balance of a long-established marriage.***

In the wake of THE ROYLE FAMILY's success, Caroline Aherne flew out to Australia to produce this comedy about a working-class, suburban couple who have been married for 40 years. Joe Bailey, approaching 65, has just retired from his lifelong car factory job and is now clearly at a loose end at home, where he cramps the style of his Irish-descendant wife, Dossa. She has become used to busying herself with charity work and now he's getting in her way. Their whole relationship has been turned upside down by the simple act of retirement and now Dossa and Joe seek assistance from a marriage counsellor. However, this is something Joe struggles to find useful. In sessions with the unseen counsellor, Claire, he drifts off into memories of his working days and the card games and other leisure moments he shared with his colleagues, Big Sean, Chook and Wayne. Surrounding the couple are their 22-year-old son, Bobby (daughter Giselle is away, working in London), and neighbour Vanessa. The six-part comedy was also directed by Aherne.

Dotto ✶

UK (ATV) Quiz. ITV 1958–60

Presenters **Robert Gladwell, Jimmy Hanley, Shaw Taylor**

Producer **John Irwin**

● ***Join-the-dots-based game show.***

In *Dotto*, a quiz show brought over to the UK from the USA, two contestants, by answering questions, joined dots to reveal a celebrity's face. The first contestant to guess the mystery person received a cash sum for every unjoined dot left on the board (there were 50 dots at the start of each round). Robert Gladwell was the show's original host, and he was succeeded by Jimmy Hanley and then future POLICE FIVE presenter Shaw Taylor during the programme's two-year run.

The original American version was forced off the screen after being implicated in the so-called 'Quiz Show Scandal' which rocked US game shows in the late 1950s. It was alleged that certain 'interesting' contestants (those whom viewers liked and who generated good audiences) were favoured by programme sponsors and were given the answers to questions in advance so they could continue as reigning champions from programme to programme.

Double Deckers, The

See *Here Come The Double Deckers*.

Double First ✶✶

UK (BBC) Situation Comedy. BBC 1 1988

N. V. (Norman Vernon) Standish	**Michael Williams**
Mary Webster	**Ann Bell**
Louise Hobson	**Jennifer Hilary**
Ellen Hobson	**Holly Aird**
Derek	**Clive Merrison**
William	**Peter Tuddenham**

Writers **John Esmonde, Bob Larbey**
Producer **Gareth Gwenlan**

● ***A brilliant academic refuses to live up to other people's expectations.***

Who would have thought that Oxford University's most promising student of 1960 would be found 28 years later working as a hamburger cook in a Home Counties restaurant? That's the puzzle facing all those who know N. V. Standish. At university he was a champion sportsman, excelling at cricket and squash. He had already published an acclaimed novel and was destined for a high-profile career in the diplomatic service. Where did it all go wrong? Well, it seems that Standish is a bit of a layabout and a sponger, as is proved when sisters Mary and Louise, two old college girlfriends, decide to offer him a home in the hope of rehabilitating the great man. But the independent-minded Standish decides to plough his own furrow and milk the situation throughout the series' seven episodes (the first a one-hour introductory special and all shot on film, spurning a studio laugh track). Ellen is Louise's impressionable schoolgirl daughter, Derek is the next-door neighbour who sees through N. V., and William is our hero's friend.

Double Your Money ✶✶

UK (Associated-Rediffusion/Arlington) Quiz. ITV 1955–68

Host **Hughie Green**

Creator **John Beard**

● ***Extremely popular double-or-quit quiz show.***

Airing first on Radio Luxembourg, *Double Your Money* was brought to television by Associated-Rediffusion, with its Canadian compere, Hughie Green, once again in charge of events. Participants had the chance to win up to £1,000 by answering questions on specialized subjects. Beginning with a lowly £1 question, the contestants selected from 42 available topics and then 'doubled or quit' with each answer to a total of £32. They were then eligible to enter the Treasure Trail, which led to the jackpot prize. For the nail-biting £1,000 question, contestants were isolated in a sound-proofed booth.

As much a part of the programme as the quiz itself was Hughie Green's over-the-top showmanship, as he clowned around, telling corny jokes and poking fun at his contestants. The show's hostesses were also part of the act. The most prominent were Valerie Drew, Jean Clarke, Alice Earrey (a 77-year-old former charlady who had appeared as a contestant), Nancy Roberts, Barbara Roscoe, Anita West (also briefly a BLUE PETER presenter), Julie de Marco and chirpy Cockney teenager Monica Rose, who became Hughie's sidekick for most of the 1960s. Robin Richmond was the programme's resident organist.

Along with TAKE YOUR PICK, *Double Your Money* was a stalwart of ITV's earliest programme schedules and ran until Associated-Rediffusion lost its franchise in 1968. One edition, in 1966, was recorded in Moscow and, because the Communist Party banned cash prizes, the winner picked up a television set instead. In 1971 the concept was revived by Yorkshire Television as *The Sky's the Limit*, in which air miles (up to 21,000) and spending money (£600) replaced pure cash as prizes. Monica Rose was again seen at Hughie Green's side.

Double Your Money was based on the American show *The $64,000 Question*, which, somewhat confusingly, also aired in the UK in 1956–8 as *The 64,000 Question*, hosted by Jerry Desmonde and, for a while, Robin Bailey. Impoverished Britain offered only multiples of sixpence a question instead of dollars, with the top prize fixed at £1,600 (later doubled). Nevertheless, matters were taken extremely seriously and retired copper Detective Supt. Robert Fabian was employed as custodian of the questions. With its original title of *The $64,000 Question*, it was revived in 1990 with Bob Monkhouse asking the questions.

Dougall, Robert

MBE (1913–99)

Distinguished and genial BBC newsreader, one of the Corporation's first TV news presenters. Croydon-born Dougall joined the BBC via its accounts department, before moving to the Empire Service as an announcer in the early 1930s. After spending the war with the Royal Naval Volunteer Reserve, he returned to the BBC in 1946, working as a reporter for its European and Far Eastern services, before switching to the Light Programme, again as announcer. When TV news began in 1954, he (like his early colleagues, Richard Baker and Kenneth Kendall) was kept out of sight, reaching the limelight only when ITN pushed their newscasters into the picture. Dougall read the news until 1973 and subsequently made programmes about bird-watching (he was at one time President of the RSPB). He also hosted STARS ON SUNDAY and Channel 4's senior citizens' magazine *Years Ahead* and was seen in programmes like NATIONWIDE, GOING FOR A SONG and, famously, dancing on *The Morecambe and Wise Show*.

Douglas, Colin

(1912–91)

Northern actor whose most prominent roles were as dim-witted crook BONEHEAD in the comedy series of the same name and as Edwin Ashton, the father of A FAMILY AT WAR. Among his other credits were parts in early children's programmes like *The Children of the New Forest, The Prince and the Pauper, The Gordon Honour, Queen's Champion* and *Quick Before They Catch Us*. He was also seen in *Dick Barton – Special Agent, Dial RIX*, FIRE CRACKERS (George), *Love Story*, FOLLYFOOT, TELFORD'S CHANGE, THE SWEENEY, *God's Wonderful Railway* and NANNY (Donald Gray), with his last performance coming in Alan Bleasdale's GBH, as troubled Labour Party veteran Frank Twist.

Douglas, Jack

(1927–)

British comedian and stooge whose Alf Ippititimus act (complete with nervous tics) was much played to TV audiences in the 1960s, especially on *The Des O'Connor Show*. He was also at one time the resident comic on CRACKERJACK and was seen in *Not on Your Nellie* (Stanley Pickersgill), THE SHILLINGBURY TALES and its sequel, *Cuffy* (Jake), and *Carry On Laughing*.

Douglas, Michael

(1944–)

The son of Kirk Douglas and now a Hollywood giant in his own right, Michael Douglas came to the fore as Inspector Steve Keller, Mike Stone's (Karl Malden) partner in THE STREETS OF SAN FRANCISCO. While working on the series, he was busy furthering his film executive career, producing *One Flew over the Cuckoo's Nest*, and television has since played a poor second fiddle. He is married to actress Catherine Zeta Jones.

Douglas Fairbanks Presents ✶✶

UK (Douglas Fairbanks) Drama Anthology. ITV 1956–7

Host **Douglas Fairbanks Jr**

Producers **Douglas Fairbanks Jr, Lance Comfort, Harold Huth**

● ***Popular, filmed collection of single stories.***

Hollywood leading man Douglas Fairbanks Jr introduces, produces and occasionally stars in this anthology of dramas, which range from murders to farces. Guest stars include Buster Keaton and Christopher Lee. Production took place at the British National Studios in Elstree and around 150 half-hour episodes were made.

Down to Earth [1] **

UK (BBC) Situation Comedy. BBC 1 1995

Tony Fairfax ..... **Richard Briers**
Chris Fairfax ..... **Christopher Blake**
Molly Fairfax ..... **Kirsten Cooke**
Jim ..... **Steve Edwin**
Oswald ..... **Stephen Bent**
Ramon ..... **Sandor Elès**
Helen Thorpe ..... **Joanna Van Gyseghem**

Writers **John Esmonde, Bob Larbey**
Producer **John B. Hobbs**

A deposed diplomat is forced to work as a garden labourer.

Tony Fairfax is one of the chaps who has been handed everything on a silver platter. Thirty-seven years as a cultural attaché in a banana republic have divorced him from the real world, as he quickly discovers when a revolution in his adopted South American home forces him to return to Britain. He has no qualifications and no obvious skills. His former boss, Ramon, has no sway in this foreign land and the only people he can turn to are his younger brother, Chris, and sister-in-law Molly, who run a gardening company. For Tony, the only way to pick up the strands of his life is to pick up a spade and start digging to earn his keep. But when you're not used to dirty hands, or working-class colleagues, it's an uphill struggle, made all the more uncomfortable when ghosts from your past return to haunt you. Just one series (seven episodes) of this 'fish out of water' sitcom was produced.

Down to Earth [2] **

UK (BBC/Whistling Gypsy) Drama. BBC 1 2000–2005

Faith Addis ..... **Pauline Quirke**
Brian Addis ..... **Warren Clarke**
Marcus Addis ..... **Toby Ross-Bryant**
Sarah Addis ..... **Ellie Beaven**
Molly Addis ..... **Alexandra Stone**
Addy ..... **Pat Keen**
Mac ..... **Rowena Cooper**
Rachel ..... **Nimmy March**
Alex ..... **Rupert Ward-Lewis**
Bill Thompson ..... **David Sterne**
Mandy ..... **Caroline Hayes**
Celeste Rogers/Addis ..... **Katy Reeves**
Matt Brewer ..... **Ian Kelsey**
Frankie Brewer ..... **Angela Griffin**
Beccy Brewer ..... **Inga Brooksby**
Lucy Brewer ..... **Charlotte Redpath**
Sam Brewer ..... **Elliot Spencer Keyse**
Thomas Byrne
Wilson Clarke/Steadman ..... **Ram John Holder**
Daphne Brewer ..... **Elizabeth Bennett**
Jackie Murphy ..... **Denise Welch**
Tony Murphy ..... **Ricky Tomlinson**
Emma Murphy ..... **Zara Dawson**
Danny Wood ..... **Dominic Cooper**
Ryan Cooper ..... **Marc Jordan**
Kate Cooper ..... **Finn Atkins**
Lyn Cooper ..... **Melanie Kilburn**
Nick Christy ..... **Rob Collier**
Kerry Jamil ..... **Shelley Conn**
Vi Hughes ..... **Cherith Mellor**
PC Jim Tully ..... **Matthew Devitt**

Producers **Rosemarie Whitman, Sharon Houlihan**

A London family tries to adapt to country living.

When a VAT demand for £40,000 hits Faith and Brian Addis, it seems like the end of the world. In reality, however, it gives them the chance to start a new life, far away from the rat race. Brian gives up his struggling florist's business, Faith resigns as an English teacher at the local comprehensive and, together with their kids – teenagers Marcus and Sarah, plus young Molly – they up sticks and relocate to Oakleigh, Devon. They move into a ramshackle, thatched cottage and live off the land (growing flowers, of course, among other crops) on the fringe of a quiet village. Thus they find that rural life, while new, terrifying and amusingly unpredictable in some respects, also offers peace of mind and personal satisfaction. However, by no means all their plans work out as intended, especially when the weather is so unreliable and diseases like foot and mouth take a hold. The programme was based on Faith Addis's own autobiographical books, *The Year of the Cornflake, Green behind the Ears, Buttered Side Down, It's Better Than Work* and *Taking the Biscuit*.

In the 2003 series, following Brian's death, Faith sells up, leaving their property (Silverdale Farm) and lifestyle in the hands of the Brewer family. The Brewers share the action with local publicans Jackie and Tony Murphy (of the Black Bull) in the next series, before heading back to the city by the time of the 2005 series. The Murphys then hand the pub over to new heart-throb landlord Nick Christy in order to take over the farm themselves, with grand ideas for making their fortune. By which time, so far had things moved on from the original premise that the BBC really ought to have given it a new title.

Downwardly Mobile **

UK (Portman/Yorkshire) Situation Comedy. ITV 1994

Rosemary ..... **Frances de la Tour**
Clem ..... **Philip Jackson**
Sophie ..... **Josie Lawrence**
Mark ..... **Stephen Tompkinson**

Writers **Alistair Beaton, Barry Pilton**
Producer **Philip Hinchcliffe**

Two mismatched couples find house sharing is far from comfortable.

When Black Wednesday sends yuppies everywhere bolting for cover, there is nowhere for once-affluent Sophie and Mark to run, except to Mark's elder brother, Clem, and sister-in-law, Rosie. Clem, a craftsman, and Rosie, an over-charitable psychiatrist, are a happily impoverished couple who now have to play host in their humble house to their once affluent relations. Mark's high-flying job in the City has crashed along with the Stock Market and times are hard, too, for former designer Sophie. Sadly, now they start spreading discontent into the once quietly joyful lives of Clem and Rosie, too. The new living arrangement is far from satisfactory on all accounts, but it's only for the time being, isn't it? One series of seven episodes was made.

Doyle, Craig

(1970–)

Dublin-born presenter, seen in programmes such as TOMORROW'S WORLD, HOLIDAY and GRANDSTAND. His brother, Keith, is also a presenter and has been seen on HOLIDAY and *five News*.

Doyle, Tony

(1942–2000)

Irish actor known for a number of prominent roles, including bent policeman John Deakin in BETWEEN THE LINES, villainous George Ferguson in BAND OF GOLD, roguish Brian Quigley in BALLYKISSANGEL, struggling father Moran in *Amongst Women* and patriarch Harry Clancy in *Four Fathers*. Among his other credits were 1990 (Dave Brett), *Firm Friends* (Michael Gutteridge) and *Circle of Deceit* (Graham), plus guest spots in series like BOON, BULMAN and PEAK PRACTICE. He was also cast in the role of Michael McCready in MCCREADY AND DAUGHTER but died suddenly before production began. He was the father of actress Susannah Doyle.

Dragnet ★★

US (MCA/Mark VII) Police Drama. ITV 1955–68 (US: NBC 1951–9; 1967–70)

DVD: Alpha Video

Sgt Joe Friday	**Jack Webb**
Sgt Ben Romero	**Barton Yarborough**
Sgt Ed Jacobs	**Barney Phillips**
Officer Frank Smith	**Herb Ellis**
	Ben Alexander
Officer Bill Gannon	**Harry Morgan**
Announcer	**George Fenneman**
	Hal Gibney

Creator/Producer **Jack Webb**

● ***Documentary-style police series relating the cases of a no-nonsense, strait-laced cop.***

'Ladies and gentlemen, the story you are about to see is true. Only the names have been changed to protect the innocent.' So begins every episode of this highly successful police drama which was the first to portray a policeman's lot realistically, including the pressures of his private life. It centres on plodding bachelor cop Sgt Joe Friday, badge number 714 in the Los Angeles Police Department. His earliest colleague is Ben Romero, but following the death of actor Barton Yarborough after only three episodes, Friday is briefly accompanied by Ed Jacobs and then through the show's glory years by Officer Frank Smith (usually played by Ben Alexander). With the relaunch of the programme in 1967, after seven years off the air, Harry Morgan (later Colonel Potter in M*A*S*H) joins Friday on the beat as the hypochondriac Bill Gannon. This series is entitled *Dragnet '67* and brings the 1950s series up to date, dealing with topical issues like drug-pushing and student protest.

Dragnet had previously been a hit on US radio and was the brainchild of actor Jack Webb, who also directed the series and researched the concept tirelessly. His contacts in the real-life police department allowed him access to genuine case files, from which the programme's storylines were adapted. Right from the show's characteristic 'dum-de-dum-dum' opening bars, music is skilfully used to heighten the tension. Documentary-style camera angles are often employed, and Webb himself provides a clinical, ultra-serious narration throughout each episode, incorporating dates and times as a policeman would when relating the facts to a courtroom. An announcer winds up the show, explaining the fate of the captured criminals.

Friday became known for his frank dialogues. He demands 'just the facts, ma'am', and matter-of-factly explains, 'My name's Friday, I'm a cop.' Towards the end of the first run of the series, he is promoted to lieutenant, although, strangely, with the 1967 revival he is a sergeant again. Harry Morgan paid tribute to his time in *Dragnet* (which was the first American police drama to be seen on British television) by appearing in a 1987 film parody which starred Dan Aykroyd and Tom Hanks. Prior to this, the series had been brought back in syndication in the USA (1989–90), with Jeff Osterhage as Det. Vic Daniels and Bernard White as Det. Carl Molina the two leading men. Another revival aired in 2003, this time casting MARRIED . . . WITH CHILDREN's Ed O'Neill as Joe Friday and Ethan Embry as Frank Smith.

Drake, Charlie

(Charles Springall; 1925–)

Short, ginger, cherubic comedian, fond of slapstick routines and mispronunciations. It was as The Worker that he became a 1960s TV favourite, turning up at the Labour Exchange to make Henry McGee's life (as Mr Pugh – or, rather, 'Mr Peeyew') a misery. Drake's TV break came in the 1950s, when he appeared with Bob Monkhouse and Dennis Goodwin in *Fast and Loose* (in which Monkhouse blew off part of his left ear when a stunt went wrong). He also starred in children's shows, often as part of an unlikely double act, *Mick and Montmorency*, with lanky comedian Jack Edwardes. His own series, *Drake's Progress, Charlie Drake in* . . . and *The Charlie Drake Show*, followed. In one episode of the last (entitled *Bingo Madness*), Drake was knocked unconscious when a stunt went wrong during a live transmission. After a period of 'retirement', the jaunty Londoner bounced back and *The Worker* arrived in 1965. Drake also appeared in the marriage-agency sitcom *Who is Sylvia?* (which he co-wrote with Donald Churchill) and the vaudeville series, *Slapstick and Old Lace*, before switching to straight roles in dramas like CRIME AND PUNISHMENT, *Endgame*, BLEAK HOUSE (Smallweed) and *Filipina Dreamgirls*. However, he did revive *The Worker* in 1978 as a segment of *Bruce Forsyth's Big Night*. At the peak of his comedy career, Drake ventured into films, with limited success, and even into the pop charts, notching up a run of novelty hits. 'Hallo, my dahlings' became his catchphrase.

Drake, Gabrielle

(1944–)

British actress, born in Pakistan and much seen on television from the late 1960s onwards. Having appeared in action series like THE AVENGERS, THE SAINT and THE CHAMPIONS, Drake was cast as Lt. Gay Ellis in another ITC romp, UFO, and then appeared as Jill Hammond in the road-haulage saga THE BROTHERS. However, it was as motel supremo Nicola Freeman in CROSSROADS that she made a name for herself in the world of soap, staying with the series for a couple of years and rejoining it again very briefly just before the programme was cancelled (for the first time). Among her other credits have been the sitcom *Ffizz*, KELLY MONTEITH (playing his wife), *No. 10, The Importance of being Earnest* and MEDICS (Diana Hardy). Guest appearances have been made in PEAK PRACTICE,

THE INSPECTOR LYNLEY MYSTERIES and HEARTBEAT in recent years.

Drama Playhouse ★★

UK (BBC) Drama Anthology. BBC 1 1970; 1972

A collection of drama pilot programmes.

Taking its lead from COMEDY PLAYHOUSE, which had already proved its worth as the testing ground for new sitcoms, the short-lived *Drama Playhouse* looked to pilot potential drama series. Though only six dramas aired during the two runs, the success rate was good, with three – THE REGIMENT, THE ONEDIN LINE and SUTHERLAND'S LAW – making it into prime-time series of their own. The other three dramas were *The Befrienders*, by Harry W. Junkin, which starred Faith Brook and Megs Jenkins in a story about the Samaritans; *The Venturers*, by Donald Bull, with Douglas Wilmer and James Kerry in a banking tale; and Terry Nation's *The Incredible Robert Baldick*, featuring Robert Hardy as a man haunted by fear.

Drama-Doc

Short for dramatized documentary, the style of programming that reconstructs historical events using actors working from a script built around a number of known facts. It is a style of programming that has brought much confusion in the past, with facts sometimes embroidered or assumptions introduced. Consequently, some viewers have been unsure of the real or fictional nature of the programme. Genuinely fictional dramas, made using documentary camera techniques and editing in a search for extra realism, have clouded the issue even further, although this convention is now widely accepted and acknowledged.

Dream On ★★★

US (HBO) Situation Comedy. Channel 4 1991–2 (US: HBO 1990–6)
DVD: Universal (Region 1 only)

Martin Tupper .... **Brian Benben**
Judith Tupper/Stone .... **Wendie Malick**
Toby Pedalbee .... **Denny Dillon**
Jeremy Tupper .... **Chris Demetral**
Eddie Charles .... **Jeffrey Joseph**

Creators/Writers **David Crane, Marta Kauffman**
Executive Producers **John Landis, Kevin Bright**
Producers **Ribb Idels, David Crane, Marta Kauffman**

A hapless American's life is dominated by old television programmes.

Martin Tupper is a 36-year-old New York publishing executive recently divorced from Judith, the psychiatrist mother of his 11-year-old son, Jeremy. Martin, however, finds it difficult to adapt to his refound bachelorhood. Stumbling from one-night stand to one-night stand, and always keeping an eye on Judith's new relationship with 'Mr Perfect', Dr Richard Stone, Martin seeks guidance in the ways of the single man from his friend, Eddie Charles, a local talk show host. There is little comfort at work, however, from his bulldog secretary, Toby.

Martin, a neurotic type, rides an emotional rollercoaster, and for every emotion there is a TV clip from his youth. Having been sat in front of the television as a child in the 1950s, Martin's mind now works overtime, dredging up moments from classic black-and-white series that encapsulate his prevailing moods and feelings. For viewers, the clips (usually just one-liners) act as Martin's thought-bubbles.

Dream On was created to make use of a library of old material that could no longer find a market in syndication. The writers viewed hundreds of classic programmes in the search for snappy lines around which they could build a story. Sometimes the story came first and the lines followed. Among the vintage cuttings were pieces by Ronald Reagan, Lee Marvin, Jack Benny, Groucho Marx, Bette Davis, George Burns and Vincent Price. The series was not networked in the USA but aired on the HBO cable channel, giving the producers greater freedom with sexual content. In the UK, later series were shown on Sky One. Its executive producer, John Landis, is better known for feature films like *The Blues Brothers*, *Trading Places* and *An American Werewolf in London*.

Dressing for Breakfast ★★★

UK (Warner Sisters) Situation Comedy. Channel 4 1995; 1997–8

Louise .... **Beatie Edney**
Carla .... **Holly Aird**
Liz .... **Charlotte Cornwell**
Dave .... **Nigel Lindsay**
Fabrizio ('Fab') .... **Robert Langdon Lloyd**
Rose .... **Sophie Stanton**
Graham .... **Richard Durden**
Mike .... **Mark Aiken**
Sarah .... **Lucy Robinson**

Creator **Stephanie Calman**
Writers **Stephanie Calman, Nick Revell, Ian Brown**
Producer **Jane Wellesley**

A single girl's life is still fun, even if she is unlucky in love.

Louise has plenty going for her: she is young (twentysomething), attractive, makes jewellery for a living, has her own flat and is a damn good cook, but sadly for her there is no man in her life. This is partly because she lacks confidence and judgement. Her slightly zany but strong-willed best friend, Carla, does have a bloke, what's more a calm, gentle, live-in bloke named Dave, who is happy to play second fiddle. He is content to cook, to clean, to do more or less whatever he is told. He even wants to marry Carla (against her best instincts). To make matters worse for Louise, her insensitive mother, Liz, has a sex life, too. She has just remarried and now Louise has an Italian named Fab as her new stepdad. Egged on and set up by Carla, and mismatched by her mum, Louise stumbles her way through a series of unsuccessful relationships. In later episodes, Fab has died and Liz is once again available, which means she gets in Louise's way more than ever. Throughout, however, there are plenty of girlie-giggle moments and some shrewd observations of the male psyche. The series grew out of a book written by creator Stephanie Calman. Sharing the same title, this was a collection of humorous notes on the life of a single woman.

Driscoll, Patricia

(1927–)

A familiar face with younger viewers in the 1950s, it was Cork-born Patricia Driscoll who originally related the contents of Picture Book for Monday's WATCH WITH MOTHER. However, in 1957, she left to replace Bernadette O'Farrell as Maid Marian in THE ADVENTURES OF ROBIN HOOD, allowing Vera McKechnie to take over as page-turner for the toddlers. Later roles included small parts in MARK SABER, DANGER MAN and *Kidnapped*, as well as the part of Connie in the sitcom *Second Time Around*.

Driver, Betty

MBE (1920–)

Although universally known today as Betty Turpin/Williams, homely barmaid and queen of the hotpot, Leicester-born Betty Driver's TV career predates even CORONATION STREET by a number of years. As a child star she took over from Gracie Fields on a stage tour and later spent seven years as singer with Henry Hall's band, entertaining the troops in World War II. After appearing in a number of stage plays and Ealing comedies, Driver was given her own variety programme, *The Betty Driver Show*, by the BBC in 1952. She later turned to drama and appeared as the bossy canteen manageress, Mrs Edgeley, in the *Coronation Street* spin-off PARDON THE EXPRESSION (with Arthur Lowe), and then in Granada's *Love on the Dole*, before being signed by the company in 1969 to appear in the *Street* proper as policeman Cyril Turpin's wife.

Driver, Harry

(1931–73)

British scriptwriter and producer, one-time partner of Jack Rosenthal and later in collaboration with Vince Powell on sitcoms. As well as contributing to CORONATION STREET, Driver also penned (with Rosenthal) a few episodes of the crime drama THE ODD MAN, and some scripts for TAXI. He worked with Powell on the comedies *Bulldog Breed*, BOOTSIE AND SNUDGE, HERE'S HARRY and PARDON THE EXPRESSION, although his straight-drama work continued through series like ADAM ADAMANT LIVES! Driver and Powell's best-remembered contributions were still to come, however. Among their later creations were GEORGE AND THE DRAGON, TWO IN CLOVER, NEVER MIND THE QUALITY, FEEL THE WIDTH, *The Best of Enemies*, BLESS THIS HOUSE, FOR THE LOVE OF ADA, NEAREST AND DEAREST, SPRING AND AUTUMN and *Mike and Bernie*, with certainly the most controversial of all being the racist comedy LOVE THY NEIGHBOUR.

Driving Ambition ✱✱

UK (BBC) Drama. BBC 1 1984

Donna Hewitt .... **Rosemary Martin**
Jen Robinson .... **Anne Carroll**
Ray Hewitt .... **Mark Kingston**
Mick Robinson .... **Donald Gee**
Ken Lark .... **Gavin Richards**
David .... **Andrew Rigby**
Joanna .... **Eileen Fletcher**
Nigel .... **Adam Kotz**
Bill .... **Brian Bovell**

Writer **Paula Milne**
Producer **Carol Robertson**

● ***Two married women decide to enter the macho world of motor sport.***

With husbands always glued to sport on TV, two housewives in their late thirties decide they need more in life. Donna Hewitt hatches a particularly ambitious plan to rebuild her banger of a Mini and enter it in major saloon car races, with herself at the wheel. Her friend and neighbour, Jen Robinson, can't drive but she is handy beneath the bonnet and so joins Donna as her mechanic. They find an ally in former racing driver Ken Lark, a man of few words who agrees to sponsor their efforts and becomes their team supremo. The two husbands grudgingly tag along. An early offering from dramatist Paula Milne, this eight-part series employed Stirling Moss as its motor sport consultant.

Driving School ✱✱

UK (BBC) Documentary. BBC 1 1997

Producer **Mark Fielder**

● ***Thrills and spills with a group of learner drivers.***

Driving School was the series that introduced the nation to Maureen Rees, a 55-year-old police station cleaner from Cardiff who had failed seven driving tests. Maureen was one of seven pupils from driving schools in Bristol that featured in this six-episode docu-soap. Using small in-car cameras to record their efforts, programmes offered a mixture of horror and hilarity as the earnest learners battled to make the grade, sometimes putting the wider world at risk. Quietly spoken Paul Farrell and Pam Carr were the ultra-patient instructors but pupils were also seen practising with partners who were not so relaxed – Maureen's long-suffering, bus driver husband Dave, for instance. For Maureen, however, the series was a life-changer. She was drafted on to chat shows and magazine programmes, was featured on THIS IS YOUR LIFE and even achieved a minor hit with a version of the Madness hit 'Driving in my Car'. Other pupils included teenager Danny Waring, twins James and Victoria Sibson, and grandmother Joan Rodwell. Officers from Thames Valley police were also shown taking their advanced driving tests.

Drop the Dead Donkey ✱✱✱

UK (Hat Trick) Situation Comedy. Channel 4 1990–1; 1993–4; 1996; 1998
DVD: Cinema Club

Gus Hedges .... **Robert Duncan**
George Dent .... **Jeff Rawle**
Alex Pates .... **Haydn Gwynne**
Henry Davenport .... **David Swift**
Sally Smedley .... **Victoria Wicks**
Damien Day .... **Stephen Tompkinson**
Dave Charnley .... **Neil Pearson**
Joy Merryweather .... **Susannah Doyle**
Helen Cooper .... **Ingrid Lacey**

Creators/Producers **Guy Jenkin, Andy Hamilton**
Executive Producer **Denise O'Donoghue**

● ***Topical satire based around the staff of a TV newsroom.***

It would be difficult to make comedy more up to date than *Drop the Dead Donkey*. By recording each episode the night before transmission and editing it on the day, with voice-overs on the closing credits for up-to-the-minute comment on breaking news, this was a situation comedy with a difference. However, considering the 'situation' was a TV newsroom, it needed to be hypertopical to succeed.

The newsroom in question is that of Globelink News, owned by the unseen Sir Roysten Merchant but run by his responsibility-shirking, yuppie yes-man Gus Hedges. Editor of the news team is George Dent, a hypochondriac divorcé and father of a rebellious teenager. His assistant in the first two series is wily Alex Pates, whose mum is seldom off the phone. The rest of the team consists of a cynical production secretary (the inappropriately named Joy Merryweather), an alcoholic, toupee-wearing news anchor, Henry Davenport, and his sanctimonious on-air colleague, Sally Smedley, plus reporters Dave Charnley (the office Romeo and compulsive gambler) and unscrupulous Damien Day (known to fabricate tragedy to enliven a story). Helen Cooper, a lesbian single mother, later joins the news team as Alex's replacement.

Drop the Dead Donkey was an instant hit and quickly picked up a cult following, with the result that celebrities and politicians queued up for cameo roles. However, as the characterizations became more defined, reliance on real-life news for humour decreased, and the programme focused more on its characters, using topical stories more as fillers. There were no series in 1995 or 1997, but *Drop the Dead Donkey* returned for a final fling at the end of 1998. In a world grappling with the arrival of digital TV, the future for Globelink and its news team appeared bleak; the series showed the characters scrabbling for new careers as the station headed for closure.

Creators Andy Hamilton and Guy Jenkin wrote the vast majority of episodes.

Drovers' Gold ✶✶

UK (BBC) Drama. BBC 1 1997

Ruth Jones	**Geraldine James**
Aaron Jones	**Andrew Howard**
Daniel Jones	**Aneirin Hughes**
Vaughan	**David Calder**
Handl Williams	**Robert Pugh**
Moc Morgan	**Freddie Jones**
Armstrong	**Ray Stevenson**
Elizabeth	**Emma Fielding**
Mary	**Ruth Jones**
Rebecca	**Sharon Geater**
Dafydd	**Alun Jones**
Sir Huw	**John Standing**
Sir Thomas	**Keith Barron**
Markby	**Robert Glenister**
Ma Whistler	**Liz Fraser**

Writer **Michael Chaplin**
Producers **Ruth Caleb, Anji Dyer**

● ***A desperate Welsh farmer takes her cattle to London in search of a better price.***

The year is 1843, the place the fictitious West Wales valley of Cwm Cadarn. Widow Ruth Jones runs a small farm. Life is tough and getting tougher by the minute, especially as Vaughan, the unscrupulous English drover, has refused to offer a good price for her cattle. In desperation, she decides to take the cows to market herself, helped by her sons, Aaron and Daniel, and a motley crew of celtic cowboys. Their destination is prosperous London but the 300 miles they need to cross – over the River Wye into England, through Berkshire and Buckinghamshire and eventually to Smithfield Market – form a difficult terrain, filled with unforeseen costs, cattle disease, cholera, complicated romances and folk bent on greed or revenge, with the spiteful Vaughan always attempting to scupper their progress. Their voyage is one of adventure, tempered by the fact that it was on such a drive that Ruth's husband went missing 14 years before. This five-part, semi-epic drama – directed by Tristram Powell and Lesley Manning, and originally planned with the title of *Harvest Moon* – begins with a feature-length episode.

Drumbeat ✶

UK (BBC) Pop. Music 1959

Presenters **Gus Goodwin, Trevor Peacock**

Producer **Stewart Morris**

● ***The BBC answer to an ITV rock 'n' roll hit.***

As if to prove that imitation is indeed the sincerest form of flattery, this early pop music showcase for Saturday evenings was the BBC's response to ITV's ground-breaking OH BOY! Billed in typically stuffy *Radio Times*-speak as 'Thirty fast-moving minutes of music in the ultra-modern manner', its regular artists were Bob Miller and the Millermen, Vince Eager, The John Barry Seven, Adam Faith, Roy Young and Sylvia Sands, with guests during the four-month run including Russ Conway, Billy Fury, Paul Anka, Cliff Richard, Marti Wilde and The Poni-Tails. Female vocal support was provided by The Barry Sisters. Gus Goodwin was first presenter, replaced by Trevor Peacock. The BBC had much more luck with another new pop show in 1959: JUKE BOX JURY continued through to 1967.

Drury, James

(1934–)

As the classic strong, silent cowboy, James Drury was TV's THE VIRGINIAN, the eastern ranch foreman who travelled west to bring new ideas to the Shiloh estate in Wyoming. Drury first played the role in 1958, when he starred in the pilot. But, in that seldom-seen episode, the Virginian was a dandy, dressed in fancy clothes and sporting short pistols, and it took four years before the series was revamped and accepted by the network. Drury's TV fame arrived after some teenage theatre work and films like *Forbidden Planet, Love Me Tender* and *Pollyanna*. His other television peformances included episodes of GUNSMOKE and THE RIFLEMAN, but little was seen of him after *The Virginian* ended its nine-year run. He did star in *Firehouse*, a short-lived adventure series, and he has also been seen in TV movies (including the pilot for ALIAS SMITH AND JONES) and guest spots.

Dry Run

A rehearsal in which the crew merely observe the script and the movement of the performers, without the equipment running.

Dubbing Mixer

The technician responsible for mixing the soundtracks on a programme.

Duce, Sharon

(1950–)

Sheffield-born actress much seen on TV as the star of series like BIG DEAL (Jan Oliver), GROWING PAINS (Pat Hollingsworth, both opposite Ray Brooks) and *Coming Home* (Sheila Maddocks). She also appeared as Carole, the other woman, in HELEN – A WOMAN OF TODAY, was WPC Cameron in Z CARS, and played Emily Jessop in FIRST BORN, Maggie Fell in the three-part thriller *Natural Lies*, and Anita in another drama, *Into the Fire*. Among her other credits have been MINDER, WYCLIFFE, CLOCKING OFF (Vicky Sullivan), *The Law* (Linda Farrer QC), LONDON'S BURNING, EMMERDALE, CASUALTY, CONVICTION (Sandra Buliegh) and DALZIEL AND PASCOE.

Duchess of Duke Street, The ✶✶✶

UK (BBC/Time-Life) Drama. BBC 1 1976–7
DVD: Universal

Louisa Leyton/Trotter .... **Gemma Jones**
Charlie Tyrrell .... **Christopher Cazenove**
Mary Phillips .... **Victoria Plucknett**
Merriman .... **John Welsh**
Joseph Starr .... **John Cater**
Major Toby Smith-Barton .... **Richard Vernon**
Lizzie .... **Maureen O'Brien**
Irene Baker .... **Jan Francis**
Augustus Trotter .... **Donald Burton**
Mrs Violet Leyton .... **June Brown**
Mr Ernest Leyton .... **John Rapley**
Lord Henry Norton .... **Bryan Coleman**
Mrs Catchpole .... **Doreen Mantle**
Monsieur Alex .... **George Pravda**
Major Johnny Farjeon .... **Michael Culver**
Prince of Wales .... **Roger Hammond**
Mrs Wellkin .... **Kate Lansbury**
Mrs Cochran .... **Mary Healey**
Violet .... **Holly De Jong**
Lottie .... **Lalla Ward**

Creator/Producer **John Hawkesworth**
Executive Producer **Richard Beynon**

● ***A cook works her way out of the kitchen to become owner of a select hotel.***

Loosely based on the life-story of Rosa Lewis, a kitchen maid who became manageress of the fashionable Cavendish Hotel in Jermyn Street, this series introduces viewers to Louisa Leyton, a gruff, hard-working, Cockney girl determined to better herself. The series begins in the year 1900 with Louisa's arrival as assistant chef to Monsieur Alex in the household of Lord Henry Norton. There she meets sommelier Augustus Trotter and the Honourable Charles Tyrrell, who admires her cooking and her ambition. Deputizing for the chef when the Prince of Wales calls for dinner, Louisa finds herself courted by royalty. Pressurized by the Prince's supporters, Louisa is badgered into marrying Gus Trotter (the Prince cannot consider compromising a single woman, and her career faces ruin if she rejects him). The Trotters are financially supported and buy the Bentinck Hotel at 20 Duke Street, but the marriage falls apart amid soaring bills and Gus's heavy drinking. Louisa works herself sick to save the hotel but is rescued by Charlie Tyrrell – soon to inherit the title of Lord Haslemere – who buys up the premises and employs Louisa to run it. Without her husband's hindrance, she bustles around, barking out orders, and turns the Bentinck into one of the best hotels in London, with the help of her loyal staff, principally Mary, the Welsh maid; Starr, the hall porter (and his fox-terrier, Fred); doddery butler Merriman; and Major Smith-Barton, a penniless military man who works for his keep by smooth-talking the aristocratic guests.

As the series progresses, personal and commercial calamities befall the staff, most notably Louisa's pregnancy by Charlie (resulting in baby Lottie, who is brought up secretly in the country), and reminders of her working-class background that never fail to dog our heroine.

If the programme had more than an echo of UPSTAIRS, DOWNSTAIRS about it, that wasn't coincidental. It was also created by John Hawkesworth and featured theme music by the same composer, Alexander Faris. The mouth-watering displays of traditional English food were created by chef Michael Smith.

Duchovny, David

(1960–)

American actor – a Masters graduate in English Literature from Yale – who gained international stardom in his role of FBI agent Fox Mulder in THE X-FILES. His TV break came in TWIN PEAKS, playing transvestite FBI agent Denis/Denise. He has also narrated the erotic series *Red Shoe Diaries*. He is married to actress Téa Leoni.

Duck Patrol ✶

UK (LWT) Situation Comedy. ITV 1998

Prof .... **Richard Wilson**
Darwin .... **David Tennant**
Gillian Monroe ('Marilyn') ...... **Samantha Beckinsale**
Ollie .... **Trevor Cooper**
Hero .... **Craig Fairbrass**
Sarge .... **Geoffrey Hutchings**
Taz .... **Jason Watkins**
Val .... **Sue Johnston**
Stan .... **John Biggins**
Angie .... **Jan Ravens**

Creators **Jan Etherington, Gavin Petrie**
Writers **Jan Etherington, Gavin Petrie, Peter Tilbury, Peter Tinniswood, Peter Spence**
Producer **Jamie Rix**

● ***A motley band of coppers keeps law and order on a quiet stretch of the Thames.***

Richard Wilson swaps his Victor Meldrew angst for a quiet time on the Thames in this short-lived sitcom. Recorded without a laugh track, as if to underline the gentle nature of the comedy and the relaxed setting, *Duck Patrol* focuses on the river police unit based at Ravensbeck Station (action was shot near Sunbury Lock). Although Sarge is the one supposedly in charge, he prefers to go fishing and it falls to the dedicated Prof to lead his team on a daily basis, although there is never much to get excited about in this sleepy part of the suburbs. Prof is partnered in his rounds by young Darwin, an ingenuous lad with a crush on fellow PC Marilyn. Prof himself is courted by local pub landlady Val. Just one series of seven episodes was produced.

Due South ✶✶✶

Canada (Alliance) Comedy Drama. BBC 1 1995–8 BBC 2 1999
DVD: Network

Constable Benton Fraser .... **Paul Gross**
Det. Ray Vecchio .... **David Marciano**
Capt./Lt. Harding Welsh .... **Beau Starr**
Det. Louis Guardino .... **Daniel Kash**
Det. Jack Huey .... **Tony Craig**
Elaine .... **Catherine Bruhier**
Fraser Sr .... **Gordon Pinsent**
Francesca Vecchio .... **Ramona Milano**

Insp. Meg Thatcher	**Camilla Scott**
Det. Stanley Raymond Kowalski	**Callum Keith Rennie**
Det. Thomas E. Dewey	**Tom Melissis**

Creator **Paul Haggis**
Executive Producer **Paul Gross**

A Canadian mountie always gets his man in Chicago.

Mountie Benton Fraser abandons his Rockies patch when he sets out to find the killer of his father. He ends up in Chicago, where he stays as an attachment at the Canadian consulate, somehow always getting involved in local law-enforcement. Here he applies his own moral code – not to mention heightened animal instincts – and cuts through the corruption and cynicism that dog the city justice scene. Joining the ultra-polite, and often naïve, Fraser – still in his scarlet Mountie uniform – on his adventures in the Windy City are his deaf (but lip-reading) white husky-wolf cross, Diefenbaker, and his street-wise, local cop pal, Ray Vecchio. Three seasons along, Fraser gains a new police partner when Stanley Raymond Kowalski replaces Vecchio, assuming the latter's identity while Vecchio goes undercover. Leslie Nielsen guests early on as Mountie Sgt Buck Frobisher.

With its dry humour and quirky feel (reminiscent of NORTHERN EXPOSURE), *Due South* pokes gentle fun at both American and Canadian stereotypes. It was produced in Canada, with a grimed-up and newly graffiti-ridden Toronto doubling for the real Chicago. In the UK, the series was initially shown on Sky One but suffered badly at the hands of terrestrial TV schedulers, despite its considerable popularity, jumping days, skipping weeks and even switching channels during its sporadic four-year run.

Duel, Pete

(Peter Deuel; 1940–71)

Popular and handsome leading American actor of the 1960s, whose TV high spot (and, sadly, last role) was as Hannibal Heyes in ALIAS SMITH AND JONES. Originally using his real name, Deuel, he appeared in shows like COMBAT, THE BIG VALLEY and THE FUGITIVE, and then gained more fame as a regular in the popular US sitcom *Gidget*. His own comedy, *Love on a Rooftop*, followed, as well as a handful of movie roles. During the first season of *Alias Smith and Jones*, Duel, always highly ambitious and politically sensitive, was found dead of a bullet wound to his head. That was on New Year's Eve 1971 and, although some contend that it was an accident, or even murder, it was judged that he was a suicide victim. His role as Heyes was taken over by the show's narrator, Roger Davis.

Duffy, Patrick

(1949–)

A 1970s and 1980s heart-throb, Patrick Duffy's most celebrated role was as Bobby Ewing, JR's brother, in DALLAS. Such was his importance to the series that, after leaving the show in 1985 (and being killed off in a car accident), he was coaxed back to boost the viewing figures, his death (and the whole of one season) being bizarrely explained away as just a dream experienced by his screen wife, Pam. Previously, Duffy had starred as the amphibious hero (Mark Harris) of THE MAN FROM ATLANTIS, and since *Dallas* he has appeared in the sitcom *Step by Step* (Frank Lambert), with guest spots in series like DIAGNOSIS MURDER and *Touched by an Angel*.

Dukes of Hazzard, The ✶

US (Warner Brothers/Piggy) Adventure. BBC 1 1979–85 (US CBS 1979–85)
DVD: Warner Home Video

Luke Duke	**Tom Wopat**
Bo Duke	**John Schneider**
Daisy Duke	**Catherine Bach**
Uncle Jesse Duke	**Denver Pyle**
Sheriff Roscoe P. Coltrane	**James Best**
Jefferson Davis 'Boss' Hogg	**Sorrell Booke**
Deputy Enos Strate	**Sonny Shroyer**
Cooter	**Ben Jones**
Deputy Cletus	**Rick Hurst**
Lulu Hogg	**Peggy Rea**
Miz Emma Tisdale	**Nedra Volz**
Sheriff Little	**Don Pedro Colley**
Laverne	**Lila Kent**
Emery Potter	**Charlie Dell**
Coy Duke	**Byron Cherry**
Vance Duke	**Christopher Mayer**
The Balladeer	**Waylon Jennings** *(voice only)*

Creator **Guy Waldron**
Producers **Joseph Gantman, Paul Picard**

High-speed, slapstick action with two modern-day Robin Hoods.

The Dukes of Hazzard are cousins Luke and Bo Duke, who live with their third cousin, stunning Daisy, and their wise old Uncle Jesse somewhere east of the Mississippi and south of the Ohio. Avoiding traps set by their corrupt adversaries – the fat, white-suited Boss Hogg (a local politician) and his incompetent brother-in-law, Sheriff Coltrane – the Dukes ride to the rescue of the good folk of Hazzard County. They race around in a beefed-up, red-and-white, 1969 Dodge Charger, known as 'General Lee', often getting involved in spectacular chases and crashes, and becoming extremely popular with younger viewers.

After a year or so, Sonny Shroyer, who played Coltrane's grinning deputy, Enos Strate, was given his own spin-off series on US TV, temporarily making way for Rick Hurst in the new role of Deputy Cletus. However, more substantial cast changes were required when stars Tom Wopat and John Schneider fell out with producers over merchandising royalties. For a while they were replaced by Byron Cherry and Christopher Mayer as two other Duke cousins (the storyline has it that Luke and Bo go to try their luck in a motor-racing circuit), but they were brought back when ratings fell, the two new boys leaving at the same time. Banjo-picking country music accompanied all the action and Waylon Jennings, who acted as narrator, also performed the show's theme song. In 2005 Warner Brothers released a new feature film based on the series, starring Johnny Knoxville as Luke, Seann William Scott as Bo, Jessica Simpson as Daisy, Willie Nelson as Uncle Jesse and Burt Reynolds as Boss Hogg.

Dumont, Allen B.

(1901–65)

American TV pioneer, strongly involved in the development of the cathode ray tube. He founded the DuMont TV network in 1946 but the channel struggled to survive and, when comprehensively beaten by CBS for status as America's third network, DuMont closed in 1955. In its short time it had specialized in sports events, political coverage and quiz and variety shows.

Duncan, Lindsay

(1950–)

Edinburgh-born actress best remembered for her roles in TRAFFIK (Helen), GBH (Barbara Douglas), A YEAR IN PROVENCE (Annie Mayle), *The Rector's Wife* (Anna), *Jake's Progress* (Monica), *Just William* (Lady Walton), TOM JONES (Lady Bellaston), SHOOTING THE PAST (Marilyn Truman), OLIVER TWIST (Elizabeth Leeford), *Dirty Tricks* (Alison), PERFECT STRANGERS (Alice) and ROME (Servilia). Other credits include DICK TURPIN, KIT CURRAN, TECX, TRAVELLING MAN, REILLY – ACE OF SPIES, COLIN'S SANDWICH, SPOOKS, AGATHA CHRISTIE'S POIROT and numerous single dramas. She is married to actor Hilton McRae.

Dunlop, Lesley

(1956–)

Newcastle-born actress with an extensive television portfolio. Although probably best known as Zoe Callender in MAY TO DECEMBER (replacing Eve Matheson), Dunlop has also appeared as Lydia Holly in SOUTH RIDING, Ruth Fullman in ANGELS and Sarah Harger in *Capstick's Law*, as well as in the dramas *Rich Deceiver* (Ellie Freeman), THE PHOENIX AND THE CARPET (Eliza), WOKENWELL (Lucky Whiteside), TESS OF THE D'URBERVILLES (Joan Durbeyfield), *Pure Wickedness* (Mo Healy) and WHERE THE HEART IS (Anna Kirkwall). Among her other credits have been *Penmarric*, THE ADVENTURES OF BLACK BEAUTY, OUR MUTUAL FRIEND, SMUGGLER (Sarah Morton), DOCTOR WHO, SILENT WITNESS, *The Many Lives of Albert Walker* (Jean Crowley) and *My Uncle Silas*.

Dunn, Clive

OBE (1920–)

Clive Dunn has been playing old men for five decades. He will always be remembered principally as the senile butcher Jack Jones, panicky veteran of Kitchener-era conflicts, in DAD'S ARMY, but he also brought his doddery charms to kids' TV as Charlie Quick, aka GRANDAD. Dunn had come to light on children's TV in the 1950s, before appearing on *The Tony Hancock Show*, *The Dickie Henderson Half-Hour*, IT'S A SQUARE WORLD and *The World of Beachcomber*. In 1960 he took the part of Old Johnson in BOOTSIE AND SNUDGE, and 14 years later starred as Sam Cobbett in the YTV sitcom *My Old Man*, with his real-life wife Priscilla Morgan taking the role of his daughter, Doris. He was also seen in the gag show *Jokers Wild*.

Durbridge, Francis

(1912–98)

British writer of suspense serials, working for the BBC from the early 1950s. Among his most prominent contributions were *The Broken Horseshoe*, *Operation Diplomat* (both 1952), *Portrait of Alison* (1955), *The Scarf* (1959), THE WORLD OF TIM FRAZER, *The Desperate People* (1963), *Melissa* (1964, remade in 1974 and reworked by Alan Bleasdale in 1997), *A Man Called Harry Brent* (1965), *A Game of Murder* and *Bat out of Hell* (both 1966), *The Passenger* and *Stupid Like a Fox* (both 1971), *The Doll* (1975) and *Breakaway* (1980) – many packaged under the umbrella title *Francis Durbridge Presents*. Durbridge was also the creator of wealthy sleuth Paul Temple.

Dustbinmen, The ✶✶

UK (Granada) Situation Comedy. ITV 1969–70
DVD: Network

'Cheese and Egg' Petty	**Bryan Pringle**
Winston Platt	**Graham Haberfield**
'Smellie' Ibbotson	**John Barrett**
'Heavy Breathing'	**Trevor Bannister**
Eric	**Tim Wylton**
Bernard ('Bloody Delilah')	**John Woodvine**
	Brian Wilde

Creator **Jack Rosenthal**
Producers **Jack Rosenthal, Richard Everitt**

● ***The misadventures of a team of refuse collectors.***

Based on a 1968 play by Jack Rosenthal, entitled *There's a Hole in Your Dustbin, Delilah*, *The Dustbinmen* was Rosenthal's series about a gang of northern binmen, watching them shirking work or lusting after housewives (like 'Mrs 15 Sheba Street'). Leader of the number 3 gang in the Corporation Cleansing Department is beret-wearing Cheese and Egg (his initials are C. E.) and riding with him on their bin lorry (affectionately dubbed *Thunderbird 3*) are Manchester City fanatic Winston (the driver), slow-witted Welshman Eric (a CORONATION STREET fan), ladies' man Heavy Breathing (who wears a bowler hat) and the toothless, unfortunately nicknamed Smellie. Their exasperated boss at the corporation depot is the so-called Bloody Delilah. The cameras follow the lads on their rounds and see them react to various crises in their life which sometimes lead to temporary Damascus-style conversions from minor sins and bad habits.

Despite its vulgarity and coarse ('pigging') language, *The Dustbinmen* was a big hit with viewers, and all six first series episodes topped the ratings. Rosenthal opted out after the first two seasons, leaving the scriptwriting to others, having already passed the producer's chair over to Richard Everitt. The original one-off play had various cast differences: Frank Windsor played Bloody Delilah, Jack MacGowran played Cheese and Egg and Harold Innocent was Heavy Breathing. The series theme music was provided by Derek Hilton.

Duttine, John

(1949–)

Barnsley-born actor in many lead and supporting roles. Highlights of his career – after early parts in Z CARS, SOFTLY, SOFTLY and WARSHIP – have included JESUS OF NAZARETH (John the Evangelist), *People Like Us* (Archie Carver), SPEND, SPEND, SPEND (Keith Nicholson), *The Devil's Crown* (King John), THE MALLENS (Donald Radlet), TO SERVE THEM ALL MY DAYS (David Powlett-Jones), THE DAY OF THE TRIFFIDS (Bill Masen), THE OUTSIDER (Frank Scully), *Psy-Warriors*, LAME DUCKS (Brian Drake), A WOMAN OF SUBSTANCE (Joe Lowther), AIN'T MISBEHAVIN' (Dave Drysdale), OUT OF THE BLUE (DI Eric Temple), *This is Personal: the Hunt for the Yorkshire Ripper* (Det. Chief Supt. Jim Hobson), *Sweet Revenge* (DI Briars), *The Jury* (Mark Waters), *The Courtroom* (Gavin Street) and HEARTBEAT (Sgt George Miller). Guest roles have come in such series as THE RUTH RENDELL MYSTERIES, DANGERFIELD, PILGRIM'S REST, MIDSOMER MURDERS, TOUCHING EVIL, PEAK PRACTICE, THE BILL, CASUALTY, WHERE THE HEART IS and DALZIEL AND PASCOE.

Duty Free ★★

UK (Yorkshire) Situation Comedy. ITV 1984–6
DVD: Cinema Club

David Pearce .... **Keith Barron**
Amy Pearce .... **Gwen Taylor**
Robert Cochran .... **Neil Stacy**
Linda Cochran .... **Joanna Van Gyseghem**
Carlos .... **Carlos Douglas**

Writers **Eric Chappell, Jean Warr**
Producer **Vernon Lawrence**

● ***Two couples toy with adultery in the Spanish sun.***

When David Pearce is made redundant, he and his wife, Amy, use some of the pay-off for a holiday in Spain, where they pal up with Robert and Linda Cochran. Through various compromising and farcical situations, including much hiding in wardrobes and under beds, the series exposes David and Linda's attempts at adultery, with Robert and Amy remaining rather strait-laced throughout. Carlos is the bemused waiter who witnesses the bizarre goings-on. Their package holiday lasted seven weeks on screen and indeed was not completed until a second series ended, a year later. A third season saw the foursome reunited on a winter holiday in the same hotel, and there was also a Christmas special in the same location.

Dyke, Greg

(1947–)

English TV executive, the BBC's Director General from January 2000 until 2004, when he resigned following criticism of the Corporation in the Hutton Report into the death of Dr David Kelly. Previously, Dyke had been credited with saving TV-am (by introducing Roland Rat, among other moves) as its Editor-in-Chief from 1983, and had been Chief Executive of LWT, Programme Controller of TVS, Chairman of GMTV and Chief Executive of Pearson Television.

Dynasty ★★

US (Aaron Spelling/Fox-Cat) Drama. BBC 1 1982–9
(US: ABC 1981–9)
DVD: Fox (Region 1 only)

Blake Carrington .... **John Forsythe**
Krystle Jennings/Carrington .... **Linda Evans**
Alexis Carrington/Colby/Dexter .... **Joan Collins**
Fallon Carrington/Colby .... **Pamela Sue Martin**, **Emma Samms**
Steven Carrington .... **Al Corley**, **Jack Coleman**
Adam Carrington/Michael Torrance .... **Gordon Thomson**
Cecil Colby .... **Lloyd Bochner**
Jeff Colby .... **John James**
Claudia Blaisdel .... **Pamela Bellwood**
Matthew Blaisdel .... **Bo Hopkins**
Lindsay Blaisdel .... **Katy Kurtzman**
Walter Lankershim .... **Dale Robertson**
Joseph Anders .... **Lee Bergere**
Kirby Anders/Colby .... **Kathleen Beller**
Andrew Laird .... **Peter Mark Richman**
Sammy Jo Dean/Carrington/Fallmont .... **Heather Locklear**
Michael Culhane .... **Wayne Northrop**
Dr Nick Toscanni .... **James Farentino**
Mark Jennings .... **Geoffrey Scott**
Congressman Neal McVane .... **Paul Burke**
Farnsworth 'Dex' Dexter .... **Michael Nader**
Amanda Carrington .... **Catherine Oxenberg**, **Karen Cellini**
Dominique Deveraux .... **Diahann Carroll**
Gerard .... **William Beckley**
Gordon Wales .... **James Sutorius**
Daniel Reece .... **Rock Hudson**
Lady Ashley Mitchell .... **Ali MacGraw**
Danny Carrington .... **Jameson Sampley**
Joel Abrigore .... **George Hamilton**
King Galen .... **Joel Fabiani**
Prince Michael .... **Michael Praed**
Clay Fallmont .... **Ted McGinley**
Ben Carrington .... **Christopher Cazenove**
Caress Morell .... **Kate O'Mara**
Dana Waring/Carrington .... **Leann Hunley**
Krystina Carrington .... **Jessica Player**
Sable Colby .... **Stephanie Beacham**
Sgt Johnny Zorelli .... **Ray Abruzzo**
Virginia Metheny .... **Liza Morrow**
Capt. William Handler .... **John Brandon**
Rudy Richards .... **Lou Beatty Jr**
Joanna Clauss/Sills .... **Kim Terry-Costin**
Monica Colby .... **Tracy Scoggins**

Creators **Richard Shapiro, Esther Shapiro**
Executive Producer **Aaron Spelling**
Producer **Douglas Cramer**

● ***Oil, money and family rivalries in a Denver setting.***

Closely modelled on Dallas, *Dynasty* almost bettered it in the ratings. As with the saga of the Ewings, the wealth of the featured parties comes from oil (indeed, the programme's working-title was *Oil*), with the beneficiaries this time the Carrington family and the setting Denver, Colorado. Head of the family is Blake Carrington, who marries his blonde secretary, Krystle Jennings, in the first episode. His children by previous marriages are a man-hungry, precocious daughter named Fallon and a bisexual son, Steve. Other original cast members include geologist Matthew Blaisdel, once a lover of Krystle, Claudia, his disturbed wife, and their attractive young daughter, Lindsay.

From the start Krystle's unhappiness in her marriage is clear, as Blake devotes most of his time to keeping his empire intact. Her problems are only beginning, however, for at the end of the first season Blake's vindictive ex-wife, Alexis, arrives, seeking to regain her share of the family fortune. From this point on, the programme hinges around this female JR's attempts to remove Krystle or unseat Blake himself. Alexis marries Blake's great rival, Cecil Colby, and, though he dies of a heart-attack soon after, she inherits the power of his oil company, Colbyco, and becomes even more formidable. Meanwhile, daughter Fallon continues her promiscuous ways, having affairs with all and sundry, including Jeff Colby, whom she marries, producing LB ('Little Blake'). Steve marries Sammy Jo Dean and conceives a son, Danny. He also gets involved with Claudia, endures a period of exile in Indonesia and undergoes plastic surgery following an explosion (actor Al Corley left the series). This clumsy switch of actors is later repeated with Fallon, who strangely loses three inches in height, becomes 14 years younger and begins to speak with an English accent.

As in *Dallas*, new characters are constantly being introduced, some of them members of the Carrington clan, keen to get their hands on the family silver. These include Adam Carrington, Blake's illegitimate son (it is later proven that this is not so), who arrives using the name Mark Torrance; black singer Dominique Deveraux, one of Tom's (Blake's dad) unplanned offspring; and Blake's younger brother, Ben. Alexis is far from pleased to see the arrival of her sister, Caress, who tries to publish a damaging book about her called *Sister Dearest*. Alexis buys the publishers to prevent her doing so.

Always keen to better its mentor, *Dynasty* took the high road, introducing world statesmen and royalty into its plots. Ex-President Gerald Ford and his wife, Betty, are joined in one episode by former Secretary of State Henry Kissinger. The royalty comes in the form of the fictitious Prince Michael of Moldavia, who plans to wed Alexis's daughter, Amanda. But, in a sensational cliffhanger, the Carringtons are 'massacred' at the European wedding reception by gun-toting revolutionaries. However, it turns out that only two guests have died and the action returns once more to Denver.

Other highlights of the show's run are the conviction of Alexis for murdering Mark Jennings (Krystle's former husband), although the deed is actually committed by Congressman Neal McVane in an Alexis disguise; the birth of Blake and Krystle's daughter, Krystina; Krystle's affair with Daniel Reece (Rock Hudson's last role); the abduction of Krystle and her replacement by a lookalike actress, so good she even fools Blake; Alexis finally wresting power from Blake, before kicking him and Krystle out of the 48-room Carrington mansion; and the destruction in a fire of Blake's hotel, La Mirage, in which Claudia, who has started it, is killed. Marriages come and go, Blake loses his memory and thinks he is still married to Alexis, little Krystina needs a heart transplant and is then abducted, and Blake finally regains his company.

Sensational to the end, the last season sees a mummified body dragged from the Carringtons' lake (it turns out to be one of Alexis's old flames, but who has killed him?). Cousin Sable arrives from Los Angeles to sort out Alexis, Krystle sinks into a coma in a Swiss hospital, Blake and a bent policeman shoot each other, Alexis and her husband, Dex, are pushed off a balcony by Adam, and Fallon and little Krystina are trapped down an old mineshaft with a Nazi art collection! A two-hour special, *Dynasty: The Reunion*, seen in 1992, aimed to conclude matters. This reveals that Alexis has survived, somehow, and explains how Fallon and Krystina are pulled free, how Krystle returns from her sanitarium, and how Blake both loses and wins back his business empire, going to prison for murder in between.

In the pilot for *Dynasty*, the role of Blake was filled by George Peppard but, for the series proper, he was replaced by John Forsythe, the man who had earlier provided the voice for Charlie in Charlie's Angels. *Dynasty* was also responsible for the spin-off, THE COLBYS, which temporarily took Jeff and Fallon away from the original series.

E4

Digital sister channel to Channel 4, which started broadcasting on 18 January 2001. Targeting the 16–34 age group, E4 includes first runs of popular US series like SCRUBS, ER and THE WEST WING, along with original drama and comedy that often makes its way later to Channel 4.

Eagle of the Ninth, The ★★

UK (BBC) Drama. BBC 1 1977

Marcus Flavius Aquila .... **Anthony Higgins**
Marcus's father .... **Peter Whitbread**
Drusillus .... **Bernard Gallagher**
Hilarion .... **Matthew Long**
Cradoc .... **Patrick Malahide**
Aulus .... **Brian Carey**
Aquila .... **Patrick Holt**
Esca .... **Christian Rodska**
Cottia .... **Gillian Bailey**
Claudius .... **Martin Heller**
Stephanos .... **W. H. D. Joss**
Guern .... **Victor Carin**
Tradui .... **Moultrie Kelsall**
Gault .... **Robert Docherty**

Writer **Bill Craig**
Producer **Pharic MacLaren**

● ***A Roman soldier searches for the standard lost by his father's missing legion.***

History reports that, around the year AD 117, the Roman Ninth Legion (the Hispana), which was based at Eboracum (today's York), was sent north to head off a revolt by Caledonian tribesmen. The legion was never heard of again, but its eagle (standard) was eventually unearthed hundreds of miles away at Silchester, Hampshire. How it got there and the truth about the legion's disappearance remain a mystery, but novelist Rosemary Sutcliff could see the potential of linking the two. In her 1954 book *The Eagle of the Ninth*, she filled in the gaps. Her story is adapted here in six episodes, directed by Michael Simpson and pitched at the Sunday teatime drama market.

The hero is Marcus, a young Roman officer whose father disappeared while serving with the Ninth. He makes his way to Britain and takes command of a frontier fort. Marcus is keen to make an alliance with local warlord Cradoc, but, despite this, the fort is attacked and many are killed. Marcus himself is badly injured and is forced to relinquish his military duties. He moves to Calleva (Silchester) to spend time with his uncle, Aquila, and while here saves a local gladiator, Esca, from death in the arena. Esca reveals some information about the fate of the Ninth and together they set out to discover the truth and rescue the eagle. Along the way they encounter Guern, once a centurion with the Ninth now living as a local tribesman. He tells them that the legion was slaughtered. Undeterred, Marcus continues with his quest and finally finds the elusive standard.

Early Doors ★★★★

UK (Ovation/Granada/Phil McIntyre) Situation Comedy. BBC 2 2003–4
DVD: BBC

Ken Dixon .... **John Henshaw**
Joe .... **Craig Cash**
Nigel 'Duffy' .... **Phil Mealey**
Jean Dixon .... **Rita May**
Melanie Dixon .... **Christine Bottomley**
Eddie Bell .... **Mark Benton**
Joan Bell .... **Lorraine Cheshire**
Old Tommy .... **Rodney Litchfield**
Phil .... **James Quinn**
Nige .... **Peter Wight**
Liam .... **James McAvoy**
Winnie .... **Joan Kempson**
Tanya .... **Susan Cookson**
Debbie .... **Lisa Millett**
Janice .... **Maxine Peake**
Dean .... **Lee Ingleby**
Nicola .... **Susan McArdle**

Writers **Craig Cash, Phil Mealey**
Producers **Lucy Ansbro, John Rushton**

● ***Life through the eyes of the customers in a northern pub.***

It's 5.30 p.m. at The Grapes in Manchester and the regulars are banging on the door. Landlord Ken keeps them waiting while he finishes his opening-up routine then welcomes them in with a volley of genial insults. Best mates Joe and Duffy chew the fat after a day's work (or less than a day if they can get away with it), philosophizing about their relationships with wives and other women. Tight-fisted Old Tommy counts out the pennies for his round of one and takes his seat grouchily in the corner. Eddie and Joan occupy their own usual table close by, once gormless Eddie has told Ken about the latest hiccup with the traffic management on Samuel Street and Joan has lit the first of many cigarettes. A knock at the back door signals the arrival of skiving coppers Phil and Nige, who cadge a couple of drinks and tell Ken all about the latest scams at the nick. Later visitors are likely to be part-time bar maid Tanya and her friend Debbie, who pay lip service to a healthy lifestyle through the aerobics classes hosted by Ken's adopted daughter, Melanie. They may share a table with Janice, if Janice can find someone to sit for the baby that just might be Duffy's. Liam is usually another late arrival. He's Melanie's well-meaning Scottish boyfriend but it looks like he's being corrupted by the macho bar-room crowd over a hand of cards or the latest discussion of fag-ends in the urinal. Meanwhile, upstairs, Ken's idle mum, Jean, rules the roost, chatting to daily help Winnie about the latest local gossip while picking over the contents of a chocolate box.

These are the people whose lives we share in the engaging *Early Doors*, a sort of ROYLE FAMILY for the licensed trade. Not much happens in each episode, but plans are being laid for a lads' beano, involving a trip to York Races and an hour or two in a stripclub on the way home, while Ken has plenty of personal worries, especially when Mel announces she wishes to meet her real dad.

By the time of series two, personal relationships have

progressed, or perhaps regressed. Liam has cleared off, leaving Melanie in the hands of a new young lothario named Dean. She's also tracked down her dad, much to Ken's distress, and Ken himself just cannot declare his own feelings for Tanya, leading to frustration and anger on both sides.

The series was initially a joint venture by *The Royle Family*'s Craig Cash and Caroline Aherne, but Aherne backed out of both scripting and playing the pub's landlady, and Cash brought in old friend Phil Mealey to share the writing chores and also to make his first acting appearance. Good gags, thoughtful direction by Adrian Shergold (series one) and Cash (series two), well-developed characterization and sympathetic lighting were just four parts of the package that made this unorthodox comedy succeed.

EastEnders ★★★★

UK (BBC) Drama. BBC 1 1985–
DVD: BBC

Arthur Fowler	**Bill Treacher**
Pauline Fowler	**Wendy Richard**
Michelle Fowler/Holloway	**Susan Tully**
Mark Fowler	**David Scarboro**
	Todd Carty
Lou Beale	**Anna Wing**
Pete Beale	**Peter Dean**
Kathy Beale/Mitchell	**Gillian Taylforth**
Ian Beale	**Adam Woodyatt**
Dennis Watts	**Leslie Grantham**
Angie Watts	**Anita Dobson**
Sharon Watts/Mitchell/ Rickman	**Letitia Dean**
Dot Cotton/Branning	**June Brown**
Nick Cotton	**John Altman**
Charlie Cotton	**Christopher Hancock**
Ethel Skinner	**Gretchen Franklin**
Simon Wicks	**Nick Berry**
Pat Wicks/Butcher/Evans	**Pam St Clement**
George 'Lofty' Holloway	**Tom Watt**
Mary Smith	**Linda Davidson**
Dr Harold Legg	**Leonard Fenton**
Ali Osman	**Nejdet Salih**
Sue Osman	**Sandy Ratcliff**
Mehmet Osman	**Haluk Bilginer**
Guizin Osman	**Ishia Bennison**
Tony Carpenter	**Oscar James**
Cassie Carpenter	**Delanie Forbes**
Hannah Carpenter	**Sally Sagoe**
Kelvin Carpenter	**Paul J. Medford**
Andy O'Brien	**Ross Davidson**
Debbie Wilkins	**Shirley Cheriton**
Naima Jeffery	**Shreela Ghosh**
Saeed Jeffery	**Andrew Johnson**
Martin Fowler	**Jon Peyton Price**
	James Alexandrou
Vicki Fowler/Watts	**Samantha Leigh Martin**
	Scarlett Johnson
James Willmott-Brown	**William Boyde**
Cindy Williams/Beale	**Michelle Collins**
Tom Clements	**Donald Tandy**
Donna Ludlow	**Matilda Ziegler**
Colin Russell	**Michael Cashman**
Barry Clark	**Gary Hailes**
Duncan Boyd	**David Gillespie**
Jan Hammond	**Jane How**
Danny Whiting	**Saul Jephcott**
Rod Norman	**Christopher McHallem**
Carmel Roberts/Jackson	**Judith Jacob**
Matthew Jackson	**Steven Hartley**
Darren Roberts	**Gary MacDonald**
Junior Roberts	**Aaron Carrington**
Aisha Roberts	**Aisha Jacob**
Ashraf Karim	**Aftab Sachak**
Sufia Karim	**Rani Singh**
Shireen Karim	**Nisha Kapur**
Sohail Karim	**Ronnie Jhutti**
Dr David Samuels	**Christopher Reich**
Magda 'Mags' Czajkowski	**Kathryn Apanowicz**
Frank Butcher	**Mike Reid**
Mo Butcher	**Edna Doré**
Diane Butcher	**Sophie Lawrence**
Ricky Butcher	**Sid Owen**
Sam Mitchell/Butcher/ Hunter	**Danniella Westbrook/Morgan**
	Kim Medcalf
Janine Butcher/Evans	**Rebecca Michael**
	Alexia Demetriou
	Charlene/Charlie Brooks
Paul Priestley	**Mark Thrippleton**
Trevor Short	**Phil McDermott**
Disa O'Brian	**Jan Graveson**
Marge Green	**Pat Coombs**
Julie Cooper	**Louise Plowright**
Eddie Royle	**Michael Melia**
Grant Mitchell	**Ross Kemp**
Phil Mitchell	**Steve McFadden**
Peggy Mitchell/Butcher	**Jo Warne**
	Barbara Windsor
Rachel Kominsky	**Jacquetta May**
Jules Tavernier	**Tommy Eytle**
Celestine Tavernier	**Leroy Golding**
Etta Tavernier	**Jacqui Gordon-Lawrence**
Clyde Tavernier	**Steven Woodcock**
Hattie Tavernier	**Michelle Gayle**
Lloyd Tavernier	**Garey Bridges**
Kofi Tavernier	**Marcel Smith**
Christine Hewitt	**Elizabeth Power**
Mandy Salter	**Nicola Stapleton**
Aidan Brosnan	**Sean Maguire**
Steve Elliot	**Mark Monero**
Richard 'Tricky Dicky' Cole	**Ian Reddington**
Nigel Bates	**Paul Bradley**
Debbie Tyler/Bates	**Nicola Duffett**
Clare Tyler	**Gemma Bissix**
Gill Fowler	**Susannah Dawson**
Shelley	**Nicole Arumugam**
Sanjay Kapoor	**Deepak Verma**
Gita Kapoor	**Shobu Kapoor**
Carol Jackson	**Lindsey Coulson**
Alan Jackson	**Howard Antony**
Bianca Jackson/Butcher	**Patsy Palmer**
Robbie Jackson	**Dean Gaffney**
Sonia Jackson/Fowler	**Natalie Cassidy**
Blossom Jackson	**Mona Hammond**
Billy Jackson	**Devon Anderson**
Natalie Price/Evans	**Lucy Speed**
Nellie Ellis	**Elizabeth Kelly**
David Wicks	**Michael French**
Geoff Barnes	**David Roper**
Ruth Aitken/Fowler	**Caroline Paterson**
Della Alexander	**Michelle Joseph**
Binnie Roberts	**Sophie Langham**
Big Ron	**Ron Tarr**
Roy Evans	**Tony Caunter**

Character	Actor
Tiffany Raymond/Mitchell	**Martine McCutcheon**
Vicki Fowler	**Samantha Leigh Martin**
Stan Dougan	**Jack Chissick**
Barry Evans	**Shaun Williamson**
Liam Tyler	**Francis Magee**
Willy Roper	**Michael Tudor Barnes**
Lydia	**Marlaine Gordon**
Ted Hills	**Brian Croucher**
Tony Hills	**Mark Homer**
Sarah Hills	**Daniela Denby-Ashe**
Felix Kawalski	**Harry Landis**
Guppy Sharma	**Lyndam Gregory**
Meena McKenzie	**Sudha Bhuchar**
Joe Wicks	**Paul Nicholls**
Lorraine Wicks	**Jacqueline Leonard**
Michael Rose	**Russell Floyd**
Dan Zappieri	**Carl Pizzie**
Alistair Matthews	**Neil Clark**
Sue Taylor	**Charlotte Bellamy**
Simon Raymond	**Andrew Lynford**
Lenny Wallace	**Desune Coleman**
Huw Edwards	**Richard Elis**
April Branning	**Debbie Arnold**
Frankie	**Syan Blake**
Mick McFarlane	**Sylvester Williams**
Stephen Beale	**Stuart Stevens**
	Edward Savage
Peter Beale	**Alex Stevens**
	Joseph Shade
	James Martin
Lucy Beale	**Casey Anne Rothery**
	Melissa Suffield
DCI Mason	**Campbell Morrison**
Neelam Kapoor	**Jamila Massey**
George Palmer	**Paul Moriarty**
Alex Healy	**Richard Driscoll**
Polly Becker	**Victoria Gould**
Annie Palmer	**Nadia Sawalha**
Lorna Cartwright	**Janet Dibley**
Irene Hills/Raymond	**Roberta Taylor**
Vanessa Carlton	**Adele Salem**
Mary Flaherty	**Melanie Clark Pullen**
Conor Flaherty	**Sean Gleeson**
Matthew Rose	**Joe Absolom**
Susan Rose	**Tilly Vosburgh**
Jessie Moore	**Chelsey Paden**
Jeff Healy	**Leslie Schofield**
Julie Haye	**Karen Henthorn**
Nick Holland	**Dominic Taylor**
Terry Raymond	**Gavin Richards**
Chris Clark	**Matthew Jay Lewis**
Louise Raymond/ Simmonds	**Carol Harrison**
Rosa di Marco	**Louise Jameson**
Gianni di Marco	**Marc Bannerman**
Beppe di Marco	**Michael Grecco**
Teresa di Marco	**Leila Birch**
Nicky di Marco	**Carly Hillman**
Lilly Mattock	**Barbara Keogh**
Melanie Healy/Owen	**Tamzin Outhwaite**
Josie McFarlane	**Joan Hooley**
Billy Mitchell	**Perry Fenwick**
Jamie Mitchel	**Jack Ryder**
Lisa Shaw/Fowler	**Lucy Benjamin**
Steve Owen	**Martin Kemp**
Saskia Duncan	**Deborah Sheridan-Taylor**
Nina Harris	**Troy Titus-Adams**
Dr Fonseca	**Jimi Mistry**

Character	Actor
Dan Sullivan	**Craig Fairbrass**
Andrea Price	**Cindy O'Callaghan**
Jackie Owen	**Race Davies**
Troy Harvey	**Jamie Jarvis**
Jim Branning	**John Bardon**
Sandra di Marco	**Clare Wilkie**
Laura Dunn/Beale	**Hannah Waterman**
Joe di Marco	**Jake Kyprianou**
Mo Harris	**Laila Morse**
Charlie Slater	**Derek Martin**
Zoë Slater	**Michelle Ryan**
Lynne Slater/Hobbs	**Elaine Lordan**
Kat Slater/Moon	**Jessie Wallace**
Little Mo Morgan/Mitchell	**Kacey Ainsworth**
Kim McFarlane	**Krystle Williams**
Ashley Cotton	**Frankie Fitzgerald**
Kerry Skinner	**Gemma McCluskie**
Asif Malik	**Ashvin Luximon**
Garry Hobbs	**Ricky Groves**
Audrey Trueman	**Corinne Skinner Carter**
Dr Anthony Trueman	**Nicholas R. Bailey**
Trevor Morgan	**Alex Ferns**
Gary Bolton	**Bruce Byron**
Marcus Christie	**Stephen Churchett**
Paul Trueman	**Gary Beadle**
Patrick Trueman	**Rudolph Walker**
Winston	**Ulric Browne**
Nathan Williams	**Doug Allen**
Derek Harkinson	**Ian Lavender**
Nita Mistry	**Bindya Solanki**
Anish Mistry	**Ali Zahoor**
Tom Banks	**Colm Ó Maonlaí**
Gus Smith	**Mohammed George**
Liam Butcher	**Nathaniel Gleed**
Revd Tom Stuart	**Shaun Dooley**
Alfie Moon	**Shane Richie**
Spencer Moon	**Christopher Parker**
Victoria 'Nana' Moon	**Hilda Braid**
Kate Tyler/Morton	**Jill Halfpenny**
Joanne Ryan	**Tara Lynne O'Neill**
Dennis Rickman	**Nigel Harman**
Minty Peterson	**Cliff Parisi**
Andy Hunter	**Michael Higgs**
Kelly Taylor	**Brooke Kinsella**
Shirley Benson	**Robyn Moore**
Tariq Larousi	**Nabil Elouahabi**
Ronny Ferreira	**Ray Panthaki**
Kareena Ferreira	**Pooja Shah**
Adi Ferreira	**Ameet Chana**
Dan Ferreira	**Dalip Tahil**
Ash Ferreira	**Raji James**
Yolande Duke/Trueman	**Angela Wynter**
Juley Smith	**Joseph Kpobie**
Sasha Perkins	**Jemma Walker**
Graham Foster	**Alex McSweeney**
Mickey Miller	**Joe Swash**
Wilfred Atkins	**Dudley Sutton**
Chrissie Watts	**Tracy-Ann Oberman**
Jane Collins	**Laurie Brett**
Rosie Miller	**Gerry Cowper**
Demi Miller	**Shana Swash**
Keith Miller	**David Spinx**
Darren Miller	**Charlie G. Hawkins**
Stacey Slater	**Lacey Turner**
Johnny Allen	**Billy Murray**
Jake Moon	**Joel Beckett**
Danny Moon	**Jake Maskall**
Tina Stewart	**Charlotte Avery**

Ruby Allen .... **Louisa Lytton**
Michael Rawlins .... **Melyvn Hayes**
Leo Taylor .... **Phillip Dowling**
Dawn Miller .... **Kara Tointon**
Joe Macer .... **Ray Brooks**
Naomi Julien .... **Petra Letang**
Honey Edwards .... **Emma Barton**
Jack Edwards .... **Nicky Henson**
Bert Atkinson .... **Dave Hill**
Carly Wicks .... **Kellie Shirley**
Chelsea Fox .... **Tiana Benjamin**
Elizabeth 'Squiggle' Fox .... **Belinda Owusu**
Denise Fox .... **Diane Parish**
Dr Oliver Cousins .... **Tom Ellis**
Bradley Branning .... **Charlie Clements**

Creators **Julia Smith, Tony Holland**
Producers **Julia Smith, Mike Gibbon, Corinne Hollingworth, Richard Bramall, Michael Ferguson, Pat Sandys, Helen Greaves, Leonard Lewis, Barbara Emile, Mike Hudson, Jane Fallon, Diana Kyle, Nicholas Hicks-Beach, Alison Davis, Jane Harris, Josephine Ward, Johnathan Young, Miriam Segal, Lis Steele, Stephen Garwood, Matthew Robinson, David Boulter, Paul Annett, Jon East, Emma Turner, Gordon Ronald, Helena Pope, Anne Edyvean, Diana Barton, Lorraine Newman, Nicky Cotton, Oliver Kent, Jeannine Jones, Belinda Campbell, Jenny Robbins, Colin Wratten, Sean O'Connor, Nicholas Copus, Jonathan Phillips, Rumu Sen-Gupta, Peter Rose, Sue Butterworth, Mark Sendell, Jamie Annett, Pam Fraser Solomon, Steve Finn, Michael Owen Morris, George Ormond, John Greening, Jyoti Fernandes, Julie Press, Jo Johnson, Pamela Hansson**

● ***The continuing story of working-class East End folk.*** *EastEnders* has succeeded where COMPACT, UNITED! and THE NEWCOMERS all failed, namely in providing a serious, lasting, 52-weeks-a-year challenger to CORONATION STREET in the great soap opera war. Set in the fictitious London borough of Walford E20, the series focuses on life in and around grimy Albert Square, a decaying Victorian residential area with a market tagged on the side. A greasy-spoon café and a downbeat pub, The Queen Victoria, see as much of the action as any of the houses. The major characters at the start are the related Beale and Fowler families. Head of the clan is crotchety Lou Beale, who lives with her daughter, Pauline Fowler, Pauline's husband, Arthur, and children, Michelle and Mark. New baby Martin arrives soon after. Pauline's twin brother, Pete Beale, runs the market fruit-and-veg stall, occasionally assisted by his blonde wife, Kathy, and schoolboy son, Ian. Den and Angie Watts are the squabbling pub landlords, fighting for the attentions of their adopted daughter, Sharon. Café Osman is run by Turk Ali Osman and his English wife, Sue; and other major characters in the early days include gossipy hypochondriac Dot Cotton; her villainous son, Nick; daffy old Ethel Skinner; barman Simon 'Wicksy' Wicks; dopey Lofty Holloway; yuppie boy- and girlfriend Andy O'Brien and Debbie Wilkins; Naima and Saeed Jeffery, two Asian grocers; and the Carpenters, a West Indian family. As the cast list above shows, many other characters have taken up residence in Albert Square since.

EastEnders has always kept up a good pace, bustling along twice a week, with an omnibus edition on Sundays. A third weekly episode was added in 1994 and a fourth in 2001. The best-remembered storylines generally revolve around love triangles, infidelity and deceit, with more than a pinch of medical crisis and gangsterish crime for good measure. Michelle's pregnancy by 'Dirty' Den and her subsequent jilting of Lofty is one. Arthur's endless unemployment and eventual nervous breakdown is a long-running saga, and Kathy's rape at the hands of smoothie Willmott-Brown is another pot-boiler. Further high spots are the break-up of Den and Angie's marriage; Den's abrupt disappearance (although thought to be dead, he later returns); Nick's attempts to poison his mother; the break-up of hardman Grant Mitchell's marriage to Sharon, following his cuckoldry by his own brother, Phil; the break-up of Grant's next marriage, to Tiffany, involving his sleeping with her mother, Louise; Ian and Cindy Beale's child-custody battle (after she arranges to have him shot); and the attempted murder trial of Little Mo Morgan. To boost viewing figures, the series occasionally ventures abroad – to Spain, Paris, Italy and Ireland, for example, with episodes sometimes extended to five nights a week to cover the foreign action.

Never afraid to court controversy, *EastEnders* has bravely tackled touchy issues such as prostitution (through unmarried mum Mary); homosexuality (with lovers Colin and Barry); homelessness (of teenagers Mandy and Aidan); abortion (Michelle's unborn child by Lofty); Alzheimer's Disease (the mental deterioration of Mo Butcher); alcoholism (Phil Mitchell); AIDS (the HIV infection of Mark Fowler); and euthanasia (the assisted death of Ethel). Murder was the first subject on the programme's lips, and the series raced to a flying start with the death of resident Reg Cox in episode one (killed, it is revealed later, by Nick Cotton). But through all the doom and gloom that has dominated *EastEnders*, there have also been many lighter and funnier moments.

The series was the brainchild of producer Julia Smith and script editor Tony Holland, who had worked together on dramas like ANGELS and DISTRICT NURSE. Legend has it that the idea was concocted in 45 minutes in a Shepherd's Bush wine bar. The execution of the idea was far more thorough, however, and saw the flimsy working titles of *East 8* and *London Pride* quickly dropped. With its enormous initial publicity push, *EastEnders* was a hit from day one. It has gained more than its share of moral critics, but the audience figures have spoken for themselves. Not only matching *Coronation Street*, *EastEnders* has often knocked its northern rival off the top of the ratings.

EastEnders trivia is boundless. Fans can reveal that the beer served at The Vic has been brewed by Luxford & Copley, that the pub poodle was Roly, and Ethel's dog was named Willy. They'll tell you the name of Willmott-Brown's pub (The Dagmar) and the man who owns the grotty launderette (Mr Opidopoulous), as well as the numbers of the houses where the characters have lived: the Fowlers at number 45 and Dr Legg at number 1, for instance. And they'll recall the spin-off records that made the UK charts: 'Anyone Can Fall in Love' (a vocal version of the theme music by Simon May) by Anita Dobson, 'Every Loser Wins' by Nick Berry and 'Something Outa Nothing' by Letitia Dean and Paul Medford (known as The Banned in the series). All were hits in 1986. There have also been *EastEnders* spin-off programmes: *Civvy Street*, a special screened in 1988, looked back to the Albert Square of 1942, and featured a young Lou Beale, played by Karen Meagher, and her friend Ethel, played by Alison Bettles; *Ricky and Bianca*, in 2002, saw estranged husband and wife arguing it out in Manchester; and *Dot's Story*, another special in 2003, reflected on Dot Cotton's childhood during the war, with Tallula Pitt-Brown as the young Dot.

Eastwood, Clint

(1930–)

Legendary movie-cowboy turned award-winning director, whose rise to fame was greatly assisted by his seven-year portrayal of trail rider Rowdy Yates in RAWHIDE. Previously,

Eastwood had gained parts only in B-movies and guest spots in minor TV series.

Ebsen, Buddy

(Christian Rudolf Ebsen; 1908–2003)

Versatile American actor who appeared to be typecast when his marathon stint as country bumpkin Jed Clampett in THE BEVERLY HILLBILLIES came to an end, but who branched out effectively into detective work as the ageing private eye BARNABY JONES, and returned yet again in the 1980s as retired investigator Roy Houston in MATT HOUSTON. In his pre-TV days (which effectively comprised most of his career), Ebsen had been a Hollywood song-and-dance man, appearing in lavish stage and movie musicals in the 1930s and 1940s. His first foray on to the small screen came in Walt Disney's DAVY CROCKETT, playing Crockett's sidekick, Georgie Russell, and this led to parts in Western series such as MAVERICK, HAVE GUN, WILL TRAVEL, BONANZA, RAWHIDE and GUNSMOKE, as well as the adventure series *Northwest Passage*. When *The Beverly Hillbillies* beckoned, Ebsen was already in his mid-fifties. Among his other TV appearances were guest spots in HAWAII FIVE-O, ALIAS SMITH AND JONES and HARDCASTLE AND MCCORMICK. He was also a published song writer.

Eccleston, Christopher

(1964–)

Salford-born actor, favouring gritty roles, whose most notable work has been as welfare officer Sean Maddox in *Friday on My Mind*, DCI David Bilborough in CRACKER, teacher Drew McKenzie in *Hearts and Minds*, Nicky Hutchinson in OUR FRIENDS IN THE NORTH, Trevor Hicks in HILLSBOROUGH, Joe Broughton in *Flesh and Blood*, Steven Baxter in *The Second Coming* and the ninth DOCTOR WHO. Other prominent parts have been in CLOCKING OFF, OTHELLO, *Wilderness Men* (explorer Alexander von Humboldt), LINDA GREEN, *Strumpet* (Strayman), *Sunday* (General Ford) and *The King and Us* (Anthony). CASUALTY, BOON and AGATHA CHRISTIE'S POIROT feature among his earlier credits. He also narrated the documentaries *Motorway Life* and *Dubai Dreams*.

Echo Four-Two ✶

UK (Associated-Rediffusion) Police Drama. ITV 1961

DI Harry Baxter	**Eric Lander**
DS Joe York	**Geoffrey Russell**
Acting Supt. Dean	**Geoffrey Chater**

Producer **Richard Matthews**

● NO HIDING PLACE ***spin-off, showcasing bright young detective Harry Baxter.***

Promoted from sergeant to inspector, Harry Baxter, Lockhart's sidekick in *No Hiding Place*, becomes the star of this short-lived series. He is now placed in charge of E Division's Q-cars, a squad of unmarked vehicles used for surveillance, and, with his assistant, Joe York, tackles various assignments from an office in Bow Street. A strong female following for Eric Lander instigated this series, but an actors' strike hastened its downfall before all 13 planned episodes were produced. Lander then returned to the mother series.

Eddington, Paul

CBE (1927–95)

British actor whose TV work began in the 1950s when he played Will Scarlett in THE ADVENTURES OF ROBIN HOOD. A plethora of other ITC adventures followed, and Eddington was easily spotted in the likes of THE AVENGERS, THE PRISONER and THE CHAMPIONS. He also popped up as a bent copper in DIXON OF DOCK GREEN, played Brutus in *The Spread of the Eagle* presentation of *Julius Caesar*, was a reporter in the Raj series *Frontier*, took the role of civil servant Strand in SPECIAL BRANCH and featured as Astor Harris in HINE. However, it was as Jerry Leadbetter, husband of Margo and neighbour of the Goods, in THE GOOD LIFE that he at last achieved top billing. This was followed by the enormously successful YES, MINISTER and *Yes, Prime Minister* (in which he starred as the bamboozled MP and PM Jim Hacker), the sitcom LET THERE BE LOVE (bachelor Timothy Love) and numerous other high-profile performances. These included the play OUTSIDE EDGE, MISS MARPLE and THE CAMOMILE LAWN (Uncle Richard). His last appearance was as Justice Shallow in BBC 2's *Henry IV*. He was the father of actress Gemma Eddington.

Eden, Mark

(1928–)

Shakespearean stage and film actor whose most dramatic television role has been as Alan Bradley in CORONATION STREET. Moving in with Rita Fairclough, Bradley's persona gradually changed from gentle man-friend to psychotic misogynist, making him one of the *Street*'s most evil creations. Eden's earlier TV appearances had been as crusading sports writer Ray Saxon in the 1968 series *Crimebuster*, DC Peter Bradfield in the anthology series DETECTIVE, Detective Inspector Parker in Lord Peter Wimsey, Spencer in THE TOP SECRET LIFE OF EDGAR BRIGGS, plus parts in dramas like THE AVENGERS, SIR FRANCIS DRAKE, THE SAINT, MAN IN A SUITCASE, THE PRISONER, SPYDER'S WEB, SPECIAL BRANCH, ARTHUR OF THE BRITONS, WILDE ALLIANCE, CRIBB, POLDARK and JESUS OF NAZARETH, as well as a pre-Bradley incarnation in *Coronation Street* as one of Elsie Tanner's boyfriends, Wally Randle. A recent guest appearance came in DOCTORS. He is married to *Street* star Sue Nicholls.

Edge of Darkness ✶✶✶✶

UK (BBC) Drama. BBC 2 1985

DVD: BBC

Ronald Craven	**Bob Peck**
Emma Craven	**Joanne Whalley**
Darius Jedburgh	**Joe Don Baker**
James Godbolt	**Jack Watson**
Grogan	**Kenneth Nelson**
Bennett	**Hugh Fraser**
Pendleton	**Charles Kay**
Det. Chief Supt. Ross	**John Woodvine**
Harcourt	**Ian McNeice**
Terry Shields	**Tim McInnerny**
Clemmy	**Zoë Wanamaker**
Chilwell	**Alan Cuthbertson**
Childs	**Trevor Bowen**

Writer **Troy Kennedy Martin**
Producer **Michael Wearing**

● ***A Yorkshire policeman, following up the murder of his daughter, is drawn into nuclear subterfuge.***

When Detective Inspector Ronald Craven's scientist daughter, Emma, is gunned down at his side by a shotgun-wielding Irishman, he initially believes the murder is a botched attempt to kill him. After all, he has been involved with terrorist informers in Northern Ireland. However, the more he considers the case, and the more he discovers about his daughter's links with an environmental action group called Gaia, the less certain he becomes. Branching out into some lone detective work, Craven finds himself immersed in political intrigue, egged on by two devious civil servants, Pendleton and Harcourt, and drawing in interested parties from around the globe. The trail leads to Northmoor, a disused coal mine, which is revealed to be a secret nuclear waste dump that has been infiltrated by Gaia activists, including Emma, shortly before her death. With the assistance of Darius Jedburgh, an abrasive Texan CIA agent, Craven penetrates the site. Both are fatally contaminated and the whole affair is eventually swept under the carpet by the authorities. The only hope of exposing the scandal then rests with Gaia, with whom Craven files a report.

Edge of Darkness was one of the BBC's most successful drama series of all time. Screened initially to great acclaim on BBC 2, it earned itself a repeat showing on BBC 1 just a few weeks later, before picking up various awards the following year. Its dark, gloomy imagery enhanced the gravity of its subject matter; the ghostly appearances of Craven's dead daughter, supplying him with snippets of information, added to the 'out of our hands' atmosphere, and Eric Clapton's bluesy electric guitar provided powerful incidental music.

Editor

The creative technician who cuts and arranges the recorded material into the finished form. The term is also applied to the ultimate decision-maker or chief producer of a current affairs, news, sport or magazine programme.

Edmonds, Noel

(1948–)

Bearded disc jockey turned TV presenter, fond of gentle pranks and hidden camera routines. A Radio Luxembourg DJ as a teenager, Edmonds quickly moved to Radio 1, where his breakfast show was a huge success, 1972–7. His TV breaks came with TOP OF THE POPS, *Z-Shed* and then a new-style Saturday morning programme for kids, MULTI-COLOURED SWAP SHOP. Moving on from *Swap Shop*, Edmonds dominated Saturday teatimes for many years, with (mostly live) programmes like *Lucky Numbers*, THE LATE, LATE BREAKFAST SHOW, *The Saturday Roadshow* and NOEL'S HOUSE PARTY. After a period away from the screen, he resurfaced in 2005 as host of Channel 4's daily quiz DEAL OR NO DEAL. He has also presented Top Gear (reflecting his interest in motor sports); a revival of JUKE BOX JURY; COME DANCING; the junior MASTERMIND series, *Hobby Horse*; the nostalgic *Time of Your Life* and *Noel's Telly Years*; the guessing game *Whatever Next?*; the TV quiz TELLY ADDICTS; *Noel's Addicts*; *Noel's Christmas Presents*; and *The World of the Secret Camera*. His dazzling shirts and sweaters have become a trademark. Despite his success in the UK, an attempt at a talk show in the USA in 1986 failed to work out. In 1985, Edmonds founded the Unique media group.

Edmondson, Adrian

(1957–)

English comedian and comic actor, once part of an act known as 20th Century Coyote with Rik Mayall. As Vyvyan in THE YOUNG ONES he perfected his violent moron character, which he carried through into FILTHY, RICH AND CATFLAP (Eddie Catflap) and BOTTOM (Eddie Hitler). He is married to Jennifer Saunders, with whom he appeared in HAPPY FAMILIES (idiot Guy Fuddle), GIRLS ON TOP, *French and Saunders* and assorted COMIC STRIP satires. He has also appeared in BLACKADDER (Baron Von Richthoven), SATURDAY LIVE (with Rik Mayall, as the Dangerous Brothers), the futuristic comedy *Snakes and Ladders* (Giles), the Richard Briers comedy-drama IF YOU SEE GOD, TELL HIM (Gordon Spry), ANNA LEE, *Doctors and Nurses* (Roy Glover), *The Young Indiana Jones Chronicles*, JONATHAN CREEK (Brendan Baxter), *Twisted Tales*, HOLBY CITY and *Surviving Disaster* (Valeri Legasov). In addition, Edmondson sang the theme song, 'This Wheel's on Fire', with Julie Driscoll (now Julie Tippetts), for ABSOLUTELY FABULOUS.

Edna, The Inebriate Woman ★★★

UK (BBC) Drama. BBC 1 1971

Edna .... **Patricia Hayes**
Josie .... **Barbara Jefford**
Irene .... **Pat Nye**

Writer **Jeremy Sandford**
Producer **Irene Shubik**

● ***A homeless woman is let down by society's attempts at welfare.***

Having shaken up the Establishment with his bleak depiction of the plight facing homeless families in his 1966 play CATHY COME HOME, writer Jeremy Sandford moved on to homeless single people in 1971. Edna, the eponymous star of this PLAY FOR TODAY offering, is the sort of society victim everyone wants to forget. Unable to cope with life after a spell in HMP Holloway, she suffers from schizophrenia and considers herself to be a malfunctioning piece of machinery. Her mind 'gets cloudy', she says, which leads her to cause havoc almost everywhere she goes. She's been banned from countless hostels because she throws food, gets drunk and wets the bed, and wandering the streets she cuts a tragicomic figure, yelling 'I am not the vagrant' to anyone who will listen. Flashbacks to her horrific earlier life suggest the causes of Edna's current predicament. She is undesirable, a person no one is willing to get close to, but someone desperately in need of care. Sandford claimed to have developed the character from meetings with real people like Edna. Ted Kotcheff directed.

Educating Marmalade/Danger – Marmalade at Work ★★

UK (Thames) Children's Situation Comedy. ITV 1982–4

Marmalade Atkins .... **Charlotte Coleman**
Mrs Atkins .... **Lynda Marchal**
Carol Macready
Mr Atkins .... **John Bird**
Mrs Allgood .... **Gillian Raine**
Dr Glenfiddick .... **John Fortune**
Wendy Wooley .... **Elizabeth Estensen**

Executive Producer **Pamela Lonsdale**
Producers **Sue Birtwistle, Marjorie Sigley**

● ***There's no hope for a teenage tearaway, in school or at work.***

Marmalade Atkins is the naughtiest schoolgirl in the world, much to the despair of her long-suffering parents. In a bid to kerb her outrageous behaviour, they pass her round a number of educational establishments (she's already been expelled from ten), from the local school to a convent, Eton, boarding school, finishing school and even into the care of an animal trainer, before she ends up with an old-fashioned nanny. None of these, of course, is able to handle the fiery carrot top, as education officer Mrs Allgood sadly discovers. In the second series, billed as *Danger – Marmalade at Work*, the troublesome Miss Atkins has thankfully left school and is now chaperoned by an ultra-eager social worker, Wendy Wooley, who tries to place her in an assortment of jobs and training schemes. The results are disastrously the same. Marmalade is seen joining the police, the secret service, the army and the navy, and working as a housemaid and an air hostess. She also takes lessons in cookery, art and eventually showbiz, at a Fame-type school in New York City. For this series, Carol Macready replaced Lynda Marchal as Marmalade's mum (Marchal, as Lynda La Plante, was building a new career in writing).

The pilot episode, *Marmalade Atkins in Space*, appeared as part of 1981's anthology series *Theatre Box*, for which special scripts and instruction books were prepared to allow young theatre groups to present their own interpretation of each play. Bad Manners sang the theme song to the 1982 series.

Edward and Mrs Simpson ★★★

UK (Thames) Historical Drama. ITV 1978
DVD: Network

Edward .... **Edward Fox**
Mrs Wallis Warfield Simpson . **Cynthia Harris**
Queen Mary .... **Peggy Ashcroft**
Stanley Baldwin .... **David Waller**
George, Duke of York .... **Andrew Ray**
Duchess of York .... **Amanda Reiss**
Ernest Simpson .... **Charles Keating**
King George V .... **Marius Goring**
Lady Thelma Furness .... **Cherie Lunghi**
Walter Monckton .... **Nigel Hawthorne**
Aunt Bessie Merryman .... **Jessie Matthews**
Lady Diana Cooper .... **Patricia Hodge**
Duff Cooper .... **Trevor Bowen**
Archbishop of Canterbury ...... **Maurice Denham**
Chips Channon .... **Gary Waldhorn**
Major John Aird .... **Simon Cadell**
Major Alexander Hardinge ..... **John Shrapnel**
Clement Atlee .... **Patrick Troughton**

Writer **Simon Raven**
Producer **Andrew Brown**

● ***The Story of King Edward VIII's abdication.***

This expensive seven-part drama relates events leading up to the abdication crisis of 1936, with particular focus on the controversial affair between Prince Edward (later King Edward VIII) and American divorcée Wallis Simpson. Based on the biography by Frances Donaldson, the series portrays Mrs Simpson as a calculating schemer, something that distressed the real Duchess of Windsor, who was still alive and residing in France when it was first broadcast. Edward Fox won much acclaim for his performance as the emotionally torn king.

Edward the Seventh ★★★★

UK (ATV) Historical Drama. ITV 1975
DVD: Network

Edward .... **Timothy West** *(adult)*
Charles Sturridge *(teenager)*
Queen Victoria .... **Annette Crosbie**
Prince Albert .... **Robert Hardy**
Princess Alexandra .... **Deborah Grant**
Helen Ryan
Princess Vicky .... **Felicity Kendal**
Duchess of Kent .... **Alison Leggatt**
Col. Bruce .... **Harry Andrews**
Lord Palmerston .... **André Morell**
Benjamin Disraeli .... **John Gielgud**
William Gladstone .... **Michael Hordern**
Princess Dagmar .... **Jane Lapotaire**
Lillie Langtry .... **Francesca Annis**
Prince Eddy .... **Charles Dance**
Lord Salisbury .... **Richard Vernon**
Lord Coventry .... **Robert Flemyng**
Lady Brooke .... **Carolyn Seymour**
Kaiser Wilhelm .... **Christopher Neame**
Herbert Asquith .... **Basil Dignam**
Sir Henry Campbell-Bannerman .... **Geoffrey Bayldon**

Writers **David Butler, John Gorrie**
Producer **Cecil Clarke**

● ***A detailed dramatization of the life of King Edward VII.***

Edward was 60 years of age when he succeeded his long-reigning mother, Queen Victoria, to the throne, which meant that his better years were behind him. This 13-part biopic looks closely at the life and loves of the Prince and also focuses on the personality of the great Queen herself and other members of the royal family. With scenes filmed within Osborne House, Sandringham and other royal properties, by permission of the present Queen, the series was much applauded for its attention to detail, production techniques and the performances of the lead actors. Based on a biography by Philip Magnus, it was largely written by David Butler, formerly Dr Nick Williams in EMERGENCY – WARD 10. Butler went on to co-write LILLIE for LWT in 1978, in which Francesca Annis reprised her Lillie Langtry role. *Edward the Seventh* was retitled *Edward the King* when shown in the USA.

Edwardian Country House, The

See *1900 House, The*.

Edwardians, The ★★

UK (BBC) Drama. BBC 2 1972–3

Producer **Mark Shivas**

● ***Eight dramatizations of the lives of turn-of-the-century British pioneers.***

This series of drama-documentaries looks closely at nine early 20th-century figures of note: Messrs Charles Rolls and Frederick Royce (played by Michael Jayston and Robert Powell); writers E. Nesbit (Judy Parfitt) and Arthur Conan Doyle (Nigel Davenport); Daisy, mistress of Edward VII (Virginia McKenna); scout-founder Robert Baden-Powell (Ron Moody); music hall star Marie Lloyd (Georgia Brown); journalist and MP Horatio

Bottomley (Timothy West); and Prime Minister David Lloyd George (Anthony Hopkins).

Edwards, Anthony

(1962–)

California-born actor best known as Dr Mark Greene in ER, but also seen as murderer Dick Hickock in the dramatization of Truman Capote's *In Cold Blood*. His early credits included a sitcom, *It Takes Two*, and NORTHERN EXPOSURE (boy in the bubble Mike Monroe).

Edwards, Huw

(1961–)

Welsh news anchor, beginning his career as a newsreader with the Swansea Sound commercial radio station. He then joined the BBC's news trainee scheme, becoming eventually a political correspondent, progressing into presenting the BBC's main news bulletins, most notably the nightly *Six O'Clock News* from 1999 and the *10 O'Clock News* from 2002. Edwards has also hosted NEWSNIGHT, PANORAMA, *The Story of Wales*, SONGS OF PRAISE and various state occasion broadcasts, plus, in 2005, a special week of NEWSROUND.

Edwards, Jimmy

DFC (1920–88)

English comedian whose handlebar moustache became a trademark. Awarded the DFC for his wartime RAF efforts, Edwards broke into radio in the late 1940s, when, as Pa Glum, he appeared in *Take It from Here*. This ran for 12 years and The Glums were revived on TV as part of *Bruce Forsyth's Big Night* in 1978. However, it is as Professor Jimmy Edwards, the corrupt principal of Chiselbury School in WHACK-O!, that he will always be remembered by viewers, and, after playing the role for four years, 1956–60, he donned his gown and picked up his cane once more for a revival in 1971. His other TV starring roles were in SEVEN FACES OF JIM, *Six More Faces of Jim, More Faces of Jim, Bold as Brass* (musician Ernie Briggs), *Mr John Jorrocks* (Jorrocks, Master of Foxhounds), and THE FOSSETT SAGA (Victorian writer James Fossett), and as the cowardly knight *Sir Yellow*. The famous moustache was apparently grown to obscure facial injuries received when one of his aircraft crashed in the war.

Edwards, Vince

(Vincento Eduardo Zoine; 1928–96)

American leading man of the 1960s, an international heartthrob thanks to his star status in BEN CASEY. He was generally seen in the UK only in guest spots and in TV movies (including the pilot for KNIGHT RIDER) after the series ended in 1966, moving more into directing, although he did pop up in a couple of lesser dramas in the USA (notably *Matt Lincoln*). His earliest TV performances came in shows such as ALFRED HITCHCOCK PRESENTS and THE UNTOUCHABLES.

Eerie, Indiana ✱✱

US (Unreality, Inc./Cosgrove-Meurer/Hearst) Science Fiction. Channel 4 1993 (US: NBC 1991–2)
DVD: BMG Special Products (Region 1 only)

Marshall Teller	**Omri Katz**
Simon Holmes	**Justin Shenkarow**
Marilyn Teller	**Mary-Margaret Humes**
Edgar Teller	**Francis Guinan**
Syndi Teller	**Julie Condra**
Mr Bartholomew J. Radford	**John Astin**

Creators **Karl Schaefer, Jose Rivera**

● ***A teenager witnesses strange goings-on in his new town.***
Hot on the heels of the mysterious TWIN PEAKS came *Eerie, Indiana*, a light comedy based around the eccentric inhabitants of a small Midwestern community. New kid in town is adolescent Marshall Teller (played by DALLAS's John Ross, Omri Katz), who has just arrived from New Jersey with his dad, Edgar (an inventor), mum, Marilyn and older sister, Syndi. Marshall's new buddy is Simon, a few years his junior but equally interested in the wacky events that take place in this appropriately named settlement (population 16,661 – most as nutty as fruitcakes). Together the boys keep a record of the strange happenings – sightings of Elvis as Marshall delivers the *Eerie Examiner*; the neighbour who seals her kids in a kind of Tupperware each night to keep them young; the dogs whose plans for rebellion are overheard on a dental brace; the secret repository for the lost items of the world, such as odd socks. The boys stow away the evidence in the Tellers' loft because no one else turns a hair at the weirdness out there. To underline the kookiness of the community, former Addams Family lead John Astin is later added as a shopkeeper. *Gremlins* director Joe Dante acted as consultant for the series, also directing some episodes, but, despite its originality, only one series (19 episodes) of *Eerie, Indiana* was produced. However, a revamp, entitled *Eerie, Indiana: the Other Dimension* and featuring new actors and characters, was developed in 1998.

Egan, Peter

(1946–)

Suave English actor whose many roles have encompassed both drama and comedy. Following his performance as a violent gangster in 1969's BIG BREADWINNER HOG, he took the somewhat different part of the Earl of Southampton in ELIZABETH R in 1971 and remained in period costume for PRINCE REGENT in 1979. In the 1980s he charmed sitcom viewers as the super-smooth Paul Ryman in EVER DECREASING CIRCLES, before becoming Hannah Gordon's house husband, David Braithwaite, in the banking comedy JOINT ACCOUNT. He also won acclaim as Magnus Pym in the BBC's adaptation of Le Carré's A PERFECT SPY and as a war cripple in the one-off play *A Day in Summer*, for YTV. Among his other credits have been Seth Starkadder in COLD COMFORT FARM, Oscar Wilde in LILLIE, MOTHER LOVE, REILLY – ACE OF SPIES (Major Fothergill), THE DARK SIDE OF THE SUN (Raoul Lavalliere), *The Organisation*, TALES OF THE UNEXPECTED, THRILLER, PARADISE POSTPONED (Henry Simcox), THE RUTH RENDELL MYSTERIES and A WOMAN OF SUBSTANCE. In recent years, Egan has been seen in *The Peacock Spring* (Sir Gwithiam), the *Screen One* comedy *Gobble* (Peter Villiers), *Chiller* (Richard Cramer), AMBASSADOR (Michael Cochrane) and *Cry Wolf* (Dr Hook), as well as making guest appearances in *The Inspector Pitt Mysteries*, A TOUCH

OF FROST, THE INSPECTOR LYNLEY MYSTERIES, MY FAMILY and JERICHO.

Ehle, Jennifer
(1969–)

British actress, born in North Carolina, the daughter of actress Rosemary Harris. Undoubtedly her biggest role to date has been as Elizabeth Bennet in PRIDE AND PREJUDICE, although she also made the headlines with her portrayal of Calypso in THE CAMOMILE LAWN. Later work has included *Melissa* (title role), and other credits take in both *Rik Mayall Presents* and *Alan Bleasdale Presents.*

El C.I.D. ✶✶

UK (Granada) Comedy. Drama. ITV 1990–2

Douglas Bromley .... **John Bird**
Bernard Blake .... **Alfred Molina**
Frank .... **Tony Haygarth**
Metcalf .... **Donald Churchill**
Delgado .... **Simon Andreu**
Mercedes .... **Viviane Vives**
Stevie Blake .... **Robert Reynolds**
Rosie Bromley .... **Amanda Redman**
Gus Mercer .... **Kenneth Cranham**
Graham .... **Niven Boyd**
Señora Sanchez .... **Maria Isbert**

Creators **Chris Kelly, Iain Roy**
Executive Producer **Sally Head**
Producer **Matthew Bird**

● ***Two former Scotland Yard officers move to the Costa del Crime.***

When police clerk Douglas Bromley is told he is being relocated to Derbyshire, the idea doesn't greatly appeal, so he encourages his beefy CID colleague, Bernard Blake, to join him in early retirement and a voyage of adventure to Spain. Setting out in a motorized yacht, aptly named *El C.I.D.*, they moor up on the Costa del Sol, near Marbella, where they quickly immerse themselves in the area's dodgy goings-on. The bar they intend to open is criminally destroyed and the hapless duo join forces with Delgado and Mercedes, father and daughter detectives, in a long-running battle with the local underworld (and, in particular, nasty Gus Mercer and his henchman, Graham). Metcalf is the bombastic owner of the marina where their boat is berthed and Frank is the expat proprietor of the snappily named Chez Frank restaurant. Blake's troublesome brother, Stevie, turns up in the second season, before Blake himself leaves in the third series, to be replaced by Rosie, Bromley's long-lost daughter. She arrives in Marbella after being dumped by her boyfriend and joins her dad as an accomplice in Delgado and Partners.

Eldorado ✶✶

UK (Cinema Verity/J Dy T) Drama. BBC 1 1992–3

Gwen Lockhead .... **Patricia Brake**
Drew Lockhead .... **Campbell Morrison**
Blair Lockhead .... **Josh Nathan**
Nessa Lockhead .... **Julie Fernandez**
Trish Valentine .... **Polly Perkins**
Dieter Schultz .... **Kai Maurer**
Joy Slater .... **Leslee Udwin**
Snowy White .... **Patch Connolly**
Roberto Fernandez .... **Franco Rey**
Rosario Fernandez .... **Stella Maris**
Maria Fernandez .... **Maria Sanchez**
Abuela Fernandez .... **Maria Vega**
Javier Fernandez .... **Iker Ibanez**
Ingrid Olsson .... **Bo Corre**
Marcus Tandy .... **Jesse Birdsall**
Pilar Moreno .... **Sandra Sandri**
Olive King .... **Faith Kent**
Isabelle Leduc .... **Framboise Gommendy**
Philippe Leduc .... **Daniel Lombart**
Arnaud Leduc .... **Mikael Philippe**
Lene Svendsen .... **Nanna Moller**
Per Svendsen .... **Kim Romer**
Trine Svendsen .... **Marchell Betak**
Clare Wilkie
Gavin Hindle .... **Darren Newton**
Allan Hindle .... **Jon Morrey**
Gerry Peters-Smith .... **Buki Armstrong**
Bunny Charlson .... **Roger Walker**
Freddie Martin .... **Roland Curram**
Fizz Charlson .... **Kathy Pitkin**
Stanley Webb .... **William Lucas**
Rosemary Webb .... **Hilary Crane**
Tracy .... **Hayley Bromley**
Antonio .... **Jose Antonio Navarro**
'Razor' Sharpe .... **Kevin Hay**
Sergio Munoz D'Avila .... **Alexander Torriglia**
Alex Morris .... **Derek Martin**

Creators **Julia Smith, Tony Holland**
Executive Producers **Verity Lambert, John Dark**
Producers **Julia Smith, Corinne Hollingworth**

● ***Drama with an expatriate community in Spain.***

In 1992, the year of falling European barriers, the BBC did its bit for the cause by launching a thrice-weekly 'soap for Europe'. Trailed in the tabloids as 'sex, sun and sangria', *Eldorado* was set in the Spanish fishing village of Los Barcos and focused on its community of expatriate Brits, Frenchmen and Danes, all 'living their dream' of a home in the sun but discovering that their new life was not one long holiday after all.

The community's mother figure is Gwen Lockhead, a teacher who runs the English-language newspaper. Gwen's husband, Drew, is a lazy, hard-drinking Glaswegian, her son, Blair, is a typically troublesome teenager and her daughter, Nessa, although wheelchair bound, is determinedly independent. The Lockheads' neighbours are retired military man Stanley Webb, who lives with his young-at-heart wife, Rosemary, Olive King, the local nosy parker, and another ex-army man, Bunny Charlson, who is shacked up with Fizz, a 17-year-old runaway. Charmer Marcus Tandy is the 'Costa del Crime' villain in hiding, gay Freddie Martin knocks about with the rebellious Gerry (a girl), and Snowy White is the Los Barcos handyman. Brothers Gavin and Allan Hindle run the beach bar, Joy Slater owns the wine bar and Trish Valentine is the ageing nightclub singer who enjoys a stormy relationship with Dieter Schultz, a 19-year-old German windsurfing teacher. The French are represented by tennis coach Philippe Leduc, his flirty wife, Isabelle, and their 16-year-old romantic son, Arnaud. The Svendsen family offer the Danish input. Dad Per owns a chandlery business, mum Lene is a beautician and their 14-year-old daughter is called Trine. Completing the line-up of Los Barcos principals are Swedish tour guide Ingrid Olssen and a handful of local Spaniards, mostly from the

Fernandez family: Roberto, the town doctor, his wife, Rosario, and two teenage children, Maria and Javier. Abuella is Roberto's traditionally minded mother. Pilar Moreno is the other native and she works at Marcus Tandy's stables, eventually becoming his girlfriend. The interaction of this motley band of retirees, escapees from the rat race, old bigots and young new Europeans is the source of the series' drama.

Eldorado was the biggest and most ambitious series yet awarded to an independent production company (Cinema Verity) by the BBC. A whole village was specially constructed in Spanish woodland for filming and the cast and crew took up residence locally. Sadly, *Eldorado* did not capture the public's imagination in the way Julia Smith and Tony Holland's earlier creation, EASTENDERS, had, and critics piled on the agony. Although viewing figures were on the mend, it was cancelled by new BBC 1 boss Alan Yentob just a year after it had begun.

Electronic News Gathering

See *ENG*.

11 O'Clock Show, The ★★

UK (Talkback) Comedy. Channel 4 1998–2000

Fred MacAulay, Brendon Burns, Iain Lee, Ali G, Tommy Vance, Rich Hall, Mackenzie Crook, Daisy Donovan, Ricky Gervais, Paul Garner, Alan Francis, Alex Lowe, Sarah Alexander, Jon Holmes

Executive Producer **Peter Fincham**
Producers **Harry Thompson, Nick Martin, Dan Mazer, John Rowlands, Paul Gilheany, Dominic English, Richard Hopkins, Phil Clarke**

● ***Late-night send up of the latest news and current affairs.***
This collection of sketches, gags, spoof reports, daft vox pops and animations ran for five series but is probably best known for the number of rising stars who gained exposure from it. Most notable was Sacha Baron Cohen in his guise of Ali G, bamboozling interview guests with leading questions and innuendo. Having a similar effect on MPs was The Angel of Delight, a reporter played by Daisy Donovan, daughter of photographer Terence Donovan, later to appear in MY FAMILY and other series of her own such as DAISY DAISY. Add to this the pre-OFFICE pairing of Mackenzie Crook and Ricky Gervais, and future COUPLING star Sarah Alexander, and it's easy to see why *The 11 O'Clock Show* had its fans.

The series ran for three consecutive weeknights, with shows written and recorded on the day of transmission for ultra-topicality. First hosts in a trial run that extended to only two weeks were Fred MacAulay and Brendon Burns, supported by Iain Lee. Lee (later seen hosting the ill-fated *RI:SE* breakfast show on Channel 4) took over from the next series, supported mostly by Daisy Donovan (brought in from reporting), with other performers chipping in with taped or studio items. By the time of the last series, Sarah Alexander and Jon Holmes were at the helm. Some later episodes were billed as *The 11 O'Clock Show: the News Alternative*. Compilations of Ali G material from the programme were broadcast in 1999 as *Da Best of Ali G*.

Elizabeth R ★★★

UK (BBC) Historical Drama. BBC 2 1971
DVD: BBC/Warner Home Video (Region 1 only)

Elizabeth I .... **Glenda Jackson**
Robert Dudley .... **Robert Hardy**
William Cecil .... **Ronald Hines**
Mary Tudor .... **Daphne Slater**
Thomas Cranmer .... **Bernard Hepton**
Kat Ashley .... **Rachel Kempson**
Edward VI .... **Jason Kemp**
Catherine Parr .... **Rosalie Crutchley**
Count de Feria .... **Leonard Sachs**
Bishop de Quadra .... **Esmond Knight**
Sir James Melville .... **John Cairney**
Mary, Queen of Scots .... **Vivian Pickles**
Sir Francis Walsingham .... **Stephen Murray**
Duke of Alençon .... **Michael Williams**
Catherine de Medici .... **Margareta Scott**
Earl of Essex .... **Robin Ellis**
Sir Anthony Babington .... **David Collings**
Phillip II, King of Spain .... **Peter Jeffrey**
Sir Francis Drake .... **John Woodvine**
Sir Walter Raleigh .... **Nicholas Selby**
Francis Bacon .... **John Nettleton**
Father Robert Parsons .... **Paul Hardwick**
Lettice Knollys .... **Angela Thorne**
O'Neill, Earl of Tyrone .... **Patrick O'Connell**
Sir Robert Cecil .... **Hugh Dickson**
Earl of Southampton .... **Peter Egan**

Writers **John Hale, Rosemary Anne Sisson, Julian Mitchell, Hugh Whitemore, John Prebble, Ian Rodger**
Producer **Roderick Graham**

● ***The troubled life of England's Virgin Queen.***
In six self-contained episodes, each of 90 minutes' length, *Elizabeth R* dramatizes the tortuous life of the famous 16th-century monarch, beginning with her difficult road to the throne and ending with her lonely death. In doing so, it also affords viewers an insight into court life in Tudor times.

Following hot on the heels of the enormously successful THE SIX WIVES OF HENRY VIII, *Elizabeth R* had much to achieve but, thanks to its large (for the time) budget of £237,000, close attention to detail and an excellent cast (some reprising the roles they had taken in *Six Wives*), it enjoyed similar acclaim. For her role as Elizabeth, Glenda Jackson shaved her forehead, donned eccentric hairpieces and wore a false nose. Courtesy of hours in the make-up room, she was seen to age from a youthful, determined 15 to a grotesque, pallid 70-year-old over the course of the series.

Ellen ★★★

US (Black/Marlens/Touchstone) Situation Comedy. Channel 4 1994–9 (US: ABC 1994–8)
DVD: A&E Home Video (Region 1 only)

Ellen Morgan .... **Ellen DeGeneres**
Adam Greene .... **Arye Gross**
Holly .... **Holly Fulger**
Anita .... **Maggie Wheeler**
Joe Farrell .... **David Anthony Higgins**
Paige Clark .... **Joely Fisher**
Audrey Penney .... **Clea Lewis**
Spence Kovak .... **Jeremy Piven**

Creators **Neal Marlens, Carol Black, David Rosenthal**
Executive Producers **Neal Marlens, Carol Black**

An insecure single woman runs a bookshop in LA.

Blonde Ellen Morgan is manager of a Los Angeles bookstore-cum-coffee-shop called Buy the Book. Being slightly wacky, she spends most of her days and evenings observing the finer points of life with her photographer flatmate, Adam Greene, and girlfriends Holly and Anita – although the last two are written out after the very earliest episodes (which aired in the USA under the title *These Friends of Mine*). Taking their place are new confidants Joe Farrell, who brews ace coffee at the shop (now owned by Ellen), and Paige Clark. Audrey Penney is introduced as a niggling neighbour at the same time. Spence Kovak, Ellen's cousin, eventually replaces Adam as her flatmate. Later episodes see Buy the Book damaged by an earthquake and then rebuilt, only to be sold by Ellen to a major chain, but the big story of this series came in a groundbreaking 1997 double episode. In this Ellen 'comes out', aided by her therapist (played by Oprah Winfrey). It was the first time in US TV history that the lead character in a series had openly professed homosexuality, outraging right-wing America but also creating a new gay TV icon.

Ellery Queen **

US (Universal/Fairmont-Foxcroft) Detective Drama. BBC 1 1976 (US: NBC 1975–6)

Ellery Queen	**Jim Hutton**
Insp. Richard Queen	**David Wayne**
Sgt Velie	**Tom Reese**
Simon Brimmer	**John Hillerman**
Frank Flannigan	**Ken Swofford**

Producers **Peter S. Fischer, Michael Rhodes**
Executive Producers **Richard Levinson, William Link**

A crime writer helps his policeman father solve mysteries in New York.

Ellery Queen, the 1920s literary creation of cousins Frederic Dannay and Manfred Bennington Lee, moved into US radio in 1939, graduating to television in 1950. Since his debut, he has been played by six different actors: Richard Hart, Lee Bowman, Hugh Marlowe, George Nader, Lee Philips and Jim Hutton, the last in this series, which made it on to UK screens in 1976. The brilliant, if a bit forgetful, Queen is, on the face of it, a mystery novelist. However, he is usually called in to help out his father, Richard, who works for the NYPD. The setting is 1947 and also seen are plain-clothes cop Velie, radio criminologist Simon Brimmer and newspaper reporter Frank Flannigan. As a trademark, Queen always asks the viewing audience if it can guess whodunnit, before proceeding to the denouement. The series also aired in the UK as *Ellery Queen Whodunnit*. Music was by Elmer Bernstein.

Elliot, John

(1918–97)

Early BBC documentary maker, writer, producer and director (1954's WAR IN THE AIR was his greatest achievement) who went on to script some influential dramas, including A FOR ANDROMEDA and *The Andromeda Breakthrough* (both with Fred Hoyle, the latter also as producer). Elliot also created MOGUL and FALL OF EAGLES, co-wrote *A Stranger on the Hills*, and penned some episodes of Z CARS and THE BRACK REPORT. He later became a BBC executive.

Elliott, Denholm

CBE (1922–92)

Actor readily cast as a distinguished, but slightly dodgy or sinister Englishman in many films and TV dramas. His major television performances were in THE MAN IN ROOM 17 (Imlac Defraits), MYSTERY AND IMAGINATION (Count Dracula), CLAYHANGER (Tertius Ingpen), *The Signalman, Blade on the Feather, Hôtel du Lac*, BLEAK HOUSE (John Jarndyce), *Scoop*, RIPPING YARNS, *Codename Kyril* and the mini-series *Marco Polo* (Niccolò Polo). He also played George Smiley in *A Murder of Quality* and William Filmore in CATHERINE COOKSON'S *The Black Candle*. His first wife was Virginia McKenna.

Elphick, Michael

(1946–2002)

Chichester-born actor, headlining in a range of comedies and dramas, especially as German petty crook PRIVATE SCHULZ, fireman-turned-adventurer Ken BOON, working-class taxidermist Sam Tyler in THREE UP, TWO DOWN, and news agency boss Harry Salter in *Harry*. Among his many other credits were the comedy *Pull the Other One* (Sidney Mundy), AUF WIEDERSEHEN, PET (Irish labourer Magowan), CORONATION STREET, Z CARS, CROWN COURT, BLUE REMEMBERED HILLS (Peter), *This Year, Next Year*, THE SWEENEY, SHOESTRING, *Roger Doesn't Live Here Anymore* (wrestler Stanley), MASADA, SUPERGRAN, *Jenny's War, Stanley and the Women, The One and Only Phyllis Dixey, The Fix* (Peter Campling), THE BILL, DAVID COPPERFIELD (Barkiss) and *Metropolis* (Andrew Kaplan). His last role was in EASTENDERS (Harry Slater).

Elton, Ben

(1959–)

British stand-up comic and comedy scriptwriter. Among his writing credits have been THE YOUNG ONES (with Rik Mayall and Lise Mayer), GIRLS ON TOP (script editor), HAPPY FAMILIES, FILTHY RICH AND CATFLAP, *Lenny Henry Tonite*, THE THIN BLUE LINE, *Blessed* (also as director) and, with Richard Curtis, BLACKADDER (apart from the first series). In front of the camera (often complete with sparkling jacket), he has hosted *South of Watford* and SATURDAY LIVE, appeared in Granada's ALFRESCO and once stood in for *Wogan*. Elton has also been *The Man from Auntie* in a monologue and sketch show (later revamped as *The Ben Elton Show*) that has given a thorough airing to his sharp social and political observations. Outside television, he has had several novels published (including *Stark*, in which he appeared on its adaptation for BBC 2) and has scripted West End plays.

Emergency – Ward 10 **

UK (ATV) Drama. ITV 1957–67

Nurse Pat Roberts	**Rosemary Miller**
Nurse/Sister Carole Young	**Jill Browne**
Sister Cowley	**Elizabeth Kentish**
Nurse/Sister/Matron Mary Stevenson	**Iris Russell**
Dr Alan Dawson	**Charles Tingwell**
Dr Patrick 'Paddy' O'Meara	**Glyn Owen**
Potter	**Douglas Ives**
Dr Chris Anderson	**Desmond Carrington**

Dr Simon Forrester	**Frederick Bartman**
Mr Stephen Brooks	**John Brooking**
Dr Peter Harrison	**Peter Howell**
RSO Hughes	**John Paul**
Nurse Ann Guthridge	**Norah Gorsen**
Staff Nurse Jane Morley	**Ann Sears**
Dr John Rennie	**Richard Thorp**
Nurse Jo Buckley/Anderson	**Barbara Clegg**
Nurse Julie Wayne	**Jean Aubrey**
Sister Shelley	**Gene Anderson**
Nurse O'Keefe	**Kerry Marsh**
Donald Latimer	**John Carson**
Jake O'Dowd	**Shaun O'Riordan**
Staff Nurse Craigie	**Shirley Thieman**
Mr Harold de la Roux	**John Barron**
Margaret de la Roux	**Kathleen Byron**
Dr Whittaker	**Robert Macleod**
Sister Crawford	**Cicely Hullett**
Audrey Blake/Dawson	**Jane Downs**
RSO Miller	**John Barrie**
Dr Don Nolan	**Ray Barrett**
Dr Nick Williams	**David Butler**
Miss Nesbitt	**Ann Firbank**
Nurse Gregg	**Felicity Young**
Derek Bailey	**Brian Nissen**
Sister Rhys	**Joan Matheson**
Mr Lester Large	**John Carlisle**
Dr Frances Whitney	**Paula Byrne**
Dr Richard Moone	**John Alderton**
Sister MacNab	**Dorothy Smith**
Rupert Marsden	**Ian Colin**
Andrew Shaw	**John Line**
Dr Ted Bryan	**Richard Bidlake**
Dr Bob Coughlin	**Desmond Jordan**
Dr Griffiths	**Robert Lang**
Nurse Ann Webb	**Jean Trend**
Sally Bowen	**Carol Davies**
Linda Stanley	**Jennifer Wright**
Dr Beckett	**Geoffrey Colvile**
Dr James Gordon	**Michael McKevitt**
Elizabeth Benskin	**Sheila Fearn**
Sister Mary Doughty	**Pamela Duncan**
Staff Nurse Jill Craig	**Anne Brooks**
Mr Fitzgerald	**John Arnatt**
Nurse Kate Ford	**Jane Rossington**
Nurse Michaela Davies/ Large	**Tricia Money**
Mr Giles Farmer	**John White**
Nurse Kwe Kim-Yen/Kwei	**Pik-Sen Lim**
Estelle Waterman	**Pauline Yates**
Mr Victor	**Richard Carpenter**
Jean Twillow	**Elisabeth Murray**
Tim Birch	**Frazer Hines**
Mr Guy Marshall	**Tom Adams**
Mr Barrett	**Geoffrey Russell**
Dr Rex Lane Russell	**Basil Hoskins**
Lena Hyde	**Caroline Blakiston**
Staff Nurse/Sister Jane Beattie	**Anne Lloyd**
Amanda Brown	**Hilary Tindall**
Dr Alex Grant	**Michael Baxter**
Sister Ransome	**Stella Tanner**
Mr Booth	**Jonathan Newth**
Mr Bacon	**David Pinner**
Mr Dorsey	**David Garth**
Dr Brook	**William Wilde**
Dr Louise Mahler	**Joan Hooley**
Dr Murad	**Salmaan Peer**
Prof. Jenkins	**John Welsh**
Staff Nurse Lyle	**Colette Dunne**
Helen Booth	**Rosemary Frankau**
Nurse Parkin	**Therese McMurray**
Dr Fairfax	**Victor Winding**
Elizabeth Fairfax	**Honor Shepherd**
Sister Wright	**Zulema Dene**
Nurse Jones	**Janet Lees Price**
Mr Bailey	**David King**
Mr Verity	**Paul Darrow**
Dr Richmond	**Noel Coleman**
Mr Kent	**Ian Cullen**
Staff Nurse Amy Williams	**Sonia Fox**
Dr Green	**Langton Jones**

Creator **Tessa Diamond**
Producers **Antony Kearey, Rex Firkin, Hugh Rennie, John Cooper, Cecil Petty, Josephine Douglas, Pieter Rogers**

● ***Britain's first twice-weekly, long-running drama series, focusing on staff and patients in a general hospital.***

Emergency – Ward 10, the brainchild of ATV staff writer Tessa Diamond, ran for ten years and drew huge audiences. Its cancellation in 1967 was, according to Lew Grade, boss of ATV, one of his biggest mistakes. The series initially focused on trainee nurse Pat Roberts, a farm girl getting to grips with life in a city hospital. She was quickly joined in the limelight by a host of budding stars. Jill Browne as her roommate, Nurse (later Sister) Carole Young, won most male admirers, although some of her male colleagues also became heart-throbs for female viewers. These included Charles Tingwell as surgeon Alan Dawson, Desmond Carrington as Dr Chris Anderson, Ray Barrett as Dr Don Nolan, and Dr John Rennie, who was played by a youngster by the name of Richard Thorp, now better known as EMMERDALE's Alan Turner. John Alderton joined the cast in 1963 as youthful Dr Richard Moone (he was later to marry his co-star, Jill Browne).

The action took place at Oxbridge General Hospital and, although drama was high, tragedy was scarce; of more concern were the lives and loves of the hospital staff. Patient deaths were strictly limited to five per year, and this was later reduced to just two. That was good news for emerging names like Ian Hendry, Albert Finney and Joanna Lumley, who all signed up for treatment. *Emergency – Ward 10*'s success spawned a feature film, *Life in Emergency Ward 10*, in 1958, and also one spin-off series, *Call Oxbridge 2000*. This saw Dr Rennie heading off into private practice and itself led to another series, entitled *24-Hour Call*. *Emergency – Ward 10*, for all intents and purposes, was resurrected by ATV in the 1970s in the guise of GENERAL HOSPITAL.

Emery, Dick

(1917–83)

British comedian, fond of outrageous characterizations and drag sketches. His *Dick Emery Show*, which began in 1963 and ran for nearly two decades, saw him adopting the guises of a sex-starved spinster (always 'Miss' not 'Madam'); an effeminate swinger ('Hello, Honky Tonk'); a toothy vicar; a camp sailor; a dim bovver-boy; Farmer Finch; a classy tramp; the conniving, chortling old codger, Lampwick; and Mandy, the brassy blonde who always misunderstood the interviewer, so providing Emery with his catchphrase, 'Ooh, you are awful, but I like you!' After radio (and, later, TV) success in *Educating Archie*, Emery had arrived on the small screen in the 1950s, in *The Tony Hancock Show* and with Libby Morris in *Two's Company*. He also supported Michael Bentine in IT'S A SQUARE

WORLD and played Chubby Catchpole in THE ARMY GAME. In 1964 he took the role of Mr Hughes in the early version of the TV station comedy *Room at the Bottom*. Emery hosted *The Dick Emery Hour* for Thames in 1979, but returned to the BBC in 1982 to star in a comedy-thriller series entitled simply *Emery*, playing the part of investigator Bernie Weinstock (and several of his suspects) in cases entitled *Legacy of Murder* and *Jack of Diamonds*.

Emmerdale Farm/Emmerdale ★★

UK (Yorkshire) Drama. ITV 1972–
DVD: Granada Ventures

Annie Sugden/Kempinski	**Sheila Mercier**
Jack Sugden	**Andrew Burt**
	Clive Hornby
Joe Sugden	**Frazer Hines**
Sam Pearson	**Toke Townley**
Peggy Skilbeck	**Jo Kendall**
Matt Skilbeck	**Frederick Pyne**
Amos Brearly	**Ronald Magill**
Henry Wilks	**Arthur Pentelow**
Marian Wilks	**Gail Harrison**
Alec Saunders	**Alan Tucker**
Sharon Crossthwaite	**Louise Jameson**
Revd Edward Ruskin	**George Little**
Liz Ruskin	**Daphne Green**
Dr Clare Scott	**Joanna Tope**
Dr Grant	**Arthur Hewlett**
Penny Golightly	**Louisa Martin**
David Rhys	**Martin Howells**
Nicholas Phelps	**John Bown**
Alison Gibbons	**Carolyn Moody**
Andrew Watson	**Malcolm Terris**
Frank Blakey	**Eric Allan**
Janey Blakey	**Diane Grayson**
Ruth Merrick	**Lynn Dalby**
Tom Merrick	**David Hill**
	Edward Peel
	Jack Carr
Beattie Dowton	**Barbara Ogilvie**
Ben Dowton	**Larry Noble**
Dryden Hogben	**Roy Boyd**
Diana Prescott	**Zibba Mays**
Franklin Prescott	**Donald Morley**
Norah Norris	**Barbara Ashcroft**
Kathy Davis/Gimbel	**Polly Hemingway**
Jim Gimbel	**John Atkinson**
Freda Gimbel	**Mary Henry**
Martin Gimbel	**George Fenton**
James Bonfills	**Tom Browne**
Tom Raistick	**Leonard Trolley**
Rosemary Kendall	**Lesley Manville**
Ernie Shuttleworth	**John Comer**
	Peter Schofield
Winnie Purvis	**Kathy Staff**
Hilda Semple	**Liz Smith**
Bob Matthews	**William Ellis**
Sarah Foster	**Patricia Brake**
Mel Openshaw	**Richard Borthwick**
Lily Cropper	**Gwen Harris**
Lucy Stubbs	**Adrienne Frank**
Dolly Acaster/Skilbeck	**Katherine Barker**
	Jean Rogers
Revd David Cowper	**John Abbott**
Gladys Bullock	**Sandra Voe**
Revd Donald Hinton	**Hugh Manning**
Richard Roper	**David Horovitch**
Ruth Hepton	**Stephanie Turner**
Ian Hepton	**Tim Preece**
Clive Hinton	**Martin Potter**
Anthony Moeketsi	**Oscar James**
Nellie Ratcliffe	**Gabrielle Blunt**
Seth Armstrong	**Stan Richards**
Revd Hugh Chadband	**Ted Richards**
Francesca Zorelli	**Jasmina Hilton**
Major Vivien Denyer	**Kevin Stoney**
Trevor Thatcher	**Michael Cadman**
Rachel Wellow	**Susan Carpenter**
Naomi Clough	**Pat Beckett**
Maurice Westrop	**Edward Dentith**
Florrie Arnold	**Sheila Fay**
Tober Moore	**Richard Beale**
Martha Moore	**Enid Irvin**
Irene Madden	**Kathleen Byron**
Phil Fletcher	**Kenneth Watson**
Maggie Fletcher	**Margaret John**
Terry Fletcher	**Bernard Padden**
Richard Anstey	**Carl Rigg**
Judy Westrop	**Jane Cussons**
Pat Merrick/Sugden	**Helen Weir**
Jackie Merrick	**Ian Sharrock**
Sandie Merrick	**Jane Hutcheson**
Alan Turner	**Richard Thorp**
Archie Brooks	**Tony Pitts**
Caroline Bates	**Diana Davies**
Bill Middleton	**Johnny Caesar**
Sam Skilbeck	**Benjamin Whitehead**
Sita Sharma	**Mamta Kash**
Kathy Bates/Merrick/Tate/Glover	**Malandra Burrows**
Karen Moore	**Annie Hulley**
Phil Pearce	**Peter Alexander**
Drew Dawson	**Jock MacDonald**
Nick Bates	**Cy Chadwick**
Eric Pollard	**Christopher Chittell**
Ruth Pennington	**Julia Chambers**
Robert Sugden	**Christopher Smith**
	Karl Davies
Kate Hughes/Sugden	**Sally Knyvette**
Mark Hughes	**Craig McKay**
Rachel Hughes	**Glenda McKay**
Dennis Rigg	**Richard Franklin**
Pete Whiteley	**Jim Millea**
Lynn Whiteley	**Fionnuala Ellwood**
Bill Whiteley	**Teddy Turner**
Stephen Fuller	**Gregory Floy**
Frank Tate	**Norman Bowler**
Christopher Tate	**Peter Amory**
Zoë Tate	**Leah Bracknell**
Kim Tate/Barker/Marchant	**Claire King**
Sarah Connolly/Sugden	**Madeleine Howard**
	Alyson Spiro
Michael Feldmann	**Matthew Vaughan**
Elizabeth Feldmann/Pollard	**Kate Dove**
Elsa Feldmann	**Naomi Lewis**
Revd Tony Charlton	**Stephen Rashbrook**
Sangeeta Parmar	**Razia McGann**
Jayesh Parmar	**John Leary**
Leonard Kempinski	**Bernard Archard**
Carol Nelson	**Philomena McDonagh**
Julie Bramhope	**Ruth Whitehead**
Vic Windsor	**Alun Lewis**
Viv Windsor/Hope	**Deena Payne**

Character	Actor
Scott Windsor	**Toby Cockerell**
	Ben Freeman
Kelly Windsor/Glover	**Adele Silva**
Donna Windsor	**Sophie Jeffrey**
	Verity Rushworth
Shirley Foster/Turner	**Rachel Davies**
Bernard McAllister	**Brendan Price**
Angharad McAllister	**Amanda Wenban**
Jessica McAllister	**Camilla Power**
Luke McAllister	**Noah Huntley**
Betty Eagleton	**Paula Tilbrook**
Britt Woods	**Michelle Holmes**
Terry Woods	**Billy Hartman**
Nellie Dingle	**Sandra Gough**
	Maggie Tagney
Butch Dingle	**Paul Loughran**
Sam Dingle	**James Hooton**
Tina Dingle	**Jacqueline Pirie**
Zak Dingle	**Steve Halliwell**
Ned Glover	**Johnny Leeze**
Jan Glover	**Roberta Kerr**
Roy Glover	**Nicky Evans**
David Glover	**Ian Kelsey**
Linda Glover/Fowler	**Tonicha Jeronimo**
Biff Fowler	**Stuart Wade**
Emma Nightingale	**Rachel Ambler**
Mandy Dingle	**Lisa Riley**
Sean Rossi	**Mark Cameron**
Susan Wilde	**Louise Heaney**
Marcus Ellis	**Richard Burke**
Andy Hopwood/Sugden	**Kelvin Fletcher**
Steve Marchant	**Paul Opacic**
Lisa Clegg/Dingle	**Jane Cox**
Albert Dingle	**Bobby Knutt**
Marlon Dingle	**Mark Charnock**
Sophie Wright	**Jane Cameron**
Will Cairns	**Paul Fox**
Emma Cairns	**Rebecca Loudonsack**
Anthony Cairns	**Edward Peel**
Rebecca Cairns	**Sarah Neville**
Lord Alex Oakwell	**Rupam Maxwell**
Lady Tara Oakwell/Thornfield	**Anna Brecon**
Billy Hopwood	**David Crellin**
Dee Pollard	**Claudia Malkovich**
Patrick 'Paddy' Kirk	**Dominic Brunt**
Graham Clark	**Kevin Pallister**
Heather Hutchinson	**Siobhan Finneran**
Lyn Hutchinson	**Sally Walsh**
Laura Johnstone	**Louise Beattie**
Tricia Stokes/Fisher/Dingle	**Sheree Murphy**
Revd Ashley Thomas	**John Middleton**
DI Spalding	**Davyd Harries**
Stella Jones	**Stephanie Schonfield**
Bernice Blackstock/Thomas	**Samantha Giles**
Gavin Ferris	**Robert Beck**
Sean Reynolds	**Stephen McGann**
Emily Wylie/Dingle/Kirk	**Kate McGregor**
John Wylie	**Seamus O'Neill**
Frankie Smith	**Gina Aris**
	Madeleine Bowyer
Pete Collins	**Kirk Smith**
Alice Bates	**Rachel Tolboys**
Claudia Nash	**Susan Duerden**
Elsa Chappell	**Natasha Gray**
Richie Carter	**Glenn Lamont**
Angie Reynolds	**Freya Copeland**
Diane Blackstock/Sugden	**Elizabeth Estensen**
Adam Forrester	**Tim Vincent**

Character	Actor
Cain Dingle	**Jeff Hordley**
Ollie Reynolds	**Vicky Binns**
Jason Kirk	**James Carlton**
Edna Birch	**Shirley Stelfox**
Carlos Diaz	**Gary Turner**
Marc Reynolds	**Anthony Lewis**
Gloria Weaver/Pollard	**Janice McKenzie**
Rodney Blackstock	**Patrick Mower**
Joe Fisher	**Edward Baker-Duly**
Virginia West	**Bridget Fry**
Nicola Blackstock	**Nicola Wheeler**
Carol Wareing	**Helen Pearson**
Charity Dingle/Tate	**Emma Atkins**
Bev Mansfield	**Sarah Malin**
Andrew Fraser	**Mark Elstob**
Victoria Sugden	**Hannah Midgley**
Chloë Atkinson	**Amy Nuttall**
Len Reynolds	**Peter Martin**
Ed Wills	**James Midgley**
Bob Hope	**Antony Audenshaw**
Joseph Tate	**Oliver Young**
Cynthia Daggert	**Kay Purcell**
Danny Daggert	**Cleveland Campbell**
Latisha Daggert	**Danielle Henry**
Louise Appleton	**Emily Symons**
Katie Addyman/Sugden	**Sammy Winward**
Brian Addyman	**Martin Reeve**
Eve Birch	**Raine Davison**
Ray Mullan	**Seamus Gubbins**
Maggie Calder	**Dee Whitehead**
Craig Calder	**Jason Hain**
Lucy Calder	**Elspeth Brodie**
Peg Dingle	**Jeanne Hepple**
Jess Weston	**Ruth Abram**
Phil Weston	**Mark Jardine**
Jerry Mackinley	**Rob Dixon**
Sydney Woolfe	**Nathan Gladwell**
Rhona Goskirk	**Zoe Henry**
Laurel Potts	**Charlotte Bellamy**
Stephanie Stokes	**Lorraine Chase**
Debbie Jones/Dingle	**Charley Webb**
Ronnie Marsden	**Ray Ashcroft**
Frances Marsden	**Sandy Walsh**
Alistair Marsden	**Danny Tennant**
Paul Marsden	**Matthew Booth**
Elaine Marsden	**Samantha McCarthy**
Siobhan Marsden	**Abigail Fisher**
Dawn Hope/Woods	**Julia Mallam**
Wilf Butler	**Peter Armitage**
Stephen Butler	**William Snape**
Shadrach Dingle	**Andy Devine**
Jarvis Skelton	**Richard Moore**
Shelly Williams	**Carolyn Pickles**
Darren 'Daz' Eden/Hopwood	**Luke Tittensor**
Pearl Ladderbanks	**Meg Johnson**
Chastity 'Chas' Dingle	**Lucy Pargeter**
Ethan Blake	**Liam O'Brien**
Tom King	**Ken Farrington**
Carl King	**Tom Lister**
Sadie King	**Patsy Kensit**
Jimmy King	**Nick Miles**
Matthew King	**Matt Healy**
Max King	**Charlie Kemp**
Simon Meredith	**Dale Meeks**
Lesley Meredith	**Sherrie Hewson**
Paul Lambert	**Matthew Bose**
Val Lambert	**Charlie Hardwick**
Belle Dingle	**Eden Taylor-Draper**

Jean Tate	**Megan Pearson**
Libby Charles	**Ty Glaser**
Tamsin Charles	**Jenny Gleave**
Jasmine Thomas	**Jemma-Louise Coleman**
Tonicha Daggert	**Kerry Stacey**
Sandy Thomas	**Freddie Jones**
Dr Adam Forsythe	**Richard Shelton**
Jean Hope	**Susan Penhaligon**

Creator **Kevin Laffan**
Executive Producers **Peter Holmans, David Cunliffe, Michael Glynn, Keith Richardson**
Producers **David Goddard, Robert D. Cardona, Michael Glynn, Anne W. Gibbons, Richard Handford, Michael Russell, Stuart Doughty, Morag Bain, Nicholas Prosser, Mervyn Watson, Kieran Roberts, Steve Frost, Tim Key, Kathleen Beedles, Jonathan Phillips**

Long-running saga of Yorkshire farming folk.

Airing twice a week, *Emmerdale Farm* began life as one of the dramas commissioned by ITV to fill its afternoon schedules. It quickly attracted sizeable audiences and was moved to an early-evening slot in 1977, eventually becoming fully networked in 1988 and so developing into one of the UK's major soaps.

The focus of the series was, for many years, the Sugden family, inhabitants of Emmerdale Farm itself, set on the fringes of the fictitious rural village of Beckindale (the name of the village has since been changed to Emmerdale). The first-ever episode saw the funeral of Jacob Sugden, the family's wastrel father, leaving his wife Annie to take charge of farm affairs. Annie, a wholesome farmer's wife in the old tradition, was supported by her sons, Jack and Joe, daughter Peggy, and crusty old Sam Pearson, Annie's dad, who was known to all as Grandad. Also on hand was Peggy's husband, shepherd Matt Skilbeck. Down in the village, the local hostelry (purveyor of Ephraim Monk ales) was The Woolpack, jointly owned and managed by stroppy Amos Brearly (a part-time columnist for the *Hotten Courier*) and kindly, pipe-smoking Henry Wilks, whose daughter Marian was also seen. Storylines generally followed the farming calendar, with worries over crop yield, river pollution or lamb sickness merging with the usual stresses and strains of family life.

Unavoidable in such soap marathons, cast changes followed aplenty. Peggy was killed off, leaving Matt to marry Dolly Acaster. Jack disappeared to Rome and resumed his career as a writer, only to return (played by a different actor) several years later. And Joe spent some time in France. New characters came and went. Among the most durable have been poacher-turned-gamekeeper Seth Armstrong and Alan Turner, once-hated manager of NY Estates, who displayed more geniality as The Woolpack's landlord, on the retirement of Amos Brierly. The Emmerdale farmhouse resounded to the bickering of several new families as the Sugden boys brought home their latest wives and step-offspring. But, through it all, until her death, Annie remained the matriarchal figure, barking words of advice to her wayward children between cooking meals and doing the ironing. However, major changes were afoot.

In the mid-1980s the programme was taken by the neck and given a good shake. In came grittier plots and meaner characters. Now the lads not only baled the hay but rolled in it, too. Extra-marital liaisons became a speciality, much to the dismay of the programme's creator, Kevin Laffan. Finally, in recognition of the changes that had swept through the series, the name was shortened to the snappier *Emmerdale* in November 1989. Even since then, there have been new brooms at work and, in an effort to boost viewing figures, increasingly sensational storylines – from murders to a siege at the post office – have been introduced. The Christmas 1993 plot, involving a plane crashing on the village, provoked much controversy but enabled the producers to clear out the dead wood and bring in some fresh faces. This 'coming of age' of *Emmerdale* has been much lamented by those viewers who enjoyed the slow-paced, pastoral pleasures of the early years. A third weekly episode was introduced in January 1997 and the series settled into a Tuesday–Thursday schedule, before the series went five nights a week in 2000.

For many years, the screen Beckindale was actually the Yorkshire village of Esholt, near Bradford (although initially another village, Arncliffe, was used), and The Woolpack's exterior was really that of Esholt's Commercial Inn (and previously The Falcon at Arncliffe). However, in order to relieve the real-life village of tourist congestion, a lookalike film set was constructed in the 1990s.

Empire Road ★★

UK (BBC) Drama. BBC 2 1978–9

Everton Bennett	**Norman Beaton**
Walter Isaacs	**Joe Marcell**
Hortense Bennett	**Corinne Skinner-Carter**
Marcus Bennett	**Wayne Laryea**
Ranjanaa Kapoor	**Nalini Moonasar**
Miss May	**Rosa Roberts**
Desmond	**Trevor Butler**
Royston	**Vincent Taylor**
Mr Kapoor	**Melan Mitchell**
Sebastian Moses	**Rudolph Walker**

Writer **Michael Abbensetts**
Producer **Peter Ansorge**

Life in a racially mixed Midlands street.

Filmed in the Handsworth area of Birmingham, *Empire Road* focuses on the relationship between the West Indian and Asian inhabitants of a residential street. At the centre of the action are Guyanan grocer Everton Bennett, owner of four of the houses, and his stuttering brother-in-law, Walter Isaacs. Through the romance of Everton's son, Marcus, and their Asian neighbour, Ranjanaa, the series exposes inter-racial friction. It also reveals the different outlooks and mentalities of the various generations.

Empire Road broke new ground in being the first drama to be written, performed and directed entirely by black artists. Its writer was Guyanan Michael Abbensetts. The 1978 first season consisted of only five episodes, but ten more episodes followed a year later. In the second series, two white women are added to provide balance, and former LOVE THY NEIGHBOUR star Rudolph Walker is introduced as Sebastian Moses, a new and menacing landlord. The final episode revolves around Marcus and Ranjanaa's wedding and the hopes it brings for racial harmony in Empire Road.

Empty Nest ★★

US (Witt-Thomas-Harris/Touchstone) Situation Comedy. Channel 4 1989–92 (US: NBC 1988–95)

Dr Harry Weston	**Richard Mulligan**
Barbara Weston	**Kristy McNichol**
Carol Weston	**Dinah Manoff**
Nurse LaVerne Todd	**Park Overall**
Charley Dietz	**David Leisure**

Creator **Susan Harris**

Executive Producers **Paul Junger Witt, Tony Thomas, Susan Harris, Rod Parker, Hal Cooper, Gary Jacobs**

● ***A widower doctor shares his Miami home with two demanding daughters.***

Paediatrician Harry Weston does not have long to get used to the emptiness of his Florida home after the death of his wife, Libby. Thinking they are helping out the old man, two of Harry's daughters move right in, bringing their own problems. Carol is a neurotic, job-jumping divorcée, and Barbara is a plain-clothes police officer (a third daughter, Emily, is away at college). Also taking up valuable space is giant dog Dreyfuss. Charley Dietz is Harry's scrounging neighbour and LaVerne Todd is the drawling nurse from Arkansas at the Miami Community Medical Center, where Harry works. Occasional visitors are the cast of THE GOLDEN GIRLS (from which the series was a spin-off). Indeed, Estelle Getty, as Sophia Petrillo, became a regular cast member in the final two seasons, which were not shown by Channel 4.

Encryption

The scrambling of a TV signal, allowing it to be decoded only by those who have paid the relevant subscription and have the appropriate equipment or viewing card. It is the everyday working basis for most satellite and cable channels.

Endemol

Multi-national TV production company, founded in 1994 from a merger of Joop van den Ende Productions and John de Mol Produkties, two major Dutch TV production firms. Its head office remains in the Netherlands but now controls subsidiary companies in 22 countries. In the UK its acquired businesses and brands include Endemol UK (formerly Bazal), Brighter Pictures, Initial and Hawkshead. Among its major contemporary successes are BIG BROTHER, READY STEADY COOK, RESTORATION and *Fear Factor*. Since 2000, Endemol has been part of the Telefónica communications group.

Enemy at the Door ★★

UK (LWT) Drama. ITV 1978; 1980
DVD: Goldhil Home Media (Region 1 only)

Major Richter	**Alfred Burke**
Clare Martel	**Emily Richard**
Olive Martel	**Antonia Pemberton**
Dr Philip Martel	**Bernard Horsfall**
Oberleutnant Kluge	**John Malcolm**
Hauptmann Reinicke	**Simon Cadell**
Major Freidel	**Simon Lack**
Peter Porteous	**Richard Heffer**

Creator/Writer **Michael Chapman**
Producers **Michael Chapman, Jonathan Alwyn**
Executive Producer **Tony Wharmby**

● ***Life in the Channel Islands during the German occupation.***

The Channel Islands were the only part of the United Kingdom to be occupied by the Germans during World War II. This 13-part drama analyses the effect the occupation had on the day-to-day life of the local residents, looking particularly at the Guernsey-based Martel family and especially their 20-year-old daughter, Clare. The action begins in June 1940, with the islanders awaiting with trepidation the impending invasion, and continues through the darkest days of the war itself.

The Channel Islands invasion was revisited by ITV 1 in 2004 with ISLAND AT WAR.

Enfield, Harry
(1961–)

Sussex-born comedian coming to the fore on SATURDAY LIVE with his characterization of Stavros, the Greek kebab-shop owner. On the back of Stavros he created the brash plasterer Loadsamoney, and his antithesis, hard-up Geordie Buggerallmoney. Enfield then gained his own BBC series, *Harry Enfield's Television Programme*, in which a host of new characters were introduced (some in collaboration with Paul Whitehouse and Kathy Burke), most notably the sadistic Old Gits, Tim Nice-but-Dim, Wayne and Waynetta Slob, the constantly surprised Double-Take Brothers, mechanics Lee and Lance, and Miles Cholmondely-Warner, whose cracked and jumpy bits of old documentary inspired Enfield's commercials for the Mercury telephone company. There were also The Scousers (a send-up of Brookside), sensational DJs Mike Smash and Dave Nice from Radio Fab FM and the constantly interfering father-in-law ('Only me . . . You don't want to do that'). Once bored with his creations, Enfield has tended to drop them and introduce new characters. His later series, *Harry Enfield and Chums*, gave birth to, among others, the Lovely Wobbly Randy Old Ladies, the Self-Righteous Brothers, a war-contrite young German tourist, a pair of gay Dutch policemen, Harry the naughty toddler and Kevin the sulky teenager (who eventually gained his own special, *Kevin's Guide to being a Teenager*, in 1999, and was spun-off into a feature film, *Kevin & Perry Go Large*, in 2000). Enfield also provided voices for SPITTING IMAGE (Jimmy Greaves, Douglas Hurd, etc.) and starred as Little Jim Morley in GONE TO THE DOGS and as Dermot in the first series of MEN BEHAVING BADLY. In 1989 he presented the old thespian send-up *Norbert Smith – A Life* and in 1993 hosted the mostly serious *Harry Enfield's Guide to Opera*. In yet further contrast, in the 1980s Enfield was seen in the fashion show *Frocks on the Box*, played the title role in *Norman Ormal: a Very Political Turtle* and the Revd Tony Blair in *Sermon from St Albion's* in 1998, and in 2000 presented a documentary on teenagers, *Harry Enfield's Real Kevins*, before moving to Sky One for a new series entitled *Harry Enfield's Brand Spanking New Show*. Enfield has also fronted *Harry Enfield's Big Arts* and, in 2002, returned to BBC 1 with a new sitcom about an ageing rock star, CELEB (Gary Bloke). His guest appearances take in *The Young Indiana Jones Chronicles*, *Look Around You* and AGATHA CHRISTIE'S MARPLE.

ENG
(Electronic News Gathering)

For decades, news departments relied on filmed reports from correspondents, which were slow to process and required a large crew to produce. With the development of videotape technology, including smaller, lighter cameras and camcorders, and the use of microwave or satellite links back to the studio (collectively known as ENG), news coverage became more immediate and much more flexible.

English, Arthur
(1919–95)

Veteran British entertainer who arrived in television after years on the music hall boards, playing wide-boy characters. In the early 1970s he took the part of Slugger in the horsey series FOLLYFOOT, which led to roles in series like *Copper's End* and CROWN COURT. He played Ted Cropper in *How's Your Father*, Bodkin in THE GHOSTS OF MOTLEY HALL and caretaker Mr Harman in ARE YOU BEING SERVED?, and became Arthur, one of Alf Garnett's new sparring partners, in IN SICKNESS AND IN HEALTH. English was also seen in the drama *Funny Man*, and played Sid in Channel 4's 1987 retirement home sitcom *Never Say Die* and Fred Whattle in the seaside comedy *High and Dry*.

Englishman Abroad, An ★★★

UK (BBC) Drama. BBC 1 1983

Guy Burgess .... **Alan Bates**
Coral Browne .... **Coral Browne**

Writer **Alan Bennett**
Producer **Innes Lloyd**

● ***A British actress is approached by an exiled spy.***

This single drama, directed by John Schlesinger, recalls the meeting between actress Coral Browne and the traitor Guy Burgess, who had defected to the Soviet Union with Donald Maclean in 1951. Browne (playing herself) is in Moscow on tour with a production of *Hamlet* in 1958 when she is visited in her dressing room by Burgess, now rather dishevelled and down on his luck. They strike up a relationship and continue to correspond on her return home to Britain.

Englishman's Castle, An ★★

UK (BBC) Drama. BBC 2 1978

Peter Ingram .... **Kenneth More**
Sally/Jill .... **Isla Blair**
Frank Worth/Arthur .... **Anthony Stafford**
Bert Worth/Adrian .... **Rob Edwards**
Jimmy .... **Brian Peck**
Mrs Worth/Connie .... **Noël Dyson**
Mr Worth/John .... **Peter Hughes**
Henry Ingram .... **David Meyer**
Harmer .... **Anthony Bate**
Mrs Ingram .... **Kathleen Byron**
Mark Ingram .... **Nigel Havers**
Susan .... **Fiona Gray**
Inspector .... **Philip Bond**
Lonsdale .... **Frederick Treves**
German Officer/Heinz .... **Louis Sheldon**

Writer **Philip Mackie**
Producer **Innes Lloyd**

● ***A TV producer fights with his conscience in an England ruled by Germany.***

Peter Ingram is a successful TV producer and writer. His soap opera has earned him fame and fortune and allows him and his family to enjoy the good life. The twist in this particular tale is that, while the story is set in contemporary 1970s England, it is an England that in 1940 lost the war to Germany. The country is now a satellite of Germany and, although the overt aggression has subsided and an air of normality enshrouds the country, Nazi ideology still perniciously pervades society. Jews are conspicuous by their absence and infringement of the laws on racial purity is punishable by death. History has been rewritten and the media is rigidly controlled.

Ingram, while he has benefited under the new regime, nevertheless struggles with his conscience. Will it perhaps find an outlet in his TV drama, which is set during World War II? In this show within a show, the central family are the Worths, with Frank and Bert two brothers with opposing views on the hostilties. Bert is a conscientious objector, while Frank is proudly patriotic and keen to show his bravery. Sally is the girl torn between the two. Then there's the difficulty for the family of having a German soldier billeted at their home.

Paul Ciappessoni directs this three-part PLAY OF THE WEEK presentation, with each episode 50 minutes long.

Ennal's Point ★★

UK (BBC) Drama. BBC 2 1982

Jack Tustin .... **Philip Madoc**
Animal Morgan .... **Glyn Owen**
Stick Watts .... **Gerald James**
Harry Quentin .... **James Warrior**
Geoffrey Hannah .... **David Lyn**
Snowy White .... **John Cording**
George Peace .... **Philip Rowlands**
Len Dance .... **Huw Ceredig**
Ben Dance .... **Mici Plwm**
Ned Spelling .... **Cadfan Roberts**
Amy Tustin .... **Denise Buckley**
Nance Grail .... **Rachel Thomas**
Jenny Grail .... **Beth Morris**
Billy John Grail .... **Alun Lewis**
Luke Grail .... **Hugh Thomas**
Dr Stafford .... **Gareth Armstrong**
Mrs Ivy Morgan .... **Mal Henson**

Creator/Writer **Alun Richards**
Producer **John Hefin**

● ***Occupational and personal dramas with a lifeboat crew.***

Jack Tustin is the coxswain of the *Samuel Grail*, the Ennal's Point lifeboat. With quiet authority, he leads his crew out onto the wild ocean to rescue those in peril, keeping everyone calm and clear-headed and inspiring those about him to do their best. But this six-part drama is not simply a tale of courage beyond the call of duty. Drama on the sea is underscored by drama in the personal lives of the Ennal's Point crew: the fears of their wives and families who are left behind whenever there's a 'shout'; the strains this extraordinary voluntary service places on the crewmen themselves; their hopes and ambitions within the lifeboat service.

A BBC Wales production, *Ennal's Point* was filmed in and around Mumbles, using the real Mumbles lifeboat for action shots. The series was inspired by writer Alun Richards's own novel of the same title from 1977. Hazel O'Connor's 'Will You' was used as the theme music.

Enterprise
See *Star Trek: Enterprise*.

Epilogue

A tailpiece to the day's viewing (now seldom seen, thanks to 24-hour TV), in which usually some religious or moral reflection was delivered by a guest speaker.

Equalizer, The ✶✶

US (Universal) Detective Drama. ITV 1986–90 (US: CBS 1985–9)

Robert McCall	**Edward Woodward**
Control	**Robert Lansing**
Lt. Burnett	**Steven Williams**
Lt. Isadore Smalls	**Ron O'Neal**
Scott McCall	**William Zabka**
Mickey Kostmayer	**Keith Szarabajka**
Sgt Alice Shepherd	**Maureen Anderman**
Pete O'Phelan	**Chad Redding**
Harley Gage	**Richard Jordan**

Creators **Michael Sloan, Richard Lindheim**
Executive Producers **Michael Sloan, James McAdams**
Producer **Alan Barnette**

● ***A former secret agent hires himself out to those seeking justice.***

Robert McCall is retired from the world of US Government espionage, in which he was given the name 'The Equalizer'. Now, somewhat ashamed of his duplicitous past, he seeks to make amends with his son and ex-wife for the neglect he has shown them over the years, and also hires himself out, via newspaper classified ads, to clients in big trouble. The ads read: 'Got a problem? Odds against you? Call The Equalizer. Tel: 212 555 4200.' Weeding out the callers on his answering machine, he then sets out to adjust the balance of good and evil on their behalf, acting as a private eye, or simply as a bodyguard, but often bringing his gun into play. His fee is small, if he charges one.

Despite his tough, streetwise exterior, McCall is really compassionate, intelligent and articulate. Always immaculately turned-out, he lives in a stylish Manhattan apartment, loves music and drives a swish black Jaguar. In his work he is supported by Mickey Kostmayer (who does much of the running around) and from time to time he links up with Control, his former agency boss. His son, Scott, a music student, also appears, as does Pete O'Phelan, an old friend from his spying days, who runs the bistro where McCall relaxes. Stewart Copeland of The Police rock group composed the theme music.

ER ✶✶✶

US (Constant c/Amblin/Warner Brothers) Medical Drama. Channel 4 1995– (US: NBC 1994–)
DVD: Warner Home Video

Dr Mark Greene	**Anthony Edwards**
Dr Douglas Ross	**George Clooney**
Dr Susan Lewis	**Sherry Stringfield**
Dr Peter Benton	**Eriq La Salle**
Dr John Carter	**Noah Wyle**
Dr David Morgenstern	**William H. Macy**
Dr William 'Wild Willy' Swift	**Michael Ironside**
Head Nurse Carol Hathaway	**Julianna Margulies**
Jerry Markovic	**Abraham Benrubi**
Jennifer Greene	**Christine Harnos**
Dr John 'Tag' Taglieri	**Rick Rossovich**
Dr Angela Hicks	**C. C. H. Pounder**
Dr Deborah/Jing-Mei Chen	**Ming-Na Wen**
Jeanie Boulet	**Gloria Reuben**
Harper Tracy	**Christine Elise**
Dr Kerry Weaver	**Laura Innes**
Chloe Lewis	**Kathleen Wilhoite**
Ray Shepherd	**Ron Eldard**
Dr Carl Vucelich	**Ron Rifkin**
Dr Abby Keaton	**Glenne Headly**
Dr Donald Anspaugh	**John Aylward**
Carla Harris	**Lisa Nicole Carson**
Al Grabarsky	**Mark Genovese**
Nurse Lydia Wright	**Ellen Crawford**
Nurse Rhonda Sterling	**Jenny O'Hara**
Dennis Gant	**Omar Epps**
Dr Anna Del Amico	**Maria Bello**
Dr Elizabeth Corday	**Alex Kingston**
Lucy Knight	**Kellie Martin**
Dr Maggie Doyle	**Jorja Fox**
Dr Robert 'Rocket' Romano	**Paul McCrane**
Dr Luka Kovac	**Goran Visnjic**
Dr Gabriel Lawrence	**Alan Alda**
Nurse Haleh Adams	**Yvette Freeman**
Dr Cleo Finch	**Michael Michele**
Nurse Abby Lockhart	**Maura Tierney**
Dr Dave Malucci	**Erik Palladino**
Maggie Wyczenski	**Sally Field**
Nicole	**Julie Delpy**
Dr Michael Gallant	**Sharif Atkins**
Dr Gregory Pratt	**Mekhi Phifer**
Dr Jing-Mei Chen	**Ming-Na**
Dr Neela Rasgotra	**Parminder Nagra**
Nurse Samantha Taggart	**Linda Cardellini**
Dr Ray Barnett	**Shane West**
Dr Dubenko	**Leland Orser**
Dr Archie Morris	**Scott Grimes**

Creator **Michael Crichton**
Executive Producers **John Wells, Michael Crichton, Lydia Woodward**

● ***Breathless action in the casualty unit of a Chicago hospital.***

'ER' stands for Emergency Room, and this ground-breaking medical drama is set in that vital section of Chicago's Cook County General Hospital. What was so innovative, when *ER* arrived, was the sheer relentlessness of the action, with new characters arriving every minute and countless storylines woven into each episode, defying the received wisdom that American audiences would not be able to follow such complexity. (The series went on to top the annual ratings, with an audience reach of some 33 million.) Unlike earlier, heart-warming doctors-and-nurses series, *ER* is not afraid to show the staff failing in their efforts to preserve life, hand-held cameras racing around after them as they exhaustingly dash from patient to patient. Complex technical language is not forsaken, and there is no shortage of spurting blood and organ close-ups.

The series' heart-throb at the outset is womanizing paediatrician Doug Ross, sometimes a victim of his own attitude but at other times a genuine hero. His romantic past with Nurse Carol Hathaway is a running theme. Attracting equal attention is level-headed chief resident Dr Mark Greene (whose terminal illness dominates later episodes), with other key figures over the years including Greene's lawyer wife Jennifer and his potential lover, Dr Susan Lewis; junkie intern John Carter; fearsome black surgeon Peter Benton; English doctor Elizabeth Corday; an older version of M*A*S*H's Hawkeye Pierce in Dr

Gabriel Lawrence (Alan Alda returning to the operating theatre); chief resident Kerry Weaver, abrasive surgeon Robert Romano; Croatian Luka Kovac; and intensive care nurse Abby Lockhart.

The series was created by *Jurassic Park* writer Michael Crichton, himself a junior doctor in his youth. One episode was 'guest' directed by Quentin Tarantino; another episode was transmitted live – another brave departure from the US television norm. In the UK, since 2001 new episodes have aired first on E4 before being broadcast a few weeks later by Channel 4.

Eskimo Day/Cold Enough for Snow ***

UK (Greenpoint/BBC) Drama. BBC 1 1996/1997

Shani Whittle .... **Maureen Lipman**
Bevis Whittle .... **David Ross**
Neil Whittle .... **Benedict Sandford**
Hugh Lloyd .... **Tom Wilkinson**
Harriet Lloyd .... **Anna Carteret**
Pippa Lloyd .... **Laura Howard**
Simon Poole .... **James Fleet** *(Eskimo Day)*
James Poole .... **Alec Guinness** *(Eskimo Day)*
Malcolm Judd .... **Grant Warnock** *(Eskimo Day)*
Mrs Judd .... **Kathryn Pogson** *(Eskimo Day)*
Miss Samantha Bodley .... **Cheryl Fergison**
Gordon Callow .... **Nicholas Le Prevost** *(Cold Enough)*

Writer **Jack Rosenthal**
Executive Producer **Tessa Ross**
Producer **Ann Scott**

Overprotective parents flounder as their children start to flee the nest.

Jack Rosenthal's single drama about the 'letting go' of children as they make their way in the world revolves around three would-be students who arrive in Cambridge for interviews. Regrettably, their parents are also in tow, exhibiting a mix of pride, anxiety and concern that is overbearing to the point of comedy. A day of embarrassment and revelation is in store as the parents kill time during the interviews. The Whittles are from Blackburn, son Neil chaperoned by his parents, the superstitious Shani and the overwhelmed Bevis. The wealthy Lloyds are from Cheltenham, daughter Pippa and mother Harriet driven insane by father Hugh's pompous bullying. Malcolm Judd is a bit forgetful, which means he, too, has a parent watching over him, as his mother secretly follows him to Cambridge. In a parallel subplot, former academic James Poole – the father of Simon Poole, the hapless man conducting some of the student interviews – is a candidate himself (albeit an unwilling one) on the same day, for a place in a retirement home, so presenting another take on the parent–child relationship. *Eskimo Day*'s strange title was derived from part of Shani Whittle's dialogue in which she reflected on how Eskimos, when they are old and of no further use to their offspring, simply shuffle off into the snow. On New Year's Eve 1997, the BBC broadcast a sequel. Again penned by Jack Rosenthal, *Cold Enough for Snow* revisits the Whittles and the Lloyds as A-level results are posted and the kids are about to finally leave home. Piers Haggard directed both films (*Screen One* presentations).

Esmonde, John

(1937–)

London-born comedy writer, usually in collaboration with Bob Larbey. Their joint successes have included sketches for Dick Emery then their own sitcoms, *Room at the Bottom*, PLEASE SIR!, *The Fenn Street Gang*, *Bowler*, THE GOOD LIFE, GET SOME IN!, THE OTHER ONE, *Feet First*, *Just Liz*, DON'T ROCK THE BOAT, *Now and Then*, EVER DECREASING CIRCLES, BRUSH STROKES, DOUBLE FIRST, HOPE IT RAINS, MULBERRY and DOWN TO EARTH. Since Esmonde's retirement, Larbey has continued writing solo.

Espionage *

UK (Herbert Brodkin/ATV/Plautus) Spy Drama Anthology. ITV 1963–4

Executive Producer **Herbert Hirschman**
Producer **George Justin**

Collection of spy dramas based on true stories.

This series, filmed throughout Europe, treats the subject of espionage much more sombrely than its spoofy successors like THE MAN FROM U.N.C.L.E., especially as it gleans its facts from real events (some newsreel footage is also used in production). The gloom is lightened somewhat by the appearances of talented guest-stars like Patrick Troughton, Bernard Bresslaw, Peter Vaughan, Anthony Quayle, Jim Backus and Bernard Lee ('M' from the James Bond films).

Eurosport

Trans-continental sports channel owned and operated by the French network TF 1. It broadcasts, unscrambled and free of charge in 18 languages, from the Astra satellites, offering a variety of sports from soccer to basketball. Its digital descendant in the UK is British Eurosport.

Eurotrash *

UK (Rapido) Magazine. Channel 4 1993–
DVD: Warner Vision International

Presenters **Antoine de Caunes, John-Paul Gaultier, Lolo Ferrari**

Producers **Peter Stuart, John Godfrey, Ian Dunkley**

Irreverent look at eccentric activity across the English Channel.

The title says it all: this late-night selection of lewd and offbeat continental goings-on is not to everyone's taste. French host Antoine de Caunes (initially alongside fashion designer John-Paul Gaultier) smirks his way through a series of smutty reports, overlaid with a cheeky commentary, that investigates the most bizarre pastimes enjoyed by our European neighbours. The first programme featured a Belgian rat restaurant and an amateur pornographer, which nicely set the tone for the weeks to come. Later features involved a nude cleaning service, an Italian ugly club and rabbit showjumping. A big, brash, cartoon-like set underlines the ridiculousness of the whole affair, complemented by the equally cartoon-like, mammoth figure of later co-presenter Lolo Ferrari (who tragically died in 2000). Other regulars have included toy giraffes Pee Pee & Po Po, Mr Penguin, the Romeo Cleaners, Eddy Wally, and Eva and Adele. Katie Boyle joined de Caunes in 1998 for a one-off review of Eurovision's most memorable moments entitled *A Song for Eurotrash*.

Eurovision

The international network of cable and satellite links established by the European Broadcasting Union in 1954 to facilitate the transfer of programmes, news items and sports events between countries and to allow simultaneous broadcasts across the Continent.

Eurovision Song Contest ✶✶

Europe (including BBC) Entertainment. BBC 1 1956–

● ***Annual Europe-wide song competition.***

Much ridiculed but nevertheless a big crowd-puller (if only for the voting at the end), the *Eurovision Song Contest* has been a fixture of the television calendar for nearly 50 years. Originally devised as a showcase for the new Eurovision network, which linked broadcasters across the Continent, its popularity has now increased to the point where over 40 nations wish to compete, and countries such as Israel, Turkey and members of the former Eastern Bloc have joined the fray. To accommodate all comers, a semi-final, qualifying stage has been introduced.

The format involves each country presenting an original song in turn and then voting (via the Eurovision link) on each other's contributions to find the winner, allocating marks from 12 points down to one. The winning country stages the next year's *Contest*. Scores are conveyed multilingually by the show's compere, with individual, voice-only commentaries provided for each country (the drily sarcastic Terry Wogan has become associated with this role for the UK, although the likes of David Jacobs, Rolf Harris, David Gell, Dave Lee Travis, Pete Murray, Michael Aspel and John Dunn have also performed this task). Technical hiccups, unavoidable in a live, pan-European link-up of this magnitude, have become part of the attraction.

The United Kingdom did not participate in the inaugural *Contest* in 1956, but soon initiated its own monthly competition, known as the *Festival of Popular Songs*. The 1956 *Festival* winner, 'All', sung by Patricia Bredin, went on to represent the UK (and finish seventh) in the 1957 *Contest*. In recent years, the British entry has been selected through an annual *Song for Europe* showdown.

Ireland has become the king of the contest, with four wins in the 1990s and seven in all; the UK has won the competition on five occasions, and the *Contest*'s whipping boys traditionally have been the Norwegians, thanks to their glorious nil scores (brilliantly matched by the UK's entry, 'Cry Baby', by Jemini, in 2003). *Eurovision* has been roundly condemned for not moving with the times, for its overtly political voting biases that now make the contest a travesty, and for rewarding countries who regurgitate the established 'Boom-bang-a-puppet-in-a-box' catchy-song formula. Only on rare occasions has the real music world peeped through – Abba's 1974 victory with 'Waterloo', for instance, and Love City Groove's rap contribution for the UK in 1995.

EUROVISION SONG CONTEST WINNERS

Year	*Winning Country*	*Winning song*	*Winning Singer*	*UK Song*	*UK Singer*
1956	Switzerland	*Refrain*	Lys Assia	–	–
1957	Netherlands	*Net Als Toen*	Corry Brokken	*All* (7th)	Patricia Bredin
1958	France	*Dors, mon amour*	André Claveau	–	–
1959	Netherlands	*Een Beetje*	Teddy Scholten	*Sing Little Birdie* (2nd)	Teddy Johnson and Pearl Carr
1960	France	*Tom Pillibi*	Jacqueline Boyer	*Looking High High High* (2nd)	Bryan Johnson
1961	Luxembourg	*Nous, les amoureux*	Jean-Claude Pascal	*Are You Sure?* (2nd)	The Allisons
1962	France	*Un premier amour*	Isabelle Aubret	*Ring a Ding Girl* (4th)	Ronnie Carroll
1963	Denmark	*Dansevise*	Grethe and Jørgen Ingmann	*Say Wonderful Things* (4th)	Ronnie Carroll
1964	Italy	*Non ho l'età per amarti*	Gigliola Cinquetti	*I Love the Little Things* (2nd)	Matt Monro
1965	Luxembourg	*Poupée de cire, poupée de son*	France Gall	*I Belong* (2nd)	Kathy Kirby
1966	Austria	*Merci chérie*	Udo Jurgens	*A Man without Love* (9th)	Kenneth McKellar
1967	UK	*Puppet on a String*	Sandie Shaw	*Puppet on a String* (1st)	Sandie Shaw
1968	Spain	*La, la, la*	Massiel	*Congratulations* (2nd)	Cliff Richard
1969	4 countries tied:				
	Spain	*Viva cantando*	Salome	*Boom Bang-A-Bang* (joint 1st)	Lulu
	UK	*Boom Bang-A-Bang*	Lulu		
	Holland	*De Troubadour*	Lennie Kuhr		
	France	*Un jour, un enfant*	Frida Boccara		
1970	Ireland	*All Kinds of Everything*	Dana	*Knock Knock Who's There* (2nd)	Mary Hopkin
1971	Monaco	*Un banc, un arbre, une rue*	Severine	*Jack in the Box* (4th)	Clodagh Rodgers
1972	Luxembourg	*Après toi (Come What May)*	Vicky Leandros	*Beg, Steal or Borrow* (2nd)	New Seekers

1973	Luxembourg	*Tu te reconnaîtras (Wonderful Dream)*	Anne-Marie David	*Power to All Our Friends* (3rd)	Cliff Richard
1974	Sweden	*Waterloo*	Abba	*Long Live Love* (joint 4th)	Olivia Newton-John
1975	Netherlands	*Ding-Dinge-Dong (Ding-a-Dong)*	Teach-In	*Let Me be the One* (2nd)	The Shadows
1976	UK	*Save Your Kisses for Me*	Brotherhood of Man	*Save Your Kisses for Me* (1st)	Brotherhood of Man
1977	France	*L'Oiseau et l'enfant*	Marie Myriam	*Rock Bottom* (2nd)	Lynsey De Paul and Mike Moran
1978	Israel	*A Ba Ni Bi*	Izhar Cohen and Alphabeta	*Bad Old Days* (11th)	Co-Co
1979	Israel	*Hallelujah*	Milk and Honey	*Mary Ann* (7th)	Black Lace
1980	Ireland	*What's Another Year?*	Johnny Logan	*Love Enough for Two* (3rd)	Prima Donna
1981	UK	*Making Your Mind Up*	Bucks Fizz	*Making Your Mind Up* (1st)	Bucks Fizz
1982	West Germany	*Ein bisschen Frieden (A Little Peace)*	Nicole	*One Step Further* (7th)	Bardo
1983	Luxembourg	*Si la vie est cadeau*	Corinne Hermès	*I'm Never Giving Up* (6th)	Sweet Dreams
1984	Sweden	*Diggy Loo-Diggy Ley*	The Herreys	*Love Games* (7th)	Belle and the Devotions
1985	Norway	*La Det Swinge (Let It Swing)*	The Bobbysocks	*Love is . . .* (4th)	Vikki
1986	Belgium	*J'aime la vie*	Sandra Kim	*Runner in the Night* (7th)	Ryder
1987	Ireland	*Hold Me Now*	Johnny Logan	*Only the Light* (13th)	Rikki
1988	Switzerland	*Ne partez pas sans moi*	Céline Dion	*Go* (2nd)	Scott Fitzgerald
1989	Yugoslavia	*Rock Me*	Riva	*Why Do I Always Get It Wrong?* (2nd)	Live Report
1990	Italy	*Insieme: 1992 (Altogether: 1992)*	Toto Cotugno	*Give a Little Love Back to the World* (6th)	Emma
1991	Sweden	*Fangad av en Stormvind (Captured by A Love Storm)*	Carola	*A Message to Your Heart* (10th)	Samantha Janus
1992	Ireland	*Why Me?*	Linda Martin	*One Step Out of Time* (2nd)	Michael Ball
1993	Ireland	*In Your Eyes*	Niamh Kavanagh	*Better the Devil You Know* (2nd)	Sonia
1994	Ireland	*Rock 'n' Roll Kids*	Paul Harrington and Charlie McGettigan	*We Will be Free (Lonely Symphony)* (10th)	Frances Ruffelle
1995	Norway	*Nocturne*	Secret Garden	*Love City Groove* (joint 10th)	Love City Groove
1996	Ireland	*The Voice*	Eimear Quinn	*Ooh Aah . . . Just a Little Bit* (8th)	Gina G
1997	UK	*Love Shine a Light*	Katrina and the Waves	*Love Shine a Light* (1st)	Katrina and the Waves
1998	Israel	*Diva*	Dana International	*Where are You?* (2nd)	Imaani
1999	Sweden	*Take Me to Your Heaven*	Charlotte Nilsson	*Say It Again* (joint 12th)	Precious
2000	Denmark	*Fly on the Wings of Love*	Olsen Brothers	*Don't Play That Song Again* (16th)	Nicki French
2001	Estonia	*Everybody*	Tanel Padar and Dave Benton	*No Dream Impossible* (15th)	Lindsey Dracass
2002	Latvia	*I Wanna*	Marie N	*Come Back* (joint 3rd)	Jessica Garlick
2003	Turkey	*Every Way That I Can*	Sertab Erener	*Cry Baby* (26th-last)	Jemini
2004	Ukraine	*Wild Dances*	Ruslana Lyzhichko	*Hold on to Our Love* (16th)	James Fox
2005	Greece	*My Number One*	Helena Paparizou	*Touch My Fire* (22nd)	Javine
2006	Finland	*Hard Rock Hallelujah*	Lordi	*Teenage Life* (19th)	Daz Sampson

Eustace Bros, The

See *Paradise Heights*.

Evans, Barry

(1943–97)

Fresh-faced British actor whose major roles were in situation comedy. He starred in DOCTOR IN THE HOUSE and *Doctor at Large* as naïve young Michael Upton, although he didn't stay with the series' sequels, relinquishing the lead to Robin Nedwell. He also played Jeremy Brown, the hapless evening class teacher in the controversial MIND YOUR LANGUAGE, and was seen in the Dick Emery comedy-thriller *Legacy of Murder*, among other programmes.

Evans, Chris

(1966–)

Bespectacled, ginger, controversial DJ, media entrepreneur and presenter of light entertainment shows such as DON'T FORGET YOUR TOOTHBRUSH, TFI FRIDAY and OFI SUNDAY, plus the golf travelogue *Tee Time*. Evans began in radio with Piccadilly in Manchester, before moving to GLR in London and then Radio 1. His television work commenced with the satellite channel The Power Station, before he switched to Channel 4's THE BIG BREAKFAST, where he quickly established himself as one of TV's most adaptable live-programme presenters. Evans has also provided the voice of guest rock star Lenny Lazenby in BOB THE BUILDER. In 2002 he produced Channel 5's early-evening entertainment show *Live with . . . Chris Moyles* and was later executive producer of the game show *Boys and Girls, The Terry and Gaby Show* and *Johnny Vegas: 18 Stone of Idiot*. In 2001 he married singer/actress Billie Piper, but they have since separated.

Evans, Linda

(Linda Evanstad; 1942–)

Blonde American actress who endured a 12-year wait between starring roles. Her TV career began with bit parts in popular US series like *Bachelor Father* and MY FAVORITE MARTIAN, but her major break arrived with THE BIG VALLEY, in which she was cast as Audra Barkley. *The Big Valley* ended in 1969, and the 1970s proved more difficult for Evans. She appeared for a while in a spy series called *Hunter* and made a few TV movies, but it wasn't until DYNASTY arrived in 1981 that she regained a high profile, starring as Krystle Jennings/Carrington. Ironically, she had been earmarked for an undefined role which turned out to be that of Pam in DALLAS, but the concept took too long to reach the studio and Evans was released from her contract. Later, she was seen in NORTH AND SOUTH BOOK II (Rose Sinclair). Her first husband was film director John Derek.

Eve, Trevor

(1951–)

Birmingham-born actor, largely seen in the theatre but coming to television prominence in the role of the radio detective SHOESTRING. Eve's subsequent TV work (often seeing him cast as unpleasant, untrustworthy characters) has included *Jamaica Inn*, LACE, *The Corsican Brothers, Shadow Chasers* (Professor Jonathan MacKensie), the steamy drama A SENSE OF GUILT (irresponsible writer Felix Cramer), *Parnell and the Englishwoman* (Charles Stewart Parnell), *A Doll's House, Screen One's* MURDER IN MIND (policeman Malcolm Iverson), *Screen Two's Black Easter* (detective Alex Fischer), THE POLITICIAN'S WIFE (MP Duncan Matlock), *Heat of the Sun* (Supt. Albert Tynan), *An Evil Streak* (scheming uncle Alex Kyle), DAVID COPPERFIELD (Mr Murdstone), WAKING THE DEAD (DCI Peter Boyd) and LAWLESS (John Paxton). He is married to actress Sharon Mughan, with whom he runs a production company called Projector.

Evening Shade ★★

US (Bloodworth-Thomason/Mozark/MTM) Situation Comedy. Channel 4 1992–4 (US: CBS 1990–4)

Wood Newton	**Burt Reynolds**
Ava Newton	**Marilu Henner**
Taylor Newton	**Jay R. Ferguson**
Molly Newton	**Melissa Martin**
	Candace Hutson
Will Newton	**Jacob Parker**
Evan Evans	**Hal Holbrook**
Frieda Evans	**Elizabeth Ashley**
Ponder Blue	**Ossie Davis**
Dr Harlan Elldridge	**Charles Durning**
Merleen Elldridge	**Ann Wedgeworth**
Herman Stiles	**Michael Jeter**
Fontana Beausoleil/Evans	**Linda Gehringer**
Nub Oliver	**Charlie Dell**
Emily Newton	**Alexa Vega**

Creator **Linda Bloodworth-Thomason**

● ***A former football star goes back to his country roots.***

In this easy-going, thoughtful sitcom, Wood Newton is a retired professional footballer returning to his home town of Evening Shade, Arkansas, to coach the hopeless high school team (the Mules). He brings back to this rural hinterland his wife, Ava (keen to stand for a major attorney's job), and kids Taylor, Molly and Will. A fourth child, Emily, arrives later. Helping Wood coach the team is naïve maths teacher Herman Stiles, while other wacky townsfolk include Ava's lusty dad, *Evening Shade Argus* proprietor Evan Evans (who marries stripper Fontana Beausoleil). Evan's forthright sister, Frieda, doctor Harlan Elldridge and his wife, Merleen, and confused newspaper delivery man Nub Oliver also feature prominently. Events are narrated by Ponder Blue, the owner of the local rib shack. Wood is eventually elected mayor of the town. Star Burt Reynolds also directed many episodes.

Ever Decreasing Circles ★★★

UK (BBC) Situation Comedy. BBC 1 1984; 1986–7; 1989
DVD: Network

Martin Bryce	**Richard Briers**
Ann Bryce	**Penelope Wilton**
Paul Ryman	**Peter Egan**
Howard Hughes	**Stanley Lebor**
Hilda Hughes	**Geraldine Newman**

Creators/Writers **John Esmonde, Bob Larbey**
Producers **Sydney Lotterby, Harold Snoad**

● ***A pedantic neighbourhood do-gooder is upstaged by the smoothie next door.***

Martin Bryce, employee of Mole Valley Valves, former REME regiment member, and driver of a light blue Dormobile, likes things done properly. And because no one else can be trusted, he likes to do them himself. By immersing himself in the well-being of his local suburban community, endlessly chairing meetings, organizing functions, tackling bureaucracy and generally leading from the front, Martin would severely test the patience of Job, let alone his long-suffering wife, Ann. For Martin, bedtime means only one thing – drawing up rotas. Next door to the Bryces (who live at 'Brooksmead', in The Close) moves Paul Ryman, the suave proprietor of a beauty salon, for whom things seem to fall very nicely. Without the slightest effort, he always manages, unintentionally, to steal the limelight and rob Martin of all the credit. From the way he flirts with Ann, it is clear that he could also steal Martin's wife, but Paul is too nice for that, and Ann too loyal. Friends to all are their childlike neighbours, Howard and Hilda Hughes, who usually dress in matching sweaters.

Everett, Kenny

(Maurice Cole; 1944–95)

Zany, controversial DJ turned TV comedian. After working for the pirate radio station Radio London and for Radio Luxembourg, Liverpudlian Kenny Everett became one of Radio 1's first presenters and quickly moved into television. In 1968 he was one of the presenters of NICE TIME (with Germaine Greer and Jonathan Routh), was given his own series, *The Kenny Everett Explosion*, in 1970 and subsequently became a familiar face on panel games, also announcing the prizes on CELEBRITY SQUARES. He appeared in the satire show UP SUNDAY and then, in 1978, along came the comedy series *The Kenny Everett Video Show*, which he hosted in front of a bank of TV monitors. Sketches involved his own characterizations like Cupid Stunt (the buxom movie star who did everything 'in the best possible taste'), Sid Snot (the greaser), hairdresser Marcel Wave and the space animation *Captain Kremmen*. Arlene Phillips's Hot Gossip writhed around between sketches, and Everett was also supported by Miss Whiplash, Cleo Rocos. In 1982, after numerous guest appearances on BLANKETY BLANK, Everett returned to the BBC, where his show was renamed *The Kenny Everett Television Show* but his larger-than-life characters remained to the fore (including some new faces like punk Gizzard Puke). Among his other series were *Making Whoopee*, *Ev* and the game shows *Gibberish* and *Brainstorm*.

Every Second Counts ★★

UK (BBC) Quiz. BBC 1 1986–93

Presenter **Paul Daniels**

Producers **David Taylor, Stanley Appel**

● ***Light-hearted quiz for married couples.***

Hosted by Paul Daniels, *Every Second Counts* invited three married couples to answer questions which earned them vital seconds on a clock. The highest-scoring couple then progressed to the final, in which they used the seconds they had accrued to answer yet more questions and win progressively better prizes. Each set of questions related to a subject and, in the 'true or false' fashion, contestants had to state whether Daniels was reading a correct answer. Red herrings and contrived gags abounded. For the final stage, the couple needed to extinguish a series of triangular lamps with quick and accurate responses to tricky little posers.

Every Silver Lining ★

UK (BBC) Situation Comedy. BBC 1 1993

Nathaniel 'Nat' Silver .... **Andrew Sachs**
Shirley Silver .... **Frances de la Tour**
Lorraine Silver .... **Sarah Malin**
Leonard .... **David Yip**
Spencer .... **Roger Hyams**
Willie .... **Oscar Quitak**
Dean .... **Danny Swanson**

Writer **Simon Block**
Producer **Richard Boden**

● ***A Jewish couple disagree about running their business and their private lives.***

Nat and Shirley Silver run the Silver Diner, a greasy spoon café in London's East End. While Nat spends much of his time playing chess with Leonard, his gambler friend who runs a Chinese take-away, or caring for the tropical fish he names after showbiz stars like Frank Sinatra and Bing Crosby, bossy wife Shirley longs for holidays in Israel. She also schemes to marry off her student daughter, Lorraine, and has far-reaching plans for the business, but these somehow never quite come off. Helping the Silvers – and ensuring their dreams are never realized – are 70-year-old 'head waiter' Willie and his junior, Dean. Spencer is Lorraine's nosy boyfriend. Just six episodes were made.

Executive Producer

The chief overseer of a programme or a series of programmes, usually responsible for the control of budgets. Sometimes the executive producer is the head of the department in a television company. In other cases, it is the programme creator or the star performer, who has vested interests in the direction the series takes.

Executive Stress ★★

UK (Thomas) Situation Comedy. ITV 1986–8

Caroline Fairchild .... **Penelope Keith**
Donald Fairchild .... **Geoffrey Palmer**
Peter Bowles
Anthea Duxbury .... **Elizabeth Counsell**
Edgar Frankland III .... **Harry Ditson**
Andrew Morgan .... **Ben Aris**
Peter Stuart .... **Timothy Carlton**
David Neville
Sylvia .... **Wanda Ventham**
Gordon .... **Donald Pickering**
Peter Davenport .... **Geoffrey Whitehead**
Mrs Bently .... **Jo Warne**

Creator/Writer **George Layton**
Producer **John Howard Davies**

● ***Using a false name, a wife takes a job in her husband's publishing company.***

When the last of Caroline Fairchild's five children leaves home for university, she decides to resurrect her publishing career after 20 years. Once credited with discovering the hugely successful *Dartington Trilogy*, she confidently applies for a job at Oasis Publishing using her maiden name, Caroline Fielding. Oasis, however, takes over Ginsberg Publishing, the struggling company for which her husband, Donald, works as sales and marketing manager. Caroline gets the job the same fateful day and starts work as editorial director, much to hubby's surprise. As Donald has been retained and American boss Edgar Frankland has a 'no couples' rule, they resolve to keep their relationship a secret (commuting separately into London from their Buckinghamshire home). However, there is inevitably much suspicion from colleagues like Peter Stuart, the personnel director, and Anthea Duxbury, Caroline's former secretary, now export sales director. The truth eventually comes out in the second series when the Fairchilds are made joint managing directors of Oasis and attention switches to their rivalry at work. Tim Rice and Andrew Lloyd Webber composed the theme song, 'Remember How We Fell in Love', which was sung by Julie Covington.

Expert, The ★★

UK (BBC) Detective Drama. BBC 2 1968–9; 1971; 1976

Prof. John Hardy .... **Marius Goring**
Dr Jo Hardy .... **Ann Morrish**
DCI Fleming .... **Victor Winding**
Jane Carter .... **Sally Nesbitt**
DS Ashe .... **Michael Farnsworth**
Sandra Hughes .... **Valerie Murray**
Susan Bartlett .... **Virginia Stride**

Creators **Gerard Glaister, N. J. Crisp**
Producers **Gerard Glaister, Andrew Osborn**

● ***A pathologist digs deep to help police with their investigations.***

John Hardy is a Warwickshire pathologist who, with the help of his somewhat younger wife, Jo (a GP), and his receptionist, Jane Carter, turns up vital evidence needed by police to secure tricky convictions. Detective Chief Inspector Fleming is his police ally, and the two men enjoy a strong mutual respect and a close friendship.

Meticulously researched by actor Marius Goring (formerly TV's Sir Percy Blakeney in THE ADVENTURES OF THE SCARLET PIMPERNEL), the character was the invention of producer Gerard Glaister, whose own uncle had been Professor of Forensic Science at Glasgow University. *The Expert* ran from 1968 to 1971, before returning for one more run in 1976. With its modest, thoughtful tone, it contrasted sharply with TV's other major pathologist series from that era, QUINCY.

Extras ★★★

UK (BBC/HBO) Situation Comedy. BBC 2 2005–
DVD: Universal

Andy Millman .... **Ricky Gervais**
Maggie Jacobs .... **Ashley Jensen**
Greg .... **Shaun Pye**
Barry .... **Shaun Williamson**
Agent .... **Stephen Merchant**

Creators/Writers **Ricky Gervais, Stephen Merchant**
Executive Producer **Jon Plowman**
Producer **Charlie Hanson**

● ***A bit-part actor battles to win himself a bigger role.***

Repeating the phenomenal success of THE OFFICE was never going to be easy for Ricky Gervais and Stephen Merchant. By most accounts, however, they made a pretty good fist of it with *Extras*. The scenario this time is the film and television business and, in particular, the frustrations of one Andy Millman, a professional extra. After five years of standing in the shadows, he'd love to break into the big time, but he's hampered by various problems, not least by an over-inflated view of his own talents but also by having a particularly inept agent. So instead of taking centre stage, Andy is forced to play the smallest supporting roles to some of the biggest names around, and in so doing he discovers their 'true' personalities. The various guest stars who appear as 'themselves' (in essence, grossly exaggerated caricatures) in series one are Ben Stiller, Ross Kemp, Vinnie Jones, Kate Winslet, Les Dennis, Samuel L. Jackson and Patrick Stewart. Andy's confidante is best friend Maggie Jacobs, one of the few extra colleagues he doesn't bitch about. Inevitably echoes of *The Office* abound, particularly in the absence of PC, and in the toe-curling moments of embarrassment and humiliation. Gervais and Merchant also direct.

F Troop ✶✶

US (Warner Brothers) Situation Comedy. ITV 1968–74
(US: ABC 1965–7)
DVD: Warner Home Video (Region 1 only)

Capt. Wilton Parmenter .... **Ken Berry**
Sgt Morgan O'Rourke .... **Forrest Tucker**
Cpl. Randolph Agarn .... **Larry Storch**
Wrangler Jane .... **Melody Patterson**
Chief Wild Eagle .... **Frank DeKova**
Crazy Cat .... **Don Diamond**
Bugler Hannibal Dobbs .... **James Hampton**
Trooper Duffy .... **Bob Steele**
Trooper Vanderbilt .... **Joe Brooks**
Trooper Hoffenmuller .... **John Mitchum**
Roaring Chicken .... **Edward Everett Horton**

Creator **Richard M. Bluel**
Producers **Richard M. Bluel, Hy Averback**

● ***The farcical exploits of a cavalry troop on the Indian front line.***

Fort Courage, a cavalry outpost somewhere in deepest Kansas, is commanded by Captain Wilton Parmenter. Well, that's what he thinks. Parmenter was a laundry orderly in the Union army at the end of the Civil War, but one day a simple sneeze changed his life. The loud snort apparently sounded just like 'Charge!' to his own side's cavalry, which sped into action just in time to thwart an attack by the Confederacy. Parmenter was commended for his initiative, promoted to captain and given the posting at Fort Courage. Unfortunately, he is not the real boss of the outfit. That honour is usurped by his sergeant, Morgan O'Rourke, a kind of Wild West Bilko figure who runs the show with his sidekick, Corporal Agarn, but always gives the credit to his nominal camp commander. O'Rourke has even agreed a secret pact with the supposedly hostile Hekawi Indians, headed by the canny Chief Wild Eagle. Between them, O'Rourke and Wild Eagle run an Indian souvenir racket and protect their business interests by staging fake attacks on the fort whenever top brass arrive for an inspection.

O'Rourke's work-shy soldiers are as incompetent as the fort's captain. The bugler, Dobbs, always plays a bum note, one private, Hoffenmuller, is a German who speaks no English, and Vanderbilt, the look-out, is officially blind. Little wonder the Indians can't be bothered to fight them. Also on the scene is Wrangler Jane, a sharp-shooting cowgirl who runs the post office and chases after the boyish Parmenter.

Fabian of Scotland Yard ✶

UK (Trinity/Charles Wick/Telefilm Enterprises) Police Drama. BBC 1954–6

DI Robert Fabian .... **Bruce Seton**

Producers **John Larkin, Anthony Beauchamp**

● ***The cases of a po-faced London detective.***

Screaming around the streets of the capital in a heavy, black Humber Hawk squad car, pipe-smoking Detective Inspector Robert Fabian was one of TV's first police heroes. Based on the life of a real Detective Inspector Fabian (a Flying Squad officer who, on retirement from the force, went on to be 'Guardian of the Questions' on ITV's big-money quiz show, *The 64,000 Question*), this was strait-laced, by-the-book, 1950s detective work, dramatizing cases from the files of Scotland Yard.

Fabian's success is largely down to his innovative detection methods, as he drags the police force into the 1950s with all its forensic advances. The real Inspector Fabian pops up at the end of each programme to deliver some personal homilies on the events taking place. The series, made on film and heavily laden with plummy accents, was also screened in the USA as *Patrol Car*, and included brief tourism guides for American viewers, explaining where and what were Hampton Court or Somerset House, for instance, if the plot required Fabian to visit them. Some episodes were re-edited into feature films for cinema release. These went out as *Fabian of the Yard* (1954) and *Handcuffs, London* (1955).

Face the Music ✶✶

UK (BBC) Quiz. BBC 2/BBC 1 1967–84

Presenter **Joseph Cooper**

Producer **Walter Todds**

● ***High-brow, but light-hearted music quiz.***

Hosted at the piano by the jovial Joseph Cooper, *Face the Music* was the BBC's long-running music quiz for celebrities, focusing mainly on the classical world but also drawing on other musical styles. Regular panel members who attempted to identify snippets of tunes included Joyce Grenfell, Richard Baker and Robin Ray.

Face to Face ✶✶

UK (BBC) Interview Programme. BBC 1959–62; BBC 2 1995–7

Presenters **John Freeman, Jeremy Isaacs**

Producers/Editors **Hugh Burnett, Michael Poole, David Herman, Julian Birkett**

● ***Incisive interviews with famous people, probing their personalities and lifestyles.***

Face to Face broke new ground in TV interviewing. Although celebrities had faced the camera before, the public had never seen them so exposed by what was essentially a cross-examination. The interrogator was Panorama presenter John Freeman. As he probed he never wavered from the courteous and polite, but his assault on the interviewee was relentless and seldom failed to open up the real person behind the famous front. Strangely, the victims seemed quite happy to bare their souls.

Each programme began with caricature sketches of the week's guest by Felix Topolski, which faded into the real image to the lilting strains of a Berlioz overture. The set was stark – simply two uncomfortable chairs a yard apart – and the whole atmosphere one of interrogation. Seldom was Freeman himself seen, and then usually only the back of his head. The focus was always on the interviewee as he or she was gradually dissected. Over 30 guests in all appeared, although only a couple of them were women. Guests included Martin Luther King, Adam Faith, Stirling Moss, Bertrand Russell, Dame Edith Sitwell, King Hussein of Jordan, Tony Hancock, John Osborne, Evelyn Waugh, Carl Gustav Jung, John Huston, Augustus John, Cecil Beaton, Lord Reith and Henry Moore, but by far the most controversial appearance was by Gilbert Harding. The WHAT'S MY LINE? panellist was notorious for being gruff, rude and intolerant, but Freeman exposed a gentler, more humane side. During the interview, Harding was even reduced to tears when questioned about his mother who, unknown to Freeman, had just died.

The highlights of the series were repeated in 1988 with introductions by Joan Bakewell and, in a special episode, Freeman himself was quizzed by Dr Anthony Clare. In the interim years he had been editor of the *New Statesman*, Ambassador to the USA and head of London Weekend Television. *Face to Face* resurfaced in the 1990s as an occasional segment of *The Late Show*, with Jeremy Isaacs as interrogator, and then as a series in its own right. Among Isaac's interviewees were Arthur Miller, Lauren Bacall, Ken Dodd, Anthony Hopkins, Norman Mailer, Germaine Greer, Stephen Sondheim, Harold Pinter, Kate Adie, Roddy Doyle, Diana Rigg, Bob Monkhouse and, shortly before his death, Paul Eddington.

Fainthearted Feminist, The ✶✶

UK (BBC) Situation Comedy. BBC 2 1984

Martha .... **Lynn Redgrave**
Josh .... **Jonathan Newth**
Mary .... **Sarah Neville**
Mo .... **Helen Cotterill**
Jane .... **Sara Sugarman**
Ben .... **Andrew Paley**
Irene .... **Polly Adams**
Mother .... **Joan Sanderson**
Bess .... **Linda Polen**
May .... **Julia Swift**

Writers **Jill Tweedie, Christopher Bond**
Executive Producer **Alan J. W. Bell**
Producer **Zanna Beswick**

● ***A wife and mother struggles to assert her feminist principles.***

How does a woman's libber manage when she has a husband and three kids to look after? That's the dilemma facing Martha, whose radical days seem long behind her as middle age approaches and domestic chores take over her life. Nevertheless, she tries to be true to her principles through her involvement with the Sebastopol Women's Centre, while struggling to keep up with the ironing, entertaining husband Josh's boss and caring for two teenagers and a new baby. Mary and Mo are Martha's more militant friends, whose reckless escapades draw Martha into further hot water. This short-lived series (five episodes) was inspired by the *Letters from a Faint-hearted Feminist* column in *The Guardian* newspaper that had started up, anonymously, some three years earlier. It eventually transpired that the column's author was Jill Tweedie, who worked with Christopher Bond to bring her idea to the small screen. Mandie Fletcher directs.

Fairbanks, Douglas, Jr

KBE (Hon.) (1909–2000)

American actor, the son of silent film star Douglas Fairbanks. After a career in films and distinguished service during World War II, he turned to television in the 1950s, hosting and sometimes acting in an anthology series of half-hour dramas entitled DOUGLAS FAIRBANKS PRESENTS, which was made in the UK (where he lived for a number of years) but seen around the world. The stories generally had the theme of people caught up in unusual circumstances. His later TV performances included a guest spot on THE LOVE BOAT. Fairbanks's first wife was Joan Crawford.

Fairly Secret Army ✶✶

UK (Video Arts) Situation Comedy. Channel 4 1984; 1986

Major Harry Kitchener
Wellington Truscott .... **Geoffrey Palmer**
Nancy .... **Diane Fletcher**
Beamish .... **Jeremy Child**
Sgt Major Throttle .... **Michael Robbins**
Doris Entwistle .... **Liz Fraser**
Stubby Collins .... **Ray Winstone**
Crazy Colin Carstairs .... **James Cosmo**
Jill .... **Diana Weston**
Peg Leg Pogson .... **Paul Chapman**
Ron Boat .... **Richard Ridings**

Writer **David Nobbs**
Producer **Peter Robinson**

● ***A retired military man sets up his own right-wing army to keep moral standards high.***

With the influence of left-wing sympathizers, anarchists and feminists increasing in Britain – or so he perceives – Major Harry Kitchener Wellington Truscott, a quite unemployable old army bigot, once of the Queen's Own West Mercian Lowlanders, decides to combat growing subversion by forming a private army of sympathizers. Rallying to his cause are a motley crew of half-wits, National Front supporters, ex-military colleagues and people with nothing better to do. To take on the loony left, Truscott assembles the raving right and, as he tries to whip them into shape, sounds not unlike a latter-day Alf Garnett.

Faith, Adam

(Terence Nelhams; 1940–2003)

Cockney teen singer of the later 1950s/early 1960s, much seen on pop shows of the day, including OH BOY! and *Boy Meets Girls*. He later branched out into acting, appearing in the anthology series SEVEN DEADLY SINS in 1966 and earning his own series, BUDGIE, in 1971. After a couple of years as Soho's perennial loser, Budgie Bird, Faith didn't return to the small screen, apart from the odd guest appearance, until LOVE HURTS arrived in 1991. As Frank Carver opposite Zoë Wanamaker's Tessa Piggott, he found himself with yet another hit on his hands. In 2000, Faith ventured into sitcom, playing Jack Squire in *The House That Jack Built*.

Faith in the Future

See *Second Thoughts*.

Faking It ★★★

UK (RDF Media) Channel 4 2000–

Narrator **Michael Kitchen**

Creator/Executive Producer **Stephen Lambert**

● ***Job-swap novices aim to fool professional experts.***

Can a poshly spoken Oxford student pass himself off as a nightclub bouncer in London? Would a Yorkshire girl prove convincing as a society deb? These are the two questions asked in the short first series of the fly-on-the-wall documentary series *Faking It*. Alex Geikie is the would-be streetwise doorman, Lisa Dickinson-Grey the provincial girl receiving the *My Fair Lady* treatment: together they lay the groundwork for future longer series that sees a host of unlikely characters taking up the challenge of becoming something they most certainly are not. Along the way, each brave volunteer is given training and the help of a mentor, someone who knows what is required to make the grade, but eventually it falls upon the imposter to do the business in the company of professionals. Along the way to each tense finale, there are tears, tantrums, embarrassment, ridicule, bullying, frustration and disappointments aplenty. Cellist Sian Evans takes it upon herself to become a night club DJ; country vicar Nigel Done tries his hand as a used-car salesman; Liverpudlian decorator Paul O'Hare becomes a conceptual artist; Newcastle burger vendor Ed Devlin finds things hot in the kitchen as a professional chef; Irish sheep shearer Gavin Freeborn competes as a leading hair stylist; gentle ballet dancer Kasper Cornish trains as a wrestler; club dancer Shelley Elvin dares to rub shoulders with the show jumping fraternity; naval officer Spence Bowdler grits his teeth and dresses up as a drag queen; Lynn Hurst, a fire service control operator, calls the shots as a TV director; George Lubega, a lawyer in the City, learns the swagger and spiel of a garage MC; Jo Weatherill, a tomboyish kick boxer, forces herself into sequins to be a competitive ballroom dancer; acrophobic insurance salesman Matt Davies fights back his fears as a film stuntman; web designer Stuart Matheson attempts a tougher kind of surfing in Cornwall; radiographer David Keith learns the ropes of fashion photography; Phil Deane, a tester of computer games, revs up as a racing driver; ferry hostess Lucy Craig faces the elements as a yachtswoman; punk singer Chris Sweeney aims to impress as a classical music conductor; Malcolm Woodcock, a pool-playing bicycle courier, hops aboard a polo pony; choirgirl Laura-Jane Foley tries it on as a raunchy rock singer; management consultant Rob Archer turns dog trainer, despite never having owned a mutt; newsagent Jatinder Sumal swaps selling the news to writing it as a showbiz journalist; quiet chess player Maximillion Devereaux gives it a go as a bawling soccer manager; physicist Kevin McMahon turns illusionist on a London cabaret stage; and Kate Harding, a shy girl whose idea of fun is dressing up for historical re-enactments, has to call the shots as a music video director for Liberty X. A special edition, first shown in 2005 and billed as *When Blue Peter Became Abba*, sees four former presenters of the children's programme – Peter Duncan, Janet Ellis, Romana D'Annunzio and Stuart Miles – groomed as an Abba tribute band for a performance at an Irish rock festival.

One-off, 'where are they now' programmes, entitled *Faking It Changed My Life*, have also been screened and an American version, *Faking It USA*, was shown by Channel 4 in 2003. Special episodes of *Faking It* were also made for Channel 4's teenage strand, T4, in 2004.

Falcon Crest ★★

US (Lorimar) Drama. ITV 1982–91 (US: CBS 1981–90)

Angela Channing/Stavros .... **Jane Wyman**
Chase Gioberti .... **Robert Foxworth**
Maggie Gioberti/Channing .... **Susan Sullivan**
Lance Cumson .... **Lorenzo Lamas**
Tony Cumson .... **John Saxon**
Cole Gioberti .... **William R. Moses**
Victoria Gioberti/Hogan/Stavros .... **Jamie Rose**
Dana Sparks
Julia Cumson .... **Abby Dalton**
Gus Nunouz .... **Nick Ramus**
Phillip Erikson .... **Mel Ferrer**
Emma Channing .... **Margaret Ladd**
Douglas Channing .... **Stephen Elliott**
Sheriff Turk Tobias .... **Robert Sampson**
Mario Nunouz .... **Mario Marcelino**
Chau-Li .... **Chau-Li Chi**
Melissa Agretti/Cumson/Gioberti .... **Ana Alicia**
Carlo Agretti .... **Carlos Romero**
Richard Channing .... **David Selby**
John Costello .... **Roger Perry**
Diana Hunter .... **Shannon Tweed**
Jacqueline Perrault .... **Lana Turner**
Nick Hogan .... **Roy Thinnes**
Darryl Clayton .... **Bradford Dillman**
Lori Stevens .... **Maggie Cooper**
Sheriff Robbins .... **Joe Lambie**
Linda Caproni/Gioberti .... **Mary Kate McGeehan**
Vince Caproni .... **Harry Basch**
Dr Michael Ranson .... **Cliff Robertson**
Pamela Lynch .... **Sarah Douglas**
Terry Hartford/Ranson .... **Laura Johnson**
Joseph Gioberti .... **Jason Goldberg**
Norton Crane .... **Jordan Charney**
Francesca Gioberti .... **Gina Lollobrigida**
Greg Reardon .... **Simon MacCorkindale**
Lorraine Prescott .... **Kate Vernon**
Joel McCarthy .... **Parker Stevenson**
Gustav Riebmann .... **J. Paul Freeman**
Father Bob .... **Bob Curtis**
Jordan Roberts .... **Morgan Fairchild**
Father Christopher .... **Ken Olin**
Cassandra Wilder .... **Anne Archer**
Robin Agretti .... **Barbara Howard**
Apollonia .... **Patricia 'Apollonia' Kotero**
Peter Stavros .... **Cesar Romero**
Eric Stavros .... **John Callahan**
Erin Jones .... **Jill Jacobson**
Kit Marlowe .... **Kim Novak**
Dan Fixx .... **Brett Cullen**
Meredith Braxton .... **Jane Badler**
Dina Wells .... **Robin Greer**
Guy Stafford .... **Jeff Kober**
Mrs Whitaker .... **Laurel Schaefer**
Carly Fixx .... **Mariska Hargitay**
Garth .... **Carl Held**
Frank Agretti .... **Rod Taylor**
Pilar Ortega/Cumson .... **Kristian Alfonso**
Nick Agretti .... **David Beecroft**
Ben Agretti .... **Brandon Douglas**
Tommy Ortega .... **Dan Ferro**
Cesar Ortega .... **Castulo Guerra**

Gabriel Ortega	**Danny Nucci**
R. D. Young	**Allan Royal**
Michael Channing	**Robert Gorman**
Michael Sharpe	**Gregory Harrison**
Julius Karnow	**Norman Parker**
Ed Meyers	**Philip Baker Hall**
Brian	**Thom Adcox**
Lauren Daniels	**Wendy Phillips**
Walker Daniels	**Robert Ginty**
Jace Sampson	**Stuart Pankin**
Genele Ericson	**Andrea Thompson**

Creator **Earl Hamner**
Executive Producers **Earl Hamner, Michael Filerman**

Family and business rivalries in Californian wine country.

Hot on the heels of Dallas and Dynasty came *Falcon Crest*, an American soap born of the same stock as its predecessors. The setting this time is California's Napa Valley ('Tuscany Valley' in the series), the industry providing the opulence is wine production and the central character is ruthless Angela Channing. Angela's rival is Chase Gioberti, who has moved from New York to take up his share of the Falcon Crest vineyard fortune. He is the son of her late brother, Jason, and the two spar, fight and tussle over power and prestige. The difference between them is that where Angela is hard and cruel, Chase is essentially good, caring for his employees and the people of the valley. Other principals include Chase's wife, Maggie, his son, Cole, and daughter, Victoria. There is also Angela's family, consisting of daughters Julia and Emma (the former mentally deranged, the latter a man-eater), Julia's son, Lance Cumson, and his wife, Melissa Agretti, daughter of another big wine family. As the series progresses, Angela's tyranny is challenged by a new rival, newspaper magnate Richard Channing, the son of her former husband, Douglas. Richard has inherited half of *The Globe* newspaper in San Francisco (Julia and Emma each have 25 per cent) and fights unscrupulously for yet more power, including control of the vineyards (which he eventually achieves).

The series becomes more and more violent as the years pass, stretching credulity as it does so. First a sinister business co-operative called 'The Cartel', led by Gustav Riebmann, is introduced. Then another treacherous institution, an underworld gang described as 'The Thirteen', makes its bow. Like *Dallas* and *Dynasty, Falcon Crest* is well endowed with shootings, framings, trials, stormy marriages, unknown heirs, disputed fathers, amnesiacs, schizophrenics, bombings, plane crashes, white slave rings and numerous skeletons which pop out of cupboards. It does, however, allow its cast a happy ending.

In the final episode, after years of wrangling, attempted murders and the like, the family are reunited and reconciled. Richard (who turns out to be Angela's son after all) marries newcomer Lauren Daniels and sells the vineyard back to Angela, whom he recognizes at last as its 'rightful owner'. Plans are made for Falcon Crest to be handed down after her death, hopefully without recrimination.

Falcon Crest was the brainchild of THE WALTONS creator Earl Hamner. Interestingly, it made a point of casting famous film stars who seldom appeared on television, and the likes of Rod Taylor, Gina Lollobrigida, Kim Novak and Lana Turner all made appearances.

Falk, Peter

(1927–)

New York-born actor who arrived on US television in the late 1950s, moving on to play gangster roles in series like THE UNTOUCHABLES and NAKED CITY. He picked up an Emmy for a performance on *The Dick Powell Show* and was given his first star billing in the legal drama series *The Trials of O'Brien*. However, in 1968, Falk won the part of a character that was to change his life. In the TV movie *Prescription: Murder*, he donned the grubby mac and picked up the stubby cigar of offbeat detective Lt. Columbo, after Bing Crosby had turned down the part. Columbo proved popular and returned in another movie in 1971, before steady production began and the series became part of the MYSTERY MOVIE anthology. With his grouchy voice, scruffy appearance and sad squint (Falk had lost an eye as a child), Columbo became one of TV's classic creations, resurfacing again in the 1980s. Falk has also been seen more recently in *The Lost World* (Theo Kerr).

Falklands Play, The ★★

UK (BBC) Drama. BBC 2 2002

Margaret Thatcher	**Patricia Hodge**
Lord Carrington	**James Fox**
William Whitelaw	**John Standing**
Francis Pym	**Jeremy Child**
Nicholas Ridley	**Michael Cochrane**
John Nott	**Clive Merrison**
Richard Luce	**Jonathan Coy**
Robert Armstrong	**Rupert Vansittart**
Gen. Alexander Haig	**Colin Stinton**
Sir Nicholas Henderson	**Jeremy Clyde**
President Ronald Reagan	**Bob Sherman**
Sir Anthony Parsons	**Robert Hardy**

Writer **Ian Curteis**
Producer **Jeremy Howe**

The Falklands War, as seen from the heart of the British government.

Although written to mark the fifth anniversary of the Falklands conflict, this single drama was not shown until 20 years after that war ended. Despite being commissioned by BBC Director-General Alasdair Milne in the mid-1980s, the play was never made as intended. A bitter exchange of views between writer Ian Curteis, BBC management and politicians of the time suggested various reasons for its cancellation, from an impending general election to alleged left-wing bias within the BBC. The play tells the story of the Argentinian invasion of the Falkland Islands and the British government's reaction and response. War footage was shunned in favour of heated ministerial debate, bringing in also the various shuttle diplomacy missions of President Reagan's envoy, General Haig. When finally produced (directed by Michael Samuels), it was shown first on the digital Channel BBC 4, although Radio 4 broadcast an audio version a few days before it reached television (same cast except with Hugh Fraser replacing James Fox as Lord Carrington).

Fall and Rise of Reginald Perrin, The/The Legacy of Reginald Perrin ★★★

UK (BBC) Situation Comedy. BBC 1 1976–9/BBC 1 1996
DVD: Second Sight

Reginald Perrin	**Leonard Rossiter** *(Fall)*
Elizabeth Perrin	**Pauline Yates**
CJ (Charles Jefferson)	**John Barron**
Joan Greengross	**Sue Nicholls**
David Harris-Jones	**Bruce Bould**
Tony Webster	**Trevor Adams** *(Fall)*
Jimmy	**Geoffrey Palmer**
Linda	**Sally-Jane Spencer**
Tom	**Tim Preece**
	Leslie Schofield *(Fall)*
Doc Morrissey	**John Horsley**
Prue Harris-Jones	**Theresa Watson**
McBlane	**Joseph Brady** *(Fall)*
Geraldine Hackstraw	**Patricia Hodge** *(Legacy)*
Hank	**Michael Fenton-Stevens** *(Legacy)*
Welton Ormsby	**David Ryall** *(Legacy)*

Creator/Writer **David Nobbs**
Producers **Gareth Gwenlan, John Howard Davies**

● ***When a mid-life crisis strikes, a suburban commuter fakes his death and seeks new horizons under another identity.***

Reginald Iolanthe Perrin works for Sunshine Desserts in a boring office job. He travels to work each morning from his Norbiton home on the same crowded commuter train, always arriving eleven minutes late for a variety of wacky British Rail reasons (including dead dog on the line). There, despite the attentions of his loyal secretary, Joan Greengross, his career is going nowhere (perhaps symbolized by the crumbling letters on the company sign) and he is constantly browbeaten by his bumptious boss, CJ, who regales him with advice beginning 'I didn't get where I am today . . .' Home life has become rather mundane, too, with his wife's day revolving around waving him off in the morning and greeting him in the evening, and the thought of visiting his mother-in-law inexplicably fills him with images of a waddling hippopotamus.

It all becomes too much and Reggie plans a way out. He takes himself off to the seaside, abandons his clothes on the beach to fake drowning and branches out into a new life. After a period wandering Britain's country lanes, he resurfaces back in suburbia, courting his wife, Elizabeth, under the new identity of Martin Wellbourne. He soon reassumes his true name, although by now he has developed an anarchic streak.

Perrin sets up his own chain of shops, Grot, which specializes in selling useless objects – cruet sets without holes, square footballs, etc. – and recruits his former colleagues from the defunct Sunshine Desserts. Joan once again becomes his secretary, tempting him with her womanly wiles, and he takes delight in employing CJ as a minor executive. There is also room for his two sycophantic juniors from the old company, Tony 'Great' Webster and David 'Super' Harris-Jones, as well as Elizabeth. But things go too well for Grot and, resenting the success, Reggie sets out to bring the company to its knees before, once again, embarking on a new existence. This time the whole cast joins him in a mock seaside suicide. When they resurface in a third series, Reggie has opened Perrins, a rehabilitation commune for stressed executives, finding room for all the usual cronies, including his military-minded brother-in-law, Jimmy (who is always apologizing for something, claiming there has been a 'bit of a cock-up'), and an indecipherable Scottish cook, McBlane.

The role was a marvellous vehicle for Leonard Rossiter, who won acclaim for his portrayal of the highly agitated, stuttering eccentric. Filled with memorable catchphrases, it was scripted by David Nobbs from his original novel, *The Death of Reginald Perrin*, which, some claim, inspired MP John Stonehouse to fake his death in the same way.

In 1996, the BBC bravely decided to resurrect the concept. Considered by some at the time as an attempt to perform *Hamlet* without the prince, *The Legacy of Reginald Perrin* brought together most of the original cast members, but failed to excite the critics. In the new series, Reggie has died once and for all – in the series a billboard advertising the insurance company to which he subscribed had fallen on him; in real life actor Leonard Rossiter had died in 1984 – and is commemorated in the opening titles which show his RIP headstone marked with the tribute 'Forever Revolting'. Reggie may have gone, but his spirit lives in his will, which bequeaths £1 million to each of his associates if they can prove they have done something totally absurd. To achieve their goal, the team forms a new company named Broscor – the Bloodless Revolution of Senior Citizens and the Occupationally Rejected – with the intention of reclaiming the world for those cast aside by thrusting society. Actor Trevor Adams, who had played Tony Webster, could not be traced, so a new, but similar, character named Hank (catchphrase 'wicked') fills his shoes. Another key addition to the cast is solicitor Geraldine Hackstraw. Writer David Nobbs released a novel of the same name to coincide with the new series.

Fall Guy, The ★★

US (Twentieth Century-Fox) Adventure. ITV 1982–7
(US: ABC 1981–6)

Colt Seavers	**Lee Majors**
Howie Munson	**Douglas Barr**
Jody Banks	**Heather Thomas**
Samantha 'Big Jack' Jack	**Jo Ann Pflug**
Terri Shannon/Michaels	**Markie Post**
Pearl Sperling	**Nedra Volz**

Creator/Producer **Glen A. Larson**

● ***A movie stuntman doubles up as a modern-day bounty hunter.***

Colt Seavers is the Fall Guy, a courageous, daring movie stunt double who tops up his income by acting as a bounty hunter, tracking down bail jumpers and other fugitives who have a price on their heads. The spectacular stunts he perfects in films often come in handy when apprehending the runaways. Seavers is assisted by beautiful stuntwoman Jody Banks, as well as by his cousin, Howie Munson, who acts as his business manager. Big Jack, the bail bondswoman, hands out the orders, until she is replaced by Terri Shannon (her surname is later changed to Michaels), who then gives way in turn to a grumpy old lady named Pearl Sperling. Star Lee Majors also sings the theme song.

Fall of Eagles ✶✶

UK (BBC/Time-Life) Drama. BBC 1 1974
DVD: DD Home Entertainment

Otto von Bismarck	**Curt Jurgens**
Princess Victoria ('Vicky')	**Gemma Jones**
Kaiser Wilhelm I	**Maurice Denham**
Emperor Franz Josef	**Miles Anderson** *(young)*
	Laurence Naismith
Empress Elizabeth ('Sisi')	**Diane Keen** *(young)*
	Rachel Gurney
Fritz	**Denis Lill**
Tsar Alexander III	**Tony Jay**
Vladimir Lenin	**Patrick Stewart**
Kaiser Wilhelm II	**Barry Foster**
Tsar Nicholas II	**Charles Kay**
Paul von Hindenburg	**Marius Goring**
Narrator	**Michael Hordern**

Creator **John Elliot**
Producer **Stuart Burge**

● ***The collapse of the great European dynasties of the 19th and early 20th centuries.***

In some detail, *Fall of Eagles* re-creates developments in Austria–Hungary, Russia and Germany before, during and immediately after World War I. In 13 episodes, each 50 minutes in length, the drama relates the romances, political crises and eventual fall from power of the ruling families of those countries – the Romanovs (represented largely by Tsar Nicholas II), the Hohenzollerns (Kaiser Wilhelm II) and the Habsburgs (Emperor Franz Josef). The series begins in the mid 19th century and continues through to the abdication of Wilhelm in 1918. Writers include Hugh Whitemore, John Elliot, Trevor Griffiths, Jack Pulman, Troy Kennedy Martin and Robert Muller.

Fallen Hero ✶✶

UK (Granada) Drama. ITV 1978–9

Gareth Hopkins	**Del Henney**
Dorothy Hopkins	**Wanda Ventham**
Martin Hopkins	**John Wheatley**
Joe Harris	**Barry Stanton**
Sally Jones/Hopkins	**Marged Esli**
Wilf Calder	**Frank Crompton**
Alan Field	**Brian Miller**
Rebecca Westgate	**Prunella Gee**
Baby Dorothy Hopkins	**Caroline Mooney**
Suzie Crossley	**Vicky Williams**

Creator/Writer **Brian Finch**
Executive Producer **Michael Cox**
Producer **June Howson**

● ***A rugby league star's life hits rock bottom when his career is wrecked by injury.***

Gareth Hopkins, a boy from the Welsh valleys, was about to collect his first rugby union cap when he decided to turn professional and move north to the rugby league circuit. Nine years later, at the age of 35, his life comes crashing down around him when he suffers a career-ending leg injury. This two-series drama follows Hopkins through the subsequent months as he attempts to come to terms with a less than rosy future. As he struggles with loss of earnings and self-respect, his marriage also turns into a ruck. A job pulling pints at the Pigeon pub hardly helps and, to make matters worse, his stepson, Martin, is then accused of murder. Hopkins, the fallen hero, begins to reflect on what might have been.

Falsey, John

(1951–)

See *Brand, Joshua.*

Fame ✶✶✶

US (MGM/United Artists) Drama. BBC 1 1982–5
(US: NBC 1982–3; Syndicated 1983–7)
DVD: MGM

Lydia Grant	**Debbie Allen**
Coco Hernandez	**Erica Gimpel**
Danny Amatullo	**Carlo Imperato**
Leroy Johnson	**Gene Anthony Ray**
Bruno Martelli	**Lee Curreri**
Doris Schwartz	**Valerie Landsburg**
Julie Miller	**Lori Singer**
Montgomery MacNeil	**P. R. Paul**
Mr Benjamin Shorofsky	**Albert Hague**
Elizabeth Sherwood	**Carol Mayo Jenkins**
Mr Greg Crandall	**Michael Thoma**
Mrs Charlotte Miller	**Judy Farrell**
Angelo Martelli	**Carmine Caridi**
Dwight	**David Greenlee**
David Reardon	**Morgan Stevens**
Mrs Gertrude Berg	**Ann Nelson**
Holly Laird	**Cynthia Gibb**
Christopher Donlon	**Billy Hufsey**
Quentin Morloch	**Ken Swofford**
Cleo Hewitt	**Janet Jackson**
Jesse Valesquez	**Jesse Borrego**
Nicole Chapman	**Nia Peeples**

Creator **Christopher Gore**
Producer **Stanley C. Rogow**

● ***Energetic musical drama featuring students and staff at a performing arts college.***

Based on Alan Parker's film of the same name, *Fame* is set in New York's School of the Arts and focuses on a group of talented youngsters learning how to take their place in the world of show business. The emphasis is on sweat, the only way to the top being through dedication and hard work, and the series traces the students' ambitions, their progress, their personal crises and their hard-earned successes, beginning with their arrival as freshers and running through to graduation.

The teachers and instructors are led by sultry Lydia Grant, the demanding dance teacher. She is supported by the much-revered, white-bearded Mr Shorofsky, the music teacher; no-nonsense English tutor Elizabeth Sherwood; and drama teacher Mr Crandall, who is later replaced by David Reardon. Quentin Morloch is the stuffy Principal and the dippy school secretary is Mrs Berg.

The real stars, however, are the kids themselves: Leroy, an agile, creative dancer from Harlem; Coco, an over-ambitious, impetuous singer and dancer; Bruno, a keyboard genius; Doris, a talented comedienne and actress; and Danny, another comic. Julie is a brilliant cellist from the backwoods of Grand Rapids, Michigan, who struggles to come to terms with life in the city, while Montgomery is the son of a successful actress. Characters introduced later include a second influx of students. Among these are dancers Jesse and Christopher; Holly, who concentrates on drama; Dwight, a chubby tuba player; and singer/dancer Nicole.

Four of the original film's stars reprised their roles in this TV version, namely Gene Anthony Ray, Lee Curreri, Albert Hague and Debbie Allen (who also took charge of the show's choreography). The theme song from the film had been a number one hit for Irene Cara in 1982, but Erica Gimpel, her successor as Coco, provided the vocals on the TV version. The programme also spun off several British chart hits, performed by The Kids from Fame, with 'Hi-Fidelity' and 'Starmaker' being the most successful. There were no hits in the States, but *Fame* was always more successful in the UK than in its native USA.

Fame Academy ★★

UK (Initial) Talent Show. BBC 1 2002–5
DVD: Vision Video/Universal-Island

Presenters **Cat Deeley, Patrick Kielty**

Executive Producers **Richard Hopkins, Louise Rainbow**

● ***Trained hopefuls do battle for showbiz stardom.***

Hot on the heels of ITV's success with POPSTARS and POP IDOL, the BBC introduced *Fame Academy*, a similar sort of talent contest but with an element of hard graft thrown in. In the US drama series FAME, performing arts students were told that sweat, dedication and hard work were the only ways to make it to the top. *Fame Academy* added that particular dimension to the usual mix of embarrassing auditions, tears, tantrums and vote-'em-off phone-ins that we now recognize as 'reality TV'. Eleven candidates were already accepted out of the 10,000 who applied by the time of the first programme, with viewers given the chance to select the 12th and final hopeful as the series got underway. Billeted in Witanhurst, a 19th-century North London mansion equipped with dance studio and music suites, the aspiring stars rose at 6.30 each morning and endured three hours of choreography and three hours of vocal training each day, building up to staged performances in the live broadcast at the end of the week. In the glare of the spotlight, each performer then sang to survive, with viewers kicking out one of the three worst performers and the inmates getting rid of another of their own gang. At the end of ten gruelling weeks, David Sneddon was declared overall winner. Head of the Academy was former Capital Radio executive Richard Park, vocal coach was Carrie Grant (joined later by husband David Grant), dance teacher was Kevin Adams, songwriting tutor was Pam Sheyne, and personal development coach was Jeremy Milnes. Celebrity visiting lecturers also gave classes.

The series was followed up by *Comic Relief Does Fame Academy*, a week-long charity special in March 2003 featuring nine celebrities, which was won by actor Will Mellor. In summer 2003, a second full series aired under the title *Fame Academy II*. This time viewers voted initially for the best 13 contestants out of a pool of 25 and Bee Gee Robin Gibb joined the coaching team. Alex Parks won the final. While there was no proper series in 2004, *Comic Relief Does Fame Academy* resurfaced in March 2005, with Radio DJ Edith Bowman taking the honours.

Fame Academy was based on a European format that was particularly successful in Spain under the title *Operación Triunfo*.

Fame is the Spur ★★

UK (BBC) Drama. BBC 1 1982

John/Hamer Shawcross .... **Tim Pigott-Smith**
Arnold Ryerson .... **David Hayman**
Tom Hannaway .... **George Costigan**
Ann Artingstall .... **Joanna David**
Ellen Stansfield .... **Paola Dionisotti**
Gordon Stansfield .... **David Collings**
Aunt Lizzie .... **Phyllida Law**
Pen Muff .... **Julia McKenzie**
Polly .... **Susan Edmonstone**
Lady Lettice .... **Elizabeth Counsell**

Writer **Elaine Morgan**
Producer **Richard Beynon**

● ***Three childhood pals play their part in shaping 20th-century British society.***

Using the development of the Labour Party, from its roots up to the Spanish Civil War, as a backdrop, *Fame is the Spur* tells the story of three ambitious friends from the slum backstreets of Manchester. Each is determined to make an impact on society. The story begins in 1877 and out of such humble origins Tom, Arnold and John quickly make their way in the world. Tom is a wideboy whose business fortunes begin in a rag and bone yard and progress through the local council. For his capitalist efforts, he is eventually knighted. Arnold takes a quite different path, becoming active in the trade union movement and going out of his way to care for his peers. John, or Hamer as he likes to be known in later years, joins the Labour Party and builds himself a political career. He becomes a cabinet minister in the Ramsay MacDonald government and then heads for the House of Lords. With music by former Animal Alan Price, *Fame is the Spur* was dramatized by Elaine Morgan in eight parts from the 1940 novel by Howard Spring.

Family, The ★★★

UK (BBC) Documentary. BBC 1 1974

Producer **Paul Watson**

● ***Fly-on-the-wall documentary series about a working-class Reading family.***

The Wilkins family enjoyed temporary stardom through this warts-and-all, 12-part look at their turbulent domestic life. Terry Wilkins was a bus conductor living with his outspoken wife, Margaret. Sons Gary and Christopher, daughters Marion and Heather, plus Gary's wife, Karen, and two-year-old son, Scott, and Marion's live-in boyfriend, Tom Bernes, completed the crowded family group housed in a maisonette above a greengrocer's shop in Whitley Street, Reading. Also seen was Heather's teenage boyfriend, Melvin Applethwaite. A camera crew virtually lived with the family for three months and recorded their high spots and their lowest ebbs. Blazing rows made colourful viewing and the Wilkinses' flair for letting family skeletons out of the cupboard added to the drama. Later, one-off retrospectives revealed how the family had gradually drifted apart once the series had ended.

Producer Paul Watson repeated the experiment nearly 20 years later, although in rather sunnier climes, in his Australian documentary series SYLVANIA WATERS.

Family at War, A ✶✶

UK (Granada) Drama. ITV 1970–2
DVD: Acorn Media

Edwin Ashton .... **Colin Douglas**
Jean Ashton .... **Shelagh Fraser**
Margaret Ashton/Porter .... **Lesley Nunnerley**
Philip Ashton .... **Keith Drinkel**
Sheila Ashton .... **Coral Atkins**
David Ashton .... **Colin Campbell**
Freda Ashton .... **Barbara Flynn**
Robert Ashton .... **David Dixon**
Sefton Briggs .... **John McKelvey**
Tony Briggs .... **Trevor Bowen**
John Porter .... **Ian Thompson**
Celia Porter .... **Margery Mason**
Harry Porter .... **Patrick Troughton**
Michael Armstrong .... **Mark Jones**
Ian McKenzie .... **John Nettles**

Creator **John Finch**
Producers **Richard Doubleday, Michael Cox, James Brabazon**

● ***Glum portrayal of 1930s and 1940s hardships in the lives of a Liverpool family.***

Granada's most expensive ever serial at the time, *A Family at War* focuses on the middle-class Ashton family as they struggle through the lean war years. Starting in May 1938 and running on to 1945, it sees them emerge from the decay of the Depression to face the even more bitter realities of World War II, and witnesses family and romantic relationships disintegrate along the way. Never a day passes without a new worry for the Ashtons, headed by morose Yorkshire dad Edwin, who is beholden at work to his pompous brother-in-law, Sefton Briggs. Sefton and his sister, Edwin's wife Jean, have inherited the family printing works. Eldest child is David, a docks worker who has married too young to Sheila, produced two children, Peter and Janet, and is constantly in debt until he joins the RAF. Next comes schoolteacher Margaret, who marries John Porter, who goes missing in action. Philip is the 21-year-old Oxford student who fights in the Spanish Civil War, while Freda, the youngest daughter, is just starting work and Robert, the youngest son, is away at nautical school.

The programme's symbolic titles-sequence, showing a demolished sandcastle, is as well remembered as the series itself.

Family Fortunes ✶✶

UK (ATV/Central/Carlton) Game Show. ITV 1980–5; 1987–2002

Presenters **Bob Monkhouse, Max Bygraves, Les Dennis, Andy Collins**

Producers **William G. Stewart, Graham C. Williams, Tony Wolfe, Dennis Liddington, Andrew Wightman, Mike Morrisey**

● ***Game show in which families guess what the public thinks.***

Based on the American quiz *Family Feud, Family Fortunes* uses a giant computer (initially known as Mr Babbage – after the inventor of the first computer) to display the findings of a public survey. One hundred members of the public are asked to name various items – a song you sing at parties, things you find at the seaside, etc. – and the two competing families (each consisting of five contestants) try to work out which answers have been given. The most popular answers provide the most points. There are cash prizes and other valuables to be won. Bob Monkhouse was the first host, succeeded in 1983 by Max Bygraves. After a two-year gap in production, the series returned with Les Dennis as host. Dennis quit when the series moved into a daytime slot in 2002, with Andy Collins taking his place. *Family Fortunes* has become famous for the off-beam answers given by some contestants. Among the best remembered have been: 'Name something you do in the bathroom' *Answer*: 'Decorate'; 'Name a famous Royal' *Answer*: 'Mail'; 'Name something that flies without an engine' *Answer*: 'A bicycle with wings'. Such out-takes have been celebrated in occasional episodes of *Family Misfortunes*. An 'all-star' version has also been produced. *Family Fortunes* was briefly revived as one instalment of ANT & DEC's *Game Show Marathon* in 2005, a series that celebrated the best-loved game shows in ITV's 50-year history.

Family Ties ✶✶

US (UBU/Paramount) Situation Comedy. Channel 4 1985–6 (US: NBC 1982–9)

Elyse Keaton .... **Meredith Baxter-Birney**
Steve Keaton .... **Michael Gross**
Alex P. Keaton .... **Michael J. Fox**
Mallory Keaton .... **Justine Bateman**
Jennifer Keaton .... **Tina Yothers**
Andrew Keaton .... **Brian Bonsall**
Irwin 'Skippy' Handelman .... **Marc Price**
Nick Moore .... **Scott Valentine**
Ellen Reed .... **Tracy Pollan**
Lauren Miller .... **Courteney Cox**

Creator/Executive Producer **Gary David Goldberg**

● ***Politics divide a family but love conquers all.***

The Keatons are a middle-class family living happily in Columbus, Ohio. Dad Steve works for a TV station (WKS); mum Elyse is an architect. They are liberal children of the 1960s, which puts them genially at odds with their own conservative offspring, who are growing up in the get-rich-quick world of the 1980s. Reaganesque values are particularly welcomed by smart teenage son Alex, who delves deeply into economics and finance, and later heads off to further such interests at Leland College. Mallory is Alex's younger sister, a high school underachiever, while Jennifer is the youngest of the pack at only nine (a fourth child, baby Andrew, appears in later episodes). Generation gap and political humour are the hallmarks of this long-running series that made a star out of Michael J. Fox (although it was snapped up by Channel 4 only after he had headlined in the blockbuster movie *Back to the Future*). The future real-life Mrs Fox, Tracy Pollan, appeared as Alex's college girlfriend, Ellen Reed.

Fantasy Island ✶

US (Spelling-Goldberg) Drama. ITV 1978–85 (US: ABC 1978–84)
DVD: Sony

Mr Roarke .... **Ricardo Montalban**
Tattoo .... **Herve Villechaize**
Julie .... **Wendy Schaal**
Lawrence .... **Christopher Hewett**

Executive Producers **Aaron Spelling, Leonard Goldberg**

● ***Dreams come true for visitors to a mysterious tropical island.***

Fantasy Island, owned and run by the enigmatic Mr Roarke, is the place where, temporarily at least, dreams really can come true. By paying a mere $10,000 for their trip, each visitor can have one wish fulfilled, provided it isn't *too* fanciful. Whether it is to date attractive women or to make lots of money, this is the chance of a lifetime, and the customers are not short-changed. Things always work out and endings tend to be happy, even if a few problems or hiccups are encountered along the way. What's more, all the guests go away having learned some valuable lessons about themselves.

Helping Mr Roarke to keep the customer satisfied are his assistants, initially the midget, Tattoo, and then Lawrence. Roarke's goddaughter, Julie, also features for a while. Roarke himself becomes more and more obscure as the series progresses. It is ultimately revealed that it is his sorcery that lies behind the fantasy factory and in one episode he is seen to face up to the Devil. Each hour-long programme is built around two or three separate fantasies, and the series was modelled on THE LOVE BOAT, also a hit for the Aaron Spelling production team.

Fantasy Island was remade in 1998 with Malcolm McDowell as Mr Roarke. This time there was a more sinister air about proceedings and greater use of special effects to convey the supernatural. It was screened on satellite TV in the UK.

Far from the Madding Crowd ★★★

UK (Granda/WGBH Boston) Drama. ITV 1998
DVD: Cinema Club

Gabriel Oak	**Nathaniel Parker**
Sgt Frank Troy	**Jonathan Firth**
Mr Boldwood	**Nigel Terry**
Bathsheba Everdene	**Paloma Baeza**
Fanny Robin	**Natasha Little**
Joseph Poorgrass	**Sean Gilder**
Jan Coggan	**Phillip Joseph**
Mrs Coggan	**Elizabeth Estensen**
Liddy Smallbury	**Tracey Keating**
Billy Smallbury	**Kevin Kibbey**
Cain Ball	**Luke Redbond**
Mark Clark	**Andy Robb**
Henery Fray	**Robin Soans**
Maryann Money	**Linda Bassett**
Laban Tall	**Neil Caple**
Old Malter	**Charles Simon**
Soberness Miller	**Sarah Tansey**
Temperance Miller	**Victoria Alcock**

Writer **Philomena McDonagh**
Producer **Hilary Bevan Jones**

● ***Victorian country tale of ill-chosen marriage and reckless romance.***

Nicholas Renton directs this four-part, loyal adaptation of Thomas Hardy's 1874 novel that deals with various intertwined romances. The story – contrasting the virtue of honest, patient love with the unreliability of heated passion – is of headstrong young farm owner Bathsheba Everdene, who relies heavily on her good shepherd Gabriel Oak but cannot see beyond her class prejudices to reciprocate his love for her, especially when there's a rival for her attention in the shape of dull neighbouring farmer Mr Boldwood. In a second love story, Bathsheba's servant Fanny Robin falls for another of Bathsheba's suitors, the dashing Sgt Troy, but their affair has a tragic ending and Troy eventually marries Bathsheba. That, too, is a troubled relationship and more drama unfolds as a major character disappears and then resurfaces with shocking consequences.

Far Pavilions, The ★★

UK (Geoff Reeve and Associates/Goldcrest) Drama. Channel 4 1984
DVD: Acorn Media

Ashton Pelham-Martyn	**Ben Cross**
Princess Anjuli	**Amy Irving**
Kaka Ji Rao	**Christopher Lee**
Koda Dad	**Omar Sharif**
Major Sir Louis Cavagnari	**John Gielgud**
Lt. Wally Hamilton	**Benedict Taylor**
The Rana of Bhithor	**Rossano Brazzi**
Biju Ram	**Saeed Jaffrey**
Major Jenkins	**Robert Hardy**
Princess Shushila	**Sneh Gupta**
Belinda Harlowe	**Felicity Dean**
George Garforth	**Rupert Everett**
Mrs Viccary	**Jennifer Kendal**

Writer **Julian Bond**
Producer **Geoffrey Reeve**

● ***Sumptuous story from the days of the Raj.***

Costing some £8 million to make, *The Far Pavilions*, like THE JEWEL IN THE CROWN, capitalized on the interest in Raj India generated by Richard Attenborough's film *Gandhi*. In three two-hour episodes, it tells of a young British army officer, Ash Pelham-Martyn, in service with the élite Corps of Guards. Because of his Indian upbringing, Ash is torn between the British and Indian cultures, and his forbidden love for former childhood playmate Princess Anjuli adds to the torment. On a wider stage, political intrigue and civil unrest lead to battles galore. The series was adapted by Julian Bond from the novel by M. M. Kaye. Music was provided by Carl Davis.

Farrow, Mia

(Maria Farrow; 1945–)

The daughter of actress Maureen O'Sullivan, Mia Farrow owes much of her movie fame to her single prime-time TV role, that of Allison McKenzie in PEYTON PLACE. Even though she stayed only two years with the series, it allowed her to gain important exposure and led to a succession of film roles. However, once she had left the series, her character was not forgotten, and the mysterious whereabouts of Allison continued to pervade the storylines of *Peyton Place* right through to its end. More recently, Farrow was seen in the mini-series *A Girl Thing*. Her two husbands were Frank Sinatra and André Previn.

Farson, Daniel

(1927–97)

Effective Anglo-American TV journalist/scriptwriter of the 1950s and early 1960s, when, for ITV, he presented some of the channel's more revealing documentaries. A groundbreaking live TV interviewer who went for the jugular, his credits included THIS WEEK, *People in Trouble, Success Story, Dan Farson Meets, Now What Do I Do?* and *Pursuit of Happiness*, plus a film on pub entertainers entitled *Time, Gentlemen, Please!*

He also introduced *SMS*, a series of adaptations of stories by Somerset Maugham, in 1960, and penned *The Frighteners*, a WEDNESDAY PLAY shown in 1964.

Fast Show, The ✱✱✱✱

UK (BBC) Comedy. BBC 2 1994; 1996–7; 2000
DVD: BBC

Paul Whitehouse, Charlie Higson, Caroline Aherne, John Thomson, Arabella Weir, Mark Williams, Simon Day

Producers **Paul Whitehouse, Charlie Higson**
Executive Producer **Geoffrey Perkins**

Inventive, pacy, character- and punchline-driven sketch show.

The Fast Show was born out of Harry Enfield's TV programmes. Enfield's close associates, Paul Whitehouse and Charlie Higson, were watching a package of Enfield's sketches which had been edited down for a press preview. They realized that these quick, straight-to-the-punchline highlights were all that was needed to get a laugh. They picked up the idea and, supported by Caroline Aherne, John Thomson, Arabella Weir, Mark Williams and Simon Day, created *The Fast Show*: as its name suggests, a swiftly moving barrage of short skits in which recurring characters never failed to delight viewers by churning out their favourite catchphrases.

The major players are: music hall comedian Arthur Atkinson ('How queer!'), often introduced by fellow veteran Tommy Cockles; Lord of the Manor Ralph, who has a crush on his Irish estate worker, Ted (later stars of a one-off special in December 1998); romantic car salesman Swiss Toni (his smoothie lines written by Bob Mortimer; the character later resurfacing in his own series for BBC 3); rambling toff Rowley Birkin QC ('I was very, very drunk'); Unlucky Alf ('Oh bugger!'); diet- and fashion-conscious Jesse ('This week I shall be mostly eating . . .'); Kenneth and Kenneth, the provocative menswear assistants ('Suit you, sir!); Colin Hunt, the office nerd; TV pundit Ron Manager (allegedly based on former Luton boss Alec Stock); the Oz-TV presenters of 'That's Amazing'; the consumptive country TV host Bob Fleming; Andy, the paranoid shirker of office romances; Sir Geoffrey Norman, a deny-everything Tory MP; Louis Balfour, host of 'Jazz Club' ('Nice'); hen-pecked Roy and his wife, Renee ('What did I say, Roy?'); the Fat Sweaty Coppers; US TV reporter Ed Winchester; the caddish 13th Duke of Wymborne, usually to be found in a schoolgirl dormitory; cop/doctor Monkfish; US mobsters 'The Unpronouncables'; the crew of Chanel 9, a Mediterranean TV station ('Chrissie Waddle', 'Scorchio'); Dave Angel, Eco-Warrior; deaf stuntman Chip Cobb; Cockney Chris, the would-be thief ('I'm a geezer, a little bit whoor, a little bit waay'); the squeamish zoo-keeper; manic-depressive painter Johnny ('Black!'); middle-class liar Patrick Nice ('Which was nice'); incompetent Californian Professor Denzil Dexter; the competitive dad; a band of itinerant pan-pipers; the equally restless family with luggage; a vampire-cum-racing-tipster; and Archie, the intrusive pub codger who's done everything ('Hardest game in the world'). There are also other assorted unnamed characters such as Weir's insecure girl ('Does my bum look big in this?'), rude South African cosmetics assistant ('No offence!'), and the woman with the good idea that men always ignore; Day's 'Someone's sitting there, mate' man and his pub know-all, Billy Bleach (later spun-off into his own series, *Grass*); Aherne's tactless supermarket checkout girl and easily impressed, gum-chewing teenager; Williams's man on the run ('You ain't seen me, right?'); and Whitehouse's excited Northern youth ('brilliant'). Funny as they are, there is always something sad and pathetic about these novel characters.

The show's theme music is 'Release Me'. Three instalments comprising *The Last Fast Show Ever* were screened at Christmas 2000.

Fat Friends ✱✱

UK (Rollem/Yorkshire/Tiger Aspect) Comedy Drama. ITV 1 2000; 2002; 2004–5
DVD: Columbia Tri-Star Home Video

Betty Simpson	**Alison Steadman**
Kelly Simpson/Chadwick	**Ruth Jones**
Lauren Harris	**Gaynor Faye**
Alan Ashburn	**Richard Ridings**
Jamie Rymer	**James Corden**
Carol McGary	**Janet Dibley**
Val Lorrimer	**Kathryn Hunt**
Julia Fleshman	**Josie Lawrence**
Joan Kirk	**Rita May**
Kevin Chadwick	**Jonathan Ryland**
Mrs Chadwick	**Sandra Gough**
Douglas Simpson	**Barrie Rutter**
Joanne Simpson	**Jessica Harris**
Lynette Pickering	**Susan Cookson**
Aysha Kapoor	**Meera Syal**
Pippa	**Caroline Pegg**
Jose	**Adam Zane**
Liz Ashburn	**Barbara Marten**
Beverley Ashburn	**Holly Scourfield**
Marilyn Harris	**Eleanor Bron**
Leonard Harris	**Allan Corduner**
Carl Whittaker/Watkinson	**Jason Merrells**
Norma Patterson	**Lynda Baron**
Rebecca Patterson	**Lisa Riley**
Paul Thompson	**Paul Warriner**
Sid	**Bill Rodgers**
Max Robertson	**David Harewood**
Russell Simpson	**Oliver Pickering**
Simon de Vier	**Ian Kershaw**
Clare Hart	**Christine Tremarco**
Sean Hurst	**Julian Kerridge**
Mercedes	**Janine Mellor**

Creator **Kay Mellor**
Executive Producers **Kay Mellor, David Reynolds, Greg Brenman**
Producers **Gareth Morgan, Yvonne Francas, Josh Dynevor**

Light-hearted but emotional insights into the lives of northern slimmers.

The weekly meetings of the Leeds branch of the Superslimmers dieting club provide a rallying point for a group of cheerful but unfortunately troubled people. At each 'Count with Carol' class the scales do their bit and the pounds added or lost are totalled up, but beyond the facts and figures of weight loss, and the pressure of slimming competitions, lie a host of sorry tales. Some members are barely overweight; others are in dire need of shedding a few stone, but in most cases there is a good reason for their weight gain. Not that this is a dark drama in any way, as this ribald, earthy comedy has colourful, larger-than-life characters at its core, but there are some tear-jerking moments along the way. The story of bullied schoolboy Jamie is a good example. His secret is the depressed mother he needs to care for. Then there's chubby Alan Ashburn, whose marriage is in tatters; aspiring actress Lauren whose Jewish family tells her she's thin and whose boyfriend calls her a pudding; Betty Simpson, wife of a chip shop owner, who reveals on television that she once gave up a son for adoption; Betty's daughter, Kelly, whose initial concerns revolve around being two sizes too big for her wedding dress but then suffers frustration at her inability to conceive; and bossy, bulimic teacher Carol herself, whose family background is far from happy. Later additions to the cast – in a world where the women are feisty and bold and the men feeble and inept – include shy garden centre worker Rebecca and her domineering mother, Norma. Guest stars (playing themselves) include Richard Whiteley, Richard and Judy and Trisha Goddard, the last in a 90-minute special screened on New Year's Day 2004 as the first episode of series three.

Fat Friends is almost a family project for creator Kay Mellor, who pens most episodes. Daughter Gaynor Faye not only stars in the series but also scripts some parts (as Gaynor Mellor), while producer Yvonne Francas, another of Kay's daughters, appears in a small role in the first series (as Yvonne Mellor).

Father Brown ✶✶

UK (ATV) Detective Drama. ITV 1974
DVD: Acorn Media

Father Brown .... **Kenneth More**
Flambeau .... **Dennis Burgess**

Writer **Hugh Leonard**
Producer **Ian Fordyce**

● ***The cases of a clerical detective in the 1920s.***
Fifteen years before Father Dowling began investigating, this quaint, period series featured Father Brown, TV's first detective in holy orders. Wily and perceptive, Brown is a mild-mannered, easy-going criminologist who solves cases using a mixture of human understanding and conventional detection. Whether it is identifying a decapitated corpse at a garden party or helping a young girl to avoid blackmail, the saintly sleuth shines through. His motto is 'Have Bible, will travel' and Flambeau is his close friend. The series was based on the short stories of G. K. Chesterton.

Father, Dear Father ✶✶

UK (Thames) Situation Comedy. ITV 1968–73
DVD: Clear Vision Video

Patrick Glover .... **Patrick Cargill**
Anna Glover .... **Natasha Pyne**
Karen Glover .... **Ann Holloway**
Matilda 'Nanny' Harris .... **Noël Dyson**
Barbara Mossman .... **Ursula Howells**
Mrs Glover .... **Joyce Carey**
Georgie .... **Sally Bazely**
Dawn Addams
Bill Mossman .... **Patrick Holt**
Tony Britton

Creators/Writers **Johnny Mortimer, Brian Cooke**
Producer **William G. Stewart**

● ***A womanizing novelist struggles to keep his family and friends in check.***
Patrick Glover, writer of spy novels, is divorced and a free spirit – in principle. However, plagued by his dotty mother, his agent (Georgie), his ex-wife (Barbara), her new, scrap-metal-merchant husband (Bill), a fussy nanny and two trendy daughters (Anna and Karen), his life is never his own. Although he drives a swish sports car and lives in a spacious, well-appointed house in Hillsdown Avenue, Hampstead, complete with a cuddly St Bernard named H. G. Wells, his peace and privacy are constantly being shattered by the household entourage. This archetypal TV farce was produced by future FIFTEEN-TO-ONE host William G. Stewart. An Australian version (with only Patrick Cargill and Noël Dyson from the original cast) was shown in the UK in 1978–80. A spin-off feature film was released in 1973.

Father Dowling Investigates ✶✶

US (Viacom) Detective Drama. ITV 1990–94 (US: NBC 1989; ABC 1990–1)

Father Frank Dowling .... **Tom Bosley**
Sister Stephanie ('Sister Steve') .... **Tracy Nelson**
Marie Brody .... **Mary Wickes**
Father Philip Prestwick .... **James Stephens**
Sgt Clancy .... **Regina Krueger**

Creators **Ralph McInerny, Dean Hargrove, Joel Steiger**
Executive Producers **Fred Silverman, Dean Hargrove**
Producer **Barry Steinberg**

● ***A Catholic priest has a nose for crime.***
Amiable Father Frank Dowling is the parish priest of St Michael's in Chicago, but he finds his true vocation in amateur detective work. Joined in his investigations by a nun, Sister Stephanie (or Sister Steve as she prefers to be known), the detective in the dog collar is drawn into the most complicated murder mysteries, which he unravels with great aplomb. Steve, a street-kid-turned-nun, is a more than useful ally. She still knows all the tricks of the trade, from picking locks to gathering information. She even drops her nun's habit, on occasions, to go incognito. The unlikely duo drive around in Dowling's run-down old station wagon and, using their clerical appearances, are able to go where normal detectives fear to tread. In the background are bumbling Father Prestwick, a junior priest dispatched by the Bishop to keep an eye on the wayward Dowling, and Marie, the loyal housekeeper at the St Michael's vicarage. Sgt Clancy acts as Dowling's police contact.

The character was created by novelist Ralph McInerny and the series – known as *The Father Dowling Mysteries* in the USA – gave Tom Bosley his first starring role after HAPPY DAYS.

Father Ted ✶✶✶✶

UK (Hat Trick/Channel 4) Situation Comedy. Channel 4 1995–6; 1998
DVD: VCI

Father Ted Crilly .... **Dermot Morgan**
Father Dougal McGuire .... **Ardal O'Hanlon**
Father Jack Hackett .... **Frank Kelly**
Mrs Doyle .... **Pauline McLynn**
Father Noel Furlong .... **Graham Norton**

Writers **Graham Linehan, Arthur Mathews**
Producers **Geoffrey Perkins, Lissa Evans**

● ***The surreal adventures of three delinquent Irish priests.***
Bleakly set on fictitious Craggy Island, somewhere off the coast of Galway, this cult comedy focuses on the stressed life of Father Ted Crilly, a heavy-smoking, bad-mouthed ('Feck!') Catholic priest with more of a lust for the temporal world

than for the spiritual. Fast cars and fast women are more his cup of tea than faith and funerals, but they remain just distant dreams to the generally good-natured, slightly wayward cleric. However, Ted's patience is sorely tried by his young assistant, the enthusiastic but ultra-thick (actually profoundly unworldly) Father Dougal McGuire, the sort of man who takes instructions literally, with disastrous consequences. The senior priest in the house is the blasphemous Father Jack Hackett, an angry, often wheelchair-bound psychopath who is perhaps a future version of Ted himself, having finally descended without hope into the mire of 'Drink!' (literally anything, from toilet cleaner to engine oil) and 'Girls!' It seems that the Church is already well aware of this dubious trio, for they have all been 'exiled' to the island, for various reasons: Ted for the embezzlement of a charity fund (the sick child hoping for a visit to Lourdes was deprived and Ted went to Las Vegas on the proceeds); Dougal for some incident involving nuns; and Jack for an unspecified wedding ceremony outrage. The three live in a particularly grim-looking parochial house (actually a building near Ennistymon, County Clare), where they are dutifully looked after by the equally bizarre Mrs Doyle, forever insisting that they have a cup of tea ('Oh go on!').

Adding to this explosive mix are the inbred islanders, who never fail to cause Ted grief, and occasional religious visitors like the phlegmatic, unentertainable Father Stone and incessantly irritating Father Noel Furlong. The thought of nuns coming to the house is just too much to bear.

The Catholic church does not escape lightly in *Father Ted* – its conventions, sacred places and even its very creed are held up to ridicule, but always in a fashion that is so over the top that it has no grounding in reality. The action is always farcical, with moments of violent slapstick. Nor are the stars ever shown conducting major ceremonies or taking confession.

Three seasons of wild acclaim were brought suddenly to an end with the premature death of star Dermot Morgan from a heart attack in March 1998 (just days before the third series was due to be screened). The only consolation was that at least the series ended while still in its prime. The Father Ted character had previously been performed in stand-up by co-writer Arthur Mathews.

Fawcett, Farrah

(1947–)

Shaggy-haired American actress, the face of 1977 after starring as one of CHARLIE'S ANGELS (sporty Jill Munroe). On a wave of lookalike dolls and merchandising, Fawcett left the series after just one season but was forced to make occasional return appearances (to avoid contractual difficulties). Previously, she had gained bit parts in series like THE FLYING NUN, MARCUS WELBY, MD and THE SIX MILLION DOLLAR MAN, and had also appeared as David Janssen's neighbour in HARRY-O. Little television has come her way after leaving *Charlie's Angels*, apart from a short-lived sitcom, *Good Sports*, in 1991, and guest spots in series like Ally McBeal, SPIN CITY and *The Guardian*, but she has won a fair amount of film work. She was at one time married to actor Lee Majors and was known as Farrah Fawcett-Majors when *Charlie's Angels* began.

Fawlty Towers ✱✱✱✱

UK (BBC) Situation Comedy. BBC 2 1975; 1979
DVD: BBC

Basil Fawlty	**John Cleese**
Sybil Fawlty	**Prunella Scales**
Manuel	**Andrew Sachs**
Polly Sherman	**Connie Booth**
Major Gowen	**Ballard Berkeley**
Miss Tibbs	**Gilly Flower**
Miss Ursula Gatsby	**Renee Roberts**
Terry	**Brian Hall**

Writers **John Cleese and Connie Booth**
Producers **John Howard Davies, Douglas Argent**

Chaos in a seaside hotel, courtesy of its manic owner.
Fawlty Towers, a modest little Torquay hotel, is run by husband and wife Basil and Sybil Fawlty. Modest the hotel may be, but Basil has ambitious plans for his small empire and runs it with great enthusiasm. Sadly, the guests tend to get in the way. Inhibited also by his nagging, droning, gossiping wife and by Manuel, a useless Spanish waiter from Barcelona who understands little English ('I know nathing'), Fawlty's best-laid plans always end in disaster.

Fawlty is a master at turning the simplest procedures – like serving dinner to late guests – into complete chaos, and his patronizing air, biting sarcasm and bouts of rage all contrive to make matters worse. When practising a fire drill, he refuses to allow a real kitchen fire to interrupt the flow of proceedings; when entertaining German guests, a blow on the head encourages the already unbalanced hotelier to goosestep around the dining room, magnificently failing not to 'mention the war'. When an undercover hotel inspector comes to town, Fawlty unctuously fawns over every guest except the right one, and on a planned gourmet evening, Terry, his chef, gets blind drunk.

Hovering on the fringe at all times are the hotel's permanent guests, two doddery old ladies (Miss Tibbs and Miss Gatsby) and the senile and deaf Major Gowen. But, thankfully, there is also Polly, the chambermaid, who attempts to bring some order back to the hotel. Hers is generally only a limited success, with her lanky, hot-headed boss screwing things up time and again. He can't even keep control of the hotel's name plate, which is constantly tampered with by meddling hands to offer Fatty Owls, Farty Towels, Watery Fowls or other anagrammatic names.

The series combines the best aspects of farce – misconstrued conversations, physical stunts, well-timed exits and entrances, etc. – with some classic one-liners and insults. Very few series manage to imbue the viewers with so much tension, frustration and exasperation, but *Fawlty Towers* has been generally accepted as one of the gems of British TV comedy. It was allegedly inspired by a visit by the Monty Python team to a Torquay hotel and their discovery of a rude hotelier who threw Eric Idle's briefcase into the street, thinking it was a bomb. The character was written into one of John Cleese and Graham Chapman's *Doctor at Large* (see DOCTOR IN THE HOUSE) scripts, before finally achieving greatness in his own right in this sitcom, several years later. After the acclaim of the first six *Fawlty Towers* episodes, the second series took four years to arrive (partly because Cleese and his co-writer wife, Connie Booth, had split up), but most people thought it well worth the wait.

FBI, The ✱✱

US (Warner Brothers/Quinn Martin) Police Drama. ITV 1965–75 (US: ABC 1965–74)

Insp. Lewis Erskine .... **Efrem Zimbalist Jr**
Agent Arthur Ward .... **Philip Abbott**
Barbara Erskine .... **Lynn Loring**
Special Agent Jim Rhodes .... **Stephen Brooks**
Special Agent Tom Colby .... **William Reynolds**
Agent Chris Daniels .... **Shelly Novack**
Narrator .... **Marvin Miller**

Executive Producer **Quinn Martin**
Producer **Charles Lawton**

Successful series highlighting the cases of a fictitious FBI agent.

Inspector Lew Erskine works for the Federal Bureau of Investigation and travels the length and breadth of the USA, seeking out criminals and fraudsters and unearthing political subversives and other enemies of the state. During the course of the programme's run he is assisted by a number of different colleagues. One of these, Jim Rhodes, is romantically entwined with Barbara, Erskine's daughter, in the first series, but she is then dropped from the cast. (This was a deliberate ploy by the producers, who wanted to isolate the cold, methodical Erskine even further – his wife had already been killed in a shoot-out.) Not that Erskine, a dedicated, businesslike operator, appears to mind. He insists his work *always* takes precedence over his private life. A career detective, he has been with the Bureau for 30 years, right from the turbulent days of the 1930s, when he helped round up gangsters. Now he reports to Arthur Ward, assistant to the Bureau's Director.

The series won the approval of the real FBI chief, J. Edgar Hoover, who permitted filming at their Washington headquarters. Many of the stories were allegedly based on true cases and, in America, appeals for assistance in tracking down real villains were sometimes made at the end of the show.

Feldman, Marty

(1933–82)

Mop-haired, wide-eyed English comedian, a companion of Mel Brooks and Gene Wilder in the cinema but, before his movie days, a success on the small screen. Feldman's career began in writing. His collaborator was Barry Took and between them they penned scores of scripts for radio series like *Round the Horne* and *Educating Archie*, and TV comedies such as THE ARMY GAME, BOOTSIE AND SNUDGE, *Scott On . . ., The Walrus and the Carpenter, Barney is My Darling, Broaden Your Mind* and ON THE BRADEN BEAT. They also wrote for comics like Dick Emery, Harry Secombe and Frankie Howerd, and Feldman (with John Law) provided the famous 'class' sketch, featuring Ronnie Barker, Ronnie Corbett and John Cleese, for THE FROST REPORT. He also co-produced Corbett's comedy, NO – THAT'S ME OVER HERE! Moving in front of the camera, he starred in the manic AT LAST THE 1948 SHOW and out of this gained his own BBC 2 series, *Marty*, which developed the zany visual humour that was to characterize his later movie work. Other series followed, such as *The Marty Feldman Comedy Machine* and *Marty Back Together Again*. Feldman died of a heart attack while filming in Mexico in December 1982.

Fell Tiger ✱✱

UK (BBC) Drama. BBC 1 1985

Joe Borrow .... **David Hayman**
Kath Borrow .... **Alyson Spiro**
Susan Harvey .... **Jan Harvey**
Don Stanforth .... **Neil Phillips**
Dave Ashton .... **Eamon Boland**
Mal Fleet .... **Mark Drewry**
Martin Cunningham .... **Ian Marter**

Writer **Christopher Green**
Producer **Bob McIntosh**

A top climber needs to rebuild his life after an accident.

Joe Borrow is a leading mountaineer. During an expedition to the Himalayas he saves the life of a colleague and returns to Britain as a hero. Sadly, he has reached the peak of his climbing career. A major accident means he now needs to face up to a less mobile future. His personal life – undermined by deceit and duplicity – is also in turmoil, and his marriage to Kath is on the rocks. But Joe determinedly sets about creating himself a future, accepting a job at Whinn Rigg in the Lake District, presenting climbing courses for young executives. The job is offered by Don Stanforth, but Stanforth turns out to be less than reliable and the new challenges in Borrow's life are more daunting than they first seem. This six-part drama was produced by BBC Scotland.

Fellows, The ✱✱

UK (Granada) Detective Drama. ITV 1967

Oldenshaw .... **Richard Vernon**
Dimmock .... **Michael Aldridge**
Mrs Hollinsczech .... **Jill Booty**
Thomas Anthem .... **James Ottaway**
Alec Spindoe .... **Ray McAnally**

Creator **Robin Chapman**
Producers **Robin Chapman, Peter Plummer**

Two academic criminologists solve crimes from a Cambridge college.

A follow-up series to THE MAN IN ROOM 17 (and indeed subtitled *Late of Room 17*), *The Fellows* focuses on two Government-financed crime-crackers, Oldenshaw and Dimmock, who have, at last, left the famous Room 17 to take up residence at All Saints' College, Cambridge. Appointed by the Home Office to the Peel Research Fellowship, their role now is to study how the nature of crime changes as society evolves. However, they soon re-established themselves as formidable detectives, calling on the assistance of number-cruncher Mrs Hollinsczech and servant Thomas Anthem. Alec Spindoe, a gangster convicted during the series, was later given his own TV spin-off series, *Spindoe*.

Felton, Norman

(1913–)

London-born producer, raised from a teenager in America. He was responsible for such hits as *Robert Montgomery Presents*, DR KILDARE, THE MAN FROM U.N.C.L.E. (also as co-creator), STRANGE REPORT and *Executive Suite*.

Feltz, Vanessa

(1962–)

London-born, Cambridge graduate presenter, hosting her own talk shows, *Vanessa* and *The Vanessa Show*, until the latter was axed amid a scandal over planted studio guests. Feltz has also fronted *Watchdog: Value for Money* and the quiz *Quotation Marks*, appeared on programmes like *Good Morning* and *The Wright Stuff*, and, in 1996, was 'on the bed' in THE BIG BREAKFAST. She also played Mrs Fitzwarren in ITV's celebrity pantomime *Dick Whittington* and was a contestant in the first *Celebrity* BIG BROTHER.

Fenn Street Gang, The

See *Please Sir!*

Fennell, Albert

(1920–88)

British producer, closely associated with THE AVENGERS, THE NEW AVENGERS and, later, THE PROFESSIONALS, all in collaboration with Brian Clemens.

Ferris, Pam

(1948–)

British actress, famous as Ma Larkin in THE DARLING BUDS OF MAY and also starring as district nurse Peggy Snow in WHERE THE HEART IS, and gardening sleuth Laura Thyme in ROSEMARY AND THYME. Other credits have included *Meantime* (Mavis), CONNIE (Nesta), *All Change* (Maggie Oldfield), HARDWICKE HOUSE (Cynthia Crabbe, the French mistress), ORANGES ARE NOT THE ONLY FRUIT (Mrs Arkwright), *Mr Wakefield's Crusade* (Mad Marion), *Performance*'s *Roots* (Mrs Bryant), CLUEDO (Mrs White), MIDDLEMARCH (Mrs Dollop), *The Rector's Wife* (Eleanor Ramsay), *Death of a Salesman* (The Woman), *Screen Two*'s *Mrs Hartley and the Growth Centre* (Alice Hartley), OUR MUTUAL FRIEND (Mrs Boffin), THE TENANT OF WILDFELL HALL (Mrs Markham) and *The Turn of the Screw* (Mrs Grose). Ferris has also been seen in *Sweet Revenge* (Denise Williams), PARADISE HEIGHTS (Marion Eustace) and *Pollyanna* (Mrs Snow), as well as making guest appearances in series like CASUALTY, LINDA GREEN and AGATHA CHRISTIE'S MARPLE. She is married to actor Roger Frost.

Fiddlers Three ✶

UK (Yorkshire) Situation Comedy. ITV 1991

Ralph West .... **Peter Davison**
Ros West .... **Paula Wilcox**
Harvey .... **Peter Blake**
Osborne .... **Tyler Butterworth**
Mr J. J. Morley .... **Charles Kay**
Norma .... **Cindy Day**

Writer **Eric Chappell**
Executive Producer **Vernon Lawrence**
Producer **Graham Wetherell**

● ***Office politics in a provincial outpost of a big business.***

Hapless Ralph West works in an office where petty squabbles and rivalries are part of everyday life. Fifteen years with the company, with no prospect of promotion, have left him frustrated, so he follows every avenue to try and make some progress in his career. Joining him as one of the 'fiddlers' (accountants) are the scheming Harvey and dreamy junior Osborne. Their day is taken up by efforts to get the better of each other or their boss, J. J. Morley. Norma is the office secretary. At home, supportive wife Ros looks after the Wests' three children. Just one series (but consisting of 14 episodes) was produced. Writer Eric Chappell had explored a similar situation in his early comedy THE SQUIRRELS.

Fifteen to One ✶✶

UK (Regent) Quiz. Channel 4 1988–2003

Presenter **William G. Stewart**

Creator **John M. Lewis**
Producers **William G. Stewart, Mark Noades**

● ***Fast-moving daily general knowledge quiz involving 15 contestants.***

Drily compered by experienced producer William G. Stewart (formerly of FATHER, DEAR FATHER, BLESS THIS HOUSE and THE PRICE IS RIGHT, among other popular series), *Fifteen to One*'s aim was to whittle down 15 hopefuls into one daily winner. Arranged in an arc around Stewart, the contestants were asked two questions in turn. Those failing to get at least one right were eliminated. For the next stage, the contestants defended what remained of their initial three lives by nominating one another to answer questions. The last three contestants, with a life intact, progressed to the last round. In this, they battled head to head, trying to eliminate each other through nomination and also looking to notch a high score for themselves. The 15 highest-scoring daily winners competed in the grand final at the end of the series. As in MASTERMIND, no flashy prizes were on offer, just a simple but tasteful commemorative trophy and the prestige of being a *Fifteen to One* champion.

55 Degrees North ✶✶

UK (Zenith North) Police Drama. BBC 1 2004–

DS Dominic 'Nicky' Cole .... **Don Gilet**
Claire Maxwell .... **Dervla Kirwan**
Sgt Rick Astel .... **Andrew Dunn**
Errol Hill .... **George Harris**
DI Dennis Carter .... **Christian Rodska**
PC Martin Clark .... **Mark Stobbart**
DS Frank Maguire .... **Michael Hodgson**
DS Patrick Yates .... **Darren Morfitt**
Sgt Brookes .... **Emma Cleasby**
James Wren .... **Brian Protheroe**
Matty Cole .... **Jaeden Burke**
Georgina Hodge .... **Jacqueline King**

Writer **Timothy Prager**
Executive Producers **Adrian Bate, Barbara McKissack**
Producer **Jo Wright**

● ***A young black cop fights crime and prejudice on the streets of Newcastle.***

The archetypal 'fish out of water' detective, Nicky Cole takes up an appointment with the police in Newcastle upon Tyne, the geographical location of which is – if you care to look it up in an atlas – 55 degrees north. But, as well as over-fastidiously pinpointing the focus of the action, the title seems designed to suggest that the lead man is some distance away from his preferred latitude, in this case London. He is also, if the racist attitude of his new colleagues is a good indicator, the first black man ever to have been seen this far north.

Faced with these niggling challenges, and also an inevitably hard-handed boss in the shape of DI Carter, the virtuous Cole makes a good fist of it. He works the night shift, taking an unorthodox but successful approach to putting hookers, extortionists and date rapists in their place, and having so many run-ins with ambitious Crown Prosecution Service lawyer Claire Maxwell that it seems inevitable that they're going to become an item. Instilling good family and moral values into the maverick cop is his Uncle Errol, with whom Cole is joint guardian of his seven-year-old nephew, Matty.

Applauded for its pace and neat lines in places, but slated for its pedestrianism and crass dialogue in others, the schizophrenic *55 Degrees North* gave critics a headache, not sure whether, overall, it was good or bad. The general feeling was the former.

Film ✳✳

UK (BBC) Film Review. BBC 1 1971–

Presenters **Jacky Gillott, Joan Bakewell, Barry Norman, Frederic Raphael, Jonathan Ross**

Producers **Iain Johnstone, Patricia Ingram, Don Bennetts, Barry Brown, Jane Lush, Bruce Thompson, Allan Campbell, Tom Webber**

● ***Topical review of the cinema world.***

Beginning in 1971 as a programme for the south-east only, the *Film* series has since established itself as the most valuable cinema review on television, incorporating appraisals of the latest releases, interviews with major stars about their forthcoming films and details of the current box-office hits. In its early days, as *Film 71*, the presenter was Jacky Gillott. However, Barry Norman took over the hot seat in 1972, alternating with Joan Bakewell and Frederic Raphael, then claimed the series as his own the following year. When he stood down briefly in 1982 to front OMNIBUS, a succession of temporary stand-ins (including producer Iain Johnstone) held the fort, pending his return. When Norman moved to Sky, he was succeeded by Jonathan Ross (from 1999). The programme's title has changed with each year, becoming *Film 72*, etc.

Filthy Rich and Catflap ✳✳

UK (BBC) Situation Comedy. BBC 2 1987
DVD: Universal

Ralph Filthy	**Nigel Planer**
Richard Rich	**Rik Mayall**
Eddie Catflap	**Adrian Edmondson**

Writer **Ben Elton**
Producer **Paul Jackson**

● ***Aggression and anarchy dominate the lives of a TV performer, his minder and his agent.***

This send-up of television celebrity sees comedian and 'TV star' Richie Rich striving to keep in with his peers (the likes of 'Brucie' and 'Tarby'), but continually hampered by his useless hypochondriac agent, Ralph Filthy, who can never get him any work, and his mindless minder, Eddie Catflap. The sketches are punctuated by various asides to the camera. Penned by Ben Elton, the series offers more than an echo of the team's earlier success with THE YOUNG ONES.

Fimbles ✳✳

UK (Novel Entertainment) Children's Entertainment. BBC 1 2002–4
DVD: BBC

Executive Producers **Mike Watts, Claire Elstow**
Producer **Lucinda Whiteley**

● ***Fun, games and education with a family of striped creatures.***

Aimed at the 2–4-year-old market, *Fimbles* is a colourful preschool education and entertainment show that aired first on the digital channel CBeebies. Its stars are three brightly coloured, striped, podgy, hippo-like creatures named Fimbo, Florrie and Baby Pom. Fimbo (aged five) is the busy one, always looking for things to do and getting into scrapes. Florrie (four) is inquisitive and enjoys singing and dancing, while Baby Pom, being the youngest of the trio (two), is excitable, independent and keen. Together they inhabit Fimble Valley, a place of wonder that has welcoming features called Purple Meadow, the Happy Hollow, the Comfy Corner, the Play Dips, the Busy Base, the magical Tinkling Tree and the Bubble Fall. Their friends are Rockit the frog and Ribble the chick and parental guidance is provided by Bessie the bird and Roly Mo the mole (later given his own spin-off short, *The Roly Mo Show*: BBC 2 2004–). The Fimbles' days are spent singing songs, listening to stories and discovering interesting new things – the last usually imminent when the trio declare they have a 'Fimbling feeling' that sets their fingers a-twinkling.

The Fimble characters were created by illustrator Sarah Hayes and are brought to television using actors in costume – Adam Blaug, Samantha Dodd, Denise Dove, Leah Green, Holli Hoffman and John Tobias. The Fimbles' heads, meanwhile, are animatronically controlled. Inevitably, a new children's magazine and a raft of cuddly merchandise accompanied the series' launch.

Final Cut, The

See *House of Cards*.

Finch, John

Liverpool-born scriptwriter whose work has generally focused on Northern working-class situations. Among his credits have been A FAMILY AT WAR, SAM, *This Year, Next Year, Flesh and Blood, Spoils of War* and episodes of THE ODD MAN, *The Villains, The Hard Word, Nightingale's Boys, Capstick's Law* and CORONATION STREET (also as producer).

Fine Romance, A ✳✳

UK (LWT) Situation Comedy. ITV 1981–4
DVD: Network

Laura Dalton	**Judi Dench**
Mike Selway	**Michael Williams**
Helen Barker	**Susan Penhaligon**
Phil Barker	**Richard Warwick**
Harry	**Geoffrey Rose**

Creator/Writer **Bob Larbey**

Producers **James Cellan Jones, Don Leaver**

● ***A middle-aged couple fumble their way through a relationship.***

Laura Dalton, a linguist from Fulham, and Mike Selway, a landscape gardener, are perfect for each other, or so it seems to their friends and relations. They themselves are unsure, though, which leads to much humming and ha-ing and an on-off romance. In their early 40s and each set in their ways, they are incapable of grasping the nettle and, despite much prompting from Laura's sister, Helen, and her husband, Phil (who instigates their meeting by arranging a party), it takes them three years to make the right decision.

Things proved simpler in real life, where stars Judi Dench and Michael Williams were husband and wife. Judi Dench also sang the theme song.

Fingerbobs ✳

UK (Q3) Children's Entertainment. BBC 1 1972
DVD: Contender Entertainment

Presenter **Rick Jones**

Writers **Joanne and Michael Cole**

● ***Simple puppetry, music and songs for toddlers.***

The original digital television. In the guise of Yoffy, a maker of finger puppets, bearded PLAY SCHOOL refugee Rick Jones uses this series to introduce preschool children to such creations as Fingermouse, Scampi, Flash (a tortoise) and Gulliver (a seagull). With the little paper puppets fitting snugly on his gloved fingers ('Yoffy lifts a finger, and a mouse is there'), Jones moves on to examine the shapes and textures of assorted other materials, from feathers and stones to string and paint, over the course of the 13 episodes. These items often then feature in an animated story, with simple songs to help fill the 15-minute WATCH WITH MOTHER lunchtime strand. A similar series, *Fingermouse*, followed in 1985.

Finlay, Frank

CBE (1926–)

Lancashire-born actor, often in controversial roles. His portrayal of CASANOVA in Dennis Potter's 1971 series enraged Mrs Whitehouse, and he followed it up with performances as publisher Peter Manson in the equally sensational BOUQUET OF BARBED WIRE and *Another Bouquet*. He was the Führer in the drama *The Death of Adolf Hitler*, and among his many other appearances have been parts in plays and series like TARGET LUNA, *Doctor Knock, This Happy Breed, Candide, The Adventures of Don Quixote* (Sancho Panza), *84 Charing Cross Road*, COUNT DRACULA (Van Helsing), *Saturday, Sunday, Monday, The Last Campaign*, TALES OF THE UNEXPECTED, BLACKADDER, *Aspects of Love, The Other Side*, LOVEJOY, HEARTBEAT, COMMON AS MUCK (Derek), HOW DO YOU WANT ME? (Astley Yardley), LONGITUDE (Admiral Wager), *The Sins* (Uncle Irwin Green), *Station Jim* (Riorden Sr), THE LOST PRINCE (Anthony Asquith), EROICA (Haydn), PRIME SUSPECT (Arnold Tennison), LIFE BEGINS (Eric Thornhill) and *Johnny and the Bomb* (Tom Maxwell), as well as assorted Shakespearean roles. He also starred in the ARMCHAIR THEATRE pilot for the comedy NEVER MIND THE QUALITY, FEEL THE WIDTH (Patrick Kelly).

Finney, Albert

(1936–)

Salford-born, RADA-trained actor whose TV appearances have increased later in his career. Among his small-screen credits have been *Pope John Paul II* (title role), *The Biko Inquest, The Endless Game* (Alec Hillsden), *The Image* (Jason Cromwell), THE GREEN MAN (Maurice Allington), KARAOKE/COLD LAZARUS (Daniel Feeld), *Screen Two*'s *A Man of No Importance* (Alfie Byrne), *Nostromo* (Dr Monygham), the award-winning single drama A RATHER ENGLISH MARRIAGE (Reggie Conyngham-Jervis), *My Uncle Silas* (title role) and THE GATHERING STORM (Winston Churchill). Finney has been married to two actresses, Jane Wenham and Anouk Aimée.

Finnigan, Judy

(1948–)

Daytime TV presenter, for many years co-host of ITV's *This Morning* with her second husband, Richard Madeley, and for a while a live evening chat show, *Tonight with Richard Madeley and Judy Finnigan*. They have since taken their daytime chat show, *Richard and Judy*, to Channel 4. Finnigan's career began as a researcher with Granada and progressed via the company's regional news magazines. She also reported for Anglia TV. *Classic Coronation Street* saw her introduce epic moments from the long-running soap, while, as first presenter of *We Can Work It Out*, she fronted ITV's answer to WATCHDOG.

Fire Crackers ✳✳

UK (ATV) Situation Comedy. ITV 1964–5

Charlie	**Alfred Marks**
Jumbo	**Joe Baker**
Weary Willie	**Sidney Bromley**
Loverboy	**Ronnie Brody**
Hairpin	**Cardew Robinson**
Tadpole	**Clive Elliott**
George	**Colin Douglas**
Station Officer Blazer	**John Arnatt**
Leading Fireman Piggott	**Norman Chappell**

Producer **Alan Tarrant**

● ***The slapstick adventures of a village fire brigade.***

Set in the fictitious settlement of Cropper's End (population 70), *Fire Crackers* concerns the inept local firemen and their decrepit 1907 engine, which is known as Bessie. Somehow this particular band of fire-fighters have been forgotten by the powers that be, so, even though they happily draw their salary, they never need to man the pumps. Instead, in times of trouble they call out Station Officer Blazer and his crew from the neighbouring town, allowing Charlie, the fire chief, and his work-shy team to spend more time cadging pints in The Cropper's Arms. It is just as well, as their token attempts at fire drills usually end in disaster anyway.

Fireball XL5 ★★

UK (AP Films/ATV/ITC) Children's Science Fiction. ITV 1962–3
DVD: Carlton

Voices:
Col. Steve Zodiac .... **Paul Maxwell**
Prof. Matthew Matic .... **David Graham**
Venus .... **Sylvia Anderson**
Commander Zero .... **John Bluthal**
Lt. 90 .... **David Graham**
Zoonie .... **David Graham**
Robert the Robot .... **Gerry Anderson**

Creators **Gerry Anderson, Sylvia Anderson**
Producer **Gerry Anderson**

● ***The crew of a state-of-the-art spacecraft protects Earth from invaders.***

Gerry Anderson's second venture into Supermarionation (high-tech puppetry) centres on the exploits of dashing Steve Zodiac, the handsome, blond, dare-devil commander of the spacecraft *Fireball XL5*, one of the XL series of faster-than-light rockets. Working for World Space Patrol in the year 2063, the ship is assigned to Sector 25 of the Solar System to counter the aggressive advances and cunning subterfuge of extraterrestrials like Mr and Mrs Spacespy. Zodiac is ably supported by Venus, his French girlfriend, who is also a Doctor of Space Medicine, and Professor Matt Matic, the navigator, technical genius and designer of *XL5*. Robert, a transparent robot, is the co-pilot and a 'lazoon' named Zoonie is also aboard. Missions are co-ordinated by Commander Zero and his junior, Lt. 90, from Space City. The adventures take Zodiac and his crew all across the galaxy. If a planetary landing is in order, the rocket's nose-cone (*Fireball Junior*) detaches itself and flies the team to the surface. On the planet, they travel on souped-up scooters known as jet-mobiles.

Fireball XL5 was the only Gerry Anderson series to be fully networked in the USA. Its theme song, 'Fireball', by Don Spencer, narrowly missed the UK Top 30 in 1963.

Fireman Sam ★★

UK (Bumper/HIT) Animation. BBC 1 1987–8; 1990; 1994; BBC 2 1997; 2005
DVD: HIT Entertainment

Narrator/Voices **John Alderton, John Sparkes, Joanna Ruiz, Sarah Hadland**

Creator **Rob Lee**
Producers **Ian Frampton, John Walker, Robin Lyons**

● ***The adventures of a Welsh fireman and his colleagues.***

'The hero next door', Fireman Sam is the daring and caring central figure in the small but dedicated Pontypandy fire service. On the word of the whiskery Station Officer Steele (a ringer for Windsor Davies), Sam, with colleagues Trevor Evans and Elvis Cridlington, hops aboard his engine, Jupiter (registration J999), and rides to the rescue of cats up trees, kids stranded on thin ice and shops about to be engulfed with flames. Adventures in the Welsh valleys usually centre on Bella Lasagne's café or Dilys Price's grocery store, with Dilys's mischievous son, Norman, all too often at the heart of affairs. His delinquency contrasts with the good, but occasionally misguided, behaviour of twins Sarah and James – personal favourites of action man Sam himself. The series first aired in Welsh on S4C, under the title *Sam Tân*. Maldwyn Pope sings the theme song. A new series of 26 episodes (with new-look figures and new song words) was produced in the new millennium, introducing new characters such as the Flood family, Dusty the dog and bush pilot Tom! Comedian John Sparkes stepped in as narrator, joined by the vocal talents of Joanna Ruiz and Sarah Hadland.

First Born ★★★

UK (BBC/Australian Broadcasting Corporation/Television New Zealand) Science Fiction. BBC 1 1988

Edward Forester .... **Charles Dance**
Ann Forester .... **Julie Peasgood**
Lancing .... **Philip Madoc**
Chris Knott .... **Peter Tilbury**
Nancy Knott .... **Rosemary McHale**
Dr Graham .... **Roshan Seth**
Marais .... **Marc de Jonge**
Jessop .... **Niven Boyd**
Emily Jessop .... **Sharon Duce**
Gor .... **Jamie Foster**
Young Gor .... **Peter Wiggins**
Gerry .... **Nina Zuckerman**
Nell Forester .... **Gabrielle Anwar**
Young Nell .... **Beth Pearce**

Writer **Ted Whitehead**
Producer **Sally Head**

● ***A scientist creates a man/gorilla hybrid, with dangerous consequences.***

It is genetics specialist Edward Forester's God-like desire to create a new breed of creature, one endowed with all man's intelligence but without the aggressive instincts associated with humankind. To this end, he begins experimenting with female gorilla cells and his own sperm. The result is the birth of a man-gorilla, which he names Gordon, or Gor. After losing his infantile ape hair, Gor matures into a model son but, eventually confronted with facts about his birth, demands to see his mother, a gorilla named Mary, who beats him to death in a violent rage. The consequences of Forester's genetic tamperings are not at an end, however, as his daughter, Nell, then gives birth to Gor's child, a baby clearly of mixed species.

This three-part series was an adaptation of the novel *Gor Saga* by Maureen Duffy.

First Churchills, The ★★

UK (BBC) Historical Drama. BBC 2 1969
DVD: Acorn Media

John Churchill .... **John Neville**
Sarah Churchill .... **Susan Hampshire**
Sidney Godolphin .... **John Standing**
Charles II .... **James Villiers**
York .... **John Westbrook**
Princess Mary .... **Lisa Daniely**
Princess Anne .... **Margaret Tyzack**
Shaftesbury .... **Frederick Peisley**

Writer/Producer **Donald Wilson**

● ***Period drama charting the distant ancestry of the famous 20th-century prime minister.***

Long before Sir Winston was even a twinkle in his father's eye, his family was heavily entwined with British politics – as far back as Stuart times, when John Churchill wrestled for power in the court of King Charles II. Putting his military skills to good use in assorted European battles, Churchill won from the sovereign the title of the first Duke of Marlborough and, with his wife, Sarah (a lady-in-waiting to the future Queen Anne), instigated the famous line of statesmen bearing his name. Written, directed and produced by Donald Wilson, the series ran to 12 episodes.

First of the Summer Wine

See *Last of the Summer Wine.*

First Tuesday ★★

UK (Yorkshire) Documentary. ITV 1983–93

Presenters **Jonathan Dimbleby, Olivia O'Leary**

Powerful series of documentaries on wide-ranging subjects of contemporary significance.

Shown in a post-*News at Ten* slot, *First Tuesday* offered a collection of influential documentaries on subjects as diverse as housewife strippers, joy riders, radioactive pollution and Siamese twins. One notable programme followed a Geordie living and working in China and another investigated the man who shot John Lennon. Using pictures to tell their own story, the series also exposed the abuse dished out in old people's homes, went behind the scenes of the Hillsborough disaster and looked again at the case of the Guildford Four. Jonathan Dimbleby was the first presenter, succeeded by Olivia O'Leary in later years. The name was derived from the fact that the programme was screened on the first Tuesday of the month.

Firth, Colin

(1960–)

Hampshire-born actor whose most celebrated role has been as Mr Darcy in PRIDE AND PREJUDICE. His other credits have included *Camille, Dutch Girls, Lost Empires* (Richard Herncastle), TUMBLEDOWN (Robert Lawrence), *Hostages*, THE RUTH RENDELL MYSTERIES, *Master of the Moor* (Stephen Whalby), *Performance*'s *The Deep Blue Sea* (Freddie Page) and *The Widowing of Mrs Holroyd* (Charles Holroyd), *Screen Two*'s *The Hour of the Pig* (Richard Courtois), plus *Nostromo* (Charles Gould), *The Turn of the Screw* (Master), *Donovan Quick* (title role) and CONSPIRACY (Wilhelm Stuckart). He is the brother of actor Jonathan Firth.

Firth, Peter

(1953–)

Bradford-born former child actor, who played Archie Weeks in THE FLAXTON BOYS and Scooper in HERE COME THE DOUBLE DECKERS. Today, he is best known as tough MI5 supremo Harry Pearce in SPOOKS. In between, Firth played Dorian Gray in a PLAY OF THE MONTH version of *The Picture of Dorian Gray*, Dominick Hide in two PLAYS FOR TODAY, THE FLIPSIDE OF DOMINICK HIDE and *Another Flip for Dominick*, Henry Tilney in *Northanger Abbey*, Dr James Radcliffe in HEARTBEAT and Alex Turnbull in THE BROKER'S MAN. Other roles have come in ARTHUR OF THE BRITONS, THE PROTECTORS, TALES OF THE UNEXPECTED, *Tickets for the Titanic*, ANNA LEE, SOLDIER, SOLDIER, AND THE BEAT GOES ON, KAVANAGH QC, HOLDING ON and THE VICE, among other programmes. Firth has also featured in US series like THAT'S LIFE and LAW AND ORDER: SPECIAL VICTIMS UNIT.

Fish, Michael

MBE (1944–)

Long-serving BBC weatherman (1974–2004), the presenter who unfortunately assured viewers that there were no hurricanes on the way in 1987. He has also made guest appearances on other shows.

Fisher, Gregor

(1953–)

Scottish comic actor, best known as the string-vested philosopher, Rab C. Nesbitt, a spin-off character from NAKED VIDEO. Another *Naked Video* product which Fisher took into its own off-shoot was THE BALDY MAN. Fisher also starred in *Scotch and Wry* and as Para Handy in THE TALES OF PARA HANDY, Hector Robertson in *Brotherly Love*, The Fly in GORMENGHAST, Perks in THE RAILWAY CHILDREN and James Stewart in *Kidnapped*, with earlier appearances coming in such series as FOXY LADY (Hector Ross), *City Lights*, THE BILL, BOON and CHANCER.

Fist of Fun ★★

UK (BBC) Comedy. BBC 2 1995–6

Stewart Lee, Richard Herring, Peter Baynham, Kevin Eldon

Writers **Stewart Lee, Richard Herring**
Producer **Sarah Smith**

Off-beat sketches from a young comic duo and colleagues.

Successful radio comics Lee and Herring made the transition to television in this sketch series in which they were primarily supported by Peter Baynham and, later, Kevin Eldon. Hobbies played a big part in the often surreal humour as did such diverse and wacky subjects as the people of Somerset, the theory of relativity, driving instructors and a girl who smells of Spam. Baynham offered the character of Welsh Peter, a lonely chef living in Balham. In series two, news for people called Ian was presented by Ian Lewis and Ian Ketterman.

Fitzgerald, Tara

(1967–)

Sussex-born actress whose early television credits included the parts of Dollie Stokesay in *Anglo-Saxon Attitudes*, Victoria Mordaunt in CATHERINE COOKSON'S *The Black Candle*, and Emily in *Six Characters in Search of an Author*. She featured as Polly in THE CAMOMILE LAWN, took the title role in *The Vacillations of Poppy Carew*, and appeared as Catherine in *Fall from Grace* and as Adele Rice in *Screen Two*'s *A Man of No Importance*. Later major roles include Helen Graham in THE TENANT OF WILDFELL HALL, Marian Halcombe in THE WOMAN IN WHITE, Grace in *The Student Prince*, Beth in *Little White Lies*, Lady Dona St Columb in *Frenchman's Creek*, Zoe Walters in *In the Name of Love*, DI Harkness in *Like Father, Like Son* and Kat Ashley in *The Virgin Queen*. Among her guest appearances are parts in CADFAEL, MURDER IN MIND, AGATHA CHRISTIE'S MARPLE and ROSE AND MALONEY.

five

The UK's fifth terrestrial TV channel finally arrived in 1997, after years of uncertainty over the viability of such a service. The channel was first proposed in the late 1980s, when it was suggested that a couple of channels then devoted to non-broadcasting concerns could be freed up for transmissions – although there was a fly in the ointment, in that domestic video recorders in some parts of the country would need retuning to prevent interference from the new signal. This imposed a heavy financial commitment on prospective broadcasters, as they would have had to pay for the retuning exercise.

The ITC advertised the Channel 5 franchise in 1992, but only one application was received and this was declined. After a thorough review of the prospects for the channel, the franchise was re-advertised in 1994, the winning bid announced a year later as coming from C5 Broadcasting, which satisfied the Commission with regard to both programming commitments and commercial viability – including the cost of retuning video recorders. Despite rival bidder Virgin TV gaining a judicial review, C5 Broadcasting took to the air on 30 March 1997, employing the then five Spice Girls to publicize the launch. After a half-hour introductory slot, the first scheduled programme was the new soap, *Family Affairs*. Only about 60 per cent of UK homes were able to receive the channel at first, but its coverage has increased since (helped by the fact it is now available on digital services).

Initial response to Channel 5's programming from the ITC was good, with the freshness and vitality it brought to children's, religious and news programming being especially welcomed. However, in 2000 there was widespread criticism of the channel's late-night programming, which had come to rely heavily on 'adult' material. The channel fought back, however, and gained new respect for its treatment of history and art in particular. In 2002, the on-air name of the channel was shortened to five.

Channel 5 is now owned by the RTL Group. David Elstein was the channel's first chief executive (1997–2000), succeeded by Dawn Airey and then, in 2003, by Jane Lighting.

Five Children and It ✳✳

UK (BBC) Children's Drama. BBC 1 1991
DVD: BBC

Cyril	**Simon Godwin**
Anthea	**Nicole Mowat**
Robert ('Bob')	**Charlie Richards**
Jane	**Tamzen Audas**
Martha	**Laura Brattan**
Psammead	**Francis Wright** *(voice only)*
The Lamb	**Lewis and Alexander Wilson**
Andrew Beale	**Paul Shearer**
Mother	**Mary Conlon**
Lady Chittenden	**Penny Morrell**

Writer **Helen Cresswell**
Producer **Richard Callanan**

Victorian brothers and sisters discover a sand fairy that grants them wishes.

Cyril, Anthea, Bob, Jane and baby brother Hilary (commonly known as 'The Lamb') have arrived at their family's country home (The White House) after living a stuffy life in London. Their father is away and their mother also must now leave them, to look after their sick grandmother. The excited children are left in the care of young housekeeper Martha and are allowed to play anywhere on the estate. They discover an ancient sandpit and, while digging, unearth a strange, hairy, grumpy creature (portrayed by an animatronic puppet) that explains it is a psammead, or sand fairy. It is the last survivor of the species, the others having died of colds when the seas rose and soaked their sandy homes. The psammead also reveals that it has the power to grant one or two wishes each day to the children and thus the adventures begin. Inevitably there is little pleasure in what the over-ambitious siblings gain from their wishes, and plenty of lessons about what is right/wrong/sensible to desire. Among the wishes (some careless) that are granted are to be as beautiful as the day, to be rich and to have wings. They also summon up a real medieval castle, complete with besieging soldiers, and see their baby brother fully grown up. Thankfully each wish fades away at sunset and normality returns. Wrapped up in the children's escapades are Martha's suitor, Andrew Beale, and snooty, child-hating local aristocrat Lady Chittenden.

This six-part fantasy, with music by Michael Omer, was directed by Marilyn Fox, with the script adapted by Helen Cresswell from the 1902 novel of the same name by E. Nesbit. It had previously been dramatized in two episodes by the BBC in 1951. A sequel, *The Return of the Psammead* (BBC 1 1993, starring Anna Massey), which featured different children, was not the invention of Nesbit, but was penned entirely by Cresswell.

Five O'Clock Club ✳✳

UK (Associated-Rediffusion) Children's Entertainment.
ITV 1963–6

Presenters **Muriel Young, Howard Williams, Wally Whyton**

Twice-weekly light magazine for younger viewers.

Taking its cue from the earlier series *Lucky Dip* and *Tuesday Rendezvous*, very much in the same vein, *Five O'Clock Club* was a popular Tuesday and Friday offering for the under-12s. Its hosts, Muriel Young, Howard Williams and, later, Wally Whyton, presented a mixed bag of pop singers and other guests, and gently sparred with their puppet co-stars, Fred Barker (a dog voiced by Basil Brush man Ivan Owen) and Ollie Beak (an opinionated Liverpudlian owl in a school cap, voiced by Whyton, who resurfaced in the 1970s pop show *Get It Together*). Additional items included guitar tips from Bert Weedon, hobbies with Jimmy Hanley and animals with Grahame Dangerfield. The programme became *Ollie and Fred's Five O'Clock Club* in 1965. The same year, the cheeky puppets popped up alongside presenter Marjorie Sigley in *Five O'Clock Funfair*.

Flambards ✳✳

UK (YTV) Drama. ITV 1979
DVD: Cinema Club

Christina Parsons/Russell	**Christine McKenna**
Mr Russell	**Edward Judd**
Mark Russell	**Steven Grives**
William Russell	**Alan Parnaby**
Dick Wright	**Sebastian Abineri**
Violet Wright	**Gillian Davey**
Mary	**Rosalie Williams**
Fowler	**Frank Mills**
Aunt Grace	**Olive Pendleton**

Dorothy .... **Carol Leader**
Sandy Hardcastle .... **Peter Settelden**
Percy Adams .... **John Ringham**
Joe .... **David Huscroft**

Executive Producer **David Cunliffe**
Producer **Leonard Lewis**

● ***A teenage orphan is forced to live with her angry uncle and cousins.***

In 1909 plucky Christina Parsons, a 16-year-old orphan, is taken under the wing of boozy, grouchy Mr Russell, her mother's crippled half-brother. She goes to live at Flambards, his decaying estate near Hornhill in the Essex countryside. It is a horsey household, and she learns to ride with the local hunt but there are few other pleasures at Flambards. She finds more in common with housekeeper Mary and young groom Dick than her cousin, Mark, who is a sadistic bully who wants her for his wife. However, Mark's gentler younger brother, William, is altogether more sympathetic. He hates horses and is fascinated by the new craze of aviation. William and Christina grow ever closer and eventually leave Flambards together to start a new life in London. William becomes an aircraft mechanic/flying instructor and Christina takes a job in The Chase Hotel, owned by the father of a new friend, Dorothy, whose boyfriend is also a flyer. The series follows their lives, through her marriage to William, the difficulties of the World War I years, and the tragedy that strikes everyone. She finally returns as mistress to Flambards, having inherited the money her mother left in trust until she was 21.

Based on a trilogy of romantic novels by Kathleen Peyton, the 13-part series was adapted by various writers, including Alan Plater. David Fanshawe provided the eerie music (some whistled).

Flame Trees of Thika, The ✶✶

UK (Euston Films/Thames) Drama. ITV 1981
DVD: Fremantle Home Entertainment

Tilly Grant .... **Hayley Mills**
Robin Grant .... **David Robb**
Elspeth Grant .... **Holly Aird**
Major .... **John Nettleton**
Mr Roos .... **Morgan Sheppard**
Mrs Nimmo .... **Carol Macready**
Ian Crawfurd .... **Ben Cross**
Lettice Palmer .... **Sharon Mughan**
Hereward Palmer .... **Nicholas Jones**
Alec .... **Dai Bradley**

Writer **John Hawkesworth**
Producers **John Hawkesworth, Christopher Neame**
Executive Producer **Verity Lambert**

● ***A young English girl charts her new life in East Africa.***

Rattling across the sun-baked plains in an ox cart loaded with their worldly possessions are 11-year-old Elspeth Grant and her mother, Tilly. They are on their way to Thika, said to be a 'place on a map where two rivers meet', somewhere in deepest Kenya. The year is 1913 and the country is known at the time as the East African Protectorate. The Grants, including coffee-farmer husband Robin, are heading into a new life, thousands of miles away from home, where the lights are beginning to dim as World War I approaches. What they discover is a life-changing experience among the proud wild beasts of the bush and beneath the glorious scarlet canopies of the indigenous flame trees. Elspeth enjoys a magical childhood, with Twinkle her pet duiker (antelope) for company. Less happy with the rigours of African life is neighbour Lettice Palmer, who accompanies her husband, Hereward, in this adventure but is, it is all too obvious, more at home in the comfortable middle-class drawing rooms of England. There are further complications when Lettice's looks attract the attentions of local big-game hunter Ian Crawfurd. The seven-part drama, directed by Roy Ward Baker, was based on the autobiographical novel of the same name by Elspeth Huxley, which, it was reported, inspired writer John Hawkesworth as he flew off on a safari holiday. Filmed over 18 weeks in 1980, all footage was original, which meant hours of patient waiting for animals to oblige with required behaviour and hundreds of miles of driving to capture the sporadically flowering flame trees wherever they happened to be in bloom.

Flamingo Road ✶✶

US (Lorimar/MF) Drama. BBC 1 1981–3 (US: NBC 1981–2)

Sheriff Titus Semple .... **Howard Duff**
Sam Curtis .... **John Beck**
Claude Weldon .... **Kevin McCarthy**
Eudora Weldon .... **Barbara Rush**
Skipper Weldon .... **Woody Brown**
Constance Weldon/Carlyle ..... **Morgan Fairchild**
Fielding Carlyle .... **Mark Harmon**
Lane Ballou .... **Cristina Raines**
Lute-Mae Sanders .... **Stella Stevens**
Sande Swanson .... **Cynthia Sikes**
Elmo Tyson .... **Peter Donat**
Michael Tyrone .... **David Selby**

● ***Greed, corruption and scandal in a sleepy Southern town.***

Based on the 1949 film starring Joan Crawford, *Flamingo Road* was another of the DALLAS/DYNASTY clones that attempted to secure a permanent prime-time slot. In the event, the series was short-lived, lasting only two seasons.

The stories are set in the small town of Truro, Florida, where the wealthiest street is Flamingo Road. On Flamingo Road lives Claude Weldon, proprietor of the local paper mill, together with his wife Eudora, son Skipper (who runs the mill) and spoiled adopted daughter Constance. Constance marries Fielding Carlyle, a local politician, whose advancement is owed in no small measure to the manipulative sheriff of Truro, Titus Semple. Semple knows the ins and outs of the whole neighbourhood, including the sort of secrets that make him all-powerful. Fielding really loves Lane Ballou, singer at Lute-Mae's casino-cum-brothel, but is badgered into the marriage that will best suit his – or, rather, Semple's – plans. Lane is now romantically entwined with construction developer Sam Curtis.

Also featured is Elmo Tyson, the owner of the town's newspaper, *The Clarion*, and another major character arrives in the shape of Michael Tyrone, an angry tycoon out to avenge the execution of his innocent father. His schemes introduce murder and voodoo to the dozy old town, spicing up the family jealousies, business rivalries and political intrigue that dominate the sleazy storylines.

Flashing Blade, The ★★

France (Pathé Cinema Paris) Children's Historical Drama. BBC 1 1969
DVD: Network

François de Recci .... **Robert Etcheverry**
Guillot .... **Jacques Balutin**
Isabelle de Sospel .... **Geneviève Casile**
Mazarin .... **Gianni Esposito**
Duke de Sospel .... **Jean Martinelli**
Don Alonso .... **Mario Pilar**
Bodinelli .... **Angelo Bardi**
Mireille .... **Claude Gensac**

● ***A French knight rides to the rescue of his beleaguered countrymen.***

This 12-part swashbuckler is devoted to the daring exploits of one François de Recci, a French chevalier dedicated to the overthrow of the iniquitous Spanish. His story begins when he arrives at Casal fort and finds it besieged by the enemy. But efforts to bring help to his countrymen lead him into scrape after scrape, encountering adversaries such as Don Alonso and finding brave allies like Mireille. All the while, Guillot is de Recci's loyal companion. The series – directed by Yannick Andréi and known in the original French as *Le Cavalier Tempête* – was dubbed into English.

Flaxton Boys, The ★★

UK (Yorkshire) Children's Drama. ITV 1969–71; 1973

1969
Jonathan Flaxton .... **David Smith**
Lucy Flaxton .... **Penelope Lee**
Nathan .... **James Hayter**
Archie Weeks .... **Peter Firth**
Flora .... **Molly Urquhart**
Sir Peregrine Stilgoe .... **Richard Gale**

1970
Andrew Flaxton .... **Moultrie Kelsall**
Archie Weekes .... **Hugh Cross**
Peter Weekes .... **Dai Bradley**
Sarah Weekes .... **Lila Kaye**
David Stilgoe .... **Philip Maskery**
Sir Tarquin Stilgoe .... **Richard Gale**
Barnaby Sweet .... **Victor Winding**
Jacklin Flaxton .... **Gerry Cowan**

1971
Jonathan Flaxton .... **Alan Guy**
William Pickford .... **John Ash**
Benjamin Sweet .... **Victor Winding**
Lady Jane Flaxton .... **Veronica Hurst**
Mary Porter .... **Heather Page**
Miles Osborne .... **Richard Gale**
Roger Grafton .... **Gerry Cowan**
Revd Albermarle Dobson Partridge .... **Nicholas Pennell**
Sgt Cornfield .... **Royston Tickner**

1973
Matthew Flaxton .... **Andrew Packett**
Terry Nichols .... **Philip Baldwin**
Elizabeth Flaxton .... **Joanna Jones**
Benjamin Sweet .... **Victor Winding**
Edith .... **Pamela Duncan**

Narrator **Gerry Cowan** *(all series)*

Executive Producer **Jess Yates**
Producer **Robert D. Cardona**

● ***The adventures of four generations of boys living in a creepy Yorkshire hall.***

Flaxton Hall is a large, castellated country house near the village of Carliston, between Harrogate and Hull. The imposing, creaky structure has a gloomy, spooky atmosphere, as young Jonathan Flaxton and his mother, Lucy, discover when they inherit the old pile in mysterious circumstances. The year is 1854 and the boy's father, Captain Andrew Flaxton, is missing in action in the Crimea. Rumours abound that there is a fortune hidden somewhere within the ivy-covered hall and keen to get his evil hands on it is the local tyrant, Sir Peregrine Stilgoe, of neighbouring Stilgoe Hall. However, when Captain Flaxton finally returns home from the war, Sir Peregrine is sent to jail and the family themselves unearth the treasure that secures their future. In the meantime, Jonathan and his best friend, Archie Weeks, have plenty of adventures exploring the hall, its grounds and the moorland around it.

In series two (1970), set in 1890, a new generation of 'Flaxton boys' takes up residence. Peter Weekes is the son of Archie, and he is joined in his adventures by David Stilgoe, ward of Sir Tarquin Stilgoe, the equally despicable son of the disgraced Sir Peregrine. A sworn enemy of the Flaxton family, Tarquin has plans to take over the hall in order to release the coal reserves located beneath it. He finds a willing ally in the ruthless Jacklin Flaxton, a distant member of the ancestral family who, on the death of old Captain Andrew, has claimed the house in the absence of Jonathan Flaxton. Jonathan (now in his thirties) had stormed out after a row with his father and has since disappeared. However, when Peter sneaks into Jonathan's old room, he finds evidence to suggest that Jonathan may still be alive and so, along with David, embarks on a quest to find the rightful heir to Flaxton Hall. The boys are assisted in their search by lovable rogue Barnaby Sweet.

The 1971 series moved the Flaxton story on to 1928. Young Jonathan Flaxton brings a close schoolfriend, Londoner William Pickford, back to Yorkshire for the summer holidays. Despite the demise of the Stilgoes (there are plans to turn Stilgoe Hall into an orphanage), there are still villains abroad to add intrigue and excitement to life in the hall. Particularly troublesome are a pair of forgers, Miles Osborne and Roger Grafton. On the boys' side is Benjamin Sweet, the amiable son of old Barnaby.

Benjamin resurfaces in the final series (1973). The year is now 1945 and Flaxton Hall has been used as an army camp during the war. As the troops begin to leave, one visitor decides to stay. He is Londoner Terry Nichols, an evacuee who has no home to return to. Terry and Matthew Flaxton, son of Jonathan (away with the war), become the new Flaxton boys. Benjamin has been in the navy and his return helps restore some normality to life at Flaxton Hall, but there is still much excitement in the boys' lives.

Using Prokofiev's *Classical Symphony* as its rousing theme music, *The Flaxton Boys* was an early children's drama offering from Yorkshire Television. Educational in tone, it proved to be popular Sunday teatime fare. Among its writers was BBC's darts commentator Sid Waddell. A number of cast members featured in more than one series, one of whom was narrator Gerry Cowan. The series was filmed at Ripley Castle, near Harrogate.

Fletcher, Cyril

(1913–2005)

THAT'S LIFE's 'odd ode' performer. Cyril Fletcher's TV career stretches way back to the medium's earliest days. It was in 1936 that he appeared on the fledgling BBC service, reciting his novel poems and participating in the Corporation's first pantomime, *Dick Whittington*. He also appeared in revues like *Tele-Ho!* After the war, he was often seen on TV in the company of his wife, Betty Astell. His seaside pier show, *Saturday Night Attraction*, was screened in 1949, and he went on to join the panel of WHAT'S MY LINE?, take part in the religious series *Sunday Story* and star in his own ITV show. He joined *That's Life* in the 1970s, composing his odd odes and selecting bizarre newspaper clippings. He also presented gardening programmes.

Flextech

International media company which merged with cable TV provider Telewest in 2000 and is now NTL's content division, following the merger of NTL and Telewest in 2006. It has notable television holdings in the UK, including the cable/digital channels Bravo, Living TV, Trouble, Challenge TV and Ftn. In addition, Flextech/Telewest owns 50 per cent of UKTV (the other 50 per cent belonging to BBC Worldwide), provider of UKTV Gold, UKTV Style, UKTV Drama, UKTV History, UKTV Food, UKTV People, UKTV Documentary, UKTV G2 and UKTV Bright Ideas.

Flintstones, The ✱✱✱

US (Hanna-Barbera) Cartoon. ITV 1961–6 (US: ABC 1960–6)
DVD: Warner Home Video

Voices:

Fred Flintstone .... **Alan Reed**
Wilma Flintstone .... **Jean Vander Pyl**
Barney Rubble .... **Mel Blanc**
Betty Rubble .... **Bea Benaderet**
Gerry Johnson
Dino .... **Mel Blanc**
Pebbles Flintstone .... **Jean Vander Pyl**
Bamm Bamm Rubble .... **Don Messick**

Creators/Executive Producers **William Hanna, Joseph Barbera**

● ***Comic animation imaginatively placing 1960s lifestyles in a Stone Age setting.***

The Flintstones are Fred and Wilma, with little daughter Pebbles an addition to the family in later years. They live (with their pet dinosaur, Dino) in the city of Bedrock some time around one million years BC. Loud-mouthed, hapless Fred works as a crane operator at the Rockhead & Quarry Construction Co., alongside his next-door neighbour and best buddy, Barney Rubble. Barney's wife, Betty, is a close friend of Wilma's and the Rubbles soon extend their family, too, when they adopt a baby boy, Bamm Bamm.

The cartoon's humour is largely derived from the fanciful idea of presenting prehistoric man with 20th-century mod cons. The primitive inhabitants of Bedrock have the lot, if in a very basic form. Fred's hi-fi system, for example, consists of a bird with a large beak scratching out sounds from a stone disc, and the Flintstones' car, complete with tail fins, runs only when they run (it is feet-powered). The household waste-disposal system is a gluttonous buzzard hidden under the sink; a baby elephant on roller skates acts as Wilma's vacuum cleaner, while Fred's crane at work is a dinosaur. Their newspaper, *The Daily Slate*, arrives on heavy stone slabs and, of course, they own a Stoneway piano. Several famous 'guest stars' make appearances, including Perry Masonry, the crack barrister, actor Stony Curtis and TV host Ed Sullystone.

The Flintstones (originally planned as *The Flagstones*) had the honour of being the first animation to be made specifically for US TV's prime time, and is still being run on TV stations across the world, Fred's yell of 'Yabba Dabba Do!' becoming one of TV's best-remembered catchphrases. The Stone Age setting apart, it borrowed much from the hit American series THE HONEYMOONERS, which starred Jackie Gleason and revolved around pal-neighbours who were constantly in hot water. A feature film, *A Man Called Flintstone*, reached the cinema in 1966 and a spin-off series, *Pebbles and Bamm Bamm*, premiered in 1971. In 1994 John Goodman starred in a live-action film version, which was eventually followed in 2000 by *The Flintstones in Viva Rock Vegas*, with Mark Addy taking the lead. *The Flintstones* concept was reworked in another Hanna-Barbera production, THE JETSONS. This time the 20th-century way of life was applied to the space age.

Flip Side of Dominick Hide, The/ Another Flip for Dominick ✱✱

UK (BBC) Science Fiction. BBC 1 1980/1982
DVD: BBC

Dominick Hide .... **Peter Firth**
Jane .... **Caroline Langrishe**
Ava .... **Pippa Guard**
Caleb Line .... **Patrick Magee**
Great Aunt Mavis .... **Sylvia Coleridge**
Helda .... **Jean Trend**

Writers **Alan Gibson, Jeremy Paul**
Producer **Chris Cherry**

● ***A time traveller from the future is bewildered by 1980s London.***

This PLAY FOR TODAY achieved almost cult status with its tale of a friendly but naïve lad from 150 years in the future who visits Britain in the 1980s. By sending his flying saucer through a time warp, Dominick Hide leaves the year 2130 and returns to London in 1980 to do some historical research. He discovers a city far removed from the one he has just left. In his time, the world is a hygienic place of order and calm, and Hide is bemused and confused by the hustle and bustle he now encounters. Happily, he is befriended by a girl named Jane who becomes his lover and, in a quirk of fate, gives birth to Dominick's own great-great-grandfather.

Hide resurfaced in a second *Play for Today* two years later entitled *Another Flip for Dominick*, in which his boss, Caleb Line, sends him back to 1982 to find a missing researcher. Once again Dominick meets up with Jane (and his two-year-old son/ancestor), before returning to his wife, Ava, in his own time.

Flipper ✱✱

US (MGM/Ivan Tors) Adventure. ITV 1966–9 (US: NBC 1964–8)

Porter 'Po' Ricks .... **Brian Kelly**
Sandy Ricks .... **Luke Halpin**
Bud Ricks .... **Tommy Norden**

Hap Gorman	**Andy Devine**
Ulla Norstrand	**Ulla Stromstedt**

Creator/Executive Producer **Ivan Tors**
Producer **Stanley Colbert**

The adventures of two young boys and their pet dolphin at a Florida marine park.

Fifteen-year-old Sandy Ricks and his ten year-old brother, Bud, live at the Coral Key Park in Florida, where their widower father, Po Ricks, is Chief Ranger. In early episodes, carpenter Hap Gorman, an old sea-dog, also hangs around, regaling the boys with tall stories, but he is replaced by glamorous Scandinavian biochemist Ulla Norstrand. The family has a pet labrador, Spray, and even a pet pelican, Pete, but it is with Flipper, their tame dolphin, that they have the most fun. This incredibly intelligent sea mammal leads Bud and Sandy into a host of maritime adventures and is often at hand to help them out of awkward or dangerous situations. Together they flush out crooks, avert disasters and swim to the rescue of struggling sailors.

The bottle-nosed dolphin was played most often by an animal named Suzy, and the series was based on the 1963 film of the same name, which starred Chuck Connors as dad alongside son Luke Halpin. In 1996, Paul Hogan and Elijah Wood starred in a feature-film remake with the same title.

Flockhart, Calista

(1964–)

American theatre actress who shot to fame as neurotic lawyer ALLY MCBEAL, after previously taking only minor roles in a couple of low-key US programmes.

Flockton Flyer, The ✶✶

UK (Southern) Children's Drama. ITV 1977–8

Bob Carter	**David Neal**
Jan Carter	**Gwyneth Strong**
Jimmy Carter	**Peter Duncan**
Kathy Carter	**Sheila Fearn**
Jessica Carter	**Annabelle Lanyon**
	Catrin Strong
Bill Jelly	**Geoffrey Russell**
Commander Frost	**Anthony Sharp**

Writer **Peter Whitbread**
Producer **Colin Nutley**

A wholesome family restores a derelict railway line and its flagship loco.

The *Flockton Flyer* is an old GWR engine that appears to have steamed its last. Then the Carter family take over the Flockton Lane End Railway and restore the iron horse to its former glory. However, running and maintaining a private railway line is not without its problems as the Carters (dad Bob, mum Kathy and kids Jimmy, Jan and Jessica) discover. But, helped out by Bill Jelly and old sea dog Commander Frost, they overcome sabotage and go on to open a nature trail alongside the line. They even catch crooks and ensure the railway and its famous engine are a boon to all the neighbourhood. When the series returned for a second run, the Carters were motherless, Kathy having temporarily headed for Canada. *The Flockton Flyer* was notable for early starring roles for Peter Duncan (BLUE PETER) and Gwyneth Strong (ONLY FOOLS AND HORSES' Cassandra).

Floor Manager

The person who takes charge on the studio floor during production, passing on instructions given through headphones by the director in the control room. It is the floor manager who cues the presenters, etc. The term is often abbreviated to FM.

Flower Pot Men ✶✶

UK (BBC) Children's Entertainment. BBC 1952–4

Voices **Peter Hawkins**

Creators **Freda Lingstrom, Maria Bird**
Writer **Maria Bird**

The secret adventures of two flowerpot dwellers at the bottom of a garden.

Airing in Wednesday's WATCH WITH MOTHER slot, *Flower Pot Men* exposed the covert activities of identical puppets Bill and Ben. Made out of pots themselves, their hands covered in big gardening gloves and their feet in hobnail boots, Bill and Ben live in two giant (normal size to humans) flowerpots down by a potting shed. Whenever the gardener pops home for a spot of lunch, the two rascals slowly raise their heads out of the pots to see if the coast is clear, before leaping out to play. Adventures generally centre around whatever object they can find, but a constant guessing game for viewers is which of the twin puppets has done this or that in the programme. 'Was it Bill or was it Ben?' toddlers are asked, and the truth comes out when the culprit turns around to reveal his name on his back. (Older viewers know instantly, as Bill's voice is a few octaves higher than his friend's.) When the man who works in the garden has finished his lunch and is on his way down the garden path, the Flower Pot Men scramble back into their pots in the nick of time. Keeping counsel is their neighbour, Weed, who kindly alerts them to signs of danger. Also in on the boys' secret is the little house, which probably 'knows something about it, too', if its smile is anything to go by.

Flower Pot Men was *Watch with Mother*'s second offering, hot on the heels of ANDY PANDY. Behind the project were *Andy Pandy*'s creators, Freda Lingstrom and Maria Bird, with Audrey Atterbury and Molly Gibson once again pulling the strings and Gladys Whitred and Julia Williams adding the songs. Bill and Ben's 'flobbalot' gibberish was provided by master voicer Peter Hawkins, later to add his talents to THE WOODENTOPS and CAPTAIN PUGWASH, among other animations. A new, 'string-free' version, entitled *Bill and Ben*, was launched in the new millennium (BBC 1 2001–2), with John Thomson voicing Bill and Jimmy Hibbert speaking for Ben.

Floyd, Keith

(1943–)

Somerset-raised restaurateur turned TV celebrity Keith Floyd made his name in a series of programmes for the BBC that dissected the culinary traditions of various corners of the world. These included *Floyd on France, Floyd on Spain, Floyd on Italy, Floyd on Britain and Ireland, Floyd's American Pie, Floyd on Oz* and *Far Flung Floyd*. Other series included *Floyd on Fish* and *Floyd on Food*. He later moved into independent production for series like *Floyd on Africa, Capital Floyd, Floyd's Fjord Fiesta, Floyd's India* and *Floyd around the Med*. Establishing himself as a popular, if garrulous frontman, he barked out orders to his camera crew while clutching his trademark glass of wine. Floyd was also chosen to succeed Clive James in what became *Floyd on TV*, before himself making way for Chris Tarrant. His first flirtation with television came in a regional (West of England) programme called *RPM*.

Flumps, The ✶✶

UK (David Yates/BBC) Animation. BBC 1 1977
DVD: Contender Entertainment

Narrator **Gay Soper**

Creator/Writer **Julie Holder**
Producer **David Yates**

● ***The domestic adventures of a fur ball family.***

The Flumps: Grandfather, Father, Mother, Perkin, Posey and Pootle. This family of round, furry creatures, each with a distinctive hat (or in Posey's case a blue bow), provided preschool fun for 1970s toddlers as they went about their daily business. Domestically regimented like THE WOODENTOPS 20 years before, each Flump knows his/her role: Dad digs the garden and does the DIY, Mum cooks and cleans, Grandfather dozes most of the time or plays his Flumpet, and the kids are up to mischief or just learning the rules of life. Fun is had with magnets, roller skates, rockets and more. Animation was by David Kellahar; music was provided by Paul Reade. Just 13 episodes were made but repeats were countless.

Flying Doctor, The ✶

UK (Associated British Picture/ABC) Adventure. ITV 1959–60

Dr Greg Graham .... **Richard Denning**
Mary Meredith .... **Jill Adams**
Dr Jim Harrison .... **Peter Madden**
Charley Wood .... **Alan White**

Producer **David MacDonald**

● ***Adventures in the bush with an American doctor.***

Nearly 30 years before THE FLYING DOCTORS took off from Cooper's Crossing, tall, handsome American medic Greg Graham, his blind assistant, Dr Harrison, and his trusty nurse, Mary, were life-savers in the Australian outback. Responding to urgent radio messages, they wing their way (always in the nick of time) to remote patients in a small plane piloted by their friend, Charley. Graham has arrived in Australia on leave from a research institute in San Francisco. The series was filmed partly at Elstree and partly on location in Australia.

Flying Doctors, The ✶✶

Australia (Nine Network/Crawford) Drama. BBC 1 1988–97

Dr Tom Callaghan .... **Andrew McFarlane**
Dr Chris Randall .... **Liz Burch**
Sister Kate Wellings/
Standish .... **Lenore Smith**
Ron Miller .... **Mark Little**
Annie Rogers .... **Tammy Macintosh**
Dr Geoff Standish .... **Robert Grubb**
Sam Patterson .... **Peter O'Brien**
Emma Plimpton/Patterson .... **Rebecca Gibney**
Paula Patterson .... **Vikki Blanche**
Demetris Goannides ('DJ') .... **George Kapiniaris**
Maggie Hutton .... **Marie Redshaw**
Marty Jarvis .... **Mark Neal**
Vic Buckley .... **Maurie Fields**
Nancy Buckley .... **Val Jellay**
George Baxter .... **Bruce Barry**
Violet Carnegie .... **Pat Evison**
Hurtle Morrison .... **Max Cullen**
Nick Cardaci .... **Alex Papps**
Sgt Jack Carruthers .... **Terry Gill**
Dr Rowie Lang .... **Sarah Chadwick**
Dr Guy Reid .... **David Reyne**
Debbie O'Brien .... **Louise Siversen**
Dr David Ratcliffe .... **Brett Climo**
Dr Magda Heller .... **Melita Jurisic**
Claire Bryant .... **Beverley Dunn**
'Johno' Johnson .... **Christopher Stollery**
Luke Mitchell .... **Gerard Kennedy**

Executive Producers **Hector Crawford, Ian Crawford, Terry Ohlsson, Ian Bradley**
Producers **Charles 'Bud' Tingwell, Graham Moore, Stanley Walsh, Oscar Whitbread**

● ***Tense adventures with a team of airborne medics.***

The town of Coopers Crossing is the setting for this collection of tales about Australia's Royal Flying Doctors Service (RFDS). The team doctors (first Tom Callaghan, then his replacement Geoff Standish, plus others like Chris Randall and rookie David Ratcliffe) are winged across the outback to treat farmers, miners, tourists and other folk in distress, for whom conventional medics are simply too distant. Hopping aboard a Nomad light aircraft (call sign: 'Victor Charlie Charlie'), they risk life and limb touching down in the inhospitable, parched bush, racing against time to save lives in peril. Supporting the daring docs are nurse Kate Wellings (eventually to marry widower Standish), radio operator DJ, and pilots Sam Patterson (married to garage mechanic Emma) and 'Johno' Johnson. Other townsfolk include publicans Vic and Nancy Buckley, odd job man Nick Cardaci, miserable grazier George Baxter, town mother figure Violet Carnegie and police officer Jack Carruthers. Such locals, and indeed the medical staff themselves, often provide as much colour and intrigue as the stricken guests who grace each episode.

The series grew out of a six-hour, three-part mini-series produced in 1984 and was filmed in the little farming town of Minyip, a few hours' drive north-west of Melbourne. Scripts were vetted by the real-life RFDS, which also picked up a handsome royalty from the success of the series.

Flying Lady ✶✶

UK (Yorkshire) Drama. ITV 1987; 1989

Harry Bradley .... **Frank Windsor**
Jean Bradley .... **Anne Stallybrass**
Mrs Burrows .... **Gabrielle Daye**
Rita Bradley .... **Anna Lindup**
Elizabeth Edmonds
Andy Gregson .... **Billy Fellows**
Moira .... **Gillian Martell**

Writer **Brian Finch**
Executive Producer **Keith Richardson**
Producer **Anne W. Gibbons**

● ***A Yorkshire family is drawn into other people's troubles through its car hire firm.***

Harry Bradley receives a cheque for £14,000 and decides to buy a Rolls-Royce. He plans to hire it out as a new business venture, setting up Bradley Car Hire. However, each person who signs up for Harry's services seems to have a story to tell and the Bradleys (Harry, wife Jean and daughter Rita) find themselves in some peculiar situations. All in all there is plenty for Harry to contemplate as he chews his pipe. Mrs Burrows is Jean's mum, Moira is the barmaid at the village pub, and Rita's boyfriend, Andy Gregson, is Harry's mechanic. Peter Skellern sang the theme song. A pilot episode had a couple of cast differences: Anna Wing played Mrs Burrows and Prue Clark was Rita.

Flying Nun, The ✳

US (Screen Gems) Situation Comedy. ITV 1968–70
(US: ABC 1967–70)

Sister Bertrille (Elsie Ethrington) .... **Sally Field**
Sister Jacqueline .... **Marge Redmond**
Reverend Mother Plaseato ...... **Madeleine Sherwood**
Carlos Ramirez .... **Alejandro Rey**
Sister Sixto .... **Shelley Morrison**
Sister Ana .... **Linda Dangcil**
Capt. Gaspar Formento .... **Vito Scotti**
Marcello .... **Manuel Padilla Jr**

Producers **Harry Ackerman, William Sackheim**

● ***A young novice has the ability to take to the air and find adventure.***

Young Elsie Ethrington joins the order of nuns at the convent of San Tanco in Puerto Rico, where she is given the name of Sister Bertrille. However, a chance combination of the convent's location (on a high, windy mountain top), her wing-like headdress and her light frame (she weighs not much more than six stone), contrive to give her the power of flight. Not that she is always able to control this gift, much to the consternation of the prim Mother Superior Plaseato and the amusement of her colleagues, Sister Jacqueline and Sister Sixto. Watching in admiration is local casino owner Carlos Ramirez, a convent benefactor who takes a shine to the petite airborne novice. The series was based on the novel *The Fifteenth Pelican*, by Tere Rios.

Flynn, Barbara

(Barbara McMurray; 1948–)

Sussex-born actress whose most memorable performances have been as Freda Ashton in Granada's A FAMILY AT WAR, schoolteacher Jill Swinburne in the BEIDERBECKE trilogy and the feminist Dr Rose Marie in A VERY PECULIAR PRACTICE, although she has many other programme credits to her name. These include KEEP IT IN THE FAMILY, OPEN ALL HOURS, THE LAST SONG (Shirley), *Second Chance*, MAYBURY, THE BARCHESTER CHRONICLES (Mary Bold), *Day To Remember* and INSPECTOR MORSE. She also played Mme Maigret in the 1990s revival of MAIGRET and was seen as Judith, Fitz's wife, in CRACKER, private investigator Dee Tate in CHANDLER AND CO., Miss Jeffries in the pilot of *The Vanishing Man*, Miss Sally Browning in WIVES AND DAUGHTERS, Sarah Ridd in *Lorna Doone*, Maria in *Night Flight*, Imogen in *Perfect*, Emily in THE FORSYTE SAGA, Mrs French in HE KNEW HE WAS RIGHT, Mary, Queen of Scots in ELIZABETH I and Julia Bickleigh in MALICE AFORETHOUGHT. Other recent appearances have come in *The Law*, HORNBLOWER, MURDER IN MIND, AGATHA CHRISTIE'S POIROT, *Sweet Medicine*, THE INSPECTOR LYNLEY MYSTERIES and SEA OF SOULS.

Flynn, Jerome

(1963–)

British actor, best known for his work alongside Robson Green in SOLDIER, SOLDIER (Paddy Garvey) and AIN'T MISBEHAVIN' (Eddie Wallis). The pair also enjoyed a run of hugely successful pop records. A keen environmentalist, Flynn was well suited to the later role of wildlife policeman Tom McCabe in BADGER. Other credits have included *The Fear*, BETWEEN THE LINES (DS Eddie Hargreaves) and *Ruth Rendell's The Lake of Darkness* (Martin Urban). He is the son of actor Eric Flynn and the brother of actor Daniel Flynn.

Follyfoot ✳✳

UK (Yorkshire) Children's Drama. ITV 1971–3

Dora .... **Gillian Blake**
Steve .... **Steve Hodson**
Slugger .... **Arthur English**
The Colonel .... **Desmond Llewelyn**
Ron Stryker .... **Christian Rodska**
Lewis Hammond .... **Paul Guess**

Executive Producer **Tony Essex**
Producer **Audley Southcott**

● ***Eventful days at a home for neglected horses in Yorkshire.***

Follyfoot Farm is a retirement home for old and unwanted horses at Harewood, near Leeds. It is owned by a patrician former army man known as The Colonel and run by his niece, Dora, and Steve, a formerly wayward youth turned reliable stable hand. The farm kitchen is in the hands of a rough-and-ready old boxer named Slugger (once The Colonel's batman), and also in the action is daily help Ron Stryker, a layabout biker with a heart of gold beneath an abrasive exterior.

Adventures at Follyfoot revolve around the rehabilitation of distressed and neglected horses. These are broadly based on the novels by Monica Dickens (particularly the first one, *Cobbler's Dream*, published in 1963). In the farmyard stands a burnt-out tree, victim of a lightning bolt. The Colonel reckons it will bloom again if given enough attention, so everyone who passes by is required to throw a bucket of water on to its roots. The tree becomes a good luck charm to the farm folk (and a symbol of hope for worn-out horses) and is featured in the programme's theme song, 'The Lightning Tree', performed by The Settlers, which was a minor chart hit in 1971.

Food and Drink ✳✳

UK (BBC/Bazal) Food Magazine. BBC 2 1982–2002

Presenters **Simon Bates, Gillian Miles, Henry Kelly, Susan Grossman, Jilly Goolden, Chris Kelly, Michael Barry, Oz Clarke, Paul Heiney, Antony Worrall Thompson, Emma Crowhurst**

Producers **Henry Murray, Peter Bazalgette, Alison Field, Tim Hincks, Elaine Bancroft, Geraldine McClelland, Gloria Wood, Lyndsay Davis**

● ***Eating and drinking magazine.***

Crafty recipes, drink reviews and the latest news from the

catering world formed the basis of this popular BBC 2 programme for many years. Simon Bates and Gillian Miles were the original hosts, succeeded by Henry Kelly and Susan Grossman, but the main line-up in its hey-day was Chris Kelly as anchor, Michael Barry in charge of cooking and Jilly Goolden judging various drinks from wines to teas, conveying her findings in an avalanche of over-the-top adjectives. Goolden was later joined by Oz Clarke. In 1997, Barry was succeeded as resident chef by Antony Worrall Thompson. Paul Heiney hosted one series (1991–2) while Chris Kelly was working on another project, and when Kelly finally left the programme in 1999 Goolden took over as host, assisted by Leith's cookery school headteacher Emma Crowhurst. Goolden herself left in 2000, when topical features were abandoned in favour of prerecordings.

Football Focus

See *Grandstand*.

Footballers' Wives ✶✶

UK (Shed) Drama. ITV 2002–6
DVD: VCI

Kyle Pascoe	**Gary Lucy**
Jackie Pascoe/Webb	**Gillian Taylforth**
Chardonnay Lane/Pascoe	**Susie Amy**
Ian Walmsley	**Nathan Constance**
Donna Walmsley	**Katharine Monaghan**
Jason Turner	**Cristian Solimeno**
Tanya Turner/Laslett	**Zoë Lucker**
Frank Laslett	**John Forgeham**
Stefan Hauser	**Philip Bretherton**
Holly Walmsley	**Billie Wackrill**
Marie Minshull	**Micaiah Dring**
Salvatore Biagi	**Daniel Schutzmann**
Archie Malloch	**Sam Graham**
Ronald Bateman	**Chad Shepherd**
Lara Bateman	**Leanne Baker**
Tel Harper	**Nick Lopez**
Nurse Dunkley	**Julie Legrand**
Marguerite Laslett	**Paula Wilcox**
Darius Fry	**Peter Ash**
Federica Hauser	**Jess Brooks**
Roger Webb	**Jesse Birdsall**
Conrad Gates	**Ben Price**
Amber Gates	**Laila Rouass**
Harley Lawson	**Jamie Davis**
Shannon Donnelly/Lawson	**Sarah Barrand**
Noah Alexander	**Marcel McCalla**
Hazel Bailey	**Alison Newman**
Elaine Hardy	**Caroline Chikezie**
Bruno Milligan	**Ben Richards**
Lucy Milligan	**Helen Latham**
Katie Jones	**Elaine Glover**
Bethany Mortimer	**Camilla Beeput**
Seb Webb	**Tom Swire**
Garry Ryan	**Nicholas Ball**
Tremaine Gidigbi	**Chucky Venice**
Liberty Baker	**Phina Oruche**
Urszula Rosen	**Lucia Giannecchini**
Callum Watson	**Craig Gallivan**
Trisha Watson	**Angela Ridgeon**
Paolo Bardosa	**Jay Rodan**

Creators **Maureen Chadwick, Ann McManus**

Producers **Brian Park, Paul Marquess, Liz Lake, Claire Phillips, Sean O'Connor, Cameron Roach**

The tacky world of top soccer stars and their spoilt partners.

In the world of the Premiership footballer, the rewards are great, the lifestyle is extravagant and the people are shallow: that's the message offered by this sex-and-soccer pot boiler. At the heart of affairs (in every sense) is the fictitious Earls Park club, run by chairman Frank Laslett and managed by German Stefan Hauser. However, very little action takes place on the field, with the bedroom a favoured alternative.

The story begins with the arrival of new striker Ian Walmsley from Bolton and, with his wife, Donna, he provides an introduction to the club's overpaid and oversexed stars, plus their equally self-indulgent, designer-clad wives and partners, who are never far from the scandal of a tabloid exposure. Among the glamorous other halves is topless model Chardonnay, soon to marry star player Kyle Pascoe (in a Beckham-esque ceremony complete with thrones), and the devious druggie Tanya, whose husband, Jason, later has a fling with Kyle's mother. Later recruits include Roger Webb, the new manager; Conrad Gates, England captain; Conrad's Bollywood actress wife, Amber; new teenage genius Harley Lawson; Harley's girlfriend, Shannon Donnelly; gay player Noah Alexander; Hazel Bailey, the hard-nosed footballers' agent; physio Elaine Hardy; angry team member Bruno Milligan; and Bruno's wife, Lucy. Guests making cameo appearances include Desmond Lynam, Antony Worrall Thompson, Neil Fox, Lionel Blair and David Seaman. The (few) footballing scenes were shot at Selhurst Park, the home of Crystal Palace. In one intriguing storyline the character of Tanya is sent to prison and ends up briefly in the equally tacky and sensational BAD GIRLS.

In 2005, ITV 2 launched a spin-off series featuring some of the original cast, plus new characters. Called *Footballers' Wives Extra Time*, it was later repeated on ITV 1 (2006).

Footprint

The area of the Earth that a satellite's transmissions reach. If you live outside the footprint area, you can't pick up the signals.

For the Children ✶

UK (BBC) Children's Entertainment. BBC 1946–51

Producers **Mary Adams, Andrew Miller Jones**

Early entertainment for school-age children.

Among the items offered under this umbrella title were features on stamp collecting and other wholesome pursuits, classic stories and tales and, from August 1946, music and fun with MUFFIN THE MULE and his piano-playing escort, Annette Mills. Muffin was originally just one of the puppets Annette (and her puppeteer, Ann Hogarth) worked with, but he quickly outshone the likes of Peregrine the Penguin, Sally the Sea Lion, Oswald the Ostrich and Louise the Lamb, to the point where he was given his own series. Only Prudence and Primrose Kitten came close to equalling his popularity, also appearing in their own series in the 1950s. *For the Children*, meanwhile, gave way to ANDY PANDY and the WATCH WITH MOTHER crew.

For the Love of Ada ✶✶

UK (Thames) Situation Comedy. ITV 1970–1

Ada Cresswell/Bingley .... **Irene Handl**
Walter Bingley .... **Wilfred Pickles**
Leslie Pollitt .... **Jack Smethurst**
Ruth Pollitt .... **Barbara Mitchell**

Creators/Writers **Vince Powell, Harry Driver**
Producer **Ronnie Baxter**

● ***Romance in the twilight years with two game pensioners.***
When Ada Cresswell buries her late husband, little does she know that the man who has dug the grave will be her next spouse. Beginning a gentle love affair with fellow senior citizen Walter Bingley, Ada moves into his home at Cemetery Lodge, much to the surprise of her daughter, Ruth, and Manchester Utd fanatic son-in-law, Leslie. The sprightly 70-year-olds are eventually married. A feature-film version was released in 1972 and a US copy, *A Touch of Grace*, starring J. Pat O'Malley and Shirley Booth, followed in 1973.

Forbes, Emma
(1965–)

London-born presenter, first seen in a cookery slot on GOING LIVE!, which led to her co-presenting the Saturday morning programme's successor, LIVE AND KICKING, with Andi Peters. She then co-hosted the game show *Talking Telephone Numbers* with Phillip Schofield and a regional version of WHAT'S MY LINE? Her other credits have included *Speakeasy*, LWT's *The Weekend Show*, *Esther* (standing in for Esther Rantzen), *Tip Top Challenge* and *The Club*. Her parents are film director Bryan Forbes and actress Nanette Newman.

Ford, Anna
(1943–)

Gloucestershire-born newsreader and presenter, one of TV-am's 'Famous Five'. Prior to her short stint on breakfast television, Ford had been an ITN newscaster (on *News at Ten*), TOMORROW'S WORLD presenter and a reporter on MAN ALIVE and *Reports Action*, arriving on TV after a time as an Open University tutor. She has guest-hosted both *Wogan* and HAVE I GOT NEWS FOR YOU, and has presented *Understanding Toddlers* and an arts programme for the Performance cable channel. Ford was one of the BBC's senior newsreaders until retiring in 2006.

Fordyce, Keith
(1928–)

Former Radio Luxembourg and Light Programme disc jockey, a Cambridge law graduate who presented some of the early 1960s pop shows, especially *Wham!!*, THANK YOUR LUCKY STARS and READY, STEADY, GO! He also hosted COME DANCING, a few gardening programmes and Westward's regional quiz *Treasure Hunt*.

Foreign Bodies ✶✶

UK (BBC) Situation Comedy. BBC 2 1987; 1989

Tom .... **Dan Gordon**
Roisin .... **Hilary Reynolds**
Alex .... **Colum Convey**
Septa .... **Maeve Germaine**
Mrs Fogarty .... **Eileen Colgan**
Harry .... **John Hewitt**
Soup .... **Louis Rolston**
Elaine .... **Catherine Brennan**
Madge .... **Trudy Kelly**
Carol .... **Tracey Lynch**
Mrs Parker .... **Margaret D'Arcy**
Sammy .... **B. J. Hogg**
Bootlace .... **Walter McMonagle**

Writers **Bernard Farrell, Graham Reid**
Producer **Sydney Lotterby**

● ***Catholic Irish girls and Protestant Unionist boys enjoy a Northern Irish friendship.***
Given its history of sectarian violence, Northern Ireland has never been an obvious place to locate a situation comedy (1991's SO YOU THINK YOU'VE GOT TROUBLES being a rare exception). FOREIGN BODIES looked to break the mould with its story of Roisin and Septa, two Catholic girls from Dublin, who take up nursing positions at a Belfast hospital. When Roisin meets and falls for car mechanic Tom, it's not just a north–south divide that causes problems, but other social conventions, too, challenged by the fact that she is Catholic and he is Protestant. The fourth party in the equation is Tom's best mate, Alex, who usually causes trouble for everyone else. The series – which enjoyed three runs – was a joint effort between Ulsterman Graham Reid and Dublin writer Bernard Farrell. Sydney Lotterby directed as well as produced, for BBC Northern Ireland.

Forest Rangers ✶✶

Canada (ASP) Children's Adventure. ITV 1964–6

Ranger George Keeley .... **Graydon Gould**
Peter Keeley .... **Rex Hagon**
Joe Two Rivers .... **Michael Zenon**
Sgt Scott .... **Gordon Pinsent**
Chub Stanley .... **Ralph Endersby**
Mike Forbes .... **Peter Tully**
Uncle Raoul .... **Rolland Bedard**
Gaby LaRoche .... **Syme Jago**
Denise LaGarde .... **Barbara Pierce**
Ted .... **George Allan**
Matt Craig .... **Eric Cryderman**
Johnny O'Reilly .... **Michael Tully**
Kathy .... **Susan Conway**
Zeke .... **Ronald Cohoon**
Aggie Apple .... **Barbara Hamilton**
Macleod .... **Joe Austin**

Producer **William Davidson**

● ***Adventurous kids have fun in the Canadian wilderness.***
The Forest Rangers (members of an outdoor activities organization known as the Junior Ranger Club) include Chub (a fostered city kid), Mike, Peter, Ted, Denise, Matt, Johnny, Zeke and Kathy. Based in a disused Hudson Bay fort, in the town of Indian River, they spend their time helping folk in trouble.

Bears, wolves, snakes, poachers and bandits feature prominently in their day-to-day affairs, as they investigate trouble in disused mines or rescue civilians trapped in the wild. Friends and associates include a Native American by the name of Joe Two Rivers, plus Sgt Scott, a Royal Canadian Mounted Policeman. George Keeley is their chief ranger mentor and they also have a pet fawn, named Lady.

Forever Green ★★

UK (LWT/Picture Partnership) Drama. ITV 1989; 1992

Jack Boult	**John Alderton**
Harriet Boult	**Pauline Collins**
Freddy Boult	**Daisy Bates**
Tom Boult	**Nimer Rashed**
Lady Patricia Broughall	**Paola Dionisotti**
Hilly	**Wendy Van Der Plank**

Writers **Terence Brady, Charlotte Bingham, Douglas Watkinson**
Executive Producer **Nick Elliott**
Producer **Brian Eastman**

A town family moves to the country and discovers rural life is tougher than it looks.

Jack and Harriet Boult, concerned for the health of their asthmatic daughter, Freddy, decide to up sticks from London and head for the country. Taking up residence at the run-down Meadows Green Farm, somewhere in deepest Gloucestershire, the townies soon realize that country life has its downs as well as its ups. They find themselves immersed in protests against toxic waste, battling against horse rustlers and protecting barn owls in danger. Tom is their son, and also seen are cranky aristocrat Lady Pat and animal-loving local girl Hilly. Two series of this slow-moving, sentimental drama were made, three years apart.

Forrest, Steve

(William Forrest Andrews; 1924–)

The brother of actor Dana Andrews, Steve Forrest was one of TV's action men in the 1960s, taking the part of Texas antiques-dealer-cum-investigator John Mannering, aka THE BARON. He followed this up with the role of Lt. 'Hondo' Harrelson in S.W.A.T. in the mid-1970s and resurfaced in the 1980s as Ben Stivers in DALLAS. He also has plenty of TV movies to his name.

Forrester, Philippa

(1968–)

Winchester-born presenter with two degrees (English, and Ecology and Environmental Science) who started out in the Children's BBC presenters' 'broom cupboard' and in programmes like *The O Zone*, GOING LIVE! and *Zoo Watch*, before appearing regularly on *This Morning* and GMTV. Her best-known work is as presenter of TOMORROW'S WORLD and ROBOT WARS, but she has also been a team captain in the karaoke show *Night Fever* and hosted programmes as varied as *The World's Strongest Man, The Disney Club, The Heaven and Earth Show, Barking Mad, Dreamwheels* and *Making Animal Babies*. Forrester has also been a producer for *Natural World*.

Forsyte Saga, The [1] ★★★★

UK (BBC/MGM) Drama. BBC 2 1967
DVD: BBC

Jolyon 'Jo' Forsyte	**Kenneth More**
Soames Forsyte	**Eric Porter**
Irene Heron/Forsyte	**Nyree Dawn Porter**
Jolyon 'Old Jolyon' Forsyte	**Joseph O'Conor**
James Forsyte	**John Welsh**
Winifred Forsyte/Dartie	**Margaret Tyzack**
Ann Forsyte	**Fay Compton**
Montague Dartie	**Terence Alexander**
Hélène Hilmer/Forsyte	**Lana Morris**
Philip Bosinney	**John Bennett**
Michael Mont	**Nicholas Pennell**
Frances Crisson/Forsyte	**Ursula Howells**
Swithin Forsyte	**George Woodbridge**
Mrs Heron	**Jenny Laird**
Fleur Forsyte	**Susan Hampshire**
Annette Lamotte/Forsyte	**Dallia Penn**
Jolyon 'Jolly' Forsyte	**Michael York**
Jolyon 'Jon' Forsyte	**Martin Jarvis**
June Forsyte	**Susan Pennick**
	June Barry

Producer **Donald Wilson**

Family squabbles and scandals in the Victorian and Edwardian ages.

The Forsyte Saga was the BBC's last major drama to be produced in black and white, which probably explains why it has not been repeated in recent years, despite its enormous worldwide success. It was the serial which put BBC 2 on the map, attracting six million viewers on Sunday evenings, disrupting church services and emptying pubs. A year later, it was repeated on BBC 1, gaining an audience of 18 million. It was the first serial the BBC ever sold to the Soviet Union and was purchased by stations all over America. And yet *The Forsyte Saga* almost never happened. Producer Donald Wilson had longed to televise John Galsworthy's novels for years, but a combination of problems over rights and stubbornness at the BBC had thwarted him. However, putting together a star cast, Wilson got his way and the series was produced in 26 episodes, each presented as a separate act but with a cliffhanger ending to draw viewers back the following week.

The television script extends the time-scale of Galsworthy's novels, running from 1879 to 1926 and charting the feuding and fighting of the Forsytes, a London merchant family headed by Jolyon (Jo) and his cousin, Soames. Other notable family members include Old Jolyon, the ageing patriarch, and Irene, Soames's wife in a loveless marriage, who is cruelly raped by her husband in one memorably shocking scene. Irene is romantically linked to architect Philip Bosinney and later marries Jo, giving birth to Jon, who becomes illicitly entwined with Fleur, Soames's daughter by a second marriage.

The series confirmed the BBC's reputation for costume dramas and spawned a host of lookalikes, such as THE FIRST CHURCHILLS and THE PALLISERS. Its influence was also seen in the glossy American soaps of the next decade (like DALLAS). More immediately, it revived the flagging career of Kenneth More and made a star out of Susan Hampshire. Eric Porter reaped the accolades, too. ITV presented a new adaptation of Galsworthy's work in 2001.

Forsyte Saga, The [2] ★★★

UK (Granada) Drama. ITV 1 2002–3
DVD: Cinema Club

Soames Forsyte	**Damian Lewis**
Irene Heron/Forsyte	**Gina McKee**
Philip Bosinney	**Ioan Gruffudd**
June Forsyte	**Gillian Kearney**
Young Jolyon Forsyte	**Rupert Graves**
Hélène Hilmer/Forsyte	**Amanda Ooms**
Frances Crisson/Forsyte	**Sarah Winman**
Jolyon 'Old Jolyon' Forsyte	**Corin Redgrave**
Swithin Forsyte	**Robert Lang**
George	**Alistair Petrie**
Montague Dartie	**Ben Miles**
Winifred Forsyte/Dartie	**Amanda Root**
Aunt Juley	**Wendy Craig**
Aunt Ann Forsyte	**Judy Campbell**
Aunt Hester	**Ann Bell**
James Forsyte	**John Carlisle**
Emily	**Barbara Flynn**
Mrs Heron	**Joanna David**
Parfitt	**Malcolm Raeburn**
Bilson	**Maggie Fox**
Jolyon 'Jolly' Forsyte	**Christian Coulson**
Holly	**Amanda Ryan**
Val	**Julian Ovenden**
Annette Lamotte/Forsyte	**Beatriz Batarda**
Fleur Forsyte	**Aimee Brigg** *(young)*
	Emma Griffiths Malin
Jon Forsyte	**Toby Parkes** *(young)*
	Lee Williams
Dora	**Bella Hamblin**
Farmer Maple	**Brian Southwood**
Michael Mont	**Oliver Milburn**
Prosper Profond	**Michael Maloney**
Gradman	**Richard Hope**
Smither	**Jowanna Rose**

Writers **Stephen Mallatratt, Jan McVerry, Kate Brooke, Phil Woods**
Executive Producers **Andy Harries, Rebecca Eaton, Sita Williams**
Producers **Sita Williams, David Boulter**

● ***A second television treatment of Galsworthy's epic tale of family scandal.***

Granda's 2002 adaptation of John Galsworthy's *chef d'oeuvre* was sure to draw comparisons with its illustrious 1967 predecessor. However, starting in 1874, the new version, for its initial six-episode run, focused only on the first two of the nine Forsyte works (*The Man of Property* and *In Chancery*), the idea being to pick up the story in future series. It did return, a year later, with four more episodes that cover the stories contained in Galsworthy's third novel, *To Let*, but there the tale concludes.

Stars Damian Lewis and Gina McKee offer up a pale, simmering tyrant and a cold fish as their interpretations of Soames and Irene, in the footsteps of Eric Porter and Nyree Dawn Porter. The triangular relationship of these two characters and the flighty architect Bosinney takes centre stage in series one. Other family debacles concern the artistic Young Jolyon, who runs off with his daughter's governess, Hélène, and Winifred's marriage to the financially feckless Montague Dartie. In series two, a new generation of Forsytes takes the lead, headed by Soames's daughter, Fleur, and Irene's son, Jon, whose love affair further divides this splintered family.

Welsh operatic star Bryn Terfel sings the theme song.

Forsyth, Brigit

(1940–)

Edinburgh-born actress, much seen in supporting roles, such as Bob's bossy wife, Thelma, in WHATEVER HAPPENED TO THE LIKELY LADS? However, she has enjoyed lead roles of her own, particularly in the sitcoms, *Tom, Dick and Harriet* (Harriet Maddison) and SHARON AND ELSIE (Elsie Beecroft), and the drama *Holly*. She also played Veronica Haslett in THE GLAMOUR GIRLS, Dr Judith Vincent in THE PRACTICE, Miss Maitland in *Dark Season*, Rosemary Dobson in *Nice Town*, Mrs Wells in SPARK, Sylvia Dickinson in CHILDREN'S WARD and Francine Pratt in PLAYING THE FIELD, and among her other appearances have been parts in *Adam Smith*, HOLDING THE FORT, *The Master of Ballantrae*, BOON, *Running Wild*, AGATHA CHRISTIE'S POIROT, THE BILL, CASUALTY, DOWN TO EARTH and assorted plays.

Forsyth, Bruce

CBE (Bruce Forsyth-Johnson; 1928–)

Highly popular British entertainer whose career stretches back to stage variety performances as Boy Bruce, The Mighty Atom (aged 14). He broke into television in the 1950s and became the main compere of SUNDAY NIGHT AT THE LONDON PALLADIUM in 1958, where he demonstrated his unique and gently aggressive style of handling live audiences and nervous amateur contestants, gaining one of his many catchphrases, 'I'm in charge.' (Forsyth revived the show as *Tonight at the London Palladium* in 2000.) Becoming one of TV's top entertainers, he was given his own variety series, *The Bruce Forsyth Show*, by ATV and proceeded to develop a one-man cabaret routine, singing, dancing, playing the piano and cracking jokes along the way. 'Nice to see you, to see you nice' became another of his catchphrases. In the 1970s he hosted The Generation Game (picking up yet more gimmicks: 'Didn't he do well!', 'Good game. Good game', etc.) and then, moving to ITV, presented *Bruce Forsyth's Big Night*, PLAY YOUR CARDS RIGHT, *Hollywood or Bust* and YOU BET! Back with the BBC, he hosted the game show *Takeover Bid* and a relaunched *Generation Game*, before switching again to ITV to revamp *Play Your Cards Right* and Leslie Crowther's THE PRICE IS RIGHT. Back at the BBC, he has fronted a quiz called *Didn't They Do Well!*, STRICTLY COME DANCING and *Bruce Goes Dancing*. Bruce has also tried his hand at situation comedy, replacing the late Leonard Rossiter in the supermarket farce TRIPPER'S DAY (as Cecil Slinger in the renamed *Slinger's Day*), and drama, in a 1960s version of Oscar Wilde's *The Canterville Ghost*. His first wife was actress/dancer Penny Calvert and his second wife was *Generation Game* hostess Anthea Redfern. Forsyth's third wife is Miss World 1975, Wilnelia Merced. His daughter Julie is a singer with the Guys and Dolls vocal group.

Forsythe, John

(John Freund; 1918–)

American actor well versed in father-figure roles. A one-time baseball commentator, Forsythe switched to acting, appearing on stage, radio and film, before – on Alfred Hitchcock's advice – concentrating on television. He appeared as a guest in ALFRED HITCHCOCK PRESENTS and other anthology series, before headlining in *Bachelor Father* from 1957 to 1962. *The John Forsythe Show* followed and then another comedy, *To Rome with Love*. Neither of these made it on to British screens. A quiet spell as narrator and voice-over actor resulted in the role of Charlie in CHARLIE'S ANGELS, a part in which he was never seen, only heard. In 1981 he was enticed back in front of the camera as tycoon Blake Carrington in DYNASTY and became an international celebrity. His most recent starring role was as Senator William Powers in the sitcom *The Powers That Be*.

Fortunes and Misfortunes of Moll Flanders, The ✻✻✻

UK (Granada/WGBH) Drama. ITV 1996
DVD: Anchor Bay

Moll Flanders	**Alex Kingston**
Mr Richardson	**Struan Rodger**
Mrs Richardson	**Maureen O'Brien**
Rowland Richardson	**Colin Buchanan**
Maria Richardson	**Caroline Harker**
Robin Richardson	**Ian Driver**
Mr Baggot	**Kenneth McDonald**
Mrs Baggot	**Mary Healey**
James 'Jemmy' Seagrave	**Daniel Craig**
Daniel Dawkins	**Christopher Fulford**
Lemuel 'Lemmy' Golightly	**Tom Ward**
Mrs Golightly	**Diana Rigg**
Sir Richard Gregory	**Ronald Fraser**
Lucy Diver	**Nicola Walker**
Mrs Riordan	**Patti Love**
Mrs Seagrave	**Trevyn McDowell**
Mr Bland	**James Fleet**

Writer **Andrew Davies**
Executive Producer **Gub Neal**
Producer **David Lascelles**

● ***Daniel Defoe's bodice-ripping tale of an opportunistic orphan girl.***

Andrew Davies's TV version of *Moll Flanders* was noted for its bawdy scenes, nudity and strong language. In four parts, it follows the story of an urchin girl born in Newgate Prison and brought up by gypsies, who falls on her feet when adopted by Mr Richardson, the Mayor of Colchester, as part-family, part-servant. Flanders (who reveals all through intimate asides to the camera) then uses her womanly wiles to shape the course of her life. She marries several times, crashes into bankruptcy and travels to the New World of America in the company of a Virginian seaman and plantation owner, who turns out to be her natural half-brother. She eventually marries lover Jemmy, a highwayman, and ends up in poverty before being sentenced to hang at Tyburn for thieving. Shown first in the USA, the dramatization made a star out of Alex Kingston, who shortly afterwards headed for Hollywood and the role of Dr Elizabeth Corday in ER. Purists were annoyed that a new lesbian lover, Lucy Diver, was introduced into the plot, but Kingston defended the move as it highlighted, through genuine love and tenderness, how Flanders mostly used sex to manipulate men. David Attwood directed; Jim Parker composed the music.

Fortunes of War ✻✻✻✻

UK (BBC/WGBH Boston/Primetime) Drama. BBC 1 1987
DVD: Cinema Club

Guy Pringle	**Kenneth Branagh**
Harriet Pringle	**Emma Thompson**
Prince Yakimov	**Ronald Pickup**
Dobson	**Charles Kay**
Prof. Inchcape	**James Villiers**
Clarence Lawson	**Richard Clifford**
Sasha Drucker	**Harry Burton**
Bella Niculesco	**Caroline Langrishe**
Prof. Lord Pinkrose	**Alan Bennett**
Simon Boulderstone	**Robert Graves**
Edwina Little	**Diana Hardcastle**
Toby Lush	**Christopher Strauli**
Bill Castlebar	**Robert Stephens**
Sophie Oresanu	**Elena Secota**
Galpin	**Desmond McNamara**
Dubedat	**Mark Drewry**
Charles Warden	**Jeremy Brudenell**
Alan Frewen	**Peter Tilbury**
Sgt Ridley	**Jeff Rawle**
Capt. Aidan Pratt	**Greg Hicks**
Angela Hooper	**Ciaran Madden**
Lord Peter Lisdoonvarna	**Jeremy Sinden**

Writer **Alan Plater**
Producer **Betty Willingale**

● ***A young couple's life and relationship are thrown into turmoil by global conflict.***

Opening in September 1939, at the outset of World War II, and running through to 1943, *Fortunes of War* is the story of newlyweds Guy and Harriet Pringle. Naïve, outgoing Guy works as an English lecturer for the British Council in Bucharest, and with his sensible, more reserved wife lives in a cosy little academic community, seemingly oblivious to the events unfolding outside. However, as the conflict deepens, Romania turns fascist and the Pringles are forced to flee. They find themselves separated from home (in Greece and in Egypt, behind the German front), continually bumping into a small coterie of acquaintances who are in the same isolated situation (happily out of harm's way for some). These include the lazy, parasitic clown Prince Yakimov, foreign office executive Dobson, young army officer Simon Boulderstone, Jewish refugee Sasha Drucker, poet Bill Castlebar, flighty Edwina Little, pompous visiting lecturer Lord Pinkrose, and devious socialist Dubedat. However, the Pringles' love for each other is put to the test, especially when they are forcibly parted by events and when Guy repeatedly puts his work ahead of their relationship. As a result, their characters and personalities are forced to change.

Costing £6 million, *Fortunes of War* was the BBC's response to Granada's success with lavish dramas like BRIDESHEAD REVISITED and THE JEWEL IN THE CROWN. It was adapted in seven parts by Alan Plater from Olivia Manning's two trilogies, comprising the novels *The Great Fortune, The Spoilt City, Friends and Heroes* (*The Balkan Trilogy*), *The Danger Tree, The Battle Lost* and *The Sum of Things* (*The Levant Trilogy*).

Forty Minutes ✶✶

UK (BBC) Documentary. BBC 2 1981–94

Editors **Roger Mills, Edward Mirzoeff, Caroline Pick, Paul Watson**

Acclaimed documentary series tackling a variety of offbeat subjects.

With each programme lasting, as expected, 40 minutes, this collection of documentaries (a successor to MAN ALIVE) looked at subjects as varied as child prostitution, lavatories, gifted children, homing pigeons, battered husbands, amateur dramatics and prize-winning leeks. A well-remembered 1986 contribution was Paul Watson's *The Fishing Party* that focused on four well-bred, controversially right-wing men having a laugh on an angling trip, while another, *Away the Lads* in 1994, followed boisterous English youths on holiday in Benidorm.

Fossett Saga, The ✶

UK (LWT) Situation Comedy. ITV 1969

James Fossett .... **Jimmy Edwards**
Herbert Quince .... **Sam Kydd**

Writer **Dave Freeman**
Producer **David Askey**

A writer of cheap literature sees a better future for himself.

Setting aside his schoolmaster's cape and cane, Jimmy Edwards branched out as a writer of penny dreadfuls in late-Victorian times in this short-lived sitcom. James Fossett is nothing if not ambitious and is seldom without a crackpot scheme to make himself wealthy. However, the extent of his over-optimism is regularly exposed by his sidekick, Herbert Quince, a window cleaner-cum-unofficial valet. Also seen on one occasion is music hall singer Millie Goswick, played by June Whitfield.

Foster, Barry

(1931–2002)

Fair, curly-haired, Nottinghamshire-born actor whose TV high spot was the VAN DER VALK series of the early 1970s, in which he played the lead character, a Dutch police detective. The series was briefly revived in 1991. Among his other credits were parts in *Skyport*, MOGUL (Robert Driscoll), *Divorce His, Divorce Hers*, FALL OF EAGLES (Kaiser Wilhelm II), *The Three Hostages* (Richard Hannay), SMILEY'S PEOPLE (Saul Enderby), *A Woman Called Golda*, P. D. JAMES's *Death of an Expert Witness*, *Hôtel Du Lac*, BERGERAC, INSPECTOR MORSE, *The Free Frenchman* and ROGER ROGER (Pieter Eugene).

Foster, Julia

(1941–)

Fair-haired British actress. She appeared in EMERGENCY – WARD 10, starred as Angie Botley in *Good Girl*, played Amy Wilde in WILDE ALLIANCE and took the title role in a version of *Moll Flanders*. She was also Janet in the domestic sitcom *The Cabbage Patch*, Carol Bolitho in *Virtual Murder*, Liz Weldon in LATE STARTER and Doris Doyle, the mum, in the kids' fantasy *News at Twelve*. Among her other credits have been roles in CASUALTY, HOLBY CITY and numerous single dramas, some in anthologies like LOVE STORY and *Play for Tomorrow*. She was once married to PLAY SCHOOL presenter Lionel Morton and is the mother of CASTAWAY 2000 star Ben Fogle.

Fosters, The ✶✶

UK (LWT) Situation Comedy. ITV 1976–7

Samuel Foster .... **Norman Beaton**
Pearl Foster .... **Isabelle Lucas**
Vilma .... **Carmen Munro**
Sonny Foster .... **Lenny Henry**
Shirley Foster .... **Sharon Rosita**
Benjamin Foster .... **Lawrie Mark**

Producer **Stuart Allen**

Fun and games with a black family in south London.

Breaking new ground as the first British series to feature an all-black cast, *The Fosters* was based on an American sitcom entitled *Good Times* (a spin-off from *Maude*, itself a spin-off from ALL IN THE FAMILY). Using anglicized original scripts, it featured an immigrant family living in a south London tower block. The Fosters are harassed dad Samuel, coping mum Pearl, artistic eldest son Sonny, 16-year-old Shirley and young Benjamin. In the same block lives Vilma, Pearl's friend and confidante. The programme was also notable for giving Lenny Henry (then aged 17) his first series role, but was attacked by some critics for reinforcing racial stereotypes.

Four Feather Falls ✶✶

UK (AP Films/Granada) Children's Western. ITV 1960
DVD: Network

Voices:
Tex Tucker .... **Nicholas Parsons**
Rocky .... **Kenneth Connor**
Dusty .... **Kenneth Connor**
Pedro .... **Kenneth Connor**
Grandpa Twink .... **David Graham**
Fernando .... **David Graham**
Ma Jones .... **Denise Bryer**
Little Jake .... **Denise Bryer**

Producer **Gerry Anderson**

Cowboy puppetry featuring a fair but tough sheriff who keeps order with the help of a little magic.

Tex Tucker is the sheriff of the Western town of Four Feather Falls, but he is no ordinary lawman. His job is made considerably more comfortable by four magical feathers that he wears in his stetson. The feathers, given to Tex by Indian Chief Kalamakooya for rescuing his lost son, Makooya, each have a function: one feather enables Tex's dog, Dusty, to speak (albeit with an English accent); another gives the power of speech to his horse, Rocky. The last two feathers control his two pistols, which independently swivel and fire whenever the sheriff is in danger. Should any of these feathers get lost, however, then the respective magical power also disappears.

Ably supported by Rocky and Dusty, his unofficial deputies, Tex is a true Western hero, standing for no nonsense in a typical cowboy town (founded on a site where the Indian chief had restored a dry waterfall). Among the villains are Fernando, Big Bad Ben and Pedro the Bandit, and the townsfolk who rely on their hero include Doc Haggerty, Ma Jones the storekeeper, Grandpa Twink and his grandson, Little Jake. Short on killing and big on songs (Michael Holliday provided Tex's singing voice, including for the theme song, 'Two Gun Tex of Texas'; Barry Gray composed the music; and Tommy Reilly provided harmonic accompaniment), the 15-minute series ran to 39 episodes. Producer Gerry Anderson also directed.

Four Just Men, The ✶✶

UK (Sapphire/ITC) Adventure. ITV 1959–60

Ben Manfred MP .... **Jack Hawkins**
Tim Collier .... **Dan Dailey**
Jeff Ryder .... **Richard Conte**
Ricco Poccari .... **Vittorio De Sica**
Nicole .... **Honor Blackman**
Vicky .... **June Thorburn**
Giulia .... **Lisa Gastoni**
Jock .... **Andrew Keir**

Executive Producer **Hannah Fisher (Weinstein)**
Producers **Sidney Cole, Jud Kinberg**

● ***Four wartime colleagues reunite to combat crime.***

The Four Just Men, as they style themselves, are MP and amateur detective Ben Manfred; American reporter Tim Collier, who is based in Paris; New York lawyer Jeff Ryder; and wealthy Roman hotelier Ricco Poccari. They were all members of the same Allied unit during the war and have been brought together again by Manfred at the dying request of their wartime leader, Colonel Bacon, to tackle injustice around the world. The men generally work alone (with each episode featuring only one star), although Manfred's men are also supported by their personal assistants: Nicole for Collier, Vicky for Ryder and Giulia for Poccari. The series was based on the 1906 novel by Edgar Wallace and the 1939 film, which cast the men in a more sinister light.

Fourth Arm, The ✶✶

UK (BBC) Drama. BBC 1 1983

Major Gallagher .... **Paul Shelley**
Col. Gwillim .... **Philip Latham**
Lt. Col. Squires .... **Neil Stacy**
Lamboit (Ferdy) .... **Roy Boyd**
Simone Portales (Rossignol) ... **Eve Adam**
Solange Rohr (Chardonneret) . **Susan Kyd**
Stephen Lovell (Hibout) .... **Rob Edwards**
Sgt Birkett (Hirondelle) .... **Angela Cheyne**
Wilson (Corbeau) .... **Stuart Black**
Ellen (Merle) .... **Carole Nimmons**
George Macklin (Choucas) ...... **Dean Harris**
Sgt Cameron (Grive) .... **Michael MacKenzie**
Capt. Macaulay (Mesange) ..... **Robert Swales**
Soltysyk (Warsaw) .... **Boris Isarov**
Cpl Moffat (Miff) .... **Leonard Fenton**
Prof. Evans .... **Gerald James**

Creators **John Brason, Gerard Glaister**
Writer **John Brason**
Producer **Gerard Glaister**

● ***An undercover squad aims to sabotage Hitler's last-chance strike weapon.***

It is 1944. The war is drawing to a close but Hitler, it appears, still has one final trick up his sleeve. His new secret weapon, the feared V-1, could be launched on Britain at any time. British intelligence is aware of this, however, and sets out to destroy the new flying bomb, or at least delay its impact, by putting together a team of specialists to sabotage the German plans. Members are recruited from every walk of life, and from various nationalities, and each is assigned a codename for the operation. This 12-part series follows their mission, from initial training to action in the field, showing how they deal with internal feuds and possible infiltration into their camp. A book of the same title was issued at the same time as the series aired.

Fowlds, Derek

(1937–)

British actor whose career has veered between reading stories to an animal puppet, manoeuvring a confused politician and supervising young policemen. It was as Basil Brush's straight man that Fowlds first became known, a role he followed up with appearances in dramas such as EDWARD THE SEVENTH, CLAYHANGER, STRANGERS, CRIBB, TRIANGLE, *Affairs of the Heart* (heart-attack victim Peter Bonamy), *My Son, My Son, Rules of Engagement*, BOON, INSPECTOR MORSE, CHANCER and *Firm Friends* (John Gutteridge), as well as comedies such as *After This, That*, MISS JONES AND SON, ROBIN'S NEST and RINGS ON THEIR FINGERS. As private secretary Bernard Wooley in YES, MINISTER and its sequel, *Yes, Prime Minister*, he helped keep Paul Eddington's Jim Hacker on the straight and narrow, and in HEARTBEAT, as the fatherly if set-in-his-ways Sgt Blaketon, he kept an eye on young coppers like Nick Berry's PC Rowan. His second wife was BLUE PETER presenter Lesley Judd. His son, Jeremy, is also an actor.

Fowler, Harry

MBE (Henry Fowler, 1926–)

Chirpy Cockney actor and presenter, a star of THE ARMY GAME (Corporal Flogger Hoskins) and OUR MAN AT ST MARK'S (Harry the Yo Yo), before branching out into children's programmes, hosting *Going a Bundle* with Kenny Lynch and *Get This* with James Villiers. He has also appeared in series like SPOONER'S PATCH (Jimmy the Con), *Dead Ernest* (Cherub Fred), *Dramarama*, SCARECROW AND MRS KING, SUPERGRAN, *Davro's Sketch Pad*, THE BILL, CASUALTY, IN SICKNESS AND IN HEALTH, WORLD'S END and LOVE HURTS, as well as around 80 films.

Fox ✶✶

UK (Thames/Euston Films) Drama. ITV 1980

Billy Fox .... **Peter Vaughan**
Connie Fox .... **Elizabeth Spriggs**
Kenny Fox .... **Ray Winstone**
Joey Fox .... **Larry Lamb**
Vin Fox .... **Bernard Hill**
Ray Fox .... **Derrick O'Connor**
Phil Fox .... **Eamon Boland**
Renie Fox .... **Rosemary Martin**
Andy Fox .... **Richard Weinbaum**
Nan .... **Cindy O'Callaghan**

Writer **Trevor Preston**
Executive Producer **Verity Lambert**
Producer **Graham Benson**

● ***The singular and collective lives of a south London family with shady connections.***

This 13-part filmed drama revolves around the Fox family,

headed by local Mr Big, Billy Fox, who celebrates his 70th birthday in the opening episode. The same episode introduces his clan, made up of his second wife, Connie, his five sons and their respective wives, mistresses and offspring. The boys are Vin, working in the construction industry; Kenny, an aspiring welterweight boxer; Joey, a womanizing taxi-driver; Phil, a student; and finally Ray. Also prominent are Vin's wife, Renie, and their deaf son, Andy (Billy's pride and joy). The drama unfolds in two phases: before and after 'King' Billy's death, showing how the family struggles to deal with the loss of this larger-than-life figure who terrifies other villains but is kind to the ordinary folk on his manor.

Fox, Edward

OBE (1937–)

Upright British actor, star of EDWARD AND MRS SIMPSON. Among his other credits have been parts in THE AVENGERS, MAN IN A SUITCASE, JOURNEY TO THE UNKNOWN, *Hard Times* (Harthouse), *Shaka Zulu*, *Quatermaine's Terms* (St John Quatermaine), GULLIVER'S TRAVELS (General Limtoc), A DANCE TO THE MUSIC OF TIME (Uncle Giles), *I was a Rat* (Prof. Prosser), FOYLE'S WAR, DANIEL DERONDA (Sir Hugo Mallinger) and AGATHA CHRISTIE'S POIROT, although he has been more prolific in the cinema. He is the brother of actor James Fox and father of actress Emilia Fox.

Fox, Emilia

(1974–)

British actress, the daughter of actors Edward Fox and Joanna David. Emilia's TV debut came in the role of Georgiana Darcy in PRIDE AND PREJUDICE, while she was still an English student at Oxford. Other major parts have been in REBECCA (Mrs de Winter), *Bright Hair* (Ann Devenish), CATHERINE COOKSON'S *The Round Tower* (Vanessa Ratcliffe), RANDALL AND HOPKIRK (DECEASED) (Jeannie Hurst), SHOOTING THE PAST (Spig), *Bad Blood* (Jackie Shipton), DAVID COPPERFIELD (Clara), *Other People's Children* (Dale), *Henry VIII* (Jane Seymour), SILENT WITNESS (Nikki Alexander), *Gunpowder, Treason and Plot* (Lady Margaret), and *The Virgin Queen* (Amy Dudley), with guest appearances in THE SCARLET PIMPERNEL, *Verdict*, COUPLING and AGATHA CHRISTIE'S MARPLE. Fox is married to actor Jared Harris, son of the late Richard Harris.

Fox, Michael J.

(Michael Andrew Fox; 1961–)

Canadian actor, best known for Hollywood blockbusters like *Back to the Future* and *Teen Wolf*, whose major TV credits have been in the comedies FAMILY TIES (Alex Keaton) and SPIN CITY (Deputy Mayor Michael Flaherty). His well-publicized fight against Parkinson's disease led him to retire from the latter, although he later made occasional appearances in the series and acted as a consultant. Fox had previously been seen in *Leo and Me*, and *Palmerstown, USA* (Willy-Joe Hall), as well as taking small roles in such shows as *Trapper John, MD*. He also provided the voice of Marty in the cartoon version of *Back to the Future* and starred alongside Woody Allen in the single drama *Don't Drink the Water*. A recent guest credit came in SCRUBS. He is married to actress Tracy Pollan (a former FAMILY TIES co-star).

Fox, Sir Paul

CBE (1925–)

Former paratrooper and journalist Paul Fox joined the BBC in 1950 as holiday relief writer on BBC TELEVISION NEWSREEL, but he quickly put down roots. He was influential in the setting-up of the SPORTSVIEW unit and was the programme's editor from 1953. Fox went on to edit PANORAMA and then progressed up the ladder to the position of Controller of BBC 1 in 1967. He was lured away to Yorkshire Television in 1973, to succeed Donald Baverstock as programme controller, becoming the company's managing director in 1977. He also chaired ITN for two years. In 1988 Fox returned to the BBC on a three-year contract as Managing Director of BBC Television.

Fox Broadcasting Company

America's fourth network, making inroads where others (particularly DuMont in the 1940s and 1950s) failed. The company is owned by News Corporation, and takes its name from the old Twentieth Century-Fox studios, which are now part of the company. Fox went on air in November 1986 and soon began to eat into the market share of America's big three networks (CBS, NBC and ABC), adopting a trendier attitude and cleverly launching new programmes in August when the other stations have traditionally scheduled reruns. While Fox is still not in the same league as the established networks, it is having its successes (including poaching the Superbowl) and among its innovative programmes have been BEVERLY HILLS 90210, THE SIMPSONS, MARRIED . . . WITH CHILDREN, THE X-FILES, 24 and MALCOLM IN THE MIDDLE, HOUSE and *American Idol*. It is a sister channel to Fox News.

Foxy Lady ★★

UK (Granada) Situation Comedy. ITV 1982; 1984

Daisy Jackson .... **Diane Keen**
Joe Prince .... **Geoffrey Burridge**
J. P. Schofield .... **Patrick Troughton**
Ben Marsh .... **Milton Johns**
Tancred Taylour .... **Alan David**
Hector Ross .... **Gregor Fisher**
Owen Buckley .... **Steven Pinder**
Acorn Henshaw .... **Tom Mennard**

Writer **Geoffrey Lancashire**
Producer **John G. Temple**

A female editor rides to the rescue of an ailing northern newspaper.

Set in 1959, *Foxy Lady* relates how Daisy Jackson gamely takes on the editorship of the *Ramsden Reminder*, a weekly local rag tottering on the brink of bankruptcy following the death of the previous incumbent. Her all-male team consists of accountant Joe Prince, feature writer J. P. Schofield, gambling sports writer Ben Marsh, women's page editor Hector Ross, arts editor Tancred Taylour, print trainee Owen Buckley and odd-job man Acorn Henshaw. Circulation initially picks up, but life is never easy for Daisy.

The cast list makes interesting reading today. Not only did it feature veterans like former DOCTOR WHO Patrick Troughton and Tom Mennard (CORONATION STREET's Sam Tindall), but also a pre-CROSSROADS and BROOKSIDE Steven Pinder, and Gregor Fisher before he donned the string vest of Rab C. Nesbitt.

Foyle's War ★★★

UK (Greenlit) Police Drama. ITV 2002–4; 2006–
DVD: Acorn Media

Det. Chief Supt. Christopher Foyle .... **Michael Kitchen**
Samantha Stewart .... **Honeysuckle Weeks**
DS Paul Milner .... **Anthony Howell**
Andrew Foyle .... **Julian Ovenden**

Creator **Anthony Horowitz**
Writers **Anthony Horowitz, Matthew Hall, Michael Russell, Rob Heyland**
Producers **Jill Green, Simon Passmore, Keith Thompson**

● ***Blackmail behind blackouts, robbery among ration books and murder in mufti: the cases of a wartime detective.***

The heart-warming idea that the nation pulled unanimously together during World War II and that crime was something temporarily forgotten is well and truly laid to rest in *Foyle's War*. A detective series in the INSPECTOR MORSE/MIDSOMER MURDERS mould, it begins in May 1940 with the Germans seemingly poised to make their assault on England's southern coast. Detective Chief Superintendent Christopher Foyle lives and works for the police in Hastings, but feels his talents could be more wisely used elsewhere during the conflict. His superiors disagree, and Foyle realizes that they are right when the first of a sequence of murders and other serious crimes rears its ugly head. The diligent but understated Foyle is a widower, whose student son, Andrew, is now a pilot in the RAF. At work, his number two, DS Paul Milner, has already done his bit, tragically losing part of a leg during the fight to save Norway. Now Milner has to cope with physical handicap, a reluctant return to civvy street and a wife who shows him less affection than he deserves after his injury, even to the point of fleeing to the country and leaving him to fend for himself. As Foyle doesn't drive, his chauffeuse is Samantha Stewart, a vicar's daughter who has been seconded from the army's MTC (Mechanised Transport Corps) to help out Foyle during a driver shortage. Her clipped speech and gauche manner fail to conceal an eagerness to prove her worth as an investigator herself. The action progresses gradually, episode by episode, through the war years, bringing in real-life contemporary events as a backdrop to each crime mystery.

Fraggle Rock ★★

UK (TVS/Jim Henson/CBC) Children's Entertainment. ITV 1984–92
DVD: HIT Entertainment

The Captain .... **Fulton Mackay**
PK .... **John Gordon-Sinclair**
BJ .... **Simon O'Brien**

Creator **Jim Henson**
Executive Producers **Anna Home, Jim Henson, J. Nigel Pickard**
Producers **Duncan Kenworthy, Lawrence S. Mirkin, Victor Pemberton**

● ***A wonderful world of music and adventure exists beneath a weather-beaten lighthouse.***

On Fraggle Rock, a bare rugged outcrop off the south coast of England, stands a lighthouse. The lighthouse keeper is an old sea dog called simply The Captain, who has no one for company but his faithful old hound, Sprocket. But beneath this lonely outpost lurks a fantastic subterranean world. Unknown to The Captain, in a maze of tunnels live the Fraggles, a colourful species of big-eyed, bushy creatures who have bags of energy and enjoy lots of song and dance. They even have their own resident band, the Fraggle Five, consisting of the hesitant Wembley, the depressed Boober, the bohemian Mokey, the straight-talking Red and the adventurous Gobo. Adventure, in fact, runs in Gobo's family, for it was his Uncle Matt who discovered the door to the human world ('outer space') and now sends back postcards describing the latest discoveries on his journey among the 'silly creatures'. Joining the Fraggles down below are the Doozers, an industrious, hard-hatted race of builders whose fabulous constructions are inevitably eaten by the Fraggles, plus the last survivors of the Gorg royal family, Pa, Ma and Junior. These impoverished noble giants live in a crumbling castle whose garden is raided for radishes by the hungry Fraggles. Completing the line-up is Marjorie, a rubbish heap that not only talks and sings but is a venerable source of wisdom for her underground neighbours. She is protected by helpers Philo and Gunge. In 1988, The Captain returned to sea and was replaced by his nephew, PK, who himself gave way to the even more youthful BJ a year later.

In Canada, where the series was shot, and the USA, the human oblivious to the Fraggles' existence was an inventor named Doc (played by Gerry Parkes) and the Fraggles lived beneath his house. Some of these episodes were shown in the UK after the original British episodes ended. A cartoon version was also made.

Francis, Clive

(1946–)

The son of NO HIDING PLACE star Raymond Francis, Clive Francis has enjoyed a successful (and more varied) TV career of his own. Among his major roles have been Francis Poldark in POLDARK, DS Dexter in NEW SCOTLAND YARD, Miles Henty in MAY TO DECEMBER, Major Maurice Drummond in THE PIGLET FILES and Dominic Eden in THE 10%ERS. He has also been seen in STRANGE REPORT, THE BRETTS, BULMAN, THE FAR PAVILIONS, *David Copperfield*, YES, PRIME MINISTER, *Old Flames*, LIPSTICK ON YOUR COLLAR (Major Hedges), SHARPE, *The Plant* (DCI Pinker), *Giving Tongue* (Llewellyn Groves), LONGITUDE (Captain Digges), *Reversals* and ROSEMARY AND THYME.

Francis, Jan

(1951–)

Dark-haired English actress, seen in both dramatic and comedy roles. Her most prominent performance was as Penny Warrender in the sitcom JUST GOOD FRIENDS. However, she has enjoyed several other starring roles, as resistance worker Lisa Colbert in SECRET ARMY, newly widowed Sally Hardcastle in STAY LUCKY, and Maggie Perowne in *Under the Hammer*, for instance. Her ballet training came in useful for her part in *A Chance to Sit Down*, and among the many other programmes she has contributed to have been JACKANORY, SUTHERLAND'S LAW, LOOKING FOR CLANCY, *The Long Chase* (Susan Fraser), ANNE OF GREEN GABLES (Diana Barry), *Rooms, Couples*, THE DUCHESS OF DUKE STREET, RAFFLES, *A Play for Love*, THE RACING GAME, TARGET, RIPPING YARNS, *The Good Companions*, TALES OF THE UNEXPECTED, Alan Plater's PREMIERE offering, *Give Us a Kiss, Christabel*, *The Ghostbusters of East Finchley* (Grace Pullen), SPARK (Colette Parkerwell), HEARTBEAT, SUNBURN, MICAWBER, *The Alan Clark Diaries* (Barbara Lord), *According to Bex*, *Bloodlines* (Elaine Hopkin), *Twisted Tales* and WHERE THE HEART IS.

Francis, Raymond

(1911–87)

One of British television's earliest coppers, London-born Raymond Francis played the snuff-taking Tom Lockhart in three different series: MURDER BAG in 1957, CRIME SHEET in 1959, and finally NO HIDING PLACE, which ran for eight years up to 1967. Francis had previously appeared in a handful of TV plays and starred as Dr Watson in a 1951 BBC version of *Sherlock Holmes*. Not long before he died he returned to make a cameo appearance as Lockhart in THE COMIC STRIP PRESENTS *Five Go Mad in Dorset* (one of several such appearances for Lockhart over the years). Francis was also seen in series like *Thomas and Sarah*, EDWARD AND MRS SIMPSON, MISS MARPLE and ME AND MY GIRL. He was the father of actor Clive Francis.

Franciscus, James

(1934–91)

American leading man who guested in various 1950s series like HAVE GUN, WILL TRAVEL and THE TWILIGHT ZONE, before winning a lead role in NAKED CITY. As Detective Jim Halloran, he stayed with the series for just one year but, throughout the 1960s and 1970s, he was never short of work. US dramas, including *The Investigators* and *Mr Novak*, plus smaller parts in programmes like THE FBI, kept him busy for most of the time. In 1971 he played blind private detective LONGSTREET, and later appeared in a couple of other series, *Doc Elliott* and *Hunter*. He had several TV movies to his name, too.

Frank Stubbs Promotes/Frank Stubbs ✳✳

UK (Carlton/Noel Gay) Comedy Drama. ITV 1993–4

Frank Stubbs	**Timothy Spall**
Petra Dillon	**Lesley Sharp**
Dawn Dillon	**Danniella Westbrook**
Archie Nash	**Trevor Cooper**
Dave Giddings	**Nick Reding**
Karen Lai	**Choy-Ling Man**
Diane Stubbs	**Hazel Ellerby**
Blick	**Roy Marsden**

Creator **Simon Nye**
Producer **Hilary Bevan Jones**

● ***An aspiring showbiz promoter never quite makes it big.***

Ticket-tout Frank Stubbs is tired of pacing the West End streets hawking overpriced tickets for the top shows. He is even more tired of being nicked and having to spend the night in the cells. Inspired by the success of smooth young Dave Giddings, he decides that promotion is to be the name of the game from now on. His first break comes with an Australian country and western singer, whom he stages despite the best efforts of his more established rivals. Predictably, she then leaves him for a real professional. After that, the ever-optimistic Frank and his colleague, Archie, find themselves ducking and diving in and out of schemes to promote kit cars, Russian skaters, graffiti artists, hopeful actresses, ambitious film directors, a low-profile politician and an American evangelist. Frank has just as many troubles in his personal life, too. He lives with his recently widowed (and virtually bankrupted) sister, Petra, and her daughter, Dawn, in a flat above a betting shop. His own wife, Diane, has kicked him out after his much-regretted fling with a teenager. In the second series, shown in 1994, Stubbs has moved to a swish new office-block, owned by a character named Blick.

Borrowing heavily from the Arthur Daley school of wheeling and dealing, the series was based on Simon Nye's novel *Wideboy*. Nye also wrote some of the episodes.

Frankenstein Jr and the Impossibles ✳

US (Hanna-Barbera) Cartoon. BBC 1 1967 (US: CBS 1966–8)

Voices:

Frankenstein Jr	**Ted Cassidy**
Buzz Conroy	**Dick Beals**
Prof. Conroy	**John Stephenson**
Multi Man	**Don Messick**
Fluid Man	**Paul Frees**
Coil Man	**Hal Smith**

Executive Producers **William Hanna, Joseph Barbera**

● ***Cartoon package featuring a giant Frankenstein robot and a vigilante pop group.***

Frankenstein Jr is the invention of red-headed boy scientist Buzz Conroy, son of the eminent Professor Conroy. A huge, talking, thinking, rocket-powered robot, Frankenstein Jr looks just like his horror movie namesake but is used entirely for good causes, defeating supervillains like Dr Shock and Birdman. Buzz controls Jr with a special radar ring and also joins the robot on his missions. Clambering up on his back, Buzz utters the magic command 'Allakazoom!', which blasts them off from the Professor's mountain lab. Once in action, Buzz dons his rocket-belt, which enables him to fly, and Jr employs an armoury of ingenious weapons.

The Impossibles are a three-man, touring pop-group whose performances are constantly interrupted by their boss, Big D, who speaks to them from a video screen hidden in a guitar. With the cry of 'Rally-Ho!', the trio bound into action against crooks, making full use of their incredible abilities. Coil Man has spring-loaded, extending limbs, Fluid Man has the power to become any kind of liquid (allowing him to trickle under doors, for example) and Multi Man can make instant and unlimited copies of himself. The 'Impossicar' takes them from gig to gig.

Any actors worried about typecasting ought to consider Ted Cassidy's role in this series. Fresh from playing Lurch in THE ADDAMS FAMILY, he now found himself voicing a Frankenstein robot. The giant robot idea was derived from a Japanese series called *Gigantor*.

Franklin, Gretchen

(1911–2005)

London-born actress familiar in down-to-earth, dithery female roles, most notably as Ethel Skinner in EASTENDERS. She played Alf Garnett's wife (then Alf *Ramsey*) in the COMEDY PLAYHOUSE pilot of TILL DEATH US DO PART, but didn't continue into the series because of stage commitments. Programmes she appeared in, in a varied career, included QUATERMASS, *The Artful Dodger*, COMPACT, *The Dick Emery Show*, GEORGE AND MILDRED, *Bowler*, *Churchill's People*, plus various single dramas. She was also Sarah Meek in *Castle Haven*, Myrtle Cavendish in CROSSROADS, Auntie Lil in I DIDN'T KNOW YOU CARED and Alice in *Dead Ernest*.

Franklyn, William

(1926–)

For all his TV work, smoothie William Franklyn may be best remembered as the 'Schh! You know who' man, after his commercials for Schweppes soft drinks. However, he entered television in the mid-1950s, taking roles in series like DOUGLAS FAIRBANKS PRESENTS, THE COUNT OF MONTE CRISTO and INTERNATIONAL DETECTIVE, before securing star billing in the 1961 adventure series TOP SECRET, in which he played undercover agent Peter Dallas. He was a familiar face in the 1960s and 1970s, cropping up in action series like THE AVENGERS and THE BARON, and detective stories like MAIGRET and PUBLIC EYE, fronting the sketch show *What's On Next?*, and taking parts in the comedies *Paradise Island* (shipwrecked entertainments officer Cuthbert Fullworthy) and *The Steam Video Company*. He hosted the panel game *Masterspy* and was also seen in *Moon and Son*, THE UPPER HAND, LOVEJOY, GBH and *The Courtroom* (Judge Matthew Johnson). He is the father of actress Sabina Franklyn.

Fraser, Bill

(1908–87)

Busy British character actor, best remembered as Sgt Claude Snudge in THE ARMY GAME and its sequels, BOOTSIE AND SNUDGE and *Foreign Affairs*, as well as the slightly different *Vacant Lot* (builder William Bendlove). His other performances included Barney Pank in *Barney is My Darling*, a defrocked priest in Joe Orton's play *Funeral Games*, undertaker Basil Bulstrode in *That's Your Funeral* and stationmaster Hedley Green in THE TRAIN NOW STANDING. Fraser was also seen as one of Alf Garnett's buddies in TILL DEATH US DO PART, and played Mr Micawber in a BBC version of *David Copperfield*, Henry Brassington in *Flesh and Blood*, Bert Baxter in THE SECRET DIARY OF ADRIAN MOLE, Dr Fellows-Smith in *Doctors' Daughters* and Mr Justice Bullingham in RUMPOLE OF THE BAILEY. He also appeared in P. D. JAMES's *Cover Her Face*, although his TV credits dated way back to the 1940s. His wife was actress Pamela Cundell (DAD'S ARMY's Mrs Fox).

Fraser, Ronald

(1930–97)

Lancashire-born actor, star of the 1970 sitcom THE MISFIT, in which he played Basil 'Badger' Allenby-Johnson. Fraser also took the role of Inspector Spooner in the first series of SPOONER'S PATCH and enjoyed plenty of other TV credits, popping up in drama anthologies like *Rogues' Gallery* and *Conceptions of Murder*, comedies such as LIFE WITHOUT GEORGE (senile pianist Mr Chambers), and adventure series like *The Young Indiana Jones Chronicles*, as well as taking parts like Major Archibald Paxville MP in PENNIES FROM HEAVEN, Sid Dawes in *Follow Me*, Dr Porter in *The Blackheath Poisonings*, Van Helsing in *Virtual Murder* and Sir Richard Gregory in MOLL FLANDERS (one of his last roles).

Frasier ★★★★

US (Grub Street/Paramount) Situation Comedy. Channel 4 1994–2004 (US: NBC 1993–2004)
DVD: Paramount

Dr Frasier Crane .... **Kelsey Grammer**
Dr Niles Crane .... **David Hyde Pierce**
Daphne Moon/Crane .... **Jane Leeves**
Martin Crane .... **John Mahoney**
Roz Doyle .... **Peri Gilpin**
Bob 'Bulldog' Briscoe .... **Dan Butler**

Creators **David Angell, Peter Casey, David Lee**
Executive Producers **David Angell, Peter Casey, David Lee, Kelsey Grammer, Christopher Lloyd, Joe Keenan, Mark Reisman, Jon Sherman, Dan O'Shannon, Sam Johnson**

● ***The turbulent life of a pompous radio psychiatrist.***
Frasier Crane, formerly the intellectual at the bar of CHEERS, has divorced wife Lilith, left Boston and returned to his home town of Seattle. Settling into a new job as resident shrink on the radio station KACL, he is just beginning to enjoy life in his luxurious new apartment in Elliott Bay Towers when his independence is shattered by the arrival of his invalid father. Martin is an ex-cop who has taken a bullet on duty, and moving in with him are his physical therapist, a semi-psychic Mancunian named Daphne Moon, and an irritatingly intelligent terrier named Eddie (played by a dog called Moose – later retired and replaced by his son, Enzo). Not that this is the limit of Frasier's extended family, as his even more effete brother, Niles (also an analyst), is seldom away from his doorstep, bemoaning his life with his never-seen, extremely wealthy, hypochondriac wife, Maris. At work, too, Frasier's sanity is tested during his daily phone-in, this time by wacky callers (played by celebrities like Art Garfunkel and Mel Brooks), nymphomaniac producer Roz and vulgar, practical-joking sports presenter Bulldog. The strain also spills over to the aptly named local coffee shop, Café Nervosa.

Although exhibiting all the best traits of the US sitcom – precise characterization, sharp dialogue and rich farce among them – *Frasier* is also a comedy of manners. The upper-class pretensions of Frasier (who is considerably more refined here than in his latter days at *Cheers*) and Niles are sharply contrasted with the working-class ethics of their good-hearted dad – designer furniture opposite a tatty old armchair, expensive wines against cans of Ballantine's beer, snooty restaurant dinners before the opera versus a hot dog at the ball game, etc. Recurring strands include Frasier's struggle to find a new woman, Roz's similar unhappiness in her single life and Niles's crush on the oblivious Daphne.

As the series develops, the storylines move on. Maris divorces Niles, Martin dates a barmaid named Sherry, Roz becomes a single mum and Niles marries a demandingly fussy plastic surgeon named Mel. In one memorable season-closer, Daphne's wedding to attorney Donny Douglas is wrecked when she and Niles finally get it together and head off in Martin's Winnebago (they later marry). Also seen at times is Daphne's brother Simon, played with an atrocious Cockney accent by Anthony LaPaglia. In the final episode, Martin gets married, Roz becomes station manager, Niles and Daphne's baby boy arrives and Frasier – after toying with a new job in San Francisco – leaves Seattle to *chercher la femme* in Chicago.

Cheers had been lauded by both viewers and critics, but its spin-off proved even more successful, being showered with Emmys and attracting massive audiences.

Fraud Squad ★★

UK (ATV) Police Drama. ITV 1969–70

DI Gamble .... **Patrick O'Connell**
DS Vicky Hicks .... **Joanna Van Gyseghem**

Helen Gamble .... **Elizabeth Weaver**
Lucy Gamble .... **Katherine O'Connell**
Supt. Proud .... **Ralph Nossek**

Creator **Ivor Jay**
Producer **Nicholas Palmer**

The inquiries of Scotland Yard's Fraudulent Crimes Squad.

The featured members of the Fraud Squad are Detective Inspector Gamble and his assistant, DS Hicks (one of TV's first prominent female detectives). Together they tackle fraud in all areas, from the activities of con men to the dubious financial status of a religious sect. Problems within Gamble's own family also come to the fore. The series was created by Ivor Jay, a former DIXON OF DOCK GREEN and CROSSROADS scriptwriter.

Freeman, Right Hon. John

MBE (1915–)

Serious, determined British interviewer (almost interrogator) of the late 1950s/early 1960s, mostly on FACE TO FACE. A former Panorama contributor and Labour MP for Watford, he went on to edit the *New Statesman* and to become British High Commissioner in India, Ambassador to the USA and chairman of both London Weekend Television and ITN.

Freeman, Martin

(1971–)

English actor best known as Tim in THE OFFICE. He has since appeared as Lord Shaftesbury in CHARLES II – THE POWER AND THE PASSION, Mike in HARDWARE, Terry Ross in *The Debt*, DS Stringer in *Margery and Gladys*, and Ed Robinson in *The Robinsons*. Other work has included contributions to the comedy shows *Bruiser*, *World of Pub* and *TV to Go*, plus small roles in CASUALTY, *Lock, Stock . . .*, BLACK BOOKS and LINDA GREEN.

Freetime

See *Magpie*.

Freeview

Package of digital channels put together by the BBC, Crown Castle International and BSkyB to replace the service formerly provided by ITV Digital. Unlike the latter, however, as its name suggests, all channels available in Freeview do not entail subscriptions and can be received without payment via a terrestrial digital receiver. The complete package was not initially available through Sky Digital or digital cable providers but most of the channels, individually, could be received. The first channels to feature in the Freeview package when launched on 30 October 2002 (apart from digital versions of the main terrestrial channels) were BBC News 24, Sky News, ITV News Channel, Sky Sports News, BBC 4, BBC Parliament, UK History, UK TV, BBC Choice, ITV 2, CBBC, CBeebies, the charity-based Community Channel, plus music, travel and shopping channels. The service is now run by DTV Services Ltd., a company jointly owned by the BBC, BSkyB, National Grid Wireless (the new name for Crown Castle) and ITV and Channel 4, who joined the consortium in 2005.

Freewheelers ★★

UK (Southern) Children's Adventure. ITV 1968–73

Col. Buchan .... **Ronald Leigh-Hunt**
Karl August Von Gelb .... **Geoffrey Toone**
Bill Cowan .... **Tom Owen**
Terry Driver .... **Mary Maude**
Chris Kelly .... **Gregory Phillips**
Nick Carter .... **Christopher Chittell**
Olga Yevchenko .... **Jeanne Moody**
Fiona .... **Carole Mowlam**
Prof. Craig .... **Eric Dodson**
Bryant .... **Ivan Beavis**
Mike Hobbs .... **Adrian Wright**
Col. Aristides .... **Pamela Ann Davy**
Major Tom Graham .... **Eric Flynn**
Max Prentiss .... **John Colclough**
Sue Craig .... **Wendy Padbury**
Ryan .... **Richard Shaw**
Burke .... **Michael Ripper**
Steve Walker .... **Leonard Gregory**
Dr Jo Bell .... **Jenny Till**
Colin Wade .... **Ray Armstrong**
Jill .... **Caroline Ellis**
Gen. Grant .... **Michael Barrington**
Prof. Kirov .... **Gerard Heinz**
Morris .... **Donald Morley**
Eva .... **Katarina Granlund**
Dave .... **Martin Neil**
Phil .... **Sam Kydd**
Naylor .... **Robert Gillespie**
Crouch .... **Neil McCarthy**
Cunliffe .... **Bernard Horsfall**

Creator **Chris McMaster**
Producer **Chris McMaster**

Teenagers help British Intelligence defeat global crime.

Fast cars, helicopters and speedboats, these are the hallmarks of *Freewheelers*, an all-action series for kids with more than a hint of James Bond in its conception. The Freewheelers are a group of daring teenagers, but the personnel changes from series to series. Initially, Bill Cowan (played by Tom Owen, later star of LAST OF THE SUMMER WINE), Terry Driver and Chris Kelly are the intrepid trio who aid Colonel Buchan of MI6 in his quest to pin down vengeful Nazi Von Gelb. Von Gelb is a man whose evil knows no bounds: he even has plans to freeze Britain into an ice cube if he doesn't get his way. Thankfully the Freewheelers win through, but Von Gelb is not done for and reappears in later episodes. The suave, good-living Buchan remains centre stage (except for one series when – on assignment – he is temporarily replaced by Formula 3 driver Major Graham). However, the Freewheelers themselves come and go, adding at various times Nick (played by Christopher Chittell, EMMERDALE's Eric Pollard), Mike, Max, Sue, Steve, Jill, Eva and Dave to their number. Also brought into the action are Fiona, Buchan's Scottish oceanographer colleague, fellow scientist Dr Jo Bell and young intelligence agent Colin Wade. Among the numerous villains who outstay their welcome are the glamorous Colonel Aristides, skulduggerous Ryan and Blake, and the devious General Grant. With its cliffhanger endings, relentless pace and assorted European locations, *Freewheelers* provided a thrilling segment of children's hour for five years.

FremantleMedia

FremantleMedia is a division of the RTL Group that includes some of British television's best-known production companies. The business was previously known as Pearson Television, which started the portfolio by acquiring Thames Television, the former ITV franchisee for London weekdays. Later acquisitions were Alomo (BIRDS OF A FEATHER, GOODNIGHT SWEETHEART), Witzend (AUF WIEDERSEHEN, PET), Grundy (NEIGHBOURS, GOING FOR GOLD), Regent Television (FIFTEEN TO ONE) and Talkback (THEY THINK IT'S ALL OVER). Pearson was also a major shareholder in Channel 5 and merged with fellow shareholder CLT-UFA in 2000 to create the RTL Group. Pearson later abandoned television altogether, selling its stake in the new company to Bertelsmann in December 2001, heralding the name change for the British television division to FremantleMedia.

French, Dawn

(1957–)

British comic actress, long-time writing and performing partner of Jennifer Saunders and wife of Lenny Henry. After a spell as a teacher and some club work with Saunders, she broke into television as part of the COMIC STRIP team, appearing in all their films. With Saunders, Ruby Wax and Tracey Ullman, she featured as Amanda in GIRLS ON TOP (also as co-writer) and then starred in the comic mystery plays MURDER MOST HORRID. She has headlined as GERALDINE GRANGER, THE VICAR OF DIBLEY, Lisette in *Let Them Eat Cake*, murdering nurse Elaine Dobbs in the *Screen One* presentation *Tender Loving Care*, Bev Bodger in the drama *Sex and Chocolate*, Alice Putkin in TED AND ALICE and Mary Trewednack in WILD WEST, as well as hosting the food and fashion programmes *Scoff* and *Swank*, providing voices for *Pongwiffy* and *Bosom Pals*, and being seen in THE YOUNG ONES, THE STORYTELLER, HAPPY FAMILIES (the cook), DAVID COPPERFIELD (Mrs Crupp), AGATHA CHRISTIE'S MARPLE and, of course, *French and Saunders*.

French, Michael

(1962–)

British actor who sprang to fame as David Wicks in EASTENDERS, moving on to roles such as Jeff Slade in CRIME TRAVELLER, Nick Jordan in HOLBY CITY (with cross-over appearances in CASUALTY), DS Alexander Murchison in *The Fabulous Bagel Boys*, Ellis Bride in *The Gentleman Thief*, and Dr Tom Gilder in BORN AND BRED. French has also contributed to *The Afternoon Play* series.

French Fields

See *Fresh Fields*.

Fresh Fields/French Fields ✶✶

UK (Thames) Situation Comedy. ITV 1984–6/1989–91

Hester Fields	**Julia McKenzie**
William Fields	**Anton Rodgers**
Sonia Barratt	**Ann Beach**
Nancy Penrose	**Fanny Rowe**
Guy Penrose	**Ballard Berkeley**
Peter Richardson	**Philip Bird**
Emma Richardson	**Debbie Cumming**
	Sally Baxter *(French Fields)*
	Karen Ascoe *(French Fields)*
Monsieur Dax	**Oliver Pierre** *(French Fields)*
Marie-Christine	**Victoria Baker** *(French Fields)*
Madame Remoleux	**Valerie Lush** *(French Fields)*
Chantal Moriac	**Pamela Salem** *(French Fields)*
Jill Trendle	**Liz Crowther** *(French Fields)*
Hugh Trendle	**Robin Kermode** *(French Fields)*

Creators/Writers **John Chapman** *(Fresh Fields/French Fields)*, **Ian Davidson** *(French Fields)*
Producers **Peter Frazer-Jones** *(Fresh Fields)*, **James Gilbert** *(French Fields)*

A middle-aged couple spice up their life after the kids leave home.

With the children, Tom and Emma, having flown the nest, Hester and William Fields need new challenges and new zest in their life. They embark on a rejuvenated relationship, enjoying each other's company and bouncing along in their new-found freedom, trying out new hobbies and pastimes. They live in Barnes, west London. The slightly scatty Hester (a cordon bleu cook) works one day a week at Lucy's Kitchen, and William is an accountant in the City, but their lives are playfully entwined, even if interrupted (especially at mealtimes) by nosy, scrounging neighbour Sonia and by Nancy, Hester's mum, who lives in the granny flat in the garden. Nancy's former husband (and Hester's father), Guy, is also seen from time to time. In 1989, the programme was revived after a three-year hiatus, but with its format and title changed. William is now headhunted for a job in France, so the Fields jump on the foreign property bandwagon and grapple with the language across the Channel. Their tactless, yuppie neighbours there are the Trendles, with Mme Remoleux the Fields' interfering housekeeper.

Fresh Prince of Bel-Air, The ✶✶

US (Stuffed Dog/Quincy Jones/David Salzman/NBC) Situation Comedy. BBC 2 1991–6 (US: NBC 1990–6)
DVD: Warner Home Video

Will Smith	**Will Smith**
Philip Banks	**James Avery**
Vivian Banks	**Janet Hubert-Whitten**
	Daphne Maxwell Reid
Carlton Banks	**Alfonso Ribeiro**
Hilary Banks	**Karyn Parsons**
Ashley Banks	**Tatyana M. Ali**
Nicky Banks	**Ross Bagley**
Geoffrey	**Joseph Marcell**
Jazz	**Jeff Townes**

Executive Producers **Quincy Jones, Kevin Wendle, Susan Borowitz, Andy Borowitz, Winifred Hervey-Stallworth, Gary H. Miller**

A Philadelphia rap artist is exiled to prosperous Los Angeles.

Young rapper Will Smith lives in a rough, tough district of west Philadelphia, but when he becomes a bit too involved in local gang culture, his parents ship him off to relatives on the west coast for his well-being. Comedy comes from both class and race – from the awkward situation of a poor boy trying to fit in with a snooty family that lives in a mansion, even though they are all black. Refined Uncle Philip, a lawyer (later judge), seems the very antithesis of black street cred, but has done his time with the brothers and is always able to point Will in the right direction. Aunt Vivian plays the loyal wife and family peacemaker and there are three kids: studious Carlton, spoilt, self-centred Hilary and young Ashley, Will's best friend in the house. A fourth child, Nicky, arrives later in the series' run. The family's butler, Geoffrey, proves a useful ally to the reluctant cuckoo in the nest. Will attends the Bel-Air Academy (later the University of Los Angeles) and struggles to fit in, palling up with Jazz (played by Will Smith's real-life rapping partner Jeff Townes, aka DJ Jazzy Jeff). Noted for its youthful feel and vibrant, cartoonish tone, yet with a moralistic undercurrent, the series was screened as part of the DEF II youth strand in the UK. Smith also performed the title track as he began his transformation from successful rap artist to Hollywood superstar.

Freud ✶✶

UK (BBC) Drama. BBC 2 1984

Sigmund Freud .... **David Suchet**
Anna Freud .... **Alison Key**
Martha Bernays .... **Helen Bourne**
Minna Bernays .... **Suzanne Bertish**
Jacob Freud .... **Howard Goorney**
Amalie Freud .... **Eliza Hunt**
Joseph Breuer .... **David Swift**
Teresa .... **Claire Davenport**
Carl Jung .... **Michael Pennington**

Writer **Carey Harrison**
Producer **John Purdie**

The father of psychoanalysis looks back on his remarkable life.

This six-part biopic of Sigmund Freud begins with the psychiatrist aged 83, dying in exile in England at the start of World War II. As he looks back over his eventful life, he reflects on personal affairs, his early work in Vienna in the 1870s and 1880s, his collaboration with doctor Joseph Breuer, his experiments in Paris, and his time in practice back in Austria. He remembers the way in which his pre-eminence in his field was established when the concept of psychoanalysis took hold in the USA in the early 20th century and also considers the turbulence his bold theories caused in society.

Freud, Sir Clement

(1924–)

TV personality, writer, humorist and gourmet, much seen on dog food adverts. For many years Freud was a Liberal MP. He is the father of radio and TV presenter Emma Freud.

Friday Night Armistice, The

See *Saturday Night Armistice, The*.

Friday Night Live

See *Saturday Live*.

Friel, Anna

(1976–)

Actress born in Belfast and raised in Rochdale, achieving star status as Beth Jordache in BROOKSIDE. Earlier, she had appeared in small roles in a variety of series, including *8:15 From Manchester*, EMMERDALE, CORONATION STREET, MEDICS, *In Suspicious Circumstances* and GBH (Susan Nelson). Since leaving *Brookside*, she has been seen in *Shakespeare Shorts: A Midsummer Night's Dream* (Hermia), OUR MUTUAL FRIEND (Bella Wilfer), CADFAEL, *Tales from the Crypt, The Tribe* (Lizzie), *Fields of Gold* (Lucia Merritt) and the single dramas *All for Love* (Flora) and *Watermelon* (Claire Ryan). In 2004, she played Megan Delaney in an American series called *The Jury*.

Friends ✶✶✶✶

US (Bright/Kauffman/Crane/Warner Brothers) Situation Comedy. Channel 4 1995–2004 (US: NBC 1994–2004)
DVD: Warner Home Video

Rachel Green .... **Jennifer Aniston**
Monica Geller/Bing .... **Courteney Cox Arquette**
Phoebe Buffay/Hannigan .... **Lisa Kudrow**
Joey Tribbiani .... **Matt LeBlanc**
Chandler Bing .... **Matthew Perry**
Ross Geller .... **David Schwimmer**
Gunther .... **James Michael Tyler**
Mike Hannigan .... **Paul Rudd**

Creators **Marta Kauffman, David Crane**
Executive Producers **Kevin S. Bright, Marta Kauffman, David Crane, Adam Chase, Greg Malins, Michael Curtis, Shana Goldberg-Meehan, Scott Silveri, Ted Cohen**

Six twentysomethings share life in New York City.

This hugely successful sitcom, noted for its sharp one-liners, focuses on a group of six friends who live in the Big Apple and hang out at Central Perk, a Greenwich Village coffee-shop. The three girls are rather spoilt Rachel Green, now – having walked out of her wedding and alienating her father – struggling to make her own way in the world as a waitress (and, later, as a fashion buyer); assistant-chef Monica Geller, in whose apartment Rachel seeks refuge; and their off-beat, New Age, masseuse pal, Phoebe Buffay. The three boys are museum worker Ross Geller, Monica's brother, who has just divorced his wife, Carol; dim, would-be actor Joey Tribbiani; and Joey's clownish, office worker roommate, Chandler Bing. The last two live across the hall from Rachel and Monica. The friends' lives revolve around career ambitions, romantic tie-ups and memories of their past (complete with flashbacks).

The biggest traumas seem to involve Ross, who discovers his wife is having his baby while living with her lesbian lover. He then begins an affair with Rachel, whom he had a crush on at school. He later marries English girl Emily, but the marriage is not a success. He returns to Rachel, who eventually has his baby, Emily. Of the others, Chandler and Monica became more than 'friends' and try desperately for a while to keep their relationship from the rest of the gang. This is after Monica has had a fling with Dr Richard Burke, a friend of her parents. Actress Lisa Kudrow also occasionally appears as Phoebe's twin sister, Ursula, who is a cross-over character from another sitcom, *Mad About You*. One other (thankfully unseen) regular is the Ugly Naked Guy, spied on by the gang from Monica's apartment.

By the time of the last episode, Monica and Chandler leave the scene to raise a family, Phoebe marries boyfriend Mike Hannigan and Ross and Rachel reach yet another understanding. Which leaves Joey all on his lonesome, but not for long. Barely had *Friends* disappeared off the air but a spin-off series entitled simply *Joey* (five 2005–) reached the screen, in which the eponymous hero moves to Hollywood to further his acting career.

Almost all *Friends* episodes are titled 'The One with . . .' (fill in the gap). The show's theme song, 'I'll Be There for You', was a UK hit for The Rembrandts in 1995.

Front Line, The ★★

UK (BBC) Situation Comedy. BBC 1 1984–5

Malcom ..... **Paul Barber**
Sheldon ..... **Alan Igbon**
Earl ..... **Ronnie Cush**

Creator/Writer **Alex Shearer**
Producer **Roger Race**

Two black brothers have different takes on life.

Having explored the comic potential of two incompatible brothers living together in his earlier sitcom, SINK OR SWIM, Alex Shearer returned to the idea with *The Front Line*, but this time taking the humour into the black community. The brothers (actually half-brothers) this time are Malcom and Sheldon. Malcom is earnest and ambitious. He works as a security guard but soon realizes his dream of becoming a police officer. This is a total sell-out as far as Rasta Sheldon is concerned, especially when Malcom's beat is the local front line (the place where blacks hang out). Inevitably, Sheldon's minor criminal antics get Malcom into hot water, but, through it all, brotherly love still shines through. Earl is Sheldon's mate; Maria is Malcom's WPC friend. The six episodes were filmed in Bristol and Cardiff, with producer Roger Race also directing.

Front Man

The main presenter of a news, sports or magazine programme, the link between the various items that make up the programme. Also known as anchor.

Frontier House

See *1900 House, The.*

Frost, Sir David

OBE (1939–)

Kent-born broadcaster who became an overnight success (or 'rose without trace', as Malcolm Muggeridge's wife is alleged to have put it) on the revolutionary satire show THAT WAS THE WEEK THAT WAS, in 1962. Having presented a few low-key programmes for ITV, Frost, the Cambridge graduate son of a Beccles minister, was thrust into the *TW3* host's chair when Brian Redhead pulled out. His unflappability shone through and he also took the show to the USA, where it established itself but failed to win the same acclaim. Back in the UK, Frost compered *TW3*'s less successful offspring, NOT SO MUCH A PROGRAMME, MORE A WAY OF LIFE, and then married comedy with hard-hitting interviews, hosting THE FROST REPORT (complete with sketches from Messrs Ronnie Barker, Ronnie Corbett and John Cleese) on the BBC and *The Frost Programme* (instigating 'trials by television') on ITV. He was executive producer of AT LAST THE 1948 SHOW, NO – THAT'S ME OVER HERE! and *The Ronnie Barker Playhouse*, and starred in his own *Frost on Saturday* and *Frost on Sunday* (while commuting across to the USA), plus various *Frost over . . .* programmes on countries like New Zealand and Australia. In 1974 he presented *Frost's Weekly* for the BBC and two years later secured a series of exclusive interviews with disgraced President Nixon which were screened on both sides of the Atlantic and offered some important revelations and disclosures. In 1982 he formed part of TV-AM's 'Famous Five' as they launched commercial breakfast television in the UK. With the company's problems spilling over into the public domain, he soon found himself the last of the five still at the station. His TV-am Sunday morning show established itself as an important weekly focal point for the political world and he was enticed to take it across to the BBC as *Breakfast With Frost*. However, he did briefly return to ITV in a regional late-night discussion show, again called *The Frost Programme*, in 1993. To underline his versatility, Frost has also produced a couple of TV movies, hosted the panel game THROUGH THE KEYHOLE, and presented superlative facts and feats in special editions of THE GUINNESS BOOK OF RECORDS. As an executive, Frost has been a member of the LWT and TV-am boards and owns his own company, David Paradine Productions (using his middle name). 'Hello, good evening and welcome' has been his much-mimicked catchphrase. His first wife was late actress Lynne Frederick.

Frost Report, The ★★★

UK (BBC) Comedy. BBC 1 1966–7

David Frost, Ronnie Barker, Ronnie Corbett, John Cleese, Julie Felix, Tom Lehrer, Nicky Henson, Sheila Steafel

Producer **James Gilbert**

Topical satire show, debunking a different subject every week.

Whereas David Frost's 1968 offering, *The Frost Programme*, focused on in-depth interviews and exposés, the earlier *Frost Report* was a light-hearted affair. It took a different topic each week – holidays, Parliament, sin, etc. – and reviewed it satirically through sketches performed by the likes of John Cleese and Ronnies Barker and Corbett, complemented by a suitable song from Julie Felix. Offerings included the famous 'class' sketch in which the tall, upper-class Cleese looked down on the shorter, middle-class Barker who in turn looked down on the diminutive, working-class Corbett. The programme's writers included the MONTY PYTHON team of Eric Idle, John Cleese, Graham Chapman, Michael Palin and Terry Jones (in tandem for the first time), as well as Tim Brooke-Taylor, John Law and Marty Feldman. A compilation of the best moments, *Frost Over England*, won the Golden Rose at the Montreux Festival in 1967.

Fry, Stephen

(1957–)

Hampstead-born comedian and actor, the partner of Hugh Laurie in SATURDAY LIVE, *A Bit of Fry and Laurie*, and JEEVES AND WOOSTER (Jeeves). He played the conniving Lord Melchett in BLACKADDER II and his descendant, the booming GENERAL MELCHETT, in *Blackadder Goes Forth*; and his other contributions have come in ALFRESCO, THE YOUNG ONES, FILTHY RICH AND CATFLAP, HAPPY FAMILIES (Dr De Quincy), ALAS SMITH AND JONES, WHOSE LINE IS IT ANYWAY?, *Old Flames, In the Red* (Radio 2 Controller), THE MAGICIAN'S HOUSE (voice of Jasper the Owl), GORMENGHAST (Professor Bellgrove) and the investigative reporter spoof *This is David Lander*. Fry also appeared in *Stalag Luft* (Wing Commander James Forrester), LONGITUDE and as Mybug in COLD COMFORT FARM and Breton in *Surrealissimo*. His voice-over talents have been well employed for factual programmes such as *Paddington Bear: the Early Years*, *Reading the Decades*, *Natural World* and *The Two Loves of Anthony Trollope*, as well as the pre-school animation *Pocoyo*. More recently, Fry has hosted the magic show *Dirty Tricks* and the comedy quiz QI, played Dr Arnold in TOM BROWN'S SCHOOLDAYS and starred in the sitcom *Absolute Power* (Charles Prentiss). While a student at Cambridge, Fry appeared as a contestant on UNIVERSITY CHALLENGE and reworked the musical *Me and My Girl*, which was taken to the West End with great success. He has also written some best-selling novels.

Fugitive, The ★★★★

US (QM) Drama. ITV 1964–7 (US: ABC 1963–7)

Dr Richard Kimble	**David Janssen**
Lt. Philip Gerard	**Barry Morse**
Donna Taft	**Jacqueline Scott**
Fred Johnson ('The One-Armed Man')	**Bill Raisch**
Helen Kimble	**Diane Brewster**
Narrator	**William Conrad**

Creator **Roy Huggins**
Executive Producer **Quinn Martin**

● ***A doctor wrongly convicted of murder goes on the run, trying to find the real killer.***

Dr Richard Kimble returns home one evening to find his wife dead and a mysterious one-armed man running from the direction of the house. Kimble is arrested for murder and convicted on circumstantial evidence – no one else has seen the intruder, but the neighbours did hear the Kimbles quarrelling. Fortunately for Kimble, the train taking him to prison for execution is derailed and he seizes the chance to slip his unconscious guard, Lt Gerard, and makes a break. Realizing his only chance of redemption lies in finding the real culprit, he starts to comb the entire United States for the one-armed man, all the while knowing that Gerard is always only one step behind him.

Plagued by Gerard's relentless pursuit, Kimble is forced to shift from town to town, from low-paid job to low-paid job and from identity to identity, only occasionally making contact with his sister, Donna Taft. His tense life on the run even takes him to Mexico and Canada, and the different setting for each episode keeps the show fresh, giving producers the scope to try out new ideas and bring in guest stars.

Unlike most suspense series, *The Fugitive* is allowed a proper conclusion in its final episode, which drew massive audiences all round the world. Kimble at last quarries the one-armed man in a deserted amusement park. As the two men struggle, Gerard arrives to shoot the man he now realizes is the real murderer. This day, 29 August 1967, is, as narrator William Conrad affirms, 'the day the running stopped'. (The episode was shown a day later in the UK.)

The Fugitive was inspired by Victor Hugo's 19th-century French classic *Les Misérables*, and the real-life case of Dr Sam Sheppard, who was convicted of killing his wife in 1954. The concept was revived in 1993, when Harrison Ford starred in a new cinema version of the Kimble story. A TV remake, starring Timothy Daly, was aired on E4 in the UK in 2001.

Full Circle

See *Around the World in 80 Days*.

Fullerton, Fiona

(1956–)

Fair-haired actress, born in Nigeria, progressing from youthful roles in the 1970s to star in series like ANGELS (Patricia Rutherford), THE CHARMER (Clarice Mannors) and various other dramas. She also hosted *Great Country Houses*. Her first husband was actor Simon MacCorkindale.

Further Adventures of Lucky Jim, The ★★

UK (BBC) Situation Comedy. BBC 2 1967; 1982

Jim Dixon	**Keith Barron** *(1967)*
	Enn Reitel *(1982)*
Lucy	**Glynis Barber** *(1982)*
Philip	**David Simeon** *(1982)*
Joanna	**Barbara Flynn** *(1982)*

Writers **Dick Clement, Ian La Frenais**
Producers **Duncan Wood** *(1967)*, **Harold Snoad** *(1982)*

● ***A north country lad finds it hard to settle in Swinging London.***

Based on, and updated from, Kingsley Amis's 1954 novel *Lucky Jim*, this series related happenings in the life of Jim Dixon, a cautious lad from Eckersley, Yorkshire, new in London in the permissive 1960s. Not liking what he saw, and finding it hard to fit in, Jim indulged himself in Walter Mitty-like fantasies and private rants about the state of society around him. In 1982 the series was revived with Enn Reitel as Dixon, returning to London in 1967 after a year in Holland, and resuming his position as a teacher of Medieval History at a red-brick university. Another remake, entitled just *Lucky Jim*, scripted by Jack Rosenthal and starring Stephen Tompkinson, aired on ITV 1 in 2003.

Futurama ★★★

US (The Curiosity Company/Twentieth Century-Fox) Cartoon. Channel 4 2000–2 (US: Fox 1999–2003)
DVD: Fox

Voices:

Philip J. Fry	**Billy West**
Prof. Hubert J. Farnsworth	**Billy West**
Turanga Leela	**Katey Sagal**
Bender	**John DiMaggio**
Amy Wong	**Lauren Tom**
Dr John Zoidberg	**Billy West**
Hermes Conrad	**Phil LaMarr**
Zapp Brannigan	**Billy West**
Nibbler	**Frank Welker**
Kif Kroker	**Maurice LaMarche**

Creator **Matt Groening**
Executive Producers **Matt Groening, David X. Cohen, Ken Keeler**

● ***A 20th-century delivery boy wakes up 1,000 years into the future.***

Dopey, 25-year-old pizza courier Philip Fry has an accident at work on 31 December 1999. Delivering to a company called Applied Cryogenics, he tumbles into a capsule in the laboratory and is frozen. He wakes up in New York in the year 3000, where, in a world dominated by aliens, androids and far-out inventions, he finds himself a job aboard an intergalactic cargo vessel. His new colleagues are Bender, a heartless, boozy, cigar-puffing, gambling, former girder-bending robot who is addicted to pornography, and Leela, a pony-tailed cyclops who specializes in martial arts. She also pilots the ship and is Fry's occasional girlfriend. Together, they wander the universe, delivering goods for the Planet Express company. Their decrepit scientific guru/employer is Prof. Farnsworth, a far distant nephew of Fry himself, and also seen are their inept, alien company physician Dr Zoidberg; young Martian colleague Amy Wong; her bone-less boyfriend, Lt. Kif Kroker; Kroker's he-man commanding officer in the Democratic Order of Planets, Zapp Brannigan; Jamaican bureaucrat Hermes Conrad; and Leela's ever-hungry, nappy-wearing pet, Nibbler. Using the wonders of the future to comment on today's world, Matt Groening's creation is, like his more successful THE SIMPSONS, gag-rich and fast-moving, with a typically surreal and black side. Guest voices belong to John Goodman, Al Gore and Steven Hawking among others.

Gaffer

The chief electrician in a team.

Gaffer, The ✳

UK (Yorkshire) Situation Comedy. ITV 1981–3

Fred Moffat .... **Bill Maynard**
Harry .... **Russell Hunter**
Betty .... **Pat Ashton**
Charlie .... **Don Crann**
Ginger .... **David Gillies**
Henry Dodd .... **Keith Marsh**
Joe Gregory .... **Alan Hockey**

Creator/Writer **Graham White**
Producer **Alan Tarrant**

● ***A hapless businessman struggles to keep his family firm afloat.***

Fred Moffat is the cunning, sardonic owner of Moffat Engineering Company, a modest light engineering firm permanently hovering on the edge of collapse. Despite his best efforts to drum up trade and avoid the VAT man, and his various get-rich schemes, Moffat's motley band of employees live in a state of endless insecurity. Harry is their shop steward, Betty the secretary and Charlie the best worker. Moffat's great business rival is Joe Gregory, who, like Moffat, becomes a local councillor. In the end, Moffat concedes defeat, throws in the towel and emigrates Down Under. The series was created by Graham White, himself the managing director of a light engineering company in Derby.

Gall, Sandy

CBE (1927–)

Former ITN newscaster and foreign correspondent, joining the organization from Reuters in 1963. In his 29 years with ITN, he gained a reputation for venturing behind the front lines and into trouble spots like Uganda, Vietnam and Afghanistan, presenting his findings in a series of important documentaries. He is also a well-published author.

Gallery

The control room: home of the director, production assistant, vision mixer and other technicians during recording or live transmission.

Galloping Galaxies! ✳

UK (BBC) Children's Situation Comedy. BBC 1 1985–6

SID .... **Kenneth Williams** *(voice only)*
Capt. Pettifer .... **Robert Swales**
Second Officer Morton .... **Paul Wilce**
Communications Officer Webster .... **Nigel Cooke**
Miss Mabel Appleby .... **Priscilla Morgan**
Dinwiddy Snurdle .... **James Bree**
Robot 7 .... **Michael Deeks**
Robot 20 .... **Matthew Sim**
Robot 35 .... **Julie Dawn Cole**
SID Junior .... **Kenneth Williams** *(voice only)*
Mr Elliott .... **James Mansfield**
Murphy .... **Sean Caffrey**
Niall Buggy

Writer **Bob Block**
Producer **Jeremy Swan**

● ***Mishap and mayhem on a turbulent cruise through the cosmos.***

It's a bumpy ride for the crew of the *Voyager* spacecraft as it powers across the universe in the 25th century. Because its domineering computer, SID, is none too reliable, the ship blasts through time warps, skirts black holes and clatters into asteroid belts, sometimes stopping to pick up assorted aliens to make life on board even more unpredictable. Hot on their heels is space pirate Murphy and his team of robots. Nominal commander of the *Voyager* is Captain Pettifer and he is accompanied by officers Morton and Webster. Joining the crew is Miss Appleby, a 20th-century citizen picked up by accident when the ship encounters a time warp wobble. Other new recruits are Junior (SID's little computer colleague) and, in the second series, Elliott (replacing Webster). Also caught up in affairs is Dinwiddy Snurdle, the owner of a malfunctioning time machine.

Galton, Ray

OBE (1930–)

British comedy scriptwriter, usually in collaboration with Alan Simpson. After meeting while both were convalescing from TB, Galton and Simpson were jointly responsible for Tony Hancock's scripts on HANCOCK'S HALF HOUR on radio and television, later moving on to pen CITIZEN JAMES for Sid James and then, in 1962, an episode of COMEDY PLAYHOUSE entitled *The Offer*. This proved to be the pilot for STEPTOE AND SON, a series they wrote for 12 years (with a five-year hiatus in the middle). Their later work (scripts for Frankie Howerd and Spike Milligan, scores of individual comedies – some billed under the *Galton & Simpson Comedy* umbrella – and efforts like *Casanova '73*, *Dawson's Weekly* and episodes of *Mr Aitch*) by common consent was not, understandably, in the same league, although they did win fans with their 1972 adaptation of Gabriel Chevalier's CLOCHEMERLE and there was plenty of interest in 1996–7 when Paul Merton resurrected a number of their scripts in *Paul Merton in Galton & Simpson's . . .* Galton, without Simpson, joined forces with Johnny Speight to write the police comedy SPOONER'S PATCH in 1979, and with John Antrobus to script *Room at the Bottom* in 1986 and GET WELL SOON – which recalled his meeting with Simpson in hospital – in 1997.

Gambon, Sir Michael

CBE (1940–)

Dublin-born actor best known for his award-winning portrayal of Philip Marlow in Dennis Potter's THE SINGING DETECTIVE. Subsequently, he starred in the revival of MAIGRET. Gambon's other television work has included the 1968 adventure series *The Borderers* and dramas like *The Seagull, Eyeless in Gaza, Oscar Wilde* (Wilde), *The Heat of the Day, The Entertainer* (Archie Rice), the thriller *Faith* (Peter John Moreton), and *Screen Two's A Man of No Importance* (bigoted butcher Carney), although he also starred as Brian in the sitcom THE OTHER ONE, and appeared in series like *About Face*, MINDER, BERGERAC and Jim Henson's GREEK MYTHS. More recently, he was Squire Hamley in WIVES AND DAUGHTERS, clockmaker John Harrison in LONGITUDE, Raymond Symon in PERFECT STRANGERS, King Edward VII in THE LOST PRINCE, and Prior's first ancestor in *Angels in America*.

Game for a Laugh ★★

UK (LWT) Comedy. ITV 1981–5

Presenters **Jeremy Beadle, Henry Kelly, Matthew Kelly, Sarah Kennedy, Rustie Lee, Martin Daniels, Lee Peck, Debbie Rix**

Executive Producer **Alan Boyd**
Producers **Phil Bishop, Keith Stewart, Brian Wesley, Bob Merrilees**

● ***Practical jokes and silly stunts designed to make a fool out of the public.***

In the vein of CANDID CAMERA, *Game for a Laugh* was a combination of pre-filmed hidden-camera pranks and studio-based stunts, all aimed at catching out Joe Public. Victims' embarrassment was glossed over by shrieks of laughter from the studio audience. Each week the hosts – perched on four high stools – signed off with a contrived 'Watching us, watching you' farewell. Rustie Lee, Lee Peck, Debbie Rix and Martin Daniels later joined the team, and Jeremy Beadle moved on to even greater practical joking in *Beadle's About. Game for a Laugh* was based on the 1950s US game show *People are Funny*.

Game On ★★★

UK (Hat Trick) Situation Comedy. BBC 2 1995–6; 1998
DVD: VCI

Matthew Malone	**Ben Chaplin**
	Neil Stuke
Martin Henson	**Matthew Cottle**
Mandy Wilkins	**Samantha Janus**
Clare Monohan	**Tracy Keating**
Jason	**Mark Powley**
Archie Glenister	**Crispin Bonham-Carter**

Writers **Andrew Davies, Bernadette Davis**
Executive Producer **Denise O'Donoghue**
Producers **Geoffrey Perkins, Sioned Wiliam**

● ***Three London flatmates battle their way through life.***

Game On is like a dysfunctional, cruder version of *Friends*. It focuses on three young flatsharers, each with his or her own personal problems. Most screwed-up is 'double hard' Matthew, whose parents have died, leaving him the money to buy his Battersea flat, but who now suffers from agoraphobia and never ventures outside its door. He whiles away his days watching TV, dressing up as macho film characters or polishing his surfboard, if not exploring the secret contents of the drawers in the room he lets to Mandy. Blonde but not dumb, Mandy from Herne Bay works as a temp and struggles to combat her bimbo image and build a real career, always finding herself taken advantage of, and never being able to say no to a man's advances. Dating losers is her way of life. The third member of this Sartre-esque trio is ingenuous Martin, a ginger-haired, freckly bank worker, a 'sad bastard' whose mother still sends him frozen meals and who is desperate to find a girlfriend and savour his first sexual experience. He is constantly bullied by his life-long 'mate', Matthew. Martin does eventually find a girl, in the shape of Irish nurse Clare, and is heart-broken when she dumps him and then gives birth to his child. Mandy almost marries into the aristocracy through Archie, and Matthew inadvertently hooks up with the gay Jason.

Game On was a return to comedy for co-writer Andrew Davies and helped make a star out of Ben Chaplin, who left for Hollywood after one series and was replaced as Matthew by Neil Stuke. The theme song, 'Where I Find My Heaven', was performed by the Gigolo Aunts and was a UK hit in 1995.

Game, Set and Match ★★★

UK (Granada) Spy Drama. ITV 1988

Bernard Samson	**Ian Holm**
Fiona Samson	**Mel Martin**
Erich Stinnes	**Gottfried John**
Werner Volkmann	**Michael Degen**
Dicky Cruyer	**Michael Culver**
Gloria Kent	**Amanda Donohoe**
Bret Rensselaer	**Anthony Bate**
Frank Harrington	**Frederick Treves**
Silas Gaunt	**Michael Aldridge**
Julian MacKenzie	**John Wheatley**
Morgan	**Struan Rodger**
Zena Volkmann	**Brigitte Karner**
David Kimber-Hutchinson	**Peter Vaughan**
Henry Tiptree	**Jeremy Child**

Writer **John Howlett**
Producer **Brian Armstrong**

● ***A desk-bound intelligence agent is sent back into action.***

After allegedly bungling a counter-espionage mission in Poland and losing his nerve, loner Bernard Samson has been retired to desk duty. Earlier, he had formed a secret agency known as the Brahms Network and, when this is infiltrated by an enemy activist, Samson is called back into the front line to sort it out. He ends up in East Berlin, confronting his long-time friend, Werner Volkmann, and his own KGB-agent wife, Fiona, who heads an underground intelligence unit called Yellow Submarine.

The 13-part series was based on a trilogy of books by Len Deighton, *Berlin Game, Mexico Set* and *London Match*, and was filmed in all three locations.

Gangster Show, The ★★

UK (BBC) Drama. BBC 2 1972

Arturo Ui	**Nicol Williamson**
O'Casey	**Sam Wanamaker**

Sheet .... **Larry Cross**
Clark .... **Phil Brown**
Butcher .... **Robert O'Neil**
Bowl .... **James Berwick**
Dogsborough .... **Peter Frye**
Ernesto Roma .... **Weston Gavin**
Ragg .... **Bob Sherman**
Dockdaisy .... **Marcella Markham**

Writer **George Tabori**
Producer **Tony Garnett**

● ***A Hitler-like figure rises to power in crime-ridden Chicago.***
The Gangster Show was the name given to an adaptation of Bertold Brecht's 1941 play *The Resistible Rise of Arturo Ui*. Jack Gold directs this hour and three-quarters drama which draws a sardonic parallel between German Nazis and Chicago gangsters, pitching the lead figure, Arturo Ui, a Hitler look-alike, into a mobster's shoes. Carl Davis supplies the music.

Gangsters ✶✶

UK (BBC) Crime Drama. BBC 1 1976; 1978

John Kline .... **Maurice Colbourne**
Khan .... **Ahmed Khalil**
Anne Darracott .... **Elizabeth Cassidy**
Dermot Macavoy .... **Paul Antrim**
Malleson .... **Paul Barber**
Sarah Gant .... **Alibe Parsons**
Rafiq .... **Saeed Jaffrey**
Rawlinson .... **Philip Martin**
Lily Li Tang .... **Chai Lee**
Shen Tang .... **Robert Lee**
Red Stick .... **Kahjoo Chua**
Iqbal Khan .... **Zia Moyheddin**

Writer **Philip Martin**
Producer **David Rose**

● ***The violent face of the underworld in 1970s Birmingham.***
Gangsters focuses on former SAS man John Kline, freed from prison to work for DI6 agent Khan in monitoring and manipulating events in the Birmingham underworld. Installed as the manager of The Maverick nightclub, Kline mixes with all manner of seedy characters, including Chinese triad members, pimps, whores, extortionists, terrorists, drug-pushers and illegal-immigrant smugglers.

Shot on video using a roving camera, *Gangsters* won acclaim for effectively conveying the tension in the city's underworld and the menace of its low life. However, its graphic violence was heavily criticized. The 12-part series resulted from a one-off PLAY FOR TODAY of the same title in 1975, also written by Philip Martin. Chris Farlowe sang the theme song and Dave Greenslade composed the music.

Gannon, Lucy

(1949–)

One-time military policewoman and care worker who has become one of UK television's most prolific screenwriters. Her creations have included SOLDIER, SOLDIER, PEAK PRACTICE, BRAMWELL, *Insiders*, HOPE AND GLORY, *Servants* and *Blue Dove*. She also wrote *Screen One's Tender Loving Care* and *Trip Trap*, *Pure Wickedness, Plain Jane* and the single dramas, *Big Cat*, *The Gift* and *Dad*.

Garden, Graeme

(1943–)

Aberdeen-born, Cambridge-educated doctor who began writing for television in the mid-1960s, eventually appearing on screen in a sketch show entitled *Twice a Fortnight* (with Tim Brooke-Taylor, Bill Oddie, *et al.*). This was followed by another sketch show, *Broaden Your Mind*, before Garden and Oddie set about preparing scripts for LWT's DOCTOR IN THE HOUSE and two of its sequels. In 1970 Garden, Brooke-Taylor and Oddie were offered their own series, based around three crazy do-gooders. In THE GOODIES, Garden, playing an over-the-top version of himself, was the trio's mad scientist. Since then, he has continued writing (for shows such as *Rory Bremner*, SMITH AND JONES, SURGICAL SPIRIT, *Shoebox Zoo* and, with Oddie, the sci-fi spoof *Astronauts*); acting (among his appearances have been episodes of YES, MINISTER, STRANGERS, PEAK PRACTICE and HOLBY CITY, plus the single dramas *The Student Prince* and *My Summer with Des*); panel gaming (*Tell the Truth* and *If I Ruled the World*); presenting TV pop-science programmes (he was one of the hosts of *Bodymatters*); and hosting the daily quiz *Beat the Nation* (with Brooke-Taylor). With his *Goodies* colleagues, he also voiced the BANANAMAN cartoon series.

Gardeners' World ✶✶

UK (BBC/Catalyst) Gardening. BBC 2 1968–

Presenters **Percy Thrower, Peter Seabrook, Clay Jones, Stefan Buczacki, Geoffrey Smith, Geoff Hamilton, Alan Titchmarsh, Monty Don**

Executive Producers **Stephanie Silk, Tony Laryea, Owen Gay**
Producers **Paul Morby, Bill Duncalf, Barry Edgar, Rosemary Forgan, Laurence Vulliamy, Betty Talks, John Percival, Colette Foster, Carrie Tooth, Sarah Davis, Richard Simkin, Sarah Moors, Rosemary Edwards**

● ***Long-running gardening magazine.***
This full-colour successor to the highly popular GARDENING CLUB was launched by the much-respected Percy Thrower in 1968, using his own garden as a backdrop. Over the years, reports on shows and garden visits have intercut the sound gardening basics the programme places at its core, although the range and scope of plants and plots has expanded considerably, thanks to the garden centre boom of the past 25 years. Alan Titchmarsh took over as host in 1996, following the death of Geoff Hamilton, and he was supported by presenters like Pippa Greenwood, Gay Search, Stephen Lacey, Joe Swift, Chris Beardshaw, Sarah Raven and Rachel de Thame. When Titchmarsh retired, he was succeeded in 2003 by Monty Don, joined by Beardshaw, Raven, Swift and newcomer Carol Klein.

Gardening Club ✶✶

UK (BBC) Gardening. BBC 1 1955–67

Presenter **Percy Thrower**

Producers **John Furness, Paul Morby**

● ***Gardening tips and news.***
Gardening Club, the forerunner of today's many gardening programmes, was originally screened from a rooftop garden

at the BBC's Lime Grove, where Percy Thrower offered useful advice to growers nationwide. Each week he was joined by specialist guests and enthusiastic amateurs. With the arrival of colour television, *Gardening Club* gave way to GARDENERS' WORLD, again hosted by Percy Thrower.

Gardner, Andrew

(1932–99)

Tall, respected ITN newscaster, one of the first two presenters of *News at Ten* (with Alastair Burnet), having anchored ITN's earlier offerings: *Dateline*, *Reporting '66* and *Reporting '67*. His earlier career was in broadcasting in Rhodesia and then with the BBC. After leaving ITN in 1977, he worked for Thames, presenting regional news magazines, before retiring in 1992.

Garner, James

(James Baumgarner; 1928–)

American actor who entered television in the 1950s, playing small roles in series like CHEYENNE while under contract to Warner Brothers. Warners then gave him his own vehicle, the Western spoof MAVERICK, which more and more began to reflect Garner's own understated sense of humour. However, tied to a limiting contract, Garner fell into conflict with the studio and walked out in 1960. He remained out of major TV work for 11 years, until he was cast as lead in another *Maverick*-like series entitled *Nichols*, made by his own Cherokee Productions. Three years later he achieved greater success as Jim Rockford, the ex-con private investigator in THE ROCKFORD FILES, before he returned to *Maverick* in a TV movie and a short-lived revamp which went out under the name of *Bret Maverick*. He later played Senator Norman Grant in SPACE and in 1991 he starred in a US sitcom entitled *Man of the People* (politician Jim Doyle). In the mid-1990s he took on the role of Woodrow F. Call in the LONESOME DOVE sequel, *Streets of Laredo*, and appeared in TV movie revivals of *The Rockford Files*. He has since made guest appearances in CHICAGO HOPE and starred in the US series *First Monday* and *8 Simple Rules*.

Garnett, Tony

(1936–)

Birmingham-born, one-time actor who became a script editor on THE WEDNESDAY PLAY and thus moved into TV production. As a producer, his political sympathies have manifested themselves in plays like UP THE JUNCTION, CATHY COME HOME, *The Lump*, THE GANGSTER SHOW and *The Gamekeeper*, and the series DAYS OF HOPE and LAW AND ORDER. He also produced the comedy shorts THE STAGGERING STORIES OF FERDINAND DE BARGOS and the *Screen One* drama *Born Kicking*. Since the 1990s, as head of World Productions, he has produced major series such as BETWEEN THE LINES, THIS LIFE, CARDIAC ARREST, THE COPS, BALLYKISSANGEL and ATTACHMENTS.

Garrison's Gorillas ✱✱

US (Selmur) War Drama. ITV 1968 (US: ABC 1967–8)

Lt. Craig Garrison .... **Ron Harper**
Actor .... **Cesare Danova**
Casino .... **Rudy Solari**
Chief .... **Brendon Boone**
Goniff .... **Christopher Cary**

Executive Producer **Selig J. Seligman**

A gang of criminals is freed from US prisons to help in the war effort.

Lt. Craig Garrison is the man who pieced together this crack squad (a kind of early A-Team), which is used on highly dangerous missions behind enemy lines during World War II. Based secretly in England, the enlisted crooks are offered a tempting productivity deal: a pardon after the war if their efforts are successful, execution if they fail. The men are each chosen for their distinctive skills and talents. They are Actor (a good-looking, smooth-talking con merchant), Casino (an expert safe-cracker), Chief (a Native American knife expert) and Goniff (an agile cat-burglar and pick-pocket). Their undercover work takes them all across Europe: to Germany, Holland, France, Italy, Yugoslavia and other locations. Similarities with the movie *The Dirty Dozen* are obvious.

Garry Halliday ✱✱

UK (BBC) Children's Drama. BBC 1959–62

Garry Halliday .... **Terence Longdon**
Bill Dodds .... **Terence Alexander**
Jean Wills .... **Ann Gudrun**
Jennifer Wright
The Voice .... **Elwyn Brook-Jones**
Kurt .... **Maurice Kaufmann**
Insp. Franks .... **Michael Collins**
Dr Edmundo .... **Richard Warner**
Insp. Potter .... **Nicholas Meredith**
Edward Jewesbury
Martha Blair .... **Jennifer Jayne**
Vicky Fox .... **Audrey Nicholson**
Nigel Fox .... **Frederick Treves**
Eddie Robbins .... **Bill Kerr**
Sgt Adolph Traumann .... **Maurice Kaufmann**

Creator **Justin Blake**
Producer **Richard West**

A civilian pilot foils the evil plans of an international criminal.

In this Saturday teatime thriller series, Garry Halliday is a pilot with a commercial airline who tumbles into all kinds of intrigue. When first encountered he is regularly flying the Amsterdam route, assisted by co-pilot Bill Dodds and hostess Jean Wills. Spotting something strange out of the cabin window, the daring airman uncovers a fiendish plot that has been hatched by a criminal mastermind known as The Voice. It is by no means the last time that Halliday finds himself face to face with this particular villain, who on this occasion is abetted by his henchman Kurt. Halliday in all appears in eight different adventures (most lasting six episodes each and airing simply under the title of *Garry Halliday*, though two have fuller titles: *Garry Halliday and the Secret of Omar Khayyam* and *Garry Halliday and the Gun-Runners* – both 1962). In later stories, Halliday has a new co-pilot, Australian Eddie Robbins, plus a replacement stewardess, Vicky Fox, daughter of Garry's new business partner, Nigel Fox. The series was partly filmed at Lydd airfield in Kent, with action sequences provided initially by real-life Silver City Airways, then Skyways and finally British United Air Ferries.

Gascoigne, Bamber

(1935–)

Erudite Bamber Gascoigne was host of UNIVERSITY CHALLENGE for 25 years (1962–87). He has also presented CINEMA, his own 13-part history of Christianity, *The Christians*, the cultural quiz *Connoisseur*, and various other high-brow documentaries. He has also appeared as a guest in JONATHAN CREEK.

Gascoine, Jill

(1937–)

London-born actress-turned-novelist, seen in series like THE GENTLE TOUCH and C.A.T.S. EYES (both as female copper Maggie Forbes) and THE ONEDIN LINE (Letty Gaunt). Among her other credits have been parts in DIXON OF DOCK GREEN, DR FINLAY'S CASEBOOK, GENERAL HOSPITAL, RAFFLES, Z CARS, SOFTLY, SOFTLY, WITHIN THESE WALLS, BERYL'S LOT, JUSTICE, BOON, TAGGART, *Virtual Murder* (Victoria Fleming), EL C.I.D. and *Screen One*'s *Trust Me* (Vivien Empson), the last two opposite her husband, Alfred Molina.

Gathering Storm, The ★★★

UK (BBC/HBO/Scott Free) Historical Drama. BBC 2 2002
DVD: Warner Home Video

Winston Churchill .... **Albert Finney**
Clementine 'Clemmie' Churchill .... **Vanessa Redgrave**
Ralph Wigram .... **Linus Roache**
Ava Wigram .... **Lena Headey**
Desmond Morton .... **Jim Broadbent**
David Inches .... **Ronnie Barker**
Violet Pearman ('Mrs P') .... **Celia Imrie**
Sir Robert Vansittart .... **Tom Wilkinson**
Brendan Bracken .... **Anthony Brophy**
Randolph Churchill .... **Tom Hiddleston**
Stanley Baldwin .... **Derek Jacobi**
Ivo Pettifer .... **Hugh Bonneville**

Writer **Hugh Whitemore**
Executive Producers **Tracey Scoffield, Ridley Scott, Tony Scott, Julie Payne**
Producers **Frank Doelger, David M. Thompson**

● ***The life of Churchill in the 1930s, frustrated and powerless as war beckons.***

Retracing ground covered to some degree in the earlier WINSTON CHURCHILL – THE WILDERNESS YEARS, this multi-award-winning single drama reflects on life for the maverick MP during the 1930s. Churchill is seen by many as a spent force, a man whose high office days are over. But Winston is a fighter, and from his country retreat – Chartwell, in Kent – which he shares with his beloved wife, Clemmie, he takes up the cause of the British Empire, opposing Indian independence. He then shrewdly perceives the threat building under new German Chancellor Adolf Hitler while his Conservative allies conveniently turn a blind eye, hoping that war will not return. Aided by conscientious civil servant Ralph Wigram, Churchill acquires detailed information about how the Nazi war effort is mounting. When he is proved right and war is finally declared, he is recalled to the Cabinet in glory as First Lord of the Admiralty, becoming Prime Minister within months and leading Britain to victory through the dark days of the early 1940s. Star Albert Finney received much acclaim for walking the walk and talking the talk of the great man and the drama was also notable for coaxing Ronnie Barker out of retirement to play Churchill's defiant butler, Inches. Richard Loncraine directed; Howard Goodall provided the music.

Gaunt, William

(1937–)

Yorkshire-born actor whose baby-faced looks helped make him popular in the late 1950s and 1960s, giving him parts in *Colonel Trumper's Private War* (Lt. Hastings), SERGEANT CORK (Sgt Bob Marriott), HARPERS WEST ONE, PROBATION OFFICER, THE AVENGERS, THE SAINT, SOFTLY, SOFTLY and *The Tenant of Wildfell Hall* (Mr Lawrence), culminating in the role of Richard Barrett in the supernatural spy series THE CHAMPIONS. In the 1980s and 1990s he resurfaced as foster-parent Tony Hunter in CLAIRE, juror Andrew Cook in JURY, harassed dad Arthur Crabtree in the sitcom NO PLACE LIKE HOME, solicitor Edward Capstick in *Capstick's Law*, old buffer Aubrey in *A Gentlemen's Club*, Mr Hunningdon in GBH and grandfather Andrew Prentice in NEXT OF KIN. Also in his portfolio are performances in CROWN COURT, *Cottage to Let, Holly* (Gordon Godolphin), *Nobody's House* (Peter Sinclair), *The Foundation, Love and Marriage*, THE FAR PAVILIONS, *The Preventers* (a *Champions* spoof), HEARTBEAT, MIDSOMER MURDERS, DOCTORS, *La Femme Musketeer* (Trevoux), *Cathedral* (John Browne) and HOLBY CITY.

Gay Cavalier, The ★

UK (George King/Associated-Rediffusion) Adventure. ITV 1957

Capt. Claude Duval .... **Christian Marquand**
Dinny O'Toole .... **Larry Burns**
Major Mould .... **Ivan Craig**

Producer **George King**

● ***The rousing adventures of a Royalist hero during the English Civil War.***

The Gay Cavalier is Captain Claude Duval, a man of action and great courage. Together with his friend and accomplice, Dinny O'Toole, Duval flamboyantly thwarts the advances of Cromwell's Roundhead army and, in particular, its chief intelligence officer, Major Mould. This series was, however, a far cry from the more historically precise BY THE SWORD DIVIDED. Its French star, Christian Marquand, later became a film director, with *Candy* (1968) one of his offerings.

Gazette

See *Hadleigh*.

GBH ★★★★

UK (GBH Films) Drama. Channel 4 1991

Michael Murray .... **Robert Lindsay**
Stephen Hall *(young)*
Jim Nelson .... **Michael Palin**
Barbara Critchley/Douglas .... **Lindsay Duncan**
Michelle Atkinson
Mrs Lillian Murray .... **Julie Walters**
Laura Nelson .... **Dearbhla Molloy**
Eileen Critchley .... **Jane Dawson (Danson)**
Franky Murray .... **Philip Whitchurch**
Peter .... **Andrew Schofield**

Martin Niarchos	**Michael Angelis**
Diane Niarchos	**Julia St John**
Mr Matthew Weller	**David Ross**
Lou Barnes	**Tom Georgeson**
Mervyn Sloan	**Paul Daneman**
Bubbles	**Peter-Hugo Daly**
Geoff Heaps	**Bill Stewart**
Teddy	**Alan Igbon**
Frank Twist	**Colin Douglas**
Philip	**Jimmy Mulville**
Mr Grosvenor	**Daniel Massey**
Susan Nelson	**Anna Friel**

Writer **Alan Bleasdale**
Executive Producer **Verity Lambert**
Producers **Alan Bleasdale, David Jones**

An ambitious council leader and a gentle schoolteacher cross swords against a backdrop of political subversion.

Michael Murray, a former electrician, is the newly installed leader of a northern city council (Liverpool in all but name). Power, fame and women are the keystones of his life and militancy is his watchword. Jim Nelson, in contrast, is the caring headteacher of a school for children with special needs, a hypochondriacal family man whose ambitions are modest. When Nelson's Hanley Grange Primary School defies a Murray strike call, the two men become bitter enemies, to the detriment of Murray's career and Nelson's sanity. However, *GBH* is far more complicated than that. This seven-part drama has various sub-plots and undercurrents. It reveals how the two men are just pawns in a sinister political game, with right-wing Establishment figures infiltrating left-wing activist groups to give them a bad name, and shows how Murray's murky and tormented past comes back to haunt him in the form of the beautiful but mysterious Barbara Douglas. Other key figures include Murray's Irish mother; his brother/chauffeur, Franky; the Nelsons' best friends Martin and Diane Niarchos; Mr Weller, Murray's old headmaster; Geoff, the manager of the Royal Imperial Grand Hotel, where much of the double-dealing takes place; Trotskyite Mervyn Sloan; and particularly devious Lou Barnes and his henchman Peter. The *GBH* of the title did not stand, as many initially believed, for Grievous Bodily Harm, but for supposedly Great British Holiday, referring to a sequence when Nelson – his mental health breaking up – heads off on vacation (at a Welsh holiday camp run by crazy Mr Grosvenor), returning to find the family home trespassed upon.

GBH was a labour of love for Alan Bleasdale. He had already abandoned attempts to script the idea as a film and as a novel. As a tense piece of television drama it won many plaudits although, in established Bleasdale fashion, it ruffled a few feathers at the same time. Former Liverpool Council Deputy Leader Derek Hatton sought legal advice over what he saw as a fictionalization of his time in power, but Bleasdale denied that Michael Murray had been based on anyone in particular. Rather, as star Robert Lindsay explained, *GBH* was a reminder to the public that our lives are manipulated by activists from both left and right. Bleasdale, in the *Radio Times*, described the drama as 'one caring, liberal madman's odyssey through the appalling farce of life in Britain today; trying to make some sense of the place'. Robert Young directed; Elvis Costello and Richard Harvey composed the music. Two young future stars featuring among the notable cast were Anna Friel and Jane Danson (billed as Dawson).

Gee, Dustin

(Gerald Harrison; 1942–86)

British comedian and impersonator, for some time partner of Les Dennis, with whom he starred in *Go For It* and *The Laughter Show*. His TV break came with WHO DO YOU DO? in the mid-1970s, and he followed it up with regular appearances in *Russ Abbot's Madhouse*. Among his best-remembered take-offs were Larry Grayson and CORONATION STREET's Vera Duckworth. He died of a heart attack in 1986.

Gemini Man ✶

US (Universal) Adventure. BBC 1 1976 (US: NBC 1976)

Sam Casey	**Ben Murphy**
Leonard Driscoll	**William Sylvester**
Dr Abby Lawrence	**Katherine Crawford**

Executive Producer **Harve Bennett**
Producer **Leslie Stevens**

An invisible man works as a secret agent for a Government think-tank.

When NBC's INVISIBLE MAN series, starring David McCallum, was not a success, the company reworked the formula with a new cast and some subtle changes. The result was *Gemini Man*, which fared even worse in the US ratings war. It centres on Sam Casey, an agent for INTERSECT, who has been exposed to underwater radiation and rendered invisible. Thanks to the efforts of his superior, Leonard Driscoll (played by Richard Dysart in the pilot episode), and computer specialist Abby Lawrence, Casey is able to restore his appearance using a special watch-like device. He can, when required, turn the device off and return to invisibility – a very useful ploy for a secret agent; but if he does this for more than 15 minutes in one day, he will die.

General Hospital ✶✶

UK (ATV) Drama. ITV 1972–9

Dr Matthew Armstrong	**David Garth**
Dr William Parker Brown	**Lewis Jones**
Dr Martin Baxter	**James Kerry**
Sister Edwards	**Monica Grey**
Dr Peter Ridge	**Ian White**
Arnold Capper	**John Halstead**
Dr Robert Thorne	**Ronald Leigh-Hunt**
Dr Neville Bywaters	**Tony Adams**
Sister Ellen Chapman	**Peggy Sinclair**
Dr Joanna Whitworth	**Patricia Maynard**
Nurse Hilda Price	**Lynda Bellingham**
Dr Richard Kirby	**Eric Lander**
Nurse Katy Shaw	**Judy Buxton**
Dr Knight	**Carl Rigg**
Dr Guy Wallman	**Tom Adams**
Dr Chipapo	**Jason Rowe**
Sister Washington	**Carmen Munro**
Staff Nurse/Sister Holland	**Pippa Rowe**
Nurse Stevens	**Amber Thomas**
Dr Mayhew	**Archie Tew**
Dr Helen Sanders	**Judy Loe**
Staff Nurse Nelson	**Victoria Burton**

Producers **Ian Fordyce, Royston Morley**

● ***Day-to-day drama with staff and patients at a major hospital.***

Although sharing its name with a long-running American soap, *General Hospital* was effectively EMERGENCY – WARD 10 revisited, albeit with a new cast and setting. Having cancelled *Ward 10* in 1967 and living to regret it, Lew Grade and his ATV associates decided to revamp the idea. They wanted an afternoon series to fill space newly made available after restrictions on broadcasting hours had been lifted. The result was a drama set in Midland General Hospital.

While not quite achieving the cult following *Ward 10* had enjoyed, the series still picked up a sizeable audience, enough to earn a transfer to an evening time-slot three years into its run. Episode length increased from a half-hour to a full hour at the same time, and two programmes a week became one. As in its predecessor, it was the lives and loves of the *General Hospital* staff that took centre stage, as well as internal power struggles. Housewives were offered a new generation of heart-throb doctors, most notably Martin Baxter and Neville Bywaters (the latter played by Tony Adams, later Adam Chance in CROSSROADS), while veterans like Drs Armstrong and Parker Brown seldom saw eye to eye and added sparks of tension and excitement.

Generation Game, The ★★★

UK (BBC) Game Show. BBC 1 1971–82; 1990–2002

Presenters **Bruce Forsyth, Larry Grayson, Jim Davidson**

Producers **Alan Tarrant, James Moir, Terry Heneberry, Robin Nash, Alan Boyd, Marcus Plantin, David Taylor, Guy Freeman, Jonathan Beazley, Sue Andrew, Jonathan Glazier, Ben Kellett**

● ***Family couples compete in silly games and challenges.***

The Generation Game is the number-one game show in British TV history, enjoying two lengthy prime-time runs. Simple in format, it involved four couples (each composed of an elder and a younger member of a family – father and daughter, aunt and nephew, etc.) competing in two heats and a semi-final. The heats consisted of two games based on little quizzes and challenges – guessing film themes and miming the answer to a partner, spotting personalities in disguise, etc. Demonstrations by experts (making pots, icing cakes, spinning plates, performing a dance, etc.), which the contestants had to copy, proved particularly popular. Points were awarded for performance and the two heat-winning couples then competed in a semi-final. This often took the form of a comic playlet, with celebrity judges allocating marks for performances. The winning duo progressed to a final 'conveyor belt' round in which a succession of household goodies (always including a cuddly toy) passed before their eyes. Everything that they could recall in a set time was taken home as prizes.

The Generation Game was devised by a Dutch housewife who was inspired by game shows like *Beat the Clock* (part of SUNDAY NIGHT AT THE LONDON PALLADIUM), and when it was televised in Holland as *Een Van De Acht* (*One From Eight*) it topped the ratings. Former *Beat the Clock* host Bruce Forsyth was the obvious choice to take charge of the UK version and he quickly established the programme as an integral part of Saturday evening viewing. Forsyth revelled in the party game format. With a twinkle in his eye, he bullied and coerced the hapless contestants through each show, combining words of encouragement with false anger and gentle mockery. The contestants loved it. Assisting Bruce was the leggy Anthea Redfern, who was soon to be his second wife.

When Bruce was lured away to ITV in 1978, it seemed that *The Generation Game*'s heyday was over. Camp comedian Larry Grayson was not an obvious replacement, yet he made the show an even bigger hit. Sensibly avoiding Forsyth's aggressive approach, Grayson instead brought his own effete style to proceedings, in which he was assisted by Scottish folk singer Isla St Clair. *The Generation Game* was cancelled in 1982 but was brought back, with Bruce Forsyth again at the helm, in 1990. Once more, his skilful manipulation of the studio audience and his ease with contestants ensured that the programme was as popular as ever. Dancer Rosemarie Ford became his Girl Friday. In 1994, Bruce retired once more, leaving Jim Davidson to take over a year later, supported by Sally Meen and, subsequently, Melanie Stace, then Lea Kristensen.

The Generation Game has aired under several titles. In the early days, it was known as *Bruce Forsyth and the Generation Game*. It then became *Larry Grayson's Generation Game*, and the latest incarnation has been called *Bruce Forsyth's Generation Game* or *Jim Davidson's Generation Game*. It has also given us catchphrases galore – from 'Let's meet the eight who are going to generate' and 'Let's see the scores on the doors' to 'Good game, good game' and 'What's on the board, Miss Ford?'. King of the catchphrases, however, has been 'Didn't he do well?' – just like the programme itself.

On New Year's Eve 2005, Graham Norton hosted *Generation Fame*, a one-off revival featuring celebrity contestants.

Gentle Ben ★★

US (Ivan Tors) Children's Adventure. ITV 1968–9
(US: CBS 1967–9)

Tom Wedloe .... **Dennis Weaver**
Mark Wedloe .... **Clint Howard**
Ellen Wedloe .... **Beth Brickell**
Henry Boomhauer .... **Rance Howard**
Willie .... **Angelo Rutherford**

Producers **Andy White, George Sherman**

● ***A Florida family has a giant brown bear as its pet.***

The Wedloes live in the Florida Everglades, where the central feature of their existence is the family pet, a giant American brown bear named Ben. Though the bear is usually very 'gentle', especially in the company of eight-year-old Mark, he is regularly provoked by outsiders, which leads to numerous boy-and-bear adventures. Mark's dad, Tom, played by Dennis Weaver, is a wildlife officer who travels around the swamplands on an airboat, but child actor Clint Howard's real father also appears, in the role of backwoodsman Henry Boomhauer. (Clint's brother, Ron Howard, is even better known as an actor/director.) Willie, a friend of Mark's, is added to the cast in later episodes. The series – shown in the USA from 1967 but only sporadically seen in the UK – was based on the film *Gentle Giant*, which was set in Alaska. The inspiration for the film was Walt Morey's book *Gentle Ben*.

Gentle Touch, The ★★

UK (LWT) Police Drama. ITV 1980–4

DI Maggie Forbes .... **Jill Gascoine**
DCI Bill Russell .... **William Marlowe**
DS Jake Barratt .... **Paul Moriarty**
Steve Forbes .... **Nigel Rathbone**

DI Bob Croft	**Brian Gwaspari**
DS Jimmy Fenton	**Derek Thompson**
DS Peter Philips	**Kevin O'Shea**
DI Mike Turnbull	**Bernard Holley**
DI Jack SlaterMichael	**Graham Cox**
Sgt Sid Bryant	**Michael Cronin**

Creator **Terence Feely**
Executive Producers **Tony Wharmby, Nick Elliott**
Producers **Kim Mills, Jack Williams, Michael Verney-Elliott**

● *Softly, softly crime-busting with a female police officer.*
Maggie Forbes is a former police cadet who has worked her way up through the ranks and is now posted to London's Seven Dials police station, covering the areas of Soho and Covent Garden. As the series begins she finds herself almost simultaneously promoted to the rank of detective inspector and widowed by the murder of Ray, her PC husband (Leslie Schofield). Despite being ordered to take time off, she drags herself back into action to pursue her husband's killers but then resigns from the force. Persuaded to rejoin, she finds the subsequent months difficult, as problems with Steve, her teenage son, interfere with her progress at the station. Eventually, she and the series settle down into a catalogue of routine crime stories, with the 'gentle touch' of the title always evident in Maggie's investigations. Forbes's colleagues at Seven Dials are Detective Insp. Bob Croft, DS Jake Barratt, DS Jimmy Fenton and, later, DS Peter Philips. Their grouchy boss is DCI Russell. After four years, Maggie leaves Seven Dials, only to resurface in C.A.T.S. EYES.

George and Mildred ★★

UK (Thames) Situation Comedy. ITV 1976–9
DVD: Network

George Roper	**Brian Murphy**
Mildred Roper	**Yootha Joyce**
Jeffrey Fourmile	**Norman Eshley**
Ann Fourmile	**Sheila Fearn**
Tristram Fourmile	**Nicholas Bond-Owen**
Ethel	**Avril Elgar**
Humphrey	**Reginald Marsh**
Jerry	**Roy Kinnear**

Writers **Johnnie Mortimer, Brian Cooke**
Producer **Peter Frazer-Jones**

● *The further adventures of a feuding landlord and landlady.*
In this MAN ABOUT THE HOUSE spin-off, George and Mildred Roper have moved from their ground-floor flat to a middle-class housing development (46 Peacock Crescent, Hampton Wick). There, the pushy, man-hungry Mildred strives to be upwardly mobile and the weedy, shiftless George – with his motorcycle and sidecar – defiantly proclaims his working-class roots. Next door live the Fourmiles: snooty Jeffrey, his likeable wife, Ann, and their bespectacled young son, Tristram, who is constantly corrupted by George. The Fourmiles later add baby Tarquin to their family. Regular visitors, much to Mildred's embarrassment, are her materialistic sister Ethel and brother-in-law Humphrey. Jerry is George's layabout pal and Truffles is Mildred's pampered Yorkshire Terrier.

Like *Man about the House*, which became *Three's Company* in the USA, this series was also translated into an American version. *The Ropers* starred Norman Fell and Audra Lindley.

George and the Dragon ★★

UK (ATV) Situation Comedy. ITV 1966–8
DVD: Network

George Russell	**Sid James**
Gabrielle Dragon	**Peggy Mount**
Col. Maynard	**John Le Mesurier**
Ralph	**Keith Marsh**

Creators/Writers **Vince Powell, Harry Driver**
Producers **Alan Tarrant, Jack Williams**

● *A lecherous chauffeur has his style cramped by a formidable new housekeeper.*
Randy George Russell is driver and general handyman to the distinguished Colonel Maynard and enjoys his privileged position in the stately household. That all changes, however, when a new housekeeper is appointed. George's wandering hands have already seen off 16 domestics, but when Miss Gabrielle Dragon arrives, recommended by the Premier Domestic Agency, there is little chance of George making unwanted advances to *her*. A bellowing battleaxe of a widow, Gabrielle has reverted to her (appropriate) maiden name on the death of her husband, and now battle duly commences between George and the Dragon. Also seen is Ralph, the smelly, sloppy gardener.

George Burns and Gracie Allen Show, The

See *Burns and Allen Show, The*.

Georgeson, Tom

(1941–)

Liverpudlian actor, probably best known as Harry Naylor in BETWEEN THE LINES, one of the BOYS FROM THE BLACKSTUFF (Dixie Dean) or DI Howard Jones in LIVERPOOL ONE. Georgeson's other credits have been many, with the major offerings being *The Peppermint Pig* (James Greengrass), THE MANAGERESS (Eddie Johnson), *Les Girls* (Conrad), SCULLY (Isiah), *The Last Place on Earth*, GBH (Lou Barnes), WUTHERING HEIGHTS (Joseph), BLEAK HOUSE (Clamb), *Under the Greenwood Tree* (Geoffrey Day), *The English Harem* (Eric Pringle) and QED's dramatization *Cause of Death* (bereaved parent Ray Peters). Guest appearances have been in series like WHEN THE BOAT COMES IN, TURTLE'S PROGRESS, MAYBURY, THE PROFESSIONALS, DEMPSEY AND MAKEPEACE, THE BILL, STAY LUCKY, RESNICK, *The Locksmith*, BRAMWELL, HOLBY CITY, DALZIEL AND PASCOE, ULTIMATE FORCE, FOYLE'S WAR, WAKING THE DEAD, AGATHA CHRISTIE'S POIROT, A TOUCH OF FROST, and MIDSOMER MURDERS.

Georgian House, The ★★

UK (HTV) Children's Science Fiction. ITV 1975–6

Dan	**Spencer Banks**
Abbie	**Adrienne Byrne**
Ngo	**Brinsley Forde**
Ellis	**Jack Watson**
Leadbetter	**Peter Schofield**
Mistress Anne	**Constance Chapman**
Lady Cecilia	**Valerie Lush**
Sir Jeremy	**Michael Gover**

Ariadne	**Janine Duvitski**
Cook	**Ruth Kettlewell**
Miss Humphreys	**Anna Quayle**

Writers **Jill Laurimore, Harry Moore**
Executive Producer **Patrick Dromgoole**
Producer **Leonard White**

Two students are transported back to the 18th century to help a young slave boy.

When teenagers Abbie and Dan take part-time jobs at a Georgian house museum in Bristol, working for the curator, Ellis, they discover more than they had bargained for. Picking up a strange wooden carving, they find it has magical properties that draw them back to the year 1772, to the house as it was during its Georgian heyday. The property belongs to the wealthy Leadbetter family and, with no immediate hope of return to their own time, the kids adopt positions in the household, Abbie 'above stairs' and Dan as a kitchen boy. They meet a mysterious young black slave, Ngo, who, it appears, has called them back in time to help him return to his homeland, Sierra Leone. By setting Ngo free, they eventually return with clear consciences to the 20th century. Star Spencer Banks featured prominently on children's TV in the 1970s, appearing in such series as TIMESLIP and *Tightrope*.

Gerber, David

(1925–)

Prolific American producer of the 1970s, working on shows like CADE'S COUNTY, NANNY AND THE PROFESSOR, THE GHOST AND MRS MUIR, *Born Free*, POLICE STORY, POLICE WOMAN, *Joe Forrester, Gibbsville, David Cassidy – Man Undercover* and THE QUEST. In 1986 he joined the newly merged MGM and United Artists, introducing new blood and building up the company's prime-time share through such series as THIRTYSOMETHING and IN THE HEAT OF THE NIGHT. He went on to become head of the MGM Worldwide Television Group. In the 1990s, he headed up All American Television, the company that produced BAYWATCH among other series. In 2003 he was executive producer of a small-screen revival of *Tarzan*.

Gervais, Ricky

(1961–)

Reading-born Ricky Gervais made a few TV appearances as part of the unsuccessful 1980s pop duo Seona Dancing and once managed the pop group Suede before joining the radio station XFM, where he presented a show with his writing partner, Stephen Merchant. He broke into television as part of the team on THE 11 O'CLOCK SHOW and was then given his own chat show, *Meet Ricky Gervais*. Stardom beckoned, however, when he and Merchant wrote and directed THE OFFICE in 2001, with Gervais starring as self-deluding boss David Brent (a character first introduced on radio). At Christmas 2002, he donned the gloves and boxed Grant Bovey in a charity TV match and added his voice to the *Robbie the Reindeer* animation, *Legend of the Lost Tribe*. In 2005, he and Merchant launched EXTRAS, their second foray into the world of sitcom, this time set in the world of celebrity also-rans, with Gervais playing film extra Andy Millman. Gervais has also made a guest appearance in *Alias* and written and appeared (vocally) in an episode of THE SIMPSONS.

Get Back ★★

UK (Alomo) Situation Comedy. BBC 1 1992–3

Martin Sweet	**Ray Winstone**
Loretta Sweet	**Carol Harrison**
Albert Sweet	**Larry Lamb**
Prudence Sweet	**Jane Booker**
Bernie Sweet	**John Bardon**
Eleanor Sweet	**Kate Winslet**
Joanna Sweet	**Michelle Cattini**
Bungalow Bill	**Zoot Money**
Lucy	**Shirley Stelfox**

Creators **Laurence Marks, Maurice Gran**
Producer **Bernard McKenna**

A recession victim is forced to return to his lowly roots.

The go-ahead days of the 1980s are over, as Martin Sweet suddenly discovers. He is a self-made man in the Thatcherite mould, but his career crashes along with the economy in the early 1990s and he, wife Loretta and daughters Eleanor and Joanna are left penniless with the closure of his fashion boutique. The swish, five-bedroomed house in Hatch End has to be sold and the only roof that can be placed over their heads belongs to the cramped council flat in north London that is rented by Martin's conniving dad. It may be handy for the Arsenal, but it's not where Martin wants to live these days. To make matters worse, brother Albert still manages to make a pretty penny and has to be tapped for loans that might help Martin get up and running once again. Martin is, however, a fighter and whether he needs to sell dog food or collect debts, he intends to bounce back. A running theme of the series was the use of references to Beatles' songs, not only in the programme title itself but in the titles of individual episodes, plus the names of the main characters ('Sweet Loretta Martin' is name-checked in the track 'Get Back'; other songs like 'Dear Prudence' and 'The Continuing Story of Bungalow Bill' also feature in this way). Two series, totalling 15 episodes, were made.

Get Smart ★★★

US (Talent Associates/Heyday) Situation Comedy. BBC 1 1965–7 (US: NBC 1965–9; CBS 1969–70; Fox 1995)

Maxwell Smart	**Don Adams**
Agent 99	**Barbara Feldon**
Thaddeus ('The Chief')	**Edward Platt**
Agent 13	**Dave Ketchum**
Prof. Carlson	**Stacy Keach**
Conrad Siegfried	**Bernie Kopell**
Starker	**King Moody**
Hymie, the robot	**Dick Gautier**
Agent 44	**Victor French**
Agent Larrabee	**Robert Karvelas**
Charlie Watkins	**Angelique Pettyjohn**
99's mother	**Jane Dulo**

Creators **Mel Brooks, Buck Henry**
Executive Producer **Leonard Stern**

Spoof espionage capers, featuring an incompetent secret agent and his useless colleagues.

At a time when James Bond and THE MAN FROM U.N.C.L.E. were all the rage, *Get Smart* offered the funny side of spying. It features Maxwell Smart, Agent 86 for CONTROL, an intelligence service with headquarters ten storeys beneath Main

Street in Washington, DC. The offices are entered through the bottom of a telephone kiosk. Disaster-prone, but always enthusiastic, Smart operates undercover as a salesman for the Pontiac Greeting Card Company and winds up in the most embarrassing predicaments for a spy. He usually blunders his way through, but not before saying, 'Sorry about that, Chief,' umpteen times to Thaddeus, his long-suffering boss.

CONTROL's adversaries are KAOS, run by the megalomaniac Siegfried and his sidekick, Starker. Against them, Smart works closely with his attractive and intelligent partner, Agent 99 (her real name is never revealed), who later becomes his wife and bears him twins. Another colleague is Agent 13, who takes his undercover role rather too seriously, hiding in the most unusual places, like mailboxes and vending machines. There are also Agent Larrabee, who is even dimmer than Smart, Charlie Watkins, a spy in drag (but that is some make-up!), and Fang, a dog, code-numbered Agent K13.

Smart is generously supplied with gadgetry to help him perform his duties, although these devices (such as a telephone hidden in his shoe) never function quite as intended. For top-secret discussions, CONTROL uses an anti-bugging device known as the Cone of Silence, a clear dome which descends from the ceiling. While the intention is that people *outside* the dome cannot hear the conversation, unfortunately those *inside* are similarly excluded. In addition, CONTROL has an intelligent robot, Hymie, which takes every command literally, with disastrous results.

After a feature film outing in 1989 called *Get Smart, Again!*, the series was briefly revived by Fox in the US in 1995, with Max now head of CONTROL and 99 moving into politics as a Congresswoman.

Get Some In! ✶✶

UK (Thames) Situation Comedy. ITV 1975–8

Cpl Percy Marsh .... **Tony Selby**
Jakey Smith .... **Robert Lindsay**
Karl Howman
Ken Richardson .... **David Janson**
Bruce Leckie .... **Brian Pettifer**
Matthew Lilley .... **Gerard Ryder**
Alice Marsh .... **Lori Wells**
Min .... **Madge Hindle**
Cpl Wendy Williams .... **Jenny Cryst**

Creators/Writers **John Esmonde, Bob Larbey**
Producer **Michael Mills**

● ***Four young RAF conscripts are bullied by a brainless corporal.***

Like THE ARMY GAME before it, *Get Some In!* focuses on the National Service years, when thousands of unwilling and often unsuitable young men were drafted into the forces. This time the action takes place in 1955, at RAF Skelton, where the motley draftees include teddy boy Jakey Smith, dim Scotsman Bruce Leckie, wet vicar's son Matthew Lilley and clean-living grammar school boy Ken Richardson. On arrival at the camp, their worst nightmare is realized when they are assigned to the care of Corporal Marsh, a vindictive, cowardly bully-boy who treats his charges like lackeys and makes their training period a misery. However, it is usually Marsh who suffers in the end, as the lads, led by 'Poof House' Richardson, easily outwit their stupid NCO.

After subsequent training as nursing assistants at RAF Midham (again alongside Marsh), the lads are posted to Malta but are immediately recalled to RAF Hospital Druidswater. There, they find themselves intimidated yet again by Marsh, who now enjoys hero status, having allegedly carried a superior officer 84 miles to safety in the snows of Labrador. Marsh's demanding wife, Alice, is also seen, as are NAAFI serving girl Min and Leckie's butch girlfriend (later wife), Corporal Wendy.

Get Well Soon ✶✶

UK (BBC) Situation Comedy. BBC 1 1997

Roy Osborne .... **Matthew Cottle**
Brian Clapton .... **Eddie Marsan**
Mrs Ivy Osborne .... **Anita Dobson**
Mrs Howell .... **Samantha Beckinsale**
Mrs Clapton .... **Patsy Rowlands**
Mr Bernard Walpole .... **Neil Stacy**
Sister Shelley .... **Kate O'Toole**
Jeffry .... **William Osborne**
Squadron Leader Fielding .... **Robert Bathurst**
Norman Tucker .... **Hugh Bonneville**
Padre .... **Michael Troughton**

Writers **Ray Galton, John Antrobus**
Producer **Philip Kampff**

● ***Two teenagers make the best of a long convalescence.***

In the late 1940s, as if the ravages and privations of war and its aftermath were not enough, Britain was still plagued by the deadly TB virus. Across the country, hospital beds were occupied by sick young men and women who sometimes took years to recuperate. *Get Well Soon* is the story of two such men, but also recalls the meeting of comedy giants Ray Galton and Alan Simpson, who first encountered each other in such desperate circumstances. While they convalesced from the effects of TB, the two men laid the groundwork for such sitcoms as HANCOCK'S HALF-HOUR and STEPTOE AND SON by forging their writing partnership. Here, in this six-part comedy penned by Galton himself, with new collaborator John Antrobus, although the premise is similar, the names have been changed and the characters are not strictly built on the real Galton and Simpson.

In 1947, naïve Roy Osborne arrives at a sanitorium and is naturally glum at the prospect of many months in such a dreary hole. Trying to cheer him up (after initial disagreements) is his gluttonous ward-neighbour, Brian Clapton. Their blossoming friendship provides the backdrop for a series of tales involving a nutty padre, an unhinged RAF squadron leader and numerous romantic liaisons, including one between Bernard Walpole (the husband of a fellow patient) and Roy's flighty mother, Ivy. Sister Shelley is the dragon who keeps everyone in order.

Ghost

A distortion or double image on a TV picture, generally caused by signals bouncing off another building, or badly positioned aerials.

Ghost and Mrs Muir, The ✶✶

US (20th Century-Fox) Situation Comedy. ITV 1969–71
(US: NBC 1968–9/ABC 1969–70)

Capt. Daniel Gregg .... **Edward Mulhare**
Mrs Carolyn Muir .... **Hope Lange**
Martha Grant .... **Reta Shaw**
Candice 'Candy' Muir .... **Kellie Flanagan**

Jonathan Muir .... **Harlen Carraher**
Claymore Gregg .... **Charles Nelson Reilly**

Creator **Jean Holloway**
Producers **Howard Leeds, Gene Reynolds**

The ghost of a 19th-century seafarer haunts the family that rents his old home.

The late Captain Daniel Gregg was a blustery old sea dog of the worst sort. As a ghost, his speciality is scaring off anyone who dares to rent his beloved Gull Cottage in Schooner Bay from his dopey, mortal nephew, Claymore. However, he meets his match when winsome widow Carolyn Muir, a writer, takes up residence with her two children, Candy and Jonathan, plus housekeeper Martha and dog Scruffy. Eventually the living and the dead declare a truce and live in comparative harmony on the New England shoreline. The captain even becomes rather protective of his new family. The series was based on the 1947 film starring Rex Harrison and Gene Tierney, which itself was derived from the novel by R. A. Dick.

Ghost Squad/GS5 ★★

UK (Rank/ATV) Police Drama. ITV 1961–5/1964

Nick Craig .... **Michael Quinn**
Sir Andrew Wilson .... **Donald Wolfit**
Helen Winters .... **Angela Browne**
Tony Miller .... **Neil Hallett**
Geoffrey Stock .... **Anthony Marlowe**
Jean Carter .... **Claire Nielson**
Peter Clarke .... **Ray Barrett**

Producers **Connery Chappell, Antony Kearey, Dennis Vance**

The dangerous adventures of a small group of undercover policemen.

The 'Ghost Squad', officially the International Investigation Division of Scotland Yard, operates in total secrecy. The job of its operatives is to infiltrate underworld gangs, spy rings or other secret societies, lying low for possibly months at a time and using an alias which only they and their direct superior knows about. They work in places as far afield as Marseilles and Hong Kong and they cannot rely on the regular police force or other governmental agencies for their salvation: their lives are on the line, and this contributes to the suspense of each episode. Number one agent is American Nick Craig, a master of disguise. Tony Miller is his friend and colleague seen later, and their superior is Sir Andrew Wilson, supported by his 23-year-old secretary, Helen Winters. When Wilson and Winters are posted to another department, they are succeeded by Geoffrey Stock and his Scottish secretary, Jean Carter, who also becomes an agent.

The dangers of the job are poignantly illustrated at the end of the second season, when Craig is killed by an explosion at sea. When the programme returned, he was replaced by the meeker, more methodical Peter Clarke, who offered quite a contrast to Miller, his tough and physical partner. The programme title also changed, to GS5. The series was based on the book *The Ghost Squad*, an account of real police undercover activity, by former detective John Gosling.

Ghost Story for Christmas, A ★★

UK (BBC) Drama Anthology. BBC 1 1971–8

Inspired by the stories of M. R. James, this was the BBC's late-night attempt to run a little ice down the spine of viewers who had had things a touch too cosy over the Christmas period. Each year, a new (usually 35-minute) tale was presented, with details as below. The 1976 story was not actually billed as *A Ghost Story for Christmas*, while the 1977 and 1978 offerings were billed as *Christmas Ghost Story*.

1971: *The Stalls of Barchester* by M. R. James, adapted by Lawrence Gordon Clark, starring Robert Hardy and Clive Swift
1972: *A Warning to the Curious* by M. R. James, adapted by Lawrence Gordon Clark, starring Peter Vaughan and Clive Swift
1973: *Lost Hearts* by M. R. James, adapted by Robin Chapman, starring Joseph O'Conor and Susan Richards
1974: *The Treasure of Abbot Thomas* by M. R. James, adapted by John Bowen, starring Michael Bryant and John Herrington
1975: *The Ash Tree* by M. R. James, adapted by David Rudkin, starring Edward Petherbridge and Lalla Ward
1976: *The Signalman* by Charles Dickens, adapted by Andrew Davies, starring Denholm Elliott and Bernard Lloyd
1977: *Stigma* by Clive Exton, starring Kate Binchy and Peter Bowles
1978: *The Ice House* by John Bowen, starring John Stride and David Beames

Ghosts of Motley Hall, The ★★

UK (Granada) Children's Situation Comedy. ITV 1976–8
DVD: Network

Sir George Uproar .... **Freddie Jones**
Sir Francis 'Fanny' Uproar ...... **Nicholas Le Prevost**
Bodkin .... **Arthur English**
Matt .... **Sean Flanagan**
The White Lady .... **Sheila Steafel**
Mr Gudgin .... **Peter Sallis**

Creator/Writer **Richard Carpenter**
Producer **Quentin Lawrence**

The ghostly inhabitants of a stately home resent the presence of intruders.

Created and written by CATWEAZLE and ROBIN OF SHERWOOD author Richard Carpenter, *The Ghosts of Motley Hall* introduces the spectral inhabitants of a disused country mansion. Patrolled by caretaker/estate agent Mr Gudgin, 400-year-old Motley Hall has stood derelict for more than 20 years. It is the ancestral home of the Uproar family, who are still represented by the spirits of Sir George Uproar, a Victorian army general, and his ancestor Fanny, an 18th-century fop and a gambler. Their ghostly colleagues are former family servants Bodkin (an Elizabethan jester) and Matt (a stable boy from the Regency era), along with the mysterious White Lady (who can't even remember herself who she was when alive). Any attempt to attract new buyers or residents is scuppered by the supernatural beings, with the aid of television special effects. Wilfred Josephs contributed the music.

Gideon's Way ✶✶

UK (New World/ITC) Police Drama. ITV 1965–6
DVD: Network

Commander George Gideon .. **John Gregson**
Chief Insp. David Keen .... **Alexander Davion**
Kate Gideon .... **Daphne Anderson**

Producers **Robert S. Baker, Monty Berman**

● ***Determined detection with a talented Scotland Yard sleuth.***

Filmed in documentary fashion, with much location shooting, the gritty, somewhat violent *Gideon's Way* tells of the CID investigations of Commander George Gideon and his partner, Chief Inspector David Keen, two men who have worked their way up through the force. The series, transmitted in the USA under the title *Gideon CID*, and based on the novels by John Creasey, aka J. J. Marric, followed a 1958 film version, *Gideon's Day*, starring Jack Hawkins.

Gilbert, James

(1923–)

British producer, with the BBC from the early 1960s, although also in the independent sector later, responsible for comedies like *On the Bright Side*, IT'S A SQUARE WORLD, *Moody in . . .*, THE SEVEN FACES OF JIM, *The Big Noise*, *Barney is My Darling*, NOT ONLY . . . BUT ALSO . . ., *The Walrus and the Carpenter*, THE FROST REPORT, *The Illustrated Weekly Hudd*, *The Old Campaigner*, ME MAMMY, *Tales from the Lazy Acre*, WHATEVER HAPPENED TO THE LIKELY LADS?, LAST OF THE SUMMER WINE, SEVEN OF ONE, EXECUTIVE STRESS, FRENCH FIELDS, THE LABOURS OF ERICA and AIN'T MISBEHAVIN'.

Giles, Bill

OBE (1939–)

Devon-born meteorologist, a BBC weather presenter from 1975 and head of the BBC Weather Centre, 1983–2000.

Gill, Michael

(1923–2005)

British producer/director of documentaries, most notably in charge of Kenneth Clark's CIVILISATION and Alistair Cooke's AMERICA. After working for *The Scotsman* newspaper, Gill joined the BBC in 1954 as an arts producer in schools programmes. He was father of restaurant and TV critic A. A. Gill.

Gilligan's Island ✶

US (Gladasaya/United Artists) Situation Comedy. ITV 1965 (US: CBS 1964–7)
DVD: Warner Home Video (Region 1 only)

Gilligan .... **Bob Denver**
Jonas Grumby ('The Skipper') **Alan Hale Jr**
Thurston Howell III .... **Jim Backus**
Mrs Lovey Howell .... **Natalie Schafer**
Roy Hinkley ('The Professor') .. **Russell Johnson**
Ginger Grant .... **Tina Louise**
Mary Ann Summers .... **Dawn Wells**

Creator/Executive Producer **Sherwood Schwartz**

● ***A group of castaways tries to escape from a tropical island.***

A rough time is in store for the motley band of tourists on board the good ship *Minnow*. During their three-hour charter cruise from Honolulu a storm blows up, the boat is lost and they are shipwrecked on a desolate South Pacific island. Their futile attempts to escape and return home provide this sitcom's storylines.

The castaways include two members of the boat's crew, the genial, chubby Skipper and the incompetent First Mate, Gilligan, who is usually responsible for the failure of escape bids. Other members of the party are obnoxious millionaire Thurston Howell III and his dim wife, Lovey; 'The Professor', a science teacher and the group's escape planner; Mary Ann Summers, a simple country girl from Horners Corners, Kansas; and glamorous movie starlet Ginger Grant. However, realism is not *Gilligan's Island*'s strong point. Numerous guest stars turn up to help the party to get off the island, but how these visitors come and go is never explained, nor is the cast's changes of clothes or the presence of a reference library used by The Professor. If the cruise was meant to be only three hours long, how come they are now so far from civilization?

Gilligan's Island enjoyed only a sporadic screening in the UK. As a result, star Alan Hale Jr has always been better known in Britain as CASEY JONES. Two or three revivals were made for American audiences in the late 1970s and early 1980s.

Gilmore, Peter

(1931–)

German-born, Yorkshire-raised actor, a hit in the 1970s as handsome sea captain James Onedin in THE ONEDIN LINE. Previously, Gilmore had been a singer with the George Mitchell Singers and, in addition to stage and film work, had appeared in TV series like HUGH AND I, as well as having his own song-and-dance act. Since *The Onedin Line* ended, Gilmore's work has become less obvious, though he did play safari park supremo Ben Bishop in ONE BY ONE, starred in the drama *A Man Called Intrepid* and made guest appearances in CASUALTY and HEARTBEAT. His three marriages have all been to actresses, to Una Stubbs, Jan Waters and Anne Stallybrass.

Gimme Gimme Gimme ✶✶

UK (Tiger Aspect) Situation Comedy. BBC 2 1999–2000; BBC 1 2001
DVD: Vision Video

Linda La Hughes .... **Kathy Burke**
Tom Farrell .... **James Dreyfus**
Suze .... **Beth Goddard**
Jez .... **Brian Bovell**
Beryl Merit .... **Rosalind Knight**

Writer **Jonathan Harvey**
Executive Producers **Mark Chapman, Peter Bennett-Jones**
Producers **Sue Vertue, Matthew Francis**

● ***Daily battles with two mismatched flatmates.***

Redhead Linda La Hughes shares Flat B at Rectory House with Tom Farrell. She is slovenly, dresses garishly and is seriously deluded about her own beauty (she thinks she is 'the ginger Jerry Hall'). She drifts between temporary jobs while on the lookout for sex; she adores Liam Gallagher and hates Patsy Kensit. Tom is a vain, pretentious, out-of-work actor and an outrageous homosexual, constantly lusting after Simon Shepherd from PEAK PRACTICE (who guests in one episode). Most plots centre on their search for sex and/or stardom, with vulgarity well to the fore. Jez and Suze live in the flat below, while Beryl Merit, a former prostitute, is their landlady. After two series on BBC 2, *Gimme Gimme Gimme* was promoted to BBC 1.

Ginger Tree, The ✶✶✶

UK (BBC/NHK) Drama. BBC 1 1989

Mary Mackenzie .... **Samantha Bond**
Richard Collingsworth .... **Adrian Rawlins**
Count Kentaro Kurihama .... **Daisuke Ryu**
Isabelle de Chamonpierre .... **Cécile Paoli**
Father Anthony .... **Nicholas Farrell**
Sir Claude MacDonald .... **Nicholas Le Prevost**
Baroness Aiko Onnodera .... **Fumi Dan**
Alicia .... **Joanna McCallum**
Taro .... **Hironori Wada**
Hirushi Tsushima .... **Tetsuro Tamba**
Minagawa .... **Shigeru Muroi**
Bob Dale .... **Colin Stinton**

Writer **Christopher Hampton**
Executive Producer **Alan Shallcross**
Producer **Tim Ironside Wood**

● ***A Scots girl finds love and tragedy in early-20th-century China and Japan.***

The year is 1903. Headstrong 19-year-old Mary Mackenzie sets out on an arduous voyage to Mukden, Manchuria, to marry her dashing fiancé, Richard Collingsworth, who is a military attaché. Sadly, the region finds itself on the brink of war, as Russia and Japan fight for control of the Chinese territory, and Mary's life there proves to be rather different from what she had hoped. The marriage immediately runs into trouble, and, when her husband is sent away for a year, Mary falls in love with a Japanese nobleman, Count Kentaro Kurihama, becoming pregnant with his child. Her son is later abducted on his father's orders and, as Mary's tale closes with World War II looming, his whereabouts remain concealed. However, she has remained in Japan and, against all odds, has forged herself a successful career in fashion design and retail, something she will have to relinquish if, as advised, she returns to Europe to avoid the inevitable horrors of war.

Filmed in Japan, Taiwan and the Isle of Man, at a cost of £4 million, *The Ginger Tree* was the first BBC drama to be shot for High Definition Television. Anthony Garner directs the four episodes, which were based on the novel of the same name by Oswald Wynd. Music was composed by Dominic Muldowney.

Gingerbread Girl, The ✶

UK (Yorkshire) Situation Comedy. ITV 1993

Linda .... **Janet Dibley**
Matt .... **John Diedrich**
Eddie .... **Tyler Butterworth**
Kerry .... **Isabella Marsh**
Stella .... **Tracie Bennett**

Writer **Alex Shearer**
Producer **Robin Carr**

● ***A single mum tries to make ends meet and start a new life.***

Linda is struggling to bring up daughter Kerry without former husband Matt, who can't even make his maintenance payments on time. But Linda is a determined type and, while calling on help and advice from best friend Stella and neighbour Eddie, does her best to ensure a good future for herself and the sometimes difficult Kerry. The laughs in such a grim situation come from Linda's move back into dating circles (and the jealousy it brings out in Matt), her work in a Greek restaurant and her problems with the DSS. Just seven episodes were made.

Girl from U.N.C.L.E., The ✶

US (Arena/MGM) Secret Agent Drama. BBC 1 1966–7
(US: NBC 1966–7)

April Dancer .... **Stefanie Powers**
Mark Slate .... **Noel Harrison**
Alexander Waverly .... **Leo G. Carroll**
Randy Kovacs .... **Randy Kirby**

Producer **Douglas Benton**

● ***A female secret agent and her British partner fight an anarchic global crime syndicate.***

In this spin-off from THE MAN FROM U.N.C.L.E., *The Girl from U.N.C.L.E.* is April Dancer, paired on assignments with British agent Mark Slate (played by Rex Harrison's son, Noel). Like their counterparts in the original series, they collect their orders from agency supremo Mr Waverly and work to combat the efforts of THRUSH to take over the world. Robert Vaughn, as Napoleon Solo, made the odd cross over appearance, but this series, coming hot on the heels of the campy BATMAN, was even more far-fetched than the original *U.N.C.L.E.* adventures and quickly died a death.

Dancer and Slate first appeared in a *Man from U.N.C.L.E.* episode entitled *The Moonglow Affair*, but the roles were filled at the time by former Miss America Mary Ann Mobley and veteran actor Norman Fell. In the UK, *The Girl from U.N.C.L.E.* and *The Man from U.N.C.L.E.* shared the same BBC 1 time-slot, appearing in alternate weeks.

Girls About Town ✶✶

UK (ATV) Situation Comedy. ITV 1970–1

Rosemary Pilgrim .... **Julie Stevens**
Brenda Liversedge .... **Denise Coffey**
George Pilgrim .... **Robin Parkinson**
Harold Liversedge .... **Peter Baldwin**
Mrs Pilgrim .... **Dorothy Reynolds**

Creator/Writer **Adele Rose**
Producer **Shaun O'Riordan**

● ***Two bored housewives try to spice up their lives.***

Suffering from a severe case of marriage tedium, housewife friends Rosemary Pilgrim and Brenda Liversedge decide to add some zest to their lives by getting out and about. They hope to make their husbands sit up and take notice, but with little success. Adding to Rosemary's frustration is her interfering, true-blue mother-in-law.

The series sprang from a 1969 single drama starring Anna Quayle and Barbara Mullaney (later CORONATION STREET's Rita Fairclough), in which Rosemary and Brenda join an escort agency. When the series began, another future *Street* name, Peter Baldwin (Derek Wilton), was added to the cast, and the roles of Rosemary and Brenda were filled by former PLAY SCHOOL presenter Julie Stevens and DO NOT ADJUST YOUR SET star Denise Coffey.

Girls on Top ✶✶

UK (Witzend/Central) Situation Comedy. ITV 1985–6
DVD: BFS Entertainment

Candice Valentine .... **Tracey Ullman**
Amanda Ripley .... **Dawn French**
Jennifer Marsh .... **Jennifer Saunders**
Shelley Dupont .... **Ruby Wax**
Lady Carlton .... **Joan Greenwood**

Writers **Dawn French, Jennifer Saunders, Ruby Wax**
Producer **Paul Jackson**

● ***Four zany, but incompatible, girls share a London flat.***
Described by some as a female equivalent of THE YOUNG ONES, *Girls on Top* concerns four wacky girls who share a comfortably appointed Chelsea flat, owned by Lady Carlton, a batty romantic novelist who lives downstairs. The four are the mendacious Candice (a blonde hypochondriac); domineering feminist Amanda (who works for a magazine called *Spare Cheeks*); slouchy, slow-witted Jennifer, and rich, brash American Shelley (who has come to London to be an actress). When the second season begins, Candice is no longer around (actress Tracey Ullman had departed for the USA), and the other three soldier on without her.

Give Us a Break ✶✶

UK (BBC) Comedy Drama. BBC 1 1983

Mickey Noades .... **Robert Lindsay**
Mo Morris .... **Paul McGann**
Tina Morris .... **Shirin Taylor**
Ron Palmer .... **David Daker**

Creator/Writer **Geoff McQueen**
Producer **Terence Williams**

● ***An East End wide boy takes a snooker prodigy under his wing.***
Mickey Noades is a 36-year-old waster who has never made anything of his life. For a living, he gambles and does a spot of wheeling and dealing, spending much of his time in Ron Palmer's pub, The Crown & Sceptre, where his girlfriend, Tina, is a barmaid. When Tina's young brother, Mo, arrives from jobless Liverpool, Mickey makes him less than welcome, until he realizes that Mo is an exceptional snooker player. With plenty of money to be made from hustling in London's snooker halls, Mickey sees his life opening up before him and his 'big break' just around the corner.

The series was the first drama written by former carpenter Geoff McQueen, who later went on to create THE BILL. A Christmas special was produced in 1984. Snooker coaching for the series was provided by professional Geoff Foulds.

Give Us a Clue ✶✶

UK (Thames) Game Show. ITV 1979–91; BBC 1 1997

Presenters **Michael Aspel, Michael Parkinson, Tim Clark**

Producers **Juliet Grimm, David Clark, Robert Reed, Keith Beckett**

● ***Light-hearted celebrity charades game.***
Michael Aspel and, from 1984, Michael Parkinson tried to keep order in this TV version of the ancient parlour game Charades. A team of male celebrities (led by Lionel Blair) took on a team of women (captained by Una Stubbs and, later, Liza Goddard), with each member of the team having to perform a mime in turn, hoping to convey to their colleagues the title of a book, film, TV programme, show, song, etc. To spice things up, a number of risqué titles were dropped in, daring the stars to be a bit cheeky. The series was revived for a daytime outing on BBC 1 in 1997, with new host Tim Clark and team captains Julie Peasgood and Christopher Blake.

Gladiators ✶✶

UK (LWT) Entertainment. ITV 1992–2000

Presenters **Ulrika Jonsson, John Fashanu, Jeremy Guscott**

Producers **Nigel Lythgoe, Ken Warwick**
Executive Producers **John Kaye Cooper, Nigel Lythgoe**

● ***Members of the public do battle with superfit athletes in a contest of strength and technique.***
Gladiators, recorded at Birmingham's National Indoor Arena, was a mix of IT'S A KNOCKOUT and THE SUPERSTARS, with a lot more muscle and considerably more posing. Body-builders, wrestlers and athletes of all kinds and both sexes were recruited as the resident team of 'Gladiators', all squeezed into leotards and given names like Wolf, Hunter, Nightshade (athlete Judy Simpson), Amazon (swimmer Sharron Davies) and Jet (Diane Youdale). Their job was to see off the challenges of four daring viewers each week in a series of stamina-sapping contests involving running, climbing, swinging and beating each other with big, cushioned clubs. John Sachs provided the commentary. The series proved surprisingly popular with younger viewers, and international challenge matches were also staged (hosted by Kimberley Joseph and Mike Adamle). The inspiration was the US series *American Gladiators*.

Glaister, Gerard

DFC (1915–2005)

Hong Kong-born former RAF squadron leader and decorated bomber and Spitfire pilot who became a prolific BBC drama producer/director. His most prominent work was in a common vein, namely behind-the-scenes business sagas, as typified by OIL STRIKE NORTH, THE BROTHERS, BUCCANEER, HOWARDS' WAY and TRAINER, although probably his greatest achievement was COLDITZ, which he devised with Brian Degas. N. J. Crisp was another of Glaister's collaborators. Among his early work were STARR AND COMPANY and *The Dark Island*, and other production credits included *The Men from Room 13*, DR FINLAY'S CASEBOOK, *Moonstrike*, *The Revenue Men*, THE EXPERT, *Codename*, *The Long Chase*, SECRET ARMY, *Kessler*,

MORGAN'S BOY, THE FOURTH ARM and the CAPT. PERCIVAL trilogy, BLOOD MONEY, SKORPION and COLD WARRIOR.

Glam Metal Detectives, The ✶✶

UK (Comic Strip Metal) Comedy. BBC 2 1995

Gary Beadle, Mark Caven, Phil Cornwell, Doon Mackichan, Sara Stockbridge, George Yiasoumi, Mac McDonald, Barry Stanton, Steve Marcus, David Schneider

Producer **Nira Park**

Innovative sketch show based on the superficial world of cable television.

Zapping between channels (and therefore saving the viewer the effort of squeezing the remote control), *Glam Metal Detectives* introduces a selection of old monochrome movies, naff commercials and bizarre stations like the Bloodsports Channel. Over seven episodes, there are snippets from such programmes as *The Big Me*, *Betty's Mad Dash* and *Colin Corleone* but, above all, the series showcases the Glam Metal Detectives themselves, a rock band determined to save the world through the power of their hit records. Their targets range from environmental issues to the awful fizzy drink Splat, and their efforts take them all across the globe, from London and Hollywood to Tibet and Bavaria (where one of their members is abducted by witches). Peter Richardson directed. A track from the series, 'Everybody Up!', briefly charted in the UK in 1995.

Glamour Girls, The ✶✶

UK (Granada) Situation Comedy. ITV 1980; 1982

Veronica Haslett	**Brigit Forsyth**
Debbie Wilkinson	**Sally Watts**
Ernest Garstang	**Duggie Brown**
Brian Frodsham	**Tom Price**
Mr Dylan Meredith	**James Warrior**

Writer **David Nobbs**
Producer **John G. Temple**

Hopes of a better life are dashed for two northern girls who join the promotions industry.

When seedy businessman Ernest Garstang opens his own sales promotion agency, Glamgirl Ltd, it seems like the start of a new life for Veronica Haslett and Debbie Wilkinson. While hardly the best of friends, they do share a desire to do something more with their lives, to have a bit of fun and adventure. Becoming promotions models could be the answer, although it doesn't quite turn out that way. Despite the fact that they are the only two girls on Garstang's books, he struggles to find them work, and when it does arrive it's not the sort of job they really want – like demonstrating non-stick frying pans, or having to parachute from a plane to advertise perfume. Helping out Garstang in the office is his young gofer, Brian Frodsham, and also seen is Mr Meredith, who runs the Casablanca Club and has his eyes set on Veronica. Two series were produced. Derek Hilton supplied the music.

Glaser, Paul Michael

(1943–)

Dark-haired American actor and director whose claim to fame has been the role of Detective Dave Starsky in the 1970s cop series STARSKY AND HUTCH. Glaser's earliest TV work came in daytime soaps and through guest appearances in shows like THE WALTONS. After hanging up Starsky's chunky cardigans, he turned more to directing, although he has cropped up in a number of TV movies, including *The Great Houdinis*, in which he played escapologist Harry Houdini.

Glenister, Philip

Son of director John Glenister and brother of actor Robert Glenister, Philip Glenister has a number of high-profile TV roles to this name, many of them as police officers. He was DS Danny Curtis in *Frontiers*, Phil in ROGER ROGER, William Dobbin in VANITY FAIR, 'Mack' Mackintosh in CLOCKING OFF, DCI Daniel Lloyd in *Lloyd and Hill*, Rob Campbell in *The Hunt*, William Stafford in *The Other Boleyn Girl*, DCI Bell in STATE OF PLAY, Von Rheingarten in ISLAND AT WAR, Dougie Molloy in *The Stepfather*, Eddie in *The Walk*, DCI Driscoll in VINCENT, John Speers in *Last Rites* and DCI Gene Hunt in LIFE ON MARS. Other credits include DROP THE DEAD DONKEY, BERGERAC, LOVE HURTS, HEARTBEAT, THE DETECTIVES, BLUE HEAVEN, SOLDIER, SOLDIER, SILENT WITNESS, *Have Your Cake and Eat It* (Joe Martin), SHARPE, MY WONDERFUL LIFE (Phil), WYCLIFFE, HORNBLOWER (Hobbs), THE VICE and *Byron* (William Fletcher). He is married to actress Beth Goddard.

Glenister, Robert

Brother of Philip Glenister and son of director John Glenister. He played Steve Webber in SINK OR SWIM, Ken in *The Lonelyhearts Kid*, Colin Morris in CHANCER, Sgt Ian Anderson in SOLDIER, SOLDIER, Markby in DROVERS' GOLD, Tubes in DIRTY WORK and 'Squeal' Blake in MY FRAGILE HEART. Glenister also featured as DS Terry Reid in A TOUCH OF FROST, Clive Wilson in SIRENS, Robert Weldon in MURDER, Dr Geoff in ROGER ROGER, Gerhardt in EROICA, Anton Drexler in HITLER: THE RISE OF EVIL, Clive Stevenson in BETWEEN the SHEETS, Ash Morgan in HUSTLE, Frank Thompson in CLASS OF '76 and Simon Carter in *Legless*. Among his guest roles are parts in DOCTOR WHO, P. D. JAMES, THE BILL, BOON, ONLY FOOLS AND HORSES, CASUALTY, PIE IN THE SKY, KAVANAGH QC, PRIME SUSPECT, BRAMWELL, MIDSOMER MURDERS and HEARTBEAT. He was once married to Amanda Redman.

Gless, Sharon

(1943–)

Blonde American actress, Detective Christine Cagney in CAGNEY AND LACEY. Earlier, Gless had broken into television playing secretaries and other secondary roles. She was Holly Barrett in the detective series *Faraday and Company*, nurse Kathleen Faverty in MARCUS WELBY, MD, receptionist Maggie in *Switch* and took minor parts in MCCLOUD, *Cool Million* and other shows. When Meg Foster was dropped from *Cagney and Lacey* in 1982, Gless was called up to take her place. She later starred in the legal drama series *The Trials of Rosie O'Neill*, produced, like *Cagney and Lacey*, by Barney Rosenzweig, whom she married in 1991. More recently she appeared in the American version of QUEER AS FOLK.

Glittering Prizes, The ✳✳✳

UK (BBC) Drama. BBC 2 1976

Adam Morris .... **Tom Conti**
Barbara Morris .... **Barbara Kellerman**
Lionel Morris .... **Leonard Sachs**
Joyce Hadleigh/Bradley .... **Angela Down**
Dan Bradley .... **Malcolm Stoddard**
Barbara Ransome/Parks .... **Anna Carteret**
Mike Clode .... **Mark Wing-Davey**
Anna Cunningham .... **Emily Richard**
Alan Parks .... **John Gregg**
Bill Bourne .... **Clive Merrison**
Stephen Taylor .... **Eric Porter**
Gavin Pope .... **Dinsdale Landen**

Writer **Frederic Raphael**
Producer **Mark Shivas**

● ***The changing lives of a group of Cambridge students.***
Beginning in 1953, when its chief characters are all Cambridge undergraduates, *The Glittering Prizes* follows a group of young intellectuals through to their middle-age in the 1970s, charting the ups and downs in their varied lives. The central character is Adam Morris, a scholarship student who becomes a wealthy novelist. Taking the form of six 80-minute plays, the series won much critical acclaim. On a similar theme, author Frederic Raphael followed up with OXBRIDGE BLUES, seven plays screened in 1984.

Glover, Brian

(1934–97)

Yorkshire-born actor, presenter and writer, a one-time teacher and professional wrestler (under the name of Leon Arras). A familiar face on television, Glover asked the questions on the science show DON'T ASK ME, played dimwit Heslop in PORRIDGE, featured as the frightening Tommy Beamish in *Lost Empires* and carried Peter Davison's bags in CAMPION, as the detective's manservant, Magersfontein Lugg. In addition, he starred as Edgar Rowley in the comedy *South of the Border*, appeared as Yorkie in MINDER and Selwyn Price in ANNA LEE, and was also seen in *Sez Les, Sounding Brass*, ALL CREATURES GREAT AND SMALL, WHATEVER HAPPENED TO THE LIKELY LADS?, DIXON OF DOCK GREEN, THE REGIMENT, SECRET ARMY, RETURN OF THE SAINT, FOXY LADY, DOCTOR WHO, BOTTOM and the wrestling drama *Rumble*, among many offerings. He was the voice of the Tetley teafolk in their various commercials and also wrote scripts for PLAY FOR TODAY and other dramas.

Glynis ✳

US (Desilu) Situation Comedy. BBC 1 1964 (US: CBS 1963)

Glynis Granville .... **Glynis Johns**
Keith Granville .... **Keith Andes**
Chick Rogers .... **George Mathews**

Producers **Jess Oppenheimer, Edward H. Feldman**

● ***An attorney and his novelist wife stumble into adventure.***
Glynis Granville, a writer of mystery stories, often dabbles in amateur sleuthing, assisted by Keith, her lawyer husband. In the tried and tested style of Lucy and Ricky in I LOVE LUCY (also produced by Jess Oppenheimer), these comic Thin Man-type detectives goof around in search of clues, usually solving cases only by luck. Chick Rogers is the retired policeman who occasionally lends a hand. This vehicle for comedy star Glynis Johns survived only one short season, however.

GMTV

(Good Morning Television)

Breakfast television station which – under the consortium name of Sunrise Television – won the early-morning ITV franchise from TV-am in the 1991 auctions with a bid of £34.6 million. The company is currently owned by ITV plc (75 per cent) and Disney (25 per cent). Broadcast from London's South Bank television centre, its output is a mixture of news, reaction, general magazine items and cartoons. Transmissions began on 1 January 1993. On the sofa in the early days were Fiona Armstrong and Michael Wilson, but since then the main presenters have included Eamonn Holmes, Anthea Turner, Lorraine Kelly, Penny Smith, Kate Garraway, Ben Shephard, Fiona Phillips, John Stapleton, Andrew Castle, Carla Romano and Richard Gaisford, with Alastair Stewart, and later Steve Richards, fronting Sunday's political programme.

Gnomes of Dulwich, The ✳✳

UK (BBC) Situation Comedy. BBC 1 1969

Big .... **Terry Scott**
Small .... **Hugh Lloyd**
Old .... **John Clive**

Creator/Writer **Jimmy Perry**
Producers **Sydney Lotterby, Graeme Muir**

● ***Pearls of wisdom from a trio of garden gnomes.***
Big, Small and Old are three stone gnomes in a Dulwich garden who spend their time discussing the state of the human race, prompted by the actions (unseen) of people who pass them by. The gnomes also enjoy a rivalry with their plastic counterparts in the neighbouring gardens.

God Slot

The irreverent term for early Sunday evening when religious programmes have historically been scheduled on British TV. However, the slot has been eroded over the years and ITV has now abandoned it altogether, leaving BBC 1 to uphold the tradition with SONGS OF PRAISE.

Goddard, Liza

(1950–)

Smethwick-born actress, some of whose earliest appearances were in Australia alongside SKIPPY, THE BUSH KANGAROO (Clancy Merrick). Moving back to the UK, she was Victoria in TAKE THREE GIRLS (and reprised the role for a 1982 update, *Take Three Women*), worked with her future husband, Colin Baker, in THE BROTHERS (April Winter/Merroney) and played Lily Pond/Browne in YES – HONESTLY. In the 1980s she starred as mistress Nellie Bligh in PIG IN THE MIDDLE, Claire in the advertising sitcom *Watch This Space*, piano teacher Belinda Purcell in ROLL OVER BEETHOVEN and Laurel Manasotti in THAT'S LOVE, as well as being a frequent guest in BERGERAC, playing diamond thief Philippa Vale. Among her many other credits have been parts in *The Befrienders, Holding On*, WODEHOUSE PLAYHOUSE, TALES OF THE UNEXPECTED, *Brendon Chase*,

Woof!, DOCTOR WHO, WILD WEST (Gilly) and numerous panel games, including GIVE US A CLUE (team captain). Her second husband was pop star/actor Alvin Stardust.

Goddard, Trisha

(1957–)

London-born talk show presenter, the host of ITV's *Trisha* daytime series from 1998 and the similar *Trisha Goddard* for five from 2005. Previously, Trisha had presented Australia's version of PLAY SCHOOL.

Going for a Song ★★

UK (BBC) Game Show. BBC 1 1965–77; 1995–2001

Presenters **Max Robertson, Michael Parkinson, Anne Robinson, Michael Aspel**

Producers **John Irving, John King, Paul Smith**

Subdued quiz in which panellists attempt to guess the value of an antique.

Produced by the BBC in Bristol, *Going for a Song* was the forerunner to ANTIQUES ROADSHOW but with echoes of the earlier ANIMAL, VEGETABLE, MINERAL? Chairman Max Robertson offered an intriguing piece of antiquity to his distinguished guests (Customers versus Connoisseurs), who worked out what the item was and then estimated its sales value. Points were awarded for the closest guess. Arthur Negus made his name as a regular pundit and the programme was characterized by the twittering of a caged mechanical bird over the opening and closing credits. The series returned with Michael Parkinson in the chair, expert assistance from Eric Knowles, and team captains Tony Slattery and Leslie Ash (later Mariella Frostrup, Kit Hesketh-Harvey, Lucinda Lambton and Penny Smith), at lunchtimes in 1995. In 2000, Anne Robinson took over as presenter. She was succeeded by Michael Aspel a year later, when new team captains Rachel de Thame and Mark Porter were added.

Going for Gold ★

UK (Grundy) Quiz. BBC 1 1987–96

Presenter **Henry Kelly**

Executive Producers **Bill Mason, Michael Whyte**

Elimination contest to find 'the quiz champion of Europe'.

This daytime show pitched seven contestants from 14 countries (later expanded to more than 20) into international general knowledge combat. The fact that all the questions were asked in English (with the added complication of Henry Kelly's Irish brogue) seemed a little unfair when, for most contestants, English was a second language at best. This didn't seem to affect the outcome, however, as British entrants were often soundly beaten by their continental rivals. The quiz was shaped over three rounds, entitled 'Beat the Buzzer', 'Four in a Row' and 'Head to Head', with daily winners eventually returning to fight for a place in the semifinals and final later in the year. Each day's losers, however, were given a couple more chances to make the grade, thanks to a kind of *repêchage* system. The prize for the overall winner of the first series (hence the programme title) was a trip to the 1988 Olympic Games in South Korea. Later prizes were of similar magnitude. The series was modelled on the popular French quiz, *Questions pour un champion*, and was itself repackaged as *One to Win* (Channel 5 2000).

Going Gently ★★

UK (BBC) Drama. BBC 2 1981

Bernard Flood	**Norman Wisdom**
Sister Scarli	**Judi Dench**
Austin Miller	**Fulton Mackay**
Gladys Flood	**Stephanie Cole**
Sister Marvin	**Margaret Whiting**
George Flood	**Peter Attard**

Writer **Thomas Ellice**
Producer **Innes Lloyd**

Two dying men live out their last days in a hospital ward.

Setting aside his comic antics for once, Norman Wisdom was showered with praise after this single drama – based on the novel by Robert C. S. Downs – was broadcast as part of BBC 2's *Playhouse* series. Wisdom plays Bernard Flood, a retired salesman who is now dying of cancer in hospital and spends his last days bickering with fellow sufferer Austin Miller and nurse Sister Scarli. Stephen Frears directed the emotional performances, with music from George Fenton.

Going Live! ★★

UK (BBC) Children's Entertainment. BBC 1 1987–93

Presenters **Phillip Schofield, Sarah Greene, Kristian Schmid**

Editor **Chris Bellinger**

Saturday morning children's magazine.

The successor to MULTI-COLOURED SWAP SHOP and *Saturday Superstore*, *Going Live!* brought the Saturday morning TV idea up to date and abandoned the cheesy 'swapping' and 'department store' concepts that had marked its two predecessors. Sarah Greene held her place from the *Superstore* crowd and was now joined, from the Children's BBC's 'broom cupboard', by Phillip Schofield and his puppet pal, Gordon the Gopher. Later, ex-Neighbour Kristian Schmid was roped in to help out when Schofield's West End job as Joseph (of the *Dreamcoat*) scuppered his early-morning routine.

Regular features included the 'Double Dare' action trivia quiz with Peter Simon; the chance to ring in and 'Ask the Expert', quiz guests in 'Press Conference', or have your say in 'Soapbox'; plus roving reports from Mark Chase and items from the 'Newsround Newshounds'. Studio 7's odd-job men, Simon Hickson and Trevor Neal, provided the laughs, and imported colour came from a selection of cartoons (*Thundercats, Teenage Mutant Hero Turtles*, THE JETSONS, etc.). In later series, slots included 'All About Me' (where kids told their own life-story and discussed their hobbies), 'Greenline' (an ecology slot with Jonathon Porritt), 'Check It Out' (consumerism with Emma Freud), cookery instruction from Emma Forbes and the new game, 'Run the Risk' (with Peter Simon and Shane Richie). After six years, the series finally relinquished the Saturday morning slot to LIVE AND KICKING.

Going Straight

See *Porridge*.

Gold Robbers, The ★★

UK (LWT) Police Drama. ITV 1969

Det. Chief Supt. Cradock .... **Peter Vaughan**
DS Tommy Thomas .... **Artro Morris**
Richard Bolt .... **Richard Leech**

Creators **John Hawkesworth, Glyn Jones**
Producer **John Hawkesworth**

An aircraft load of gold bullion is stolen in a breathtaking crime.

This 13-part serial, created by John Hawkesworth (UPSTAIRS, DOWNSTAIRS) and Glyn Jones, cast Peter Vaughan in an unusual role. Now famed for his arch-criminal performances (especially 'Genial' Harry Grout in PORRIDGE), he found himself on the other side of the law in this earlier outing, with his character, formidable CID man Cradock, totally committed to cracking this dare-devil crime, recovering gold ingots worth £5½ million and, one by one, bringing the perpetrators to book. Not so surprising was George Cole, who appeared as a guest star in one episode, playing a second-rate con man.

Golden Girls, The ★★★

US (Witt-Thomas-Harris/Touchstone) Situation Comedy.
Channel 4 1986–93 (US: NBC 1985–92)
DVD: Buena Vista

Dorothy Zbornak .... **Beatrice Arthur**
Blanche Devereaux .... **Rue McClanahan**
Rose Nylund .... **Betty White**
Sophia Petrillo .... **Estelle Getty**
Stanley Zbornak .... **Herb Edelman**
Miles Webber .... **Harold Gould**

Creator **Susan Harris**
Executive Producers **Paul Junger Witt, Tony Thomas, Marc Sotkin, Susan Harris**

Four mature Florida ladies enjoy their 'golden years' together.

The four sparky 'Golden Girls' are out to prove one thing: not only does life begin at 40, but it gets better in one's 50s and 60s. The girls share a roomy bungalow in Miami, owned by Blanche Devereaux, a widowed Southern belle with an enormous appetite for men. Her friends are Dorothy Zbornak, a divorced, level-headed schoolteacher; Rose Nylund, a scatty widow of Scandinavian descent; and Sophia Petrillo, Dorothy's resourceful mother, who has moved in with the others after her Shady Pines retirement home burned down.

Blanche is the genuine merry widow, openly flirtatious and scandalously brazen, while Dorothy is tall, cynical and a touch domineering. She is visited occasionally by Stan, the hapless husband who left her after 38 years to live with an air hostess. Naïve Rose is prone to misunderstandings, and the others dread her long-winded and pointless tales about her home town, St Olaf, Minnesota. Sicilian-born Sophia, meanwhile, is dry and forthright. Having suffered a stroke which has damaged the tact cells of her brain, she pulls no punches and everyone receives the sharp end of her tongue.

Although the girls live life to the full, the more worrying side of growing old is never forgotten. Grouped around the kitchen table for midnight ice-cream feasts, the foursome openly discuss their feelings and their worries: about men, about their families, about themselves. What comes through more than anything is the special relationship they enjoy, echoed in the theme song, 'Thank You for being a Friend'.

The Golden Girls comes to an end when Dorothy marries Blanche's Uncle Lucas (played by Leslie Nielsen) and moves away from Miami. The three others also move – into a hotel and a spin-off series entitled *The Golden Palace*.

Scripts from the series were later adapted for UK audiences and remade as BRIGHTON BELLES, though quite why when the original was on air over here remains a mystery. Sheila Hancock starred as Frances (the Dorothy figure), Wendy Craig was Annie (Rose), Sheila Gish played Bridget (Blanche) and Jean Boht appeared as Josephine (Sophia).

Golden Oldie Picture Show, The ★

UK (BBC) Pop Music. BBC 1 1985–8

Presenter **Dave Lee Travis**

Producer **John King**

New videos of famous pop hits from the past.

Hopping aboard the rock video bandwagon that began to roll in the 1980s, Radio 1 DJ Dave Lee Travis introduced this novel programme, which showcased purpose-made videos based around the hits of yesteryear. Even if a record had charted way back in 1958, it could enjoy the 1980s treatment with a video of its very own. Three series, plus Christmas specials, were produced.

Golden Shot, The ★★

UK (ATV) Game Show. ITV 1967–72; 1974–5

Presenters **Jackie Rae, Bob Monkhouse, Norman Vaughan, Charlie Williams**

Producers **Colin Clews, John Pullen, Edward Joffe, Mike Lloyd, Les Cocks, Dicky Leeman**

Colourful crossbow-shooting for prizes.

In this popular live game show, contestants fired crossbows at cartoon targets in an effort to win cash and other prizes. Hosted initially by Canadian SPOT THE TUNE veteran Jackie Rae, *The Golden Shot* was not an immediate hit. In the hands of Rae's successor, Bob Monkhouse, however, it became one of the biggest shows of its day, notching up large audiences for its Sunday teatime slot (having transferred from Saturday nights). Monkhouse was himself succeeded by Norman Vaughan and then by Charlie Williams, before returning to administer the last rites to a tired and dying show in 1975.

Based on a successful German concept, the programme consisted of a series of shooting games. Viewers at home, by way of telephone, could direct a blindfolded marksman to fire at the target, using basic directions like 'Up a bit, down a bit, left a bit, fire'. Other games involved studio contestants taking over control of the crossbows themselves. They shot at bright, humorous pictures and scored by piercing targets made of apple. The ultimate prize was a treasure chest of gold coins that spilled out on to the studio floor when a slender thread was broken. Celebrities mingled with participants and TV cameras were built into the crossbows to show viewers at home how the contestants were aiming.

Supporting the hosts were the 'Golden Girls', initially Andrea Lloyd, Carol Dilworth (later mother of pop star Chesney Hawkes) and Anita Richardson, but most famously dizzy blonde Anne Aston (whose maths, as she added up the target totals, always left room for improvement). Aston was later assisted by a guest 'Maid of the Month'. Bernie the Bolt was the silent man who loaded the crossbows, although there were in fact three 'Bernies' employed during the programme's eight-year run (Derek Young, Alan Bailey and, best remembered, Johnny Baker).

The Golden Shot was briefly revived as one instalment of ANT & DEC's *Game Show Marathon* in 2005, a series that celebrated the best-loved game shows in ITV's 50-year history.

Gone to Seed ★★

UK (Central) Comedy Drama. ITV 1992

Hilda Plant .... **Alison Steadman**
Winston Plant .... **Warren Clarke**
Monty Plant .... **Jim Broadbent**
Mag .... **Sheila Hancock**
Wesley Willis .... **Peter Cook**
Billy .... **Rufus Sewell**
Faith .... **Sheila White**
Lucy Lastic .... **Sara Stockbridge**
Batman .... **Jon Strickland**
Robin .... **Cliff Parisi**
Miss Pringle .... **Hilda Fenemore**
Big Ron .... **Andy Linden**

Writer **Tony Grounds**
Producer **Tim Whitby**

● ***Eccentric triplets help their domineering mum run a garden centre in London's yuppiefied Docklands.***

Hilda is a 42-year-old spinster, whose life revolves around gardening and Millwall FC; Winston is an out-of-work builder and part-time wrestler, complete with eye patch and hair extension; and Monty is a country and western singer who harbours dreams of turning the London Docklands into a sea of flowers. Together the Plant siblings work in the family garden centre, assisting Mag, their miserable matriarch. She controls the cash-strapped business and is under pressure from con man and old flame Wesley Willis to sell up. The troubles of the business and personal woes are covered in this six-episode follow-up to GONE TO THE DOGS that pitched the same main cast members into new roles.

Gone to the Dogs ★★

UK (Central) Comedy Drama. ITV 1991
DVD: Network

Lauren Patterson .... **Alison Steadman**
Larry Patterson .... **Warren Clarke**
Jim Morley .... **Jim Broadbent**
Little Jim Morley .... **Harry Enfield**
Pilbeam .... **Martin Clunes**
Margaret .... **Rosemary Martin**
Stanley .... **Cliff Parisi**
Popeye .... **Jon Strickland**
Jean .... **Sheila Hancock**

Writer **Tony Grounds**
Producer **Michele Buck**

● ***A jailbird tries to outmanoeuvre a rich old schoolmate.***

Jim Morley, freshly released from jail, is a loser who has little going for him. Out of a job, he sees an opportunity to improve his situation in Larry Patterson, a former school chum who has made his fortune in the video business. Larry's also a successful racing greyhound owner and, with his son, Little Jim (Larry's errand boy), Morley sets out to grab a piece of the action. However, the greyhound world is a rough place in which to do battle. Equally tough is the personal relationship between the leading parties, with newly separated Jim looking to press his attentions on Larry's wife, Lauren. She's another former schoolmate and is herself looking for a way of undermining her smug, flashy prat of a husband of 25 years. The six-part, one-hour series (the last two parts shown as a double episode) was set in Essex and featured dog racing scenes from Walthamstow. It was also noted for giving Harry Enfield his first straight drama role and for guest appearances from the West Ham World Cup winners Bobby Moore, Geoff Hurst and Martin Peters. The main cast (with the exception of Enfield) were reunited a year later for GONE TO SEED, in which they played different characters.

Gonet, Stella

(1963–)

Scottish actress best known as Bea in THE HOUSE OF ELIOTT, but also seen in dramas like *The Advocates* (Alex Abercorn), *Screen One's Trip Trap* (abused wife Kate Armstrong), THE CROW ROAD (Fiona), SUPPLY AND DEMAND (DCI Jane Leyland), *Verdict* (Alex Horton-Smith) and *The Secret* (Nadia). Guest appearances have come in series like CASUALTY, MIDSOMER MURDERS, FOYLE'S WAR, THE INSPECTOR LYNLEY MYSTERIES, MURDER IN SUBURBIA, WHERE THE HEART IS, TAGGART, and *Julian Fellowes Investigates*.

Good, Jack

(1931–)

TV's Mr Pop Music. Beginning with SIX-FIVE SPECIAL in 1957, Jack Good revolutionized television coverage of the music scene. At last here was someone (who had joined the BBC as a trainee only in 1956) actually producing programmes for teenage music fans, even if he cautiously sold it to the stuffy Corporation as a young person's magazine. One of its unusual and pioneering features was use of the audience, not ignoring them but bringing them into the proceedings. Controversially sacked a year later, he moved to ABC to produce a rival show, OH BOY!, which ultimately saw the end of the by now staid *Six-Five Special*. In 1959 he created *Boy Meets Girls*, a vehicle for Marty Wilde, and, a year later, *Wham!!* Good was a hit even across the Atlantic, devising *Shindig* and numerous other pop successes. *Oh Boy!* was briefly revived in the late 1970s.

Good Guys, The ★★

UK (LWT/Haverhall) Comedy Drama. ITV 1992–3

Guy MacFadyean .... **Nigel Havers**
Guy Lofthouse .... **Keith Barron**

Executive Producer **Nick Elliott**
Producers **Andrew Montgomery, Michael Whitehall**

● ***Two well-meaning, out-of-work characters join forces to help others, but without much success.***

When Guy Lofthouse walks out on both his marriage and his job in Leeds, he ends up in Richmond, Surrey – and somewhat bewildered by life in the south. Meeting his equally unemployed namesake, Guy MacFadyean, the two Guys strike up a friendship and agree to share a flat. To put some purpose into their empty lives, they set about helping other people, with unpredictable results.

The series was specially created for Nigel Havers and Keith Barron, to enable the two actors to work together. It was made for LWT by Nigel Havers's own production company, Haverhall.

Good Life, The ✱✱✱✱

UK (BBC) Situation Comedy. BBC 1 1975–8
DVD: Acorn Media

Tom Good .... **Richard Briers**
Barbara Good .... **Felicity Kendal**
Margo Leadbetter .... **Penelope Keith**
Jerry Leadbetter .... **Paul Eddington**
Andrew ('Sir') .... **Reginald Marsh**

Creators/Writers **John Esmonde, Bob Larbey**
Producer **John Howard Davies**

● ***A young couple go self-sufficient in Surbiton.***
Tom Good has become tired of the rat race. On his 40th birthday, sick of commuting to his draughtsman's job in the City (where he creates cereal gifts for the JJM company), he throws it all in to concentrate on home farming. Ably and inventively assisted by Barbara, his perky wife, the buoyant Tom turns his back garden into an allotment, growing fruit and vegetables and housing chickens, pigs, a cockerel named Lenin and even a goat named Geraldine. For heating and cooking they restore an old cast-iron range, and for power they run a generator in the cellar. Living off the land, and bartering away the surplus with local shopkeepers, the Goods thrive on the joys of self-sufficiency, even if there are moments of deep despair.

It is at times like these that their true-blue neighbours, Jerry and Margo, ride to the rescue. Although they consider Tom and Barbara to be completely insane, and to have brought 'The Avenue' into disrepute, they remain loyal friends. Even if Margo hates donning wellies to feed the pigs, she still does so, and she and Jerry (a former work colleague of Tom's) always take great interest in events next door. In return, the Goods bring a ray of wholesome sunshine into the depressingly snobbish life of their wealthier neighbours. Occasionally seen is Jerry's overbearing boss, 'Sir'.

Good Morning Britain

See *TV-am*.

Good Morning Television

See *GMTV*.

Good Old Days, The ✱✱

UK (BBC) Variety. BBC 1 1953–83

Chairmen **Don Gemmell, Leonard Sachs**

Producer **Barney Colehan**

● ***The days of the music hall re-created.***
Indelibly associated with its loud and wordy compere, Leonard Sachs (who took over from first chairman Don Gemmell), *The Good Old Days* owed just as much to its long-serving producer, Barney Colehan, who was responsible for developing this music hall revival show. Broadcast (somewhat irregularly) from one of the true surviving music halls, the City Varieties in Leeds, the programme lasted over 30 years and provided older viewers with a happy slice of golden age nostalgia. Its guest stars (the likes of Roy Hudd, Danny La Rue, Ray Alan, Ken Dodd, etc.) performed music hall acts in the style of Marie Lloyd and others, and dressed for the part in 1890s costume. So did the studio audience, who donned false sideburns and frilly hats and were encouraged to join in the proceedings by singing along or waving a handkerchief. And then there was the polysyllabic Leonard Sachs himself, filled with vociferous verbosity, never using one word when 27 would do, smashing down his gavel and rousing the audience to a rapturous welcome for even the most unheard-of performers. The Players' Theatre Company and the Northern Dance Orchestra were the resident supporting artists and each edition ended with the cast and audience joining together in a chorus of 'The Old Bull and Bush'.

Good Sex Guide, The ✱✱

UK (Carlton) Comedy/Information. ITV 1993–4

Presenter **Margi Clarke**

Producer **Vicki Barrass**

● ***Forthright advice on sex, with humorous sketches to ease embarrassment.***
Margi Clarke's colourful commentary added a down-to-earth matter-of-factness to the 'awkward' and intimate subjects considered by this late-night programme, which tackled the taboo subject of 'getting the most out of sex', with the help of acknowledged experts. Among the actors offering light relief through assorted comedy sketches were Tony Robinson, Linda Robson, Pauline Quirke, Stephanie Cole, Bernard Hill, Roger Lloyd Pack, Julia Hills, Haydn Gwynne and Timothy Spall. Clarke returned with a second series in 1994, with the likes of Leslie Grantham, Nigel Planer and Martin Clunes contributing to the fun.

Goodbye Mr Chips ✱✱

UK (BBC) Drama. BBC 1 1984
DVD: Granada Ventures (2002 version)

Mr Chipping ('Chips') .... **Roy Marsden**
Katherine .... **Jill Meager**
Mrs Wickett .... **Anne Kristen**
Meldrum .... **George Baker**
Dr Merivale .... **Peter Baldwin**
Sir John Rivers .... **Paul Williamson**
Kemp .... **John Harding**
Max Staefel .... **Stephen Jenn**
Terris .... **Daniel Flynn**
Staines .... **Andrew Groves**
Prescote .... **Peter Doran**

Writer **Alexander Baron**
Producer **Barry Letts**

● ***A dedicated schoolteacher reveals his memoirs.***
With an eye on the Sunday teatime audience, Gareth Davies directs this six-part adaptation of James Hilton's 1934 novella

of the same name. Set in Brookfield School, this is the lifestory of one Mr Chipping, affectionately known as Mr Chips, one of the establishment's most devoted teachers. Events are recalled by the hero himself, as he lies on his deathbed in his 80s and looks back to the days when he arrived at Brookfield as a callow, nervous youth. Covering the last 30 years of the 19th century, and the first three decades of the 20th, it tells how Chips fell in love with the school and its life, how he matured as a classics teacher and housemaster, and how personal tragedy and the outbreak of war scarred his time there. His marriage to Katherine, the girl he meets on holiday, and the transformation it brings to his life as a confirmed bachelor are chronicled, as is her tragic death during childbirth. Finally, his tale told, Chips passes peacefully away within sight of the school he called home.

In order to appear convincing as the octogenarian Chips, star Roy Marsden (bravely stepping into shoes worn by an Oscar-winning Robert Donat in the famous 1939 film version) faced an arduous five-and-a-half hours per day in make-up. Extras for the series were supplied by Christ College, Brecon, and Repton School. Dudley Simpson composed the music. As if to prove that a good tale always deserves another telling, Frank Delaney penned a new two-hour adaptation of the book for airing on ITV 1 on Boxing Day 2002. Martin Clunes starred as Chips, with Victoria Hamilton his beloved Kathie. Stuart Orme directed.

Goodbye Mr Kent ★★

UK (BBC) Situation Comedy. BBC 1 1982

Travis Kent .... **Richard Briers**
Victoria Jones .... **Hannah Gordon**
Lucy Jones .... **Talla Hayes**

Writers **Peter Vincent, Peter Robinson**
Producer **Gareth Gwenlan**

● ***An unexpected lodger turns a widow's life upside down.***

Times are hard for divorced, working mum Victoria Jones and she decides to advertise for a quiet female companion to share the bungalow she lives in with her teenage daughter, Lucy. Instead, Travis Kent shows up. He's an extremely annoying, over-optimistic freelance journalist, who always thinks he's on the brink of some huge success and blames everyone else for his many failings. Despite his natural flair for irritation, Victoria finds him strangely compelling and somehow agrees that he can move in. It is a move that she regrets on more than one occasion later. But, although Kent is truly a pain, when he causes daily havoc and interferes in Victoria's social life, there is no doubt that he brightens up her world at the same time.

Writers Peter Vincent and Peter Robinson acknowledged in *Radio Times* that the inspiration for the hapless Travis was the character of Oscar Madison, the self-centred slob in THE ODD COUPLE. Just one series of seven episodes was produced, with Ronnie Hazlehurst supplying the music.

Goodies, The ★★★

UK (BBC/LWT) Comedy. BBC 2 1970–7; 1980/ITV 1981–2
DVD: Network

Graeme .... **Graeme Garden**
Tim .... **Tim Brooke-Taylor**
Bill .... **Bill Oddie**

Creators/Writers **Graeme Garden, Tim Brooke-Taylor, Bill Oddie**
Producers **John Howard Davies, Jim Franklin, Bob Spiers (LWT)**

● ***Zany humour with a trio of do-gooders.***

Graeme, Tim and Bill are benefactors to society, available to do anything, anywhere and at any time to help humanity. Taking on the weirdest assignments, they find themselves guarding the Crown Jewels, rescuing London from the advance of a giant kitten, and in other bizarre situations. Sometimes they cook up their own world improvement schemes and attempt to put them into action. Energetically charging around on a three-seater bicycle (a 'trandem'), the three form an unlikely team.

Tim is a weedy royalist sporting a Union Jack waistcoat, Graeme is a mad scientist type and Bill is an unkempt, hairy socialist-cum-cynic. They live in a typical 1970s flat, dominated by portraits of the Queen (for Tim) and Chairman Mao (for Bill), plus Graeme's computer. Their adventures are punctuated with crazy sight gags, slapstick sketches and spoof TV commercials.

There are send-ups galore as the trio take contemporary fads or issues and place them surreally in different contexts – a north country spoof on the Kung Fu craze, for instance. Bill Oddie's original music features prominently (The Goodies had five real-life hits in the 1970s – most notably, alas, 'Funky Gibbon' in 1975).

Originally planned as *Super-Chaps Three, The Goodies* was one of BBC 2's biggest successes of the 1970s, enjoying repeat showings on BBC 1. However, disillusioned with the Corporation's lack of commitment to the programme, the team moved to LWT for a short run in 1981–2, by which time the concept had dated somewhat.

The team was finally reunited at Christmas 2005 in *Return of the Goodies* (BBC 2), a one-off celebration of the series.

Goodman, John

(1952–)

Giant American comic actor, achieving star status as Dan Conner in the blue-collar sitcom ROSEANNE. With his film career really taking off, he has not featured in any other major TV offerings, save a few TV movies and *Saturday Night Live*. Guest appearances have included roles in programmes like MOONLIGHTING, THE EQUALIZER and THE WEST WING (as politician Glenallen Walken).

Goodness Gracious Me ★★★

UK (BBC) Comedy. BBC 2 1998; 2000
DVD: Fremantle

Sanjeev Bhaskar, Meera Syal, Kulvinder Ghir, Nina Wadia

Producer **Anil Gupta**
Executive Producer **Jon Plowman**

● ***Award-winning cross-cultural sketch show.***

Beginning on BBC Radio, *Goodness Gracious Me* soon transferred to television, bringing with it a novel approach to cultural humour. 'Sacred cows' in more than one sense are slaughtered as the four second-generation Indian stars lampoon their own ethnic traditions and at the same time dig away at Britishness and the British treatment of Asians.

Recurring characters include the Coopers (an Indian couple named Kapoor who believe they are pukka English); two Indian mothers who try to outdo each other in terms of what their respective sons have achieved; a pseudo-Maharishi character who fakes his mystic knowledge; two confused youths known as the Bhangramuffins; and an Indian dad who insists everyone who has achieved anything in this world has been Indian. There are also spoofs of the hyper-dramatic 'Bollywood' films, starring wonderstar Chunky, reports from fading showbiz gossip columnist Smeeta Smitten, and the latest infelicity from the tactless Mr 'Cheque please', who never fails to insult his lady dinner-guests. Memorable sketches include the send-up 'Delhitubbies' and one about a group of young Indians visiting a restaurant for an 'English', boorishly ordering 'something bland'. Although the series ended in 2000, a special in 2001, entitled *Goodness Gracious Me – Back Where They Came From*, saw the team take their comic creations to India.

Goodnight Mister Tom ★★★

UK (Carlton) Drama. ITV 1998
DVD: Carlton

Tom Oakley .... **John Thaw**
Willie Beech .... **Nick Robinson**
Mrs Beech .... **Annabelle Apsion**
Ralph Briggs .... **Geoffrey Hutchings**
Mr Greenway .... **Charles Kay**
Dr Stelton .... **William Armstrong**

Writer **Brian Finch**
Producer **Chris Burt**

● ***A grumpy widower becomes a father to a lonely evacuee.***

As bombs threaten to rain down on wartime London, nine-year-old Willie Beech is evacuated along with other children to the East Anglian village of Little Weirwold. He is billeted with the grouchy and extremely unwilling Tom Oakley, a man whose curmudgeonly exterior is gradually scratched away to reveal a heart of gold. What draws out Mister Tom's sensitivity is the discovery that the boy has been badly abused – something that jars with memories of the dear young son he himself had lost many years before. When Willie returns to London and a bleak future, Oakley seeks him out to return him to a better life in the country. This heart-warming, award-winning single drama was based on the children's novel of the same name by Michelle Magorian.

Goodnight Sweetheart ★★

UK (Alomo) Situation Comedy. BBC 1 1993; 1995–9
DVD: Revelation

Gary Sparrow .... **Nicholas Lyndhurst**
Yvonne Sparrow .... **Michelle Holmes**
Emma Amos
Phoebe Bamford/Sparrow ...... **Dervla Kirwan**
Elizabeth Carling
Eric .... **David Ryall**
Ron Wheatcroft .... **Victor McGuire**
PC Reg Deadman .... **Christopher Ettridge**
Noël Coward .... **David Benson**

Creators **Laurence Marks, Maurice Gran**
Executive Producer **Allan McKeown**
Producers **John Bartlett, Nic Phillips**

● ***An unhappily married TV engineer wanders through a time warp and picks up a 1940s girlfriend.***

London television repair man Gary Sparrow and Yvonne, his personnel officer wife, are going through a sticky patch. She wants more from life and is heavily involved in her Open University pyschology degree; he has more interest in simpler matters, like the physical side of their relationship. One day, on his rounds, he wanders down Ducketts Passage, an East End alleyway, finds himself lost and pops into The Royal Oak pub in Stepney for directions. Having been charged tuppence-farthing for his half-pint, he assumes he has discovered a theme pub but, stepping outside again, realizes that he has actually slipped back in time to 1940. Taking a shine to Phoebe, the landlord's daughter, Gary soon makes a habit of popping back to the war years, where the locals (and particularly Phoebe's dad, Eric) distrust this strange young man with weird ideas who claims to be a songwriter (his hits include 'Your Song', 'I Can't Get No Satisfaction' and 'When I'm Sixty-Four'). Meanwhile Yvonne is increasingly bemused by Gary's new interest in wartime nostalgia. Gary's only confidant is his printer pal, Ron.

After the death of her dad, Phoebe runs the pub with the help of inept local bobby PC Deadman (actor Christopher Ettridge is also seen occasionally as Deadman's grandson, a 1990s policeman). Gary marries Phoebe and a son, Michael, is born. They move to a plush West End flat for security, where one of their neighbours is Noël Coward. There are changes in the 1990s, too. Gary opens a wartime nostalgia shop ('Blitz and Pieces'), on the site of the now-developed Ducketts Passage, to provide a cover for his time-travelling activities, while Yvonne first joins a Korean company, then sets up a holistic cosmetics business that makes her a fortune and earns her a peerage. In the finale to the series, Gary saves the life of the Prime Minister, Clement Attlee, and then discovers his time portal is permanently blocked, implying that he has now fulfilled the mission for which he has been allowed to travel through time. Trapped in 1945, he scribbles a note beneath the wallpaper of his West End flat, explaining his predicament to Yvonne and Ron, knowing it will be discovered during decorating work in 1999.

Goodson, Mark

MBE (1915–92)

Prolific American inventor of TV quizzes and panel games, often in conjunction with his partner, Bill Todman. Together they were responsible for the likes of WHAT'S MY LINE?, *I've Got a Secret*, *Beat the Clock*, CALL MY BLUFF, THE PRICE IS RIGHT and FAMILY FORTUNES. Goodson–Todman Productions was their company, formed after Goodson had worked as a radio announcer and Todman as a scriptwriter. Their ventures into drama productions were not so successful.

Goodyear, Julie

MBE (1942–)

Inseparable from bold, brassy Bet Lynch/Gilroy, her character in CORONATION STREET until 1995 (and occasions since), Lancashire-born Julie Goodyear arrived in Weatherfield in 1966, although it wasn't until 1970 that she became a Rover's Return regular. Among her other TV credits have been Granada series like PARDON THE EXPRESSION (the 1966 *Street* spin-off), A FAMILY AT WAR, *City '68*, *The War of Darkie Pilbeam*, THE DUSTBINMEN and NEAREST AND DEAREST, plus the sketch show *Revolver*.

Goolden, Jilly

(1956–)

Sussex-born TV wine and drinks expert, first gaining recognition on FOOD AND DRINK for her much-mimicked 'over the top' tasting descriptions, and later extending into other programming, including as host of *The Great Antiques Hunt*, and as a contributor to HOLIDAY. She later appeared in I'M A CELEBRITY . . . GET ME OUT OF HERE!

Gordon, Hannah

(1941–)

Scottish actress seen in both dramatic and comedy roles. Among her best-remembered performances have been as Suzy Bassett, with John Alderton, in MY WIFE NEXT DOOR; as Victoria Jones, Richard Briers's landlady, in GOODBYE MR KENT; Peter Barkworth's wife (Sylvia Telford) in TELFORD'S CHANGE; and as Belinda Braithwaite in another banking series, JOINT ACCOUNT, with Peter Egan. She played Virginia Hamilton, Lord Bellamy's second wife, in UPSTAIRS, DOWNSTAIRS and her other credits have included parts in THE RAT CATCHERS, LADYKILLERS, MIDDLEMARCH, DR FINLAY'S CASEBOOK, HADLEIGH, THE PERSUADERS!, *Miss Morrison's Ghosts*, THE PROTECTORS, *My Family and Other Animals*, TAGGART, JONATHAN CREEK, MIDSOMER MURDERS, ONE FOOT IN THE GRAVE, MONARCH OF THE GLEN, HEARTBEAT and some Dickens adaptations. She was also seen with Morecambe and Wise, as one of their harassed guests, and has presented the series *Gardeners' Calendar* and *Watercolour Challenge*.

Gordon, Noele

(1923–85)

Famous as CROSSROADS proprietor Meg Richardson/Mortimer, Noele Gordon became a household name after a long and varied career on stage and television. She first appeared in a BBC play way back in 1938 and shortly afterwards assisted John Logie Baird by appearing in one of his colour TV experiments. In the 1950s, with a string of stage plays and musicals to her name, Gordon formally studied the new medium of television in the USA and returned to the UK to work for the embryonic ATV as an adviser on women's programmes. This led to on-screen presentation work on programmes such as *Tea with Noele Gordon*, *Fancy That* and *Hi-T!*, some sports shows, the admag *About Homes and Gardens*, a part in the sitcom *The Most Likely Girl* (Eve Edwards) and, in 1957, the well-remembered magazine *Lunch Box*. In 1964 she was cast as the queen bee of the company's new daily soap opera, and she remained with *Crossroads* until being surprisingly axed in 1981.

Gordon-Sinclair, John

(1962–)

Scottish comedy actor, starring in series such as HOT METAL (Bill Tytla), YOUR CHEATIN' HEART (journalist Frank McClusky), *Snakes and Ladders* (Gavin), AN ACTOR'S LIFE FOR ME (hopeful thespian Robert Neilson), NELSON'S COLUMN (reporter Gavin Nelson), LOVED BY YOU (newlywed film-maker Michael Adams) and the single comedy *My Summer with Des* (Cameron). Guest appearances have been in series like MURDER IN MIND. He also played Macbeth in the *Shakespeare Shorts* series of extracts, David Hanson in *Goodbye Mr Steadman*, Dr George Meyrick in *The Many Lives of Albert Walker*, Ted in *Mad About Alice* and Matt Bancroft in *Roman Road*. In the 1980s he took over as the human face of FRAGGLE ROCK (PK) from Fulton Mackay.

Goring, Marius

CBE (1912–98)

Isle of Wight-born actor with a flair for accents and dialects. A prolific film performer, Goring's first television appearance came in a Chekhov play in 1938. In 1956 he became TV's master of disguise, Sir Percy Blakeney, alias The Scarlet Pimpernel (in THE ADVENTURES OF . . .), saver of aristocratic French souls, in a series which he also co-produced. Goring's next starring role came 13 years later and was in quite a different vein. On this occasion he played Midlands pathologist John Hardy in THE EXPERT. He resurfaced in 1983 as Dr Emile Englander, one of THE OLD MEN AT THE ZOO, and among his other credits were episodes of series as varied as FALL OF EAGLES (Paul von Hindenburg), EDWARD AND MRS SIMPSON (King George V), MAN IN A SUITCASE and WILDE ALLIANCE, plus many single dramas.

Gormenghast ★★★

UK (BBC/WGBH) Drama. BBC 2 2000

DVD: BBC

Lady Gertrude, Countess of Groan	**Celia Imrie**
Dr Prunesquallor	**John Sessions**
Barquentine	**Warren Mitchell**
Lord Sepulchrave, Earl of Groan	**Ian Richardson**
Lady Fuchsia Groan	**Neve McIntosh**
Nannie Slagg	**June Brown**
Flay	**Christopher Lee**
Swelter	**Richard Griffiths**
Steerpike	**Jonathan Rhys Meyers**
Clarice Groan	**Zoë Wanamaker**
Cora Groan	**Lynsey Baxter**
Irma Prunesquallor	**Fiona Shaw**
Mollocks	**Eric Sykes**
Poet	**Sean Hughes**
Keda	**Olga Sosnovkska**
Bookman	**George Yiasoumi**
Rottcodd	**Windsor Davies**
Titus Groan	**Cameron Powrie**
	Andrew N. Robertson
Prof. Bellgrove	**Stephen Fry**
Prof. Perch	**Mark Williams**
Prof. Fluke	**James Dreyfus**
Prof. Shred	**Phil Cornwell**
Prof. Mule	**Steve Pemberton**

Prof. Flower .... **Martin Clunes**
De'ath .... **Spike Milligan**
The Fly .... **Gregor Fisher**

Writer **Malcolm McKay**
Producer **Estelle Daniel**

A kitchen hand worms his way up the ladder of power in a decrepit old castle.

Adapted from Mervyn Peake's novels *Titus Groan* and *Gormenghast*, this acclaimed, four-part series took five years to reach the screen once the rights had been secured, so difficult was it to marry the extravagant visual imagery of Peake's work with a modest television budget. When it finally arrived, *Gormenghast* proved to be a visually striking wallow in classic fantasy. The setting is the spectacular Gormenghast castle, a daunting architectural combination of the Oriental and Gothic, presided over by the melancholy 76th Earl of Groan (who descends into madness, believing himself to be an owl) and his fat, lazy wife, Gertrude (whose pet is an albino rook). The story concerns a kitchen boy named Steerpike, who crawls his way up through the household, plotting the removal of all who block his road to power, particularly Titus Groan, heir to the earldom. The cast of grotesque characters is brought to life by a roll call of acting heavyweights, including Warren Mitchell as Master of the Ritual Barquentine; Richard Griffiths as Swelter, the grotesque cook; Christopher Lee as Flay, a veteran servant; Zoë Wanamaker and Lynsey Baxter as Clarice and Cora, Lord Groan's crazed twin sisters; June Brown as Nannie Slagg; and John Sessions and Fiona Shaw as castle doctor Prunesquallor and his equally barking spinster sister. Cameos from some of Britain's top comic talents as a team of schoolmasters provide the icing on the cake. Andy Wilson directed the serial.

Governor, The ✶✶

UK (La Plante/Samson Films) Drama. ITV 1995–6
DVD: Contender

Helen Hewitt .... **Janet McTeer**
Gary Marshall .... **Derek Martin**
Russell Morgan .... **Ron Donachie**
'Jumbo' Jackson .... **Dave Nicholls**
Moira Levitt .... **Sophie Okonedo**
Dr Thomas .... **Jeremy Sheffield**
James Malahide .... **Paul Kynman**
Governor Lyons .... **Eric Allan**
Victor Braithwaite ('Tarzan') .. **Terry O'Neill**
Brian Samora .... **Jake Abraham**
Snoopy Oswald .... **Eamonn Walker**
John Bunny .... **Mal Whyte**
Dr Davyd Harris .... **Bob Blythe**
Annette Bullock .... **Charlotte Cornwell**
Eugene Buffy .... **Craig Charles**
Jason Hully .... **Oliver Montgomery**
Officer Chiswick .... **Idris Elba**
Governor Syons .... **Pat Laffan**

Writer **Lynda La Plante**
Executive Producer **Steve Lanning**
Producer **Lynda La Plante**

A woman governor tries to streamline a tough men's prison.

Thirty-three-year-old Helen Hewitt has just been appointed governor of the high security, all-male Barfield prison. Suspicions about her likely new regime are rife: the prison has just experienced a riot, all the staff are on edge and she is the youngest-ever female governor in the UK. Hewitt herself sees her role as a firm manager. She is fair but, it must be said, not always an angel and, while she is prepared to encourage offenders to return to the straight and narrow she does not fall into the trap of being an easily swayed liberal – especially when dealing with the likes of the dangerous 'Tarzan' and other devious inmates. During Hewitt's tenure, there are many serious problems and incidents – including prisoner death and corruption among her warders – that ensure her job is always on the line. Hewitt leaves the prison at the end of series one, but returns at the start of series two, when a hostage situation arises. The ex-governor, having now become an expert in dealing with such cases, is the perfect person to sort it out. It is not long before she is back in her old job.

Gower, David

(1957–)

Former England batsman and Test captain, retiring in 1993 and now one of the leading commentators on the sport, working for both the BBC and Sky Sports, and for a while presenting Grandstand's *Cricket Focus* and BBC 2's *Gower's Cricket Monthly*. Gower has also been a team captain in the comedy quiz THEY THINK IT'S ALL OVER.

Grace and Favour

See *Are You Being Served?*

Grace Under Fire ✶✶

US (Carsey-Werner) Situation Comedy. BBC 2 1994–9
(US: ABC 1993–8)

Grace Kelly .... **Brett Butler**
Quentin Kelly .... **Jon Paul Steuer**
Sam Horrigan
Elizabeth 'Libby' Kelly .... **Kaitlin Cullum**
Russell Norton .... **Dave Thomas**
Nadine Swoboda .... **Julie White**
Wade Swoboda .... **Casey Sander**
Faith Burdette .... **Valri Bromfield**
Dougie .... **Walter Olkewicz**
Vic .... **Dave Florek**
Bill Davis .... **Charles Hallahan**
John Shirley .... **Paul Dooley**
Rick Bradshaw .... **Alan Autry**
Floyd Norton .... **Tom Poston**

Creator **Chuck Lorre**

A mother of three defies the male of the species and fends for her family alone.

Grace Kelly lives in Missouri and has a pretty low opinion of men. Considering she has just broken up with her boozy, abusive husband, Jimmy, and has been left to care for her three kids (Quentin, Libby and baby Patrick), that's hardly surprising. But she's a resilient sort and takes a job at an oil refinery to support her family, giving as good as she gets from red-necked workmates like Dougie, Vic, Bill and John. Lending a helping hand are her friends Nadine (four times married) and Wade, plus divorcé pharmacist Russell, until she acquires a boyfriend, Rick, who works for the same company. Later episodes (not screened on terrestrial TV in the UK) saw Grace moving to an advertising agency in St Louis and then to a building firm.

Grace Under Fire was seen by many as an updated version of ROSEANNE, with its blue-collar settings and straight-to-the-point humour. The character's sharp, Southern tongue and aggressive attitude made the choice of her name particularly ironic. A version of The Beatles' 'Lady Madonna' by Aretha Franklin was used as the theme song.

Grade, Lord Lew

(Louis Winogradsky; 1906–98)

Grade was born in the Ukraine. His showbiz career began in the world of dance (he was World Charleston Champion in 1926) but then moved into talent-spotting and management. He set up the Lew and Leslie Grade agency with his younger brother and took care of many of the world's finest acts of the 1940s and 1950s. In 1955 he formed a consortium to bid for one of the ITV franchises. The resulting company, Associated Television (ATV), was given the Midlands weekday and the London weekend ITV contracts. Grade and his colleagues also established ITC (Incorporated Television Production Company) at the same time, with a view to producing films for television. The company was responsible for such dramas as THE ADVENTURES OF ROBIN HOOD, THE SAINT, JESUS OF NAZARETH, MOSES – THE LAWGIVER and the Gerry Anderson puppet series, all aimed purposefully at the American market. Throughout ATV's time on air and ITC's time in production, Grade's influence was enormous, and his personality and presence ensured his programmes were never short of publicity. His ventures into the movie business, primarily in the 1970s and 1980s, proved less lucrative. He was the uncle of TV executive Michael Grade (Leslie's son) and brother of the late Lord Bernard Delfont.

Grade, Michael

CBE (1943–)

British TV executive with experience on both sides of the Atlantic. Grade began as a sports writer, before joining his family's theatrical agency and subsequently moving into television. At LWT, he was Head of Light Entertainment and Director of Programmes and, crossing to the States, spent some time with Embassy Television. He became Controller of BBC 1 in 1984 and, later, Director of Programmes, and during his four years at the Corporation was given credit for rejuvenating both BBC television networks, with his scheduling expertise widely acclaimed. He repositioned existing shows to their greater benefit (drawing on his intimate knowledge of ITV competition) and was responsible for commissioning and nurturing a host of new ideas. EASTENDERS was a classic case, with Grade firmly committed to its early success. EDGE OF DARKNESS, TUTTI FRUTTI and THE SINGING DETECTIVE were other notable achievements. Grade's BBC years were not without controversy, however. In 1986 he added to the storm over THE MONOCLED MUTINEER by passing a press release which wrongly stated that all the facts were authentic; and, a year earlier, he had angered sci-fi fans by postponing a season of DOCTOR WHO and cancelling THE TRIPODS two-thirds of the way through. From 1988 to 1997 he was Chief Executive of Channel 4, controversy following him back into the independent sector. He later became Non-Executive Chairman of Pinewood Studios UK and was then appointed Chairman of the BBC, succeeding Gavyn Davies, in 2004. Grade is the son of talent agent the late Leslie Grade and nephew of the late Lord Lew Grade.

Graef, Roger

OBE (1936–)

Acclaimed, New York-born documentary maker, working in Britain and responsible for landmark contributions such as POLICE and *Feltham Sings!* Among his dozens of other films are *Inside the Brussels HQ, Decision: British Communism* and *In Search of Law and Order*, plus comedy films like *The Secret Policeman's Ball, Look at the State We're In* and the original COMIC RELIEF show. More recent credits include *The Protectors, Rail Cops* and *Secrets of the Iraq War*. He also wrote and directed the 1988 drama *Closing Ranks*. Graef was a founding member of the board of Channel 4 and now runs his own production company, Films of Record.

Grafters ✶✶

UK (Coastal/Granada) Comedy Drama. ITV 1998–9

Joe Purvis .... **Robson Green**
Trevor Purvis .... **Stephen Tompkinson**
Paul .... **Neil Stuke**
Laura .... **Emily Joyce**
Henry .... **Pip Miller**
Simon Purvis .... **Darren Morfitt**
Lennie Purvis .... **Maurice Roëves**
Viv Casey .... **Lesley Vickerage**
Nick Costello .... **David Westhead**
Clare Costello .... **Katherine Wogan**
Alan Purvis .... **Berwick Kaler**
Pippa .... **Marian McLoughlin**
Geoff .... **Stephen Boxer**
Becky .... **Stacy Hart**
Lizzie .... **Heather Bleasdale**
Sam .... **William Parker**

Producers **Helen Gregory, Jonathan Curling**

Mismatched brothers are building partners.

Geordie brothers Joe and Trevor Purvis talk themselves into a major building job in London. They are to convert a house for yuppie couple Paul and Laura, but soon realize they've bitten off more than they can chew. Trevor, after all, is not even a qualified builder: he's just filling in time after losing his office job. He is, naturally, rather concerned – unlike his super-confident, older brother, who can charm the birds out of the trees. Both brothers have a chequered past, with offspring from previous relationships to worry them. They also look like having a chequered future, as both enter a relationship with the unfaithful Laura. Even with the help (hindrance?) of rowdy young cousin Simon, the end of this particular job seems a long way off. This provides many opportunities for exploring relationships within the complex Purvis family that extends to father Lennie and his affluent brother Alan, manager of a building society. After the initial eight-part series, the brothers returned for another eight episodes of light-hearted drama a year later. This time the setting is Brighton, where the boys live in a camper van on the beach and Joe has set his sights on making a fortune by converting a derelict school. He has recruited a divorced architect, Viv Casey, to his cause (and to his bed), and befriended her ten-year-old son, but trouble is on the horizon, not least from rival developer Nick Costello, whose sister, Clare, becomes the object of the romantic Trevor's attentions.

Grammer, Kelsey
(1955–)

American actor, born in the US Virgin Islands. After minor roles in soaps, Grammer made the decisive move from stage to small screen when offered the part of psychiatrist Frasier Crane in CHEERS, a character who was then spun off into his own even more successful series, FRASIER, making Grammer an international star. He has also provided the voice of Sideshow Bob for THE SIMPSONS and *Gary the Rat*, the star of a US series for which he is also executive producer.

Grampian Television

Taking to the air on 30 September 1961, Grampian Television is the independent television contractor for North Scotland (basically from Fife north to Shetland and west to the Hebrides – the largest of all ITV franchise regions). Its main production centre is in Aberdeen, but the company also operates smaller studios in Stornoway, Dundee and Inverness. Since 1976 some regional programmes have been made in Gaelic, but, while the company has a good reputation for local news and current affairs, it is not renowned for contributions to the ITV national network. Grampian is now part of Scottish Media Group, which also owns Scottish Television.

Gran, Maurice
(1949–)

British comedy scriptwriter, in collaboration with partner Laurence Marks. Together Marks and Gran, whose early work included writing for Marti Caine, have been responsible for some of the most popular sitcoms and comedy-dramas since the 1980s, many produced by their own company, Alomo (bought by Pearson Television, now FremantleMedia, in 1996). These have included SHINE ON HARVEY MOON, *Roots*, HOLDING THE FORT, *Relative Strangers*, THE NEW STATESMAN, ROLL OVER BEETHOVEN, *Young, Gifted and Broke*, *Snakes and Ladders*, SO YOU THINK YOU'VE GOT TROUBLES, BIRDS OF A FEATHER, LOVE HURTS, GOODNIGHT SWEETHEART, GET BACK, *Unfinished Business*, *Dirty Work*, MEN OF THE WORLD (as producers) and BELIEVE NOTHING. After setting up the premiss in early episodes, Marks and Gran have often passed the writing of their comedies into other hands. Alomo also produced the Adam Faith sitcom *The House That Jack Built*. In contrast, the duo also scripted *Screen One's Wall of Silence* and the historical drama MOSLEY, having earlier contributed to THE BRETTS.

Granada Television

Granada Television was formed in 1955 by Sidney (later Lord) Bernstein and his brother, Cecil, to operate the North of England ITV weekday franchise (ABC was given the weekends). Following the London ITV companies on to the air, its first programmes went out on 3 May 1956. With restructuring and the arrival of Yorkshire Television in 1968, its transmission area was recentred on the north-west, but for the full seven days a week.

Granada always occupied a hallowed position among ITV companies, managing to combine commercial astuteness with a commitment to high-quality programming, an attribute not often recognized in commercial broadcasting. The company fostered young writers and producers in all areas of programming, from the mass-market appeal of CORONATION STREET to the weaker audience potential of award-winning documentaries like WORLD IN ACTION and DISAPPEARING WORLD. Granada also showed itself to be a rival to the BBC in classic drama. BRIDESHEAD REVISITED and THE JEWEL IN THE CROWN were lavish productions in the early 1980s, and equal acclaim was later afforded to productions such as THE ADVENTURES OF SHERLOCK HOLMES, PRIME SUSPECT and CRACKER. However, the company was also happy to exploit cheap and cheerful, viewer-spinning concepts, including THE COMEDIANS, BUSMAN'S HOLIDAY, STARS IN THEIR EYES, YOU'VE BEEN FRAMED and THE KRYPTON FACTOR. In the 1980s Granada opened up its studios to the public, creating for a number of years one of Britain's major tourist attractions (now closed).

Despite its impressive record, there were fears that Granada would lose its franchise in the 1991 auctions, when Phil Redmond's Mersey Television outbid it by several millions. This was one decision that went in favour of quality instead of cash, however, and Granada survived. After that time, Granada began producing programmes for the BBC, notably WHAT THE PAPERS SAY, UNIVERSITY CHALLENGE and THE ROYLE FAMILY. The longest surviving ITV company, Granada gradually took overall control of its fellow ITV franchisees, LWT, Yorkshire, Tyne Tees, Anglia, Meridian and Border, before merging with Carlton to create ITV plc in 2004.

The name Granada was dreamt up by Sidney Bernstein for his theatre business in the 1920s, following a breathtaking visit to the Spanish city of that name.

Grand, The ★★★

UK (Granada) Drama. ITV 1997–8

John Bannerman	**Michael Siberry**
Sarah Bannerman	**Julia St John**
Marcus Bannerman	**Mark McGann**
Mr Jacob Collins	**Tim Healy**
Miss Esme Harkness	**Susan Hampshire**
Kate Morris	**Rebecca Callard**
Stephen Bannerman	**Stephen Moyer**
	Ifan Meredith
Mary Bannerman	**Louie Ramsay**
Ruth Manning/Bannerman	**Amanda Mealing**
	Victoria Scarborough
Adele Bannerman	**Camilla Power**
Mrs Sylvia Harvey	**Christine Mackie**
Clive Evans	**Paul Warriner**
Monica Jones	**Jane Danson**
Lynne Milligan	**Naomi Radcliffe**
Brenda Potter	**Maria Mescki**
Lark Rothery	**Julia Haworth**
Fred Willets	**Richard Standing**
Christina Lloyd-Price	**Emily Hamilton**
Bob Jessop	**John Henshaw**
Tom Corbett	**Ian Kershaw**

Writers **Russell T. Davies, Chris Thompson, Julian Roach**
Executive Producer **Gub Neal**
Producer **Antony Wood**

Drama in the lives of the guests and management of a luxurious 1920s hotel.

The investment has been made, the refurbishment complete: all that is needed now is for the Grand to be a success. That's the position facing the Bannerman family at the start of this series. John Bannerman and his wife, Sarah, have ploughed their savings into restoring the family hotel, making it the plushest in Manchester. But there's an element of risk involved. It is New Year's Eve, 1919, the lights still barely back on across Europe after the horrors of the Great War, so custom is not guaranteed. Besides this, unforeseen financial traumas are about to strike and these quickly lead to the involvement of James's caddish brother, Marcus, whose investment in the business is badly needed. What isn't so welcome is his reason for getting involved: he sees it as a way to Sarah's heart, despite having a girlfriend, Ruth Manning, of his own. Then there is John and Sarah's dispirited son, Stephen, who has returned home from the conflict but remains at a loose end, plus easily led, 17-year-old daughter Adele. Prominent among the guests is resident Miss Harkness, a lady of independent means whose background turns out to be less respectable than implied. These are the troubles upstairs. Down below, all is not sweetness and light among the staff, either. Hall porter is Jacob Collins, a man of few words but well endowed with common sense. If he appears distracted and morose, it is because his son was shot as a deserter in 1915. Mrs Harvey is the prudish housekeeper, always chivvying the rebellious parlour and kitchen maids, among whom teenagers Kate Morris and Monica Jones stand out. Despite her sharp tongue, Kate is destined to make progress in her job and her life, but for Monica, who fantasizes about rising above her station, tragedy lurks on the horizon.

The series was filmed on a specially constructed, period set (Art Deco) at Granada's studios. Eighteen episodes were produced over two years and among the guest stars was the late rock singer Ian Dury.

Grandad ✳

UK (BBC) Children's Situation Comedy. BBC 1979–80; 1982; 1984

Charlie Quick	**Clive Dunn**
Dighy Righy	**Maurice Thorogood**
Mildred	**Jane Waddell**
Mr Watkins	**Geoffrey Russell**
Capt. Flint	**Laura Macaw**
Bert Barnford	**James Marcus**
Miss Crampton	**Helen Cotterill**

Creator **Clive Dunn**
Writer **Bob Block**
Executive Producer **Anna Home**
Producer **Jeremy Swan**

● ***An enthusiastic but hapless pensioner runs a community hall.***

From Bob Block, writer of some of the most popular children's comedies of the 1970s, came *Grandad*, based on an idea by star Clive Dunn. Donning old man's clothing yet again, Dunn becomes Charlie Quick – affectionately known to all as 'Grandad' – who works as caretaker of the Parkview Rehearsal Hall. It is his misdirected efforts to assist everyone who hires the hall (musicians, dancers, etc.) that raise most of the juvenile laughs. The title echoes Dunn's 1970 chart topper of the same name, which he performed on TOP OF THE POPS sitting in a rocking chair surrounded by devoted chanting kids.

Grandstand ✳✳✳

UK (BBC) Sport. BBC 1 1958–

Presenters **Peter Dimmock, David Coleman, Frank Bough, Desmond Lynam, Steve Rider**

● ***The BBC's Saturday afternoon sports showcase.***

Now approaching its 50th birthday, *Grandstand*, the world's longest-running live sports programme, is a national institution, and Saturday afternoons, one would think, would not be the same without it – despite the BBC's loss of many major sporting events in recent years. However, the BBC has announced that the programme is to be phased out by 2009. It will be replaced by programming dedicated to individual sports, rather than the Grandstand all-in-one package. Grandstand's format has changed little over the years. Live horse racing has been mixed with boxing, rugby union, rugby league, cricket, motor sports and occasional other events, and all the day's soccer and rugby details have been rounded up to provide a full results service at the end, including reports from the major matches. The final scores, as they happen, have been reported on the Teleprinter and, in latter years, its replacement, the Videprinter.

Peter Dimmock was the first host but quickly gave way to David Coleman. Frank Bough took over in 1968, and from the 1980s Desmond Lynam and Steve Rider shared the honours, until Lynam's departure to ITV in 1999. Rider himself headed in the same direction in 2005. Other presenters have been drafted in as relief cover over the years, including Harry Carpenter, Harry Gratian, Bob Wilson, David Icke and, more recently, the late Helen Rollason (first female presenter), Sue Barker, Ray Stubbs, Dougie Donnelly, John Inverdale, Hazel Irvine, Clare Balding and Jill Douglas. The main specialist commentators have been as follows: boxing, Harry Carpenter and Jim Neilly; rugby union, Cliff Morgan, Bill McLaren, Nigel Starmer-Smith, Nick Mullins, Andrew Cottes, Eddie Butler and Jonathan Davies; rugby league, Eddie Waring and Ray French; racing, Peter O'Sullevan, Clive Graham, Julian Wilson, Jimmy Lindley, Richard Pitman, Peter Scudamore, Clare Balding, Willie Carson and Jim McGrath; motor sports, Murray Walker and Barry Nutley; winter sports, Alan Weeks, David Vine and Julian Tutt; golf, Henry Longhurst and Peter Alliss; swimming, Alan Weekes and Hamilton Bland; cricket, Richie Benaud, Jim Laker, Peter West, Tony Lewis and David Gower; darts, Sid Waddell and Tony Green; snooker, Ted Lowe, Clive Everton, Ray Edmonds, Dennis Taylor and John Virgo; tennis, Dan Maskell and John Barrett; athletics, Ron Pickering, Stuart Storey, David Coleman, Brendan Foster, Paul Dickenson, Steve Cram and Roger Black. *Football Preview*, the look ahead to the day's soccer, was hosted for many years by Sam Leitch. *Football Focus*, its successor, was fronted by Bob Wilson until his departure to ITV in 1994 and his replacement by Ray Stubbs and Gary Lineker. This strand has been a stand-alone, pre-*Grandstand* programme since 2001, latterly fronted by Manish Bhasin. The sports results have been read by the famous voices of the late Len Martin (soccer) and Tim Gudgin (most of the others).

Variations on the *Grandstand* theme have included *Sunday Grandstand* (inaugurated in 1981) and extended versions for the Olympic Games, the World Cup, etc.

Grange Hill ✳✳✳

UK (BBC/Mersey) Children's Drama. BBC 1 1978–

Peter 'Tucker' Jenkins	**Todd Carty**
Mr Tony Mitchell	**Michael Percival**
Justin Bennett	**Robert Craig Morgan**
Benny Green	**Terry Sue Patt**
Trisha Yates	**Michelle Herbert**
David Lewis	**Gary Fetterplace**
Jackie Heron	**Miriam Mann**
Thomas Watson	**James Jebbia**
Hughes	**Donald Waugh**
Mr Foster	**Roger Sloman**

Character	Actor
Ann Wilson	**Lucinda Duckett**
Penny Lewis	**Ruth Davies**
Judy Preston	**Abigail Brown**
Alan Hargreaves/Humphries	**George Armstrong**
Lucinda	**Letitia Dean**
Mr Graham Sutcliffe	**James Wynn**
Mr Baxter	**Michael Cronin**
Mr Llewellyn	**Sean Arnold**
Simon Shaw	**Paul Miller**
Andrew Stanton	**Mark Chapman/Eadie**
Michael Doyle	**Vincent Hall**
Cathy Hargreaves	**Lyndy Brill**
Mary Johnson	**Kim Benson**
Karen Stanton	**Carey Born**
Susi McMahon	**Linda Slater**
Clare Scott	**Paula Ann Bland**
Sudhamani Patel	**Sheila Chandra**
Tommy Watson	**Paul McCarthy**
Matthew Cartwright	**Nicholas Pandolfi**
Mr Hopwood	**Brian Capron**
Mrs Bridget McCluskey	**Gwyneth Powell**
Mr Keating	**Robert Hartley**
Pogo Patterson	**Peter Moran**
Michael Green	**Mark Bishop**
'Gripper' Stebson	**Mark Savage**
Duane Orpington	**Mark Baxter**
'Stewpot' Stewart	**Mark Burdis**
Pamela Cartwright	**René Alperstein**
Annette Firman	**Nadia Chambers**
Anita Unsworth	**Joanne Boakes**
Precious Matthews	**Dulice Liecier**
Suzanne Ross	**Susan Tully**
Samuel 'Zammo' McGuire	**Lee MacDonald**
Roland Browning	**Erkan Mustafa**
Miss Mooney	**Lucinda Gane**
Mr 'Scruffy' McGuffy	**Fraser Cains**
Mr Bronson	**Michael Sheard**
Jonah Jones	**Lee Sparke**
Mr Smart	**Simon Haywood**
Janet St Clair	**Simone Nylander**
Fay Lucas	**Alison Bettles**
Jimmy Flynn	**Terry Kinsella**
Julie Marchant	**Lisa York**
Sarah Wilks	**Joanne Bell**
Jackie Wright	**Melissa Wilks**
Robbie Wright	**John Alford**
Diane Cooney	**Julie-Ann Steel**
Mandy Firth	**Anita Savage**
Ronnie Birtles	**Tina Mahon**
Miss Booth	**Karen Ford**
Gonch Gardner	**John Holmes**
Cheryl Webb	**Amma Asante**
Imelda Davis	**Fleur Taylor**
'Hollo' Holloway	**Bradley Sheppard**
Mrs Reagan	**Lucinda Curtis**
Vince Savage	**Steve West**
'Mauler' McCaul	**Joshua Fenton**
Helen Kelly	**Ruth Carraway**
Georgina Hayes	**Samantha Lewis**
Danny Kendall	**Jonathan Lambeth**
Ted	**Ian Congdon-Lee**
Matthew Pearson	**Paul Adams**
Ant Jones	**Ricky Simmonds**
Ziggy Greaves	**George Wilson/Christopher**
Mr Mackenzie	**Nicholas Donnelly**
Mr Griffiths	**George A. Cooper**
Mr Max Hargreaves	**Kevin O'Shea**
Mr Geoff Hankin	**Lee Cornes**
Mr Peter Robson	**Stuart Organ**
Caroline 'Calley' Donnington	**Simone Hyams**
Chrissy Mainwaring	**Sonya Kearns**
'Tegs' Ratcliffe	**Sean Maguire**
Mrs Keele	**Jenny Howe**
Trevor Cleaver	**John Drummond**
Mrs Monroe	**Anna Quayle**
Fiona Wilson	**Michelle Gayle**
Natasha Stevens	**Clare Buckfield**
Natalie Stevens	**Julie Buckfield**
Becky Stevens	**Natalie Poyser**
Justine Dean	**Rachel Roberts**
Maria	**Luisa Bradshaw-White**
Jacko Morgan	**Jamie Lehane**
Robyn	**Nina Fry**
Miss Jayne Carver	**Sally Geoghegan**
Julie Corrigan	**Margo Selby**
Anna Wright	**Jenny Long**
Gordon	**Andrew Henry**
Wendy Wright	**Amelda Brown**
Con	**Daniel O'Grady**
Mrs Jenkins	**Madelaine Newton**
Sarah-Jane Webster	**Laura Hammett**
Dudley	**Steven Hammett**
Kevin Jenkins	**George Stark**
Poppy Silver	**Ayesha Antoine**
Wayne Sutcliffe	**Peter Morton**
Colin Brown	**Colin Ridgewell**
Sam	**Kevin Bishop**
Delia 'Dill' Lodge	**Rochelle Gadd**
Josh Davis	**Jamie Groves**
Joe Williams	**Martino Lazzeri**
Lucy Mitchell	**Belinda Crane**
Dennis Morris	**Alan Cave**
Jessica Arnold	**Amy Simcock**
James 'Arnie' Arnold	**Aidan J. David**
Jerome	**Nicholas Pinnock**
Mr Mitchell	**Tim Bentinck**
Chris Longworth	**Ben Freeman**
Mr Brisley	**Adam Ray**
Mr Parrot	**Peter Leeper**
Paula	**Abigail Hart**
Lauren	**Melanie Joseph**
Judi Jeffries	**Laura Sadler**
Mrs Margaret Holmes	**Rachel Bell**
Mr Phillips	**Don Warrington**
Mr Dai 'Hard' Jones	**Clive Jones**
Laurie Watson	**Sian Welsh**
Joanna	**Fiona Wade**
Andy	**Ashley Walters**
Tom 'Speedy' Smith	**Oliver Elmidoro**
Sam 'Cracker' Bacon	**Jonathon Marchant-Heatley**
Lisa West	**Charlotte McDonagh**
Alec Jones	**Thomas Carey**
Matt Singleton	**Robert Stuart**
Rachel	**Francesca Martinez**
Adam Hawkins	**Sam Bardens**
Gemma Lyons	**Maggie Mason**
Franco Savi	**Francesco Bruno**
Carlene	**Lorraine Woodley**
Max Abassi	**Michael Obiora**
Sean Pearce	**Iain Robertson**
Nathan Charles	**Marcel McCalla**
Darren Clarke	**Adam Sopp**
Amy Davenport	**Lindsey Ray**
Becky	**Emma Pierson**
Zoe	**Jade Williams**
Ben Miller	**Daniel Lee**

Ian Hudson	**John Hudson**
Kamal Hussain	**Taylor Scipio**
Spencer Hargreaves	**Colin White**
Ray	**Kelly George**
Calvin Braithwaite	**Arnold Oceng**
Anika Modi	**Jalpa Patel**
Evelyn Wright	**Diana Magness**
Kelly Bradshaw	**Kate Bell**
Tracy Long	**Sally Morton**
Miss Fraser	**Judith Wright**
Simon	**Dominic Power**
Danny Hartson	**Max Brown**
Kieran 'Ozzie' Osborne	**Jon Newman**
Frankie Abbott	**Mark Lewis**
Martin Miller	**Matthew Buckley**
Shannon Parks	**Amanda Fahy**
Leah Stewart	**Jessica Staveley-Taylor**
Shona West	**Sophie Shad**
Vikki Meedes	**Emma Willis**
Clare Chaplin	**Naomi Osei-Mensah**
Josh Irving	**Shane Leonidas**
Maddie Gilks	**Kacey Barnfield**
Tom Smith	**Oliver Elmidoro**
Kathy McIlroy	**Sammy O'Grady**
Briony Jones	**Renee Montemayor**
Mr Stephen Deverill	**Nicolas Tizzard**
Carl Fenton	**Reggie Yates**
Harriet Davenport	**Jenny Galloway**
Patrick 'Togger' Johnson	**Chris Perry-Metcalfe**
Andy Turner	**Chris Crookall**
Abel Benson	**Lucas Lindo**
Annie Wainwright	**Lauren Bunney**
Emma Bolton	**Daniella Fray**
Max Humphries	**James Wignall**
Matthew 'Mooey' Humphries	**Jonathan Dixon**
Mel Adams	**Sarah Lawrence**
Karen Young	**Holly Quin-Ankrah**
Mr Chris Malachay	**Edward Baker-Duly**
Barry 'Baz' Wainwright	**Thomas Hudson**
Tanya Young	**Kirsten Cassidy**
Nick Edwards	**Tom Graham**
Miss Dyson	**Nikki Grosse**
Mrs Bassinger	**Jacqueline Boatswain**
Mrs Knuckle	**Valerie Lilley**
Wally Scott	**Simon O'Brien**
Jeremy Bishop	**Max Friswell**
Mr Steve Green	**Celyn Jones**
Taylor Mitchell	**Reece Noi**
Tim 'Tigger' Johnson	**Jack McMullen**
Sammy Lee	**Holly Mann**
Ed Booth	**Alex Sheldon**
Chloe Moore	**Mia Smith**
Andrea O'Malley	**Darcy Isa**
Alex Pickering	**Josh Brown**
Alison Simmons	**Georgia Foote**
Dawn O'Malley	**Hollie-Jay Bowes**
Donnie	**Rob Norbury**
Eleanor	**Amber Hodgkiss**
Holly Parsons	**Rebecca Anne Withey**
Katrina Simpson	**Chantelle Latham**
Miss Adams	**Terri Dwyer**
Mr Fox	**Paul Orchard**
Mr McDonnell	**Paul Gilmore**
Mrs Rawlinson	**Kim Hartman**

Creator **Phil Redmond**
Executive Producers **Anna Home, Richard Callanan, Phil Redmond**
Producers **Colin Cant, Susi Hush, Kenny McBain, Ben Rea, Ronald Smedley, Albert Barber, Christine Secombe, Lee Hardman**

Realistic tales of life in a city comprehensive school.

In the days when the nearest thing to unruly behaviour on children's television was an elephant wetting itself in the BLUE PETER studio, it would have been quite unthinkable to have switched on at five o'clock and watched a schoolboy trying to kick his heroin addiction. But times move on and kids' TV certainly caught up with its viewers when the BBC launched *Grange Hill* in 1978.

The brainchild of Liverpudlian writer Phil Redmond (later to take BROOKSIDE to Channel 4), *Grange Hill* (screened twice a week as a children's soap opera) was school as it really was, with none of the jolly japes and wizard wheezes of BILLY BUNTER's days. The action took place at Grange Hill Comprehensive and, to make its intended audience feel at home, low, kid-height camera-angles were used. The series showed pupils (mostly Form 1 Alpha) out of control, insulting teachers, truanting, bullying weaklings, smoking and shoplifting. It covered subjects as intense as child abuse, racism, sex, pregnancy, job hunting and, yes, drugs; and, while it received no thanks from Mary Whitehouse, its audience, aged between six and 16, loved it. Critics also failed to note that no one ever benefited from any of the hell-raising. Punishments were suitably doled out and the moral angles were well publicized. The programme's educational value was equally overlooked. In 1986, on the back of pupil Zammo's fight with heroin addiction, the cast released a hit record, 'Just Say No', and the relevant episode of the series was followed by a special factual programme on the subject. Within the unfolding drama, one other major turn of events involved the merger of Grange Hill with arch-rival schools Brookdale and Rodney Bennett in 1981.

Although lead and supporting characters have come and gone as pupils have progressed through school (the major players are listed above), the best remembered is Tucker Jenkins (played by future *EastEnder* Todd Carty), who also earned his own spin-off series, *Tucker's Luck* (1983–5), on leaving school. Carty's EASTENDERS sister, Susan Tully, was another early star, playing Suzanne Ross, and several other members of the prime-time soap cut their TV teeth in the classrooms of *Grange Hill*. Oscar-winning writer Anthony Minghella was the series' script editor, 1983–8. Phil Redmond returned to the series as executive producer in 2003, relocating the school out of London and to nowhere in particular (filming took place in Liverpool, as Mersey Television took over production), and aiming to re-introduce lighter elements to the format. Also guesting at this time was Todd Carty as Tucker, bringing in his rascally nephew, 'Togger' Johnson.

Grant, Richard E.

(Richard Esterhuysen; 1957–)

Actor born and raised in Swaziland who, having earned cult status through the film *Withnail and I*, soon acquired major TV roles, too, especially as the new face of THE SCARLET PIMPERNEL (Sir Percy Blakeney). Grant's other television credits take in dramas and comedies, among them *Honest, Decent, Legal and True*, *Codename: Kyril* (Sculby), *Here is the News*, *Suddenly Last Summer* (George Holly), *Hard Times* (Harthouse), *Bed*, *Butter*, KARAOKE/COLD LAZARUS (Nick Balmer), *A Royal Scandal* (George, Prince of Wales), TRIAL AND RETRIBUTION (Stephen Warrington), *A Christmas Carol* (Bob Cratchit), the animation *The Miracle Maker* (voice of John the Baptist) and *Hound of the Baskervilles* (Stapleton). He also narrated the comedy series PALLAS and his guest appearances include parts in ABSOLUTELY

FABULOUS, *Let Them Eat Cake* and FRASIER (as one of Daphne's brothers). In 2003 he starred as Simon Marchmont in the spoof cookery series *Posh Nosh*.

Grant, Rob

British comedy writer, most often in collaboration with partner Doug Naylor. Undoubtedly, Grant and Naylor's biggest success has been with the space sitcom RED DWARF, although they have also been major contributors to THREE OF A KIND, SPITTING IMAGE, ALAS SMITH AND JONES, CARROTT'S LIB and numerous radio series. Another sitcom product of theirs was THE 10%ERS. Grant also penned the sitcom *Dark Ages* and Sky One's sci-fi comedy *The Strangerers*.

Grant, Russell

(1952–)

Bouncy TV astrologer and contributor to magazine programmes, an early star of the BBC's BREAKFAST TIME. Other credits have included *Russell Grant's Postcards* and *House Busters*.

Grantham, Leslie

(1947–)

London-born actor who shot to fame as EASTENDERS' Dirty Den Watts. During his time in the series, it was revealed that Grantham had spent 11 years in prison for a murder he had committed while a soldier in Germany. In confinement he took up acting and, on release, he trained at drama school. His earliest TV roles came with minor parts in THE JEWEL IN THE CROWN, DOCTOR WHO and BULMAN. On leaving *EastEnders*, capitalizing on his new-found status as a TV sex-symbol, Grantham moved on to star in *Winners and Losers* (boxing promoter Eddie Burt), THE PARADISE CLUB (nightclub manager Danny Kane), *99–1* (undercover cop Mick Raynor), CLUEDO (Colonel Mustard), *The Uninvited* (Chief Supt. Gates, also as creator and executive producer) and Sky One's *The Stretch* (Terry Greene).

He has also co-hosted the game show *Fort Boyard* and was seen in *Time Keepers of the Millennium* before returning briefly to *EastEnders* in 2003. Guest appearances include roles in series like WYCLIFFE and HEARTBEAT.

Grass

See *The Fast Show*.

Graves, Peter

(Peter Aurness; 1926–)

Tall American actor, the brother of GUNSMOKE star James Arness. The brothers' TV breaks came at about the same time. In the mid-1950s, while James was beginning a long career in the guise of Dodge City lawman MATT DILLON, Peter launched into a five-year run as Jim Newton, the father figure in the horsey kids' series *Fury*. In 1960 Graves starred as Chris Cobb, an American stagecoach owner, in the Australian Western WHIPLASH, and, five years later, appeared in the drama series COURT MARTIAL. Around this time he also popped up in series like ALFRED HITCHCOCK PRESENTS and *Route 66*. However, it is as Jim Phelps, team leader of the Impossible Missions Force in MISSION: IMPOSSIBLE, that he is best remembered. Moving on to TV movies and mini-series, Graves later played Fred 'Palmer' Kirby in the blockbusters THE WINDS OF WAR and *War and Remembrance*. In recent times, he has made regular guest appearances as John 'The Colonel' Camden in the US drama series *7th Heaven*.

Gravy Train, The/The Gravy Train Goes East ★★★

UK (Portman) Situation Comedy. Channel 4 1990/1991

Hans-Joachim Dorfmann	**Christoph Waltz**
Michael Spearpoint	**Ian Richardson**
Villeneuve	**Jacques Sereys**
Hilda Spearpoint	**Judy Parfitt**
Gianna	**Anita Zagaria**
Nadine	**Almanta Suska** *(Gravy Train)*
Milcic	**Alexei Sayle** *(Gravy Train)*
Gustave	**Geoffrey Hutchings** *(Gravy Train)*
Delise	**Mandy Mealing** *(Gravy Train)*
Katya Princip	**Francesca Annis** *(Goes East)*
Steadiman	**Jeremy Child** *(Goes East)*
Larson Parson	**John Dicks** *(Goes East)*
Tankic	**Henry Goodman** *(Goes East)*
Galina	**Cecile Paoli** *(Goes East)*
Plitplov	**Roger Lloyd Pack** *(Goes East)*

Writer **Malcolm Bradbury**
Executive Producers **Tom Donald, Victor Glen**
Producers **Ian Warren, Philip Hinchcliffe**

● ***Black comedy about inefficiencies and corruption in the EEC.***

In this four-part satirical story of bribery and criminality at the heart of the European Community, naïve young German Hans-Joachim Dorfmann takes up a junior position in the EEC's Directorate of Information and Culture. Surprisingly, he is immediately very popular. Colleagues flatter him, women fawn over him and he is rapidly promoted. It is only when he is charged with disposing of the European plum mountain that he begins to realize that he is being manipulated, not least by the Machiavellian Milcic and cynical British emissary Michael Spearpoint. When Dorfmann re-emerges a year later, in the four-episode sequel, *The Gravy Train Goes East*, he is embroiled in relations between the EEC and the fictitious country of Slaka, an ex-Communist Balkan state that is hoping to join the Community against Britain's wishes. Its president is former romantic novelist Katya Princip. This second series was largely filmed in Budapest.

Gray, Linda

(1942–)

Model turned actress whose earliest TV credits came in such series as MARCUS WELBY, MD and MCCLOUD. From 1978 to 1989 Gray starred as Sue Ellen, J. R. Ewing's boozy wife in DALLAS, also trying her hand at directing some episodes. When Ian McShane guested in the Texan super soap, Gray repaid the compliment by accepting a part in his somewhat less flashy LOVEJOY series. Her most prominent role since has been as Hillary Michaels in *Melrose Place* and its spin-off, *Models Inc.* She has also been seen in numerous TV movies and a few American programmes that were not screened in the UK, most notably the comedy show *All That Glitters* and the soap *The Bold and the Beautiful*.

Grayson, Larry

(William White; 1923–95)

Camp British comedian, once a music hall drag performer known as Billy Breen. With stories of friends like Everard, Apricot Lil and Slack Alice, Grayson earned himself TV celebrity status in the early 1970s through one-off guest performances (on shows like *Saturday Variety*) and his own ITV series, *Shut That Door* (named after his catchphrase). A close friend of Noele Gordon, he made a famous cameo appearance in CROSSROADS in 1973, playing a disgruntled motel guest, and returned two years later to act as chauffeur at Noele's TV wedding to John Bentley, when Meg married Hugh Mortimer. However, the high spot of his career came when Bruce Forsyth moved to ITV in 1978 and Grayson was chosen to succeed him as host of the hugely popular GENERATION GAME. With Isla St Clair as his partner, Grayson matched Forsyth's success, and the series continued for another three years. A tell-the-truth guessing game, *Sweethearts*, in 1987, proved less durable and little was seen of Grayson afterwards, except as a team captain in *A Question of Entertainment*. His last TV appearance was in the 1994 Royal Variety Performance.

Great British Quiz, The

See *Masterteam*.

Great Britons ✶✶✶

UK (BBC) Documentary. BBC 2 2002

Presenter **Anne Robinson**

Producer **Mark Harrison**

● ***Viewers vote to select the greatest Briton of all time.***

In 2002 the BBC organized a national poll to find the greatest Briton who has ever lived. From votes by members of the public a shortlist of 100 names was drawn up, which was showcased in the initial programme in the series. The 'top ten' were then granted entire, hour-long programmes to themselves. Among the 100 were expected faces (Margaret Thatcher, King Arthur, William Blake, David Livingstone, Captain Scott and Queen Victoria), but also less obvious choices (David Beckham, Boy George, John Lydon, Freddie Mercury, J. K. Rowling and John Peel). Each of the final ten nominees was championed by a celebrity or expert who illustrated his/her case with examples of their favoured contender's achievements, asking viewers to vote once more and put their choice top of the pile. The ultimate winner was Winston Churchill, promoted by Mo Mowlam, beating Jeremy Clarkson's selection, Isambard Kingdom Brunel, into second place. The other finalists (and their spokespeople) were Oliver Cromwell (Richard Holmes), John Lennon (Alan Davies), Princess Diana (Rosie Boycott), Charles Darwin (Andrew Marr), Horatio Nelson (Lucy Young), Isaac Newton (Tristram Hunt), William Shakespeare (Fiona Shaw) and Queen Elizabeth I (Michael Portillo).

Great Expectations ✶✶✶

UK (BBC) Drama. BBC 2 1999

Philip Pirrip ('Pip') .... **Gabriel Thomson** *(young)*
Ioan Gruffudd
Miss Havisham .... **Charlotte Rampling**
Abel Magwitch .... **Bernard Hill**
Estella .... **Gemma Gregory** *(young)*
Justine Waddell
Joe Gargery .... **Clive Russell**
Mrs Joe .... **Lesley Sharp**
Mr Jaggers .... **Ian McDiarmid**
Wemmick .... **Nicholas Woodeson**
Pumblechook .... **Terence Rigby**
Biddy .... **Emma Cuniffe**
Herbert Pocket .... **Daniel Evans**
Bentley Drummle .... **James Hillier**

Writer **Tony Marchant**
Producer **David Snodin**

● ***Dark and moody adaptation of Dickens's famous novel.***

Tony Marchant's take on *Great Expectations* contrasts sharply with many previous film and television adaptations of this Dickens classic. Whereas other dramatists have played up the eccentricity and light-heartedness of certain characters, to sugar the meaner sides of the story, this BBC production majors on the darker elements, as it spins out the tale of a young boy's progression through society. Casting Charlotte Rampling as the deranged and Machiavellian jilted bride, Miss Havisham, was another departure, as the actress filling this tragic role has customarily been much older. That said, the two episodes (directed by Julian Jarrold) remain faithful to the Dickens tale, as orphan Pip encounters the escaped convict Magwitch in a churchyard, visits Miss Havisham and her ward, Estella, at Satis House, leaves his home with the Gargerys and becomes a lawyer in London, making friends with Herbert Pocket. Eventually the mystery of who has bequeathed a fortune to set our hero on the road to becoming a gentleman is solved and, as the good times fade, Pip learns the lessons of adversity.

Previous television versions of *Great Expectations* are as follows: BBC 1959 (Dinsdale Landen as Pip, Helen Lindsay as Estella); BBC 1 1967 (Christopher Guard and Gary Bond as Pip, Francesca Annis as Estella, John Tate as Magwitch); BBC 1 1981 (Gerry Sundquist as Pip, Joan Hickson as Miss Havisham, Stratford Johns as Magwitch, Patsy Kensit as young Estella); and ITV (HTV) 1991 (Anthony Calf as Pip, Anthony Hopkins as Magwitch, Jean Simmons – Estella in David Lean's classic 1946 film version – as Miss Havisham). There was also a TV movie made in 1974, starring Michael York as Pip, Sarah Miles as Estella and James Mason as Magwitch.

Great Railway Journeys of the World/Great Railway Journeys ✶✶✶

UK (BBC) Documentary. BBC 2 1980; 1994; 1996; 1999

Executive Producers **Roger Laughton, David Taylor**

● ***Lyrical exploration of the world's most spectacular and intriguing rail transits.***

It's generally a rule in television that if a format is worth repeating, it's worth repeating quickly. *Great Railway Journeys of the World* bucks that trend. Although the first series of six rail documentaries aired in 1980, it took 14 years for the concept to return to our screens (and then with the shortened title of *Great Railway Journeys*). The idea is simple: place someone with wit – and usually no shortage of wisdom – on a train and follow a timetabled route, taking in the glory of the landscape, the foibles of fellow travellers and the mini-disasters along the way. Setting the journey in its political, historical and geographical contexts adds depth.

Tie-in books were published to coincide with the transmission of some series. The featured personalities and the routes they covered are listed below:

1980

Ludovic Kennedy (journalist)	**New York–Los Angeles**
Michael Frayn (playwright)	**Sydney–Perth**
Brian Thompson (playwright)	**Bombay–Cochin**
Michael Palin (comedian)	**London–Kyle of Lochalsh**
Michael Wood (historian)	**Cape Town–Victoria Falls**
Miles Kington (journalist)	**Lima–La Paz**
Eric Robson (broadcaster)	**Paris–Budapest**

1994

Clive Anderson (chat show host)	**Hong Kong–Ulan Bator**
Natalia Makarova (ballerina)	**St Petersburg–Tashkent**
Rian Malan (author)	**Cape Town–Bophutatswana**
Michael Palin (comedian)	**Derry–Kerry**
Lisa St Aubin (novelist–poet)	**Santos–Santa Cruz**
Mark Tully (journalist)	**Karachi–Khyber Pass**

1996

Victoria Wood (comedian)	**Crewe–Crewe (via northern Britain)**
Alexei Sayle (comedian)	**Aleppo–Aqaba**
Henry Louis Gates Jr (educationist)	**Great Zimbabwe–Kilimatinde**
Buck Henry (screenwriter–actor)	**High Andes–Patagonia**
Benedict Allen (explorer)	**Mombasa–Mountains of the Moon**
Ben Okri (novelist)	**London–Arcadia**
Chris Bonington (mountaineer)	**Halifax–Porteau Cove**

1999

Ian Hislop (satirist)	**India: East–West**
Michael Portillo (politician)	**Granada–Salamanca**
Fergal Keane (journalist)	**Tokyo–Kagoshima**
Rick Stein (chef)	**Los Mochis–Veracruz**
Nick Hancock (comedian)	**Guantanamo–Pinar Del Rio**
Danny Glover (actor)	**St Louis–Dogon Country**
Stephen Tompkinson (actor)	**Singapore–Bangkok**

Great War, The ★★★★

UK (BBC/CBC/ABC) History. BBC 2 1964
DVD: DD Home Entertainment

Narrator	**Sir Michael Redgrave**
Douglas Haig	**Sir Ralph Richardson** *(voice only)*
Lloyd George	**Emlyn Williams** *(voice only)*
Other voices	**Marius Goring, Cyril Luckham, Sebastian Shaw**

Producers **Tony Essex, Gordon Watkins**

Graphic account of the misery of World War I.

Billed as 'A BBC Tonight production', *The Great War* was one of the first major programmes to be screened on BBC 2 (with a repeat later in the year on BBC 1 for most of the country, which still could not receive the new channel). In 26 parts it told the horrific story of World War I, assisted by eyewitness accounts from all sides and early photographs. Primitive film gathered from over 20 countries was restored and adjusted to run at contemporary speed to replay what was possibly the first photographic record of an active war. Notable actors' voices helped illustrate events, complementing Sir Michael Redgrave's narrative. The series was produced in collaboration with the Imperial War Museum, CBC in Canada and Australia's ABC. Antony Jay and Robert Kee featured among the writers and Wilfred Josephs scored the music, which was performed by the BBC Northern Orchestra. The programmes were rerun on BBC 2 in 2003.

Greatorex, Wilfred

(1922–2002)

British scriptwriter, editor and producer, responsible for creating series like THE PLANE MAKERS (later *The Power Game*), *Front Page Story* (with Rex Firkin), HINE, *The Man from Haven, The Inheritors*, SECRET ARMY (with Gerald Glaister), 1990 and AIRLINE. In 1987 Greatorex tried unsuccessfully to sue advertising agency J. Walter Thompson over the use of *Airline* star Roy Marsden in a look-alike TV commercial for the British Airports Authority.

Green, Hughie

(1920–97)

Canadian showman, talent spotter and quiz show host, one of ITV's earliest stars. After a career in radio and on stage and screen as a child performer (among his film credits were *Midshipman Easy* and *Tom Brown's Schooldays*), Green spent the war as a pilot in the Canadian air force, continuing in civil aviation after the hostilities. He also returned to radio, hosting OPPORTUNITY KNOCKS for both the BBC and Radio Luxembourg and then DOUBLE YOUR MONEY for the latter. Both shows transferred to television with the arrival of ITV, *Opportunity Knocks* running for a marathon 21 years from 1956 and *Double Your Money* for 13 years from 1955. In 1971 Green hosted the quiz's natural successor, *The Sky's the Limit*, which was, effectively, *Double Your Money* with air miles. In the early days, Green also compered SUNDAY NIGHT AT THE LONDON PALLADIUM. His contrived gags and his catchphrase, 'I mean that most sincerely, folks', were much mimicked. On his death in 1997, it was revealed that he was the real father of TV presenter Paula Yates.

Green, Robson

(1964–)

A Northumberland-born, Byker-raised, one-time shipyard draughtsman who entered television via a local theatre company. His major roles have included Jimmy Powell in CASUALTY, Dave Tucker in SOLDIER, SOLDIER, Rory Connor in CATHERINE COOKSON'S *The Gambling Man*, Owen Springer in RECKLESS, DI Dave Creegan in TOUCHING EVIL, Eric Trapp in AIN'T MISBEHAVIN', Joe Purvis in GRAFTERS, John Close in CLOSE AND TRUE and Barry Grimes, Michael Flynn, Steve McTear and Richard Thomas in the single productions *The Student Prince, Rhinoceros, The Last Musketeer* and *Blind Ambition*, respectively. More recently, Greene has starred in *Take Me* (Jack Chambers), *Trust* (lawyer Stephen Bradley), WIRE IN THE BLOOD (Dr Tony Hill), *Unconditional Love* (Pete Gray), *The Afternoon Play, Christmas Lights* and its follow-up series, *Northern Lights* (Colin), *Like Father, Like Son* (Dominic Milne), *Beaten* (Michael) and *Rocket Man* (George Stevenson). He runs his own company, Coastal Productions, and has often appeared alongside his acting (and singing) partner, Jerome Flynn.

Green Acres ★★★

US (Filmways) Situation Comedy. BBC 1 1966–8
(US: CBS 1965–71)
DVD: MGM (Region 1 only)

Oliver Wendell Douglas	**Eddie Albert**
Lisa Douglas	**Eva Gabor**
Eb Dawson	**Tom Lester**
Mr Eustace Haney	**Pat Buttram**
Hank Kimball	**Alvy Moore**
Fred Ziffel	**Hank Patterson**
Doris Ziffel	**Barbara Pepper**
Sam Drucker	**Frank Cady**
Alf Monroe	**Sid Melton**
Ralph Monroe	**Mary Grace Canfield**

Creator **Jay Sommers**
Producers **Jay Sommers, Paul Henning**

A wealthy New York lawyer and his wife opt for a life in the country.

The Beverly Hillbillies back to front, *Green Acres* tells the story of Oliver Douglas, who, despite the objections of his trendy, Hungarian wife Lisa (played by Zsa Zsa Gabor's sister, Eva), gives up the rat race and moves to the sticks in pursuit of nature. They buy – unseen – a farm ('Green Acres') from local con merchant Mr Haney and find it badly in need of repair. The farmhouse itself is no more than a run-down shack. Employing dopey handyman Eb Dawson and sibling carpenters Alf and Ralph (yes, a girl!) Monroe, they gradually get the sickly farm back on its feet. All the while the Douglases are bemused by the quirky logic of the locals and are forced to learn the habits and customs of the backwoods. Nevertheless, Lisa continues to swan around the place in designer gowns, affecting the social airs and graces of her former life on Park Avenue. Sam Drucker is the local shopkeeper, Hank Kimball the agricultural rep and Fred Ziffel the pig breeder, whose star porker, Arnold, can perform tricks like a dog and is treated like a son. The series was closely linked to another American comedy, PETTICOAT JUNCTION, which was set in the same town, Hooterville, Illinois. Cast members often showed up in both shows. Critics liked *Green Acres*, seeing it as more than just another rural comedy and commenting on its skilful absurdity and surreal air. A TV movie follow-up, *Return to Green Acres*, reuniting most of the original cast, was aired in the USA in 1990.

Green Green Grass, The

See *Only Fools and Horses*.

Green Man, The ★★★

UK (BBC/A&E) Drama. BBC 1 1990

Maurice Allington	**Albert Finney**
Gramps	**Michael Hordern**
Dr Underhill	**Michael Culver**
Joyce	**Linda Marlowe**
Diana	**Sarah Berger**
Jack	**Nicky Henson**
Lucy	**Josie Lawrence**
Nick	**Michael Grandage**
Amy	**Natalie Morse**
David	**Robert Schofield**
Sonnenschein	**Nickolas Grace**

Writer **Malcolm Bradbury**
Producer **David Snodin**

A boozy restaurateur thinks he's seen a ghost.

Maurice Allington is a rather unpleasant chap who runs a hotel-restaurant called The Green Man in the Cambridgeshire countryside. In order to drum up trade, he claims the premises are haunted, but no one has seen the ghost for many a year – until Maurice himself stumbles upon him. The ghost's name is Underhill and he takes Allington into his confidence, making him an intriguing promise. However, Joyce, Allington's wife, and Diana, his mistress, find it hard to believe that all this talk of the supernatural is anything more than Maurice's over-indulgence in alcohol coming to the fore.

Green Wing ★★★

UK (Talkback Thames) Situation Comedy. Channel 4 2004; 2006
DVD: Channel 4

Dr Caroline Todd	**Tamsin Greig**
Dr Guillaume 'Guy' Secretan	**Stephen Mangan**
Dr 'Mac' Macartney	**Julian Rhind-Tutt**
Joanna Clore	**Pippa Haywood**
Dr Alan Statham	**Mark Heap**
Dr Angela Hunter	**Sarah Alexander**
Sue White	**Michelle Gomez**
Dr Martin Dear	**Karl Theobald**
Boyce	**Oliver Chris**
Harriet Schulenburg	**Olivia Colman**
Kim Alabaster	**Sally Bretton**
Naughty Rachel	**Katie Lyons**
Karen Ball	**Lucinda Raikes**
Cordelia	**Saskia Wickham**

Creator/Producer **Victoria Pile**

Petty rivalries and sexual shenanigans in an unruly hospital.

A sitcom set in a hospital? A world weary of ONLY WHEN I LAUGH and *Carry on Nurse* would be only too justified in thinking that this was the last thing television in the new millennium required. Thankfully, *Green Wing* comes from a different direction altogether and dumps bed pan gags and bossy matrons in the hospital incinerator. While a hospital may indeed be the setting (and a real hospital is used for shooting), the humour derives from the strained relationships between its core of characters.

It all begins when Caroline Todd, the new surgical registrar, turns up for duty at East Hampton Hospital Trust, dishevelled after spending the night sleeping in her car. When she accepts anaesthetist Guy Secretan's offer of a bed at his place, she soon regrets this error, as the scheming womanizer uses her indiscretion to his full macho advantage. Secretan's great rival is Dr Macartney, the man in the sights of unpredictable staff liaison officer Sue White. Hospital administrator is Joanna Clore, a sex- and self-obsessed woman who shares a kinky relationship with dopey consultant radiologist Alan Statham. Trying to make his presence felt, but failing miserably, is the team's perennial loser, Martin Dear, while Angela Hunter is the sparky doctor who becomes Caroline's new flatmate.

Green Wing deals lightly with narrative and puts its weight behind absurdity. Blink and you miss another daft sight gag; cough and the latest oddball remark gets drowned out. The use of speeded up and slow-down camera work also keeps viewers on their toes, and the pace seldom lets up. The net result is a surreal, wacky, highly inventive spin on the situation comedy genre (each episode at least 50 minutes long), produced by the team behind SMACK THE PONY. While producer Victoria Pile also devised the series, its creation was in truth a team effort. A band of eight writers worked with the actors to develop the characters, taking their improvised lines and working them into the script.

Greene, Hugh Carleton
Sir Hugh Greene (1910–87)

The brother of novelist Graham Greene and one of the BBC's most famous directors-general. Greene, a former *Daily Telegraph* journalist, was editor of the BBC's German Service during the war and, when hostilities ceased, helped to reorganize broadcasting in Germany. He became the BBC's Director of News and Current Affairs and then was appointed Director-General in 1960, holding the post for over nine years. During this period, a decade of technological advances and social change, Greene was credited with allowing the BBC to move with the times. Under his guidance, the Corporation drifted away from the starchy proprieties of the 1950s and floated into innovative, more permissive waters. The Hugh Greene era was the era of THAT WAS THE WEEK THAT WAS, STEPTOE AND SON, CATHY COME HOME and TILL DEATH US DO PART. It was also the era that prompted Mary Whitehouse's first criticisms of broadcasting standards, although Greene quite happily shrugged off complaints from her fledgling 'Clean-up TV' campaign. However, on one notable occasion Greene did err on the side of caution, refusing to screen the realistic nuclear war drama THE WAR GAME, in 1966, fearing it would alarm the public (it was eventually shown in 1985). Although, generally, Greene remained steadfast in his protection of the independence of the BBC, his postponement of an episode of *Steptoe and Son* on election night in 1964, allegedly at the request of Harold Wilson, did rather tarnish his reputation with observers. Greene was knighted the same year, but his relationship with the Labour Party later deteriorated. When Wilson appointed Lord Hill, Chairman of the Independent Television Authority, to the position of Chairman of the BBC in 1967, it was seen as a means of keeping Greene in check and a response to some perceived anti-Labour programming controversies. Greene eventually left his post in 1969, but became the first ex-DG to take a seat on the board of Governors, a seat he maintained until 1971.

Greene, Lorne
(1915–87)

Whether as a roving merchant seaman, a reassuring father-figure in the Wild West or an intergalactic space commander, Lorne Greene won the respect of more than one generation of TV viewers. Greene was born in Ottawa, and his first field of expertise was radio. Failing to find much acting work, he became an announcer for CBC and during the war established himself as the authoritative 'Voice of Canada'. Moving south to the USA in the 1950s, he began to pick up small TV roles, in programmes like ALFRED HITCHCOCK PRESENTS, WAGON TRAIN and CHEYENNE, and then, in 1957, in the UK, won the part of Captain Grant 'Mitch' Mitchell in the adventure series SAILOR OF FORTUNE. However, it was his next major role which proved definitive. He was cast as Ben Cartwright, patriarch of the Ponderosa, in the classic Western BONANZA, which ran for 14 years up to 1973. He moved into police work with the short-lived detective drama *Griff* the same year, added his voice to two long-running nature series, *Lorne Greene's Last of the Wild* and *Lorne Greene's New Wilderness*, and in 1978 was launched into outer space to be the Moses-like Commander Adama in the *Star Wars* clone, BATTLESTAR GALACTICA. His last starring role was in a fire-fighting caper called *Code Red*. Among his other credits were TV movies and mini-series such as ROOTS (slave-owner John Reynolds).

Greene, Richard
(1918–85)

Plymouth-born leading man in Hollywood films of the 1930s, who found new fame as the swashbuckling Robin Hood in THE ADVENTURES OF ROBIN HOOD, an early ITV success. The show's 143 episodes proved such a hit that Greene made few TV appearances afterwards (most notably in episodes of THE PROFESSIONALS and TALES OF THE UNEXPECTED), choosing to settle down to a retirement of horse breeding in Ireland.

Greene, Sarah
(1958–)

London-born presenter, a former child actress/model, the daughter of TV DIY man and actor Harry Greene and actress Marjie Lawrence, and now the wife of presenter/DJ Mike Smith. Greene's TV break came with the children's drama series *The Swish of the Curtain*, playing Sandra Fayne. The same year (1980) she joined BLUE PETER, from which she progressed to SATURDAY SUPERSTORE, GOING LIVE!, *Posh Frocks and New Trousers*, the game show *Happy Families*, the swap shop *The Exchange, Good Morning Summer*, PEBBLE MILL, Sky One's afternoon chat show, programmes for Carlton Food Network, and numerous documentary specials. She has also made guest appearances in DOCTOR WHO and CASUALTY, and appeared in the spoof documentary *Ghostwatch*. Her sister is weather presenter Laura Greene.

Gregson, John
(1919–75)

British actor who, after many film appearances (most notably in *Genevieve*), took the role of Commander George Gideon in the police series GIDEON'S WAY, in 1965. Six years later he resurfaced in Shirley MacLaine's photojournalist sitcom *Shirley's World*, playing her editor, Dennis Croft, and in 1976 he was Kirby, the risk-taking insurance agent, in Southern's thriller serial *Dangerous Knowledge*, a series screened a year after his death.

Greig, Tamsin

British actress, mostly in comedy roles and most notably as Fran in BLACK BOOKS, Dr Caroline Todd in GREEN WING and Alice Chenery in LOVE SOUP. Other roles have come in series such as BLUE HEAVEN, NEVERWHERE (Lamia), FAITH IN THE FUTURE, *Blind Men* (Valerie), *High Stakes*, HAPPINESS (Emma), *People Like Us, World of Pub, Falling Apart* (Jackie), JONATHAN CREEK, *When I'm Sixty-Four* (Denny), DOCTOR WHO and READY WHEN YOU ARE MR MCGILL (Lianne). Tamsin also plays Debbie Aldridge in Radio 4's *The Archers*. She is married to actor Richard Leaf.

Griffiths, Leon

(1928–92)

British scriptwriter, best remembered as the creator of MINDER. Griffiths's early TV writing included episodes of THE FOUR JUST MEN, OUT OF THIS WORLD, OUT OF THE UNKNOWN, GHOST SQUAD, TALES OF MYSTERY, NO HIDING PLACE and RED-CAP, plus the Roy Kinnear sitcom *A Slight Case of* . . . While working on single plays such as the boxing drama *Dinner at the Sporting Club* in the 1970s, he was advised to adapt one of his stories so that it concentrated on just two of its characters, a dodgy wheeler-dealer and his jailbird bodyguard. *Minder* was born and with it one of TV's classic creations, Arthur Daley. (Ironically, Daley's fluent Cockney patter was provided by a writer who had been born in Sheffield and brought up in Glasgow.) Griffiths, however, suffered a stroke and the second season had to be written by others, although the Writers' Guild award that the programme won was still presented to him personally. Inspired, Griffiths fought his way back to work and resumed his involvement, right up to his death in 1992. His other contributions included the six-part adaptation of PIECE OF CAKE, plus scripts for series like HAZELL, THE RETURN OF THE SAINT and THE RACING GAME.

Griffiths, Richard

(1947–)

Versatile Cleveland-born actor, star of the sitcom NOBODY'S PERFECT (Sam Hooper, alongside Elaine Stritch), the bizarre comedy WHOOPS APOCALYPSE (Soviet leader Dubienkin), the thriller BIRD OF PREY (snoopy civil servant Henry Jay), the wine comedy *Ffizz* (Jack Mowbray), and the unsuccessful historical drama THE CLEOPATRAS (the grotesque Potbelly). Griffiths also starred as Trevor Beasley in another comedy, A KIND OF LIVING, appeared as the porter in the murder-mystery *Mr Wakefield's Crusade*, played the policeman-chef Henry Crabbe in PIE IN THE SKY, and took the parts of Geoffrey Crichton Potter in *In the Red*, Swelter the cook in GORMENGHAST and Leo Wheeldon in HOPE AND GLORY. He played medical consultant Mr Ron in *TLC*, politician William Whitelaw in *Jeffrey Archer – the Truth*, Sir Edward Marshall-Hall in THE BRIDES IN THE BATH and Mr Bayham Badger in BLEAK HOUSE. Among his many guest appearances have been parts in WHEN THE BOAT COMES IN, BERGERAC, MINDER, INSPECTOR MORSE and THE VICAR OF DIBLEY.

Griffiths, Trevor

(1935–)

Manchester-born playwright, one of TV's most political dramatists, espousing left-wing causes, particularly in his most notable series, BILL BRAND. His first contribution was *Adam Smith* (written under the pen name of Ben Rae) and among his other offerings have been *Occupations, Comedians, Through the Night, Country, The Last Place on Earth* (the story of Captain Scott) and the skinhead drama *Oi for England*. He has also adapted D. H. Lawrence's *Sons and Lovers* for the small screen.

Grimleys, The ✶✶✶

UK (Granada) Situation Comedy. ITV 1999–2001

Gordon Grimley .... **James Bradshaw**
Miss Geraldine Titley .... **Amanda Holden**
Mr Doug Digby .... **Brian Conley**
Mr Neville Holder .... **Noddy Holder**
Darren Grimley .... **Ryan Cartwright**
Lisa Grimley .... **Corrieann Fletcher**
Janet Grimley .... **Jan Ravens**
Baz Grimley .... **Nigel Planer**
Nan .... **Barbara Keogh**
Shane Titley .... **Simon Lowe**
Reg Titley .... **Paul Angelis**
John Arthur
Miss Thing .... **Ruby Snape**
Wayne .... **Richard Rowbotham**
Dave Trebilcock .... **Craig Kelly**

Writer **Jed Mercurio**
Producers **Spencer Campbell, Saurabh Kakkar**

● ***Retro-comedy reflecting on adolescence in the West Midlands in the 1970s.***

Riding the wave of 1970s nostalgia that broke at the end of the 1990s, *The Grimleys* is set on the Jericho Council Estate, Dudley, in 1975. Young Gordon Grimley hopes to go to university one day (against the wishes of his slobby dad, Baz) but, in the meantime, has visions of a romance with his attractive English teacher, Miss Titley, who also happens to be a neighbour. As if this ambition is not already too great, standing obstinately in the way is his sadistic gym teacher, Doug Digby. More amenable is Mr Holder, the music teacher (whom thirty-something viewers thought bore more than a passing resemblance to the former lead singer of pop group Slade). Littered with 1970s references, from Vauxhall Vivas to Angel Delight, *The Grimleys* is a nostalgic wallow for anyone who was a teenager at the time. It followed a 1997 pilot episode in which Samantha Janus played Miss Titley and Jack Dee played Doug Digby. Apart from the aforementioned Mr Holder, there were also cameo appearances by 1970s figures Alvin Stardust (as a barman), William Woollard (science teacher), Frank Bough (newsreader), Jim Bowen (shop steward), Stephen Lewis (bus-driver), Patrick Mower (hero), Johnny Ball (teacher) and Tony Blackburn (swinger).

Grindl ✶

US (Screen Gems/David Swift) Situation Comedy. ITV 1964 (US: NBC 1963–4)

Grindl .... **Imogene Coca**
Anson Foster .... **James Millhollin**

Creator **David Swift**
Producers **Harry Ackerman, Winston O'Keefe**

● ***An agency domestic worker finds trouble in every job she's allocated.***

Grindl is a middle-aged professional domestic helper, listed on the books of an employment agency. Each week Anson Foster, head of the agency, assigns her latest job, which takes her to all manner of places and drops her in all kinds of situations. One week she may be babysitting, another she could be a cook. One thing is certain, however, something is always likely to happen to make Grindl's life that little bit more difficult. This sitcom was devised for Imogene Coca, for many years staunch support to Sid Caesar in the classic American variety programme *Your Show of Shows*. Just one season of 32 episodes was made.

Grip

The technician responsible for production hardware like props, camera mountings, dollies and cranes. Where a large crew is involved, the head man is known as the key grip.

Grossman, Loyd

OBE (1950–)

Boston, Massachusetts-born presenter working on British TV. Grossman's first attempts to enter the entertainment business came as a member of the punk band Jet Bronx and the Forbidden, but he achieved far greater success snooping around celebrities' homes in THROUGH THE KEYHOLE and dissecting amateur cooks' dinners in MASTERCHEF. Other credits have included various food programmes, the quiz *Relative Knowledge*, the shopping documentary series *Off Your Trolley with Loyd Grossman* and *The History of British Sculpture with Loyd Grossman*.

Ground Force ✶✶

UK (Bazal/Endemol/BBC) Lifestyle. BBC 2 1997–8; BBC 1 1998–2005

Presenters **Alan Titchmarsh, Charlie Dimmock, Tommy Walsh, Will Shanahan, Kirsty King**
Producer **John Thornicroft**
Executive Producer **Carol Haslam**

● ***Garden make-overs for unsuspecting householders.***
Inviting viewers to nominate gardens that could do with a make-over (and whose owners probably wouldn't mind) was the basis of this CHANGING ROOMS meets GARDENERS' WORLD cross. The unsuspecting owner was then summoned away, leaving Alan Titchmarsh and his team two days in which to transform an ugly patch of land into a domestic paradise. Titchmarsh provided the designs, Charlie Dimmock (quickly becoming a cult figure because, always bra-less, she displayed a cult figure) specialized in water features, and landscaping builder Tommy Walsh organized the infrastructure with the help of Will Shanahan. With a budget of no more than £1,000, the team set about creating dream gardens and then waited anxiously for the bewildered owner to return. On one famous occasion in 1999, the team set off for South Africa and surprised ex-President Nelson Mandela by redeveloping his back yard. Other overseas excursions saw the team working in India, the West Indies, the South Atlantic, New York and Ethiopia.

Like its sister programme, *Changing Rooms*, *Ground Force* began quietly on BBC 2, moving into the BBC 1 limelight after two years. The two programmes merged for a special in 2000 entitled *When Changing Rooms Met Ground Force*, in which the interior decorating and gardening specialists switched jobs. Titchmarsh left the series in 2002 and new girl Kirsty King was added from 2003. *Ground Force America* (BBC 1 2003–4) saw the team tackle garden refurbishments in the USA.

Grove Family, The ✶✶

UK (BBC) Drama. BBC 1954–7

Bob Grove .... **Edward Evans**
Gladys Grove .... **Ruth Dunning**
Pat Grove .... **Sheila Sweet**
Carole Mowlam
Jack Grove .... **Peter Bryant**
Daphne Grove .... **Margaret Downs**
Lennie Grove .... **Christopher Beeny**
Gran .... **Nancy Roberts**

Writers **Michael Pertwee, Roland Pertwee**
Producer **John Warrington**

● ***Ups and downs in the life of Britain's first soap family.***
The Grove Family was the BBC's first attempt at a grown-up soap, although the Corporation had already produced a children's equivalent in THE APPLEYARDS. The Groves (named after the BBC's Lime Grove studios) were lower middle class, just about comfortably off, and had come through the post-war shortages like most other 'ordinary' families. This enabled viewers to relate to the characters and made the series very popular.

The family lived in Hendon and consisted of dad Bob, a jobbing builder; housewife Gladys; elder daughter and assistant librarian Pat; Jack, who was doing National Service and was a bit of a lad; teenage schoolgirl Daphne; and cheeky young Lennie (a youthful Christopher Beeny). Completing the household was the hunched, crotchety Gran, a grumble forever on her lips. Cousin Rodney was added for youth interest as the younger Groves grew up.

Drawing heavily on the likes of *Mrs Dale's Diary* and *The Archers* in style, there was very little drama in *The Grove Family*. Reassuringly British (with no intruding US culture), its action focused instead on petty squabbles and occasional domestic strife, but a 'public service' element was also built in. Viewers were made acutely aware of the need to purchase a TV licence, for example, or to protect themselves from burglaries. One story even warned of the dangers of sailing! Scripts were provided by father and son Roland and Michael Pertwee and, when they asked for a short break after three years of solid writing, the BBC declined and, much to viewers' dismay, closed down the series altogether.

Little footage of the series is known to exist today, although there was a film spin-off, entitled *It's a Great Day*, in 1955. Also, as part of the BBC's Lime Grove commemorations in 1991, modern-day soap stars stepped in to re-create extracts from original scripts. Mum was played by Sue Johnston, Dad by Leslie Grantham, Gran by Anna Wing, Pat by Sally Ann Matthews, Jack by Nick Berry, Daphne by Kellie Bright and Lennie by Paul Parris.

Growing Pains ✶✶

UK (BBC) Drama. BBC 1 1992–3

Tom Hollingsworth .... **Ray Brooks**
Pat Hollingsworth .... **Sharon Duce**
Mark Hollingsworth .... **Tat Whalley**
Lisa Hollingsworth .... **Rosie Marcel**
Simon Hollingsworth .... **Peter Lloyd**
Joan Craddock .... **Rosemary Leach**
Miriam Craddock .... **Lill Roughley**
George Critchley .... **Trevor Peacock**
Sandra Philips .... **Liz Crowther**
Caroline Thornley .... **Clare Byam Shaw**
David Wain .... **Martin Gower**
Andy Drayton .... **Julian Wadham**
Jotinder Bholla .... **Kamilla Blanche**
Jason Begley .... **Sean Maguire**

James Blake	**Barry Birch**
Trudy	**Emily Aston**

Creator **Steve Wetton**
Writers **Steve Wetton, Roger Davenport**
Producer **Richard Bramall**

A hard-working couple experience the pleasures and pains of fostering children.

Pat Hollingsworth reaches a crossroads in her life. She has seen three children grow up and is wondering what to do next. Then she spots an advert for foster parents and somehow persuades her reluctant husband, Tom, who works (unhappily) as a carpet salesman, to climb on board. So, in addition to their own kids – Mark, Lisa and Simon – they soon become temporary parents to a host of other children, of various ages, each having their own, often tragic, story to tell. Naturally, things do not always go to plan, and some of the children have problems fitting in, but for the Hollingsworths this new vocation adds another, welcome dimension to life. Also involved in the usually hectic goings-on are Pat's sister, Miriam (a college lecturer), and her secretly racy mum, Joan. Tom's work colleagues include his boss, George Critchley, and secretary Sandra Philips. Caroline Thornley is the fostering officer who oversees the Hollingsworths' work.

The series was devised as a sitcom for Radio 4 in 1989, by real-life fosterer Steve Wetton. Ray Brooks (who starred in the radio version, again with Sharon Duce) saw its potential as a television drama, bought the rights and persuaded the BBC to commission the concept. Two series, totalling 20 episodes, were then produced. Episode titles and snippets of music used in each programme reflected Tom's passion for the Hollywood musicals of the 1930s. The theme song was 'I Could Care for You'.

Growing Pains of Adrian Mole, The

See *The Secret Diary of Adrian Mole, Aged 13 ¾*.

Growing Pains of PC Penrose, The/ Rosie ★★

UK (BBC) Situation Comedy. BBC 1 1975/BBC 1 1977–9; 1981

PC Michael 'Rosie' Penrose	**Paul Greenwood**
Sgt Flagg	**Bryan Pringle** *(Growing Pains)*
PC Buttress	**David Pinner** *(Growing Pains)*
PC Toombs	**Alan Foss** *(Growing Pains)*
Insp. Fox	**Christopher Burgess** *(Growing Pains)*
WPC Dean	**Catherine Chase** *(Growing Pains)*
PC Wilmot	**Tony Haygarth** *(Rosie)*
Gillian Chislehurst	**Frankie Jordan** *(Rosie)*
Millie Penrose	**Avril Elgar** *(Rosie)*
	Patricia Kneale *(Rosie)*
Uncle Norman	**Allan Surtees** *(Rosie)*
Auntie Ida	**Lorraine Peters** *(Rosie)*
Bill Chislehurst	**Don McKillop** *(Rosie)*
Glenda Chislehurst	**Maggie Jones** *(Rosie)*
Chief Insp. Dunwoody	**Paul Luty** *(Rosie)*
Sgt West	**Barry Hart** *(Rosie)*
WPC Brenda Whatmough	**Penny Leatherbarrow** *(Rosie)*
Merv	**Robert Gillespie** *(Rosie)*
	John Cater *(Rosie)*

Creator/Writer **Roy Clarke**
Producers **Douglas Argent, Bernard Thompson**

The misadventures of a hapless young constable and his associates.

Viewers were introduced to young PC Penrose, or 'Rosie' as he was familiarly known, in the series *The Growing Pains of PC Penrose*. A friendly but exceptionally naïve copper, he is based in this series alongside PCs Toombs and Buttress at the police station in Slagcaster, Yorkshire, where he is cruelly bullied by his blustering superior, Sgt Flagg. However (when the series' title was shortened to *Rosie*), he is given a compassionate move back to his home town of Ravens Bay, to be near his 'invalid' mother, Millie. He now resides with his flighty mum at his Auntie Ida's house, where his Uncle Norman spends most of his time in the garden (whether he likes it or not). At work, Rosie is paired with PC Wilmot, a more experienced but also more reckless bobby, whom Rosie often has to bail out of trouble and protect from the clutches of WPC Whatmough. Cigar-puffing Chief Inspector Dunwoody is their no-nonsense boss and Merv their short-sighted, inept supergrass. Rosie also has a girlfriend, the demanding, clinging Gillian, whose snooty, factory-owning dad has little time for her PC boyfriend.

This gentle comedy was written by Roy Clarke (who used to be a policeman himself) and introduced up-and-coming actor Paul Greenwood. Greenwood returned to police ranks a decade later, but this time much further up the ladder, when he took the part of SPENDER's by-the-book boss, Supt. Yelland. Greenwood also co-wrote and sang the theme song for *Rosie*.

Gruffudd, Ioan

(1973–)

Welsh actor noted for his lead roles in dramas like HORNBLOWER (Horatio Hornblower), GREAT EXPECTATIONS (Pip), WARRIORS (Lt. John Feeley), *Man and Boy* (Harry Silver) and THE FORSYTE SAGA (Philip Bosinney). Gruffudd has also been seen in *Love in the 21st Century* (Jack), the 1996 sequel to POLDARK (Jeremy Poldark), *Happy Now* (Max Bracchi), and the US sci-fi/legal drama *Century City* (Lukas Gold), plus Welsh-language dramas like *Pobol y Cwm*.

GS5

See *Ghost Squad*.

Guardians, The ★★

UK (LWT) Science Fiction. ITV 1971

Tom Weston	**John Collin**
Clare Weston	**Gwyneth Powell**
Sir Timothy Hobson	**Cyril Luckham**
Christopher Hobson	**Edward Petherbridge**
Frank Benedict	**David Burke**
Eleanor	**Lynn Farleigh**
Norman	**Derek Smith**

Creators **Rex Firkin, Vincent Tilsley**
Producer **Andrew Brown**

Futuristic tale of oppressive government and organized rebellion.

Sometime in the near future, with Britain in chaos following industrial unrest, soaring inflation and the collapse of a coalition government, control of the country is given to a body of so-called 'experts' whose powers are enforced by state police known as the Guardians. But even though calm is quickly restored, an organized resistance movement is formed to undermine the new totalitarian regime that masquerades behind the slogan 'Make Britain Great'. This movement is known as Quarmby and its struggle is chronicled in this 13-part drama. Notable characters are Guardian officer Tom Weston and his wife, Clare; the Prime Minister, Timothy Hobson; his son, Christopher; and psychiatrist Frank Benedict.

Guinness, Sir Alec

CBE (1914–2000)

Distinguished British film actor whose television work came late in life. By far his most acclaimed role was as spycatcher George Smiley in John Le Carré's TINKER, TAILOR, SOLDIER, SPY and *Smiley's People*. Among his other credits were *Caesar and Cleopatra*, *Conversations at Night*, *Gift of Friendship*, *Little Lord Fauntleroy*, *Monsignor Quixote* and the *Screen One* presentations *A Foreign Field* (war veteran Amos) and ESKIMO DAY (academic James Poole).

Gulliver's Travels ★★

UK/US (Channel 4/NBC/RHI) Drama. Channel 4 1996 (US: NBC 1996)
DVD: Cinema Club

Dr Lemuel Gulliver	**Ted Danson**
Mary Gulliver	**Mary Steenburgen**
Dr Bates	**James Fox**
Tom Gulliver	**Thomas Sturridge**
Farmer Grultrud	**Ned Beatty**
Rajah	**Shashi Kapoor**
Empress Munodi	**Geraldine Chaplin**
Gen. Limtoc	**Edward Fox**
Prof. of Politics	**Graham Crowden**
Prof. of Sunlight	**John Gielgud**
Dr Parnell	**Robert Hardy**
Drunlo	**Edward Woodward**
Clustril	**Nicholas Lyndhurst**
Emperor of Lilliput	**Peter O'Toole**
Empress of Lilliput	**Phoebe Nicholls**
Immortal Gatekeeper	**Kristin Scott Thomas**
Sorcerer	**Omar Sharif**
Prof. of Language	**Richard Wilson**

Writer **Simon Moore**
Producer **Duncan Kenworthy**

A traveller recounts his fantastic voyages to a sceptical audience.

This ambitious rendition of Jonathan Swift's famous satire cast CHEERS star Ted Danson in the title role alongside a host of British acting greats. Filming the whole of Swift's book, and not just the familiar Lilliput and Brobdingnag sections, the production also added a new dimension in which Gulliver aims to convince his peers of the truth of his adventure (and of his sanity) on his return home after eight years a-wandering. Out to ensnare him is the devious Dr Bates, who has set his sights on stealing Gulliver's wife, Mary. A feast of special effects helped swallow up the reported $20 million budget for the four-hour drama, directed by Charles Sturridge, which was split into two episodes.

Gun Law

See *Gunsmoke*.

Gunsmoke/Gun Law ★★★

US (CBS) Western. ITV 1956–70 (US: CBS 1955–75)

Marshal Matt Dillon	**James Arness**
Kitty Russell	**Amanda Blake**
Dr Galen ('Doc') Adams	**Milburn Stone**
Chester Goode	**Dennis Weaver**
Quint Asper	**Burt Reynolds**
Sam	**Glenn Strange**
Festus Haggen	**Ken Curtis**
Thad Greenwood	**Roger Ewing**
Newly O'Brien	**Buck Taylor**
Mr Jonas	**Dabbs Greer**
Hank	**Hank Patterson**
Louie Pheeters	**James Nusser**
Barney	**Charles Seel**
Howie	**Howard Culver**
Ed O'Connor	**Tom Brown**
Percy Crump	**John Harper**
Ma Smalley	**Sarah Selby**
Miss Hannah	**Fran Ryan**

Creators **Norman Macdonnell, John Meston, Charles Marquis Warren**
Producers **Norman Macdonnell, Philip Leacock, John Mantley**

A strong and virtuous marshal maintains law and order in a Wild West town.

Gunsmoke hinges on the fictional figure of Matt Dillon, the strong, no-nonsense marshal of Dodge City in 1870s Kansas. Standing six and a half feet tall, he is a giant physically and inspirationally, a man of great integrity and principle. He is tough but fair, and outlaws quickly realize that they are not welcome on his patch. But Dillon is not flawless. A rather intense and occasionally uncertain man, he is seen to worry and anguish over the right course to take, and he doesn't always make the correct decision. However, Dillon knows he can rely on the support of the Dodge City townsfolk. His closest confidants are Doc Adams and Kitty Russell, proprietress of the Longbranch Saloon. Adams is tetchy but kind; Russell is tough, with a soft centre, an early tart with a heart who seems to have a crush on Dillon, although the relationship is never taken any further. Dillon is also assisted by his deputies, Chester Goode (who brings a touch of comic relief with his limp) and, later, Festus Haggen (a drawling hillbilly). Also seen at various times are rugged half-Indian blacksmith Quint Asper, gunsmith Newly O'Brien and Dillon's friend, Thad Greenwood. Other Dodge City residents include shopkeeper Jonas; rancher O'Connor; Percy Crump, the undertaker; a hotel clerk called Howie; Hank, the stable keeper; Ma Smalley, who runs the boarding house; Barney, the telegraph man; and the local drunkard, Louie Pheeters. A year before the series ends, Kitty Russell is replaced in the saloon by a new landlady, Miss Hannah.

Dillon himself does not appear in many later episodes, leaving the stage to the townsfolk and one-off guest stars, although the series always stays true to its principles of portraying the realistic side of Wild West life. That's what John Wayne promised when he introduced the very first episode, even though he himself declined the role of the marshal. With William Conrad (who had provided Dillon's voice for years on radio) lacking the looks the part demanded, Wayne recommended the relatively unknown actor James Arness. Long after the series ended, Arness returned to the role of Dillon for a succession of TV movies in the 1980s and 1990s.

When *Gunsmoke* arrived in the UK, as an early ITV import,

it was screened under the title of *Gun Law*, although later episodes and reruns carried the original programme name.

Gutteridge, Reg

OBE (1924–)

Long-serving ITV boxing commentator, a one-time amateur champion himself before his career was ended by the loss of a leg during the Normandy campaign in World War II. He turned instead to journalism and eventually to boxing writing. Gutteridge also dabbled in coverage of greyhound racing. In the 1990s, he was paired with his old commentating 'rival', Harry Carpenter, for a nostalgic sports series on satellite TV.

Guyler, Deryck

(1914–99)

Deep-voiced, Cheshire-born radio comedian who moved into television as a foil for Eric Sykes. Playing the part of policeman Corky, Guyler stayed with Sykes for many years. He is also remembered as the Desert Rat school caretaker, Norman Potter, in PLEASE SIR! and was much seen on television playing his specialist musical instrument, the washboard. Among his other credits were supporting roles for the likes of Charlie Chester, Fred Emney, Dick Emery and Eric Barker, plus the Michael Bentine shows IT'S A SQUARE WORLD and *All Square*, and the sitcoms *Something in the City*, HERE'S HARRY, *Three Live Wires*, *Room at the Bottom* and *The Best of Enemies*.

Gwynne, Fred

(1926–93)

Tall (6 foot 5 inch) American comic actor, for ever remembered as Herman, the lumbering Frankenstein's monster look-alike in THE MUNSTERS. Previously Gwynne had starred in another successful sitcom, playing inept cop Francis Muldoon in CAR 54, WHERE ARE YOU? That role followed appearances in THE PHIL SILVERS SHOW and other series, plus films like *On the Waterfront*. Gwynne also made a living writing and illustrating children's books and was once a copywriter for the J. Walter Thompson advertising agency, a position which gave him financial security while he worked his way into acting in his spare time.

Gwynne, Haydn

British actress who came to the fore in David Lodge's drama NICE WORK, playing Dr Robyn Penrose. Her later credits include *Time Riders* (Dr B. B. Miller), DROP THE DEAD DONKEY (Alex Pates), *The Merchant of Venice* (Portia), PEAK PRACTICE (Dr Joanna Graham), MERSEYBEAT (Supt. Susan Blake), *The Secret* (Emma Faraday) and ROME (Calpurnia). Guest appearances have been in such series as A VERY PECULIAR PRACTICE, LOVEJOY, AGATHA CHRISTIE'S POIROT, DANGERFIELD, MIDSOMER MURDERS, DALZIEL AND PASCOE, and ABSOLUTE POWER.

Hadleigh ★★

UK (Yorkshire) Drama. ITV 1969; 1971; 1973; 1976

James Hadleigh	**Gerald Harper**
Susan Jackson	**Gillian Wray**
Maxwell	**Alastair Hunter**
Lady Helen Hadleigh	**Ambrosine Phillpotts**
Mrs Jackson	**Margery Mason**
Anne Hepton	**Jane Merrow**
Jennifer Caldwell/Hadleigh	**Hilary Dwyer**
Joanna Roberts	**Jenny Twigge**
Charles Caldwell	**Gerald James**

Creator **Robert Barr**
Executive Producers **Peter Willes, David Cunliffe**
Producers **Terence Williams, Jacky Stoller**

● ***The life and times of a laid-back Yorkshire squire.***

James Hadleigh is the classic smoothie, a refined country gentleman who occasionally has to stoop as low as to work to finance his rich tastes. A former civil servant who inherits his wealth and his mansion, Melford Park in the West Riding of Yorkshire, from his father, Hadleigh still farms himself out to the Treasury now and again when times grow 'hard' – when his racehorse stable is threatened with closure, for example. At first a most eligible bachelor with a flat in Knightsbridge, the suave, charming Hadleigh finally succumbs to marriage when the attractive (and independently wealthy) Jennifer Caldwell walks his way. The series was a spin-off from a series called *Gazette* (ITV 1968), the story of a weekly newspaper owned by Hadleigh's father.

Haggard ★★

UK (Yorkshire) Situation Comedy. ITV 1990; 1992

Squire Haggard	**Keith Barron**
Roderick	**Reece Dinsdale**
Grunge	**Sam Kelly**
Sir Joshua	**Michael Jayston**
Fanny	**Sara Crowe**

Writer **Eric Chappell**
Producer **Vernon Lawrence**

● ***An impoverished squire and his randy son go looking for wealth.***

In the 18th century, the house of Haggard is under siege. The family finances have been frittered away and now the devious Squire Haggard needs to marry off his licentious son, Roderick, to a wealthy bride. With their lowly manservant, Grunge, in tow, the two set off across England, rampaging through the countryside, leering and boozing as they search for the perfect woman. It seems a young blonde girl named Fanny might be suitable, and the optimistic Haggard and son will do everything to get her, even resorting to love potions if necessary. When all fails, there's always gambling, swindling and robbery as other means of getting some cash. The series was based on the book *Squire Haggard's Journal*, by Michael Green. Robert Hartley provided the theme music.

Hagman, Larry

(1931–)

The son of musical star Mary Martin, Larry Hagman broke into showbiz in the early 1950s, finding work in New York's theatreland. He appeared with his mother in London as an extra in *South Pacific* in 1951 and spent some time in the USAF before working his way into television. His first prominent role was in the US daytime serial *The Edge of Night* in 1961, and then in 1965 Hagman was chosen to play genie master Tony Nelson in the sitcom I DREAM OF JEANNIE. The show was a hit and ran for five years, and Hagman followed it with film roles and two other US comedies, *The Good Life* and *Here We Go Again*, both of which failed to take off. Then, just when it seemed his career had peaked and was on the slide, up popped the part of TV's all-time Mr Nasty, J. R. Ewing, in the hugely successful DALLAS. Hagman soon became vital to the series. He directed as well as starred in it, also becoming joint executive producer; and when JR was shot in 1980 the world stopped to find out who had pulled the trigger. The series ran until 1991. Since then Hagman has made few excursions into prime time, most notably with the US series *Orleans*.

Hale, Alan, Jr

(1918–90)

Cheerful American light and comic actor, best remembered by British TV audiences as CASEY JONES in the 1950s railroad Western. In the 1960s he was a stalwart of the farce GILLIGAN'S ISLAND, playing Jonas Grumby, the skipper of the shipwrecked cruise ship. His dad, whom Alan Jr resembled physically, was a silent movie star.

Hale, Gareth

(1953–)

London-born former teacher who turned comedian and formed a successful, if at times controversial, double act with another ex-teacher, Dudley-born Norman Pace. After writing for THREE OF A KIND and appearances in THE YOUNG ONES, *The Entertainers, The Laughter Show, Pushing Up Daisies, Coming Next . . .*, SATURDAY LIVE and *Saturday Gang*, the duo were given their own series by LWT. Never afraid to put pressure on the boundaries of taste, they found themselves at the centre of a storm over a sketch involving a cat and a microwave oven. Their act also included an impersonation of a pair of Cockney gangster bodyguards, the two Rons (who gained their own series, *The Management*, in 1988), and a parody of kids' TV (as Billy and Johnny, the patronizing presenters). Hale and Pace also tried their hand at straight acting in DOCTOR WHO and the three-part crime drama *A Pinch of Snuff* (an ITV forerunner of DALZIEL AND PASCOE). Moving to the BBC, they took the challenges presented by the documentary series *Jobs for the Boys*, starred in the silent comedy *Oddbods*, and hosted their own comedy/variety series, *h&p@bbc*. Gareth has since been seen as Doug McKenzie in the soap opera *Family Affairs*, while Norman has made a guest appearance in CASUALTY.

Hall, Robin
(1937–98)

Popular Scottish folksinger of the 1950s and 1960s, in partnership with Jimmie MacGregor. Their big break came on TONIGHT, for which they performed a number every week. They were then given the chance to branch out in THE WHITE HEATHER CLUB and were also seen on the ITV series *Hullabaloo*. After their partnership broke up in 1979 Hall became an occasional folk performer back in Scotland. MacGregor has since worked for Radio Scotland and Scottish television.

Hall, Stuart
(1934–)

News and sports presenter born and based in Manchester, known for his loquacious football reporting and his hysterical hosting of IT'S A KNOCKOUT/JEUX SANS FRONTIÈRES. Hall has also fronted WHAT THE PAPERS SAY, QUIZ BALL, a children's quiz called *How Right Can You Be?*, the pub-based *Quiz Night*, the antiques game show *Going, Going, Gone*, and the regional news magazine *Look North/North West Tonight*.

Hall, Willis
(1929–2005)

British scriptwriter, often in collaboration with Keith Waterhouse. Among their many joint credits were INSIDE GEORGE WEBLEY, QUEENIE'S CASTLE, BUDGIE, BILLY LIAR, *The Upper Crusts, Our Kid* and WORZEL GUMMIDGE, plus sketches for THAT WAS THE WEEK THAT WAS, BBC-3 and THE FROST REPORT, and shows starring Dick Emery, Dora Bryan, Millicent Martin and Roy Hudd. They also contributed plays for anthologies like *The Sunday Play* and *Studio '64*. Additionally, Hall worked solo on the sitcoms *The Fuzz* and *The Bright Side*, wrote the children's dramas *The Danedyke Mystery* and *The Return of the Antelope* and episodes of ROBIN'S NEST, SECRET ARMY, THE CREZZ, MINDER, *Moving Story* plus other series, and penned notable single dramas like *The Villa Maroc*. His first wife was actress Jill Bennett.

Hallelujah! ✶

UK (Yorkshire) Situation Comedy. ITV 1983–4

Capt. Emily Ridley	**Thora Hird**
Sister Alice Meredith	**Patsy Rowlands**
Sister Dorothy Smith	**Rosamund Greenwood**
Brigadier Charles Langton	**Garfield Morgan**
Brother Benjamin	**David Daker**

Writer **Dick Sharples**
Producer **Ronnie Baxter**

A Salvation Army captain is determined to clean up her patch.

Although she has served 42 years in the Salvation Army, Emily Ridley's enthusiasm knows no bounds. Unfortunately, she is rather mishap-prone and has probably her best days behind her, which leads her superiors to contrive a means of ensuring her retirement. She is asked to take over the unit in the sinful Yorkshire town of Brigthorpe. If she doesn't turn the place around in four weeks, she will be forced to go. Rattling collecting tins in pubs, staging lunch clubs for OAPs and acting as an agony aunt for the whole neighbourhood, Ridley battles to render the disused bingo hall/citadel into a meaningful centre for the wayward folk of the town. In her efforts, she is aided and abetted by her niece, Alice Meredith, newly enrolled after the death of her husband, Arthur. Their first recruit is another widow, Dorothy Smith, whose main aim in life is to discover another man. By the time of the second series, Emily's work in Brigthorpe has been done and she is now installed at the Mill Street Citadel in Blackwick. Providing 'assistance' is Brother Benjamin, a convert from the vices of drinking and smoking but always likely to revert to former habits. The programme's titles showed Ridley and Meredith fronting a marching Salvation Army band as it boomed out 'When the Saints Go Marching In'.

Hamilton, Andy
(1954–)

London-born actor, producer, director and comedy writer, often in conjunction with Guy Jenkin, with whom he worked on NOT THE NINE O'CLOCK NEWS, ALAS SMITH AND JONES, WHO DARES, WINS . . ., SHELLEY and THE KIT CURRAN RADIO SHOW and, most notably, created DROP THE DEAD DONKEY. Hamilton's solo work has included the sports comedies *Eleven Men against Eleven* and *Trevor's World of Sport*, the comedy-thriller *Underworld*, and BEDTIME, plus sketches for *The Dawson Watch* and *The Marti Caine Show*. On screen, he was seen in CHELMSFORD 123, played editor Robin Sanders in Guy Jenkin's *Screen One* drama *The Lord of Misrule*, and also featured in the dramas *Crossing the Floor* and *Mr White Goes to Westminster*.

Hamish Macbeth ✶✶✶

UK (Zenith) Drama. BBC 1 1995–7
DVD: BBC

Hamish Macbeth	**Robert Carlyle**
TV John McIver	**Ralph Riach**
Lachlan	**Jimmy Yuill**
	Billy Riddoch
Lachie Jr	**Stuart Davids**
Alex MacLaine	**Valerie Gogan**
Rory Campbell	**Brian Pettifer**
Esme	**Anne Lacey**
Doc Brown	**Duncan Duff**
Barney	**Stuart McGugan**
Agnes	**Barbara Rafferty**
Jimmy Soutar	**Rab Christie**
Major Roddy Maclean	**David Ashton**
Isobel Sutherland	**Shirley Henderson**
Neil the Bus	**Iain McColl**

Producers **Deirdre Keir, Charles Salmon**

Unconventional policing with a Highland bobby.

Hamish Macbeth is the unambitious community copper in the dozy, eccentric-populated Highland village of Lochdubh (pronounced 'Lochdoo' – real-life Plockton). Laid back about most things (salmon poaching never exercises him, pub lock-ins are community events, pirate radio is a service not a felony, and he likes to smoke a bit of pot himself now and again), he nevertheless proves more than a handful for any prospective criminals (usually outsiders up to no good). Stories reflect the timeless, parochial nature of the village where key characters include Doc Brown, grocer Rory Campbell and the second-sighted TV John (so named for having the first set in the village). However, Macbeth's best pal is his West Highland terrier, Wee Jock (real name Zippy) who, to much grief, does not survive the first series after a hit-and-run incident. Wee Jock Two (real name Fraoch, later replaced by Dex) is appointed for future episodes. Human love for the lawman comes from journalist Isobel and Alex, a former girlfriend.

The series, a first starring role for Robert Carlyle, was based on the novels by M. C. Beaton (Marion Chesney), in which Macbeth's dog was a mongrel called Towser. Less twee than HEARTBEAT, with more bite than BALLYKISSANGEL, and not far removed from a Wild West drama – sheriff rounding up invading outlaws, etc. – this darkly humorous series appealed to more than the usual Sunday night light-drama crowd.

Hammer House of Horror ✶✶

UK (ATV/Hammer/Chips/Cinema Arts) Thriller Anthology. ITV 1980
DVD: Granada Ventures

Producer **Roy Skeggs**

● ***A collection of suspense tales produced with the cinema horror specialists.***

The gory one-hour films grouped together as *Hammer House of Horror* feature guest stars like Diana Dors, Denholm Elliott, Anthony Valentine, Siân Phillips and Hammer favourite Peter Cushing. The 13 stories (under the control of Hammer directors such as Peter Sasdy, Don Sharp and Alan Gibson) revolve around such subjects as voodoo, cannibalism, werewolves, witchcraft and other manifestations of the supernatural.

Hamner, Earl, Jr

(1923–)

American writer whose own life story formed the basis of THE WALTONS, which he created. Hamner also acted as narrator on the series. Later, he created and produced the glossy soap FALCON CREST and co-produced *Snowy River: the McGregor Saga*. Among his other work were the scripts of some episodes of THE TWILIGHT ZONE.

Hampshire, Susan

OBE (1937–)

British actress whose TV debut came as Andromeda in *The Andromeda Breakthrough*, the sequel to the sci-fi classic, A FOR ANDROMEDA, thanks to Julie Christie's decision to leave the role. However, most people's earliest recollection of Hampshire is as the headstrong Fleur in THE FORSYTE SAGA. She followed it up with Forsyte look-alikes THE FIRST CHURCHILLS (Sarah Churchill) and THE PALLISERS (Lady Glencora Palliser). She has also starred in THE BARCHESTER CHRONICLES (Madeline Neroni), *Vanity Fair* (Becky Sharp), THE GRAND (Esme Harkness), COMING HOME and NANCHERROW (Miss Catto in both), MONARCH OF THE GLEN (Molly MacDonald) and *Sparkling Cyanide* (Lucilla Drake), plus a musical version of *Dr Jekyll and Mr Hyde*, as well as taking the lead in Carla Lane's LEAVING (Martha Ford) and Roy Clarke's DON'T TELL FATHER (Natasha Bancroft). She has numerous guest appearances to her name, in programmes as diverse as THE TIME TUNNEL and *The Morecambe and Wise Show*. Hampshire also once hosted a gardening programme called *Going to Pot*. She has been an active campaigner for dyslexia awareness (she is a sufferer herself).

Hancock, Nick

(1962–)

Stoke-on-Trent-born actor and comedian, once a Cambridge Footlights member. He was the original host of ROOM 101 and chairman of the comedy quiz THEY THINK IT'S ALL OVER, and also fronted the biographical comedy *You Only Live Once*. He was star of the series of comedy shorts called *Nights* (Bob), and the sitcoms ME, YOU AND HIM (John, as well as co-writer) and HOLDING THE BABY (Gordon Muir), plus the soccer drama *Bostock's Cup* (Mike Tonker). Guest appearances take in series as diverse as *Great Railway Journeys* (see GREAT RAILWAY JOURNEYS OF THE WORLD) and MR BEAN. Hancock also co-wrote the sitcom *Blind Men* and, in contrast, presented *Sex and Stopping: A History of Contraception*. As a narrator he has worked on docu-soaps like *The Zoo Keepers* and *Pleasure Beach*.

Hancock, Sheila

OBE (1933–)

Isle of Wight-born actress, the wife of the late John Thaw and mother of actress Melanie Thaw. Among her sitcom credits have been THE RAG TRADE (Carole), THE BED-SIT GIRL (Sheila), MR DIGBY DARLING (devoted secretary Thelma Teesdale), *Now Take My Wife* (Claire Love), GONE TO SEED (Mag), and BRIGHTON BELLES (Frances). Hancock has also proved her versatility through serious dramas like 1989's JUMPING THE QUEUE and other credits have included *Entertaining Mr Sloane*, the 1972 version of Waugh's *Scoop, Horizontal Hold, The Mating Machine*, DOCTOR WHO, *Dramarama, God Our Help, But Seriously – It's Sheila Hancock, The Buccaneers* (Duchess of Trevenick), *Dangerous Lady* (Sarah Ryan), *Alice in Wonderland* (Cook), *Close Relations* (Dorothy Hammond), *Love or Money* (Teresa), and *The Thing about Vince . . .* (Pat Skinner). More recently she has been seen in BEDTIME (Alice Oldfield), *The Russian Bride* (Dora), *Bait* (Pam Raeburn), *Feather Boy* (Edith Sorrel), *Forty-something* (Gwendolen) and BLEAK HOUSE (Mrs Guppy), as well as making guest appearances in EASTENDERS (Barbara Owen). Her first husband was actor Alec Ross.

Hancock, Tony

(1924–68)

'The lad himself', as he was dubbed, Birmingham-born Tony Hancock has been widely acclaimed as one of Britain's funniest ever comedians and a pioneer of TV situation comedy. A member of *Ralph Reader's Gang Show* during the war, Hancock remained on the stage when the hostilities ceased, becoming resident comic at the Windmill and touring other theatres. In 1951 he joined the cast of radio's *Educating Archie* and was such a success that he began appearing on TV (in series like KALEIDOSCOPE) and was given his own radio show, HANCOCK'S HALF HOUR, in 1954. Two years later the series transferred to television, although not before Hancock had made a couple of sketch series for ITV under the banner of *The Tony Hancock Show*. *Hancock's Half Hour* (finally just known as *Hancock*) ran until 1961, making Hancock the country's number-one comic. He even turned his hand to straight drama, appearing in the 1958 play *The Government Inspector* (part of the *Television World Theatre* anthology). In 1963 he switched to ITV, leaving behind him his scriptwriters, Ray Galton and Alan Simpson, and with them the peak of his success. A career in film fizzled out and Hancock grew more and more depressed. His drink problem was well documented and, always highly self-critical, he took his own life while working on a series for Australian

TV in 1968. His last British offering had been *Hancock's* in 1967, in which he played a nightclub owner. In 1991 Alfred Molina starred in a *Screen One* production, *Hancock*, which dramatized his tragic last seven years.

Hancock's Half Hour/ Hancock ****

UK (BBC/ATV) Situation Comedy. BBC 1956–60/1961; ITV 1963
DVD: BBC

Anthony Aloysius Hancock ..... **Tony Hancock**
Sidney James ..... **Sidney James** *(Half Hour)*

Creators/Writers **Ray Galton, Alan Simpson**
Producers **Duncan Wood** (BBC), **Tony Hancock** (ATV)

The highs and lows in the life of a perpetual dreamer.

Hancock's Half Hour, its title announced in breathless, stammering fashion by 'the lad himself', was one of Britain's first major comedy series and remains in the eyes of many a true classic. Beginning on radio in 1954, it quickly transferred to television and introduced to viewers the complex personality of Anthony Aloysius Hancock, inhabitant of 23 Railway Cuttings, East Cheam. The character is a moody, bumptious type, sporting a Homburg hat and a heavy overcoat, a man prone to constant questioning of the whys and wherefores of the world and a gloomy ponderer of his personal circumstances. Life's petty injustices and annoyances are guaranteed to generate a torrent of observations and criticisms. For instance, what could be worse than reading a thriller novel only to find the last page torn out? Similarly frustrating is the way in which his ambitious plans to improve his station always end in failure and humiliation, as prophesied by his cynical room mate, played by Sid James.

James, the man who pricks Hancock's bubbles, left the series in 1960 to pursue his own starring roles, and the last season went out simply under the title of *Hancock*, the star having moved to a new address. These episodes include such classics as *The Radio Ham* and *The Blood Donor* (with its oft-quoted exclamation: 'A pint? That's very nearly an armful!'). Hancock subsequently broke up his partnership with writers Galton and Simpson and moved to ITV, where he produced himself one (notably less successful) series of *Hancock*.

In 1996–7, Galton and Simpson revamped some of the classic scripts (including the above-mentioned) for the ITV series *Paul Merton in Galton & Simpson's . . .*, with the deadpan HAVE I GOT NEWS FOR YOU panellist filling the Hancock role.

Handl, Irene

(1901–87)

Cheerful Cockney character actress, in her latter years well versed in daffy old lady parts. She did not begin acting until she was nearly 40 but soon secured herself plenty of film, stage and radio work. On television in the 1950s she was seen in variety shows like CHELSEA AT NINE and in the screen version of *Educating Archie*, as well as in HANCOCK'S HALF HOUR and in *Laughter in Store* and *Drake's Progress* (both with Charlie Drake). However, her biggest TV success was opposite Wilfred Pickles in the OAP sitcom FOR THE LOVE OF ADA (Ada Cresswell). Among her other major roles were *Barney is My Darling* (Ramona Pank), *Mum's Boys* (Mrs Crystal Pallise), MAGGIE AND HER (Julia McKenzie's nosy neighbour, Mrs Perry), METAL MICKEY (the granny) and *Never Say Die* (Dorothy). Handl also enjoyed scores of guest appearances, ranging from THE ADVENTURES OF ROBIN HOOD and THE RAG TRADE to *Dramarama* and SUPERGRAN.

Hanged Man, The **

UK (Yorkshire) Thriller. ITV 1975

Lewis Burnett ..... **Colin Blakely**
Alan Crowe ..... **Michael Williams**
John Quentin ..... **Gary Watson**

Creator/Writer **Edmund Ward**
Executive Producer **Peter Willes**
Producers **Marc Miller, Edmund Ward**

A businessman plays dead to find out who has been trying to kill him.

Ruthless construction entrepreneur Lew Burnett has gained many bitter enemies on his way to the top, so many in fact that there have been three attempts on his life. After the third attempt, he decides to go along with the idea, for what better way is there to seek out your enemies than if they think you are already dead? Joined by a friend, an ex-mercenary named Alan Crowe, who has discovered his secret, Burnett begins to track down nine potential assassins, scouring his life for people who have loved or hated him. Being 'dead', he has no money or resources at his fingertips, just the wit and guile that have helped him build his empire. Despite this, his search takes him to Switzerland and other countries, where he confronts various crime barons and finds that there is a hired assassin by the name of John Quentin still on his trail. Eight episodes were produced.

Hangin' with Mr Cooper *

US (Bickley-Warren/Jeff Franklin/Lorimar) Situation Comedy. Channel 4 1993–7 (US: ABC 1992–7)

Mark Cooper ..... **Mark Curry**
Vanessa Russell ..... **Holly Robinson**
Robin Dumars ..... **Dawnn Lewis**
Earvin Rodman ..... **Omar Gooding**
Tyler Foster ..... **Marquise Wilson**
Geneva Lee ..... **Saundra Quarterman**
Nicole Lee ..... **Raven-Symone**
P. J. Moore ..... **Nell Carter**

Creator **Jeff Franklin**

A fun-loving teacher shares his home with attractive women.

In this black update of *Three's Company* (the US version of MAN ABOUT THE HOUSE), Mr Cooper is Mark, a tall former basketball star who returns home to Oakland, California, to become a high school coach and relief teacher. Sharing his house are platonic friends Vanessa (a music teacher and a childhood buddy) and the sassy Robin (the object of Mark's lust), although from the second series Robin has moved out to be replaced by Mark's cousin, Geneva, and her plain-speaking little girl, Nicole. Never able to resist a bit of fun, Cooper is often in hot water at school, especially when strict headteacher P. J. Moore arrives to frown upon his mischief. A new dimension is added when Geneva succeeds PJ as principal, becoming both his boss and his flatmate.

Hanging Gale, The ★★★

UK (Little Bird/BBC) Drama. BBC 2 1998
DVD: Acorn Media

Sean Phelan	**Joe McGann**
Conor Phelan	**Mark McGann**
Liam Phelan	**Paul McGann**
Daniel Phelan	**Stephen McGann**
Townsend	**Michael Kitchen**
Maeve Phelan	**Fiona Victory**
Mary Dolan	**Tina Kellegher**
James Phelan	**Joe Pilkington**
Joseph Phelan	**Ciaran Fitzgerald**
Molly Phelan	**Ciara Marley**
Ferry	**Sean McGinley**
Coulter	**Gerard McSorley**

Writer **Allan Cubitt**
Executive Producers **Robert Copper, James Mitchell, David Blake Knox**
Producer **Jonathan Cavendish**

● ***Four brothers battle to feed their family in the face of tyranny and famine.***

In 1846, Ireland is being plundered by absentee English landlords, leaving the hard-working locals with but a pittance on which to live. When Townsend, a new land agent, arrives in the County Donegal settlement of Brannocktown, he does so knowing that the last person to take on his job was murdered, such is the hatred the greedy landowners inspire. However, just as relations with the newcomer begin to settle down, in sweeps the horrendous potato famine to devastate the Irish people once more. This four-part drama, of a nation's fight to stave off starvation and ruin, sees the four doughty Phelan brothers in conflict with the brutal authorities as they seek every means possible to preserve their Galready homestead. Sean has a wife and kids to protect; Con takes up fighting to earn some money; teacher Daniel also adopts the physical approach, joining the growing band of rebels; and all this is a bitter trial for peaceful parish priest Liam. The brainchild of Stephen McGann, *The Hanging Gale* was largely conceived as a vehicle for himself and his three brothers, who had never worked together on television before. Diarmuid Lawrence directed.

Hanley, Jimmy

(1918–70)

Former child star Jimmy Hanley was a versatile showman, notching up a series of films for Rank in the 1940s and becoming a hit on radio and TV in the 1950s. His most prominent role was as the landlord of *Jim's Inn*, a fictitious pub that he ran with his second wife, Maggie. The series was TV's most popular admag, a vehicle for promoting various goods and services. Customers used to stroll in to discuss their latest bargains at the bar. The series started in 1957, but in 1963 admags were banned by Parliament and Hanley was out of a job, although he was later seen on the kids' series FIVE O'CLOCK CLUB, talking about hobbies. His first wife was actress Dinah Sheridan, with whom he had two children, actress/presenter Jenny and Conservative politician Jeremy.

Hanna, William

(1910–2001)

With his partner, Joseph Barbera, William Hanna created two of animation's most memorable characters in TOM AND JERRY for film producer MGM. However, after setting up their own studio called Hanna-Barbera in 1957, they were later responsible for a cavalcade of TV cartoons that enlivened many a childhood. Their first creations, a cat and dog named Ruff and Reddy, were soon followed by the much more successful HUCKLEBERRY HOUND, *Quick Draw McGraw*, YOGI BEAR, THE FLINTSTONES, BOSS CAT and THE JETSONS. Among the studio's later offerings were JONNY QUEST, *Secret Squirrel, Space Kidettes*, FRANKENSTEIN JR AND THE IMPOSSIBLES, SHAZZAN!, THE BANANA SPLITS, WACKY RACES, SCOOBY DOO, WHERE ARE YOU?, *It's the Wolf, The Harlem Globetrotters*, JOSIE AND THE PUSSYCATS, HELP! IT'S THE HAIR BEAR BUNCH, *The Amazing Chan and the Chan Clan*, WAIT TILL YOUR FATHER GETS HOME, *Goober and the Ghost Chasers*, INCH HIGH, PRIVATE EYE, HONG KONG PHOOEY, *Valley of the Dinosaurs, The Great Grape Ape* and *Captain Caveman*.

Hannah, John

(1962–)

Scottish actor with numerous starring and supporting parts to his name. He played the title roles of both MCCALLUM (pathologist Iain McCallum) and REBUS (detective John Rebus), shared the limelight as DS Franky Drinkall in OUT OF THE BLUE, and appeared in Steve Coogan's *Three Fights, Two Weddings and a Funeral* (comically echoing his role in the film *Four Weddings and a Funeral*). Other credits have included *Bookie* (Johnny Dawson), *Civvies* (Don Walker), BETWEEN THE LINES (DC Mellis), *Faith* (Nick Simon), *Circles of Deceit* (Jason Sturden), *Screen One's Truth or Dare* (Nick), *Amnesia* (DS Mackenzie Stone) and *Cold Blood* (Jake Osbourne), as well as narration work on *Predators, The Natural World* and *Deep Jungle*. Hannah has also featured in the American series *MDs* and as a guest in *Alias*, FRASIER, AGATHA CHRISTIE'S MARPLE and SEA OF SOULS. He is married to actress Joanna Roth.

Hannay ★★

UK (Thames) Drama. ITV 1988–9
DVD: Delta Music

Richard Hannay	**Robert Powell**
Count Otto von Schwabing	**Gavin Richards**
Reggie Armitage	**Christopher Scoular**
Eleanor Armitage	**Jill Meager**

Writers **Michael Robson, Robin Miller, Richard Carpenter, Paul Wheeler**
Executive Producers **Lloyd Shirley, Richard Bates**
Producers **Richard Bates, Robert Banks Stewart**

● ***An officer-adventurer does battle with the Hun and others.***

Richard Hannay has returned to the UK after nearly 30 years as a mining engineer, prospector and military intelligence officer in South Africa. He wants to settle down, find a wife and take things easy for a while. Regrettably, it is not to be. In the preamble to World War I, Europe is in a state of flux, politics are reshaping the continent and Imperial Germany is on the rise. For the tweed-suited Hannay, with his unfailing nose for intrigue, retirement must wait as he embarks on a series of mysteries that all too often seem to involve the devious German Count von Schwabing. The videotaped series was based on John Buchan's dashing hero, played here as in the 1978 feature film *The Thirty-Nine Steps* by Robert Powell. Music was by Denis King. Thirteen episodes were made, over two series.

Hanrahan, Brian

(1949–)

British journalist, who joined BBC TV News as a reporter in 1980. After notable achievements alongside ITN's Michael Nicholson in the Falklands conflict (in one memorable report he declared that, while he couldn't comment on British aircraft losses, he had 'counted them all out and counted them all back in'), Hanrahan became the BBC's Far East Correspondent, 1983–6, and Moscow Correspondent, 1986–8. Since 1989 he has been the BBC's Diplomatic Correspondent.

Happiness ★★★

UK (BBC) Situation Comedy. BBC 2 2001; 2003
DVD: BBC

Danny Spencer	**Paul Whitehouse**
Terry Roche	**Mark Heap**
Rachel Roche	**Fiona Allen**
Angus	**Clive Russell**
Charlie	**Johnny Vegas**
Sid	**Pearce Quigley**
Toby X	**Michael Wildman**
Toby C	**Tim Plester**
Emma	**Tamsin Greig**
Neela	**Amita Dhiri**

Writers **Paul Whitehouse, David Cummings**
Producers **Rosemary McGowan, Paul Whitehouse**

● *An actor's life takes a turn for the worse as he approaches middle age.*

Danny Spencer is 39 and a successful voice artist. He's created the animated character of Dexter the bear, a kung fu nurse that has become a favourite with kids everywhere. However, this apart, things are not going so well. Firstly, his wife has just died in a road accident and he is forced to balance his genuine sadness with the exciting prospect of new-found freedom. Secondly, while Dexter may be exceptionally well-known, Danny remains reluctantly anonymous. Even the various guest stars who appear on his programme (Dawn French, Cat Deeley and Bob Geldof among them) largely ignore poor Danny, which adds to his mid-life crisis. Concerns grow about his bald patch and facial wrinkles, and visions of his uncertain life ahead contrast with the enjoyable days of his past (hence much use of old chart music as a soundtrack). Danny leans heavily on his friends, Terry and the pregnant Rachel, but gets little positive support from Angus (who has reinvented his life and now pulls birds again, despite his advancing years) or the gormless duo of Charlie and Sid. Tobys X and C are Danny's disrespectful studio engineers.

With a version of Ken Dodd's 1964 hit of the same title (sung by Danny in Dexter's lisping voice) as its ironic theme music, the series features Plasticine animation from Aardman Animations, creators of Wallace & Gromit. Further guests include star Paul Whitehouse's FAST SHOW colleagues Charlie Higson, Simon Day and Mark Williams, plus radio/TV presenters Jonathan Ross, Angus Deayton and Steve Wright.

Happy Apple, The ★★

UK (Thames) Situation Comedy. ITV 1983

Nancy Gray	**Leslie Ash**
Charles Murray	**Nicky Henson**
Arthur Spender	**John Nettleton**
Freddie Maine	**Jeremy Child**
Mr Bassington	**Derek Waring**
Kenilworth	**Peter-Hugo Daly**

Writer **Keith Waterhouse**
Producer **Michael Mills**

● *A secretary has the know-how to save a struggling advertising agency.*

The Happy Apple, a stage play by Jack Pulman, was adapted into this sitcom with seven episodes by Keith Waterhouse. Events focus on life at Murray, Maine and Spender, a small, failing advertising agency. It seems that they are about to go out of business with office furniture being repossessed and their single client, Bassington's Ice Cream, unhappy with the company's performance. However, things take a remarkable turn for the better when the firm's three partners discover that their secretary, Nancy Gray, is more than just a pretty face. It seems she has hidden talents, especially in the line of market research, and her input turns the business round. It's not all plain sailing, though, as the vultures at rival agency, Dobson and Dobson, try to poach the firm's prize asset.

Happy Days ★★★

US (Paramount/Miller-Milkis) Situation Comedy. ITV 1976–85
(US: ABC 1974–84)
DVD: Paramount (Region 1 only)

Richie Cunningham	**Ron Howard**
Arthur Fonzarelli ('Fonzie')	**Henry Winkler**
Howard Cunningham	**Tom Bosley**
Marion Cunningham	**Marion Ross**
Joanie Cunningham	**Erin Moran**
Warren 'Potsie' Webber	**Anson Williams**
Ralph Malph	**Donny Most**
Chuck Cunningham	**Gavan O'Herlihy**
	Randolph Roberts
Arnold (Matsuo Takahashi)	**Pat Morita**
Alfred Delvecchio	**Al Molinaro**
Charles 'Chachi' Arcola	**Scott Baio**
Lori Beth Allen/Cunningham	**Linda Goodfriend**
Jenny Piccalo	**Cathy Silvers**
Roger Phillips	**Ted McGinley**
K. C. Cunningham	**Crystal Bernard**
Ashley Pfister	**Linda Purl**
Heather Pfister	**Heather O'Rourke**

Creator **Garry K. Marshall**
Executive Producers **Thomas L. Miller, Edward K. Milkis, Garry K. Marshall**
Producers **Tony Marshall, Jerry Paris**

● *Nostalgic sitcom featuring a middle-class Milwaukee family and their teenage children.*

Laced with contemporary pop hits, *Happy Days* follows the Cunningham family throughout the late years of the 1950s and into the 1960s, with particular focus on their teenage son, Richie, and his pals. The Cunninghams live in Milwaukee, Wisconsin, where chubby, hapless dad Howard owns a hardware store. His red-haired wife, Marion, is a typical housewife of the time, bringing up the children and supporting her husband, but always with a youthful spring in her step. Son Richie is the classic all-American boy, complete with apple-pie looks, and viewers share his growing pains as he starts dating girls and progresses through school. Apart from Richie, there are two other Cunningham kids, Chuck and Joanie. Chuck, however, appears in only the earliest episodes before moving off to college, to be strangely forgotten by everyone in the cast, including his own mother and father. Joanie, on the other hand, genuinely grows up with the show. At the start, she is just a freckly little kid with only a few lines, but by the end of the run she has developed into one of the star names and even has her own spin-off series, JOANIE LOVES CHACHI.

The show was originally intended to focus on Richie and his chum Potsie as they negotiated teenage life in the rock 'n' roll era. However, while Richie remains central to the show, the rather slow-witted Potsie is gradually pushed into the background, alongside wisecracking redhead Ralph Malph, as an unexpected star is born. That star is Fonzie, the show's leather-jacketed hell-raiser, who cruises the streets on a cherished motorcycle. There is always something special about 'The Fonz'. He is cool with a capital C, an expert mechanic with a magic touch and the dream date of every girl in Milwaukee. He moves into the flat above the Cunninghams' garage and, as the series develops, his rough edges become considerably smoother.

Richie, Potsie, Ralph and Fonzie are all regulars at Arnold's, a drive-in diner and soda store run initially by Japanese proprietor Arnold, then by the sad-faced but kind-hearted Al Delvecchio. The boys attend Jefferson High School, before graduating and moving on to the University of Wisconsin in Milwaukee. As they grow older, the emphasis switches to kids of Joanie's generation. Richie and Ralph join the army and are dispatched to Greenland (Ron Howard and Donny Most left the series), while Potsie takes a job at the Cunningham hardware store. New faces include Fonzie's cousin, Chachi, who becomes Joanie's boyfriend, and Roger, Marion's nephew, the school's new basketball coach. Howard's niece, KC, lives with the family for a while and Joanie's much-talked-about, boy-mad friend, Jenny Piccalo, is eventually seen (played by Cathy Silvers, daughter of comedian Phil Silvers). Other characters introduced over the years include Fonzie's divorcée girlfriend, Ashley Pfister, and her little daughter, Heather. Rock singer Leather Tuscadero, played by Suzi Quatro, is an occasional guest.

Richie eventually marries his college sweetheart, Lori Beth (by telephone, with Fonzie acting as proxy groom), and a Richie Junior appears on the scene. Fonzie joins Al as a partner in Arnold's and even teaches at the High School. In the final episode, Joanie and Chachi are married, the whole family (except Chuck) reassemble and Howard thanks viewers for being part of their lives for over ten years.

Apart from *Joanie Loves Chachi*, *Happy Days* led to two other spin-offs, LAVERNE AND SHIRLEY and MORK AND MINDY. The programme was not, as often surmised, based on the film *American Graffiti* (in which Ron Howard had starred), but on an episode of LOVE, AMERICAN STYLE entitled *Love and the Happy Day*, which had featured Howard and Anson Williams as 1950s schoolkids. The original series theme music was Bill Haley's 'Rock around the Clock', although an original title track soon superseded it, becoming a minor hit itself for a group called Pratt and McLain with Brotherlove.

Happy Ever After ★★

UK (BBC) Situation Comedy. BBC 1 1974; 1976–8

Terry Fletcher .... **Terry Scott**
June Fletcher .... **June Whitfield**
Aunt Lucy .... **Beryl Cooke**
Susan Fletcher .... **Pippa Page**
Debbie Fletcher .... **Caroline Whitaker**

Creators **John Chapman, Eric Merriman, Christopher Bond, John Kane**
Producers **Peter Whitmore, Ray Butt**

A middle-aged couple are saddled with a geriatric aunt.

Middle-class suburban couple Terry and June Fletcher are just settling down to life on their own after 23 years of marriage. Their two daughters have, at last, flown the nest. Then, out of the blue, June's frail, 73-year-old Aunt Lucy arrives, looking for somewhere to put up for two weeks. With her squawking pet mynah bird (Gunga Din) also in attendance, Lucy puts down roots and makes sure the Fletchers' burdensome days are far from over. The daughters, Susan and Debbie, pay occasional visits to cheer up their patient, resilient mum and blustering, hapless dad.

The series, which was spun off a 1974 COMEDY PLAYHOUSE pilot, eventually evolved into TERRY AND JUNE, in which the old bird (and the mynah) have disappeared and the Fletchers are known as the Medfords.

Happy Families ★★

UK (BBC) Situation Comedy. BBC 1 1985

Edith/Joyce/Cassie/Roxanne/ Madelaine Fuddle .... **Jennifer Saunders**
Guy Fuddle .... **Adrian Edmondson**
Cook .... **Dawn French**
Dr De Quincy .... **Stephen Fry**
Flossie .... **Helen Lederer**

Writer **Ben Elton**
Producer **Paul Jackson**

A crazy, crotchety grandmother summons her grandchildren to her deathbed.

Barmy Edith Fuddle, being about to pop her clogs, demands the presence of her four granddaughters at her bedside. Unfortunately, they are now scattered around the world. To bring them together, their imbecile brother, Guy, is dispatched on his travels. Despite constantly losing his way, Guy eventually tracks them all down, one per episode. Cassie is working as a Hollywood soap actress; Madelaine is living with a randy poet in a French artists' commune; Joyce is a novice nun inspired by *The Sound of Music*; and Roxanne is in jail.

All the sisters and the grandmother are played by Jennifer Saunders, and the series, made by the BBC in Manchester, cleverly varies its camera techniques to reflect the granddaughters' situations. The Hollywood scenes are shot in soap style, arty pastels are used for France, a jolly 1940s style is employed for the convent episode and a hard documentary edge pervades the prison sequences.

Harben, Philip

(1906–70)

A familiar face on British television from the 1940s through the 1960s, small, bearded Philip Harben was one of the UK's first TV cooks. Presenting in his striped butcher's apron, his major series were *Cookery, Cookery Lesson* (a back-to-basics guide), *Man in the Kitchen* (cookery tips for men), *Continental Cookery, What's Cooking, Headway* (cookery theory) and *The Tools of Cookery*.

Harbour Lights ✱✱

UK (Valentine/BBC) Drama. BBC 1 1999–2000

Mike Nicholls .... **Nick Berry**
Jane Ford .... **Matilda Ziegler**
WPC/DC Melanie Rush .... **Tina Hobley**
Aunt Nicholls .... **Paola Dionisotti**
Tony Simpson .... **Gerard Horan**
Elvis .... **Louis Mahoney**
George Blade .... **Freddie Davies**
Rita Blade .... **Margot Leicester**
Steve Blade .... **Tim Matthews**
Jason Blade .... **Francis Pope**
Kelly Blade .... **Emma Pike**
Nancy Ford .... **Gillian Raine**
Jake Ford .... **Liam Tattershall**

Creators **David Martin, Steve Lanning**
Executive Producer **Mal Young**
Producer **Steve Lanning**

● ***A naval officer opts for the quiet life as harbour master at his home port.***

Mike Nicholls has returned home. Raised by his aunt, who runs the Pier's Hotel in the seaside town of Bridehaven, he had left to join the navy at 16. However, after many eventful seafaring years, a diving accident claimed the life of a friend and forced Mike to rethink his life. Still blaming himself (needlessly) for the tragedy, Nicholls is now the harbour master in his home town. His job is to help protect those in peril on the sea, but also to keep the peace between locals who make their living from the ocean and thoughtless tourists who intrude upon their patch. Taking his position as part of the emergency services to the extreme, he is also closely involved on the land side, helping out police, residents and visitors alike when the need arises. There are two women in his life, single mother Jane Ford (sister of his dead friend) and WPC Mel Rush, but our thoroughly decent hero has little time for petty emotional matters. Other locals include Jane's boss, dodgy bingo hall and amusement arcade owner Tony Simpson, the scruffy but good-hearted Blade family (whose son, Steve, becomes Mike's deputy harbour master), and music-loving, Caribbean café owner Elvis. In series two, Jane has left to marry an old flame, leaving Mel in pole position for Mike's affections. With the departure of Elvis, too, George Blade (played by Freddie 'Parrot Face' Davies) has taken over the Harbour Café.

Harbour Lights was filmed in the Dorset village of West Bay, near Bridport – home of creators David Martin and Steve Lanning – where the Bridport Arms pub doubled up as the series' Bridehaven Arms. Fifteen episodes in total were made.

Hardcastle & McCormick ✱✱

US (Paramount) Detective Drama. ITV 1983–5 (US: ABC 1983–6)

Judge Milton C. Hardcastle .... **Brian Keith**
Mark 'Skid' McCormick .... **Daniel Hugh-Kelly**
Sarah Wicks .... **Mary Jackson**
Lt. Michael Delaney .... **John Hancock**
Lt. Frank Harper .... **Joe Santos**

Creators/Executive Producers **Stephen J. Cannell, Patrick Hasburgh**

● ***A retired judge tracks down criminals who were wrongfully acquitted during his career.***

Hard-line, poker-playing judge Milton C. Hardcastle is a youthful 65 and a fitness fanatic, but his real obsession is with 'ones that got away' – guilty men who have squirmed through a legal loophole or employed a cunning brief to avoid conviction. Hanging up his gavel, 'Hardcase' abandons his official impartiality and sets about tracking down these refugees from justice. He needs a young partner to help with the legwork and chooses his last defendant, promising to help Mark 'Skid' McCormick to beat a technical conviction for car crime in return for help. Hardcastle makes full use of his contacts in the legal trade, but calls upon McCormick's knowledge of shadier dealings (and driving skills), and the two enjoy a sparkling repartee. Plenty of car chases ensue, with the judge tearing around in a red prototype 'Coyote' sports car (licence plates DE JUDGE), wearing T-shirts that openly declare his hatred of villains. But though he holds a grudge against bad guys, and longs to get even, it is only for current misdemeanours and not past events that Hardcastle pursues his enemies. Sarah Wicks is the sharp-tongued housekeeper at the judge's mansion in Malibu.

Harding, Gilbert

(1907–60)

British TV celebrity of the 1950s, earning a reputation for acute rudeness through appearances on panel games like WHAT'S MY LINE? A one-time schoolmaster and police officer, Harding had used his skill at languages to enter the BBC's monitoring service. From there, via service overseas, he became host of the radio quizzes *Round Britain Quiz, The Brains Trust* and *Twenty Questions*. Initially earmarked to host *What's My Line?* on alternate weeks, Harding found being a panel member infinitely more suitable and allowed Eamonn Andrews to keep the chairman's job full time. In one famous television moment in 1960, Harding appeared on FACE TO FACE, only to admit readily that his bad manners and temper were 'quite indefensible'. In the same interview, he broke down when interrogator John Freeman inadvertently touched on the recent death of Harding's mother. The same year Harding collapsed and died on the steps of the BBC.

Hardware ✱✱

UK (Talkback Thames) Situation Comedy. ITV 1 2003–4

Mike .... **Martin Freeman**
Kenny .... **Peter Serafinowicz**
Rex .... **Ken Morley**
Anne .... **Susan Earl**
Steve .... **Ryan Cartwright**
Julie .... **Ella Kenion**

Writer **Simon Nye**
Producer **Margot Gavan Duffy**

● ***The staff at an ironmonger's store while away their day with pranks and dreams.***

At Hamway's Hardware shop, customers can expect a hard time. Unless they happen to be consummate DIYers or professional tradesmen, they are guaranteed to receive a handful of sarcasm and wedge of mickey-taking from the frustrated salesmen along with their washers and nails. The team is headed up by Mike, a hapless underachiever who tries in vain to rise above the puerility of his best friend, the smug Kenny, and young student trainee Steve. If it's not the customers who bear the brunt of their wasted lives and failed ambitions, it's their boss, the immature, by-the-book boss Rex, a man unhappily married for 40 years. Brightening up Mike's life is girlfriend Anne, who runs the Nice Day Café across the road with the help of man-hungry Julie.

After a BAFTA-nominated first series that was praised for its pace and wit in the teeth of an overbearing laugh track, *Hardware* returned for a disappointing second outing that left critics less impressed.

Hardwicke House ★★

UK (Central) Situation Comedy. ITV 1987

R. G. Wickham	**Roy Kinnear**
Paul Mackintosh	**Roger Sloman**
Cynthia Crabbe	**Pam Ferris**
Peter Philpott	**Nick Wilton**
Herbert Fowl	**Granville Saxton**
Harry Savage	**Tony Haygarth**
Moose Magnusson	**Duncan Preston**
Dick Flashman	**Gavin Richards**
Slasher Bates	**Kevin Allen**

Writers **Richard Hall, Simon Wright**
Producer **Paula Burdon**

● ***Anarchy rules at a violent secondary school.***

Although, when viewed today, this chaotic comedy seems rather par for the course, in its day it sparked outrage. Indeed, the series caused so much uproar that it was cancelled after a mere two of the recorded seven episodes had been shown. The setting is Hardwicke House, a school in the care of ineffectual, boozy headmaster R. G. Wickham, which leaves unruly staff trying to outperform unruly pupils. Among the main characters are the sycophantic deputy head Mackintosh, environmentalist French teacher Ms Crabbe, sadistic English master Herbert Fowl, gruff Scottish sports teacher Harry Savage, spivvy gambler Dick Flashman of the history department, and Icelandic maths teacher Moose Magnusson. Smoking in class, getting kids to run errands, leering after sixth-form girls, siphoning off stationery for onward sale and electrocuting pupils are just a few of the masters' vices, as new and naïve geography teacher Peter Philpott discovers. Kids ring-led and bullied by Slasher Bates support the teachers in their crimes against education. John Stroud directed and Peter Brewis provided the music.

Hardy, Robert

CBE (1925–)

Cheltenham-born actor whose most prominent TV roles have been as Dudley, Earl of Leicester, in ELIZABETH R, Siegfried Farnon in ALL CREATURES GREAT AND SMALL and the title part in WINSTON CHURCHILL – THE WILDERNESS YEARS. He also played Fred Potter in the sitcom *If the Crown Fits*, Alec Stewart in THE TROUBLESHOOTERS, Abwehr Sergeant Gratz in MAN-HUNT, Prince Albert in EDWARD THE SEVENTH, *Daily Crucible* editor Russell Spam (and its proprietor, Twiggy Rathbone) in HOT METAL, Arthur Brooke in MIDDLEMARCH, Sir Herbert Hamilton in BRAMWELL, Dr Parnell in GULLIVER'S TRAVELS, Viscount Berryann in NANCHERROW, Illingworth in *The Lost World*, Sir James Caird in SHACKLETON, Mr Justice Morland in *Justice in Wonderland*, and Sir Anthony Parsons in THE FALKLANDS PLAY. In addition, since the early 1960s, Hardy has been seen in many other single dramas and series such as AN AGE OF KINGS, MYSTERY AND IMAGINATION, *The Dark Island* (Nicolson), THE BARON, SUPERNATURAL, DANIEL DERONDA, UPSTAIRS, DOWNSTAIRS, THE DUCHESS OF DUKE STREET, THE CLEOPATRAS, THE FAR PAVILIONS, *Jenny's War*, *The Shooting Party*, INSPECTOR MORSE, MIDSOMER MURDERS, FOYLE'S WAR, *Lucky Jim*, SPOOKS, P. D. JAMES and WAR AND REMEMBRANCE (again as Winston Churchill).

Hargreaves, Jack

OBE (1911–94)

Yorkshire-raised Jack Hargreaves was one of TV's gentler personalities. Whether it was explaining scientific facts to kids on HOW! or delving into the wonders of nature and practising rural crafts in his series *Out of Town* and *Country Boy*, he was a presenter who moved at his own pace, drawing calmly on his pipe and offering (usually adlibbed) opinions in a relaxed, natural, unhurried way. A former vet's assistant and journalist (managing editor of *Picture Post*), his first TV series was *Gone Fishing* for Southern, for whom he was also Deputy Programme Controller in the late 1960s and early 1970s. When Southern lost its franchise in 1981, *Gone Fishing*'s successor, *Out of Town*, was cancelled, although Hargreaves did follow it up with a similar effort, *Old Country*, for Channel 4.

Hark at Barker/His Lordship Entertains ★★★

UK (LWT/BBC) Situation Comedy. ITV 1969–70/BBC 2 1972

Lord Rustless	**Ronnie Barker**
Badger	**Frank Gatliff**
Mildred Bates	**Josephine Tewson**
Dithers	**David Jason**
Cook	**Mary Baxter**
Effie	**Moira Foot**

Producers **Humphrey Barclay** *(Hark)*, **Harold Snoad** *(Entertains)*

● ***The misadventures of a lecherous old peer and his inept staff.***

Hark at Barker was based on Alun Owen's single play *Ah, There You Are*, which was screened as part of *The Ronnie Barker Playhouse* in 1968. It features the lusty, opinionated, cigar-puffing Lord Rustless, as he meanders around his stately home, Chrome Hall. His staff consists of Badger the butler, Dithers the gardener, Mildred the secretary, Effie the maid and Cook. Other occasional characters are also played by Ronnie Barker. After two seasons on ITV, Rustless and his employees switched to BBC 2 in 1972 to star in the series *His Lordship Entertains*, in which the old buffer's stately pile has been turned into a hotel. These seven episodes were written by Barker himself under the pseudonym Jonathan Cobbald.

Harker, Caroline

(1966–)

Younger sister of Susannah Harker, and daughter of actress Polly Adams. Caroline has been seen in such dramas and comedies as *Growing Rich* (Laura), JILLY COOPER'S RIDERS (Tory Lovell), MIDDLEMARCH (Celia Brooke), A TOUCH OF FROST (WPC Hazel Wallace), HONEY FOR TEA (Hon. Lucy Courtney), *Holding On* (Vicky), A DANCE TO THE MUSIC OF TIME (Priscilla), MOLL FLANDERS (Maria), *I Saw You* (Lucy), AUF WIEDERSEHEN, PET (Pru Scott-Johns) and *The Queen's Sister* (Rachel Burke). Guest appearances have been in series like CASUALTY, KAVANAGH QC, MIDSOMER MURDERS, FOYLE'S WAR and MURDER IN SUBURBIA.

Harker, Susannah

(1965–)

London-born actress, the daughter of actress Polly Adams and sister of actress Caroline Harker. Her major TV credits have included *The Fear* (Linda Galton), CHANCER (Jo Franklyn), *Adam Bede* (Dinah Morris), HOUSE OF CARDS (Mattie Storin), PRIDE AND PREJUDICE (Jane Bennet), *Ultraviolet* (Angie), *Heat of the Sun* (Emma Fitzgerald), MURDER IN MIND and WAKING THE DEAD. She is married to actor Iain Glen.

Harlech Television

See *HTV*.

Harper, Gerald

(1929–)

Smooth-talking actor and radio presenter, the epitome of a country gent when portraying HADLEIGH, a character given his own series after appearances in *Gazette*. Earlier, Harper had been the more flamboyant ADAM ADAMANT, a frozen Edwardian adventurer reawakened in the Swinging Sixties. Although a number of smaller TV parts had come his way pre-*Adamant* (in series such as SKYPORT), and Harper had also guested in action series like THE AVENGERS and THE CHAMPIONS, since *Hadleigh* he has concentrated on radio and stage work, although a recent cameo role was in the sitcom *Mr Charity*.

Harpers West One ✶✶

UK (ATV) Drama. ITV 1961–3

Mike Gilmore	**Tristram Jellinek**
Edward Cruickshank	**Graham Crowden**
Harriet Carr	**Jan Holden**
Aubrey Harper	**Arthur Hewlett**
Albert Fisher	**Frederick Peisley**
Jackie Webb	**Pauline Stroud**
Julie Wheeler	**Vivian Pickles**
Roger Pike	**Norman Bowler**
Oliver Backhouse	**Philip Latham**
Philip Nash	**Bernard Horsfall**
Frances Peters	**Jayne Muir**
Jeff Tyson	**Gordon Ruttan**
Susan Sullivan	**Wendy Richard**

Creators **John Whitney, Geoffrey Bellman**
Producers **Hugh Rennie, Rex Firkin, Royston Morley**

● ***Behind the scenes at a fictional London department store.***

'Shopping with the lid off', as the programme blurb put it, *Harpers West One* focused on events in the lives of the team at Harpers department store in the West End. From customer liaison to personal liaisons, this series looked at all aspects of life in the store, but lasted a mere two seasons. Among the major players were PR man Mike Gilmore, staff controller Edward Cruickshank, personnel officer Harriet Carr, chairman Aubrey Harper and, in later episodes, secretary Susan Sullivan. It was co-created by future IBA Director-General John Whitney. *Harpers West One* was also responsible for one of 1961's biggest hit singles, 'Johnny Remember Me' by John Leyton, who turned up in the series playing the character Johnny St Cyr.

Harriott, Ainsley

(1957–)

Flamboyant, London-born TV chef fronting series like *Can't Cook, Won't Cook, Ainsley's Barbecue Bible, Ainsley's Meals in Minutes, Ainsley's Big Cook Out, Party of a Lifetime* and *Ainsley's Gourmet Express*, after making his TV cooking debut on *Good Morning with Anne and Nick* and following this up with spots on FOOD AND DRINK. He has also been a regular competitor (later host) in *Ready, Steady, Cook* and fronted *The Hidden Camera Show*. His lively presentation recalls his previous part-time career as a stand-up comedian at The Comedy Store while working shifts as a sous-chef (which led to his supporting Bobby Davro in the series *Davro*). In his catering past, Harriott was head chef at Lord's cricket ground's famous Long Room for nine years. He is the son of pianist Chester Harriott.

Harris, Rolf

CBE (1930–)

Bearded Australian TV personality, a musician, singer, comedian and painter rolled into one. Former Junior Backstroke Champion of Australia, Harris arrived in the UK in 1952 to study art but soon took up showbiz as a career, making his TV debut in WHIRLIGIG alongside his animated drawing board, Willoughby. In 1959 he appeared with Tony Hancock in HANCOCK'S HALF HOUR and in the same year continued in children's TV with *Musical Box*, an animated nursery rhyme show, made with Peter Firmin. During the early 1960s Rolf's regular partner was Coojee Bear, a koala puppet. From 1967 Harris starred in his own Saturday night variety show, inevitably conjuring up a giant painting (using large pots of paint and decorating brushes) to illustrate one of his novel songs. Viewers could also count on odd musical instruments, be they didgeridoos, wobble boards, piano accordions or Stylophones. In the 1980s he hosted *Rolf Harris's Cartoon Time* and in the 1990s he began a new lease of life as presenter of ANIMAL HOSPITAL, moving on to *Zoo Watch Live, Rolf's Amazing World of Animals* and *Test Your Pet*. Among his other series have been *Rolf's Walkabout, Rolf on Saturday, OK?, Hey Presto, It's Rolf, Rolf's Here! OK?* and *Rolf's Cartoon Club*. A more recent credit has been *Rolf on Art*, in which he introduced viewers to great painters and their masterpieces, and he followed this up with *Star Portraits with Rolf Harris*, in which celebrities posed for professional artists, and *Rolf on African Art*.

Harris, Susan

American comedy writer (on sitcoms like ALL IN THE FAMILY and THE PARTRIDGE FAMILY) who broke through in the 1970s by creating SOAP and its spin-off, BENSON. In the 1980s and 1990s she was responsible for THE GOLDEN GIRLS, *The Golden Palace*, NURSES and EMPTY NEST, all made by Witt-Thomas-Harris, the production company she founded with her husband, Paul Junger Witt, and another partner, Tony Thomas.

Harrison, Kathleen

(1892–1995)

Veteran British actress, fond of Cockney charlady roles, even though she was born in Lancashire. Her big TV success came in 1966, after a lengthy career in films (most notably in the *Huggett* series), when she was cast as MRS THURSDAY, a cleaner who inherited a fortune and a controlling interest in a large company. After that, her appearances were confined to guest spots in series like DANGER UXB and a couple of Dickens adaptations (including the 1978 version of *Our Mutual Friend* as Henrietta Boffin), having turned down the part of EDNA, THE INEBRIATE WOMAN, which won Patricia Hayes much acclaim.

Harry and the Hendersons ✶✶

US (Amblin/Universal) Situation Comedy. BBC 1 1991–5
(US: Syndicated 1990–3)

Harry	**Kevin Peter Hall**
	Dawan Scott
	Brian Steele
George Henderson	**Bruce Davison**
Nancy Henderson	**Molly Cheek**
Ernie Henderson	**Zachary Bostrom**
Sara Henderson	**Carol-Ann Plante**
Samantha Glick	**Gigi Rice**
Tiffany Glick	**Cassie Cole**
Walter Potter	**David Coburn**
Bret Douglas	**Noah Blake**
Darcy Payne	**Courtney Peldon**
Hilton Woods	**Mark Dakota Robinson**

Executive Producer **Lin Oliver**

A family takes in a 'missing link' as a pet.

The Henderson family is enjoying a vacation in the woodlands of America's Pacific Northwest when their car hits a strange creature. It turns out to be a 'sasquatch', otherwise known as a 'bigfoot' – an eight-foot-tall ape-like missing segment of the human evolutionary chain. They take the gentle giant home to Seattle to recuperate and, when ten-year-old Ernie wants to keep him, parents George and Nancy acquiesce. Apart from 17-year-old sister Sara, the only other people in the know about Harry's existence are TV reporter neighbour Samantha Glick, her daughter Tiffany and biologist Walter Potter, and humour comes from the family's attempts to keep Harry's presence under wraps and the well-meaning but clumsy ape's endless domestic disasters. New characters are introduced as the series progresses: Bret Douglas is Nancy's brother who moves in with the Hendersons, and Darcy Payne is the girl with designs on young Ernie. By the end of the series' run, the Hendersons' secret is out, however, and Harry has become a local celebrity. The man inside the bigfoot suit changed twice: original actor Kevin Peter Hall (who had played the same part in the 1987 film *Bigfoot and the Hendersons* – the only member of the film cast carried over to the TV version) died after one series and was replaced by Dawan Scott and then Brian Steele. Former HAPPY DAYS star Scott Baio directed some episodes.

Harry O ✶✶

US (Warner Brothers) Detective Drama. BBC 1 1974–7
(US: ABC 1974–6)

Harry Orwell	**David Janssen**
Det. Lt. Manny Quinlan	**Henry Darrow**
Lt. K. C. Trench	**Anthony Zerbe**
Sgt Don Roberts	**Paul Tulley**
Lester Hodges	**Les Lannom**
Dr Fong	**Keye Luke**

Creator **Howard Rodman**
Executive Producer **Jerry Thorpe**
Producers **Robert E. Thompson, Robert Dozier, Buck Houghton, Alex Beaton**

A retired cop lives in a beach shack and works as a private detective.

Former marine Harry Orwell has been pensioned out of the police force after being shot in the back. Despite constant pain from a bullet lodged in his body, he still works as a private detective, taking on cases that both arouse his interest and supplement his income. A drop-out among detectives, the grumpy, whisky-swilling Orwell is, all the same, a lot more dependable than his temperamental car, which forces him to make good use of public transport. Based in San Diego, and living in a beach-front house, he works closely with his by-the-book former colleague Lt. Manny Quinlan, of the local police; but when Quinlan is killed off Orwell moves to Santa Monica. Here, life is even less comfortable, as Harry has to deal with the sarcastic Lt. Trench.

Actress Farrah Fawcett made her TV debut in this series, appearing as Orwell's next-door neighbour.

Harry's Game ✶✶✶

UK (Yorkshire) Thriller. ITV 1982
DVD: Network

Capt. Harry James Brown	**Ray Lonnen**
Davidson	**Benjamin Whitrow**
Bannen	**Nicholas Day**
Billy Downes	**Derek Thompson**
Theresa McCorrigan	**Linda Robson**
Seamus Duffryn	**Charles Lawson**
Minister of Defence	**Denys Hawthorne**
Col. George Frost	**Geoffrey Chater**
Capt. Arthur Fairclough	**Andy Abrahams**
Insp. Howard Rennie	**Sean Caffrey**
Mrs Downes	**Margaret Shevlin**
Josephine Laverty	**Gil Brailey**
Frankie	**Christopher Whitehouse**

Writer **Gerald Seymour**
Executive Producer **David Cunliffe**
Producer **Keith Richardson**

An army captain infiltrates terrorist ranks to track down a killer.

This three-part thriller, screened on consecutive nights, centres on 34-year-old Captain Harry Brown, a specialist called up on the orders of the Prime Minister (against the advice of military and local experts) to go undercover in Northern

Ireland. Born in Portadown (and therefore knowing the territory) and with wide military experience under his belt, Brown's mission is to mingle with the IRA and to hunt down the assassin of government minister Henry Danby. The tense, cat-and-mouse action was penned by former ITN reporter Gerald Seymour from his own novel, with the haunting theme song a hit for Clannad in 1982.

Hart, Tony

(1925–)

Maidstone-born children's TV artist and presenter of VISION ON, the programme for youngsters with hearing difficulties. He subsequently gained his own series, *Take Hart*, HARTBEAT and *The Artbox Bunch*, although some of his early work was as operator of *Quackers* in Ray Alan's *Tich and Quackers*. He also appeared in the long-running series WHIRLIGIG and *Playbox*, and drew the Packi adventures for BLUE PETER in the late 1950s (as well as designing the BLUE PETER ship logo).

Hart of the Yard ✶

US (Universal) Situation Comedy. ITV 1980–1 (US: ABC 1980)

Det. Insp. Roger Hart	**Ron Moody**
Det. Jennifer Dempsey	**Cassie Yates**
Lt. Vince de Gennaro	**Michael Durrell**
Det. Jacobi	**Victor Brandt**
Det. Ramsey	**Renny Roker**
Det. Grauer	**Tom Williams**

Creators **Arne Sultan, Chris Hayward**
Executive Producer **Norman Barasch**

● ***The misadventures of a Scotland Yard detective on secondment in San Francisco.***

Det. Insp. Roger Hart is a man of many talents in this half-hour comedy series – an accomplished swordsman, a master of disguise, an explosives specialist and more. Sadly, most of these skills are hidden beneath a veneer of gross clumsiness. When he is offered a tour of duty with the San Francisco Police Department, such ineptness, combined with his over-refined English mannerisms, render him an appalling ambassador for the British police service. His boss, Lt. de Gennaro, in desperation pairs him with another 'difficult' officer, Det. Jennifer Dempsey, in San Francisco's 22nd Precinct, but the mishaps just keep on coming. This US-made sitcom (known Stateside as *Nobody's Perfect*, but retitled in the UK because of the Elaine Strich/Richard Griffiths sitcom of the same name) failed to find an audience in America and was cancelled after just ten episodes.

Hart to Hart ✶✶

US (Aaron Spelling) Detective Drama. ITV 1980–5 (US: ABC 1979–84)
DVD: Columbia TriStar (Region 1 only)

Jonathan Hart	**Robert Wagner**
Jennifer Hart	**Stefanie Powers**
Max	**Lionel Stander**

Creator **Sidney Sheldon**
Executive Producers **Aaron Spelling, Leonard Goldberg**

● ***A self-made millionaire and his journalist wife spice up their life by chasing crooks.***

Jonathan Hart, head of Jonathan Hart Industries, and his wife, Jennifer (a former world-famous journalist), live in a mansion in Bel-Air, where they have everything they need – except excitement. They don't need to work, so, to add some zest to their sad, pampered lives, they spend most of their time dashing around the world in a private jet, acting as a pair of amateur sleuths. They are supported by Max, their gruff, wrinkled chauffeur, and their dog, Freeway.

The series was created by novelist Sidney Sheldon and borrowed heavily from *The Thin Man* films of the 1930s and 1940s, which starred William Powell and Myrna Loy as Nick and Nora Charles.

Hartbeat

See *Vision On*.

Hartnell, William

(1908–75)

London-born actor, for ever remembered as the first DOCTOR WHO, playing the role as a mysterious, tetchy, headstrong old man in an Edwardian frock-coat. He stayed with the series from its beginnings in 1963 to 1966, when a combination of dissatisfaction with the series and illness saw him leave. He made one further appearance in the series, in the story called 'The Three Doctors', in which Jon Pertwee's version was given the assistance of his previous incarnations. Previously, Hartnell had starred in THE ARMY GAME, as the blustery Sgt Major Bullimore, a similar performance to his Sgt Grimshaw in the film *Carry On Sergeant* (just one of over 60 films he made). One of Hartnell's last TV performances was in the anthology series CRIME OF PASSION.

Harty, Russell

(1934–88)

Northern presenter and chat show host who worked his way from schoolteaching and producing BBC radio arts programmes to national status through shows such as *Russell Harty Plus* and *Harty*. Along the way, his distinctive 'you are, are you not?' style of questioning was much mimicked. One of his earliest production (and presentation) successes was AQUARIUS in 1969, and Harty continued in front of the cameras for a series of chat shows for LWT (*Eleven Plus*, which became *Russell Harty Plus*). He switched channels in 1980 and gained his own peak-time slot on BBC 2 with the show *Russell Harty*. In one famous instance, model/singer Grace Jones whacked him about the head, believing he was ignoring her. Among his other credits were *Saturday Night People* (with Janet Street-Porter and Clive James, for the London ITV region), *All About Books*, SONGS OF PRAISE, *Harty Goes to Hollywood*, *Russell Harty at the Seaside* and *Favourite Things*. Harty died in 1988 of hepatitis, an illness he picked up while filming a series on the Grand Tour of Europe.

Harvey, Jonathan

(1968–)

Liverpool-born writer, responsible for GIMME GIMME GIMME, *Birthday Girl*, *Von Trapped*, *Best Friends*, *The Big Brother Panto*, and episodes of CORONATION STREET, MURDER MOST HORRID, AT HOME WITH THE BRAITHWAITES, *Spine Chillers* and *Twisted Tales*.

Hass:

HANS (1919–) and LOTTE (1929–)

Austrian husband-and-wife diving team who pioneered underwater filming for television in the 1950s and 1960s. In 1956 they brought the wonders of the deep to BBC viewers in *Diving to Adventure*, although their longer-running series was *The Undersea World of Adventure*. Their films were dubbed into German, as well as English, to cover both markets. In 1966 Hans presented a different kind of nature programme. Entitled *Man*, it looked at the behaviour of the human race as if observed by outsiders.

Hasselhoff, David

(1952–)

American actor who shot to fame as co-star (with a car!) of KNIGHT RIDER, playing do-gooder Michael Knight. After four years behind the wheel of the world's cleverest motor, Hasselhoff moved to the seaside to star in the hugely popular BAYWATCH, as lifeguard Lt. Mitch Buchannon. When the network decided to drop the series, Hasselhoff used his own money to produce more episodes under the title of *New Baywatch* and sold them into syndication. These were followed by a detective spin-off, *Baywatch Nights*. His earlier TV career included guest spots in THE LOVE BOAT and POLICE STORY, as well as a seven-year run in a US daytime soap, *The Young and the Restless*.

Have Gun Will Travel ★★★

US (CBS) Western. ITV 1959–64 (US: CBS 1957–63)
DVD: Paramount (Region 1 only)

Paladin .... **Richard Boone**
Hey Boy .... **Kam Tong**
Hey Girl .... **Lisa Lu**

● ***A mysterious Wild West troubleshooter hires himself out to those seeking justice.***

Paladin is an enigmatic figure. A cultured, well-educated former West Point student, he now lives at the classy Hotel Carlton in San Francisco. A loner, dressed menacingly in black, he appears cynical and somewhat threatening, but he is also warm and sensitive at the same time, a good man at heart. His work, after all, involves righting wrongs – even if it is for a fee. His love of the good things in life means that he needs to earn his keep, and he operates as a bodyguard, a courier, a private detective, or whatever is asked of him. But, although his gun is for hire, the inscrutable Paladin is a man of principle and is even known to turn on his employers if it appears that they are the real bad guys. He is a slick operator and far removed from the other, rough-and-ready ranch-bound TV cowboys of his time.

'Paladin' means 'knightly hero' and is a name given to the knight chess piece, which appears in white on Paladin's holster and also on his calling-card, which bears the words 'Have Gun, Will Travel . . . Wire Paladin, San Francisco'. Any wires received are delivered by Hey Boy, the Chinese hotel hand (replaced by Hey Girl for a short period). Duane Eddy had a UK hit with an instrumental version of the theme song, 'The Ballad of Paladin', in 1962.

Have I Got News for You ★★★★

UK (Hat Trick) Comedy Quiz. BBC 2 1990–2000/BBC 1 2000–
DVD: VCI

Angus Deayton, Paul Merton, Ian Hislop

Producers **Harry Thompson, Colin Swash, Richard Wilson, Giles Pilbrow, Nick Martin, Steve Doherty, Rebecca Papworth, Jo Bunting**

● ***Ultra-topical current affairs satire/quiz.***

The television version of Radio 4's *The News Quiz, Have I Got News for You* is a mock contest between comedian Paul Merton (for one season replaced by stand-in captains owing to other commitments) and *Private Eye* editor Ian Hislop, each accompanied by celebrity guests from the worlds of entertainment, journalism or politics. The format relies heavily on the speed of thought and quick wit of its contestants (not to mention a little forward planning) as they adlib answers and jokes to various clips about the week's events. Blacked-out words in newspaper headlines, odd ones out and a caption competition are regular features. Comics such as Alexei Sayle, Vic Reeves and Frank Skinner have been called in as team members, as have writers like Andrew Morton and Will Self, and TV folk like Anne Robinson, Jonathan Ross and Trevor McDonald. Among the political guests have been Neil Kinnock, Cecil Parkinson, Charles Kennedy, Ken Livingstone, Boris Johnson and Sir Rhodes Boyson. When Roy Hattersley failed to show up, his place alongside Paul Merton was taken by a tub of lard. Even though scoring is totally haphazard, it is Hislop's team that usually loses. Events were chaired by Angus Deayton until tabloid exposures of his private life led to his sacking in 2002 and replacement by guest hosts, and he contributed as much ribald and risqué humour as the panellists themselves. Thankfully, by prerecording the show the night before transmission, the slanderous bits have been cut out – allegedly.

Havers, Nigel

(1949–)

One of TV's aristocratic smoothies, Nigel Havers, son of the late former Attorney-General Sir Michael Havers, has seldom been short of television work. From early appearances in dramas such as UPSTAIRS, DOWNSTAIRS, SHABBY TIGER, *Black Arrow* and *Nicholas Nickleby*, Havers moved on to THE GLITTERING PRIZES, PENNIES FROM HEAVEN (salesman Conrad Baker), NANCY ASTOR (Bobbie Shaw) and WINSTON CHURCHILL – THE WILDERNESS YEARS (Randolph Churchill). He starred as Paul Craddock in A HORSEMAN RIDING BY, Roy Calvert in STRANGERS AND BROTHERS and Dr Tom Latimer in DON'T WAIT UP. He also took the title role (Ralph Gorse) in THE CHARMER, played one of THE GOOD GUYS (Guy McFadyean), was Hugh Fleming in *A Perfect Hero* and Richard in the thriller *Element of Doubt*, and in 1998 succeeded Nigel Le Vaillant as star of DANGERFIELD (Dr Jonathan Paige). He also headlined in *Chiller, The Heart Surgeon* (Alex Marsden), *Gentleman Thief* (A. J. Raffles), *Manchild* (Terry) and MURDER IN MIND, and has hosted *OK! TV*. Among his other credits have been *A Raging Calm*, AN ENGLISHMAN'S CASTLE (Mark Ingram), *Coming Out, Unity, Goodbye Darling, After the Party*, CATHERINE COOKSON'S *The Glass Virgin* (Edmund Lagrange), *A Little Princess*, MURDER MOST HORRID, LITTLE BRITAIN, BORN AND BRED (Henry Williamson) and *Open Wide* (Peter Hillman).

Hawaii Five-O ✶✶

US (CBS/Leonard Freeman) Police Drama. ITV 1970–82 (US: CBS 1968–80)

Det. Steve McGarrett .... **Jack Lord**
Det. Danny 'Danno' Williams . **James MacArthur**
Det. Chin Ho Kelly .... **Kam Fong**
Det. Kono Kalakaua .... **Zulu**
Governor Philip Grey .... **Richard Denning**
Wo Fat .... **Khigh Dhiegh**
Det. Ben Kokua .... **Al Harrington**
Che Fong .... **Harry Endo**
Doc Bergman .... **Al Eben**
May .... **Maggi Parker**
Jenny Sherman .... **Peggy Ryan**
Duke Lukela .... **Herman Wedemeyer**
Attorney General John Manicote .... **Glenn Cannon**
James 'Kimo' Carew .... **William Smith**
Lori Wilson .... **Sharon Farrell**
Tom 'Truck' Kealoha .... **Moe Keale**

Creator/Executive Producer **Leonard Freeman**
Producers **Bill Finnegan, Bob Sweeney, Philip Leacock, Richard Newton, Douglas Green, B. W. Sandefur**

The cases of a special police unit and its self-righteous leader on the islands of Hawaii.

Five-O is not your normal police force. These guys (a special division of the Hawaiian State Police) work separately from the Honolulu Police Department and are directly answerable to the Governor. They operate from the Iolani Palace, the supposed seat of the Hawaiian Government, and their tight-lipped, no-nonsense boss is Steve McGarrett.

The blue-suited McGarrett loathes crooks and seems to have no other passion in life. He is ably supported by his main men, 'Danno' Williams ('Book 'em, Danno' became a catch-phrase) and Chin Ho Kelly. Another original colleague, Kono Kalakaua, is written out after a few years, although most of the cast stay with the show for much of its very long run. When Williams and Kelly eventually leave, new officers like Lori Wilson, Truck Kealoha and 'Kimo' Carew are added to see the series through to its close.

Five-O, being independent, is able to avoid the petty bureaucracies of normal police work. Its brief is to keep this tropical paradise clean, to mop up vermin that disrupt the life of Honolulu and the other islands. Consequently, McGarrett and his boys target spivs, hoodlums and, more purposefully, the organized underworld, especially an elusive oriental villain by the name of Wo Fat.

As well as taking the star role, Jack Lord was also heavily involved in the series behind the scenes. He became a Hawaiian resident and, to many viewers, became synonymous with the islands.

Hawaiian Eye ✶

US (Warner Brothers) Detective Drama. ITV 1960–3 (US: ABC 1959–63)

Thomas Jefferson (Tom) Lopaka .... **Bob Conrad**
Tracy Steele .... **Anthony Eisley**
Cricket Blake .... **Connie Stevens**
Kazuo Kim .... **Poncie Ponce**
Lt. Quon .... **Mel Prestidge**
Greg MacKenzie .... **Grant Williams**
Moke .... **Doug Mossman**
Philip Barton .... **Troy Donahue**

Executive Producer **William T. Orr**
Producers **Stanley Niss, Charles Hoffman, Ed Jurist**

A trio of detectives work from a Hawaiian hotel.

Another product off the 1950s Warner Brothers detective series conveyor belt, this offering focuses on the Hawaiian Eye agency, a private investigation firm that operates out of the swish Hawaiian Village Hotel in Honolulu. Its main men are Tom Lopaka and Tracy Steele, with Greg MacKenzie joining a year after the series begins. Cricket Blake is their attractive singer/photographer friend and also seen is Kim, a zany local cab driver, who strums a ukulele and drags his whole family into the firm's investigations. When actor Anthony Eisley left the series, Troy Donahue, fresh from another Warner Brothers clone, *Surfside 6*, became part of the team, playing the hotel's social secretary, Philip Barton. Also seen from time to time was Stu Bailey (Efrem Zimbalist Jr) from the show's sister series, 77 SUNSET STRIP. The theme music was composed by Mack David and Jerry Livingston.

Hawes, Keeley

(1977–)

London-born actress prominent on TV since the mid-1990s, taking major roles in dramas such as KARAOKE (Linda Langer), *The Moonstone* (Rachel Verinder), *The Beggar Bride* (Angela Harper), OUR MUTUAL FRIEND (Lizzie Hexham), *The Blonde Bombshell* (Diana Dors), *The Inspector Pitt Mysteries*, MURDER IN MIND, OTHELLO (Dessie Brabant), WIVES AND DAUGHTERS (Cynthia Kirkpatrick), SPOOKS (Zoe Reynolds), *A Is for Acid* (Gillian Rogers), TIPPING THE VELVET (Kitty Butler), *Lucky Jim* (Christine Callaghan), CANTERBURY TALES (Emily), DATE RAPE: SEX AND LIES (Kate), *Macbeth* (Ella Macbeth) and *Under the Greenwood Tree* (Fancy Day). Guest appearances have come in PIE IN THE SKY and AGATHA CHRISTIE'S MARPLE. She is married to actor Matthew Macfadyen.

Hawk, Jeremy

(Cedric Lange; 1918–2002)

A former music hall straight man to stars like Arthur Askey, Arthur Haynes and Norman Wisdom, South Africa-born Jeremy Hawk also supported Benny Hill and American comic Sid Caesar on TV, but he found his niche in the early days of television as a quiz master. As host of CRISS CROSS QUIZ and *Junior Criss Cross Quiz* from 1957 to 1962, he was a familiar face in most households. He then presented the improvisation comedy *Impromptu*, but found little TV work later (save guest spots in THE NEW AVENGERS and THE PROFESSIONALS, and a memorable Cadbury's Whole Nut commercial in the 1970s: 'Nuts who-ole Ha-azelnuts; Cadbury's take 'em and they cover 'em in chocolate') and returned to the stage. Hawk was the father of actress Belinda Lang, with whom he briefly appeared in 2 POINT 4 CHILDREN. Another guest appearance was in AGATHA CHRISTIE'S POIROT.

Hawkesworth, John

(1920–2003)

British writer/producer, a one-time Rank film scriptwriter, chiefly remembered for period pieces such as UPSTAIRS,

DOWNSTAIRS and THE DUCHESS OF DUKE STREET (also as creator). In addition, he produced and co-scripted THE GOLD ROBBERS and the sitcom *In for a Penny*, created/adapted *The Short Stories of Conan Doyle*, BY THE SWORD DIVIDED, DANGER UXB and THE FLAME TREES OF THIKA, and worked on episodes of THE ADVENTURES OF SHERLOCK HOLMES, CRIME OF PASSION and CAMPION.

Hawkeye and the Last of the Mohicans ✶

Canada (Normandie) Adventure. ITV 1957
DVD: Platinum Disc (Region 1 only)

Nat 'Hawkeye' Cutler .... **John Hart**
Chingachgook .... **Lon Chaney Jr**

Producer **Sigmund Neufeld**

● ***Escapades in the American wilderness with a trapper and his Indian comrade.***

This drama series, loosely based on the novel by James Fenimore Cooper, features Nat Cutler, known familiarly as 'Hawkeye', a trapper, fur trader and scout for the US cavalry. His adventures in the northern frontierland, and encounters with the Huron Indians during the 1750s, are shared by his redskin blood-brother, Chingachgook. Star John Hart had previously enjoyed brief TV fame when temporarily taking over the role of the LONE RANGER from Clayton Moore.

Hawkins, Peter

(1924–2006)

London-born actor best known for voicing children's animated characters. His vocal talents were put to good use in programmes like FLOWER POT MEN, THE WOODENTOPS, CAPTAIN PUGWASH, SIR PRANCELOT, TIN TIN, RAINBOW, NOAH AND NELLY, *The Perishers* and SUPERTED; and Hawkins also spoke for DOCTOR WHO's Daleks and Cybermen. In vision, he appeared in WHIRLIGIG and *Stranger from Space*, among other programmes.

Hawthorne, Sir Nigel

CBE (1929–2001)

Coventry-born, South Africa-raised actor, acclaimed for his tongue-twisting performances as Sir Humphrey Appleby in YES, MINISTER and *Yes, Prime Minister*. Hawthorne also played Pierre Curie in MARIE CURIE, Dr Grantly in THE BARCHESTER CHRONICLES and the sadistic examiner of would-be taxi-drivers in Jack Rosenthal's play *The Knowledge*. Among his other credits were EDWARD AND MRS SIMPSON (Walter Monckton), *Warrior Queen, The Hunchback of Notre Dame, A Tale of Two Cities, The World Cup – A Captain's Tale, Jukes of Piccadilly* (Brinsley Jukes), *Jenny's War*, MAPP AND LUCIA (Georgie Pillson), *The Miser, The Fragile Heart* (heart surgeon Edgar Pascoe), *Victoria and Albert* (Lord Melbourne) and the *Everyman* documentary *Canterbury* (presenting a history of Canterbury Cathedral). Over the years, he also guested in series like DAD'S ARMY, THOMAS AND SARAH, HADLEIGH and GOING STRAIGHT.

Hayes, Melvyn

(1935 –)

Diminutive English actor, initially a jockey. As a teenager he played one of the boys in BILLY BUNTER OF GREYFRIARS SCHOOL and also in the 1950s appeared in QUATERMASS *II*, plus other dramas like *The Silver Sword* (Edek Balicki). He was the Artful Dodger in BBC's 1962 adaptation of *Oliver Twist*, and in 1971 he was seen as Albert, the grown-up, in HERE COME THE DOUBLE DECKERS. Hayes was also cast as Gregory in the Jimmy Edwards comedy *Sir Yellow*, and played Melvyn Didsbury in the kids' series POTTER'S PICTURE PALACE, as well as providing the voice of Skeleton for the SUPERTED cartoons. Other early roles included assorted crooks in DIXON OF DOCK GREEN and Z CARS, and supporting roles in *Mr Pastry* and THE SEVEN FACES OF JIM. However, by far his most successful part has been as Bombardier 'Gloria' Beaumont, the drag artist in IT AIN'T HALF HOT MUM. He has since made guest appearances in DROP THE DEAD DONKEY, DOCTORS and EASTENDERS (Mr Rawlins), was part of the team of senior comic actors in *Revolver* and provided voices for the animation *Pongwiffy*. His second wife was actress Wendy Padbury and they are the parents of actress Charlie Hayes (Ruth in WYCLIFFE).

Hayes, Patricia

OBE (1909–98)

London-born actress, on stage from the age of 12 and generally seen as a foil or support to comedians like Arthur Askey, Tony Hancock, Arthur Haynes, Eric Sykes, Ken Dodd and Benny Hill. In contrast, her dramatic skills were brought to the fore in an award-winning PLAY FOR TODAY, EDNA, THE INEBRIATE WOMAN. Hayes was also seen as neighbour Griselda Wormold in HUGH AND I, Lillian in *The Trouble with Lillian*, Mrs Basket in LAST OF THE BASKETS, traffic warden Mrs Cantaford in SPOONER'S PATCH, mother Alice Tripp in MARJORIE AND MEN, Old Pat in THE LADY IS A TRAMP and in programmes as varied as *Educated Evans*, TILL DEATH US DO PART (Min), *The World of Beachcomber, The Corn is Green*, THE AVENGERS, THE VERY MERRY WIDOW, *Mr Pye, The Witches and the Grinnygog* (Miss Bendybones), *Screen One's The Lord of Misrule* and CASUALTY. Her son is actor Richard O'Callaghan.

Haygarth, Tony

(1945–)

Liverpudlian actor seen in scores of dramas and comedies, particularly ROSIE (PC Wilmot), KINVIG (Des Kinvig), OUR FRIENDS IN THE NORTH (Roy Johnson) and WHERE THE HEART IS (Vic Snow). Other credits have come in WHATEVER HAPPENED TO THE LIKELY LADS?, I, CLAUDIUS, THE GHOSTS OF MOTLEY HALL, SHOESTRING, HARDWICKE HOUSE (Harry Savage), LOVEJOY, *Farrington of the FO* (Fidel Sanchez), *All Change* (Brian Oldfield), *The December Rose* (Tom Gosling), SCULLY (Dracula), EL C.I.D. (Frank), THE BORROWERS (Mildeye), MAKING OUT (Kip), A TOUCH OF FROST, PRESTON FRONT, BETWEEN THE LINES, CHILLER, SHARPE, PIE IN THE SKY, INSPECTOR MORSE, KAVANAGH QC, MIDSOMER MURDERS, MURDER IN MIND, *Fields of Gold* (George Hurst), HORNBLOWER, *The Mayor of Casterbridge* (Solomon Longways), FOYLE'S WAR, DOCTORS, THE ROYAL, THE BILL, *The Afternoon Play, The Rotters Club* (Jack Forrest), *Twenty Thousand Streets under the Sky* (Governor), *Class of '76* (DS Pritchard), THE INSPECTOR LYNLEY MYSTERIES, BLEAK HOUSE (Gridley) and *Under the Greenwood Tree* (Reuben).

Haynes, Arthur

(1914–66)

One of TV's first star comedians, former radio comic Arthur Haynes specialized in social nuisance characters like the manipulative, silent Oscar Pennyfeather and a disgruntled, bemedalled tramp. These appeared in *The Arthur Haynes Show* (written by Johnny Speight and co-starring Nicholas Parsons as his straight man), which was launched in 1956 after Haynes had stolen the spotlight in a series called *Strike a New Note* and had appeared in *The Charlie Chester Show*. He was still starring in his own series when he died suddenly in 1966.

Hazell ★★

UK (Thames) Detective Drama. ITV 1978–80
DVD: Network

James Hazel .... **Nicholas Ball**
'Choc' Minty .... **Roddy McMillan**
Cousin Tel .... **Desmond McNamara**
Graham Morris .... **Peter Bourke**

Creators **Terry Venables, Gordon Williams**
Producers **June Roberts, Tim Aspinall**

A crocked London policeman becomes a private eye.

When James Hazell is forced to retire from the police force in his early 30s because of a damaged ankle, he turns to drink and destroys his marriage. Reformed and dried out, he becomes a private investigator, helped by his cousin Tel, with his main sparring partner a Scottish CID officer named 'Choc' Minty.

Even if the series errs on the violent side, Hazell is a fun character, a Jack the Lad with a flair for the telling phrase. A true Cockney, he enjoys the glamour of his profession and bustles along in life, mixing it with the best, but not always coming out on top. In spoof *film noir* fashion, Hazell provides a commentary voice-over for each episode. The series was based on books by football manager Terry Venables and Gordon Williams, who also contributed to the TV version.

HDTV

(High Definition Television)

A system that produces sharper television pictures (up to 1,080 lines), more realistic colours and better sound than existing digital services. Analogue versions have been trialled for years in Japan, in particular, but only with the advent of digital technology and plasma screens has HDTV really taken off. HD-ready sets and HD receivers are required to view the new transmissions, which are now being offered by major broadcasters. However, unless programmes have been filmed in HD, viewers will see no benefit. American series like CSI: CRIME SCENE INVESTIGATION and LOST are already shot the new way, and BBC productions such as BLEAK HOUSE[2] and ROME have also been made in HD. The Corporation plans to make all new programmes in HD by 2010. Sports coverage is increasingly available in the new format.

He Knew He was Right ★★★

UK (BBC/WGBH Boston/Deep Indigo) Drama. BBC 1 2004
DVD: BBC Warner (Region 1 only)

Louis Trevelyan .... **Oliver Dimsdale**
Emily Trevelyan .... **Laura Fraser**
Col. Frederick Osborne .... **Bill Nighy**
Miss Jemima Stanbury .... **Anna Massey**
Sir Marmaduke Rowley .... **Geoffrey Palmer**
Nora Rowley .... **Christina Cole**
Lady Rowley .... **Geraldine James**
Lady Milborough .... **Jane Lapotaire**
Mr Glascock .... **Raymond Coulthard**
Hugh Stanbury .... **Stephen Campbell Moore**
Dorothy Stanbury .... **Caroline Martin**
Priscilla Stanbury .... **Amy Marston**
Mrs Stanbury .... **Joanna David**
Mr Gibson .... **David Tennant**
Martha .... **Maggie Ollerenshaw**
Mr Samuel Bozzle .... **Ron Cook**
Mrs Susan Bozzle .... **Patsy Palmer**
Camilla French .... **Claudia Blakley**
Arabella French .... **Fenella Woolgar**
Mrs French .... **Barbara Flynn**
Mr Oliphant Outhouse .... **John Alderton**
Mrs Outhouse .... **Lynn Farleigh**
Brooke Burgess .... **Matthew Goode**
Caroline Spalding .... **Anna-Louise Plowman**
Mr Crump .... **James Bolam**

Writer **Andrew Davies**
Producer **Nigel Stafford-Clark**

Suspicion, pride and jealousy combine to wreck a happy society marriage.

This first dramatization of a rather overlooked novel from 1869 by Anthony Trollope imbues 19th-century aristocratic life with more than a sprinking of modern-day woes. The story tells of a young married couple, Louis and Emily Trevelyan, whose domestic bliss is shattered by a sharp pin-prick of Othellian jealousy. When the rakish MP Colonel Osborne pays a visit on Emily, Louis is overcome with suspicion; when Emily stubbornly refuses to apologize for seeing her old family friend, their marriage irretrievably breaks down. Emily is first banished to Wells to stay with the Stanbury family, mother and sisters of Louis's best friend, journalist Hugh Stanbury, and when Osborne cheekily calls on her there, she is brought back to lodge with dour vicar Mr Outhouse in the East End of London. Meanwhile, Louis slides catastrophically off the rails. He kidnaps their young son and heads for Italy, leaving others to seek him out. Nora is Emily's young sister, who initially lives with the couple; Sir Marmaduke is Emily's blustering old father, a former governor of the Mandarin Islands; Miss Stanbury is Hugh's hard-headed, meddling maiden aunt; Mr Bozzle is the devious private detective Louis employs to tail his wife; Mr Glascock is Nora's wealthy suitor; and Camilla and Arabella French are two sisters vying for the attentions of slimy parson Mr Gibson, a man who himself takes a shine to Emily during her sojourn in the West Country.

Sumptuously staged in four parts, with location scenes shot in Italy and characters occasionally baring their souls directly to camera, *He Knew He was Right* is directed by Tom Vaughan.

Head, Anthony

(1954–)

British actor best known as Rupert Giles in BUFFY THE VAMPIRE SLAYER (billed as Anthony Stewart Head) and as Sebastian's Prime Minister in LITTLE BRITAIN, if not for the series of Gold Blend coffee adverts he shared with Sharon Mughan. He was also William Le Breton in LILLIE, Oliver Sampson in *VR.5*, James in *Manchild* and Chester Grant in MONARCH OF THE GLEN.

Other credits include roles in ENEMY AT THE DOOR, THE MALLENS, SECRET ARMY, BERGERAC, *Love in a Cold Climate*, C.A.T.S. EYES, HOWARDS' WAY, BOON, ROCKLIFFE'S BABIES, THE COMIC STRIP PRESENTS . . ., THE DETECTIVES, *Highlander*, *The Ghostbusters of East Finchley*, NYPD BLUE, JONATHAN CREEK, SILENT WITNESS, SPOOKS, MY FAMILY, NEW TRICKS, MURDER INVESTIGATION TEAM, ROSE AND MALONEY and *Hotel Babylon*. His brother is actor/singer Murray Head.

Head Over Heels ★★

UK (Carlton) Drama. ITV 1993

Gracie Ellis .... **Ann Bell**
Camilla De La Mer .... **Jackie Morrison**
Catherine Ellis .... **Sally Geoghegan**
Heather Brook .... **Diana Morrison**
Bernadette Brennan .... **Kathy Kiera Clarke**
Patsy Willoughby .... **Elena Ferrari**
Alice Willoughby .... **Jessica Lloyd**
Stella Dunn .... **Gemma Page**
Suni .... **Pinky Amadour**
Jack Ellis .... **Michael Thomas**
Jimmy Ellis .... **Ian Embleton**
Flora Dunn .... **Alison Skilbeck**
Daniel Dunn .... **Nicholas Haverson**

Creator **Jane Prowse**
Producers **Brian Eastham, Jane Prowse**

● ***The girls of a 1950s finishing school discover rock 'n' roll.***

The Gracie Ellis Academy of Elegance in Notting Hill Gate educates daughters of the *nouveaux riches* in the rules and conventions of high society, through lessons in deportment and etiquette. However, things are turned 'head over heels' with the arrival of new pupil Camilla De La Mer, a Scottish tearaway who brings rock 'n' roll to the school. She even converts the local café into a trendy hang-out called The Rockit. The girls skip classes and flout school rules once the rock 'n' roll bug bites, learning to express their own personalities and question the social conventions imposed upon them. *Head Over Heels* emphasized the novelty and fun of the 1950s. Underscored by a good assortment of rock 'n' roll tracks, it drew on dated filming techniques and nostalgic special effects to re-create the feel of the time. Jaunty Ealing comedy-type incidental music and archaic screen wipes linked the action, and a clever use of faded colour stock distinguished the series, which was Carlton's first drama contribution to the ITV network. The theme song was sung by Nick Haverson, who also played the part of aspiring vicar-turned-rock 'n' roll hero Daniel Dunn.

Health and Efficiency ★★

UK (BBC) Situation Comedy. BBC 1 1993–5

Dr Michael Jimson .... **Gary Olsen**
Dr Kate Russell .... **Felicity Montagu**
Rex Regis .... **Roger Lloyd Pack**
Diana Ewerts .... **Deborah Norton**
Dr Phil Brooke .... **Victor McGuire**
Sister Beth Williams .... **Adjoa Andoh**

Creator/Writer **Andrew Marshall**
Producer **Richard Boden**

● ***Doctors battle accountants in a comic struggle for the soul of the NHS.***

This two-series comedy, set in St James's General Hospital, arrived against a real-life backdrop of ever-tighter resources for the National Health Service and government pressure to find increased efficiencies within the system. Representing the new emphasis on money is administrator Diana Ewerts, a Thatcherite, save-money-at-all-costs, non-medical member of staff who is constantly at odds with the more caring doctors and nurses. Michael Jimson is the leading man amongst the medics, a gambler and the registrar leader of Surgical Team B, whose day-to-day working life is hindered by a failed relationship with fellow consultant Kate Russell (they were once engaged). Phil Brooke is the junior doctor delegated to do all the unpleasant work and his chaotic love life only adds to the stresses on the wards. More in tune with Diana (in more ways than one) is sour-faced surgeon Rex Regis, a man who will wield the scalpel at the drop of a hat if there's a bob or two in it. Twelve episodes were produced.

Healy, Tim

(1952–)

Geordie actor, familiar from a number of light comedy-dramas. It was as Denis in AUF WIEDERSEHEN, PET that Healy first grabbed the viewers' attention, although he had already appeared in programmes like CORONATION STREET, EMMERDALE FARM, MINDER, *The World Cup – A Captain's Tale* and WHEN THE BOAT COMES IN. His other credits have included A KIND OF LIVING (Brian Thompson), A PERFECT SPY, CRACKER, HEARTBEAT, TOM JONES (Mr Nightingale Sr), CATHERINE COOKSON'S *A Dinner of Herbs* (Mr Mulcaster), *The Lost World* (McArdle), *The Jury* (Eddie Fannon), PETER KAY'S PHOENIX NIGHTS, *Breeze Block* (Ralph Breeze), the kids' show *Tickle on the Tum*, DEAD MAN WEDS (Paul King), VIC AND BOB IN CATTERICK (Ian), *The All Star Comedy Show*, DALZIEL AND PASCOE, THE LAST DETECTIVE and *Murder Investigation Team*. Healy also headlined as expatriate Cockney Reg Toomer in THE BOYS FROM THE BUSH, Foxy in the dustbinmen comedy COMMON AS MUCK, Mr Collins in THE GRAND, seedy hotelier Harry Springer in HEARTBURN HOTEL, Bertie Masson in *Bostock's Cup* and Malcolm Cromer in the play *King Leek*. He was also narrator of *Disaster Masters*. He is married to actress Denise Welch.

Hearne, Richard

OBE (1909–79)

Acrobatic Richard Hearne was one of British TV's first clowns, playing the part of a nimble but accident-prone old man in numerous slapstick sketches. The character was Mr Pastry, complete with walrus moustache, long coat-tails and gold-rimmed spectacles perched half-way down the nose. Mr Pastry first appeared in one of Hearne's many stage performances and arrived on television in 1946. He went on to star in series such as *Mr Pastry's Progress*, *Leave It to Mr Pastry*, *Ask Mr Pastry* and *Mr Pastry's Pet Shop*, as well as guesting on CRACKERJACK and SUNDAY NIGHT AT THE LONDON PALLADIUM. Pre-Pastry, Hearne had featured in a number of early BBC comedy programmes. He also starred in several films.

Heartbeat ★★

UK (Yorkshire) Drama. ITV 1992–

PC/Sgt Nick Rowan .... **Nick Berry**
Dr Kate Rowan .... **Niamh Cusack**

Sgt Oscar Blaketon .... **Derek Fowlds**
Claude Jeremiah Greengrass .. **Bill Maynard**
Dr Alex Ferrenby .... **Frank Middlemass**
PC Alf Ventress .... **William Simons**
PC Phil Bellamy .... **Mark Jordon**
George Ward .... **Stuart Golland**
Gina Ward .... **Tricia Penrose**
Dr James Radcliffe .... **Peter Firth**
Maggie Bolton .... **Kazia Pelka**
Eileen Reynolds .... **Anne Stallybrass**
Jo Weston/Rowan .... **Juliette Gruber**
Bernie Scripps .... **Peter Benson**
Dr Neil Bolton .... **David Michaels**
PC/DC Mike Bradley .... **Jason Durr**
Sgt Raymond Craddock .... **Philip Franks**
Auntie Mary .... **Arbel Jones**
Jackie Lambert/Bradley .... **Fiona Dolman**
Andy Ryan .... **Martin Ledwith**
Vernon Scripps .... **Geoffrey Hughes**
Dr Tricia Summerbee .... **Clare Calbraith**
David Stockwell .... **David Lonsdale**
PC Tom Nicholson .... **Ryan Early**
Jenny Latimer .... **Sarah Tansey**
Sgt Dennis Merton .... **Duncan Bell**
Lord Ashfordly .... **Rupert Vansittart**
Dr Liz Merrick .... **Aislin McGuckin**
PC Steve Crane .... **James Carlton**
PC Rob Walker .... **Jonathan Kerrigan**
Rosie Cartwright .... **Vanessa Hehir**
Dr Helen Trent .... **Sophie Ward**
PC Geoff Younger .... **Steven Blakeley**
Sgt George Miller .... **John Duttine**
Peggy Armstrong .... **Gwen Taylor**

Creator **Johnny Byrne**
Executive Producer **Keith Richardson**
Producers **Stuart Doughty, Steve Lanning, Keith Richardson, Carol Wilks, Gerry Mill, Archie Tait**

Nostalgic drama about a constable patrolling a Yorkshire moorland beat.

Beginning in 1964, *Heartbeat* is the story of PC Nick Rowan and his doctor wife, Kate (the programme's title is derived from a combination of their two professions). Having left their London base to return to Kate's home area of the North Yorkshire moors, the Rowans take up residence in the police house in the village of Aidensfield, where Nick becomes the village bobby. He reports to the grouchy Sgt Blaketon at the Ashfordly police station, and his PC colleagues are the skiving, chain-smoking veteran, Alf Ventress, and the somewhat reckless Phil Bellamy. Kate becomes a partner in the Aidensfield general practice headed by old friend Alex Ferrenby and, following his death, she takes over as the village's only doctor. Tragedy strikes, however, when Kate dies shortly after giving birth to a daughter, Katie. Bane of Rowan's life is lovable rogue Claude Jeremiah Greengrass, who, with his loyal mutt, Alfred, is usually at the heart of some scam or other. George Ward, assisted by Gina, his trendy Liverpudlian niece, runs The Aidensfield Arms, the local pub. Later arrivals are district nurse Maggie Bolton, Nick's Auntie Eileen and schoolteacher Jo Weston, the new girl in the PC's life. Following their marriage, Nick's promotion to sergeant (when Blaketon retires to run the post office and later the pub) and the Rowans' subsequent departure from Aidensfield (Nick goes to Canada to become a Mountie, taking his family with him), attention focuses on new copper Mike Bradley. Freshly dispatched from the Met aboard a Triumph Bonneville motorbike, Bradley has a lot to learn about rural policing. Also new is Dr Neil Bolton, Maggie's former husband; Nick's replacement, Sgt Raymond Craddock; and Jackie Lambert, Mike's girlfriend. In later series, the role of village rascal is handed to Vernon Scripps, while new doctors are Tricia Summerbee, Liz Merrick and Helen Trent. PCs Nicholson, Crane and Walker, plus Sgts Merton and Miller, join the team at the nick.

Heartbeat was based on the *Constable* novels by Nicholas Rhea, the pen-name of former Yorkshire policeman Peter Walker. With its liberal use of contemporary pop hits and careful selection of period furniture and other items, this gentle, nostalgic drama attracted a huge audience. Buddy Holly's 'Heartbeat', sung by Nick Berry, was the programme's theme song. As a series cash-in, Nick Rowan's transatlantic adventure was chronicled in a one-off video production entitled *Heartbeat: Changing Places*, which was eventually screened by ITV in 1999. In 2003, a spin-off series called THE ROYAL, about a neighbouring cottage hospital, was launched by ITV 1, with cross-over appearances from *Heartbeat* characters.

Heartburn Hotel ★★

UK (BBC) Situation Comedy. BBC 1 1998; 2000

Harry Springer .... **Tim Healy**
Duggie Strachan .... **Clive Russell**
Simon Thorpe .... **Peter Gunn**
Mrs Muskett .... **Madaleine Moffatt**
Debbie .... **Zita Sattar**
Rina Mahony
Baker .... **Kim Wall**
Morgan .... **Ifan Huw Dafydd**
Scouse .... **Stephen Aintree**
Mr Chander A Singh .... **Kaleem Janjua**
Mrs Chander A Singh .... **Adlyn Ross**
Mr Hussan .... **Karzan Krekar**

Writers **John Sullivan, Steve Glover**
Producer **Gareth Gwenlan**

A run-down Birmingham hotel is a home for losers – including its management.

When ex-army chef Harry Springer (a Falklands veteran, as he proudly makes clear) splashed all his money into the Olympic Hotel in Smethwick, it was in anticipation of Birmingham winning the right to stage the 1992 Olympic Games. With the games going to Barcelona instead, Springer is now stuck with a crumbling establishment that, despite having bedrooms glamorously named after leading athletes, is little more than a doss house for the most unfortunate in society. Except that Harry does not quite see his guests in this light. While happy to accept their DSS rent cheques, he takes great pleasure in poking fun at the motley collection of unemployed people, asylum seekers and mentally sick who now have to call the Olympic their home. Such is the essence of this deliberately downbeat comedy. Another victim of the tight-fisted Springer's spite is his old army buddy, Duggie Strachan, a teacher and gambler who is so shy of women that his feet squelch with perspiration whenever he's in their company. Then there is Harry's anoraky nephew, Simon, who gets on everyone's nerves by banging on about his estranged wife. With plots arranged around visiting guests as well as the sad inmates, *Heartburn Hotel* ran to 13 episodes, including a Christmas special.

Hearts and Bones ✶✶

UK (United/BBC) Drama. BBC 1 2000–1

Emma Rose .... **Dervla Kirwan**
Richard Rose .... **Hugo Speer**
Louise Slaney .... **Amanda Holden**
Mark Rose .... **Damian Lewis**
Sinead Creagh .... **Rose Keegan**
Michael Owen .... **Andrew Scarborough**
Amanda Thomas .... **Sarah Parish**
Robbie Rose .... **Kieran O'Brien**
Sam Rose .... **Joel Pitts**
Donna Slaney .... **Anita Dobson**
Liz Booth .... **Pippa Guard**
Stuart Gee .... **Andrew Woodall**
Rachel Heath .... **Sylvestra Le Touzel**
Dominic Morris .... **Mark Bazeley**
James Norton .... **Lloyd Owen**
Hermann .... **Michael Fassbender**

Writer **Stewart Harcourt**
Producer **Sally Haynes**

● ***The complicated personal lives of a group of friends in London.***

Eight friends in their late twenties and early thirties have known each other for a long time, most since their schooldays in Coventry. Now they live in south London and remain close. However, trouble is brewing. Emma has lived with Mark for a number of years. They even have a young son, Sam. Despite the fact that their relationship is not as strong as it has been, they decide to get married. However, when Emma declares her passion for Mark's quiet brother, Rich, and receives an incriminating lovebite on her wedding day, the cat is well and truly among the pigeons. Other friends in the group can't help but be drawn into the drama, as well as coping with problems of their own. Rich's girlfriend is Louise, a beauty consultant, and their relationship is tested by the painful death of her mother. Amanda works as a parliamentary adviser but drives away her insecure partner, Michael, with her sharp tongue. Lone wolf Sinead is the slightly wacky friend to all but really fancies Mark. Eventually, the truth about Emma and Rich is revealed and Mark decides to walk away from her and the rest of the group. He is absent for the more upbeat series two (set three months later), in which he is replaced by James, a manipulative Labour councillor who makes advances to Amanda, Emma and Louise. Rich feels the weight of guilt after his brother's departure, Amanda looks like becoming a politician, but falls pregnant, and Louise, looking for greater social standing, joins the police force. Sinead, meanwhile, has met a German lover, Hermann, on holiday and he follows her back to London, with not-so-happy consequences. With surprises a-plenty and comic relief throughout, *Hearts and Bones* won acclaim for its portrayal of tangled personal relationships and the crises that strike those who discover they are not so young any longer. Thirteen episodes were produced.

Hearts of Gold ✶

UK (BBC) Entertainment. BBC 1 1988–96

Presenters **Esther Rantzen, Michael Groth, Joy Aldridge, Mike Smith, Carol Smillie, Mickey Hutton**

Creator **Esther Rantzen**
Producers **Bryher Scudamore, Richard Woolfe, Jane Elsdon-Dew, Nick Vaughan-Barratt**

● ***Deserving members of the public receive achievement awards.***

Heart-warming, tear-jerking or, to some, just plain cringeworthy, *Hearts of Gold* – a sort of unofficial honours agency – cheerfully handed out gongs to ordinary people who had performed outstanding acts of kindness or bravery. Viewers provided nominations and Esther Rantzen donned disguises as varied as charwoman, shop assistant and even punk rocker to surprise unsuspecting guests. With Michael Groth (later Joy Aldridge, then Mike Smith, Carol Smillie and Mickey Hutton) she then bestowed Hearts of Gold awards in recognition of their achievements.

Hec Ramsey ✶✶

US (Universal/Mark VII) Western/Detective Drama. ITV 1973–4 (US: NBC 1972–4)

Hec Ramsey .... **Richard Boone**
Sheriff Oliver B. Stamp .... **Richard Lenz**
'Doc' Amos Coogan .... **Harry Morgan**
Arne Tornquist .... **Dennis Rucker**

Executive Producer **Jack Webb**
Producers **Douglas Benton, Harold Jack Bloom**

● ***The cases of a cowboy detective at the turn of the 20th century.***

Hec Ramsey is a renowned sharpshooter who has discovered an interest in criminology. Taking on the job of deputy in the town of New Prospect, Oklahoma, he still totes his gun but also employs rather more subtle methods of bringing outlaws to book. In a special trunk Ramsey gathers together all the latest pieces of crime-busting 'technology', from fingerprinting paraphernalia to magnifying glasses, which he puts to good use in his search for justice. Working alongside Hec is reliable old Doc Coogan and a young, inexperienced sheriff, Oliver B. Stamp, who is initially worried by his partner's reputation as a gunslinger. *Hec Ramsey* was screened as part of the MYSTERY MOVIE anthology. The pilot was called *The Century Turns*.

Hector Heathcote ✶✶

US (Terrytoons) Cartoon. BBC 1 1965–6 (US: NBC 1964–5)

Voices:
Hector Heathcote .... **John Myhers**

Creator **Eli Bauer**
Executive Producer **Bill Weiss**

● ***A cartoon time traveller turns up in vital places in history.***

Created for a series of theatrical releases, beginning with *The Minute and a 1/2 Man* (1959), Hector Heathcote moved to television a few years later, already known as the cartoon character who plays an important part in famous scenes from history. Each story is set in a different time and place: the American War of Independence, the French Revolution, etc., which allows our hero – always sporting a tricorn hat and supported by his dog, Winston – to pop up and lend a hand in shaping the course of events. In this series, Heathcote was supported by filler cartoons about Sidney, a clumsy elephant, and Hashimoto, a martial arts mouse from Japan.

Hector's House **

France (Europe 1/Télécompagnie) Children's Entertainment. BBC 1 1968–70
DVD: Contender

Creator **Georges Croses**

The domestic adventures of a dog, a cat and a frog.

In this five-minute puppet animation (much used as pre-news filler) the Hector in question is a large, sensible-looking dog with floppy ears who shares his home with Zaza, a cat dressed in a red pinafore. Their next-door neighbour (forever nipping over the fence by ladder) is Mrs Kiki, a giggly frog in a gingham overall, who displays a talent for weather forecasting. The trio enjoys mild mirth around the house and garden, the two females playing silly jokes on the gullible hound and Hector never failing to act gallantly as a true gentleman, courteously assisting his friends at every turn. His catchphrase is a variation on 'I'm just a big, silly old Hector', adapted according to circumstance into 'big sensible old Hector', 'big sad old Hector', etc. The only other regular is a bird that twitters in a tree at the start and finish of each programme. The series was known in its native France as *La Maison de Tou Tou*.

Hedley, Jack

(Jack Hawkins; 1930–)

Solid British actor whose starring status in the Francis Durbridge thriller THE WORLD OF TIM FRAZER in 1960 was not followed up with another lead role until COLDITZ in 1972, in which he played Lt. Colonel Preston. However, he did play Corrigan Blake in the 1962 Alun Owen play *You Can't Win 'Em All*, which led to the *Corrigan Blake* series (although John Turner then assumed the title role). Hedley was also seen in KATE, as Kate Graham's editor, Donald Killearn, the TV movie of *Brief Encounter* and scores of other series, from WHO PAYS THE FERRYMAN?, ONE BY ONE and REMINGTON STEELE to the dramas *Gentlemen and Players*, *A Quiet Conspiracy*, *Hard Cases* and DALZIEL AND PASCOE.

Heggessey, Lorraine

(1956–)

British television executive, beginning as a BBC news trainee after work as a junior newspaper reporter, and progressing to produce programmes like PANORAMA, *Sixty Minutes* and NEWSNIGHT. Moving into independent production, she worked on THIS WEEK, *Hard News* and *Dispatches*, before returning to the BBC in 1992 to edit/produce such series as *Biteback*, *The Underworld*, QED, THE HUMAN BODY and ANIMAL HOSPITAL. Heggessey was appointed Head of Children's Production in 1997 and Director of Programmes in 1999. In 2000 she became the first female Controller of BBC 1, where one of her first acts was to commission a fourth episode of EASTENDERS a week, a move partly responsible for the fact that the channel outperformed ITV in audience terms that year for the first time since 1955. She remained in the post until leaving in 2005 to become chief executive of Talkback Thames.

Heimat ****

West Germany (WDR/SFB) Drama. BBC 2 1986
DVD: Tartan Video

Paul Simon	**Michael Lesch** *(young)*
	Dieter Schaad
Maria Wiegand/Simon	**Marita Breuer**
Katharina Simon	**Gertrud Bredel**
Mathias Simon	**Willi Burger**
Eduard Simon	**Rüdiger Weigang**
Pauline Simon/Kröber	**Karin Kienzler** *(young)*
	Eva Marie Bayerwaltes
Alois Wiegand	**Johannes Lobewein**
Robert Kröber	**Arno Lang**
Marie-Goot Schirmer	**Eva-Marie Schneider**
Lucie	**Karin Rasenack**
Lotti	**Andrea Koloschinski** *(young)*
	Anke Jendrychowski *(young)*
	Gabriele Blum
Glasisch	**Kurt Wagner**
Wilfried Wiegand	**Hans Jürgen Schatz**
Otto Wohlleben	**Jörg Hube**
Pieritz	**Johannes Metzdorf**
Anton Simon	**Markus Reiter** *(young)*
	Mathias Kniesbeck
Ernst Simon	**Roland Bongard** *(young)*
	Michael Kausch
Martha Wiegand	**Sabine Wagner**
Horst Simon	**Andreas Merters**
Hermann	**Frank Kleid** *(young)*
	Jörg Richter *(young)*
	Peter Harding

Creator **Edgar Reitz**
Writers **Edgar Reitz, Peter Steinbach**

Epic saga of German families caught up in the turbulent events of the 20th century.

Although initially a major theatrical release, spanning some 16 hours and screened with meal breaks in its native Germany, *Heimat* became one of the TV events of 1986 when broadcast by BBC 2 over 11 consecutive nights. The sweeping saga of three families (the Simons, the Wiegands and the Schirmers), covering the years 1919 to 1982, the film is set in the fictional village of Schabbach in the Hunsrück region of Germany (an upland area between the Rhine and Mosel), which was the homeland of creator/director Edgar Reitz.

In May 1919, Paul Simon returns home after World War I and everyone expects that he will continue to work in the family forge. Paul, however, has other ideas and sets out to build a new life in America, abandoning wife Maria and sons Anton and Ernst. Those left behind now have to contend with the rise to power of Hitler and the Nazis. Brother Eduard Simon welcomes the change and soon becomes mayor of neighbouring Rhaunen. By 1938, Maria has found a new love, Otto Wohlleben, an engineer, working on the new autobahn. Together they have a son, Hermann. War breaks out and Maria's brother, Wilfried, joins the SS on the home front, while Anton and Ernst are sent away to battle. The families are divided by the conflict and eventually Schabbach is taken by American troops. Just as they had embraced Nazism, the locals now easily shed their fascist pasts and begin to create a new life for themselves in the post-war years. The story ends with the death of Maria, her funeral bringing together surviving family members to reflect on their troubled lives. The name *Heimat*, meaning literally 'home', signifies more, however, suggesting that all the leading players have been searching for a place in which to belong. Shot mainly in monochrome, and broadcast here with English subtitles, the film employed a largely non-professional cast.

Reitz, however, had not finished with the concept. *The Second Heimat*, released in 1992, tells the story of young Hermann Simon who leaves the village to develop a musical career in Munich, meets a Chilean friend, Juan, and falls in love with a cellist named Clarissa. Other artistic colleagues also fall under the spotlight, as the series advances year by year from 1960 to 1970. The saga of Hermann (now a famous conductor) and Clarissa is revisited in *Heimat 3*, completed in 2004, set initially at the time of the collapse of the Berlin Wall and concluding in the new millennium. These two sequels were screened on BBC 4 in 2005.

Heiney, Paul

(1949–)

Yorkshire-born TV reporter and presenter, the husband of broadcaster Libby Purves. He first came to light as one of Esther Rantzen's supporting crew on THAT'S LIFE and THE BIG TIME, before sharing the limelight with Chris Serle in IN AT THE DEEP END. He presented *The Travel Show* for BBC 2 and once stepped in as host of FOOD AND DRINK while Chris Kelly took a season off. Other credits include WATCHDOG, a regional programme about the *Pilgrim's Way* and *Animal Park*.

Helen – A Woman of Today ★★

UK (LWT) Drama. ITV 1973

Helen Tulley .... **Alison Fiske**
Frank Tulley .... **Martin Shaw**
Carole .... **Sharon Duce**
Chris Tulley .... **Christopher Ballantyne**
Diana Tulley .... **Diana Hutchinson**

Producer **Richard Bates**

A wife and mother divorces her cheating husband and seeks a new life of her own.

Reflecting the increasingly feminist mood of the time, and for once making the woman in a broken marriage the centre of attention, *Helen – a Woman of Today* relates the story of Helen Tulley, a middle-class, thirtysomething mother of two young children (Chris and Diana) who decides to strive for more from life. It all begins with an affair between Frank, her husband, and another woman, Carole. Despite being urged by friends and families to stand by her man, Helen turns instead to study, becoming self-reliant and battling her own way through a cold world. There were 13 episodes.

Hello Girls, The ★★

UK (BBC/Diverse Fiction) Drama. BBC 1 1996; 1998

Chris Cross .... **Letitia Dean**
Sylvia Sands .... **Amy Marston**
Ronni Ferrari .... **Helen Sheals**
Val Pepper/Latimer .... **Samantha Seager**
Susi Simmons .... **Samantha Hardcastle**
Pamela Heath .... **Kate Lonergan**
Miss Annie Armitage .... **Stephanie Turner**
Miss Dolly Marriott .... **Maggie McCarthy**
Dick Mandeville .... **Colin Wells**
Rick Hollister .... **Daniel Newman**
Jim .... **Paul Parris**
Dave Curtis .... **Mark Aiken**
Mike Simmons .... **Stephen Lord**

Writers **Ruth Carter, Jo O'Keefe, David Ashton, Julie Rutterford**
Producers **Laurence Bowen, Jacinta Peel**

Fun and games with a team of switchboard girls at the turn of the 1960s.

Based on the novel *Switchboard Operators* by Carol Lake, this light drama is based around the lives of a rather naïve group of teenage GPO employees in Derby. Ringleader of the switchboard girls is confident blonde Chris Cross, who takes under her wing new girl Sylvia Sands. For Sylvia – nicknamed 'Fruity' – it is the first job and the start of a learning curve about adult life. Also in the team are streetwise Ronni Ferrari, who joins Chris and Sylvia as part of a singing group called The Teletones; married, former hairdresser Pam Heath; union rep Val Pepper; and gossipy farmer's daughter Susi Simmons. Overseeing their work – and underlining the generation chasm that is opening up at the time – are dowdy Miss Marriott and prim Miss Armitage. Also seen are Dick Mandeville, Chris's boyfriend ('a thousand-a-year man' at Rolls-Royce), who is engaged to another girl; telegraph boy Jim; and Sylvia's young Marxist friend, Rick Hollister.

Beginning in 1959, stories follow everyday dramas at the exchange, friendly rivalry with the male engineers, and events after work at the Locarno ballroom. A second series, set two years later, sees the girls coming to terms with the new liberation of the 1960s and, at work, battling against job losses through automation. New characters include journalist Mike Simmons and engineer Dave Curtis.

Hello Goodbye Man, The ★★

UK (BBC) Situation Comedy. BBC 2 1984

Denis Ailing .... **Ian Lavender**
Jennifer Reynoldston .... **Mary Tamm**
Ken Harrington .... **Paul Chapman**
Glenn Harris .... **Dominic Guard**

Writer **David Nobbs**
Producer **Alan J. W. Bell**

A nervous sales rep is clearly in the wrong job.

It's amazing what a few pep pills can do. Denis Ailing is a fumbling, self-conscious 42-year-old who has never been assertive in his life. But, with the help of a few tablets, he somehow secures a new position as a salesman for Cookham's Cures, a role for which he is psychologically unfit. Over six episodes, Ailing (in more than just name) struggles to make a success of his job and the spotlight falls on his painfully hopeless attempts to make a sale or find common ground with his feminist colleague, Jennifer Reynoldston. Also on the company's books is Glenn Harris, a super-salesman who effortlessly casts Ailing's efforts into the shade.

Hell's Kitchen ★★

UK (Granada) Reality. ITV 1 2004–5

Presenter **Angus Deayton**

Executive Producers **Natalka Znak, Richard Cowles, Tim Miller, Layla Sabih**

Producers **Rachel Arnold, Michelle Langer, Rachel Watson**

Aspiring chefs taste the pressures of a restaurant kitchen.

In a variation on the 'take a bunch of celebrities, humiliate them and vote them off' reality show, *Hell's Kitchen* was based in a temporary London restaurant. The aim was to train the hapless celebs in top culinary skills, which would be tested nightly, over two weeks, by food critics, other famous folk and members of the public. Gordon Ramsay was their take-no-nonsense teacher. Feeling the heat of the kitchen and Ramsay's fiery tongue were Edwina Currie, James Dreyfuss, Belinda Carlisle, Dwain Chambers, Abi Titmuss, Amanda Barrie, Matt Goss, Roger Cook, Al Murray and the winner, ex-Brookside star Jennifer Ellison.

For the second series a year later, Ramsay gave way to Gary Rhodes and Jean-Christophe Novelli, who headed up two teams of non-celebrity chef wannabes. The winner was Newcastle caterer Terry Miller.

Help! ✶✶

UK (BBC) Situation Comedy. BBC 1 1986–7

Tex .... **Stephen McGann**
Lenny .... **David Albany**
Davva .... **Jake Abraham**
Annie .... **Sheila Fay**
Jimmy Galbraith .... **Paddy Ward**

Writer **Joe Boyle**
Producer **Mike Stephens**

The only way is up for three jobless Merseysiders.

Everyone knows that Liverpool in the 1980s was riddled with unemployment. This comedy set out to prove, however, that there was plenty of spirit left in the city, personified by the eternal optimism of three out-of-work youths named Tex, Lenny and Davva. Tex is the entrepreneur of the three, a chancer whose luck tends to run out prematurely. Lenny is the resident brain box, having a Grade 4 CSE in English Literature, which allows him to dabble in poetry and philosophy. Davva is just plain thick. At the green and golden age of 19, the lads agree they have plenty to look forward to: they just need a little help along the way. Each episode begins and ends in the shelter in Wavertree Park where a meeting of minds to discuss the way forward takes place. In between, with long days to kill, Annie's café provides a temporary refuge.

Help! It's the Hair Bear Bunch ✶

US (Hanna-Barbera) Cartoon. BBC 1972–3 (US: CBS 1971–4)

Voices:
Hair Bear .... **Daws Butler**
Bubi Bear .... **Paul Winchell**
Square Bear .... **Bill Callaway**
Mr Eustace E. Peevly .... **John Stephenson**

Executive Producers **William Hanna, Joseph Barbera**

Three bears in a zoo live the life of Riley.

If you're a caged-up bear you should at least expect decent living conditions, and the ursine residents of Cave Block No. 9 at the Wonderland Zoo make sure as hell that they don't miss out on life's little luxuries. The Hair Bear Bunch are ring-led by Hair Bear himself (so-named after his frizzy locks). A grizzly equivalent of Top Cat (BOSS CAT), he is loyally supported by his sidekick buddies, little Bubi Bear and the rather dim, sun-hatted Square Bear. Together they fight deportation to the hardships of the wild and dream up ways of getting the better of mean zookeeper Mr Peevly and his appropriately named assistant, Botch.

He-Man and the Masters of the Universe ✶

US (Filmation) Cartoon. ITV 1983–6 (US: Syndicated 1983–5)
DVD: Contender

Voices:
He-Man .... **John Erwin**
Skeletor .... **Alan Oppenheimer**
Teela .... **Linda Gary**
Man-at-Arms .... **Erik Gunden**
Orko .... **Lou Scheimer**
The Sorceress .... **Linda Gary**
Evil-Lyn .... **Linda Gary**
She-Ra .... **Melendy Britt**

Producer **Lou Scheimer**

A dashing blond superhero saves his bleak planet from a skull-faced tyrant.

Add a touch of Arthurian legend to *Star Wars* and you get this animation, which was developed to promote a range of Mattel toys but became a big earner in itself. It concerns the mighty He-Man, a Herculean figure who defends the Castle Grayskull from the evil clutches of his enemy, Skeletor, the witch Evil-Lyn and their brutal cronies, dubbed the Masters of the Universe. Foremost among our hero's many allies are warrioress Teela, her adoptive father, Man-at-Arms, and the comical magician Orko, plus a pet orange and green tiger, Cringer (aka Battlecat). Crucial to He-Man's well-being is a magic sword, handed to him years before when he was merely Prince Adam by the spiritual, bird-like Sorceress. Adam now waves the sword to draw strength from the elements, yelling 'By the power of Grayskull' and so transforming himself into his athletic alter-ego to preserve the planet of Eternia, to which he is heir. Adam's sister, Princess Adora, is added to the cast later. She, too, has superhuman skills that she flexes under the guise of She-Ra (Princess of Power). A spin-off series was soon hers. A live-action feature-film version called simply *Masters of the Universe* was released in 1987 (with Dolph Lundgren as He-Man, Frank Langella as Skeletor and Meg Foster as Evil-Lyn) and the series was revived for television in 2002, with new actors voicing the parts.

Henderson, Dickie

OBE (1922–85)

Versatile British entertainer, the son of Dick Henderson, a Yorkshire-born vaudeville comic. Dickie's peak television years were undoubtedly the mid-1950s to the early 1970s. After a decade and a half on the stage, he broke into television alongside Arthur Askey in BEFORE YOUR VERY EYES and was given his own series, *The Dickie Henderson Show*. He then compered SUNDAY NIGHT AT THE LONDON PALLADIUM, starred in *The Dickie Henderson Half-Hour* and in 1960 embarked on the long-running *The Dickie Henderson Show*. In this song-and-dance sitcom he played himself, with June Laverick (later Isla Blair) cast as his wife. This was followed by another comedy, entitled *A Present for Dickie*, in which he found himself entrusted with an Indian elephant. His other notable TV credits were in *I'm Bob, He's Dickie* (with Bob Monkhouse) and *I'm Dickie – That's Showbusiness.*

Henderson, Don

(1932–97)

Softly spoken British actor, the glove-wearing, inhaler-sniffing star of BULMAN and other series. His character of George Bulman first appeared in THE XYY MAN and then in STRANGERS, with his ever-present scarf employed to hide scars left by Henderson's cancer surgery. His weak voice, often put down to a cold in the series, was another by-product of Henderson's illness. Post-*Bulman*, Henderson moved into THE PARADISE CLUB (ex-priest Frank Kane) alongside Leslie Grantham. Among Henderson's many other appearances were parts in POLDARK, CROSSROADS, DICK TURPIN, NEW SCOTLAND YARD, DIXON OF DOCK GREEN, VAN DER VALK, THE ONEDIN LINE, WARSHIP (Master-at-Arms Heron), RIPPING YARNS, DOCTOR WHO, KNIGHTS OF GOD (Colley), HOT METAL, MINDER, *The Boy Who Won the Pools* (Mr Baverstock), *The Secret Life of Polly Flint* (Old Mazy), DEAD HEAD (DI Malcolm), *Dramarama, Merlin of the Crystal Cave* (Galapas), *Dandelion Dead* (Chief Insp. Crutchett), *Three Seven Eleven* (Empire Sam), and 2 POINT 4 CHILDREN (Frank, Ben's dad). He was married to actress Shirley Stelfox, with whom he appeared in MAKING OUT (Mr Beachcroft).

Hendry, Ian

(1931–84)

Determined-looking British actor whose showbusiness debut was as stooge to Coco the clown. After some notable stage performances, he broke into films in the 1950s, then secured himself some minor roles in such series as THE INVISIBLE MAN, PROBATION OFFICER and EMERGENCY – WARD 10. His first starring part was as Dr Geoffrey Brent in POLICE SURGEON, a series which quickly evolved into THE AVENGERS, the character becoming Dr David Keel and linking up with Patrick Macnee's John Steed, as a couple of crime fighters. Hendry left *The Avengers* in 1962, to be replaced eventually by Honor Blackman, triggering a major change of direction for the series. He waited four years for his next major role, which arrived in THE INFORMER, when he played disbarred barrister Alex Lambert, who worked as a police informer, and he was then cast as astronaut Captain Don Quick in the sci-fi fantasy comedy THE ADVENTURES OF DON QUICK in 1970. THE LOTUS EATERS, in which he took the part of alcoholic expatriate Erik Shepherd, followed in 1972. Among Hendry's other credits were guest spots in series like THE PROTECTORS, THE PERSUADERS!, THE SWEENEY and SUPERNATURAL. His most prominent last roles were in *For Maddie with Love*, opposite Nyree Dawn Porter, and a stint in BROOKSIDE as hard-drinking sailor Davey Jones.

Henry, Lenny

CBE (Lenworth Henry; 1958–)

Dudley-born comedian whose rise to fame began on NEW FACES (and appearances in *The Summer Show*, a showcase for the best finds of the series) in 1975. Majoring initially on gags and impressions, Henry graduated to sitcom in the short-lived THE FOSTERS (Sonny Foster). Then came TISWAS and its late-night offspring *OTT*, before Henry joined Tracey Ullman and David Copperfield in the sketch show THREE OF A KIND. He appeared in THE YOUNG ONES and SATURDAY LIVE and secured his own BBC series, *The Lenny Henry Show*, which fluctuated between stand-up comedy, sketches and sitcom, allowing him to develop characters like Fred Dread, Minister for Reggae; Algernon the Rasta; Theophilus P. Wildebeeste; Deakus the old Jamaican; Reverend Nat West; PC Ganja and his dog, Selassie; and the 'crucial' Brixton pirate radio DJ, Delbert Wilkins (who enjoyed a later series all to himself). A series of comedy playlets, *Lenny Henry Tonite*, followed. Soon Henry became a linchpin of the COMIC RELIEF appeals and was also seen as the temperamental Gareth Blackstock in CHEF! In 1996 he provided the voice for cartoon cat *Famous Fred* (a later voice credit was for the animation *Little Robots*). In 1997 he headed into the jungle for *Lenny Henry's Big Amazon Adventure* and a year later he took his humour on the road for a series of shows from provincial theatres in *Lenny Henry Goes to Town*. Later he played superheadteacher Ian George in the drama series HOPE AND GLORY and sailed the ocean for the documentary *Lenny's Big Atlantic Adventure*. In 2000 he returned to character comedy with *Lenny Henry in Pieces* and then, in 2004, revived *The Lenny Henry Show*. Other credits include major parts in *Screen One's Alive and Kicking* (Stevie 'Smudger' Smith), *The Man* (Dennis Jackson), *Goodbye Mr Steadman* (Roy Buchanan) and *War at the Door* (narrator). He is married to comedian Dawn French and used to run the Crucial Films independent production company.

Henry's Cat ★★

UK (Bob Godfrey) Cartoon. BBC 1 1983–7; 1992
DVD: Delta Music

Narrator **Bob Godfrey**

Creator/Writer **Stan Hayward**
Producers **Bob Godfrey, Mike Hayes**

● ***A lazy cat and his friends have colourful adventures.***

Henry's Cat is a plump yellow beast who, with a bunch of animal chums, enjoys lots of surreal adventures in this wobbly-image animation from Roobarb creator Bob Godfrey (who both directs and narrates here). The rather lazy feline gets into all sorts of scrapes with chums like Chris Rabbit, Pansy Pig, Mosey Mouse, Sammy Snail, Douglas Dog, Ted Tortoise and Denise Duck, usually to the disapproval of Establishment figures like Constable Bulldog or Farmer Giles. When all is said and done, however, it does appear that such excitement has been just another of the cat's fanciful daydreams. As for his owner, Henry, he is never seen.

Henshaw, John

(1951–)

Manchester-born actor whose major break came when playing PC Roy Bramell in THE COPS. He has starred since as pub landlord Ken Dixon in EARLY DOORS, Lol O'Toole in NICE GUY EDDIE, stationmaster Wilf Bradshaw in BORN AND BRED, Councillor Seeley in *Johnny and the Bomb*, and Brian in *Open Wide*. He was also Ezra Dingle in EMMERDALE and other smaller roles have come in GBH, CRACKER, THE GRAND, HEARTBEAT, THE BILL, CASUALTY, THE ROYLE FAMILY, LINDA GREEN and LIFE ON MARS.

Henson, Jim

(1936–90)

American puppeteer and TV executive, the man responsible for the Muppets (a combination of marionettes and hand puppets). Henson's puppetry was first featured on television in Washington, DC, through a series called *Sam and Friends*, which ran for six years from 1955. This gave him the exposure to send his creations on to national programmes like *The Tonight Show* and *The Ed Sullivan Show*. In 1969 his Muppet empire really began to move, thanks to a starring role in the new educational kids' series SESAME STREET. Creatures like Big Bird, Oscar the Grouch and Kermit the Frog helped youngsters worldwide to learn their numbers and letters. However, in order to win his puppets a prime-time slot, Henson was forced to move to the UK, where Lord Grade put up funds for the phenomenally successful THE MUPPET SHOW. Henson himself voiced some of the characters, including the show's emcee, Kermit. On the back of the Muppets Henson created FRAGGLE ROCK and the award-winning THE STORYTELLER, starring John Hurt. *Dinosaurs* was his last completed project before he died prematurely in 1990. He was succeeded at the helm of Jim Henson Productions by his son, Brian Henson.

Hepton, Bernard
(1925–)

Stern-looking British actor/director whose performance as Archbishop Thomas Cranmer in THE SIX WIVES OF HENRY VIII was followed by a spell in COLDITZ as the kind Nazi Kommandant. He switched sides to play café owner/Resistance fighter Albert Foiret in SECRET ARMY, was Pallus in I, CLAUDIUS, played estate agent Donald Stimpson, trying to nail down Nigel Havers, in THE CHARMER, and was Mr Woodhouse in JANE AUSTEN'S EMMA. Hepton has also taken to comedy in THE SQUIRRELS (Mr Fletcher) and *Sadie It's Cold Outside* (Norman Potter), plus a guest appearance in SOME MOTHERS DO 'AVE 'EM. His other credits have included THE TROUBLESHOOTERS, TINKER, TAILOR, SOLDIER, SPY and *Smiley's People* (Toby Esterhase), *Mansfield Park*, BLOOD MONEY (Chief Supt. Meadows), BLEAK HOUSE (Krook), BERGERAC, *The Woman in Black, A Perfect Hero* (Arthur Fleming), *The Old Devils* (Malcolm Cellan-Davies), *Dandelion Dead* (Davies) and MIDSOMER MURDERS.

Herbs, The ★★

UK (Filmfair) Children's Entertainment. BBC 1 1968
DVD: 4 Front Video

Narrator **Gordon Rollings**

Creator/Writer **Michael Bond**
Executive Producer **Graham Clutterbuck**

● ***Fragrant happenings in an English country garden, with its herbs as the stars.***

Relating the surreal happenings in the garden of Sir Basil and Lady Rosemary, *The Herbs* features such memorable creations as Constable Knapweed; schoolteacher Mr Onion and his wife, Mrs Onion; the Chives (their children/pupils); Bayleaf the gardener; Aunt Mint, an avid knitter; Sage the owl; Tarragon the dragon; Pashana Bedi the snake-charmer; and Belladonna the evil witch. Other characters are neatness fanatic Miss Jessop and her suitor, Good King Henry, and Signor Solidago, the Italian singing teacher. However, the undoubted stars are a manic, tail-chasing dog named Dill and a 'very friendly' lion called Parsley – later to gain his own spin-off series, *The Adventures of Parsley* (BBC 1 1970). 'Herbidacious' is the magic word that opens the gate to the garden. The action is narrated by Gordon Rollings (Arkwright in the John Smith's beer commercials) and the series aired under the WATCH WITH MOTHER banner.

Hercules: The Legendary Journeys ★★

US (Renaissance/MCA) Adventure. Channel 5 1997–2002 (US: Syndicated 1995–9)
DVD: Anchor Bay Entertainment

Hercules .... **Kevin Sorbo**
Iolaus .... **Michael Hurst**

Creator **Christian Williams**
Executive Producers **Sam Raimi, Robert G. Tapert, Christian Williams**

● ***A half-mortal, half-god fights for good in ancient times.***

Filmed in New Zealand, this tongue-in-cheek, all-action series returns to the theme of Greek myths and legends. The eponymous hero is the son of Zeus (sometimes seen portrayed by Anthony Quinn). Half-man and half-god, Hercules uses his extraordinary strength and fighting skills to battle for good on Earth, partly in revenge for the murder of his wife and children by the evil goddess Hera, his stepmother. His enemies are many, from corrupt gods to awesome, computer-generated monsters, but, with his loyal companion, Iolaus, Hercules usually saves the day. The series was developed from a collection of TV movies shown in the USA in 1994 and led to its own spin-off, XENA: WARRIOR PRINCESS, which, like *The Legendary Journeys*, aired first on Sky One in the UK before transferring to Channel 5.

Here Come the Double Deckers ★★

UK (Twentieth Century-Fox/Century Films) Children's Entertainment. BBC 1 1971

Scooper .... **Peter Firth**
Billie .... **Gillian Bailey**
Brains .... **Michael Audreson**
Doughnut .... **Douglas Simmonds**
Spring .... **Brinsley Forde**
Sticks .... **Bruce Clark**
Tiger .... **Debbie Russ**
Albert .... **Melvyn Hayes**

Creators **Roy Simpson, Harry Booth**
Producer **Roy Simpson**

● ***A group of do-gooder kids stumble into musical adventures.***

Using a disused double-decker bus housed in a London junkyard as their HQ, the Double Deckers are a bunch of game kids who find themselves wrapped up in lots of zany escapades. Leader of the gang is Scooper (played by a young Peter Firth) and the other members are swotty Brains (usually inventing something), chubby Doughnut, American Sticks (so named after his drumming skills), Billie (played by Gillian Bailey, later Jinny Martin in POLDARK), Spring (future Aswad reggae group-member and VH-1 presenter Brinsley Forde) and tiny Tiger. Albert is their grown-up friend. With its jaunty 'Get on board' theme song, the series, made in the UK, was screened first in the USA before being bought by the BBC.

Here's Harry ✶✶

UK (BBC) Situation Comedy. BBC 1960–5

Harry Worth .... **Harry Worth**

Producers **John Ammonds, John Street**

● ***A well-meaning bumbler tackles bureaucracy.***

Playing himself, trilby-hatted Harry Worth starred as a clumsy, ineffective, dithering complainer who ended up confusing all around him. Living with his cat, Tiddles, in the northern town of Woodbridge, Harry makes plenty of references to his aunt, Mrs Amelia Prendergast, but she is never seen. Other characters come and go. *Here's Harry* was the series for which Worth created his famous shop-window opening sequence in which he waved one arm and one leg in the air and, because of the reflection in the glass, made it look as if he was completely off the ground.

Here's Lucy ✶

US (CBS/Lucille Ball) Situation Comedy. BBC 1 1969–71
(US: CBS 1968–74)
DVD: Shout! Factory

Lucy Carter .... **Lucille Ball**
Harrison Carter .... **Gale Gordon**
Mary Jane Lewis .... **Mary Jane Croft**
Kim Carter .... **Lucie Arnaz**
Craig Carter .... **Desi Arnaz Jr**

Producer **Gary Morton**

● ***Lucille Ball's third family sitcom, with the action now set in California.***

Here's Lucy is in many ways no more than a name change for THE LUCY SHOW, with Lucy still aided in her slapstick routines by Mary Jane Croft, and Gale Gordon still around to provide the foil. However, Lucy has now moved to Los Angeles and her surname is Carter, although she is still a widow. Her new children, Kim and Craig, are played by her own son and daughter, while Gale Gordon this time plays Uncle Harry, Lucy's brother-in-law and owner of the Unique Employment Agency, where she works as a secretary.

Hergé's Adventures of Tintin ✶✶

France (Télé-Hachette) Animation. BBC 1 1962–4
DVD: Anchor Bay Entertainment

Narrator **Peter Hawkins**

Producer (UK) **Peggy Miller**

● ***A young reporter and his pet dog lurch from scrape to scrape.***

Created in 1929 and first seen as a comic strip in the Belgian weekly *Le Petit Vingtième*, Tintin was the brainchild of Hergé, alias cartoonist George Rémi. Over the years, the character appeared in over 20 books and made his TV bow in France in 1961 in this series of episodic adventures. Dubbed into English, Tintin arrived in the UK a year later, and British viewers were treated to the hair-raising (in more ways than one, considering his tufty locks) escapades of the red-headed cub reporter. Loyally at Tintin's side is his white fox-terrier, Snowy (Milou in the original French), and also lending a hand is grog-sodden Captain Haddock, the black-bearded skipper of the ship *Karaboudjan*. Other characters seen from time to time are the bowler-hatted Thompson Twins (who gave their name to the 1980s pop group), the deaf and forgetful Professor Calculus and the conspiratorially minded General Alcazar.

With each adventure chopped up into breathless five-minute episodes, complete with cliffhanger endings, Tintin is forever immersed in investigations like *The Crab with the Golden Claw*, *Star of Mystery*, *Red Rackham's Treasure*, *Black Island*, *Objective Moon* and *The Calculus Case*. With so many repeat showings over the years, who could now forget the announcer's booming voice heralding another instalment of *Hergé's Adventures of . . . Tintin*?

Hetty Wainthropp Investigates ✶✶

UK (BBC) Drama. BBC 1 1996–8
DVD: Acorn Media

Hetty Wainthropp .... **Patricia Routledge**
Robert Wainthropp .... **Derek Benfield**
Geoffrey Shawcross .... **Dominic Monaghan**
DCI Adams .... **John Graham Davies**
Janet .... **Suzanne Maddock**

Creators **John Bowen, David Cook**
Executive Producers **Michael Wearing, Jo Wright**
Producer **Carol Parks**

● ***A pensioner housewife turns private detective.***

Set in deepest Lancashire (as the mournful cornet theme music pre-warns), this unusual series of investigations features redoubtable 60-year-old Hetty Wainthropp, the happily married, but rather bored, wife of redundant Robert. Donning her worn beret and raincoat, and using her natural talent for snooping to the full, she begins to dig into more serious matters than local tittle-tattle, starting her own Wainthropp Detective Agency with the help of her 17-year-old sidekick, Geoffrey, a reformed shoplifter, who carries his boss pillion on a scooter. Her first case arises from an instance of pension fraud involving the post office where she works part-time; and from then on, by infiltrating knitting circles or posing as a dinner lady, she constantly bemuses the local constabulary's DCI Adams with her success rate. A fifth regular character, Geoffrey's girlfriend Janet, is introduced in later episodes.

The series was co-devised by David Cook, who had created the character of Hetty in his novel *Missing Persons*.

H. G. Wells' Invisible Man ✶✶

UK (Official Films/ITP) Science Fiction. ITV 1958–9
DVD: ILC

Dr Peter Brady .... **Tim Turner** *(voice only)*
Diane .... **Lisa Daniely**
Sally .... **Deborah Watling**
Sir Charles Anderson .... **Ernest Clarke**

Producer **Ralph Smart**

● ***An invisible scientist works for the secret service.***

Dr Peter Brady has become a victim of his own experiments into light refraction at Castle Hill Laboratories and has lost his visibility. Unable to reverse the process and condemned to a life of transparency, he becomes an intelligence agent and works for the UK Government in places where more obvious spies literally cannot tread. He also helps out friends, the police and other needy persons who learn of his unusual attribute while, at the same time, always seeking an antidote for his affliction. Often bandaged up and wearing sunglasses to give him some recognizable form, he is supported by his widowed sister, Diane, and niece, Sally.

The series was acclaimed for some of its special effects, which included a self-smoking cigarette and a self-drinking glass of wine. The man who played Brady was never credited, although the voice turned out to belong to actor Tim Turner.

Hickson, Joan

OBE (1906–98)

Although synonymous with Agatha Christie's geriatric sleuth MISS MARPLE, Northants-born Joan Hickson didn't arrive in St Mary Mead until she was nearly 80 years old. Her earlier TV credits included the roles of the receptionist in the 1950s series *The Royalty*, housekeeper Mrs Peace in OUR MAN AT ST MARK'S, Mrs Morrow in *Good Girl* and Lady Harriet in *Poor Little Rich Girls*, plus a host of appearances in series like THE INVISIBLE MAN, BACHELOR FATHER, WHATEVER HAPPENED TO THE LIKELY LADS? (Thelma's mother), THE CREZZ (Emily Bronte), NANNY and *Time for Murder*.

Hi-De-Hi! ★★★

UK (BBC) Situation Comedy. BBC 1 1981–8
DVD: Universal

Ted Bovis	**Paul Shane**
Gladys Pugh	**Ruth Madoc**
Jeffrey Fairbrother	**Simon Cadell**
Spike Dixon	**Jeffrey Holland**
Peggy Ollerenshaw	**Su Pollard**
Fred Quilley	**Felix Bowness**
Mr Partridge	**Leslie Dwyer**
Yvonne Stewart-Hargreaves	**Diane Holland**
Barry Stewart-Hargreaves	**Barry Howard**
Sylvia	**Nikki Kelly**
Betty	**Rikki Howard**
Mary	**Penny Irving**
Squadron Leader Clive Dempster, DFC	**David Griffin**
The Twins (Bruce and Stanley)	**The Webb Twins**
Tracey	**Susan Beagley**
April	**Linda Regan**
Dawn	**Laura Jackson**
Julian Dalrymple-Sykes	**Ben Aris**
Uncle Sammy Morris	**Kenneth Connor**

Creators/Writers **David Croft, Jimmy Perry**
Producers **David Croft, John Kilby, Mike Stephens**

● ***High jinks in a British holiday camp at the turn of the 1960s.***

Beginning in the summer of 1959, this thinly veiled send-up of Butlins, Pontins and the like focuses on events at Maplins holiday camp at Crimpton-on-Sea, progressing season by season into the early 1960s. The pilot programme (screened in 1980) sees the arrival of the members of staff. The new Entertainments Officer is the ineffective Jeffrey Fairbrother, a Cambridge archaeologist who decides to seek pastures new when his wife leaves him. Also new is young camp comic Spike Dixon, quickly corrupted when taken under the wing of wily camp host Ted Bovis. Fairbrother's assistant is valleys girl Gladys Pugh, who triples up as sports organizer and Radio Maplin announcer (rousing campers from their slumbers with a lilting 'Morning, campers'). Fairbrother instantly warms her frigid heart, although her smouldering advances are never welcomed. Other members of the entertainments team are bent jockey Fred Quilley, now in charge of the camp horses; grouchy, boozy Punch-and-Judy man Mr Partridge ('Jolly Uncle Willie' to the kids he detests); snooty, fading ballroom stars Yvonne and Barry Stewart-Hargreaves; and a small group of Yellowcoats, whose job it is to cajole the campers into having fun, whether they like it or not. Desperate to get in the thick of the action is daffy chalet maid Peggy Ollerenshaw, who longs to abandon her dustpan and brush in favour of a yellow jacket. Always in the background, issuing edicts but never showing his face, is the all-powerful but illiterate boss man, Joe Maplin. In later series, ex-RAF man Clive Dempster replaces Fairbrother in the entertainments hot seat, among other cast changes.

Action centres on the glorious coarseness of everyday holiday camp life. In the daytime, campers gather around the Olympic-sized swimming pool to witness beauty contests and various slapstick competitions. In the evening they repair to the Hawaiian Ballroom to be entertained by Ted's vulgar jokes and Spike's silly costumes. Unfortunately for real-life holiday camps, who were trying to live down their primitive past, the series was a huge hit and ran for eight years. Nostalgia was a key to its success, but so was authenticity, with co-writer Jimmy Perry drawing inspiration for the series from his time as a Butlins Redcoat. Perry also composed the theme song, 'Holiday Rock'.

High & Dry ★

UK (Yorkshire) Situation Comedy. ITV 1987

Ron Archer	**Bernard Cribbins**
Richard Talbot	**Richard Wilson**
Trevor Archer	**Angus Barnett**
Miss Baxter	**Vivienne Martin**
Fred Whattle	**Arthur English**

Writers **Alan Sherwood, Michael Knowles**
Producer **Ronnie Baxter**

● ***Father and son try to revive a derelict seaside pier.***

It's 1946 and resourceful Ron Archer spots a bargain. The long pier at Midbourne is up for sale at a ridiculous price and he can see its potential. The only trouble is, he doesn't have the finances to bring back the glory days and so he applies pressure on reluctant bank manager Richard Talbot to see him through. The pier is bought and the two, together with Ron's dopey son, Trevor, and Talbot's secretary, Miss Baxter, attempt to revive its fortunes. However, with money always desperately short, it's a constant battle that sometimes requires the assistance of Fred Whattle, the pier's resident squatter, and the Friends of Midbourne Pier Association (FOMPA).

This studio-bound comedy was initially a spin-off from DAD'S ARMY. Writers Michael Knowles (best known as Capt. Ashwood in IT AIN'T HALF HOT MUM) and Harold Snoad penned a BBC Radio sequel to the great BBC sitcom and called it *It Sticks Out Half a Mile*. Airing on Radio 2 in 1983–4, it featured John Le Mesurier, Ian Lavender and Bill Pertwee in their familiar roles of Wilson, Pike and Hodges, now, in the post-war years, getting together to save the derelict Frambourne Pier. The concept transferred to television via a BBC 1 pilot called *Walking the Planks*, starring Michael Elphick as Ron and Gary Raynsford as Trevor, alongside Richard Wilson and Vivienne Martin. When the pilot was not taken up for a series, the writers approached Yorkshire Television and *High & Dry* was born (with Snoad – better known as a BBC comedy producer

– now scripting under the near-anagrammatic pen-name of Alan Sherwood).

High Chaparral, The ★★

US (NBC/David Dortort) Western. BBC 2 1967–71
(US: NBC 1967–71)

Big John Cannon .... **Leif Erickson**
Buck Cannon .... **Cameron Mitchell**
Billy Blue Cannon .... **Mark Slade**
Manolito Montoya .... **Henry Darrow**
Victoria Cannon .... **Linda Cristal**
Don Sebastian Montoya .... **Frank Silvera**
Sam Butler .... **Don Collier**
Reno .... **Ted Markland**
Pedro .... **Roberto Contreras**
Joe .... **Robert Hoy**
Vasquero .... **Rodolfo Acosta**
Wind .... **Rudy Ramos**

Creator/Producer **David Dortort**

A family struggles to make a living from its ranch.

In BONANZA the Cartwrights have their Ponderosa in Nevada. The Cannons in this series live on The High Chaparral in Arizona Territory, some time in the 1870s. Head of the family is gritty, hard-working Big John Cannon, assisted in his efforts to establish a cattle ranch by his blond son, Billy Blue, and by Buck, John's gruff but fun-loving younger brother. John's first wife is killed by Apaches in the first episode, but he then marries Victoria Montoya, daughter of Mexican nobleman Don Sebastian Montoya. When she moves to The High Chaparral, so does her brother, Manolito.

Despite constant Indian attacks, wrangles with Mexicans and hassles from rustlers and other outlaws, Big John and his family never flinch from their fight with the land. Reno, Pedro and Joe are their ranch hands, working under the supervision of Sam Butler. When the naïve Blue is written out of the series towards its close, he is replaced by Wind, a half-breed who comes to live with the Cannons. The programme's creator, David Dortort, was also the man behind *Bonanza*.

High Definition Television

See *HDTV*.

High Life, The ★★

UK (BBC) Situation Comedy. BBC 2 1995
DVD: Network

Sebastian Flight .... **Alan Cumming**
Steve McCracken .... **Forbes Masson**
Shona Spurtle .... **Siobhan Redmond**
Capt. Duff .... **Patrick Ryecart**

Writers **Alan Cumming, Forbes Masson**
Producer **Tony Dow**

Two frustrated air stewards dream of bigger things.

This fast-moving, six-part sitcom sprang out of a pilot episode shown in 1994 as one of BBC 2's *Comic Asides*. Sebastian Flight and Steve McCracken are in-flight stewards working for Air Scotia. Their job is to keep customers happy on the low-cost shuttle service between London and Prestwick, though they dream of a more exotic long-haul route that seems destined never to come their way. Indeed, if only they'd keep their feet on the ground and their heads out of the clouds, life would be much less stressful, as camp Sebastian always has a fruitless scheme up his sleeve to escape from the humdrum routine of this supposedly glamorous life, and libidinous Steve is similarly thwarted in his more earthy ambitions. Adding to their woes are vicious head stewardess Shona Spurtle and the perpetually confused pilot, Captain Duff.

Highway ★★

UK (Various) Religion. ITV 1983–93

Presenter **Harry Secombe**

Executive Producer **Bill Ward**

Easy-going Sunday evening hymns and chat from various locations around the British Isles.

Hosted by Harry Secombe from a different venue each week, *Highway* was a roving version of STARS ON SUNDAY, produced in turn by all the different ITV companies for the network. Harry (later Sir Harry) invited guests to sing religious songs, give readings or just chat about their lifestyles and spiritual feelings. Secombe himself provided a number of the songs in every programme. For the last series, in 1993, the programme was displaced to early afternoons, as ITV looked for programmes with bigger audiences at Sunday teatimes. Secombe returned with a new series, *Sunday Morning with Secombe*, in 1994, in which he chatted to guests at the venue for the week's *Morning Worship*, which then followed.

Highway Patrol ★★

US (Ziv) Police Drama. ITV 1956–62 (US: Syndicated 1955–9)

Chief Dan Mathews .... **Broderick Crawford**
Narrator .... **Art Gilmore**

Executive Producer **Vernon E. Clark**

No-nonsense crimebusting with an American squad car officer.

There is only one regular in *Highway Patrol* and that is Chief Dan Matthews. Matthews, a chunky, determined, fast-talking police officer with a broken nose, works for an unnamed force in an unnamed state (the emblems on the patrol cars read simply 'Highway Patrol'). His targets are criminals of all kinds – murderers, bank robbers, smugglers, hijackers and petty thieves – and by posting all-points bulletins, yelling 'Ten-Four' ('Message received and understood') and 'Ten-Twenty' ('Report your position') into his car intercom, the gravel-voiced Matthews always gets his man. With nearly all the action taking place out on the road, involving bikes and occasionally helicopters as well as cars, little is seen of Matthews's office base.

Highway Patrol was one of the founding fathers of TV cop shows, even though it came together on a minuscule budget. Over 150 half-hour episodes were made.

Highway to Heaven ★★

US (NBC) Drama. ITV 1987–90 (US: NBC 1984–9)
DVD: A&E Home Video (Region 1 only)

Jonathan Smith .... **Michael Landon**
Mark Gordon .... **Victor French**

Creator/Executive Producer **Michael Landon**

An angel in training is sent to Earth to help people in trouble.

When Arthur Morton dies, he goes to Heaven and is groomed as an angel. With his name changed to Jonathan Smith, he is sent back to Earth to gain some experience of helping sad and worried people. He travels the globe as a wandering labourer, accompanied by one of his first converts, a cynical cop named Mark Gordon. Smith opts for counselling, moral support and leadership by example as means of lightening the loads of others, but he can always call upon his angelic powers, if required. Both lead actors had previously appeared in Michael Landon's earlier success, LITTLE HOUSE ON THE PRAIRIE.

Hilary ★★

UK (BBC) Situation Comedy. BBC 2 1985–6

Hilary Myers	**Marti Caine**
Lyn	**Caroline Moody**
Wesley	**Philip Fox**
Kimberley	**Jack Smethurst**
George	**Philip Madoc**
Angela	**Sandra Carrier**

Writers **Peter Robinson, Peter Vincent**
Producers **Harold Snoad, Ray Butt**

A TV researcher's life is a battlefield.

Despite the trappings of a successful career, life is always uphill for Hilary, a scatty, disorganized divorcée (mother of a 19-year-old son) who works as a researcher on a TV chat show. At home at her flat in Putney, she is a lousy cook and is hassled by her neighbours, the man-hungry Lyn and the suicidal, drippy Wesley. When things get tough, she does at least have the company of her pet mynah bird, Arthur (voiced by Percy Edwards). At work, on Eagle Television's *Searchlight* show, she is beholden to demanding producer George and puts up with catty comments from colleague Angela. The series follows Hilary from personal disaster to personal disaster as the best-laid plans always go awry. A pilot episode was screened in 1984.

Hilda Lessways

See *Clayhanger.*

Hill, Benny

(Alfred Hawthorne Hill; 1924–92)

Celebrated British funnyman whose saucy postcard style of humour made him a favourite around the world. Benny Hill was one British comedy export who made even the Americans laugh, and his cheeky grin and feigned air of innocence enabled him to get away with smutty jokes and innuendoes that would have died in the hands of other comics. They certainly wouldn't have been aired in peak hours. The hallmarks of his shows were send-ups of other TV personalities (whether they were Moira Anderson, Fanny Cradock or Jimmy Hill); comic creations like the saluting half-wit, Fred Scuttle; bawdy songs that exhibited his skill with words – such as his number-one hit, 'Ernie (The Fastest Milkman in the West)'; and, most provocatively, slapstick chases involving scantily-clad women. Most of the time he was ably supported by stooges like Bob Todd, Henry McGee and Jack Wright. Hill's career began in music hall (including a period as a straight man to Reg Varney) and progressed to television via the radio comedy *Educating Archie*. His TV debut came in 1949 and his first series for the BBC was shown in 1955. In 1964 he won plaudits for his portrayal of Bottom in *A Midsummer Night's Dream* and then, in 1969, Hill switched to Thames TV, where he stayed until his show was axed amid rows over sexism in 1989 (even though he had already toned down the voyeurism and ditched the steamy Hill's Angels dance troupe). Central was prepared to give him another bite of the cherry three years later but Hill died of a heart attack before he could finish the series.

Hill, Bernard

(1944–)

Manchester-born actor who won acclaim for his portrayal of Yosser 'Gissa Job' Hughes in BOYS FROM THE BLACKSTUFF. Previously Hill had played Gratus in I, CLAUDIUS and appeared in FOX (Vin Fox). He later starred as Lech Walesa in Channel 4's *Squaring the Circle* and as Mike in *Olly's Prison*, and appeared as DS Gavin Douglas in *Telltale*, Uncle Fred in LIPSTICK ON YOUR COLLAR, and Joe in the *Stages* presentation *Speaking in Tongues*. He also played Len Tollit in the sitcom ONCE UPON A TIME IN THE NORTH, Frank Nickle in CATHERINE COOKSON'*s The Gambling Man*, Edward Tulliver in *The Mill on the Floss*, Magwitch in GREAT EXPECTATIONS, MI5 agent Derek Jennings in *The Grid* and former minister David Blunkett in *A Very Social Secretary*. He has been seen in many single dramas, including television Shakespeare, and presented a factual series, *The Real History Show*.

Hill, Lord Charles

(1904–89)

Fondly remembered from the war years as the Radio Doctor, Charles Hill, one-time secretary of the British Medical Association, became Member of Parliament for Luton in 1950, serving in the Ministries of Food, Housing and Local Government, and Welsh Affairs, as well as occupying the positions of Postmaster-General and Chancellor of the Duchy of Lancaster. He left Parliament in 1963 (a victim of Macmillan's 'Night of the Long Knives') and took over as Chairman of the Independent Television Authority. At the ITA he insisted that the ITV companies offered more time to ITN (a move that resulted in *News at Ten*) and oversaw the important 1967 franchise reviews. Surprisingly, he was transferred virtually overnight to the chairmanship of the BBC in the same year. This appointment was seen as an attempt by the Prime Minister, Harold Wilson, to discipline the BBC's Director-General, Sir Hugh Greene (Greene and Wilson had fallen out). Hill remained with the Corporation until 1972, before becoming Chairman of Abbey National Building Society and Laporte Industries. During his time as BBC Chairman he was criticized for unhinging the delicate relationship between the Director-General and the Chairman, intervening in day-to-day decisions and concentrating greater power in the hands of the Governors.

Hill, Harry

(Matthew Hall; 1964–)

Kent-born, bespectacled, surreal/off-beat comedian, a qualified doctor, who has made an obsession with badgers his trademark (along with pointy-collared shirts and pockets full of pens) and created a catchphrase out of 'What are the chances of that happening, eh?' His first TV series, *Harry Hill's*

Fruit Fancies, was a collection of six 15-minute, silent monochrome films, but vocal lunacy was re-established with the series *Harry Hill*, in which he was supported by Al Murray, Bert Kwouk and others. Hill then moved to ITV to send up the week's television programmes in *Harry Hill's TV Burp* and star in *The All-New Harry Hill Show*. He also appeared in the TV pantomime *Dick Whittington*, and has hosted *New* YOU'VE BEEN FRAMED, as well as making guest appearances in programmes like *A Bear's Tale*.

Hill, Jimmy

OBE (1928–)

British soccer pundit, a former Brentford and Fulham footballer, and later manager of Coventry City, who broke into television with LWT, for which he became Head of Sport and Deputy Controller of Programmes. Via *On the Ball* (part of WORLD OF SPORT) and *The Big Match*, Hill arrived at the BBC, becoming its football expert during the 1970s and 1980s, and hosting MATCH OF THE DAY and other major events. He retired from the Corporation in 1998 and has since worked for Sky Sports. In the mid-1960s Hill was a consultant on the soccer soap UNITED!

Hill Street Blues ✱✱✱✱

US (MTM) Police Drama. ITV/Channel 4 1981–9
(US: NBC 1981–7)

Capt. Frank Furillo .... **Daniel J. Travanti**
Sgt Phil Esterhaus .... **Michael Conrad**
Officer Bobby Hill .... **Michael Warren**
Officer Andy Renko .... **Charles Haid**
Joyce Davenport .... **Veronica Hamel**
Det. Mick Belker .... **Bruce Weitz**
Lt. Ray Calletano .... **Rene Enriquez**
Det. Johnny 'JD' LaRue .... **Kiel Martin**
Det. Neal Washington .... **Taurean Blacque**
Lt. Howard Hunter .... **James B. Sikking**
Sgt/Lt. Henry Goldblume .... **Joe Spano**
Officer/Sgt Lucy Bates .... **Betty Thomas**
Grace Gardner .... **Barbara Babcock**
Fay Furillo .... **Barbara Bosson**
Det./Lt. Alf Chesley .... **Gerry Black**
Officer Leo Schnitz .... **Robert Hirschfield**
Officer Joe Coffey .... **Ed Marinaro**
Chief Fletcher P. Daniels .... **Jon Cypher**
Officer Robin Tataglia/ Belker .... **Lisa Sutton**
Assistant DA Irwin Bernstein .... **George Wyner**
Jesus Martinez .... **Trinidad Silva**
Det. Harry Garibaldi .... **Ken Olin**
Det. Patricia 'Patsy' Mayo .... **Mimi Kuzyk**
Mayor Ozzie Cleveland .... **J. A. Preston**
Sgt Stanislaus Jablonski .... **Robert Prosky**
Lt. Norman Buntz .... **Dennis Franz**
Celeste Patterson .... **Judith Hansen**
Sidney Thurston ('Sid the Snitch') .... **Peter Jurasik**
Officer Patrick Flaherty .... **Robert Clohessy**
Officer Tina Russo .... **Megan Gallagher**
Officer Raymond .... **David Selburg**

Creators/Executive Producers **Steven Bochco, Michael Kozoll**
Producers **Gregory Hoblit, David Anspaugh, Anthony Yerkovich**

Life with the officers of a busy police station on the seedier side of town.

The Hill Street Station is based in the wrong side of a large, unnamed eastern American city (the exteriors were done in Chicago). Surrounded by the worst elements – drug-pushers, prostitutes, racketeers, and more – the policeman's lot at Hill Street is not a happy one. This series reveals how the motley band of law-enforcers struggle to cope with daily trauma, and witnesses its effect on their personal lives and working relationships.

In semi-serial form, the programme follows a day's events in Hill Street, from the morning roll-call to last thing at night. The show's own roll-call is as follows. Head of the station is Captain Frank Furillo, a patient, quietly spoken, firm commander. Dedicated and responsible, he deals not only with events on the streets but also with police bureaucracy and turmoil in his personal life. Plagued for alimony by his ex-wife, Fay, he strikes up an affair with defence attorney Joyce Davenport that turns into marriage. At work, however, they remain professional adversaries.

Beneath Furillo is Sgt Phil Esterhaus, a fatherly head sergeant who urges his troops, 'Let's be careful out there.' When actor Michael Conrad died, three years into the run, Esterhaus was written out (having had a heart attack while making love to widow Grace Gardner). Then there are scruffy undercover detective Mick Belker (known to bite those he arrests); SWAT squad lieutenant Howard Hunter; toothpick-chewing plain-clothesman Neal Washington; his alcoholic partner J. D. LaRue; Detective Alf Chesley; and the sensitive community affairs officer, Henry Goldblume. Completing the team are the station's hispanic second-in-command, Ray Calletano, the black/white patrolman team of Bobby Hill and Andy Renko (who are shot in the opening episode), and Lucy Bates, with her partner, Joe Coffey. Leo Schnitz is the desk officer and Fletcher Daniels is the smarmy, ambitious police chief who later runs for mayor.

Added over the years are Robin Tataglia (an officer who marries Belker); Detective Harry Garibaldi, Sgt Stan Jablonski (Esterhaus's replacement); Detective Patsy Mayo; Officer Tina Russo; Officer Pat Flaherty; Officer Raymond; and the abrasive Lt. Norman Buntz, on the face of it a lout, but in fact nobody's fool. The local underworld is also represented, by informer Sid the Snitch and cocky Jesus Martinez, leader of the Diablos gang, as are the city's legal eagles by prosecutor Irwin Bernstein (as well as by Joyce Davenport).

Hill Street Blues was applauded by critics but was not a hit in the ratings. Nevertheless, it won eight Emmys in one season (a record) and attracted a dedicated following. Its success came from its subtle juxtaposition of humour and human drama, and from its realistic characterizations. The storylines are equally true to life. The cops do not always come out on top. Sometimes the cases are never resolved. On other occasions, the cops themselves are seen to be the bad guys. Hand-held, news-style camerawork added to the realism. In short, the '*Blues*' changed the face of American cop shows: car chases and shoot-outs were no longer enough after this series. The theme music, by Mike Post, was a UK hit in 1982. Buntz and Sid the Snitch eventually went on to a short-lived spin-off, *Beverly Hills Buntz*.

Hillsborough ✱✱✱

UK (Granada) Drama. ITV 1996

Trevor Hicks .... **Christopher Eccleston**
Jenni Hicks .... **Annabelle Apsion**

John Glover .... **Ricky Tomlinson**
Theresa Glover .... **Rachel Davies**
Joe Glover .... **Scot Williams**
Ian Glover .... **Stephen Walters**
Eddie Spearritt .... **Mark Womack**
Jan Spearritt .... **Tracey Wilkinson**
Chief Supt. David Duckenfield **Maurice Roëves**
Dr Stefan Popper .... **Ian McDiarmid**

Writer **Jimmy McGovern**
Producer **Nicola Shindler**

● ***Three families fight to expose the truth about a disaster that claimed the lives of their children.***

On 15 April 1989, 95 football supporters lost their lives at the FA Cup semifinal match between Liverpool and Nottingham Forest. The game was staged at Sheffield Wednesday's Hillsborough stadium and the fans died because a gate was opened to allow a rush of supporters into an already heavily congested area. The event was a tragedy of the deepest kind in itself, but what followed, to many people closely involved with the case, added grave insult to grievous injury, as responsibility for the incident was, it was claimed, ducked by the police. This single drama explores the aftermath of that horrendous day, examining the subsequent enquiries that sought an explanation for the disaster from the viewpoint of three families who lost teenage children at the match. Writer Jimmy McGovern, who had already touched on the issue in one memorable CRACKER storyline, claimed that all the facts in his script were true, based on evidence given by witnesses or documented statements. Charles McDougall directed.

Himalaya with Michael Palin

See *Around the World in 80 Days*.

Hine ✶✶

UK (ATV) Drama. ITV 1971

Joe Hine .... **Barrie Ingham**
Walpole Gibb .... **Colin Gordon**
Astor Harris .... **Paul Eddington**
Susannah Gray .... **Sarah Craze**
Jeremy Windsor .... **John Steiner**

Creator/Producer **Wilfred Greatorex**

● ***The tough, grimy world of an international arms dealer.***

Joe Hine sells weapons for a living and makes enemies along the way. A lone trader, he battles against giant corporations, chancing his arm in a multi-billion-pound undercover market in defence equipment. His chief rivals are Walpole Gibb and Astor Harris, men who set out to destroy him. Sick of the hypocritical business, Hine always seeks to pull off the last big deal that will allow him to retire in style. One series of 13 episodes was produced.

Hines, Frazer

(1944–)

Yorkshire-born actor, best known as EMMERDALE's Joe Sugden, a role he played off and on for over 20 years. His TV debut came as Jan in *The Silver Sword*, and he also played Toby in *Queen's Champion*, Tim in *Smugglers' Cove*, Tim Birch in EMERGENCY – WARD 10, and John Trenchard in *Smuggler's Bay*, before travelling with DOCTOR WHO as Highland warrior Jamie McCrimmon. Among his other credits have been appearances in COMPACT, Z CARS, CORONATION STREET and DUTY FREE. His first wife was actress Gemma Craven and his second wife is sportswoman Liz Hobbs.

Hippies ✶✶

UK (Talkback) Situation Comedy. BBC 2 1999

Ray Purbbs .... **Simon Pegg**
Jill Sprint .... **Sally Phillips**
Alex Picton-Dinch .... **Julian Rhind-Tutt**
Hugo Yemp .... **Darren Boyd**
Dad .... **John Benfield**
Mum .... **Geraldine McNulty**
Prof. Rickman .... **Simon Kunz**

Creators **Graham Linehan, Arthur Mathews**
Writer **Arthur Mathews**
Executive Producer **Peter Fincham**
Producer **Geoffrey Perkins**

● ***The team behind a counter-culture newspaper attempt to change the world.***

The time is late 1969, a couple of years after the Summer of Love, and hippiedom is well on the wane. Not that that inhibits the editorial team of *Mouth*, London's underground paper for the flower people, run from a flat in Notting Hill Gate. Founder and editor of the organ is Ray Purbbs, begetter of unlikely schemes to change the world for the better and always likely to end up with egg on his face. More wary but still wrapped up in Ray's crazily idealistic world is posh Alex Picton-Dinch, a laid-back Mr Cool who can't quite divorce himself from his privileged upbringing, his Harrow school education or his love of golf. The paper's tea girl, and Ray's girlfriend, is Jill Sprint, a feminist/hippie more in principle than practice to the point where she espouses free love but blocks Ray's carnal advances. The fourth member of the team is dense dopehead Hugo Yemp. Together, the long-haired, peace-pleading, kaftan-clothed quartet put their efforts into such surreal ventures as staging a musical, publishing attacks on the police, protesting against sandpaper and attending a nude rock festival. One episode, in which schoolkids are given the chance to edit *Mouth*, is a direct reference to the real-life obscenity trial that faced *Oz* magazine when it made the same error of judgement during the same era. Despite being heralded as from the team that brought us Father Ted, *Hippies* failed to turn on the viewers that tuned in, and dropped out after just six episodes were produced.

Hird, Dame Thora

OBE (1911–2003)

Morecambe-born actress Thora Hird became a national institution. Although much of her work fell into the comedy vein, she proved herself possibly even more adept in straight drama, as evidenced by her moving monologues, *A Cream Cracker under the Settee* and *Waiting for the Telegram*, for Alan Bennett's TALKING HEADS series. In the world of sitcoms, Hird will be remembered, to a lesser and greater degree, for her performances as disgruntled housewife Thora Blacklock in MEET THE WIFE, boarding-house proprietor Thora Parker in *Ours is a Nice House*, funeral director Ivy Unsworth in IN LOVING MEMORY, Salvation Army Captain Emily Ridley in HALLELUJAH! and Edie Pegden, the tutting ringleader of the ladies, in LAST OF THE SUMMER WINE. Among her many other credits were the hymn series *Praise Be* (host), and roles in series as varied as THE ADVENTURES OF ROBIN HOOD, ALL CREATURES GREAT AND SMALL, *The First Lady* (councillor Sarah Danby), *Flesh and Blood* (Mabel Brassington) and *Goggle Eyes* (Mrs Harrington). There were also numerous single dramas like A KIND OF LOVING in 1962, *Memento Mori* in 1992 and *Lost for Words* in 1999, in which she returned to the part of the mother (this time a stroke victim) of writer Deric Longden that she had first played in the *Screen One* presentation *Wide-Eyed and Legless*, in 1993. Her daughter is actress Janette Scott.

His Lordship Entertains

See *Hark at Barker*.

Hislop, Ian

(1960–)

British humorist, comic writer and satirist, editor of *Private Eye* for over a decade and a team captain on HAVE I GOT NEWS FOR YOU. Hislop's other TV work has included scripts for THREE OF A KIND and, with Nick Newman, *About Face*, SPITTING IMAGE, *Harry Enfield and Chums* and MURDER MOST HORRID. He and Newman also penned the *Screen One* comedy *Gobble* and the sitcom MY DAD'S THE PRIME MINISTER. In quite a different vein, Hislop also presented *Canterbury Tales*, Channel 4's review of the Church of England in the 20th century, and *Not Forgotten*, the same channel's insight into the lives of men and women killed in World War I.

History Man, The ★★★

UK (BBC) Drama. BBC 2 1981

Dr Howard Kirk	**Antony Sher**
Barbara Kirk	**Geraldine James**
Flora Beniform	**Isla Blair**
Annie Callendar	**Laura Davenport**
Henry Beamish	**Paul Brooke**
Myra Beamish	**Maggie Steed**
Anne Petty	**Chloe Salaman**
Melissa Tordoroff	**Miriam Margolyes**
Felicity Phee	**Veronica Quilligan**
Martin Kirk	**Jonathan Bruton**
Celia Kirk	**Charlotte Enderby**
Moira Milikin	**Elizabeth Proud**
John McIntosh	**Graham Padden**
Jane McIntosh	**Judy Liebert**
Miss Ho	**Zienia Merton**

Writer **Christopher Hampton**
Producer **Michael Wearing**

● ***A trendy, self-serving academic gets his comeuppance.***
Malcolm Bradbury's novel of varsity vices was brought to television in four parts by Christopher Hampton. The story, set in October 1972, concerns one Howard Kirk, a manipulative sociology lecturer at Watermouth University. A 'sideboards and flares' he-man, Kirk thinks nothing of abusing his position to seduce students, using the cover of sexual liberation, or to fill their brains with left-wing ideals. However, allegations of 'gross moral turpitude' soon threaten his lifestyle. Barbara is his long-suffering, hippyish wife and among his academic colleagues are the equally sexually generous Flora Beniform, new young English lecturer Annie Callendar and the hapless Henry Beamish. Robert Knights directed the serial, which scandalized some viewers with its sex content. George Fenton provided the music.

History of Britain by Simon Schama, A ★★★

UK (BBC) History. BBC 2 2000–2
DVD: BBC

Presenter **Simon Schama**

Writer **Simon Schama**
Executive Producer **Martin Davidson**

● ***Lively, personal account of Britain through the ages.***
In the footsteps of BBC academics Kenneth Clark and Jacob Bronowski stepped Simon Schama, a lecturer charged with writing and presenting an historical overview of his native country, even though he had not lived in Britain for 20 years. Schama, a professor of art history and history at New York's Columbia University, was chosen, it seems, as much for his infectious enthusiasm and ability to tell a tale as his deep knowledge of the subject. Making the past come to life by dragging up seemingly insignificant parts of the story proved his forte. Recognizing that this is a personal selection of historical highlights by deliberately titling the series '*A* History' rather than '*The* History', Schama moved from pre-Roman times right through to Winston Churchill in 17 episodes that were transmitted in three series over two years. With the help of reconstructions and site visits, he exposed kings and queens, the Black Death, the Civil War, Cromwell, the Empire and social and religious change. A more detailed, three-volume book accompanied the production.

Hitchcock, Sir Alfred

(1899–1980)

Celebrated British film director whose television work, although limited, is listed among TV's all-time classics. In the US-made ALFRED HITCHCOCK PRESENTS (later extended into *The Alfred Hitchcock Hour*) he gave viewers an anthology of thrillers, not all directed, but at least all overseen, by the Master of Suspense himself. He also appeared on screen to top and tail each story, mostly with short quirky or bizarre anecdotes which had little to do with the main feature. In the mid-1980s, after his death, he resurfaced as host of a new run of *Alfred Hitchcock Presents*, his appearances coming courtesy of colourized old footage from the original series.

Hitch-Hiker's Guide To The Galaxy, The ★★

UK (BBC) Situation Comedy. BBC 2 1981
DVD: BBC

Arthur Dent	**Simon Jones**
Ford Prefect	**David Dixon**
The Book	**Peter Jones** *(voice only)*
Zaphod Beeblebrox	**Mark Wing-Davey**
Trillian	**Sandra Dickinson**
Marvin	**David Learner**
	Stephen Moore *(voice)*

Creator/Writer **Douglas Adams**
Producer **Alan J. W. Bell**

An intergalactic-guidebook compiler and his human friend flee Earth's destruction and hitch rides across the universe.

Ford Prefect was a researcher for the electronic *Hitch-Hiker's Guide to the Galaxy*, the ultimate universal reference book. With the book badly needing an update, he was dispatched to Earth to gather information, remaining there for 15 years and making friends with Arthur Dent. One day, learning that the Earth is in imminent danger of demolition to make way for a hyperspace bypass, Prefect reveals that he is not from Guildford after all and urges Dent to escape with him aboard the demolition spacecraft. Unfortunately, the ship is manned by the ugly, sadistic Vogons, a race of green aliens who terrorize others with appalling poetry. Fleeing their clutches, Prefect and Dent join the *Heart of Gold*, a spaceship in the hands of two-headed former con man and part-time Galactic President Zaphod Beeblebrox, who is heading for the lost planet of Magrathea. His crew consists of pilot Trillian (actually a former Earthling named Trisha McMillan) and a manic-depressive robot, Marvin the Paranoid Android, who suffers from pains in his diodes.

As the duo thumb their way around the galaxy, and the bemused Arthur hunts for a good cup of tea, they encounter Slartibartfast (architect of the fjords), the Golgafrinchians (former middle-managers and telephone operatives who have been banned from their planet because of their uselessness) and pan-dimensional beings dressed up as white mice who are desperately seeking the Ultimate Question to Life, the Universe and Everything. They already know the answer: it is 42. The hitch-hikers also visit Milliways, the Restaurant at the End of the Universe, and are entertained by the talking Dish of the Day and galactic rock star Hotblack Desiato, before ending up on prehistoric Earth, contemplating the events that are to engulf the planet in the aeons ahead.

A mixture of fantasy, satire and pun, the series employed some innovative special effects, including the use of video games to stage space battles and mock computer graphics to show pages from the book. It needed such efforts, since the original Radio 4 version – with that medium's decidedly cheaper advantage of mere suggestion – had enjoyed a cult following. The theme music was a version by Tim Souster of The Eagles track 'Journey of the Sorcerer'.

A feature film version, starring Martin Freeman, Mos Def and Stephen Fry, was released in 2005.

HMS Brilliant

See *Sailor*.

Hobley, McDonald

(Dennys Jack Valentine McDonald-Hobley; 1917–87)

One of Britain's earliest on-screen TV announcers, McDonald Hobley, complete with bow tie and dinner jacket, first appeared on the BBC in 1946, sharing announcing shifts with Jasmine Bligh, Sylvia Peters and, later, Mary Malcolm. During the same period he also presented the magazine programme KALEIDOSCOPE and COME DANCING, and appeared with Mr Pastry (Richard Hearne), this coming after a pre-war stint in the theatre, and radio work in the Far East during the hostilities. After ten years with the BBC, Hobley moved to ABC. He later made guest appearances in programmes like THE SAINT and OUT OF THE UNKNOWN. Hobley was born in the Falkland Islands, and one of his last TV contributions came in a Channel 4 programme about the South Atlantic dependencies.

Hodge, Patricia

(1946–)

British actress, cast in comedy as well as straight drama roles. Among her TV highlights have been the part of the plummy barrister Phyllida Trant in RUMPOLE OF THE BAILEY, Mary Fisher in THE LIFE AND LOVES OF A SHE DEVIL, TV presenter/detective Jemima Shore in JEMIMA SHORE INVESTIGATES, Lady Julia Verinder in *The Moonstone*, and the title role in *The Cloning of Joanna May*. Hodge played Lady Diana Cooper in EDWARD AND MRS SIMPSON, Sybilla Howarth in THE OTHER 'ARF, Penny Milburn in HOLDING THE FORT, Julia Merrygrove in RICH TEA AND SYMPATHY, Margaret Thatcher in THE FALKLANDS PLAY, solicitor Geraldine Hackstraw in THE LEGACY OF REGINALD PERRIN and Georgina Sweet in *Sweet Medicine*. She has also popped up in episodes of SOFTLY, SOFTLY, THE PROFESSIONALS, *Disraeli*, NANNY (Mrs Sackville), ROBIN OF SHERWOOD, THE ADVENTURES OF SHERLOCK HOLMES, INSPECTOR MORSE, WAKING THE DEAD and more, and was seen in the dramas THE NAKED CIVIL SERVANT and *The One and Only Phyllis Dixey*, among others.

Hogan, Paul

(1939–)

Australian comedian, a former construction-worker who hit the box office big time in the 1980s with the film *Crocodile Dundee*. In between, *The Paul Hogan Show* was extremely popular Down Under and was imported to the UK by Channel 4. Supported by the likes of Delvene Delaney and John Cornell, Hogan used the 'Benny Hill'-type sketch show to introduce a range of wacky characters like Leo Wanker and Hoges, a 'no-poofters' man-of-the-world, always dressed in sleeveless shirts, shorts and football socks. It helped put Foster's lager and Vegemite on the UK map. Hogan married actress Linda Kozlowski in 1990.

Hogan's Heroes ★★★

US (Bing Crosby) Situation Comedy. ITV 1967–71
(US: CBS 1965–71)
DVD: Paramount (Region 1 only)

Col. Robert Hogan	**Bob Crane**
Col. Wilhelm Klink	**Werner Klemperer**
Sgt Hans Schultz	**John Banner**
Cpl Louis LeBeau	**Robert Clary**
Cpl Peter Newkirk	**Richard Dawson**
Cpl James Kinchloe	**Ivan Dixon**
Sgt Andrew Carter	**Larry Hovis**
Helga	**Cynthia Lynn**
Hilda	**Sigrid Valdis**

Creators **Bernard Fein, Albert S. Ruddy**
Producer **Ed Feldman**

Allied soldiers rule the roost at a Nazi POW camp.

Somewhere in the Nazi empire is Stalag 13, a prisoner-of-war camp nominally commanded by the monocled Colonel Klink and his inept, fat sidekick, Sgt Schultz. In actuality, although their captors don't realize it, the camp is run by its inmates and the true supremo is the shrewd, wisecracking American, Colonel Robert Hogan. Hogan is ably supported by a troop of versatile Allied soldiers. These are LeBeau, a Frenchman with culinary skills; Newkirk, a brash Cockney; Sgt Carter, the skilful but slow farmboy; and a black electronics genius, Corporal

Kinchloe. Between them, the prisoners run a useful Allied operational base. They supply intelligence, assist refugees and print counterfeit money, but, above all, they have a wonderful time. This is more of a hotel than a prison. By lifting the wire fence in garage-door style, they can pop out to take the air or seek entertainment in the town. They also have their own sauna in which to sweat off the delights of LeBeau's wonderful Gallic cuisine. Little wonder they never look to escape.

The series echoes the far more serious Billy Wilder film *Stalag 17*, which was released in 1953, starred William Holden and blended humour with moments of drama and realism.

Hogg's Back ✶

UK (Southern) Children's Situation Comedy. ITV 1975–6

Dr Hogg .... **Derek Royle**
Pearl .... **Jackie Piper**
Pearl .... **Wendy Richard**
Gen. Balding .... **Robert Dorning**
Vicar .... **Eric Dodson**
Mrs Mac .... **Pat Coombs**

Creator/Writer **Michael Pertwee**
Producer **Peter Croft**

● ***A seaside GP is not only behind the times but accident-prone, too.***

Eccentric Dr Hogg is called out of retirement to provide care for the residents of Belling-on-Sea. Unfortunately, his medical skills are a little bit rusty and he himself is forgetful and prone to disaster, resulting in much slapstick and many pratfalls. Pearl is Hogg's assistant, but she soon gets married and is replaced by another girl . . . named Pearl. In the second series, Mrs Mac arrives as Hogg's housekeeper. The series was created for star Derek Royle by Michael Pertwee, who had long recognized the actor's acrobatic skills. Royle consequently performed all his own stuntwork.

Holby City ✶✶

UK (BBC) Medical Drama. BBC 1 1999–

Anton Meyer .... **George Irving**
Nick Jordan .... **Michael French**
Kirstie Collins .... **Dawn McDaniel**
Jasmine Hopkins .... **Angela Griffin**
Julie Fitzjohn .... **Nicola Stephenson**
Ray Sykes .... **Ian Curtis**
Paul Ripley .... **Luke Mably**
Victoria Merrick .... **Lisa Faulkner**
Karen Newburn .... **Sarah Preston**
Ellie Sharpe .... **Julie Saunders**
Muriel McKendrick .... **Phyllis Logan**
James Roberts .... **Bryan Murray**
Danny Shaughnessy .... **Jeremy Edwards**
Kath Shaughnessy/Fox .... **Jan Pearson**
Tushara 'Tash' Bandara .... **Thusita Jayasundera**
Mike Barratt .... **Clive Mantle**
Alex Adams .... **Jeremy Sheffield**
Sandy Harper .... **Laura Sadler**
Steve Waring .... **Peter de Jersey**
Keri McGrath .... **Anna Mountford**
Stan Ashleigh/Hill .... **Paul Shane**
Liam Evans .... **Adrian Lewis Morgan**
Anil Banerjee .... **Kulvinder Ghir**
Janice Taylor .... **Siobhan Redmond**
Guy Morton .... **Paul Blackthorne**
Samantha Kennedy .... **Colette Brown**
Chrissie Williams .... **Tina Hobley**
Ric Griffin .... **Hugh Quarshie**
Owen Davis .... **Mark Moraghan**
Alistair Taylor .... **Dominic Jephcott**
Marija Ocvar .... **Ana Sofrenovic**
Mubbs Hussein .... **Ian Aspinall**
Lisa Fox .... **Luisa Bradshaw-White**
Jess Griffin .... **Verona Joseph**
Ben Saunders .... **David Paisley**
Pam McGrath .... **Denise Welch**
Diane Lloyd .... **Patricia Potter**
Jan Goddard .... **Judy Loe**
Tom Campbell-Gore .... **Denis Lawson**
Ed Keating .... **Rocky Marshall**
Terry Fox .... **Miles Anderson**
Anita Forbes .... **Kirsty Mitchell**
Tricia Williams .... **Sharon Mughan**
Rosie Sattar .... **Kim Vithana**
Zubin Khan .... **Art Malik**
Nic Yorke .... **Liam Garrigan**
Kelly Yorke .... **Rachel Leskovac**
Helen Grant .... **Susannah York**
Paul Rose .... **Andrew Lewis**
DI Jane Archer .... **Christine Entwistle**
Will Curtis .... **Noah Huntley**
Donna Jackson .... **Jaye Jacobs**
Mickie Hendrie .... **Kelly Adams**
Mark Williams .... **Robert Powell**
Dean West .... **Paul Henshall**
Matt Parker .... **Adam Best**
Connie Beauchamp .... **Amanda Mealing**
Michael Beauchamp .... **Anthony Calf**
Carlos Fashola .... **David Bedella**
Sean Thompson .... **Chinna Wodu**
Lola Griffin .... **Sharon D. Clarke**
Elliot Hope .... **Paul Bradley**

Creator/Executive Producer **Mal Young**
Producers **Mervyn Gill-Dougherty, Yvon Grace, Stephen Garwood, Sally Avens, Caroline Levy, Lisa Williams, Philip Leach, Matt Tombs, Richard Stokes, Julie-Ann Robinson, Anne Edyvean, Sharon Houlihan, Emma Turner, Paul Goodman, Rebecca Hedderly, Huw Kennair-Jones, Sharon Hughff, Michael Offer, Chris Ballantyne, Roberto Troni, Emma Kingsman-Lloyd, Oliver Kent, Johann Knobel, Simon Meyers, Claire Armspach**

● ***Clinical and personal crises on the wards of a city hospital.***

Set in the same fictitious hospital as its mother series, CASUALTY, *Holby City* takes viewers beyond the doors of the A&E department and into one of the surgical wards. Here life and death situations are everyday fare and personal relationships wrap themselves around medical matters. Head of the care team is consultant surgeon Anton Meyer, a monstrous stickler for the highest standards. Working alongside Meyer are keen, womanizing surgeon Nick Jordan; firm and ambitious senior house officer Kirstie Collins; house officer Victoria Merrick (always in the shadow of her doctor father); heart consultant Muriel McKendrick; ward clerk Paul Ripley, plus nurses Ray Sykes (prankster), Karen Newburn (icy but sympathetic, later married to Jordan), Julie Fitzjohn (single mother of daughter Rosie) and her friend, new junior ward sister Jasmine Hopkins (from a hippy background). Some of the characters (Jordan, Fitzjohn and senior surgeon James

Roberts) were introduced in an episode of *Casualty* shown in November 1998.

Among later arrivals are Catholic sister Kath Shaughnessy; her student nurse son, Danny; lesbian registrar Tash Bandara; and unorthodox registrar Alex Adams. These are joined by novice nurse Sandy Harper; charge nurse Steve Waring; out-reach nurse Keri McGrath; and army-bore care assistant Stan Ashleigh (later renamed Hill). Further recruits include popular nurse Liam Evans; paediatrician Janice Taylor; her locum husband, Alistair; senior house officer Samantha Kennedy; plain-speaking sister Chrissie Williams; obstetrician Owen Davis; consultant surgeon Ric Griffin; his daughter, Jess, a student nurse; obstetrics registrar Mubbs Hussein; and midwives Lisa Fox and Ben Saunders. Tom Campbell-Gore is a new, self-righteous heart surgeon and Diane Lloyd a new registrar. Team members also include later midwife Mickie Hendrie; nurse Donna Jackson; charge nurse Mark Williams (former husband of nurse Tricia); student doctors Dean West and Matt Parker; consultant surgeon Connie Beauchamp; Ric's ex-wife, registrar Lola Griffin; and cardio-thoracic surgeon Elliot Hope. *Casualty* characters also regularly drop into Darwin Ward, including heartthrob Mike Barratt, who returns to head up the surgery team on the adjoining Keller Ward (one of a few new wards introduced as the series progressed).

Unlike *Casualty*, however, which is shot in Bristol, *Holby City* is filmed in an office block, close to the set of EASTENDERS in Hertfordshire. The first series consisted of just nine episodes, but inside three years *Holby City* was being screened nearly every week of the year. Guest stars have included David Soul, Patsy Kensit, Phill Jupitus, Madhur Jaffrey and Adrian Edmondson.

Hold the Back Page! ✶✶

UK (BBC) Drama. BBC 1 1985–6

Ken Wordsworth .... **David Warner**
Reg .... **Eric Allan**
Alison .... **Gil Brailey**
Charlie Wordsworth .... **Lee Whitlock**
Russell de Vries .... **David Horovitch**
Steve Stevens .... **Peter-Hugo Daly**
Frank McNab .... **Richard Ireson**
Ruby .... **Tilly Vosburgh**

Writers **Andrew Nickolds, Stan Hey**
Producer **Evgeny Gridneff**

● ***A journalist struggles when he moves downmarket to earn more money.***

Ken Wordsworth is a sports journalist on a quality Sunday newspaper. However, when Alison, his ex-wife, sues for alimony, he is forced to look for more lucrative employment and starts writing for a tabloid daily. There he is dubbed 'The Poet Laureate of Sport', because of his use of big words, but Ken is not happy in his new job. Petty Fleet Street squabbles with his deputy editor, Frank McNab, and rivals like Steve Stevens get him down and, torn between what he wants to write and what he has to, his enthusiasm wanes and his cynicism grows. This is manifested in his personal life, too. A heavy drinker, he now finds himself trying to balance a bachelor lifestyle with the need to be a good father to his teenage son, Charlie. Ten episodes charted Wordsworth's journey around Britain's sporting venues.

Holden, Amanda

(1971–)

Hampshire-born actress whose earliest TV appearance came as a contestant on BLIND DATE. This was followed by a small role in EASTENDERS, playing market stall holder Carmen. Holden has since starred in a mix of comedies and dramas, including KISS ME KATE (Mel), THE GRIMLEYS (Geraldine Titley), *Happy Birthday Shakespeare* (Alice), SMACK THE PONY, HEARTS AND BONES (Louise Slaney), *The Hunt* (Sarah Campbell), *Now You See Her* (Jessica), CUTTING IT (Mia Bevan), CELEB (Debs), *Mad About Alice* (Alice) and *Wild at Heart* (Sarah Trevanion), also making guest appearances in dramas like JONATHAN CREEK and AGATHA CHRISTIE'S MARPLE. Amanda was famously once married to actor/comedian Les Dennis.

Holding the Baby ✶

UK (Granada) Situation Comedy. ITV 1997–8

Gordon Muir .... **Nick Hancock**
Hugh Bonneville
Rob Muir .... **Joe Duttine**
Daniel Muir .... **Joshua Atherton**
Jacob Atherton
Adam Sandford
Laura .... **Sally Phillips**
Ian .... **Paul Mark Elliott**
Claire .... **Lou Gish**

Creator **Mark Wadlow**
Writers **Mark Wadlow, Dominic Minghella, Paul Dornan, Chris Niel, Georgia Pritchett**
Producers **Justin Judd, Rob Bullock**

● ***A harassed single dad tries to keep his home, work and social lives alive.***

Creator Mark Wadlow based this sitcom partly on his own experience of being traded in by a girlfriend for a younger man, and partly on the time he spent helping a friend named Gordon Muir look after his young daughter while Gordon's wife was travelling on business. Here he presents us with the real Gordon's namesake, a thirtysomething employee of *Carpet Review* magazine whose wife has jilted him for a 21-year-old lover, leaving him in charge of their two-year-old son, Daniel. Gordon's a good and capable dad on the whole, but his new predicament has dire consequences for his professional and social lives. Plots revolve around his hunt for a nanny, attending a mum-and-toddler group and juggling work commitments. Not helping matters is Rob, his tactless, philandering slob of a brother, who now shares Gordon's house, although the company of friend Laura is somewhat more comforting.

After an initial run of seven episodes, *Holding the Baby* returned for a second outing. In this series, Hugh Bonneville replaces Nick Hancock as the downtrodden Gordon, with young Adam Sandford taking over from twins Joshua and Jacob Atherton as Daniel. Also introduced is Claire, one of Rob's intended dates, who instead becomes Gordon's new girlfriend. Poor ratings, to some degree resulting from the series being broken into two chunks three months apart, led to its cancellation after five episodes, leaving two instalments unscreened. All the same, a US version with the same title, starring Jon Patrick Walker, aired on the Fox network in 1998.

Holding the Fort ★★

UK (LWT) Situation Comedy. ITV 1980–2

Russell Milburn .... **Peter Davison**
Penny Milburn .... **Patricia Hodge**
Fitzroy 'Fitz' .... **Matthew Kelly**

Creators/Writers **Laurence Marks, Maurice Gran**
Producer **Derrick Goodwin**

● ***A husband and wife try role-reversal.***

Young married couple Russell and Penny Milburn have a baby daughter, Emma. However, instead of Russell being the breadwinner, it is Penny who returns to work, reclaiming her old job as a captain with the army. Russell stays at home, looks after Emma and dabbles with his own brewery, housed in the basement, generally hindered by his lifelong pal, Fitz. With Russell and Fitz both ardent pacifists, Penny's source of income is a cause of constant friction.

When *Holding the Fort* ended, after three seasons, Fitz was given his own spin-off, *Relative Strangers* (Channel 4 1985–7), in which he is surprised by John, his 18-year-old son (played by Mark Farmer), a child he has never known about.

Holiday ★★

UK (BBC) Travel. BBC 1 1969–

Presenters **Cliff Michelmore, Joan Bakewell, Anne Gregg, Frank Bough, John Carter, Desmond Lynam, Eamonn Holmes, Anneka Rice, Jill Dando, Craig Doyle, Ginny Buckley, Laurence Llewelyn-Bowen**

● ***Long-running holiday magazine.***

A tourism brochure of the air, *Holiday* is now the oldest travel review programme on British television. Initially its title incorporated the year in question, beginning with *Holiday 69*, but that idea has now been dropped. Throughout, its concept has been quite simple: holiday destinations at home and abroad have been featured and appraised in pre-filmed reports, with plaudits given to the best features and less generous comments made about the limitations of each resort. The very first programme included an item on Torremolinos; however, some destinations over the years have been attacked as being too fanciful and beyond the limits of the ordinary viewer's pocket. To complement the recorded inserts, *Holiday* has also offered general advice for travellers, publicized last-minute bargains and investigated tourist complaints.

Holiday was once a stalwart of BBC 1's Sunday evening schedules and its Gordon Giltrap theme music, 'Heartsong', led nicely into the God slot during the dark winter months. It has since moved to a peak-time week-night position. Cliff Michelmore was the chief presenter for 17 years, but his successors have proved less durable, some, like Desmond Lynam and Anneka Rice, lasting only one or two seasons. Anne Gregg spent ten years with the programme, enjoying varying degrees of prominence; and among the show's many contributing reporters have been Fyfe Robertson, Kieran Prendiville, Sarah Kennedy, Bill Buckley, John Pitman, Kathy Tayler, Kevin Woodford, Sankha Guha and Monty Don. John Carter was one of the 'experts' in the first series and remained close to the programme for many years. From 1988 Carter was involved with Thames TV's rival programme, *Wish You Were Here . . . ?* (ITV 1974–2003). *Wish You Were Here . . . ?* was introduced chiefly by Judith Chalmers, who was partnered over several series by Chris Kelly. Mary Nightingale and Ruth England were later presenters. It has been succeeded by a daytime equivalent, *Wish You Were Here . . . Today?* (ITV 1 2001–).

Holiday has been complemented by various spin-off series, most notably *Summer Holiday* (BBC 1 1994–2002) a sister programme providing more topical information during the summer season. There was also a budget version, *Holiday on a Shoestring*, in 1999. Another spin-off was *Holiday: Fasten Your Seatbelt* (BBC 1 1996–8), in which the programme's presenters and other celebrities attempted to perform holiday jobs such as air stewardess, chalet maid or cast member at Walt Disney World.

Holland, Jeffrey

(1946–)

Midlands-born comedian and comic actor, much seen in company with Russ Abbot on his *Madhouse* shows and on *The Les Dennis Laughter Show*. Holland played up-and-coming holiday-camp comedian Spike Dixon in HI-DE-HI! and remained with the Perry/Croft repertory company for YOU RANG, M'LORD?, taking the role of head of the household James Twelvetrees, and OH, DOCTOR BEECHING!, as station master Cecil Parkin. Early roles came in episodes of DIXON OF DOCK GREEN, CROSSROADS and DAD'S ARMY.

Holland, Jools

OBE (Julian Holland; 1958–)

Deptford-born presenter, formerly keyboards player with the group Squeeze. Holland moved into television as host of the controversial rock show THE TUBE, following this up with the more eclectic and long-running LATER WITH JOOLS HOLLAND and its New Year extension, *Jools's Annual Hootenanny*. Holland has also chaired a relaunch of JUKE BOX JURY, played himself in the comedy *The Groovy Fellers*, hosted the music and comedy show *The Happening*, supported Chris Evans on DON'T FORGET YOUR TOOTHBRUSH, introduced the musical travelogue *Beat Route*, and contributed to the architectural series *Building Sites*. In 2002, he presented *Jools Holland's Piano*, a two-part celebration of the instrument's importance to popular music.

Holland, Mary

British actress famed not for a television series but for her role in a long-running commercial. As Katie, Mary was TV's Oxo mum for 18 years from 1958. When the advert was eventually dropped in 1976, Holland was snapped up by Electrolux and later made a commercial for Oxo rivals Bovril.

Hollyoaks ★★

UK (Mersey) Drama. Channel 4 1995–
DVD: Carlton

Kurt Benson .... **Jeremy Edwards**
Ollie Benson .... **Paul Leyshon**
Lucy Benson .... **Kerrie Taylor**
Natasha Andersen .... **Shebah Ronay**
Greg Andersen .... **Alvin Stardust**
Sarah Andersen .... **Anna Martland**
Louise Taylor .... **Brett O'Brien**
Maddie Parker .... **Yasmin Bannerman**
Tony Hutchinson .... **Nick Pickard**

Jambo Bolton .... **William Mellor**
Lisa Bolton .... **Isabel Murphy**
Dawn Cunningham .... **Lisa Williamson**
Angela Cunningham .... **Liz Stooke**
Max Cunningham .... **Matthew Littler**
Jude Cunningham .... **Davinia Taylor**
Cindy Cunningham .... **Stephanie Waring**
Bazz .... **Toby Sawyer**
Lewis Richardson .... **Ben Hull**
Mandy Richardson/
Hutchinson .... **Sarah Jayne Dunn**
Ruth Osborne/Benson .... **Terri Dwyer**
Jack Osborne .... **James McKenna**
Mrs Osborne .... **Lynda Rooke**
Julie Matthews .... **Julie Buckfield**
Rob Hawthorn .... **Warren Derosa**
Dermot Ashton .... **Lauren Beales**
Susi Harrison .... **Deborah Chad**
Carol Groves .... **Natalie Casey**
Benny Stringer .... **Matthew Morgan**
Sol Patrick .... **Paul Danan**
Kate Patrick .... **Natasha Symms**
Gina Patrick .... **Dannielle Brent**
Mr Richardson .... **David McAlister**
Mrs Richardson .... **Kathryn George**
Finn .... **James Redmond**
Jasmine Bates .... **Elly Fairman**
Sean Tate .... **Daniel Pape**
Sam 'OB' O'Brien .... **Darren Jeffries**
Emily Taylor .... **Lorna Pegler**
Adam Morgan .... **David Brown**
Luke Morgan .... **Gary Lucy**
Beth Morgan .... **Elizabeth O'Grady**
Kate Baines
Zara Morgan .... **Kelly Greenwood/Condron**
Andy Morgan .... **Ross Davidson**
Sue Morgan .... **Eve White**
Darren Osborne .... **Ashley Taylor-Dawson**
Paul Millington .... **Zander Ward**
Sam Smallwood .... **Tim Downie**
Nikki Sullivan .... **Wendy Glenn**
Anna Green .... **Lisa M. Kay**
Mark Gibbs .... **Colin Parry**
Alex Bell .... **Martino Lazzeri**
Geri Hudson .... **Joanna Taylor**
Ben Davies .... **Marcus Patric**
Izzy Cornwell/Davies .... **Elize du Toit**
Taylor James .... **Michael Price**
Lorraine Wilson .... **Jo-Anne Knowles**
Victoria Hutchinson/
Finnigan .... **Fiona Mollison**
Jacqui Hudson .... **Julie Peasgood**
Chloe Bruce .... **Mikyla Dodd**
Matt Musgrove .... **Kristian Ealey**
Brian Drake .... **Jonathan Le Billon**
Jess Holt .... **Frankie Hough**
Steve Holt .... **Conor Ryan**
Theo .... **Andrew Somerville**
Steph Webster/Dean .... **Carley Stenson**
Laura Burns .... **Lesley Johnston**
Helen Cunningham .... **Kathryn George**
Gordon Cunningham .... **Bernard Latham**
Abby Davies .... **Helen Noble**
Will Davies .... **Barny Clevely**
Lisa Hunter .... **Gemma Atkinson**
Les Hunter .... **John Graham Davies**
Dan Hunter .... **Andy McNair**
Lee Hunter .... **Alex Carter**
Sally Hunter .... **Katherine Dow Blyton**
Ellie Hunter/Mills .... **Sarah Baxendale**
John Stuart .... **Andy Henderson**
Becca Hayton/Dean .... **Ali Bastian**
Jamie Nash .... **Stefan Booth**
Jodie Nash .... **Katie McEnery**
Toby Mills .... **Henry Luxemburg**
Nick O'Connor .... **Darren Bransford**
Norman Sankofa .... **Jamie Luke**
Eve Crawford .... **Natasha Lund**
Bombhead .... **Lee Ottway**
Jake Dean .... **Kevin Sacre**
Debbie Dean .... **Jodi Albert**
Craig Dean .... **Guy Burnett**
Frankie Dean/Osborne .... **Helen Pearson**
Johnno Dean .... **Mark Powley**
Cameron Clark .... **Ben Gerrard**
Scott Anderson .... **Daniel Hyde**
Kristian Hargreaves .... **Max Brown**
Joe Spencer .... **Matt Milburn**
Robbie Flynn .... **Andrew Newton Lee**
Natalie Osborne .... **Tiffany Mulheron**
Sophie Burton .... **Connie Powney**
Melanie Burton .... **Cassie Powney**
Justin Burton .... **Chris Fountain**
Dannii Carbone .... **Christina Baily**
Tom Cunningham .... **Ellis Hollins**
Darlene Taylor .... **Sarah Lawrence**
Richard Taylor .... **Richard Calkin**
Ali Taylor .... **Luti Fagbenie**
Nicole Owen .... **Ciara Janson**
Liam/Sam Owen .... **Louis Tamone**
Carrie Owen .... **Jaq Croft**
Rob Owen .... **David Prosho**
Zak Barnes .... **Kent Riley**
Candy Browne .... **Laura Handley**
Nathan Haywood .... **Robert Norbury**
Stuart Harding .... **Dan Cryer**
Russell Owen .... **Stuart Manning**
Liz Taylor/Burton .... **Andrée Bernard**
Nancy Hayton .... **Jessica Fox**
Jeremy Peterson .... **Simon Cole**
Rhys Ashworth .... **Andrew Moss**
Hannah Ashworth .... **Emma Rigby**
Josh Ashworth .... **Sonny Flood**
Suzanne Ashworth .... **Suzanne Hall**
Dominic Reilly .... **John Pickard**
Andy Holt .... **Warren Brown**
Jessica Harris .... **Jennifer Biddall**
Freddy Watson .... **Greg Kelly**
Jamie ('Fletch') .... **Sam Darbyshire**
Gilly Roach .... **Anthony Quinlan**
Louise Summers .... **Roxanne McKee**
Olivia Johnson .... **Rochelle Gadd**
Sarah Barnes .... **Loui Batley**
Kathy Barnes .... **Sarah Jane Buckley**
Mark Jury .... **Ash Newman**
Clare Devine .... **Samantha Rowley**
Michaela Jones/McQueen .... **Hollie-Jay Bowes**
Sean Kennedy .... **Matthew Jay Lewis**

Creator **Phil Redmond**
Producers **Phil Redmond, Jo Hallows, David Hanson**

Teen soap set in a comfortable northern suburb.
Unlike creator Phil Redmond's earlier angst-ridden offerings, GRANGE HILL and BROOKSIDE, *Hollyoaks* initially played on the lighter side of life, following the social scene among a group

of middle-class kids in a pleasant suburb of Chester. The thrust of the action centred on teen crushes, clothes, cars and other adolescent worries; but darker themes have emerged as the series has progressed, with broken marriages, law-breaking, drugs, death and other less wholesome activities getting into the picture.

The main characters at the outset were motor-mad Kurt Benson, confident Natasha Andersen (soon to meet a sad end); theatrically minded Louise Taylor; trendy Maddie Parker; social struggler Tony Hutchinson; rebellious joker Jambo Bolton; and interior-design shop-worker Dawn Cunningham. New kids arrived on the block as the series advanced to twice a week (five nights a week from 2003). Among the more mature members of the cast was Greg Andersen, Natasha's dad, who was landlord of the local boozer, The Dog in the Pond, and who (in keeping with his actor's glitzy past) was well into 1960s and 1970s music. Some 'adult' episodes, screened later in the evening or on the sister channel, E4, have also been shown, occasionally with spin-off titles like *Hollyoaks Let Loose*, *Hollyoaks: No Going Back* and *Hollyoaks: Back from the Dead*. Considering the programme's close production links with *Brookside*, it was perhaps not so surprising that one character, Matt Musgrove, appeared in both dramas.

Hollywood ★★★

UK (Thames) Historical Documentary. ITV 1980

Narrator **James Mason**

Writers/Producers **Kevin Brownlow, David Gill**

● ***A detailed study of the age of the silent movie.***

Subtitled *A Celebration of the American Silent Film* when shown in the USA, *Hollywood* won much acclaim as a well-researched, thoughtful history of the great days of the US film industry. Project masterminds Kevin Brownlow and David Gill take the trouble to explore in depth the background to the world of the silent movie, explaining the context of certain films and, most importantly, screening them in the best possible condition, with appropriate music and at the proper speed. This reveals how these early pieces of cinema were really artistic jewels and not the jumpy, jerky bits of footage most people think them to be. The contributions of the directors, writers, cameramen and performers of the day are also evaluated in this 13-part documentary. Carl Davis supplies the grand theme music.

Hollywood Greats, The ★★

UK (BBC) Documentary. BBC 1 1977–85; 1999; 2001–

Narrators **Barry Norman, Ian McShane, Jonathan Ross**

Producers **Margaret Sharp, Richard Downes, Allan Campbell, Pauline Law**

● ***Warts-and-all documentary portraits of Hollywood's legendary film stars.***

Intermittently, over eight years, BBC film critic Barry Norman compiled a collection of biographies of the biggest names in the movie world. Using film clips and interviews to illustrate his points, Norman was not afraid to destroy a few myths in his interpretation of the stars' work and private lives. Among those featured were Judy Garland, Charles Laughton, Ronald Coleman, Joan Crawford, Clark Gable, Errol Flynn, Spencer Tracy, Jean Harlow, Humphrey Bogart, Groucho Marx, Charlie Chaplin, Marilyn Monroe, Edward G. Robinson, John Wayne, Henry Fonda and Steve McQueen. The last contribution by Norman was a one-off film on Bing Crosby, shown in 1985.

In 1999 the series was resurrected as simply *Hollywood Greats* for profiles of Cary Grant, Bette Davis, Robert Mitchum and Katharine Hepburn. Barry Norman having departed for Sky TV, the narration was handled by Ian McShane. In 2001, the series returned once more, with Jonathan Ross at the helm, profiling Audrey Hepburn, Judy Garland (again), Gene Kelly and Sammy Davis Jr. Later series celebrated Steve McQueen (again), Doris Day, Tony Curtis, Burt Lancaster, Michael Caine, Kirk Douglas, James Stewart, Dustin Hoffman, Richard Harris, John Wayne, Anthony Hopkins, Tom Cruise, Lauren Bacall, Jane Fonda, David Niven, Harrison Ford, Jack Lemmon and Marlon Brando.

Holm, Sir Ian

CBE (Ian Holm Cuthbert; 1931–)

British actor, largely on stage and screen but also prominent on television, including as narrator on programmes like TELEVISION, SURVIVAL, *Natural World, How To Build a Human* and *D Day*. The highlight to date has been the part of disgraced spy Bernard Samson in GAME, SET AND MATCH. Holm also starred in *Frankenstein* (a MYSTERY AND IMAGINATION story), played Paul Presset in the intense drama *We, the Accused*, and took the parts of Napoleon in *Napoleon and Love* and Himmler in HOLOCAUST. He appeared as Michael in the trilogy *Conjugal Rites*, assumed the guise of J. M. Barrie in the *Play of the Week* trilogy *The Lost Boys*, played Hercule Poirot in a one-off thriller *Murder by the Book*, and was seen as Zerah in JESUS OF NAZARETH, Pod in THE BORROWERS and Patrick in LAST OF THE BLONDE BOMBSHELLS, in addition to parts in a host of heavyish dramas and classics like *Uncle Vanya* (Astrov), *The Misanthrope*, *The Deep Blue Sea* (William Collyer) and *King Lear* (Lear). His third wife was actress Penelope Wilton.

Holmes, Eamonn

(1959–)

Belfast-born presenter of news, current affairs, sport and magazine programmes, chiefly associated with GMTV until his departure for Sky News in 2005. His TV career began with Ulster Television, where he covered farming and sport after training as a journalist. He took over as host of *Good Evening Ulster* from Gloria Hunniford and followed her to the UK mainland to host *Open Air, Pot Black Timeframe*, HOLIDAY, *Oddballs, Garden Party*, HOW DO THEY DO THAT?, SONGS OF PRAISE, POINTS OF VIEW, *TV Scrabble, Pass the Buck, Remotely Funny* and THE NATIONAL LOTTERY LIVE, *The Christmas Show, Hard Spell* and *Star Spell, Sudo-Q* and *City Hospital*, among other programmes.

Holmes and Yoyo ★

US (Universal) Situation Comedy. BBC 1 1976–7
(US: ABC 1976–7)

Det. Alexander Holmes .... **Richard B. Shull**
Gregory 'Yoyo' Yoyonovich ..... **John Schuck**
Capt. Harry Sedford .... **Bruce Kirby**
Officer Maxine Moon .... **Andrea Howard**

Creators **Jack Sher, Lee Hewitt**
Executive Producer **Leonard Stern**

● ***A hapless cop's new partner is a temperamental robot.***
Despite his name, Alexander Holmes is not the world's greatest detective. In fact the dopey policeman's record is so poor (particularly when it comes to getting his patrol partners injured) that his superiors foist on him a robot colleague. Yoyo is a remarkably human-looking creation who brings a new dimension to crime cracking, thanks to his photographic memory, colour-print production and other technological advances. But, like all mechanoids, he is prone to malfunction at times, which gives rise to much of the humour. Holmes soon learns Yoyo's secret but this doesn't prevent him being as inept as ever on the streets. In contrast, policewoman Maxine Moon is blissfully unaware that Yoyo doesn't have a heart and keeps making passes at the electronic cop. Just 13 episodes were made: John Astin, former star of THE ADDAMS FAMILY, directed some.

Holness, Bob

(1928–)

Radio and television personality, beginning his career in his native South Africa in 1955. After a number of years with Radios 1 and 2, Radio Luxembourg and LBC in London, Holness found himself an unlikely cult figure among teenagers in the 1980s, thanks to his long-running quiz show, BLOCKBUSTERS. He later hosted another quiz, *Raise the Roof*, and the revival of CALL MY BLUFF. Among his earlier TV credits were the game shows TAKE A LETTER and JUNIOR CRISS CROSS QUIZ, and, more seriously, WORLD IN ACTION and WHAT THE PAPERS SAY.

Holocaust ★★★

US (NBC/Titus) Drama. BBC 1 1978 (US: NBC 1978)

Dr Josef Weiss	**Fritz Weaver**
Berta Weiss	**Rosemary Harris**
Karl Weiss	**James Woods**
Inga Helms/Weiss	**Meryl Streep**
Rudi Weiss	**Joseph Bottoms**
Anna Weiss	**Blanche Baker**
Moses Weiss	**Sam Wanamaker**
Erik Dorf	**Michael Moriarty**
Marta Dorf	**Deborah Norton**
Kurt Dorf	**Robert Stephens**
Reinhard Heydrich	**David Warner**
Heinrich Himmler	**Ian Holm**
Adolf Eichmann	**Tom Bell**

Writer **Gerald Green**
Executive Producer **Herb Brodkin**
Producer **Robert Berger**

● ***Controversial dramatization of the persecution of the Jews by the Nazis.***
This grim, four-part drama, screened on consecutive nights by the BBC, recounts the atrocities of World War II, with particular focus on the plight of European Jews and their persecution and extermination by the Nazis. The Weiss family from Berlin, headed by Dr Josef Weiss, represent the Judaic race, and the character of lawyer Erik Dorf is seen as a manifestation of Nazi ambition. Their respective lives are charted from the year 1935 to the end of hostilities. Despite criticism for turning one of the most horrific periods in history into a semi-soap opera, with sentimental music, pointless dialogue and inevitably subdued horrors, the series was a moving experience for most viewers and won numerous awards.

Home, Anna

OBE (1938–)

British TV producer/director and executive working in children's programming from the early 1960s. Home began with the BBC, where she helped develop PLAY SCHOOL, JACKANORY and GRANGE HILL (the last as executive producer of all the Corporation's children's drama output). She joined the fledgling TVS to create its children's department in 1981, and was responsible for ITV network output that included NO. 73, FRAGGLE ROCK and KNIGHTS OF GOD, but she returned to the BBC in 1986 as Head of Children's Programmes, eventually retiring in 1997 and becoming chief executive of the Children's Film and Television Foundation.

Home and Away ★★

Australia (Network 7) Drama. ITV 1989–2000/Channel 5 2001–

Tom Fletcher	**Roger Oakley**
Pippa Fletcher/Ross	**Vanessa Downing**
	Debra Lawrance
Celia Stewart	**Fiona Spence**
Alf Stewart	**Ray Meagher**
Ruth 'Roo' Stewart	**Justine Clarke**
Ailsa Hogan/Stewart	**Judy Nunn**
Donald Fisher	**Norman Coburn**
Lance Smart	**Peter Vroom**
Sally Keating/Fletcher/Saunders	**Kate Ritchie**
Carly Morris/Lucini	**Sharyn Hodgson**
Lynn Davenport/Fletcher	**Helena Bozich**
Floss McPhee	**Sheila Kennelly**
Neville McPhee	**Frank Lloyd**
Al Simpson	**Terence Donovan**
Bobby Simpson/Morgan/Marshall	**Nicolle Dickson**
Martin Dibble	**Craig Thompson**
Sophie Simpson	**Rebekah Elmaloglou**
Viv Newton	**Mouche Phillips**
Morag Bellingham	**Cornelia Frances**
Frank Morgan	**Alex Papps**
Steven Matheson	**Adam Willits**
Matt Wilson	**Greg Benson**
Marilyn Chambers/Fisher	**Emily Symons**
Emma Jackson	**Dannii Minogue**
Grant Mitchell	**Craig McLachlan**
Ben Lucini	**Julian McMahon**
Adam Cameron	**Mat Stevenson**
Michael Ross	**Dennis Coard**
Blake Dean	**Les Hill**
Karen Dean	**Belinda Jarrett**
Nick Parrish	**Bruce Roberts**
Simon Fitzgerald	**Richard Norton**
Haydn Ross	**Andrew Hill**
David Croft	**Guy Pearce**
Lucinda Croft	**Dee Smart**
Shane Parrish	**Dieter Brummer**
Damian Roberts	**Matt Doran**
Sam Marshall	**Ryan Clark**
Greg Marshall	**Ross Newton**
Finlay Roberts	**Tina Thomsen**
Irene Roberts	**Lynne McGranger**
Luke Cunningham	**John Adam**
Tug O'Neale	**Tristan Bancks**
Roxanne Miller	**Lisa Lackey**

Sarah Taylor	**Laura Vazquez**
Angel Brooks/Parrish	**Melissa George**
Jack Wilson	**Daniel Amalm**
Rob Storey	**Matthew Lilley**
Shannon Reed	**Isla Fisher**
Curtis Reed	**Shane Ammann**
Donna Bishop	**Nicola Quilter**
Selina Cook	**Tempany Deckert**
Travis Nash	**Nic Testoni**
Joel Nash	**David Woodley**
Natalie Nash	**Antoinette Byron**
Tom Nash	**Graeme Squires**
Gypsy Nash	**Kimberley Cooper**
Rebecca Nash	**Belinda Emmett**
Jesse McGregor	**Ben Unwin**
Peta Janossi	**Aleetza Wood**
Hayley Smith	**Rebecca Cartwright**
Ella	**Scott Lynch**
Will Smith	**Zac Drayson**
Ken Smith	**Anthony Phelan**
Justine Welles	**Bree Desborough**
Vinnie Patterson	**Ryan Kwanten**
Chloe Fraser	**Kristy Wright**
James Fraser	**Michael Piccirilli**
Duncan Stewart	**Brendan McKensy**
Mitch McColl	**Cameron Welsh**
Harry Keller/Reynolds	**Justin Melvey**
Shauna Bradley	**Kylie Watson**
Nick Smith	**Matt Juarez**
	Chris Egan
Colleen Smart	**Lyn Collingwood**
Rhys Sutherland	**Michael Beckley**
Shelley Sutherland	**Paula Forrest**
Dani Sutherland	**Tammin Sursok**
Kirsty Sutherland/Phillips	**Christie Hayes**
Jade Sutherland	**Kate Garvey**
Noah Lawson	**Beau Brady**
Leah Poulos/Patterson/ Patterson-Baker	**Ada Nicodemou**
Dr Charlotte Adams	**Stephanie Chaves-Jacobson**
Sebastian Miller	**Mitch Firth**
Dr Flynn Saunders	**Martin Dingle-Wall**
	Joel McIlroy
Max Sutherland	**Sebastian Elmaloglou**
Alex Poulos	**Danny Raco**
Josh West	**Daniel Collopy**
Kane Phillips	**Sam Atwell**
Beth Hunter/Sutherland	**Clarissa House**
Katherine 'Kit' Hunter	**Amy Mizzi**
Scott Hunter	**Kip Gamblin**
Robbie Hunter	**Jason Smith**
Henry Hunter	**Tobi Atkins**
Matilda Hunter	**Indiana Evans**
Tasha Andrews	**Isabel Lucas**
Ric Dalby	**Mark Furze**
Barry Hyde	**Ivar Kants**
Kim Hyde	**Chris Hemsworth**
Dan Baker	**Tim Campbell**
Amanda Vale	**Holly Brisley**
Cassie Turner	**Sharni Vinson**
Tony Holden	**Jon Sivewright**
Jack Holden	**Paul O'Brien**
Lucas Holden	**Rhys Wakefield**
Martha Mackenzie	**Jodi Gordon**

Creator/Executive Producer **Alan Bateman**

● ***Life with troubled kids in the fictitious Australian resort of Summer Bay.***

Home and Away was developed by Australia's Seven Network, the station which gave away NEIGHBOURS in 1985. It was seen as a rival to that series not only in its native country but also in the UK, where it was purchased by ITV to run head to head with *Neighbours* at lunchtimes and in the early evening.

Set in the coastal town of Summer Bay (it is *always* summer), near Sydney, *Home and Away* initially focuses on foster-parents Tom and Pippa Fletcher, who have moved to a run-down caravan park after Tom has lost his job. Tom dies of a heart attack in his car early on, and his wife, Pippa, then soldiers on alone (albeit with a different actress in the role) before marrying Michael Ross. Among the other prominent citizens of Summer Bay are local headmaster Donald Fisher; know-all grocer/bait-shop owner Alf Stewart; his wife Ailsa; and teacher Grant Mitchell (played by Craig McLachlan, poached from *Neighbours*). The kids are initially headed by Bobby Simpson (one-time co-owner with Ailsa of the local restaurant, The Summer Bay Diner); Carly Morris (later married to former soldier Ben Lucini); orphan Adam Cameron; and studious Steven Matheson, but new generations of youngsters make their way to Summer Bay over the years as, melodramatically, the series mingles tales of romance, death, family secrets and other scandals. One episode was filmed in Ironbridge, Shropshire. In summer 2001, the series switched to Channel 5/five in the UK.

Home Improvement ★★

US (Wind Dancer/Touchstone) Situation Comedy. Channel 4 1994–9 (US: ABC 1991–9)
DVD: Buena Vista

Tim Taylor	**Tim Allen**
Jill Taylor	**Patricia Richardson**
Brad Taylor	**Zachery Ty Bryan**
Randy Taylor	**Jonathan Taylor Thomas**
Mark Taylor	**Taran Noah Smith**
Wilson Wilson	**Earl Hindman**
Al Borland	**Richard Karn**
Lisa	**Pamela Anderson**
Heidi	**Debbe Dunning**

Executive Producers **Matt Williams, Carmen Finestra, David McFadzean**

● ***The star of a DIY TV show wields less power at home.***

Expanding on his stand-up act, which majored on the macho fascination with motors and power tools, Tim Allen branched out into sitcom with *Home Improvement*. In it he plays Tim Taylor, the tool-belted host of a TV DIY show (*Tool Time*, sponsored by Binfords Tools) in Detroit. Taylor is a man whose solution to every problem is to bring out a more powerful tool. Al Borland is nominally Tim's assistant on the show but is the guy who really knows how to use a workbench. Also seen are glamorous Tool Time Girls, first Lisa (a pre-Baywatch Pamela Anderson) and then Heidi. Taylor is also a family man, with an intelligent, ambitious wife, Jill (a psychologist), to keep him in check and run the house, plus three young kids, Brad, Randy and Mark, who progress through their teenage years as the show continues. They despair whenever the cack-handed home improver threatens to dig out one of his famous tools. Wilson is the next-door neighbour, whose face is never seen behind the garden fence but who is always quick with advice on dealing with women – an area in which Tim is notably deficient.

Home James ✶

UK (Thames) Situation Comedy. ITV 1987–90

Jim London .... **Jim Davidson**
Robert Palmer .... **George Sewell**
Henry Compton .... **Harry Towb**
Sarah .... **Vanessa Knox-Mawer**
Paula .... **Sherrie Hewson**
Terry .... **Owen Whittaker**
Connie .... **Cecilia-Marie Carreon**
Eleanor Hayward .... **Juliette Grassby**

Executive Producer **Anthony Parker**
Producers **Anthony Parker, David Askey, Martin Shardlow**

A chirpy Cockney falls on his feet as a private chauffeur.

Jim London, having seen his little house in UP THE ELEPHANT AND ROUND THE CASTLE demolished, has at last found paid employment. He's a delivery driver for Palmer Electronics plc, but is soon accused of failing to do his duty and is sacked on the spot. The truth is, however, that Jim is innocent, and he is brought back onto the payroll by company boss Robert Palmer, who shares Jim's East End upbringing. Jim becomes Palmer's personal chauffeur and takes up residence in his swanky mansion, where he instantly ruffles the feathers of snooty butler Henry Compton. Also in service at the house are Paula, Terry and au pair Connie, and mucking in is Palmer's attractive daughter, Sarah. Thus the scene is set for three series of domestic farce. Eventually, however, Palmer's business goes belly up and the staff is downsized, leaving only Jim and his sparring partner Compton to care for their struggling boss. Palmer, however, bounces back as a business consultant, taking on pushy Eleanor Hayward as his new PA during the final series.

Home to Roost ✶✶

UK (Yorkshire) Situation Comedy. ITV 1985–7; 1989–90
DVD: BFS Entertainment (Region 1 only)

Henry Willows .... **John Thaw**
Matthew Willows .... **Reece Dinsdale**
Enid Thompson .... **Elizabeth Bennett**
Fiona Fennell .... **Joan Blackham**

Writer **Eric Chappell**
Producers **Vernon Lawrence, David Reynolds**

A father's life is turned upside down when his grown-up son returns home.

With his parents divorced, 17-year-old Matthew Willows lived with his mother – until she threw him out. In him she recognizes the same stubbornness and other character traits that led to her separation from his father, Henry. Now the homeless Matthew decides to move in with his dad and the sparks begin to fly. Henry has long been accustomed to living life at his own pace, in his own grumpy way and only for himself. Now there is a cuckoo in the nest, and what's more this cuckoo is a younger version of himself. The result is a series of generation-gap conflicts, as father and son do domestic battle. Enid is Henry's housekeeper (actress Elizabeth Bennett reprised the role for the American version, *You Again*, starring Jack Klugman), replaced in later editions by new daily Fiona Fennell. Rebecca Lacey occasionally drops in as Julie, Matthew's sister.

Homicide: Life on the Street ✶✶✶

US (Baltimore Pictures/Fatima/Reeves/Fremantle) Police Drama. Channel 4 1993–9 (US: NBC 1993–9)
DVD: A&E Home Video (Region 1 only)

Det. Stanley Bolander .... **Ned Beatty**
Det. John Munch .... **Richard Belzer**
Det. Frank Pembleton .... **Andre Braugher**
Det. Tim Bayliss .... **Kyle Secor**
Det. Beau Felton .... **Daniel Baldwin**
Lt. Al Giardello .... **Yaphet Kotto**
Det./Sgt Kay Howard .... **Melissa Leo**
Det. Meldrick Lewis .... **Clark Johnson**
Det. Steve Crosetti .... **Jon Polito**
Lt./Capt./Det. Megan Russert .... **Isabella Hofmann**
Det. Mike Kellerman .... **Reed Diamond**
J. H. Brodie .... **Max Perlich**
Dr Julianna Cox .... **Michelle Forbes**
Det. Paul Falsone .... **Jon Seda**
Det. Stuart Gharty .... **Peter Gerety**
Det. Laura Ballard .... **Callie Thorne**
Det. Terri Stivers .... **Toni Lewis**
Det. Rene Sheppard .... **Michael Michele**
Agent Mike Giardello .... **Giancarlo Esposito**

Creator **Paul Attanasio**
Executive Producers **Barry Levinson, Tom Fontana**

Glamour-free insight into the workings of an inner-city murder squad.

Baltimore is the setting for this gritty police drama. Taking hand-held cameras out into the heart of the city, and shunning excessive car chases and shoot outs, realism was the aim of the production team. The focus is on a motley bunch of detectives as they work over murder cases or perhaps just kill time at the station. Divided into four operational teams, the cops include Det. Stanley Bolander (nicknamed 'The Big Man'), who works with world-weary Munch, and the skilful Pembleton who tours with novice Bayliss, but there's a large turnover of cast members. Edgy relationships, political incorrectness and often inappropriate behaviour shine through, alongside a genuine commitment to make their work pay. Al Giardello is the superior officer (a black Italian) who yells out the commands to keep his officers in check. He later shares his job with Megan Russert, who, having climbed the police ladder, is then busted back down to detective. A white board in the office lists the cases under investigation, the ink colour being changed from red to black whenever the case is put to bed. The series was based on the book *Homicide: A Year on the Killing Streets*, by journalist David Simon, who spent time researching with the real-life Baltimore murder squad.

Honey for Tea ✶

UK (BBC) Situation Comedy. BBC 1 1994

Nancy Belasco .... **Felicity Kendal**
Prof. Simon Latimer .... **Nigel Le Vaillant**
Sir Dickie Hobhouse .... **Leslie Phillips**
Jake Belasco .... **Patrick McCollough**
Hon. Lucy Courtney .... **Caroline Harker**
Dr Basil Quinn .... **Alan David**
Charlie Chadwick .... **Crispin Bonham-Carter**

Writer **Michael Aitkens**
Producer **Gareth Gwenlan**

A Californian widow and her son claim their inheritance at an English university.

In this seven-episode, culture-clash comedy, recently bereaved American Nancy Belasco is left penniless but does have some idea of how to benefit from her late husband's 'business dealings'. His less than honest transactions have included support for his alma mater, St Maud's College, Cambridge, and now Nancy seizes the chance to call in a favour. Her 20-year-old son, Jake, is far from academically brilliant but, as far as Nancy is concerned, he deserves his chance and so, by hook or by crook, she installs him as a student among the brightest young people in England. Jake proceeds to take his opportunity with both hands, winning the affections of the aristocratic Lucy Courtney, secretary to wacky college master Sir Dickie Hobhouse. Meanwhile, Nancy finds herself a job at the university, working as assistant bursar alongside stick-in-the-mud don Dr Basil Quinn, and sharing hall residence with tutor Simon Latimer, who helps her through the arcane customs and practices of English varsity life.

Honey Lane

See *Market in Honey Lane*.

Honey West ★

US (Four Star) Detective Drama. ITV 1965–6 (US: ABC 1965–6)

Honey West .... **Anne Francis**
Sam Bolt .... **John Ericson**
Aunt Meg .... **Irene Hervey**

Creator **G. G. Fickling**
Executive Producer **Aaron Spelling**

Private investigations with a feminine kick.

Spun-off from an episode of BURKE'S LAW, this series introduced one of the first female private eyes on TV. Honey West takes over the family investigation agency following the death of her father and makes a pretty good fist of it, assisted by adoring legman Sam Bolt, who scolds her for getting into trouble, and her pet ocelot, Bruce. Emma Peel-type martial arts skills, James Bond gadgetry and a TV repair van (branded 'H. W. Bolt & Co., TV Service'), fitted out with the latest surveillance equipment, also help no end. Aunt Meg casts a parental eye over her daring niece and occasionally gets caught up in the private detection. The character of Honey West first appeared in the 1957 novel *This Girl for Hire*, penned by husband and wife Forest and Gloria Fickling under the pen name of G. G. Fickling. Star Anne Francis had previously been best known for her role in the cult movie *Forbidden Planet*.

Honeycombe, Gordon

(1936–)

Versatile Gordon Honeycombe is remembered by most viewers as one of ITN's longest-serving newscasters, joining the network in 1965. Honeycombe entered broadcasting in radio in Hong Kong and then became a member of the Royal Shakespeare Company. After 12 years at ITN, he left after a dispute over a firefighters' strike, which he publicly supported, and concentrated instead on his successful writing career. He has had a number of books published and has scripted TV plays. A keen genealogist, he hosted *Family History* for the BBC in 1979 and also acted as narrator on Arthur C. Clarke's MYSTERIOUS WORLD for YTV. In 1984 he resumed newsreading with TV-am, staying five years before returning to the stage.

Honeymooners, The ★★★★

US (Jackie Gleason Enterprises) Situation Comedy. BBC 2 1989–91 (US: CBS 1955–6)
DVD: Paramount (Region 1 only)

Ralph Kramden .... **Jackie Gleason**
Ed Norton .... **Art Carney**
Alice Kramden .... **Audrey Meadows**
Sheila MacRae
Trixie Norton .... **Joyce Randolph**
Jane Kean

Executive Producer **Jack Philbin**

A bus driver and his best mate dream of a better life, but their wives are more realistic.

A belated late-night screening in the UK undervalues the significance of *The Honeymooners* in television history. This simple domestic sitcom is always cited as one of TV's comedy milestones but, strangely, it took over 30 years to get a decent airing in Britain. The series features a New York bus driver, Ralph Kramden, who shares a dingy apartment in Chauncey Street, Brooklyn, with his long-suffering wife, Alice. Big Ralph is an angry, blustery sort. His rage is essentially the cry of the frustrated urban blue-collar worker, destined to live in a modest little world all his life. As a means of escape, Kramden dreams up countless get-rich-quick schemes, all of which come to naught, as the more down-to-earth and pragmatic Alice could have predicted. There's plenty of rough and tumble in the Kramden house, and many's the time that Ralph jokingly threatens to take a swipe at his missus (sending her 'right to the moon'), but they realize they are in this together. The programme title may be ironic (even at the start they are many years into married life), but there's a wholesome bond between the spouses that Ralph recognizes at the end of each show when he tells Alice that she's the greatest (star Jackie Gleason's own nickname was 'The Great One'). Providing a further dimension to the Kramdens' little world are their upstairs neighbours, the Nortons. Ed is a sewage worker, cheerfully far more content with his lot than Kramden and ever-optimistic. He is 'Ralphie-boy's' best buddy and hapless co-conspirator, a man whose ineptitude only raises Kramden's blood pressure still further. Ed's wife, Trixie, is a housewife like Alice, but she dotes on her husband and is less likely to kick up a storm over the boys' trips to the Raccoon Lodge or other bids for freedom. (If the situation sounds familiar, think Fred and Barney: *The Honeymooners* is often credited as providing the basics of THE FLINTSTONES.)

The main core of *Honeymooners'* episodes is a package of 39 filmed half-hours first shown in 1955–6. However, the Kramdens and the Nortons first appeared in live sketches around 1951 in *Cavalcade of Stars*, one of the big shows made by the long-defunct DuMont network. In these skits, the part of Alice was played by Pert Kelton. When Jackie Gleason was offered *The Jackie Gleason Show*, his own variety programme, by CBS in 1952, *The Honeymooners* filled part of each show. They returned in the same format after the filmed series, in 1956–7. Further *Honeymooners* sketches appeared from time to time in *Jackie Gleason and His American Scene Magazine* (1962–6, with Sue Ane Langdon as Alice and Patricia Wilson as Trixie) but the next time *The Honeymooners* properly resurfaced was in 1966, in a revamp of *The Jackie Gleason Show*. With Sheila MacRae in the role of Alice and Jane Kean as Trixie, these sporadic sketches spread over four years often included musical numbers. In the 1970s, four *Honeymooner* reunions were produced, and in the 1980s Jackie Gleason released primitive recordings of some of the earliest sketches, which, edited together, were successfully syndicated in the USA. A man of many talents, Gleason also co-wrote *The Honeymooners*' theme song, 'You're My Greatest Love'.

Hong Kong Beat, The ★★

UK (BBC) Documentary. BBC 1 1978

Producer **John Purdie**

● ***A nine-part study of policing in the cramped colony of Hong Kong.***

Focusing on the activities of the British Colonial Force as they provided law and order in Hong Kong's busy, lively streets, *The Hong Kong Beat* won much acclaim and also gave rise to its fair share of controversy. It watched as local policemen rounded up the illegal immigrants, drug-pushers and other social nuisances which made policing this part of the world so complicated, hazardous and unique. The programme's theme music was a Top 30 hit for Richard Denton and Martin Cook in 1978.

Hong Kong Phooey ★★

US (Hanna-Barbera) Cartoon. BBC 1 1975 (US: ABC 1974–5)

Voices:

Penrod 'Penry' Pooch/ Hong Kong Phooey .... **Scatman Crothers**
Sgt Flint .... **Joe E. Ross**
Rosemary .... **Kathy Gori**
Spot .... **Don Messick**

Executive Producers **William Hanna, Joseph Barbera**
Producer **Iwao Takamoto**

● ***The clumsy canine janitor at a police station is actually a superhero trained in martial arts.***

Penrod Pooch (or Penry as he is known to Rosemary, the switchboard operator) works as the flunky in a big city police station. Unknown to his colleagues, especially the grouchy Sgt Flint, this is no ordinary dog but a crimebuster extraordinaire who operates under the guise of Hong Kong Phooey. Leaping into a filing cabinet, Penry dons his oriental superhero costume before dashing out in the Phooeymobile (garaged in a rubbish bin behind the station) to confront the weirdest criminals in the world. By banging a gong, he can convert his vehicle into other forms of transport, or even into hiding places. Phooey is accompanied only by Spot, the station's striped cat. Once in action, our hero demonstrates the martial arts he has learned from a correspondence course, dipping into the *Hong Kong Book of Kung Fu* to attempt manoeuvres like the slow-motion Hong Kong Phooey Chop (much to the exasperation of his feline companion). Among the Mutt of Steel's adversaries are Mr Tornado, the Gum Drop Kid and Professor Presto.

Hooperman ★★

US (Adam/20th Century-Fox) Police Drama. ITV 1988–90 (US: ABC 1987–9)

Det. Harry Hooperman .... **John Ritter**
Capt. Celeste ('CZ') Stern .... **Barbara Bosson**
Susan Smith .... **Debrah Farentino**
Officer Boris 'Bobo' Pritzger .... **Clarence Felder**
Officer Maureen 'Mo' DeMott .... **Sydney Walsh**
Officer Rick Silardi .... **Joseph Gian**
Insp. Clarence McNeil .... **Felton Perry**
Betty Bushkin .... **Alix Elias**

Creators **Steven Bochco, Terry Louise Fisher**
Executive Producers **Robert Myman, Leon Tokatyan, Rick Kellard**

● ***Life with a thoughtful San Francisco cop.***

In this half-hour mix of fast action and light humour, Harry Hooperman is a gun-shy detective in the San Francisco Police Department who, for leisure, plays saxophone in a local nightclub. He works for a tough but troubled boss, C. Z. Stern, and among his colleagues are gay cop Rick Silardi and Rick's protective partner, Mo DeMott. Home for Hooperman is a run-down apartment block bequeathed to him (together with its angry tenants) in an early episode by his murdered landlady, who also left him a noisy Jack Russell terrier, Bijoux. Susan Smith, the apartment's handyperson, is also a would-be writer. She has an affair with Harry, but leaves town after miscarrying his baby. This 'dramedy' – with a theme tune by Mike Post – came from the creators of HILL STREET BLUES and LA LAW. Its star, John Ritter, was the son of country singer Tex Ritter and had previously played the Richard O'Sullivan role in *Three's Company*, the American version of MAN ABOUT THE HOUSE.

Hopalong Cassidy ★★

US (William Boyd) Western. BBC 1955–6 (US: NBC 1949–51; Syndicated 1952–3)
DVD: Platinum Disc (Region 1 only)

Hopalong Cassidy .... **William Boyd**
Red Connors .... **Edgar Buchanan**

Producer **William Boyd**

● ***A cowboy samaritan rides to the rescue on his snow-white charger.***

The character of Hopalong Cassidy was created by Clarence E. Mulford around the start of the 20th century. But that was a different Hopalong from the one the kids knew and loved in the 1950s. Mulford had portrayed Cassidy as a rough, mean vagabond with a bad limp, a man who drank, swore and smoked. Actor William Boyd turned him into a faultless hero, an idol for the children, immaculately turned out in black to contrast dramatically with his silver hair, his silver spurs, his pearl-handled revolvers and his white steed, Topper. No longer troubled by the limp, he lived at the Bar 20 ranch and was accompanied in his adventures by Red Connors.

William Boyd had already played the role in the cinema, and he picked up the rights to these old B-movies when no one else was interested. He and his associate, Toby Anguish, re-edited them and repackaged them for TV. The first TV Hopalong, therefore, was actually the cinema version revisited. Eventually Boyd produced this new series specifically for television. It became an instant hit with younger viewers and went on to be one of the first great merchandising successes of the small screen.

Hope and Glory ✶✶

UK (BBC) Drama. BBC 1 1999–2000

Ian George .... **Lenny Henry**
Debbie Bryan .... **Amanda Redman**
Phil Jakes .... **Clive Russell**
Jan Woolley .... **Pippa Guard**
Colin Ward .... **William Gaminara**
Tony Elliot .... **Lee Warburton**
Sally Bell .... **Sara Stephens**
Mike Waters .... **Martin Trenaman**
Elaine Rawlings .... **Valerie Lilley**
Dennis Hill .... **Philip Whitchurch**
Jude Jakes .... **Julia Deakin**
Kitty Burton .... **Gillian Kearney**
Leo Wheeldon .... **Richard Griffiths**
Liana Andrews .... **Senya Roberts**
Keeley Porter .... **Sarah French**
Annie Gilbert .... **Phyllis Logan**
Matt Bennett .... **Gresby Nash**

Creator **Lucy Gannon**
Writers **Lucy Gannon, Ann Marie Di Mambro, Lisa Hunt**
Producers **Nicolas Brown, Chrissy Skinns**

● ***A dedicated young headmaster turns around a failing inner-city comprehensive.***

Hope Park School in London has been 'named and shamed' as one of the worst schools in the country. When 'superhead' Ian George is sent to investigate its failings, he surprisingly ends up accepting the position of its new head teacher, forgoing a big-salary job with the government inspectorate to breathe new life into the crumbling edifice. His task is immense: the pupils are unruly, the staff are indolent, the buildings in a poor state of repair. But, such are his idealism and commitment, George soon begins to turn things around, despite initial obstruction from certain colleagues like appalling geography teacher Jan Woolley and bitter and frustrated Scottish deputy head Phil Jakes. Support comes from the caring but headstrong maths teacher, Debbie Bryan, who becomes George's second deputy head (and later lover). But George has little time for play. A workaholic, he only wants the best for the school and its pupils, whom he views as having had a raw deal. So that the kids can meet their part of the bargain, he even tours the local estate every morning to round up latecomers and truants. When faced with outside opposition, such as from obstructive LEA man Leo Wheeldon in series two, George's stubbornness comes into play: he is a principal with principles. George's revolution even continues after the loss of both his deputies, when, in series three, new staff members Annie Gilbert and Matt Bennett are selected to fill their shoes.

Hope and Glory was a series that divided its audience. Some viewers felt truly inspired to meet the government's call for those who can to teach; others derided its over-simplistic and sentimental approach to the problems facing the nation's secondary schools.

Hope It Rains ✶✶

UK (Thames) Situation Comedy. ITV 1991–2

Harry Nash .... **Tom Bell**
Jace .... **Holly Aird**
Dennis .... **Eamon Boland**

Creators/Writers **John Esmonde, Bob Larbey**
Producer **John Howard Davies**

● ***A teenage girl and her stick-in-the-mud godfather don't see eye to eye.***

There's trouble in store for bachelor Harry Nash, when he agrees to provide a home for his 18-year-old goddaughter on the death of her parents. When Jace arrives, she turns his world upside down, for Harry is a well-ordered fellow, happy in his own company (miserable, in other words). He's about as animated as the exhibits in the ropey Empire Wax Museum he runs at a downtrodden seaside resort (the programme's title comes from Harry's wish for inclement weather, to bring in the punters). Jace, on the other hand, is lively, disorganized and rebellious. She stays in bed late and has plenty of other annoying habits that rub Harry up the wrong way. What they do have in common is stubbornness – which can only mean trouble. Caught in the middle of the bunfight is Dennis, Harry's easy-going photographer pal. Thirteen episodes were made, over two series.

Hopkins, Anthony

KBE (1937–)

Welsh-born cinema grandee, now an American citizen, who, before Hollywood beckoned, focused on television, appearing in work as varied as WAR AND PEACE (Pierre), THE EDWARDIANS (David Lloyd-George), QB VII (Dr Adam Kelno), *The Lindberg Kidnapping Case, Kean* (Edmund Kean), *Victory at Entebbe, Othello* (the Moor himself), *A Married Man, The Bunker* (Hitler), *Great Expectations* (Magwitch), *The Hunchback of Notre Dame* (Quasimodo), *Hollywood Wives* and *Across the Lake* (Donald Campbell), many of which were mini-series. Guest appearances in series like DEPARTMENT S characterized Hopkins's early career.

Hopkins, John

(1931–98)

Acclaimed London-born writer, the first script editor on Z CARS, a series for which he himself penned over 50 episodes. His work on the programme (and an earlier thriller series, *A Chance of Thunder*, in 1961) was followed by a couple of notable TV plays, *Fable* (1965) and *Horror of Darkness* (1966), before he contributed a four-part series entitled *Talking to a Stranger* (also 1966), which depicted the break-up of a family from various viewpoints. It was showered with praise and led to a growing involvement in the cinema, although Hopkins continued to script television material, including the hugely expensive *Divorce His, Divorce Hers* for HTV, SMILEY'S PEOPLE (with John Le Carré) and *Codename Kyril*. Other credits included episodes of DETECTIVE and two early Campion serials, *Dancers in Mourning* (1959) and *Death of a Ghost* (1960). His second wife was actress Shirley Knight.

Horace ✶✶

UK (Yorkshire) Comedy Drama. ITV 1982

Horace .... **Barry Jackson**
Mother .... **Jean Heywood**
Mr Frankel .... **Anthony Wingate**
Mrs Tiddy .... **Daphne Heard**

Writer **Roy Minton**
Executive Producer **David Cunliffe**
Producer **Keith Richardson**

Laughter and tears with a backward middle-aged man.

This six-part, twice-weekly offering was a risky venture into the realm of disability. Horace is a middle-aged man who, sadly, has the rather simple mind of a ten-year-old. His life revolves around working in a joke factory and spending a somewhat isolated existence somewhere between the worlds of adults and children. It is an existence in which sadness and humour walk side by side, as misunderstanding and muddle make even straightforward events chaotic and complicated, and in which Horace's long-suffering mother and Yorkshire neighbours like the bed-ridden Mrs Tiddy have to pick up the pieces. Based on a BBC 2 play from 1972, *Horace* stars former screen fight arranger Barry Jackson, now most familiar as pathologist Dr Bullard in MIDSOMER MURDERS. Richard Holmes supplies the music.

Hordern, Sir Michael

CBE (1911–95)

Grand old man of the English stage and screen, whose television work was occasional but notable, if focused at the heavier end of the drama market. His small-screen work stretched back to the 1940s (he appeared in a production of *Rebecca* in 1947, for instance) and his major roles were as Willie in *Cakes and Ale*, Friar Domingo in SHOGUN and the Reverend Simeon Simcox in PARADISE POSTPONED, with other credits including EDWARD THE SEVENTH (Gladstone), THE HISTORY MAN, *Ivanhoe*, *Mistress of Suspense*, TALES OF THE UNEXPECTED, *Scoop*, THE GREEN MAN and the ghost story *Whistle, and I'll Come to You*, for OMNIBUS. He also appeared in the *Screen Two* presentation *Memento Mori* (Godfrey Colston), INSPECTOR MORSE and MIDDLEMARCH (Peter Featherstone), as well as narrating FALL OF EAGLES. Hordern also performed Shakespeare for television, including *King Lear*, *Romeo and Juliet* and *The Tempest*. At the other end of the scale, he appeared with Richard Briers in the sketch anthology *Tall Stories*, acted as narrator for PADDINGTON and *The Secret World of Polly Flint*, voiced the part of Badger in the 1980s animation of THE WIND IN THE WILLOWS and told stories on JACKANORY.

Horizon ★★★

UK (BBC) Science Documentary. BBC 2 1964–

Award-winning popular-science programme.

Beginning monthly but now seen more frequently, *Horizon* has been a centrepiece of BBC 2's schedules since the channel's inception. Its brief has been science, but the scope has been broad and the treatment flexible. The usual pattern has been to devote a whole programme to one particular issue. Often using remarkable footage, the programme discusses a topic of general scientific interest or reviews the latest scientific advance. On occasions, dramatizations have been used, perhaps to illustrate events in the life of an inventor or chemist. Topics in recent years have included ice mummies, mosquitoes, asteroid impacts, the lost city of Atlantis, the collapse of the World Trade Centre towers, the Atkins Diet and Stephen Hawking. See also LIFE STORY.

Hornblower ★★★

UK (United/Meridian/A&E) Drama. ITV 1998–9; 2002–3

DVD: Cinema Club

Midshipman/Lt. Horatio Hornblower .... **Ioan Gruffudd**
Captain/Admiral Sir Edward Pellew .... **Robert Lindsay**
Matthews .... **Paul Copley**
Styles .... **Sean Gilder**
Oldroyd .... **Simon Sherlock**
Lt. Bracegirdle .... **Jonathan Coy**
Master Bowles .... **Colin McClachlan**
Finch .... **Chris Barnes**
Midshipman/Lt. Archie Kennedy .... **Jamie Bamber**
Midshipman Cleveland .... **Frank Boyce**
Lt. Bush .... **Paul McGann**
Capt. Hammond .... **Ian McElhinney**

Producer **Andrew Benson**
Executive Producers **Vernon Lawrence, Delia Fine, Michele Buck**

Rousing tales of life on the high seas.

Beginning with a series of four two-hour films, *Hornblower* is based on the book *Mr Midshipman Hornblower* by C. S. Forester and features the exploits of one Horatio Hornblower. A callow, seasick, 17-year-old youth new on board HMS *Justinian* in the first film – set in 1794 – Hornblower matures into a more than able seaman and works his way up the naval ladder to the rank of lieutenant. Taking the raw recruit under his wing, and recognizing his talent, is the redoubtable Captain Pellew, skipper of Hornblower's second ship, HMS *Indefatigable*. Guest stars include Denis Lawson as Captain Foster, Cherie Lunghi as the Duchess of Wharfedale and Peter Vaughan as Admiral Lord Hood. The films, costing £12 million, were filmed off the coasts of Yalta in the Ukraine and Portugal, using two authentic vessels – a Baltic trader called the *Julia* and the newly built 22-gun *Grand Turk*. These and some 11 scale models were employed to re-create some of the fiery battles of the late 18th century. But, as well as the glory, the often sheer misery and discomfort of life at sea were also shown. Hornblower returned to ITV in 2002 in a new two-parter, this time filmed in a dry-land mocked-up ship. This was followed a year later by two new two-hour adventures.

Horowitz, Anthony

(1956–)

British screenwriter (and successful children's novelist), specializing in crime drama. After working on series such as ROBIN OF SHERWOOD, THE SAINT (the 1980s revival), WILLIAM TELL, *Dramarama*, BOON, *The Gift*, AGATHA CHRISTIE'S POIROT, ANNA LEE and MURDER MOST HORRID, Horowitz was influential in setting up MIDSOMER MURDERS (being its first writer) and then created his own series THE VANISHING MAN, CRIME TRAVELLER, MURDER IN MIND and FOYLE'S WAR. He also adapted his own kids' book *South by South East* for ITV and wrote a two-part thriller for Channel 5 called *Menace*. Horowitz is married to TV producer Jill Green.

Horseman Riding By, A ★★★

UK (BBC) Drama. BBC 1 1978
DVD: Acorn Media

Paul Craddock	**Nigel Havers**
John Rudd	**Glyn Houston**
Grace Lovell/Craddock	**Fiona Gaunt**
Claire Derwent/Craddock	**Prunella Ransome**
Rose Derwent	**Valerie Phillips**
Dr O'Keefe	**Glyn Owen**
Dr Maureen O'Keefe/Rudd	**Gillian McCutcheon**
Arabella Codsall	**Madge Ryan**
Martin Codsall	**Joby Blanshard**
Will Codsall	**David Delve**
Sydney Codsall	**Kevin Cope**
	Terence Budd
Elinor Willoughby/Codsall	**Sarah Porter**
Lord Gilroy	**Jack May**
Tamer Potter	**Forbes Collins**
Meg Potter	**Pam St Clement**
Smut Potter	**Martin Fisk**
Cissie Potter	**Valerie Holloway**
Violet Potter	**Wendy Holloway**
Arthur Pitts	**Robert Vahey**
Martha Pitts	**Maryann Turner**
Gloria Pitts	**Christine Hargreaves**
Henry Pitts	**Christopher Reeks**
Mrs Ada Handcock	**Julie May**
James Grenfell	**Frank Moorey**
Revd Horsey	**Milton Johns**

Writer **Arden Winch**
Producer **Ken Riddington**

A young invalid soldier becomes the liberal new squire of a Devon estate.

In 1902 young, well-to-do Paul Craddock, a former Boer War lieutenant suffering from a shrapnel wound to his leg, arrives on the Devon coast to view an estate that is on the market. He wants a new role in life and has money to invest after inheriting his father's scrap business in London. The Shallowford Estate on the River Sorrel has been badly run by its previous owners, the Lovells; but Craddock likes what he sees and, encouraged by very capable estate manager John Rudd, he accepts the challenge to become the new squire. His new title involves keeping a close eye on the various farming families who rent property in 'The Valley'. These include rough-and-ready poachers the Potters, the pushy Codsalls, the modest Pitts family and the very pleasant Derwents (particularly pleasant is daughter Claire, who becomes Paul's assistant and eventually his second wife). Craddock impresses the locals with his fairness and liberality, but these traits are not so popular with his Conservative neighbour, Lord Gilroy.

The story – based on the novel by R. F. Delderfield – progresses in 13 parts through various personal ups and downs and through times of difficulty and happiness in the estate right up to and beyond World War I, when many of the men are called away to duty, with tragic consequences.

Horsfield, Debbie

(1955–)

Eccles-born dramatist, writer of light dramas like MAKING OUT, THE RIFF RAFF ELEMENT, *Born to Run*, SEX, CHIPS AND ROCK 'N' ROLL and *Cutting It*.

Horton, Robert

(Mead Howard Horton; 1924–)

Rugged American leading man of the 1950s and 1960s, seen to best effect as trail scout Flint McCullough in WAGON TRAIN, following a year in an American soap called *King's Row*. After five years in *Wagon Train*, Horton left the series, allegedly because he was fed up with Westerns. All the same, his next – and, to date, last – starring role was in another Western, the short-lived A MAN CALLED SHENANDOAH in 1965. Among Horton's other TV credits have been episodes of ALFRED HITCHCOCK PRESENTS and another US soap, *As the World Turns*.

Hoskins, Bob

(1942–)

British actor whose film career has largely overshadowed his television record, the early highlights of which were the leading parts of George Dobbs in THICK AS THIEVES, Arthur Parker in PENNIES FROM HEAVEN and Arnie Cole in *Flickers*. Hoskins started out with minor roles in dramas like *Villains*, CROWN COURT and NEW SCOTLAND YARD, plus various single plays. He later appeared in THRILLER, VAN DER VALK and ROCK FOLLIES, among other series, before narrating the comedy BIG JIM AND THE FIGARO CLUB and featuring as removals man Alf in the educational series ON THE MOVE. Subsequent TV credits include the role of De Flores in a BBC *Performance* presentation of *The Changeling*, providing the voice of Teddy in *The Forgotten Toys* and playing Mr Micawber in DAVID COPPERFIELD and Prof. George Challenger in *The Lost World*. He also guest-starred in FRASIER.

Hot Metal ★★★

UK (LWT) Situation Comedy. ITV 1986; 1988

Terence 'Twiggy' Rathbone/ Russell Spam	**Robert Hardy**
Harry Stringer	**Geoffrey Palmer**
Greg Kettle	**Richard Kane**
Bill Tytla	**John Gordon-Sinclair**
Max	**Geoffrey Hutchings**
Father Teasdale	**John Horsley**
Richard Lipton	**Richard Wilson**

Writers **Andrew Marshall, David Renwick**
Producer **Humphrey Barclay**

An ailing tabloid newspaper falls victim to an unscrupulous media baron.

The Daily Crucible, a flabby newspaper at the tabloid end of the market, is being strangled by its competitors and its circulation is plummeting. Its proprietors, Rathouse International, a global media conglomerate headed by the ruthless 'Twiggy' Rathbone, consequently take remedial action, installing a new editor, Rathbone's lookalike, Russell Spam. Spam radically alters the nature of the paper, introducing sex exposés, majoring on political scandals and adding titillation to page three, much to the disgust of managing editor Harry Stringer. But it works, and circulation roars ahead. Stringer (mysteriously lost in a flying incident) is replaced by a new MD, Richard Lipton, in the second and last series.

Hot Shoe Show, The ✶

UK (BBC) Entertainment. BBC 1 1983–4

Presenter **Wayne Sleep**

Producer **Tom Gutteridge**

Introduction to dance for the masses.

In an attempt to bring performance dance to the people, this light-hearted dip into the terpsichorean world was fronted by diminutive Wayne Sleep and featured a resident company of hoofers. Most came from London stage shows of the time; others from the Royal Ballet. In their number were Bonnie Langford, Finola Hughes and Cherry Gillespie (formerly of TOP OF THE POPS' Pan's People). Short routines were combined with songs and comedy for a dance mix with populist appeal.

Hotel ✶

US (Aaron Spelling) Drama. ITV 1983–9 (US: ABC1983–8)

Victoria Cabot .... **Anne Baxter**
Peter McDermott .... **James Brolin**
Christine Francis .... **Connie Sellecca**
Mark Danning .... **Shea Farrell**
Billy Griffin .... **Nathan Cook**
Dave Kendall .... **Michael Spound**
Megan Kendall .... **Heidi Bohay**
Julie Gillette .... **Shari Belafonte-Harper**

Executive Producers **Aaron Spelling, Douglas S. Cramer**

The lives and loves of visitors to a swish San Francisco hotel.

From the creators of THE LOVE BOAT, this series adopts a similar format – introducing guest stars to supply the main action in each episode, with a small supporting permanent cast to provide the background. Events centre around the St Gregory Hotel and the regulars are manager Peter McDermott; his attractive assistant, Christine Francis; Mark Danning, the hotel's PR executive; and Billy Griffin, an ex-con turned security officer. Bette Davis was scheduled to star in the series, playing hotel owner Laura Trent, but, through illness, she appeared in only the first episode. Anne Baxter was brought in to take over in the guise of her sister-in-law, Victoria Cabot. The series was based on the novel by Arthur Hailey.

House ✶✶✶

US (Heel and Toe/Bad Hat Harry/Universal) Drama. five 2005– (US: Fox 2004–)
DVD: Universal

Dr Gregory House .... **Hugh Laurie**
Dr Lisa Cuddy .... **Lisa Edelstein**
Dr James Wilson .... **Robert Sean Leonard**
Dr Allison Cameron .... **Jennifer Morrison**
Dr Taylor Eric Foreman .... **Omar Epps**
Dr Robert Chase .... **Jesse Spencer**
Sela Ward .... **Stacy Warner**

Creator **David Shore**
Executive Producers **Paul Attanasio, Katie Jacobs, David Shore, Bryan Singer**

A medical consultant has no time for his patients but is brilliant at his job.

Physically, Dr Greg House is a bit of a wreck. He walks with a limp, supported by a stick, he's never clean shaven, he suffers from hay fever and he has trouble sleeping. No wonder he's grumpy and has a woeful bedside manner. Mentally, however, he's as sharp as a tack, as his small cohort of junior doctors can testify. House's career is not so much medical as detective. He specializes in infectious diseases and his diagnostic skills are second to no one's. Putting emotion firmly to one side, and employing a systematic process of elimination, he's able to root out the cause of the most baffling ailments. The bright young doctors in House's team are immunologist Allison Cameron, intensive-care specialist Robert Chase and neurologist Eric Foreman. Oncology specialist James Wilson is House's old friend and the one person he sometimes turns to for advice. Lisa Cuddy is the hospital administrator and the source of tension (romantic and otherwise) for the dishevelled main man.

Creator David Shore has admitted to basing the character of Greg House on Conan Doyle's Sherlock Holmes. There are clues to the inspiration scattered through the series, from the similarity of both men's surnames to their shared addiction to drugs (Vicodin in House's case). It is even revealed that House lives at number 221B, the same as Holmes's address in Baker Street. For star Hugh Laurie to win a Golden Globe award by playing an American doctor (complete with convincing American accent) in an American series was quite an achievement but Laurie was not the only import. Jesse Spencer, who plays Chase, had previously starred as Billy Kennedy in NEIGHBOURS.

House of Cards/To Play the King/ The Final Cut ✶✶✶✶

UK (BBC/WGBH Boston) Drama. BBC 1 1990/1993/1995
DVD: BBC

Francis Urquhart .... **Ian Richardson**
Mattie Storin .... **Susannah Harker** *(Cards)*
Elizabeth Urquhart .... **Diane Fletcher**
Tim Stamper .... **Colin Jeavons** *(Cards/King)*
Roger O'Neill .... **Miles Anderson** *(Cards)*
Henry Collingridge .... **David Lyon** *(Cards)*
Anne Collingridge .... **Isabelle Amyes** *(Cards)*
Penny Guy .... **Alphonsia Emmanuel** *(Cards)*
Lord Billsborough .... **Nicholas Selby** *(Cards)*
Charles Collingridge .... **James Villiers** *(Cards)*
Patrick Woolton .... **Malcolm Tierney** *(Cards)*
John Krajewski .... **William Chubb** *(Cards)*
Stephen Kendrick .... **Tommy Boyle** *(Cards)*
The King .... **Michael Kitchen** *(King)*
Sarah Harding .... **Kitty Aldridge** *(King)*
David Mycroft .... **Nicholas Farrell** *(King)*
Chloe Carmichael .... **Rowena King** *(King)*
John Stroud .... **Leonard Preston** *(King)*
Ken Charterhouse .... **Jack Fortune** *(King)*
Lord Quillington .... **Frederick Treves** *(King)*
Princess Charlotte .... **Bernice Stegers** *(King)*
Bryan Brynford-Jones .... **John Bird** *(King)*
Sir Bruce Bullerby .... **David Ryall** *(King/Cut)*
Commander Corda .... **Nick Brimble** *(King/Cut)*
Claire Carlsen .... **Isla Blair** *(Cut)*
Tom Makepeace .... **Paul Freeman** *(Cut)*
Geoffrey Booza Pitt .... **Nickolas Grace** *(Cut)*

Writer **Andrew Davies**
Producer **Ken Riddington**
Executive Producer **Michael Wearing**

A scheming Government whip aims to become Prime Minister – by hook or by crook.

House of Cards, a four-part tale of political intrigue and infighting, was dramatized by Andrew Davies from the novel by the Conservative Party's Chief of Staff, Michael Dobbs, and benefited from being screened originally at the time of Mrs Thatcher's downfall. It went on to become the BBC's best-selling drama of the early 1990s, with sales to some 24 countries.

The drama focuses on the Government Chief Whip, Francis Urquhart ('FU'), a highly ambitious but untrustworthy man (his stock answer to a leading question is: 'You might think that, but I couldn't possibly comment'). The viewer is taken into the character's confidence and left in no doubt about his unscrupulous behaviour through regular asides to the camera. The story picks up with the demise of Margaret Thatcher and her replacement with a wimpy male successor. This gives Urquhart all the motivation he needs to put his Machiavellian plans into action, ably assisted by devious whip Tim Stamper. By the end of the serial Urquhart is installed in Number 10, at the expense of the life of investigative journalist (and FU's lover) Mattie Storin.

Urquhart's troubles are just beginning, however. In a sequel, *To Play the King*, produced by the same team from another Michael Dobbs novel, Urquhart finds himself under pressure from a newly enthroned monarch with liberal tendencies. He employs opinion pollster Sarah Harding as his adviser (and lover) and battles with the King and his PR team led by covert homosexual David Mycroft. Stamper, elevated only as far as party chairman, though deeming himself worthy of greater reward, seeks to blackmail his mentor over the death of Mattie Storin.

The Final Cut provides the last instalment in the FU saga. Despite having seen off the King and Stamper, Urquhart is now clinging on to power, beleaguered by memories of his military past in Cyprus, where he callously murdered two local men. Among his pursuers are the Foreign Secretary, Tom Makepeace, and his lover, backbencher Claire Carlsen, who takes the job as FU's Parliamentary Private Secretary.

Michael Dobbs, unhappy at Andrew Davies's adaptation of this series, had his name removed from *The Final Cut* credits.

House of Eliott, The ★★★

UK (BBC) Drama. BBC 1 1991–2; 1994
DVD: Acorn Media

Beatrice Eliott .... **Stella Gonet**
Evangeline Eliott .... **Louise Lombard**
Lady Lydia Eliott .... **Barbara Jefford**
Arthur Eliott .... **Peter Birch**
Jack Maddox .... **Aden Gillett**
Penelope Maddox .... **Francesca Folan**
Sebastian Pearce .... **Jeremy Brudenell**
Peregrine 'Piggy' Garstone .... **Robert Daws**
Tilly Watkins/Foss .... **Cathy Murphy**
Lady Dolly Haycock .... **Jill Melford**
Mr Duroque .... **Colin Jeavons**
Victor Stride .... **Anthony Valentine**
Daphne Haycock .... **Kelly Hunter**
Sir Desmond Gillespie .... **David De Keyser**
Madge Howell/Althorpe .... **Judy Flynn**
Gerry Althorpe .... **Jamie Foreman**
Betty Butcher .... **Diana Rayworth**
Agnes Clarke .... **Victoria Alcock**
Chalmers .... **Kate Paul**
Florence Ranby .... **Maggie Ollerenshaw**
Ralph Saroyan .... **Michael Culver**
Lord Alexander Montford .... **Rupert Frazer**
Lady Elizabeth Montford .... **Elizabeth Garvie**
Alice Burgoyne .... **Kate Fahy**
Joseph Wint .... **Stephen Churchett**
Charles Quance .... **Bill Thomas**
Grace Keeble .... **Melanie Ramsey**
Larry Cotter .... **Ian Redford**
Miles Bannister .... **Robert Hands**
Daniel Page .... **Richard Lintern**
Katya Beletsky .... **Caroline Trowbridge**
Norman Foss .... **Toby Whitehouse**

Creators **Jean Marsh, Eileen Atkins**
Producers **Jeremy Gwilt, Ken Riddington**

Two impoverished sisters set up their own fashion house in the 1920s.

When their 'respectable' doctor father suddenly dies in 1920, leaving a host of debts and a mistress to boot, Beatrice (Bea) and Evangeline (Evie) Eliott are shaken out of their somewhat sheltered existence in Highgate by the need to find their own way in the world. Thirty-year-old Bea takes a job with photographer Jack Maddox, while Evie (12 years her junior) becomes an apprentice dressmaker. Despite the hindrance of their devious solicitor cousin Arthur, their efforts culminate in the setting-up of their own London fashion company, The House of Eliott. Their battles to survive in a competitive world, to see off their unscrupulous banker, Ralph Saroyan, and to meet head-on the social prejudices facing independent women at that time provide the focus for later episodes. The personal lives of the girls and their workshop assistants also come to the fore. In the second series, the sisters briefly move to Paris to learn about international fashion. Bea marries Jack but, as his film-making/journalistic/political career begins to take off, cracks develop in their relationship. A third series sees the birth of Bea's baby, Lucy, and Evie's liaison with portrait painter Daniel Page.

Costing some £6 million in its first series alone, *The House of Eliott* was devised by UPSTAIRS, DOWNSTAIRS creators Jean Marsh and Eileen Atkins and bore many of the hallmarks of that popular period drama. Costumes featured in the series were exhibited at the Victoria and Albert Museum in 1992.

House of Windsor, The ★★

UK (Granada) Situation Comedy. ITV 1994

Max Kelvin .... **Warren Clarke**
Lord Montague Bermondsey .. **Leslie Phillips**
Caroline Finch .... **Serena Gordon**
Sir Nicholas Foulsham .... **Neil Stacy**
Giles Huntingdon .... **Jeremy Sinden**
Lady Sharpcott .... **Margaret Courtenay**
Danny Jackson .... **Barry Howard**
Ray Barker .... **Sean Gallagher**
Kate Hargreaves .... **Louise Germaine**

Writers **Mark Wadlow, Russell T. Davies, Chris Fewtrell, Zeddy Lawrence, Luke Freeman**
Producer **Antony Wood**

Wry glimpse below stairs at Buckingham Palace.

In the early 1990s the British monarchy was ripe for taunting.

A series of tabloid scandals meant that there were plenty of obvious gags up for grabs, and this six-part sitcom made the most of them. Without ever showing the Windsors themselves, the series takes the viewer backstage, so to speak, to witness the activities of the household – the equerries, ladies-in-waiting, press team and other vital cogs that make the royal wheel revolve. At the helm is the Lord Chamberlain, Montague Bermondsey, one of the old school, soon joined at the heart of affairs (in more ways than one) by modern PR honcho Max Kelvin (a thinly veiled amalgam of *Sun* editor Kelvin Mackenzie and publicist Max Clifford). Private Secretary Sir Nicholas Foulsham tries to keep the peace. However, with the ineptitude of Bermondsey's adjutant, Giles Huntingdon, and bitter resentment from Kelvin's assistant, Caroline Finch, it is not an easy peace to keep. Plenty of gossip from limp footman Danny Jackson, Jackson's roguish number two, Ray Barker, and chambermaid Kate Hargreaves, plus unhelpful contributions from boozy lady-in-waiting Lady Sharpcott, add to the turmoil below stairs. Although recorded on a Friday and transmitted on the following Sunday evening for topicality, the series never quite grabbed the audience's attention and just one series was the result.

How!/How 2 ✱✱

UK (Southern/TVS/Meridian/Scottish) Children's Entertainment. ITV 1966–81/1990–2004; 2006

Presenters (How!/How 2) **Fred Dinenage;** *(How!)* **Jack Hargreaves, Jon Miller, Bunty James, Jill Graham, Dr Tom Gaskell, Marian Davies;** *(How 2)* **Carol Vorderman, Gareth Jones, Sian Lloyd, Gail Porter, Gail McKenna**

Producers **Angus Wright** *(How!)*, **Tim Edmunds, Adrian Edwards, Jonathan Sanderson** *(How 2)*

● ***Educational children's series explaining how things happen.***

Always popular, *How!* managed to combine science with humour. Its four studio-bound presenters took turns to explain the scientific reasons why certain things happen. These might be of vital importance or of the most trivial nature. Tricks and experiments involving matchsticks, coins and water were favourite items. The main hosts (palms raised in Red Indian greeting at the beginning and end of each programme) in the early years were jokey Fred Dinenage, thoughtful Jack Hargreaves, gadget-minded Jon Miller and Bunty James, who was later replaced by Jill Graham and then Marian Davies. Dr Tom Gaskell was another early contributor. The series was revived in 1990 under the title of *How 2*. Dinenage returned for the relaunch and was joined by COUNTDOWN girl Carol Vorderman (with various later replacements) and kids' TV presenter Gareth 'Gaz Top' Jones.

How Do They Do That? ✱✱

UK (Grundy/Telepictures) Factual. BBC 1 1994–7

Presenters **Desmond Lynam, Jenny Hull, Eamonn Holmes, Esther McVey**

Producers **John Longley, Martin Lucas, Gill Stribling-Wright**

● ***Tricks of many trades revealed.***

How do stunt men survive big falls? How does air traffic control work? How is a giant oilrig positioned precisely in the North Sea? How can penguins dance in TV commercials for beer? These were just some of the questions posed by *How Do They Do That?* This light-hearted factual series, looking at the way technology and skilful people work, delved into worlds where the impossible seems to happen. Viewers were asked to submit queries that would stand up to TV examination. First host Desmond Lynam quit after two series, to be replaced by Eamonn Holmes, and Lynam's co-presenter Jenny Hull left one series later, with Esther McVey stepping into her shoes.

How Do You Want Me? ✱✱

UK (Kensington Films) Situation Comedy. BBC 2 1998–9

Ian Lyons .... **Dylan Moran**
Lisa Lyons .... **Charlotte Coleman**
Astley Yardley .... **Frank Finlay**
Helen Yardley .... **Emma Chambers**
Dean Yardley .... **Peter Serafinowicz**
Pam Yardley .... **Diana Fairfax**
Derek Few .... **Mark Heap**
Warren Yardley .... **Simon Bateso**
Norriswood .... **Clive Merrison**
John .... **Jasper Holmes**
Gavin .... **Will Barton**
Jill .... **Philippa Stanton**
Phil .... **Gary Sefton**

Writer **Simon Nye**
Producer **Margot Gavan Duffy**

● ***A city boy finds country life impossible.***

Ian Lyons is the proverbial fish out of water in this rustic comedy. Irishman Ian has just moved down from London to the Sussex countryside along with his new wife, Lisa, to be close to her family. Sadly, his metropolitan ways and moods do not sit comfortably in the hostile, inbred village community of Snowle and he cannot help doing or saying something that will alienate his in-laws, especially Lisa's monstrous father, Astley Yardley (not a difficult task). The hideous Yardleys are very much the controlling influence in this community and the sarcastic Ian proves to be a real embarrassment and inconvenience to them, especially when he sets up as the local photographer. While there are inevitable slapstick moments, the humour here is dry, generally understated and often dark, helped along by the pleasant absence of a laugh track. Creator Simon Nye is also seen, making a guest appearance as a postman. Two series of six episodes were produced.

Howard, Ron

(1954–)

American child actor, today one of Hollywood's most successful directors. Following early appearances in shows like *Dennis the Menace* and THE TWILIGHT ZONE, Ron (or Ronny) Howard's TV career began to move when he was aged six and was cast for the part of Opie Taylor, Andy's son in the extremely popular US sitcom *The Andy Griffith Show*. The series ran from 1960 to 1968 and, in between episodes, Howard took time off to appear in dramas such as THE FUGITIVE. In the early 1970s he was a member of *The Smith Family* (Bob Smith), another US comedy, which starred Henry Fonda, and around this time he also took the part of a young wounded soldier in an episode of M*A*S*H. However, he then secured his biggest TV role, that of Richie Cunningham in HAPPY DAYS. Howard had played the role of the fresh-faced 1950s teenager in a pilot episode, seen as part of LOVE, AMERICAN STYLE, and he stayed with *Happy*

Days for six years, making occasional return appearances later while establishing himself in the movie world. He has since worked on the TV version of his feature film PARENTHOOD, was executive producer of 24, and was executive producer and narrator of the comedy series *Arrested Development*.

Howard, Ronald

(1918–96)

A former journalist and the son of Leslie Howard, Ronald Howard was a familiar face in two diverse series, a 1954 version of *Sherlock Holmes* (in the title role) and the action adventure *Cowboy in Africa* (Wing Commander Howard Hayes) more than a decade later. He also briefly played Will Scarlett in THE ADVENTURES OF ROBIN HOOD.

Howards' Way **

UK (BBC) Drama. BBC 1 1985–90

Tom Howard	**Maurice Colbourne**
Jan Howard	**Jan Harvey**
Jack Rolfe	**Glyn Owen**
Avril Rolfe	**Susan Gilmore**
Ken Masters	**Stephen Yardley**
Leo Howard	**Edward Highmore**
Lynne Howard/Dupont	**Tracey Childs**
Polly Urquhart	**Patricia Shakesby**
Abby Urquhart/Hudson	**Cindy Shelley**
Gerald Urquhart	**Ivor Danvers**
Kate Harvey	**Dulcie Gray**
Charles Frere	**Tony Anholt**
Bill Sayers	**Robert Vahey**
Sir John Stevens	**Willoughby Grey**
Davy	**Kulvinder Ghir**
Dawn	**Sally Farmiloe**
Claude Dupont	**Malcolm Jamieson**
Richard Shellet	**Oscar Quitak**
Admiral Redfern	**Michael Denison**
David Lloyd	**Bruce Bould**
Orrin Hudson	**Ryan Michael**
	Jeff Harding
Sarah Foster	**Sarah-Jane Varley**
Mark Foster	**Graham Pountney**
Curtis Jaeger	**Dean Harris**
Sir Edward Frere	**Nigel Davenport**
Robert McIntyre	**Fraser Kerr**
Amanda Parker	**Francesca Gonshaw**
Anna Lee	**Sarah Lam**
Emma Neesome	**Sian Webber**
Richard Spencer	**John Moulder-Brown**
Michael Hanley	**Michael Loney**
Vanessa Andenberg/Rolfe	**Lana Morris**
Laura Wilde	**Kate O'Mara**
Vicki Rockwell	**Victoria Burgoyne**
James Brooke	**Andrew Bicknell**
Robert Hastings	**Paul Jerricho**
Jenny Richards	**Charmian Gradwell**

Creators **Gerard Glaister, Allan Prior**
Producer **Gerard Glaister**

Glossy soap centring on boats, boardrooms and bedrooms. Redundant 44-year-old aircraft designer Tom Howard decides to take the plunge and buys into a boat-building business, inspired by the work he has done on his own yacht, *The Flying Fish*. His wife, Jan, having given her life to establishing the family and home, and fearing for the future, is less than impressed with Tom's new venture. Tom's partner in the struggling Mermaid Yard, where they perfect swish boats like the *Barracuda*, is boozy craftsman Jack Rolfe. Rolfe's obsolete business knowledge is supplemented with advice from his shrewd daughter, Avril, soon to be Tom's new lover. In response, Jan becomes manageress of a fashion house and embarks on affairs with her posing boss Ken Masters and ageing businessman Sir Edward Frere, father of smarmy tycoon Charles Frere. Tom's racing-mad but kind-hearted mother-in-law, Kate Harvey, lends a hand whenever called upon, but the Howards' children, drop-out student Leo and spoilt, sailing-obsessed Lynne, cause more than a few headaches. Lynne marries Frenchman Claude Dupont, but he is killed while water-skiing. Languid Leo's on/off girlfriend is prickly Abby Urquhart, whose squabbling parents are also featured.

Howards' Way, set on the River Hamble in fictional Tarrant (real-life Bursledon), is a series about dodgy business deals, gaudy lifestyles, brave men and flashy women. It has been described as the 'first Thatcherite soap' and survived not only the years of boom and bust but also the tragic death of its main star. When Maurice Colbourne died of a heart attack in 1989, Tom Howard was written out and the rest of the cast bravely soldiered on for one more year. Singer Marti Webb, backed by the Simon May Orchestra, took the programme's theme song, 'Always There', into the Top 20 in 1986.

Howerd, Frankie

OBE (Francis Howard; 1917–92)

British comedian, known for his 'oohs', 'aahs', 'please yourselves' and stuttering, bumbling delivery (caused by a natural childhood stammer, which he exaggerated for effect). Eventually breaking into showbiz at the end of World War II, and making a name for himself on radio shows like *Variety Bandbox*, Howerd was given his first TV show in 1952. It was entitled *The Howerd Crowd* and was followed by numerous variety spots and guest turns over the years. Although his popularity faltered at the turn of the 1960s, and Howerd appeared not to be moving with the times, he was thrown a lifeline with an appearance on THAT WAS THE WEEK THAT WAS, which resulted from a successful appearance in Peter Cook's Establishment Club. Howerd never looked back. He went on to star in a London stage version of *A Funny Thing Happened on the Way to the Forum*, which led to a TV lookalike, UP POMPEII!, in 1969. In this, as Lurcio the slave, Howerd meandered his way through double entendres and innuendoes (some allegedly too strong for the man himself), trying to deliver a prologue. The series led to a run of film spin-offs, as well as a similar TV outing set in the Middle East, *Whoops Baghdad!*, in 1973. In all, Howerd was seldom off TV screens in the 1960s and 1970s, thanks to programmes such as *The Frankie Howerd Show*, *The Howerd Confessions*, *Frankie Howerd Strikes Again* and *A Touch of the Casanovas* (the pilot for a never-realized series). His wartime sitcom, *Then Churchill Said to Me*, made in 1982, was not broadcast (because of the Falklands conflict) until UK Gold screened it 11 years later. In 1992 he entertained selected audiences in a short series called *Frankie's on . . .* (the gap filled by words to reflect his location, like *Board* for the *Ark Royal* or *the Coals* for a mining community). One of his last series was the kids' comedy *All Change*, in 1989, in which he played the ghostly Uncle Bob.

Howman, Karl

(1953–)

British comic actor, well versed in Jack the Lad-type roles. After appearing in the kids' drama *The Jensen Code* (Jacko), Howman eventually succeeded Robert Lindsay in the guise of Jakey Smith in the RAF sitcom GET SOME IN!, before securing his own series, BRUSH STROKES, playing the gentle womanizer/decorator Jacko (no relation to his earlier role with the same name). He went on to star with Geraldine McEwan as the mysterious MULBERRY, as villainous barman Wayne Todd in *Bad Boys*, and as Charlie in BABES IN THE WOOD. Among his other credits have been episodes of ANGELS, MINDER, THE SWEENEY, HAZELL, PORRIDGE, FOX, SHELLEY, THE PROFESSIONALS, A FINE ROMANCE, JULIET BRAVO, DEMPSEY AND MAKEPEACE, BOON, THE BILL, HOLBY CITY and THE LAST DETECTIVE. He was also in the play THE FLIPSIDE OF DOMINICK HIDE. He is the father of *Family Affairs* actress Chloe Howman.

How's Your Father? ✱

UK (Yorkshire) Situation Comedy. ITV 1979–80

Harry Matthews .... **Harry Worth**
Shirley Matthews .... **Debby Cumming**
Martin Matthews .... **Giles Watling**
Vera Blacker .... **Fanny Carby**
Mrs Simkins .... **Sonia Graham**

Writers **Pam Valentine, Michael Ashton**
Producer **Graeme Muir**

A dithering banker tries to keep his kids on the straight and narrow.

Middle-aged bank clerk Harry Matthews – a man sadly out of touch with the youth of today – has recently been widowed and now must face up to the challenge of raising his two teenage children alone. However, looking after son Martin (19) and daughter Shirley (16) is way beyond the capabilities of the well-meaning, enthusiastic but unfortunately disaster-prone Harry, for whom every day offers nothing but trouble and strife. Two series were produced.

HR Pufnstuf ✱✱

US (Krofft) Children's Comedy. ITV 1970 (US: NBC 1969–71)
DVD: Freemantle Home Entertainment

Jimmy .... **Jack Wild**
Witchiepoo .... **Billie Hayes**

Writers **Lennie Weinrib, Howard Morris**
Producers **Sid Krofft, Marty Krofft**

A young boy is lured to a magic island by an evil witch.

This lively musical cross between *Robinson Crusoe* and *The Wizard of Oz* tells the story of Jimmy, a young lad who owns a talking golden flute named Freddie. To steal the flute, a nasty sorceress by the name of Witchiepoo lures Jimmy to her island home, enticing him into a boat then leaving him shipwrecked. Thankfully, HR Pufnstuf, the genial dragon mayor of Living Island (as the theme song said: 'He's your friend when things get rough') spots the boy in distress and brings him ashore. Thereafter, Jimmy shares the company of Pufnstuf and his humorous friends – Judy the Frog, Cling and Clang, Ludicrous Lion and Dr Blinky (a white owl). Also seen are Horsey and Grandfather and Grandmother Clock, and the voices of the Four Winds are heard from time to time. Living with Witchiepoo in her spooky castle are her three sidekicks: a yellow spider named Seymour, a green vulture called Orson and the grey Stupid Bat. She also controls the Evil Trees and Mushrooms in the Evil Forest and darts around on her rocket-powered Vroom Broom. With the help of her cronies, and by spying on events around the island through her Image Machine, Witchiepoo scuppers all Jimmy's attempts to return home, but she never gains control of the magic flute.

The programme's non-human characters were represented by colourful, lifelike puppets, with voices supplied by Joan Gerber, Felix Silla and Walker Edmiston, among others. Seventeen episodes were made and a feature-film version was released in 1970.

HTV

(Harlech Television)

HTV was the ITV contractor for Wales and the West of England from 4 March 1968, after winning the franchise from TWW. Initially Harlech Television, the name of the successful bidding consortium (which included Lord Harlech), was used on air, but this was soon shortened to HTV. The company later retained its franchise on two occasions and offered two separate services for viewers. HTV West (based in Bristol) covered the West of England, with specifically targeted news, sports and features programmes dropped into the general output, while HTV Cymru/Wales (based in Cardiff) did the same for Welsh viewers. The Welsh side of the company also produced Welsh-language programmes. These were screened on S4C, but before the Welsh fourth channel was established in 1982 Welsh programmes replaced certain English-language programmes in the HTV Wales schedules. HTV West made a name for itself for innovative children's science fiction in the 1970s. Programmes such as THE GEORGIAN HOUSE, SKY and THE CHILDREN OF THE STONES all made it to the national network. It also contributed game shows like MR AND MRS, *Definition*, *Cuckoo in the Nest* and *Three Little Words*. ROBIN OF SHERWOOD and WYCLIFFE were other network successes. HTV was later acquired by Carlton, eventually becoming part of ITV plc. Station idents now present the region as ITV Wales.

Huckleberry Hound Show, The ✱✱

US (Hanna-Barbera/Screen Gems) Cartoon. ITV 1960–4 (US: Syndicated 1958–62)
DVD: Warner Home Video (Region 1 only)

Voices:
Huckleberry Hound .... **Daws Butler**
Pixie .... **Don Messick**
Dixie .... **Daws Butler**
Mr Jinks .... **Daws Butler**
Yogi Bear .... **Daws Butler**
Boo Boo .... **Don Messick**
Hokey Wolf .... **Daws Butler**
Ding-a-Ling .... **Doug Young**

Creators/Executive Producers **William Hanna, Joseph Barbera**

The adventures of an easy-going, never-flustered Southern pooch.

Huckleberry Hound takes things as they come. He always sees the good things in life and makes little criticism of the bad – and this despite the cruellest of luck, which invites trees to fall on him and bombs to blow up beneath him. He just carries on cheerfully singing his favourite song, 'Clementine'.

Painfully slow in thought and speech, this is a dog with all the time in the world and the spirit to give anything a go. The baggy-eyed bloodhound assumes various guises throughout his successful series: he is seen as a French legionnaire, a professor, a fireman and also the dashing Purple Pumpernickel, for instance. Huckleberry Hound was one of the small screen's first cartoon heroes. Sharing his limelight, in their own segments of the show, were *Pixie and Dixie* and YOGI BEAR. Pixie and Dixie are two Southern mice who torment Mr Jinks, the cat (who hates 'those meeces to pieces'). Yogi, in conjunction with his sidekick, Boo Boo, is the perennially hungry picnic-snatcher of Jellystone National Park (so popular he was given his own series, leading to his replacement here by the Bilko-like Hokey Wolf, a sharp-talking conwolf, aided and abetted by the fox, Ding-a-Ling).

The Huckleberry Hound Show was the programme that launched former Tom and Jerry animators William Hanna and Joseph Barbera into the TV bigtime.

Hudd, Roy
OBE (1936–)

Croydon-born entertainer in the music hall tradition, a former Butlin's Redcoat whose TV career kicked off with guest appearances in sitcoms like OUR HOUSE but really progressed through regular work on NOT SO MUCH A PROGRAMME, MORE A WAY OF LIFE. His own series for the BBC and ITV followed, including *Hudd, The Illustrated Weekly Hudd* and *The Roy Hudd Show*, all of which exhibited his versatility and demonstrated his fondness for the music hall greats. These days, whenever a nostalgic programme is on the air, Roy Hudd is never far away. Hudd's dramatic skills were also given the chance to shine when, in 1993, he played Harold Atterbow in Dennis Potter's LIPSTICK ON YOUR COLLAR. He followed this with the parts of John Parry in COMMON AS MUCK, Beach in *P. G. Wodehouse's Heavy Weather*, Ben Baglin in Potter's swan-song, KARAOKE, and the part of undertaker Archie Shuttleworth in CORONATION STREET. Hudd also appeared in *The Quest* trilogy of dramas (Charlie) and made guest appearances in RANDALL AND HOPKIRK (DECEASED) and *All About George*. He has been just as familiar on radio, thanks to his long-running series *The News Huddlines*.

Hudson, Rock
(Roy Scherer; 1925–85)

Hollywood heart-throb of the 1950s and 1960s, whose television work was reserved until the end of his career (save for the odd guest appearance in shows like I LOVE LUCY and ROWAN AND MARTIN'S LAUGH-IN). In 1971 (the same year as he allegedly turned down the Tony Curtis role in THE PERSUADERS!), Hudson starred in a TV movie, *Once Upon a Dead Man*, which proved to be the pilot for the MYSTERY MOVIE series MCMILLAN AND WIFE, in which he appeared with Susan Saint James. The series ran for six years, and when it ended, Hudson stayed with TV, taking roles in an assortment of miniseries, including *Wheels* (Adam Trenton) and THE MARTIAN CHRONICLES (Colonel John Wilder). In 1982 he was cast as another detective, Brian Devlin, in a short-lived series entitled *The Devlin Connection* (it was cancelled because Hudson underwent heart surgery), before he resurfaced as Daniel Reece in DYNASTY in 1984. It proved to be Hudson's last major role before his well-publicized death from an Aids-related illness a year later.

Huggins, Roy
(1914–2002)

Prolific American producer and writer, the creator of series like MAVERICK, 77 SUNSET STRIP, THE FUGITIVE, *Run for Your Life* and THE ROCKFORD FILES. He also produced CHEYENNE, THE VIRGINIAN, ALIAS SMITH AND JONES, BARETTA and HUNTER, among numerous other action series. His own production company was known as Public Arts.

Hugh and I ★★

UK (BBC) Situation Comedy. BBC 1962–7

Terry Scott	**Terry Scott**
Hugh Lloyd	**Hugh Lloyd**
Mrs Scott	**Vi Stevens**
Mr Crispin	**Wallas Eaton**
Mrs Crispin	**Mollie Sugden**
Norma Crispin	**Jacquie Wallis**
	Jill Curzon
Arthur Wormold	**Cyril Smith**
	Jack Haig
Griselda Wormold	**Patricia Hayes**

Creator/Writer **John Chapman**
Producers **David Croft, Duncan Wood**

Two friends seek to improve their lot, with disastrous results.

Lobelia Avenue, Tooting, is the home of Mrs Scott, her troublesome, unemployed son, Terry, and their lodger, Hugh Lloyd, a worker at a local aircraft factory. Forming a Laurel-and-Hardy-like double act, the two lads constantly find themselves in hot water, with the bumptious, over-ambitious Terry leading the timid, fretful Hugh astray. Usually 'get rich quick' schemes are to blame. Next to the Scotts, on one side, live the Crispins, he a loud-mouth, she a snob, and their daughter, Norma, an object of lust for the boys. On the other side are the Wormolds. For their final fling in 1966, the lads are sent on a cruise to the Far East, paid for out of the £5,000 Hugh has won with a Premium Bond. Terry and Hugh then embark on more adventurous escapades in the murky world of espionage in their 1968 follow-up series, *Hugh and I Spy*, in which each episode is given a cliffhanger ending.

Hughes, Geoffrey
(1944–)

Liverpudlian actor often cast in slobby, layabout roles. For eight years he was kind-hearted binman Eddie Yeats in CORONATION STREET, with more recent highlights being Onslow, Hyacinth Bucket's vest-wearing brother-in-law, in KEEPING UP APPEARANCES, iffy-goods dealer Twiggy in THE ROYLE FAMILY and rascally Vernon Scripps in HEARTBEAT. He also played Mr Lithgow in the Channel 4 sitcom *The Bright Side*, Ray Hartley in *Coasting* and Dilk in MAKING OUT, and he has popped up in a range of other series from Z CARS, THE LIKELY LADS, YOU RANG, M'LORD? and CURRY AND CHIPS to THE MIND OF MR J. G. REEDER, NO – HONESTLY, DOCTOR WHO and SPENDER. He provided the voice for Paul McCartney's character in the cartoon film *Yellow Submarine*.

Hughes, Nerys

(1941–)

Welsh actress most notable on TV as Sandra Hutchinson in THE LIVER BIRDS and Megan Roberts in THE DISTRICT NURSE. She played Maisie, the barmaid, in the comedy drama *The Flying Swan* in 1965, Beth Jenkins in a short-lived YTV sitcom called *Third Time Lucky* in 1982, and Diana in Ruth Rendell's *Gallowglass*, and has also appeared in *How Green was My Valley*, presented kids' series like PLAY AWAY, *Alphabet Zoo* and JACKANORY, made guest appearances in DOCTOR WHO and hosted the practical magazine programme *Bazaar*. More recent credits have included *The Queen's Nose* (Glenda), *The Secret* (Gwen) and a small role in DOCTORS. One of her earliest starring roles was in the 1964 serial *Diary of a Young Man*.

Hull, Rod

(1935–99)

British entertainer with Australian connections, not least his aggressive, giant Emu puppet, which Hull first spotted in 1969 when working on a children's TV show in Australia. Armed with this uncontrollable beast, Hull returned to the UK a year later and was, throughout the 1970s and 1980s, a big name in children's television. He devised and hosted the first *Children's Royal Variety Performance* and starred in series like *Rod Hull and Emu, EBC* (Emu's Broadcasting Company), *Emu's World* and *Emu's Pink Windmill Show*. On one celebrated appearance on *Parkinson*, Emu very clearly ruffled the interviewer's feathers, violently attacking Parky and pushing him on to the floor. Hull also enjoyed success across the Atlantic.

Human Body, The ★★★

UK (BBC/Learning Channel) Documentary. BBC 1 1998
DVD: BBC

Presenter **Prof. Robert Winston**

Producer **Richard Dale**

A journey through the life of the human body in seven instalments.

Professor (Lord) Robert Winston was the host of this acclaimed series which explored the changes that take place in the body during the course of a lifetime. Beginning with ovulation and showing the very moment of conception – the actual fusion of sperm and ovum – and continuing through birth, infancy, puberty and beyond, right up to the point of death (the series controversially filmed the death of a 63-year-old man), it aimed to provide viewers with a new insight into how the body works. With the aid of some brave volunteers and ground-breaking camerawork, the series provoked thought and won awards.

Human Jungle, The ★★

UK (Independent Artists/ABC) Medical Drama. ITV 1963; 1965

Dr Roger Corder	**Herbert Lom**
Dr Jimmy Davis	**Michael Johnson**
Jennifer Corder	**Sally Smith**
Jane Harris	**Mary Steele**
Nancy Hamilton	**Mary Yeomans**

Creator **Julian Wintle**
Producers **Julian Wintle, Leslie Parkyn**

The professional and domestic troubles of a London psychiatrist.

Widower Dr Roger Corder is a specialist in emotional distress and his counselling helps many disturbed patients back to health. He enjoys a good relationship with his junior colleague, Dr Jimmy Davis, and his supportive assistants, Jane Harris and Nancy Hamilton, and stories revolve around the various cases they undertake, with Corder heading out and about to meet his patients in their own surroundings (where he can understand them better). However, the workaholic doctor is less successful in his private life, seldom being able to communicate with his determined teenage daughter, Jennifer.

Human Remains ★★★

UK (Baby Cow) Comedy. BBC 2 2000
DVD: BBC

Writers **Rob Brydon, Julia Davis**
Executive Producers **Steve Coogan, Henry Normal**
Producer **Alison Macphail**

Spoof documentary series about various couples with bizarre relationships.

Taking one couple per episode, *Human Remains* exposes the rather disturbing nature of some people's private lives. Writers Rob Brydon and Julia Davis, po-faced, don the mantle of each character, gradually revealing embarrassing and often repulsive traits as the camera hovers, documentary-style, to monitor their offbeat lifestyles. This dark comedy, based on shrewd observation, introduces such grotesque creations as perverted guest house owners Gordon and Sheila, decrepit flower shop proprietors Ray and Les, Christian zealots Tony and Beverlee (whom even the local vicar avoids), and Stephen and Michelle, a Welsh couple panicking about their forthcoming wedding day.

Humphries, Barry

(1934–)

Australian entertainer, the creator of larger-than-life housewife megastar Dame Edna Everage and boozy cultural attaché Sir Les Patterson. His first TV appearances came in comedies like NOT ONLY . . . BUT ALSO . . . and *The Late Show*, and his own series have included *Barry Humphries' Scandals*, *The Dame Edna Experience*, *Dame Edna's Neighbourhood Watch* and *Dame Edna's Work Experience*. Humphries has also organized more than one AUDIENCE WITH *Dame Edna*. Additionally, he was seen in the single drama DOCTOR FISCHER OF GENEVA (Richard Deane) and the serial SELLING HITLER (as Rupert Murdoch), plus a famous guest spot in ALLY MCBEAL.

Humphrys, John

(1943–)

Cardiff-born seasoned journalist, newsreader and presenter, one of the Radio 4 *Today* team since 1987 but still active on television. After a grounding in newspapers, Humphrys entered television with HTV and then, in 1970, became a BBC foreign correspondent, working in the USA and South Africa up to 1980. He then took over as diplomatic correspondent, before joining the new-look *Nine O'Clock News* team as one of its chief presenters a year later. He stayed with the news until 1986 and returned occasionally later as a newsreader on the BBC's main bulletins. Humphrys also hosted the Sunday political programme *On the Record*, has chaired numerous debates and discussion programmes, and, since 2003, has been the questionmaster for MASTERMIND. His brother Bob is a sports presenter with BBC Wales.

Hunniford, Gloria

(1940–)

Northern Ireland-born radio and TV presenter. Hunniford's showbusiness career began in singing (she made her debut at the age of nine), before progressing into radio work in Canada and Northern Ireland, then television (*Good Evening Ulster*). From a base as a Radio 2 presenter in the early 1980s, she moved into UK TV, hosting shows like *Sunday, Sunday*, SONGS OF PRAISE, *We Love TV, Wogan, Gloria, Family Affairs* (with her late daughter, Caron Keating), *Gloria Live, Sunday Live, Good Fortune, Ladies of the House*, CHILDREN IN NEED, PEBBLE MILL and *Open House with Gloria Hunniford*. She was also a regular panellist in *That's Showbusiness* and made a guest appearance in AUF WIEDERSEHEN, PET.

Hunt, Gareth

(1943–)

London-born actor who came to light as Frederick, the footman, in UPSTAIRS, DOWNSTAIRS and later headlined in THE NEW AVENGERS, playing Mike Gambit. He then turned to comedy and starred in the sitcom *That Beryl Marston*, playing Gerry Bodley, and, later, SIDE BY SIDE, as plumber Vince Tulley. Hunt has also appeared in MINDER, DOCTOR WHO, *Enid Blyton's Castle of Adventure* (Bill Cunningham), *Night and Day* (Charlie Doyle), *Harry and the Wrinklies* (Priestly), *Powers* (Tom Watkins) and DOCTORS, plus countless coffee commercials.

Hunter ✶

US (Stephen J. Cannell/Lorimar) Police Drama. ITV 1985
(US: NBC 1984–91

DS Rick Hunter .... **Fred Dryer**
DS Dee Dee McCall .... **Stepfanie Kramer**
Sgt Bernie Terwilliger .... **James Whitmore Jr**
Capt. Lester Cain .... **Arthur Rosenberg**
Capt. Dolan .... **John Amos**
Capt. Charlie Devane .... **Charles Hallahan**
Arnold 'Sporty' James .... **Garrett Morris**

Executive Producers **Stephen J. Cannell, Fred Dryer, Roy Huggins, Lawrence Kubik**

● ***A tough, maverick cop carries a powerful gun.***
Though surviving only a few months on British TV (satellite stations excepted), *Hunter* was a big earner in its native USA, lasting a good seven years. The premise was quite simple: just take Clint Eastwood's hard-nosed, violent cop 'Dirty Harry' Callahan and remodel him for television. The result was Rick Hunter, the son of a mobster whose unorthodox methods of closing loopholes in the law were highly effective. Like Callahan, Hunter carries a Magnum, the powerful handgun that can rip criminals apart. Hunter names his Simon. However, whilst Dirty Harry tends to work best on his own, Rick Hunter is usually seen as part of a duo, teaming up on the Los Angeles streets with an attractive but equally brutal female cop named Dee Dee McCall, affectionately known as 'The Brass Cup Cake'. Star Fred Dryer was a former New York Giants and LA Rams footballer. The theme music was by Mike Post.

Hunter's Walk ✶✶

UK (ATV) Police Drama. ITV 1973–4; 1976

DS Smith .... **Ewan Hooper**
Sgt Ken Ridgeway .... **Davyd Harries**
PC Fred Pooley .... **Duncan Preston**
DC 'Mickey' Finn .... **David Simeon**
PC Harry Coombes .... **Charles Rea**
Betty Smith .... **Ruth Madoc**

Creator **Ted Willis**
Producer **John Cooper**

● ***A small police force keeps the peace in a provincial town.***
Set in the modest Midlands settlement of Broadstone (actually Rushden, Northants), *Hunter's Walk* focuses on the team at the local police station, namely po-faced DS 'Smithy' Smith, 'Mickey' Finn, his junior detective colleague, PCs Pooley and Coombes, and station officer Ken Ridgeway. Faced with routine police investigations, mostly of a domestic nature, they successfully patrol the streets in steady, DIXON OF DOCK GREEN fashion (not surprisingly, as this was also created by Lord Ted Willis). Smith's wife was played by future HI-DE-HI! star Ruth Madoc.

Hurt, John

CBE (1940–)

Award-winning Derbyshire-born actor who, after appearances in series like GIDEON'S WAY and THE SWEENEY, shot to fame as Quentin Crisp in Thames TV's THE NAKED CIVIL SERVANT in 1975. He followed this with the roles of Caligula in I, CLAUDIUS and Raskolnikov in CRIME AND PUNISHMENT and was THE STORYTELLER in Jim Henson's acclaimed children's series. Other credits have included the VJ Day drama *Prisoners in Time* (Eric Lomax), *Bait* (Jack Blake) and *The Alan Clark Diaries* (title role). He also provided voices for the animation *Pride* and narrated the drama-documentary *Hiroshima*.

Hustle ✶✶

UK (Kudos) Drama. BBC 1 2004–
DVD: Warner Home Video

Michael 'Mickey' Stone .... **Adrian Lester**
Danny Blue .... **Marc Warren**
Ashley 'Ash' Morgan .... **Robert Glenister**
Stacie Monroe .... **Jaime Murray**
Albert Stroller .... **Robert Vaughn**
Eddie .... **Rob Jarvis**

Creator **Tony Jordan**
Writers **Tony Jordan, Matthew Graham, Ashley Pharoah, Howard Overman, Julie Rutterford**
Producers **Simon Crawford Collins, Karen Wilson, Lucy Robinson**

● ***A group of confidence tricksters target the corrupt wealthy.***
They say there's one born every minute, and this team of well-groomed con merchants aims to prove just that. Suave Michael Stone (familiarly known as Mickey Bricks) is the

leader of this gang of endearing crooks, bringing them back together once he's been released from a two-year prison sentence for beating up his wife's new boyfriend (he's never been collared for any of the scams he's perpetrated). His associates are American Albert Stroller, an ex-shoe salesman and a hardened gambler whose job in the team is to find the marks (mugs) they can take for a ride; Ash Morgan, a computer buff and fixer who finds the rooms, offices, etc. the gang need to make their cons plausible; and Stacie Monroe, whose feminine wiles and sultry looks provide a useful distraction when necessary. Joining the gang is wannabe big player Danny Blue, till now a cocky, small-time playing-card trickster. Eddie is their barman associate.

These cool operators are major league players who aim high and take great pains to ensnare their victims. Their speciality is the 'long con', in which the rewards are enormous but the time and effort required are considerable. Against a background of racy incidental music, freeze frames and slow motions, and offering occasional asides to the camera to ensure that the viewer doesn't take things too seriously, the slick team ransack their way through the bank accounts of some of the most gullible and greedy people in Britain, be they bent coppers, dodgy art dealers or men with friends in high places. Occasionally daft, and stylistically harking back to the good old days of ITC adventure series, *Hustle* focuses on the nicer side of villainry.

Hylton, Jack

(1892–1965)

British bandleader who became one of ITV's earliest light entertainment producers, working with Arthur Askey, Tony Hancock, Alfred Marks, Dickie Henderson, Anne Shelton and others.

I

I, Claudius ✱✱✱✱

UK (BBC/London Films) Historical Drama. BBC 2 1976
DVD: BBC

Claudius	**Derek Jacobi**
Livia	**Siân Phillips**
Augustus	**Brian Blessed**
Tiberius	**George Baker**
Drusus	**Ian Ogilvy**
Marcellus	**Christopher Guard**
Julia	**Frances White**
Antonia	**Margaret Tyzack**
Agrippa	**John Paul**
Lucius	**Simon MacCorkindale**
Caligula	**John Hurt**
Germanicus	**David Robb**
Livilla	**Patricia Quinn**
Agrippina	**Fiona Walker**
Postumus	**John Castle**
Herod	**James Faulkner**
Sejanus	**Patrick Stewart**
Piso	**Stratford Johns**
Messalina	**Sheila White**
Drusilla	**Beth Morris**
Nero	**Christopher Biggins**
Castor	**Kevin McNally**
Gratus	**Bernard Hill**
Marcus	**Norman Eshley**
Narcissus	**John Cater**
Pallas	**Bernard Hepton**
Caractacus	**Peter Bowles**

Writer **Jack Pulman**
Producer **Martin Lisemore**

● ***The power struggles of Imperial Rome as seen through the eyes of an innocent.***

Depicting the debauchery and duplicity of life in ancient Rome, *I, Claudius*, directed by Herbert Wise, was a 12-part dramatization of two novels by Robert Graves: *I, Claudius* and *Claudius the God*. It focuses on Emperor Claudius, who relates events in his lifetime via flashbacks, taking up the story in the time of the Emperor Augustus (24 BC) when the stammering, limping Claudius is a sickly child. It progresses through the reigns of the despotic Tiberius and the deranged Caligula to reveal how, quite against his desires, Claudius himself becomes ruler of the empire. Murder and manoeuvring lie at every turn, interspersed with perverse orgies and gluttonous feasts, with the chief manipulator Claudius's cruel grandmother, the arch-poisoner Livia.

The snake that writhed across the mosaic in the opening titles aptly set the tone for this colourful, often gory series which won much acclaim, not least for the performance of Shakespearean actor Derek Jacobi.

I Didn't Know You Cared ✱✱✱

UK (BBC) Situation Comedy. BBC 1 1975–6; 1978–9
DVD: Second Sight

Uncle Mort	**Robin Bailey**
Les Brandon	**John Comer**
Annie Brandon	**Liz Smith**
Carter Brandon	**Stephen Rea**
	Keith Drinkel
Pat Partington/Brandon	**Anita Carey**
	Liz Goulding
Uncle Staveley	**Bert Palmer**
	Leslie Sarony
Linda Preston	**Deirdre Costello**
Mrs Partington	**Vanda Godsell**
Sid Skelhorn	**Ray Dunbobbin**
	Bobby Pattinson

Creator/Writer **Peter Tinniswood**
Producer **Bernard Thompson**

● ***The battle of the sexes in a morose northern household.***

The Brandons are a miserable-go-unlucky Yorkshire family living in an industrial town. They consist of Les and Annie (unhappily married for 25 years); their son, Carter; his wife, Pat; and Annie's mufflered brother, Mort, who 'served all through First World War' and who is forced to move in when his wife, Edna, dies. While the womenfolk harass and bully, the men try desperately to slink away to the pub or Mort's allotment, where he hoists a Union Jack above his converted railway-carriage shed. There Les and Mort aim to protect young Carter from his socially ambitious new wife over a brew of tea and a hand of dominoes. Carter's response is usually a hesitant 'Aye ... Well ... Mmm ...' Visits by the terrifying Three Great-Aunts from Glossop, much-dreaded works outings and encounters with Unsworth's lively pork pies give the family plenty to battle over, with only funerals and opposition to 'London beer' likely to bring any harmony. Also seen is senile army veteran Uncle Staveley, who carries the ashes of his 'oppo', Cpl Parkinson, in a box around his neck and whose best conversation is, 'I heard that, pardon?' Linda Preston is the local Jezebel who seeks to seduce Carter at every turn.

Creator Peter Tinniswood had earlier introduced the Brandons in a trilogy of novels, and Uncle Mort and Carter have also been heard on BBC Radio.

I Dream of Jeannie ✱✱

US (Sidney Sheldon/Screen Gems) Situation Comedy. ITV 1966–71 (US: NBC 1965–70)

Jeannie	**Barbara Eden**
Capt./Major Tony Nelson	**Larry Hagman**
Capt./Major Roger Healey	**Bill Daily**
Dr Alfred Bellows	**Hayden Rorke**
Gen. Martin Peterson	**Barton MacLane**
Amanda Bellows	**Emmaline Henry**

Creator/Executive Producer **Sidney Sheldon**

● ***An astronaut is the master of a beautiful young genie.***

When his test mission is aborted, NASA astronaut Tony Nelson parachutes back to Earth and finds himself marooned on a desert island. There, he picks up a bottle, uncorks it and lets loose a beautiful genie, appropriately named Jeannie, who promises him his every wish. Naturally, the first thing he calls for is a rescue helicopter and then returns home to his base at Cocoa Beach, Florida, taking Jeannie along for the ride.

The fun of this series comes from the fact that only Tony and his playboy buddy Roger Healey know about Jeannie and only they can see her. NASA's psychiatrist, Alfred Bellows, thinks Tony is nuts, of course, and looks for every opportunity to prove it. With Jeannie supposedly being 2,000 years old, she has some difficulty interpreting 20th-century expressions and figures of speech, and this leads to even more confusion and chaos whenever she steps in to 'help' her master. She is also in love with Tony, and takes every opportunity to spoil his chances with other women. Somewhat ironically, it is Jeannie whose wish finally comes true, when she and Tony are married towards the end of the series.

I Love Lucy ★★★★

US (CBS/Desilu) Situation Comedy. ITV 1955–61
(US: CBS 1951–61)
DVD: Paramount (Region 1 only)

Lucy Ricardo	**Lucille Ball**
Ricky Ricardo	**Desi Arnaz**
Ethel Mertz	**Vivian Vance**
Fred Mertz	**William Frawley**
Little Ricky Ricardo	**Richard Keith**

Writers **Jess Oppenheimer, Madelyn Pugh, Bob Carroll**
Producers **Jess Oppenheimer, Desi Arnaz**

A dance-band leader's patience is sorely tried by his scatterbrained wife.

I Love Lucy was a pioneer among TV programmes. It set the pattern for the 'domestic' sitcom and was the first series to be filmed (before a live audience), rather than transmitted live. This has also contributed to its longevity, since all the original programmes are still available in good condition. It centres on the life of Lucy Ricardo (née MacGillicuddy), a zany, rather immature redhead of Scottish descent, for whom nothing goes right. Her Cuban husband, Ricky, is a dance-band leader and Lucy longs to follow him into show-business, despite her lack of talent. Failing this, she at least wants to be more than an ordinary housewife and consequently cooks up endless hare-brain schemes to make money or to improve life around the home, most of them prone to disaster. But, as the programme's title reveals, Ricky really does love Lucy and, although extremely annoyed, he is remarkably forgiving, considering the amount of hassle she causes him.

The Ricardos live in an apartment on the East Side of Manhattan, where their frumpy landlord and landlady are Fred and Ethel Mertz. Lucy finds a willing ally and accomplice in Ethel, who is years younger than her wisecracking, irascible husband, and the two girls often wage a battle of the sexes with the guys. But they are all good friends at heart. In one season, Ricky finds fame in Hollywood and the foursome set off on a famous car trek across America; in another, they tour Europe with Ricky's band.

One of the highlights of the series is the birth of Little Ricky in the second season, an event planned to coincide with Lucille Ball's own second pregnancy (the episode was screened the night that Ball's real baby was born). Other developments include Ricky moving on from the Tropicana Club, where he works, to owning his own nightspot, the Babaloo Club, and then starring in his own TV show.

Lucille and Desi Arnaz were married in real life and owned the programme's production company, Desilu. After their divorce, Lucille developed another two successful comedies in the same vein, THE LUCY SHOW and HERE'S LUCY, while Desi went on to produce THE UNTOUCHABLES, among other programmes.

I Married Joan ★★

US (Volcano) Situation Comedy. BBC 1955–8 (US: NBC 1952–5)
DVD: VCI

Joan Stevens	**Joan Davis**
Judge Bradley Stevens	**Jim Backus**
Minerva Parker	**Hope Emerson**
Beverly Grossman	**Beverly Wills**
Charlie	**Hal Smith**
Mabel	**Geraldine Carr**
Janet Tobin	**Sheila Bromley**
Kerwin Tobin	**Dan Tobin**

Producer **P. J. Wolfson**

A judge relates his wacky wife's mishaps as a lesson in court.

Although it was first seen in Britain at almost exactly the same time as I LOVE LUCY, *I Married Joan* was, in its native USA, a clinger to Lucy's coat-tails, first airing a year after the scatterbrained redhead made her bow. The premiss is much the same, with Joan a well meaning but disaster-prone housewife, but this time the weary husband is a judge, Bradley Stevens. In every episode he presides over court and starts to recount to those present the latest exploits of his dearly beloved, but very trying, other half, ultimately drifting off into a flashback of her latest frenetic escapade. Like Lucy, Joan has a co-conspirator, in the shape of neighbour Minerva Parker. She is later replaced by star Joan Davis's real-life daughter, Beverly Wills, as Joan's student sister, Beverly Grossman. Also seen are various other friends and neighbours who inevitably get caught up in Joan's crazy life.

I Spy ★★

US (Sheldon Leonard) Secret Agent Drama. ITV 1967–9
(US: NBC 1965–8)
DVD: Image Entertainment (Region 1 only)

Kelly Robinson	**Robert Culp**
Alexander 'Scotty' Scott	**Bill Cosby**

Producers **Sheldon Leonard, Mort Fine, David Friedkin**

A tennis professional and his trainer are really American spies.

Alexander 'Scotty' Scott and Kelly Robinson are two American secret agents, travelling around the world on various assignments using the international tennis circuit as cover. Scotty, to all intents and purposes, is the coach. In reality, he's a high-flying academic achiever (a Rhodes Scholar) and a multilinguist. Kelly is the 'tennis pro', extremely well-educated (this time in law at Princeton) like his partner, but, as he really has to be, also a first-rate tennis player. Although there are plenty of tense moments, a little tongue-in-cheek humour runs through every episode.

I Spy has a place in TV history for being the first US drama series to star a black person – Bill Cosby. Co-star Robert Culp also wrote some of the episodes. A TV movie, *I Spy Returns*, brought the duo back together in 1994.

I Woke Up One Morning ✱✱

UK (BBC) Situation Comedy. BBC 1 1985–6

Derek .... **Frederick Jaeger**
Max .... **Michael Angelis**
Danny .... **Peter Caffrey**
Zero .... **Robert Gillespie**
Eddie .... **Jonathan Kydd**
'Irrelevant' .... **Tim Potter**
Sister May .... **Frances White**
Rosa .... **Shirin Taylor**

Writer **Carla Lane**
Producer **Robin Nash**

● ***Four alcoholics help each other kick the habit.***

Not an obvious subject for humour, but this Carla Lane comedy is built around four alcoholics who struggle to come to terms with their addiction. The four meet at a hospital, where they are each undergoing psychotherapy to help them beat the booze. They soon learn to depend on each other in their fight against the bottle. Derek is a gentleman farmer, whose wife has been having an affair with a farm hand, though whether this was a cause or consequence of his addiction is not clear. Max, on the other hand, just cannot handle reality. He is well placed to have a job, a wife and a steady home life, but the thought of it is just too much. Danny, the Irishman, is a dreamer, whose life went downhill when the girl he loved, Mary Malone, failed to notice him, while the fourth addict, Zero, his marriage in tatters, feels 'washed out by life'. The laugh track conspicuous by its absence, this series – despite Carla Lane's witty lines – had a genuine darker side. Two series, totalling 12 episodes, were produced.

IBA

See *ITC*.

Ident Board

A board displaying details of the programme being recorded. Often incorporating a countdown clock, it is shown to the camera or imposed on the screen at the start of recording to confirm the title, episode, scene, date, etc.

Idiot Board

A cue card, displaying lines or instructions, held next to the camera to help forgetful presenters and actors.

Idle, Eric

(1943–)

British comedy actor and writer, best known for his work as part of the MONTY PYTHON team. Previously, Idle had scripted sketches for THE FROST REPORT with Tim Brooke-Taylor and other Pythons. He had also written episodes of the Ronnie Corbett comedy NO – THAT'S ME OVER HERE and been seen in AT LAST THE 1948 SHOW, *We Have Ways of Making You Laugh* and the children's comedy DO NOT ADJUST YOUR SET. He later worked as script editor on early episodes of THE LIVER BIRDS, wrote for THE TWO RONNIES, created and starred in RUTLAND WEEKEND TELEVISION and its spin-off, *The Rutles*, and headlined as Grant Pritchard in the short-lived American sitcom *Nearly Departed*, also appearing as Ian Maxtone-Graham in SUDDENLY SUSAN. Idle also wrote and sang the theme song for ONE FOOT IN THE GRAVE, making one guest appearance on screen, too.

If You See God, Tell Him ✱✱

UK (BBC) Situation Comedy. BBC 1 1993

Godfrey Spry .... **Richard Briers**
Gordon Spry .... **Adrian Edmondson**
Muriel Spry .... **Imelda Staunton**

Writers **David Renwick, Andrew Marshall**
Producer **Marcus Mortimer**

● ***A man's life is structured around TV commercials.***

'God', or, to give him his full name, Godfrey Spry, is a retired widower who, because of a freak accident with a runaway wheelbarrow, is confined to a wheelchair and now has an attention span of only 30 seconds. This means that the only world he fully comprehends is that of the television commercial and, because of his affliction, his belief in whatever these promotions offer is total. Not surprisingly, this leads to trouble with 'listening banks', aftershaves that promise success with women and government opportunity schemes. Picking up the pieces are Godfrey's son and daughter-in-law, Gordon and Muriel. Although critics commented that building a comedy around a character with a disability was not funny, for writers David Renwick and Andrew Marshall the concept did provide the scope to lampoon the TV advertising industry. Even the title parodied commercials that once encouraged viewers to buy shares in British Gas (the 'If you see Sid' campaign). Four episodes of 45 minutes were produced.

I'm a Celebrity . . . Get Me Out of Here! ✱✱

UK (LWT/Granada) Documentary. ITV 1 2002–
DVD: Granada Ventures

Presenters **Ant and Dec**

Executive Producers **Richard Cowles, Natalka Znak, Alex Gardiner**

● ***Personalities compete in a game of jungle endurance.***

The North Queensland rainforest in Australia is the location for this celebrity survival experience. Over two weeks, a group of famous (and not-so-famous) faces brave the jungle, imposed hardships, physical challenges, bush tucker trials (forced eating of grubs and other unpalatables), the unblinking camera and, toughest of all, each other's company. They are gradually whittled down by voting viewers to one winner. First 'King of the Jungle' was DJ Tony Blackburn, whose weary career found new legs as a result. Battling it out with Blackburn were Darren Day, Uri Geller, Tara Palmer-Tomkinson, Christine Hamilton, Nell McAndrew, Nigel Benn and Rhona Cameron. All hoped to raise money for favourite charities. Cricketer Phil Tufnell won the 2003 version, outstaying Antony Worrall Thompson, Toyah Willcox, Wayne Sleep, Danniella Westbrook, Linda Barker, Siân Lloyd, John Fashanu, Catalina Guirado and Chris Bisson. Former Atomic Kitten singer Kerry McFadden triumphed in early 2004, seeing off challenges from Jennie Bond, Peter André, Katie Price (Jordan), Alex Best, Neil Ruddock, Lord Brocket, Diane Modahl, Mike Read and John Lydon (Johnny Rotten). The second 2004 series was won by comedian Joe Pasquale. His rivals were Janet Street-Porter, Paul Burrell, Fran Cosgrave, Sophie Anderton, Sheila Ferguson, Natalie Appleton, Vic Reeves, Nancy Sorrell (Vic's wife), Antonio Fargas and Brian Harvey. The winner in 2005 was Carol Thatcher, defeating Sheree Murphy, Sid Owen, Jimmy Osmond, Tommy Cannon, Bobby Ball, Antony Costa, Jenny Frost, David Dickinson, Jilly Goolden, Kimberley Davies and Elaine Lordan (the last two dropping out early through medical problems).

Programmes, hosted by Ant and Dec, are transmitted live each evening, recapping on the struggles endured in the previous 24 hours. Supporting programmes like *I'm a Celebrity . . . Jungle Diary* and ITV 2's *I'm a Celebrity . . . Get Me Out of Here Now!* fill in at other times for viewers who could not get enough of B-list humiliation.

I'm Alan Partridge ✶✶✶

UK (Talkback/BBC) Situation Comedy. BBC 2 1997; 2002
DVD: BBC

Alan Partridge .... **Steve Coogan**
Lynn .... **Felicity Montagu**
Susan .... **Barbara Durkin**
Sophie .... **Sally Phillips**
Michael .... **Simon Greenall**
Dave Clifton .... **Phil Cornwell**
Tony Hayers .... **David Schneider**
Sonja .... **Amelia Bullmore**

Writers **Peter Baynham, Steve Coogan, Armando Iannucci**
Producer **Armando Iannucci**

● ***A former TV chat show host struggles to regain the limelight.***

Alan Partridge, previously seen as sports anchor of THE DAY TODAY and as host of his own talk show, KNOWING ME, KNOWING YOU . . . WITH ALAN PARTRIDGE ('Aha!'), had almost sunk without trace. His TV career having ended in a flurry of chaotic programmes and collapsing ratings, he has been banished to the backwater of Radio Norwich, where he presents the early-morning show, between 4.30 and 7 a.m. Although he resents this change of fortune, Partridge still considers himself prime-time material and is determined to force his way back into television – despite an astonishing lack of tact and talent. In the meantime, having been kicked out by his wife, Carol, he lives as a guest at the Linton Travel Tavern, where he is (at best) humoured by manager Susan and smirking receptionist Sophie, but where he can at least patronize the indecipherable Geordie maintenance man, Michael. The obnoxious Partridge's only friend is his loyal doormat of a PA, Lynn. Dave Clifton is the 'hand-over' DJ at the station, who effortlessly wins the morning exchanges, and Tony Hayers is the BBC programming commissioner who turns down all Partridge's ideas. The series follows the doyen of sports casual as he recites unworkable TV formats into a dictaphone and tries to turn the cold shoulders of showbiz celebrities. After five years in the Norfolk wilderness, Partridge returned in a new series with the same title in 2002. Having moved out of the hotel, he now lives in a mobile home while waiting for his new house to be finished. He has somehow attracted a Ukrainian girlfriend named Sonja but, while Lynn still tends to his every need, his only other 'friend' is Michael, who has switched jobs to work at a petrol station. Partridge himself is still in career stasis, hosting Radio Norwich's late night show and a cable TV game show called *Skirmish*.

I'm Dickens, He's Fenster ✶✶

US (Heyday) Situation Comedy. ITV 1962–4 (US: ABC 1962–3)

Arch Fenster .... **Marty Ingels**
Harry Dickens .... **John Astin**
Kate Dickens .... **Emmaline Henry**
Mel Warshaw .... **Dave Ketchum**
Mulligan .... **Henry Beckman**
Myron Bannister .... **Frank DeVol**

Producer **Leonard Stern**

● ***The misadventures of a pair of carpenters.***

No job is too simple for the cack-handed carpenter duo of Arch Fenster (dim, carefree and single) and Harry Dickens (married – or perhaps anchored – to Kate and therefore frustratingly more level-headed). They work for vain, toupee-topped Myron Bannister on various construction jobs, aided and abetted in their clumsy antics by colleagues Mulligan and Mel. Star John Astin had more success with his next sitcom, THE ADDAMS FAMILY.

I'm the Law ✶

US (Cosman) Police Drama. BBC 1954–5 (US: Syndicated 1953)

Lt. George Kirby .... **George Raft**

Executive Producer **Pat Costello**
Producer **Jean Yarborough**

● ***Very early American cop show set in New York City.***

Gangster actor George Raft swapped sides for this half-hour foray into primitive TV policing. Taking on the mantle of Lt. George Kirby of the NYPD, Raft's beat is the Big Apple and he patrols the city streets in search of thugs, murderers and thieves, dishing out knuckle sandwiches and bullets aplenty. Raft also acts as narrator. Lou Costello's brother, Pat, was the show's executive producer, maintaining a very tight budget.

Imrie, Celia

(1952–)

British actress in dramatic and comedy roles. Apart from scores of guest appearances – taking in major series like ABSOLUTELY FABULOUS, RANDALL AND HOPKIRK (DECEASED), HEARTBEAT, DALZIEL AND PASCOE, MIDSOMER MURDERS, JONATHAN CREEK, AGATHA CHRISTIE'S MARPLE and AGATHA CHRISTIE'S POIROT – her many credits have included BERGERAC (Marianne Bellshade), *A Question of Guilt*, ORANGES ARE NOT THE ONLY FRUIT (Miss Jewsbury), THE RIFF RAFF ELEMENT (Joanna Tundish), *A Very Open Prison, A Dark Adapted Eye* (Vera Hillyard), *Boswell and Johnson's Tour of the Western Isles* (Lady MacDonald), *Black Hearts in Battersea* (Duchess of Battersea), WOKENWELL (June Bonney), TOM JONES (Mrs Miller), *The Writing on the Wall* (Kirsty), *Into the Blue* (Nadine), *Mr White Goes to Westminster* (Victoria), GORMENGHAST (Lady Gertrude), and various Victoria Wood offerings, including DINNERLADIES (Philippa Moorcroft). Imrie also played Lucretia Otis in *The Canterville Ghost*, Aunt Sadie in *Love in a Cold Climate*, Violet Pearman in THE GATHERING STORM, Kate Lawton in *Sparkhouse*, Rose Henderson in *A is for Acid*, Miss Frazier in *Station Jim*, Ellen Reynolds in *Plain Jane*, Mrs Meyrick in DANIEL

DERONDA, Anna Gromeko in DOCTOR ZHIVAGO, Gail Forrester in *The Planman*, Lady Susan Brading in DOC MARTIN and Fran Davies in *Mr Harvey Lights a Candle*.

In at the Deep End **

UK (BBC) Documentary. BBC 1 1982–4; 1987

Presenters **Chris Serle, Paul Heiney**

Executive Producer **Edward Mirzoeff**
Producer **Nick Handel**

● ***Two reporters take crash courses in other people's professional skills.***

THAT'S LIFE presenters Chris Serle and Paul Heiney alternated as stars of this light-hearted series which saw them attempting to acquire professional skills and put them to the test – all within a matter of weeks. For instance, Serle was called upon to partner snooker star Steve Davis in a doubles match against Tony Meo and Alex Higgins after receiving coaching from the likes of Ray Reardon, Terry Griffiths and Cliff Thorburn. He also underwent intense training to become a press photographer and then covered a royal assignment for the *Daily Mirror*. Between them Serle and Heiney tried their hand at numerous occupations, including auctioneer, actor, shepherd, opera singer, bookmaker and fashion designer.

In Deep **

UK (Valentine) Police Drama. BBC 1 2001–3

Liam Ketman	**Nick Berry**
Garth O'Hanlon	**Stephen Tompkinson**
Pamela Ketman	**Lisa Maxwell**
Nicola Ketman	**Karianne Henderson**
Max Ketman	**Buster Reece**
Marta Drusic	**Meera Syal**
Kelly	**Carli Norris**
Sophie	**Fiona Allen**

Writers **Peter Jukes, Stephen Brady**
Executive Producer **Mal Young**
Producer **Steve Lanning**

● ***Two plain-clothes cops infiltrate Britain's nastiest crime rings.***

Liam Ketman and Garth O'Hanlon are special-operations detectives working undercover to root out the dregs of society: paedophiles, pimps, drug pushers, racists, bent coppers and the like. Ketman is married, but his job makes his home life sticky when he is forced to lie to his wife, Pamela, and kids, Nicola and Max. To keep himself sane in the horrific world he inhabits, he regularly consults police analyst Marta Drusic. O'Hanlon, on the other hand, is very much a lone wolf, reckless and headstrong. Being single, he doesn't suffer as badly from the guilt and depression that bug his colleague and is altogether a meaner cookie. The series, airing as part of BBC 1's *Crime Doubles* season, opened with three stories in 2001 and returned with four more a year later. This time the duo are supported, or rather hindered, by incompetent assistant Kelly, and Marta has given way to replacement psychiatrist Sophie. Four more stories followed in 2003.

In Loving Memory **

UK (Yorkshire) Situation Comedy. ITV 1979–80; 1982–4; 1986

Ivy Unsworth	**Thora Hird**
Billy Henshaw	**Christopher Beeny**
Amy Jenkinson	**Avis Bunnage**
Ernie Hadfield	**Colin Farrell**
Mary Braithwaite/Henshaw	**Sherrie Hewson**

Writer **Dick Sharples**
Producer **Ronnie Baxter**

● ***A widow and her nephew run a northern undertaker's.***

When Jeremiah Unsworth dies in the first episode of this series, he leaves his wife, Ivy, as sole proprietor of his funeral director's business in the Lancashire mill-town of Oldshaw. The year is 1929. For help in running the business, Ivy enlists her gormless nephew, Billy. Other local characters, like bachelor Ernie Hadfield, are also on the scene.

The pilot for this series had been screened some ten years earlier (and indeed topped the ratings). Written by Dick Sharples and produced by Ronnie Baxter, this one-off comedy for Thames cast Edward Chapman and Marjorie Rhodes in the lead roles of Jeremiah and Ivy.

In Sickness and in Health

See *Till Death Us Do Part*.

In the Heat of the Night **

US (MGM) Police Drama. ITV 1988–90 (US: NBC 1988–92; CBS 1992–4)

Chief Bill Gillespie	**Carroll O'Connor**
Chief of Detectives Virgil Tibbs	**Howard Rollins**
Althea Tibbs	**Anne-Marie Johnson**
Sgt Bubba Skinner	**Alan Autry**
Deputy Parker Williams	**David Hart**
Deputy Lonnie Jamison	**Hugh O'Connor**
Deputy Willson Sweet	**Geoffrey Thorne**
Deputy Junior Abernathy	**Christian Le Blanc**

Creator **James Lee Barrett**
Executive Producers **Fred Silverman, Juanita Bartlett, David Moessinger, Jeri Taylor, Carroll O'Connor, Hugh Benson, Ed Ledding**

● ***TV version of the Oscar-winning film of the same name.***

Reprising the roles played by Rod Steiger and Sidney Poitier in the classic movie, Carroll O'Connor, formerly of ALL IN THE FAMILY, becomes Police Chief Bill Gillespie and Howard Rollins black cop Virgil Tibbs. Together they aim to fight crime in the small town of Sparta, Mississippi. Tibbs is a native of the town but has only just returned home, having worked in the high-tech police circles of Philadelphia. He finds himself appointed to the role of Chief of Detectives, alongside Gillespie, although the crusty old cop resents the appointment, which has been made by a black mayor seeking black votes. His resentment is not racial (the series had little of the tension of the original film) but centres on his dislike of the modern police methods Tibbs introduced. It is the familiar experience-versus-youth argument. However, as a team they achieve results and a healthy mutual respect develops between the two men.

Carroll O'Connor was forced to withdraw from a few episodes because of ill-health, and his place was taken by Joe Don Baker in the guise of Acting Chief Tom Dugan. Actor Hugh O'Connor, who played Deputy Jamison, was Carroll O'Connor's son.

Inch High, Private Eye ✳

US (Hanna-Barbera) Cartoon. BBC 1 1975 (US: NBC 1973–4)

Voices:
Inch High .... **Lennie Weinrib**
Lori .... **Kathy Gori**
Gator .... **Bob Lutell**
Mr Finkerton .... **John Stephenson**
Braveheart .... **Don Messick**

Executive Producers **William Hanna, Joseph Barbera**

● ***Crime-busting with the world's smallest sleuth.***

Inch High, Private Eye is, as his name makes clear, a pocket-size private investigator. Clothed in a dark green raincoat, a pork-pie hat on his head, the tiny tec works for the Finkerton Detective Agency, headed by doubting boss Mr Finkerton. Helping Inch High in his work are his blonde niece, Lori, and the dopey, blue-suited Gator, the muscles of the unit – both, happily, full-sized persons. Together with sloppy St Bernard dog Braveheart, they head off searching for clues in a bright red motor known as the Hushmobile, which is otherwise hidden in an underground bunker. With gadgets galore and a practised line in dry understatement, the animation acknowledges the influence of GET SMART in its conception. Just 13 25-minute films were made.

Incorporated Television Production Company

See *ITC*[1].

Incredible Hulk, The ✳✳

US (Universal) Science Fiction/Adventure. ITV 1978–82 (US: CBS 1978–82)
DVD: Universal

Dr David Banner .... **Bill Bixby**
The Incredible Hulk .... **Lou Ferrigno**
Jack McGee .... **Jack Colvin**

Executive Producers **Glen A. Larson, Kenneth Johnson**
Producers **James D. Parriott, Chuck Bowman**

● ***A mild-mannered scientist turns into an angry green monster when provoked.***

Scientist David Banner becomes a victim of his own experiments on human strength by accidentally exposing himself to a massive dose of gamma rays. The effects of the radiation mean that he now turns into a raging green giant whenever he gets angry. Banner can feel the change coming on but, after the Hulk has indulged in an orgy of violence and then reverts to his true self, Banner, unfortunately, can never remember what has happened 'during his absence'.

With the world believing him to be dead, Banner runs from town to town in search of a cure for his weird malady. On his tail is *National Register* reporter Jack McGee, who has guessed Banner's secret and is looking for concrete evidence to back up his suspicions. Inevitably, something always manages to irk the docile Dr Jekyll, releasing the shirt-busting, roaring Mr Hyde figure of the Hulk.

Lou Ferrigno, who played the monster, was a former Mr Universe, and the series was based on the early 1960s *Marvel* comic strip by Stan Lee, in which Banner's Christian name was Bruce, not David.

Independent Television Commission

See *ITC*[2].

Independent Television News

(ITN)

ITN was established by the 1954 Television Act as a news-gathering organization jointly owned by the various ITV companies. Its first news bulletin was aired on 22 September 1955, when Christopher Chataway read the headlines in a 12-minute programme. Following the introduction of new regulations in the 1990 Broadcasting Act, ITN was refounded as a profit-making news business with commercial contracts to the ITV companies and other broadcasters. It is now owned by a consortium made up of ITV plc, Daily Mail & General Trust, Reuters, and United Business Media. Also in 1990, ITN moved to new purpose-built headquarters in London's Gray's Inn Road. In 2001, ITN retained the contract to provide news to ITV until 2009.

ITN now provides news 24 hours a day, with the main bulletins being *Lunchtime News* at 12.30 (launched in 1972 under the title *First Report* and now monitoring the day's developing stories), *ITV Evening News* at 6.30 (a 30-minute review of the day's events so far), *Channel 4 News* (the 7 p.m. in-depth bulletin), and a late bulletin between 10 and 11 p.m., since 1999 the successor to the highly regarded *News at Ten* (Britain's first 30-minute news programme when introduced in 1967, and still a name applied on some evenings to this late bulletin). In addition to these, ITN offers news headlines through the night and a half-hour round-up at 5.30 a.m. known as *Morning News*. The company also provides news services for other broadcasters, including radio bulletins for IRN (Independent Radio News) and Classic fM.

Over and above formal news reports, ITN has also produced a number of feature programmes, which have been broadly news- and current affairs-based. Between 1957 and 1964, for instance, ROVING REPORT was a series of topical documentaries compiled by ITN correspondents around the world. More recently, *House to House*, fronted by Maya Even on Channel 4, reported the business of the day from the Houses of Commons and Lords. There have been programmes on royalty, elections, budgets and other state occasions, too.

In 1997 ITN acquired 49 per cent of the pan-continental *Euronews* channel, but sold its interest in 2001. In August 2000 the 24-hour, digital ITN News Channel was launched. This was sold and renamed ITV News Channel in 2002. However, its new owner, ITV plc, closed down the channel in December 2005.

See also NEWS.

Indoor League, The ✳✳

UK (Yorkshire) Sport. ITV 1973–8
DVD: Network

Presenters **Fred Trueman, Fred Dinenage**

Executive Producers **John Fairley, John Wilford**
Producers **Sid Waddell, John Meade**

Bar-room Olympics, Yorkshire style.

'Nah then!' Thus quoth cricket legend Fred Trueman, insisting daytime audiences pay attention because the battle of the bar-room was about to begin. With mug of ale in hand, Trueman presided over six series of pub game contests in a fake boozer, handing over his bar stool only briefly to Fred Dinenage for a few instalments in 1975. Trueman impressed on viewers the seriousness of shove-ha'penny, bar billiards, arm wrestling, table football, table skittles, pool and especially darts, as the series went on to do for 'arrers' what POT BLACK had once achieved for snooker. Masterminding proceedings was producer/commentator Sid Waddell, with other commentators including Dave Lanning, Keith Macklin, Kent Walton, Neil Cleminson, Bill Maynard, Fraser Davy, Hector O. Meades and Neil Hawke. But the last word always went to the pipe-chomping Trueman, who bid his guests a fond Yorkshire farewell: 'I'll see thee.'

Informer, The ★★

UK (Rediffusion) Adventure. ITV 1966–7

Alex Lambert .... **Ian Hendry**
Janet Lambert .... **Heather Sears**
Sylvia Parrish .... **Jean Marsh**
DS Piper .... **Neil Hallett**
Tony Cass .... **Tony Selby**

Creators **John Whitney, Geoffrey Bellman**
Executive Producer **Stella Richman**
Producers **Stella Richman, Peter Collinson, John Whitney**

The risky life of a professional informer.

Disgraced and disbarred barrister Alex Lambert has begun to rebuild his life and his shaky marriage. Using the excellent contacts he has made over the years on both sides of the law, he branches out into a new career as a paid informer. Passing on information to Piper, his police contact, Lambert lives off the substantial rewards offered by insurance companies. But secrecy is vital and his life is continually under threat. Not even his wife is party to his true profession and he masquerades under the guise of a business consultant.

Inherited Audience

An audience that a programme gains from the previous show on the same channel, with viewers not bothering to switch over. Planners make use of inherited audiences to give new series a launch-pad.

Inigo Pipkin/Pipkins ★★

UK (ATV) Children's Entertainment. ITV 1973/ITV 1974–81
DVD: Network

Inigo Pipkin .... **George Woodbridge**
Johnny .... **Wayne Laryea**
Hartley Hare .... **Nigel Plaskitt**
Tortoise .... **Nigel Plaskitt**
Topov .... **Heather Tobias**
Loraine Bertorelli
Elizabeth Lindsay
Pig .... **Heather Tobias**
Loraine Bertorelli
Anne Rutter
Alex Knight
Octavia Ostrich .... **Heather Tobias**
Loraine Bertorelli
Elizabeth Lindsay
Fred Pipkin .... **Royce Mills**
Mrs P .... **Diana Eden**
Charlie .... **Charles McKeown**
Bertha .... **Jumoke Debayo**
Tom .... **Jonathan Kydd**
Peter .... **Paddy O'Hagan**
Uncle .... **Nigel Plaskitt**
Pigeon .... **Loraine Bertorelli**
Moony .... **Nigel Plaskitt**
Narrator .... **Nigel Plaskitt**

Creator **Michael Jeans**
Writers **Susan Pleat, Anna Standon, David Cregan**
Producer **Michael Jeans**

Comical adventures in a puppeteer's workshop.

This long-running, pre-school entertainment was set in the workshop of one Inigo Pipkin, a craftsman who specializes in glove puppets called Pipkins. But these are no ordinary puppets: they can sing, dance and behave like humans, and stories follow their adventures in and around the workshop and the fun they have with the items therein, usually drawing an educational conclusion. Often they head out into the big wide world, travelling in the Pipkin Puppet Van (a black Morris Minor). Most fondly remembered are toothy, ever-so-camp Hartley Hare, Topov the monkey, Tortoise and Pig, each character having such failings that can be corrected on air, thus presenting a moral message. Initially titled *Inigo Pipkin*, the series was renamed *Pipkins* for most of its eight years on air after the death of its leading man, George Woodbridge. Care of his puppets then passed to his apprentice, Johnny.

Inman, John

(1935–)

Preston-born actor, a stage pantomime dame, known for his camp roles of menswear assistant Mr Humphries in ARE YOU BEING SERVED? (through which 'I'm free!' became his catchphrase), rock factory proprietor Neville Sutcliffe in *Odd Man Out* and male secretary Graham Jones in *Take a Letter, Mr Jones*. The character of Mr Humphries resurfaced in the *Are You Being Served?* revival, *Grace and Favour*, in 1992, while Inman has otherwise been seen recently in DOCTORS and the sketch show *Revolver*.

Innes Book of Records, The ★★

UK (BBC) Comedy/Music. BBC 2 1979–81

Host **Neil Innes**

Producer **Ian Keill**

Sketches and musical parodies with the former Bonzo Dog man.

In the late 1960s Neil Innes mixed easily with the new breed of alternative comedians, working with the Monty Python team and inspiring the wacky pop group The Bonzo Dog Doo Dah Band. In this, his own series, a decade later, he demonstrated his talent for deadpan humour and his flair for uncannily accurate musical send-ups. Anyone who saw *The Rutles* would vouch for this rare ability.

Inside George Webley ★★

UK (Yorkshire) Situation Comedy. ITV 1968; 1970

George Webley .... **Roy Kinnear**
Rosemary Webley .... **Patsy Rowlands**

Creators/Writers **Keith Waterhouse, Willis Hall**
Producers **Bill Hitchcock, John Duncan**

A man's life is dominated by worry.

Bank clerk George Webley is one of life's know-alls and the archetypal worryguts. He frets over the silliest matters and, in his mind, something is always about to go wrong. Has he left the gas on, for example? In contrast, his dozy, ever-hungry wife, Rosemary, is far more relaxed.

There was more than an echo of *Inside George Webley* in Paul Smith and Terry Kyan's comedy COLIN'S SANDWICH 20 years later.

Inspector Alleyn Mysteries, The ★★

UK (BBC) Police Drama. BBC 1 1993–4
DVD: Acorn Media

Chief Insp. Roderick Alleyn ..... **Patrick Malahide**
Insp. Brad Fox .... **William Simons**
Agatha Troy .... **Belinda Lang**

Creator **Ngaio Marsh**
Producer **George Gallaccio**

A well-bred, academically brilliant detective works for Scotland Yard in the late 1940s.

New Zealand author Dame Ngaio Marsh's toff detective was first brought to television in the 1960s as part of the DETECTIVE anthology, in which he was played by Michael Allinson. Simon Williams donned Alleyn's trilby for a 90-minute special in 1990, but when a series was cast in 1993 it was Patrick Malahide – already familiar as MINDER's Sgt Chisholm – who was offered the role. He portrays Roderick Alleyn as a true gentleman, unfailingly polite but a steely adversary for law-breakers. A man with a double first in Classics from Oxford, Alleyn is a policeman almost out of a sense of duty. He moves in aristocratic circles but is never a snob. He is supported in his work by the loyal Inspector Fox and in his private life by his artistic lady friend, Agatha Troy (both William Simons and Belinda Lang had taken the same roles in the 1990 offering).

In the original novels, Alleyn's cases cover the period 1933 to 1980 (two years before his creator's death). For this television rendition, the action is confined to 1948. After a run of five mysteries, Alleyn returned in 1994, not in another series but in the first of a collection of one-off investigations.

Inspector Lynley Mysteries, The ★★

UK (BBC/WGBH Boston) Police Drama. BBC 1 2001–
DVD: WGBH Boston (Region 1 only)

DI Thomas Lynley .... **Nathaniel Parker**
DS Barbara Havers .... **Sharon Small**
Helen Clyde/Lynley .... **Lesley Vickerage**

Producers **Ruth Baumgarten, Jenny Robins, Christopher Aird**

The cases of an upper-crust detective and his working-class sidekick.

Thomas Lynley is an aristocrat. He is, in fact, the eighth earl of Asherton and lives in a swish Chelsea house, but his blue blood hangs like a millstone around his neck. Now in his 30s, he wants to contribute more to society than such nobility is generally seen to do and so has become a policeman. In Scotland Yard, his background marks him out like a sore thumb but he's a solid, thorough detective so his place is assured. Joining him in his investigations is a girl from the other end of the social rainbow. Barbara Havers, in her late 20s, lives in a little house in Acton with her sick mother and father. Her brother died as a teenager and she feels his loss keenly. Unlike Lynley, who has been handed grace and style on a plate, Havers is a fashion disaster, with an almost pathological fear of contact with the opposite sex. From the start, the chip on her shoulder sets her and her posh superior at odds, and her sharp tongue provokes reproach, but at least they get results, using Lynley's brilliant, Oxford-educated mind and Havers's terrier-like groundwork. Criminal profiler Helen Clyde (played by Emma Fielding in the pilot episode) is Lynley's posh girlfriend (later wife). Gabrielle Drake is occasionally seen as Lynley's mother, Lady Asherton. The series was based on novels written by American Elizabeth George.

Inspector Morse ★★★★

UK (Zenith/Central/Carlton) Police Drama. ITV 1987–93; 1995–8; 2000
DVD: Granada Ventures

Chief Insp. Endeavour
Morse .... **John Thaw**
DS Robbie Lewis .... **Kevin Whately**
Max .... **Peter Woodthorpe**
Dr Grayling Russell .... **Amanda Hillwood**
Chief Supt. Bell .... **Norman Jones**
Chief Supt. Strange .... **James Grout**
Dr Laura Hobson .... **Clare Holman**
Adele Cecil .... **Judy Loe**

Executive Producer **Ted Childs**
Producers **Kenny McBain, Chris Burt, David Lascelles, Deirdre Keir**

The complicated cases of a cerebral Oxford detective.

Chief Inspector Morse (first name concealed for many years) of the Thames Valley Police is an Oxford graduate and a lover of culture. Poetry, Wagnerian opera and cryptic crosswords are his passions, along with gallons of real ale to oil the cogs of his brilliant detective mind. Somewhat squeamish for a copper, and always with an eye for the ladies (although seldom a success with the opposite sex), Morse cruises the dreaming-spired streets of Oxford in his 1960 Mark 2 red Jaguar, accompanied by his ingenuous sergeant, Lewis, a Geordie making his way up the CID ladder. Unlike the crotchety bachelor Morse, genial Lewis is a family man, and the contrast between the two is well contrived. The pair enjoy a good working relationship, even if Morse is cruelly patronizing at times.

The investigations are unfailingly multidimensional and Morse always needs time to collar his man, or woman. His theories regularly go awry, and one murder turns into two or three before he finally pieces together the solution (often with the help of a chance remark from Lewis), much to the dissatisfaction of his boss, Chief Supt. Strange. Indeed, seldom is there an episode when pathologists like Max or Dr Russell do not have to appear more than once.

With each beautifully photographed episode at feature length, there is bags of scope for both character and plot development. Stories initially came from the original novels by Oxford academic Colin Dexter, who endowed Morse with his own love of classics, culture, crosswords and booze. Indeed, Morse's name was derived from Sir Jeremy Morse, then Chairman of Lloyds Bank and one of Dexter's crossword rivals. Lewis, too, was christened after a crossword setter, although in the books he was Welsh and nearing retirement age. When the novels ran out, Dexter penned a series of new plots for TV, before finally handing over the invention to other writers. His involvement with the series continued, however – as an extra, he walked on in every episode, as Hitchcock used to do.

The series of *Inspector Morse* ended in 1993, but one-off specials (generally following new books by Colin Dexter) were produced in each of the years 1995–8, with the last-ever episode, based on Dexter's *The Remorseful Day*, being aired in 2000. However, in 2006 Kevin Whately returned to Oxford in a new drama called *Lewis*, picking up the good sergeant's life after the death of his mentor, and also his wife, killed in a hit-and-run incident. Laurence Fox plays his bag carrier, DS James Hathaway.

In the 1997 story *Death is Now My Neighbour*, Morse's Christian name is finally revealed as being 'Endeavour'. The programme's sweeping theme music by Barrington Pheloung is cleverly based on the Morse Code beat for the letters M-O-R-S-E.

Inspector Wexford

See *Ruth Rendell Mysteries, The*.

Interceptor

See *Treasure Hunt*.

Interference

Sound or picture distortion caused by external electrical signals.

International Detective ✶✶

UK (Delry/ABC) Detective Drama. ITV 1959–61

Ken Franklin .... **Arthur Fleming**

Producer **Gordon L. T. Scott**

● ***The adventures of a calm, systematic detective-agency man.***

Ken Franklin works for the William J. Burns International Detective Agency in New York and jets around the world on various assignments. Given his briefing by W. J. Burns himself (a character never properly seen), Franklin then uses intellect rather than brute force to bring home results. Each episode is entitled *The . . . Case* (fill in the blank) and is shot in documentary style.

The series was supposedly based on the files of a real William J. Burns agency. Star Arthur (Art) Fleming went on to host one of American TV's most popular quiz shows, *Jeopardy*.

Interpol Calling ✶

UK (Rank/Wrather/ATV) Police Drama. ITV 1959–60

Insp. Paul Duval .... **Charles Korvin**
Insp. Mornay .... **Edwin Richfield**

Executive Producer **F. Sherwin Green**
Producers **Anthony Perry, Connery Chapell**

● ***Cases from the files of the International Criminal Police Organization, Interpol.***

Inspectors Duval and Mornay, two detectives operating out of Interpol's Paris headquarters, investigate murders, foil blackmailers, arrest hijackers, dupe drug-pushers and apprehend would-be assassins all around the world in this half-hour series. Each episode opens with a speeding car crashing through a checkpoint, setting the pace for the action to follow. Thirty-nine stories were filmed.

Intrigue ✶✶

UK (ABC) Detective Drama. ITV 1966

Gavin Grant .... **Edward Judd**
Val Spencer .... **Caroline Mortimer**

Creator **Tony Williamson**
Producer **Robert Banks Stewart**

● ***An industrial troubleshooter prevents the theft of business secrets.***

Suave Gavin Grant, a gourmet, wine buff and general *bon viveur*, works as a freelance management consultant. But he doesn't get paid to generate marketing ideas or cost-cutting measures: his skills are employed in tackling industrial espionage, providing stability in the dog-eat-dog world of commerce – and he is rewarded accordingly. Val Spencer is his attractive partner. The 13-part series was based on an idea by experienced ITC writer Tony Williamson and numbered acclaimed adventure writers like Robert Holmes and Brian Clemens among the script team.

Invaders, The ✶✶✶

US (Quinn Martin) Science Fiction. ITV 1967 (US: ABC 1967–8)

David Vincent .... **Roy Thinnes**
Edgar Scoville .... **Kent Smith**
Narrator .... **William Conrad**

Creator **Larry Cohen**
Executive Producer **Quinn Martin**
Producer **Alan A. Armer**

● ***An architect tries to alert the world to an alien invasion.***

Most people think David Vincent is paranoid: he believes the world is under threat from a race of aliens whose planet is dying. In the style of Richard Kimble in THE FUGITIVE, he moves from town to town, attempting to warn the human race, but at the same time keeping himself clear of the Invaders' clutches.

Vincent, an architect, was driving down a deserted country road and pulled over to get some sleep. He was awakened by the arrival of a spaceship and the realization that an invasion was taking place. He ran to bring help, but the police discovered only a young courting couple who denied everything

Vincent had said. This was the first of many brick walls to confront him during the course of the series.

Because the Invaders assume human form, Vincent has great difficulty persuading people to believe his story. Usually, those in whom he placed his trust turn out to be aliens themselves, as even he has problems spotting them. He soon gathers, though, that they are not complete human clones and that they have some strange defects, most notably a crooked little finger. Another giveaway is the fact that, having no hearts, they have no pulse or emotions.

After many narrow escapes, Vincent manages to convince a small group of citizens that his story is true, and he is thus given seven colleagues (known as 'The Believers') to finance and support his mission to save the planet. The leader of the group is Edgar Scoville, a millionaire electronics executive.

The story never is brought to a climax, but Vincent does have his successes. He thwarts various alien plans and kills a number of Invaders during the course of the series, seeing them glow red then evaporate, leaving behind just a burnt outline on the ground. But the aliens, too, are killers, using either ray guns or a small disc device which, when applied to the back of the neck, gives the victim heart failure. Only once is the Invaders' true likeness revealed, and even then it is blurred, leaving the viewer truly mystified about these sinister spacemen. The series was rerun on BBC 2 in 1984 and 1992.

Invasion: Earth ✶✶

UK (BBC/Sci-Fi Channel) Science Fiction. BBC 1 1998
DVD: A&E Home Video (Region 1 only)

Flt Lt. Chris Drake	**Vincent Regan**
Dr Amanda Tucker	**Maggie O'Neill**
Major Gen. David Reece	**Fred Ward**
Squadron Leader Helen Knox	**Phyllis Logan**
Lt. Charles Terrell	**Anton Lesser**
Nick Shay	**Paul J. Medford**
Flt Lt. Jim Radcliffe	**Jo Dow**
Sgt Tuffley	**Gerard Rooney**
Group Capt. Susan Preston	**Sara Kestelman**
Emily Tucker	**Laura Harling**
Wing Commander Friday	**Chris Fairbank**
Flt Lt. Stewart	**Bob Barrett**
Gran	**Diana Payan**
Nurse Louise Reynolds	**Zoe Telford**
DS Holland	**Nicola Grier**
Dr Vickers	**Hugh Ross**
Jenny Marchant	**Sheila Grier**

Writer **Jed Mercurio**
Producers **Jed Mercurio, Chrissy Skins**

Scientists and the military combine to thwart an alien invasion.

When RAF pilot Chris Drake rather over-eagerly shoots down an unidentified flying object, it is but the start of Earth's woes. As the ship crashes into the Scottish Highlands, an alien emerges, confirming not only the existence of life beyond our planet but also the fact that Earth is about to be caught up in a struggle between two extraterrestrial races, the Echoes and the nDs. Drake is disciplined by the authorities but begins the fight-back personally, joining forces with determined scientist Amanda Tucker, who works for a body called SETI (the Search for Extra-Terrestrial Intelligence), monitoring signals from outer space. They gain the support of both the RAF and NATO, bringing into play the mysterious Lt. Charles Terrell; Flight Lt. Jim Radcliffe, leader of the RAF's land team; Squadron Leader Helen Knox, who suspects Russian involvement; Group Capt. Susan Preston, a formidable neurologist; and fellow scientist Nick Shay, with NATO's Major Gen. David Reece calling the shots. The action meanders between London during the Blitz and the present-day Highland village of Kirkhaven, as the malevolent nDs turn their eyes on our humble little planet.

Invasion: Earth was a high-budget production (£750,000 reportedly spent on each of the six 50-minute episodes), jointly funded with the US Sci-Fi Channel. Writer Jed Mercurio had previously created both CARDIAC ARREST and THE GRIMLEYS. His inspiration, he claimed, was the notorious Roswell incident of 1947, when aliens were thought to have crash-landed in New Mexico.

Inverdale, John

(1957–)

Devon-born sports presenter, moving from Radio 5 Live to front programmes like *On Side, Rugby Special, Britain's Strongest Man*, POINTS OF VIEW, *High Stakes, In the Know* and GRANDSTAND for the BBC.

Invisible Man, The [1]

See *H. G. Wells' Invisible Man*.

Invisible Man, The [2] ✶

US (Universal) Science Fiction. BBC 1 1975 (US: NBC 1975–6)

Dr Daniel Westin	**David McCallum**
Walter Carlson	**Craig Stevens**
Dr Kate Westin	**Melinda Fee**

Executive Producer **Harve Bennett**
Producer **Leslie Stevens**

An invisible scientist undertakes covert missions for a West Coast think-tank.

Dr Daniel Westin has perfected the means of making things invisible, but when he hears that the Government wishes to use his achievement for military purposes, he destroys all his equipment, memorizes the formula and makes himself invisible in order to escape. However, with the reversing procedure ineffective, he is stranded in invisibility.

In an effort to pursue a normal life, Westin has a wig, a realistic face mask and rubber hands created, which he pulls off in times of trouble. So that he can continue his experiments and find a way back to normality, he and his wife, Kate, go to work for the KLAE Corporation (a Californian research unit), occasionally performing undercover missions for his boss, Walter Carlson. KLAE finances Westin's attempts to resume normality, and Westin uses the codename 'the KLAE Resource' whenever he is in action.

Invisible Man, The [3] ✶✶

UK (BBC) Drama. BBC 1 1984
DVD: BBC Worldwide

Griffin, the Invisible Man	**Pip Donaghy**
Revd Bunting	**Michael Sheard**
Dr Cuss	**Gerald James**
Teddy Henfrey	**Jonathan Adams**
Mr Hall	**Ron Pember**
Mrs Hall	**Lila Kaye**

Sandy Wadgers .... **Roy Holder**
Mrs Roberts .... **Anna Wing**
Constable Jaffers .... **John Quarmby**
Thomas Marvel .... **Frank Middlemass**
Dr Samuel Kemp .... **David Gwillim**
Lucy .... **Merelina Kendall**

Writer **James Andrew Hall**
Producer **Barry Letts**

● ***A deformed scientist becomes increasingly power-crazed.***
Unlike the ITV fanciful interpretation of the same name from the 1950s, or Universal's take on the theme from the 1970s, this BBC dramatization of H. G. Wells's 1897 novel looks to follow the original storyline. Over six episodes, it relates the tale of unscrupulous scientist Griffin, who has become invisible through his experiments. Wearing bandages to give him some form, he arrives in the village of Iping and takes up lodging with Mr and Mrs Hall. However, Griffin is intent on using his new-found freedom for improper ends. He robs the local vicarage and, when this is discovered, he goes on the run, roping in a tramp named Thomas Marvel to help him out. He eventually seeks refuge with fellow scientist Dr Samuel Kemp, but Griffin is by now a homicidal maniac. The message from author Wells is that, however far science advances mankind, human morality must advance with it to ensure there is never power without control. Stephen Deutsch supplies the music.

Ireland: A Television History ✶✶

UK/Ireland (BBC/RTE) Historical Documentary. BBC 2 1980–1

Presenter/Writer **Robert Kee**

Producers **Jeremy Isaacs, Jenny Barraclough**

● ***A 13-part account of the development of Ireland.***
Bravely attempting to portray the history of this country on television for the first time, Robert Kee's Irish documentary began 800 years earlier, at the point when the English first became involved with their island neighbour. It progressed through to the recent troubles and the days of violence, using eye-witness accounts and old film footage to analyse the underlying causes of the unrest. For its efforts, the series won the BAFTA Best Documentary Series award. Kee also supplied an accompanying book.

Irish RM, The ✶✶

UK (James Mitchell/Rediffusion Films/Ulster/RTE/Little Bird) Drama. Channel 4 1983–5
DVD: Acorn Media

Major Sinclair Yeates .... **Peter Bowles**
Philippa Butler/Yeates .... **Doran Godwin**
Florence Macarthy 'Flurry' Knox .... **Bryan Murray**
Sally Knox .... **Lise-Ann McLaughlin**
Slipper .... **Niall Toibin**
Mrs Cadogan .... **Anna Manahan**
Peter Cadogan .... **Brendan Conroy**
Lady Knox .... **Faith Brook**
Mrs Knox .... **Beryl Reid**
Dr Jerome Hickey .... **Jonathan Ryan**
Bridget Brickley/Cadogan .... **Virginia Cole**
Julia .... **Deirdre Lawless**

Writers **Rosemary Anne Sisson, Alfred Shaughnessy, Hugh Leonard, Julia Jones**
Executive Producer **James Mitchell**
Producer **Adrian Hughes**

● ***An army major resigns his commission to become a Resident Magistrate in colonial Ireland.***
Prim and proper Major Sinclair Yeates has retired to the rural west coast of Ireland at the end of the 19th century, with the aim of enjoying peace in his new role of local magistrate, helping to administer British rule. But his hopes of pastoral calm are rudely shattered by parochial disputes, arguments over livestock and sheer, unfathomable blarney, leaving the rather gullible Yeates deep in hot water, especially if his mischievous landlord, Flurry Knox, is involved. The series was based on the 1899 book *Some Experiences of an Irish RM*, by Somerville and Ross (Edith Somerville and Violet Florence Martin).

Iron Horse ✶

US (Screen Gems) Western. BBC 1 1967–8 (US: ABC 1966–8)

Ben Calhoun .... **Dale Robertson**
Dave Tarrant .... **Gary Collins**
Barnabas Rogers .... **Bob Random**
Nils Torvald .... **Roger Torrey**
Julie Parsons .... **Ellen McRae**

Producers **Fred Freiberger, Matthew Rapf**

● ***A playboy-gambler becomes a railroad pioneer in the 1880s.***
Ben Calhoun has won the Buffalo Pass, Scalplock and Defiance railroad line in a poker game. However, the line is in difficulty, only half constructed and on the verge of bankruptcy. Undaunted, Ben, together with his pet racoon, Ulysses, construction engineer Dave, brawny crewman Nils and Barnabas, an orphan clerk, sets about reviving the company's fortunes and getting the trains to run on time through the untamed West. Julie Parsons is introduced later as proprietor of the Scalplock General Store. (Actress Ellen McRae found greater success after changing her name to Burstyn; she picked up an Oscar for *Alice Doesn't Live Here Anymore* in 1974.)

Irons, Jeremy

(1948–)

Isle of Wight-born actor, now a Hollywood name but successful on TV first in such series as *Notorious Woman* (Franz Liszt), THE PALLISERS (Frank Tregear), *Love for Lydia*, Pinter's adaptation of *Langrishe, Go Down* (Otto Beck), *Tales from Hollywood* (Odon Von Horvath) and BRIDESHEAD REVISITED. In the last, his portrayal of Charles Ryder was widely acclaimed. He returned to television in 2000, playing Rupert Gould in LONGITUDE and was later seen as the Earl of Leicester in *Elizabeth I*. Early exposure was gained in the children's series PLAY AWAY. His second wife is actress Sinéad Cusack.

Ironside

See *Man Called Ironside, A.*

Is It Legal? ★★

UK (Hartswood/Carlton) Situation Comedy. ITV 1995–6/ Channel 4 1998

Bob	**Patrick Barlow**
Stella Phelps	**Imelda Staunton**
Colin Lotus	**Richard Lumsden**
Dick Spackman	**Jeremy Clyde**
Alison	**Kate Isitt**
Darren	**Matthew Ashforde**
Sarah	**Nicole Arumugam**

Writer **Simon Nye**
Producer **Beryl Vertue**

● ***Fumbling and farce in a workshy solicitors' office.***

Set in the old-fashioned Hounslow office of Lotus, Spackman & Phelps, a firm of solicitors, *Is It Legal?* is a tale of executive ineptitude and staff in-fighting. Senior partner is Dick, an aloof man who fails to understand the minutiae of day-to-day work and would rather not be there at all. Stella, meanwhile, is the moody senior partner, man-hungry but disorganized. Bob, their clerk, is a drippy, long-term bungler with a complicated personal life. Alongside these, Darren is the dopey office junior, Sarah is the sandwich girl who turns Bob's head, and Alison is the lazy secretary who knows how to wrap her male colleagues around her little finger. They are joined by Colin, the new junior partner, who has landed his position through nepotism and certainly not because of his legal knowledge. Indeed, with precious little legal input, the series majors on the personal relationships within this claustrophobic office and the little pranks the staff play on each other.

Much like writer Simon Nye's MEN BEHAVING BADLY, the series was dropped after two runs by ITV and then picked up by another channel (when the series moved to Channel 4 in 1998, Dick had left and Stella was in charge). However, *Is It Legal?* failed to achieve the same success even when resurrected.

Isaacs, Sir Jeremy

(1932–)

Scottish-born producer and TV executive, initially with Granada working on programmes like WHAT THE PAPERS SAY and ALL OUR YESTERDAYS, and then with the BBC (PANORAMA, etc.) and Thames. Among the highlights of his television career have been the acclaimed THE WORLD AT WAR and Robert Kee's IRELAND: A TELEVISION HISTORY (both as producer). He later became Programme Controller at Thames and was the first Chief Executive of Channel 4. Isaacs has also been seen in front of the cameras, as the inquisitor in the revival of FACE TO FACE. After becoming General Director of the Royal Opera House in Covent Garden, 1988–97, he returned to television production with his own company, creating the factual series *Cold War* and *Millennium: A Thousand Years of History*. He is currently chairman of Artsworld, the digital television cultural channel.

Island at War ★★

UK (Granada) Drama. ITV 1 2004
DVD: Acorn Media (Region 1 only)

James Dorr	**James Wilby**
Felicity Dorr	**Clare Holman**
Baron Von Rheingarten	**Philip Glenister**
Wilf Jonas	**Owen Teale**
Kathleen Jonas	**Julia Ford**
Colin Jonas	**Sean Ward**
Ada Jonas	**Ann Rye**
Mary Jonas	**Amy Ginsburg Harvey**
Cassie Mahy	**Saskia Reeves**
Urban Mahy	**Julian Wadham**
Angelique Mahy	**Joanne Froggatt**
June Mahy	**Samantha Robinson**
Sheldon Leveque	**Sean Gallagher**
Francis La Palotte	**Benjamin Whitrow**
Capt. Muller	**Daniel Flynn**
Lt. Walker	**Conor Mullen**
Philip Dorr	**Sam Heughan**
Margaret	**Caroline Strong**
Delphine	**Sarah Kirkman**
Ronald	**Nicholas Roud**
Eugene La Salle	**Richard Dempsey**
Zelda Kay	**Louisa Clein**
Bernhardt Telleman	**Laurence Fox**
Oberwachtmeister Wimmel	**Colin Tierney**
Oberleutnant Flach	**Andrew Havill**

Creator/Writer **Stephen Mallatratt**
Executive Producer **Sita Williams**
Producer **John Rushton**

● ***Channel Islanders struggle under Nazi invasion.***

Covering similar ground to 1978's ENEMY AT THE DOOR, *Island at War* depicts the German occupation of the Channel Islands during World War II. The precise setting this time is the fictitious island of St Gregory (the Isle of Man was used for filming), and the lives of three families are used to highlight the miseries and hardships experienced under an occupation force. First there are the Dorrs. James Dorr is Deputy Bailiff in the island's government. He is conscientious and devoted to his wife, Felicity, who is not an island native and finds life there all too claustrophobic. Their son, Philip, is away in the army but finds himself dropped back onto St Gregory for a reconnaissance mission. Wilf Jonas is a policeman who leaves the running of the family farm to his wife, Kathleen. Their young children are Colin and Mary, while Ada is Wilf's old mum. Kathleen's brother, Sheldon Leveque, leads a charmed life as a wheeler-dealer trading with both sides of the conflict. The third family are the Mahys. Ill-fated husband Urban runs a grocery with his wife, Cassie. Their daughters are Angelique, who works alongside James Dorr, and June, an easily led singer. Across the battlelines they face island commander Von Rheingarten, a tough man, but a man who still has something of a conscience. He also has an eye for Felicity. His subordinates include Walker, a true Nazi, and Telleman, an intellectual airman sucked into actions he doesn't believe in. Also central to the action is young Jewish German Zelda Landau, who is stranded on St Gregory and needs to keep both her identity and faith a secret. The islanders' story, beginning in June 1940 shortly before the Germans arrive, is told over six 90-minute episodes, but not without controversy. In the Channel Islands themselves, the series was attacked for its alleged inaccuracies.

It Ain't Half Hot Mum ✶✶✶

UK (BBC) Situation Comedy. BBC 1 1974–8; 1980–1
DVD: BBC

RSM B. L. Williams	**Windsor Davies**
Gunner/Bombardier 'Gloria' Beaumont	**Melvyn Hayes**
Bombardier 'Solly' Solomons	**George Layton**
Rangi Ram	**Michael Bates**
Gunner 'Lofty' Sugden	**Don Estelle**
Col. Reynolds	**Donald Hewlett**
Capt. Ashwood	**Michael Knowles**
Gunner 'Paderewski' Graham	**John Clegg**
Gunner Mackintosh	**Stuart McGugan**
Gunner 'Nobby' Clark	**Kenneth MacDonald**
Gunner Nigel Parkin	**Christopher Mitchell**
Gunner 'Nosher' Evans	**Mike Kinsey**
Char Wallah Muhammed	**Dino Shafeek**
Punka Wallah Rumzan	**Babar Bhatti**

Creators/Writers **Jimmy Perry, David Croft**
Producers **David Croft, Graeme Muir**

● ***Life with an army concert party in the Indian subcontinent.***

Set during World War II, *It Ain't Half Hot Mum* relates the farcical exploits of the Royal Artillery Concert Party as they entertain the active men, and takes its name from the content of letters written home by one of its recruits, Gunner Parkin. Joining Parkin in the troupe are Bombardier Solomons (written out after the early episodes); drag artist Gunner Beaumont (known to all as Gloria); intellectual pianist Gunner Graham; diminutive chief vocalist Gunner 'Lofty' Sugden; Scotsman Gunner Mackintosh; and Gunners Clark and Evans. Their out-of-touch COs are snooty Colonel Reynolds and his idiotic sidekick, Captain Ashwood, but bane of their lives is the Welsh Sgt Major Williams. 'Old Shut Up', as they know him, considers the concert party to be a bunch of 'pooftahs' (especially Gloria and 'Mr Lah-de-dah Gunner Graham'). He does, however, have more respect for young Parkin, a Colchester lad who, in the Sgt Major's eyes, has a fine pair of shoulders and always sets a good example to the rest of the unit (Williams thinks he is the boy's father). The local wallahs, genuinely considering themselves to be true Brits, provide the racial humour. (The late Michael Bates was blacked up as the comical bearer Rangi Ram and, on Bates's death, Dino Shafeek's loyal char wallah gained more prominence, warbling 'Land of Hope and Glory' after each programme's closing credits.) The show opens to the troupe's rousing theme song, inviting viewers to 'Meet the gang 'cos the boys are here, the boys to entertain you'.

Windsor Davies and Don Estelle capitalized on their roles for a spin-off single, 'Whispering Grass', which surprisingly topped the UK charts in 1975.

It Takes a Thief ✶✶

US (Universal) Spy Drama. ITV 1968–71 (US: ABC 1968–70)

Alexander Mundy	**Robert Wagner**
Noah Bain	**Malachi Throne**
Wallie Powers	**Edward Binns**
Alister Mundy	**Fred Astaire**

Creator **Collier Young**
Producer **Jack Arnold**

● ***An expert thief is freed from jail to work for the Government.***

Sophisticated, handsome Al Mundy is the perfect cat-burglar, yet, somehow, he has been caught and confined in San Jobel prison. Realizing his potential, the US Government offers him a degree of liberty, inviting him to steal for the SIA intelligence agency. Between missions, Mundy is forced to return to custody, but when he is out he certainly makes the most of it, travelling all round the world and making contact with hordes of glamorous women, most of whom fall for his style and charm. His father, Alister, another master thief, is introduced later. He has taught his son the tricks of the trade and now finds himself joining Alexander on certain missions. Mundy's SIA chief in the early days is Noah Bain. In later episodes (when Mundy is no longer locked up between assignments), Wallie Powers is his agency contact.

It Takes a Worried Man ✶✶

UK (Thames) Situation Comedy. ITV 1981; 1983/Channel 4 1983

Philip Roath	**Peter Tilbury**
Ruth	**Diana Payan**
Simon	**Nicholas Le Prevost**
Napley	**Andrew Tourell**
Old Man	**Christopher Benjamin**
Liz	**Sue Holderness**

Creator **Peter Tilbury**
Writers **Peter Tilbury, Barry Pilton, Colin Bostock-Smith**
Producers **Anthony Parker, Douglas Argent**

● ***Life is particularly stressful for a lazy insurance man.***

Philip Roath is suffering from a mid-life crisis. He is 35 years old, his wife, Ellen, has just left him and his hair and teeth appear to be going the same way. He's formally employed as an insurance salesman, but such are his personal worries that he rarely manages to get any work done at all. It's hardly surprising, therefore, that his colleagues, Ruth, Napley and the Old Man, rarely have cause to bolster his confidence with a compliment or two. When Roath starts talking to himself, he knows he's in a bad way and manages to overcome his endless indecision to visit an analyst, Simon. It's a bad move, however, as Simon is more insecure than his patient and burdens Philip with his own cares and worries. Thus, Roath meanders from one personal disaster to another. Things seem to be looking up in series two, when he finds himself a girlfriend, Liz, although the fact that she can't make up her mind whether to keep her independence or move in with Philip does not bode well. For its third series, the programme – created by and starring Peter Tilbury, writer of SHELLEY and CHEF! – switched channels, from ITV to Channel 4.

ITA

See *ITC (Independent Television Commission).*

ITC [1]

(Incorporated Television Programme Co.)

ITC was the company founded in 1954 by theatrical businessmen Lew and Leslie Grade, Prince Littler and Val Parnell to bid for one of the first ITV franchises. Initially unsuccessful, ITC turned instead to independent production and distribution, with THE ADVENTURES OF ROBIN HOOD the first commissioned programme. However, the group was soon asked to join another consortium, which had won a franchise but was having difficulty getting on air. The resulting company became ATV. To avoid conflicts of interest between the broadcasting company and the production company, ATV took over full control of ITC in 1957, making it a wholly owned subsidiary. ITC went on to specialize in action series like DANGER MAN, THE SAINT, THE CHAMPIONS, RANDALL AND HOPKIRK (DECEASED) and THE PRISONER, as well as most of the Gerry Anderson puppet series and, in the 1970s, THE MUPPET SHOW. ITC was sold to Australian businessman Robert Holmes à Court in 1982, who in turn sold it to another Australian, Alan Bond. A management buy-out later conferred control into yet newer hands. In 1995 it was taken over by Polygram, and later by Carlton Communications, now part of ITV plc.

ITC [2]

(Independent Television Commission)

The ITC was the public organization responsible for licensing and regulating commercially funded television services in the UK until its replacement by new super-regulator Ofcom in December 2003.

The ITC replaced both the IBA (Independent Broadcasting Authority) and the Cable Authority on 1 January 1991. It not only granted broadcasting licences to Channel 3 (ITV) companies, Channel 4, Channel 5, cable channels and satellite services but also monitored their progress, ensuring they adhered to the strict standards and guidelines it laid down for programming and advertising. Those failing to do so were liable to penalities. The Chairman, Deputy Chairman and the eight Members of the Commission were all appointed by the Secretary of State for Culture, Media and Sport, and the ITC was funded by licence fees payable by contracting broadcasters.

The ITC's predecessor, the IBA, was responsible for both independent television and independent radio. It had a greater 'hands-on' approach to programme monitoring, with the various contractors needing to agree schedules with the IBA (in accordance with the Broadcasting Act). As a result, the IBA was the legally accountable broadcaster. Under the new system it is the programme company that is legally accountable. The IBA, inaugurated in 1971, was a descendant of the ITA (Independent Television Authority), which was established by Parliament under the Television Act of 1954 and concerned itself solely with the appointment and output of ITV companies in the days before the advent of independent radio.

It'll be Alright on the Night ★★★

UK (LWT) Comedy. ITV 1977–2006

Presenter/Writer **Denis Norden**

Producers **Paul Smith, Paul Lewis, Sean Miller, Simon Withington**

● ***Sporadic collections of out-takes and bloopers from the worlds of film and TV.***

When the clipboard clutching Denis Norden, in an avalanche of puns and corny wisecracks, launched *It'll be Alright on the Night* in 1977, he tapped into a new vein of television comedy. Previously, fluffs and foul-ups by professional actors and TV presenters had been discreetly kept away from the viewing public (although, for years, they had been mischievously edited together by TV technicians for private viewing). Now everything came out into the open and the public loved seeing their word-perfect announcers and performers brought crashing down to earth by a Freudian slip of the tongue or the lapse of an imperfect memory. Clips of actors 'corpsing' (creasing up into uncontrollable laughter) were particularly popular. Because such infelicities are everyday occurrences in TV and film production, Norden was able to gather up the best scraps from the cutting-room floor at least once every couple of years since, and the best bits were recycled into various compilation programmes to fill the gaps between new episodes. The BBC has withheld its own out-takes for use in its similar offering, *Auntie's Bloomers* (1991–2001), hosted by Terry Wogan, which spawned its own spin-off series, *Auntie's Sporting Bloomers* (1995–7).

ITN

See *Independent Television News*.

It's a Knockout/Jeux Sans Frontières ★★★

UK (BBC/Ronin) Game Show. BBC 1 1966–82/Channel 5 1999–2001

Presenters **David Vine, Eddie Waring, Stuart Hall, Keith Chegwin, Frank Bruno**

Producers **Barney Colehan, Cecil Korer, Geoff Wilson, Richard Hearsey, Robin Greene**

● ***Inter-town silly games contests.***

Greasy poles, daft costumes, giant beach balls and impossible obstacle courses were the order of the day in *It's a Knockout*. Very loosely based on a 1950s series called *Top Town*, in which amateur entertainers competed for their home town, this series pitched willing and athletic citizens into combat for the right to represent the United Kingdom in the European finals. These finals went out under the title of *Jeux Sans Frontières*.

Each *It's a Knockout* contest consisted of a variety of races and battles in which teams struggled to jump through hoops, climb sticky slopes or splash through water while dressed as outsize cartoon figures. There was usually a theme (often medieval) to link events, and a 'joker' could be played to double the points won in any one game. Interspersed throughout was the Mini-Marathon (the Fil Rouge in the Euro-edition), a drawn-out, multi-element game presided over by rugby league's Eddie Waring. Hosting proceedings initially was David Vine, but he gave way to laugh-a-minute Stuart Hall in 1972. Veteran announcer McDonald Hobley and Katie Boyle were also involved in the very early days, and Arthur Ellis acted as tournament referee for the duration.

Jeux Sans Frontières began in 1967 and was hosted by a different country each week, but always in the presence of international arbiters Gennaro Olivieri and Guido Pancaldi. After a series of international heats, a grand final was held, featuring the top-scoring team from each country. The UK's first representatives were Bridlington, who took on the rest of the Continent in France.

There were numerous *It's a Knockout* celebrity specials, the most notable being *The Grand Knockout Tournament* in 1987, when the four teams competing for charity were captained by HRH the Prince Edward, HRH the Princess Anne, HRH the Duke of York and HRH the Duchess of York. *It's a Knockout* also transferred to the USA in 1975, where it was renamed *Almost Anything Goes*. This survived only one year before being superseded by a celebrity series entitled *All-Star Anything Goes*.

Back in the UK, Channel 5 resurrected the series in summer 1999, with Keith Chegwin the excitable host, assisted by guffawing referee Frank Bruno and scorers Lucy Alexander and Nell McAndrew.

It's a Square World ★★★

UK (BBC) Comedy. BBC 1960–4

Michael Bentine, Clive Dunn, Frank Thornton, Benny Lee, Len Lowe, Dick Emery, Leon Thau, Ronnie Barker, Louis Mansi, Anthea Wyndham, Janette Rowselle, John Bluthal, Freddie Earie, Joe Gibbons

Creator **Michael Bentine**
Writers **Michael Bentine, John Law**
Producers **G. B. Lupino, James Gilbert, John Street, Joe McGrath**

● ***Madcap, surreal, early sketch show.***

Collating fictitious reports from the four corners of the world and adding much more besides, *It's a Square World* was a direct ancestor of MONTY PYTHON and other bizarre comedies. Former Goon Michael Bentine was the brains behind the project, and he and an extensive supporting cast starred in a series of zany visual sketches which pushed back the boundaries of TV comedy. Bentine had a penchant for scale models, using them to weird effect. Boats were a favourite: he caused the Woolwich Ferry to sink in one stunt, and in another famous episode sent a Chinese junk to attack the House of Commons. Bentine also planted a 40-foot whale outside the Natural History Museum, much to the dismay of local drivers, and, on another occasion, sent the BBC Television Centre into space.

A follow-up series, *All Square*, appeared courtesy of ATV in 1966–7 and there was a one-off *It's a Square World* revival back on BBC 1 in 1977.

It's Awfully Bad for Your Eyes, Darling . . . ★★

UK (BBC) Situation Comedy. BBC 1 1971

Gillian Page-Wood ('Pudding')	**Jane Carr**
Virginia Watter	**Jennifer Croxton**
Clover Mason	**Elizabeth Knight**
Samantha Ryder-Ross	**Joanna Lumley**
Bobby Dutton	**Jeremy Lloyd**
Dominic	**Jonathan Cecil**

Creators/Writers **Jilly Cooper, Christopher Bond**
Producer **Leon Thau**

● ***Four disorganized girls share a London flat.***

Although now noted for blockbuster novels, at the turn of the 1970s Jilly Cooper was best known as the author of a popular column for the *Sunday Times* newspaper. *It's Awfully Bad for Your Eyes, Darling* . . . was her first attempt at television success, penned in association with Christopher Bond. The concept was based on her own experience of sharing dreary, untidy flats in London with other like-minded girls who generally worked as secretaries by day and dressed up for cocktail parties at night. Here Cooper pitches together four rather well-to-do girls in that mould – Pudding, Viriginia, Clover and Samantha – with storylines and dialogue based around their experiences with men, interfering parents and other such issues. Ken Jones provided the music. The series was spun off a COMEDY PLAYHOUSE presentation in 1971, in which there were a couple of cast differences. Firstly, there was no Clover. Secondly, the character of Virginia had a different surname (Walker) and was played by Anna Palk.

It's Dark Outside ★★

UK (Granada) Police Drama. ITV 1964–5

Chief Insp. Charles Rose	**William Mervyn**
DS Swift	**Keith Barron**
Anthony Brand	**John Carson**
Alice Brand	**June Tobin**
DS Hunter	**Anthony Ainley**
Claire	**Veronica Strong**
Fred Blaine	**John Stratton**
Sebastian	**Oliver Reed**

Producer **Derek Bennett**

● ***The return of the sharp-tongued detective, Mr Rose.***

It's Dark Outside formed the middle segment of a trilogy of series featuring the acerbic Inspector Rose. Rose had first appeared in THE ODD MAN six months earlier, as did the character of Detective Sgt Swift, a soft-hearted, pensive copper. Here they are joined by Anthony and Alice Brand, a barrister and his journalist wife, though not for long. By the second season the Brands and Swift are gone, leaving the calm, cold Rose in prime position, supported by newcomers DS Hunter (Anthony Ainley, a future DOCTOR WHO Master), his girlfriend, Claire, and her boozy reporter friend, Fred Blaine. A young actor named Oliver Reed appears in some episodes as Sebastian, the ringleader of a bunch of tearaways. The programme gained a cult following for its grim, tense, almost *film noir* atmosphere and it also generated a chart-topping single, Jackie Trent's 'Where are You Now (My Love)'. For more adventures with the refined investigator, see MR ROSE.

It's Garry Shandling's Show ★★★

US (Showtime) Situation Comedy. BBC 2 1987–90 (US: Showtime 1986–90)

Garry Shandling	**Garry Shandling**
Mrs Ruth Shandling	**Barbara Cason**
Nancy Bancroft	**Molly Cheek**
Pete Schumaker	**Michael Tucci**
Jackie Schumaker	**Bernadette Birkett**
Grant Schumaker	**Scott Nemes**
Leonard Smith	**Paul Willson**
Phoebe Bass	**Jessica Harper**

Creators **Garry Shandling, Alan Zweibel**
Executive Producers **Bernie Brillstein, Brad Grey, Garry Shandling**

● ***Unusual comedy series in which the star plays himself and talks directly to the studio audience.***

This show is based around the fictitious life of neurotic comic Garry Shandling, with the set modelled around his real-life sitting-room. There is a plot (of sorts) in each episode, usually centring on Garry's lack of success with women or other paranoia. He confides in viewers and positively encourages the studio audience to welcome the guest stars he introduces. Other members of the cast also engage the audience, and the whole show is put together so that it parodies the techniques and conventions of television.

Regular droppers-by to his Sherman Oaks condominium

are his mother, his friend Nancy Bancroft and neighbours the Schumakers, with intelligent young son Grant. Nosy Leonard Smith, manager of the building, also appears. Just before the series ends, Garry marries his girlfriend, Phoebe Bass.

This break-all-the-rules type of television was not new. The inspiration was very clearly THE BURNS AND ALLEN SHOW in the 1950s, in which George Burns drew himself aside from the plots to discuss the show with viewers. This technique has become known as 'breaking the fourth wall'.

It's Only TV . . . But I Like It ★★

UK (Open Mike) Comedy Quiz. BBC 1 1999–2002

Presenter **Jonathan Ross**

Producers **Andy Davies, Jon Naismith, Shaun Pye**

● ***Celebrity TV quiz for laughs.***

Doing for classic television what HAVE I GOT NEWS FOR YOU does for topicality, THEY THINK IT'S ALL OVER for sport and NEVER MIND THE BUZZCOCKS for pop, this comedy quiz initially featured Jack Dee alongside Julian Clary as a team captain. His place from series two, however, was taken by Phill Jupitus. The captains each led two fellow celebrities through a series of humorous rounds of questions based on TV trivia. Among the features were Granny Knows Best (guessing the people or programmes described by pensioners) and Opportunity Knockers (spotting which talent show contenders are still in the business). Added to this were theme tune mimes, BLUE PETER makes and other such mirth.

ITV

(Channel 3)

Independent television arrived in the UK in 1955 after years of debate. There were widespread fears that commercial television would turn out to be a vulgar and gimmicky concept, fears that were stimulated by the American experience, where sponsors and game shows ruled the airwaves. Nevertheless, the Television Act of 1954 bravely opened up the television market to an advertising-led channel.

This channel was controlled and regulated by a public body, the Independent Television Authority (ITA), who owned the transmitters, oversaw programme standards and monitored advertising. A federal system was conceived for broadcasters. For coverage, the UK was carved up into regions; independent companies then applied for sole transmission rights, selling advertising to generate revenue and paying a levy to the ITA for their licences. The first ITV region to go on air was London, where the franchise was split into weekdays and weekends. Associated-Rediffusion was awarded the Monday-to-Friday contract, with ATV handling Saturday and Sunday. The first transmission was on 22 September 1955, when Associated-Rediffusion and ATV jointly held a Gala Opening Night, beginning with a formal inauguration ceremony at London's Guildhall. The new channel was known by a number of names, the most common being CTV, Channel 9 or ITA.

Piecemeal, the other elements of the ITV network fell into place until, by 1962, nearly all of the UK, including the Channel Islands, was covered (the one exception, the Isle of Man, followed in 1965). The ITV companies were closely monitored for performance and over the years several franchise reviews were held. In 1964 all the companies passed muster (except for Wales West and North, which had gone out of business). In 1967 there were several changes. ATV was given the Midlands on a seven-days-a-week basis, and Associated-Rediffusion and ABC (the contractor for the Midlands and the North at weekends) were asked to merge to take on the London weekday franchise. This they did under the name of Thames Television. London at weekends was given to London Weekend Television (LWT). In Wales and the West TWW lost its licence to Harlech Television, and in the North Granada was allowed to extend its transmission times from five to seven days a week, but had to relinquish the area east of the Pennines to a new franchisee (ultimately Yorkshire Television). In 1980 there were more changes. Out went Westward Television (the contractor for the South-West) and Southern (Southern England), to be replaced by TSW and TVS respectively. At the same time ATV was obliged to reconstitute itself as Central Independent Television to hang on to the Midlands area.

For the next round of franchise renewals a new system was brought into play by the Conservative Government. Instead of merely applying for the licence to broadcast, prospective ITV companies were asked to bid for the franchise. This was designed to extract more money from ITV companies, which the Government felt were operating advertising monopolies in their individual areas. Under the new system, the highest bidder would get the franchise, provided that the new regulatory body, the ITC, was happy with the business plan and the commitment to programme quality. In highly controversial circumstances, Thames was outbid by Carlton Communications and lost its franchise. However, Granada was outbid by Mersey Television but retained its franchise. Other losers were TVS and TSW (both deemed to have overbid) and these gave way to Meridian and Westcountry respectively. TV-am, the breakfast-time contractor appointed in 1980, lost out to Sunrise Television (soon to be renamed GMTV). The farcicality of the situation was further outlined when it was revealed that Central (unopposed in its application) secured the profitable Midlands area with a bid of just £2,000. After this restructuring, ITV was officially known as Channel 3. Subsequently, there was much consolidation in the industry, gradually leading to just two major players dominating the ITV stage – Granada (owner of LWT, Tyne Tees, Yorkshire, Anglia, Meridian, Border and some of GMTV) and Carlton (owner of Central, Westcountry, HTV and also part of GMTV). The companies merged in 2004 to form ITV plc. (The regions covered by Grampian and Scottish (Scottish Media), Ulster and Channel remain independent.) ITV 2 – a digital channel with a notably young slant supporting ITV partly through spin-off and follow-up programming – was launched digitally in 1998 and ITV itself was rebranded ITV 1 in summer 2001. In 2004 ITV 3, centred on reruns of major ITV dramas, came on air, followed by ITV 4, focusing on male interests, sports and films, in 2005.

ITV Digital

See *ONdigital*.

Ivanhoe [1] ★★

UK (Screen Gems/Sydney Box) Adventure. ITV 1958–9

Ivanhoe .... **Roger Moore**
Gurth .... **Robert Brown**
Bart .... **John Pike**
Prince John .... **Andrew Keir**
King Richard .... **Bruce Seton**

Executive Producer **Peter Rogers**
Producers **Herbert Smith, Bernard Coote**

● ***The chivalrous hero of Sir Walter Scott's novel takes on a 'Robin Hood' mantle.***

Ivanhoe returns home after the Crusades to find that good King Richard has been usurped by his wicked brother, Prince John, who is now tyrannizing the people. Freeing Gurth and Bart, two doomed serfs who become his squires, he sets about righting wrongs and helping those in distress. This swashbuckling series was Roger Moore's first starring role and he bravely performed his own stunts. Its executive producer, Peter Rogers, went on to develop the *Carry On* series of films.

The original *Ivanhoe* tale has been dramatized twice since by the BBC, in 1970 starring Eric Flynn (father of Jerome), and again in 1997, starring Steven Waddington.

Ivanhoe ² ✳✳✳

UK (BBC/A&E) Drama. BBC 1 1997

Wilfred of Ivanhoe .... **Steven Waddington**
Sir Brian de Bois-Guilbert .... **Ciaran Hinds**
Rowena .... **Victoria Smurfit**
Cedric of Rotherwood .... **James Cosmo**
Prince John .... **Ralph Brown**
Waldemar Fitzurse .... **Ronald Pickup**
Rebecca .... **Susan Lynch**
Isaac of York .... **David Horovitch**
Athelstane of Coningsburgh .... **Chris Walker**
Gurth .... **Trevor Cooper**
Wamba .... **Jimmy Chisholm**
King Richard .... **Rory Edwards**
Robin of Locksley .... **Aden Gillett**
Little John .... **David J. Nicholls**
Sir Reginald Front de Boeuf ... **Nick Brimble**
Sir Maurice de Bracy .... **Valentine Pelka**
Lucas de Beaumanoir .... **Christopher Lee**
Queen Eleanor .... **Siân Phillips**

Writer **Deborah Cook**
Producer **Jeremy Gwilt**

● ***Earthy dramatization of Sir Walter Scott's famous novel.***

With the aim of depicting the 12th century as a time of hardship, misery and brutal cruelty, this six-part adaptation of *Ivanhoe* is deliberately grimier than the flamboyant, 'flashing sword' versions seen previously in film and on TV. Although expanding Scott's storyline in places, the drama generally follows the original plot, with Ivanhoe returning from the Crusades in disguise, his reputation damaged by false accusations of betrayal against King Richard. On arrival home, to a land ruled cruelly by Prince John, he finds his sweetheart, Rowena, about to become betrothed to fellow Saxon Athelstane. Thus his battles are many: to re-establish his good name, to reclaim his inheritance, to win back his bride and to defeat the hated regent. Matters are then complicated by his attraction to Rebecca, the beautiful daughter of a Jewish moneylender (anti-Semitism rears its ugly head); the presence of his great rival Sir Brian de Bois-Guilbert (a Norman champion); the religious rage of Lucas de Beaumanoir (Grand Master of the Knights Templar); and various skirmishes, sieges and important jousting tournaments.

Ivor the Engine ✳✳

UK (Smallfilms) Cartoon. ITV 1959; 1962–3/BBC 1 1976–7; 1979
DVD: 4 Front Video

Narrators **Oliver Postgate, Olwen Griffiths, Anthony Jackson**

Creator/Writer **Oliver Postgate**
Producer **Oliver Postgate**

● ***The homely adventures of a little Welsh steam train.***

'In the top left-hand corner of Wales there was a railway called the Merioneth and Llantissily Rail Traction Company Ltd', so viewers of this animation are told before being introduced to the railway's star employee, Ivor the Engine. Bearing the M&LRT Co. Ltd livery, the little green puffer is driven by Jones the Steam, who works in conjunction with colleagues like Owen the Signal and Dai Station, the man who looks after Llaniog Station. Ivor's boiler is fired by Idris, a small dragon with a high-pitched voice who takes up residence when his volcano home is rendered uninhabitable. In a series of quaint little adventures, Ivor and Jones chug around the mountainous landscape of Wales helping out citizens in trouble and longing to sing in the choir, like Ivor's friend, Evans the Song.

Ivor the Engine was produced by the Smallfilms partnership of Oliver Postgate and Peter Firmin, with Firmin drawing all the pictures. It was first screened at lunchtime on ITV via Associated-Rediffusion, before transferring to the BBC in 1976, who commissioned new films and colour versions of the original tales.

Ivory, William

(1964–)

Nottinghamshire-born actor/writer William Ivory is possibly still best known for playing gormless Eddie Ramsden in CORONATION STREET, although his script work has been widely acclaimed, too. On screen he has been seen in RESNICK (DC Mark Divine), the single drama *Care* (DC Devlin) and as a guest in a number of series, including ALL CREATURES GREAT AND SMALL, BOON, CHEF!, *Lock, Stock . . .* and ROSE AND MALONEY. As a writer, his contributions have included *King Leek*, COMMON AS MUCK (also appearing as Vinny), *The Sins* (also guesting in a small role), *Night Flight* (also as Sergeant Stan), *A Thing Called Love* and *Faith*.

J

Jack the Ripper

See *Second Verdict*.

Jackanory ✳✳✳

UK (BBC) Children's Entertainment. BBC 1/BBC 2 1965–96
DVD: Acorn Media

Executive Producers **Anna Home, Angela Beeching**
Producers **Joy Whitby, David Coulter, Anna Home, Daphne Jones, David Turnball, Angela Beeching, Christine Secombe, Margie Barbour, Roger Singleton-Turner, Nel Romano**

● ***Celebrity storytime for younger viewers.***
Jackanory took its name from the nursery rhyme which begins 'I'll tell you a story of Jackanory . . .', and that effectively sums up what the programme was about – simple storytelling. The success and longevity of the programme (although initially only scheduled for a six-week run) stemmed from this most basic of formats, with just a few illustrations and the narrative skills of the guest reader as embellishments.

Characterized in its golden age by twirling kaleidoscope images in its opening and closing credits, *Jackanory* usually presented just one book a week, its contents abridged to fit over five 15 minute editions with the same reader employed for the duration (later episodes were shown on BBC 2 on Sunday mornings). The first story to be featured was *Cap of Rushes*, told by Lee Montague. Over the years, more than 700 books were read, by over 400 storytellers. Bernard Cribbins holds the record for most appearances, followed by the late Kenneth Williams. Many children's favourites were aired, some more than once, with Roald Dahl recognized as the viewers' top author (his *Charlie and the Chocolate Factory* was voted number one in a poll on the occasion of *Jackanory*'s 20th birthday). In 1979, Tolkien's *The Hobbit* was read to celebrate the programme's 3,000th edition. In 1984, HRH the Prince of Wales narrated his own story, *The Old Man of Lochnagar*.

A sister programme of playlets, *Jackanory Playhouse*, was also developed (BBC 1 1972–85).

Jackson, Glenda

MP, CBE (1936–)

Birkenhead-born actress and latterly Labour MP for Hampstead and Highgate, whose television highlight was her Emmy-award-winning title role in ELIZABETH R, though a later appearance as Cleopatra with Morecambe and Wise in a play 'wot Ernie wrote' ironically is just as well remembered by viewers. One of Jackson's last TV performances before taking her seat in the House came in the 1991 John Le Carré drama *A Murder of Quality*. She has since returned to narrate the documentary series *Boss Women*.

Jackson, Gordon

OBE (1923–90)

With his soft Scottish burr and impeccable comportment, Gordon Jackson became one of TV viewers' favourite personalities in the early 1970s in his guise of the reliable butler, Hudson, in UPSTAIRS, DOWNSTAIRS. His next starring role, however, was in quite a different vein, as George Cowley, the demanding boss of Bodie and Doyle in THE PROFESSIONALS. All this came after a lengthy career as a character actor in the British film and theatre industries and television appearances in plays and series like DR FINLAY'S CASEBOOK and MYSTERY AND IMAGINATION. Jackson was one of the hosts of STARS ON SUNDAY and also popped up in programmes and TV movies such as *Spectre, The Last Giraffe*, THE NEW AVENGERS, *Noble House* (Supt. Armstrong), *My Brother Tom*, CAMPION and *A Town Like Alice* (Noel Strachan).

Jackson, Kate

(1948–)

American actress, one of the original three CHARLIE'S ANGELS, a role she was awarded after appearing in the supernatural daytime soap *Dark Shadows* and another US action series, *The Rookies*. Jackson stayed with *Charlie's Angels*, playing the part of team leader Sabrina Duncan, for three years, eventually leaving to concentrate on film work and TV movies. She returned to US prime-time TV in 1983, playing secret agent Amanda King in SCARECROW AND MRS KING, a role which lasted four years. In 1988 she played the lead in the TV series version of the film *Baby Boom*.

Jackson, Michael

(1958–)

Macclesfield-born programme maker, turned TV executive. His career began in independent production, where he created *The Media Show* for Channel 4. In 1988, he joined the BBC to work on *The Late Show*, rising rapidly through the ranks to become controller of BBC 2 in 1993, then BBC 1 in 1996. A year later, he was appointed Chief Executive of Channel 4, where he was credited with making the channel more commercial and won acclaim for new quality programming at the same time. He left Channel 4 in 2001 to work for the USA Entertainment Group in America, later becoming Chairman of the Universal Television Group.

Jacobi, Sir Derek

CBE (1938–)

Distinguished British thespian acclaimed for his portrayal of the stammering, bumbling Claudius in I, CLAUDIUS. Previously, Jacobi had appeared in THE STRAUSS FAMILY (Josef Lanner) and THE PALLISERS (Lord Fawn), and post-Claudius he has starred as spy Guy Burgess in PHILBY, BURGESS AND MACLEAN, *Mr Pye*, George Salisbury in the *Screenplay* presentation *The Vision Thing*, Alan Turing in BREAKING THE CODE, Squire Fairfield in *The Wyvern Mystery* and as the monastic sleuth CADFAEL. Other major credits have included *The Jury* (George Cording QC), THE GATHERING STORM (Stanley Baldwin), *Inquisition* (Cardinal), THE LONG FIRM (Lord Teddy Thursby) and *Jason and the Argonauts* (Phineas), plus narration work on series like *The History of Britain from the Air* and guest spots in FRIENDS, FRASIER, RANDALL AND HOPKIRK (DECEASED) and AGATHA CHRISTIE'S MARPLE. He also contributed to THE BBC TELEVISION SHAKESPEARE (Richard II). In TV movies, Jacobi was seen as Frollo in *The Hunchback of Notre Dame* and Hitler in *Inside the Third Reich*.

Jacobs, David [1]

CBE (1926–)

Silken-voiced, London-born radio and television personality, one of the original presenters of TOP OF THE POPS when it started in 1964, although Jacobs had already been host of the successful JUKE BOX JURY since 1959. Jacobs also chaired *Tell the Truth* in the 1950s, hosted a brief revival of WHAT'S MY LINE? in 1973, and compered COME DANCING. He is the younger brother of drama director the late John Jacobs and the father of actress Emma Jacobs.

Jacobs, David [2]

American writer/producer, creator of DALLAS and its spin-off, KNOTS LANDING, among other prime-time TV credits, most of which never aired in the UK.

Jacques, Hattie

(Josephina Edwina Jacques; 1924–80)

Kent-born actress, seen most often in matronly roles in the cinema (particularly in *Carry On* films) and as a foil for Eric Sykes on TV. She played Eric's sister in SYKES for many years from 1960, having previously worked with him on the radio series *Educating Archie*. However, Hattie did once have a series of her own, MISS ADVENTURE in 1964, in which she played investigator Stacey Smith, who haplessly stumbled into global escapades. She also starred as Georgina Ruddy in the communal comedy OUR HOUSE in 1960, played Miss Manger in the shortlived sitcom *Charley's Grants* in 1970, and appeared in HANCOCK'S HALF HOUR, *The World of Beachcomber* and as a guest on THAT WAS THE WEEK THAT WAS as well as many other shows. She was once married to John Le Mesurier.

Jake and the Fatman ✳

US (Dean Hargrove/Fred Silverman/Viacom) Legal Drama. ITV 1989–91 (US: CBS 1987–92)

Jason Lochinvar 'Fatman' McCabe	**William Conrad**
Jake Styles	**Joe Penny**
Derek Mitchell	**Alan Campbell**
Gertrude	**Lu Leonard**
Judge Smithwood	**Jack Hogan**
Lisbeth Berkeley-Smythe	**Olga Russell**
Sgt Rafferty	**George O'Hanlon Jr**

Creators **Dean Hargrove, Joel Steiger**
Executive Producers **Fred Silverman, Dean Hargrove, David Moessinger**

● ***A fat ex-cop becomes a determined district attorney.***

J. L. 'Fatman' McCabe was once a police officer known for plain talk, resilience, cunning and a tendency to bend rules when it suited him. Having left the force, he now operates as a district attorney in an unnamed Californian city (a thinly disguised Los Angeles). He is joined in his practice by Jake Styles, a fit, girl-happy private investigator who does most of the legwork, though McCabe can't resist getting back on the streets himself when the opportunity arises. Also part of the team are rookie Assistant DA Derek Mitchell, Gertrude, the office secretary, and Fatman's pet, partly deaf bulldog Max, who looks just like him. After the first season, the format changes and McCabe, Jake and Derek ship out to Hawaii, Fatman's home state, to work as investigators for the Honolulu prosecutor's office. But it is not long before they return to California and the old set-up, taking with them their new secretary, Lisbeth. Dick Van Dyke appeared as Dr Mark Sloan in one episode, which led to a spin-off series, DIAGNOSIS MURDER. *Jake and the Fat Man* was itself a spin-off from another detective series, MATLOCK.

James, Clive

(1939–)

Perceptive, wry Australian journalist, commentator and TV personality, one-time member of the Cambridge Footlights. His series *Saturday Night People, Clive James on Television, The Late Clive James, Postcard From . . ., Saturday Night Clive, The Talk Show with Clive James*, CLIVE JAMES – FAME IN THE TWENTIETH CENTURY and *The Clive James Show*, as well as regular New Year's Eve parties, have amply demonstrated his self-effacing wit, droll humour and keenness to poke gentle fun (particularly at foreign television programmes). In addition, James was a familiar guest on UP SUNDAY and presented the rock show *So It Goes*. He has also contributed numerous single features (such as *Clive James and the Calendar Girls, Clive James Meets Roman Polanski* and *Clive James Finally Meets Frank Sinatra*). James also presented the film magazine CINEMA for a while and has his own production company, Watchmaker Productions.

James, Geraldine

OBE (1950–)

English actress seen in a variety of prominent dramas. After a TV debut in THE SWEENEY, these have included *Dummy* (Sandra X), THE HISTORY MAN (Barbara Kirk), THE JEWEL IN THE CROWN (Sarah Layton), *I Remember Nelson* (Emma Hamilton), BLOTT ON THE LANDSCAPE (Lady Maud Lynchwood), *Stanley and the Women* (Dr Trish Collings), *The Healer* (Dr Mercedes Honeysett), *Over Here* (Lady Beatrice Billingham), INSPECTOR MORSE, BAND OF GOLD (Rose Garrity), DROVERS' GOLD (Ruth), KAVANAGH QC (Eleanor Harker) and *The Sins* (Gloria Green), plus *Screen One*'s *Ex* (Alice), *Losing Track* (Mrs Dewey) and *Doggin' Around* (Sarah Williams), and *Performance's A Doll's House* (Mrs Linde). More recent credits have been in CRIME AND PUNISHMENT (Pulcheria), *White Teeth* (Joyce Malfen), *An Angel for May* (Susan Higgins), *Hound of the Baskervilles* (Mrs Mortimer), STATE OF PLAY (Yvonne Shaps), LITTLE BRITAIN, HE KNEW HE WAS RIGHT (Lady Rowley) and AGATHA CHRISTIE'S POIROT.

James, P. D.

See *P. D. James*.

James, Sid

(1913–76)

South African comic actor, a stalwart of the *Carry On* films. On television (and radio) in the 1950s, James was the perfect foil for Tony Hancock in HANCOCK'S HALF HOUR, which led to his own sitcom, *East End – West End*, in 1958. From this base, he went on to star in a succession of comedies. These included CITIZEN JAMES (champion of the underdog Sid James), TAXI (cabbie Sid Stone), GEORGE AND THE DRAGON (chauffeur George Russell), TWO IN CLOVER (rat race escapee Sid Turner) and BLESS THIS HOUSE (frustrated family man Sid Abbott), all of which gave him ample opportunity to exercise his trademark dirty chuckle. James's earliest contributions came in single dramas in the 1940s.

Jameson, Louise

(1951–)

London-born actress with a number of prominent roles to her name. These have included Leela in DOCTOR WHO, Dr Anne Reynolds in THE OMEGA FACTOR, Blanche Simmons in TENKO, Susan Young in BERGERAC and Rosa di Marco in EASTENDERS. Jameson has also appeared in Z CARS, EMMERDALE FARM (Sharon Crossthwaite), CASUALTY, THE SECRET DIARY OF ADRIAN MOLE AGED 13¾, THE GENTLE TOUCH, *Cider With Rosie, The Boy Dominic*, THE BILL, RIDES (Janet), *Agatha Christie's The Pale Horse* (Florence) and WYCLIFFE, among other series.

Jamie ✶✶

UK (LWT) Children's Science Fiction. ITV 1971

Jamie Dodger .... **Garry Miller**
David Dodger .... **Ben Aris**
Molly Dodger .... **Jo Kendall**
Mr Zed .... **Aubrey Morris**
Tink Bellow .... **Nigel Chivers**

Writer **Denis Butler**
Executive Producer **Francis Coleman**
Producer **Antony Kearey**

● ***A young boy travels back in time on a magic carpet.***

On a visit to a junk shop, 13-year-old Jamie Dodger discovers an old 'magic' carpet. Egged on by the mysterious shopkeeper, Mr Zed, he buys it and takes it home. There he learns that the carpet has unusual powers, enabling him to ride back in time and meet some of history's most colourful characters. These include Guy Fawkes, Robert the Bruce, Samuel Pepys and Horatio Nelson, and the boy also visits the Battle of Hastings, Victorian London, old Baghdad and the Great Fire of London. Prompted by the ageless Mr Zed (a master of disguise), Jamie looks behind the scenes of the major events in history (helpfully his dad is a historian), sometimes accompanied by his cautious friend, Tink Bellow. On one occasion he even meets his parents when they are still kids. This 13-part series filled ITV's Sunday teatime adventure slot. The harmonica theme music was provided by Larry Adler.

Jamie and the Magic Torch ✶✶

UK (Cosgrove Hall/Thames) Children's Entertainment. ITV 1977–80
DVD: Fremantle Home Entertainment

Narrator **Brian Trueman**

Writer **Brian Trueman**
Producers **Brian Cosgrove, Mark Hall**

● ***The nightly adventures of a young boy and his loyal pooch.***

A suburban street at night. A mother's call of 'Sleep well, Jamie' is hopelessly optimistic, for her young offspring promptly gets out of bed, collects his magic torch and, with his Old English sheepdog, Wordsworth, sets off for another adventure. By training his torch onto the carpet, thereby opening up a hole through which a helter-skelter descends, Jamie arrives in Cuckoo Land, a magical, psychedelic world where the fun starts. Meeting the likes of law enforcer Officer Gotcha, amnesiac, whiskery old codger Mr Boo, odd-job man Jo-Jo Help, a rag doll called Nutmeg, plus Wellibob the cat, villainous rabbit Bulli Bundy and drop out Strumpers (with a trumpet for his nose), night time is always exciting. With the help of his magic torch, Jamie never fails to provide assistance wherever required. Joe Griffiths supplies the music. Three series (39 episodes) were made.

Jane ✶✶

UK (BBC) Comedy. BBC 2 1982

Jane .... **Glynis Barber**

Producer **Ian Keill**

● ***Ten-minute short based on the wartime cartoon heroine.***

Featuring a pre-DEMPSEY AND MAKEPEACE Glynis Barber, this inventive filler placed live actors and actresses against cartoon backgrounds to re-create the adventures of the *Daily Mirror*'s forces favourite. Jane, originally drawn by Norman Pett, had a disconcerting habit of losing her outer clothing, which left her struggling through various escapades in nothing but her underwear. The episodes were screened on five consecutive nights and an omnibus edition was shown the following weekend. Two years later, Jane returned in another five episodes entitled *Jane in the Desert*.

Jane Austen's Emma ✶✶✶

UK (Meridian) Drama. ITV 1996
DVD: A&E Home Video (Region 1 only)

Emma Woodhouse .... **Kate Beckinsale**
Mr Knightley .... **Mark Strong**
Miss Bates .... **Prunella Scales**
Mr Woodhouse .... **Bernard Hepton**
Harriet Smith .... **Samantha Morton**
Frank Churchill .... **Raymond Coulthard**
Mr Elton .... **Dominic Rowan**
Mrs Elton .... **Lucy Robinson**
Mrs Weston .... **Samantha Bond**
Mr Weston .... **James Hazeldine**
Jane Fairfax .... **Olivia Williams**

Writer **Andrew Davies**

Producer **Sue Birtwistle**

● ***Love comes as a shock for a society matchmaker.***

Twenty-one-year-old Emma Woodhouse is clever and intelligent, and lives with her crotchety old father. An arch-self-deluder, she herself has no intention of marrying but she does have plans for almost all her associates in the introspective village of Highbury. Unfortunately, she is so busy fixing up romantic liaisons for others that she doesn't realize how her own heart is being gradually stolen. Particularly subject to Emma's interference are naïve young Harriet Smith and vicar Mr Elton, while the one person to really pinpoint the failings of Miss Woodhouse is bachelor Mr Knightley. Other key characters include Emma's former governess, Mrs Weston; the local gossip, Miss Bates; her accomplished niece Jane Fairfax; and Jane's fiancé, Frank Churchill. This one-part dramatization, by the PRIDE AND PREJUDICE team of Andrew Davies and Sue Birtwistle, was partly filmed in the Wiltshire National Trust village of Lacock. Directed by Diarmuid Lawrence, it followed previous versions in 1960 (BBC: Diana Fairfax as Emma, Paul Daneman as Mr Knightley) and 1972 (BBC 2: Doran Godwin as Emma, John Carson as Mr Knightley).

Jane Eyre ★★★

UK (LWT/A&E) Drama. ITV 1997

Jane Eyre	**Samantha Morton**
Mr Rochester	**Ciaran Hinds**
Mrs Fairfax	**Gemma Jones**
Mason	**Richard Hawley**
Mrs Reed	**Deborah Findlay**
Miss Temple	**Emily Joyce**
Helen Burns	**Gemma Eglinton**
Blanche Ingram	**Abigail Cruttenden**
Adèle	**Timia Berthome**
Grace Poole	**Val McLane**
St John Rivers	**Rupert Penry-Jones**
Diana Rivers	**Elizabeth Garvie**

Writer **Kay Mellor**
Executive Producers **Delia Fine, Sally Head**
Producer **Greg Brenman**

● ***A young governess wins the heart of her pupil's father, a man with a mysterious past.***

Jane Eyre is an impoverished orphan girl raised by her aunt, Mrs Reed. After teenage trauma, she eventually becomes a teacher and accepts a position as governess to Adèle, the daughter of Mr Rochester, the lord of Thornfield Hall. At first, he is curt and blunt, but gradually relations between the two begin to warm. However, as a mutual attraction builds, and Jane's journey to womanhood is well underway, there is a barrier to their happiness: the mystery regarding Rochester's long-lost wife. Various television adaptations of Charlotte Brontë's emotional novel preceded this one-off, two-hour presentation. They came in 1956 (BBC: Daphne Slater as Jane, Stanley Baker as Rochester); 1963 (BBC: Ann Bell as Jane, Richard Leech as Rochester); 1973 (BBC 2: Sorcha Cusack as Jane, Michael Jayston as Rochester); and 1983 (BBC 1: Zelah Clarke as Jane, Timothy Dalton as Rochester). A 1971 TV movie version starred Susannah York and George C. Scott.

Janssen, David

(David Meyer; 1930–80)

For four years in the 1960s, TV audiences worldwide sweated with David Janssen in his guise of Dr Richard Kimble, aka THE FUGITIVE, as his nemesis, Lt. Philip Gerard, closed in time and again. It was a role that made Janssen one of TV's biggest stars and followed another lead role as *Richard Diamond, Private Detective*, between 1957 and 1960. All the same, Janssen had to wait nearly ten years after *The Fugitive* ended for a series to approach the success of his 1960s hit. That was HARRY O, in which he played wounded private eye Harry Orwell, one of the 1970s' quirky investigators. In between had come a largely unnoticed drama, *O'Hara, US Treasury*. Janssen's last dramatic contribution to television was the expensive mini-series *Centennial*, in which he played Paul Garrett. He died of a heart attack just before his 50th birthday.

Janus, Samantha

(1972–)

British actress whose TV highlights have included DEMOB (Hedda), PIE IN THE SKY (Nicola), GAME ON (Mandy Wilkins), the pilot for THE GRIMLEYS (Geraldine Titley), *Imogen's Face* (Imogen), BABES IN THE WOOD (Ruth) and LIVERPOOL ONE (DC Isobel De Pauli). Other credits have come in *Sharman*, MINDER, *Strange*, JUDGE JOHN DEED and *The Afternoon Play*. In 1991 she represented the UK in the Eurovision Song Contest, singing 'A Message to Your Heart' and finishing tenth.

Jarvis, Martin

OBE (1941–)

British actor seen in dramas like *Nicholas Nickleby* (title role), *Breakaway* (Sam Harvey), DOCTOR WHO, CRIME OF PASSION, THE RIVALS OF SHERLOCK HOLMES, THE PALLISERS (Frank Greystock), WITHIN THESE WALLS, JULIET BRAVO, ENEMY AT THE DOOR, RUMPOLE OF THE BAILEY, P. D. JAMES's *The Black Tower*, MURDER MOST HORRID, INSPECTOR MORSE, *Sex 'n' Death* (Neil Biddle), MICAWBER, THE INSPECTOR LYNLEY MYSTERIES, A TOUCH OF FROST and DOCTORS. His major roles have been in THE FORSYTE SAGA (Jon Forsyte) and the sitcom RINGS ON THEIR FINGERS (Oliver Pryde). He also played Godfrey Ablewhite in the BBC's 1972 adaptation of *The Moonstone*, Uriah Heep in its 1975 DAVID COPPERFIELD, M. de Rênal in its 1993 SCARLET AND BLACK, Baron de Whichehalse in *Lorna Doone*, Mr Blades in *Bootleg*, Frank in *The Queen's Nose* and Leonard in *Much Ado about Nothing*. As narrator, his voice has added authority to such series as SURVIVAL and HORIZON, and fun to the *Huxley Pig* animations. He is married to actress Rosalind Ayres.

Jason, Sir David

OBE (David White; 1940–)

One of British television's biggest stars since the 1980s, Finchley-born David Jason came late into the acting world, having first trained as an electrician. He was discovered in a play on Bournemouth pier by producer Humphrey Barclay and his TV break arrived in 1968, in the bizarre children's comedy DO NOT ADJUST YOUR SET. One role he played in the series was 'superhero' Captain Fantastic, who also appeared later in MAGPIE. From there he moved into sitcom, with the kids' series *Two Ds and a Dog* (chauffeur Dingle Bell), and then with Ronnie Barker in HARK AT BARKER, *His Lordship Entertains* (both as Dithers the gardener) and *Six Dates with Barker*. He appeared in the Richard Gordon '*Doctor*' series, was a gardener in CROSSROADS, made guest appearances in Z CARS and then gained his own vehicles, THE TOP SECRET LIFE OF EDGAR BRIGGS, playing an inept spy, and *Lucky Feller*, as shy plumber Shorty Mepstead. As the wily old lag Blanco in PORRIDGE and the hapless and frustrated shop boy Granville in OPEN ALL HOURS Jason almost became Ronnie Barker's protégé, but was then given another series of his own, playing Peter Barnes for three years in A SHARP INTAKE OF BREATH. In 1981 Jason was offered a role which took him to the top of his trade, that of wide-boy Del Boy Trotter in ONLY FOOLS AND HORSES. After this, Jason never looked back and branched out into straight(er) drama as the porter Skullion in PORTERHOUSE BLUE, Ted Simcock in A BIT OF A DO, chirpy Pop Larkin in THE DARLING BUDS OF MAY, Billy Mac in the *Screen One* presentation *The Bullion Boys*, and the morose copper, Jack Frost, in A TOUCH OF FROST (which also featured his real-life brother, Arthur White). He starred in the one-off dramas *March in Windy City* (Steven March) and ALL THE KING'S MEN (Captain Frank Beck), and, in contrast, took viewers on scuba tours of the Caribbean Sea in *David Jason: in His Element* and the Pacific in *David Jason in Search of Paradise*, and then looked at Australian wildlife in *David Jason with Killers and Koalas*. He also voiced the part of Toad in the 1980s animation of *The Wind in the Willows*, the DANGERMOUSE, *Count Duckula* and *Angelmouse* cartoon characters, and Rola Pola Bear in the kids' series *The Adventures of Dawdle*. More recently, he played Dave in (and directed) *The Quest* and its sequels, starred as MICAWBER, narrated the documentary *Infested* and played Des in the drama *Diamond Geezer*.

Jason King ★★

UK (Scoton/ITC) Detective Drama. ITV 1971–2
DVD: Granada Ventures

Jason King	**Peter Wyngarde**
Nicola Harvester	**Ann Sharp**
Sir Brian	**Dennis Price**
Ryland	**Ronald Lacey**

Creators **Dennis Spooner, Monty Berman**
Producer **Monty Berman**

● ***Light-hearted* DEPARTMENT S *spin-off featuring novelist Jason King.***

Jason King was the prominent member of the *Department S* team. This was hardly surprising, given the extravagant lifestyle he enjoyed and the outrageous 1970s fashions he favoured. Now out on his own, he continues writing his 'Mark Caine' mysteries and indulging in investigations of his own, usually surrounded by beautiful girls. Nicola Harvester is his publisher, and Sir Brian, together with his assistant, Ryland, are civil servants who blackmail King (over tax evasion) into working for the Government from time to time. His assignments are considerably more down-to-earth than the baffling *Department S* cases, despite being set in exotic locations.

Jay, Sir Antony

(1930–)

Former TONIGHT journalist who helped launch THAT WAS THE WEEK THAT WAS in 1962 and later wrote for THE GREAT WAR and THE FROST REPORT as well as the script for the 1969 documentary ROYAL FAMILY. He also served on the Annan Committee, which looked into the future of British broadcasting in the 1970s. However, Jay's greatest success came in collaboration with Jonathan Lynn when he created and wrote YES, MINISTER (and, later, *Yes, Prime Minister*). The show became a firm favourite with politicians, and Jay picked up a knighthood in 1987.

Jay, Peter

(1937–)

British journalist, for a while in the late 1990s the BBC's Economics Editor. The son of Labour cabinet minister Douglas Jay, he worked in the Treasury and then became Economics Editor of *The Times*. From 1972 Jay was the presenter of WEEKEND WORLD, ITV's Sunday political programme, until leaving in 1977 to take up an appointment as British Ambassador to the USA, bestowed on him by his father-in-law, premier James Callaghan. He returned to television in 1983 as head of TV-am, bringing with him a 'mission to explain', as the new station set out to provide news and information to early-morning viewers. However, with audiences and advertising woefully low, Jay was forced to leave after six weeks, and with his departure the tone of the programming became less serious. Other credits have included *A Week in Politics*.

Jayston, Michael

(Michael James; 1935–)

British stage and screen actor whose television work has majored on adaptations of classics (he was Edward Rochester in the BBC's 1980 version of *Jane Eyre*) but also extends to comedy, as well as dramas like THE POWER GAME and CALLAN. He took the part of Charles Rolls in THE EDWARDIANS episode *Mr Rolls and Mr Royce*, and then, in 1975, starred as QUILLER. Among his later credits have been parts in *About Face*, TINKER, TAILOR, SOLDIER, SPY (Peter Guillam), A BIT OF A DO (Neville Badger), HAGGARD (Sir Joshua), DOCTOR WHO (The Valeyard), THE DARLING BUDS OF MAY, THE GOOD GUYS, OUTSIDE EDGE (Bob Willis), EASTENDERS (Alistair), CATHERINE COOKSON'*s A Dinner of Herbs* (Justice Craig), ONLY FOOLS AND HORSES (Raquel's father), THE ROYAL, MURDER IN SUBURBIA and THE BILL.

Jeeves and Wooster ★★★

UK (Granada/Picture Partnership) Comedy Drama. ITV 1990–3
DVD: Granada Ventures

Jeeves	**Stephen Fry**
Bertie Wooster	**Hugh Laurie**
Aunt Agatha	**Mary Wimbush**
	Elizabeth Spriggs
Aunt Dahlia	**Brenda Bruce**
	Vivian Pickles
	Patricia Lawrence
	Jean Heywood
Roderick Spode	**John Turner**
Madeline Bassett	**Francesca Folan**
	Diana Blackburn
	Elizabeth Morton
Gussie Fink-Nottle	**Richard Garnett**
	Richard Braine
Oofy Prosser	**Richard Dixon**
Sir Watkyn Bassett	**John Woodnutt**
Tuppy Glossop	**Robert Daws**

Barmy Fotheringay Phipps ..... **Adam Blackwood**
Martin Clunes
Stiffy Byng ..... **Charlotte Attenborough**
Amanda Harris

Writer **Clive Exton**
Executive Producer **Sally Head**
Producer **Brian Eastman**

An aristocratic airhead is bailed out by his savvy butler.
This adaptation of P. G. Wodehouse's tales of upper-class twit Bertie Wooster and his redeeming valet, Jeeves, was tailor-made for the comedy double act of Stephen Fry and Hugh Laurie, who donned period costume for their 1930s roles. As the socializing Wooster stumbles from social disaster to social disaster, sometimes in trepidation of his London aunts Agatha and Dahlia, it is the calm, resourceful Jeeves who rides to the rescue. Later episodes are set in New York.

An earlier (1965–7) BBC version, entitled *The World of Wooster*, starred Ian Carmichael as Wooster and Dennis Price as Jeeves.

Jemima Shore Investigates ★★

UK (Thames) Detective Drama. ITV 1983

Jemima Shore ..... **Patricia Hodge**

Creator **Antonia Fraser**
Producer **Tim Aspinall**

A TV journalist discovers blackmail and murder among the upper classes.
Jemima Shore is a TV reporter, the writer and presenter of Megalith Television's *Jemima Shore Investigates*. In her spare time, as well as indulging her love of music, her inquiring mind leads her into amateur detective work, prowling around her own high-class social circles and sniffing out crime amid the aristocracy and the *nouveaux riches*. The stories were based on the novels by Antonia Fraser.

Shore made her TV bow as early as 1978 when, portrayed by Maria Aitken, she appeared in an *Armchair Thriller* presentation entitled *Quiet as a Nun*.

Jenkin, Guy

British producer, director and comedy writer, often in conjunction with Andy Hamilton (see Hamilton's entry for joint credits). Jenkin's solo work has included sketches for A KICK UP THE EIGHTIES, SPITTING IMAGE, SATURDAY LIVE and *Now – Something Else*, plus an episode of *Look at the State We're In!* He also wrote the detective series *Sharman*, *Screen Two's A Very Open Prison* and *Crossing the Floor*, *Screen One's The Lord of Misrule*, and Channel 4's *Mr White Goes to Westminster*, plus *Sex 'n' Death*, *Jeffrey Archer: the Truth* and *The Private Life of Samuel Pepys*.

Jennie, Lady Randolph Churchill ★★★

UK (Thames) Historical Drama. ITV 1974

Jennie Jerome/Lady Randolph Churchill ..... **Lee Remick**
Lord Randolph Churchill ..... **Ronald Pickup**
Duchess of Marlborough ..... **Rachel Kempson**
Duke of Marlborough ..... **Cyril Luckham**
Count Kinsky ..... **Jeremy Brett**
Sir Henry Wolff ..... **Charles Lloyd Pack**
Prince of Wales ..... **Thorley Walters**
Arthur Balfour ..... **Adrian Ropes**
George Cornwallis-West ..... **Christopher Cazenove**
Mrs Patrick Campbell ..... **Siân Phillips**
Winston Churchill ..... **Warren Clarke**
Mr Leonard Jerome ..... **Dan O'Herlihy**
Mrs Jerome ..... **Helen Horton**
Leonie Jerome ..... **Barbara Parkins**
Pearl Craigie ..... **Zoë Wanamaker**

Writer **Julian Mitchell**
Executive Producer **Stella Richman**
Producer **Andrew Brown**

The life and career of the mother of Sir Winston Churchill.
This seven-part drama was produced as part of the celebrations to mark the centenary of Churchill's birth, and it focused on the life of his mother, an American born into a wealthy family. It follows her rise into aristocratic circles after meeting her future husband, Lord Randolph Churchill, at a party off Cowes in 1873. It shows the daring, flirtatious lady campaigning politically on her husband's behalf, giving birth to Winston and progressing her own career by launching a literary magazine. Scripts were vetted by Lady Spencer Churchill, Sir Winston's widow, and filming took place at family homes, including Blenheim Palace. Warren Clarke, playing Winston, was required to age from 16 to 47 during the series.

Jericho ★★★

UK (Granada/WGBH Boston) Police Drama. ITV 1 2005–

DI Michael Jericho ..... **Robert Lindsay**
DS Clive Harvey ..... **David Troughton**
DC John Caldicott ..... **Ciarán McMenamin**
WPC Penny Collins ..... **Kellie Bright**
AC Graham Cherry ..... **Nicholas Jones**
Rita Harvey ..... **Eve Matheson**
Jenny Harvey ..... **Zoe Colton**
Juliette ..... **Aurélie Bargème**
Angela ..... **Lydia Leonard**

Creator/Writer **Stewart Harcourt**
Producer **Cameron McAllister**

A maverick detective is London's most famous policeman.
It's not so much the detective as London in 1958 that is the star of this atmospheric crime series. Trilby-hatted DI Michael Jericho plies his trade in the seedy streets of Soho, beneath winking neon lights and through a swirl of dense, relentless smog. He's a dedicated, if moody, copper, indeed a bit of a hero who is about to be given his own TV show, which is the source of less than pleasant rivalry at the nick. Still, Jericho can always count on the resigned support of his old mucker Sgt Harvey, an honest family man who is the one person who can tell his boss where he's going wrong, having worked alongside him for nearly 20 years. The duo take under their wing young DC Caldicott, a new CID officer about to get married to his girlfriend, Angela. Action takes place in bars, cinemas, night clubs and often in Harvey's own house, until his long-suffering but genially supportive wife, Rita, sends Jericho back onto the streets. A less-than-welcoming home for Jericho is a modest flat above an apartment used by French prostitute Juliette. They strike up a relationship, that is later to be used against our hero – as if he doesn't have enough

personal problems, haunted, as he is, by his own dad's death on duty as a copper in 1926.

Jesus of Nazareth ★★★★

UK (ITC/RAI) Drama. ITV 1977
DVD: Granada Ventures

Jesus Christ	**Immad Cohen** *(boy)*
	Robert Powell *(adult)*
Virgin Mary	**Olivia Hussey**
Joseph	**Yorgo Voyagis**
Mary Magdalene	**Anne Bancroft**
Simon	**Peter James Farentino**
Judas Iscariot	**Ian McShane**
John the Baptist	**Michael York**
Nicodemus	**Laurence Olivier**
Simeon	**Ralph Richardson**
Herodias	**Valentina Cortese**
Balthazar	**James Earl Jones**
Melchior	**Donald Pleasence**
Gaspar	**Fernando Rey**
Joseph of Arimathea	**James Mason**
Herod the Great	**Peter Ustinov**
Salome	**Isabel Mestres**
Herod Antipas	**Christopher Plummer**
Caiaphas	**Anthony Quinn**
Pontius Pilate	**Rod Steiger**
Barabbas	**Stacy Keach**
Zerah	**Ian Holm**
The Adulteress	**Claudia Cardinale**
Yehuda	**Cyril Cusack**
Amos	**Ian Bannen**
Elizabeth	**Marina Berti**
Anna	**Regina Bianchi**
Joel	**Oliver Tobias**
Centurion	**Ernest Borgnine**

Writers **Anthony Burgess, Suso Cecchi d'Amico, Franco Zeffirelli**
Executive Producer **Bernard J. Kingham**
Producer **Vincenzo Labella**

The life of Jesus as seen by Franco Zeffirelli and Lord Lew Grade.

This much-publicized epic centres on Jesus as a man, not a myth. By playing down the supernatural, Lew Grade's ITC hoped to present the life of Christ to all religions, and not just to Christians. And, although chock-full of star names, the production was not simply a vehicle for celebrities, with the glitzy sensationalism of early Hollywood versions steadfastly avoided.

The story (in two two-hour episodes) follows Christ from his boyhood (with plenty of footage devoted to his time with Joseph in the carpentry shop), through the inspirational, public part of his life (with the gathering of the disciples and the delivering of the sermons and parables) and on to the crucifixion and resurrection. In line with the Gospels, the miracles are featured, but special effects are minimal and it is the words, not the spectacular deeds, of Jesus which become the focus of his greatness.

In conjunction with Italy's RAI network, the film was shot on location in Tunisia and Italy at great expense over three years, and the attention to detail in costumes and backdrops was much applauded. The idea for the epic allegedly came from Pope Paul, who had mentioned it to Lew Grade at an audience some years earlier.

Jetsons, The ★★

US (Hanna-Barbera/Screen Gems) Cartoon. ITV 1963–4
(US: ABC 1962–3)
DVD: Warner Home Video (Region 1 only)

Voices:

George Jetson	**George O'Hanlon**
Jane Jetson	**Penny Singleton**
Judy Jetson	**Janet Waldo**
Elroy Jetson	**Daws Butler**
Astro	**Don Messick**
Cosmo G. Spacely	**Mel Blanc**
Rosie	**Jean Vander Pyl**

Executive Producers **William Hanna, Joseph Barbera**

THE FLINTSTONES ***inverted: an animation taking 20th-century lifestyles and applying them to the future.***

The Jetsons live in the 21st century, in the push-button world of Orbit City. Head of the household is 35-year-old George Jetson, who works at Spacely Space Sprockets, owned by Cosmo Spacely, where the three-hour day is still far too long. With his shopping-mad wife, Jane, and two children, George lives in the Skypad Apartments, which can be conveniently raised above the clouds to avoid bad weather. George also owns a nuclear-powered space car, while Jane has the assistance of a sarcastic robot maid named Rosie to help with the housework. The Jetsons' two children are 15-year-old Judy, a teenybopper, and nine-year-old Elroy, an electronics whizzkid who travels to school (the Little Dipper School) down a pneumatic tube. The family's Scooby-Doo-like dog is called Astro.

Whereas the Flintstones enjoy 20th-century comforts *à la* Stone Age, the Jetsons have high-tech benefits which were only imaginable when the series was created in the 1960s. Some, such as the video phone, are already now in use, but devices like the 'Foodarackacycle', which provides a selection of meals at the touch of a button, are still a little ahead of us.

The Jetsons' voices sound familiar: Penny Singleton played Blondie in the 1940s films, Daws Butler was the voice behind YOGI BEAR, and Don Messick went on to further canine success when voicing SCOOBY-DOO. Jean Vander Pyl was Wilma Flintstone. New episodes were produced in 1985, and a full-length cinema version was released a few years later.

Jeux Sans Frontières

See *It's a Knockout*.

Jewel, Jimmy

(James Marsh; 1909–95)

Sheffield-born music hall comedian who successfully took his double act with cousin Ben Warriss into radio and then on to the small screen in the early 1950s. Variety series like *Re-turn It Up* and *The Jewel and Warriss Show*, the sitcoms *Double Cross* and *It's a Living*, and appearances on SUNDAY NIGHT AT THE LONDON PALLADIUM made the duo popular and wealthy, keeping them at the forefront of TV comedy until the 1960s, when their act began to seem rather dated. Jewel left showbusiness but was tempted back by Frank Muir with a part in a BBC comedy in 1967. This encouraged him to look away from gags and sketches and more seriously at acting roles, and he secured the part of pickle factory owner Eli Pledge in the popular sitcom NEAREST AND DEAREST in 1968. He followed up with guest spots in series like THE AVENGERS and two further sitcoms, *Thicker Than Water* (widower father Jim Eccles) and SPRING AND AUTUMN (pensioner Tommy Butler). Among his later credits were WORZEL GUMMIDGE, ONE FOOT IN THE GRAVE, *Look at It This Way*, CASUALTY and the 1981 13-part drama *Funny Man*, which was based around the life of Jimmy's comedian father (also known as Jimmy Jewel) in the 1920s.

Jewel in the Crown, The ✱✱✱✱

UK (Granada) Drama. ITV 1984
DVD: Granada Ventures

Ronald Merrick	**Tim Pigott-Smith**
Hari Kumar	**Art Malik**
Daphne Manners	**Susan Wooldridge**
Sgt Guy Perron	**Charles Dance**
Dr Anna Klaus	**Renee Goddard**
Lady Lili Chatterjee	**Zohra Segal**
Pandit Baba	**Marne Maitland**
Barbie Batchelor	**Peggy Ashcroft**
Sarah Layton	**Geraldine James**
Susan Layton/Bingham/Merrick	**Wendy Morgan**
Capt. Teddie Bingham	**Nicholas Farrell**
Mildred Layton	**Judy Parfitt**
Lady Ethel Manners	**Rachel Kempson**
Mabel Layton	**Fabia Drake**
Fenny Grace	**Rosemary Leach**
Major/Col. Arthur Grace	**James Bree**
Count Dimitri Bronowsky	**Eric Porter**
Cpl 'Sophie' Dixon	**Warren Clarke**
Capt. Nigel Rowan	**Nicholas Le Prevost**
Major Gen. Rankin	**Bernard Horsfall**

Writer **Ken Taylor**
Producer **Christopher Morahan**

● ***Race and class conflict in wartime India.***

Based on *The Raj Quartet*, four books by Paul Scott, *The Jewel in the Crown* (the title of the first book – the 'jewel' allegorically standing for India) traces growing unrest in the Indian subcontinent during World War II, by following the lives of certain Britons and locals. The story begins in Mayapore in 1942 and continues in various Indian locations, including Mirat, Pankot and Calcutta. At the forefront is sadistic Ronald Merrick, a devious, bigoted police officer (later army officer) who frames Hari Kumar, an English-raised Indian reporter for the *Mayapore Gazette*, for the rape of Daphne Manners, an ungainly orphan-girl hospital worker who has shunned Merrick's advances. Although the rape outrage happens early on in the story, and Hari and Daphne are soon written out, the incident – and its consequences – come to symbolize the cauldron of race hatred and distrust which was boiling up in India at that time. The plot then switches to the Layton family (particularly level-headed Sarah Layton), ageing missionary Barbie Batchelor and other associates, and the series rolls steadily, dramatically and colourfully on to 1947 and the eve of Indian independence, all the while introducing new facets of the cultural problem, particularly growing Muslim/Hindu conflicts.

Drawing obvious comparisons with the contemporary feature film *A Passage to India* (which also starred Art Malik and Peggy Ashcroft), *The Jewel in the Crown* was made in both India and the UK, at great expense, but not without a catalogue of production problems, from freak weather conditions in India to a fire at the TV studio in Manchester. Its TV inspiration had been a 1982 Granada play, *Staying On*, featuring Trevor Howard and Celia Johnson. Newsreel footage was used to help establish the context for the complicated storyline.

Jilly Cooper's Riders ✱✱

UK (Anglia) Drama. ITV 1993
DVD: Cinema Club

Rupert Campbell-Black	**Marcus Gilbert**
Jake Lovell	**Michael Praed**
Helen Macaulay/Campbell-Black	**Arabella Tjye**
Tory Lovell	**Caroline Harker**
Billy Lloyd-Foxe	**Anthony Calf**
Lavinia Greenslade	**Belinda Mayne**
Granny Maxwell	**Brenda Bruce**
Fenella 'Fen' Maxwell	**Sienna Guillory**
Malise Gordon	**John Standing**
'Humpty' Hamilton	**Timothy Morand**
Molly Carter	**Stephanie Beacham**
Col. Carter	**Anthony Valentine**
Nigel	**Andrew Hall**
Laura Duparru	**Cecile Paoli**
Janey Henderson	**Serena Gordon**
Dudley Drabble	**Ian Hogg**

Writers **Terence Brady, Charlotte Bingham**
Producer **Roger Gregory**

● ***Personal and sporting rivalries among the upper classes.***

Jake Lovell still has nightmares about his days at prep school. Because he is of Romany origin and his mother was the school cook, he was bullied, and once badly injured, by a group of boys led by the sadistic Rupert Campbell-Black. Now, many years on, as Jake makes his way up the hierarchy of showjumping, their paths cross yet again. Campbell-Black is the golden boy of the sport but now his position is jeopardized by his old adversary and he doesn't like it one bit, especially as the Olympic Games are on the horizon. An intense rivalry ensues, complicated by Rupert's many affairs – despite his marriage to American animal-rights activist Helen Macaulay – and family strains on all sides. Billy Lloyd-Foxe is Campbell-Black's best buddy and Malise Gordon is the UK showjumping team manager. Fen is the young sister of Jake's wife, Tory, and Col. and Molly Carter are her wealthy but indignant parents, who see the penniless Jake's career as a good investment. Sports writer Janey Henderson is the girl who turns the heads of both Billy and Rupert. With plenty of 'riding' scenes (in every sense), this two-part potboiler – loosely based on Jilly Cooper's blockbuster novel and directed by Gabrielle Beaumont – is as much a tale of bedroom gymnastics as it is of equestrianism.

Jim Henson's Greek Myths

See *Storyteller, The*.

Jim'll Fix It ✱✱✱

UK (BBC) Children's Entertainment. BBC 1 1975–94

Presenter **Jimmy Savile**

Producer **Roger Ordish**

● ***Long-running children's programme making viewers' dreams come true.***

A favourite with adults as well as youngsters, *Jim'll Fix It* was a popular segment of Saturday evening viewing for 19 years. Its premiss was simple: children (and some adults) wrote in with a special wish and the BBC, fronted by Jimmy Savile from a gadget-loaded armchair, fulfilled the most enterprising requests. The dreams-made-reality varied from meeting favourite pop stars to piloting Concorde and interviewing the Prime Minister. The Osmonds and Pan's People were among the first guests. Featured viewers were presented with a 'Jim Fixed It for Me' medallion to commemorate the occasion.

Jimmy's ✶✶

UK (Yorkshire) Documentary. ITV 1987–96

Executive Producer **Chris Bryer**
Producers **Richard Handford, Irene Cockroft**

The stresses, strains, tears and smiles at a major general hospital.

This fly-on-the-wall documentary series lasted longer than most critics would have dared to suggest. Centring on events at St James's Hospital in Leeds (the largest general hospital in Europe), it witnessed highs and lows in the lives of its numerous patients, doctors and nurses. With its delicate observation of the skill and care of staff, and the heartaches and joys of inmates, *Jimmy's*, originally only a daytime programme, so intrigued viewers that it soon earned itself an evening slot. Over the years, the production crew became almost part of the hospital team. No patient was obliged to appear and, even if giving initial consent, all had the right to pull out halfway through filming or to ask for edits to be made. Later series were screened by Sky One. In 2004, ITV 1 ran a Sunday morning docu-soap series entitled *St Jimmy's*, focusing on the work of the chaplaincy services at the hospital.

Jim's Inn

See *admags*.

Joanie Loves Chachi ✶

US (Miller-Milkis-Boyett/Henderson/Paramount) Situation Comedy. ITV 1983–6 (US: ABC 1982–3)

Joanie Cunningham	**Erin Moran**
Charles 'Chachi' Arcola	**Scott Baio**
Alfred Delvecchio	**Al Molinaro**
Louisa Delvecchio	**Ellen Travolta**
Uncle Rico	**Art Metrano**
Bingo	**Robert Peirce**
Mario	**Derrel Maury**
Annette	**Winifred Freedman**

Executive Producers **Garry Marshall, Edward K. Milkis, Thomas L. Miller, Robert L Boyett, Lowell Ganz, Ronnie Hallin**

Teenage sweethearts sing in a band in early 1960s Chicago.

Richie's little sister has grown up. In this HAPPY DAYS spin-off Joanie 'Shortcake' Cunningham is deemed to be adult enough to leave home and she heads for Chicago. There, with boyfriend Chachi, she performs in a band that includes drummer Bingo, plus Chachi's cousins, Mario and Annette. Keeping everything above board, they live with Chachi's mom, Louisa, who has just married Al Delvecchio (erstwhile owner of Arnold's diner) and together they run a family restaurant. Also seen is Louisa's Uncle Rico, the band's untrustworthy manager. Sadly, despite a promising start in the US ratings, the series – which featured plenty of music – fell away and the main characters returned to the comforts of Milwaukee. Stars Erin Moran and Scott Baio also sang the theme song, 'You Look at Me.'

Joe ✶✶

UK (Q3) Animation. BBC 1 1966; 1971

Narrators **Lee Montague, Colin Jeavons**

Writer **Alison Prince**

A little boy grows up in a transport café.

A new Monday show for WATCH WITH MOTHER in 1966, *Joe* relates the adventures of a big-eyed boy with rosy cheeks and a pudding-basin haircut. Joe, who always wears practical dungarees, lives with his mum and dad at a transport café – a good source of adventures for an inquisitive little lad like Joe. In the second series, five years later (narrated now by Colin Jeavons), Joe acquires a new baby sister, Rosie. Each episode is titled 'Joe and the . . .' (fill in the gap with nouns as disparate as 'Fog', 'Goulash' and 'Dust-Cart'). The pictures were drawn by Joan Hickson, Diana Potter directed and Laurie Steele added the soundtrack.

Joe Forrester

See *Police Story*.

Joe 90 ✶✶

UK (Century 21/ITC) Children's Science Fiction. ITV 1968–9
DVD: Carlton

Voices:

Joe McClaine/Joe 90	**Len Jones**
Prof. Ian McClaine	**Rupert Davies**
Commander Shane Weston	**David Healy**
Sam Loover	**Keith Alexander**
Mrs Ada Harris	**Sylvia Anderson**

Creators **Gerry Anderson, Sylvia Anderson**
Executive Producer **Reg Hill**
Producer **David Lane**

The leading agent for a global protectorate is a nine-year-old boy.

Brilliant scientist Professor Ian 'Mac' McClaine has developed a machine which allows the transfer of people's brain-patterns. Known as BIG RAT – Brain Impulse Galvanoscope, Record And Transfer – the equipment is tested and then regularly used on Mac's nine-year-old adopted son, Joe, who becomes Most Special Agent for World Intelligence Network (WIN), an agency dedicated to keeping peace around the globe. Furnished with the expert knowledge of an airline pilot, an astronaut, an explosives specialist or even a brain surgeon, Joe McClaine adopts the guise of Joe 90, a special operative whose schoolboy looks enable him to venture where other agents fear to tread. To activate the new brain-patterns and pick up the specialist skills or knowledge he needs, Joe simply dons a pair of scientific glasses, making him look more like the class swot than a secret agent. To help him on his assignments, he is equipped with a special 'school bag', containing a transmitter, a gun and, of course, his magic glasses. Contacts at WIN are its deputy head, Commander Weston, and Weston's assistant, Sam Loover. Mrs Harris is the McClaines' housekeeper. The programme's opening titles show BIG RAT at work, with Joe's chair lifted into a metal cage which revolves at high speed. Around him, sophisticated computers whiz and sparkle as they transfer brain-patterns into the boy's mind.

Joe 90 was Gerry Anderson's ninth puppet series, but was considerably less successful than the three which immediately preceded it, STINGRAY, THUNDERBIRDS and CAPTAIN SCARLET AND THE MYSTERONS. Among the actors lending their vocal cords were MAIGRET's Rupert Davies and Keith Alexander, formerly the voice of the Italian mouse puppet Topo Gigio.

John Craven's Newsround

See *Newsround*.

John Silver's Return to Treasure Island ✱✱

UK (Primetime/HTV) Adventure. ITV 1986

Long John Silver	**Brian Blessed**
Jim Hawkins	**Christopher Guard**
Ben Gunn	**Ken Colley**
Van Der Brecken	**Reiner Schöne**
Squire Trelawney	**Bruce Purchase**
Dr Livesey	**Peter Copley**
Revd Morgan	**Artro Morris**
Isabella	**Deborah Poplett**
Abed	**Peter Lloyd**
Hallows	**Donald Pickering**
Gaynes	**Dicken Ashworth**
Conchita	**Aixa Moreno**

Writer **John Goldsmith**
Executive Producer **Patrick Dromgoole**
Producer **Alan Clayton**

● ***Television sequel to R. L. Stevenson's classic tale.***

Having graduated from Oxford, ten years after the original *Treasure Island* adventure, Jim Hawkins returns briefly to his mother's inn, The Admiral Benbow, before taking up a job as plantation agent in Jamaica for Squire Trelawney. He stumbles across his old mate Long John Silver, who has broken into the pub to recover the celebrated treasure map, believing there is more booty to be unearthed with its help. The two soon find themselves once again on the high seas, setting sail for Treasure Island and more swashbuckling escapades. The series, with music by Terry Oldfield and Tom McGuinness, was mostly filmed in Jamaica.

Johnny Jarvis ✱✱

UK (BBC) Drama. BBC 1 1983

Johnny Jarvis	**Mark Farmer**
Alan Lipton	**Ian Sears**
Stella	**Johanna Hargreaves**
Mr Jarvis	**John Bardon**
Mrs Jarvis	**Catherine Harding**
Mrs Lipton	**Diana Davies**
Paul Turner	**Alrick Riley**
Manning	**Jamie Foreman**
Jake	**Maurice Colbourne**
Colonel	**Nick Stringer**
Kenny	**Jim Findley**
Pauline	**Sarah London**
Guy	**Gary Shail**

Writer **Nigel Williams**
Producer **Guy Slater**

● ***Two unlikely classmates continue their turbulent friendship after leaving school.***

Seen through the eyes of one Alan Lipton, this serial relates the early adult lives of himself and his sparky school friend Johnny Jarvis. Jarvis and Lipton are pupils at a Hackney comprehensive in the school year 1977–8. Jarvis is the classroom buffoon, with a smart mouth, but he does possess a talent for welding – at least something to build on as he is about to enter the big wide world. The bespectacled Lipton, however, is markedly without skills. He is an introvert and a dreamer, his one goal in life being to meet the father he has never known. On leaving school, the boys run into a girl called Stella, who shares a squat with Alan, but then decides she prefers Johnny and eventually moves in with Johnny and his mother. Alan drifts on to a hostel, gets drawn into crime and forms a rock band with a new pal, Guy. Eventually, the friends are reunited when Johnny and Stella join Alan in a new flat he has found, but relationships remain tense. The series ends in the then present day of 1983, against a grim backdrop of recession and widespread unemployment, the lads having experienced six years (one per episode) of an up-and-down friendship.

Johns, Stratford

(Alan Stratford Johns; 1925–2002)

South African actor, best remembered in the guise of Charlie Barlow of Z CARS, SOFTLY, SOFTLY and BARLOW AT LARGE fame, following early guest appearances in series like THE AVENGERS. Later he was cast as Piso, the head of the guards, in I, CLAUDIUS, union-boss-turned-peer Lord Mountainash in the sitcom *Union Castle*, the evil killer in Channel 4's *Brond*, Mr A. B. Noon BA in *The Life and Times of Henry Pratt*, Abbé Pirard in SCARLET AND BLACK and Mr Stockton in NEVERWHERE, among many other roles in series like MINDER, DOCTOR WHO and MURDER MOST HORRID. He also played Barlow in JACK THE RIPPER, a 1973 investigation into the mysterious case of the Victorian murderer, which led to a series, SECOND VERDICT, in 1976, with Barlow and his colleague John Watt (Frank Windsor) taking a look at other unsolved crimes. His last TV appearance was as a guest in HEARTBEAT.

Johnson, Don

(1949–)

Despite appearing in films as early as 1970, Don Johnson failed to make TV inroads (apart from failed pilots, some guest appearances and one role in a version of *From Here to Eternity*) until 1984, when he was cast as Detective James 'Sonny' Crockett in the all-action cop series MIAMI VICE. Running for five years, it made Johnson one of the biggest names of the 1980s, his ultra-casual dress, stubbled chin and permanent scowl inspiring a generation of look-alikes. In the 1990s he returned to the limelight as star (and executive producer) of the cop show *Nash Bridges*, returning to prime time yet again in 2005 as lawyer Grant Cooper in *Just Legal*. He has twice married (and divorced) actress Melanie Griffith.

Johnston, Sue
(1943–)

Warrington-born actress who gained national prominence through her portrayal of BROOKSIDE matriarch Sheila Grant. Previously, Johnston had played Mrs Chadwick in CORONATION STREET among other smaller TV roles. Since leaving Brookside Close, she has been cast as Barbara Grade in *Goodbye Cruel World*, was the mother in a celebratory remake of THE GROVE FAMILY, starred as Miriam Johnson in *Screenplay's Bitter Harvest*, took the part of Grace Robbins in the limousine drama *Full Stretch*, and featured as rich but frustrated housewife Terese Craven in LUV. Starring roles have kept coming and she has headlined in MEDICS (Ruth Parry), *Into the Fire* (Lyn Candy), CRIME TRAVELLER (Grisham), DUCK PATROL (Val), *The Jump* (Maeve Brunos), THE ROYLE FAMILY (Barbara Royle), SEX, CHIPS AND ROCK 'N' ROLL (Irma Brookes), WAKING THE DEAD (DI Grace Foley), *Face* (Alice), *My Uncle Silas* (Mrs Betts), *Happy Together* (Val) and *Score* (Maggie), as well as narrating the documentary series *Children's Hospital* and appearing in series like INSPECTOR MORSE, A TOUCH OF FROST and CUTTING IT (Caroline Ferraday).

Joint Account ✱✱

UK (BBC) Situation Comedy. BBC 1 1989–90

Belinda Braithwaite	**Hannah Gordon**
David Braithwaite	**Peter Egan**
Ned Race	**John Bird**
Louise	**Lill Roughley**
Jessica	**Ruth Mitchell**
Charles Ruby	**Richard Aylen**

Writer **Don Webb**
Producer **Mike Stephens**

A husband and wife swap traditional roles: she works; he stays at home.

As the labour market changes, so does family life, as this role-reversal comedy proves. Belinda Braithwaite is the manager of a bank and, quietly dominating their relationship, wears the trousers around the house she shares with her guileless house-husband David. Two series were built around the idea that the woman has the career while hubby cooks and cleans.

Joking Apart ✱✱✱

UK (Pola Jones/Peter Jones/BBC) Situation Comedy. BBC 2 1993; 1995

Mark Taylor	**Robert Bathurst**
Becky Johnson/Taylor	**Fiona Gillies**
Tracy Glazebrook	**Tracie Bennett**
Robert Glazebrook	**Paul Raffield**
Trevor	**Paul-Mark Elliott**

Writer **Steven Moffat**
Producer **Andre Ptaszynski**

A stand-up comic recalls his failed marriage.

'My wife left me,' drily declares comedian and TV scriptwriter Mark Taylor. This preludes a series of flashbacks which recall his fleeting marriage to Becky Johnson. After they had met at a funeral (which Mark gatecrashed by accident), their romance developed apace, but then fell apart just as quickly, as Mark's stand-up humour took over their relationship. When he cracked one joke too many, Becky left him, tired of being his 'lawfully wedded straight man'. Mark's efforts to win her back from boring estate agent Trevor form the basis of the rest of the first series and all the second (shown in 1995). Also involved in this farcical comedy of errors are Robert and Tracy, their increasingly bizarre and totally dim friends. Chris Rea's 'Fool If You Think It's Over' (sung by Kenny Craddock) provided the theme music. *Joking Apart* was developed from a one-off *Comic Aside*, screened in 1991.

Joly, Dom
(1968–)

Lebanon-born comedian and TV prankster, responsible for TRIGGER HAPPY TV, *Being Dom Joly*, *This is Dom Joly* and *World Shut Your Mouth*, also writing, producing and directing.

Jonathan Creek ✱✱✱

UK (BBC) Comedy Drama. BBC 1 1997–9; 2001; 2003–4
DVD: BBC

Jonathan Creek	**Alan Davies**
Madelaine 'Maddy' Magellan	**Caroline Quentin**
Adam Klaus	**Anthony Head**
	Stuart Milligan
Carla Borrego	**Julia Sawalha**
Brendan Baxten	**Adrian Edmondson**

Creator/Writer **David Renwick**
Producers **Susan Belbin, Verity Lambert**

Lateral-thinking detective work from a stage magician's assistant.

Nerdy Jonathan Creek lives in an East Anglian windmill, has wild, curly hair, wears a duffel coat and works for smarmy top illusionist Adam Klaus. In fact, he is the brains behind Klaus's act, devising all the tricks and building the elaborate equipment needed to perform the 'magic'. It turns out that the sort of mind which excels at this work is also pretty good at solving baffling crimes – body in a sealed room, etc. – a fact that is immediately grasped by devious journalist Maddy Magellan. Using Creek to supply her with great copy, Maddy manipulates him into obscure investigations where logic seems to go out of the window and only the impossible seems possible. Thus begins not only their sparky working relationship but also a 'will they, won't they' romantic scenario, all laced together with a wry humour that viewers have come to expect from writer David Renwick. Renwick claims to have plucked the name of his hero from a place he visited in Kentucky. There was no series in 2000 or 2002 but Creek did feature in a two-hour special in 2001. With Maddy apparently away on a book tour, this time he is assisted by theatrical agent (later TV presenter) Carla Borrego, who returns as Creek's contentious sidekick in later episodes. The theme tune is an extract from Saint-Saëns's *Danse Macabre*.

Jones, Carolyn
(1929–83)

American actress in films from the late 1940s. On television, after some early appearances in shows like DRAGNET, Jones was cast as Morticia Addams, the sultry wife in THE ADDAMS FAMILY, in 1964. A few years later, she was also seen in BATMAN, playing Marsha, the Queen of Diamonds. Later in her career,

Jones focused on daytime soaps, TV movies and mini-series, including ROOTS. At one time, she was the wife of TV executive Aaron Spelling.

Jones, Chuck

(Charles M. Jones; 1912–2002)

American animation producer/director, for 24 years with Warner Brothers, where he created the characters of Roadrunner and Pepe Le Pew among others, and contributed to Daffy Duck, Sylvester and Tweety Pie, Porky Pig and Bugs Bunny adventures. He also worked on later TOM AND JERRY cartoons and became head of children's programmes at the USA's ABC network.

Jones, Davy

(David Jones; 1945–)

Diminutive Manchester-born actor, a would-be jockey but tempted on to the stage instead. One of his first TV breaks came with CORONATION STREET, in which he played Ena Sharples's grandson, Colin Lomax, in 1961. Moving to America, he starred on Broadway as the Artful Dodger in *Oliver* and took a guest part in BEN CASEY. However, global fame awaited. In 1966 he successfully auditioned for a role in a new zany comedy about a pop group, becoming the lead singer of THE MONKEES and embarking on a few years of frenzied touring and filming. Since those days, Jones has resurfaced only sporadically, appearing in TV movies and series such as LOVE, AMERICAN STYLE, THE BRADY BUNCH, TRAINER and MY TWO DADS, as well as occasionally piecing together The Monkees for nostalgia tours. He is the father of actress Sarah Jones.

Jones, Elwyn

(1923–82)

British screenwriter, script editor and producer, with contributions to *Jacks and Knaves*, Z CARS, SOFTLY, SOFTLY, DOCTOR WHO, GAZETTE, DOOMWATCH and JACK THE RIPPER among other scripting credits. He also produced Alun Owen's 1963 sitcom *Corrigan Blake* and created the police series PARKIN'S PATCH.

Jones, Freddie

(1927–)

Versatile British actor whose television work has varied between the classics, general drama, sitcom and kids' programmes. These have included *Treasure Island*, *Uncle Vanya*, VANITY FAIR (Sir Pitt Crawley), THE CAESARS (Claudius), MYSTERY AND IMAGINATION (Sweeney Todd), THE DISTRICT NURSE (Dr Emlyn Isaacs), THE AVENGERS, MENACE, THE RETURN OF SHERLOCK HOLMES, INSPECTOR MORSE, THE GHOSTS OF MOTLEY HALL (Sir George Uproar), PENNIES FROM HEAVEN, CHILDREN OF THE STONES (Dai), IN LOVING MEMORY (pilot episode), *The Strange Affair of Adelaide Harris* (Selwyn Raven), THE SECRET DIARY OF ADRIAN MOLE, *Sob Sisters* (Leo), *Screen One's Adam Bede* (Squire), *The True Adventures of Christopher Columbus* (Herald), MR WROE'S VIRGINS (Tobias), NEVERWHERE (The Earl of Earl's Court), COLD COMFORT FARM (Adam Lambsbreath), DROVERS' GOLD (Moc), *The Young Indiana Jones Chronicles*, MIDSOMER MURDERS, HEARTBEAT, THE ROYAL, CASANOVA (Bragadin) and EMMERDALE (Sandy Thomas). Actor Toby Jones is his son.

Jones, Gemma

(1942–)

As the gruff cook and proprietress of The Bentinck Hotel, Louisa Trotter, British actress Gemma Jones found instant fame in THE DUCHESS OF DUKE STREET IN 1976. Since that time she has made guest appearances in series like INSPECTOR MORSE, AN UNSUITABLE JOB FOR A WOMAN, MIDSOMER MURDERS, AGATHA CHRISTIE'S POIROT and JUDGE JOHN DEED, and appeared as Miss Menzies in THE BORROWERS, Mrs Fairfax in JANE EYRE, Mrs Biddle in THE PHOENIX AND THE CARPET, Beatrice Kyle in *An Evil Streak*, Elizabeth Harrison in LONGITUDE, Mrs Bubby in *Bootleg*, Dr Jean Mullins in TRIAL AND RETRIBUTION, and Kay in *All about George*. Previously, she had played Fleda Vetch in the Henry James drama *The Spoils of Poynton*, and PRINCESS VICTORIA in Fall of Eagles. Gemma's father is actor Griffith Jones and her brother is actor Nicholas Jones.

Jones, Griff Rhys

(1953–)

Cardiff-born comedian and actor, partner of Mel Smith. A Cambridge Footlights performer (alongside the likes of Rory McGrath and Clive Anderson), Jones was working as a radio producer before he joined Smith, Pamela Stephenson and Rowan Atkinson in NOT THE NINE O'CLOCK NEWS in 1980, replacing Chris Langham, who had left the series after one run. In 1984, Griff and Mel branched out into ALAS SMITH AND JONES, their own sketch show, which later became simply *Smith and Jones*. They also presented *The World According to Smith and Jones* (voicing over old film clips) for ITV and a series of semi-dramas entitled *Smith and Jones in Small Doses* for BBC 2. Jones also played Bamber Gascoigne in one memorable episode of THE YOUNG ONES, and, while always a stalwart of Comic Relief, he has also turned his hand to straight drama, playing Cornelius Carrington in PORTERHOUSE BLUE, Ian Deasey in DEMOB and Max Vivaldi in MINE ALL MINE. Other credits are as host of the literary review *Bookworm*, the annual *Nation's Favourite Poem* contest and RESTORATION, and as narrator of the children's series *Tales from the Poop Deck*. Jones also presented and co-wrote *The Secret Life of Arthur Ransome* and joined Rory McGrath and Dara O'Briain to recreate Jerome K. Jerome's tale of *Three Men in a Boat*. He has appeared in TV pantomimes and also made a guest appearances in *Casualty*, AGATHA CHRISTIE'S MARPLE and *Monkey Trousers*. With Smith, Jones founded Talkback, the production company responsible for some of their series, plus other comedy hits, which has since been sold.

Jones, Ken

(1930–)

Liverpudlian comic actor and writer, often cast in shifty working-class roles. He played prison officer Leslie Mills in *Her Majesty's Pleasure*, Detective Sgt Arnold Nixon in *The Nesbitts are Coming*, 'Orrible Ives in PORRIDGE, Archangel Derek in *Dead Ernest*, boxing trainer Dave Locket in SECONDS OUT, park-keeper Tom in *Valentine Park*, Whistle Willy in the kids' comedy BEHIND THE BIKE SHEDS, and, more memorably, Rex in THE SQUIRRELS, Billy Clarkson in *The Wackers* and Clifford Basket in LAST OF THE BASKETS. Jones has also been seen in THE LIVER BIRDS, *Struggle*, THE BOUNDER, BOON, WATCHING, HUNTER'S WALK and MURPHY'S LAW, among numerous series.

Jones, Peter

(1920–2000)

Shropshire-born comedy actor and writer, on television from the 1950s. Peter Jones is probably best remembered as Mr Fenner in THE RAG TRADE, although he also starred as Gerald Garvey in BEGGAR MY NEIGHBOUR, Roland Digby in MR DIGBY, DARLING, Clive Beauchamp in the airline sitcom *From a Bird's Eye View*, Sidney in the busking comedy *Kindly Leave the Kerb*, Eddie, the petty crook, in *Mr Big* (also as co-writer), Gerald, the frustrated dad, in the shortlived *I Thought You'd Gone* (again with writing credits), the mad Prime Minister, Kevin Pork, in WHOOPS APOCALYPSE and the Voice of The Book in THE HITCH-HIKER'S GUIDE TO THE GALAXY. Additionally, Jones appeared in *Mild and Bitter*, *Q6* and *One-Upmanship* and had a wealth of guest appearances behind him, in series as diverse as STRANGE REPORT, C.A.T.S. EYES, THE GOODIES, RUMPOLE OF THE BAILEY, HOLBY CITY and MIDSOMER MURDERS.

Jones, Terry

(1942–)

Welsh comedian, actor and writer, most famously a member of the MONTY PYTHON team. Jones began his career writing in partnership with Michael Palin, contributing to THE FROST REPORT, *A Series of Bird's*, *The Late Show*, *Broaden Your Mind*, *Horne A'Plenty* and MARTY. The two also wrote for and appeared in *Twice a Fortnight*, DO NOT ADJUST YOUR SET and THE COMPLETE AND UTTER HISTORY OF BRITAIN. With Palin, after the success of *Monty Python*, Jones also wrote RIPPING YARNS and for THE TWO RONNIES. More recently, he has been seen in *The Young Indiana Jones Chronicles* and writing/presenting *The Crusades*, *Ancient Inventions*, *Terry Jones's Medieval Lives* and *The Story of 1*. He also created, and provided voices for, *Blazing Dragons*, an animation based on King Arthur's quest for the Holy Grail.

Jonny Briggs ✶✶

UK (BBC) Children's Drama. BBC 1 1986

Jonny Briggs	**Richard Holian**
Mam Briggs	**Jane Lowe**
Dad Briggs	**Leslie Schofield**
Rita Briggs	**Sue Devaney**
Albert Briggs	**Tommy Robinson**
Humphrey Briggs	**Jeremy Austin**
Mavis	**Debbie Norris**
Miss Broom	**Karen Meagher**
Pam	**Georgina Lane**
Jinny	**Adèle Parry**
Mr Badger	**John Forbes-Robertson**

Writer **Valerie Georgeson**
Producer **Angela Beeching**

● ***Life is never simple for a young Yorkshire lad and his family.***

Aimed at the younger end of the junior audience, Joan Eadington's stories of little Jonny Briggs established themselves on TV in numerous episodes of JACKANORY (read by Bernard Holley) before being spun off into a light drama series. Jonny and his dog Razzle have to make sense of a complicated home life near Leeds, in which strange things often happen, his big brother Albert keeps inventing things and there's always a queue for the bathroom in the morning. Humphrey is Jonny's other brother, Rita is his griping elder sister and Mavis is Rita's best friend. Miss Broom is Jonny's teacher.

Jonny Quest ✶✶

US (Hanna-Barbera) Cartoon. BBC 1 1965 (US: ABC 1964–5)
DVD: Warner Home Video (Region 1 only)

Voices:

Jonny Quest	**Tim Matthieson**
Dr Benton Quest	**John Stephenson**
	Don Messick
Roger 'Race' Bannon	**Mike Road**
Hadji	**Danny Bravo**
Bandit	**Don Messick**

Creator/Writer **Doug Wildey**
Executive Producers **William Hanna, Joseph Barbera**

● ***Four scientific adventurers travel the world explaining natural phenomena.***

Jonny Quest is the bright 11-year-old son of bearded scientist Dr Benton Quest, leader of a small team of intelligence specialists. With Jonny, an Indian chum named Hadji, their pilot-cum-bodyguard Race Bannon, and miniature bulldog Bandit, Dr Quest whizzes around the globe in a supersonic plane, following up reports of strange happenings and unearthing rare treasures in the style of Indiana Jones. Whether it is the sighting of an alien creature or another bizarre event, Quest and his crew soon get to the bottom of it, more often than not battling against the clock in the process. They usually conclude their adventures by explaining the scientific reasons for the phenomena encountered.

This sensibly constructed, well-liked, educational cartoon was aired during evening prime time in the USA, just like its Hanna-Barbera predecessors, THE FLINTSTONES, THE JETSONS and TOP CAT.

Jonsson, Ulrika

(1967–)

Swedish TV personality, branching out from a position as secretary at TV-am to become one of the station's weather presenters. She has since moved into light entertainment, appearing in a quiz called *Who's Bluffing Who?* and hosting GLADIATORS, the 1998 EUROVISION SONG CONTEST, THE NATIONAL LOTTERY, *Dreamworld* and the game/lifestyle shows *Mother Knows Best*, *Dog Eat Dog*, *The Property Shop: Des Res*, *How Do I Look?* and *Mr Wright*, as well as acting as a team captain in the spoof quiz SHOOTING STARS. Her *Shooting Stars* colleagues, Vic Reeves and Bob Mortimer, also wrote her a one-off sketch show called *It's Ulrika!* Jonsson has also ventured into politics, interviewing John Major prior to the 1997 election and fronting *Ulrika in Euroland*.

Joseph, Lesley

(1946–)

British actress, most familiar as the man-hungry Dorien Green in BIRDS OF A FEATHER, but with other credits including *Sadie, It's Cold Outside*, *Les Girls*, AND MOTHER MAKES FIVE, MINDER, HORIZON, *Roots* (Melanie Goldblatt in the ITV comedy, not the US mini-series), the wrestling comedy *Rumble* (Ma Pecs), and the schools drama *Spywatch* (Miss Millington). More recently, she has played Rachel Culgrin in *Night and Day*.

Josie and the Pussycats/Josie and the Pussycats in Outer Space ✶

US (Hanna-Barbera) Cartoon. BBC 1972–3/1973–4 (US: CBS 1970–2/1972–4)

Voices:

Josie .... **Janet Waldo**
Cathy Douglas (*singing*)
Melody .... **Jackie Joseph**
Cherie Moore (*singing*)
Valerie .... **Barbara Pariot**
Patricia Holloway (*singing*)
Alan .... **Jerry Dexter**
Alexander Cabot III .... **Casey Kasem**
Alexandra Cabot .... **Sherry Alberoni**
Sebastian .... **Don Messick**
Bleep .... **Don Messick**

Executive Producers **William Hanna, Joseph Barbera**

A female rock group saves the world, and then the universe.

Josie and the Pussycats are a trio of teenage rock musicians who find that adventure dogs them while they tour the world. Many's the time the girls are called upon to thwart the ambitions of evil megalomaniacs, still dressed in their stage-show kitty ears and tails. Redhead Josie is lead singer with the band and she is supported by African-American Valerie and dippy blonde Melody. Adding muscle is their roadie, Alan, but generally getting in the way is the band's hapless manager, Alexander Cabot, and his interfering sister, Alexandra (whose badger hair streak could have won her a part in THE MALLENS). She is also jealous of Alan's closeness to Josie, and Josie's success, and it is through her petty revenges that many of the adventures begin. Completing the crew is Sebastian, Alexandra's equally black and white cat. The girls' singing voices were provided by Cathy Douglas, Patricia Holloway and Cherie Moore (later famous as CHARLIE'S ANGELS' Cheryl Ladd). After two years, the concept of the series was modified and the title changed to *Josie and the Pussycats in Outer Space*. Not content with outwitting the finest villains this planet has to offer, now the starlets conquer the cosmos, having been accidentally fired off into the big blue yonder aboard a NASA rocket. Joining the team is a cute alien creature (a duck of some sort) named Bleep.

In 2001 the concept was floated off into a live-action feature film entitled *Josie and the Pussycats*, starring Rachael Leigh Cook.

Jossy's Giants ✶✶

UK (BBC) Situation Comedy. BBC 1 1986–7

Jossy Blair .... **Jim Barclay**
Albert Hanson .... **Chistopher Burgess**
Bob Nelson .... **John Judd**
Tracey Gaunt .... **Julie Foy**
Ross Nelson .... **Mark Gillard**
Ricky Sweet .... **Paul Kirkbright**
Harvey McGuinn .... **Julian Walsh**
Glenn Rix .... **Stuart McGuinness**
Ian 'Selly' Sellick .... **Ian Sheppard**
Councillor Glenda Fletcher .... **Jenny McCracken**
Dave Sharkey .... **Tony Melody**
Wayne Chapman .... **Oliver Orr**
Daz .... **Lee Quarmby**
Shaz .... **Jenny Luckraft**
Opal .... **Suzanne Hall**
Noleen .... **Jo-Anne Green**
Lisa .... **Angela Freear**
Melanie .... **Lucy Keightley**

Creator/Writer **Sid Waddell**
Producer **Paul Stone**

An ex-professional restores the fortunes of a teenage soccer team.

Glipton Grasshoppers are a team of 13-year-old footballers, although 'team' is perhaps not quite the correct word. Their success rate is pretty miserable until they are taken over by Jossy Blair, a former professional who was badly injured in his first-ever match and can never play at the top level again. The youngsters respond to the Geordie's coaching skills and 'Jossy's Giants' start to climb the ladder of junior soccer, with young Ross the star striker. By the time of the second series, the Giants have gone off the boil. Girls have entered the boys' lives and Jossy has problems getting the lads to keep their eye on the ball. Mind you, he doesn't set the best example himself, as local councillor Glenda Fletcher can vouch. With the young cast chosen for their footballing skills ahead of any professional acting status, *Jossy's Giants* (created by darts commentator Sid Waddell) ran for two series.

Journey to the Center of the Earth ✶

US (Filmation/Twentieth Century-Fox) Cartoon. BBC 1 1968–9 (US: ABC 1967–9)

Voices:

Prof. Oliver Lindenbrook .... **Ted Knight**
Cindy Lindenbrook .... **Jane Webb**
Alec McEwen .... **Pat Harrington Jr**
Lars .... **Pat Harrington Jr**
Count Saccnuson .... **Ted Knight**
Torg .... **Pat Harrington Jr**

Executive Producers **Louis Scheimer, Norman Prescott**

A party of explorers tries to reach the legendary centre of the Earth.

In an attempt to retrace the steps of explorer Arnie Saccnuson, archaeologist Professor Oliver Lindenbrook gathers together a small team of adventurers, consisting of his niece, Cindy; student Alec McEwen; a guide, Lars; and Gertrude, Cindy's pet duck. Entering a cavern to look for clues, they are trapped when an explosion blocks the entrance. They soon discover the blast to be the work of the malevolent Count Saccnuson, the last living descendant of the renowned explorer who, with Torg, his dim henchman, has his own plans for the Earth's core. For the Professor and his team there is no alternative: they just have to follow Arnie's trail (marked 'AS') and hope to find a way back to the surface. As they do so, not only are they hindered by the Count and Torg (who have also been trapped by the bungled explosion), but they also encounter a variety of prehistoric monsters, lost civilizations and assorted natural phenomena. The series was based very loosely on Jules Verne's 1865 novel and the 1959 film starring James Mason.

Journey to the Unknown ✳

UK (Hammer/Twentieth Century-Fox) Drama. ITV 1968–9

Producer **Anthony Hinds**
Executive Producers **Joan Harrison, Norman Lloyd**

● ***An anthology of supernatural suspense tales.***

Financed by Twentieth Century-Fox but produced in Britain by Hammer, this anthology of 17 stories embraces both science fiction and psychological horror with its varied tales of murder, twisted minds, sorcery, ESP, medical experimentation and the afterlife. The tone is set by sinister opening titles, which depict a spooky abandoned fairground. American stars usually take the lead (the likes of Joseph Cotten, Julie Harris, Barbara Bel Geddes, Roddy McDowall and Stefanie Powers are seen), with familiar UK faces in support. Producers Joan Harrison and Norman Lloyd both worked on ALFRED HITCHCOCK PRESENTS and the influence of the Master of Suspense is very apparent.

Joyce, Yootha

(1927–80)

British comic actress, imprinted in viewers' minds as the sex-starved Mildred Roper in MAN ABOUT THE HOUSE and GEORGE AND MILDRED. Joyce came to the role on the back of a run of guest appearances in the 1960s (in programmes like THE AVENGERS and in the comedies BROTHERS IN LAW and *Corrigan Blake*). She had also starred in the Milo O'Shea sitcom ME MAMMY, in which she played his willing secretary, Miss Argyll, and ON THE BUSES, as Jessie the clippie. She was once married to actor Glynn Edwards.

Judge Dee ✳✳

UK (Granada) Detective Drama. ITV 1969

Judge Dee	**Michael Goodliffe**
Ma Joong	**Arne Gordon**
Tao Gan	**Garfield Morgan**
Hoong	**Norman Scace**

Writer **John Wiles**
Producer **Howard Baker**

● ***A powerful judge unravels mysteries in the ancient Orient.***

A Chinese takeaway. Judge Dee was created in novels by Dutch diplomat Robert van Gulik and his tales of deduction in the Far East were adapted for television by John Wiles. Based on the life of a real magistrate, who solved crimes by acting as a mix of detective, prosecutor, judge and jury in seventh-century China, the series features the dignified Dee as he uncovers intrigue in monasteries, religious festivals and the like, assisted by his cohorts Ma Joong, Tao Gan and Hoong. The real Dee, it is said, later became a minister of state in the T'ang Empire.

Judge John Deed ✳✳

UK (BBC/One-Eyed Dog) Legal Drama. BBC 1 2001–3; 2005–

Judge John Deed	**Martin Shaw**
Jo Mills QC	**Jenny Seagrove**
Charlie Deed	**Louisa Clein**
Rita 'Coop' Cooper	**Barbara Thorn**
Stephen Ashurst	**Dave Norman**
Row Colemore	**Christopher Cazenove**
Georgina 'George' Channing QC	**Caroline Langrishe**
Lady Francesca Rochester	**Jemma Redgrave**
Sir Joseph Channing	**Donald Sinden**
Sir Ian Rochester	**Simon Chandler**
Sir Michael Nivan	**Trevor Bowen**
Brian Harrison	**Michael Eaves**
Norman Children	**Tim Munro**
Sir Monty Everard	**Simon Ward**
Laurence James	**Fraser James**
Rachel Crawcheck	**Amita Dhiri**
Lady Vera Everard	**Joan Blackham**
Sir Tim Listfield	**Anthony Barclay**
Marc Thompson	**Adrian Lukis**
Morag Hughes	**Mary Woodvine**
Sir Alan Peasmarsh	**Jeremy Child**
Neil Haughton	**Aneirin Hughes**

Creator/Writer/Producer **G. F. Newman**

● ***A High Court judge can't help bending the law to accommodate his own views.***

John Deed is a maverick, a former crusading barrister now promoted to the bench. Leaving none of his passion behind, he believes that justice means more than the law, which results in his handling each case on his own terms, rather than by the book – not a way to endear yourself to the Lord Chancellor. Divorced from QC George Channing, with a wayward student daughter (Charlie), the dynamic judge also has an eye for the ladies. Jo Mills is the prosecuting barrister who becomes his girlfriend but still appears in numerous cases over which he presides. Behind the scenes, there is always some Establishment figure waiting to whisper words of warning into the radical judge's ears whenever he strays too far from the accepted norm. The series followed a feature-length pilot screened in January 2001.

Juke Box Jury ✳✳

UK (BBC/Noel Gay) Pop Music. BBC 1 1959–67; 1979; BBC 2 1989–90

Presenters **David Jacobs, Noel Edmonds, Jools Holland**

Creator **Peter Potter**
Producers **Stewart Morris, Harry Carlisle, Neville Wortman, Barney Colehan, Barry Langford, Terry Henebery, Colin Charman, Roger Ordish**

● ***A celebrity panel reviews new record releases.***

Along with DOCTOR WHO and DIXON OF DOCK GREEN, *Juke Box Jury* was one of the stalwarts of Saturday teatime television in the early 1960s. The name of its instrumental theme music, 'Hit and Miss' (a Top Ten entry for the John Barry Seven in 1960), summed up what the programme was all about. Host David Jacobs played a selection of brand-new records to a panel of four knowledgeable personalities, who then declared whether the records would be 'hits' or 'misses'. While the records played, the cameras focused on the faces of the studio audience, gauging their reaction to the new discs. If the jury's overall conclusion was a 'hit', Jacobs rang a bell; if it was a 'miss' he sounded a klaxon. To add to the excitement, a mystery guest usually lurked in the background, waiting to confront pundits who gave their record the thumbs down.

The very first panel consisted of disc jockey Pete Murray, singers Alma Cogan and Gary Miller, and 'typical teenager' Susan Stranks (later wife of Robin Ray and presenter of MAGPIE). In December 1963, a massive audience was generated by the fact that The Beatles filled all four pundits' chairs and, a year later, the jury was temporarily increased to five, to accommodate the Rolling Stones. Although cancelled in 1967 (when the last panel again included Murray and Stranks, as well as Eric Sykes and Lulu), *Juke Box Jury* was briefly revived with Noel Edmonds as chairman in 1979, and once more in 1989, when former THE TUBE presenter Jools Holland became host.

Julia ✱✱

US (Twentieth Century-Fox) Situation Comedy. ITV 1969–71 (US: NBC 1968–71)

Julia Baker .... **Diahann Carroll**
Corey Baker .... **Marc Copage**
Dr Morton Chegley .... **Lloyd Nolan**
Hannah Yarby .... **Lurene Tuttle**
Marie Waggedorn .... **Betty Beaird**
Earl J. Waggedorn .... **Michael Link**
Len Waggedorn .... **Hank Brandt**
Melba Chegley .... **Mary Wickes**
Sol Cooper .... **Ned Glass**
Carol Deering .... **Allison Mills**
Paul Cameron .... **Paul Winfield**
Steve Bruce .... **Fred Williamson**
Kim Bruce .... **Stephanie James**

Producer **Hal Kanter**

Landmark comedy about a young black widow living in an integrated world.

After the death of her pilot husband in the Vietnam War, nurse Julia Baker – left as sole parent for young son Corey – takes up an appointment in the medical office of a Los Angeles aerospace firm. There she teams up with fellow nurse Hannah Yarby and grouchy boss Dr Morton Chegley. The laughs come from typical office situations and also from Julia's personal life, where her boyfriends include Paul Cameron and Steve Bruce. Sol Cooper is Julia's landlord. Although the general situation of this comedy broke little in the way of new ground, what was significant was the casting of a black woman in a lead role for the first time in the USA since the series *Beulah* in the early 1950s. Like I SPY in 1965, it marked a major step forward in the representation of blacks on TV (albeit quite affluent blacks), bringing them out of the supporting cast and offering professional roles instead of the accustomed blue-collar jobs of the past (even Beulah was a housemaid). The integration of races – Earl, Corey's best friend is white and they all live in a racially mixed apartment block – worried ratings-conscious network executives at first. They wrote off the series by pitching it against the massive, long-running *Red Skelton Show*, but it proved to be a surprise hit.

Juliet Bravo ✱✱

UK (BBC) Police Drama. BBC 1 1980–5
DVD: BBC

Insp. Jean Darblay .... **Stephanie Turner**
Tom Darblay .... **David Hargreaves**
Sgt Joseph Beck .... **David Ellison**
Sgt George Parrish .... **Noel Collins**
PC Roland Bentley .... **Mark Drewry**
Supt. Hallam .... **James Grout**
PC Gallagher .... **Gerard Kelly**
DCI Logan .... **Tony Caunter**
PC Sims .... **David Gillies**
PC Helmshore .... **David Straun**
Insp. Kate Longton .... **Anna Carteret**
PC Brian Kelleher .... **C. J. Allen**
PC Danny Sparks .... **Mark Botham**
DCI Perrin .... **Edward Peel**
DS Maltby .... **Sebastian Abineri**

Creator **Ian Kennedy Martin**
Producers **Terence Williams, Jonathan Alwyn, Geraint Morris**

Community policing with a female inspector.

Reminiscent of Z CARS in its setting, tone and content, *Juliet Bravo* focuses on Jean Darblay and Kate Longton, female police inspectors in the small, fictional town of Hartley in Lancashire. Darblay, career copper and housewife, battles against sexism from the start. Her arrival is greeted by distrust and resentment from her fellow officers (especially the obnoxious CID mob), but she rapidly earns respect, enjoying particular support from her solid, dependable sergeants, Joe Beck and George Parrish, as well as her husband, Tom, a social worker. Juliet Bravo is her police call-sign. When, after three years, Darblay accepts promotion and moves on, she is replaced by Kate Longton, who takes over not only her patch but also the headaches that go with it.

Cosy and reassuring, with an emphasis on human drama rather than sensational crime, *Juliet Bravo* was written by Ian Kennedy Martin, creator of THE SWEENEY. He brought Stephanie Turner with him (she had played George Carter's wife and, incidentally, was once a WPC in *Z Cars*).

Jumping the Queue ✱✱✱

UK (BBC) Drama. BBC 1 1989

Matilda .... **Sheila Hancock**
Hugh Warner .... **David Threlfall**
Huw Jones .... **Don Henderson**
Tom .... **John Stride**
Louise .... **Joanne Pearce**
Piers .... **Terence Harvey**

Writer **Ted Whitehead**
Producer **Sally Head**

A suicidal widow resconsiders her life after meeting a man on the run.

Star Sheila Hancock was instrumental in getting this adaptation of Mary Wesley's first novel (1983) onto the TV screen. Hancock had discovered the book while an Open University student and promptly bought up the rights. She then sold them to the BBC. The story concerns Matilda, an unhappy middle-aged widow who decides to take her own life. She prepares to go out in style and organizes a final picnic for herself. Shortly before she is about to commit suicide she bumps into Hugh, a younger man on the run from the police, who suspect him of killing his mother. Wrapped up in his plight, she postpones her death and tries to help him, his troubles helping her to come to terms with the many miseries in her own life. Claude Whatham directed this two-part thriller.

Junior Criss Cross Quiz

See Criss Cross Quiz.

Junior Showtime ✶

UK (Yorkshire) Children's Entertainment. ITV 1969–74

Presenter **Bobbie Bennett**

Executive Producer **Jess Yates**

Child entertainers relive the good old days of variety theatre.

This relentlessly cheerful children's talent show was recorded at the City Varieties Theatre in Leeds (also home to BBC's THE GOOD OLD DAYS). Although hosted by grown-up Bobbie Bennett (known as 'Mr Interlocutor'), the stars were all juniors, as its title implied. Over the show's five-year run legions of precocious young performers took the stage – singing, dancing, telling jokes, doing impressions, ventriloquizing and displaying other such talents – while comic asides came from the puppets Fred Barker, Kitty the theatre cat, and Mr Albert, an ostrich who was also the stage manager. Resident song-and-dance troupe the Showtime Minstrels blacked up to emulate George Mitchell's prime-time Black and White Minstrels, and the stars came together for a grand finale that was broadly based on a different theme each week (schooldays, farms, Hans Christian Andersen, Mexico, etc.). The most prominent artists to spring from the series were Jack Wild (HR PUFNSTUF), Mark Curry (BLUE PETER), Bonnie Langford (JUST WILLIAM and DOCTOR WHO), Joe Longthorne (his own variety shows), plus soap actors Julie Shipley (Christine Millward in CORONATION STREET), Kathryn Apanowicz (Mags Czajkowski in EASTENDERS), Malandra Burrows (Kathy Glover in EMMERDALE, then still known as Malandra Newman) and Charles Dale (Dennis Stringer in *Coronation Street*). Regular contributors were the Poole family from Castleford, most notably Glyn Poole, who co-hosted the series with Mark Curry, Bonnie Langford and Marjorie Phillips for a while. Other guest hosts were Ken Dodd, Billy Dainty and Joe Brown. Before *Junior Showtime* finally bit the dust, it was moved from a weekday slot to Sunday teatime. This longer programme aimed to amuse and entertain the whole family and included the New Generation dance group.

Junkin, John

(1930–2006)

Ealing-born actor and comedy writer, also working as a programme consultant/script editor. On screen he was seen supporting stars like Tommy Cooper and Marty Feldman, and in sitcoms as Wally, Alf Garnett's milkman, in TILL DEATH US DO PART; boozy husband Sam Marshall in *Sam and Janet*; Bert Ryding in the Stanley Holloway comedy *Thingumybob*; building foreman Charlie Cattermole in *On the House*; Odius in UP POMPEII!; Tim Brooke-Taylor's flatmate, Harold King, in *The Rough with the Smooth* (also as co-writer); Tommy Wallace in SHARON AND ELSIE; and legal clerk Steven in LAW AND DISORDER. Junkin also revealed his skill in straight drama in the crime thriller OUT, and in series like *Penmarric*, DICK TURPIN, ALL FOR LOVE, ALL CREATURES GREAT AND SMALL, MCCREADY AND DAUGHTER, *The Sins* (Archie Rogers) and EASTENDERS (Ernie). Other credits included BLOTT ON THE LANDSCAPE, LOOKING FOR CLANCY (Jim Clancy), *Scoop*, SHELLEY, *The Ravelled Thread* (Dobbs), INSPECTOR MORSE, *The Thing about Vince* and HOLBY CITY, while his own comedy series, *Junkin*, ran for four seasons and his radio show *Hello Cheeky* also transferred to TV for a while. In 1969 he hosted a panel game called *Give Me Your Word*. Junkin's many writing credits included episodes of THE ARMY GAME, *The World of Beachcomber, Mr Aitch, Langley Bottom, Paradise Island*, QUEENIE'S CASTLE and the sketch show *What's on Next?*, plus scripts for many top comedians, including Ted Ray, Bob Monkhouse, Morecambe and Wise, Leslie Crowther, Jim Davidson and Mike Yarwood.

Jury ✶✶

UK (BBC) Drama. BBC 1 1983

The Jurors

John Bannister	**Desmond McNamara**
Christine Cywinska	**Debbie Farrington**
Louise Barrett	**Corinne Skinner-Carter**
Gerald Sadler	**Hugh Lloyd**
David Farrell	**David Simeon**
Mary Matthews	**Gabrielle Lloyd**
Andrew Cook	**William Gaunt**
Julian Spears	**Charles Shaughnessy**
Mick Thompson	**Richard Piper**
Steve Jackson	**Steve Alder**
Elizabeth Robbins	**Angela Morant**
Ann Coombes	**Margaret Whiting**

In Court

Donald Fleming	**Grant Cathro**
Judge	**Alan Judd**
Defence Counsel	**Hugh Ross**
Prosecution Counsel	**Sam Dastor**
Clerk of Court	**Bronwen Gray**

Writers **Andrew Lynch, Dave Simpson, Peter Whalley, Ken Blakeson**
Producer **Colin Turner**

The private lives of a team of jurors.

Using the courtroom trial of one Donald Fleming as a backdrop, this 13-part series moves away from legal eagles and into the troubled lives of the selected jury members. Flicking through their personal experiences and day-to-day concerns, exposing their shortcomings and vulnerabilities, the series provides an insight into the sort of people that have to decide a defendant's guilt or otherwise. One episode is devoted to each juror (although two, Steve Jackson and Elizabeth Robbins, are jointly covered), with the concluding two parts focusing on complicated courtroom deliberations and, eventually, the verdict.

Just a Gigolo ✶✶

UK (Central) Situation Comedy. ITV 1993

Nick Brim	**Tony Slattery**
Simon Brim	**Paul Bigley**
Natalie	**Rowena King**

Writers **Carl Gorham, Michael Hatt, Amanda Swift**
Producer **Paul Spencer**

The misadventures of a reluctant male escort.

Soon after losing his job, school teacher Nick Brim is propelled into a new career as a male escort, when a woman mistakes him for her paid consort. He joins an escort agency and, operating under the pseudonym of Giorgio, becomes involved with a variety of rich spinsters and widows, all the while dreaming of a date with Natalie, waitress at the local wine bar. Nick shares a flat with Simon, his unemployed, reckless, TV addict brother. But the fact that they are both broke means that Nick is forced to persevere with his new 'profession' and all its pitfalls.

Just Amazing! ✱✱

UK (Yorkshire/Action Time) Factual. ITV 1983–4

Presenters **Barry Sheen, Kenny Lynch, Jan Ravens, Suzanne Danielle**

Producer **John Fanshawe**

Cornucopia of wacky human behaviour.

This Saturday evening slice of light entertainment took as its theme spectacular stunts from around the world, mixed in bizarre human-interest stories and then showcased people with ridiculously strange skills. Viewers had the chance to meet a family that kept a pig in the house as a pet, or see daredevil motorcyclists leap double-decker buses, followed up by a man who eats bicycles. Former world motorcycling champion Barry Sheene, comedian Kenny Lynch and impressionist Jan Ravens provided the links, hamming it up and dishing out cheesy gags. Ravens was later replaced by actress Suzanne Danielle. The theme music was by Alan Parker and Robert Hartley. A compilation of programme highlights was screened in 1985.

Just Good Friends ✱✱✱

UK (BBC) Situation Comedy. BBC 1 1983–4; 1986
DVD: Universal

Vince Pinner .... **Paul Nicholas**
Penny Warrender .... **Jan Francis**
Daphne Warrender .... **Sylvia Kay**
Norman Warrender .... **John Ringham**
Rita Pinner .... **Ann Lynn**
Les Pinner .... **Shaun Curry**
Clifford Pinner .... **Adam French**
Georgina Marshall .... **Charlotte Seely**

Creator/Writer **John Sullivan**
Producer **Ray Butt**

A jilted girl meets her former fiancé and they embark on a new on-off romance.

Jack-the-Lad Vincent Pinner met prim-and-proper Penny Warrender at a Rolling Stones concert in Hyde Park. Romance blossomed and they decided to get married. But, on the day, Vince chickened out. Five years later, he and Penny meet by accident in a pub and are drawn into a new love-hate relationship, exasperated by their different class roots and chosen professions. Cheeky, working-class Vince is assistant manager at Eddie Brown's Turf Accountants, while prissy, middle-class Penny works for the Mathews, Styles and Lieberman advertising agency. Other major characters are Penny's snooty mum, Daphne, her unemployed, hen-pecked dad, Norman, and Vince's gloriously vulgar parents, Rita, a keen rock 'n' roll fan, and Les, a scrap-metal merchant. Also seen is Vince's accident-prone younger brother, Cliffy. After numerous false dawns, Vince (now in charge of his dad's business) and Penny (now working in Paris) do indeed manage to tie the knot.

A letter from a girl in the same situation as Penny, published on the problems page of a women's magazine, allegedly inspired John Sullivan to create the series.

Just Jimmy ✱✱

UK (ABC) Situation Comedy. ITV 1964–8

Jimmy Clitheroe .... **Jimmy Clitheroe**
Mrs Clitheroe .... **Mollie Sugden**
Danny .... **Danny Ross**

Producer **Ronnie Baxter**

The misadventures of an unruly schoolboy.

Translated from BBC Radio, *Just Jimmy* was the television manifestation of *The Clitheroe Kid*, in which 4-foot 3-inch Lancastrian comedian Jimmy Clitheroe performed his naughty-schoolboy routines. He was supported in this series by Mollie Sugden as his over-the-top mum and by Danny Ross as Danny, his older, girls- and motorbikes-mad cousin.

Just William ✱✱

UK (LWT) Situation Comedy. ITV 1977–8

William Brown .... **Adrian Dannatt**
Mr Brown .... **Hugh Cross**
Mrs Brown .... **Diana Fairfax**
Ethel Brown .... **Stacy Dorning**
Robert Brown .... **Simon Chandler**
Violet Elizabeth Bott .... **Bonnie Langford**
Mrs Bott .... **Diana Dors**
Mr Bott .... **John Stratton**
Douglas .... **Tim Rose**
Ginger .... **Michael McVey**
Henry .... **Craig McFarlane**

Writer **Keith Dewhurst**
Executive Producer **Stella Richman**
Producer **John Davies**

A mischievous schoolboy is a handful for his parents.

Richmal Crompton's colourful adventures of trying schoolboy William Brown were first brought to the screen by the BBC in *William* in 1962–3, with Dennis Waterman and then Dennis Gilmore in the title role. Fifteen years later, William was back, with Adrian Dannatt filling Master Brown's shoes.

William is the mischievous type, fond of pranks and tricks and never far from trouble. His band of followers, known as the Outlaws, consist of Douglas, Ginger and Henry. William has a sister, Ethel, and an older brother, Robert, though his arch-enemy is the dreadful, lisping Violet Elizabeth Bott. She has set her heart on marrying him and promises to scream until she makes herself sick whenever she fails to get her way.

Just William made yet another return to the small screen in 1994–5, when the BBC cast young Oliver Rokison in the lead role. Over two series, he was joined by Polly James, Lindsay Duncan and Joan Sims, among other stars.

Justice ✱✱

UK (Yorkshire) Legal Drama. ITV 1971–4

Harriet Peterson .... **Margaret Lockwood**
Sir John Gallagher .... **Philip Stone**
Dr Ian Moody .... **John Stone**

Bill .... **John Bryans**
James Eliot .... **Anthony Valentine**

Executive Producer **Peter Willes**
Producers **James Ormerod, Jacky Stoller**

The cases of a junior barrister.

Middle-aged Harriet Peterson is a devoted, dedicated lawyer doing the rounds of the courtrooms of northern England. After the first 13 episodes, and following encouragement from her boss, Sir John Gallagher, she moves to London, where she ultimately discovers a rival in barrister James Eliot, whom she regularly upstages. With the scripts (penned by the likes of James Mitchell, Ian Curteis and Edmund Ward) checked by a real lawyer, the programme is careful in its detail and depicts the legal system in all its colours. Harriet, for instance, is no Perry Mason and is certainly not infallible.

The role provided a triumphant return to the small screen for Margaret Lockwood, who had previously been seen as lawyer Julia Stanford in a one-off play, *Justice is a Woman*, in 1969.

Kaleidoscope ✳

UK (BBC) Magazine. BBC 1946–53

Host **McDonald Hobley**

Producer **John Irwin**

● ***Easy-going magazine programme calling on viewer involvement.***

This television manifestation of the 1930s radio series *Monday Night at Eight* comprised a variety of light-hearted items, from competitions and puzzles to comedy and games. Among the features were Word Play (an early version of GIVE US A CLUE), Be Your Own Detective (an observation game), Collectors' Corner (antiques with Iris Brooke), contributions from Memory Man Leslie Welch and Puzzle Corner with Ronnie Waldman (with viewers asked to spot the deliberate mistake). Anyone at home wishing to take part in the 'which year' tune medley competition had to place a copy of the *Radio Times* in their window by noon on broadcast day in order to be spotted and selected. Assisting host McDonald Hobley with events were the likes of Max Kester, Dorothy Ward, Lind Joyce, Garry Miller, John Slater, Diana Decker, Elizabeth Welch and Carole Carr. *Kaleidoscope* was screened once a fortnight.

Kaplinsky, Natasha

(1972–)

BBC Breakfast and news bulletin presenter, formerly with Sky News and, before that, Carlton and Meridian local news programmes. Natasha has also hosted STRICTLY COME DANCING and CHILDREN IN NEED. Before turning to television, she worked in the press office of Labour leaders Neil Kinnock and John Smith.

Karaoke/Cold Lazarus ✳✳✳

UK (Whistling Gypsy/BBC/Channel 4) Drama. BBC 1/Channel 4 1996

Daniel Feeld .... **Albert Finney**
Nick Balmer .... **Richard E. Grant**
Arthur 'Pig' Mailion .... **Hywel Bennett**
Sandra Sollars .... **Saffron Burrows**
Ben Baglin .... **Roy Hudd**
Linda Langer .... **Keeley Hawes**
Anna Griffiths .... **Anna Chancellor**
Mrs Baglin .... **Liz Smith** *(Karaoke)*
Oliver Morse .... **Ian McDiarmid**
Lady Ruth Balmer .... **Julie Christie** *(Karaoke)*
Mrs Haynes .... **Alison Steadman**
Peter (*movie*) .... **Neil Stuke** *(Karaoke)*
Waiter (*movie*) .... **Steven Mackintosh** *(Karaoke)*
Prof. Emma Porlock .... **Frances de la Tour** *(Cold Lazarus)*
Martina Masdon .... **Diane Ladd** *(Cold Lazarus)*
Fyodor Glazunov .... **Ciaran Hinds** *(Cold Lazarus)*
David Siltz .... **Henry Goodman** *(Cold Lazarus)*
Luanda .... **Ganiat Kasumu** *(Cold Lazarus)*
Tony Watson .... **Grant Masters** *(Cold Lazarus)*
Kaya .... **Claudia Malkovich** *(Cold Lazarus)*
Nat .... **Jonathan Cake** *(Cold Lazarus)*
Karl .... **Rob Brydon** *(Cold Lazarus)*

Writer **Dennis Potter**
Executive Producers **Peter Ansorge, Michael Wearing**
Producers **Kenith Trodd, Rosemarie Whitman**

● ***Two linked, four-part dramas depicting the dying days of a writer and the exploitation of his mind in the future.***

In an unprecedented display of collaboration, the BBC and Channel 4 jointly brought the final works of acclaimed TV playwright Dennis Potter to the screen. It was Potter who had instigated the arrangement. Speaking in his last TV interview, with Melvyn Bragg, the pain-racked author requested on air that the two broadcasting companies should come together and co-produce his final two, linked works, *Karaoke* and *Cold Lazarus*. They were dramas that Potter had fought hard to finish as his death from pancreatic cancer loomed large. With a determination few authors possess, he ground away at his scripts, often forgoing painkillers to keep his head clear, and completed the works just weeks before he died. Potter chose the director, Renny Rye, and the two producers with whom he had enjoyed greatest success over the years, Kenith Trodd and Rosemarie Whitman, to see the project through. *Karaoke* was screened first on BBC 1, with a repeat a day later on Channel 4. *Cold Lazarus* aired first on Channel 4, with BBC 1 offering the rerun the next day.

Karaoke concerns a writer named Daniel Feeld, a man suffering from a serious illness and alcoholism who finds his written lines suddenly issuing from the mouths of real people and his fiction becoming fact. Comic relief is provided by his spoonerizing agent, Ben Baglin. The serial is resonant in Potter themes: an author – a thinly disguised version of Potter himself – haunted by his work and his past; repressed sexuality; a beautiful girl (nightclub hostess Sandra Sollars); some particularly nasty villains (the vile Arthur 'Pig' Mailion); and, of course, no shortage of strong language.

Cold Lazarus takes the action way into the future, to the year AD 2368. There, scientists at the Masdon Science Centre in London, headed by Professor Porlock, are successfully reviving the head of Daniel Feeld, which has been preserved cryogenically. They manage to release memories of the 20th century and extracts from Feeld's life and work that soon become of interest to international media tycoon David Siltz – a final attack by Potter on the manipulation of authors and their work by commercial media. In this future age, people move around the lab in thought-powered, semi-organic wheelchairs called auto-cubes and drive hovering bubble cars down the streets, while a terrorist group known as RON (Reality or Nothing) wages war on the way the world is now run.

Karlin, Miriam

OBE (Miriam Samuels; 1925–)

London-born actress who satirized militant trade-unionists in her portrayal of Paddy, the whistle-blowing shop steward in THE RAG TRADE. Earlier, Karlin had appeared in the 1946 production of *Alice* and then starred with Sid James in his first (post-Hancock) sitcom, *East End – West End*. She returned to television in the 1990s in the sitcom SO HAUNT ME, playing Jewish ghost Yetta Feldman, and has been seen more recently in HOLBY CITY, DOCTORS, DALZIEL AND PASCOE and AGATHA CHRISTIE'S MARPLE.

Karloff, Boris

(William Pratt; 1887–1969)

Although a master of the horror genre in the cinema, Boris Karloff's major television role was quite different. He played Colonel March of Scotland Yard in 1956, head of the Department of Queer Complaints. In a more familiar vein, he also hosted OUT OF THIS WORLD, an anthology of science-fiction stories in the early 1960s, and he continued to make guest appearances, in series like THE GIRL FROM U.N.C.L.E. and *Route 66*, until his death in 1969.

Kate ★★

UK (Yorkshire) Drama. ITV 1970–2

Katherine 'Kate' Graham	**Phyllis Calvert**
Donald Killearn	**Jack Hedley**
Wenda Padbury	**Penelope Keith**
Stephen Graham	**Marcus Hammond**
Mr Winch	**Preston Lockwood**
Ellen Burwood	**Elizabeth Baker**
Bruce Rogers	**Tony Anholt**
Lillian Coates	**Barbara Markham**

Producers **Stanley Miller, Pieter Rogers**

● ***An agony aunt has problems of her own.***

Kate Graham, aged around 50, the widowed mother of teenage son Stephen, works as the 'Dear Monica' problem-page editor for *Heart and Home* magazine. But, as well as dispensing advice to her readers, Kate is in demand among her colleagues, particularly her friend, editor Donald Killearn, the boss of Killearn Enterprises, who has encouraged Kate to take the job. Furthermore, her own home life in Chelsea – where housekeeper Ellen Burwood keeps things ship-shape – is far from settled. Also prominent in the office are Wenda Padbury, the heiress daughter of Lord Padbury, who has turned to journalism as a hobby and is at times quite insufferable; respected company secretary Mr Winch; features editor Lillian Coates; and new-blood journalist Bruce Rogers. As the series unfolds, Donald moves on up, and Kate and Wenda go on to share the editor's chair.

Kate & Allie ★★★

US (Reeves Entertainment) Situation Comedy. Channel 4 1986–93 (US: CBS 1984–9)

Kate McArdle	**Susan Saint James**
Allie Lowell	**Jane Curtin**
Emma McArdle	**Ari Meyers**
Chip Lowell	**Frederick Koehler**
Jennie Lowell	**Allison Smith**
Ted Bartelo	**Gregory Salata**
Bob Barsky	**Sam Freed**
Lou Carello	**Peter Onorati**

Creator **Sherry Coben**

Executive Producers **Mort Lachman, Merrill Grant, Saul Turteltaub, Bernie Orenstein**

● ***Two old schoolfriends, both divorced, share a New York apartment.***

Kate McArdle and Allie Lowell have been friends for donkey's years. After both suffer marriage breakdowns, they decide to pool resources, share a flat in Greenwich Village and provide each other with emotional support on tap. Kate keeps her job as a travel agent, while Allie runs the home. Also along for the ride are Kate's daughter Emma and Allie's two kids, Chip and Jennie, making domestic life always colourful. Ex-husbands Max (McArdle) and Charles (Lowell) also occasionally drop by, to be cut to shreds by the newly independent women. There is a hint of THE ODD COUPLE about the two leads: dark-haired Kate is lively and glamorous, while blonde Allie is more down to earth and frumpy – but deep friendship is the oil that keeps the cogs of their lives turning. Their love lives enter the equation on a regular basis, especially when Kate dates plumber Ted Bartelo and Allie finds romance with radio sports reporter Bob Barsky. Allie and Bob eventually marry, move to a new home and invite Kate – now partner with Allie in a catering business – to join them, the kids gradually flying the coop (Emma and Jennie sign up at Columbia University). It is figured that Allie will need the company while Bob is working weekdays in his new TV job in Washington. Lou Carello is the manager of the new condominium who has designs on Kate.

Kavanagh QC ★★★

UK (Carlton) Drama. ITV 1995–9; 2001
DVD: Carlton

James Kavanagh QC	**John Thaw**
Lizzie Kavanagh	**Lisa Harrow**
Julia Piper/Piper-Robinson	**Anna Chancellor**
Peter Foxcott QC	**Oliver Ford Davis**
Jeremy Aldermarten QC	**Nicholas Jones**
Tom Buckley	**Cliff Parisi**
Kate Kavanagh	**Daisy Bates**
Matt Kavanagh	**Tom Brodie**
Alex Wilson	**Jenny Jules**
Helen Ames	**Arkie Whiteley**
Emma Taylor	**Valerie Redmond**
Eleanor Harker QC	**Geraldine James**

Producer **Chris Kelly**
Executive Producer **Ted Childs**

● ***The cases of a brilliant lawyer with a complicated personal life.***

Fresh from playing INSPECTOR MORSE and a less successful excursion in A YEAR IN PROVENCE, John Thaw grew his hair and became battling barrister James Kavanagh. Kavanagh is a talented, working-class, liberal-minded, Mancunian brief with a penchant for defending the underdog. However, in tried and tested TV fashion, his own personal life is less well organized. His wife, Lizzie, is having an affair with another lawyer and his teenage kids are up to the usual adolescent tricks. His free time is devoted to his hobby of sailing. Julia Piper is Kavanagh's junior colleague at work.

As the series progresses, Julia moves to the States (once recruiting her old boss to help with a trial in Florida) and Lizzie dies, leaving Kavanagh mournful but free to build a sparky new working relationship with Scots colleague Emma Taylor and a romantic liaison with fellow barrister Eleanor Harker. Kavanagh's head of chambers is Peter Foxcott; Tom Buckley is the firm's clerk. The series was applauded for its legal accuracy and producer Chris Kelly (of FOOD AND DRINK fame) has admitted that certain aspects of the lead character were inspired by real-life defence barrister Michael Mansfield QC.

Kay, Peter

(1973–)

Bolton-born comedian, writer and actor who made a big impression with his spoof documentary series, *That Peter Kay Thing*, in which he played no fewer than 15 different characters. One of these characters, social club proprietor Brian Potter, then gained his own series, known as PETER KAY'S PHOENIX NIGHTS, which Kay also directed and which ran to a sequel, MAX & PADDY'S ROAD TO NOWHERE (with Kay as Max). Among his guest appearances are roles in CORONATION STREET (drayman Eric Gartside), LINDA GREEN and *The Catherine Tate Show*, and some time as a presenter of THE BIG BREAKFAST.

Kay, Vernon

(1974–)

Lancashire-born presenter of mostly youth-orientated lifestyle, reality and game shows. These have included *Top of the Pops Plus*, *FBI*, *T4*, *The Mag*, *The Grill*, *A Wife for William*, *Head Jam*, *Girls and Boys*, *Celebrities under Pressure*, *Hit Me Baby One More Time*, *California Dreaming* and *Record of the Year*. A former fashion model, his break came when he won 'Model of the Week' in THE BIG BREAKFAST and was snapped up by Channel 4. Kay is married to presenter Tess Daly with whom he hosted the singing contest *Just the Two of Us*.

Kaye, Gorden

(1941–)

British comedy actor, much seen on TV, especially as the reluctant Resistance hero, René Artois, in 'ALLO 'ALLO. Previously, Kaye had popped up in a host of other comedies, including TILL DEATH US DO PART, ARE YOU BEING SERVED?, IT AIN'T HALF HOT MUM, THE GROWING PAINS OF PC PENROSE, OH HAPPY BAND and COME BACK MRS NOAH. He was Ray Benge in the black comedy *Born and Bred*, neighbour Mr Chatto in *Just Liz*, Jem in *God's Wonderful Railway*, Frank Broadhurst in *Codename Icarus*, and was also seen in LAST OF THE SUMMER WINE as Maynard Lavery, a TV presenter, and in dramas like the *Screen One* presentation *Bullion Boys* (Nickson), SHOESTRING, ALL CREATURES GREAT AND SMALL, FAME IS THE SPUR, *The Foundation* and CORONATION STREET (Bernard Butler, Elsie Tanner's nephew). In 1987 he narrowly escaped death in the gales which ravaged southern England, sustaining severe head injuries, but made a full recovery. Recently he has been seen in the *Revolver* sketch show.

Kaye, Paul

(1965–)

Wembley-born comedian/actor whose alter-ego, Dennis Pennis, sent celebrities running for cover with his disdainful interviews (to Joan Collins: 'You look a million lire'; to Demi Moore: 'If it was under the right circumstances, and it was not gratuitously done, would you ever consider leaving your clothes on in a movie?'). The flame-haired, nerdy character was first seen in a BBC 2 programme called *The Sunday Show* and then headlined in *Anyone for Pennis* and *Very Important Pennis*, as well as an ITV music series called *Pennis Pops Out*. Kaye later starred in the one-off punk rock satire, *Wrath*, co-starred with Michelle Collins as Kenny Marsh in TWO THOUSAND ACRES OF SKY, and played self-absorbed marketing man Bob Slay in the sitcom *Perfect World*. He has also hosted the game show *Liar* and made guest appearances in WAKING THE DEAD and DOWN TO EARTH.

Keach, Stacy

(1941–)

American cinema and television actor, known for Shakespearean roles in the 1960s, but famous as tough detective MIKE HAMMER in the 1980s. Previously, Keach had starred in the shortlived detective series *Caribe* and in the Civil War drama *The Blue and the Grey*, as well as playing Barabbas in JESUS OF NAZARETH. He later appeared in the mini-series *Mistral's Daughter* and *Hemingway*, plus the US series *Titus* and *Prison Break* (Warden Henry Pope), and has narrated numerous factual programmes in the USA. Unfortunately, his big-time period in Mickey Spillane's *Mike Hammer* was punctuated by a much-publicized spell in Reading prison for drugs offences. His father, Stacy Keach Sr, played Professor Carlson in GET SMART

Kearney, Gillian

(1972–)

Coming to the fore as runaway schoolgirl Debbie McGrath in BROOKSIDE in the 1980s, Liverpool-born Gillian Kearney has since moved on to star in a number of prime-time series. These have included CATHERINE COOKSON'S *The Tide of Life* (Emily Kennedy), SEX, CHIPS AND ROCK 'N' ROLL (Ellie Brookes), LIVERPOOL ONE (Julie Callaghan), HOPE AND GLORY (Kitty Burton), CLOCKING OFF (Lynne Watson), MURDER IN MIND, THE FORSYTE SAGA (June Forsyte), *The Real Jane Austen* (title role) and *Sweet Medicine* (Deb Sweet). Guest appearances have been in programmes like WATERFRONT BEAT, CASUALTY, HEARTBEAT, HETTY WAINTHROPP INVESTIGATES, MEN OF THE WORLD, *Black Cab*, MIDSOMER MURDERS, BLUE MURDER, SHAMELESS and WHERE THE HEART IS.

Kee, Robert

(1919–)

British journalist, a reporter on PANORAMA and THIS WEEK in the 1950s and 1960s, who also contributed as a writer to the acclaimed documentary series THE GREAT WAR. He joined ITN in the mid-1970s to present the novel lunchtime news bulletin *First Report*. In 1980 he wrote and presented IRELAND: A TELEVISION HISTORY and in 1983 was a member of TV-am's 'Famous Five', presenting *Daybreak*, the station's news and information reveillé.

Keel, Howard

(Harry Leek; 1919–2004)

American musical star for whom television celebrity arrived late. His earliest TV appearances were as a guest in series like HERE'S LUCY and THE QUEST, but it wasn't until he arrived in DALLAS in 1981, as silver-haired Clayton Farlow, that Keel became an established TV performer. Later guest appearances came in MURDER, SHE WROTE and *Walker, Texas Ranger*.

Keen, Diane

(1946–)

British actress starring as Fliss Hawthorne in THE CUCKOO WALTZ sitcom, though she had already enjoyed credits in SOFTLY, SOFTLY, CROSSROADS (Sandra Gould), PUBLIC EYE, THE SWEENEY, CROWN COURT, FALL OF EAGLES (Empress Elizabeth) and a BBC version of *The Legend of Robin Hood* (Maid Marian), among other programmes. During and after *The Cuckoo Waltz*, Keen played Empress Chimalma in *The Feathered Serpent*, Laura Dickens in THE SANDBAGGERS, Sandy Bennett in RINGS ON THEIR FINGERS, Sally Higgins in SHILLINGBURY TALES, provincial newspaper editor Daisy Jackson in FOXY LADY and novelist-housewife Alice Hammond in *You Must Be the Husband*. More recently, she has been seen as Jenny Burden in THE RUTH RENDELL MYSTERIES, Connie French in SEPTEMBER SONG, Mollie Marchbank in BROOKSIDE, Julia Parsons/McGuire in DOCTORS, and Hilary Galway in *The Deputy*, with guest roles in series like A TOUCH OF FROST and CITY CENTRAL.

Keep It in the Family ✶✶

UK (Thames) Situation Comedy. ITV 1980–3

Dudley Rush	**Robert Gillespie**
Muriel Rush	**Pauline Yates**
Duncan Thomas	**Glyn Houston**
Susan Rush	**Stacy Dorning**
Jacqui Rush	**Jenny Quayle**
	Sabina Franklyn

Creator **Brian Cooke**
Producers **Mark Stuart, Robert Reed**

● ***Upstairs-downstairs, generation-gap comedy.***

The Rush family live in Highgate Avenue, Highgate. Nominal head of the household is Dudley, a slightly eccentric professional cartoonist (drawer of the 'Bionic Bulldog' cartoon). His caricature family consists of dutiful wife Muriel and problematic daughters Susan (aged 17) and Jacqui (21), who are constantly tapping him for cash, bringing home unsuitable boyfriends and indulging in reckless pursuits. When the Rushes' old lodger dies and his downstairs flat becomes vacant, the girls take it over, giving themselves more independence and their parents more grey hairs. Duncan is Dudley's Welsh boss, who also moves in with the family, and another regular is the old glove-puppet Dudley talks to while drawing.

The series gave rise to an American cover version entitled *Too Close for Comfort*, starring Ted Knight.

Keeping Mum ✶✶

UK (BBC) Situation Comedy. BBC 1 1997–8

Peggy	**Stephanie Cole**
Andrew	**Martin Ball**
Richard	**David Haig**
Tina	**Meera Syal**
Kate	**Carol Starks**

Creator/Writer **Geoffrey Atherden**
Producer **Stephen McCrum**

● ***A frustrated divorcé is a carer for his ailing old mother.***

Andrew has just been divorced from wife Kate and has moved back in with his ageing mum. This is partly to gain a roof over his head and partly to keep an eye on her. Although Peggy is mostly sound of body, her brain doesn't quite function as it should – simple chores like making a cup of tea are problematic and her memory is not what it should be. Not that this stops her from indulging in mischief when she feels like it. For Andrew, his new life is all rather a headache. He doesn't only need to ensure that Peggy is safe but also has to find a way of reasserting his independence – a move that his confused but headstrong mum is determined to suppress. Poor Andrew (a journalist) cannot even rely on his selfish older brother, Richard (a dentist), and catty sister-in-law, Tina, for help.

Keeping Mum was based on a long-running Australian series called *Mother and Son*, written by Geoffrey Atherden, who adapted and extended his scripts for the British audience (with the help of Paul Mayhew-Archer). Despite criticisms of bad taste in the way that senile dementia was treated as a humorous subject, a second series was produced. *Keeping Mum* was the BBC's first comedy to be specifically shot in widescreen.

Keeping up Appearances ✶✶

UK (BBC) Situation Comedy. BBC 1 1990–5
DVD: Universal

Hyacinth Bucket	**Patricia Routledge**
Richard Bucket	**Clive Swift**
Elizabeth	**Josephine Tewson**
Emmet Hawksworth	**David Griffin**
Daisy	**Judy Cornwell**
Onslow	**Geoffrey Hughes**
Rose	**Shirley Stelfox**
	Mary Millar
Vicar	**Jeremy Gittins**
Daddy	**George Webb**

Creator/Writer **Roy Clarke**
Producer **Harold Snoad**

● ***A socially climbing housewife lives in fear of letting herself down.***

Only one thing matters to Hyacinth Bucket (pronounced 'bouquet') and that is what other people think of her. From her suburban base in Blossom Avenue, she moves heaven and earth to mix with the right crowd and to ensure that her image remains intact. Sadly, her council-house sisters, slutty Daisy and tarty Rose, plus her shirtless brother-in-law, Onslow, ensure it is a battle she is doomed to lose. They look after Hyacinth's loopy old dad and are always likely to pop round in Onslow's S-reg Cortina (complete with furry dice). Undaunted, Hyacinth badgers her meek, long-suffering husband, Richard, into helping with her candlelight suppers and other socially aspirant schemes and talks up the brilliance of her son, Sheridan (who is away at polytechnic), to all who will listen. She answers the telephone with a ringing 'The Bucket residence: the lady of the house speaking', and hounds Elizabeth, her nervous neighbour, and Elizabeth's divorced brother, Emmet, to the point where they become prisoners in their own home. Generally, though, it is Hyacinth's own social gaffes that scupper her rise to the top.

Keith, Penelope

OBE (1940–)

Surrey-born comedy actress often in plummy, snooty parts. Having appeared in series like THE AVENGERS, *Six Shades of Black*, HADLEIGH, KATE (Wenda Padbury) and THE PALLISERS

(Mrs Hittaway), it was as the socially paranoid Margo Leadbetter, neighbour of the self-sufficient Goods, in THE GOOD LIFE, that Keith found her forte. This led to a series of her own, TO THE MANOR BORN, in which she played Audrey fforbes-Hamilton, cruelly ejected from her stately home on the death of her husband. Her later sitcom work has included *Moving* (would-be house mover Sarah Gladwyn), SWEET SIXTEEN (Helen Walker, a love-struck owner of a building firm), EXECUTIVE STRESS (publisher Caroline Fairchild), NO JOB FOR A LADY (novice Labour MP Jean Price), LAW AND DISORDER (barrister Phillippa Troy) and NEXT OF KIN (stressed grandmother Maggie Prentice). Other credits have included *The Norman Conquests*, SPYDER'S WEB, *On Approval*, JACKANORY, COMING HOME (Aunt Louise) and *Margery and Gladys* (Margery Heywood). She briefly hosted WHAT'S MY LINE? on the death of Eamonn Andrews, and, in complete contrast, provided the voice of the bear in TELETUBBIES.

Keith Barret Show, The

See *Marion and Geoff*.

Kelly, Barbara

(1923–)

Canadian actress and television personality, a familiar face in the 1950s as a panellist on WHAT'S MY LINE? With her husband, the late Bernard Braden, Kelly moved to Britain in 1949 and, together, they made a name for themselves on BBC Radio and then TV, including the shortlived sitcom *B and B*. Kelly was also seen in assorted plays and in programmes like CRISS CROSS QUIZ and *Kelly's Eye*, and provided the voice of the computer in SPACE: 1999. She returned to the screen in the 1984 revival of *What's My Line?* Kelly is the mother of actress Kim Braden.

Kelly, Chris

(1940–)

Cheshire-born presenter, writer and producer, for many years at Granada, and previously at Anglia, working on programmes like WORLD IN ACTION (narrator), CINEMA and the children's series ZOO TIME, *Sixth Form Challenge*, JUNIOR CRISS CROSS QUIZ, CLAPPERBOARD and *Anything You Can Do*. He was Judith Chalmers's partner on WISH YOU WERE HERE . . . ? for many years and host of BBC 2's FOOD AND DRINK for another lengthy period. He is also a published writer, wrote the drama *The Zero Option* that led to the series SARACEN, co-created EL C.I.D., and produced the dramas, SOLDIER, SOLDIER, KAVANAGH QC and *Without Motive*.

Kelly, Henry

(1946–)

Irish journalist turned presenter of game shows, whose major TV break came with GAME FOR A LAUGH in 1981. Since then, he has appeared on TV-am and *Monkey Business* and also hosted the inter-European quiz GOING FOR GOLD.

Kelly, Lorraine

(1959–)

Breakfast TV presenter who joined TV-am as its Scottish correspondent after working in local newspapers and as a researcher at BBC Scotland. She went on to become one of the anchors of *Good Morning Britain* from 1988, before joining GMTV when it acquired the breakfast franchise in 1993. She has also presented a programme simply titled *Lorraine* for Sky One, *Design Wars*, *This Morning* and *Can't Sing Singers*, and was a team captain in *A Question of TV*.

Kelly, Matthew

(1950–)

Tall British presenter and actor, coming to the fore through GAME FOR A LAUGH and subsequently host of *Kelly's Eye*, YOU BET! and STARS IN THEIR EYES. Kelly earlier appeared in the drama *Funny Man*, the hotel sitcom *Room Service* (Dick Sedgewick) and the comedy HOLDING THE FORT, playing the part of Fitz, which was later spun off into another series, *Relative Strangers*, in which he starred. Other credits have included fronting Children's ITV (the first presenter) and roles in *The Rather Reassuring Programme*, *The Critic*, *Madabout*, *Quandaries*, *The Sensible Show*, *Adventures of a Lifetime*, *Give a Pet a Home*, *Animal Champions*, *City Hospital*, *Never Had It So Good* and *After They were Famous* (narrator). Since leaving STARS IN THEIR EYES, Kelly has returned to acting in a major way, with credits in *Cold Blood* (serial killer Brian Wicklow), BLEAK HOUSE (Old Mr Turveydrop) and *Egypt* ('The Great Belzoni').

Kelly, Sam

(1943–)

Prolific British actor, often seen in incompetent or slightly stupid parts, such as the illiterate Warren in PORRIDGE and the inept Captain Hans Geering in 'ALLO 'ALLO. Among his earliest opportunities were episodes of EMERGENCY – WARD 10 and THE LIVER BIRDS. He played Norman Elston in the flashback sitcom *Now and Then*, Les Brooks in the unemployment comedy *We'll Think of Something*, Grunge in HAGGARD, Sam the chauffeur in ON THE UP and Adolf Hitler in *Stalag Luft*, and he supported *Paul Merton in Galton & Simpson's . . .* He has also been seen in more serious roles in INSPECTOR MORSE, BOYS FROM THE BLACKSTUFF and CHRISTABEL, and other credits have included CORONATION STREET (decorator Bob Challis), THIN AIR (Henry Campbell), THE BILL, MAKING OUT, STAY LUCKY, MARTIN CHUZZLEWIT (Mr Mould), *Holding On* (Bernard), OLIVER TWIST (Giles), *Where There's Smoke* (DI Collins), BARBARA (Ted Liversidge), MICAWBER (Mr Cudlipp), LIFE BEGINS, BLACK BOOKS (Manny's dad), *Pat and Mo* (Stan), CASUALTY, HEARTBEAT, *Beauty* (Bernard), A TOUCH OF FROST, the remake of READY WHEN YOU ARE, MR MCGILL, *Northern Lights*, and MIDSOMER MURDERS. Kelly also provided voices for *PC Pinkerton*.

Kelly Monteith ★★★

UK (BBC) Situation Comedy. BBC 2 1979–84

Kelly Monteith, Gabrielle Drake

Writers **Kelly Monteith, Neil Shand**
Producers **James Moir, Bill Wilson, Geoff Posner, John Kilby**

A stand-up comic reflects on the humorous things that take place in his life.

Predating both IT'S GARRY SHANDLING'S SHOW and SEINFELD, which cover similar ground, *Kelly Monteith* is a sitcom about a comedian who works at home. His days are filled with observations on the absurdities of life and the unfortunate events that befall him. Monologues to the camera are complemented by journeys outside the apartment for sketches that illustrate the star's message about this little grievance or that strange predicament. Sharing his flat for the first two series is his wife (played by Gabrielle Drake), but thereafter the marriage breaks up and Monteith pursues a bachelor lifestyle (in an echo of events taking place in the star's real life at around the same time), but not without many a mishap. By the time of the last series, it is openly conceded that his home is actually a television stage and a production team is introduced to underline this. This adds another dimension – a show within a show – with Monteith seen as the comedian in the flat, and then as himself off set. Support throughout comes from the likes of Victor Spinetti, Tony Anholt, Michael Stainton, Barry Gosney, Jacqueline Clarke, Percy Edwards, Louis Mansi, Philip Trewinnard, Joanna Van Gyseghem, Enn Reitel, John Barron, Trudie Styler, Pippa Page and Donald Gee.

American Kelly Monteith first caught the eye in the UK when he appeared a couple of times on Des O'Connor's chat show, and the stand-up comedian from St Louis, Missouri, gained a writing collaborator at the same time. Neil Shand was working on the O'Connor programme, helping guests shape their acts for the show, and it was with Shand that Monteith went on to develop this series. Ronnie Hazlehurst provides the music.

Kemp, Martin
(1961–)

Islington-born actor, now on his second career having run up 20 hit singles with Spandau Ballet, a group that also featured his older brother, Gary. As boys, the brothers had trained at the Anna Scher drama club, securing bit parts in TV series like JACKANORY, THE GLITTERING PRIZES and RUMPOLE OF THE BAILEY, and Kemp moved back into acting on the demise of the band. He secured roles in *Growing Rich, Highlander, Murder Between Friends*, THE BILL and SUPPLY AND DEMAND (DI Eddie McEwan) before joining the cast of EASTENDERS as Steve Owen. Since leaving Walford, he has starred in the dramas *Daddy's Girl* (Chris Cooper), *Serious and Organised* (DC Jack Finn), *Family* (Joey Cutler), THE BRIDES IN THE BATH (George Joseph Smith), *Can't Buy Me Love* (Alan Harris) and *Love Lies Bleeding* (Mark Terry), with guest spots in WHERE THE HEART IS and AGATHA CHRISTIE'S MARPLE. Kemp is married to Shirlie Holliman, one-time member of pop duo Pepsi and Shirlie.

Kemp, Ross
(1964–)

English actor, best known as the bullish Grant Mitchell in EASTENDERS (for ten years from 1989 and returning later). Previously, Kemp had played Graham Lodsworth, the son of Dolly Skilbeck, in EMMERDALE FARM and had been seen in various programmes, including BIRDS OF A FEATHER, LONDON'S BURNING, THE MANAGERESS and THE CHIEF. More recently, he has ventured into the wild for the survival documentary *Ross Kemp Alive in Alaska* and starred in the security guard story *Hero of the Hour* (Richie Liddle), the legal drama *In Defence* (Sam Lucas), as DC Jack Mowbray in *Without Motive* and in A CHRISTMAS CAROL (Eddie Scrooge). He was also Sgt Henno Garvie in ULTIMATE FORCE, Harry Fielding in *The Crooked Man* and Gavin Hughes/Frank Perry in *A Line in the Sand*. Other credits have included *One Foot in the Past*, a cameo in CITY CENTRAL (as a transvestite), the docu-soap *Paddington Green* (narrator) and EXTRAS (parodying himself).

Kendal, Felicity
CBE (1946–)

British actress, born in Warwickshire into a showbiz family and raised in India while her parents toured theatrically. Felicity, as a matter of course, joined them in their productions but found it hard, on return to Britain, to break into television. Among her earliest TV work was a WEDNESDAY PLAY entitled *The Mayfly and the Frog* and episodes of LOVE STORY, MAN IN A SUITCASE, THE PERSUADERS!, CRIME OF PASSION and EDWARD THE SEVENTH (Princess Vicky). However, her future was secured when she was cast in the first of a series of whimsical, independent female roles, beginning with Barbara Good in THE GOOD LIFE and continuing with Gemma Palmer in SOLO and Maxine in THE MISTRESS. In 1978 she appeared as Dorothy Wordsworth in *Clouds of Glory*, Ken Russell's biopic of the Lakeland poets. In the 1990s she was seen in THE CAMOMILE LAWN (Aunt Helena) and played Nancy Belasco, an American widow in Cambridge, in the sitcom HONEY FOR TEA. In 2003 she made her debut as gardening sleuth Rosemary Boxer in ROSEMARY AND THYME.

Kendall, Kenneth
(1924–)

A teacher immediately after the war, Kenneth Kendall joined the BBC in 1948 and became one of the Corporation's first three 'on screen' newsreaders in 1955. He stayed until 1961, when he left to go freelance and made rare guest appearances in dramas like THE TROUBLESHOOTERS, DOCTOR WHO and ADAM ADAMANT LIVES! He returned to the BBC in 1969 and left again 12 years later, after a shake-up of the main news bulletins, soon resurfacing in regional television and as host of Channel 4's popular TREASURE HUNT series. After retiring from television, he opened a restaurant on the Isle of Wight.

Kennedy, Sir Ludovic
(1919–)

British writer, journalist and presenter, one of ITN's first newscasters back in 1956. In 1958 and 1959 Kennedy stood unsuccessfully as Liberal parliamentary candidate for Rochdale (the first occasion being a by-election). In the 1960s he became a reporter on PANORAMA and also worked on TONIGHT, 24 HOURS, THIS WEEK and *Midweek*. He was the first host of the review programme DID YOU SEE . . . ? and has also presented QUESTION TIME. In 1972 he chaired the controversial debate *A Question of Ulster*, and, in 1979, he secured a frank interview with Lord Mountbatten only weeks before his untimely death. Kennedy also contributed to the BBC's GREAT RAILWAY JOURNEYS OF THE WORLD (New York–Los Angeles). He married ballerina Moira Shearer in 1950, has written numerous books (including the exposé of the Christie murders, *10 Rillington Place*) and has been a campaigner against miscarriages of justice and for voluntary euthanasia.

Kennedy, Sarah
MBE (1950–)

Blonde British presenter of GAME FOR A LAUGH, BUSMAN'S HOLIDAY, *Classmates, Daytime, Collector's Lot* and various animal series. She was one of the shortlived *Sixty Minutes* team which took over from NATIONWIDE, and also broadcasts regularly on radio.

Kerr, Graham

(1934–)

As host of *Entertaining With Kerr: the Galloping Gourmet* in the late 1960s, Sussex-raised Graham Kerr became a housewives' favourite and made swilling wine part of a TV cook's repertoire long before Keith Floyd raised a glass in anger. His 'Galloping Gourmet' nickname came from his mad-dash cooking style and the fact that he tore around the set. Kerr's rise to fame began in New Zealand after a career in military catering, picking up pace when he moved to Australia. His TV series were largely produced by his wife, Treena Kerr. In later years, Kerr reined back his ultra-rich recipes and began to present low-fat cookery programmes in the USA.

Key Grip

See *Grip*.

Kick up the Eighties, A ★★★

UK (BBC) Comedy. BBC 2 1981; 1984

Richard Stilgoe, Tracey Ullman, Ron Bain, Miriam Margolyes, Roger Sloman, Rik Mayall, Robbie Coltrane

Producers **Tom Gutteridge, Colin Gilbert**

● ***Comedy sketch show introducing a host of new talent.***

A product of BBC Scotland's comedy department, which was later to contribute NAKED VIDEO among other programmes, *A Kick up the Eighties* featured humorist Richard Stilgoe anchoring a series of offbeat sketches. Tracey Ullman, Miriam Margolyes and Robbie Coltrane (who replaced Stilgoe in the second series) all gained valuable early exposure from the series, as did Rik Mayall, billed under his alter ego of Kevin Turvey, a boring Brummie who delivered a pointless monologue each week. Turvey was also featured in a one-off spoof documentary, *Kevin Turvey – the Man behind the Green Door* (1982).

Kids from 47A, The ★★

UK (ATV) Children's Comedy Drama. ITV 1973–5

Jess Gathercole	**Christine McKenna**
Willy Gathercole	**Nigel Greaves**
Binny Gathercole	**Gaynor Hodgson**
George Gathercole	**Russell Lewis**
Mrs Gathercole	**Mary MacLeod**
Mrs Batty	**Maryann Turners**
Mrs Grubb	**Peggyann Clifford**
Miss East	**Joan Newell**
Mr Stephens	**Lloyd Lamble**
Miss Hayes	**Susan Brown**

Creator **Charlotte Mitchell**
Producer **Alan Coleman**

● ***Four children survive on their own after their mother is taken ill.***

When their widowed mother suddenly needs to go into hospital, the four Gathercole children believe they can cope at home until Aunt Olive arrives to look after them. Unfortunately, their aunt never shows up, which presents the kids with a dilemma: should they struggle on alone, or would they be better off in the care of social services? There is only one answer as far as they are concerned, so they decide to battle it out, trying to quell intra-family squabbles and at the same time keep the authorities off their backs as much as possible. Luckily, Jess (16) works in an office, so there is some income, plus a more or less adult voice in the household (flat 47A). She is supported by 14-year-old Willy, when he is not playing soccer. Binny (12) does her bit around the house while dreaming of becoming a romantic novelist, which leaves eight-year-old George to act more than his age and to cause as little trouble as he can for his elder siblings (easier said than done). Balancing the multiple concerns of schoolwork, shopping, bill paying and other domestic chores with the help of social workers, friends and colleagues, the kids muddle through until tragedy strikes at the start of series two. Mum dies and the kids know they are in this for the long term. Mrs Batty is their annoying neighbour at first, but she is soon replaced by Mrs Grubb.

Creator Charlotte Mitchell insisted that this was no fairy tale, stressing that social workers would rather maintain a parentless family as a unit than see it dispersed over several homes and therefore that the underlying premiss of *The Kids from 47A* was quite authentic. Writers included Phil Redmond, John Kane and Lynda Marchal (Lynda La Plante).

Kielty, Patrick

(1971 –)

Northern Irish comedian and presenter of reality, game and chat shows. In his home province, he has hosted *PK Tonight*, while nationwide he has been seen at the helm of programmes like *After the Break, Last Chance Lottery*, THE NATIONAL LOTTERY BIG TICKET, *Patrick Kielty Almost Live, Stupid Punts*, FAME ACADEMY and *Celebrity Love Island*.

Killer

See *Taggart*.

Killer Net ★★

UK (La Plante) Drama. Channel 4 1998
DVD: Contender

Scott Miller	**Tam Williams**
Joe Hunter	**Paul Bettany**
Susie	**Emily Woof**
Charlotte 'Charlie' Thorpe	**Cathy Brolly**
'Scruffy'	**Simon Meacock**
Dome	**Gareth Marks**
DJ Brent	**Jason Orange**
Robin Butler-Cook	**Mark Tandy**
DS Collingwood	**Christopher Neame**
DI Colby	**Richard McCabe**

Writer/Producer **Lynda La Plante**

● ***A student discovers the dangers that lurk on the Internet.***

Scott Miller is a psychology student in Brighton. However, his work begins to suffer when he spends more and more time wrapped up in his computer. It is a pastime that eventually leads him into serious trouble, especially when he discovers Killer Net, a sinister Web game that helps users carry out the perfect murder. As he browses the Web, Scott meets the mysterious and erotic Charlotte. The prospect is exciting at first but his life changes for ever when Charlotte is found murdered and he is a key suspect, having played the on-line game. A study of the seedier side of the Internet, this four-part Lynda La Plante drama was directed by Geoff Sax. However, it received much flak from some quarters for its excessive sex scenes and technical errors.

Kilroy-Silk, Robert

(1942–)

Former Labour MP who, after the publication of his book, *Hard Labour*, branched out into daytime TV talk shows with *Day by Day*, which was soon renamed *Kilroy*. He also hosted the quickly cancelled quiz *Shafted*. He returned to politics by becoming a Member of the European Parliament, initially representing the UK Independence Party, and later founded a new party, Veritas, resigning its leadership soon after the 2005 general election.

Kind of Living, A ✱✱

UK (Central) Situation Comedy. ITV 1988; 1990

Trevor Beasley	**Richard Griffiths**
Carol Beasley	**Frances de la Tour**
Brian Thompson	**Tim Healy**
Ken Dixon	**C. J. Allen**
Og	**Christopher Rothwell**
Tedstill	**Alec Christie**
Linda	**Anita Carey**
Baby Joe	**Luke Freeman**

Writer **Paul Makin**
Producer **Glen Cardno**

● ***A frustrated schoolmaster fails to look on the bright side of life.***

Trevor Beasley is a stick-in-the mud. A middle-aged schoolteacher, with a lot on his plate, he can't help whinging about his lot, at home and in the staffroom. (Others might say he has much to look forward to: a new house, a new job and a new baby – so far only named 'Og'.) Beasley has just moved south to London from Bolton with his downtrodden wife, Carol, but she eventually has her fill of Trevor's chauvinism, finds a new career and heads off for a new life. This leaves Trevor to return north alongside his long-time friend, Brian Thompson. Back in Bolton, he meets up with Brian's sister, Linda, who Brian thinks might make a good match for his stuffy pal. Baby Joe is Linda's young son. Three series were produced.

Kind of Loving, A ✱✱

UK (Granada) Drama. ITV 1982

Vic Brown	**Clive Wood**
Ingrid Rothwell/Brown	**Joanne Whalley**
Mr Brown	**Robert Keegan**
Mrs Brown	**Constance Chapman**
Jim Brown	**Richard Tolan**
Jimmy Slade	**Bernard Strother**
Albert Conroy	**Neil Phillips**
David Lester	**Patrick Nyland**
Christine Lester	**Cherith Mellor**
Willy Lomas	**Ashley Barker**
Mrs Rothwell	**Clare Kelly**
Mr Van Huyten	**John Gabriel**
Donna Pennyman	**Susan Penhaligon**
Franklyn	**Derek Benfield**
Miriam Graham	**Hilary Tindall**
Hedley Graham	**Peter Halliday**
Janice Wheeler	**Karen Davies**

Creator/Writer **Stan Barstow**
Producer **Pauline Shaw**

● ***A Yorkshire lad's life is dominated by a strained marriage.***

In ten episodes, taking the story from December 1957 through till October 1973, *A Kind of Loving* relates events in the life of Vic Brown, a miner's son from the West Riding of Yorkshire. Brown's life soon takes a wayward course when he falls for Ingrid Rothwell, a young typist in the engineering firm where he works as a draughtsman. A shotgun marriage ensues but the relationship struggles as the years pass, not least because of Ingrid's mother's interference. Brown is offered a job and the chance to move south, to Longford, Essex, but this adds to his marital stress, especially when he begins an affair with local rep actress Donna Pennyman. The years continue to tick by and we ultimately encounter Vic in 1973, when, as a high-flying businessman, his eye for the ladies remains unshielded, leading to yet more trouble.

The series, directed by Jeremy Summers, was scripted by Stan Barstow from his own successful novel and its two sequels, *The Watchers on the Shore* and *The Right True End*. Music was supplied by Derek Hilton. Twenty years earlier, *A Kind of Loving* had been turned into a film by John Schlesinger, with a script from Keith Waterhouse and Willis Hall. It starred Alan Bates, June Ritchie and Thora Hird.

King, Claire

(1963–)

Yorkshire-born actress whose major roles have been as Kim Tate in EMMERDALE and Karen Betts in BAD GIRLS. Other parts have been in series such as BABES IN THE WOOD, DOWN TO EARTH, DALZIEL AND PASCOE, *The Courtroom*, *The Afternoon Play*, HOLBY CITY, DONOVAN and HOLLYOAKS.

King, Dave

(1929–2002)

Middlesex-born comedian, actor and singer, a big name in the 1950s and early 1960s. He hosted his own series, *The Dave King Show*, for both BBC and ITV, and, after some time in the States, returned to star in another comedy, *Dave's Kingdom*. After small roles in THE SWEENEY, HAZELL, PENNIES FROM HEAVEN and MINDER, he once again took centre stage in *Fancy Wanders*, an off-beat comedy in which he played Fancy, a philosophizing unemployed man. He was later seen in THE PROFESSIONALS, BERGERAC, RUMPOLE OF THE BAILEY, BLEAK HOUSE (Sgt George), PERFECT SCOUNDRELS, CORONATION STREET (Jack Duckworth's brother, Clifford) and HEARTBEAT, among other offerings.

King, Larry

(Lawrence Zeiger; 1933–)

American journalist and radio and TV presenter, since 1985 host of the influential *Larry King Live* for CNN, which attracts all the top political names and allows viewers telephone access to them.

King and Castle ✶✶

UK (Thames) Drama. ITV 1986; 1988

Ronald King .... **Derek Martin**
David Castle .... **Nigel Planer**
Deirdre Aitken .... **Laura Davenport**
Mr Hodinett .... **Andrew Cruickshank**
Miss Wilmott .... **Mary Healey**

Creator **Ian Kennedy Martin**
Writers **Ian Kennedy Martin, Andy de la Tour, Nigel Planer**
Executive Producer **Lloyd Shirley**
Producers **Chris Burt, Peter Duguid**

● ***An unlikely duo run a debt collection agency in London.***
Bent copper Ronald King runs into trouble in the force and decides to form The Manor Debt Collection Agency with martial arts instructor David Castle. Castle, however, prefers his sideline in genealogical investigation and is initially reluctant to get involved. It turns out his concerns are justified. The work the partnership picks up extends well beyond the run-of-the-mill rent arrears, or even slow payment of catalogue money: one week it's intervening in a bitter divorce, the next recovering a floppy disk that can lead to a big pay day. Touted by some as a replacement for MINDER, thanks to its London humour and black economy setting, *King and Castle* sprang out of a pilot episode seen as part of the STORYBOARD anthology in 1985. Music was provided by Sound Lab, with vocals added by star Nigel Planer.

King of the Hill ✶✶✶

US (3 Arts/Film Roman/Deedle-Dee/Twentieth Century-Fox) Cartoon. Channel 4 1997–2000 (US: Fox 1997–2000)
DVD: Fox (Region 1 only)

Voices:
Hank Hill .... **Mike Judge**
Peggy Hill .... **Kathy Najimy**
Bobby Hill .... **Pamela Segall Adlon**
Luanne Platter .... **Brittany Murphy**
Dale Gribble .... **Johnny Hardwick**
Nancy Gribble .... **Ashley Gardner**
Joseph Gribble .... **Brittany Murphy**
Bill Dauterive .... **Stephen Root**
Boomhauer .... **Mike Judge**

Creators/Executive Producers **Mike Judge, Greg Daniels**

● ***Family life with a Texan redneck.***
Set in Arlen, Texas, *King of the Hill* is the story of Hank Hill, a 40-year-old, bespectacled salesman for Strickland Propane who harbours typically forthright Texan values. Hank shares his home with plain-looking, plain-speaking, supply-teacher wife Peggy, podgy 12-year-old son Bobby and Peggy's niece Luanne, a beauty student who has quit her own family's trailer home. Next door live the Gribbles: conspiracy theorist Dale, promiscuous wife Nancy and son Joseph. Among Hank's beer-guzzling buddies are slob divorcé Bill and the incomprehensible Boomhauer. Simply animated, *King of the Hill* is more a traditional suburban sitcom than a mere cartoon. The show's creators already had a track record: Mike Judge was responsible for *Beavis and Butthead*, while Greg Daniels had worked on THE SIMPSONS. In the UK, episodes aired first on Sky One.

King Rollo ✶

UK (King Rollo) Children's Entertainment. BBC 1980

Narrator **Ray Brooks**

Writer **David McKee**

● ***Whimsical stories about a genial king and his court.***
This collection of homely, colourful tales, crudely animated to give a jerky, quirky feel, concerns the good King Rollo, a bearded ruler who shares his castle with the auburn-haired Queen Gwen, the industrious Cook and the mysterious Magician – a bespectacled man sporting flowing hooped robes and a giveaway pointed hat. Little excitement is to be found in each five-minute episode, unless the mischievous royal cat, Hamlet, has his way.

King's Royal ✶✶

UK (BBC) Drama. BBC 1 1982

Sir Fergus King .... **Tom Bell**
Rita King .... **Louie Ramsay**
Robert King .... **Eric Deacon**
Mrs Veitch .... **Anne Kristen**
Tom Hoey .... **John Vine**
Gwen Hoey .... **Sally Osborn**
Fiona Fraser .... **Heather Moray**
Roderick Fraser .... **James Copeland**
Mary Devine .... **Alyson Spiro**
Father Campbell .... **Patrick Troughton**
Morrison .... **Andrew Keir**
James King .... **Simon Cowell-Parker**

Writers **Ewart Alexander, Michael Elder**
Producer **Geraint Morris**

● ***The fortunes of a Scottish whisky dynasty.***
Fergus King lives in Glasgow during Victorian times. An orphan, he has used the city's prosperity, gained through sugar and tobacco trading, and exploited the poor, to earn himself a respectable place in society. His family, however, is not so admiring. Son Robert is shrewd. He's the man who creates blended whisky, mixing cheap and quality spirits to produce a refined bottled drink that greatly enhances the family's wealth. Tom Hoey, married to Fergus's daughter, Gwen, is even less trustworthy. He uses the King empire to furnish himself with a comfortable lifestyle but indulges himself in women and wine. Family spats bubble to the top as King's Royal Whisky becomes all the rage and Fergus is knighted from above but undermined from below. This ten-part serial was based on a novel by John Quigley.

Kingston, Alex
(1963–)

English Shakespearean actress seen in series like THE KNOCK (Katherine Roberts) and CROCODILE SHOES (Caroline Carrlson), but making her mark in the title role of MOLL FLANDERS. She then moved to America to take the part of Dr Elizabeth Corday in ER. Back in Britain, she assumed the title role in the drama BOUDICA. Earlier small roles had come in GRANGE HILL, THE BILL and SOLDIER, SOLDIER, while a recent guest appearance was in *Without a Trace*. Her first husband was actor Ralph Fiennes.

Kinnear, Roy

(1934–88)

Wigan-born comedian and actor, originally a member of the THAT WAS THE WEEK THAT WAS team and later moving on to star in his own sitcoms, usually portraying breathless, sweaty types. The highlights were *A Slight Case of . . .* (smooth talker H. A. Wormsley), *A World of His Own* (daydreamer Stanley Blake), INSIDE GEORGE WEBLEY (George, a perpetual worrier), *Cowboys* (building firm manager Joe Jones), *The Clairvoyant* (title character Arnold Bristow), *No Appointment Necessary* (greengrocer/hairdresser Alf Butler) and the ill-fated HARDWICKE HOUSE (headmaster Mr R. G. Wickham). Kinnear also supported hosts of other actors (such as Dick Emery and then Willie Rushton in *Rushton's Illustrated*) in their series. His credits included TILL DEATH US DO PART, THE AVENGERS, THE GOODIES, THE SWEENEY, CASUALTY, MINDER (Whaley), GEORGE AND MILDRED (George's friend, Jerry). *The Incredible Mr Tanner* (Sidney) and the animations *Bertha* (narrator) and SUPERTED (voice of Bulk). Kinnear died in 1988 while shooting the film *The Return of the Musketeers* in Spain, when his horse slipped and fell, throwing him to the ground.

Kinvig ✱✱

UK (LWT) Situation Comedy. ITV 1981

Des Kinvig .... **Tony Haygarth**
Netta Kinvig .... **Patsy Rowlands**
Jim Piper .... **Colin Jeavons**
Miss Griffin .... **Prunella Gee**
Mr Horsley .... **Patrick Newell**
Buddo .... **Simon Williams**

Creator/Writer **Nigel Kneale**
Producer **Les Chatfield**

● ***An electrical repairman is whisked off to Mercury by a sexy spacewoman.***

Des Kinvig leads a mundane life. Running a back-street electrical repair shop in Bingleton, married to the suffocating Netta and sharing his home with a giant dog named Cuddley, this is one man in urgent need of excitement. It arrives in the form of shapely alien Miss Griffin, who persuades Des to join her on trips to Mercury. There, they and the 500-year-old Buddo team up against an ant-like race called the Xux, who aim to take over Earth by giving humans the power to bend cutlery and by flooding the planet with humanoid robots.

Played for laughs, the storyline leaves viewers wondering whether it has all been a figment of Des's imagination, sparked off by UFO discussions with his anoraky friend, Jim Piper. Creator Nigel Kneale was the writer of 1984 and QUATERMASS in the 1950s.

Kirwan, Dervla

(1971–)

Dublin-born actress who appeared in the series *Troubles* as a teenager but whose first major role was in Melvyn Bragg's controversial drama *A Time to Dance* (Bernadette Kennedy). She then starred as Phoebe Bamford in GOODNIGHT SWEETHEART and as Assumpta Fitzgerald in BALLYKISSANGEL, quitting both roles before the series ended. She has also featured in *The Dark Room* (Jinx Kingsley), *Mr White Goes to Westminster* (Pam), *Eureka Street* (Aoirghe). *The Flint Street Nativity* (Gabriel), *The Greatest Store in the World* (Geraldine), *Happy Birthday Shakespeare* (Kate Green), Sky One's *The Bombmaker*, HEARTS AND BONES (Emma Rose), *The Deputy* (Terri Leonard), 55 DEGREES NORTH (Claire Maxwell) and CASANOVA (Casanova's mother). Guest appearances have come in series like RANDALL AND HOPKIRK (DECEASED) and DALZIEL AND PASCOE.

Kiss Me Kate ✱✱

UK (BBC Carlton) Situation Comedy. BBC 1 1998–2000

Kate Salinger .... **Caroline Quentin**
Douglas .... **Chris Langham**
Mel .... **Amanda Holden**
Craig .... **Darren Boyd**
Tony .... **Cliff Parisi**
Alex .... **Holly Atkins**
Iain .... **Bill Nighy**
Jo .... **Elizabeth Renihan**

Writers **Chris Langham, John Morton**
Producer **Nick Symons**
Executive Producer **Geoffrey Perkins**

● ***A counsellor finds more trouble in her own life than in her clients'.***

Kate Salinger, a single psychotherapist in her thirties, runs a counselling service but is called on to help her colleagues in the office more than her fee-paying clients. Of greatest concern is business partner Douglas, a man with a ton of worries on his shoulders and an unrequited passion for Kate. Completely disorganized, Douglas even manages to lose his home and ends up sharing Kate's flat above the office. Also needing a careful hand is Mel, their slightly dippy receptionist, especially when she is in the company of Craig, the completely dense travel agent who becomes her boyfriend, after unsuccessfully pursuing Kate. To escape from the mental pressures of the office, the troupe often decamp to the local wine bar, run by Tony, although a more sober alternative is offered in later episodes when Café Coffee, with its stoic serving girl Jo, becomes the break-time hangout. Also seen is Iain, Douglas's effortlessly over-achieving brother, a heart surgeon who instantly steals Kate's heart. Painstakingly compiled by co-star Chris Langham and his writing colleague, John Morton. *Kiss Me Kate* is a running farce, deriving its humour from complicated misunderstandings and smart cross-talk.

Kit Curran Radio Show, The/Kit Curran ✱✱

UK (Thames) Situation Comedy. ITV 1984/Channel 4 1986

Kit Curran .... **Denis Lawson**
Les Toms .... **Paul Brooke**
Damien Appleby .... **Clive Merrison**
Roland Simpson .... **Brian Wilde**
Sally Beamish .... **Debbi Blythe**
Pamela Scott .... **Lindsay Duncan** *(Kit Curran)*

Writers **Andy Hamilton, Guy Jenkin**
Producers **Derrick Goodwin, Anthony Parker** *(Kit Curran)*

● ***An ignorant radio presenter is a small time conman.***

Kit Curran is the top DJ at the modest independent station Radio Newtown – the archetypal big fish in a small pond. However, he's an arrogant, self-obsessed sort, a compulsive liar with no respect for his listeners. All that concerns him is how to make a fast buck and if it means bending the rules to do so, that won't bother him, as he proves time and again over six episodes, much to the disapproval of his new boss, Roland Simpson. For series two, Kit has been ousted from his job and, while planning to set up his own station, uses his communication skills as a 'businessman', joined by two of his former colleagues, Les Toms and newsreader Damien Appleby. They form Curran Associates Incorporated and set up base in Brentford, where they dabble in assorted money-grabbing schemes, from double glazing to matchmaking. Disapproval comes from new 'associate' Pamela Scott. This second run of six episodes was simply titled *Kit Curran* and aired on Channel 4.

Kitchen, Michael

(1948–)

Leicester-born actor in many lead and supporting roles. Highlights include *The Brontës of Haworth* (Branwell), Stephen Poliakoff's single drama CAUGHT ON A TRAIN (Peter), *The Guilty* (Steven Vey), TO PLAY THE KING (The King), *Dandelion Dead* (Major Herbert Armstrong), *The Buccaneers* (Sir Helmsley Thwaite), *Wilderness* (Luther Adams), THE HANGING GALE (Townsend), SUNNYSIDE FARM (Ezekiel Letchworth), RECKLESS (Richard Crane), *A Royal Scandal* (Lord Malmesbury), *The Secret World of Michael Fry* (Herbie), OLIVER TWIST (Mr Brownlow), *Lorna Doone* (Judge Jeffreys), A&E (Jack Turner), THE RAILWAY CHILDREN (Father), *Alibi* (Greg), *Falling* (Henry Kent) and FOYLE'S WAR (Det. Chief Supt. Christopher Foyle). Other roles have come in offerings such as FALL OF EAGLES, *Beasts*, *Kidnapped*, *Brimstone and Treacle*, *The Browning Version*, *Doomsday Gun*, FREUD, *Love Song*, *Ball-Trap on the Côte Sauvage*, *Rik Mayall Presents*, INSPECTOR MORSE, PIE IN THE SKY, A TOUCH OF FROST, DALZIEL AND PASCOE and SECOND SIGHT. Kitchen has also narrated FAKING IT.

Klugman, Jack

(1922–)

American actor, star of TV version of THE ODD COUPLE (Oscar Madison) and even better known as the grouchy pathologist QUINCY. In a long television career, Klugman has appeared in kids' shows, plays and early cult series like THE TWILIGHT ZONE, NAKED CITY, BEN CASEY and THE DEFENDERS. His first starring role was in a comedy not seen in the UK, *Harris against the World*. Klugman also played Henry Willows in *You Again?*, a US translation of the sitcom HOME TO ROOST.

Kneale, Nigel

(1922–)

Isle of Man-born BBC staff writer and script reader who helped shift the goal posts of TV drama through his adventurous 1953 thriller *The* QUATERMASS *Experiment*. A year later, Kneale was responsible for the graphic adaptation of Orwell's *1984*, which caused a storm in Parliament. His next major work was *Quatermass II* in 1955, joined by *Quatermass and the Pit* in 1958. Kneale continued to lean on the boundaries of acceptability with plays like THE YEAR OF THE SEX OLYMPICS and *Wine of India* (a WEDNESDAY PLAY, 1970), before leaving the BBC in 1975 to work for ITV. *Beasts*, an anthology of chillers involving animals, was aired in 1976, and *Quatermass* was revived for Euston Films in 1979, before Kneale attempted comedy with the sci-fi sitcom KINVIG in 1981. *The Quatermass Experiment* was brought back again as a live TV experiment in 2005 and among Kneale's other more recent works have been *The Woman in Black*, *Stanley and the Women* and episodes of SHARPE and KAVANAGH QC, with other notable credits over the years including an adaptation of *Wuthering Heights* (1953), *The Creature* (1955), *The Road* (part of the *First Night* anthology, 1963), *The Crunch* (from *Studio '64*, 1964), *The Chopper* (for *Out of the Unknown* in 1971) and THE STONE TAPE.

Knight Errant ✶✶

UK (Granada) Adventure. ITV 1959–61

Adam Knight	**John Turner**
Liz Parrish	**Kay Callard**
Peter Parker	**Richard Carpenter**
Toby Hollister	**William Fox**
Stephen Drummond	**Hugh David**
Frances Graham	**Wendy Williams**
Gregory Wilson	**Stephen Cartwright**
Col. Cope-Addams	**Alan Webb**

Creator **Philip Mackie**
Producers **Warren Jenkins, Kitty Black**

A newspaper advertisement leads to a life of adventure for a modern-day crusader.

Adam Knight, a meanderer between jobs, bites the bullet and decides to work for himself, placing a newspaper advert which reads: 'Knight Errant '59. Quests undertaken, dragons defeated, damsels rescued. Anything, anywhere, for anyone, so long as it helps. Fees according to means.' The result is a series of interesting and diverse cases, revolving around other people's problems.

Joining Adam in his Knight Errant agency are ex-*Daily Clarion* journalist Liz Parrish and young writer Peter Parker. A later addition to the team is Adam's new business consultant, Toby Hollister, a spirits tycoon. When Adam leaves for Canada to run his uncle's farm, he is replaced as agency boss by Stephen Drummond, a publisher with little time for his true profession. Drummond's secretary, Frances Graham, also arrives. Peter Parker then returns to his writing and is substituted by Greg Wilson and a retired army man, Colonel Cope-Addams, adds military experience to the set-up.

The first series was entitled *Knight Errant '59*, becoming *Knight Errant '60* when the year changed. After Adam Knight's departure, the programme was renamed *Knight Errant Limited*. Richard Carpenter, who played Peter Parker, switched career himself, from acting to writing, moving on to create series like CATWEAZLE and DICK TURPIN.

Knight Rider ✶✶

US (Universal/Glen A. Larson) Science Fiction. ITV 1983–7
(US: NBC 1982–6)
DVD: Universal

Michael Knight	**David Hasselhoff**
Devon Miles	**Edward Mulhare**
Bonnie Barstow	**Patricia McPherson**
April Curtis	**Rebecca Holden**
KITT	**William Daniels** *(voice)*
Reginald Cornelius III ('RC3')	**Peter Parros**

Creator/Producer **Glen A. Larson**

An ex-cop rights wrongs with the help of a supercar.

Michael Long, a young police officer, is shot in the face and left for dead. To his rescue comes Wilton Knight, a millionaire industrialist (played in the opening episode by Richard Basehart) who himself has little time to live. Long undergoes plastic surgery to repair his features and, in respect for his saviour, changes his name to Michael Knight. When the millionaire dies, he leaves his estate to Michael for the benefit of the fight against crime, and Michael accepts the bequest with relish.

As part of the inheritance, Michael takes possession of an amazing, computerized black car, known as the Knight Industries Two Thousand, or KITT for short. KITT is not only capable of speeds over 300 m.p.h. and equipped with an armoury of lethal weapons, it also talks, has a moody personality and comes whenever Michael needs it. With such a trusty steed, Knight, not surprisingly, often succeeds in his fight for justice.

Knight's helpers are Devon Miles, manager of the dead millionaire's estate, and a mechanic, Bonnie Barstow, who is temporarily replaced by April Curtis and then the laid-back RC3. They operate from a base known as the Foundation for Law and Government in California and follow KITT and Knight in a large support van. (KITT, despite its flashy appearance, was no more than a souped-up Pontiac Trans Am.)

Knightmare ✶✶

UK (Anglia/Broadsword) Children's Game Show. ITV 1987–94

Treguard .... **Hugo Myatt**
Merlin/Mogdred .... **John Woodnutt**
Olgarth/Granitas/Troll .... **Guy Standeven**
Lillith/Mildread .... **Mary Miller**
Monk/Casper/Cedric .... **Lawrence Werber**
Folly/Gibbet .... **Alec Westwood**
Dwarf/Olaf/Mrs Grimwold .... **Tom Karol**
Gretel .... **Audrey Jenkinson**
Sir Gumboil/The Knight .... **Edmund Dehn**
Golgarach/McGrew .... **David Verrey**
Mellisandre/Oracle .... **Zoe Loftin**
Velda/Brangwen/Morghanna **Natasha Pope**
Motley .... **Paul Valentine**
Hordriss the Confuser .... **Clifford Norgate**
Pickle .... **David Learner**
Michael Cule
Gundrada .... **Samantha Perkins**
Erin Geraghty
Gwendoline .... **Juliet Henry-Massey**
Lord Fear/Ah Wok .... **Mark Knight**
Skarkill/Julius Scaramonger ... **Rayner Bourton**
Elita .... **Stephanie Hesp**
Sidriss/Greystagg .... **Iona Kennedy**
Capt. Nemanor/Ridolfo .... **Adrian Neil**
Majida .... **Jackie Sawiris**
The Brollachan .... **Anthony Donovan** *(voice)*

Creator/Writer **Tim Child**
Producers **Sally Freeman, Tim Child**

● ***Dungeons and dragons for kids.***

Taking advantage of emerging computer-generated imagery and well-established chroma key techniques, *Knightmare* was an adventure game for four children. One donned a special helmet and was sent off into a superimposed labyrinth of castle rooms, caves, forests, dungeons, etc. to follow a quest, while the other three guided him/her from a studio, aided by Treguard, the Dungeon Master, assisted at various times by Pickle the elf and Majida, an Arabic genie. By working out riddles and overcoming challenges the team hoped to win a prize (not something that happened often). Standing in their way was a repertory company of actors adopting various magical disguises (some benign, some malevolent) such as Mogdred the necromancer, Morghanna and Sidriss the sorceresses, Folly and Motley the jesters, Gretel the maid, Gundrada the swordmistress, Skarkill the Goblin Master and Lord Fear.

The brainchild of reporter and producer Tim Child, the series was initially made by Anglia before Child's own company, Broadsword, took over production.

Knights of God ✶✶

UK (TVS) Children's Science Fiction. ITV 1987

Gervase .... **George Winter**
Julia .... **Claire Parker**
Owen .... **Gareth Thomas**
Mordrin .... **John Woodvine**
Hugo .... **Julian Fellowes**
Arthur .... **Patrick Troughton**
Beth .... **Shirley Stelfox**
Colley .... **Don Henderson**
Williams .... **John Vine**
Brig. Clarke .... **Barrie Cookson**
Dai .... **Owen Teale**
Tyrell .... **Peter Childs**

Writer **Richard Cooper**
Executive Producer **Anna Home**
Producer **John Dale**

● ***In the chaotic future, a teenager joins a rebellion against the autocratic ruling regime.***

The year is 2020. Britain has experienced a bitter civil war, seen its royal family deposed and is now ruled by the so-called Knights of God. But this brutal, dictatorial regime has plenty of enemies and the people begin to fight back against its religious and social impositions. The Resistance plots to overthrow the rulers and restore the monarchy, but these are dangerous times and there are many casualties. Prominent in the rebellion is Gervase, a young man who has been hypnotized by the evil Mordrin, leader of the Knights. He has been instilled with an important command, but will he carry it out? Julia is the girl to whom our hero is devoted. Part-medieval, part-futuristic, this well-received, adventurous, 13-part series – a rare Sunday teatime offering from TVS – was written by one-time Tyneside drama lecturer Richard Cooper.

Knock, The ✶✶

UK (LWT/Bronson/Knight) Drama. ITV 1994; 1996–7; 1999–2000

Bill Adams .... **Malcolm Storry**
Gerry Birch .... **David Morrissey**
George Webster .... **Anthony Valentine**
Nicki Lucas .... **Suzan Crowley**
Barry Christie .... **Steve Toussaint**
Jo Chadwick .... **Tracy Whitwell**
Arnie Rheinhardt .... **Marston Bloom**
George Andreotti .... **Enzo Squillino Jr**
Diane Ralston .... **Caroline Lee Johnson**
Eddie Barton .... **Jack Ellis**
Kevin Butcher .... **Andrew Dunn**
Tommy Maddern .... **Ian Burfield**
Katherine Roberts .... **Alex Kingston**
Allan Montfort .... **Oliver Tobias**
Alex Murray .... **Daniel Brown**
Jake Munro .... **Daniel O'Grady**
David Ancrom .... **Mark Lewis Jones**

Lynn Hickson	**Sarah Malin**
Glen Vaughan	**Peter O'Brien**
Rob Maguire	**Jonathan Kerrigan**
Jessica Haworth	**Michelle Morris**

Executive Producer **David Newcombe**
Producers **Anita Bronson, Paul Knight, Philip Leach**

A team of customs officers go undercover to foil smuggling rackets.

The Knock focuses on the London-based City and South team of Customs and Excise officers, whose job it is to root out the most sophisticated attempts to bring drugs, arms, jewellery and other illegal or counterfeit goods into the UK. Head of the squad is Bill Adams, later replaced by David Ancrom. In a selection of mostly three- and four-part stories, the team travel the world in search of their prey, hoping to nail such villains as gold smuggler George Webster, gangster Tommy Maddern and wheeler-dealer Allan Montfort. Other guest criminals are played by Dennis Waterman, Cherie Lunghi and Michael Brandon. In 2000 a new task force is introduced. Codenamed Indigo, it features stalwarts Diane Ralston, Barry Christie and Alex Murray, alongside new colleagues, under new, hard-line boss Glen Vaughan. The series was supposedly inspired by the documentary series *The Duty Men*.

Knots Landing **

US (Lorimar/Roundlay/MF) Drama. BBC 1 1980–3; 1986–94 (US : CBS 1979–93)

Gary Ewing	**Ted Shackleford**
Valene Ewing/Gibson/Waleska	**Joan Van Ark**
Sid Fairgate	**Don Murray**
Karen Fairgate/MacKenzie	**Michele Lee**
Richard Avery	**John Pleshette**
Laura Avery/Sumner	**Constance McCashin**
Kenny Ward	**James Houghton**
Ginger Ward	**Kim Lankford**
Diana Fairgate	**Claudia Lonow**
Michael Fairgate	**Pat Petersen**
Eric Fairgate	**Steve Shaw**
Jason Avery	**Justin Dana**
	Danny Gellis
	Danny Ponce
	Matthew Newmark
Abby Cunningham/Ewing/Sumner	**Donna Mills**
Brian Cunningham	**Bobby Jacoby**
	Brian Austin Green
Olivia Cunningham/Dyer	**Tonya Crowe**
Roy Lance	**Steven Hirsch**
Lilimae Clements	**Julie Harris**
Amy	**Jill Cohen**
Joe Cooper	**Stephen Macht**
M. Patrick (Mack) MacKenzie	**Kevin Dobson**
Ciji Dunne	**Lisa Hartman**
Chip Roberts	**Michael Sabatino**
Ben Gibson	**Douglas Sheehan**
Gregory Sumner	**William Devane**
Cathy Geary/Rush	**Lisa Hartman**
Mary-Frances Sumner	**Danielle Brisebois**
	Stacy Galina
Joshua Rush	**Alec Baldwin**
Paul Galveston	**Howard Duff**
Ruth Galveston	**Ava Gardner**
Peter Hollister	**Hunt Block**
Linda Martin	**Leslie Hope**
Jill Bennett	**Teri Austin**
Paige Matheson	**Nicollette Sheridan**
Tina	**Tina Lifford**
Peggy	**Victoria Ann-Lewis**
Marsha	**Marcia Solomon**
Anne Winston/Matheson	**Michelle Phillips**
Jean Hackney	**Wendy Fulton**
Russell Winston	**Harry Townes**
Al Baker	**Red Buttons**
Bobby Gibson	**Joseph Cousins**
	Christian Cousins
Betsy Gibson	**Kathryn and Tiffany Lubran**
	Emily Ann Lloyd
Carlos	**Carlos Cantu**
Jody Campbell	**Kristy Swanson**
Charles Scott	**Michael York**
Barbara	**Ronne Troup**
Ana	**Movita Castenada**
Johnny Rourke	**Peter Reckell**
Patricia Williams	**Lynne Moody**
Frank Williams	**Larry Riley**
Julie Williams	**Kent Masters-King**
Harold Dyer	**Paul Carafotes**
Bob Phillips	**Zane Lasky**
Mort Tubor	**Mark Haining**
Danny Waleska	**Sam Behrens**
Linda Fairgate	**Lar Park-Lincoln**
Virginia Bullock	**Betsy Palmer**
Paula Vertosick	**Melinda Culea**
Ted Melcher	**Robert Desiderio**
Amanda Michaels	**Penny Peyser**
Claudia Whittaker	**Kathleen Noone**
Kate Whittaker	**Stacy Galina**
Nick Schillace/Dimitri Pappas	**Lorenzo Caccialanza**
Jason Lochner	**Thomas Wilson Brown**
Dick Lochner	**Guy Boyd**
Tom Ryan	**Joseph Gian**
Steve Brewer	**Lance Guest**
Charlotte Anderson	**Tracy Reed**

Creator **David Jacobs**
Executive Producers **Lee Rich, Michael Filerman, David Jacobs**

Life, love, death and deception in a Californian cul-de-sac.

Having fled the excesses of DALLAS, Gary Ewing, his family's alcoholic black sheep, arrives in the small town of Knots Landing in California. Remarried to his estranged wife, Val, he settles down in a pleasant cul-de-sac, taking a job at Knots Landing Motors, a classic car dealership owned by one of his neighbours, Sid Fairgate. Sid and his wife, Karen, live with their three teenage children, Diana, Michael and Eric. Also on the close are scheming, lecherous attorney Richard Avery and Laura, his estate agent wife, as well as music executive Kenny Ward and his partner, Ginger. Soon to arrive is Sid's divorcée sister, Abby Cunningham. She moves into the cul-de-sac with her two children, Brian and Olivia, and quickly begins to spread gossip and seduce the menfolk.

So the scene is set, and against this backdrop the usual soap storylines develop, pitting characters against each other in romance, business and intrigue. Typically, there are murders, scandals, adulterous affairs and bitchy in-fighting, but *Knots Landing* doesn't stray too far off what is realistically possible, unlike its glossier contemporaries. Characters come, make a big splash and then disappear. Gregory Sumner stays longer than most. He is a dodgy senator with underworld connections who marries both Laura (divorced from Richard) and, later, Abby. The Williamses are other new arrivals, a black family hiding out under a witness protection scheme. Gradually, the neighbourhood's younger generation push their way to the fore, especially Michael Fairgate, Olivia Cunningham and Paige Matheson, the illegitimate daughter of Karen's new husband, attorney Mack MacKenzie (Sid is killed when his car drives off a cliff). Gary's brothers from *Dallas* pop into some episodes, and Gary and Val return the compliment by occasionally visiting Texas to see their wayward daughter, Lucy.

Despite winning praise for its 'ordinariness' (well, at least when compared with DYNASTY), *Knots Landing* didn't really catch on in the UK. The series was dropped by the BBC after just a few years, and when picked up again in 1986, it was given only an afternoon time-slot, not the Saturday evening prime time with which it began.

Knowing Me, Knowing You . . . With Alan Partridge ★★★

UK (Talkback/BBC) Comedy. BBC 2 1994–5
DVD: BBC

Alan Partridge	**Steve Coogan**
Glen Ponder	**Steve Brown**

Writers **Steve Coogan, Armando Iannucci, Patrick Marber**
Executive Producer **Peter Fincham**
Producer **Armando Iannucci**

Spoof chat show with an obnoxious host.

In this series, thematically inspired by the music of Abba, the hapless sports anchor from THE DAY TODAY branches out on his own. Alan Partridge, freshly blazered and slacked, is the host of a celebrity chat show played out on a set consciously modelled on the foyer of a posh hotel. Regrettably, events quickly descend into chaos every week, largely because of Partridge's ego, prejudices and incompetence. Interviewees – forced to respond with an 'Aha!' to a contrived greeting of 'Knowing me Alan Partridge, knowing you (guest's name), aha!' – are little aware at the outset of the grim experience facing them. Roped into cheesy stunts, they are also brutally embarrassed by tactless revelations from the crass host, but it is inevitably Partridge himself who has most egg on his face by the end of proceedings. The only named support is band leader Glen Ponder (played by real-life musical director Steve Brown), whose house band is given a different name each week and whom Partridge tries to engage in cringeworthy celebrity banter at the top of the show. Backing star Steve Coogan, by adopting a variety of guest disguises, are Patrick Marber, John Thomson, Rebecca Front, Doon Mackichan, David Schneider and others. As well as one series of six shows in 1994, a Christmas special (*Knowing Me, Knowing Yule*) was screened in 1995. After this debacle, the next viewers saw of the self-deluding front man was in the series I'M ALAN PARTRIDGE.

Knowles, Nick

(1962–)

Middlesex-born presenter of lifestyle programmes and quizzes. A former accounts clerk with the BBC, he became a researcher and then talked his way into news reporting for Australian television. Returning to the UK, he joined the TVS newsroom, later working also for Meridian and presenting regional programmes like *Ridge Riders*. His major credits include *Straight Up, 5's Company, Put It to the Test, Find a Fortune, Judgemental, DIY SOS, Historyonics, City Hospital, Secrets of Magic, Beckham Back in Time, A Land Worth Loving, You be the Judge* and *Departure Lounge*.

Knox, Barbara

(1933–)

Oldham-born actress, famous as CORONATION STREET's Rita Bates/Littlewood/Fairclough/Sullivan. Pre-Weatherfield, Knox (as Barbara Mullaney) had appeared in rep and on radio, as well as in series like EMERGENCY – WARD 10 (Nurse Fulton), MRS THURSDAY, THE DUSTBINMEN, NEVER MIND THE QUALITY, FEEL THE WIDTH, A FAMILY AT WAR and the pilot play for GIRLS ABOUT TOWN. Mullaney changed her name on marrying businessman John Knox in the late 1970s.

Kojak ★★

US (Universal) Police Drama. BBC 1 1974–8 (US: CBS 1973–8)
DVD: Universal

Lt. Theo Kojak	**Telly Savalas**
Capt. Frank McNeil	**Dan Frazer**
Lt. Bobby Crocker	**Kevin Dobson**
Det. Stavros	**George Savalas**
Det. Rizzo	**Vince Conti**
Det. Saperstein	**Mark Russell**
Det. Prince	**Borah Silver**

Creator **Abby Mann**
Executive Producer **Matthew Rapf**

Unorthodox police work with a no-nonsense, plain-clothes cop in New York City.

Theo Kojak is a distinctive kind of police officer. For starters, he sucks lollipops and wears fancy waistcoats. He calls people 'Pussycat' and, even more unusually, when he lifts his trilby, he reveals a magnificent shaven head. Once seen, he is never forgotten. His policing methods are rather unconventional, too. He works in the Manhattan South, 13th Precinct of the New York Police Department, where his boss, Frank McNeil, was once his partner. Kojak's refusal to play the police game by the book means that promotion has never come his way. Dry and cynical, he is always too ready to bend the rules, which needles his superiors. On the streets, Kojak is supported by another plain-clothes cop, Bobby Crocker, though his sharpest banter is reserved for Stavros, the overweight, bushy-haired detective played by Telly Savalas's brother, George (originally credited as 'Demosthenes', his middle name).

Kojak became a cult figure in the UK. Lollipop sales boomed and bald became beautiful. Kids strolled around asking, 'Who loves ya, baby?' echoing Kojak's catchphrase. Telly Savalas, although already an established character actor, was propelled to international stardom by the series and even broke into the pop charts, mumbling his way to number one in 1975 with a depressing rendition of David Gates's 'If'. After a couple of sequels in the mid-1980s, the character returned to the screens in a series of TV movies, by which time he had at last gained promotion to inspector. A revival of *Kojak*, starring black actor Ving Rhames, was broadcast from 2005 (ITV 4 in the UK).

Kolchak: The Night Stalker ★★

US (Francy/Universal) Science Fiction. ITV 1983–5 (US: ABC 1974–5)
DVD: Universal (Region 1 only)

Carl Kolchak .... **Darren McGavin**
Tony Vincenzo .... **Simon Oakland**
Ron Updyke .... **Jack Grinnage**
Emily Cowles .... **Ruth McDevitt**
Gordy Spangler .... **John Fielder**
Monique Marmelstein .... **Carol Ann Susi**

Creator **Jeff Rice**
Executive Producer **Darren McGavin**
Producers **Paul Playdon, Cy Chermak**

● ***A news reporter tracks down supernatural murderers.***

Carl Kolchak works for the Chicago-based Independent News Service (INS) as an investigative reporter. His speciality is murder and he finds himself stalking the most vicious, the most twisted and the most famous of killers, reciting his findings into a portable tape recorder. However, because Kolchak claims the guilty parties all belong to the supernatural world, his ulcer-prone boss, Tony Vincenzo, constantly spikes his reports. Tales of Jack the Ripper, out-of-control robots, werewolves and swamp monsters are just a little too hard to swallow, especially as these grisly fiends are seldom actually seen and Kolchak never produces photographic evidence. To add to Kolchak's discomfort, the authorities, too, are keen to hush things up. The series sprang from the success of two TV movies, *The Night Stalker* (in which Kolchak tracks down a Las Vegas vampire) and *The Night Strangler* (with the star on the trail of an ancient alchemist who lives in the eerie underground world of old Seattle). These in turn had been based on Jeff Rice's 1970 novel *The Kolchak Papers*. However, Rice objected when the weekly series began, claiming he hadn't given permission, and, consequently, only 20 episodes were made.

Kossoff, David

(1919–2005)

Softly spoken British actor/writer, prominent in the 1950s as hen-pecked Alf in THE LARKINS and in the 1960s as Marcus Lieberman, boss of the family furniture company, in A LITTLE BIG BUSINESS. Kossoff also took the role of the Sheriff of Nottingham in a 1953 version of *Robin Hood* and appeared in the very first ARMCHAIR THEATRE production, *The Outsider*, in 1956, among other plays. His guest appearances came in series like INTERPOL CALLING, THE SAINT, ESPIONAGE and LOVEJOY. Much later, he was seen telling Bible stories on STARS ON SUNDAY. He was the father of the late Paul Kossoff, guitarist with the rock band Free.

Krypton Factor, The ★★

UK (Granada) Quiz. ITV 1977–95

Presenters **Gordon Burns, Penny Smith**

Creator **Jeremy Fox**
Producers **Jeremy Fox, Stephen Leahy, David Jenkins, Geoff Moore, Patricia Pearson, Rod Natkiel, Kieran Roberts, Caroline Gosling, Wayne Garvie**

● ***Physical and mental contest to find Britain's 'superperson'.***

Taking its name from Superman's home planet, *The Krypton Factor* aimed to find Britain's brainiest and fittest quiz show contestant. Four contenders took part in each heat, progressing to semi-finals and then the Grand Final, in which *The Krypton Factor* champion was declared. They were subjected to tests of mental agility, intelligence, general knowledge and observation (using film clips and, for many years, an identity parade). An army assault course was used to assess physical strength and fitness (age and sex handicaps levelled the playing field), and a flight simulator was employed to gauge 'response'. Each contestant's final score was known as his or her Krypton Factor. Gordon Burns presented the show throughout its long run and was joined by Penny Smith as co-presenter in the final series in 1995.

A number of celebrity specials were produced over the years, as well as a few international challenge editions (this was the first UK quiz format to be sold to America). Ross King hosted a short-lived junior version, *Young Krypton*, in 1988.

Kumars at No. 42, The ★★★

UK (Hat Trick) Comedy. BBC 2 2001–4; BBC 1 2005
DVD: VCI

Sanjeev Kumar .... **Sanjeev Bhaskar**
Sushila .... **Meera Syal**
Madhuri Kumar .... **Indira Joshi**
Ashwin Kumar .... **Vincent Ebrahim**

Writers **Sanjeev Bhaskar, Richard Pinto, Sharat Sardana**
Executive Producers **Jimmy Mulville, Denise O'Donoghue, Anil Gupta**
Producers **Lissa Evans, Richard Pinto, Sharat Sardana, Anil Gupta, Helen Williams**

● ***Irreverent, Asian-style 'chat show'.***

Inevitably conjuring up the image of GOODNESS GRACIOUS ME meeting MRS MERTON, *The Kumars at No. 42* is part-sitcom, part-spoof chat show featuring an Asian family who live in the eponymous number 42 somewhere in Wembley. Behind the house they have constructed a TV studio to allow spoilt only son Sanjeev to conduct his own talk show. Fussy mum Madhuri, cash-obsessed dad Ashwin and crazy granny Sushila help to make his celebrity guests welcome and then join Sanjeev on the set, armed with barbed questions to hurl at the week's patsies, and largely improvising from a basic script. Among the famous faces that have rung the doorbell at number 42 and been ushered into the family home and then like lambs to the slaughter onto the studio stage are Michael Parkinson, Richard E. Grant, Graham Norton, Minnie Driver, Melvyn Bragg, Cliff Richard and Richard and Judy. Some episodes aired first on BBC Choice before being shown on BBC 2.

An attempt at a US version, featuring Mexicans and entitled *The Ortegas*, didn't even make it to air, although there was greater success around the world. In Australia, the series became *Greeks on the Roof* and similar nationality swaps took place as other countries picked up the concept.

Kung Fu ✶✶

US (Warner Brothers) Western. ITV 1973–6 (US: ABC 1972–5)
DVD: Warner Home Video

Kwai Chang Caine .... **David Carradine** *(adult)*
Radames Pera *(boy)*
Master Po .... **Keye Luke**
Master Kan .... **Philip Ahn**

Creator **Ed Spielman**
Executive Producer **Jerry Thorpe**
Producers **Herman Miller, Alex Beaton**

● ***A Chinese half-breed seeks his long-lost brother across the Wild West.***

A man of few words, peace-loving Kwai Chang Caine was born in Imperial China, son of an American sea-captain and a local woman. He grew up in a strict Buddhist temple, becoming a Shaolin priest and benefiting from the wisdom of great sages. There, he also learnt the martial art of Kung Fu. Having killed a member of the Chinese royal family (in self-defence), he flees to America in the 1870s to seek out his half-brother. However, with a price on his head, he is pursued from town to town by oriental hitmen and other bounty-hunters.

The softly spoken, somewhat spaced-out drifter enjoys the freedom of his own company and the pleasure of his own thoughts. He finds himself helping folk in trouble at every turn, but he is a reluctant hero and always the last to resort to violence, turning the other cheek as often as possible. However, a half-breed stumbling around in the violent Wild West is an easy target for bullies. So, when the situation calls for it (every episode), he is forced to draw on his fighting skills. With much of the action filmed in slow motion for effect, Caine effortlessly kicks and chops down his aggressors, often more than one at a time.

Intercut with flashbacks to his childhood, the programme also shows Caine learning his philosophical approach to life from Master Kan and the blind Master Po, the Buddhist priests who call him 'Grasshopper'. Each episode begins by recalling the tortuous initiation ceremony at the temple, Caine lifting a burning-hot cauldron with his wrists and so branding them with the mark of the dragon. The series stemmed from the success of the Kung Fu films made by master of the art, Bruce Lee. The concept was revived in 1993, in *Kung Fu: The Legend Continues*. Carradine this time played Caine's modern-day grandson, also called Kwai Chang Caine.

Kydd, Sam

(1917–82)

British character actor, a supporting player for many big names (from Arthur Askey to Tony Hancock) and a star in his own right on more than one occasion. Probably the highlight of his television career was the 1960s children's series ORLANDO, in which he played former smuggler Orlando O'Connor, a character first seen in the drama series CRANE. Among his earliest contributions was a 1950 version of *Toad of Toad Hall*. Kydd went on to appear in Harry Worth's first sitcom, *The Trouble with Harry*, play Bosun 'Croaker' Jones in *Mess Mates*, take the part of Smellie in the controversial Johnny Speight comedy CURRY AND CHIPS, and star as Herbert Quince, valet to Jimmy Edwards, in THE FOSSETT SAGA. He was Sam Weller in *The Pickwick Papers*, was seen in the kids' comedy TOTTERING TOWERS, and appeared in several ITV action series in the 1960s. One of his last appearances was as Mike Baldwin's father in CORONATION STREET. He was the father of actor Jonathan Kydd.

KYTV ✶✶

UK (BBC) Situation Comedy. BBC 2 1990; 1992–3

Mike Channel .... **Angus Deayton**
Mike Flex .... **Geoffrey Perkins**
Anna Daptor .... **Helen Atkinson Wood**
Martin Brown .... **Michael Fenton Stevens**
various characters .... **Philip Pope**

Writers **Angus Deayton, Geoffrey Perkins**
Producer **Jamie Rix**

● ***Mock satellite broadcasting with a fictitious TV station.***

KYTV is a spoof on the emerging satellite TV networks of the time, satirizing the programming, poking fun at their technical problems and parodying their broadcasters. The station is named after Sir Kenneth Yellowhammer, its founder and chairman, and the main presenters are Mike Channel, Mike Flex, Anna Daptor and the bumbling Martin Brown. Phil Pope provides the music as well as appearing as continuity announcer. The team sends up every aspect of programming, from travelogues and crime reports to God slots and election coverages. The one-off special *The Making of David Chizzlenut* gives viewers the chance to look behind the scenes of a TV classic.

KYTV was a follow-up to the same team's Radio 4 series, *Radio Active*, in which they mocked the standard of programming at some commercial radio stations.

L

L For Lester ✶✶

UK (BBC) Situation Comedy. BBC 2 1982

Lester Small	**Brian Murphy**
Mrs Davies	**Hilda Braid**
Sally Small	**Amanda Barrie**
Alf Bayley	**John Forgeham**
Bert	**Colin Spaull**
Mr Davies	**Richard Vernon**
Sid	**Tony Millan**
Chief Insp. Rodgers	**James Cossins**

Writer **Dudley Long**
Producer **Dennis Main Wilson**

● ***Townsfolk suffer at the hands of the local driving instructor.***

Lester Small is proprietor of a one-man driving school, The Lester Small School of Motoring. Regrettably, his haplessness and the ineptitude of his students means that no one is safe in the small West Country town in which he operates. Confrontations with local lawman Chief Inspector Rodgers inevitably ensue. Mrs Davies, wife of the local bank manager, is undoubtedly Lester's worst client. Just six episodes were made.

La Frenais, Ian

(1937–)

See *Clement, Dick.*

LA Law ✶✶✶

US (Twentieth) Legal Drama. ITV 1987–92 (US: NBC 1986–94)

Leland McKenzie	**Richard Dysart**
Douglas Brackman Jr	**Alan Rachins**
Michael Kuzak	**Harry Hamlin**
Arnie Becker	**Corbin Bernsen**
Grace Van Owen	**Susan Dey**
Ann Kelsey	**Jill Eikenberry**
Stuart Markowitz	**Michael Tucker**
Victor Sifuentes	**Jimmy Smits**
Abby Perkins	**Michele Greene**
Roxanne Melman	**Susan Ruttan**
Benny Stulwicz	**Larry Drake**
Jonathan Rollins	**Blair Underwood**
Dave Meyer	**Dann Florek**
Rosalind Shays	**Diana Muldaur**
Cara Jean (C. J.) Lamb	**Amanda Donohoe**
Tommy Mullaney	**John Spencer**
Zoey Clemmons	**Cecil Hoffman**

Creators **Steven Bochco, Terry Louise Fisher**
Executive Producers **David Kelley, Gregory Hoblit**

● ***The cases of a prominent Los Angeles law firm.***

LA Law has been described as HILL STREET BLUES in a courtroom. Indeed, there are many similarities between the two programmes, not least because *Law*'s co-creator Steven Bochco was also one of the brains behind the *Blues*. He brought with him much the same format: a large, well-defined cast, interweaving storylines and the ability to mix serious business with the lightest of humour. His collaborator on this series was former CAGNEY AND LACEY producer Terry Louise Fisher, herself a former Deputy District Attorney.

The law firm in question is that of McKenzie, Brackman, Chaney and Kuzak. McKenzie is the paternal senior partner, Brackman the penny-pinching, balding son of one of the founding partners, and Kuzak the hard-working, compassionate litigation partner. Chaney dies in the opening episode. Working with them are Ann Kelsey (another litigation partner), Stuart Markowitz (the tax partner and Ann's future husband), and the philandering divorce partner, Arnie Becker. Also in the team are their associates, hispanic Victor Sifuentes, new arrival Abby Perkins and Roxanne Melman, Becker's secretary. Grace Van Owen is Kuzak's Deputy DA girlfriend who sometimes has to oppose him in the courtroom. Black lawyer Jonathan Rollins and mentally retarded office boy Benny Stulwicz are added later.

Political and romantic ambitions punctuate the legal activities of the company, with associates vying to become partners and workmates trying to become bedmates. Abby sets up on her own but finds life hard away from the practice and soon returns. New litigator Roz Shays is brought in and proves too disruptive, before she falls into an empty elevator shaft and is killed. Grace is promoted to a judge, but decides she prefers attorney work and packs it in to join the firm. Later, Kuzak leaves to form his own company, resulting in a name change for the firm to McKenzie, Brackman, Chaney and Becker, and the arrival of three new attorneys. These are freelancer Tommy Mullaney, his former wife, Zoey, and English litigation lawyer C. J. Lamb.

Combining soapy storylines with responsible handling of touchy subjects like AIDS and racial abuse, *LA Law* also proves that TV lawyers are not infallible. Like the cops on Hill Street, the legal eagles in LA are not always successful. In the UK, the series was dropped by ITV in 1992, but further episodes were seen on Sky One. A reunion feature TV film, *LA Law: the Movie*, was released in 2002.

La Plante, Lynda

(Lynda Titchmarsh; 1946–)

Liverpudlian actress turned dramatist, billed as Lynda Marchal when seen in series like THE SWEENEY, RENTAGHOST (Tamara Novek), MINDER, FOX, *Coming Home* (Muriel Maddocks) and EDUCATING MARMALADE (Mrs Atkins), and also for her first script credits in THE KIDS FROM 47A. She made a major impression with her first prime time TV offering, WIDOWS, which she followed up with *Widows 2* and then the highly acclaimed PRIME SUSPECT series of police dramas. Her other work has included *Seekers, The Lifeboat, Framed, Civvies, Comics, She's Out* (the revival of *Widows*), SUPPLY AND DEMAND, THE GOVERNOR – the first major series from her own production company, La Plante Productions – TRIAL AND RETRIBUTION (which introduced revolutionary split-screen imagery), the Internet thriller KILLER NET, *Mind Games* and THE COMMANDER. For the States, she has written a revamp of *Widows*, adapted her own novel *Bella Mafia* and scripted *The Prosecutors* with Tom Fontana.

La Rue, Danny

OBE (Daniel Patrick Carroll; 1927–)

Britain's most famous drag artist, Danny La Rue (actually born in Cork, Ireland) was almost a regular on THE GOOD OLD DAYS and other variety shows in the 1960s and 1970s. His other TV work has been confined to guest appearances and adaptations of his stage shows.

Labours of Erica, The ★★

UK (Thames) Situation Comedy. ITV 1989–90

Erica Parsons .... **Brenda Blethyn**
Clive Bannister .... **Clive Merrison**
Dexter Rook .... **Geoffrey Davies**
Jeremy Parsons .... **Paul Spurrier**
Myrna Burton .... **Rona Anderson**
Robert Beresford .... **Simeon Pearl**

Writers **Richard Fegen, Andrew Norriss**
Producers **John Howard Davies, James Gilbert**

Life begins at 40 for a frustrated single mum.

Erica Parsons is a lone parent with a 14-year-old son, Jeremy. As her 40th birthday approaches, a long-term relationship with her boss, Dexter Rook, comes to an end, giving her two good reasons to take stock of her life. Rediscovering the diaries she penned as a teenager, she realizes that she still has so many dreams and ambitions to fulfil. Now is the time to put that right, she thinks, and so she sets herself a series of ambitious tasks – from taking up fishing to daring to smoke a cigarette in front of her strict old headmistress. However, this is the start of a troublesome time for young Jeremy, whose mum sees his homework as a chance to improve her own education, for Dexter, whose new advances are rejected by the born-again adventurer, and for everyone else who knows Erica and wonders what on earth she'll be getting up to next.

Lace ★★

US (Lorimar) Drama. ITV 1984 (US: ABC 1984)

Lili .... **Phoebe Cates**
Judy Hale .... **Bess Armstrong**
Jennifer 'Pagan' Tralone .... **Brooke Adams**
Maxine Pascale .... **Arielle Dombasle**
Prince Abdullah .... **Anthony Higgins**
Pierre Boursal .... **François Guetary**
Dr Geneste .... **Anthony Quayle**

Writer **Elliott Baker**

A pornographic actress tries to find her real mother.

Epitomizing the 1980s 'bonkbuster' mini-series, the two-part lingerie commercial known as *Lace* is based on the novel of the same name by Shirley Conran. The story concerns a vengeful porn star, Lili, who sets out to discover which of three women – Maxine (French), Judy (American) or Pagan (English) – is the real mother that abandoned her at birth. Inevitably there was a follow-up, *Lace II* (ITV 1985), which focuses on her efforts to find her true father, again from a trio of likely contenders. This time the part of the woman revealed to be her mother (Judy) was played by Deborah Raffin. William Hale directed both series.

Lacey, Rebecca

(1969–)

British actress, the daughter of the late Ronald Lacey and actress Mela White. Among her numerous high-profile roles, the parts of Hilary in MAY TO DECEMBER and Dr George Woodman in CASUALTY stand out, but other notable credits include THE BRETTS (Emily), HOME TO ROOST (Julie Willows), *News at Twelve* (Sharon Doyle), BADGER (Claire Armitage) and MONARCH OF THE GLEN (Irene). Guest roles have been likewise in drama and comedy, in programmes like LOVEJOY, THE DARLING BUDS OF MAY, THE RUTH RENDELL MYSTERIES, *Vice Versa* (Dulcie Grimstone), P. G. Wodehouse's *Heavy Weather*, GAME ON, THE BILL, A TOUCH OF FROST, MURDER IN MIND, MURDER IN SUBURBIA, HEARTBEAT, HUSTLE and MURDER INVESTIGATION TEAM.

Ladd, Cheryl

(Cheryl Stoppelmoor; 1951–)

American leading lady, wife of Alan Ladd's son, David. Her first television work involved providing one of the singing voices for the cartoon series JOSIE AND THE PUSSYCATS (under the name Cherie Moore). She later appeared on US TV under her maiden name of Cheryl Stoppelmoor, before, as Cheryl Ladd, she was cast as Kris Munroe, sister of Farrah Fawcett-Major's character, Jill, in CHARLIE'S ANGELS. After the series ended, Ladd moved into films and TV movies but returned to US prime time in 1994 in the detective series *One West Waikiki*. More recently, she has been seen as Jillian Deline in *Las Vegas*.

Ladies in Charge ★★

UK (Thames) Drama. ITV 1986

Babs Palmer .... **Julia Hills**
Diana Granville .... **Carol Royle**
Vicky Barton .... **Julia Swift**

Writers **Fay Weldon, Paula Milne, Julia Jones, Anne Valery**
Executive Producer **Lloyd Shirley**
Producer **Peter Duguid**

A trio of young women set up an agency to help people in the aftermath of World War I.

When three young women return home after serving as ambulance drivers during the Great War life seems to lack an edge. Having witnessed appalling scenes and suffering, they feel that they cannot simply drop back into their comfortable former existences. They also miss the buzz of doing good deeds and so decide to give up their time to help people less fortunate than themselves. Defying convention, which says that women should not go out to work, particularly in a time of great unemployment like the early 1920s, they set up an agency to provide a helping hand to fellow citizens in need. This might be a spot of childminding, or something more demanding. The trio are the lively Babs, Diana, whose husband has been killed on the Somme, and Vicky, the least upper-class of the three (who replaced a girl called Polly, played by Amanda Root, in the pilot episode shown in 1985 as part of the STORYBOARD anthology). The pilot was written by Alfred Shaughnessy, from an idea by Kate Herbert-Hunting, and the story was loosely based on that of the Universal Aunts organization.

Lady Chatterley ★★★

UK (London Films/Global Arts/BBC) Drama. BBC 1 1993
DVD: Metrodome

Lady Connie Chatterley .... **Joely Richardson**
Mellors .... **Sean Bean**
Sir Clifford Chatterley .... **James Wilby**
Mrs Bolton .... **Shirley Anne Field**
Hilda .... **Hetty Baynes**
Field .... **David Sterne**
Sir Michael Reid .... **Ken Russell**

Writers **Michael Haggiag, Ken Russell**

● ***A frustrated aristocrat finds physical comfort with one of her estate's gamekeepers.***

Attractive young Lady Connie Chatterley is nursemaid to her disabled husband. Sir Clifford is confined to a wheelchair after World War I injuries and caring for him has left his wife exhausted, not to mention sexually frustrated. To find some freedom, she takes to walking the extensive grounds and woodlands of the family stately home (Wragby Hall – real-life Wrotham Park, Hertfordshire in this dramatization) and in doing so encounters the earthy, muscular charms of handsome gamekeeper Mellors, a man for whom she cannot control her desires. The affair is consummated and Connie's marriage spirals down to destruction. She aims to escape by spending some time at Mandalay, her father's house by the sea, but can't resist one final night of passion with Mellors. This four-part adaptation of D. H. Lawrence's controversial novel – subject of an infamous obscenity trial in 1960 – was co-written and directed by Ken Russell, who also appeared in the cast list.

Lady is a Tramp, The ★★

UK (Regent) Situation Comedy. Channel 4 1983–4

Old Pat .... **Patricia Hayes**
Lanky Pat .... **Pat Coombs**
Davey .... **Peter Cleall**

Writer **Johnny Speight**
Producer **William G. Stewart**

● ***Two bag ladies defy authority.***

With the sitcom pedigrees of producer William G. Stewart, writer Johnny Speight and stars Patricia Hayes and Pat Coombs, Channel 4 had high hopes for this vagrant comedy, but only two series were eventually forthcoming. Old Pat is, as the Matt Monro theme song explains, a tramp, a garrulous taker-on of authority. Her less strident accomplice is Lanky Pat, usually cast as a sounding board for Old Pat's rhetoric. Together they take up residence in a rusty old van, propped up on bricks in a derelict London yard. But this is a step forward from the chilly park benches they have been used to, so things are on the up. To earn a few bob, they put on an act for queues at bus stops, but they maintain their dignity by always fighting their corner. Davey is their younger friend and he, plus the assorted other tramps who cross the old ladies' realm, provide much of the inspiration for their scheming fun and games.

Ladykillers/Lady Killers ★★

UK (Granada) Legal Drama Anthology. ITV 1980–1

Host **Robert Morley**

Producer **Pieter Rogers**

● ***Drama collection recalling the crimes of some notorious murderers.***

This anthology of reconstructions of famous murder trials focuses chiefly on the 'gentler sex' – perhaps not a fair description, after close scrutiny of the crimes the featured women committed. The seven *causes célèbres* concern Marie Marguerite Fahmy (played by Barbara Kellerman), Kate Webster (Elaine Paige), Ruth Ellis (Georgina Hale), Mary Eleanor Pearcey (Joanna David), Charlotte Bryant (Rita Tushingham), Madeleine Smith (Elizabeth Richardson) and Amelia Elizabeth Dyer (Joan Sims). When the series returned for seven more episodes the following year (using the subtly different title of *Lady Killers*), the female monopoly was broken, although all the cases strongly featured a woman – as a victim, if not a murderer or accomplice. These cases involve Dr Crippen (John Fraser), Frederick and Margaret Seddon (Michael Jayston and Carol Drinkwater), George Joseph Smith (Kenneth Haigh), Ronald True (Christopher Cazenove), Frederick Bywaters and Edith Thompson (Christopher Villiers and Gayle Hunnicutt), Neville Heath (Ian Charleson) and Sidney Harry Fox (Tim Brierley). Robert Morley introduced each hour-long episode, in which fact merged with fiction to create a tale fit for TV consumption. Writers included Jeremy Sandford, Arden Winch, Frances Galleymore and Nemone Lethbridge. Paul Lewis provided the theme music.

Lakes, The ★★★★

UK (BBC/Company) Drama 1997; 1999
DVD: Second Sight

Danny Kavanagh .... **John Simm**
Emma Quinlan/Kavanagh .... **Emma Cunniffe**
Bernie Quinlan .... **Mary Jo Randle**
Peter Quinlan .... **Paul Copley**
Pete Quinlan .... **James Thornton**
Annie/Jessica Quinlan .... **Jessica Perry**
Grandad .... **Tony Rohr**
Sheila Thwaite .... **Elizabeth Rider**
Arthur Thwaite .... **David Westhead**
Paula Thwaite .... **Jenna Scruton**
Father Matthew .... **Robert Pugh**
Gary Alcock (Chef) .... **Charles Dale**
John Parr/Fisher .... **Kevin Doyle**
Simone Parr/Fisher .... **Clare Holman**
Ruth Alcock .... **Elizabeth Berrington**
Mr Archer .... **Nicholas Day**
Lucy Archer .... **Kaye Wragg**
Doreen Archer .... **Elizabeth Bennett**
Joey .... **Robin Laing**
Tharmy .... **Lee Oakes**
Albie .... **Matt Bardock**
Robert .... **Ryan Pope**
Sgt Eddie Slater .... **Bob Mason**
Dr Sarah Kilbride .... **Barbara Wilshere**
Juliet Bray .... **Sally Rogers**
Susan Charles .... **Sam Hall**
Jo Jo Spiers .... **Amanda Mealing**

Ged Hodson .... **Marshall Lancaster**
Charles Kilbride .... **Robert Morgan**
Beverly .... **Annabelle Apsion**
Thomas Alcock .... **Joel Philimore**
Billy Jennings .... **Justin Brady**

Writer **Jimmy McGovern**
Executive Producer **George Faber**
Producers **Charles Pattinson, Matthew Bird**

An unemployed Liverpool lad moves to Cumbria and becomes the catalyst for local tensions.

Poetry-loving tearaway Danny Kavanagh is on the dole, addicted to gambling and becoming less welcome at home. He decides to make a new life in the Lake District, meeting local girl Emma on the coach journey north. He takes a job as a kitchen slave under a brutal, bigoted chef in an Ullswater hotel and proceeds to make Emma pregnant. After marriage, a brief return to Liverpool, and a period in jail for theft, inspired by gambling-induced poverty, Danny returns to the Lakes to find Emma, hoping to repair their relationship and promising never to gamble again. A family accident on the lake leads to the finger being pointed again at Danny and a spotlight being trained on the hypocrisy, deceit, wavering Catholicism and sexual profligacy that permeates the tight-knit local community.

Semi-autobiographical, in that writer Jimmy McGovern had himself been a gambler in youth, had taken a job in a lakeside hotel kitchen and met his wife along the way, *The Lakes* was promoted as 'a Britpop serial for the nineties', and featured music from bands like Stone Roses and Primal Scream. Although the series won rave reviews, Lake District inhabitants were not impressed with the image it portrayed of Cumbrian life.

More controversy followed the second series, which focuses less on Danny and more on characters like flirty hotelier's daughter Lucy Archer, Emma's mother (Bernie) and the local priest. Police complained of similarities between a real crime and events in the programme and, while producers declared the circumstances to be purely coincidental, the names of two characters, local headteacher John Parr and his wife Simone, were changed to reflect sensitivities.

Lamarr, Mark

(Mark Jones; 1967–)

Swindon-raised comedian and presenter, the host of the pop quiz NEVER MIND THE BUZZCOCKS, *Mark Lamarr Leaving the 20th Century* and *Lamarr's Attacks*. Previously he was seen as team captain in SHOOTING STARS, presenter of *Saturday Review*, THE WORD and *Planet Showbiz*, and interviewer on THE BIG BREAKFAST. Lamarr also made a guest appearance in *15 Storeys High*.

Lambert, Verity

(1935–)

Verity Lambert was one of Britain's earliest female producers. She was the first producer (1963–5) of DOCTOR WHO and was fundamental in establishing the series as a popular 'bug-eyed monster' show, instead of the educational series its creator, Sydney Newman, intended. Lambert was also the first producer of THE NEWCOMERS, then, in 1966, she co-created and produced ADAM ADAMANT LIVES! In 1968 she worked on DETECTIVE and in 1969 produced *W. Somerset Maugham*, a series of stories by the famous author, before moving to LWT, where she was responsible for BUDGIE. Later Head of Drama at Thames and an executive with Euston Films, Lambert nurtured MINDER from its shaky beginnings into a classic and had other hits with series like ROCK FOLLIES, HAZELL, THE FLAME TREES OF THIKA and the trilogy *The Norman Conquests*. She now runs her own independent production company, Cinema Verity, makers of *Coasting*, BOYS FROM THE BUSH, GBH, MAY TO DECEMBER, *Sleepers, Class Act, She's Out*, A PERFECT STATE, THE CAZALETS and the ill-fated ELDORADO. Other productions have included JONATHAN CREEK and LOVE SOUP.

Lame Ducks ✶✶

UK (BBC) Situation Comedy. BBC 2 1984–5

Brian Drake .... **John Duttine**
Tommy .... **Patric Turner**
Angie .... **Lorraine Chase**
Maurice .... **Tony Millan**
Ansell .... **Brian Murphy**
Mrs Drake .... **Primi Townsend**
Mrs Kelly .... **Cyd Hayman**

Creator/Writer **Peter J. Hammond**
Producer **John B. Hobbs**

A man on the brink of divorce sells his house and moves to the country, taking a motley band of losers with him.

Brian Drake, hit by a lorry and convalescing in hospital, is told by his wife that she wants a divorce. On release, he sells his house and takes off with the proceeds to find a new home in the country. Accompanying him is a reformed arsonist, Tommy, whom he met in hospital, and soon they are joined by the promiscuous Angie and by Maurice, a postman who wants to walk round the world on a 6-foot ball. Completing this collection of lame ducks is Ansell, the incompetent private eye sent by Drake's wife to track him down. They all move into a cottage in the village of Scar's Edge, where Mrs Kelly is their glamorous but somewhat unpredictable neighbour. For the second series, the setting has changed to a disused railway station at Stutterton Stop.

Lame Ducks was the first venture into comedy by drama writer P. J. Hammond, the creator of SAPPHIRE AND STEEL among other programmes.

Lancashire, Sarah

(1964–)

Blonde English actress, the daughter of CORONATION STREET scriptwriter the late Geoffrey Lancashire, and it was in the soap that she became famous, playing Raquel Wolstenhulme/Watts. Since leaving the *Street*, she has headlined in a number of roles, including the parts of Liz Deakin in BLOOMIN' MARVELLOUS, Ruth Goddard in WHERE THE HEART IS, Anne Cloves QC in *Verdict*, Yvonne Kolakowski in CLOCKING OFF, Coral Atkins in *Seeing Red*, Ruth Quirke in CHAMBERS and Trina Lavery in *My Fragile Heart*. Lancashire has also starred in *Gentlemen's Relish* (Violet Askey), *The Glass* (Carol Parker), *Back Home* (Peggy Dickinson), *The Cry* (Meg Bartlet), ROSE AND MALONEY (Rose Linden), *Birthday Girl* (Rachel Jones), *Sons and Lovers* (Gertrude Morel), *The Rotters Club* (Barbara Chase) and *Cherished* (Angela Cannings).

Lancer ✶✶

US (Twentieth Century-Fox) Western. BBC 2 1969–71
(US: CBS 1968–71)

Murdoch Lancer	**Andrew Duggan**
Johnny Madrid Lancer	**James Stacy**
Scott Lancer	**Wayne Maunder**
Teresa O'Brien	**Elizabeth Baur**
Jelly Hoskins	**Paul Brinegar**

Creators **Samuel Peeples, Dean Riesner**
Producer **Alan A. Armer**

Survival is the name of the game for a ranching family in the Old West.

In 1870s California, the sprawling San Joaquin Valley – already showcased in THE BIG VALLEY – is home to veteran rancher Murdoch Lancer. Age is taking its toll, however, and Murdoch, with only his ward, Teresa (daughter of a former ranch hand), to assist, is struggling to prevent ambitious locals from taking their share of his estate. The only option is to send for the cavalry, in the form of his two sons, half-brothers with precious little in common except their father's blood. Johnny is of Mexican stock, a wandering firebrand; Scott is part-Irish and a college graduate from refined Boston. Somehow they pull together and preserve the ranch for the Lancer clan. Reinforcement comes later from new ranch hand Jelly Hoskins (played by Paul Brinegar, who, you would think, had surely seen enough desert dust and dirt as Wishbone in RAWHIDE).

Land of Hope and Gloria ✶

UK (Thames) Situation Comedy. ITV 1992

Gloria Hepburn	**Sheila Ferguson**
Gerald Hope-Beaumont	**Andrew Bicknell**
Nanny Princeton	**Joan Sanderson**
Evelyn Spurling	**Daphne Oxenford**
Crompton	**John Rapley**
Vanessa	**Vivien Darke**

Writer **Simon Brett**
Producer **Peter Frazer-Jones**

A pushy American businesswoman takes a new broom to an English stately home.

Feisty American Gloria Hepburn is set to ruffle feathers when she takes up a position as business manager at Beaumont House, the crumbling stately home of Gerald Hope-Beaumont. The marriage of shrewd, dynamic marketing ideas and crusty, restrained Englishness is not a happy one, but nevertheless Gloria ploughs on, updating the guided tours, sprucing up the gift shop and introducing murder-mystery weekends. Casting disapproving looks is long-serving Nanny Princeton (a swan song for actress Joan Sanderson, who died a month before the series aired). The lead role of Gloria was a first major acting job for former Three Degrees vocalist Sheila Ferguson, but just six episodes were produced.

Land of the Giants ✶✶

US (Twentieth Century-Fox/Irwin Allen) Science Fiction. ITV 1968–72 (US: ABC 1968–70)

Capt. Steve Burton	**Gary Conway**
Mark Wilson	**Don Matheson**
Barry Lockridge	**Stefan Arngrim**
Dan Erickson	**Don Marshall**
Commander Alexander Fitzhugh	**Kurt Kasznar**
Valerie Scott	**Deanna Lund**
Betty Hamilton	**Heather Young**
Insp. Kobrick	**Kevin Hagen**

Creator/Executive Producer **Irwin Allen**

The crew and passengers of a stricken airliner are stranded on a planet inhabited by giants.

On 12 June 1983, a sub-orbital commercial flight from America to London flies through a mysterious cloud and crash-lands on a planet resembling Earth but which is home to people 12 times normal height. The series follows the space castaways' efforts to repair their ship, the *Spindrift*, and return home, while fending off monster insects and animals, or fleeing from the giants, who want them for experiments.

The crew are Captain Steve Burton, his co-pilot, Dan Erickson, and stewardess Betty Hamilton. The passengers are engineering executive Mark Wilson, wealthy heiress Valerie Scott, 12-year-old Barry Lockridge and Barry's dog, Chipper. There is one joker in the pack, however: the intriguing, unscrupulous Commander Fitzhugh, who is wanted by the police. Their adversaries in the Land of the Giants are headed by Inspector Kobrick, who works for the SIB security service.

The series was noted for its elaborate special effects (particularly the use of giant-size props) and was created by Irwin Allen, the inspiration behind VOYAGE TO THE BOTTOM OF THE SEA, THE TIME TUNNEL and the similar LOST IN SPACE. It was repeated on Channel 4 from 1989.

Landau, Martin

(1928–)

American actor, the husband of Barbara Bain, who starred with him in his two big successes, MISSION: IMPOSSIBLE (in which he played Rollin Hand) and SPACE: 1999 (Commander John Koenig). Previously, Landau had made guest appearances in episodes of THE TWILIGHT ZONE, BONANZA, I SPY and THE WILD, WILD WEST, but has found little TV work of note in recent years, save the odd movie and guest spots in *Without a Trace*.

Landen, Dinsdale

(1932–2003)

British actor in comedy as well as straight drama. The highlights of his TV career were the part of Pip in *Great Expectations* and the title roles in *Mickey Dunne* and *Devenish*. He also starred as Barty Wade in PIG IN THE MIDDLE, Colonel Farrier in CATHERINE COOKSON*'s The Wingless Bird*, and Lord Brightlingsea in *The Buccaneers*, and appeared in *World in Ferment*, *The Mask of Janus*, THE GLITTERING PRIZES and *Arms and the Man*, with guest roles in the likes of THE AVENGERS, THE PROTECTORS, CROWN COURT, THE IRISH RM, LOVEJOY and THE INSPECTOR LYNLEY MYSTERIES.

Landon, Michael

(Eugene Orowitz; 1936–91)

American actor, writer, director and producer, who entered the business through bit parts in the 1950s, an injury having brought to an end a promising sports career. He starred in the cult movie *I was a Teenage Werewolf* and took parts in series like *Wanted Dead or Alive* and WELLS FARGO, before he was spotted by David Dortort, creator of BONANZA, and pitched into the role of Little Joe Cartwright, which was to last for 14 years. When *Bonanza* ended, Landon (who had already gained behind-the-camera experience in the series) created a programme of his own, LITTLE HOUSE ON THE PRAIRIE, in which he also starred (dad Charles Ingalls). When *Little House* finished after eight years, Landon's versatility proved itself yet again as he launched into another of his own productions, HIGHWAY TO HEAVEN, playing probationary angel Jonathan Smith. The series ended in 1988 and Landon, the producer, followed it with the prime-time series *Father Murphy*, plus a few TV movies.

Lane, Carla

OBE (1937–)

Liverpudlian comedy writer whose first major success was THE LIVER BIRDS, created with her former scripting partner, Myra Taylor. With Taylor, Lane also contributed numerous episodes to BLESS THIS HOUSE before embarking on a string of hits of her own. These have included *No Strings*, THE LAST SONG, SOLO, THE MISTRESS, BUTTERFLIES, LEAVING, I WOKE UP ONE MORNING, BREAD, SCREAMING, LUV and SEARCHING. Much of her work has focused on mid-life crises and, in particular, the pressures on a woman, with pathos mixing readily with humour throughout.

Lang, Belinda

(Belinda Lange; 1955–)

London-born actress, the daughter of 1960s quiz show host Jeremy Hawk and actress Joan Heal. Among her more prominent roles have been Beth Marwood/Powlett-Jones in TO SERVE THEM ALL MY DAYS, Kate in DEAR JOHN, Martha Brett in THE BRETTS, Liza in SECOND THOUGHTS, Agatha Troy in THE INSPECTOR ALLEYN MYSTERIES and Bill Porter in 2 POINT 4 CHILDREN. Other credits have included *The Cabbage Patch* (Susie), *Bust* (Sheila Walsh), *Making News*, STAY LUCKY (Lady Karen), MIDSOMER MURDERS, ROSEMARY AND THYME, and an acclaimed portrayal of Christine Hamilton in the drama *Justice in Wonderland*. She is married to actor Hugh Fraser (POIROT's Captain Hastings).

Langford, Bonnie

(Bonita Langford; 1964–)

Flame-haired singer, dancer and actress, a former child star seen on OPPORTUNITY KNOCKS (aged six), JUNIOR SHOWTIME and as Violet Elizabeth Bott in JUST WILLIAM. Later credits have included *The Saturday Starship*, THE HOT SHOE SHOW, AGATHA CHRISTIE'S MARPLE and DOCTOR WHO, in which she played Mel, one of his assistants. She is married to actor Paul Grunert.

Langrishe, Caroline

(1958–)

British actress probably best known as auctioneer Charlotte Cavendish in LOVEJOY but with a TV career stretching back to the mid-1970s. She appeared in THE GLITTERING PRIZES, ANNA KARENINA and THE BROTHERS, as well as playing Jane in the PLAY FOR TODAY productions THE FLIPSIDE OF DOMINICK HIDE and *Another Flip for Dominick*. She was also Kate Smith in PULASKI, Bella Niculesco in FORTUNES OF WAR, Penny Nichols in CHANCER, Jane Bewley in MOSLEY, Kate Cameron in *Brotherly Love*, Miss Bozek in *Justice in Wonderland*, George Channing QC in JUDGE JOHN DEED and Lady Carnarvon in *Egypt*. The RETURN OF SHELLEY, BOON, TRAINER, PEAK PRACTICE, SHARPE, CLUEDO and *The Afternoon Play* have been other credits.

Lansbury, Angela

CBE (1925–)

British actress enjoying a late lease of life as novelist-cum-amateur-sleuth Jessica Fletcher in MURDER, SHE WROTE. Lansbury's showbusiness debut came after she was evacuated out of England in 1940. Three years later, she caught the eye in *Gaslight* and embarked on a successful film career. Television work beckoned in the 1950s, with appearances in assorted plays and anthology series, but she soon moved on to the stage instead, notching up hits on Broadway, breaking off in between for more film work. She returned to the small screen in the 1980s, taking parts in some TV movies before being offered her most celebrated role to date, as the perceptive Miss Fletcher, in 1984. Recent guest appearances have come in the LAW AND ORDER spin-offs *Special Victims Unit* and *Trial by Jury*.

Laramie ★★

US (Revue) Western. BBC 1959–64 (US: NBC 1959–63)

Slim Sherman	**John Smith**
Andy Sherman	**Bobby Crawford Jr**
Jess Harper	**Robert Fuller**
Jonesy	**Hoagy Carmichael**
Mike Williams	**Dennis Holmes**
Daisy Cooper	**Spring Byington**
Gandy	**Don Durant**
Mort Corey	**Stuart Randall**

Two friends run a ranch and trading post in the Wild West.

In the 1870s Slim Sherman and his 14-year-old brother, Andy, are orphaned by an outlaw who shoots their father on their Wyoming ranch. Rather than leave, they decide to keep up the estate and, with the help of an old friend, Jonesy (played by songwriter Hoagy Carmichael), and Jess Harper, a drifter who puts down roots, they set about scratching out a living from the never-too-fruitful property. Andy is eventually written out, and Jonesy leaves after a year or so, leaving Slim and Jess as partners. As well as raising cattle, they offer a staging-post for traffic on the Great Overland Mail Stage Line, which ensures that a host of interesting and troublesome characters pass their way. Later additions to the cast are young Mike Williams, who has been orphaned by Indians, housekeeper Daisy Cooper and ranch-hand Gandy. The town sheriff, Mort Corey, is also seen on a regular basis.

Larbey, Bob

(1934–)

London-born comedy writer, often in conjunction with John Esmonde (see Esmonde's entry for joint work). Larbey, singly, has also penned A FINE ROMANCE, AS TIME GOES BY, ON THE UP, AIN'T MISBEHAVIN', MY GOOD FRIEND, a Channel 4 film called THE CURIOUS CASE OF SANTA CLAUS, and episodes of THE DARLING BUDS OF MAY.

Large, Eddie

(Eddie McGinnis; 1942–)

As his stage name suggests, the bigger half of the Manchester comedy duo Little and Large, with Syd Little. Discovered on OPPORTUNITY KNOCKS in 1971, the pair later worked on CRACKERJACK, the impressionists' show WHO DO YOU DO?, and their own prime-time series for Thames (*The Little and Large Tellyshow*) and then the BBC (*The Little and Large Show*). They have been guest stars in numerous variety programmes and game shows, and Large also appeared in the football drama *The King and Us*.

Larkins, The ★★

UK (ATV) Situation Comedy. ITV 1958–60; 1963–4

Alf Larkins	**David Kossoff**
Ada Larkins	**Peggy Mount**
Eddie Larkins	**Shaun O'Riordan**
Joyce Rogers	**Ruth Trouncer**
Jeff Rogers	**Ronan O'Casey**
Sam Prout	**George Roderick**
Hetty Prout	**Barbara Mitchell**
Myrtle Prout	**Hilary Bamberger**
Vicar	**Charles Lloyd Pack**
Major Osbert Rigby-Soames	**Hugh Paddick**
Mrs Gannett	**Hazel Coppen**
Georgie	**Hugh Walters**

Creator/Writer **Fred Robinson**
Producers **Bill Ward, Alan Tarrant**

Life with a lively Cockney family.

The Larkins are hen-pecked but shrewd dad Alf, his battleaxe wife, Ada, unemployable son Eddie, daughter Joyce, and her American husband, Jeff Rogers, an out-of-work writer of cowboy comics. They live at 66 Sycamore Street, somewhere in the London suburbs, and Alf works in the canteen at a plastics factory. Also seen are snoopy neighbour Hetty Prout, her husband, Sam, and their daughter, Myrtle. Together they find themselves in a variety of farcical situations that proved popular with viewers at the turn of the 1960s (so much so that a spin-off film, *Inn for Trouble*, was released in 1959 and saw the Larkins in charge of a country pub). In the last series, shown three years after the main run, Sycamore Street has been demolished, Alf and Ada (now alone) take over a nearby café and gain a lodger, Osbert Rigby-Soames.

Shaun O'Riordan, who played Eddie Larkins, went on to be one of ATV's major drama and comedy producers.

Larry Sanders Show, The ★★★★

US (Brillstein-Grey/Columbia Tristar) Comedy. BBC 2 1993–9 (US: HBO 1992–8)
DVD: Sony Pictures Home Entertainment

Larry Sanders	**Garry Shandling**
Arthur	**Rip Torn**
Hank Kingsley	**Jeffrey Tambor**
Jeannie Sanders	**Megan Gallagher**
Jerry	**Jeremy Piven**
Phil	**Wallace Langham**
Paula	**Janeane Garofalo**
Darlene	**Linda Doucett**
Beverly	**Penny Johnson**
Francine	**Kathryn Harrold**
Brian	**Scott Thompson**

Executive Producers **Garry Shandling, Brad Grey**

A revealing glimpse behind the scenes of a late-night talk show.

After the success of the innovative IT'S GARRY SHANDLING'S SHOW, its star became a popular replacement host of Johnny Carson's *Tonight Show*, and was once in the running to take the place of David Letterman. The experience gave Shandling the idea for a sitcom based on the late-night chat show concept, in which he was cast as the host of such a show.

The Larry Sanders Show is split between on- and off-air action. On air, the programme (shot on videotape) plays like a real-life chat show, featuring genuine celebrity guests like Roseanne and David Duchovny. Off air (shot on film), the backroom business reveals the bickering, bad language and cynicism behind making such a programme, and these segments are recorded without the customary US laugh-track to emphasize the difference between the two worlds. Sanders himself is a perfectionist and smarmily self-absorbed. His confident, generous on-screen persona contrasts with his insecure, demanding real personality. His team includes a devious producer-cum-protective-manager, Artie; guest booker Paula; chief writer Jerry and his scripting colleague, Phil; and Sanders's dim, sycophantic stooge, Hank, whose catchphrase 'Hey, now!' caught on big in the States.

Although winning critical acclaim, the series was never given a fair crack of the whip in the UK, being shunted into late-night slots on BBC 2.

Larson, Glen A.

(1937–)

Highly successful American writer, producer and director, working on such hits as IT TAKES A THIEF, THE VIRGINIAN, ALIAS SMITH AND JONES, MCCLOUD, THE SIX MILLION DOLLAR MAN, THE FALL GUY, QUINCY, BATTLESTAR GALACTICA, BUCK ROGERS IN THE 25TH CENTURY, AUTOMAN, MANIMAL, MAGNUM PI and KNIGHT RIDER, many as creator and also as composer of the theme music. In the 1950s he was a member of the Four Preps vocal group, who had three UK hits, most notably 'Big Man'.

Lassie ★★

US (Lassie Television) Children's Adventure. ITV 1956–75 (US: CBS 1954–71; Syndicated 1971–4)

Jeff Miller	**Tommy Rettig**
Ellen Miller	**Jan Clayton**
Gramps Miller	**George Cleveland**
Sylvester 'Porky' Brockway	**Donald Keeler**
Matt Brockway	**Paul Maxey**
Timmy Martin	**Jon Provost**
Doc Weaver	**Arthur Space**
Ruth Martin	**Cloris Leachman**
	June Lockhart
Paul Martin	**Jon Shepodd**
	Hugh Reilly
Uncle Petrie Martin	**George Chandler**
Boomer Bates	**Todd Ferrell**
Cully Wilson	**Andy Clyde**

Corey Stuart	**Robert Bray**
Bob Erickson	**Jack De Mave**
Scott Turner	**Jed Allan**
Garth Holden	**Ron Hayes**
Ron Holden	**Skip Burton**
Mike Holden	**Joshua Albee**
Dale Mitchell	**Larry Wilcox**
Keith Holden	**Larry Pennell**
Lucy Baker	**Pamelyn Ferdin**
Sue Lambert	**Sherry Boucher**

Executive Producers **Robert Maxwell, Jack Wrather**
Producers **Rudy Abel, Sherman Harris, Bob Golden, William Beaudine Jr, Bonita Granville Wrather**

An intelligent and heroic collie dog saves lives and averts disasters.

In this long-running series, based on the 1943 film *Lassie Come Home*, starring Elizabeth Taylor and Roddy McDowall, the lovable Lassie moves from owner to owner. Initially, she lives with young Jeff Miller and his widowed mother and grandfather on a farm near the town of Calverton. When the Millers move to the city, Lassie is taken in by the Martin family, who have bought the farm, with Lassie's best friend now Timmy, an adopted orphan. The next home for Lassie is provided by oldtimer Cully Wilson, after the Martins emigrate to Australia (it seems like these people just can't wait to get away from the dog), but Wilson suffers a heart attack and Lassie's new master is ranger Corey Stuart. After a few years, Corey is hurt in a fire and care of the collie is handed on to two of his colleagues, Scott Turner and Bob Erickson, though Lassie is already beginning to find her own freedom. Eventually, she becomes a real loner and takes to wandering across the USA. At one point, she gives birth to a litter of pups (quite an achievement as the dog playing Lassie was always male). The last *Lassie* series sees the old collie at home with yet another new family, the Holdens, whose friends are Sue Lambert, a vet, and deaf girl Lucy Baker. Throughout the run, the storylines were always much the same: heartwarming tales of Lassie saving the day, looking after the injured and raising the alarm in times of trouble.

An animated version, *Lassie's Rescue Rangers*, was also produced, before a revival, *The New Lassie*, appeared in 1989. In this series Lassie lives in California with the McCulloch family, whose Uncle Steve is really young Timmy from the earliest episodes (actor Jon Provost), now grown up and using his real name (Timmy apparently was a name given to him as an orphan). Lassie resurfaced again in a 1997 Canadian TV version (the family were the Cabots), and then starred in a new feature film released in 2006 entitled simply *Lassie*. The character was created by author Eric Knight.

Last Detective, The ✶✶

UK (Granada) Police Drama. ITV 1 2003–
DVD: Acorn Media

DC 'Dangerous' Davies	**Peter Davison**
Mod Lewis	**Sean Hughes**
DI Ray Aspinall	**Rob Spendlove**
Julie Davies	**Emma Amos**
DS Steve Pimlott	**Charles De'Ath**
DC Darren Barrett	**Billy Geraghty**
Mrs Fulljames	**Elizabeth Bennett**
Sgt Stone	**Colin MacLauchlan**
WPC Maya Kapoor	**Vineeta Rishi**

Creator **Richard Harris**
Producers **Nick Hurran, Deirdre Keir**

An old-fashioned, courteous policeman is the butt of station jokes.

In 1981, ITV presented a one-off dramatization of Leslie Thomas's 1976 novel *Dangerous Davies The Last Detective* (the first of a series of books). It starred Bernard Cribbins as an amiable, but ultimately not ineffective, suburban copper, and Bill Maynard as his offbeat, philosophizing friend and confidant, Mod Lewis. When the idea was reincarnated in 2003, the humour was toned down a notch and Peter Davison was brought in to do his usual sterling job of playing a slightly harassed, downtrodden, likeable hero.

DC 'Dangerous' Davies works the streets of Willesden. His nickname stems from the fact that he's as inoffensive as a policeman can get. His other monicker, the one giving its name to the title of the series, has arisen because Davies is the detective who is handed the jobs colleagues don't want. He's also the last member of the team to be given the chance to shine when something urgent crops up. But shine Davies always manages to do, even though there is never even as much as a brownie point added to his CV for his efforts. So the daily routine for Davies is to take on spitefully assigned menial cases – looking after the victim of a burglary, inquiring into the disappearance of a tramp, refereeing a dispute over a leylandii hedge, or teaching kids road safety – but very often these lead to deeper investigations. These Davies handles deftly if at his own plodding pace, much to the astonishment of his practical-joking colleagues, Pimlott and Barrett, and bullying boss, Aspinall.

Dangerous's reputation as a push-over extends into his private life, where his marriage to flirtatious Julie has broken down and, initially at least, he has the advances of man-eating landlady Mrs Fulljames to negotiate. But there's always Mod to provide some strange comfort. The fussy Irish friend, and later flatmate, with always a new job on the go, is usually there to allow Davies to talk over his troubles. The other star of the show is Davies's lumbering dog (initially a Newfoundland and later a St Bernard) who drags the hapless policeman around the avenues and commons of North London.

Last of the Baskets, The ✶✶

UK (Granada) Situation Comedy. ITV 1971–2

Bodkin	**Arthur Lowe**
Clifford Basket	**Ken Jones**
Mrs Basket	**Patricia Hayes**

Creator/Writer **John Stevenson**
Producer **Bill Podmore**

A factory worker inherits an earldom and all its debts.

When the 12th Earl of Clogborough decides to abdicate after 93 years of holding the title, an heir to the earldom has to be found. It turns out to be Clifford Basket, a boiler-tender in a northern factory and as unlikely a peer as ever there was. Sadly, what the uncouth Clifford inherits is a run-down mansion and an ever-increasing mound of unpaid bills. At least Bodkin, the Earl's last remaining servant, is still around to guide the unfortunate Basket and his mother through their new, demanding lifestyle. The setting is the fictitious Little Clogborough-in-the-Marsh, and two series were produced.

Last of the Blonde Bombshells, The ✱✱

UK (WTTV/BBC) Drama. BBC 1 2000
DVD: HBO Home Video (Region 1 only)

Elizabeth	**Judi Dench**
Patrick	**Ian Holm**
Gwen	**Cleo Laine**
Betty	**Joan Sims**
Annie	**June Whitfield**
Evelyn	**Billie Whitelaw**
Madeleine	**Leslie Caron**
Dinah	**Olympia Dukakis**
Vera	**Thelma Ruby**
Joanna	**Millie Findlay**
Paul	**Dom Chapman**

Writer **Alan Plater**
Producer **Su Armstrong**

● ***A young-at-heart pensioner re-forms a band she played in more than 50 years before.***

Recently widowed Elizabeth played in a girl band during the war. Encouraged by her young granddaughter, Joanna, and a busker she sees playing an old Hoagy Carmichael number, she once again picks up her saxophone. After bumping into Patrick, an old rascal who was the only male member of the troupe (he played the drums in drag), she begins to think about the old days. Remembering the fun they all had when she was the youngest member of the Blonde Bombshells, she agrees to try to re-form the band to raise money for Joanna's school. Tracing her former colleagues proves a little difficult. One (Joan) has died, one (Vera) is in a nursing home, one (Evelyn) is in prison, one (Dinah) has returned to America and another (Madeleine) is back home in France. She has more luck with Annie, who has kept her music alive in a Salvation Army band, with Betty, the former bandleader, who is now a bar-room pianist, and with professional singer/trumpet player Gwen. Somehow she persuades all available ladies to come together and the scene is set for a final, nostalgic performance in which the significance of the number of rose prints on Patrick's drumkit is finally revealed. Gillies MacKinnon directed this light-hearted single drama.

Last of the Mohicans, The ✱✱

UK (BBC) Drama. BBC 1 1971

Hawkeye	**Kenneth Ives**
Chingachgook	**John Abineri**
Uncas	**Richard Warwick**
Col. Munro	**Andrew Crawford**
Cora Munro	**Patricia Maynard**
Alice Munro	**Joanna David**
David	**David Leland**
Major Heyward	**Tim Goodman**
Magua	**Philip Madoc**
Lt. Otley	**Michael Cullen**

Writer **Harry Green**
Producer **John McRae**

● ***Frontier adventures with the members of a threatened Indian tribe.***

North America, 1757: Cora and Alice Munro are making their way to meet their father, a colonel stationed at Fort William. Their guide is the Huron Indian Magua, but Magua is treacherous and the sisters' lives are in danger. To their rescue comes Indian scout Hawkeye and two members of the Mohican tribe, Chingachgook and Uncas (the 'Last of the Mohicans'). Thus Native American is set against Native American in a land afflicted by battles between the colonial British and French. James Fenimore Cooper's famous story of 1826 (part of his *Leatherstocking* collection) was filmed in Scotland and broadcast in eight parts directed by David Maloney. Dudley Simpson provided the soundtrack. A follow-up series, *Hawkeye, the Pathfinder*, was made by the same team a couple of years later (BBC 1 1973). See also HAWKEYE AND THE LAST OF THE MOHICANS.

Last of the Summer Wine ✱✱

UK (BBC) Situation Comedy. BBC 1 1973; 1975–6; 1978–9; 1981–93; 1995–
DVD: Universal

Norman Clegg	**Peter Sallis**
William 'Compo' Simmonite	**Bill Owen**
Cyril Blamire	**Michael Bates**
Walter 'Foggy' Dewhurst	**Brian Wilde**
Seymour Utterthwaite	**Michael Aldridge**
Nora Batty	**Kathy Staff**
Wally Batty	**Joe Gladwin**
Sid	**John Comer**
Ivy	**Jane Freeman**
Crusher (Milburn)	**Jonathan Linsley**
Wesley Pegden	**Gordon Wharmby**
Edie Pegden	**Thora Hird**
Howard	**Robert Fyfe**
Marina	**Jean Fergusson**
Pearl	**Juliette Kaplan**
Glenda	**Sarah Thomas**
Barry	**Mike Grady**
Eli Duckett	**Danny O'Dea**
Clem 'Smiler' Hemingway	**Stephen Lewis**
Auntie Wainwright	**Jean Alexander**
Herbert 'Truly' Truelove	**Frank Thornton**
Tom Simmonite	**Tom Owen**
Roz	**Dora Bryan**
Billy Hardcastle	**Keith Clifford**
Mrs Avery	**Julie T. Wallace**
Alvin Smedley	**Brian Murphy**
Miss Davenport	**Josephine Tewson**
Entwistle	**Bert Kwouk**
Nelly	**June Whitfield**

Creator/Writer **Roy Clarke**
Producers **James Gilbert, Bernard Thompson, Sydney Lotterby, Alan J. W. Bell**

● ***Geriatric delinquents while away their retirement with childish games and pranks.***

Last of the Summer Wine is the world's longest-running sitcom. It began as a COMEDY PLAYHOUSE presentation in 1973 and then emerged as a series in its own right the same year. Filmed in the Yorkshire village of Holmfirth, it has focused for most of its life on three mischievous but lovable pensioners who pass their twilight years energetically engaging themselves in a second childhood of assorted romps and antics. The original trio are seedy, tramp-like Compo, laconic widower (and lifelong Co-op furniture operative) Cleggy and former Royal Signals sergeant Cyril Blamire. Blamire is replaced by another ex-military man, army sign-writer Foggy Dewhurst (actor Michael Bates was taken ill). He, in turn, is substituted for a few seasons by schoolteacher turned crackpot inventor Seymour Utterthwaite. Former policeman Herbert Truelove ('Truly of the Yard') later becomes the third man behind Compo and Clegg.

As the men lurch from scrape to scrape, desperately trying to keep them in check are the town's disapproving womenfolk, particularly the redoubtable Nora Batty, the object of Compo's desires. Also seen in this battle of the sexes have been Wally, Nora's hen-pecked husband; Seymour's sister, Edie, and her mechanic husband, Wesley; and fiery Pearl and her wimpy husband, Howard (with the brassy Marina as his fancy woman). Auntie Wainwright, the junk-shop owner who never misses a sale, has also been in the action, as have café-proprietor Ivy and her husband, Sid. Edie's daughter, Glenda, and her husband, Barry; the short-sighted Eli; and the inappropriately named Smiler have also contributed as the character ensemble has extended over the years.

The spring 2000 series was a tribute to actor Bill Owen, who died after filming only three episodes. His character suffered a fatal seizure after seeing Nora Batty not in her usual wrinkled stockings but in black tights. Compo's funeral was shown, and other episodes revealed how his ageing chums coped with his loss, with Owen's own son, Tom (once star of FREEWHEELERS), playing Compo's long-lost offspring.

In 1988, the series spawned a prequel, which showed the old folk in their formative years. Entitled *First of the Summer Wine*, it featured Peter Sallis as Cleggy's dad, with David Fenwick as the young Norman, Paul Wyett as Compo, Richard Lumsden as Foggy and Paul McLain as Seymour.

Last Resort with Jonathan Ross, The ✶✶

UK (Channel 4/Callender/Channel X) Chat Show. Channel 4 1987–8

Presenter **Jonathan Ross**

Producers **Colin Callender, Katie Lander**

American-style celebrity chat show.

The show that brought fame to a young, snappy-dressing programme researcher named Jonathan Ross was a David Letterman-clone chat and music show. *The Last Resort* featured high-profile celebrity guests who were prepared to take as much from their wisecracking host as they gave. Among the stars gracing the set were Donald Sutherland, Elton John, Steve Martin, Tom Jones, Paul McCartney, George Harrison, Peter Cook, Sean Connery, Ricki Lake, Phil Collins and Donny Osmond. Rowland Rivron, in the guise of Dr Martin Scrote, provided regular sketches. Four series were produced, the later programmes just bearing the title *The Last Resort*.

Last Song, The ✶✶

UK (BBC) Situation Comedy. BBC 2 1981; 1983

Leo Bannister .... **Geoffrey Palmer**
Liz Carroll .... **Nina Thomas**
Alice .... **Caroline Blakiston**
Shirley .... **Barbara Flynn**
Jane .... **Hetty Baynes**
Alison .... **Gay Wilde**

Writer **Carla Lane**
Producer **Sydney Lotterby**

An estranged wife makes life a misery for her husband and his new love.

This generation-gap romantic comedy features 50-year-old Leo Bannister, a surgeon who has separated from his wife, Alice, and now shares a flat with Liz Carroll, a 24-year-old who has surprisingly stolen his heart. However, with his divorce not finalized, the scene is set for plenty of hassle from his loud and deliberately awkward wife, who attempts to wreck his new happiness. Shirley is Liz's best friend, and Jane and Alison are Leo's daughters. In the second series, Liz has flown the coop but Leo is still having a miserable time with Alice. Thirteen episodes were made in total.

Late Expectations ✶✶

UK (BBC) Situation Comedy. BBC 1 1987

Ted Jackson .... **Keith Barron**
Liz Jackson .... **Nanette Newman**
Suzie Jackson .... **Caroline Mander**
Polly Jackson .... **Sara Griffiths**
George Jackson .... **Paul McCarthy**
Harry .... **Norman Ashley**
Joyce .... **Sally Hughes**

Writer **John Gleason**
Producer **John B. Hobbs**

A surprise pregnancy sends shock waves through a middle-aged couple's life.

After 23 years of marriage, a second honeymoon seems an appropriate celebration for Ted and Liz Jackson. However, a shock is in store when, shortly after their return, Liz discovers she is pregnant. Not only that, but twins are on the way. Panic sets in, not just because of Liz's age (43) but also because their child-rearing days are long behind them: the three kids they already have are now well into their teens. So Liz and Ted begin the parental learning curve all over again, attending antenatal classes, finding clothes no longer fit and having sleepless nights over the cost of the new arrivals. Just one series was produced, however, so we never saw how the born-again parents coped with their extended family.

Late, Late, Breakfast Show, The ✶✶

UK (BBC) Entertainment. BBC 1 1982–6

Presenters **Noel Edmonds, Mike Smith**

Producer **Michael Hurll**

Saturday evening collection of silly stunts, pranks and gags.

A halfway house between MULTI-COLOURED SWAP SHOP and NOEL'S HOUSEPARTY, *The Late, Late Breakfast Show* represented Noel Edmonds's successful transition from children's TV to adult programming. Despite becoming popular for regular features like the Hit Squad (hidden-camera jokes staged by former Candid Camera man Peter Dulay), bizarre contests like Mr Puniverse and a feature on out-takes entitled The Golden Egg Awards, the series is unfortunately now best remembered for the death of a member of the public in one of the show's action sequences. In a section entitled Give It a Whirl, a willing viewer was chosen each week to attempt (with prior training) a daredevil stunt for a live outside broadcast hosted by Mike Smith. Sadly, one 'Whirly Wheeler' was killed during practice for a high-rise escapology trick. This led to major ructions within the BBC and the inevitable cancellation of the series after four years on air. The programme's theme music was provided by Gary Kemp of the pop group Spandau Ballet.

Late Night Line-Up

See *Line-Up*.

Late Starter ✶✶

UK (BBC) Drama. BBC 1 1985

Edward Brett	**Peter Barkworth**
Mary Brett	**Rowena Cooper**
Liz Weldon	**Julia Foster**
Helen Magee	**Beryl Reid**
Simon Brett	**Simon Cowell-Parker**
Jack Owen	**Michael Elphick**
Penny Johnson	**Carol Leader**
Colin Johnson	**John Flanagan**
Nicki	**Akosua Busia**

Writer **Brian Clark**
Producer **Ruth Boswell**

● ***Retirement spells disaster for a college lecturer.***
Edward Brett has spent a long and contented career immersed in the world of academia but, when he decides to give up his position as professor of English Literature, his circumstances dramatically take a turn for the worse. On the day he retires, his personal and financial affairs both fall into disarray. His wife vanishes, and proves very hard to track down, leaving Brett to start both his career and romantic life all over again. This time it is in the 'real world', with few of the trappings his cosy university job once provided. To make ends meet he takes a job as a barman but the road that might lead back to the warmth and happiness of middle-class life is long and steep.

Later with Jools Holland ✶✶✶✶

UK (BBC) Music. BBC 2 1992–
DVD: Warner Music Vision

Presenter **Jools Holland**

Executive Producer **Mark Cooper**
Producers **Mark Cooper, Alison Howe**

● ***Uncomplicated live music showcase, with all styles represented.***
Beginning modestly as just one strand of the BBC 2 post-NEWSNIGHT arts magazine, *The Late Show, Later with Jools Holland* has become a widely respected vehicle for live music from right across the spectrum. The simple format – assorted artists arranged in a circle inside a bare studio, performing pieces in turn, as well as jamming together for the show's theme music – has been enhanced by intelligent questioning and a little droll wit from the former TUBE frontman. Holland has also plonked in on keyboards to accompany contributors. From jazz to country, via soul, gospel, blues, funk, rock and Britpop, the cosmopolitan musical mix has enjoyed wide appeal. Artists gracing the show have included Smokey Robinson, Björk, Robert Plant, Blur, Willie Nelson, Dusty Springfield, David Bowie, Manic Street Preachers, Sting, Tony Bennett, Robbie Williams, Ladysmith Black Mambazo, Van Morrison, Kirsty MacColl, Craig David, REM, P. J. Harvey and Paul McCartney. Stereophonics, Portishead, Macy Gray and Catatonia were just some of the performers to make their TV debuts on the show. Occasional specials have devoted the entire proceedings to artists like kd lang, Johnny Cash, Mark Knopfler, Elvis Costello, The Beautiful South, Noel and Liam Gallagher, and Paul Weller.

Latham, Philip

(1929–)

British actor, familiar in the 1960s and 1970s through his portrayals of Willy Izard in MOGUL and THE TROUBLESHOOTERS and Plantagenet Palliser in THE PALLISERS. Among his many other credits have been *The Treasure Seekers* (Mr Bastable), HARPERS WEST ONE (Oliver Backhouse), *The Cedar Tree* (Arthur Bourne), MAIGRET, SERGEANT CORK, JUSTICE, LOVE STORY, *Killers*, HAMMER HOUSE OF HORROR, DOCTOR WHO, *No. 10*, NANNY, THE PROFESSIONALS, THE FOURTH ARM (Colonel Gwillim) and LEAVING (Mr Raphael).

Laugh??? I Nearly Paid My Licence Fee ✶✶

UK (BBC) Comedy. BBC 2 1984

Robbie Coltrane, John Sessions, Ron Bain, Louise Gold

Producer **Colin Gilbert**

● ***Gags and skits made in Scotland.***
This short-lived BBC Scotland sketch show (chronologically between A KICK UP THE EIGHTIES and NAKED VIDEO, but broadly following the same pattern) is primarily notable for early appearances from Robbie Coltrane and John Sessions. David McNiven provided the songs. Just six programmes were made.

Laugh Track

Also known as canned laughter. Prerecorded audience laughter that is added to programmes (particularly filmed programmes) to provide atmosphere. The idea is said to have originated in 1950 with an American series called The Hank McCune Show. Studio-produced shows generally have live audiences which are 'warmed up' before recording starts.

Laura and Disorder ✶

UK (BBC) Situation Comedy. BBC 1 1989

Laura Kingsley	**Wendy Craig**
Oberon	**Stephen Persaud**
Howard Kingsley	**Graham Sinclair**
Helen Kingsley	**Sally Hughes**
Holly	**Marie Berry**

Writers **Jonathan Marr, Ross Bentley**
Producer **John B. Hobbs**

● ***A dippy divorcée's return home means misery for her starchy son.***
Laura Kingsley is newly divorced and a free woman again. She decides to leave her home of the past ten years in California and return to England to see her son, Howard, and his wife, Helen. Unfortunately, Laura is one of those people who are

dogged by calamity and her return sends Howard and Helen's life into turmoil. To make matters worse for her stuffy son, Laura discovers a new black soulmate named Oberon, who lives in a squat with his girlfriend, Holly. Despite the fact that star Wendy Craig penned much of the material herself (under her usual pseudonym of Jonathan Marr), and the rest was scripted by her son, Ross Bentley, the programme only ran to one series of six episodes. Jack Parnell supplied the theme music.

Laurie, Hugh
(1959–)

Eton- and Cambridge-educated actor who rowed in the 1980 Boat Race and starred alongside Emma Thompson, Tony Slattery and others in the 1981 Footlights Revue. It was at Cambridge that Laurie joined forces with Stephen Fry, with whom he entered television in the sketch show ALFRESCO. There followed appearances in THE YOUNG ONES, GIRLS ON TOP, FILTHY RICH AND CATFLAP, HAPPY FAMILIES, SATURDAY LIVE, *Look at the State We're In!* and, most prominently, BLACKADDER (Prince George in *Blackadder the Third* and Lt. George in *Blackadder Goes Forth*). The duo also appeared in their own sketch show, *A Bit of Fry and Laurie*, and in Granada's dramatization of JEEVES AND WOOSTER (with Laurie as Bertie Wooster). Laurie has also been seen in serious parts, as in the dramas *All or Nothing at All* (Leo Hopkins), *Fortysomething* (Paul Slippery, also as director), *The Young Visiters* (Lord Bernard Clark), *Life with Judy Garland* (Vincente Minnelli) and HOUSE (Dr Greg House), as well as a guest spot in SPOOKS. Laurie also narrated *The Tale of Jack Frost* and has provided voices for cartoons like *Preston Pig*.

Laurie, John
(1897–1980)

As Mr Frazer, the gloomy, penny-pinching undertaker in DAD'S ARMY, John Laurie became a household name, 'We're doomed' becoming his catchphrase. But this eye-rolling Scottish actor had already enjoyed decades of showbusiness success by the time the small screen beckoned. Some viewers will recall him in the classic Hitchcock version of *The Thirty-Nine Steps* back in 1935, just one of dozens of film roles, in addition to extensive stage work. Laurie was also seen on television in the 1930s, though his first major role didn't arrive until 1961, when he played the thriller writer Algernon Blackwood in hosting the anthology series TALES OF MYSTERY. Later in the 1960s he was the mad scientist, McTurk, in the kids' adventure series THE MASTER, and he also appeared in THE AVENGERS and DR FINLAY'S CASEBOOK.

Lavender, Ian
(1946–)

British actor, usually in comic roles, and easily best remembered for his portrayal of mummy's boy Frank Pike in DAD'S ARMY. As Clive Cunliffe, he was stranded in space with Mollie Sugden in COME BACK MRS NOAH, and he also played Ginger in *Mr Big*, gormless Ron in the revival of the radio series *The Glums*, for *Bruce Forsyth's Big Night* (and later in their own short series), Denis Ailing, the failing salesman, in THE HELLO GOODBYE MAN, and Tom, the dentist, in the sitcom *Have I Got You . . . Where You Want Me?* Lavender has also provided voices for the animation *PC Pinkerton*, made guest appearances in CASUALTY, PEAK PRACTICE, GOODNIGHT SWEETHEART and DOCTORS, and played Professor Plum in a special edition of CLUEDO. More recently, he was seen as Derek Harkinson in EASTENDERS.

Laverne and Shirley ★★

US (Paramount/Miller-Milkis) Situation Comedy. ITV 1977–84 (US: ABC 1976–83)
DVD: Paramount (Region 1 only)

Laverne De Fazio	**Penny Marshall**
Shirley Feeney	**Cindy Williams**
Carmine Ragusa	**Eddie Mekka**
Frank De Fazio	**Phil Foster**
Andrew 'Squiggy' Squigman	**David L. Lander**
Lenny Kosnowski	**Michael McKean**
Edna Babish/De Fazio	**Betty Garrett**
Sonny St Jacques	**Ed Marinaro**
Rhonda Lee	**Leslie Easterbrook**

Creator **Garry K. Marshall**
Executive Producers **Thomas L. Miller, Edward K. Milkis, Garry K. Marshall**
Producers **Lowell Ganz, Tony Marshall, Mark Rothman**

Two incident-prone girl flatmates work at a brewery but long for something better.

Laverne De Fazio and Shirley Feeney work in the bottling section of the Shotz brewery in Milwaukee in the late 1950s. They also room together in the basement of a town house. They are ambitious, seek fun and fame, but are always short of cash. Tall Laverne (sporting a large, looping 'L' on her sweater) is rather loud, but very insecure. Petite, dark-haired Shirley is naïve and easily taken in. Together they lurch from scrape to scrape.

Their friends feature prominently, particularly the womanizing Carmine, Shirley's on-off boyfriend who likes to be known as 'The Big Ragu' and is always liable to burst into his signature song, 'Rags to Riches'. There are also the well-meaning but very dim brewery truck-drivers, Squiggy and Lenny. Laverne's father, Frank, owns the Pizza Bowl, where the girls bowl and dance. He later marries Mrs Babish, Laverne and Shirley's landlady.

Well into its run, *Laverne and Shirley* changes location. It is now the early 1960s and the action has moved to California, where Laverne and Shirley are hoping for a career in films. True to form, they end up working only as shop assistants, in Bardwell's Department Store. All the friends move with them, and a couple of new neighbours, Rhonda, a dancer and model, and Sonny, a stuntman, are introduced. Laverne's father and new stepmother take over a restaurant, Cowboy Bill's. A couple of years later, Shirley is married off to army doctor Walter Meany (actress Cindy Williams asked to be written out, after a dispute over working hours) and the show continues for one last season with just Penny Marshall starring and Laverne now working at the Ajax Aerospace Company.

Laverne and Shirley was a very successful spin-off from HAPPY DAYS, in which the girls had made a couple of fleeting appearances. Penny Marshall was the sister of *Happy Days* creator Garry Marshall and has since made a name for herself as a Hollywood director. 'Making Our Dreams Come True', the theme song performed by Cyndi Grecco, was an American hit single in 1976. The series, originally seen sporadically around the ITV network, has also been rerun on the BBC as a daytime filler.

Law and Disorder ✶

UK (Thames/Central) Situation Comedy. ITV 1994

Phillippa Troy	**Penelope Keith**
Gerald Triggs	**Simon Williams**
Judge Wallace	**Charles Kay**
Arthur Bryant	**Eamon Boland**
Steven	**John Junkin**
Susan	**Emma Davies**

Writer **Alex Shearer**
Producer **John Howard Davies**

A talented barrister/writer is handed the most unlikely civil cases.

As barristers go, Phillippa Troy does appear to have a peculiar workload. When a balloonist frightens a bull to death, Phillippa has to dispute claims for damages; when a football fan gets the wrong tattoo, again it is left to Phillippa to fight his corner; when a man is accused of eating his shipmate, poor Phillippa must somehow ensure charges of cannibalism are dismissed. But, so effective is her no-nonsense style, she always manages to get the better of her old adversary, Gerald Triggs, with the help of Steven, her clerk, Susan, their junior, and Arthur Bryant, her instructing solicitor. Wallace is the judge on all occasions. As a second string to her life, Phillippa doubles up as a children's author, writing books about Prickly Peter, a hedgehog. Just one series was made, consisting of six episodes.

Law and Order [1] ✶✶

UK (BBC) Legal Drama. BBC 2 1978

DI Fred Pyall	**Derek Martin**
Alex Gladwell	**Ken Campbell**
Clifford Harding	**Alan Ford**
DS Eric Lethridge	**Billy Cornelius**
Micky Fielder	**Roy Sone**
DCI Tony Simmons	**Fred Haggerty**
Jack Lynn	**Peter Dean**
Cathy Lynn	**Deirdre Costello**
Judge Robert Quigley	**André Van Gyseghem**
Horace MacMillan QC	**Michael Griffiths**
Brian Harpenden-Smith QC	**Peter Welch**
Michael Messick QC	**Terence Bayler**
Stanley Eaton QC	**Jeffrey Segal**
Governor Maudling	**Edward Cast**
Chief Officer Carne	**Roger Booth**
Principal Officer McClean	**Farrell Sheridan**
Principal Officer Allen	**Gil Sutherland**

Creator/Writer **G. F. Newman**
Producer **Tony Garnett**

Straight-talking drama exploring crime from both sides of the story.

A Detective's Tale, A Villain's Tale, A Brief's Tale, A Prisoner's Tale: the titles of the four films in this short series sum up four facets of the criminal justice system. *Law and Order* was novelist G. F. Newman's first television commission. It started out simply as a one-off police drama that producer Tony Garnett wanted to pull no punches and show the true face of policing in the 1970s, blowing away the froth of established cops-and-robbers shows. But, as the work came together, Newman was encouraged to add further dimensions, to analyse the lot of not just the policeman but also that of others who complete the crime equation, namely the criminal, the lawyer and the prisoner. His series focuses on three individuals. The first is DI Fred Pyall, a 43-year-old, grim-faced, hard detective whose family life has fallen foul of the long hours and stresses of his job. Pyall's adversary is Jack Lynn, a sharp-dressing, 40-year-old, right-wing crook, who, when he gets his comeuppance, is also seen as the prisoner of the series. The third major player is 35-year-old Alex Gladwell, a cunning brief who demands a high fee for getting hardened criminals off the hook.

Law and Order broke new ground in exposing imperfections in the police service and the frailties and occasional duplicity of the men who do the law enforcing. It also explores the failings of the prison service, offers an insight into why criminals behave as they do, and reveals the way in which bent lawyers can twist justice for their own personal gain. Perhaps most disturbing for the Establishment is the suggestion that cops and robbers are made of the same stuff and it is just circumstance that leads them to fall on one or other side of the fence. Predictable howls of protest from the police and the prison service followed the initial broadcast. The four-letter words that Newman had scattered throughout his scripts for authenticity were censored by the BBC, but he did at least succeed in introducing many viewers to a whole new vocabulary of 'trade' terms from the shady world of crime and punishment. Leslie Blair directs the four films that run to around 80 minutes each.

Law & Order [2] ✶✶✶

US (Wolf Films/Universal) Police/Legal Drama. BBC 1 1991; Channel 5 2002– (US: NBC 1990–)
DVD: Universal

DS Max Greevey	**George Dzundza**
Det. Mike Logan	**Christopher Noth**
Det. Phil Cerreta	**Paul Sorvino**
Capt. Donald Cragen	**Dann Florek**
Det. Lennie Briscoe	**Jerry Orbach**
Lt. Anita Van Buren	**S. Epatha Merkerson**
Asst DA Ben Stone	**Michael Moriarty**
Asst DA Paul Robinette	**Richard Brooks**
Asst DA Claire Kincaid	**Jill Hennessy**
DA Adam Schiff	**Steven Hill**
Asst DA Jack McCoy	**Sam Waterston**
Det. Reynaldo 'Rey' Curtis	**Benjamin Bratt**
Asst DA Jamie Ross	**Carey Lowell**
Asst DA Abbie Carmichael	**Angie Harmon**
Det. Eddie Green	**Jesse L. Martin**
Asst DA Serena Southerlyn	**Elisabeth Röhm**
DA Arthur Branch	**Fred Dalton Thompson**

Creator **Dick Wolf**
Executive Producers **Dick Wolf, Michael Chernuchin, William M. Finkelstein, Edwin Sherin, Joseph Stern, Peter Jankowski, Arthur Penn, Barry Schindel**

Two halves of a crime story: the detective work and the legal prosecution.

Following a similar format to the 1960s series ARREST AND TRIAL, each episode of *Law & Order* divides into two parts. The first half deals with the discovery of a crime and the police response; the second sees the police hand the files over to the district attorney's office for prosecution, culminating in a dramatic court case. Filled with twists and turns, the series is a breathless ride through the American judicial system, cramming so many plots and sub-plots into each slick, 50-minute episode that an 'edited highlights' atmosphere is conveyed. The hand-held cameras and 'news-report'-style filming add to the pace and realism. The main characters on the NYPD side are chunky cop Max Greevey and his younger colleague, Mike Logan, plus their replacements, Phil Cerreta, wily old Lennie Briscoe, his idealistic right-hand man Rey Curtis and later compulsive Eddie Green. The cops are answerable at various times to Capt. Donald Cragen and Lt. Anita Van Buren. On the legal side Ben Stone and Paul Robinette eventually give way to Claire Kincaid then Jack McCoy, Jamie Ross, Abbie Carmichael and Serena Southerlyn, all responsible to gruff, politically motivated DA Adam Schiff, later replaced by DA Arthur Branch. Mike Post provided the theme music. After an early run on BBC 1, and then doing the rounds of various digital/satellite stations, the series returned to UK terrestrial TV in 2002, courtesy of Channel 5, picking up with episodes from 1997.

In 1999 NBC launched the first spin-off series, entitled *Law & Order: Special Victims Unit* (five 2003–), starring Christopher Meloni as Det. Elliot Stabler, Richard Belzer as Det. John Munch and Mariska Hargitay as Det. Olivia Benson. Capt. Cragen also features and the focus here is on sexual crimes. In 2001 *Law & Order: Criminal Intent* arrived (five 2004–), with the attention given to New York's Major Case Squad and its handling of high-profile investigations, with detectives trying to work through the psyche of criminals to crack the cases. Vincent D'Onofrio stars as Det. Robert Goren, with Kathryn Erbe as Det. Alexandra Eames, Jamey Sheridan as Capt. James Deakins and Courtney B. Vance as Asst DA Ron Carver. In 2005 NBC aired the first series of *Law & Order: Trial by Jury*, a third offshoot, giving more attention to the work of defence teams, jurors, judges and other folk wrapped up in the judicial system. Bebe Neuwirth (Lilith in CHEERS) stars as Asst DA Tracey Kibre, supported by Amy Carlson as Asst DA Kelly Gaffney, with Arthur Branch and Lennie Briscoe crossing over from the mother series. *Trial by Jury* was screened by ITV 3 from 2006.

Lawley, Sue
OBE (1946–)

Midlands-born journalist and current affairs presenter, originally seen on NATIONWIDE and TONIGHT. She has also chaired QUESTION TIME; the BBC right-to-reply programme, *Biteback*, and other debates; stood in for Terry Wogan on his chat show; read the main BBC news bulletins; presented some interview shows for ITV; and fronted *Hospital Watch*, *Review of the Year* and the news magazine *Here and Now*. In 1995 she anchored the special 50th anniversary BBC news programmes which commemorated events leading up to VE and VJ Day. Lawley is also host of the radio series *Desert Island Discs*.

Lawrence, Josie
(Wendy Lawrence; 1959–)

British actress and comic, one of the stars of the improvisation series WHOSE LINE IS IT ANYWAY? Previously, Lawrence had been seen on FRIDAY NIGHT LIVE (with her Florence from Cradley characterization) and among her other appearances have been parts in AGATHA CHRISTIE'S POIROT, CAMPAIGN (film-maker Linda Prentice), Harry Enfield's *Norbert Smith – A Life*, THE GREEN MAN (Lucy), the kids' comedy *Jackson Pace: The Great Years* (Ryveeta Tusk), *Paul Merton in Galton & Simpson's . . .*, WHERE THE HEART IS, HOLBY CITY, DOWN TO EARTH and AGATHA CHRISTIE'S MARPLE. She was Janet Wilkins in the apocalyptic comedy *Not with a Bang*, Lottie in the *Screen Two* film *Enchanted April*, Maggie Costello in the cricketing comedy OUTSIDE EDGE, Sophie in DOWNWARDLY MOBILE, Mary in *The Flint Street Nativity*, fitness guru Julia Fleshman in FAT FRIENDS and Camilla in *A Many Splintered Thing*. She has also starred in her own series, *Josie*, appeared in THE COMIC STRIP PRESENTS and voiced numerous cartoon characters.

Lawson, Denis
(1947–)

Glaswegian actor, writer and director, seen on TV as DJ Kit Curran in THE KIT CURRAN RADIO SHOW, Eddie Cass in the thriller DEAD HEAD, Rossi in *The Justice Game*, John Stone in AMBASSADOR, Greg in BOB MARTIN, Tom in *Other People's Children*, Tom Campbell-Gore in HOLBY CITY, Julius Gore-Urquhart in LUCKY JIM, Al Jackson in *Sensitive Skin* and John Jarndyce in BLEAK HOUSE. Other credits include BERGERAC, BOON, *That Uncertain Feeling*, EL C. I. D., *Screen One's Born Kicking*, *Natural Lies*, CATHERINE COOKSON*'s The Round Tower*, PIE IN THE SKY, COLD FEET, HORNBLOWER and *Solid Geometry*, a short film he directed and co-wrote. He is an uncle to actor Ewan McGregor.

Layton, George
(1943–)

British actor, comedian and writer, some of his earliest appearances coming as striker Jimmy Stokes in the soccer soap UNITED!, and as Paul Collier in the various DOCTOR series (some episodes of which he also wrote, initially under the name of Oliver Fry). Layton was one of the first three presenters of THAT'S LIFE (with Esther Rantzen and Bob Wellings) and played Bombardier Solomons in the earlier seasons of IT AIN'T HALF HOT MUM. He was Brian Booth in *My Brother's Keeper* (again also as writer), popped up now and again as Des in MINDER and as the Aussie crook Ray in THE SWEENEY, hosted the quiz show *Pass the Buck*, and provided voices for the animation *Pigeon Street*. Later, Layton played Alan Brooks in SUNBURN and Mr Jacobs in *Metropolis*, with guest appearances in DOCTORS and HOLBY CITY. Among his other writing credits have been DON'T WAIT UP and EXECUTIVE STRESS, and episodes of ON THE BUSES, ROMANY JONES, ROBIN'S NEST and *My Name is Harry Worth*.

Le Mesurier, John
(John Elton Halliley; 1912–83)

Elegant British actor, raised in Bury St Edmunds and initially training in law. Le Mesurier has been immortalized as the ineffective Sgt Wilson in DAD'S ARMY but was a prominent performer on TV for four decades. In the 1950s he starred on children's television (including in WHIRLIGIG) and went on to be a regular guest on HANCOCK'S HALF HOUR, appeared as Colonel Maynard in GEORGE AND THE DRAGON, and headlined as the hard-up aristocrat, Lord Bleasham, in *A Class by Himself*. His performance in the Dennis Potter play *Traitor*, based on spy Kim Philby, was much acclaimed. Le Mesurier (his stage name was his mother's maiden name) was also seen in such programmes as THE AVENGERS, THE TROUBLESHOOTERS, THE GOODIES, DOCTOR AT LARGE, WORZEL GUMMIDGE and BRIDESHEAD REVISITED, and his voice was as familiar as his face, thanks to numerous Homepride flour commercials and the children's animation BOD, for which he was narrator. His second wife was actress Hattie Jacques.

Le Vaillant, Nigel
(1958–)

British actor born in Pakistan. Oxford-educated, Le Vaillant is best known as Drs Julian Chapman in CASUALTY and Paul Dangerfield in DANGERFIELD. Other credits have included BRIDESHEAD REVISITED, JEMIMA SHORE INVESTIGATES, CHRISTABEL, *Call Me Mister*, WISH ME LUCK, AGATHA CHRISTIE'S POIROT, MINDER, HANNAY, LADIES IN CHARGE, *Poor Little Rich Girl*, THE BILL and HONEY FOR TEA (Professor Simon Latimer).

Leach, Rosemary
(1925–)

Shropshire-born actress much seen on television as a supporting player in sitcoms and straight drama, but also with some notable starring parts to her name. She appeared with Ronnie Corbett in NO – THAT'S ME OVER HERE, NOW LOOK HERE . . . and *The Prince of Denmark*, was Sadie Potter in *Sadie, It's Cold Outside*, Queen Victoria in *Disraeli*, Katy Bunting, a late first-time mother, in *Life Begins at Forty*, Fenny Grace in JEWEL IN THE CROWN, Joan Craddock in GROWING PAINS, swindled widow Joan Plumleigh-Bruce in THE CHARMER, Mavis Hunt in AN UNGENTLEMANLY ACT, and Mary in *Screen One's Tender Loving Care*. She was also Lady Brightlingsea in *The Buccaneers*, Nanny Collins in BERKELEY SQUARE, Mrs Forefoot Meadows in CATHERINE COOKSON*'s Tilly Trotter*, Vera in *Perfect*, Mrs Dickinson in *Back Home*, Irene in *Down to Earth* and Carol Samson in *The Secretary Who Stole £4 Million*. The 1971 version of *Cider With Rosie* gave her another chance to shine, and among other credits have been parts in ARMCHAIR THEATRE productions and other plays, THE POWER GAME, RUMPOLE OF THE BAILEY, JACKANORY, THE ROADS TO FREEDOM, *When We Are Married*, *Summer's Lease*, TITMUSS REGAINED, *Blood and Peaches*, *Chiller*, *Frighteners*, MIDSOMER MURDERS, *Bosom Pals* (voices), HEARTBEAT, MY FAMILY, DOCTORS, HOLBY CITY, AFTERLIFE, *The Afternoon Play* and various TV adaptations of classics.

League of Gentlemen, The ★★★★

UK (BBC) Comedy. BBC 2 1999–2000; 2002
DVD: BBC

Mark Gatiss, Steve Pemberton, Reece Shearsmith

Writers **Jeremy Dyson, Mark Gatiss, Steve Pemberton, Reece Shearsmith**
Producers **Sarah Smith, Jemma Rodgers**

● ***Darkly comic goings-on in a bleak northern town.***

Having secured awards at the Edinburgh Festival and then enjoyed success on BBC Radio, *The League of Gentlemen* team switched seamlessly to television in 1999. Their surreal series, set in the bleak northern town of Royston Vasey ('You'll Never Leave!') and involving sketches plus a continuing storyline, focuses on the in-bred local townsfolk, all seemingly hiding a deep, dark, desperate secret. Among the oddball creations – all played by the trio of Steve Pemberton, Mark Gatiss and Reece Shearsmith – are sadistic, pen-obsessed careers adviser Pauline; dim, unemployed lad Mickey; Edward and Tubbs, whose shop is only for the use of locals; Barbara, the transsexual taxi-driver; Mr Chinnery, the lethal vet; dubious butcher Hilary Briss; gun-toting businessman Geoff and his colleagues, Mike and Brian; alcoholic vicar Bernice; German exchange teacher Herr Lipp; forgotten pop star Les McQueen and his band, Crème Brûlée; inept theatre group Legz Akimbo; joke shop owner Lance King; Kenny Harris, who runs a cinema that only shows films featuring dogs; amateur magician Dean Tavalouris; useless debt collectors Big Barry and Glen; *Knight Rider* fan Neds; weird Dr Carlton; and Judee Levinson, proprietor of a beauty salon called Spit & Polish. The only sanity comes from outsiders like back-packer Benjamin, whose local aunt and uncle, Harvey and Val Denton, have some peculiar domestic rules concerning bodily functions. A guest character, foul-mouthed Mayor Vaughan, is played by comedian Roy 'Chubby' Brown, whose real name is Royston Vasey. The series was filmed in the Derbyshire town of Hadfield.

Lear, Norman
(1922–)

Influential American producer, a former scriptwriter who, in the 1970s, was responsible for introducing a more adult attitude to American situation comedy. The break came with ALL IN THE FAMILY and its outspoken lead character, Archie Bunker, based on TILL DEATH US DO PART and Alf Garnett. The series was a huge hit and broke new ground in exploring what was acceptable in American television. Its spin-offs, *Maude* and *The Jeffersons*, were just as challenging to the 'Honey, I'm home' tradition of US comedies, as was *Sanford and Son* (another UK clone, this time of STEPTOE AND SON). Lear was also responsible for the cult comedies *Mary Hartman, Mary Hartman* and DIFF'RENT STROKES, and became a shrewd media businessman. Much of his early TV (and film) work was in collaboration with Bud Yorkin.

Leaving ★★

UK (BBC) Situation Comedy. BBC 1 1984–5

Daniel Ford	**Keith Barron**
Martha Ford	**Susan Hampshire**
Mr Chessington	**Richard Vernon**
Gina Ford	**Lucy Aston**
Matthew Ford	**Gary Cady**
Mrs Ford	**Elizabeth Bradley**
Josephine	**Caroline Dennis**
Mr Raphael	**Philip Latham**
Freda	**Norma Streader**
Ray Huntingdon	**John Arthur**

Writer **Carla Lane**
Producer **John B. Hobbs**

● ***A couple's divorce is anything but smooth.***

In their middle age, Daniel and Martha Ford, despite having a nice home and family, are not seeing eye to eye. At Martha's suggestion they decide to part on good terms but all does not go to plan. People and things – their kids, Gina and Matthew, Daniel's mum and even the dog – become obstacles and the pair have difficulty going their separate ways. By the time of the second series, Daniel and Martha have finally divorced. They now set out to make new lives for themselves, all the while trying to keep things amicable and attempting to hold the family together. Freda is Daniel's new girlfriend. Written in Carla Lane's wordy, thoughtful style, *Leaving* was described as not so much a situation comedy as a situation tragedy. It had its moving moments, as well as humour.

Legacy of Reginald Perrin, The
See *Fall and Rise of Reginald Perrin, The.*

Leigh, Mike

OBE (1943–)

Award-winning British screenwriter and director whose television work has centred on comedies derived from social observation (particularly of the middle classes) with a strong leaning on his actors' improvisational skills, including those of one-time wife Alison Steadman. His most acclaimed works have been NUTS IN MAY and ABIGAIL'S PARTY, with other credits including *Hard Labour* (1973), *Kiss of Death* (1977), *Grown-Ups* (1980) and *Home Sweet Home* (1982).

Lenny The Lion Show, The ✱✱

UK (BBC) Children's Entertainment. BBC 1956–63

Producers **Ronald Eyre, Johnny Downes, Peter Whitmore**

● ***Fun, games and pop music with a soppy ventriloquist's lion.***

Ventriloquist Terry Hall and his Lenny the Lion puppet were one of the hottest properties in children's television in the late 1950s and early 1960s. Somewhat languid in appearance, failing to pronounce his 'r's, and prone to burying his maned head in his paw, the wide-eyed Lenny was unusual in being an animal dummy rather than the run-of-the mill talking boy. He was also one of the first dummies to be given arm-movements, which added to his novelty factor. As well as gags, Lenny's programmes (first seen under the *Children's Television* banner), had a strong pop-music element. Indeed, his 1962 series was entitled *Pops and Lenny* and listed The Beatles as guests on one occasion.

Lenska, Rula

(Roza Maria Lubienska; 1947–)

Tall, flame-haired, British actress of noble Polish descent who first came to light in ROCK FOLLIES (playing 'Q' – or Nancy Cunard de Longchamps – of The Little Ladies rock band) and has since been seen in programmes like *Take a Letter, Mr Jones* (Mrs Warner, John Inman's boss), *Family Pride*, PRIVATE SCHULZ (Gertrude Steiner), MINDER, ROBIN OF SHERWOOD, BOON, AN ACTOR'S LIFE FOR ME, CLUEDO (Mrs Peacock), the kids' series *Kappatoo*, STAY LUCKY, ONE FOOT IN THE GRAVE and EASTENDERS (Krystal). Earlier credits included DIXON OF DOCK GREEN, THE BROTHERS, EDWARD THE SEVENTH, THE SAINT and SPECIAL BRANCH. Her second husband was Dennis Waterman.

Let There be Love ✱✱

UK (Thames) Situation Comedy. ITV 1982–3

Timothy Love	**Paul Eddington**
Judy	**Nanette Newman**
Dennis Newberry	**Henry McGee**
Charles	**Stephen Nolan**
Edward	**Ian Morrison**
Elizabeth	**Claudia Gambold**

Writers **Johnnie Mortimer, Brian Cooke, Brian Platt, John Seaton, John Chapman**
Producer **Peter Frazer-Jones**

● ***A single man's comfortable life is turned upside down when he inherits a family.***

Timothy Love has everything going for him. A happy-go-lucky, middle-aged bachelor, he has few responsibilities, until, that is, he meets widow Judy and Love by name experiences love by nature. Timothy doesn't realize at first that Judy has three children (plus an Alsatian dog, Rusty) and when this is revealed he has to weigh up the consequences of the discovery. If he goes ahead with their planned wedding, his carefree days will be over and his pocket will take a pounding. However, the attraction is just too great and the long meander to the altar begins. By series two, Timothy and Judy are married and kids Charles, Edward and Elizabeth are firmly part of Love's life. Also seen is Dennis Newberry, Timothy's friend and work colleague at an advertising agency, who, in contrast, sees his own marriage collapse.

Letterman, David

(1947–)

American comedian, talk show host and producer, a former announcer, weatherman, children's presenter and writer who, after working with Mary Tyler Moore, eventually broke into the big time courtesy of Johnny Carson's *Tonight* (as a regular guest and stand-in host). This led indirectly to his own series, *Late Night with David Letterman*, in 1982. This cult chat show, famous for its offbeat stunts and camera trickery, has also been screened in the UK.

Levinson, Richard

(1934–87)

American executive, a writer and producer, working closely with William Link to create action series like COLUMBO, ELLERY QUEEN, MANNIX, BANACEK, TENAFLY and MURDER, SHE WROTE, as well as many TV movies. They also contributed episodes to ALFRED HITCHCOCK PRESENTS, THE FUGITIVE, BURKE'S LAW and other dramas.

Lewis

See *Inspector Morse*.

Lewis, Damian

(1971–)

Eton-educated British actor starring in the dramas WARRIORS (Lt. Neil Loughrey), *Life Force* (Glemser), HEARTS AND BONES (Mark Rose), BAND OF BROTHERS (Major Richard Winters), THE FORSYTE SAGA (Soames Forsyte), COLDITZ (Nicholas McGrade), *Much Ado about Nothing* (Benedick) and *Friends and Crocodiles* (Paul). He also narrated the documentary *Soldier, Husband, Daughter, Dad*. Earlier appearances came in AGATHA CHRISTIE'S POIROT and A TOUCH OF FROST.

Lewis, Martyn

CBE (1945–)

Prominent Welsh newsreader and presenter, formerly with the BBC in Northern Ireland, HTV Wales and ITN but for many years from 1986 back at the BBC as one of its main frontmen. He has also hosted special reports, SONGS OF PRAISE, *Crime Beat* and the daytime game show *Today's the Day*, and, after leaving BBC News in 2000, fronted the retrospective *News 40: the Battle of Britain*. Other recent credits have included *Dateline Jerusalem* (news of the first Easter) and *Ultimate Questions*.

Lewis, Shari

(Shari Hurwitz; 1934–98)

New York-born ventriloquist who had her own show on British television in the 1960s and 1970s, featuring her glove puppets Lamb Chop (first seen on US TV in 1957), Hush Puppy and Charlie Horse. She also wrote dozens of children's books.

Liberace

(Wladziu Valentino Liberace; 1919–1987)

Flamboyant American pianist and entertainer whose variety shows were very popular in the 1950s and 1960s. Although he had been classically trained, 'Lee' Liberace forwent all the starchy trappings of a concert pianist and, instead, he made brightly sequined costumes, shiny candelabra and a sparkling toothy smile his trademarks. He may have been panned by the critics, but he was loved by his audience and was so unperturbed by all the flak that he coined the memorable phrase, 'I cried all the way to the bank.' Fully aware of his outrageous persona, Liberace was happy to camp it up in BATMAN, playing the villainous Chandell. His later television work was focused on specials and guest appearances.

Library Film

Stock footage used to illustrate a news item or another feature.

Licence Fee

The annual fee payable to the Government for the use of radio and television receivers in the UK. This provides the funding for the BBC. The licence (initially wireless only, of course) was introduced at ten shillings (50p) in 1922. The fee remained static until 1946, when it was doubled to £1. It has gradually increased over the years and a two-tier licence fee, for monochrome or colour viewing, was instigated in 1967, on the arrival of colour television.

Life and Legend of Wyatt Earp, The ✻✻

US (Louis F. Edelmann/Wyatt Earp Enterprises) Western. ITV 1956–62 (US: ABC 1955–61)
DVD: Rhino (Region 1 only)

Wyatt Earp	**Hugh O'Brian**
Bat Masterson	**Mason Alan Dinehart III**
Ben Thompson	**Denver Pyle**
Abbie Crandall	**Gloria Talbot**
Doc Fabrique	**Douglas Fowley**
Marsh Murdock	**Don Haggerty**
Jim 'Dog' Kelly	**Paul Brinegar**
	Ralph Sanford
Doc Holliday	**Douglas Fowley**
	Myron Healey
Shotgun Gibbs	**Morgan Woodward**
Morgan Earp	**Dirk London**
Virgil Earp	**John Anderson**
Nellie Cashman	**Randy Stuart**
Old Man Clanton	**Trevor Bardette**
Sheriff John Behan	**Lash La Rue**
	Steve Brodie
Doc Goodfellow	**Damian O'Flynn**

Producer **Robert F. Sisk**

Early Western depicting the colourful life of the famous marshal.

Broadly based on fact, this series follows Wyatt Earp's career in almost serial form and catalogues his encounters with the famous outlaws of the Wild West. It begins with the murder of his friend Marshal Whitney, and Earp agreeing to take on his badge in Ellsworth, Kansas. The rugged lawman later moves to Dodge City, where he confronts the infamous Doc Holliday and is assisted by his deputy, Bat Masterson. The mayor, Jim 'Dog' Kelly, is also a friend, and Earp's brothers Virgil and Morgan appear now and again (but not Matt Dillon who, according to GUNSMOKE, was also Marshal of Dodge City at that time).

In his last posting, Earp takes over as Marshal of Tombstone, Arizona, meeting some of his most fearsome adversaries, the Clanton 'Ten Percent Gang'. With the Tombstone sheriff, Johnny Behan, in the pocket of Old Man Clanton, Earp is forced to call up frontiersman Shotgun Gibbs, a friend from Dodge City, to be his new deputy. Doc Holliday also shows up, and the series comes to a conclusion with the celebrated 'Gunfight at the OK Corral'. Nellie Cashman, owner of the Birdcage Saloon, is Earp's romantic attachment. Throughout the series, Earp's trademark is a pair of 'Buntline Special' pistols with extended barrels. They allow him to shoot his enemies from a long distance – very useful when dealing with such a nasty crowd.

Life and Loves of a She Devil, The ✻✻✻

UK (BBC) Drama. BBC 2 1986
DVD: Network

Ruth	**Julie T. Wallace**
Bobbo	**Dennis Waterman**
Mary Fisher	**Patricia Hodge**
Mrs Fisher	**Liz Smith**
Nurse Hopkins	**Miriam Margolyes**
Father Ferguson	**Tom Baker**

Writer **Ted Whitehead**
Producer **Sally Head**

A spurned wife uses supernatural powers to wreak revenge on her husband and his mistress.

Ruth is a pathetic specimen. Hideously ugly and devoid of self-confidence, she discovers that her accountant husband, Bobbo, has only married her out of pity and simply uses her to look after the kids and run the home. When one day he walks out to live with Mary Fisher, a best-selling divorcée authoress of romantic fiction, in her luxurious converted lighthouse, Ruth's hurt and anger manifests itself supernaturally. Remembering his parting words, in which he dubbed her a 'she devil', Ruth burns down the family home and sets out on the road of revenge. Using a selection of disguises and identities to weave her spell, Ruth manipulates other people into destroying Bobbo's life and career. Along the way, she strikes a powerful blow for womankind.

The Life and Loves of a She Devil, directed by Philip Saville and adapted by Ted Whitehead in four parts from Fay

Weldon's novel, gave unknown actress Julie T. Wallace her big break. 'Uglified' to fit the bill, Wallace stole the show but still wasn't asked to appear in the 1989 US film version, *She Devil*, which starred Roseanne Barr.

Life and Times of David Lloyd George, The ✶✶

UK (BBC) Historical Drama. BBC 2 1981

David Lloyd George	**Philip Madoc**
	Dylan Jones *(young)*
Margaret Owen/Lloyd George	**Lisabeth Miles**
William George	**William Thomas**
	Euros Jones *(young)*
Richard Lloyd	**Meredith Edwards**
Betsy George	**Beryl Williams**
William Ewart Gladstone	**Roland Culver**
Lizzie Davies	**Ruth Madoc**
Richard Lloyd George	**Iestyn Garlick**
	Jac Wynne-Williams *(young)*
Herbert Henry Asquith	**David Markham**
Winston Churchill	**William Hootkins**
Anita Williams/George	**Gillian Elisa Thomas**
Megan Lloyd George	**Sue Jones-Davies**
	Lisa Grug *(young)*
Frances Stevenson	**Kika Markham**
Sara	**Elen Roger Jones**
John Redmond	**Dermot Tuohy**
John Dillon	**Denys Hawthorne**
Gwilym Lloyd George	**John Francis**
Lord Grey of Falloden	**Anthony Sharp**
Reginald McKenna	**Hugh Morton**
Sir Edward Carson	**Kevin Flood**
Maurice Hankey	**Jonathan Elsom**
J. T. Davies	**Ioan Meredith**
Andrew Bonar Law	**Fulton Mackay**
Georges Clémenceau	**Michael Anthony**
Sir Max Aitken	**Ed Deveraux**
Lord Curzon	**John Gill**
A. J. Sylvester	**David Troughton**
Aneurin Bevan	**Ray Smith**

Writer **Elaine Morgan**
Producer **John Hefin**

A poor Welsh boy becomes one of the most influential statesmen of the 20th century.

This nine-part biopic of Liberal politician Lloyd George was produced by BBC Wales and is possibly best known for spawning a number two hit single in its evocative theme tune, 'Chi Mai' by Ennio Morricone. The drama itself begins with the future prime minister's impoverished Baptist upbringing in a Welsh-speaking village, underlining how unlikely and meteoric his rise to power was to be. It follows his election to Parliament in 1890, revealing his ability to inspire both extreme admiration and deep hatred through his intelligence and oratory, and then charts his progress into the Cabinet. As Chancellor of the Exchequer he lays the foundation for the welfare state, his redistributive policies enraging the House of Lords in the process. Lloyd George becomes premier in 1916 and his significant role in the World War I victory is explored, as is his stance against the suffragette movement and his problems dealing with the Irish Question. There is also the less salubrious side of his life: his incessant womanizing. Despite marrying early, Lloyd George becomes known for his string of mistresses, most notably his secretary, Frances Stevenson, who becomes his second wife on the death of his first wife, Margaret.

Life and Times of Grizzly Adams, The ✶✶

US (Sunn Classic) Adventure. ITV 1978–9 (US: NBC 1977–8)

James Capen 'Grizzly' Adams	**Dan Haggerty**
Mad Jack	**Denver Pyle**
Nakuma	**Don Shanks**
Robbie Cartman	**John Bishop**

Executive Producer **Charles E. Sellier Jr**
Producers **Leonard B. Kaufman, Jim Simmons, Art Stolnitz**

Accused of a crime he did not commit, a man flees to a satisfying life in the wilderness.

The Life and Times of Grizzly Adams was based on the exploits of a real 19th-century refugee who lived in the Sierra Nevada and struck up a rapport with animals. In the TV version, Grizzly lives in a log cabin, at one with nature, wearing only cloth garments. He fishes to eat but never hunts. He is befriended by Mad Jack (also the show's narrator), an Indian named Nakuma and a young lad, Robbie Cartman, who lives on a nearby farm. Adams's constant companion is a wild bear named Ben, which he rescued as a cub. Their heartwarming adventures are built around the call of the wild, the trials of nature and the disruptive visits of strangers. The real Adams died in 1860 while touring with P. T. Barnum's circus. The theme song, 'Maybe', was a UK hit for Tom Pace in 1979.

Life Begins ✶✶

UK (Granada) Drama. ITV 1 2004–5
DVD: Granada Ventures

Maggie Mee/Thornhill	**Caroline Quentin**
Phil Mee	**Alexander Armstrong**
Eric Thornhill	**Frank Finlay**
Brenda Thornhill	**Anne Reid**
Clare	**Claire Skinner**
Guy	**Stuart McQuarrie**
Becca Mee	**Ace-Destiny Ryan**
James Mee	**Elliot Henderson-Boyle**
Kathleen	**Ellie Haddington**
Samantha	**Abby Ford**
George	**Alan Williams**
Jeff	**Paul Thornley**
Helen	**Chloe Howman**
Karen	**Sarah Ozeke**
Anna Daniels	**Naomi Allisstone**
Carl	**Huw Rhys**
Paul	**Danny Webb**
Keiron	**Nicholas Boulton**
Genevieve	**Michelle Holmes**
Kevin	**Finlay Robertson**
Frank	**Roy Dotrice**

Creator **Mike Bullen**
Writers **Mike Bullen, John Forte**
Producer **John Chapman**

A jilted middle-aged mum needs to find a new man and a new job.

A family holiday in a picture-postcard Suffolk cottage doesn't quite turn out as Maggie Mee has planned. Husband Phil seems rather edgy and, before they can even settle down to enjoy the break, he announces that he's going to move out. Thus Maggie, a woman on the brink of her forties, finds herself in a new world – one without a husband and, as she soon discovers, without much money. Ten years of raising kids Becca and James has taken Maggie far away from the cut and thrust of the employment world, so she needs to learn new tricks if she's to keep the family afloat. Resourcefulness could well be her middle name, however, and she cheeks her way into a job at a St Albans travel agency. But holding this down while coping with troubled children, 'supportive' ageing parents Eric and Brenda, and assorted domestic crises is never easy, especially when the ex-hubby seems to be doing just fine in his new life with new girlfriend Anna (at least at first). Shoulders to cry on belong to friend Clare and neighbour Kathleen, but Maggie is resilient and keeps bouncing back, always hoping, but never dreaming, that things are soon to change dramatically for the better. A ray of hope breaks through at the end of the six-part first series when she starts to date her son's history teacher, Paul, but an awkward relationship triangle featuring Maggie, Paul and Phil goes on to dominate the eight-part second run, shown in 2005.

From the pen of COLD FEET creator Mike Bullen, *Life Begins* was originally offered to Sarah Lancashire, who declined, but second-choice Caroline Quentin effortlessly made the role her own.

Life of Birds, The ✱✱✱✱

UK (BBC) Natural History. BBC 1 1998
DVD: BBC

Presenter **David Attenborough**

Executive Producer **Mike Salisbury**
Producers **Mike Salisbury, Fergus Beeley, Nigel Marven, Peter Bassett, Miles Barton**

● ***The secrets of our feathered friends.***

Painstakingly filmed over three years, in over 40 countries and at a cost in excess of £7 million, this acclaimed series from the BBC's Natural History Unit provides an insight into the diverse and surprising world of our airborne neighbours. Beginning with flightless birds, the comprehensive package moves on to explore the aerodynamics of flight, then feeding, hunting and mating habits, plus bird language and the way in which these creatures adapt to new environments and testing climates. Over ten 50-minute episodes, it is convincingly revealed that there is far more to our feathered friends than colourful plumage and a sweet song.

Life of Bliss, A ✱✱

UK (BBC) Situation Comedy. BBC 1960–1

David Bliss	**George Cole**
Zoe Hunter	**Sheila Sweet**
Tony Fellows	**Colin Gordon**
Anne Fellows	**Isabel Dean**
Pam Batten	**Frances Bennett**
Bob Batten	**Hugh Sinclair**

Creator/Writer **Godfrey Harrison**
Producers **Graeme Muir, Godfrey Harrison**

● ***A shy and confused young bachelor's life is riddled with misunderstanding.***

It's hard to imagine George Cole playing a bashful young bachelor prone to verbal gaffes, but that was his role in this long-running radio series which enjoyed some television exposure in 1960 and 1961. As the constantly confused David Bliss, he stumbles from one mishap to another, finding solace in the company of Psyche, his wire-haired fox-terrier (barked for by Percy Edwards). Also seen are Bliss's girlfriend, Zoe, and his sister and brother-in-law, Anne and Tony Fellows, the last two replaced by Pam and Bob Batten (also Bliss's sister and brother-in-law) in the second series.

Life on Earth ✱✱✱✱

UK (BBC/Warner Brothers) Natural History. BBC 2 1979
DVD: BBC

Presenter/Writer **David Attenborough**

Producers **Christopher Parsons, John Sparks, Richard Brock**

● ***Painstaking insight into how life-forms developed on our planet.***

Reflecting on the geological development of the Earth from the earliest times to the present day, naturalist/broadcaster David Attenborough lucidly explains in this ambitious series how different species of plants and animals came into being and evolved as the planet changed climate. Assisted by spectacular photography (over a million feet of film were shot) and visits to more than 30 countries in three years, Attenborough's colourful, 13-part history of 3,500 million years of nature won acclaim from all quarters, with probably the best-remembered scene his frolics with friendly gorillas in a tropical jungle.

Life on Earth was, at the time, the biggest project ever undertaken by the BBC's Natural History Unit in Bristol, and it prompted two sequels, THE LIVING PLANET in 1984 and TRIALS OF LIFE in 1990.

Life on Mars ✱✱✱

UK (Kudos) Police Drama. BBC 1 2006–

DCI/DI Sam Tyler	**John Simm**
DCI Gene Hunt	**Philip Glenister**
WPC Annie Cartright	**Liz White**
DS Ray Carling	**Dean Andrews**
DC Chris Skelton	**Marshall Lancaster**
Nelson	**Tony Marshall**
Phyllis Dobbs	**Noreen Kershaw**

Creators **Tony Jordan, Ashley Pharoah, Matthew Graham**
Writers **Matthew Graham, Ashley Pharoah, Tony Jordan, Chris Chibnall**
Executive Producers **Jane Featherstone, Matthew Graham**
Producer **Claire Parker**

● ***A successful CID man finds himself transported back to the 1970s.***

Sam Tyler works as a detective chief inspector in Manchester. One day, while investigating the abduction of his colleague, he is mown down by a car. Knocked unconscious, he wakes up back in 1973. The David Bowie song that gives its name to the series was playing on his iPod at the time of the accident and now it's belting out of the 8-Track in his state-of-the-art 1970s Rover. Tyler discovers that he's just been transferred to the city's police force and, with nowhere else to go, turns up at the office to find out what the hell is going on. Apparently, he's now only a DI and has a boss of his own to deal with.

That man is DCI Gene Hunt, a cartoon-like re-creation of the 1970s cops seen in THE SWEENEY, SPECIAL BRANCH and the ilk. His policing methods are primitive and corrupt, to say the least, which alarms Tyler, who is used to 21st-century methodology and open-minded investigations. Hunt's also a bully, a bigot and a boozer, who encourages the rest of his team to follow suit. All of which leaves Tyler as a true fish out of water, not only trying to get to grips with an era when, in reality, he was only four years old, but also struggling to gain respect for his unorthodox (for the time) policing techniques. The only source of comfort is WPC Annie Cartright, to whom Tyler bares his soul and reveals his predicament. Gradually, through voices permanating from his real time zone, Tyler realizes that he is, in fact, in a coma, and can't escape from the time-warp in which his damaged body has engulfed him.

Life Story ✳✳✳

UK (BBC) Drama. BBC 2 1987

Jim Watson .... **Jeff Goldblum**
Francis Crick .... **Tim Pigott-Smith**
Maurice Wilkins .... **Alan Howard**
Rosalind Franklin .... **Juliet Stevenson**
Raymond Gosling .... **Nicholas Fry**
Sir Lawrence Bragg .... **Geoffrey Chater**
Vittorio Luzzati .... **John Moreno**
Erwin Chargaff .... **Lyndon Brook**
Elizabeth Watson .... **Betsy Brantley**
Odile Crick .... **Petronella Ford**

Writer **William Nicholson**
Producer **Mick Jackson**

Scientists race to discover the secrets of DNA.

This 110-minute HORIZON special dramatizes the real-life battle to unlock the secrets of DNA – the key to life itself. The year is 1951 and, in Cambridge, Watson (an American) and Crick (British), two brilliant but brash young researchers, feel they are close to unravelling one of science's greatest mysteries and discovering the double helix structure of DNA. Eternal fame is the prize. The men are relentless in their efforts and bond well as a team, but their work is a series of highs and lows. At one stage they announce to the world that they have found the answer, only to suffer the embarrassment of being proved wrong. Meanwhile, at King's College, London, two rivals are also close to making this monumental discovery. Maurice Wilkins and Rosalind Franklin are less excitable in their work and are also hampered by the fact that they don't get on, rendering their approach to the job less cohesive. The friction in their relationship plays a large part in their failure to beat Watson and Crick to their goal, which is achieved soon after vital data from the London research team falls into the hands of the boys in Cambridge. The drama was retitled *The Race for the Double Helix* in the USA. Producer Mick Jackson also directs.

Life with the Lyons ✳✳

UK (BBC/Associated-Rediffusion) Situation Comedy. BBC 1955–6; ITV 1957–60

Ben Lyon .... **Ben Lyon**
Bebe Daniels Lyon .... **Bebe Daniels Lyon**
Barbara Lyon .... **Barbara Lyon**
Richard Lyon .... **Richard Lyon**
Aggie Macdonald .... **Molly Weir**
Florrie Wainwright .... **Doris Rogers**

Producers **Bryan Sears** *(BBC)*, **Barry Baker** *(ITV)*

At home with an American family in Britain.

The Lyons family of entertainers – dad Ben, his wife, Bebe Daniels, son Richard and daughter Barbara – endeared themselves to the British public by staying on in the UK during the war years, instead of fleeing back to their native USA. They remained popular in the 1950s through their BBC radio sitcom, in which they played themselves. *Life with the Lyons* then transferred to television, initially on the BBC and then on ITV. Assisting the Lyons was their Scottish housekeeper, Aggie, with Florrie their nosey neighbour. Their dog was called Skeeter. Many of the scripts were penned by Bebe.

Life Without George ✳✳✳

UK (BBC) Situation Comedy. BBC 1 1987–9

Jenny Russell .... **Carol Royle**
Larry Wade .... **Simon Cadell**
Amanda .... **Rosalind March**
Elizabeth Estensen
Ben Morris .... **Michael Thomas**
Sammy .... **Kenny Ireland**
Campbell Morrison
Carol .... **Cheryl Maiker**
Mr Harold Chambers .... **Ronald Fraser**
Josie .... **Selina Cadell**

Writers **Penny Croft, Val Hudson**
Executive Producer **Robin Nash**
Producer **Susan Belbin**

Love on the rebound for a dance instructor and an estate agent.

When George Stanton, her live-in lover of five years' standing, walks out, Jenny Russell, owner of Russell's dance and fitness studio, is understandably distraught. Then a one-night stand with drippy, Marmite-drinking estate agent Larry Wade sets her on course for a new on-off love affair. Larry, a partner in Morris, Morris and Wade, is divorced and lives with his dog, Napoleon. Although his intentions towards Jenny are transparent, he is constantly frustrated by her memories of George, and this leads him to binge on cheese-and-onion crisps. Jenny's best friend is her neighbour, Amanda, who is having trouble with her womanizing husband, Patrick. They console each other. Larry's friend and business partner, Ben, is altogether more ruthless when it comes to women and never fails to give Larry worthless advice. Carol is Jenny's receptionist at the studio, where senile Mr Chambers plays the piano and country girl Josie is an assistant. The main social rendezvous in this setting of Primrose Hill is the local singles bar, run by gay barman Sammy.

Co-writer Penny Croft (daughter of comedy producer David Croft) also wrote and sang the programme's theme song.

Lifesense

See *Supersense*.

Lift Off/Lift Off with Ayshea ✶✶

UK (Granada) Pop Music. ITV 1969–74

Presenters **Ayshea Brough, Graham Bonney, Wally Whyton**

Producer **Muriel Young**

● ***Pop-music magazine for younger viewers.***

Airing as part of ITV's children's programming, *Lift Off* was no rival to TOP OF THE POPS but was still one of the few outlets for pop on TV in the early 1970s. Although co-hosted initially by Graham Bonney and later by Wally Whyton, the programme's star was actress Ayshea Brough (also seen in UFO) and, from 1972, the programme's title was changed to reflect this, becoming *Lift Off with Ayshea*. Ayshea also kept youngsters in touch with the latest pop news via a weekly column in the 'Junior *TV Times*', *Look-in*. As well as highlighting the top bands of the day, *Lift Off* also featured a resident team of dancers called The Feet. It was produced, like other similar Granada pop shows – *Discothèque*, *Get It Together*, *Shang-A-Lang*, *Arrows* and *45* – by former FIVE O'CLOCK CLUB hostess Muriel Young.

Light Entertainment

The generic term given to programmes like variety shows, quizzes and comedies.

Likely Lads, The/Whatever Happened to the Likely Lads? ✶✶✶✶

UK (BBC) Situation Comedy. BBC 2 1964–6/BBC 1 1973–4
DVD: Warner Home Video/BBC

Bob Ferris	**Rodney Bewes**
Terry Collier	**James Bolam**
Audrey Collier	**Sheila Fearn**
Thelma Chambers/Ferris	**Brigit Forsyth**

Creators/Writers **Dick Clement, Ian La Frenais**
Producers **Dick Clement** *(The Likely Lads)*, **James Gilbert, Bernard Thompson** *(Whatever Happened to)*

● ***Life in the 1960s and 1970s with a couple of north-eastern lads-about-town.***

In *The Likely Lads*, Bob Ferris and Terry Collier are two young pals who work in a factory making electrical parts. Bob is ingenuous, ambitious and keen to see the good side of people (especially those in authority). Terry is a cynic, proud of his working-class roots and a true Jack the Lad figure. Theirs is an unusual but solid friendship which sees them tour the pubs of Newcastle in search of beer and birds, chewing the fat over several pints of brown ale and ending up in all manner of scrapes, usually at Terry's instigation and against Bob's better judgement. The series became a surprise hit, even though only screened on BBC 2, but it ended after just two years. Bob, disillusioned with his lot, decides to join the army and Terry resolves to keep him company. But Bob's flat feet keep him in civvy street and he and Terry part company.

The duo were back together again seven years later, thanks to a remarkably successful revival entitled *Whatever Happened to the Likely Lads?* With the turn of the 1970s, Bob's bourgeois dreams have begun to be realized. Now an executive on the point of marriage to his boss's daughter, Thelma (seen at the end of *The Likely Lads*), he owns his own house and has taken to holidays on the Costa Brava and Saturday nights in the trattoria. Terry, on the other hand, escaping a disastrous marriage in Germany, has not changed, except perhaps to bury himself even further into his proletarian origins and deep-rooted chauvinism. The two meet up by chance on a train, inadvertently chatting to each other in the dark when the train's lighting fails, before each suddenly realizing who the other is. Their revived friendship is just as loyal, if more strained than before, with Bob and the fierce Thelma cosseting themselves with middle-class comforts and Bob kicking his heels like some latter-day Andy Capp. The lads' altered relationship echoes the social changes that swept Britain between the 1960s and the 1970s, changes stressed time and again as they reminisce about their heyday and pay dispiriting visits to old stamping grounds that are sadly now unrecognizable or even demolished. A feature-film version was released in 1976.

In 2002, ITV paid homage to Bob and Terry in a one-off called *Ant and Dec in a Tribute to the Likely Lads*, which saw the popular young entertainers filling the shoes of Rodney Bewes and James Bolam in a remake of one of the classic scripts. Bewes offered a cameo appearance as a news vendor.

Lillie ✶✶

UK (LWT) Drama. ITV 1978
DVD: Cinema Club

Lillie Le Breton/Langtry	**Francesca Annis**
Edward Langtry	**Anton Rodgers**
William Le Breton	**Anthony Head**
Dean Le Breton	**Patrick Holt**
Clement Le Breton	**Adam Bareham**
Mrs Le Breton	**Peggy Ann Wood**
Reggie Le Breton	**Simon Turner**
Arthur Jones	**David Gwillim**
Prince Louis of Battenberg	**John Castle**
Dominique	**Catherine Feller**
Frank Miles	**Brian Deacon**
Oscar Wilde	**Peter Egan**
James Whistler	**Don Fellows**
Morten Frewen	**Philip York**
Edward, Prince of Wales	**Denis Lill**
Princess/Queen Alexandra	**Ann Firbank**
Patsy Cornwallis-West	**Jennie Linden**
King Leopold of Belgium	**Derek Smith**
Crown Prince Rudolf	**Patrick Ryecart**
Sarah Bernhardt	**Cheryl Campbell**
Henrietta Labouchere	**Annette Crosbie**
Agnes Langtry	**Stephanie Cole**
Jeanne Marie	**Joanna David**
Sir Hugo De Bathe	**James Warwick**

Writers **David Butler, John Gorrie**
Executive Producer **Tony Wharmby**
Producer **Jack Williams**

● ***The colourful life of actress Lillie Langtry.***

From her birth as the daughter of a clergyman in the Channel Islands, the life of the beautiful 'Jersey Lily' was always eventful. The highlight was her scandalous relationship with Edward, Prince of Wales ('Bertie'), although she was known to have dallied with other royals, while being married to the weak-willed Edward Langtry. In true rags-to-riches style, she rose determinedly from humble beginnings to become one of the most glamorous women of her time (late 19th/early 20th century), along the way having the honour of being the first celebrity to promote a commercial product (Pears soap). She became the darling of America and socialized closely with the likes of Oscar Wilde and James Whistler, conceiving an illegitimate daughter, Jeanne Marie, and eventually marrying for a second time, to Hugo De Bathe.

For this biopic, actress Francesca Annis reprised the role she had played in ATV's EDWARD THE SEVENTH three years earlier. Over the 13 parts, she was called upon to age from 16 to 70. The series was based on the book *The Prince and the Lily*, by James Brough.

Limbo

The use of no scenery in the studio. Plain white/black flooring combines with a plain white/black background to give an infinity effect.

Lincoln, Andrew

(Andrew Clutterbuck; 1973–)

English actor and director, one of the stars of THIS LIFE (Egg) who has since appeared in THE WOMAN IN WHITE (Walter Hartright), *Bomber* (Capt. Willy Byrne), *State of Mind* (Julian Latimer), CANTERBURY TALES (Alan King), TEACHERS (Simon), *Whose Baby?* (Barry), *Lie with Me* (Will Tomlinson) and *Afterlife* (Robert Bridge). He has also narrated series like *Mersey Blues*, *The Trench* and *No Waste Like Home*, and made guest appearances in programmes such as DROP THE DEAD DONKEY and *Trevor's World of Sport*.

Linda Green ★★

UK (Red) Comedy Drama. BBC 1 2001–2
DVD: BBC

Linda Green	**Liza Tarbuck**
Michelle Fenton	**Claire Rushbrook**
Jimmy McKenzie	**Sean Gallagher**
Darren Alexander	**Daniel Ryan**
Iris Green	**Rachel Davies**
Frank Green	**Dave Hill**
Katy Green	**Jessica Harris**
Fizz Green	**Bruno Langley**
Ricky Pinder	**John Donnelly**

Creator **Paul Abbott**
Writers **Paul Abbott, Catherine Johnson, Daniel Brocklehurst, Russell T. Davies, Chris McHallern, Tom Higgins, Chris Bucknall**
Executive Producers **Jane Tranter, Nicola Shindler, Paul Abbott**
Producers **Nicola Shindler, Matthew Bird, Phil Collinson**

● ***Sex and a single girl in her thirties.***

Linda Green: a northern lass with a modern outlook on life. Bold and daring by nature, she lives alone. During the day, she works as a finance adviser in a car salesroom; in the evenings, she sings in a club. The rest of the time, she's busy chasing a new man. When there's not one to be found, she falls back on her mechanic colleague Jimmy McKenzie for casual sex. Michelle Fenton is Linda's best friend, a chiropodist and confidante. Darren Alexander is Michelle's boyfriend. In the background hover Linda's family: former teacher turned union rep dad Frank, mum Iris and younger sister and brother Katy and Fizz. Mixing poignancy with bawdy humour, *Linda Green* attracts major guest stars, including Christopher Eccleston, David Morrissey, Peter Kay, Jane Horrocks, Jamie Theakston and star Liza Tarbuck's own father, Jimmy Tarbuck, who plays her Uncle Vic (with suggestions that he is in fact our heroine's real father). Among the writers are creator Paul Abbott and award-winning Russell T. Davies. Two ten-part series have been produced.

Lindsay, Robert

(Robert Stevenson; 1949–)

Derbyshire-born actor whose television break came in 1975 with the sitcom GET SOME IN!, in which he played teddy-boy Jakey Smith. Lindsay was then signed up to star as Tooting's Che Guevara, Wolfie Smith, in CITIZEN SMITH. He was later cast as boxer Pete Dodds in SECONDS OUT, played wheeler-dealer Mickey Noades in GIVE US A BREAK and took the part of Carter in Channel 4's security guard comedy, NIGHTINGALES, as well as topping the bill as rising political star Michael Murray in Alan Bleasdale's GBH. Jack Higgins's drama *Confessional* was another of his credits, as were *Screen Two's Genghis Cohn* (former SS man Otto Schatz), *The Wimbledon Poisoner* (Henry Farr), *Brazen Hussies* (Billy Bowmans), *Goodbye My Love* (Derek Humphry), *Jake's Progress* (Jamie Diadoni), OLIVER TWIST (Fagin), HORNBLOWER (Captain/Admiral Edward Pellew), MY FAMILY (Ben Harper), *Hawkins* (Luke Hawkins), *Masterworks* (Vince), the puppet series *Don't Eat the Neighbours* (voices), JERICHO (1950s detective Michael Jericho) and *Friends and Crocodiles* and *Gideon's Daughter* (Sneath in both). Lindsay has also been seen in numerous Shakespearean roles, made a guest appearance in ABSOLUTELY FABULOUS, played Tony Blair in *A Very Social Secretary*, and had a small role in one episode of THE GOOD LIFE. His narration work includes the series *Space Race*. His first wife was actress Cheryl Hall (also seen in *Citizen Smith*).

Line Producer

See *Associate Producer*.

Linehan, Graham

(1968–)

Irish comedy writer/director, usually in partnership with compatriot Arthur Mathews. Their greatest creation has been undoubtedly FATHER TED, but their other series have included PARIS, HIPPIES and the sketch show BIG TRAIN. They have also contributed to *The All New Alexei Sayle Show*, *Alexei Sayle's Stuff*, *Harry Enfield and Chums*, SMITH AND JONES, THE DAY TODAY, *Coogan's Run*, THE FAST SHOW (the 'Ted and Ralph' sketches), BRASS EYE, THE SATURDAY/FRIDAY NIGHT ARMISTICE, *Jam* and BLACK BOOKS. Guest roles in I'M ALAN PARTRIDGE saw them appear the other side of the camera for a change. Linehan has also written and directed *The IT Crowd*.

Lineker, Gary

(1960–)

Former England soccer captain (and his country's second-highest goal-scorer) turned TV sports presenter, the host of MATCH OF THE DAY and GRANDSTAND's *Football Focus* slot. He has also been a team captain in the comedy quiz THEY THINK IT'S ALL OVER.

Line-Up/Late Night Line-Up ★★

UK (BBC) Arts Magazine. BBC 2 1964–72

Presenters **Denis Tuohy, John Stone, Michael Dean, Joan Bakewell, Nicholas Tresilian, Sheridan Morley, Tony Bilbow**

● ***Late-night magazine programme covering most aspects of the arts and popular culture.***

Beginning as no more than a ten-minute preamble to the evening's programmes on the fledgling BBC 2, *Line-Up* was soon extended and moved to a new, end-of-the-evening time-slot. In doing so, it became a popular arts magazine and a lively talking shop, looking at films, literature and music of all kinds on most nights of the week. Segments of the programme became series in their own right. *Film Night* began as a strand called *The Film World Past and Present*, and the adventurous late-1960s rock show *Colour Me Pop* was another *Late Night Line-Up* spin-off. *Disco 2* (a progressive rock show, despite its name) arrived via the same route and eventually led to the durable OLD GREY WHISTLE TEST. In all nearly 3,000 editions were produced.

Link, William

(1933–)

See *Levinson, Richard.*

Lipman, Maureen

CBE (1946–)

Yorkshire-born actress, usually in comedy parts (often scripted by her late husband, Jack Rosenthal). Her earliest credits include roles in THE LOVERS, *Rooms*, CROWN COURT, *Regan* (the pilot for THE Sweeney), *Couples*, the dramas ROGUE MALE, *The Evacuees*, *The Knowledge*, *Absent Friends* and *Absurd Person Singular*, and the sketch show *Don't Ask Us*. After taking the part of Alison Holmes in the short-lived sitcom *A Soft Touch* in 1978, Lipman was given her own series, AGONY, playing Jane Lucas, an agony aunt (revived in 1995 as *Agony Again*). She then featured as Stella Craven in SMILEY'S PEOPLE and starred as Maggie Costello in the original production of OUTSIDE EDGE, as well as hard-up landlady Sheila Haddon in ALL AT NO. 20. Lipman played 12 different roles in *About Face*, featured as Miss Minchin in *A Little Princess*, and was cast as Shani Whittle in Rosenthal's *Screen One* films ESKIMO DAY and *Cold Enough for Snow*. Ironically, greatest praise came after her commercials for British Telecom and her characterization of the classic worry-ridden Jewish mother (Beattie). Lipman's stage tribute to Joyce Grenfell, *Re-Joyce!*, has also reached the small screen. More recently, she has appeared in *Oklahoma!* and played Lillian Spencer in CORONATION STREET, Marcia in *Winter Solstice* and bag lady Maggie Wych in *The Fugitives*, as well as making guest appearances in JONATHAN CREEK and WHERE THE HEART IS. Away from acting, she is a successful writer of books and a magazine columnist.

Lipstick on Your Collar ★★★

UK (Whistling Gypsy) Musical Drama. Channel 4 1993

Pte Francis Francis .... **Giles Thomas**
Pte Mick Hopper .... **Ewan McGregor**
Sylvia Berry .... **Louise Germaine**
Cpl Peter Berry .... **Douglas Henshall**
Col. Harry Bernwood .... **Peter Jeffrey**
Major Wallace Hedges .... **Clive Francis**
Major Archie Carter .... **Nicholas Jones**
Major Johnnie Church .... **Nicholas Farrell**
Lt. Col. 'Truck' Trekker .... **Shane Rimmer**
Aunt Vickie .... **Maggie Steed**
Uncle Fred .... **Bernard Hill**
Harold Atterbow .... **Roy Hudd**
Lisa .... **Kymberley Huffman**

Writer **Dennis Potter**
Producer **Rosemarie Whitman**

● ***The final part of Dennis Potter's semi-autobiographical, musical trilogy.***

Having caused a stir with previous nostalgic 'drama with music' offerings PENNIES FROM HEAVEN and THE SINGING DETECTIVE, Dennis Potter brought *Lipstick on Your Collar* to Channel 4 in 1993. This time he focused on the social changes sweeping Britain in the 1950s, and particularly on the growing awareness among young people of their own identities. At the heart of the story is Pte Mick Hopper, a national serviceman working in War Office boredom, having to seek permission to speak and spending his days translating Russian documents as the Cold War gathers momentum. In the background the Suez Crisis is breaking and the atom bomb proliferating. But the younger generation are now looking to the west and the exciting, glitzy possibilities off-loaded by an influential USA. While his days remain dreary, Hopper breaks free in the evenings to play drums in a rock 'n' roll band. A new sexual promiscuity is pervading the country and Hopper falls for the beautiful, dark-haired Lisa, while his Welsh friend, Francis, is dangerously drawn to Sylvia, the blonde bombshell who is badly abused by her bullying husband, Corporal Berry, and agitated by the odious Harold Atterbow.

Lisemore, Martin

(1940–77)

British TV executive, the producer of classics like THE PALLISERS and I, CLAUDIUS, and other adaptations such as *The Spoils of Poynton, Jude the Obscure, Cousin Bette, The Golden Bowl, Emma, How Green was My Valley*, OUR MUTUAL FRIEND and MURDER MOST ENGLISH.

Little, Natasha

(1970–)

Liverpool-born actress whose major roles have been in THIS LIFE (Rachel), FAR FROM THE MADDING CROWD (Fanny Robin), VANITY FAIR (Becky Sharp), *Love in the 21st Century, Man and Boy* (Gina Silver), *Dickens* (Ellen Ternan), MURDER IN MIND, *Byron* (Augusta Leigh), *The Crooked Man* (Lisa Talbot) and SPOOKS (Dr Vicki Westbrook). Other credits include parts in CADFAEL, *Big Women* and EXTRAS.

Little, Syd

(Cyril Mead; 1942–)

See *Large, Eddie.*

Little Big Business, A ★★

UK (Granada) Situation Comedy. ITV 1964–5

Marcus Lieberman	**David Kossoff**
Simon Lieberman	**Francis Matthews**
Lazlo	**Martin Miller**
Charlie	**Billy Russell**
	Jack Bligh
Naomi Lieberman	**Diana Coupland**
	Constance Wake
Basil Crane	**David Conville**
Miss Stevens	**Joyce Marlowe**

Writer **Jack Pulman**
Producer **Peter Eton**

● ***Business and family conflicts coincide at a furniture factory.***

Marcus Lieberman is the proprietor of a furniture workshop and a stubborn traditionalist at heart. However, when he introduces Simon, his educated and ambitious son, into the business, he is forced to modernize his ways. Such innovation doesn't please craftsmen Lazlo and Charlie either. On Simon's side is colleague Basil Crane. This series, with its light Jewish humour, followed a pilot screened in 1963, in which the role of Simon was played by James Maxwell.

Little Big Time ★★

UK (Southern) Children's Entertainment. ITV 1968–74

Presenter **Freddie Garrity**

Oliver in the Overworld	
Freddie Garrity	**Himself**
The Undercog	**Graham Haberfield**
The Mighty Dictaphone	**David King**
The Grim Gramophone	**Blake Butler**
Oliver the Clock	**Pete Birrel**
Chief High Pipe	**Gordon Clyde**
Princess Necessity	**Debbie Bowen**
The Deferential Gearbox	**Bob McBain**
The Clockwork King	**Philip Ray**
Other series	
Stupid Nana	**Peter Birrel**
Prof. Frantic	**Frankie Holmes**
Sir Jasper Nastybonse	**Kevork Malikyan**
Mr InOut Pending	**Bob McBain**
Miss Penny	**Penelope Nice**
Taff	**Talfryn Thomas**

Writer **David McKellar**
Producer **Angus Wright**

● ***Songs and laughter for kids, plus a pop opera.***

This lively vehicle for eccentric pop band Freddie and the Dreamers was one of Southern Television's most successful contributions to the ITV network. The series was initially conceived as a combination of jokes, sketches, dances and musical interludes, performed by lead singer Freddie Garrity and other members of his group (Peter Birrel, Roy Crewsdon, Bernie Dwyer and Derek Quinn), plus guests. Recorded at Southampton University's Nuffield Theatre, in front of 400 schoolkids, it showcased leading club acts. A five-minute segment in each programme was later devoted to a serial pop opera called *Oliver in the Overworld*. This little fantasy – penned by Mike Hazelwood and Albert Hammond (the songs were first issued as a Freddie and the Dreamers album) – explored the mysterious Overworld, a land with no sky, just a painted tin roof, ruled over by the Clockwork King, who had created it thousands of years before. It is the place where machines are born, so, appropriately, the King's wife is Queen Necessity, the Mother of Invention. The royals travel around their kingdom on a special 'Overmotive' train. Into this world step Freddie and his grandfather clock, Oliver. Oliver has lost his memory and Freddie tries to help him retrieve it, combating the villainous Undercog, who – with his sidekicks Spoke-in-the-Wheel and Spanner-in-the-Works – has tampered with Oliver's mechanism. Other major characters are Harry the Heater, who has a cold, and a metronome that has lost her ding (the song 'Gimme Dat Ding' was later a hit for The Pipkins). The musical proved so popular that the next (1971) series was entirely given over to a sequel. In this extended *Oliver in the Overworld* (performed live), Freddie and Oliver return to find the Clockwork King under pressure from a sinister business tycoon called The Mighty Dictaphone, who lives in Dictaphone Hall, and his accomplice, The Grim Gramophone. Encountering characters like Chief High Pipe, leader of the man-eating Hungry Drains, they battle to stop the villains stealing the key on the Clockwork King's crown – the key that assigns power in the Overworld.

The Overworld theme exhausted, subsequent series returned to music and comedy, with a central plank being the Joke Hall of Fame. In this, Freddie was joined by wacky characters like Sir Jasper Nastybonse, Stupid Nana and Professor Frantic. Ian Curry acted as announcer and among the contributors was Tony Robinson. The series theme tune was composed by Mitch Murray and Peter Callander.

Little Britain ★★★★

UK (BBC) Comedy. BBC 2 2003; BBC 1 2004–5
DVD: BBC

Matt Lucas, David Walliams

Narrator **Tom Baker**

Creators/Writers **Matt Lucas, David Walliams**
Producers **Myfanwy Moore, Geoff Posner**

● ***Britain through the lives of its most eccentric citizens.***

Another product of Radio 4's comedy department, *Little Britain* first transferred to television courtesy of the digital channel BBC 3, where it helped underline the new network's reputation for breaking comedy. It was soon repeated to a wider audience on BBC 2. However, by the time of series two, BBC 2 was bypassed completely, and the series jumped from first outing on BBC 3 to a slightly revised second showing on BBC 1. The BBC knew it had a hit on its hands.

'Britain, Britain, Britain,' intones quirky announcer Tom Baker, introducing viewers to a colourful congregation of characters strutting their stuff in a series of short sketches, each set in a (usually fictitious) town or village somewhere in the UK. Creators Matt Lucas and David Walliams take all the lead roles, bringing to life individuals whose personalities wander between the grotesque and the simply daft.

Chubby Marjorie Dawes (a Lucas creation seen earlier in SHOOTING STARS) is the patronizing leader of a Fat Fighters slimming class, for instance, while Kenny Craig is the stage hypnotist from Troby who uses his 'powers' to spice up his empty private life. In Sneddy, Jeremy Rent is a theatrical agent whose most annoying client is diminutive Dennis Waterman, who always wants to write and sing the theme song to any production in which he is cast. In Flatley, deranged Anne's rehabilitation into the community by the over-confident Dr Lawrence is always a disaster; in Downing Street, obsessive personal assistant Sebastian Love has a huge crush on his boss, the Prime Minister (played by Anthony Head); and there are always strange goings-on at Kelsey Grammar School in Flange. Elsewhere, Jason is an otherwise normal lad who has a thing about his best mate's gran; former Olympian Denver Mills thrives on past glory, making totally inappropriate public speeches; Peter Andre is an overenthusiastic royal reporter; and Des Kaye is a former kids' TV star now employed at DIY Universe in Little Tokyo – all further examples of the barking population of this sceptred isle. And there's something rather sinister about quirky Scottish hotelier Ray McClooney with his little tin whistle.

However, the most popular creations are the ever-caring Lou and his lazy, fake invalid friend Andy, who live in Herby; Daffyd Thomas, proud to declare himself the only gay in the village of Llandewi Breffi, despite ample evidence to the contrary; useless Old Haven transvestite Emily Howard ('I'm a lady'), who later acquires an equally inept associate named Florence; and shell-suited, gobby teenager from Darkley Noone Vicky Pollard ('Yeah, but no, but . . .').

Later creations include Bubbles DeVere, an obese health club resident who won't pay her bills; young toff Harvey who is still breast feeding from his mum (Geraldine James); hopeless drug counsellor Doug; and shire Tories Judy and Maggie for whom the merest hint of anything that is not truly British induces a bout of vomiting.

Almost rivalling THE FAST SHOW with its number of recurring catchphrases, *Little Britain* instantly tickled the ribs of the public and raced into the national consciousness. Behind the scenes help for Lucas and Walliams came from THE LEAGUE OF GENTLEMEN's Mark Gatiss, who was script editor on series one, and comedian Rob Brydon, who filled the same role from series two.

Little House on the Prairie/Little House: A New Beginning ★★

US (NBC) Drama. BBC 1 1975; ITV 1976–84 (US: NBC 1974–83)
DVD: Universal

Charles Ingalls .... **Michael Landon**
Caroline Ingalls .... **Karen Grassle**
Laura Ingalls/Wilder .... **Melissa Gilbert**
Mary Ingalls/Kendall .... **Melissa Sue Anderson**
Carrie Ingalls .... **Lindsay Greenbush**
Sidney Greenbush
Isaiah Edwards .... **Victor French**
Grace Edwards .... **Bonnie Bartlett**
Nels Oleson .... **Richard Bull**
Harriet Oleson .... **Katherine MacGregor**
Nellie Oleson/Dalton .... **Alison Arngrim**
Willie Oleson .... **Jonathan Gilbert**
Lars Hanson .... **Karl Swenson**
Dr Baker .... **Kevin Hagen**
Revd Robert Alden .... **Dabbs Greer**
Eva Beadle/Simms .... **Charlotte Stewart**
Ebenezer Sprague .... **Ted Gehring**
Jonathan Garvey .... **Merlin Olsen**
Alice Garvey .... **Hersha Parady**
Andy Garvey .... **Patrick Laborteaux**
Adam Kendall .... **Linwood Boomer**
Albert Ingalls .... **Matthew Laborteaux**
Grace Ingalls .... **Wendy Turnbeaugh**
Brenda Turnbeaugh
Hester Sue Terhune .... **Ketty Lester**
Almanzo Wilder .... **Dean Butler**
Eliza Jane Wilder .... **Lucy Lee Flippin**
Percival Dalton .... **Steve Tracy**
James Cooper .... **Jason Bateman**
Cassandra Cooper .... **Missy Francis**
Nancy Oleson .... **Allison Balson**
Jenny Wilder .... **Shannen Doherty** *(New Beginning)*
John Carter .... **Stan Ivar** *(New Beginning)*
Sarah Carter .... **Pamela Roylance** *(New Beginning)*
Jeb Carter .... **Lindsay Kennedy** *(New Beginning)*
Jason Carter .... **David Friedman** *(New Beginning)*
Etta Plum .... **Leslie Landon** *(New Beginning)*

Creator **Michael Landon**
Executive Producers **Michael Landon, Ed Friendly**

● ***A family struggles to make a living on the American plains in the late 19th century.***

Here is a Western with a difference. Instead of engaging in squabbles with Indians and bandits, the main characters in this series enjoy a peaceful existence, their only fight being with nature in an effort to maintain a comfortable home. *Little House on the Prairie* was based on the autobiographical books by Laura Ingalls Wilder. She appears as a character in the series and, acting as narrator, leads viewers through the changes taking place in the Ingalls household.

The family live on a smallholding in Walnut Grove, Plum Creek, Minnesota, in the 1870s. Head of the household is Charles Ingalls, hardworking and trustworthy. His wife, Caroline, has borne him three children: Laura, her elder sister Mary, and little Carrie, and the family owns a dog, Jack. In their efforts to scratch out a living they are supported by their friends, the tough-looking Mr Edwards, Mr Hanson, who owns the mill, and Nels Oleson, the local shopkeeper. Edwards is later replaced by Jonathan Garvey, his wife Alice, and son Andy.

Over the years, the Ingalls have their ups and downs, leading to numerous cast changes. They are blessed with a fourth daughter, Grace, but tragedy strikes when Mary loses her sight and is forced to attend a special blind school. There she meets blind tutor Adam Kendall, later to be her husband. As times grow even harder, the Ingalls are forced to sell up and move temporarily to Winoka, Dakota, where they adopt a young orphan, Albert. Mary gives birth to a baby boy, who is tragically killed in a fire which also takes the life of Alice Garvey.

Laura marries Almanzo Wilder, after becoming a teacher, and Nels Oleson's spiteful daughter, Nellie, is also married, to a Jew named Isaac Cohen who hides his religion under the name of Percival Dalton. Adam miraculously regains his sight and heads for New York to work for his father's law company, taking Mary with him. The Ingalls take in two more orphans, Charles and Caroline Cooper; and another orphan, Nancy, is adopted by Mrs Oleson and proves to be as dislikeable as Nellie. Meanwhile, Laura gives birth to a daughter, Rose.

In the programme's final season, its star and executive producer, Michael Landon, decided to call it a day, and much rejigging was required before the show could continue. It was renamed *Little House: A New Beginning* and centred on Laura, Almanzo and little Rose. Charles sells the Little House and moves to a job in Burr Oak, Iowa, leaving the homestead to local newspaper proprietors John and Sarah Carter and their two sons.

These heartwarming tales of honest labour and strong family values were similar in flavour to those seen in THE WALTONS, but *Little House* was very much Michael Landon's baby. Not only did he star and produce, he also directed and wrote some of the episodes. The series lasted only one year after his departure. The programme, somewhat unusually, changed channels in the UK, from BBC 1 to ITV, during the course of its initial run. It was rerun on Channel 4 in the 1990s. Radio 4 broadcast its own adaptation of Wilder's tales in 2001.

Littlest Hobo, The ★

Canada (Storer/McGowan/Canamac) Children's Drama. ITV 1964–5
DVD: VCI

Creator **Dorrell McGowan**

● ***An itinerant dog is a friend and saviour to all.***

His real name is London, but no one ever knows that. This genial Alsatian dog is the most helpful stray that ever wandered up your driveway. Not only is he docile and friendly, but, like Lassie, he usually prevents accidents, defeats crime, averts tragedies and leaves behind a sound moral message for good measure. With no regular human partner, the canny canine drifts from town to town, all across Canada, and just when those that take him in start to consider him their pet, off he goes again, to another town, another adventure. The series, shot first in 1963, was remade in colour from 1979, when the catchy 'Maybe Tomorrow' theme song was added.

All this followed a low-key 1958 film. Although billed in some publications as an 'adult action series', there's no mistaking where its real audience lay.

Live Aid ★★★★

UK (BBC) Music. BBC 2/BBC 1 1985
DVD: Warner Vision

Presenters **Janice Long, Richard Skinner, David Hepworth, Andy Batten-Foster, Mike Smith, Mark Ellen, Andy Kershaw, Paul Gambaccini, Steve Blacknell**

Producers **John Burrowes, Trevor Dann**

● ***Legendary big-name pop concert in aid of the African famine appeal.***

Following the success of Band Aid's chart-topping charity single, 'Do They Know It's Christmas?', 'Feed the World' campaigner Bob Geldof conjured up the idea for a globally transmitted live concert. This came to fruition on Saturday, 13 July 1985. Beginning at noon (UK time) at Wembley Stadium and continuing through to 4 a.m. from JFK Stadium in Philadelphia, *Live Aid* was simply the biggest rock festival ever to be staged over one day. Satellites beamed pictures from one stadium to the other so that the live audiences could view the staggered events on both sides of the Atlantic. On television, DJs interviewed the stars, who urged viewers to ring in with cash pledges. A total of over £60 million was raised as a result. Status Quo set the ball rolling with a rendition of 'Rocking All Over the World', Phil Collins appeared at both stadia, courtesy of Concorde, and the full list of acts billed to appear was as follows: at Wembley, Status Quo, Style Council, Ultravox, Boomtown Rats, Adam Ant, Spandau Ballet, Elvis Costello, Nik Kershaw, Sade, Sting, Phil Collins, Julian Lennon, Howard Jones, Bryan Ferry, Paul Young, Alison Moyet, U2, Dire Straits, Queen, David Bowie, The Who, Elton John, Wham and Paul McCartney; at Philadelphia, Bryan Adams, The Beach Boys, Tears for Fears, Simple Minds, The Pretenders, Santana, Pat Metheny, The Thompson Twins, Nile Rodgers, Madonna, Tom Petty, The Cars, Kenny Loggins, Neil Young, Power Station, Eric Clapton, Phil Collins, Robert Plant, Jimmy Page, Paul Martinez, Duran Duran, Patti Labelle, Hall and Oates, The Temptations, Mick Jagger, Tina Turner and Bob Dylan. Not originally billed, but appearing, were Kiki Dee, George Michael, INXS and B. B. King (Wembley), and George Thorogood and the Destroyers (Philadelphia).

Live and Kicking ★★

UK (BBC) Children's Entertainment. BBC 1 1993–2001

Presenters **Andi Peters, Emma Forbes, John Barrowman, Zoë Ball, Jamie Theakston, Steve Wilson, Emma Ledden, Ortis Deley, Trey Farley, Katy Hill, Sarah Cawood, Heather Suttie**

Editors **Chris Bellinger, Angela Sharp, Annette Williams, Simon Parsons**

● ***All-action Saturday morning magazine, majoring on music, jokes and showbiz.***

Picking up where GOING LIVE! left off, *Live and Kicking* introduced new presenters Andi Peters, Emma Forbes and John Barrowman, but carried over several familiar features. These included the game 'Run the Risk' (with Peter Simon and Shane Richie – later replaced by John Eccleston, then Bobby Davro) and comic capers with Trev and Simon (Trevor Neal and Simon Hickson). Over a number of series Trev and Simon also hosted items called 'Daft as a Brush', 'Video Garden', 'Star Driving Test', 'Video Goldmine', 'Video Galleon', and 'Transmission Impossible'. Slots introduced later included 'Famous for Five Minutes' (viewers at home grab a chance of stardom), 'It's My Life' (people with unusual lifestyles), the 'Hot Seat' (celebrities take questions), 'Big Bang', 'Up Your Jumper' and 'Electric Circus' (latest film and TV news – presented by John Barrowman as he eased his way out of the programme; the feature was later presented by Dannii Minogue and Toby Anstis, then Kate Sanderson, among others). Additional games and features were 'Nobble the Wobble', 'Hit, Miss or Maybe' (Juke Box Jury-style record reviews), 'Talk to the Hand' and 'Trey-Spotting'. Among the cartoons, viewers could enjoy *The Addams Family*, *The Chipmunks*, *Eek the Cat*, *Rugrats*, *The X-Men*, *Spider-Man*, *Terrible Thunder Lizards*, *Godzilla*, THE SIMPSONS, *Monster Ranchers*, *Big Wolf on Campus*, *Roswell Conspiracies*, *The Wild Thornberrys* and *Mona the Vampire*. Live action comedies and dramas took in *Clarissa Explains It All*, *Kenan and Kel*, *Smart Guy* and *Sweet Valley High*. In the studio, at various times, Dr Aric Sigman offered his services as an agony uncle and Trude Mostue answered questions on pet care. Computer games were reviewed in 'J: Drive'.

In autumn 1996, Zoë Ball and Jamie Theakston replaced Andi Peters and Emma Forbes as anchors, and a year later THE MEN IN TROUSERS (Gez Foster, Ben Ward and Richard Webb) took over the slapstick from Trev and Simon, sharing the limelight each week with Mr Blobby and two leprechaun puppets. In autumn 1999, Ball and Theakston gave way to Steve Wilson and Emma Ledden, but a year later (after a mauling in the ratings by Ant and Dec's SM:TV LIVE) it was all change again, with Ortis Deley, Trey Farley, Katy Hill and Sarah Cawood fronting a new-look series. Heather Suttie replaced Hill towards the end, which came in September 2001 (after the programme's first run through the summer), when it was replaced by *The Saturday Show* (2001–).

Live 8 ✳✳✳

UK (BBC) Music. BBC2/BBC1 2005
DVD: EMI Studios

Presenters **Jonathan Ross, Jo Whiley, Fearne Cotton**

Producers **Lorna Dickinson, Elaine Paterson, Cerrie Frost, Kim Ross**

● ***Rock and pop marathon to 'Make Poverty History'.***

Twenty years on from the memorable LIVE AID rock telethon in aid of the starving of Africa, Bob Geldof, Midge Ure, Harvey Goldsmith, Richard Curtis and others joined forces to stage this free concert on 2 July 2005 in London's Hyde Park (tickets were offered via a texting lottery). The aim was to put pressure on the leaders of the G8 countries, who were shortly to meet for a summit in Edinburgh, to cancel Third World debt, increase aid budgets and reform world trading arrangements to benefit struggling African economies (the Make Poverty History campaign). Assembled musicians included Paul McCartney, Sting, Elton John, U2, The Who, Pink Floyd, Keane, Snow Patrol, Coldplay, Dido, Madonna, Snoop Dogg, Robbie Williams, REM, Mariah Carey, UB40, Travis, Velvet Revolver, Stereophonics, Joss Stone, Razorlight, Scissor Sisters, The Killers, Ms Dynamite, Annie Lennox and Geldof himself, plus the African Children's Choir. Highlights of simultaneous concerts held in other major cities around the world were screened during intervals, comedians like Ricky Gervais, Matt Lucas, David Walliams, Lenny Henry, Dawn French and Peter Kay helped introduce the acts, and Jonathan Ross anchored the TV coverage from a glass pod. Graham Norton later introduced events at the corresponding gig at the Museum of Art in Philadelphia, USA. *Radio Times* produced eight different commemorative covers to mark the event.

Liver Birds, The ✳✳

UK (BBC) Situation Comedy. BBC 1 1969; 1971–2; 1974–9; 1996
DVD: Universal

Beryl Hennessey .... **Polly James**
Dawn .... **Pauline Collins**
Sandra Hutchinson/Paynton .. **Nerys Hughes**
Carol Boswell .... **Elizabeth Estensen**
Mrs Hutchinson .... **Mollie Sugden**
Mr Hutchinson .... **Ivan Beavis**
Mrs Hennessey .... **Sheila Fay**
Carmel McSharry
Mr Hennessey .... **Cyril Shaps**
Bill Dean
Paul .... **John Nettles**
Robert .... **Jonathan Lynn**
Mrs Boswell .... **Eileen Kennally**
Carmel McSharry
Lucien Boswell .... **Michael Angelis**
Grandad .... **Jack Le White**
Mr Boswell .... **Ray Dunbobbin**
Father O'Leary .... **Patrick McAlinney**
Derek Paynton .... **Tom Chadbon**
Rex .... **Geoffrey Leesley**
Gwyn .... **Lee Oakes**

Creators **Carla Lane, Myra Taylor, Lew Schwarz**
Producers **Sydney Lotterby, Douglas Argent, Roger Race, Philip Kampff**

● ***The ups and downs in the life of two Liverpudlian flatmates.***

Seen by some as a female version of THE LIKELY LADS, *The Liver Birds* centres on two perky single girls who share a bedsit in Huskisson Street, Liverpool, where their life revolves around romance, finance and family troubles. Initially, the two girls are wacky Beryl and prim Dawn, but this first series (resulting from a 1969 COMEDY PLAYHOUSE pilot) runs to only four episodes. With the return of *The Liver Birds* (in 1971), Dawn has disappeared and in her place is the naïve and ingenuous Sandra. A year later, the girls move to a more spacious apartment and, when Beryl leaves (to marry Robert, a Londoner played by Jonathan Lynn) at the end of the fourth season, Sandra gains a new flatmate, Carol, whose voice and dress sense both need volume controls. Also seen over the years are Sandra's boyfriend, Paul (a pre-BERGERAC John Nettles), her snooty mother and various members of Beryl's and Carol's families. Possibly best remembered is Carol's brother, Lucien, who keeps and loves rabbits, but her Catholic mother is another notable creation, as she proves to be a forerunner of BREAD's Nellie Boswell (writer Carla Lane even gave her the same surname). Before the series ends, Sandra has married Derek, her vet boss, and Carol has moved in as their lodger.

Although very much associated with Carla Lane, the series was in fact co-created with her former writing partner, Myra Taylor, and Lew Schwarz, and the early episodes were script-edited by Eric Idle. From the fourth season, however, Lane was in sole charge. The jaunty theme song, with its 'You dancing? You asking? I'm asking. I'm dancing' tag, was performed by The Scaffold.

In 1996, BBC I revived the series, bringing back Beryl as a lodger in Sandra's house. Beryl has been married three times, while Sandra is now looking after her demanding mother and trying to maintain a relationship with boyfriend Rex. Also seen is Beryl's son, Gwyn. Somewhat confusingly, actress Carmel McSharry is brought back to play Beryl's mum (she had played Carol's mum previously), and Michael Angelis returns as Lucien, this time Beryl's brother.

Liverpool One ✳✳

UK (Lime Street) Drama. ITV 1998–9

DC Isobel De Pauli .... **Sam Janus**
DC Mark Callaghan .... **Mark Womack**
DI Howard Jones .... **Tom Georgeson**
DC Joanna McMullan .... **Katy Carmichael**
DC Frank White .... **Paul Broughton**
Ch. Insp. Graham Hill .... **Eamon Boland**
John Sullivan .... **Paul Usher**
DC Tomaszewski .... **Simon O'Brien**

Writer **Simon Burke**
Producer **Colin McKeown**

● ***An attractive, intelligent policewoman finds life hard on the streets of Liverpool.***

Moving from the Metropolitan Police to the Merseyside Police's vice squad is not a soft option for DC Isobel De Pauli. De Pauli – a psychology graduate – discovers that her new patch in Liverpool is tough and violent, with gangsters, drugs and prostitutes the everyday fare. Working for boss DI Jones and partnered by DC 'Cally' Callaghan, she finds herself in close pursuit of the Sullivan family in particular, a hard-nosed family of drug-pushers headed by the devious John Sullivan who, to complicate matters, is also Cally's cousin. But her arrival also causes resentment in the force, possibly not helped by her glamorous looks and the rather skimpy tops she wears. Typical of what is now known as a 'gritty drama', *Liverpool One* was well received by viewers and critics.

Living Planet, The ★★★★

UK (BBC) Natural History. BBC 1 1984
DVD: BBC

Host **David Attenborough**

Executive Producer **Richard Brock**
Producer **Ned Kelly**

● ***The exhaustive follow-up to*** **LIFE ON EARTH.**
Employing the same stunning photography and imbued with the same infectious enthusiasm as in *Life on Earth*, *The Living Planet* saw David Attenborough now turn his attention away from the evolution of plants and animals and fix his gaze instead on the way life-forms have learned to live in the modern world. Again, there was no stinting on travel – the team filmed at the edge of volcanic craters, in the baking heat of the Sahara and in the freezing wastes of the Arctic – to graphically portray just how well flora and fauna have learned to adapt to today's Earth with all its diverse environments. It revealed that nowhere on the planet was devoid of life.

Living TV

One-time sister channel to UK Gold – when it was known as UK Living – Living TV is a cable/digital channel owned by Flextech and dedicated mostly to women's interests, although widening its appeal in recent years. As a result, programming has majored on cookery (repeats of Keith Floyd, Delia Smith, etc.), talk shows, fashion, agony aunts, romance, gardening, health and female-orientated game shows. Imports shown have often had a female bias and have included series like CAGNEY AND LACEY, KATE AND ALLIE, CHARLIE'S ANGELS, THE GOLDEN GIRLS, ALLY MCBEAL and WILL AND GRACE. Feature films have usually been of the emotional type.

Lizzie Dripping ★★

UK (BBC) Children's Drama. BBC 1 1973; 1975

Lizzie Dripping .... **Tina Heath**
Aunt Blodwen .... **Jane Lowe**
Miss Platt .... **Ann Morrish**
Witch .... **Sonia Dresdel**
Albert Arbuckle .... **Geoffrey Matthews**
Patty Arbuckle .... **Barbara Mitchell**
Toby Arbuckle .... **Candida Lucy Rowe**
Gramma .... **Sheila Raynor**
Jonathan .... **Keith Allingham**

Creator/Writer **Helen Cresswell**
Executive Producer **Anna Home**
Producer **Angela Beeching**

● ***A teenage girl lives in a dream world.***
In Nottinghamshire, home of creator Helen Cresswell, 'Lizzie Dripping' is apparently an affectionate name given to dozy girls who daydream their life away – hence the inspiration for this series and the books that preceded it. Lizzie Dripping made her TV debut in a 1972 *Jackanory Playhouse* production, *Lizzie Dripping and the Orphans*, narrated by Hannah Gordon and starring the cast that went on to make the series only a few months later. Filmed, appropriately, in Eakring, Nottinghamshire, the stories tell of young Lizzie (played by a 17-year-old, pre-Blue Peter Tina Heath), for whom the divide between fantasy and reality is slight and who tends to make up adventures that somehow come true – such as when she makes friends with a witch, who becomes a useful ally.

Lloyd, Innes
(1925–91)

Innovative British drama producer, for many years with the BBC, initially in outside broadcasts and then working on series like DOCTOR WHO (in the Patrick Troughton era) and the anthology *Dead of Night*, as well as many one-off plays. Lloyd also contributed the mini-series WAUGH ON CRIME, for the *Thirty-Minute Theatre* collection, and produced dramas in the PREMIERE series. Among other offerings were THE SNOW GOOSE (1971), THE STONE TAPE, *Orde Wingate* (1976), AN ENGLISHMAN'S CASTLE, *Speed King* (1979), *Fothergill* (1981), GOING GENTLY, *East of Ipswich* (1987), *Across the Lake* (1988), BOMBER HARRIS (1989) and *102 Boulevard Haussman* (1991). His last production was Alan Bennett's *A Question of Attribution* (1991), telling the story of an encounter between spy Anthony Blunt and The Queen. Lloyd had previously produced many of Bennett's works, including *A Day Out* (1972), *Sunset across the Bay* (1974), AN ENGLISHMAN ABROAD, *The Insurance Man* (1985) and the series TALKING HEADS.

Lloyd, Jeremy
(1932–)

British comedy actor and scriptwriter, once a cast member of ROWAN AND MARTIN'S LAUGH-IN and also seen in the comedy IT'S AWFULLY BAD FOR YOUR EYES, DARLING. Among his early contributions were small roles in THE AVENGERS and CALLAN. On the writing side, in conjunction with David Croft, Lloyd was responsible for ARE YOU BEING SERVED? (and its sequel, *Grace and Favour*), COME BACK MRS NOAH, OH HAPPY BAND! and 'ALLO 'ALLO. Earlier collaboration with Jimmy Grafton resulted in scripts for *The Dickie Henderson Show*, the sketch show *New Look*, and the sitcoms *Vacant Lot* and *Mum's Boys*. Lloyd also co-devised the panel game WHODUNNIT? with Lance Percival. He was once married to Joanna Lumley.

Lloyd, John
(1951–)

Radio-producer-turned-TV-producer, responsible for some of the major TV comedies since the 1980s. These have included NOT THE NINE O'CLOCK NEWS, SPITTING IMAGE and the BLACKADDER series. Lloyd nearly became first host of HAVE I GOT NEWS FOR YOU, but, having recorded a pilot episode, decided to stay behind the camera. Later he created and produced the comedy quiz show QI.

Lloyd, Kevin
(1949–98)

Best known as THE BILL's DC 'Tosh' Lines, Derby-born actor Kevin Lloyd was a familiar face on British television for some 20 years. He was Oscar in *Misfits* and Ricky in DEAR JOHN, and other credits came in programmes as varied as AUF WIEDERSEHEN, PET, BY THE SWORD DIVIDED, Z CARS, ALL IN GOOD FAITH, *Sounding Brass*, THE BORGIAS, MINDER, HAZELL, ANDY CAPP, DEMPSEY AND MAKEPEACE, BOON and CORONATION STREET (Don Watkins). He was the brother of ITN journalist Terry Lloyd, who was tragically killed in the 2003 Iraq War.

Lloyd Pack, Roger

(1944–)

British actor immortalized as the slow-witted Trigger in ONLY FOOLS AND HORSES. However, Lloyd Pack (the son of actor Charles Lloyd Pack and father of actress Emily Lloyd) has been much seen on TV. He was David Irving in SELLING HITLER, Jimmy Ryan in *Moving*, Albert Mason in SPYDER'S WEB, Beckett in BYKER GROVE, Quentin in *Archer's Goon*, Plitplov in THE GRAVY TRAIN GOES EAST, Phillips in *Dandelion Dead*, Rex Regis in HEALTH AND EFFICIENCY, Owen Newitt in THE VICAR OF DIBLEY, Sir Baldwin De'Ath in the kids' comedy *Knight School*, Ken Thompson in *The Missing Postman*, Anderson in TOM JONES, Mr Sowerberry in OLIVER TWIST, Captain Man in LONGITUDE and Norman Pendleton in BORN AND BRED. He has also appeared in series like PRIVATE SCHULZ, STAY LUCKY, MR BEAN, BOON, INSPECTOR MORSE, THE KRYPTON FACTOR, THE CHIEF, *Paul Merton in Galton & Simpson's . . .*, THE BILL, MURDER ROOMS: THE DARK BEGINNINGS OF SHERLOCK HOLMES, DALZIEL AND PASCOE, *Margery and Gladys*, WHERE THE HEART IS, DOC MARTIN, AGATHA CHRISTIE'S POIROT, DOCTOR WHO and 2 POINT 4 CHILDREN (practical joker/plumber Jake).

Loach, Ken

(1936–)

British drama director, fond of the documentary style, noted for his realism and responsible for emotive pieces like UP THE JUNCTION, CATHY COME HOME, *In Two Minds* (1967), *The Rank and File* (1971), *The Price of Coal* (1977) and the series DAYS OF HOPE, among other offerings. Earlier he had worked on Z CARS and the serial *Diary of a Young Man*. Loach returned to the small screen with a Channel 4 film, *The Navigators*, in 2001.

Lockwood, Margaret

CBE (Margaret Mary Lockwood Day; 1916–90)

British actress for whom television success arrived late. After a long and respectable career in the movies, dating back to the 1930s, Margaret Lockwood only really found her TV niche in 1971, when she donned the wig of barrister Harriet Peterson in JUSTICE. Seven years earlier she had starred in the pub series *The Flying Swan*, playing landlady Mollie Manning, and before that, in 1957, she played a similar role as Mollie Miller, proprietress of the Royalty Hotel in the drama series *The Royalty*. Lockwood also enjoyed numerous other TV drama credits, including *Pygmalion*, as early as 1948.

Loe, Judy

(1947–)

British actress, seen in comedy as well as straight drama roles. She was Lulli in the children's series ACE OF WANDS, Celia Kemp in the game-show sitcom *Good Night and God Bless*, abandoned wife Alison Reynolds in *Missing from Home*, Pam in SINGLES and Dr Elizabeth Stafford in THE CHIEF. Among her numerous other credits have been Z CARS, MAN AT THE TOP, EDWARD THE SEVENTH, WHEN THE BOAT COMES IN, *Yesterday's Dreams*, THE UPCHAT LINE, *Couples*, ROBIN'S NEST, MISS JONES AND SON, RIPPING YARNS, *Heartland*, INSPECTOR MORSE (Adele Cecil), PEAK PRACTICE, CATHERINE COOKSON*'s The Moth* (Kate Thorman), *Eurocops*, *Revelations*, CASUALTY/HOLBY CITY (Jan Goddard) and SILENT WITNESS. Her first husband was the late Richard Beckinsale and her second husband is director Roy Battersby. Loe is the mother of actress Kate Beckinsale.

Logan, Gabby

(Gabrielle Logan; 1973–)

Pioneering female presenter of TV football, first at Sky Sports then with ITV, where she has hosted *On the Ball*, *The Premiership* and the *World Cup*. The daughter of former Wales football captain and manager Terry Yorath, Gabby represented Wales in rhythmic gymnastics at the 1990 Commonwealth Games. In 2001 she married Scottish rugby international Kenny Logan. Other credits include hosting *The Vault* quiz show.

Logan, Phyllis

(1956–)

Scottish actress still probably best known as Lovejoy's girlfriend, Lady Jane Felsham, even though she has starred in numerous other dramas, most notably *Bust* (Sheila Walsh), *Love and Reason* (Lou Larson MP), INVASION EARTH (Squadron Leader Helen Knox), HOLBY CITY (Muriel McKendrick), ALL THE KING'S MEN (Mary Beck), NCS: MANHUNT (Inspector Anne Warwick), HOPE AND GLORY (Annie Gilbert), *Fields of Gold* (Rachel Greenlaw), *Dickens* (Georgina Hogarth), *Alibi* (Linda) and *Beneath the Skin* (DCI Grace Shilling). Other parts have come in *And a Nightingale Sang*, *Rik Mayall Presents*, HANNAY, KAVANAGH QC, INSPECTOR MORSE, HEARTBEAT, *Chiller*, AN UNSUITABLE JOB FOR A WOMAN, MIDSOMER MURDERS, RANDALL AND HOPKIRK (DECEASED), AGATHA CHRISTIE'S POIROT, DALZIEL AND PASCOE, MURDER IN SUBURBIA, SILENT WITNESS, SPOOKS and SEA OF SOULS.

Logan's Run ✶

US (MGM) Science Fiction. ITV 1978 (US: CBS 1977–8)

Logan .... **Gregory Harrison**
Jessica .... **Heather Menzies**
Rem .... **Donald Moffat**
Francis .... **Randy Powell**

Executive Producers **Ivan Goff, Ben Roberts**
Producer **Leonard Katzman**

● ***In the 24th century, two refugees flee from certain death.***
This series, based on the book by William F. Nolan and George Clayton Johnson, and the film starring Michael York, is set in the year 2319 on an Earth devastated by nuclear war. No longer one civilization, the planet exists only as a series of individual cities, separated by stretches of wilderness. In one such settlement, the City of Domes, all the citizens have a wonderful lifestyle – they live only for fun. However, there is one drawback: life is terminated at the age of 30.

Logan, a high-ranking police officer, or a Sandman as they are known, has reached the critical age and is about to undergo the 'Carousel' death ceremony when he decides to make a run for it. He is assisted by Jessica, a young rebel girl, and a humorous android, Rem, whom they meet early on in their travels. Together, they seek a legendary haven known as Sanctuary, but they are pursued all the way by another Sandman, Logan's former partner, Francis, as they brave the outside world and its hostile inhabitants.

Lois & Clark – The New Adventures of Superman

See *New Adventures of Superman, The.*

Lollipop Loves Mr Mole/Lollipop ★★

UK (ATV) Situation Comedy. ITV 1971–2

Maggie Robinson	**Peggy Mount**
Reg Robinson	**Hugh Lloyd**
Bruce Robinson	**Rex Garner**
Violet Robinson	**Pat Coombs**

Creator/Writer **Jimmy Perry**
Producer **Shaun O'Riordan**

● ***A husband and wife's happy little life is disrupted by their close family.***

Although she is big, bold and domineering, Maggie Robinson is the perfect partner for her meek and timid husband, Reg. They give each other the soppy nicknames referred to in the programme's title and their life together in Fulham is a peaceful one. Then, out of the blue, Reg's brother, Bruce, returns from Africa with his wife, Violet, supposedly for a few days' holiday. However, the visitors outstay their welcome and soon upset Lollipop and Mr Mole's domestic bliss. The second series – with Bruce and Violet still *in situ* – aired under the truncated title of *Lollipop*.

Lombard, Louise

(Louise Perkins; 1970–)

Essex-born actress best known for her role as Evie in THE HOUSE OF ELIOTT, although with several other TV parts to her name. Her earliest credits came in dramas like CAPITAL CITY (Louise), CHANCER (Anna), THE BILL and CATHERINE COOKSON*'s Black Velvet Gown*, and more recently she has starred in *Shakespeare Shorts* (Lady Macbeth), BODYGUARDS (Liz Shaw) and *Metropolis* (Charlotte Owen). Now based in Los Angeles, Lombard has also been seen in CSI: CRIME SCENE INVESTIGATION (Sofia Curtis).

London Weekend Television

See *LWT.*

London's Burning ★★

UK (LWT) Drama. ITV 1988–2002
DVD: Network

Roland 'Vaseline' Cartwright	**Mark Arden**
Mike 'Bayleaf' Wilson	**James Hazeldine**
Station Officer Sidney Tate	**James Marcus**
Sub-Officer John Hallam	**Sean Blowers**
Tony Sanders	**Treva Etienne**
Malcolm Cross	**Rupert Baker**
Bert 'Sicknote' Quigley	**Richard Walsh**
Leslie 'Charisma' Appleby	**Gerard Horan**
Josie Ingham	**Katharine Rogers**
George Green	**Glen Murphy**
Gerry	**Eric Deacon**
Kevin Medhurst	**Ross Boatman**
David	**Gil Taper Myers**
Maggie	**Shirley Greenwood**
Donna	**Paddy Navin**
Clare	**Valerie Holliman**
Jean Quigley	**Amanda Dickinson**
Marion Cartwright	**Helen Blizard**
Sandra Hallam	**Kim Clifford**
Scase	**Cliff Howells**
Colin Parrish	**Stephen North**
Kate Stevens	**Samantha Beckinsale**
Nick Georgiadis	**Andrew Kazamia**
Stuart 'Recall' Mackenzie	**Ben Onwukwe**
Kelly	**Vanessa Pett**
Laura MacKenzie	**Ona McCracken**
Geoff 'Poison' Pearce	**Michael Garner**
Billy Ray	**John Alford**
Ariadne	**Katerina Jugati**
Ben MacKenzie	**Gordon Calliste**
	Fraser Ayres
	Graham Bryan
Jack Morgan	**Clive Wood**
Clingfilm	**Chris Larner**
Jaffa	**Alan Talbot**
Cyril	**Frederick Warder**
Pitbull	**Al Hunter Ashton**
Skip	**Brad Clayton**
Carole Webb	**Zoë Hayes**
Gregg	**Steven Houghton**
Beattie	**Christine Ellerbeck**
Nanny Ray	**Pamela Lyne**
Evgenia	**Sonia Graham**
Costas	**Peter Birrel**
	Marcus Katsantonis
DO Chapman	**Graham Sinclair**
Tiggy	**Anouka Brook**
Nancy	**Kim Taylforth**
Nicky	**Katy Stephens**
Jo	**Natalie Ratcliff**
Marianne	**Minna Aaltonen**
Sally 'Gracie' Fields	**Heather Peace**
Daniel Barratt	**Brad Gorton**
Joe Walker	**Jim Alexander**
Chris Hammond	**Jonathan Guy Lewis**
Yvonne Bradley	**Jane Hazlegrove**
Lisa Hammond	**Melanie Barker**
Jacqui Parker	**Sharon Gavin**
Fiona	**Helen Anderson**
Rob 'Hyper' Sharpe	**Connor Byrne**
Ronnie 'Hi-Ho' Silver	**Fuman Dar**
DO Griggs	**Simon Merrells**
John Coleman	**Edward Peel**
Adam Benjamin	**Sam Callis**
Alison Hemmings	**Liz Crowther**
Sean Bateman	**Dominic Taylor**
Flatty	**Mark Leadbetter**
Steve Prentiss	**Scott Lane**
Elaine Reeve	**Sharon Duce**
Melissa	**Katy Odey**
Andie	**Joanne Adams**
Kate	**Natalie Robb**
Charlie Mead	**Terry Anderton**
Mick Callaghan	**Anthony Green**
Frank Mooney	**Tristan Gemmill**

Shauna Callaghan .... **Liza Walker**
Craig Ross .... **Leon Black**
Lisa Hall .... **Jan Anderson**
Dexter Ross .... **Oscar James**

Creator **Jack Rosenthal**
Executive Producers **Linda Agran, Nick Elliott, Sarah Wilson**
Producers **Paul Knight, Gerry Poulson, David Shanks, David Newcombe, Angus Towler**

● ***High drama with the chirpy crew of a London fire station.***
The firefighters of Blue Watch B25, Blackwall, made their bow in Jack Rosenthal's 1986 TV film *London's Burning*. It focused on the brave men and women of this undervalued emergency service. Watching them at home and at work, the play introduced such lively characters as Vaseline (a slippery customer), Charisma (who had none) and Sicknote (always ill). The public took to this motley crew of loafers and mickey-takers who selflessly risked life and limb, irrespective of personal problems, and a series was commissioned in 1988.

Other members of Blue Watch – a mixture of senior firefighters and rookies – are Sidney Tate (the father figure), Bayleaf (the mess manager who dreams of opening a restaurant), Josie and Kate (women in a predominantly man's world), Tony, Malcolm, Kevin, George and Colin. Recall (because of his photographic memory), the motorbike-loving Nick, Geoff 'Poison' Pearce, wide-boy Billy Ray, sub-officer Carole Webb and temporary station officer Chris Hammond are among the later additions. Incidents are based on real-life events and include plane crashes, petrol-tanker explosions, tube disasters and hostel fires. The stunts are spectacular and carefully choreographed. The late James Hazeldine (Bayleaf) also directs a number of episodes.

Lone Ranger, The ★★

US (Apex/Lone Ranger Television) Western. BBC 1956–62 (US: ABC 1949–57)
DVD: Cinema Club

The Lone Ranger .... **Clayton Moore**
John Hart
Tonto .... **Jay Silverheels**
Dan Reid .... **Chuck Courtney**
Jim Blaine .... **Ralph Littlefield**

Creators **George W. Trendle, Fran Striker**
Executive Producers **Jack Chertok, Jack Wrather**
Producers **Harry Poppe, Sherman Harris**

● ***Cult Western series featuring a mysterious masked hero and his Indian companion.***
The Lone Ranger's story begins when a group of six Texas Rangers is ambushed by a band of outlaws known as the Butch Cavendish Hole in the Wall gang. Only one survives, John Reid, and he is nursed back to health by an Indian, Tonto, whose life Reid has already saved. Swearing to avenge the death of his colleagues, who include his own brother, Reid tracks down the killers. He then embarks on a life as an intriguing Robin Hood character, dedicated to helping those in trouble. He wears a white hat and a black mask to conceal his identity and he rides a white stallion named Silver. His loyal companion, Tonto (who rides a horse called Scout), knows him as 'Kemo Sabe', meaning 'trusty scout'.

The Lone Ranger's identity is never revealed and, as he wanders from town to town routing villains, people are left to wonder, 'Who was that masked man?' as he lets out a cry of 'Hi-yo Silver' and speeds away, refusing payment and gratitude for the help he has provided. The Lone Ranger does have one base which he touches from time to time: the silver mine he owned with his dead brother. Looked after by old Jim Blaine, this provides him with the wealth to continue his travels and also the silver bullets that he uses in his pistol (although the squeaky-clean Lone Ranger never shoots to kill; the outlaws usually shoot each other or die by accident). Occasionally, Dan Reid, John's nephew, joins the duo, riding a horse called Victor.

The Lone Ranger was played for most of its run by Clayton Moore, though John Hart took over the role for a couple of years. Jay Silverheels, the one and only TV Tonto, was a real Mohawk Indian, who later spoke out against the humbling way Native Americans had always been portrayed on television. The TV series followed the success of *The Lone Ranger* on American radio in the 1930s. A cartoon version was produced in the 1960s, using the same *William Tell Overture* by Rossini as its theme music.

Lonesome Dove ★★★★

US (Motown) Western. BBC 1 1991 (US: CBS 1989)
DVD: Acorn Media

Augustus 'Gus' McCrae .... **Robert Duvall**
Woodrow F. Call .... **Tommy Lee Jones**
Jake Spoon .... **Robert Urich**
Joshua Deets .... **Danny Glover**
Newt Dobbs .... **Ricky Schroder**
Lorena Wood .... **Diane Lane**
Clara Allen .... **Anjelica Huston**
Blue Duck .... **Frederic Forrest**
Dish Boggett .... **D. B. Sweeney**
July Johnson .... **Chris Cooper**
Pea Eye Parker .... **Tim Scott**

Writer **Bill Wittliff**
Executive Producers **Bill Wittliff, Suzanne de Passe**
Producer **Dyson Lovell**

● ***Epic tale of a cattle drive north from Texas.***
In this multi-Emmy-winning mini-series, directed by Simon Wincer, two former Texas Rangers are seduced away from their modest ranching and livery business (the Hat Creek Cattle Company) in the Rio Grande town of Lonesome Dove by old buddy Jake Spoon. He enchants the rather indolent Gus McCrae and the highly moral Woodrow Call with tales of fortunes to be made driving cattle through uncharted territory up to Montana. The four episodes expose a tale of hardship and deprivation on the 2,500-mile trail through the wild and barren plains, spiced with petty jealousies and the more malignant threat of Indian attacks and the spiteful wickedness of renowned outlaws. Lorena Wood is the whore who follows the Hat Creek outfit north and eventually introduces friction between Gus and Jake. Also on the trail is naïve young Newt Dobbs, rapidly becoming a man and desperate to unearth the true identity of his father. The series, which was credited with bringing the serious Western back to the small screen, was adapted from the Pulitzer Prize-winning novel by Texan author Larry McMurtry. A sequel, *Return to Lonesome Dove*, was aired by CBS in 1993 and screened in the UK in 1994. Only Ricky Schroder remained from the original cast, but new stars included Oliver Reed and Jon Voight. In 1994, *Lonesome Dove: the Series* was syndicated in the USA. By this time, Schroder had also left, but his character continued (played by Scott Bairstow), having set up home in the Montana town of Curtis Wells. A second sequel, the two-part *Streets of Laredo*, with James Garner as Woodrow Call, was broadcast in 1995 on CBS

(UK: BBC 2 1998). There was also a prequel, *Dead Man's Walk*, showing McCrae (David Arquette) and Call (Jonny Lee Miller) in their younger days, screened by ABC in 1996.

Long Firm, The ★★★

UK (BBC) Drama. BBC 2 2004
DVD: BBC

Harry Starks	**Mark Strong**
DI George Mooney	**George Costigan**
Lord Teddy Thursby	**Derek Jacobi**
Ruth Thursby	**Judy Parfitt**
Ruby Ryder	**Lena Headey**
Tommy	**Joe Absolom**
Jimmy	**Phil Daniels**
Lenny	**Shaun Dingwall**
Karen	**Kaye Wragg**
Manny	**Neil Conrich**
Jock McClusky	**Geoff Bell**

Writer **Joe Penhall**
Producer **Liza Marshall**

A ruthless gay gangster dominates 1960s Soho.

Bille Eltringham directs the four instalments of this stylish adaptation of Jake Arnott's novel of the same name. The drama centres on one Harry Starks, a London gangster who mingles with the great and the good of society, gaining undue influence and celebrity. Four facets of his life are depicted, episode by episode, beginning in 1964. The first focuses on his relationship with impecunious Tory Lord Teddy Thursby, a man who shares Harry's homosexual leanings, something that Harry can easily use against the naïve peer when their 'business' relationship breaks down. That business revolves around the use of Thursby's name to add weight to Harry's dubious companies. (One particular con-trick Harry masterminds is known as 'The Long Firm', hence the drama's title.) In episode two, Harry makes use of fading movie star Ruby Ryder to boost his ailing Stardust nightclub, and in episode three boozy drug-pusher Jimmy is enrolled as Harry's leg man when Harry tries to find the killer of a young rent boy. In the last part, Harry is in prison, but still spreading his malevolent influence, as ingenuous sociology lecturer Lenny finds to his cost. Slithering around in the background throughout is crooked copper George Mooney.

The Long Firm was acclaimed by critics and reviewers, although some stomach-churning moments of unspeakable brutality understandably offended many viewers.

Long John Silver

See *Adventures of Long John Silver, The.*

Longitude ★★★★

UK (Granada/Channel 4/A&E) Historical Drama. Channel 4 2000
DVD: Cinema Club

John Harrison	**Michael Gambon**
Rupert Gould	**Jeremy Irons**
William Harrison	**Ian Hart**
Elizabeth Harrison	**Gemma Jones**
Muriel Gould	**Anna Chancellor**
Sir Frank Dyson	**Alec McCowen**
George Graham	**Peter Vaughan**
John Jeffries	**Peter-Hugo Daly**
Agnes 'Dodo' Gould	**Barbara Leigh Hunt**
Capt. Campbell	**Nick Reding**
Revd Neville Maskelyne	**Samuel West**
Dr Bliss	**Ian McNeice**
Lord Sandwich	**Bill Nighy**
Lord Morton	**Brian Cox**
Christopher Irwin	**Tim McInnerny**
Sir Charles Pelham	**Nigel Davenport**
Admiral Wager	**Frank Finlay**
Capt. Proctor	**John Standing**
Admiral Balchen	**Charles Gray**
Capt. Man	**Roger Lloyd Pack**
Sir Edmund Halley	**John Wood**
Commodore Forrest	**Gary Waldhorn**
Capt. Digges	**Clive Francis**
Capt. Bourke	**Darragh O'Malley**
King George	**Nicholas Rowe**
Grace Ingram	**Lucy Akhurst**

Writer **Charles Sturridge**
Executive Producers **Pippa Cross, Anthony Root, Delia Fine**
Producer **Selwyn Roberts**

A clock-maker's hopes of improving life for mariners are hindered by the authorities.

But for the actions of 18th-century Yorkshire carpenter John Harrison, the lives of thousands of men at sea would have been lost. This two-part, star-studded drama sumptuously recalls the life Harrison dedicated to developing an accurate timepiece that, in conjunction with the position of the sun, would enable mariners to correctly calculate their longitude, thus avoiding shipwrecks and many disastrous weeks lost at sea. Harrison spends 50 years trying to claim a £20,000 prize offered by the Government for a solution to the problem, but finds his every move scuppered by the assessing body, the Royal Astronomical Society, whose bigwigs favour more celestial ways out of the naval predicament. Even when Harrison's various clocks prove their worth time and again, helping ships navigate and saving lives, the Society raises new obstacles to his success. For the later part of his life, the sick Harrison has to rely on his son, William, to take his inventions on their required sea trials. Harrison's progress is paralleled in this film by the efforts of early 20th-century naval officer Rupert Gould to reconstruct Harrison's venerable timepieces. Gould, a casualty of World War I, has suffered a nervous breakdown and his marriage collapses as he devotes his life to studying Harrison's work. With big name cameo appearances galore, *Longitude* – adapted and directed by Charles Sturridge from Dava Sobel's book – was Channel 4's major presentation to welcome the new millennium. Geoffrey Burgon composed the music.

Longstreet ★★

US (Paramount) Detective Drama. ITV 1973 (US: ABC 1971–2)

Mike Longstreet	**James Franciscus**
Nikki Bell	**Marlyn Mason**
Duke Paige	**Peter Mark Richman**
Mrs Kingston	**Ann Doran**

Creator/Executive Producer **Stirling Silliphant**

Blindness does not deter a Louisiana insurance snoop.

In the 1970s, nearly all TV detectives needed some distinctive trait and for Mike Longstreet it, regrettably, was blindness. His life shattered by villains who set off a blast that both kills his wife and robs him of his sight, this insurance investigator refuses to lie down. With the help of an Alsatian guide dog named Pax and an electronic stick that helps him gauge distances, Longstreet loses none of his detective nous, successfully hounding out thieves and fraudsters in steamy New Orleans. Relying on his remaining four senses, he tends to notice odd smells, sounds, tastes and textures that provide vital clues. Close friend and assistant is Nikki Bell, Mrs Kingston is his housekeeper and Duke Paige works for the same insurance firm. Bruce Lee is occasionally seen as Longstreet's self-defence guru, Li Tsung. The series was slated by some critics for its over-casual treatment – unintentionally comic it was said – of a major physical handicap.

Longthorne, Joe

(1955–)

British singer and impressionist, well known for his take-offs of Shirley Bassey, Johnny Mathis and other vocalists. Longthorne was a regular on the kids' variety series JUNIOR SHOWTIME while a teenager in the early 1970s and emerged into the adult market via the talent show *Search for a Star*. He then joined *The Les Dennis Laughter Show*, before being given his own ITV series in the late 1980s.

Look ★★

UK (BBC) Natural History. BBC 1 1955–69

Host **Peter Scott**

Producers **Brandon Acton-Bond, Tony Soper, Eileen Molony, Jeffrey Boswell**

● ***Innovative British wildlife series.***

This pioneering, long-running, in-depth view of the natural world was presented for most of its life by the famous naturalist Peter Scott, founder of the Severn Wildfowl Trust at Slimbridge. Predating Anglia's SURVIVAL by six years, *Look* was produced by the BBC's wildlife specialists in Bristol, and a children's version was also aired. Repeats were at one time shown under the title of *Look Again*. When Scott travelled to Oceania and the Galapagos Islands, the series briefly took the title of *Faraway Look*.

Looking for Clancy ★★

UK (BBC) Drama. BBC 2 1975

Frank Clancy .... **Robert Powell**
Steve Fletcher *(young)*
Dick Holt .... **Keith Drinkel**
Tommy Pender *(young)*
Lucy Caldwell .... **Eileen Helsby**
Ted Shatto .... **John Blythe**
Penny Clancy .... **Catherine Schell**
Jim Clancy .... **John Junkin**
Eileen Clancy .... **Barbara Young**
Dai Owen .... **James Grout**
Marcus Selby .... **T. P. McKenna**

Writer **Jack Pulman**
Producer **Richard Beynon**

● ***The death of a boyhood friend encourages a devious journalist to reconsider his life.***

Frank Clancy is the son of an Irish policeman, growing up in Hoxton, east London, during World War I. His best friend is Dick Holt, as ambitious as Clancy himself, both lads aiming to be leading Fleet Street journalists one day. Clancy takes every opportunity that presents itself, even if it means compromising his early principles. He throws in a job as the editor of a socialist journal to become the political editor of a tabloid and makes plenty of enemies on his rise to the top. Others see him as manipulative, but Clancy fails to recognize the trait in himself until forced to think back over his life when he discovers that Holt has committed suicide because of his behaviour. By this time Clancy is 50 and a newspaper editor. The five-part serial, telling Clancy's story in flashbacks, was an adaptation of a novel by Frederic Mullally. Bill Hays directed and the catchy theme song was composed by Brian Wade and Tony Cliff.

Lord, Jack

(John Joseph Ryan; 1920–98)

New York-born leading man who found his niche (and fortune) as Steve McGarrett, the no-nonsense head of detectives on HAWAII FIVE-O. He played McGarrett for 12 years, making Hawaii his home in the process. He was also an exhibited artist. Lord's other TV work was confined to guest appearances (usually as baddies) in series like THE UNTOUCHABLES, THE FBI, HAVE GUN WILL TRAVEL, NAKED CITY, RAWHIDE, GUNSMOKE, THE FUGITIVE, DR KILDARE, BONANZA, THE MAN FROM U.N.C.L.E. and A MAN CALLED IRONSIDE, as well as the lead role in an early 1960s Western series *Stoney Burke*.

Lord Peter Wimsey ★★

UK (BBC) Drama. BBC 1 1972–5
DVD: Acorn Media

Lord Peter Wimsey .... **Ian Carmichael**
Bunter .... **Glyn Houston**
Derek Newark
DCI Charles Parker .... **Mark Eden**

Producers **Richard Beynon, Bill Sellars**

● ***Classy crime-solving with an elegant aristocrat.***

Lord Peter Wimsey was the scourge of all murderers in the 1920s. Created in novels by Dorothy L. Sayers, he came to life in this period-TV outing through the monocled impersonation of Ian Carmichael. Wimsey is prim, proper and always a gentleman. He tends to appear a bit of an upper-class twit, but this is a deliberate ploy to fool his adversaries. In truth, he possesses a sharp analytical mind, enhanced by an encyclopaedic knowledge of classical music. He loves cricket, enjoys good conversation and savours the best food and drink, just part of the *bon viveur* lifestyle he pursues at his home in Piccadilly.

With never a financial worry, and desperate to restore order to an untidy world, Wimsey is regularly on hand to pick up the pieces of a murder mystery in the most unusual of settings. Invaluable on these occasions is his loyal manservant, Bunter (a former army sergeant colleague), a man who can easily mix with the lower classes and extract information denied to his employer. Police presence is provided by Wimsey's brother-in-law, Inspector Parker (played by future CORONATION STREET villain Mark Eden).

Five of Sayers's novels were dramatized for this TV version: *Clouds of Witness*, *The Unpleasantness at the Bellona Club*, *Murder Must Advertise*, *The Nine Tailors* and *Five Red Herrings*. Three more – *Strong Poison*, *Have His Carcase* and *Gaudy Night*

– were adapted for a series entitled *A Dorothy L. Sayers Mystery*, screened on BBC 2 in 1987, with Edward Petherbridge as Wimsey, Richard Morant as Bunter and David Quiller as Parker. Also featured in this revamp was Harriet Walter as Harriet Vane, Wimsey's crime-writer friend.

Lost ★★★

US (Touchstone) Drama. Channel 4 2005– (US: ABC 2004–)
DVD: Buena Vista Home Entertainment

Dr Jack Shepherd	**Matthew Fox**
Kate Austin	**Evangeline Lilly**
Charlie Pace	**Dominic Monaghan**
Shannon	**Maggie Grace**
Michael Dawson	**Harold Perrineau Jr**
Hugo 'Hurley' Reyes	**Jorge Garcia**
James 'Sawyer' Ford	**Josh Holloway**
Walt Lloyd	**Malcolm David Kelley**
Jin-Soo Kwon	**Daniel Dae Kim**
Boone Carlyle	**Ian Somerhalder**
Sayid Jarrah	**Naveen Andrews**
John Locke	**Terry O'Quinn**
Sun Kwon	**Yunjin Kim**
Claire Littleton	**Emilie de Ravin**
Libby	**Cynthia Watros**
Ana Lucia Cortez	**Michelle Rodriguez**
Mr Eko	**Adewale Akinnuoye-Agbaje**

Creators **J. J. Abrams, Damon Lindelof, Jeffrey Lieber**
Executive Producers **J. J. Abrams, Damon Lindelof, Bryan Burk, Carlton Cuse**

The survivors of a plane crash are trapped on a bizarre Pacific island.

After huge success in its native USA, *Lost* arrived in the UK via Channel 4 in 2005. To ensure the series hit the ground running (like most of its characters), the broadcaster launched its biggest ever promotional campaign for a new programme, with director David LaChapelle hired to fly to Hawaii to film special adverts with the stars.

Lost begins with Oceanic Air flight 815 from Sydney to Los Angeles veering 1,000 miles off course, breaking up in mid-air and crash-landing on a remote island in the South Pacific. There are initially 48 survivors, who, once the wounded have been cared for, have to try to get along in order to stay alive and remain sane. It falls to Dr Jack Shepherd to take the lead and he provides a moral anchor for the disparate community. His colleagues include Kate Austin, the girl he takes a shine to, but, it transpires, like everyone else, she has a secret past. Vying with Jack for Kate's attentions is Sawyer, a man who takes delight in antagonizing others. Charlie Pace is the has-been rock star, a bass player with a band called Drive Shaft; Michael Dawson and Walt Lloyd are father and nine-year-old son, who have only just come together after a custody battle; and Jin and Sun are a young Korean couple. Alongside these are spoilt girl Shannon and her over-bearing half-brother Boone; Sayid, a former member of Iraq's Republican Guard; Claire who is pregnant; Locke, who is particularly enigmatic; and Hurley, the chubby joker in the pack. We learn more about this motley band via flashbacks as the series progresses. However, *Lost* is more than a Robinson Crusoe tale for the 21st century. There appears to be something sinister at work on the island and there's more than a suggestion that the survivors are mere pawns in a giant game. The constantly rustling undergrowth, the howls of unseen animals and the inclement weather combine to unsettle the survivors as they try to find out where they are, how to get home, and, particularly, how to get along with each other. Newcomers Libby, Ana Lucia and Mr Eko appear in series two.

Lost in Space ★★

US (Twentieth Century-Fox/Irwin Allen) Science Fiction. ITV 1965–9 (US: CBS 1965–8)
DVD: Fox Home Entertainment

Prof. John Robinson	**Guy Williams**
Maureen Robinson	**June Lockhart**
Dr Zachary Smith	**Jonathan Harris**
Major Don West	**Mark Goddard**
Judy Robinson	**Marta Kristen**
Will Robinson	**Billy Mumy**
Penny Robinson	**Angela Cartwright**
The Robot	**Bob May**
	Dick Tufeld *(voice)*

Creator/Executive Producer **Irwin Allen**
Producers **Jerry Briskin, William Faralla**

A pioneering family is stranded in outer space.

In 1997 an over-populated Earth sends the Robinson family on a five-year mission to a planet in the Alpha Centauri system to plan for colonization. But their spaceship is sabotaged and they become *Lost in Space*. The family consists of father John Robinson, an astrophysicist; his biochemist wife, Maureen; and children Judy, Will and Penny. Geologist Don West is the pilot of their spaceship, the *Jupiter II*, and a genial, somewhat sarcastic robot provides scientific expertise and controls the spacecraft. The joker in the pack is Dr Zachary Smith, a foreign agent who sabotaged the mission by interfering with the robot, but who found himself trapped on board when the ship took off. He was forced to wake the family from their suspended animation to try to rectify the situation.

For most of the first season, the Robinsons survive on a barren planet on which their ship crash-lands. Stories revolve around their attempts to repair the *Jupiter II* and find a way home, but each week some strange alien intelligence arrives to throw them into danger. The aliens are always treacherously assisted by the cowardly, work-shy Dr Smith, whose sole aim is to find a quick way back to civilization, preferably without the Robinsons. His plans consistently backfire and, just as you think all was well, the programme ends with another sinister turn of events, a cliffhanger to be resolved next time. In later seasons, the Robinsons do manage to take off, but still Earth eludes them.

At first, *Lost in Space* is straight science fiction, but it becomes very lighthearted (it was forced into competition with BATMAN on American TV). The plots are somewhat predictable, with the arrogant Dr Smith constantly bringing trouble to the extremely accommodating and surprisingly forgiving family. His closest friend, nine-year-old Will, a wholesome, electronics whizz-kid, often ruins Smith's indulgent schemes by staying loyal to his family. Will's blonde sister, Judy, spends much of her time romantically entwined with action man Don West, while his other sister, dark-haired, 11-year-old Penny, dotes on her pet space monkey, which is known as 'The Bloop'.

The character of Dr Smith was scheduled for only six episodes, but actor Jonathan Harris, a late addition to the cast, quickly became the show's star and Smith stayed. Guy Williams had previously starred as the swashbuckling ZORRO, and Angela Cartwright was one of the Von Trapp children in *The Sound of Music*. Child actor Billy Mumy has more recently been seen (grown up) in another sci-fi series, BABYLON 5. The robot, which had no name, closely resembled Robbie the robot in the 1956 Walter Pidgeon film *Forbidden Planet*. Gary Oldman played Dr Smith in a 1997 feature film based on the series, with William Hurt as John Robinson and Matt LeBlanc as Don West.

Lost Prince, The ✳✳✳

UK (Talkback/BBC/WGBH Boston) Historical Drama. BBC 1 2003
DVD: BBC

Johnnie .... **Daniel Williams** *(young)*
Matthew Thomas
Georgie .... **Brock Everitt-Elwick** *(young)*
Rollo Weeks
Lalla .... **Gina McKee**
Queen Mary .... **Miranda Richardson**
Edward VII .... **Michael Gambon**
George V .... **Tom Hollander**
Queen Alexandra .... **Bibi Andersson**
Stamfordham .... **Bill Nighy**
Asquith .... **Frank Finlay**
Lloyd George .... **Ron Cook**
Mr Hansell .... **John Sessions**
Fred .... **David Westhead**
Tsar Nicholas .... **Ivan Marevich**
Tsarina Alexandra .... **Ingeborga Dapkunaite**
Kaiser Wilhelm .... **David Barrass**
Callender .... **Graham Crowden**

Writer **Stephen Poliakoff**
Producer **John Chapman**

A young prince with behavioural difficulties is hidden away from the world.

Prince John, or Johnnie to his immediate family, is the youngest son of King George V and Queen Mary. Sadly, his epilepsy, autism and naïve plain speaking do not make him a fit person to have around the court, so Johnnie is banished to Sandringham in the care of his devoted nanny, Lalla. Lalla it is who provides the love and affection that is regrettably lacking from Johnnie's relationship with his protocol- and duty-constrained parents, and it is she who does her best to protect and nurture her delicate charge. Johnnie's other key ally is his elder brother, Georgie, who is groomed for the sort of duties that the plucky Johnnie will never be allowed to undertake but who recognizes the support his brother needs. Bringing in appearances by leading politicians of the day and visits from the extended Royal Family throughout Europe, *The Lost Prince* is a sad and moving look at the conventions and expectations of aristocracy in the early decades of the 20th century and World War I, as well as a tribute to misunderstood children with learning difficulties and social handicaps. Stephen Poliakoff also directs his own sympathetic, two-part film, which was based on true events. The real Prince John died in 1919, aged 13.

Lotterby, Sydney

Prolific British comedy producer/director, working for the BBC on series of varying success, like *Broaden Your Mind*, THREE OF A KIND (1967 version), THE LIVER BIRDS, THE GNOMES OF DULWICH, ME MAMMY, UP POMPEII, SYKES, *Now Take My Wife*, SOME MOTHERS DO 'AVE 'EM, PORRIDGE, *Going Straight*, LAST OF THE SUMMER WINE, OPEN ALL HOURS, BUTTERFLIES, YES, MINISTER (and *Yes, Prime Minister*), *Coming Home*, THE LAST SONG, EVER DECREASING CIRCLES, THE MAGNIFICENT EVANS, BRUSH STROKES, FOREIGN BODIES, MAY TO DECEMBER, *A Gentleman's Club*, AS TIME GOES BY, BLOOMIN' MARVELLOUS and, for Central, *Old Boy Network*.

Lotus Eaters, The ✳✳

UK (BBC) Drama. BBC 2 1972–3

Erik Shepherd .... **Ian Hendry**
Ann Shepherd .... **Wanda Ventham**
Nestor Turton .... **Maurice Denham**
Major Edward Woolley .... **Thorley Walters**
Mrs Miriam Woolley .... **Sylvia Coleridge**
Donald Culley .... **James Kerry**
Ruth Stewart .... **Cyd Hayman**
Capt. Krasakis .... **Stefan Gryff**
Philip Mervish .... **Karl Held**
Leigh Mervish .... **Carol Cleveland**
Nikos .... **Antony Stamboulieh**
Katerina .... **Karan David**
Gerald Mace .... **Timothy Carlton**
Dr Dartington .... **Ronald Howard**
Sam Webber .... **Paul Maxwell**
Imogen Lundqvist .... **Susan Engel**
Cotton .... **Frank Duncan**
Ariadne Mazonaki .... **Calliope Petrohilos**

Creator/Writer **Michael J. Bird**
Producers **Anthony Read, Michael Glynn**

Expatriate drama set in the sunny climes of Crete.

'To eat the fruit of the lotus is to lose the desire to return home. But everyone who does has a reason.' So read the promotional blurb for this 15-part drama over two series. Focusing on a little tavern (Shepherd's Bar) in the Cretan resort of Aghios Nikolaos, *The Lotus Eaters* tells tales of its proprietors, Erik (an alcoholic) and Ann Shepherd, and the various emigrants who use the bar as a home from home. These include a crusty old major and his wife, scrounging hobo Nestor Turton and squabbling American siblings Philip and Leigh Mervish. Their lives and secrets unfold as the series progresses. It is revealed for instance that Erik was once acquitted of the murder of a 15-year-old schoolgirl but is still haunted by the experience.

Lou Grant ✳✳✳

US (MTM) Drama. ITV 1979–83 (US: CBS 1977–82)

Lou Grant .... **Edward Asner**
Charlie Hume .... **Mason Adams**
Joe Rossi .... **Robert Walden**
Billie Newman/McCovey .... **Linda Kelsey**
Margaret Pynchon .... **Nancy Marchand**
Art Donovan .... **Jack Bannon**
Dennis 'Animal' Price .... **Daryl Anderson**
Adam Wilson .... **Allen Williams**
Carla Mardigian .... **Rebecca Balding**
Reuben Castillo .... **Emilio Delgado**

Executive Producers **Gene Reynolds, James L. Brooks, Allan Burns**

Dramas unfold in the newsroom of a Los Angeles daily newspaper.

Lou Grant was a spin-off from the highly successful sitcom THE MARY TYLER MOORE SHOW, but it was far more serious than its predecessor. Its lead character, Lou Grant, is News Director at WJM-TV in Minneapolis, in the Mary Tyler Moore series. However, when that show finishes, Grant and the other members of the news team are fired. At the age of 50, knowing little else but news, he takes a job as City Editor of the *Los Angeles Tribune*, working under Managing Editor Charlie Hume but often in conflict with the paper's outspoken proprietor, widow Margaret Pynchon. Colleagues at the newspaper are investigative reporter Joe Rossi, Art Donovan the Assistant City Editor, and photographer 'Animal'. Also featured is independent young reporter Billie Newman. As an informative, crusading team, they cover all manner of news stories, including sensitive issues such as Vietnamese refugees, child abuse and gun control. It is believed that Ed Asner's outspoken views on such matters may have contributed to the cancellation of the series after five years.

Love, American Style ★★

US (Paramount) Comedy. ITV 1970–5 (US: ABC 1969–74)

Creators **Douglas S. Cramer, Tom Miller**
Executive Producers **Arnold Margolin, Jim Parker**

● ***An anthology of comedy skits (three or four per show) characterizing love and the American way of life.***

There are no regular stars in *Love, American Style*. Guest artistes are called in to perform all the sketches. Each sketch is titled '*Love and . . .*' (fill in the blank with the subject-matter), and romance of all kinds is featured: among old people, among young people, extra-marital, intra-marital, and in all sorts of settings. The only familiar faces belong to a repertory company that performs short comic interludes. One other regular feature is 'Lovemate of the Week' (an attractive bathing beauty).

Guest stars attracted to the series included the likes of Sonny and Cher, Tiny Tim and Burt Reynolds, and one episode proved particularly fruitful. *Love and the Happy Day*, starring Ron Howard and Anson Williams, was the pilot for the 1950s nostalgia comedy HAPPY DAYS. *Love, American Style* proved to be a useful filler programme for a number of ITV regions.

Love Boat, The ★

US (Aaron Spelling) Comedy. ITV 1978–87 (US: ABC 1977–86)

Capt. Merrill Stubing	**Gavin MacLeod**
Burl 'Gopher' Smith	**Fred Grandy**
Dr Adam Bricker	**Bernie Kopell**
Isaac Washington	**Ted Lange**
Julie McCoy	**Lauren Tewes**
Vicki Stubing	**Jill Whelan**
Ashley Covington ('Ace') Evans	**Ted McGinley**
Judy McCoy	**Pat Klous**

Executive Producers **Aaron Spelling, Douglas S. Cramer**

● ***Romantic sketches set aboard a luxurious cruise ship.***

Three years after LOVE, AMERICAN STYLE (in its native USA) came *The Love Boat*, another anthology series centring on romance. The setting this time is the *Pacific Princess* cruise liner, with the storylines provided by each week's passengers. Like its predecessor, *The Love Boat* attracts a wealth of Hollywood talent as guest stars: Jane Wyman, Raymond Burr and Greer Garson, for instance; but it also has a cast of regulars as the ship's crew, and they featured in the various playlets. Headed by Captain Stubing, the staff include the ship's doctor, Adam Bricker, purser Gopher Smith, bartender Isaac Washington, photographer Ace and social director Julie McCoy, later replaced by Judy McCoy. The Captain's 12-year-old daughter, Vicki, is also introduced. The Love Boat Mermaids, a troupe of female singers and dancers, are added to the show later, performing a different musical number each week. Much of the series was filmed on real cruises, with fare-paying passengers performing as extras. The series closed when Captain Stubing married a lady called Emily Heywood, played by Marion Ross of HAPPY DAYS fame. The theme song, 'The Love Boat', was sung by Jack Jones (by Dionne Warwick in the last series). A revamp, *The Love Boat: the Next Wave*, began on US TV in 1998, with Robert Urich as Captain Jim Kennedy.

Love Hurts ★★

UK (Alomo) Drama. BBC 1 1992–4
DVD: Delta Music

Frank Carver	**Adam Faith**
Tessa Piggott	**Zoë Wanamaker**
Diane Warburg	**Jane Lapotaire**
Hugh Marriner	**Stephen Moore**
Max Taplow	**Tony Selby**
Mrs Marjory Piggott	**Hilary Mason**
Dr A. T. Piggott	**Richard Pearson**
Bob Pearce	**John Flanagan**
Jade Carver	**Robin Weaver**
Malcolm Litoff	**Richard Cordery**
Grace Taplow	**Edna Doré**
Simon Friedman	**David Horovitch**
Anthony Friedman	**Ben Fisher**
Jonathan Friedman	**Laurence Amias**
Sandra	**Belinda Davison**
Alex Friedman	**Carl Morris**
Marshall Baumblatt	**Olivier Pierre**
David Ben-Ari	**Sasson Gabi**
Sam Levison	**Rolf Saxon**
Mirav Levison	**Suzanne Bertish**

Creators **Laurence Marks, Maurice Gran**
Executive Producers **Allan McKeown, Michael Pilsworth, Joanna Willett**
Producers **Guy Slater, Tara Prem, Irving Teitelbaum**

● ***A disillusioned businesswoman and a millionaire plumber try to make a relationship work.***

Forty-one and single, Tessa Piggott is a media/marketing high-flyer in the City. But, seeking pastures new, having been dumped by Hugh Marriner, her boss/lover of seven years, she moves into her own flat and becomes a director of SEED (Society for Environmental and Ecological Development), a Third World aid charity. At the same time, she meets 49-year-old divorcé Frank Carver. A rough-diamond, Carver is, on the face of it, a lowly plumber but is in fact a millionaire businessman, whose Carver Corporation has just bought the little plumbing firm that Tessa calls out to fix her bathroom. They, somewhat inconveniently, fall in love, with all its emotional consequences. The series then traces the development of Tessa and Frank's relationship, as work pressures and time apart take their toll. In the second series, they get married while on business together in Russia, but married life proves just as tricky, as Tessa continues her development work, this time for the Baumblatt Foundation. By the third and final season, she is pregnant, giving birth to baby Alice. Juggling work and parenthood is equally fraught with tension. Other major characters include rabbi Diane Warburg, who is chairman of SEED and also Tessa's confidante; Diane's duplicitous husband, Simon, a polytechnic lecturer; and Tessa's work rival,

SEED's Overseas Director, Bob Pearce. Jade is Frank's 19-year-old student daughter whose untidiness drives him to distraction, and Max is his chauffeur/aide. Peter Polycarpou sings the theme song (which is not the old Everly Brothers hit of the same title). Alan Hawkshaw supplies the music.

Love Soup ✳✳✳

UK (BBC) Situation Comedy. BBC 1 2005
DVD: BBC

Alice Chenery .... **Tamsin Greig**
Gil Raymond .... **Michael Landes**
Cleo Martin .... **Sheridan Smith**
Milly Russell .... **Montserrat Lombard**
Irene .... **Trudie Styler**
Bob .... **Brian Protheroe**
Lloyd Drewitt .... **Owen Brenman**

Creator/Writer **David Renwick**
Producer **Verity Lambert**

Two lonely romantics seem perfect for each other: but will they ever meet?

Alice Chenery lives in Brighton and works on the cosmetics counter of a London department store. Sadly, she's a little low on confidence and self-esteem, and when it comes to men, her life is a bit of a disaster zone. Gil Raymond, meanwhile, lives in the country and is a successful TV scriptwriter – or was for eight years in his native America. He had followed his girlfriend across the Atlantic, only to be jilted within three hours of landing. Consequently, his love life is also in turmoil.

A quirky, romantic comedy, *Love Soup* handles Alice and Gil's stories separately, running parallel storylines within each episode, revealing their latest mishaps and romantic faux-pas, and underscoring their similar outlook on the world. The burning question for viewers is: Will these potential soul mates ever actually meet? Alice is egged on in her quest for a man by her shop colleagues, pushy Cleo and dim Milly, while Gil finds trouble on his doorstep from next-door neighbour Irene, who has just kicked out her husband, Bob, and now seems to have her eye on Gil. Lloyd Drewitt is Gil's unhelpful agent. Writer David Renwick (who makes a cameo appearance in one episode) revealed that the concept was based on his own experiences. He had placed an advertisement in a lonely hearts column which was answered by a cosmetic consultant at Harrod's who lived in Brighton. She later became his wife. The title *Love Soup* – while suggesting that finding the right partner in life is dependent on what a bubbling cauldron of emotions and circumstance throws up – is also the name of a series of TV comedies to which Gil is asked to contribute.

Love Story ✳✳

UK (ATV) Drama Anthology. ITV 1963–9; 1972–4

Single dramas in the romantic vein.

Love Story was the umbrella title for a collection of one-off plays that had romance as their linchpin. Among its most prominent contributing writers were Robert Muller, Edna O'Brien, Doris Lessing, Mordecai Richler, Robert Holles, Alfred Shaughnessy, Roman Polanski and the French novelist and screenwriter Marguérite Duras. Judi Dench, Patrick Macnee, Vanessa Redgrave, Jeremy Kemp, Dudley Moore, Julia Foster and Robert Hardy were some of the featured performers.

Love Thy Neighbour ✳

UK (Thames) Situation Comedy. ITV 1972–6
DVD: Fremantle

Eddie Booth .... **Jack Smethurst**
Joan Booth .... **Kate Williams**
Bill Reynolds .... **Rudolph Walker**
Barbie Reynolds .... **Nina Baden-Semper**
Arthur .... **Tommy Godfrey**
Jacko Jackson .... **Keith Marsh**
Nobby Garside .... **Paul Luty**

Creators/Writers **Harry Driver, Vince Powell**
Producers **Stuart Allen, Ronnie Baxter, Anthony Parker, William G. Stewart**

A bigot's life is turned upside down when a black man moves in next door.

There have been few more controversial sitcoms than *Love Thy Neighbour*, which takes delight in the predicament facing white trade-unionist Eddie Booth whose new next-door neighbour in Maple Terrace is Bill Reynolds, a true-blue Tory and, even worse, a black man. It was intended, according to its producers, to take the sting out of racial conflict. Others saw it as a barrage of cheap colour jokes that reinforced racial stereotypes. It is quite true, however, that the bigot always loses out. Eddie is never prepared to give Bill a chance, yet Bill always comes up trumps, delighting in humiliating Eddie and always giving as good as he gets. Meanwhile, to underline the futility of it all, the two wives, Joan and Barbie, become good friends. Arthur, Jacko ('I'll have a half') and Nobby are their pals down at the Jubilee Social Club. Remarkably, the series was a huge ratings success. The theme song was sung by Stuart Gillies. A feature-film version was released in 1973, and the series was revamped in 1980 in Australia. *Love Thy Neighbour in Australia*, as it was titled when screened in the UK two years later, depicts Eddie embroiled in the same racial conflict on his emigration Down Under. There was also a short-lived American version, starring Ron Masak and Harrison Page, in 1973.

Loved by You ✳✳

UK (Carlton) Situation Comedy. ITV 1997–8

Michael Adams .... **John Gordon-Sinclair**
Kate Adams .... **Trevyn McDowell**
Lander .... **Gary Love**
Becky Edwards .... **Kim Thomson**
Ruth Jackson .... **Gillian Bevan**
Tom Jackson .... **Steven Alvey**
Dave .... **Gary Webster**

Writers **Danny Jacobson, Paul Reiser, Steve Paymer, Billy Grundfest, Daryl Rowland, Lisa DeBenedictus, Sally Lapiduss, Pamela Eells**
Executive Producer **Richard Boden**
Producer **Steve Bailie**

The course of true love fails to run smoothly for a newlywed couple.

Michael and Kate Adams have been married only five months. They have good, interesting jobs (he's a documentary film-maker, she's a PR officer) and they live in a swish flat. However, there's always something getting in the way of wedded bliss – usually intrusions from Kate's sister, Becky, or Michael's slobby best mate, Lander, or even visits from Kate's ex-boss,

Ruth, and her gynaecologist husband, Tom – which gives the newlyweds plenty to argue about when they're finally on their own. To drive the wedge in further, fantasy sequences and flashbacks help the bickering duo picture their former lives, or the lives they just might wish they now had. By the time of series two, Lander has departed to be replaced by the equally irksome Dave.

The series was adapted (by Gary Sinyor, then David Wolstencroft) from the US series *Mad About You* (NBC 1992–9), introducing British references in place of American where relevant, but largely following the script closely, which meant lots of sharp one-liners. The original series was co-created by its star Paul Reiser and Danny Jacobson and the lead characters' names were Paul and Jamie Buchman (Helen Hunt shared top billing).

Lovejoy ✶✶

UK (Tamariska/Witzend/McShane) Comedy Drama. BBC 1 1986; 1991–4
DVD: Delta

Lovejoy .... **Ian McShane**
Tinker Dill .... **Dudley Sutton**
Eric Catchpole .... **Chris Jury**
Lady Jane Felsham .... **Phyllis Logan**
Lord Felsham .... **Pavel Douglas**
Charlie Gimbert .... **Malcolm Tierney**
Dandy Jack .... **Geoffrey Bateman**
Beth .... **Diane Parish**
Charlotte Cavendish .... **Caroline Langrishe**

Creator **Ian La Frenais**
Producers **Robert Banks Stewart, Richard Everitt, Emma Hayter, Jo Wright, Colin Schindler**

● ***A shady antiques dealer stumbles into intrigue in the East Anglian countryside.***

Dubbed by some 'The Antiques Rogue Show', *Lovejoy* was based on the novels of Jonathan Gash and concerned a slightly dodgy dealer in antiquities. Lovejoy's patch is rural Essex and Suffolk, which he combs for underpriced treasures to sell on with a nice mark-up. Being what is known as a 'divvie', he instinctively knows when an antique is rare and valuable. At his side are Tinker, his tweedy, beret-hatted old friend, and young gofer Eric Catchpole. When Eric leaves to run his uncle's pub, he is replaced by Beth, another 'trainee'. Leather-jacketed Lovejoy (who lives in a picturesque country cottage and drives a battered Morris Minor affectionately named Miriam) enjoys the company of local aristocrat Lady Jane Felsham and, though flirtation is the name of the game, wedding bells never chime. On Lady Jane's departure, in comes university-educated auctioneer Charlotte Cavendish, and she almost succeeds in getting the lovable wheeler-dealer to the altar in the very last episode of the series.

Played in humorous-thriller style, *Lovejoy* also employs the television technique known as 'breaking the fourth wall'. As seen earlier in programmes like THE GEORGE BURNS AND GRACIE ALLEN SHOW and IT'S GARRY SHANDLING'S SHOW, this calls on Lovejoy, in an aside to the camera, to explain events directly to the viewers.

Lovers, The ✶✶

UK (Granada) Situation Comedy. ITV 1970–1

Geoffrey Scrimgeor .... **Richard Beckinsale**
Beryl Battersby .... **Paula Wilcox**
Mrs Battersby .... **Joan Scott**
Roland Lomax .... **Robin Nedwell**

Creator **Jack Rosenthal**
Writers **Jack Rosenthal, Geoffrey Lancashire**
Producers **Jack Rosenthal, Les Chatfield**

● ***Two teenagers have different hopes for their relationship.***

Geoffrey (or 'Geoffrey Bubbles Bon Bon', as Beryl, his girlfriend, likes to call him) is very concerned with the physical side of their romance – or, more precisely, with the fact that there is no physical side. No matter how hard he tries to consummate their relationship (egged on by his pal, Roland, with whom he works at Westland Bank), the scheming Beryl (watched over by her prudish widowed mum) is always too virtuous to give in. 'Percy Filth', as she knows it, is not for her, despite the permissive age in which they live. Marriage, in her eyes, is a far better objective.

The Lovers proved to be the break that both Paula Wilcox and Richard Beckinsale needed in their fledgling careers. A feature-film version followed in 1972.

Lowe, Arthur

(1915–82)

Derbyshire-born actor, for ever the bumptious Captain Mainwaring in DAD'S ARMY, but the star of numerous other sitcoms and dramas. These included POTTER (Redvers Potter), BLESS ME FATHER (Father Duddleswell) and A. J. WENTWORTH, BA (schoolmaster Wentworth). In the 1960s he was draper Leonard Swindley, the man jilted by Emily Nugent at the altar in CORONATION STREET – a character which he took into the spin-off series PARDON THE EXPRESSION and *Turn Out the Lights*. Lowe also voiced the *Mr Men* cartoons, starred with Richard Briers in *Ben Travers Farces*, appeared in Harold Pinter's first TV play (an ARMCHAIR THEATRE production called *A Night Out*) and was Dr Maxwell in *Doctor at Large* (see DOCTOR IN THE HOUSE), Bodkin in LAST OF THE BASKETS, Micawber in a 1975 BBC version of DAVID COPPERFIELD and Louis Pasteur in MICROBES AND MEN. Lowe was also seen in the dramas PHILBY, BURGESS AND MACLEAN (Herbert Morrison) and *A Voyage Around My Father*, and appeared as a guest in THE AVENGERS, among other series. He was married to actress Joan Cooper, who was cast as Godfrey's sister Dolly in *Dad's Army*.

Lucas, Matt

(1974–)

London-born writer, comedian and actor, now a household name thanks to his partnership with David Walliams in writing and appearing in LITTLE BRITAIN. The duo had worked together previously on *Rock Profiles*, a series of spoof documentaries and interviews with music names. Lucas first came to light as manic drummer George Dawes, the scorer dressed in a babygrow in SHOOTING STARS, and he has been seen with that programme's creators, Reeves and Mortimer, in several of their other series, including *Catterick* (Roy Oates). He also appeared in SUNNYSIDE FARM (Mr Mills), *Sir Bernard's Stately Homes* (Sir Bernard Chumley, one of his earliest comic creations), *Surrealissimo*, *The All Star Comedy Show*, *Look Around You* and CASANOVA (Villars). Lucas also provided the voice of Merlin for the animation *King Arthur's Disasters*.

Lucky Jim

See *The Further Adventures of Lucky Jim*.

Lucy Show, The ✶✶

US (CBS/Desilu) Situation Comedy. BBC 1 1962–8
(US: CBS 1962–8)
DVD: Oracle Home Entertainment

Lucy Carmichael	**Lucille Ball**
Vivian Bagley	**Vivian Vance**
Chris Carmichael	**Candy Moore**
Jerry Carmichael	**Jimmy Garrett**
Mr Barnsdahl	**Charles Lane**
Theodore J. Mooney	**Gale Gordon**
Harry Conners	**Dick Martin**
Sherman Bagley	**Ralph Hart**
Harrison Cheever	**Roy Roberts**
Mary Jane Lewis	**Mary Jane Croft**

● ***A bored widow seeks a new husband and thinks up hare-brained schemes to improve her life.***

In this follow-up to I LOVE LUCY, Lucille Ball stars without her husband, Desi Arnaz. Having said that, the format is essentially much the same, with Lucy playing Lucy Carmichael, a scatterbrained widow living with her two children, Chris and Jerry, in Danfield, Connecticut. She is once again supported by Vivian Vance, this time in the guise of Vivian Bagley, a divorcée friend who, with her son, Sherman, shares a house with the Carmichaels. Lucy's main aspiration is to find herself a new husband, but, as ever, all her best plans crumble around her. Lucy finds a perfect foil for her slapstick antics in her no-nonsense boss, Mr Mooney, who succeeds the cantankerous Mr Barnsdahl seen in the earliest episodes. Mooney is President of the Danfield First National Bank and Lucy is his part-time secretary.

After a few seasons, the location of the series is switched to San Francisco, with major cast-changes. Lucy still works for Mr Mooney, who is now Vice-President of the Westland Bank, under boss Harrison Cheever, but her daughter, Chris, no longer features. Also gone is Vivian Bagley, to appear only occasionally as a visitor. Lucy's new accomplice is neighbour Mary Jane Lewis.

See also I LOVE LUCY and HERE'S LUCY.

Luke's Kingdom ✶✶

UK/Australia (Yorkshire/TCN9) Adventure. ITV 1976

Luke Firbeck	**Oliver Tobias**
Jason Firbeck	**James Condon**
Jassy Firbeck/Elliot	**Elisabeth Crosby**
Samuel Firbeck	**Gerard Maguire**
Lt. Robarts	**Edmund Pegge**
Lt. Elliot	**Alfred Bell**
Kate	**Helen Morse**
Molly	**Shirley Cameron**
Rosie	**Victoria Anoux**
Anna Louise	**Bettina Kenter**

Executive Producer **Tony Essex**

● ***An immigrant family battles for survival in the untamed Australia of the 1830s.***

When former naval lieutenant Jason Firbeck loses his wife in 1829, he takes his family from Yorkshire to Australia to seek a new life, hoping to claim land bequeathed to them by a rich friend. When they arrive in New South Wales, they find their land occupied by others, leaving them to scratch out a living in the bush. Squatting on Crown land, they live outside the colony's judicial control and face the animosity of other settlers, aborigines, outlaws and soldiers. Injustice and hardship are rife, and the family's life is always on the line. Jason's family consists of a daughter, Jassy, and two sons, Samuel and Luke, the latter the hero of the series who leads them in their pursuit of a peaceful home. Two years in the making, the 13-part drama – described as 'The Lives and Loves of the Firbeck Family' – featured music by Francis Essex, brother of executive producer Tony Essex. Tony sadly died shortly after the series was completed.

Lumley, Joanna

OBE (1946–)

British actress and former model, born in India and typically seen in classy, sophisticated roles, though offering a game alternative as Patsy in ABSOLUTELY FABULOUS. Lumley's TV career has veered between lead roles and strong supporting parts, with the highlights being the athletic Purdey in THE NEW AVENGERS and the mysterious Sapphire in SAPPHIRE AND STEEL. She was Samantha Ryder-Ross in Jilly Cooper's sitcom IT'S AWFULLY BAD FOR YOUR EYES, DARLING; played Elaine Perkins, a girlfriend of Ken Barlow, in CORONATION STREET; and starred as Mrs Smiling in COLD COMFORT FARM, Kate Swift in *Class Act*, Diana Carey-Lewis in COMING HOME/NANCHERROW, Donna Sinclair in DR WILLOUGHBY, Liz Franks in A RATHER ENGLISH MARRIAGE and Davina Jackson in *Sensitive Skin*. One of her earliest performances was in EMERGENCY – WARD 10 and other credits have included parts in STEPTOE AND SON, THE PROTECTORS, ARE YOU BEING SERVED?, OXBRIDGE BLUES, *The Glory Boys*, *Mistral's Daughter*, *A Perfect Hero* (Loretta Stone), LOVEJOY, CLUEDO (Mrs Peacock), ROSEANNE (as Patsy again), AGATHA CHRISTIE'S MARPLE and the cartoon *The Forgotten Toys* (voices). In 1989 she stood in as host of *Wogan*; in 1994 she appeared in the documentary *Girl Friday*, which recounted her nine-day 'survival' on the uninhabited island of Tsarabajina, off Madagascar; and in 1997 she retraced her grandparents' trek through the Himalayas in *Joanna Lumley in the Kingdom of the Thunder Dragon*. Lumley has also presented a *Born to be Wild* nature documentary. She delivered monologues in *Up in Town*, co-produced THE CAZALETS, and over the years has been a regular panellist in CALL MY BLUFF. Her first husband was comedy actor/writer Jeremy Lloyd.

Lunghi, Cherie

(1952–)

Nottingham-born actress, as Gabriella Benson the star of the football drama THE MANAGERESS, but also seen as Alex Ferguson in BILL BRAND, Princess Charlotte in PRINCE REGENT, Dorothy in THE MONOCLED MUTINEER, Margaret Van de Merwe in *Master of the Game*, Julia in *Little White Lies*, Laura Testvalley in *The Buccaneers*, Mrs Steerforth in DAVID COPPERFIELD, Merle Kirschman in *A Likeness in Stone*, Jennet Jourdemayne in *The Lady's Not for Burning*, Zinnia Raggitt in CUTTING IT, and Cleo Steyn QC in *The Brief*. Lunghi has also appeared in TALES OF THE UNEXPECTED, *Praying Mantis*, STRANGERS AND BROTHERS, *Harem*, THE RUTH RENDELL MYSTERIES, HORNBLOWER (Duchess of Wharfedale), THE INSPECTOR LYNLEY MYSTERIES, WAKING THE DEAD, MIDSOMER MURDERS, NEW TRICKS and AGATHA CHRISTIE'S MARPLE, among other dramas, plus, briefly, EASTENDERS (Jan Sherwood).

Luv ✱✱

UK (BBC) Situation Comedy. BBC 1 1993–4

Harold Craven	**Michael Angelis**
Terese Craven	**Sue Johnston**
Lloyd	**Peter Caffrey**
Hannah Craven	**Sandy Hendrickse**
Victor Craven	**Russell Boulter**
	Stefan Escreet
Darwin Craven	**Stephen Lord**
Bernie	**Jackie Downey**
Carro	**Debbie Andrews**
Eden	**Julie Peasgood**
Martinique	**Jan Ravens**
Antonio	**Zubin Varla**
Tone	**Gerard O'Hare**
Arthur	**Raymond Coulthard**
Chezz	**Akim Mogaji**

Creator/Writer **Carla Lane**
Producer **Mike Stephens**

A successful Liverpool businessman finds that money can't buy him love or peace at home.

Harold Craven, self-made proprietor of Craven's Ornamental Garden Requisites (mostly plastic flowerpots), cares deeply for his wife and children and showers them with gifts. Nevertheless, he finds himself head of a family that struggle to express their need for each other. His wife, Terese, is a bored housewife who wants only one thing – for her husband to say he loves her – and their adopted children bring even more heartache into their stressed lives. Elder son Victor is gay and lives with his boyfriend in an 'out of the way' cottage Harold has bought for them. Daughter Hannah endures a stormy marriage with a dim Italian named Antonio, and whining younger son Darwin still lives at home, dossing his way through life, espousing the animal rights cause and indulging in pseudo-paramilitary manoeuvres to free livestock. Away from the bedlam of home life, Harold relaxes in the company of Lloyd, his perceptive Irish chauffeur, and in the arms of Eden, a beautiful blonde whom he employs as his secretary. Bernie and Carro are the workers who give Harold a hard time on the factory floor, especially when he insists on playing them classical music.

In the second series, Harold abandons Eden, only to find his former mistress bent on revenge, and the factory goes through financial difficulties that have repercussions for all the Craven family.

LWT

LWT (formerly London Weekend Television) won the ITV franchise for London weekends in 1967 (under the application name of London Television Consortium), and went on air on 2 August 1968. It retained its franchise in 1980 and again in 1992, generally broadcasting to London from 5.15 p.m. on Friday to closedown on Sunday, as well as making many programmes for the ITV network at its South Bank studios. Among its most notable contributions over the years were sitcoms like DOCTOR IN THE HOUSE and ON THE BUSES, arts programmes like AQUARIUS and THE SOUTH BANK SHOW, drama such as UPSTAIRS, DOWNSTAIRS and BOUQUET OF BARBED WIRE, current affairs series like WEEKEND WORLD and game shows such as GAME FOR A LAUGH and PLAY YOUR CARDS RIGHT. LWT was later taken over by Granada and is now part of ITV plc.

Lynam, Desmond

(1942–)

Laid-back Irish-born sports frontman whose charm and style have led him into other presentation work. Beginning his broadcasting career in radio sport, working particularly on boxing commentaries, Lynam's TV break came in the late 1970s with NATIONWIDE's Friday night sports segment and led to GRANDSTAND, SPORTSNIGHT, MATCH OF THE DAY and all the BBC's major sporting events coverage, before he defected to anchor ITV's soccer coverage in 1999, subsequently hosting *The Premiership* but retiring after the Euro 2004 competition. He tried one season as presenter of HOLIDAY, was also seen as co-host of HOW DO THEY DO THAT? and made a guest appearance as himself in the play *My Summer with Des*. In 2005 he took over from the late Richard Whiteley as host of COUNTDOWN.

Lynch, Joe

(1925–2001)

Irish comedy actor, chiefly recalled as the tailor Patrick Kelly in NEVER MIND THE QUALITY, FEEL THE WIDTH. He was later seen as Paddy O'Brien in another sitcom, *Rule Britannia*, and in guest appearances in RETURN OF THE SAINT. He was also narrator of the children's series CHORLTON AND THE WHEELIES, and appeared in CORONATION STREET, playing two different roles in the 1970s.

Lyndhurst, Nicholas

(1961–)

Although widely recognized as plonker Rodney Trotter from the hugely successful ONLY FOOLS AND HORSES, Nicholas Lyndhurst began his showbiz career as a child actor. He was seen in numerous youthful dramas, including ANNE OF AVONLEA (Davy Keith), *Heidi* and THE TOMORROW PEOPLE, and took the dual lead roles in *The Prince and the Pauper*. He was one of the hosts of the Saturday morning magazine *Our Show* (along with Susan Tully and others), and played Fletch's son, Raymond, in GOING STRAIGHT, before maturing into adult parts through BUTTERFLIES, in which he was Ria's son, Adam. Once *Only Fools and Horses* had begun, Lyndhurst became a popular choice for sitcom producers. He was Ashley in THE TWO OF US, Peter Chapman in THE PIGLET FILES and Gary Sparrow in GOODNIGHT SWEETHEART. Among his other credits have been *Round and Round*, *Spearhead*, *Slimming Down*, TO SERVE THEM ALL MY DAYS, *Stalag Luft* ('Chump' Cosgrove), GULLIVER'S TRAVELS (Clustril), MURDER IN MIND, DAVID COPPERFIELD (Uriah Heep) and *Thin Ice* (Graham Moss).

Lynn, Jonathan

(1943–)

British actor, writer and director, a Cambridge Footlights graduate, acclaimed in particular for YES, MINISTER and *Yes, Prime Minister*, which he scripted in collaboration with Antony Jay. In front of the cameras, he appeared in the sketch show *Twice a Fortnight*, and played Danny Hooley in DOCTOR IN THE HOUSE, Beryl's husband (Robert) in THE LIVER BIRDS and Pete Booth in *My Brother's Keeper* (also as writer). Other acting parts have come in BAR MITZVAH BOY (Harold), *Turnbull's Finest Hour* (Roddy Cheever-Jones), OUTSIDE EDGE (Kevin Costello in the 1982 one-off), *The Knowledge* and DIANA. Among

Lynn's other writing credits (usually with George Layton) have been episodes of the *Doctor* series, ON THE BUSES and *My Name is Harry Worth*. Lynn has more recently turned to directing, calling the shots for films like *Nuns on the Run* and *Sgt Bilko*.

Lytton's Diary **

UK (Thames) Drama. ITV 1985–6

Neville Lytton .... **Peter Bowles**
Henry Field .... **Bernard Lloyd**
Ian .... **Bernard Archard**
Catherine Lytton .... **Fiona Mollison**
Laura Gray .... **Anna Nygh**
Colin .... **Lewis Fiander**
David Edding .... **Adam Norton**
Dolly .... **Holly de Jong**
Norman .... **David Ryall**
Pandora .... **Jane Laurie**
Henry Field .... **Bernard Lloyd**
Wayne Munroe .... **John Stride**
Mark .... **James Aubrey**
Helena .... **Barbara Kellerman**
Trevor Bates .... **Joseph Young**
Jenny .... **Harriet Keevil**

Creators **Peter Bowles, Philip Broadley**
Writer **Ray Connolly**
Producers **Chris Burt, Derek Bennett**
Executive Producer **Lloyd Shirley**

Incidents in the life of a newspaper diarist.

Partly created by its star, Peter Bowles, *Lytton's Diary* began life as part of Thames Television's anthology series *Storyboard* in 1983. Two years later, it became a series. Bowles plays Neville Lytton, the gossip columnist for *The Daily News*. His investigations into society scandals provide ample titbits for his features and draw him into intrigue. Office colleagues include editors Ian and Mark, and lawyer Colin. His Fleet Street rival is Henry Field, who also lives with Lytton's wife, Catherine. Lytton's girlfriend is Laura Gray.

M Squad ★★

US (Latimer/Revue/Universal) Police Drama. ITV 1958–60 (US: NBC 1957–60)

Lt. Frank Ballinger .... **Lee Marvin**
Capt. Grey .... **Paul Newlan**

Executive Producer **Richard Lewis**

● ***A no-nonsense plain-clothes cop is on the trail of big city criminals.***

M is for Murder and these half-hour tales provide an insight into Chicago's elite M Squad. More particularly, they focus on the work of the laconic Lt. Frank Ballinger, a dedicated undercover member of the team who patrols the streets of the Windy City alone, answering to boss Captain Grey. Little is known about Ballinger's private life, such is his devotion to duty. The character also narrates the action, in the style of DRAGNET's Joe Friday. Count Basie provided the best-remembered theme music (there was an earlier version).

McAnally, Ray

(1926–89)

Irish actor who, after years of supporting roles in the cinema and on TV, became a star late in life. Although he had appeared as gangster Alec Spindoe in SPINDOE in 1968, and was seen in ME MAMMY and *Pollyanna* (John Pendleton), it was as Rick, Peter Egan's deceitful dad, in A PERFECT SPY that he began to steal the show, and he capped that with a BAFTA award-winning performance as left-wing Labour Prime Minister Harry Perkins in Channel 4's A VERY BRITISH COUP. He later appeared as Sir William Gull in a version of *Jack the Ripper* and one of his last performances came in ITV's adaptation of GREAT EXPECTATIONS (Mr Jaggers), shown in 1991, two years after his death. Other early appearances had been as a guest in series like THE AVENGERS, MAN IN A SUITCASE, STRANGE REPORT, CROWN COURT, DICK TURPIN and STRANGERS.

McCall, Davina

(1967–)

London-born presenter of light-entertainment series such as *Streetmate, Beachmate, The Real Holiday Show, Don't Try This at Home*, THE BRITS, BIG BROTHER, *Closure, The Vault*, POP-STARS*: the Rivals, Reborn in the USA, Love on a Saturday Night, He's Having a Baby* and a STARS IN THEIR EYES special. She has also hosted THE BRIT AWARDS and starred in the sitcoms *Sam's Game* (Sam) and *A Bear's Tale* (Dave Ian McCall). Davina – a former booker of male models – was given her TV break by MTV in 1992. In 2006 she hosted her own chat show, *Davina*, for the BBC. Davina is married to former *Pet Rescue* presenter Matthew Robertson.

McCallum ★★★

UK (Scottish) Police Drama. ITV 1997–8
DVD: Cinema Club

Dr Iain McCallum .... **John Hannah**
DI Bracken .... **Gerard Murphy**
Joanna Sparkes .... **Suzanna Hamilton**
Dr Angela Moloney .... **Zara Turner**
Sir/Prof. Paddy Penfold .... **Richard Moore**
Dr Fuzzy Brightons .... **James Saxon**
Bobby Sykes .... **Richard O'Callaghan**
DC Small .... **Alex Walkinshaw**
Dr Aidan Petit .... **Hugo Speer**
Clare Gilmore .... **Charlotte Randle**
Rory O'Neil .... **Jason Barry**
Dr Dan Gallagher .... **Nathaniel Parker**
Dr Charley Fielding .... **Eva Pope**

Creator **Stuart Hepburn**
Writers **Stuart Hepburn, Ben Rostul, Mike Cullen, Jane Hollowood, Russell Gascoigne**
Producers **Murray Ferguson, Robert Banks Stewart**

● ***A pathologist turns detective but is deeply saddened by the carnage he witnesses.***

Iain McCallum is a forensic pathologist, a working-class Scots boy made good, who now holds an important position at St Patrick's hospital in London. Faced with the results of the most sickening murders, he finds his job hard to bear, not least when he is forced to challenge assumed causes of death and lead the hunt for serial killers – or even, on one occasion, someone out to kill McCallum himself. After all, wasn't he trained to look after the living, not poke around among the dead? The moody and introspective hero finds temporary solace in girlfriend Joanna Sparkes, but the gruesome murders roll on and the stresses of the job keep taking their toll. Eventually, after two series, the soul-searching doctor falls for his colleague, Dr Angela Moloney, and they head off to manage a department in California. In their place (in a one-off, second pilot keeping the name *McCallum*, which was shown in December 1998), St Patrick's gains a new pathologist in Dr Dan Gallagher, an ex-army doctor, supported by the brusque Dr Charley Fielding. A series didn't follow and star Nathaniel Parker went on to become toff detective INSPECTOR LYNLEY instead. The original pilot was screened in 1995. The series theme song was a version of 'Cry Me a River' by Mari Wilson.

McCallum, David

(1933–)

Blond Scottish actor, busy on both sides of the Atlantic and once a heart-throb as secret agent Illya Kuryakin in THE MAN FROM U.N.C.L.E.. *U.N.C.L.E.* followed his arrival in the USA in the early 1960s and roles in series like PERRY MASON and THE OUTER LIMITS. Later, he was airman Simon Carter in COLDITZ, Dr Daniel Westin aka THE INVISIBLE MAN, Steel in SAPPHIRE AND STEEL, Alan Breck in *Kidnapped*, Alex Vesey in MOTHER LOVE, John Grey in TRAINER, Professor Plum in CLUEDO and Billy Fawcett in COMING HOME. More recently, McCallum has enjoyed success again in the USA, appearing as Dr Joseph

Bloom in *VR.5*, Walter Thornhill in *The Education of Max Bickford* and Donald 'Ducky' Mallard in *Navy NCIS*. Additionally, McCallum appeared in *March in Windy City* and numerous TV movies, and has made guest appearances in series as varied as BOON, HEARTBEAT and SEX AND THE CITY. He has also turned his hand to directing. His first wife was actress Jill Ireland.

McCaskill, Ian

(1938–)

Quirky Scottish meteorologist who joined the BBC forecasting team in 1978 and quickly attracted the attentions of impressionists. He worked for a while at Central Television in the early 1980s and has also been seen as a guest on numerous other programmes. He retired from the BBC in the late 1990s.

McClain's Law ✳✳

US (MGM) Police Drama. BBC 1 1982 (US: NBC 1981–2)

Det. Jim McClain .... **James Arness**
Det. Harry Gates .... **Marshall Colt**
Det. Jerry Cross .... **Carl Franklin**
Lt. Edward DeNisco .... **George DiCenzo**
Vangie Cruise .... **Conchata Ferrell**

Creator **Eric Bercovici**
Producers **Mark Rafters, Robert H. Justman**

A retired detective rejoins the police to hunt for his friend's killer.

Forced to leave the police force in San Pedro, California, some 13 years earlier because of a leg injury, Jim McClain is dragged back into detective work when his fishing partner is brutally murdered. Convinced that only he is capable of tracking down the killer, McClain – now aged 52 – persuades the authorities to take him back into the force, even though detection methods have changed dramatically in his absence. But, with excellent support from colleagues Harry Gates and Jerry Cross, McClain quickly drops back into the routine. Even though his rough-and-tumble ways seem rather archaic at times (and wind up his boss, Lt. DeNisco), he proves reasonably effective. Off duty, Jim returns to his waterside hang-out, Vangie Cruise's bar.

A welcome change in direction for James Arness, after his 20-odd years in GUNSMOKE, this series was partly inspired by a 1952 film in which he had starred with John Wayne. Called *Big Jim McLain*, it featured Wayne in the title role as a right-wing special agent rooting out communists in Hawaii.

McClanahan, Rue

(1934–)

After plenty of supporting roles, Rue McClanahan was at last able to claim some of the limelight when she was cast as the man-hungry Southern belle, Blanche Devereaux, in THE GOLDEN GIRLS and *The Golden Palace*. The former brought her back into contact with Bea Arthur, with whom she had appeared in the ALL IN THE FAMILY offshoot, *Maude*. Among McClanahan's other credits have been parts in LOU GRANT, THE LOVE BOAT and numerous TV movies, as well as the US series *Apple Pie*, *Mama's Family*, *Safe Harbor* and *The Lot*.

McCloud ✳✳

US (Universal) Police Drama. ITV 1972–6 (US: NBC 1970–7)
DVD: Universal (Region 1 only)

Sam McCloud .... **Dennis Weaver**
Peter B. Clifford .... **J. D. Cannon**
Sgt Joe Broadhurst .... **Terry Carter**
Chris Coughlin .... **Diana Muldaur**
Sgt Grover .... **Ken Lynch**

Creator/Executive Producer **Glen A. Larson**

A cowboy becomes a cop in New York City.

Deputy Marshal Sam McCloud arrives in New York in pursuit of a refugee prisoner. Nailing his man, he decides to stick around for a while and learn the ways of a big-city police force, operating in a world far removed from his usual beat of Taos, New Mexico. Riding a horse through the New York traffic and sporting a sheepskin jacket, cowboy boots and a stetson, he joins Manhattan's 27th Precinct, working alongside Sgt Joe Broadhurst. Although McCloud is meant to be the learner, it is Broadhurst who enjoys the greater education, as the determined Western lawman drags him into the thick of the action, shunning the subtler approach to policing usually employed in the city. This does little to endear either of them to their superior, Chief Clifford. But, as our hero would put it, 'There you go.' Chris Coughlin is McCloud's writer girlfriend.

Based on the Clint Eastwood film *Coogan's Bluff*, and derived from a pilot called *Who Killed Miss USA* (aired as *Who Killed Merri-Ann* in the UK), the series was part of ITV's MYSTERY MOVIE package. A TV movie, *The Return of Sam McCloud*, was made in 1989, with McCloud having become a US senator.

MacCorkindale, Simon

(1952–)

Successful British actor, also working behind the camera. His most notable TV performances have been as Lt. Carter in *Hawkeye, the Pathfinder*, Lucius in I, CLAUDIUS, Joe Kapp in the 1979 revival of QUATERMASS, Jonathan Chase, hero of the sci-fi detective series, MANIMAL, Greg Reardon in FALCON CREST (also with directing credits), Peter Sinclair in *Counterstrike* and Harry Harper in CASUALTY. Other appearances have come in *The Doombolt Chase* (Lt. Commander Madock), JUST WILLIAM, JESUS OF NAZARETH, *Beasts*, WILL SHAKESPEARE, *The Mannions of America* and THE DUKES OF HAZZARD. MacCorkindale is married to Susan George (his first wife was Fiona Fullerton). Together they founded the Amy International production company.

McCoy, Sylvester

(James Kent-Smith; 1943–)

Scottish actor, dealing in both comic and straight drama roles. Undoubtedly his most famous character has been DOCTOR WHO (the seventh incarnation, 1987–9). Previously (often under the name of Sylveste McCoy) he had been seen in children's offerings like VISION ON, TISWAS, *Jigsaw*, *Dramarama* and *Eureka*, sitcoms such as BIG JIM AND THE FIGARO CLUB (Turps, the painter) and dramas like *The Last Place on Earth* (Birdie Bowers), *Beyond Fear* (Michael Sams) and TOM JONES (Mr Dowling). More recently, he has played the Lord High Chamberlain in the kids' comedy *See It Saw It*, and made guest appearances in CASUALTY, THE BILL and HOLLYOAKS.

McCready and Daughter ★★

UK (Ecosse Films/BBC) Detective Drama. BBC 1 2000–1

Michael McCready	**Lorcan Cranitch**
Clare Cooper/McCready	**Patsy Palmer**
Donal McCready	**Brendan Coyle**
DCI Alan Kendall	**David Westhead**
Laura Cooper	**Kim Thomson**

Creators **Robert Jones, Ming Ho**
Writers **Robert Jones, Ted Gannon, John Flanagan, Andy McCulloch, John Martin Johnson**
Executive Producers **Douglas Rae, Kate Triggs, Robert Cooper**
Producers **Louise Berridge, Nick Pitt**

A private eye allows his daughter to help with his cases. Michael McCready is an ex-policeman who runs a private detective agency in the Kilburn area of London. He lives alone in an office/flat above a second-hand shop, following the breakdown of his marriage some years ago. His daughter, Clare, has frittered away the money he has set aside for her college education, deepening the chasm that already exists between them, but reconciliation arrives when he helps her avoid an arson conviction. Taking her into his employ, to keep her out of trouble, McCready finds himself indebted to the feisty, independent redhead on more than one occasion. Donal is Michael's wheeling-dealing younger brother who runs McCready's Hotel and Hogan's pub; Alan Kendall is the amenable local CID man; and Laura is Clare's mother, an ex-teacher now a civil servant.

The role of Michael McCready was originally earmarked for Tony Doyle, who died shortly after rehearsals began. BALLYKISSANGEL colleague Lorcan Cranitch stepped in at short notice. After a pilot episode in 2000, five more programmes were shown in 2001.

McCutcheon, Martine

(1976–)

London-born actress who shot to fame as Tiffany Raymond/Mitchell in EASTENDERS, using her success to branch out into a singing career (beginning with the hit, 'Perfect Moment'). After stage musical acclaim she returned to TV for a special entitled *Martine Sings the Musicals* in 2002. She also played Tracy Pringle in *The English Harem* and guest appearances have come in THE BILL, THE KNOCK and SPOOKS.

McDonald, Sir Trevor

OBE (1939–)

Trinidadian newscaster, for years the main anchor for NEWS AT TEN, until December 2005. He joined ITN in 1973 and, after working as a reporter and sports correspondent, became its diplomatic correspondent and diplomatic editor, also spending seven years with *Channel 4 News*. McDonald had previously worked in radio and television in the West Indies and for the BBC World and Caribbean services in London. His other work includes fronting awards ceremonies and *Tonight – with Trevor McDonald*.

McDowall, Roddy

(1928–98)

London-born actor/celebrity photographer, formerly a Hollywood child star (particularly remembered with Lassie and Flicka), whose most memorable TV role was as Galen in THE PLANET OF THE APES. His earliest TV credits were in episodes of THE TWILIGHT ZONE, NAKED CITY, ARREST AND TRIAL, ALFRED HITCHCOCK PRESENTS and THE INVADERS, and he also played The Bookworm in BATMAN. After *The Planet of the Apes*, McDowall enjoyed a run of US dramas and TV movies, such as *The Rhinemann Exchange*, *Fantastic Journey* and *Tales of the Gold Monkey* (Bon Chance Louie), and guest spots in series like WONDER WOMAN.

McEwan, Geraldine

(Geraldine McKeown; 1932–)

English actress much seen on television in roles like Miss Farnaby in MULBERRY, Anne Dickens in TEARS BEFORE BEDTIME, Mrs Proudie in THE BARCHESTER CHRONICLES, Emmeline Lucas (aka Lucia) in MAPP & LUCIA, Jess's religious mother in ORANGES ARE NOT THE ONLY FRUIT, Mrs Gotobed in CARRIE'S WAR, and the title characters of *The Prime of Miss Jean Brodie* and AGATHA CHRISTIE'S MARPLE, plus many single dramas, including *Thin Ice* (Mrs Violet Jerome).

McFadden, Joseph

(1975–)

Scottish actor whose TV debut came in an episode of TAGGART (aged 12). He later joined the cast of TAKE THE HIGH ROAD (Gary McDonald) and from there moved on to star in such dramas as THE CROW ROAD (Prentice McHoan), *Bumping the Odds* (Andy), SEX, CHIPS AND ROCK 'N' ROLL (Dallas McCabe), *The Glass* (Paul Duggan) and *Sparkhouse* (Andrew Lawton). Other credits have come in *Macbeth, The Law, Raphael – Mortal God* (Raphael), *The Afternoon Play* and JUDGE JOHN DEED.

MacFadyen, Matthew

(1974–)

Glasgow-born actor featuring or starring in a number of top dramas from WUTHERING HEIGHTS (Hareton Earnshaw), WARRIORS (Pte Alan James) and MURDER ROOMS: THE DARK BEGINNINGS OF SHERLOCK HOLMES to PERFECT STRANGERS (Daniel Symon), THE WAY WE LIVE NOW (Sir Felix Carbury), SPOOKS (Tom Quinn) and THE PROJECT (Paul Tibbenham). He is married to *Spooks* co-star Keeley Hawes.

McGann:

JOE (1958–), PAUL (1959–), MARK (1961–), STEPHEN (1963–)

Four acting brothers much seen on British TV since the 1980s. Joe has starred in ROCKLIFFE'S BABIES as PC Gerry O'Dowd, in THE CHRONICLES OF NARNIA as Lord Glozelle, in THE UPPER HAND as Charlie Burrows, in *Madame Bovary* as Paul, and in *Night and Day* as Alex Wells, and also appeared in *Harry Enfield's Television Programme* (one of 'The Scousers').

Paul has been Mo Morris in GIVE US A BREAK, Percy Toplis in THE MONOCLED MUTINEER, Joe Thompson in *Nice Town*, Cpl Chris Ryan in the SAS drama *The One That Got Away*, the eighth DOCTOR WHO, Steve in *Nature Boy*, Eugene Wrayburn in OUR MUTUAL FRIEND, Jonathan Vishnevski in *Fish*, Patrick Vine in *Sweet Revenge*, Lt. Bush in HORNBLOWER, Gerry Henson in *Lie with Me* and Col. MacNab in *Kidnapped* (he was also pencilled in for the title role in SHARPE but missed out through injury). Guest appearances include roles in SEA OF SOULS and AGATHA CHRISTIE'S MARPLE.

Mark has played Mad Dog in SCULLY, Detective C. J. Brady in YELLOWTHREAD STREET, Gary Halliwell in THE MANAGERESS, Marcus Bannerman in THE GRAND, Crean in SHACKLETON, DC David Ingram in *Blood Strangers*, Joseph Bazalgette in *Seven Wonders of the Industrial World* and Sextus Roscius in the *Timewatch* presentation *Murder in Rome*, as well as making guest appearances in INSPECTOR MORSE and WHERE THE HEART IS.

Stephen has taken the roles of Bob in *Streetwise*, Tex in HELP! and Sean Reynolds in EMMERDALE. All four have many other credits to their names and appeared together (as the Phelan brothers) in the 1995 drama series THE HANGING GALE.

McGee, Henry

(1929–2006)

British actor and straight man to leading comics, particularly Benny Hill, Tommy Cooper, Dick Emery, Frankie Howerd, Reg Varney and Charlie Drake (Mr Pugh in THE WORKER). In sitcom, he was Lt. Raleigh in TELL IT TO THE MARINES, appeared with Ronnie Corbett in NO – THAT'S ME OVER HERE, and played Dicky Bligh in UP THE WORKERS and Dennis in LET THERE BE LOVE. His other credits have included parts in THE SAINT, THE AVENGERS, THE GOODIES, RISING DAMP, SYKES, DOCTOR AT LARGE and a 2003 appearance in LAST OF THE SUMMER WINE.

McGoohan, Patrick

(1928–)

American-born, British-raised actor whose earliest television credits were in series like THE ADVENTURES OF AGGIE, THE ADVENTURES OF SIR LANCELOT and MARK SABER. He became a big name in the 1960s thanks to his starring roles as John Drake in DANGER MAN and Number 6 in his own cult series, THE PRISONER (he created it and wrote and directed some episodes). At one point, it is claimed, McGoohan was the richest man on TV and allegedly turned down the part of THE SAINT, before it was offered to Roger Moore, because Simon Templar was too promiscuous. In the 1970s he returned to the small screen as medical man *Rafferty* and in TV movies, but he also worked behind the scenes, directing an episode of COLUMBO, for instance (as well as guest starring in the series).

McGovern, Jimmy

(1949–)

Acclaimed, Liverpool-born dramatist, known for tackling difficult subjects and for creating gritty characters. After working as a bus conductor and in insurance, he qualified as a teacher, but then started writing for local theatre. He was given a chance to write for BROOKSIDE and stayed for six years. Since then his major works have included CRACKER, *Hearts and Minds*, *Screen Two's Priest*, HILLSBOROUGH, THE LAKES, DOCKERS, *Sunday* and *Gunpowder, Treason and Plot*.

McGowan, Alistair

(1965–)

British actor/comedian/impressionist, specializing in take-offs of sports personalities like Alan Hansen, David Beckham and Naseem Hamed, but also successful with innovative characterizations, such as newsreader Huw Edwards, actor Nigel Havers, presenter Richard Madeley and interior designer Laurence Llewelyn-Bowen. All of these were highlighted in his own series, *Alistair McGowan's Big Impression*, in which he was supported by Ronni Ancona. Previously, McGowan had provided voices for SPITTING IMAGE, THE STAGGERING STORIES OF FERDINAND DE BARGOS, *Klinik!* (Dr Werther) and the *Robbie the Reindeer* cartoons, and, as an actor, appeared in CHILDREN'S WARD, PRESTON FRONT (Spock), SPARK (Mike Parkerwell) and *Dark Ages* (Redwald), as well as making guest appearances in MURDER MOST HORRID and JONATHAN CREEK. More recently, McGowan has been a team captain for 29 *Minutes of Fame*, appeared in the sketch show *Monkey Trousers*, fronted a wildlife documentary, *Alistair McGowan Goes Wild with Rhinos*, and played Mr Kenge in BLEAK HOUSE. He has also starred as DI Gil Mayo in *Mayo*.

McGrath, Rory

(1956–)

British comedian, writer and presenter, a member of the Cambridge Footlights troupe before becoming a writer for BBC Radio comedy programmes and then scripting for NOT THE NINE O'CLOCK NEWS (and its spin-off, ALAS SMITH AND JONES). He later appeared in WHO DARES, WINS ... and co-founded Hat Trick Productions (for whom he co-wrote – and played Badvoc in – CHELMSFORD 123). He has also taken part in WHOSE LINE IS IT ANYWAY?, fronted *Rory McGrath's Commercial Breakdown* and *Killer Queens*, hosted the quizzes *Trivial Pursuit* and *Sports Anorak of the Year*, narrated the series *It Shouldn't Happen to a . . .*, and, most prominently, been a regular on THEY THINK IT'S ALL OVER. He has also presented *Rory McGrath's Bloody Britain*, a history series for the digital channel Discovery, and joined Griff Rhys Jones and Dara O'Briain to re-create Jerome K. Jerome's tale of *Three Men in a Boat*.

MacGregor, Jimmie

(1930–)

See *Hall, Robin*.

MacGyver ★★

US (Paramount) Secret Agent Drama. UK 1987–94 (US: ABC 1985–92)

DVD: Paramount

MacGyver	**Richard Dean Anderson**
Peter Thornton	**Dana Elcar**
Jack Dalton	**Bruce McGill**
Nikki Carpenter	**Elyssa Davalos**
Murdoc	**Michael Des Barres**

Creator **Lee David Zlotoff**
Executive Producers **Henry Winkler, John Rich**

A resourceful secret agent saves the world with the clever use of everyday items.

MacGyver works for the Phoenix Foundation, a special unit

that sends him on seemingly impossible missions across the world to defeat crime and subterfuge. But this is an agent who much prefers brains to brawn. For MacGyver a caseful of high-tech gadgets or the latest weaponry is not an option: this hero is a master of improvisation, employing everyday objects – paper clips, newspapers, etc. – to help him defeat the bad guys, often with only seconds to spare. His boss is Peter Thornton, a man whose eyesight deteriorates as the series progresses, adding to the challenges facing the smart MacGyver. Jack Dalton is an unreliable buddy and Nikki Carpenter is MacGyver's girlfriend (for a while). Sometimes seen is MacGyver's arch-enemy, Murdoc. No Christian name is given for the lead man, except in one dream sequence when it is suggested that 'Angus' may be, in fact, his first name. HAPPY DAYS star Henry Winkler was co-creator and one of the executives driving the project. Randy Edelman provided the theme music.

McHale's Navy ★★

US (Sto-Rev) Situation Comedy. BBC 1963 (US: ABC 1963–6)

Lt. Commander Quinton McHale .... **Ernest Borgnine**
Capt. Wallace B. Binghamton .... **Joe Flynn**
Ensign Charles 'Chuck' Parker .... **Tim Conway**
Lt. Elroy Carpenter .... **Bob Hastings**
Torpedoman Lester Gruber .... **Carl Ballantine**
Quartermaster George 'Christy' Christopher .... **Gary Vinson**
Harrison 'Tinker' Bell .... **Billy Sands**
Virgil Edwards .... **Edson Stroll**
Nurse Molly Turner .... **Jane Dulo**
Joseph 'Happy' Haines .... **Gavin MacLeod**
Fuji Kobiaji .... **Yoshio Yoda**

Creator **Edward Montagne**

A scheming naval officer calls the shots in the South Seas.

Bilko-on-sea, *McHale's Navy* reports the farcical exploits of a US Navy patrol torpedo ship (PT 73) stationed at the stunning South Pacific island of Taratupa during World War II. Captain of the vessel is Wallace Binghamton, but it is really Lt. Commander Quinton McHale who mans the bridge. Though he bends every rule in the book, making Binghamton (nicknamed 'Old Lead Bottom') bluster, McHale's superiors are forced to keep him in place because of his in-depth knowledge of the region. Besides, the men love him. Like Bilko, McHale can seldom resist a fast buck or the chance to swindle someone; gambling is his life. Carpenter is Binghamton's right-hand man; the bumbling and fumbling Ensign Parker is McHale's number two; and Fuji is the Japanese POW (unofficial) who cooks the crew's gourmet meals. The series ran for 139 episodes in its native USA (including a final season when the crew was transferred to Italy), but only enjoyed a short run in the UK. It was a spin-off from a drama in the *Alcoa Premiere* anthology in 1962, which starred Ernest Borgnine and Joe Flynn, and itself engendered two film releases: *McHale's Navy* (1964) and *McHale's Navy Joins the Air Force* (1965, without Borgnine). An up-to-date movie version, *McHale's Navy*, was released in 1997, with Tom Arnold in the title role and Borgnine supporting.

McInnerny, Tim

(1956–)

British actor whose most prominent roles have been as Lord Percy and, later, Captain Darling in BLACKADDER. However, he has also been seen in programmes as varied as EDGE OF DARKNESS (Terry Shields), THE ADVENTURES OF SHERLOCK HOLMES, *Shadow of the Noose*, A VERY BRITISH COUP (Fiennes), THE COMIC STRIP PRESENTS, THE VICE, LONGITUDE (Christopher Irwin), TRIAL AND RETRIBUTION, *Gunpowder, Treason and Plot* (Lord Robert Cecil), SPOOKS (Oliver Mace), AGATHA CHRISTIE'S MARPLE and *The Strange Case of Sherlock Holmes and Arthur Conan Doyle* (Selden). Actress Lizzie McInnerny is his sister.

McIntire, John

(1907–91)

John McIntire's craggy looks were very familiar to viewers in the 1950s and 1960s, courtesy of his starring roles in NAKED CITY (Lt. Dan Muldoon) and WAGON TRAIN (Christopher Hale). A few years later, McIntire turned up in another Western, THE VIRGINIAN, taking the role of Clay Grainger, new owner of the Shiloh Ranch. With guest appearances in the 1970s in series like LOVE, AMERICAN STYLE and THE LOVE BOAT, plus roles in prime-time American series right up to 1981, McIntire enjoyed a remarkable television career, especially if you consider that he didn't start working in the medium until he was nearly 50, having concentrated earlier on radio acting.

Mackay, Fulton

OBE (1922–87)

Scottish actor, PORRIDGE's by-the-book prison officer Mr Mackay. Previously, he was Willie in *Mess Mates* and a regular guest as Jamie in DR FINLAY'S CASEBOOK, played Det. Supt. Inman in SPECIAL BRANCH and featured in the sketch show *Between the Lines*. Among his later work were roles in the kids' sci-fi adventure *King of the Castle* (Hawkspur, a mad scientist), the single dramas GOING GENTLY (Austin Miller) and *A Sense of Freedom*, a Channel 4 sitcom called *Mann's Best Friends* (lodger Hamish Ordway), and FRAGGLE ROCK (the Captain). Other appearances over the years were in series such as THE AVENGERS, THE SAINT, THE EDWARDIANS, THE TROUBLESHOOTERS, *The Foundation*, SOME MOTHERS DO 'AVE 'EM, CROWN COURT, GOING STRAIGHT and STRANGERS.

McKee, Gina

(1964–)

British actress who holds the rare honour of appearing in the first ever TV advertisement for condoms, playing a chemist's shop assistant. Her TV debut came as teenager Jane in *Quest of Eagles*, but, much more significantly, she went on to win acclaim for her portrayal of Mary Cox in OUR FRIENDS IN THE NORTH (ageing from 18 to 52). She has also been seen as kidnap victim Stephanie Slater in *Beyond Fear*, insecure wife Beth Murray in *Element of Doubt*, Mary Leslie in *The Treasure Seekers*, drunken single mum Caroline in *Screen Two's Mothertime*, Ellie, the older woman in love with a young man (Paul Nicholls), in *The Passion*, and nanny Lalla in THE LOST PRINCE. McKee also featured in the comedies BRASS EYE and *The Chest*, and played Julie and Sue Bishop in the sitcoms *The Lenny Henry Show* and AN ACTOR'S LIFE FOR ME, respectively. More recently, she starred as Irene in the remake of THE FORSYTE SAGA and as Lauren Armstrong in *The Baby War*.

Mackenzie ★★

UK (BBC) Drama. BBC 1 1980

Robert Mackenzie	**Jack Galloway**
Jean Mackenzie	**Kara Wilson**
Ruth Isaacs	**Lynda Bellingham**
David Isaacs	**Toby Salaman**
Diana Crawley	**Sheila Ruskin**
George Kovacs	**Richard Marner**
Jamie Mackenzie	**Derek Gray**
	Andrew Gray
	Ewan Stewart
Duncan Mackenzie	**Michael McLaughlin**
	David Donaldson
Lisa Isaacs	**Debra Langerman**
	Harriet Collins
	Georgia Slowe
	Tracey Ullman

Writer **Andrea Newman**
Producer **George Gallaccio**

● ***A Scottish builder puts sex and success before his family.***
This steamy saga examining intra-family relationships begins in October 1955. Robert Mackenzie is a Scottish builder and fiercely ambitious. He aims to get to the top, no matter what it takes, and immediately upsets his family by taking wife Jean off to London. Although the Mackenzies have two sons, Jamie and Duncan, it doesn't stop Robert from indulging in affairs with younger women. Bound up in Mackenzie's story are the Isaacs – husband David, wife Ruth and daughter Lisa – and the Kovacs – George and his neurotic model daughter, Diana Crawley. The 12 episodes, penned by Andrea 'Bouquet of Barbed Wire' Newman, cover 19 turbulent years in Mackenzie's life and at the time stretched existing boundaries of censorship with their sexual content. Anthony Isaac supplied the music.

McKenzie, Julia
(1941–)

Middlesex-born actress, star of the sitcoms MAGGIE AND HER (Maggie), *That Beryl Marston . . . !* (Georgie Bodley) and FRESH/FRENCH FIELDS (Hester Fields). She was Mrs Forthby in BLOTT ON THE LANDSCAPE and her singing voice has occasionally been heard in series like *Song by Song*. Among her numerous other credits have been appearances in *Battle of the Sexes, Frost's Weekly, Adam Bede, Absent Friends*, FAME IS THE SPUR (Pen Muff), *Hôtel du Lac*, THE TWO RONNIES, *The Stanley Baxter Show*, P. D. JAMES and MIDSOMER MURDERS, as well as her own programme, *Julia and Company*.

McKenzie, Robert
(1917–81)

Enthusiastic Canadian political commentator who brought his 'Swingometer' into BBC election coverages. Though chiefly an academic, his other work included pieces for PANORAMA, TONIGHT and 24 HOURS, as well as a series of his own, *The Pursuit of Power*, shortly before he died.

McKern, Leo
(Reginald McKern; 1920–2002)

Australian actor, identified by most viewers as the irascible legal rogue RUMPOLE OF THE BAILEY. However, McKern's TV appearances were many. He was one of the actors to play the mysterious Number 2 in the cult series THE PRISONER, popped up in early series like THE ADVENTURES OF ROBIN HOOD, and played Mr Boffin in OUR MUTUAL FRIEND and Zaharov in REILLY – ACE OF SPIES. He also had numerous guest appearances and TV films to his name and earned acclaim in single dramas like *The Tea Party*, Jonathan Miller's *Alice In Wonderland, The Sun is God* (playing the artist Turner), *On the Eve of Publication, Screen One's A Foreign Field* (Cyril), and *Screen Two's The Last Romantics* (Sir Arthur Quiller-Couch). He was a familiar face in the 1980s, advertising Lloyds Bank. Actress Abigail McKern is his daughter.

Mackie, Philip
(1918–85)

British playwright and producer whose long career's highlights (most as writer) were *Maupassant, Saki* and *The Victorians* (all as producer), MR ROSE, *Paris 1900, The Liars*, THE CAESARS (all as writer/producer), *Napoleon and Love, Conjugal Rites, Good Girl*, THE NAKED CIVIL SERVANT, RAFFLES, AN ENGLISHMAN'S CASTLE, *The Organisation*, MALICE AFORETHOUGHT, THÉRÈSE RAQUIN, THE CLEOPATRAS, *Praying Mantis* and episodes of THE RIVALS OF SHERLOCK HOLMES and JEMIMA SHORE INVESTIGATES. A former documentary-maker, Mackie joined the BBC as a contract writer in 1954 and later worked for Granada (where he became Head of Drama), among other companies.

McLachlan, Craig
(1965–)

Australian actor who shot to fame as Henry Ramsay in NEIGHBOURS before switching soaps and taking on the role of Grant Mitchell in HOME AND AWAY. He had earlier appeared in *Sons and Daughters*. Later credits have included the mini-series *Heroes II* and the part of Ed in BUGS, as well as the Australian dramas *Tribe, McLeod's Daughters* and *Through My Eyes*. McLachlan has had some hit singles in the UK, most notably 'Mona'.

McManus, Mark
(1935–94)

Scottish actor, a former boxer, whose first major role was as the eponymous lead in the northern mining saga SAM, although in his latter years he was known to viewers as the gritty Glasgow detective TAGGART, making 30 episodes of the series from 1983. McManus was another policeman, DCI Jack Lambie, in STRANGERS and also appeared in MAN AT THE TOP, COLDITZ, THE BROTHERS, CROWN COURT, *The Foundation*, TARGET, *Union Castle*, MINDER, *Dramarama* and other dramas. The late Brian Connolly, lead singer of The Sweet pop group, was his foster-brother (some reports claim half-brother).

McMillan and Wife ★★

US (Universal) Police Drama. ITV 1972–9 (US: NBC 1971–7)
DVD: Universal (Region 1 only)

Commissioner Stewart McMillan .... **Rock Hudson**
Sally McMillan .... **Susan Saint James**
Sgt/Lt. Charles Enright .... **John Schuck**
Mildred .... **Nancy Walker**
Agatha .... **Martha Raye**
Sgt Steve DiMaggio .... **Richard Gilliland**
Maggie .... **Gloria Stroock**

Creator/Executive Producer **Leonard B. Stern**
Producer **Jon Epstein**

A San Francisco police chief and his wife stumble across crime at every turn.

Loosely based on *The Thin Man* series of films, *McMillan and Wife* concerns a hapless police commissioner who is continually dragged into detective work by his attractive wife. Stewart and Sally McMillan have a successful marriage, a witty rapport and a nose for crime, which means that there is no chance of this policeman leaving his work at the office. Whether they are doing the shopping, going to a party or taking a holiday, *something* is bound to arouse their curiosity. Even in bed all they talk about is murder. Little wonder they need the sharp-tongued Mildred to do their housework.

McMillan and Wife was part of the MYSTERY MOVIE collection of crime capers and was derived from a pilot movie called *Once upon a Dead Man*. When, after five years, Susan Saint James and Nancy Walker decided to leave the series, Rock Hudson soldiered on alone, with the title shortened to *McMillan*. Sally is killed off in a plane crash and Stewart is furnished with a new assistant, in the shape of Sgt Steve DiMaggio, who replaces the well-intentioned but slow-witted Sgt Charles Enright, now promoted to lieutenant. Mildred's sister, Agatha, arrives to be his housekeeper, and Maggie is his new secretary. The new format didn't last long, however.

McNally, Kevin

(1956–)

Birmingham-raised actor and writer whose on-screen credits (sometimes as Kevin R. McNally) include CROWN COURT, I, CLAUDIUS (Castor), POLDARK (Drake Carne), DIANA (Jan Leigh), DOCTOR WHO, WE'LL MEET AGAIN, THIN AIR (Mark Gentian), *Tygo Road* (Adam Hartley), *A Masculine Ending* (Andrew Gardner), *Full Stretch* (Baz Levick), *Chiller, Frontiers* (Supt. Graham Kirsten), *Underworld* (Jezzard), DAD (Alan Hook), *Uprising* (Terry Gaines), SHACKLETON (Worsley), CONSPIRACY (Martin Luther), BEDTIME (Simon), *Dunkirk* (Major Gen. Alexander) and *Bloodlines* (James Hopkin). Guest appearances have been in series like MURDER MOST HORRID, MIDSOMER MURDERS and SPOOKS. As a writer, McNally has penned episodes of *Lock, Stock* . . .

Macnee, Patrick

(1922–)

Old Etonian Patrick Macnee, a cousin of David Niven, will probably be remembered for one television role – debonair, gentleman agent John Steed in THE AVENGERS and THE NEW AVENGERS – although he has contributed to numerous TV movies and mini-series since. He played the head of U.N.C.L.E. in the one-off *Return of the Man from U.N.C.L.E.* in 1983, was cast in the US series *Empire* (Calvin Cromwell), *Gavilan* (Milo Bentley) and *Thunder in Paradise* (Edward Whitaker), and appeared as Lord Peter Awliscombe in *Nancherrow* (see COMING HOME). More recently he has been seen in America in the series *Night Man*. Macnee has appeared as a guest in dramas like BATTLESTAR GALACTICA, DICK TURPIN, MAGNUM PI and MURDER, SHE WROTE. Most of Macnee's earliest television work was gained in Canada and the USA (including one role in RAWHIDE), following some stage and film work in Britain.

McPartlin, Anthony

(1975–)

One half of Ant and Dec, popular TV presenters hosting series like *The Ant and Dec Show, Ant and Dec Unzipped, SM:TV* and *Friends Like These*, after they both came to fame in BYKER GROVE, in which Ant played PJ and Dec (Donnelly) played Duncan. (McPartlin had also been seen in the BBC's holiday ideas programme *Why Don't You?*) These roles also took them into the record charts with a series of PJ and Duncan hits like 'Let's Get Ready to Rhumble' and 'Stuck on U'. Other hosting credits include *Slap Bang with Ant and Dec, CD:UK, Record of the Year*, POP IDOL, *Ant & Dec's Secret Camera Show, Ant and Dec's Saturday Night Takeaway*, I'M A CELEBRITY . . . GET ME OUT OF HERE!, and *Ant & Dec's Gameshow Marathon*. These likely lads also appeared in *Ant and Dec in a Tribute to the Likely Lads*, a remake of a classic episode from the 1970s series, and provided voices for the animation *Engie Benjy*. In case readers ever wonder which is which, Ant always appears on the left side of the screen.

McQueen, Geoff

(1947–94)

British scriptwriter, a former manager with an electrical company who broke into television with an episode of THE GENTLE TOUCH and then his own snooker-room drama, GIVE US A BREAK. Soon afterwards, McQueen penned a single play for Thames TV's STORYBOARD anthology. Entitled *Woodentop*, it proved to be the pilot for THE BILL. McQueen's later offerings included the light-hearted dramas BIG DEAL and STAY LUCKY, and episodes of UP THE ELEPHANT AND ROUND THE CASTLE and HOME JAMES. He also devised the David Jason drama *March in Windy City*. His last TV work was *Rules of Engagement* (shown posthumously).

McShane, Ian

(1942–)

Blackburn-born actor, prominent on both sides of the Atlantic. McShane starred as Joc Lunn in a series called *You Can't Win* in 1966 and as Heathcliff in a 1967 version of *Wuthering Heights*. He then appeared in the Joe Orton play *Funeral Games* in 1968 and later played Judas in JESUS OF NAZARETH, Sir Eric Russell in ROOTS, Benjamin Disraeli in *Disraeli* and Bert in *Dirty Money*. His other major credits have been in WILL SHAKESPEARE and plays and mini-series like *Grand Larceny, The Pirate*, WAR AND REMEMBRANCE, *Bare Essence, Evergreen* and *Man and Boy* (Marty Mann). From 1986 he became familiar as the roguish antiques dealer LOVEJOY, a series that he also co-produced through his own company, McShane Productions. The company was also responsible for a two-part drama, *Soul Survivors*, in which McShane played DJ Otis Cooke, and the legal series *Madson*, with McShane, who devised the series, as prisoner-turned-lawyer John Madson. More recently, McShane has starred as barkeeper Al Swearengen in the Western series *Deadwood*. Narration work on SURVIVAL, *The Natural World* and HOLLYWOOD GREATS, plus guest appearances in series like REDCAP, SPACE: 1999, MINDER, COLUMBO, PERRY MASON, DALLAS (Don Lockwood), IN DEEP, *Trust* (Alan Cooper-Fozard) and THE WEST WING add to his varied portfolio. He is married to actress Gwen Humble.

Mad Death, The ★★

UK (BBC) Drama. BBC 1 1983

Michael Hilliard	**Richard Heffer**
Dr Ann Maitland	**Barbara Kellerman**
Johnny Dalry	**Richard Morant**
Tom Siegler	**Ed Bishop**
Bill Stanton	**Jimmy Logan**
Miss Stonecroft	**Brenda Bruce**
Bob Nicol	**Paul Brooke**
Jane Stoddard	**Debbi Blythe**

Writer **Sean Hignett**
Producer **Bob McIntosh**

● ***An unprepared Britain is thrown into panic by a rabies epidemic.***

When a rich French woman decides to smuggle her pampered pet cat into Britain, she unwittingly sparks a national disaster. The cat, it transpires, has been in contact with a rabid fox and has now introduced the dreaded disease into the UK. Its spread remains undetected until the first human victim is struck down. Immediately, an area of the country is quarantined off and it is left to one Michael Hilliard to keep the disease under control, with the help of Dr Ann Maitland, who strives to detect the origin of the outbreak. When their efforts are deliberately sabotaged, it becomes all the more obvious what a catastrophic effect this disease might have on the country. This three-part drama from BBC Scotland was based on a novel by Nigel Slater.

Madeley, Richard

(1956–)

British presenter, largely associated with daytime television where, with his wife, Judy Finnigan, he has presented *This Morning* on ITV and *Richard and Judy* on Channel 4 (they also hosted the evening chat show, *Tonight with Richard Madeley and Judy Finnigan*). Madeley has also chaired the quizzes *Runway* and *Connections*, plus the panel game CLUEDO, and previously worked as a journalist, reporting for Border, Yorkshire and Granada TV news.

Madigan ★★

US (Universal) Police Drama. ITV 1973 (US: NBC 1972–3)

Sgt Dan Madigan	**Richard Widmark**

Executive Producer **Frank Rosenberg**
Producers **Dean Hargrove, Roland Kibbee**

● ***An abrasive New York cop prefers his own company.***

Madigan is one of TV's great loners, one of the quirky cops of the 1970s. Living in a spartan one-room flat, he works for the NYPD during the day, but has little social life at night. Perhaps it is his hard, cool indifference that puts people off, with his genuinely soft centre just too well concealed. At least, having no attachments, he is free to travel, and his work does take him a long way from the busy streets of New York City.

The concept was inspired by a 1968 film of the same name. After a pilot movie called *Brock's Last Case, Madigan* became part of the MYSTERY MOVIE crime anthology series, showing in feature-length episodes. However, only six were ever made, each known by its setting, for example *The Manhattan Beat*, *The Naples Beat* and *The Lisbon Beat*.

Madoc, Philip

(1934–)

Welsh actor normally cast in somewhat sombre or menacing roles. He was Magua in the BBC's 1972 version of LAST OF THE MOHICANS, Det. Chief Supt. Tate in TARGET, Jack Brewer in *Flickers*, Lloyd George in THE LIFE AND TIMES OF DAVID LLOYD GEORGE, newspaper baron Fison in A VERY BRITISH COUP, TV producer George in HILARY and Lancing in FIRST BORN. Madoc was also seen in MANHUNT (Lutzig) and both BOUQUET OF BARBED WIRE and its sequel, *Another Bouquet*, plus the lifeboat drama, ENNAL'S POINT (Jack Tustin), and a kids' drama serial called *Moonacre* (Sir Benjamin). He has enjoyed guest roles in TV movies and series like THE AVENGERS, DOCTOR WHO, THE BARON, MAN IN A SUITCASE, RANDALL AND HOPKIRK (DECEASED), DEPARTMENT S, FORTUNES OF WAR, SINGLES, CAPITAL CITY, BROOKSIDE, DOCTORS and DAD'S ARMY, often playing a villain. In recent years Madoc has been seen in the single drama *Thin Ice* (headmaster), as a QC in HE KNEW HE WAS RIGHT, and made several appearances as Welsh detective DCI Noel Bain in *A Mind to Kill*. He was once married to actress Ruth Madoc.

Madoc, Ruth

(1943–)

British actress, popular in the 1980s as HI-DE-HI!'s Welsh camp announcer, Gladys Pugh. Previously, Madoc had appeared in HUNTER'S WALK, as policeman's wife Betty Smith, and in the series *Leave It to Charlie* and THE LIFE AND TIMES OF DAVID LLOYD GEORGE (as Lizzie Davies, alongside her first husband, Philip Madoc). She has since been seen in the dramas *Oliver's Travels* (Mrs Evans), *Agatha Christie's The Pale Horse* (Sybil Stamfordis), *Jack of Hearts* (Jean Pryce) and MINE ALL MINE (Myrtle Jones), and as presenter of SONGS OF PRAISE. A guest appearance in LITTLE BRITAIN and a part in the sketch series *Revolver* are other recent credits.

Maelstrom ★★★

UK (BBC) Drama. BBC 1 1985

Catherine Durrell	**Tusse Silberg**
Anders Bjornson	**David Beames**
Anna Marie Jordahl	**Susan Gilmore**
Lars Nilsen	**Christopher Scoular**
Ingrid Nilsen	**Edita Brychta**
Astrid Linderman	**Ann Todd**

Writer **Michael J. Bird**
Producer **Vere Lorrimer**

● ***A young English girl is caught up in a Norwegian mystery.***

Catherine Durrell is surprised to hear that she has been left an inheritance by a total stranger. To claim it, she needs to travel to Norway, but when she arrives she finds herself trapped in a whirlpool of intrigue and terror as she tries to navigate her way to the truth about her obscure benefactor. Also wrapped in the 'maelstrom' – an allusion to the area of viciously eddying winds and currents off the north-west coast of Scandinavia – is a local family. The scenery may be stunning (the series was filmed among the blue fjords and snow-capped peaks of the Alesund region of Norway) but there is menace at work, casting a shadow over several lives. This six-part drama came from the same production team as the similarly enigmatic DARK SIDE OF THE SUN and THE LOTUS EATERS.

Magazine

A programme made up of assorted features of various lengths and on numerous topics, some inserted on film or video, others presented in the studio.

Maggie and Her ✶✶

UK (LWT) Situation Comedy. ITV 1978–9

Maggie Brooks .... **Julia McKenzie**
Mrs P (Perry) .... **Irene Handl**

Writer **Leonard Webb**
Producers **David Askey, Simon Brett**

A pensioner intrudes in the life of her younger neighbour.
Teacher Maggie Brooks, in her mid-thirties, is happily divorced from husband Fred. She moves into a flat in Argyle Mansions, London, but discovers a new irritant in her nosey neighbour, Mrs P. Mrs P is a plucky, plain speaking pensioner, with an unfortunate flair for malapropisms and a tendency to come out with incongruously youthful sayings. She considers it her job to take Maggie under her wing, and thus bluntly interferes with Maggie's day-to-day affairs. While this would seem to be purgatory for Maggie, she can't help having a soft spot for Mrs P – probably because they share the same East End roots – and cares for her like her own mum. Most of the humour comes from Maggie's man troubles, community hiccups in the block of flats and Mrs P's struggles to cope with the modern world. Laurie Holloway provided the theme music. The series followed a 1976 pilot entitled *Poppy and Her*.

Magic Boomerang, The ✶

Australia (ABC/Pacific/Fremantle) Children's Adventure. ITV 1966

Tom Thumbleton .... **David Morgan**
Wombat .... **Rodney Pearlman**
Dan Thumbleton .... **Telford Jackson**
Mrs Thumbleton .... **Penelope Shelton**

Producer **Chris Stewart**

A young lad discovers a boomerang with special qualities.
Tom Thumbleton is a useful kid to know. He owns a magic boomerang that comes in ever so handy in tackling cattle thieves and bank robbers, saving stranded sailors or perhaps just giving a helping hand to friends and family in a spot of bother. When there's so much to be wary of in the wilds of Australia, he's definitely a boy to have on your side.

Magic Roundabout, The ✶✶✶✶

France (Serge Danot) Children's Entertainment. BBC 1 1965–8; 1970–1; 1974–7/Channel 4 1992–3

Narrators/Writers **Eric Thompson, Nigel Planer**

Creator **Serge Danot**
Producer (UK) **Ursula Eason**

A girl and her friends enjoy surreal adventures in a magic garden.
Few series are more fittingly described as 'cult' than *The Magic Roundabout*. Although each episode was just five minutes long and, almost as an afterthought, tagged on to the end of children's hour, this animation became a firm favourite not only with kids but also with adult audiences. Consequently, there were howls of protest when transmission was switched to an earlier time-slot.

The Magic Roundabout was produced in France by Serge Danot as *Le Ménage enchanté* and shown first on French television in 1964. When the series arrived in the UK, the narration was drily and wittily redubbed by Eric (father of Emma) Thompson, who also rewrote the scripts for British consumption. The first episode tells of how sad Mr Rusty, is. Mr Rusty, is the whiskery owner of a carousel, a man whose barrel-organ provides the show's theme music. Unfortunately, he is sad because his roundabout is deserted: there is no magic to bring in the children. Then he receives a parcel containing the jack in a box figure of Zebedee who is capable of magic and promises to put everything right. Thereafter, the storyline goes as follows. Young Florence arrives at the roundabout on a regular basis. Zebedee, who is a strange, freckle-faced creature with a waxed moustache and a bedspring for feet, then bounces into the picture and, in a cascade of harp strings, the 'real' nature of life around the roundabout disappears and all manner of odd things begin to happen. New characters drift into the action, primarily a pompous, sleek-haired dog known as Dougal, a quirky snail called Brian and a laid-back rabbit named Dylan. There are also Ermintrude, a camp, flower-chewing cow, manic cyclist Mr Machenry, a talking train and, occasionally, Florence's friend Paul, plus one or two other chums. When it all gets a bit too frenetic, up bounces Zebedee to declare it is 'Time for bed.'

Children loved the series for its visual humour. Adults enjoyed Thompson's 'in' references to topical issues and personalities of the day. With the arrival of colour television, the surreality of it all became even more apparent, and some viewers began to question just what lay behind the series. Fingers were pointed at the almost hallucinogenic nature of the concept, with The Magic Roundabout itself declared to be an allegory for a 'trip' and Mr Rusty some kind of drug-peddler. It may seem ludicrous – and has always been firmly denied – but there was plenty of evidence to support this theory. After all, everything is perfectly normal until Florence arrives at the roundabout, Dylan is always spaced out and Dougal's favourite food is sugar cubes (with all their LSD connections). But even if you dismiss the 'drug culture' theory, *The Magic Roundabout* will still be fondly remembered by today's parents and grandparents as a cheerful part of everyday life in the 1960s.

A cinema version, *Dougal and the Blue Cat*, was released in the UK in 1972 and the series was revived by Channel 4 in 1992, with previously unscreened episodes adapted (very much in the Eric Thompson vein) for British audiences by Nigel Planer. A further cinema film was released in 2005. This time just called *The Magic Roundabout*, it featured the vocal talents of

Jim Broadbent (Brian), Robbie Williams (Dougal), Bill Nighy (Dylan), Joanna Lumley (Ermintrude), Kylie Minogue (Florence), Lee Evans (The Train) and Ian McKellen (Zebedee).

Magic Wands

The flippant term used for programmes that make viewers' dreams and wishes come true. One of the first such programmes in the UK was *Ask Pickles* in the 1950s, but the longest-running example was JIM'LL FIX IT, which notched up 20 years of giving kids the chance to meet pop stars, drive trains, interview politicians, etc. Some adults' hopes were also fulfilled. Esther Rantzen's THE BIG TIME was another such vehicle, and among more recent offerings were the heavily sentimental SURPRISE, SURPRISE and *Noel's Christmas Presents*.

Magical Mystery Tour ✶✶

UK (Apple Films) Musical Drama. BBC 1 1967
DVD: MPI Home Video

Paul McCartney, John Lennon, George Harrison, Ringo Starr

Creators/Writers/Producers **The Beatles**

● ***Dreamy, colourful, chaotic showcase for the music of the Fab Four.***

After the success of their earlier two feature films, *A Hard Day's Night* and *Help!*, a new visual offering from The Beatles was greatly anticipated. It arrived in the form of a film for television, on Boxing Day 1967. Whereas previously The Beatles had been guided by director Dick Lester and manager Brian Epstein, then recently deceased, this time they were on their own, writing the script (what little there was), composing and performing the music and directing the whole piece. In fact, the 50-minute work was put together in a completely unorthodox, unstructured fashion. A multi-coloured coach was hired and filled with friends and associates, plus one or two names from showbusiness (those aboard included Ivor Cutler, Jesse Robins, Mandy West, Nat Jackley and Victor Spinetti). It then took off for the West Country, stopping as appropriate to shoot various scenes. The finished project inevitably reflects this and was roundly criticized by those in the know for being self-indulgent and unprofessional. Perhaps if the BBC had screened it first on BBC 2, where colour transmissions were available, instead of on dreary, old black and white BBC 1, it might have made more of an impression. In the heady year of psychedelia, the vibrant colours and the dreamy sequences may have made more sense. As it was, a colour repeat was shown on BBC 2 on 5 January, 1968. A double EP was released of the film's soundtrack.

Magician, The ✶✶

US (Paramount) Adventure. ITV 1974–5 (US: NBC 1973–4)

Anthony Blake	**Bill Bixby**
Max Pomeroy	**Keene Curtis**
Dennis Pomeroy	**Todd Crespi**
Jerry	**Jim Watkins**
Dominick	**Joseph Sirola**

Executive Producer **Lawrence Heath**

● ***An illusionist uses his talents to assist the cause of justice.***

Conjuror Tony Blake was wrongfully convicted of a crime early in his life. Bitter about the experience, he left prison vowing to make sure that the same thing won't happen to other innocent people. He now aims to help folk in trouble or under threat, preventing crime wherever he can, making full use of the sleight-of-hand and other illusionary skills he employs in his stage act. His assistants in his crusade are journalist Max Pomeroy (who gives Blake his leads) and Max's wheelchair-bound son, Dennis. Jerry is the pilot of Blake's private plane, *The Spirit*. Later, the setting switched to the Magic Castle, a Hollywood nightclub where Blake has a residency. Actor Bill Bixby performed many of the illusionist's tricks himself.

Magician's House, The ✶✶

UK (Kudos/Forefront/BBC) Science Fiction Drama. BBC 1 1999–2000

Stephen Tyler/The Magician	**Ian Richardson**
Jack Green	**Neil Pearson**
Meg Lewis	**Siân Phillips**
Mary Green	**Katie Stuart**
Matthew Morden	**Christopher Redman**
Alice Constant	**Olivia Coles**
William Constant	**Steven Webb**
Phoebe Taylor	**Kate Greenhouse**
	Kendall Cross
Kev	**Martin Evans**
Rat	**Jennifer Saunders** *(voice only)*
Jasper the Owl	**Stephen Fry** *(voice only)*
Charles Morden	**Robert Wisden**

Writer **William Corlett**
Producers **Helena Cynamon, Stephen Garrett, Mickey Rodgers, Karen Troubetzkoy**

● ***Three children battle to preserve a Welsh wilderness from developers on behalf of a 500-year-old sorcerer.***

Young Mary Green is to spend Christmas with her dad, Jack, his pregnant girlfriend, Phoebe, and her two cousins, Alice and William, in a 500-year-old house deep in the unspoilt Golden Valley in Wales. It is not a prospect the American girl relishes. However, supernatural events conspire to bring the sulky Mary back into the family fold. In the year 1600 magician Stephen Tyler has discovered a means of time travel, but it is his rebellious sidekick Matthew Morden who decides to use it first. His curiosity getting the better of him, he sends a rat into the future, a move that is likely to distort the balance of good and evil. The rat speaks directly to Mary and encourages her to prevent her future stepmother from giving birth to the valley's first baby for 400 years – an event that would foil the plans of those plotting the destruction of the wilderness. Other talking animals (Jasper, Tyler's owl; Cinnabar, a fox; and Spot, a dog) also help or hinder the children, while the oblivious Jack sets about transforming Golden House into a hotel. There's also sound advice from local ecologist Meg Lewis, whose family shares a long history with that of Stephen Tyler. The story concludes with Tyler's battle for supremacy with his young upstart assistant, security for Golden Valley the prize. A new threat to the lovely valley is witnessed in the second series. This time it is summer and a theme park is planned by one of Matthew's descendants, Charles Morden. Tyler, having created a powerful new substance called black gold, travels to the future to try to prevent the destruction. However, the magician is sent spiralling back in time, leaving behind his magical pendant and, with his powers failing, getting trapped between worlds. It is a situation that can only spell bad news for Golden Valley and its population of badgers, especially when Matthew is once again called forward to stop the children hampering his family's progress. All 12 episodes of this Emmy-winning, Sunday teatime series (filmed in Canada) were penned by William Corlett from his own novels.

Magnificent Evans, The ★★★

UK (BBC) Situation Comedy. BBC 1 1984
DVD: BBC

Plantagenet Evans	**Ronnie Barker**
Rachel	**Sharon Morgan**
Willie	**Dickie Arnold**
Bron	**Myfanwy Talog**
Probert	**William Thomas**
Home Rule O'Toole	**Dyfed Thomas**

Creator/Writer **Roy Clarke**
Producer **Sydney Lotterby**

The shameless philandering of a flamboyant Welsh photographer.

Plantagenet Evans, modestly describing himself as a 'genius, photographer and man of letters', is the most colourful character in a sleepy Welsh town. So colourful, in fact, that the local chapel folk openly disapprove. Just one of his many scandalous activities is his relationship with Rachel, a local beauty who, as his fiancée and assistant, has her own apartment at his home/studio, much to the concern of her sister, Bron, and Bron's husband, Probert. While modest Rachel plays down their affair, Evans himself, dressed in flowing cape and wide-brimmed hat, never shirks attention. As the local franchise-holder for Scandinavian log stoves and a part-time antiques dealer, he is also a man of many means, devoted to the cause of making money. Bullying Willie, his loyal but silent sidekick, into doing all the donkey work, he parades around in his vintage motor, leering at girls, defying the local gossips, plying his artistic trade and disparaging his customers. Also seen from time to time is the town's fervent nationalist, Home Rule O'Toole.

Magnum, PI ★★

US (Universal/Bellisarius/Glen A. Larson) Detective Drama. ITV 1981–7 (US: CBS 1980–8)
DVD: Universal

Thomas Sullivan Magnum	**Tom Selleck**
Jonathan Quayle Higgins III	**John Hillerman**
Theodore 'TC' Calvin	**Roger E. Mosley**
Orville 'Rick' Wright	**Larry Manetti**
Robin Masters	**Orson Welles** *(voice only)*
Mac Reynolds	**Jeff MacKay**
Lt. Maggie Poole	**Jean Bruce Scott**
Lt. Tanaka	**Kwan Hi Lim**
Agatha Chumley	**Gillian Dobb**
Francis Hofstetler ('Ice Pick')	**Elisha Cook Jr**
Assistant DA Carol Baldwin	**Kathleen Lloyd**

Creators **Donald P. Bellisario, Glen A. Larson**

A private eye looks after the Hawaiian estate of a mysterious millionaire.

Womanizing Thomas Sullivan Magnum (TS to his friends) is a former naval intelligence officer turned private investigator. He is based on the Hawaiian islands, where his main contract is to protect the estate of writer Robin Masters, who is perpetually away from home and, hence, never seen, only heard. In return, Magnum is provided with luxurious accommodation on the Oahu seafront and the use of his employer's Ferrari. However, all is not plain sailing, thanks to the presence of Jonathan Quayle Higgins III, Masters's crusty English manservant. A former sergeant major, his strict military background jars with Magnum's easygoing approach to life and, while a professional respect develops over the years, there is always much friction between them. Higgins particularly dislikes Magnum's abuse of the millionaire's generosity, but he does have the consolation of knowing that his two Doberman Pinscher guard-dogs, Zeus and Apollo, share his feelings about the private investigator.

Magnum (who also narrates the series) takes on other assignments, too, many thrust upon him by Assistant DA Carol Baldwin. For these, he is assisted by two Vietnam veteran colleagues, TC and Rick, but the cases seldom pay their way and Magnum often fouls up. TC runs the Island Hoppers helicopter company, while Rick (real name Orville, which he refuses to use) is owner of a bar based on Rick's Café in the film, *Casablanca*. He later moves to the exclusive King Kamehameha Beach Club, in joint ownership with Robin Masters. Rick also has some handy connections in the local underworld, such as the dodgy businessman Ice Pick.

With the end of the series in sight, the studio shot a two-hour special in which the hero is killed off and goes to Heaven. However, the show continued for one more season and so it had to be explained away as a dream. When the finale does eventually come, Magnum rediscovers a lost daughter and rejoins the navy. But a degree of ambiguity veils the denouement. Robin Masters, it is suggested, is none other than Higgins himself but, as this is never properly confirmed, the audience is left in some doubt.

Magnum, PI used the same production facilities as HAWAII FIVE-O and the scripts often referred to the Five-O police unit and its leader, Steve McGarrett.

Magnusson, Magnus

KBE (Hon.) (Magnus Sigursteinnson 1929–)

Icelandic TV presenter, famous for his 'I've started so I'll finish' role as questionmaster on MASTERMIND. He is also a keen historian and an expert on Viking matters, resulting in series like *Vikings!*, CHRONICLE, *Unsolved Mysteries*, *BC: The Archaeology of the Bible Lands*, *Living Legends* and *The Balloon Game*. His earliest TV work was on TONIGHT, after a journalistic career in Scotland, where he was raised, and in the early 1970s he hosted a debate programme entitled *Mainly Magnus*. Magnusson has also worked on Icelandic television. He is the father of news presenter Sally Magnusson and TV producer Jon Magnusson.

Magpie ★★★

UK (Thames) Children's Magazine. ITV 1968–80

Presenters **Susan Stranks, Pete Brady, Tony Bastable, Douglas Rae, Mick Robertson, Jenny Hanley, Tommy Boyd**

Executive Producer **Lewis Rudd**
Producers **Sue Turner, Tony Bastable, David Hodgson, Randal Beattie, Tim Jones, Leslie Burgess**

Lively children's-hour magazine.

Transmitted live twice a week from Thames TV's Teddington studios, *Magpie* was conceived as a rival to the BBC's well-established BLUE PETER. Its trendy trio of presenters,

Susan Stranks, Tony Bastable and former Radio 1 DJ Pete Brady, set out to bring kids' TV up to date, with features on pop music (even the theme music was rock-based), fashions and genuinely interesting pastimes. Specialist educational segments like *A Date with Tony* (a regular in-depth look at a historical event), the *ABC of Football*, and items of space news with ITN's Peter Fairley were introduced and, for humour, the zany Captain Fantastic character (David Jason) from DO NOT ADJUST YOUR SET was given a five-minute slot. *Magpie* also had a motor-launch (called *Thames Magpie* – the Thames studios were at the side of Teddington Lock). All this might have been viewed as radical, given the wholesome, almost puritan, fare served up by its BBC competitor, but, having said that, the format of the two programmes was remarkably similar and many ideas were shared.

There were plenty of making and cooking projects, animals featured strongly (*Magpie* had its own pony, Puff) and, each Christmas, *Magpie* annuals accompanied *Blue Peter* books on the newsagents' shelves. Both programmes offered badges as prizes and both organized yearly appeals. *Magpie*, however, offered ten different badges, awarded for various achievements or contributions, and the *Magpie* appeal was subtly different, too. Instead of calling for used paperback books or milk bottle tops, it asked directly for cash, and the totals raised were indicated by a red line that ran around the entire Thames studio complex. Early efforts were modest in their ambitions and were known as *Magpie Sixpence* appeals, kids being asked to donate a tanner (2½p) out of their pocket money.

However, *Magpie* and *Blue Peter* seemed to grow further apart over the years. While the BBC show seemed firmly rooted in the 1960s, *Magpie* became more 'with it' by the day and enjoyed a far more relaxed studio atmosphere. Captain Fantastic was quickly dropped and new presenters were gradually drafted in. Quiet Scotsman Douglas Rae, mop-haired Mick Robertson, actress Jenny Hanley and disc jockey Tommy Boyd were later recruits. When *Magpie* ended in 1980, Robertson went on to present a similar, leisure-based series entitled *Freetime* (1980–5; 1988).

The *Magpie* name – apparently chosen to admit that it was a direct 'steal' from *Blue Peter* – was derived from the old rhyme which featured in the rocky theme music – 'One for sorrow, Two for joy, Three for a girl and Four for a boy, Five for silver, Six for gold, Seven is a secret never to be told. Eight's a wish and Nine a kiss, Ten is a bird you must not miss'. The track was performed by The Murgatroyd Band, a pseudonym for The Spencer Davis Group (the programme's fat magpie mascot was known as Murgatroyd).

Maid Marian and Her Merry Men ★★★

UK (BBC) Children's Comedy. BBC 1 1989–90; 1993–4

Maid Marian .... **Kate Lonergan**
Robin Hood .... **Wayne Morris**
Sheriff of Nottingham .... **Tony Robinson**
Barrington .... **Danny John-Jules**
Rabies .... **Howard Lew Lewis**
Little Ron .... **Mike Edmonds**
King John .... **Forbes Collins**
Gary .... **Mark Billingham**
Graeme .... **David Lloyd**

Creator/Writer **Tony Robinson**
Producer **Richard Callanan**

● ***Robin Hood with a difference: now Maid Marian is in charge and Robin is a wimp.***

This off-beat, award-winning children's comedy, penned by BLACKADDER star Tony Robinson, turns the tales of Sherwood Forest inside out. It casts Robin Hood as an ineffective yuppie figure (known as Robin of Islington) and bestows command of the Merry Men on the bold Maid Marian, who eggs them on like a school hockey captain. In her ineffective troupe are midget Little Ron, Rastafarian Barrington and Rabies. Tony Robinson himself appears as the Sheriff of Nottingham.

Maigret ★★★

UK (BBC/Winwell) Police Drama. BBC 1960–3
DVD: Cinema Club (Gambon version)

Insp. Jules Maigret .... **Rupert Davies**
Lucas .... **Ewen Solon**
Madame Maigret .... **Helen Shingler**

Creator **Georges Simenon**
Executive Producer **Andrew Osborn**

● ***The investigations of the celebrated French detective.***

Hero of some 150 stories by Belgian novelist Georges Simenon, and already played in the cinema by Jean Gabin, Maigret, the Paris detective, reached the TV screen in 1960. Produced not by a French company but by the BBC, whom Simenon had approached because of its reputation for drama, this hugely successful series made a star – if a chronically typecast one – out of Rupert Davies. Renowned for his pipe, raincoat and trilby trademarks, Maigret, like INSPECTOR MORSE and company over 20 years later, is a thinking man's detective. He solves cases by analysing the characters and personalities of his suspects, and by visiting them at home, where he can learn more about them, rather than calling them into the sterile atmosphere of his office (where a photograph of his beloved Madame Maigret holds pride of place on his desk). In his investigations, he was assisted by his sidekick, Lucas.

Although it failed as a stage play, and despite a disastrous attempt to film the character (Rupert Davies walked off the set), *Maigret* has lingered pleasantly in viewers' minds. Ron Grainer's theme music and the classic opening sequence, showing Maigret striking a match against a wall to light his pipe, are particularly fondly remembered. Davies returned for a one-off 90-minute production, *Maigret at Bay*, in 1969; Richard Harris took over for an HTV film in 1988; and a new TV adaptation, produced by Granada with Michael Gambon in the lead role and Geoffrey Hutchings as Lucas, ran in 1992–3. On this occasion, filming took place in Budapest, rather than Paris (it was cheaper and looked more like 1950s Paris than the real thing).

Main Chance, The ★★

UK (Yorkshire) Legal Drama. ITV 1969–70; 1972; 1975

David Main .... **John Stride**
Julia Main .... **Kate O'Mara**
Sarah Courtenay/Lady Radchester .... **Anna Palk**
Margaret Castleton .... **Margaret Ashcroft**
Henry Castleton .... **John Wentworth**

Creator/Writer **Edmund Ward**
Executive Producers **Peter Willes, David Cunliffe, John Frankau, Derek Bennett**

● *A successful young lawyer strives to reach the top.*

David Main, a lawyer in his early 30s, is brash, keen and hungry for success. But although he shops around for the best, most profitable cases, he also finds himself drawn to the defence of the most humble. Very often his impetuosity leads him into precarious situations, but his energy and knowledge of the law carry him through. A stickler for efficiency, Main is also forward-thinking and works out of an office filled with the latest high-tech gadgetry. Julia, his wife, appears only in the first series, but his 23-year-old little-rich-girl secretary, Sarah Courtenay, later to become Lady Radchester, stays with him throughout the show's lengthy run.

Main Event, The ✶

UK (Grundy) Quiz. BBC 1 1993

Presenter **Chris Tarrant**

Creator **Alan Boyd**
Producer **Danny Greenstone**

● *Manic panel game-cum-quiz show for early Saturday evenings.*

Two families were paired with two teams of celebrities in this all-action series of charades, observation games, general knowledge quizzes and against-the-clock challenges. A nightmare of technology, the programme – a mix of GIVE US A CLUE, TREASURE HUNT and THE KRYPTON FACTOR, played very much for fun – came from three separate locations: the two family homes and a BBC studio, where the celebrities were based. Domestic sitting rooms, kitchens and bedrooms were glimpsed draped in heavy-duty cabling, and cameras, microphones and production staff were always well in view. Neighbours and friends appeared and were dragged into the proceedings, as the eager families of four sat on their sofas behind their giant toadstool buzzer. Preventing the show from descending into absolute chaos was host Chris Tarrant, who typically whipped up the hysteria and ensured the game ran at a furious pace. The three celebrities in each team usually represented TV programmes, from THE BILL to DROP THE DEAD DONKEY.

Maisie Raine ✶✶

UK (Fair Game/BBC) Police Drama. BBC 1 1998–9

DI Maisie Raine	**Pauline Quirke**
Chief Supt. Jack Freeman	**Ian McElhinney**
DCI Susan Askey	**Anna Patrick**
TI/DC George Kyprianou	**Steve John Shepherd**
Kelvin	**Paul Reynolds**
DC Stephen Holmes	**Brian Bovell**
DC Helen Tomlin	**Rakie Ayola**
DS Mickey Farrel	**Richard Graham**
TI Chris Mallory	**Dean Lennox Kelly**
Joan	**Stella Moray**

Producers **Irving Teitelbaum, Ian Scaife**

● *A no-nonsense female detective finds her methods questioned by her graduate boss.*

Allotment-digging widow Maisie Raine is a down-to-earth London copper who has risen through the ranks to the position of detective inspector, answerable to station boss Jack Freeman, an old friend. However, life in the Bessomer Street nick is never straightforward, thanks to her direct superior, Susan Askey, a yuppie-ish fast-track recruit with modern methods. Into the same bracket falls trainee detective George Kyprianou, who initially rubs Maisie up the wrong way but soon gains her respect, while in the background are the other team members, Holmes, Farrel and Tomlin. Maisie's private life is similarly eventful, as her slightly shifty brother, Kelvin, keeps filling her flat with dodgy goods.

Based on the experiences, if not precisely the career, of real-life policewoman Carol Bristow, this series abandons car chases and sensationalism in favour of the human approach to policing, with Maisie always seeking a reason for a crime and taking time to consider the consequences for all those involved. The second series sees the arrival of a new recruit named Chris Mallory for Maisie to knock into shape. Askey and Kelvin are both safely out of Maisie's hair, and Joan, a maternal new cleaner, arrives, giving our heroine someone to confide in.

Majors, Lee

(Harvey Lee Yeary II; 1939–)

American actor Lee Majors has seldom been short of a prime-time TV role since making his TV debut in 1965. After appearances in series like *The Alfred Hitchcock Hour* and GUNSMOKE, he was cast as Heath Barkley, Barbara Stanwyck's third son, in THE BIG VALLEY. The series ran for four years and, when it ended, Majors quickly moved on to another Western, THE MEN FROM SHILOH. In this revamped version of THE VIRGINIAN he played Roy Tate. A less notable series, *Owen Marshall, Counselor at Law*, followed and then, in 1974, came his biggest role, that of bionic man Colonel Steve Austin in THE SIX MILLION DOLLAR MAN. In 1981 Majors was THE FALL GUY, stuntman Colt Seavers, in a series that ran for five years and for which Majors also sang the theme song. In 1990, he joined the Vietnam drama series, *Tour of Duty* ('Pop' Scarlet), moving on to the martial arts action series *Raven* (Herman Jablonski, or 'Ski'). He has also appeared in numerous TV movies and was once married to actress Farrah Fawcett.

Making Out ✶✶

UK (BBC) Comedy Drama. BBC 1 1989–91

Queenie	**Margi Clarke**
Jill	**Melanie Kilburn**
Rex	**Keith Allen**
Carol May	**Shirley Stelfox**
Stella	**Sheila Grier**
Pauline	**Rachel Davies**
Chunky	**Brian Hibbard**
Norma	**Tracie Bennett**
Bernie	**Alan David**
Donna	**Heather Tobias**
Gordon	**Jonathan Barlow**
Ray	**Tim Dantay**
Klepto	**Moya Brady**
Bella Grout	**Deborah Norton**
Simon	**Gary Beadle**
Frankie	**John Forgeham**
Mr Beachcroft	**Don Henderson**
Nicky	**William Ash**
Colin	**David Hargreaves**
Sharon	**Claire Quigley**
Gavin	**John Lynch**
Kip	**Tony Haygarth**

Rosie .... **Jane Hazlegrove**
Avril .... **Susan Brown**
Maureen .... **Alexandra Pigg**
Dilk .... **Geoffrey Hughes**
Hetty .... **Pat Mills**

Creator **Franc Roddam**
Writer **Debbie Horsfield**
Producers **John Chapman, Carol Wilks**

● ***Ups and downs in the lives of a group of factory workers.*** Set in a converted Manchester mill, home of New Lyne Electronics, *Making Out* revolves around the tumultuous lives of the company's shop-floor workers as they battle against bosses, fight with their menfolk and generally try to make more of their lives. Nominal shop steward is Pauline, but the group's ringleader is the fiery Queenie, whose petty-criminal husband, Chunky, is always looking for a quick buck. Carol May is the lady-like granny who chases sexy boss Rex, well-educated fellow worker Donna longs to have a baby and Klepto is a teenage romantic in conflict with her Orthodox Greek family. Then there is Jill, the new girl, who embarks on an affair with Gavin, a Northern Irish Manchester United footballer, while her husband, Ray, becomes involved with Rosie, a hairdresser. Among the New Lyne bosses are ineffective Bernie, secretary Norma and chairman Mr Beachcroft. By the time the series ends after three runs, new management has taken over and the company is known as Shangri-La Electronics. Music for the programme was provided by New Order.

Malahide, Patrick

(Patrick G. Duggan; 1945–)

Berkshire-born actor/writer featured as DS Chisholm in MINDER, Raymond/Mark Binney/Finney in THE SINGING DETECTIVE and Arthur Starkey in the kids' fantasy *News at Twelve*. In 1977 he was Cradoc in THE EAGLE OF THE NINTH, in 1984 he played Saul in *Charlie*, in 1986 he was Hastymite in *The December Rose*, in 1988 he starred in the sci-fi series *The One Game*, in 1992 he was both the Assistant Commissioner in *The Secret Agent* and Robert Dangerfield in *The Blackheath Poisonings*, and in 1993 he became Inspector Roderick Alleyn in THE INSPECTOR ALLEYN MYSTERIES. He has since played Reverend Edward Casaubon in MIDDLEMARCH, Bailie Creech in *Screen One's Deacon Brodie*, Captain Claude Howlett in ALL THE KING'S MEN, Sir John Conroy in *Victoria and Albert*, Ralston in GOODBYE MR CHIPS, Patrick Brontë in *In Search of the Brontës*, DI Sean Brennan in *Amnesia*, Sir Francis Walsingham in *Elizabeth I* and Anders in *Friends and Crocodiles*. Other credits have included episodes of *Theatre Box*, SHOESTRING, *Dramarama*, INSPECTOR MORSE, BOON, LOVEJOY, THE RUTH RENDELL MYSTERIES, AGATHA CHRISTIE'S POIROT, and the *Performance* presentation of *A Doll's House* (Dr Rank). He runs the production company Ryan Films and writes under his real name of P. G. Duggan – his works have included the *Screen Two* offering *Reasonable Force* and the thriller series *The Writing on the Wall*.

Malcolm, Mary

(1918–)

Former radio announcer who became one of the BBC's on-screen continuity announcers after the war. In 1958 she left to go freelance and later worked for German television (making programmes about Britain). One of her last prominent appearances on UK TV was as a guest in an episode of THE GOODIES in 1976. Malcolm is the granddaughter of actress Lillie Langtry.

Malcolm in the Middle ★★★

US (Satin City/Regency/Fox) Situation Comedy. BBC 2 2001– (US: Fox 2000–)
DVD: Fox (Region 1 only)

Malcolm .... **Frankie Muniz**
Lois .... **Jane Kaczmarek**
Hal .... **Bryan Cranston**
Reese .... **Justin Berfield**
Dewey .... **Erik Per Sullivan**
Francis .... **Christopher Kennedy Masterson**
Caroline Miller .... **Catherine Lloyd Burns**
Stevie Kenarban .... **Craig Lamar Traylor**

Creator **Linwood Boomer**
Executive Producers **Linwood Boomer, David Richardson, Al Higgins, Todd Holland**

● ***A super-intelligent kid is stuck at the centre of a crazy world.***
A mad but just about functional family; a class full of nerdy chums at school; a generally chaotic life: all these revolve around poor Malcolm. Malcolm is a child genius (IQ 165) transplanted at school into the Krelboyne class for gifted students, which is not such a good move as it means he spends most of his day with a load of geeks. Things aren't much better at home. Eldest brother Francis is a delinquent and, as punishment for past sins, has been banished to military school. This leaves three boys still permanently in the nest, of which the cynical Malcolm is the middle one. Youngest is the easily pushed around Dewey, and oldest is the thuggish Reese, who resents Malcolm's privileged treatment and takes it out on him. Abdicating control of the squabbling clan is dim and hairy dad Hal, a keen sports fan (especially skating), but thankfully family life is firmly held together by plain-speaking mum Lois, who is prone to walking round the house naked and who works at the Lucky Aide drug store. Stevie Kenarban is Malcolm's smart, wheelchair-bound buddy. This hugely successful (in its native USA), quirky comedy was first seen on Sky One in the UK before airing on the BBC. The theme song, 'Boss of Me' was provided by the band They Might Be Giants and was a UK Top 30 hit in 2001.

Malden, Karl

(Karl Mladen Sekulovich; 1912–)

American actor of Yugoslav descent whose television career did not take off until the early 1970s, despite having first appeared on the Broadway stage in the 1930s and in the movies in 1940. It was his role as Det. Lt. Mike Stone in a TV movie called THE STREETS OF SAN FRANCISCO which proved the catalyst, with a full-blown series following and running for five years. Malden was later seen in numerous TV movies, though a second series of his own, entitled *Skag*, proved to be a flop. One of his later guest appearances came in an episode of THE WEST WING.

Malice Aforethought ★★

UK (BBC) Drama. BBC 2 1979
DVD: WGBH Boston (Ben Miller version; Region 1 only)

Dr Bickleigh .... **Hywel Bennett**
Julia Bickleigh .... **Judy Parfitt**

Madeleine Cranmere	**Cheryl Campbell**
Reverend Hessary Torr	**Harold Innocent**
Quarnian Torr	**Briony McRoberts**
Denny Bourne	**Christopher Guard**
William Chatford	**David Ashford**
Sir Francis Lee-Bannerton	**Thorley Walters**
Sir Bernard Deverell	**Michael Aldridge**

Writer **Philip Mackie**
Producer **Richard Beynon**

A country doctor is suspected of killing his wife.

Potted meat sandwiches never seemed so suspicious as in this dark tale of wife murder set in the 1930s. Mild-mannered Dr Bickleigh has been the victim of incessant bullying and contempt from his wife, Julia, for ten years. His only escape has been to dream of a real romance and flight from this marital torment. He meets a girl called Madeleine Cranmere and falls in love. Regrettably, Julia will not allow him a divorce, so it seems the only alternative is murder. However, things go somewhat awry when Madeleine marries rival Denny Bourne. Bickleigh's wife is found dead – poisoned – and the doctor is subsequently brought to trial, when those potted meat sandwiches come under investigation. The four-part serial, directed by Cyril Coke and shot in and around Winchester, was based on the novel of the same name written in 1929 by Anthony Berkeley, using the pen name of Francis Iles. Ron Grainer provided the music.

Malice Aforethought was remade in two parts with a new script from Andrew Payne (ITV 1 2005). This time Ben Miller stars as Bickleigh, with Barbara Flynn as Julia.

Mallens, The ★★

UK (Granada) Drama. ITV 1979–80
DVD: Bfs Entertainment (Region 1 only)

Thomas Mallen	**John Hallam**
Donald Radlet	**John Duttine**
Dick Mallen	**David Rintoul**
Jane Radlet	**Gillian Lewis**
Michael Radlet	**John Southworth**
Mary Peel	**Mary Healey**
Barbara Farrington	**Pippa Guard**
Constance Farrington/Radlet	**Julia Chambers**
	June Ritchie
Anna Brigmore	**Caroline Blakiston**
Matthew Radlet	**Ian Saynor**
Barbara Mallen	**Juliet Stevenson**
Michael Radlet	**Gerry Sundquist**

Writer **Jack Russell**
Producer **Roy Roberts**

A rogue Victorian squire is the father of numerous bastard children.

Ruthless Thomas Mallen is the lord of High Banks Hall, set amid the Northumberland moors (filming actually took place in Dovedale, Derbyshire). Living with his weak-willed gambler son Dick, he is a man with scant regard for women and, having lusted and raped most of his life, is now the father of several illegitimate sons, all easily identified by the trademark Mallen white streak in their hair. As the feuding children begin to emerge from the woodwork, and his fortunes become intertwined with the Radlet family of Wolfbur Farm, where Donald Radlet is one of his bastard offspring, so Thomas's troubles increase. It soon emerges that Mallen has mortgaged the hall and frittered away the proceeds. He eventually moves in with his nieces, Barbara and Constance Farrington, and their governess (soon to be his new lover), Anna Brigmore.

The first seven episodes were based on the novels *The Mallen Litter* and *The Mallen Streak* by CATHERINE COOKSON. These were followed by a second series (entitled *Catherine Cookson's The Mallens*) which focuses on Barbara Mallen (the illegitimate, deaf daughter of Thomas and Barbara Farrington) and her lover, Michael Radlet (the illegitimate son of Constance). These episodes were derived from another Cookson novel, *The Mallen Girl*.

Man about the House ★★★

UK (Thames) Situation Comedy. ITV 1973–6
DVD: Network

Robin Tripp	**Richard O'Sullivan**
Chrissy Plummer	**Paula Wilcox**
Jo	**Sally Thomsett**
George Roper	**Brian Murphy**
Mildred Roper	**Yootha Joyce**
Larry Simmons	**Doug Fisher**

Creators/Writers **Johnnie Mortimer, Brian Cooke**
Producer **Peter Frazer-Jones**

Two girls and a boy share a flat at a time when co-habitation was a novelty.

Needing a third sharer to help pay the rent on their Earl's Court flat, two young, attractive girls, dark-haired Chrissy and blonde, toothy Jo, plan to find another girl. But when Robin Tripp, a catering student, is found sleeping in the bath the morning after a party, they decide to let him move in, especially as he can cook. The new arrangement understandably raises a few eyebrows, particularly with the girls' landlords, George and Mildred Roper, who live downstairs.

Although there is much mock-sexual bravado, this *ménage à trois* is definitely not of the murky kind, despite Robin's attempts to bed the far too sensible Chrissy. The well-signalled humour comes from domestic squabbles (like hogging the bathroom), their respective boyfriends/girlfriends, and Robin and Chrissy's attempts to follow Jo's weird logic. There are also nosy interruptions from the Ropers, he a work-shy weakling, she a man-devouring social climber with an eye on young Robin.

Two spin-offs followed: ROBIN'S NEST, in which Robin opens his own bistro, and GEORGE AND MILDRED, following the Ropers' new life on a middle-class housing estate. The series also spawned a feature film of the same title and was translated for American audiences in a less subtle version called *Three's Company*.

Man Alive ★★

UK (BBC) Current Affairs. BBC 2 1965–82

Editors **Desmond Wilcox, Bill Morton**
Producer **Michael Latham**

Social pains and pleasures examined through the lives of ordinary people.

This long-running documentary series took an interest in the problems and sometimes the happier experiences of ordinary citizens, tackling awkward and difficult subjects in the process. Each film focused on one topic, which could be as varied as agoraphobia and homosexuality. Its production team, originally headed by Michael Latham, comprised such notables as

Desmond Wilcox, Trevor Philpott, Esther Rantzen, John Pitman and Harold Williamson. Variations on the theme included *The Man Alive Report* in 1976 and *The Man Alive Debate* in 1982.

Man at the Top **

UK (Thames) Drama. ITV 1970–2

Joe Lampton .... **Kenneth Haigh**
Susan Lampton .... **Zena Walker**
Margaret Brown .... **Avice Landon**

Creator **John Braine**
Producers **George Markstein, Lloyd Shirley, Jacqueline Davis**

An unscrupulous businessman fights to stay ahead of the game.

Picking up the story related in John Braine's novel *Room at the Top*, and the 1958 Laurence Harvey film of the same name (plus its 1965 sequel, *Life at the Top*), *Man at the Top* concerns Joe Lampton, a pushy, aggressive northerner who has battled his way up the ladder to relative prosperity. Thirteen years on, Lampton now lives in Surrey's stockbroker belt, working as a management consultant. He is determined to stay there and is prepared to pull any stroke to do so. He is also keen on pulling women, as his wife, Susan, is only too aware. In 1973 the series spawned a feature film of its own, also called *Man at the Top* and starring Kenneth Haigh.

Man Called Ironside, A **

US (Harbour/Universal) Police Drama. BBC 1 1967–76 (US: NBC 1967–75)

Chief Robert T. Ironside .... **Raymond Burr**
DS Ed Brown .... **Don Galloway**
Officer Eve Whitfield .... **Barbara Anderson**
Mark Sanger .... **Don Mitchell**
Officer Fran Belding .... **Elizabeth Baur**
Commissioner Dennis Randall **Gene Lyons**
Lt. Carl Reese .... **Johnny Seven**
Diana Sanger .... **Joan Pringle**

Creator **Collier Young**
Executive Producers **Joel Rogosin, Cy Chermak**

A wheelchair-bound cop still gets his man.

Raymond Burr followed up his enormously successful PERRY MASON role with this series about a top detective who faces early retirement after receiving a crippling injury. Robert T. Ironside is Chief of Detectives in the San Francisco Police Department, but his career is placed on the line when, at the age of 46, he is badly injured by a bullet from a would-be assassin. He is expected to quit the force but, although confined to a wheelchair, he persuades his superior, Commissioner Randall, to allow him to stay on in a consultative capacity.

So it is that, paralysed from the waist down, the grouchy Ironside is still able to put his 25 years of experience to good use. Living in and working from a converted attic above the police department, he travels to the scenes of crime in a modified police van, assisted and minded by Mark Sanger. Sanger used to be a juvenile delinquent, a street rebel, but he mellows so much during the series that he even graduates from law school before it ends. Two other colleagues, Sgt Ed Brown and policewoman Eve Whitfield, help put Ironside's ideas into action, with Eve replaced after a few seasons by new policewoman Fran Belding. In America, the show was known simply as *Ironside*. In the UK, some episodes aired under the umbrella title of *The Detectives*.

Man Called Shenandoah, A **

US (MGM) Western. ITV 1966–7 (US: ABC 1965–6)

Shenandoah .... **Robert Horton**

Creator/Executive Producer **E. Jack Neuman**
Producer **Fred Freiberger**

A cowboy with amnesia wanders the Wild West looking for his true identity.

Some time after the American Civil War has ended, a man wounded in a gunfight is found by two buffalo-hunters, who take him to the nearest town in the hope of claiming a bounty. As it happens, he is not on the wanted list, but no one actually knows who he is. He recovers but continues to suffer from memory loss. He adopts the name of Shenandoah and sets out to find his real self. Drifting from town to town, he searches in vain for clues that will help him discover his identity. Fortunately, star Robert Horton was no stranger to travelling the prairies, having previously appeared in WAGON TRAIN.

Man Dog *

UK (BBC) Children's Science Fiction. BBC 1 1972

Kate .... **Carol Hazell**
Sammy .... **Jane Anthony**
Duncan .... **Adrian Shergold**
Henry .... **Roy Boyd**
Halmar .... **Jonathan Hardy**
Mrs Morris .... **Mollie Sugden**
Mr Morris .... **John Rapley**
Gala .... **Derek Martin**
Levin .... **Christopher Owen**

Writer **Peter Dickinson**
Producer **Anna Home**

Three kids and their dog assist refugees from the future.

A period of detention at school is the start of an amazing adventure for teenagers Kate and Sammy. Spotting something bizarre – a man walking through a closed door – they investigate further and, with Kate's brother, Duncan, they are soon embroiled in something dark and mysterious. It transpires that aliens known as The Group, from 600 years into the future, are at large on Earth, apparently pursued by police from their own time. They force the children to say nothing about their presence and one of the aliens takes over the mind of Sammy's dog, Radnor. Anna Home and Paul Stone directed the six episodes between them.

Man from Atlantis **

US (Solow) Science Fiction. ITV 1977–8 (US: NBC 1977–8)

Mark Harris .... **Patrick Duffy**
Dr Elizabeth Merrill .... **Belinda J. Montgomery**
C. W. Crawford .... **Alan Fudge**
Mr Schubert .... **Victor Buono**
Brent .... **Robert Lussier**

Executive Producer **Herbert F. Solow**
Producer **Herman Miller**

● *An underwater man works for the secret services.*

When a half-man, half-fish is washed up on the California shore, it is believed that he is the last survivor of the lost continent of Atlantis. Nursed back to health by naval doctor Elizabeth Merrill, Mark Harris (as she christens him) stays on to work with her and the Foundation for Oceanic Research in their efforts to learn more about the seas. He is also employed by the US Government to help combat marine crime (and, on occasion, even space aliens).

Green-eyed Mark looks human but benefits from extra-sharp senses and superhuman strength. His webbed feet and hands allow him to swim faster than a dolphin. He also has gill tissue instead of lungs, which forces him to return to the sea to breathe every 12 hours. Mark and Elizabeth use a submersible known as the *Cetacean* on their sea patrols and work for Foundation head C. W. Crawford. Their biggest adversaries are mad scientist Mr Schubert and his inept sidekick, Brent.

Man from Interpol, The ✱

UK (Danziger) Police Drama. ITV 1960–1

Commander Anthony Smith ..	**Richard Wyler**
Supt. Mercer	**John Longden**

Producers **Edward J. Danziger, Harry Lee Danziger**

● *The cases of a top Interpol agent.*

Tony Smith is one of Interpol's leading men. His investigations take him all around the world, tracking down international criminals and, occasionally, spies. He specializes in cases where crime crosses national borders, pursuing his targets from country to country. Despite scripts by the likes of Brian Clemens, and guest appearances from John Le Mesurier, Peter Vaughan, Rolf Harris and others, the low-budget productions later gained a reputation for being somewhat unexciting.

Man from U.N.C.L.E., The ✱✱✱

US (MGM/Arena) Secret Agent Drama. BBC 1 1965–8
(US: NBC 1964–8)
DVD: Warner Home Video

Napoleon Solo	**Robert Vaughn**
Illya Kuryakin	**David McCallum**
Mr Alexander Waverly	**Leo G. Carroll**
Lisa Rogers	**Barbara Moore**

Creators **Norman Felton, Sam Rolfe**
Executive Producer **Norman Felton**

● *The counter-conspiracy assignments of a secret agent and his partner.*

The 'Man from U.N.C.L.E.' is Napoleon Solo, a suave, relaxed American agent working for an undercover, international, anti-crime organization. U.N.C.L.E. stands for United Network Command for Law and Enforcement, and head of its agents is elderly Englishman Alexander Waverly. Solo is accompanied on most of his missions by Illya Kuryakin, a sullen blond Russian. Their efforts chiefly centre on foiling the ambitious plans of THRUSH, an eccentric global crime syndicate. Each episode is entitled '*The . . . Affair*' (fill in the blank as appropriate).

U.N.C.L.E. headquarters are located in Manhattan, with a secret entrance behind the Del Floria tailor's shop. Agents enter the shop and the tailor lifts a clothes press to open a hidden door in a changing cubicle. Once inside, the agents don special triangular badges to allow them to pass through the corridors of the office. Each agent has his own numbered badge: Solo's is 11, Waverly's 1 and Kuryakin's 2. Solo and Kuryakin never go into action without a collection of electronic gadgetry, including two-way radios concealed in fountain pens. 'Open Channel D' paves the way for a message back to HQ. Yet, for all this technology, the pair constantly require help from ordinary civilians (often a beautiful girl falling for Solo's charms) in achieving their goals.

The Man from U.N.C.L.E. came to TV on the back of the James Bond craze. The name Napoleon Solo was actually borrowed from a gangster in *Goldfinger*, and producer Norman Felton consulted Bond author Ian Fleming before developing the series. Catching the secret agent wave, *The Man from U.N.C.L.E.* was, all the same, played with tongues firmly in cheeks (more so even than the Bond originals). However, a couple of years later, following criticism of its spoofiness, the series was firmed up, and a new character, that of Mr Waverly's secretary, Lisa Rogers, was introduced. The show also spawned a spin-off, THE GIRL FROM U.N.C.L.E. (with which it alternated weekly in the UK), and a series of eight full-length movies, collated from the TV footage.

The acronym 'U.N.C.L.E.' was given its meaning only after the series had started, in response to viewers' requests for an explanation of the letters. 'THRUSH' was never spelt out.

Man in a Suitcase ✱✱

UK (ITC) Detective Drama. ITV 1967–8
DVD: Network

McGill	**Richard Bradford**

Creators **Richard Harris, Dennis Spooner**
Producer **Sidney Cole**

● *A discredited CIA agent turns to detective work.*

McGill is a grim, tough man of few words. A former US intelligence agent, he was wrongly accused of allowing a top scientist to defect to the USSR and, framed and sacrificed in the name of international diplomacy, was dismissed from his post, his reputation in tatters. With only a battered suitcase and a gun to his name, he now operates as a private detective and bounty-hunter in Britain and on the Continent, never relenting in his search for the evidence which will clear his name.

McGill (whose first name is supposedly John but is never used) charges $500 a day (plus expenses) for his work, although he is sometimes cheated by shady employers. Having a dodgy past himself, and lacking friends in authority, there is very little he can do about it. And that is not the only complication. His former CIA colleagues are always lurking in the background, blackmailing him into doing jobs or threatening to drop him in it at any moment.

Man in Room 17, The ✱✱

UK (Granada) Detective Drama. ITV 1965–6

Oldenshaw	**Richard Vernon**
Dimmock	**Michael Aldridge**
Sir Geoffrey Norton	**Willoughby Goddard**
Imlac Defraits	**Denholm Elliott**

Creator **Robin Chapman**
Producer **Richard Everitt**

● ***Two top criminologists solve the most baffling crimes without even leaving their office.***

Room 17, based near the Houses of Parliament, was set up by the Government to house the Department of Social Research, a secret unit for investigating the criminal mind. The actual 'Man' is Oldenshaw, a barrister, ex-war correspondent and crime specialist, who recruits as his partner the younger Dimmock, a former student of the Ohio University Institute of Criminology. Together the two men out-think the most experienced police and counter-intelligence brains in the country. If Scotland Yard or the Government ever find themselves in need of assistance, they call upon this far-from-dynamic duo, whose brain power always delivers the goods. Civil servant Sir Geoffrey Norton is their link with the outside world.

In the second season, Dimmock is replaced by a new specialist, Defraits, but the original pairing are reunited in a follow-up series, THE FELLOWS. To firmly detach the 'Men' and their cerebral work from the sweat and grime of street detection, two film crews with different directors were employed. One handled the scenes inside the Room, the other the rest of the action.

Man of the World ★★

UK (ATV) Adventure. ITV 1962–3

Mike Strait .... **Craig Stevens**
Maggie .... **Tracey Reed**
Hank .... **Graham Stark**

Producer **Harry Fine**

● ***The adventurous life of a globe-trotting photo-journalist.***

American Mike Strait enjoys a glamorous lifestyle. His freelance assignments (mostly for fashion magazines) take him to the four corners of the world (or rather Shepperton Studios). However, instead of merely photographing or reporting his story, Strait unfailingly becomes involved in the action, finding himself up to his neck in murder, blackmail, espionage and intrigue of all kinds. *Man of the World* gave rise to a spin-off series, THE SENTIMENTAL AGENT, drawn from an episode of the same title, in which Carlos Thompson played the part of import–export agent Carlos Varela.

Manageress, The ★★

UK (Zed) Drama. Channel 4 1989–90

Gabriella Benson .... **Cherie Lunghi**
Camilla Power *(young)*
Martin Fisher .... **Warren Clarke**
Eddie Johnson .... **Tom Georgeson**
Sergio Rebecchi .... **Sergio Fantoni**
Gary Halliwell .... **Mark McGann**
Jim Wilson .... **Stephen Tompkinson**
Simon Benson .... **Paul Geoffrey**
Charlie O'Keefe .... **David Cheesman**
Tony Morris .... **Robbie Gee**
Terry Moir .... **Joe Dixon**
Perry Gardner .... **Mark Adams**
Trevor Coughlan .... **Glyn Grimstead**
Willie Young .... **James Grant**

Writers **Stan Hey, Neville Smith**
Producers **Glenn Wilhide, Sophie Balhetchet**

● ***An inexperienced woman is appointed manager of a professional soccer team.***

It seems the height of folly and personal indulgence when a wealthy Italian businessman buys a club in the English second division and installs his daughter as manager. The press has a field day, considering it a publicity stunt, the club's rivals laugh behind their hands and the players feel personally insulted. However, Gabriella Benson is no fool, despite her closest working experience being as a teacher of aerobics. Crazy about soccer since she was a slip of a girl, she knows her onions and manages not only to win over her critics and shrug off sexist taunts, but to bring respectability to a struggling team, too. Among the prominent players are captain Gary Halliwell and strikers Charlie O'Keefe and Tony Morris. Eddie Johnson assists Gabriella as team coach during her first season at the helm, giving way in season two to Willie Young. Simon is the 'soccer widower' husband. It was decided that most of the 'playing' actors would be chosen for their footballing ability first, and their acting skills second, in the search for realism on the pitch. To avoid a 'Roy of the Rovers' artificiality, the football club was never actually named. Two series of six episodes were made, directed by Christopher King.

Mancuso, FBI ★★

US (Steve Sohner) Police Drama. BBC 1 1990–1 (US: NBC 1989–90)

Nick Mancuso .... **Robert Loggia**
Kristen Carter .... **Lindsay Frost**
Eddie McMasters .... **Fredric Lehne**
Dr Paul Summers .... **Charles Siebert**
Jean St John .... **Randi Brazen**

Creator **Steve Sohner**
Executive Producers **Steve Sohner, Jeff Bleckner**

● ***A cynical FBI man has a unique approach to tackling high-level crime.***

Nick Mancuso has served the FBI long and well, albeit in his own disrespectful and independent way. When he is about to retire, however, he is asked to stay on to take on the dirty tasks regular officers can't handle, such as rooting out corruption in government circles or putting a lid on international crises. Helping the grouchy veteran are secretary Jean St John, lawyer Kristen Carter and forensics specialist Dr Paul Summers, while monitoring his progress is his young boss, Eddie McMasters. Robert Loggia had first played Mancuso in a 1988 mini-series called *Favorite Son.*

Manhunt ★★

UK (LWT) Drama. ITV 1970

Jimmy Porter .... **Alfred Lynch**
Vincent .... **Peter Barkworth**
Nina .... **Cyd Hayman**
Adelaide .... **Maggie Fitzgibbon**
Abwehr Sgt Gratz .... **Robert Hardy**
Lutzig .... **Philip Madoc**

Creator/Executive Producer **Rex Firkin**
Producer **Andrew Brown**

● ***Heroic tales of French Resistance activity during World War II.***

Using Beethoven's Fifth Symphony as its theme tune (echoing its use as a wartime code by the Allies), *Manhunt* tells of the daring exploits of Resistance workers who seek to sabotage German activities and smuggle stranded airmen or vital supplies to Britain from occupied France. The principals are agents Vincent and Nina, plus downed RAF pilot Jimmy. Together, they are on the run from the Nazis, headed by Abwehr Sgt Gratz. Fear, conscience, loyalty and suspicion compete for control of their minds, and a tense atmosphere pervades all 26 episodes.

Manimal ✳

US (Glen A. Larson/Twentieth Century-Fox) Science Fiction. BBC 1 1984 (US: NBC 1983)

Prof. Jonathan Chase .... **Simon MacCorkindale**
Det. Brooke McKenzie .... **Melody Anderson**
Tyrone 'Ty' Earle .... **Michael D. Roberts**
Lt. Nick Rivera .... **Reni Santoni**

Narrator **William Conrad**

Creators/Producers **Glen A. Larson, Donald R. Boyle**

● ***A zoologist catches criminals by adopting animal forms.***

Jonathan Chase is a professor at New York University, where he specializes in animal behaviour. As a sideline, he doubles up as consultant to the NYPD on animal use in criminology, but he proves more useful to the force than they know. Because he is able to transform himself into any animal at will (a trick his late father picked up in the jungle), he can temporarily mutate into cats, snakes, hawks or whatever to work undercover, or even to physically corner crooks. Ty Earle is Chase's streetwise buddy and a former colleague from Vietnam; Brooke McKenzie is the female officer who takes a shine to our hero. Only these two know Chase's secret. Nick Rivera is their boss. This short-lived series of just seven episodes swiftly followed a pilot in which Glynn Turman played the part of Earle.

Mannix ✳✳

US (Paramount) Detective Drama. ITV 1968–76 (US: CBS 1967–75)

Joe Mannix .... **Mike Connors**
Lou Wickersham .... **Joseph Campanella**
Peggy Fair .... **Gail Fisher**
Lt. Adam Tobias .... **Robert Reed**
Lt. George Kramer .... **Larry Linville**
Lt. Art Malcolm .... **Ward Wood**

Creators **Richard Levinson, William Link**
Executive Producer **Bruce Geller**
Producers **Ivan Goff, Ben Roberts**

● ***A private eye prefers fists to computers when trying to get results.***

Joe Mannix works for Lou Wickersham, head of an enterprising, high-tech Los Angeles detective firm known as Intertect. Despite being equipped with the latest crime-prevention technology (including a car computer that transmits and receives photographs and fingerprints of suspects), Mannix is more at home using the tried and tested combination of his own detective nous and the good, old-fashioned knuckle sandwich.

After leaving Intertect he becomes his own boss, setting up a detective agency on the first floor of his apartment block at 17 Paseo Verdes in West LA, and employing widow Peggy Fair as his personal assistant. Her husband (a police officer and a friend of Mannix's) was killed in action and she turns out to be more than just a secretary herself, lending a hand in investigations and often being held hostage for her pains. Several LA cops also chip in from time to time, most notably Lieutenants Adam Tobias, Art Malcolm and George Kramer (the last played by the late Larry Linville, better known as Frank Burns in M*A*S*H)

Manville, Lesley

(1956–)

Brighton-born actress who first gained prominence as teenager Rosemary Kendall in EMMERDALE FARM. She has since moved on to a mix of comedy and dramatic roles, including Helen Wyatt in *A Bunch of Fives*, Nikki in *King Cinder*, Rachel Elliot/Fortune in SOLDIER, SOLDIER, Rosie in *Goggle Eyes*, Margot in *The Mushroom Picker*, Melissa Quigley in AIN'T MISBEHAVIN', Beattie Freeman in TEARS BEFORE BEDTIME, Ellie in *The Bite* and Susannah Peel in *Painted Lady*. Lesley also played Hilary in *Holding On*, Karen in REAL WOMEN, Nadine in *Other People's Children*, Villy in THE CAZALETS, Dora Bruce in *Plain Jane*, Mandy Greenfield in *Bodily Harm*, Salvation Army captain Annie Walsh in *Promoted to Glory* and Maria Hale in *North and South*. Guest appearances have come in series like THE GENTLE TOUCH, BULMAN, CORONATION STREET, KAVANAGH QC, SILENT WITNESS, ROSE AND MALONEY and AGATHA CHRISTIE'S POIROT. Manville was once married to actor Gary Oldman.

Many Wives of Patrick, The ✳✳

UK (LWT) Situation Comedy. ITV 1976–8

Patrick Woodford .... **Patrick Cargill**
Harold Randall .... **Robin Parkinson**
Elizabeth Woodford .... **Ursula Howells**
Nancy Grenville .... **Elspet Gray**
Gerald Grenville .... **Thorley Walters**
Josephine Fabré .... **Wendy Williams**
Laura Ryder .... **Bridget Armstrong**
Betsy Vanderhoof .... **Lorna Dallas**
Helen Woodford .... **Elizabeth Counsell**
Amanda Woodford .... **Wendy Padbury**
Madeleine Woodford .... **Julie Dawn Cole**
Richard Woodford .... **David Simeon**
Edgar Ryder .... **Brian Wilde**
David Woodford .... **Patrick Ryecart**
Mother .... **Agnes Lauchlan**

Creators **William G. Stewart, Patrick Cargill, Colin Frewin**
Writer **Richard Waring**
Producer **William G. Stewart**

● ***A wealthy antiques dealer has trouble with his numerous wives and offspring.***

Henry VIII probably had the right idea by bumping some of them off. It's all very well having six wives, but if they're all still alive and likely to descend upon you at any moment, life suddenly becomes very complicated. Such is the world of Patrick Woodford, the well-to-do proprietor of the Woodford Gallery antiques emporium in Bond Street and driver of a yellow Rolls-Royce. Though he lives in luxury in Chester Square, Belgravia, and claims to be in his mid-to-late 40s, he certainly hasn't aged too well, probably thanks to the hassle inflicted upon him by his assorted wives and nine children. So complicated is his personal life, he needs to consult various charts and a family tree every day to help him keep track of all the birthdays, wedding anniversaries, etc., often falling back on the loyal attentions of his manservant/secretary, Harold, to help him out of a hole. The six wives are Elizabeth, whom he married at the age of 18 and now wants back; Nancy, now married to Gerald; Josephine, a French girl; Laura, now wed to Edgar; American Betsy; and his current but estranged wife, Helen, who refuses to grant him a divorce without an avalanche of alimony. His nine children are: Victoria, David, Madeleine, Margaret, Amanda, Gordon, Nicholas and two Richards (all seen only rarely, or not at all). Not far removed from the situation explored in Father, Dear Father, *The Many Wives of Patrick* was yet another farce vehicle for Patrick Cargill. Johnny Johnston wrote the music.

Mapp & Lucia ✶✶

UK (LWT) Comedy Drama. Channel 4 1985–6
DVD: Acorn Media/Cinema Club

Elizabeth Mapp/Mapp-Flint ... **Prunella Scales**
Emmeline 'Lucia' Lucas .... **Geraldine McEwan**
Georgie Pillson .... **Nigel Hawthorne**
'Quaint' Irene Cole .... **Cecily Hobbs**
Major Benjamin 'Benjy' Flint . **Denis Lill**
Mr Algernon Wyse .... **Geoffrey Chater**
Mrs Susan Wyse .... **Marion Mathie**
Grosvenor .... **Geraldine Newman**
Cadman .... **Ken Kitson**
Padre (Revd Kenneth Bartlett) .... **James Greene**
Godiva 'Diva' Plaistow .... **Mary MacLeod**

Writer **Gerald Savory**
Executive Producer **Nick Elliott**
Producer **Michael Dunlop**

● ***Two women battle to be top dog in a seaside village.***

Elizabeth Mapp and Lucia Lucas are social rivals in the well-to-do circles of 1930s England. Lucia's home village of Riseholme, in the Cotswolds, has become rather too claustrophobic after the death of her dear Peppino (late husband), so she decides to rent Miss Mapp's house (Mallards) in the Sussex resort of Tilling-on-Sea. She takes with her a simpering, toupéed twit of a friend named Georgie, a fop charmed by her little diversions into the Italian language but scared rigid that she might ask for his attentions in a physical way. The scene is set for a long-drawn-out game of social oneupmanship, with the practical Mapp trying to outfox her affected but cunning new acquaintance. Playing their parts are the eccentric locals, such as rumbustious Major Benjy (later Mapp's new husband), his monocled drinking companion Mr Wyse, the Birmingham-born Padre who insists on speaking with a Scottish accent, and the androgynous artist 'Quaint' Irene Cole. The series was based on the novels by E. F. Benson that began with *Queen Lucia* in 1920. Jim Parker provided the sweeping theme music.

Marchant, Tony

British dramatist whose acclaimed, uncompromising work has included TAKE ME HOME, *Goodbye Cruel World, Into the Fire, Holding On*, GREAT EXPECTATIONS, *Kid in the Corner, Bad Blood, Never, Never, Swallow*, CRIME AND PUNISHMENT, *The Knight's Tale* for CANTERBURY TALES and *Passer By*.

Marcus Welby, MD ✶✶

US (Universal) Medical Drama. ITV 1969–77 (US: ABC 1969–76)

Dr Marcus Welby .... **Robert Young**
Dr Steven Kiley .... **James Brolin**
Consuelo Lopez .... **Elena Verdugo**
Myra Sherwood .... **Anne Baxter**
Kathleen Faverty .... **Sharon Gless**
Janet Blake/Kiley .... **Pamela Hensley**

Creator/Executive Producer **David Victor**

● ***Doctors-and-patients drama, a kind of* DR KILDARE *or* BEN CASEY *in reverse.***

Thoroughly dedicated, silver-haired GP Marcus Welby runs a practice from his home in Santa Monica, California. After suffering a heart attack, he is forced to take on a younger doctor to help with the workload. That younger man is Steven Kiley, a motorcycling student neurologist. He signs up for a year's experience but never leaves. Unlike previous medical dramas, in which revered old docs had to keep young hothead physicians in check, this series turns the youngster into the level-headed one and makes the older man a bit of a maverick. Kind, reassuring Welby employs an unusual technique in dealing with sickness. He believes in treating the whole patient, not just the precise ailment, convinced that psychological and other factors have some bearing in each case. This is all new to the outspoken Kiley, who plays it by the book.

Both men lead a bachelor existence, though there is a romantic liaison early on for Welby in the form of Myra Sherwood, and Kiley eventually marries Janet Blake, a PR director at the local Hope Memorial Hospital. Other cast regulars are nurses Consuelo Lopez and Kathleen Faverty (the latter played by Sharon Gless, later of CAGNEY AND LACEY).

Margolyes, Miriam

OBE (1941–)

Oxford-born character and comic actress, a Cambridge Footlights graduate (and UNIVERSITY CHALLENGE contestant). Her TV appearances have been many and varied, taking in FALL OF EAGLES, *Ken Dodd's World of Laughter, Kizzy* (Mrs Doe), THE GLITTERING PRIZES, THE WATER MARGIN (voices), THE HISTORY MAN (Melissa Tordoroff), *Take a Letter Mr Jones* (Maria), A KICK UP THE EIGHTIES, FREUD, OLIVER TWIST (Mrs Bumble), THE LIFE AND LOVES OF A SHE DEVIL (Hopkins), BLACKADDER (various roles), MR MAJEIKA (Wilhelmina Warlock) and THE COMIC STRIP PRESENTS ... She also appeared in the US comedy *Frannie's Turn* (Frannie Escobar), COLD COMFORT FARM (Mrs Beetle), THE PHOENIX AND THE CARPET (Cook), *A Little Princess* (Miss Amelia), VANITY FAIR (Miss Crawley), *Moonacre* (Old Elspeth), SUPPLY AND DEMAND (Edna Colley), *Dickens* (Catherine Dickens), AGATHA CHRISTIE'S MARPLE and *Wallis and Edward* (Aunt Bessie). Margolyes has also narrated programmes such as *The Way We Cooked* and presented *Dickens in America*.

Marie Curie ✶✶✶

UK (BBC/Time-Life) Drama. BBC 2 1977

Marie Curie .... **Jane Lapotaire**
Pierre Curie .... **Nigel Hawthorne**
Prof. Lippmann .... **James Berwick**
Prof. Sklodowski .... **Denis Carey**
Eugène Curie .... **Maurice Denham**

Prof. Appell	**Richard Bebb**
Paul Langevin	**Peter Birrel**
Jean Perrin	**Hugh Dickson**
Henriette Perrin	**Sally Home**
Ernest Rutherford	**Clive Graham**
Bronya	**Penelope Lee**
Irène Curie	**Rebekah O'Neill** *(young)*
	Hannah Isaacson *(teenager)*
	Isabelle Aymes
Eve Curie	**Gillian Bailey**

Writer **Elaine Morgan**
Producer **Peter Goodchild**

A poor Polish girl becomes one of the world's greatest scientists.

John Glenister directs this award-winning lifestory of brilliant scientist Marie Curie. The story begins in 1886 with Marya Sklodowska (as she was then) working as a governess on an estate in the countryside around Warsaw. The job is a means to an end: she only wants to earn enough money to follow her elder sister, Bronya, to France and study science. She has family and personal hurdles to clear first, however, and then there is the not insubstantial fact that, as a woman, her career possibilities are limited. Nevertheless, Marie fights on. Once in France, she progresses her studies against all odds and meets the already distinguished Pierre Curie, who initially distracts her from her work. They marry in 1895 and soon they are a powerful team, discovering the radioactive element polonium in pitchblende (uranium ore). Their work is sceptically received, however, and Marie determines to make the great breakthrough, namely to prove the existence of radium – a painstaking feat that eventually wins her a Nobel Prize. The fame this brings does the Curies no favours, alas, and their work is continually hampered. Pierre's health is also worryingly on the wane before he is tragically killed in a road accident. As the series builds to its climax, there is scandal in the air when personal letters between Marie and Paul Langevin, a married colleague, are stolen. Irène and Eve are the Curies' two daughters. Carl Davis supplies the incidental music for the five episodes.

Marine Boy ✶

Japan (Japan Telecartoons/Seven Arts) Cartoon. BBC 1 1969–70

Voices:

Marine Boy	**Corinne Orr**
Dr Mariner	**Jack Curtis**
Bulton	**Peter Fernandez**
Piper	**Jack Grimes**
Neptina	**Corinne Orr**
Cli Cli	**Corinne Orr**

Producer **Hinoru Adachi**

The adventures of a young aquatic hero.

Marine Boy is the son of Dr Mariner, head of Ocean Patrol, an international body dedicated to preserving peace beneath the waves. But Marine Boy is also one of the organization's top agents. Diving into danger, he battles it out with a host of sea foes, including Captain Kidd and Dr Slime, keeping his air-supply alive by chewing Oxygum, a revolutionary oxygen-generating bubblegum. This amazing gum was invented by oceanographer Dr Fumble, who also created Marine Boy's other gadgets, which include an electric boomerang, a bullet-proof wetsuit and jet-propelled flying boots. Assisting our hero are Bulton and Piper, his colleagues in the flying submarine known as the P-1, as well as a pet white dolphin called Splasher, a fishy friend called Cli Cli and a mermaid, Neptina (possessor of a magic pearl).

Marion and Geoff ✶✶✶

UK (Baby Cow) Comedy. BBC 2 2000; 2003
DVD: BBC

Keith Barret	**Rob Brydon**

Writers **Rob Brydon, Hugo Blick**
Producer **Hugo Blick**

The video diaries of a heartbroken but resilient taxi driver.

Keith Barret is a minicab driver who has lost everything he cared for in life, namely his wife, Marion, and his two sons, Rhys and Alun (his 'little smashers'). Nevertheless, the lonely Keith refuses to be put down, as he relates to the video camera installed in his cab. An eternal optimist, he bravely takes viewers through the whole painful course of his marriage breakdown, recalling the happier days he shared with Marion in Cardiff, then the fateful barbecue in which he discovered her affair with her boss, Geoff, through to the trauma of divorce proceedings – all in a series of agonizingly self-deluding ten-minute monologues. To flesh out the story, the unfortunate barbecue is then revisited in a one-off, 50-minute film called *A Small Summer Party* (BBC 2 2001), with Steve Coogan in the role of successful executive Geoff and Tracy-Ann Oberman as the brazenly adulterous Marion. The ever-cheerful Keith returned in 2003, now working as a chauffeur for a wealthy family but still pining for his lost children. The character was then spun-off into a series of spoof talk shows, under the title of THE KEITH BARRET SHOW (BBC 2 2004–5), in which our jovially hapless hero interviews celebrity couples about their relationships in front of a studio audience ('It's just a bit of fun', as he describes it).

Marjorie and Men ✶✶

UK (Anglia) Situation Comedy. ITV 1985

Marjorie Belton	**Patricia Routledge**
Alice Tripp	**Patricia Hayes**
George Banthorpe	**Timothy West**
Henry Bartlett	**James Cossins**
Sid Parkin	**Ronnie Stevens**

Writers **John Gorrie, Peter Spence**
Producer **John Rosenberg**

A middle-aged woman can't find romance – thanks to her meddlesome mum.

Marjorie Belton is a free and easy divorcée, or at least she would be if her interfering old mum would let her be. Every time Marjorie seems on the brink of a new relationship (one per episode), up pops Alice to unwittingly strangle it at birth through her unfortunate matchmaking. During the day, Marjorie works at a bank, under the direction of manager Henry Bartlett, and alongside platonic friend Sid Parkin. In the evenings, she's on the prowl for a new man in her life. *Marjorie and Men* was an early starring role for Patricia Routledge, and a rare sitcom from Anglia Television, but just six episodes were produced.

Mark Saber/Saber of London ✳

UK (Danziger) Detective Drama. ITV 1957–9/1959–61

Mark Saber ..... **Donald Gray**
Stephanie Ames ..... **Diana Decker**
Insp. Brady ..... **Patrick Holt**
Insp. Chester/Parker/Price ..... **Colin Tapley**
Insp. Chester ..... **Frank Hawkins**
Barney O'Keefe ..... **Michael Balfour**
Judy ..... **Teresa Thorne**
Pete Paulson ..... **Neil McCallum**
Larry Nelson ..... **Gordon Tanner**
Bob Page ..... **Robert Arden**
Eddie Wells ..... **Garry Thorne**
Ann Somers ..... **Jennifer Jayne**

Producers **Edward J. Danziger, Harry Lee Danziger**

● ***The cases of a one-armed Scotland Yard detective turned private eye.***

Mark Saber has had a chequered TV history. The character first reached the small screen in the USA as a British detective in the New York Police Department (in series entitled *Mystery Theatre* and *Inspector Mark Saber – Homicide Squad*, both with Tom Conway in the title role). However, when he came to Britain in a production called simply *Mark Saber*, things had changed considerably. For a start he only had one arm! He now worked as a private detective, supported by his blonde secretary, Stephanie ('Stevie') Ames. Two police officers were also prominent, Inspectors Brady and Chester (although Chester was also known as Parker or even Price at times). Later into the action come sidekick Barney O'Keefe and a girl named Judy. This series was not networked in the UK and for US consumption it was retitled *The Vise*.

To add to the confusion, after a couple of years the concept was reworked yet again, with the title switched to *Saber of London* and our hero now undertaking assignments on the Continent. O'Keefe was replaced by Canadian Pete Paulson, who was in turn replaced by Larry Nelson, then Bob Page and then Eddie Wells, a reformed crook. Ann Somers was introduced as Saber's girlfriend.

The programme's star, Donald Gray, was a former BBC announcer who had lost an arm in World War II. He later provided the voice for Colonel White in CAPTAIN SCARLET AND THE MYSTERONS.

Market in Honey Lane/Honey Lane ✳✳

UK (ATV) Drama. ITV 1967–9

Billy Bush ..... **John Bennett**
Sam English ..... **Michael Golden**
Dave Sampson ..... **Ray Lonnen**
Mike Sampson ..... **Iain Gregory**
Jacko Bennet ..... **Peter Birrel**
Jimmy Bentall ..... **Jack Bligh**
Polly Jessel ..... **Pat Nye**
Danny Jessel ..... **Brian Rawlinson**
Harry Jolson ..... **Ivor Salter**
Gervase Lorrimer ..... **Gabriel Woolf**
Carol Frazer ..... **Veronica Hurst**
Al Dowman ..... **Derren Nesbitt**
Tom Mount ..... **Michael Ripper**
Alf Noble ..... **James Culliford**
Stella Noble ..... **Patricia Denys**
Dawn ..... **Julie Samuel**

Creator **Louis Marks**
Producer **John Cooper**

● ***Events in the lives of London market stall-holders.***

Set in London's East End, *Market in Honey Lane* was a rare commodity in the 1960s, in that it challenged CORONATION STREET's supremacy in the ratings for a while. The series focused on the vibrant Cockney workers at the fictitious Honey Lane market, with a different character highlighted in each episode. The characters included fruit-and-veg merchant Billy Bush and the mother and son duo of Polly and Danny Jessel. In September 1968 the title was shortened to *Honey Lane* and transmission was switched to afternoons. The series was cancelled a year later.

The programme was staged and recorded at ATV's Elstree studios. When the BBC took over Elstree, it, too, produced a drama series centred chiefly around London market folk. EASTENDERS, however, has been considerably more resilient than its 1960s predecessor.

Marks, Alfred

OBE (1921–96)

London-born comedian and comic actor, big in the 1950s and 1960s through series like *Don't Look Now*, *Alfred Marks Time* and SUNDAY NIGHT AT THE LONDON PALLADIUM (which he compered). He was Charlie, the fire chief, in FIRE CRACKERS in 1964 and starred as Albert Hackett in another sitcom, *Albert and Victoria*, in 1970. Marks was also a regular on panel games like *Jokers Wild* and appeared in *Paris 1900*, *Funny Man*, MAYBURY, *Lost Empires*, CHILDREN'S WARD and *Virtual Murder* (Professor Zeff), with guest spots in THE PERSUADERS!, JASON KING, THE ADVENTURER, THE SWEENEY, *Dramarama* and LOVEJOY, among other series. One of his last appearances came in *The All New Alexei Sayle Show*.

Marks, Laurence

(1948–)

See *Gran, Maurice*.

Marks, Louis

(1928–)

British writer, script editor and producer, working prominently on science fiction and thriller series like DOCTOR WHO, *Dead of Night* and DOOMWATCH, THE FOUR JUST MEN and the soap MARKET IN HONEY LANE (which he created). He has also produced a number of other notable single and serial dramas, such as *The Lost Boys*, *Grown-ups*, SILAS MARNER, *Bavarian Night*, *The Trial*, *Memento Mori*, MIDDLEMARCH, *Plotlands* and, most recently, DANIEL DERONDA.

Marlowe – Private Eye

See *Philip Marlowe*.

Marr, Andrew

(1959–)

Glasgow-born journalist, the BBC's political editor 2000–5. Marr began his career as a trainee with *The Scotsman*, became a parliamentary correspondent and moved to London, later working for *The Economist* and editing *The Independent*. Immediately prior to joining the BBC he wrote for the *Daily Express* and *The Observer*. Marr has also presented BBC Four's *The Talk Show* and argued the case for Charles Darwin in GREAT BRITONS. Since leaving BBC News, Marr has hosted the *Sunday AM* political programme. His wife is former ITN political journalist Jackie Ashley.

Marriage Lines, The ✶✶

UK (BBC) Situation Comedy. BBC 1 1963–6

George Starling .... **Richard Briers**
Kate Starling .... **Prunella Scales**
Peter .... **Ronald Hines**
Norah .... **Christine Finn**

Creator/Writer **Richard Waring**
Producers **Graeme Muir, Robin Nash**

● ***The highs and lows of newly wed life.***

Recently married George and Kate Starling live in a flat in Earl's Court. George works in the City as a lowly paid clerk and Kate used to be his secretary, but, in keeping with the mood of the times, she now stays at home. This series focuses on their domestic and financial problems, with their compatibility severely tested by endless petty rows that usually see George heading for the pub. Two neighbours, Peter and Norah, are around for the first season, before they move away and up market, leaving the Starlings depressingly stuck on the first rung of the property ladder. Kate later gives birth to a baby daughter, Helen, whom George describes as 'The Cuckoo', because her presence adds to his domestic duties and interferes with his already restricted social life.

The Marriage Lines – known later simply as *Marriage Lines* – was specifically created by writer Richard Waring for the talents of young Richard Briers, who had appeared with him in BROTHERS IN LAW.

Married for Life

See *Married . . . with Children.*

Married . . . with Children ✶✶✶

US (Columbia) Situation Comedy. ITV 1989–94
(US: Fox 1987–97)
DVD: Columbia TriStar (Region 1 only)

Al Bundy .... **Ed O'Neill**
Peggy Bundy .... **Katey Sagal**
Kelly Bundy .... **Christina Applegate**
Bud Bundy .... **David Faustino**
Steve Rhoades .... **David Garrison**
Marcy Rhoades/D'Arcy .... **Amanda Bearse**
Jefferson D'Arcy .... **Ted McGinley**

Creators **Ron Leavitt, Michael G. Moye**

● ***A Chicago family is constantly at war with itself over money and sex.***

Fifteen years of married life, with a demanding wife, two demanding kids and a totally undemanding job as a shoe salesman, is enough to sap the energy from any man, as Al Bundy will testify. Al is the sort of guy who will do anything for an easy life – as long as it doesn't mean giving in to the physical demands of his frustrated, indolent wife, Peggy, for whom the word 'housework' holds no meaning. The teenage kids – bimbo daughter Kelly and lusty son Bud – he can usually buy off with a few bucks, but the daily grind at Gary's shoe store in Chicago – and those horrible feet – is something he just has to live with. All he really wants is the right to be able to drink with his buddies and lust chauvinistically after anything in a short skirt, even if it is only in a glossy magazine. In contrast, next door to the Bundys live Steve and Marcy Rhoades, a young couple who actually enjoy each other's company and the carnal exercise that goes with it. But the Bundy curse eventually takes a hold and Steve leaves. Marcy later marries Jefferson D'Arcy, who sponges off her wages as a banker. Buck is the Bundy family pooch. Frank Sinatra's 'Love and Marriage' is the ironic theme song. *Married . . . with Children* mostly aired in a late-night slot in the UK (presumably because of its adult, some would say 'vulgar', content), with transmissions varying around the ITV regions. It has been seen more frequently, however, on satellite and digital channels. In 1996, Carlton produced a British version of the series for ITV. Entitled *Married for Life*, it starred Russ Abbot as Ted Butler and Susan Kyd as his wife, Pam, but only seven episodes were made.

Marsden, Roy

(Roy Mould; 1941–)

British actor now best known as detective Adam Dalgliesh in the P. D. JAMES mysteries. Otherwise, Marsden has played George Osborne in the BBC's 1967 version of VANITY FAIR, Neil Burnside in The SANDBAGGERS, Jack Ruskin in AIRLINE, Charles Edward Chipping in GOODBYE MR CHIPS, Blick in FRANK STUBBS and Capt. Good in *King Solomon's Mines*. He also appeared in the series of dramatic reconstructions of real events, *Against All Odds*, and played Sir William Boyd-Templeton in *Dangerous Lady*. Guest appearances have come in series like SPACE: 1999, THE NEW AVENGERS, TALES OF THE UNEXPECTED, ONLY FOOLS AND HORSES, VINCENT and *Eleventh Hour*. Marsden was once married to *Airline* co-star Polly Hemingway and is the brother of actor/director Michael Mould.

Marsh, Jean

(1934–)

English actress, best remembered as parlourmaid Rose in UPSTAIRS, DOWNSTAIRS, a series she created with Eileen Atkins in 1971. Twenty years later, Marsh and Atkins also devised THE HOUSE OF ELIOTT. On screen, Marsh has also been seen in the TV version of the film 9 TO 5, playing Roz Keith, in the Sidney Sheldon drama *Master of the Game* (Mrs Talley), the *Screen One* adaptation of *Adam Bede* (Lisbeth Bede) and *The All New Alexei Sayle Show*, as well as starring as Rosie Tindall in a short-lived sitcom called *No Strings*. Other credits include *Agatha Christie's The Pale Horse* (Thyrza Grey), *The Ghost Hunter* (Mrs Croker), THE MAYOR OF CASTERBRIDGE (a vagrant) and guest appearances in THE TOMORROW PEOPLE, KAVANAGH QC, HOLBY CITY, DOCTORS and *Julian Fellowes Investigates*. She was also an early guest in DOCTOR WHO (Sara Kingdom) and appeared in other 1960s series such as *Blackmail* and THE INFORMER (Sylvia Parrish). Marsh was once married to actor Jon Pertwee.

Marsh, Reginald

(1926–2001)

London-born actor, often in sitcoms as someone's boss. After working as a quiz contestant researcher for Granada, Marsh appeared in CORONATION STREET (Dave Smith), GEORGE AND MILDRED (Mildred's brother-in-law, Humphrey), with Harry Worth in HERE'S HARRY and *My Name is Harry Worth*, and with Les Dawson in *The Loner*. Among his many other credits were CROSSROADS (Reg Lamont), THE PLANE MAKERS and THE POWER GAME (Arthur Sugden), *The New Forest Rustlers, The Handy Gang, The Old Campaigner* ('LB'), *How's Your Father* (Mr Winterbottom), *Never Say Die* (Mr Hebden), THE RAT CATCHERS, THE BARON, MRS THURSDAY, BLESS THIS HOUSE, TERRY AND JUNE (Sir Dennis Hodge), THE GOOD LIFE ('Sir'), CROWN COURT, WHODUNNIT?, BARLOW, *The Ravelled Thread* (Higby), THE SWEENEY, *Scarf Jack* (Sir William Wynne), SEARCHING and HELP! Marsh also starred in Joe Orton's play *The Erpingham Camp* and in Nigel Kneale's THE STONE TAPE, as well as his own drama, *The Man Who Came to Die*.

Marshall, Andrew

(1954–)

British comedy writer, for many years in collaboration with David Renwick. Together they worked on BBC Radio before moving into television and providing scripts for NOT THE NINE O'CLOCK NEWS, *Russ Abbot's Madhouse, Alexei Sayle's Stuff, There's a Lot of It About, The Steam Video Company* and *The Kenny Everett Television Show*, as well as creating *End of Part One*, WHOOPS APOCALYPSE and HOT METAL. While Renwick has since scored solo with ONE FOOT IN THE GRAVE and JONATHAN CREEK, Marshall has developed *Sob Sisters*, 2 POINT 4 CHILDREN, HEALTH AND EFFICIENCY, DAD and *Strange*. They joined forces again in 1993 for the Richard Briers comedy IF YOU SEE GOD TELL HIM.

Marshall, Garry K.

(Gary Masciarelli; 1934–)

American actor, writer, director and producer with a string of TV hits behind him and now active in the cinema. After working as a writer on THE DICK VAN DYKE SHOW and THE LUCY SHOW in the 1960s, Marshall went on to greater things in the 1970s, producing THE ODD COUPLE, then creating and producing series like HAPPY DAYS and its spin-offs, LAVERNE AND SHIRLEY, MORK AND MINDY and JOANIE LOVES CHACHI, plus *Makin' It* and the poorly received *Me and the Chimp*. On screen, Marshall has taken small roles in dozens of programmes, most notably MURPHY BROWN, in which he played Stan Lansing. His sister is actress/director Penny Marshall, who appeared in *The Odd Couple* and *Laverne and Shirley* (Laverne).

Marshall, Kris

(1973–)

British actor most familiar as Nick Harper in MY FAMILY. Previously Marshall had made minor appearances in TRIAL AND RETRIBUTION and THE BILL, and played Frank Green in *Metropolis*. After *My Family*'s huge successes, he moved on to star as Pasha in DOCTOR ZHIVAGO, DS Luke Stone in *Murder City*, Art in *My Life in Film* and Dudley Sutton in *Funland*.

Martian Chronicles, The ✶✶

US (Charles Fried) Science Fiction. BBC 1 1980 (US: NBC 1980)
DVD: MGM (Region 1 only)

Col. John Wilder	**Rock Hudson**
Ruth Wilder	**Gayle Hunnicutt**
Sam Parkhill	**Darren McGavin**
Elma Parkhill	**Joyce Van Patten**
Father Stone	**Roddy McDowall**
Genevieve Seltzer	**Bernadette Peters**
Anna Lustig	**Maria Schell**
Father Peregrine	**Fritz Weaver**

Writer **Richard Matheson**
Producers **Andrew Donally, Milton Subotksy**

Man finds a new home on Mars, to the detriment of the indigenous population.

Telling the story of Earth's gradual colonization of Mars, this three-part drama was based on Ray Bradbury's 1951 book *The Silver Locusts* (later renamed *The Martian Chronicles*). The creatures alluded to in Bradbury's original title are the spacecraft that descend on the planet and, like their earthly namesakes, proceed to ravage the local environment. The story begins in 1999 and concludes in 2006, the central figure being Colonel John Wilder, leader of one of the expeditions, who is sent to discover what has happened to his predecessors. Wilder is a man sensitive to the rape of this new world and keen to find a genuine Martian, a race that earlier expeditions, it is believed, have wiped out. But, when the Earth is destroyed by nuclear war, there are few options open to the small colony of humans who now inhabit Mars. Michael Anderson directed.

Martin, Dave

(1935–)

See *Baker, Bob*.

Martin, Dick

(1922–)

American comedian, the writing and performing partner of Dan Rowan from 1952. A stand-in spot for Dean Martin in the summer of 1966 proved to be their big break. As a result, they were given their own gag-and-sketch show, LAUGH-IN, which became a massive international hit. Martin (the dumb one) had earlier been seen in THE LUCY SHOW, playing Lucy's friend Harry Conners, and, post-*Laugh-in*, he made guest appearances in series like THE LOVE BOAT and DIAGNOSIS MURDER, as well as involving himself in directing. Rowan decided upon retirement when *Laugh-in* ended after five years, but died in 1987.

Martin, Ian Kennedy

(1936–)

British screenwriter, usually on crime series, and the creator of *Letters from the Dead*, THE SWEENEY, JULIET BRAVO, THE CHINESE DETECTIVE, KING AND CASTLE and *The Fourth Floor*. Among his other writing credits have been episodes of THE PROTECTORS, THE TROUBLESHOOTERS, *This Man Craig*, SPECIAL BRANCH, *Parkin's Patch*, THE RIVALS OF SHERLOCK HOLMES, HADLEIGH, COLDITZ, THE ONEDIN LINE, *Scorpion Tales*, *Madson* and THE KNOCK. He was also story editor of REDCAP and is brother to fellow writer Troy Kennedy Martin.

Martin, Millicent

(1934–)

Essex-born singer seen as a guest on numerous variety and comedy shows (including with Morecambe and Wise) but chiefly remembered for her contributions (and particularly her topical intros) to THAT WAS THE WEEK THAT WAS. She was later given her own series, *Mainly Millicent*, *Millicent* and *The Millicent Martin Show*, and starred as stewardess Millie Grover in the airline sitcom *From a Bird's Eye View*. She returned to UK TV in 1992, starring as clairvoyant Gladys Moon in the thriller series *Moon and Son*, and has since made prominent cameo appearances as Daphne's mum in FRASIER, as well as appearing in the US daytime soap DAYS OF OUR LIVES. Her first husband was singer Ronnie Carroll and her second actor Norman Eshley.

Martin, Quinn

(Martin Cohn; 1922–87)

American producer, initially with Desilu, for whom he produced THE UNTOUCHABLES. Branching out on his own, Martin founded QM Productions and was responsible for some of the biggest hits of the 1960s and 1970s, including THE FUGITIVE, THE FBI, THE INVADERS, CANNON, DAN AUGUST, *Most Wanted*, THE STREETS OF SAN FRANCISCO and BARNABY JONES.

Martin, Troy Kennedy

(1932–)

British writer, the creator of Z CARS, although he left after three months, allegedly concerned at the direction the series was taking. He did, however, return to write the last episode. Among his other notable credits have been *Diary of a Young Man* (with John McGrath), *If It Moves, File It*, REILLY – ACE OF SPIES, the acclaimed EDGE OF DARKNESS, THE OLD MEN AT THE ZOO and episodes of REDCAP, OUT OF THE UNKNOWN, FALL OF EAGLES, COLDITZ and THE SWEENEY. Martin has also worked as a writer in Hollywood. He is the brother of writer Ian Kennedy Martin.

Martin Chuzzlewit ★★★

UK (BBC) Drama. BBC 2 1994
DVD: BBC Warner (Region 1 only)

Old Martin Chuzzlewit	**Paul Scofield**
Seth Pecksniff	**Tom Wilkinson**
Jonas Chuzzlewit	**Keith Allen**
Young Martin Chuzzlewit	**Ben Walden**
Montague Tigg	**Pete Postlethwaite**
Tom Pinch	**Philip Franks**
Mercy Pecksniff/Chuzzlewit	**Julia Sawalha**
Charity Pecksniff	**Emma Chambers**
Anthony Chuzzlewit	**Paul Scofield**
Mrs Lupin	**Lynda Bellingham**
Mary Graham	**Pauline Turner**
Mrs Todgers	**Maggie Steed**
Mark Tapley	**Steve Nicolson**
David Crimple	**David Bradley**
John Westlock	**Peter Wingfield**
Mrs Sarah Gamp	**Elizabeth Spriggs**
Mr Chuffey	**John Mills**
Mr Mould	**Sam Kelly**
Betsy Prig	**Joan Sims**
Nadgett	**Graham Stark**
Ruth Pinch	**Cordelia Hayes O'Herlihy**

Writer **David Lodge**
Producer **Chris Parr**

A disinherited young man seeks his own fortune while his family destroys itself with greed.

In this adaptation of Charles Dickens's *The Life and Adventures of Martin Chuzzlewit*, Old Martin Chuzzlewit is a very rich man, but he distrusts almost everyone around him, fearing they are greedy for his fortune. Only his ward, Mary Graham, is close to him and when his grandson, Young Martin, has the audacity to fall in love with her, the old man conspires to get him fired from his job with his scheming architect cousin, Mr Pecksniff. Thus Martin has to make his way in the world (assisted by young companion Mark Tapley), even heading off to America. The lessons he learns make him a reformed character, to the point where, eventually, Old Martin is reconciled with his grandson and Mary's hand is assured. Among the other major characters are the ironically named Charity and Mercy, Pecksniff's daughters; Mercy's devious thug of a husband, Jonas Chuzzlewit (Old Martin's nephew); Tom Pinch, Pecksniff's goodly helper; con merchant Montague Tigg; London boarding house keeper Mrs Todgers; Mrs Gamp, an old nurse who swills gin from a teapot, and her equally sodden friend Betsy Prig.

To re-create the cobbled lanes of Dickens's London, filming of this acclaimed six-part adaptation took place in King's Lynn, Norfolk. Star Paul Scofield played both Old Martin and his estranged brother, Anthony. Pedr James directed. The novel was previously televised by the BBC in 1964 with Barry Jones as Old Martin, Gary Raymond as Young Martin and Ilona Rodgers as Mary Graham.

Martin Kane, Private Investigator ★★

UK (Towers of London/ABC) Detective Drama. ITV 1957–8

Martin Kane	**William Gargan**
Supt. Page	**Brian Reece**

Producer **Harry Alan Towers**

An American private eye moves to London.

Martin Kane is an investigator in New York City. However, now taking up residence in England, he brings his transatlantic talents to bear in the capture of British and European criminals, working closely with Supt. Page of Scotland Yard. Although this odd combination of wise-cracking gumshoe and staid English copper rarely strays outside the office, they still get results.

William Gargan had been the first actor to portray Kane on US television and radio at the turn of the 1950s, and had himself been a private investigator before turning to the stage. He didn't stay with the show for the whole of its US run (three other Martin Kanes – Lloyd Nolan, Lee Tracy and Mark Stevens – were introduced) but, being the original and best, he was brought back for this British version. Ironically, considering the American series had been sponsored by a tobacco company, Gargan later underwent surgery for throat cancer and subsequently dedicated his life to warning others about the dangers of smoking. He died in 1979. The real Martin Kane had not been a detective at all, but was an advertising executive for the J. Walter Thompson agency, producers of the American version.

Mary, Mungo and Midge ✶

UK (John Ryan) Animation. BBC 1 1969
DVD: Contender

Narrators **Richard Baker, Isabel Ryan**

Writer **Daphne Jones**
Producer **John Ryan**

● ***A girl, a dog and a mouse find adventure in a busy town.*** From the Captain Pugwash/John Ryan school of animation came *Mary, Mungo and Midge*, a new offering in the Tuesday WATCH WITH MOTHER slot for 1969. Mary is a little girl who lives with her parents on the top floor of a block of eight flats in a suburban town. Her flat is the one with the flowers in the window box. Mary's two friends are Mungo, a sensible dog, and Midge, a mischievous mouse (usually introduced by a shrill blast of the flute). Their simple adventures largely involve trips up and down in the lift, Midge riding on Mungo's nose, although visits to the toy shop, the fairground, the garage and the hospital also feature. John Ryan drew and animated the series himself, which was filmed by Bura and Hardwick, with music supplied by Johnny Pearson.

Mary Tyler Moore Show, The ✶✶✶✶

US (MTM) Situation Comedy. BBC 1 1971–2 (US: CBS 1970–7)
DVD: Fox (Region 1 only)

Mary Richards	**Mary Tyler Moore**
Lou Grant	**Edward Asner**
Ted Baxter	**Ted Knight**
Murray Slaughter	**Gavin MacLeod**
Rhoda Morgenstern	**Valerie Harper**
Phyllis Lindstrom	**Cloris Leachman**
Bess Lindstrom	**Lisa Gerritsen**
Gordon 'Gordy' Howard	**John Amos**
Georgette Franklin/Baxter	**Georgia Engel**
Sue Ann Nivens	**Betty White**

Creators/Writers/Executive Producers **James L. Brooks, Allan Burns**
Producers **Ed Weinberger, Stan Daniels**

● ***Life at work and at home with an independent single girl.*** This award-winning sitcom is set in the newsroom of a fictitious Minneapolis TV station, WJM-TV, Channel 12, and focuses on the working and domestic lives of Mary Richards, the assistant producer of its news programme. Mary, single, friendly, level-headed and very genuine, is also independently minded, a sensible career woman of the 1970s. She arrives at WJM-TV following a break-up with her boyfriend. Her boss at the station is Lou Grant, the blustering news producer, with other staff members including the chief news-writer, Murray Slaughter, weatherman Gordy Howard, and Ted Baxter, the dim, conceited anchorman. The newsroom is a real family, even if it is the worst TV news set-up in America.

Mary's best friend is window-dresser Rhoda Morgenstern, a girl far more in fear of being left on the shelf than Mary. She is eventually written out into her own series, RHODA. Another spin-off was *Phyllis*, based around Mary's highly strung, nosey landlady, Phyllis Lindstrom, who moves to San Francisco with her daughter, Bess, after the death of her never-seen husband, Lars. A later addition to the cast is Sue Ann Nivens, the man-eating hostess of the station's *Happy Homemaker Show*.

When Mary Tyler Moore decided to call it a day, the series was concluded by introducing new management who sack virtually all the staff. Only bumbling newsreader Ted keeps his job. Lou Grant is another survivor, moving on to Los Angeles and his own drama series, LOU GRANT. After success in the 1960s as Laura Petrie in THE DICK VAN DYKE SHOW, Mary Tyler Moore confirmed her star status with this role. Not only that, but the programme established her powerful MTM production company and provided valuable early experience for the creators and performers of many top sitcoms of the 1980s (including producer James L. Brooks, the brains behind TAXI and THE SIMPSONS).

Mary Whitehouse Experience, The ✶✶

UK (Spitting Image) Comedy. BBC 2 1991–2

Hugh Dennis, David Baddiel, Steve Punt, Rob Newman

Producer **Marcus Mortimer**

● ***Irreverent topical sketch show.*** Nothing to do with the clean-up-TV campaigner mentioned in its title, *The Mary Whitehouse Experience* arrived on BBC 2 heaped with acclaim after its time as a late-night comedy offering on Radio 1. A pilot episode in 1990 was quickly followed by two series of fast-moving sketches and satirical, studenty gags, often built around one theme per programme. To some critics, it was the NOT THE NINE O'CLOCK NEWS of the 1990s.

Masada ✶✶✶

US (Universal) Historical Drama. BBC 1 1983 (US: ABC 1981)

Gen. Flavius Silva	**Peter O'Toole**
Eleazar Ben Yair	**Peter Strauss**
Sheva	**Barbara Carrera**
Vespasian	**Timothy West**
Merovius	**Anthony Valentine**
Falco	**David Warner**
Quadratus	**Dennis Quilley**
Rubrius Gallus	**Anthony Quayle**

Writer **Joel Oliansky**
Executive Producers **Jennings Lang, George Eckstein**

● ***A Roman officer's career is blighted by his failure to defeat a group of rebellious Jews.*** In the year AD 70, the Romans launch an attack on Jerusalem. Though the incursion is mostly successful, some resistance fighters, led by one Eleazar Ben Yair, take refuge in the hills. They defend a seemingly impregnable rock fortress at the summit of Mount Masada and hold out long enough to humiliate the forces of the Roman general, Flavius Silva, who is eventually sent in to disperse the rebellion. Silva is on the brink of retirement, and needs a speedy resolution to this problem, especially when a young and brutal new officer called Falco arrives from Rome and threatens his position. With challenges on two fronts, Silva, reluctantly, finds he has no room for compromise. For his adversary, Ben Yair, the choice is between capture or mass suicide. This four-part, eight-hour mini-series, directed by Boris Sagal, was broadly based on true events and used Ernest Gann's book *The Antagonists* as its template.

Maschwitz, Eric

OBE (1901–69)

Versatile British light entertainment producer, with the BBC from 1926 and holding various posts, including Editor of *Radio Times*, Head of Light Entertainment (1958–61) and Assistant and Adviser to Controller of Television Programmes (1961–3). Maschwitz also worked as a novelist, writing thrillers with Val Gielgud (Sir John's brother) under the pen-name of Holt Marvell. He was an accomplished dramatist and, wearing his lyricist's hat, wrote the words to the songs 'These Foolish Things' and 'A Nightingale Sang in Berkeley Square'. Away from the BBC, he worked for MGM in Hollywood, on films like *Goodbye Mr Chips*, before surprisingly returning to the Corporation in 1958. Those who thought he was of the wrong generation for the new era were quickly proved wrong when he commissioned, among other successes, JUKE BOX JURY, THE BLACK AND WHITE MINSTREL SHOW, WHACK-O! and STEPTOE AND SON. He left the BBC for Associated-Rediffusion in 1963 (for whom he had already produced DESTINATION DOWNING STREET), where he became producer of special projects and worked on programmes like OUR MAN AT ST MARK'S. His first wife was actress Hermione Gingold.

M*A*S*H ★★★★

US (Twentieth Century-Fox) Situation Comedy. BBC 2 1973–84 (US: CBS 1972–83)
DVD: Fox

Capt. Benjamin Franklin 'Hawkeye' Pierce	**Alan Alda**
Capt. 'Trapper John' McIntyre	**Wayne Rogers**
Major Margaret 'Hot Lips' Houlihan	**Loretta Swit**
Major Frank Burns	**Larry Linville**
Cpl. Walter 'Radar' O'Reilly	**Gary Burghoff**
Lt. Col. Henry Blake	**McLean Stevenson**
Father Francis Mulcahy	**William Christopher**
Cpl./Sgt Maxwell Klinger	**Jamie Farr**
Col. Sherman T. Potter	**Harry Morgan**
Capt. B. J. Hunnicut	**Mike Farrell**
Major Charles Emerson Winchester III	**David Ogden Stiers**
Dr Sidney Freedman	**Alan Arbus**
Gen. Clayton	**Herb Voland**
Nurse Kellye	**Kellye Nakahara**
Igor Straminsky	**Jeff Maxwell**
Nurse Bigelow	**Enid Kent**
Sgt Zale	**Johnny Haymer**
Sgt Luther Rizzo	**G. W. Bailey**
Roy	**Roy Goldman**
Soon-Lee	**Rosalind Chao**

Creator **Larry Gelbart**
Executive Producers **Gene Reynolds, Burt Metcalfe**

● ***Life with an anarchic army hospital during the Korean War.***

*M*A*S*H* was based on the film of the same name, starring Donald Sutherland and Elliott Gould. It is rare for a TV spin-off to achieve the success of a mother film, let alone surpass it, but *M*A*S*H* was an exceptional series, as nearly all TV critics agreed. Many have paid tribute to the writing, acting and production skills that enabled it to extract laughter from the most unlikely scenario of a blood-sodden war.

The series is set in the early 1950s, when the American involvement in Korea resulted in the draft not only of soldiers but also of medical men and women, most serving in MASH (Mobile Army Surgical Hospital) units. It follows everyday events in the fictitious 4077th MASH, reflecting and never neglecting the tragedy and futility of war and the seemingly needless loss of life. It is, indeed, an unusual setting for a comedy, but in such numbing circumstances as these, where a sense of humour is vital, it appears very apt.

Bringing mirth out of madness is Captain Benjamin Franklin Pierce, commonly known as 'Hawkeye'. Drafted from his home town of Crabapple Cove, Maine, where he lives with his father, he is Chief Surgeon and is desperately sickened by the pointless bloodshed. Diligent and dedicated to his vocation, at the same time he spurns military discipline and refuses to doff his cap to the powers that be. Master of the wisecrack and the quick retort, Hawkeye can also bring tears to viewers' eyes with his human reflections on the carnage around him.

His roommate, in a tent known as 'The Swamp', is 'Trapper John' McIntyre. Together they alleviate the heaviness of war by playing practical jokes, making advances to nurses and distilling their own liquor. Butt of their humour is the self-centred, by-the-book jerk, Frank Burns, who tries to pull rank but never succeeds. Someone who has more time for Frank is Chief Nurse Margaret 'Hot Lips' Houlihan, a gutsy blonde with a voice like a foghorn. Despite Frank's well-publicized marriage, the two conduct a covert love affair that is the worst-kept secret of the whole war.

In charge of this mayhem is easy-going commanding officer Lt. Colonel Henry Blake. His only concern is discipline within the operating theatre and he is admirably supported by his shy company clerk, Walter O'Reilly, nicknamed 'Radar' after his uncanny clairvoyance, especially when choppers bearing wounded soldiers are due to arrive. Cuddly, bespectacled Radar brings out mothering instincts in all the nurses. He sleeps with a teddy bear and drinks only Grape Nehis on his visits to the well-frequented Rosie's Bar. Spiritual comforter to the unit is chaplain Francis Mulcahy, mild-mannered but never afraid to speak his mind.

After the first season, a new arrival adds extra colour. He is Corporal Max Klinger, a reluctant soldier of Lebanese extraction from Toledo, Ohio. In an effort to wangle a 'Section Eight' (a discharge for madness) he dresses in women's clothing.

*M*A*S*H* also sees other important cast-changes over the series. Colonel Blake is discharged and leaves for home, only for his plane to be shot down over the Sea of Japan with no survivors. His replacement is the horse-loving, ex-cavalry officer Colonel Sherman Potter. Potter is a genial commander with plenty of bark, but his bite is reserved, like Blake's, for medical discipline, allowing the madness instigated by Hawkeye and Trapper John to continue – at least until Trapper ships out. Actor Wayne Rogers left the series to be replaced by Mike Farrell as B. J. Hunnicut, Hawkeye's new accomplice. B. J. (the initials are never explained) is a real family man, shunning all advances and longing to rejoin his wife, Peg, and their little daughter, Erin. Nevertheless, he is as much a joker as Hawkeye, so Frank Burns finds no respite here.

Indeed, Frank's days are numbered. The beginning of the end comes when Margaret marries Lt. Colonel Donald Penobscot. Although he is seldom seen and the marriage is short-lived, it brings her involvement with Frank to an end. After the break-up of her marriage, Margaret mellows somewhat and finds herself more in tune with the rest of the camp; but by this time Frank has gone AWOL and then is dispatched to another unit, to be replaced by an aristocratic Bostonian, Major Charles Emerson Winchester III. Pompous Winchester, like Frank, rooms with Hawkeye and B.J. and he is just as easy a victim. He genuinely believes his blue blood places him in a higher circle than his army colleagues, and he bitterly resents the waste of his enormous medical talents in the 'patch-up' operating theatres of a MASH unit. He does, however, earn a modicum of respect, which sly, sneaky Frank was never able to do.

When Radar is allowed home to help his elderly mother run their country smallholding, his place as clerk goes to Klinger, who abandons his female wardrobe and switches back to traditional military attire. In addition to these primary characters, *M*A*S*H* also sees the comings and goings of many temporary personnel, including psychiatrist Sidney Freedman, who pays occasional visits to check the mental health of both patients and staff.

*M*A*S*H* was deliberately conceived to shame Americans over their involvement in the Vietnam War, which was still under way when the programme started. But its tactics changed over the years and the last episodes are quite different in style from the first. The blatant anarchy has gone and the show has become less a comedy with dramatic moments and more a drama with comic touches. In its two-hour-special finale (which gained America's biggest-ever TV audience), Hawkeye harrowingly suffers a nervous breakdown, Winchester is gutted by the senseless killing of the POW musicians he has befriended, and, while everyone else returns home, Klinger, ironically, decides to stay in Korea, having met and married beautiful local girl Soon-Lee. It wasn't quite the end, though. Potter, Mulcahy and Klinger resurfaced in the spin-off series, *After MASH*. There had been an earlier spin-off, too, entitled *Trapper John MD*, but not featuring Wayne Rogers (it was set 28 years later).

Gary Burghoff was the only leading member of the cast to star in the film version, and Jamie Farr was the only cast member actually to have served in the Korean War. In the pilot for the TV series, the unit chaplain was Father *John* Mulcahy, played by George Morgan. More notable is the fact that Alan Alda won Emmy awards for his contributions as actor, writer and director in the series – a unique achievement. The concept was based on Richard Hooker's novel *M*A*S*H*, which drew on his own experience as a medic in the Korean War. A cover version of Johnny Mandel's theme tune, 'Suicide is Painless', was a UK number one hit for a group called The MASH in 1981.

Massey, Anna

CBE (1937–)

Born in Surrey, the daughter of actors Raymond Massey and Adrianne Allan, Anna Massey's later career has been characterized by her roles as irascible older ladies and maiden aunts. Her leading TV credits have included parts in DAVID COPPERFIELD (Jane Murdstone), THE PALLISERS (Laura Kennedy), THE MAYOR OF CASTERBRIDGE (Lucetta Templeman), REBECCA (Mrs Danvers), *I Remember Nelson* (Lady Nelson), *Mansfield Park* (Aunt Norris), *Hôtel du Lac* (Edith Hope) and *A Tale of Two Cities* (Miss Pross). She was also seen in *Sea Dragon* (Prioress), THE RETURN OF THE PSAMMEAD (Aunt Marchmont), *Emily's Ghost* (Miss Rabstock), NICE DAY AT THE OFFICE (Janice Troutbeck), *A Respectable Trade* (Sarah Cole), HE KNEW HE WAS RIGHT (Miss Stanbury), *Belonging* (Brenda), *Agatha Christie – a Life in Pictures* (older Agatha) and *The Robinsons* (Pam Robinson). Guest spots have come in, among other series, HAZELL, TALES OF THE UNEXPECTED, THE DARLING BUDS OF MAY, INSPECTOR MORSE, THE INSPECTOR ALLEYN MYSTERIES, MIDSOMER MURDERS, *Strange* and THE WORST WEEK OF MY LIFE. Anna's brother was actor Daniel Massey, and her first husband was Jeremy Brett.

Master, The ★★★

UK (Southern) Children's Drama. ITV 1966

The Master	**Olaf Pooley**
Dr Totty McTurk	**John Laurie**
Chinaman	**Terence Soall**
Judy	**Adrienne Poster**
Nicky	**Paul Guess**
Father	**Richard Vernon**
Squadron Leader Frinton	**George Baker**
Pinkie	**Thomas Baptiste**
Jim	**John Woodnutt**

Writer **Rosemary Hill**
Producer **John Braybon**

● ***Two children outwit a despotic genius on a barren Atlantic island.***

Some 500 miles out in the Atlantic sits the craggy outpost of Rockall, windswept, cold and apparently deserted. Two kids and a dog – Judy, Nicky and terrier Jokey – discover, however, that there is more to this inhospitable isle than just a mention in the shipping forecast. While sailing in the vicinity, they clamber ashore and unearth the truth – that this is the base for The Master, a 150-year-old megalomaniac who intends to use his telepathy and advanced scientific equipment to hold the world to ransom. Whom to trust with their secret is the big dilemma facing the kids, and the role eventually falls to supportive Squadron Leader Frinton. Among their enemies are the eccentric scientist McTurk and the Chinaman, The Master's malevolent sidekick. The six-part series was based on a novel by E. H. White (author of *The Sword in the Stone*) and featured a cameo appearance by astronomer Patrick Moore. It was a major network production for Southern TV, launching the company's golden era of action adventure serials for kids, and also provided early exposure for actress Adrienne Posta (billed with the original spelling of her name, 'Poster').

Masterchef/Masterchef Goes Large ★★

UK (Union Pictures/BBC) Cookery. BBC 1 1990–2000; BBC 2 2001/BBC 2 2005–

Presenters **Loyd Grossman, Gary Rhodes; John Torode, Gregg Wallace** *(Goes Large)*
Creator **Franc Roddam**
Executive Producers **Bradley Adams, Richard Kalms, Richard Bryan**
Producers **Phillippa Robinson, Richard Bryan, Melanie Jappy; Karen Ross, Paolo Proto** *(Goes Large)*

● ***Long-running contest for amateur chefs.***

This annual knock-out tournament showcased the very best in home cooking, inviting the viewing public to don their aprons and prove to the experts that top cuisine was not just the preserve of the professional chef. Three contestants each week individually planned and executed a menu to a budget (in an edited-down two and a half hours) which would be tasted and reviewed by Grossman and a pair of celebrity guests (top chefs and showbiz stars). The anxious contenders to the *Masterchef* title waited patiently while the judges 'deliberated, cogitated and digested'. Regional heats led to an end-of-series grand final. One of the 1993 finalists, Ross Burden, has since progressed to TV chef status. A spin-off version for 10–15-year-olds, *Junior Masterchef*, was also seen.

In 2001 the series switched to BBC 2, Gary Rhodes was installed as new host and rules were changed so that contestants needed to prepare two dishes inside two hours. However, the new format lasted only one series. For a few years *Masterchef* was confined to the archives until the success of reality TV shows prompted executives to bring it back, this time with a more ruthless edge. Contestants are now taken to different styles of restaurants and asked to learn the ropes and show their skills within a day. With episodes running daily, the series – now retitled *Masterchef Goes Large* – also employs critics John Torode and Gregg Wallace to praise or lambast the would-be chefs.

Mastermind ★★★

UK (BBC) Quiz. BBC 1 1972–81; 1983–97; BBC 2 2003–

Presenters **Magnus Magnusson, John Humphrys**

Creator **Bill Wright**
Producers **Bill Wright, Roger Mackay, Penelope Cowell Doe, Peter Massey, David Mitchell, Pam Cavannagh, Sally Evans**

High-brow quiz tournament.

Mastermind proved to be one of television's most unlikely hits. Initially airing late at night, because schedulers considered it too academic for the viewing masses, it quickly gained a cult following. When it was brought into peak hours as a short-term replacement, it clocked up huge audience figures, so there it remained.

Each programme (often staged at a university) featured four contenders (never 'contestants'), all taking turns to answer questions on a nominated specialist subject and then facing a round of general knowledge posers. The highest scorer (and sometimes the highest-scoring loser) progressed to a semi-final, in which a different specialist subject had to be chosen. On reaching the four-contender grand final, the participants were able to revert to their original or second-choice topics or opt for a brand-new subject. Chosen topics over the years varied from British Moths, The Works of Dorothy L. Sayers and Old Time Music Hall to Drama in Athens, 500–388 BC, English Cathedrals and the Sex Pistols and Punk Rock. The relentless questioning of host Magnus Magnusson was likened to interrogation. Indeed, creator Bill Wright brought his World War II past into play by echoing the standard interrogation procedure – 'Name, Rank, Serial Number' – in the series' 'Name, Occupation, Specialist Subject' contender introductions. With the lights dimmed, the contender (spot-lit in a lonely black leather chair) was faced with a barrage of notoriously difficult questions for a keenly timed two minutes.

Mastermind was responsible for a couple of over-used catchphrases in the English language. 'Pass' (used to skip a question and save time) became a common reply when someone didn't know an answer to something, and 'I've started so I'll finish' (Magnus's quip when interrupted by the time-up buzzer) was open to all sorts of interpretation. The programme's threatening theme music was called 'Approaching Menace', by Neil Richardson.

On its retirement from television in 1997, *Mastermind* switched to Radio 4, installing Peter Snow as questionmaster. It was revamped for television by the Discovery Channel in 2001, with Clive Anderson asking the questions. *Mastermind* was dusted off (on BBC 2) at Christmas 2002 with a one-off, 40th anniversary contest featuring celebrities Vic Reeves, Adam Hart-Davies, Janet Street-Porter and Jonathan Meades, before returning as a series in 2003, with John Humphrys in the interrogator's chair. *Celebrity Mastermind* later returned for short runs (BBC 1 2004–), soon followed by *Junior Mastermind* (also BBC 1 2004–).

Probably the best-remembered *Mastermind* champions were taxi-driver Fred Housego and train-driver Christopher Hughes, but the following all won the cut-glass *Mastermind* trophy:

Mastermind Winners

1972	**Nancy Wilkinson**
1973	**Patricia Owen**
1974	**Elizabeth Horrocks**
1975	**John Hart**
1976	**Roger Prichard**
1977	**Sir David Hunt**
1978	**Rosemary James**
1979	**Philip Jenkins**
1980	**Fred Housego**
1981	**Leslie Grout**
1982	**No contest**
1983	**Christopher Hughes**
1984	**Margaret Harris**
1985	**Ian Meadows**
1986	**Jennifer Keaveney**
1987	**Jeremy Bradbrooke**
1988	**David Beamish**
1989	**Mary Elizabeth Raw**
1990	**David Edwards**
1991	**Stephen Allen**
1992	**Steve Williams**
1993	**Gavin Fuller**
1994	**Dr George Davidson**
1995	**Kevin Ashman**
1996	**Richard Sturch**
1997	**Anne Ashurst**
2003	**Andy Page**
2004	**Shaun Wallace**
2005	**Patrick Gibson**

Masterteam ★★

UK (BBC) Quiz. BBC 1 1985–7

Presenter **Angela Rippon**

Producer **Dave Ross**

Teatime team tournament for quiz buffs.

This daily contest (shown before the early-evening news) pitted two teams of three quiz enthusiasts head to head, with the ultimate aim of finding the 'Masterteam' of the series. Angela Rippon fired the questions ('Let's play'), which began and ended with a rapid general knowledge buzzer round called 'Team Challenge'. In between, four of the contestants (chosen by their opponents) were placed under the 'Spotlight' and made to answer questions on categories selected from a board of six subjects, ranging from Sport, Cinema, Television or Pop Music to Transport, Food and Drink, Literature or Living World and others. (After a category was selected it was no longer available, diminishing the choice for later contestants.) A letters game called 'In a Spin' punctuated proceedings. For this a team needed to make the longest word possible containing three given letters in sequence, the word by necessity starting with the first letter. Unfinished *Masterteam* games were often carried over to the next day. A team winning two games earned bronze medals; three wins resulted in silver medals, and there were gold medals for teams successful four times (who then retired). The eight highest-scoring teams over the series battled it out in a final knockout tournament. Modest book and record tokens were the material prizes.

The format was later rehashed into *The Great British Quiz* (daytime BBC 1 1994–5, hosted by Janice Long, then Philip Hayton). Angela Rippon moved on to host *Matchpoint*, a contrived, tennis-themed general knowledge quiz from the same BBC production team (daytime BBC 1 1990).

Match of the Day ✶✶✶

UK (BBC) Football. BBC 2/BBC 1 1964–6/1966–

Presenters **Kenneth Wolstenholme, David Coleman, Jimmy Hill, Bob Wilson, Desmond Lynam, Gary Lineker**

Commentators **Kenneth Wolstenholme, David Coleman, Wally Barnes, John Motson, Barry Davies, Idwal Robling, Tony Gubba, Alan Parry, Gerald Sinstadt, Clive Tyldesley, Jon Champion, Jonathan Pearce, Guy Mowbray**

● ***Recorded highlights, and occasional live action, from the day's top football matches.***

In these days when soccer is a prized commodity among TV stations, it is hard to believe that regular football coverage did not begin until 1964, and even then was relegated to BBC 2, the minority-interest channel. (It was felt that the greater clarity of BBC 2's 625-line system would allow the use of more wide shots instead of the close-ups most commonly seen previously.) However, once England had won the World Cup in 1966, the mood changed and *Match of the Day* was switched to BBC 1.

The original format involved the playback of highlights of just one of the day's top games. Not to deter spectators, details of the match being covered were not publicized in advance. The first game televised was Liverpool versus Arsenal at 6.30 p.m. on 22 August 1964 (Liverpool won 3–2, Roger Hunt scored the first *Match of the Day* goal and only 50,000 viewers bothered to tune in). Over the years, a second and then a third match were added, with eventually all the important goals scored in the Premiership reviewed as well. During the late 1960s and 1970s, a regional format was pioneered whereby, after the main match, some BBC studios around the country broadcast highlights of local interest.

The programme's chief commentator for many years was Kenneth Wolstenholme, with other contributors including Wally Barnes, David Coleman, Alan Weeks and Idwal Robling (who primarily covered Welsh action). From 1971 John Motson and Barry Davies (the latter till September 2004) took charge of matches, supported by the likes of Tony Gubba, Alan Parry, Gerald Sinstadt, Clive Tyldesley, John Champion, Jonathan Pearce and Guy Mowbray. The programme's presenters have varied, too, the current frontman being Gary Lineker, and expert analysts have been introduced to highlight the key moments. Jimmy Hill (as well as anchoring the programme for many years) was one. Others have included Alan Hansen, Trevor Brooking, Mark Lawrenson, Gordon Strachan, Peter Schmeichel, Alan Shearer and Graeme Le Saux. With ITV buying up rights to Premiership action (screened in *The Premiership*, ITV 1 2001–4, hosted by Des Lynam and later Gaby Logan), *Match of the Day*'s coverage was confined largely to cup ties for three seasons, before returning to Premiership duty in 2004. This time it was supported by *Match of the Day 2*, a Sunday evening edition for BBC 2, fronted by Adrian Chiles.

The title *Match of the Day* has also been used by the BBC for highlights of the Wimbledon tennis championships.

Matchpoint

See *Masterteam*.

Mathews, Arthur

(1959–)

See *Linehan, Graham*.

Matlock ✶✶

US (Strathmore/Viacom) Legal Drama. ITV 1987–92 (US: NBC 1986–92; ABC 1992–5)

Benjamin L. Matlock	**Andy Griffith**
Tyler Hudson	**Kene Holliday**
Charlene Matlock	**Linda Purl**
Michelle Thomas	**Nancy Stafford**
Cassie Phillips	**Kari Lizer**
Asst DA Julie March	**Julie Sommars**
Les 'Ace' Calhoun	**Don Knotts**
Conrad McMaster	**Clarence Gilyard Jr**
Leanne McIntyre	**Brynn Thayer**
Cliff Lewis	**Daniel Roebuck**
Jerri Stone	**Carol Huston**

Creator **Dean Hargrove**
Executive Producers **Dean Hargrove, Fred Silverman, Andy Griffith**

● ***A brilliant Georgia lawyer disarms opponents with his casual country manners.***

For American audiences, Andy Griffith is a reassuring figure. Having packed in eight years as kindly policeman Andy Taylor in *The Andy Griffith Show*, he returned to the screens in this series as an attorney who never fails. Ben Matlock is like a Southern Perry Mason, a man highly esteemed by everyone, it seems, except his adversaries, who inevitably fall for his homespun charm hook, line and sinker. His easy-going manner and bumpkin drawl fool cocky criminals in every episode as the razor-sharp brief liberally doles out rope and lets the villains hang themselves. Helping Matlock work his wonders are his daughter Charlene, a junior partner in his Atlanta-based firm, and stockbroker Tyler Hudson, who doubles up as Matlock's leg man. These are later replaced by other assistants, including Leanne McIntyre, another of Ben's lawyer daughters, and Conrad McMaster as his new investigator. Also seen is next-door neighbour Les Calhoun, played by Don Knotts, Griffith's former co-star in *The Andy Griffith Show*. A number of episodes took the form of feature-length TV movies. A spin-off series from Matlock was JAKE AND THE FATMAN.

Matt Houston ✶

US (Aaron Spelling/Warner Brothers) Detective Drama. BBC 1 1983–7 (US: NBC 1986–92; ABC 1992–5)

Matlock 'Matt' Houston	**Lee Horsley**
C. J. Parsons	**Pamela Hensley**
Bo	**Dennis Fimple**
Lamar Pettybone	**Paul Brinegar**
Lt. Vince Novelli	**John Aprea**
Rosa 'Mama' Novelli	**Penny Santon**
Det. Lt. Michael Hoyt	**Lincoln Kilpatrick**
Chris	**Cis Rundle**
Roy Houston	**Buddy Ebsen**

Creator **Lawrence Gordon**
Executive Producer **Aaron Spelling**
Producer **Michael Fisher**

A super-rich playboy tracks criminals in his spare time.
Matt Houston hails from a wealthy family, a very wealthy family. Having managed their cattle and oil empire in Texas, he moves to California to look after the family's off-shore exploration rigs. However, Matt spends less and less time in the job once he discovers a new, more exciting hobby: detective work. He proves to be an effective semi-professional sleuth. Helped by his beautiful lawyer friend C.J. and an amiable Los Angeles cop, Lt. Novelli (whose mama often invites Matt for dinner), Matt revels in this new adventure. With Bo and Lamar, a couple of squabbling Texan ranch-hands, also in tow, Houston Investigations is never going to be a lucrative enterprise, but what does that matter to a loaded young guy like Matt, who is surrounded by gorgeous women and all the trappings of a playboy lifestyle, including a luxurious penthouse, his own private helicopter and flashy cars (an Excalibur, a Rolls or a Mercedes)?

In later seasons, Matt gives up his oil interests and devotes himself full time to his hobby. Lt. Hoyt is the new police officer on the scene, and Matt's uncle, Roy, also turns up. A retired detective, he joins his nephew back on the streets, linking up with C.J. and the team's state-of-the-art computer (known as Baby), in pursuit of villains.

Matthews, Francis

(1927–)

British actor, star of the late 1960s/early 1970s detective series PAUL TEMPLE, and the voice of Captain Scarlet in CAPTAIN SCARLET AND THE MYSTERONS. He also appeared in the sitcoms *My Man Joe* (Lord Peregrine Hansford), A LITTLE BIG BUSINESS (Simon Lieberman), *A Roof over My Head* (Jack Askew), TEARS BEFORE BEDTIME (Geoffrey Dickens) and DON'T FORGET TO WRITE (Tom Lawrence). He starred as Eric the Prologue in Alan Plater's TRINITY TALES, was seen in THE WORLD OF TIM FRAZER (Lewis Richards) and *Brat Farrar*, and made guest appearances in NO HIDING PLACE, THE SAINT, THE AVENGERS, *The Morecambe and Wise Show*, CROWN COURT, THE DETECTIVES, TAGGART and JONATHAN CREEK, among other series. More recently he has joined the cast of HEARTBEAT and THE ROYAL as Dr James Alway, and appeared in *All About George* (Ted).

Maughan, Sharon

(Sharon Mughan; 1951–)

British actress as well known for her coffee commercials as for her programme credits, which have included BY THE SWORD DIVIDED (Anne Lacey/Fletcher), THE FLAME TREES OF THIKA (Lettice Palmer), SHABBY TIGER (Rachel Rosing), *Dombey and Son*, HANNAY, THE RETURN OF THE SAINT, INSPECTOR MORSE, THE RUTH RENDELL MYSTERIES and HOLBY CITY (Tricia Williams) – billed in some under her real name of Sharon Mughan. She is married to Trevor Eve.

Maverick ★★★

US (Warner Brothers) Western. ITV 1959–63 (US: ABC 1957–62)
DVD: Warner Home Video (Region 1 only)

Bret Maverick .... **James Garner**
Bart Maverick .... **Jack Kelly**
Samantha Crawford .... **Diane Brewster**
Cousin Beauregard Maverick . **Roger Moore**
Brent Maverick .... **Robert Colbert**

Creator **Roy Huggins**
Producers **Roy Huggins/William L. Stewart**

Two cowardly brothers are professional poker-players in the Wild West.
Maverick is a Western with a difference – it is played for laughs. It features wisecracking Texan Bret Maverick, a full-time card-shark who earns a living by preying on losers. It begins as a traditional cowboy series but soon turns into a spoof on the Old West, despite the introduction of Bret's more serious younger brother, Bart. (Bart was actually added to ease production problems. With two film crews and two stars alternating as leads, twice as many programmes could be produced.)

The Mavericks are wanderers, stumbling into towns with ridiculous names like Bent City and Ten Strike. Unlike other cowboy heroes, these guys are true yellowbellies. When in trouble they follow their pappy's earnest advice: 'Run!' Both are lazy, untrustworthy and self-centred, yet they often find time to help people in trouble. They generally don't cheat at cards and, in case things turn nasty during a game, they keep a $1,000 bill pinned inside their jackets. For a while, Bret has a female rival, attractive swindler Sam Crawford, and the duo spend several episodes trying to out-con each other.

Maverick's gentle mockery of the conventional Western is highlighted when guest stars like Clint Walker (from CHEYENNE) and Ty Hardin (from BRONCO) drop by. Some episodes are also parodies of BONANZA and GUNSMOKE. Like Clint Walker, James Garner fell out with Warner Brothers and was replaced by Roger Moore as Cousin Beau, who, unusually for a Maverick, had won a commendation in the Civil War before moving to England to soak up the culture. A third Maverick brother, Brent, arrived later but, without Garner, it wasn't long before the series came to an end. A few revivals were attempted in the 1970s and 1980s, none with the success of the original.

Max & Paddy's Road to Nowhere

See *Peter Kay's Phoenix Nights*.

Max Headroom ★★★

US (Chrysalis/Lakeside/Lorimar) Science Fiction. Channel 4 1989 (US ABC 1987)

Edison Carter/Max Headroom **Matt Frewer**
Theora Jones .... **Amanda Pays**
Bryce Lynch .... **Chris Young**

Creator **Peter Wagg**

A TV reporter and his computer alter-ego unearth corruption in the bleak future.
This science fiction romp takes the computer-enhanced character of Max Headroom (based on, and voiced by, actor Matt Frewer) back to his dramatic roots. *Headroom* was devised for a one-off TV film in 1984 but shot to fame when developed into his own pop music series for Channel 4 (*The Max Headroom Show*, 1985–7). In this he linked rock videos, his staccato, stuck-screen delivery (in the days when PCs were still rather scarce) engendering cult status. The character was then taken to America where the sci-fi setting was re-explored. In it Frewer continues to play Max, but also Edison Carter, a

TV reporter for Network 23. It is while Carter is recovering from a bad motorcycle accident ('max headroom' being the last words he sees on a warning sign) that a computer version of him is concocted to take his place. Once recovered, Carter continues to nose his way into the underbelly of society, looking for scandals that will boost his channel's performance. Max, meanwhile, indulges himself by popping up on the omnipresent TV screens that, by law, can't be switched off, and haranguing viewers with his wit and sarcasm. Indeed, television spookily dominates this particularly grim view of the world ahead ('20 minutes into the future'). Not only do ratings mean everything but commercials have been condensed into intense short bursts known as 'blipverts'. Theora Jones is Carter's assistant and Bryce Lynch the young researcher who instigated the 'cloning' of Carter.

Max continued to host a music and chat show on US TV while this science-fiction series was running and Matt Frewer cashed in as the new face of Coca-Cola.

May to December ***

UK (Cinema Verity) Situation Comedy. BBC 1 1989–94
DVD: Acorn Media

Alec Callender .... **Anton Rodgers**
Zoe Angell/Callender .... **Eve Matheson**
Lesley Dunlop
Jamie Callender .... **Paul Venables**
Miles Henty .... **Clive Francis**
Vera Flood/Tipple .... **Frances White**
Hilary .... **Rebecca Lacey**
Dot Burgess .... **Kate Williams**
Debbie Burgess .... **Chrissie Cotterill**
Roy Morgan-Jones .... **Paul Raynor**
Simone .... **Carolyn Pickles**
Mr Burgess .... **Ronnie Stevens**
Rosie MacConnachy .... **Ashley Jensen**

Creator/Writer **Paul A. Mendelson**
Executive Producer **Verity Lambert**
Producers **Sydney Lotterby, Sharon Bloom**

Generation-gap romance between a middle-aged lawyer and a young schoolteacher.

When 26-year-old games mistress Zoe Angell arrives in the Pinner offices of Semple, Callender and Henty to make arrangements for her divorce, little does she know that she will eventually marry Alec Callender, the 53-year-old senior partner (and ardent PERRY MASON fan) who handles her case. For sprightly Zoe and lumbering Alec, it isn't love at first sight but, seeing each other out of business hours, their relationship begins to blossom, much to the surprise of Zoe's greengrocer mum, Dot, and her frustrated sister, Debbie. Even more shocked are Alec's prim daughter, Simone, his wise-cracking son, Jamie (who works with him in the office), and the other members of the office staff. These are frumpy secretary Miss Flood and over-familiar typist Hilary. While Zoe and Alec move on to marriage and its inherent difficulties, plus the birth of their daughter, Fleur, so changes take place at the law firm. Jamie is made a partner after the departure of Miles Henty (the company name changes to Semple, Callender and Callender); Miss Flood secures herself a husband, hospital plasterer Gerald Tipple; and the daffy Hilary eventually makes way for an eccentric Scots girl by the name of Rosie MacConnachy.

Mayall, Rik

(Richard Mayall; 1958–)

Anarchic Essex-born comedian/comic actor/writer, whose reputation was established by his role as Rick in THE YOUNG ONES (also co-writer) and its echoes in FILTHY RICH AND CATFLAP (Richie Rich) and BOTTOM (Richie Richard; again co-writer). Earlier, Mayall (once part of an act called 20th-Century Coyote with Adrian Edmondson) had established the character of boring Brummie Kevin Turvey in the sketch series A KICK UP THE EIGHTIES, and also featured in THE COMIC STRIP PRESENTS. He then starred as MP Alan B'Stard in THE NEW STATESMAN and played Lord Flashheart in assorted episodes of BLACKADDER. With Edmondson, he appeared as one of the Dangerous Brothers on SATURDAY LIVE, and among his numerous other credits have been the anthology *Rik Mayall Presents*, *Grim Tales*, *The Lenny Henry Show*, JACKANORY, HAPPY FAMILIES, *In the Red* (Dominic De'Ath), THE BILL, LOVE HURTS, *The Canterville Ghost* (Dampier), JONATHAN CREEK, MURDER ROOMS: THE DARK BEGINNINGS OF SHERLOCK HOLMES, *How to Be a Little S*d* (voice only), THE KNOCK and, in complete contrast, the musical *Horse Opera*. In 2002 he introduced a new character, Professor Adonis Cnut in the Marks and Gran sitcom BELIEVE NOTHING. Since then he has added his voice to the children's series *Shoebox Zoo* and *King Arthur's Disasters*, and starred as George Kinsey in another sitcom, *All About George*.

Maybury ***

UK (BBC) Drama. BBC 2 1981–3

Dr Edward Roebuck .... **Patrick Stewart**
Dr Jennifer Brent .... **Judy Riley**
Sister Barbara Bowley .... **Yvonne Brewster**
Nurse Barry Donovan .... **Michael Melia**
Fred Tarkey .... **Stuart Fox**

Producer **Ruth Boswell**

The cases of patients at a mental hospital.

This adventurous series aimed to paint a more positive picture of mental illness and its related problems by looking closely at a number of psychiatric cases at a fictitious hospital (Maybury General). It was intended that patients were seen as not 'mad people' but as ordinary people suffering from an illness. Central to each case is Dr Edward Roebuck (played by a pre-STAR TREK Patrick Stewart). Various stories overlap during the programme's 13 episodes and, on the whole, reveal how psychiatrists can help but also hinder the recovery of some patients. Among the guest sick are Juliet Stevenson and Kenneth Branagh. A second series of seven episodes was screened in 1983, with Maybury General being demolished and Roebuck relocating to another hospital. Music was by Daryl Runswick. Writers included Anthony Minghella and Douglas Watkinson.

Maynard, Bill

(Walter Williams; 1928–)

Yorkshire-born actor, primarily in comic roles. His TV career was launched in the 1950s, when he shared top billing with Terry Scott in *Great Scott – It's Maynard!*, and then gained his own series, *Mostly Maynard*. After a career downturn, he resurfaced in the 1970s and early 1980s, and was much in demand as Frank Riley in *The Life of Riley*, Stan the Fryer in TRINITY TALES and the accident-prone Selwyn Froggitt in OH NO! IT'S SELWYN FROGGITT and *Selwyn*. He was also the

Reverend Alexander Goodwin in the sitcom *Paradise Island* and Fred Moffat, otherwise known as THE GAFFER. More recently, he has been seen as the petty crook Claude Jeremiah Greengrass in HEARTBEAT and THE ROYAL. Maynard also has plenty of guest appearances to his name, in series as varied as UP POMPEII!, HUNTER'S WALK, FATHER BROWN, WORZEL GUMMIDGE, MINDER, DALZIEL AND PASCOE and CORONATION STREET (music agent Micky Malone), and has made his mark in single dramas (particularly *Kisses at Fifty* in 1973).

Mayor of Casterbridge, The ✶✶

UK (BBC) Drama. BBC 2 1978
DVD: BBC

Michael Henchard .... **Alan Bates**
Susan Henchard .... **Anne Stallybrass**
Mrs Goodenough .... **Avis Bunnage**
Donald Farfrae .... **Jack Galloway**
Abel Whittle .... **Peter Bourke**
Elizabeth-Jane .... **Janet Maw**
Lucetta Templeman/Farfrae .. **Anna Massey**
Jopp .... **Ronald Lacey**

Writer **Dennis Potter**
Producer **Jonathan Powell**

A man's reckless past ruins his highly successful career.
Drunkard Michael Henchard sells his wife, Susan, and baby for five guineas during a fit of pique at Weydon-Priors Fair. Once sober, he deeply regrets his actions and abandons the bottle. Eighteen years later, Henchard has risen to become the Mayor of Casterbridge, wealthy and widely respected. When Susan returns, he insists that they remarry as a matter of honour but this is just the start of Henchard's new woes. He discovers his young manager, Donald Farfrae, is seeing Elizabeth-Jane, the girl he believes to be his daughter, andfires him, only for Farfrae to marry Henchard's own mistress, Lucetta. Susan dies and Henchard's secret past is revealed, reducing his business and his good name to tatters. His life collapses around him, especially when he learns that Elizabeth-Jane is not his real daughter after all, and he turns once more to drink as Farfrae assumes more and more of what was once his, including the position of Mayor of Casteridge. Dennis Potter's adaptation of Thomas Hardy's classic novel of 1886 was directed in seven parts by David Giles. Carl Davis supplied the score.

A new adaptation, by Ted Whitehead, was directed by David Thacker and screened in two parts by ITV 1 in 2003 (Ciaran Hinds as Henchard; Juliet Aubrey as Susan; James Purefoy as Farfrae).

Me & My Girl ✶

UK (LWT) Situation Comedy. ITV 1984–5; 1987–8

Simon Harrap .... **Richard O'Sullivan**
Derek Yates .... **Tim Brooke-Taylor**
Nell Cresset .... **Joan Sanderson**
Samantha Harrap .... **Joanne Ridley**
Madeleine 'Maddie' Dunnock **Leni Harper**
Isobel McClusky .... **Sandra Clarke**
Liz .... **Joanne Campbell**

Creator **John Kane**
Writers **Colin Bostock-Smith, John Kane, Bernard McKenna**
Executive Producer **Humphrey Barclay**
Producers **John Reardon, Malcolm Taylor**

A widower struggles to bring up his teenage daughter.
Simon Harrap, an executive at the Eyecatchers advertising agency in Covent Garden, found himself alone and in sole charge of three-year-old daughter Samantha when his wife passed away. Now Samantha is a teenager and to help him cope with the problems of adolescence, his snooty mother-in-law, Nell Cresset, is part of the household (she is also a director of his company). They also have a housekeeper: initially goofy Scots girl Maddie, later replaced by fellow Scot Isobel. Humour comes from Simon's attempts to set an example and to keep Samantha on the straight and narrow (particularly with regard to homework and boys) while, at the same time, failing to curb his own recklessness. His friend and work-colleague is the heavily married-with-three-kids Derek Yates, and Liz is his secretary. The theme song is sung by Peter Skellern.

Me Mammy ✶✶

UK (BBC) Situation Comedy. BBC 1 1969–71

Bunjy Kennefick .... **Milo O'Shea**
Mrs Kennefick .... **Anna Manahan**
Miss Argyll .... **Yootha Joyce**
Cousin Enda .... **David Kelly**
Father Patrick .... **Ray McAnally**

Creator/Writer **Hugh Leonard**
Producers **James Gilbert, Sydney Lotterby**

An Irishman's style is cramped by his clinging mother.
Forty-year-old Bunjy Kennefick is an Irishman living and working in London. An executive with a large West End company, he drives a flash car and lives in an expensive Regent's Park flat. His secretary, Miss Argyll, doubles up as his girlfriend. Unfortunately, his widowed mother has also crossed the Irish Sea and, being a devout Catholic, is reluctant to give up her innocent son to the heady delights of the English capital – and Miss Argyll in particular. A later addition to the cast is Bunjy's Cousin Enda, another exile from the Emerald Isle. The series began life as a COMEDY PLAYHOUSE pilot in 1968.

Me, You and Him ✶

UK (Thames) Situation Comedy. ITV 1992

John .... **Nick Hancock**
Mark .... **Steve Punt**
Harry .... **Hugh Dennis**
Helen .... **Harriet Thorpe**
Todd .... **Ron Donachie**

Writers **Nick Hancock, Steve Punt, Hugh Dennis**
Producer **John Stroud**

The frustrations of life after college with three old friends.
John is an uncommitted schoolteacher, Mark is hopelessly unemployed and Harry is a thrusting business executive who has just returned from spending three years working abroad: together this trio of flatsharing ex-schoolfriends comprise the Me, You and Him of the programme title. Coming to terms with the real world after the carefree debauchery of student life provides plenty of scope for fallings-out, juvenile behaviour and nostalgic reminiscences in this unusual, partly surreal comedy, the main point being that the three twenty-somethings no longer have very much in common. Just one series of six episodes was produced.

Mears, Ray
(1964–)

English specialist in 'bushcraft', the art of survival and exploration in the wild outdoors. He appeared as the outdoor expert in a BBC series called *Tracks* and then his own series ensued, some telling tales of real-life survival against the odds in the most extreme areas of the planet. These have included *Ray Mears's World of Survival, The Essential Guide to Rocks, Ray Mears's Extreme Survival, Ray Mears's Real Heroes of Telemark* and *Ray Mears's Bushcraft.*

Medics ✶✶

UK (Granada) Medical Drama. ITV 1990; 1992–5

Prof. Geoffrey Hoyt	**Tom Baker**
Ruth Parry	**Sue Johnston**
Dr Robert Nevin	**James Gaddas**
Dr Claire Armstrong	**Francesca Ryan**
Jess Hardman	**Penny Bunton**
Dr Gail Benson	**Emma Cunningham**
Dr Alison Makin	**Teddie Thompson**
Dr Jay Rhaman	**Jimmi Harkishin**
Toby Maitland-Evans	**Jo Stone-Fewings**
Dr Alex Taylor	**Peter Wingfield** **Edward Atterton**
Dr Tom Carey	**Hugh Quarshie**
Gavin Hall	**Ian Redford**
Helen Lomax	**Dinah Stabb**
Dr Sarah Kemp	**Patricia Kerrigan**
Billy Cheshire	**Clarence Smith**
Derek Foster	**Nick Dunning**
Diana Hardy	**Gabrielle Drake**
Janice Thornton	**Susan McArdle**
Stuart Bevan	**Rupert Frazer**
Peter Vance	**Ian Shaw**

Executive Producer **Sally Head**
Producers **Tony Dennis, Alison Lumb, Louise Berridge**

● ***The pressures of work on the doctors and staff at a busy general hospital.***
Described by Tony Dennis, one of the show's producers, as a programme 'about people doing an impossible job', *Medics* focuses on the staff of fictitious Henry Park Hospital, examining the stresses and strains of their intense employment. At the heart of much of the action are Geoffrey Hoyt and Ruth Parry. Hoyt is the flamboyant and eccentric professor of surgery and Parry the embattled chief executive. Contemporary NHS politics thrust their way to the top of the agenda, and personal problems, like the death of Hoyt's wife and his near-fatal car accident, also come to the fore. Increasing attention is also paid to younger members of staff, like student doctor Alex Taylor, house officer Jess Hardman, new mother Claire Armstrong and lesbian doctors Sarah Kemp and Alison Makin, as the series progresses.

Meet the Wife ✶✶

UK (BBC) Situation Comedy. BBC 1 1964–6

Thora Blacklock	**Thora Hird**
Freddie Blacklock	**Freddie Frinton**

Creators/Writers **Ronald Wolfe, Ronald Chesney**
Producers **John Paddy Carstairs, Graeme Muir, Robin Nash**

● ***A northern couple bicker their way through married life.***
Thora and Freddie Blacklock are not unhappily married: they just don't always see eye to eye. Thora is bossy and domineering and Freddie, a plumber by profession, likes to rebel now and again; but whatever divides them is soon forgotten. Theirs is a marriage much like many others, really, allowing viewers to feel comfortable with the characters. *Meet the Wife* was, consequently, a popular series. It stemmed from a 1963 COMEDY PLAYHOUSE presentation entitled *The Bed*, in which the Blacklocks, having just celebrated their silver wedding anniversary, argue over whether to buy twin beds to replace their lumpy and uncomfortable matrimonial double.

Mellor, Kay
(1952–)

English writer and actress, whose scripts have included BAND OF GOLD, PLAYING THE FIELD, JANE EYRE, *Just Us*, FAT FRIENDS, *Gifted* and *Between the Sheets*, as well as episodes of *Dramarama*, BROOKSIDE, CORONATION STREET, CHILDREN'S WARD and FAMILIES (which she created). She is the mother of actress Gaynor Faye (the *Street*'s Judy Mallet), who has appeared in several of Kay's dramas. Mellor herself sometimes appears, too, as in 2002's *A Good Thief*, in which she starred as Rita. She was also seen in *Stan the Man* (Margaret).

Memoirs of Sherlock Holmes, The
See *Adventures of Sherlock Holmes, The.*

Men Behaving Badly ✶✶✶✶

UK (Hartswood/Thames) Situation Comedy. ITV 1992; BBC 1 1994–8
DVD: Fremantle Home Entertainment

Dermot Povey	**Harry Enfield**
Gary Strang	**Martin Clunes**
Tony Smart	**Neil Morrissey**
Deborah	**Leslie Ash**
Dorothy	**Caroline Quentin**
Les	**Dave Atkins**
George	**Ian Lindsay**
Anthea	**Valerie Minifie**
Ken	**John Thomson**

Creator/Writer **Simon Nye**
Producer **Beryl Vertue**

● ***Two friends flatshare in typically squalid bachelor fashion.***
In this series, based on writer Simon Nye's own novel, Dermot and Gary, a pair of overgrown adolescents, are the men behaving badly. This involves sharing a flat in South London, neglecting the washing-up, using colourful language, ogling the girl upstairs (Deborah), drooling over aerobics videos, swilling beer and having limited success with women. After the first season, Dermot leaves to travel the world and is replaced by drippy, unemployed Tony, who instantly falls in love with Deborah. Also seen is Dorothy, Gary's cynical girlfriend (a nurse), Les, slovenly landlord of the local boozer, The Crown (later replaced by the dim, stone-faced Ken), and George and Anthea, Gary's limp colleagues at the security firm where he works. Although initially an ITV sitcom, from the third season the programme was screened on BBC 1, at a later transmission time. This allowed the men to behave just that little bit more badly. The final three episodes were shown over Christmas

1998 and explored Gary and Dorothy's attempts to conceive a child.

Men from Shiloh, The

See *Virginian, The*.

Men into Space ✶

US (United Artists/CBS) Science Fiction. BBC 1960 (US: CBS 1959–60)

Col Edward McCauley .... **William Lundigan**

Producer **Lewis Rachmil**

● ***The adventures of early space-pioneers.***

One of TV's first 'space race' series, reaching American screens less than two years after the first Sputnik was launched, *Men into Space* centres on the exploits of brave astronaut Colonel Edward McCauley, who travels the solar system, landing on other planets, working at the moon base and orbiting Earth in a space station. Dramas and crises revolve around equipment failure or personal problems, rather than alien attacks or visits from bug-eyed monsters. Although many of the series' ideas have yet to come to fruition, this was generally regarded as a sensible, realistic science-fiction series and was produced in semi-documentary style in conjunction with the US armed forces.

Men of the World ✶✶

UK (Alomo) Situation Comedy. BBC 1 1994–5

Lenny Smart .... **David Threlfall**
Kendle Bains .... **John Simm**
Gilby Watson .... **Daniel Peacock**
Mrs Daff .... **Brenda Bruce**
Becky .... **Eva Pope**

Writer **Daniel Peacock**
Producers **Maurice Gran, Laurence Marks, Claire Hinson**

● ***A cuckolded travel agent teaches his lodger how to deal with women.***

Abandoned in his thirties by his promiscuous wife, Lenny Smart has fallen back on the laddish, chauvinistic ways of his youth. Lenny is manager of Tymans Travel in Manchester and, bruised by his marriage experience, decides to educate his young colleague and lodger, Kendle Bains, in the ways and means of handling women – with disrespect high on the list of requirements. Lenny also regales his junior with tales of a golden past littered with sporting, boozing and womanizing triumphs, but Kendle is more sensible and closer to the 1990s image of a 'new man'. Optimistic and ever romantic, he can't help straying from the path his mentor sets out for him, such as when he falls for the lovely Becky in series two. Writer Daniel Peacock also appears as Lenny's pal and partner in crime, Gilby, a window cleaner. Twelve episodes were produced. Stars David Threlfall and John Simm also sang the theme song.

Menace ✶✶

UK (BBC) Drama Anthology. BBC 2 1970; BBC 1 1973

Producer **Jordan Lawrence**

● ***A collection of suspense plays by top writers.***

This anthology of thrillers ran to two series that were one channel and three years apart. The first series offered 13 spine-tinglers, with ten plays in the second series, both including contributions from leading contemporary scriptwriters like Alun Richards, Hugh Whitemore, Ken Taylor, Roy Clarke and Fay Weldon. Each 75-minute story explores the concept of menace, from whatever source it originates, and some include supernatural elements. Stars include Freddie Jones, Gwen Watford, Robert Lang, Sheila Hancock, Peter Sallis, Hannah Gordon, George Cole, Annette Crosbie and Patrick Mower. The second play, *Good Morning, Yesterday!*, featuring Roddy McMillan as a Glaswegian detective, was later developed into a series called THE VIEW FROM DANIEL PIKE. The *Menace* theme music was composed by Don Harper.

Men's Room, The ✶✶✶

UK (BBC) Drama. BBC 2 1991

Charity Walton .... **Harriet Walter**
Prof. Mark Carleton .... **Bill Nighy**
James Walton .... **Patrick Drury**
Jane Carleton .... **Mel Martin**
Sally .... **Amanda Redman**
Margaret Lacey .... **Charlotte Cornwell**
Mavis McDonald .... **Cheryl Hall**
Alan Pascoe .... **David Ryall**
Tessa Pascoe .... **Kate Hardie**
Dr Ivan Swinhoe .... **Bill Stewart**
Mack MacKinnon .... **Philip Croskin**
Steve Kirkwood .... **James Aubrey**
Delia .... **Tilly Vosburgh**
Shelley .... **Victoria Scarborough**
Eric .... **Ian Redford**

Writer **Laura Lamson**
Producer **David Snodin**

● ***Steamy saga of academic adultery.***

Beginning in 1980 and spanning most of the Thatcher years (to 1989), *The Men's Room* is the story of sociologist Charity Walton, a mother of four whose life is turned upside down by an affair with Mark Carleton, the deceitful, womanizing new head of department at Queen's College, University of London, where she works as a researcher. Sex and betrayal are the hallmarks of this acclaimed five-part drama, which also features Charity's best friend, Sally, a publisher; Margaret, an outspoken feminist; Swinhoe, a shoplifting criminologist; and Mavis, Carleton's boozy secretary. The story was adapted by Laura Lamson from the novel by Ann Oakley.

Mercer, David

(1928–80)

Prolific British socialist playwright, one of the so-called 'angry young men' of 1960s drama. Mercer brought his own political experiences, his criticisms of the failures of Communist Bloc regimes and a fascination with psychiatry to his many television dramas (some seen as WEDNESDAY PLAYS and PLAY FOR

TODAYS). He began with a trilogy (now known as *The Generations*), comprising the plays *Where the Difference Begins* (1961), *A Climate of Fear* (1962) and *The Birth of a Private Man* (1963), interrupted by *A Suitable Case for Treatment* (1962) and *The Buried Man* (1963). He later penned another trilogy made up of *On the Eve of Publication* (1968), *The Cellar and the Almond Tree* and *Emma's Time* (both 1970). Among other memorable works over the years were *And Did Those Feet?* (1965), *In Two Minds* (1967), *The Parachute* (1968), *Let's Murder Vivaldi* (1968) and *Huggy Bear* (1976). He also contributed to *Wessex Tales*. His last offering was *Rod of Iron* for Yorkshire TV in 1979.

Meridian Television

Meridian was the ITV franchise-holder for the South and South-East of England, winning the contract from TVS in 1991 and taking to the air on 1 January 1993. Meridian operated from three studios, in Southampton, in Newbury and near Maidstone, and its most notable contributions to the ITV network were the dramas *Harnessing Peacocks*, *Under the Hammer* and THE RUTH RENDELL MYSTERIES, the comedy *Tracey Ullman: A Class Act* and the travelogue *Coltrane in a Cadillac*. Meridian later became part of the Granada Media group, now itself subsumed into ITV plc, but the Meridian name lives on in the regional news programme *Meridian Tonight*.

Mersey Beat/Merseybeat ✳

UK (BBC) Police Drama. BBC 1 2001–4

Supt. Susan Blake	**Haydn Gwynne**
Insp./Supt. Jim Oulton	**John McArdle**
PC Steve Traynor	**Jonathan Kerrigan**
WPC/Sgt Connie Harper	**Michelle Holmes**
PC Larry 'Tiger' Barton	**Chris Walker**
Sgt Bill Gentle	**David Hargreaves**
WPC Miriam 'Mim' Da Silva	**Shelley Conn**
Sgt Danny Jackson	**Danny Lawrence**
Maddie Wright	**Eileen O'Brien**
Dr Al Blake	**Paul Bown**
Dawn Oulton	**Kathy Jamieson**
Chief Constable Bishop	**Stephen Moore**
Jenny Oulton/Lyndon	**Julia Haworth**
WPC Jodie Finn	**Josephine d'Arby**
WPC Jackie Brown	**Joanna Taylor**
Guy Morgan	**Mark Aiken**
Blue McCormack	**Yasmin Bannerman**
Phil Brack	**Louis Emerick**
Mark Salt	**Bernard Merrick**
Insp. Charlie Eden	**Lesley Ash**
DI Pete Hammond	**Mark Womack**
PC Glenn Freeman	**Scot Freeman**
Cust. Sgt Lester Cartwright	**Gary Cargill**
Natalie Vance	**Tupele Dorgu**
DC Vince Peterson	**Kevin Harvey**
DS Roz Kelly	**Claire Sweeney**

Producers **Ken Horn, Kay Patrick, Chris Ballantyne, Maria Ward**

● ***A female superintendent leads a troubled team of officers at a northern police station.***

This series is set in Newton Park police station in Runcorn, Cheshire, where Supt. Susan Blake is in charge of the shop. Married for six years to Al, a doctor, 35-year-old Blake has just returned from maternity leave (second child) and is now struggling to balance her twin career of mother and fast-track graduate police officer, all the while battling against bureaucracy and the advance of computers. Thankfully, old head Inspector Jim Oulton is able to keep things ticking over at the nick whenever the two clash, not that his own home life, in which money is tight and his marriage to big spender Dawn is on the rocks, is at all perfect. Also part of Blake's noisy team is over-eager 26-year-old copper Steve Traynor, a man in emotional turmoil following the death of his girlfriend. Then there are veteran Sgt Bill Gentle, a yachting enthusiast, who feels threatened by the success of younger members of the force; cell manager Danny Jackson, unhappily single; kick-boxing, ultra-keen new WPC Mim Da Silva; whinging golf buff 'Tiger' Barton; determined WPC Connie Harper; and maternal receptionist Maddie Wright. Thus the action is largely focused on how the police officers cope with the strains of their jobs, rather than merely following a succession of robberies and murders. From the second series, which sees the arrival of new recruits Jodie Finn and Jackie Brown, plus a vicious assault on Susan Blake, the programme is renamed *Merseybeat*. Blake is replaced in series three by new hard-nosed (on the surface) inspector Charlie Eden (who has jilted four boyfriends at the altar), with Jim promoted to superintendent. From series four, shown in 2003–4, the action is relocated to Liverpool (although the nick is still Newton Park), the camera work is given a grittier edge and new characters include ambitious PC Glenn Freeman and DI Pete Hammond as the CID side of station life is told for the first time. Jonathan Kerrigan, who plays PC Steve Traynor, also provides the theme music.

Merton, Paul

(Paul Martin; 1957–)

South London-born comedian, a former civil servant. Merton is best known as one of the regulars in the topical quiz HAVE I GOT NEWS FOR YOU, although he has also been seen on WHOSE LINE IS IT ANYWAY?, in two series of his own surreal sketch show for Channel 4, in the comedy *An Evening with Gary Lineker* (Ian), in *Paul Merton in Galton & Simpson's . . .* (two series reworking classic *Hancock* and other scripts), and as host of ROOM 101. In 1994 he presented a history of the London Palladium for the BBC and a year later hosted *Paul Merton's Life of Comedy*. He has also appeared in TV pantomimes, provided voices for the *Rex the Runt* animation, and made a guest appearance in ONE FOOT IN THE GRAVE. Among his writing credits are scripts for *Terry and Julian*. Merton was once married to actress Caroline Quentin.

Mervyn, William

(William Mervyn Pickwood; 1912–76)

British actor whose earliest TV parts (after years on the stage) included Captain Crocker-Dobson in the naval comedy *The Skylarks* in 1958 and Sir Hector in *Saki* in 1962. In 1963 he adopted the guise of Chief Inspector Rose in THE ODD MAN, which led to a rather weird spin-off, IT'S DARK OUTSIDE, in 1964 and finally to the character's own series, MR ROSE, in 1967. A year earlier, Mervyn played Sir Gerald in *The Liars* and embarked on a five-year clerical career as the Bishop in ALL GAS AND GAITERS. In 1971 he starred as the 43rd Duke of Tottering in the kids' comedy TOTTERING TOWERS and was later seen as Mr Justice Campbell in CROWN COURT. Guest roles came in series like THE ADVENTURES OF ROBIN HOOD, THE FOUR JUST MEN, NO HIDING PLACE, THE PERSUADERS! and RAFFLES.

Messiah ***

UK (BBC/Paramount/Great Meadow) Police Drama. BBC 1 2001; 2003–5
DVD: BBC

DCI Red Metcalfe .... **Ken Stott**
DI Duncan Warren .... **Neil Dudgeon**
DS Kate Beauchamp .... **Frances Grey** *(1, 2, 3)*
Susan Metcalfe .... **Michelle Forbes** *(1, 2, 3)*
DCS Emerson .... **Art Malik** *(1, 2)*
Helen Warren .... **Gillian Taylforth** *(1, 2)*
Eric Metcalfe .... **Kieran O'Brien** *(1, 2)*
DS Jez Clifton .... **Jamie Draven** *(1)*
DCI Charlie MacIntyre .... **Alun Armstrong** *(2)*
Dr Carl Henderson .... **Michael Maloney** *(3)*
Pace Tierney .... **Liam Cunningham** *(3)*
DS Vickie Clarke .... **Maxine Peake** *(4)*
Rachel Price .... **Helen McCrory** *(4)*
Jack Price .... **Hugo Speer** *(4)*

Writers **Lizzie Mickery** *(1, 2, 3)*, **Boris Starling** *(1)*, **Terry Cafolla** *(4)*
Producers **Louise Berridge** *(1)*, **Joshua St Johnston** *(2)*, **Sophie Gardiner** *(3)*, **Sanne Wohlenberg** *(3)*, **Peter Norris** *(4)*

A dedicated detective faces the most horrific of murder cases.

If you have the stomach for mutilated bodies, then *Messiah* may be the programme for you. The first outing for DCI Red Metcalfe, a troubled, brooding police officer, is based on a novel by Boris Starling. Metcalfe's gruesome case centres on a series of murders in which the victims' tongues have been cut out and a spoon inserted in their mouths. It is not until he establishes a Biblical connection that he begins to make progress. Warren is his plain-speaking number two, with Clifton and Beauchamp the young detective sergeants.

Messiah 2 was finally screened (after a postponement due to real-life crimes) early in 2003. Once again, it is in two parts like the original drama and once again a serial killer is on the loose. The methods are equally brutal. Another two-parter, *Messiah 3*, arrived in 2004, with a murderer on the rampage in a hospital. Equal amounts of blood and gore feature in *Messiah 4*, broadcast in three parts in 2005. Throughout all stories, there are shocks and twists aplenty, and even if you think you can close your eyes through the nasty bits, there are graphic explanations of what's happening in the dialogue. Critics continue to praise the classy production values, the sharp storylines and, in particular, star Ken Stott's riveting performance as Metcalfe. However, many viewers fail to get beyond the opening scenes, so grisly are their contents.

Messick, Don

(1926–97)

American cartoon voicer, specializing in canine creations, including SCOOBY-DOO, Muttley in WACKY RACES and the JETSONS' dog, Astro. He was also Bamm Bamm in THE FLINTSTONES, Dr Benton Quest in JONNY QUEST, Boo Boo in YOGI BEAR, Snorky in THE BANANA SPLITS, Aramis in *The Three Musketeers*, Multi Man in FRANKENSTEIN JR AND THE IMPOSSIBLES, Spot the cat in HONG KONG PHOOEY, Pixie in *Pixie and Dixie*, plus Atom Ant, Touché Turtle and many more characters. Messick was originally a ventriloquist, then a radio actor in the 1940s and 1950s.

Metal Mickey **

UK (LWT) Children's Comedy. ITV 1980–3

Mr Wilberforce .... **Michael Stainton**
Mrs Wilberforce .... **Georgina Melville**
Granny .... **Irene Handl**
Ken Wilberforce .... **Ashley Knight**
Haley Wilberforce .... **Lucinda Bateson**
Janey Wilberforce .... **Lola Young**
Steve Wilberforce .... **Gary Shail**

Writer **Colin Bostock-Smith**
Producer **Michael Dolenz**

A family's home life is disrupted by a zany robot.

Invented by boy scientist Ken Wilberforce to help out around the home, Metal Mickey brings nothing but chaos to Ken's family. A five-foot-tall, magical robot in the R2D2 (*Star Wars*) mould, Mickey spouts the catchphrase 'Boogie boogie' and turns the household upside down with his space-age antics, which include trips to the future, teleportation and conversations with aliens. There are also more mundane happenings, like Mickey trying to become a pop star or Mickey finding himself kidnapped. The show is possibly best remembered, however, for another Mickey – its producer/director was the former Monkee Micky Dolenz.

Miami Vice **

US (Universal) Police Drama. BBC 1 1985–90 (US: NBC 1984–9)
DVD: Universal

Det. James 'Sonny' Crockett ... **Don Johnson**
Det. Ricardo Tubbs .... **Philip Michael Thomas**
Lt. Martin Castillo .... **Edward James Olmos**
Det. Gina Navarro/Calabrese . **Saundra Santiago**
Det. Trudy Joplin .... **Olivia Brown**
Det. Stan Switek .... **Michael Talbott**
Det. Larry Zito .... **John Diehl**
Izzy Moreno .... **Martin Ferrero**
Caitlin Davies .... **Sheena Easton**

Creators **Michael Mann, Anthony Yerkovich**
Executive Producer **Michael Mann**

Two trendy cops patrol the glitzy but drug-poisoned streets of Miami.

Very much a 1980s programme in its feel, with generous use of contemporary rock music, *Miami Vice* delves behind the cool, pastel shades of this glamorous Florida city and unearths a seedier side, heavily dependent on the drug culture. Its stars are cops Crockett and Tubbs. Stubble-chinned, heavy-smoking Crockett is an ex-football star, aggressive and straight-talking. He works under the street name of Sonny Burnett and lives on a houseboat called *St Vitus' Dance*, which he shares with a pet alligator named Elvis. Separated from his wife, Caroline, Crockett now enjoys the attentions of many of the city's beautiful women, although most of his girlfriends tend to meet a grisly end. Even one he marries, rock star Caitlin Davies (played by real-life singer Sheena Easton), is murdered.

Dressed in a crumpled light jacket and a T-shirt, Crockett's casual scruffiness contrasts sharply with the silk-shirted, double-breasted, sartorial elegance of his hip partner, Tubbs, a black New York cop, who has come to Miami to flush out the drugs-pusher who murdered his brother. Tubbs's undercover identity is Rico Cooper and the duo cruise the tropical streets in Crockett's flash Ferrari Spider, or the Testarossa that replaces it. They are assisted by undercover policewomen Trudi Joplin and Gina Calabrese and detectives Stan Switek and Larry Zito, and their boss is temperamental Lt. Castillo.

Miami Vice was conceived as a sort of MTV cops show, hence the rock-video-style photography and the liberal helpings of chart music. The pounding theme tune, by Jan Hammer, became a hit on both sides of the Atlantic in 1985 and numerous guest stars from the rock world dropped in for cameo roles, including Phil Collins, Ted Nugent, James Brown, Glenn Frey and Little Richard. Also featured were celebrities like Bianca Jagger, boxer Roberto Duran and comedian Tommy Chong.

In 2006 Colin Farrell and Jamie Foxx starred in a feature film revival, also called *Miami Vice*.

Micawber ✶✶

UK (Yorkshire) Drama. ITV 2001–2
DVD: Cinema Club

Wilkins Micawber .... **David Jason**
Emma Micawber .... **Annabelle Apsion**
Mr Cudlipp .... **Sam Kelly**
Milton .... **Michael Troughton**
Henry .... **Sean Gallagher**
Wilkins Micawber Jr .... **Andrew Quigley**
Lily Micawber .... **Lucinda Dryzek**

Writer **John Sullivan**
Producer **Vernon Lawrence**

● ***The further adventures of Dickens's impecunious eccentric.***
When the ONLY FOOLS AND HORSES team of writer John Sullivan and stars David Jason and Nicholas Lyndhurst was mooted as part of the BBC's plans for a new dramatization of DAVID COPPERFIELD, there was understandably much excitement. Regrettably, the plans fell through and only Lyndhurst took his place among the credits of the lavish 1999 adaptation. Undaunted, however, Sullivan and Jason switched their talents to ITV. This four-part series picks up the tale of Copperfield's chum, the impoverished but relentlessly cheerful Wilkins Micawber and his ever-supportive wife, Emma. Episodes revolve around the desperate family's pursuit by a vicious moneylender, a job in the theatre, a court case and our hero's appointment as an under-butler in a noble household. Street scenes were filmed in Edinburgh.

Michael Hayes ✶✶

US (Trotwood/Baumgarten Prophet/New Regency/Columbia) Legal Drama. Channel 4 1998 (US: CBS 1997–8)

Michael Hayes .... **David Caruso**
Eddie Ruiz .... **Ruben Santiago-Hudson**
Caitlin Hayes .... **Mary B. Ward**
Danny Hayes Jr .... **Jimmy Galeota**
Danny Hayes .... **David Cubitt**
Jenny Nevins .... **Hillary Danner**
John Henry Manning .... **Peter Outerbridge**
Lindsay Straus .... **Rebecca Rigg**

Writers **Nicholas Pileggi, Joe Romano**
Executive Producers **Paul Haggis, John Romano, Nicholas Pileggi, Craig Baumgarten**

● ***A working-class former cop accepts one of America's most powerful legal jobs.***
Michael Hayes used to be a cop in New York, but turned it all in to study law. Rising through the legal ranks, he has made his way to the post of deputy attorney. Then, one day, his boss is almost killed and Hayes finds himself installed as the acting US Attorney for the Southern District of New York City. As this area covers quarters like theatreland and Wall Street, there is plenty of crime to keep the prosecutors busy. Carrying aloft the sword of justice and the shield of decency, the incorruptible, brooding Hayes leads a moral crusade for right in cases that involve terrorists, drug-pushers, informers, the Mob and more, never fearing to make waves or upset the Establishment. Eddie Ruiz is Michael's colleague and buddy. Inevitably, however, the main man's personal life is not quite so straightforward. His brother, Danny, is a jailbird and Michael has, in his absence, taken under his wing Danny's estranged wife, Caitlin, and her young son, Danny Jr. Despite gaining a reputation for being a classy, easy-to-watch series, *Michael Hayes* was quickly cancelled by CBS and only 22 episodes were made.

Michell, Keith

(1926–)

Australian Shakespearean actor, a former art teacher, whose finest hour came in 1970 as the legendary king in THE SIX WIVES OF HENRY VIII, ageing and fattening up as the series progressed (it was a role he resumed in 1996 for the BBC's adaptation of *The Prince and the Pauper*). Michell also starred in the 1972 film version, *Henry VIII and His Six Wives*, and took up singing on the back of his acting success, notching up one minor hit in 1971 with 'I'll Give You the Earth' and then resurfacing with the novelty single 'Captain Beaky', in 1980. Later credits have been few, apart from appearances in some TV movies and guest spots in MURDER, SHE WROTE, although his earliest parts date from 1951 (a production of R. L. Stevenson's *The Black Arrow*) and 1962 (Heathcliff in *Wuthering Heights*).

Michelmore, Cliff

CBE (1919–)

British presenter, on TV from the 1950s when he fronted *Highlight* and, more notably, TONIGHT, as well as contributing some early sports commentaries. He joined the BBC after working for British Forces radio on *Family Favourites* (through which he met his wife, the late Jean Metcalfe), and moved into television to write, direct and produce children's programmes like ALL YOUR OWN. His other notable credits have included PANORAMA, 24 HOURS, *Talkback, Wheelbase, Chance to Meet*, STARS ON SUNDAY, *Home on Sunday*, SONGS OF PRAISE, the charity programme *Lifeline*, and the pioneering global satellite link-up, OUR WORLD. He was the first presenter of HOLIDAY, in 1969, worked on the nightly magazine *Day by Day* for Southern Television and hosted the BBC's space and election coverages, as well as the occasional information panel game *So You Think . . . ?* He is the father of TV presenter/composer Guy Michelmore.

Mickey Spillane's Mike Hammer

See *Mike Hammer*.

Microbes and Men ✶✶

UK (BBC) Drama. BBC 2 1974

Ignaz Semmelweis .... **Robert Lang**

Louis Pasteur	**Arthur Lowe**
Robert Koch	**James Grout**
Emile Roux	**Charles Kay**
Paul Ehrlich	**Milo O'Shea**
Marie Pasteur	**Antonia Pemberton**
Emmy Koch	**Patricia Heneghan**
Loir	**Keith Drinkel**
Emil Behring	**David Swift**
Virchow	**Frank Gatliff**

Writers **Martin Worth, John Wiles, Bruce Norman**
Producer **Peter Goodchild**

Tales of scientific dedication to conquering disease.

Microbes and Men is a tribute to some of the brightest medical men of history. Over six episodes it traces the careers of Louis Pasteur, Ignaz Semmelweis, Robert Koch and Paul Ehrlich, exploring the remarkable breakthroughs they made in eradicating disease. Pasteur's work with typhoid, rabies and anthrax comes under the spotlight, along with his discoveries about immunology and inoculation. Semmelweis is celebrated for pioneering antiseptic treatment that dramatically reduced the number of mothers dying from puerperal (childbed) fever in 1840s Europe. Koch's contributions to the debates about TB and anthrax are highlighted and his assistant, Ehrlich, is featured for his development of chemotherapy and for creating the world's first synthetic drug (salvarsan for syphilis). Music is supplied by Dudley Simpson and an accompanying book, by Robert Reid, was published by the BBC to coincide with the initial broadcast.

Middlemarch ★★★★

UK (BBC/WGBH Boston) Drama. BBC 2 1994
DVD: BBC

Dorothea Brooke	**Juliet Aubrey**
Arthur Brooke	**Robert Hardy**
Dr Tertius Lydgate	**Douglas Hodge**
Peter Featherstone	**Michael Hordern**
Nicholas Bulstrode	**Peter Jeffrey**
Revd Edward Casaubon	**Patrick Malahide**
Rosamond Vincy	**Trevyn McDowell**
Will Ladislaw	**Rufus Sewell**
Celia Brooke	**Caroline Harker**
Revd Camden Farebrother	**Simon Chandler**
Sir James Chettam	**Julian Wadham**
Fred Vincy	**Jonathan Firth**
Mrs Dollop	**Pam Ferris**
Mrs Vincy	**Jacqueline Tong**
Mary Garth	**Rachel Power**
Mayor Vincy	**Stephen Moore**
Mrs Cadwallader	**Elizabeth Spriggs**
Mr Standish	**Ronald Hines**
Caleb Garth	**Clive Russell**
Raffles	**John Savident**
Voice of George Eliot	**Judi Dench**

Writer **Andrew Davies**
Producer **Louis Marks**
Executive Producers **Rebecca Eaton, Michael Wearing**

Acclaimed, six-part dramatization of George Eliot's best-known work.

Costing £6 million to produce, *Middlemarch* was a risky enterprise for the BBC, but the corporation had no need to worry, as this venture into elaborate costume drama was exceptionally well received. Indeed, it acted as a catalyst for a host of other 1990s period-pieces, including PRIDE AND PREJUDICE.

Opening in 1829, at a time of political and industrial change, the story centres on idealistic, well-meaning Dorothea Brooke, who mistakenly marries mean-minded Revd Edward Casaubon and then falls for his artist cousin, Will Ladislaw. Other prominent characters include feckless Rosamond Vincy and her future husband, Tertius Lydgate, a forward-thinking young doctor. Members of the old establishment, like Dorothea's landowning uncle, Arthur Brooke, Rosamund's father, Mayor Vincy, and unscrupulous banker Nicholas Bulstrode exemplify the generation gap that was beginning to grow in this era of social upheaval. The series was filmed in Stamford, Lincolnshire. The BBC had previously adapted the novel for the small screen in 1968.

Midnight Caller ★★

US (December 3rd/Lorimar) Detective Drama. BBC 1 1989–92 (US: NBC 1988–91)

Jack 'Nighthawk' Killian	**Gary Cole**
Devon King	**Wendy Kilbourne**
Billy Po	**Dennis Dun**
Lt. Carl Zymak	**Arthur Taxier**
Deacon Bridges	**Mykel T. Williamson**
Nicky Molloy	**Lisa Eilbacher**

Creator **Richard Di Lello**
Executive Producer **Robert Singer**
Producer **John F. Perry**

An ex-cop becomes a radio presenter but can't leave his former life behind.

When Jack Killian accidentally kills his patrol partner while pursuing a crook, his life is turned upside down. Although officially cleared of all blame by the police, he decides to quit the force. At a loose end, he accepts the offer of working for beautiful Devon King, as a late-night phone-in host on her radio station, KJCM (98.3 FM) in San Francisco. There (using the nickname of 'Nighthawk') he finds himself in contact with all manner of shady people who call him up and leave intriguing cases to solve, which he either passes on to his policeman friend, Carl Zymak, or to a newspaper contact, Deacon Bridges, or, more likely, sets out to handle himself, often at great personal danger. The phone-in also covers intense moral issues like AIDS and drugs, and Killian proves to be a thoughtful but straight-talking host, if a touch too moody and flip outside the studio. On the other side of the glass is engineer Billy Po. Nicky Molloy later takes over as Nighthawk's boss.

Midsomer Murders ★★★

UK (Bentley) Police Drama. ITV 1997–
DVD: Acorn Media

DCI Tom Barnaby	**John Nettles**
DS Gavin Troy	**Daniel Casey**
Joyce Barnaby	**Jane Wymark**
Cully Barnaby	**Laura Howard**
Dr George Bullard	**Barry Jackson**
DS Daniel Scott	**John Hopkins**
PC/DC Ben Jones	**Jason Hughes**

Producers **Brian True-May, Betty Willingale, Peter Cregeen**

Murder investigations in picture-postcard England.

Overtly aimed at the international audience with its overdose of traditional English village imagery (rose gardens, churches, cricket, fetes, pubs, hunts, stately homes, red phone-boxes, etc.), *Midsomer Murders* is a two-hour detective series steeped in the colours of AGATHA CHRISTIE and INSPECTOR MORSE, but always played with the tongue ever-so-slightly in cheek. The focal point is easy-going DCI Tom Barnaby, a more than competent career copper – strangely bereft of quirky traits and personal problems – based in the town of Causton, which is the urban hub of the beautiful, timeless yet strangely sinister fictional county of Midsomer. With the ambitious, though still a little wet behind the ears, Sgt Troy at his side, Barnaby is called out into the glorious English countryside to solve heinous crimes involving eccentric folk in villages with provocative names like Badger's Drift, Midsomer Worthy and Morton Fendle. Providing moral support, if rather resigned to disrupted mealtimes and abandoned social evenings, are Barnaby's wife, Joyce, and his theatrically minded daughter, Cully. When Troy gains promotion to inspector and is transferred to Middlesbrough, he is replaced by townie Dan Scott, who finds life in the countryside hard to get used to. Scott in turn is later replaced by keen-as-mustard rookie DC Ben Jones.

The series, filmed in and around Buckinghamshire and Oxfordshire, was inspired by novels by Caroline Graham, five of which have been adapted for storylines. Series writers include Anthony Horowitz, Douglas Watkinson, P. J. Hammond, Alan Plater and Andrew Payne. John Nettles and Daniel Casey, in their guises of Barnaby and Troy, made cameo appearances in the Christmas 2003 edition of *French and Saunders Actually*.

Mike Hammer ✶✶

US (Columbia) Detective Drama. ITV 1984–6 (US: CBS 1984–7)
DVD: Tango Entertainment (Region 1 only)

Mike Hammer .... **Stacy Keach**
Velda .... **Lindsay Bloom**
Capt. Pat Chambers .... **Don Stroud**
Assistant DA Lawrence Barrington .... **Kent Williams**
Ozzie the Answer .... **Danny Goldman**
Jenny .... **Lee Benton**
The Face .... **Donna Denton**

Executive Producer **Jay Bernstein**
Producer **Lew Gallo**

● ***Violent, leering private eye series, based on the colourful books by Mickey Spillane.***

Spillane's Mike Hammer is a hard New York detective fighting crime in a tough city. His investigations into the underworld, among drug-pushers, murderers, kidnappers and other such lively characters, are glossily depicted in this series. Assisted by his buxom secretary, Velda, the chain-smoking Hammer can also call on the help of his friend, Pat, a captain in the New York Police Department. On the streets, he has several contacts, including Ozzie the Answer, and among the parade of very shapely females on view is Jenny, the bartender at Hammer's regular drinking hole, the Light 'n' Easy bar. Lawrence Barrington, Hammer's legal adversary, is an assistant district attorney who operates by the book and dislikes the brawling gumshoe's unorthodox methods. The most intriguing character, however, is a beautiful brunette known as 'The Face'. Hammer catches sight of her in nearly every episode but never manages to meet her. Finally, it is revealed that she is a writer looking to use his exploits as the basis for a series of novels.

When criticism of the show's sexist attitude grew too heavy, the glamorous women were 'toned down'; but the violence, if anything, increased, with Hammer's hatred of the criminal fraternity exposed in an orgy of killings and maimings. It says it all that Hammer gives a pet name – Betsy – to his hand-gun.

Ironically, filming of the series was interrupted for a year or so because of real-life crime matters, when actor Stacy Keach spent time in Reading prison for a drugs offence. Keach resumed the role in 1997 in a short-lived series entitled *Mike Hammer: Private Eye*. He was not TV's first Mike Hammer, however. This honour went to Darren McGavin, star of an American adaptation in the 1950s.

Miles, Michael

(1919–71)

New Zealand-born 'quiz inquisitor' of TAKE YOUR PICK, conducting the quickfire 'yes/no interlude' and asking contestants to 'take the money or open the box' from the very start of ITV broadcasts in 1955. Miles had brought the show over from Radio Luxembourg, where it had been a hit for three years. It proved extremely popular on television, too, and ran for 13 years. Undaunted by its cancellation in 1968, Miles returned with a similar format in *Wheel of Fortune* a year later, but died in 1971. He was the father of radio presenter Sarah Lucas.

Miller, Sir Jonathan

CBE (1934–)

Multi-talented British writer, director and producer, who is also a qualified doctor. A product of the Cambridge Footlights troupe that included the likes of David Frost and Peter Cook, Miller arrived in television via the *Beyond the Fringe* revue. Among other TV contributions, he edited MONITOR, produced a version of Plato's *Symposium* and an acclaimed adaptation of ALICE IN WONDERLAND, worked on OMNIBUS, took charge of the BBC's ambitious Shakespeare project in 1980 and merged his medical and television knowledge in *The Body in Question* in 1978 (writer and presenter). In 1997 he hosted *Jonathan Miller's Opera Works*, a series of workshops for aspiring singers. Later credits have included *Jonathan Miller's Brief History of Disbelief*, *Absolute Rubbish with Jonathan Miller* and a guest appearance in *Sensitive Skin*.

Milligan, Spike

KBE (Hon.) (Terence Milligan; 1918–2002)

Offbeat British comedian, born in India. Through his work with THE GOONS on radio in the 1950s, Milligan established a reputation for bizarre, quirky humour, which later translated to television in the form of the animated TELEGOONS. He also starred with fellow Goon Peter Sellers in *Idiot Weekly, Price 2d* in 1956, and wrote its sequels, A SHOW CALLED FRED and *Son of Fred*. He made guest appearances in NOT ONLY . . ., BUT ALSO . . . in the mid-1960s, and then, in 1968, appeared in *The World of Beachcomber*, before launching into his run of innovative *Q* programmes in 1969, beginning with *Q5* and working his way up to *Q9*. The early episodes predated even MONTY PYTHON with their free-form sketches, often lacking beginnings and proper endings. Less successful was his interpretation of Pakistani Kevin O'Grady (Paki-Paddy) in Johnny Speight's controversial sitcom CURRY AND CHIPS (Milligan had previously popped up in Speight's TILL DEATH US DO PART). He wrote the mini-saga *The Phantom Raspberry-Blower of Old London Town* (first seen as one of *Six Dates for Barker*) for

THE TWO RONNIES, and was a regular on *The Marty Feldman Comedy Machine*. Among Milligan's numerous other contributions were *Milligan's Wake*, *Muses With Milligan*, *Oh in Colour*, *The Last Turkey in the Shop Show*, *There's a Lot of It About*, GORMENGHAST (headmaster De'Ath) and voices for the children's animations *Wolves, Witches and Giants*, *The Great Bong* and *Badjelly the Witch*.

Mills, Annette

(1894–1955)

The sister of John Mills, Annette Mills was a children's favourite in the 1940s and 1950s when introducing popular puppets like Prudence and Primrose Kitten, Sally the Sealion, Oswald the Ostrich, Louise the Lamb, Monty the Monkey, Mr Peregrine the Penguin and, most famous of all, MUFFIN THE MULE. As Muffin danced on top of her piano, Mills sang and played. They first appeared together in 1946, as part of the BBC's *For the Children* series, after Mills had been forced to give up her song-and-dance career following a couple of bad accidents. She died just eight days after her last appearance with Muffin in 1955.

Mills, Sir John

CBE (1908–2005)

Stalwart of the British cinema John Mills enjoyed relatively few television credits. Most notable were the offbeat Western *Dundee and the Culhane* (as barrister Dundee), the Resistance revival THE ZOO GANG (Tommy Devon or 'The Elephant'), the 1979 version of QUATERMASS (Professor John Quatermass), the retirement sitcom *Young at Heart* (Albert Collyer), the mini-series A WOMAN OF SUBSTANCE (Henry Rossiter), the single drama *Harnessing Peacocks* (Bernard), MARTIN CHUZZLEWIT (Mr Chuffey) and *Gentleman Thief* (Arthur Rosehip). Mills was also a guest in numerous programmes, most famously with Morecambe and Wise, but also in TALES OF THE UNEXPECTED and PERFECT SCOUNDRELS. He was the father of actresses Juliet and Hayley Mills.

Mills, Roger

Award-winning British documentary producer and editor, working for the BBC on programmes like *Inside Story*, SAILOR, HONG KONG BEAT, *Strangeways*, FORTY MINUTES and Michael Palin's extravagant voyages, AROUND THE WORLD IN 80 DAYS, *Pole to Pole*, *Full Circle*, *Michael Palin's Sahara* and *Himalaya with Michael Palin*.

Milne, Alasdair

(1930–)

BBC current affairs producer and director in the 1950s and 1960s, working on programmes like *Highlight*, TONIGHT and THAT WAS THE WEEK THAT WAS, who later became the Corporation's Director of Programmes, Managing Director and Director-General (1982–7). Milne was the first Director-General to come from a production background, and under his auspices the BBC opened up its breakfast television and daytime television services. His resignation in 1987, at the behest of the Chairman, led to a period of upheaval and change at the BBC.

Milne, Paula

British dramatist whose TV creations have included ANGELS, *A Bunch of Fives*, DRIVING AMBITION, *The Gemini Factor*, CHANDLER AND CO., SECOND SIGHT and *State of Mind*. Among her other acclaimed work has been the 1982 play *John David*, and the serials THE POLITICIAN'S WIFE, *The Fragile Heart* and *The Virgin Queen*, plus episodes of CORONATION STREET, CROSSROADS, Z CARS, JULIET BRAVO, *Girl Talk*, GRANGE HILL, *Dramarama*, *The Squad*, LADIES IN CHARGE and THE RUTH RENDELL MYSTERIES.

Mind of Mr J. G. Reeder, The ★★

UK (Thames) Detective Drama. ITV 1969; 1971

Mr J. G. Reeder	**Hugh Burden**
Sir Jason Toovey	**Willoughby Goddard**
Mrs Houchin	**Mona Bruce**
Margaret Belman	**Gillian Lewis**

Executive Producer **Lloyd Shirley**
Producers **Kim Mills, Robert Love**

● ***A mild-mannered office clerk solves crimes in his own unassuming way.***

It is the 1920s and Mr J. G. Reeder works for the Department of Public Prosecutions. Although his everyday appearance is quite innocuous (bespectacled, slightly downmarket in dress, and totally unthreatening in manner), he nevertheless possesses a mind capable of cracking the most enigmatic of crimes. As he himself puts it, he sees evil in everything, much to the misfortune of crooks up and down the country. Sir Jason Toovey is his department head, and Reeder is assisted first by Mrs Houchin and later by Margaret Belman. The series was based on the stories of Edgar Wallace, published in 1925.

Mind Your Language ★

UK (LWT/Tri Films) Situation Comedy. ITV 1977–9; 1986
DVD: Cinema Club

Jeremy Brown	**Barry Evans**
Miss Courtney	**Zara Nutley**
Danielle Favre	**Françoise Pascal**
Ali Nadim	**Dino Shafeek**
Jamila Ranjha	**Jamila Massey**
Anna Schmidt	**Jacki Harding**
Juan Cervantes	**Ricardo Montez**
Giovanni Cupello	**George Camiller**
Chung Su-Lee	**Pik-Sen Lim**
Taro Nagazumi	**Robert Lee**
Maximillian Papandrious	**Kevork Malikyan**
Ranjeet Singh	**Albert Moses**
Sid	**Tommy Godfrey**
Zoltan Szabo	**Gabor Vernon**
Ingrid Svenson	**Anna Bergman**
Gladys	**Iris Sadler**

Creator/Writer **Vince Powell**
Producer **Stuart Allen**

● ***Mayhem and misunderstanding in an English-for-foreigners class.***

English teacher Jeremy Brown bit off more than he could chew when enrolling as instructor of an evening class for mature foreign students. His multinational pupils include amorous

French girl Danielle Favre, humourless German Anna Schmidt, Italian romeo Giovanni Cupello, and other similarly well-defined racial stereotypes, all of whom have clearly never considered the concept of ethnic tolerance. Misunderstanding and abuse are rife in the classroom, leading to constant aggression and turning the naïve, inoffensive Brown into a quivering, frustrated wreck. Miss Courtney is the dragon-like principal who has the knack of entering the class at just the wrong moment, and Sid is the Cockney caretaker.

Mind Your Language was revived in 1986 by independent production company Tri Films. The series was not fully networked but did bring back together most of the original cast, along with several new faces playing characters in the same mould.

Minder ✶✶✶✶

UK (Euston Films/Thames/Central) Comedy Drama. ITV 1979–80; 1982–5; 1988–9; 1991; 1993–4
DVD: Clear Vision Video

Arthur Daley	**George Cole**
Terry McCann	**Dennis Waterman**
Dave	**Glynn Edwards**
Des	**George Layton**
DS Albert 'Charlie' Chisholm	**Patrick Malahide**
Sgt Rycott	**Peter Childs**
Maurice	**Anthony Valentine**
DC Jones	**Michael Povey**
Ray Daley	**Gary Webster**
DS Morley	**Nicholas Day**
DC Park	**Stephen Tompkinson**
DC Field	**Jonty Stephens**

Creator **Leon Griffiths**
Executive Producers **Verity Lambert, Lloyd Shirley, Johnny Goodman**
Producers **Lloyd Shirley, George Taylor, Ian Toynton**

The dodgy dealings of one of London's great survivors and his beefy assistant.

Arthur Daley is a name that has become synonymous with shady deals, for this cowardly but lovable rogue specializes in less than reliable, marginally hooky produce dished out at a bargain price. Whether it is mutton-dressed-as-lamb motors from his used-car showroom or crates of *appellation noncontrôlée* from his lock-up, Arthur has the knack of twisting suckers' arms and getting them to buy. Of course, they soon return the goods, or the law intervenes to ensure that Daley's pockets are once again as empty as when they started. But this trilby-sporting, cigar-chewing master of Cockney slang is never far away from another 'nice little earner'.

Arthur's right hand is Terry McCann, a former professional boxer and occasional jailbird. Now on the straight and narrow (as far as Arthur will allow), McCann – one of life's losers – is easy meat for Daley, who pays him a pittance and promises him the earth. Hired out as a commodity by Arthur to be a bodyguard, bouncer, fetcher or carrier, Terry nevertheless is always there to protect his guv'nor from someone with a grievance – and such people are not hard to find. The wonderful repartee between Daley and his uncomfortable, generally kind-hearted 'minder' as they work their way around the fringes of the underworld is even more important than the stories themselves.

Off duty, the pair can be found in the Winchester Club, run by its genial steward, Dave. This refuge from ' 'er indoors' (as Daley refers to his wife) is also the setting for many 'business' meetings. On the side of justice are policemen Chisholm, Rycott and Jones. Just like Wyle E. Coyote and the Road Runner, their sole aim is to catch up with Arthur Daley, the crook with the Teflon finish.

The series was nearly brought to a close on many occasions, as both George Cole and Dennis Waterman contemplated a way out. But when Waterman finally called it a day in 1991, Gary Webster was introduced in the role of Arthur's second cousin's son, Ray, and Daley's schemes and scams continued apace. Pursuit this time came from coppers Morley and Park.

Dennis Waterman also co-wrote (with Gerard Kenny) and performed the theme song, 'I Could be So Good for You', which he took to number three in the charts in 1980. Cole joined him on a novelty hit, 'What are We Gonna Get 'Er Indoors' at Christmas 1983, and the partnership was celebrated in a hit for The Firm, 'Arthur Daley ('E's Alright)', in 1982.

Mine All Mine ✶✶✶

UK (Red) Comedy Drama. ITV 1 2004
DVD: Cinema Club

Max Vivaldi	**Griff Rhys Jones**
Val Vivaldi	**Rhian Morgan**
Maria Vivaldi	**Siwan Morris**
Candy Vivaldi	**Joanna Page**
Leo Vivaldi	**Matthew Berry**
Gethin Morris	**Jason Hughes**
Danny Baveystock	**Jo Stone-Fewings**
Myrtle Jones	**Ruth Madoc**
Bronwen Thomas	**Jennifer Hill**
Sam Benyon	**Simon Gregor**
Iris Price	**Lynn Hunter**
Thomas Roberts	**Glyn Morgan**
Mr Collier	**Robin Griffith**
Big Claire	**Debbie Chazen**
Mrs Digby	**Ri Richards**
Stella Craven	**Sharon Morgan**
Rico Vivaldi	**John Scott Martin**

Writer **Russell T. Davies**
Producer **Annie Harrison-Baxter**

An eccentric failed entrepreneur claims he owns the city of Swansea.

Bumbling Max Vivaldi is a bit of a crackpot, always looking for a new get-rich-quick scheme. He currently runs a mini-cab business, but, as with all his other ventures, this is going nowhere. Pulsing within his veins, however, is the chance to prove that he is the rightful owner of the whole of his beloved Swansea, where this comedy drama is set. He possesses a will written in 1710 that seems to indicate that, passing down through several generations, the city really is his, all his. No one takes him seriously, of course – not even his wife Val, and children Maria, Candy and Leo – until a London auctioneer named Danny Baveystock steps off a train and is immediately absorbed into the riotous Vivaldi clan (shades of THE DARLING BUDS OF MAY). He's come to inspect a bakelite telephone that Max thinks is worth a fortune. It is, of course, valueless but Danny spots the framed 18th-century document and decides to look into the validity of Max's claim, thinking there may just be some legal basis to it. As Max's star begins to rise, he realizes that the hard work is yet to be done, not least within his own family, where Val runs off with Sam, the egg man, sister Stella wants her share of the inheritance and lecherous dad Rico needs to be certified to annul his greater claim to the booty. Meanwhile other family members have their problems to deal with. Feisty Maria has been dumped by banker boyfriend Gethin and has taken a shine to their London visitor;

dopey Candy thinks she can be a pop star but has no talent whatsoever; and studious young Leo is hiding his homosexuality while secretly building up his own little business empire. The story is told over five noisy episodes.

Mini-Series

A term generally given to glossy dramas (often adaptations of blockbuster novels) spread over a handful of episodes, which are usually scheduled on consecutive nights. The genre was initiated in the 1970s by concepts like RICH MAN, POOR MAN and others in the *Best Sellers* collection.

Minogue, Kylie

(1968–)

Australian actress and singer, shooting to fame as Charlene Robinson in NEIGHBOURS before quitting the series to concentrate on a pop music and film career. Previously Minogue had appeared in series like THE SULLIVANS and *The Henderson Kids*. Her sister, Dannii, is also an actress/singer.

Mirren, Dame Helen

(Ilynea Lydia Mironoff; 1945–)

London-born actress who scored some notable TV successes with the PRIME SUSPECT mini-series, playing DCI Jane Tennison. Earlier, she was Valerie in the 1972 adaptation of *Cousin Bette*, took roles in numerous classic plays and single dramas, like *The Duchess of Malfi* and THE BBC TELEVISION SHAKESPEARE (*As You Like It*), and also appeared in Dennis Potter's acclaimed BLUE REMEMBERED HILLS (Angela). *Mrs Reinhard, Behind the Scenes*, THRILLER, *Miss Julie, The Serpent Son, After the Party, Coming Through* and JACKANORY number among her other credits. More recent work includes the mini series *Painted Lady* (blues singer Maggie Sheridan), voices for the animation *Pride*, and the title role in *Elizabeth I*.

Misfit, The ✶✶

UK (ATV) Situation Comedy. ITV 1970–1

Basil 'Badger' Allenby-Johnson .... **Ronald Fraser**
Ted Allenby-Johnson .... **Simon Ward**
Alicia Allenby-Johnson .... **Susan Carpenter**
Stanley Allenby-Johnson .... **Patrick Newell**

Creator/Writer **Roy Clarke**
Producer **Dennis Vance**

An expat returns from the Far East and finds Britain has changed for the worse.

Fifty-year-old Basil Allenby-Johnson, nicknamed 'Badger' during his many years of rubber planting in Malaya, returns to live with his son, Ted, and daughter-in-law, Alicia, in 1970s London. While he has been in the Orient, the permissive society has by-passed Badger, rendering him shocked and bewildered on arrival back in the old country. The liberal and open-minded attitudes of his hosts are equally baffling. In the second series he links up with his brother, Stanley, but, wherever he goes, Badger is the complete Misfit of the title. Written by LAST OF THE SUMMER WINE and OPEN ALL HOURS creator Roy Clarke, episodes were one hour in length.

Miss Adventure ✶

UK (ABC) Detective Drama. ITV 1964

Stacey Smith .... **Hattie Jacques**
Henry Stanton .... **Jameson Clark**
Philip Costain .... **John Stone**
Alexei Adamov .... **Paul Whitsun-Jones**

Creators **Peter Yeldham, Marjorie Yeldham**
Producer **Ernest Maxin**

A female investigator finds herself constantly in hot water.

Lively Stacey Smith works for the hard-up, London-based Stanton Detective Agency, run by Henry Stanton. Henry sends her off on rather tepid assignments but these always offer more excitement than they promise, leading her to confront blackmailers, murderers and jewel thieves in locations as exotic as Greece and Denmark. But what Stacey is really looking for is a man. This was an unusual role for distinguished comedy actress Hattie Jacques and one that lasted only 13 episodes (three investigations).

Miss Jones and Son ✶✶

UK (Thames) Situation Comedy. ITV 1977–8

Elizabeth Jones .... **Paula Wilcox**
Mrs Jones .... **Charlotte Mitchell**
Joan Scott
Mr Jones .... **Norman Bird**
Geoffrey .... **Christopher Beeny**
Rose Tucker .... **Cass Allen**
David .... **David Savile**
Penny .... **Catherine Kirkwood**
Roly Jones .... **Luke Steensil**

Creator/Writer **Richard Waring**
Producer **Peter Frazer-Jones**

A young, unmarried mum struggles to bring up her baby.

Elizabeth Jones was shocked when her boyfriend left her after a four-year relationship. She was even more surprised to discover she was pregnant. Despite failing to make the appropriate arrangements for claiming benefit, and consequently finding herself short of income, she happily gives birth to a baby son whom she christens Roland Desmond Geoffrey Jones. Her prudish parents are less than pleased with the situation at first but soon rally round to support their daughter, as do her neighbour, Geoffrey, and friend, Rose Tucker. This daring (for the time) comedy focuses on Elizabeth's attempts to make ends meet and do the best by her son. In the second series, Geoffrey moves out and a new neighbour, David (a widower), and his daughter, Penny, move in. David, a writer, and Elizabeth, an illustrator, begin to pool their talents and gradually their relationship becomes less platonic and rather more intimate.

Miss Marple ✶✶✶

UK (BBC) Detective Drama. BBC 1 1984–7; 1989; 1991–2
DVD: BBC

Miss Jane Marple .... **Joan Hickson**
DI/DCI Slack .... **David Horovitz**

Producers **Guy Slater, George Gallaccio**

● *The cases of Agatha Christie's celebrated female sleuth.*
In an interpretation far removed from the blustery character portrayed by Margaret Rutherford in 1960s films, Joan Hickson plays the role of geriatric detective Miss Marple much closer to the written original, dressed heavily in tweed, with a crocodile-skin handbag draped over her arm. Frail, gentle and self-effacing, she relies on a softly-spoken investigative technique with a well-chosen query, followed by intense periods of listening. This, combined with a flair for analysing personality traits and an uncanny skill of spotting the out-of-the-ordinary, endows this elderly, gardening-loving spinster with the talent to suss out even the cleverest murderer. In doing so, she suitably embarrasses the police force in her home of St Mary Mead and other picturesque 1930s villages. In true Christie tradition, the gory side of murder and the cruelty involved are always quickly overlooked, as each case develops into a complex, mind-bending puzzle that only our heroine can solve. The first adaptation to be screened was *The Body in the Library*, with *The Mirror Crack'd from Side to Side* concluding the sporadic, drawn-out series at Christmas 1992, when Joan Hickson retired at the tender age of 86.

In the new millennium the nosey old girl was brought back into action. *Agatha Christie's Marple* (ITV 1 2004–) stars Geraldine McEwan as the eponymous geriatric sleuth, and a host of big-name guest stars, reviving assorted tales already covered in the BBC offering.

Miss World ✶

UK (BBC/Thames) Beauty Contest. BBC 1 1951–79/ITV 1980–8/ Channel 5 1999–2000/ITV 1 2004

Producers **Bryan Cowgill, Humphrey Fisher, Philip Lewis, Michael Begg, Ken Griffin** *(BBC)*, **Steve Minchin** *(Thames)*, **Lisa Chapman** *(Channel 5)*

● *Long-running beauty pageant aiming to discover the world's most attractive girl.*
Miss World was one of the television highlights of the year in the UK for over three decades until being dropped from the schedules in 1988 as political correctness gathered speed. After a revival on Sky One in the late 1990s, the beauty pageant returned to terrestrial TV in 1999, televised by Channel 5 until 2000. In 2001, ITV 2 broadcast the event. The 2002 event, hastily staged at London's Alexandra Palace, was not covered by any UK channel, following riots (and deaths) sparked by the contest in the original chosen venue of Nigeria. In 2003, Sky One resumed coverage, but ITV 1 pitched in for the rights to show a recording of the 2004 event in the early hours of the morning, with live coverage restricted to the backwaters of Sky Travel, which also carried the 2005 event.

Conceived by Eric and Julia Morley of Mecca in 1951, its unashamed purpose has been to choose the most beautiful and charming girl from a collection of national representatives to reign as Miss World for the next 12 months. Vital statistics have been quoted, tears have been shed, there has been much talk of working with children and animals, and, in the contest's heyday, the British public backed their fancies like horses in the Grand National. There have been controversial moments, too, such as when Helen Morgan (UK), Miss World 1974, was forced to resign only days after being crowned when newspapers revealed she was actually the mother of a young child. Miss Sweden, Kiki Haakonson, won the first contest, and among the other well-remembered Miss Worlds are Eva Reuber-Staier (Austria, 1969), Marjorie Wallace (USA, 1973), Wilnelia Merced (Puerto Rico, 1975 – later wife of Bruce Forsyth), Cindy Breakspeare (Jamaica, 1976) and Mary Stavin (Sweden, 1977). Rosemarie Frankland (1961), Ann Sydney (1964), Lesley Langley (1965) and Sarah-Jane Hutt (1983) were other UK winners. Rosanna Davison, Miss Ireland and winner of the 2003 event, is the daughter of singer Chris de Burgh.

The venue in the early days was London's Lyceum Ballroom, with music supplied by the Joe Loss Orchestra but, from 1964, the Royal Albert Hall hosted proceedings for many years and the Phil Tate Orchestra provided accompaniment. Among the main comperes (some for just single years) were David Coleman, Peter West, David Jacobs, Michael Aspel, Simon Dee, Keith Fordyce, Pete Murray, David Vine, Terry Wogan, Ray Moore, Patrick Lichfield, Andy Williams, Paul Burnett, Sacha Distel and Esther Rantzen. When coverage was transferred to ITV via Thames TV from 1980, Judith Chalmers, Peter Marshall, Anne Diamond, Mary Stavin and Alexandra Bastedo were seen in charge at various times. Jerry Springer hosted the 2000 event from the Millennium Dome and returned to compere the following year's contest alongside Claire Smith in South Africa.

Mission: Impossible ✶✶✶

US (Paramount) Spy Drama. BBC 1 1970–5 (US: CBS 1966–73; ABC 1988–90)

Daniel Briggs .... **Steven Hill**
Jim Phelps .... **Peter Graves**
Cinnamon Carter .... **Barbara Bain**
Rollin Hand .... **Martin Landau**
Barney Collier .... **Greg Morris**
Willy Armitage .... **Peter Lupus**
Voice on the tape .... **Bob Johnson**
Paris .... **Leonard Nimoy**
Dr Doug Lane .... **Sam Elliott**
Dana Lambert .... **Lesley Ann Warren**
Casey .... **Lynda Day George**
Mimi Davis .... **Barbara Anderson**

Creator/Executive Producer **Bruce Geller**

● *A highly skilled task force undertakes ridiculously dangerous assignments.*
These tales of international intrigue feature the Los Angeles-based IMF (Impossible Missions Force). This is a team of remarkable individuals, each renowned for his or her distinctive skills, and it is led by Jim Phelps, who took over from Daniel Briggs, the man seen in charge in the very earliest episodes. It is Phelps who collects the team's briefings, which arrive in a parcel containing a self-destructing audio tape. The tape bursts into flames five seconds after delivering its message. Along with the tape comes a series of photographs to help with the mission, but, beyond these, the team know they are always on their own. The secret government body issuing the assignment offers no assistance whatsoever and even promises to deny all knowledge of the agents.

Although the tape never orders the team into action (it simply states: 'Your mission, should you choose to accept it . . .'), Phelps always agrees to take on the job. He then devises a complicated plan of attack and chooses his task force from a sheaf of possible agents. However, with the exception of occasional guest stars, he always selects the same team. The agents are strong man Willy Armitage, electronics wizard Barney Collier (who creates most of their high-tech gadgets), master of disguise Rollin Hand, and fashion model Cinnamon Carter, whose main function is distraction. The last two leave after a couple of series and are replaced by Dana Lambert in the glamour role and new disguise expert Paris (played by 'Mr Spock', Leonard Nimoy).

The ultra-cool squad's outrageous missions usually centre on thwarting Communist plots in banana republics and tiny European states, although they also confront more conventional crime in the United States. By restricting dialogue and characterization to a minimum, and by the use of snappy editing, the producers turn out a series of high-paced, all-action adventures.

Mission: Impossible (mostly billed as *Mission Impossible* – without the colon – in the UK) was revived briefly in 1988 to fill gaps in US TV schedules caused by a Hollywood writers' strike. Filmed in Australia, it again starred Peter Graves as head of a new team of operators, with the self-destructing audio tape now updated to a digital disc. A film version, starring Tom Cruise, was released in 1996 and was followed by two sequel movies. The well-remembered theme music was composed by Lalo Schifrin.

Mister Ed ✶✶

US (Filmways) Situation Comedy. ITV 1962–5 (US: CBS 1961–6)
DVD: MGM (Region 1 only)

Wilbur Post .... **Alan Young**
Carol Post .... **Connie Hines**
Roger Addison .... **Larry Keating**
Kay Addison .... **Edna Skinner**
Gordon Kirkwood .... **Leon Ames**
Winnie Kirkwood .... **Florence MacMichael**
Mister Ed's Voice .... **Allan 'Rocky' Lane**

Creator **Al Simon**
Executive Producers **Al Simon, Arthur Lubin**
Producer **Herbert W. Browar**

● ***A talking horse gives his master headaches.***

When architect Wilbur Post decides to give up the city in favour of the countryside around Los Angeles, little does he know what awaits him. With his newlywed wife, Carol, he buys a large country house and discovers in the barn an eight-year-old palomino, named Mister Ed (played by a horse called Bamboo Harvester). However, this is no ordinary horse: this one can talk and, to prove the point, he introduces every episode with the whinnied words, 'Hello, I'm Mister Ed.'

But Mister Ed will talk only to Wilbur, since Wilbur (or 'Buddy Boy', as the horse nicknames him) is the only human being Ed has found worth talking to. Predictably, this tends to land his master in hot water, particularly when he is overheard talking to the horse. As if that isn't enough, the cynical and grumpy Mister Ed is also keen on giving Wilbur advice (from the horse's mouth, so to speak), which usually leads to even more trouble.

The cast is completed by the Posts' bemused next-door neighbours, Roger and Kay Addison. When actor Larry Keating died, his screen wife, Edna Skinner, continued alone for a while until she was replaced with a new couple, the Kirkwoods. The series was created by Arthur Lubin, who had directed the *Francis* (the talking mule) films, starring Donald O'Connor, in the 1950s.

Mistress, The ✶✶

UK (BBC) Situation Comedy. BBC 2 1985; 1987

Maxine .... **Felicity Kendal**
Luke Mansel .... **Jack Galloway**
 Peter McEnery
Helen Mansel .... **Jane Asher**
Jenny .... **Jenny McCracken**
Simon .... **Tony Aitken**
Jamie .... **Paul Copley**

Creator/Writer **Carla Lane**
Producer **Gareth Gwenlan**

● ***The pitfalls of an extra-marital affair.***

The Mistress is more a situation tragedy than a situation comedy, dealing, as it does, with the touchy subject of adultery and all its drawbacks and dangers. At the apex of this particular eternal triangle is Maxine, an independent, single-minded woman who lives alone (apart from pet rabbits) in a comfortable pink flat. Her lover is Luke Mansel, a married businessman, torn between the demanding Maxine and his suspecting wife, Helen. Secret meetings, snatched moments of passion and longed-for dirty weekends are balanced by pangs of guilt and desperate attempts to keep the illicit affair under wraps. Jenny is an old school friend with whom Maxine owns the Flora florist's shop, while Simon is Luke's envious work-colleague and confidant who suffers chronically from marital boredom.

MIT

See *The Bill*.

Mitchell, Denis

(1912–)

Pioneering British documentary-maker, noted for his impressionistic studies of human life, the highlights of his career being *In Prison* (1957), *On Tour* (1958), MORNING IN THE STREETS, *A Soho Story* (1959), *The Wind of Change* (1960), *Chicago – Portrait of a City* (1961), *A Wedding on Saturday* (1964), *Seven Men* (1971), *European Journey* (1972 and 1973) and *Private Lives* (1975). His first contribution (after beginning in BBC radio) was *On the Threshold* in 1955, and he also worked on *This England* and WORLD IN ACTION.

Mitchell, James

(1926–2002)

North-eastern English scriptwriter, the creator of CALLAN, WHEN THE BOAT COMES IN and SPYSHIP, and the co-creator of JUSTICE, but also contributor to THE TROUBLESHOOTERS and THE AVENGERS, among other series.

Mitchell, Leslie

(1905–85)

British television's first regular announcer, Leslie Mitchell opened up the BBC service from Alexandra Palace in 1936, welcoming viewers to 'the magic of television'. As a sideline in those early days, he also interviewed guests for PICTURE PAGE. The Scots-born former actor and radio presenter turned freelance after the war (during which he had worked for British Movietone News), commentating on state and political events for the BBC, but also working for ITV. He was the first presenter of THIS WEEK, in 1956, briefly Head of Talks at Associated-Rediffusion and, in the 1970s, resurfaced as chairman of the Tyne Tees nostalgia quiz *Those Wonderful TV Times*.

Mitchell, Warren

(Warren Misell; 1926–)

RADA-trained British actor, infamous as the bigoted Alf Garnett in TILL DEATH US DO PART. Mitchell's showbusiness career began on the stage and progressed via radio (Radio Luxembourg, plus BBC shows like *Educating Archie*) to television, where some of his first roles were to support Tony Hancock in HANCOCK'S HALF HOUR and Charlie Drake in *Drake's Progress*. He also appeared as Cromwell in the 1955 adaptation of *The Children of the New Forest* and starred in an early sitcom, *Three Tough Guys*. In 1961 Mitchell played Pan Malcov in a short-lived Granada sitcom called *Colonel Trumper's Private War*. More successfully, in 1965 he was cast as the outspoken Alf Ramsey in a COMEDY PLAYHOUSE episode that proved to be the pilot for *Till Death Us Do Part*. Ramsey became Garnett and the series ran from 1966 to 1968 and returned for another three years in 1972. It was briefly revived as *Till Death* . . . by ATV in 1981, and then revamped as IN SICKNESS AND IN HEALTH by the BBC for seven years from 1985. *The Thoughts of Chairman Alf* were still being broadcast as recently as 1998. Mitchell's other TV work has included performances in classic dramas such as *The Caretaker*, *The Merchant of Venice* and *Death of a Salesman*, *Screen One's Wall of Silence* (Hassidic Jew Schmuel Singer), *Screen One*'s *Gobble* (Waterboard Chairman), and two further sitcoms – an early sort of YES, MINISTER called *Men of Affairs* (Sir William) in 1973, and SO YOU THINK YOU'VE GOT TROUBLES (Ivan Fox, a Jew in Northern Ireland) in 1991 – plus smaller roles in many series like OUT OF THE UNKNOWN, THE AVENGERS, THE SAINT, THE SWEENEY, AIN'T MISBEHAVIN' (Ray Smiles), GORMENGHAST (Barquentine) and A CHRISTMAS CAROL (Eddie Scrooge's dad). More recent guest roles have been in series like LOVEJOY, KAVANAGH QC, WAKING THE DEAD and LAST OF THE SUMMER WINE.

Mixed Blessings ✶

UK (LWT) Situation Comedy. ITV 1978; 1980

Thomas Simpson	**Christopher Blake**
Susan Lambert/Simpson	**Muriel Odunton**
Aunt Dorothy	**Joan Sanderson**
Edward Simpson	**George Waring**
Annie Simpson	**Sylvia Kay**
William Lambert	**Stefan Kalipha**
Matilda Lambert	**Carmen Munro**
Winston Lambert	**Gregory Munroe**
Mrs Beasley	**Pauline Delany**
Mr Huntley	**Ernest Clark**

Creator **Sid Green**
Writers **Sid Green, Derrick Goodwin**
Producer **Derrick Goodwin**

A racially mixed couple struggle to make their marriage acceptable to others.

This adventurous comedy focuses on two university graduates, Thomas Simpson and Susan Lambert. It sees them getting engaged, being married and then starting a family; but what makes this relationship unusual (for the time) is that Thomas is white and Susan is black. Both sets of parents are convinced the marriage will not work, other relatives disapprove and only Thomas's Aunt Dorothy has confidence in the liaison. Realizing that money is scarce (Susan is a social worker, but Thomas is initially unemployed), Dorothy even offers them a home in her basement flat. The programme's theme music – sung by star Christopher Blake – was written by actor Peter Davison.

Moffat, Steven

(1961–)

Scottish writer (a former teacher) of mainly sitcoms, although perhaps his greatest success has come with the kids' drama PRESS GANG. Moffat is the man behind JOKING APART, CHALK and COUPLING, but he also scripted the one-off comedies *Exam Conditions* and *The Office* (not the BBC sitcom) and has contributed to MURDER MOST HORRID and DOCTOR WHO. Moffat is married to producer Sue Vertue.

Mogul/The Troubleshooters ✶✶

UK (BBC) Drama. BBC 1 1965–72

Brian Stead	**Geoffrey Keen**
Willy Izard	**Philip Latham**
Peter Thornton	**Ray Barrett**
Alec Stewart	**Robert Hardy**
Robert Driscoll	**Barry Foster**
Derek Prentice	**Ronald Hines**
Steve Thornton	**Justine Lord**
Jane Webb	**Philippa Gail**
Roz Stewart	**Deborah Stanford**
Mike Szabo	**David Baron**
Eileen O'Rourke	**Isobel Black**
Charles Grandmercy	**Edward De Souza**
Claire Cooke	**Camilla Brockman**
Julie Serres	**Virginia Wetherell**
Ginny Vickers	**Jayne Sofiano**
Miss Jenkins	**Beryl Cooke**
Ghislaine Foss	**Dora Reisser**
James Langely	**John Carson**
Britte Langely	**Anna Matisse**
Lita Perez	**Barbara Shelley**

Creator **John Elliot**
Producers **Peter Graham Scott, Anthony Read**

Power struggles and other excitement in the oil industry.

Mogul International is a major oil production company, headed by managing director Brian Stead and his financial controller, Willy Izard. In the first series, which is simply entitled *Mogul*, much of the action takes place at executive level but, as attention shifts to the younger and more dynamic members of staff, the title is changed to *The Troubleshooters* and the drama moves out of the office and on to rigs scattered around the world. The key, globetrotting 'troubleshooters' are Peter Thornton and Alec Stewart.

The 'soapy' boardroom and bedroom elements apart, the series was much respected in the real oil world for its attention to detail and accuracy in technical matters. Issues covered in the storylines, such as explosions, earthquakes, racial tension, company takeovers and the discovery of new oilfields, uncannily foretold real events, and this no doubt contributed to its seven-year residence on UK screens. The Mogul company was allegedly based on BP.

Molina, Alfred

(1953–)

British actor, the husband of Jill Gascoine, with whom he made a guest appearance in C.A.T.S. EYES. Molina has also been seen in CASUALTY, played Nigel the wrestler in the Leonard Rossiter comedy *The Losers*, Gen. Carmona in ASHENDEN, Tony Havens in A YEAR IN PROVENCE, musician John Ogden in the drama *Virtuoso*, and retired crook Hamish in *Alan Bleasdale Presents Requiem Apache*. He also appeared in the TV movies *The Accountant, Drowning in the Shallow End, Trust Me, A Very Polish Practice, Hancock* ('the lad himself'), *The Trial* and *Nervous Energy*. Probably his most prominent role has been as the retired copper, Blake, in EL C.I.D., although he has also headlined in American series called *Ladies Man* and *Bram and Alice*, and made a guest appearance in *Law & Order: Special Victims Unit*.

Moll Flanders

See *Fortunes and Misfortunes of Moll Flanders, The*.

Monarch of the Glen ★★

UK (BBC/Ecosse Films) Drama. BBC 1 2000–5
DVD: Acorn Media

Hector MacDonald	**Richard Briers**
Molly MacDonald	**Susan Hampshire**
Archie MacDonald	**Alastair Mackenzie**
Katrina Finlay	**Lorraine Pilkington**
Golly Mackenzie	**Alexander Morton**
Alexandra 'Lexie' McTavish/ MacDonald	**Dawn Steele**
Duncan McKay	**Hamish Clark**
Justine	**Anna Wilson-Jones**
Lord Angus Kilwillie	**Julian Fellowes**
Fergal Maclure	**Jason O'Mara**
Stella Moon	**Alexandra Gilbreath**
Irene Stuart	**Rebecca Lacey**
Badger	**Angus Lennie**
Lady Dorothy Trumpington Bonnet	**Richenda Carey**
Paul Bowman-MacDonald	**Lloyd Owen**
Andrew Booth	**Paul Freeman**
Hermione Trumpington Bonnet	**Hermione Gulliford**
Jessica 'Jess' Mackenzie	**Rae Hendrie**
Ewan Brodie	**Martin Compston**
Isobel Anderson	**Simone Lahbib**
Donald Ulysses MacDonald	**Tom Baker**
Dr McKendrick	**Donald Douglas**
Meg Paterson	**Karen Westwood**
Chester Grant	**Anthony Head**
Lucy Ford	**Lucy Akhurst**
Iona MacLean	**Kirsty Mitchell**
Amy McDougal	**Kellyanne Farquhar**

Creator **Michael Chaplin**
Producers **Nick Pitt, Paddy Higson, Jeremy Gwilt, Stephen Garwood, Rob Bullock**
Executive Producers **Barbara McKissack, Douglas Rae**

● ***A noble Scottish family struggles to meet its responsibilities.***

Fourteen generations of the MacDonald family have run the Glenbogle estate in the Highlands of Scotland. For more than 400 years they have looked after a magnificent multi-turreted mansion on the side of a loch, caring for the grounds and wildlife, harvesting the timber and genially dispensing justice for the locals. The present head of the clan, Hector Naismith MacDonald, is a curmudgeonly old stick, stubbornly tethered to tradition and roguishly eccentric. His dotty wife, Molly, is softly spoken but not without spirit, her particular vice being gambling. Supporting them in the upkeep of the estate are feisty housekeeper Lexie (a notoriously bad cook), odd job boy Duncan and veteran gamekeeper Golly. Regrettably, things have taken a turn for the worse. The grand old house now has a leaking roof and faulty electrics, bills have not been paid and it looks like the clan will have to sell up. It is lucky then that Molly tricks son and heir Archie back to Glenbogle to see the state of affairs for himself. Archie, in his late twenties, has been building a successful restaurateur career in London with his girlfriend, Justine. However, when faced with the crisis back home and the fact that he has, unknowingly, inherited the title of laird from Hector (as a tax dodge), he reluctantly stays on to rebuild the fortunes of the estate. An emotional note is struck with the revelation that the true heir, Archie's elder brother Jamie, was killed in an accident on the loch in 1985. Despite this, with bolshie local headteacher/conservationist Katrina Finlay on hand to add romantic friction (especially when Justine follows Archie north and when a new ranger, Fergal Maclure, is taken on), the scene is set for seven series of light-hearted, quirky, Sunday evening dramas in which the spectacular Scottish scenery has a starring role.

To disrupt the pastoral harmony, there are occasional grudge matches with Kilwillie, laird of the next-door estate, while various officials are sent from Lascelles Bank in London to steer the MacDonalds on a course to solvency, most notably the dictatorial Stella Moon. At the end of the third series, the death of Hector casts a pall over the engagement of Archie to Lexie and in the next series a new cook, Irene, arrives to take Lexie's place 'below stairs'. By series four, Lexie and Archie are married and Kilwillie's stuffy old sister, Lady Dorothy, and Archie's half-brother, Paul, an ex-soldier, have arrived to stir up things. Paul eventually takes over the laird's role as Archie moves away. The next series sees the return after 40 years of family black sheep Donald MacDonald, brother of the late Hector. By the time *Monarch of the Glen* finally draws to a close, Glenbogle is once again financially embarrassed and on the market.

A Hogmanay special in 2003 allowed the MacDonalds to explore their family's history, with the cast taking dual roles as today's characters and their 19th-century ancestors. The series – filmed on the Ardverikie estate, near Laggan – was inspired by the Highland novels by Compton McKenzie.

Monitor [1]

A television display showing camera output. Monitors are used by the director to line up and select the next shot and also by presenters to see what is going out while they are on air.

Monitor [2]

UK (BBC) Arts Magazine. BBC 1 1958–65

Hosts **Huw Wheldon, Jonathan Miller**
Producers **Peter Newington, Nancy Thomas, Humphrey Burton**

● ***Britain's first successful arts programme.***

During its seven-year run, *Monitor* became a Sunday night institution for the learned classes. Screened at around 10 p.m., and presented for the most part in relaxed, authoritative fashion by its editor, Huw Wheldon, the programme spanned all artistic fields and laid the foundations for later successes like TEMPO, OMNIBUS, AQUARIUS and THE SOUTH BANK SHOW. *Monitor* also broke new ground by commissioning film profiles of artists from emerging film-makers like Ken Russell and John Schlesinger. These have since become archive classics.

Russell, for instance, made biopics of Elgar, Debussy, Rousseau and Bartók, while Schlesinger contributed pieces on Britten and others. Melvyn Bragg co-scripted some of Russell's work.

Monkees, The ★★★

US (Raybert/Screen Gems) Situation Comedy. BBC 1 1966–8 (US: NBC 1966–8)
DVD: Rhino (Region 1 only)

Davy	**Davy Jones**
Mickey	**Micky Dolenz**
Peter	**Peter Tork**
Mike	**Mike Nesmith**
Miss Purdy	**Jesslyn Fax**
Mr Babbitt	**Henry Corden**

Creators/Producers **Bert Schneider, Robert Rafelson**

Zany humour with a quartet of pop musicians.

In the wake of the success of The Beatles and, particularly, their madcap films *A Hard Day's Night* and *Help!*, a couple of American producers, Bert Schneider and Robert Rafelson, developed an idea for a TV version and advertised for four young lads to fashion into a pop group. The advert called for 'Four insane boys, aged 17–21'. After auditioning over 400 applicants, they settled on three Americans and one Englishman. Davy Jones was an actor from Manchester who had appeared briefly in CORONATION STREET as Ena Sharples's grandson. He was joined by another actor, Micky Dolenz, formerly Mickey Braddock of CIRCUS BOY fame, and the group was completed by Peter Tork and Michael Nesmith, both of whom did have some musical experience, albeit in the folk medium. Stephen Stills, later of supergroup Crosby, Stills and Nash, was one of the hopefuls turned down for the series.

Musically, their early recordings were made by session musicians, masterminded by producer Don Kirschner, and the series spawned some huge hits on both sides of the Atlantic. 'Last Train to Clarksville', 'I'm a Believer', 'Daydream Believer', 'Pleasant Valley Sunday' and 'A Little Bit Me, A Little Bit You' were the group's biggest successes, and all premièred on the TV show. In the group, the calm, bobble-hatted Nesmith and lank-haired, dozy Tork were the guitarists, the manic Dolenz sang and played the drums, and the hopeless romantic Jones mainly sang but sometimes tapped a tambourine or rattled a maraca.

The series, although borrowing heavily from Dick Lester's Beatles films in concept, was quite original in its own way. This was the first time that comedy had been treated to unusual camera-angles (often hand-held), blurred focuses, cranked-up or overexposed film and really snappy editing. The plots were less remarkable and featured the band getting into various scrapes and nearly always ending up in some kind of chase sequence.

After the break-up of the band and the end of the series, the most musically active was Nesmith, who became a respected performer/producer in the country rock sphere. Dolenz went on to produce and direct the METAL MICKEY series, Jones also returned to acting, but little was heard of Tork. The band reformed for a major concert tour in the late 1990s.

Monkey

See *Water Margin, The.*

Monkhouse, Bob

OBE (1928–2003)

Quick-witted British comedian, actor, writer, presenter, cartoonist and game show host. Multi-talented Monkhouse's showbiz career began to take off when he started selling jokes to comedians like Max Miller in the early 1940s, while still a schoolboy. With his partner, Denis Goodwin, he worked in radio and then broke into television. Their first series, *Fast and Loose*, in 1954, was an instant success and they also worked together on the sitcom *My Pal Bob* and *The Bob Monkhouse Hour*. Monkhouse, heading off solo, compered SUNDAY NIGHT AT THE LONDON PALLADIUM and fronted CANDID CAMERA. His love of silent films led to his own retrospective, *Mad Movies*, and he also tackled another sitcom, playing Bob Mason, a disc jockey, in *The Big Noise* in 1964. A few years later, Monkhouse replaced Jackie Rae as host of THE GOLDEN SHOT and turned it into a huge Sunday teatime hit. He went on to chair CELEBRITY SQUARES in 1975 (and its revival in 1993), did three years in charge of FAMILY FORTUNES from 1980, and switched to the BBC to host the bingo quiz *Bob's Full House*, and the revived talent show *Bob Says* OPPORTUNITY KNOCKS, in the middle of that decade. Back on ITV, he was the questionmaster on *The $64,000 Question* and star of the newlywed game show *Bob's Your Uncle*. Among his other contributions were *I'm Bob, He's Dickie* (with Dickie Henderson), the slapstick show *Bonkers!*, the cartoon contest *Quick on the Draw*, a BBC 2 chat show majoring on top comics, the fast-moving joke panel-game *Gagtag*, the quick recall quiz *Monkhouse's Memory Masters*, the audience-inspired *Bob Monkhouse on the Spot*, periods hosting both NATIONAL LOTTERY LIVE and THE BIG BREAKFAST, and various other quizzes over the decades, from *Do You Trust Your Wife?* to *Wipeout*. Straight drama credits included parts in *All or Nothing at All* and JONATHAN CREEK, and Monkhouse also provided the voice of Mr Hell for *Aaagh! It's the Mr Hell Show*. Among his last contributions were *Bob Monkhouse's Comedy Heroes* and a two-part career retrospective entitled *Behind the Laughter*.

Monocled Mutineer, The ★★★

UK (BBC) Drama. BBC 1 1986

Percy Toplis	**Paul McGann**
Charles Strange	**Matthew Marsh**
Cruikshank	**Nick Reding**
Geordie	**Billy Fellows**
Brigadier Gen. Thomson	**Timothy West**
Lady Angela Forbes	**Penelope Wilton**
Strachan	**Ron Donachie**
Guiness	**Anthony Calf**
Dorothy	**Cherie Lunghi**
Woodhall	**Philip McGough**

Writer **Alan Bleasdale**
Producer **Richard Broke**

A rebellious private leads a coup on the eve of a World War I battle.

Based on true events recalled in a book by William Allison and John Fairley, *The Monocled Mutineer* is the story of dashing rogue Percy Toplis. The cynical Nottinghamshire miner, a private in the British army, is stationed at the Etaples training camp in France and, on the night before the Battle of Passchendaele in 1917, instigates a mutiny among his harshly treated fellow recruits. His partner in the action is Charles Strange, a political idealist. This four-part dramatization by Alan Bleasdale (whose own grandfather had died at Passchendaele) adds fiction to the bare facts and depicts how Toplis escapes into the French hills, takes to impersonating an army officer and leads a group of renegades in the taking of a bridge. He then returns to England and falls in love with Dorothy, a young widow, before being captured in the Lake District and 'executed' for his crimes by MI5 assassin Woodhall.

The series proved to be the most provocative of Alan Bleasdale's works up to that time and roused the ire of Establishment figures and old soldiers. The suggestion that deserters were executed by their own side (exemplified in the drama by the shooting of an officer named Cruikshank) was heavily condemned. The fact that Michael Grade, the BBC's Director of Programmes, had passed a press release stating that the story was totally factual only made matters worse. According to Grade, the fuss detracted from the quality of the drama itself.

Monsignor Renard ★★★

UK (Carlton) Drama. ITV 2000

Monsignor Augustin Renard	**John Thaw**
Madeleine Claveau	**Cheryl Campbell**
Hélène Claveau	**Juliette Caton**
Albert Claveau	**Andrew McCulloch**
Malo Gagnepain	**Jimmy Yuill**
Etienne Rollinger	**Dominic Monaghan**
Louis Cavailles	**Geoffrey Hutchings**
Yves Renard	**Des McAleer**
Antoine Cabache	**Timothy Walker**
Jean Marie Vercors	**Jamie Lee**
Sgt Roger Duclos	**John Axon**
Henri Baquet	**Adam Kotz**
Clara Baquet	**Teresa Banham**
Alain Baquet	**Edward Hewitt**
Daniel Flandin	**Jay Villiers**
David Lavalle	**Patrick Nielsen**
Madame Dufosse	**Barbara Kellerman**
Monsieur Dufosse	**Michael Attwell**
Major Drexler	**Bernd-Uwe Reppenhagen**
Lt. Beckmann	**Anatole Taubman**
Rudi Brandt	**Klaus Schreiber**
Alois	**Torben Liebrecht**

Writers **Russell Lewis, Charles Wood, Stephen Churchett**
Executive Producer **Ted Childs**

A priest helps his home townsfolk to brave the German occupation.

Augustin Renard, a Roman Catholic priest, returns after 20 years to the little French town of St Josse-des-Bois, the place where he grew up, in the Pas de Calais. It is the early days of the German occupation during World War II and the townsfolk are in a panic about the prospect of invasion. Mayor Louis Cavailles is of little use in uniting the people, so the unorthodox Monsignor Renard needs to extend his duties beyond the spiritual. Sickened by the brutality of the eventual occupiers, the priest – a former soldier, decorated in World War I – finds himself drawn into active resistance, even to the point of being, for a while, incarcerated. One typical act of defiance is the use of a religious procession to stage a protest against the German treatment of Jews. Among the most prominent townsfolk are Madeleine, a former lover of Renard who now runs Café L'Etoile with husband Albert and attractive daughter Hélène; Renard's brother, Yves; Gagnepain, a petty thief; Henri Baquet, the local pharmacist, and his family; police chief Antoine Cabache; the mayor's deputy, Daniel Flandin; and a reckless youth called Etienne. The series meanders through 1940 over four 90-minute episodes, culminating in Christmas that year, when the Germans are firmly in control and ensure the locals know it. Filmed at a cost of £6 million, the series was shot in the Picardy town of St Valery-sur-Somme. To ensure that corny accents didn't detract from the seriousness of the plot, the French characters spoke plain English and the Germans communicated in their native language (subtitled in English).

Monsters, The ★★

UK (BBC) Science Fiction. BBC 1962

Prof. John Brent	**William Greene**
Felicity Brent	**Elizabeth Weaver**
Prof. Cato	**Robert Harris**
Wilf Marner	**Howard Douglas**
Van Halloran	**Alan Gifford**
Hopkins	**Mark Dignam**
Esmee Pulford	**Helen Lindsay**
Smetanov	**George Pravda**

Writers **Evelyn Frazer, Vincent Tilsley**
Producer **George R. Foa**

The sighting of a monster in a lake leads to a complex murder enquiry.

Inspired by a PANORAMA documentary about the Loch Ness monster, this four-part drama, directed by Mervyn Pinfield, was set on the banks of fictional Lake Kingswater in 1952. Zoology professor John Brent is staying with his wife, Felicity, at a lakeside hotel on their honeymoon when local man Wilf Marner reports seeing a strange creature in the lake. He had first spotted the beast ten years earlier but was a member of the local Home Guard at the time and had dared not risk his position by discussing it too widely. Now, however, he's a civilian again and is keen to reveal his discovery. Brent is intrigued by the man's tale, even more so when a government agent is found dead in the water and the dead man's sister, Esmee Pulford, arrives on the scene. Is there really a monster in the lake, or could the mysterious Professor Cato, who owns a mini-submarine, have something to do with these enigmatic events? As well as offering sci-fi thrills, the series also claimed to raise the moral question about how human and animal life can successfully survive together on Earth.

Montgomery, Elizabeth

(1933–95)

Betty Grable insured her legs, so perhaps Elizabeth Montgomery should have sought cover for her nose, for as winsome witch Samantha Stephens in BEWITCHED, she relied on its twitching to cast her benign spells. Samantha was a role she played for eight years from 1964 and the series was produced by her husband, William Asher. Keeping it in the family, it was her dad, actor Robert Montgomery, who, somewhat reluctantly, gave Elizabeth her TV break, offering her a part in his anthology series *Robert Montgomery Presents* in the early 1950s. She followed this with appearances in dozens of other series but, after leaving *Bewitched*, Montgomery was generally seen only in TV movies.

Monty Python's Flying Circus ★★★★

UK (BBC) Comedy. BBC 1 1969–73; BBC 2 1973–4
DVD: BBC

John Cleese, Michael Palin, Eric Idle, Graham Chapman, Terry Jones, Terry Gilliam, Carol Cleveland

Writers **John Cleese, Michael Palin, Eric Idle, Graham Chapman, Terry Jones, Terry Gilliam**
Producers **John Howard Davies, Ian MacNaughton**

● ***Cerebral wit, visual humour and slapstick bound together by anarchy.***

When it first reached the TV screen in 1969, filling a former religious slot, late on Sunday night, *Monty Python's Flying Circus* understandably met with some bemusement. However, it soon acquired a fervent global following and genuine cult status. Each programme was well endowed with sketches and held together with animation and one-liner humour; but, essentially, anything went in this manic collage of comedy styles.

The sketches relied heavily on off-beat domestic situations and spoof TV interviews or documentaries, although the series seldom lacked invention. Swaying between incomprehensibility and bad taste, it was a show that shocked and confused, but was always inspired. The Oxbridge background of its writers/performers surfaced in the show's literary and artistic allusions, yet there was always room for juvenile pranks, vulgar asides and general silliness. Among the highlights were skits like *The Dead Parrot*, in which John Cleese confronted Michael Palin, a shopkeeper, with the corpse of a bird he had just purchased. Another classic was *The Lumberjack Song*, a rousing Canadian chorus of machismo which unravelled into a celebration of transvestism. There was also *The Argument Clinic*, *Upper Class Twit of the Year*, *The Ministry of Silly Walks*, *Spam*, *The Spanish Inquisition*, *The Fish-Slapping Dance*, and *Blackmail* (a sadistic game show). Classic characters included Graham Chapman's stuffy army officer, Terry Jones's piercingly vocal women, Eric Idle's seedy men, and the cerebrally challenged Gumby, complete with knotted handkerchief on head.

Wrapped around the sketches were Terry Gilliam's chaotic, surreal cartoons which 'stole' images from classical art. Sometimes they picked up from the end of the previous sketch (which seldom had a punchline), in the same way that sketches themselves occasionally merged when a character from an earlier skit wandered into the action. Snappily cut together, it was a programme without a beginning and without an end which broke all the rules of television structure. Its opening titles, bouncing along on the music of Sousa's *Liberty Bell*, could appear anywhere in the show, even after the closing credits, and along the way there was plenty of time for developing catchphrases, from Michael Palin's succinct 'It's' (possibly the shortest catchphrase ever) to John Cleese's 'And now for something completely different.'

Yet if *Monty Python* broke new ground, it could at the same time be seen as the culmination of the unconventional comedy trend that had begun with THAT WAS THE WEEK THAT WAS, and developed through THE FROST REPORT, NOT ONLY ... BUT ALSO ..., AT LAST THE 1948 SHOW and DO NOT ADJUST YOUR SET. The Pythons had all learned their craft in such programmes, a craft which was to stand them in good stead in individual projects long after *Monty Python* was laid to rest. John Cleese did not appear in the final season (which went out under the simple title of *Monty Python*).

A series of stage shows and feature films was also produced, the earliest films reprising the best of the TV sketches but the later ones taking the Python manic humour to new bounds in mock epics like *Monty Python and the Holy Grail* and the notorious *Life of Brian*.

Moody, Ron

(Ronald Moodnick; 1924–)

British actor whose television work has failed to achieve the heights of his cinema and stage performances. Indeed, his TV outlets have been few. These have included a 1961 BBC series entitled *Moody in ...* (various contrived 'lands', such as *Storeland*), a show for YTV in 1968 entitled *Moody*, and the odd single drama (such as Jack Rosenthal's *Mr Ellis versus the People* in 1974). There have also been TV movies, a couple of kids' series (*Into the Labyrinth*, playing sorcerer Rothgo, and *Mike and Angelo*, as Angelo's father), plus a sitcom, HART OF THE YARD (DI Roger Hart, a London detective working in San Francisco – the series was called *Nobody's Perfect* in the US). Moody has, however, made guest appearances in numerous other programmes, including THE AVENGERS, THE BILL, HOLBY CITY and EASTENDERS (Edwin Caldicot), and added his vocal talents to various animations, such as *The Telebugs* and THE ANIMALS OF FARTHING WOOD (Badger).

Moonbase 3 ★★

UK (BBC) Science Fiction. BBC 1 1973
DVD: Second Sight

Dr David Caulder	**Donald Houston**
Tom Hill	**Barry Lowe**
Michel Lebrun	**Ralph Bates**
Dr Helen Smith	**Fiona Gaunt**

Producer **Barry Letts**

● ***The inhabitants of a lunar station strive to build a new future for mankind.***

This six-part drama trades on a more feasible approach to science fiction than most space series. The year is 2003 and Earth has begun to colonize the moon. However, since the Apollo lunar landings, progress has been slow and man is still only living in primitive pods. Moonbase 1 belongs to the USA; the USSR has Moonbase 2; China runs Moonbase 4 and Moonbase 5 is controlled by Brazil. Moonbase 3 is the domain of Europe, and therefore has a multinational crew. With lunar living still in the experimental stage and highly claustrophobic, the pressures on the team are enormous, as new base director David Caulder – a Welsh former Oxford University professor – discovers. With the assistance of his French number two, Michel Lebrun, scientific director Tom Hill and psychiatrist Helen Smith, Caulder aims to keep his charges in good shape. Unfortunately, constant worries over technical problems, competition from other bases, low budgets and the need to justify their experimental existence mean they are fighting a losing battle. Consultant for the series was BBC science boffin James Burke.

Moonlighting ★★★

US (Picturemaker) Comedy Drama. BBC 2 1986–9
(US: ABC 1985–9)
DVD: Universal

Maddie Hayes	**Cybill Shepherd**
David Addison	**Bruce Willis**
Agnes Dipesto	**Allyce Beasley**
Herbert Viola	**Curtis Armstrong**
Virginia Hayes	**Eva Marie Saint**
Alex Hayes	**Robert Webber**
MacGilicuddy	**Jack Blessing**

Creator/Executive Producer **Glenn Gordon Caron**
Producer **Jay Daniel**

● ***Off-beat sleuthing with a squabbling but romantically linked pair of investigators.***

When top fashion model Maddie Hayes is swindled by her financial managers, she discovers that one of the few investments she still owns is City of Angels Investigations, a private detective agency set up to make a loss to offset against her tax bills. Running the business is cocky David Addison, a flippant, streetwise young private eye. Although Maddie intends to sell off the company, Addison ensures that she holds on to it, renaming the firm the Blue Moon Detective Agency, after the Blue Moon shampoo she used to market. With her modelling career now behind her, Maddie decides to take a hand in the running of the business and the aloof, classy blonde and the smirking, stubble-chinned punk became unlikely partners.

From the start, their relationship is electric. They come from widely differing backgrounds and they have different ways of working. Yet they also have chemistry. Although they spar and fight their way through investigations, there is always a restrained romance behind their bickering. Maddie toys with other suitors (even marrying a stranger on a train) and David plays the field, but the two eventually cave in and get together. All the same, even while pregnant with his child (later miscarried), the animosity between the partners remains and explodes into violent verbal exchanges (the sharp repartee is the highlight of the programme).

At work, they are successful, taking on a variety of unusual cases and usually gaining positive results, at the same time turning the Blue Moon Detective Agency into a viable business. They are assisted by their scatty receptionist, Agnes Dipesto, who answers the telephone with a little rhyme, and Herbert Viola, the object of Agnes's desires, who joins the team as a clerk but longs to be a detective. His office rival is MacGilicuddy. Maddie's parents, Alex and Virginia, are also seen.

With its witty dialogue style gleaned from the 1940 film *His Girl Friday*, starring Cary Grant and Rosalind Russell, *Moonlighting* is one of those programmes that breaks every law of television. Characters speak to camera, out-takes are shown over the closing credits and actors drop out of character and address the audience as themselves. The surreal air is enhanced with episodes like *Atomic Shakespeare*, based on *The Taming of the Shrew*, written in iambic pentameters and performed in period costume. However, the programme was plagued with production problems, and reruns had to be inserted when the latest episodes failed to arrive on time. Stars Shepherd and Willis didn't always see eye to eye, and this all contributed to a rather scrappy finish to the series. It faded away rather than going out with a bang. The theme song was a UK hit for Al Jarreau in 1987, and Bruce Willis followed up with hits of his own.

Moore, Brian

(1932–2001)

Experienced British soccer commentator and general sports presenter whose main credits were *The Big Match*, WORLD OF SPORT (the *On the Ball* segment), *Who's the Greatest?*, *Midweek Sports Special* and other major sport coverage. Before joining ITV in 1968, Moore worked as a journalist for *The Times* and BBC radio (from 1961). He retired after the 1998 soccer World Cup finals, but was later seen on satellite TV.

Moore, Clayton

(Jack Carlton Moore; 1914–99)

Television's LONE RANGER, Clayton Moore began his movie career in 1938 as a stuntman (he was previously a circus performer). He was offered the part of the masked Western hero ten years later and, as soon as the series hit US TV screens, Moore became a huge celebrity. After three years, he fell out of favour with the show's producers over contractual matters and John Hart was brought in as a replacement for 52 episodes, before Moore returned to the role he now felt to be his own. In 1979, the Wrather Corporation, which owned the rights to the character, took legal action to prevent Moore from continuing to wear the Lone Ranger mask. He adopted mask-shaped sunglasses instead.

Moore, Dudley

CBE (1935–2002)

Oxford educated classical pianist, jazz performer, actor and comedian, in the early days in collaboration with Peter Cook. Moore, together with Cook, Alan Bennett and Jonathan Miller, was one of the *Beyond the Fringe* team in 1960–1. TV work soon followed. When the BBC asked him to do a special, he enrolled Cook to compile a couple of sketches. The BBC liked what it saw and gave them their own series, NOT ONLY . . . BUT ALSO . . . Among Moore's other credits were assorted variety shows, an episode of the drama anthology LOVE STORY, and his own *Not to Mention Dudley Moore*. In the 1970s, however, Moore concentrated mainly on film work, becoming a Hollywood name through his role in *10*. His later TV work was confined to two unsuccessful US sitcoms, *Dudley* and *Daddy's Girls*, and to providing the voice for Oscar the piano in the cartoon *Oscar's Orchestra*. The first of Moore's four wives was actress Suzy Kendall; the second was actress Tuesday Weld.

Moore, Mary Tyler

(1936–)

American actress and television executive whose MARY TYLER MOORE SHOW was one of the USA's biggest successes in the 1970s. A former dancer, her TV break came in unusual circumstances. After a few commercials and small roles, she was cast as Sam, the secretary, in David Janssen's 1959 series *Richard Diamond, Private Detective*, although the only parts of her that viewers saw were her legs. She quit after three months in favour of appearances in dramas like HAWAIIAN EYE. Two years later, her role as Laura Petrie, the wife in THE DICK VAN DYKE SHOW, established Moore as a major sitcom star, but her career seemed to be going no further when the series ended in 1966. After a few stage and film disappointments, she was given another chance to shine in her own *Mary Tyler Moore Show* in 1970 and this time didn't let the opportunity pass. It was a ratings hit and its portrayal of an independent, career-minded female (Mary Richards) matched the general mood of the 1970s. Moore and her then husband, Grant Tinkler, founded the production company MTM (Mary Tyler Moore Enterprises, responsible for such series as LOU GRANT, REMINGTON STEELE and HILL STREET BLUES), which was later sold to the UK's TVS. She has since returned to the small screen in the unsuccessful 1985 and 1988 sitcoms *Mary* and *Annie McGuire*, and the 1995 drama series *New York News*.

Moore, Sir Patrick

CBE (Patrick Caldwell-Moore; 1923–)

Britain's number one stargazer, Patrick Moore has been presenting his monthly series THE SKY AT NIGHT since 1957, making it one of the BBC's longest-running programmes. His fascination with astronomy began at an early age and he became a member of the British Astronomical Association when just 11. After working as a navigator in the wartime RAF, Moore was commissioned to write his first books on space and set up his own observatory. All this led to a call from the BBC and, eventually, *The Sky at Night*. He also hosted the series about eccentrics *One Pair of Eyes*, in 1969, hosted a kids' astronomy series, *Seeing Stars*, in 1970, and was the resident expert on the BBC's coverage of the lunar missions in the 1960s and 1970s. In the 1990s Moore was seen as *The Gamesmaster* in Channel 4's computer game contest. Additionally, he has been a popular guest in numerous light entertainment shows, often exhibiting his prowess on the xylophone. Moore also made a cameo appearance in the 1966 kid's sci-fi classic, THE MASTER.

Moore, Sir Roger

CBE (1927–)

London-born leading man who arrived on television in 1958, wearing the chain mail of Sir Walter Scott's IVANHOE, having already made one film in Hollywood and others in England. In 1959 he played Silky Harris in the gold rush caper *The Alaskans*, and a year later was cast as Cousin Beauregard in MAVERICK. He even introduced SUNDAY NIGHT AT THE LONDON PALLADIUM. Then, in 1962, came his most celebrated TV characterization, that of Simon Templar, debonair hero of THE SAINT. The series ran for seven years and made Moore – a former film cartoonist and model – an international star. Although he didn't really capitalize on the situation with his next TV outing, THE PERSUADERS! (Lord Brett Sinclair), in 1971, he soon made up for it by making seven films as James Bond. Apart from guest appearances, that mostly put paid to Moore's television career, as he fixed his quizzical gaze (and much-mimicked raised eyebrows) firmly on the movie world, although he did resurface in a US series called *The Dream Team*. Moore's second wife was the late singer Dorothy Squires.

More, Kenneth

(1914–82)

British actor, a 1950s cinema favourite who also enjoyed a couple of notable TV roles. These came in 1967, as Jolyon Forsyte in THE FORSYTE SAGA, and seven years later as G. K. Chesterton's cleric-detective, FATHER BROWN. More also starred in THE WHITE RABBIT, a 1967 dramatization of the heroics of resistance fighter Wing-Commander Yeo-Thomas, and played Peter Ingram in AN ENGLISHMAN'S CASTLE in 1978. However, one of his earliest small-screen performances came in 1946 as Badger in *Toad of Toad Hall* and he enjoyed numerous other single-drama credits, too. More's third wife was actress Angela Douglas.

More 4

Digital channel launched by Channel 4 on 10 October 2005. It's stated aim was to redefine the term 'adult entertainment' by focusing on films, documentaries, current affairs, news and drama.

More Tales of the City

See *Armistead Maupin's Tales of the City*.

Morecambe, Eric

OBE (Eric Bartholomew; 1926–84)

Possibly Britain's most popular comedian to date, Eric Morecambe took his stage name from his home town. His career began in variety theatres before the war and, when auditioning for a new-talent show in 1941, he met a young entertainer from Leeds by the name of Ernest Wiseman, otherwise known as Ernie Wise. They forged an enterprising double-act, but their progress was shattered by war service. However, meeting again by chance in 1947, they were able to resume their joint career. Their first television forays came in the early 1950s and led, in 1954, to their own disastrous series called *Running Wild*, which set back their hopes of stardom. Undaunted, the pair continued to improve their act on stage and radio and were chosen to support Winifred Atwell in her TV series, this resulting in another short series of their own, *Double Six*, and appearances on SUNDAY NIGHT AT THE LONDON PALLADIUM, which encouraged ATV to give them *The Morecambe and Wise Show* in 1961, scripted by Sid Green and Dick Hills. This time they didn't squander their chance and quickly established themselves and the characteristics of their act – Ernie's pomposity, Eric's boyish anarchy, their Abbot-and-Costello-like exchanges, all underscored by impeccable comic timing. Viewers took to their many sight gags: Eric slipping his glasses askew, for instance, slapping Ernie around the face or pretending to be strangled behind the stage curtain. The public began to refer to Ernie as Little Ern and 'the one with the short, fat, hairy legs'. Unfortunately, their attempts to make it in the movies proved fruitless. Their films, *The Intelligence Men*, *That Riviera Touch* and *The Magnificent Two*, flopped.

In 1968, after Eric had suffered a heart attack, they were tempted over to the BBC where, by common consent, they produced their best work (most scripted by Eddie Braben). A regular feature of their shows was a play 'wot Ernie wrote' which never failed to attract a big-name guest star. Among those who giggled their way through proceedings were Glenda Jackson, Diana Rigg, John Mills, Eric Porter, Peter Cushing (to return many times still looking for payment) and Hannah Gordon. Shirley Bassey sang in a hobnail boot. The duo were seen in domestic situations (even innocently sharing a double bed). They cruelly disparaged Des O'Connor's singing and were constantly upstaged at the end of each show by the outsize Janet Webb or Arthur Tolcher with his mouth-organ. Ernie's alleged hairpiece ('You can't see the join') provided many gags and Eric flicked non-existent pebbles into a paper bag. Most shows closed with a neck-slapping rendition of 'Bring Me Sunshine' (their ITV theme song had been 'Two of a Kind'). If Eric had put one of his catchphrases, 'What do you think of it so far?', to the nation, he would not have received the usual reply of 'Rubbish!'. *The Morecambe and Wise Christmas Show* became a national institution. Angela Rippon kicked away her news desk and danced at Christmas 1976 and a team of newsreaders and sports presenters staged an acrobatic version of 'There is Nothing Like a Dame' a year later.

The partners switched back to ITV in 1978 with less success (Eddie Braben was not immediately released by the BBC), while the BBC countered by screening repeats of their best material. However, they soon knew they would have to start treading carefully. Eric's heart problems resurfaced in 1979 and, after surgery, he was forced to take things somewhat easier. The partnership was brought to an end when Eric suffered another, this time fatal, heart attack in 1984. Their last work together was a TV movie, *Night Train to Murder*, which was aired in 1985. Ernie soldiered on alone, making stage and television appearances, becoming a member of the revived WHAT'S MY LINE? panel and even writing on gardening for the *News of the World*. He died in 1999.

Morgan, Elaine
(1920–)

Welsh dramatist whose most notable works have included 1960's *A Matter of Degree* (and a spin-off sitcom, *Lil*, five years later), *Epitaph for a Spy*, *A Pin to See the Peepshow*, the single drama *Joey* (1974), ANNE OF AVONLEA, *How Green was My Valley*, MARIE CURIE, TESTAMENT OF YOUTH, THE LIFE AND TIMES OF DAVID LLOYD GEORGE, FAME IS THE SPUR and episodes of DR FINLAY'S CASEBOOK, *Sanctuary*, THE DOCTORS, THE ONEDIN LINE and THE BROTHERS.

Morgan, Harry
(Harry Bratsburg; 1915–)

American actor who arrived in television in the early 1950s, after acting in films (as Henry Morgan) since 1942. In the USA, he has notched up plenty of prime-time roles, beginning with the part of Pete Porter in a comedy, *December Bride*, which was spun off into its own series, *Pete and Gladys*. For UK viewers, however, Morgan will be remembered for two roles in particular. In 1967 he joined Jack Webb in a revival of DRAGNET, becoming Officer Bill Gannon. Then, in 1974, he made a one-off guest appearance in M*A*S*H and proved such a hit that he was asked back as the unit's new CO, Colonel Sherman Potter. Morgan's character lived on in the sequel, *After M*A*S*H*. In 1987, he starred in another US sitcom, *You Can't Take It with You*. Viewers may also recall him as Phil Jensen in *My World and Welcome to It*, Doc Amos B. Coogan in HEC RAMSEY, Bob Campbell in *Roots: The Next Generations*, Harry S. Truman in *Backstairs at the White House*, and as a guest star in numerous series, from GUNSMOKE and THE PARTRIDGE FAMILY to THIRD ROCK FROM THE SUN.

Morgan's Boy ★★

UK (BBC) Drama. BBC 1 1984

Morgan Thomas	**Gareth Thomas**
Lee Turner	**Martyn Hesford**
Val Turner	**Marjorie Yates**
Pugh Davies	**Jack Walters**
Matthew Gibbs	**John Skitt**
Louise Gibbs	**Tracey Childs**
Harry Gregory	**Alan Rowe**
Eileen Gregory	**Maxine Audley**
Tom Griffiths	**James Warrior**
Sarah Griffiths	**Pippa Hinchley**
Price	**Charles Dale**
Les	**Artro Morris**
Alan	**Stephen Yardley**
Tom Duncan	**David Quilter**
Graham	**Robbin John**

Writer **Alick Rowe**
Producer **Gerard Glaister**

A city kid is forced to live with his uncle in the wilds of Wales.

There are problems facing teenager Lee Turner. His mother has taken up with a new lover, a man with whom the boy does not see eye to eye, so to resolve the situation Lee is packed off to live with his uncle on a farm in the Black Mountains of Wales. It is initially not a happy relationship. Sullen city boy Lee resents having to stay in this backwater and is insecure in his new home. His uneducated, taciturn uncle, Morgan, is equally uncertain about how things will pan out. However, the seemingly incompatible youth and middle-aged man somehow form a bond that is strong enough to withstand cross-generation spats and their different outlooks on life. It keeps them close when times are hard in the village of Blainau and particularly when the local estate wants to repossess the farm. Lonely Morgan, with his parents dead and his sister living away, discovers at last that he does have a family.

Mork and Mindy ★★★

US (Miller-Milkis/Henderson/Paramount) Situation Comedy. ITV 1979–81 (US: ABC 1978–82)
DVD: Paramount (Region 1 only)

Mork	**Robin Williams**
Mindy McConnell	**Pam Dawber**
Frederick McConnell	**Conrad Janis**
Cora Hudson	**Elizabeth Kerr**
Orson	**Ralph James** *(voice only)*
Eugene	**Jeffrey Jacquet**
Exidor	**Robert Donner**
Franklin Delano Bickley	**Tom Poston**
Nelson Flavor	**Jim Staahl**
Remo Da Vinci	**Jay Thomas**
Jean Da Vinci	**Gina Hecht**
Glenda Comstock	**Crissy Wilzak**
Mearth	**Jonathan Winters**
Miles Sternhagen	**Foster Brooks**

Creators **Garry K. Marshall, Joe Glauberg, Dale McRaven**
Executive Producers **Garry K. Marshall, Tony Marshall**
Producers **Bruce Johnson, Dale McRaven**

A naïve alien arrives on Earth and pals up with a pretty young girl.

Fifteen years after MY FAVORITE MARTIAN had created comedy from an alien–human friendship, *Mork and Mindy* came to the TV screen and did the same thing – in subject-matter, at least. This time the style is much more frenetic and the alien far less predictable than Uncle Martin in the earlier series. Mork comes from the planet Ork, bleems and bleems away from Earth (as he puts it). There, he is considered odd because he has a sense of humour and, when he went too far and poked fun at Orson, their leader, the Orkans sent him to our planet as a punishment, to file reports on the weird lifestyles of Earth's inhabitants. He arrives in a large eggshell-like spacecraft near Boulder, Colorado, and is discovered by Mindy McConnell, a genial single girl who works in her dad's music store. She finds him intriguing and amusing, is entertained by his child-like ways and is touched by his kindness. Consequently, Mork takes up residence in Mindy's attic, much to the consternation of her crusty father.

Although he looks human, Mork is prone to talking gibberish and doing wacky things like wearing a suit back to front, sitting on his head or drinking water with his fingers. There are always aspects of Earth life that he just cannot comprehend and, at the end of every episode, he reports back his experiences to the unseen Orson, before signing off, twisting his ears and saying 'Nanu Nanu', Orkan for goodbye.

In later episodes, Mindy's father, Fred, her hip grandmother, Cora Hudson, and Eugene, a black youth who frequents the music store, are written out. Fred later returns and some new characters are introduced when a brother and sister, Remo and Jean Da Vinci, arrive from the Bronx. Remo works at the New York Deli and pays for Jean to attend medical school. Also new are Mindy's politically ambitious cousin, Nelson, and Mork's UFO-prophet friend, Exidor, leader of the invisible Friends of Venus clan. Mr Bickley, the crotchety neighbour who writes greeting cards for a living, comes into the action a little more, and Mindy takes a job in the newsroom of a television station, KTNS, working for boss Mr Sternhagen.

Mork and Mindy's friendship grows deeper and deeper until they eventually marry, taking a honeymoon on Ork. Soon after, Mork gives birth by releasing a tiny egg from his navel. The egg grows in size until it bursts open to reveal the baby, a fully grown, middle-aged man. He, in the Orkan tradition, will grow younger, not older, and will never want for love and care in his later years. They call the 'baby' Mearth; he calls Mork 'Mommy' and Mindy 'Shoe'.

Mork and Mindy was a spin-off from an episode of HAPPY DAYS where, in a dream, Mork arrives in Milwaukee and tries to kidnap Richie Cunningham. It made a star out of the relatively unknown Robin Williams, whose unpredictably quirky humour was perfect for the character of Mork. One of his childhood heroes had been comedian Jonathan Winters, and Williams was able to pay his mentor a tribute by helping to cast him as Mearth.

Morley, Ken

(1943–)

British actor, a former teacher who became a cult hero with his portrayal of self-important supermarket manager Reg Holdsworth in CORONATION STREET from 1990, but whose TV career has also encompassed programmes like 'ALLO 'ALLO (the German Flockenstuffen), YOU RANG, M'LORD?, THE FALL AND RISE OF REGINALD PERRIN, BULMAN, *Who Dares, Wins . . .*, *All Passion Spent*, *Les Girls*, WATCHING, *The Return of the Antelope*, THE GRAND and HARDWARE (Rex). Other guest appearances have been in RED DWARF and *Margery and Gladys*.

Mornin' Sarge ★★

UK (BBC) Situation Comedy. BBC 2 1989

Ted	**Robin Driscoll**
Ben	**Tony Haase**
Kevin Robinson	**Pete McCarthy**
Wendy	**Rebecca Stevens**
'Sarge'	**Paul Brooke**

Writers **Tony Haase, Rebecca Stevens, Peter McCarthy**
Producers **Jamie Rix, John Kilby**

● ***Wacky comedy with the crew of a suburban police station.***

Set in the chaotic Middleford Broadway police station, this farcical comedy – with echoes of the *Naked Gun* movies – features a collection of misfit officers who each have their own character flaws. Lazy CID man Ted is a bigot and hates children, Wendy is obsessed with holidays, and the pivotal figure, Sarge, also runs the station bar. Ben is the (allegedly) superior officer and into this mad world has stepped former geography teacher Kevin Robinson, a new graduate recruit constable. Just six episodes were made, plus a pilot.

Morning in the Streets ★★★

UK (BBC) Documentary. BBC 1959

Producer **Denis Mitchell**

● ***The dawn of a new day in Britain's industrial heartlands.***

Shot in Liverpool, Salford, Stockport and Manchester, this 35-minute film is one of TV's landmark documentaries. Jointly directed by influential producer Denis Mitchell and cameraman Roy Harris, it focuses on early stirrings in these northern cities, beginning with empty wet streets that slowly fill up with men going to work, children heading for school, women gossiping at the back door. This 'impression of life and opinion', created by letting ordinary people speak for themselves, ends when the kids break for lunch. The BBC Northern Orchestra provides the mood music, with harmonica soloist Tommy Reilly to the fore.

Morris, Chris

(1965–)

Bristol-born actor, comedian and writer whose work has often pushed the boundaries of TV comedy and stirred up plenty of controversy. His programmes include THE DAY TODAY, BRASS EYE and *Jam*. He played Denholm in *The IT Crowd* and has also been seen in I'M ALAN PARTRIDGE. Additionally, Morris wrote and produced the comedy *Nathan Barley*.

Morris, Colin

(1916–96)

British writer and producer, creator of *Jacks and Knaves*, THE NEWCOMERS and THE DOCTORS. Among his other contributions were drama-documentaries like *The Wharf Road Mob* (1957), *Who, Me?* (1959) and *Walk with Destiny* (a Winston Churchill biography, 1974), plus episodes of series like *King of the River* and WHEN THE BOAT COMES IN. He also produced a number of editions of Z CARS.

Morris, Johnny

OBE (1916–99)

Fondly remembered for making animals talk, Welsh-born Johnny Morris presented ANIMAL MAGIC for 21 years from 1962. Before moving into television, he had managed a farm in Wiltshire and presented a radio series, in which he did other people's jobs for a day and travelled around the south-west. On TV, he appeared as *The Hot Chestnut Man*, which made full use of his flair for telling a tale. When *Animal Magic* came along, Morris donned a zoo-keeper's uniform and spent many days at Bristol Zoo, adding a whimsical vocal track to the films he made, putting casual quips in the mouths of his animal subjects. It was a trick he used when narrating another children's favourite, the Canadian series TALES OF THE RIVERBANK. In 1970 Morris took a journey through South America for a series entitled *A Gringo's Holiday* and followed this with *Series in the Sun*, a look at Captain Cook's Pacific. In 1976 he presented *Oh to be in England*, a tourist's-eye view of the country. Another credit was for a series called *Follow the Rhine*. He was working on a new animal series, *Wild Thing*, for ITV when he was taken ill and died in 1999.

Morris, Jonathon

(John Morris; 1960–)

Manchester-born actor whose most prominent role has been as the poetic Adrian Boswell in BREAD but who has had plenty of other TV credits to his name since the early 1980s, among them BEAU GESTE (John), *That Beryl Marston . . . !* (Phil), THE PROFESSIONALS, *The Prisoner of Zenda, Hell's Bells, The Consultant*, THE AGATHA CHRISTIE HOUR, DOCTOR WHO and THE PRACTICE. For kids, Morris has presented JACKANORY and chaired *The Movie Game*.

Morris, Juliet

(1965–)

English factual programme presenter, beginning in BBC regional news in the West Country and moving on to front NEWSROUND, *BBC Breakfast News, The Six O'Clock News, Here and Now, 999, The House Detectives, The Heaven and Earth Show, The Travel Show, Mysteries* and *The Good Food Show*, among other offerings, as well as narrating series such as *The Stress Factor*.

Morrissey, David

(1963–)

Liverpool-born actor and director whose early television roles included those of Billy in *One Summer*, George Bowman in *Cause Célèbre*, Theseus in JIM HENSON'S GREEK MYTHS, Rob in *The Widowmaker*, Lawrence Jackson in *Framed* and *Finney* in the series of the same name. He later starred as Gerry Birch in THE KNOCK, Ride in *Into the Fire*, DS 'Lew' Lewyn in OUT OF THE BLUE, Shaun in *Holding On*, Bradley Headstone in OUR MUTUAL FRIEND, Frank Healy in *Pure Wickedness*, Dave Dewston in *Murder*, prison officer Mike in *Out of Control*, Richie MacGregor in *This Little Life*, Stephen Collins in STATE OF PLAY, Gordon Brown in *The Deal* and Ripley Holden in BLACKPOOL. His notable guest credits take in BETWEEN THE LINES, LINDA GREEN and CLOCKING OFF. One of his directing credits was Tony Marchant's play *Passer By*. Morrissey is married to novelist Esther Freud.

Morrissey, Neil

(1962–)

Midlands-born actor, usually in comic roles, such as Rocky Cassidy in BOON, Tony in MEN BEHAVING BADLY and Barry in CARRIE AND BARRY. He featured regularly in NOEL'S HOUSE PARTY as window cleaner Sammy the Shammy, played art student David in *A Woman's Guide to Adultery*, and John Croft and Martin in the one-off comedies, *The Chest* and *My Summer with Des*, respectively. Morrissey also played Paul Rochet in PARIS, Phil in the pilot of ROGER ROGER, the New Romantic transsexual Charlie/Charlotte in *Hunting Venus*, Nick Cameron aka THE VANISHING MAN, bus-driver Will Green in *Happy Birthday Shakespeare*, and Charlie Eustace in PARADISE HEIGHTS/THE EUSTACE BROTHERS. He has also supplied voices for the animations BOB THE BUILDER and MAISY, hosted *TV's Naughtiest Blunders*, and donned an oxygen tank to present *Dive to Shark City*. Other credits have included the mini-series ELLIS ISLAND, *Travellers by Night* (Flick), JULIET BRAVO, FAIRLY SECRET ARMY, ROLL OVER BEETHOVEN, C.A.T.S. EYES, PULASKI, *Gentlemen and Players, The Flint Street Nativity* (a Wise Man), MURDER IN MIND, *The Morph Files* (narrator), *Men Down Under* and the quiz *Petrolheads* (host).

Morse, Barry

(1918–)

London-born actor who made his name on the Canadian stage before moving into television. He has enjoyed major roles on both sides of the Atlantic, not least as the relentless Lt. Philip Gerard on the trail of Dr Richard Kimble, THE FUGITIVE. Later, Morse took on the role of Mr Parminter in the secret agent caper THE ADVENTURER and played Alec Marlowe (The Tiger) in THE ZOO GANG, Professor Victor Bergman in SPACE: 1999, Adam Verver in an adaptation of Henry James's *The Golden Bowl*, Wolf Stoller in THE WINDS OF WAR, Murgatroyd in A WOMAN OF SUBSTANCE, Dr Harley in *Master of the Game* and the US President, former actor Johnny Cyclops, in WHOOPS APOCALYPSE. More recently, he has made guest appearances in DOCTORS and WAKING THE DEAD.

Mortimer, Bob

(1959–)

See *Reeves, Vic*.

Mortimer, Sir John

CBE (1923–)

British barrister, writer and dramatist, the creator of RUMPOLE OF THE BAILEY. Among his other offerings have been WILL SHAKESPEARE, *A Voyage Round My Father*, PARADISE POSTPONED, TITMUSS REGAINED, *A Summer's Lease, Under the Hammer, Cider With Rosie* and the hugely successful adaptation of Evelyn Waugh's BRIDESHEAD REVISITED. Mortimer also contributed to the 1965 satire show BBC-3. He is the father of actress Emily Mortimer.

Mortimer, Johnnie

(1930–92)

British comedy scriptwriter, usually in collaboration with Brian Cooke. Together they created series such as FATHER, DEAR FATHER, MAN ABOUT THE HOUSE, GEORGE AND MILDRED, ROBIN'S NEST, *Alcock and Gander, Full House*, LET THERE BE LOVE, *Tom, Dick and Harriet, Kindly Leave the Kerb* and *The Incredible Mr Tanner* (the last two extensions of an episode they penned for *The Ronnie Barker Playhouse*). The duo also wrote episodes of AND MOTHER MAKES FIVE, *Bernie, Life With Cooper* and *Cribbins*. In addition, Mortimer created NEVER THE TWAIN.

Moses – The Lawgiver ✶✶

UK/Italy (ITC/RAI) Drama. ITV 1977

Moses .... **Burt Lancaster**
William Lancaster *(young)*
Aaron .... **Anthony Quayle**
Miriam .... **Ingrid Thulin**
Jethro .... **Shmuel Rodensky**
Bithia .... **Mariangela Melato**
Zipporah .... **Irene Papas**
Dathan .... **Yousef Shiloah**
Joshua .... **Aharon Ipale**
Eliseba .... **Marina Berti**
Pharaoh Mernefta .... **Laurant Terzieff**

Narrator **Richard Johnson**

Writers **Anthony Burgess, Vittorio Bonicelli, Gianfranco de Bosio**
Producer **Vincenzo Labella**

● ***The biblical story of the liberator of the Hebrews.***

Costing nearly £3 million, and four years in the making, this six-part biblical drama had a troubled conception. Production was halted by the outbreak of the Yom Kippur War in 1973 and then, once complete, the serial sat on the shelf for two years before being screened. A straightforward account of the life of Moses, the drama begins with the Israelites entering Egypt, after plague and famine have destroyed their homeland. These people become strong and powerful to the point where Pharaoh Ramses II orders them into slavery and kills all the male babies. However, one – Moses – survives, hidden in the bulrushes until discovered by Egyptian princess Bithia. Moses grows into a strong and determined man. He marries Zipporah and is told by God, through the Burning Bush, to lead his people out of captivity. When Pharaoh Mernefta, a childhood friend of Moses, refuses to set the Israelites free, God inflicts ten plagues on the Egyptians and parts the Red Sea so Moses and his followers can flee. The Ten Commandments are handed down, but Moses smashes the tablets on discovering how his own people have begun to worship false idols. Still, the Promised Land beckons and Moses continues to lead the way. Gianfranco de Bosio directs. An abridged version of the series was packaged for theatrical release in 1975.

Mosley ✶✶✶

UK (Alomo/Channel 4) Historical Drama. Channel 4 1998

Sir Oswald 'Tom' Mosley .... **Jonathan Cake**
Lady Cynthia 'Cimmie' Curzon/Mosley .... **Jemma Redgrave**
David Lloyd George .... **Windsor Davies**
Robert Boothby .... **Hugh Bonneville**
Lord Curzon .... **Robert Lang**
Ramsey MacDonald .... **Ralph Riach**
Jane Bewley .... **Caroline Langrishe**
J. H. Thomas .... **Ken Jones**
Philip Snowden .... **Eric Allan**
Diana Guinness/Mosley .... **Emma Davies**
Mussolini .... **Stefano Gressieux**
Count Grandi .... **Arturo Venegas**
Lord Rothermere .... **Nigel Davenport**

Writers **Laurence Marks, Maurice Gran**
Producer **Irving Teitelbaum**

● ***Four-part biopic of Britain's own fascist figurehead.***

Based on the books *Rules of the Game* and *Beyond the Pale*, by Mosley's own son, Nicholas Mosley, Laurence Marks and Maurice Gran's biography of the *bête noire* of pre-war British politics uncovers a complex, brilliant man whose thirst for power and eye for the ladies scupper a promising career. Beginning in 1918, and Oswald Mosley's election to parliament as a member of the Conservative Party (the youngest MP at the time), the serial exposes the political impatience of the man as he quits the Tories over the suppression of the Irish, briefly becomes independent and then joins the Labour Party. Despite becoming a government minister in Ramsey MacDonald's 1929 administration, two years later he is back in the political wilderness, leaving Labour because of its inactivity, as he sees it, over unemployment. In 1932 he sets up the British Union of Fascists (the thuggish 'Blackshirts'), drawing far-right-wing support and embarking on a misjudged campaign against Jews. A controversial march through London's East End eventually leads to the party's disbandment by law. By the outbreak of the war, despite flirtations with Hitler and Mussolini, Mosley is discredited and destined to spend most of the conflict in internment. Along this eventful political journey, Mosley also displays notoriously philanderous instincts. Despite marrying Lady Cimmie Curzon, he cannot resist the attentions of others and, after her death, weds his long-time mistress, Diana Guinness, in Nazi Germany. Music was provided by Barrington Pheloung.

Mosley, Bryan

OBE (1931–99)

Leeds-born actor, a former stunt-fight choreographer and keen fencer who was best known as Alf Roberts in CORONATION STREET, a part he first played in 1961. Not being a long-term contract-holder, Mosley was forced to leave the series the same year, during an actors' strike, but returned in 1968 and was in Weatherfield continuously until his character died of a heart attack just 40 days before Mosley himself died of the same cause. His other TV work included *The Villains*, ARMCHAIR THEATRE, IT'S A SQUARE WORLD, Z CARS, THE PLANE MAKERS, THE SAINT, THE AVENGERS, NO HIDING PLACE, A FAMILY AT WAR, THE WORKER, QUEENIE'S CASTLE, DOCTOR WHO, THE DUSTBINMEN and CROSSROADS (Denis Rutledge).

Mother Love ✶✶✶

UK (BBC) Drama. BBC 1 1989

Helena Vesey .... **Diana Rigg**
Kit Vesey .... **James Wilby**
Alex Vesey .... **David McCallum**
Angela .... **Friona Gillies**
Ruth .... **Isla Blair**
George .... **James Grout**

Writer **Andrew Davies**
Producer **Ken Riddington**

● ***A mother's overbearing love for her son ruins their lives.***

Helena Vesey is the ultra-possessive mother cited in the title of this four-part tale of deception and revenge, adapted by Andrew Davies from the novel by Domini Taylor. Her suffocating affection for her son, Kit, an ex-Charterhouse schoolboy and recently qualified barrister who still lives at home in Wimbledon, allied to her loathing for her former husband, famous musical conductor Alex, are the catalysts for the disruption of all their lives. Drawn into the tangled web is Angela, an art gallery assistant from a wealthy family in rural Berkshire whom Kit has agreed to marry after only three weeks' acquaintance. Diana Rigg picked up a BAFTA for her sinister performance. Simon Langton directs.

Mother's Ruin ✶

UK (Granada) Situation Comedy. ITV 1994

Leslie H. Flitcroft .... **Roy Barraclough**
Kitty Flitcroft .... **Dora Bryan**
Brucella Pashley .... **Julia Deakin**
Wendy Watson .... **Kay Adshead**
Clive Watson .... **Jason Done**

Writer **John Stevenson**

A mother makes life miserable for a frustrated bachelor.

A vehicle created for the popular Roy Barraclough on his departure from CORONATION STREET, *Mother's Ruin* returns to the familiar bachelor son–interfering mother routine often visited by Ronnie Corbett. Here Barraclough stars as 50-year-old Leslie Flitcroft, a man trying desperately to sever his mother Kitty's apron strings but boxed in by his job as manager of the family's health food store (Nurse Nature). He'd like to spend more time with the love of his life, Wendy Watson (mother of teenager Clive), but the scheming Kitty has other ideas. Brucella Pashley is the plain woman who works with Leslie in the shop and, thinks Kitty is a far more fitting lady-companion than Wendy. The programme title plays on the fact that Kitty, a long faded actress, enjoys a regular tipple of gin and primrose. The vehicle did not run far – only to six episodes.

Motormouth ✶✶

UK (TVS) Children's Entertainment. ITV 1988–92

Presenters **Neil Buchanan, Tony Gregory, Andrea Arnold, Julian Ballantyne, Caroline Hanson, Gaby Roslin, Steve Johnson, Andy Crane**

Executive Producers **Janie Grace, J. Nigel Pickard**
Producers **Adrian Edwards, Tim Edmunds, Sue Morgan, J. Nigel Pickard, Vanessa Hill**

Saturday morning mix of education, entertainment, pop, prattle, games and gunge.

ITV's response to BBC's Saturday morning domination in the 1980s was spearheaded by TVS. Following on from the fun and games of NO. 73 were the fun and games of *Motormouth* (identified by a giant inflatable mouth), which proved to be an important career stepping-stone for Gaby Roslin in particular. A typically vibrant mix of features, news reviews, chart music, games, phone-ins and cartoons was interspersed with a little original drama/comedy. A segment called *Spin Off*, about the alleged production crew at the TV studios, starred actors Roger Sloman, Richard Waiter, Pippa Michaels and Joe Greco; the idea was revived for the fourth and final series with Siobhan Finneran, Carla Mendonça, Cal McCrystal and Gary Parker. Among the featured cartoons were *She-Ra, Princess of Power, The Real Ghostbusters, The Mysteries of Scooby Doo, Police Academy, Samurai Pizza Cats* and *Beetlejuice*, plus perennials *Sylvester, Bugs Bunny* and *Daffy Duck*. Games and features included Trap Door, It's Torture, Gunge 'Em in the Dungeon, Mousetrap, Letters in the Loo and Me and My Mate. Early presenter Andrea Arnold took off and sent back reports from a tour of the world; Terry Nutkins frequently dropped in to talk animals; Jason Donovan was a regular musical guest; and Rustie Lee cooked up popular recipes. Series two and three went out as *Motormouth 2* and *3*, respectively (as the concept was continually modified). On its cancellation, *Motormouth* was succeeded by the similar *What's Up Doc?* (ITV 1992–5).

Motson, John

OBE (1945–)

Salford-born, long-serving BBC soccer commentator (covering well over 1,000 matches). He is known and much mimicked for his sheepskin coat and endless supply of match trivia.

Mount, Peggy

OBE (Margaret Mount; 1916–2001)

Powerful Essex-born actress, usually cast as a domineering wife or colleague. Her first major TV role set the trend. In THE LARKINS, first seen in 1958, she played Ada, battleaxe wife of David Kossoff's Alf Larkins. Earlier, Mount had featured as Polly Sutherland in a children's drama serial called *The Cabin in the Clearing*. In 1961 she was Martha, one of the *Winning Widows*, and in 1966 she teamed up with Sid James as the appropriately named Gabrielle Dragon in GEORGE AND THE DRAGON. Somewhat changing tack, Mount played sleuth Virginia Browne in 1969's *John Browne's Body*, but was back on form in 1971, as Maggie in LOLLIPOP LOVES MR MOLE. From brow-beating men she made the weedy Pat Coombs her next target when playing Flora Petty in YOU'RE ONLY YOUNG TWICE, but after that series ended in 1981, Mount was largely seen in straight roles. She played Mrs Weaver in *Virtual Murder* and accepted guest spots in dramas like INSPECTOR MORSE, CASUALTY and DOCTOR WHO, although, as if to prove that old habits die hard, she did also appear as Aunt Fanny in the kids' sitcom *All Change* in 1991.

Mower, Patrick

(1940–)

British actor, a 1970s favourite following his roles as lecturer Michael West in *Haunted*, agent Cross in CALLAN, DCI Tom Haggerty in SPECIAL BRANCH, Det. Supt. Steve Hackett in TARGET, and many panel game appearances (WHODUNNIT?, WHAT'S MY LINE?, etc.). In addition to the above, Mower also appeared as reporter John Brownhill in the newspaper drama *Front Page Story*, featured in the biography of *Marco Polo*, and played Don Tierney in THE DARK SIDE OF THE SUN. He also took smaller roles in series like DIXON OF DOCK GREEN, THE AVENGERS, THE PROTECTORS, UFO, THE SWEENEY and STRANGERS. In 2000 he returned to the small screen as Rodney Blackstock in EMMERDALE and has also been seen as Mr Thripp in the kids' comedy *There's a Viking in My Bed*.

Mr and Mrs ✶

UK (HTV/Border/Action Time) Quiz. ITV 1969–88; 1999

Presenters **Alan Taylor** *(HTV)*, **Derek Batey** *(Border)*, **Julian Clary** *(Action Time)*

Creator **Roy Ward Dickson**

Producers **Derek Clark** *(HTV)*, **Derek Batey, William Cartner** *(Border)*, **Jo Sargent** *(Action Time)*

● ***Couples win money by answering questions about their partners.***

'Which shoe does your husband put on first?' and 'Does your wife carry a handbag – always, sometimes or never?' were typical *Mr and Mrs* questions. This quiz, which had been running in the HTV area before being networked, demanded no more of married couples than that they knew their partner's little habits and foibles. Three questions were put to the husband and three to the wife. While one was answering questions, the spouse was asked to leave the studio. He/she was then brought back to put the record straight and give the correct answers themselves. Each matching response earned the couple some cash and all six correct answers won the jackpot. Three couples were usually featured in each programme.

The series was produced alternately by HTV and Border (it has been one of the latter company's few contributions to the ITV network). Alan Taylor hosted the HTV programmes and Derek Batey those from Border. A Welsh-language version, *Sion a Sian*, was also made. The idea returned to television in the early 1990s when the satellite channel UK Living broadcast *The New Mr and Mrs Show*. In 1999 ITV presented *Mr and Mrs with Julian Clary*, in which the couples no longer needed to be married to participate. Stacey Young was Clary's assistant.

Mr Bean ✶✶✶

UK (Thames/Central/Tiger) Comedy. ITV 1990–5
DVD: Universal

Mr Bean .... **Rowan Atkinson**

Writers **Rowan Atkinson, Richard Curtis, Robin Driscoll**
Producers **John Howard Davies, Sue Vertue, Peter Bennett-Jones**

● ***The virtually silent adventures of a walking disaster zone.***

Effectively a vehicle for Rowan Atkinson's mime skills, this near-silent comedy revolves around the accident-prone Mr Bean, a gormless, friendless, brainless little chap with a flair for causing havoc. A trip to the sales, a spot of DIY or a day at the seaside are all likely to bring threats to life and limb for Mr Bean or those around him. Numerous specials were made, as well as regular series. Such was the international appeal of this modern-day Monsieur Hulot that a feature film, *Bean – the Ultimate Disaster Movie*, was produced in 1997. A cartoon version appeared on ITV in 2002.

Mr Benn ✶✶

UK (Zephyr/United) Children's Entertainment. BBC 1 1971–2
DVD: Contender

Narrator **Ray Brooks**

Creator/Writer **David McKee**

● ***A man discovers magical adventures at the back of a costume shop.***

Mr Benn, resident of 52 Festive Road, London, enjoys escapism. In each episode, he indulges his hobby by walking along to the local fancy-dress shop, where he is greeted by a shopkeeper who arrives 'as if by magic' and escorts him through to the changing rooms. Donning the outfit of the day, Mr Benn then exits through a special door and into a land of adventure, which is always related to the clothes he is wearing. He is seen as a knight in armour, a caveman, a spaceman, a pirate, a cowboy and a hunter, among other guises. Inevitably, the courteous and genial Mr Benn is able to provide some valuable assistance to the people he meets before the shopkeeper suddenly pops up to lead him back into the changing room. Switching back into his business suit and bowler hat, Mr Benn then strolls off home, taking with him a souvenir of his day's work.

Although the series has been repeated endlessly on the BBC, only 13 episodes of this WATCH WITH MOTHER animation were ever produced. Creator David McKee came up with the idea when he lived in a street called Festing Road in Putney.

Mr Digby, Darling ✶

UK (Yorkshire) Situation Comedy. ITV 1969–71

Roland Digby .... **Peter Jones**
Thelma Teesdale .... **Sheila Hancock**
Mr Trumper .... **Brian Oulton**
Olive .... **Beryl Cooke**
Mr Bailey .... **Peter Stephens**
Joyce .... **Janet Brown**
Norman Stanhope .... **Michael Bates**

Creators/Writers **Ken Hoare, Mike Sharland**
Producers **Chris Hodson, Bill Hitchcock**

● ***An executive is cosseted by his loyal and devoted secretary.***

Thelma Teesdale works for the Rid-O-Rat pest extermination company as secretary to Mr Roland Digby, the firm's assistant public relations officer. From the time he arrives in the morning until he leaves for home in the evening, Thelma caters for his every need, cooking his breakfast on a stove hidden in a filing cabinet, bringing out his slippers, darning his socks and pulling out all the stops to protect him from the outside world. However, her ambitious plans to secure his advancement are usually ill advised and doomed to failure. For Digby the fourth-floor office is a home from home, a refuge from his domineering wife, Eleanor, and the three kids whose names he can never remember (Dominic, Gwendolyn and Robin). Thelma's colleagues include Norman Stanhope (in later episodes), while Mr Trumper is the confused boss and Olive is his secretary. Bob Leaper provided the theme music.

Mr Magoo ✶✶

US (UPA) Cartoon. BBC 1962–4 (US: Syndicated 1960–2; NBC 1964–5)
DVD: Sony (Region 1 only)

Voices:
Mr Quincy Magoo .... **Jim Backus**
Waldo .... **Jerry Hausner**
Daws Butler
Millie .... **Julie Bennett**

Executive Producer **Henry G. Saperstein**

● ***The misadventures of a short-sighted old codger.***

Created in the 1940s, myopic Mr Magoo appeared in various TV packages, from half-hour compilations to this series of five-minute shorts. Most of the mirth comes from the fact that he can't tell a telephone box from a police officer, or an ugly woman from a moose – although, with his surly, irascible manner and bulbous nose, there is more than an echo of W. C. Fields. Whereas Fields disliked children intensely, Magoo hates dogs, for instance. (Indeed, it is reputed that Fields used the name Primrose Magoo when checking into hotels.)

Semi-regulars in these short TV animations are Magoo's stupid nephew, Waldo, and Waldo's girlfriend, Millie, although other relatives show up from time to time. In the longer programmes made later, Magoo sometimes appears in a historical or literary guise, such as Rip Van Winkle or William Tell. Assorted cinema versions were also produced, beginning in 1949 with *Ragtime Bear*, which saw Magoo in a supporting role.

Mr Majeika ★★

UK (TVS) Children's Situation Comedy. ITV 1988–90

Mr Majeika	**Stanley Baxter**
Melanie Brace-Girdle	**Claire Sawyer**
Thomas Grey	**Andrew Read**
Mr Potter	**Roland MacLeod**
Bunty Brace-Girdle	**Fidelis Morgan**
Pam Bigmore	**Eve Ferret**
Hamish Bigmore	**Simeon Pearl**
Ron Bigmore	**Chris Ellison**
	Chris Mitchell
Worshipful Wizard	**Richard Murdoch**
Flavia Jelley	**Pat Coombs**
Prince	**Sanjiv Madan**

Writer **Jenny McDade**
Executive Producer **J. Nigel Pickard**
Producers **Roger Cheveley, John Price**

A disgraced wizard has fun and games on Earth.

Strange things start to happen in Class III of St Barty's School when new teacher Mr Majeika takes charge – not surprisingly, because he is in fact a wizard, expelled to Britland from Wizardland (Walpurgis) by the Worshipful Wizard for failing his magic exams no fewer than 17 times. Majeika is not supposed to use his magical powers while he's here but he can't resist the odd spell or two to help maintain discipline in the classroom. Most impressed are pupils Thomas Grey (replaced by Prince for the third and final series) and Melanie Brace-Girdle, and before long the genial sorcerer is astonishing the whole population of Much Barty with bizarre goings-on and comical adventures. The programme was based on the *Mr Majeika* books by Humphrey Carpenter, who also guested in the series; other guests included Miriam Margolyes, Hugh Lloyd and Frank Thornton. Music was by Paul Hart.

Mr Palfrey of Westminster ★★

UK (Thames) Spy Drama. ITV 1984–5

Mr Palfrey	**Alec McCowen**
The Co-ordinator	**Caroline Blakiston**
Blair	**Clive Wood**

Executive Producer **Lloyd Shirley**
Producer **Michael Chapman**

The cases of a master spycatcher.

Mr Palfrey (first name never given) works for a secret Government department from an office close to the Houses of Parliament. His 'Iron Lady' boss is the similarly unnamed Co-ordinator, and his legwork is done by a vicious action man named Blair. Through the studious, inquisitorial Mr Palfrey viewers learn much about the mysterious world of counter-espionage. The ten-episode series was spun off *The Traitor*, a play in Thames TV's STORYBOARD anthology, shown in 1983, and Mr Palfrey was also seen in another *Storyboard* production called *A Question of Commitment* in 1989.

Mr Rose ★★

UK (Granada) Detective Drama. ITV 1967–8

Mr Charles Rose	**William Mervyn**
John Halifax	**Donald Webster**
Drusilla Lamb	**Gillian Lewis**
Jessica Dalton	**Jennifer Clulow**
Robert Trent	**Eric Woolfe**

Creator **Philip Mackie**
Producers **Philip Mackie, Margaret Morris**

A retired police officer can't escape from his previous life.

Chief Inspector Rose, formerly of THE ODD MAN and IT'S DARK OUTSIDE, has inherited the wealth of two maiden aunts and taken retirement from the force to concentrate on his cottage garden in Eastbourne and the writing of his memoirs. Having kept copies of all his case files, he has a personal library of crime, and the fear that he is about to reveal all brings some of his former adversaries – and colleagues – back into his life. Gratefully picking up the scent and rejecting the boredom of his retirement years, Mr Rose wallows once again in investigation after investigation. Rose's assistants are his manservant, former detective John Halifax, and his attractive secretary, Drusilla Lamb. Drusilla is later replaced by Jessica Dalton, and Robert Trent takes over as Rose's sidekick for the last series.

Mr Wroe's Virgins ★★★

UK (BBC) Drama. BBC 2 1993

John Wroe	**Jonathan Pryce**
Joanna	**Lia Williams**
Leah	**Minnie Driver**
Hannah	**Kerry Fox**
Martha	**Kathy Burke**
Dinah	**Moya Brady**
Rachel	**Catherine Kelly**
Rebekah	**Ruth Kelly**
Tobias	**Freddie Jones**
Moses	**Nicholas Woodeson**
Samuel Walker	**Stefan Escreet**

Writer **Jane Rogers**
Producer **John Chapman**

A self-styled prophet of doom demands seven virgins from the local community.

Broadly based on a true-life incident, this drama is set in the mill town of Ashton-under-Lyne, near Manchester. The central figure is John Wroe, founder of a Christian Israelite church in readiness for an impending apocalypse. In 1830 he asks the townsfolk to give him seven virgins for his 'comfort and succour', and the unfolding events are then seen through the eyes of four of the women, one per episode. They are Joanna, a woman of absolute religious conviction and the spiritual leader of the commune, whom Wroe chooses to father a new messiah; Leah, beautiful, shapely and sexually precocious, who joins Wroe to escape from everyday life but who finds herself rejected by him; Hannah, the educationally liberated, socialist-minded member of the group, who is greatly attracted to the grotesque Wroe; and Martha, a devastated, badly beaten mute who has been treated like an animal on her father's farm and whom Wroe transforms through care and attention. The other girls are Dinah, Rachel and Rebekah. The drama – adapted by Jane Rogers from her own novel – is set against a backdrop of great industrial change and religious impropriety, tempered by an epidemic of cholera.

Mrs Bradley Mysteries, The ★★

UK (BBC/WGBH) Detective Drama. BBC 1 2000
DVD: WGBH Boston (Region 1 only)

Mrs Adela Bradley .... **Diana Rigg**
George Moody .... **Neil Dudgeon**
Insp. Christmas .... **Peter Davison**

Writers **Simon Booker, Julie Rutterford, Gwyneth Hughes**
Producer **Deborah Jones**

● ***A sophisticated amateur sleuth lifts the lid on society crimes.***

Mrs Adela Bradley is a divorced, well-read lady of independent means who spends her spare time solving country house mysteries in the late 1920s (an era made obvious not only by the fashions but also by the jazzy musical accompaniment). Employing her knowledge of psychoanalysis, her expertise in poisons and her study of handwriting, among many skills, she is able to fathom out the most enigmatic crime. Whenever more mundane or practical assistance is needed, she can always call upon her trusted chauffeur, George Moody. With plenty of pithy asides to the camera, the stylish, worldly wise Mrs Bradley ensures the audience is well informed of her progress. Inspector Christmas is the police investigator she happily outshines on most occasions. *The Mrs Bradley Mysteries*, adapted from the novels by Gladys Mitchell (a contemporary of Agatha Christie), was trialled with a pilot in 1998. The series proper, however, ran only to a further four episodes.

Mrs Merton and Malcolm

See *Mrs Merton Show, The.*

Mrs Merton Show, The ★★★

UK (Granada) Comedy. BBC 2 1995/BBC 1 1996–8

Mrs Dorothy Merton .... **Caroline Hook/Aherne**

Producers **Peter Kessler, Mark Gorton, Kenton Allen, Spencer Campbell**

● ***Celebrities squirm as their personal life is probed by a 'little old lady'.***

Success late at night on BBC 2 quickly led to a prime-time BBC 1 slot for this award-winning spoof chat show. Caroline Aherne stars as the bespectacled, blue-rinsed geriatric, Mrs Merton, belying her sweet, homely looks by terrorizing guests with 'innocent' double entendres and cheeky personal questions. Empathizing with her studio audience regulars (real Oldham and Wigan pensioners – friends and family – who became minor celebrities through their involvement), the diminutive hostess harks back fondly to the good old days and swoons over an assortment of showbiz heart-throbs. Celebrities – George Best, Michael Parkinson, Boy George, Des Lynam, Sacha Distel, Ian Botham, Joanna Lumley, Bernard Manning and Michael Winner among them – who have foolishly agreed to take a seat on her sofa are then subjected to a barrage of irony and pointed questions that would simply sound impertinent from another, less 'harmless' mouth. Classic lines include the seemingly innocuous query to Debbie McGee: 'So what first attracted you to millionaire Paul Daniels?' Halfway through each programme, the audience is cajoled into a 'heated debate', offering an opportunity for plain-speaking senior citizens like Horace, Roy, Bernard, Anne, May, Sylvia, Liz and Enid to shine. Such regulars also featured among the 50 audience stalwarts Mrs Merton once took to Las Vegas to record the show before an American audience. These shows, plus a video record of the trip (produced and directed by Philippa Robinson), were screened on BBC 1 in 1997.

Mrs Merton's live music comes initially from Hooky and the Boys (featuring Aherne's then husband, Peter Hook) and later from the Patrick Trio. Also appearing from time to time is the star's childlike son, Malcolm (Craig Cash). The two characters were later spun off into a sitcom, *Mrs Merton and Malcolm* (BBC 1 1999, Aherne and Cash supported by Brian Murphy as pensioner Arthur Capstick), which peered into their suburban home life in Heaton Norris. Caroline Aherne first adopted the guise of Mrs Merton – then a spoof agony aunt – for local radio in Stockport.

Mrs Thursday ★★

UK (ATV) Comedy Drama. ITV 1966–7

Alice Thursday .... **Kathleen Harrison**
Richard B. Hunter .... **Hugh Manning**

Creator **Ted Willis**
Producer **Jack Williams**

● ***A charlady inherits a fortune.***

When millionaire tycoon George Dunrich dies, he leaves his estate not to his four grasping ex-wives but to his long-serving and loyal charlady, Alice Thursday. Inheriting his wealth, his multinational property empire, his Rolls-Royce and his Mayfair mansion, Mrs Thursday moves out of her Mile End home and into the privileged classes. But, until the kind-hearted char learns to distinguish her friends from her enemies, she is chaperoned and protected by the genial Richard Hunter, her aide and business adviser.

Allegedly created by Ted Willis specifically as a vehicle for Kathleen Harrison (cinema's Mrs Huggett), *Mrs Thursday* was a surprise hit, knocking shows like CORONATION STREET off the top of the ratings and giving Harrison a late taste of TV stardom.

MTV

MTV, or Music Television, was established as a cable channel in the USA in 1981 by Warner Amex Satellite Entertainment, with the aim of focusing on the rock and pop markets. During its first decade on air it helped establish the music video as a major source of entertainment for the teens and twenties, and coined a new term, VJ (video jockey), for the presenter linking each item. The first video seen (on 1 August 1981) was 'Video Killed the Radio Star' by Buggles. MTV Europe (kicking off on 1 August 1987 with the video 'Money For Nothing' by Dire Straits) became part of a series of global stations comprising also MTV Japan, MTV Brasil, MTV Internacional and MTV Latino, and in 1997 MTV UK and Ireland was launched. MTV has been broadcast from the Astra satellites since 1989 and it now has several sister channels. Foremost is VH1, which was started in 1985 to cater specifically for older, thirtysomething music fans. There are also MTV 2, MTV Base, MTV Dance, MTV Hits, VH1 Classic and VH2, all reflecting different shades of the rock and pop spectrum. As well as music videos, MTV features interviews, concert news, items on film and fashion, and original programming, including an upbeat version of BLIND DATE called *Singled Out*. Among the channel's biggest successes have been the cartoon characters *Beavis and Butt-head*, THE OSBOURNES and the *Unplugged* series, in which rock stars play mostly without electronic amplification. The company is currently owned by Viacom, which took control in 1987.

Muck and Brass ✶✶

UK (Central) Drama. ITV 1982

Tom Craig	**Mel Smith**
Jamal	**Darien Anghadi**
John Roman	**Johnny Allan**
Reg Palmer	**Raymond Mason**
Maurice Taylor	**James Faulkner**
Basil Bastedes	**Simon Jones**

Writer **Tom Clarke**
Producer **Margaret Matheson**

● ***A determined novice fights his way to the top of the property business.***

Tom Craig is a man seeking vengeance: he is after the crooks that framed his father over a property deal. During his investigations Craig discovers that he has inherited a group of derelict houses in an urban area that is ripe for redevelopment. Thus begins his rise up the slippery ladder of business. Craig uses his windfall as a way into the market and embarks on a bruising battle to defeat bureaucracy, civic corruption and the guile of the established big players. Never afraid to bully if necessary, Craig also falls back on gentle persuasion to get his way. His leading adversaries in this mean game are John Roman, Basil Bastedes and Reg Palmer.

The programme was set in a fictional city, a loose amalgam of Birmingham, Coventry, Nottingham and Leicester, and its working title – underlining the financial wheeling and dealing involved – was *City*. Marek Kanievska directed the six episodes, which provided a rare opportunity for comedian Mel Smith – fresh from NOT THE NINE O'CLOCK NEWS – to slip into straight drama.

Muffin the Mule ✶

UK (BBC/Parthian) Children's Entertainment. BBC 1946–57
DVD: Maverick Entertainment

Presenters/Writers **Annette Mills, Jan Bussell**
Producers **David Boisseau, Joy Harington, Peter Thompson, Dorothea Brooking, Nan McDonald, John Warrington, Gordon Murray, Peggy Bacon**

● ***Song and dance with a puppet mule.***

One of the earliest favourites of children's television, the legendary Muffin the Mule made his TV debut in 1946, in a five-minute FOR THE CHILDREN slot in which he danced atop a grand piano while his co-star, Annette Mills, sang. Muffin and Mills (sister of actor John Mills) were subsequently given their own series and other puppets were introduced, like Oswald the Ostrich, Peregrine the Penguin, Herbert the Hippo, Katie the Kangaroo, Peter the Pup, Prudence and Primrose Kitten, Sally the Sealion, Louise the Lamb and Monty the Monkey. The strings were pulled by puppeteer Ann Hogarth from behind a screen on top of the piano (the puppet had been made for Hogarth and her husband, Jan Bussell, in the 1930s for their puppet circus, along with a clown called Crumpet). Muffin's last TV appearance with Annette Mills came in 1955, just days before she died.

Muffin's day was not done, however. Forty years later, the stubborn mule resurfaced in a computer-generated, ten-minute cartoon series from Maverick Entertainment that maintains much of the character of the puppet original and also features Muffin's old buddies, Oswald the Ostrich, Peregrine the Penguin and Louise the Lamb (BBC 2 2005–).

Muggeridge, Malcolm

(1903–90)

London-born journalist and commentator, working as an interviewer for PANORAMA in the 1950s and later for Granada. Much of his work involved spiritual matters, initially as a sceptic in many instances, but later as a firm Catholic, gaining the nickname of St Mugg. Muggeridge was never afraid to bring important people, historical and modern, down to earth, and his documentaries included *The Thirties*, *Pilgrimage to Lourdes*, *Twilight of Empire* (about India), *Ladies and Gentlemen, It is My Pleasure* (reflecting on his own US lecture-tour), *A Socialist Childhood* (his own), *Remembering Virginia* (Woolf), *Lord Reith Looks Back*, *A Life of Christ*, *A Quest for Gandhi*, *Something Beautiful for God* (about Mother Teresa) and *Tolstoy. Rags to Riches*. He was also seen in *Press Conference*, THE BRAINS TRUST, *Appointment With . . .*, LET ME SPEAK, BBC-3, *The Late Show*, Jonathan Miller's ALICE IN WONDERLAND and his own retrospective, *Muggeridge Ancient and Modern*. Outside of broadcasting, Muggeridge had been a teacher in India and Egypt, reporter for the *Manchester Guardian* and the *Daily Telegraph*, and Editor of *Punch*.

Muir, Frank

CBE (1920–98)

To many viewers, Frank Muir is best remembered as a team captain on the BBC 2 word game CALL MY BLUFF, the one in the bow tie who couldn't sound his 'r's. However, Muir's TV background was far more complex than that. With his writing partner, Denis Norden (having already scripted *Take It from Here* and other comedies for radio), Muir penned Dick Bentley's sitcom *And So to Bentley* and the Jimmy Edwards series WHACK-O! and THE SEVEN FACES OF JIM. They also wrote Richard Briers's first major outlet, BROTHERS IN LAW (and its spin-off, *Mr Justice Duncannon*), and the Bob Monkhouse comedy *The Big Noise*, as well as episodes of *Early to Braden* and material for THE FROST REPORT. Muir presented a talent show entitled *New to You* way back in 1946, two decades later made guest appearances in NOT ONLY . . . BUT ALSO . . ., and over the years brought his wit and wisdom to numerous panel games. In 1964, with Norden, he wrote and presented a sketch show, *How to be an Alien*, and they joined forces again to revive their *Take It from Here* creations, *The Glums*, for *Bruce Forsyth's Big Night* in 1978. Behind the scenes, Muir was, at one time, Assistant Head of Comedy at the BBC and, later, Head of Light Entertainment at LWT (where he also fronted *We Have Ways of Making You Laugh*). In 1992 he plundered the small-screen archives for 13 weeks of *TV Heaven* on Channel 4.

Mulberry ✳✳✳

UK (BBC) Situation Comedy. BBC 1 1992–3

Mulberry .... **Karl Howman**
Miss Rose Farnaby .... **Geraldine McEwan**
Bert Finch .... **Tony Selby**
Alice Finch .... **Lill Roughley**
Mary Healey
The Stranger .... **John Bennett**

Creators/Writers **John Esmonde, Bob Larbey**
Producer **John B. Hobbs**

● ***A mysterious manservant enriches the life of a dowdy spinster.***

Cantankerous Rose Farnaby lives alone in her musty family home, Farnaby Manor, with only her well-entrenched, conniving servants, Bert and Alice Finch, for company. Then, one day, an enigmatic new figure arrives. Mulberry instantly brightens up the household, sweet-talking the frumpy Miss Farnaby into making more of her life, adding zest to each day and encouraging her to break habits of a lifetime and try her hand at unusual pursuits. He genially ensures that the Finches know their place and also protects Miss Farnaby from other detractors like her scheming sisters, Adele and Elizabeth. Where the lovable Mulberry comes from no one seems to know, but his paranormal connections with a figure known only as The Stranger make the mystery even deeper.

Mullard, Arthur

(Arthur Mullord; 1913–95)

Cockney comic actor – a former professional boxer – popular for his down-to-earth, working-class roles in the 1970s. In particular, he was Wally Briggs in ROMANY JONES and its sequel, *Yus My Dear*. Additionally, Mullard guested in HANCOCK'S HALF HOUR, played Mr Rossiter, the neighbour, in *The Arthur Askey Show*, supported Alfie Bass and Bill Fraser in *Vacant Lot*, appeared in the kids' comedies *On the Rocks* and *Whizzkid's Guide*, and backed up Spike Milligan in *The World of Beachcomber* and *Oh in Colour*. At his peak, he was a popular panellist on programmes like CELEBRITY SQUARES.

Multi-Coloured Swap Shop ✳✳✳

UK (BBC) Children's Entertainment. BBC 1 1976–82

Presenters **Noel Edmonds, Keith Chegwin, Maggie Philbin, John Craven**

Producer **Rosemary Gill**

● ***Live, interactive kids' magazine.***

Opening a new front in Saturday-morning children's programming, and allowing younger viewers to actually participate in events for once, *Multi-Coloured Swap Shop* was a light-hearted magazine which bound together cartoons, pop music, sport, phone-ins and competitions with a loose 'swapping' theme. Kids were encouraged to ring in with details of toys, books, clothes, etc. (but definitely no pets) they wished to swap, naming the item they were looking for in return. The most interesting exchanges were highlighted in the list of Top Ten Swaps. Celebrity guests were also asked to donate a 'swap' as a competition prize, and John Craven organized the 'News Swap', which gave viewers the chance to air their opinions on news items of the day. Maggie Philbin helped out around the studio, Delia Smith dropped in for a spot of cooking, and Keith Chegwin was out on the road, secretly visiting a different venue each week and calling on locals to turn out in force and bring along their swaps. However, *Multi-Coloured Swap Shop* was very much a vehicle for Noel Edmonds, who relished this early opportunity to show off his live-TV skills. (For the record, Edmonds's co-star, the *Swap Shop* dinosaur mascot, was called Posh Paws and the unseen studio crane operator was Eric.)

The series was initially intended as a six-week filler. But it was only after six *years*, when Edmonds decided to move on, that the *Multi-Coloured Swap Shop* came to an end (for the last two years it was known simply as *Swap Shop*). It was replaced by the similarly styled *Saturday Superstore* (1982–7). This was hosted by 'General Manager' Mike Read, assisted by Chegwin (still out and about, this time in the 'Delivery Van') and John Craven, plus 'Saturday Girl' Sarah Greene. Vicky Licorish and David Icke held court in the 'Coffee Shop' and the 'Music and Sports Departments'. Also seen was the puppet Crow.

Multiplex

The name given to a collection of digital channels, six services that use up only the same space as one old analogue channel. When Digital Terrestrial Television was launched in the UK, six multiplexes were developed: one for the BBC; one for ITV, Channel 4 and Teletext; one for Channel 5, S4C and Scottish Gaelic programming; and three for new service provider, ONdigital (these multiplexes are now run by Freeview).

Mulville, Jimmy

(1955–)

Liverpool-born actor, comedian and TV executive, a former Cambridge Footlights performer and co-founder of Hat Trick Productions. He was a member of *The Steam Video Company* and the WHO DARES, WINS ... teams, co-wrote and appeared as Aulus Paulinus in the Roman spoof CHELMSFORD 123, took the part of Donald Redfern in the sitcom THAT'S LOVE and played Philip, the researcher, in GBH and Monica's husband in *Jake's Progress*. More recently, he was Jonathan in *Life Isn't All Ha Ha Hee Hee*. Mulville has also been programme consultant on HAVE I GOT NEWS FOR YOU, a writer/producer on ALAS SMITH AND JONES, producer of the sitcom *The Big One* and Simon Mayo's series CONFESSIONS, and host of *The Brain Game*, and has contributed reports for HOLIDAY. Other credits include producing or directing one-off dramas like *Eleven Men against Eleven*, *Lord of Misrule* and *Gobble*.

Munsters, The ✳✳✳

US (Universal) Situation Comedy. BBC 1 1965–7
(US: CBS 1964–6)
DVD: Universal

Herman Munster .... **Fred Gwynne**
Lily Munster .... **Yvonne De Carlo**
Grandpa .... **Al Lewis**
Edward Wolfgang ('Eddie') Munster .... **Butch Patrick**
Marilyn Munster .... **Beverly Owen**
Pat Priest

Creators **Joe Connelly, Bob Mosher**

● *A ghoulish family scare the living daylights out of their neighbours.*

The Munsters hit the TV screen at the same time as THE ADDAMS FAMILY and there are many similarities between the two series. If anything, *The Munsters* is less subtle than its rival, for while the Addams family look more or less normal and just act odd, the Munsters are real monsters, although of the friendly, kind-hearted type.

Nominal head of the household is timid giant Herman, a Frankenstein's monster look-alike, complete with bolted-on head and leaden boots. His wife, Lily, is a vampire who walks around the house in shrouds, wearing a bat necklace. Her father, Grandpa, sometimes known as 'The Count', is an experimental magician who conjures up potions in his cellar laboratory and then struggles to find an antidote. He is known to disappear and hide, or even change into a bat. The Munsters' son is Eddie, a werewolf with a pronounced V-shaped haircut and pointed ears. He is often seen playing with his wolfman doll. With the family live Herman's niece, Marilyn, pitied by all for her plainness (in fact, she is an attractive blonde and the only human-looking member of the household).

Stories revolve around the family's contacts with the outside world and the misconception that they are normal and everyone else is strange. Visitors to their rambling Gothic mansion at 1313 Mockingbird Lane, Mockingbird Heights, are at first bemused and then terrified by its contents: heavy cobwebs, suits of armour, secret passages, an electric chair, a coffin telephone-booth, and a black cat that roars like a lion. For the Munsters, life is seen in reverse. They talk about noises 'loud enough to wake the living', are worried when the shutters don't creak at night and adorn the house with weeds instead of flowers. They cruise around town in a souped-up hearse. At night, Lily sleeps like a corpse, with her arms crossed over her chest, clutching a flower to her bosom. In the day, Herman works for a funeral home, Gateman, Goodbury & Graves. At all times, Grandpa longs for the Old Country (Transylvania).

Beverly Owen, who played Marilyn, left after the first series and was replaced by Pat Priest. Fred Gwynne, Yvonne De Carlo and Al Lewis reprised their roles in a one-off TV movie entitled *The Munsters' Revenge*, made in 1981, before new actors took over for a limp revival in 1988 (from 1990 in the UK) called *The Munsters Today*.

Muppet Show, The/Muppets Tonight! ★★★★

UK (*Show*: ITC/Henson; *Tonight!*: Henson) Variety. ITV 1976–81/ BBC 1 1996

DVD: Buena Vista Home Entertainment

Voices:

Kermit the Frog .... **Jim Henson**
Steve Whitmire *(Tonight!)*
Miss Piggy Lee .... **Frank Oz**
Fozzie Bear .... **Frank Oz**
Zoot .... **Dave Goelz**
Gonzo .... **Dave Goelz**
Statler .... **Richard Hunt**
Jerry Nelson *(Tonight!)*
Waldorf .... **Jim Henson**
Dave Goelz *(Tonight!)*
Sweetums .... **Richard Hunt**
Sam the Eagle .... **Frank Oz**
The Swedish Chef .... **Jim Henson**
Dr Teeth .... **Jim Henson**
Sgt Floyd Pepper .... **Jerry Nelson**
Rowlf .... **Jim Henson**
Animal .... **Frank Oz**
Capt. Link Hogthrob .... **Jim Henson**
Dr Julius Strangepork .... **Jerry Nelson**
Dr Bunsen Honeydew .... **Dave Goelz**
Beaker .... **Richard Hunt**
Steve Whitmire *(Tonight!)*
Scooter .... **Richard Hunt**
Beauregard .... **Dave Goelz**
Pops .... **Jerry Nelson**
Lew Zealand .... **Jerry Nelson**
Janice .... **Richard Hunt**
Rizzo the Rat .... **Steve Whitmire**
Robin the Frog .... **Jerry Nelson**
Spamela Hamderson .... **Leslie Carrara**
Bill the Bubble Guy .... **Dave Goelz**
Clifford .... **Kevin Clash**
Sal .... **Brian Henson**
Pepe .... **Bill Barretta**
Seymour .... **Brian Henson**
Bob .... **Bill Barretta**
Randy .... **Dave Goelz**
Andy .... **Steve Whitmire**
Johnnie Fiama .... **Bill Barretta**

Creators **Jim Henson, Frank Oz**
Executive Producer **David Lazer**
Producers **Jack Burns, Jim Henson**

● *A wacky troupe of puppet animals tries to stage a variety show.*

The Muppets were devised and christened by Jim Henson in America in the 1950s. They were half marionette and half glove puppet, hence their name, and they appeared intermittently on US TV for more than a decade before coming to the fore in the children's educational series SESAME STREET. The chance of a major show of their own eluded them in America, but Lew Grade put his trust in their abilities and financed the production of *The Muppet Show* in Britain.

The premiss of each programme is that the Muppets organize and perform a variety show, before a live audience. Master of Ceremonies is Kermit the Frog, operated and voiced by Henson himself. He is supported (or hindered) by a large cast of weird animal and humanoid performers and stage-hands. Fozzie Bear is a stand-up comedian with a pointed head, small hat and lame jokes. Rowlf is a shaggy dog piano-player, and other music comes from Dr Teeth and the Electric Mayhem, featuring Animal on drums and laid-back guitarist Floyd. Gonzo is a hook-beaked stuntman and trumpeter whose instrument explodes at the start of each show.

Soon to become co-star with Kermit is blonde Miss Piggy. Her unrequited love for the frog means she is constantly trying to ensnare him, and anyone who stands in her way feels the power of her left hook. Other notable characters are mad scientist Dr Bunsen Honeydew, a crazy Swedish chef, and a pair of crotchety old men, Statler and Waldorf, who heckle the show from their box seats. More barracking comes from Sam, a right-wing American eagle. A regular slot in the show is given to the serial *Pigs in Space*, which pits Captain Link Hogthrob, commander of the starship *Swinetrek*, against the evil Dr Strangepork.

A host of famous stars also appeared as the Muppets' guests, Elton John, Peter Sellers, George Burns, Peter Ustinov, Raquel Welch and Rudolf Nureyev among them, and, apart from the technical mastery of the puppet form, the show's success came from the human nature of its characters, their attempts to succeed and their tendency to fail. The inventiveness of the musical numbers also played a part. Buffalo Springfield's 'For What It's Worth', for instance, was performed with pathos against a field sports backdrop, and the show spawned a couple of chart hits, 'The Muppet Show Music Hall EP' and A. A. Milne's 'Halfway Down the Stairs' (by Kermit's nephew, Robin).

The Muppets also made a couple of feature films before returning to the small screen in 1996. In *Muppets Tonight!* (made and screened first in the US), the manic creatures have abandoned their variety theatre in favour of a local TV station, K-MUP TV. Among the characters added to the troupe are mob-linked lounge crooner Johnny Fiama and his bodyguard monkey, Sal; Bob, a security bear; elevator flunkies Seymour and Pepe, an elephant and a prawn; Miss Piggy's stupid nephews, Randy and Andy; and Bill the Bubble Guy, whose party-piece amounts to blowing bubbles out of the top of his head. The new host is allegedly streetwise Clifford and the *Bay of Pigs Watch* saga features curvy porker Spamela Hamderson. Guest stars like Michelle Pfeiffer, Pierce Brosnan and John Goodman flocked to appear.

Muppets Tonight!

See *Muppet Show, The.*

Murder Bag ✱✱

UK (Associated-Rediffusion) Police Drama. ITV 1957–9

Det. Supt. Tom Lockhart .... **Raymond Francis**

Creator **Glyn Davies**
Producer **Barry Baker**

● ***Half-hour detective series introducing long-serving Detective Superintendent Lockhart.***

In this early series, snuff-sniffing Tom Lockhart is assisted in his investigations by different police officers each week, but always present is the 'Murder Bag' of the title. This black briefcase, seen in close-up behind the opening titles, provides Lockhart with the equipment he needs to gather forensic evidence. Over 70 items are held in the case, ranging from airtight jars to tweezers, and each week it is called into play in pursuit of yet another murderer. The first 30 episodes did not have separate titles but case numbers, and were listed as *Murder Bag – Case One*, etc. All subsequent programmes carried titles such as *Lockhart Sets a Trap* and *Lockhart Misses a Clue*, and most transmissions were live. Barry Baker and Peter Ling scripted most episodes between them. From here, the character of Lockhart went on to CRIME SHEET (where he could investigate more than murder) and then his *pièce de résistance*, NO HIDING PLACE.

Murder in Mind ✱✱✱

UK (BBC/Paul Knight) Drama Anthology. BBC 1 2001–3
DVD: BBC

Creator **Anthony Horowitz**
Executive Producer **Mal Young**
Producer **Paul Knight**

● ***Murder – from the killer's point of view.***

This collection of murder stories provides a break from traditional whodunnits and detective capers. Instead, the process of murder is viewed through the eyes of each of the killers: normal people, on the face of it, who are driven to commit the ultimate crime by distressing circumstances. Glossing over violence and gratuitous gore, each drama homes in on the psychology of the murder act, witnessing events that lead to the decision to commit the crime and the impact of its aftermath on the protagonists. Among the major guest performers are David Suchet, Steve McFadden, Timothy West, Kevin Whateley, Pauline Quirke, Rob Brydon, Nigel Havers, Neil Pearson, Nicholas Lyndhurst and Adam Faith, in his last television role. Writers include creator Anthony Horowitz, Stephen Leather, Simon Sharkey, Guy Burt and J. C. Wilsher. The fact that series two and three were broken up, with episodes shown only sporadically, on different days on BBC 1, didn't help this offering achieve longevity.

Murder in Suburbia ✱

UK (Granada) Police Drama. ITV 1 2004–5

DI Kate Ashurst .... **Caroline Catz**
DS Emma Scribbins .... **Lisa Faulkner**
DCI Sullivan .... **Jeremy Sheffield**
Gallimore .... **Glen Davies**

Executive Producer **Sharon Bloom**
Producers **Joy Spink, Tim Whitby**

● ***A couple of female detectives mop up mayhem among the middle classes.***

With MIDSOMER MURDERS hoovering up all the heinous crimes the country can commit, ITV needed something that did the same for the residential suburbs. Enter fictitious Middleford and its chief crime fighters, buddy cops Ashurst and Scribbins ('Scribbs'). The duo are chalk and cheese types, as flagged up by the fact that one (Ashurst) is a brunette and the other is a blonde. They lead different lifestyles: Ashurst is efficient and organized, while Scribbins subscribes to the chaos theory. Nevertheless, despite drowning in a sea of girlie gossip, they work well together, combining Ashurst's by-the-book authority with Scribbins's natural feel for the job. Their boss, DCI Sullivan, is a bit of all right in their books, but is very much a man of mystery. Their work takes them into the seedy middle-class world of singles clubs, wife-swapping circles, golf clubs, charity balls and residential homes. ITV's launch description of the series as 'murder mysteries for the speed dating generation' underscores its depth.

Murder Investigation Team

See *The Bill.*

Murder Most English ✱✱

UK (BBC) Drama. BBC 2 1997

DI Purbright .... **Anton Rodgers**
DS Love .... **Christopher Timothy**
Chief Constable Chubb .... **Moray Watson**
Sgt Malley .... **John Comer**
Warlock .... **John Tordoff**
Miss Lucilla Teatime .... **Brenda Bruce**
Dr Meadow .... **Derek Waring**
Mrs Helen Carobleat .... **Caroline Blakiston**
Dr Rupert Hillyard .... **Antony Carrick**

Writer **Richard Harris**
Producer **Martin Lisemore**

● ***Crime mysteries set in a surprisingly offbeat English village.***

The Flaxborough Chronicles by Colin Watson (which began with the 1958 novel *Coffin, Scarcely Used*) provide the inspiration for this seven-part series directed by Ronald Wilson. Set in a small rural town in Lincolnshire, the action centres on one DI Purbright, a determined, shrewd, polite detective with a subtle sense of humour. His nose for intrigue leads him to investigate missing spies, absent ladies, the mysterious Flaxborough Crab and the baffling death of a local person. With fine supporting performances from the likes of Peter Sallis, Lesley Dunlop, Barbara Flynn, Patrick Newell, Stephanie Cole and James Grout, as some of the rebellious locals, the series revels in a uniquely British brand of gentle humour, taking its lead from the rich heritage of the Ealing comedy, and bringing to television the quirky, subversive, light touch of the original books.

Murder Most Horrid ★★★

UK (Talkback/BBC) Comedy Anthology. BBC 2 1991; 1994; 1996; 1999

Dawn French

Producers **Jon Plowman, Sophie Clarke-Jervoise**
Executive Producers **Peter Fincham, Jon Plowman**

● ***Series of spoof murder playlets.***

Dawn French stars in this colourful pastiche of the TV mystery/thriller genre. Adopting a new character every episode – kids' TV presenter Bunty Breslaw, social worker Tina Mellish, secretary Sally Fairfax, surgeon Kate Marshall, abattoir-staffer Daisy Talwinning, policewoman-turned-gangster Whoopi Stone, dinner lady Tiffany Drapes, etc. – French finds herself embroiled in the most grisly and gruesome situations yet always manages to prove that murder is a funny business. Among the major guest stars are Nigel Havers, Timothy Spall, Amanda Donohoe, Timothy West, Jim Carter, Sarah Lancashire and Frances Barber. Scripts were penned by writers such as Anthony Horowitz, Ian Hislop and Nick Newman, Paul Smith and Terry Kyan, and Steven Moffat.

Murder One ★★★★

US (Steven Bochco Productions/Twentieth Century-Fox) Drama. BBC 2 1996–7 (US: ABC 1995–7)
DVD: Fox

Theodore 'Teddy' Hoffman ..... **Daniel Benzali**
Justine Appleton ..... **Mary McCormack**
Richard Cross ..... **Stanley Tucci**
Neil Avedon ..... **Jason Gedrick**
Chris Docknovich ..... **Michael Hayden**
Lisa Gillespie ..... **Grace Phillips**
Miriam Grasso ..... **Barbara Bosson**
Arnold Spivak ..... **J. C. Mackenzie**
Arthur Polson ..... **Dylan Baker**
Lila Marquette ..... **Vanessa Williams**
Julie Costello ..... **Bobbie Phillips**
Annie Hoffman ..... **Patricia Clarkson**
Louis Heinsbergen ..... **John Fleck**
Francesca Cross ..... **Donna Murphy**
Det. Raymond Velacek ..... **Joe Spano**
Dr Graham Lester ..... **Stanley Kamel**
Judge Beth Bornstein ..... **Linda Carlson**
DA Roger Garfield ..... **Gregory Itzin**
James Wyler ..... **Anthony LaPaglia**
Det. Vince Biggio ..... **Clayton Rohner**
Aaron Mosely ..... **D. B. Woodside**
Sharon Rooney ..... **Missy Crider**
Caroline Van Allen ..... **Romy Walthall**
Malcolm Dietrich ..... **Ralph Waite**
Rickey Latrell ..... **Rick Worthy**
Clifford Banks ..... **Pruitt Taylor Vince**
Lynette Banks ..... **Karen Austin**
Gary Blondo ..... **John Pleshette**

Creators **Steven Bochco, Charles H. Eglee, Channing Gibson**
Executive Producers **Steven Bochco, Charles H. Eglee**

● ***The cases of a rich person's law firm, exploring all aspects of the American justice system.***

Murder One broke new ground when, for its first series, all 23 episodes focused on just one criminal trial. In the dock is Neil Avedon, a young film star with a serious attitude problem, pleading not guilty to the murder of teenager Jessica Costello. However, before getting to the trial, the series looks at preliminary police inquiries, jury selection and other important background details, as well as the effect on the personal lives of those involved, and it doesn't end when the verdict is announced. Head of the defending team from Hoffman & Associates is bald-headed, bespectacled Teddy Hoffman, a brilliant advocate with enormous respect in the business. Sadly, his marriage is falling apart. Joining Teddy in the firm are reliable Chris Docknovich, ambitious Lisa Gillespie, impetuous Justine Appleton, quirky Arnold Spivak and gay PA Louis Heinsbergen. On the other side of the bench are hard-nosed Assistant District Attorney Miriam Grasso, an old friend of Teddy's, and vengeful local cop Arthur Polson. Key figures in the case are slimy businessman Richard Cross, dubious doctor Graham Lester and untrustworthy District Attorney Roger Garfield.

Despite winning rave notices from viewers and critics, the series failed in the US ratings, thanks to being allocated the suicide slot against ER. It was, however, given a second bite of the cherry and returned a year later with a new lead man. Teddy has been written out (to work on his marriage) and has handed over control of the firm to his junior partners, who bring on board slick but devious lawyer James Wyler to give their image a bit more clout. Lisa has also left, to be replaced by Aaron. This time there are three separate trials under the microscope during the season's run, involving the murder of the Californian governor and his mistress, the future of a serial murderer and an O. J. Simpson-style case concerning a basketball star.

Murder Rooms: The Dark Beginnings of Sherlock Holmes ★★★

UK (BBC/WGBH) Detective Drama. BBC 1 2001
DVD: Mosaic Movies

Dr Joseph Bell ..... **Ian Richardson**
Dr Arthur Conan Doyle ..... **Charles Edwards**
Insp. Warner ..... **Simon Chandler**

Writers **David Pirie, Paul Billing, Stephen Gallagher, Daniel Boyle**
Producers **Ian Madden, Alison Jackson**

A Victorian pathologist provides the inspiration for 'the greatest detective'.

In a bid to shed light on the origins of Arthur Conan Doyle's celebrated literary sleuth, this collection of murder mysteries focuses on Dr Joseph Bell, said to be the real-life model for Sherlock Holmes. Bell was Conan Doyle's tutor at Edinburgh University's medical school, but he was more than a lecturer: he was also a part-time forensic pathologist, from whom the future author no doubt learned much about the science of detection. This four-episode series was founded on a pilot (BBC 2 2000, with Robin Laing as Conan Doyle) that followed a fictitious investigation in Edinburgh in 1878. In the series itself, Conan Doyle, now in general practice in Southsea, finds he has need of his mentor to solve a succession of typically baffling cases, one of which again returns him to the Scottish capital.

Murder, She Wrote **

US (Universal) Detective Drama. ITV 1985–97 (US: CBS 1984–96)
DVD: Universal

Jessica Fletcher	**Angela Lansbury**
Sheriff Amos Tupper	**Tom Bosley**
Grady Fletcher	**Michael Horton**
Dr Seth Hazlitt	**William Windom**
Mayor Sam Booth	**Richard Paul**
Sheriff Mort Metzger	**Ron Masak**

Creators **Richard Levinson, William Link, Peter S. Fischer**
Executive Producer **Peter S. Fischer**
Producers **Robert F. O'Neill, Robert E. Swanson**

A middle-aged novelist solves murder cases in her spare time.

Widow Jessica Beatrice Fletcher lives in Cabot Cove, Maine, and used to be a substitute teacher until writing brought her fame and wealth. (Her first book, a detective thriller called *The Corpse Danced at Midnight*, had been submitted to a publisher by Grady, her accountant nephew, and became a huge success.) However, when one of her relatives is suspected of murder, Jessica is able to bring her own detective skills into play. She clears his name and thus begins her investigative career.

Jessica becomes a sort of American Miss Marple. Travelling the world to promote her books or to visit her many relations, she finds herself constantly embroiled in murder mysteries that the local police cannot resolve. Piecing together the clues in often very complicated plots, Jessica proves to be a thorough and quick-witted sleuth, bringing many a culprit to book, much to the amazement of the local law-enforcers. When not travelling, her acquaintances in Cabot Cove (which itself has more than its fair share of murders) include local sheriff Amos Tupper (later replaced by Sheriff Mort Metzger), Mayor Sam Booth and Dr Seth Hazlitt. In later episodes, Jessica moves part-time to New York, living weekdays in a Manhattan apartment while teaching criminology at Manhattan University. On some occasions, Jessica herself does not appear at all, other than to introduce the episode's 'guest sleuth'. After the series proper ended, Angela Lansbury resumed her role as Jessica for a handful of TV movies. A spin-off series from *Murder, She Wrote* was *The Law and Harry McGraw*, based on a disorganized Boston detective played by Jerry Orbach who had appeared in a few episodes.

Murdoch, Rupert

(1931–)

One of the world's media barons, Australian-born Rupert Murdoch, the head of the News Corporation empire, has left his mark on the television world as well as in newspapers and publishing. In 1985 he became an American citizen for business reasons and took control of Twentieth Century-Fox and a string of regional TV stations in order to establish a fourth US television network (Fox). Then, in 1989, he pre-empted the launch of British Satellite Broadcasting (BSB), the official UK satellite station, by opening up his own Sky network, which, in 1990, merged with (in many ways absorbed) BSB, becoming British Sky Broadcasting. News Corporation also owns the Asian satellite station Star TV, the American digital provider DirecTV, and Sky Italia.

Murnaghan, Dermot

(1957–)

Devon-born former ITN newscaster, who also read the news for *Channel 4 Daily* and presented ITV series like *Police Action Live* and *The Big Story*. Since moving to the BBC, he has hosted *Breakfast*, *The State We're In*, a revamp of TREASURE HUNT and the quiz *Eggheads*. He is married to journalist/producer Maria Keegan.

Murphy, Ben

(1942–)

American actor, in television since 1968, initially taking small parts in series like IT TAKES A THIEF, THE VIRGINIAN and *The Name of the Game*. He waited until 1971 to earn a starring role, which came as Thaddeus Jones (aka Kid Curry) in ALIAS SMITH AND JONES, a bigger hit in the UK than in its native USA, leaving Murphy still looking for a TV breakthrough back home. He followed it with a series of similarly prominent but not overwhelming parts, including the title role in THE GEMINI MAN (Sam Casey). Among other dramas, Murphy was also seen in THE WINDS OF WAR (Warren Henry), and in *Griff*, *The Chisholms*, *The Dirty Dozen* and *Lottery*.

Murphy, Brian

(1933–)

Isle of Wight-born comic actor chiefly remembered as the hen-pecked, work-shy George Roper in MAN ABOUT THE HOUSE and GEORGE AND MILDRED. However, Murphy has also starred in other comedies: *Sez Les*, *The Incredible Mr Tanner* (busker Ernest Tanner), L FOR LESTER (hapless driving instructor Lester Small), and LAME DUCKS (inept private eye Ansell). In 1995 he was seen as con man George Manners in BROOKSIDE and in 1999 played Arthur Capstick in MRS MERTON AND MALCOLM. More recently he has played Alvin in LAST OF THE SUMMER WINE and Maurice in *The Booze Cruise*. Among many guest appearances, Murphy has been seen in THE AVENGERS, CALLAN, *Theatre Box*, BOON, ONE FOOT IN THE GRAVE, JONATHAN CREEK, CASUALTY, THE BILL, SUNBURN, *The All Star Comedy Show* and *The Catherine Tate Show*.

Murphy Brown ✶✶

US (Shukovsky-English/Warner Brothers) Situation Comedy. BBC 2 1994 (US: CBS 1988–98)
DVD: Warner Home Video (Region 1 only)

Murphy Brown .... **Candice Bergen**
Jim Dial .... **Charles Kimbrough**
Frank Fontana .... **Joe Regalbuto**
Corky Sherwood/Forrest .... **Faith Ford**
Miles Silverberg .... **Grant Shaud**
Eldin Bernecky .... **Robert Pastorelli**
Phil .... **Pat Corley**

Creators **Diane English, Joel Shukovsky**

An independent-minded career journalist works for a TV news magazine.

Murphy Brown is a presenter for the Washington DC-based TV magazine *F.Y.I. (For Your Information)*. She is a tough, plain-speaking divorcée and doesn't suffer fools gladly. She is also very successful at her job, but her personal life is not without problems, as visits to the Betty Ford Clinic in a bid to kick booze and cigarettes prove. The hard-case exterior conceals a soft, vulnerable centre. Foremost among Murphy's colleagues are inexperienced producer Miles Silverberg; humourless news anchor Jim Dial; airhead reporter Corky Sherwood (a former Miss America); and investigative reporter Frank Fontana. (Murphy never has a regular secretary and a running joke sees her trying out a new assistant every week.) Off-air, the bar at which the gang wash away the cares of the day is Phil's Place; at home, Murphy shares her load with her long-term decorator, Eldin Bernecky, whom she later installs as nanny when she gives birth to baby Avery. This decision to raise a child as a single mother provoked the most significant event surrounding the series. US Vice-President Dan Quayle picked on the storyline in a speech on family values in 1992, criticizing its 'bad' children-out-of-wedlock example. Like some of his other utterances, it was a comment that blew up in Quayle's face and rocketed *Murphy Brown* to the top of the US ratings. Despite its popularity Stateside, the series only enjoyed a short taste of terrestrial airtime in the UK, but there has been much greater exposure on satellite channels.

Murphy's Law ✶✶

UK (Tiger Aspect). BBC 1 2003–
DVD: DD Home Entertainment

DS Tommy Murphy .... **James Nesbitt**
DI Annie Guthrie .... **Claudia Harrison**
DC Alan Carter .... **Del Synnott**
Father McBride .... **Mark Benton**
Hilary Clarke .... **Sarah Berger**
DS Paul Allison .... **Owen Teale**
Dep. Supt. Rees .... **Michael Feast**
Dave Callard .... **Mark Womack**
Caz Miller .... **Michael Fassbender**
Ellie Holloway .... **Georgia MacKenzie**
Richard Holloway .... **Ramon Tikaram**
George Garvey .... **Larry Lamb**
Leedham .... **Maggie Lloyd Williams**
Ollington .... **Shaun Dooley**

Creator **Colin Bateman**
Producers **Tom Sherry, Sanne Craddick, Jemma Rodgers**

An undercover cop with nothing to lose puts his life on the line.

Tragedy took over Northern Ireland policeman Tommy Murphy's life when his eight-year-old daughter was murdered by the terrorists he was chasing. Now, relocated to London, with a marriage in tatters, he has nothing left to live for but his work. Despite being psychologically scarred by the experience, the scruffy detective with a sense of humour as dark as his harrowing past is put back to work as an undercover detective. Because of his experience, he now has no fear: the worst has already happened. Therefore he calmly rubs shoulders with prisoners, gangsters, Russian hoods, homeless people, an elite police unit – whatever it takes to get a result for the force. There are hopes that his personal life may take a turn for the better as sexual tension with his boss Annie Guthrie begins to crackle, but their relationship is viciously ended early in series two. Young DC Carter supports Murphy in his cases, while a recurring character, Father McBride, is a close friend. Series three takes on more of a serial quality, with Murphy adopting the same undercover persona throughout as he homes in on gangland boss Dave Callard and his politician associate, George Garvey. Murphy also has a cold fish new boss in the form of Dep. Supt. Rees, with DS Allison his new police liaison officer.

The series was specially written for star James Nesbitt by novelist Colin Bateman, an old friend from Northern Ireland, and began with a pilot episode in 2001.

Murray, Bryan

(1949–)

Irish actor seen in a variety of series, usually in 'dodgy' roles. The highlights have been THE IRISH RM (Flurry Knox), BREAD (Shifty), PERFECT SCOUNDRELS (con man Harry Cassidy), BROOKSIDE (wife-beater Trevor Jordache), THE BILL (Harry Fullerton), *Proof* (Irish politician Myles Carrick) and *The Baby War* (Connor). Guest appearances include roles in HOLBY CITY, CASUALTY and SILENT WITNESS.

My Cousin Rachel ✶✶

UK (BBC) Drama. BBC 2 1983

Contessa Rachel Sangalletti ... **Geraldine Chaplin**
Philip Ashley .... **Christopher Guard**
Ambrose Ashley .... **John Shrapnel**
Nick Kendall .... **John Stratton**
Louise Kendall .... **Amanda Kirby**
Seecombe .... **Bert Parnaby**
John .... **Jamie Cresswell**
Rainaldi .... **Charles Kay**

Writer **Hugh Whitemore**
Producer **Richard Beynon**

Love and mystery in Victorian Cornwall.

This four-part adaptation of Daphne du Maurier's novel focuses on Rachel Sangalletti. Rachel is the widow of Ambrose Ashley. They had met overseas and had been married for only a short time. She is now suspected of having poisoned her husband, but this is just one of the intrigues that surface as she embarks on a relationship with Philip, cousin and ward of her late husband. Also featuring strongly in the plot are Rainaldi, Rachel's lawyer, and Nick Kendall, Philip's godfather.

My Dad's the Prime Minister ✶✶

UK (BBC) Situation Comedy. BBC 1 2003–4
DVD: Maximum Entertainment

Prime Minster Michael Phillips	**Robert Bathurst**
Dillon Phillips	**Joe Prospero**
Clare Phillips	**Carla Mendonça**
Sarah Phillips	**Emma Sackville**
Duncan Packer	**Jasper Britton**
Det. Andy Sharp	**Brian Bovell**
Lighthouse	**Luke Newberry**
Flash	**Leagh Conwell**
Geezer	**Joe Gunn**
JJ	**Simone Gunn**
Harry	**Eugene Simon**
Granny Phillips	**Marcia Warren**
Gary McRyan	**Paterson Joseph**
Chancellor	**Rupert Vansittart**
Opposition Leader	**Albert Welling**
Home Secretary	**Michael Fenton Stevens**
Mr Speaker	**Michael Cronin**

Creators/Writers **Ian Hislop, Nick Newman**
Producer **Francis Matthews**

● ***A schoolboy suffers because of his father's rather important job.***
Parents are a huge embarrassment when you're aged 12, as we all know, but for Dillon Phillips the cringe factor is simply enormous because his dad's the leader of the country. He's always on TV and in the papers, not always for the right reasons; he makes far too big an entrance on school sports day – in a helicopter, surrounded by security men; and when elections come around, everyone has an opinion about your old man. To make matters worse, mum is a high-flying businesswoman, who never has the time to share with you or your obnoxious older sister, Sarah. You can't even be your juvenile self, as everything you do takes on magnified proportions. Asking the Home Office for help with your geography homework is not that naughty, is it? Then there's Duncan Packer, dad's spin doctor, and your personal bodyguard, Andy Sharp, to keep you in your place, too. (Sharp gives way to Gary McRyan in series two.) All this in front of schoolmates Lighthouse and Geezer, and school enemy Flash.

Ian Hislop and Nick Newman's comedy pokes plenty of fun at the proprieties and vanities of the top job in government, and especially at the concept of a family man holding down that role, à la Tony Blair. Lots of cameo performances come from the likes of Jeremy Paxman, John Humphrys, John Sergeant, Sue Barker and Melvyn Bragg. The series was first shown on the digital children's channel CBBC before transferring to a Sunday teatime slot on BBC 1. Series two, in 2004, gained promotion to peak time, with a more adult tone adopted. A Christmas special followed the same year.

My Family ✶

UK (DLT/Rude Boy) Situation Comedy. BBC 1 2000–
DVD: VCI

Ben Harper	**Robert Lindsay**
Susan Harper	**Zoë Wanamaker**
Nick Harper	**Kris Marshall**
Janey Harper	**Daniela Denby-Ashe**
Michael Harper	**Gabriel Thomson**
Brigitte	**Daisy Donovan**
Abi Harper	**Siobhan Hayes**
Roger Bailey Jr	**Keiron Self**
Alfie	**Rhodri Meilir**

Creator **Fred Barron**
Producer **John Bartlett**

● ***Home means harassment for an immature dentist.***
Although on the face of it a typical British domestic sitcom, in the NO PLACE LIKE HOME vein, *My Family* has its roots in American comedy. Creator Fred Barron had written for shows like SEINFELD, THE LARRY SANDERS SHOW and CAROLINE IN THE CITY and wanted to create a programme about his own family. However, feeling that American executives would have made it rather too twee, he brought the idea to Britain, and with it the concept of ensemble writing. The UK method normally just sees one or two writers penning a whole series, but in the States a whole roomful of scribes contributes to each episode, and that's what Barron introduced with *My Family*, employing a mix of British and American writers. As for the storyline, it's another tale of household crises, intra-family friction, misunderstandings and double-takes built around the middle-class Harpers. Childish, incompetent dad Ben is a dentist (a character based on creator Barron's own father), his organized wife Susan is a tour guide and their three kids bring more than their fair share of problems into the house. Elder son Nick is both jobless and clueless; fashion-crazy teenager Janey is manipulative (she eventually heads for Manchester University but soon returns, complete with baby Kenzo); and junior son Michael is a computer genius who has trouble at school. Student cousin Abi is another part of the household and she's keen on Ben's dull dentist colleague, Roger. Because of the number of writers involved, series have included up to 14 episodes in one run. There was no series in 2005, but there was a Christmas special.

My Favorite Martian ✶✶

US (Jack Chertok) Situation Comedy. ITV 1963–4
(US: CBS 1963–6)
DVD: Rhino (Region 1 only)

Uncle Martin	**Ray Walston**
Tim O'Hara	**Bill Bixby**
Lorelei Brown	**Pamela Britton**
Angela Brown	**Ann Marshall**
Mr Harry Burns	**J. Pat O'Malley**
Det. Bill Brennan	**Alan Hewitt**

Creator **John L. Greene**
Producer **Jack Chertok**

● ***A journalist befriends a Martian who has crash-landed on Earth.***
Los Angeles Sun reporter Tim O'Hara is on the way to an assignment when he discovers a crashed spacecraft and its occupant, a Martian anthropologist who has been studying Earthmen. Seeing the alien is stunned and in need of help, Tim takes him home and makes him comfortable in his boarding-house room, while he works on the amazing story for his boss, Mr Burns. But, being almost human-like and speaking English, the Martian makes a strong impression on Tim, who scraps the story and decides to keep the alien's identity a secret. He passes him off as his Uncle Martin and finds him a room in the house, to give Martin time to repair his ship. No one else knows Martin's secret, though Bill Brennan, a police officer, who arrives in the second series, is always fishing

around. Brennan is also Martin's rival for the attentions of their landlady, Mrs Brown. Her teenage daughter, Angela, appears in the first season.

Preceding MORK AND MINDY by a decade and a half, *My Favorite Martian* has many similarities. Martin is not as zany as Mork but he does have unusual powers, such as telepathy and the ability to make himself invisible. He can move objects by pointing at them, is a technological genius, can talk to animals and has little retractable antennae on his head.

My Friend Flicka ★★

US (Twentieth Century-Fox) Children's Adventure. ITV 1957–8 (US: CBS 1956–7)

Ken McLaughlin .... **Johnny Washbrook**
Rob McLaughlin .... **Gene Evans**
Nell McLaughlin .... **Anita Louise**
Gus Broeberg .... **Frank Ferguson**
Hildy Broeberg .... **Pamela Beaird**

Executive Producer **Buddy Adler**
Producers **Alan A. Armor, Peter Packer, Sam White, Herman Schlom**

● ***A boy's best friend is his horse.***

Eleven-year-old Ken McLaughlin lives with his parents, Rob and Nell, ranch-hand Gus and, most importantly, his horse, Flicka, on the Goose Bar Ranch near Coulee Springs in turn-of-the-century Montana. In the Lassie vein, boy and horse fall into all manner of adventures, although the drama is not always as intense, and much of the action centres on the family's struggles on the northern American frontier. Hildy is Gus's niece.

My Friend Flicka (one of the first children's series to be filmed in colour) was based on the book by Mary O'Hara and the 1943 film starring Roddy McDowall. 'Flicka' is Swedish for 'little girl', and the equine star was a horse called Wahama.

My Good Friend ★★★

UK (Hartswood/Anglia) Situation Comedy. ITV 1995–6

Peter Banks .... **George Cole**
Harry King .... **Richard Pearson**
Ellie .... **Minnie Driver**
Lesley Vickerage
Betty .... **Matilda Ziegler**
Annabelle Apsion
Brian .... **Michael Lumsden**
Neil .... **Caleb Lloyd**
Jamie O'Brien
Miss Byron .... **Joan Sims**
Maria .... **Nimmy March**

Writer **Bob Larbey**
Producer **Beryl Vertue**

● ***Two senior citizens refuse to be overwhelmed by retirement.***

In this gentle comedy, Peter Banks is a widower who misses his late wife. He also misses his job as a postal worker and finds enforced retirement a trial. However, when he bumps into former librarian Harry King, another lonely but more bashful pensioner, he finds a new soulmate. More than that, he finds an accomplice to help while away his long days in little bouts of mischief and rebellion. The pals do not always see eye to eye, but their friendship becomes strong as they embark on short outings and new ventures, and set themselves little challenges in order to keep vital. Unfortunately for Peter, he has to live with his fussy (and understandably exasperated) daughter, Betty, and son-in-law, Brian. He would rather share the same digs as bachelor Harry, who has a room with a warm-hearted young landlady named Ellie, single mum of young Neil, but it is not to be, because also sharing Ellie's home is the eccentric old Miss Byron (affectionately known as 'Pickles'). Maria is a waitress at a wine bar the old gents frequent.

The two series were directed by Martin Dennis and Jeremy Ancock. For the second series, major cast changes were needed when Minnie Driver, Matilda Ziegler and Caleb Lloyd left, to be replaced by former SOLDIER, SOLDIER stars Lesley Vickerage and Annabelle Apsion, plus young Jamie O'Brien.

My Good Woman ★★

UK (ATV) Situation Comedy. ITV 1972–4

Clive Gibbons .... **Leslie Crowther**
Sylvia Gibbons .... **Sylvia Syms**
Philip Broadmore .... **Keith Barron**
Bob Berris .... **Glyn Houston**
Revd Martin Hooper .... **Richard Wilson**

Creator/Writer **Ronnie Taylor**
Producers **Les Chatfield, William G. Stewart, Ronnie Baxter**

● ***A husband suffers because his wife is a compulsive charity-worker.***

Antiques dealer Clive Gibbons is a charity widower. His wife, Sylvia, is so concerned with raising money for good causes and helping out the less fortunate that their life together is rather barren. Despite his efforts to convince her that charity begins at home, the hapless Clive is forced to seek solace in the company of his neighbour, Philip Broadmore, and then, in later episodes, his darts colleague, Bob Berris, as Sylvia arranges yet another jumble sale. Martin Hooper is the vicar benefiting from most of Sylvia's worthy deeds.

My Hero ★★

UK (Big Bear) Situation Comedy. BBC 1 2000–3; 2005–
DVD: IMC Vision

George Sunday ('Thermoman') .... **Ardal O'Hanlon**
Janet Dawkins .... **Emily Joyce**
Mrs Raven .... **Geraldine McNulty**
Dr Piers Crispin .... **Hugh Dennis**
Tyler .... **Philip Whitchurch**
Ella Dawkins .... **Lill Roughley**
Stanley Dawkins .... **Tim Wylton**
Arnie .... **Lou Hirsch**
Ollie .... **Finlay Stroud** *(voice only)*
George Monday .... **James Dreyfus**

Executive Producers **Geoffrey Perkins, Sophie Clarke-Jervoise**
Producers **Marcus Mortimer, John Stroud, Jamie Rix**

● ***A dim alien with superpowers struggles to save the world.***

George Sunday is not what he seems. Far from being a mild-mannered health-food shopkeeper in Northolt, he is in fact a superhero, masquerading under the alter-ego of Thermoman. George is 326 years old and comes from the planet Ultron. Here on Earth he is bestowed with special powers *à la* Superman, which he endeavours to put to good use rescuing stricken souls and averting global disasters. Unfortunately, by saving nurse Janet Dawkins from certain death at the Grand Canyon and falling in love, he has made life a little more complicated for himself. Living with a girlfriend means he has to adapt more to society, presenting a 'normal' front to her family, friends and workmates who (unlike Janet) can never know his secret. George is also a bit slow in picking up the little nuances of human life and understanding earthly customs – which leads to countless gaffes, double-takes and misunderstandings lifted from the well-thumbed sitcom book of laughs. Typically long-suffering Janet is, on the other hand, level-headed and down to earth (in the conventional sense). She works at a health centre for the deceitful and egocentric Piers Crispin and alongside tactless receptionist Mrs Raven. Ella is Janet's demanding mum and Stanley is her dad. Tyler is the Liverpudlian UFO fantasist who lives in the same block of flats as George and Janet, and Arnie is George's fraudulent cousin from Ultron who now works at the shop. At the end of the second series, Janet (after a six-day pregnancy) gives birth to brilliant baby Ollie, like his father equipped with superhuman powers, which means he's always likely to fly out of the nursery window on a mission to save the world. When Ardal O'Hanlon left the series in 2006 he was replaced by James Dreyfus as George in a new body. The many writers have included Paul Mendelson and Paul Mayhew-Archer.

My Mother the Car ✳

US (United Artists/Cottage Industries/NBC) Situation Comedy. ITV 1965 (US: NBC 1965–6)

Dave Crabtree .... **Jerry Van Dyke**
Abigail Crabtree .... **Ann Sothern** *(voice only)*
Barbara Crabtree .... **Maggie Pierce**
Cindy Crabtree .... **Cindy Eilbacher**
Randy Crabtree .... **Randy Whipple**
Capt. Bernard Mancini .... **Avery Schreiber**

Creators **Allan Burns, Chris Hayward**
Producer **Rod Amateau**

A man buys a vintage motor car, only to find it is his mother reincarnated.

When lawyer Dave Crabtree visits a second-hand car lot in his small Californian town to look for a cheap new car, he is inexplicably drawn to a rickety 1928 Porter. He soon discovers why: the car is actually a reincarnation of his late mother. Understandably, he buys the car and restores it, much to the disgust of his wife, Barbara, and two children, Cindy and Randy, who really want a station-wagon. They can't understand why Dave is so protective of the old boneshaker and why he resists villainous attempts by classic-car dealer Captain Mancini to take the Porter off his hands. Of course, *they* can't hear his mother's voice bellowing out of the car radio, nagging and domineering him just as she used to when she was alive.

Jerry Van Dyke is Dick Van Dyke's brother, but he failed to achieve the same kind of sitcom success. *My Mother the Car* was almost universally panned by critics and lasted only one season. For some, it was the worst US sitcom of the 1960s.

My Three Sons ✳✳

US (Don Fedderson) Situation Comedy. ITV 1961–8 (US: ABC 1960–5/CBS 1965–72)

Steve Douglas .... **Fred MacMurray**
Mike Douglas .... **Tim Considine**
Robbie Douglas .... **Don Grady**
Richard 'Chip' Douglas .... **Stanley Livingston**
Michael 'Bub' O'Casey .... **William Frawley**
'Uncle' Charley O'Casey .... **William Demarest**
Sally Morrison/Douglas .... **Meredith MacRae**
Ernie Douglas .... **Barry Livingston**
Katie Miller/Douglas .... **Tina Cole**
Barbara Harper/Douglas .... **Beverly Garland**
Dodie Harper/Douglas .... **Dawn Lyn**
Polly Williams/Douglas .... **Ronnie Troup**

A widowed father is devoted to his three kids.

This warm-hearted suburban family comedy – as American as apple pie – ran for 12 years in its native USA, making it the country's second longest-running sitcom (after *The Adventures of Ozzie* and *Harriet* – not screened in the UK). Aircraft engineer Steve Douglas is a widower, solidly bringing up his three well-mannered sons in the pleasant district of Bryant Park, somewhere in a Midwest conurbation. His kids are Mike (18), Robbie (14) and Chip (7). Completing the household are Steve's late wife's father, 'Bub' O'Casey, a gruff but kind-hearted old codger who takes care of most of the cooking and cleaning, and lovable dog Tramp. Ensuring his boys grow up on the straight and narrow is what occupies most of Steve's time, and he's always willing to drag them all away on camping holidays and other wholesome adventures. As for the boys, their attention gradually turns to girls and one by one they get married. Mike is the first to tie the knot, with girlfriend Sally Morrison (a device for writing actor Tim Considine out of the series). Robbie weds next but stays close to home with his new wife, Katie, and their 'three sons' (triplets), and, not long before the series ends, Chip gets hitched, to college girlfriend Polly Williams. Along the way, however, there are several cast changes. When Bub decides to move to Ireland (actor William Frawley was ill), his brother Charley takes his place as live-in curmudgeon, and when Mike is married off, a new third 'son' is introduced, in the form of orphan Ernie, who had already been seen as a chum of Chip's. Steve – having relocated the family to north Hollywood – himself remarries. Teacher Barbara Harper is his new wife, bringing her young daughter, Dodie, into the household, and, by the time the series winds up, the Douglas family tree has become quite complicated.

My Two Dads ✳

US (Michael Jacobs/Columbia) Situation Comedy. Channel 4 1990–1 (US: NBC 1987–90)

Michael Taylor .... **Paul Reiser**
Joey Harris .... **Greg Evigan**
Nicole Bradford .... **Staci Keenan**
Judge Margaret Wilbur .... **Florence Stanley**
Ed Klawicki .... **Dick Butkus**
Cory Kupkus .... **Vonni Ribisi**
Shelby Haskell .... **Amy Hathaway**
Zack Nichols .... **Chad Allen**

Creators **Michael Jacobs, Danielle Alexandra**
Executive Producer **Michael Jacobs**

Two incompatible men are the guardians of a teenage girl.

Nicole Bradford is 12 and alone in the world following the death of her single mother. She does, however, have a dad, but who he is remains unknown. It could be high-flying financial adviser Michael Taylor, or it could be laid-back artist Joey

Harris, both of whom had relationships with Nicole's mother all those years ago. The two men had fallen out over this love triangle but have now been brought together by their responsibilities to their possible daughter. Michael and Joey are appointed joint guardians and set up an unusual *ménage à trois* in Joey's New York apartment. The two men are quite different creatures. Michael is jumpy and conservative, Joey relaxed and liberal, but spirited Nicole loves them both, which is an advantage as they try to guide her through the trials of teenage life. They do, however, have the assistance of their supervising judge Margaret Wilbur, who, fortunately, owns and lives in the same building. Ed Klawicki runs the local diner they frequent, while Shelby is Nicole's best friend and Cory and Zack two of her boyfriends. Star Greg Evigan co-wrote and sang the theme song.

My Wife Next Door ✶✶

UK (BBC) Situation Comedy. BBC 1 1972

George Bassett .... **John Alderton**
Suzy Bassett .... **Hannah Gordon**

Creators **Brian Clemens, Richard Waring**
Writer **Richard Waring**
Producer **Graeme Muir**

● ***A freshly divorced couple live side by side in the country.***

When George Bassett is divorced by his wife, Suzy, he decides to make a fresh start. He moves out of London and into the countryside. Unfortunately for George, Suzy has also escaped from the city and they find themselves living as next-door neighbours in numbers 1 and 2 Copse Cottages, near Stoke Poges. To preserve their independence they draw up an 'Atlantic Charter' of rules and regulations which they attempt to follow on a day-by-day basis, while all the time prying into each other's affairs (domestic and romantic). They are clearly still in love but are terrified to admit it, to their mutual cost.

My Wonderful Life ✶✶

UK (Granada) Comedy Drama. ITV 1997–9

Donna .... **Emma Wray**
Shirley .... **Vicky Connett**
Rhiannon .... **Amanda Riley**
Marina .... **Elizabeth Berrington**
Alan .... **Tony Robinson**
Lawrie .... **Gary Webster**
Simon .... **Oliver Furness**
Roger .... **Hamish Clark**
Bridget .... **Claire Perkins**
Phil .... **Philip Glenister**
Gail .... **Nicola Stephenson**
Briedha .... **Aingeal Grehan**
Joan Kempson

Creator **Simon Nye**
Writers **Simon Nye, Amanda Swift, Paul Dornan**
Producers **Mark Redhead, Sophie Clarke-Jervoise, Spencer Campbell**

● ***Children, romance or career are the three options facing a single mum.***

Donna has reached a crossroads in her life. A feisty single mother of two young daughters (Shirley and Rhiannon), she is torn between devoting all her time to their well-being, finding a new man and building her career as a nurse. Regrettably those around her don't seem to be of much help, from patronizing neighbour Marina and her eco-warrior husband Alan to her two suitors, Lawrie (a paramedic) and Roger (a doctor). Phil is the bad-penny husband Donna has thrown out. By the time of the second series, Lawrie has disappeared and Donna has temporarily plumped for Roger, although she finds herself outshone by Phil's new trendy girlfriend, Gail. With its thoughtful tone and absence of a laughter track, *My Wonderful Life* is more a comedy drama than an outright sitcom. The series resulted from an hour-length pilot episode shown in 1996 called *True Love* (produced by Brian Park), in which Shirley and Rhiannon were played by Elizabeth Earl and Hannah McVeigh, respectively. This pilot apart, 23 episodes were produced over three series. An American version, starring Ally Walker, was piloted in 2002.

Mystery and Imagination ✶✶

UK (ABC/Thames) Thriller Anthology. ITV 1966; 1968; 1970

Richard Beckett .... **David Buck**

Creators **Jonathan Alwyn, Terence Feely**
Producer **Jonathan Alwyn**

● ***Dramatizations of Victorian chillers.***

Hosted by David Buck in the guise of Victorian adventurer Richard Beckett (who also appears in some of the stories), *Mystery and Imagination* presented three series of 19th-century thrillers. These included works by Robert Louis Stevenson and Edgar Allan Poe, as well as lesser-known writers, but most were in the spine-tingling Gothic tradition. The classics *Frankenstein* and *Dracula* were both featured, as were *Sweeney Todd*, *The Canterville Ghost* and *The Fall of the House of Usher*. Episodes until 1968 were produced by ABC, with Thames taking over after ABC lost its ITV franchise.

Mystery Movie ✶✶

US (Universal) Mystery. ITV 1972–8 (US: NBC 1971–7)

● ***Rotating series of TV movies featuring various sleuths and law-enforcers.***

The *Mystery Movie* umbrella title covered the adventures of COLUMBO, MCCLOUD, MCMILLAN AND WIFE, MADIGAN, QUINCY, *The Snoop Sisters*, HEC RAMSEY, *Faraday and Company*, TENAFLY, AMY PRENTISS, *Cool Million*, *McCoy* and BANACEK, which aired in sequence on ITV. The most successful concepts (like *Columbo, McMillan and Wife, Quincy* and *McCloud*) were later billed simply under their own titles, whereas others (like *McCoy* and *Cool Million*) faded away very quickly. In the USA, the series was broken down into *Sunday Mystery Movie* and *Wednesday Mystery Movie* blocks for airing on NBC.

Nail, Jimmy

(James Bradford; 1954–)

Geordie actor, writer, producer and singer, coming to fame as Oz in AUF WIEDERSEHEN, PET and later turning to his own ideas for starring roles. These have come in SPENDER, as the maverick Newcastle copper, and CROCODILE SHOES, playing singer/songwriter Jed Shepperd. He now runs his own production company, Big Boy. Nail has also been seen in BLOTT ON THE LANDSCAPE, *Shoot for the Sun*, MINDER and SPYSHIP (Metcalfe). His stage name allegedly comes from an accident when he worked in a glass factory: he stood on a six-inch nail and gained the nickname 'Jimmy the Nail'.

Naked City ★★★

US (Shelle/Screen Gems) Police Drama. ITV 1959–64
(US: ABC 1958–63)
DVD: Image Entertainment (Region 1 only)

Det. Lt. Dan Muldoon .... **John McIntire**
Det. Jim Halloran .... **James Franciscus**
Janet Halloran .... **Suzanne Storrs**
Patrolman/Sgt Frank Arcaro .... **Harry Bellaver**
Lt. Mike Parker .... **Horace McMahon**
Det. Adam Flint .... **Paul Burke**
Libby .... **Nancy Malone**

Creator **Sterling Silliphant**
Executive Producer **Herbert B. Leonard**

● ***Grimy, realistic police dramas set in New York City.***

'There are eight million stories in the Naked City', the narrator of this programme reveals. Most of them, it seems, revolved around crime, as the city's police officers (by no means all of them angels) come under the spotlight, combing the seedy streets in search of muggers, murderers and other assorted felons. Veteran cop Dan Muldoon of the 65th Precinct is the programme's first main man, but he is killed off early on when his car crashes into a petrol tanker. His younger partner, Jim Halloran, and Jim's wife, Janet, don't last much longer and are also written out after only one season. Muldoon is replaced by Mike Parker, a tough, determined operator, who is later assisted by Detective Adam Flint and Sgt Frank Arcaro (promoted from his patrolman status in the earlier episodes). Flint's girlfriend, Libby, is also seen. But, in many ways, the real star of the programme is the city itself. The series was filmed entirely on location, with long shots drawing the attention of the viewer away from the personalities and focusing it instead on the bustling metropolis, the hub of all this villainous activity. The jazzy score by Billy May added to the moody atmosphere.

Naked City also specialized in weird episode titles. Examples included *The King of Venus Will Take Care of You*, *Howard Running Bear is a Turtle* and *No Naked Ladies in Front of Giovanni's House*. Guest stars abounded, most just fledgling actors at the time. Dustin Hoffman, Robert Redford, Jon Voight, Gene Hackman, Peter Falk, George Segal and Peter Fonda were the most notable. The story on which *Naked City* was based was written by Broadway columnist Mark Hellinger, and an Oscar-winning film version, starring Barry Fitzgerald and Don Taylor, appeared in 1948.

Naked Civil Servant, The ★★★

UK (Thames) Drama. ITV 1975
DVD: Network

Quentin Crisp .... **John Hurt**

Writer **Philip Mackie**
Producer **Barry Hanson**

● ***The biography of an outspoken homosexual.***

This 90-minute dramatization by Philip Mackie of Quentin Crisp's revealing autobiography was initially turned down by the BBC before being accepted, with caution, by Thames and the IBA. It portrayed events in the life of Crisp, a prominently homosexual government employee and former art school model (hence the title), from the late 1920s to the mid-1970s. John Hurt played the lead with flamboyant effeminism, and the work proved influential in opening stubbornly closed eyes to the predicament of gay men in society, thanks to its balanced combination of humour and tenderness. Viewers were shocked; critics doled out awards.

Naked Video ★★

UK (BBC) Comedy. BBC 2 1986–7; 1989; 1991

Helen Lederer, Gregor Fisher, Tony Roper, Ron Bain, Andy Gray, Elaine C. Smith, Jonathan Watson, John Sparkes, Louise Beattie

Producers **Colin Gilbert, Philip Differ**

● ***Pot-pourri of comic sketches from north of the border.***

A comedy offering from BBC Scotland, *Naked Video* helped establish the careers of Helen Lederer and Gregor Fisher in particular and also gave the world a handful of well-defined new comic characters. These included Rab C. Nesbitt, the aggressive, Glaswegian street philosopher, and the follically challenged Baldy Man (both played by Fisher and later graduating to their own series). Another innovation was Siadwell, the simple-minded Welsh poet, portrayed by John Sparkes. These appeared amid a collection of running sketches, some of which satirized topical issues. *Naked Video* was derived from a radio programme entitled *Naked Radio*.

Name That Tune

See *Spot the Tune*.

Nancy Astor ★★

UK (BBC) Drama. BBC 2 1982

Nancy Langhorne/Shaw/Astor **Lisa Harrow**
Chillie Langhorne .... **Dan O'Herlihy**
Nanaire Langhorne .... **Sylvia Syms**

Phyllis Langhorne/Brand .... **Lise Hilboldt**
Robert Gould Shaw .... **Pierce Brosnan**
Waldorf Astor .... **James Fox**
Lord Revelstoke .... **Julian Glover**
Philip Kerr .... **David Warner**
Robert Brand .... **Bernard Brown**
Bobbie Shaw .... **Nigel Havers**
Wissie Astor .... **Marsha Fitzalan**

Writer **Derek Marlowe**
Producer **Philip Hinchcliffe**

Biography of Britain's first female MP.

In nine episodes, this series traces the ups and downs in the life of Nancy Langhorne, an ambitious southern belle, the daughter of a tobacco auctioneer from Virginia. It follows her marriage to Robert Gould Shaw, a wealthy Boston playboy, and its subsequent collapse; her move to Europe with her sister, Phyllis; and her new romance with a British millionaire politician, Waldorf Astor, proprietor of *The Observer*, whom she goes on to marry and with whom she sets up home at Cliveden. When he is elevated to the House of Lords in 1919, Nancy assumes his place in the House of Commons, thereby carving herself a niche in history as the first woman to take her seat as a Member of Parliament. In the House, her sharp American tongue earns many enemies.

Nanny ★★

UK (BBC) Drama. BBC 1 1981–3

Barbara Gray/Taverner .... **Wendy Craig**
Donald Gray .... **Colin Douglas**
Mrs Sackville .... **Patricia Hodge**
Mrs Rudd .... **Anna Cropper**
Mr Rudd .... **Frank Mills**
Duke of Broughton .... **Richard Vernon**
Duchess of Broughton .... **Judy Campbell**
Lord Somerville .... **John Quayle**
Lady Somerville .... **Jane Booker**
Twomey .... **Jim Norton**
Lillian Birkwith .... **Jayne Lester**
Sam Taverner .... **David Burke**
Frank Hailey .... **Stephen Sweeney**
Major Fancombe .... **Geoffrey Chater**
Capt. Marsh .... **Allan Cuthbertson**

Creator **Wendy Craig**
Producers **Guy Slater, Bernard Krichefski**

The life of a children's nurse in the 1930s.

Dreamt up by actress Wendy Craig, who submitted the idea under the pen-name of Jonathan Marr, *Nanny* is the story of Barbara Gray, a traditional children's carer, working in the homes of the rich and noble. She begins her new career in 1932, having trained as a nanny after the break-up of her marriage (Barbara has been unable to have children of her own). Her enlightened approach makes her a popular and trustworthy choice for wealthy parents, although she regularly moves from home to home. On her new marriage, to Sam Taverner, Barbara is generally expected to give up her vocation but, contrary to the mood of the times, she prefers to continue in her profession. Craig's idea was developed into three series of scripts, most penned by the NO – HONESTLY husband-and-wife writing team of Charlotte Bingham and Terence Brady.

Nanny and the Professor ★★

US (Twentieth Century-Fox) Situation Comedy. ITV 1970–3 (US: ABC 1970–1)

Phoebe Figalilly .... **Juliet Mills**
Prof. Howard Everett .... **Richard Long**
Hal Everett .... **David Doremus**
Bentley 'Butch' Everett .... **Trent Lehman**
Prudence Everett .... **Kim Richards**
Aunt Henrietta .... **Elsa Lanchester**

Creators **A. J. Carothers, Thomas L. Miller**

A young English nanny tames three American brats.

There's more than a hint of Mary Poppins about Phoebe Figalilly. She's an English nanny who turns up in Los Angeles at just the right moment to take charge of the three unruly children (Hal, Butch and Prudence) of widowed American maths professor Howard Everett. What's more, she appears to have a certain psychic ability that gives her a slightly magical aura and helps her communicate with the family's pets. Or could it be that she's just a calm, very loving person? Whatever her secret may be, it definitely spells success, for tranquillity and happiness are restored to what was once a manic household. Also seen is Phoebe's Aunt Henrietta, who joins her in LA for a while. Harry Nilsson sings the theme song.

Nardini, Daniela

(1967–)

Scottish actress coming to the fore as Anna Forbes in THIS LIFE, after small parts in series like TAKE THE HIGH ROAD, TAGGART and DR FINLAY. Her later credits have included RECKLESS (Viv Reid), *Big Women* (Layla), *Undercover Heart* (Lois Howarth), *Rough Treatment* (Eve Turner), *Love in the 21st Century* (Ellie), *Table 12* (Eve), *Outside the Rules* (Natalie Vine), *Sirens* (Jay Pearson), *Quite Ugly One Morning* (Sara Slaughter) and *Gunpowder, Treason and Plot* (Lady Huntly).

Nation, Terry

(1930–97)

Welsh comedy scriptwriter (sometimes in collaboration with John Junkin), working in BBC Radio in the 1950s, then on Tony Hancock's ITV series in 1963. Nation then switched more to drama and, in particular, to science fiction, with significant results. He will primarily go down in television history as the man who invented the Daleks, the pepperpot megalomaniacs from DOCTOR WHO, but he also created the 1970s sci-fi classics SURVIVORS and BLAKE'S 7. In addition, Nation contributed to NO HIDING PLACE, THE BARON, DEPARTMENT S, THE SAINT, THE CHAMPIONS, THE AVENGERS, THE PERSUADERS!, THE PROTECTORS, OUT OF THE UNKNOWN, OUT OF THIS WORLD and other anthologies, and dramatized Isaac Asimov's *The Caves of Steel* for BBC 2 in 1964.

National Lottery Live, The ★★

UK (BBC). BBC 1 1994–

Presenters **Anthea Turner, Gordon Kennedy, Bob Monkhouse, Ulrika Jonsson, Dale Winton, Carol Smillie, Terry Wogan, Patrick Kielty, Bradley Walsh, Brian Conley, Angela Griffin, Simon Mayo, Claudia Winkelman, Eamonn**

Holmes, Lulu, Terry Alderton, Des O'Connor, Suzi Perry, Shauna Lowry, Phillip Schofield, Ian Wright, Julian Clary, Mark Durden-Smith

● ***Light entertainment around the week's National Lottery draws.***

Launched with great fanfares on 19 November 1994, the National Lottery was an immediate TV hit, as viewers switched on in millions to check their tickets. The first draw was wrapped up in the glitz of a lively game show, hosted by Noel Edmonds, supported by former ABSOLUTELY comic Gordon Kennedy and (as she was then known) ex-BLUE PETER girl Anthea Turner. Kennedy and Turner took over the show from the second week, visiting places of interest around the UK where the draw would take place (first port of call was the Rhondda Heritage Park in South Wales). Kennedy was the first to move on, while Turner continued to use the draw as a springboard to TV stardom, as did the resident psychic predictor, Mystic Meg.

The introduction of a midweek draw on Wednesdays on 5 February 1997 temporarily produced a shorter equivalent of the Saturday show. The formats of both editions have been revamped regularly since (indeed, the Wednesday event is now simply restricted to the draws themselves), to incorporate new quizzes, games, music and other entertainment, adopting titles like *The National Lottery Big Ticket* (Anthea Turner and Patrick Kielty), *The National Lottery on Tour* (Bradley Walsh; concert venues around the UK), *The National Lottery Dreamworld* (Ulrika Jonsson making people's dreams come true; midweek), *The National Lottery: Amazing Luck Stories* (Carol Smillie and, later, Shauna Lowry; midweek), *The National Lottery Greatest Hits* (Angela Griffin; midweek, from Manchester), *The National Lottery: Local Heroes* (Carol Smillie; championing charitable individuals around the country), *The National Lottery: We've Got Your Number* (Brian Conley), *National Lottery Winning Lines* (Simon Mayo and later Phillip Schofield; produced by the WHO WANTS TO BE A MILLIONAIRE? team), *National Lottery Love Songs* (Claudia Winkelman; midweek), *The National Lottery Stars* (Dale Winton and big names), *National Lottery Third Degree* (Eamonn Holmes and a quiz for charities; midweek), *Red Alert with the National Lottery* (Lulu and Terry Alderton), *Dale's All Stars with the National Lottery* (Dale Winton with music and chat; midweek), *The National Lottery: UK 2000* (Carol Smillie looking at lottery-funded projects; midweek), *The National Lottery: on the Spot* (Des O'Connor and Suzi Perry), *The National Lottery Jet Set* (Eamonn Holmes with a quiz offering a rich and famous lifestyle), *The National Lottery: In It to Win It* (Dale Winton game show), *The National Lottery – Wright around the World* (Ian Wright quiz with travel prizes), *The National Lottery Come and Have a Go* (Julian Clary big cash quiz) and *The National Lottery Millionaire Manor* (Mark Durden-Smith quiz on the rich and famous).

In addition to the regular hosts mentioned above, Charles Nove and Alan Dedicoat ('the Voice of the Balls') have acted as announcers, interviews have been conducted by the likes of Krishnan Guru-Murthy and Toby Anstis, and there have been many guest and short-term presenters, including Jimmy Tarbuck, Adam Woodyatt, Gary Barlow, Carol Vorderman, Ainsley Harriott, Michael Ball, Bruce Forsyth, Ronnie Corbett, Hale and Pace, Shirley Bassey, Bob Monkhouse, Rolf Harris and Brenda Emmanus.

Nationwide ★★

UK (BBC) Current Affairs. BBC 1 1969–83

Presenters **Michael Barratt, Bob Wellings, Sue Lawley, Richard Stilgoe, Frank Bough, Dilys Morgan, Brian Widlake, Glyn Worsnip, Valerie Singleton, John Stapleton, Hugh Scully, Sue Cook, Richard Kershaw, Laurie Mayer, Fran Morrison, David Dimbleby**

Creator **Derrick Amoore**
Producers/Editors **Derrick Amoore, Michael Bunce, Phil Sidey, Ron Neil, Andrew Clayton, Tim Gardam, Paul Corley, Richard Tait, John Gau, Paul Woolwich, Hugh Williams, Roger Bolton**

● ***Light-hearted early evening news magazine.***

For a decade and a half *Nationwide* was an integral part of British teatime. Following on from the main early-evening news bulletin, Monday to Friday, the 50-minute programme was a mixed bag of newsy items, political discussions, consumer affairs and light entertainment. After the introductory headlines, viewers were sent 'nationwide', i.e. the BBC regions opted out to present their own 20-minute or so local news round-ups (*Points West, Look North, Wales Today*, etc.). When these programmes finished, they handed back to London and the *Nationwide* studio, although the regions stayed 'live' to feed back reports and local reactions to the day's news, and to allow interviews to take place across the network. Technical problems abounded, with sound or vision going down on a regular basis.

Nationwide seemed to be obsessed with the great British eccentric and was always looking for unusual stories about skateboarding ducks or men who claimed they could walk on eggs. Regular features included the programme's Consumer Unit (headed behind the scenes by Bernard Wiggins who, as Bernard Cornwell, later wrote the Sharpe novels), which developed into a separate series called WATCHDOG, and Price Check, which monitored the cost of living. Richard Stilgoe performed topical songs, Susan Stranks took a stroll down Memory Lane and numerous politicians were put On the Spot. On Fridays, the weekend sporting action was previewed by Desmond Lynam, Peter Walker and other sports presenters in Sportswide and, most Decembers, there was a *Nationwide* Carol Competition.

Michael Barratt, Sue Lawley and Bob Wellings were the mainstays of the programme for many years, with Valerie Singleton and Frank Bough joining from BLUE PETER and GRANDSTAND later. A young John Stapleton and David Dimbleby also acted as anchors. *Nationwide*'s best-remembered reporters included Jack Pizzey, Bernard Falk, Philip Tibenham, Bernard Clarke, Martin Young, and the late Pattie Coldwell, and among the frequent contributors from the regional studios were Tom Coyne and Alan Towers (Birmingham), Mike Neville (Newcastle), Bruce Parker (Southampton), Stuart Hall (Manchester), Ian Masters (Norwich) and Hugh Scully (Plymouth). In all, 3,131 editions were produced before *Nationwide* gave way to a look-alike programme entitled *Sixty Minutes* in 1984. Hosted by Desmond Wilcox, Sally Magnusson, Nick Ross, Beverly Anderson and Sarah Kennedy, it lasted only one year.

Naylor, Doug

(1955–)
See *Grant, Rob.*

NBC

America's NBC, standing for National Broadcasting Company, was established by RCA to help sell the radio (and later television) equipment it manufactured. Its first radio broadcast came in 1926, with a regular TV service following in 1939, and NBC's history remained indelibly linked to the fortunes of RCA for decades. In the 1950s, for instance, the network became the first to broadcast all its programmes in colour, in an effort to boost sales of the newly developed RCA colour system. Among the company's most influential early executives was David Sarnoff, powerful head of RCA for 40 years.

As a network, NBC has nearly always run behind its great rival, CBS, but all that has changed in recent years, thanks to huge success with series like ER, SEINFELD, FRIENDS, FRASIER and THE WEST WING. Earlier hits included DRAGNET, BONANZA, DR KILDARE, THE MAN FROM U.N.C.L.E., THE COSBY SHOW and CHEERS. Of the three main US broadcasters, NBC has also been the most innovative. It launched the first dual-anchor news programme, for example, and also developed the TV movie concept.

NBC, which was sold to General Electric in 1985, took a majority holding in the European satellite station Super Channel in 1993. However, NBC Super Channel, as it became known, has since been replaced in digital packages by CNBC, a business and financial channel, set up in the USA in 1989. In 2004 NBC merged with Vivendi Universal Entertainment to create NBC Universal, a corporation that also owns Universal Studios and its associated theme parks. General Electric still owns 80 per cent, while Vivendi Universal has the other 20 percent.

NCS Manhunt ★★★

UK (BBC) Police Drama. BBC 1 2002

DI John Borne	**David Suchet**
DS Maureen Picasso	**Samantha Bond**
Supt. Bob Beausoleil	**Keith Barron**
DS Ruby Sparks	**Melanie Hill**
DS Peter Moon	**Jonny Phillips**
DC Charlie Spanish	**Gerard Horan**
DC Mary D'Eye	**Sara Stewart**
DC Johnny Khan	**Ashen Bhatti**
DC Karen Bogard-Black	**Jenny Jules**
DC Chrissie Crowe	**Paul McKay**
DC Jack Silver	**Michael Fassbender**

Writer **Malcolm McKay**
Producer **Sue Austen**

An elite squad of police officers targets society's cruellest criminals.

NCS stands for National Crime Squad. This is a crack team of police officers whose mission is to seek out the big boys, the really nasty villains who call all the shots in the world of crime – drug barons, serial murderers, preachers of racial hatred, that sort of nice person. But the pressure is enormous, which makes the team particularly humourless and grouchy, no one more so in fact than its obsessive leader, DI John Borne, one of television's finest shouting cops. Borne also tends to get rather hot under the collar when his team is landed in it by his boozy and devious branch commander Beausoleil, whose decision making leaves much to be desired. Borne's number two is the icy Maureen Picasso, while a third key member of the unit is the rather warmer 'mother hen'-type figure of DS Ruby Sparks. The disturbing nature of the cases they investigate makes their daily lives intense and distressing. Of course, another reason for the prevalent bad temper among the squad may just be that they've been saddled with some of the strangest surnames in TV police history.

After a two-part pilot, screened as part of BBC 1's *Crime Doubles* season in 2001, slick and stylish *NCS Manhunt* returned for three further two parters a year later.

Nearest and Dearest ★★

UK (Granada) Situation Comedy. ITV 1968–73
DVD: Network

Nellie Pledge	**Hylda Baker**
Eli Pledge	**Jimmy Jewel**
Lily	**Madge Hindle**
Walter	**Edward Malin**
Stan	**Joe Gladwin**
Bert	**Bert Palmer**
Grenville	**Freddie Rayner**

Creators **Vince Powell, Harry Driver**
Producers **Peter Eckersley, Bill Podmore**

A middle-aged brother and sister grudgingly share control of a northern pickle factory.

Eli and Nellie Pledge, bachelor and spinster, are brought back together on the death of their father, who bequeaths them his Pledge's Purer Pickles business. Bickering and fighting, the pair somehow manage to keep the company afloat, although there is just as much vinegar in their relationship as in the pickle jars. The plots often play second fiddle to the boundless insults they trade, which range from 'big girl's blouse' to 'knock-kneed knackered old nosebag'. The show was essentially a vehicle for Hylda Baker's distinctive line in comedy, littered with malapropisms and doubles entendres. It allowed her a few gems along the way, such as when Nellie remarked that Eli reminded her of that beautiful song from *The Sound of Music*. 'Which one,' responded Eli, ' "My Favourite Things?" ' 'No,' came back the put-down, ' "Idleswine." '

The Pledges are ably supported in the factory by their down-to-earth but rather decrepit foreman, Stan, and often have to play host at home to cousin Lily and her silent, quivering husband, Walter, who is plagued with waterworks trouble. The burning question is always 'Has he been?', although we are all assured that 'He knows, you know' (one of Baker's oldest catchphrases). A cinema version was made in 1972. Hylda Baker moved on to another sitcom in a similar vein. Entitled *Not on Your Nellie* (ITV 1974–5), it saw her cast as Fulham publican Nellie Pickersgill.

Nedwell, Robin

(1946–99)

Birmingham-born comic actor, popular in the 1970s as the hero of most of the DOCTOR series (Duncan Waring). Nedwell also appeared in THE LOVERS, playing Geoffrey's friend Roland and, when John Alderton left the role of Mike Upchat in THE UPCHAT LINE, Nedwell stepped in for the sequel, *The Upchat Connection*. He was also pop musician Peter Higgins in SHILLINGBURY TALES, Fiddler in a shortlived comedy called *West End Tales*, Harry Lumsdon, THE CLIMBER, in the 1983 BBC sitcom, and Reverend Green for one season of CLUEDO. Nedwell returned to the small screen in the 1991 *Doctor* revival, *Doctor at the Top*.

Negus, Arthur

OBE (1903–85)

Amiable, silver-haired antiques expert, prominent in GOING FOR A SONG, ANTIQUES ROADSHOW and the travelogue *Arthur Negus Enjoys*. His gentle, informative manner encouraged viewers to regard their family heirlooms in quite a different light.

Neighbours ✳✳

Australia (Grundy) Drama. BBC 1 1986–
DVD: Fremantle Home Entertainment

Helen Daniels	**Anne Haddy**
Jim Robinson	**Alan Dale**
Paul Robinson	**Stefan Dennis**
Julie Robinson/Martin	**Vikki Blanche**
	Julie Mullins
Scott Robinson	**Darius Perkins**
	Jason Donovan
Lucy Robinson	**Kylie Flinker**
	Sasha Close
	Melissa Bell
Terri Inglis/Robinson	**Maxine Klibingaitis**
Max Ramsay	**Francis Bell**
Maria Ramsay	**Dasha Blahova**
Shane Ramsay	**Peter O'Brien**
Danny Ramsay	**David Clencie**
Tom Ramsay	**Gary Files**
Eileen Clarke	**Myra De Groot**
Des Clarke	**Paul Keane**
Daphne Lawrence/Clarke	**Elaine Smith**
Dan Ramsay	**Syd Conabere**
Edna Ramsay	**Jessica Noad**
Nikki Dennison	**Charlene Fenn**
Mike Young	**Guy Pearce**
Dr Clive Gibbons	**Geoff Paine**
Madge Mitchell/Ramsay/Bishop	**Anne Charleston**
Charlene Mitchell/Robinson	**Kylie Minogue**
Henry Mitchell/Ramsay	**Craig McLachlan**
Rosemary Daniels	**Joy Chambers**
Nell Mangel/Worthington	**Vivean Gray**
Zoe Davis	**Ally Fowler**
Jane Harris	**Annie Jones**
Susan Cole	**Gloria Ajenstat**
Rob Lewis	**Ernie Bourne**
Gail Lewis/Robinson	**Fiona Corke**
Malcolm Clarke	**Noel Trevarthen**
Jamie Clarke	**S. J. Dey**
	Ryder Susman
	James Mason
	Nicholas Mason
	Angus McLaren
Harold Bishop	**Ian Smith**
Bronwen Davies	**Rachel Friend**
Sharon Davies	**Jessica Muschamp**
Nick Page	**Mark Stevens**
Sally Wells	**Rowena Mohr**
Edith Chubb	**Irene Innescourt**
Todd Landers	**Kristian Schmid**
Katie Landers	**Sally Jensen**
David Bishop	**Kevin Harrington**
Lou Carpenter	**Tom Oliver**
Josh Anderson	**Jeremy Angerson**
Melissa Jarrett	**Jade Amenta**
Joe Mangel	**Mark Little**
Toby Mangel	**Finn Greentree Keene**
	Ben Guerens
Kerry Bishop/Mangel	**Linda Hartley**
Melanie Pearson/Mangel	**Lucinda Cowden**
Sky Bishop/Mangel	**Mirander Fryer**
	Stephanie McIntosh
Gemma Ramsay	**Beth Buchanan**
Hilary Robinson	**Anne Scott-Pendlebury**
Matthew Williams/Robinson	**Ashley Paske**
Dr Beverly Marshall	**Lisa Armytage**
	Shaunna O'Grady
Caroline Alessi	**Gillian Blakeney**
Christina Alessi/Robinson	**Gayle Blakeney**
Tiffany 'Lochy' McLachlan	**Amber Kilpatrick**
Ryan McLachlan	**Richard Norton**
Eddie Buckingham	**Bob La Castra**
Gemma Ramsay	**Beth Buchanan**
Doug Willis	**Terence Donovan**
Pam Willis	**Sue Jones**
Adam Willis	**Ian Williams**
Cody Willis	**Amelia Frid**
	Peta Brady
Brad Willis	**Scott Michaelson**
Gaby Willis	**Rachel Blakely**
Dorothy Burke	**Maggie Dence**
Michael Daniels	**Brian Blain**
Glen Donnelly	**Richard Huggett**
Brenda Riley	**Genevieve Lemon**
Guy Carpenter	**Andrew Williams**
Phoebe Bright/Gottlieb	**Simone Robertson**
Cameron Hudson	**Benjamin Mitchell**
Faye Hudson	**Lorraine Bailey**
Beth Brennan/Willis	**Natalie Imbruglia**
Marco Alessi	**Felice Arena**
Rick Alessi	**Dan Falzon**
Philip Martin	**Ian Rawlings**
Hannah Martin	**Rebecca Ritters**
Debbie Martin	**Marnie Reece-Wilmore**
Benito Alessi	**George Spatels**
Cathy Alessi	**Elspeth Ballantyne**
Amy Robinson	**Sheridan Compagnino**
Stephen Gottlieb	**Lochie Daddo**
Lauren Carpenter	**Sarah Vandenbergh**
Michael Martin	**Troy Beckwith**
Mark Gottlieb	**Bruce Samazan**
Fiona Hartman	**Suzanne Dudley**
Annalise Hartman	**Kimberley Davies**
Wayne Duncan	**Jonathan Sammy-Lee**
Cheryl Stark	**Caroline Gillmer**
Dannielle 'Danni' Stark	**Eliza Szonert**
Brett Stark	**Brett Blewitt**
Darren Stark	**Todd MacDonald**
Colin Taylor	**Frank Bren**
Sam Kratz	**Richard Grieve**
Marlene Kratz	**Moya O'Sullivan**
Serendipity 'Ren' Gottlieb	**Raelee Hill**
Karl Kennedy	**Alan Fletcher**
Susan Kennedy	**Jackie Woodburne**
Billy Kennedy	**Jesse Spencer**
Libby Kennedy/Kirk	**Kym Valentine**
Malcolm Kennedy	**Benji McNair**
Kevin 'Stonefish' Rebecchi	**Anthony Engleman**
Jarrod 'Toadfish' Rebecchi	**Ryan Moloney**
Kev Rebbechi	**Don Bridges**
Jen Handley	**Alyce Platt**

Luke Handley .... **Bernard Curry**
Mike Healey .... **Andrew Blackman**
Bianca Zanotti .... **Anne Gagliardi**
Joanna Hartman/Evans .... **Emma Harrison**
Catherine O'Brien .... **Rhada Mitchell**
Steve George .... **Alex Dimitriades**
Angie Rebecchi .... **Lesley Baker**
Louise 'Lolly' Carpenter .... **Tessa Taylor**
Jiordan Anna Tolli
Lisa Elliot .... **Kate Straub**
Shannon Jones .... **Diana Glenn**
Drew Kirk .... **Dan Paris**
Teresa Bell .... **Krista Vendy**
Joel Samuels .... **Daniel MacPherson**
Ruth Wilkinson/Martin .... **Ailsa Piper**
Anne Wilkinson .... **Brooke Satchwell**
Lance Wilkinson .... **Andrew Bibby**
Ben Atkins .... **Brett Cousins**
Caitlin Atkins .... **Emily Milburn**
Amy Greenwood .... **Jacinta Stapleton**
Sarah Beaumont .... **Nicola Charles**
Paul McClair .... **Jansen Spencer**
Wayne 'Tad' Reeves .... **Jonathon Dutton**
Joe Scully .... **Shane Connor**
Lyn Scully .... **Janet Andrewartha**
Stephanie 'Steph' Scully/ Hoyland .... **Carla Bonner**
Felicity Scully .... **Holly Valance**
Michelle Scully .... **Katie Keltie**
Jack Scully .... **Jay Bunyan**
Dione 'Dee' Bliss .... **Madeleine West**
Dr Darcy Tyler .... **Mark Rafferty**
Tim Collins .... **Ben Anderson**
Elly Conway .... **Kendall Nunn**
Gino Esposito .... **Shane McNamara**
Jess Fielding .... **Elisha Gazdowicz**
Stuart Parker .... **Blair McDonough**
Evan Hancock .... **Nicholas Opolski**
Maggie Hancock .... **Sally Cooper**
Matt Hancock .... **Stephen Hunt**
Emily Hancock .... **Isabella Oldham**
Leo Hancock .... **Josh Jay**
Anthony Hammer
Daniel Clohesy .... **Thomas Blackburne**
Taj Coppin .... **Jaime Robbie Reyne**
Tahnee Coppin .... **Anna Jennings Edquist**
Lori Lee .... **Michelle Ang**
Connor O'Neill .... **Patrick Harvey**
Ruby Dwyer .... **Maureen Edwards**
Valda Sheergold .... **Joan Sydney**
Trixie Tucker/Carpenter .... **Wendy Stapleton**
Kat Riley .... **Gemma Bishop**
Oscar Scully .... **Ingo Dammer-Smith**
Charlie Cassidy .... **Cliff Ellen**
Liljana Bishop .... **Marcella Russo**
Serena Bishop .... **Lara Sacher**
Gus Cleary .... **Ben Barrack**
Lana Crawford .... **Bridget Neval**
Luka Dokich .... **Keelan O'Hehir**
Svetlanka Ristic .... **Deidre Rubenstein**
Max Hoyland .... **Stephen Lovatt**
Boyd Hoyland .... **Kyal Marsh**
Summer Hoyland .... **Marisa Siketa**
Izzy Hoyland .... **Natalie Bassingthwaighte**
Janelle Timmins .... **Nell Feeney**
Scott 'Stingray' Timmins .... **Ben Nicholas**
Dylan Timmins .... **Damien Bodie**
Bree Timmins .... **Sianoa Smit-McPhee**
Janae Timmins .... **Elize Taylor-Cotter**
Alex Kinski .... **Andrew Clarke**
Rachel Kinski .... **Caitlin Stasey**
Zeke Kinski .... **Matthew Werkmeister**
Katya Kinski .... **Dichen Lachman**
Ned Parker .... **Dan O'Connor**
Elle Robinson .... **Pippa Black**

Creator/Executive Producer **Reg Watson**

Middle-class ups and downs for the residents of a Melbourne cul-de-sac.

From shaky beginnings, *Neighbours* has become one of the success stories of Australian TV. Created by former CROSSROADS producer Reg Watson, it initially aired in 1985 on the country's Seven Network but dwindling audiences resulted in its cancellation after only six months. The programme's producers, Grundy, however, decided to fight on and sold the show to the rival Ten Network. With a complete facelift, including new sets and new, predominantly younger, actors (only five remained from the Seven Network episodes), *Neighbours* slowly began to take off. The series arrived in the UK in 1986, as one of the BBC's first daytime offerings. It was originally scheduled at 10 a.m. and 1.30 p.m. each day but, on the advice of his schoolgirl daughter, BBC 1 Controller Michael Grade moved the 10 a.m. showing to 5.35 p.m. There it captured a massive children, housewives and home-from-work audience and never looked back.

Neighbours is set in Ramsay Street, a semi-affluent cul-de-sac in the fictitious Melbourne suburb of Erinsborough (the name is actually an anagram of 'Or Neighbours'). The street takes its name from the ancestors of one of its most prominent families, the Ramsays, who dominate the action in the early days along with the Robinsons and the Clarkes. The most noteworthy characters over the years have been widower Jim Robinson, his supportive mother-in-law, Helen Daniels, and his assorted kids, including pompous Paul and teenager Scott (a role which launched Jason Donovan into celebrity status). The rival Ramsays are at first headed by Max, a plumber, but he quickly gives way to his sister, Madge Mitchell, and her wayward children, former jailbird Henry and car mechanic Charlene (Kylie Minogue's big break). The Clarkes are primarily hapless bank manager Des and his ex-stripper wife, Daphne. These families have been expanded in the course of time to bring in various errant children, ex-wives, forgotten parents, etc., and numerous other residents have come and gone, too. Tittle-tattling Mrs Mangel and her loud son, Joe, the twins Christina and Caroline Alessi, dithery Harold Bishop (Madge's new husband), Lou Carpenter, and the Willis brood are representative of these later arrivals.

The concerns of Ramsay Street residents have varied from the life-threatening to the banal, but the sun has always shone and things have generally turned out well. The younger element (the kids of Erinsborough High School) and their middle-aged parents and grandparents have happily shared the limelight, ensuring interest for viewers old and young, and, apart from the school and the close itself, the main focal point has been the Lassiters complex and, in particular, its bar (initially The Waterhole and later Chez Chez, Lou's Place and Scarlet Bar), coffee shop and hairdresser's. Among the big names whose careers were helped along by *Neighbours* are Russell Crowe and Guy Pearce. The programme's theme song was composed by Tony Hatch and Jackie Trent, and sung by Barry Crocker.

Nelson's Column ★★

UK (BBC) Situation Comedy. BBC 1 1994–5

Gavin Nelson .... **John Gordon-Sinclair**
Clare Priddy .... **Sophie Thompson**
Jackie Spicer .... **Elizabeth Counsell**
Mike Walker .... **Steven O'Donnell**
Lorraine Wilde .... **Camille Coduri**

Writer **Paul Mayhew-Archer**
Producer **Susan Belbin**

● ***A newspaper reporter is frustrated at work and in love.***
Gavin Nelson is a journalist with a provincial newspaper, the *Herald*. He has two goals for every day: to find something interesting to include in his column in the paper, and to impress his junior colleague, Clare Priddy. Unfortunately, he lives in a town where news is at a premium, which means he often has to bend the rules to get an exclusive, and Clare is oblivious to his charms and finds it easy to resist his advances. Eventually, Gavin starts to date the new receptionist, Lorraine Wilde, but still dreams of sharing his life with Clare. Jackie Spicer is the demanding editor of the rag, while Mike Walker is the photographer who accompanies Nelson on his assignments. The series was recorded in and around Oxford.

Nero Wolfe ★★

US (Paramount) Detective Drama. ITV 1983 (US: NBC 1981)
DVD: A&E Home Video (Chaykin version; Region 1 only)

Nero Wolfe .... **William Conrad**
Archie Goodwin .... **Lee Horsley**
Saul Panzer .... **George Wyner**
Fritz Brenner .... **George Voskovec**
Theodore Horstman .... **Robert Coote**
Insp. Cramer .... **Allan Miller**

Executive Producers **Ivan Goff, Ben Roberts**

● ***A reclusive epicurean solves mysteries from his New York townhouse.***
As his portly frame suggests, wealthy Nero Wolfe enjoys the good life, particularly the gourmet food served up by his butler, Fritz. But he is also a brilliant detective. Despite hardly ever venturing onto the streets, he is able to crack the most puzzling of cases, thanks to evidence dragged up by his henchmen, Archie Goodwin and Saul Panzer. For a pastime, Wolfe cultivates orchids with the help of horticulturalist Theodore Horstman. Inspector Cramer is the contact at the NYPD. The short-lived series (13 episodes only) was based on the character created by novelist Rex Stout in the 1930s and provided star William Conrad with a more restful role than he had endured in Cannon. *Nero Wolfe* returned to US TV (A&E) in 2001, with Maury Chaykin in the title role and Timothy Hutton as Archie Goodwin.

Nesbitt, James

(1965–)

Northern Irish actor whose major roles have been as Adam Williams in COLD FEET and Thomas Murphy in MURPHY'S LAW, although he has also been seen in SEARCHING (Duncan), BALLYKISSANGEL (Leo), PLAYING THE FIELD (John Dolan), TOUCHING EVIL (Laney), BLOODY SUNDAY (MP Ivan Cooper), CANTERBURY TALES (Nick Zakian), *Wall of Silence* (Stuart Robe), *Passer By* (Joe Keyes), *Quite Ugly One Morning* (Jack Parlabane), *Big Dippers* (Barry) and the TV film *Hear My Song*. Nesbitt has also narrated series like *Life on the List* and lent his voice to the animation *Tractor Tom*. His first TV appearance came in an episode of BOON and other early roles came in LOVEJOY, BETWEEN THE LINES and SOLDIER, SOLDIER.

Nesmith, Michael

(1942–)

American actor and musician, one of The Monkees. When the series ended, Nesmith drifted off into ambitious musical projects with his First National Band, writing the song 'Different Drum' for Linda Ronstadt, plus other tracks, mostly in a country rock vein. He became a pioneer in rock videos which, ironically, brought him back to TV in *Michael Nesmith in Television Parts* in 1985. Its combination of avant-garde humour and music videos proved familiar to Monkees fans.

Nettles, John

(1943–)

Some of Cornish actor John Nettles's earliest television performances came in series like A FAMILY AT WAR (Ian Mackenzie) and THE LIVER BIRDS (Paul, Sandra's boyfriend), after his debut in an episode of THE EXPERT. Via appearances in series like THE ADVENTURES OF BLACK BEAUTY, DICKENS OF LONDON, *Holding On*, ENEMY AT THE DOOR and some single dramas, he arrived in 1981 at his first starring role, the part of Jim BERGERAC, the Jersey detective with a drink problem and a gammy leg. It was a role Nettles played for over ten years, making Jersey his home in the process and doing wonders for its tourist trade. He has since become known as another detective, the thoughtful DCI Tom Barnaby in MIDSOMER MURDERS. Nettles has also narrated docu-soaps like AIRPORT and *Disaster*, and appeared in the BBC's 2002 version of *Hound of the Baskervilles* (Dr Mortimer). He also appeared – as Barnaby – in a cameo in FRENCH & SAUNDERS ACTUALLY, with other guest spots coming in BOON and HEARTBEAT.

Network

A chain of TV stations linked by cable or satellite in order to broadcast programmes over a larger area. The term is given to the USA's big stations (NBC, ABC, CBS, Fox, UPN and WB), which are able to transmit their programmes across the country via the transmitters of their affiliated independent stations. In the UK, a programme transmitted by all the ITV regions (as opposed to only one or two) is described as being 'networked'.

Never Come Back ★★★

UK (BBC) Drama. BBC 2 1990
DVD: BFS Entertainment (Region 1 only)

Desmond Thane .... **Nathaniel Parker**
Foster .... **James Fox**
Anna Raven .... **Suzanna Hamilton**
Marcus .... **Jonathan Coy**
Sarah .... **Ingrid Lacey**
Mr Poole .... **Timothy Bateson**
Wellman .... **David Becalick**
Luke .... **Martin Clunes**

Aunt Olivia .... **Mary Wimbush**
Sir John .... **John Woodnutt**
Embury .... **Anthony Dawes**
Dr Carver .... **Nigel Pegram**

Writer **David Pirie**
Producer **Joe Waters**

A feckless writer's obsession for a mysterious girl puts his life on the line.

Never Come Back was the title of John Mair's only novel. He died in an air accident just a year after it was first published in 1941, but the book went on to gain cult status. Ben Bolt directs this three-part adaptation by David Pirie in atmospheric *film noir* style, with music supplied by Stanley Myers. The story is set in 1939 and concerns one Desmond Thane, an aspiring novelist. He works for a magazine but there's not enough excitement in his job, nor in the easy virtues of most of the women he conquers. However, this heartless cynic then encounters a mysterious girl named Anna Raven. He knows nothing about her but becomes infatuated. Anna is a rebel and he likes her approach to life. However, she is bad news. Thane tries to find out more about Anna and thus changes his life for ever. He soon finds himself wanted for murder and on the run, tortured and almost killed by unknown enemies. When he tries to unearth why all this should be happening to him, there is nothing but silence from the authorities and further threats from his adversaries.

Never Mind the Buzzcocks ★★

UK (Talkback Thames) Comedy Quiz. BBC 2 1996–

Presenter **Mark Lamarr**

Executive Producers **Peter Fincham, Alan Brown**
Producers **Jim Pullin, Richard Wilson, Simon Bullivant, Warren Prentice, Steve Doherty, Lucy Clarke**

Anarchic quiz show based around pop and rock music.

Combining in its title a controversial 1977 Sex Pistols album and the name of a Manchester-based New Wave band, *Never Mind the Buzzcocks* was a logical progression from HAVE I GOT NEWS FOR YOU and its sports follow-up, THEY THINK IT'S ALL OVER. The subject this time is the world of rock and pop. Mark Lamarr sees fair and unfair play, and installed as team captains initially were comedians Sean Hughes and Phill Jupitus, with Bill Bailey replacing Hughes in 2002. Together with guests from the music business and comedy, the regulars do light-hearted battle over rounds that include guessing hummed record introductions, working out obscure words in a well-known hit, spotting faded stars in an identity parade and adding the next line to a given lyric. For the early 2006 series, host Lamarr was absent and his place was filled by various guest presenters, including Jonathan Ross and Dale Winton.

Never Mind the Quality, Feel the Width ★★

UK (ABC/Thames) Situation Comedy. ITV 1967–71

Emmanuel 'Manny' Cohen .... **John Bluthal**
Patrick Kelly .... **Joe Lynch**
Rabbi Levy .... **Cyril Shaps**
Father Ryan .... **Eamon Kelly**

Creators **Vince Powell, Harry Driver**
Producers **Ronnie Baxter, Stuart Allen**

Genial ethnic comedy set in an East End tailor's shop.

Manny Cohen and Patrick Kelly are partners in a small tailoring enterprise in the East End of London. Their religious differences provide the chief source of conflict and comedy, as coat-maker Manny, the Jew, always considers Patrick, the trouser-maker, to be a bigoted Catholic. Similar sentiments flow in the opposite direction and often the local rabbi and priest need to intervene. The series stemmed from a one-off ARMCHAIR THEATRE production in 1967, in which Frank Finlay took the part of Patrick Kelly. Thames TV took over production of the series in 1968, when ABC lost its ITV franchise. A film version was released in 1972.

Never the Twain ★★

UK (Thames) Situation Comedy. ITV 1981–4; 1986–91
DVD: Clear Vision Video

Simon Peel .... **Donald Sinden**
Oliver Smallbridge .... **Windsor Davies**
David Peel .... **Robin Kermode**
Christopher Morris
Lyn Smallbridge/Peel .... **Julia Watson**
Tacy Kneale
Veronica Barton .... **Honor Blackman**
Aunt Eleanor .... **Zara Nutley**
Ringo .... **Derek Deadman**

Creator **Johnnie Mortimer**
Writers **Johnnie Mortimer, Vince Powell, John Kane**
Producers **Peter Frazer-Jones, Anthony Parker**

Two neighbouring antiques dealers are the best of enemies.

Simon Peel and Oliver Smallbridge are old adversaries. Despite the fact that Simon's son, David, and Oliver's daughter, Lyn, are in love, the squabbling antiques experts are never able to patch up their quarrel. Not even when David and Lyn are married. Nor when Martin, their mutual grandson, is born. Exacerbating their rivalry is the occasional appearance of Veronica Barton, the lady both men want in their lives. When David and Lyn emigrate to Canada, Simon's Aunt Eleanor arrives to keep the two old fools in check.

Neverwhere ★★★

UK (BBC/Crucial) Science Fiction. BBC 2 1996
DVD: A&E Home Video (Region 1 only)

Richard Mayhew .... **Gary Bakewell**
Door .... **Laura Fraser**
Mr Croup .... **Hywel Bennett**
Mr Vandemar .... **Clive Russell**
Marquis de Carabas .... **Paterson Joseph**
Old Bailey .... **Trevor Peacock**
Jessica .... **Elizabeth Marmur**
Mr Stockton .... **Stratford Johns**
Angel Islington .... **Peter Capaldi**
Hunter .... **Tanya Moodie**
The Earl of Earl's Court .... **Freddie Jones**
Lamia .... **Tamsin Greig**
Hammersmith .... **Tony Pritchard**
The Abbot .... **Earl Cameron**
Serpentine .... **Julie T. Wallace**

Creators **Neil Gaiman, Lenny Henry**
Writer **Neil Gaiman**
Producer **Clive Brill**

A young man finds himself transported to a bizarre and dangerous subterranean world.

Good Samaritan Richard Mayhew soon regrets coming to the aid of an injured young girl. The girl is Door, appropriately named because she can open up an entrance to a hidden city: London Below. She is also in trouble. Someone has attacked her noble family and Richard, a Scot who works in the City, now finds himself helping to track down the assailants in a peculiar underground world. There are plenty of sinister faces lurking in the dark corners of this strange land. Most menacing are the devilish double act Mr Croup and Mr Vandemar, vicious hitmen. Then there are Serpentine, a rubber fetishist; the Earl of Earl's Court, who travels with his entourage on a tube train to disused stations; the blind Abbot and his Black Friars; the luminous Angel Islington; Hammersmith, a skilled blacksmith; and Old Bailey, who lives on the rooftops and eats rooks. Other macabre beings can be found at the Floating Market, which changes its location on a regular basis – anywhere from Battersea Power Station to HMS Belfast. To help nail her family's killers, Door also hires the mysterious Marquis de Carabas, plus a bodyguard, Hunter, and the icy Lamia, one of the beautiful so-called Velvets, who becomes their guide. The six-part fantasy was jointly created by comedian Lenny Henry – whose Crucial Films produced the series – and top adult comic writer Neil Gaiman. Gaiman also penned the subsequent novel based on the series.

New Adventures of Black Beauty, The

See *Adventures of Black Beauty, The.*

New Adventures of Charlie Chan, The ✶

UK (TPA/ITC) Detective Drama. ITV 1957–8

Charlie Chan	**J. Carrol Naish**
Barry Chan	**James Hong**
Insp. Duff	**Rupert Davies**
Insp. Marlowe	**Hugh Williams**

Executive Producer **Leon Fromkess**
Producers **Rudolph Flothow, Sidney Marshall**

Tales of the oriental detective created by Earl Derr Biggers.

Charlie Chan originally found fame in the cinema (played by the likes of Warner Oland, Sydney Toler and Roland Winters) as a smart, proverb-quoting detective from Honolulu who had numerous children. In this series, he has moved to London, but is still supported by his ever-eager 'Number One Son', Barry. As before, the oriental investigator is polite, calm, diligent and very successful.

Earl Derr Biggers's character was allegedly based on Chang Apana, a real Hawaiian police detective. He reappeared in cartoon form in the 1970s, in a series called *The Amazing Chan and the Chan Clan.*

New Adventures of Superman, The ✶✶

US (Roundelay/December 3rd/Warner Brothers) Science Fiction. BBC 1 1994–7 (US: ABC 1993–7)
DVD: Warner Home Video

Superman/Clark Kent	**Dean Cain**
Lois Lane	**Teri Hatcher**
Perry White	**Lane Smith**
Jimmy Olsen	**Michael Landes**
	Justin Whalin
Catherine 'Cat' Grant	**Tracy Scoggins**
Lex Luthor	**John Shea**
Jonathan Kent	**Eddie Jones**
Martha Kent	**K. Callan**

Executive Producers **Deborah Joy Levine, Robert Singer**

'Man of Steel' revamp with a romantic twist.

The full American title, *Lois & Clark – the New Adventures of Superman*, sums up the extended emphasis on the will-they, won't-they love facet of the Superman story that comes to the fore in this updated, camp remake of the 1950s series. The story has it that *Daily Planet* reporter Lois Lane continually spurns the fumbled advances of bespectacled, country-boy colleague Clark Kent, not realizing that he is really the superhero she secretly adores. Otherwise, the usual features are all there – basically an indestructible guy saving Metropolis from destruction time and again, with a supporting cast of blustering editor Perry White and keen cub reporter Jimmy Olsen, plus, now and again, the hero's adoptive parents, Jonathan and Martha Kent. Also returning is billionaire ultra-villain Lex Luthor, who deceives Lois into an affair, but new is society columnist Cat Grant, keen to show Clark the ways of the world. Eventually, Ms Lane susses out Kent's true alter-ego and their relationship blossoms while the world around them lurches from one near-disaster to another. An interesting guest star, playing Lois's mother, is Phyllis Coates, who played Lois herself in the 1950s version.

New Adventures of Wonder Woman, The

See *Wonder Woman.*

New Avengers, The ✶✶

UK (Avengers Enterprises/IDTV) Adventure. ITV 1976–7
DVD: A&E Home Video (Region 1 only)

John Steed	**Patrick Macnee**
Purdey	**Joanna Lumley**
Mike Gambit	**Gareth Hunt**

Producers **Albert Fennell, Brian Clemens**

Further adventures of John Steed and his daring assistants.

In *The New Avengers*, John Steed is called up once more to thwart extravagant plots by the world's most eccentric saboteurs and assassins. Working undercover for the British Secret Service, as in THE AVENGERS, Steed, however, now spends more time on his private stud-farm, where he indulges his hobbies of breeding horses and entertaining beautiful women. Ageing a little, but as suave and sophisticated as ever, he is typically supported by a glamorous female, but also, this time, by a tough young male, someone to do the running around.

The newcomers are Purdey and Gambit. Purdey, a former ballerina with a much-copied page-boy haircut, is classy, elegant and as hard as nails. Like her predecessors Gale, Peel and King, she knows how to fight. Her strength is in her kick, and many an assailant feels the power of her long, shapely legs. She is also a good shot and extremely fit. Mike Gambit provides the muscle which Steed now lacks. A former mercenary, he is a weapons specialist and a practitioner of kung fu. Both young colleagues show Steed the respect he deserves and rely on his wealth of experience and knowledge.

The series being produced in association with a French TV company and also with some Canadian input, three episodes were filmed in France and four in Canada, although the majority was made in the UK.

New Dick Van Dyke Show, The

See *Dick Van Dyke Show, The.*

New Faces ✳✳

UK (ATV/Central) Talent Show. ITV 1973–8; 1986–8

Hosts **Derek Hobson, Nicky Martin, Marti Caine**

Producers **Les Cocks, Albert Stevenson, Richard Holloway**

Talent show in which hopefuls are openly criticized by a professional panel.

Branded as cruelly frank and downright insensitive, *New Faces* was OPPORTUNITY KNOCKS with bite. It aimed to feature artists who had never appeared on television before, and those who dared to participate found their acts subjected to the views of four 'experts'. These included established showbusiness names, record producers, DJs, agents and critics. Among regular pundits were Mickie Most, Clifford Davis, Alan A. Freeman, Martin Jackson, Ted Ray, Tony Hatch, Hilary Kingsley, George Elrick, Ed Stewart, John Smith and Peter Prichard. Awarding marks out of ten in categories such as Presentation, Content and Star Quality, the panel's forthright comments were known to reduce artists to tears at times. Some were awarded no points at all. Arthur Askey, on the other hand, thought every act was fantastic. Some were, indeed, good enough to make the grade: Lenny Henry, Les Dennis, Jim Davidson, Victoria Wood, Showaddywaddy, Patti Boulaye and Gary Wilmot were the most prominent. EMMERDALE star Malandra Burrows (using the name of Malandra Newman) appeared as a singer at the age of nine and became the series' youngest winner. Like other heat-winners, she progressed to the grand final, where the series winner was decided.

One *New Faces* champion, Marti Caine, went on to host a revival of the series, entitled *New Faces of 86* (then *87* and *88*). Among the new celebrity critics was newspaper columnist Nina Myskow. The Johnny Patrick Orchestra provided musical support in the early days, with Harry Rabinowitz's Orchestra taking over in the 1980s. The show's original 'You're a Star' theme song was performed by former Move vocalist Carl Wayne.

New Phil Silvers Show, The

See *Phil Silvers Show, The.*

New Scotland Yard ✳✳

UK (LWT) Police Drama. ITV 1972–4

Det. Chief Supt. John Kingdom	**John Woodvine**
DS Alan Ward	**John Carlisle**
Det. Chief Supt. Clay	**Michael Turner**
DS Dexter	**Clive Francis**

Executive Producer **Rex Firkin**
Producer **Jack Williams**

Two CID officers investigate serious crimes in London.

Kingdom and Ward are two quietly efficient detectives, working from New Scotland Yard. Kingdom is the more thoughtful, Ward the tougher, less approachable partner. Together – and not without friction – they inquire into cases of murder, blackmail, extortion and the new, violent crimes of the 1970s. After two series, they are replaced for the final run by experienced Chief Supt. Clay and his junior colleague, DS Dexter, but, throughout, the series avoids the plain 'cops-and-robbers' stereotype of many police series, and depicts police work, more truthfully, as hard and personally distressing.

New Statesman, The ✳✳✳

UK (Yorkshire) Situation Comedy. ITV 1987; 1989; 1991–2
DVD: Cinema Club

Alan Beresford B'Stard	**Rik Mayall**
Sarah B'Stard	**Marsha Fitzalan**
Piers Fletcher-Dervish	**Michael Troughton**
Bob Crippen	**Nick Stringer**
Norman Bormann	**R. R. Cooper**
Beatrice Protheroe	**Vivien Heilbron**
Sir Stephen Baxter	**John Nettleton**
Sir Greville	**Terence Alexander**
Roland Gidleigh-Park	**Charles Gray**
Mrs Thatcher	**Steve Nallon**
Neil Kinnock	**Johnny More**
Sidney Bliss	**Peter Sallis**

Creators/Writers **Laurence Marks, Maurice Gran**
Producers **David Reynolds, Tony Charles, Andrew Benson, Bernard McKenna**

The unscrupulous manoeuvrings of an ambitious MP.

Alan B'Stard is the Conservative Member of Parliament for the North Yorkshire constituency of Haltemprice. Styling himself as a country squire, he is not so much a confirmed Thatcherite as a rampant right-winger, a man who has maimed his electoral opponents in a car crash to win a 27,000-vote majority and become the youngest MP in the House. Riding roughshod over all who stand in his way (physically as well as metaphorically), sleaze means nothing to the mean and vicious B'Stard, who lines his own pockets, cynically hides behind his parliamentary scapegoat, Piers Fletcher-Dervish, and wriggles his way up the ladder. B'Stard's lesbian wife, Sarah, daughter of the odious Roland Gidleigh-Park, is heiress to a fortune and only stays with her husband for appearances' sake. Also seen is B'Stard's sex-changing business consultant, Norman Bormann (actress Rowena Cooper was billed as R. R. Cooper so as not to give the game away too early). Eventually leaving Parliament, B'Stard finds himself imprisoned in a Russian gulag before returning to the political fray as a Euro MP.

Although the series – which used Mussorgsky's *Pictures at*

an Exhibition as its theme music – ended in 1992, a one-off special in which B'Stard was interviewed by Brian Walden was screened on BBC 1 at Christmas 1994.

New Tricks ✶✶

UK (Wall to Wall) Police Drama. BBC 1 2004–
DVD: BBC

Brian Lane	**Alun Armstrong**
Jack Halford	**James Bolam**
Det. Supt. Sandra Pullman	**Amanda Redman**
Gerry Standing	**Dennis Waterman**
PC Clark	**Chiké Okonkwo**
DAC Donald Bevan	**Nicholas Day**
Esther Lane	**Susan Jameson**
DAC Robert Strickland	**Anthony Calf**

Creators **Roy Mitchell, Nigel McCrery**
Producers **Gina Cronk, Tom Sherry, Francis Matthews**

● ***Three retired detectives are brought back to solve old crimes.***

When you think about it, there's a lot of expertise that is lost when someone retires from work, most so, perhaps, within the police force. That's why Brian Lane, Jack Halford and Gerry Standing have been brought back into action, forming a division known as UCOS (Unsolved Crime and Open Case Squad). Still officially civilians, the trio share a long and chequered history of policing and, while they may not be up to much running and chasing these days, they are still capable of exercising the little grey cells in order to get their man.

There are two downsides, however: each of the men has his own personal problems, and they are all just a little out of touch with modern policing methods, which makes them a liability almost as much as an asset. Brian Lane, for instance, is a former detective inspector with 35 years of service. He lost his job and was forced into retirement when a drug dealer died in custody. Brian carried the can, but is convinced that he was set up, which has turned him into a paranoid, nervous wreck, a condition for which he needs medication. Esther is his very long-suffering wife. Jack Halford doesn't have a wife to fall back on. Mary Halford was killed in a hit-and-run accident and is now buried in the family garden. He still considers she's around though, and offloads his worries to her at every turn. Gerry Standing's problems are very much of his own making. Not only is he bankrupt, he is a serial womanizer with a track record of three divorces and three daughters. They all remain on good terms with the old rascal, but do give him more than his share of headaches – especially when he learns he's going to be a grandad. In charge of this maverick triumvirate is Sandra Pullman. It's her penance for fluffing a hostage rescue and now she has to make them toe the line while pleasing her manipulative boss, DAC Bevan (played by Tim Woodward in the 2003 pilot episode; Bevan is replaced in series two by DAC Strickland). Pullman doesn't find this easy and needs a psychiatrist to help her separate private life and job. PC Clark is the team's gofer, a sharp young copper who keeps them in touch with 21st-century techniques.

If it wasn't for the seriousness of their work, these old guys would really be a comic bunch – eccentric, quirky and full of rebellion. Fortunately the gravity of the situation usually carries them through as together they tackle such crimes as the murder of a young WPC, fraud in the Queen's art collection, the death of a peace protestor and a multi-million-pound theft of jewellery. Dennis Waterman, somewhat inevitably, sings the theme song, written by Mike Moran.

Newcomers, The ✶✶

UK (BBC) Drama. BBC 1 1965–9

Ellis Cooper	**Alan Browning**
Vivienne Cooper	**Maggie Fitzgibbon**
Gran Hamilton	**Gladys Henson**
Philip Cooper	**Jeremy Bulloch**
Maria Cooper	**Judy Geeson**
Lance Cooper	**Raymond Hunt**
Janet Langley/Cooper	**Sandra Payne**
Jeff Langley	**Michael Collins**
Arnold Tripp	**Gerald Cross**
Arthur Huntley	**Tony Steedman**
Cornwallis	**Philip Ray**
George Harbottle	**Glynn Edwards**
Tom Lloyd	**Michael Standing**
Betty Lloyd	**Helen Cotterill**
Peter Connolly	**Patrick Connor**
Dick Alderbeach	**Keith Smith**
Ted Rumble	**Anthony Wager**
Mrs Katie Heenan	**Vanda Godsell**
Andrew Heenan	**Jonathan Bergman**
Celia Blatchford	**Barbara Keogh**
Sydney Huxley	**Anthony Verner**
Eunice Huntley	**Sally Lahee**
Amelia Huntley/Malcolm	**Naomi Chance**
Paul Bose	**Mahav Sharma**
Frank Claw	**Thomas Heathcote**
Cora Brassett	**Eileen Way**
Bert Harker	**Robert Brown**
Vera Harker	**June Bland**
Joyce Harker	**Wendy Richard**
Jimmy Harker	**David Janson**
James Neal	**David Knight**
Charlie Penrose	**Victor Platt**
Mary Penrose	**Megs Jenkins**
Prudence Penrose	**Eileen Helsby**
Jacob Penrose	**George Woodbridge**
Herbert Button	**J. G. Devlin**
Celia Stuart/Murray	**Beryl Cooke**
Henry Burroughs	**Campbell Singer**
Sally Burroughs	**Alysoun Austin**
William Pargeten	**Julian Somers**
Gordon Pargeter	**Colin Stepney**
Rufus Pargeter	**Michael Redfern**
Minnie Pargeter	**Cindy Wright**
Andrew Kerr	**Robin Bailey**
Caroline Kerr	**Heather Chasen**
Kirsty Kerr	**Jenny Agutter** **Maggie Don**
Margot Kerr	**Sally-Jane Spencer**
Charles Turner	**Neil Hallett**
Robert Malcolm	**Conrad Phillips**
Eric Crutchley	**John Kidd**
Peter Metcalfe	**Gil Sutherland**
Hugh Robertson	**Jack Watling**
Olivia Robertson	**Mary Kenton**
Julie Robertson	**Deborah Watling**
Michael Robertson	**Robert Bartlett**
Adrian Robertson	**Paul Bartlett**

Creator **Colin Morris**
Producers **Verity Lambert, Morris Barry, Ronald Travers, Bill Sellars**

● ***A London family are uneasy about their new life in the country.***

The Newcomers, a twice-weekly soap, centred around the Coopers, a London family who moved out of the Smoke into the sticks and set up home in the fictitious Suffolk village of Angleton (real-life Haverhill). The series' petty dramas revolved around life at work with dad Ellis (a supervisor at Eden Brothers' computer parts factory – boss: Arthur Huntley) and at home, on a new housing estate, as well as other focal points of the town, including the pubs The Crown and primarily The Bull (landlord: Peter Connolly, then Henry Burroughs), Burroughs' Supermarket and St Peter's Church. Mum Vivienne struggled to cope with their three teenage children (17-year-old Philip, 16-year-old Maria and 13-year-old troublemaker Lance), as well as her glum, live-in mum, as the difficulties of settling into a new neighbourhood and integration with locals like the Langleys and the indigenous farming community became all too evident. Throughout, the problems facing the fast-developing town – such as the need for a by-pass – were prominently reported in the *Angleton Advertiser* (editor: Arnold Tripp). Among the Coopers' later neighbours was brash, 20-year-old Cockney Joyce Harker, played by a pre-EastEnders Wendy Richard. Another actress gaining experience in the series was Jenny Agutter, as Kirsty Kerr, young daughter of another new family. Ellis Cooper was written out in 1968, dying of a heart attack, and Vivienne emigrated to New Zealand with new lover Charles Turner. Another family, the Robertsons, subsequently took over the role of 'the newcomers'.

Newhart ★★★

US (MTM) Situation Comedy ITV 1983–4/Channel 4 1984–7 (US: CBS 1982–90)

Dick Loudon .... **Bob Newhart**
Joanna Loudon .... **Mary Frann**
George Utley .... **Tom Poston**
Kirk Devane .... **Steven Kampmann**
Leslie Vanderkellen .... **Jennifer Holmes**
Stephanie Vanderkellen/
Harris .... **Julia Duffy**
Larry .... **William Sanderson**
First Darryl .... **Tony Papenfuss**
Second Darryl .... **John Voldstad**
Michael Harris .... **Peter Scolari**

Creator **Barry Kemp**

A writer and his wife run an inn in an eccentric New England town.

Dick Loudon is a successful author, making his money out of 'How to' books. Quitting New York in favour of a new life in New England, he and his wife, Joanna, decide to refurbish and run a country inn, The Stratford, in Vermont. The staff they inherit include dim handyman George Utley and part-time maid/student Leslie Vanderkellen (replaced by her spoilt cousin, Stephanie, after one season). Next door is a café/gift shop called the Minuteman, run by a compulsive liar named Kirk Devane. Thus the scene is set for a series of mishaps and misunderstandings characterized by star Bob Newhart's easy-going manner, double-takes and perplexed stare, with the Loudons depicted as the only sane people in a mad world. However, things change after a couple of years when Loudon begins hosting *Vermont Today*, a talk show on the local TV station. This introduces producer Michael Harris, who marries Stephanie – an ideal match since they are equally shallow. Also added to the show are three bumpkin brothers who take over the café (two mute ones with the name Darryl, the other, their spokesman, Larry) and constantly surprise everyone with nuggets of highbrow culture or learning. In the series' last-ever episode, it is implied that the whole venture has been a dream, as Newhart is seen waking up as Bob Hartley, the character he had played so successfully in the acclaimed *Bob Newhart Show* (seldom seen in the UK). Henry Mancini provided the theme tune.

Newman, Andrea

(1938–)

British novelist and TV writer, known for controversial series (often exploring middle-class mores) such as BOUQUET OF BARBED WIRE, *Another Bouquet*, MACKENZIE, A SENSE OF GUILT, *Imogen's Face*, *An Evil Streak* and *Pretending to be Judith*. She also wrote episodes of HELEN – A WOMAN OF TODAY and has contributed single dramas to anthologies like *Tales of Unease* and *The Frighteners*.

Newman, Nanette

(1934–)

British actress and presenter who is probably better known for her detergent commercials than her programme credits. Among her TV contributions have been the dramas *Stay with Me till Morning* (Robin Lendrick) and *Jessie* (title role), and the comedies LET THERE BE LOVE (widow Judy) and LATE EXPECTATIONS (middle-aged mother-to-be Liz Jackson). Newman also appeared in *Prometheus* and *The Endless Game*, and has made guest appearances in numerous series, including MARK SABER, SIR FRANCIS DRAKE, THE SAINT and JOURNEY TO THE UNKNOWN. She is married to film director Bryan Forbes and is the mother of TV presenter Emma Forbes.

Newman, Sydney

(1917–97)

Canadian drama specialist who joined ABC in 1958 to produce the influential ARMCHAIR THEATRE series of plays. While there, as Head of Drama, Newman was also co-creator of THE AVENGERS (and its forerunner, POLICE SURGEON), as well as the TARGET LUNA/PATHFINDERS sci-fi adventures for kids. Five years later, he was enticed over to the BBC, where he became its Head of Drama and gained a reputation as a tough overseer. Among the BBC's most notable achievements under his auspices were DOCTOR WHO (creator), THE WEDNESDAY PLAY (including classics like UP THE JUNCTION and CATHY COME HOME) and THE FORSYTE SAGA. His own productions over the years included Alun Owen's *Lena, O My Lena* (1960), John Wyndham's *Dumb Martian* (1962) and Harold Pinter's *Tea Party* (1965). He subsequently returned to Canada to work in film and TV.

News

Television presentation of the news was initially a voice-only affair. Announcers simply regurgitated radio bulletins. While BBC Television Newsreel, which began in 1948, was an advance into moving pictures (if not up-to-the-minute stories), it took until 1954 for the first television news bulletin as we now know it to reach the air. Richard Baker was the first presenter of *BBC Television News*, on 5 July, although, for a further 14 months, no newsreader was seen in vision while delivering the news. It was feared that their facial expressions would detract from their impartiality. Kenneth Kendall became the first newsreader in shot, in September 1955. The same month, not coincidentally, ITV took to the air, bringing with it the more dynamic forces of ITN (Independent Television News). It was ITN who pioneered the American two-presenter format in the UK when it launched the half-hour *News at Ten* on 3 July 1967. The programme was a huge success, being axed – amid great controversy – only on 5 March 1999. The first presenters were Alastair Burnet and Andrew Gardner. The last (with the bulletin now back to single-presenter format) was Trevor McDonald. The name *ITV News at Ten* has since been revived for some late-evening bulletins.

Over the years, technical developments have changed the face of television news presentation. Autocues have allowed presenters to directly face the viewers, satellites have provided instant international coverage, computer graphics have added colour and variety to dull items and brightened up studio sets, and Electronic News Gathering (ENG) has enabled reporters and cameramen to send on-the-spot reports directly back to the studio, with small, lightweight camera equipment and camera phones allowing access to hitherto impossible situations. Non-stop satellite and digital news channels have been established to provide information on breaking events around the clock. At the forefront of these was CNN, followed by Sky News and, later, BBC News 24.

It is believed by many that Angela Rippon was the first national female newsreader, but in fact there were others before her. Barbara Mandell appeared on ITN's lunchtime news as early as 1955, and Nan Winton was seen on the BBC for six months from 1960. Other prominent newsreaders (or newscasters, as ITN has traditionally called them) have been Michael Aspel, Corbett Woodall, Bob Langley, John Edmunds, Richard Whitmore, Peter Woods, John Humphrys, John Simpson, Andrew Harvey, Sue Lawley, Jan Leeming, Michael Buerk, Philip Hayton, Frances Coverdale, Nicholas Witchell, Jeremy Paxman, Chris Lowe, Moira Stuart, Jennie Bond, Debbie Thrower, Laurie Mayer, Jill Dando, John Tusa, Edward Stourton, Justin Webb, Huw Edwards, Jon Sopel, George Alagiah, Sian Williams, Fiona Bruce, Darren Jordon, Jane Hill, Sophie Raworth, Bill Turnbull, Matthew Amroliwala and Natasha Kaplinsky (all for the BBC); Christopher Chataway, Robin Day, Anthony Brown (father of BBC correspondent Ben Brown), Ian Trethowan, Ludovic Kennedy, Andrew Gardner, Reginald Bosanquet, Sandy Gall, Gordon Honeycombe, Alastair Burnet, Leonard Parkin, Ivor Mills, Peter Snow, Robert Kee, Trevor McDonald, Rory MacPherson, Michael Nicholson, Alastair Stewart, Selina Scott, Pamela Armstrong, Fiona Armstrong, John Suchet, Carol Barnes, Jon Snow, Sue Carpenter, Anne Leuchars, Nicholas Owen, Anya Sitaram, Denis Tuohy, Katie Derham, Mark Austin, Andrea Catherwood, Mary Nightingale, Shiulie Ghosh, Leyla Daybelge, Fiona Foster, Bill Neely, James Mates, Felicity Barr, Steve Scott and Nina Hossain (for ITN). Martyn Lewis, Peter Sissons, Anna Ford, Julia Somerville and Dermot Murnaghan are some of the newsreaders who have worked for both channels. Peter Sissons was also an early anchor of Channel 4 News, but Jon Snow has been in that hot seat since 1989, supported by Zeinab Badawi, Shahnaz Pakravan, Cathy Smith, Jane Bennett-Powell, Phil Gayle, Daljit Dhaliwal, Tanya Sillem, Krishnan Guru-Murthy, Sue Turton, Alex Thomson, Kirsty Lang, Bridgid Nzekwu, Sarah Smith, Samira Ahmed, Keme Nzerem, Lindsay Taylor, Carl Dinnen and Katie Razzall. The newest national service, Channel 5 News (now Five News), was launched by Kirsty Young, who was backed up by Rob Butler and Charlie Stayt and eventually succeeded, when she left for ITN's ITV news, by Andrea Catherwood and Katie Ledger (Young has since returned to Channel 5). Other Five News readers include Kate Sanderson, Julie Etchingham, Helen Fospero, Barbara Serra and Anjali Rao.

News at Ten

See *News*.

Newsnight ★★★★

UK (BBC) Current Affairs. BBC 2 1980–

Presenters **Peter Snow, Peter Hobday, Charles Wheeler, John Tusa, Olivia O'Leary, Jenni Murray, Donald MacCormick, Gavin Esler, Jeremy Paxman, Francine Stock, Kirsty Wark, Jeremy Vine**

Editors **George Carey, Ron Neil, Sian Keevil, George Entwistle, Peter Barron**

● ***Late-night current affairs round-up.***

Much acclaimed, *Newsnight* (initially four nights a week, later five) has performed the task of reviewing in detail the major news stories of the day, with special emphasis on political and foreign affairs. Its conception in 1980 was revolutionary in that it brought together the BBC's news and current affairs departments for the first time. After industrial disputes had postponed the launch on various occasions, the original team of presenters comprised Peter Snow (with the programme until 1997), Peter Hobday, Charles Wheeler and John Tusa, with news bulletins read by Fran Morrison and sports reports from David Davies (later David Icke). The format was later changed to incorporate just one host/interviewer. Jeremy Paxman, Kirsty Wark, Jeremy Vine and Gavin Esler have held this position in recent years, relieved occasionally by Sue Cameron, John Simpson, James Cox, Huw Edwards, Gordon Brewer, Sarah Montague, Martha Kearney, Allan Little, Mark Urban, John Sopel, Eddie Mair and others.

Newsnight's challenging interviewing techniques have made it both admired and feared by politicians, some of whom openly questioned the programme's 'patriotism' during international conflicts such as the Falklands and Gulf Wars, when presenters deliberately aimed to present a balanced picture of events. One of the most memorable moments in the programme's history came when Jeremy Paxman unsuccessfully pressed the then Home Secretary, Michael Howard, 14 times for an answer to the question, 'Did you threaten to overrule him?', referring to Howard's dispute with Prison Chief Derek Lewis.

Newsnight Review (BBC 2 2001–) is an extension of the Friday night edition of *Newsnight* in which Mark Lawson discusses the cultural week with well-read guests.

Newsround ★★★

UK (BBC) Children's News. BBC 1 1972–

Presenters **John Craven, Lucy Mathen, Roger Finn, Helen Rollason, Paul McDowell, Juliet Morris, Krishnan Guru-Murthy, Julie Etchingham, Chris Rogers, Kate Sanderson, Lizo Mzimba, Matthew Price, Becky Jago, Adam Smyth, Lizzie Greenwood, Adam Fleming, Laura Jones, Rachel Horne, Ellie Crisell, Thalia Pellegrini, Sonali Gudka**

● ***A bulletin of topical news for juniors.***

This innovative series has aimed to make important news stories more accessible to younger viewers. Lasting just five or ten minutes and dropped into the children's schedule on weekday evenings (just two to start, now five nights), *Newsround* (*John Craven's Newsround* until 1987, Craven eventually leaving in 1989) has presented snippets of real news, explaining the background in fine detail for young minds to grasp. There has always been an emphasis on subjects of youth interest, but the programme has never been patronizing. On some occasions, *Newsround* has even beaten adult news programmes to the punch with breaking stories, such as the *Challenger* space-shuttle disaster. The first programme on 4 April 1972 was intended to be the start of only a six-week trial. In those early days, the programme carried details of an earthquake in Iran and the build-up to the launch of *Apollo 16*. More recent initiatives have included mock elections for children in the run-up to a general election and the introduction of the monthly Doc Slot, in which Dr David Bull discussed children's health. In October 2005 prime-time BBC newsreader Huw Edwards took over the programme for a week.

A round-up programme, *Newsround Weekly* (presented by Lucy Mathen), was added in 1977 and the longer *Newsround Extra* (an investigative series introduced in 1975) has been aired on some Fridays. With the arrival of CBBC in 2002, extra daily bulletins were added for that channel. In 2005 a Saturday morning extension entitled *Sportsround* (presented by Jake Humphrey) took to the air.

Next of Kin ✱✱

UK (BBC) Situation Comedy. BBC 1 1995–7

Maggie Prentice .... **Penelope Keith**
Andrew Prentice .... **William Gaunt**
Liz .... **Tracie Bennett**
Georgia .... **Ann Gosling**
Philip ('Pip') .... **Matthew Clarke**
Jake .... **Jamie Lucraft**
Tom .... **Mark Powley**
Rosie .... **Wanda Ventham**
Hugh .... **Timothy Carlton**
Roxanne .... **Diana Magness**

Writers **Jan Etherington, Gavin Petrie**
Producer **Gareth Gwenlan**

A middle-aged couple find themselves parents of a young family once again.

An early retirement in France is on the horizon for suburban couple Maggie and Andrew Prentice, but their carefully laid plans are about to be thrown to the winds when their son, Graham, and daughter-in-law, 'Bootface', are killed in a car accident. Although shocked, they shed few tears because, frankly, they never liked them very much anyway. However, there is the question of the children – Georgia (13 and a vegetarian), Pip (11) and Jake (5) – and where they will now live. In truth, the kids are strangers but they – and their pets – have no other home than with their grandparents (the 'next of kin'), and so Maggie and Andrew find themselves with a family to raise all over again. The Prentices do their best to overcome such problems as an overcrowded house, the generation gap, trouble at school, the sheer cussedness of their new charges and, of course, the trauma of lost parents, with some youthful guidance from Liz, the family's daily help. Such new worries, however, mean that Maggie is unlikely ever to give up smoking and Andrew will similarly remain in hock to the bottle. 'Tea for Two' is the ironic theme tune.

Nice Day at the Office ✱✱

UK (BBC) Situation Comedy. BBC 1 1994

Phil Bachelor .... **Timothy Spall**
Tippit .... **John Sessions**
Janice Troutbeck .... **Anna Massey**
Chris Selwyn .... **David Haig**
Dave Morrison .... **Brian Pettifer**
Lizzie Kershaw .... **Nicola Stephenson**

Writers **Paul Shearer, Richard Turner**
Producer **Stephen McCrum**

A loudmouthed clerical worker rails against the claustrophobia of office life.

In this six-part exposé of office politics and petty rivalries, Phil Bachelor is a frustrated executive who has given ten years of his life to the same company. And for what? To turn up every day and face the same tedium, that's what. Waging battles over paper clips and waste-paper bins, his eccentric colleagues in the data processing office include frumpy Janice, fashion disaster secretary Lizzie, contemptible boss Chris and inept Dave, but the biggest bugbear in Phil's life is the aggressive security man, Tippit. It's all too much for the bolshie Phil to bear. He knows that there is more to life than this, and he does his best to find some distraction. Regrettably, his only escape is usually to the pub to drown his sorrows.

Nice Guy Eddie ✱✱

UK (BBC) Drama. BBC 1 2002

Eddie McMullen .... **Ricky Tomlinson**
Frank Bennett .... **Tom Ellis**
Veronica 'Ronnie' McMullen .... **Rachel Davies**
Vera McMullen .... **Elizabeth Spriggs**
Angela Jones .... **Christine Tremarco**
Becca McMullen .... **Emma Vaudrey**
Laura McMullen .... **Stephanie Waring**
Lawrence 'Lol' O'Toole .... **John Henshaw**
Sharon .... **Joanne Sherryden**
Neil Jones .... **Scot Williams**

Creators **Johanne McAndrew, Elliot Hope**
Writers **Johanne McAndrew, Elliot Hope, Steve Lawson**
Producers **Colin McKeown, Paddy Higson**

A Liverpudlian detective leads complicated work and family lives.

Fifty-three-year-old Eddie McMullen is a private detective with a shambolic personal life. A large part of the problem is the stranger who knocks on his door and declares Eddie is his father. Whether 24-year-old former army lad Frank Bennett really is his son or not plays on Eddie's mind, but he keeps refusing to take that all-conclusive paternity test. In the meantime, Frank comes in handy doing Eddie's leg work. Meanwhile, the rest of his family – Ronnie (ambitious wife of 25 years who runs the Bridal Enchantment shop), overbearing mum Vera (a widowed former Tiller Girl) and demanding daughters Ange (loudmouth assistant to her mum; always fighting with husband Neil), Becca (policewoman) and Laura (A-level student) – are not amused. Eddie's professional life is not much simpler, either, as the various cases he undertakes invariably lead him into hot water. But, as the title says, Eddie is a decent and likeable sort – albeit a hypochondriac with a penchant for kebabs – who just gets overtaken by events. Lol

O'Toole is his lawyer buddy (once married to Ronnie's sister), and Sharon is Lol's dolled-up blonde secretary. The six-part series, produced by BBC Northern Ireland and screened in 2002, followed a 90-minute pilot episode a year earlier.

Nice Time ***

UK (Granada) Comedy. ITV 1968–9

Presenters **Germaine Greer, Jonathan Routh, Kenny Everett, Sandra Gough**

Producer **John Birt**

Anarchic and bizarre sketch show.

Originally a programme just for the Granada region, *Nice Time* proved so popular that it was extended to the ITV network. It comprised a collection of wacky sketches and inventive stunts, built around viewers' requests for favourite moments from comedy films. However, it is best remembered today for giving young DJ Kenny Everett his TV break, for promoting the then Warwick University lecturer Germaine Greer, and for being produced by future BBC Director-General John Birt. Sandra Gough (ex-CORONATION STREET) joined the team in series two.

Nice Work ***

UK (BBC) Drama. BBC 2 1989

Vic Wilcox	**Warren Clarke**
Dr Robyn Penrose	**Haydn Gwynne**
Prof. Philip Swallow	**Christopher Godwin**
Marjorie Wilcox	**Janet Dale**
Brian Everthorpe	**John Forgeham**
Charles Bennett	**Martin Jacobs**
Stuart Baxter	**David Calder**
Basil Penrose	**Patrick Pearson**

Writer **David Lodge**
Producer **Chris Parr**

A ruthless industrialist and a bluestocking embark on an unlikely but steamy affair.

It is January 1986 and Robyn Penrose has taken up a three-year appointment in the English department of the University of Rummidge in the Midlands. At a time of recession, and with cuts to education budgets on the horizon, academia is being urged to forge closer links with industry. Each faculty is asked to nominate a member of staff to shadow a figure in local industry. As Robyn has just written a book on the 'Victorian industrial novel', she seems an appropriate choice. Reporting back to Prof. Swallow, the Head of English and Dean of the Faculty of Arts, she joins the executives at a local foundry, J. Pringle & Co., and finds herself assigned to the boss, Vic Wilcox. Wilcox has been in charge for nine months and is trying to streamline the business. However, his methods and philosophy appal the liberal Robyn, who finds it hard to remain merely an observer. The two figures are poles apart physically and socially: she is lean, fit, cerebral and drives a red Renault 5; he is overweight, a chain-smoker, pig-headed and sits behind the wheel of a flash car with a personalized number plate. Somehow, however, a bond forms between the two, the relationship spirals out of control and they become unlikely lovers. The four-part series was penned by David Lodge, from his own novel. Rachel Portman provided the music and Christopher Menaul directed.

Nicholas, Paul

(Paul Beuselinck; 1945–)

British singer and actor who used his charm to good effect as Vince Pinner in the sitcom JUST GOOD FRIENDS in the 1980s. Before that, his biggest role was in a short-lived 1979 BBC comedy entitled *Two Up, Two Down* in which, as Jimmy, he starred with Su Pollard. Nicholas had also taken smaller roles in numerous drama series (like Z CARS and LADY KILLERS), appeared in assorted films and stage musicals, and notched up a few pop chart hits (also hosting *Paul*, his own kids' pop show). He was later seen as the financially embarrassed Neil Walsh in *Bust* (1987) and as vet James Shepherd in the comedy *Close to Home* (1989), as well as singing and dancing in variety shows. He returned to the small screen in 2000, as Ronnie Buchan in *Burnside* and David Janus in SUNBURN, continuing with guest spots in DOCTORS, THE BILL and HOLBY CITY. Nicholas was also narrator of the *Spot* cartoons.

Nicholls, Paul

(1979–)

Bolton-born actor coming to light in the kids' series *Earthfasts* (David Wix) and *The Biz!* (drama student Tim), and then being cast as Joe Wicks in EASTENDERS. His next move was into CITY CENTRAL (PC Terry Sydenham), and he followed this with *The Passion* (passion play actor Daniel), *Table 12* (Ol), CANTERBURY TALES (Jerome), *A Thing Called Love* (Gary Scant), *Blue Dove* (Nick Weston) and *Gunpowder, Treason and Plot* (Lord Darnley). Nicholls has also made guest appearances in OUT OF THE BLUE and *Fully Booked*.

Nicholls, Sue

(Susan Harmar-Nicholls; 1943–)

Known today as Audrey Roberts in CORONATION STREET (a role she has played since 1979), Sue Nicholls's TV appearances have been many and varied. Some viewers may recall her in CROSSROADS, as waitress Marilyn Gates, a part which gave her a hit single, 'Where Will You Be?', in 1968. Others may recall her performances as Joan Greengross, Reggie Perrin's devoted secretary, or as Wanda Pickles, Jim Davidson's neighbour in UP THE ELEPHANT AND ROUND THE CASTLE. Her other credits have included *Not on Your Nellie* (barmaid Big Brenda), PIPKINS (Mrs Muddle), RENTAGHOST (Nadia Popov), THE DUCHESS OF DUKE STREET, *Village Hall, Heartland*, THE PROFESSIONALS, *Doctor on the Go* (see DOCTOR IN THE HOUSE), THE GENTLE TOUCH and WODEHOUSE PLAYHOUSE. She is the daughter of one-time Conservative MP Lord Harmar-Nicholls and is married to former *Street* bad guy Mark Eden.

Nichols, Dandy

(Daisy Nichols; 1907–86)

British actress, famous for one role, that of Else, Alf Garnett's much-abused wife in TILL DEATH US DO PART and *In Sickness and in Health*. Her one other major part was as Madge in the 1971 sitcom *The Trouble with Lillian* (opposite Patricia Hayes), although she also appeared in series like *Ask Mr Pastry*, EMERGENCY – WARD 10, DIXON OF DOCK GREEN, NO HIDING PLACE, MRS THURSDAY, MAN IN A SUITCASE, BERGERAC and the kids' comedy *The Bagthorpe Saga* (Mrs Fosdyke).

Nicholson, Michael

OBE (1937–)

Award-winning ITN journalist, with the company since 1963, having previously worked as a political writer with D. C. Thompson. Nicholson has the distinction of covering more wars than any other British TV reporter. These have included the conflicts in Vietnam, Biafra (eastern Nigeria), the Falklands and in the Gulf. He was ITN's Southern Africa correspondent, 1976–81, and presenter of *News at 5.45* for three years from 1982. He is currently the chief foreign affairs correspondent. In 2001, he presented *Back to the Front with Michael Nicholson*, in which he revisited former war zones.

Nickelodeon

Children's channel originating on cable TV in the USA in 1979, when it was founded by the Warner Amex company. It was later taken over by Viacom. From the start, the focus of its programming has been on variety for younger viewers, combining cartoons with live programming, youth drama and game shows. Since 1993 it has broadcast to Europe from the Astra satellite system, and is also now available via cable companies. Its programming remains heavily American, with hit series like SABRINA THE TEENAGE WITCH and *Rugrats* to the fore. A younger children's service is provided by a sister channel, Nick Jr, and a further addition has been Nicktoons TV. In the USA, Nickelodeon's daytime service is complemented by Nick at Night, a grown-ups channel which features vintage TV shows (although the trend is now to focus on 'modern classics' like ROSEANNE and CHEERS, with the older series now covered by a related channel called TV Land).

Nielsens

The all-important US league table of TV audiences, collated by the A. C. Nielsen company (using meters attached to television receivers). The term has become synonymous with 'ratings' in America. A. C. Nielsen was also active in the UK TV industry for a while in the 1950s.

Nightingales ★★★

UK (Alomo) Situation Comedy. Channel 4 1990; 1992–3

Carter .... **Robert Lindsay**
Bell .... **David Threlfall**
Sarge .... **James Ellis**
The Inspector .... **Peter Vaughan**
Eric Swan .... **Ian Sears**
Piper .... **Edward Burnham**

Creator/Writer **Paul Makin**
Producers **Esta Charkham, Rosie Bunting**

● ***Three security guards while away the hours with conversation and practical jokes.***

Carter, Bell and Sarge are the stars of this ambitious surreal comedy. Though they work as security guards, little of note ever happens to disrupt the long nights they spend in the rest room, trapped in each other's company. The result is a television equivalent of *Waiting for Godot*. Occasional visitors to antagonize the crew and intrude upon their fantasies include The Inspector and Eric the Werewolf. Otherwise, their constant cry is 'There's nobody here but us chickens!'

Nighty Night ★★★

UK (Baby Cow) Situation Comedy. BBC 2 2004; 2006
DVD: BBC

Jill Tyrell .... **Julia Davis**
Don Cole .... **Angus Deayton**
Cath Cole .... **Rebecca Front**
Terry Tyrell .... **Kevin Eldon**
Linda .... **Ruth Jones**
Glen Bulb .... **Mark Gatiss**
Sue 2 .... **Felicity Montagu**

Creator/Writer **Julia Davis**
Producers **Alison MacPhail, Ted Dowd**

● ***A beauty consultant pretends her husband is dead to start a new life.***

Taking situation comedy into darker waters than ever before, *Nighty Night* is about as PC as a party in a crematorium. The central thrust is that poor Terry Tyrell is told he is suffering from cancer. This shattering discovery does have a bright side, however. His selfish wife, Jill, now believes she has a chance to kick-start her disappointing life. However, it turns out that Terry has been misdiagnosed and is not terminally ill after all, but, having set out on her new journey, Jill is reluctant to turn back. Consequently, she fails to pass on the good news to Terry, whom she packs off to a hospice while she tries various far from subtle moves to attract the attentions of new neighbour Don Cole. Don, a doctor, is not as unresponsive as he should be, considering he has a wheelchair bound wife (Cath) who is suffering from MS and needs his daily care, but Jill doesn't quite get things her own way. Usually taking the brunt of Jill's sarcasm and spite is Linda, her asthmatic assistant at the beauty salon. The creation of such an inhumane monster as Jill – a woman so evil and self-preoccupied that she even stages a mock funeral for her husband – inevitably drew an avalanche of criticism from viewers offended by such a casual treatment of illnesses that have caused distress for millions. Nevertheless, *Nighty Night* was showered with awards and was commissioned for a second series, in which Jill follows Don and Cath to Cornwall, where they are trying to repair their marriage. Both series went out first on BBC 3.

Nighy, Bill

(1949–)

Surrey-born actor whose major roles have been as Prof. Mark Carleton in THE MEN'S ROOM, Cameron Foster in STATE OF PLAY, Col. Osborne in HE KNEW HE WAS RIGHT and Gideon in *Gideon's Daughter*. Nighy also played Vincent Fish in AGONY, Tom Frewen in *Eye of the Storm*, Cecil Meares in *The Last Place on Earth*, Sam Courtney in *Making News*, Lord Sandwich in LONGITUDE, James in CANTERBURY TALES, the Earl of Clincham in *The Young Visiters*, Jeffrey Grainger in AUF WIEDERSEHEN, PET, Stamfordham in THE LOST PRINCE and Lawrence in *The Girl in the Café*. He has also been seen in FOX, MINDER, BERGERAC, REILLY – ACE OF SPIES, BOON, PEAK PRACTICE, WYCLIFFE, KAVANAGH QC, *People Like Us*, KISS ME KATE and READY WHEN YOU ARE MR MCGILL.

Nimmo, Derek

(1932–99)

Liverpudlian actor often seen in rather dithery roles. He enjoyed great success with his clerics, the Reverend Mervyn

Noote in ALL GAS AND GAITERS, Brother/Father Dominic in OH BROTHER and *Oh Father*, and Dean Selwyn Makepeace in *Hell's Bells* (plus the Reverend Green in a CLUEDO special). He also played David in THE BED-SIT GIRL, Frederick in the comedy *Blandings Castle*, Bingo Little in *The World of Wooster*, David in another sitcom, *Sorry I'm Single*, Henry Prendergast in the political comedy *My Honourable Mrs*, Chris Bunting in *Life Begins at Forty* and George Hutchenson in *Third Time Lucky*. Nimmo also made a well-publicized cameo appearance in NEIGHBOURS and, in the 1970s, was host of the chat shows *If It's Saturday, It Must be Nimmo* and *Just a Nimmo*.

Nimoy, Leonard

(1931–)

American actor/director who will always be Star Trek's pointy-eared Vulcan, Mr Spock, even though he has enjoyed plenty of other TV work. Nimoy's TV debut came in the 1950s, with parts in series like DRAGNET and LARAMIE. More guest appearances came in the 1960s, including in THE MAN FROM U.N.C.L.E. and GET SMART, before he was cast as Spock, which he followed with the role of Paris, master of disguise, in MISSION: IMPOSSIBLE. Nimoy has since been seen in TV movies and mini-series (such as *Marco Polo*) and has also worked as a programme narrator.

9 to 5 ★★

US (IPC/Twentieth Century-Fox) Situation Comedy. ITV 1982–4; 1988–9 (US: ABC 1982–3; Syndicated 1986–8)

Violet Newstead .... **Rita Moreno**
Doralee Rhodes .... **Rachel Dennison**
Judy Bernly .... **Valerie Curtin**
Roz Keith .... **Jean Marsh**
Franklin Hart .... **Jeffrey Tambor**
Peter Bonerz
Harry Nussbaum .... **Herb Edelman**
Linda Bowman .... **Leah Ayres**
Michael Henderson .... **George Deloy**
Marsha McMurray Shrimpton .... **Sally Struthers**
William 'Bud' Coleman .... **Edward Winter**
Charmin Cunningham .... **Dorian Lopinto**
Russ Merman .... **Peter Evans**
Morgan .... **Art Evans**
E. Nelson Felb .... **Fred Applegate**

Creator **Patricia Resnick**

Three secretaries outmanoeuvre their chauvinistic bosses.

A spin-off from the 1980 movie of the same title, which starred Jane Fonda, Dolly Parton and Lily Tomlin as three sparky secretaries who get the better of their sexist boss. Fonda maintains her involvement, this time as one of the executive producers, and Dolly Parton's theme song is also used, although initially voiced by Phoebe Snow. To add to the continuity, Parton's own sister, Rachel Dennison, takes over the part of curvy country girl Doralee Rhodes, one of the feisty females who run the office at Consolidated Companies. Her workmates are single mother Violet (many years with the company and frustrated) and college graduate Judy (bright but lacking common sense), and together they fight the snide chauvinism of boss Franklin Hart, who is intent on using the girls as a doormat. Hart is assisted in his subterfuge by sneaky office manager Roz. Cast changes see the introduction of a couple of salesmen, Harry and Michael, and also the departure of Judy, who is briefly replaced by new girl Linda. Such alterations were not welcomed, however, and the series was quickly cancelled. It was revived in 1986 for syndication in the USA. Back comes Judy, joined by Doralee and new secretary Marsha, a hapless divorcée. They now work for Barkley Foods International and have three new bosses to confront: Russ Merman for Judy, Bud Coleman for Doralee, and Charmin Cunningham, then E. Nelson Felb, for Marsha. With changes behind the scenes, too (Fonda had long departed), the feminist slant is considerably watered down, rendering this just another office politics comedy.

1984 ★★★

UK (BBC) Science Fiction. BBC 1954

Winston Smith .... **Peter Cushing**
O'Brien .... **André Morell**
Julia .... **Yvonne Mitchell**
Syme .... **Donald Pleasence**
Emmanuel Goldstein .... **Arnold Diamond**
Parsons .... **Campbell Gray**

Writer **Nigel Kneale**
Producer **Rudolph Cartier**

Controversial adaptation of George Orwell's portentous novel.

Variously criticized and praised by the politicians of the day, this one-off drama shocked the nation. As its title suggests, it focuses on life in 1984 (30 years ahead), at a time when a totalitarian regime known as Big Brother is watching over all of Britain. Society is divided into clearly defined groups. First there is the Inner Party, then comes the Outer Party. Beyond these 'privileged' citizens are the ordinary masses, the Proles. Language has been eroded away, limiting individual expression by the abolition of words, and videoscreens watch people as they go about their everyday chores, checking for signs of dissent.

At the heart of the action is Winston Smith, a member of the Outer Party who works as a rewriter of history in the Ministry of Truth. It is his growing rebellion, encouraged by a girlfriend, Julia, and then viciously curbed by the devious O'Brien in the dreaded Room 101, that exemplifies the control of the authorities and the nightmare of life under such a regime. The torture sequence involving live rats is well remembered.

Transmitted live on a Sunday night, *1984* was repeated – again live – four days later, drawing the biggest audience since the CORONATION (largely as a result of the clamour which followed the first showing). The play was written by Nigel Kneale and produced by Rudolph Cartier, two adventurous BBC men who, a year or so earlier, had created the groundbreaking QUATERMASS *Experiment*. Kneale revived *1984* in 1965, with David Buck, Jane Merrow and Joseph O'Connor in the lead roles of Smith, Julia and O'Brien, but, unlike its predecessor, it passed virtually unnoticed.

1940s House, The

See *1900 House, The*.

1900 House, The ★★★

UK (Wall to Wall) Documentary. Channel 4 1999
DVD: PBS Home Video (Region 1 only)

Producer **Simon Shaw**

● ***A modern family endures the living conditions of a century ago.***

As a social experiment, *The 1900 House* pitched a British family back in time by asking them to live in an authentic Victorian home. Number 50 Elliscombe Road, in Charlton, London, was selected as a suitable property for the experiment. A terraced house, built in 1900, it was stripped of all modern conveniences and refitted with the trappings of life at the turn of the 20th century. Gas lighting replaced electricity. For heating water and cooking, an old range was added to the kitchen; for laundry, a copper was provided to boil water with a washboard and soap for the wash itself. The outside lavatory was furnished with torn-up newspaper in place of toilet tissue. Braving this return to the past, with only a little training, were the Bowler family from Somerset, who – selected from some 400 applicants – found themselves having not just to survive in the house for three months, but also to really live in it – coping with meagre food supplies typical of the time, wearing the restrictive clothes of the day and making their own entertainment through musical soirees, charades and playing cards. Father Paul, a Royal Marines warrant officer, was forced to miss part of the experience through calls of duty, but mum Joyce battled on with 16 year-old Kathryn, twins Ruth and Hilary (12) and Joseph (9). Being relatively well off, they were able to employ a maid (Elizabeth). However, for a middle-class family from the late 20th century this proved to be an awkward experience, albeit just one of many stresses. To let off steam, the family privately recorded video diaries to a specially installed camera. Historian and programme consultant Daru Rooke occasionally dropped by to offer advice. Following the nine-part series, a one-off programme at Christmas 1999 spoke to the family a year after their ordeal had ended to collate their thoughts on this life-changing experience.

Continuing the theme, the same production company later came up with the five-part *The 1940s House* (Channel 4 2001). This time 17 Braemar Gardens, West Wickham, Kent, was stripped back 60 years to the days of the Blitz. The Haymers family from Yorkshire (dad Michael, mum Lyn, daughter Kirstie and Kirstie's two sons, Ben aged ten and Tom, seven) took up residence for nine weeks and experienced the delights of powdered egg, blackouts and fake air-raids. A special 'war cabinet' of period experts was set up to impose a regime on the family.

The Edwardian Country House (Channel 4 2002, producer: Caroline Ross Pirie) was a return to the early years of the 20th century (broadly 1905–14), but moving the setting into gentrified circles. Creating a real-life UPSTAIRS, DOWNSTAIRS, it assembled two teams of inmates and confined them to Manderston, a large country house just south of Edinburgh. Upstairs were the Olliff-Cooper family from Hampshire, cast as lords of the manor (dad John, mum Anna, kids Jonty (18) and Guy (nine), plus Anna's sister, Avril Anson). Downstairs were butler Hugh Robert Edgar, housekeeper Jean Davies, chef Denis Dubiard, ladies' maid Eva Morrison, footman Charlie Clay, children's tutor Reji Raj-Singh, plus assorted parlour maids among a staff of a dozen in total. Over six programmes, covering three months at the house, the series explored the strained relationship between the 'classes', the constraints of aristocratic life and the hardships below stairs. In a six-part companion series, *Treats from the Edwardian Country House* (Channel 4 2002), Hugh Fearnley-Whittingstall showcased the culinary and other pleasures enjoyed by the wealthy families of the period.

The six-part *Frontier House* (Channel 4 2002) took the concept to the USA, bringing together in Montana three families for a six-month taste of life as 1883 pioneers. The task for each was to construct their own log cabin home, live in it and make it work, hopefully setting themselves up to survive the misery of a winter in the wilderness, surrounded by dangerous animals. Featured were the Clune family from California (parents Gordon and Adrienne, kids Aine, Justin and Connor, plus niece Tracy), Karen and Mark Glenn from Tennessee (with children Erin and Logan), and Nate Brooks from Boston. Nate was accompanied initially by his dad, Rudy, then by his fiancée, Kristin, who arrived for a frontier wedding.

1990 ★★

UK (BBC) Drama. BBC 2 1977–8

Jim Kyle .... **Edward Woodward**
Faceless (Maudsley) .... **Paul Hardwick**
Herbert Skardon .... **Robert Lang**
Dave Brett .... **Tony Doyle**
Delly Lomas .... **Barbara Kellerman**
Dan Mellor .... **John Savident**
Henry Tasker .... **Clifton Jones**
Greaves .... **George Murcell**
Jack Nichols .... **Michael Napier Brown**
Kate Smith .... **Yvonne Mitchell**
Lynn Blake .... **Lisa Harrow**
PCD Insp. MacRae .... **David McKail**
Tony Doran .... **Clive Swift**

Creator **Wilfred Greatorex**
Producer **Prudence Fitzgerald**

● ***An Orwellian vision of the future, in all its depressing glory.***

This drama centred on the hypothesis that at the end of the 20th century Britain would be ruthlessly controlled by a government that suppressed all resistance in the name of the common good. Looking just 13 years into the future, *1990* foresees a Britain where rationing and identity cards are back on the agenda and where *emi*gration, not *immi*gration, is the problem, as scientists and other dissidents seek to flee the totalitarian state. Overseeing the oppression is a Home Office division known as the Public Control Department (PCD), with the cruel Herbert Skardon at its head, supported by a deputy, Delly Lomas (later replaced by Lynn Blake). Opposing them is resistance leader Jim Kyle, a Home Affairs reporter for one of the three surviving newspapers. With his colleagues, Kyle aims to smuggle dissidents out of the country and subvert the powers of the PCD by operating an underground press and hindering their every movement.

Nip/Tuck ★★★

US (Warner Brothers) Comedy Drama. Channel 4 2004–5
(US: Fox 2003–)
DVD: Warner Home Video

Sean McNamara .... **Dylan Walsh**
Christian Troy .... **Julian McMahon**
Julia McNamara .... **Joely Richardson**
Matt McNamara .... **John Hensley**

Annie McNamara .... **Kelsey Lynn Batelaan**
Liz Winters/Cruz .... **Roma Maffia**
Grace Santiago .... **Valerie Cruz**
Vanessa .... **Kate Mara**
Kimberly Henry .... **Kelly Carlson**
Jude .... **Phillip Rhys**
Merril Bobolit .... **Joey Slotnick**
Megan O'Hara .... **Julie Warner**
Gina Russo .... **Jessalyn Gilsig**
Claire Grubman .... **Ruth Williamson**
Alla Korot
Dr Erica Noughton .... **Vanessa Redgrave**

Creator **Ryan Murphy**
Executive Producers **Ryan Murphy, Michael M. Robin, Greer Shephard**

Two Florida plastic surgeons have troubles in and out of their operating theatre.

Miami plastic surgeon Christian Troy is anything but what his forename implies. He'll take advantage of any situation for his carnal or financial gain – and he's not very good at his work, either, as the number of botched operations underlines. His partner, Sean McNamara, is the conscience of the team, a man troubled by Christian's attitude and antics and finding his family life hard, with a disgruntled wife, Julia, and a dismissive son, Matt. These are the stars of this black comedy drama that offers up absurd storylines involving people who want to look like their idols, desire enlarged bodily parts, or have committed some foolish and rather gory act upon their personage. A liberal helping of sex scenes are interspersed with loads of bloody, squelchy surgical moments in this fast-moving, smartly written, glossy production that underlines that the beauty business can be painful, expensive and frankly ridiculous. Each episode is named after one of the patients the doctors treat.

One interesting point is that star Joely Richardson's real mum, Vanessa Redgrave, plays her screen mum, Dr Erica Noughton, from series two. Episodes were screened first on Sky One in the UK, before a terrestrial launch on Channel 4.

Nixon, David

(1919–78)

Popular British conjuror and game show panellist of the 1950s–1970s. A former stage partner of Norman Wisdom, Nixon became one of UK TV's earliest celebrities, appearing on the children's show *Sugar and Spice*, and using his charm to good effect as a regular panellist on shows like WHAT'S MY LINE? and *My Wildest Dream*. In the late 1950s he starred in *It's Magic* and went on to host *Showtime* and *Comedy Bandbox*. In the late 1960s and 1970s, he was given his own shows, *Nixon at Nine-Five, Now for Nixon, The Nixon Line, David Nixon, Tonight with David Nixon, The David Nixon Show* and *David Nixon's Magic Box*, some of which helped introduce an aristocratic foxy puppet by the name of Basil Brush to an enthusiastic audience.

No Angels ★★

UK (World) Drama. Channel 4 2004–
DVD: VCI

Lia Costoya .... **Louise Delamere**
Beth Nicholls .... **Jo Joyner**
Anji Mittel .... **Sunetra Sarker**
Kate Oakley .... **Kaye Wragg**
Jamie .... **Derek Riddell**
Callum .... **James Frost**
McManus .... **Francis Magee**
Emma .... **Charlotte Leach**
Pamela 'Grizzly' Adams .... **Judy Flynn**
Ajesh .... **Emil Marwa**
Neil .... **Dean Andrews**
Stella .... **Lynn Ferguson**
Paul .... **Mark Aiken**
Clare Fletcher .... **Lisa Millett**
Daisy .... **Clare Kerrigan**
Marcus .... **James Thornton**
Justyn .... **Tom Ellis**
Dr Peter Compton .... **Matt Bardoc**

Creator **Toby Whithouse**
Producers **Helen Gregory, Steve Lightfoot, Tim Baker**

Four nurses share a job, a flat and a raucous private life.

Likely to damage nursing recruitment, was what the Royal College of Nursing concluded on seeing the first episodes of this raunchy drama series, declaring that the programme's depiction of professional nursing was not in the least bit accurate. The programme makers responded by declaring that an NHS nurse with 20 years' experience worked as consultant on the series, and that many of the unorthodox goings-on were actually drawn from real-life instances. It was this consultant's view that, while the image of nursing conveyed was not very flattering, it was, nonetheless, an honest one.

No Angels is set in St Margaret's Hospital in Leeds, where Lia, Beth, Anji and Kate work as nurses. Their daily routine revolves around sparring and flirting with doctors like Callum, Jamie and McManus, dealing with stroppy patients and colleagues, and finding a release somehow from the stresses of the job. In such situations, a black sense of humour often comes in very handy, as does the odd practical joke lifted seemingly straight from a *Carry On* film – drugging a junior doctor at a party, retrieving missing false teeth from a corpse, a prostitute working the wards, etc. However, *No Angels* is not really a medical drama. The emphasis is more on the personal lives of the four girls, who also share a flat and party every night. Liberal doses of booze, drugs and sex litter their out-of-hours existence. Kate, a career nurse, is rather sweet but wholly insecure, after a bad near-wedding experience. She works as an acting sister on the Medical Assessment Unit (MAU). Unambitious Anji, meanwhile, is particularly promiscuous, despite awaiting her arranged marriage. Scalpel-tongued Lia is a former wild child and mother of 12-year-old Emma (who lives with her dad), while fourth flatmate Beth is a rather lazy but cunning blonde with an insatiable appetite for lager. To keep the pace lively, Motown and northern soul thud along as a soundtrack. Three series, totalling 26 episodes, have so far been produced.

No Bananas ★★★

UK (BBC) Drama. BBC 1 1996

Evelyn Hamilton .... **Alison Steadman**
Arthur Hamilton .... **Michael Elwyn**
Mary Hamilton/Slater .... **Rachel Power**
William Hamilton .... **Tim Matthews**
Dorothea Grant .... **Stephanie Beacham**
Edward Grant .... **Michael Byrne**
Rose Grant .... **Paloma Baeza**
Thomas Slater .... **Tom Bell**

Grandma Slater .... **Edna Doré**
Ellen Slater .... **Linda Bassett**
Tom Slater .... **Dorian Healy**
Harry Slater .... **Dominic Rowan**
Frank Slater .... **Gregor Truter**
Clifford Slater .... **Paul Williams**
Geoffrey Slater .... **Ryan Davenport**
Kaye Bentley .... **Rachel Pickup**
Moira Barnes .... **Keeley Gainey**

Creator **Ginnie Hole**
Writers **Ginnie Hole, Lisa Evans, Sam Snape, Stan Hey, Brian Thompson**
Producer **Peter Norris**

Trials-and-tribulations-of-war drama, featuring two incompatible but related Kent families.

A hasty, eventful wedding sets the scene for this Sunday evening period drama. Opening on 2 September 1939, a largely carefree time for most of Britain, it focuses on the union through marriage of the well-to-do Hamilton family of Chittenden and the working-class Slaters from Gillingham – the result of the unplanned pregnancy of Mary Hamilton by Harry Slater. A day later war is declared and the story of these reluctantly intertwined families through the conflict begins to unfold. The Slater family is headed by the fiercely patriotic Thomas and his chain-smoking wife, Ellen, their sons including ex-jailbird Tom, who still hasn't mended his ways, dragging younger brother Clifford into the mire with him. Third brother Frank is an ex-boxer with a good heart, while the newly wed Harry, the first of the family to graduate from university, is still in love with his ex-girlfriend, Kaye Bentley. The Hamiltons comprise dad Arthur, a local newspaper editor, happily married wife Evelyn and their children, adolescent William and the newly wed Mary, a former Cambridge student. Also seen is roguish Grandma Slater, plus Evelyn's snooty and overdressed sister, Dorothea, with her much older, fascist husband, Edward (a doctor), and spoilt teenage daughter, Rose. The ten episodes take events up to the Blitz, in September 1940, looking at the hardships of the early war years, active service, romances – licit and otherwise – and the stresses on each household. John Altman provided the music.

No Hiding Place ★★

UK (Associated-Rediffusion) Police Drama. ITV 1959–67

Det. Chief Supt. Tom Lockhart **Raymond Francis**
DS/DI Harry Baxter .... **Eric Lander**
DS Russell .... **Johnny Briggs**
DS Perryman .... **Michael McStay**
DS Gregg .... **Sean Caffrey**

Producers **Ray Dicks, Richard Matthews, Jonathan Goodman, Peter Willes, Geoffrey Nugus, Michael Currer-Briggs**

More adventures with top detective Lockhart.

After earlier exploits in the MURDER BAG and CRIME SHEET, Detective Chief Superintendent Lockhart of Scotland Yard returned to the screen in this long-running series in which he was assisted by keen young DS Baxter. Baxter's popularity was so great that he was later given his own spin-off series, ECHO FOUR TWO, before returning to Lockhart's side when that programme failed to take off. When Baxter moved on yet again, replacement sergeants Russell and Perryman were introduced, with DS Gregg eventually added as the final partner for this genial, snuff-taking sleuth.

The series was popular with both the public and the police, particularly for its authenticity. Over 230 episodes were produced, many of them transmitted live. When it was taken off in 1965, such was the furore that the producers were forced to extend Lockhart's career by a couple more years. One 1962 episode saw a guest appearance by Patrick Cargill in the guise of TOP SECRET's Miguel Garetta. Supporting actor Johnny Briggs, of course, has since found fame as CORONATION STREET's Mike Baldwin, but for the part of Russell the rather short actor had to wear built-up shoes. The *No Hiding Place* theme music, performed by Ken Mackintosh and his orchestra, entered the pop charts in 1960.

No – Honestly ★★

UK (LWT) Situation Comedy. ITV 1974–5

Charles 'CD' Danby .... **John Alderton**
Clara Burrell/Danby .... **Pauline Collins**

Writers **Terence Brady, Charlotte Bingham**
Producer **Humphrey Barclay**

A couple look affectionately back to the early days of their courtship and marriage.

Clara and CD Danby are a well-matched, romantic couple. She is a children's novelist, the daughter of peer Lord Burrell and author of the 'Ollie the Otter' books. He is a comic actor and together they have become a success. But life hasn't always been so generous. Their early relationship (ten years before) was pitted with minor disasters, and these are introduced in flashback form in each episode, after the couple's introductory chat to the camera. Their whimsical approach to life and their fondness for social pranks form a backdrop to most of the plots, as does Clara's scatty, convoluted logic which both bemuses and amuses her patient, caring husband. The duo then wrap up each episode with another piece to camera.

This was very much a 'married couples' series, as both the writers, Terence Brady and Charlotte Bingham, and the stars, John Alderton and Pauline Collins, were real-life husbands and wives. With its pieces to camera and Clara's weird logic, it owed more than a little to THE BURNS AND ALLEN SHOW. When Alderton and Collins called it a day, Donal Donnelly and Liza Goddard were brought in as Matt Browne and Lily Pond, a songwriter and his secretary, and the title became *Yes – Honestly* (it was screened 1976–7). The *No – Honestly* theme song, by Lynsey De Paul, reached the Top Ten in 1974, but 'Yes – Honestly' by Georgie Fame was not a hit.

No Job for a Lady ★★

UK (Thames) Situation Comedy. ITV 1990–2

Jean Price .... **Penelope Keith**
Sir Godfrey Eagan .... **George Baker**
Ken Miller .... **Paul Young**
Norman .... **Garfield Morgan**
Geoff Price .... **Mark Kingston**
Harry .... **Nigel Humphreys**
Richard .... **Michael Cochrane**

Creator/Writer **Alex Shearer**
Producer **John Howard Davies**

A new, ambitious female MP discovers the House of Commons is a bit of a jungle.

When newly elected Labour MP Jean Price takes her seat at Westminster, she quickly realizes that its operations are far from straightforward. In dealings with her Tory opposite number, Sir Godfrey Eagan, and her Labour whip, Norman, she soon learns to pick her friends carefully. Principles and practicality, she finds, are not always compatible. Advising her is her office share, Scottish MP Ken Miller, while hubby Geoff provides support at home.

No Place Like Home ★★

UK (BBC) Situation Comedy. BBC 1 1983–4; 1986–7

Arthur Crabtree .... **William Gaunt**
Beryl Crabtree .... **Patricia Garwood**
Nigel Crabtree .... **Martin Clunes**
Andrew Charleson
Paul Crabtree .... **Stephen Watson**
Tracy Crabtree .... **Dee Sadler**
Lorraine Codd .... **Beverley Adams**
Raymond Codd .... **Daniel Hill**
Vera Botting .... **Marcia Warren**
Ann Penfold
Trevor Botting .... **Michael Sharvell-Martin**
Roger Duff .... **Roger Martin**

Creator/Writer **Jon Watkins**
Producer **Robin Nash**

● ***A middle-aged couple's plans for a quiet life are ruined by children who refuse to leave home.***

Arthur and Beryl Crabtree have raised four children and now look forward to the day when their time, once again, will be their own. A second honeymoon is planned as the last of their offspring finally leaves home. However, their hopes are soon dashed as one by one the fledglings return to the nest, disillusioned with life in the outside world. For the children, there simply is no place like home. Eldest of the kids is Lorraine, who has married Raymond Codd but has quickly cast him aside. There are also Nigel, Paul and Tracy (and their assorted boy- and girlfriends), while the Crabtrees' domestic bliss is disturbed as well by their nosey neighbours, the Bottings, particularly the shrieking, animal-loving Vera. Arthur and Vera's husband, Trevor, often escape to the greenhouse when things become unbearable, seeking solace in a glass of home-made sherry.

Actress Beverley Adams, who played Lorraine, is the daughter of former CRACKERJACK hostess Jillian Comber.

No. 73/7T3 ★★

UK (TVS) Children's Entertainment. ITV 1982–8

Ethel Davis .... **Sandi Toksvig**
Dawn Lodge .... **Andrea Arnold**
Harry Stern .... **Nick Staverson**
Percy Simmons .... **Patrick Doyle**
Martin Edwards .... **Richard Addison**
Hazel Edwards .... **Jeannie Crowther**
Alec Simmons .... **Patrick Doyle**
Neil .... **Neil Buchanan**
Fred the Postman .... **Tony Aitken**
Kim .... **Kim Goody**
Tony Deal .... **Nick Wilton**
Eazi .... **Tony Hypolyte**
Maisie McConachie .... **Kate Capstick**
Jules .... **Julian Callaghan**
Nadia .... **Nadia de Lemeny**
Hamilton Dent .... **Richard Waites**

Creator/Producer **John Dale**

● ***Wacky characters welcome guests to their lively suburban house.***

Behind a bright red door daubed with a vibrant yellow number 73 lay a madcap world of Saturday morning entertainment. Rooms in the house were used for various purposes – interviewing celebrity guests, meeting animal expert David Taylor, staging live music from pop bands, etc. – or simply to introduce assorted drop-in items like cartoons and quizzes (including the Sandwich Quiz – a correct answer added another layer to the sandwich). The house also had residents: Ethel was the landlady (played at first as an old lady) and her lodgers at the outset were nutty Percy (later replaced by Scot Alec, played by the same actor), Dawn (a roller-skating fashion addict) and nephew Harry (a bit of a daredevil). With the Edwardses living next door and numerous regular callers, including conman Tony Deal and Fred the Postman, the hosts of the show enacted a mini-soap opera/sitcom. Stories revolved, for instance, around bits of the house falling apart and, notably, Ethel getting married. They also screened little 'am-dram' films of their own making, like *Roman Around* and the Spaghetti Western *Ricochet*. Ethel (Sandi Toksvig) left in 1986.

No. 73 was launched in the TVS area only in 1982, spreading to the ITV network a year later. An extra helping of the madness, *Sunday at No. 73*, was added in 1986 and the format of the original show was changed a year later. An outdoor Wild West set (replacing former homes in the Southampton and Maidstone studios) was introduced. The programme's title was then changed to *7T3* in 1988, but the show lasted only one series in this guise, giving way to the more conventional MOTORMOUTH.

No – That's Me over Here ★★

UK (Rediffusion/LWT) Situation Comedy. ITV 1967–8; 1970

Ronnie .... **Ronnie Corbett**
Laura .... **Rosemary Leach**
Henry .... **Henry McGee**
Secretary .... **Jill Mai Meredith**

Writers **Graham Chapman, Eric Idle, Barry Cryer**
Executive Producer **David Frost**
Producers **Bill Hitchcock, Marty Feldman**

● ***A middle-class commuter seeks social status.***

Life is never straightforward for Ronnie. The little man, smartly attired in three-piece suit, bowler hat, brolly and briefcase, aims high, but somehow always falls well short. This is particularly the case when he strives to outdo his patronizing next-door neighbour, Henry, who commutes alongside him to their City offices. Laura is Ronnie's long-suffering wife.

Although dropped after one season in 1968 when Rediffusion lost its ITV franchise, the series was picked up two years later by LWT. Corbett went on to play numerous other 'little man' roles, often accompanied, as here, by Rosemary Leach (see NOW LOOK HERE . . . !).

No Time for Sergeants ★★

US (Warner Brothers) Situation Comedy. ITV 1964–5 (US: ABC 1964–5)

Pte Will Stockdale .... **Sammy Jackson**
Sgt King .... **Harry Hickox**
Pte Ben Whitledge .... **Kevin O'Neal**
Millie Anderson .... **Laurie Sibbald**

Capt. Martin .... **Paul Smith**
Col. Farnsworth .... **Hayden Rorke**
Grandpa Jim Anderson .... **Andy Clyde**
Capt. Krupnick .... **George Murdock**
Pte Langdon .... **Michael McDonald**
Pte Blanchard .... **Greg Benedict**
Pte Neddick .... **Joey Tata**

Creator **Mac Hyman**
Executive Producer **William T. Orr**

● ***A hillbilly's homespun logic is more than a match for his military superiors.***

First a novel (by Mac Hyman), next a 1955 TV play, then a Broadway stage play (by Ira Levin) and a 1958 film (all with Andy Griffith in the lead): *No Time for Sergeants* had done the rounds by the time it became a small-screen sitcom. The story concerns simple country boy Will Stockdale who is enrolled in the US Air Force. It is not his scene at all. But the yokel constantly makes good by using his natural common sense and resourcefulness to outwit the cynical NCOs (especially Sgt King) and officers on the base. Ben Whitledge is Will's pal, Millie is Will's girlfriend and Jim is Millie's grandad.

Noah and Nelly ✶✶

UK (Roobarb Enterprises) Animation. BBC 1 1976

Voices **Richard Briers, Peter Hawkins**

Creator/Writer **Grange Calveley**

● ***Colourful adventures with the crew of an all-terrain ark.***

'All aboard the *SkylArk*!' From the same stable as ROOBARB (but without the famous wobbles) came *Noah and Nelly*, travelling the world in their highly adaptable vessel, the *SkylArk*. Usually wafting through the air beneath a big pink balloon, the *SkylArk* can also plummet to the depths of the ocean or find adventure on land, too, if required. It is shaped like a large spotted creature with two heads – very appropriate as most of the inmates are also two-headed. No messing about with 'two by two' on this ark: one animal with two heads saves space, although the two heads don't always agree with one another. Thus we are presented with Humphrey the pigs, George the rhinos, Brian the lions, Cynthia the snakes, Rose the elephants, Maureen the giraffes, William the hippos, Ahmed the camels, Ronald the gorillas, Cedric the crocodiles, Cyril the tigers, and Mildred the geese. Hosts to these wacky creatures are Nutty Noah, an old sea dog with a ginger beard bushing out from under his sou'wester, and Niggly Nelly, whose own rainwear conceals blue frizzy hair and, as often as not, a pair of versatile knitting needles. Whenever a problem presents itself, good old Nelly sets to with her needles and knits up a device that will provide the answer. As to where the *SkylArk* is destined to travel each day, that is often a matter of chance, as the ship's map is totally blank. If prodded, however, it will send the *SkylArk* to yet another intriguing destination. The titles of the five minute episodes all begin with 'During . . .' ('During a Stay at Reservoir Desert', 'During a Smashing Time', etc.).

Noah's Ark ✶✶

UK (Whitehall Films/Carlton) Drama. ITV 1997–8

Noah Kirby .... **Anton Rodgers**
Valerie Kirby .... **Angela Thorne**
Tom Kirby .... **Peter Wingfield**
Clare Somers .... **Orla Brady**
Mr Jasper .... **Frederick Treves**
Anna Lacey .... **Kate Alderton**
Nicky Baldwin .... **Chris Jury**
Cath Baldwin .... **Emily Morgan**
Jake Henshaw .... **Paul Warriner**
Simon Morton .... **Michael Carter**
Linda Morton .... **Cathryn Harrison**
Emma Pearson .... **Amy Robbins**

Creator **Johnny Byrne**
Writers **Johnny Byrne, Sam Lawrence, Joe Turner**
Producers **Sue Bennett-Urwin, Michael Whitehall**

● ***Animal welfare and family friction in a country setting.***

Noah Kirby is the vet in the Worcestershire village of Melton. He is vastly experienced but also has an old-fashioned, instinctive feel for animal medicine. His son, Tom, however, while he has all the right qualifications and is very methodical, is not a natural healer like his disorganized dad, so there is always tension between the two. Nevertheless, Noah needs help, as his wife Valerie points out, and Tom is the obvious person to assist, although it is only the arrival of local wildlife specialist Clare Somers that convinces Kirby junior to stick around this rural backwater. The pull of a career does eventually prove too strong and Tom leaves before the start of series two. His place is taken by motorbiking northerner Jake Henshaw, a trainee vet with a fear of spiders. Such comings and goings play second fiddle to the everyday drama of life in Melton – a place where badly treated horses, dog fights, poisoned fish, and occasionally more exotic stricken beasts inevitably mean cruel humans that Noah and his colleagues are determined to bring to book.

Noakes, John

(1934–)

Yorkshire-born actor whose greatest role was as the resident daredevil in BLUE PETER. Noakes joined the series in 1966, after acting in a number of TV series and working on stage as a 'feed' to Cyril Fletcher. He stayed with *Blue Peter* for 12 years, forming part of the series' golden-age trio with Valerie Singleton and Peter Purves. Accompanied by his playful collie, Shep ('Get down, Shep' became a catchphrase), he even secured his own spin-off series, *Go With Noakes*, in which he continued his hair-raising stunts such as climbing chimneys, leaping out of aircraft and tearing around in racing cars. Later, he worked for YTV and then for TV-am, on its Saturday morning show, but more or less retired to Majorca thereafter. In 1994 he was reunited with Valerie Singleton to present the over-50s afternoon magazine *Next* and returned again in 1999 as host of *Mad About Pets*. Noakes also hosted *The Dinosaur Trail*.

Nobbs, David

(1935–)

British novelist and screenwriter, responsible for series like THE FALL AND RISE OF REGINALD PERRIN, THE LEGACY OF REGINALD PERRIN, FAIRLY SECRET ARMY, A BIT OF A DO and *The Life and Times of Henry Pratt*. Among his other TV work have been scripts for THAT WAS THE WEEK THAT WAS, *The Roy Hudd Show*, THE FROST REPORT and *The Dick Emery Show* (all with the late Peter Tinniswood), plus *Sez Les*, THE TWO RONNIES and *Lance at Large* (for Lance Percival). Nobbs has also scripted *Shine a*

Light (with David McKellar and Peter Vincent), *Keep It in the Family* (with Peter Vincent), *Whoops Baghdad!* (with Sid Colin and David McKellar), *Dogfood Dan and the Carmarthen Cowboy*, THE GLAMOUR GIRLS, THE HELLO GOODBYE MAN, *The Sun Trap*, RICH TEA AND SYMPATHY, *Stalag Luft*, *Gentlemen's Relish* and adaptations of *Love on a Branch Line* and Malcolm Bradbury's *Cuts*.

Nobody's Perfect ★★

UK (LWT) Situation Comedy. ITV 1980; 1982

Bill Hooper	**Elaine Stritch**
Sam Hooper	**Richard Griffiths**
Henry Armstrong	**Moray Watson**
Liz Parker	**Kim Braden**
Sammy Parker	**Simon Nash**
Mrs Whicker	**Ruby Head**

Writer **Elaine Stritch**
Producer **Humphrey Barclay**

● ***Marriage second time around for an American woman and her English husband.***

Brash, middle-aged American Bill Hooper has been married for eight years. Her husband, Sam, is a dowdy English doctor and it is the ups and downs of their transatlantic relationship that take centre stage. In the background are the Hoopers' housekeeper, Mrs Whicker, and Liz, Sam's divorcée daughter from his previous marriage, with her seven-year-old son, Sammy. But, when home life becomes just too demanding, Sam escapes in the company of his friend and neighbour Henry Armstrong. The series was based on stories adapted by star Elaine Stritch herself from the scripts of the US sitcom *Maude*, a spin-off from ALL IN THE FAMILY. Title caricatures of the lead characters were drawn by US artist Al Hirschfeld and music was by Denis King.

Noddy

A familiar, contrived shot in news interviews where the interviewer is seen to nod in acknowledgement to the interviewee's answers. These shots are usually recorded at the end of the interview and then dropped in between questions during editing, to smooth over ugly breaks.

Noel's House Party ★★

UK (BBC) Entertainment. BBC 1 1991–9

Presenter **Noel Edmonds**

Executive Producer **Michael Leggo**
Producers **Michael Leggo, Jonathan Beazley, Guy Freeman, John McHugh, Philip Kampff**

● ***Live Saturday-evening mélange of gags and silly games.***

Following the demise of THE LATE, LATE BREAKFAST SHOW in 1986, Noel Edmonds returned to Saturday teatime telly in 1988 with *Noel Edmonds' Saturday Road Show*, in which he pretended to present each programme from a different and exotic location. The emphasis was on silly games, lots of laughs and a few hidden-camera tricks. Some elements he then took on to *Noel's House Party*, based at a mock stately home in the fictitious village of Crinkley Bottom. The show went from strength to strength, benefiting from Edmonds's coolness with live television. Among the favourite features were the Gotcha Oscars (in which a celebrity was conned into making a spoof TV programme or personal appearance), Grab a Grand (celebrities clutching at banknotes in a wind machine to earn money for a lucky viewer), NTV (hidden cameras in people's homes), The Pork Pie (a member of the audience trying to deny a shameful incident in his/her life), Wait Till I Get You Home (precocious kids telling secrets about their parents), and My Little Friend (where an inanimate object started talking to children). There were also little quizzes like The Lyric Game, surprise guests, psychedelic drenchings courtesy of the gunge tank, and the show's own soap opera, *Crinkley Bottom*, featuring the Weeks family, headed by Liszt and Newt publican George Weeks (played by Brian Croucher). Veteran DJ Tony Blackburn was seen as the butler on many occasions. One newcomer introduced by the show – Mr Blobby, a bloated pink dummy with yellow spots – went on to take the country by storm.

The last series of *Noel's House Party* were not happy ones for Noel Edmonds. In January 1998, he demanded that the show did not go out, as the quality was well below what he considered suitable (compilation programmes filled the slot for two weeks). Nevertheless, the *House Party* returned the following autumn, only to be finally cancelled in March 1999.

Noggin the Nog

See *Saga of Noggin the Nog, The*.

Norden, Denis

CBE (1922–)

British comedy writer, the former partner of Frank Muir and with him responsible for many TV scripts (see Frank Muir for their joint credits). Norden was also seen on the satire show, BBC-3, and, in the 1970s, hosted the nostalgia game, *Looks Familiar*. Since 1977 he has become best known for presenting television out-takes under the title IT'LL BE ALRIGHT ON THE NIGHT, as well as occasional programmes involving nostalgic/funny TV clips, under the title of *Denis Norden's Laughter File*. Norden announced his retirement from television in 2006

Norman, Barry

CBE (1933–)

The son of British film director Leslie Norman, Barry Norman was born into the world of cinema. Since leaving a position with the *Daily Mail*, he has brought his love of the silver screen into TV via programmes such as THE HOLLYWOOD GREATS and the long-running FILM series, which he quit in 1999 to work for Sky. He was, for a while in 1982, presenter of OMNIBUS and, in 1988, hosted the Olympic Games for Channel 4. His other series have included *The British Greats*, *The Rank Charm School*, *Barry Norman's Hong Kong*, *Barry Norman on Broadway/in Chicago/in Celebrity City*, plus work on LATE NIGHT LINE-UP. Trivia buffs will know that he once appeared with Morecambe and Wise and that he also directed an episode of THE SAINT. He is father of fellow film critic Emma Norman and TV presenter Samantha Norman.

North and South/North and South Book II ✱✱

US (ABC/David L. Wolper) Historical Drama. ITV 1986–7 (US: ABC 1985–6)
DVD: Warner Home Video

Orry Main	**Patrick Swayze**
George Hazard	**James Read**
Madeline Farbray/LaMotte/Main	**Lesley-Anne Down**
Frederick Douglass	**Robert Guillaume**
Maude Hazard	**Inga Swenson**
Stanley Hazard	**Jonathan Frakes**
Justin LaMotte	**David Carradine**
Clarissa Main	**Jean Simmons**
Brett Main/Hazard	**Genie Francis**
Ashton Main/Huntoon	**Terri Garber**
Virgilia Hazard	**Kirstie Alley**
Elkanah Bent	**Philip Casnoff**
Constance Flynn/Hazard	**Wendy Kilbourne**
Charles Main	**Lewis Smith**
James Huntoon	**Jim Metzler**
Madame Conti	**Elizabeth Taylor**
Isabel Hazard	**Wendy Fulton**
	Mary Crosby *(Book II)*
Billy Hazard	**John Stockwell**
	Parker Stevenson *(Book II)*
Abraham Lincoln	**Hal Holbrook** *(Book II)*
Jefferson Davis	**Lloyd Bridges** *(Book II)*
Miles Colbert	**James Stewart** *(Book II)*
Burdetta Halloran	**Morgan Fairchild** *(Book II)*
Rose Sinclair	**Linda Evans** *(Book II)*
Mrs Neal	**Olivia de Havilland** *(Book II)*
Congressman Sam Greene	**David Ogden Stiers** *(Book II)*
Dorothea Dix	**Nancy Marchand** *(Book II)*

Executive Producer **David L. Wolper**

● ***The American Civil War turns two friendly families into political enemies.***

America, just before the Civil War: two families find their lives intermingling, even though they are on opposite sides of the oncoming conflict. The Mains own a cotton plantation in South Carolina and are Confederates, while the Hazards are factory owners from Philadelphia and are defenders of the Union. But, politics apart, with skeletons rattling out of cupboards, and passionate love affairs all the rage, there is as much conflict in each household as there is likely to be on the battlefield in this *Gone with the Wind* clone, which has Hollywood names dropping by at every turn. A sequel, *North and South Book II*, was produced a year later, taking the story deep into the Civil War years. When patriarchs Orry Main and George Hazard – once interns together at West Point – become officers in the opposing armies, long-standing friendships come under extreme pressure. The saga concludes in a third instalment, *Heaven and Hell: North and South Book III* (US: ABC 1994), set during the post-war reconstruction. All were based on novels by John Jakes.

North Square ✱✱✱

UK (Company) Legal Drama. Channel 4 2000

Peter McLeish	**Phil Davis**
Alex Hay	**Rupert Penry-Jones**
Billy Guthrie	**Kevin McKidd**
Rose Fitzgerald	**Helen McCrory**
Morag Black	**Ruth Millar**
Wendy De Souza	**Kim Vithana**
Tom Mitford	**Dominic Rowan**
John (Bob)	**James Midgley**
Johnny Boy	**James Murray**
Dr Helen Fernyhough	**Victoria Smurfit**
Stevie Goode	**Sasha Behar**
Hussein Ali	**Robert Mountford**
Michael Marlowe	**Tony Monroe**
Leo Wilson	**Jack Fortune**

Creator **Peter Moffat**
Writers **Peter Moffat, Simon Block, Andrew Holden**
Producer **Alison Davis**

● ***The members of a new legal practice seek to win at all costs.***

The history of TV legal drama is littered with compassionate, brilliantly articulate barristers who fight to the death for the underdog simply because of their love of justice. *North Square* offers a rather different view of the wigged brief. In a world far removed from PERRY MASON, RUMPOLE OF THE BAILEY and KAVANAGH QC, the setting this time is the newly founded North Square Chambers in Leeds. Head of chambers is ambitious Wendy De Souza but the power behind the throne is the devious chief clerk, Peter McLeish. It is this chain-smoking, modern-day Machiavelli who brings in the business, rubbing shoulders alternatively with solicitors and villains in order to bag the best jobs, often sending his protégés, John and Johnny Boy, out to do his dirty work. There is seemingly no underhand method he won't employ if it ensures the chambers keeps rolling along – and he gets his cut. De Souza apart, leading the team of barristers are unscrupulous young turks Alex Hay and Billy Guthrie. The rights and wrongs of a case don't enter the equation for them, with truth playing a weak second fiddle to the chance to earn big money. Out of their wigs and gowns they could easily pass for some of the yobs they represent. Billy is a particular liability, a hothead who has a court case of his own to fight. Billy's partner, Rose Fitzgerald, is also part of the practice, returning to work just days after giving birth to their new baby. Morag is a trainee barrister, fighting to keep her job.

This smart, glossy drama was created by Peter Moffat, who was himself a barrister for eight years. Despite good reviews, and a handful of awards, just one series of ten 50-minute episodes was made.

Northern Exposure ✱✱✱

US (Finnegan-Pinchuk/Falahey/Austin Street/Cine-Nevada/Universal) Drama. Channel 4 1992–7 (US: CBS 1990–5)
DVD: Universal

Dr Joel Fleischman	**Rob Morrow**
Maggie O'Connell	**Janine Turner**
Maurice Minnifield	**Barry Corbin**
Chris Stevens	**John Corbett**
Ed Chigliak	**Darren E. Burrows**
Holling Vincoeur	**John Cullum**
Shelly Tambo	**Cynthia Geary**
Marilyn Whirlwind	**Elaine Miles**
Ruth-Anne Miller	**Peg Phillips**
Dr Phillip Capra	**Paul Provenza**
Michelle Capra	**Teri Polo**

Creators **Joshua Brand, John Falsey**

Executive Producers **John Falsey, Andrew Schneider**

● ***Events in the off-beat life of an isolated Alaskan town.***

Set in the fictional settlement of Cicely, Alaska, miles from civilization, *Northern Exposure* focuses on the interrelationships of its mildly eccentric townsfolk. At the forefront is Jewish New Yorker Joel Fleischman, a newly qualified doctor whose arrival heralds the start of the series. Much against his will, but obliged because the Alaskan state has subsidized his college fees, Fleischman moves to the town to take over the vacant local practice. His escape attempts are always thwarted, but Fleischman's real reason for staying on (though never admitting it) is his love-hate relationship with his landlady, Maggie O'Connell, the air-taxi pilot. However, messing with O'Connell is fraught with danger, as her five previous boyfriends all died in tragic circumstances. Others in the cast are Ed Chigliak, a young Native American film-buff, and Maurice Minnifield, former NASA astronaut and the town's patriarch. One-time adventurer Holling Vincoeur is proprietor of the local bar/restaurant (The Brick), which he runs with his teenage girlfriend, Shelly (whom he stole from Maurice). Chris 'In The Morning' Stevens is the town's philosophizing radio DJ and part-time minister, sensible Ruth-Anne runs the all-purpose shop and Marilyn is Fleischman's unflappable, monosyllabic Eskimo assistant. Occasional visitors to town are Adam, a sort of missing-link backwoodsman with a talent for *cordon bleu* cookery; his hypochondriac wife, Eve; Bernard, Chris's black half-brother; and Mort, a moose that wanders down the main street during the titles and credits.

Star Rob Morrow left the series after five years and was replaced by Paul Provenza and Teri Polo, as new doctor Phillip Capra and his journalist wife, Michelle. The series ended a few months later. With its stunning scenery and quirky feel, *Northern Exposure* was often likened to the spooky TWIN PEAKS, but with a much more wholesome atmosphere.

Norton, Graham

(Graham Walker; 1963–)

Camp Irish comedian and chat show host (*V Graham Norton*) whose big break came after standing in as presenter of *The Jack Docherty Show*, which led to his own talk show, *So Graham Norton*. Norton later switched to the BBC to present STRICTLY DANCE FEVER and *The Bigger Picture with Graham Norton*. He has also hosted the quizzes *Carnal Knowledge* and *Bring Me the Head of Light Entertainment*, played Father Noel Furlong in FATHER TED, narrated *Paul Daniels in a Black Hole* and fronted *Graham Goes to Dollywood*. Norton has also hosted a series for US TV called *The Graham Norton Effect*.

Not in Front of the Children ★★

UK (BBC) Situation Comedy. BBC 1 1967–70

Jennifer Corner .... **Wendy Craig**
Henry Corner .... **Paul Daneman**
Ronald Hines
Trudi Corner .... **Roberta Tovey**
Verina Greenlaw
Robin Corner .... **Hugo Keith-Johnston**
Amanda Corner .... **Jill Riddick**
Mary .... **Charlotte Mitchell**

Creator/Writer **Richard Waring**
Producer **Graeme Muir**

● ***A mother tries to cope with her troublesome family.***

Beginning as a 1967 COMEDY PLAYHOUSE presentation called *House in a Tree*, *Not in Front of the Children* was Wendy Craig's first excursion into the daffy, harassed-housewife role she was to perfect in later series like AND MOTHER MAKES THREE/FIVE and BUTTERFLIES. Here she holds together a middle-class household comprising her husband, Henry, and growing children, Trudi, Robin and Amanda, trying all the while to moderate between disagreeing parties. The series also ran on BBC radio.

Not on Your Nellie

See *Nearest and Dearest*.

Not Only . . . But Also . . . ★★★★

UK (BBC) Comedy. BBC 2 1965–6; 1970

Peter Cook, Dudley Moore

Creators **Peter Cook, Dudley Moore**
Producers **Joe McGrath, Dick Clement, James Gilbert**

● ***Innovative comedy revue, renowned for its offbeat humour.***

Not Only . . . But Also . . . resulted from a one-off show that the BBC commissioned from musician/comedian Dudley Moore. Enlisting the help of his *Beyond the Fringe* partner, Peter Cook, for a couple of sketches, Moore came up with a formula that worked, and the duo were rewarded with this series which initially ran on BBC 2 but was quickly repeated on BBC 1 to much acclaim. Mixing manic comedy with jazzy interludes, each programme began in the most unusual of settings, including underwater. One regular insert was Poets Cornered, an opportunity for comics like Spike Milligan and Barry Humphries to show off their spontaneous rhyming skills on pain of being dropped into a gunge tank (long before TISWAS popularized this form of punishment). For many viewers, however, the highlights were Cook and Moore's Pete and Dud routines, the so-called 'Dagenham Dialogues', in which they played two ordinary but rather dim blokes who discussed issues of the day, cultural matters and flights of fantasy over a sandwich or a pint. Although largely scripted, these sequences were prone to bouts of adlibbing, particularly from Cook. Like Poets Cornered, Pete and Dud found their echo in later comedy work, especially in Mel Smith and Griff Rhys Jones's head-to-head dialogues. Programmes ended with the closing song, 'Goodbye-ee', which, when released as a single, reached number 18 in the 1965 charts.

Although the series ended in 1966 after just two seasons, *Not Only . . . But Also . . .* was revived in 1970 as part of BBC 2's *Show of the Week* showcase, and in 1971 two programmes recorded in Australia were also screened by the BBC.

Not So Much a Programme, More a Way of Life ★★

UK (BBC) Comedy. BBC 1 1964–5

John Bird, Eleanor Bron, Michael Crawford, John Fortune, David Frost, Roy Hudd, P. J. Kavanagh, Cleo Laine

Producer **Ned Sherrin**

● ***Direct descendant of*** **THAT WAS THE WEEK THAT WAS.**

The ground-breakingly irreverent *That was the Week That Was*

was taken off the air in advance of the 1964 general election, and was eventually replaced by this similar show of topical satire, running three times a week. Equally aggressive in its sardonic treatment of politics and current affairs, it, in turn, gave way to a successor series, BBC-3, in 1965.

Not the Nine O'Clock News ***

UK (BBC) Comedy. BBC 2 1979–80; 1982
DVD: BBC

Mel Smith, Griff Rhys Jones, Pamela Stephenson, Rowan Atkinson, Chris Langham

Producers **Sean Hardie, John Lloyd**

Topical satire with a new generation of Fringe comedians.
Squared up against BBC 1's main bulletin, as its title suggested, this was BBC 2's spoof of current events, presented from a very familiar, newsy studio set. Interspersed with the 'headlines' were topical send-ups of anything from the proposed Advanced Passenger Train to Miss World, providing the young stars of *Not the Nine O'Clock News* with ample opportunity to show off the talents that were to make them household names in the decade to follow.

The team consisted of Pamela Stephenson (with her astute Angela Rippon take-offs), Rowan Atkinson (flexing his facial muscles in portrayals of aliens and other odd-bods), Mel Smith and fourth partner, Chris Langham. By series two, Langham had left, to be replaced by Griff Rhys Jones, who quickly forged a successful liaison with Smith.

Throughout, the humour ranged from honest, TWO RONNIES-ish gags to the positively outrageous. Dubbing spoof headlines over existing news footage was one running theme, mocking pop videos was another, and there was also biting satire, wicked parody and skits on other TV programmes like UNIVERSITY CHALLENGE, POINTS OF VIEW and even MONTY PYTHON'S FLYING CIRCUS. Among the writers were Richard Curtis, David Renwick, Clive Anderson, Andy Hamilton and Guy Jenkin. A selection of books, records and concerts followed to capitalize on the show's enormous success.

Notes and Queries with Clive Anderson **

UK (Celandine) Factual. BBC 2 1993

Presenters **Clive Anderson, Carol Vorderman**

Producer **Philippe Bassett**

Light-hearted 'answers' show.
Based on the *Guardian*'s 'Notes and Queries' column, this short-lived series provided answers to life's annoying little questions and worries. Clive Anderson, Carol Vorderman and celebrity guests explained to a studio audience how to survive in a plummeting lift, why water is wet, why there are no green mammals and other imponderable matters, eliciting yet more ludicrous enquiries in response.

Now Look Here . . . **

UK (BBC) Situation Comedy. BBC 1 1971; 1973

Ronnie .... **Ronnie Corbett**
Mother .... **Madge Ryan**
Gillian Lind
Laura .... **Rosemary Leach**
Keith .... **Richard O'Sullivan**
Col. Sutcliffe .... **Donald Hewlett**

Writers **Graham Chapman, Barry Cryer**
Producers **Bill Hitchcock, Douglas Argent**

A mummy's boy finds himself at odds with the world.
Seen off to work by his mum each morning, bachelor Ronnie lives in the suburban town of Bramley and works in an office where he rails against everything in sight (while, at the same time, pretending to be liberal-minded). His chief adversary is his colleague, Keith. In the second and last series, Ronnie finally flees the nest (though not entirely his mother's attentions) by marrying a girl called Laura. The story resumes in a spin-off series called *The Prince of Denmark* (1974), in which he and his new wife run a pub she has inherited.

NTL

NTL Incorporated was created in 2006 with the merger of cable TV providers NTL and Telewest. The company is the UK's largest cable operator and also supplies broadband and other communications services to domestic residences and businesses. NTL began life as International CableTel in 1993 and expanded by acquiring other cable operating companies around the UK. It changed its name to NTL in 1996 after taking over National Transcommunications Ltd. NTL's content division is known as Flextech (see also Telewest and Flextech).

NTSC

Standing for National Television System Committee (the body which introduced it as standard), NTSC is the system of television transmission used in the USA. It is based on 525 lines, unlike the British PAL system which operates on 625 lines. NTSC is also standard in Canada and Japan, among other countries.

Nurses **

US (Witt-Thomas-Harris/Touchstone) Situation Comedy. Channel 4 1992–6 (US: NBC 1991–4)

Nurse Sandy Miller .... **Stephanie Hodge**
Nurse Annie Roland .... **Arnetia Walker**
Nurse Julie Milbury .... **Mary Jo Keenen**
Nurse Greg Vincent .... **Jeff Altman**
Nurse Gina Cuevas .... **Ada Maris**
Dr Hank Kaplan .... **Kenneth David**
Kip Gilman
Paco Ortiz .... **Carlos LaCamara**
Dr Riskin .... **Florence Stanley**
Nurse Luke Fitzgerald .... **Markus Flanagan**
Jack Trenton .... **David Rasche**
Casey MacAfee .... **Loni Anderson**

Creator **Susan Harris**
Executive Producers **Paul Junger Witt, Tony Thomas, Susan Harris**

Five nurses chew the fat at a Miami hospital.
Set in the Miami Community Medical Center, this verbal comedy focuses on the staff of the third floor nurses' station,

picking up with the arrival of new, scalpel-tongued, divorcée nurse Sandy Miller. Around her, Sandy discovers an array of wacky characters, from the neurotic nurse with various phobias (Julie Milbury) to an insubordinate and rather dangerous male nurse (Greg Vincent). In charge of the section is harassed mum Annie Roland; Gina is the plain-speaking immigrant, Paco is the flunky who knows everything that is going on, Dr Hank Kaplan is the industrious but financially embarrassed medic and Riskin is the grumpy doctor. Later arrivals are Luke Fitzgerald, who prefers his own company, and Jack Trenton, a convicted criminal, doing community service as an orderly. In the final season, the hospital is sold and a new manager, Casey MacAfee is appointed. Like already successful comedies from the same stable (and set in the same city), The GOLDEN GIRLS and EMPTY NEST (with some cross-over appearances from stars of those shows), *Nurses* relies more on the dialogue between the main characters – and particularly woman-talk – than farcical action.

Nuts in May ✳✳✳

UK (BBC) Drama. BBC 1 1976
DVD: Meridian Entertainment

Keith .... **Roger Sloman**
Candice Marie .... **Alison Steadman**
Ray .... **Anthony O'Donnell**
Honky .... **Sheila Kelley**
Finger .... **Stephen Bill**
Miss Beale .... **Richenda Carey**
Quarryman .... **Eric Allan**

Writer **Mike Leigh**
Producer **David Rose**

● ***A country break proves stressful for a city couple.***

When city dwellers think it's a good idea to leave the rat race (at least for a while) and take to the country, all too rarely do things turn out as planned, as Mike Leigh's PLAY FOR TODAY demonstrates. Shot on film in documentary style, with actors working from a script originally based on improvisation (as in Leigh's later ABIGAIL'S PARTY), *Nuts in May* tells of Keith and Candice Marie's short break in rural Dorset. Banjo-plucking Keith is a pompous council bureaucrat; guitar-strumming wife Candice Marie is considerably more introvert, an earth-child pacifist and vegetarian. Optimistically pitching their tent on a basic campsite, and 'treating' fellow campers to their music, they look forward to savouring the country air and tranquillity, but friction with locals, other visitors and not least between themselves results in a holiday from hell. Leigh also directs, with his then wife, Alison Steadman, starring as Candice Marie.

Nutt House, The ✳✳

US (Brooksfilms) Situation Comedy. BBC 2 1989 (US: NBC 1989)

Reginald J. Tarkington .... **Harvey Korman**
Ms Frick .... **Cloris Leachman**
Mrs Edwina Nutt .... **Cloris Leachman**
Freddy .... **Mark Blankfield**
Charles Nutt III .... **Brian McNamara**
Sally Lonnaneck .... **Molly Hagan**

Creators/Executive Producers **Mel Brooks, Alan Spencer**

● ***A New York hotel lives up to its portentous name.***

This typically wacky comedy from Mel Brooks and Alan Spencer is set in a once grand, now crummy, New York hotel, called appropriately Nutt House. Mrs Edwina Nutt is the doddery owner but its incompetent manager is Reginald Tarkington, 'assisted' by lusty German housekeeper Ms Frick (a second role for Cloris Leachman). Charles is Mrs Nutt's dopey playboy son, while Freddy is the short-sighted lift boy and Sally is Mrs Nutt's secretary. Together they ensure guests have a stay to remember – for all the wrong reasons. However, the riotous slapstick assault proved too much for US audiences and the show was cancelled after only ten episodes had been made.

Ny-Lon ✳✳

UK (Touchpaper) Drama. Channel 4 2004

Edie Miller .... **Rashida Jones**
Michael Antonioni .... **Stephen Moyer**
Astrid .... **Rachel Milner**
Lauren Antonioni .... **Emily Corrie**
Raph .... **Navin Chowdhry**
Luke .... **David Rogers**
Katherine .... **Christine Adams**
Tabitha .... **Anna Wilson Jones**
Kristin .... **Marit Kile**
Seth .... **Bo Poraj**
Callum .... **Finlay Robertson**
Angelo .... **James Bird**
Kenny .... **Jonah Lotan**
Claudia .... **Pandora Colin**
Marlon .... **Kirris Riviere**
Gemma .... **Claire Nicholson**
Tara .... **Lucianne McEvoy**
Rachna .... **Stephanie Street**

Creators **Simon Burke, Anya Camilleri**
Writers **Simon Burke, Gary Parker**
Producer **Peter Norris**

● ***A London banker and a New York sales girl fight to make a trans-atlantic romance work.***

Long-distance love affairs are always tricky, but when they extend the breadth of the Atlantic they can screw up your life – as young lovers Mike and Edie soon discover. Edie is an American girl, a sales assistant in a record store and part-time literacy teacher, who is on a trip to London when her handbag is stolen. City broker Mike rides to the rescue and romance blossoms. When she returns to New York the reality sinks in. How do they manage to maintain their relationship when work, opinionated friends, awkward family members, different cultures and, particularly, 3,000 miles of ocean lie between them? Astrid is Edie's hard-headed flat-mate in the Big Apple, Lauren is Mike's student sister, and Kristin is his ex-girlfriend, now pregnant. Luke is Edie's former feller. This fast-moving, slick drama, beautifully shot on location in the two cities, offers a clever use of time shifts and narratives. Co-creator Simon Burke, who wrote all but one of the seven episodes, was inspired by a similar relationship of his own.

Nye, Simon

(1958–)

British novelist and screenwriter, a former translator and the creator of MEN BEHAVING BADLY, FRANK STUBBS PROMOTES, IS IT LEGAL?, the one-off comedy drama *True Love* (which led to the series MY WONDERFUL LIFE), HOW DO YOU WANT ME?, BEAST, THE SAVAGES, WILD WEST, HARDWARE and CARRIE AND BARRY. Nye also co-wrote the comedy drama *The Last Salute* with Tim Binding. Other work includes the single dramas *Beauty*, *Tunnel of Love* and *Open Wide*, the animation *Pride*, TV pantomimes and recent adaptations of THE RAILWAY CHILDREN, *Pollyanna* and *My Family and Other Animals*.

NYPD Blue ★★★

US (Steven Bochco) Police Drama. Channel 4 1994–2000; 2003–4 (US: ABC 1993–2005)
DVD: Fox

Det. John Kelly .... **David Caruso**
Det. Andy Sipowicz .... **Dennis Franz**
Lt./Capt. Arthur Fancy .... **James McDaniel**
Laura Hughes Kelly .... **Sherry Stringfield**
Officer Janice Licalsi .... **Amy Brenneman**
Officer/Det./Sgt James Martinez .... **Nicholas Turturro**
Asst District Attorney Sylvia Costas .... **Sharon Lawrence**
Det. Greg Medavoy .... **Gordon Clapp**
Donna Abandando .... **Gail O'Grady**
Det. Bobby Simone .... **Jimmy Smits**
Det. Diane Russell .... **Kim Delaney**
Det. Adrienne Lesniak .... **Justine Miceli**
Det. Jill Kirkendall .... **Andrea Thompson**
John Irvin .... **Bill Brochtrup**
Det. Danny Sorenson .... **Rick Schroder**
James Sinclair .... **Daniel Benzali**
Det. Baldwin Jones .... **Henry Simmons**
Theo Sipowicz .... **Austin Majors**
Asst District Attorney Valerie Haywood .... **Garcelle Beauvais-Nilon**
Det. Connie McDowell .... **Charlotte Ross**
Lt. Tony Rodriguez .... **Esai Morales**
Det. John Clark Jr .... **Mark-Paul Gosselaar**
Det. Rita Ortiz .... **Jacqueline Obradors**

Creators **Steven Bochco, David Milch**

Executive Producers **Steven Bochco, David Milch, Mark Tinker, Bill Clark, Gregory Hoblit**

● ***The stresses and strains of policing the Big Apple.***

This classy police drama devotes as much attention to the personal lives of the cops of New York's 15th Precinct as to their heroic anti crime activities. At the front of the action is red-haired, fast achiever John Kelly, who still has a soul despite 15 years of gritty police work and continues to carry a torch for his ex-wife, Laura, a lawyer, even though he becomes dangerously involved with fellow cop Janice Licalsi. Under Kelly's wing is streetwise trainee cop James Martinez. Kelly is partnered by overweight alcoholic Andy Sipowicz, who is forced to reappraise his life after being shot while in the company of a prostitute and who eventually marries assistant DA Sylvia Costas. In the background is by-the-book station boss Lt. Fancy, unreliable officer Greg Medavoy and attractive clerk Donna Abandando. Kelly leaves in the second season and is replaced by Bobby Simone, a sensitive cop still grieving after the death of his wife. Simone is kicked off the force for a while but returns, cleared of accusations made against him, before sensationally dying of a heart attack. His replacement is youthful Danny Sorenson, a keen ex-drugs cop, who becomes a surrogate son for Sipowicz, whose own son has been murdered. When Sorenson goes missing, he is replaced as Sipowicz's partner by eager young cop John Clarke. At the same time, Fancy is succeeded by new station supremo Tony Rodriguez.

Hand-held camerawork adds an air of authenticity to recordings, and the series received a record 26 Emmy nominations for its first year, this despite being boycotted by dozens of TV stations because of its much-touted bad language and graphic sex (neither of which proved heavy by British standards). Sadly, as for numerous other quality American shows, *NYPD Blue*'s UK audience slipped away and it ended up in a midnight graveyard slot. The series ended in the USA in 2005, but it had already run out of time on Channel 4.

Oater

A familiar term for a television Western, much in use in the 1960s when series like BONANZA, RAWHIDE, WAGON TRAIN and LARAMIE were the order of the day. Another nickname is 'horse opera'.

O'Brien, Richard

(Richard Smith; 1942–)

British actor, writer and presenter with a trademark shaven head. He is probably best known for his work as host of Channel 4's game show THE CRYSTAL MAZE, though he has also been seen in series like THE RACING GAME, *Rushton's Illustrated*, ROBIN OF SHERWOOD (druid Gulnar) and the kids' fantasy *The Ink Thief*. O'Brien also wrote a 1977 PREMIERE film, *A Hymn from Jim*. The theatre remains important, and among the plays and musicals he has scripted has been *The Rocky Horror Show*.

O.C., The ★★

US (Twentieth Century-Fox) Drama. Channel 4 2004–
(US: Fox 2003–)
DVD: Warner Home Video

Ryan Atwood	**Benjamin McKenzie**
Sandy Cohen	**Peter Gallagher**
Kirsten Cohen	**Kelly Rowan**
Seth Cohen	**Adam Brody**
Marissa Cooper	**Mischa Barton**
Jimmy Cooper	**Tate Donovan**
Julie Cooper/Nichol	**Melinda Clarke**
Summer Roberts	**Rachel Bilson**
Luke Ward	**Chris Carmack**
Dawn Atwood	**Daphne Ashbrook**
Caleb Nichol	**Alan Dale**
Rachel	**Bonnie Somerville**
Anna Stern	**Samaire Armstrong**
Taryn	**Kim Oja**
Oliver Trask	**Taylor Handley**
Hailey Nichol	**Amanda Righetti**
Theresa	**Navi Rawat**
Lindsay Gardner	**Shannon Lucio**
Alex Kelly	**Olivia Wilde**
Zach	**Michael Cassidy**
Trey Atwood	**Bradley Stryker**
	Logan Marshall-Green

Creator **Josh Schwartz**
Executive Producers **Josh Schwartz, McG, Bob DeLaurentis, Dave Bartis, Doug Liman**

● ***A young tearaway adds a new dimension to a prosperous Californian settlement.***

Sixteen-year-old Ryan Atwood meets soft-touch lawyer Sandy Cohen while in police custody, having attempted to steal a car. Sandy offers to help Ryan, an offer which turns into providing a bed for the night, something Sandy's wife, Kirsten, is not too happy about. The youth immediately recognizes where he's well off. Newport Beach in Orange County ('The O. C.'), California, is where the rich and beautiful live. Ryan is particularly struck by the girl next door, Marissa Cooper, and he soon gets on well with the Cohen's teenage son, Seth, too. It's not long before Ryan is a fixture in the Cohen house and it's only a matter of time before he becomes legally adopted by the family. Ryan may be a wild one but he's good news for the rather insecure Seth, whose eyes are opened to the exciting side of life by his new brother. Marissa's best friend, Summer Roberts, is the girl Seth desperately wants to get close to, but she's a party animal and is hard to pin down.

But it's not just the kids who dominate this glossy soap opera. Kirsten and Sandy are no longer seeing eye to eye, largely because Kirsten's career as an architect has drawn her apart from her family. It's even worse next door, where Marissa's dad, Jimmy, is in deep financial doo-doo. When his marriage to Julie breaks down, she turns to the wealthiest man in town, Caleb Nichol, who happens to be Kristen's dad. And so the drama unfolds, with new, temporary characters (like Hailey, Kirsten's disruptive sister, and Trey, Ryan's elder brother) arriving to stir up the pot.

Described as 'Beverly Hills 90210 with an edge', this teen soap proved a big hit for the Fox network in the USA. In the UK, episodes were seen first on the digital channel E4, a few days before airing on Channel 4.

O'Connor, Carroll

(1924–2001)

In his guise of bigot Archie Bunker in ALL IN THE FAMILY, American actor Carroll O'Connor was the USA's Alf Garnett. The role came in O'Connor's middle age, after decades of treading the boards in Europe as well as America. His first TV appearances arrived in series like THE RIFLEMAN, BONANZA, VOYAGE TO THE BOTTOM OF THE SEA and I SPY, playing rather modest roles. But in 1968 he starred in a risky pilot for *All in the Family*, which became a full series three years later and, with its sequel, *Archie Bunker's Place*, ran for 12 years in all. In contrast, in 1988, O'Connor was cast as Bill Gillespie, Chief of Police, in the TV version of IN THE HEAT OF THE NIGHT. He was also seen in TV movies and among his last roles were parts in the sitcom *Mad About You* and the drama series *Party of Five*.

O'Connor, Des

(1932–)

London-born singer, comedian, presenter and talk show host who came to the fore in the 1950s in series like SPOT THE TUNE. *The Des O'Connor Show* (for ATV, featuring comic Jack Douglas in support) ran through most of the 1960s (a time when Des was notching up a string of hit singles) and O'Connor's other series for ITV in the 1960s and 1970s included *Des* and *Des O'Connor Entertains*. O'Connor then switched to the BBC for *Des O'Connor Tonight*, a chat/variety show, but that, too, transferred to ITV. He was once compere of SUNDAY NIGHT AT THE LONDON PALLADIUM and, in more recent years, has hosted a revival of TAKE YOUR PICK, the talent show *Pot of Gold*, *The National Lottery – on the Spot* and *Today with Des and Mel* (with Melanie Sykes). Despite being mercilessly pilloried for his singing by Morecambe and Wise, O'Connor has remained one of the UK's favourite entertainers.

O'Connor, Tom

(1939–)

Liverpudlian comic who found his niche as a variety and game show presenter in the 1970s and 1980s. A former teacher, O'Connor broke out of the nightclub circuit and into the big time after winning OPPORTUNITY KNOCKS. He also appeared on THE COMEDIANS before compering *Wednesday at Eight* and *London Night Out*. One element of these was the NAME THAT TUNE quiz, which soon became a series in its own right, with O'Connor at the helm. He has also had his own series, *Tom O'Connor*, fronted *Night Out at the London Casino* and has been seen on numerous panel games (many as host), including *Zodiac, Password, Gambit, I've Got a Secret, Cross Wits* and *A Question of Entertainment*. O'Connor has also appeared in DOCTORS, playing Father Tom.

Odd Couple, The ***

US (Paramount) Situation Comedy. ITV 1971–3 (US: ABC 1970–5)

Felix Unger .... **Tony Randall**
Oscar Madison .... **Jack Klugman**
Murray Greshner .... **Al Molinaro**
Speed .... **Garry Walberg**
Vinnie .... **Larry Gelman**
Roy .... **Ryan McDonald**
Dr Nancy Cunningham .... **Joan Hotchkis**
Gloria Unger .... **Janis Hansen**
Blanche Madison .... **Brett Somers**
Myrna Turner .... **Penny Marshall**
Miriam Welby .... **Elinor Donahue**

Executive Producers **Garry K. Marshall, Sheldon Keller**
Producer **Tony Marshall**

● ***Two incompatible friends share an apartment and get on each other's nerves.***

Felix Unger and Oscar Madison used to be childhood friends. They are brought together again when both are divorced, and they decide to share Oscar's apartment in Manhattan. The only trouble is that the two are totally incompatible. Felix is a hard-working, cultured photographer, a hypochondriac with an over-the-top need to see everything in its place and lead an organized life. In contrast, Oscar is a slobbish sportswriter for the *New York Herald*. He lives sloppily, eats messily and litters his room with empty beer cans and dirty laundry. Not surprisingly, there is a great deal of friction between the two 'friends'.

Other regulars are Oscar's Thursday night poker partners, Murray the inept cop, Speed and Vinnie. Myrna is Oscar's secretary, and Nancy Cunningham is his sporty girlfriend in early episodes. Felix's girlfriend is Miriam Welby, who lives in the same building, but he is later reunited with his wife, Gloria, and when he moves out to live with her again the series ends, leaving Oscar to revel in his regained squalid freedom.

Based on Neil Simon's successful comedy, and the 1968 film starring Jack Lemmon and Walter Matthau, the series also generated a cover version of its own, entitled *The New Odd Couple*, with the same characters now played by black actors (Ron Glass as Felix, Demond Wilson as Oscar). There was also an animated adaptation, featuring a tidy cat and a lazy dog, entitled *The Oddball Couple*.

Odd Man, The **

UK (Granada) Police Drama. ITV 1962–3

Steve Gardiner .... **Edwin Richfield**
Chief Insp. Gordon .... **Moultrie Kelsall**
DS Swift .... **Keith Barron**
Judy Gardiner .... **Sarah Lawson**
South .... **Christopher Guinee**
Chief Insp. Rose .... **William Mervyn**
Anne Braithwaite .... **Sarah Lawson**
Ruth Jenkins .... **Anna Cropper**

Creator **Edward Boyd**
Producer **Stuart Latham**

● ***Weirdly atmospheric detective series, introducing the character of Chief Inspector Rose.***

The Odd Man initially centres on five main characters, all involved in or around the murky world of crime. These are Steve Gardiner, a theatrical agent and part-time private eye; his wife, Judy; grim Chief Inspector Gordon; his amiable colleague DS Swift; and a mysterious villain named South. Although each programme is self-contained, the episodes run in a serial format, culminating in the murder of Judy by South, and Steve's pursuit of her killer.

Although this series is credited with bringing Inspector Rose (later of IT'S DARK OUTSIDE and MR ROSE) to our screens, in fact he does not appear until the second season, taking over from Gordon and teaming up with Swift. He is also a rather different character from the one seen later, considerably more unpleasant. Actress Sarah Lawson, although written out in the first season, returns in the third as Judy's twin sister, and the cult series continues its bizarre tales of crime and intrigue.

Creator Edward Boyd specialized in husband-and-wife sleuths, having written such stories for BBC Radio before moving to television.

Oddie, Bill

OBE (1941–)

Cambridge Footlights graduate, a contemporary of his writing partners, Tim Brooke-Taylor and Graeme Garden. Lancashire-born Oddie broke into television by writing for THAT WAS THE WEEK THAT WAS and through appearances on BBC-3 and then, more significantly, AT LAST THE 1948 SHOW, *Twice a Fortnight* and *Broaden Your Mind*. He also contributed scripts to HARK AT BARKER, but it was when he joined Brooke-Taylor and Garden in THE GOODIES in 1970 that viewers really began to take notice. Oddie was seen as the hairy, aggressive, cynical member of the trio of do-gooders. He also wrote the music for the show. With Garden, Oddie had already scripted episodes of DOCTOR IN THE HOUSE (he went on to write for some of its sequels) and when *The Goodies* ended, the two penned the short-lived sitcom *Astronauts*. Oddie has since brought his love of bird watching and the wide outdoors to TV in series like *Birding with Bill Oddie, Bill Oddie Goes Wild, Dinosaur Island, Wild in Your Garden with Bill Oddie, Britain Goes Wild with Bill Oddie, Bill Oddie in Tiger Country* and *Spring Watch*. He also co-wrote (with second wife Laura Beaumont), and starred in, the comedies *From the Top* (William Worthington) and *The Bubblegum Brigade* (William), fronted the kids' show *The Saturday Banana*, and hosted the religious celebration *Festival*, as well as *Bill Oddie's History Hunt*. Other credits have included the drama TITMUSS REGAINED (Hector Bolitho Jones) and *Natural World*, which he has narrated. He is the father of actress Kate Hardie.

Ofcom

(Office of Communications)

The regulatory body set up in 2003 to take over the functions of the Independent Television Commission (see ITC), also handling the former remit of the Broadcasting Standards Commission, Oftel, the Radio Authority and the Radio Communications Agency. In broad terms, it is Ofcom's job to regulate the quality, variety, decency and legality of broadcasting in the UK.

Office, The ★★★★

UK (BBC) Situation comedy. BBC 2 2001–3
DVD: BBC

David Brent	**Ricky Gervais**
Gareth Keenan	**Mackenzie Crook**
Tim Canterbury	**Martin Freeman**
Dawn Tynsley	**Lucy Davis**
Jennifer Taylor-Clarke	**Stirling Gallacher**
Malcolm	**Robin Hooper**
Donna	**Sally Bretton**
Chris 'Finchy' Finch	**Ralph Ineson**
Karen Roper	**Nicola Cotter**
Keith Bishop	**Ewan MacIntosh**
Neil Godwin	**Patrick Baladi**
Rachel	**Stacy Roca**
Trudy	**Rachel Isaac**

Writers **Ricky Gervais, Stephen Merchant**
Producer **Ash Atalia**

● ***Spoof documentary set in paper products company.***
David Brent is the regional manager of Wernham Hogg, a paper firm with an office on Slough Industrial Estate. Brent considers himself the ultimate professional manager, 12 years in the business and a man who knows when to clown around with his juniors and when to lay down the law – that's what he tells the hand-held cameras in this fly-on-the-wall send-up. The truth is that Brent is a prat of the highest order, an untrustworthy, sad individual for whom no one in the office has the slightest respect, except his weaselly number two, Gareth Keenan. Gareth, who claims to be a former Territorial Army volunteer, is anoraky, fastidious, and similarly derided by his colleagues. His chief antagonizer is frustrated sales rep Tim Canterbury. Dawn is the receptionist who fancies Tim (the attraction is mutual but never acted upon), and Finchy is Brent's sexist boozing partner. These are the key members of a depressed office where no one has achieved, or is ever likely to achieve, their career goals. The series documents life in the company as the threat of branch closure and mass redundancy rears its ugly head. In series two, the Slough office is still open but the rival Swindon branch has moved in and Brent now answers to former Swindon boss Neil Godwin. The whole story is wrapped up in a two-part Christmas special (shown in 2003), in which Brent (now redundant) infiltrates the office party and there's a moving twist in the Dawn/Tim relationship. The theme song is 'Handbags and Gladrags'.

Star Ricky Gervais – who wrote and directed the series with Stephen Merchant – also appeared as Brent in a short film for BBC 1's coverage of the 2002 FA Cup Final. In 2005 BBC 3 broadcast *The Office: an American Workplace*, a US adaptation of the concept, starring Steve Carell as Brent's transatlantic equivalent, Michael Scott, manager of paper company Dunder Mifflin, based in Scranton, Pennsylvania.

Office of Strategic Services

See *OSS*.

Ogilvy, Ian

(1943–)

British actor whose major TV role has been as Simon Templar in RETURN OF THE SAINT. Ogilvy was also seen as Rupert in *The Liars*, Lawrence Kirbridge in UPSTAIRS, DOWNSTAIRS, Drusus in I, CLAUDIUS and Richard Maddison in the comedy *Tom, Dick and Harriet*. Ogilvy also featured in dramas like *The Spoils of Poynton*, *Moll Flanders*, ANNA KARENINA, and the three-part thriller *Menace Unseen*. Other credits include the US series *Generations* (Reginald Hewitt) and *Malibu Shores*, plus smaller parts in the likes of THE AVENGERS, STRANGE REPORT, RIPPING YARNS, ROBIN OF SHERWOOD and DIAGNOSIS MURDER.

O'Grady, Paul

(1955–)

British drag comedian and chat show host, the real identity of Lily Savage, the towering peroxide bombshell from Birkenhead. As his brassy, ex-prostitute creation, which he launched in a London pub, appropriating his mother's maiden name, he has appeared in countless TV programmes, including THE BIG BREAKFAST, *The Lily Savage Show*, BROOKSIDE (guest), *Lily Live* and as host of the revival of BLANKETY BLANK. Out of his famous disguise, O'Grady made his TV debut in THE BILL. He has also fronted the documentary series *Paul O'Grady's Orient* and *Paul O'Grady's America*, and hosted *Screen Tests of the Stars* and *Outtake TV*. He has also starred as Ray in the bingo sitcom *Eyes Down*, and has been given his own daily chat shows, *The Paul O'Grady Show* (ITV 1 2004–5) and *The New Paul O'Grady Show* (Channel 4 2006–).

Oh Boy! ★★★

UK (ABC/ATV) Pop Music. ITV 1958–9; 1979–80

Hosts **Tony Hall, Jimmy Henny**

Creator **Jack Good**
Producers **Jack Good, Ken O'Neill**
Executive Producer **Richard Leyland**

● ***Britain's first total rock 'n' roll programme.***
Oh Boy! was created by TV pop pioneer Jack Good after a dispute had led him to pull out of his earlier success, SIX-FIVE SPECIAL. Whereas the latter had featured magazine items and intrusions of other kinds of music, *Oh Boy!* was pure rock 'n' roll and, as direct competition on Saturday nights, hastened *Six-Five Special*'s demise. It was the programme that made a star out of Cliff Richard, who had been installed by Good as the featured artist; and other regular contributions came from Marty Wilde, the Vernons Girls, the Dallas Boys, Cherry Wainer, Red Price, Tony Hall, Ronnie Carroll and Neville Taylor and the Cutters. Harry Robinson's band (which provided the music) was remodelled by Good into Lord Rockingham's XI and went on to have chart hits of its own (most notably 'Hoots Mon' in 1958). All programmes were staged at the Hackney Empire. The programme was briefly revived by ATV in 1979–80, with Les Gray of Mud, Alvin Stardust, Freddie 'Fingers' Lee, Joe Brown and Shakin' Stevens among the regulars.

Oh Brother!/Oh Father! ✱✱

UK (BBC) Situation Comedy. BBC 1 1968–70/1973
DVD: DD Home Entertainment

Brother/Father Dominic .... **Derek Nimmo**
Father Anselm .... **Felix Aylmer**
Father Matthew .... **Derek Francis**
Master of the Novices .... **Colin Gordon** *(Oh Brother!)*
Father Harris .... **Laurence Naismith** *(Oh Father!)*
Mrs Carr .... **Pearl Hackney** *(Oh Father!)*
Walter .... **David Kelly** *(Oh Father!)*

Writers **David Climie, Austin Steele**
Producers **Duncan Wood, Harold Snoad, Johnny Downes** *(Oh Brother!)*, **Graeme Muir** *(Oh Father!)*

● ***A bumbling novice is accepted into a priory.***
Oh Brother! sees the return of Derek Nimmo's plummy but good-hearted cleric character, first exhibited as Noote in ALL GAS AND GAITERS. This time his identity is Brother Dominic, a sincere but hapless novice at Mountacres Priory. Dominic is eventually 'promoted' to Father Dominic for a follow-up series, *Oh Father!*, in which he leaves the monastery to become curate to Father Harris.

Oh Doctor Beeching! ✱✱✱

UK (BBC) Comedy. BBC 1 1996–7
DVD: DD Home Entertainment

Jack Skinner .... **Paul Shane**
Ethel Schumann .... **Su Pollard**
Cecil Parkin .... **Jeffrey Holland**
May Skinner .... **Julia Deakin**
Vera Plumtree .... **Barbara New**
Harry Lambert .... **Stephen Lewis**
Arnold .... **Ivor Roberts**
Ralph .... **Perry Benson**
Percy .... **Terry John**
Gloria Skinner .... **Lindsay Grimshaw**
Wilfred Schumann .... **Paul Aspden**
Amy Matlock .... **Tara Daniels**
Mr Orkindale .... **Richard Spendlove**

Creators **David Croft, Richard Spendlove**
Producers **David Croft, Charles Garland**

● ***The staff of a steam railway station fight for its survival.***
Set at rural Hatley station (real-life Arley, on the Severn Valley Railway), *Oh Doctor Beeching!* was another of David Croft's nostalgic ensemble comedies, this time penned in collaboration with former railwayman Richard Spendlove. The time is 1963, with Beeching's swingeing cuts to the railway network about to come into force. Fearful for their jobs, the station crew do their best to keep things alive. They are headed by new-broom station master Cecil Parkin; ticket collector/announcer Jack Skinner, whose days of scamming are coming to an end; Skinner's wife, May, who runs the station buffet and, it seems, is one of Cecil's old flames; the Skinners' teenage daughter (possibly Cecil's), Gloria; and ticket clerk Ethel Schumann. Ethel's dim son, Wilfred (his US serviceman dad having long disappeared), lends a hand here and there, while miserable Harry Lambert (a revival of Stephen Lewis's Blakey character from ON THE BUSES) mans the signal box, cuts the men's hair and grows vegetables all at the same time. Engine-driver's widow Vera Plumtree lives in one of the cottages behind the station, next door to Ethel and Wilfred. Regular callers at the station are engine-driver Arnold, his hopeless fireman, Ralph, and guard Percy.

The series followed a 1995 pilot episode, in which May was played by Sherrie Hewson. Partly rerecorded, it was transmitted again as the first episode of series one a year later.

Oh Happy Band! ✱

UK (BBC) Situation Comedy. BBC 1 1980

Harry Worth .... **Harry Worth**
Mr Herbert .... **Jonathan Cecil**
Mr Braithwaite .... **John Horsley**
Mr Sowerby .... **Billy Burden**
Mr Pilgrim .... **Tom Mennard**
Mr Giles .... **Tony Sympson**
Mrs Draper .... **Jan Holden**
Glenda .... **Moira Foot**
Vicar .... **Harold Bennett**
Mrs Tickford .... **Peggyann Clifford**
Miss Mayhew .... **Margaret Clifton**

Writers **Jeremy Lloyd, David Croft**
Producer **David Croft**

● ***A band leader also conducts community affairs.***
Harry Worth is the leader of the brass band in the little town of Nettlebridge. So small is the community that this dithering bungler seems to be at the heart of all its activities. Wanting the best for his troupe of musicians, he gets them to record a track for Terry Wogan's radio programme, with typical lack of success, and even tries to enter the band in the *Guinness Book of Records* by playing at high altitude in a series of hot air balloons. But his responsibilities don't end with band life, as he becomes ringleader of protests against the construction of a new airport on the town's doorstep. Despite scripts and production from Jeremy Lloyd and David Croft, this series only ran to six episodes. It appears that Harry Worth's era had now passed (*Oh Happy Band!* proved to be his last sitcom). Music provision was by the Aldershot Brass Ensemble.

Oh No It's Selwyn Froggitt/ Selwyn ✱✱

UK (Yorkshire) Situation Comedy. ITV 1976–7/1978

Selwyn Froggitt .... **Bill Maynard**
Mrs Froggitt .... **Megs Jenkins**
Maurice Froggitt .... **Robert Keegan**
Ray .... **Ray Mort**
Clive .... **Richard Davies**
Jack .... **Bill Dean**
Harry .... **Harold Goodwin**
Vera Parkinson .... **Rosemary Martin**
Lynda Baron
Mervyn Price .... **Bernard Gallagher** *(Selwyn)*

Creator/Writer **Alan Plater** (not *Selwyn*)
Producer **Ronnie Baxter**

● ***The misadventures of an irrepressible but inept handyman.***
Bachelor Selwyn Froggitt lives with his long-suffering mum and brother Maurice (whose girlfriend is the much-married Vera Parkinson) in the fictitious Yorkshire town of Scarsdale. Employed by the local council in its Public Works department, Froggitt fancies himself as a handyman, but his

self-confidence is tragically misplaced. Every job he undertakes ends in disaster. Froggitt also considers himself a bit of an intellectual, reading the *Times Literary Supplement* for fun, and is secretary of the Scarsdale Workingmen's Club and Institute where he drinks pints of 'cooking' and socializes with the likes of Clive, Jack and Ray, the barman. A thumbs-up cry of 'Magic' and an inane grin are his trademarks.

After three seasons of mayhem in Scarsdale, Froggitt was uprooted for a spin-off series simply called *Selwyn*. This pitches him into the role of Entertainments Officer at the Paradise Valley holiday camp on the Yorkshire coast, where the predictable consequences are witnessed by manager Mervyn Price. Alan Plater created the character of Selwyn Froggitt for a one-off play in 1974 and continued to write most of the scripts for the resultant series (but not *Selwyn*). Actor Bill Dean wrote the topical lyrics for each programme's theme song.

O'Hanlon, Ardal

(1965–)

Irish stand-up comedian and comic actor, the son of a former Irish health minister. It was as the idiotic Father Dougal Maguire in FATHER TED that O'Hanlon made his name, following the role with the parts of journalist Eamon Donaghy in *Big Bad World*, George Sunday (alias superhero Thermoman) in MY HERO, and stressed new father Gary in *Blessed*. O'Hanlon has also hosted *The Stand-Up Show* and provided the voice of cartoon reindeer Robbie.

Oil Strike North ✱✱

UK (BBC) Drama. BBC 1 1975

Jim Fraser .... **Nigel Davenport**
Frank Ward .... **Michael Whitney**
Julie Ward .... **Angela Douglas**
Elaine Smythe .... **Barbara Shelley**
Angus Gallacher .... **Callum Mill**
Shona Campbell .... **Angela Cheyne**
Charles Wayman .... **Richard Hurndall**
Donald Cameron .... **Andrew Robertson**
Jack Mullery .... **Glyn Owen**

Creators **N. J. Crisp, Gerard Glaister**
Producer **Gerard Glaister**

● ***High drama in the North Sea with the crew of an oil-rig.***

This 13-part serial concerns the company Triumph Oil, which is battling against the elements to extract oil from the cold and bleak North Sea, using rig *Nelson One*. Three months before its Government concession expires, the company discovers that there just might be oil in an area it hasn't yet considered, so the race is on to find the black gold. Episodes tend to involve helicopters and divers, usually with a heightened sense of danger, and attention is also paid to the pressures facing the 70 men cooped up on the rig, as well as the commercial side of the venture.

The top men are Fraser, the Operations Area Manager, and Frank Ward, the American drilling superintendent. Ward's wife Julie is also seen. Angus Gallacher is editor of the local *Muirport Gazette*, campaigning against the environmental and cultural damage being wreaked on this part of Scotland. After creators Gerard Glaister and N. J. Crisp had spent two years in research, filming took place in Peterhead.

Old Boy Network ✱✱

UK (Clement-La Frenais/SelecTV/Central) Situation Comedy. ITV 1992

Lucas Frye .... **Tom Conti**
Peter Duckham .... **John Standing**
Sir Roland White .... **Robert Lang**
Tamsin .... **Georgia Allen**
Parker Morrow .... **Jayne Brook**

Creators **Dick Clement, Ian La Frenais**
Writers **Dick Clement, Ian La Frenais, Steve Coombes, Dave Robinson**
Executive Producers **Tony Charles, Allan McKeown**
Producer **Sydney Lotterby**

● ***The best of enemies start their own espionage service.***

Two spies come in from the cold in this seven-episode sitcom from Clement and La Frenais. Lucas Frye is an MI5 double agent whose posting in Moscow has melted away with the end of the Cold War. Returning to England, he meets up with an old public school adversary, Peter Duckham, whose path has crossed with Frye's more than once thanks to his work for MI6. But Duckham is now retired and, with both men out of work, they reluctantly agree to set up their own spy agency, Frye–Duckham Associates, taking commissions from wherever they may come, be it from Middle Eastern sheiks or Third World soccer teams. The pair make extremely uncomfortable bedfellows – not least because Frye had once had an affair with Duckham's wife – and their missions are not as profitable as they might have expected.

Old Grey Whistle Test/Whistle Test ✱✱✱✱

UK (BBC) Rock Music. BBC 2 1971–88
DVD: BBC

Presenters **Ian Whitcomb, Richard Williams, Bob Harris, Anne Nightingale, David Hepworth, Mark Ellen, Richard Skinner, Andy Kershaw, Ro Newton**

Producer **Michael Appleton**

● ***Cult rock-music programme.***

Taking its name from the old adage that if the grey-haired doorman whistles your tune you've a hit on your hands, *Old Grey Whistle Test* developed out of a progressive-rock programme called *Disco 2*, which in turn was a derivative of LATE NIGHT LINE-UP. Unlike TOP OF THE POPS, *Whistle Test* did not pander to the pop charts but focused instead on developments in the album and live-music worlds. Two bands generally played live in the (unfurnished) studio, with interviews, film inserts and gig news completing the package. Its initial hosts were Ian Whitcomb and Richard Williams, but it was under the guidance of 'Whispering' Bob Harris that the programme's glory years arrived. Harris's laid-back, understated intros and genuine feel for the music added an air of authenticity and authority to proceedings and helped to ensure that the programme became a must for every self-respecting rock-music fan. A succession of other DJs and journalists, beginning with Anne Nightingale, filled the presenter's chair in the 1980s and, from 1983, the title was officially shortened to *Whistle Test*. The jaunty theme music, played over the 'star-kicker' opening titles, was 'Stone Fox Chase', by Area Code 615.

Old Men at the Zoo, The ★★

UK (BBC) Drama. BBC 2 1983

Simon Carter .... **Stuart Wilson**
Lord Godmanchester .... **Robert Morley**
Dr Edwin Leacock .... **Maurice Denham**
Dr Emile Englander .... **Marius Goring**
Sir Robert Falcon .... **Robert Urquhart**
Mr Sanderson .... **Andrew Cruickshank**
Dr Charles Langley-Beard .... **John Phillips**
Matthew Price .... **Richard Wordsworth**
Lord Oresby .... **Roland Culver**
Diana Price .... **Shelagh Fraser**
Martha Carter .... **Toria Fuller**
Harriet Leacock .... **Jan Harvey**

Writer **Troy Kennedy Martin**
Producer **Jonathan Powell**

● ***An ineptly run British zoo is a metaphor for the country as a whole.***

This five-part adaptation of Angus Wilson's satirical, futuristic novel of the same name concerns Simon Carter, the recently appointed secretary of Britain's National Zoo. His first day in the job, however, is dramatic to say the least. On a basic level, a giraffe runs amok and a young zookeeper is killed, but, while Carter tries to cope with the old zealots who run the place, in the wider world a major global crisis is brewing. One of the zoo's directors, Lord Godmanchester, a press magnate megalomaniac, then donates his Welsh estate for the purpose of setting up a major wildlife reserve, but this collapses, and eventually Carter is forced to move the animals back to London. All the while the international situation worsens. Finally, there is a nuclear strike on the city and Carter is badly hurt. It takes him two years to recover and when he does he learns that England is now under totalitarian control.

Among the other key characters are Dr Edwin Leacock, another director of the National Zoo; Sir Robert Falcon, curator of mammals; Matthew Price, curator of birds; Mr Sanderson, curator of insects; and Dr Emile Englander, who becomes director of the zoo in the aftermath of the nuclear attack. Using the contrast of humans and animals, images of the free and the oppressed form a central theme of the serial. Action and rhetoric are also juxtaposed as the zoo and its directors become a metaphor for ineffective government. In Wilson's 1961 novel, the 'enemy' is a united Europe; in this version it is the Arab races. Stuart Burge directed.

O'Leary, Dermot

(1973–)

Essex-born DJ and presenter of mostly youth- and music-oriented programmes, including *Fully Booked*, *T4*, BIG BROTHER'S LITTLE BROTHER, *SAS: Are You Tough Enough?*, *Re:Covered, Born to Win*, *Shattered* and *UK Music Hall of Fame*. He runs his own production company, Murphia.

Oliver, Jamie

MBE (1975–)

If cookery is the new rock 'n' roll, as some people rather unimaginatively claim, then Jamie Oliver must be the new Mick Jagger. Oliver was born in Southend and gained his culinary experience in the kitchen of his parents' pub in Clavering, Essex. He went on to catering college and then took jobs in two top London restaurants. He was spotted working at the River Café and offered his own TV series, *The Naked Chef*, in 1999, so named because of his down-to-earth enthusiasm for a simple style of cooking in which he claimed to take everyday ingredients and make them more tasty, stripping food back to its fundamentals. Supermarket adverts followed, as did a recording contract for his band, Scarlet Division, in which he plays drums. *Jamie's Kitchen*, in 2002, saw him offer a chance of a catering career to a group of unemployed youths. This was followed by *Return to Jamie's Kitchen*. In 2005 he caused quite a stir with *Jamie's School Dinners* in which he lambasted the standard of school catering in the UK, resulting in changes in approach from the Government down. Later the same year he presented *Jamie's Great Escape*, in which he toured Italy and its kitchens in his old campervan.

Oliver Twist ★★★

UK (Diplomat/United/WGBH/HTV) Drama. ITV 1999

Oliver Twist .... **Sam Smith**
Agnes Fleming .... **Sophia Myles**
Mr Fleming .... **Alun Armstrong**
Mr Bumble .... **David Ross**
Mrs Mann .... **Julie Walters**
Edwin Leeford .... **Tim Dutton**
Monks .... **Marc Warren**
Mr Brownlow .... **Michael Kitchen**
Elizabeth Leeford .... **Lindsay Duncan**
Fagin .... **Robert Lindsay**
Bill Sikes .... **Andy Serkis**
Nancy .... **Emily Woof**
Artful Dodger .... **Alex Crowley**
Mrs Bedwin .... **Annette Crosbie**
Mr Grimwig .... **John Grillo**
Sally .... **Liz Smith**
Mr Sowerberry .... **Roger Lloyd Pack**
Mrs Sowerberry .... **Ger Ryan**
Noah Claypole .... **James Bradshaw**
Giles .... **Sam Kelly**
Toby Crackitt .... **Andrew Schofield**
Mr Ferguson .... **Clive Russell**
Mr Fang .... **David Ryall**

Writer **Alan Bleasdale**
Executive Producers **Alan Bleasdale, Michele Buck, Rebecca Eaton**
Producer **Keith Thompson**

● ***Dickens's orphan hero gets the Bleasdale treatment.***

An orphan of unknown parentage, Oliver Twist suffers the harshest of childhoods. Raised in a workhouse dominated by a brutal beadle, Mr Bumble, he is then sold into an apprenticeship with undertaker Mr Sowerberry, but runs away to London and falls into a life of crime. His new mentor is Fagin, an arch-thief who has a gang of boys to do his dirty work. Although briefly rescued by the kindly Mr Brownlow, Oliver is recaptured by Fagin's gang, inspired by the villainous Bill Sikes and the mysterious Monks. Wounded while burgling, Oliver eventually rediscovers his lost family, while the criminal element get their just desserts. Alan Bleasdale's four-part reworking of the classic Dickens novel brings to the fore the story of Oliver's parents, Agnes Fleming and Edwin Leeford, which Dickens himself largely confines to the end of his tale. Another character whose role is enhanced is the boy's benefactor, Mr Brownlow, while Fagin is portrayed as a pied piper figure rather than the ugly Jewish caricature painted by his creator. The serial was partly shot in Prague and was directed by Renny Rye. Previous adaptations include: BBC 1962 (Bruce Prochnik as Oliver, Max Adrian as Fagin, Melvyn Hayes as the Artful Dodger and Peter Vaughan as Bill Sikes – the violent murder of Nancy by Sikes provoked outrage) and BBC 1 1985 (Scott Funnell and Ben Rodska as Oliver, Eric Porter as Fagin, David Garlick as the Artful Dodger and Michael Attwell as Sikes).

Olivier, Lord Laurence

(1907–89)

Lord Olivier's glorious theatrical and cinematic biography has been well presented in other publications, but his television work, though sparse, was no less well received. His first contribution was a play, *John Gabriel Borkman*, in 1958. Fifteen years later, he was narrator on the award-winning WORLD AT WAR and then appeared in JESUS OF NAZARETH as Nicodemus. In the 1980s he starred in a series of dramas, all of which attracted high praise. He was Lord Marchmain in BRIDESHEAD REVISITED, played *King Lear* for Channel 4 and starred in *A Voyage Round My Father* (Clifford Mortimer) and *The Ebony Tower*. There were also TV movies and mini-series, with his last TV role coming in *Lost Empires*, as fading comedian Harry Burrard. His wives were actresses Jill Esmond, Vivien Leigh and Joan Plowright.

Olsen, Gary

(1957–2000)

British comedy actor, best known as dad Ben Porter in 2 POINT 4 CHILDREN, but also star of *Prospects* (Pincy), *Wilderness Road* (Keith), THE BILL (PC Dave Litten), HEALTH AND EFFICIENCY (Dr Michael Jimson) and PILGRIM'S REST (café owner Bob Payne). He also appeared in Steve Coogan's *Three Fights, Two Weddings and a Funeral*, and took small roles in series such as MINDER, BOON, VAN DER VALK and CASUALTY.

Omaar, Rageh

(1967–)

Television journalist, born in Somalia. Omaar shot to fame through his coverage of the Iraq War for the BBC in 2003, during which he earned the cheeky nickname of the 'Scud Stud'. After beginning his career in print media, he moved to Ethiopia in 1991 and began contributing to the BBC World Service. Returning to London, Omaar worked again for the World Service and, moving into television, was later appointed a Middle East correspondent and then Africa correspondent. He is now freelance.

O'Mara, Kate

(1939–)

British actress who appeared in numerous drama series, including THE AVENGERS, *The Troubleshooters* (see MOGUL), THE SAINT, Z CARS, NO HIDING PLACE, DANGER MAN, WEAVERS GREEN (Mick Armstrong), MARKET IN HONEY LANE, COURT MARTIAL, PAUL TEMPLE, THE CHAMPIONS, DEPARTMENT S, THE PROTECTORS, THE PERSUADERS! and THE MAIN CHANCE (Julia Main), while building a career in the British cinema (particularly in Hammer horror films). In the 1970s and 1980s, however, she gradually made TV her forte with roles like air-freight magnate Jane Maxwell in THE BROTHERS, Katherine Laker in TRIANGLE, The Rani (a renegade Time Lord) in DOCTOR WHO, Caress Morell in DYNASTY and Laura Wilde in HOWARDS' WAY. O'Mara has also appeared in panel games (including as Mrs Peacock in CLUEDO) and with comedians like THE TWO RONNIES and Morecambe and Wise. More recently, she has played Virginia O'Kane in BAD GIRLS and Jackie Lawrence in *Family Affairs*, and appeared as a guest in ABSOLUTELY FABULOUS (Jackie) and CROSSROADS. Kate is a daughter of actress Hazel Bainbridge and sister of actress Belinda Carroll.

Omega Factor, The ✶✶

UK (BBC) Drama. BBC 1 1979
DVD: DD Home Entertainment

Tom Crane	**James Hazeldine**
Dr Anne Reynolds	**Louise Jameson**
Roy Martindale	**John Carlisle**
Michael Crane	**Nicholas Coppin**
Edward Drexel	**Cyril Luckham**
Andrew Scott-Erskine	**Brown Derby**
Julia Crane	**Joanna Tope**
Morag	**Natasha Gerson**

Creator **Jack Gerson**
Producer **George Gallaccio**

● ***A secret Scottish agency investigates paranormal activity.***

Department 7, based in a large Victorian house in Edinburgh, is a psychical research centre, looking into the paranormal. Actually, it is a front for MI5, who see paranormal activity as having massive potential in the espionage game. Interrogation could be so much easier if minds could be read, and the uses of supernatural bugging would be endless. Co-opted to work for the department is Tom Crane, an investigative reporter who happens to be a natural psychic. His associate is Dr Anne Reynolds, who introduces a sceptical angle to his work. Together they seek out instances of seemingly paranormal activity – children with special powers, unexplained deaths, mishaps when students play with a ouija board, that sort of thing. The shadowy world in which they work unfolds over ten episodes. The series was produced by BBC Scotland. Music is supplied by Anthony Isaac.

Omnibus ✶✶

UK (BBC) Arts. BBC 1 1967–2003

● ***Long-running BBC arts programme.***

The natural successor to MONITOR, *Omnibus* – with its declared aim of providing 'television to remember' – proved even more durable than its predecessor. Its creative weekly films and essays won much acclaim, among the best recalled being Ken Russell's *Dante's Inferno* (about Dante Gabriel Rossetti) in 1967, Tony Palmer's pop-music critique, *All My Loving*, in 1968, and the spooky Jonathan Miller adaptation of M. R. James's *Whistle, and I'll Come to You* in the same year. In 1993, to commemorate the programme's silver jubilee, a series of the best films was repeated on BBC 1. These included works on Kathleen Ferrier, David Bowie, Leonard Bernstein's *West Side Story*, cinematographer Vittorio Storaro, the Brothers Grimm and Ken Russell's 1968 profile of Frederick Delius. More recent subjects have included Reeves and Mortimer, Darcey Bussell, Mrs Gaskell, Sir Norman Foster, Roddy Doyle, Deborah Harry and Stephen King. Henry Livings was the programme's first presenter, though other hosts included Humphrey Burton,

Richard Baker and Barry Norman (who briefly chaired proceedings in the early 1980s).

On Safari

See *Denis, Armand and Michaela.*

On the Braden Beat ✱✱

UK (ATV) Consumer Affairs. ITV 1962–7

Presenter **Bernard Braden**

Producers **Jock Watson, Francis Coleman**

● ***Consumer affairs and light entertainment magazine.***

On the Braden Beat was ITV's Saturday night answer to THAT WAS THE WEEK THAT WAS. However, this programme combined general entertainment and topical humour with consumer investigations and battles against bureaucracy. After five years with ITV, Braden took the show to the BBC, creating BRADEN'S WEEK, in which he was assisted by reporter/researcher Esther Rantzen. Its clear descendant, THAT'S LIFE (without Braden), followed in 1973.

On the Buses ✱✱

UK (LWT) Situation Comedy. ITV 1969–73
DVD: Cinema Club

Stan Butler .... **Reg Varney**
Mrs Butler .... **Cicely Courtneidge**
Doris Hare
Olive .... **Anne Karen**
Arthur .... **Michael Robbins**
Jack Harper .... **Bob Grant**
Insp. Cyril Blake .... **Stephen Lewis**

Creators **Ronald Chesney, Ronald Wolfe**
Producers **Stuart Allen, Derrick Goodwin, Bryan Izzard**

● ***A bus-driver and his conductor lark about on their travels.***

Stan Butler is a driver for the London-based Luxton Bus Company, usually working with his conductor mate Jack on the number 11 route to the cemetery gates. Bane of his life is humourless Inspector Blake, who is always desperate to catch the chirpy pair up to no good. (Blakey's catchphase, 'I 'ate you, Butler,' was quickly adopted by the viewing public.)

Stan lives with his widowed mother, his dowdy sister, Olive, and her gruff, layabout husband, Arthur, but life is somewhat brighter at the depot, where there are always busty clippies to chase and jokes to play on the much-maligned Blakey. In keeping with the humour of the time, leering and innuendo dominate the series, although there is seldom any serious sexual activity – living with his mum, Stan never has the opportunity, much to his frustration.

Cicely Courtneidge was the first actress to play Stan's mum, although Doris Hare is best remembered in the role, while Stephen Lewis, who played Blakey, took his character into a spin-off series. Entitled *Don't Drink the Water* (ITV 1974–5), it saw Blakey moving into a retirement home in Spain with his spinster sister, Dorothy (Pat Coombs).

Three feature film versions (*On the Buses*, *Mutiny on the Buses* and *Holiday on the Buses*) were released in the 1970s, reflecting the popularity of this cheerfully vulgar comedy, and a US copy, set in New York and entitled *Lotsa Luck*, was also produced.

On the Move ✱✱

UK (BBC) Education. BBC 1 1975–6

Alf .... **Bob Hoskins**
Bert .... **Donald Gee**

Writer **Barry Took**
Producer **David Hargreaves**

● ***Light-hearted attempt to encourage illiterate viewers to learn to read and write.***

This series of award-winning ten-minute programmes, shown at Sunday teatimes, featured Bob Hoskins and Donald Gee as removals men Alf and Bert, who travelled around Britain and, with the help of famous guest stars in each episode, remarked on strange words in the English language. The aim was to stimulate people who couldn't read to do something about it. *On the Move* was partly inspired by an Italian series from the 1950s and 1960s, *Non E Mai Troppo Tardi* (*It's Never Too Late*), which tackled that country's chronic illiteracy problem.

On the Up ✱✱

UK (BBC) Situation Comedy. BBC 1 1990–2
DVD: Cinema Club

Tony Carpenter .... **Dennis Waterman**
Sam .... **Sam Kelly**
Mrs Fiona Wembley .... **Joan Sims**
Ruth Carpenter .... **Judy Buxton**
Maggie .... **Jenna Russell**
Stephanie Carpenter .... **Vanessa Hadaway**
Dawn .... **Michelle Hatch**
Mrs Carpenter .... **Dora Bryan**
Pauline Letts

Creator/Writer **Bob Larbey**
Producer **Gareth Gwenlan**

● ***A self-made millionaire has wife and domestic-staff troubles.***

East Ender Tony Carpenter is somewhat ill at ease with the sumptuous trappings of wealth, even though his own graft has made them possible. Forced to live in a posh Surrey neighbourhood (Esher) by Ruth, his socially superior wife of 16 years' standing (who keeps walking out on him), he employs a trio of home-based assistants who also give him a few headaches (but remain his only true friends). These are Sam, a childhood pal, who has become his butler and chauffeur; widow Mrs Wembley, his tipsy, old-movie-loving housekeeper; and Maggie, the Scottish personal assistant who helps with his car hire company (TC Luxury Cars). Tony struggles to justify his extravagant lifestyle, especially to his own mum, an avowed socialist who does her best to disown him. Adding to the conflict are Stephanie, Tony's problematic, public school-based daughter, and Dawn, the rather dim model Tony dates in later episodes.

Star Dennis Waterman also wrote and sang the programme's closing theme song.

Once upon a Time in the North ✱✱

UK (Philip Partridge) Situation Comedy. BBC 1 1994

Len Tollit .... **Bernard Hill**
Pat Tollit .... **Christine Moore**

Siobhan Tollit	**Susan McArdle**
Sean Tollit	**Andrew Whyment**
Mr Bebbington	**Bryan Pringle**
Morris Tollit	**Bob Mason**
Bob Carling	**Bill Stewart**

Writer **Tim Firth**
Producer **Philip Partridge**

A northern man has high hopes for his family's future.

Len Tollit is ever the optimist. He's desperate to create a better world for his Yorkshire family (wife Pat and kids Sean and Siobhan) and goes to extreme lengths to make this happen. Sadly, although he always aims high, he inevitably falls a long way short, in work and in leisure. Never mind, the resilient, defiantly working-class Len will try again. The family live in the fictitious town of Sutton Moor, where Morris is Len's dopey brother and Mr Bebbington a pensioner who occupies the granny flat next to the Tollit house. Each episode title begins 'The Time . . .', as in the first episode's 'The Time Len Spent His Redundancy Cheque', revealing how newly unemployed Len starts making plans for a more colourful future by setting up a company selling mobile phones. One series of six episodes was produced, all scripted by PRESTON FRONT creator Tim Firth.

ONdigital

ONdigital was the UK's first Digital Terrestrial Television provider. Operating three multiplexes and broadcasting a wide range of channels through a normal domestic aerial (although not as many as supplied by Digital Satellite Television broadcaster BSkyB or Digital Cable Television operators), ONdigital was the first company in the world to offer terrestrial digital TV, launching its service on 15 November 1998 (shortly after its satellite rival, but ahead of cable competitors). The company, jointly owned by Carlton Communications and Granada Media Group, later changed its name to ITV Digital but the business collapsed in 2002 after bidding too much for coverage of Nationwide League football. The multiplexes are now controlled by Freeview.

One by One ✶✶

UK (BBC) Drama. BBC 1 1984–5; 1987

Donald Turner	**Rob Heyland**
Maurice Webb	**Peter Jeffrey**
Paddy Reilly	**James Ellis**
Gran Turner	**Liz Smith**
Howard Rundle	**Garfield Morgan**
Ethel Ledbetter	**Sonia Graham**
Jenny Blount	**Rosie Kerslake**
Peter Raymond	**Jack Hedley**
Maggie Raymond	**Heather James**
Ben Bishop	**Peter Gilmore**
Lady Ann	**Catherine Schell**
Jock Drummond	**Andrew Robertson**
Liz Collier	**Christina Nagy**

Producer **Bill Sellars**

A newly qualified vet transforms the treatment of exotic animals.

Donald Turner, fresh from veterinary school, returns to his home town as assistant to the local practitioner, Maurice Webb. However, most of his time seems to be spent at the local zoo, and his first case involves treating an elephant with the 'skitters'. This is an era (the 1960s) when exotic creatures are little understood. The vet's job is no more than to keep them alive, rather than assisting in their general wellbeing. Dedicated medications are unheard of and the animals are treated with human or domestic pets' drugs. Turner recognizes the problems and gradually becomes a specialist in the care of exotic beasts. Paddy Reilly is the resident head zookeeper.

In the second series, set eight years later, Turner is a full partner in the practice (Webb soon leaves altogether) and the action switches to a safari park – supposedly Britain's first – run by new character Ben Bishop. The final instalments in this ALL CREATURES GREAT AND SMALL-type, amusing drama are fixed in 1971, with Turner now set up as freelance international vet, handling exotic species. The programme was based on the experiences recalled by vet David Taylor in his *Zoo Vet* books.

One Foot in the Grave ✶✶✶✶

UK (BBC) Situation Comedy. BBC 1 1990–7; 2000
DVD: BBC

Victor Meldrew	**Richard Wilson**
Margaret Meldrew	**Annette Crosbie**
Mrs Jean Warboys	**Doreen Mantle**
Patrick Trench	**Angus Deayton**
Pippa Trench	**Janine Duvitski**
Mr Nick Swainey	**Owen Brenman**

Creator/Writer **David Renwick**
Producers **Susan Belbin, Esta Charkham, Jonathan P. Llewellyn**

An accident-prone pensioner is the world's greatest whinger.

Unceremoniously retiring from his job as a security guard, 60-year-old amateur ventriloquist Victor Meldrew settles down to long days at home, much to the distress of his Scottish wife, Margaret. For Victor (a deliberately ironic first name) is the world's number one complainer. Litter in his front garden is one of his pet hates; the failure of mail order firms to supply the correct goods is another. His curmudgeonly attitude to life is soon recognized by their new neighbours when the Meldrews move from their demolished home at 37 Wingate Drive to 19 Riverbank, a more modern development. On one side live bus-driver Pippa and her cynical, professional husband, Patrick – proud master of the tiny dog Denzil – who, from the strange happenings next door, is firmly convinced that Victor is insane. On the other side live the very cheerful, but extremely boring, Mr Swainey and his invalid mother. The insensitive Mrs Warboys – whose unseen husband, Chris, deserts her – is another close associate (rather too close at times).

Although the series centres on ridiculous misunderstandings and gentle forms of farce, *One Foot in the Grave* also has its surreal elements and more than a touch of pathos (it is once barely mentioned that the Meldrews long before lost a young son named Stuart). Tender moments intermingle with Victor's yells of outrage ('I don't believe it!') and Margaret's cries of despair. All this made *One Foot in the Grave* the BBC's most popular sitcom in the early 1990s. For Christmas 1993, a feature-length special, *One Foot in the Algarve*, was produced, and after January 1995 only Christmas specials were made for a couple of years. In the last, Patrick and Pippa finally escape and the Meldrews' new neighbours are Derek and Betty McVitie (played by Tim Brooke-Taylor and Marian

McLoughlin). Patrick and Pippa are back for the final series (screened in 2000), when Victor is – unusually for a sitcom character – killed off.

The theme song for the series was written and sung by Eric Idle. An American version, beginning in 1996, starred Bill Cosby and was simply entitled *Cosby*.

100% ✶✶

UK (Grundy) Quiz. Channel 5 1997–2001

Announcer **Robin Houston**

Creator **Tom Atkinson**
Producer **Mark Noades**

● ***Quiz show without a host.***

Three contestants took part in each edition of this 100-question general knowledge daily (weekdays) quiz, a stalwart of Channel 5's schedules from its first week on air for four years. There were a number of novelty factors to capture the viewer's attention. Firstly, there was no visible host, just the voice of Robin Houston to introduce the contestants and read the questions and scores. Secondly, each contestant's score was given as a percentage of correct answers against the total number of questions asked. Thirdly, for the latter half of the game, contestants were not able to see who was leading. All questions were displayed on the screen, together with three possible answers, some of which were included for humour. Subject categories helped to break up the 100 questions. A modest £100 was awarded to the daily winner, but he/she was able to return to accumulate more money.

The simple format was easily applied to spin-off series and specials. A mid-afternoon quiz called *100% Gold* included questions aimed at the 50+ age-group, while *100% Sex* was a late-night variation for the younger generation. Specials were devised to slot into Channel 5 'theme days' and included quizzes dedicated to the likes of Abba, Queen and Elvis Presley.

One Man and his Dog ✶✶

UK (BBC) Sheep Dog Trials. BBC 2 1976–

Presenters **Phil Drabble, Robin Page, Clarissa Dickson Wright**

Producers **Philip S. Gilbert, Ian Smith, Joy Corbett, Daniel Brittain-Catlin**

● ***Shepherds and their faithful hounds compete for the BBC Television Trophy.***

An unlikely hit, *One Man and His Dog* was hosted by flat-capped Phil Drabble for 18 years, before he handed over his crook and wellies to new presenter Robin Page. Loyal viewers on a Sunday teatime appreciated the traditional, rural skills of dog-handling, exhibited by shepherds who, with just a few whistles, could instruct their charges to herd the most unruly sheep through gates, round posts and into wooden pens. No doubt the beautiful rural landscapes, with their rolling fields and dry-stone walls, added to the attraction. Trials experts Eric Halsall, Ray Ollerenshaw and Gus Dermody also contributed over the years. More recent offerings have just been Christmas specials, hosted by Clarissa Dickson Wright and, later, Ben Fogle and Shauna Lowry.

199 Park Lane ✶

UK (BBC) Soap Opera. BBC 1 1965

Tony Ashman	**Philip Bond**
Sgt Baines	**Geoffrey Toone**
Harry	**Jerold Wells**
Claire Bell	**Caroline Hunt**
Lord Caister	**Derek Bond**
Anne Faulkner	**Ellen McIntosh**
Ben Graham	**Edwin Richfield**
Stella Graham	**Isabel Dean**
Derek Farrow	**Leonard Cracknell**
Kate Harvester	**Brenda Kaye**
Constantine Petrakos	**Henry Gilbert**
Caroline Petrakos	**Ann Firbank**
Jeremy Quest	**Hugh Latimer**
Colin Gage	**Paul Grist**
Alexa Kovacs	**Yvette Rees**
Prescott	**Frederick Piper**

Creator **William Fairchild**
Producer **Morris Barry**

● ***The intriguing lives of the wealthy residents at a London apartment block.***

199 Park Lane is one of the best addresses in London and this twice-weekly (Tuesday and Friday) serial takes a look at some of the people who live in this trendy block of flats. New arrival is MP Anne Faulkner and she encounters a mixed group of residents who include ambitious industrialist Ben Graham (unhappily married to wife Stella); dashing womanizer Lord Caister; Greek millionaire Constantin Petrakos and his stunning English wife, Caroline; and fashion designer Jeremy Quest, who is charged with teaching the trade to his Welsh nephew, Colin Gage. There are also Alexa, Jeremy's assistant; Tony Ashman, a gossip columnist always ready to dig out some dirt; and Derek Farrow, son of a successful stockbroker who is secretly dating Claire Bell, the working-class girl from the flower shop downstairs. Kate Harvester is the block's manageress and porter Sgt Baines, a former Brigade of Guards officer, is her enforcer. After 18 episodes of society parties, dinners in the building's top-notch restaurant and cosy drinks in its Harry's Bar, the series wound up to be replaced by THE NEWCOMERS.

Onedin Line, The ✶✶

UK (BBC) Drama. BBC 1 1971–4; 1976–80
DVD: Universal

Capt. James Onedin	**Peter Gilmore**
Robert Onedin	**Brian Rawlinson**
	James Garbutt
Elizabeth Onedin/Frazer/Lady Fogarty	**Jessica Benton**
Anne Webster/Onedin	**Anne Stallybrass**
Capt. Baines	**Howard Lang**
Sarah Onedin	**Mary Webster**
Mr Callon	**Edward Chapman**
Capt. Webster	**James Hayter**
Emma Callon/Fogarty	**Jane Seymour**
Matt Harvey	**Ken Hutchison**
Albert Frazer	**Philip Bond**
Daniel Fogarty	**Michael Billington**
	Tom Adams
Mr Jack Frazer	**John Phillips**

Charlotte Onedin .... **Laura Hartong**
Victoria Thomas
Leonora Biddulph .... **Kate Nelligan**
Caroline Maudslay .... **Caroline Harris**
Margarita Juarez/Onedin .... **Roberta Iger**
Mr Dunwoody .... **John Rapley**
Letty Gaunt/Onedin .... **Jill Gascoine**
Samuel Onedin .... **Timothy Slender**
Christopher Douglas
William Frazer .... **Marc Harrison**
Josiah Beaumont .... **Warren Clarke**
Max Van Der Rheede .... **Frederick Jaeger**
Caroline .... **Jenny Twigge**
Tom Arnold .... **Keith Jayne**

Creator **Cyril Abraham**
Producers **Peter Graham Scott, Peter Cregeen, Geraint Morris**

The saga of a Liverpool shipping line.

Twenty-eight-year-old James Onedin is a determined, hard-driving ship's captain. On returning from a voyage in 1860, he learns of his shopkeeper father's death and that he has inherited little of his estate. The business goes instead to his elder brother, Robert, but James doesn't really mind as his heart remains at sea. Unhappy at his treatment by his boss, Mr Callon, and brim-full of enterprise, he sets out to start his own rival business, acquiring the decrepit three-masted schooner *Charlotte Rhodes* from the penniless, boozy Captain Webster, largely in return for marrying Webster's sour-faced, determined daughter, Anne (played by Sheila Allen in the pilot). Anne immediately involves herself in the business as an active partner.

The late 1800s are precarious times and running a merchant ship is not a comfortable business, even with a whiskery old sea-dog like Captain Baines (who constantly objects to his master's methods) as first mate. The series follows the commercial and personal exploits of the quick-tempered Onedin, as well as his life on the cruel sea. In the background, adding domestic and business complications, are his wealthy, but penny-pinching brother – whom James has roped in as partner – and his attractive sister, Elizabeth. Later problems are provided by his troublesome daughter, Charlotte, and his next two wives (when Anne dies in childbirth, James marries Charlotte's governess, Letty Gaunt, who also dies, before he weds a Spanish widow, Margarita Juarez).

Running for nine years (and taking the period up to 1886), *The Onedin Line* was derived from a one-off DRAMA PLAYHOUSE presentation in 1970 and became a stalwart of BBC 1's Sunday nights. Its evocative theme music came from Khachaturyan's ballet *Spartacus*, intended for a situation far removed from the Dartmouth docksides where this series was filmed.

O'Neill, Maggie

(1967–)

British actress whose major TV credits have included TAKE ME HOME (Kathy), *Friday on My Mind* (Louise Ross), *The Life and Times of Henry Pratt* (Auntie Doris), *Killing Me Softly* (Sara Thornton), INVASION: EARTH (Dr Amanda Tucker), BIRTHS, MARRIAGES AND DEATHS (Alex) and *Hero of the Hour* (Alison Liddle), plus *Chiller*, *Screen One's Blore – MP*, *Screen Two's Defrosting the Fridge* and *The Fix*. In 2000 she joined the cast of PEAK PRACTICE as Dr Alex Redman. O'Neill has also been seen in *White Teeth* (Poppy Burt-Jones), INSPECTOR MORSE, BOON, CADFAEL, MURDER IN MIND, THE ROYAL, SHAMELESS (Sheila Jackson), *Family Business* (Elaine Tobelem), MIDSOMER MURDERS, BLUE MURDER and VINCENT.

Only Fools and Horses ★★★★

UK (BBC) Situation Comedy. BBC 1 1981–3; 1985–93; 1996; 2001–3
DVD: BBC

Derek 'Del Boy' Trotter .... **David Jason**
Rodney Trotter .... **Nicholas Lyndhurst**
Grandad Trotter .... **Lennard Pearce**
Uncle Albert Trotter .... **Buster Merryfield**
Raquel Slater/Trotter .... **Tessa Peake-Jones**
Cassandra Parry/Trotter .... **Gwyneth Strong**
Aubrey 'Boycie' Boyce .... **John Challis**
Marlene Boyce .... **Sue Holderness**
Trigger .... **Roger Lloyd Pack**
Mike Fisher .... **Kenneth MacDonald**
Mickey Pearce .... **Patrick Murray**
Denzil .... **Paul Barber**
Jevon .... **Steven Woodcock**
Sid .... **Roy Heather**
Roy Slater .... **Jim Broadbent**
Alan Parry .... **Denis Lill**
Pam Parry .... **Wanda Ventham**
Damien Trotter .... **Grant Stevens**
Robert Liddement
Jamie Smith
Benjamin Smith

Creator/Writer **John Sullivan**
Producers **Ray Butt, Gareth Gwenlan**

The misadventures of a flashy London spiv and his hapless brother.

Only Fools and Horses was *the* British sitcom of the 1980s. From humble beginnings as a slow-moving idea for a series called *Readies*, it grew into one of the best-loved comedies the BBC has ever produced, ranking alongside STEPTOE AND SON, TILL DEATH US DO PART, HANCOCK'S HALF HOUR and FAWLTY TOWERS. Testimony to its popularity is the fact that its Christmas Day specials were the highlight of the BBC's festive season.

Taking its name from the old adage that 'only fools and horses work', the series is constructed around Derek 'Del Boy' Trotter, a market fly-pitcher with an endless supply of hooky goods fresh off the back of a lorry. Ever the optimist ('this time next year, we'll be millionaires' and 'he who dares, wins' are his catchphrases), Del Boy is the sole provider for his close-knit family, which consists of his lanky 'plonker' of a brother, Rodney, and his dim old Grandad. Together they share a high-rise council flat in Nelson Mandela House on the Nyerere estate in Peckham. Swathed in gold, heavily splashed with Brut and puffing a chunky cigar, Del enjoys the good life, which effectively means a night down The Nag's Head drinking Drambuie-and-grapefruit cocktails, followed by a Ruby Murray (a curry). Lovely jubbley, as he puts it. His choice of women leaves a lot to be desired, although occasionally he does stumble across a classier girl, which warrants a trip to a Berni Inn for a steak meal.

Rodney, left orphaned when his mother died and his dad cleared off, relies on Del for his wellbeing, although this effectively scuppers any hopes he harbours of a life of his own. It is Rodney who, despite having two GCEs (Maths and Art), is the dogsbody of Trotter's Independent Trading (Titco), and the driver of the firm's decrepit, yellow three-wheeled van (emblazoned with Del's dreams of empire: 'New York, Paris, Peckham'). Grandad is the silly old sod who runs the home and does the (bad) cooking, in between bouts of sulking or simultaneously watching two TV sets. With the death of actor

Lennard Pearce, Grandad also passes away and in his place his equally wily brother, the boys' Uncle Albert, is introduced. An old sea-dog with a Captain Birdseye beard, Albert can instantly break up any party with the ominous words 'During the war . . .'

The Trotters are also well blessed with friends and associates. These include dense road-sweeper Trigger (so named not because he carries a gun but because he looks like a horse), who always thinks Rodney's name is Dave; flashy car salesman Boycie and his flirty wife, Marlene; Mike, landlord of the pub; Denzil, a lorry driver; and Sid, the unhygienic owner of the Old Oak Café. Rodney's pals include brainless Mickey Pearce and snappily-dressed Jevon. The Trotters' nemesis is bent copper Roy Slater.

Writer John Sullivan allows his characters to mature as the series progresses and moments of pathos are introduced – such as when Rodney marries yuppie banker Cassandra and Del is left isolated and, for once, alone. However, Del's momentary introspection soon gives way to love for actress/stripogram girl Raquel, who bears him a son, portentously named Damien, much to Rodney's terror.

After a three-year hiatus, *Only Fools and Horses* returned at Christmas 1996 with a three-part story that revealed how Del and Rodney did, at last, become millionaires by rediscovering a watch in their lock-up garage that was worth £6 million. It was a universally acclaimed revival that many considered to be a glorious finale. With the death of actor Buster Merryfield, who played Albert, in 1999, it seemed that the Trotters had done their last dodgy deal but the gang resurfaced for a Christmas special in 2001 which saw the family's wealth disappear and Del and Rodney once again back on their uppers. The untimely death, too, of Kenneth Macdonald (Mike), meant promotion for Sid as he took over The Nag's Head. Further Christmas specials followed in 2002 and 2003, rounding off the Trotter saga.

Echoes of *Only Fools and Horses* live on, however, in *The Green Green Grass* (BBC 1 2005–), a spin-off sitcom in which Boycie and Marlene (with teenage son Tyler, played by Jack Doolan) flee Peckham (and the notoriously vengeful Driscoll Brothers) to acquire Winterdown Farm in Shropshire, taking with them incongruous city ways and prejudices.

Only When I Laugh ★★

UK (Yorkshire) Situation Comedy. ITV 1979–82
DVD: Bfs Entertainment

Roy Figgis	**James Bolam**
Archie Glover	**Peter Bowles**
Norman Binns	**Christopher Strauli**
Dr Gordon Thorpe	**Richard Wilson**
Staff Nurse Gupte	**Derrick Branche**

Creator/Writer **Eric Chappell**
Producer **Vernon Lawrence**

● ***The petty squabbles of a trio of long-term hospital patients.***

Bolshy lorry-driver Roy Figgis, snooty, upper-class hypochondriac Archie Glover and naïve young Norman Binns are long-stay patients in this hospital comedy. They battle over the best beds, put the wind up new patients, complain about the hospital radio service and wrangle with the medical staff. These include haughty, irascible surgeon Gordon Thorpe and frustrated male Indian nurse Gupte. The ironic 'H.A.P.P.Y.' theme song sets the tone.

Open All Hours ★★★★

UK (BBC) Situation Comedy. BBC 2 1976; BBC 1 1981–2; 1985
DVD: BBC

Arkwright	**Ronnie Barker**
Granville	**David Jason**
Nurse Gladys Emmanuel	**Lynda Baron**
Milkwoman	**Barbara Flynn**
Mrs Delphine Featherstone	**Stephanie Cole**

Creator/Writer **Roy Clarke**
Producer **Sydney Lotterby**

● ***Penny-pinching with a north country shopkeeper and his ha-ha-hapless nephew.***

Adopting yet another characterization that showed off his comic gifts to great effect, Ronnie Barker in this series introduced viewers to Arkwright, the tightest grocer in the north of England. Constantly battling with an entrenched stammer and the advances of 1970s shopkeeping, Arkwright is mean, devious and conniving. He is particularly hard on his young nephew, Granville, the son of Arkwright's sister by an unnamed Hungarian, who has grown up as the grocer's errand boy, shop assistant and general skivvy. But Granville is also a daydreamer and pictures himself in better situations, usually in the arms of some beautiful woman.

Arkwright, too, has romantic aspirations, in his case to fall into the bosom of buxom Gladys Emmanuel, the Morris Minor-driving nurse who lives across the street with her ailing mother. Although she needs to fend off Arkwright's wandering hands and turn a deaf ear to his practised innuendo, she nevertheless harbours genuine affection for the stingy old grocer.

The days are long in this shop. From well before dawn to well after dusk the lights are on and the door is open. Each programme begins with Arkwright setting out his special offers on stalls at the front, winding up with his taking them back in again. In between, confused customers come and go (usually with goods Arkwright has conned them into buying), and Granville has suffered another day of abuse and frustration. But it never prevents him from answering back to his mentor or smirking whenever Arkwright catches his fingers in the shop's temperamental till.

The characters first appeared in the Ronnie Barker anthology of pilot shows, *Seven of One*, in 1973 (with Sheila Brennan in the role of Nurse Emmanuel) but three years passed before a series followed (on BBC 2). This was repeated on BBC 1 in 1979 and new episodes eventually appeared in 1981 and 1982. However, the last series was not transmitted until 1985, four years after David Jason had switched trading places to Peckham market, and taken on the role of Del Boy in ONLY FOOLS AND HORSES. An American version of *Open All Hours* was also made, entitled *Open All Night*.

Operation Good Guys ★★

UK (Fugitive/BBC) Situation Comedy. BBC 2 1997–2000
DVD: BBC

DI Beach	**David Gillespie**
DS Ray Ash	**Ray Burdis**
Gary Barwick	**Gary Beadle**
Mark Kemp	**Mark Burdis**
'Strings'	**John Beckett**
'Bones'	**Perry Benson**
Roy Leyton	**Roy Smiles**

Sgt Dominic de Sade .... **Dominic Anciano**
Kim Finch/'Boo-Boo' .... **Kim Taylforth**
Hugo 'Smiler' McCarthy .... **Hugo Blick**
Bill Zeebub .... **William Scully**
Hugo Crippen .... **Hugo Blick**

Narrator **Hugo Blick**

Creators **Ray Burdis, Dominic Anciano**
Writers/Producers **Dominic Anciano, Ray Burdis, Hugo Blick**

Fly-on-the-wall spoof about a team of inept police officers.

Operation Good Guys is the codename for a secret mission headed up by the incapable DI Beach and his team of hopeless detectives. The task force's job is to investigate and convict one of Britain's biggest known criminals, 'Smiler' McCarthy, but their mission repeatedly collapses into chaos, when they arrest the wrong suspects and find themselves on the end of multi-million-pound lawsuits. Unfortunately, the whole shambles has been recorded by a BBC documentary team so there is no hiding place for the Beach boys. By the second series, the team has rightly been demoted and is back in uniform, having to undergo training at college. They are then sent off on a new mission to Spain, where the delights of the holiday trade prove much too distracting. In series three, among other debacles, the team is shipped out to a remote island to take part in a survival experience and is later charged with protecting an extremely important family (think corgis). Martin Kemp, Christopher Biggins, Victor Kiam, Jude Law, Denise Van Outen, Frank Warren and Patsy Palmer – plus members of the BBC top brass like Geoffrey Perkins, Paul Jackson, Alan Yentob and Will Wyatt – are among the guest stars, most playing themselves. Partially scripted but largely improvised, this documentary send-up, shot on video, pre-empted the similar but more subtle THE OFFICE by four years.

Oppenheimer ★★★

UK (BBC) Drama. BBC 2 1980

Robert Oppenheimer .... **Sam Waterston**
Kitty Harrison/Oppenheimer . **Jana Shelden**
Jean Tatlock .... **Kate Harper**
Frank Oppenheimer .... **Garrick Hagon**
Robert Serber .... **Peter Whitman**
Charlotte Serber .... **Erica Stevens**
Enrico Fermi .... **Edward Hardwicke**
Gen. Leslie Groves .... **Manning Redwood**
Robert Wilson .... **John Morton**
Jacky Oppenheimer .... **Liza Ross**
Haakon Chevalier .... **Peter Marinker**
Isidor Rabi .... **Barry Dennen**
Edward Teller .... **David Suchet**
Hans Bethe .... **Matthew Guinness**
George Kistiakowsky .... **Milton Johns**
Robert Bacher .... **Blair Fairman**
Ernest Lawrence .... **Bob Sherman**
Ed Condon .... **Shane Rimmer**
James Tuck .... **Dave Hill**
Henry Stimson .... **Alexander Knox**
Lewis Strauss .... **Phil Brown**
Joseph Volpe .... **Peter Banks**
Roger Robb .... **Philip O'Brien**
Lloyd Garrison .... **James Maxwell**
Gen. Kenneth Nichols .... **Christopher Muncke**
Herbert Marks .... **Stuart Milligan**
Narrator .... **John Carson**

Writer **Peter Prince**
Producer **Peter Goodchild**

Personal, professional and political problems persecute the father of the atom bomb.

If there's one event in the 20th century that changed the course of humanity for ever, it was the dropping of the first atomic bomb. This series explores the life of the man who developed that bomb. Julius Robert Oppenheimer's story is picked up in 1938, when he is working as an inspirational professor of physics in Berkeley, California, and dabbles mildly in politics. He has known connections – via family and friends – with the American Communist Party, including through the woman who will be his new wife, Kitty Harrison. When war breaks out, Oppenheimer is thrust into the race to produce the first atomic bomb, heading up a secret laboratory near Los Alamos, New Mexico, to research into nuclear fission. Dealing with the technology is not his only worry, however, as internal disputes among his team put pressure on its leader, and external interest by the FBI – tipped off about his Communist links – makes life even more difficult. After the dropping of the bomb and the end of the war, Oppenheimer faces up to the new reality he has created. He becomes a senior adviser to the US Government, as part of the Atomic Energy Commission, but his left-wing past continues to haunt him. It is the era of the McCarthy witch-hunts, and in 1953 he is accused of being a Soviet agent. His security clearance is rescinded, pending a hearing into his conduct. Major figures featuring in Oppenheimer's story are Robert Serber, his closest friend and one-time pupil; Robert Wilson, another long-time colleague; Teller and Lawrence, who lobby to take Oppenheimer's work to a new level by developing the H bomb; Isidor Rabi, a Nobel Prize-winning physicist who joins Oppenheimer in calling for control of atomic weapons to be held in international civilian, not US military, hands; and Haakon Chevalier, a Communist friend whose association with Oppenheimer causes mighty waves in the US administration. Carl Davies provides the music; Barry Davis directs the seven episodes. An accompanying book, entitled *J. Robert Oppenheimer and the Story of the Atomic Bomb*, was written by producer Peter Goodchild and published by BBC Books.

Opportunity Knocks/Bob Says 'Opportunity Knocks' ★

UK (Associated-Rediffusion/ABC/Thames/BBC) Talent Show. ITV 1956–78; BBC 1 1987–90

Hosts **Hughie Green, Bob Monkhouse, Les Dawson**

Producers **Peter Dulay, Milo Lewis, Royston Mayoh, Robert Fleming, Keith Beckett, Stewart Morris**

Long-running talent show in which viewers at home elect the top act.

Beginning on Radio Luxembourg in the early 1950s, *Opportunity Knocks* and its ebullient host, Hughie Green, were brought to television soon after ITV began. There had been talent shows on TV before – *Carroll Levis Discoveries* was one – but none proved to have the stamina of *Opportunity Knocks*, which not only survived the ITV franchise swap of 1968 but was resurrected by the BBC in 1987, having been cancelled by Thames in 1978.

The format was simple. Green introduced half-a-dozen acts per week ('Friends, we want to hear them,' Green declared), each 'sponsored' by a studio guest who offered background information about the performers. At the end of the show, all the acts gave a short reprise of their routine which the studio audience evaluated by applauding. The highest scorers on the 'clapometer' were declared the studio winners, but this counted for nothing. What mattered ('And I mean that most sincerely, folks,' Green was known to swear) were the votes of viewers at home, expressed by the mailing in of postcards. At the start of the following week's programme, the winners were announced and were given the chance to repeat their success. A winning contestant could return literally week after week and, at the end of each series, an all-winners show was put together. Telephone voting replaced postal votes when the BBC revived the show under the title of *Bob Says 'Opportunity Knocks'* (the new host being Bob Monkhouse). Les Dawson, himself probably the programme's greatest find, presented the final season, with the title reverting to *Opportunity Knocks*.

Other notable performers given their showbusiness break by *Opportunity Knocks* were Russ Abbot (as part of the Black Abbots group), Freddie Starr, The Bachelors, Frank Carson, Mary Hopkin, Little and Large, Paul Daniels, Freddie Davies, Peters and Lee, Lena Zavaroni, Ken Goodwin, Pam Ayres, Bonnie Langford, Paul Melba, Tom O'Connor and Paper Lace. But whatever happened to winners like Bobby Crush, Neil Reid, Gerry Monroe, Millican and Nesbitt, Stuart Gillies, Berni Flint and 1960s muscle man Tony Holland? There were hard-luck stories, too. Su Pollard was allegedly beaten by a singing dog and a singer called Gerry Dorsey even failed the audition. He changed his name to Engelbert Humperdinck and did rather better for himself.

Opt Out

The term given to the practice by regional TV stations of leaving national output and screening local programmes/inserts instead.

Oranges are Not the Only Fruit ✱✱✱

UK (BBC) Drama. BBC 2 1990
DVD: Second Sight

Jessica ('Jess')	**Emily Aston**
	Charlotte Coleman
Mother	**Geraldine McEwan**
Pastor Finch	**Kenneth Cranham**
May	**Elizabeth Spriggs**
Mrs Green	**Freda Dowie**
Elsie Norris	**Margery Withers**
Miss Jean Jewsbury	**Celia Imrie**
Cissy	**Barbara Hicks**
Mrs Netty Arkwright	**Pam Ferris**
Melanie	**Cathryn Bradshaw**

Writer **Jeanette Winterson**
Producer **Phillippa Giles**

A young Lancashire girl rebels against her mother's religious ambitions.

Adapted for television in three parts by Jeanette Winterson from her own Whitbread Prize-winning novel, *Oranges are Not the Only Fruit* is the story of Jess, an adopted northern lass who refuses to yield to her mum's religious fanaticism. Earmarked as a future missionary, Jess is subjected to oppressive preaching from the bigoted Pastor Finch and made to join in thunderous hymn-singing with her mother's geriatric friends. A lesbian encounter with Melanie, a teenage acquaintance, provokes the wrath of the assembled Pentecostals, but their primitive and brutal efforts to drive the Devil out of the girl backfire and she is lost to them for ever.

Despite seeming a risky undertaking by the BBC, as neither the director, Beeban Kidron, nor the producer, Phillippa Giles, had conducted a TV drama before, the serial was widely acclaimed and went on to collect several awards.

Origami ✱

UK (Yorkshire) Children's Entertainment. ITV 1968–72

Presenter **Robert Harbin**

Executive Producer **Jess Yates**

An ancient Japanese art form revealed.

The venerable skill of origami (paper folding) was the unlikely subject of this series of 15-minute programmes dropped into ITV's children's hour. Conjuror Robert Harbin (whose TV pedigree dates back to the 1950s through shows like WHIRLIGIG) deftly creased and pressed pieces of paper 8–10 inches square into not only flowers and animals but also more adventurous items like boomerangs, a space module and a Noah's Ark, complete with Mr and Mrs Noah. An accompanying column appeared in the children's *TV Times*, *Look-In*.

Orlando ✱✱

UK (Associated-Rediffusion) Children's Adventure. ITV 1965–8

Orlando O'Connor	**Sam Kydd**
Long John Turner	**Gregory Phillips**
Triss Fenton	**Margo Andrew**
Steve Morgan	**David Munro**
Jenny Morgan	**Judy Robinson**
Shish Kebab	**Arthur White**

Producer **Ronald Marriott**

Spin-off for children from the adult series CRANE.

Orlando O'Connor was Crane's right-hand man in the earlier tales of smuggling and petty crime on the North African coast. Now he returns to Britain and, after failing to establish a boat-building business, and having instead a series of adventures with two kids, Long John and Triss, seeks out an old Navy friend. His friend, however, has been killed and Orlando, with the help of Steve and Jenny Morgan, two teenagers who have inherited their uncle's detective agency, sets about finding his murderer. Thus begin many adventures for this particular trio, in which Orlando's life is saved on many an occasion by a magical Arabic charm called the Gizzmo. The action takes place mostly around London's docklands.

'Orrible ✱✱

UK (BBC/Union Pictures) Situation Comedy. BBC 2 2001
DVD: BBC

Paul ''Orrible' Clark	**Johnny Vaughan**
Sean Orlov	**Ricky Grover**
Di Clark	**Di Botcher**
Lee	**Lee Oakes**
Shiv Clark	**Angel Coulby**

Tim .... **William Boyde**
Noel .... **Clint Dyer**

Writers **Johnny Vaughan, Ed Allen**
Producers **Michael Jacob, Bradley Adams**

A self-deluding East Ender has ambitions to become part of the local crime scene.

Paul Clark, 32, is an optimist who sets his sights high. His aim: to find recognition among the local villains and, to this end, he willingly runs errands for and curries favour with some of London's nastiest crooks. As he is always accompanied, and usually hindered, by Sean, his dopey best mate/bodyguard, things usually go awry and Clark finds himself on the run from the thugs he tries to impress. Not that Clark is alone in his ambition: all the regulars (especially arch-rival Noel) at his boozer, the Fox and Hounds (stewarded by actor William Boyde, formerly Willmott-Brown of the Dagmar in EastEnders), are also in awe of the local heavies. Consequently, his career ambition can be perceived as a desire to gain respect – which, when your only work is as a part-time (dangerous) minicab driver and you live with your mum (a hard-nosed bailiff), is not always easy to come by. Poking fun at our hero's ineptitude and his many lies and exaggerations are teenage sister Shiv and her druggie boyfriend, Lee. Star Johnny Vaughan was said to have based the series on characters he met during his much-publicized stretch behind bars.

Osbournes, The ***

US (MTV) Docu-Soap. Channel 4 2002–5 (US: MTV 2002–5)
DVD: Buena Vista Home Entertainment

Executive Producers **Greg Johnston, Jeff Stilson, Lois Clark Curren, Sharon Osbourne**

The startling lifestyle of a rock star and his family.

Forget THE SIMPSONS and THE ADDAMS FAMILY: meet *The Osbournes*. When Sharon Osbourne, manager of rock singer Ozzy, met MTV executives to discuss some music specials, she couldn't help relating some of the crazy things that happen at home. The MTV guys took the bait and signed the Osbourne family up for a fly-on-the-wall documentary that took America by storm. Home is a luxury mansion in Beverly Hills, into which Sharon, Ozzy and their two teenage kids, Kelly and Jack, move in the first instalment (elder daughter Aimee refused to take part). What follows is an extraordinary insight into an extraordinary family, the patriarch of which is a 53-year-old, shambling and confused rock star with a short attention span. He bears the scars of rock 'n' roll excess but clearly loves his nearest and dearest, which comes as a shock to those who still picture Ozzy as a hell-raising Black Sabbath frontman who bites the heads off bats and doves. Yet this is a take-as-you-find household. There are countless arguments about domestic issues and endless friction over touring arrangements, with expletives bouncing off the walls (when brought to Channel 4 after earlier airing on MTV in the UK, some of the bad language was bleeped out, although those who desired the unexpurgated version could see a complete repeat a few days later). A visit to the Osbournes' is not for the faint-hearted or those who, on medical grounds, have been ordered not to laugh out loud.

Osmonds, The

ALAN (1949–), WAYNE (1951–), MERRILL (1953–), JAY (1955–), DONNY (1957–), MARIE (1959–) and JIMMY (1963–)

American singing family, possibly the world's most famous Mormons, who first found TV fame in the 1960s on *The Andy Williams Show*. In the 1970s they were extremely popular, both on television and in the pop charts, with *Donny and Marie* their longest-lasting series. They also sang the theme song for the Western *The Travels of Jaimie McPheeters*, a series in which they once made guest appearances. In 1995 Marie starred with Betty White in the sitcom *Maybe This Time*, while Jimmy entered the challenge of I'M A CELEBRITY ... GET ME OUT OF HERE! in 2005.

Osoba, Tony

British actor with some memorable supporting roles behind him. He was the Scottish heavy, McLaren, in PORRIDGE, DS Chas Jarvis in DEMPSEY AND MAKEPEACE, Freddie in *Making News*, and rag-trade boss Peter Ingram in CORONATION STREET. Among his other credits have been THE FLAME TREES OF THIKA, THE PROFESSIONALS, DOCTOR WHO, MINDER, THE CLEOPATRAS, *Churchill's People*, BERGERAC, THE BILL, *Crown Prosecutor, Arabian Nights*, BROOKSIDE, A DANCE TO THE MUSIC OF TIME, WAKING THE DEAD and the EastEnders bubble *Perfectly Frank*.

OSS/Office of Strategic Services **

UK (Robert Siodmak/LSQ/Buckeye/ITP) Spy Drama. ITV 1957–8

Capt. Frank Hawthorne .... **Ron Randell**
The Chief .... **Lionel Murton**
Sgt O'Brien .... **Robert Gallico**

Executive Producers **Joseph Harris, William Eliscu**
Producer **Jules Buck**

World War II espionage tales, based on true events.

OSS stands for Office of Strategic Services, the USA's precursor to the CIA, whose top man is Captain Frank Hawthorne. Against a wartime backdrop, Hawthorne and his colleague, Sgt O'Brien, work on the Continent to expose foreign spies, rescue stranded personnel and mount sabotage missions, often in conjunction with the French Resistance. The stories were drawn from the files of the real OSS, which was disbanded after the war, and authenticity was ensured by co-producer William Eliscu, who had himself served in the agency. In the UK the series was often billed in full as *Office of Strategic Services*. Each episode was entitled 'Operation ...' (fill in the blank).

O'Sullevan, Sir Peter

CBE (1918–)

Irish-born horse-racing commentator, the voice of the BBC's racing coverage for over 50 years. O'Sullevan called the horses for the Corporation from 1947 to 1997, initially while racing correspondent for the Press Association. He later wrote for the *Daily Express*.

O'Sullivan, Richard
(1944–)

British actor, once a child performer and seen on TV from the 1950s in series like *Little Lord Fauntleroy, All Aboard*, DIXON OF DOCK GREEN and THE ADVENTURES OF ROBIN HOOD (Prince Arthur). In 1966 he played mail-room boy Taplow in the sitcom *Foreign Affairs*, and in the early 1970s played the sneaky Dr Bingham in *Doctor at Large* and *Doctor in Charge* (see DOCTOR IN THE HOUSE), which led to other sitcom roles, most notably that of Robin Tripp in MAN ABOUT THE HOUSE and ROBIN'S NEST. He appeared with Ronnie Corbett in NOW LOOK HERE! (Keith), and was Richard Gander with Beryl Reid in *Alcock and Gander*. Switching briefly back to drama, O'Sullivan starred as DICK TURPIN in the series of the same name in 1979, but was tempted back to comedy with ME AND MY GIRL in 1984, playing widower Simon Harrap. In 1991 he was psychiatrist Adam Charlesworth in *Trouble in Mind*. Other credits have included DANGER MAN, REDCAP, STRANGE REPORT and FATHER, DEAR FATHER.

Othello ★★

UK (LWT/WGBH/CBC) Drama. ITV 2001
DVD: Acorn Media (Region 1 only)

John Othello .... **Eamonn Walker**
Ben Jago .... **Christopher Eccleston**
Dessie Brabant .... **Keeley Hawes**
Michael Cass .... **Richard Coyle**
Sinclair Carver .... **Bill Paterson**
Lulu .... **Rachael Stirling**

Writer **Andrew Davies**
Producers **Julie Gardner, Anne Pivcevic**

● ***Envy and jealousy combine to undermine a successful black police officer.***

This one-off, two-hour modernization of Shakespeare's tragedy brings the action forward five centuries, with the location switched to London from Venice and Cyprus.

John Othello is a black officer in the Metropolitan Police. When he is fast-tracked over his white mentor, Ben Jago, and, in a piece of political expediency, becomes commissioner, Jago is incensed and plots Othello's downfall. While pretending to be still the best of buddies, he latches on to Othello's obsession for wife Dessie Brabant and, by worming young detective Michael Cass into Dessie's life, provokes an outburst of jealousy that ends in desperate circumstances. The victory belongs to the smarmy, sneering Jago, who confides his true emotions directly to the camera while springing the trap for his former comrade.

Other 'Arf, The ★★

UK (Witzend/ATV/Central) Situation Comedy. ITV 1980–2; 1984

Lorraine Watts .... **Lorraine Chase**
Charles Latimer MP .... **John Standing**
Brian Sweeney .... **Steve Adler**
Sybilla Howarth .... **Patricia Hodge**
George Watts .... **John Cater**
Lord Freddy Apthorpe .... **James Villiers**
Bassett .... **Richard Caldicot**
Mrs Lilley .... **Sheila Keith**

Creator **Terence Howard**
Writers **Terence Howard, Paul Makin**
Executive Producer **Allan McKeown**
Producers **Tony Charles, Douglas Argent**

● ***A Tory MP has an affair with a Cockney model.***

The course of love never does run smooth for upper-class Tory MP Charles Latimer and Cockney model Lorraine Watts who meet in a restaurant. Sybilla Howarth and Brian Sweeney, the partners they ditch, remain on the scene to make life uncomfortable, and ultimately Charles loses his parliamentary seat, forcing him and Lorraine to open up his home, Dormer House, to paying guests. Bassett and Mrs Lilley are his domestic staff, George is Lorraine's dad and Lord Freddy Apthorpe an aristocratic chum of Charles's.

The Other 'Arf capitalized on model Lorraine Chase's success as the Cockney girl in adverts for Campari. When asked by her smoothie suitor, 'Were you truly wafted here from Paradise?', she responded, 'No. Luton Airport', and so launched her acting career.

Other One, The ★★★

UK (BBC) Situation Comedy. BBC 1 1977; 1979

Brian Bryant .... **Michael Gambon**
Ralph Tanner .... **Richard Briers**
Sue Bainbridge .... **Jill Kerman**

Writers **John Esmonde, Bob Larbey**
Producers **John Howard Davies, Roger Race**

● ***Two social misfits form an unlikely friendship.***

Brian Bryant, from Cricklewood, is a clerk with a recording company, handling long-forgotten back issues. His life is mundane, but then so is he. His wife, Jill, divorced him on grounds of mental cruelty – he bored her. To add a little spice to his existence he decides to take a holiday in Spain and at the airport bumps into Ralph Tanner, a confident, know-it-all sales rep from Luton, who takes Brian under his wing. Describing himself as a 'lone wolf', Ralph makes out that he has the world at his fingertips, but the truth is he is as lonely, sad and naïve as his new friend. The first series follows their exploits in Spain, in which Tanner's *braggadocio* falls flatter than the local tortillas and it is obvious that he needs Brian more than Brian needs him. Sue Bainbridge is their holiday courier. In series two, shown in 1979, the pair are back in Britain and Ralph has secured a salesman's job for Brian in the packaging company where he works. The duo then shamble their way around the UK looking for orders, with Ralph supposedly in the driving seat and Brian his timid apprentice. Ronnie Hazelhurst provided the theme music.

OTT

See *Tiswas*.

Our Friends in the North ★★★★

UK (BBC) Drama. BBC 2 1996
DVD: Bmg Music Programming

Nicky Hutchinson .... **Christopher Eccleston**
Mary Soulsby/Cox .... **Gina McKee**
Terry 'Tosker' Cox .... **Mark Strong**
George 'Geordie' Peacock .... **Daniel Craig**
Felix Hutchinson .... **Peter Vaughan**
Austin Donohue .... **Alun Armstrong**

Florrie Hutchinson	**Freda Dowie**
Eddie Wells	**David Bradley**
John Edwards	**Geoffrey Hutchings**
Benny Barratt	**Malcolm McDowell**
Deputy Chief Constable Roy Johnson	**Tony Haygarth**
Commissioner Colin Blamire	**Peter Jeffrey**
Commander Harold Chapple	**Donald Sumpter**
DI/Det. Chief Supt. John Salway	**David Schofield**
DS Ron Conrad	**Danny Webb**
Julia Allen	**Louise Salter**
Claud Seabrook	**Julian Fellowes**
Anthony Cox	**Matthew Baron**
	Adam Pearson
	Daniel Casey
Elaine Craig/Cox	**Tracey Wilkinson**
Claudia Seabrook	**Saskia Wickham**

Writer **Peter Flannery**
Producer **Charles Pattinson**

Socio-political change in Britain illustrated by the lives of four friends from Newcastle.

The widely acclaimed *Our Friends in the North* is the nine-part story of four teenage friends, beginning in 1964 and tracing their vastly differing lives through to the 1990s, providing an insight into the social and political developments that shape the country along the way. The foursome begin with idealistic young socialist Nicky Hutchinson, who gives up his education to work for local politician Austin Donohue at a time when a Labour government is being elected and new hope is spreading through the working classes. His girlfriend, Mary Soulsby, a university student, is forced to abandon academia when she falls pregnant to Tosker Cox, an objectionable 'pal' of Nicky's who has unrealistic pretensions of becoming a pop star. The fourth member of the gang is Geordie Peacock, Nicky's best mate, who is destined to run away from home and his violently abusive father.

Progressing through the 1960s and 1970s, the drama unfolds as Nicky angrily walks out on corrupt local politics and turns to anarchy; the self-sacrificing Mary and the self-centred Tosker become unhappily married parents of two kids, living in an uninhabitable new tower block; and Geordie finds himself living the high life in the pay of London vice baron Benny Barratt.

Things come to a head in the Thatcherite 1980s. Nicky unsuccessfully returns to the political arena as a parliamentary candidate and then makes his mark as a photo-journalist; Mary finds her own voice and is voted on to the council; womanizing Tosker joins the 'me first' band of wealth-gatherers, buying council houses and running his own businesses; and sad Geordie slides into a miserable spiral of prison and homelessness. Nicky finally marries, and then cheats on, Mary, and Tosker finds a new wife, too, named Elaine.

In the more harmonious 1990s there is an air of reconciliation. Now in their middle ages, the four friends have experienced the trauma of raising kids and watching parents grow old and die (notably the Alzheimer's tragedy of Nicky's dad, Felix). The idealism and hopes of youth have been transformed into scepticism born out of bitter experience. And, though the four continue on their individual paths in life – Nicky again solo, Mary riding high in politics, Tosker scrabbling back up from near-bankruptcy and buying a boat nightclub on the Tyne, and Geordie, the loner, resignedly walking away from it all yet again, they do at least seem to have learned to understand each other.

As intriguing as its personal storylines are, the serial was also recognized for the way in which it explored social upheavals in the late 20th century – from political and police corruption in the 1960s and union militancy in the 1970s to uncompromising Thatcherism (especially concerning the miners' strike) in the 1980s and the more subdued, post-recession 1990s. It began life as a stage play, in which events ended in 1979 at the start of the Thatcher years. When its writer, Peter Flannery, was eventually commissioned to develop it for television (after 15 years), he extended the action up to 1995 and the threshold of another new political era.

Our House ★★

UK (ABC) Situation Comedy. ITV 1960–1

Georgina Ruddy	**Hattie Jacques**
Simon Willow	**Charles Hawtrey**
Daisy Burke	**Joan Sims**
Capt. Iliffe	**Frank Pettingell**
Mrs Iliffe	**Ina de la Haye**
Gordon Brent	**Norman Rossington**
Herbert Keene	**Frederick Peisley**
Stephen Hatton	**Trader Faulkner**
Marcia Hatton	**Leigh Madison**
William Singer	**Bernard Bresslaw**
Henrietta	**Hylda Baker**
Marina	**Eugenie Cavanagh**

Writers **Norman Hudis, Brad Ashton, Bob Block**
Producer **Ernest Maxin**

Comic capers with the oddball residents of a large house.

Carry On under One Roof may have been a more appropriate title for this farcical comedy, partly written by *Carry On* scriptwriter Norman Hudis and starring several of the big-screen performers. It features a rag-bag of nine people who meet in an estate agent's office and, by pooling their funds, manage to buy a house big enough to accommodate them all. The cohabitors are librarian Georgina Ruddy; council official Simon Willow; unemployable Daisy Burke; the artistic, newly wed Hattons; Yorkshire sea-dog Captain Iliffe and his French violinist wife; bank clerk Herbert Keene; and law student Gordon Brent. When the second series begins, some new house-sharers, including William Singer, Marina and Henrietta, are added.

After the introductory first episode, which was billed as *Moving in to Our House*, not all the characters appear in each story.

Our Man at St Mark's/Our Man from St Mark's ★★

UK (Associated-Rediffusion) Situation Comedy. ITV 1963–5/1966

Revd Andrew Parker	**Leslie Phillips**
Revd Stephen Young	**Donald Sinden**
Mrs Peace	**Joan Hickson**
Anne Gibson	**Anne Lawson**
Harry the Yo Yo	**Harry Fowler**

Creators/Writers **James Kelly, Peter Miller**
Producer **Eric Maschwitz**

Humorous happenings in the daily life of a country vicar.

St Mark's, a rural parish centring around the village of Felgate, is blessed with the Reverend Andrew Parker as its slightly eccentric vicar. This series focuses on his day-to-day exploits, taking in the amusing incidents and, occasionally, the sentimental. Parker is assisted by his girlfriend, Anne Gibson, and housekeeper, Mrs Peace. When St Mark's gains a new vicar, Stephen Young, after one series, Mrs Peace remains *in situ* and a reformed crook by the name of Harry the Yo Yo (on account of the fact that he is in and out of prison) is employed as sexton/gravedigger. Stephen also brings with him a Scottie dog named Mr Robertson. The title changes slightly for the fourth and final season. Becoming *Our Man from St Mark's*, it sees Stephen promoted to archdeacon and transferred to a cathedral.

Our Man at St Mark's began a year after a similar series had aired in the USA. Entitled *Going My Way*, it starred Gene Kelly and was a small-screen version of the classic 1944 Bing Crosby film.

Our Mutual Friend ★★★

UK (BBC/CBC) Drama. BBC 2 1998
DVD: BBC

Eugene Wrayburn	**Paul McGann**
Lizzie Hexam	**Keeley Hawes**
John Rokesmith/Harmon	**Steven Mackintosh**
Bella Wilfer/Harmon	**Anna Friel**
Mr Boffin	**Peter Vaughan**
Mrs Boffin	**Pam Ferris**
Silas Wegg	**Kenneth Cranham**
Mr Venus	**Timothy Spall**
Rogue Riderhood	**David Bradley**
Gaffer Hexam	**David Schofield**
Charley Hexam	**Paul Bailey**
Mortimer Lightwood	**Dominic Mafham**
Lady Tippins	**Margaret Tyzack**
Mr Tremlow	**Robert Lang**
Alfred Lammle	**Anthony Calf**
Sophronia Lammle	**Doon Mackichan**
Bradley Headstone	**David Morrissey**
Jenny Wren	**Katy Murphy**
Betty Higden	**Edna Doré**
Mr Sloppy	**Martin Hancock**
Mr Veneering	**Michael Culkin**
Mrs Veneering	**Rose English**

Writer **Sandy Welch**
Producer **Catherine Wearing**

● ***Acclaimed dramatization of Dickens's last complete novel.***

Two love stories form the centrepiece of this four-part adaptation of Dickens's final and, for many, greatest novel. The first concerns self-deluding barrister Eugene Wrayburn, who falls in love with lowly boatman's daughter, Lizzie Hexam, but has a rival for her attentions in obsessive schoolmaster Bradley Headstone. The second involves wealthy John Harmon, who pretends to be dead in order to check out the girl he is supposed to marry if he is to claim his inheritance. The girl is Bella Wilfer, the feckless, adopted daughter of Mr Boffin, a kind-hearted foreman from the dust company once run by Harmon's father. Boffin has acquired his property in John's absence. However, the deeper romance behind the main stories is the love of money, as greed and grime go hand in hand and the meek, it is hoped, will inherit the earth. The serial was filmed in the Cotswolds and also on Cardiff Bay (doubling for the Thames-side London of the 1860s). Previous adaptations of *Our Mutual Friend* have come in 1958–9 (BBC: Rachel Roberts as Lizzie, Zena Walker as Bella, David McCallum as Wrayburn, Paul Daneman as John Harmon) and 1976 (BBC 2: Lesley Dunlop as Lizzie, Jane Seymour as Bella, Nicholas Jones as Wrayburn, John McEnery as John Harmon).

Our World ★★

UK (BBC) Entertainment. BBC 1 1967

Presenter **Cliff Michelmore**

Producer **Ray Colley**

● ***Satellite link-up featuring contributions from TV companies around the world.***

This celebration of satellite technology, sponsored by the European Broadcasting Union, was broadcast between 8 and 10 p.m. on the evening of Sunday, 25 June 1967. Hosted by Cliff Michelmore, it employed four satellites and over a million miles of cabling to bring together live pictures from most parts of the globe (the Soviet Union and Poland were notable exceptions, having pulled out because of the Israeli Six-Day War earlier in the month). In all, 18 countries contributed a (non-political) televisual message or other item. The BBC's offering was a live performance of The Beatles singing 'All You Need is Love'.

Out ★★★

UK (Thames/Euston Films) Drama. ITV 1978

Frank Ross	**Tom Bell**
Anne Ross	**Lynn Farleigh**
Evie	**Pam Fairbrother**
DI Bryce	**Norman Rodway**
Rimmer	**Robert Walker**
Cimmie	**Katharine Schofield**
Ralph Veneker	**John Junkin**
Chris Cottle	**Brian Croucher**
Vic Lee	**Frank Mills**
Bernie Machen	**Oscar James**
Pretty Billy Binns	**Peter Blake**

Writer **Trevor Preston**
Executive Producer **Johnny Goodman**
Producer **Barry Hanson**

● ***A vicious, bitter criminal is released from jail and looks for revenge.***

Tough, intense bank-robber Frank Ross, a hardman among hardmen, has only one aim in life. Now back on the streets after eight years in prison, he is looking for the person who shopped him. Nothing gets in his way in his quest for the informer, and his obsessed meanderings through London's underworld are punctuated by encounters with numerous sad and evil characters. The violence is heavy and the police Ross confronts are as grubby and miserable as the villains they set out to catch. Frank's wife, mentally wrecked by his bleak life of crime, is also seen. A powerful, six-part drama, *Out* won much acclaim.

Out of the Blue ★★★

UK (BBC) Police Drama. BBC 1 1995–6

DI Eric Temple	**John Duttine**

DS Franky Drinkall	**John Hannah**
DC Ron Ludlow	**Peter Wight**
DC Marty Brazil	**Neil Dudgeon**
DS Rebecca Bennett	**Orla Brady**
DC Warren Allen	**Darrell D'Silva**
DC Bruce Hannaford	**Lennie James**
CID Aide/DC Tony Bromley	**Andy Rashleigh**
PC Alex Holder	**Stephen Billington**
Dr Innocent Adesigbin	**Pauline Black**
Kath Ludlow	**Sally Edwards**
DS Jim 'Lew' Lewyn	**David Morrissey**
Lucy Shaw	**Nicola Stephenson**

Creators/Writers **Peter Bowker, Bill Gallagher**
Executive Producers **Michael Wearing, Caroline Oulton**
Producers **Jo Wright, Laura Mackie**

● ***A team of Yorkshire detectives grapple with brutal inner-city crimes.***

Billed as a return to the ensemble police drama, in the mould of Z CARS, and borrowing stylistically from US series like HILL STREET BLUES, *Out of the Blue* studies the interaction between members of the CID team at Brazen Gate police station in South Yorkshire. Creators Peter Bowker and Bill Gallagher set out to produce a drama of equals, with no deliberate pecking order among the main core of characters. However, the nominal head of the team, though always fighting to keep control, is DI Eric Temple. He is flanked by the strongly ambitious Franky Drinkall, who sees his career put on hold because of epilepsy problems; volatile Marty Brazil, whose marriage is dogged by the fact that he and his wife can't have kids; and smart alec Warren Allen, who has the hots for his partner, Rebecca Bennett. There are also reliable Ron Ludlow, whose family life is falling apart; self-critical Bruce Hannaford; and late-achiever Tony, who has just broken into CID ranks. The crimes they confront are bleak and heinous, ranging from child abduction to male rape, but the focus is always on how the team deals with each problem – usually with black humour – and its effects on their personal lives. The shocking murder of one of their number at the end of the first series leaves a huge emotional scar. New in the team in series two is DS 'Lew' Lewyn, who hides a colourful past. Twelve episodes were produced in total. The programme title symbolically describes the move police officers make when they leave uniform for plain-clothes work.

Out of the Unknown ★★

UK (BBC) Science Fiction. BBC 2 1965–7; 1969; 1971

Producers **Irene Shubik, Alan Bromly**

● ***Well-respected sci-fi anthology series.***

Initially taking works by renowned science-fiction authors like John Wyndham, Ray Bradbury and Isaac Asimov, this collection of spooky tales proved to be Britain's definitive answer to THE TWILIGHT ZONE. It employed skilled TV writers like Troy Kennedy Martin, Terry Nation and Leon Griffiths as adaptors, and was masterminded by former ARMCHAIR THEATRE story editor Irene Shubik, who had already attempted a similar concept when working on ABC's OUT OF THIS WORLD. The tales were not all thrillers, some were satires and comedies, but fantastic space creatures and bug-eyed monsters were steadfastly avoided. The series also attracted some of the best contemporary acting talents – the likes of Marius Goring, George Cole, Warren Mitchell, Donald Houston, David Hemmings and Rachel Roberts – as well as aspiring directors like Ridley Scott. In 1969, after a two-year gap, the series was revived in colour and the emphasis switched from pure sci-fi to horror and psychological suspense, as new producer Alan Bromly picked up the reins.

Out of This World ★★

UK (ABC) Science Fiction. ITV 1962

Host **Boris Karloff**

Producer **Leonard White**

● ***An innovative British series of hour-long science-fiction plays.***

Produced by ABC, already highly successful with its ARMCHAIR THEATRE collection of single dramas, this series was British TV's first attempt at a science-fiction anthology. Many of the trends it set, such as using the works of established sci-fi authors, employing first-rate adaptors and leading performers, and varying the style of each play from pure suspense to black comedy, were continued through to its natural successor, the BBC's OUT OF THE UNKNOWN. Thirteen episodes were made, and were shown on Saturday nights, with introductions by the softly sinister Boris Karloff. Among the writing talent on show were Terry Nation, Leon Griffiths, Clive Exton, Julian Bond and Richard Waring.

Outer Limits, The ★★★★

US (Daystar/United Artists) Science Fiction. ITV 1964; BBC 2 1995–9 (US: ABC 1963–5; Showtime 1995–2001; Sci-Fi 2001–2)
DVD: MGM

The Control Voice	**Vic Perrin**
	Kevin Conway

Creator/Executive Producer **Leslie Stevens**
Producers **Joseph Stefano, Ben Brady**

● ***Stylish anthology of sci-fi thriller stories.***

In the 1950s and 1960s, video static and picture distortion were annoyingly familiar to TV viewers. However, there was always an announcer at hand to confirm that normal programming would resume as soon as possible – unless you happened to be watching *The Outer Limits*. Playing on the poor reliability of TV signals and television equipment, *The Outer Limits* set out to frighten viewers from the start, opening with the loss of the picture and a voice that declared ominously: 'There is nothing wrong with your television set. Do not attempt to adjust the picture. We are controlling transmission. We will control the horizontal. We will control the vertical. For the next hour, sit quietly and we will control all you see and hear. You are about to experience the awe and mystery that reaches from the inner mind to the Outer Limits.'

What followed was one of the 49 sci-fi thrillers that made up *The Outer Limits* anthology. Most concerned Earth invasions by extraterrestrial life-forms and are best remembered for their catalogue of terrifying aliens, which varied from giant insects to intelligent rocks and invisible parasites. But there was much more to *The Outer Limits* than bug-eyed monsters. The camera work applied a stark, *film noir* veneer to the imaginative stories and, though the monsters took centre stage, it was the humans – or, rather, human nature – that stole the show, with a moral always drawn from proceedings. Thankfully, the announcer – or Control Voice (the person was never seen) – then restored normality, concluding with the words: 'We now return control of your television set to you, until next week at the same time, when the Control Voice will take you to . . . the Outer Limits.'

The show's first producer, Joseph Stefano, certainly knew how to chill; he had already written the screenplay for Hitchcock's *Psycho*. Being an anthology series, *The Outer Limits* called upon guest artists every week, with stars like Leonard Nimoy, William Shatner, Martin Sheen, Donald Pleasence and David McCallum taking on lead roles. BBC 2 reran the entire series in 1980–1. A new version aired sporadically on BBC 2 from 1995, with Kevin Conway assuming the Control Voice role.

Outhwaite, Tamzin

(1970–)

One of Ilford-born Tamzin Outhwaite's earliest TV roles was as a presenter of the youth show *No Limits* (billed as Tammi Outhwaite). Later there were small parts in both MEN BEHAVING BADLY and THE BILL. However, joining EASTENDERS as Melanie Healy/Beale/Owen proved to be her big break, which she followed up with the lead roles in the military police drama RED CAP (Sgt Jo McDonagh) and an improvised drama about young offenders called *Out of Control* (Dean's mum). She was later seen in *Final Demand* (Natalie Bingham), *When I'm Sixty-Four* (Caz), *Frances Tuesday* (Frances West), *Walk Away and I Stumble* (Claire Holmes) and *Hotel Babylon* (Rebecca), and, in 2001, featured in *Tamzin Outhwaite Goes Wild with Dolphins*.

Outside Broadcast

Abbreviated to OB, an outside broadcast is a programme or part of a programme that takes place outside the controlled environment of a television studio. An OB at a major sporting event or state occasion, for example, is a complex operation, involving numerous strategically placed cameras and microphones, all co-ordinated by a director and his/her team working from a mobile control room.

Outside Edge ★★★

UK (Central) Situation Comedy. ITV 1994–6
DVD: Network

Miriam ('Mim') Dervish	**Brenda Blethyn**
Roger Dervish	**Robert Daws**
Maggie Costello	**Josie Lawrence**
Kevin Costello	**Timothy Spall**
Dennis Broadley	**Denis Lill**
Bob Willis	**Jeremy Nicholas**
	Michael Jayston
Alex Harrington	**Ben Daniels**
	Christopher Lang
Nigel	**Nigel Pegram**
Ginnie Willis	**Tracy Brabin**
Shirley Broadley	**Hilary Crane**

Writer **Richard Harris**
Producer **Paula Burdon**

● ***Middle-class tensions run high at an English cricket club.***

While the concept of early-middle-aged men playing cricket at weekends, supported by their tea-making wives, forms the hub of this popular ITV comedy, the real focus is on class, sex and marital harmony. The major players – an otherwise incompatible foursome – at Brent Park Cricket Club are stuffy chauvinist Roger Dervish (club captain) and his frustrated, mousy wife, Mim, and the more earthy Maggie and Kevin Costello, she an ever-practical nymphomaniac who thinks her husband the best thing since sliced bread, he enjoying their lusty relationship but also slobbishly indulging in real kitchen activities, not to mention a good few pints with the rest of the lads.

The series was spun off a stage play which had already been made into a TV drama in 1982, starring Paul Eddington and Prunella Scales as the Dervishes and Maureen Lipman and Jonathan Lynn as the Costellos.

Outsider, The ★★

UK (Yorkshire) Drama. ITV 1983

Frank Scully	**John Duttine**
Fiona Neave	**Carol Royle**
Sylvia Harper	**Joanna Dunham**
Donald Harper	**Norman Eshley**
Lord Wrathdale	**Peter Clay**
Lady Wrathdale	**Elizabeth Bennett**
Miss Banner	**Pauline Letts**
Reuben Flaxman	**Michael Sheard**
Tom Holliday	**Ted Morris**

Writer **Michael J. Bird**
Executive Producer **David Cunliffe**
Producer **Michael Glynn**

● ***A hard-nosed journalist stirs up trouble in a Yorkshire town.***

Frank Scully is an uncompromising journalist. He pays a visit to the small market town of Micklethorpe (real life Knaresborough), in Wrathdale, initially just to see old friends. However, he decides to stay and takes over as editor of the local rag, *The Messenger*, much to the concern of several local townsfolk, who, it transpires, harbour a number of social secrets. Scully's arrival and his nose for a story certainly cause a flutter, as skeletons start rattling in cupboards and illicit affairs come out into the open. Among the women in Scully's life are Fiona Neave, who runs the local printing factory, and his old friend Sylvia Harper. Alan Hawkshaw provided the music for the series.

Out-takes

Material shot but not used in the finished programme, often because of gaffes and blunders. These have proved particularly popular with viewers when grouped in humorous collections like IT'LL BE ALRIGHT ON THE NIGHT and *Auntie's Bloomers*.

Over the Rainbow ★★

UK (SelecTV/Meridian) Situation Comedy. ITV 1993

Finnoula ('Finn')	**Angeline Ball**
Michelle	**Bronagh Gallagher**
Neil	**Peter Sullivan**
Spence	**Ian Targett**
Uncle Roddy	**Eamon Morrissey**

Creators **Dick Clement, Ian La Frenais**

Writers **Dick Clement, Ian La Frenais, Geoff Rowley**
Producer **Bernard McKenna**

● ***Two Irish girls try to break into the music business, hampered by their inept male friends.***
Having lived together in London for two years, Finn and Neil decide to get married. However, things don't go quite to plan when Neil and his flatmate, Spence, take part in a safe robbery on the day of the wedding. Neil is imprisoned for a year and, when released, makes his way to Brighton, where Finn has rented a flat over her Uncle Roddy's pub, The Rainbow. With fellow Irish girl Michelle, she has taken up singing in a rock band, and Neil and Spence (who had been living with Finn) now decide that there's money to be made by hanging on to the shirt-tails of the girls' talent as managers of 'Wicked Cleavage'. Always in the background, however, is Finn's randy uncle – the man who had orchestrated the ill-fated robbery. Finn, meanwhile, has to choose between the lads and decides on neither. The series was loosely based on the hugely successful film *The Commitments*, also co-penned by writers Dick Clement and Ian La Frenais, and featuring stars Angeline Ball and Bronagh Gallagher, but just one, eight-part series was produced.

Owen, Alun

(1925–94)

Welsh dramatist, one of UK TV's major early playwrights. For ARMCHAIR THEATRE he penned *No Trams to Lime Street* in 1959, quickly followed by *After the Funeral, Lena, O My Lena* (both 1960) and *The Rose Affair* (1961). *The Strain* (1963) and *Shelter* (1967) were among other acclaimed 1960s offerings, as was *You Can't Win 'Em All* (1962), which led to a six-part series, *Corrigan Blake*, the following year. Similarly, another play, *Ah – There You Are* (part of *The Ronnie Barker Playhouse* collection), created the character of Lord Rustless and resulted in the series HARK AT BARKER, in 1969. The same year, his trilogy comprising *MacNeil*, *Cornelius* and *Emlyn* aired under the *Saturday Night Theatre* banner. His later work included *Norma* (1974), *Forget-Me-Not* (1976) and *Kisch, Kisch* (1983), plus a serial adaptation of R. F. Delderfield's *Come Home Charlie and Face Them*. Owen also wrote the screenplay for The Beatles' film *A Hard Day's Night*.

Owen, Bill

MBE (Bill Rowbotham; 1914–99)

Few actors have held down the same television role for over 20 years, but Bill Owen was one of them, thanks to his marathon stint as the seedy Compo in LAST OF THE SUMMER WINE. (His son, Tom, has since succeeded him in the cast.) Owen's TV career, however, stretched way back. In 1951 he played Inspector Lestrade in an ambitious BBC adaptation of the Sherlock Holmes mysteries. In 1963 he starred as Fred Cuddell, alongside Sid James, in TAXI and, eight years later, played the conniving Sgt Sam Short in *Copper's End*. Among his other credits were WHATEVER HAPPENED TO THE LIKELY LADS? (Thelma's dad, George Chambers), TALES OF THE UNEXPECTED, BRIDESHEAD REVISITED (Lunt) and CORONATION STREET. Owen also wrote several plays and the lyrics for numerous songs.

Owen, Clive

(1964–)

Midlands-born actor, the star of CHANCER (Stephen Crane), *Lorna Doone* (John Ridd), *Sharman* (Nick Sharman), *Split Second* (Michael Anderson) and SECOND SIGHT (DCI Ross Tanner), as well as *An Evening with Gary Lineker* (Bill), and *Screen Two's Bad Boy Blues*. His dad, Jess, once won New Faces with his country band, The Gingerbreads. Owen is married to actress Sarah-Jane Fenton.

Owen, Ivan

(1927–2000)
See *Brush, Basil.*

Owen, MD

See *Doctors, The.*

Owen, Nicholas

(1947–)

ITN newscaster and reporter, working on all the main bulletins (including *Channel 4 News*) and the company's royal correspondent, 1994–2000. He has also fronted Channel 4's *The Parliament Programme* and hosted the quiz show *Watching the Detectives*. Owen's career began in newspapers. He joined the BBC in the north of England in 1981 and transferred to ITN in 1984.

Owen, Nick

(1947–)

Berkhamsted-born journalist and presenter, coming to the fore as host of TV-am's GOOD MORNING BRITAIN in 1983, following work as a news and sports frontman for ATV and Central (as well as TV-am). Owen has also hosted the quizzes *Sporting Triangles* and *Hitman*, *Midweek Sports Special* and other sporting events. His breakfast-time partnership with Anne Diamond was poached by the BBC for *Good Morning with Anne and Nick* in the 1990s. In recent years he has been presenting *Midlands Today* for the BBC.

Oxbridge Blues ✶✶✶

UK (BBC) Drama Anthology. BBC 2 1984

Narrator **Norman Rodway**

Writer **Frederic Raphael**
Producer **James Cellan Jones**

● ***Further tales from the lives of Oxbridge graduates.***
Based on his own short stories, THE GLITTERING PRIZES author Frederic Raphael penned this collection of seven plays that featured actors like David Suchet, Michael Elphick, Joanna Lumley, John Bird, Geoffrey Palmer, Ben Kingsley, Ian Charleson, Alfred Marks, Diane Keen and Carol Royle. Some appeared in more than one play, assuming new characters each time.

Pace, Norman

(1953–)
See *Hale, Gareth.*

Packet of Three/Packing Them In ✶✶

UK (Jon Blair/Fine Time) Comedy. Channel 4 1991/1992

Frank .... **Frank Skinner**
Jenny .... **Jenny Eclair**
Henry .... **Henry Normal** *(of Three)*
Reg .... **Roger Mann** *(Them In)*
Boyle .... **Kevin Eldon** *(Them In)*

Producers **Jon Blair, John Stroud** *(of Three)*, **Jo Sargent** *(Them In)*

● ***Behind the scenes and on-stage at 'Britain's newest venue'.***

Taking a variety theatre as its setting (the Crumpsall Palladium), *Packet of Three* boldly merged sitcom and stand up. Running the theatre were its inept owner Henry, ticket seller Jenny and stage manager Frank. This trio provided the background laughs while top guest performers from the comedy and cabaret circuits did their turns in the limelight. With Henry Normal departing before the second series, and the number of guests varying from the original three per show, the second run was retitled *Packing Them In*. Roger Mann and Kevin Eldon were added as crew members Reg and Boyle. The 16 late-night shows over the two series featured such guests as Al Murray, Lily Savage, Mark Lamarr and Alistair McGowan.

Packing Them In

See *Packet of Three.*

Paddington ✶✶

UK (Filmfair) Animation. BBC 1 1976; 1979

Narrator **Michael Hordern**

Creator/Writer **Michael Bond**
Producer **Graham Clutterbuck**

● ***The adventures of a somewhat disorientated Peruvian bear in London.***

Paddington, the hero of books by Michael Bond since 1958, finally arrived on television in 1976. As a result, a new generation of youngsters was able to appreciate the cuddly bear in the blue duffle coat, floppy hat and wellies who loves marmalade sandwiches and lives with the Brown family at 32 Windsor Gardens. Mr Henry Brown is the head of the family, along with his wife and children Jonathan and Judy. Mrs Bird is the family cook.

The Browns found the bear at Paddington station (hence his name) wearing a tag reading 'Please look after this bear'. Looking after this bear, however, proves increasingly difficult, as the rather bemused but always inquisitive Paddington stumbles from mishap to mishap. Paddington's best friend is antiques dealer Mr Gruber, like Paddington a refugee from his own country.

These five-minute episodes, shown in the 'Magic Roundabout slot' just before the early evening news, featured a model Paddington animated by Ivor Wood against a static drawn background. One-off specials followed the two series, in 1983, 1986 and 1987. A more advanced, technically superior, updated series entitled *Paddington Bear* was seen on ITV in 1990 but failed to charm audiences like the original series.

Pagett, Nicola

(Nicola Scott; 1945–)

Cairo-born actress, popular on TV in the 1970s in particular, during which time she played Miss Elizabeth in UPSTAIRS, DOWNSTAIRS and took the title role in ANNA KARENINA. In the 1980s she was Adele Fairley in A WOMAN OF SUBSTANCE and Liz Rodenhurst in A BIT OF A DO. In 1994 she starred as hairdresser Sonia Drysdale in AIN'T MISBEHAVIN' and in 2000 she took the part of Sally Kegworth in *Up Rising*. Among her other credits have been THE CAESARS, THE PERSUADERS!, BARLOW AT LARGE, *Napoleon and Love*, THE SWEENEY, THE RIVALS OF SHERLOCK HOLMES, WAR AND PEACE, *French Without Tears*, LOVE STORY, *Shadow on the Sun*, *Scoop* and the Dennis Potter play *Visitors*. She is married to playwright Graham Swannell.

PAL

Phase Alternate Line colour-television system, developed in Germany and now in use throughout western Europe, except for France, which uses its own SECAM system. PAL, an adaptation of the American NTSC system (using 625 lines in the UK instead of the USA's 525, and with built-in colour correction), is also the standard in Brazil and China, among other countries.

Palin, Michael

CBE (1943–)

Sheffield-born actor, comedian, writer and presenter, famously one of the MONTY PYTHON troupe but with many other strings to his bow. Among his first writing credits were sketches for THE FROST REPORT, which brought Palin and his writing partner, Terry Jones, in touch with John Cleese, Graham Chapman and Eric Idle. They also scripted for John Bird's comedy *A Series of Bird's*, *The Late Show*, *Horne A'Plenty*, *Broaden Your Mind* and *Marty*. In 1967 Palin appeared in *Twice a Fortnight*, a late-night sketch show, and was then given the chance to shine in the wacky children's comedy, DO NOT ADJUST YOUR SET. This led to THE COMPLETE AND UTTER HISTORY OF BRITAIN, a spoof history series he compiled and presented with Jones in 1969. MONTY PYTHON'S FLYING CIRCUS, the same year, was a natural progression. While a serving Python, Palin continued to write elsewhere, with one of his regular outlets THE TWO RONNIES, and, when the Python team decided to call it a day in 1974, his next TV project was RIPPING YARNS, a send-up of *Boy's Own* tales, again in collaboration with Terry Jones. In the 1980s Palin drifted away from the small screen and focused more on cinema work. He was tempted back by the chance to emulate Phileas Fogg's attempt to go AROUND THE WORLD IN 80 DAYS, for a 1988 BBC documentary series. It proved to be an enormous success and the accompanying book sold over half a million copies – enough to call for several sequels, *Pole to Pole, Full Circle, Sahara with Michael Palin* and *Himalaya with Michael Palin* (see AROUND THE WORLD IN 80 DAYS, plus another travelogue, *Michael Palin's Hemingway Adventure*, celebrating the centenary of Ernest Hemingway's birth. Palin also demonstrated his dramatic skills with an acclaimed performance as schoolteacher Jim Nelson in Alan Bleasdale's GBH. Among his other credits have been *Three Men in a Boat* (Harris), GREAT RAILWAY JOURNEYS OF THE WORLD, *Michael Palin and the Ladies Who Loved Matisse, Michael Palin and the Mystery of Hammershøi* and the scripts for the TV films *East of Ipswich* and *Number 27*. Palin was also a founder director of Meridian Television, for whom he compiled *Palin's Column*, a series about the Isle of Wight, and starred in *A Class Act* (alongside Tracey Ullman).

Pallas ★★

UK (Noel Gay) Comedy. Channel 4 1991–2

Narrator **Richard E. Grant**

Producer **Geoff Atkinson**

● ***Humorous take on the everyday lives of the Royal Family.***

In the style of THE STAGGERING STORIES OF FERDINAND DE BARGOS, *Pallas* takes as its spoof subject matter the British royal family. Using news footage, dubbed with actors' voices, a ten-part soap is created, with episodes lasting either five or ten minutes and storylines including Fergie hosting karaoke contests, the Queen abdicating and Prince Charles running for cover. This series was shown over Christmas 1991. For Christmas 1992, a sequel, *Pallas 2* – a series of three, 25-minute episodes – was produced.

Pallisers, The ★★★

UK (BBC) Drama. BBC 2 1974
DVD: Acorn Media

Lady Glencora M'Cluskie/ Palliser .... **Susan Hampshire**
Plantagenet Palliser MP .... **Philip Latham**
Duke of Omnium .... **Roland Culver**
Burgo Fitzgerald .... **Barry Justice**
Countess of Midlothian .... **Fabia Drake**
Alice Vavasor/Grey .... **Carole Mortimer**
George Vavasor .... **Gary Watson**
Laura Kennedy .... **Anna Massey**
Lady Dumbello .... **Rachel Herbert**
Marie Goesler/Finn .... **Barbara Murray**
Marchioness of Auld Reekie ... **Sonia Dresdel**
John Grey .... **Bernard Brown**
Dolly Longstaffe .... **Donald Pickering**
Duke of St Bungay .... **Roger Livesey**
Lord Chiltern .... **John Hallam**
Phineas Finn .... **Donal McCann**
Lord Fawn .... **Derek Jacobi**
Lizzie Eustace/Emilius .... **Sarah Badel**
Barrington Erle .... **Moray Watson**
Robert Kennedy .... **Derek Godfrey**
Lawrence Fitzgibbon .... **Neil Stacy**
Collingwood .... **Maurice Quick**
Mr Monk .... **Bryan Pringle**
Violet Effingham/Chiltern .... **Mel Martin**
Mrs Bunce .... **Brenda Cowling**
Mary Flood/Finn .... **Máire Ní Ghráinne**
Mrs Hittaway .... **Penelope Keith**
Lord Brentford .... **Lockwood West**
Revd Emilius .... **Anthony Ainley**
Frank Greystock .... **Martin Jarvis**
Lord George .... **Terence Alexander**
Mr Gresham .... **Robin Bailey**
Mr Bonteen .... **Peter Sallis**
Mrs Bonteen .... **June Whitfield**
Adelaide Palliser .... **Jo Kendall**
Gerard Maule .... **Jeremy Clyde**
Frank Tregear .... **Jeremy Irons**
Earl of Silverbridge .... **Anthony Andrews**
Lady Mabel Grex .... **Anna Carteret**
Emily Wharton/Lopez .... **Sheila Ruskin**
Abel Wharton .... **Brewster Mason**
Ferdinand Lopez .... **Stuart Wilson**
Quintus Slide .... **Clifford Rose**
Isabel Boncasson .... **Lynne Frederick**
Sir Orlando Drought .... **Basil Dignam**

Writer **Simon Raven**
Producer **Martin Lisemore**

● ***Six of Anthony Trollope's novels merged into one TV series.***

Tracing the rise to power of snooty Plantagenet Palliser, his arranged marriage to the flighty Lady Glencora, and ending with the political emergence of his son, the Earl of Silverbridge, this series follows the ups and downs of the wealthy Palliser family and their associates in Victorian times. This is a family of near-noble birth that strives for power under the Liberal banner, echoing Trollope's own parliamentary yearnings. Dwelling also on personalities, social conflicts and the battle for family supremacy, this dramatization becomes a reflection of life in Trollope's time. However, made up of 26 episodes, the series was badly disrupted by a BBC labour dispute in July 1974. When filming was finally completed, the Corporation was forced to repeat five earlier episodes in order to enable viewers to catch up on events. Consequently, although the first part went out in January, the long-awaited finale did not arrive until November.

Palmer, Geoffrey

OBE (1927–)

London-born actor, in a range of supporting and starring roles, usually of a lugubrious nature. In the 1970s, he played Jimmy, Reggie's brother-in-law, in THE FALL AND RISE OF REGINALD PERRIN (also in the 1990s revival, *The Legacy of Reginald Perrin*) and Ben, Ria Parkinson's husband, in BUTTERFLIES. Later, Palmer starred as Leo Bannister in Carla Lane's THE LAST SONG and loony right-winger Harry Truscott in FAIRLY SECRET ARMY. He also appeared as Donald Fairchild in EXECUTIVE STRESS and as Lionel Hardcastle in AS TIME GOES BY. In addition, Palmer has been seen in *Bulldog Breed*, THE AVENGERS, EDWARD THE SEVENTH, BILL BRAND, FAWLTY TOWERS, DOCTOR WHO, BERGERAC, INSPECTOR MORSE, CHRISTABEL (Mr Burton), *After the War, Stalag Luft* (Kommander), THE INSPECTOR ALLEYN MYSTERIES and *Absolute Power*, as well as taking the roles of Field Marshal Haig in BLACKADDER GOES FORTH, Harry Stringer in HOT METAL, the Foreign Secretary in WHOOPS APOCALYPSE, Robert Crane in RECKLESS*: The Sequel*, grandfather Robert in STIG OF THE DUMP, Donald Savage in THE

SAVAGES, Thackeray in *Dickens*, Minnit in *The Young Visiters* and Sir Marmaduke Rowley in HE KNEW HE WAS RIGHT. He also narrated THE 1940 HOUSE, as he did the early 1960s serial GARRY HALLIDAY.

Palmer, Tony

(1935–)

British writer, director, rock-music critic and documentary-maker. His early contributions included the sketch show *Twice a Fortnight*, and teenage pop shows like *How It Is* and *How Late It Is*. These changed the way pop was presented on TV, using music as a background to arts features, politics and other world events. He produced *All My Loving* for Omnibus in 1968, which aimed to dispel the myth that rock stars were all delinquents, and has also supplied profiles of Benjamin Britten, Peter Sellers, William Walton, Stravinsky, Richard Burton and Margot Fonteyn (the last for THE SOUTH BANK SHOW). Palmer's ALL YOU NEED IS LOVE, a 17-part history of popular music, was screened in 1977.

Pan

The movement of a camera horizontally from left to right or vice versa, as opposed to tilt, which is its up-and-down manoeuvre.

Panorama ★★★

UK (BBC) Current Affairs. BBC 1 1953–

Presenters **Patrick Murphy, Max Robertson, Richard Dimbleby, James Mossman, Robin Day, Alastair Burnet, David Dimbleby, Charles Wheeler, Fred Emery, Robert Kee**

Editors **Dennis Bardens, Michael Barsley, Rex Moorfoot, Michael Peacock, Paul Fox, David Wheeler, Jeremy Isaacs, John Grist, David J. Webster, Brian Wenham, Frank Smith, Christopher Capron, Roger Bolton, George Carey, Peter Ibbotson, David Dickinson, Tim Gardam, Robert Rowland, Peter Pagnamenta, Mark Thompson, Glenwyn Benson, Steve Hewlett, Peter Horrocks, Mike Robinson**

● ***The world's longest-running current affairs programme.***

Although noted today for its hard-hitting investigations and reports into matters of political and social concern, *Panorama* began in quite a different vein. It was launched in 1953 as 'a fortnightly reflection of the contemporary scene', a magazine programme produced by Andrew Miller Jones and hosted by newspaper journalist Patrick Murphy, who quickly made way for Max Robertson, as anchor. Malcolm Muggeridge was the resident interviewer, Denis Mathews was the art critic, Nancy Spain reviewed books and Lionel Hale discussed events in the theatre. After two years, however, *Panorama* was completely revamped to become a 'window on the world'. In came respected commentator Richard Dimbleby, and he fronted the programme through its glory days in the late 1950s and early 1960s. Other notable anchormen are listed above (although the studio has lately been abandoned in favour of prerecorded reports). Dimbleby's team included John Freeman (later of FACE TO FACE) and Christopher Chataway. Later contributors included Michael Barratt, Trevor Philpott, Michael Charlton and Leonard Parkin.

As well as being noted for its longevity, *Panorama* has also provided some memorable items for the TV archives. In 1961 the Duke of Edinburgh became the first member of the royal family to be interviewed on television when quizzed by Richard Dimbleby. Four years earlier, on 1 April 1957, Dimbleby and his crew sprang a celebrated April Fools' prank on the viewing public, when it presented a documentary on the spaghetti harvest in southern Switzerland. A massive audience was attracted on 20 November 1995 for (the then unknown) Martin Bashir's explosive interview with Diana, Princess of Wales.

Para Handy – Master Mariner ★★

UK (BBC) Comedy Drama. BBC 1959–60

Para Handy McFarlane	**Duncan Macrae**
Dan Macphail	**John Grieve**
Dougie	**Roddy McMillan**
Sunny Jim (Davey Green)	**Angus Lennie**

Writer **Duncan Ross**
Producer **Pharic MacLaren**

● ***Easy-going tales of a roguish merchant seaman.***

The *Para Handy* stories written by Neil Munro (initially under the pen-name of Hugh Foulis in 1905 editions of the *Glasgow Evening News*) have become some of the most televised pieces of literature. This series from the turn of the 1960s featured Duncan Macrae as Captain Peter 'Para Handy' McFarlane, the wily skipper of the tiny Clyde steamer known as *The Vital Spark*, which plied its trade along the lochs and channels of western Scotland, delivering goods to isolated communities. Para Handy was notoriously unreliable and his crew were equally inept.

Under the name of *The Vital Spark, Para Handy* was revived for a COMEDY PLAYHOUSE presentation in 1965, and a series with the same title followed in 1966–7. Roddy McMillan took the lead role in both, and John Grieve was once again cast as Macphail, the chief engineer. Walter Carr took the part of Dougie the mate and cabin boy/cook Sunny Jim was played by Alex McAvoy. The series was revived again in 1974 and then completely recast for a 1994–5 version, *The Tales of Para Handy*, starring Gregor Fisher as the boozy old sea-dog. Rikki Fulton was seen as Macphail, Sean Scanlan as Dougie and Andrew Fairlie as Sunny Jim. The stories were now set in the 1930s.

Paradise Club, The ★★

UK (Zenith) Drama. BBC 1 1989–90

Danny Kane	**Leslie Grantham**
Father Frank Kane	**Don Henderson**
DI Rosy Campbell	**Kitty Aldridge**
Carol Kane	**Barbara Wilshere**
Jonjo O'Brady	**Peter Gowen**
Polish Joe	**Leon Herbert**
Ginger	**Jack Ellis**
Eddie Cleary	**Peter Gunn**
DS Tommy Cooper	**Malcolm Raeburn**
DC Webster	**Ben Daniels**
DI Sarah Turnbull	**Caroline Bliss**
DS Nesbit	**Jack Galloway**
Peter Noonan	**Philip Martin Brown**

Creator/Writer **Murray Smith**
Producer **Selwyn Roberts**

● ***Two dodgy brothers run a seedy dance-hall.***

Francis (Frank) and Danny Kane are two brothers who have drifted apart. Frank, a one-time boxing champ, ran away to the Foreign Legion and then became a priest, but is troubled by gambling addiction; Danny lives a yuppie lifestyle with his young family in Docklands, his earnings enhanced by his position in the family 'firm' (their dad was the infamous 'Hatchet Jack' Kane). They are brought together for the first time in eight years by the death of their mother, the vicious head of 'The Paradise Mob', who bequeaths Frank her Paradise Club, in Paradise Street, Rotherhithe. Having just left his seamen's mission in Liverpool, following false accusations of theft against him, Frank decides to make a go of running the club, with Danny as his partner. As proprietors of this drinking and dancing den, they become further immersed in the activities of the south London underworld. Two series were made of their murky adventures.

Paradise Heights/The Eustace Bros ★★

UK (BBC) Drama. BBC 1 2002–3

Clive Eustace	**Charles Dale**
Charlie Eustace	**Neil Morrissey**
Richard Eustace	**Ralf Little**
Marion Eustace	**Pam Ferris**
Julia Sawyer	**Joanne Froggatt**
Claire Eustace	**Lindsey Coulson**
Jack Edwards	**David Troughton**
Yvonne Edwards	**Mary Tamm**
Toby Edwards	**Rupert Evans**
Sam Eustace	**Nicholas Harvey**
	Matthew Beard *(Eustace Bros)*
Eddie Aspen	**Nigel Betts**
Davey Robinson	**Lee Oakes**
Terry Hennessy	**Bruce Byron**
DI Hannington	**Michael Hadley**
Angie James	**Marcia Mantack**
Mandy Cutler	**Nicky Ladanowski**
Melissa Garvey	**Beth Goddard**

Creator **Ashley Pharoah**
Writers **Ashley Pharoah, Adrian Mead, Dan Sefton**
Producer **Polly Hill**

Three brothers battle to keep their business afloat – by hook or by crook.

Clive Eustace runs his family's discount warehouse, Paradise Heights, in Nottingham. He's a nice bloke, probably too nice to ever make a success of the business, but he does have a bit of a temper, and it is often one of his younger brothers who provokes it. Next in line is reckless Charlie (always a sucker for a scam) while baby of the family is hapless Richard (in line to go to university). Widowed mum Marion is the steely-eyed matriarch who keeps everyone in line. It's a close-knit family, but they do annoy each other and they do have plenty of worries. The business – retailing anything from baked beans to bargain beer – is not in the best of shape, financially, and is hampered by being hugely in debt to the local Mr Big, Jack Edwards. The fact that Charlie is sleeping with Jack's wife, Yvonne, is another issue destined to make another day in Paradise more difficult. Also seen are Claire, Clive's estranged wife; Sam, his 12-year-old son; Julia, the brothers' adopted sister and fiancée of Edwards's son, Toby; plus assorted inept warehouse employees.

Mixing humour and sharp dialogue with scenes of violent aggression, *Paradise Heights* sits in the middle ground between comedy and drama, and received a lukewarm response from both critics and viewers. Nevertheless, the series returned for a second run in 2003, but with the revised title of *The Eustace Bros*. This time around, the warehouse has gone and the trio are jointly running an auction and house clearing business. Melissa Garvey, a fellow reclamations dealer, is the new female interest in the business but, with other family members and Jack Edwards out of the picture, the action focuses more tightly on the three brothers and their complicated business and social lives.

Paradise Postponed ★★★

UK (Thames) Drama. ITV 1986
DVD: Acorn Media

Revd Simeon Simcox	**Michael Hordern**
Dorothy Simcox	**Annette Crosbie**
Henry Simcox	**Paul Hawkins** *(young)*
	Peter Egan
Fred Simcox	**Graham McGrath** *(young)*
	Paul Shelley
Agnes Salter/Simcox	**Zoë Hart** *(young)*
	Eleanor David
Dr Salter	**Colin Blakely**
Leslie Titmuss	**Eli Nathenson** *(young)*
	David Threlfall
Charlotte Fanner/Titmuss	**Zoë Wanamaker**
Lady Grace Fanner	**Jill Bennett**
Sir Nicholas Fanner	**Richard Vernon**
Arthur Nubble	**Matthew Verrey** *(young)*
	Kenny Ireland
Francesca Simcox	**Amy Wetmore** *(young)*
	Leonie Mellinger
Lonnie Simcox/Hope	**Claire Oberman**
Doughty Strove	**Thorley Walters**
Terry Fawcett	**Tom Chadbon**
Glenys Bigwell/Fawcett	**Lill Roughley**
Magnus Strove	**Dominic Jephcott**
Benjamin K. Bugloss	**William Hootkins**
Jennifer Battley/Strove	**Marsha Fitzalan**
Bridget Bigwell	**Ann Davies**
Maggie Fawcett	**Gabrielle Blunt**
Tina Fawcett/Kitson	**Rowena Snaith** *(young)*
	Gwyneth Strong
Elsie Titmuss	**Sylvia Kay**
George Titmuss	**Colin Jeavons**
Gary Kitson	**Ewan Stewart**
Lord Naboth	**George Belbin**
Lady Naboth	**Margaret Courtenay**
Wyebrow	**Alan Rowe**
Ted Lawless	**Dave Atkins**
Revd Kevin Bulstrode	**Albert Welling**
Monica Bulstrode	**Frances White**
Tom Nowt	**Thomas Heathcote**
Mrs Mallard-Greene	**Jacqueline Hill**
'Malley' Mallard-Greene	**David Savile**
Simon Mallard-Greene	**Jeremy Gilley**
	Gerald McArthur
Sara Mallard-Greene	**Araminta Craig-Hall**
Dora Nowt	**Eileen Way**

Creator/Writer **John Mortimer**
Executive Producers **Johnny Goodman, Lloyd Shirley**
Producer **Jacqueline Davis**

The death of a vicar leads to family skeletons being unearthed.

In 1985, the Revd Simeon Simcox, the rather secular vicar of Rapstone, breathes his last breath. However, his impact on his family is not over by any means. In his will it is revealed that his fortune has been left to arrogant politician Leslie Titmuss. It seems the odd bequest has something to do with the fact that Titmuss, when young, used to help Simcox in his garden, but the fact that, as well as being Tory MP for Harstcombe, Titmuss is now a greedy property developer queers the pitch no end, especially as Simcox, himself, was a lifelong socialist and a campaigner for CND. Simcox's family has mixed emotions about the contents of the will. His wife, Dorothy, seems rather unconcerned at being left penniless, and one of the sons, Fred, a country doctor, is easy-going enough to not let it worry him. Fred's brother, on the other hand, is incandescent. Henry is a pompous novelist and Hollywood screenwriter and he is determined to prove that his father was insane in order to annul the will. To explain the background to the turn of events, the action drifts back to 1948, at a time when a new dawn for English society was promised by the post-war era, a dawn that failed to break as the years progressed, leaving 'Paradise postponed'.

For his 11-part drama, writer John Mortimer created his own piece of rural Oxfordshire, rural communities (now largely weekend retreats for City folk) like Rapstone Fenner, Picton Principal and Skurfield, in the Rapstone Valley. *Paradise Postponed* later generated a three-part sequel, *Titmuss Regained* (ITV 1991), in which the rapacious MP has advanced to Secretary of State for Housing, Ecological Affairs and Planning. With Rapstone under threat of development, where will his sympathies lie, with his constituents or his Thatcherite free-market beliefs?

Paramount Comedy Channel

Digital channel specializing in reruns of sitcoms, drawing on a major catalogue of past hits. A typical evening's viewing might consist of US series like M*A*S*H, SPIN CITY, THE LARRY SANDERS SHOW, FRASIER, SEINFELD and MARRIED . . . WITH CHILDREN, supported by British contributions like *Harry Hill*, FATHER TED, WHOSE LINE IS IT ANYWAY? and DROP THE DEAD DONKEY. There is also room for US comedies that have not aired on UK terrestrial networks, such as *Mad About You*, *Becker* and *Clueless*. Jointly owned by Viacom and BSkyB, the channel was launched in the UK in 1995 as simply The Paramount Channel, acquiring the word 'Comedy' when it narrowed down its content from general entertainment to pure humour. It has since been joined by Paramount Comedy 2, a second channel dealing in the same fare.

Paras, The ★★

UK (BBC) Documentary. BBC 1 1983

Narrator **Glyn Worsnip**

Writer **Glyn Worsnip**
Producer **Bill Jones**

Recruits to the Parachute Regiment battle to make the grade.

This early fly-on-the-wall documentary series follows 41 hopefuls as they begin their gruelling training with the 480 Recruit Platoon of the Parachute Regiment. Over seven episodes, Glyn Worsnip observes their progress and interviews would-be Red Berets as they endure 22 weeks of some of the hardest training in the military world. While they tough it out, and the less suitable begin to fall by the wayside, the outbreak of the Falklands War casts a shadow over the induction process.

Pardon My Genie ★★

UK (Thames) Children's Situation Comedy. ITV 1972–3

The Genie ..... **Hugh Paddick**
Arthur White
Mr Thomas Cobbledick ..... **Roy Barraclough**
Hal Adden ..... **Ellis Jones**
Patricia Cobbledick ..... **Lynette Earving**
PC Appleby ..... **Joe Dunlop**

Creator **Bob Block**
Writers **Bob Block, Larry Parker**
Producer **Daphne Shadwell**

A young shop assistant accidentally releases a genie into his world.

In this children's version of I DREAM OF JEANNIE, Hal Adden works in a hardware shop in the fictional town of Widdimouth. One day, Hal picks up an old watering can and starts to clean it, thereby releasing a 4,000-year-old genie, whose magic is as behind the times as the genie himself. But the wish-bestowing spirit is a genial sort and keeps 'helping out' Hal during his daily chores, with predictably unfortunate consequences. In the second series, the genie has changed shape and personality. He's now a darker, more sinister servant (star Hugh Paddick was replaced by Arthur White) but the results of his meddling remain much the same. Mr Cobbledick is Hal's portly, harassed boss, Fred is Hal's shaggy dog and PC Appleby is the local copper constantly bemused by events.

Pardon the Expression ★★

UK (Granada) Situation Comedy. ITV 1965–6

Leonard Swindley ..... **Arthur Lowe**
Ernest Parbold ..... **Paul Dawkins**
Miss Sinclair ..... **Joy Stewart**
Mrs Edgeley ..... **Betty Driver**
Walter Hunt ..... **Robert Dorning**

Executive Producer **H. V. Kershaw**
Producers **Harry Driver, Derek Granger**

A pompous draper joins a large chain store and assumes extra responsibility.

A spin-off series from CORONATION STREET, *Pardon the Expression* follows the fortunes of Leonard Swindley, the teetotal, lay-preaching, one-time proprietor of Weatherfield's Gamma Garments boutique. Mr Swindley is now assistant manager of a branch of the Dobson and Hawks chain store, a position guaranteed to exaggerate his pomposity. Ernest Parbold is his buck-passing boss, Miss Sinclair is the staff manageress and Mrs Edgeley (played by Betty Driver, the *Street*'s future Betty Turpin) is in charge of the canteen. When Mr Parbold leaves after the first series, Walter Hunt takes his place.

Pardon the Expression, taking its name from Mr Swindley's catchphrase of 'If you'll pardon the expression', gave birth to a spin-off series of its own, *Turn Out the Lights* (1967), in which Swindley and Hunt team up as a duo of amateur ghost-hunters.

Parenthood ✳✳

US (Imagine) Situation Comedy. BBC 2 1993 (US: NBC 1990–1)

Gil Buckman .... **Ed Begley Jr**
Karen Buckman .... **Jayne Atkinson**
Kevin Buckman .... **Max Elliott Slade**
Taylor Buckman .... **Thora**
Justin Buckman .... **Zachery LaVoy**
Helen Buckman .... **Maryedith Burrell**
Julie Buckman/Hawks .... **Bess Meyer**
Garry Buckman .... **Leonardo DiCaprio**
Tod Hawks .... **David Arquette**
Susan Buckman-Merrick .... **Susan Norman**
Nathan Merrick .... **Ken Ober**
Patty Merrick .... **Ivyann Schwan**
Frank Buckman .... **William Windom**
Marilyn Buckman .... **Sheila MacRae**
Great Grandma Greenwell ..... **Mary Jackson**

Creators **Ron Howard, Lowell Ganz, Babaloo Mandel**

● ***Childcare as seen through the eyes of three generations of an American family.***

Spun-off from the 1989 movie of the same name (director Ron Howard returning as executive producer), *Parenthood* is a feelgood family comedy based around the joys (*sic*) of watching your kids grow up. The Buckmans are the extended family at the heart of affairs. Gil is husband of Karen and father of ten-year-old Kevin, eight-year-old Taylor and little Justin, four. Gil's sisters' families are also featured. Helen is divorced and bringing up teenagers Garry (an early role for Leonardo DiCaprio) and Julie, who is married to painter and decorator Tod Hawks. Second sister Susan is a teacher, hitched to academic Nathan and mother of potential genius Patty, aged four. Above and beyond are Gil's own parents, whose example he is always trying to better when dealing with his kids. Frank is his workaholic dad, mum Marilyn joins him in casting an eye over their offspring's parenting techniques but Great Grandma is usually too deaf to keep up. Although the big names of the original film did not reappear (Steve Martin, Mary Steenburgen, Jason Robards, Rick Moranis, Keanu Reeves), some of the younger members of the cast did reprise their roles for television. Not in the movie, but billed here simply as 'Thora', is Thora Birch, later famous as the daughter in the film *American Beauty*.

Paris ✳✳

UK (Talkback) Situation Comedy. Channel 4 1994

Alain Degout .... **Alexei Sayle**
Paul Rochet .... **Neil Morrissey**
Minotti .... **Allan Corduner**
Madame Ovary .... **Beverley Klein**
Pilo .... **Simon Godley**
Beluniare .... **James Dreyfus**
Valerie .... **Liz Kettle**
Mirielle .... **Clare Cathcart**
Hugo .... **Walter Sparrow**

Writers **Graham Linehan, Arthur Mathews**
Producer **Sioned Wiliam**

● ***A struggling artist and his cronies try to make a living in decadent Paris.***

Paris, the 1920s: a colourful city in a decade of change. Alain Degout is an impoverished but optimistic artist, part of the city's lingering bohemian sect. Any day now he will be discovered and his paintings will sell for vast sums. Regrettably it's taking longer than he has hoped. To drown his sorrows, he frequents the Café Hugo, where his drinking buddies include foppish fellow painter Paul Rochet, mad Italian Minotti and a suicidal poet, Valerie, all of whom suffer from delusions and pretensions akin to those that assail the frustrated Degout. This six-part comedy was a pre-FATHER TED offering from writers Graham Linehan and Arthur Mathews.

Parish, Sarah

(1969–)

Somerset-born actress who gained early television exposure as one of the girls in the Boddington's beer commercials. Her major roles have been as Dawn Rudge in PEAK PRACTICE, Jane in THE VICE, Amanda Thomas in HEARTS AND BONES, Ali Pearson in *Sirens*, Allie Henshall in CUTTING IT, Annie Naylor in *Trust*, Lydia Gray in *Unconditional Love*, Dr Charlotte Woods in *Reversals*, Natalie Holden in BLACKPOOL, Maggie Joy Blunt in *Our Hidden Lives* and Beatrice in *Much Ado about Nothing*. Sarah also appeared in the *Table 12* series of short films, and other roles have come in CITY CENTRAL, AGATHA CHRISTIE'S MARPLE and the sitcoms BABES IN THE WOOD, BEAST and *Brotherly Love*.

Parker, Fess

(1925–)

American actor, an instant hit as Disney's DAVY CROCKETT. Enjoying his American hero status, Parker followed up with tales of another pioneer, DANIEL BOONE, ten years later. In between he starred as Senator Eugene Smith in *Mr Smith Goes to Washington*.

Parker, Nathaniel

(1962–)

English actor, the son of former British Rail chairman the late Sir Peter Parker. Parker's earliest starring roles came in A PIECE OF CAKE ('Flash' Gordon), NEVER COME BACK (Desmond Thane), CATHERINE COOKSON'S *The Black Candle* (Lionel Filmore) and *Look at It This Way* (Miles Goodall), although he is best known as the toff detective Thomas Lynley in THE INSPECTOR LYNLEY MYSTERIES. He has also starred as Gabriel Oak in FAR FROM THE MADDING CROWD, Dr Dan Gallagher in MCCALLUM, Capt. Rawdon Crawley in VANITY FAIR, Andrew Pearce in *Trust*, Charles II in *The Private Life of Samuel Pepys*, James in *Pretending to be Judith* and Harold Skimpole in BLEAK HOUSE. Smaller roles have come in INSPECTOR MORSE, AGATHA CHRISTIE'S POIROT, *Rik Mayall Presents* and A TOUCH OF FROST, among other series. Parker is married to actress Anna Patrick.

Parkin, Leonard

(1929–93)

British reporter and newscaster, with ITN for many years. Initially working as a newspaper journalist in his native Yorkshire, Parkin joined the BBC news team in 1954, later becoming its Canadian and then Washington correspondent. As such, he was the first British reporter to break the news of President Kennedy's assassination. For the BBC, he also worked on PANORAMA and 24 HOURS. In 1967, the year that NEWS *at Ten* was launched, he switched to ITN, for whom he also presented election programmes and, later, the lunchtime news (*First Report* and *News at One*) and *News at 5.45*, eventually leaving in 1987.

Parkinson, Michael

CBE (1935–)

Undoubtedly king of the chat shows in the 1970s, Barnsley-born Michael Parkinson's career began in newspaper journalism, graduating to work for Granada, where he contributed to local news magazines, WORLD IN ACTION, WHAT THE PAPERS SAY and CINEMA. He then joined the BBC's 24 HOURS team, produced sports documentaries for LWT and ventured into talk shows with *Tea Break*, before, in 1971, embarking on his 11-year run as host of *Parkinson*. BBC 1's extremely popular Saturday night series specialized in featuring the biggest names in Hollywood and elsewhere, providing memorable moments such as Muhammad Ali at his verbal best, some classic early exposure for Billy Connolly and, much to the host's displeasure, a rough-and-tumble encounter with Rod Hull's Emu. In 1983 he became one of TV-am's 'Famous Five', largely working on the weekend output, and later sharing the limelight with his wife, Mary. Parkinson has since chaired the quiz and game shows GIVE US A CLUE, *All Star Secrets*, GOING FOR A SONG and *2000 to 1*, worked on *The Help Squad*, written and narrated the animation *The Woofits*, presented a history of rugby league in *A League Apart*, appeared in *Ghostwatch* (a *Screen One* special), and resurrected *Parkinson* with no little success.

Parsons, Nicholas

OBE (1928–)

Grantham-born actor and presenter, first seen on TV in guest roles in series like THE ADVENTURES OF ROBIN HOOD, sketch shows like *Look at It This Way* and *Here and Now*, and, more, prominently, as stooge to Arthur Haynes, Eric Barker and, later, Benny Hill. At around the same time he was providing the voice for Gerry Anderson's puppet cowboy, Tex Tucker, in FOUR FEATHER FALLS, and pursuing a bright career in British film comedies. In the late 1960s Parsons appeared in an American sitcom, *The Ugliest Girl in Town*, and in the BBC comedy THE VERY MERRY WIDOW (Francis). More successfully, in the 1970s, Parsons hosted the remarkably popular quiz show SALE OF THE CENTURY. In the 1990s, he chaired TV versions of his successful radio series *Just a Minute*. His has also been a familiar face on other panel games, and Parsons has never been afraid to mock his own smoothie image with cameo roles in THE COMIC STRIP PRESENTS, THE NEW STATESMAN and other comedies, plus the game shows CLUEDO (Reverend Green) and *The Alphabet Quiz*. His first wife was actress Denise Bryer.

Partridge Family, The ✶✶

US (Screen Gems) Situation Comedy. BBC 1 1971; ITV 1972–4 (US: ABC 1970–4)
DVD: Sony

Shirley Partridge	**Shirley Jones**
Keith Partridge	**David Cassidy**
Laurie Partridge	**Susan Dey**
Danny Partridge	**Danny Bonaduce**
Christopher Partridge	**Jeremy Gelbwaks**
	Brian Forster
Tracy Partridge	**Suzanne Crough**
Reuben Kinkaid	**Dave Madden**

Creator **Bernard Slade**
Executive Producer **Bob Claver**

● ***Life at home and on the road with a family pop group.***
When suburban widow Shirley Partridge casually joins her children's band as a singer, little does she know that a career as a pop star beckons. Putting together a song called 'I Think I Love You' in the family's garage-cum-rehearsal-room, the group sells the track to a record company. It becomes a hit and turns the family into top performers. Climbing aboard a painted-up old school bus, Shirley and her kids then head off on tour across America from their home in San Pueblo, California. Apart from Mom, the family consists of 16-year-old Keith, 15-year-old Laurie, freckly Danny, aged ten (who organizes the band), Chris, aged seven, and five-year-old Tracy. Their agent (who dislikes children) is Reuben Kinkaid. The family has a dog called Simone.

Like THE MONKEES before them, The Partridge Family grew into a real-life pop group and had hits on both sides of the Atlantic. However, they never claimed to perform on the actual recordings, apart from vocals by Shirley Jones and David Cassidy. Their biggest hits in Britain were cover versions of 1960s classics like 'Breaking Up is Hard to Do', 'Looking through the Eyes of Love' and 'Walking in the Rain'. David Cassidy quickly outgrew the series, branching out on his own and becoming one of the 1970s' first teenage idols. Shirley Jones was his real-life stepmother. Cast members Susan Dey, Danny Bonaduce, Brian Forster and Suzanne Crough reprised their roles vocally for animated parts in the cartoon series *Goober and the Ghost Chasers*. There was also a Partridge Family cartoon series set in the future and entitled *Partridge Family: 2200 AD*. The same four actors contributed, with other actors filling the remaining cast parts.

The Partridge Family was inspired by the experiences of the Cowsills, a Rhode Island family of a mom and her kids who had American hits in the 1960s.

Pastry, Mr

See *Hearne, Richard.*

Paterson, Bill

(1945–)

Glasgow-born actor in a variety of prominent dramas and comedies. These have included *Licking Hitler*, UNITED KINGDOM, *Smiley's People* (Lander Strickland), THE SINGING DETECTIVE (Dr Gibbon), DUTCH GIRLS, AUF WIEDERSEHEN, PET (Ally Fraser), TRAFFIK (Jack Lithgow), *Yellowbacks, Shrinks* (Matt Hennessey), *Tell Tale Hearts* (Anthony Steadman), *Lenny Henry: in Dreams, The Writing on the Wall* (Bull), *Oliver's Travels* (Baxter) and *The Ghostbusters of East Finchley* (Mr Small). Paterson has also been seen in THE CROW ROAD (Kenneth McHoan), *Melissa* (DCI Cameron), *Mr White Goes to Westminster* (Ben White MP), *Rebel Heart* (James Connolly), *The Whistle-Blower* (DI Neil Sleightholme), *Swallow* (Angus Tighe), OTHELLO (Sinclair Carver), WIVES AND DAUGHTERS (Mr Gibson), DOCTOR ZHIVAGO (Alexander Gromeko), *Ed Stone is Dead* (Nigel Winterbourne), *Danielle Cable: Eyewitness* (DI Nick Biddis), CANTERBURY TALES (Theo), SEA OF SOULS (Dr Douglas Monaghan), BORN AND BRED (Harry Woolf), *Lie With Me* (DCI Collman) and *A Midsummer Night's Dream* (Theo). He also provided voices for SHOEBOX ZOO. Guest appearances have come in series like BOON, MURDER MOST HORRID, *Trust* and FOYLE'S WAR.

Pathfinders in Space/Pathfinders to Mars/Pathfinders to Venus

See *Target Luna*.

Paul Temple ✶✶

UK (BBC/Taurus) Detective Drama. BBC 1 1969–71

Paul Temple .... **Francis Matthews**
Steve Temple .... **Ros Drinkwater**
Kate Balfour .... **June Ellis**
Eric .... **Blake Butler**

Creator **Francis Durbridge**
Producers **Alan Bromly, Peter Bryant, Derrick Sherwin**

● ***A writer of detective novels is also a part-time private eye.***

Paul Temple, aged 30, impeccably bred, suave, cool and sophisticated, is also amazingly wealthy. Living in a swish Chelsea apartment with his 25-year-old wife, Steve, he needs to write only one book a year (three months' work) to maintain his extravagant lifestyle. Consequently, the couple spend the rest of their time touring Britain and Europe, using Paul's finely honed analytical mind to root out international criminals. Temple drives a Rolls-Royce Silver Shadow Coupé and thoroughly enjoys his opulent existence, but he abhors violence of all kinds.

The character of Paul Temple was created by writer Francis Durbridge back in the 1930s, and the inspiration is said to have been a fellow passenger on a train, who looked like a private detective. By 1938 Paul Temple had appeared on BBC Radio, conceived as a Canadian-born, Rugby School- and Oxford-educated son of an army officer. With some three dozen novels to his name, Temple had turned to amateur detection, helping out Scotland Yard with some of their more baffling crimes, and had met up with Steve Trent, a Fleet Street journalist whom he went on to marry. Six actors played the role on radio but some critics have suggested that the TV version (one of the BBC's first colour productions) was tailor-made for the urbane Francis Matthews.

Paxman, Jeremy

(1950–)

Leeds-born journalist and presenter, frontman of NEWSNIGHT since 1989 and previously a reporter in Northern Ireland. Among his credits have been PANORAMA, TONIGHT, BREAKFAST TIME, *The Six O'Clock News* and regional programmes. Paxman took over from Ludovic Kennedy as chairman of the review programme DID YOU SEE . . . ? and has since been questionmaster in the revival of UNIVERSITY CHALLENGE, as well as chairing the debate show *You Decide*.

Pay Per View

A system devised to allow viewers to watch certain additional programmes (films, sporting events, etc.) on the payment of an on-the-spot fee. Whereas the primitive concept looked at coins and slots as a method of payment, today's sophisticated technology uses interactive digital networks.

P. D. James ✶✶

UK (Anglia) Police Drama. ITV 1983–5; 1988; 1991; 1993; 1995; 1997–8; BBC 1 2003; 2005
DVD: Universal

Chief Supt./Commander Adam Dalgliesh .... **Roy Marsden**
.... **Martin Shaw** *(BBC)*
Insp. John Massingham .... **John Vine**
Emma Lavenham .... **Janie Dee** *(BBC)*
DI Kate Miskin .... **Victoria Scarborough** *(BBC)*
Tilly Blackwood *(BBC)*

Producers **John Rosenberg, Hilary Bevan Jones, Andrew Benson, Martyn Auty; Margaret Enefer, Richard Broke** *(BBC)*

● ***The assignments of pensive Scotland Yard detective Adam Dalgliesh.***

Unlike Jim TAGGART or INSPECTOR MORSE, Adam Dalgliesh never had his name in lights. All his adventures, adaptations of P. D. James's novels, aired under their individual book titles, but everyone knew he was the star. In fact, he had only one regular companion, an ambitious copper named John Massingham, and that was just for the first three investigations.

A Scotland Yard chief superintendent, Dalgliesh is promoted to commander in the story entitled *The Black Tower* and holds the rank thereafter. He lives partly in London and partly in Norfolk, where the country lanes are leafy and the seaside towns quiet, but where, nevertheless, murders come thick and fast. His first TV case, *Death of an Expert Witness*, aired in seven parts in 1983 (predating his fellow cerebral cops Morse, Taggart and Wexford). Then followed *Shroud for a Nightingale*, *Cover Her Face*, *The Black Tower*, *A Taste for Death*, *Devices and Desires*, *Unnatural Causes*, *Mind to Murder*, *Original Sin* and *A Certain Justice*, most in serial form and filled with guest stars like Joss Ackland, Phyllis Calvert, Pauline Collins, Maurice Denham and Susannah York. The stories also all feature more than one murder for the tall, confident, morally sound detective to tackle and, true to the books, the plots are complicated and involved. Furthermore, in the best tradition of TV cops, Dalgliesh is not denied his quirks. Behind his rather formal, stuffy image, the calm, quietly spoken sleuth is a competent poet, the son of an Anglican vicar. He is also a widower and lives alone in a converted windmill.

The character was revived by BBC 1 in 2003, with Martin Shaw taking over the role in P. D. James's *Death in Holy Orders*. University lecturer Emma Lavenham is introduced as Dalgliesh's new romantic interest. Both returned in 2005 for another two-parter, *The Murder Room*.

Peacock, Michael

(1929–)

British news and current affairs producer (PANORAMA, etc.) who joined the BBC as a trainee in 1952 and was given the responsibility of launching BBC 2 in 1964. He later became Controller of BBC 1 and then was LWT's managing director in the late 1960s. After some time as an independent producer and consultant, Peacock joined Warner Brothers for a few years in the 1970s. From 1989 to 2005 he was chairman of the production company Unique Broadcasting (later UBC Media Group).

Peacock, Trevor

(1931–)

Born in London, Trevor Peacock is one of TV's most familiar character actors. His most prominent role has been as Jim Trott in THE VICAR OF DIBLEY, although he has also been seen in scores of other roles. These have included Tommy Hollister in THICK AS THIEVES, Daniel Quilp in *The Old Curiosity Shop*, Dennis Tonsley in *Born and Bred*, Renard in WISH ME LUCK, Charlie Penfold in *Dodgem*, Ralf in *Merlin of the Crystal Cave* and George Critchley in GROWING PAINS. He also played Acky Belcher in THE RIFF RAFF ELEMENT, Old Bailey in NEVERWHERE, Dad Middlemass in *Underworld*, Trevor in *The Gift*, Rouault in *Madame Bovary*, Maurie in *The Sins*, Parson Bowden in *Lorna Doone*, Marlobe in *Armadillo*, Mr Ruggles in THE WAY WE LIVE NOW, William Barker in *Dickens*, Christopher Coney in THE MAYOR OF CASTERBRIDGE, Arthur in *Family Business*, and Mr Martin in *The Legend of the Tamworth Two*. Among the other programmes he has contributed to in a career stretching back to the early 1960s are *The Villains*, MAN IN A SUITCASE, EDWARD THE SEVENTH, THE GENTLE TOUCH, JIM HENSON'S GREEK MYTHS, THE BILL, BOON, VAN DER VALK, MAIGRET, BETWEEN THE LINES, CHEF!, WHERE THE HEART IS, MY FAMILY, JONATHAN CREEK, WAKING THE DEAD, MIDSOMER MURDERS and EASTENDERS, plus presentations of Shakespeare. One of his earliest TV appearances was as presenter of the 1959 pop music series DRUMBEAT and his musical interests continued into the 1960s, when he composed Herman's Hermits' 1965 US hit 'Mrs Brown You've Got a Lovely Daughter'. Trevor is the father of actor Daniel Peacock.

Peak Practice ★★

UK (Central/Carlton) Drama. ITV 1993–2002
DVD: Network

Dr Jack Kerruish	**Kevin Whately**
Dr Beth Glover	**Amanda Burton**
Dr Will Preston	**Simon Shepherd**
Sarah Preston	**Jacqueline Leonard**
Dr Daniel Acres	**Tom Beard**
Dr John Reginald	**Andrew Ray**
Kim Beardsmore	**Esther Coles**
Ellie Ndebala	**Sharon Hinds**
Isabel de Gines	**Sylvia Syms**
James White	**Richard Platt**
Chloe White	**Hazel Ellerby**
Sandy	**Melanie Thaw**
Trevor Sharpe	**Shaun Prendergast**
Alice North	**Margery Mason**
Francine Sinclair	**Veronica Quilligan**
Dr Andrew Attwood	**Gary Mavers**
Dr Erica Matthews	**Saskia Wickham**
Kate Webster/Preston	**Shelagh McLeod**
Kirsty Attwood	**Sukie Smith**
Russ Skinner	**James Kerr**
Laura Elliott	**Veronica Roberts**
Dr Pat Hewland	**Elisabeth Sladen**
Dr David Shearer	**Adrian Lukis**
Clare Shearer	**Yolanda Vazquez**
	Fiona Gillies
Emma Shearer	**Jenni Gallagher**
Tom Shearer	**Nicholas Harvey**
Norman Shorthose	**Clive Swift**
Dawn Rudge	**Sarah Parish**
Dr Joanna Graham	**Haydn Gwynne**
Patricia Davey	**Annette Ekblom**
Dr Sam Morgan	**Joseph Millson**
Bridgit Mellors	**Siobhan O'Carroll**
Rita Barratt	**Anne Reid**
Dr Tom Deneley	**Gray O'Brien**
Kate Turner	**Lynsey Baxter**
Richard Turner	**David Mallinson**
Kerri Davidson	**Susannah Corbett**
Dr Alex Redman	**Maggie O'Neill**
Tony Preston	**Adam Croasdell**
Charlie Webster	**George Wells**
Claire Brightwell	**Eva Pope**
Carol Johnson	**Deborah Grant**
Dr Matt Kendal	**Jamie Bamber**
Shaun Carter	**Victor McGuire**

Creator **Lucy Gannon**
Producers **Tony Virgo, Michele Buck, Damien Timmer, Mervyn Gill-Dougherty, Phil Collinson, Neil Zeiger**

Professional and personal problems for the staff of a Derbyshire general practice.

Dr Jack Kerruish is disillusioned with city life and city medicine. Having enjoyed a fulfilling three years establishing a medical centre in Africa, he returns to London in search of a new career direction. He wants to join a country practice and is eventually accepted into a somewhat wobbly partnership in the Peak District village of Cardale (real-life Crich). His colleagues are Beth Glover and Will Preston, two local doctors who have decided to keep their independence and fight on in their dilapidated Beeches surgery when threatened by competition from a new, flashy health-centre. Kerruish's financial input is important, but he also brings new technology and dynamism to the practice. However, Kerruish soon discovers that, if the city has its problems, so does the country, as he comes face to face with the everyday hardships of rural life and the emotional problems of the local community. There is also the practice to re-establish, the bank to stave off, and the rival health-centre to keep an eye on.

Kerruish is very much his own man. Sometimes selfish and insensitive, he is often at odds with his partners, even though he becomes romantically linked with Beth and, by the end of the second series, they have married. In the third series, Kerruish's wanderlust has returned, and he and Beth eventually leave Cardale for Africa. From the next series, their places alongside senior partner Will Preston are taken by newly qualified former electrician Andrew Attwood, a Liverpudlian, and idealistic Erica Matthews, both of whom bring new inner-city ideas – and with them no shortage of friction – into the country backwater. A series later, Attwood temporarily moves to Manchester and is replaced by Preston's friend, David Shearer, whose wife, Clare, suffers from manic depression. Attwood later returns to replace Preston and begin a romance with Erica. This ends with her jilting him at the altar. Her replacement is hospital surgeon Joanna Graham. Joining the Beeches after the death of the adulterous Shearer is Sam Morgan. Another new arrival is ex-army medic Alex Redman, soon followed by former military colleague Claire Brightwell, who, it transpires, has reasons other than mere employment to be in Cardale. Young new doctor Matt Kendal also takes his place at the Beeches in due course. However, *Peak Practice* ends under rather a cloud, with ITV cancelling it in 2002 without resolving a cliff-hanger ending.

Peak Time/Prime Time

The hours when TV audiences are at their greatest, and so the time of day of particular importance to advertisers. Known generally as peak time in the UK, the hours are 7.00–10.30 p.m. Prime time in the USA covers 7.30–11 p.m.

Pearson, Neil

(1959–)

London-born actor, best known as hot-headed CIB detective Tony Clark in BETWEEN THE LINES and newsroom romeo Dave Charnley in DROP THE DEAD DONKEY. Other credits have included *Submariners* ('Cock' Roach), CHELMSFORD 123 (Mungo), THAT'S LOVE (Gary), *Les Girls*, *This is David Lander*, the single drama *Oi for England*, RHODES (Dr Jameson), *Screen Two's Crossing the Floor* (New Labour leader Tom Peel), SEE YOU FRIDAY (Greg), *Bostock's Cup* (Gerry Tudor), *Heaven on Earth* (Richard Bennett), THE MAGICIAN'S HOUSE (Jack Green), *Dirty Work* (Leo Beckett), *The Whistle-Blower* (Dominic Tracey), *A Lump in My Throat* (John Diamond), *Armadillo* (Rintoul), MURDER IN MIND, *Trevor's World of Sport* (Trevor Heslop) and *The Booze Cruise* (Rob Sewell). Pearson also narrated the documentary series BACK TO THE FLOOR.

Peasgood, Julie

Blonde British actress with a host of drama and sitcom credits to her name. Among the most notable parts have been Fran Pearson in BROOKSIDE, Roxy in SEPTEMBER SONG, Eden in LUV, Anne in FIRST BORN and Jacqui Hudson in HOLLYOAKS. Others have included SURVIVORS, *Seven Faces of Woman*, CLAYHANGER (Ada), LORD PETER WIMSEY, *This Year Next Year* (Kath Shaw), BOON, TAGGART, BRUSH STROKES, 2 POINT 4 CHILDREN, VAN DER VALK, THE 10%ERS, SPENDER, CHANDLER & CO., *A Woman's Guide to Adultery* (Sandra), PERFECT SCOUNDRELS, THE RUTH RENDELL MYSTERIES, EMMERDALE (Jo Steadman), DOCTORS, HOLBY CITY and *Can't Buy Me Love* (Janice). She was TV critic for *Good Morning with Anne and Nick*, team captain in the BBC's revamp of GIVE US A CLUE, and hosted *Tall Tales and Antique Sales*, plus the regional offerings *Party of Your Life* and *Boot Sale Challenge*.

Pebble Mill at One/Pebble Mill ★★

UK (BBC) Magazine. BBC 1 1972–86; 1991–6

Presenters **Bob Langley, Tom Coyne, Marian Foster, David Seymour, Donny MacLeod, Jan Leeming, Bob Hall, Tony Francis, Philip Tibenham, Jonathan Fulford, Marjorie Lofthouse, David Freeman, Paul Gambaccini, Anna Ford, Paul Coia, Josephine Buchan, Magnus Magnusson; (1991–6) Judi Spiers, Alan Titchmarsh, Gloria Hunniford, Ross King, Sarah Greene**

Producers/Editors **Terry Dobson, Roy Ronnie, Roger Ecclestone, Roger Laughton, Malcolm Nisbet, Jim Dumighan, Peter Hercombe**

● ***Light-hearted early-afternoon magazine.***

This frivolous lunchtime filler was the BBC's response to ITV's new afternoon series like CROWN COURT and EMMERDALE FARM. Broadcast live from the foyer of Pebble Mill, the BBC's Birmingham TV centre, it featured, among other items, music, celebrity interviews, fashion news, gardening with Peter Seabrook, keep fit with Eileen Fowler, *Collectors' Corner* with Arthur Negus, and cookery with Michael Smith and Glyn Christian. The title was shortened to *Pebble Mill* in later years and a few spin-off programmes were created. *Saturday Night at the Mill* ran from 1976, Norman Vaughan hosted *Pebble Mill Showcase* in 1978 and *Pebble Mill on Sunday* appeared in 1979. Although cancelled in 1986 to make way for the *One O'Clock News* and programmes like NEIGHBOURS, the series was revived as part of the BBC's daytime package in 1991, becoming more of a chat show, broadcast from a studio rather than the entrance hall.

Peck, Bob

(1945–99)

English Shakespearean actor whose major TV credit came in EDGE OF DARKNESS (Ronald Craven). He also appeared in dramas like AN UNGENTLEMANLY ACT (Major Mike Norman), *After Pilkington*, *Who Bombed Birmingham?*, *Natural Lies* (Andrew Fell), *Deadly Summer* (Donald Hardcourt), CATHERINE COOKSON'S *The Black Velvet Gown* (Percival Miller) and *The Scold's Bridle* (DS Cooper). He was married to actress Jill Baker.

Penhaligon, Susan

(1949–)

British actress born in the Philippines who has enjoyed a number of prominent roles on television. Most notably, she was Prue Sorenson in A BOUQUET OF BARBED WIRE in 1976 and in 1987 starred as Natalie Harris in *Heart of the Country*. She was Helen in A FINE ROMANCE, made guest appearances in PUBLIC EYE, UPSTAIRS, DOWNSTAIRS, COUNTRY MATTERS, RETURN OF THE SAINT, THE RACING GAME, REMINGTON STEELE and BERGERAC, and has also appeared in single dramas like Jack Rosenthal's *Polly Put the Kettle On* and the BBC's 1977 adaptation of COUNT DRACULA. Since the 1990s Penhaligon has been seen as Julia Charlesworth in *Trouble in Mind* and in *Teenage Health Freak*, THE RUTH RENDELL MYSTERIES, WYCLIFFE, DOCTORS and A TOUCH OF FROST (Pam Hartley), among other series.

Pennies From Heaven ★★★

UK (BBC) Drama. BBC 1 1978

DVD: BBC

Arthur Parker .... **Bob Hoskins**
Eileen Everson .... **Cheryl Campbell**
Joan Parker .... **Gemma Craven**
The Accordian Man .... **Kenneth Colley**
Mr Warner (The Headmaster) .... **Freddie Jones**
Davey Everson .... **Philip Jackson**
Maurice Everson .... **Spencer Banks**
Mr Everson .... **Michael Bilton**
Irene .... **Jenny Logan**
Conrad Baker .... **Nigel Havers**
Tom .... **Hywel Bennett**
Major Archibald Paxville, MP .... **Ronald Fraser**
The Inspector .... **Dave King**

Writer **Dennis Potter**
Producer **Kenith Trodd**

● ***A music salesman's life is not as joyful as his songs make out.***

It is 1935 and 35-year-old Londoner Arthur Parker works as a self-employed sheet music salesman. He really loves his music. Given the chance, he drifts away from the suburban drudgery of his life with frigid wife Joan, and into the fantasy world of song lyrics. A sales trip to Gloucestershire and a chance meeting with a young teacher named Eileen leads him to be unfaithful, but the consequences of his actions haunt everyone. As Arthur's marriage collapses, Eileen falls pregnant and, to spare her poor mining family the shame, quits her job and heads for London. There she is befriended by Tom, a pimp, who advises an abortion and puts Eileen on the game. In circumstances of some distress, she and Arthur again meet up and they go on the run when Arthur is suspected of murdering a blind girl in the country. The real culprit, it seems, is a mysterious accordion player who frequently crosses the path of both Arthur and Eileen. Piers Haggard directs.

What is innovative about *Pennies From Heaven* is the use of contemporary 1930s tunes to underpin the plot, their banal words given new meaning when contrasted with the serious goings-on. As in Hollywood pictures, the actors suddenly break into song and dance, miming to the original recordings. Sometimes, men mime to women's voices and vice versa. It is a technique that Dennis Potter re-employs in THE SINGING DETECTIVE eight years later and again in the third part of his musical trilogy, LIPSTICK ON YOUR COLLAR, in 1993. A film version of *Pennies From Heaven*, also scripted by Potter and starring Steve Martin and Bernadette Peters, was made in 1981.

Penry-Jones, Rupert

(1970–)

English actor, son of Angela Thorne and Peter Penry-Jones, and brother of Laurence Penry-Jones. His most prominent roles have been as Dick Hawk-Monitor in COLD COMFORT FARM, The Prince in *The Student Prince*, Stanley Thorman in CATHERINE COOKSON'S *The Moth*, St John Rivers in JANE EYRE, Dietrich in *The Tribe*, Alex Hay in NORTH SQUARE, Donald Maclean in CAMBRIDGE SPIES, Grimani in CASANOVA and Adam Carter in SPOOKS. Other credits have come through programmes like KAVANAGH QC, FAITH IN THE FUTURE and AGATHA CHRISTIE'S POIROT.

People's Century ★★★

UK (BBC/WGBH) Historical Documentary. BBC 1 1995–7

Narrator **Sean Barrett**

Executive Producer **Peter Pagnamenta**
Producers **Jonathan Lewis, Bill Treharne Jones, Daniel Brittain-Catlin, Mark Davis, Graham Chedd, James De Vinney, Archie Baron, John Bridcut, Angus Macqueen, Sally Doganis, Jennifer Clayton, Charles Furneaux, Marian Marzynski, Max Whitby, Peter Ceresole, Anne Moir, Ben Loeterman**

● ***A citizens'-eye view of a century of drama, trauma and change.***

This expansive history of the 20th century considers monumental global events through the eyes of the common people. Taking 1900 as its beginning, the series progresses to cover major social and political changes, wars, economic crises, technological and industrial advances, sport and the development of mass media, not purely from a UK/American perspective but, sometimes uncomfortably, from parties on all sides. Costing some £10 million to produce, the 26-part series took four years to research and collate. One of its major achievements was to find remarkable witnesses to key moments in the century. People who appeared in archive footage of the time were rediscovered – genuine witnesses to events as diverse as Queen Victoria's funeral, the establishment of Henry Ford's production lines, the trenches of World War I, the rise of Nazi Germany, the civil rights marches, the rise and fall of the Iron Curtain and more. This was achieved by staging special screenings of rare films in the places in which they were shot and asking locals to come forward for interview if they were featured. Their poignant memories were then dropped into a programme framework built by a team of specialist historians to create a vibrant view of history out of small personal details. The first series of ten programmes takes the story up to World War II; the eight programmes in series two cover events up to the 1950s; and the final eight programmes of series three carry through to the mid-1990s. Zbigniev Preisner composed the theme music.

Peppard, George

(1928–94)

American actor, popular in the cinema in the 1960s, after making his first TV appearances a decade earlier, in series like ALFRED HITCHCOCK PRESENTS. In the 1970s Peppard returned to the small screen, taking the role of MYSTERY MOVIE detective BANACEK. Two years into the series, he moved on to another prime-time drama, *Doctors' Hospital*, but left a year later. He then played Blake Carrington in the pilot for DYNASTY but was not given the series role and, just when it seemed that his career was petering out, up popped the character of cigar-chomping A-TEAM leader, Colonel John 'Hannibal' Smith, which made him a favourite with youngsters all over the world. Peppard was also seen in numerous TV movies.

Perfect Scoundrels ★★

UK (TVS) Comedy Drama. ITV 1990–2

Guy Buchanan .... **Peter Bowles**
Harry Cassidy .... **Bryan Murray**

Creators **Ray Connolly, Peter Bowles, Bryan Murray**
Executive Producer **Graham Benson**
Producers **Tim Aspinall, Terence Williams, Tony Virgo**

● ***Two sophisticated con men swindle shadier members of society.***

Meeting at the funeral of a master con man, suave Guy Buchanan and rough diamond Harry Cassidy are coaxed into joining forces to avenge the death of their old ally. Executing an elaborate sting on the alleged murderer, the two lovable rogues discover they themselves have been swindled when the 'dead' man duly takes care of the proceeds. However, realizing how well they perform in tandem, Guy and Harry make their double act permanent, despite personal differences that threaten their partnership. For instance, Harry, an Irish parrot-fancier, lacks vital discipline, which angers smooth-talking Guy, and an element of mutual distrust pervades their business dealings. They work as latter-day Robin Hoods, for the most part picking only on those who rip off others. The third and final season, though, shows the perfect scoundrels in a new light, as they occasionally target less-deserving victims.

Actors Peter Bowles and Bryan Murray, who had worked

together in THE IRISH RM, devised this series as a vehicle for their own talents.

Perfect Spy, A ✱✱✱

UK (BBC) Drama. BBC 2 1987
DVD: BBC

Magnus Pym	**Peter Egan**
	Jonathan Haley *(young)*
	Nicholas Haley *(young)*
	Benedict Taylor *(young)*
Rick Pym	**Ray McAnnally**
Dorothy Pym	**Caroline John**
Mary Pym	**Jane Booker**
Makepeace Watermaster	**Iain Cuthbertson**
Syd Lemon	**Tim Healy**
Jack Brotherhood	**Alan Howard**
Mr Muspole	**Andy de la Tour**
Perce Loft	**Jack Ellis**
Axel	**Rüdiger Weigang**
Miss Dubber	**Peggy Ashcroft**

Writer **Arthur Hopcraft**
Producer **Colin Rogers**

● ***A top-level spy disappears and the search for his whereabouts is on.***

When British intelligence officer Magnus Pym goes missing, the hunt begins to find the lifelong secret agent. Pym had been brought up without a mother by his domineering conman of a father, Rick, whose cockney crony Syd Lemon had been a mentor to the young Magnus. Now, having served his country in central Europe, Magnus has sought solace in his seaside bolthole, Farleigh Abbot (real-life Dawlish), at Miss Dubber's guest house. There he looks back over his life and reflects on his career as a master of deception. Pym's wife, Mary, plus Lemon and other agents attempt to find the elusive spy. Other key characters include Dorothy (Magnus's 20-year-younger sister), Czech agent Axel, lawyers Perce Loft and Makepeace Watermaster, and accountant Muspole. The seven episodes were directed by Peter Smith.

Perfect State, A ✱

UK (Cinema Verity) Situation Comedy. BBC 1 1997

Laura Fitzgerald	**Gwen Taylor**
Bert Figgis	**Trevor Cooper**
Malcolm Batley	**Matthew Cottle**
Mayor Winston Wainwright	**Rudolph Walker**
Julie Fitzgerald	**Jacqueline Defferary**
Gareth Jones	**Alan David**
Simon Watson	**Richard Hope**
Johnny Pearce	**Danny Webb**
Deidre Pearce	**Emma Amos**

Writer **Michael Aitkens**
Executive Producers **Verity Lambert, Geoffrey Perkins**
Producer **Sharon Bloom**

● ***A dead-end coastal town declares UDI.***

Flatby is a quiet little seaside town quietly minding its own boring business until the EU decides to destroy its fishing fleet – one man and his boat. The town is up in arms and, orchestrated by publican/deputy mayor Laura Fitzgerald, decides to declare itself independent of the UK and the EU. Aiding and abetting the effort are Laura's solicitor daughter, Julie, and teacher Malcolm Batley (who discovers that Flatby has never formally been annexed to the UK). Also involved are laid-back, golfing mayor Winston Wainwright; philosophical butcher Bert Figgis; and London estate agent Johnny Pearce (who foresees money-making ventures in the new circumstances) with his dippy wife, Deidre. The UK government is not easily deterred, however, and sends envoys in the shape of civil servants Gareth Jones and Simon Watson. The scene is set for farcical battles over sovereignty in which the cunning locals regularly outfox the emissaries of Westminster. Dewi Humphreys directed the seven episodes.

Perfect Strangers [1] ✱✱

US (Miller-Boyett/Lorimar) Situation Comedy. BBC 1 1987–92 (US: ABC 1986–93)

Larry Appleton	**Mark Linn-Baker**
Balki Bartokomous	**Bronson Pinchot**
Donald 'Twinkie' Twinkacetti	**Ernie Sabella**
Edwina Twinkacetti	**Belita Moreno**
Susan Campbell	**Lise Cutter**
Mary Anne Spencer/ Bartokomous	**Rebeca Arthur**
Jennifer Lyons/Appleton	**Melanie Wilson**
Harriette Winslow	**Jo Marie Payton-France**
Lydia Markham	**Belita Moreno**
Sam Gorpley	**Sam Anderson**
Tess Holland	**Alisan Porter**

Executive Producers **Thomas L. Miller, Robert L. Boyett**

● ***Culture-clash cousins are best buddies.***

Larry Applegate is a single guy working for the Ritz Discount Store and living happily in Chicago, until his distant cousin, Balki, shows up. Balki, an innocent abroad, is a shepherd from the primitive Mediterranean island of Mypos and now sees Uncle Sam as his passport to a fortune. The two guys share an apartment and become good friends, with most of the laughs coming from Balki's fractured English and hapless misunderstanding of the American way of life. Susan Campbell is their neighbour and Twinkie is Larry's boss at the store. The lads later get jobs at a newspaper, the *Chicago Chronicle*, where Larry becomes a reporter and Balki works in the mailroom. Lydia Markham (played by Belita Moreno, who had previously been seen as Twinkie's wife) is the resident agony aunt and Harriette Winslow is the smart-mouthed elevator operator who gains her own spin-off series, *Family Matters* (US: ABC 1989–98). The boys' new neighbours are air hostesses Jennifer Lyons and Mary Anne, destined to be their brides as the series unwinds.

Perfect Strangers [2] ✱✱✱

UK (Talkback/BBC) Drama. BBC 2 2001
DVD: BBC

Raymond	**Michael Gambon**
Daniel	**Matthew Macfadyen**
Alice	**Lindsay Duncan**
Rebecca	**Claire Skinner**
Charles	**Toby Stephens**
Esther	**Jill Baker**
Irving	**Timothy Spall**
Poppy	**Kelly Hunter**
Stephen	**Anton Lesser**

Richard .... **J. J. Feild**

Writer **Stephen Poliakoff**
Executive Producers **Peter Fincham, David M. Thompson**
Producer **John Chapman**

Languid account of a family reunion and the mysteries it unfolds.

In a gathering of the clan, the Symons, a family of London Jews, have been called together for three days of getting to know each other at Claridges Hotel. Organizer Poppy tries to keep everyone in order and Stephen, the genealogist, marks out the family tree for all to peruse. But, while these people may be connected by blood, that's about all that binds them. Some have never even met before, as young surveyor Daniel Symon finds out. Daniel is one of the Hillingdon Symons, the only child of Esther and the belligerent Raymond – who doesn't want to be there at all. For Daniel, the experience is a voyage of discovery as he meets new cousins, unearths secrets about his relations, does his best to mend family fences and is haunted by flickering memories of his own childhood. The rift between the elegant Alice and her nephew and niece, Charles and Rebecca, is particularly intriguing, as are the wide-boy antics of odd cousin Irving. Pictures of his late grandfather posing ridiculously on a lawn and himself dressed as a little prince inspire Daniel to delve even deeper into family history when the party is reconvened a few days later in the grounds of a large country house. The luxurious, three-part story was inspired by a reunion of writer/director Stephen Poliakoff's own family. Adrian Johnson provided the music.

Perils of Penelope Pitstop, The

See *Wacky Races*

Perrie, Lynne

(Jean Dudley; 1931–2006)

Pint-sized, Yorkshire-born actress and cabaret performer who played Ivy Tilsley/Brennan in CORONATION STREET from 1971 until written out in 1994. Previously, Perrie (sister of comic/actor Duggie Brown) had been seen in series like QUEENIE'S CASTLE (Mrs Petty), CROWN COURT and FOLLYFOOT, as well as in a number of single dramas, such as *Leeds United* and *Slattery's Mounted Foot*.

Perry, Jimmy

OBE (1923–)

British actor and comedy scriptwriter, usually in collaboration with David Croft, with whom he created the doyen of British sitcoms, DAD'S ARMY (based on his own misadventures as a youth in the Home Guard). With Croft, Perry went on to script other comedy favourites like IT AIN'T HALF HOT MUM (echoing his time as a Royal Artillery concert-party manager), HI-DE-HI! (Perry was a Butlin's Redcoat) and YOU RANG, M'LORD? Perry also penned THE GNOMES OF DULWICH, LOLLIPOP LOVES MR MOLE, *Room Service* and, with Robin Carr, the shopkeeping sitcom *High Street Blues*.

Perry Mason ★★★

US (Paisano) Legal Drama. BBC 1 1961–7 (US: CBS 1957–66)

Perry Mason .... **Raymond Burr**
Della Street .... **Barbara Hale**
Paul Drake .... **William Hopper**
Hamilton Burger .... **William Talman**
Lt. Arthur Tragg .... **Ray Collins**
Lt. Anderson .... **Wesley Lau**
Lt. Steve Drumm .... **Richard Anderson**

Creator **Erle Stanley Gardner**
Executive Producers **Gail Patrick Jackson, Arthur Marks**
Producers **Ben Brady, Art Seid, Sam White**

The cases of an almost invincible Los Angeles defence lawyer.

Created by writer-lawyer Erle Stanley Gardner in 1933, defence attorney Perry Mason is remarkable. His brilliant analytical mind, his vast experience in the legal field and his finely honed powers of advocacy enable him to succeed in even the most hopeless cases. With any other attorney, dozens of defendants would be destined for the electric chair. With Perry Mason, not only are they acquitted but the real culprits are unearthed. Admirably supported by his loyal and efficient secretary, Della Street, and his hard-working case investigator, Paul Drake, Mason is virtually unbeatable. It's true that he does, in fact, lose three cases, but all have mitigating circumstances, such as the defendant who refuses to give evidence to clear her name.

Mason's technique is based on methodical, painstaking collation of all the evidence, relying heavily on Drake's ability to dig up some new facts. Very often the vital clues do not arrive until the last minute, with Drake charging into the courtroom to pass the information to his burly boss. It is then that Mason's verbal skills are put to the test, to extract a confession from one of the witnesses, or even one of the spectators. All this is particularly frustrating for prosecuting attorney Hamilton Burger, Mason's chief adversary, and the testifying police officer, Lt. Tragg (later replaced by Lt. Drumm). And just in case the audience has not been able to keep up with events, Perry, Paul and Della gather together in the finale to talk through and explain each case.

In the very last episode, *The Case of the Final Fade-out*, creator Erle Stanley Gardner guest-starred as the judge. However, the series was revived in 1973 under the title of *The New Perry Mason*, with Monte Markham in the lead role. It bombed, but Raymond Burr picked up the reins again for a 1985 TV movie that saw Della accused of murder and Perry leaving his new-found place on the judges' panel to defend her. An intermittent run of feature-length episodes followed, in which Mason was assisted by Della and Paul Drake Jr, son of the original investigator (actor William Hopper had died and Barbara Hale's real-life son, William Katt, was drafted in to do the running around). Drake was later replaced by Ken Malansky, played by William R. Moses. William Talman, who had played Ham Burger, had also died and Mason now encountered a new opponent in Michael Reston, played by M*A*S*H's Major Winchester, David Ogden Stiers.

Persuaders!, The ★★

UK (Tribune/ITC) Adventure. ITV 1971–2
DVD: Carlton

Danny Wilde .... **Tony Curtis**
Lord Brett Sinclair .... **Roger Moore**
Judge Fulton .... **Laurence Naismith**

Creator/Producer **Robert S. Baker**

Two playboys tackle corruption among the jet-set.

Danny Wilde is a rough diamond, a fun-loving American from the streets of Brooklyn. But he is also rich. Through skilful buying and selling of oil stocks, he has made himself into a multi-millionaire. In contrast, Harrow- and Oxford-educated Lord Brett Sinclair has found things rather easy. Born into the English aristocracy and heir to a fortune, he has never needed to work. Together, they comprise an unlikely team of investigators, tracking down villains in the glamour spots of the world.

Their liaison stems from a party on the French Riviera at which they are coerced by a retired judge named Fulton into joining his fight for justice. He wants them to use their spare time and many millions to help him catch those criminals who fall through the usual legal nets, realizing that they can work in places where conventional detectives cannot go. Wilde and Sinclair take up the challenge as a bit of a lark, enjoying visiting Europe's high spots, wining and dining in all the best places and meeting scores of beautiful women along the way. As they come from totally different backgrounds and upbringings, the rapport between the two stars is one of the keystones of the programme.

Glossy and expensively produced, *The Persuaders!* was deliberately aimed at the American market. Sadly, it failed to take off in the States and as a result didn't last long in Britain. The theme music, by John Barry, was a Top 20 hit in the UK in 1971.

Pertwee, Bill

(1926–)

British actor, usually in comic roles and best remembered as the obnoxious ARP Warden, Hodges, in DAD'S ARMY. He has also been seen in other Jimmy Perry and David Croft productions, including YOU RANG, M'LORD?, as the scrounging policeman, PC Wilson. He had earlier played another policeman, in the Sid James/Victor Spinetti sitcom TWO IN CLOVER and among his other credits are roles in *The Norman Vaughan Show*, *Frost's Weekly*, *The World of Beachcomber*, SYKES, BILLY LIAR, CHANCE IN A MILLION and *Tom, Dick and Harriet*. Bill was a cousin of the late Jon Pertwee.

Pertwee, Jon

(John Pertwee; 1919–96)

British actor, much heard in BBC Radio comedy in the postwar years and also making a few inroads into the cinema. However, it was television that gave Pertwee his finest hours. In 1970 he took over one of the classic roles on UK TV, namely that of DOCTOR WHO, succeeding Patrick Troughton. It was a part he played for four years. Pertwee was largely responsible himself for his next major series. He recalled Barbara Euphan Todd's WORZEL GUMMIDGE books and sold the concept of a series to Southern Television, securing himself the role of the famous talking scarecrow in the process. His other credits were as varied as the panel game WHODUNNIT? (host), SIX-FIVE SPECIAL, IVANHOE, JACKANORY, THE AVENGERS, THE GOODIES, SUPERTED (voice of Spottyman), *Virtual Murder* (Luis Silverado), a 1946 version of *Toad of Toad Hall*, and the early comedies *Round the Bend* and *Evans Abode*. He was the son of writer Roland Pertwee, cousin of actor Bill Pertwee, brother of playwright Michael Pertwee and father of actors Sean and Dariel Pertwee. Jon's first wife was UPSTAIRS, DOWNSTAIRS star Jean Marsh.

Peter Kay's Phoenix Nights ★★★★

UK (Ovation/Goodnight Vienna/Channel 4) Situation Comedy. Channel 4 2001–2
DVD: VCI

Brian Potter	**Peter Kay**
Max	**Peter Kay**
Jerry St Clair	**Dave Spikey**
Ray Von	**Neil Fitzmaurice**
Holy Mary	**Janice Connolly**
Alan	**Steve Edge**
Les	**Toby Foster**
Marion	**Bea Kelley**
Kenny	**Archie Kelly**
Young Kenny	**Justin Moorhouse**
Patrick ('Paddy')	**Patrick McGuinness**
Denzil 'Den' Perry	**Ted Robbins**

Writers **Peter Kay, Neil Fitzmaurice, Dave Spikey**
Executive Producer **Phil McIntyre**
Producers **Mark Herbert, John Rushton**

● ***The owner of a northern social club aspires to greatness.***

If ever a club was appropriately named it is the Phoenix, Bolton's answer to the WHEELTAPPERS' AND SHUNTERS'. On two separate occasions the premises have burned down but its owner, wheelchair-bound Brian Potter, will not let it die and defiantly resurrects the business from the ashes. Potter will do anything to make the club a success, although the efforts of his willing but hapless staff tend to get in the way. His chief cohort is compere/singer Jerry St Clair, a man whose talents have reached their rightful plateau, but there are also enthusiastic DJ Ray Von and assorted other barmaids and potmen, plus dense bouncers Max and Paddy and resident musical duo Les Alanos, to ensure Potter's plans never materialize quite as expected. Quiz nights, 'free and easy' singalongs, talent contests, bingo, Chinese suppers (cooked by illegal immigrants) and *Stars in Their Eyes* evenings all collapse in chaos. Potter's great rival is Den Perry, the Mr Big owner of the Banana Grove club, whom Potter believes torched the Phoenix.

The series was spun-off from an episode of a fly-on-the-wall spoof collection called *That Peter Kay Thing* (Channel 4 2000), a multi-character vehicle for the rising northern comic. It itself generated an offshoot series, when the two bouncers' eventful journeys in a camper van were covered in *Max & Paddy's Road to Nowhere* (Channel 4 2004).

Peter Principle, The ★

UK (Hat Trick) Situation Comedy. BBC 1 1997; 2000

Peter Duffley	**Jim Broadbent**
Susan Harvey	**Claire Skinner**
Geoffrey Parkes	**Stephen Moore**
Bradley Wilson	**David Schneider**
David Edward	**Daniel Flynn**
Iris	**Janette Legge**
Brenda	**Tracy Keating**
Barbara	**Beverley Callard**
Evelyn Walker	**Wendy Nottingham**

Writers **Mark Burton, John O'Farrell, Dan Patterson**
Executive Producer **Denise O'Donoghue**
Producer **Dan Patterson**

An over-promoted manager sends a provincial bank branch into chaos.

According to 'the Peter Principle', everyone is promoted to their level of incompetence – a fact amply demonstrated by this particular Peter, Peter Duffley. Duffley is the manager of the Aldbridge branch of C&P (County and Provincial) Bank and displays such complete ineptitude, pomposity and greed that it's a wonder he has any customers left. Most of the credit for keeping the ship afloat must go to his efficient assistant, Susan Harvey, because the rest of the bank staff are not much brighter or industrious than the leader they rightly distrust. For Susan, working for such an underachiever who relegates office life to the level of farce is a wholly frustrating experience.

After a pilot episode in 1995 (in which the lead character was called Peter Duff and Lesley Sharp took the role of Susan, among other cast changes), the series kicked off with six episodes in 1997, but did not re-emerge until 2000. Never a critical success, it was then quickly shunted to a late-night slot to play out this second run of six.

Peters, Sylvia

British television personality of the 1940s and 1950s, working as one of the BBC's on-screen continuity announcers (in rota with Mary Malcolm and McDonald Hobley). She joined the Corporation in 1947, making use of her talents as a former dancer to also introduce TELEVISION DANCING CLUB with Victor Sylvester and COME DANCING in its formative years. For children's television she read the *Bengo* stories. Peters eventually left the BBC to freelance for commercial television.

Petrocelli ★★

US (Paramount) Legal Drama. BBC 1 1978–9 (US: NBC 1974–6)

Tony Petrocelli	**Barry Newman**
Maggie Petrocelli	**Susan Howard**
Pete Ritter	**Albert Salmi**
Lt. John Ponce	**David Huddleston**

Creators **Sidney J. Furie, Harold Buchman, E. Jack Neuman**
Executive Producers **Thomas L. Miller, Edward J. Milkis**

A Harvard-educated lawyer of Italian descent opens a legal practice for ranchers.

Tony Petrocelli and his wife, Maggie, have given up their lucrative city life and moved west into the fictitious town of San Remo, setting up home in a camper-van. Hiring ranch-hand Pete Ritter as an investigator, Petrocelli opens up a legal practice, providing help for the local cattle-farmers. Unfortunately, his sophisticated eastern methods are not always appreciated and many clients cannot afford to pay him at the end of the day. As a result, the Petrocellis are not the richest attorney family in America. Lt. Ponce is Tony's friend, despite being the police officer who works against him on many cases.

Based on the 1970 film *The Lawyer*, in which Barry Newman played the part of Petrocelli, the series was innovative in using flashback sequences to show how crimes had occurred from the viewpoints of various characters. It was filmed in Tucson, Arizona.

Petticoat Junction ★★

US (Filmways) Situation Comedy. ITV 1964 (US: CBS 1963–70)
DVD: MPI Home Video

Kate Bradley	**Bea Benaderet**
Uncle Joe Carson	**Edgar Buchanan**
Billie Jo Bradley	**Jeannine Riley**
	Gunilla Hutton
	Meredith MacRae
Bobbie Jo Bradley	**Pat Woodell**
	Lori Saunders
Betty Jo Bradley/Elliott	**Linda Kaye Henning**
Charlie Pratt	**Smiley Burnette**
Floyd Smoot	**Rufe Davis**
Sam Drucker	**Frank Cady**
Homer Bedloe	**Charles Lane**
Newt Kiley	**Kay E. Kuter**
Selma Plout	**Virginia Sale**
	Elvia Allman
Henrietta Plout	**Lynette Winter**
Steve Elliott	**Mike Minor**
Dr Janet Craig	**June Lockhart**
Wendell Gibbs	**Byron Foulger**

Creator **Paul Henning**

Bumpkin humour at the terminus of an old steam train.

In the 1960s, American television considered there to be much mileage in the yokel comedy. Like its predecessor, THE BEVERLY HILLBILLIES, *Petticoat Junction* takes the rise out of the home-spun wisdom, offbeat logic and strange customs of 'backward' country folk – not surprisingly, as both shows were created by the same man, Paul Henning. Henning even brought an actress from *The Beverly Hillbillies* to star in his new show: Bea Benaderet, who had played Jed Clampett's cousin Pearl, stepped up to headline after years of supporting roles (including the voice of Betty Rubble in THE FLINTSTONES). Here she plays widow Kate Bradley, the owner of the Shady Rest Hotel in fictional Hooterville. Kate is 'helped' around the hotel by workshy Uncle Joe, who spends most of his time dreaming up fruitless get-rich-quick schemes, and her three lovely daughters, Billie Jo, Bobbie Jo and Betty Jo, for whom she needs to find husbands. Betty Jo (played by Paul Henning's own daughter) does soon find her beau, in the shape of pilot Steve Elliott. Other notable townsfolk include general storekeeper Sam Drucker and Kate's arch-rival, Selma Plout, who will find a husband for her own daughter, Henrietta, if it kills her – preferably before Kate's daughters marry. Otherwise, most of the excitement in town comes with the arrival of the *Cannonball*, the veteran locomotive that steams into Hooterville crewed by engineers Charlie Pratt and Floyd Smoot (and later Wendell Gibbs). Apart from the travellers it brings, there is much controversy about the train itself because Homer Bedloe of the C. F. & W. Railroad wants to close down the line. Following the illness and untimely death of Bea Benaderet, Dr Janet Craig was introduced as a matriarchal figure for the town but the series only lasted a couple more years. The show's obscure title is explained by showing the three Bradley girls swimming in the water tank used to replenish the train, their petticoats hung over the side. Another Paul Henning comedy, GREEN ACRES, was later set just outside Hooterville and characters from that series (like handyman Eb Dawson, played by Tom Lester) tended to wander into *Petticoat Junction* from time to time.

Pettifer, Julian

(1935–)

Wiltshire-born journalist and presenter, working for programmes like TONIGHT, PANORAMA and 24 HOURS after appearing on Southern Television. As well as award-winning reports from the Vietnam War and a raft of documentaries and nature programmes (including narrating *The Natural World* and presenting *Safari UK*), Pettifer has also hosted *Bite-back* (the BBC viewers' response programme) and the quiz BUSMAN'S HOLIDAY, and contributed to *Assignment*.

Peyton Place ***

US (Twentieth Century-Fox) Drama. ITV 1965–70 (US: ABC 1964–9)

Constance MacKenzie/ Carson	**Dorothy Malone**
	Lola Albright
Allison MacKenzie	**Mia Farrow**
Dr Michael Rossi	**Ed Nelson**
Leslie Harrington	**Paul Langton**
Rodney Harrington	**Ryan O'Neal**
Norman Harrington	**Christopher Connelly**
Matthew Swain	**Warner Anderson**
Betty Anderson/Harrington/ Cord/Harrington	**Barbara Parkins**
Julie Anderson	**Kasey Rogers**
George Anderson	**Henry Beckman**
Dr Robert Morton	**Kent Smith**
Steven Cord	**James Douglas**
Hannah Cord	**Ruth Warrick**
Elliott Carson	**Tim O'Connor**
Eli Carson	**Frank Ferguson**
Nurse Choate	**Erin O'Brien-Moore**
Dr Clair Morton	**Mariette Hartley**
Dr Vincent Markham	**Leslie Nielsen**
Rita Jacks/Harrington	**Patricia Morrow**
Ada Jacks	**Evelyn Scott**
Mrs Dowell	**Heather Angel**
Stella Chernak	**Lee Grant**
Gus Chernak	**Bruce Gordon**
Dr Russ Gehring	**David Canary**
DA John Fowler	**John Kerr**
Marian Fowler	**Joan Blackman**
Martin Peyton	**George Macready**
	Wilfred Hyde-White
Sandy Webber	**Lana Wood**
Chris Webber	**Gary Haynes**
Lee Webber	**Stephen Oliver**
Rachael Welles	**Leigh Taylor-Young**
Jack Chandler	**John Kellogg**
Adrienne Van Leyden	**Gena Rowlands**
Eddie Jacks	**Dan Duryea**
Carolyn Russell	**Elizabeth 'Tippy' Walker**
Fred Russell	**Joe Maross**
Marsha Russell	**Barbara Rush**
Revd Tom Winter	**Bob Hogan**
Susan Winter	**Diana Hyland**
Dr Harry Miles	**Percy Rodriguez**
Alma Miles	**Ruby Dee**
Lew Miles	**Glynn Turman**
Jill Smith/Rossi	**Joyce Jillson**

Creator/Producer **Paul Monash**

The inhabitants of a small New England town have many dark secrets to hide.

Based on the novel by Grace Metalious, which had already been adapted for two feature films, *Peyton Place* found its way to the small screen courtesy of the success of CORONATION STREET in the UK. Realizing that a TV soap opera could be sustained in prime time on a twice-a-week basis and was not just worthy of daytime filler status, producer Paul Monash took up Metalious's tale of sexual intrigue and closet skeletons to develop this hugely successful series. It turned out to be the programme which made stars of Ryan O'Neal and Mia Farrow, and was the first American soap to be sold to Britain.

The setting for the series is the small, fictitious town of Peyton Place in New England. The central characters are bookstore-keeper Constance MacKenzie and her illegitimate daughter, Allison, who is romantically involved with Rodney Harrington, the son of wealthy mill manager Leslie Harrington. There are also handsome, young GP Mike Rossi (Constance's heart-throb); Betty Anderson (Rodney's wife on two occasions, who, in between, marries drunken lawyer Steven Cord); and Elliot Carson (Allison's secret father, who spent 18 years in prison and later runs the town newspaper). Throughout the show's run, well over a hundred actors and actresses are introduced, and the storyline wanders from trivial family scandals and illicit romances right through to sensational murders and nail-biting court cases.

The most significant event in the show's early years is the disappearance of Allison MacKenzie. (When Mia Farrow left the series, her character was written out, lost on a foggy night.) Other notable storylines see Rodney acquitted of murder, the marriage of Norman Harrington (Rodney's younger brother) to Rita Jacks, daughter of barkeeper Ada Jacks, and the death and funeral of the town's father figure, Rodney's mill-owning grandfather, Martin Peyton. When the series ends, Mike Rossi is in the dock, on trial for murder, and Rodney is confined to a wheelchair.

Viewers of reruns may be confused by seeing Lola Albright as Constance MacKenzie in some early episodes. She temporarily replaced Dorothy Malone, who was seriously ill. Wilfred Hyde-White did the same for George Macready, the actor who played Martin Peyton. *Return to Peyton Place*, a daytime sequel employing different actors, reached US screens in 1971, and several members of the original cast resurfaced in a couple of TV movies, *Murder in Peyton Place* (1977) and *Peyton Place: The Next Generation* (1985).

Phil Silvers Show, The ****

US (CBS) Situation Comedy. BBC 1957–60 (US: CBS 1955–9)

M/Sgt Ernest Bilko	**Phil Silvers**
Cpl Rocco Barbella	**Harvey Lembeck**
Cpl Henshaw	**Allan Melvin**
Col John T. Hall	**Paul Ford**
Pte Duane Doberman	**Maurice Gosfield**
Pte Sam Fender	**Herbie Faye**
Sgt Rupert Ritzik	**Joe E. Ross**
Pte Dino Paparelli	**Billy Sands**
Pte Fielding Zimmerman	**Mickey Freeman**
Mrs Nell Hall	**Hope Sansberry**
Sgt Grover	**Jimmy Little**
Sgt Joan Hogan	**Elisabeth Fraser**

Creator/Writer **Nat Hiken**
Producers **Nat Hiken, Edward J. Montagne**

A sharp-witted, scheming sergeant is head of a US Army platoon.

Master Sgt Ernie Bilko is an inmate of the fictitious Fort Baxter army camp, near Roseville, Kansas (and later at Camp Freemont, California), although inmate is probably not the right word. Nominal head of the base is Colonel John Hall, but it is Bilko who pulls all the strings, certainly as far as his own comfortable lifestyle is concerned. Not many army sergeants can sleep in late, come and go as they please, avoid physical labour or drive around in their CO's car. But not every sergeant is Sgt Bilko.

This balding, bespectacled motor-pool NCO is the master of the money-making scam. He'll bet on anything, from drill competitions to shooting practices. If a good singer turns up in his platoon, he'll use him to win a choir contest or secretly tape his voice to sell to a record company. He has an eagle eye for losers and sets out to take them to the cleaners. However, his best-laid plans often backfire, mostly because, behind his brash exterior, Bilko is just too kind-hearted and can't go through with the kill.

Assisting Bilko with his schemes are his corporals, Barbella and Henshaw, and his inept company of enlisted men, most notably the fat, dozy Doberman (regularly employed as a fall-guy) and the pessimistic Pte Fender. Although loyal to Bilko, the platoon is also wary of its sergeant, knowing his conniving ways; but, in fairness, Bilko is always very protective of his boys. One of his easier preys is superstitious Mess Sgt Ritzik, another compulsive gambler.

The series comprises a run of poker games, betting coups and other outrageous money-making ventures, all doomed to failure. But the highlight is quick-thinking, smooth talking Bilko himself, who can extricate himself from the tightest of corners with a phoney smile, a sackful of charm and a few empty promises. Joan Hogan provides Bilko's romantic interest, although he is not averse to flattering Mrs Hall, the Colonel's wife, if doing so opens a few doors.

Originally titled *You'll Never Get Rich* when first screened in America, *The Phil Silvers Show* has also been billed as *Sgt Bilko*. It has enjoyed rerun after rerun all over the world and helped establish many careers, especially among its writers, who included creator Nat Hiken and future Broadway playwright Neil Simon. The show also gave opportunities to up-and-coming young actors like Dick Van Dyke and Alan Alda. The casting director for the series was ex-world boxing champion Rocky Graziano, whose real name, incidentally, was Rocco Barbella, the same as one of Bilko's corporals. Maurice Gosfield, who played Doberman, later provided the voice for Benny the Ball in the Bilko cartoon spoof BOSS CAT (*Top Cat*).

Four years after the series ended, Phil Silvers resurfaced in the role of Harry Grafton, a devious factory foreman, in *The New Phil Silvers Show* (ITV 1963–4), but the programme lasted only one season.

Philbin, Maggie

(1955–)

Manchester-born presenter, coming to light on MULTI-COLOURED SWAP SHOP, on which she appeared with Keith Chegwin, to whom she was married for several years. Philbin later hosted *The Show Me Show*, TOMORROW'S WORLD, *Hospital Watch*, *Bodymatters Roadshow* and *The Living Earth*, as well as lifestyle programmes such as *Countdown to Christmas*.

Philby, Burgess and Maclean ★★

UK (Granada) Drama. ITV 1977

Kim Philby	**Anthony Bate**
Guy Burgess	**Derek Jacobi**
Donald Maclean	**Michael Culver**
Sir Stuart Menzies	**Richard Hurndall**
Philby's Control	**Peter Vaughan**
Herbert Morrison	**Arthur Lowe**

Writer **Ian Curteis**

Exposé of the double lives of three of Britain's most famous traitors.

Beginning in the late 1940s, Ian Curteis's single drama – directed by Gordon Flemyng – analysed the way in which Kim Philby, Guy Burgess and Donald Maclean coped with their lives as Soviet agents deeply embedded within the British Foreign Office. Philby is portrayed as the most level-headed, chief of the UK's Soviet counter-espionage unit, based in London, and then as CIA liaison in Washington. Burgess is seen as very reckless, his openly bourgeois lifestyle and drunken binges taken as evidence that he could not possibly be a security risk, while Maclean, unhappily posted to the Cairo embassy, is a haunted man, also prone to the excesses of drink. When evidence begins to emerge that there are double agents at the highest level who have been passing nuclear secrets to the Soviets, the net begins to draw in and eventually Maclean (now back in London after a nervous breakdown) and Burgess (on leave from his Washington posting) pack their bags and defect to Moscow. Philby battles it out, denying he is the 'third man' but knowing that his close association with his former Cambridge University colleagues has put him in the spotlight. Despite questions being asked in the House, an internal inquiry – lacking convincing evidence – clears Philby, and he retires to Beirut as a journalist, from where, we learn, he defects eight years later.

Philip Marlowe ★

US (ABC) Detective Drama. BBC 1960 (US: ABC 1959–60)

Philip Marlowe	**Philip Carey**

Raymond Chandler's famous detective given a rather smoother edge.

This TV portrayal of Chandler's celebrated gumshoe transforms Marlowe from a rough diamond into a softer, more gentlemanly type. His name and his devoutly independent status are the only echoes of the hard-bitten character made famous by Humphrey Bogart. A truer interpretation followed in 1984, in *Marlowe – Private Eye*, a five-episode LWT series starring Powers Boothe. Six more episodes, again featuring Boothe, were made in Canada in 1986.

Phillips, Conrad

(Conrad Philip Havord; 1930–)

One of British TV's first action heroes, Conrad Phillips played the title role in THE ADVENTURES OF WILLIAM TELL in 1958. Previously, apart from small parts in series like THE COUNT OF MONTE CRISTO and THE NEW ADVENTURES OF CHARLIE CHAN, Phillips had worked in the theatre, and it was to the stage that he returned for most of the 1960s. He resurfaced to play Robert Malcolm in THE NEWCOMERS and, in the 1970s and

1980s, was a guest in numerous series, from SUTHERLAND'S LAW, CRIBB, *The Return of Sherlock Holmes* (see THE ADVENTURES OF . . .) and HOWARDS' WAY to FAWLTY TOWERS, NEVER THE TWAIN, KELLY MONTEITH and SORRY! He appeared in the 1973 drama *The Man Who was Hunting Himself*, played NY Estates' MD Christopher Meadows in EMMERDALE FARM and was also seen in children's dramas like *Into the Labyrinth*, mini-series like *The Master of Ballantrae* and TV movies such as *Arch of Triumph*. He was back in William Tell country in the late 1980s for a Franco-American version entitled *Crossbow*, in which he played Tell's mentor, Stefan.

Phillips, Fiona

(1961–)

Kent-born presenter, joining GMTV (soon taking over as its Hollywood correspondent) after spells at BBC South and East, and Sky. She has also presented *OK! TV*, *Rich and Famous*, *Start the Weekend*, *Sunday Night* and *Baby House*, and is married to GMTV editor Martin Frizell.

Phillips, Leslie

OBE (1924–)

London-born star of comedy films, once a boy actor. His TV career has spanned more than 50 years, one of his earliest roles being Tom Bridger in the 1952 sitcom *My Wife Jacqueline*. His most recent work includes the role of Hal Porter in the *Crime Doubles* drama *Outside the Rules*, a contribution to the sketch show *Revolver*, and guest spots in MONARCH OF THE GLEN, HOLBY CITY, MIDSOMER MURDERS, WHERE THE HEART IS and AGATHA CHRISTIE'S MARPLE. In between, Phillips has blended both comedy and straight drama in productions like OUR MAN AT ST MARK'S (Revd Andrew Parker), *Foreign Affairs* (Dennis Proudfoot), *Casanova '73* (Henry Newhouse), *Summer's Lease*, CHANCER (James Blake), *Love on a Branch Line* (Lord Flamborough), HONEY FOR TEA (Sir Dickie Hobhouse), THE HOUSE OF WINDSOR (Lord Montague Bermondsey), *Agatha Christie's The Pale Horse* (Lincoln Bradley), TAKE A GIRL LIKE YOU (Lord Archie Edgerstone) and SWORD OF HONOUR (Gervase Crouchback). Other guest roles have been in the likes of THE ADVENTURES OF ROBIN HOOD, MARK SABER, BOON, THE COMIC STRIP PRESENTS . . ., RUMPOLE OF THE BAILEY, THE RUTH RENDELL MYSTERIES, *Days Like These* and DALZIEL AND PASCOE.

Phillips, Siân

CBE (1934–)

Welsh actress, winning much acclaim for her portrayal of the manipulative Livia in I, CLAUDIUS. She also played Clemmie in WINSTON CHURCHILL – THE WILDERNESS YEARS, George Smiley's wife Ann in TINKER, TAILOR, SOLDIER, SPY and SMILEY'S PEOPLE, and appeared in the dramas *Siwan* (title role), *How Green was My Valley* (Beth Morgan), *Shoulder to Shoulder* (Emmeline Pankhurst), JENNIE, LADY RANDOLPH CHURCHILL (Mrs Patrick Campbell), *Warrior Queen* (Boudicca), CRIME AND PUNISHMENT (Katerina Ivanova), *Barriers* (Mrs Dalgleish), *The Snow Spider* (Nain), CATHERINE COOKSON'S *The Black Candle* (Daisy Bennett), THE BORROWERS (Mrs Driver), *The Vacillations of Poppy Carew*, IVANHOE (Queen Eleanor), *The Scold's Bridle* (Mathilda Gillespie), ARISTOCRATS (Lady Emily) and THE MAGICIAN'S HOUSE (Meg Lewis). Among her other offerings have been *The Quiet Man*, *Heartbreak House*, *Off to Philadelphia in the Morning*, VANITY FAIR and P. D. JAMES'S *The Murder Room*, plus guest spots in the likes of JACKANORY, PERFECT SCOUNDRELS and THE LAST DETECTIVE. Her second husband was actor Peter O'Toole.

Philpott, Trevor

(1924–98)

Northampton-born reporter and trend-setting documentary-maker, once with TONIGHT, PANORAMA and MAN ALIVE, but then given his own series, including *The Philpott File* (from 1969).

Phoenix, Patricia

(Patricia Pilkington; 1923–86)

As CORONATION STREET'S brassy Elsie Tanner, Irish-born, Manchester-raised Pat Phoenix became one of TV's favourite scarlet women. She joined the series at its outset in 1960, having worked her way through the theatre and performed as a youngster on radio's *Children's Hour*. She had even written scripts for Harry Worth and Terry Hall and LENNY THE LION. Phoenix played the fiery Elsie for 24 years (apart from a few years away in the 1970s) and, when she left the *Street* in 1984, she remained on our screens in the sitcom CONSTANT HOT WATER (playing Phyllis Nugent, a seaside landlady), and as an agony aunt for TV-am. Her last TV role was in *Hidden Talents*, a drama in the *Unnatural Causes* anthology series, in which she played a bedridden actress. Phoenix was at one time married to her screen partner, Alan Browning, but they had separated before he died. Shortly before she herself died, of lung cancer in 1986, she wed her companion and old friend, actor Tony Booth.

Phoenix and the Carpet, The ✶✶

UK (BBC) Children's Drama. BBC 1 1997
DVD: Walt Disney Video (Region 1 only)

Robert	**Ivan Berry**
Jane	**Charlotte Chinn**
Anthea	**Jessica Fox**
Cyril	**Ben Simpson**
Phoenix	**David Suchet** *(voice only)*
Eliza	**Lesley Dunlop**
Cook	**Miriam Margolyes**
Father	**Ian Keith**
Mother	**Mary Waterhouse**
The Psammead	**Francis Wright**
Mr Tonks	**Christopher Biggins**
Lily	**Jean Alexander**
Mrs Biddle	**Gemma Jones**
Uncle Felix	**Mark Powley**
Selina	**Selina Cadell**
Amelia	**Nicola Redmond**
Revd Blenkinsop	**Philip Bird**

Writer **Helen Cresswell**
Executive Producer **Anna Home**

Four children have fun with a magical bird and a Persian carpet.

When Edwardian children Robert, Jane, Anthea and Cyril discover an egg wrapped up in their new nursery carpet, they are obviously intrigued. By accidentally dropping it into the fireplace, however, a whole world of adventure is suddenly opened to them. Out of the egg hatches a phoenix that encourages them to mount the carpet and fly out of their London home to exotic lands like India where they meet unusual people. However, having to contend with housekeeper Eliza and the awful Mrs Biddle, getting away is not always so easy. Animatronics and chroma key made the phoenix and the flight sequences come to life in this six-part adaptation of E. Nesbit's 1904 novel of the same name, which had previously been dramatized by John Tully for BBC 1, 1976–7 (produced by Dorothea Brooking).

Pickering, Ron
(1930–91)

London-born athletics coach who became a highly respected BBC sports commentator. Pickering's break came when he discovered young Welsh long-jumper Lynn Davies, whom he coached to a gold medal at the Tokyo Olympics in 1964. He joined the BBC for coverage of the 1968 Olympics and never looked back, becoming the Corporation's main athletics pundit and covering other events such as basketball. Pickering was also seen as host of THE SUPERSTARS and WE ARE THE CHAMPIONS.

Pickles, Wilfred
OBE (1904–78)

British actor and presenter whose Yorkshire accent caused some consternation when he began reading the news on national radio in the 1940s. Pickles was also popular a decade later, when he hosted (together with his wife, Mabel) *Ask Pickles* for the BBC. A sort of heavily sentimental SURPRISE, SURPRISE of its day, it specialized in reuniting members of families. Pickles also took to acting, gaining guest spots in series like DR FINLAY'S CASEBOOK before securing a starring role in the senior citizens' romantic comedy FOR THE LOVE OF ADA (gravedigger Walter Bingley). Pickles also hosted STARS ON SUNDAY for a while. One of his last TV roles was as Bernard King in an ITV drama series called *The Nearly Man* in 1975.

Pickup, Ronald
(1940–)

English actor with a long career combining Shakespeare, period and modern drama, and comedy. He played Lord Randolph Churchill in JENNIE, LADY RANDOLPH CHURCHILL, Andrew Maiby in *Tropic*, Frank Gladwyn in *Moving*, Prince Yakimov in FORTUNES OF WAR, Brian Appleyard in *Not with a Bang*, Felix D'Arcy in A MURDER OF QUALITY, Andrew Powell in *A Time to Dance*, Roger Tundish in THE RIFF RAFF ELEMENT and the Duke of Battersea in *Black Hearts in Battersea*. He was also seen as Waldemar Fiturse in IVANHOE, Col. Winters in CAMBRIDGE SPIES, Ernest Sorrel in *Feather Boy*, Fraser in THE WORST WEEK OF MY LIFE, Prof. Meadows in CHERISHED and Handey in SUPERNOVA. He provided the voice of the lion, Aslan, for the BBC's CHRONICLES OF NARNIA and guest roles have come in series such as FATHER BROWN, BOON, INSPECTOR MORSE, LOVEJOY, *Milner*, SILENT WITNESS, HETTY WAINTHROPP INVESTIGATES, CASUALTY, HORNBLOWER, DALZIEL AND PASCOE, MURDER ROOMS: THE DARK BEGINNINGS OF SHERLOCK HOLMES, THE INSPECTOR LYNLEY MYSTERIES, WAKING THE DEAD, MIDSOMER MURDERS, FOYLE'S WAR, HUSTLE, HOLBY CITY and SEA OF SOULS. He is the father of actress Rachel Pickup.

Picture Book ✶

UK (BBC) Children's Entertainment. BBC 1955–63

Presenters **Patricia Driscoll, Vera McKechnie**

Writer **Maria Bird**
Producers **Freda Lingstrom, David Boisseau**

● ***Early toddlers' magazine programme.***
The Monday segment of the WATCH WITH MOTHER strand belonged to *Picture Book* from 1955 to the mid-1960s (including reruns). Hosted initially by Patricia Driscoll, with stories read by Charles E. Stidwill, the programme was taken over by Vera McKechnie when Driscoll left to star as Maid Marian in THE ADVENTURES OF ROBIN HOOD.

Picture Book was more of a magazine programme than an early JACKANORY, with Driscoll and McKechnie turning the pages to introduce various items. One page showed how to make something – paper lanterns, for instance. Another introduced the puppet adventures of Bizzy Lizzy, a wispy-haired little girl with a magic wishing flower on her dress (later given her own series). *Picture Book* also had a page for animals, and more puppets, the Jolly Jack Tars, filled another. These sailors in their berets and hooped shirts drifted across the ocean to strange lands like Bottle Island, sometimes in search of the 'Talking Horse'. The principals were the Captain (complete with bushy moustache), Mr Mate, Jonathan the deck-hand and Ticky the monkey. Before the last page was turned and it was time to 'put the *Picture Book* away' for another day, Sossidge, the programme's marionette dachshund, was also usually seen.

Picture Page ✶

UK (BBC) Magazine. BBC 1936–9; 1946–52

Presenters **Joan Miller, Joan Gilbert, Mary Malcolm**

Creator/Editor **Cecil Madden**
Producers **George More O'Ferrall, Royston Morley, Harold Clayton, John Irwin, Stephen McCormack, Michael Mills**

● ***Early magazine programme curiously based around a telephone switchboard.***
Canadian actress Joan Miller was the presenter of *Picture Page*, and for this role she took the part of a telephone operator. In very contrived fashion, she called up the guests who had been booked to appear and patched them into vision. As 'The Switchboard Girl', Miller became one of TV's earliest personalities, predating even the official opening of the BBC television service (*Picture Page* began life as an experimental test programme before 'real' programming began). Miller was assisted in proceedings by Leslie Mitchell, who took care of the interviews, and also seen were Jasmine Bligh and John Snagge. About 20 items were packed into each hour-long edition and two programmes a week were transmitted. Among the guests persuaded to appear were Danny Kaye, Maurice Chevalier, Will Hay, Sabu, Dinah Sheridan and Sophie Tucker. When the television service was revived after the war, *Picture Page* came back, too, with Joan Gilbert taking over as presenter.

Pie in the Sky ✳✳✳

UK (Witzend) Detective Drama. BBC 1 1994–7
DVD: Acorn Media

Henry Crabbe	**Richard Griffiths**
Margaret Crabbe	**Maggie Steed**
ACC Freddy Fisher	**Malcolm Sinclair**
WPC/Sgt Sophia Cambridge	**Bella Enahoro**
Steve Turner	**Joe Duttine**
Linda	**Alison McKenna**
John	**Ashley Russell**
Henderson	**Nick Raggett**
Nicola	**Samantha Janus**
Gary Palmer	**Nicholas Lamont**
PC Ed Guthrie	**Derren Litten**
PC Jane Morton	**Mary Woodvine**
Sally	**Marsha Thomason**

Creator **Andrew Payne**
Producers **Jacky Stoller, David Wimbury, Chrissy Skinns**

A detective-turned-restaurateur is called back into action against his will.

After 25 years in the police force, podgy Det. Inspector Henry Crabbe decides to retire from Barstock CID and pursue a new career based on his hobby, gastronomy (and, in particular, traditional British cooking). Unfortunately, his accountant wife is not so keen, and nor is Freddy Fisher, the Assistant Chief Constable who values Crabbe's investigative skills. Despite opening his own restaurant, named Pie in the Sky, in the fictitious town of Middleton, Henry is not allowed to take full retirement. A little unfortunate incident in his last case is used by Fisher to blackmail Crabbe into staying on part-time, resulting in the rotund chef being constantly dragged away from his kitchen and once again into police matters.

At his restaurant, Crabbe is a perfectionist, carefully choosing his vegetables from Henderson, a local grower who also works as washer-up. In addition, Crabbe keeps his own chickens, whose nerves he soothes with extracts from Elgar. Steve Turner, an ex-con, and later Gary Palmer are taken on as co-chefs. WPC Cambridge is usually the bringer of bad tidings from the local nick.

In the final series, Crabbe is forced to take charge of the PDS (Public Duties Squad) and against his best instincts is obliged to hire himself out to private companies as a means of raising money for the police. He is joined by two similarly sidelined officers, upper-class Jane Morton and northerner Ed Guthrie.

The series was created by Andrew Payne specifically for star Richard Griffiths, and Griffiths was closely involved in the development of the programme and its characters. With a recipe or cooking tip included in every episode, *Pie in the Sky* proved popular with foodies as well as crime fans.

Piece of Cake ✳✳✳

UK (Holmes Associates/LWT) War Drama. ITV 1988
DVD: Bfs Entertainment (Region 1 only)

'Fanny' Barton	**Tom Burlinson**
'Moggy' Cattermole	**Neil Dudgeon**
'Ram' Ramsey	**Jack McKenzie**
'Dicky' Starr	**Tom Radcliffe**
'Pip' Patterson	**George Anton**
'Sticky' Stickwell	**Gordon Lovitt**
'Flip' Moran	**Gerard O'Hare**
'Flash' Gordon	**Nathaniel Parker**
'Mother' Cox	**Patrick Bailey**
'Fitz' Fitzgerald	**Jeremy Northam**
'Moke' Miller	**Mark Womack**
Squadron Leader Rex	**Tim Woodward**
Chris Hart	**Boyd Gaines**
'Uncle' Kellaway	**David Horovitch**
'Skull' Skelton	**Richard Hope**
Air Commodore Bletchley	**Michael Elwyn**
Eng Officer Marriott	**Stephen MacKenna**
LAC 'Harry' Gullett	**John Bleasdale**
Trevelyan	**Jason Calder**
Steele-Stebbing	**Julian Gartside**
Zardanowski	**Tomek Bork**
Haducek	**Ned Vukovic**

Writer **Leon Griffiths**
Executive Producer **Linda Agran**
Producer **Andrew Holmes**

A squadron of Spitfire pilots prepares for the Battle of Britain.

This six-part drama, based on a controversial book by Derek Robinson, angered some veterans of the armed forces by depicting the heroic Spitfire pilots of World War II not as the accustomed 'golden boys' but as raw, not always likeable, novices. Beginning in 1939, it focuses on the young men of fictitious 1020 Hornet Squadron (motto: 'Beware Our Sting') as they prepare for war at their base in the village of Kingsmere (real life South Cerney, Gloucestershire). Many are still teenagers, inevitably inexperienced and immature, and uncertain about the road ahead. To knock them into a successful fighting unit they are placed in the hands of Squadron Leader Rex, an eccentric landed gent who fails to adapt to the technological and social changes that the war brings. Among the keen pilots are Scottish public schoolboy 'Pip' Patterson, Australian 'Fanny' Barton, American Chris Hart and the youngest of the young, 'Sticky' Stickwell. Reilly is Rex's faithful pooch. The series follows the squadron as they prepare for action during the 'phoney war' of autumn 1939 and as they move to a chateau close to the French–German border to await action. Finally, the lads, noticeably less relaxed and carefree than before the onset of hostilities, return to England to swelter in the chaotic hot summer of 1940 in the run-up to the Battle of Britain. Inevitably, not all the team makes it through and new recruits like Steele-Stebbing, Zardanowski and Haducek sadly have to take the place of those falling in action. Re-creating aerial action with restored Spitfires and other period aircraft, the series was a delight for plane enthusiasts at least, if not for those with warmer memories of 'the Few'.

Pig in the Middle ✳✳

UK (LWT) Situation Comedy. ITV 1980–1; 1983

Nellie Bligh	**Liza Goddard**
Bartholomew 'Barty' Wade	**Dinsdale Landen** **Terence Brady**
Susan Wade	**Joanna Van Gyseghem**

Creators/Writers **Charlotte Bingham, Terence Brady**
Producer **Les Chatfield**

A middle-aged man drifts between his wife and his mistress.

Barty and Susan Wade are a middle-class couple living in East Sheen. Sadly, Barty's life is not his own and he is constantly nagged by his fussy wife. At one of Susan's many parties, Barty meets fun-loving Nellie Bligh and, taking her as his 'other woman', is able to indulge himself in many of the happy pursuits Susan has banned. However, despite Nellie's advances, Barty remains celibate. Even when he eventually walks out on his wife, it is only to move in next door to Nellie. When Dinsdale Landen left the series, the programme's co-writer, Terence Brady, stepped into the lead role. A US version, entitled *Oh Madeline* and starring Madeline Kahn, was screened by ABC 1983–4.

Piglet Files, The ★★

UK (LWT) Situation Comedy. ITV 1990–2
DVD: Bfs Entertainment (Region 1 only)

Peter Chapman	**Nicholas Lyndhurst**
Major Maurice Drummond	**Clive Francis**
Major Andrew Maxwell	**John Ringham**
Sarah Chapman	**Serena Evans**
Dexter	**Michael Percival**
Lewis	**Steven Law**
Trueman	**Paul Cooper**
Flint	**Louise Catt**

Writers **Brian Leveson, Paul Minett**
Producer **Robin Carr**

● ***A polytechnic teacher is seconded into MI5.***

Life is about to change for college lecturer Peter Chapman. He is suddenly sacked by his polytechnic and sent for an interview with MI5, who have earmarked the 32 year-old as a potential agent. They want to use his teaching skills as a link between ministry boffins and inept agents struggling to cope with new technology. However, when his boss, Prof. Shawcross, defects, Chapman immediately inherits his job. Given the codename 'Piglet', and taking orders from Majors Drummond and Maxwell, he embarks on a life of subterfuge alongside blockheads for whom British intelligence is an obvious misnomer. Sarah is Peter's bemused wife, an employee of a publishing company. Three series, totalling 21 episodes, were produced. The theme music was penned by Rod Argent and Peter Van Hooke, and co-star Clive Francis drew the caricatures that featured in the title sequence.

Pigott-Smith, Tim

(1946–)

British actor, an award-winner for his portrayal of bigot Ronald Merrick in THE JEWEL IN THE CROWN. He also starred in FAME IS THE SPUR (Hamer Shawcross), was Brendan Bracken in WINSTON CHURCHILL – THE WILDERNESS YEARS, Hardy in *I Remember Nelson*, Steve Marsh in the sitcom *Struggle*, King Ferdinand in *The True Adventures of Christopher Columbus*, Hubert in *Screen One's The Bullion Boys*, Chief Constable John Stafford in THE CHIEF, James Wisheart in the drama-doc *Innocents*, and DS Frank Vickers in THE VICE. Other appearances have come in classic plays (including Shakespeare) and in dramas like WINGS, THE GLITTERING PRIZES, *The Hunchback of Notre Dame, The Lost Boys*, DANGER UXB, *The Secret Case of Sherlock Holmes*, LIFE STORY (Francis Crick), *Ghosts* and, like many other actors, DOCTOR WHO. Apart from lots of narration work, more recent credits have come in programmes like KAVANAGH QC, DR TERRIBLE'S HOUSE OF HORRIBLE, THE INSPECTOR LYNLEY MYSTERIES, SPOOKS and as Major General Ford in BLOODY SUNDAY, Count Dietrichstein in *Eroica*, Pliny the Elder in *Pompeii – The Last Day*, Lord Shaftesbury in *The Private Life of Samuel Pepys* and Richard in *North and South* (he also played Richard's son, Frederick, in a 1975 version of the same drama).

Pilger, John

(1939–)

Award-winning Australian journalist working in the UK since 1958 and specializing in hard-hitting investigations. From a background with the *Daily Mirror* and on WORLD IN ACTION, Pilger has gone on to expose the atrocities of Cambodia in *Year Zero – The Silent Death of Cambodia* and the treatment of Vietnam War veterans back home in the USA, and to compile reports on hidden matters in Nicaragua, Japan and other countries. In 1974 he was given his own series, *Pilger*, and more recent exposés have included *Death of a Nation* (focusing on Indonesian brutality in East Timor); the *Network First* report *Inside Burma: Land of Fear*; *Apartheid Did Not Die* (a return to South Africa); *Paying the Price: the Killing of the Children of Iraq*; *The New Rulers of the World* (the power of giant corporations); *Palestine is Still the Issue*; *Breaking the Silence* (about the war on terror); and *Stealing a Nation* (the expulsion of the residents of the Chagos Islands in the 1960s and 1970s.

Pilgrim's Rest ★★

UK (Tiger Aspect) Situation Comedy. BBC 1 1997

Bob Payne	**Gary Olsen**
Tilly	**Gwen Taylor**
Didier	**Pierre Forest**
Ronnie	**Jay Simpson**
Drew	**John Arthur**
Quentin	**Jonathan Aris**
Pamela	**Nina Young**
Mo	**Michael Fenton Stevens**

Creator **Bernard McKenna**
Writers **Bernard McKenna, Simon Block, Paul Mayhew-Archer**
Producer **Mark Chapman**

● ***An isolated truck stop is the perfect rendezvous for losers.***

Pilgrim's Restaurant in Kent is a transport café lacking one vital attribute: transport. Former rock band roadie Bob Payne bought it just before a major bypass opened, leaving the greasy spoon stranded high and dry – much like the human debris that still frequents it or works there. Didier is a romantic French trucker who makes the detour off the main carriageway to be with others similarly deluded: people like Ronnie, who dreams of making a fast buck but never will; Drew, the dopey policeman; Quentin, Drew's graduate sidekick; and, of course, Bob himself, who can only shrug his shoulders at the way misfortune has treated him and lust despairingly after his student waitress, Pamela. However, there is more misery about to be inflicted on this motley crew with the arrival of Bob's haughty elder sister, Tilly. She owns half the café, though she has been under the illusion that it is a posh restaurant, and only when her wealthy husband, Duncan, leaves her to her own devices does she discover the truth. Over six episodes, these assorted characters go in search of a life over plates of egg and chips. For anyone foolish enough to think of dropping in, there is always a warning to be read in the café's malfunctioning neon sign, which shorts out to offer alternative names like 'Grim Rest', 'Pig's Aunt' and 'Grim Start' (echoing a similar device used in FAWLTY TOWERS).

Pilot

A trial programme for a possible series. A pilot is used to see if the idea works, to iron out any previously unforeseen problems and, if aired, to gauge public response. Sometimes the pilot is then used as the first episode of the series or is repeated as a prologue to the series. Pilots are also sometimes aired as part of an anthology, with COMEDY PLAYHOUSE a classic example. This series of pilots has resulted, over the years, in sitcoms like STEPTOE AND SON, TILL DEATH US DO PART and THE LIVER BIRDS. In the 1970s the trend in the USA was to produce feature-length TV movies as pilots. Consequently, *The Marcus Nelson Murders* served as the pilot for KOJAK, *Smile Jenny You're Dead* for HARRY O, etc.

Pingu ★★

Switzerland/UK (Trickfilmstudio/HIT) Children's Animation. BBC 1 1990–1; 1993; 1995; 1997; BBC 2 2004–
DVD: HIT Entertainment

Voices:
Pingu .... **Carlo Bonomi**
Marcello Magni

Creator **Silvio Mazzola**

A young penguin learns about life the hard way.
This series of five-minute moral adventures features the rather wayward young penguin named Pingu, who lives on the ice cap with his mum, his pipe-smoking postman dad and baby sister, Pinga. The family home is an igloo with all mod cons. Each day Pingu goes out to play and usually ends up in some kind of scrape through his somewhat reckless behaviour. But fear not, no harm ensues and the cheeky young penguin is sure to have learned his lesson by the close of the programme. Sometimes penguin friends like Pingo get involved; at other times it is Robbie the seal who is Pingu's accomplice. This stop-frame, claymation series was initially produced in Switzerland from 1986, directed by Otmar Gutmann, but BOB THE BUILDER producer HIT bought the rights and developed new episodes in the UK in 2004, with Italian Marcello Magni brought in to replace Carlo Bonomi, the original artist behind Pingu's strange Penguinese language (none of which was ever scripted). Such was the popularity of the mischievous little chap that a *BBC Pingu* magazine was also published.

Pingwings, The ★

UK (Associated-Rediffusion/Smallfilms) Animation. ITV 1962–3

Narrators **Oliver Postgate, Olwen Griffiths**

Writer **Oliver Postgate**

A family of penguins have fun on a farm.
Inspired by a knitted penguin left to dry on a washing line, *The Pingwings* was Oliver Postgate's first attempt at stop-frame puppet animation, a move that would eventually lead to POGLES' WOOD, CLANGERS and BAGPUSS. Airing under ITV's *Small Time* banner, each little film told of the adventures of a family of woolly waddlers – Mr and Mrs Pingwing, children Paul and Penny and the tiny Baby – who lived a landlubber's life on a farm (the series was shot outdoors among real livestock). Vernon Elliott provided the music.

Pink Panther Show, The ★★

US (DePatie-Freleng) Cartoon. BBC 1 1970–7
(US: NBC 1969–78; ABC 1978–9)

The Inspector .... **Pat Harrington Jr** *(voice only)*

Executive Producers **David DePatie, Friz Freleng**

The animated misadventures of a hapless pink cat.
The Pink Panther was originally created for the Blake Edwards film of the same name, starring Peter Sellers as the bungling Inspector Henri Clouseau on the trail of a stolen gemstone called the Pink Panther. The cartoon cat appeared only in the titles sequence, and then for only a few seconds. However, the exposure was enough to earn some cinema releases of his own, before this TV version began in America in 1969.

The series initially contained some puppet sketches and was hosted by comedian Lenny Schultz. More familiar to UK viewers, however, were the 100 per cent cartoon packages that followed, with the series' name changing a number of times as its animated components alternated. The classic combination comprises two Panther cartoons sandwiching the latest case of the Inspector, an inept Clouseau clone. Other notable partners for the Panther are the Ant and the Aardvaark, and Crazylegs Crane. Yet there is only one star, the Pink Panther himself – 'the one and only, truly original panther, Pink Panther, from head to toe'.

Plodding around on his hind legs, the flat-footed pink cat with a long, looping tail is a compulsive do-gooder, a character whose best-laid plans are guaranteed to go awry. Stoically accepting every disaster Nature hurls his way (apart from an occasional gnashing of the teeth or the raising of an eyebrow), the stone-faced, silent feline is completely resigned to the catastrophes in his life. He is so accident-prone that on a bright, sunny day, a single cloud is known to hover over his head, spouting rain. All this as Henry Mancini's 'durrum, durrum' theme music wafts along in the background.

The opening and closing sequences are familiar, too, showing the Panther being ushered in and out of a flashy (real-life) sports car, parked outside the show's theatre. Although it earned some lengthy runs in the BBC's Saturday teatime slot, the show was also well employed as a filler programme, plugging gaps when sporting events overran or another series finished early. In addition, the programme generated an enormous amount of cheap merchandising, ranging from pencil cases to sickly pink chocolate bars.

Pinky and Perky ★★

UK (BBC/Thames) Children's Entertainment. BBC/ITV 1957; 1960–8; ITV 1970–1

Creators **Jan Dalibor, Vlasta Dalibor**
Producers **Trevor Hill, Stan Parkinson**

Pop music and fun with two puppet piglets.
Created by Czech immigrants Jan and Vlasta Dalibor, Pinky and Perky were Britain's favourite string puppets in the late 1950s and early 1960s. The twin pigs were identical in all respects, except that Pinky wore red and Perky wore blue (not much use on black-and-white TV), and that Perky usually donned a beret in front of the cameras. Their repertoire consisted of high-pitched (fast-forwarded tape) jokes and songs, including versions of contemporary pop hits. Their theme song was 'We Belong Together'. The piglets ran their own

fictitious television station, PPC TV, which employed some of their animal friends, the likes of Horace Hare, Ambrose Cat, Conchita the cow, Morton Frog, Basil Bloodhound, Bertie Bonkers (a baby elephant), Vera Vixen and a bird pop group called The Beakels. The various human straight men keeping them company (at different times) were John Slater, Roger Moffat, Jimmy Thompson, Bryan Burdon and Fred Emney. The prancing porkers' series were given various titles, including *Pinky and Perky's Pop Parade, Pinky and Perky's Island, Pinky and Perky Times* and *Pinky and Perky's American Journey*.

Pinter, Harold

CH (1930–)

British dramatist, widely applauded for his dialogues but criticized by some for the obscure nature of his plays. He was initially commissioned for stage and radio, but came to the fore via ARMCHAIR THEATRE in 1960 with his first television play, *A Night Out*. After further dramas for ITV – *Night School* (also 1960), *The Collection* (1961) and, more controversially, *The Lover* (1963) – Pinter switched to the BBC. He wrote *Tea Party* for a pan-European anthology series entitled *The Largest Theatre in the World* in 1965, which he followed with *The Basement*, a visually adventurous offering for BBC 2's *Theatre 625* in 1967. Although Pinter then branched out into cinema work, he returned to the small screen in 1973 with a contribution entitled *Monologue* and, three years later, his drama *The Collection* was screened in the prestigious *Laurence Olivier Presents* . . . anthology, with Olivier himself in the cast. Pinter's adaptation of Aidan Higgin's *Langrishe, Go Down* was shown as a *Play of the Week* in 1978 (Pinter himself playing Barry Shannon), and *The Hothouse* followed in 1982 with, at the end of the decade, *The Heat of the Day*, adapted from Elizabeth Bowen's novel. In 1992 his *Old Times* was a *Performance* presentation, and a year later his adaptation of Kafka's *The Trial* was shown as a *Screen Two* film. Pinter's first wife, Vivien Merchant, starred in some of his earliest works and, as with *Langrishe, Go Down*, Pinter himself occasionally appeared, too, under the stage name of David Baron. He was also seen in the 1964 adaptation of Sartre's *In Camera* and in the 1976 drama ROGUE MALE. Pinter later married novelist/historian Lady Antonia Fraser. He was made a Companion of Honour in 2002 and won the Nobel Prize for Literature in 2005.

Piper, Billie

(1982–)

Swindon-born singer who, before her 18th birthday, scored three number 1 hits in the UK ('Because We Want To', 'Girlfriend' and 'Day & Night'). She then turned to acting, starring as Alison Crosby in CANTERBURY TALES and Bella in *Bella and the Boys*, before clinching the lead role of Rose Tyler in the re-vamp of DOCTOR WHO. In 2005 she played Hero in *Much Ado about Nothing*. In 2001 she married DJ/presenter Chris Evans, though they have since separated.

Pipkins

See *Inigo Pipkin*.

Plane Makers, The/The Power Game ✱✱

UK (ATV) Drama. ITV 1963–5/1965–6; 1969
DVD: Network

John Wilder	**Patrick Wymark**
Pamela Wilder	**Barbara Murray**
	Ann Firbank
Don Henderson	**Jack Watling**
Arthur Sugden	**Reginald Marsh**
Kay Lingard	**Norma Ronald**
Henry Forbes	**Robert Urquhart**
Sir Gordon Revidge	**Norman Tyrrell**
James Cameron-Grant, MP	**Peter Jeffrey**
Sir Gerald Merle	**William Devlin**
Caswell Bligh	**Clifford Evans**
Kenneth Bligh	**Peter Barkworth**

Producers **Rex Firkin, David Reid**

● ***Friction between unions and bosses at an aircraft factory.***
The Plane Makers was set in the hangars and workshops of the fictitious Scott Furlong aircraft factory and focuses on industrial strife and management quandaries among the 5,000 staff as they develop the exciting new Sovereign aircraft. In the first series, the cast varies week by week but, from the start of the second season, the company's managing director, John Wilder, is the man everyone is beginning to hate, outshining other characters like works manager Arthur Sugden and chief test pilot, Henry Forbes. Wilder takes on even greater prominence when the programme is renamed *The Power Game* after two series. With the action transferred off the shop floor and into the boardroom, more attention is given to Wilder's wheelings and dealings. After the failure of a vertical take-off aircraft (Veetol) project, the bullying businessman leaves Scott Furlong, takes a seat on the board of a bank and picks up a knighthood. He begins scheming in pastures new and encounters fresh rivals in the shape of north country tycoon Caswell Bligh and his son, Kenneth. For the final series (shown three years after the previous run), Sir John is ensconced in diplomatic circles as a member of the Foreign Office (Ambassador for Special Situations and Trade), burrowing away for Britain around the world (each episode title is prefixed with his role, 'Special Envoy'). The series ended with the sudden death of its star, PATRICK WYMARK (father of MIDSOMER MURDERS actress Jane Wymark).

Planer, Nigel

(1953–)

British actor and writer, usually in comedy roles. His break came with *The Comic Strip* (which he helped to found with Peter Richardson, his partner in an act called The Outer Limits) and he subsequently appeared in the troupe's run of TV films. He broke into television by writing for NOT THE NINE O'CLOCK NEWS and playing Lou Lewis in SHINE ON HARVEY MOON. Then came THE YOUNG ONES, in which he created the role of the hippy Neil, which won him a cult following. Planer followed this with a more conventional sitcom in ROLL OVER BEETHOVEN (rock 'n' roll star Nigel Cochrane), but returned to anarchy as Filthy in FILTHY RICH AND CATFLAP. He moved on to light drama in KING AND CASTLE (debt-collector David Castle; also singing the theme song) and heavier matters in Dennis Potter's BLACKEYES (advertising executive Jeff). Planer was also seen in BLACKADDER, played a pregnant man in the drama

Frankenstein's Baby, George Pepperly in *Unnatural Pursuits* and Jocelyn Pride in the single drama *Cuts*, and offered viewers acting advice in *Nicholas Craig – The Naked Actor* and its various sequels. In 1992 he took over from the late Eric Thompson as writer and narrator of THE MAGIC ROUNDABOUT and a year later starred as hapless French teacher Laurence Didcott in BONJOUR LA CLASSE. Planer also played Malvolio in the schools' series *Shakespeare Shorts* and featured in THE GRIMLEYS (Baz Grimley). Guest appearances include roles in JONATHAN CREEK, THE BILL and THE LAST DETECTIVE.

Planet of the Apes, The ★★

US (Twentieth Century-Fox) Science Fiction. ITV 1974–5
(US: CBS 1974)
DVD: Fox

Galen .... **Roddy McDowall**
Alan Virdon .... **Ron Harper**
Pete Burke .... **James Naughton**
Urko .... **Mark Lenard**
Zaius .... **Booth Colman**

Executive Producer **Herbert Hirschman**
Producer **Stan Hough**

● ***Two astronauts crash-land on a planet ruled by apes, where man is the subservient race.***

On 19 August 1980, three American astronauts are approaching the Alpha Centauri system when they run into radioactive turbulence. Activating an automatic homing device, they are sent spinning back to Earth, but through a time-warp that dumps them over 1,100 years into the future. One of the crew, Jonesy, dies on impact but there are two survivors, Alan Virdon and Pete Burke. They discover an Earth with a remarkably different social structure from the planet they have left. In the year 3085, man is no longer in control. A holocaust has come and gone, during which apes took over the planet. Orangutans are the ruling species, gorillas are the violent law-enforcers and chimpanzees the more gentle intellectuals. The apes talk, wear clothes, ride horses and tote guns. Humans are simply slaves and menial workers.

Virdon and Burke begin a life on the run, steering clear of gorilla guerrillas and seeking a way of returning to their own time. Only an inquisitive, peace-loving chimpanzee named Galen affords them any assistance as they hide from angry Urko, the gorilla chief of security. Zaius is the more rational orangutan councillor who tries to keep Urko in check. However, the series ends without conclusion after only 14 episodes: it was not a success in the USA.

The programme was based on the successful film series that began with *Planet of the Apes* and ended with *Battle for the Planet of the Apes*, in which Roddy McDowall played various lead ape roles similar to Galen. The original idea came from Pierre Boulle's book *The Monkey Planet*.

Planets, The ★★★

UK (BBC/A&E) Documentary. BBC 2 1999
DVD: BBC

Executive Producer **John Lynch**
Producer **David McNab**

● ***Acclaimed introduction to the wonders of the solar system.***

Using archive footage, images returned by space probes, special effects and computer simulations, and featuring interviews with space technicians and leading astronomers, *The Planets* presents a televisual journey through our solar system. Over eight episodes, all the major bodies orbiting the sun – plus the star itself – are analysed, discussing their origins, composition, geography, ferocious climates and potential for harbouring life.

Plater, Alan

CBE (1935–)

North-eastern writer with many credits. Plater has contributed to series like Z CARS, SOFTLY, SOFTLY, CRANE, CRIBB, FLAMBARDS, THE ADVENTURES OF SHERLOCK HOLMES, CAMPION, MAIGRET, MISS MARPLE, FRANK STUBBS, THE RUTH RENDELL MYSTERIES (*Simisola*), DALZIEL AND PASCOE and MIDSOMER MURDERS, as well as presenting his own original series like *The First Lady*, OH NO! IT'S SELWYN FROGGITT, TRINITY TALES, *The Loner*, *Get Lost!*, *Middlemen* and *Oliver's Travels*, plus THE BEIDERBECKE AFFAIR and its two sequels, *The Beiderbecke Tapes* and *The Beiderbecke Connection*. He has also penned original plays like *Ted's Cathedral*, *To See How Far It Is* (a 1968 trilogy for *Theatre 625*), *Close the Coalhouse Door*, *Seventeen Per Cent Said Push Off*, *The Land of Green Ginger*, the 1977 PREMIERE film *Give Us a Kiss, Christabel*, LAST OF THE BLONDE BOMBSHELLS and *Belonging*. Plater has also adapted other works for the small screen, like A. J. Cronin's THE STARS LOOK DOWN, Trollope's THE BARCHESTER CHRONICLES, Olivia Manning's FORTUNES OF WAR, L. P. Hartley's *Feet Foremost*, J. B. Priestley's *The Good Companions* and Chris Mullin's A VERY BRITISH COUP. Other notable scripts have included *A Day in Summer*, *Misterioso*, *The Referees* and *Orwell on Jura*.

Play Away ★★

UK (BBC) Children's Entertainment. BBC 2 1971–84

Presenters **Brian Cant, Derek Griffiths, Chloe Ashcroft, Lionel Morton, Toni Arthur, Julie Stevens, Carol Chell, Rick Jones, Miranda Connell, John Styles, Johnny Silvo, Johnny Ball, Norman Norman, David Wood, Julie Covington, Tony Robinson, Anita Dobson, Floella Benjamin, Nerys Hughes, Alex Norton, Delia Morgan, Jeremy Irons**

Producers **Cynthia Felgate, Ann Reay, John Smith, Anne Gobey, Jeremy Swan**

● ***Entertainment and education for younger children.***

A natural progression from PLAY SCHOOL, *Play Away* was a Saturday afternoon programme aimed at children up to the age of seven. Accordingly, it featured somewhat less infantile games and songs than were seen in its well-established sister programme and also threw in a few jokes. The series did, however, share many of the same presenters (the most prominent mentioned above), although some new faces were also introduced (including a young Jeremy Irons). A studio audience added to the fun. Music was provided by pianist Jonathan Cohen and the Play Away Band, and the theme song was written by Lionel Morton.

Play for Today ✱✱✱

UK (BBC) Drama Anthology. BBC 1 1970–84

Influential collection of single dramas.

Play for Today was effectively THE WEDNESDAY PLAY under a different name (the transmission day having moved to Thursday) and what the latter had contributed to 1960s TV drama, the former emulated in the 1970s and early 1980s. The *Play for Today* collection featured tragedies, comedies and fantasies, with, among its most celebrated offerings, Jim Allen's *The Rank and File*, Jeremy Sandford's EDNA, THE INEBRIATE WOMAN (both 1971), Hugh Whitemore's *84 Charing Cross Road* (1975), Mike Leigh's NUTS IN MAY (1976) and ABIGAIL'S PARTY (1977), Jack Rosenthal's BAR MITZVAH BOY (1976), Dennis Potter's BLUE REMEMBERED HILLS (1979) and Jeremy Paul and Alan Gibson's THE FLIPSIDE OF DOMINICK HIDE and *Another Flip for Dominick* (1980 and 1982). The series also introduced RUMPOLE OF THE BAILEY in 1975 and won notoriety for two plays that were initially banned: Dennis Potter's *Brimstone and Treacle* (1976, eventually screened in 1987) and Roy Minton's *Scum* (1977, screened in 1991).

Play of the Month ✱✱✱

UK (BBC) Drama Anthology. BBC 1 1965–79; 1982–3

Sunday-night collection of old and new plays.

Airing originally once a month, as its title suggests, but then more sporadically, this anthology of single dramas won much acclaim for its treatment of established works and also for its new commissions. Noted offerings included John Osborne's *Luther* in 1965, Rudolph Cartier and Reed de Rouen's *Lee Oswald – Assassin* in 1966, Arthur Miller's *Death of a Salesman* also in 1966, David Mercer's *The Parachute* in 1968, and adaptations of E. M. Forster's *A Passage to India* in 1965 and *A Room with a View* in 1973, by Santha Rama Rau and Pauline Macauley, respectively.

Play School ✱✱

UK (BBC) Children's Entertainment. BBC 2 1964–88

Presenters **Patrick Abernethy, Bruce Allen, Mike Amatt, Nigel Anthony, Stan Arnold, Toni Arthur, Chloe Ashcroft, Johnny Ball, Janine Barry, Ben Bazell, Floella Benjamin, Stuart Bradley, Christopher Bramwell, Brian Cant, Stephen Cartwright, Carol Chell, Gordon Clyde, John Colclough, Miranda Connell, Kate Copstick, Hilary Crane, Brian Croucher, Paul Danquah, Simon Davies, Ray C. Davis, Jonathan Dennis, Susan Denny, Marian Diamond, Diane Dorgan, Heather Emmanuel, Sheelagh Gilbey, Jon Glover, John Golder, Gordon Griffin, Derek Griffiths, Elvi Hale, Jane Hardy, David Hargreaves, Fred Harris, Maggie Henderson, Terence Holland, Wayne Jackman, Emrys James, Brian Jameson, Colin Jeavons, Kerry Jewell, Lloyd Johnson, Jona Jones, Rick Jones, Dawn Keeler, Judy Kenny, Robin Kingsland, Robert Kitson, Marla Landi, Ian Lauchlan, Phyllida Law, Carole Leader, Sarah Long, Bridget McCann, Stuart McGugan, Nigel Makin, Michael Mann, Dibbs Mather, Nick Mercer, Elizabeth Millbank, Mary Miller, Delia Morgan, Ann Morrish, Lionel Morton, Susan Mosco, Carmen Munroe, Libby Murray, Jennifer Naden, Lesley Nightingale, Janet Palmer, Angela Piper, Valerie Pitts, Karen Platt, Peter Reeves, Gordon Rollings, Beryl Roques, Sheila Rushkin, Dev Sagoo, Michael Scholes, Andrew Secombe, Shireen Shah, Johnny Silvo, Lucie Skeaping, Evelyn Skinner, Jon Skolmen, Don Spencer, Julie Stevens, Virginia Stride, Ben Thomas, Eric Thompson, Christopher Tranchell, Valerie Turnbull, Miguel Villa, Carole Ward, Liz Watts, John White, Mela White, Wally Whyton, Rod Wilmott, Heather Williams, Barry Wilsher, Fraser Wilson, Rosalind Wilson, Lesley Woods, Sam Wyse, Lola Young**

Creator **Joy Whitby**

Fun and games for the pre-school age.

'Here is a house. Here is a door. Windows: one, two, three, four. Ready to knock? Turn the lock. It's *Play School*.' These were the words that introduced the under-fives to *Play School*, the first programme seen on BBC 2. It wasn't meant to be the first, but a celebration outside broadcast from Paris the night before had been wiped out by a power cut and the honour of opening up Britain's third TV channel fell to the first programme in the next day's schedule (*Play School* went out at 11 a.m.).

A mixture of songs, mimes and stories, *Play School* provided a daily dose of mild education and entertainment for the youngest viewers for 24 years. In its heyday there were two presenters per programme (one male, one female), aided by William Blezard on piano, and each pair worked for a whole week before giving way to two of their colleagues. They were ably assisted by the *Play School* toys: two bears, Little Ted and Big Ted; two dolls, the frumpy Hamble (retired and replaced in 1986 by Poppy, a black doll) and raggy Jemima; and the villain of the piece, Humpty, a stuffed egg with arms, legs and a face. Dressed up and bounced on many a knee, these toys became known to every child in the land. The show also had a rocking horse, Dapple, and real animals. Katoo, the cockatoo, was the best known, alongside rabbits George and Peter, a guinea-pig called Elizabeth, Henry and Henrietta mice and two goldfish, Bit and Bot.

The programme opened with a study of the calendar, with the day, month and date carefully spelled out, and each day had a theme. Monday was Useful Box Day, Tuesday was Dressing-up Day, Wednesday was Pets Day, Thursday was Ideas Day, and Friday Science Day. A central feature was the glance at the clock and a chance to tell the time, using the 'big hand, little hand' system, followed by a look at the models at the base of the clock that set the scene for the daily story (sometimes told by a guest reader: the first tale was *Little Red Hen*, read by Athene Seyler). After all this came the dilemma of which window to look through – the arched, the square or the round – before a film about some outside activity or workplace. All these features were held together by a series of songs, dances, mimes and games of pretend, led by presenters who tended to overuse the prompt: 'Can you do that?' Songs about catching fishes alive and wibbly, wobbly walks were used over and over again, and some renditions were more tuneful than others.

The programme brought to light many notable performers whose talents were only hinted at by their monosyllabic duties here. The first show's presenters were Virginia Stride and Gordon Rollings (later Arkwright in the John Smith's beer commercials), and among other fondly remembered hosts were the whimsical Brian Cant, mime specialist Derek Griffiths, ex-Four Pennies vocalist Lionel Morton, quirky Johnny Ball and dreadlocked Floella Benjamin. Emma Thompson's parents, Phyllida Law and Eric (MAGIC ROUNDABOUT) Thompson, were also prominent in the show's early days, as was musician Rick Jones, subsequently presenter of *Fingerbobs*.

Elements of *Play School* (including the windows and the

clock) were incorporated in a new BBC pre-school series, *Tikkabilla*, in 2002.

Play Your Cards Right **

UK (LWT/Talbot) Game Show. ITV 1980–7; 1994–9; 2002

Presenter **Bruce Forsyth**

Creator **Chester Feldman**
Producers **David Bell, Alasdair Macmillan, Paul Lewis, Dean Jones**

● ***Game show involving some general knowledge and a lot of luck with cards.***

A 'higher or lower' card game, *Play Your Cards Right* combined knowledge of public opinion with a little gambling technique. Contestant couples guessed how many people out of a survey sample of 100 believed this or that. The first couple's guess was used as a marker by the second couple, who then simply stated 'higher' or 'lower'. The winners took control of the card game and progressed along a board, turning over playing cards, guessing whether the next card would be higher or lower than the one before. A wrong answer gave control to their opponents. For contestants successfully negotiating the final card round, and amassing enough points by gambling along the way, the prize was a new car. Enthusiastically hosted as ever by Bruce Forsyth, the series generated plenty of new Brucie catchphrases, most notably 'You get nothing for a pair – not in this game', 'What do points make? Prizes!' and 'It could still be a big night, if you play your cards right.'

Under the name of *Bruce Forsyth's Play Your Cards Right* the show returned to the screen in 1994, after an absence of seven years. *Play Your Cards Right* was then included as one instalment of ANT & DEC's *'s Game Show Marathon* in 2005, a series that celebrated the best-loved game shows in ITV's 50-year history.

The concept was derived from the US game show, *Card Sharks*.

Playing the Field **

UK (Tiger Aspect/BBC) Drama. BBC 1 1998–2000; 2002

Theresa Mullen	**Lesley Sharp**
Jo Mullen	**Jo McInnes**
Luke Mullen	**Ralph Ineson**
Matthew Mullen	**Chris Walker**
Mrs Mullen	**Elizabeth Spriggs**
Mr Mullen	**James Ellis**
Eddie Ryan	**John Thomson**
Rita Dolan	**Melanie Hill**
John Dolan	**James Nesbitt**
Geraldine Powell	**Lorraine Ashbourne**
Dave Powell	**Tim Dantay**
Diane Powell	**Debra Stephenson**
Rick Powell	**Nicholas Gleaves**
Sharon 'Shazza' Pearce/ Mullen	**Marsha Thomason**
Gabrielle Holmes	**Saira Todd**
Angie Gill	**Tracey Whitwell**
Jim Pratt	**Ricky Tomlinson**
Francine Pratt	**Brigit Forsyth**
Garry McGreer	**Dorian Healy**
Kate Howard	**Olivia Caffrey**
Mikey	**Emma Rydal**
Ryan Pratt	**Lee Ross**
Scott Bradley	**James Thornton**
Holly Quinn	**Gaynor Faye**
Pauline Pearce	**Annette Bentley**
Kelly Powell	**Claudie Blakley**
Lizzy Makin	**Kelli Hollis**
Gordon	**Antony Byrne**
Martin Dolan	**Tom Moore**
Raquel Pearce	**Naomi Hurtault**

Creator **Kay Mellor**
Executive Producers **Charles Brand, Tessa Ross**
Producers **Greg Brenman, Hugh Warren, Kathleen Hutchison, Lis Steele**

● ***More off- than on-the-field drama with a team of women footballers.***

Although a South Yorkshire women's football team lies at the heart of this emotional drama, most of the action takes place away from the pitch and inside the personal lives of the players and their families. In the first episode, for instance, Theresa Mullen is due to marry long-time lover Eddie Ryan, but the weak-willed Ryan bails out at the last minute. All this while Theresa is summoning up the courage to tell her young sister, Jo, that she is really her natural mother, and while Theresa's mum struggles against agoraphobia. Captain of the Castlefield Blues is Geraldine Powell, battling to get out of an extra-marital affair with her brother-in-law, Rick; and also prominent is mother-of-two Rita Dolan, whose husband John, an ex-pro, is coerced into taking the job of team coach by sponsor Jim Pratt. Pratt's company, J. P. Electrics, funds the team against the wishes of his snooty wife, Francine. Other players include Rick's glamorous wife Diane, lesbian Angie Gill, drugtaker Shazza and policewoman-goalkeeper Gabby Holmes. In later series, new players like Irish midwife Kate, loner Mikey and firewoman Holly, plus new coaches Scott and Gordon, are introduced, as is the Pratts' untrustworthy son, Ryan, and man-eater Lizzy Makin.

Plaza Patrol *

UK (Yorkshire) Situation Comedy. ITV 1991

Bernard Cooney	**Tommy Cannon**
Trevor Purvis	**Bobby Ball**

Writers **Richard Lewis, Louis Robinson**
Producer **Graham Wetherell**

● ***Bungling security men are in charge of a northern shopping centre.***

Bernard Cooney and Trevor Purvis are the two security guards charged with patrolling a shopping mall overnight. Regrettably, their firm, H&L Security, has made a bad choice, their ineptitude only adding to the risks facing shoppers and shopkeepers alike. This sitcom vehicle for stage comics Cannon and Ball only ran to one series of six episodes – too long, claimed critics, although the final episode in fact gained the highest viewing figures of all. The duo had previously played similar roles (clumsy village policemen) in the 1983 film *The Boys in Blue*.

Please Sir! ✶✶✶

UK (LWT) Situation Comedy. ITV 1968–72
DVD: Cinema Club

Bernard Hedges	**John Alderton**
Norman Potter	**Deryck Guyler**
Miss Doris Ewell	**Joan Sanderson**
Mr Morris Cromwell	**Noel Howlett**
Mr Price	**Richard Davies**
Mr 'Smithy' Smith	**Erik Chitty**
Eric Duffy	**Peter Cleall**
Frankie Abbott	**David Barry**
Dennis Dunstable	**Peter Denyer**
Maureen Bullock	**Liz Gebhardt**
Sharon Eversleigh	**Penny Spencer**
	Carol Hawkins
Peter Craven	**Malcolm McFee**
	Leon Vitali
Penny Wheeler/Hedges	**Jill Kerman**
Mr Dix	**Glynn Edwards**
Mr David Ffitchett-Brown	**Richard Warwick**
Miss Petting	**Vivienne Martin**
Gobber	**Charles Bolton**
Terry Stringer	**Barry McCarthy**
Daisy	**Rosemary Faith**
Des	**Billy Hamon**
Celia	**Drina Pavlovic**

Creators/Writers **John Esmonde, Bob Larbey**
Producers **Mark Stuart, Phil Casson**

● ***A hesitant, naïve teacher's first job is in a rough inner-city school.***

Recent graduate Bernard Hedges secures his first appointment as English and History teacher at Fenn Street Secondary Modern, under the auspices of headmaster Mr Cromwell. From the start, his unruly class, 5C, go out of their way to make life difficult for him, but they soon come to respect the bashful yet dedicated master, whom they nickname 'Privet'.

Behind the desks the youths include loudmouth Frankie Abbott, who acts hard but always runs to his mother; slow-witted Dennis, who comes from a deprived home; brash class-leader Eric Duffy; flirtatious Sharon; and Maureen, an evangelical Christian who has a crush on her teacher. The staff are just as unhelpful. Apart from the incompetent headmaster, there are thick-skinned Welshman Pricey teaching maths and science; formidable deputy-head Doris Ewell; dithery old Smithy; and former Desert Rat caretaker Norman Potter, who is terrified of the kids but enjoys great influence with the headmaster. After a couple of years, Hedges acquires a girlfriend, Penny Wheeler, who eventually becomes his wife.

Please Sir!, LWT's first big comedy success, was inspired by the 1967 film *To Sir, with Love*. Its own feature film was released in 1971 and a spin-off, *The Fenn Street Gang*, followed on TV, tracing the lives of the teenagers after leaving school. *Please Sir!* continued simultaneously for one more year, but the new kids and teachers introduced failed to catch on. The American version was WELCOME BACK KOTTER, featuring a young John Travolta among the pupils.

Pleasence, Donald

(1919–95)

British actor, a specialist in macabre and sinister roles. In addition to his long film career, Pleasence was seen in numerous TV dramas, including Dennis Potter's *Blade on the Feather*, Joe Orton's *The Good and Faithful Servant*, the tabloid satire *Scoop*, and Gerald Savory's adaptation of *Double Indemnity*. He was Syme in the classic Nigel Kneale version of 1984, Prince John in THE ADVENTURES OF ROBIN HOOD, Melchior in JESUS OF NAZARETH, Reverend Septimus Harding in THE BARCHESTER CHRONICLES and also starred in THE RIVALS OF SHERLOCK HOLMES, in which he played Carnacki, the ghost-hunter. He made a number of mini-series and TV movies (one of his last appearances was as Victor in *Screen Two's Femme Fatale*) and was seen as a guest in THE OUTER LIMITS, DICK TURPIN and COLUMBO. Occasionally, he appeared with his actress daughter, Angela Pleasence.

Plowright, David

CBE (1930–)

Distinguished British TV executive, closely associated with Granada Television, which he joined in 1957 having previously been a newspaper journalist. With Granada, he worked on regional news magazines before moving up to edit WORLD IN ACTION. In 1968 he was made the station's Programme Controller, in 1975 its Managing Director and in 1987 Chairman of the company. He has also been an important figure in the ITV network and was once Chairman of the Independent Television Companies Association and a director of ITN. In his time at Granada, Plowright – brother of actress Dame Joan Plowright – was widely respected and involved himself closely in programming matters. He even produced episodes of CORONATION STREET. However, in 1992, to the dismay of many of his colleagues, he left in controversial circumstances, reputedly concerned at the company's lack of commitment to, and investment in, quality programming. From then until 1997 he was Deputy Chairman of Channel 4. Plowright was later an outspoken supporter of regional ITV programming as moves to create one national ITV company gathered pace.

Pogles' Wood ✶✶

UK (Smallfilms) Children's Entertainment. BBC 1 1966–7

Voices **Oliver Postgate, Olwen Griffiths, Steve Woodman**

Creator/Writer/Producer **Oliver Postgate**

● ***The fairy-tale adventures of a woodland family.***

Pogles' Wood focuses on day-to-day happenings in the yokel life of the industrious Mr Pogle, his domesticated wife, their young son Pippin and pet squirrel/rabbit Tog, all of whom live in a treetrunk in the heart of a forest. Film footage of the countryside and rural activities is cut into each episode.

This fondly remembered contribution, with puppets by Peter Firmin, was originally conceived as *The Pogles*, in which the little couple were unwittingly ensnared by all kinds of magic involving a special bean plant and a malevolent witch. The BBC liked the idea but felt the witch too scary, and only screened the programme as part of another series called *Clapperboard* in 1965. More wholesome adventures were therefore drummed up by creator Oliver Postgate, with Pippin and Tog added to help Mr and Mrs Pogle appreciate the wonders of nature. The series – now part of the WATCH WITH MOTHER strand – proved so popular that it gave birth to a children's comic, *Pippin*.

Points of View ★★

UK (BBC) Viewer Response. BBC 1 1961–71; 1979–

Presenters **Robert Robinson, Kenneth Robinson, Barry Took, Anne Robinson, Carol Vorderman, Terry Wogan**

● ***Fast-moving viewer-response programme.***

This sprightly little offering was originally conceived as a five-minute filler for dropping in before the news, but it has become one of the BBC's longest-running programmes. It has consisted chiefly of viewers' moans and groans about the Corporation's output, though not all feedback has been negative. Extracts from letters have been read out on air by announcers and, strangely, most contributions seem to have begun with the words 'Why, oh why, oh why?' Critics have knocked the programme for offering only token criticism of the BBC and for being of little constructive benefit. The presenters' cheery put-downs have perhaps fostered this idea.

Robert Robinson was the original host, followed by Kenneth Robinson. Barry Took picked up the reins in the late 1970s and Anne Robinson was in the hot seat for a number of years. Having the name Robinson obviously helps if you want to host *Points of View* (Tony Robinson was also once a stand-in – one of many guest presenters).

Robert Robinson also presented a children's version, *Junior Points of View* (1963–70), a job he shared with Sarah Ward, Gaynor Morgan Rees and Cathy McGowan.

Poirot

See *Agatha Christie's Poirot.*

Poldark ★★★

UK (London Films/BBC) Drama. BBC 1 1975–7
DVD: Universal

Capt. Ross Poldark	**Robin Ellis**
Elizabeth Chynoweth/Poldark/Warleggan	**Jill Townsend**
George Warleggan	**Ralph Bates**
Francis Poldark	**Clive Francis**
Verity Poldark/Blamey	**Norma Streader**
Charles Poldark	**Frank Middlemass**
Demelza Carne/Poldark	**Angharad Rees**
Caroline Penvenen/Enys	**Judy Geeson**
Jud Paynter	**Paul Curran**
Prudie	**Mary Wimbush**
Nicholas Warleggan	**Nicholas Selby**
	Alan Tilvern
Dr Dwight Enys	**Richard Morant**
	Michael Cadman
Sir Hugh Bodrugan	**Christopher Benjamin**
Lady Constance Bodrugan	**Cynthia Grenville**
Capt. Malcolm McNeil	**Donald Douglas**
Mr Nat Pearce	**John Baskcomb**
Harris Pascoe	**Ralph Nossek**
	Preston Lockwood
Zacky Martin	**Forbes Collins**
Paul Daniel	**Pip Miller**
Sam Carne	**David Delve**
Drake Carne	**Kevin McNally**
Geoffrey Charles Poldark	**Stefan Gates**
	Richard Gibson
Agatha Poldark	**Eileen Way**
Revd Osborne Whitworth	**Christopher Biggins**
Morwenna Chynoweth/Whitworth	**Jane Wymark**
Hugh Armitage	**Brian Stirner**
Rowella Chynoweth/Solway	**Julie Dawn Cole**
Monk Adderley	**Malcolm Tierney**

Producers **Morris Barry, Anthony Coburn, Richard Beynon, Colin Tucker**

● ***An 18th-century Cornish squire fights to keep his estate in order and his emotions in check.***

Returning home (believed dead) from doing battle with the Americans in their War of Independence, dashing Cornish squire Ross Poldark discovers his late father's estate in ruins, the tin mines up for sale and the love of his life, Elizabeth, betrothed to his cousin Francis. Determined to rectify matters, Ross sets about tackling the local powers that be, especially loathsome George Warleggan. He aims to re-establish the Poldark name and to bring justice to his workers and other oppressed Cornish folk. He even takes on the invading French. However, one battle he struggles to win is with his heart over the fair Elizabeth, even after she is married to Francis and he to Demelza, the fiery, nit-ridden, urchin servant-girl he has made pregnant. Poldark's feud with Warleggan continues into series two, which also sees Ross arrested as a spy in France before being elected a Member of Parliament. He still carries a torch for Elizabeth, a matter that destabilizes his marriage to Demelza.

Winston Graham's novels were adapted by the BBC into 29 serial episodes and, thanks in no small part to the good looks of its leading man, *Poldark* was one of the most popular dramas of its time. The story was revived by HTV in 1996 in a two-hour sequel costing around £1.5 million and set ten years after the close of the BBC serial. John Bowe and Mel Martin took over the roles of Ross and Demelza in the Winston Graham story, *Strangers from the Sea.*

Pole to Pole

See *Around the World in 80 Days.*

Poliakoff, Stephen

(1952–)

London-born dramatist/director, writing for the theatre and film, as well as television. Much of his work is autobiographical and centred around London, reflecting social change, family conflicts and sexual taboos. Highlights include *Hitting Town* (1976), *Stronger Than the Sun* (1977), *City Sugar* (1978), *Bloody Kids* (1979), CAUGHT ON A TRAIN (1980), *Soft Targets* (1982), *Hidden City* (1988), *Screen One*'s *She's Been Away* (1989) and *The Tribe* (1998), plus the series/serials *Frontiers* (with Sandy Welch), SHOOTING THE PAST, PERFECT STRANGERS, THE LOST PRINCE, *Friends and Crocodiles* and *Gideon's Daughter.*

Police ★★

UK (BBC) Documentary. BBC 1 1982

Editor **John Shearer**

● ***Out and about with the officers of the Thames Valley Police.***

This warts-and-all documentary series focused on E Division of the Thames Valley Police as they patrolled the streets of

Reading and its environs over a nine-month period. Among various incidents, it showed the force organizing a stake-out for a planned robbery and, at the other extreme, saw officers accused of beating up a drunk. One detective broke down in tears after being demoted, but the most controversial of the 11 episodes dealt with a rape case in which police treatment of the victim brought howls of protest. The series was directed by Roger Graef and Charles Stewart. Two decades on, Graef returned with a new documentary called *Police 2001* (BBC 2 2001), which looked at how things had changed in the Thames Valley Police.

Police Five ★★

UK (ATV/LWT) Factual. ITV 1962–90

Presenter **Shaw Taylor**

● ***Short filler programme in which police request help in solving crimes.***

With questions like 'Were *you* in the neighbourhood', host Shaw Taylor appealed for viewers' assistance in tracking down criminals and preventing future incidents. Produced in conjunction with New Scotland Yard, this series focused on crimes in the capital, although regional equivalents were also shown in other ITV areas. Taylor's parting advice was, 'Keep 'em peeled.' LWT also produced *Junior Police Five* in the 1970s.

Police Squad! ★★★★

US (Zucker/Zucker/Abrahams/Paramount) Situation Comedy. ITV 1983 (US: ABC 1982)

Frank Drebin .... **Leslie Nielsen**
Capt. Ed Hocken .... **Alan North**
Ted Olson .... **Ed Williams**
Johnny the Snitch .... **William Duell**
Officer Norberg .... **Peter Lupus**
Al .... **John Wardell**

Creators/Executive Producers **Jerry Zucker, David Zucker, Jim Abrahams**
Producer **Bob Weiss**

● ***Ridiculous satire on all established cop shows.***

Police Squad!, from the team that produced the cinema hit *Airplane*, is a zany, over-the-top collection of word-plays and sight gags that parodies every cliché and action sequence of 'serious' police programmes. Its star, Leslie Nielsen, plays stone-faced Frank Drebin, whose rank varies from lieutenant down to sergeant. Gathered around him are his boss, Captain Hocken, lecherous lab technician Ted Olson, Officer Norberg and Johnny the Snitch, a shoeshine boy with all the latest words on the street (in fact he can answer questions on anything, as long as someone is paying). There is also Al, an officer so tall his face never fits on the screen. Old TV gimmicks are ripe for the picking: the narrator reads out a different episode title from that shown on the screen, 'Tonight's Guest Star' is instantly murdered and forgotten for the rest of the show, and the programme ends with the classic freeze-frame finish seen in many early series, only this time it is the actors themselves who do the freezing, struggling to hold their poses as the credits roll by.

Only six episodes of *Police Squad!* were made, however, and its ratings were low, probably because the programme demanded so much attention from viewers with its many puns and background jokes. All the same, the series did spawn a few successful feature films, *The Naked Gun: From the Files of Police Squad!*, *The Naked Gun 2½: The Smell of Fear* and *Naked Gun 33⅓: The Final Insult*, not to mention a collection of Red Rock cider commercials.

Police Story ★★★

US (Columbia) Police Drama Anthology. ITV 1974–80 (US: NBC 1975–7; ABC 1988)

Creator **Joseph Wambaugh**
Executive Producer **David Gerber**

● ***Individual stories about police officers, their families and the stresses of the job.***

Adopting a different approach from established police series, *Police Story* offers, well, a story about police – not so much about the crooks they chase, nor the subsequent trials and convictions, but about the stresses and strains of being a police officer. Its creator, former Los Angeles Police Department officer-turned-novelist Joseph Wambaugh, used his own experiences and those of his colleagues to inspire the show's scriptwriters. They came up with issues like tensions in a police officer's marriage, concerns over shooting a criminal, the death of a patrol partner, alcoholism on the force and other such difficulties, but without entirely forgoing adrenaline-moments like car chases. More than a decade after the programme officially ended, US viewers were treated to a handful of new episodes. A writers' strike meant that every resource was plundered to keep shows on the air and some unused *Police Story* scripts were therefore picked up and shot for transmission on ABC. The series, however, is perhaps best remembered for a spin-off, POLICE WOMAN, derived from an episode called *The Gamble*, in which Angie Dickinson played female officer Lisa Beaumont (changed to Pepper Anderson in the resultant series). This overshadowed another spin-off, *Joe Forrester*, starring Lloyd Bridges (ITV 1976–7).

Police Surgeon ★★

UK (ABC) Police Drama. ITV 1960

Dr Geoffrey Brent .... **Ian Hendry**
Insp. Landon .... **John Warwick**
Amanda Gibbs .... **Ingrid Hafner**

Producers **Julian Bond, Leonard White**

● ***A police doctor gets too involved in his cases.***

Geoffrey Brent is a doctor with the Bayswater police who has the knack of solving cases that baffle his detective colleagues. The programme was seen by many as the basis for THE AVENGERS, as Ian Hendry soon went on to fill the similar role of Dr David Keel in the first episodes of that long-running series. This British-made *Police Surgeon* should not be confused with the Canadian series of the same name, starring Sam Groom.

Police Woman ★★

US (David Gerber/Columbia) Police Drama. ITV 1975–9 (US: NBC 1974–8)

Sgt Suzanne 'Pepper' Anderson .... **Angie Dickinson**
Lt. Bill Crowley .... **Earl Holliman**
Det. Joe Styles .... **Ed Bernard**

Det. Pete Royster .... **Charles Dierkop**
Cheryl .... **Nichole Kallis**
Lt. Paul Marsh .... **Val Bisoglio**

Creator **Robert Collins**
Executive Producer **David Gerber**
Producer **Douglas Benton**

A glamorous policewoman works undercover for the Los Angeles Police Department.

Blonde divorcée Pepper Anderson works for the criminal conspiracy bureau of the LAPD, as part of the vice squad, taking on unusual undercover roles. Posing as a prostitute, a stripper, a gangster's moll and other ladies of the underworld, she infiltrates the seamier side of LA society, backed up by her colleagues, Joe Styles and Pete Royster. Drama comes from the highly risky (and risqué) situations in which she is placed. The squad chief, and Pepper's best friend, is Lt. Bill Crowley. In the earliest episodes, Pepper's autistic sister, Cheryl, a student at a special school, is occasionally seen.

Police Woman was a spin-off from an American anthology series called POLICE STORY, in which Angie Dickinson once appeared as an officer named Lisa Beaumont.

Politician's Wife, The ★★★

UK (Producers Films/Channel 4) Drama. Channel 4 1995
DVD: Cinema Club

Flora Matlock .... **Juliet Stevenson**
Duncan Matlock .... **Trevor Eve**
Mark Hollister .... **Anton Lesser**
Sir Donald Frazier .... **Ian Bannen**
Clive Woodley .... **Frederick Treves**
Jennifer Caird .... **Minnie Driver**
Rosalind Clegg .... **Diana Fairfax**
Ian Ruby-Smith .... **Patrick Drury**
Colin Fletcher .... **Stephen Boxer**
Mrs Lucas .... **Charmian May**

Writer **Paul Milne**
Producers **Jenny Edwards, Jeanna Polley, Neal Weisman**

The cheated wife of a leading Tory plots his downfall.

Duncan Matlock is a cabinet minister. He is also unfaithful to his wife, Flora. When news breaks of his extra-marital affair with vice girl Jennifer Caird, the woman scorned overcomes initial feelings of hurt to unleash the fury that proverbially hell cannot match. But she plays it cool. Under pressure from Conservative Party grandees to 'stand by her man' – who, embarrassingly, is Minister for the Family – she dutifully presents a dignified, loyal facade. But, beneath this calm exterior, she begins to manufacture her husband's fall from grace, starting with an act of sabotage on his plans to privatize child benefit. However, politicians tend to stick together and she finds that retribution is not going to be easy. This award-winning, three-part drama was directed by Graham Theakston.

Pollard, Su

(1949–)

British actress, comic and singer, specializing in daffy females. It was as Peggy, the ambitious chalet maid in HI-DE-HI!, that she made her name, having earlier appeared on OPPORTUNITY KNOCKS and with Paul Nicholas in a short-lived sitcom entitled *Two Up, Two Down*. She played Peggy for eight years and followed it with virtually the same role in YOU RANG, M'LORD?, this time in the guise of parlourmaid Ivy Teasdale, and again in OH DOCTOR BEECHING!, as ticket clerk Ethel Schumann. Pollard also sang the theme song ('Starting Together') for a fly-on-the-wall documentary series, *The Marriage*, and other credits have included the kids' comedy *Clock On*, THE COMEDIANS, *Summer Royal* and *Get Set for Summer*, as well as a guest role in GIMME GIMME GIMME and the voice of Noisy in the animation *Little Robots*.

Pop Idol ★★★

UK (Thames/19 TV) Talent Show. ITV 2001–3
DVD: Fremantle Home Entertainment

Presenters **Ant and Dec**

Executive Producers **Richard Holloway, Nigel Lythgoe, Simon Fuller, Richard Holloway**
Producers **Claire Horton, Ken Warwick**

The search for a new pop superstar.

This staggeringly successful follow-up to POPSTARS (produced by that show's notorious Nigel Lythgoe) set about unearthing a new chart giant. Would-be Pop Idols from all over the UK were whittled down by a quartet of judges (not known for mincing words) consisting of Simon Cowell (Head of A&R at RCA records), DJ Neil (Dr) Fox, publicist Nicki Chapman (from *Popstars*) and record producer Pete Waterman. Then the onus was placed on the viewing audience to select ten finalists from a short list of 50, over five live heats, after comments on their performance by the judges. The final ten were then eliminated weekly, one by one, to leave ultimate 'Pop Idol' Will Young to narrowly shade it over Gareth Gates. The other eight finalists were Korben (Chris Niblett), Jessica Garlick, Aaron Bayley, Laura Doherty, Rosie Ribbons, Hayley Evetts, Zoë Birkett and Darius Danesh (an unsuccessful *Popstars* contender who became a late replacement for finalist Rik Waller, who was ruled out by a throat infection). All finalists later toured together and a recording of the final performance, at London's Earl's Court, was screened by ITV in April 2002. They also jointly released an album of big band songs. Success proved immediate for Will Young and Gareth Gates, who both secured instant chart-toppers, while Jessica Garlick went on to represent the UK in the 2002 Eurovision Song Contest.

Pop Idol returned in 2003 for a contest won by Michelle McManus, defeating Mark Rhodes, Sam Nixon, Chris Hide, Susanne Manning, Roxanne Cooper, Kim Gee, Marc Dillon, Brian Ormond, Andy Scott Lee, Kirsty Crawford and Leon McPherson. The format of *Pop Idol* was sold around the world, becoming massive in the USA as *American Idol*, for which Simon Cowell was again a judge. In December 2003, ITV 1 screened *World Idol*, a one-off contest for the winners of series from 11 countries, with Will Young representing the UK. It was won by Norwegian Kurt Nilsen.

Pop Quest ★★

UK (Yorkshire) Quiz. ITV 1975–8

Presenters **Steve Merike, Kid Jensen, Sally James, Mike Read, Megg Nicol**

Producers **Ian Bolt, Peter Max-Wilson**

● *Teenagers show off their extensive rock and pop knowledge.*

This searching quiz aimed to find the teenagers with the best knowledge of the pop music movement, but covering the whole history of the rock 'n' roll era and not just the contemporary scene. Series one was organized as a contest involving teams from the various ITV regions, with Steve Merike firing the questions. From series two, however, *Pop Quest* became an individual knockout contest hosted by Kid Jensen and Sally James, who gave way in series three to Mike Read and Megg Nicol. Questions ranged from quick-fire, on-the-buzzer introductory and final rounds to selections from a category board containing such topics as Progressive Music, Rock 'n' Roll, Black Music, New Wave and Hit Picks (three snippets of hits to identify from a given year or artist). In the grand final, the four survivors also had to endure time in the 'Hot Seat' under a barrage of tricky questions. In a diversion from the main contest, different star artists appeared each week in series one. A regular feature in series two was 'Track Facts', looking at the making of a record, from signing the artist through to the sale of the disc. This was replaced in series three by 'Feed Back', a mini-discussion about rock issues such as electric guitars, jukeboxes and record collecting.

Popstars/Popstars: The Rivals ★★

UK (LWT/Screentime) Documentary. ITV 2001/ITV 2002
DVD: Granada Media

Executive Producers **Nigel Lythgoe, Bob Massie**
Producers **James Breen, Tim Quicke, David O'Neill, Conrad Green**

● *Fly-on-the-wall look at the making of a chart pop group.*

This 13-part series leered behind the scenes of the creation of a new pop group. It voyeuristically followed proceedings from the placing of the first advertisement for would-be stars, through auditions across Britain to the release of the first single, including along the way tuition sessions on style, choreography and media relations. Tension was high as the last group of ten contenders was whittled down to a final fab five. Judges (ruthless executive producer Nigel Lythgoe – a former Young Generation dancer and experienced choreographer and producer – publicist/manager Nicki Chapman and Paul Adam, A&R Director of Polydor Records) travelled to each contender's home to break the good or bad news. The lucky quintet were Kym Marsh from Wigan (who only revealed the fact that she had children after being selected), Myleene Klass from Wood Green, Suzanne Shaw from Bury, Noel Sullivan from Cardiff and Danny Foster from Hackney. The group then headed for a secret venue to record their first album. Given the name of Hear'Say, they performed their first live set at The Brits awards at Earl's Court and went straight to number 1 with their first single release, 'Pure and Simple'. The programme then went on to explore the new pressures of their changed lives. The five runners-up (Jessica Taylor, Kevin Simm, Kelli Young, Tony Lundun and Michelle Heaton) also found themselves with a recording deal, when they were shaped into the band Liberty X and signed to Richard Branson's V2 label. (Later the same year, the same production team followed up with *Soapstars*, charting the progress of wannabe soap opera actors and actresses, with the prize a role as part of a new family in the cast list of Emmerdale.)

Popstars was based on an Australian format that has been sold to more than 40 countries. In 2002, the follow-up series *Popstars: the Rivals* was a contest to find members for two new five-piece groups, one male and one female. The bands that eventually emerged were called One True Voice and Girls Aloud. Davina McCall hosted with judges Pete Waterman, Geri Halliwell and Louis Walsh.

Porridge ★★★★

UK (BBC) Situation Comedy. BBC 1 1974–7
DVD: BBC

Norman Stanley Fletcher .... **Ronnie Barker**
Lennie Godber .... **Richard Beckinsale**
Mr Mackay .... **Fulton Mackay**
Mr Barrowclough .... **Brian Wilde**
Ingrid Fletcher .... **Patricia Brake**
Harry Grout .... **Peter Vaughan**
Lukewarm .... **Christopher Biggins**
McLaren .... **Tony Osoba**
Warren .... **Sam Kelly**
Mr Geoffrey Venables .... **Michael Barrington**
Blanco Webb .... **David Jason**
Harris .... **Ronald Lacey**
Cyril Heslop .... **Brian Glover**
Ives .... **Ken Jones**
Judge Stephen Rawley .... **Maurice Denham**

Writers **Dick Clement, Ian La Frenais**
Producer **Sydney Lotterby**

● *Fun behind bars with a wise old lag and his ingenuous young cell-mate.*

Norman Stanley Fletcher is a habitual criminal who accepts imprisonment as an occupational hazard, according to his trial judge. So it is that this Muswell Hill wide-boy with a heart of gold is sentenced to a five-year term in HMP Slade, an isolated prison in deepest Cumbria. Much against his wishes, he is forced to share a cell with young Lennie Godber, a first-time offender from Birmingham, embarking on a two-year stretch for breaking and entering. Fletch becomes a father-like figure to the amiable Godber, helping him to weather his first period of confinement, showing him the tricks of survival and leading him through the vagaries of prison etiquette.

Fletcher's considerable experience in incarceration earns him respect from most of the criminals around him, the likes of 'Bunny' Warren, illiterate and easily led; decrepit Blanco; 'Black Jock' McLaren, the Glaswegian heavy; and Lukewarm, the gay cook. But there are also less agreeable inmates like 'Orrible' Ives, slimy Harris and 'genial' Harry Grout, the wing's Mr Big, who runs all the rackets and enjoys life's little luxuries in his own comfortably appointed private room. On the other side of the fence is Mr Mackay, the chief warder. Despairing of the ineffective governor, Mr Venables, he longs to regiment the prisoners and rule the prison with an iron jackboot. But, like his easily conned, hen-pecked assistant, Mr Barrowclough, he is never a match for our hero.

Laced together with Fletcher's sparkling wit and skilful repartee, *Porridge* extols the ironies and paradoxes of prison life, never glorifying life inside but cleverly commenting on the difficulties and pressures endured by convicted criminals. The series – which grew out of a play called *Prisoner and Escort*, seen as part of the *Seven of One* Ronnie Barker anthology in 1973 – became a firm favourite in jails all across Britain. However, a short-lived TV sequel, *Going Straight* (BBC 1 1978), featuring Fletcher's life back on the outside, failed to reach the heights of the original, despite reintroducing Fletch's daughter, Ingrid, allowing Godber to make visits and casting a young Nicholas Lyndhurst as Fletch's teenage son, Raymond. A cinema version of *Porridge* was released in 1979.

Porter, Eric
(1928–95)

London-born actor who won acclaim for his TV portrayal of Soames in THE FORSYTE SAGA. He was later seen in dramas like *Churchill and the Generals* (Sir Alan Brooke), ANNA KARENINA (Alexei Karenin), WINSTON CHURCHILL – THE WILDERNESS YEARS (Neville Chamberlain), *The Canal Children* (Col. Russell), THE GLITTERING PRIZES (Stephen Taylor), OLIVER TWIST (Fagin), THE ADVENTURES OF SHERLOCK HOLMES (Moriarty) and THE JEWEL IN THE CROWN (Count Dimitri Bronowski). His television appearances dated back to the 1950s.

Porter, Nyree Dawn
OBE (1940–2001)

New Zealand-born actress seen on British TV in single dramas and series like *Madame Bovary* (title role), THE FORSYTE SAGA (Irene), *The Liars* (Hermione), *Never a Cross Word* (Deirdre Baldock), The PROTECTORS (the Contessa di Contini) and *For Maddie with Love* (Maddie). Lesser roles came in THE MAN FROM INTERPOL, DANGER MAN, THE AVENGERS and *Doctor in Charge* (see DOCTOR IN THE HOUSE), among other programmes.

Porterhouse Blue ★★★

UK (Picture Partnership) Comedy. Channel 4 1987
DVD: Cinema Club

John Skullion .... **David Jason**
Sir Godber Evans .... **Ian Richardson**
The Dean .... **Paul Rogers**
Senior Tutor .... **John Woodnutt**
The Bursar .... **Harold Innocent**
The Praelector .... **Ian Wallace**
Cornelius Carrington .... **Griff Rhys Jones**
Lionel Zipser .... **John Sessions**
Prof. Siblington .... **Willoughby Goddard**
Sir Cathcart D'eath .... **Charles Gray**
Mrs Biggs .... **Paula Jacobs**
Lady Mary Evans .... **Barbara Jefford**
The Chaplain .... **Lockwood West**
Walter .... **Bob Goody**

Writer **Malcolm Bradbury**
Producer **Brian Eastman**

● ***A new principal attempts to drag an ancient college into the modern world but finds his efforts resisted.***

Porterhouse is the most archaic of Cambridge colleges, firmly rooted in tradition and privilege. 'Porterhouse Blue' is the term given to a stroke brought on by over-indulgence, such a fate being suffered by the college's Master who dies without an agreed successor. So it falls on the Prime Minister, as protocol demands, to choose the new Master. It turns out to be Sir Godber Evans, a former Minister for Social Security, who, of course, is a Porterhouse old boy. Unfortunately, his background is otherwise not quite in keeping with the traditions of the college, he being the son of a butcher and a grammar school boy. But to make matters worse, egged on by his domineering, reforming wife, Lady Mary, he decides to bring the college into the 20th century. He'd like to admit women, introduce scholars, stop the many extravagant feasts and wipe out corruption. Evans, however, reckons without one notable adversary. For head porter Skullion, Porterhouse is his life. Steeped in college tradition, he is only five years away from retirement but is determined to fight the Master's plans. Caught up in the developments is ultra-conscientious student Lionel Zipser, who is fixated by his widowed cleaner, Mrs Biggs. To avoid the embarrassment of her finding his cache of condoms, Zipser inflates them with gas and sends them up his chimney, leading to the bizarre sight of dozens of the rubber items floating among the spires and lawns of the college in the drama's best-remembered scene. Tom Sharpe's black comedy, adapted in four parts by Malcolm Bradbury, was directed by Robert Knights. The theme song was performed by The Flying Pickets.

Postgate, Oliver
(1925–)

Born in London, the son of *Good Food Guide* founder Raymond Postgate, Oliver Postgate has been responsible for some of the most fondly remembered children's animation series on British television. A former actor and keen inventor, Postgate fell into television work by accident, after working as a stage manager and props man. Seeing the poor quality of the material he often worked on, he set out to create his own programme and came up with *Alexander the Mouse*, drawn by his new collaborator, Peter Firmin, with whom Postgate was to work for most of his TV career. *Alexander the Mouse* was a crude magnetic animation (voiced, like future offerings, by Postgate himself), but better was to come in Postgate's next project, a series of silent films for deaf children called *The Journey of Master Ho*, which was shot and animated in single frames. This paved the way for Smallfilms' (Postgate and Firmin's company) big break, the adventures of IVOR THE ENGINE, and then the atmospheric SAGA OF NOGGIN THE NOG. Later creations were *The Seal of Neptune*, THE PINGWINGS (a first step into animating puppets), *The Pogles* and POGLES' WOOD, CLANGERS, BAGPUSS, *Tottie – the Story of a Doll's House* and finally *Pinny's House* in 1986.

Postlethwaite, Pete
OBE (1945–)

Northern English actor whose recent success in the cinema has overshadowed his TV work. On the small screen his major roles have included parts in *Horse in the House* (Uncle Doug), *The Muscle Market* (Danny), MARTIN CHUZZLEWIT (Montague Tigg), SHARPE (Obadiah Hakeswill), *Lost for Words* (Deric Longden), *Butterfly Collectors* (DI John McKeown) and *The Sins* (Len Green). Lesser parts have been in series like BOON, BETWEEN THE LINES, MINDER, LOVEJOY and CASUALTY.

Postman Pat/Postman Pat and Friends ★★

UK (BBC/Woodlands Animation/Entertainment Rights) Animation. BBC 1 1981–2; 1991–2; 1995; 1997/BBC 2 2004; 2006
DVD: Universal

Narrator **Ken Barrie**

Creator/Writer **John Cunliffe**
Producers **Michael Cole, Ivor Wood**

● ***The daily rounds of a rural postman.***

Accompanied by Jess, his black-and-white cat, Postman Pat Clifton does the rounds of the countryside around Greendale (based on the Lake District), providing assistance above and beyond the call of duty to the local residents. These include postmistress Mrs Goggins; the Reverend Peter Timms; the bike-riding Miss Rebecca Hubbard; Granny Dryden; twins Katy and Tom Pottage; farmers George Lancaster and Alf Thompson (plus wife Dorothy); builder Ted Glen; shepherd Peter Fogg; mobile shopkeeper Sam Waldron; lady doctor Sylvia Gilbertson; PC Selby; and Major Forbes, who lives at Garner Hall. Pat's family, with whom he shares Forge Cottage, are also seen: wife Sara and six-year-old son Julian. His red post-van bears the registration number PAT 1. The stories were written by John Cunliffe, also seen as the canalboat-owning master of ROSIE AND JIM. Bryan Daly provided the music and narrator Ken Barrie's rendition of the catchy theme song entered the UK charts no fewer than three times between 1982 and 1983, but on no occasion climbing higher than number 44. However, when the song was played as a joke on Terry Wogan's radio show, it brought the programme to the attention of a wider audience and sparked a merchandising boom on which the real-life Post Office capitalized with glee.

After a seven-year absence, *Postman Pat* returned to children's television in 2004 in new episodes entitled *Postman Pat and Friends*, produced by Entertainment Rights. New characters included the Bains family – Ajay, Nisha, Meera and Nikhil – who look after the village steam train, the *Greendale Rocket*, and broaden the programme's ethnic scope.

Post-production

The work done on a programme after the recording has finished. This principally involves editing and sound dubbing.

Pot Black/Pot Black Timeframe ★★

UK (BBC/White Rabbit) Snooker. BBC 2 1969–86; 1991–3

Presenters **Keith Macklin, Alan Weeks, David Icke, Eamonn Holmes, David Vine**

Creator/Commentator **Ted Lowe**
Producers **Philip Lewis, Reg Perrin, David Kenning, John G. Smith**

Innovative TV snooker championship.

An ideal exhibition vehicle for colour television, *Pot Black*, a popular, one-frame, annual snooker tournament, was devised by 'whispering' commentator Ted Lowe. The series, unexpectedly, ran and ran but was eventually overshadowed by the extensive televising of 'real' snooker. As such, it became a victim of its own success and was taken off in 1986. *Junior Pot Black* was produced instead. *Pot Black* returned, hosted by Eamonn Holmes, in 1991. A year later it was revamped as *Pot Black Timeframe*, and saw players having to pocket the balls in a set time. The original format was revived in 1993, with David Vine as emcee. The theme tune was entitled 'Black and White Rag'.

Pot Black returned in 2005, not as a programme in its own right but as a feature of GRANDSTAND. A single-frame tournament, featuring eight contemporary snooker stars, was played out during one Saturday's programme.

Pot the Question

See *Big Break*.

Potter ★★

UK (BBC) Situation Comedy. BBC 1 1979–80; 1983

Redvers Potter .... **Arthur Lowe**
Robin Bailey
Aileen Potter .... **Noël Dyson**
The Vicar .... **John Barron**
'Tolly' Tolliver .... **John Warner**
Diana .... **Honor Shepherd**
Harry Tooms .... **Harry H. Corbett**
Jane .... **Brenda Cowling**

Creator/Writer **Roy Clarke**
Producers **Peter Whitmore, Bernard Thompson**

A cantankerous former businessman can't help interfering in other people's affairs.

Redvers Potter, former MD of Pottermints ('the hotter mints'), a firm founded by his grandfather, is in need of new horizons after selling his share in the company. He takes up jogging, noses his way into other people's business and strikes up friendships with Tolly, his antiques dealer neighbour, and the local vicar, who seems as out of touch with reality as the bumbling Potter himself. Potter's independent wife, Aileen (though she prefers to be called Madge), takes regular rollockings from her pedantic husband but remains defiant, while the Vicar's largely silent wife, Jane, is no more than an unpaid housekeeper. Also seen is a sad local villain Harry Tooms, who tries to reinvent his life in the company of the curmudgeonly old buffers.

The title role unfortunately had to be recast when Arthur Lowe died between series. Robin Bailey stepped into the breach.

Potter, Dennis

(1935–94)

Controversial but innovative British playwright, responsible for some of the most acclaimed dramas seen on television, but also for some of the most criticized. Much of Potter's writing had autobiographical undertones, echoing a childhood in the Forest of Dean and a life dogged by illness (psoriatic arthropathy, later exemplified in THE SINGING DETECTIVE). The susceptibility of youth, patriotism, the power of religion and nostalgia of all kinds (particularly musical) pervaded his bold screenplays, and he seldom shunned multilayered storylines and frank sexual content. An Oxford graduate, Potter once stood as Labour parliamentary candidate, wrote for THAT WAS THE WEEK THAT WAS and worked on the *Daily Herald* in the early 1960s as a reporter and TV critic. His understanding of television matters was exhibited in his own screenwriting, as he sought to move the barriers of TV convention. His first offering was a WEDNESDAY PLAY, *The Confidence Course*, in 1965. The same year he contributed *Alice*, STAND UP, NIGEL BARTON and VOTE, VOTE, VOTE FOR NIGEL BARTON. His *Son of Man* (1969), in which he humanized Christ, brought howls of disapproval from the Establishment and, in a way, his CASANOVA (1971), with its nudity, was not unexpected by those who raised the clamour. *Brimstone and Treacle*, made in 1976, was deemed to be too upsetting with its rape of a handicapped girl and was not screened until 1987; but Potter won new fans with his PENNIES FROM HEAVEN in 1978. BLUE REMEMBERED HILLS (1979) famously put actors like Colin Welland, Michael Elphick and Helen Mirren into children's clothing, but it is THE SINGING DETECTIVE, shown in 1986, which many consider to be his most fitting memorial. Later efforts such as

BLACKEYES (1989, also as director) and LIPSTICK ON YOUR COLLAR (1993) were not as well received, although still attracting their share of protest. Among Potter's many other works were *Emergency – Ward 9* (1966), *Message for Posterity* (1967), *A Beast with Two Backs* (1968), *Angels are So Few* (1970), *Traitor* (1971), *Follow the Yellow Brick Road* (1972), *Double Dare* (1976), *Where Adam Stood* (1976), THE MAYOR OF CASTERBRIDGE, *Rain on the Roof, Cream in My Coffee, Blade on the Feather* (all 1980), F. Scott Fitzgeralds's TENDER IS THE NIGHT (1985), *Visitors* (1987), CHRISTABEL (1988) and *Screen Two's Midnight Movie* (1994). He also set up his own production company, Whistling Gypsy. Potter's last dramas, KARAOKE and *Cold Lazarus*, were chiselled out under great strain in his dying days, and were screened, according to the author's wishes, consecutively on BBC 1 and Channel 4 in spring 1996. To the end he expressed his love of television and his sadness at increased commercialization which, he felt, was ruining the medium.

Potter's Picture Palace ★★

UK (BBC) Children's Situation Comedy. BBC 1 1976; 1978

Peter Potter	**Eden Phillips**
Reggie Turpin	**David Lodge**
Frank Plank	**Colin Edwynn**
Melvyn Didsbury	**Melvyn Hayes**
Sidney 'Bogie' Bogart	**John Comer**
Joan Biddle	**Angela Crow**
The Kid	**Bruce Watt**
Desmond Bagshaw	**Mark Dempsey**

Writers **Brian Finch, Phil Redmond, Dick Sharples**
Executive Producer **Anna Home**
Producer **John Buttery**

● ***A new owner tries to breathe life into a struggling cinema.***

On the death of his Aunt Mattie, Peter Potter inherits her crumbling old cinema, the Picture Palace. Despite interference from his cousin Reggie (who wants the fleapit for his own), Potter raises the curtain and bravely attempts to rejuvenate the business. With his team of employees and friends (such as plumber Frank Plank), he conjures up a series of stunts and schemes designed to raise the profile of the Palace. Sadly, most badly backfire. Two series were produced.

Powell, Robert

(1944–)

Salford-born actor whose first major TV role was as Toby Wren in DOOMWATCH in 1970. He soon followed it with the lead in Thomas Hardy's *Jude the Obscure*, but it wasn't until he played Christ in the blockbuster JESUS OF NAZARETH in 1977 that Powell became a major star. His other credits have included *Pygmalion*, the EDWARDIANS episode *Mr Rolls and Mr Royce* (as Royce), *The Four Feathers*, LOOKING FOR CLANCY (Frank Clancy), *The First Circle* and *Merlin of the Crystal Cave* (Ambrosius). He was Dr Henry Fynn in the mini-series *Shaka Zulu*, and was cast as John Buchan's hero, HANNAY, having already taken the role in a film version of *The Thirty-Nine Steps*. In the 1990s Powell was seen in company with Jasper Carrott, playing inept copper Dave Briggs in *Canned Carrott* and its spin-off, THE DETECTIVES. More recently, he has been seen as nurse Mark Williams in HOLBY CITY and in guest roles in AGATHA CHRISTIE'S MARPLE and DALZIEL AND PASCOE. Powell's wife, Barbara 'Babs' Lord, is a former Pan's People dancer.

Powell, Vince

Prolific British scriptwriter, for many years in collaboration with his former comedy partner, Harry Driver (see entry for Driver for their work together). Since Driver's death in 1973, Powell has devised and written *The Wackers, Rule Britannia, Home Sweet Home, My Son Reuben*, MIND YOUR LANGUAGE, *Odd Man Out, Young at Heart, Father Charlie* and BOTTLE BOYS, and contributed episodes of *Paradise Island*, A SHARP INTAKE OF BREATH, NEVER THE TWAIN, SLINGER'S DAY and *Full House*, among other series. Powell has also scripted numerous episodes of CORONATION STREET.

Power Game, The

See *Plane Makers, The.*

Powers, Stefanie

(Stefania Federkiewicz; 1942–)

American actress who shot to international stardom as April Dancer, THE GIRL FROM U.N.C.L.E., in 1966, after just a few small roles in series like BONANZA. The fame didn't last, however, when the series was cancelled after just one year, and Powers was forced to climb her way back to the top in the theatre and through guest spots in programmes like LOVE, AMERICAN STYLE and MARCUS WELBY, MD. It worked and, although one prime-time drama, *The Feather and Father Gang*, was not a huge success, Powers did find her métier as millionairess adventurer Jennifer Hart in HART TO HART. She has also been seen in numerous mini-series and TV movies, notably *Mistral's Daughter* and WASHINGTON: BEHIND CLOSED DOORS, and, in 2001, made a guest appearance in DOCTORS.

Practice, The ★★

UK (Granada) Drama. ITV 1985–6

Dr Lawrence Golding	**John Fraser**
Dr Judith Vincent	**Brigit Forsyth**
Dr David Armitage	**Tim Brierley**
Pauline Kent	**Judith Barker**
Carol Stansfield	**Eileen O'Brien**
Dorothy Fuller	**Joyce Kennedy**
Peter Bishop	**Steve Halliwell**
Debra Bates	**Rachel James**
Susan Turner	**Michelle Holmes**
Gwen Bryce	**Lesley Nightingale**
Sheila Jessop	**Frances Cox**
Dr Reginald Biddy	**Ronald Fraser**
Dr Chris Clark	**Rob Edwards**

Executive Producer **June Howson**
Producer **Sita Williams**

● ***Day-to-day melodrama in an inner-city medical centre.***

In the search for another CORONATION STREET (and to forestall the BBC's launch of EASTENDERS), Granada devised this twice-weekly (Friday and Sunday) soap opera set in a modern doctors' surgery. The location is the fictitious Castlehulme Health Centre in Manchester where the senior GP is Lawrence Golding. Twenty years a local doctor, Golding, while conservative and fatherly, is inclined to be a little brusque with some patients. Alongside Golding works Judith Vincent, an unmarried doctor with men problems, the sort of practitioner who, unfortunately, gets emotionally drawn into too many of her cases. The third strand of the medical hierarchy is filled by ambitious, new-ideas man David Armitage, like Drs Kildare and Casey before him, always likely to make female patients swoon. With the help of a social worker, health visitor, receptionists and nursing staff, these three treat a recurring cast of local sufferers augmented by guests, with stories viewed from both the medical and the patients' own perspectives. All stories, it was stated, were based on true instances, as reported in the medical press but with the names changed. Human predicaments counted for as much as physical ailments. By the time of the second series, there was only one episode a week, shown an hour later in the evening (Granada seemed to see more promise in ALBION MARKET) and Armitage had been replaced by a dashing new doctor by the name of Chris Clark.

Praed, Michael
(1960–)

British actor seen in series like THE PROFESSIONALS and THE GENTLE TOUCH before hitting the big time as ROBIN OF SHERWOOD, which in turn led to his being cast (after a stint on the Broadway stage) as Prince Michael of Moldavia in DYNASTY. In 1993 Praed played Jake Lovell in JILLY COOPER'S RIDERS and in 1995 was seen as Marty James in the legal drama series *Crown Prosecutor*. More recently he has starred as Phileas Fogg in a US series called *The Secret Adventures of Jules Verne* and made guest appearances in CASUALTY, THE BILL and DOCTORS, as well as narrating *The Natural World*.

Premiere ★★

UK (BBC) Drama Anthology. BBC 2 1977–80

Producers **Graham Benson, Innes Lloyd, John Norton, Terry Coles**

● ***Collection of half-hour films by new directors.***

In May 1976 the BBC announced it was to give people the chance to direct their first film for television. The six people chosen from the 200 or so applicants were half BBC employees and half outsiders. Their professions included a director of commercials and a cameraman. In autumn 1977, their efforts made it to the small screen under the *Premiere* banner. The experiment was then repeated over three further years (the second season billed as *Premiere 2* and the fourth season as *Premiere IV*). Among the directing 'discoveries' were Frederic Raphael (already an established screenwriter) and Micky Dolenz (an ex-MONKEE).

The first season consisted of: *Pit Strike* by Alan Sillitoe, directed by Roger Bamford, starring Brewster Mason, Jennie Linden and Bernard Hill; *A Hymn for Jim* by Richard O'Brien, directed by Colin Bucksey, starring Harry H. Corbett and Christopher Guard; *There's No Place* by Brian Clark, directed by Graham Baker, starring Linda Robson and Peter-Hugo Daly; *The Obelisk* by E. M. Forster, adapted by Pauline Macaulay, directed by Giles Foster, starring Rosemary Martin and Peter Sallis; *A Little Outing* by Alan Bennett, directed by Brian Tufano, starring John Comer and Philip Jackson; and *Give Us a Kiss, Christabel* by Alan Plater, directed by Peter Farrell, starring Dennis Waterman and Jan Francis.

Premiership, The
See *Match of the Day*.

Prendiville, Kieran
(1947–)

Although perhaps still best known to many viewers as one of Esther Rantzen's male sidekicks on THAT'S LIFE, Lancashire-born Kieran Prendiville is now one of British television's most successful drama writers. He created ROUGHNECKS, BALLYKISSANGEL and BADGER, and also penned the single dramas *Vicious Circle* and *Care*, plus episodes of BOON and THE BILL. In front of the cameras, he also hosted TOMORROW'S WORLD and *The Television Show*.

Prequel

Follow-up to a drama in which the action predates that in the original programme, often introducing younger versions or ancestors of the original's main characters. Examples have included *First of the Summer Wine* and *Dallas: The Early Years*.

Press Gang ★★★★

UK (Richmond Films/Central) Children's Adventure. ITV 1989–93
DVD: Network

Lynda Day	**Julia Sawalha**
'Spike' Thomson	**Dexter Fletcher**
Kenny Phillips	**Lee Ross**
Sarah Jackson	**Kelda Holmes**
Matt Kerr	**Clive Wood**
Colin Mathews	**Paul Reynolds**
Danny McColl	**Charlie Creed-Miles**
Tiddler	**Joanna Dukes**
Billy Homer	**Andy Crowe**
Julie Craig	**Lucy Benjamin**
Frazz Davis	**Mmoloki Chrystie**
Sam Black	**Gabrielle Anwar**
Mr Sullivan	**Nick Stringer**

Creator **Bill Moffat**
Writer **Steven Moffat**
Producer **Sandra C. Hastie**

● ***The trials and tribulations of running a school newspaper.***

In this highly acclaimed children's drama, the GCSE pupils of Norbridge High run a youth newspaper called the *Junior Gazette*, an offshoot of the local press. The idea is the brainchild of local journalist Matt Kerr, who enlists English teacher Mr Sullivan to get the project off the ground. The team he puts together is talented and dedicated, although not all are academic achievers. Some pupils are roped in as means to keep them on the straight and narrow. The *Gazette*'s hard-nosed editor is Lynda Day. American Spike Thomson is the number-one reporter, genial Kenny Phillips the deputy editor, and slippery Colin Mathews the advertising manager.

Adopting a far more adult approach than previous efforts in the same vein (ADVENTURE WEEKLY, *A Bunch of Fives*, etc.), *Press Gang* draws comparisons with HILL STREET BLUES, LOU GRANT and other thoughtful US dramas, thanks to its realism and its level-headed treatment of touchy subjects like child abuse, drugs and even local politics and corruption. Serious press issues like censorship, morality and privacy are prominent, too. The series also explores relationships between its characters, particularly the Lynda and Spike will-they, won't-they tease, and allows its characters to mature season by season. Filmed cinematically, it also dabbles in dream sequences, flashbacks and fantasies. By turns witty and touching, *Press Gang* lays claim to being the best children's drama ever in the minds of many critics, and its heritage has been considerable. Both its stars, Julia Sawalha and Dexter Fletcher, have moved on to bigger things, while former teacher Steven Moffat, who made his TV writing debut with *Press Gang*, is now one of UK TV's most successful writers.

Preston Front ★★

UK (BBC) Comedy Drama. BBC 1 1994; 1996–7

Dave Gadd ('Hodge') .... **Colin Buchanan**
Wayne Disley ('Eric') .... **Paul Haigh**
Simon Matlock ('Spock') .... **Stephen Tompkinson**
Alistair McGowan
Ally .... **Kate Gartside**
Tony Lloyd ('Lloydy') .... **Adrian Hood**
Des Moyle ('Diesel') .... **Tony Marshall**
Dawn Lomax .... **Caroline Catz**
Laura .... **Lucy Akhurst**
Peter Polson .... **David MacCreedy**
Carl Rundle .... **Kieran Flynn**
Bob Betty .... **Mark Fletcher**
Lennox .... **Sam Graham**
Doyle .... **Darren Brown**
Jeanetta .... **Susan Wooldridge**
Caroline Pickles
Mr Wang .... **Ozzie Yue**
Kirsty .... **Holly Grainger**
Greg Scarry .... **Nicky Henson**
Mel .... **Angela Lonsdale**
Declan .... **Oliver Cotton**
Mrs Ruddock .... **Maytelock Gibbs**

Writer **Tim Firth**
Executive Producers **Barry Hanson, Chris Parr**
Producers **Chris Griffin, Bernard Krichefski**

● ***Ups and downs in the lives of a group of Territorial Army soldiers.***

As this series humorously reveals, the Territorial Army, the UK's reserve force, takes its recruits from all walks of life. Butchers, bakers and candlestick-makers during the week are transformed into a fighting unit at weekends. *All Quiet on the Preston Front* (simply *Preston Front* in its second and third series) focuses on a reserve unit in Roker Bridge, Lancashire. It exposes how a bickering squad of twentysomething civilians become brothers and sisters in arms in their spare time, and follows each individual's (often wayward) attempts at life fulfilment.

The main characters are teenage father Hodge – his nickname derived from his middle names of Howard Roger – who lives in a caravan and works at Roker Bridge Garden Centre; his best mate, Wayne Disley, known only as Eric, who lives with his elderly parents; Spock, a nerdy history teacher, who provides the brains for the unit; the hapless Lloydy, whose occupation is deemed to be 'classified' but who at one time breeds koi carp for a millionaire, and then invents a successful boardgame called Gurkha Tank Battle; Dawn, Eric's student-hating, student-teacher girlfriend; Ally, an unhappily married solicitor's wife; optimistic Diesel, who runs a garage but is always looking for a new venture; mean corporal Polson; and Laura, Hodge's ingenuous girlfriend, who sings (badly) in a Chinese restaurant and works in a wholefood shop.

In the interests of accuracy, the cast was made to endure a five-day training exercise with the real-life TA so that they knew how to ford rivers, load a rifle and generally act like real soldiers. However, as writer Tim Firth conceded, the army was only a device to introduce the characters, and, increasingly, TA activity was pushed into the background in favour of a closer look at the personal lives of the characters. Comparisons were drawn with the US series FRIENDS as relationships between the characters grew ever stronger.

Price is Right, The/Bruce's Price is Right ★★

UK (Central/Talbot/Yorkshire/TalkbackThames) Game Show. ITV 1984–8; 1995–2001; 2006

Presenters **Leslie Crowther, Bruce Forsyth, Joe Pasquale**

Producers **William G. Stewart, Howard Huntridge**

● ***Manic game show in which contestants win prizes by knowing the price of goods in the shops.***

'Come on down' was the gimmicky catchphrase employed by Leslie Crowther when hosting this all-action game show. Selecting contestants at random from a hyped-up studio audience, Crowther urged the chosen ones to join him in a series of games that shared one theme – guessing the value of household items. The contestants with the closest guesses picked up the prizes. After a gap of seven years, the series was brought back as *Bruce's Price is Right*, with Bruce Forsyth calling the shots.

The Price is Right was briefly revived again as one instalment of ANT & DEC's *Game Show Marathon* in 2005, a series that celebrated the best-loved game shows in ITV's 50-year history, before a new series began in 2006 with comedian Joe Pasquale as host. Before arriving in the UK, *The Price is Right* had been one of America's most popular game shows, first airing in 1956.

Pride and Prejudice ★★★★

UK (BBC/A&E) Drama. BBC 1 1995
DVD: BBC

Mr Fitzwilliam Darcy .... **Colin Firth**
Miss Elizabeth Bennet .... **Jennifer Ehle**
Mrs Bennet .... **Alison Steadman**
Lydia Bennet .... **Julia Sawalha**
Mr Bennet .... **Benjamin Whitrow**
Jane Bennet .... **Susannah Harker**
Kitty Bennet .... **Polly Maberly**
Mary Bennet .... **Lucy Briers**
Miss Bingley .... **Anna Chancellor**
Mr Bingley .... **Crispin Bonham-Carter**
Mr Hurst .... **Rupert Vansittart**
Mrs Louisa Hurst .... **Lucy Robinson**
Sir William Lucas .... **Christopher Benjamin**
Lady Lucas .... **Norma Streader**
Charlotte Lucas .... **Lucy Scott**
Maria Lucas .... **Lucy Davis**
George Wickham .... **Adrian Lukis**
Mr Collins .... **David Bamber**
Lady Catherine de Bourgh ...... **Barbara Leigh-Hunt**
Anne de Bourgh .... **Nadia Chambers**
Georgiana Darcy .... **Emilia Fox**
Mr Gardiner .... **Tim Wylton**
Mrs Gardiner .... **Joanna David**

Writer **Andrew Davies**
Producer **Sue Birtwistle**

● ***An eligible bachelor and a bright young woman's mutual attraction is spoiled by bad first impressions and social etiquette.***

Universally acclaimed as one of the BBC's most successful costume romps, *Pride and Prejudice*, remarkably, became cult viewing. Jane Austen's 19th-century story of the lowly but respectable Bennet sisters, their ambitions to marry into higher society and the various husbands they court along the way caught the public imagination. However, much of the attraction must have come from the engaging lead couple of Jennifer Ehle and Colin Firth and their celebrated mix of coy glances, smouldering looks, heaving bosoms and skin-tight wet shirts.

The stars assumed the identities of Miss Elizabeth Bennet and Mr Fitzwilliam Darcy, she level-headed, intelligent but of rather rustic origins; he restrained, seemingly arrogant and much more wealthy. Although their relationship has a rocky start, their mutual attraction grows by the episode. Pemberley, Darcy's stately pile, is destined to be shared with the independent-minded Miss Bennet.

Other characters who add depth to the tale include the excitable Mrs Bennet, stoical Mr Bennet and Elizabeth's sisters Jane (kind, but shy), Lydia (flirty and reckless), Kitty and Mary. The first two marry Darcy's rich friend, Mr Bingley (who rents Netherfield Hall near the Bennets' home in Longbourne), and the caddish ex-army officer, Mr Wickham, respectively. Unctuous, sycophantic ecclesiast Mr Collins also hopes for the hand of Elizabeth, while Bingley's sister – another contender for the key to Pemberley – does everything she can to discredit Elizabeth.

Hot on the heels of the immensely successful MIDDLEMARCH, *Pride and Prejudice* continued the 1990s revival in costume dramas. It had been dramatized on four previous occasions (BBC 1952: Peter Cushing as Darcy, Daphne Slater as Elizabeth; BBC 1958: Alan Badel and Jane downs; BBC 1 1967: Lewis Fiander and Celia Bannerman; BBC 2 1980: David Rintoul and Elizabeth Garvie).

Prime Suspect ★★★★

UK (Granada/WGBH Boston) Police Drama. ITV 1991–3; 1995–6; 2003

DVD: Cinema Club

DCI/Det. Supt. Jane Tennison .... **Helen Mirren**
DS Bill Otley .... **Tom Bell** *(1 and 3)*
Det. Chief Supt. Mike Kernan .... **John Benfield** *(1, 2 and series)*
George Marlow .... **John Bowe** *(1)*
Tim Woodward *(series)*
Moyra Henson .... **Zoë Wanamaker** *(1)*
DI Tony Muddyman .... **Jack Ellis** *(1, 2 and series)*
DI Frank Burkin .... **Craig Fairbrass** *(1 and 2)*
DC/DI Richard Haskons .... **Richard Hawley** *(1, 2 and series)*
DS Terry Amson .... **Gary Whelan** *(1)*
WPC Maureen Havers .... **Mossie Smith** *(1)*
DCI John Shefford .... **John Forgeham** *(1)*
Peter Rawlins .... **Tom Wilkinson** *(1)*
DS Oswalde .... **Colin Salmon** *(2)*
DC Lillie .... **Philip Wright** *(1, 2, and 3)*
DC Jones .... **Ian Fitzgibbon** *(1 and 2)*
DC/DS Rosper .... **Andrew Tiernan** *(1 and 2)*
Vera Reynolds .... **Peter Capaldi** *(3)*
Jimmy Jackson .... **David Thewlis** *(3)*
Commander Chiswick .... **Terrence Hardiman** *(3)*
Insp./Det. Chief Supt. Larry Hall .... **Mark Strong** *(3, 2003)*
WPC Norma Hastings .... **Karen Tomlin** *(3)*
Supt. Halliday .... **Struan Rodger** *(3)*
WPC Kathy Bibby .... **Liza Sadovy** *(3)*
DI Dalton .... **Andrew Woodall** *(3)*
DI Ray Hebdon .... **Mark Drewry** *(3)*
DS Rankine .... **David O'Hara** *(5)*
DI Devanney .... **Julia Lane** *(5)*
DC Henry Adeliyeka .... **John Brobbey** *(5)*
Det. Chief Supt. Ballinger .... **John McArdle** *(5)*
The Street .... **Steven Mackintosh** *(5)*
DCI Simon Finch .... **Ben Miles** *(2003)*
DC Michael Philips .... **Barnaby Kay** *(2003)*
DS Alun Simms .... **Robert Pugh** *(2003)*
DAC Charles Evans .... **Tony Pritchard** *(2003)*
DS Lorna Greaves .... **Tanya Moodie** *(2003)*
DC David Butcher .... **Sam Hazeldine** *(2003)*
DC Sean Firth .... **Steve Gibbs** *(2003)*
Milan Lukic .... **Oleg Menshikov** *(2003)*
Elizabeth Lukic .... **Clare Holman** *(2003)*
Robert West .... **Liam Cunningham** *(2003)*
Jasmina Blekic .... **Ingeborga Dapkunaite** *(2003)*

Creator **Lynda La Plante**
Executive Producer **Sally Head**
Writers **Lynda La Plante** *(1 and 3)*, **Allan Cubitt** *(2)*, **Paul Billing** *(series)*, **Eric Deacon** *(series)*, **Guy Hibbert** *(series)*, **Guy Andrews** *(5)*, **Peter Berry** *(2003)*
Producers **Don Leaver** *(1)*, **Paul Marcus** *(2, 3 and series)*, **Brian Park** *(series)*, **Lynn Horsford** *(5)*, **David Boulter** *(2003)*

● ***An ambitious female detective fights sexism within the force.***

Jane Tennison is a single-minded, career policewoman whose progress through the ranks has been impeded by male prejudice – until, that is, she wins the battle to take charge of a major case – the brutal murder of a prostitute – following the sudden death of main man DCI Shefford. At long last her abilities are given the chance to shine through, though there is still plenty of resentment and obstruction from colleagues like Sgt Bill Otley at the Southampton Row nick. George Marlow is the man in Tennison's sights, even though he has an alibi from girlfriend Moyra Henson. Peter Rawlins is Jane's own long-suffering lover.

Such was the success of the two-part original *Prime Suspect* that *Prime Suspect 2* followed a year later. A second sequel, *Prime Suspect 3*, shown in 1993, saw Tennison moving from her base at Southampton Row to Soho's vice squad. A subsequent series of three single dramas (entitled simply *Prime Suspect*) was screened in 1995, and then another two-parter, *Prime Suspect 5*, in 1996, in which Tennison had been transferred to Manchester and was dealing with drug crime. In 2003, again in two parts, the drama returned, simply billed as *Prime Suspect*, with Tennison investigating the death of an illegal Bosnian immigrant.

Taking the role of this hard-nosed, heavy-smoking copper signalled a major change in career direction for former Shakespearean actress Helen Mirren. Her new severe haircut and sober suits were a world away from the roles she once enjoyed on stage. But Mirren had little difficulty in convincing viewers and went on to collect the BAFTA Best Actress award for three consecutive years. It was not enough for Hollywood, however, and when Universal bought the film rights to *Prime Suspect*, she was not considered for the lead role. The series was inspired by real policewoman Jackie Malton, who contributed as a script advisor.

Prime Time

See *Peak Time.*

Prince Regent ★★

UK (BBC) Historical Drama. BBC 1 1979

George, Prince of Wales	**Peter Egan**
King George III	**Nigel Davenport**
Mrs Maria Fitzherbert	**Susannah York**
Charles James Fox	**Keith Barron**
Queen Charlotte	**Frances White**
Frances, Lady Jersey	**Caroline Blakiston**
William Pitt	**David Collings**
Princess Caroline	**Dinah Stabb**
Isabella, Lady Hertford	**Barbara Shelley**
Princess Charlotte	**Cherie Lunghi**

Producer **Colin Tucker**

● ***Eight-part biopic of the future King George IV.***

Spanning 37 years, this costume romp takes the lead character from being a vibrant, young prince up to his days as an old, gout-ridden ruler. The tale begins in 1782, as drunkard, waster, lecher George Augustus Frederick, the Prince of Wales, comes of age. He considers himself to be witty, a lover of fine things and a talented, sensitive soul; his father believes otherwise. The Prince falls in love with widow Mrs Fitzherbert, who is quite an unsuitable match, being both older and a Catholic, but he nevertheless marries her in secret. The marriage not being officially recognized, the Prince then weds Princess Caroline, whom he grows to hate. His wait for the throne is almost terminal. Despite becoming Prince Regent, he ascends to the throne himself only in 1820, by which time he is fat and sick. Carl Davis provides the music.

Pringle, Bryan

(1935–2002)

Staffordshire-born, RADA-trained actor, a familiar face in situation comedies. He was Cheese and Egg in THE DUSTBINMEN and Sgt Flagg in THE GROWING PAINS OF PC PENROSE. He was also seen in THE PALLISERS (Mr Monk), *Room Service* (Charles Spooner), AUF WIEDERSEHEN, PET, *The Good Companions*, LOVE STORY, *The Management* (Mr Crusty), PARADISE POSTPONED, *Blind Justice*, ONCE UPON A TIME IN THE NORTH (Mr Bebbington), KING AND CASTLE, FLYING LADY, INSPECTOR MORSE, ALL CREATURES GREAT AND SMALL, AFTER HENRY, PRIME SUSPECT, PERFECT SCOUNDRELS, RUMPOLE OF THE BAILEY, BOON, *P. G. Wodehouse's Heavy Weather* (Pirbright), *A Prince Among Men* (Vince), TESS OF THE D'URBERVILLES (Kail), VANITY FAIR (Raggles), WOKENWELL (Sadly Stan Potter), BARBARA and plenty more series, including *The Young Indiana Jones Chronicles* and *My Uncle Silas*.

Prisoner, The ★★★★

UK (Everyman/ATV) Adventure. ITV 1967–8
DVD: Granada Ventures

The Prisoner (Number 6)	**Patrick McGoohan**
The Butler	**Angelo Muscat**

Creator/Executive Producer **Patrick McGoohan**
Producer **David Tomblin**

● ***A secret agent is held captive in a mysterious Italianate village.***

In the opening titles of *The Prisoner*, a sports car races through the streets of London beneath a thundery sky. An unnamed British intelligence agent steps out and bursts into a Whitehall office, abruptly handing in his resignation. Returning home to pack a suitcase, he is overcome by a puff of gas, waking up in a quaint, turreted village, surrounded by mountains and sea. As each episode then makes clear, the agent is trapped. There is no escape from the village and he is constantly pumped for information, mostly about his sudden resignation. He has even lost his identity and is now known simply as Number 6, though he continues to claim, 'I am not a number. I am a free man.'

And that, on the face of it, is all *The Prisoner* is about: a man held against his will, subjected to interrogation and attempting to escape. But there is far more to this series and so many questions are left unanswered. Who are his captors? Why are they holding him? Indeed, who is our hero? And will he ever be able to get away? All that viewers know is that head of the village is Number 1, and he is never seen, leaving his chief operative, Number 2, to deal with Number 6. But even Number 2 changes from episode to episode and the only face Number 6 can always recognize is that of a silent, dwarf butler.

Number 6 is not the only captive, but he is the only one who still has the will to break out. The others have already been brainwashed, going through the motions of their everyday life, playing human chess on a giant board in the village square, saying 'Be seeing you' and staggering on with their purposeless existence. And who are they anyway? In contrast, Number 6's mind is firmly set on escape, slipping away from the village's penny-farthing bicycles, its golf-cart taxis, piped blazers, closed-circuit security cameras and the floating, bouncing, white balloon-like guard known as Rover. Inevitably, his plans are foiled.

Enigmatic to the end, *The Prisoner* concludes with a story that sees Number 6 being invited to take over the community and at last revealing the face of Number 1 – it is his own. A missile is launched to destroy the village, and Number 6 flees with the butler and two other inmates. As he races through London in his sports car, with the skies once again thundery, a certain familiarity shines through. With the doors of his house slamming closed behind him, can it be that the nightmare really is over, or has it just begun again?

Many conclusions have been drawn from this classic series. Was the village a sort of retirement home for burned-out secret agents, or was it some kind of enemy intelligence centre? Or could it have been that The Prisoner was really trapped only in his own mind, a victim of a severe nervous breakdown, a theory supported by the circular pattern of events, including the conclusion, and the revelation of Number 1's face as his own. Certainly there were statements about democracy, personal freedom and social engineering in there, but the surreal nature of the series made it difficult for anyone to pin it all down.

The star of the series, Patrick McGoohan, was also the creator and driving force. Many fans believed *The Prisoner* to be a sequel to his previous success, DANGER MAN, although this was never stated. Instead, McGoohan has subsequently agreed that the programme was an allegorical conundrum. Not for nothing was his independent production company called Everyman, in direct reference to medieval morality plays.

Actors who played Number 2 included Leo McKern, Anton Rodgers, Peter Wyngarde and Patrick Cargill. The village used for filming was Portmeirion in North Wales, created as an Italian fantasy by architect Sir Clough Williams-Ellis.

Prisoner: Cell Block H ★★

Australia (Grundy) Drama. ITV 1979–87
DVD: Fremantle Home Entertainment

Lynn Warner .... **Kerry Armstrong**
Bea Smith .... **Val Lehman**
Vera Bennett .... **Fiona Spence**
Freida 'Franky' Doyle .... **Carol Burns**
Karen Travers .... **Peita Toppano**
Jeanette 'Mum' Brooks .... **Mary Ward**
Erica Davidson .... **Patsy King**
Meg Jackson/Morris .... **Elspeth Ballantyne**
Dr Greg Miller .... **Barry Quin**
Doreen Anderson/Burns .... **Collette Mann**
Marilyn Mason .... **Margaret Laurence**
Elizabeth Birdsworth .... **Sheila Florance**
Eddie Cook .... **Richard Moir**
Jim Fletcher .... **Gerard Maguire**
Pat O'Connell .... **Monica Maughan**
Chrissie Latham .... **Amanda Muggleton**
Noeline Burke .... **Jude Kuring**
Steve Wilson .... **Jim Smillie**
Jean Vernon .... **Christine Amor**
Barbara Davidson .... **Sally Cahill**
Jock Stewart .... **Tommy Dysart**
Judy Bryant .... **Betty Bobbit**
Margo Gaffney .... **Jane Clifton**
Helen Smart .... **Caroline Gillmer**
Colleen Powell .... **Judith McGrath**
Steve Faulkner .... **Wayne Jarratt**
Maxine Daniels .... **Lisa Crittenden**
Joan Ferguson .... **Maggie Kirkpatrick**
Pixie Mason .... **Judy McBurney**
Myra Desmond .... **Ann Phelan**
Joyce Barry .... **Joy Westmore**
Lexie Patterson .... **Pepe Trevor**
Ann Reynolds .... **Gerda Nicholson**
Rita Connors .... **Glenda Linscott**

Creator/Executive Producer **Reg Watson**
Producers **Phil East, Marie Trevor, Ian Bradley, John McRae, Sue Masters**

● ***Low-budget, grim soap set in an Australian women's jail.***

The Wentworth Detention Centre houses some of Melbourne's toughest female criminals and, through a series of rather far-fetched plots, this programme examines the inter-relationships of these inmates, their warders, and fringe characters such as partners on the outside, prison doctors and other officials. The series deals openly with issues such as lesbianism and wanton assault (by both prisoners and guards) and in its own melodramatic way strips the front off hard-bitten prisoners to reveal personal tragedies that have led them into a life of crime. It shows how some mature to rehabilitate themselves successfully on their release, although it also makes it clear that, for others, prison life is the only option.

Principal characters early on are Governor Erica Davidson, her deputy Jim Fletcher, brutal warder Vera Bennett and the more sympathetic guard, Meg Jackson. Ringleader of the prisoners is Bea Smith (doing time for the murder of her husband), and other characters are lesbian biker and armed robber Franky Doyle, Karen Travers, a deeply religious ex-schoolteacher (also convicted of the murder of her husband), and dumb blonde Lynn Warner, a convicted nanny. Thumb-sucking Doreen Anderson is the easily led unmarried-mother-turned-forger; Marilyn Mason is a prostitute and the prison nympho; 'Mum' Brooks the gentle, well-respected gardening lover (yet another imprisoned for killing her husband); and Lizzie Birdsworth the alcoholic, chain-smoking mass-murderer who is hell-bent on escape. Greg Miller is the prison doctor.

The show, originally entitled simply *Prisoner*, was renamed *Prisoner: Cell Block H* to avoid confusion with Patrick McGoohan's cult series of the 1960s in the UK and USA. Its creator, Reg Watson (a former CROSSROADS producer), and one of its producers, Marie Trevor, later moved on to the rather more successful NEIGHBOURS. Maggie Kirkpatrick, who played Joan Ferguson, appeared with Lily Savage in a spoof stage version, which opened in London in 1995.

Private Investigator ★★

UK (BBC) Detective Drama. BBC 1958–9

John Unthank .... **Campbell Singer**
Bill Jessel .... **Douglas Muir**
Mrs Layton .... **Ursula Camm**
Peter Clarke .... **Ian White**
James Wilson .... **Allan McClelland**

Creator/Writer/Producer **Arthur Swinson**

● ***The cases of a mundane private eye.***

Keeping himself to himself, with a view to avoiding attention and preserving his cover, Scottish private investigator John Unthank was rolled out by the BBC for two series of detective work. Unthank is in demand with governments, companies and individuals, and his assignments see him working against smugglers and currency fraudsters, and even for the National Canine Defence League on the Mediterranean. His restrained approach, polished manners and smart appearance place him an ocean apart from that of the wisecracking American sleuths of his era. Christopher Barry directed.

Private Schulz ★★★

UK (BBC) Comedy Drama. BBC 2 1981

Pte Gerhard Schulz .... **Michael Elphick**
Major Neuheim .... **Ian Richardson**
Bertha Freyer .... **Billie Whitelaw**
Iphraim 'Solly' Solikoff .... **Cyril Shaps**
Schumacher .... **Terence Suffolk**
Gertrude Steiner .... **Rula Lenska**
Prof. Bodelschwingh .... **David Swift**

Writer **Jack Pulman**
Producer **Philip Hinchcliffe**

● ***A German fraudster reluctantly works for the SS.***

Cowardly, small-time wheeler-dealer Gerhard Schulz has spent two spells in Spandau prison for fraud. In summer 1939 he applies for a role in the Postal Censorship department, so he can use his knowledge of five languages, but is seconded instead to SS Counter Espionage. Headed by mad Major Neuheim, the division is charged with developing novel ideas that will be useful in war – schemes like dropping forged £5 notes on Britain. Although such ideas are masterminded by Schulz, it is Neuheim who takes the credit. Solly is the master forger Schulz employs to make his plans work, while the Dietrich-esque Bertha Freyer is the good-time girl at Salon Kitty, where the stoical Schulz listens in to bugged bedroom conversations. Schulz's lively war also sees him on duty under-cover in England. Each episode opens with newsreel footage highlighting the stage of the war that has been reached at the time. In addition to Neuheim, actor Ian Richardson plays a number of other roles in the series.

Private Secretary ✶✶

US (Jack Chertok) Situation Comedy. ITV 1957–60 (US: CBS 1953–7)
DVD: Alpha Video

Susie McNamara .... **Ann Sothern**
Peter Sands .... **Don Porter**
Vi Praskins .... **Ann Tyrrell**
Mickey 'Cagey' Calhoun .... **Jesse White**
Sylvia Platt .... **Joan Banks**

Producer **Jack Chertok**

The secretary of a theatrical agent usually saves the day.
This early sitcom is set in New York's theatreland. Susie McNamara is on-the-ball secretary to actors' agent Peter Sands, but, like Thelma in MR DIGBY, DARLING many years later, is not quite sure where her paid duties end. The result is that Peter's well-being becomes of paramount importance to the loyal Susie as she dabbles in his extramural affairs as well as his business interests. Nevertheless, Susie and Peter work well together and enjoy plenty of success. Vi is the receptionist who is Susie's best friend, Sylvia is another friend and Cagey Calhoun an untrustworthy rival agent. The series is also known as *Susie*, the name it was given when first repeated in the USA to avoid confusion with new episodes. Stars Ann Sothern and Don Porter were reunited in *The Ann Sothern Show* (US: CBS 1958–61), a sitcom in which they ran a New York hotel.

Probation Officer ✶✶

UK (ATV) Drama. ITV 1959–62

Philip Main .... **John Paul**
Jim Blake .... **David Davies**
Iris Cope .... **Honor Blackman**
Bert Bellman .... **John Scott**
Maggie Weston .... **Jessica Spencer**
Andrew Wallace .... **Jack Stewart**
Stephen Ryder .... **Bernard Brown**
Bill Morgan .... **Windsor Davies**

Creator **Julian Bond**
Producers **Antony Kearey, Rex Firkin, Hugh Rennie**

Drama in the lives of a team of probation officers.
Charged with the welfare of delinquents, criminals and other social unfortunates, members of the probation service constantly find themselves dragged into the affairs of others. This series depicts – in semi-documentary style – some typical problems faced by a team from inner London, and originally features Philip Main, Jim Blake and Iris Cope as its chief characters. Numerous other semi-regular characters are introduced during the programme's three-year run and the cast lists change frequently.

Producer

The executive in charge of a programme, taking the original idea and drawing together the resources to make it happen. These resources include the budget and the crew, from the director and camera team to the performers. Sometimes, particularly in non-drama programming, the producer may provide more 'hands-on' creative input. Otherwise, he or she delegates this to the director but still assumes overall responsibility for the finished project.

Production Assistant

The production assistant, or PA, is the producer and director's right-hand person. PAs work on a programme from its very earliest days, helping in the planning and staging, and continue their involvement through to the eventual recording or live transmission.

Professionals, The ✶✶

UK (Avengers Mark 1/LWT) Spy Drama. ITV 1977–80; 1982–3
DVD: Contender

George Cowley .... **Gordon Jackson**
William Bodie .... **Lewis Collins**
Ray Doyle .... **Martin Shaw**
Murphy .... **Steve Alder**

Creator **Brian Clemens**
Executive Producers **Albert Fennell, Brian Clemens**
Producers **Sidney Hayers, Raymond Menmuir**

The violent activities of a secret crime-busting unit.
'The Professionals' are the men and women of CI5 (Criminal Intelligence 5), a covert agency set up by the Government to specialize in criminal intelligence in the way that MI5 centres on military intelligence. The aim is to pre-empt trouble and so nip crime in the bud. Head of the section is no-nonsense, ex-MI5 man George Cowley. He assembles around him a team of the toughest operatives, none more resilient and respected than Bodie, a former SAS and Parachute Regiment hero brimming with confidence. Bodie's partner is Doyle, an ex-copper with a curly perm. Fresh from an East End CID division, he is calm on the outside but harbours a rage within which threatens to burst out at any second. The pair are affectionately known as 'The Bisto Kids' to Cowley, whom they know as 'The Cow'.

The programme was created by Brian Clemens, the brains behind some of THE AVENGERS' best adventures, although this all-action, macho series did not share the light-hearted, tongue-in-cheek, quirky qualities of his earlier work. It was parodied by members of *The Comic Strip* in a one-off satire, *The Bullshitters*. In 1999, Sky One launched an updated version of *The Professionals*. Entitled *CI5: the New Professionals*, it starred Edward Woodward, Kal Weber, Colin Wells and Lexa Doig.

Prompter

See *Autocue*.

Properties or Props

Studio or set furnishings/decorations intended to provide realism or convey a certain atmosphere.

Protectors, The [1] ★★

UK (ABC) Adventure. ITV 1964

Ian Souter .... **Andrew Faulds**
Robert Shoesmith .... **Michael Atkinson**
Heather Keys .... **Ann Morrish**

Producer **Michael Chapman**

Three professional troubleshooters nip crime in the bud.

'We sell security. Object: To prevent crime.' This is the motto of The Protectors, a trio of crime specialists working from a swish London office. The three are former insurance claims inspector Ian Souter, ex-policeman Robert Shoesmith and their girl Friday, Heather Keys. Operating in the twilight zone between the underworld and the security services, this determined trio act to prevent crimes from taking place. The bearded, relaxed Souter, a Scotsman, is intelligent, experienced and decisive, Shoesmith has an understanding of the criminal mind which borders on admiration, and Keys has an expert's eye for art forgeries. After placing an advertisement in newspapers, encouraging potential clients to 'Call Welbeck 3269', they find themselves protecting people in fear of an imminent crime, or those who have already fallen victim. They call themselves SIS, standing for Specialists in Security, and their assignments lead them into murder, espionage and other forms of intrigue.

Two of the stars headed off in rather different career directions when this short-lived series came to an end. Andrew Faulds became a Member of Parliament and Ann Morrish went on to present PLAY SCHOOL, among other television roles.

Protectors, The [2] ★★

UK (Group Three/ITC) Adventure. ITV 1972–4
DVD: Carlton

Harry Rule .... **Robert Vaughn**
Contessa di Contini .... **Nyree Dawn Porter**
Paul Buchet .... **Tony Anholt**
Suki .... **Yasuko Nagazumi**
Chino .... **Anthony Chinn**

Producers **Gerry Anderson, Reg Hill**

Three top investigators join forces to save the world from international crime.

The Protectors are Harry Rule, the Contessa di Contini and Paul Buchet. Together they blaze around Europe's top resorts, darting from flashy cars into private jets and meeting crime head on. They tackle spies, drug-pushers, smugglers, thieves and murderers. Rule is their leader, a suave, ultra-cool American working from a high-tech office in London. He lives in a country mansion with an Irish wolfhound named Gus and is looked after by his au pair, Suki (a martial arts expert). The Contessa di Contini is Lady Caroline Ogilvy, an elegant English widow whose late Italian husband has left her a villa in Rome. Her speciality is art and antiques fraud, and she is chauffeured by a karate-chopping driver named Chino. Fresh-faced Paul Buchet is an amorous Frenchman who operates out of a Paris apartment. The trio's glossy, rather violent adventures were produced by puppet-master Gerry Anderson. Tony Christie belted out the closing theme song, 'Avenues and Alleyways', a UK chart hit in 1973. Music was composed by John Cameron.

Public Eye ★★

UK (ABC/Thames) Detective Drama. ITV 1965–6; 1968–9; 1971–3; 1975
DVD: Network

Frank Marker .... **Alfred Burke**
Mrs Helen Mortimer .... **Pauline Delany**
DI Percy Firbank .... **Ray Smith**
Ron Gash .... **Peter Childs**

Creators **Roger Marshall, Anthony Marriott**
Executive Producers **Lloyd Shirley, Robert Love**
Producers **Don Leaver, John Bryce, Richard Bates, Michael Chapman, Kim Mills, Robert Love**

The poorly paid investigations of a grimy private detective.

Frank Marker is an unambitious detective, a sad character who dips in and out of the murky underworld pond. He works for next to nothing, sometimes not even getting paid for his troubles; but his satisfaction comes from a job well done and the escapism it provides from his own drab world. Marker operates out of seedy, backstreet offices, firstly in London, then Birmingham and, finally, Brighton. He is a one-man band whose professional trust is often abused – such as when he goes to jail for handling stolen jewellery, even though he is only acting as a go-between for the insurers and the thieves.

Marker is joined later in the series by Mrs Mortimer, his landlady, as well as by Inspector Firbank, a copper whose feathers Marker repeatedly ruffles. Ron Gash is a fellow detective who wants Marker to join him in a partnership. The first three seasons (with quirkily named episode titles like *They Go Off in the End, Like Fruit* and *I Went to Borrow a Pencil, and Look What I Found*) were produced by ABC TV but, when it lost its ITV franchise, production was taken over by its successor, Thames Television.

Pulaski ★★

UK (BBC) Drama. BBC 1 1987

Larry Summers/Pulaski .... **David Andrews**
Kate Smith/Briggsy .... **Caroline Langrishe**
Paula Wilson .... **Kate Harper**
Jerome .... **Rolf Saxon**
Hilary .... **Timothy Carlton**
Jane .... **Deborah Grant**
Brad .... **Terry Cade**
Director .... **Nigel Pegrum**
Charles .... **Donald Hewlett**
Celia .... **Elspet Gray**
Millie .... **Helen Burns**
DS Ford .... **Ray Winstone**

Creator **Roy Clarke**
Writers **Roy Clarke, Andrew Payne, Geoffrey Case, Richard Carpenter**
Producer **Paul Knight**

An actor's private life is as eventful as that of the detective he plays on TV.

This is a series about a private eye called Pulaski. Well . . . part of the time. It's actually a series within a series. Pulaski is a TV detective, a Polish-American priest turned private investigator. Where he once called on the Good Book to right wrongs, he now falls back on a gun and his handy pair of fists. His adoringly supportive English assistant in his battles against low life is Briggsy. However, once the camera stops turning, life begins to imitate art as the actor playing Pulaski comes into his own. He's Larry Summers, a lecherous, hard-drinking American who is married to Kate Smith, the actress who plays Briggsy and who is far from being the devoted partner she plays on the small screen. Life away from the set is as eventful as it is on, as fact and fiction merge, Summers is drawn into real-life intrigue, and transatlantic tensions with his other half seethe and bubble. Paula is the programme's producer. Comedy writer Roy Clarke created this novel light drama which runs to eight episodes. The title theme, written by Brian Bennett, was performed by his band, The Shadows.

Pulman, Jack

(1925–80)

British writer, first on TV in the 1950s with his own dramas, but later better known for his adaptations. The highlights were I, CLAUDIUS, WAR AND PEACE and CRIME AND PUNISHMENT. Of his own creations, PRIVATE SCHULZ and the David Kossoff sitcom A LITTLE BIG BUSINESS were among the most notable, as well as the plays *A Book with Chapters in It, Nearer to Heaven* and *You Can't Have Everything*. Other credits include LOOKING FOR CLANCY and episodes of FALL OF EAGLES and POLDARK. One of his stage plays, THE HAPPY APPLE, became a TV series, developed by Keith Waterhouse.

Punch Drunk ✶✶

UK (BBC) Situation Comedy. BBC 1 1993

Vinnie Binns .... **Kenny Ireland**
Vikki Brown .... **Diana Hardcastle**
Hance Gordon .... **John Kazek**
Pat Hunter .... **Sean Scanlan**
Neillie .... **Jake D'Arcy**
Norman Banks .... **Jonathan Kydd**
Danny .... **Grant Smeaton**
Slug .... **Gilbert Martin**
Mrs Gordon .... **Claire Nielson**

Writer **Clayton Moore**
Producer **Colin Gilbert**

● ***Comedy set amidst Glasgow's boxing fraternity.***

Vinnie Binns is a failed boxing manager, master of the crummy Maharg gym but tired of being only known as 'Jimmy Binns's son', in deference to his successful father. Every good fighter he has signed has been stolen, by the likes of his flashy rival Pat Hunter. When Vinnie discovers 19-year-old Hance Gordon – his best prospect yet – fighting in a pub, Hunter once again schemes to poach him. However, Vinnie unearths an unlikely ally in Vikki Brown, a former psychiatrist researching a PhD in the morality of boxing. She finds herself drawn into supporting the amiable Binns rather than her pompous boyfriend, Norman Banks, who, to further his Doctors Against Boxing (DAB) campaign, links up with rival Hunter. Neillie is Vinnie's long-serving assistant and drinking pal, Danny is the dim gym worker and Slug is Hunter's hard man.

Pursuers, The ✶

UK (Crestview/ABC) Police Drama. ITV 1961–2

DI John Bollinger .... **Louis Hayward**
DS Steve Wall .... **Gaylord Cavallaro**
DS Dick Anderson .... **Geoffrey Hibbert**

Creator/Executive Producer **Donald Hyde**

● ***The cases of two Scotland Yard detectives and a loyal Alsatian police dog.***

Middle-aged Detective Inspector John Bollinger patrols the streets of London, assisted by DS Wall and, usually, a large, black Alsatian dog named Ivan. Occasional assistance is provided by DS Anderson. Its human star, the South African Louis Hayward, arrived on television, having been a Hollywood actor since the 1930s. Thirty-nine episodes were made of this half-hour series, with guest stars including Barry Foster, John Le Mesurier, Honor Blackman and Rosalie Crutchley.

Purves, Peter

(1939–)

Northern English actor/presenter, undoubtedly best known as one of the three hosts, along with John Noakes and Valerie Singleton, during BLUE PETER's 'golden age'. However, he also has the rare honour of playing two separate parts in one story of DOCTOR WHO, the second being space pilot Steven Taylor, who went on to become one of the Doctor's regular companions. Since leaving *Blue Peter*, Purves has hosted the game show *Babble* and series such as *Stopwatch* and *Kick Start*, as well as annual events like darts tournaments, Crufts and other animal shows.

Pyke, Dr Magnus

OBE (1908–92)

British scientist turned TV presenter in the 1970s, thanks to the YTV series DON'T ASK ME and *Don't Just Sit There*, in which he was a resident pundit. His natural enthusiasm, fast talking and flailing arms made him an instant celebrity.

QB VII ✶✶

US (Screen Gems) Legal Drama. BBC 1 1976 (US: ABC 1974)
DVD: Columbia TriStar (Region 1 only)

Dr Adam Kelno .... **Anthony Hopkins**
Abe Cady .... **Ben Gazzara**
Angela Kelno .... **Leslie Caron**
Samantha Cady .... **Juliet Mills**
Lady Margaret Alexander Weidman .... **Lee Remick**
David Shawcross .... **Dan O'Herlihy**
Tom Bannister .... **Anthony Quayle**
Clinton-Meek .... **John Gielgud**
Justice Gilroy .... **Jack Hawkins**
Natalie .... **Judy Carne**

Writer **Edward Anhalt**
Producer **Douglas Cramer**

● ***A doctor fights to clear his name of war crime allegations.***

When, 20 years after the end of World War II, an American author publishes a claim that successful Jewish doctor Adam Kelno committed crimes against humanity in Poland during the conflict, the doctor sues for libel. In the resulting court case, however, Kelno's whole life comes under intense scrutiny, his saintly reputation is questioned and his role in concentration camp experimentation is thoroughly examined. This lengthy, two-part drama, based on the novel by Leon Uris and directed by Tom Gries, was a forerunner of the popular mini-series format. The title refers to the courtroom where the legal drama unfolds (Queens' Bench VII).

QED ✶✶

UK (BBC) Documentary. BBC 1 1982–98

Editors **David Filkin, Simon Campbell-Jones, Susan Spindler, Lorraine Heggessey, Michael Mosley**

● ***Wide-ranging documentary series with a scientific bent.***

Spontaneous combustion, overcoming drug addiction, the intense training of children to be sporting superstars, the effect of smoking on the human body and the chemistry of sexual attraction were all typical subjects aired in this ambitious series of sometimes light-hearted science documentaries. Occasional dramatizations helped sugar the scientific pill. In 1999, the series was replaced with the similar *Living Proof*, from the same production team. The logic was that – even after 16 years – the public did not understand the significance of the abbreviation 'QED'.

QI ✶✶✶

UK (Talkback Thames) Comedy Quiz. BBC 2 2003–

Presenter **Stephen Fry**
Creator/Producer **John Lloyd**

● ***High-brow quiz with a humorous common touch.***

The erudite Stephen Fry was an obvious choice to host this comedy game show based around impossible-to-know pieces of knowledge (the title apparently standing for 'quite interesting'). The fun comes from seeing the four comedian panellists floundering for answers and the surreal twist they often put on the questions posed. It doesn't matter whether they get the answers right, because points can be scored for embroidering their answers with 'quite interesting' snippets of information. Further dimensions are added through a liberal sprinkling of intriguing anecdotes and famous quotes, and from the debunking of perceived wisdom. Points are deducted from panellists who offer predictable but wholly wrong answers, with regular contributor Alan Davies usually the fall guy for this particular infelicity. Other comics featured throughout the series include Hugh Laurie, Bill Bailey, Danny Baker, John Sessions, Jeremy Hardy, Linda Smith, Rich Hall, Clive Anderson, Rob Brydon, Gyles Brandreth, Jo Brand and Sean Lock. Series one deals with topics beginning with A; series two moves on to B, series three to C, and so on.

Quantum Leap ✶✶

US (Bellisarius) Science Fiction. BBC 2 1990–4
(US: NBC 1989–93)
DVD: Universal

Dr Sam Beckett .... **Scott Bakula**
Al Calavicci .... **Dean Stockwell**

Creator/Producer **Donald Bellisario**

● ***A time-travelling scientist is stranded in the past.***

Scientist Sam Beckett is heavily involved in a secret time-travel project known as Quantum Leap. One day, turning himself into a human guinea-pig, he uses the machine to go spinning back in time. But there he becomes stranded, thrown forwards and backwards to different eras within a period of 30 years of his own birth (1953). In each episode, he finds himself trapped in the body of another person which could be male or female. One week he is a trapeze artist who has to prevent his sister suffering a tragic fall, another week a high school quarterback trying to stop two team-mates from throwing an important game. While he is allowed to meddle with time in such minor instances, Sam is prohibited from altering anything major, such as Kennedy's assassination. In his temporary persona, though he looks the part to all concerned, to viewers he still appears as the same old Sam.

While waiting to be returned to his own time, Sam's only hope is to fulfil his temporary roles as flawlessly as possible, trying not to arouse suspicions and aiming to win the day for the person concerned. To this end, he is aided by the hologrammatic image of a colleague, a cigar-chewing admiral called Al. Al (seen only by Sam) brings news of efforts to return Sam home, as well as assorted tit-bits about the people and the times in which Sam is stranded, using a hand-held terminal linked to a computer named Ziggy. But Al's information is always incomplete, with key details left out until the last possible moment. Having averted disaster, or at least having carried off his historical impersonation without too much distress, Sam, wailing a tremulous 'Oh boy!', is whisked away into another time zone and another body. Unfortunately, the final episode does not make happy viewing for fans of Sam Beckett, who learns that there is simply no way back to the present day. This is one hero who isn't coming home. Mike Post composed the theme music.

Quatermass ★★★

UK (BBC/Thames/Euston Films) Science Fiction. BBC 1 1953; 1955; 1958–9; ITV 1979
DVD: BBC

The Quatermass Experiment (BBC, 1953)
Prof. Bernard Quatermass ...... **Reginald Tate**
Judith Carroon ...... **Isabel Dean**
Victor Carroon ...... **Duncan Lamont**
John Paterson ...... **Hugh Kelly**
James Fullalove ...... **Paul Whitsun-Jones**
Dr Gordon Briscoe ...... **John Glen**
Chief Insp. Lomax ...... **Ian Colin**
DS Best ...... **Frank Hawkins**

Quatermass II (BBC, 1955)
Prof. Bernard Quatermass ...... **John Robinson**
Paula Quatermass ...... **Monica Grey**
Dr Leo Pugh ...... **Hugh Griffiths**
Capt. John Dillon ...... **John Stone**
Vincent Broadhead ...... **Rupert Davies**

Quatermass and the Pit (BBC, 1958–9)
Prof. Bernard Quatermass ...... **André Morell**
Barbara Judd ...... **Christine Finn**
Dr Matthew Roney ...... **Cec Linder**
Sladden ...... **Richard Shaw**
Col. Breen ...... **Anthony Bushell**
Capt. Potter ...... **John Stratton**
James Fullalove ...... **Brian Worth**

Quatermass (ITV, 1979)
Prof. Bernard Quatermass ...... **John Mills**
Joe Kapp ...... **Simon MacCorkindale**
Clare Kapp ...... **Barbara Kellerman**
Kickalong ...... **Ralph Arliss**
Caraway ...... **Paul Rosebury**
Bee ...... **Jane Bertish**
Hettie ...... **Rebecca Saire**
Marshall ...... **Tony Sibbald**
Sal ...... **Toyah Willcox**
Annie Morgan ...... **Margaret Tyzack**

Writer **Nigel Kneale**
Executive Producer **Verity Lambert** *(Thames)*
Producers **Rudolph Cartier** *(BBC)*, **Ted Childs** *(Thames)*

● ***The alien-thwarting adventures of Professor Bernard Quatermass, grandfather of all TV science-fiction heroes.***

The name 'Quatermass' has become synonymous with early TV sci-fi, yet relatively few viewers would have seen the original ground-breaking series. Transmitted live in 1953, when homes with TVs were few and repeats impossible, the six-part story nevertheless managed to set the trend for TV horror-fantasy leading to three follow-ups, the last 26 years later. The brains behind the project was Nigel Kneale, a BBC staff-writer given the chance to branch out with his own ideas. What he foresaw in *The Quatermass Experiment* was a new kind of TV thriller, adventurous in both its subject matter and presentation. The story concerns astronaut Victor Carroon, who returns to Earth contaminated by an alien life-form. As the alien vegetable gradually takes over Carroon's body and threatens to reproduce in devastingly vast quantities, it falls to space scientist Professor Quatermass to track him down. Cornering Carroon at Westminster Abbey, Quatermass appeals to what remains of his human nature, urging Carroon to destroy himself and save the planet.

When Quatermass resurfaced, two years later, production techniques had advanced somewhat. This time (again over six episodes) the Professor is called upon to protect Earth from aliens that have infiltrated people's minds and bodies. Identifying the alien base as being an asteroid on the other side of the planet, Quatermass and his colleague, Dr Pugh, set off in the Professor's own latest space rocket to destroy it. The original Quatermass, Reginald Tate, died just weeks before this second series, leaving John Robinson to take over the character.

The third six-part element in the saga, *Quatermass and the Pit*, was the most sophisticated of the BBC versions, concentrating on the idea that Martians had arrived on Earth millions of years earlier and had imparted certain attributes to man's ancestors, a process that explained away phenomena like ghosts, demons and ESP. This comes to light as the last traces of blitzed London are being redeveloped and a five-million-year-old skull is discovered next to an alien capsule in a deep pit. The Professor (now played by André Morell), aided by palaeontologist Matthew Roney, is brought in to restore order.

No more was heard of Quatermass until Thames and Euston Films picked up the reins in 1979. In a four-episode story Kneale had first penned around ten years earlier, John Mills became the fourth actor to play the scientist, who returns to London from a Scottish retirement to look for his missing granddaughter, Hettie. Once again, aliens are at the heart of the problem, bringing chaos to society and harvesting and taking away hordes of young people (hippies known as 'Planet People') at places as diverse as Wembley Stadium and ancient stone circles. Teaming up with Joe Kapp, a young Jewish astronomer, Quatermass not only foils the aliens but retrieves Hettie along the way.

In 2005, BBC 4 offered a rare experiment in live television when it re-created the original *Quatermass* story in one episode, adapted by Richard Fell. *The Quatermass Experiment* this time starred Jason Flemyng (as Quatermass), supported by Adrian Dunbar, Mark Gatiss, David Tennant and Andrew Tiernan, and attracted more than 500,000 viewers, the highest audience for that channel in a year.

The first three *Quatermass* stories were also filmed by Hammer and released on the cinema circuit, two with Brian Donlevy in the title role. The films were given new titles for American audiences: *The Creeping Unknown*, *Enemy from Space* and *Five Million Years to Earth* (starring Andrew Keir), respectively.

Quayle, Sir Anthony

CBE (1913–89)

Anthony Quayle's finest hours definitely came on the stage and in the cinema, but he made his contribution to television's archives as well. He starred as criminologist Adam Strange in the 1968 series STRANGE REPORT, acted as narrator for many series (including THE SIX WIVES OF HENRY VIII), and appeared in numerous TV movies, plays and mini-series, including QB VII (Tom Bannister), MOSES – THE LAWGIVER (Aaron), MASADA (Rubrius Gallus), *The Last Days of Pompeii*, *The Endless Game* (Glanville), *Confessional* (The Pope), and THE BBC TELEVISION SHAKESPEARE (*Henry IV* parts I and II). Guest roles were in MAN OF THE WORLD, THE SAINT, ESPIONAGE and TALES OF THE UNEXPECTED, among other series.

Queenie's Castle ★★

UK (Yorkshire) Situation Comedy. ITV 1970–2

Queenie Shepherd .... **Diana Dors**
Raymond Shepherd .... **Freddie Fletcher**
Douglas Shepherd .... **Barrie Rutter**
Bunny Shepherd .... **Brian Marshall**
Jack .... **Tony Caunter**
Mrs Petty .... **Lynne Perrie**

Creators **Keith Waterhouse, Willis Hall**
Producers **Graham Evans, Ian Davidson**

A Yorkshire matriarch rules her family with a rod of iron.

Queenie Shepherd is the undoubted head of the impoverished Shepherd clan. Dominating her motley trio of sons (Raymond, Douglas and Bunny), she lives in the Buckingham flats, a Yorkshire housing development. Also part of the household is Queenie's brother-in-law, Jack, and poking her nose in – and risking Queenie's ready wrath – is their neighbour, Mrs Petty (a pre-CORONATION STREET Lynne Perrie). Another *Street* star, Bryan Mosley, is seen as their landlord.

Queer as Folk ★★★

UK (Red) Drama. Channel 4 1999–2000
DVD: Channel 4 Video

Stuart Jones .... **Aidan Gillen**
Vince Tyler .... **Craig Kelly**
Nathan Maloney .... **Charlie Hunnam**
Hazel Tyler .... **Denise Black**
Phil Delaney .... **Jason Merrells**
Janice Maloney .... **Caroline O'Neill**
Romey Sullivan .... **Esther Hall**
Bernard Thomas .... **Andy Devine**
Donna Clarke .... **Carla Henry**
Rosalie Cotter .... **Caroline Pegg**
Lisa Levene .... **Saira Todd**
Marcie Finch .... **Susan Cookson**
Marie Jones .... **Maria Doyle Kennedy**
Cameron Roberts .... **Peter O'Brien**
Lance Amponah .... **John Brobbey**
Roy Maloney .... **Paul Copley**
Graham Beck .... **Pearce Quigley** *(2)*
Claire Fletcher .... **Judy Holt** *(2)*
Mickey Smith .... **Clinton Kenyon** *(2)*

Writer **Russell T. Davies**
Producer **Nicola Shindler**

The lives and lifestyles of three gay men in Manchester.

Inevitably controversial, *Queer as Folk* did not disappoint critics with its graphic sex scenes and fierce language. Set in Manchester, and particularly in the gay quarter around Canal Street, the eight-part series tells of three gay lads, all comfortable with their sexuality, but having different expectations from it. Stuart Jones is the central character, an arrogant, well-paid PR executive who is always on the prowl for a new conquest. His best mate is old school friend Vince Tyler, an assistant manager at a supermarket, who holds a torch for Stuart but finds his devotion unreciprocated. To make matters worse, Vince has not come out at work and is therefore pursued by female colleagues. The third side of the gay triangle is provided by 15-year-old Nathan Maloney, a naïve schoolboy who develops a crush on Stuart and leaps illegally out of the closet. Naturally, parental problems ensue. The series was followed up a year later by a two-part sequel, *Queer as Folk 2*. Russell T. Davies's scripts were also adapted for American TV, the subsequent series shown in the UK as *Queer as Folk: USA* (BBC Choice 2002).

Quentin, Caroline

(1961–)

Surrey-born actress whose major TV series have included MEN BEHAVING BADLY (Dorothy), DON'T TELL FATHER (Kate Bancroft), *All or Nothing at All* (Rebecca), JONATHAN CREEK (Maddy Magellan), KISS ME KATE (Kate Salinger), BLUE MURDER (DCI Janine Lewis) and LIFE BEGINS (Maggie Mee), as well as the comedy-drama *An Evening with Gary Lineker* (Monica). Quentin also presented the first series of the interior design programme *Home Front* and played Beth Pastorov in *The Innocent*, Gina in *Goodbye Mr Steadman*, Bridget Watmore in *Hot Money*, Lin Beresford in *Blood Strangers*, Maria Moogan in *Von Trapped* and Julie Hill in *Footsteps in the Snow*. She has been seen in many other series, from CASUALTY, *Shadow of the Noose, Up Line* and WHOSE LINE IS IT ANYWAY? to MR BEAN, *This Is David Lander* and *Harry Enfield's Television Programme*, and has narrated documentaries such as *Living Famously*. She was once married to comedian Paul Merton.

Quest, The ★★

US (Columbia) Western. BBC 1 1976–7 (US: NBC 1976)

Morgan Beaudine .... **Kurt Russell**
Quentin Beaudine .... **Tim Matheson**

Creator **Tracy Keenan Wynn**
Executive Producer **David Gerber**
Producers **Mark Rodgers, James H. Brown**

In the Wild West of the 1880s, two brothers set out to find their long-lost sister.

Morgan Beaudine and his sister, Patricia, were taken captive when children by Cheyenne Indians, but they became separated. Morgan was raised by his captors and given the name of 'Two Persons' and, although he has now returned to white society, he still trusts Indians more than his own kind. He also dresses like a Native American and speaks their language – a useful asset in the Wild West. His brother, Quentin, has enjoyed a quite different upbringing, living with an aunt and being educated in San Francisco. He plans to be a doctor, but first things first. Their sister is still missing, so the brothers hit the road in an attempt to track her down and reunite the family. Their 'Quest' proves long and largely fruitless.

Question of Sport, A ★★★

UK (BBC) Quiz. BBC 1 1970–

Presenters **David Vine, David Coleman, Sue Barker**

Producers **Nick Hunter, Mike Adley, Kieron Collins,**

Carl Doran, Caroline Roberts, Sally Evans, Gareth Edwards

● ***Light-hearted quiz featuring sporting personalities.***

A Question of Sport has achieved an audience appeal that reaches beyond the realms of traditional sports fans. The relaxed, jokey atmosphere and flippant banter have made the series into a popular light entertainment show, with high viewing figures to boot. Two teams of three sporting celebrities (each containing a resident captain) have worked their way through several rounds of sporting teasers, answering questions on their own individual events as well as general sporting matters. Favourite rounds have included the picture board (identifying the personality from an obscure picture), what happened next? (guessing the sequence of events after the film has stopped), the mystery personality (revealed only in short glimpses through unusual camera-angles) and the 60-second rapid-fire section (worth up to nine points).

David Vine was the first host, succeeded in 1979 by David Coleman, who in turn gave way to Sue Barker in 1997. Excluding guest captains, *A Question of Sport* teams have been led by Cliff Morgan, Henry Cooper, Fred Trueman, Brendan Foster, Gareth Edwards, Emlyn Hughes, Willie Carson, Bill Beaumont, Ian Botham, Ally McCoist, John Parrott, Frankie Dettori and Matt Dawson. In 1987 the programme achieved a rare coup, when HRH the Princess Anne was recruited on to Emlyn Hughes's team to celebrate the 200th edition.

Question Time ★★★

UK (BBC/Mentorn) Debate. BBC 1 1979–

Presenters **Robin Day, Peter Sissons, David Dimbleby**

● ***Studio-audience-led political debate.***

Question Time has been based on a simple formula: take three politicians of different persuasions, plus one or two 'neutrals' – often industrialists or academics – and throw them to the lions (in the form of a studio audience of mixed political views). Without pre-knowledge, the panellists have to answer tricky, topical questions put to them by the gathered masses. Keeping order, and helping to put the panellists on the spot, was initially Robin Day, whose inimitably gruff style helped establish the series. When he retired in 1989, his seat was taken, amid much publicity, by then Channel 4 newscaster Peter Sissons. Sissons has subsequently handed over control to David Dimbleby. Over the years, several fill-in hosts have also been employed to cover for sickness. These have included Sue Lawley and Ludovic Kennedy. The idea for *Question Time* was based on Radio 4's *Any Questions*.

Quiller ★★

UK (BBC) Secret Agent Drama. BBC 1 1975

Quiller	**Michael Jayston**
Angus Kinloch	**Moray Watson**
Loman	**Nigel Stock**
Rosalind	**Sinead Cusack**
Diane	**Prunella Gee**

Producer **Peter Graham Scott**

● ***The cases of a stubborn and determined secret agent.***

Broadly based on the 1966 film *The Quiller Memorandum*, starring George Segal, and the novels by Adam Hall, this series focuses on the exploits of hard-nosed secret agent Quiller, a man on his own against the world. Often at odds with his boss, Angus Kinloch, Quiller works for an undercover government body known only as The Bureau and officially does not exist. His missions – to protect VIPs, destroy a politically sensitive cargo, spring a political prisoner, save a condemned man, assist a defector to get to the UK, etc. – are covered in 13 episodes. Writers included Michael J. Bird and Brian Clemens.

Quilley, Denis

OBE (1927–2003)

British actor seen in a variety of series from the kids' sci-fi thriller TIMESLIP (Commander Traynor), to the sitcom RICH TEA AND SYMPATHY (biscuit magnate George Rudge). He played Richard Shelton in a 1951 version of R. L. Stevenson's *The Black Arrow*, Gladstone in *No. 10*, Quadratus in the mini-series MASADA, Peter in another mini-series, *AD*, and among his other credits were MARK SABER, THE MAN IN ROOM 17, DIXON OF DOCK GREEN, THE AVENGERS, CLAYHANGER (George Cannon), TALES OF THE UNEXPECTED, THE BRETTS, *After the War* and *Family Album*, plus single dramas.

Quincy, ME ★★

US (Universal/Glen A. Larson) Detective Drama. ITV 1977–85 (US: NBC 1976–83)

DVD: Universal

Quincy, ME	**Jack Klugman**
Lt. Frank Monahan	**Garry Walberg**
Sam Fujiyama	**Robert Ito**
Danny Tovo	**Val Bisoglio**
Lee Potter	**Lynette Mettey**
Dr Robert J. Asten	**John S. Ragin**
Sgt Brill	**Joseph Roman**
Eddie	**Ed Garrett**
Marc	**Marc Scott Taylor**
Diane	**Diane Markoff**
Dr Emily Hanover	**Anita Gillette**

Creators **Glen A. Larson, Lou Shaw**
Executive Producer **Glen A. Larson**
Producers **Lou Shaw, Peter Thompson, Robert F. O'Neill, Michael Star**

● ***An inquisitive pathologist keeps unearthing new clues and frustrating the local police.***

Widower Quincy works for the Los Angeles County Coroner's Office as a medical examiner (ME) and has abandoned a profitable medical practice in order to take on this demanding job. But he is born to it. The quick once-over of the corpse is not for Quincy. He goes into every detail and, just when the cops think they have a 'natural causes' case on their hands, the pushy pathologist uncovers something more suspicious. So pushy is Quincy that the police can hardly ignore him. But, just in case they do, much to the consternation of his boss, Dr Asten, Quincy often turns detective himself and heads out looking for clues, assisted by his young colleague, Sam Fujiyama.

In his private life, Quincy has a girlfriend, Lee Potter, though such is his dedication to his job, their romance never quite takes off. He therefore lives alone, on a boat moored near a bar called Danny's Place, where he spends whatever free time he has. Lee soon leaves the scene, but Quincy later meets psychiatrist Emily Hanover, whom he subsequently marries.

Quincy's Christian name is never given, though a once-seen business card does give his initial as R.

The series began life as a part of the MYSTERY MOVIE anthology, but proved so popular in the USA that it was given its own regular slot.

Quirke, Pauline

(1959–)

A teenage performer in the 1970s, Pauline Quirke has now developed into an adult star, thanks largely to roles in ANGELS (Vicki Smith), SHINE ON HARVEY MOON (Veronica), BIRDS OF A FEATHER (Sharon), THE SCULPTRESS (murderess Olive Martin), REAL WOMEN (Mandy), MAISIE RAINE (title role), DOWN TO EARTH (Faith Addis), *Office Gossip* (Jo) and *Being April* (April). With her *Birds* co-star, Linda Robson, she also featured in the challenge series *Jobs for the Girls*; and other notable credits have included the dramas *Deadly Summer* (Linda Topping), *The Canterville Ghost* (medium Madame Murielle), *The Story of the Treasure Seekers* (Eliza), *Our Boy* (Sonia), *Last Christmas* (Gwen), DAVID COPPERFIELD (Peggotty), MURDER IN MIND, CARRIE'S WAR (Hepzibah Green) and *North and South* (Dixon). She appeared in DIXON OF DOCK GREEN as a child, and worked in all manner of kids' shows for Thames, including YOU MUST BE JOKING! and her own series, *Pauline's Quirkes* and *Pauline's People*. She has also been seen in THE DUCHESS OF DUKE STREET, CROWN COURT, *Lovely Couple*, GIRLS ON TOP, ROCKLIFFE'S BABIES, THE GOOD SEX GUIDE, CASUALTY, RANDALL AND HOPKIRK (DECEASED) and THE BILL, and narrated the docu-soap *Lakesiders*.

Quiz Ball ★★

UK (BBC) Quiz. BBC 1 1966–72

Presenters **David Vine, Barry Davies, Stuart Hall**

Creator **George Woolley**
Producers **Bill Wright, Mary Evans**

● ***Light-hearted soccer quiz involving football league teams.***

Quiz Ball was a game show in the QUESTION OF SPORT vein, but with its sporting content confined to association football. In each match, two professional soccer teams competed for the right to advance through the knock-out tournament. Arsenal played Nottingham Forest in the very first programme. Teams were composed of players, management and celebrity supporters and they answered questions of varying degrees of difficulty to progress along an electronic scoreboard (designed like a football pitch) towards goal. A hard question was the equivalent of a 'long ball', catapulting the team into their opponents' penalty box if answered correctly, whereas easier questions could be pieced together like a passing game for a slower approach. The team with the most goals won the match. There was even an international element to the tournament, with special Home International matches taking place between England, Wales, Scotland and Northern Ireland. David Vine was the first chairman and questionmaster, followed by Barry Davies and, finally, Stuart Hall.

John Witty was the announcer.

R3 ✶✶

UK (BBC) Science Fiction. BBC 1 1964–5

Sir Michael Gerrard	**John Robinson**
Miss Brooks	**Brenda Saunders**
Dr George Fratton	**Moultrie Kelsall**
Dr May Howard	**Elizabeth Sellars**
Dr Peter Travers	**Richard Wordsworth**
Dr Jack Morton	**Simon Lack**
Betty Mason	**Janet Kelly**
Pomeroy	**Edwin Richfield**
Tom Collis	**Derek Benfield**
Porter	**Maxwell Foster**
Phillip Boult	**Michael Hawkins**
Dr Richard Franklin	**Oliver Reed**

Creator **N. J. Crisp**
Producers **Andrew Osborn, John Robins**

● ***The private and professional lives of a team of scientists.***

Focusing on the staff of R3 (short for Research Centre No. 3, a division of the Ministry of Research), this series examines how scientists cope with the responsibilities and demands of their jobs, and how these affect their domestic lives. Effectively, it takes eggheads and boffins and gives them a human dimension. Sir Michael Gerrard (played by a former Professor QUATERMASS, John Robinson) is director of the unit, supported by his number two, Dr George Fratton. Beneath him work a team of dedicated scientists, struggling to cope with the morality of certain experiments and the social consequences of new discoveries. In the second season the focus moves to the department's trouble-shooting agency, a specialist team geared up to solving problems beyond normal human knowledge. It is led by Phillip Boult, aided by a young Oliver Reed in the role of Dr Richard Franklin.

Rab C. Nesbitt ✶✶

UK (BBC) Situation Comedy. BBC 2 1990–4; 1996–9
DVD: John Williams Productions

Rab C. Nesbitt	**Gregor Fisher**
Mary Nesbitt	**Elaine C. Smith**
Gash Nesbitt	**Andrew Fairlie**
Burney Nesbitt	**Eric Cullen**
Jamesie Cotter	**Tony Roper**
Ella Cotter	**Barbara Rafferty**
Andra	**Brian Pettifer**
Dodie	**Iain McColl**
Norrie	**John Kazek**
Bridie	**Nicola Park**
Natalie	**Elaine Ellis**
Screech Nesbitt	**David McKay**
Mr Grogan	**Jimmy Logan**

Creator/Writer **Ian Pattison**
Producer **Colin Gilbert**

● ***The downs and downs of tenement life with a Glasgow street-philosopher.***

Sporting a string vest and a grubby headband, and brandishing a rolled-up newspaper, Rab C. Nesbitt made his name in the NAKED VIDEO sketch show, taking the Establishment to task in an opinionated drunken stupor. Following a New Year's special in 1989 (*Rab C. Nesbitt's Seasonal Greet*), this series was launched. It showcases the aggressive waster at home and at play, battling with his wife, Mary, and obnoxious kids, Gash and Burney, squabbling with his drinking chums (including his best mate, Jamesie) and bamboozling the forces of law and order with unfathomable Scottish gibberish. Bouts of prison, illness and family strife allow the giro-king to reflect on his unhappy lot.

Racing Game, The ✶

UK (Yorkshire) Detective Drama. ITV 1979–80
DVD: Lance (Region 1 only)

Sid Halley	**Mike Gwilym**
Chico Barnes	**Mick Ford**

Executive Producer **David Cunliffe**
Producer **Jacky Stoller**

● ***A disabled jockey turns to private detective work.***

Horse racing has never fared well in TV drama. Like the much-criticized TRAINER a decade later, this attempt to bring the colour of the sport of kings into viewers' living rooms was doomed to failure. Based on the hugely successful novels by former Royal jockey Dick Francis, this six-part series focuses on one Sid Halley, a jump jockey who has suffered a bad riding accident and lost a hand. Denied a return to his true vocation, Halley does the next best thing – he hovers around the fringes of racing society, setting himself up as a private investigator and mingling with some of the murkier characters in the racing world. Despite successes against dopers and nobblers, betting-coup merchants and horsenappers, he and his assistant, Chico Barnes, failed to win over viewers, and a second series didn't come under starter's orders.

Raffles ✶✶

UK (Yorkshire) Crime Drama. ITV 1977
DVD: Acorn Media

L. J. Raffles	**Anthony Valentine**
Bunny Manders	**Christopher Strauli**
Insp. Mackenzie	**Victor Carin**

Writer **Philip Mackie**
Executive Producer **David Cunliffe**
Producer **Jacky Stoller**

● ***Audacious robberies performed with aplomb by a turn-of-the-century gentleman thief.***

A first-class cricketer, man-about-town and a general good egg, Raffles has, all the same, but one excitement in life: the buzz that comes from pulling off risky thefts from his upper-class associates, often under the noses of the authorities. Part of the pleasure lies in seeing his police adversary, Inspector Mackenzie, humiliated time and again. From his first daring theft of a £10,000 diamond necklace at a stately home, Raffles is loyally supported by reliable Bunny Manders, his former public school fag and the only man in the world who knows of his old friend's escapades.

The series was based on the original stories of E. W. Hornung, with the pilot episode, *Raffles – the Amateur Cracksman*, screened as a one-off in 1975. In this pilot, Mackenzie was played by James Maxwell. In 2001 the character was exhumed for a one-off drama called *Gentleman Thief* (BBC 1), which cast Nigel Havers in the lead, although without the assistance of Bunny this time.

Rag Tag and Bobtail ✶

UK (BBC) Children's Entertainment. BBC 1953–5

Narrators **Charles E. Stidwill, David Enders, James Urquhart**

Writer **Louise Cochrane**
Producers **Freda Lingstrom, David Boisseau**

The hedgerow adventures of a trio of country animals.
Rag Tag and Bobtail was the Thursday segment of the WATCH WITH MOTHER strand and featured the little escapades of glove puppets Rag (a hedgehog), Tag (a mouse) and Bobtail (a clover-chewing buck rabbit). The puppets were created and controlled by Sam and Elizabeth Williams, and 26 episodes were made. Episodes one and two were never screened, but the remaining 24 were repeated endlessly until the programme was replaced in 1965.

Rag Trade, The ✶✶

UK (BBC/LWT) Situation Comedy. BBC 1961–3; ITV 1977–8
DVD: DD Home Entertainment

Mr Fenner	**Peter Jones**
Reg	**Reg Varney**
Paddy	**Miriam Karlin**
Carole	**Sheila Hancock**
Little Lil	**Esma Cannon**
Judy	**Barbara Windsor**
Shirley	**Wanda Ventham**
Janet	**Amanda Reiss**
Sandra	**Sheena Marshe**
Betty	**Patricia Denys**
Myrtle	**Claire Davenport**
Olive	**Stella Tanner**
Gloria	**Carmel Cryan**
Tony	**Christopher Beeny** *(LWT)*
Olive	**Anna Karen** *(LWT)*
Kathy	**Diane Langton** *(LWT)*
Lyn	**Gillian Taylforth** *(LWT)*
Jojo	**Lucita Lijertwood** *(LWT)*
Mabel	**Deddie Davies** *(LWT)*

Creators/Writers **Ronald Chesney, Ronald Wolfe**
Producers **Dennis Main Wilson** *(BBC)*, **Bryan Izzard, William G. Stewart** *(LWT)*

Union strife at a clothing factory.
Set in the East End dressmaking workshop of Fenner Fashions, *The Rag Trade* depicts the him-and-us relationship between the unscrupulous, scheming boss, Mr Fenner, and his work-shy employees, with militant Paddy, the shop steward, always ready to blow her whistle and order, 'Everybody out!' Carole is the shop treasurer, with Little Lil the button-holder and tea-maker. Other girls come and go during the series' run, but always stuck in the middle is Reg, the factory foreman.

A huge hit in the early 1960s, *The Rag Trade* was revived with less success in 1977. Only Peter Jones and Miriam Karlin survived from the original cast, and newcomers like Christopher Beeny (as foreman Tony) and Anna Karen (reprising her ON THE BUSES role of Olive) were added to the roll-call of workers. Lynsey de Paul provided the updated theme song.

Railway Children, The ✶✶✶

UK (Carlton) Drama. ITV 2000
DVD: Granada Ventures (2000 version); DD Home Entertainment (1968 version)

Mother	**Jenny Agutter**
Roberta ('Bobbie')	**Jemima Rooper**
Peter	**Jack Blumenau**
Phyllis	**Clare Thomas**
Perks	**Gregor Fisher**
Mrs Perks	**Sophie Thompson**
Old Gentleman	**Richard Attenborough**
Station Master	**Clive Russell**
Father	**Michael Kitchen**
Ruth	**Melanie Clark-Pullen**
Dr Forrest	**David Bamber**
Cook	**Valerie Minifie**

Writer **Simon Nye**
Producer **Charles Elton**

Three children discover a new life in the country after their father is suddenly arrested.
The year is 1903 and the lives of Bobbie, Peter and Phyllis are about to be shaken up. Things appear very comfortable: Father works for the Foreign Office and Mother writes poetry; the children have a happy existence in London. One day, however, two mysterious men arrive to take away their father and the family is forced to move out to the country. They find a new home in a little cottage called Three Chimneys and, to make ends meet, Mother tries to sell stories to magazines. The children have a long summer ahead of them and settle well into their new home. They discover the joys of the local railway and wave to the *Green Dragon* as it steams into the station every morning. Through their love of the trains, they are able to enlist station staff such as porter Perks and other locals, including a notable old gentleman, in their efforts to secure the return of their father.

This single drama, directed by Catherine Morshead, was based on the 1906 E. Nesbit novel that had been adapted for television three times before (BBC 1951: Marian Chapman as Bobbie, Carole Lorimer as Phyllis, Michael Croudson as Peter, Jean Anderson as Mother; BBC 1957: Anneke Wills (billed as Willys) as Bobbie, Sandra Michaels as Phyllis, Cavan Kendall as Peter, Jean Anderson again as Mother; and BBC 1 1968: Jenny Agutter as Bobbie, Gillian Bailey as Phyllis, Neil McDermott as Peter, Ann Castle as Mother). The interesting casting this time around was Jenny Agutter's switch to the Mother role.

Rainbow/Rainbow Days ★★

UK (Thames/HTV/Tetra Films) Children's Entertainment. ITV 1972–92; 1994–5; 1996–7
DVD: Fremantle Home Entertainment

Presenters **David Cook, Geoffrey Hayes, Dale Superville**

Creator **Pamela Lonsdale**
Executive Producers **Charles Warren, Alan Horrox**
Producers **Pamela Lonsdale, Vic Hughes, Charles Warren, Lesley Burgess, Sheila Kinany, Paul Cole**

● ***Education and entertainment for the pre-school age.***

Although effectively ITV's answer to PLAY SCHOOL, *Rainbow* was more a British SESAME STREET. It was hosted originally by David Cook but more famously by former Z CARS actor Geoffrey Hayes (from 1973). Guest celebrities read stories, but better remembered are the *Rainbow* puppet characters. Taught and instructed as if they were kids (indeed they acted as surrogate children to convey the educational angle), the first puppets were Moony, a sad-looking mauve creature, and his antithesis, Sunshine, a livelier, yellow one. For many years, however, the puppet cast comprised Zippy, an oval-headed, wide-eyed creation with a painful-looking zip for a mouth, George, a pink hippopotamus, and Bungle, a good-natured bear (originally played by actor John Leeson). Music was provided first by a group called Telltale, then by the trio of Rod (Burton), Jane (Tucker) and Matthew (Corbett of SOOTY fame), with Freddy (Marks) later taking the place of Matthew. Roger Walker was also once a member of the musical team. The singers were later given their own spin-off series, appropriately entitled *Rod, Jane and Freddy* (1981–5; 1989–91). New host Dale Superville joined up when the show was revamped as *Rainbow Days* (1996–7).

Ramsay, Gordon

OBE (1966–)

Fiery-tempered, Scottish TV chef, the star of *Ramsay's Boiling Point, Ramsay's Kitchen Nightmares*, HELL'S KITCHEN and *The F Word*. He's a former professional footballer with Glasgow Rangers.

Randall

LESLIE (1924–) and JOAN

One of TV's first husband-and-wife couples, the Randalls starred in their own mid-1950s sitcom, appropriately titled *Joan and Leslie* but later changed to *The Randall Touch*, which evolved from a series called *Leslie Randall Entertains*. They later appeared as investigators Jane and Dagobert Brown in the DETECTIVE anthology and advertised Fairy Snow before heading for Australia to re-create their sitcom success. Leslie also worked in the USA and Australia, but returned in the 1970s to write plays and work in radio. He later featured as Reggie Wilkie in EMMERDALE and has made guest appearances in programmes like CASUALTY, MY FAMILY and DOCTORS. Joan was often billed under her maiden name of Joan Reynolds.

Randall and Hopkirk (Deceased) 1 ★★★

UK (Scoton/ITC) Detective Drama. ITV 1969–70
DVD: Carlton

Jeff Randall .... **Mike Pratt**
Marty Hopkirk .... **Kenneth Cope**
Jean Hopkirk .... **Annette Andre**
Insp. Large .... **Ivor Dean**

Creator **Dennis Spooner**
Producer **Monty Berman**

● ***Unorthodox investigations by a private eye and his partner, a ghost.***

Jeff Randall and Marty Hopkirk are partners in a private detection agency – or, rather, they were, until Marty was murdered in a hit-and-run incident. Returning as a ghost, he helps Jeff bring his killers to book, but, from that time onward, Marty is obliged to remain on Earth (for 100 years), having broken a rule of the afterlife by staying down here after daybreak. As the old rhyme goes: *Afore the sun shall rise anew/Each ghost unto his grave must go./Cursed be the ghost who dares to stay/ And face the awful light of day./He shall not to the grave return/Until a hundred years be gone.*

Being a ghost, Marty is visible to only one person, Jeff. Not even his bemused widow, Jean, who is Jeff's secretary, knows of his presence. But this renders him remarkably useful in the detection game, as a valuable source of information, despite the fact that he cannot get physically involved. Sadly, he is also rather unreliable and very frustrating: many a time Jeff is left waiting for his white-suited, deceased partner to show up with a vital clue, or to warn him of impending danger. Inspector Large is the programme's token grumpy copper.

The series, played with a generous slice of humour, was shown in the USA under the title *My Partner the Ghost* but was not a great success across the Atlantic. BBC 2 reran the series in 1994.

Randall and Hopkirk (Deceased) 2 ★★★

UK (Working Title) Detective Drama. BBC 1 2000–1
DVD: Vision Video

Jeff Randall .... **Bob Mortimer**
Marty Hopkirk .... **Vic Reeves**
Jeannie Hurst .... **Emilia Fox**
Wyvern .... **Tom Baker**

Writers **Charlie Higson, Paul Whitehouse, Gareth Roberts, Kate Woods**
Producer **Charlie Higson**
Executive Producer **Simon Wright**

● ***Humorous update of the classic 1960s series.***

Stylishly and colourfully shot for the digital age, the new *Randall and Hopkirk* was not a simple retread of the earlier series. For a start it starred Reeves and Mortimer and so, as straight as they hoped to play it, the revamp was never likely to be taken too seriously. Secondly, Charlie Higson, a long-time associate of Vic and Bob and best known for his work on THE FAST SHOW, was drafted in to write the scripts (with a little help from Paul Whitehouse and others), which again meant that humour was unlikely to be far away. The third major point was that special effects had come a long way in 30 years and the producers now had the opportunity to play around a lot more with the supernatural world inhabited by the deceased Marty. To explore this dimension further, a new character, Wyvern – a sort of ghostly godfather for the newly dead – was introduced. In all, there was more fantasy fun and less hard detective work, classier production values and a flippancy that even the original series couldn't match.

Range Rider, The ★★

US (Flying A) Western. BBC 1955 (US:Syndicated 1951–3)
DVD: Alpha Video

The Range Rider .... **Jock Mahoney**
Dick West .... **Dick Jones**

Executive Producer **Armand Schaefer**
Producer **Louis Gray**

A mysterious do-gooder and his friend roam the West, helping folk in trouble.

This early Western showcases the exploits of the honest, principled and tough Range Rider and his boyish sidekick, Dick West. Together they drift across the Wild West of the 1860s, putting outlaws in their place, rescuing helpless civilians and assisting the forces of law and order in their own unconventional way. They have to be the two most athletic cowboys around, for rarely do they spurn the chance to leap from their horses, rope in the criminals and perform whatever heroic feat is required. This is largely because the two stars were fit and brawny themselves and were willing to do their own stuntwork (actor Jock Mahoney later went on to play Tarzan).

Dressed in a fringed buckskin shirt and a white stetson, The Range Rider wears no boots, only Indian moccasins. His horse is called Rawhide. Dick, sporting a dark, military-style shirt and a black hat, rides a steed called Lucky. The theme song for the show is 'Home on the Range'.

Rantzen, Esther

CBE (1940–)

Doyenne of TV consumerists, Esther Rantzen began her career in radio production, arriving in television as a production assistant on BBC-3 and MAN ALIVE and as a researcher/reporter on BRADEN'S WEEK. She moved on to produce and present her own series, which looked at the quirks of everyday life and stood up for the embattled consumer. Entitled THAT'S LIFE, it ran for 21 years from 1973, making Rantzen a household name. It also gave her the opportunity to expand into other programmes. These included THE BIG TIME, HEARTS OF GOLD and CHILDREN IN NEED (associated with her main charity concern, Childline). Since the end of *That's Life*, she has presented a BBC 2 topical discussion show called *Esther*, a BBC 1 campaigning vehicle called *The Rantzen Report* and an ITV series, *That's Esther*. She was married to the late TV presenter and producer Desmond Wilcox.

Raphael, Frederic

(1931–)

Chicago-born screenwriter, author of THE GLITTERING PRIZES and its sequel, OXBRIDGE BLUES. His other credits have included ROGUE MALE (1976), *The Serpent Son, School Play* (both 1979), *After the War* (1989) and the 1978 PREMIERE film *Something's Wrong* (also as director). He also hosted FILM 72 for a while.

Rat Catchers, The ★★

UK (Associated-Rediffusion) Spy Drama. ITV 1966–7

Peregrine Smith .... **Gerald Flood**
Brigadier Davidson .... **Philip Stone**
Richard Hurst .... **Glyn Owen**

Producer **Cyril Coke**

The assignments of a top-secret counter-espionage team.

The Rat Catchers are based in Whitehall but officially have no name or number; their existence is denied by the highest authorities and they work in the greatest secrecy. Their role is to defend the country from foreign threats and to obey orders without question. As a result, they live and operate in a violent, hazardous world.

The three members of the team are wealthy playboy Peregrine Smith, cold, analytical Brigadier Davidson (the brains of the team) and newcomer Richard Hurst, a former Scotland Yard superintendent. It is with Hurst's arrival that viewers first learn about the squad, and his uncertain start reveals just how unsavoury this profession can be. Indeed, it is a far cry from the glitzy world of James Bond, their cinema contemporary.

Rather English Marriage, A ★★★

UK (Wall to Wall/BBC) Drama. BBC 2 1998
DVD: Carlton

Reggie Conyngham-Jervis .... **Albert Finney**
John Light *(young)*
Roy Southgate .... **Tom Courtenay**
Iain Jones *(young)*
Liz Franks .... **Joanna Lumley**
Mary Conyngham-Jervis .... **Ursula Howells**
Katie Carr *(young)*
Grace Southgate .... **Aileen O'Gorman**
Caroline Carver *(young)*
Lord Vivian Blythgowrie .... **Jeremy Clyde**
Alan Southgate .... **Sean Murray**
Mandy Hulme .... **Adjoa Andoh**

Writer **Andrew Davies**
Executive Producers **Alex Graham, David P. Thompson**
Producer **Jo Willett**

Two widowers agree to share their lives and develop an unlikely friendship.

Reggie and Roy meet at a hospital in Tunbridge Wells. Their wives are terminally ill and die on the same ward within minutes of each other. Both suddenly discover a void in their lives. Reggie, a retired squadron leader and incorrigible ladies' man, on the face of it seems as bluff and as boorish as ever, but the boozy bounder soon realizes he needs company, if only to help with the domestic chores at his mansion. Roy Southgate, a mild-mannered ex-milkman, feels the loneliness immediately and acutely, ploughing all his energies into his own household duties. Brought together again by social worker Mandy Hulme, the two decide to pool resources: the unassuming Roy moves into Reggie's home as cook, cleaner and unofficial 'manservant' in return for his bed and board. However, the real trade is in company and friendship – an unlikely bond that survives the ups and downs of Reggie's romance with local boutique owner Liz Franks and the misery induced by Roy's sex offender son, Alan, from his prison cell. Flashbacks to their more youthful days reflect times of both joy and great sorrow. This feature-length single drama was adapted by Andrew Davies from a novel by Angela Lambert. Paul Seed directed.

Ratings

The audience figures achieved by television programmes, arranged in order of popularity. These are of particular value to advertisers but are also a useful pointer for programme-makers when gauging the success of their projects. The statistics are compiled using various means, from simple consumer surveys and viewer diaries to electronic devices attached to television receivers. Numerous companies have collated the information in the UK over the years. The American giant, A. C. Nielsen, was active in the 1950s, but also involved have been Gallup, Pulse, TAM (Television Audience Measurement) and AGB (Audits of Great Britain), the last producing figures for the Joint Industry Committee for Television Audience Research (JICTAR), a committee representing the interests of ITV companies and their advertisers. In 1981, at the behest of the 1977 Annan Committee's review of broadcasting in the UK, the separate BBC and JICTAR ratings systems were amalgamated into the Broadcasters' Audience Research Board (BARB). The collation method in use today is complex and involves drawing data by meter from more than 5,000 sample households that are selected to provide a cross-section of ages, sex and economic and social status. Recorded programmes viewed within seven days are also included in the figures.

Raven, Simon

(1927–2001)

British novelist and screenwriter, initially scripting his own plays like *The Scapegoat* (1964), *Sir Jocelyn, the Minister Would Like a Word ...* (1965), *A Soirée at Bossom's Hotel* and *A Pyre for Private James* (both 1966), before turning to adaptations like *Point Counterpoint*, *The Outstation* for *The Jazz Age* anthology, THE WAY WE LIVE NOW, THE PALLISERS, *An Unofficial Rose* and *Love in a Cold Climate*, and series dramas such as EDWARD AND MRS SIMPSON and *Sexton Blake and the Demon God*. Among his later work was the dramatization of *The Blackheath Poisonings* in 1992.

Rawhide ★★★

US (CBS) Western. ITV 1959–67 (US:CBS 1959–66)

Gil Favor .... **Eric Fleming**
Rowdy Yates .... **Clint Eastwood**
Wishbone .... **Paul Brinegar**
Pete Nolan .... **Sheb Wooley**
Jim Quince .... **Steve Raines**
Joe Scarlett .... **Rocky Shahan**
Harkness 'Mushy' Mushgrove .... **James Murdock**
Hey Soos Patines .... **Robert Cabal**
Clay Forrester .... **Charles Gray**
Jed Colby .... **John Ireland**
Ian Cabot .... **David Watson**

Creator/Producer **Charles Marquis Warren**

The adventures of a cattle-driving team as they cross the Wild West.

Chiefly remembered for being the show that gave Clint Eastwood his first taste of stardom, *Rawhide* was a Western for men by men, a kind of WAGON TRAIN with cows and precious few women. It revolves around a team of cattle-drovers, trying to lead a herd from San Antonio, Texas, up to Sedalia, Missouri, some time in the 1860s, well before the railroad arrived to alleviate this chore. Gil Favor is the head of the team, with Eastwood's Rowdy Yates the second-in-command, later to assume control when Favor is written out. Also in the troop are trail scout Pete Nolan, cook Wishbone, Mushy the drover, and a Mexican, Hey Soos (Jesus). Their men-against-the-elements voyage is constantly interrupted by encounters with intriguing strangers, so much so that even when the series ends (seven years later), they still haven't reached the end of the trail.

The 'Keep Them Doggies Rollin'' theme song was a UK hit for Frankie Laine in 1959. Sheb Wooley, who played Pete Nolan, was also a comedian-cum-country-singer and had already broken into the UK Top 20 in 1958 with 'The Purple People Eater' (a number one in the USA).

Rawle, Jeff

(1951–)

Birmingham-born actor/writer whose biggest roles have been as Billy Fisher in BILLY LIAR and as George Dent in DROP THE DEAD DONKEY. Rawle has also been seen in FORTUNES OF WAR (Sgt Ridley), *The Gift* (John Price), *The Life and Times of Henry Pratt* (Ezra), *Lord of Misrule* (Derek), FAITH IN THE FUTURE (Paul), *Microsoap* (Colin), *Neville's Island* (Neville), *I Saw You* (Frank), TAKE A GIRL LIKE YOU (Horace Charlton), *The Deputy* (Graham Hammond) and DOC MARTIN (Robert Fenn). Among his many guest appearances have been parts in CROWN COURT, VAN DER VALK, WILDE ALLIANCE, HAMMER HOUSE OF HORROR, DOCTOR WHO, BOON, THE BILL, CASUALTY, MINDER, WYCLIFFE, EASTENDERS, DALZIEL AND PASCOE, MIDSOMER MURDERS, P. D. JAMES, THE ROYAL, HEARTBEAT, WILLIAM AND MARY, MY DAD'S THE PRIME MINISTER, ULTIMATE FORCE, HOLBY CITY, SPOOKS, A TOUCH OF FROST and SEA OF SOULS. He also narrated the *Budgie, the Little Helicopter* cartoons and co-scripted *The Young Poisoner's Handbook*.

Raworth, Sophie

(1968–)

Born in Surrey and raised in Twickenham, Sophie Raworth became a BBC trainee after studying broadcast journalism, starting in local radio in Manchester, then working in Brussels and later as a producer/presenter on *Look North*, the regional news magazine from Leeds. She moved to London in 1997 to host BREAKFAST NEWS (later *Breakfast*) for five years, switching to the early-evening news bulletin in 2002. She has also fronted *Dream Lives* and the quiz show *Judgemental*, and provided reports for TOMORROW'S WORLD.

Ray, Robin

(Robin Olden; 1935–98)

London-born actor/presenter, first seen on TV in a 1956 play, *The Guv'nor*, and then alongside his father, comedian Ted Ray. He went on to appear in the comedy show *Dig This Rhubarb*, and then began to indulge his interest in the arts and, in particular, music and the cinema. Among his credits were CALL MY BLUFF (first chairman), FACE THE MUSIC (panellist) and *Film Buff of the Year* (questionmaster). Other panel games in which he featured included *The Movie Quiz* and *Cabbages and Kings*. Robin – one of the founders of radio station Classic fM – was elder brother of actor Andrew Ray and was married to former MAGPIE presenter Susan Stranks.

Ray, Ted

(Charles Olden; 1905–77)

Music hall comedian/violinist who came to television following success with *Ray's a Laugh* on the radio. His *Ted Ray Show* was popular in the 1950s, and he also compered SPOT THE TUNE on some occasions. In the 1970s he was back on the small screen as a regular panellist on the gag show *Jokers Wild* and the talent show NEW FACES. He was the father of actors Robin and Andrew Ray.

Rayner, Claire

OBE (1931–)

One of Britain's leading agony aunts, former nurse Claire Rayner is a familiar face on UK TV. She has answered problems and proffered advice on TV-am and in her own series, *Claire Rayner's Casebook*, as well as appearing as a guest on many magazine programmes. She is also a published novelist.

Ready, Steady, Go! ★★★

UK (Associated Rediffusion) Pop Music. ITV 1963–6

Presenters **Keith Fordyce, David Gell, Michael Aldred, Cathy McGowan**

Producers **Frances Hitching, Vicki Wickham**
Executive Producer **Elkan Allan**

Influential British pop-music show, a focal point of the beat boom.

'The Weekend Starts Here' was the slogan of this lively pop showcase that opened up each week to the sound of Manfred Mann's '5–4–3–2–1', and later the same band's 'Hubble Bubble Toil and Trouble'. Airing early on a Friday evening (in most parts of the country), the weekend really did begin here for many teenagers, particularly those outside London, for whom this was one of the few opportunities to savour the heady years of British beat. The kids took their lead from *RSG!* in dance, in fashion and, of course, in musical taste.

Technically advanced for its era, particularly in the innovative camerawork, *RSG!* enjoyed the patronage of nearly all the leading acts – from The Beatles and The Rolling Stones to Stevie Wonder and Little Richard – who seldom missed the chance to appear. But it also bravely introduced lesser-known artists, including obscure bands, some from across the Atlantic (who now remembers Glenda Collins and the Orchids, Van Dyke and the Bambies or Bobby Shafto?). Far more lively than the rather static TOP OF THE POPS, *RSG!* boasted a tiny studio, crammed full with excited youths enjoying a clublike atmosphere, nudging and pressing against the featured artists as they bopped to the music.

The hosts (at various times) were Keith Fordyce, David Gell, Michael Aldred and Cathy McGowan, a young discovery who quickly mastered the art of presenting TV pop. She had answered an advertisement calling for a 'typical teenager' to act as an adviser on the show, but she was soon pushed in front of the cameras. Her success lay in the fact that she was one of the fans; the viewers could identify with her as she fluffed her lines, grinned at inappropriate moments and panicked during interviews with celebrities. She was one of the teenagers, not a long-in-the-tooth broadcaster, and she soon became a style leader herself. When the programme switched to a larger studio and bands were obliged to perform live instead of miming, McGowan was kept on as solo presenter.

The series drew to a close just as the beat boom came to an end. The fact that it was axed at the height of its popularity has clearly helped maintain its respected status as a TV pop classic. Compilations were shown on Channel 4 in the 1980s, courtesy of drummer-turned-entrepreneur Dave Clark, who now owns the rights to the tapes.

Ready When You are Mr McGill ★★★

UK (Granada) Drama. ITV 1976

Joe McGill .... **Joe Black**
Phil Shaw .... **Jack Shepherd**
Don Harris .... **Stanley Lebor**
Kenneth .... **Fred Feast**
Terry .... **Mark Wing-Davy**
Jean .... **Eileen Davies**
Nancy McGill .... **Barbara Moore-Black**
Val .... **Diana Davies**
Gaffer .... **Joe Belcher**

Writer **Jack Rosenthal**
Producer **Michael Dunlop**

An ingenuous film extra ruins a TV play.

'I've never seen that young lady in my life before and I've lived here 50 years.' It's hard to believe that one sentence – just 16 words – in a play called *The Schoolteacher* could cause so much trouble. Joe McGill is a TV extra who thinks his big moment has arrived. He's been reciting his lines (sorry, line) in his sleep and insisting his wife test him on it. Dawn breaks and the action starts, but sadly all does not go to plan. It is a cold, wet day and director Phil Shaw is over-tired and in a filthy mood. The rest of the crew are not in the best spirits either. Director of photography Don Harris has just had his prized fishing rod stolen and wardrobe mistress Jean is in floods of tears at every turn. Mr McGill is on his mettle, however, and is word perfect through a series of technical glitches that ruin every take. Then tragedy strikes. On the one occasion when everything mechanical goes to plan, amnesia afflicts our hero and he fails to cut the mustard. Described by Frank Muir as 'the television industry's favourite play' (presumably for its self-parody), this instalment of Granada's *Red Letter Day* anthology reveals the agony and the ecstasy that lie behind a day's shooting, leaving it to viewers to find the funny side. Mike Newell directs and familiar faces among the supporting cast include CORONATION STREET stalwarts Teddy Turner and Jill Summers.

In 2005, ITV1 screened a remake of *Ready When You Are Mr McGill*, starring Tom Courtenay, Amanda Holden, Phil Davis, Tamsin Greig, Bill Nighy and Sally Phillips.

Real Lives ✱✱

UK (BBC) Documentary. BBC 1 1984–5

Executive Producers **Peter Pagnamenta, Edward Mirzoeff**

● ***A series of close inspections of how people live today.***
This documentary series looked at the lives of people from all parts of society, examining what made them tick. Among those featured were a defecting Russian violinist, drug-pushers, Los Angeles street-gang members, finalists in a 'True Romances' contest and a British army unit going back to Northern Ireland as civilians. One programme due for transmission in the second series caused a major stir. Entitled *At the Edge of the Union*, it focused on two individuals at opposite extremes in the Northern Ireland troubles. The two were Gregory Campbell and Martin McGuinness. The fact that McGuinness was said to have been an IRA supporter enraged the Government, which felt that terrorists should not have been given the oxygen of publicity. Home Secretary Leon Brittan intervened (without seeing the programme) and called for it to be withdrawn. This led to a dispute between the BBC's Board of Governors (who agreed with his sentiments) and the BBC Management (who wanted it to be screened). The programme was not transmitted and, in protest at what they viewed as interference in the BBC's independence, journalists from both BBC and ITN staged a one-day strike. With some changes, the programme was finally shown in October 1985, two months late.

Real McCoy, The ✱✱

UK (BBC) Comedy. BBC 2 1991–4; 1996

Curtis Walker, Ishmael Thomas, Llewella Gideon, Collette Johnson, Meera Syal, Robbie Gee, Perry Benson, Leo Chester, Felix Dexter, Kulvinder Ghir, Fraser Downie, Leon Black, Judith Jacob, Eddie Nestor

Producers **Charlie Hanson, Bill Wilson, Paulette Randall**

● ***Quick-fire humour from Britain's top black comics.***
This fast-moving sketch show provided much-needed exposure for Britain's black and Asian comedians. Fronted initially by lifelong friends Curtis and Ishmael (previously seen in the variety series *Paramount City*), plus Llewella Gideon and Collette Johnson, *The Real McCoy* soon expanded to accommodate a whole troupe of performers, plus the Danserious dancers, guest comics from the black entertainment circuit and black musicians. Sports stars like Ian Wright, Lennox Lewis, John Barnes and Judy Simpson also dropped by. One regular sketch featured the stars of the *Rub-a-Dub* pub soap opera; other skits focused on the black and Asian culture or an ethnic view of life in Britain, paving the way for the higher-profile GOODNESS GRACIOUS ME (two stars of which, Meera Syal and Kulvinder Ghir, were part of *The Real McCoy* team). Some material was derived from Step Forward, a two-day workshop organized by Lenny Henry in 1990 to encourage black and Asian comedy writers.

Real Women ✱✱✱

UK (BBC) Drama. BBC 1 1998–9

Mandy .... **Pauline Quirke**
Susie .... **Michelle Collins**
Karen .... **Lesley Manville**
Janet .... **Gwyneth Strong**
Anna .... **Frances Barber**
Chris .... **Jane Gurnett**
Steve .... **Gary Webster**
Pete .... **Richard Graham**
Barry .... **Peter-Hugo Daly**
Doreen .... **Toni Palmer**
Bobby .... **Tony Selby**
Jonathan Bell .... **Mark Moraghan**
Lyndsay .... **Debbie Arnold**
Jo .... **Con O'Neil**
Frank .... **Brian Protheroe**
Richard Scholes .... **Peter Lindford**
Barrett .... **Aaron White**
Derek Johnson .... **Dave Hill**
Michael .... **Ray Stevenson**
Jackie .... **Juliet Cowan**

Writer **Susan Oudot**
Executive Producer **Jane Tranter**
Producer **Debbie Shewell**

● ***A wedding brings old schoolfriends together and exposes crises in their personal lives.***
Five London women in their late thirties are the focus of this earthy three-part drama, written by Susan Oudot and based on her own novel of the same title. At the centre of the action is flighty Susie, about to get married to Jo but clearly having second thoughts. The four former schoolfriends who join her for the hen night begin with Mandy, a downtrodden family woman whose husband, Pete, and sons never show her any appreciation. She has now embarked on an affair with estate agent Jonathan. Then there is Janet, a bank clerk who is desperate to have her own child, but whose efforts with husband Steve come to nothing; lonely-heart Anna, a features writer who has moved into more sophisticated circles since leaving school and is now recovering from a broken relationship; and Karen, a teacher, who is scared to introduce her lesbian lover, Chris, to the rest of the gang. Also seen is Susie's sister, Lyndsay, married with four kids.

From the first drunken night out, through the eve of the wedding to the wedding day itself, secrets start to leak out and the individual problems facing the women begin to unfold. The drama resumes in a second four-part series – based on the sequel novel, *All That I Am* – in 1999. Set 18 months further on, with Susie about to give birth, it picks up the girls' stories as they head for the landmark age of 40.

Rebecca ✱✱✱

UK (BBC) Drama. BBC 2 1979
DVD: Granada Ventures (1997 version)

Mrs de Winter .... **Joanna David**
Maxim de Winter .... **Jeremy Brett**
Mrs Danvers .... **Anna Massey**
Beatrice .... **Vivian Pickles**
Jack Favell .... **Julian Holloway**
Frank Crawley .... **Terrence Hardiman**
Col. Julyan .... **Robert Fleming**

Writer **Hugh Whitemore**
Producer **Richard Beynon**

● ***A widower's second wife is haunted by memories of his late spouse.***

This four-part adaptation of Daphne du Maurier's famous 1938 novel was directed by Simon Langton. A young orphan girl feels out of place in trendy Monte Carlo until she is befriended by the wealthy but enigmatic Maxim de Winter. They marry and return to Maxim's family home, Manderley, which he shared with his late wife, Rebecca. Living up to Rebecca's heritage is difficult, however, especially as sinister housekeeper Mrs Danvers is keen to keep her memory alive. But did Rebecca die innocently, or was she murdered? And what future does the new Mrs de Winter have at Manderley? An early adaptation of the story so notably filmed by Alfred Hitchcock in 1940 came in a single drama in 1947 (BBC: Dorothy Gordon as Mrs de Winter, Michael Hordern as Maxim, Dorothy Black as Mrs Danvers). The most recent dramatization was made in two parts by Carlton for ITV in 1997 (Emilia Fox as Mrs de Winter, Charles Dance as Maxim, Diana Rigg as Mrs Danvers).

Rebus ★★★

UK (Scottish/Clerkenwell Films) Detective Drama. ITV 2001; 2006–
DVD: Universal

DI John Rebus .... **John Hannah**
Ken Stott
DI Jack Morton .... **Ewan Stewart**
DCI Gill Templar .... **Sara Stewart**
Jennifer Black
DS McCaskill .... **Stuart Hepburn**
DS Siobhan Clarke .... **Gayanne Potter**
Claire Price
DI Ormond .... **Lewis Howden**
Janice Smee .... **Michelle Fairley**

Writers **Stuart Hepburn, Ben Brown, Philip Palmer, Mark Greig, Daniel Boyle**
Producers **Murray Ferguson, Alan J. Wands**

Sombre detective work in the Scottish capital.

John Rebus is a detective inspector working in Edinburgh. A one-time alcoholic, he's seen it all and uses his experience to his advantage by bending the rules on a regular basis. His investigations lead him into all manner of seedy situations, dealing with gangsters, paedophiles, drug pushers and para-military groups, while his private life revolves around his daughter, Sammy, and a former girlfriend, Janice, who is now married to someone else. The series of three films (made by star John Hannah's own production company, Clerkenwell Films) followed a pilot in 2000, although the last of the three was not screened with the earlier two. It eventually was given an airing as the main feature on ITV 3's opening night in 2004. Rebus returned in 2006, but with Ken Stott replacing John Hannah in the lead role, and Jennifer Black and Claire Price taking over from Sara Stewart and Gayanne Potter as his colleagues Gill Templer and Siobhan Clarke. The frowning Scottish cop was originally created in novels by Ian Rankin.

Reckless ★★

UK (Granada) Drama. ITV 1997–8
DVD: WGBH Boston (Region 1 only)

Owen Springer .... **Robson Green**
Anna Fairley .... **Francesca Annis**
Richard Crane .... **Michael Kitchen**
Arnold Springer .... **David Bradley**
Vivien Reid .... **Daniela Nardini**
Dr Danny Glassman .... **Julian Rhind-Tutt**
Dr John McGinley .... **Conor Mullen**
Dr Pall .... **David Boyce**
Irma .... **Kathryn Hunt**
Myrtle Fairley .... **Margery Mason**
Phyllis .... **Kathryn Pogson**

Writer **Paul Abbott**
Producer **Sita Williams**

A young doctor falls in love with his boss's wife – an older woman.

Owen Springer is a young, up-and-coming surgeon who decides to return to his native Manchester to care for his elderly, sick father. He applies for a job at a local hospital and is interviewed by management consultant Anna Fairley: she is unimpressed with his overconfidence; he is very impressed with her looks. Springer starts work but is immediately distracted by the presence of Anna and the mysteries she brings as a more mature woman. He spots a chink in her assertive armour and his persistence begins to pay off. Unfortunately, Anna's snooty husband, Richard Crane, is Springer's boss, so the potential for disaster is huge. When Crane himself is caught playing away, it is decision time for all three and things get extremely messy. After a six-part series in 1997, *Reckless: the Sequel*, a one-off, feature-length drama was broadcast in 1998, following the wounded party's vindictive attempts at revenge.

Record Breakers ★★

UK (BBC) Children's Entertainment. BBC 1 1972–1983; 1985–2001

Presenters **Roy Castle, Ross McWhirter, Norris McWhirter, Dilys Morgan, Fiona Kennedy, Julian Farino, Cheryl Baker, Ron Reagan Jr, Kriss Akabusi, Mark Curry, Dan Roland, Linford Christie, Jez Edwards, Kate Sanderson, Sally Gray, Fearne Cotton, Shovell**

Producers **Alan Russell, Eric Rowan, Greg Childs**

***The tallest, the shortest, the latest and the greatest: TV's answer to the* Guinness Book of Records.**

For 30 years *Record Breakers* showcased some of the world's wackiest record-setters and even claimed a few firsts of its own, by arranging record-breaking attempts in the studio (over 300). Its host, until his untimely death in 1994, was Roy Castle, a man who was a record-breaker on many occasions in his own right. In the very first programme he created the world's biggest one-man band, with over 40 instruments at his disposal. He also set records for the world's fastest tap-dance (24 beats a second) and for wing-walking across the Channel, not to mention riding on top of a 39-man motorcycle pyramid and leaping from the top of the Blackpool Tower. For such achievements, as he sang in the theme song, 'You need dedication'. The *Guinness Book of Records* founders, Norris and the late Ross McWhirter, assisted Roy in the early days, and Norris has continued to make appearances from time to time. Cheryl Baker was Castle's partner from 1987 and then she remained in charge alongside ex-athlete Kriss Akabusi, former BLUE PETER man Mark Curry and, for two seasons, Ron Reagan Jr (son of the former US President). Baker and Akabusi also presented *Record Breakers Gold* (1997–8), a compilation series of greatest moments. The programme was revamped in 1998 and retitled *Linford's Record Breakers*, when athlete

Linford Christie took control, the original name returning in 2001.

Red Cap ✶✶

UK (Stormy Pictures/BBC) Drama. BBC 1 2003–4

Sgt Josephine 'Jo' McDonagh	**Tamzin Outhwaite**
Sgt Major Kenneth Burns	**Douglas Hodge**
Staff Sgt Philip Roper	**James Thornton**
Sgt Bruce Hornsby	**Gordon Kennedy**
Lt. Giles Vicary	**Blake Ritson**
Sgt Sam Perkins	**Ian Burfield**
Capt. Gavin Howard	**Peter Guinness**
Det. Thomas Strauss	**Joachim Raaf**
Staff Sgt. Neve Kirland	**Raquel Cassidy**
Cpl. Annie Ogden	**Maggie Lloyd-Williams**
Sgt. Major Steve Forney	**William Beck**
Staff Sgt. Harriet Frost	**Poppy Miller**
Saskia Roper	**Tracy Whitwell**

Creator **Patrick Harbinson**
Producer **Sarah Wilson**

A maverick military police woman gets results in spite of internal prejudice and suspicion.
Sgt Jo McDonagh is a member of the Special Investigation Branch (SIB) of the Royal Military Police, or 'Red Caps' (the colour of the berets they wear). She's been transferred here from the Close Protection Unit, following the death of a colleague when her gun jammed at the wrong moment. She now works overtime in the armoury, honing her pistol skills. McDonagh – or McDonut, as her new colleagues dub her – is a rather intense, very determined detective, belying her fragile blond looks with steely inner strength and agile fighting skills. (Her inspiration for joining the army, she claims, was Linda Hamilton in the *Terminator* movies.) Nevertheless, she finds it hard to convince her peers that she is up to the job. Most of the men alongside her either resent her presence or fancy their chances with her. Her boss, Burns, is hard and cynical, but her partner, Hornsby, is more understanding. She, meanwhile, takes a shine to fellow sergeant Philip Roper, who, unfortunately, is still married. Based in the Hohnebruck barracks in Germany, Jo and her colleagues investigate crimes involving military personnel, often stumbling into areas of disputed authority with the local police force. Max is her spaniel dog.

Creator Patrick Harbinson, who also penned most of the episodes and has worked on US series such as ER and LAW & ORDER: *Special Victims Unit*, used his own army experience to add authenticity to the drama. Two series followed a pilot episode screened at the end of 2001.

Red Dwarf ✶✶✶

UK (Paul Jackson/Grant Naylor/BBC) Situation Comedy. BBC 2 1988–9; 1991–3; 1997; 1999
DVD: BBC

Arnold J. Rimmer, BSc, SSC	**Chris Barrie**
Dave Lister	**Craig Charles**
Cat	**Danny John-Jules**
Holly	**Norman Lovett**
	Hattie Hayridge
Kryten	**David Ross**
	Robert Llewellyn
Christine/Kristine Kochanski	**Clare/C. P. Grogan**
	Chloë Annett
Capt. Hollister	**Mac McDonald**

Creators **Rob Grant, Doug Naylor**
Executive Producers **Paul Jackson, Rob Grant, Doug Naylor**
Producers **Ed Bye, Hilary Bevan Jones, Justin Judd**

Space-age sitcom featuring the last survivor on a spaceship and his annoying non-human companions.
When Technician Third-Class Dave Lister is sentenced to a period in suspended animation (or 'stasis'), some time in the 24th century, for smuggling a pregnant cat aboard his spaceship, little does he know that he will wake up three million years later and be the sole survivor of a radiation leak. Resigned to roaming the cosmos in the five-mile-long, three-mile-wide mining ship *Red Dwarf*, Lister discovers that all 168 other crew members have died and his only companions are Holly, the ship's computer, Cat, a hybrid life-form evolved from his pet, and a hologram of his obnoxious former roommate and supervisor, Arnold J. (Judas) Rimmer.

While the deadpan Holly (seen only as a face on a TV screen) is a bit of a practical joker (for a computer), the overzealous Rimmer is devoid of humour and is the exact opposite of Lister in every way. Their incompatibility is central to the series. Desperately ambitious, Rimmer, sadly, is also a coward and unfailingly inept (it was his error that led to the fatal radiation leak). Being a hologram, he can't touch anything and relies on Holly for his existence and wellbeing. Lister, on the other hand, whiles away his time eating curry, watching videos, slagging off 'smegging' Rimmer and lounging on his bunk, perhaps dreaming of Christine Kochanski, another dead crewmate (played initially in flashbacks by one-time Altered Images singer Clare Grogan but then made flesh by Chloë Annett). However, it is Cat who proves to be the most intriguing character. Portrayed as a narcissistic, black dude in snappy dress, Cat looks human (except for his fangs and six nipples) but possesses feline instincts. Lining his stomach and looking good are paramount. He toys with a roast chicken as a cat would a bird, takes 'cat naps', licks his laundry clean and sprays perfume from an aerosol to mark out his territory.

In later seasons, a new Holly is introduced, with comedian Hattie Hayridge replacing Norman Lovett as the dry, lugubrious computer (Lovett returned in the seventh series), and an android, Kryten, is added to the cast. Discovered working as a manservant to three human girls (who had long since perished), the angular robot temporarily joins *Red Dwarf* in the second series; but, with a new actor in the role, he takes up permanent residence the following year. The only other regular characters are a couple of silent robot helpers called scutters and a few talking appliances, like an outspoken toaster. However, by dipping into parallel universes, or whizzing forward to the future or back to the past, there is no shortage of new situations for the mismatched crew to encounter. When the mining ship is somehow stolen, the team are stranded for a while in space in the pokey *Starbug* shuttle.

More than three years separated series six and seven and Chris Barrie committed to only part of that seventh series but, contrary to fans' fears, *Red Dwarf* did return in 1997, with an eighth series following in 1999. In the latter, the original *Red Dwarf* was re-created by nanobots, complete with real human crew.

Red Dwarf, though slow to pick up audiences, rapidly gained cult status. Each series' title included a number, with the second series called Red Dwarf II, etc. Its creators, Rob Grant and Doug Naylor, had previously worked with Chris Barrie on

SPITTING IMAGE. Grant, however, was not involved after Red Dwarf VI.

Redcap **

UK (ABC) Police Drama. ITV 1964–6
DVD: Network

Sgt John Mann .... **John Thaw**

Creator **Jack Bell**
Producer **John Bryce**

Investigations into crime in the armed forces, conducted by a tough, no-nonsense military policeman.

John Mann is a sergeant in the Special Investigation Branch of the Royal Military Police – the 'Redcaps' – and a thorough one at that. His forceful, demanding investigations root out army crooks all over the world, from Malaya and Borneo to Aden and Cyprus; and, although he reserves a softer side of his character for those in genuine distress, his fuse is short and regularly lit. The series provided good training for John Thaw, with John Mann's bluster carried through to Jack Regan in THE SWEENEY and his sullen solitude resurfacing in INSPECTOR MORSE.

In 2001 Tamzin Outhwaite starred as Sgt Jo McDonagh in the pilot episode of a new series about military police also called RED CAP. A full series followed in 2003.

Redgrave, Jemma

(Jemima Redgrave; 1965–)

British actress, the daughter of Corin Redgrave. Her major TV credits have included *The Real Charlotte* (Pamela), THE BUDDHA OF SUBURBIA (Eleanor), BRAMWELL (Eleanor Bramwell), MOSLEY (Cynthia Curzon/Mosley), BLUE MURDER (Gale Francombe), *Cry Wolf* (Dr Wolf), *Fish* (Joanna Morgan), JUDGE JOHN DEED (Francesca Rochester), *The Swap* (Jen Forrester), *Amnesia* (Jenny Dean), *The Grid* (Emily Tuthill), TOM BROWN'S SCHOOLDAYS (Mary Arnold), *Like Father, Like Son* (Dee Stanton) and *Cold Blood* (Eve Granger). She has also made guest appearances in JUDGE JOHN DEED, MY FAMILY, THE INSPECTOR LYNLEY MYSTERIES and LEWIS.

Rediffusion

See *Associated-Rediffusion.*

Redman, Amanda

(1959–)

Brighton-born actress seen in a number of high-profile roles, in series such as THE MEN'S ROOM (Sally), *Streets Apart* (Sylvia), EL C.I.D. (Rosie Bromley), *Body and Soul* (Lynn Gibson), DEMOB (Janet Deasey), DANGERFIELD (Dr Joanna Stevens), *Beck* (title role), *Close Relations* (Prudence), THE RUTH RENDELL MYSTERIES (Susan Townsend), *The Blonde Bombshell* (Diana Dors), HOPE AND GLORY (Debbie Bryan), AT HOME WITH THE BRAITHWAITES (Alison Braithwaite), NEW TRICKS (Sandra Pullman) and *Mike Bassett: Manager* (Karine Bassett). Other credits have come in TALES OF THE UNEXPECTED, *Richard's Things*, BERGERAC, *To Have and to Hold*, SPENDER, *Screen Two's The Lorelei, The Sight* (DS Price), *Suspicion* (Carol Finnegan), *Teen Species* and *Blame the Parents* (the last two both as narrator). Redman is also principal of a theatre school in Ealing. She was once married to actor Robert Glenister.

Redmond, Phil

(1949–)

Liverpudlian writer whose early efforts included episodes of *Doctor in Charge, Doctor at Sea* (see DOCTOR IN THE HOUSE), THE KIDS FROM 47A, POTTER'S PICTURE PALACE and THE SQUIRRELS. In 1976 he changed direction and took an idea for a realistic schooldays programme to the BBC. The idea was commissioned and GRANGE HILL was born. Redmond followed this up with *Going Out*, a programme about struggling school-leavers, for Southern Television and then began work on a major project for the BBC. Entitled *County Hall*, it aimed to dramatize the workings of a major local authority but ran for only one series. Somewhat disillusioned, Redmond moved into the independent sector. He set up Mersey Television and sold an idea for a vibrant, down-to-earth soap opera to Channel 4. As BROOKSIDE, it aired on the station's first night and has proved to be one of its major successes. Among Redmond's other work has been the police series WATERFRONT BEAT and the teen soap HOLLYOAKS. He has also been a consultant for EMMERDALE (the plane crash was his idea) and returned to *Grange Hill* as executive producer in 2003. Mersey Television also unsuccessfully challenged Granada for the ITV North-West England franchise in 1991.

Redmond, Siobhan

(1959–)

Scottish actress, probably best known for her role as Det. Sgt Maureen Connell in BETWEEN THE LINES. Earlier, Redmond had appeared in the Granada comedy ALFRESCO, before joining Don Henderson in BULMAN, playing his sidekick, Lucy McGinty. Redmond was also seen in TAGGART, *Casting Off* (Gillian), CASUALTY, *The Advocates* (Janie Naismith), THE BILL, THE HIGH LIFE (air stewardess Shona Spurtle), *Screen One's Deacon Brodie* (Jean Brodie), *Screen Two's Nervous Energy* (Joyce), the Alexei Sayle comedy *Sorry about Last Night* (Julie Cordova), *In the Red* (Ms Sin), WOKENWELL (Cheryl Cappler) and *Every Woman Knows a Secret* (Jess Arrowsmith). More recently she has played Janice Taylor in HOLBY CITY and Sharon in THE SMOKING ROOM, with guest appearances in SEA OF SOULS, *The Afternoon Play* and *The Catherine Tate Show*, plus voice credits for *Shoebox Zoo*.

Reeves, George

(George Brewer; 1914–59)

TV's first SUPERMAN, George Reeves at one time looked to have a promising film career ahead of him. He appeared in *Gone with the Wind* in 1939, but then things gradually headed downhill. Turning to television, he landed the role which was, at last, to make him a household name, that of the 'Man of Steel' in *The Adventures of Superman*, which began in the USA in 1951. He played Superman for six years, suffering cruelly from typecasting when it ended. Two years later he was found shot dead, but the official suicide verdict has been challenged by those close to him.

Reeves, Vic

(Jim Moir; 1959–)

North-eastern comedian, screen partner of Bob Mortimer. Both having failed as punk rockers, Reeves was managing an alternative comedy venue in London where Mortimer, a solicitor, was a regular heckler. Joining forces, they took the *Vic Reeves Big Night Out* act on a tour of universities. It then secured its own slot on Channel 4 in 1990, where it gained a cult following for its absurd humour, catchphrases like 'You wouldn't let it lie' and novel characters like The Man with the Stick, The Ponderers, Les, and Wavy Davy. Subsequently the duo moved to the BBC with a similarly off-beat show entitled *The Smell of Reeves and Mortimer* and new characters such as The Bra Men and a chance to visit pop group Slade at home. A departure from their 'norm' was the spoof celebrity quiz SHOOTING STARS, and they also devised a one-off showcase for team captain Ulrika Jonsson. The next outings for their anarchic, but increasingly slapstick, humour (large frying pans in the face, etc.) were *Bang, Bang, It's Reeves and Mortimer* and a surreal Saturday teatime game show called *Families at War*. The pair were also seen in the single comedies *The Weekenders* and *The Honeymoon's Over*. From 2000 they starred in the revamp of the detective caper RANDALL AND HOPKIRK (DECEASED) and returned to comedy with *Vic and Bob in Catterick* (as brothers Chris and Carl, respectively) and the *Monkey Trousers* sketch show. Reeves also appeared as Eluard in the comedy drama *Surrealissimo* and presented *Vic Reeves's Rogues Gallery* for the Discovery Channel, while Bob has hosted the comedy quiz 29 MINUTES OF FAME.

Regiment, The ✶✶

UK (BBC) Drama. BBC 1 1972–3

Lt./Capt. Richard Gaunt	**Christopher Cazenove**
Lt. Col. Gaunt-Seymour	**Richard Wordsworth**
Lt. James Willoughby	**John Hallam**
Hon. Alice Gaunt	**Wendy Williams**
Charlotte Gaunt	**Wendy Allnutt**
Capt./Major Rupert Saunders	**Bernard Brown**
Dorothy Saunders	**Maria Aitken**
Capt./Major Alfred Slingsby	**Denis Lill**
Lt./Capt. Jeffrey Sissons	**Roy Herrick**
RSM William Bright	**Michael Brennan**
Col. Cranleigh-Osborne	**Frederick Treves**
Mrs Cranleigh-Osborne	**Virginia Balfour**
Dr Mary Mitcheson/Gaunt	**Penelope Lee**
Cpl. Ernest Bright	**James Bate**
Maud Slingsby	**Shirley Dixon**
Pte. Hodge	**John Hallett**
Lt. Henry Percival	**Michael Elwyn**

Creators **Jack Gerson, Nick McCarty**
Producers **Royston Morley, Terence Dudley**

● ***The fortunes of an army regiment as seen through the eyes of two families.***

The Regiment started out as a single play (part of the DRAMA PLAYHOUSE collection in 1970), in which Richard Hurndall starred as Col. Frederick Gaunt, a regimental commander-in-chief who criticizes the army and pays a heavy social price for his actions. The series that followed focuses on the years 1895–1904 and the events that unfold around the Cotswold Regiment. With the Boer War in the first series and then the days of the Raj in India in the second as backdrops, the series particularly looks at members of two families, the Gaunts and the Brights, and their varied positions in the greater scheme of things. To the fore is Lt. Richard Grant, a man who would much rather be a writer than a soldier.

Reid, Anne

(1935–)

To more mature viewers, Newcastle-born Anne Reid is still Valerie Barlow, first wife of CORONATION STREET's Ken. Younger viewers recognize her more as the plain-speaking Jean in DINNERLADIES, but in between – despite time off to raise her son – she comfortably installed herself as a stalwart of British television comedy and drama. Among her other credits have been in *Time is the Enemy* (Patience Mee), *Victoria Wood*, RICH TEA AND SYMPATHY (Sally), THE RUTH RENDELL MYSTERIES, *Pat and Margaret* (Maeve), *Firm Friends* (Wendy Holmes), ROUGHNECKS (Renie), *Paul Merton in Galton & Simpson's . . .*, and SPARK (Mrs Rudge). Anne was also seen in CATHERINE COOKSON's *The Wingless Bird* (Alice Conway), *Lost for Words* (Gloria), PEAK PRACTICE (Rita Barratt), DALZIEL AND PASCOE (Dalziel's sister, Harriet Clifford), *The Booze Cruise* (Grace), *The Young Visiters* (Angelique Monticue), LIFE BEGINS (Brenda Thornhill) and BLEAK HOUSE (Mrs Rouncewell). She also provided the voice of Wendoline in WALLACE & GROMIT's *A Close Shave* and has taken guest parts in series such as THE ADVENTURES OF ROBIN HOOD, BOON, DOCTOR WHO, HEARTBEAT, *Rik Mayall Presents*, MIDSOMER MURDERS and ROSE AND MALONEY.

Reid, Beryl

OBE (1920–96)

British actress/comedienne who enjoyed her own series (*The Beryl Reid Show* and *Beryl Reid*), plus a host of guest parts. Her earliest credits were with Vic Wise in the comedy *Vic's Grill* and as Arethusa Wilderspin in a sitcom called *The Most Likely Girl* in 1957. She then starred as Bessie Briggs in *Bold as Brass*, played Rene Jelliot and Marigold Alcock in the sitcoms *Wink to Me Only* and *Alcock and Gander*, respectively, took the parts of Helen Magee in LATE STARTER and Mrs Knox in THE IRISH RM, and appeared as Grandma in THE SECRET DIARY OF ADRIAN MOLE. Her cameo role as Connie Sachs in TINKER, TAILOR, SOLDIER, SPY won her a BAFTA award, and she went on to act in the follow-up, SMILEY'S PEOPLE. Reid was also seen in *A-Z*, THE GOOD OLD DAYS, MINDER, DOCTOR WHO, *The Beiderbecke Tapes* (see THE BEIDERBECKE TAPES), THE COMIC STRIP PRESENTS, CRACKER and A PERFECT SPY, among numerous other series spanning four decades.

Reid, Mike

(1940–)

Cockney comedian and actor, coming to the fore in THE COMEDIANS with his 'Terr-i-fic' catchphrase and aggressive style of joke-telling. He moved into children's TV to 'manage' the hectic game show RUNAROUND and later played Arthur Mullard's brother, Benny Briggs, in YUS MY DEAR, as well as making a guest appearance in MINDER and featuring in BIG DEAL. More recently, he has become widely known as Frank Butcher in EASTENDERS. Reid has also hosted his own variety series, *Mike Reid's Mates and Music* and *Entertainment Express*, plus *Mike Reid's Late Home Video Show*.

Reilly – Ace of Spies ★★★

UK (Euston Films/Thames) Spy Drama. ITV 1983
DVD: Acorn Media

Sidney Reilly .... **Sam Neill**
Major Fothergill .... **Peter Egan**
Bruce Lockhart .... **Ian Charleson**
Cummings .... **Norman Rodway**
Dzerzhinsky .... **Tom Bell**
Stalin .... **David Burke**
Lenin .... **Kenneth Cranham**
Basil Zaharov .... **Leo McKern**
Margaret Thomas/Reilly .... **Jeananne Crowley**
Insp. Tsientsin .... **David Suchet**
Baldwin .... **Donald Morley**
Count Massino .... **John Castle**

Writer **Troy Kennedy Martin**
Executive Producer **Verity Lambert**
Producer **Chris Burt**

Dramatization of the life of one of Britain's first secret agents.

In early Revolutionary Russia, Sidney Reilly, born in Odessa and raised by an aristocratic Russian family, operated as a British agent, aiming to topple the Bolshevik regime and install a new, British-approved government with himself at its head. His attempt failed, however, and Reilly was executed at the hands of the Supreme Soviet Revolutionary Tribunal.

This lavish 12-part drama, which begins in 1901, is based on the biography of the real Reilly by Robin Bruce Lockhart. Although the character is artistically spiced up for TV, Reilly was himself a colourful and intriguing personality: suave, cool and daring, with a keen eye for the ladies. The series' acclaimed, sweeping theme music was written by Harry Rabinowitz.

Reith, Lord John

(1889–1971)

Lord Reith was effectively the BBC's founding father. Born in Scotland, Reith had served in World War I and had managed a large engineering works in Coatbridge before being appointed to the job of General Manager of the newly inaugurated British Broadcasting Company in 1922. (While this may seem a surprising background, it has to be considered that there were few people at the time with experience of broadcasting in any form.) In 1927 he became what was by then the British Broadcasting Corporation's first Director-General and was knighted the same year. He left the Corporation in 1938 to become Chairman of Imperial Airways and later a government minister during the war, having set the course of public-service broadcasting the BBC was to follow successfully for decades. Reith's view of broadcasting was as more than mere entertainment for the masses. He insisted that the new media of radio and television also contributed to the intellectual and moral fabric of society – the mission was to inform and educate as well as to entertain. He was made a baron in 1940 and, in his honour, the BBC founded the prestigious annual Reith Lectures in 1948.

Relative Strangers

See *Holding the Fort*.

Remington Steele ★★★

US (MTM) Detective Drama. BBC 1/Channel 4 1983–4/1986–7
(US: NBC 1982–7)
DVD: Fox (Region 1 only)

Remington Steele .... **Pierce Brosnan**
Laura Holt .... **Stephanie Zimbalist**
Murphy Michaels .... **James Read**
Bernice Foxe .... **Janet De May**
Mildred Krebs .... **Doris Roberts**

Creators **Michael Gleason, Robert Butler**
Executive Producers **Michael Gleason, Gareth Davies**
Producers **Glenn Gordon Caron, Lee Zlotoff**

An ambitious blonde opens a detective agency, names it after a man and then finds someone to play the part.

When Laura Holt sets up the Laura Holt Investigations detective agency, she finds work hard to come by. The problem is that no one seems to trust a female detective. So she creates an imaginary male boss for herself, renaming the company Remington Steele Investigations. At last the business begins to pay. Although it is easy at first to make excuses for her absent chief, Laura soon realizes that there would have to be a real Remington Steele to keep the customers happy. As chance would have it, a suitable candidate conveniently turns up on her doorstep. He is actually a con-man, trying to get his hands on some jewels Laura is protecting. But the couple hit it off from the start. He is suave, handsome and just the job, so they agree that he should become Remington Steele, and he joins the agency as a partner.

Nothing much is ever revealed about this dark, handsome stranger of Irish descent, least of all his real name. There are occasional hints about his murky past, but he develops into a more than useful detective and the business booms. His encyclopaedic knowledge of classic Hollywood movies proves strangely handy, enabling him to solve cases by re-creating memorable scenes from films like *The Third Man, Casablanca* and *Key Largo*. He and Laura flirt with each other, though it takes some time for a full-blown affair to take off, and even then it is not properly consummated until the final season. The romantic tension between the duo helps give the show some buzz, and their sparkling repartee introduces a comic dimension to the plot, but it is never at the same level witnessed later in MOONLIGHTING (created by one of *Remington Steele*'s producers, Glenn Gordon Caron).

Also seen are Murphy Michaels, Laura's first partner, who leaves to form his own agency, and secretary Bernice Foxe, who is replaced by former tax inspector Mildred Krebs. All episodes have titles containing 'Steele' puns, such as *Steele Crazy after All These Years, Thou Shalt Not Steele* and *You're Steele the One for Me*.

Star Stephanie Zimbalist was the daughter of THE FBI and 77 SUNSET STRIP star Efrem Zimbalist Jr, who guest-starred in one episode. Although Pierce Brosnan became a Hollywood name as a result of this series, he also found it to be an impediment to future success. It was an open secret that his name had been pencilled in as the next James Bond when Roger Moore retired, but because of his contractual commitments to *Remington Steele* the part was given to Timothy Dalton. When Dalton eventually quit the Bond role in 1994, Brosnan was free and promptly signed up as 007.

Ren & Stimpy Show, The ✱✱

US (Spümcø/Carbunkle) Cartoon. BBC 2 1994–7 (US: Nickelodeon 1991–5)
DVD: Paramount (Region 1 only)

Ren Hoek	**John Kricfalusi**
	Billy West
	Bob Camp
Stimpson J. ('Stimpy') Cat	**Billy West**

Creator **John Kricfalusi**

● ***The base adventures of an angry dog and a laid-back cat.***
One of those programmes ostensibly aimed at children but quickly a hit with their parents, *Ren & Stimpy* helped take the cartoon caper into a new dimension. Ren is a deranged chihuahua dog with bloodshot eyes and Stimpy is his dopey feline buddy; together they plumb the depths of lavatorial humour, spoofing fairy tales, legends and just generally going about their violent, scatalogical everyday business. 'You eee-diot!' became an American catchphrase after Ren's constant yell of rage. The departure of the show's creator, John Kricfalusi (also original voice of Ren), signalled the beginning of the end, as network executives pursued a less controversial image for the show. However, there are reports that Kricfalusi may produce a new series in the future. *Ren & Stimpy* aired first in the UK on Sky One, before transferring to BBC 2.

Renaldo, Duncan

(Renaldo Duncan; 1904–80)

American actor, busy in the 1930s and 1940s in a variety of film roles, including that of THE CISCO KID, a part that he brought to television in 1950. As the Western rogue with the heart of gold, he became one of TV's earliest stars.

Rentaghost ✱✱

UK (BBC) Children's Comedy. BBC 1 1976–8; 1980–4
DVD: Network

Timothy Claypole	**Michael Staniforth**
Mr Harold Meaker	**Edward Brayshaw**
Fred Mumford	**Anthony Jackson**
Hubert Davenport	**Michael Darbyshire**
Mr Mumford	**John Dawson**
Mrs Mumford	**Betty Alberge**
Mrs Ethel Meaker	**Ann Emery**
Catastrophe Kate	**Jana Sheldon**
Adam Painting	**Christopher Biggins**
Hazel the McWitch	**Molly Weir**
Tamara Novek	**Lynda Marchal**
Rose Perkins	**Hal Dyer**
Arthur Perkins	**Jeffrey Segal**
Nadia Popov	**Sue Nicholls**
Queen Matilda	**Paddie O'Neill**
Susie Starlight	**Aimi Macdonald**
Bernie St John	**Vincent White**
Dobbin	**William Perry and Roland A. Wollens**

Creator/Writer **Bob Block**
Producers **Paul Ciani, Jeremy Swan**

● ***A trio of hapless ghosts try to help those still living, with disastrous consequences.***

Recently deceased Fred Mumford is finding it hard coming to terms with being a ghost, but helping him adjust to the afterlife are Victorian spectre Hubert Davenport and mischievous medieval jester Timothy Claypole. Their earthly associates include their landlord, Mr Meaker, and Fred's middle-aged mum and dad. The ghosts decide to make themselves useful by setting up the Rentaghost agency, through which they can be hired, daily or weekly, to tackle all sorts of 20th-century activities, like running a restaurant, becoming newspaper reporters or working as security guards at a department store. The chaos they bring is reported via TV news bulletins.

Later additions to the cast include a wife for Mr Meaker (who becomes the ghosts' agent); constantly bemused new neighbours Rose and Arthur Perkins (after the Meakers move by magic carpet to a new home); department store manager Adam Painting; and assorted new ghosts. These include Hazel the McWitch, American Catastrophe Kate, nanny Tamara Novek (played by future screenwriter Lynda La Plante under her stage name of Lynda Marchal), and Tamara's scatty Eastern European replacement, Nadia Popov (who sneezes whenever she's near flowers). Adding to the confusion, there are also fairy godmother Susie Starlight, an ex-actress charlady for the Perkinses, Dobbin, a pantomime horse, and Bernie St John, a dragon that lives in the cellar. Star Michael Staniforth also sang the programme's theme song. A Christmas special in 1978 was entitled RentaSanta.

Renwick, David

(1951–)

British comedy writer, for many years in partnership with Andrew Marshall (see Marshall's entry for joint work). Renwick, without Marshall, provided gags for THE TWO RONNIES, Mike Yarwood, Little and Large, Dick Emery, Janet Brown and Les Dawson earlier in his career, and since going solo he has enjoyed his greatest success through ONE FOOT IN THE GRAVE, JONATHAN CREEK and LOVE SOUP. He has also written for AGATHA CHRISTIE'S POIROT.

Repeat

The second or subsequent showing of a TV programme, usually to fill gaps in the schedule, to cover holiday periods (when low audiences do not merit new productions) or, occasionally and increasingly, because the quality of the original warrants another screening. The new interest in classic television has made repeats (once the bane of viewers' lives, or at least claimed to be) a growing segment of the TV market. In the USA, repeats are known as reruns and have always enjoyed a regular place in the schedules. With new programmes generally aired in the States between September and May, reruns have traditionally come into their own from June to August. Furthermore, once a national network has exhausted its contract for running and rerunning a series, its producers have often sold it into syndication, giving independent stations across the country the chance to buy old episodes of popular series for screening locally. That is why viewers can always find episodes of classics from the 1950s onwards doing the rounds of the USA's smaller TV stations.

Rerun

See *Repeat*.

Researcher

A member of the production team whose job is to look into possible issues and subjects for programming, to brief presenters on background information, to investigate locations prior to shooting and to contact and vet potential contributors, be they experts, interviewees or game show contestants.

Resnick ✶✶

UK (Deco/BBC) Police Drama. BBC 1 1992–3

DI Charlie Resnick .... **Tom Wilkinson**
DS Graham Millington .... **David Neilson**
DC Lynn Kellogg .... **Kate Eaton**
DC Mark Divine .... **William Ivory**
DC Dipak Patel .... **Paul Bazely**
DC Kevin Nicholls .... **Daniel Ryan**
Supt. Jack Skelton .... **Paul Jesson**
Rachel Chaplin .... **Fiona Victory**
William Doria .... **Neil Dudgeon**
Claire Millinder .... **Diana Hardcastle**

Writer **John Harvey**
Producer **Colin Rogers**

● ***Two cases for a jazz-loving Midlands police officer.***

Charlie Resnick is a detective in Nottingham. A second-generation Pole in his mid-forties, he lives alone in a house full of cats. He has been long divorced from wife Elaine, but there are no kids to complicate his life. His penchant for unusual sandwiches has contributed to his podgy build and his other passion is jazz music. Despite his glum exterior, Resnick brings humour as well as plenty of experience and intuition into his investigations. In his first TV outing, he tackles a killer of lonely hearts and this three-parter was followed a year later by a two-episode tale featuring Resnick on the trail of two unorthodox burglars. Both stories were scripted by John Harvey from his own novels.

Restoration/Restoration Village ✶✶

UK (Endemol) Factual. BBC 2 2003–4/2006

Presenter **Griff Rhys Jones**

Series Editors/Producers **Simon Shaw, Katie Boyd, Jeremy Cross**

● ***Viewer poll to fund the refurbishment of a derelict historic building.***

Thirty historic buildings from around the UK that had fallen into decay were showcased in this preservation contest. Griff Rhys Jones introduced the contender structures – all Grade I or II listed and chosen in consultation with local heritage bodies – which were then championed by celebrities like Richard E. Grant, Michael Portillo, Fiona Bruce and John Peel. Supporting their efforts were conservation architect Ptolemy Dean and historic buildings surveyor Marianne Suhr, who helped explain why each of the buildings held merit. Phone lines were then thrown open for the viewing public to vote for the building they felt deserved restoration most. Programmes were themed regionally for heats, with the ten finalists going head-to-head in the grand final. The profits from the phone calls throughout the series were channelled into a fund to start the refurbishment of the overall winner. Featured buildings included Bank Hall at Bretherton, Lancashire; a POW camp at Harperly, Durham; Moulton Windmill in Lincolnshire; Greyfriars Tower in King's Lynn, Norfolk; and the eventual victor, the Victoria Baths in Manchester. Around 2 million people voted, raising around £3.4 million for the cause. However, the Baths was not the only winner. With their profiles raised, other buildings attracted concern and funding from other quarters as a result of the series. Series two in 2004 featured a further 21 buildings, with the public vote going to The Old Grammar School and its neighbour The Saracen's Head at King's Norton, Birmingham. In 2006 the series returned as *Restoration Village*, highlighting 21 structures in UK villages.

While certain art snobs were snooty about the idea of turning architectural preservation into a TV game show, it can't be denied that *Restoration* opened the eyes of a new audience to the destruction of historical landmarks and other pieces of our social history. Griff Rhys Jones was himself personally involved in a similar project prior to the series, through his work to renovate London's Hackney Empire theatre.

Return of Shelley, The

See *Shelley.*

Return of Sherlock Holmes, The

See *Adventures of Sherlock Holmes, The.*

Return of the Psammead, The

See *Five Children and It.*

Return of the Saint ✶✶

UK (ITC) Adventure. ITV 1978–9

Simon Templar .... **Ian Ogilvy**

Executive Producer **Robert S. Baker**
Producer **Anthony Spinner**

● ***A revival of the charming 1960s international adventurer.***

Nine years after Roger Moore hung up Simon Templar's halo, lookalike Ian Ogilvy tried it on for size. Similar in many ways, although critically less well received, this regeneration of Leslie Charteris's dashing, confident hero once again sees our hero whizzing around the globe, relaxing in the company of beautiful women and escaping from many life-threatening situations – all against a backdrop of international intrigue.

Reynolds, Burt

(1936–)

American actor who served his apprenticeship in television before becoming a Hollywood star. His breaks came in the 1950s, primarily in a series called *Riverboat*, in which he shared the lead for one season. There followed guest spots in programmes like ALFRED HITCHCOCK PRESENTS, *Route 66* and THE TWILIGHT ZONE before Reynolds joined the cast of GUNSMOKE, playing half-breed blacksmith Quint Asper. He left after three years to star in his own vehicle, *Hawk*, a police series about an Indian detective in New York. In 1970 he was cast as Dan August, another cop, this time in California, and, returning to the small screen after movie success, he was retired lawman *B. L. Stryker* in 1989. A year later Reynolds starred as football coach Wood Newton in the rustic sitcom EVENING SHADE (also as director/executive producer), and around the same time was providing the voice for the alien Troy in the comedy *Out of This World*. More recently he has appeared in a US series called *Johnson County War*. He was married to ROWAN AND MARTIN'S LAUGH-IN girl Judy Carne for three years in the 1960s and in 1988 married actress Loni Anderson.

Reynolds, Debbie

(Mary Frances Reynolds; 1932–)

Popular American actress and singer, star of the sitcom *The Debbie Reynolds Show* in the late 1960s (playing scatterbrained housewife Debbie Thompson) and later seen in the impressionists show *Kopykats* and the US comedy *Alohi Paradise* (Sydney Chase), as well as providing the voice of Lulu Pickles for *Rugrats*. She had previously been married to American singer Eddie Fisher and is the mother of actress Carrie Fisher.

Reynolds, Joan

See *Randall, Joan and Leslie*.

Rhoda ✶✶✶

US (MTM) Situation Comedy. BBC 2 1974–81 (US:CBS 1974–8)

Rhoda Morgenstern/Gerard ... **Valerie Harper**
Brenda Morgenstern .... **Julie Kavner**
Joe Gerard .... **David Groh**
Ida Morgenstern .... **Nancy Walker**
Martin Morgenstern .... **Harold J. Gould**
Carlton the Doorman .... **Lorenzo Music** *(voice only)*
Donny Gerard .... **Todd Turquand**
Myrna Morgenstein .... **Barbara Sharma**
Gary Levy .... **Ron Silver**
Sally Gallagher .... **Anne Meara**
Johnny Venture .... **Michael Delano**
Jack Doyle .... **Ken McMillan**
Ramon Diaz Jr .... **Rafael Campos**

Creators **James L. Brooks, Allan Burns**
Executive Producers **James L. Brooks, Allan Burns, Charlotte Brown**
Producers **David Davis, Lorenzo Music**

● ***Life with a single Jewish girl in New York City.***

A spin-off from THE MARY TYLER MOORE SHOW, *Rhoda* follows the fortunes of Mary's best friend, Rhoda Morgenstern. Back in her native New York, Rhoda has lost some weight and generally has a more positive outlook on life. She now lives with her podgy bank clerk sister, Brenda, after failing to settle down with her parents, Martin and Ida. Brenda, like Rhoda, is on the lookout for a husband, but Rhoda finds hers first, in the shape of Joe Gerard, divorced father of ten-year-old Donny and boss of the New York Wrecking Company.

Rhoda and Joe take an apartment in Brenda's block, where Carlton is the doom-laden doorman viewers never see. But Joe goes out to work and Rhoda is stuck at home, frustrated and bored. Not surprisingly, the marriage is doomed to failure, especially after Rhoda forms her own window-dressing business with old schoolfriend Myrna Morgenstein. Joe and Rhoda divorce and she returns to the singles bars, accompanied by Brenda and some new acquaintances, air hostess Sally Gallagher and boutique-owner Gary Levy. Also seen is Rhoda's on-off boyfriend, a Vegas lounge singer named Johnny Venture. In the final series, Rhoda works with Jack Doyle and Ramon Diaz at the struggling Doyle Costume Company.

Rhoda, like *The Mary Tyler Moore Show*, was very much a 1970s series. It was also richly ethnic, applauded for its abundant Jewishness (despite the fact that neither Valerie Harper nor Nancy Walker, who played Rhoda's mother, were Jewish themselves).

Rhodes ✶✶

UK (Zenith) Historical Drama. BBC 1 1996

Cecil Rhodes .... **Martin Shaw**
Joe Shaw *(young)*
Princess Catherine Radziwill .... **Frances Barber**
Dr Jameson .... **Neil Pearson**
Barney Barnato .... **Ken Stott**
Charles Rudd .... **David Butler**
John X. Merriman .... **Philip Godawa**
Alfred Beit .... **Frantz Dobrowsky**
Neville Pickering .... **Ray Cailthard**
Sir Hercules Robinson .... **John Carson**
Harry Currey .... **Gresby Nash**
Rochfort Maguire .... **Richard Huw**
Lobengula .... **Washington Sixolo**
Babayane .... **Ramolao Makhene**
Mtshete .... **Ken Gampu**
Frank Johnson .... **Gavin Hood**
John Grimmer .... **Alex Fearns**
Frank Dawson .... **Danny Keogh**
Henry Labouchere .... **Antony Thomas**
FC Selous .... **Paul Slabolepzsy**
Paul Kruger .... **Carel Trichardt**
Philip Jourdan .... **Jeremy Crutchley**
Dr Harris .... **Guy de Lancey**

Writer **Antony Thomas**
Producers **Scott Meek, Charles Salmon**

● ***Warts-and-all retrospective on one of Britain's great imperialists.***

This sprawling epic account of the life of arch-imperialist Cecil Rhodes took 12 years to put together, at a cost of £10 million. Regrettably, viewers and critics were not keen and the eight-part drama proved to be an expensive disappointment. Writer Antony Thomas's intention was to ensure that the whole story of this remarkable Victorian was brought to light, including his darker side. What emerges is a picture of a man who arrives in South Africa in 1871 at the age of 17 for the benefit of his health and who rapidly learns to use his guile to control affairs. It follows his life as he joins his brother in the search for diamonds and founds the de Beers company; becomes Prime Minister of the Cape; personally invades Mashonaland, massacring local tribesmen; establishes his own land, Rhodesia; lays the groundwork for apartheid; plants the seeds of the Boer War; and all the while works towards his twin visions – of enhanced personal wealth and of securing the whole of Africa for British colonial rule. Other key figures in the story are Rhodes's rival in the diamond industry, Barney Barnato; protégé Neville Pickering; accomplice Dr Jameson and Russian princess Catherine Radziwill, who sees herself as the woman in his life, although his warmth towards women is always well concealed. Antony Thomas appears himself in the series, playing antagonist MP Henry Labouchere. Another interesting piece of casting was of Martin Shaw's son, Joe, as the younger version of Rhodes.

Rhodes, Gary

OBE (1960–)

London-born TV chef with a trademark spiky haircut. His series have included *Hot Chefs*, *Rhodes Around Britain*, *More Rhodes*, *Open Rhodes*, *Classic Rhodes*, *Gary Rhodes*, *Gary Rhodes's New British Classics*, *Gary Rhodes: Cookery Year*. He also hosted MASTERCHEF and featured in HELL'S KITCHEN.

Rice, Anneka

(Annie Rice; 1958–)

British presenter, born in Wales but initially working on radio and TV in Hong Kong. After a time as personal assistant to Anna Home, at BBC's children's programmes, her UK break came with Channel 4's adventurous game show TREASURE HUNT, in 1983, in which she did much leaping from helicopters and running about looking for clues. She then became known for CHALLENGE ANNEKA, a charity-orientated programme involving unlikely feats like publishing a book or building an orphanage in a matter of days. Rice also worked on TV-am's *Good Morning Britain*, contributed to WISH YOU WERE HERE . . . ? and presented one season of HOLIDAY. She hosted *Sporting Chance*, *Passport*, *Dinner Doctors* and a wildlife painting programme called *A Brush with the Wild*, and has been seen in various panel games and special reports.

Rich, Lee

(1926–)

Former advertising executive who founded Lorimar Productions (with Merv Adelson) in 1968. The company achieved several prime-time hits, including THE WALTONS, DALLAS, KNOTS LANDING, FALCON CREST and FLAMINGO ROAD, before it was eventually taken over by Warner Brothers. Rich moved on to MGM/United Artists (as Chairman and Chief Executive) but left in 1988 to go back into independent production.

Rich Man, Poor Man ★★★

US (Universal/Harve Bennett) Drama. ITV 1976 (US: ABC 1976)
DVD: Universal

Rudy Jordache	**Peter Strauss**
Tom Jordache	**Nick Nolte**
Julie Prescott/Abbott/ Jordache	**Susan Blakely**
Axel Jordache	**Edward Asner**
Mary Jordache	**Dorothy McGuire**
Willie Abbott	**Bill Bixby**
Duncan Calderwood	**Ray Milland**
Teddy Boylan	**Robert Reed**
Virginia Calderwood	**Kim Darby**
Harold Jordache	**Bo Brundin**
Teresa Sanjoro	**Talia Shire**
Bill Denton	**Lawrence Pressman**
Kate Jordache	**Kay Lenz**
Asher Berg	**Craig Stevens**
Joey Quales	**George Maharis**
Linda Quales	**Lynda Day George**
Marsh Goodwin	**Van Johnson**
Irene Goodwin	**Dorothy Malone**
Arthur Falconetti	**William Smith**
Clothilde	**Fionnuala Flanagan**

Writer **Dean Reisner**
Executive Producer **Harve Bennett**
Producer **Jon Epstein**

Two brothers grow up in very different ways and achieve contrasting success and happiness.

Rich Man, Poor Man was one of the television events of the 1970s. With a cast list littered with big names, this adaptation of Irwin Shaw's mammoth 1970 novel of the same name can be viewed today as the original blockbuster mini-series. It captivated world audiences and led to a boom in dramatizations of popular novels, which were screened under the *Best Sellers* umbrella title (usually on consecutive nights). These included Taylor Caldwell's *Captains and Kings*, Robert Ludlum's *The Rhinemann Exchange*, Arthur Hailey's *Wheels*, John Jakes's *The Bastard* and Harold Robbins's *79 Park Avenue*.

Rich Man, Poor Man is the story of the Jordache brothers, sons of an impoverished immigrant family (dad Axel is a hard-working baker in Port Phillip, New York), and follows their lives and relationships from 1945 through to the mid-1960s. The intelligent one, Rudy, breaks free from his deprived roots to become a successful businessman and politician. Julie Prescott is the girl he loves. The brawny one, Tom, meanders from scrape to scrape, taking up boxing for a while, dabbling in crime and always likely to meet an unhappy end.

Two sequels followed. *Rich Man, Poor Man – Book II*, picking up the story in 1965, focuses on the now Senator Rudy Jordache, his fight against corporate greed and the family feuds that still engulf him. A new generation of rich and poor men are seen in the form of his surrogate kids, Wesley Jordache (Tom's son) and Billy Abbott (son of Julie). *Beggarman, Thief*, set in the late 1960s, switches attention to the boys' sister, Gretchen, a film maker who has previously not been seen.

Rich Tea and Sympathy ★★

UK (Yorkshire) Comedy Drama. ITV 1991

Julia Merrygrove	**Patricia Hodge**
George Rudge	**Denis Quilley**
Grandpa Rudge	**Lionel Jeffries**
Granny Trellis	**Jean Alexander**
Sally	**Anne Reid**
Steve Merrygrove	**Ray Lonnen**
Nikki	**Tracie Bennett**
Samantha Merrygrove	**Claudia Bryan**
John Merrygrove	**Jason Flemyng**
Colin Pink	**James Warrior**
Warren Rudge	**Chris Garner**
Karen Rudge	**Lorraine Ashbourne**
Tracey Rudge	**Sara Griffiths**

Writer **David Nobbs**
Executive Producer **Vernon Lawrence**
Producer **David Reynolds**

An unlikely romance brings two incompatible families together.

David Nobbs's six-part tale of love and family friction is set in a well-heeled Yorkshire town (like his previous A BIT OF A DO). It concerns one Julia Merrygrove, divorced mother of teenagers John and Samantha, who has returned to work after devoting years of her life to motherhood. She is also a Labour councillor. There is therefore much surprise in her budding romance with her Tory employer, George Rudge, widower boss of Rudge Brothers biscuit factory, and himself father of three: Warren, Karen and Tracey. It is an entanglement that begins when their shopping trolleys collide in a supermarket.

Keeping an eye on developments are George's sex-crazed dad, Grandpa Rudge, and Julia's snooker-mad mum, Granny Trellis.

Richard, Wendy

MBE (1943–)

Middlesbrough-born actress, in TV since the early 1960s. Her major roles have been as blouse-busting Miss Brahms in ARE YOU BEING SERVED? (and *Grace and Favour*) and, in total contrast, dowdy Pauline Fowler in EASTENDERS. However, she also played supermarket manageress Joyce Harker in THE NEWCOMERS, appeared with Dora Bryan in *Both Ends Meet* (Maudie) and Hylda Baker in *Not on Your Nellie* (Doris), and was Doreen, one of the ON THE BUSES clippies, as well as Pearl in the kids' series HOGG'S BACK. Among her many other credits have been parts in HARPERS WEST ONE (Susan Sullivan), DIXON OF DOCK GREEN, Z CARS, DANGER MAN, NO HIDING PLACE, PLEASE SIR! and DAD'S ARMY. At the start of her career, she was the girl on the Mike Sarne chart-topper 'Come Outside' (1962).

Richard the Lionheart ✳

UK (Danziger) Adventure. ITV 1962–3

King Richard	**Dermot Walsh**
Prince John	**Trader Faulkner**
Blondel	**Iain Gregory**
Sir Gilbert	**Robin Hunter**
Sir Geoffrey	**Alan Haywood**
Duke Leopold	**Francis de Wolfe**
Lady Berengaria	**Sheila Whittington**

Producers **Edward J. Danziger, Harry Lee Danziger**

● ***King Richard returns from the Crusades to stop Prince John stealing the English throne.***

Prince Richard is away with his army when news reaches him of the death of his father, King Henry. Worse still, his younger brother, John, has designs on the throne that is legally Richard's, and so Lionheart returns home to put an end to the plot. It is not to be a quick affair, however, as John and his knaves prove elusive and determined, resulting in a series of swashbuckling adventures in which Richard's life is always in danger. His other enemies include Leopold and Philip of France, as well as the Saracen, Saladin, and some of the action takes place back in the Holy Land.

Richards, Stan

(Stan Richardson; 1930–2005)

Yorkshire-born actor, a former musical-comedy entertainer on the northern clubs circuit, seen in programmes like CORONATION STREET, CROWN COURT, THE CUCKOO WALTZ, ALL CREATURES GREAT AND SMALL, LAST OF THE SUMMER WINE and various dramas (such as *The Price of Coal*), before taking the role of poacher/gamekeeper Seth Armstrong in EMMERDALE FARM in 1977.

Richardson, Ian

CBE (1934–)

Scottish actor whose portrayal of the devious Francis Urquhart in Michael Dobbs's HOUSE OF CARDS, *To Play the King* and *The Final Cut* was highly acclaimed. In a long and varied TV career, Richardson has also played Bill Haydon in TINKER, TAILOR, SOLDIER, SPY, Major Neuheim in PRIVATE SCHULZ, Ramsay MacDonald in *Number 10*, Frederick Fairlie in THE WOMAN IN WHITE, Nehru in *Lord Mountbatten: The Last Viceroy* and Michael Spearpoint in THE GRAVY TRAIN and *The Gravy Train Goes East*. He was Anthony Blunt in *Blunt*, the 1987 play about the British traitor, Haig in *The Treasure Seekers*, Rex Hunt in the Falklands drama AN UNGENTLEMANLY ACT, Sir Godber Evans in PORTERHOUSE BLUE, Sir Simon de Canterville in *The Canterville Ghost*, Stephen Tyler in THE MAGICIAN'S HOUSE, Lord Groan in GORMENGHAST, Dr Joseph Bell in MURDER ROOMS: THE DARK BEGINNINGS OF SHERLOCK HOLMES and the Chancellor in BLEAK HOUSE. Richardson has also been seen in programmes as varied as HORIZON, BRASS, SORRY!, *Mistral's Daughter, A Voyage Round My Father, Churchill and the Generals* (Montgomery), *The Master of Ballantrae, Charlie Muffin, Star Quality, Strange* (Canon Black), AGATHA CHRISTIE'S MARPLE and *The Booze Cruise* (Marcus) as well as Shakespearean offerings, and narrated the single drama *A Royal Scandal*.

Richardson, Miranda

(1958–)

Versatile British actress seen in comedies like THE COMIC STRIP PRESENTS, SMITH AND JONES, ABSOLUTELY FABULOUS and *The True Adventures of Christopher Columbus* (Queen Isabella), plus programmes such as A WOMAN OF SUBSTANCE (Paula), *Sorrell and Son, After Pilkington*, the *Performance* presentation of *Old Times* (Anna), *Redemption*, THE STORYTELLER, *Snapshots, Mr Wakefield's Crusade* (Sandra), A DANCE TO THE MUSIC OF TIME (Pamela Flitton), *The Scold's Bridle* (Dr Sarah Blakeney), *Merlin* (Mab), *Alice in Wonderland* (Queen of Hearts), THE LOST PRINCE (Queen Mary) and *Gideon's Daughter* (Stella). However, she is still remembered for her naughty schoolgirl interpretation of Queen Elizabeth I in BLACKADDER *II*. She was also seen in *Blackadder the Third* (highwaywoman Amy Hardwood) and *Blackadder Goes Forth* (Nurse Mary).

Richie, Shane

(Shane Roche; 1964–)

Former Pontin's Blue Coat who arrived on television in sketch shows like *Up to Something* and *You Gotta Be Jokin'*. He then hosted the home video show *Caught in the Act* and was seen in GOING LIVE! and LIVE AND KICKING (fronting the *Run the Risk* game), *Win, Lose or Draw, Lucky Numbers* and *The Shane Richie Experience* (later reworked as *Love Me Do*). Turning to drama, he appeared in *Burnside* (Tony Shotton) and then was cast as Alfie Moon in EASTENDERS, making guest appearances also in *Night and Day*. Richie was formerly married to Coleen Nolan, of the Nolans vocal group.

Rider, Steve

(1950–)

Unflappable British sports anchorman, the main presenter of the BBC's GRANDSTAND for several years, following work for ITV on *Midweek Sports Special* and other programmes. In 2005 he decided to make the move back to ITV to anchor its coverage of Formula 1 motor racing.

Rides ✱✱

UK (Warner Sisters) Drama. BBC 1 1992–3

Patrice Jenner .... **Jill Baker**
Hal Goldie .... **Trevor Byfield**
Beki Jenner .... **Lucy Speed**
Raquel .... **Suzan Sylvester**
Aileen .... **Lynda Steadman**
Sue-Lyn .... **Katharine Schlesinger**
Bryant .... **Judith Scott**
Aggie .... **Nimmy March**
Dale Daley .... **Erica Grant**
Scarlett .... **Caroline Blakiston**
George .... **Nicola Cowper**
Janet .... **Louise Jameson**
Julian .... **Jesse Birdsall**
James Purefoy
Sacha .... **Charlotte Avery**
Yvonne .... **Maureen Flynn**
Charmian .... **Carole Hawkins**
Lavender .... **Geraldine O'Connell**
Graham .... **Paul Copley**
Pam .... **Avril Elgar**
Rhona .... **Corinne Skinner-Carter**

Creator/Writer **Carole Hayman**
Producers **Lavinia Warner, Frances Heasman**

● ***A former soldier sets up a women-only cab company.***

Looking for a fresh start in life, Patrice Jenner, now in her forties, quits her stalled career in the army and sets up her own minicab firm, which she calls Rides. What makes this business so different from all the others in London is that it is entirely crewed by women. It might be a good hook to encourage nervous female travellers to call up Rides but it also means plenty of friction between the mixed group of drivers. The team includes a resting actress, the former owner of a model agency, even a convicted car thief – not the most compatible bunch – but they are successful enough to motor on through two series, despite the best efforts of rivals to run them off the road. Indeed, by series two, Rides is branching out into limousine hire. Among the lady cabbies is Janet, a former teacher who tries to adopt a South American baby, plus motorbike couriers Sacha and George, who are more than just work colleagues. As for Patrice, Rides apart, she has another challenge to meet – that of forging a relationship with her teenage daughter, Beki. Programme creator Carole Hayman also appears occasionally, as cabbie Stella. Twelve episodes were produced in all.

Ridley, Arnold

OBE (1896–1984)

Bath-born actor and writer, fondly remembered as the incontinent Private Godfrey in DAD'S ARMY, a role he assumed at the tender age of 72. Previously, he had played a vicar in CROSSROADS and two roles in CORONATION STREET. Other guest appearances were in series like THE AVENGERS, MRS THURSDAY and THE PERSUADERS! By far his greatest achievement, however, was his penning, in 1923, of the famous stage play *The Ghost Train* (televised as early as 1937), among other theatre scripts.

Riff Raff Element, The ✱✱✱

UK (BBC) Drama. BBC 1 1993–4

Joanna Tundish .... **Celia Imrie**
Petula Belcher .... **Mossie Smith**
Roger Tundish .... **Ronald Pickup**
Carmen .... **Jayne Ashbourne**
Declan .... **Cal Macaninch**
Acky Belcher .... **Trevor Peacock**
Granny Grogan .... **Brenda Bruce**
Boyd Tundish .... **Nicholas Farrell**
Mortimer Tundish .... **Richard Hope**
Phoenix .... **Pippa Guard**
Nathan Tundish .... **Ashley Wright**
Dearbhla .... **Kate Binchy**
Alister .... **Greg Wise**
Vincent .... **George Costigan**
Oliver Tundish .... **Stewart Pile**
Nelson .... **Dicken Ashworth**
Maggie Belcher .... **Susan Brown**
Father Casper .... **Lionel Guyett**

Creator/Writer **Debbie Horsfield**
Producer **Liz Trubridge**

● ***Families from different class backgrounds share a stately home.***

Roger Tundish, recently recalled ambassador to San Andres, upsets his family on arrival home at Tundish Hall in Lancashire. With the house falling into disrepair and finances tight, he is forced to advertise for new tenants for one of the wings. 'The riff raff element need not apply', he states. However, that is precisely what he gets when his daughter-in-law, Joanna, employs Petula Belcher as resident cook, and the rest of the common-as-muck Belcher family takes up residence. Not just class friction but adultery, pregnancy and crime, including murder too, ensue. Much acclaimed, a second series of this light drama followed in 1994.

Rifleman, The ✱✱

US (Four Star/Sussex) Western. ITV 1959–64 (US: ABC 1958–63)
DVD: Alpha Video

Lucas McCain .... **Chuck Connors**
Mark McCain .... **Johnny Crawford**
Marshal Micah Torrance .... **Paul Fix**
Milly Scott .... **Joan Taylor**
Lou Mallory .... **Patricia Blair**
Sweeney .... **Bill Quinn**
Eddie Holstead .... **John Harmon**
Hattie Denton .... **Hope Summers**

Producers **Arthur Gardner, Arnold Laven, Jules Levy**

● ***A Wild West rancher helps keep order with the aid of a specially adapted gun.***

Dour, level-headed Lucas McCain arrives in New Mexico after the death of his wife. He has purchased the Dunlap Ranch, four miles south of North Fork, and is now struggling to make it pay. At the same time, he is trying to raise his 12-year-old son, Mark, teaching him lessons in life and showing him right from wrong. But Lucas also has a third job to do. Whenever outlaws ride into town or there is a threat to law and order, it is always McCain who is called upon to save the day, bailing out the town's helpless marshal, Micah Torrance. He does have some assistance, however, in the form of his converted .44

Winchester rifle that allows rapid fire. It gives Lucas a distinct advantage over his adversaries.

Like most cowboys, Lucas is provided with a little romantic interest, first with shopkeeper Milly Scott and then with Lou Mallory, ambitious proprietress of the Mallory House Hotel. Other townsfolk include Eddie Holstead, owner of the Madera House Hotel, shopkeeper Hattie Denton and Sweeney, bartender at the Last Chance Saloon. All in all, though, this is a rather heavy, sombre half-hour Western.

Rigg, Dame Diana
(1938–)

Doncaster-born actress leaping to fame as the karate-chopping Emma Peel in THE AVENGERS in 1965, having already made appearances in programmes like ARMCHAIR THEATRE and THE SENTIMENTAL AGENT. She played Mrs Peel for three years, and later credits have included her own US sitcom, entitled *Diana*, in which she played divorcée and fashion co-ordinator Diana Smythe, plus *The Diana Rigg Show*. She also appeared in a sketch show called *Three Piece Suite*, BLEAK HOUSE (Lady Dedlock), MOTHER LOVE (Helen Vesey), *Screen Two's Genghis Cohn* (Frieda von Stangel), MOLL FLANDERS (Mrs Golightly), REBECCA (Mrs Danvers), THE MRS BRADLEY MYSTERIES (title role), *Victoria and Albert* (Baroness Lehzen), MURDER IN MIND and CHARLES II – THE POWER AND THE PASSION (Queen Henrietta Maria). Actress Rachael Stirling is her daughter.

Riley, Lisa
(1976–)

Bury-born actress, EMMERDALE's Mandy Dingle and Rebecca Patterson in FAT FRIENDS. She has also fronted the home video show YOU'VE BEEN FRAMED and appeared in the drama *Blood and Peaches*. Recent guest appearances include parts in THE AFTERNOON PLAY, DOCTORS, THE BILL and HOLBY CITY.

Rin Tin Tin
See *Adventures of Rin Tin Tin, The.*

Rings on Their Fingers ✶

UK (BBC) Situation Comedy. BBC 1 1978–80

Oliver Pryde	**Martin Jarvis**
Sandy Bennett/Pryde	**Diane Keen**
Victor	**Tim Barrett**
Mr Gordon Bennett	**John Harvey**
Mrs Bennett	**Barbara Lott**
Mr Pryde	**Keith Marsh**

Creator/Writer **Richard Waring**
Producer **Harold Snoad**

Shall-we, shan't-we marriage dilemmas for a young couple.

Oliver Pryde has been happy sharing six years of his life and his West Acton flat with his winsome girlfriend, Sandy Bennett, but he still values his independence. Sandy, on the other hand, is desperately keen on marriage. With the occasional interference of relatives and workmates, the two ditherers attempt to find a way forward, with wedding bells, unfortunately for Oliver, the ultimate answer. Subsequent episodes centre on their marital strife and preparations for the birth of their first child. With its traditionalist hubby-at-work, little-lady-at-home stance, 1970s feminists loathed it.

Ripcord ✶

US (United Artists) Adventure. BBC 1 1964–5 (US: Syndicated 1961–3)

Ted McKeever	**Larry Pennell**
Jim Buckley	**Ken Curtis**
Chuck Lambert	**Paul Comi**
Charlie Kern	**Shug Fisher**

Producers **Maurice Unger, Leon Benson**

The all-action adventures of a pair of crime-fighting skydivers.

Ted McKeever and Jim Buckley, proprietors of Ripcord Inc., are parachuting teachers who double up as crime-busters. Although they often hire themselves out for dangerous rescue and recovery work, they are more usually found apprehending criminals, dropping from the skies like avenging angels. Sometimes their battles take place in mid-air. They are supported in their work by their pilot, Chuck Lambert, later replaced by Charlie Kern.

Ripley, Fay
(1966–)

Wimbledon-born actress headlining in such dramas and comedies as COLD FEET (Jenny Gifford), *I Saw You* (Grace Bingley), *Green-Eyed Monster* (Deanna), *Stretford Wives* (Donna Massey), *Dead Gorgeous* (Rose Bell), BEDTIME (Jill) and *Fungus the Bogeyman* (Jane White), after smaller roles in THE BILL and THE BROKER'S MAN and presenting the Channel 4 discussion show *Sofa Melt*. Fay has also been seen in commercials for the National Lottery, made a guest appearance in HUSTLE, and acted as narrator for documentaries such as *Danger on the Beach* and *On the Fiddle?*. She is married to Australian actor Daniel Lapaine and is a niece of 1960s singer Twinkle (Lyn Ripley), of death disc 'Terry' fame.

Ripping Yarns ✶✶✶

UK (BBC) Comedy. BBC 2 1977; 1979
DVD: Acorn Media

Michael Palin, Terry Jones

Writers **Michael Palin, Terry Jones**
Producer **Alan J. W. Bell**

Over-the-top Boys' Own adventures satirized.

Tongue-in-cheek escapism lies at the heart of this series of playlets by Michael Palin and Terry Jones that gloriously parody classic schoolboy literature. These dashing tales of exploration, sporting excellence, wartime heroics and more celebrate every exaggeration and cliché of the Victorian and Edwardian originals. Ridiculous in true Monty Python fashion, the lead characters – Palin stars in all episodes, Jones only in one – bound with youthful exuberance and naïvety, with their creators taking an almost cruel pleasure in sending up this uniquely British form of fiction. Two series were produced, two years apart, following a one-off comedy, *Tomkinson's Schooldays*, in 1976, each episode lavishly shot on film for the highest production values. The eight other stories are *The*

Testing of Eric Olthwaite, Escape from Stalag Luft 112B, Murder at Moorstones Manor, Across the Andes by Frog, The Curse of the Claw, Whinfrey's Last Case, Golden Gordon and *Roger of the Raj.*

Rippon, Angela

CBE (1944–)

British presenter, a former newspaper journalist, generally considered to have been the UK's first female newsreader, although this honour actually belongs to Barbara Mandell, who read the ITN news way back in 1955. Rippon arrived on national TV in 1973 via news magazines in the south-west. Working initially as a reporter, she went on to front *News Review* and then *The Nine O'Clock News*. On the 1976 *Morecambe and Wise Christmas Show*, she revealed new talents, pushing aside the news desk and kicking her way through 'Let's Face the Music and Dance'. Not surprisingly, she was later recruited to present COME DANCING. In 1983 she became one of TV-am's 'Famous Five' presenters, although her time at the station was, as for the others, somewhat brief. She has never been short of radio or television work, however, and has also presented THE EUROVISION SONG CONTEST, ANTIQUES ROADSHOW, MASTERTEAM, MATCHPOINT, WHAT'S MY LINE?, TOP GEAR, *The Entertainers, Open House with Gloria Hunniford* and *Sun, Sea and Bargain Spotting* among many other programmes. Angela also read the news occasionally on THE BIG BREAKFAST and later worked for the ITV News Channel.

Rising Damp ★★★

UK (Yorkshire) Situation Comedy. ITV 1974–5; 1977–8
DVD: Granada Ventures

Rupert Rigsby .... **Leonard Rossiter**
Ruth Jones .... **Frances de la Tour**
Alan Moore .... **Richard Beckinsale**
Philip Smith .... **Don Warrington**
Brenda .... **Gay Rose**

Creator/Writer **Eric Chappell**
Producers **Ronnie Baxter, Vernon Lawrence, Len Lurcuck**

● ***The inhabitants of a seedy boarding house suffer the intrusions of its even seedier owner.***

Rupert Rigsby, grubby, lecherous, ignorant, nosey and tight-fisted (and those are just his good points), is the owner of a horribly run-down northern boarding house that is home to an odd mix of lodgers. Rigsby lives on the ground floor with his cat, Vienna. Upstairs, long-haired Alan, a medical student, shares one spartan room with Philip, the son of an African tribal chief, and another room is taken by frustrated spinster Miss Jones, a university administrator. Although liberally treated to decrepit furnishings and the eponymous rising damp, the one thing Rigsby's paying guests do not receive is privacy. Given the opportunity to catch his lodgers 'at it', the snooping Rigsby does not hesitate to barge in. Whatever secrets lie in their personal lives, Rigsby prises them out into the open, and however great their hopes and dreams, Rigsby is always ready to sneer and jeer at them. His own ambition, though, is to share a night of torrid passion with Miss Jones but, like his other plans, it is never realized. Brenda is one of Rigsby's later lodgers.

The series sprang from a one-off play entitled *The Banana Box* (in which the landlord was called Rooksby) and gave Leonard Rossiter the first chance to show off his acclaimed comic timing. Indeed, most of the series' humour came from his sharp, glib delivery. A film version was released in 1980.

Rivals of Sherlock Holmes, The ★★

UK (Thames) Detective Drama. ITV 1971; 1973

Dr Thorndyke .... **John Neville**
Barrie Ingham
Max Carrados .... **Robert Stephens**
Horace Dorrington .... **Peter Vaughan**
Jonathan Pryde .... **Ronald Hines**
Martin Hewitt .... **Peter Barkworth**
Prof. Van Dusen .... **Douglas Wilmer**
Simon Carne .... **Roy Dotrice**
Carnacki .... **Donald Pleasence**
Dixon Druce .... **John Fraser**
Lady Molly .... **Elvi Hale**
Romney Pringle .... **Donald Sinden**
Bernard Sutton .... **Robert Lang**
Polly Burton .... **Judy Geeson**
Insp. Lipinzki .... **Barry Keegan**
J. T. Laxworthy .... **Bernard Hepton**
Monsieur Valmont .... **Charles Gray**
Lt. Holst .... **John Thaw**
Dagobert Trostler .... **Ronald Lewis**
William Drew .... **Derek Jacobi**
Mr Horrocks .... **Ronald Fraser**
Hagar .... **Sara Kestelman**
Charles Dallas .... **Robin Ellis**

Executive Producers **Lloyd Shirley, Kim Mills**
Producers **Robert Love, Jonathan Alwyn, Reginald Collin**

● ***Series of literary adaptations which reveal that Sherlock Holmes was not the only great detective of Victorian times.***

The self-contained episodes of this period anthology feature investigations from the casebooks of various literary sleuths. One or two crop up more than once. Authors whose work is featured include Arthur Morrison (Horace Dorrington, Martin Hewitt and Jonathan Pryde), R. Austin Freeman (Dr Thorndyke), Baroness Orczy (Polly Burton) and Jacques Futrelle (Professor Van Dusen). Notable performances come from John Thaw as Danish detective Lt. Holst, Robert Stephens as blind detective Max Carrados, Donald Pleasence as Carnacki, a ghost-hunter, and Sara Kestelman as Hagar, a gypsy detective. The series was based on a literary collection put together by one-time BBC Director-General Sir Hugh Greene.

River, The ★★

UK (BBC) Situation Comedy. BBC 1 1988

Davey Jackson .... **David Essex**
Sarah McDonald .... **Katy Murphy**
Aunt Betty .... **Vilma Hollingbery**
Tom Pike .... **Shaun Scott**
Col. Danvers .... **David Ryall**

Creator/Writer **Michael Aitkens**
Producer **Susan Belbin**

● ***An ex-con lock-keeper and a young Scots girl fall in love on the riverbank.***

Set in the fictitious rustic settlement of Chumley-on-the-Water, *The River* centres on London-born lock-keeper Davey Jackson, revealing how his idyllic existence is thrown into turmoil by the arrival of a wayward Scots girl. Sarah

McDonald, a refugee from society, is forced to call on Davey's help when the propeller on her narrowboat is damaged in an accident. While the relevant repairs are made, Davey takes the aggressive Sarah into his cottage and a romance slowly develops, despite the best efforts of Davey's grumpy Aunt Betty (an active Marxist). It is subsequently revealed that Davey has retired to this rural backwater after serving six months in prison for allegedly forging banknotes. Tom Pike is Davey's assistant lock-keeper and Colonel Danvers the local nob and snob. Some of the action takes place in the local boozer, The Ferret, presided over by an unconscious landlord named Jim.

Star David Essex also wrote and performed the programme's theme song.

Riviera Police ✶

UK (Associated-Rediffusion) Police Drama. ITV 1965

Insp. Legrand .... **Brian Spink**
Lt. Col. Constant Sorel .... **Frank Lieberman**
Supt. Adam Hunter .... **Geoffrey Frederick**
Supt. Bernie Johnson .... **Noel Trevarthen**

Producer **Jordan Lawrence**

● ***Crime fighting on the Côte d'Azur.***

Legrand, Sorel, Hunter and Johnson are four determined police officers plying their trade against such glamorous backdrops as the Cannes Film Festival, the Monaco Grand Prix and the Nice Flower Festival. They usually work separately (except for the opening episode) to put the block on killers, thieves and other exponents of crime in the south of France. However, despite its sun, sea, sand and scantily clad beauties, the series never took a hold, not even when following CORONATION STREET in the transmission schedules.

Rix, Lord Brian

(1924–)

Yorkshire-born actor, Britain's number one farceur, largely in the theatre but seen to lose his trousers on TV on many occasions, too. Rix has also had his own series, *Dial RIX*, and presented a programme for handicapped viewers, *Let's Go* (he later became Chairman of Mencap). Rix starred with Warren Mitchell in an early form of YES, MINISTER entitled *Men of Affairs* (playing MP Barry Ovis) in 1973, and played James, opposite Lynda Baron, in the house-buying comedy *A Roof over My Head*, in 1977. Rix is the brother of EMMERDALE's Sheila Mercier, husband of actress Elspet Gray, and father of actress Louisa Rix.

Roache, William

MBE (1932–)

CORONATION STREET's Ken Barlow, William Roache has been with the series since its inception, back in 1960, making him the longest-serving cast member. His previous TV experience was confined to small parts in Granada series like SKYPORT and KNIGHT ERRANT and a single drama, *Marking Time*, and, since being in the *Street*, he has had little opportunity to work elsewhere on television. He is the father of actor Linus Roache (who once played Ken's son, Peter).

Roads to Freedom, The ✶✶

UK (BBC) Drama. BBC 2 1970

Mathieu Delarue .... **Michael Bryant**
Marcelle .... **Rosemary Leach**
Daniel .... **Daniel Massey**
Boris .... **Anthony Corlan**
Ivich .... **Alison Fiske**
Lola .... **Georgia Brown**
Brunet .... **Donald Burton**
Jacques .... **Clifford Rose**
Odette .... **Anna Fox**
Chamberlain .... **Michael Goodliffe**
Daladier .... **John Bryans**
Pinette .... **Norman Rossington**
Longin .... **John Cater**
Latex .... **Peter Wyatt**
Charlot .... **Freddie Earle**
Nippert .... **Christian Rodska**
Luberon .... **Christopher Heywood**
Guiccioli .... **Paul Henry**
Philippe .... **Simon Ward**

Writer **David Turner**
Producer **David Conroy**

● ***Young intellectuals find their lives shaken up by the advent of war.***

Jean-Paul Sartre's trilogy, published 1947–50 and made up of *The Age of Reason*, *The Reprieve* and *Iron in the Soul*, was brought to television in 13 parts, with the three elements of Sartre's work kept reasonably well defined. Like the original material, the drama highlights complicated romantic liaisons at a time when war is descending upon the world, asking how personal and political freedoms may be maintained when moral and social chaos is all around.

The story begins in Paris in 1938, leads us through the Nazi occupation of the city and runs on to June 1940. Events concern Mathieu, an intellectual who fails to build firm relationships because of his questioning attitude to life, and his various associates. His mistress is Marcelle but he soon begins a new liaison, with Ivich. The other main characters are Brunet, a declared communist, and Daniel, a reluctant homosexual. James Cellan-Jones directs.

Robbins, Michael

(1930–92)

Former straight man to comics like Dick Emery and Tommy Cooper, British actor Michael Robbins hit the big time when he was cast as Arthur, Reg Varney's layabout brother-in-law, in the hit sitcom ON THE BUSES, in 1969. His previous TV work had largely consisted of plays and guest spots in series like CALLAN, THE SAINT, THE AVENGERS and DEPARTMENT S, but thereafter Robbins was known as a solid comedy actor. Among his later credits were THICK AS THIEVES, *How's Your Father* (Eddie Cropper), *The Fuzz* (DS Marble), FAIRLY SECRET ARMY (Sgt Major Throttle), *Devenish*, THE NEW STATESMAN, Dick Emery's *Legacy of Murder* and the dramas *Operation Patch* (George Cosserat), *Brendon Chase* (Sgt Bunting), *Adam Bede*, DEMPSEY AND MAKEPEACE, RUMPOLE OF THE BAILEY and THE BILL.

Robert's Robots ✱✱

UK (Thames) Children's Situation Comedy. ITV 1973–4

Robert Sommerby .... **John Clive**
Eric .... **Nigel Pegram**
KT ('Katie') .... **Brian Coburn**
Aunt Millie .... **Doris Rogers**
Gimble .... **Richard Davies**
Marken .... **Leon Lissek**
Angie .... **Jenny Hanley**
Plummer .... **David Pugh**
Desiree .... **April Olrich**
Blabberbeak .... **Nigel Pegrum** *(voice only)*

Creator/Writer **Bob Block**
Producer **Vic Hughes**

● ***Spies are chasing the secrets of a brilliant inventor of robots.***

Robert Sommerby is a genius, if a little eccentric. The hyper-intelligent scientist has invented a range of humanoid robots that look and act so lifelike that everyone is after his secret. The government is clearly interested in the benefits they may bring, as is the villainous Marken, the boss of a foreign electronics company. Marken sends the grubby Gimble to steal the plans but the detective is so hopeless that Robert's Robots are safe in their own home. (Gimble is replaced by his assistant, Plummer, in series two.) For all his skill, however, Robert does have problems with his creations. Take Eric, for instance, a robot who gets angry whenever anyone tampers with his controls, making him sing like Maria Callas or even Elvis. Then there is KT (known as Katie), a robot so dim that he falls in love with a gas cooker and a Mini. Later creations include Blabberbeak, an annoyingly talkative parrot, and the exceedingly amorous Desiree. Angie is Robert's (human) girlfriend.

Robertson, Dale

(1923–)

One of TV's Western heroes, rugged Dale Robertson was the star of TALES OF WELLS FARGO (Jim Hardie) and IRON HORSE (Ben Calhoun). He also hosted the long-running anthology series *Death Valley Days* in the late 1960s and early 1970s and resurfaced in 1981 as Walter Lankershim in DYNASTY. A 1987 adventure series, *J. J. Starbuck*, proved short-lived.

Robertson, Fyfe

(1902–87)

Much-mimicked, distinctive Scottish roving reporter, a former newspaper journalist who was seen on TONIGHT and 24 HOURS in the 1950s and 1960s but remained on TV up to the turn of the 1980s. Some of his last contributions were nostalgic documentaries broadcast under the title of *Robbie* in the 1970s.

Robin Hood

See *Adventures of Robin Hood, The*.

Robin of Sherwood ✱✱

UK (HTV/Goldcrest) Adventure. ITV 1984–6
DVD: Network

Robin of Loxley .... **Michael Praed**
Robert of Huntingdon .... **Jason Connery**
Little John .... **Clive Mantle**
Will Scarlet .... **Ray Winstone**
Maid Marion .... **Judi Trott**
Much .... **Peter Llewellyn-Williams**
Friar Tuck .... **Phil Rose**
Nasir .... **Mark Ryan**
Sheriff of Nottingham .... **Nickolas Grace**
Guy of Gisburne .... **Robert Addie**
Abbot Hugo .... **Philip Jackson**
Herne the Hunter .... **John Abineri**
Edward of Wickham .... **Jeremy Bulloch**
Lord Owen .... **Oliver Cotton**
Sir Richard of Leaford .... **George Baker**
Gulnar .... **Richard O'Brien**
Baron Simon de Belleme .... **Anthony Valentine**

Creator **Richard Carpenter**
Executive Producer **Patrick Dromgoole**
Producers **Paul Knight, Esta Charkham**

● ***The Robin Hood legend, boosted with a dose of magic.***

In this imaginative version of the famous 12th-century legend, Robin Hood (Robin of Loxley) possesses deep spiritual powers which assist him in his fight with the Sheriff of Nottingham. His adventures begin when his home at Loxley Mill is destroyed by Norman soldiers. Swearing revenge, Robin encounters the mystical Herne the Hunter, who appears to him in the form of a man with a stag's head. He endows Robin with the sword Albion, and Robin then assumes the mantle of the Hooded Man, legendary hero of the oppressed Saxon folk ('Robin in the Hood' becoming 'Robin Hood'). Maid Marion (Lady Marion of Leaford), Little John, Will Scarlet, Friar Tuck and all the familiar names join Robin in his struggle, as the episodes combine various facets of the Robin Hood legend with the zest of pagan sorcery. The cast is predominantly young and the action suitably brisk as they fight to free the people of England.

After two seasons, Michael Praed left for the USA, Broadway and eventually DYNASTY, and was replaced by Sean Connery's son, Jason. The storyline has it that Robin of Loxley is killed in an ambush but his revolutionary spirit is assumed by a new Hooded Man, blond-haired Robert of Huntingdon, a lad of noble birth who, like his predecessor, has been inspired by Herne the Hunter.

Robin's Nest ✱✱

UK (Thames) Situation Comedy. ITV 1977–81
DVD: Network

Robin Tripp .... **Richard O'Sullivan**
Victoria Nicholls/Tripp .... **Tessa Wyatt**
James Nicholls .... **Tony Britton**
Albert Riddle .... **David Kelly**
Marion Nicholls .... **Honor Blackman**
Barbara Murray
Gertrude .... **Peggy Aitchison**

Creators **Johnnie Mortimer, Brian Cooke**
Producer **Peter Frazer-Jones**

● A catering graduate opens his own bistro with the help of his girlfriend.

Fresh from the successful MAN ABOUT THE HOUSE, Robin Tripp has now left his two female flatmates and teamed up with his live-in lover, air hostess Vicky Nicholls. They live above their own Fulham bistro – Robin's Nest – where they are not-so-ably assisted by their one-armed washer-up, Albert Riddle, an Irish ex-con with an endless line in blarney. The fly in the ointment is Vicky's disapproving dad, James Nicholls, a far from sleeping partner in the business, although her divorced mother, Marion, is far more sympathetic about her daughter's cohabitation with a long-haired cook. Tensions are eventually eased with a marriage and, eventually, the birth of twins. Also seen in later episodes is restaurant help Gertrude.

Star Richard O'Sullivan also wrote the synthesizer theme music.

Robinson, Anne
(1944–)

Red-haired, Liverpudlian presenter, a national newspaper journalist who was given her television break in BREAKFAST TIME as TV critic and then hosted POINTS OF VIEW. Since then, Robinson has also presented the consumer affairs programme WATCHDOG and hit the big time by fronting THE WEAKEST LINK, in both the UK and the US. She has since hosted *Outtake TV, Guess Who's Coming to Dinner*, and *What's the Problem? with Anne Robinson*. Other major credits have included GOING FOR A SONG, *Test the Nation* and GREAT BRITONS. In 2004, *Travels with My Unfit Mother* was a documentary about an American road trip Anne made with her daughter, Emma Wilson, a successful radio broadcaster in the USA.

Robinson, Nick
(1963–)

The BBC's political editor since 2005, Nick Robinson was born in Macclesfield and began his television career as a BBC production trainee in 1986, having graduated from Oxford and worked in local radio in Manchester. On his TV CV are behind-the-scenes credits for NEWSROUND, *Brass Tacks, On the Record* and CRIMEWATCH UK, and he was also deputy editor of PANORAMA before becoming one of the BBC's political correspondents in 1996 (later Chief Political Correspondent), in which role he presented *Westminster Live*. After this he spent three years as ITN's political editor before returning to the BBC on the retirement of Andrew Marr.

Robinson, Robert
(1927–)

British journalist and presenter, a specialist in panel games, thanks to long spells as chairman of CALL MY BLUFF and ASK THE FAMILY. Robinson also hosted POINTS OF VIEW and *The Book Programme*, and worked on *Picture Parade*, MONITOR and ALL OUR YESTERDAYS. Occasionally, he has presented his own travelogues. As interviewer on BBC-3 in 1965, it was Robinson who faced Kenneth Tynan when he famously became the first person to use the 'F' word on British TV. He is the father of actress Lucy Robinson.

Robinson, Tony
(1946–)

British comedian, actor, presenter and writer, chiefly remembered for his portrayal of Baldrick, the most menial of manservants, in the various BLACKADDER manifestations. Robinson has also been a member of the WHO DARES, WINS... team, a guest host of POINTS OF VIEW and presenter of *Stay Tooned*, TIME TEAM, *Tony Robinson's Romans, The Worst Jobs in History* and *Tony Robinson's Titanic Adventure*. He wrote and appeared in the kids' comedy MAID MARIAN AND HER MERRY MEN (playing the Sheriff of Nottingham), was the headmaster in *Teenage Health Freak*, the storyteller in *Blood and Honey* and Alan in MY WONDERFUL LIFE. On Sunday mornings, Robinson fronted *The Good Book Guide*. He has also been seen in programmes as diverse as PLAY AWAY, BIG JIM AND THE FIGARO CLUB, THE GOOD SEX GUIDE, THE YOUNG ONES, BERGERAC, *Virtual Murder, A Woman's Guide to Adultery, Fact or Fiction*, DOCTORS, CASUALTY and *Knight School* (also as script consultant) and, in 1994, made one of the BBC's *Great Journeys*. As narrator, Robinson has worked on programmes like AIRLINE.

Robinson Crusoe

See *Adventures of Robinson Crusoe, The*.

Robot Wars ✶✶

UK (Mentorn Barraclough Carey) Game Show. BBC 2 1998–2002; five 2003

DVD: ILC

Presenters **Jeremy Clarkson, Philippa Forrester, Craig Charles, Julia Reed, Jayne Middlemiss**

Producers **Stephen Carsey, Bill Hobbins, Joe Shaw**
Executive Producers **Stephen Carsey, Tom Gutteridge**

● Gladiatorial combat between home-built robots.

Inspired by a similar event held annually in San Francisco, *Robot Wars* is a demolition derby for amateur inventors. Each week teams of friends, work colleagues, even school pupils present their latest piece of malevolent hardware (cosily christened Dreadnaut, Cruella, Chaos 2, Hypno-Disc or other spiky names) in the form of a radio-controlled object of destruction. Negotiating assault courses, labyrinths, mock pinball games and other tricky challenges, and pitted against rivals, it is no holds barred as the appended chainsaws, hammers and crowbars look to inflict some serious damage, while football reporter Jonathan Pearce screams a running commentary. Adding to the mechanical carnage, as the contestants seek to be series champions, are house robots like the flame-throwing Sgt Bash, pincered Dead Metal, axe-bearing Shunt, Mr Psycho, Growler and Sir Killalot, with its pneumatic lance. Craig Charles replaced Jeremy Clarkson as main presenter after series one, Julia Reed taking over from assistant Philippa Forrester from series four (although Forrester returned later). A celebrity version was shown on BBC 1 at Christmas 2000, featuring Vic Reeves, Chris Eubank and the pop band Five. In 2003, the series switched from BBC 2 to five, with Jayne Middlemiss joining the front-of-house team.

Robson, Linda

(1958–)

London-born actress, a former child performer. Although she is well known today as Tracey Stubbs in BIRDS OF A FEATHER (alongside her lifelong friend, Pauline Quirke), Robson's TV career stretches back to the 1970s. As a 12-year-old she appeared in *Jackanory Playhouse* and went on to pop up in numerous Thames TV series, including *Pauline's Quirkes*, *Pauline's People* and YOU MUST BE JOKING!, as well as the teenage drama *Going Out* (Gerry), for Southern. Moving into adult TV, Robson was seen in WITHIN THESE WALLS, THE CREZZ (Jane Smith), CRIBB, AGONY, THE OTHER 'ARF, L FOR LESTER, HARRY'S GAME (Theresa McCorrigan), UP THE ELEPHANT AND ROUND THE CASTLE, THE BILL, SOUTH OF THE BORDER and plenty of other dramas, including SHINE ON HARVEY MOON, in which she played Harvey's daughter, Maggie. With Quirke, she took part in the challenge series *Jobs for the Girls* and THE GOOD SEX GUIDE. More recently, Linda also appeared in CROSSROADS and *The All Star Comedy Show*.

Rock Family Trees ★★★

UK (BBC) Documentary. BBC 2 1995; 1998

Narrator **John Peel**

Producer **Francis Hanly**

● ***The history of major rock groups, through the eyes of the musicians themselves.***

Based on Pete Frame's authoritative genealogies of rock bands, *Rock Family Trees* traces the genesis and development of various outfits, monitoring the numerous personnel changes and their resultant successes or failures. Using Frame's hand-drawn charts for illustration, along with record sleeves and magazine cuttings, the series interviews band members past and present for their (often amusing, sometimes tragic) perspective on band history and also features archive footage of live gigs. Themes adopted in series one are *The Fleetwood Mac Story*, *The Birmingham Beat*, *Deep Purple People*, *New York Punk*, *The British R 'n' B Boom* and *The New Merseybeat*. The second series offers *California Dreamin'*, *Sabbath, Bloody Sabbath*, *The Mersey Sound*, *Banshees and Other Creatures*, *The Prog Rock Years* plus *And God Created Manchester*.

Rock Follies ★★

UK (Thames) Drama. ITV 1976–7

Anna Wynd	**Charlotte Cornwell**
Devonia 'Dee' Rhoades	**Julie Covington**
Nancy 'Q' Cunard de Longchamps	**Rula Lenska**
Derek Huggin	**Emlyn Price**
Harry Moon	**Derek Thompson**
Kitty Schreiber	**Beth Porter**
Rox	**Sue Jones-Davies**

Writer **Howard Schuman**
Executive Producer **Verity Lambert**
Producer **Andrew Brown**

● ***Life on the road with an ambitious female rock group.***

The Little Ladies are a struggling girl rock band, lurching from gig to gig, striving to rise out of the sordid lower reaches of the rock music business. This series follows their ups and downs (mostly downs), as they fight to avoid exploitation – often sexual – and establish themselves as genuine musicians. Derek Huggin is their less than helpful manager.

Busby Berkeley-inspired fantasy sequences added extra colour to this six-part drama. The music was original and penned by Roxy Music guitarist Andy Mackay, leading to two soundtrack albums and a hit single, 'OK?', which also featured Sue Jones-Davies, whose character, Rox, joined the band in the second series. Also new was pushy American agent Kitty Schreiber. This second series was entitled *Rock Follies of '77*.

Rock 'n' Roll Years, The ★★★

UK (BBC) Documentary. BBC 1 1985–7; 1994

Producers **Ann Freer, Sue Mallinson**

● ***Historical review of events year by year played over a soundtrack of contemporary pop hits.***

Beginning in 1956, at the birth of the age of rock 'n' roll, this innovative series used old newsreel and TV clips to illustrate world events year by year. To add to the period feel, rock and pop records of the day provided the soundtrack, each track carefully selected to ensure that its lyrics tied in with the theme of the archive footage. Some concert performances were also relived. The years up to 1979 were reviewed in 1985–7 and, after a one-off special entitled *The Years That Rocked the Planet*, part of BBC 2's *One World* six-week season on ecological matters to coincide with the Rio Earth Summit in 1992, the programme returned in 1994 to update coverage to the end of the 1980s. In 2004, a one-off programme entitled *The African Rock 'n' Roll Years*, focusing on the history of the troubled continent since 1960, was screened by BBC 4. The same channel introduced a whole series with exactly the same title a year later, but this was more a general documentary about African music.

Rockface ★

UK (BBC/Union Pictures/Columbia TriStar) Drama. BBC 1 2002–3

Dr Gordon Urquhart	**Clive Russell**
Douglas McLanaghan	**Brendan Coyle**
Ben Craig	**Cal Macaninch**
Mike Bayliss	**Richard Graham**
Annie Craig	**Zoë Eeles**
Caroline Morrison	**Melanie Gutteridge**
Peter Craig	**Jamie Sives**
Jamie Doughan	**Rupert Evans**
Alice Urquhart	**Barbara Rafferty**
Danny Tunick	**Kenneth Bryans**
Betty Farinelli	**Louise Goodall**
Jane Chamberlain	**Jan Harvey**
Helen	**Kim Vithana**
Julia Seddon	**Eilidh Fraser**
Adam	**Rory McCann**

Writers **Nicholas Hicks-Beach, Shelley Miller, Steve Trafford, Alick Rowe**
Producers **Jacky Stoller, Neil Zeiger**

● ***Lives on the line with a team of mountain rescue volunteers.***

The Glentannoch Mountain Rescue team are the stars of this drama series set in the Highlands of Scotland. These brave men and women are the unpaid volunteers who risk life and limb to extract members of the public from danger, scaling mountain peaks, wading turbulent rivers, and scrabbling through dark and dangerous caves along the way. Gordon Urquhart is the team leader, a diligent but overworked local GP, supported by wife Alice. Gordon's deputy is reliable Douglas McLanaghan, while other valued team members are Peter Craig, a local bobby; Peter's teacher wife, Annie, who has the hots for Peter's brother, Ben; Mike Bayliss, owner of the town's sports shop; his best mate and local philanderer Jamie Doughan, an expert mountaineer; and Caroline Morrison, a physiotherapist and probationer. They are supported by Helen, a nurse in the A&E department of the local hospital, where Jane Chamberlain, Jamie's mother, also works. Each episode depicts a high-drama race against time, with hapless ramblers, pot-holers and such like waiting to be plucked from the jaws of doom. But wrapped around each action sequence are the tangled lives and loves of the team members themselves. Despite being shot on high-definition video for a quality image, *Rockface* failed to impress and was generally panned by critics and real-life climbers. Nevertheless a second series followed, making 14 episodes in total.

Rockford Files, The ✱✱

US (Universal/Cherokee/Public Arts) Detective Drama. BBC 1 1975–82 (US: NBC 1974–80)
DVD: Universal

Jim Rockford	**James Garner**
Joseph 'Rocky' Rockford	**Noah Beery Jr**
DS Dennis Becker	**Joe Santos**
Beth Davenport	**Gretchen Corbett**
Evelyn 'Angel' Martin	**Stuart Margolin**
John Cooper	**Bo Hopkins**
Lt. Alex Diehl	**Tom Atkins**
Lt. Doug Chapman	**James Luisi**
Gandolph Fitch	**Isaac Hayes**
Lance White	**Tom Selleck**

Creators **Roy Huggins, Stephen J. Cannell**
Executive Producers **Stephen J. Cannell, Meta Rosenberg**
Producers **Roy Huggins, Charles Johnson, David Chase**

● ***An ex-con turns private investigator, taking on cases of rough justice.***

Jim Rockford was imprisoned in San Quentin for five years for a robbery he did not commit and, when new evidence exonerates and frees him, he devotes his life to investigating other dodgy cases on which the police have closed their books. He forms the Rockford Private Detective Agency, of which he is the sole employee. Having been a jailbird himself, he can call upon his crooked connections to gather vital information (especially his weasely ex-cellmate, Angel Martin). But, because he is treading on their toes and undermining their work, he is not popular with the local cops.

Jim's chief rival (but also a good friend) is Det. Sgt Dennis Becker. John Cooper is his legal ally (albeit disbarred), and Rocky, his retired truck-driver father, also lends a hand, although he is always trying to talk his son into finding a real job. Jim's one-time girlfriend, Beth Davenport, also proves useful, being the attorney who bails him out whenever he finds himself behind bars again.

Rockford lives on a Los Angeles beach in a scruffy caravan and, unlike TV's more sophisticated private eyes, he doesn't have a fancy office or a sexy secretary. All he has is a crummy answering machine, which switches itself on at the start of each episode. Rockford charges $200 a day for his work (plus expenses), but often ends up unpaid and usually much the worse for wear. He hates violence and seldom carries a gun, so he is always looking nervously over his shoulder, relying on his wry sense of humour to carry him through the murky business of private detection. But he knows how to play dirty, too, and, if the end justifies the means, he is not averse to donning a disguise, slipping a few bribes or playing the con-man.

In the final series, Jim gains another rival, in the form of private eye Lance White, who irks Jim by solving cases with the minimum of effort and, usually, a huge slice of luck. Played by Tom Selleck, the character presaged his star role as MAGNUM, PI.

Rockliffe's Babies/Rockliffe's Folly ✱✱

UK (BBC) Police Drama. BBC 1 1987–88/1988

DS Alan Rockliffe	**Ian Hogg**
PC David Adams	**Bill Champion** *(Babies)*
PC Keith Chitty	**John Blakey** *(Babies)*
PC Steve Hood	**Brett Fancy** *(Babies)*
PC Gerry O'Dowd	**Joe McGann** *(Babies)*
PC Paul Georgiou	**Martyn Ellis** *(Babies)*
WPC Karen Walsh	**Susanna Shelling** *(Babies)*
WPC Janice Hargreaves	**Alphonsia Emmanuel** *(Babies)*
DI Charlie Flight	**Edward Wilson** *(Babies)*
Det. Supt. Munro	**Malcolm Terris** *(Babies)*
Chief Supt. Barry Wyatt	**Brian Croucher** *(Babies)*
DI Derek Hoskins	**James Aubrey** *(Folly)*
Insp. Leslie Yaxley	**Ian Brimble** *(Folly)*
DC Paul Whitmore	**Aaron Harris** *(Folly)*
WPC/Sgt Rachel Osborne	**Carole Nimmons** *(Folly)*
PC Guy Overton	**Craig Nightingale** *(Folly)*
WPC Hester Goswell	**Elizabeth Morton** *(Folly)*
PC Alfred Duggan	**John Hartley** *(Folly)*

Creator **Richard O'Keefe**
Producers **Leonard Lewis** *(Babies)*, **Ron Craddock** *(Folly)*

● ***An experienced police sergeant takes a team of rookie detectives under his wing.***

Rockliffe's Babies follows the progress of seven young police officers as they train to become detectives. It shows them venturing into some of London's seediest areas as part of the Met's Victor Tango division, coming to terms with the stresses and strains of the job and also coping with their demanding, and less than perfect, supervisor, DS Alan Rockliffe. His 'babies' consist of two WPCs, Hargreaves and Walsh, plus five male officers, Adams, Chitty, Hood, O'Dowd and Georgiou, men and women of diverse backgrounds now forced to work together.

After two successful seasons, the teetotal Rockliffe was given his own spin-off series, *Rockliffe's Folly*, in which he moves out of the capital and accepts a new appointment in Wessex, believing it to be a softer option. He soon discovers that hard crime still exists, even in this rural backwater.

Roddenberry, Gene

(Eugene Roddenberry; 1921–91)

American TV executive, one-time writer for series like HIGHWAY PATROL, NAKED CITY, DR KILDARE and particularly HAVE GUN WILL TRAVEL, but whose claim to fame was always STAR TREK, which he created and produced. Roddenberry was also responsible for STAR TREK: THE NEXT GENERATION. He was married to actress Majel Barrett, who played Nurse Christine Chapel in *Star Trek*, as well as Lwaxana Troi in *The Next Generation.*

Rodgers, Anton

(1933–)

Cambridgeshire-born actor seen on television since the late 1950s, although his major roles have been since the 1980s, primarily as William Fields in FRESH/FRENCH FIELDS, Alec Callender in MAY TO DECEMBER, vet Noah Kirby in NOAH'S ARK and Ronald Kegworthy in *Up Rising*. Earlier Rodgers played Lt. Gilmore in *The Sky Larks*, a 1958 comedy, was one of the actors to appear as Number 2 in THE PRISONER, assumed the role of Sir Percy Blakeney in *The Elusive Pimpernel*, took the part of Stanley Featherstonehaugh Ukridge in the P. G. Wodehouse series *Ukridge*, and was policeman David Gradley in the psychic series ZODIAC. He also played Edward Langtry in LILLIE, appeared in Roy Clarke's *Pictures*, was DI Purbright in MURDER MOST ENGLISH, and starred in Frederic Raphael's ten-part drama *After the War*. Guest appearances have come in series such as THE PROTECTORS, RANDALL AND HOPKIRK (DECEASED), *The Organisation*, UPSTAIRS, DOWNSTAIRS, RUMPOLE OF THE BAILEY, MAIGRET, MIDSOMER MURDERS and assorted single dramas like the *Performance* presentation of *After the Dance* (David Scott-Fowler) and *C. S. Lewis: Beyond Narnia* (Lewis).

Roger Roger ***

UK (BBC) Comedy Drama. BBC 1 1998–9; 2003

Sam .... **Robert Daws**
Dexter .... **Keith Allen**
Phil .... **Philip Glenister**
Reen .... **Pippa Guard**
Baz .... **David Ross**
Marlon .... **Ricci Harnett**
Barry .... **John Thomson**
Jonathan Moore
Rajiv .... **Paul Sharma**
André .... **Terence Maynard**
Cambridge .... **Chris Larkin**
Henry .... **Jude Akuwudike**
Tina .... **Barbara Durkin**
Chrissie .... **Helen Grace**
Marilyn .... **Joan Hodges**
Dr Geoff .... **Robert Glenister**
Kenny .... **Nicholas Gleaves**
Reece .... **Steven Meo**
Mack .... **Geff Francis**
Roland .... **Tim Preece**
May .... **Edna Doré**

Creator/Writer **John Sullivan**
Producers **Gareth Gwenlan, Tony Dow**

Misadventures in the life of the harassed boss of a minicab firm.

Sam, a widower, is co-proprietor of Cresta Cabs, a London-based minicab company. His partner, Dexter, is unreliable to say the least and proves it by throwing himself into the Thames from Blackfriars bridge and bequeathing a host of debts to the beleaguered business. His bimbo widow, Tina, fails to see the difficulty in the situation and, with as incompetent a crew of drivers as it is possible to hire, Sam is left to tear out his hair.

In the usual style of writer John Sullivan, the cast-list is large and finely honed. Among the cabbies is Phil, a frustrated rock musician whose relationship with waitress Chrissie (children Cher and Madonna) is on the rocks. (The character had featured even more prominently in the 1996 pilot episode, in which he was played by Neil Morrissey and his wife by Lesley Vickerage.) Ever-optimistic part-timer Baz also works as a postman and spends his social hours taking his latest dating-agency acquaintance to his favourite Chinese restaurant. The presence of his retarded step-son, Marlon, only makes his life more difficult. Of the other characters, André is the black stud, with children all over the place; Rajiv, the intelligent one who helps with the firm's books; Cambridge, the easily duped graduate; Barry, the loud-mouth; Henry, the African who can never find his way; and Reen, the unhappily married radio operator who still has feelings for old flame Sam.

With 18 months between pilot and series one, and the same time-span between series one and two, not to mention the major cast-changes, *Roger Roger* was slow to catch on, despite securing a peak-hour Saturday evening time-slot. It was so slow, in fact, that series three (just three episodes) did not arrive until four years after the second.

Rogers, Roy

(Leonard Slye; 1911–98)

'King of the Cowboys' Roy Rogers began his career in country and western music. He performed for a while under the name of Dick Weston before legally changing his name to Roy Rogers in 1942. In the late 1930s Rogers was groomed as a Hollywood cowboy, taught to ride and pitched into a series of Westerns, beginning with *Under Western Skies* in 1938. He became one of kids' TV's first favourites when he drifted on to the small screen, in THE ROY ROGERS SHOW, accompanied by his wife, Dale Evans (Frances Octavia Smith; 1912–2001 – the 'Queen of the West'), and his trusty steed, Trigger. Some of Rogers's old movies were also edited down for TV consumption. 'Happy Trails' was his theme song.

Rogers, Ted

(1935–2001)

Twinkly-eyed, fast-talking British comic whose finest hour arrived with the game show, 3–2–1, for which he was the finger-twiddling host for nine series. Previously, Rogers had been seen in numerous variety shows, from the *Billy Cotton Band Show* to SUNDAY NIGHT AT THE LONDON PALLADIUM, and his own brief series, *And So to Ted*.

Rogue Male **

UK (BBC/Twentieth Century-Fox) Drama. BBC 2 1976
DVD: Diamond Entertainment (Region 1 only)

Sir Robert Hunter .... **Peter O'Toole**
Quive Smith .... **John Standing**
The Earl .... **Alastair Sim**
Rebecca .... **Cyd Hayman**
Saul Abrahams .... **Harold Pinter**
Peale .... **Hugh Manning**
Jessel .... **Robert Lang**
Interrogator .... **Michael Byrne**
Vaner .... **Mark McManus**
Freda .... **Maureen Lipman**
Fisherman .... **Ray Smith**

First seaman .... **Philip Jackson**
Second seaman .... **Nicholas Ball**
Muller .... **Ian East**

Writer **Frederic Raphael**
Producer **Mark Shivas**

● ***An upper-class adventurer single-handedly tackles the rise of Fascist Germany.***

It is spring 1939 and only one man, it seems, is prepared to stand up to the greatest threat to world peace for a generation. That man is Sir Robert Hunter, a dashing gentleman hero who despairs at the indifference pervading Britain over the oncoming menace. Recognizing what needs to be done, and fuelled by the fact that his fiancée has been murdered by the Nazis, Hunter takes it upon himself to go to Germany and track down the person he describes as 'the biggest game in the world'. His plan does not succeed, however, and, on the run, Hunter is thrust into a series of life-threatening adventures and escapades.

Billed in the *Radio Times* as *Peter O'Toole in Rogue Male*, this one-off, 100-minute drama, directed by Clive Donner, was based on the novel of the same name written by Geoffrey Household in 1939, which had been filmed under the title *Man Hunt* in 1941 (starring Walter Pidgeon). Chris Gunning composed the series music.

Roll Over Beethoven ✶✶

UK (Central) Situation Comedy. ITV 1985

Belinda Purcell .... **Liza Goddard**
Nigel Cochrane .... **Nigel Planer**
Oliver Purcell .... **Richard Vernon**
Lem .... **Desmond McNamara**
Marvin .... **Emlyn Price**

Creators/Writers **Laurence Marks, Maurice Gran**
Executive Producer **Allan McKeown**
Producer **Tony Charles**

● ***A famous rock star and a demure music teacher fall in love.***

Crusty retired headmaster Oliver Purcell is not amused to hear that legendary rock star Nigel Cochrane has decided to give up touring and intends to move into his staid, peaceful village. He is even more disturbed when his own daughter, Belinda, begins to give Nigel piano lessons, and when they fall in love he very nearly needs oxygen. It is an unlikely romance. Belinda, usually the dutiful, demure daughter, hardly seems the type to turn a rock legend's head, but turn it she does. Belinda also supports Nigel by writing songs with his pal, Marvin. Eventually she cuts her own album and dad, despite his bluster, is really quite pleased. The two series were screened virtually back to back.

Rollason, Helen

MBE (1956–99)

London-born sports presenter whose brave fight against cancer proved inspiring to many. A former PE teacher, Rollason entered broadcasting with Essex Radio before joining Channel 4 to cover various sports, including the 1988 Olympics. She moved to the BBC and fronted NEWSROUND and then, in 1990, she became the first woman to present the BBC's GRANDSTAND, going on to anchor numerous other sports programmes and the sports sections of news bulletins. As her illness became widely known, she was featured in a BBC documentary, *Hope for Helen*, in 1998. Her courage in sickness was recognized with a new award for inspiration at the BBC's SPORTS REVIEW OF THE YEAR ceremony in 1999.

Romany Jones ✶

UK (LWT) Situation Comedy. ITV 1973–5

Bert Jones .... **James Beck**
Betty Jones .... **Jo Rowbottom**
Wally Briggs .... **Arthur Mullard**
Lily Briggs .... **Queenie Watts**
Jeremy Crichton-Jones .... **Jonathan Cecil**
Susan Crichton-Jones .... **Gay Soper**

Creators **Ronald Chesney, Ronald Wolfe**
Producer **Stuart Allen**

● ***Neighbour versus neighbour on a run-down campsite.***

Work-shy Bert Jones lives with his wife, Betty, in a battered, leaky, ant-ridden caravan on a grotty campsite. Their nearest neighbours are bluff Cockneys Wally and Lily Briggs and, needless to say, they don't always see eye to eye. Beginning as a one-off play in 1972, the series had just completed one successful run, with another in the can, when actor James Beck died. Recasting was necessary and snooty Jeremy and Susan Crichton-Jones were introduced as Wally and Lily's new neighbours. The Briggses were later given their own spin-off show, *Yus My Dear* (1976), in which Wally took a job as a bricklayer and they were transferred to the comfort of a council house. Wally's sponging brother, Benny (played by Mike Reid), was thrown in for company.

Rome ✶✶✶

UK/US (BBC/HBO) Historical Drama. BBC 2 2005–6

Julius Caesar .... **Ciaran Hinds**
Mark Antony .... **James Purefoy**
Lucius Vorenus .... **Kevin McKidd**
Titus Pullo .... **Ray Stevenson**
Atia of the Julii .... **Polly Walker**
Pompey Magnus .... **Kenneth Cranham**
Servilia .... **Lindsay Duncan**
Marcus Junius Brutus .... **Tobias Menzies**
Octavia of the Julii .... **Kerry Condon**
Porcius Cato .... **Karl Johnson**
Niobe .... **Indira Varma**
Marcus Tullius Cicero .... **David Bamber**
Gaius Octavian .... **Max Pirkis**
Posca .... **Nicholas Woodeson**
Scipio .... **Paul Jesson**
Timon .... **Lee Boardman**
Clarissa .... **Anna Francolini**
Eleni .... **Suzanne Bertish**
Eirene .... **Chiara Mastalli**
Calpurnia .... **Hadyn Gwynne**
Vorena the Elder .... **Coral Amiga**
Lyde .... **Esther Hall**
Quintus Pompey .... **Rick Warden**
Erastes Fulmen .... **Lorcan Cranitch**

Producer **Frank Doelger**

● ***The battle for power begins as a triumphant Caesar returns to Rome.***

Filmed over 12 months at Rome's Cinecittà studios, this

near-epic presentation of the last days of the Republic of Rome was shot on a full-size set specially created to mimic the true colour and, indeed, squalor of the Eternal City in its heyday. Directors like Michael Apted worked on scripts mostly penned by Bruno Heller to bring the $100 million joint US/UK production to the screen in 11 parts (the final two shown together as a feature-length finale in the UK). The story picks up in 52 BC, with Julius Caesar and his men returning home after a gruelling stint of active duty abroad. Caesar has subdued the Gauls and returns to the city a hero, with ambitions to take what is now a failing republic and hold it together as dictator. However, there are others like Pompey who have designs on the top job, and the scheming, plotting and murdering continue apace as the battle for the hot seat warms up. Villain of the piece is the promiscuous Atia, Caesar's niece. Her rival is Caesar's elegant former lover, Servilia. This is the scenario at the top of society. For Caesar's men, at the bottom of the social ladder, life is just as demanding, if not as comfortable. They are represented by honourable centurion Lucius Vorenus and thuggish legionnaire Titus Pullo, who find life hard now they are back with their estranged families and associates. The language is blunt and strong, violence lies at every turn, and sex scenes are coarse and plentiful.

Roobarb ***

UK (Bob Godfrey) Children's Entertainment. BBC 1 1974–5
DVD: Contender

Narrator **Richard Briers**

Creator/Writer **Grange Calveley**
Producer **Bob Godfrey**

Cat and dog one-upmanship.

Drawn in dazzling colours, and in a distinctively half-finished, wobbly style (making a virtue out of a low budget), *Roobarb* concerns the daily battles of an ambitious green dog named Roobarb and a cynical, laid-back pink cat called Custard. (Producer Bob Godfrey likened the relationship to the one shared by Tony Hancock and Sid James.) Events take place in a back garden, with a fenceful of smirking birds taking sides with the winner. Quirkily narrated by Richard Briers and filled with adult wit, the series became a favourite with all ages, although it was aimed squarely at the children's market. Thirty years after its demise, creator Grange Calveley brought back the series with new scripts as *Roobarb and Custard Too* (five 2005). Although now digitally animated, the series preserved its wobbly look and once again featured the vocal talents or Richard Briers.

Room 101 ***

UK (Hat Trick) Comedy. BBC 2 1994–

Presenters **Nick Hancock, Paul Merton**

Producers **Lissa Evans, Toby Stevens, Victoria Payne**

Celebrities name the things they detest most in life.

Taking its cue from George Orwell's 1984, in which Room 101 is the place of ultimate torture, this series (which began on Radio 5) comically explores the *bêtes noires* of its famous guests. Choosing irritating pop songs, useless domestic tools, corny books, nauseating TV programmes, or even more abstract items, participants need to convince host Paul Merton (earlier Nick Hancock) that these things they hate most should be consigned to Room 101 where they can do their worst. Each item is illustrated with snippets of music, film clips, cardboard cut-outs, etc. Merton then declines or accepts the offer, sending the offending objects down a shaft (previously along a crematorium-style conveyor-belt and through a sliding door) into this bleak TV vision of Hell.

Root, Amanda

(1963–)

Essex-born actress seen in *The House of Bernarda Alba* (Adela), CATHERINE COOKSON'S *The Man Who Cried* (Hilda Maxwell), *Love on a Branch Line* (Miss Mounsey), BREAKING THE CODE (Pat Green) and *Turning World* (Evelyn Sharples), before taking the lead role in *Mortimer's Law* (Rachel Mortimer). Amanda has also featured in *Big Cat* (Alice), ANNA KARENINA (Dolly), THE FORSYTE SAGA (Winifred Forsyte), DANIEL DERONDA (Mrs Davilow), *Love Again* (Maeve Brennan), ALL ABOUT ME (Miranda), *The Robinsons* (Maggie) and *Empire* (Noella). Smaller roles and guest appearances have come in *Time for Murder*, LADIES IN CHARGE, *Worlds Beyond*, THE BUDDHA OF SUBURBIA, P. D. JAMES, SUNNYSIDE FARM, HOLBY CITY, A SMALL SUMMER PARTY, WAKING THE DEAD, A TOUCH OF FROST, MIDSOMER MURDERS, FOYLE'S WAR, ROSE AND MALONEY, *Julian Fellowes Investigates* and *The Afternoon Play*.

Root into Europe **

UK (Central) Comedy. ITV 1992

Henry Root .... **George Cole**
Muriel Root .... **Patricia Heywood**

Writers **William Donaldson, Mark Chapman**
Producers **Mark Chapman, Justin Judd**

An irrepressible bigot challenges foreign culture.

In the late 1970s, a series of opinionated, right-wing letters elicited some revealing and amusing replies from senior Establishment figures. The writer of the missives was one Henry Root, owner of a chain of wet fish shops and a natural chauvinist. But Root was fiction, a character dreamt up by writer William Donaldson, who in 1980 collated his spoof letters and their earnest replies into a best-selling book, *The Henry Root Letters*. As 1992 approached, with trade barriers falling all across the European Community, Donaldson resurrected his obnoxious alter-ego for this five-part TV series. Casting George Cole in the lead, and Patricia Heywood as his downtrodden wife, Donaldson and co-writer/producer Mark Chapman sent Root across the Channel as a self-appointed protector of English heritage. For Root, a dark threat from foreign culture and customs lurks only a short ferry ride away and he sees himself as the man to stand up for all that is right and proper. This eventful journey takes him from his home at The Anchorage, Lakeside Avenue, Esher (changed from a London address in the original letters) to France, Belgium, Spain, Italy, Germany and Holland. Along the way, the arrogant Root defiantly squares up to Johnny Foreigner at every turn, only to come off much the worse.

Roots ★★★

US (ABC/David L. Wolper) Drama. BBC 1 1977 (US: ABC 1977)
DVD: Warner Home Video

Kunta Kinte .... **Le Var Burton**
Toby (Kunta Kinte) .... **John Amos**
Binta .... **Cicely Tyson**
Omoro .... **Thalmus Rasulala**
Nyo Boto .... **Maya Angelou**
Kadi Touray .... **O. J. Simpson**
The Wrestler .... **Ji-Tu Cumbuka**
Kintango .... **Moses Gunn**
Fiddler .... **Louis Gossett Jr**
Gardner .... **William Watson**
Kizzy .... **Leslie Uggams**
Capt. Thomas Davies .... **Edward Asner**
Third Mate Slater .... **Ralph Waite**
John Reynolds .... **Lorne Greene**
Mrs Reynolds .... **Lynda Day George**
Dr William Reynolds .... **Robert Reed**
Carrington .... **Paul Shenar**
Tom Moore .... **Chuck Connors**
Ordell .... **John Schuck**
Mingo .... **Scatman Crothers**
Stephen Bennett .... **George Hamilton**
Evan Brent .... **Lloyd Bridges**
Tom Harvey .... **Georg Stanford Brown**
Irene Harvey .... **Lynne Moody**
Sam Bennett .... **Richard Roundtree**
Ames .... **Vic Morrow**
The Drummer .... **Raymond St Jacques**
Missy Anne .... **Sandy Duncan**
Squire James .... **MacDonald Carey**
Chicken George Moore .... **Ben Vereen**
Mrs Moore .... **Carolyn Jones**
Sir Eric Russell .... **Ian McShane**
Sister Sara .... **Lillian Randolph**
Jemmy Brent .... **Doug McClure**
Justin .... **Burl Ives**
Lewis .... **Hilly Hicks**

Writers **William Blinn, Ernest Kinoy, James Lee, Max Cohen**
Executive Producer **David L. Wolper**
Producer **Stan Margulies**

● ***The saga of a black American family, from its roots in slavery to the Civil War.***

If RICH MAN, POOR MAN was the mini-series that launched the idea of dramatizing popular novels with a star-studded cast, *Roots* was the serial which ensured the concept stayed well and truly afloat. This 12-hour drama was an enormous success, telling the story of various generations of a black American family, picking up the action around 1750 with the birth of a boy in a Gambian tribe. At the age of 17, the boy, Kunta Kinte, is kidnapped by white slave-traders and taken to America. Adopting the new name of Toby, he is set to work on the southern plantations, but remains doggedly independent, even losing a foot in an attempt to escape. The series then follows the misfortunes of Kunta Kinte and his clan over a hundred-year period. It sees his daughter, Kizzy, raped by her owner and giving birth to a son later known as Chicken George (because of his prowess with fighting birds), who spends some time in slavery in England. George's son, Tom, fights in the American Civil War and with his family looks forward to the emancipation of slaves that follows. But, as they embark on a move to Tennessee and the dream of a better life, they discover that their new 'freedom', with its grim poverty, poor education and feeble rights, is not the true liberty they envisaged.

That isn't the end of the *Roots* saga, however. In 1979, a sequel, entitled *Roots: The Next Generations* (featuring top actors like Henry Fonda, Marlon Brando and Richard Thomas), picks up the story in the 1880s and runs through to the late 1960s. It sees Tom, his daughter and then his granddaughter begin to make inroads in society. At the end of the family line comes Alex (played by James Earl Jones), a noted writer who is sufficiently intrigued by his family history that he returns to Africa to learn how his great-great-great-great-grandfather, Kunta Kinte, was so cruelly robbed of his freedom.

Roots and *Roots: The Next Generations* were adapted from the book by Alex Haley – the Alex of its storyline. The success of the original series (over half the population of America watched the final episode) can be put down partly to its all-star cast, and partly to the fact that the USA was swept by blizzards on the eight consecutive nights on which the series was shown. Some critics have claimed that white Americans gave the series their time in repentance for the sins of their ancestors. Others have simply suggested that sensationalism was the reason for its success, questioning the accuracy of the facts.

Rose and Maloney ★★★

UK (Company Pictures/Storm Dog) Drama. ITV 1 2002; 2004

Rose Linden .... **Sarah Lancashire**
Maloney .... **Phil Davis**
Bea Linden .... **Anne Reid**
Wendy .... **Susan Brown**
Joyce .... **Nisha Nayar**

Creator **Bryan Elsley**
Writers **Bryan Elsley, Peter Flannery**
Producers **Tom Grieves, Catherine Wearing**

● ***Chalk-and-cheese investigators correct miscarriages of justice.***

Rose Linden is a dedicated but rather disorganized case manager for the Criminal Justice Review Agency, a body set up to analyse instances where the legal process may just have got it wrong. Her fellow caseworker is Maloney, a nervy, methodical man who has to cope with Rose's brilliant mind but also her infuriatingly headstrong way of working. Rose's personal life mirrors her professional: she drinks and smokes too much, she's been banned from driving and she suffers from diabetes. What's more, she has a boyfriend who's serving a life sentence. Maloney is on probabation in his job, so he has every reason to be concerned about Rose's 'bend the rules' style of investigating. Together, however, they make a good team, their job being to reanalyse the facts and, where appropriate, restore hope and pride to lives blighted by miscarriages of justice. Their work brings them into contact with a man imprisoned for killing his daughter; a teenager convicted for murder when aged ten but still stressing his innocence; a nanny jailed for murdering a baby in her care; and a prisoner languishing in jail for murdering a fellow inmate. Wendy (played by Jenny Howe in the pilot two-parter, screened in 2002) is their Chief Commissioner boss, who answers to the Home Office, and Joyce is a junior member of the team. Bea is Rose's mother (played by Pauline Yates in the pilot). Three two-part stories followed the pilot.

Roseanne [1]

(1952–)

Outspoken stand-up comic who quickly took control of the TV sitcom named after her. In ROSEANNE, she portrayed a shirty, sarcastic working mum (Roseanne Conner) and led the programme to the top of the US ratings. Her name changed from Barr to Arnold after she wed her second husband, comic Tom Arnold, who also worked on the show. However, following the breakdown of that marriage and her remarriage, she has preferred to be billed simply as Roseanne. Her own talk show, *The Roseanne Show*, has also been seen in the UK.

Roseanne [2] ★★★★

US (Carsey-Werner/Full Moon & High Tide) Situation Comedy. Channel 4 1989–97 (US: ABC 1988–97)
DVD: Anchor Bay Entertainment

Roseanne Conner	**Roseanne (Barr/Arnold)**
Dan Conner	**John Goodman**
Jackie Harris	**Laurie Metcalf**
Rebecca 'Becky' Conner/Healy	**Lecy Goranson** **Sarah Chalke**
Darlene Conner	**Sara Gilbert**
David Jacob 'DJ' Conner	**Michael Fishman**
Crystal Anderson/Conner	**Natalie West**
Booker Brooks	**George Clooney**
Ed Conner	**Ned Beatty**
Mark Healy	**Glenn Quinn**
Bonnie	**Bonnie Sheridan**
Leon Carp	**Martin Mull**
Bev Harris	**Estelle Parsons**
Arnie Merchant/Thomas	**Tom Arnold**
Nancy Bartlett	**Sandra Bernhard**
Nana Mary	**Shelley Winters**
David Healy	**Johnny Galecki**
Fred	**Michael O'Keefe**
Scott	**Fred Willard**
Heather	**Heather Matarazzo**

Creator **Matt Williams**
Executive Producers **Marcy Carsey, Tom Werner, Roseanne Barr/Arnold, Tom Arnold**
Producers **Matt Williams, Jeff Harris**

● ***Down-to-earth comedy of life in Middle America.***

Roseanne and Dan Conner, two heavyweight wisecrackers, live at 714 Delaware Street, in the lacklustre town of Lanford, Illinois. Dan is a dry-waller in the building industry, where work is patchy; Roseanne flits from job to job, abusing her employers and dreaming of the day when bills stop arriving. But there is not much chance of that with three demanding kids to support. Eldest is Becky, a typically precocious teenager, anxious to grow up and dismissive of her parents' efforts to keep the family afloat. Next is sports-mad tomboy Darlene, comfortable with her plainness, acerbic in her wit and always her dad's best buddy. Runt of the litter is DJ, a slightly off-beat youth, the jewel of his parents' eyes and the bane of his sisters' lives. Well into the programme's run, the Conners produce a fourth child, named Jerry Garcia, after Roseanne's Grateful Dead hero.

Hovering around the comfortable but functional home is Roseanne's unmarried sister, Jackie Harris. Moping between jobs (she is at one time a cop and then a truck-driver) and boyfriends, she is Roseanne's confidante and disrupter of Dan's mealtimes. Jackie, too, gives birth to a son, fathered by Fred, (briefly) her husband. On the fringes are Rosie's half-baked friend Crystal, who later marries Dan's absent father, Ed, and an assortment of work colleagues and bosses from Roseanne's times as plastic factory worker, sweeper-up at a beauty salon and coffee-shop waitress in a shopping mall. The Conners also try their hand at running a motorbike repair shop and, when that fails, Roseanne joins Jackie, their grating mum Bev and bisexual friend Nancy in opening The Lunch Box, a loose meat diner.

The novel thing about *Roseanne* is the sheer ordinariness of its lead characters. Here is a family that eats convenience foods, watches TV all day and lives on the telephone. They work hard yet get nowhere, but the family unit remains whole, even if it does stretch at the seams from time to time, especially when Becky runs off and marries her punk boyfriend, Mark, and Darlene also leaves home for art college and secretly moves in with Mark's brother, David. An enlightened approach to parenthood and an irrepressible sense of humour make the family tick, even in the most difficult of times.

In the final series, domestic drudgery is abandoned when Roseanne and Jackie win the state lottery and launch themselves into an unlikely world of luxury hotels and financial wheeler-dealing, which tears the family apart. The fact that ABSOLUTELY FABULOUS characters Edina and Patsy (Jennifer Saunders and Joanna Lumley) join them in one episode reveals how far they have strayed from their home in downbeat Lanford. However, this uncharacteristic final season is placed into context in the last, extended episode, in which Darlene and David's baby daughter, Harris, is brought home. In the closing minutes, Roseanne reveals that the crazy events of previous weeks were only a fantasy. Writing her memoirs, she explains that times, in fact, had continued to be hard and announces how much she misses Dan, who had died from a heart attack which viewers had previously been led to believe he had survived.

Rosemary and Thyme ★

UK (Carnival Films) Detective Drama. ITV 1 2003–6
DVD: Acorn Media

Rosemary Boxer	**Felicity Kendal**
Laura Thyme	**Pam Ferris**
Matthew Thyme	**Ryan Philpott**
Helena Thyme	**Daisy Dunlop**

Producer **Brian Eastman**

● ***Country criminality – with gardening tips.***

No doubt inspired by the massive success of MIDSOMER MURDERS, ITV commissioned this lightweight whodunnit in a similar vein, reaching out to the gardening public at the same time. Laura Thyme is a farmer's daughter, a former police officer, recently dumped by her detective husband (son Matthew is another copper; daughter Helena appears in series two). To rebuild her life, she joins forces with university horticulture lecturer Rosemary Boxer, who has just lost her job. Their gardening business (Rosemary & Thyme) takes them into the picturesque heart of rural England, where, as we know only too well from the Midsomer experience, there is nothing more dangerous than envious neighbours, families with skeletons in their closets or private schools with arcane rituals. Inevitably, our green-fingered gumshoes triumph thyme and again, their success built on a daily diet of hiding behind hedges, peering through lace curtains and eavesdropping on village gossip.

Easy on the eye, *Rosemary and Thyme* – like its contrived title – is rather easy on the brain, forced into somewhat camp, simplistic plots by its restrictive one-hour format (although the first episode of series two – in which the modern-day Snoop Sisters spend some time working the gardens and murder hotspots of the French and Italian Rivieras – is a two-hour special). That said, viewers liked what they saw, with 11 million of them making it ITV's most-watched new drama of 2003. GARDENERS' WORLD's Pippa Greenwood was the series' horticultural consultant.

Rosenthal, Jack

CBE (1931–2004)

Award-winning British screenwriter, creator of the comedy series THE DUSTBINMEN, THE LOVERS, *Sadie, It's Cold Outside* and *Moving Story*, and writer of many single dramas notable for their wry humour and clever social observation. Among the highlights were *Pie in the Sky, Green Rub* (both 1963), the *Playhouse* presentation *There's a Hole in Your Dustbin, Delilah* (1968, which proved to be the pilot for *The Dustbinmen*), *Another Sunday and Sweet FA* (1972), *Polly Put the Kettle On, Mr Ellis versus the People* and *There'll Almost Always be an England* (all 1974, the last two from the *Village Hall* anthology), *The Evacuees* (1975), READY WHEN YOU ARE MR MCGILL, BAR MITZVAH BOY (both 1976), SPEND, SPEND, SPEND, *Spaghetti Two-Step* (both 1977), *The Knowledge* (1979), *P'tang Yang Kipperbang* (1982), *Mrs Capper's Birthday* (1985), *Fools on the Hill* (1986), *And a Nightingale Sang* (1989), *Screen One's Wide-Eyed and Legless* (1993), and ESKIMO DAY/COLD ENOUGH FOR SNOW (1996/1997), plus LONDON'S BURNING (1986, which, again, led to a full series, but with no Rosenthal involvement). Rosenthal also wrote for Maureen Lipman's *About Face* series (she was his wife). His earliest TV work was on CORONATION STREET (129 episodes, plus some as producer) and he also contributed to programmes like THE ODD MAN, *Bulldog Breed*, THAT WAS THE WEEK THAT WAS, *The Villains*, PARDON THE EXPRESSION, MRS THURSDAY, BOOTSIE AND SNUDGE and COMEDY PLAYHOUSE (some with his one-time partner, Harry Driver). One of his last works was a new adaptation of *Lucky Jim* for ITV 1 in 2003.

Rosenthal, Jim

(1947–)

British sports frontman, formerly in newspapers and then with BBC Radio. For ITV Sport, he has presented coverage of athletics, soccer, boxing, motor racing and other major events.

Rosie

See *Growing Pains of PC Penrose, The.*

Rosie and Jim ★★

UK (Ragdoll/Central) Children's Entertainment. ITV 1990–2; 1995–2004
DVD: Cinema Club

Presenters **John Cunliffe, Pat Hutchins, Neil Brewer**

Creators **Anne Wood, Doug Wilcox**

● ***Two rag-doll puppets come to life when their bargee companion turns his back.***

This long-running infants' favourite is set aboard the narrowboat *Ragdoll*, home of mischievous Rosie and Jim, themselves a couple of rag dolls. The boat's owner – ignorant of their activities and bemused by the inevitable changes they bring about – also takes on the guise of presenter of the programme, drawing and telling stories and fronting filmed inserts exploring the neighbourhood where the boat has moored. In all, 175 *Rosie and Jims* were produced. First host/writer is John Cunliffe (creator of POSTMAN PAT), who was affectionately dubbed 'Fizzgog' by the dolls. He is replaced after 50 episodes by illustrator Pat Hutchins ('Loopy Lobes'), who was looking for ideas for her pictures, with musician Neil Brewer ('Tootle') hopping aboard for the final 80 editions in search of musical inspiration on the *Ragdoll*'s travels.

Roslin, Gaby

(1964–)

London-born presenter, the daughter of radio announcer Clive Roslin. She first gained attention in the children's programme MOTORMOUTH, after spending time on a cable TV show called *Hippo*, and on the back of this was chosen to be Chris Evans's co-host from the start of THE BIG BREAKFAST. Roslin then hosted the nature series *Predators*, and her own Channel 4 chat show, and began to co-present the annual CHILDREN IN NEED appeals with Terry Wogan. Her other series have included *The Real Holiday Show, Television's Greatest Hits, Whatever You Want, Watchdog Healthcheck, TV Revealed, A Question of TV*, the *BBC Animal Awards, The Terry and Gaby Show* and *Solution Street*.

Ross, David

Blackburn-born actor, largely cast in comic roles. Among his most prominent roles have been parts in *Yanks Go Home* (Harry Duckworth), *Leave It to Charlie* (Harry Hutchins), SCULLY (Steve), GBH (Mr Weller), *Jake's Progress* (Eliot), CORONATION STREET (Lester Fontayne), ESKIMO DAY (Bevis Whittle), ROGER ROGER (Baz), *Melissa* (Dr Selwyn-Swanton), VANITY FAIR (Mr Sedley), OLIVER TWIST (Mr Bumble), *Station Jim* (Chambers) and THE GREEN GREEN GRASS (Elgin Sparrowhawk). Smaller roles have been in series like THE OUTSIDER, THE ADVENTURES OF SHERLOCK HOLMES, WYCLIFFE, THE BRITTAS EMPIRE, HARBOUR LIGHTS, THE BILL, LONDON'S BURNING, WHERE THE HEART IS, HEARTBEAT, MURDER IN MIND and MIDSOMER MURDERS. Additionally, he was the first actor to play Kryten in RED DWARF, before Robert Llewellyn took over the part of the hapless robot.

Ross, Joe E.

(1914–82)

American comic actor, seen as Sgt Rupert Ritzik in THE PHIL SILVERS SHOW and later a star in his own right, playing the podgy Officer Gunther Toody in CAR 54, WHERE ARE YOU? A later series, *It's About Time* (in which he played a caveman), was less successful and he soon turned to animation voicing as a new career path (among others, he was the voice of Botch in HELP! IT'S THE HAIR BEAR BUNCH and SGT FLINT in Hong Kong Phooey).

Ross, Jonathan

OBE (1960–)

Former TV researcher (for programmes like Channel 4's *Soul Train*) who became an instant hit in the mid-1980s when he hosted his own chat show, THE LAST RESORT. His snappy suits and distinctive speech impediment (a soft 'r'), quickly helped ensure celebrity status. He has since hosted *One Hour with Jonathan Ross*, *Tonight With Jonathan Ross*, *The Saturday Zoo* and *Friday Night with Jonathan Ross*, and sat in for *Wogan*. Ross's other credits have included *The Incredibly Strange Film Show*, *Mondo Rosso* (cult films), *Jonathan Ross in Stop! Kung Fu!*, *Gagtag* (chairman), *Americana* (a documentary series about American lifestyles), *Fascinating Facts!*, *The Best of Enemies*, *The Big Big Talent Show*, *In Search of Bond*, THEY THINK IT'S ALL OVER, IT'S ONLY TV BUT I LIKE IT (questionmaster), HOLLYWOOD GREATS, *Britain's Best Sitcom*, *Secret Map of Hollywood*, and numerous award ceremonies as emcee (especially THE BRITISH COMEDY AWARDS). He set up (and then sold) the Channel X production company and in 1999 took over as host of the FILM series. His brother Paul is also a presenter.

Ross, Nick

(1947–)

British current affairs anchorman, initially working for the BBC in Northern Ireland on *Scene Around Six*. He was once presenter of BREAKFAST TIME and the NATIONWIDE successor, *Sixty Minutes*, but is best known for being at the helm of CRIMEWATCH UK since 1984. Ross has also hosted its associated programmes, *Crimewatch Files* and *Crimestoppers*, plus WATCHDOG, *On the Record*, DID YOU SEE . . . ?, *Westminster with Nick Ross*, *The Search*, *Gridlock: Bank Holiday Hell*, *So You Think You're a Good Driver?* and the quiz *The Syndicate*, as well as presenting and directing *Out of Court* and contributing to series like MAN ALIVE and HORIZON.

Rossington, Jane

(1943–)

Blonde British actress, Jill Richardson/Harvey/Chance in CROSSROADS throughout the series' entire first run. Indeed, it was Jane who uttered the first words on the programme: 'Crossroads Motel, can I help you?' Her other TV credits have been few, notably the part of nurse Kate Ford in EMERGENCY – WARD 10 before *Crossroads*, and an episode of *Dramarama* since. She returned to *Crossroads* on its revival in 2001.

Rossiter, Leonard

(1926–84)

Acclaimed British actor, a viewers' favourite as seedy landlord Rigsby in RISING DAMP. He proved just as popular when suffering a mid-life crisis in THE FALL AND RISE OF REGINALD PERRIN. Rossiter did not turn professional until his late 20s and his flair for comedy was even slower to emerge. When he first arrived on the small screen in the 1960s, after notable stage performances, he was primarily a straight actor. One of his early roles was that of DI Bamber in Z CARS, although he also appeared in the satire show BBC-3. Among his other credits were Nigel Kneale's controversial THE YEAR OF THE SEX OLYMPICS (Co-ordinator Ugo Priest), the HTV movie *Thick as Thieves*, the Andrew Davies drama *Fearless Frank*, and the Roy Clarke COMEDY PLAYHOUSE presentation *Pygmalion Smith*. He also made guest appearances in series like THE AVENGERS and STEPTOE AND SON, provided the voice for the dog Boot in *The Perishers*, and was regularly seen spilling Cinzano over Joan Collins in commercials. Rossiter's final sitcoms were *The Losers* (wrestling manager Sydney Foskett) and TRIPPER'S DAY (supermarket manager Norman Tripper). Screened posthumously, his portrayal of King John in a *BBC Shakespeare* offering was a last reminder of his versatility. Both his wives were also in the acting business: Josephine Tewson and Gillian Raine.

Rothwell, Alan

(1937–)

Oldham-born actor, seen on television for over 40 years. Undoubtedly his best-remembered part was that of the ill-fated David Barlow (Ken's brother) in CORONATION STREET, which he played for eight years up to 1968. Taking time out from the *Street*, Rothwell was also seen in the South American spy caper TOP SECRET (Mike) and OLIVER TWIST (Charley Bates), and he later moved into children's entertainment as presenter of *Picture Box*, *Hickory House* and *Daisy Daisy*. He has been seen in Z CARS, CROWN COURT, ALL CREATURES GREAT AND SMALL, HEARTBEAT, CHILDREN'S WARD (Dr Davies), HETTY WAINTHROPP INVESTIGATES, THE GRAND, EMMERDALE (John Kenyon), SHIPMAN, FAT FRIENDS and CONVICTION (Mr Lindon), among other dramas, and also played junkie Nicholas Black in BROOKSIDE and Gerry Stringer in DEAD MAN WEDS.

Roughnecks ★★

UK (First Choice) Drama. BBC 1 1994–5

Tom .... **James Cosmo**
Tessa .... **Teresa Banham**
Ceefax .... **Colum Convey**
Ian .... **Paul Copley**
Cinders .... **Ricky Tomlinson**
Chris .... **Liam Cunningham**
Hilary .... **Francesca Hunt**
Heather .... **Ashley Jensen**
Terry .... **Bruce Jones**
Drew McAllister .... **John McGlynn**
Izzy .... **Annie Raitt**
Archie .... **Clive Russell**
Davey .... **Alec Westwood**
Kevin .... **George Rossi**
Wilf ('Village') .... **Hywel Simons**
Cath .... **Katy Murphy**
Edvard .... **Martin Wenner**

Creator **Kieran Prendiville**
Writers **Kieran Prendiville, Steve Coombes, Dave Robinson, Alan Whiting, Brian Elsley**
Producers **Charles Elton, Moira Williams**

● ***The personal and professional problems facing a team of oil rig workers.***

Osprey Explorer is an oil rig anchored in the bleak North Sea; *Roughnecks* is the story of its crew. Highlighting the dangers of offshore work, the series puts the miscellaneous team members in life-and-death situations and traps them for weeks on end in a claustrophobic environment where, to make matters worse, alcohol is banned. Worries are introduced over dodgy equipment and pressure is applied to the crew, who risk finding themselves out of work if they fail to strike oil. Relief provided by time ashore is often short-lived, thanks to trouble in the personal lives they resume. Tom is the main administrator on the rig and it is his Greenacres guest house in Aberdeen, run by wife Izzy and student daughter Heather, that the crew repair to on leave. Heather is seeing the much-older Chris, a driller colleague, much to her dad's displeasure. Drew is the superintendent of the rig, Terry is its skipper and Ian is the chief engineer. Other team members are Tessa, an engineer who fancies Drew; crane operator Archie, who keeps a pet rabbit; the intellectual Ceefax, who fancies Hilary, a scientist from Surrey; and Jack-the-lad drillers Davey and Kevin. Village is the Welsh dogsbody, while Cinders is the wisecracking, chauvinistic chef and part-time cab driver. New arrivals in series two include hard-nosed new boss Edvard, from the Scandinavian owners Norsco, and Cath, a worker at the heliport. Thirteen episodes were made in total, after creator Kieran Prendiville spent two years researching rig life.

Routledge, Patricia

CBE (1929–)

Birkenhead-born actress, much seen in supporting roles until blooming as Hyacinth Bucket (pronounced 'Bouquet') in Roy Clarke's KEEPING UP APPEARANCES and then as the eponymous pensioner sleuth in HETTY WAINTHROPP INVESTIGATES. Other appearances of note have come in 1964's *Victoria Regina* (Queen Victoria, ageing from 18 to 80), the BBC's 1975 version of *David Copperfield* (Mrs Micawber), the comedy MARJORIE AND MEN (divorcée Marjorie Belton), the *Bookmark* presentation, *Miss Pym's Day Out, Anybody's Nightmare* (Sheila Bowler), and in Alan Bennett's TALKING HEADS. Routledge has also been heard narrating programmes such as *The Natural World* and has been seen in series and single offerings like Z CARS, DOCTOR AT LARGE, *Sense and Sensibility, Nicholas Nickleby*, STEPTOE AND SON, *The Cost of Loving, A Visit from Miss Protheroe*, THE TWO RONNIES, CROWN COURT, AND MOTHER MAKES FIVE, TALES OF THE UNEXPECTED, *First and Last* and *Victoria Wood – As Seen on TV*.

Roving Report ★★

UK (ITN) Documentary. ITV 1957–64

Reporters **Robin Day, George Ffitch, Tim Brinton, John Hartley, Reginald Bosanquet, Huw Thomas, Lynne Reid Banks, Ian Trethowan, Neville Barker, Elizabeth Kenrick, John Whale**

Creator/Editor **Geoffrey Cox**
Producers **Michael Barsley, Robert Verrall**

Short documentaries looking at people and places in the news around the world.

Roving Report was ITN's first programme that was not exclusively news-based. It consisted of a collection of documentary films of about 20 minutes in length, compiled by ITN reporters as they travelled the world. The films were often by-products of a news-seeking expedition but, nevertheless, had their own distinct character and aimed to paint a picture of the people of a foreign city or country at that time in the news, reflecting their views, thoughts, ways of life, etc. The first programme was recorded atop the Empire State Building. Robin Day was the chief reporter in the early days.

Rowan, Dan

(1922–87)

See *Martin, Dick*.

Rowan and Martin's Laugh-In ★★★

US (Romart) Comedy. BBC 2 1968–71 (US: NBC 1968–73)
DVD: Rhino (Region 1 only)

Dan Rowan, Dick Martin, Gary Owens, Ruth Buzzi, Judy Carne, Goldie Hawn, Arte Johnson, Henry Gibson, Eileen Brennan, Jo Anne Worley, Roddy Maude-Roxby, Larry Hovis, Pigmeat Markham, Charlie Brill, Dick Whittington, Chelsea Brown, Mitzi McCall, Alan Sues, Dave Madden, Jeremy Lloyd, Teresa Graves, Pamela Rodgers, Byron Gilliam, Lily Tomlin, Ann Elder, Dennis Allen, Johnny Brown, Barbara Sharma, Nancy Phillips, Harvey Jason

Executive Producers **George Schlatter, Ed Friendly**

Hugely popular and influential, fast-moving gag show.

Hosts of *Laugh-In* were Dan Rowan, a smooth straightman, and his grinning fool of a partner, Dick Martin, but they were more than backed up by a large cast of zany comedians who worked around them. The show itself was a cross between slapstick and satire, a sort of Keystone Cops meet THAT WAS THE WEEK THAT WAS, all fused together on bright sets by 1960s TV technology. There were gags galore, not all of them terribly funny, but the weight of numbers meant that the audience just had to find something amusing.

Long before THE FAST SHOW was conceived, catchphrases were *Laugh-In*'s speciality. From Dan and Dick's 'You bet your sweet bippy' and 'Look that up in your Funk and Wagnalls', to 'Sock it to me', a cue for Judy Carne to get a thorough soaking. Even Richard Nixon dropped in to say it. Popular features and sketches included 'Letters to *Laugh-In*', the 'Flying Fickle Finger of Fate' (a mock talent show award), and the non-stop joke wall that wound up each programme, with cast members flinging open doors to belt out one-liners. All this came after Rowan and Martin had parodied the old Burns and Allen ending ('Say goodnight, Dick': 'Goodnight Dick').

Also memorable were the man riding a toddler's tricycle; Henry Gibson, the flower-power poet; and Ruth Buzzi as Gladys, the vicious lady on the park bench thrashing Arte Johnson's Tyrone, a dirty old man, with her umbrella. Johnson also popped up from behind a pot plant, as a German soldier muttering 'Very interesting, but stupid.' Lily Tomlin appeared as Ernestine, the sarcastic telephone-operator, and Alan Sues played a gormless sports presenter. Then there was Gary Owens, hand cupped over ear, bellowing into the microphone to welcome viewers to 'Beautiful Downtown Burbank', Pigmeat Markham, whose 'Here Comes The Judge' was a UK chart hit in 1968, and Goldie Hawn establishing herself as a dumb, giggly blonde.

The jokes were topical, sometimes controversial and generally very silly, but they were held together by slick editing, cameo appearances from guest stars and the hectic pace of the show. *Laugh-In* was the world's favourite comedy programme for two or three years. When it ended, Buzzi and Owens were the only cast members (apart from the hosts) still with it. The show was revived in 1979, but its time had long passed and this version is notable only for the fact that Robin Williams was one of the supporting performers.

Rowlands, Patsy

(1934–2005)

British actress, often seen as a dowdy wife, but enjoying a long and varied TV career. Among her wifely roles were Rosemary in INSIDE GEORGE WEBLEY, Betty in BLESS THIS HOUSE and

Netta in KINVIG. In contrast, she was Sally Army Sister Alice Meredith in HALLELUJAH! and also appeared in the kids' series *Follow That Dog* (Sgt Bryant), *Raven* (Mrs Young) and *Break in the Sun* (Mrs Granger), and the sitcom *The Nesbitts are Coming* (WPC Kitty Naylor). Rowlands took the roles of Miss Twitty in another children's series, TOTTERING TOWERS, Susan in THE SQUIRRELS, actress Flossie Nightingale in *Rep*, Mrs Clapton in GET WELL SOON, Mrs Harty in *Screen Two*'s *Femme Fatale*, Mrs Tinker in VANITY FAIR and Miss Millament in THE CAZALETS. To add to the variety, she was also seen in dramas like PUBLIC EYE, JULIET BRAVO, *Père Goriot*, KATE, *The History of Mr Polly* and *Crimestrike*, as well as comedies like ROBIN'S NEST, IN LOVING MEMORY, *Carry On Laughing*, *Emery* and GEORGE AND MILDRED.

Roy Rogers Show, The ★★

US (Roy Rogers) Western. ITV 1955–7 (US: NBC 1951–7)

Roy Rogers, Dale Evans, Pat Brady

Executive Producers **Art Rush, Mike North**
Producers **Jack C. Lacey, Bob Henry, Leslie H. Martinson**

● ***Clean-cut, modern-day Western with the 'King of the Cowboys'.***

Living on the Double R Bar Ranch, near Mineral City, singing cowboy Roy Rogers is an important force in the maintenance of law and order in the neighbourhood. He also owns a diner, the Eureka Café, which is run by his wife, Dale Evans ('Queen of the West'), and he is assisted by an incompetent sidekick, Pat Brady, cook at the diner and driver of an unreliable Jeep known as Nellybelle. Roy, of course, rides Trigger, alongside Dale on Buttermilk. Bullet the Alsatian dog trots along in tow, and the Sons of the Pioneers vocal group help Roy with the musical content.

Royal, The ★★

UK (Yorkshire) Drama. ITV 2003–

Dr David Cheriton	**Julian Ovenden**
T. J. Middleditch	**Ian Carmichael**
Dr Gorden Ormerod	**Robert Daws**
Dr Jill Weatherill	**Amy Robbins**
Matron	**Wendy Craig**
Ken Hopkirk	**Michael Starke**
Dr James Alway	**Francis Matthews**
Sister Brigid	**Linda Armstrong**
Staff Nurse Meryl Taylor	**Zoie Kennedy**
Alun Morris	**Andy Wear**
Lizzie Kennoway	**Michelle Hardwick**
Mr Rose	**Denis Lill**
Nigel Harper	**John Axon**
Student Nurse Samantha Beaumont	**Anna Madeley**
Dr Jeff Goodwin	**Paul Fox**
Dr Lucy Klein	**Polly Maberly**
Tom Ormerod	**Daniel Feltham**
Katie Ormerod	**Sophie Foster**
Frankie Robinson	**Scott Taylor**
Nurse Stella Davenport	**Natalie Anderson**

Producers **Ken Horn, Carol Wilks**

● ***Nostalgic drama set in a 1960s cottage hospital.***

Unashamedly exploiting a winning formula, *The Royal* is HEARTBEAT swallowed up by the NHS. St Aidan's Royal Free Hospital is a cottage hospital in the seaside town of Elsinby (real life Whitby, although the building used for exteriors is in Scarborough), not far from the moorland village of Aidensfield, home to the characters of *Heartbeat*. To launch the series, a cross-over episode of the mother programme was aired in January 2003, *The Royal* taking over the same time slot a week later. Characters from *Heartbeat* (such as lovable rogue Claude Greengrass) continue to show their faces in the wards of St Aidan's, but *The Royal* is peopled largely with a new cast, headed by enthusiastic young doctor David Cheriton. Cheriton arrives in Elsinby to shake up the dyed-in-the-wool establishment represented by veteran hospital secretary T. J. Middleditch and experienced medic Dr Alway. Joining Cheriton on the wards are Dr Gordon Ormerod and his romantic interest, Dr Jill Weatherill; pipe-smoking surgeon Mr Rose; keen staff nurse Meryl Taylor; wily hospital porter Ken Hopkirk and his witless accomplice, Alun Morris; Ken's daughter, receptionist Lizzie Kennoway; Catholic sister Brigid; and the inevitable starchy matron. Later recruits include student nurse Samantha Beaumont, psychiatrist Lucy Klein, young doctor Jeff Goodwin, administrator Nigel Harper, ambulance driver Frankie Robinson and nurse Stella Davenport. It is, of course, the Swinging Sixties, so a liberal sprinkling of contemporary pop hits, some 'did we really wear that?' fashions, and plenty of period furnishings/motors are thrown in for a cosy, nostalgic effect. Predictable and toothless *The Royal* may be, but for millions of viewers it represents a warm, fluffy, unthreatening hour of television.

Royal Canadian Mounted Police ★

Canada/UK (CBC/Crawley Films/BBC) Police Drama. BBC 1960–1

Cpl Jacques Gagnier	**Gilles Pelletier**
Constable Scott	**John Perkins**
Constable Bill Mitchell	**Don Francks**

Producers **George Gorman, Harry Horner, Bernard Girard**

● ***Stirring adventures of the RCMP.***

As if to prove that a Mountie always gets his man, this joint Canadian/UK production brought us heroic tales from the frozen north. It centred on the town of Shamattawa and its Royal Canadian Mounted Police headquarters, following the local officers in their efforts to enforce law and order.

Royal Family ★★★

UK (BBC/ITV) Documentary. BBC 1 1969

Narrator **Michael Flanders**

Writer **Antony Jay**
Producer **Richard Cawston**

● ***A glimpse inside the private and public lives of the British royal family.***

On 21 June 1969 Britons were treated to the first-ever televised account of life behind the scenes with the royal family. The 110-minute film (screened with a two-minute interval) was a joint BBC/ITV project, the BBC concentrating on programme production and ITV selling the film throughout the world. Richard Cawston, who had been Head of Documentary Programmes at the BBC since 1965, was entrusted with the delicate task of taking cameras backstage with the Windsors, as it were, and filming commenced, with Cawston directing, on 8 June 1968. The crew accompanied the Queen on tours of Brazil and Chile, and Prince Charles on trips to Malta and Cambridge. Domestically, the royals were seen aboard the Royal Yacht and Royal Train, on holiday at Balmoral and Sandringham, on duty at ceremonial events and in the office at Buckingham Palace, as well as enjoying Christmas at Windsor. The Queen viewed the finished film before it was broadcast but apparently did not ask for any edits to be made. The documentary was repeated soon afterwards on ITV and also by BBC 1 and BBC 2 on Christmas Day the same year.

Royal Television Society

The Royal Television Society started life as simply the Television Society in 1927, when interest was essentially in the scientific and development side of the new medium. With the advent of scheduled broadcasting in 1936, the Society's remit began to expand into all areas of television and today its membership consists of more than 4,000 professionals from all across the industry, including technicians and programme makers. The organization was renamed the Royal Television Society in 1966. Its function today is to arrange conventions, lectures and debates about the medium, attracting the biggest names in the business. The RTS also hosts annual awards to celebrate broadcasting achievement. These fall into several categories, including technology, craft and design, journalism, sport and education.

Royal Variety Performance ★★★

UK (ATV/BBC) Variety. ITV/BBC 1 1960–

Annual charity concert in the presence of the Queen or other members of the royal family.

A prestigious showbusiness extravaganza, the Royal Variety Performance was instituted in 1912 and became a yearly event in 1921. It was first televised for ITV in 1960 by Lew Grade's ATV, which covered proceedings again the following year. Since 1962, however, the BBC has enjoyed the right to stage the show on alternate years. Among the stars of the first televised show (held at the Victoria Palace theatre) were Norman Wisdom, Harry Worth, Benny Hill, Frankie Howerd, Cliff Richard and The Shadows, Max Bygraves, Russ Conway, Liberace and Nat 'King' Cole. In 1963, The Beatles took the Prince of Wales Theatre by storm and, in 1980, on the occasion of her 80th birthday, the Queen Mother revelled in the tribute to music hall days paid by Chesney Allen, Arthur Askey, Charlie Chester, Billy Dainty, Charlie Drake, Arthur English, Cyril Fletcher, Stanley Holloway, Roy Hudd, Richard Murdoch, Sandy Powell, Tommy Trinder and Ben Warriss. Much of 1998's show became a tribute to Frank Sinatra, who had died that year, and in 1999 the show was taken outside London for the first time, with Birmingham's Hippodrome hosting proceedings. In 2003, the venue was Edinburgh's Festival Theatre, while in 2005 the event was staged at the Wales Millennium Centre in Cardiff. Bernard Delfont staged each show from 1961 to 1978.

Royle, Carol

(1954–)

British actress probably best recalled as Jenny in LIFE WITHOUT GEORGE, which she quickly followed with the role of Jessica in Dennis Potter's controversial BLACKEYES. Royle also starred in *Girl Talk*, LADIES IN CHARGE (Diana Granville) and in Alan Plater's version of L. P. Hartley's vampire story *Feet Foremost* (part of the *Shades of Darkness* anthology). Among her other credits have been parts in series like BLAKE'S 7, THE RACING GAME, *The Cedar Tree* (Laura Collins), THE PROFESSIONALS, *Heartland*, BERGERAC, CRIBB, THE OUTSIDER, *Oxbridge Blues*, THIEF TAKERS, SECOND SIGHT, CROSSROADS (Diane), THE BILL, HEARTBEAT (Lady Patricia Brewster) and DOCTORS. She is the daughter of actor Derek Royle and sister of actress Amanda Royle.

Royle Family, The ★★★★

UK (Granada) Situation Comedy. BBC 2/BBC 1 1998–2000; 2006
DVD: Granada Ventures

Jim Royle .... **Ricky Tomlinson**
Barbara Royle .... **Sue Johnston**
Denise Royle/Best .... **Caroline Aherne**
Dave Best .... **Craig Cash**
Antony Royle .... **Ralf Little**
Norma Speakman .... **Liz Smith**
Mary Carroll .... **Doreen Keogh**
Joe Carroll .... **Peter Martin**
Cheryl Carroll .... **Jessica Stevenson**
Twiggy .... **Geoffrey Hughes**
Darren Sinclair-Jones .... **Andrew Whyment**
Emma Kavanagh .... **Sheridan Smith**

Writers **Caroline Aherne, Craig Cash, Henry Normal, Carmel Morgan**
Producers **Glenn Wilhide, Kenton Allen**

The humdrum life of a Manchester family.

When *The Royle Family* took to the air, viewers and critics were equally suspicious about its novel approach to sitcom. However, both were quickly won over and the series became the most talked-about comedy of the late 1990s. The novelty value came from a number of key decisions: to do without a laugh track or studio audience; to film the series rather than videotape it; to keep all events on one set; and, most significantly, to forgo the contrived plots and obvious gag-lines common to other sitcoms. Instead, the series merely peeped behind council house curtains, fly-on-the-wall style, as a Manchester family went about their daily affairs (it was not that far removed from the 1974 real documentary saga THE FAMILY).

The Royle family consists of layabout dad Jim, wedged in his armchair, forever scratching his privates, making wisecracks and finding reason for complaint (usually because the immersion has been left on). Mum Barbara works part-time in a baker's shop and double-time at home, cooking for the family before flopping down with a full ashtray on the sofa. Teenager Antony (known as 'Lurch') is the awkward adolescent incessantly called upon to 'make a brew' and then criticized for his laziness ('Where does he get it from?'). Elder sister Denise is even more static than Jim, unless there is a chance of half a dozen glasses of lager, while her fiancé/husband, Dave, a mobile DJ, gormlessly allows her constant demands to wash over him. Occasional visitors are Barbara's irritating mother Norma (Nana), hooky-goods merchant Twiggy, and next door neighbours the Carrolls – taciturn Joe, bubbly Irish Mary and podgy Cheryl, Denise's best friend.

Most of the action – 'action, my arse!' – takes place in the evening or on Sunday afternoons, as the family settles down after their evening meal or heavy Sunday lunch to engage in everyday chit-chat, with the television always switched on in the background. Major excitement comes from Jim's birthday, Nana's cataract operation or Antony's new vegetarian girlfriend (Emma), although each series does build up to a real climax – Denise and Dave's wedding, for instance, or the birth of their child, Baby David.

As the programme was swiftly switched from BBC 2 to BBC 1 and began to garner the awards, other comedians confessed to being green with envy for not thinking up the concept first. Star Caroline Aherne also directed the third series. The team was brought together again for an hour-long special broadcast in autumn 2006.

Roy's Raiders ★★

UK (BBC) Situation Comedy. BBC 1 1991

Roy .... **James Grout**
Henry .... **William Vanderpuye**
Chris .... **Edward Tudor-Pole**
Daisy .... **Sara Crowe**
Bazza .... **Shane Withington**
Jill .... **Rebecca Stevens**
Winco .... **Milton Johns**
Jack .... **Mark Adams**
Gavin Bailey .... **Des McAleer**

Writer **Michael Aitkens**
Producer **Susan Belbin**

● ***Mishaps and mayhem with a team of motorbike couriers.***

Despite its *Boy's Own* comic title, this six-part sitcom does not revolve around a failing football team or a crack team of commandos. Instead, a struggling motorcycle courier firm takes centre stage. As in the earlier TAXI and the later ROGER ROGER, this bunch of drivers are social misfits, with a wacky take on life or dreams unfulfilled (such as for aspiring actress Daisy). Trying to knock the team into shape is proprietor Roy (played by James Grout who, as Chief Superintendent Strange, had just as much luck reining in INSPECTOR MORSE). Competition from devious rival company Bailey's Comets adds to the hassle. David Essex wrote the theme song, which was sung by William Vanderpuye, who played Henry. Writer Michael Aitkens guested in one episode as a theatre director. Although given plenty of opportunity to shine in a prime Saturday evening slot, *Roy's Raiders* failed to deliver more than one series.

Rumpole of the Bailey ★★★

UK (Thames) Legal Drama. ITV 1978–80; 1983; 1987–8; 1991–2
DVD: Acorn Media

Horace Rumpole .... **Leo McKern**
Claude Erskine-Brown .... **Julian Curry**
Phyllida Trant/Erskine-Brown .... **Patricia Hodge**
Guthrie Featherstone .... **Peter Bowles**
George Frobisher .... **Moray Watson**
Uncle Tom .... **Richard Murdoch**
Hilda Rumpole .... **Peggy Thorpe-Bates**
Marion Mathie
Henry .... **Jonathan Coy**
Justice Bullingham .... **Bill Fraser**
Dianne .... **Maureen Darbyshire**
Fiona Allways .... **Rosalyn Landor**
Marigold Featherstone .... **Joanna Van Gyseghem**
Samuel Ballard .... **Peter Blythe**
Liz Probert .... **Samantha Bond**
Abigail McKern
Nick Rumpole .... **David Yelland**
Justice Graves .... **Robin Bailey**
Dot Clapton .... **Camille Coduri**

Creator/Writer **John Mortimer**
Executive Producer **Lloyd Shirley**
Producers **Irene Shubik, Jacqueline Davis**

● ***The cases of a gruff old barrister with a zest for justice.***

Colourful, middle-aged Horace Rumpole differs from his legal colleagues in his distinct lack of ambition and his genuine interest in clients. His brusque, down-to-earth manner ruffles many a rival's feathers, and he revels in a joyful lack of respect for authority (he calls judges 'Old darling'). Rumpole accepts defence cases only and his clients come mainly (though not uniquely) from the lower classes. He proves a saviour on most occasions, craftily turning trials in the favour of his clients. Out of the courtroom, he lives at 38 Froxbury Mansions, enjoys smoking cigars, quoting the *Oxford Book of English Verse*, drinking the Pomeroy's Wine Bar claret ('Château Fleet Street') and disappointing his wife, Hilda, 'She who must be obeyed.' Among his more refined legal contemporaries are Samuel Ballard (his Head of Chambers), Erskine-Brown and his future wife, snobbish Phyllida Trant. The part of junior barrister Liz Probert is eventually filled by Leo McKern's own daughter, Abigail.

The series was written by real-life barrister John Mortimer and the character first appeared in a BBC 1 PLAY FOR TODAY in 1975. When the Corporation declined to take up the option of a series, Mortimer and his producer, Irene Shubik, transferred the irascible old brief to Thames Television. Rumpole was retired to Florida after a couple of seasons, but returned in a two-hour special at Christmas 1980. Further series followed intermittently.

Runaround ★★

UK (Southern) Children's Quiz. ITV 1975–81

Presenters **Mike Reid, Leslie Crowther, Stan Boardman**

Creators **Merril Heatter, Bob Quigley**
Producers **Colin Nutley, Greg Lanning, John Coxall, J. Nigel Pickard**

● ***Noisy general knowledge quiz for youngsters.***

Described as 'a cross between a circus, a quiz and a chat show', raucous *Runaround* took ten kids, placed them in a studio arena and let them battle it out for toys and games. Cockney comic Mike Reid bellowed out a series of questions to which the kids needed to find an answer. On the bark of 'Go', they raced to one of three markers representing possible answers. All those standing in the correct line stayed in the quiz; others were eliminated. However, wily kids could fool their rivals by hopping between answers at the last minute when prompted by a yell of 'Runaround'. The last remaining contestant picked up the top prize. Wrapped around the quiz element were interviews with, and demonstrations by, studio guests – anyone from pop groups to sports stars. Some programmes followed a general theme: sport or Latin America, for instance. Leslie Crowther briefly replaced Reid in 1977 before himself giving way to Stan Boardman. Reid returned in 1978. The series was brought to the UK from the USA where from 1972 it was hosted by Paul Winchell (voice of WACKY RACES' Dick Dastardly). A special celebrity revival, hosted by Johnny Vegas, was screened as part of BBC 1's *Sport Relief* night in July 2002.

Rushton, William

(1937–96)

British satirist and cartoonist, coming to the fore in THAT WAS THE WEEK THAT WAS and its follow-up, NOT SO MUCH A PROGRAMME, MORE A WAY OF LIFE. He went on to host *The New Stars and Garters* with Jill Browne, to make guest appearances in NOT ONLY . . . BUT ALSO . . . and to play Plautus in UP POMPEII!, before being given his own series, *Rushton's Illustrated*. He was also seen in programmes like *Grubstreet*, UP SUNDAY, *Don't Just Sit There* and *Dawson and Friends*, and was a popular choice for panel games such as CELEBRITY SQUARES and THROUGH THE KEYHOLE. Rushton was one of the founders of *Private Eye* magazine.

Russell, Clive

(1945–)

Tall Scottish actor seen in such dramas and comedies as HANCOCK (Alan Simpson), *Tell Tale Hearts* (Adrian Fell), CRACKER (Fitz's brother, Danny), MIDDLEMARCH (Caleb Garth), *Finney* (Tucker), ATLETICO PARTICK (Bonner), ROUGHNECKS (Archie), *The Lord of Misrule* (Arthur), NEVERWHERE (Mr Vandemar), HEARTBURN HOTEL (Duggie Strachan), GREAT EXPECTATIONS (Joe Gargery), OLIVER TWIST (Mr Ferguson), HOPE AND GLORY (Phil Jakes), HAPPINESS (Angus), THE RAILWAY CHILDREN (Station Master), *Being April* (Callum) and ROCKFACE (Gordon Urquhart). More recently, he has played Newson in THE MAYOR OF CASTERBRIDGE, Gary Turnbull in AUF WIEDERSEHEN, PET, Billy Wilson in SHAMELESS, Ricky in *Heartless*, Jack in *According to Bex*, Gordon in *Faith* and Phil Nail in CORONATION STREET. Russell also appeared in *Screen Two*'s *Crossing the Floor* (Mick Boyd) and *Flowers of the Forest* (Gordon Weir). Other credits have come in SPENDER, *The Advocates*, FRANK STUBBS PROMOTES, LOVEJOY, MURDER MOST HORRID, *Ruffian Hearts*, SUNNYSIDE FARM, THE PETER PRINCIPLE, HEARTBEAT, *Black Cab*, *Lock, Stock . . .*, SPACED, WHERE THE HEART IS, WAKING THE DEAD, SILENT WITNESS and MONARCH OF THE GLEN.

Russell, Ken

(1927–)

British director/writer responsible for some outrageous movie moments but more restrained, if just as adventurous, in his television work. Russell began by contributing material for series like MONITOR and OMNIBUS and has given the TV archives some notable documentary-drama portraits of composers including Bartók, Elgar, Wagner, Delius and Debussy, plus other artistic personalities such as Isadora Duncan (*Isadora*, 1966), Dante Gabriel Rossetti (*Dante's Inferno*, 1967) and Wordsworth and Coleridge (*Clouds of Glory*, 1978). He returned to TV with his own adaptation of LADY CHATTERLEY in 1993 and the musical *Ken Russell's Treasure Island* in 1995. In 2003, he made a rare on-screen appearance in WAKING THE DEAD and he has also been seen in AGATHA CHRISTIE'S MARPLE.

Ruth Rendell Mysteries, The ★★

UK (TVS/Blue Heaven/United/Meridian) Police Drama. ITV 1987–92; 1994–2000
DVD: Lance (Region 1 only)

DCI Reg Wexford	**George Baker**
DI Mike Burden	**Christopher Ravenscroft**
Dora Wexford	**Louie Ramsay**
Jean Burden	**Ann Penfold**
Jenny Ireland/Burden	**Diane Keen**
DS Martin	**Ken Kitson**
Dr Crocker	**John Burgess**
Sgt/DS Barry Vine	**Sean Pertwee**
	Robin Kermode
	Matthew Mills

Executive Producers **Graham Benson, Michele Buck**
Producers **John Davies, Neil Zeiger**

The investigations of a slow-speaking but sharp-thinking country policeman.

Reg Wexford was one of the great thinking coppers of the 1980s. Like P. D. JAMES'S Dalgliesh, TAGGART and INSPECTOR MORSE, Wexford eschewed the hard-hitting, screaming-tyres kind of police work much enjoyed by 1970s detectives, in favour of the painstaking, analytical, working-on-a-hunch sort of investigation. Created by novelist Ruth Rendell while on holiday in Ireland (hence the name Wexford, apparently), the Detective Chief Inspector took his first name from Ruth's uncle, Reg, although most of his character traits allegedly came from her father, a softly spoken but firm teacher.

The tales are set in the fictitious Hampshire town of Kingsmarkham (Romsey was used for filming purposes), a sleepy backwater which, like Morse's Oxford and BERGERAC's Jersey, quickly witnesses more than its fair share of murders. Out and about on investigations, the fatherly Wexford is assisted by the aptly named DI Mike Burden, a gloomy man with no smile and little to smile about (his wife has died of cancer). Even when he remarries, Burden remains rather morose. At home, Wexford's understanding wife, Dora, proves to be a rock in support and a source of great encouragement. Their grown-up daughters are also seen from time to time.

Like all good TV cops, the affable, well-heeled Wexford has his share of gimmicks, in particular a rich, Hampshire burr when he speaks, an enjoyment of good cooking and an evidently well-educated manner, manifested in his quotation from Shakespeare and other literary greats. And, like all good TV cops, he always gets his man. Sometimes it takes two or three episodes, but his tortoise-like approach ensures the right result eventually.

By the time production company TVS lost its franchise in 1992, all 13 existing Ruth Rendell novels had been covered, plus a few of her short stories and a handful of new scripts (including some from star George Baker). *The Ruth Rendell Mysteries* title has since been revived by Meridian, although these intermittent thrillers have not usually featured Inspector Wexford. The Kingsmarkham copper did return, however, in 1996, 1998 and 2000, in adaptations of new Rendell stories, *Simisola*, *Road Rage* and *Harm Done* (the last billed simply as *Inspector Wexford*).

Rutland Weekend Television ★★★

UK (BBC) Situation Comedy. BBC 2 1975–6
DVD: Prism Leisure (The Rutles)

Eric Idle, David Battley, Neil Innes, Henry Woolf, Terence Bayler, Gwen Taylor

Creator/Writer **Eric Idle**
Producer **Ian Keill**

● ***Ambitious programming from Britain's smallest television network.***

Supposedly based in Rutland, England's smallest county, which had just been swallowed up into Leicestershire, this spoof series was the brainchild of MONTY PYTHON star Eric Idle, who cast himself as the programme controller of the financially challenged Rutland Weekend Television. RWT, for short, presents a variety of programme parodies, some described as 'mini-spectaculars'. Neil Innes provides the musical content, which reaches its zenith in a one-off, 1978 documentary spin-off, *The Rutles*. Telling the story of the world's greatest pop band, known individually as Dirk, Ron, Stig and Barry, but collectively as The Rutles, it intercuts spoof interviews with celebrities like Mick Jagger with scenes from the life of the so-called Pre-fab Four. The musical numbers include all-time classics like 'All You Need Is Lunch', 'W. C. Fields Forever', 'Cheese and Onion' and 'A Hard Day's Rut' (an accompanying album, with uncannily Beatle-like vocals and soundtracks, was released). An EP, headed by the track 'I Must Be In Love' made the lower reaches of the UK charts.

Rutles, The

See *Rutland Weekend Television*.

Ryan International ★★

UK (BBC) Drama. BBC 1 1970

Hugh Ryan .... **Kieron Moore**
Henri Bersac .... **Cyril Luckham**
Madame Bersac .... **Ursula Howells**
Michelle Corbon .... **Susan Sheers**

Producer **Eric Price**

● ***A jet-setting lawyer is a hero for the legally oppressed.***

Hugh Ryan is a lawyer, based in France. However, the cases he undertakes take him all over the world. The determined, urbane brief is skilled at his job, and has an eye for the underdog, but in his own life he has suffered some tragic bereavements. Among the cases he investigates are the bequest of 15 million francs to a dead man and the deliberate destruction of a priceless work of art. Ten episodes were made.

S

S4C

(Sianel Pedwar Cymru)

The Welsh fourth channel, S4C was established by the Broadcasting Act 1980 and provides around 32 hours a week of Welsh-language programming, ten hours of which are supplied free of charge by the BBC in accordance with its obligations under the Broadcasting Act 1990. The remainder of the Welsh programmes are commissioned by S4C from ITV Wales and other independent producers. Before S4C went on air on 1 November 1982 (a day earlier than Channel 4), BBC Wales and HTV Cymru/Wales mixed Welsh-language programmes with their English-language output. Now the BBC and ITV in Wales carry only programmes in English. The English-language part of S4C's schedule (around 70 per cent) is made up of programmes also seen on Channel 4, although these are usually rescheduled to give Welsh programmes prominence during peak hours. This practice has not been overly popular with viewers in predominantly English-speaking parts of the Principality.

S4C's Welsh output takes in light entertainment, drama, news, current affairs, sports and children's programmes. Among the most popular has been BBC Wales's *Pobol y Cwm*, a daily soap opera. A subtitled version was shown on BBC 2 in the rest of the UK for a while, under the translated title of *People of the Valley*. The channel has also made a name for itself in the field of animation, commissioning some very successful cartoons from independent producers like Siriol and Bumper Films. These have included SUPERTED, *Wil Cwak Cwak* and FIREMAN SAM. S4C is funded by a grant from the Treasury and its own advertising sales. It is accountable to a public body known as The Welsh Fourth Channel Authority, whose members are appointed by the Secretary of State for Culture, Media and Sport. In 1998 it launched a digital service, S4C digidol, and a year later added the digital channel S4C-2, which focuses largely on events in the Welsh Assembly and, unlike S4C itself, is accountable to Ofcom. The channel's full name, Sianel Pedwar Cymru, means Channel Four Wales.

Saber of London

See *Mark Saber*.

Sabrina the Teenage Witch ★★

US (Finishing the Hat/Hartbreak/Viacom) Situation Comedy. ITV 1996–2004 (US: ABC 1996–2000/WB 2000–3)

Sabrina Spellman .... **Melissa Joan Hart**
Aunt Hilda Spellman .... **Caroline Rhea**
Aunt Zelda Spellman .... **Beth Broderick**
Salem .... **Nick Bakay** *(voice only)*
Ted Spellman .... **Robby Benson**
Jenny Kelly .... **Michelle Beaudoin**
Harvey Kinkle .... **Nate Richert**
Libby Chessler .... **Jenna Leigh Green**
Mr Eugene Pool .... **Paul Feig**
Valerie Birckhead .... **Lindsay Sloan**
Willard Kraft .... **Martin Mull**
The Quizmaster .... **Alimi Ballard**
Morgan Cavanaugh .... **Elisa Donovan**
Roxie King .... **Soleil Moon Frye**
Brad Alcerro .... **John Huertas**
Josh .... **David Lascher**
Miles Goodman .... **Trevor Lissauer**
Cole .... **Andrew Walker**
Leonard .... **John Ducey**
Annie .... **Diana-Maria Riva**
James .... **Bumper Robinson**
Aaron Jacobs .... **Dylan Neal**

Creator **Nell Scovell**
Executive Producers **Paula Hart, David Babcock, Bruce Ferber, Nell Scovell, Carrie Honigblum, Renee Phillips, Miriam Trogdon**

● ***Adolescence is doubly difficult for a girl with magical powers.***

Sabrina Spellman has a shock on her 16th birthday: she discovers she's really a witch and the two aunts she now lives with are witches, too. Magic is very handy at school, where you can startle friends or take unique revenge on an enemy, but there is a serious side to consider, as unintentional spells can horribly backfire – which is why Sabrina later has to take special exams set by The Quizmaster. Sabrina is a witch of the good kind and helping her come to terms with her new powers along with her aunts is her dad, Ted, who appears as a talking picture in an old book (because he's really in another dimension). Salem is the family cat who is really a mischievous sorcerer exiled into feline form. Other major characters include biology teacher Mr Pool and schoolmates Jenny and Harvey, with Valerie a later addition to the class and Libby the odious cheerleader rival. Mr Kraft is the headteacher who suspects that all is not as it should be at Westbridge High. After leaving school, Sabrina heads for college, where her new friends include Morgan and Roxie. She then becomes a journalist, working for the music magazine *Scorch* and fending for herself once her aunts move away.

The series was developed as a vehicle for former *Clarissa Explains It All* star Melissa Joan Hart by the company she ran with her mother, who was one of the executive producers. It followed a pilot TV movie screened in the USA in 1996. The character also features in a handful of spin-off movies. In the UK, some episodes were screened as part of the Saturday morning programme, SM:TV LIVE. Sabrina – originally a comic-book character – first appeared on US TV in 1969 as an animated segment of *The Archie Comedy Hour* (part of a series of cartoons that gave rise to The Archies pop group), gaining a series of her own in 1970. In those days, her school was called Riverdale High.

Sachs, Andrew

(1930–)

German-born actor whose finest hour came – after small roles in series like THE SAINT, FRAUD SQUAD, CALLAN and RANDALL AND HOPKIRK (DECEASED) – with FAWLTY TOWERS, in which he played the hapless and hopeless Spanish waiter, Manuel. On the back of this success, Sachs was given the lead role in a few other sitcoms, all of which proved rather short-lived. These were *Dead Ernest* (the late Ernest Springer), *There Comes a Time* (Tony James, who didn't have long to live) and EVERY SILVER LINING (café-owner Nat Silver). Sachs, the father of radio and TV presenter John Sachs, has, however, been seen or heard in plenty of other programmes, from dramas like *The History of Mr Polly, The Tempest*, BERGERAC and CROWN COURT to series as varied as THE WORLD ABOUT US (narrator), POINTS OF VIEW (guest presenter), SUPERSENSE (narrator), *Took and Co.*, RISING DAMP, HORIZON (Albert Einstein), the kids' comedy *Pirates* (Mr Jones), *Jack of Hearts* (Peter Pryce), ATTACHMENTS (Murray Plaskow), SILENT WITNESS, THAT PETER KAY THING (narrator), *Single Voices*, DOCTORS, *Looking for Victoria*, HOLBY CITY, plus the *When in Spain* language course. He has also presented a programme about his birthplace, *Berliners*.

Sachs, Leonard

(1909–90)

South African actor who found greater fame as the super-eloquent, gavel-smashing chairman of THE GOOD OLD DAYS, a position he held from 1953 until the series ended in 1983. Among his acting credits were parts in Nigel Kneale's *1984*, THE ADVENTURES OF ROBIN HOOD, IVANHOE, THE FOUR JUST MEN, DANGER MAN, CROWN COURT, A FAMILY AT WAR, *The Man from Haven*, THE GLITTERING PRIZES (Lionel Morris), ELIZABETH R (the Count de Feria) and CORONATION STREET (Sir Julius Berlin). His last TV play was entitled *Lost for Words*, something he never was in *The Good Old Days*.

Saga of Noggin the Nog, The ★★★

UK (Smallfilms) Children's Entertainment. BBC 1 1959; 1961; 1963–5; 1970; 1982

Narrators **Oliver Postgate, Ronnie Stevens**

Creator/Writer **Peter Firmin**
Producer **Oliver Postgate**

● ***The magical adventures of a Norse king.***

Using ten-minute episodes in serial form, this characterful animation relates the story of Noggin, Prince (later King) of the Nogs, who sails to the Land of the Midnight Sun to fetch Nooka, Eskimo Princess of the Nooks, to be his queen. His guide on this voyage is Graculus, a great, green talking bird raised from an egg by Nooka, which subsequently becomes the Royal Bird. Various other adventures befall the brave Noggin in later tales (when Ronnie Stevens joins Oliver Postgate with voices: *Noggin and the Ice Dragon, Noggin and the Flying Machine, Noggin and the Omruds* and *Noggin and the Firecake*), with more than one attempt by his wicked uncle, Nogbad the Bad, to seize his throne. Other characters like Noggin's son, Prince Knut, the mighty Thor Nogson and inventor Olaf the Lofty are also seen.

Noggin the Nog was the second offering (after IVOR THE ENGINE) from the Smallfirms duo of writer/narrator Oliver Postgate and illustrator Peter Firmin. Vernon Elliott wrote the music. Colour remakes of the *Omruds* and the *Flying Machine* appeared in 1970 and, in 1982, two further colour stories arrived – a remake of the *Ice Dragon* and a new story, *Noggin and the Pie*.

Sahara with Michael Palin

See *Around the World in 80 Days*.

Sailor ★★★

UK (BBC) Documentary. BBC 1 1976

Producer **John Purdie**
Executive Producer **Roger Mills**

● ***A frank account of life with the crew of HMS Ark Royal.***

This ten-part documentary series provided an insight into events in port and at sea with the 2,500 men who crewed the aircraft carrier *Ark Royal*. A camera team lived aboard for ten weeks, capturing the high spots and the low, starting with a boozy last night out in Devonport and continuing to the final disembarkation back home. It saw drunken sailors in disgrace after unruly nights on the town and relived dramas like the winching of a seaman off a submarine for urgent medical treatment. The sailors' antics and their language were both colourful but viewers, generally, loved it. The theme song, 'Sailing', by Rod Stewart, became a Top Three hit for a second time on the back of the series. The programme's format was recalled nearly 20 years later in the documentary series *HMS Brilliant* (BBC 1 1995).

Sailor of Fortune ★

UK (ATV/Michael Sadlier) Adventure. ITV 1956–7

Grant 'Mitch' Mitchell .... **Lorne Greene**
Sean .... **Jack MacGowran**
Alfonso .... **Rupert Davies**
Johnny .... **Paul Carpenter**

Writer **Lindsay Galloway**
Producer **Michael Sadlier**

● ***An honest sea captain is embroiled in other people's murky operations.***

American Grant 'Mitch' Mitchell is the skipper of a freighter called *The Shipwreck*. He travels the world trying to make a living shipping cargo, although intrigue follows him wherever he roams. There is always someone who needs his help and his ports of call are exotic (even though filming never ventured beyond the bounds of Elstree Studios). The series provided a springboard for both Lorne Greene and Rupert Davies, who played Mitch's engineer, Alfonso.

Saint, The ★★★

UK (New World/Bamore/ITC) Adventure. ITV 1962–9

Simon Templar .... **Roger Moore**
Chief Insp. Claude Eustace Teal .... **Ivor Dean**

Creator **Leslie Charteris**
Producers **Robert S. Baker, Monty Norman**

● ***A self-supporting amateur sleuth foils crime around the world.***

The Saint is Simon Templar (ST being his initials), an independently wealthy adventurer who travels the globe stumbling into intrigue. Using a business card depicting a matchstick man with a halo, and driving a two-seater Volvo P1800 with the number plate ST 1, Templar mingles with the élite and discovers crime at every turn. His devilishly good looks, the twinkle in his eye and his suave manner help him appear cool in almost any circumstance, whether it is rescuing blackmail victims or disrupting elaborate robberies. The unruffled, totally self-assured Templar is an unqualified success and proves a wow with the ladies, including 1960s beauties like Samantha Eggar, Dawn Addams, Julie Christie and Gabrielle Drake. Templar's friendly adversary is Chief Inspector Teal (Teal was played by three other actors – Campbell Singer, Wensley Pithey and Norman Pitt – before Ivor Dean was confirmed in the role). The now-familiar theme music was composed by Edwin Astley.

The Saint was created by writer Leslie Charteris in 1928 and had already been a hit on radio and in the cinema (most notably starring George Sanders) before the TV series began. Moore, of course, later took his adventurer character into James Bond films, with Ian Ogilvy filling his shoes for a 1970s revival, RETURN OF THE SAINT. Some years later Simon Dutton was cast in a short-lived revamp called *The Saint* (ITV 1989–90).

St Elsewhere ✶✶✶✶

US (MTM) Medical Drama. Channel 4 1983–9 (US: NBC 1982–8)

Dr Donald Westphall .... **Ed Flanders**
Dr Mark Craig .... **William Daniels**
Dr Victor Ehrlich .... **Ed Begley Jr**
Dr Jack Morrison .... **David Morse**
Dr Ben Samuels .... **David Birney**
Dr Annie Cavanero .... **Cynthia Sikes**
Dr Wayne Fiscus .... **Howie Mandel**
Dr Cathy Martin .... **Barbara Whinnery**
Dr Peter White .... **Terence Knox**
Nurse Helen Rosenthal .... **Christina Pickles**
Dr Daniel Auschlander .... **Norman Lloyd**
Dr Hugh Beale .... **G. W. Bailey**
Dr Philip Chandler .... **Denzel Washington**
Dr V. J. Kochar .... **Kavi Raz**
Dr Wendy Armstrong .... **Kim Miyori**
Nurse Shirley Daniels .... **Ellen Bry**
Luther Hawkins .... **Eric Laneuville**
Dr Bob Caldwell .... **Mark Harmon**
Dr Michael Ridley .... **Paul Sand**
Joan Halloran .... **Nancy Stafford**
Mrs Ellen Craig .... **Bonnie Bartlett**
Dr Elliot Axelrod .... **Stephen Furst**
Nurse Lucy Papandrao .... **Jennifer Savidge**
Dr Jackie Wade .... **Sagan Lewis**
Warren Coolidge .... **Byron Stewart**
Dr Emily Humes .... **Judith Hansen**
Nurse Peggy Shotwell .... **Saundra Sharp**
Dr Alan Poe .... **Brian Tochi**
Mrs Hufnagel .... **Florence Halop**
Dr Roxanne Turner .... **Alfre Woodard**
Ken Valere .... **George Deloy**
Terri Valere .... **Deborah May**
Dr Seth Griffin .... **Bruce Greenwood**
Dr Carol Novino .... **Cindy Pickett**
Dr Paulette Kiem .... **France Nuyen**
Dr John Gideon .... **Ronny Cox**

Creators **Joshua Brand, John Falsey**
Executive Producer **Bruce Paltrow**

● ***Life, death and humanity at a Boston teaching hospital.***
St Elegius is a decaying old hospital in one of Boston's roughest suburbs. Run by the municipality, it is used as a depository for patients by more élitist medical centres, hence its nickname of St Elsewhere. In HILL STREET BLUES fashion (the show was by the same production company), *St Elsewhere* takes viewers on a journey through hospital life but shuns all the old medical-drama stereotypes. Here the medics are fallible, the patients are nervous and the interactions believable. There are no miracle cures and the seediness of the environment is always apparent.

Realism is a keystone of *St Elsewhere*, with echoes of *Hill Street Blues* in its pace, style and camerawork. But it is also an adventurous show, taking chances with scripts and characters, leaving the viewer wondering what the producers will try next. A programme for baby-boomers, it is chock-full of references to pop culture, such as Tannoy messages for doctors from other TV shows, throw-away allusions to pop songs or gentle parodies of films such as *The Towering Inferno*, all played with a straight face and no explanation. In the final episode, the dénouement of THE FUGITIVE is restaged as, off-camera, a one-armed man climbs an amusement-park water tower.

Chief of staff at the hospital is Donald Westphall, the widower father of a teenage girl and an autistic son. His heart surgeon is insensitive Mark Craig, whose loyal junior is Victor Ehrlich. Wayne Fiscus is the emergency specialist, Ben Samuels a randy surgeon; Daniel Auschlander, the hospital's administrator, is a liver expert who, ironically, is suffering from liver cancer. Other members of the team include dedicated but trouble-torn Jack Morrison; psychiatrist Hugh Beale; Annie Cavanero, who tends to get over-involved with her patients; anaesthetist V. J. Kochar; obese Elliot Axelrod; insecure Philip Chandler; and much-married nurse Helen Rosenthal. More tragically, there are also Peter White, who rapes pathologist Cathy Martin only to be shot by nurse Shirley Daniels; Wendy Armstrong, who commits suicide; and Bob Caldwell, a promiscuous surgeon who contracts HIV. When the hospital is taken over by a private health-care company, the Ecumena Hospitals Corporation, the dirty word 'profit' begins to make its presence felt and, as financial pressures grow, the new Chief of Services, Dr John Gideon, forces a showdown with Westphall, who 'moons' at him and resigns.

Like *Hill Street Blues, St Elsewhere* easily won over the critics but failed to gain a big audience. Somehow, though, it clung on for six years, before, in its last episode, the producers wound up the series with a cute little twist. The hospital is seen in miniature, as a model inside a snow globe, held intently by Westphall's autistic son. In the room, Westphall and another cast member are talking but, it appears, they are no longer doctors. As his father takes the globe away from the child, viewers are led to believe that *St Elsewhere* has been just a figment of the boy's imagination.

Saint James, Susan

(Susan Miller; 1946–)

American former model who has had three big hit series to her name, principally MCMILLAN AND WIFE (as the 'Wife', Sally McMillan) in the 1970s. Her first starring role was in a collection of movies entitled *The Name of the Game* in 1968, which followed guest appearances in series like IT TAKES A THIEF and A MAN CALLED IRONSIDE. In the 1980s, Saint James was seen in KATE AND ALLIE, playing Kate McArdle. She has also starred in numerous TV movies.

Sale of the Century ✶✶

UK (Anglia) Quiz. ITV 1971–83

Presenter **Nicholas Parsons**

Producers **Peter Joy, Bill Perry**

Quiz in which the money won can be spent on bargain prizes.

'The Quiz of the Week', as it was billed in the opening announcement, *Sale of the Century* was a remarkably popular quiz game that allowed contestants to use the cash they won to buy prizes at giveaway prices. Three contestants took part, answering general-knowledge questions on the buzzer. These began at £1 in value, progressing to £3 and then £5. As they began to accumulate cash, the questions were interrupted by bargain offers, tempting contestants to spend some of their winnings on such things as a set of garden furniture for £15. At the end of the game, the person with the most money left could shop for the Sale of the Century (a choice of super-bargains). Nicholas Parsons was the questionmaster, John Benson acted as announcer, Peter Fenn provided the organ accompaniments, and assorted male and female models adorned the prizes. Peter Marshall and Keith Chegwin were hosts on revivals for satellite TV in the 1990s.

Sale of the Century was briefly revived as one instalment of ANT & DEC's *Game Show Marathon* in 2005, a series that celebrated the best-loved game shows in ITV's 50-year history.

Sallis, Peter

(1921–)

As LAST OF THE SUMMER WINE's Norman Clegg for 27 years, Twickenham-born Peter Sallis has been a familiar sight on British TV screens. He also appeared in *First of the Summer Wine*, playing Cleggy's father, and was the caretaker, Mr Gudgin, in the children's comedy THE GHOSTS OF MOTLEY HALL, insurance company manager Arthur Simister in the sitcom *Leave It to Charlie*, and Sidney Bliss in THE NEW STATESMAN. Sallis appeared with Patrick Troughton in DOCTOR WHO, and his other credits – varying between serious and humorous work – have included INTERNATIONAL DETECTIVE, DANGER MAN, THE AVENGERS, SOFTLY, SOFTLY, BARLOW, *The Culture Vultures*, *The Diary of Samuel Pepys* (title role), PUBLIC EYE, SPYDER'S WEB, *The Moonstone*, THE PALLISERS (Mr Bonteen), RAFFLES, *The Clifton House Mystery* (Milton Guest), TALES OF THE UNEXPECTED, *Yanks Go Home*, LADYKILLERS, THE RIVALS OF SHERLOCK HOLMES, STRANGERS AND BROTHERS (Leonard March), THE BRETTS, *Come Home Charlie and Face Them* (Evan), HOLBY CITY, DOCTORS and *Belonging* (Nathan). He also provided the voice for Rat in the 1980s animation THE WIND IN THE WILLOWS and for WALLACE & GROMIT.

Sam ★★★

UK (Granada) Drama. ITV 1973–5

Sam Wilson	**Kevin Moreton**
	Mark McManus
Jack Barraclough	**Michael Goodliffe**
Polly Barraclough	**Maggie Jones**
George Barraclough	**Ray Smith**
Ethel Barraclough	**Alethea Charlton**
Toby Wilson	**Frank Mills**
Dora Wilson	**Barbara Ewing**
Frank Barraclough	**James Hazeldine**
Eileen Brady	**Dorothy White**
May Dakin	**Mona Bruce**
Alan Dakin	**John Price**
Sarah Corby/Wilson	**Jennifer Hilary**

Creator/Writer **John Finch**
Producer **Michael Cox**

A young lad grows up in a poor mining town in the Pennines.

Ten-year-old Sam Wilson arrives in the Yorkshire town of Skellerton with his mother, Dora, after his dad has sailed off to Canada with another woman. There his life revolves around his grandparents, Toby Wilson, a clothier, and Jack and Polly Barraclough. Proud Jack has been out of work for eight years. Also close at hand are his uncle and aunt, George and Ethel Barraclough. George, unemployed for five years, has just regained a job at the pit. He looks upon Sam as the son he has never had. Dora and George's brother, Frank, is the brainy member of the family, kept out of the mines so he can further his academic studies.

Glumly reflecting the hardships of the 1930s and 1940s, the series sees Sam turn into a man (boy actor Kevin Moreton gives way to future TAGGART Mark McManus). As he grows older, he rebels against the mining mentality that forces him into the colliery at the age of 14. Over three series, viewers witness Sam venture out to sea and return to work in an engineering factory. He marries Sarah Corby and settles in the town of Golwick but, all the while, his poverty-ridden past remains firmly in his mind and the welfare of his family continues to haunt him.

Sam Saturday ★★

UK (LWT/Cinema Verity) Police Drama. ITV 1992

DI Sam Sterne	**Ivan Kaye**
Jim Butler	**Peter Armitage**
Rita Sterne	**Doreen Mantle**
Michael Sterne	**David Fleeshman**
CDI Simpson	**Michael Elwyn**
DI Griffiths	**Simon Slater**
DC Knights	**Paul Opacic**
WPC Daniels	**Helen Levien**
Carol Greenberg	**Tracie Hart**
Harry Greenberg	**Gareth Marks**
Miriam Sterne	**Lauren Jacobs**
Joanne Sterne	**Candice Jacobs**

Creator **Alvin Rakoff**
Writers **Stanley Price, John Milne, Arthur McKenzie, Stuart Hepburn**
Producers **Sharon Bloom, Alvin Rakoff**

A Jewish detective has a troubled personal life.

It's hard enough being a CID man on the crime-ridden streets of north London, but when you can't get any peace at home after a busy day, then life's rather demanding. That's the situation facing DI Sam Sterne, a young, Jewish cop whose social life is ruined by the fact that his mother, Rita, now lives with him after a period of illness. Sam, a divorcé father, seems destined to remain single from now on because he can't bring home any girls. At work, Sam's routine is one of murder, burglary and arson in such locations as Hampstead Heath and Golders Green. Just one series of six episodes was produced. Rick Wentworth supplied the music.

Sandbaggers, The ★★

UK (Yorkshire) Spy Drama. ITV 1978; 1980

Neil Burnside	**Roy Marsden**
C	**Richard Vernon**
	Dennis Burgess

Willie Caine .... **Ray Lonnen**
Sir Geoffrey Wellingham .... **Alan MacNaughton**
Diane Lawler .... **Elizabeth Bennett**
Laura Dickens .... **Diane Keen**
Jeff Ross .... **Bob Sherman**
Mike Wallace .... **Michael Cashman**
Karen Milner .... **Jana Sheldon**
Matthew Peele .... **Jerome Willis**
Marianne Straker .... **Sue Holderness**

Creator **Ian MacKintosh**
Executive Producer **David Cunliffe**
Producer **Michael Ferguson**

The assignments of a top-secret British security unit.

'The Sandbaggers' is the colloquial title given to the Special Intelligence Force, or SIF, a government-funded counter-espionage squad. Head of the team is tough, determined Neil Burnside. On receiving his team's missions from their boss, C, it is Burnside's decision which of the Sandbaggers to send into action, knowing full well that his colleagues would be risking life and limb in the service of their country. Accordingly, he gives his men and women every assistance he can but remains assured in the knowledge that, if they have to die, the result will still be worth it. That is the pressurized world of the Sandbaggers, depicted in a heavier, less glitzy and gimmicky style than other secret agent programmes.

Sanderson, Joan

(1912–92)

British actress, famous for her female dragon roles on television. Sanderson made her name for such characterizations in PLEASE SIR! as the redoubtable Doris Ewell, having already appeared in ALL GAS AND GAITERS and *Wild, Wild Women*, after years on the stage and some TV plays. Later, she took the part of Eleanor, Prunella Scales's mother in AFTER HENRY (radio and television) and Richard O'Sullivan's mother-in-law, Nell Cresset, in ME AND MY GIRL. She also played Mrs Richards, a deaf, never-satisfied guest in one memorable episode of FAWLTY TOWERS. In contrast to her battleaxe roles, Sanderson was the benign Aunt Dorothy in the mixed-race comedy MIXED BLESSINGS, and her other credits included UPSTAIRS, DOWNSTAIRS, RIPPING YARNS, RISING DAMP, THE GHOSTS OF MOTLEY HALL, *Full House*, THE FAINTHEARTED FEMINIST and Michael Palin's TV movie *East of Ipswich*. Her last series, screened shortly after her death in 1992, was LAND OF HOPE AND GLORIA, in which she played Nanny Princeton.

Sandford, Jeremy

(1930–2003)

A former journalist with an interest in social campaigning, Jeremy Sandford was a new name to British TV drama when he scripted the provocative and disturbing CATHY COME HOME in 1966. He followed it up five years later with the award-winning EDNA, THE INEBRIATE WOMAN and also, in the 1970s, penned an episode of LADYKILLERS, among other work. He was married to dramatist Nell Dunn.

Sapphire and Steel ★★★

UK (ATV) Science Fiction. ITV 1979; 1981–2

Sapphire .... **Joanna Lumley**
Steel .... **David McCallum**
Silver .... **David Collings**

Creator **P. J. Hammond**
Writers **P. J. Hammond, Anthony Read, Don Houghton**
Executive Producer **David Reid**
Producer **Shaun O'Riordan**

Time-travelling troubleshooters foil agents of chaos and destruction.

In this imaginative series, time is perceived as a tunnel, with different time zones spread along its length. Outside lie dark forces of chaos and destruction which take advantage of any weakness in the tunnel's fabric to enter and wreak havoc. Whenever this happens, Sapphire and Steel are sent to investigate.

Little is revealed about the two characters. From the programme's introduction viewers learn that: 'All irregularities will be handled by the forces controlling each dimension. Transuranic heavy elements may not be used where there is life. Medium atomic weights are available: Gold, Lead, Copper, Jet, Diamond, Radium, Sapphire, Silver and Steel. Sapphire and Steel have been assigned.' So, it appears, Sapphire and Steel are elements sent from above, although their forms are human.

Stunning Sapphire, true to her name, wears bright blue; blond-haired Steel, cold and humourless, dresses in grey. They each have special powers. Sapphire can see through time, gauge the history of an object just by holding it and even turn the clock back for a while. The analytical Steel enjoys phenomenal strength; he can resist the flow of time and reduce his body temperature to below zero. But sometimes these superhuman attributes are not enough and the pair need assistance. Usually it comes from another element, Silver, but Lead also joins the fray on one occasion.

The nightmarish storylines centre on the pursuit of disruptive forces. In their first outing, Sapphire and Steel are called in to arrest a time warp after the reading of historic nursery rhymes brings Roundhead soldiers to the 20th century. In another, a haunted railway station is drawn back into the era of World War I. The dark forces are seldom seen, except as faceless beings or globes of light. The longer they are allowed to remain in a dimension of time, the stronger they become, and they test the dynamic duo to the extreme.

Saracen ★★

UK (Central) Drama. ITV 1989

David Barber .... **Christian Burgess**
Tom Duffy .... **Patrick James Clarke**
Col. Patrick Ansell .... **Michael Byrne**
Nugent .... **John Bennett**
Alice .... **Ingrid Lacey**

Creators **Chris Kelly, Ted Childs**
Executive Producer **Ted Childs**
Producer **Deirdre Keir**

The cases of an elite security team.

Saracen Systems is a London-based security firm, specializing in the protection of VIPs and general bodyguard duties. Its chief operatives are action men David Barber and Tom Duffy and their work takes them to such exotic locations as the Costa del Sol, Bonn, South America and Central Africa, as well as throughout the UK, shielding diplomats, confronting rebels and thwarting terrorism. Ansell is Saracen's MD, and Nugent and Alice provide other support. The 13-part series followed a pilot episode entitled *The Zero Option*, shown in 1988. This revealed how Barber, an SAS major, bungled a mission and faced ruin until offered a new position at Saracen. Duffy didn't feature and the cast was entirely different, with Stephen Hattersley as Barber, Eric Flynn as Ansell, David Ross as Nugent and Joanna Phillips-Lane in the role of Alice.

Sarnoff, David

(1891–1971)

Belarus-born American broadcasting pioneer, a former wireless operator who, it was claimed, was the first to receive the distress call from the sinking *Titanic* in 1912. Working initially for Marconi, he was employed by RCA when it took over his former company. He eventually rose to be President of the company and created the NBC radio and TV networks as a market for selling RCA receivers. Sarnoff was also one of the earliest proponents of public service broadcasting.

Satellite

An orbiting space station used for relaying television signals round the world. In its simplest form, the satellite works by acting as a reflector. Signals can be sent to a satellite and bounced off it like a mirror to another location around the globe that would otherwise (because of the curvature of the planet) be out of direct-transmission contact (such as across the Atlantic). Modern satellites, however, actually take the signals on board, amplify them and retransmit them, carrying news reports, live and recorded programming and other items round the world in a fraction of a second. The receiving station, or household, captures the signal in a dish, which varies in size depending on its location. Nearly all satellites are of the synchronous or geostationary type, that is they maintain a fixed position above the Equator by orbiting at exactly the same speed as the Earth revolves. By so doing, synchronous satellites allow themselves to be used at all times, whereas unfixed satellites in random orbit can be called into use only at certain times of the day. The most famous of satellites have been Telstar, launched in 1962 (in random orbit, but still able to provide the first transatlantic pictures), and Early Bird, otherwise known as Intelsat I, launched in 1965. The Sky satellite network uses the various Astra satellites, beaming signals up from the UK and bouncing them back over most of Europe.

The term 'satellite' also refers to a small TV station that operates by simply retransmitting the output of a larger station (with perhaps a few local-interest programmes added for community value).

Saturday Live/Friday Night Live ★★★

UK (LWT) Comedy. Channel 4 1986–7; ITV 1996

Comperes **Ben Elton, Lee Hurst**

Producers **Paul Jackson, Geoff Posner, Geoffrey Perkins, Susie Dark**

● ***Live and dangerous, fast-moving comedy showcase.***

Emulating the success of the USA's *Saturday Night Live* (NBC 1975–), which has provided a springboard to stardom for the likes of John Belushi, Chevy Chase, Dan Aykroyd, Bill Murray, Eddie Murphy and Mike Myers, *Saturday Live* was an adrenaline-fuelled kick of alternative comedy (mainly stars of London's stand-up circuit) and live music. A pilot episode in 1985 featured Lenny Henry, Chris Barrie, Robbie Coltrane, Adrian Edmondson, Rik Mayall, French and Saunders, and Christopher Ryan, with music from Slade, Smiley Culture and The Style Council, and seemed to hit the spot. The resultant series arrived a year later, offering 90 minutes of live entertainment from London's South Bank TV centre, in an unruly studio with several stages, decorated with outsize inflatables. There was no regular host for this series, the job being shared by Tracey Ullman, Lenny Henry, Pamela Stephenson, Chris Barrie, Michael Barrymore, Hale and Pace, Ben Elton, Fascinating Aida, Peter Cook and American Steven Wright. Among the featured comics were John Bird, Stephen Fry, Hugh Laurie, Jeremy Hardy and Helen Lederer, as well as 'The Dangerous Brothers' (ik Mayall and Adrian Edmondson). For series two, in 1986, and series three, in 1987 (the latter switching evenings and being billed as *Friday Night Live*), Ben Elton was the man in charge. Elton was strongly supported by Harry Enfield and his creations Stavros (the Arsenal-supporting kebab man), Loadsamoney (the cash-flashing plasterer) and Buggerallmoney (Loadsamoney's Geordie opposite). Stephen Fry and Hugh Laurie were also on the menu weekly, until replaced in 1987 by Moray Hunter and Jack Docherty. Throughout, the series gave vital exposure to a number of up-and-coming comics (Josie Lawrence, Julian Clary, Craig Charles, Paul Merton, Jo Brand – billed as 'The Sea Monster' – and more) plus comedians from across the pond (such as eccentric Emo Phillips), but established figures of fun were not overlooked either (Spike Milligan, Jasper Carrott and Frankie Howerd). The concept was revived in 1996 (ITV), with Lee Hurst as compere and Harry Hill a regular guest, but only ran to another eight episodes.

Saturday Night Armistice, The/The Friday Night Armistice ★★

UK (BBC) Comedy. BBC 2 1995–9

Presenters **Armando Iannucci, Peter Baynham, David Schneider**

Producer **Sarah Smith**

● ***Satirical and sometimes surreal look back at the major events of the week.***

The Saturday (*Friday* from 1996) *Night Armistice* was a sort of THAT WAS THE WEEK THAT WAS for the 1990s. Recorded the night before broadcast for topicality, it featured Armando Iannucci (producer of THE DAY TODAY), assisted by co-writers Peter Baynham and David Schneider. Subjects for ridicule included the public, politicians, celebrities, big news stories and even other TV programmes. One of the absurd features was dubbed 'Styes in Their Eyes' and presented images of famous people that had been computer modified to screw up their looks. There was also a gay version of *Pride and Prejudice* and viewer games like 'Hunt the Old Woman'. A few Christmas specials were also produced and, on 1 May 1997, a special *Election Night Armistice* ran for three hours, combining humour with election results as they were announced. Steve Coogan, in the guise of Alan Partridge, made guest appearances, as did Tony Robinson, while Valerie Singleton gauged the political temperature of the nation using a bouncy castle. Writers included the presenters and the Father Ted duo of Graham Linehan and Arthur Mathews. The series wound up with another special, *The New Year Armistice*, in 1999.

Saturday Superstore

See *Multi-Coloured Swap Shop.*

Saunders, Jennifer

(1958–)

British comic, actress and writer, usually seen with Dawn French, her screen partner since their days with THE COMIC STRIP PRESENTS and before. Saunders went on to star in the Ben Elton sitcom HAPPY FAMILIES, playing various members of the Fuddle family, and she also appeared as the boring Jennifer in GIRLS ON TOP, a sitcom she co-wrote with French and Ruby Wax. The BBC 2 sketch show *French and Saunders* was launched in 1987 and one of its items proved to be the 'pilot' for Saunders's hugely successful series ABSOLUTELY FABULOUS, in which she starred as the boozy, drug-obsessed fashion promoter Edina Monsoon (also reuniting the *Abfab* team for a one-off comedy called *Mirrorball*). Again with Dawn French, she featured as Colombine, Comtesse de Vache, in *Let Them Eat Cake*. Saunders has also been seen in THE YOUNG ONES, SATURDAY LIVE and THE STORYTELLER, and provided the voices of The Rat in THE MAGICIAN'S HOUSE and Sharkadder in *Pongwiffy*. She is married to comedian Adrian Edmondson.

Savage, Lily

See *O'Grady, Paul.*

Savages, The ✶✶

UK (Hartswood) Situation Comedy. BBC 1 2001

Adam Savage	**Marcus Brigstocke**
Jessica Savage	**Victoria Hamilton**
Donald Savage	**Geoffrey Palmer**
Nicola Savage	**Liberty Morris**
Luke Savage	**Jake Fitzgerald**
Mark Savage	**Gresby Nash**
Holly	**Shauna Shim**
Maria	**Flamina Cinque**

Writer **Simon Nye**
Producer **Sue Vertue**

The strains of family life are brought to bear on a young couple.

Having kids around the home places new pressures on a relationship, as Adam and Jessica Savage well know. Their life has been turned upside down since the arrival of Nicola and Luke, but it becomes even more complicated when Adam's mother leaves her husband after 34 years of marriage. Dad Donald is therefore like another child in the attention he needs, as Adam tries to fix him up as an eligible single man, arranging dates with Maria, the waitress at their favourite Italian restaurant, and teaching him how to cook. Of little help is Mark, Adam's sales rep brother. Jessica finds temporary escape in her job as a travel agent, but it's not so easy for Adam as a cartoonist who works at home. Colin Blunstone sang the theme song, a version of The Kinks' 'Days', and six episodes were produced.

Savalas, Telly

(Aristotle Savalas; 1924–94)

Powerful American actor of Greek descent. Noted for his trademark shaven head, he became one of the 1970s' biggest stars in his guise of New York cop Lt. Theo Kojak. Savalas actually took to acting fairly late in life. A war veteran decorated with a Purple Heart, he was Director of News and Special Events for ABC before taking his first on-screen role in 1959. Through guest spots on series like NAKED CITY, THE UNTOUCHABLES, THE FUGITIVE and BURKE'S LAW, he worked his way into the cinema, where he was usually cast as a bad guy. Reportedly, it was for the part of Pontius Pilate in *The Greatest Story Ever Told* that he first shaved his head. His first major TV role was in a series called *Acapulco* in 1961, but it didn't last and he waited until *Kojak* in 1973 for a taste of small-screen stardom. His later work concentrated on mini-series and TV movies.

Savile, Sir Jimmy

OBE (1926–)

Yorkshire-born disc jockey and TV presenter, a relentless worker for charitable causes. Savile's working career began as a coal miner and as a professional wrestler, before he branched out into nightclub management. Ever the extrovert, he began broadcasting for Radio Luxembourg and arrived on television as the very first presenter of TOP OF THE POPS, in 1964. He joined Radio 1 in 1968 and continued to expand his TV work. He chaired *Quiz Bingo* and hosted *Jimmy Savile and Friends* and *Clunk Click* (based on his car seatbelt campaigns), which led to the magic wand series JIM'LL FIX IT in 1975. Jim fixed it, in all, for nearly 20 years. In addition, Savile has even hosted SONGS OF PRAISE. His trademark bleached hair, tracksuit, yodel and giant cigar have made him an easy prey for impressionists.

Saville, Philip

(1930–)

British director, responsible for many acclaimed dramas. These have included ARMCHAIR THEATRE presentations such as Harold Pinter's *A Night Out* (1960), episodes of OUT OF THE UNKNOWN, plus *Hamlet at Elsinore* (an ambitious 1964 outside broadcast from Denmark), Sartre's *In Camera* (also 1964), Alan Sharp's *The Long Distance Piano Player* (1970), GANGSTERS (the 1976 PLAY FOR TODAY which became a series), and the 1977 version of COUNT DRACULA. Saville also directed BOYS FROM THE BLACKSTUFF, THE LIFE AND LOVES OF A SHE DEVIL, *The Cloning of Joanna May, The Buccaneers, Little White Lies, My Uncle Silas* and *Screen One's Wall of Silence* and *Deacon Brodie*.

Sawalha, Julia

(1968–)

London-born actress coming to the fore in the kids' drama series PRESS GANG (junior newspaper editor Lynda Day), and then ABSOLUTELY FABULOUS (Saffron). Sawalha has been prominent in numerous other dramas and comedies, including INSPECTOR MORSE, EL C.I.D., CASUALTY, LOVEJOY, SECOND THOUGHTS and FAITH IN THE FUTURE (Hannah), MARTIN CHUZZLEWIT (Mercy Pecksniff), PRIDE AND PREJUDICE (Lydia Bennet), AIN'T MISBEHAVIN' (Dolly Nightingale), *McLibel!* (Helen Steel), *The Flint Street Nativity* (Wise Man), *Mirrorball, Time Gentlemen, Please,* JONATHAN CREEK (Carla Borrego) and

HORNBLOWER (Maria). Narration work has included the *Comedy Connections* series. She is a daughter of actor Nadim Sawalha, sister of actress/presenter Nadia Sawalha and wife of her *Jonathan Creek* co-star, Alan Davies.

Sayle, Alexei

(1952–)

Liverpudlian comedian, actor and writer, distinctive in his tight suit and skinhead haircut, whose aggressive, no-nonsense style established him at the forefront of the new stand-up comics of the 1980s. At one time the compere of the Comedy Store and Comic Strip clubs, Sayle moved into television with other members of The Comic Strip, appearing in their Channel 4 films and also taking part in the ill-fated late-night TISWAS spin-off, *OTT*. He was cast as Jerzy Balowski, THE YOUNG ONES' Russian landlord (and the rest of his family), and played another Russian, Commissar Solzhenitsyn, in WHOOPS APOCALYPSE. He has since had his own sketch series, *Alexei Sayle's Stuff*, *The All-New Alexei Sayle Show* and *Alexei Sayle's Merry-Go-Round*. Sayle has also been seen as Milcic in THE GRAVY TRAIN, a futuristic DJ in DOCTOR WHO, forger Conny Kujau in SELLING HITLER, artist Alain Degout in PARIS, the Puppeteer in TOM JONES, Bac Pac in *Arabian Nights*, Charles Frobisher in TIPPING THE VELVET, a newspaper editor in *The Legend of the Tamworth Two*, and Andy Carolides in his own romantic comedy, *Sorry About Last Night*, among other programmes.

Scales, Prunella

CBE (Prunella Illingworth; 1932–)

Surrey-born actress whose career was launched by THE MARRIAGE LINES, in which she played Kate Starling, in 1963. Scales also appeared with Jimmy Edwards in SIX FACES OF JIM and with Ronnie Barker in SEVEN OF ONE, but she remains best remembered as the grating Sybil Fawlty in FAWLTY TOWERS. She followed this with *Mr Big* (Dolly), MAPP AND LUCIA (Elizabeth Mapp) and AFTER HENRY (widow Sarah France). Earlier she played bus conductress Eileen Hughes in CORONATION STREET, and other credits have come in *The Secret Garden* (Martha), *The Rector's Wife* (Marjorie Richardson), *Signs and Wonders* (Elizabeth Palmore), TARGET, NEVER THE TWAIN, JACKANORY, BERGERAC, Alan Bennett's play *Doris and Doreen*, SEARCHING (Mrs Tilston), BREAKING THE CODE (Sara Turing), JANE AUSTEN'S EMMA (Miss Bates), MIDSOMER MURDERS, *Station Jim* (Queen Victoria), *Dickens* (Elizabeth Dickens), SILENT WITNESS, *Looking for Victoria* (Queen Victoria again), CASUALTY, WHERE THE HEART IS and the TV films *The Lord of Misrule* (Shirley) and *A Question of Attribution* (Queen Elizabeth II). She is married to actor Timothy West and mother of actor Sam West.

Scarecrow and Mrs King ✶✶

US (Shoot the Moon/Warner Brothers) Secret Agent Drama. ITV 1984 (US: CBS 1983–7)

Lee Stetson ('Scarecrow')	**Bruce Boxleitner**
Mrs Amanda King	**Kate Jackson**
Dotty West	**Beverly Garland**
Billy Melrose	**Mel Stewart**
Francine Desmond	**Martha Smith**
Philip King	**Paul Stout**
Jamie King	**Greg Morton**
Dr Smyth	**Myron Natwick**
T. P. Aquinas	**Raleigh Bond**

Creators **Brad Buckner, Eugenie Ross-Leming**
Executive Producers **Brad Buckner, Eugenie Ross-Leming, George Geiger**

A young divorcée is drawn into espionage by a handsome stranger.

Lee Stetson, codenamed 'Scarecrow', is a US government agent. Amanda King is a recently divorced mother of two boys (Philip and Jamie), living in the suburbs of Washington, DC. Their paths cross one eventful day at a railway station, when Scarecrow, fleeing from Russian agents, thrusts a package into Amanda's hands for safekeeping. Although stunned at first, Mrs King discovers she actually enjoys the thrill of working undercover for 'The Agency' and continues to work closely with the impressed Scarecrow, his boss Billy Melrose and fellow agent Francine Desmond (an ex-girlfriend). To do so, she takes up a part-time position at the Agency's front business, International Federal Film. Amanda's mother, Dotty West, proves a useful ally at home, especially as, being sworn to secrecy, Amanda can never explain the reason for her often eccentric behaviour or her relationship with this good-looking mystery man. For the final season, a new informant, T. P. Aquinas, and a new section head, Dr Smyth, join the team. Before the series concludes, Scarecrow and Mrs King develop their liaison to the point of marriage, but, of course, no one knows – it is classified information.

Scarlet and Black ✶✶✶

UK (BBC) Drama. BBC 1 1993

Julien Sorel	**Ewan McGregor**
Madame de Rênal	**Alice Krige**
Monsieur de Rênal	**Martin Jarvis**
Chélan	**Joseph O'Connor**
Napoleon	**Christopher Fulford**
Valenod	**Michael Attwell**
Mathilde	**Rachel Weisz**
Marquis de la Mole	**T. P. McKenna**
Abbé Pirard	**Stratford Johns**

Writer **Stephen Lowe**

The rise and fall of a socially aspirant youth in 19th-century France.

Julien Sorel is the son of a rural carpenter. However, he is fiercely ambitious and makes his way determinedly through society, using both the Army (the Scarlet) and the Church (the Black) as his stepping stones. Along the way he makes many waves, such as when he embarks on an affair with Mme de Rênal, wife of the local mayor, while acting as a tutor to her children, a move that returns to haunt him in years to come. Other key figures include Abbé Pirard, the firm but good-hearted priest who allows Julien into a seminary in Besançon, and Mathilde, the young heiress of the Marquis de la Mole, whose secretary Julien becomes in Paris. It is when he is on the brink of marriage to Mathilde that his world is brought tumbling down and he is forced to return to his roots to fight again. This three-part adaptation of Stendhal's classic 1830 novel, *Le Rouge et le Noir*, directed by Ben Bolt, was filmed in the Franche-Comté region of south-eastern France. Stendhal's work had previously been dramatized by the BBC in 1965 (BBC 2: John Stride as Sorel and June Tobin as Mme de Rênal).

Scarlet Pimpernel, The [1]

See *Adventures of the Scarlet Pimpernel, The.*

Scarlet Pimpernel, The [2] ★★★

UK (BBC/A&E) Drama. BBC 1 1999–2000

Sir Percy Blakeney	**Richard E. Grant**
Lady Marguerite Blakeney	**Elizabeth McGovern**
Chauvelin	**Martin Shaw**
Fumier	**Christopher Fairbank**
Sir Andrew Ffoulkes	**Anthony Green**
Robespierre	**Ronan Vibert**
Suzanne de Tourney/Lady Suzanne Ffoulkes	**Beth Goddard**
Planchet	**Gerard Murphy**
Mazarini	**Ron Donachie**
Prince of Wales	**Jonathan Coy**
Fisher	**Milton Johns**
William Wetherby	**John McEnery**

Writers **Richard Carpenter, Matthew Hall, Alan Whiting, Rob Heyland**
Producers **Julian Murphy, Richard Langridge, Colin Ludlow**

● ***More tales of outlandish heroism from the enigmatic saviour of the French nobility.***

Once again the dashing and mysterious Scarlet Pimpernel rides to the rescue of the French aristocracy, this time in moody colour and widescreen with Richard E. Grant donning the mantle of the adventurer who hides behind the cowardly facade of a fop. Nick-of-time snatches from the jaws of Madame Guillotine, devious escapes from imprisonment and plenty of run-ins with the sadistic Chauvelin add excitement to the tedious society world of Sir Percy Blakeney in stories inspired by Baroness Orczy's characters. Six feature-length episodes, mostly filmed in the Czech Republic, were produced over two years.

Schama, Simon

CBE (1945–)

London-born academic, based in the USA for 20 years (a professor of history and art history at New York's Columbia University), before being asked to present A HISTORY OF BRITAIN BY SIMON SCHAMA. Earlier he had presented *Landscape and Memory* for BBC 2.

Schofield, Phillip

(1962–)

Lancashire-born presenter who gained his first broadcasting experience while living with his family in New Zealand. Moving back to the UK, Schofield won the job of presenting Children's BBC, which led to the Saturday morning magazines SATURDAY SUPERSTORE and GOING LIVE! He proved such a hit with younger viewers that he was cast as Joseph in the stage musical *Joseph and the Amazing Technicolor Dreamcoat*. He also presented *The Movie Game* and *Television's Greatest Hits* for the BBC, before being lured over to ITV to present programmes like *Talking Telephone Numbers*, *Schofield's Quest*, *Schofield's TV Gold*, *Schofield in Hawaii* and *One in a Million*. Back with the BBC, after playing Dr Dolittle on stage, he hosted *Schofield's Animal Odyssey*, THE NATIONAL LOTTERY *Winning Lines* and *Test the Nation*. He has also hosted ITV's *This Morning*, *Have I Been Here Before?* and *Dancing on Ice*.

Scooby Doo, Where are You? ★★

US (Hanna-Barbera) Cartoon. BBC 1 1970–2 (US: CBS 1969–76; ABC 1978)

Voices:

Scooby Doo	**Don Messick**
Shaggy Rogers	**Casey Kasem**
Freddy	**Frank Welker**
Daphne Blake	**Heather North**
Velma	**Nicole Jaffe**

Creators **Ken Spears, Joe Ruby**
Executive Producers **William Hanna, Joseph Barbera**
Producer **Iwao Takamoto**

● ***The misadventures of a cowardly canine and his teenage pals.***

Although his coat is brown with black spots, Great Dane Scooby-Doo has a broad yellow streak right down his back. Far from protecting his human companions, it is Scooby who dashes for cover in times of trouble (leaving his friends to call after him and giving rise to the series' title). Scooby's colleagues are Shaggy, a fumbling youth with a stubbly chin who bribes the ever-ravenous pooch with Scooby Snacks; Velma, the bespectacled, frumpy brains of the unit; Daphne, who is always the first to find trouble; and level-headed, trendy Freddy, leader of the group. Together they travel in a transit van known as *The Mystery Machine* and, no matter where the gang arrives, problems are just around the corner. Usually the mysteries involve criminals who dress up as ghosts in order to commit heinous crimes but, one way or another, the gallant amateur detectives always put an end to their activities (with precious little help from Scooby and Shaggy). In later seasons, Scooby is joined by a pup nephew, Scrappy-Doo, and the lovable hound is also seen in *Laff-a-Lympics* among other animations. Producers Hanna–Barbera obviously liked the concept, because they soon issued another dog-and-teen detective cartoon entitled *Goober and the Ghost Chasers*.

Scotland Yard

See *Case Histories of Scotland Yard.*

Scott, Brough

(1942–)

British National Hunt jockey turned journalist and TV presenter. Brough Scott has worked for ITV and Channel 4 racing since the 1970s, hosting all the major meetings. He has also been seen in other sports coverage.

Scott, Jack

(1923–)

British meteorologist who became one of TV's best-known faces through 47 years' service as a weatherman with the Met. Office, appearing on BBC TV (1969–83) and Thames Television (1983–8). On retiring from forecasting, Scott hosted the Channel 4 senior citizens' magazine *Years Ahead*.

Scott, Mike

(1932–)

British TV executive and presenter, mostly with Granada Television. Scott joined Granada as a floor manager, eventually becoming a director. Behind or in front of the camera, he has worked on local news programmes, WORLD IN ACTION, CINEMA and, when daytime TV arrived, *The Time, The Place*. He was Programme Controller at Granada from 1979 to 1987.

Scott, Terry

(1927–94)

British comic actor, the archetypal hapless husband in cosy, domestic sitcoms. Scott starred alongside Bill Maynard in *Great Scott – It's Maynard!* in 1955 and with Norman Vaughan in *Scott Free* in 1957, but the best-remembered of his early screen partners was Hugh Lloyd, with whom he appeared in 1962 in HUGH AND I and, later, *Hugh and I Spy*. They were also seen together in THE GNOMES OF DULWICH. In 1969, in the series *Scott on . . .*, he was teamed for the first time with June Whitfield, who was to be his screen wife for many years. Together, they endured suburban silliness as the Fletchers in HAPPY EVER AFTER and the Medfords in TERRY AND JUNE. Scott was also familiar in the 1970s as the schoolboy in the Curly Wurly chocolate commercials and he was cast in *Son of the Bride*, as Mollie Sugden's mummy's boy, in 1973. In the 1980s he provided the voice for the character of Penfold in the DANGERMOUSE cartoons.

Scottish Television

(STV)

The ITV contractor for Central Scotland, on air continuously since 31 August 1957. It has survived all the franchise reorganizations, despite concerns about its local programming in the mid-1960s. The main broadcasting centre is in Glasgow, with a smaller production base in Edinburgh. Among the company's contributions to the ITV network have been the drama series TAKE THE HIGH ROAD and TAGGART, the quiz show WHEEL OF FORTUNE, and children's programmes such as HOW 2 and ART ATTACK (picked up from TVS). Some local programmes have been produced in Gaelic. Scottish is now part of Scottish Media Group, which also owns Grampian Television.

Scrambling

See *Encryption*.

Screaming ✳✳

UK (BBC) Situation Comedy. BBC 1 1992

Annie	**Gwen Taylor**
Beatrice	**Penelope Wilton**
Rachael	**Jill Baker**
Ralph	**Tim Berrington**
Shirley	**Charlotte Barker**
Toby	**Jackie Downey**
Katrina	**Katy Newell**
Paddy	**Maeve Germaine**
Jennifer	**Lucy Briers**

Writer **Carla Lane**

Producer **Mike Stephens**

● ***Three single women share a house, friendship and – unfortunately – memories of the same man.***

In a bid to express how love can make fools of us all, Carla Lane built this eight-part sitcom around the lives of three women who had all fallen for the same man. Beatrice, a single woman in early middle age, has just inherited a house from her late parents, having given up the best years of her own life to ensure their longevity. Moving in with her are Annie, an ever-youthful fortysomething on the road to divorce, who has been forced out of the flat she shared with her daughter and her boyfriend, plus Rachael, a self-deluding romantic in her thirties, who works as a keep-fit trainer at a women's psychiatric hospital. Very soon, however, it becomes clear that the three women have something very important in common, and his name is Ralph. Ralph used to be Rachael's boyfriend but, it seems, had affairs with both Beatrice and Annie. Although he is seldom seen, the deceitful Ralph continues to dominate all their lives, and a glimpse of him in the street is enough to raise emotions to fever pitch in the house. At such times, it is usually Beatrice, a level-headed philosophy graduate with a dry wit, who ends up peace-making, though in their heads at least these three women will always be screaming.

Screen Test ✳✳

UK (BBC) Children's Quiz. BBC 1 1970–84

Presenters **Michael Rodd, Brian Trueman, Mark Curry**

Producers **John Buttery, David Brown, Tony Harrison**

● ***Observation quiz for kids, based on film clips.***

The young contestants on *Screen Test* viewed a series of clips from popular films and were then tested on their observation skills and general knowledge. Interviews and features on the movie world also formed part of this long-running programme, which was hosted for many years by Michael Rodd. A young film-maker's contest was also incorporated.

Script Editor

Usually employed on a long-running series, the script editor is responsible for ensuring that scripts supplied by a team of writers conform to the style of the series as a whole, taking into account character continuity, plot developments, etc.

Scrubs ✳✳✳

UK (Doozer/Touchstone) Situation Comedy. Channel 4 2002–3; 2005– (US: NBC 2001–)

DVD: Buena Vista Home Entertainment

Dr John 'JD' Dorian	**Zach Braff**
Dr Elliot Reid	**Sarah Chalke**
Chris Turk	**Donald Fraison**
Dr Bob Kelso	**Ken Jenkins**
Dr Perry Cox	**John McGinley**
Nurse Carla Espinosa	**Judy Reyes**
Jordan Sullivan	**Christa Miller Lawrence**
The Janitor	**Neil Flynn**
Ted Buckland	**Sam Lloyd**
Nurse Laverne Roberts	**Aloma Wright**
Todd	**Robert Maschio**

Creator **Bill Lawrence**
Executive Producers **Bill Lawrence, Matt Tarses, Eric Weinberg**

A team of raw interns learn the ropes at an unorthodox teaching hospital.

'JD' Dorian is fresh out of medical school and starting an internship at the Sacred Heart Hospital. He's keen to get along but soon finds that the Sacred Heart is a crazy place to work, staffed by eccentric doctors and patients. It doesn't help that nerdy JD is a touch more squeamish than a doctor really should be, or that he has an overly fertile imagination. However, he does have Turk, his old college buddy, to help him acclimatize, and then there is fellow intern Elliot Reid to lust after. Elliot herself is ambitious but socially clumsy, which lands her in just as many awkward situations as JD. Supervising the newcomers are experienced medics Dr Kelso (po-faced chief of medicine who is always barking at his subordinates) and Dr Cox (eccentric mentor figure who has a warped wit and plenty of blistering put-downs and rants at his disposal). Jordan is Cox's ex-wife. Turk's romantic interest is sassy, confident, no-nonsense nurse Carla.

As in M*A*S*H, these carers lace their daily routines with a generous dose of cynicism – possibly the only way to get through such a depressing diet of disease, death and distress. Off-beat characters like the Janitor, who, for some reason, sees it as his duty in life to harass JD, and the gloomy hospital lawyer Ted, who leads the barber shop quartet that practises in the elevators at night, also lighten the load. Michael J. Fox is an occasional guest as the obsessive-compulsive Dr Kevin Casey.

Pieced together with surreal Ally McBeal-like fantasy sequences and low-key voice-overs in the style of THE WONDER YEARS, gag-packed *Scrubs* proved itself to be a hit from day one. Why Channel 4 left a gap of two years between series two and three is therefore anyone's guess. At least episodes did air earlier on Sky One.

Scully ✶✶

UK (Granada) Situation Comedy. Channel 4 1984

Franny Scully .... **Andrew Schofield**
Mooey .... **Ray Kingsley**
Mad Dog .... **Mark McGann**
Snotty Dog .... **Richard Burke**
Gran .... **Jean Boht**
Marie Morgan .... **Gilly Coman**
Joanna .... **Cathy Tyson**
Isiah .... **Tom Georgeson**
Mrs Scully .... **Val Lilley**
Mr Scully .... **Joey Kaye**
'Crackers' Leigh .... **Mary Cunningham**
Dracula .... **Tony Haygarth**
Henry Scully .... **Elvis Costello**
Arthur Scully .... **Jimmy Gallagher**
Tony Scully .... **Peter Christian**

Writer **Alan Bleasdale**
Producer **Steve Morrison**

A cocky Liverpool youth dreams of being a soccer star.

Teenager Franny Scully hates school life, and the last thing he wants to do is act in the school pantomime. He'd much rather be out kicking a ball around in pursuit of his ultimate dream: the chance to play for his home town club, Liverpool FC. While his ambitions remain far from realistic, he battles his way through the trials and tribulations of the adolescent years, acting the tough guy but hiding a soft interior, hanging around with his cheerful but dopey mate Mooey, and making a play for Joanna, the girl he fancies. Sadly, it is her friend, Marie, who fancies him. At home Scully has to find space for himself among his mum and dad, his gran (soused in pina coladas) and brothers Arthur (a perfect child) and the railway-mad Henry (played by Elvis Costello, who also wrote and performed the theme song, 'Turning the Town Red'). As Scully daydreams about donning the famous red jersey and hearing the Kop chanting his name, numerous members of the Liverpool set-up of the time make guest appearances, including players Kenny Dalglish (Scully's idol) and Bruce Grobbelaar, manager Bob Paisley and former Anfield hero Ian St John. The series was based on Alan Bleasdale's own novels, and followed a one-off play for the BBC in 1978 entitled *Scully's New Year's Eve*. Les Chatfield directed the seven episodes.

Sculptress, The ✶✶✶

UK (Red Rooster) Drama. BBC 1 1996

Olive Martin .... **Pauline Quirke**
Rosalind Leigh .... **Caroline Goodall**
Hal Hawksley .... **Christopher Fulford**
Geoff Wyatt .... **James McCarthy**
Father Julian .... **Dermot Crowley**
Peter Crew .... **Michael Percival**
Iris Fielding .... **Lynda Rooke**
Edward Clarke .... **David Horvitch**
Dorothy Clarke .... **Ann Davies**
Stewart Hayes .... **Ian Reddington**
Albert Hayes .... **Timothy Bateson**

Writer **Reg Gadney**
Executive Producer **Jo Wright**
Producers **Julia Ouston, Linda James**

A writer believes a woman imprisoned for grisly murder is innocent.

Olive Martin is a sad, tragic figure. When her mother and sister are brutally murdered, the 22-stone Olive confesses to the killings and gains the nickname of 'the sculptress' because of the gruesome way in which the murders were carried out. Five years later, publisher Iris Fielding feels there is a book waiting to be written about Olive's case and dispatches journalist Rosalind Leigh to do the research. It proves to be a cathartic experience, helping Rosalind overcome her grief at the death of her own daughter in a car accident. She interviews Olive plus Hal Hawksley, the detective sergeant who discovered the crime and, traumatized, has since left the force to run a restaurant. She also speaks to the Clarkes, Olive's former neighbours, and Peter Carew, the solicitor Olive despises. As a result, Rosalind becomes convinced of Olive's innocence and sets out to prove it. Olive meanwhile passes her time in prison by carving human shapes out of candles stolen from the prison chapel. Stuart Orme directed this four-part drama based on the novel by Minette Walters.

Sea Hunt ✶✶

US (Ziv/United Artists) Adventure. ITV 1958–62 (US: Syndicated 1957–61)

Mike Nelson .... **Lloyd Bridges**

Producer **Ivan Tors**

Excitement with an underwater adventurer-for-hire.

Former navy diver Mike Nelson is a freelance agent who offers his underwater skills to anyone who wishes to employ him. Working from his boat, *The Argonaut*, and travelling the globe, Nelson takes on jobs for salvage companies, insurance firms and especially the US Government, swimming into all manner of tight scrapes and always coming up with the goods. Star Lloyd Bridges was the only regular, though his two young (at the time) sons, Beau and Jeff, also made guest appearances. The real star, however, was the sea itself, with all its underwater glory. The series was briefly revived with little success in 1987, when TV's Tarzan, Ron Ely, donned Nelson's mask and flippers.

Sea of Souls ✱✱

UK (Sony/BBC) Drama. BBC 1 2004–
DVD: Sony Pictures Home Entertainment

Dr Douglas Monaghan .... **Bill Paterson**
Megan Sharma .... **Archie Panjabi**
Andrew Gemmill .... **Peter McDonald**
Rena .... **Barbara Rafferty**
Philip Crookes .... **David Ashton**
Dean Claremont .... **Hugh Ross**
Justine McManus .... **Dawn Steele**
Craig Stevenson .... **Iain Robertson**
Tina Logan .... **Louise Irwin**
Prof. Michael Holloway .... **Nigel Terry**
Dr Peter Locke .... **Colin Salmon**

Creator **David Kane**
Producers **Phil Collinson, Stephen Garwood**

● ***An academic team pursues the truth behind paranormal activity.***

At Clyde University they take the paranormal very seriously. Head of the establishment's parapsychology unit is Dr Douglas Monaghan, a clever but fatherly team leader. He is ably supported by young Megan Sharma, who is bright, streetwise and good with people, and Andrew Gemmill, a sceptic, who will turn over every stone to find a logical explanation for anything that seems out of the ordinary. The trio's attention is drawn towards bizarre, unexplained events and their aim is to help those distressed by what seems to be other-wordly activities. Their work leads them to investigate issues like reincarnation and past lives; the truth behind voodoo rituals; and twins separated at birth who meet in middle age and find they share more than identical looks. When Monaghan returns for series two, he has two new assistants: Justine McManus, a compassionate and trustworthy single mum, and hot-headed Craig Stevenson. A research colleague, Peter Locke, joins the team later. This time among the subjects under the paranormal microscope are poltergeists, curses and a stage psychic. For the first two series, each of the stories divides into two episodes, screened in the UK on consecutive nights. From series three, a single, one-hour format was employed. All deliver a mix of thought-provoking, spine-tingling moments and simple, over-the-top hokum.

Seaforth ✱✱✱

UK (Initial/BBC) Drama. BBC 1 1994

Bob Longman .... **Linus Roache**
Paula Wickham/Austen .... **Lia Williams**
Sarah Wickham .... **Rosemary Martin**
Sal Longman .... **Heather Tobias**
Brian Longman .... **Raymond Pickard**
Richard Austen .... **Richard Huw**
Penny Winter .... **Christine Kavanagh**
Andrew Winter .... **Robert Swann**
Sue .... **Sally Rogers**
Lt./Major Tony Gray .... **Andrew Woodall**
Arthur Spence .... **Gary Lydon**
Fred Spence .... **John McArdle**
Capt. Karl von Berner .... **Mark Heap**
Vera Longman .... **Joanne Wooton**
John Stacey .... **Ciaran Hinds**
Diana Stacey .... **Diana Kent**
Larry Field .... **Sean Murray**
Dr Willis .... **Michael Bertenshaw**

Creator/Writer **Peter Ransley**
Executive Producers **Michael Wearing, Clive Brill**
Producers **Alan J. Wands, Eileen Quinn**

● ***A Yorkshire tearaway and his middle-class girlfriend endure the hardships of war and its aftermath.***

This 'love conquers all' drama is set in the fictitious Yorkshire town of Seaforth (Beeston, a suburb of Leeds, for filming) during World War II and the reconstruction that follows. Running over nine episodes and beginning in 1943, it features ne'er-do-well Bob Longman, an army deserter who fends for his fatherless family through theft (posing as an ARP warden during raids). In the process of burgling one big house, he saves the life of the maid, Paula Wickham, and, against her better judgment, the two begin a turbulent relationship. Despite the fact that Bob finally gives himself up to the military police and goes to war, while Paula marries RAF NCO Richard Austen, their attraction remains strong and pervades all the privations of life at the time. Trying to end their relationship is Paula's socially aspirant mother, Sarah, while Bob's own mother, Sal, struggling to cope with three kids, is despised by her son for turning to the bottle. All the while, Bob's best mate is his nine-year-old brother, Brian, who acts as lookout and errand boy. After the war, Bob attempts to make his way as one of the dodgy entrepreneurs who see rich pickings in the shattered economy, the value of army surplus goods and the redevelopment of Mafeking Park, the slumland in which he has grown up. His great rival is John Stacey.

Seagrove, Jenny

(1958–)

Malaysian-born actress who made her TV name with the lead role (Emma Harte) in the mini-series A WOMAN OF SUBSTANCE in 1985 (and its sequel, *Hold That Dream*). Earlier, Seagrove had played Laura in Wilkie Collins's THE WOMAN IN WHITE and Diana Gaylorde-Sutton in Andrew Davies's adaptation of R. F. Delderfield's DIANA. She was also seen in THE BRACK REPORT (Angela Brack) and in the 1987 Sherlock Holmes special, *The Sign of Four*, and more recently played Jo Mills QC in JUDGE JOHN DEED, as well as making guest appearances in CASUALTY and PEAK PRACTICE.

Seaquest DSV/Seaquest 2032 ✱✱

US (Amblin/Universal) Science Fiction. ITV 1993–9
(US: NBC 1993–5)

Capt. Nathan Bridger .... **Roy Scheider**
Commander Jonathan Ford .... **Don Franklin**
Dr Kristin Westphalen .... **Stephanie Beacham**
Lucas Wolenczak .... **Jonathan Brandis**

Lt. Commander Katherine Hitchcock	**Stacy Haiduk**
Lt. Tim O'Neill	**Ted Raimi**
Lt. Ben Krieg	**John D'Aquino**
Sensor Chief Miguel Ortiz	**Marco Sanchez**
Chief Manilow Crocker	**Royce D. Applegate**
Lt. James Brody	**Edward Kerr**
Dr Wendy Smith	**Rosalind Allen**
Ensign 'Lonnie' Henderson	**Kathy Evison**
Tony Piccolo	**Michael DeLuise**
Dagwood	**Peter DeLuise**
Capt. Oliver Hudson	**Michael Ironside**
Lt. J. J. Fredericks	**Elise Neal**

Creator **Rockne S. O'Bannon**
Executive Producers **Steven Spielberg, David J. Burke, Patrick Hasburgh, Tommy Thompson**

● VOYAGE TO THE BOTTOM OF THE SEA ***for the 1990s.***

In the year 2018, *seaQuest* is a 1,000-foot-long research submarine (DSV standing for Deep Submergence Vehicle). This high-tech vessel probes the amazing, and often sinister, world of the ocean, with Capt. Nathan Bridger at the helm. Second in command is Commander Jonathan Ford, while Kristin Westphalen is the chief scientist, Hitchcock the second officer, and teenager Lucas Wolenczak the resident computer genius. Not all the crew is human, however, as there is also Darwin, a talking dolphin, to help unravel the secrets of the deep, which man has by now begun to colonize. Science apart, the ship, which is operated by the United Earth/Oceans Organization (UEO), is also a peacekeeper, heavily armed to help maintain the shaky new world order after the collapse of existing nations. Despite a massive production budget from producer Steven Spielberg's Amblin Entertainment company, changes were deemed necessary after only one season. *SeaQuest* is blown up and replaced with a new design and out go several crew members, including Westphalen and Hitchcock. Among the newcomers are telepathic Wendy Smith, and Tony Piccolo, who has gills and can breathe underwater. Before the series finally sank without trace, yet further amendments were made. The date was advanced to 2032 (reflected in the new title, *seaQuest 2032*) and a new captain, Oliver Hudson, was installed, as the vessel ventured more than ever into bug-eyed alien territory.

Search for the Nile, The ***

UK (BBC) Drama-Documentary. BBC 2 1971

Richard Burton	**Kenneth Haigh**
John Hanning Speke	**John Quentin**
Isabel Arundell/Burton	**Barbara Leigh-Hunt**
David Livingstone	**Michael Gough**
Sir Roderick Murchison	**André Van Gyseghem**
Blanche Arundell	**Elizabeth Proud**
Capt. James Grant	**Ian McCulloch**
Samuel Baker	**Norman Rossington**
Florence Baker	**Catherine Schell**
Henry Stanley	**Keith Buckley**
Bombay	**Seth Adagala**
Mutesa	**Oliver Litondo**
Narrator	**James Mason**

Writers **Derek Marlowe, Michael Hastings**
Producer **Christopher Ralling**

● ***A group of explorers is obsessed with finding the source of the Nile.***

In 19th-century colonial Africa, a group of headstrong but intrepid adventures are hell bent on discovering one of the planet's greatest mysteries, namely where the River Nile rises. Regrettably, inebriated by the potential fame and honour of such an achievement, they tend to be suspicious of each other and only too happy to discredit opponents. The men are John Hanning Speke, a crackshot, but notably treacherous; David Livingstone, a missionary/explorer; Samuel Baker, big-game hunter, who takes his wife with him on his journeys; James Grant, Speke's number two, a modest amateur biologist; Henry Stanley, a *New York Herald* journalist, who seeks out the missing Livingstone, eventually finding him at Ujiji on Lake Tanganyika; and Richard Burton, a brilliant but unpredictable rebel. Their time in the Dark Continent is marked by malaria sickness, unpredictable behaviour by locals and other difficulties and dangers. Hopes founder on many an occasion before the Nile is fully uncovered. Music is by Joseph Horovitz.

Searching **

UK (Noel Gay/Carlton) Situation Comedy. ITV 1995

Mrs Tilston	**Prunella Scales**
Chancy	**Julia St John**
Lena	**Victoria Carling**
Dora	**Clare Cathcart**
Milly	**Regina Freedman**
Hetty	**Amanda Bellamy**
Daniel	**Robert Gwilym**

Creator/Writer **Carla Lane**
Producer **Robin Nash**

● ***Emotional highs and lows with the residents of a women's help centre.***

Mrs Tilston runs the Sunfield Voluntary Therapy Centre, a refuge for women with behavioural problems. She's eccentric (carries a handbell which she rings to gain attention) and religious (wears a sweater boldly declaring 'I am His'). But, if a bit batty, she is essentially kind to her five emotionally distressed residents: Chancy, Lena, Dora, Milly and Hetty. Assistance is provided by new, easy-going male therapist, Daniel, who seems to be working wonders with the previously man-hating Chancy at least. The seven-part series (described by star Prunella Scales as mix of documentary, drama, sitcom and tragedy) explores the lives of Mrs Tilston's sad inmates and her attempts to keep the centre open in the face of council bureaucracy.

Seaside Special *

UK (BBC) Entertainment. BBC 1 1975–9

Presenters **David Hamilton, Noel Edmonds, Tony Blackburn, Dave Lee Travis, Paul Burnett, Peter Powell, Mike Smith**

Producer **Michael Hurll**

● ***Saturday night variety showcase for summer months.***

Cashing in on the end-of-the-pier summer variety show concept, *Seaside Special* was initially recorded in the big top of Gerry Cottle's Circus, pitched in various seaside resorts around the UK and northern Europe. The weekly offerings mixed circus acts with the big showbiz names of the day, with Radio 1 DJs on hand to host proceedings, and occasionally take part themselves (Tony Blackburn sang from inside a lion's cage and Noel Edmonds was carried across a wire on the shoulders of a tightrope walker – with no safety net). Among the big names guest-starring were Ken Dodd, Val Doonican, Lulu, Rolf Harris, Jimmy Tarbuck, Sacha Distel, Frankie Vaughan, Ronnie Corbett, Les Dawson, Little and Large, Des O'Connor, Peters and Lee, Dionne Warwick, Cilla Black and Cliff Richard. They were supported by lesser names like Fivepenny Piece, Wayne King, The Wurzels, Stuart Gillies, and also by Ronnie Hazlehurst and His Orchestra, and the New Edition dance troupe, later succeeded by Geoff Richer's First Edition. Occasional extras were sketches by TV comedy teams, including THE GOODIES and the cast of ARE YOU BEING SERVED? The 1977 season featured the Miss Seaside Special Natural Beauty Contest. Matt Batt with the New Edition scored a top 10 hit in 1975 with the theme song, 'Summertime City'. Resorts on the roadshow's schedule were Blackpool, Great Yarmouth, Poole, Torbay, Scarborough, Southsea, Weymouth, Cherbourg, Eastbourne, Lowestoft, Bournemouth, Honfleur, Deauville, Jersey, St Malo, Bruges, Blankenberge and the Isle of Man.

Seaside Special gave way in 1981 to a look-alike called *Summertime Special* (BBC 1 1981–2), based only in Brighton. The following year, Eastbourne was the location. There was no regular host for this programme, but both seasons featured The A Team dancers.

In 1987 *Seaside Special* (or *Seaside Special '87*) returned, recorded in Jersey. Mike Smith, supported by the Beach Belles, fronted events that included a revival of the *Beat the Clock* segment of SUNDAY NIGHT AT THE LONDON PALLADIUM. It lasted only one year, replaced in 1988 by a new summer variety show from Jersey entitled *Michael Barrymore's Saturday Night Out*.

SECAM

Séquential Couleur à Mémoire, the system of television transmission developed in and used by France. It operates off 625 lines like the British PAL system, but the two are incompatible. Countries with a French colonial interest (in Africa and the Middle East, for instance) have also adopted the SECAM system, as have East European countries (although their SECAM is modified).

Secombe, Sir Harry

CBE (1921–2001)

Swansea-born comedian, singer and presenter, coming to the fore as one of *The Goons* on BBC Radio (and, later, one of the voices of THE TELEGOONS on TV). The most popular of his series were *The Harry Secombe Show* (on both ITV and BBC, *Secombe and Friends* and *Secombe with Music*, most of them variety shows, although for much of the 1980s and early 1990s he was strongly associated with the religious travelogue HIGHWAY, which followed many appearances on STARS ON SUNDAY in the 1970s. Secombe later presented SONGS OF PRAISE. He was father of actor Andrew Secombe.

Second Sight ***

UK (Twenty Twenty) Police Drama. BBC 1 2000–1

DCI Ross Tanner .... **Clive Owen**
DI Catherine Tully .... **Claire Skinner**
DS Pewsey .... **Rupert Holiday Evans**
DS Julian .... **Alexander Morgan**
DC Holt .... **Selina Boyack**
DS Finch .... **Frank Harper**
Marilyn Tanner .... **Rebecca Egan**
Sam Tanner .... **Benjamin Smith**
Supt Lawson .... **Thomas Wheatley**
DC Chad .... **Akbar Kurtha**

Writers **Paula Milne, Antonia Hallem, Niall Leonard**
Producers **David Lascelles, Lars Macfarlaine**

● ***A senior detective battles advancing blindness while investigating cases of murder.***

At the height of a complex murder enquiry DCI Ross Tanner receives some devastating personal news: he has a degenerative sight problem. He already has moments when his vision fails but, determined to remain independent, he decides not to tell his colleagues. However, his ambitious new number two, DI Catherine Tully, discovers his secret and agrees to help him through the day, while also sharing his bed at night. Marilyn is Tanner's estranged wife and Sam his precious young son. After a two-part introduction in 2000, *Second Sight* returned for three two-episode stories a year later, although Tully only features in the first story before securing a transfer and leaving the increasingly disabled Tanner to fend for himself.

Second Thoughts **

UK (LWT) Situation Comedy. ITV 1991–4

Bill Macgregor .... **James Bolam**
Faith Grayshot .... **Lynda Bellingham**
Joe Grayshot .... **Mark Denham**
Hannah Grayshot .... **Julia Sawalha**
Liza Macgregor .... **Belinda Lang**
Richard .... **Geoffrey Whitehead**

Creators/Writers **Jan Etherington, Gavin Petrie**
Producers **David Askey, Robin Carr**

● ***Two divorcés begin a relationship, despite the attentions of teenage children and a former wife.***

Bill Macgregor is an art editor for a style magazine who begins a relationship with divorcée Faith Grayshot. However, the odds are stacked against them, thanks to the interference and the personal problems of Faith's teenage kids, Joe and Hannah, and the devious doings of Bill's promiscuous ex-wife, Liza, who happens to work in the same office as Bill. Suspicion and distrust rule at home, at work and in Harpo's Wine Bar. Weddings are arranged and postponed, and the course of true love never does run smoothly. Strangely, Faith and Liza never actually meet until the very last episode.

The series, which began on BBC Radio in 1988 and ran simultaneously on television for a while, was based on the real-life romance of its creators, *TV Times* journalists Jan Etherington and Gavin Petrie, both of whom had been divorced before beginning a new life together. A sequel series, starring Lynda Bellingham and Julia Sawalha and entitled *Faith in the Future* (1995–6; 1998), focuses on Faith's attempts to rebuild her life after saying a final goodbye to Bill and gaining a new man-friend named Paul (Jeff Rawle).

Second Verdict **

UK (BBC) Drama. BBC 1 1976

Det. Chief Supt. Charlie Barlow .... **Stratford Johns**
Det. Chief Supt. John Watt ..... **Frank Windsor**

Producer **Leonard Lewis**

● ***Two fictional detectives examine real-life murder mysteries.***

Charlie Barlow and John Watt, the Z CARS and SOFTLY, SOFTLY heavyweights, are the stars of this enigmatic series. Having joined forces to re-examine the *Jack the Ripper* story in 1973, the duo are paired up again to look at six more true-crime mysteries of the past. These included *Who Killed the Princes in the Tower?*, *Lizzie Borden* and *The Lindbergh Kidnapping*.

Seconds Out ★★

UK (BBC) Situation Comedy. BBC 1 1981–2

Pete Dodds .... **Robert Lindsay**
Tom Sprake .... **Lee Montague**
Dave Locket .... **Ken Jones**
Hazel .... **Leslie Ash**

Writer **Bill MacIlwraith**
Producer **Ray Butt**

● ***A talented amateur boxer turns professional with a wily manager.***

Pete Dodds, an amateur boxer with plenty of potential but also a tendency to clown about, turns professional and is taken under the wing of successful manager Tom Sprake. To keep him in line, Sprake pairs Dodds with irritating little trainer Dave Locket, relying on the pair's incompatibility to keep Dodds focused on the job. With Locket to nark him at every turn, Dodds begins to climb towards the top. First he claims the British middleweight title and then fights for the European crown. Hazel is Pete's girlfriend.

Secret Army ★★

UK (BBC/BRT) Drama. BBC 1 1977–9

Lisa Colbert ('Yvette') .... **Jan Francis**
Albert Foiret .... **Bernard Hepton**
Squadron Leader John Curtis . **Christopher Neame**
Sturmbannführer Ludwig Kessler .... **Clifford Rose**
Monique Duchamps .... **Angela Richards**
Natalie .... **Juliet Hammond-Hill**
Andrée Foiret .... **Eileen Page**
Erwin Brandt .... **Michael Culver**
Max Brocard .... **Stephen Yardley**
Alain .... **Ron Pember**
Dr Pascal Keldermans .... **Valentine Dyall**
Gaston .... **James Bree**
François .... **Nigel Williams**
Madeleine Duclos .... **Hazel McBride**
Reinhardt .... **Louis Sheldon**
Terrence Hardiman
Paul Vercors .... **Michael Byrne**
Ralph Bates
Nick Bradley .... **Paul Shelley**
Louise .... **Maria Charles**
Rennert .... **Robin Langford**
Jacques .... **Timothy Morand**
Insp. Delon .... **John D. Collins**
Hauptmann Müller .... **Hilary Minster**
Capt. Durnford .... **Stephan Chase**

Creators **Gerald Glaister, Wilfred Greatorex**
Producer **Gerard Glaister**

● ***The daring exploits of the Belgian Resistance.***

The activities of Lifeline, an underground Resistance movement in Belgium during World War II, are showcased in *Secret Army*. This extremely courageous secret army specializes in smuggling trapped Allied servicemen ('evaders') back to Britain, via a number of escape routes and safe houses. Head of the organization is Lisa Colbert, codenamed Yvette, a young teacher who becomes a Resistance worker after the killing of her parents. She is assisted chiefly by Albert Foiret, proprietor of Le Candide, a Brussels restaurant in the Rue Deschanel which acts as the movement's base. Ironically, it is also a hostelry favoured by German officers, which adds to the danger. The other key functionaries are Foiret's mistress, Monique, Natalie, RAF liaison John Curtis, and, later, forger/pianist Max Brocard. Chief among the Nazis are local head Brandt, his much firmer replacement, Reinhardt, and the cruel Kessler, the local Gestapo leader. Madeleine Duclos is his lover. By the end of the series the war has ended, Brussels is liberated and Kessler has assumed a new identity in order to escape trial. He resurfaces as a German businessman (using the alias Manfred Dorf) in a spin-off series, *Kessler*, in 1981, in which his wartime secrets begin to be exposed.

Secret Army was probably the most unlikely of TV series to earn itself a parody. But it did just that when 'ALLO 'ALLO came along in 1984. Although the setting had been transposed to France, all the other distinctive elements were present, from the long-suffering restaurateur to the Resistance operatives and the pompous Nazis – even some of the actors returned to send themselves up. If anything, the series has been overshadowed by this spoof successor. Robert Farnon composed the *Secret Army* music.

Secret Diary of Adrian Mole, Aged 13¾, The/The Growing Pains of Adrian Mole/Adrian Mole: The Cappuccino Years ★★★

UK (Thames/Tiger Aspect/Little Dancer) Situation Comedy. ITV 1985/1987/BBC 1 2001

Adrian Mole .... **Gian Sammarco**
Stephen Mangan *(Cappuccino Years)*
Pauline Mole .... **Julie Walters**
Lulu *(Growing Pains)*
Alison Steadman *(Cappuccino Years)*
George Mole .... **Stephen Moore**
Alun Armstrong *(Cappuccino Years)*
Grandma Mole .... **Beryl Reid**
Bert Baxter .... **Bill Fraser**
Pandora Braithwaite .... **Lindsey Stagg**
Helen Baxendale *(Cappuccino Years)*
Queenie .... **Doris Hare**
Nigel .... **Steven Mackintosh**
Mr Lucas .... **Paul Greenwood**
Doreen Slater .... **Su Elliot**
Tania Braithwaite .... **Zoë Wanamaker** *(Cappuccino Years)*
Ivan Braithwaite .... **James Hazeldine** *(Cappuccino Years)*
Nigel Hetherington .... **Roderic Culver** *(Cappuccino Years)*

William Mole	**Harry Tomes** *(Cappuccino Years)*
Rosie Mole	**Melissa Batchelor** *(Cappuccino Years)*
Glenn Bott	**Alex De-Ath** *(Cappuccino Years)*

Creator/Writer **Sue Townsend**
Executive Producer **Lloyd Shirley**
Producers **Peter Sasdy, Sarah Smith** *(Cappuccino Years)*

A teenage boy chronicles his troubles as his family self-destructs.

This series, adapted by Sue Townsend from her own best-selling novel, *The Secret Diary of Adrian Mole*, is set in the Midlands and sheds light on the adolescent woes which befall young, bespectacled Adrian. In addition to the usual teenage travails of school, spots, girls and peer-pressure, Adrian also finds himself in the midst of family turmoil. His mum, Pauline, and dad, George, have gone their separate ways and now only trade insults. Also involved are his Grandma and an elderly character he befriends named Bert Baxter, while Pandora is the girl Adrian has set his heart on. When the second series begins under the title *The Growing Pains of Adrian Mole*, with Adrian aged 15, his now pregnant mum is played by pop singer Lulu. Ian Dury performed the Adrian Mole theme song, 'Profoundly in Love with Pandora'.

A new series, based on Sue Townsend's 1990s book *Adrian Mole: the Cappuccino Years*, was broadcast in 2001. Adrian is now 31 and a single parent, working as an offal chef in a West End restaurant, Hoi Polloi, while Pandora, now Dr Braithwaite, is the 'Blair babe' MP for their home town of Ashby-de-la-Zouch.

Secret Servant, The ★★

UK (BBC) Spy Drama. BBC 1 1984

Major Harry Maxim	**Charles Dance**
Agnes Algar	**Jill Meager**
George Harbinger	**Harvey Ashby**
Prof. John Tyler	**Dan O'Herlihy**
Charley Farthing	**Harry Jones**
Komoscin	**Constantine Gregory**

Writer **Brian Clemens**
Producer **Bob McIntosh**

An SAS man drafted into the security services is mistrusted by MI5.

Based on the novel by Gavin Lyall, this three-part BBC Scotland thriller was penned by Brian Clemens, who learned a lot about secret agent work during his time with THE AVENGERS. Here Clemens offers a tale of subterfuge and intrigue, dosed with defections and mole hunts. It centres on Major Harry Maxim, an SAS officer who is seconded to work in Downing Street. There he is asked to mind an important nuclear scientist, Professor John Tyler, who is visiting the UK, but MI5 is far from happy with an outsider's involvement in such an important case.

Secret Service, The ★★

UK (Century 21/ITC) Children's Science Fiction. ITV 1969

Father Stanley Unwin	**Stanley Unwin**
Matthew Harding the gardener	**Keith Alexander** *(voice only)*
Matthew Harding (the agent)	**Gary Files** *(voice only)*
Mrs Appleby	**Sylvia Anderson** *(voice only)*
The Bishop	**Jeremy Wilkin** *(voice only)*

Creators **Gerry Anderson, Sylvia Anderson**
Executive Producer **Reg Hill**
Producer **David Lane**

Short-lived Gerry Anderson combination of live action and puppetry.

Fifty-seven-year-old parish priest Father Unwin is no ordinary country parson. In fact, he is an undercover agent for BISHOP (British Intelligence Secret Headquarters, Operation Priest). Helping him to carry out his unusual job is a special device called 'The Minimiser' (found in a book lent to Unwin by one of his late parishioners), which can reduce people and objects to one-third of their normal size. When put into use on behalf of the security services, usually it is the priest's yokel gardener, Matthew, who is shrunk, allowing him to take on dangerous missions on behalf of the country. When Matthew is minimized, the priest carries him around in a brief-case. Unwin, who drives a vintage Model-T Ford named Gabriel, also has a radio built into his mock hearing-aid, through which he is given assignments by his commander, 'The Bishop'. It is also used for contacting other BISHOP agents. Mrs Appleby is Unwin's blissfully ignorant housekeeper.

The Secret Service provided a stepping stone between the Supermarionation adventures of Stingray, Thunderbirds *et al.* and Gerry Anderson's move into live action with UFO. But it failed to attract a network audience (being screened only in the Midlands, the South and the North-West) and was limited to just 13 episodes. Double-speaking comedian Stanley Unwin played the priest in long-shots, with a puppet clone used for close-ups. The late comic's gobbledygook was a feature of the series.

Secret Society ★★

UK (BBC) Current Affairs. BBC 2 1987

Presenter/Writer **Duncan Campbell**
Producer **Brian Barr**

Highly controversial series about covert British agencies and operations.

Although six episodes of this investigative series were planned, only four made it to the screen on time. One was eventually shown a year late, and the other was assigned to the dustbin. This curtailment was a result of political sensitivity, particularly over an episode revealing plans for a secret British spy satellite known as Zircon. On 31 January 1987, the BBC offices in Glasgow were raided by Special Branch officers and over 30 boxes of tapes and material relating to the programme were confiscated. The BBC Chairman, Marmaduke Hussey, made a strong protest to the Government and there was uproar in the House of Commons. *The Zircon Affair* finally aired as a 75-minute special, introduced by Ludovic Kennedy, in 1988, but another edition, entitled *Cabinet* and alleging election dirty tricks, was never broadcast, being deemed too out of date by the time the initial fuss had died down. The four episodes which were screened concerned DHSS computer databanks, emergency laws in times of national crisis, the influence of the Association of Chief Police Officers on Government policy and the UK's radar defence network.

See You Friday ★★★

UK (Yorkshire) Comedy Drama. ITV 1997

Greg .... **Neil Pearson**
Lucy .... **Joanna Roth**
Bernie .... **Mark Benton**
Sophie .... **Hermione Norris**
Fiona .... **Daisy Bates**
Daniel .... **Hugh Bonneville**
Vanessa .... **Denise Welch**

Writer **Alan Whiting**
Producer **Lizzie Taylor**

● ***A long-distance affair is a pain for two holiday lovers.***
The problem with holiday romances is that the course of love doesn't always run smooth once the holiday is over – as Greg and Lucy find in this six-part series. The couple meet up on the last day of a trip to Greece and decide to carry on seeing each other when they return to Britain. Unfortunately, Greg is a policeman in Newcastle upon Tyne and Lucy is a student in London. Between them lie 300 miles of railway track and motorway. Nevertheless they persevere, through train delays, car breakdowns, calls of duty and other hiccups that shatter the precious little time they have together, and through the interference of friends and family (not least Greg's younger sister, Fiona, who on one occasion ruins a weekend by staging an embarrassing family party). Then comes the crunch: do they move in together, and if so where – up north or down south? And whose job/course will have to give way?

Seinfeld ★★★★

US (NBC/West-Shapiro/Castle Rock) Situation Comedy. BBC 2 1993–2001 (US: NBC 1990–8)

Jerry Seinfeld .... **Jerry Seinfeld**
Elaine Benes .... **Julia Louis-Dreyfus**
George Costanza .... **Jason Alexander**
Cosmo Kramer .... **Michael Richards**
Helen Seinfeld .... **Liz Sheridan**
Morty Seinfeld .... **Phil Bruns**
Barney Martin
Frank Costanza .... **Jerry Stiller**
Estelle Costanza .... **Estelle Harris**
Uncle Leo .... **Len Lesser**
Newman .... **Wayne Knight**

Creators **Larry David, Jerry Seinfeld**

● ***Four neurotic friends contemplate the minutiae of life.***
The widely acclaimed *Seinfeld* – America's supreme 1990s sitcom – somehow never really gained a foothold in the UK. The BBC quickly lost faith and consigned it to the backwaters of late-night BBC 2, at great loss to the viewers, said the critics. *Seinfeld* is a strange kind of programme, an eccentric comedy in which nothing important ever really happens. The basic premiss is that the four self-centred, opinionated lead characters spend their time working over some utterly trivial aspect of life – the frustration of waiting in line or being stuck in traffic, the impossibility of getting a restaurant table, etc. Plots are therefore negligible, but the dialogue is sharp and perceptive, sometimes pushing back the barriers of taste in its subject-matter.

Nominal star is stand-up Jerry Seinfeld, playing himself, an obsessively fussy man who falls out with girls because of their petty habits. Of equal importance is his ex-girlfriend, Elaine, a book editor, also unlucky in love and destined always to date a weirdo. Then there are their tight-fisted, podgy buddy, George, an insecure estate agent who tells the most outrageous lies in order to charm a woman; and the semi-crazy Kramer, an unkempt whirlwind figure (always with a bright idea for making money), who lives in the same New York apartment block as Jerry. Parents, dates, bosses and other acquaintances – including maligned mailman Newman – are other occasional characters. The 'action' is usually topped and tailed with scenes of Jerry performing his nightclub act, commenting on the same topics that are engaging the characters.

Despite allegedly being offered $5 million a show to continue, Jerry Seinfeld pulled the plug after eight seasons, ensuring the series quit at the top.

Seinfeld, Jerry

(Jerome Seinfeld; 1954–)

Brooklyn-born stand-up comedian who, as star of his own sitcom, SEINFELD (playing himself), became one of US TV's biggest names of the 1990s. Previously, Seinfeld had been occasionally seen in BENSON, playing joke-writer Frankie.

Selby, Tony

(1938–)

London-born actor, usually in comic roles. Probably his most memorable creation was the loud-mouthed Corporal Marsh in GET SOME IN!, although he has been seen in numerous other sitcoms. He played Les Robinson in the lighthouse comedy *Shine a Light*, Norman Lugg in Dick Emery's *Jack of Diamonds* and the scheming handyman, Bert Finch, in MULBERRY. Selby's earliest TV work came in single dramas like Harold Pinter's *A Night Out* and Nell Dunn's UP THE JUNCTION. He has also been seen in offerings like *Tom Grattan's War*, THE AVENGERS, DEPARTMENT S, THE INFORMER, THE GOOD LIFE, *Moody and Pegg*, C.A.T.S. EYES, MINDER, DOCTOR WHO (Glitz), THE SWEENEY, BERGERAC, CASUALTY, LOVEJOY, LOVE HURTS (Max Taplow), REAL WOMEN (Bobby), HARBOUR LIGHTS (Mike's dad), *Happy Birthday Shakespeare* (Roy), DOCTORS, *Hero to Zero* (George), EASTENDERS, *Burnside* (Jim Summers) and ROSE AND MALONEY. In the 1970s he played Sam in ACE OF WANDS.

Selleck, Tom

(1945–)

Tall American actor whose ability to combine macho action with a one-of-the-lads type of humour made him one of TV's hottest names in the 1980s, thanks largely to an eight-year stint as MAGNUM, PI. Earlier, Selleck had made occasional visits to THE ROCKFORD FILES to play the annoyingly perfect detective Lance White, although his TV career dates back to the early 1970s and he gained his first small-screen experiences in soap opera (*The Young and the Restless*), TV movies and series like CHARLIE'S ANGELS. His movie career began at about the same time. In 1989 Selleck was executive producer on the Burt Reynolds detective series *B. L. Stryker*. More recently, he has starred in an American sitcom called *The Closer* and made guest appearances in FRIENDS as Dr Richard Burke.

Sellers, Peter

CBE (1925–80)

Although he became a major movie celebrity in the 1960s and 1970s, Peter Sellers sadly left little in the TV archives. After graduating from radio work with his fellow Goons, he was seen in the 1950s comedies *And So to Bentley*, *Idiot Weekly, Price 2d*, A SHOW CALLED FRED, *Son of Fred* and *Yes, It's the Cathode-Ray Tube Show*; but, after that, sightings were restricted to occasional variety and chat shows, plus guest spots in series like NOT ONLY ... BUT ALSO ... and THE MUPPET SHOW. He was also seen in Jonathan Miller's version of ALICE IN WONDERLAND and heard on commercials for Kennomeat and PG Tips. Sellers was married to actresses Britt Ekland and Lynne Frederick.

Selling Hitler ★★★

UK (Thames) Drama. ITV 1991

Gerd Heidemann	**Jonathan Pryce**
Conny Fischer	**Alexei Sayle**
Gina Heidemann	**Alison Doody**
Edda Goering	**Alison Steadman**
Edith Lieblang	**Julie T. Wallace**
Thomas Walde	**Peter Capaldi**
Wilfried Sorge	**Philip Bowen**
Jan Hensmann	**Thomas Wheatley**
Peter Koch	**Olivier Pierre**
Henri Nannen	**Richard Wilson**
Manfred Fischer	**Tom Baker**
Maria Modritsch	**Elaine Collins**
Gerd Schulte-Hillen	**John Shrapnel**
Hugh Trevor-Roper	**Alan Bennett**
Rupert Murdoch	**Barry Humphries**
David Irving	**Roger Lloyd Pack**

Writer **Howard Schuman**
Producer **Andrew Brown**

● ***Blackly comic dramatization of the Hitler diaries hoax.***

Offering a wry look at the 1983 controversy when *The Sunday Times* bought and published what were purported to be Hitler's diaries, *Selling Hitler* is based on a book covering the affair by Robert Harris. German investigative journalist Gerd Heidemann works for *Stern* magazine and is tempted by the, apparently genuine, 60 volumes of diaries that have been forged by memorabilia merchant Conny Fischer. Heidemann's own publication, headed by MD Manfred Fischer, is keen to print them, but there is also interest in the UK, especially after the handwritten diaries are declared authentic by prominent historian Hugh Trevor-Roper (who later changes his mind). Rupert Murdoch wins the auction for serialization rights and the fake diaries are sensationally published, in part, in his Sunday flagship newspaper. Also involved in the tale is Edda, the daughter of the notorious Hermann Goering. She and Heidemann have an affair that stimulates his obsession with Nazi matters. Gina, meanwhile, is Heidemann's girlfriend/wife. Alastair Reid directs the five parts.

Selwyn

See *Oh No! It's Selwyn Froggitt.*

Sense of Guilt, A ★★★

UK (BBC) Drama. BBC 1 1990

Felix Cramer	**Trevor Eve**
Sally Hinde	**Rudi Davies**
Helen Irving	**Lisa Harrow**
Richard Murray	**Jim Carter**
Inge Murray	**Malgoscha Gebel**
Elizabeth Cramer	**Morag Hood**
Carey Hinde	**Philip McGough**
Marsha Hinde	**Kate Duchene**
Karl Murray	**David Chittenden**
Peter Murray	**Charlie Condou**
Jamal Khan	**Kulvinder Ghir**

Writer **Andrea Newman**
Producer **Simon Passmore**

● ***Steamy saga of passion and betrayal.***

A Sense of Guilt was a drama which set the TV review columns buzzing. 'With more pairing than Noah's Ark', as *Radio Times* put it, this seven-part serial by Andrea (BOUQUET OF BARBED WIRE) Newman focuses primarily on selfish, philandering writer Felix Cramer. Returning to London after years overseas, Felix seduces the stepdaughter of his best friend, making her pregnant and destroying the lives of those around him. However, there are many other covert and illicit goings-on, too, enough to attract audiences of around nine million viewers.

Sentimental Agent, The ★

UK (ATV) Adventure. ITV 1963

Carlos Varela	**Carlos Thompson**
Suzy Carter	**Clemence Bettany**
Chin	**Burt Kwouk**
Bill Randall	**John Turner**

Producer **Harry Fine**

● ***The adventures of an import-export agent.***

Smartly dressed and always charming, Carlos Varela runs an international trading company in London, but is usually seen jetting around the globe on the trail of some criminal. His outward appearance is tough but it conceals a generous heart which often leads him into trouble (hence the title). His two main accomplices are secretary Suzy Carter and valet Chin. The character originally appeared in an episode of MAN OF THE WORLD.

September Song ★★

UK (Granada) Drama. ITV 1993–5

Ted Fenwick	**Russ Abbot**
Billy Balsam	**Michael Williams**
Cilla	**Susan Brown**
Arnie	**Michael Angelis**
Roxy/Jenny	**Julie Peasgood**
Sarah Fenwick	**Barbara Ewing**
Katherine Hillyard	**Diana Quick**
Connie French	**Diane Keen**
Yannis Alexiou	**George Savides**
Philip Hathaway	**Pip Miller**
Vicky	**Rebecca Callard**
Cyril Wendage	**Frank Windsor**

Mrs Trigger .... **Jan Waters**
Tom Walker .... **Matt Patresi**

Writer **Ken Blakeson**
Producers **Gareth Morgan, Brian Park**

● ***Two unlikely friends seek adventure in Blackpool, with mixed results.***

Ted Fenwick and Billy Balsam have known each other for years. Ted, a gentle, sensitive schoolteacher, eases the strains of caring for his sick wife with a nightly drink at the pub where Billy works as barman. Billy, a chain-smoking, former stand-up comic, then decides to go back on the stage, finding himself a compere's job at a Blackpool strip club, The Magic Cat. When his wife dies, Ted agrees to spend the summer sharing Billy's camper van at the seaside. Their fortunes are mixed: Billy meets exotic dancer Cilla, is spotted by a talent scout and offered the job he's always dreamed of, as a TV audience warm-up man. Ted falls in love with a stripper named Roxy, but the feelings are not reciprocated and Billy's indiscretions about Ted's previous love life lead to a bitter argument. But when Billy suffers a life-threatening heart attack, it is Ted who returns to keep him out of trouble and ensure his recovery.

In a second series, screened in 1994, Ted takes Billy on a Greek island cruise for recuperation. Ted bumps into an old flame, Katherine Hillyard, while Billy once again turns to the bottle. For the third series, in 1995, the action switches to Cromer, where Billy finds work as a pier comic and Ted tries to come to terms with his uneasy relationship with Katherine.

The series was originally written for Radio 4 in 1991 and some material for the script was provided by the late Tom Mennard, formerly Sam Tindall in CORONATION STREET (the original story was based on Mennard's experiences as a stand-up comic). When it transferred to television, it provided Russ Abbot with his first serious acting role.

Sequel

A programme following on from another, taking members of the established cast into new situations.

Sergeant, John

(1944–)

Oxford-born John Sergeant graduated from Oxford University and first appeared on television as a comedian, supporting Alan Bennett in his 1966 sketch series *On the Margin*. Turning to journalism, however, he worked in newspapers until joining the BBC in 1970 as a radio reporter. Initially covering wars overseas, he later switched to politics, rising to become the BBC's Chief Political Correspondent in 1992. While at the BBC he also wrote and presented a documentary series about the EU called *The Europe We Joined*. In 2000 he moved to ITN to replace Michael Brunson as political editor, retiring himself in 2002. Sergeant has also been seen in numerous quizzes and game shows, from HAVE I GOT NEWS FOR YOU to *Test the Nation*.

Sgt Bilko

See *Phil Silvers Show, The.*

Sergeant Cork **

UK (ATV) Police Drama. ITV 1963–4; 1966–8

Sgt Cork .... **John Barrie**
Bob Marriott .... **William Gaunt**
Supt. Billy Nelson .... **John Richmond**
Det. Joseph Bird .... **Arnold Diamond**
Supt. Rodway .... **Charles Morgan**

Creator **Ted Willis**
Producer **Jack Williams**

● ***The cases of a detective years ahead of his time in Victorian London.***

Fortysomething bachelor policeman Sgt Cork lives in Bayswater and works for the fledgling CID at Scotland Yard. He is a man of vision who deplores bureaucracy and believes in the value of scientific evidence in tracking down criminals. His ideas are pooh-poohed by many of his contemporaries, including his obstructive superior, Detective Joseph Bird. However, he does have Supt. Nelson on his side, as well as his supportive, bright young colleague, Bob Marriott, and, when Bird is removed, another ally is found in Supt. Rodway. The series, characterized by its dark, cobbled streets, swirling cloaks, top hats, and horse-drawn cabs, found an echo in CRIBB in the early 1980s.

Sergeant Preston of the Yukon **

US (Wrather) Police Drama. ITV 1959–61 (US: CBS 1955–8; Syndicated 1958)

Sgt Preston .... **Richard Simmons**

Creators **George W. Trendle, Fran Striker**

● ***Adventures on the Alaskan border with a Mountie superhero.***

A former American radio favourite, Sgt Preston (first name never used) transferred to the small screen with Richard Simmons in the lead role. Preston works for the Royal Northwest Mounted Police in the late 1890s, dashing through the snow atop his trusty steed Rex with loyal mutt Yukon King at his side. No criminal lurking in the frozen wastes of Canada's Northwest Territory stands a chance against this one-man police force. Any thoughts they might have had of ripping off the local gold prospectors are quashed by his very presence. Emil Von Reznicek's 'Donna Diana Overture' was used as the theme tune. The series came from the creators of THE LONE RANGER and *The Green Hornet*.

Serial

Drama broken into a number of episodes with a continuous storyline.

Series

A collection of programmes featuring the same cast and situation but with storylines generally confined to one episode, rather than continuing from episode to episode.

Serle, Chris

(1943–)

British actor turned presenter, thanks to a spell as one of Esther Rantzen's assistants in THAT'S LIFE. With Paul Heiney, Serle later shared the limelight in the spin-off series, IN AT THE DEEP END, and has also been seen in *Sixty Minutes*, *People*, *Medical Express*, educational programmes like *Shoot the Video*, the quiz *Runway*, and the TV archive series *Windmill*.

Serling, Rod

(1924–75)

Anyone who has seen the cult series THE TWILIGHT ZONE will soon have realized that it was Rod Serling's series. The American writer not only scripted most of the episodes but created it, produced it and top-and-tailed each episode with explanatory dialogue. He began writing in the late 1940s and, in 1956, he joined the staff of CBS's anthology series *Playhouse 90*. His second script for the series, *Requiem for a Heavyweight*, remains one of the most acclaimed in TV history and won Serling an Emmy. *The Twilight Zone*, his own idea, ran for six years from 1959, and when it ended Serling went on to write for numerous other series. He also contributed some notable film screenplays, including *Planet of the Apes*. One of his last TV projects was another suspense anthology, *Night Gallery*, in the early 1970s.

Serpico ✳

US (Emmet G. Lavery/Paramount) Police Drama. BBC 1 1977 (US: NBC 1976–7)

Frank Serpico .... **David Birney**
Lt. Tom Sullivan .... **Tom Atkins**

Executive Producer **Emmet G. Lavery**
Producers **Don Ingalls, Barry Oringer**

● ***An undercover cop combats subversion inside and outside the force.***

This short-lived series was based on the 1973 film of the same name starring Al Pacino, which, in turn, was derived from the true-life story of a New York cop, as written up by Peter Maas. Frank Serpico works in New York's 22nd Precinct, where his target is corruption. Ethically unassailable himself, his job is to root out officers on the take and lift the lid on bent officials. Not surprisingly, he makes himself many enemies along the way. His investigations take him into the world of organized crime, sniffing around drug-dealers, smugglers and racketeers. When he heads undercover, fellow cop Tom Sullivan is his police liaison. The real Frank Serpico was forced to retire from duty after being shot in the face.

Sesame Street ✳✳✳✳

US (Children's Television Workshop) Children's Education. ITV 1971–86/Channel 4 1987–99 (US: NET 1969–70; PBS 1970–)

Bob .... **Bob McGrath**
Gordon .... **Matt Robinson**
Roscoe Orman
Mr Hooper .... **Will Lee**
Susan .... **Loretta Long**
David .... **Northern J. Galloway**
Luis .... **Emilio Delgado**
Maria .... **Sonia Manzano**
Linda .... **Linda Bove**
Gina .... **Alison Bartlett**
Lillian .... **Lillias White**
Uncle Wally .... **Bill McCutcheon**
Mr Handford .... **David Langston Smyrl**
Gabriela .... **Gabriela Rose Reagan**
Miles .... **Miles Orman**
Kermit .... **Jim Henson** *(voice only)*
Big Bird .... **Frank Oz** *(voice only)*
Carroll Spinney *(voice only)*
Cookie Monster .... **Frank Oz** *(voice only)*
Oscar the Grouch .... **Frank Oz** *(voice only)*
Carroll Spinney *(voice only)*
The Count von Count .... **Jerry Nelson** *(voice only)*
Miss Piggy .... **Frank Oz** *(voice only)*
Bert .... **Jim Henson** *(voice only)*
Ernie .... **Frank Oz** *(voice only)*
Tarah .... **Tarah Lynne Schaeffer**

Creator **Joan Ganz Cooney**
Executive Producers **David D. Connell, Jon Stone, Al Hyslop**

● ***Innovative educational programme for pre-school children.***

Acclaimed by some and slated by others, *Sesame Street* was created to address the dearth of pre-school education in the USA. Funded by the non-profit-making Children's Television Workshop, it introduced kids to numbers, letters and social skills, using a fast-paced, all-action approach to cater for short attention-spans. Heavy repetition of the main points (which were packaged up like TV commercials) was another key feature.

The setting was a fake Brooklyn brownstone street (Sesame Street – the name chosen to convey a hint of magic, as in 'Open, Sesame'), where the residents provided a degree of continuity. These included Bob, and Gordon and Susan, a young couple. The sweet shop was run by Mr Hooper in the early days, and Luis and Maria were among later additions to the crew. A row of rubbish bins lined one side of the road and in one of these lived a creature called Oscar the Grouch. Oscar was just one of Jim Henson's many Muppet characters which gained important early exposure in the series. Another was Big Bird, a dim, giant canary. Each programme contained animated inserts, filmed items, sketches, songs and games, and was 'sponsored' by a number and a letter of the alphabet: 'Today's programme is brought to you by the letter "T" and the number "6".'

Over the years, the scope of *Sesame Street* was broadened to include other aims, such as teaching cultural diversity, women's roles, health and ecology, and the pace slowed slightly, to take account of criticism for being overstimulating. The programme was originally aimed at the deprived kids of the inner cities but found favour with most of America and then earned enormous sales all round the world. Among the many guest stars were Tony Bennett, Little Richard, Ray Charles and Robin Williams.

Sessions, John

(John Marshall; 1953–)

Scottish-born actor/comedian, a specialist in improvisation and mimicry, as evidenced by his many appearances on WHOSE LINE IS IT ANYWAY? Sessions has also fronted his own series, *John Sessions on the Spot*, *John Sessions' Tall Tales* and *John Sessions' Likely Stories* and has been seen in programmes as varied as *A History of Psychiatry*, TENDER IS THE NIGHT, EDUCATING MARMALADE, THE NEW STATESMAN, PORTERHOUSE BLUE (Lionel Zipser), GIRLS ON TOP, *Life with Eliza*, HAPPY FAMILIES, BOON, LAUGH??? I NEARLY PAID MY LICENCE FEE, *In the Red* (Hercules Fortescue) and GORMENGHAST (Dr Prunesquallor), and provided some of the voices for SPITTING IMAGE. He appeared as Mr Redman in *The Treasure Seekers* and Tippit in NICE DAY AT THE OFFICE, played Boswell in *Boswell and Johnson's Tour of the Western Isles* and Mr Hansell in THE LOST PRINCE, and was George Henry Lewis in *George Eliot: a Scandalous Life* and author Henry Fielding in TOM JONES. More credits have come in THE KEY (Spencer), THE LEGEND OF THE TAMWORTH TWO, HAWKING (Dennis Sciama) and *The English Harem* (Ridley). With Phil Cornwell, he starred in the celebrity spoof STELLA STREET. Sessions has featured in countless panel games and also made guest appearances in RANDALL AND HOPKIRK (DECEASED), THE INSPECTOR LYNLEY MYSTERIES, DALZIEL AND PASCOE, MURDER ROOMS: THE DARK BEGINNINGS OF SHERLOCK HOLMES, JUDGE JOHN DEED, MIDSOMER MURDERS, *Absolute Power* and AGATHA CHRISTIE'S MARPLE.

Set

The scenic construction on which a programme is presented or a drama performed.

Seven Deadly Sins/Seven Deadly Virtues ✶✶

UK (Rediffusion) Drama Anthology. ITV 1966/1967

Executive Producer **Peter Willes**

● ***Individual dramas based on sins and virtues.***
Seven Deadly Sins, a septet of plays covering a septet of sins (one per episode), encouraged viewers to guess which vice was under the microscope, and only revealed the truth at the very end. Two plays were scripted by Anthony Skene, with others by Paul Jones, Leo Lehman, Frank Markus, Alun Falconer and Joe Orton (whose contribution was *The Erpingham Camp*). Guest stars included Patrick Allen, Nigel Stock, Vivienne Merchant, Barry Foster, Anna Massey, Robin Bailey, Julia Foster, Richard O'Sullivan, Joan Sanderson, Adam Faith and Reginald Marsh. A year later, Rediffusion returned to the theme, offering *Seven Deadly Virtues* that, it seems, can often backfire. Writers this time were Bill Naughton, Leo Lehman (two), David Hopkins, John Bowen, Bill Mcllwraith and Joe Orton (*The Good and Faithful Servant*). Colin Blakely, Donald Pleasence, Patricia Routledge, George Baker, George Cole, Terence Alexander and Liz Fraser were among the featured actors this time around.

Seven Faces of Jim, The ✶✶

UK (BBC) Situation Comedy. BBC 1961

Jimmy Edwards

Writers **Frank Muir, Denis Norden**
Producers **James Gilbert, Douglas Moodie**

● ***Anthology comedy series: a Jimmy Edwards showcase.***
With the title of each episode beginning *The Face of . . .*, this series covered the subjects of Devotion, Genius, Power, Dedication, Duty, Guilt and Enthusiasm, all in sitcom fashion, allowing the series' star, Jimmy Edwards, to show off a range of new comic creations. A second series, entitled *Six More Faces of Jim*, ran in 1962. This time the topics were Fatherhood, Renunciation, Wisdom, Perseverance, Loyalty and Tradition. This latter series saw the television première of radio's comic family THE GLUMS (of *Take It from Here* fame), with Edwards as Mr Glum, Ronnie Barker playing Ron and June Whitfield as Eth. A third and final outing was conceived under the title of *More Faces of Jim*. Airing in 1963, its episodes began 'A Matter of . . .' and featured the topics of Amnesia, Growing Up, Spreadeagling, Upbringing, Espionage and Empire.

Seven of One

See *Barker, Ronnie*.

Seven Up ✶✶✶

UK (Granada) Documentary. ITV 1964; 1970; 1977; 1984; 1991; BBC 2 1998; ITV 1 2005

Creator **Tim Hewat**
Producers **Michael Apted, Claire Lewis**

● ***Real lives monitored at seven-year intervals.***
'Give me a child until he is seven, and I will show you the man': so says the Jesuit maxim. Granada Television decided to put it to the test in this pioneering series spun off from WORLD IN ACTION. The premiss is simple: to chronicle the lives of a group of children of various classes from their seventh birthday, taking a snapshot every seven years. Not all participants, however, have been keen to reappear, and some have disappeared without trace. But, by talking once again to those who do resurface, covering major personal issues (particularly relationships and career ambitions) as they mature, and contrasting these with earlier interviews, a unique picture of how people develop has been collated. Researcher on the original series was future film director Michael Apted (*Stardust, Gorky Park, Gorillas in the Mist*, etc.) who has stuck with the programme ever since as producer and director, spending five months every seven years tracking down and interviewing the original children.

Best-remembered of the group are Tony, a wannabe jockey who turned taxi driver and part-time actor (seen in bit parts in BERGERAC, EASTENDERS and THE BILL); Nick, a Yorkshire Dales lad who became a professor at the University of Wisconsin; Paul, who emigrated to Australia; public schoolboy Bruce, who wanted to be a missionary and then worked as a teacher in Bangladesh and later the East End; and Neil, who wandered, unemployed, across the Scottish Highlands before becoming a Liberal Democrat councillor in London. Others included Charles, Sue, Symon, John, Lynn, Andrew, Peter, Michelle and Jackie. Programme titles have been *Seven Plus Seven* (1970), *21 Up* (1977), *28 Up* (1984), *35 Up* (1991), *42 Up* (1998) and *49 Up* (2005).

Copycat versions have followed in other countries, including the USA, South Africa and Russia, and in 2000 a new crop of 19 seven-year-olds were selected for a fresh version, entitled *7 Up 2000* (BBC 1).

77 Sunset Strip ✶✶

US (Warner Brothers) Detective Drama. ITV 1959–64 (US: ABC 1958–64)

Stuart Bailey .... **Efrem Zimbalist Jr**
Jeff Spencer .... **Roger Smith**

Gerald Lloyd ('Kookie') Kookson III .... **Edd Byrnes**
Roscoe .... **Louis Quinn**
Suzanne Fabray .... **Jacqueline Beer**
Lt. Gilmore .... **Byron Keith**
Rex Randolph .... **Richard Long**
J. R. Hale .... **Robert Logan**
Hannah .... **Joan Staley**

Creator **Roy Huggins**
Executive Producers **Bill Orr, Jack Webb**
Producers **Roy Huggins, Howie Horowitz, William Conrad**

A private detective partnership takes on challenges around the world from its Hollywood offices.

77 Sunset Strip, in the nightclub area of Hollywood, is the base for Stu Bailey and Jeff Spencer, college graduates who have turned to private-eye work after experience in undercover government agencies. Bailey is a language expert, Spencer has a law degree, and both are skilled in judo. However, from the outset, their exploits are overshadowed by their association with Kookie, a cool, ambitious youth who runs the car park at the neighbouring Dino's (Dean Martin's) restaurant. Obsessive hair-combing and novel turns of phrase are his trademarks, although British audiences may be bemused by such jive talk as 'making the long green' (earning money), 'piling up the Zs' (sleeping) and 'a dark seven' (a bad week). (Kookie soon became the star of the show, upstaging the two leads, and actor Edd Byrnes sought better terms. When he walked out after failing to agree a contract, he was temporarily replaced as parking-lot attendant by Troy Donohue. Byrnes soon settled his differences, however, and Kookie returned as a full member of the detective team, which had briefly taken on another partner, Rex Randolph.) Suzanne Fabray is the crew's French receptionist and Roscoe, a racetrack tout from New York, is their informant. J. R. Hale is added as Kookie's parking-lot replacement and he, like Kookie, has his quirks, one of which is talking in abbreviations.

The final series of the programme features only Stu Bailey, as a globetrotting private eye. His offices are no longer on Sunset Strip and he has a new secretary, Hannah. This restructuring was the idea of new executive producer Jack Webb, of DRAGNET fame. William Conrad, the future Frank CANNON, was also one of the show's producers.

Edd Byrnes confirmed his teen idol status by making the charts on both sides of the Atlantic in 1960 with a song called 'Kookie Kookie (Lend Me Your Comb)', which he recorded for the series with Connie Stevens. Better remembered is the programme's finger-snapping theme tune.

7T3

See *No. 73*.

Sex and the City ★★★

US (HBO/Darren Star) Situation Comedy. Channel 4 1999–2004 (US: HBO 1998–2004)

Carrie Bradshaw .... **Sarah Jessica Parker**
Samantha Jones .... **Kim Cattrall**
Miranda Hobbes .... **Cynthia Nixon**
Charlotte York/MacDougal .... **Kristin Davis**
Mr Big .... **Chris Noth**
Stanford Blatch .... **Willie Garson**
Aidan Shaw .... **John Corbett**
Steve Brady .... **David Eigenberg**
Trey MacDougal .... **Kyle Maclachlan**
Jack Berger .... **Ron Livingston**
Richard Wright .... **James Remar**
Harry Goldenblatt .... **Evan Handler**
Alexandr Petrovsky .... **Mikhail Baryshnikov**
Smith Jerrod .... **Jason Lewis**
Antonio Marentino .... **Mario Cantone**

Creator **Darren Star**
Executive Producers **Darren Star, Michael Patrick King, Sarah Jessica Parker, John Melfi, Jenny Bicks, Cindy Chupack**

A New York gossip journalist and her friends lead frank and open sex lives.

Blonde, frizzy-haired Carrie Bradshaw is a writer for the *New York Star*. Her 'Sex and the City' column is published every Wednesday and contains snippets from the sex lives of her thirtysomething friends and acquaintances, particularly her three best girlfriends, with whom she lunches regularly. Miranda is the feisty redhead lawyer, Charlotte a rather reserved brunette art dealer and Samantha, another blonde, is a promiscuous PR officer; all are initially single and sexually active. Whenever they meet, Carrie picks up the latest gossip about each of their sex lives and a liberal discussion of sexual mores takes place. The language is strong and often breathtakingly graphic. Mr Big is the main man in Carrie's own life, furniture designer Aidan Shaw is another of her romantic interests, while Stanford Blatch is her gay confidant. Trey MacDougal is the cardiologist that Charlotte eventually marries. Other male input for the girls is provided by bartender Steve Brady, writer Jack Berger, hotel magnate Richard Wright, lawyer Harry Goldenblatt, artist Alexandr Petrovsky and waiter Smith Jerrod. Throughout, the emphasis is on a woman's-eye view of sex and how women can get more out of their relationships, with these three materialistic women becoming lifestyle models for many viewing contemporaries.

The series was based on Candace Bushnell's fictitious column in the same vein for the *New York Observer*, which was eventually published as a book. Being screened on the pay-per-view HBO channel in the US allowed the series to be far more explicit than would have been possible if it had aired on one of the main networks.

Sex, Chips and Rock 'n' Roll ★★★

UK (Wall to Wall/BBC) Drama. BBC 1 1999

Eloise 'Ellie' Brookes .... **Gillian Kearney**
Arden Brookes .... **Emma Cooke**
Irma Brookes .... **Sue Johnstone**
Norman Kershawe .... **David Threlfall**
Darragh 'Dallas' McCabe .... **Joseph McFadden**
Justin Devere Montague ('The Wolf') .... **James Callis**
Larry Valentine .... **Phil Daniels**
Howard Brookes .... **Nicholas Farrell**
Tex Tunicliffe .... **Julian Kerridge**
Hayley .... **Michelle Abrahams**
Shane Riordan .... **Dermot Kerrigan**

Creator/Writer **Debbie Horsfield**
Producer **Liz Trubridge**
Executive Producers **Tessa Ross, Alex Graham, Gina Cronk**

The lives of two sisters are thrown into confusion when they meet a struggling pop group.

Beginning in summer 1965, in Eccles, Manchester, this six-part nostalgic drama is based around twin sisters Ellie and Arden

Brookes. Poetry-loving Ellie is dark-haired, studious and generous of spirit; flighty Arden is blonde, self-centred and fond of a good time, whatever the cost. They live with Irma, their frosty harridan of a grandmother. A bitter dragon with a mysterious past, she has raised the girls in lieu of Howard, their sympathetic but totally ineffectual widower father, who works as a waiter at the local posh hotel. In their dreary, joyless middle-class household, Ellie and Arden are encouraged to have few ambitions: 'I want doesn't get' is the forbidding mantra. As the girls approach the end of school life, they work evenings in one of a chain of chip shops owned by their slimy 39-year-old cousin, Norman, who pressurizes Ellie into becoming his fiancée on her 18th birthday. Then, one night, into the shop stroll a bunch of musical hopefuls called The Ice Cubes: Scottish guitarist/singer Dallas; bass player Tex; and aristocratic, Lawrence Llewellyn-Bowen-lookalike drummer Justin, better known as 'The Wolf'. These former art college students are supporting has-been balladeer Larry B. Cool (Larry Valentine), who also acts as their unscrupulous manager. While the band fights to secure a recording deal, with the help of producer Shane Riordan, both girls have flings with Dallas, with somewhat predictable, if unwanted, consequences. Action later moves to London as the band makes it big. Although pedantically criticized in some quarters for the odd anachronism, *Sex, Chips and Rock 'n' Roll* provides a useful reminder that not all Britain managed to embrace the permissive Sixties. Out in the provinces, away from Swinging London, a much more archaic concept of a woman's place in the world was still rigidly in place. Creator Debbie Horsfield also wrote the lyrics of some new 'Sixties' songs for the series, which were set to music by Mike Moran. These also featured on a soundtrack album.

Sex Traffic ★★★

UK (Granada/Channel 4/Big Motion Pictures/CBC) Drama. Channel 4 2004

Daniel Appleton	**John Simm**
Madeleine Harlsburgh	**Wendy Crewson**
Elena Visinescu	**Anamaria Marinca**
Vara Visinescu	**Maria Popistasu**
Tom Harlsburgh	**Chris Potter**
Julia	**Ana Hegyi**
Rick	**Peter Sullivan**
Lou	**Matilda Ziegler**
Sarah	**Dolly Wells**
Billy Harlsburgh	**Ephraim Ellis**
Leah Harlsburgh	**Nikki Barnett**
Araz Hinzir	**Nawzad Shuani**
Magnus Herzoff	**Len Cariou**
Ernie Dwight	**Maury Chaykin**
Callum Tate	**Luke Kirby**
Insp. Lucas Reese	**Jason Watkins**
Monica	**Irina Bucescu**

Writer **Abi Morgan**
Producer **Derek Wax**

Two Eastern European sisters are lured into a sickening life of sex slavery.

Abi Morgan's closely researched, distressing exposé of the iniquitous trade in sex slavery tells the story of two Moldovan sisters. Elena and Vara think they are heading for a better life in the West, seduced by promises of regular work and the chance to send money back to their impoverished family. The reality turns out to be grimly different, as the girls are sold into prostitution in London, having been trafficked across Europe. The horror of their existence is brought fully home to the viewer – the brutality they encounter on a daily basis, the bleak future they face when their spirit dies and they are no longer of any use to their evil controllers, and the threats and violence that prevent them from being able to break free. Investigating their situation is determined young charity worker Daniel Appleton, whose delving reveals the role corporate corruption plays in the misery inflicted on girls like Elena and Vara. Another key figure, Madeleine Harlsburgh, heads up the charitable wing of a major US company that may be less clean cut than expected.

David Yates directs this harrowing two-parter that passionately delivers a sobering message but is never easy viewing. The drama collected a BAFTA award for Best Drama Serial, with the Best Actress BAFTA going to Anamaria Marinca, who had never appeared on camera before taking the role of Elena.

Sexton Blake ★★

UK (Rediffusion/Thames) Children's Detective Drama. ITV 1967–71

Sexton Blake	**Laurence Payne**
Edward Clark ('Tinker')	**Roger Foss**
Mrs Bardell	**Dorothea Phillips**
Insp. Cutts	**Ernest Clark**
Insp. Van Steen	**Leonard Sachs**
Insp. 'Taff' Evans	**Meredith Edwards**
Insp. Cardish	**Eric Lander**
Insp. Davies	**Charles Morgan**

Producer **Ronald Marriott**

Whodunnits for kids, featuring a 1920s detective.

Sexton Blake is the great detective of the Roaring Twenties. Like his illustrious predecessor, Sherlock Holmes, he lives in London's Baker Street, has a housekeeper (Mrs Bardell) and enjoys the company of an assistant, Tinker. However, for Holmes's pipe, substitute a cigar. Solving crimes off their own bat, or called in by various Scotland Yard inspectors to succeed where they have failed, Blake, Tinker and his bloodhound, Pedro, cruise the streets of the capital in a Rolls-Royce nicknamed 'The Grey Panther'.

The character was created back in the 19th century by Harry Blyth and first appeared in a boys' weekly called *The Halfpenny Marvel*. Blake also featured in several movie versions over the years and resurfaced on TV in 1978 in a BBC serial entitled *Sexton Blake and the Demon God* (with Jeremy Clyde as Blake and Philip Davis as Tinker). This earlier series was initially produced by Rediffusion, but Thames took over production after the 1968 franchise changes.

Seymour, Jane

OBE (Joyce Frankenberg; 1951–)

British actress who has made her name in the cinema but has also been seen in various television offerings, usually glossy TV movies and mini-series. Before moving to Hollywood, Seymour appeared in British series and serials like THE STRAUSS FAMILY, THE ONEDIN LINE (Emma Callon), THE HANGED MAN, *The Pathfinders*, HERE COME THE DOUBLE DECKERS and OUR MUTUAL FRIEND (Bella Wilfer). In the USA, she has starred in *Captains and Kings, East of Eden, Jack the Ripper*, WAR AND REMEMBRANCE and *The Woman He Loved* (Mrs Wallis Simpson), among many dramas, as well as headlining as DR QUINN: MEDICINE WOMAN and making guest appearances in

Smallville. Her fourth husband is director James Keach (brother of Stacy).

Shabby Tiger ★★

UK (Granada) Drama. ITV 1973

Nick Faunt	**John Nolan**
Anna Fitzgerald	**Prunella Gee**
Rachel Rosing	**Sharon Mughan**
Piggy White	**John Sharp**
Jacob 'Mo' Rosing	**Howard Southern**
Anton Brune	**Rowland Davies**
Brian	**Alexander Edgar**
Joe Kepple	**Ray Mort**
Olga Kepple	**Christine Hargreaves**

Writers **Geoffrey Lancashire, Adele Rose, John Stevenson**
Producer **Richard Everitt**

A young artist leaves his wealthy parents and sets up home with a headstrong Irish girl.

Nick comes from a prosperous background. He is the son of a millionaire but decides to bow out from privilege and take up a bohemian lifestyle as an artist: a brave move in the depressed Manchester of the 1930s. On leaving home, he meets Anna, a wild, red-haired Irish girl. She poses for his work and they shack up together. However, Anna has not declared everything about her past, as bookmaker Piggy White can reveal. Meanwhile, another girl muscles in on Nick's life. Rachel is a socially aspirant beauty of Jewish descent. She is also cunning. When she realizes that Nick comes from money, she makes every move to ensure that their relationship moves beyond the purely physical.

This seven-part dramatization of Howard Spring's novel of the same name caused quite a few ripples with its bold nude scenes. To re-create 1930s Manchester, the production team built a city set around the tram museum at Crich, Derbyshire.

Shackleton ★★★

UK (Firstsight Films) Historical Drama. Channel 4 2002
DVD: Cinema Club

Sir Ernest Shackleton	**Kenneth Branagh**
Wild	**Lorcan Cranitch**
Crean	**Mark McGann**
Worsley	**Kevin McNally**
Emily	**Phoebe Nicholls**
Frank Hurley	**Matt Day**
Curzon	**Corin Redgrave**
Janet Stancombe Wills	**Elizabeth Spriggs**
Sir James Caird	**Robert Hardy**
Eleanor	**Eve Best**
Franks	**John Grillo**
Frank	**Mark Tandy**

Writer **Charles Sturridge**
Producer **Selwyn Roberts**

An inspirational explorer saves his crew from certain Antarctic death.

From the team that had scored magnificently with LONGITUDE just a couple of years earlier, this two-part drama captured the agony and the ecstasy of polar exploration, relating the story of Ernest Shackleton, who abandoned his lecturing career to attempt to conquer the South Pole in 1914. The call of adventure is simply too great for a man who had narrowly failed to become the first to reach the Pole several years earlier. Defying the wishes of his wife, and using his charms to the full, Shackleton pulls together the finance needed to make the expedition viable. He purchases a new ship, *Endurance*, and personally selects his crew. After a bright start, tragedy strikes when the ship becomes ice bound and, before it sinks under pressure from the ice, Shackleton has to lead his men away, across the frozen wilderness with only the slightest glimmer of salvation. Teams of dogs haul the ship's lifeboats back to the ocean, allowing the men to take temporary refuge on uninhabited Elephant Island. From there, the determined Shackleton and a handful of colleagues embark on an open-topped journey in a 22-ft boat across a perilous sea to South Georgia, in the hope of bringing help to the rest of his beleaguered crew. Writer Charles Sturridge also directs, with polar scenes filmed in Greenland.

Shadow Squad ★★

UK (Associated-Rediffusion/Granada) Detective Drama. ITV 1957–9

Vic Steele	**Rex Garner**
Ginger Smart	**George Moon**
Mrs Moggs	**Kathleen Boutall**
Don Carter	**Peter Williams**

Producers **Barry Baker, Henry Patrick**

Two private eyes solve cases with a little help from their charlady.

Detective Vic Steele has resigned from the Flying Squad, tired of the rules and regulations that hampered his work. Sprung from the bureaucratic straitjacket, he sets up his own agency, assisted by Londoner Ginger Smart, and names it Shadow Squad. Often calling on the help of their cleaner, Mrs Moggs, the pair investigate all manner of intriguing crimes. After 26 episodes, Steele is mysteriously written out and the agency is handed over to another ex-cop, Don Carter (Steele is sent off on a mission to Australia, never to return; production, at the same time, switched from Associated-Rediffusion to Granada).

It was the Carter/Smart combination that made this twice-weekly show a success, although a spin-off entitled *Skyport* (ITV 1959–60), featuring Ginger as an airport security man, failed to 'take off' and lasted less than a year.

Shadowlands ★★★

UK (BBC) Drama. BBC 1 1985

C. S. Lewis	**Joss Ackland**
Joy Davidman	**Claire Bloom**
Warnie Lewis	**David Waller**
Christopher Riley	**Alan MacNaughtan**
Harry Harrington	**Philip Stone**
Alan Gregg	**Tim Preece**

Writer **William Nicholson**
Producer **David Thompson**

An Oxford don and popular author finds love late in life.

It is January 1950. Fifty-one-year-old confirmed bachelor C. S. Lewis (creator of the magical land of Narnia) receives some fan mail from established American poet and novelist Joy Davidman, a divorcée with two sons. He replies and thus embarks on a romance that utterly changes his life, most notably when Joy is diagnosed as suffering from cancer and Lewis becomes aware that he has fallen in love for the first time. Following this feature-length film (a BBC Wales Everyman presentation, directed by Norman Stone), writer William Nicholson turned the story into a stage play and then a cinema release, director Richard Attenborough casting Anthony Hopkins as Lewis and Debra Winger as Joy (Gresham).

Shaft ★★

US (MGM) Detective Drama. ITV 1974–6 (US: CBS 1973–4)

John Shaft .... **Richard Roundtree**
Lt. Al Rossi .... **Ed Barth**

Executive Producer **Allan Balter**
Producer **William Read Woodfield**

The adventures of a smooth, streetwise private eye.

Sharp-talking, straight-shooting John Shaft is based in New York, although his assignments do not confine him to that city. Calm, efficient and ruthless, this slick, trendy, black detective helps clients in all kinds of difficulty, right across America. Lt. Al Rossi is his tame police contact. The series was inspired by the popular *Shaft* film trilogy, which also starred Richard Roundtree and used the same funky theme music by Isaac Hayes. However, with the sex and violence toned down for TV viewing, this television version lacks the edge of the cinema releases. A new feature film, pitching Samuel L. Jackson into the title role, was released in 2000.

Shameless ★★★

UK (Company Pictures) Comedy Drama. Channel 4 2004–5
DVD: VCI/Channel 4

Frank Gallagher .... **David Threlfall**
Fiona Gallagher .... **Anne-Marie Duff**
Philip 'Lip' Gallagher .... **Jody Latham**
Ian Gallagher .... **Gerard Kearns**
Steve .... **James McAvoy**
Veronica .... **Maxine Peake**
Kev .... **Dean Lennox Kelly**
Sheila Jackson .... **Maggie O'Neill**
Karen Jackson .... **Rebecca Atkinson**
Kash .... **Chris Bisson**
Debbie Gallagher .... **Rebecca Ryan**
Carl Gallagher .... **Luke Tittensor**
Elliot Tittensor
Liam Gallagher .... **Joseph Furnace**
Eddie .... **Steve Pemberton**
Tony .... **Anthony Flanagan**
Yvonne .... **Kelli Hollis**
Monica .... **Annabelle Apsion**
Norma .... **Dystin Johnson**
Carol .... **Marjorie Yates**
Marty .... **Jack Deam**
Sue .... **Gillian Kearney**
Jez .... **Lindsey Dawson**
Mandy Maguire .... **Samantha Siddall**
Stan .... **Warren Donnelly**

Creator **Paul Abbott**
Producers **Emma Burge, Matt Jones, John Griffin**

A shambolic, but close-knit family survives against all odds on a northern housing estate.

One of the drama hits of 2004, *Shameless* is the raucous story of a Manchester family living a hand-to-mouth existence and battling their way through more downs than ups. The Gallaghers live on the Chatsworth council estate. Theirs is an unusual family in that there is no mother (Monica has cleared off with a lesbian lover) nor father (Frank is still, occasionally, around, but is usually too drunk to be of any help). This leaves resourceful teenager Fiona in charge and responsible for bringing up her five younger siblings (Lip, Ian, Debbie, Carl and Liam) – as well as caring for their self-deluding, duplicitous dad whenever he shows his face. They muddle through in their own individual ways, familial love binding them together in the most trying and chaotic of circumstances. For poor Fiona, there is one bright spot in her life in the form of Steve, a sweet-talking wheeler-dealer who, regrettably, turns out to be a car thief. She later leaves care of the household to the even younger Debbie. Frank, meanwhile, lives with the Valium-popping, agoraphobic Sheila and her winsome teenage daughter, Karen. Neighbours on the estate include Kev, a barman at The Jockey, and his loud partner, Veronica; and Yvonne and Kash, a shopkeeper with whom young Ian Gallagher has a gay affair.

After an acclaimed first series of seven episodes, a Christmas special in 2004 told the one-off story of the theft by Kev and Lip (normally the family's bright spark) of contaminated meat that poisons neighbours on the estate. Soon after, a second series (ten episodes) began, introducing Veronica's brother, Marty, a sufferer from Tourette syndrome and an arsonist to boot, and Carol, their interfering mother.

The scenario may be bleak, but *Shameless* is an upbeat, rollicking ride through the undaunted human spirit, filled with larger-than-life characters and bawdy, uncompromising storylines (sex, drugs, passion, crime, fiddles – you name it). While clearly differing in many respects, the series also features strong echoes of creator Paul Abbott's own turbulent upbringing on a Burnley council estate, after first his mother, then his father, left home, leaving ten children to raise themselves. Abbott also penned most episodes. Star David Threlfall was a late addition to the cast, replacing Sean Gallagher, who was the original choice for the role of Frank.

Shane, Paul

(1940–)

Yorkshire-born comedian and actor, a miner and a comic on the northern clubs circuit before turning professional. It was as holiday camp host Ted Bovis in HI-DE-HI! that he became noticed, playing the role for eight years. As shifty butler Alf Stokes in YOU RANG, M'LORD, two years later, he more or less reprised the role but then went on to star as unscrupulous theatrical agent Harry James in VERY BIG VERY SOON, before returning to the David Croft comedy troupe as porter Jack Skinner in OH, DOCTOR BEECHING! Among Shane's early appearances were a spot in CORONATION STREET as postal worker Frank Draper and time as one of THE COMEDIANS. He was also seen in TURTLE'S PROGRESS, MUCK AND BRASS, *Woof!*, KAVANAGH QC, DOCTORS, HOLBY CITY (Stan Ashleigh) and EMMERDALE (Solomon Dingle), among other series.

Sharon and Elsie ★★

UK (BBC) Situation Comedy. BBC 1 1984–5

Elsie Beecroft .... **Brigit Forsyth**
Sharon Wilkes .... **Janette Beverley**
Stanley .... **John Landry**
Roland Beecroft .... **Bruce Montague**
Ivy .... **Maggie Jones**
Elvis Wilkes .... **Lee Daley**

Ike Hepworth	**Gordon Rollings**
Tommy Wallace	**John Junkin**

Writer **Arline Whittaker**
Producers **Roger Race, Mike Stephens**

Two female workmates don't see eye to eye.

In this generation-gap comedy, early-middle-aged Elsie Beecroft works as a supervisor in the greetings cards and calendars printing firm of James Blake and Son, based in Manchester. When Sharon Wilkes, a punk school-leaver, is taken on as secretary to the company boss, Elsie does not approve. With the slightly snooty Elsie always ready to act above her station, the scene is set for some healthy workplace conflict. However, this quickly dissolves into friendship and the two girls join forces in a long-running battle for employee rights. They even socialize outside work hours.

Sharp, Lesley

(1964–)

British actress familiar to viewers as Theresa Mullen in PLAYING THE FIELD, Trudy Graham in CLOCKING OFF and Rose Cooper in BOB AND ROSE, but also starring in many other dramas and comedies. These include FRANK STUBBS PROMOTES (Petra Dillon), *Nights* (Carol), *Dandelion Dead* (Connie Davies), PRIME SUSPECT (Anne Sutherland), *The Moonstone* (Rosanna Spearman), THE PETER PRINCIPLE (Susan Harvey in the pilot episode), COMMON AS MUCK (Christine Stranks), GREAT EXPECTATIONS (Mrs Joe Gargery), *Daylight Robbery* (Carol Murphy), *Nature Boy* (Martha), *The Second Coming* (Judith Roach), *Carla* (Helen North), CARRIE'S WAR (Lou Evans), *Planespotting* (Lesley Coppin), *Born with Two Mothers* (Laura Mayfield), *Afterlife* (Alison Mundy) and *Our Hidden Lives* (Edie Rutherford).

Sharp End, The ★★

UK (BBC) Situation Comedy. BBC 1 1991

Celia Forrest	**Gwen Taylor**
Carmichael	**James Cosmo**
Andy Barras	**Philip Martin Brown**
Mrs Forrest	**Clare Kelly**
Wendy Forrest	**Rachel Egan**
Crystal	**Gaynor Faye**

Writer **Roy Clarke**
Producer **Fiona Finlay**

Debt collection is no job for a woman, as one Yorkshire lass discovers.

When her father dies, Celia Forrest inherits more than she expects. Among the items handed down is a crummy debt collection agency, which is on its last legs. Faced with a choice of letting it close or running it herself, Celia opts for the latter, a woman bravely entering a man's world, as rival tallyman Andy Barras happily informs her. He's not the only one who thinks Celia may be biting off more than she can chew: her teenage daughter, Wendy, and her mum both frown upon the move. Still, Celia has plenty of spirit. With young Crystal as her secretary and a dyslexic former debtor named Carmichael – with whom she fails to see eye to eye – as her leg man, she intends to succeed. The setting for the eight 50-minute episodes is fictional Rawthorne.

Sharp Intake of Breath, A ★★

UK (ATV) Situation Comedy. ITV 1978–81

Peter Barnes	**David Jason**
Sheila Barnes	**Jacqueline Clarke**

Creator **Ronnie Taylor**
Producers **Les Chatfield, Stuart Allen**

A defiant little man tries to defeat the system.

Life doesn't always run smoothly, as we all know, but for some people it's a continually bumpy ride. One such person is Peter Barnes, married for seven years to Sheila, who finds that every day is a challenge. In some respects his cause is much like that which confronts Victor Meldrew of ONE FOOT IN THE GRAVE several years later, in that nothing tends to go right first time. Ironically, actor Richard Wilson (who played Meldrew), along with Alun Armstrong, is regularly seen here as a jobsworth who makes Barnes's life a misery. Nevertheless, Barnes – who narrates events to the audience – is determined to buck the system, defeat red tape and get what he wants. Regrettably, despite much effort, he is seldom better off at the end. The scripts (most by creator Ronnie Taylor) offer plenty of scope for David Jason to indulge himself in the pratfalls and sight gags he has perfected over the years, but they are also quite wordy, bringing in plays on words and plenty of misunderstandings. The cartoons used in the titles sequence were drawn by Mel Calman.

Sharpe ★★★

UK (Central/Picture Palace/Celtic Films/BBC America) Drama. ITV 1993–7; ITV 2006

Lt./Capt./Major/Col. Richard Sharpe	**Sean Bean**
Hogan	**Brian Cox**
Sgt Patrick Harper	**Daragh O'Malley**
Sir Henry Simmerson	**Michael Cochrane**
Wellesley (Wellington)	**David Troughton**
	Hugh Fraser
Lawford	**Martin Jacobs**
Tongue	**Paul Trussell**
Teresa	**Assumpta Serna**
Nairn	**Michael Byrne**
Cooper	**Michael Mears**
Hagman	**John Tams**
Harris	**Jason Salkey**
Perkins	**Lyndon Davies**
Ramona Harper	**Diana Perez**
Ducos	**Feodor Atkine**
Jane Gibbons/Sharpe	**Abigail Cruttenden**
Major Gen. Ross	**James Laurenson**
Mungo Munro	**Hugh Ross**
Lady Anne Camoynes	**Caroline Langrishe**
Lucille	**Cecile Paoli**
Rossendale	**Alexis Denisof**
Obadiah Hakeswill	**Pete Postlethwaite**
Isabella Farthingdale	**Elizabeth Hurley**

Producers **Malcolm Craddock, Simon Lewis, Chris Burt, Muir Sutherland**
Executive Producers **Ted Childs, Muir Sutherland, Stuart Sutherland, Kathryn Mitchell, Steve Wilkinson**

The battlefield and bedroom exploits of an English soldier during the Napoleonic Wars.

Based on the novels by Bernard Cornwell, this sporadic series of feature-length dramas tells the story of one Richard Sharpe, a rough-and-ready Londoner who, in 1809, is instantly promoted from the ranks to officer status after saving the life of the Duke of Wellington. Standing out like the proverbial sore thumb among the snooty other commissioned men, he needs to fight prejudice on his own side as well as his country's mortal enemies. His office requires him to do his duty in various parts of Europe, often heroically stealing behind enemy lines at the bidding of the Duke himself, but seldom does the unorthodox Sharpe fail to meet some beautiful women along the way, including Lady Anne Camoynes and Jane Gibbons, who becomes his wife. The first 14 films take the action right up to the Battle of Waterloo in 1815. The 15th film, screened in two parts nine years after the others, is set in India, a year after Wellington's defeat of Napoleon.

Sean Bean – who did his own stunts, including riding and fencing work – was not the first star selected for the role. The original Sharpe was Paul McGann, but a football match injury meant the part had to be recast and all completed scenes reshot. Some episodes were filmed in places like the Crimea and in Turkey.

Shatner, William

(1931–)

Canadian actor who will always be remembered as Captain James T. Kirk, the he-man skipper of the *USS Enterprise* in STAR TREK. Before *Star Trek* began its voyage on America's screens in 1966, Shatner had been seen in numerous drama anthologies, some Westerns and the odd cop series like NAKED CITY. He starred in the pilot of THE DEFENDERS and episodes of THE TWILIGHT ZONE and THE OUTER LIMITS, and reportedly turned down the role of Dr Kildare. Shatner did, however, take a leading part in a legal drama series, *For the People*, in 1965. Because it was cancelled after only three months, he found himself available to take on *Star Trek* a year later (Jeffrey Hunter, who had appeared in the series' pilot, was not free). In the 1970s Shatner was a familiar guest in series like A MAN CALLED IRONSIDE and HAWAII FIVE-O, and also took a role in another ill-fated programme, this time a Western called *The Barbary Coast*. In 1982 he donned the policeman's uniform of Sgt T. J. HOOKER. The series ran for five years and earned Shatner a new generation of fans. In 1989 he began narrating *Rescue 911*, which reconstructed real-life dramas, and in 1994 appeared in *Tekwar*, a sci-fi series based on his own novels (written with Ron Goulart). More recent credits have been as narrator of *Twist in the Tale* and host of *Full Moon Fright Night* in the USA, plus playing himself in a sci-fi/reality TV spoof called *Invasion Iowa* and taking the star role of lawyer Denny Crane in *Boston Legal*.

Shaughnessy, Alfred

(1916–2005)

British writer, the script editor of UPSTAIRS, DOWNSTAIRS. Shaughnessy's own aristocratic upbringing was given much of the credit for the historical accuracy in this series, for which he also penned episodes. His other major contributions were the similarly genteel afternoon drama *The Cedar Tree*, *The Haunting of Cassie Palmer*, episodes of THE INFORMER, *Sanctuary*, JOURNEY TO THE UNKNOWN, HADLEIGH, MANHUNT, SPYDER'S WEB, THE ADVENTURES OF SHERLOCK HOLMES, THE IRISH RM and the pilot for LADIES IN CHARGE. One of his earliest offerings was a musical biography of music hall star Marie Lloyd, *Our Marie* (written with Christopher Barry), which was broadcast in 1953.

Shaw, Martin

(1945–)

Versatile British actor seen in series like *Sanctuary*, FRAUD SQUAD, STRANGE REPORT, CORONATION STREET (hippie Robert Croft), DOCTOR IN THE HOUSE (Huw Evans) and HELEN – A WOMAN OF TODAY (Helen's husband, Frank Tulley), before achieving lead status in THE PROFESSIONALS in the role of CI5 agent Ray Doyle. He later played Robert Falcon Scott in *The Last Place on Earth*, starred in *The Most Dangerous Man in the World* and *Cream in My Coffee*, and made a guest appearance in ROBIN OF SHERWOOD. Other credits have included parts in *Villains*, SUTHERLAND'S LAW, *Beasts*, Z CARS, THE DUCHESS OF DUKE STREET, THE NEW AVENGERS and Shakespearean plays. More recently, he has been seen as Chief Supt. Mike Barclay in *Screen One's Black and Blue*, Chief Constable Alan Cade in THE CHIEF, Chauvelin in THE SCARLET PIMPERNEL, Robert Kingsford in A&E and Adam Dalgliesh in the revamp of the P. D. JAMES detective stories. He is the father of actor Joe Shaw, with whom he shared the lead role in RHODES, and is married to presenter Vicki Kimm.

Shazzan! ✶

US (Hanna-Barbera) Cartoon. BBC 1 1969 (US: CBS 1967–9)

Voices:

Shazzan	**Barney Phillips**
Nancy	**Janet Waldo**
Chuck	**Jerry Dexter**
Kaboobie	**Don Messick**

Creator **Alex Toth**
Executive Producers **William Hanna, Joseph Barbera**

● ***Two American kids are trapped in the old mystical East.***
Finding two halves of an old ring is just the start of an adventure for a pair of twins from Maine, Nancy and Chuck. Piecing the ring together, they unwittingly send themselves back to the days of the *Arabian Nights* where they luckily have the protection of a 60-foot genie named Shazzan, an early Mr T (THE A-TEAM) figure who is summoned by calling his name aloud. They also have the assistance of a winged camel by the name of Kaboobie but cannot return to their homeland or own time until they deliver the ring to its rightful owner. Thus their quest begins, with danger and excitement at every turn.

Shelley/The Return of Shelley ✶✶

UK (Thames) Situation Comedy. ITV 1979–84; 1988–92

James Shelley	**Hywel Bennett**
Frances Smith/Shelley	**Belinda Sinclair**
Mrs Edna Hawkins	**Josephine Tewson**
Gordon Smith	**Frederick Jaeger**
Forsyth	**Kenneth Cope**
Isobel Shelley	**Sylvia Kay**
Paul	**Warren Clarke**
Alice	**Rowena Cooper**
Desmond	**Garfield Morgan**
Carol	**Caroline Langrishe**
Graham	**Andrew Castell**

Phil	**Stephen Hoye**
Ted Bishop	**David Ryall**

Creator **Peter Tilbury**
Producer **Anthony Parker**

● ***A university graduate shirks work, battles bureaucracy and bemoans the upheavals of life.***

James Shelley, a geography graduate who looks down on those less well educated than himself, wants more from life, but not if he has to work for it. Living on social security, the 28-year-old shares a flat with girlfriend Fran in Pangloss Road, north London, from where he conducts a permanent war with the taxman and other establishment figures, as well as with Fran's dad, Gordon. Mrs Hawkins is his landlady. Over subsequent series, Shelley does find sporadic work, once as a copywriter and on another occasion with the Foreign Office, but his inability and unwillingness to hold down a job leads Fran (now his wife and mother of his daughter, Emma) to kick him out. Shelley moves into his friend Paul's flat and continuously wrangles with Desmond, the building's porter, before deciding to leave for the USA and the Middle East to teach English. Six years later, in 1988, he re-emerges with the same chip on his shoulder and petulant pout on his lips in *The Return of Shelley*. Carol and Graham are his hosts on his comeback, and this time he rails against yuppies and the Americanization of British society. Later episodes revert to the original title and see the Hancockian hero lodging with pensioner Ted Bishop.

Shelley was adapted for Radio 2 in 1997, with Stephen Tompkinson taking over the lead role.

Shepherd, Cybill
(1950–)

American actress/singer, star of MOONLIGHTING (Maddie Hayes) and CYBILL (Cybill Sheridan), as well as a 1980s US soap called *The Yellow Rose* (Colleen Champion) and a few TV movies.

Shepherd, Jack
(1940–)

Dour-looking English actor, best known as detective Charles WYCLIFFE, but also eponymous star of BILL BRAND in the 1970s. Other credits have included the sketch show *World in Ferment*, the play READY WHEN YOU ARE MR MCGILL, BUDGIE, *The Devil's Crown*, COUNT DRACULA (Renfield), *Blind Justice*, *Sons and Lovers* and *Screen One's Ball-Trap on the Côte Sauvage*. Shepherd has also appeared in *Shoot to Kill*, BETWEEN THE LINES, LOVEJOY, *Over Here*, *Lorna Doone*, CITY CENTRAL, SILENT WITNESS, *Cracking Up* (Francisco Goya), *High Stakes* (Nicholas Quinn), *The Jury* (Ron Maher), *Man and Boy* (Paddy Silver), BOUDICA (Claudius), *The Other Boleyn Girl* (Thomas Boleyn), *London* (Thomas de Quincey), P. D. JAMES, *Beethoven* (Joseph Haydn), *The Slavery Business* (Robert Dinwiddie) and *All About George* (Gordon).

Shepherd, Simon
(1956–)

Bristol-born actor, familiar as Piers Garfield-Ward in CHANCER, Duncan McAllister in *Beyond Reason*, Dr Will Preston in PEAK PRACTICE and Dr Sam Bliss in *Bliss*. He has also been seen in JACKANORY *Playhouse*, LILLIE (Lord Alfred Douglas), *My Father's House*, *A Man Called Intrepid* and *Sweet Wine of Youth*, and as Peter Taylor QC in the drama-doc *A Life for a Life*, Mark Sopwith in CATHERINE COOKSON*'s Tilly Trotter* and Major 'Brick' Stone in WARRIORS, with guest appearances in *Sorrell and Son*, CASUALTY, AGATHA CHRISTIE'S POIROT, PIE IN THE SKY, GIMME GIMME GIMME and THE RUTH RENDELL MYSTERIES.

Sherlock Holmes ★★

UK (BBC) Detective Drama. BBC 1 1965; 1968

Sherlock Holmes	**Douglas Wilmer** *(1965)*
	Peter Cushing *(1968)*
Dr Watson	**Nigel Stock**
Insp. Lestrade	**Peter Madden** *(1965)*
	William Lucas *(1968)*
Mrs Hudson	**Mary Holder** *(1965)*
	Grace Arnold *(1968)*
Mycroft Holmes	**Derek Francis** *(1965)*
	Ronald Adam *(1968)*

Producer **David Goddard** *(1965)*, **William Sterling** *(1968)*

● ***The BBC's second attempt at televising The Great Detective.***

Having put together an unlikely team of actors for a 1951 version of six Conan Doyle stories, the BBC tried again 14 years later. In the earlier series, Holmes was played by Alan Wheatley (the future Sheriff of Nottingham in THE ADVENTURES OF ROBIN HOOD), assisted by a pre-NO HIDING PLACE Raymond Francis as Watson and a young Compo, Bill Owen, as Inspector Lestrade. On this occasion, Douglas Wilmer is handed Holmes's pipe and magnifying glass and is aided – or, rather, hindered – over 12 stories by an inept Dr Watson, played by Nigel Stock. The characters and same actors were originally seen in a one-off story, *The Speckled Band*, under the DETECTIVE series banner in 1964.

Stock reprised his role three years later, when Peter Cushing replaced Wilmer. Taking his lead from the rather bastardized perception of the great detective as a thorough do-gooder and an essentially kind man, Peter Cushing dons the deerstalker and picks up the hooked pipe. There are no cocaine, no violent mood-swings and none of the rudeness which Conan Doyle perceived and which Jeremy Brett reintroduced in the 1980s. Fifteen stories comprised this rendition (billed as *Sir Arthur Conan Doyle's Sherlock Holmes*), including all the favourites, from *A Study in Scarlet* to *The Hound of the Baskervilles*. Cushing was already familiar with his character, having portrayed Holmes in the 1959 Hammer version of *The Hound of the Baskervilles*.

Sherrin, Ned
CBE (1931–)

Although associated with the Radio 4 series *Loose Ends* these days, Ned Sherrin was one of the BBC's current affairs team that brought TONIGHT to the screens in the 1950s. He also devised, produced and directed the ground-breaking THAT WAS THE WEEK THAT WAS in 1962, as well as its less successful offsprings, NOT SO MUCH A PROGRAMME, MORE A WAY OF LIFE and BBC-3. He later produced the sketch shows *Where was Spring?* and *World in Ferment*, and in the 1970s, with Caryl Brahms, he adapted French farces for Patrick Cargill's series *Ooh La La!*

She's Out
See *Widows*.

Shillingbury Tales ★★

UK (ATV) Comedy Drama. ITV 1981

Peter Higgins .... **Robin Nedwell**
Sally Higgins .... **Diane Keen**
Major Langton .... **Lionel Jeffries**
Cuffy .... **Bernard Cribbins**
Jake .... **Jack Douglas**
Harvey .... **Joe Black**
Revd Norris .... **Nigel Lambert**
Mrs Simpkins .... **Diana King**
Mandy .... **Linda Hayden**

Creator/Writer **Francis Essex**
Producer **Greg Smith**

● ***Ups and downs in a picturesque English village.***

Shillingbury Tales, set in the fictitious village of Shillingbury, was developed by Francis Essex from his own one-off play *The Shillingbury Blowers*, screened in 1980. In the single drama, the 'Blowers' are members of an inept local brass band which is kicked into life by pop musician Peter Higgins. However, when the series begins, other village events fall under the microscope. Peter has married Sally Langton, daughter of the local aristocrat, Major Langton, and has settled into the village. Also in the action is Cuffy the tinker, a scruffy, mischievous tramp who lives in a run-down caravan. (He was given his own spin-off series, *Cuffy*, in 1983, with many of the Shillingbury villagers making up the supporting cast.)

Shine on Harvey Moon ★★★

UK (Central/Witzend/Meridian) Comedy Drama. ITV 1982; 1984–5; 1995

Harvey Moon .... **Kenneth Cranham**
Nicky Henson
Rita Moon .... **Maggie Steed**
Maggie Moon/Lewis .... **Linda Robson**
Stanley Moon .... **Lee Whitlock**
Lou Lewis .... **Nigel Planer**
Violet Moon ('Nan') .... **Elizabeth Spriggs**
Veronica .... **Pauline Quirke**
Harriet Wright .... **Fiona Victory**
Erich Gottlieb .... **Leonard Fenton**
Frieda Gottlieb .... **Suzanne Bertish**
Noah Hawksley .... **Colin Salmon**
Helen .... **Wendy Morgan**
Azzopardi .... **Vincenzo Nicoli**

Creators/Writers **Laurence Marks, Maurice Gran**
Executive Producer **Allan McKeown**
Producer **Tony Charles**

● ***Post-war trouble and strife for a former serviceman and his family.***

Returning home to Hackney from wartime service in India as a corporal (stores clerk) in the RAF, former professional footballer Harvey Moon discovers his home destroyed and his family life in tatters. His flighty wife, Rita, has run off with other men, his 17-year-old daughter, Maggie, is seeing his old pal, Lou Lewis, and his mother, Nan, remains as redoubtable as ever. Add to this the problems of rationing, post-war shortages and the constraints of living in a prefab (later demolished by an unexploded bomb), and Harvey's lot is not a happy one. However, he sets about making a new life for himself, becoming a Labour councillor, dating Harriet Wright, his worldly son Stanley's headmistress, and taking up residence with Erich Gottlieb and his sister, Frieda. Eventually he and Rita are, somewhat precariously, reunited.

Beginning with six half-hour episodes, *Shine on Harvey Moon*, a nostalgic comedy drama, was later extended into 60-minute instalments and ran for three years, covering the period 1945–8. In 1995 the programme was exhumed, with Nicky Henson replacing Kenneth Cranham in the lead. The story was taken up in 1953, CORONATION year, and ran through the 1950s, with immigrants flooding into Britain looking for work and Maggie set to marry Lou (now 'One Lung Lou', having lost the other). In between, creators Laurence Marks and Maurice Gran had returned to the 1940s with another offering, GOODNIGHT SWEETHEART.

Shivas, Mark

(1938–)

Successful British executive, one-time film critic and host of CINEMA, but far better remembered for his work as producer on dramas like THE SIX WIVES OF HENRY VIII, THE EDWARDIANS, CASANOVA, THE GLITTERING PRIZES, ROGUE MALE, TELFORD'S CHANGE, *The Three Hostages*, *On Giant's Shoulders*, THE BORGIAS, WINSTON CHURCHILL – THE WILDERNESS YEARS, *The Price*, THE STORYTELLER, TALKING HEADS 2 and CAMBRIDGE SPIES (the last coming from his own production company, Perpetual Motion Pictures). He also produced the *Black and Blue* series of comedy plays in 1973. Shivas was Head of Drama at the BBC 1983–93 and Head of Films 1993–7.

Shoestring ★★★

UK (BBC) Detective Drama. BBC 1 1979–80

Eddie Shoestring .... **Trevor Eve**
Erica Bayliss .... **Doran Godwin**
Don Satchley .... **Michael Medwin**
Sonia .... **Liz Crowther**

Creator/Producer **Robert Banks Stewart**

● ***Private detective work with a local radio presenter.***

Eddie Shoestring is a radio presenter – but he is also a detective. Working for West Country-based Radio West, Shoestring uses his airtime as a springboard for detective work, asking listeners to ring in with investigations he can pursue and information he can use. Usually, the cases are run-of-the-mill affairs, all set in the Bristol area, but occasionally something juicier turns up to spur the 'private ear' into action. When the crime is solved, the outcome is related on air, with names changed to protect the innocent.

Shoestring has not always been a broadcaster. He was egged into the job by the station receptionist, Sonia, after helping the station out on an investigation. Before that he was a computer expert but suffered a nervous breakdown and spent some time in a mental institution. He now lodges with barrister Erica Bayliss, an occasional girlfriend who joins in some of the sleuthing. Don Satchley is Eddie's station manager.

Although scruffily dressed and prone to drinking sprees, Shoestring is not to be underestimated. He is multitalented: not only is he a keen sketch artist (sketching is his therapy) and a good mimic, but he enjoys an excellent, sensitive rapport with his listening public. However, when times are bad, he retreats to his run-down houseboat for moments of reflection. The boat is almost as decrepit as his car, a beaten-up red Ford Cortina estate.

After just two highly successful seasons, Trevor Eve decided to move back into the theatre. It left *Shoestring*'s creator, Robert Banks Stewart, with plenty of unused ideas, so he developed a new series about another rehabilitating detective, this time based in Jersey (see BERGERAC). *Shoestring*'s presence was not quite eradicated, however, as the name Radio West was bought up by the real-life independent radio station set up to serve the Bristol area.

Shogun ★★★

US (Paramount) Drama. BBC 1 1982 (US: NBC 1980)

John Blackthorne .... **Richard Chamberlain**
Lord Toranaga .... **Toshiro Mifune**
Lady Toda Buntaro-Mariko ..... **Yoko Shimada**
Lord Ishido .... **Nobuo Kaneko**
Vasco Rodriguez .... **John Rhys-Davies**
Friar Domingo .... **Michael Hordern**
Father Alvito .... **Damien Thomas**
Omi .... **Yuki Meguro**
Yabu .... **Frankie Sabai**
Dell' Aqua .... **Alan Badel**

Writer/Producer **Eric Bercovici**
Executive Producer **James Clavell**

● ***A 17th-century adventurer is captured by the Japanese and adapts to their culture.***

Based on the real-life story of Elizabethan seaman Will Adams, *Shogun* tells of John Blackthorne, the English pilot of a Dutch vessel that is wrecked on the Japanese coast in the early 1600s. Taken under the wing of the powerful Toranaga, one of the feudal state's great warlords, Blackthorne adopts the name of Anjin-san and quickly acclimatizes to the Japanese way of living. The series watches Blackthorne embark on a steamy affair with Lady Mariko (a married noblewoman interpreter), confront Western emissaries (traders and Jesuit preachers) and take part in the many bloody conflicts which characterize Japanese life at the time. His quest: to become the first Western-born Shogun (a supreme Samurai warrior).

This easy-paced, six-part series was adapted from James Clavell's epic novel of the same name, with Clavell working on the project as executive producer. It was filmed on location in Japan, with much of the dialogue in Japanese.

Shooting Script

A version of a programme script which details all the camera shots required.

Shooting Stars ★★★

UK (BBC/Channel X) Comedy. BBC 2 1995–7; 2002

Presenters **Vic Reeves, Bob Mortimer, Matt Lucas**

Producers **Alan Marke, Lisa Clarke**

● ***Spoof celebrity game show.***

Shooting Stars is a riotous comedy quiz show in which celebrities – headed by team captains 'Ulrika-ka-ka-ka' Jonsson and 'fifties throw-back' Mark Lamarr – are subjected to a barrage of good-natured abuse and practical jokery by questionmasters Vic Reeves and Bob Mortimer (who also sing the theme song). As one participant, Danny Baker, shrewdly remarks, the guests are not so much contestants as stooges in a sketch.

Questions are divided up into buzzer rounds ('We really want to see those fingers'), an impressions round, a true-or-false round, and a club singer round, in which Vic performs a mystery hit in the style of a club performer. There is also a category-board (or, rather, category bird, being 'the Dove from Above', which the celebs are encouraged to coax down by cooing; a later manifestation is Donald Cox, the sweaty fox, who is offered gin as an enticement to descent: 'It's the gin that brings him in'). A member of the winning team is called upon to undertake a bizarre challenge in the finale.

Matt Lucas, as drummer George Dawes, usually dressed as a big baby, keeps the scores and Graham Skidmore provides the voice-overs. Johnny Vegas became a regular panellist when the series was revived in 2002 (airing first on BBC Choice), with Will Self taking over as team captain from Mark Lamarr. The 'pilot' for the series was a segment of Reeves and Mortimer's 1993 Christmas extravaganza, *At Home with Vic and Bob*.

Shooting the Past ★★★★

UK (Talkback) Drama. BBC 2 1999

Marilyn Truman .... **Lindsay Duncan**
Oswald Bates .... **Timothy Spall**
Christopher Anderson .... **Liam Cunningham**
Spig .... **Emilia Fox**
Veronica .... **Billie Whitelaw**
Garnett .... **Arj Barker**
Nick .... **Blake Ritson**
Molly .... **Sheila Dunn**

Writer **Stephen Poliakoff**
Executive Producers **Simon Curtis, Peter Fincham**
Producer **John Chapman**

● ***The staff of a photographic archive fight to prevent its closure.***

A large 18th-century house just outside London is home to the Fallon Photo Library and Collection, run by Marilyn Truman and her small, but still grossly overstaffed, team of archivists. However, the house has just been purchased by an American company to be renovated into a business school and they insist that the library must close. Communication problems mean that advance warning has not been received by Truman and she is faced with the prospect of finding a home for the collection inside a week. Leading the fight is Marilyn's number two, the eccentric and defiant Oswald Bates, supported by the quiet Veronica and the punkish Spig. Christopher Anderson is the US executive the staff must win over. The emotional pull of some of the archive's most evocative and rare images is used to the full, but Oswald goes one step further, with dramatic consequences. Stephen Poliakoff directs his own, highly acclaimed three-part drama.

Show Called Fred, A ★★

UK (Associated-Rediffusion) Comedy. ITV 1956

Peter Sellers, Valentine Dyall, Graham Stark, Kenneth Connor, Patti Lewis, Max Geldray

Writer **Spike Milligan**

● ***Off-beat comedy sketch show.***

Written by Spike Milligan and also featuring fellow Goon Peter Sellers, assorted comics and Canadian singer Patti Lewis, *A*

Show Called Fred was one of TV's first surreal comedies. It followed hot on the heels of another Peter Sellers offering, *Idiot Weekly, Price 2d* (also 1956; both series screened only in London), in which he linked sketches as the editor of a Victorian weekly newspaper. A sequel, *Son of Fred*, performed by the same team but with Johnny Vyvyan and Cuthbert Harding added to their number, was screened in the same year (including in other parts of the UK). *The Best of Fred* was a 1963 compilation of both series. Future Beatles film director Dick Lester directed proceedings.

Shubik, Irene

(1935–)

British drama producer. Previously a historian, Shubik's first job in television was as story editor to the influential Sydney Newman on programmes like ARMCHAIR THEATRE and OUT OF THIS WORLD at ABC. Moving into production, she switched with Newman to the BBC in 1963 and worked largely on THE WEDNESDAY PLAY and PLAY FOR TODAY, although she was also responsible for the OUT OF THE UNKNOWN science-fiction anthology and the Georges Simenon collection *Thirteen Against Fate*. She left the BBC in the mid-1970s, when its drama department declined to pursue a series of RUMPOLE OF THE BAILEY, after John Mortimer's one-off play had proved a hit; she took the idea to Thames instead. Later, Shubik was influential in Granada's televising of Paul Scott's *Raj Quartet* as THE JEWEL IN THE CROWN (having produced the single drama *Staying On*, based on Scott's novel), although she was not involved in the production herself. Among her many credits have been plays like *Mrs Lawrence Will Look After It* (1968), *The Last Train through the Harecastle Tunnel* (1969), *Hearts and Flowers* (1970), EDNA, THE INEBRIATE WOMAN (1971) and *The General's Day* (1973), and the *Playhouse* and *Wessex Tales* series.

Sianel Pedwar Cymru

See *S4C*.

Side by Side ✱✱

UK (BBC) Situation Comedy. BBC 1 1992–3

Vince 'Vinnie' Tulley .... **Gareth Hunt**
Gilly Bell .... **Louisa Rix**
Stella Tulley .... **Julia Deakin**
Katie Bell .... **Mia Fothergill**
Terry Shane .... **Alex Walkinshaw**
James Hammond .... **Christopher Scoular**

Writer **Richard Ommanney**
Executive Producer **Martin Fisher**
Producers **Nic Phillips, Sue Bysh**

● ***Gentle sparring with two incompatible next-door neighbours.***

All is not well in Trebor Avenue, Kingston-upon-Thames. Next door to each other live Vinnie Tulley and Gilly Bell, neighbours from different parts of the social spectrum who clearly don't see eye to eye. Vinnie is a successful, salt-of-the-earth plumber happily married to Stella. Although he's a manual worker by trade, he's a disaster zone when it comes to DIY, and his attempts to improve his home and garden only lead to further trouble with Gilly, who thinks he's dragging the area down-market. Gilly is recently widowed, makes jewellery for a living and shares her house with her unruly teenage daughter, Katie, who fancies Terry, Vinnie's lazy nephew and apprentice. Thirteen episodes were made over two series. In the second series, Gilly acquires a new man in her life, James Hammond.

Sierra Nine ✱✱

UK (Associated-Rediffusion) Children's Science Fiction. ITV 1963

Sir Willoughby Dodd .... **Max Kirby**
Dr Peter Chance .... **David Sumner**
Anna Parsons .... **Deborah Stanford**
The Baron .... **Harold Kasket**

Writer **Peter Hayes**

● ***Three scientific troubleshooters preserve peace around the world.***

Sierra Nine is headed by Sir Willoughby Dodd, an eccentric but brilliant old scientist. From a London office he monitors the assignments of his two junior colleagues, Dr Peter Chance and Anna Parsons. Their role is to preserve the balance of scientific knowledge in the world by investigating the theft of sophisticated weaponry or important formulae. Twice they find themselves up against the sinister Baron, a devious scientist bent on wreaking havoc. On the first occasion, he devises the brain machine, a microwave radio that twists the minds of workers all around the world. The next time he surfaces he possesses a terrifying death ray. Peter and Anna also endure two other adventures in this series' relatively short run. In one, a nuclear bomb goes astray and in the other they are called upon to protect an elixir which French monks claim could offer eternal life.

Silas Marner ✱✱✱

UK (BBC) Drama. BBC 1 1985

Silas Marner .... **Ben Kingsley**
Godfrey Cass .... **Patrick Ryecart**
Dunstan Cass .... **Jonathan Coy**
Nancy Lammeter .... **Jenny Agutter**
Eppie Marner .... **Melinda Whiting** *(young)*
Patsy Kensit
Sarah .... **Natalie Ogle**
William Dane .... **Paul Copley**
Bob Dowlas .... **Nick Brimble**
Jem Rodney .... **Jim Broadbent**
Mr Snell .... **Tony Caunter**

Writers **Louis Marks, Giles Foster**
Producer **Louis Marks**

● ***An outcast adopts a young orphan and finds happiness he has long forgotten.***

Subtitled *The Weaver of Raveloe*, George Eliot's classic 1861 tale of a lonely weaver whose life is transformed when a young girl wanders into his cottage on a winter's night was brought to BBC 1 as a single drama, directed by Giles Foster. Filmed in Stanway, Gloucestershire, the story reveals how little Eppie softens the heart of the miserable Marner, bringing him back into the human race. Eppie's mother, it is revealed, was the neglected wife of future squire Godfrey Cass (whose brother, Dunstan, had once stolen all Marner's gold – thus making Marner a bitter man). It was while trying to reach Cass in the winter snow that the woman had died and Eppie had reached Marner's cottage alone. But Marner's refound happiness is jeopardized some years later when Cass, realizing Eppie's parenthood, attempts to claim her. Carl Davis supplied the soundtrack. Constance Cox had previously dramatized the novel in six parts in 1964 (BBC 1: David Markham as Marner, Jonathan Collins and Moray Watson as Godfrey Cass, Natasha Pyne as Eppie).

Silent Witness ★★★

UK (BBC/A&E) Drama. BBC 1 1996–

Dr/Prof. Samantha 'Sam' Ryan	**Amanda Burton**
DI Tom Adams	**John McGlynn**
DS Harriet Farmer	**Clare Higgins**
DC Kerry Cox	**Ruth Gemmell**
Dr Trevor Stewart	**William Armstrong**
Marcia Evans	**Janice Acquah**
Wyn Ryan	**Ruth McCabe**
Beryl Ryan	**Doreen Hepburn**
Ricky Ryan	**Matthew Steer**
PC North	**Milo Twomey**
PC Jarvis	**Ian Keith**
Fred Dale	**Sam Parks**
Det. Supt. Peter Ross	**Mick Ford**
DI Rachel Selway	**Nicola Redmond**
DS Tony Speed	**Richard Huw**
DI Michael Connor	**Nick Reding**
DS Rob Bradley	**Mark Letheren**
Dr James Reynolds	**Michael Siberry**
Dr Leo Dalton	**William Gaminara**
Dr Harry Cunningham	**Tom Ward**
Dr Nikki Alexander	**Emilia Fox**

Creator **Nigel McCrery**
Executive Producer **Caroline Oulton**
Producers **Tony Dennis, Alison Lumb, Anne Pivcevic, Lars Macfarlane, Diana Kyle, Nick Pitt, Tim Bradley**

● ***The gruesome cases of a determined female pathologist.***

Dr Sam Ryan, born in Belfast, aged 37 and now working in Cambridge, is the lead character in this collection of murder investigations. Impassionate, and almost obsessive in her work, she is not the kind of pathologist to jump to conclusions or give up on a case before the truth has been discovered. A sense of justice pervades her psyche (lightened by a little dry wit) and often places her at odds with a detective looking for a quick conviction.

Ryan's cases are not pleasant: child abuse, black magic and industrial negligence feature among the storylines, and the nature of her work calls for some stomach-churning close-ups of decaying, bloated bodies and dissected organs. Relentlessly lurking in the background is Ryan's complicated family-life: an RUC officer father murdered by terrorists, an Alzheimer's victim mother, a resentful sister, a tearaway nephew and, later, a policeman colleague (Peter Ross) who used to be her lover. In subsequent episodes, Ryan moves out of Cambridge and becomes a professor of pathology at the University of London, but she is still called out as a consultant to the scenes of grisly events. Later still, she shares the mortuary limelight with another pathologist, Leo Dalton, and a trainee, Harry Cunningham, who despite having personal problems of their own help Sam in the pursuit of the truth.

In the 2004 series a major cast change takes place. After a harrowing return visit to Northern Ireland, Sam leaves and is replaced at the heart of the stories by Nikki Alexander, an archaeo-pathologist (she likes delving into prehistoric deaths) now learning the ropes in an active mortuary. Nikki has a mind of her own and an air of unpredictability.

The series theme tune is 'Silencium', by John Harle.

Silvera, Carmen

(1922–2002)

Actress born in Canada, primarily recalled as the tuneless Madame Edith in 'ALLO 'ALLO. In the early 1960s, she played Camilla Hope in the magazine soap COMPACT, and was also seen in one episode of DAD'S ARMY, as Captain Mainwaring's fancy woman. Other credits included SERGEANT CORK, Z CARS, BEGGAR MY NEIGHBOUR, NEW SCOTLAND YARD, DOCTOR WHO, WITHIN THESE WALLS, LILLIE, WHOOPS APOCALYPSE, TALES OF THE UNEXPECTED, THE GENTLE TOUCH and the *Revolver* sketch show.

Silvers, Phil

(Philip Silversmith; 1911–85)

New York-born, former burlesque comedian, one of TV's early greats. Despite having an up-and-down stage and movie career, and failing to make the grade as a variety compere on *The Arrow Show* in 1948, his later portrayal of the wonderfully devious Sgt Bilko in *You'll Never Get Rich* was so commanding that the programme's title was changed to THE PHIL SILVERS SHOW. Four years into its run (when it was at its peak in 1959), the show was cancelled so that the studio could cash in on syndicated reruns. An attempt to revive the premiss as *The New Phil Silvers Show* in 1963 (in which he played factory foreman Harry Grafton) flopped, and his TV career never recovered. He was given a semi-regular role (Shifty Shafer) in THE BEVERLY HILLBILLIES in 1969, but otherwise his later appearances were either variety specials or guest spots in series like GILLIGAN'S ISLAND and THE LOVE BOAT. His daughter, Cathy, played flirt Jenny Piccalo in HAPPY DAYS and Silvers once dropped in to the series as her screen dad.

Simm, John

(1970 –)

Born in Leeds, raised in Lancashire, John Simm made his name as tearaway Danny Kavanagh in Jimmy McGovern's drama THE LAKES, having previously played smaller roles in McGovern's CRACKER, RUMPOLE OF THE BAILEY and HEARTBEAT. He was also seen in *Chiller* and as Kendle Baines in MEN OF THE WORLD, Cecil in *Screen One*'s *Meat*, Paul in *The Locksmith*, Theo in *Forgive and Forget* and Stuart Leach in CLOCKING OFF. Simm played John Parlour in *Never, Never*, Raskolnikov in CRIME AND PUNISHMENT, Mr Hero in *White Teeth*, journalist Cal McCaffrey in STATE OF PLAY, Ace in CANTERBURY TALES, Friedrich Engels in *London*, Daniel Appleton in SEX TRAFFIC, Dr Bruce Flaherty in *Blue/Orange* and Sam Tyler, a new millennium policeman trapped in the 1970s, in LIFE ON MARS. He also plays guitar with the band Magic Alex.

Simon & Simon ★★

US (Universal) Detective Drama. ITV 1984–5 (US: CBS 1981–8)

Andrew Jackson ('A. J.') Simon	**Jameson Parker**
Rick Simon	**Gerald McRaney**
Cecilia Simon	**Mary Carver**
Janet Fowler	**Jeannie Wilson**
Myron Fowler	**Eddie Barth**
Det. Marcel 'Downtown' Brown	**Tim Reid**

Creator **Philip DeGuere**

Executive Producers **Richard Chapman, Philip DeGuere, John Stephens**

● ***Incompatible brothers run a hit-and-miss private detective firm.***

Two more unalike brothers you could never expect to meet. A. J. Simon is an ambitious, well-groomed college graduate with a swish apartment; his brother Rick is a scruffy, laid-back Vietnam War veteran who lives on a houseboat. Yet, somehow, the pair are in business together, running the small Simon & Simon Detective Agency in San Diego. Their mother, Cecilia, is at hand to cast scolding glances at the boys' errant behaviour but they somehow manage to scrape a living, despite competition from the Peerless Detective Agency run by miserable neighbour Myron Fowler. Janet is Myron's more amenable daughter, while some mercenary assistance is provided by undercover cop 'Downtown' Brown. The series – which ran for seven years in the USA but only briefly in the UK – followed a pilot film set in Florida. In 1995, the brothers were teamed up again in a new TV movie entitled *Simon & Simon: In Trouble Again*.

Simpson, Alan

OBE (1929–)

See *Galton, Ray*.

Simpson, Bill

(1931–86)

One-time Scottish Television announcer Bill Simpson is clearly imprinted in most viewers' minds as the headstrong young GP in DR FINLAY'S CASEBOOK. His later TV work was sparse, the highlight being roles in *Scotch on the Rocks* and *Kidnapped*, but also with guest spots in WHEN THE BOAT COMES IN, RETURN OF THE SAINT and *The McKinnons*.

Simpson, John

CBE (John Fidler-Simpson; 1944–)

Distinguished British journalist who joined the BBC as a news trainee in 1966. He became its Dublin correspondent six years later, before moving to Brussels in 1975 to cover the increasingly important Common Market business. Simpson was the Corporation's Southern Africa correspondent from 1977 and then took over as diplomatic correspondent in 1978, before holding the position of political editor from 1980 to 1981. Also in the early 1980s, he presented *The Nine O'Clock News* with John Humphrys. From 1982, he was the BBC's diplomatic editor, switching in 1988 to world affairs editor.

Simpsons, The ★★★★

US (Gracie Films/Twentieth Century-Fox) Cartoon. BBC 1/BBC 2 1996–2004; Channel 4 2004– (US: Fox 1989–)

Voices:

Homer Simpson	**Dan Castellaneta**
Marge Simpson	**Julie Kavner**
Bart Simpson	**Nancy Cartwright**
Lisa Simpson	**Yeardley Smith**
Abraham 'Grampa' Simpson	**Dan Castellaneta**
Patty Bouvier	**Julie Kavner**
Selma Bouvier	**Julie Kavner**
Mr Charles Montgomery Burns	**Harry Shearer**
Waylon Smithers	**Harry Shearer**
Principal Seymour Skinner	**Harry Shearer**
Moe Szyslak	**Hank Azaria**
Milhouse Van Houten	**Pamela Hayden**
Ned Flanders	**Harry Shearer**
Todd Flanders	**Nancy Cartwright**
Rod Flanders	**Pamela Hayden**
Krusty the Clown	**Dan Castellaneta**
Apu Nahasapeemapetilon	**Hank Azaria**
Police Chief Clancy Wiggum	**Hank Azaria**
Robert Underdunk Terwilliger ('Sideshow Bob')	**Kelsey Grammer**
Edna Krabappel	**Marcia Wallace**
Barney Grumble	**Dan Castellaneta**

Creator **Matt Groening**
Executive Producers **Matt Groening, James L. Brooks, Sam Simon, Bill Oakley, Josh Weinstein, Mike Scully, Al Jean, David Mirkin, David S. Cohen, Gabor Csupo, George Meyer, Mike Reiss, Steve Tompkins**

● ***The eventful life of a blue-collar American family.***

The Simpsons, bug-eyed, yellow-fleshed, four-fingers-per-hand creations of cartoonist Matt Groening, live in Evergreen Terrace in the town of Springfield. Slobbish, doughnut-eating dad Homer ('Doh!') works for the evil Mr Burns, as a safety inspector at the local nuclear power station, and drinks Duff Beer at Moe's Tavern in his spare time. Mum Marge sports a towering blue beehive, talks hoarsely and tries to keep the house together. Eight-year-old daughter Lisa is a smart achiever who plays the sax, while baby Maggie sucks perennially on a dummy. Causing most of the trouble around the home is obnoxious, crinkly headed, ten-year-old Bart ('Eat my shorts!'), a skateboarding delinquent who drives everyone mad in his pursuit of coolness ('Don't have a cow, man'). Filling out the household are dog Santa's Little Helper and cat Snowball (the second of two Snowballs, the first one deceased). Their continual struggle to survive as a unit – they virtually invented the word 'dysfunctional' – reflects some of the worst excesses of American family life. Other notable characters include Homer's senile dad, Abe, Bart's friend Milhouse, Marge's twin, unmarried sisters Patty and Selma Bouvier, religious neighbour Ned Flanders (and kids Todd and Rod), Asian Kwik-E-Mart worker Apu, and flawed TV star Krusty the Clown, whose show features the kids' favourite violent cat-and-mouse cartoon, *Itchy and Scratchy*. Also seen is Krusty's associate, the criminal Sideshow Bob. Principal Skinner runs Springfield Elementary school, while Edna Krabappel is Lisa's teacher. Barney Gumble is one of Homer's drinking buddies. Numerous guest stars' voices also make their mark in the series, including Paul and Linda McCartney, Dustin Hoffman, Gillian Anderson, David Duchovny, Kelsey Grammer, David Hyde Pierce, Meryl Streep, Bette Midler, Tom Jones, Tony Blair, Ricky Gervais (also as writer of one episode) and Elizabeth Taylor (who speaks Maggie's first-ever word).

Groening named all the Simpsons but Bart – a thinly disguised anagram of 'brat' – after members of his own family but claimed that was where the similarities ended. The naming of the town 'Springfield' was also deliberate: the same name had been used in the decidedly more wholesome 1950s sitcom *Father Knows Best*. It is also usefully vague in terms of location, since a town called Springfield can be found in most American states.

The Simpsons made their TV debut in *The Tracey Ullman Show* before they embarked on this series of their own, which became the biggest show on the Fox network. The programme's satirical tone and cultural cross-references ensured its appeal to adults as well as children, and it became the first successful prime-time animation in the States since THE FLINTSTONES. Extensive merchandising and hit records followed ('Do the Bartman' and 'Deep Deep Trouble'). In the UK, Sky One pre-empted the BBC/Channel 4 in airing the show.

Sims, Joan

(1930–2001)

British comedy actress often seen on the small screen, as well as in films. In a long and varied career, she was a guest in THE ADVENTURES OF ROBIN HOOD in the 1950s, Daisy Burke in OUR HOUSE in 1960, and Janet with John Junkin in *Sam and Janet* in 1966, and also enjoyed major roles in *Lord Tramp* (Miss Pratt), *Born and Bred* (Molly Peglar), COCKLES (Gloria du Bois), *Farrington of the FO* (Annie Begley) and ON THE UP (Mrs Wembley). Other credits included COLONEL MARCH OF SCOTLAND YARD, THE BUCCANEERS, *Here and Now*, *Before the Fringe*, TILL DEATH US DO PART (Gran), SYKES, LADYKILLERS (Amelia Elizabeth Dyer), *Poor Little Rich Girls*, WORZEL GUMMIDGE (Mrs Bloomsbury-Barton), CROWN COURT, MISS MARPLE, *Dramarama* and ONLY FOOLS AND HORSES. Sims was seen also in AS TIME GOES BY (Madge), CLUEDO (Mrs White), MARTIN CHUZZLEWIT (Betsy Prig), *Smokescreen* (Mrs Nash), MY GOOD FRIEND (Miss Byron), JUST WILLIAM, LAST OF THE BLONDE BOMBSHELLS (Betty), and the kids' series *Tickle on the Tum* and JACKANORY *Playhouse*. Additionally, she provided strong support for comics like Dick Emery, Stanley Baxter, Kenneth Williams, Ronnie Barker and Victoria Wood, and appeared with her colleagues from the *Carry On* films.

Simulcast

A simultaneous broadcast of a programme by a television station and a radio station, usually in order to obtain better sound-quality from the radio's FM frequency (in pre-digital days). Simulcasts have been used for opera, rock concerts, stereo and quadraphonic experiments and other major events. TOP OF THE POPS was simulcast on BBC 1 and Radio 1 for a few years.

Sinden, Sir Donald

CBE (1923–)

Plymouth-born, resonant-voiced actor, generally cast in upright, snooty, typically English parts. On stage since the mid-1930s and in films since the 1950s, Sinden's first TV starring role came in 1964, in the comedy OUR MAN AT ST MARK'S, as the Revd Stephen Young, having already appeared occasionally in A LIFE OF BLISS. Twelve years later he played butler Robert Hiller in TWO'S COMPANY and followed this sitcom with another, NEVER THE TWAIN, in which he played antiques dealer Simon Peel. Sinden has also been seen in THE RIVALS OF SHERLOCK HOLMES (Romney Pringle), *The Organisation*, *The Treasure Seekers* (Old Wincott), *Nancherrow* (see COMING HOME) (Robin Jarvis), JUDGE JOHN DEED (Sir Joseph Channing), and in numerous single dramas and classic plays, like *The Canterville Ghost* (Lord Dumbleton), as well as making guest appearances in series like THE PRISONER and with Morecambe and Wise. In 1979, in complete contrast, he presented a series of documentaries, *Discovering English Churches*. He is the brother of actor Leon Sinden, and father of Marc Sinden and the late Jeremy Sinden.

Singing Detective, The ★★★★

UK (BBC) Drama. BBC 1 1986

Philip E. Marlow	**Michael Gambon**
Nurse Mills/Carlotta	**Joanne Whalley**
Mark Binney/Mark Finney/ Raymond Binney	**Patrick Malahide**
Mrs Beth Marlow/Lili	**Alison Steadman**
Philip Marlow (aged ten)	**Lyndon Davies**
Mr Marlow	**Jim Carter**
Nicola Marlow	**Janet Suzman**
Dr Gibbon	**Bill Paterson**
Schoolteacher/Scarecrow	**Janet Henfrey**
Mark Binney (aged ten)	**William Speakman**

Writer **Dennis Potter**
Producers **Kenith Trodd, John Harris**

● ***A hospitalized thriller writer hallucinates into paranoia.***

This highly complex, six-part musical drama is the story of a man suffering. Philip Marlow is an author of pulp fiction, confined to hospital with a debilitating skin disease. As his sickness worsens, paranoia overwhelms him, leading him to conjure up images of the people around him as alien to his well-being. The story meanders through time back to the 1930s; it looks at the patient as a young boy, examining his formative years; and it infiltrates the pages of fiction, as people become characters from one of his own books, *The Singing Detective*. It confuses reality and fantasy, and offers a weird psychoanalytical insight into the lead character.

Claustrophobically interned in a hospital's Sherpa Tensing ward, tortured by unbearable psoriasis, the grouchy Marlow finds his temperature sweeping up and down, causing his mind to wander. Believing his wife, Nicola, is conspiring with a lover, Mark Finney, to sell his book's film rights, he drifts back to his Forest of Dean childhood to recall a devious classmate called Mark Binney (or was it Finney?). He remembers seeing his mother make love in the woods to her fancy man, Raymond Binney, a Mark Finney look-alike. At other times, he swoons off into the pages of his own novel, picturing himself as the eponymous hero, attempting to solve the mystery of a girl dredged from the Thames, trailed all the while by two shadowy figures, in a nostalgic echo of Chandler's Philip Marlowe tales. Back in reality, the sick author fights desperate verbal battles against a doctor whose opinion he derides, and is then required to restrain his sexuality as beautiful Nurse Mills works calming ointment into his suffering, flaking body.

Brilliant to some, outrageous to many and confusing to most (at least until all the pieces fall into place), *The Singing Detective* is in part an autobiographical tale. Potter himself suffered badly from psoriasis, and he had grown up in the Forest of Dean. The evocative 1930s/1940s tunes like 'Cruising down the River' and 'Dem Bones' were also clearly from Potter's younger days. When all the fuss had subsided, the general reaction was that this was an all-time classic TV drama, skilfully crafted, magnificently produced and highly entertaining. It was shown again shortly after Potter's premature death in 1994.

Singing Ringing Tree, The

See *Tales from Europe*.

Singles ✶✶

UK (Yorkshire) Situation Comedy. ITV 1988–9; 1991

Malcolm Price .... **Roger Rees**
Pamela .... **Judy Loe**
Clive Bates .... **Eamon Boland**
Jackie Phillips .... **Susie Blake**
Dennis Duval .... **Simon Cadell**
Di .... **Gina Maher**

Creators/Writers **Eric Chappell, Jean Warr**
Producers **Vernon Lawrence, Nic Phillips, Graham Wetherell**

● ***Four lonely hearts meet in a singles' bar and begin duplicitous relationships.***

Pamela, married for 20 years but now separated, and her recently divorced friend, Jackie, attend a singles' bar as a step towards finding a new relationship. There they meet bachelor market-trader Malcolm and hospital porter Clive, whose wife has left him with three children to raise. Malcolm's claim to be 'big in imports' and Clive's fake profession of 'doctor' are exposed by Di, the club's Liverpudlian barmaid, but all the same the girls and guys strike up a friendship which lasts, through peaks and troughs, for two series. Malcolm and Pamela pair up, as do Clive and Jackie. For the third and final series, Malcolm is replaced by out-of-work thespian Dennis Duval (actor Roger Rees had moved on to play Robin Colcord in CHEERS). *Singles* was derived from a one-hour play screened in 1984, with a completely different cast, including Robin Nedwell as Malcolm.

Singleton, Valerie

OBE (1937–)

Hitchin-born actress turned TV presenter whose first appearances were in ITV admags. She moved to the BBC as an announcer in 1962 and the same year joined BLUE PETER. With Christopher Trace she inaugurated the series' golden age, which continued through her partnership with John Noakes and Peter Purves. Singleton famously joined Princess Anne on the 1971 *Blue Peter Royal Safari to Kenya*, but left *Blue Peter* a year later to work on NATIONWIDE (initially on its Consumer Unit) and later on TONIGHT, *The Money Programme* and BBC Radio. She continued to make occasional visits to the *Blue Peter* studio throughout the 1970s and was sent on *Blue Peter Special Assignments*. Singleton also presented *Val Meets the VIPs*, in which she interviewed celebrities. She returned to the screen in 1993 as host of *Travel UK* and, the next year, shared the limelight once again with John Noakes in the over-50s afternoon magazine programme *Next*. She later hosted a quiz, *Backdate*.

Sink or Swim ✶✶

UK (BBC) Situation Comedy. BBC 1 1980–2

Brian Webber .... **Peter Davison**
Steve Webber .... **Robert Glenister**
Sonia .... **Sara Corper**
Mike Connor .... **Ron Pember**
Charlotte .... **Briony McRoberts**

Writer **Alex Shearer**
Producers **Gareth Gwenlan, Roger Race**

● ***Two brothers escape the rat race on a leaky narrowboat.***

To northern brothers Brian and Steve Webber, it seems like an excellent idea to buy up a decrepit old canal boat when they are in Bristol. They plan to do it up, ship it to London and offer trips to tourists along England's waterways. Sadly, without cash on the hip, the best they can do is to make the damp and depressing barge their home. Nevertheless, the hapless Brian is nothing if not ambitious, although his enthusiasm is somewhat tempered by the loutish Steve's complete lack of interest in anything but sex. Stepping between the chalk-and-cheese siblings is Brian's rather earnest, environmentally aware girlfriend, Sonia. In the third and final series, the two lads have moved out of their boat and into Newcastle, where Brian has enrolled as a computer student at the university and Steve is, inevitably, out of work. Sonia shares a flat with student Charlotte, but it's not long before Steve makes himself at home there, too. Music is by Ronnie Hazlehurst.

Sir Arthur Conan Doyle's Sherlock Holmes

See *Sherlock Holmes*.

Sir Francis Drake ✶✶

UK (ITC) Adventure. ITV 1961–2

Sir Francis Drake .... **Terence Morgan**
Queen Elizabeth .... **Jean Kent**
Trevelyan .... **Patrick McLoughlin**
John Drake .... **Michael Crawford**
Mendoza .... **Roger Delgado**
Grenville .... **Howard Lang**

Producer **Anthony Bushell**

● ***Swashbuckling, maritime adventures with the sailor hero of Queen Elizabeth I.***

Sir Francis Drake is Admiral of the Queen's Navy and, from his flagship, *The Golden Hind*, patrols the oceans for Britain. His travels take him across the Atlantic and into conflict with our continental near-neighbours, although, whenever trouble threatens, Drake always wins through, often showing off his fencing skills in the process. Although accurate in period detail, the programme's storylines are largely fictitious.

The production is especially notable, in hindsight, for its cast, which included a young Michael Crawford, as well as Roger Delgado (the original Master in DOCTOR WHO). Guest stars are noteworthy, too, including David McCallum, Nanette Newman and Warren Mitchell.

Sir Lancelot

See *Adventures of Sir Lancelot, The*.

Sir Prancelot ✶✶

UK (John Ryan) Animation. BBC 1 1972

Voices **Peter Hawkins**

Writer/Producer **John Ryan**

● ***The road to Jerusalem is paved with adventure for a knight in shining armour.***

Billed as 'the adventures of an inventive knight on his

journeys to the Crusades', *Sir Prancelot* was a five-minute teatime filler in the CAPTAIN PUGWASH mould (indeed from the same pen of John Ryan). In jerky cardboard-cut-out scenes, the portly knight with the white moustache who has a flair for Heath Robinson inventions has many an escapade on the way to the Holy Land after fleeing his debt-ridden Crumblecreek Castle. He is unfortunately accompanied by his formidable wife, Lady Hysteria, her pet Pig William, mischievous castle kids Sue and Sim, a minstrel and servants Master Gurth, Bert and Harry. Chief among their adversaries en route are Count Otto the Blot and Duke Uglio. Music is by Alan Parker.

Sissons, Peter

(1942–)

Senior BBC newsreader who joined ITN in 1964 as a trainee. Working his way up the network's ladder, he became foreign correspondent, industrial editor and presenter of the lunchtime bulletin, *News at One*, and *Channel 4 News*. He moved to the BBC in 1989 as Robin Day's successor in the chair of QUESTION TIME (he stayed for four years) and also to present the Corporation's main bulletins.

Sitcom

Situation comedy, a humorous, episodic series of programmes in which a well-defined cast of characters, confined in one location or set of circumstances, responds predictably to new events.

TV's first comedy offerings were carry-overs from radio or the music hall, but it soon carved its own niche in the world of humour by developing the situation comedy, a type of comedy that made a virtue out of the constraints of early television production. In those primitive days, camera manoeuvrability was limited and dramas and comedies were generally played out entirely within the four walls of a studio set. Consequently, with the situation static, humour had to come from strong characterization.

Most sitcoms have centred around the family. Right from the earliest successes of THE BURNS AND ALLEN SHOW and I LOVE LUCY to THE ROYLE FAMILY and MY FAMILY, the family unit has been the cradle of the action. This is not so surprising, as the family comprises a set number of interdependent characters, living in the same location and forced to react with each other to changing events. The workplace has been another popular venue, as typified by programmes like TAXI and ON THE BUSES. However, provided the circumstances are well defined and the characterization is suitably strong, virtually any setting can be used. For THE PHIL SILVERS SHOW it was a US Army base; for CHEERS a Boston bar. As if to prove the point, the most successful of sitcoms have had the most unlikely of settings – M*A*S*H's Mobile Army Surgical Hospital in the Korean War, and the Resistance bar in occupied France in 'ALLO 'ALLO, for instance.

Whereas American sitcoms employ teams of ever-changing writers, many of Britain's most memorable sitcoms have come from a small corps of authors, the likes of Ray Galton and Alan Simpson, Johnny Speight, John Esmonde and Bob Larbey, Dick Clement and Ian La Frenais, Jimmy Perry and David Croft, Vince Powell and Harry Driver, Ronald Chesney and Ronald Wolfe, Johnnie Mortimer and Brian Cooke, Maurice Gran and Lawrence Marks, Roy Clarke, Eric Chappell, John Sullivan, Carla Lane, George Layton, David Nobbs, Simon Nye, David Renwick and Andrew Marshall. Many of their works began as pilots in the COMEDY PLAYHOUSE anthology.

Sitting Pretty ★★★

UK (BBC) Situation Comedy. BBC 1 1992–3

Annie Briggs .... **Diane Bull**
Tiffany .... **Alison Lomas**
Sylvie .... **Heather Tobias**
Kitty .... **Vilma Hollingbery**
George .... **John Cater**

Creator/Writer **John Sullivan**
Producer **Susan Belbin**

● ***A 1960s jet-setter, impoverished by her late husband, is driven back to her lowly roots.***

Annie Briggs has seen better days. A 1960s good-time girl, once known as 'the Jackie Onassis of Bethnal Green', she used to rub shoulders with the big names, drift from party to party and travel the world on the arms of rich playboys. However, when her husband, Boris, dies suddenly, he leaves her penniless and staring the realities of the 1990s in the face. Her lovely home, her cars and even her dog are repossessed and she is forced to move into her last piece of property, the pokey flat she has given to her daughter, Tiffany. Tiffany, or 'Dumpling' as her mum calls her, is a trainee nurse. She seldom saw her mother while growing up, having been packed off to boarding school while Annie toured the world. Now, claustrophobically trapped within the same four walls, she sees too much of her (and hears too many of Annie's Shirley Bassey tapes). Soon the flat, too, is taken away, and Annie and Tiffany move in with Annie's mum, Kitty, hypochondriac dad, George, and twin sister, Sylvie, at Sunnyside Farm, a small chicken ranch in the country. Frumpy Sylvie, an ex-hippie with a grown-up air steward son named Lonestar (whose dad, she reckons, was Bob Marley), particularly resents her sister's presence – or, rather, the fact that she never lifts a finger around the home, unless it is to paint the nail. 'Phenomenal', Annie would say.

Situation Comedy

See *Sitcom*.

Six English Towns ★★

UK (BBC) Documentary. BBC 2 1978

Presenter/Writer **Alec Clifton-Taylor**

Producer **Denis Moriarty**

● ***An enthusiastic analysis of building styles around England.***

Alec Clifton-Taylor, a keen admirer of architecture, took viewers on a ramble through six of the country's most interesting towns in this series for BBC 2. Paying particular attention to houses and terraces, and making clear his views on modern developments, Clifton-Taylor took in visits to Chichester, Richmond (Yorkshire), Tewkesbury, Stamford, Totnes and Ludlow. The series proved so popular that *Six More English Towns* followed in 1981. These were Warwick, Berwick-upon-Tweed, Saffron Walden, Lewes, Bradford-on-Avon and Beverley. *Another Six English Towns* – Cirencester, Whitby, Bury St Edmunds, Devizes, Sandwich and Durham – rounded off the trilogy in 1984.

Six Feet Under ★★★

US (Actual Size/Greenblatt-Janollari/HBO) Drama. Channel 4 2002–4 (US: HBO 2001–5)

Nathaniel 'Nate' Fisher .... **Peter Krause**
David Fisher .... **Michael C. Hall**
Ruth Fisher/Sibley .... **Frances Conroy**
Claire Fisher .... **Lauren Ambrose**
Federico 'Rico' Diaz .... **Freddy Rodriguez**
Keith Charles .... **Mathew St Patrick**
Brenda Chenowith .... **Rachel Griffiths**
Billy Chenowith .... **Jeremy Sisto**
Nathaniel Fisher .... **Richard Jenkins**
Gabriel 'Gabe' Dimas .... **Eric Balfour**
Vanessa Diaz .... **Justina Machado**
Lisa Kimmel/Fisher .... **Lili Taylor**
Bettina .... **Kathy Bates**
Sarah O'Conner .... **Patricia Clarkson**
Russell Corwin .... **Ben Foster**
George Sibley .... **James Cromwell**
Maggie Sibley .... **Tina Holmes**
Olivier Castro Stahl .... **Peter Macdissi**

Creator **Alan Ball**
Executive Producers **Alan Ball, Robert Greenblatt, David Janollari, Alan Poul, Bruce-Eric Kaplan**

● ***Life and death as seen through the eyes of a family of funeral directors.***

Life changes for the Fisher family one Christmas Eve when dad Nathaniel is killed in a road accident. Nathaniel was head of the family business, an independent undertaker's (Fisher and Sons) based in Los Angeles, and had over 30 years' experience to call on. Now it's up to his wife and sons to keep the firm afloat, as well as to come to terms with his loss and their own complicated personal lives. Nate Jr is the prodigal son who is forced to rein back his casual, relaxed approach to life and enter the funeral business. He is made a reluctant partner in the firm with his more professional brother, David, who has learned the business from dad, resents his brother's involvement and, on a personal level, is struggling to cope with his closet gayness. Young redhead Claire is the teenage sister who dates junkie Gabe, which, like David's homosexuality, causes plenty of headaches for their mum, Ruth. Ruth has been running the backroom business for years but now has to step forward and make her presence count – a step she finds hard to take. Working for the Fishers is talented mortician Rico Diaz, a young man whose close proximity to death leads him to worry about his wife, Vanessa, and his own young family. Cop Keith Charles is David's some-time boyfriend while Brenda Chenowith is Nate's lover, a woman troubled by her disturbed younger brother, Billy. Later characters include Lisa, a passionate vegetarian and old flame of Nate's, who becomes his wife; Ruth's hippyish younger sister, Sarah; Bettina, Ruth's closest friend; George, a geology professor who marries Ruth; George's daughter, Maggie; Claire's boyfriend, Russell; and bi-sexual artist Olivier.

An adult drama, filled with sexual scenes and strong language, *Six Feet Under* uses the juxtaposition of life and death to offer a mix of black comedy and pathos: an emotional blend that secured hit status from the outset in the USA. It was created and co-written by Alan Ball, writer of the Oscar-sweeping *American Beauty*. Although the fifth and final season was screened in the UK on digital channel E4 in 2005, its sister terrestrial channel, Channel 4, ended its involvement after season four, in 2004.

Six-Five Special ★★

UK (BBC) Youth Magazine. BBC 1957–8

Presenters **Pete Murray, Josephine Douglas, Freddie Mills, Jim Dale**

Producers **Jack Good, Josephine Douglas, Dennis Main Wilson**

● ***Pioneering youth music programme.***

With its 'Over the points, over the points' theme song (by Johnny Johnson), the *Six-Five Special* rolled into town in February 1957, initially scheduled for a six-week run. Instead it ran for nearly two years. Conceived by the BBC as a means of capturing the youth market, and filling the Saturday 6–7 p.m. vacancy created by scrapping the TODDLERS' TRUCE, it proved to be a major step forward for pop music on TV.

Co-producers Jack Good and Jo Douglas were charged by the BBC with the development of the series, being two of the younger members of staff. Good was undoubtedly the prime mover and pushed the Corporation's conservative instincts to the limit. He wanted spontaneity, movement and energy; the BBC wanted something rather more sedate. Good dragged the clapping and jiving studio audience into shot and whipped up a degree of excitement; the BBC countered by balancing rock 'n' roll with skiffle, jazz and even classical music, and filling out the show with wholesome magazine items (spotlights on film stars, comedy, sport, general interest, etc.). Such restrictions proved too much for Good and he left for ITV, where he was given the freedom he needed to produce a real rock 'n' roll show, OH BOY! When this was pitched opposite *Six-Five Special* in the schedules, the latter's days were numbered.

Hosting *Six-Five Special* in its first year were Pete Murray, Jo Douglas and boxer-turned-TV-presenter Freddie Mills. Jim Dale took over in the post-Good days. The resident band were Don Lang and His Frantic Five and among the guest performers were the likes of Tommy Steele and His Steelmen, Adam Faith (making his TV debut) and, to illustrate the wide range of musical styles covered, Lonnie Donegan, Laurie London, Humphrey Lyttelton, Johnny Dankworth and Shirley Bassey. *Six-Five Special*'s early popularity resulted in a spin-off film (of the same name) and two stage shows.

Six Million Dollar Man, The ★★

US (Universal/Harve Bennett) Science Fiction. ITV 1974–9 (US: ABC 1973–8)

Col. Steve Austin .... **Lee Majors**
Oscar Goldman .... **Richard Anderson**
Dr Rudy Wells .... **Alan Oppenheimer**
Martin E. Brooks
Peggy Callahan .... **Jennifer Darling**
Jaime Sommers .... **Lindsay Wagner**
Andy Sheffield .... **Vincent Van Patten**

Creator **Henri Simoun**
Executive Producers **Glen A. Larson, Harve Bennett, Allan Balter**
Producers **Michael Gleason, Lee Sigel, Joe L. Cramer, Fred Freiberger, Richard Irving**

● ***An astronaut, rebuilt after a horrendous accident, uses his superhuman powers to work for an intelligence service.***

Steve Austin was a NASA astronaut whose lunar landing

vehicle crashed on a test flight. The authorities decided to rebuild him at a cost of $6 million, using nuclear-powered technology devised by boffin Dr Rudy Wells. Austin was given a replacement right arm which endowed him with tremendous strength, two new legs which allowed him to run at up to 60 m.p.h., and a left eye with a built-in telescope. He became a cyborg: part-man, part-machine, a superman who was still vulnerable in the usual human ways.

The new 'bionic' man now puts his amazing abilities to work on behalf of the Office of Scientific Information (OSI), an international secret agency run by the US Government, where his boss is Oscar Goldman. Austin is joined in his adventures by his girlfriend, tennis star Jaime Sommers. She, too, has been rebuilt, following a sky-diving accident. Her first appearance is short-lived, as her body rejects the implants, and she is believed to have died. But doctors and technicians resurrect her from a coma to take part in further bionic adventures alongside Austin, before she is given her own series, THE BIONIC WOMAN. There is also a bionic boy (teenage athlete Andy Sheffield), a bionic dog and even a $7 million man, a racing driver named Barney Miller, rebuilt as Austin's back-up. However, he blows a fuse and Austin has to destroy him.

Also seen in the series is secretary Peggy Callahan, and the brains behind the bionics, Dr Wells (who must have had surgery himself, because he was played by two different actors). The series was based on a handful of TV movies that had been spun-off from the book *Cyborg* by Martin Caidin.

Six Wives of Henry VIII, The ✱✱✱

UK (BBC) Historical Drama. BBC 2 1970

Henry VIII	**Keith Michell**
Catherine of Aragon	**Annette Crosbie**
Anne Boleyn	**Dorothy Tutin**
Jane Seymour	**Anne Stallybrass**
Anne of Cleves	**Elvi Hale**
Catherine Howard	**Angela Pleasence**
Catherine Parr	**Rosalie Crutchley**
Cardinal Wolsey	**John Baskcomb**
Duke of Norfolk	**Patrick Troughton**
Thomas Cromwell	**Wolfe Morris**
Archbishop Thomas Cranmer	**Bernard Hepton**
Lady Rochford	**Sheila Burrell**
Sir Thomas Seymour	**John Ronane**
Narrator	**Anthony Quayle**

Creator **Maurice Cowan**
Writers **Rosemary Anne Sisson, Nick McCarty, Ian Thorne, Jean Morris, Beverley Cross, John Prebble**
Producers **Ronald Travers, Mark Shivas, Roderick Graham**

● ***The life and loves of King Henry VIII.***

This award-winning, six-part costume drama tells the story of England's celebrated monarch through his relationships with his six wives, one per episode. It sees Henry growing in age (and size) from a slim 17-year-old to an obese 56-year-old at the time of his death. It also helps erode the cinematic Charles Laughton 'glutton' stereotype, introducing further dimensions to the man's character.

As a lead figure, Henry VIII provides much scope for the writers. Although 400 years old, his story made good 1970s TV drama, rich in sex and violence. Here is a man who marries six different women, chiefly to give himself an heir, beheads two, divorces two and sees one die shortly after childbirth. Then there are the whispered conspiracies, the treacherous double-dealing, the bloody murders and the major religious wrangles which were prevalent in those troubled times. The series made a star out of a former artist, Australian Keith Michell, and was reworked with different actresses for a film version, *Henry VIII and His Six Wives* in 1972.

Sixpenny Corner ✱

UK (Associated-Rediffusion) Soap Opera. ITV 1955–6

Sally Sharpe/Norton	**Patricia Dainton**
Bill Norton	**Howard Pays**
Mr Sharpe	**Walter Horsbrugh**
Mrs Doris Sharpe	**Betty Bowden**
Yvonne Sharpe	**Shirley Mitchell**
Mr Chas Norton	**Robert Webber**
Stan Norton	**Robert Desmond**
Uncle Fred	**Stuart Saunders**
Aunt Mabel	**Olive Milbourne**
Tom Norton	**Bernard Fox**
Grete Edler	**Christine Pollon**
Moira O'Shea	**Jan Miller**
Dr Tim O'Shea	**Michael Collins**
Eddie Perkins	**John Charlesworth**
Julie Perkins	**Elizabeth Fraser**
Phillip Collier	**Charles Ross**
Rosie Chubb	**Vi Stevens**

Creators **Jonquil Antony, Hazel Adair**
Producers **John Lemont, Michael Westmore**

● ***Serial launched with the birth of ITV.***

Britain's first daily TV soap opera arrived in 1955 with the introduction of commercial television. This 15-minute saga was the story of newlyweds Bill and Sally Norton, who ran a garage at Sixpenny Corner in the rural town of Springwood. Events inevitably spread beyond the petrol pumps and into the personal lives of the young lovers' families. Most notable figures include their respective parents, plus Stan and Tom (Bill's brothers), Yvonne (Sally's sister) and Bill's aunt and uncle, Fred and Mabel.

$64,000 Question, The

See *Double Your Money*.

Sixty Minutes

See *Nationwide*.

Skinner, Claire

(1965–)

English actress in a mix of comedy and dramatic roles. She played Lucinda in CHEF!, Agnes Conway in CATHERINE COOKSON'S *The Wingless Bird*, Jean Duport in A DANCE TO THE MUSIC OF TIME, Susan Harvey in THE PETER PRINCIPLE, DI Catherine Tully in SECOND SIGHT, Sarah Newcombe in BEDTIME, Rebecca in Stephen Poliakoff's PERFECT STRANGERS and Gail Collins in *Swallow*. Claire was also seen in INSPECTOR MORSE, BRASS EYE, *Trevor's World of Sport* (Meryl), *The Booze Cruise* (Leone Sewell), *Eroica* (Josephine), LIFE BEGINS (Clare), *The Genius of Mozart* (Nannerl), *Class of '76* (Dr Kate Tremaine), MURPHY'S LAW and AGATHA CHRISTIE'S MARPLE.

Skinner, Frank

(Chris Collins; 1957–)

Black Country-born comedian, actor and chat show host who has a masters degree in English and allegedly 'borrowed' his stage name from a member of his dad's dominoes team. He appeared as the stage manager in PACKET OF THREE/PACKING THEM IN before starring in his own stand-up and talk shows, writing – and playing Frank in – the semi-autobiographical sitcom BLUE HEAVEN, featuring as a team captain in *Gagtag* and co-hosting *Fantasy Football League* and *Baddiel and Skinner Unplanned* with his pal, David Baddiel. Skinner also played Herod in *The Flint Street Nativity* and appeared as the eponymous mini-cab driver in another of his own comedies, SHANE.

Skippy, the Bush Kangaroo ✶✶

Australia (Norfolk International) Children's Adventure. ITV 1967–9

Matt Hammond	**Ed Devereaux**
Sonny Hammond	**Garry Parkhurst**
Mark Hammond	**Ken James**
Jerry King	**Tony Bonner**
Clarissa 'Clancy' Merrick	**Liza Goddard**
Dr Anna Steiner	**Elke Neidhardt**
Dr Alexander Stark	**Frank Thring**

Writers **Ross Napier, Ed Devereaux**
Executive Producers **John McCallum, Bud Austin**
Producers **Lee Robinson, Dennis Hill**

Heart-warming tales of a boy and his pet kangaroo.

Set in Australia's Waratah National Park, *Skippy, The Bush Kangaroo*, with its catchy sing-along theme song, relates the adventures of Sonny Hammond, son of Chief Ranger Matt Hammond and younger brother of Ranger Mark Hammond, and blonde teenager Clancy Merrick (a young Liza Goddard). But the real star of the show is Sonny's intuitive pet kangaroo, Skippy. Once injured and near to death, Skippy is nursed back to health by Sonny and remains ever loyal thereafter, to the point where the bounding marsupial even warns its master of impending danger with a distinctive 'tut tut'. Also seen are local pilot Jerry King and hordes of colourful Australian mammals. In 1993 the BBC showed *The New Adventures of Skippy*.

Skorpion ✶✶

UK (BBC) Secret Agent Drama. BBC 1 1983

Chief Supt. Franks	**Terrence Hardiman**
Gabrielle	**Marianne Borgo**
Capt. Percival	**Michael Denison**
Chief Insp. Perry	**Jack McKenzie**
Insp. Clarke	**Daniel Hill**
Agatha	**Mary Wimbush**

Creator **Arden Winch**
Writer **John Brason**
Producer **Gerard Glaister**

A counter-terrorism unit stalks an assassin across the Scottish moors.

When a plane crashes on bleak Scottish moorland in strange circumstances, eyebrows are raised in the security services. In a separate development, a bomb explodes but the intended target survives – yet more intrigue. These seemingly unconnected events form the basis for a game of cat and mouse in the Scottish Highlands, involving Gabrielle, a woman who assists refugees; her would-be assassin; and the Anti-Terrorist Squad team that tracks him down. Captain Percival (previously seen in BLOOD MONEY and reappearing later in COLD WARRIOR) is the man charged with apprehending the villains in this six-part thriller.

Sky [1]

See *BSkyB*.

Sky [2] ✶✶

UK (HTV) Children's Science Fiction. ITV 1975

Sky	**Marc Harrison**
Arby Vennor	**Stuart Lock**
Jane Vennor	**Cherrald Butterfield**
Roy Briggs	**Richard Speight**
Major Briggs	**Jack Watson**
Mr Vennor	**Thomas Heathcote**
Mrs Vennor	**Frances Cuka**
Goodchild	**Robert Eddison**

Writers **Bob Baker, Dave Martin**
Producer **Leonard White**

A stranded alien needs help to return home before the Earth overpowers him.

Sky, 'part angel, part waif', is discovered by West Country boy Arby Vennor while out on a pheasant shoot. The alien youth has arrived on Earth by accident and is desperate to return home. In the meantime, our planet begins to resist his presence and its forces are manifested in a human personage known as Goodchild. Sky retaliates by using telepathy and his supernatural powers to compel humans to follow his will. He means the planet no harm, but he's not here to help us either. When his eyes glow blue, everyone had better watch out. Arby, his sister, Jane, and a friend, Roy, decide to help Sky in his plight, the main aim being to discover the 'Juganet' that will apparently solve all Sky's problems. Sky was another of HTV West's respected range of children's sci-fi offerings of the 1970s.

Sky at Night, The ✶✶✶

UK (BBC) Astronomy. BBC 1 1957–

Presenter **Patrick Moore**

Producers **Paul Johnstone, Patricia Owtram, Patricia Wood, Pieter Morpurgo, Ian Russell, Jane Fletcher**

Small-screen astronomy.

Hosted for its entire run of nearly 50 years by Patrick Moore, *The Sky at Night* – the world's longest-running science programme, with more than 600 editions produced – charts events in the space world on a monthly basis. Its first programme went out six months before *Sputnik I*, the first man-made satellite, was launched and so it can justifiably claim to have been ahead of the space race. As well as monitoring the progress of various probes and rockets, the fast-talking, ultra-enthusiastic Moore has also guided viewers on an exploration of the heavens, pointing out unusual phenomena and revealing the location of the various constellations. The dramatic theme music has been 'At the Castle Gate', from *Pelléas et Mélisande*, by Sibelius. A children's version of the programme, under the title of *Seeing Stars*, was screened in 1970.

Skyport
See *Shadow Squad*.

Sky's the Limit, The
See *Double Your Money*.

Slater, John
(1916–75)

British character actor, in TV plays during the 1940s but more familiar in series like Z CARS (DS Tom Stone). He was also a regular partner of the puppet pigs PINKY AND PERKY and, for a number of years, was seen promoting Special K cereal (a not unfamiliar activity to Slater, who had hosted the *Slater's Bazaar* admag in the late 1950s). Other credits included small roles in INTERNATIONAL DETECTIVE and DANGER MAN.

Slattery, Tony
(1959–)

London-born comedian, actor and presenter who made his name (via the Cambridge Footlights) in the improvisation show WHOSE LINE IS IT ANYWAY?, having already appeared in the late-night comedy *Saturday Stayback* and the kids' series *Tx*. He went on to star in the sitcoms THAT'S LOVE (Tristan Beasley) and JUST A GIGOLO (Nick Brim), co-wrote the children's series BEHIND THE BIKE SHEDS, hosted the film magazine *Saturday Night at the Movies*, shared the limelight with Mike McShane in *S&M* and took over from Stephen Fry in the investigative reporter spoof *This is David Lander* (renamed *This is David Harper* to accommodate the change). He has also been much involved in panel games and quizzes, hosting *Ps and Qs*, *Tibs and Fibs*, *The Music Game* and also *Trivial Pursuit* for satellite TV, and appearing regularly in *Just a Minute* and GOING FOR A SONG. Other credits have included BOON and *Screen Two's Drowning in the Shallow End*. A period of ill health away from the screen was broken by new roles in CASUALTY, *Ahead of the Class* (Stuart Stiles), THE LAST DETECTIVE, BAD GIRLS, *Meet the Magoons*, CORONATION STREET (Eric) and *The English Harem* (Sebastian Partridge).

Slinger's Day
See *Tripper's Day*.

SM:TV Live ★★★
UK (Blaze) Children's Entertainment. ITV 1998–2003

Presenters **Ant McPartlin, Declan Donnelly, Cat Deeley, James Redmond, Brian Dowling, Tess Daly, H, Claire, Des Clarke, Shavaughn Ruakere, Stephen Mulhearn**

Executive Producer **Conor MacAnally**

● ***Anarchic fun, games and music for Saturday morning.***

Along with Cat Deeley, Ant and Dec were the stars who put ITV's Saturday morning schedule on the map in this vibrant rival to LIVE AND KICKING. Like its BBC 1 counterpart (soon seen off), *SM:TV Live* featured guests, comedy, competitions and music. Notable regular features over the years were: 'Chums', a wicked send-up of FRIENDS; 'Dr Pop', looking at chart music; the quiz 'Challenge Ant'; 'Becoming', where kids dressed up as their heroes; and the 'Wonkey Donkey' rhyming game involving mystery animals. There were also excerpts from the Irish version of POPSTARS. Live action comedies and dramas dropped into the format included SABRINA, THE TEENAGE WITCH, *Clueless, The New Addams Family, Starstreet, My Parents are Aliens* and *That's So Raven*. Cartoons featured included *Cow and Chicken, The Angry Beavers, Dexter's Laboratory, I am Weasel Pokemon, Digimon, Hey Arnold!, Men in Black, Sitting Ducks, The Adventures of Jimmy Neutron* and *SpongeBob SquarePants*. Immediately after each edition of *SM:TV Live*, the same team introduced ITV's latest response to TOP OF THE POPS, entitled *CD:UK* (ITV 1998–), which comfortably outlasted *SM:TV* itself.

Ant and Dec left in December 2001 to be replaced by ex-Hollyoaks star James Redmond. Redmond and Cat Deeley were then replaced in 2002 by BIG BROTHER winner Brian Dowling and model Tess Daly, who were temporarily augmented to a foursome with the arrival of former Steps band members H and Claire and later Des Clarke and Shavaughn Ruakere. Stephen Mulhearn replaced Ruakere as the series meandered to a finish. The programme concluded in 2003 with a run of specials entitled *SM:TV Gold*, showing highlights of the five years on air and reuniting past presenters.

Smack the Pony ★★★
UK (Talkback) Comedy. Channel 4 1999–2002

Fiona Allen, Doon Mackichan, Sally Phillips

Executive Producer **Peter Fincham**
Producer **Victoria Pile**

● ***Surreal take on the absurdities in today's world from an all-woman team.***

While aiming to avoid the extremes of feminist satire and girlie giggles, nevetheless much of the comedy in this Emmy-winning sketch show comes from the world according to the female of the species. Tackling such varied topics as video-dating agencies, bad driving, men's insensitivities and bikini lines, there are plenty of visual gags and regular comedy songs from the frontline trio of Fiona Allen, Doon Mackichan and Sally Phillips, supported by the likes of Sarah Alexander, Darren Boyd, Cavan Clerkin, Tamzin Griffin, James Lance and Michael Wildman.

Small Summer Party, A
See *Marion and Geoff*.

Smart, Ralph
(1908–2001)

Australian producer/writer/director, working largely for ITC on various action romps. He is chiefly remembered for creating and producing THE INVISIBLE MAN and DANGER MAN, but he also contributed in various ways to THE ADVENTURES OF ROBIN HOOD, THE BUCCANEERS, THE ADVENTURES OF WILLIAM TELL, THE ADVENTURES OF SIR LANCELOT, THE CHAMPIONS, THE PROTECTORS and RANDALL AND HOPKIRK (DECEASED).

Smillie, Carol

(1961–)

Glasgow-born former model now TV 'lifestyle' programme presenter, having previously worked as hostess on the WHEEL OF FORTUNE game show. Her credits have included CHANGING ROOMS, *The Travel Show*, HEARTS OF GOLD, *Smillie's People*, HOLIDAY, THE NATIONAL LOTTERY LIVE, *Dream Holiday Home* and *People's Court*.

Smith, Delia

OBE (1941–)

The modern-day queen of TV cooks, thanks to her 30-part *Delia Smith's Cookery Course* in the 1970s. Smith was raised in London and entered television after preparing food for cookery photographs and then writing a column for the *Mirror Magazine* and the *Evening Standard*. Her first programme for the BBC, *Family Fare*, came in 1973. She was also seen on Multi-Coloured Swap Shop, and other major contributions have included *One is Fun, Delia Smith's Christmas, Delia Smith's Summer Collection, Delia Smith's Winter Collection* and *Delia's How to Cook*. The books that have accompanied her series have sold in vast quantities.

Smith, Jaclyn

(1947–)

American actress who played agent Kelly Garrett throughout CHARLIE'S ANGELS' five-year run (even though her partners came and went). Previously, Smith had been seen as a guest in series as varied as MCCLOUD and THE PARTRIDGE FAMILY. She later took to TV movies, playing, among other characters, Jackie Kennedy in *Jacqueline Bouvier Kennedy* in 1981 and MYSTERY MOVIE detective *Christine Cromwell* in 1989. More recently, Smith has been seen in guest appearances in US series *Becker* and *The District*.

Smith, Julia

(1927–97)

British drama producer, script editor and director, chiefly associated with EASTENDERS, which she co-created with Tony Holland, and the much-vaunted but ultimately short-lived ELDORADO. Smith had previously produced ANGELS and THE DISTRICT NURSE (also as creator) and had contributed to BBC programmes from the 1960s, including AN AGE OF KINGS, DOCTOR WHO, *Jury Room*, DR FINLAY'S CASEBOOK, THE NEWCOMERS, THE RAILWAY CHILDREN and Z CARS.

Smith, Liz

(1925–)

English actress, arriving on television in the 1970s after bringing up her children. She has appeared in many single dramas and series (increasingly as grandmothers), with the best-remembered roles being Mrs Brandon in I DIDN'T KNOW YOU CARED, Bette in 2 POINT 4 CHILDREN, Letitia Cropley in THE VICAR OF DIBLEY and Nana in THE ROYLE FAMILY. Other credits have included BOOTSIE AND SNUDGE, THE SWEENEY, NO – HONESTLY, CROWN COURT, IN LOVING MEMORY, *Now and Then*, EMMERDALE FARM, AGATHA CHRISTIE'S PARTNERS IN CRIME, THE LIFE AND LOVES OF A SHE DEVIL, CLUEDO, KING AND CASTLE, *Bust*, THE BILL, *Valentine Park*, LOVEJOY, EL C. I. D., MAKING OUT, CASUALTY and *The Young Indiana Jones Chronicles*. Liz has been seen also in BOTTOM, CRAPSTON VILLAS (voice), KARAOKE (Mrs Baglin), *The Queen's Nose* (Grandma), OLIVER TWIST (Sally), *Alice in Wonderland* (Miss Lory), *Donovan Quick* (Gran), A CHRISTMAS CAROL (Joyce), THE BILL, TRIAL AND RETRIBUTION, *A Good Thief* (Lizzie), DOCTORS, *Between the Sheets* (Audrey Delany) and the kids' comedy *Pirates*.

Smith, Mel

(1952–)

British comedian, actor and director, first coming to prominence as a member of the NOT THE NINE O'CLOCK NEWS team in 1979, in which he forged a partnership with Griff Rhys Jones (see Jones's entry for other joint credits). Smith was also seen with comedian Bob Goody in a children's series, *Smith and Goody*, as ruthless property-developer Tom Craig in MUCK AND BRASS, worryguts Colin Watkins in COLIN'S SANDWICH, and Stephen Milner in *Milner*. He also made guest appearances in THE YOUNG ONES and MINDER.

Smith, Mike

(1955–)

Blond-haired British presenter, a former Capital Radio and Radio 1 disc jockey. His credits have included BREAKFAST TIME, THE LATE, LATE BREAKFAST SHOW (with Noel Edmonds) and *Trick or Treat* (with Julian Clary). Smith has also hosted *Transit*, TOP OF THE POPS and the celebrity quiz *That's Showbusiness*. He once sat in for Terry Wogan on his thrice-weekly chat show and has often been called up to present special programmes on motor fairs, charity events, medical matters, etc. He is married to presenter Sarah Greene, with whom he fronted *The Exchange* in 1995.

Smith, Murray

(1940–2003)

Former paratrooper turned scriptwriter and novelist. Among Smith's major TV successes were episodes of THE SWEENEY, THE XYY MAN, HAZELL, CHESSGAME, DEMPSEY AND MAKEPEACE, HAMMER HOUSE OF HORROR and MINDER. Smith was the major writer on STRANGERS and BULMAN, then moved on to create THE PARADISE CLUB. He also adapted the novelist's work for *Frederick Forsyth Presents*.

Smith, Ray

(1936–91)

Welsh actor, much seen on TV from the 1960s. Coming as he did from mining stock himself, it seemed appropriate that he appeared in SAM (collier George Barraclough) and played punch-drunk boxer Dai Bando in the BBC's 1976 adaptation of *How Green was My Valley*. As DI Firbank, Smith was partner to Frank Marker in PUBLIC EYE, and he was also seen as Albert Mundy in WE'LL MEET AGAIN and Sir Bert in the sitcom *Struggle*, although it is as Chief Supt. Gordon Spikings, the bawling boss of DEMPSEY AND MAKEPEACE, that he will be best remembered. His last screen appearance came in BBC 2's version of *The Old Devils*. Smith's career also took in series like Z CARS, A FAMILY AT WAR, CALLAN, GIDEON'S WAY and FLYING LADY and such dramas as BILL BRAND, ROGUE MALE, *The Sailor's Return*, THE HILLS OF HEAVEN and MASADA.

Smith and Jones

See *Alas Smith and Jones.*

Smoking Room, The ✶✶

UK (BBC) Situation Comedy. BBC 2 2004; 2006
DVD: BBC

Barry	**Jeremy Swift**
Robin	**Robert Webb**
Clint	**Fraser Ayres**
Lillian	**Paula Wilcox**
Annie	**Debbie Chazen**
Janet	**Selina Griffiths**
Len	**Leslie Schofield**
Sally	**Nadine Marshall**
Sharon	**Siobhan Redmond**
Gordon	**Mike Walling**
Heidi	**Emma Kennedy**

Creator/Writer **Brian Dooley**
Producer **Pete Thornton**

A group of office workers spend their break times in a designated smoking room.

Creator Brian Dooley claimed personal experience in developing this low-key office comedy. When he was in his 20s, he spent many a long hour whiling away the hours in company smoke rooms (the nicotine-stained, fuggy segregated areas where the tobacco addicted can light up). His jobs were boring, but the people he met and watched during their cigarette breaks provided plenty of material for his big writing break (originally conceived as a series of ten-minute sketches).

Not much happens in this particular smoking room. The usual topics for discussion are sex, television, personal progress within the firm, plus the usual office banalities and gossip, but each character brings his or her own colour to the party. There's Barry, a rather sad, divorced crossword puzzler; Annie a promiscuous attention seeker; Len, the blasphemous security man; Clint, the inept maintenance man; and thrice-married, confident Gordon. There's also boring Heidi, who is just back from maternity leave and devoted to husband Keith; Lillian, a very happily divorced middle-ager looking for a new Mr Right; Robin, who is bored with his job and has a secret crush on post room boy Ben; shirty, plain-speaking Sally; work-focused boss Sharon; and Janet, who is disillusioned with her lot as Sharon's PA. Between them they make issues such as the shortage of gas in pocket lighters and the long-forgotten music to THE LITTLE HOUSE ON THE PRAIRIE matters of major concern.

Filmed with no laugh track, *The Smoking Room* aired first on BBC 3 before terrestrial broadcasts on BBC 2. An eight-part first series was followed by a Christmas special in 2004 and a second series of eight programmes in 2005.

Smuggler/Adventurer ✶✶

UK (*Smuggler*: Gatetarn/HTV; *Adventurer*: Gatetarn/Thames/TV New Zealand) Drama. ITV 1981/1987

Jack Vincent	**Oliver Tobias**
Sarah Morton	**Lesley Dunlop** *(Smuggler)*
Honesty Evans	**Hywel Williams Ellis** *(Smuggler)*
Capt. Walter König	**Peter Capell** *(Smuggler)*
Silas Kemble	**George Murcell** *(Smuggler)*
William Kemble	**Simon Rouse** *(Smuggler)*
Jacob	**Michael O'Hagan** *(Smuggler)*
Lt. Anderson	**Paul Gittins** *(Adventurer)*
Pat Cassidy	**Peter Hambleton** *(Adventurer)*
George Mason	**Marshall Napier** *(Adventurer)*
Maru	**Temuera Morrison** *(Adventurer)*
Li	**Peter Chin** *(Adventurer)*

Creators **Richard Carpenter, Paul Knight, Sidney Cole**
Executive Producers **Patrick Dromgoole** *(Smuggler)*, **John McRae** *(Adventurer)*
Producers **Paul Knight, Sidney Cole**

Tales of a 19th-century smuggler.

Jack Vincent was once a naval officer; now, in 1802, he is a smuggler, plying his illegal trade across the English Channel. The business is fraught with danger, not only from the excise men who patrol the patch but also from other rebels like the infamous Kemble Gang. But Vincent is brave, clever and a fine seaman. Among his allies are Honesty Evans, Sarah Morton and Sarah's grandfather, Captain König. The 13-part saga ends with Vincent unjustly accused of the murder of a Revenue officer, but his story is continued in a sequel, *Adventurer* (shown six years later). In this follow-up, Vincent instigates a mutiny, escapes from a ship bound for the penal colonies and sails the South Seas in search of plunder, pursued by his nemesis, Lt. Anderson. Among the writers involved were co-creator Richard Carpenter, plus Bob Baker and John Kane.

Snow, Jon

(Jonathan Snow; 1947–)

Award-winning, Sussex-born newscaster, a former IRN/LBC radio news reporter who joined ITN in 1976. He became its Washington correspondent in 1983 and was later its diplomatic correspondent, before taking over as anchor for *Channel 4 News* on the departure of Peter Sissons in 1989. Snow also presented the travelogue *Jon Snow Cycles Italy*. He is the cousin of fellow journalist Peter Snow.

Snow, Peter

CBE (1938–)

Dublin-born journalist and presenter, working for many years on NEWSNIGHT and the BBC's election coverages (complete with 'swingometer') and then moving on to TOMORROW'S WORLD in 1997. While preparing a report for the science show, he was almost killed in a light aircraft crash in the USA. He later presented *Battlefield Britain* and *Whose Britain is It Anyway?* with his son, Dan Snow. Snow was formerly a reporter and newscaster for ITN, which he joined in 1962. He is the cousin of newscaster Jon Snow.

Snow Goose, The ✶✶✶

UK/US (BBC/Universal) Drama. BBC 2 1971

Philip Rhayader	**Richard Harris**
Fritha	**Jenny Agutter**
Narrator	**Gary Watson**

Writer **Paul Gallico**
Producer **Frank O'Connor**

Concern for an injured bird brings a young girl and a reclusive artist together.

Billed as *Paul Gallico's The Snow Goose*, and adapted by the author from his own novel published in 1941, this 55-minute drama was one of the highlights of the BBC's 1971 Christmas season. It features 15-year-old orphan Fritha, who, in the 1930s, as war looms, finds friendship with artist Philip Rhayader, a crippled loner who lives in a lighthouse in the Great Marsh on the Essex coast. The kindness they jointly show to the local wildlife – and in particular a sick snow goose – brings them together at a time of increasing hostility in the world. Wildlife paintings by Peter Scott are used in this moving production, along with music by Carl Davies. Patrick Garland directs. The drama was broadcast as part of NBC's *Hallmark Hall of Fame* in the USA. Star Jenny Agutter was also cast in a new film version that was in production in 2005.

Snowman, The ★★★

UK (Snowman Enterprises) Cartoon. Channel 4 1982

Executive Producer **Iain Harvey**
Producer **John Coates**

● ***A snowman takes a small boy off into a magical world.***

This dreamy animation in subdued pastel colours, a perennial favourite at Christmas, was based on the book of drawings by Raymond Briggs. Briggs claimed that one particularly heavy snowfall, and the bright, tranquil world it created, had inspired him to compose his picture story of a young boy who wakes excitedly to see the new fall of snow. Rushing out to the garden, he builds a snowman that comes to life the following night and takes the boy on a magical ride through the sky. (Adding a Christmas dimension, the film-makers extended the flight up to the North Pole for an encounter with Father Christmas.) The next morning the boy wakes to find his new friend has melted in the thaw. The 30-minute film echoes the wordless book by shunning dialogue, emotion expressed only by atmospheric music from Howard Blake, the highspot being the song 'Walking in the Air' (performed not by Aled Jones, who took the song into the top five in 1985, but by chorister Peter Auty with the backing of the Sinfonia of London, whose version was also a minor hit in 1985 and 1987).

So Haunt Me ★★

UK (Cinema Verity) Situation Comedy. BBC 1 1992–4

Yetta Feldman .... **Miriam Karlin**
Sally Rokeby .... **Tessa Peake-Jones**
Pete Rokeby .... **George Costigan**
Tammy Rokeby .... **Laura Simmons/Howard**
David Rokeby .... **Jeremy Green**
Mr Bloom .... **David Graham**
Carole Dawlish .... **Julia Deakin**

Creator/Writer **Paul A. Mendelson**
Producers **Caroline Gold, Sharon Bloom**

● ***A family discover their new home is haunted by a Jewish ghost.***

When Pete Rokeby throws in his job as an advertising executive to concentrate on full-time writing, he and his family aim to keep their overheads low by moving house, from an upmarket neighbourhood to a dowdy street. Their new home, they quickly discover, is prone to icy blasts, bumps in the night and, strangely, a lingering smell of chicken soup – all down to the ghost of one-time resident Yetta Feldman. Ever since her death (choking on a chicken bone), Yetta's spirit has driven away everyone who has taken over her home, but the Rokebys prove to be different. Gradually making herself visible to them one by one, Yetta becomes a nagging grandmother to kids Tammy and David, and an annoying cuckoo to Pete and his beleaguered wife, Sally. All the same, the family sort of adopt the old lady and help find her long-lost daughter ('Carole, with an E'). Yetta's Jewish mothering instincts are brought to the fore again later, when Sally gives birth to a new baby. Also seen is Mr Bloom, the Rokebys' melancholy neighbour.

Creator Paul A. Mendelson drew partly on autobiographical experiences when working on this comedy. He, too, was once in advertising and left to pursue a writing career. With hits like MAY TO DECEMBER and *So Haunt Me*, he was clearly more successful than Pete Rokeby. Actress Laura Howard, who played Tammy, was originally billed under her real name of Laura Simmons when the series began.

So You Think You've Got Troubles ★★

UK (Alomo) Situation Comedy. BBC 1 1991

Ivan Fox .... **Warren Mitchell**
Charley Adamson .... **James Ellis**
George Nathan .... **Harry Towb**
Anne Adamson .... **Linda Wray**
Roberta Nathan .... **Stella McCusker**
Louise Nathan .... **Emer Gillespie**
Sean Doherty .... **John Keegan**

Writers **Laurence Marks, Maurice Gran**
Producer **Tara Prem**

● ***A Jew is caught up in the Northern Ireland troubles.***

Ivan Fox is a widower who has worked happily for many years as the manager of a pipe tobacco factory in north London. Then, one day, he is relocated to Belfast. Ivan is a Jew by birth, but has long since lapsed from his faith, and his new home, he discovers, is a place in which there is no hiding place from religion. Here, the dwindling and outnumbered Jewish community is desperate to welcome him into their fold, which means he reluctantly has to confront his religious responsibilities while all around him the dispute between Protestants and Catholics rages on. Other characters include bigoted factory worker Charley Adamson, a Loyalist. Creators Maurice Gran and Laurence Marks admitted that this was a tricky series to write, because of the sensitivities of local citizens. Building plots, as they did, around protection rackets, bomb alerts and road blocks could not have made their task easier, but six episodes were produced.

Soap ★★★

US (Witt-Thomas-Harris) Situation Comedy. ITV 1978–82
(US: ABC 1977–81)

Jessica Tate .... **Katherine Helmond**
Chester Tate .... **Robert Mandan**
Corrine Tate .... **Diana Canova**
Eunice Tate .... **Jennifer Salt**
Billy Tate .... **Jimmy Baio**
Benson Dubois .... **Robert Guillaume**
Grandpa Tate ('The Major') .... **Arthur Peterson**
Mary Dallas Campbell .... **Cathryn Damon**
Burt Campbell .... **Richard Mulligan**

Jodie Dallas	**Billy Crystal**
Danny Dallas	**Ted Wass**
The Godfather	**Richard Libertini**
Claire	**Kathryn Reynolds**
Peter Campbell	**Robert Urich**
Chuck Campbell	**Jay Johnson**
Dennis Phillips	**Bob Seagren**
Father Timothy Flotsky	**Sal Viscuso**
Carol David	**Rebecca Balding**
Elaine Lefkowitz	**Dinah Manoff**
Dutch	**Donnelly Rhodes**
Sally	**Caroline McWilliams**
Det. Donahue	**John Byner**
Polly Dawson	**Lynne Moody**
Saunders	**Roscoe Lee Browne**
Carlos 'El Puerco' Valdez	**Gregory Sierra**
Announcer	**Rod Roddy**

Creator/Writer/Producer **Susan Harris**
Executive Producers **Tony Thomas, Paul Junger Witt**

Parody of US daytime soap opera, featuring two related families.

The Campbells and the Tates live in the town of Dunn's River, Connecticut. Jessica Tate and Mary Campbell are sisters but, otherwise, the families have little in common, for the Tates are wealthy and live in a mansion and the Campbells are working class and live on the other side of town. Their day-to-day lives are depicted in serial form, just like an American soap opera, but the events are always hugely exaggerated.

These families certainly have their problems. Each member has a hang-up of some kind. Jessica is married to Chester Tate, a wealthy but untrustworthy stockbroker, and they have three troublesome children. Corrine is their flirtatious daughter, Eunice is involved with a married senator, and then there is their 14-year-old adolescent brat, Billy. The household is completed by Jessica's father, the Major, whose mind is still in World War II. They are all looked after by an obnoxious black manservant, Benson, who refuses to cook anything he dislikes himself. When he leaves to star in his own spin-off series, *Benson*, he is replaced by a new butler, Saunders.

Mary lives with her impotent second husband, Burt, a nervous wreck who struggles to control his wayward stepsons, Jodie, a transvestite, and delinquent Danny, who finds himself involved with the Mob. Burt also has two sons from his previous marriage: Chuck, who thinks his ventriloquist dummy, Bob, is real, and Peter, an amorous tennis coach who is murdered in the shower.

Even before it reached the screens, *Soap* invited a torrent of criticism by pre-publicizing its open treatment of taboo issues, especially extra-marital sex, homosexuality, racism, religion and terminal illness. But, when the producers promised to tone things down a little, and the first episodes were actually seen in all their overplayed glory, criticism subsided. All the same, *Soap*'s storylines still meandered between uncomfortable topics such as divorce, voyeurism, irresponsible affairs, illegitimate children and cold-blooded murders. It also touched on cloning, abduction by aliens, and even the seduction of a priest and the exorcism of a baby.

Soap Opera

The tag given to open-ended, long-running, mainly domestic dramas involving a stable cast of characters, usually of middle- or working-class background. Each episode generally involves a number of continuous storylines at various stages of development.

The term derives from 1930s American radio, when soap and detergent companies used to sponsor the 15-minute radio series that ran daily to fill the daytime schedules. In these dramas, everyday problems assumed crisis proportions and dialogue easily outstripped action. With the arrival of television as a mass medium in the 1950s, the format transferred to the screen, although programmes now ran for 30 minutes. Soap manufacturers remained heavily involved. Procter & Gamble even set up a TV studio to produce its own.

Britain's first attempt at TV soap opera – if you discount the children's drama THE APPLEYARDS that ran from 1952 – was THE GROVE FAMILY, on BBC in 1954. Of course, the detergent makers had no involvement and, unlike many of their successors, the Groves didn't last long – a mere three years. With the birth of commercial television in 1955, Britain was treated to its first daily soap, SIXPENNY CORNER, the everyday story of a garage, run by Bill and Sally Norton in a new town called Springwood. EMERGENCY – WARD 10 added a medical dimension in 1957, but it wasn't until 1960 that the soap concept really took off in the UK, with the arrival of CORONATION STREET. Even then, the *Street* – like *The Grove Family* and *Ward 10* screened only twice a week – was not a soap in the truest sense. Nearer was CROSSROADS, transmitted five days a week from 1964, until the IBA eventually cut it back to three.

The mundane nature of the soap opera has been pushed aside since the late 1970s. The arrival of DALLAS, DYNASTY and other glitzy offerings, shot like small feature films, gave rise to the 'supersoap', where the action took place on quite another plane from the down-to-earth world of the original soaps. British versions have also changed their spots. BROOKSIDE and EASTENDERS introduced a new and vigorous reality, and issues like abortion, rape, drug abuse and gruesome murder now pervade many such series. Exceptions are the tame melodramas from Australia (such as NEIGHBOURS and HOME AND AWAY) that have filled UK screens in the afternoons.

Softly, Softly/Softly, Softly – Task Force ★★

UK (BBC) Police Drama. BBC 1 1966–76

Det. Chief Supt. Charlie Barlow	**Stratford Johns**
DCI/Det. Supt./Det. Chief Supt. John Watt	**Frank Windsor**
DS/DI/DCI 'Harry' Hawkins	**Norman Bowler**
PC Henry Snow	**Terence Rigby**
DC 'Reg' Dwyer	**Gilbert Wynne**
ACC Bill Calderwood	**John Welsh**
PC Greenly	**Cavan Kendall**
PC Tanner	**David Quilter**
DC/Insp. Gwyn Lewis	**Garfield Morgan**
Mr Blackitt	**Robert Keegan**
DC Matthew Stone	**Alexis Kanner**
DC Box	**Dan Meaden**
Sgt/DS Evans	**David Lloyd Meredith**
DC Digby	**Gavin Campbell**
Chief Constable Cullen	**Walter Gotell**
ACC Austin Gilbert	**John Barron**
DC Morgan	**Howell Evans**
Policewoman/DS Allin	**Peggy Sinclair**
Chief Constable Calderwood	**John Welsh**
DI Jim Cook	**Philip Brack**
Policewoman/DC Donald	**Susan Tebbs**
Sgt Jackson	**David Allister**

PC Ted Drake .... **Brian Hall**
Policewoman/DC Forest .... **Julie Hallam**
Policewoman/DS Green .... **Heather Stoney**
PC Knowles .... **Martin C. Thurley**
Det. Supt. Adler .... **John Franklyn-Robbins**
PC Nesbitt .... **Grahame Mallard**
DS Stirling .... **Warren Clarke**
PC Dodds .... **Nigel Humphreys**
PC Perry .... **Malcolm Rennie**
PC Lincoln .... **Peter Clough**
DS Grant .... **Peter Childs**
PC Pearson .... **John Flanagan**

Creator **Elwyn Jones**
Producers **David E. Rose, Leonard Lewis, Geraint Morris**

● ***The further cases of detectives Barlow and Watt.***

One of the most successful spin-offs ever, *Softly, Softly* ran for ten years in parallel with Z CARS, its mother series. It takes up the story of the 'nasty and nice' double act of Barlow and Watt, after they leave Newtown and head south to the fictional region of Wyvern (somewhere near Bristol). Promoted to the ranks of detective chief superintendent and detective chief inspector respectively, one of the first people they encounter is their retired former desk sergeant, Blackitt (now a newsagent), and his dog, Pandy. Among their new colleagues are jovial Welshman Sgt Evans, miserable dog-handler PC Henry Snow (and his most famous charge, Inky) and a local detective inspector, Harry Hawkins. The show's title was derived from the adage 'Softly, softly, catchee monkey'.

In 1969 *Softly, Softly* became the more cumbersome *Softly, Softly – Task Force* and saw Barlow and Watt working for Thamesford Constabulary's CID Task Force. In 1969 Barlow went his own way, branching out into BARLOW AT LARGE/BARLOW. He was reunited with Watt, however, for a novel reinvestigation of the Jack the Ripper case in 1973 and a subsequent series, SECOND VERDICT, in 1976, which looked at other such mysteries.

Soldier, Soldier ★★

UK (Central) Drama. ITV 1991–7

Major Tom Cadman .... **David Haig**
Laura Cadman .... **Cathryn Harrison**
L/Cpl/Cpl/Sgt Paddy Garvey .... **Jerome Flynn**
Cpl/Sgt Nancy Thorpe/Garvey RMP .... **Holly Aird**
CSM Chick Henwood .... **Sean Baker**
Colour Sgt Ian Anderson .... **Robert Glenister**
Cpl/Sgt Tony Wilton .... **Gary Love**
Lt. Nick Pasco .... **Peter Wingfield**
Fusilier/Lance Cpl Dave Tucker .... **Robson Green**
Lt. Col. Dan Fortune .... **Miles Anderson**
Carol Anderson .... **Melanie Kilburn**
Juliet Grant .... **Susan Franklyn**
Joy Wilton .... **Annabelle Apsion**
Donna Tucker .... **Rosie Rowell**
2nd Lt./Lt./Capt. Kate Butler ... **Lesley Vickerage**
Sgt Sally Hawkins .... **Debra Beaumont**
Sheena Bowles .... **Lena Headey**
Sgt Dennis Ryan .... **Colin Salmon**
Major Bob Cochrane .... **Simon Donald**
Fusilier 'Midnight' Rawlins ..... **Mo Sesay**
Fusilier Jimmy Monroe .... **Ian Dunn**
Rachel Elliot/Fortune .... **Lesley Manville**
Padre Simon Armstrong .... **Richard Hampton**
2nd Lt. Alex Pereira .... **Angus MacFadyen**
Lt. Col. Mark Osbourne .... **Patrick Drury**
Capt./Major Kieran Voce .... **Dorian Healy**
CSM/Lt. Michael Stubbs .... **Rob Spendlove**
Marsha Stubbs .... **Denise Welch**
Fusilier Luke Roberts .... **Akim Mogaji**
Bernie Roberts .... **Rakie Ayola**
Lt. Col. Nicolas Hammond ...... **Robert Gwilym**
Major Tim Radley .... **Adrian Rawlins**
Sandra Radley .... **Suzanne Burden**
Lt. Col. Ian Jennings .... **John Bowe**
Isabelle Jennings .... **Gabrielle Reidy**
Fusilier Eddie Nelson .... **Paterson Joseph**
Tracy Whitwell .... **Kelly Deeley**
Major James McCudden .... **John McGlynn**
Lt./Capt. Jeremy Forsythe .... **Ben Nealon**
Lilian Malanjie/Forsythe .... **Nthati Moshesh**
Fusilier/Sgt. Joe Farrell .... **David Groves**
Colette Daly .... **Angela Clarke**
Cpl. William Markham .... **Razaaq Adoti**
Fusilier Andy Butcher .... **Danny Cunningham**
L/Cpl Steve Evans .... **Shaun Dingwall**
Capt. Sadie Williams .... **Sophie Dix**
Sgt Brad Connor .... **Richard Dillane**
Major Rory Taylor .... **Dougray Scott**
Lt. Col. Paul Phillips .... **Duncan Bell**
Fusilier Mel Briggs .... **Simon Sherlock**
Deborah Osbourne/Briggs ...... **Laura Howard**
Cpl Mark Hobbs .... **Ian Curtis**
Cate Hobbs .... **Kate Ashfield**
Pte Stacey Grey/Butcher .... **Kate O'Malley**
Sgt Chris McCleod .... **Jonathan Guy Lewis**
Sgt Angela McCleod .... **Fiona Bell**
Major Tim Forrester .... **James Callis**
2nd Lt. Samantha Sheridan .... **Biddy Hodson**
Lt. Col. Mike Eastwood .... **Philip Bowen**
Dr Sarah Eastwood .... **Alison Skilbeck**
Fusilier Jacko Barton .... **Thomas Craig**
Fusilier Tony Rossi .... **Chris Gascoyne**
Lt. Col. Philip Drysdale .... **James Cosmo**
Major Jessica Bailey .... **Lucy Cohu**
CSM Alan Fitzpatrick .... **Conor Mullen**
Karen Fitzpatrick .... **Joanna Phillips-Lane**
Julie Oldroyd .... **Michelle Butterly**

Creator **Lucy Gannon**
Producers **Chris Kelly, Christopher Neame, Ann Tricklebank**

● ***The rigours of an army career and its effect on personal lives.***

Soldier, Soldier focuses on the men and women of the King's Own Fusiliers Infantry Regiment as they tour the world on active and inactive duty. The first episode sees them return to their Midlands base from a six-month tour of duty in Northern Ireland. Later series follow them to Hong Kong, New Zealand, Germany, Bosnia, Cyprus, Australia and Africa, as well as guard duty at the royal palaces in the UK. In addition to the tough routine of army life, the series examines the camaraderie of the force and witnesses the stresses and strains such an existence places on the personal lives of soldiers and their families. New additions to the battalion arrive every series as some members quit or are tragically killed. Among the most memorable characters are Paddy Garvey; his military policewoman girlfriend, Nancy Thorpe; his hapless mate, Dave Tucker; Tucker's unfaithful wife, Donna; and the ill-fated Tony Wilton.

Solo ✶✶

UK (BBC) Situation Comedy. BBC 1 1981–2

Gemma Palmer .... **Felicity Kendal**
Danny .... **Stephen Moore**
Mrs Palmer .... **Elspet Gray**
Gloria .... **Susan Bishop**
Sebastian .... **Michael Howe**

Creator/Writer **Carla Lane**
Producer **Gareth Gwenlan**

● ***A 30-year-old woman goes it alone.***
Discovering that her live-in boyfriend, Danny, has been having an affair with her best friend, Gloria, Gemma Palmer decides to reassert her independence. She turfs Danny out of her flat and her life, breaks off relations with Gloria and, for good measure, resigns from her job. Going solo is not without its problems, however, but thankfully Gemma's supportive mum is usually at hand in times of crisis. In the second series, Danny has left the scene for good and Gemma has gained a new platonic friend, Sebastian.

Some Mothers Do 'Ave 'Em ✶✶✶

UK (BBC) Situation Comedy. BBC 1 1973–5; 1978

Frank Spencer .... **Michael Crawford**
Betty Spencer .... **Michele Dotrice**
Mr Lewis .... **Glynn Edwards**

Writer **Raymond Allen**
Producers **Michael Mills, Sydney Lotterby**

● ***A kind-hearted but naïve simpleton courts disaster at every turn.***
Frank Spencer is an accident waiting to happen. Sporting a knitted tank-top, unfashionable long mac and a beret, wherever he goes he brings chaos and confusion. DIY jobs result in the systematic destruction of his house while, at work (whenever he finds any), machinery explodes and his bosses despair. And yet poor Frank, with his infantile voice, unfortunate turn of phrase, expressive shoulder-twitches and hurt looks, always tries hard and means well. He is gravely offended by criticism and deeply shocked at everything untoward. At his side through thick and thin are his over-loyal wife, Betty, and baby daughter, Jessica. Mr Lewis, the irascible neighbour seen in the last series, is just one of Frank's many adversaries.

Some Mothers Do 'Ave 'Em made a star out of Michael Crawford, but the actor worked hard for his success. His characterization was so precise that it kept impressionists in gags for years after. He also chipped in with occasional ad-libs, plotted the stories for some episodes and even performed many of his own stunts that included driving a car halfway over a cliff, and narrowly escaping a collapsing chimney stack. Series creator Raymond Allen was working as a cinema cleaner on the Isle of Wight when he began writing the scripts.

Somerville, Geraldine
(1967–)

Red-haired, Irish-born actress best recalled as 'Panhandle' in Cracker. Her other credits have included the roles of Bridget Millican in CATHERINE COOKSON*'s The Black Velvet Gown*, Deborah Bennett in *Heaven on Earth*, Lady Emily in ARISTOCRATS, Val McArdale in *Daylight Robbery*, Sam Graham in *The Safe House* and Olivia in *Jilting Jo*, as well as parts in CASUALTY, AGATHA CHRISTIE'S POIROT, *Romeo and Juliet*, MURDER IN MIND, JERICHO, and *Performance's The Deep Blue Sea* (Ann Welch) and *After Miss Julie* (title role).

Somerville, Julia
(1947–)

British journalist and news presenter, who joined the BBC as a sub-editor in 1973 after working on magazines, and who went on to become labour affairs correspondent and then, from 1984, to anchor *The Nine O'Clock News*. She was poached by ITN in 1987, for whom she was one of the mainstays of NEWS *at Ten*. She has also hosted the current affairs series *3D*.

Sometime, Never ✶✶

UK (Witzend) Situation Comedy. ITV 1996

Maxine 'Max' Bailey .... **Sara Crowe**
Bernice .... **Ann Bryson**
Ian .... **Harry Burton**
Louise .... **Lucinda Fisher**
Kev .... **John Hodgkinson**
Headmaster .... **Paul Chapman**

Writer **Jenny Lecoat**
Producers **Tony Charles, Jamie Rix**

● ***Two girlfriends try to make sense of their disparate lives.***
Max and Bernice are a couple of long-time friends in their early 30s who now need each other more than ever. Blonde Max is a teacher at an urban comprehensive, but feels that there ought to be more to her life than this. Liberal-minded and always a romantic, she'd love to settle down with her boyfriend, Ian, but the opportunity doesn't seem to be coming her way because he's too busy with his work. Brunette Bernice, on the other hand, has been settled down for too long. She has two kids, a wet husband and is bored stiff by her lot. Luckily, Max has a flat in Bernice's house, so they always have each other's shoulders to cry on – usually over a bottle of cooking sherry. *Sometime, Never* was developed out of a *Comedy First* pilot episode screened in 1995 (in which Max's headmaster was played by Saeed Jaffrey), but the seven-part series was built on the success stars Sara Crowe and Ann Bryson had enjoyed as dim secretaries in commercials for Philadelphia cheese. The snappy dialogue was penned by stand-up comedian Jenny Lecoat.

Songs of Praise ✶✶

UK (BBC) Religion. BBC 1 1961–

Creator **Donald Baverstock**

● ***Television's longest-running religious programme.***
A well-rehearsed combination of hymns, prayers, blessings and inspirational interviews, *Songs of Praise* has been an integral part of Sunday evenings for more than 40 years. A different venue has hosted proceedings each week and efforts have been made to reflect all denominations and all parts of the UK (and sometimes overseas). The first transmission came from the Tabernacle Baptist Chapel in Cardiff.

The programme's presenters have been many and diverse. In recent years they have included Cliff Michelmore, Pam Rhodes, Debbie Thrower, Roger Royle, Sally Magnusson, Gloria

Hunniford, Alan Titchmarsh, Hugh Scully, Steve Chalke, Harry Secombe, Deborah McAndrew, Diane Louise Jordan, Stephanie Hughes, Aled Jones, Huw Edwards, Jonathan Edwards and Eamonn Holmes, with Cliff Richard, Russell Harty, Jimmy Savile and even Eddie Waring listed among one-time hosts.

Sooty

See *Corbett, Harry.*

Sopranos, The ★★★★

US (Chase Films/Brillstein-Grey/HBO) Drama. Channel 4 1999–2004 (US: HBO 1999–2002; 2004; 2006–)

Anthony 'Tony' Soprano	**James Gandolfini**
Dr Jennifer Melfi	**Lorraine Bracco**
Carmela Soprano	**Edie Falco**
Meadow Soprano	**Jamie-Lynn Sigler**
Anthony Soprano Jr	**Robert Iler**
Livia Soprano	**Nancy Marchand**
Christopher Moltisanti	**Michael Imperioli**
Corrado Enrico ('Uncle Junior') Soprano	**Dominic Chianese**
Arthur 'Artie' Bucco	**John Ventimiglia**
Sal 'Big Pussy' Bonpensiero	**Vincent Pastore**
Silvio Dante	**Steven Van Zandt**
Peter Paul Gualtieri ('Paulie Walnuts')	**Tony Sirico**
Irina	**Oksana Babiy**
Herman 'Hesh' Rabkin	**Jerry Adler**
Father Phil	**Paul Schulze**
Adriana La Cerva	**Drea De Matteo**
Jimmy Altieri	**Joseph Badalucco Jr**
Janice Soprano	**Aida Turturro**
Richie Aprile	**David Proval**
Jackie Aprile Jr	**Jason Cerbone**
Charmaine Bucco	**Katherine Narducci**
Furio Giunta	**Federico Castelluccio**
Gabriella Dante	**Maureen Van Zandt**
Gloria Trillo	**Annabella Sciorra**
Dr Elliot Kupferberg	**Peter Bogdanovic**
Ralph Cifaretto	**Joe Pantoliano**
Gigi Cestone	**Jon Fiore**
Rosalie Aprile	**Sharon Angela**
Bobby 'Baccala' Baccalieri	**Steven R. Schirripa**
Patsy Parisi	**Dan Grimaldi**
Vito Spatafore	**Joseph R. Gannascoli**
Eugene Pontecorvo	**Robert Funaro**
Benny Fazio	**Max Casella**
Carmine Lupertazzi	**Tony Lip**
Little Carmine Lupertazzi	**Ray Abruzzo**
Little Paulie Germani	**Carl Capotorto**
Tony Blundetto	**Steve Buscemi**
Michele 'Feech' La Manna	**Robert Loggia**
Johnny 'Sack' Sacramoni	**Vince Curatola**
Phil Leotardo	**Frank Vincent**

Creator **David Chase**
Executive Producers **David Chase, Mitchell Burgess, Robin Green, Brad Grey, Ilene S. Landress, Terence Winter**

● ***The troubled life of a middle-aged mobster.***

Tony Soprano is the head of a waste-management company – on the face of it. In truth, he's a big cheese in the New Jersey mafia. Unfortunately, all the extortion, racketeering, violence and inter-gang rivalries are driving him nuts and giving him panic attacks. That's why he signs up with analyst Dr Jennifer Melfi, a sassy shrink who attempts to unpick his confused mind while trying desperately to avoid learning facts that she knows would place her in an uncomfortable position. Regrettably, when you're associated with the mob, in even this sort of detached way, life tends to get rather complicated, as Jennifer finds out, especially when her client starts dreaming about her. Tony, meanwhile, has his 'family' to care for – the small core of lieutenants who do his bidding in and around the Bada Bing club, namely Paulie Walnuts, Silvio Dante, 'Big Pussy' Bonpensiero and the psychotically violent Christopher Moltisanti, Tony's own nephew. Then there is the jealous Uncle Junior, with whom Tony vies for control over the district, plus the real family: independent wife Carmela, wayward teenage daughter Meadow, 13-year-old bruiser Anthony, demanding, devious mother Livia (written out after actress Nancy Marchand died) and (later) hippyish, self-centred sister Janice. Add in Tony's Russian mistress, Irina, and no wonder he keeps popping the Prozac. The troubles build in later series when the FBI closes in and veteran gangsters like Tony Blundetto are released from jail.

Despite a ponderous start and the fact it never shirked strong language, racist opinion or graphic violence, *The Sopranos* was an instant hit on both sides of the Atlantic, acclaimed for its dark humour, snappy plot lines, cinematic touch and ability to shock. It even merited a profile on THE SOUTH BANK SHOW in February 2002. The theme song, 'Woke Up This Morning', was by the Alabama Three.

Sorry! ★★★

UK (BBC) Situation Comedy. BBC 1 1981–2; 1985–8

Timothy Lumsden	**Ronnie Corbett**
Mrs Phyllis Lumsden	**Barbara Lott**
Mr Sidney Lumsden	**William Moore**
Muriel	**Marguerite Hardiman**
Kevin	**Derek Fuke**
Frank	**Roy Holder**
Freddie	**Sheila Fearn**
Chris	**Chris Breeze**
Jennifer	**Wendy Allnutt**
Pippa	**Bridget Brice**

Writers **Ian Davidson, Peter Vincent**
Producer **David Askey**

● ***A 40-year-old librarian can't break free from his overpowering mother.***

Short, bespectacled, moped-riding bachelor Timothy Lumsden lives at home in Oxfordshire with his domineering, blue-rinsed mother and his hen-pecked, timid father (if his father hasn't been banished to the shed). Although his sister, Muriel, has married and moved away, Timothy has never had the courage to do so, largely because his mother refuses to let him, not believing he has grown up. She still cajoles him with kiddy talk, badgers him with lick washes, and threatens him with all manner of kiddy treats and punishments. As a result, Timothy is bashful, rather apologetic (hence the programme title) and always a little uncertain in the company of females. He enjoys a few pints down at the pub with his friend Frank, and is well placed in the library where he works, but, whenever the prospect of his leaving the nest materializes, his mother always puts her foot down and ensures he remains firmly tied to her apron-strings.

Timothy certainly does not live at home for the comforts: Mrs Lumsden's cooking is something to avoid, with everything from starters to desserts likely to be curried. Nor is privacy a possibility. Yet it is soon clear that Timothy is as wary of leaving home as his mother is determined to keep him there. And it is this stop-go dash for independence which runs at the heart of the series. *Sorry!* is not entirely dissimilar to an earlier Ronnie Corbett vehicle, NOW LOOK HERE . . .

Soul, David

(David Solberg; 1943–)

Blond American actor/singer, once billed as the Mystery Singer on *The Merv Griffin Show* in the USA, for which he donned a hood. Moving into acting, Soul secured guest parts in various series (including STAR TREK) and minor roles in US shows like *Here Come the Brides* and *Owen Marshall, Counselor at Law*, before getting his big break with the all-action police series STARSKY AND HUTCH, in 1975. As Detective Ken 'Hutch' Hutchinson, Soul became an international star, and this led to another foray into the music world, resulting in two number one hits in the UK ('Don't Give Up on Us' and 'Silver Lady'). He co-hosted the magazine show *Six Fifty-Five Special* (with Sally James) in 1982 and played Rick Blaine in a TV remake of *Casablanca* a year later. He has since taken roles in US series *The Yellow Rose* and *Unsub*, made guest appearances in PERRY MASON, HOLBY CITY, DALZIEL AND PASCOE and AGATHA CHRISTIE'S POIROT, and has been seen in many TV movies. In 2005 he took the title role in the controversial *Jerry Springer: the Opera*.

South Bank Show, The ★★★

UK (LWT) Arts. ITV 1978–

Presenter/Editor **Melvyn Bragg**

Acclaimed Sunday-night arts programme.

The successor to AQUARIUS, *The South Bank Show* picked up where the former left off, thoughtfully and unhurriedly covering all corners of the arts world, from the classical elements through to pop culture. Conducted throughout by Melvyn Bragg, the programme has combined in-depth interviews with studio performances and film profiles, to great effect. The 2005 series, for instance, included features on subjects as varied as Margot Fonteyn, Pete and Dud, and artist Tracey Emin. The theme music has been Julian Lloyd-Webber's *Variations*.

South of the Border ★★

UK (BBC) Detective Drama. BBC 1 1988; 1990

Pearl Parker	**Buki Armstrong**
Finn Gallagher	**Rosie Rowell**
Milly	**Dinah Stabb**
Fitz	**Brian Bovell**
Rose	**Corinne Skinner-Carter**
Rufus	**Valentine Nonyela**
Krish	**James Harkishin**

Creator **Susan Wilkins**
Writers **Susan Wilkins, Tony Dennis, Ayshe Raif, Winsome Pinnock, Kwabena Manso, Barbara Machin, Michael Ellis**
Producer **Caroline Oulton**

The cases of two female private eyes.

Petty thief Finn Gallagher – fresh out of jail after a two-year stretch, but still prone to bouts of shoplifting – joins forces with ambitious black beauty Pearl Parker – a refugee from a disastrous romance – to form a team of female private investigators in this novel detective caper. With occasional help from Pearl's ex-boyfriend, Fitz, who runs a reggae and soul music shop in Deptford High Street, they turn to snooping and sleuthing as a means of staying on the right side of the law. Based in a tower block flat, the girls are offered work by a lawyer friend named Milly, but life is never easy on the mean streets of south-east London (Deptford and the Docklands).

South Park ★★★

US (Comedy Central) Animation. Channel 4 1998–2004 (US: Comedy Central 1997–)

Voices:

Stan Marsh	**Trey Parker**
Kyle Broflovski	**Matt Stone**
Eric Cartman	**Trey Parker**
Kenny McCormick	**Matt Stone**
Chef	**Isaac Hayes**
Mr Hanky	**Trey Parker**
Mr Garrison	**Trey Parker**
Leopold 'Butters' Stotch	**Matt Stone**

Creators **Trey Parker, Matt Stone**
Executive Producers **Trey Parker, Matt Stone, Anne Garefino, Deborah Liebling**

Crude (in more than one sense) animation, featuring the pupils of a Colorado school.

A new era in adult animation arrived with *South Park*. It took the provocative nature of THE SIMPSONS and advanced it a mile or two with its depiction of a bunch of vulgar kids (round-headed, quirky figures) who attend school in a snow-bound, little American town called South Park. The main characters are level-headed Stan, Jewish Kyle, fat bully Cartman and Kenny – a shy, parka-wearing character that is fated to die in every episode (to the catchphrase cry: 'Oh my God, they killed Kenny!'), usually by the most grotesque methods (ranging from Ozzy Osbourne biting off his head to the *Mir* space station crashing onto him). Also seen are Mr Hanky (a turd), teacher Mr Garrison (who toys with a hand puppet) and the school's Chef (bass-voiced by soulster Isaac Hayes). Most of the dialogue and humour is focused on bodily functions and sex, bad language is the norm and taboos are broken at every turn. All the same, guest stars have queued up to provide their voices, including Elton John, Meatloaf, Jennifer Aniston and George Clooney, who barked for a gay dog.

In the UK, the series debuted on Sky One before being picked up for terrestrial airing by Channel 4. A feature film, *South Park: Bigger, Longer, Uncut*, was released in 1999.

South Riding ★★★

UK (Yorkshire) Drama. ITV 1974

Sarah Burton	**Dorothy Tutin**
Councillor Robert Carne	**Nigel Davenport**
Alderman Mrs Beddows	**Hermione Baddeley**
Midge Carne	**Judi Bowker**
Revd Millward Peckover	**Norman Scace**
Councillor Alfred E. Huggins	**Clive Swift**
Lydia Holly	**Lesley Dunlop**
Fred Mitchell	**Milton Johns**
Alderman Astell	**Norman Jones**

Writer **Stan Barstow**

Producer **James Ormerod**

● ***A teacher finds it tough going in the poverty-stricken 1930s.***

This 13-part adaptation of Winifred Holtby's novel is set in 1932, in the fictitious South Riding of Yorkshire. It tells of a progressive schoolmistress, Sarah Burton (head of Kipling Girls High School), who finds her plans for her pupils hindered by injustices in society. Also particularly prominent are Alderman Mrs Beddows and Councillor Robert Carne. The series was repeated on Channel 4 in 1987.

Southern Television

Southern was the ITV contractor for the South of England from 30 August 1958 until 31 December 1981, when its franchise was taken over by TVS. There was, however, considerable surprise, if not shock and fury, at the decision of the IBA to terminate Southern's licence, as the company had a good record in local programming and was also a more than useful contributor to the ITV network. Its national offerings included drama series like WINSTON CHURCHILL – THE WILDERNESS YEARS and the quiz show WHEEL OF FORTUNE, but it was through children's programmes that Southern gained particular respect. FREEWHEELERS, BRIGHT'S BOFFINS, *The Saturday Banana*, RUNAROUND, HOW!, LITTLE BIG TIME and WORZEL GUMMIDGE were just some of the company's many contributions to children's viewing. In addition to its programming record, Southern had never been formally criticized by the IBA, except for some concern over the make-up of the company (62.5 per cent was owned jointly by Associated Newspapers Group and D. C. Thomson), and its perceived weak coverage in certain parts of Kent. Southern believed the latter wasn't entirely its problem since the IBA had ordered key transmitters in the area to broadcast signals from London instead of Southern's. It was interesting to note that when the new franchise was awarded to TVS, the official name of the transmission area was changed from South of England to South and South-East of England (thereby, perhaps, upholding Southern's argument).

Space [1] ✶✶

US (Dick Berg/Stonehenge/Paramount) Science Fiction. ITV 1987 (US: CBS 1985)

Norman Grant	**James Garner**
Elinor Grant	**Susan Anspach**
John Pope	**Harry Hamlin**
Penny Hardesty/Pope	**Blair Brown**
Stanley Mott	**Bruce Dern**
Rachel Mott	**Melinda Dillon**
Martin Scorcella/Leopold Strabismus	**David Dukes**
Dieter Kolff	**Michael York**
Liesl Kolff	**Barbara Sukowa**
Randy Claggett	**Beau Bridges**
Debbie Dee Claggett	**Stephanie Faracy**
Senator Glancey	**Martin Balsam**
Finnerty	**James Sutorius**
Tucker Thomas	**G. D. Spradlin**
Cindy Rhee	**Maggie Han**
Funkhauser	**Wolf Kahler**
Marcia Grant	**Jennifer Runyon**
Skip Morgan	**David Spielberg**
Paul Stidham	**Ralph Bellamy**

Writers **Dick Berg, Stirling Silliphant**
Executive Producer **Dick Berg**
Producer **Martin Manulis**

● ***Dramatization of the race into space.***

This 13-hour mini-series relates the story of America's space programme, using the lives of fictional characters to reveal the real stresses and strains brought about by the space effort. Picking up from the end of World War II, it focuses on the battle between the Americans and the Russians for Nazi Germany's top rocket specialists. It continues through US political wrangles in the 1950s to the foundation of NASA and its subsequent space race successes, including the spectacular trips to the moon. Its lead characters are naval-hero-turned-senator Norman Grant; his alcoholic wife, Elinor; her devious lover, Leopold Strabismus (a TV evangelist whose real name is Martin Scorcella); and Penny Pope, Norman's mistress, an ambitious lawyer with the Senate Space Committee. Also prominent are muck-raking reporter Cindy Rhee, German rocket scientist Dieter Kolff and dedicated astrophysicist Stanley Mott, with former Korean War pilots John Pope (Penny's husband) and Randy Claggett taking the honours as the astronauts on the lunar project. The series was based on James A. Michener's novel of the same title and cost a staggering £35 million to make. Sadly, its audience figures never justified the expense.

Space [2] ✶✶✶

UK (BBC/TLC) Documentary. BBC 1 2001

Presenter **Sam Neill**

Executive Producers **Phil Dollins, Emma Swain**
Producers **Richard Burke-Ward, Jeremy Turner, Luke Campbell**

● ***Beginner's guide to the wonders of the universe.***

Jurassic Park star Sam Neill hosts this six-part populist science show, leading viewers out beyond the big blue Earth and into the depths of savage space. Employing state-of-the-art computer graphics to bring the cosmos to life, the series starts with the evolution of the universe after the Big Bang, considers asteroid and meteorite strikes on our planet and examines the mystery of black holes. It then speculates about the possibility of alien life, suggests a way forward for when the Earth is swallowed up by our dying sun, and even flirts with science fiction in examining wormholes and ion drives as methods of travelling swiftly across the galaxies. Archive film footage of space missions and interviews with eminent scientists are cut into natural footage shot in the varied climates of New Zealand to provide a very colourful, if at times deliberately simplistic, introduction to the wonders of space.

Space: Above and Beyond ✶✶

US (Hard Eight/Twentieth Century-Fox) Science Fiction. BBC 2 1997 (US: Fox 1995–6)

Lt. Nathan West	**Morgan Weisser**
Lt. Shane Vansen	**Kristen Cloke**
Lt. Cooper Hawkes	**Rodney Rowland**
Lt. Vanessa Damphousse	**Lanei Chapman**
Lt. Paul Wang	**Joel de la Fuente**
Lt. Col. Tyrus Cassius ('T. C.') McQueen	**James Morrison**

Creators/Executive Producers **Glen Morgan, James Wong**

● ***A team of rookie space fighters take on the enemies of Earth's colonialism.***

In 2063, when an alien race destroys an Earth colony on Tellus, a new team of fighters is accelerated through training in preparation for a likely intergalactic war. These fighters form the 58th Squadron of the Marine Corps Space Cavalry (the 'Wild Cards'), sent aboard the ship *Saratoga* to confront the enemy. Their adversaries are the Chigs with their associates, the AIs (Artificial Intelligence) or Silicates, a race of rebellious androids. Chief hero is Lt. Nathan West, a man whose girlfriend is believed to be one of the dead on Tellus. He is accompanied by Lt. Cooper Hawkes, an 'In Vitro' – a laboratory-bred human with no family; Capt. Shane Vansen, orphaned young by AIs; Lt. Vanessa Damphousse, an engineer; Lt. Paul Wang, the team joker; and group leader, Lt. Col. T. C. McQueen (another In Vitro). World War II-type battles rage in the outer galaxies as the team gets to grips with their mission. Only 24 episodes were produced, shown first in the UK on Sky One but later, in an early hours slot, on BBC 2.

Space: 1999 ✶✶

UK (ITC/RAI/Gerry Anderson/Group Three) Science Fiction. ITV 1975–7

Commander John Koenig .... **Martin Landau**
Dr Helena Russell .... **Barbara Bain**
Prof. Victor Bergman .... **Barry Morse**
Capt. Alan Carter .... **Nick Tate**
First Officer Tony Verdeschi ... **Tony Anholt**
Maya .... **Catherine Schell**
Sandra Benes .... **Zienia Merton**
Yasko .... **Yasuko Nagazumi**
Paul Morrow .... **Prentis Hancock**
David Kano .... **Clifton Jones**
Dr Bob Mathias .... **Anton Phillips**
Moonbase computer .... **Barbara Kelly** *(voice only)*

Creators **Gerry Anderson, Sylvia Anderson**
Executive Producer **Gerry Anderson**
Producers **Sylvia Anderson, Fred Freiberger**

● ***A nuclear waste dump explodes and the inhabitants of a moonbase are hurled out into space.***

Space: 1999 was conceived as a kind of British STAR TREK by puppet experts Gerry and Sylvia Anderson. It centres on the adventures of the crew of Moonbase Alpha (or Alphans, as they become known) who find themselves stranded in space. On 13 September 1999, a nuclear waste depository on the far side of the moon explodes and jettisons the moon, its space research station and all 311 inhabitants out, through a black hole, into deepest space. As they whiz through the galaxies, desperately trying to find a new home before their supplies run out, the reluctant travellers encounter all manner of *Star Trek*-like aliens. One such alien, Maya, who possesses the ability to turn herself into plants or animals and is the last survivor of the planet Psychon, joins the crew and becomes the girlfriend of first officer Tony Verdeschi.

Stars of the show are ex-MISSION: IMPOSSIBLE heroes, husband and wife Martin Landau and Barbara Bain. Here, Landau plays the grim moonbase commander who has just taken up his post when the explosion occurs. Bain is the chief physician. Other prominent characters are chief pilot Alan Carter and Professor Victor Bergman, the brains behind the moonbase (written out after the first series).

Space: 1999 was made in association with Italy's RAI organization and was widely acclaimed for its advanced special effects, masterminded by expert Brian Johnson. Years of detailed model-making had taught the Andersons how to stage quite spectacular space scenes, but other aspects of the production were roundly criticized, from the wooden acting to the somewhat far-fetched concept. Not even the arrival of former *Star Trek* producer Fred Freiberger managed to save the day, and the series ended without a proper conclusion.

Space Patrol ✶✶

UK (National Interest/Wonderama) Children's Science Fiction. ITV 1963–4

Voices:
Capt. Larry Dart .... **Dick Vosburgh**
Husky .... **Ronnie Stevens**
Slim .... **Ronnie Stevens**
Col. Raeburn .... **Murray Kash**
Prof. Haggerty .... **Ronnie Stevens**
Marla .... **Libby Morris**
Cassiopea .... **Libby Morris**
Gabblerdictum .... **Libby Morris**

Creator/Writer **Roberta Leigh**
Producers **Roberta Leigh, Arthur Provis**

● ***A tri-planetary space force protects the solar system.***

In the year 2100, Space Patrol is the active unit of the United Galactic Organization, a peace-keeping body formed by the natives of Earth, Mars and Venus. This series features the exploits of its lead ship, *Galasphere 347*, and its crew of Earthman Captain Larry Dart, Martian Husky and Venusian Slim. Back at base, Colonel Raeburn gives the orders, assisted by his Venusian secretary, Marla. Professor Haggerty is the unit's somewhat erratic scientific genius, and Cassiopea is his daughter. Also seen is the Gabblerdictum, a kind of Martian parrot.

Space Patrol reached the screen just as Gerry Anderson's futuristic adventures were beginning to take off, with SUPERCAR and FIREBALL XL5 already on the air. It was scripted by Anderson's former collaborator Roberta Leigh.

Space Precinct ✶✶

UK (Gerry Anderson/Mentorn/Grove) Science Fiction. BBC 2 1995–6

Lt. Patrick Brogan .... **Ted Shackleford**
Officer Jack Haldane .... **Rob Youngblood**
Officer Jane Castle .... **Simone Bendix**
Sally Brogan .... **Nancy Paul**
Capt. Rexton Podly .... **Jerome Willis**
Officer Aurelia Took .... **Mary Woodvine**
Liz Brogan .... **Megan Olive**
Matt Brogan .... **Nic Klein**
Officer Silas Romek .... **Lou Hirsch**
Officer Hubble Orrin .... **Richard James**
Sgt Thorald Fredo .... **David Quilter**
Slomo .... **Gary Martin** *(voice only)*

Creator/Producer **Gerry Anderson**
Executive Producer **Tom Gutteridge**

● ***Two American cops join a multicultural space police force.***

In the year 2140, Brogan and Haldane are two New York cops seconded to Demeter City, on the planet Altor. There, riding above the streets in their police cruiser, they are part of an intergalactic police force made up of humans, Creons and

Tarns. Their grouchy boss at Precinct 88 is the frog-faced Creon, Captain Podly, and he is just one of the strange and reptilious aliens that make up the good citizens and the bad of this hectic metropolis. Sally is Brogan's wife, Liz and Matt his kids. Among his colleagues are English cop Jane Castle and her blue-faced Tarn patrol partner, Took, plus Creon officers Romek and Orrin. Slomo is a Shakespeare-quoting police computer. Using a mix of live actors, special effects, model work and animatronics, the 24 episodes of *Space Precinct* are played more for laughs than intensity. Screened first on Sky One, before reaching BBC 2, the series was derived from an idea creator Gerry Anderson had put forward a decade earlier. Called *Space Police*, it never resulted in a series.

Spaced ★★★★

UK (LWT/Paramount) Situation Comedy. Channel 4 1999; 2001
DVD: Channel 4

Daisy Steiner .... **Jessica Stevenson**
Tim Bisley .... **Simon Pegg**
Marsha Klein .... **Julia Deakin**
Brian Topp .... **Mark Heap**
Twist Morgan .... **Katy Carmichael**
Mike Watt .... **Nick Frost**

Creators/Writers **Jessica Stevenson, Simon Pegg**
Producers **Gareth Edwards, Nira Park**

● ***Two twentysomethings pose as a professional couple in order to share a flat.***

Daisy Steiner is an aspiring journalist. Tim Bisley is a nerdy, skateboarding sci-fi buff who wants to be a comic book artist. They are hardly kindred spirits. However, they are both homeless and meet regularly in a café where they study the week's accommodation adverts in newspapers. When they spot an entry for a comfortable flat that is only available to a professional couple, they hit upon the idea of pretending to be an item. Thus they manage to con gullible, alcoholic, wacky landlady Marsha Klein into renting out her downstairs flat at 23 Meteor Street, Tufnell Park, North London, and, after they move into their new home, are forced to keep up the appearance of being partners. The pseudo-marriage, however, becomes less important to the plot as viewers are hooked into the shrewdly observed, surreal life of Daisy and Tim. The lazy, perennial underachievers live in a world of parties, drugs, dopey friends and dogs – or rather, dog, acquired by Daisy at a time of particularly low esteem. Adventurously edited, laced with fantasy sequences and filled with contemporary pop culture references, *Spaced* was an immediate hit with young audiences – and plenty of older folk, too.

Spall, Timothy

OBE (1957–)

London-born actor who is best remembered as boring Barry in AUF WIEDERSEHEN, PET, even though he has taken countless other roles. In 1993 he donned the mantle of would-be wide-boy Frank Stubbs in FRANK STUBBS PROMOTES and, the next year, was both slovenly Kevin Costello in OUTSIDE EDGE and anarchic Phil Bachelor in NICE DAY AT THE OFFICE. Spall's other credits have included works as diverse as *The Cherry Orchard, Great Writers, Tracey Ullman: A Class Act*, the *Performance* presentations *Nona* (Chico) and *Roots* (Jimmy Beales), OUR MUTUAL FRIEND (Mr Venus), the single comedy *Neville's Island* (Gordon), SHOOTING THE PAST (Oswald Bates), PERFECT STRANGERS (Irving), *The Thing about Vince . . .* (Vince Skinner), *Vacuuming Completely Nude in Paradise* (Tommy Rag), *Bodily Harm* (Mitchel Greenfield), *Cherished* (Terry Cannings), *Mr Harvey Lights a Candle* (Malcolm Harvey), and a travelogue, *African Footsteps*. Spall also provided voices for *Bosom Pals* and made guest appearances in BOON, MURDER MOST HORRID, SPENDER, *The Young Indiana Jones Chronicles* and RAB C. NESBITT.

Spark ★★

UK (BBC) Situation Comedy. BBC 1 1997

Ashley Parkerwell .... **James Fleet**
Colette Parkerwell .... **Jan Francis**
Mrs Rudge .... **Anne Reid**
Gillian Wells .... **Rebecca Raybone**
Mike Parkerwell .... **Alistair McGowan**
Mrs Wells .... **Brigit Forsyth**

Writer **Roy Clarke**
Producer **Mike Stephens**

● ***Life begins when mother dies for a hapless middle-aged single man.***

For Ashley Parkerwell, a bachelor in his mid-40s, the death of his mother is a turning point. Up to now he's been beholden to his late mum and he now glimpses an opportunity to break free and to live life as it should be lived. Right from the day of her funeral, he begins to turn his mind to attractive women and, at the prompting of his positive sister-in-law, Colette, and his sapient housekeeper, Mrs Rudge, he begins his quest for fulfilment, overriding the wishes of his dull, long-time girlfriend, Gillian, and her pushy mother. But the women Ashley meets usually bring more trouble than he'd like and he can't expect much sympathy from his successful brother Mike. Just six episodes were made.

Special Branch ★★

UK(Thames/Euston Films) Police Drama. ITV 1969–70; 1973–4

DI Jordan .... **Derren Nesbitt**
Supt. Eden .... **Wensley Pithey**
DC Morrissey .... **Keith Washington**
Det. Supt. Inman .... **Fulton Mackay**
Charles Moxon .... **Morris Perry**
DCI Alan Craven .... **George Sewell**
DS Bill North .... **Roger Rowland**
DCI Tom Haggerty .... **Patrick Mower**
Commander Nichols .... **Richard Butler**
Commander Fletcher .... **Frederick Jaeger**
Strand .... **Paul Eddington**

Executive Producers **Lloyd Shirley, George Taylor**
Producers **Reginald Collin, Robert Love, Geoffrey Gilbert, Ted Childs**

● ***The investigations of an élite division of Scotland Yard.***

Although this series is best remembered for the exploits of snappily dressed detectives Craven and Haggerty, they were latecomers to *Special Branch*. For the first two seasons, the featured officers are Inspector Jordan and his superior, Supt. Eden (later substituted by Supt. Inman). Alongside Craven and Haggerty, DS North and Commander Nichols are also added, though they are soon replaced by Commander Fletcher and a snooty civil servant named Strand.

The thrust of *Special Branch* investigations was international crime and espionage. The team were assigned to high-pressure, undercover operations which involved plugging gaps in security, preventing murders and foiling attempts at sabotage. It was the first series to show a British copper in trendy clothing (Jordan) and is also notable for being the first programme made by Thames TV's offshoot, Euston Films, which took over production after the first two seasons had gone out on videotape.

Speed, Doris

MBE (1899–1994)

As snooty Annie Walker, landlady of the Rovers Return, Doris Speed elevated herself above other residents of CORONATION STREET for 23 years. Born into a showbiz family, Speed had worked part-time on stage, radio and early television (series like SHADOW SQUAD and *Skyport*), before she became Annie at the age of 61. It was a role that *Street* creator Tony Warren had written specifically for her; but she had to be persuaded to accept it and, in doing so, she took retirement from an office job with Guinness, having been with the brewery for over 40 years. Speed left the series in 1983, shortly after the tabloid press had revealed her true age to be 84, much to the surprise even of her bosses at Granada, who believed it to be 69.

Speight, Johnny

(1920–98)

Controversial London born comedy writer, the creator of TILL DEATH US DO PART's Alf Garnett in 1965. By putting bigoted statements and bad language into the mouth of his number one character, Speight attracted the full wrath of Establishment figures. Others, however, recognized that such frankness exposed prejudices in society and applauded the writer. But worse was to come for Speight when he penned CURRY AND CHIPS in 1969. Starring Eric Sykes and a blacked-up Spike Milligan, it was seen as a racist joke too far and did not survive longer than one season. Speight, a former milkman, also wrote for Frankie Howerd, Max Wall, Norman Evans, Cyril Fletcher, Dickie Valentine, Bernard Braden, Marty Feldman, Graham Stark and Mike Reid. Among his other major credits were *The Arthur Haynes Show*, SYKES, the early sketch show called *Two's Company, Them* (a comedy about tramps), its female counterpart, THE LADY IS A TRAMP, SPOONER'S PATCH (with Ray Galton) and *The Nineteenth Hole.*

Spelling, Aaron

(1923–2006)

American TV executive – a former actor and writer (on series like WAGON TRAIN) – specializing in glossy, glitzy dramas. Spelling's early successes as a producer included BURKE'S LAW, DANIEL BOONE and HONEY WEST. He then joined with fellow executive Leonard Goldberg to produce series like S.W.A.T., STARSKY AND HUTCH, THE LOVE BOAT, CHARLIE'S ANGELS, FANTASY ISLAND, HART TO HART and T. J. HOOKER. His next partner was Douglas S. Cramer, with whom he collaborated on popular series such as DYNASTY (and its less successful spin-off, THE COLBYS), VEGAS, HOTEL, *Savannah*, BEVERLY HILLS 90210 and *Melrose Place*, plus lots of other series not shown in the UK. With Cramer he established Aaron Spelling Productions, later renamed Spelling Entertainment Inc. He was father of actress Tori Spelling.

Spend, Spend, Spend ★★★

UK (BBC) Drama. BBC 1 1977

Vivian Nicholson .... **Susan Littler**
Keith Nicholson .... **John Duttine**
Vivian's mother .... **Helen Beck**
Vivian's father .... **Joe Belcher**
Matthew .... **Stephen Bill**
Keith's granny .... **Liz Smith**

Writer **Jack Rosenthal**
Producer **Graeme McDonald**

Rags to riches and back again with a spendthrift pools winner.

When young housewife Vivian Nicholson and her husband, Keith, won the pools in 1961, she announced how it would change her life. 'I'm going to spend, spend, spend,' she declared, and her famous words provide the title for Jack Rosenthal's PLAY FOR TODAY offering (based on her autobiography) that re-creates her story. For Vivian and Keith (a miner bringing home just £7 a week), the pools fortune of £152,319 was a mixed blessing. Keith, Vivian's second husband, died prematurely in a road crash, but Vivian enjoyed four crazy years of lavish lifestyle, frittering away her windfall on booze, cars and ill-thought-out investments. By the time the play (directed by John Goldschmidt) was made, Nicholson was back where she had started in the Yorkshire town of Castleford and living on social security, having been married five times and with four grown-up kids.

Spender ★★★

UK (BBC/Initial/Big Boy) Police Drama. BBC 1 1991–3

Freddie Spender .... **Jimmy Nail**
Stick .... **Sammy Johnson**
Supt. Yelland .... **Paul Greenwood**
DS Dan Boyd .... **Berwick Kaler**
Frances .... **Denise Welch**
Keith Moreland .... **Tony McAnaney**
Laura .... **Dawn Winlow**
Kate .... **Lynn Harrison**
Det. Chief Supt. Gillespie .... **Peter Guinness**

Creators **Jimmy Nail, Ian La Frenais**
Producers **Martin McKeand, Paul Raphael**

A maverick Geordie cop is seconded back to his home city to work undercover.

Detective Sgt Spender, a plain-clothes cop with unorthodox methods, works for the Metropolitan Police. However, his superiors are increasingly frustrated by his approach to the job and, when a partner is badly injured, they transfer Spender back to his home patch of Newcastle upon Tyne, after 15 years away. Although it is intended as a one-off assignment, Spender soon finds himself permanently back on the Tyne, snooping around where the local cops – being too well known – cannot tread. He is perfect for the job: his dishevelled looks and rough-diamond appearance, with tousled hair, pierced ear and chiselled face, hardly mark him out as a policeman, and his thick Geordie accent firmly establishes him as a local.

Despite his years away, Spender can still count on a few useful contacts, most notably Stick, a convicted building society robber, whom he drags into investigations and taps for the word on the streets. DS Dan Boyd, a ring-rusty desk clerk, is assigned as Spender's police liaison, and they occasionally meet at the music shop owned by crippled rock guitarist Keith Moreland. Not being the shy type, Spender always finds his way into the thick of the action, usually ending up on the wrong end of a bust-up. But his individual approach generally brings results (after a set-back or two along the way), satisfying his no-nonsense boss, Supt. Yelland (Det. Chief Supt. Gillespie from the second series).

There are other sides to Spender's personality, too. Beneath his gritty, determined facade he possesses a heart of gold. He remains on good terms with his ex-wife, Frances, who still lives in the city; and his two young daughters, Laura and Kate, bring out an even softer part of his nature. But Spender is committed to his job and, even when Frances is killed in the third series and Spender is given permanent custody of his children, he finds it hard to balance his responsibilities.

Spender is a series with character. Newcastle's distinctive accents and familiar streets and bridges offer an intriguing backdrop, and a driving rock soundtrack helps keep up momentum. Jimmy Nail not only starred in the programme but also co-created it with Ian La Frenais and provided scripts for a number of episodes.

Spenser: for Hire ✶✶

US (John Wilder/Warner Brothers) Detective Drama. BBC 1 1989–93 (US: ABC 1985–8)

Spenser .... **Robert Urich**
Hawk .... **Avery Brooks**
Susan Silverman .... **Barbara Stock**
Assistant DA Rita Fiori .... **Carolyn McCormick**
Lt. Martin Quirk .... **Richard Jaeckel**
Sgt Frank Belson .... **Ron McLarty**

Executive Producer **John Wilder**
Producers **Dick Gallegly, Robert Hamilton**

● ***A cultured private eye stalks the streets of Boston.***

Spenser (first name not given) is a rarity among private detectives. This ex-cop is a man of principle who knows and enjoys literature, his trademark being quotes from Wordsworth and other classic writers. He is also a former boxer, and a *cordon bleu* cook to boot. He cruises the streets of Boston in a vintage Mustang car, assisted in his work by Hawk, a bald, Magnum-toting, black street-informer who is later given his own spin-off series (*A Man Called Hawk*). Guidance counsellor Susan Silverman is Spenser's girlfriend in early and later episodes, with Assistant DA Rita Fiori keeping our hero on his toes in the interim. Lt. Quirk is the local police contact and Belson is his colleague from the homicide department. The series was based on the books by Robert B. Parker.

Spin City ✶✶

US (UBU/Lottery Hill/Dreamworks) Situation Comedy. Channel 4 1997–2002 (US: ABC 1996–2002)

Deputy Mayor Michael Flaherty .... **Michael J. Fox**
Mayor Randall Winston .... **Barry Bostwick**
Stuart Bondek .... **Alan Ruck**
Paul Lassiter .... **Richard Kind**
James Hobert .... **Alexander Gaberman/Chaplin**
Nikki Faber .... **Connie Britton**
Carter Heywood .... **Michael Boatman**
Ashley Schaeffer .... **Carla Gugino**
Janelle Cooper .... **Victoria Dillard**
Karen .... **Taylor Stanley**
Claudia Sacks/Lassiter .... **Faith Prince**
Laurie Parres .... **Paula Marshall**
Stacy Paterno .... **Jennifer Esposito**
Caitlin Moore .... **Heather Locklear**
Charlie Crawford .... **Charlie Sheen**
Angie Ordoñez .... **Lana Parrilla**

Creators **Gary David Goldberg, Bill Lawrence**
Executive Producers **Gary David Goldberg, Michael J. Fox, David Rosenthal**

● ***A resourceful deputy mayor saves his boss from media suicide.***

By the mid-1990s, the days of the candid politician were numbered. Anyone laying claim to high office needed to understand that off-the-cuff remarks were out and every word uttered to the media had to be closely considered. Sadly, New York Mayor Randall Winston has failed to grasp this concept and, allied to his natural ineptitude and meagre intelligence, this means overtime for his media advisers. Heading his team of gaffe-retrievers is Deputy Mayor Michael Flaherty, an affable, youthful spin doctor who knows how to keep the media sweet. He is assisted by sneaky Stuart Bondek; idealistic speechwriter James Hobert; accountant Nikki Faber; gay rights campaigner Carter Heywood; and personal assistant Janelle Cooper. The mayor's press secretary, noisy, naïve and tight-fisted Paul Lassiter (whose mum is played by guest star Raquel Welch), is so out of touch that the rest of the gang usually hide their plans from him. Personal lives intrude on the day-to-day running of the press office, often interfering in Mike's efforts to realign his boss's image following another PR debacle. Seen in early episodes is Mike's journalist girlfriend, Ashley Schaeffer. When she is written out, Flaherty gets involved with other women, including lawyer Laurie Parres and campaign manager Caitlin Moore. Carter's ageing dog, Rags (guest voiced by David Letterman), features later. Star Michael J. Fox – whose character was often likened to the role real-life spin guru George Stephanopoulos played in the election of President Clinton – left the show at the end of series four (which is where Channel 4 bowed out in the UK), when his much-publicized fight against Parkinson's disease became tougher. He was replaced by Charlie Sheen as charismatic new deputy mayor Charlie Crawford. However, Fox continued to make guest appearances and remained as executive producer.

Spindoe

See *The Fellows*.

Spitting Image ✶✶✶✶

UK (Central) Comedy. ITV 1984–96

Voices **Chris Barrie, Enn Reitel, Steve Nallon, Jan Ravens, Harry Enfield, Jon Glover, Jessica Martin, Rory Bremner, Hugh Dennis, Kate Robbins, Steve Coogan, Alistair McGowan, John Sessions**

Creators **Martin Lambie-Nairn, Peter Fluck, Roger Law**
Producers **Jon Blair, John Lloyd, Tony Hendra, Geoffrey Perkins, David Tyler, Bill Dare, Giles Pilbrow**

● ***Cruel satire from latex puppets.***

With respect for no one, be they the royal family, Mother Teresa or especially Margaret Thatcher, the *Spitting Image* team pulled the rug from under prominent personalities for

12 years. Using rubber puppets skilfully crafted by Peter Fluck and Roger Law, and some of the country's leading impressionists and comedians for voices, the series slaughtered holy cows while poking fun at politicians, entertainers, sportsmen and other world figures. The wit was topical and direct, if at times patchy, initially drawing controversy but later earning a degree of respect or at least resignation. Some celebrities even declared themselves honoured to have had their caricature captured in latex. Among the most memorable depictions were Kenneth Baker as a slug, Norman Tebbit as a skinhead, the Pope as a swinging dude and Gerald Kaufman as Hannibal Lecter.

Developed by Fluck and Law from an idea by LWT graphics artist Martin Lambie-Nairn, the series' early writers included the likes of Ian Hislop, Rob Grant and Doug Naylor. But, as well as humour, there was pathos, particularly in some of the musical numbers. At the other end of the scale, though, was 'The Chicken Song', a chart-topping 1986 spin-off that ridiculed the Benidorm brigade and their summer disco songs.

Sponsorship

Although common in the USA in the 1950s, sponsorship is relatively new to British television. In America, sponsors virtually owned the programmes, paying for production and the cost of the airtime, gaining editorial control and reaping the benefits of the exposure their products gained. The system went out of favour in the 1960s when production expenses increased and sponsors were forced to share costs with other advertisers. A form of sponsorship arrived in the UK in 1991 (having been banned previously), with newspapers, chocolate companies, banks and biscuit manufacturers attaching their names to soap opera, game shows, sports coverage or travel programmes. Unlike in the USA, the sponsor is allowed no editorial influence, nor can its products be prominently displayed in the programme itself. Indeed, so-called 'product placement' is prohibited in any programme, sponsored or not. News and current affairs programmes are debarred from taking sponsorship.

Spooks ★★★

UK (Kudos/BBC) Secret Agent Drama. BBC 1 2002–

Tom Quinn	**Matthew Macfadyen**
Zoë Reynolds	**Keeley Hawes**
Danny Hunter	**David Oyelowo**
Harry Pearce	**Peter Firth**
Tessa Phillips	**Jenny Agutter**
Helen Flynn	**Lisa Faulkner**
Malcolm Wyn-Jones	**Hugh Simon**
Ellie Simm	**Esther Hall**
Maisie Simm	**Heather Cave**
Jed Kelley	**Graeme Mearns**
Dr Vicki Westbrook	**Natasha Little**
Ruth Evershed	**Nicola Walker**
Colin Wells	**Rory Macgregor**
Carlo	**Enzo Cilenti**
Christine Dale	**Megan Dodds**
Sam Buxton	**Shauna MacDonald**
Adam Carter	**Rupert Penry-Jones**
Oliver Mace	**Tim McInnerny**
Will North	**Richard Harrington**
Fiona Carter	**Olga Sosnovska**
Juliet Shaw	**Anna Chancellor**
Zafar Younis	**Raza Jaffrey**
Jo Portman	**Miranda Raison**

Producers **Simon Crawford Collins, Jane Featherstone, Andrew Woodhead**

● ***The day-to-day problems of British intelligence agents.***

'Spooks' is an insider nickname for spies and this series looks at the complex lives led by various agents working for MI5. The accent is both on the demands of operational work – foiling terrorist plots, restraining racist agitators, infiltrating anarchist groups, etc. – and on the stresses of home life, where telling the girlfriend or wife what you did at the office is not an option, assuming they are aware of the job you do in the first place. At the centre of the action is Tom Quinn, a tough and resourceful (though not infallible) operative who has just begun a relationship with single-mum restaurateur Ellie Simm. Unfortunately, she only knows him under one of his cover aliases (Matthew Archer) and he is barred from telling her the truth until she has been positively vetted. Joining Quinn on his assignments are ambitious young Zoë Reynolds and surveillance specialist Danny Hunter. Harry Pearce is their immediate superior. At the end of series two, it appears time has run out for Tom, who, it seems, has turned against his colleagues and is now on the run. He manages to clear his name but his enthusiasm for the cause is dimmed to the point where he is replaced by new action-man figure, Adam Carter (Carter's wife, Fiona, also a spy, joins the crew later). At the same time devious Joint Intelligence Committee member Oliver Mace decides it's time to clean up the mess that is MI5 and the whole team is put on their mettle. Series four opens with a terrorist attack on London – uncomfortable viewing, coming, as it did, just two months after the July 2005 bombings (the scenes had already been shot and were integral to the whole series, so were difficult to take out).

Using split screens, slow motion and other camera tricks, one point that the series brings home is that life in the field is extremely demanding and calls for astonishing attention to detail. It is also seldom without danger, as a particularly shocking scene involving a deep-fat fryer makes all too clear.

Spooner, Dennis

(1932–86)

British writer and script editor who penned parts of Tony Hancock's unsuccessful ITV series *Hancock* and other comedies before finding his niche in the world of science fiction and adventure dramas. Spooner contributed episodes to DOCTOR WHO, NO HIDING PLACE, FIREBALL XL5, STINGRAY, THUNDERBIRDS, THE AVENGERS, THE BARON, THE PROTECTORS, UFO, DOOMWATCH, HAMMER HOUSE OF HORROR, BERGERAC, THE PROFESSIONALS and *Dramarama*. However, he particularly endeared himself to cult TV fans by creating or co-creating MAN IN A SUITCASE, THE CHAMPIONS, DEPARTMENT S and RANDALL AND HOPKIRK (DECEASED).

Spooner's Patch ★

UK (ATV) Situation Comedy. ITV 1979–80; 1982

Insp. Spooner	**Ronald Fraser**
	Donald Churchill
DC Bulsover	**Peter Cleall**
PC Killick	**John Lyons**
PC Goatman	**Norman Rossington**
Kelly	**Dermot Kelly**
Mrs Cantaford	**Patricia Hayes**

Jimmy the Con .... **Harry Fowler**

Creators/Writers **Johnny Speight, Ray Galton**
Producer **William G. Stewart**

Day-to-day events in a hopelessly inept police station.

Inspector Spooner, head of the small, suburban Woodley police station, craves a quiet, comfortable life. Sadly, rather than heading out on to the golf course each day, he is called down from his upstairs flat to clear up the mess his corrupt and incompetent juniors have created. DC Bulsover, for instance, is one officer to keep in check, a CID man who thinks he is Starsky or Hutch and who drives around in a flashy red and-white motor. There are also bigoted PC Goatman and sarcastic PC Killick to watch over, although some of Spooner's biggest problems come from quick-tempered traffic warden Mrs Cantaford. To add to the confusion, Kelly, an Irish grass, plagues the station with his presence, before he is replaced by another informer, Jimmy the Con.

Although it combined the writing talents of Johnny Speight (TILL DEATH US DO PART) and Ray Galton (HANCOCK'S HALF HOUR and STEPTOE AND SON), the series proved a disappointment to most viewers.

Sports Review of the Year/BBC Sports Personality of the Year ★★★

UK (BBC) Sport. BBC 1 1954–

Annual sports showcase with awards for the best achievers.

Sports Review of the Year was launched way back in 1954 and has become one of the BBC's major annual events. Transmitted live, early in December, it has focused on the sporting year just passed, replaying the key action and interviewing the winners and losers. In a light-hearted diversion, good 'sports' like Frank Bruno have tried their hands at silly stunts, such as fairground shooting stalls, taking hockey penalties, performing snooker tricks, changing the tyres on a Formula One racing car and pitting their wits against electronic games. The 'Sports Personality of the Year' award has provided the climax to the evening (a full list of winners is given below), with other presentations made to 'Overseas Personality of the Year' and the best team. In 1999, new awards were introduced: 'Coach of the Year' and the 'Helen Rollason Award' for inspiration (in tribute to the late BBC sports presenter). The 1999 programme was actually titled *Sports Personality of the Century* and saw Muhammad Ali collect the eponymous award. Cool-headed hosts Sue Barker and Gary Lineker have held the show (now known as *BBC Sports Personality of the Year*) together in recent years, succeeding the likes of Peter Dimmock, David Coleman, Harry Carpenter, Frank Bough, Desmond Lynam and Steve Rider.

'Sports Personality of the Year' Winners

1954 .... **Chris Chataway**
1955 .... **Gordon Pirie**
1956 .... **Jim Laker**
1957 .... **Dai Rees**
1958 .... **Ian Black**
1959 .... **John Surtees**
1960 .... **David Broome**
1961 .... **Stirling Moss**
1962 .... **Anita Lonsbrough**
1963 .... **Dorothy Hyman**
1964 .... **Mary Rand**
1965 .... **Tommy Simpson**
1966 .... **Bobby Moore**
1967 .... **Henry Cooper**
1968 .... **David Hemery**
1969 .... **Ann Jones**
1970 .... **Henry Cooper**
1971 .... **HRH The Princess Anne**
1972 .... **Mary Peters**
1973 .... **Jackie Stewart**
1974 .... **Brendan Foster**
1975 .... **David Steele**
1976 .... **John Curry**
1977 .... **Virginia Wade**
1978 .... **Steve Ovett**
1979 .... **Sebastian Coe**
1980 .... **Robin Cousins**
1981 .... **Ian Botham**
1982 .... **Daley Thompson**
1983 .... **Steve Cram**
1984 .... **Torvill and Dean**
1985 .... **Barry McGuigan**
1986 .... **Nigel Mansell**
1987 .... **Fatima Whitbread**
1988 .... **Steve Davis**
1989 .... **Nick Faldo**
1990 .... **Paul Gascoigne**
1991 .... **Liz McColgan**
1992 .... **Nigel Mansell**
1993 .... **Linford Christie**
1994 .... **Damon Hill**
1995 .... **Jonathan Edwards**
1996 .... **Damon Hill**
1997 .... **Greg Rusedski**
1998 .... **Michael Owen**
1999 .... **Lennox Lewis**
2000 .... **Steve Redgrave**
2001 .... **David Beckham**
2002 .... **Paula Radcliffe**
2003 .... **Jonny Wilkinson**
2004 .... **Kelly Holmes**
2005 .... **Andrew Flintoff**

Sportsnight ★★★

UK (BBC) Sport. BBC 1 1968–97

Presenters **David Coleman, Frank Bough, Tony Gubba, Harry Carpenter, Steve Rider, Desmond Lynam, Ray Stubbs**

Producers **Bob Duncan, Jonathan Martin, John Philips, Vivien Kent**
Editors **Sam Leitch, Brian Barwick, Niall Sloane**

Midweek sports magazine.

The BBC's replacement for SPORTSVIEW (starting a week after its predecessor ended) was initially billed as *Sportsnight With Coleman*, David Coleman dominantly filling the anchor's chair. The intention was to create a sports news magazine, an equivalent to PANORAMA with its current affairs brief. As well as major outside broadcasts (either live or recently recorded), it offered sporting features, interviews, reviews and previews, and Coleman's own slant on the issues of the moment. Sam Leitch, best known as host of Grandstand's *Football Preview*, was the first programme editor; Niall Sloane was the last, with Brian Barwick editing for many years in between.

Sportsview ✶✶✶

UK (BBC) Sport. BBC 1954–68

Presenters **Peter Dimmock, Brian Johnston, Frank Bough**

Editors **Paul Fox, Ronnie Noble, Cliff Morgan, Alan Hart**
Producers **Dennis Monger, Cecil Petty, Alan Rees, Bryan Cowgill, A. P. Wilkinson, Alec Weeks, Alan Mouncer, Fred Viner**

● ***Early midweek sports round-up.***

Replaced after 14 years on air by SPORTSNIGHT in 1968, *Sportsview* was the BBC's first major sports showcase, predating GRANDSTAND by four years. Peter Dimmock was the programme's first host, introducing such sporting milestones as Roger Bannister's four-minute mile on 6 May 1954. *Sportsview* was also adventurous technically. It was the first BBC programme to use a teleprompter and among its other innovations was the placing of cameras inside racing cars. A younger viewers' version, *Junior Sportsview*, with hosts including Peter Dimmock, Billy Wright and Kenneth Wolstenholme, ran between 1956 and 1962, and the annual SPORTS REVIEW OF THE YEAR was another by-product.

Spot the Tune ✶

UK (Granada) Quiz. ITV 1956–62

Presenters **Ken Platt, Ted Ray, Jackie Rae, Pete Murray**

Producers **Wilfred Fielding, Johnny Hamp**

● ***Musical quiz game.***

In this self-explanatory quiz, contestants were asked to spot the tune, given only a few bars to work on. There was a jackpot (increasing by £100 a week), to be won by those with an ear for music. Singer Marion Ryan (mother of 1960s pop stars Paul and Barry Ryan) helped pose the questions, accompanied by the Peter Knight Orchestra.

The format was revived in the 1970s as *Name That Tune*, a segment of the variety show *Wednesday at Eight*, and subsequently a programme in its own right. Tom O'Connor and, later, Lionel Blair hosted proceedings, Maggie Moone was the resident songstress and the Alan Braden band struck up the tunes.

Spriggs, Elizabeth

(1929–)

English actress, often cast in matriarchal roles, such as in FOX (Connie Fox), SHINE ON HARVEY MOON (Violet 'Nan' Moon) and PLAYING THE FIELD (Mrs Mullen). Other major parts have been in THE GLITTERING PRIZES, *We, the Accused*, *Frost in May*, STRANGERS AND BROTHERS (Lady Muriel Royce), *The Haunting of Cassie Palmer* (Mrs Palmer), *Simon and the Witch* (the Witch), ORANGES ARE NOT THE ONLY FRUIT (May), *The Old Devils* (Dorothy Morgan) and *Anglo Saxon Attitudes* (Inge Middleton). Elizabeth was also seen in JEEVES AND WOOSTER (Aunt Agatha), MARTIN CHUZZLEWIT (Mrs Gamp), MIDDLEMARCH (Mrs Cadwallader), TAKIN' OVER THE ASYLUM (Grandma), *Alice in Wonderland* (Duchess), *The Sleeper* (Cath Marks), WIVES AND DAUGHTERS (Mrs Goodenough), SHACKLETON (Janet Stancombe Wills), NICE GUY EDDIE (Vera McMullen), SWISS TONI (Toni's mother) and WREN – THE MAN WHO BUILT BRITAIN (Queen Anne). Guest appearances take in the likes of CRIBB, DOCTOR WHO, SOLDIER, SOLDIER, SHERLOCK HOLMES, THE TOMORROW PEOPLE, THE RUTH RENDELL MYSTERIES, HEARTBEAT, LOVEJOY, *A Pinch of Snuff*, MIDSOMER MURDERS, CASUALTY, RANDALL AND HOPKIRK (DECEASED), THE ROYAL, WHERE THE HEART IS and JERICHO.

Spring and Autumn ✶✶

UK (Thames) Situation Comedy. ITV 1973–4; 1976

Tommy Butler	**Jimmy Jewel**
Charlie Harris	**Charlie Hawkins**
Vera Reid	**June Barry**
Brian Reid	**Larry Martyn**
Betty Harris	**Jo Warne**

Creators/Writers **Vince Powell, Harry Driver**
Producers **Ronnie Baxter, Mike Vardy, Anthony Parker**

● ***A lonely old man finds company with a 12-year-old lad.***

It seems life is over for 70-year-old former railway worker Tommy Butler when his home is demolished and he is forced to live with his daughter and son-in-law, Vera and Brian Reid, in a high-rise flat. It is clear that he isn't really wanted in their home and, to be fair, the cantankerous old moaner makes little effort to fit in. His only friend is Nelson, a stuffed green parrot. However, Tommy discovers a new soul-mate in Charlie Harris, a cheeky, somewhat wayward young Cockney lad who is neglected by his hard-up, divorced mother, Betty. Tommy and Charlie become firm friends and share many an outing. Their mutual interest in football and railways binds them together, and Charlie loves Tommy's far-fetched tales of the past.

This gentle comedy, with moments of sentimentality, followed on from a one-off 1972 play in which Tommy's daughter and son-in-law were Betty and Joe Dickinson (played by Gaye Brown and Larry Martyn).

Springer, Jerry

(1944–)

London-born host of sensational US daytime talk shows, a career he has pursued after success in American politics – he was an aide to Robert Kennedy and was later elected Mayor of Cincinnati. Springer has also hosted chat shows for ITV in the UK. In 2000 and 2001 he presented MISS WORLD.

Spy-Catcher ✶✶

UK (BBC) Secret Agent Drama. BBC 1959–61

Lt. Col. Oreste Pinto	**Bernard Archard**

Writer **Robert Barr**
Producer **Terence Cook**

● ***A Dutch security specialist weeds out spies from genuine asylum seekers.***

Charged with unearthing foreign spies who tried to enter Britain, Dutchman Lt. Col. Oreste Pinto was a key figure in World War II. This series is based on his true counterespionage experiences (some already published) as he uses wit and guile, patience and psychological warfare, to expose bogus refugees and other immigrants, quietly testing their identities, background and other claims they put forward. Twenty-four stories were filmed, over four series.

Spyder's Web ★★

UK (ATV) Spy Drama. ITV 1972

Charlotte 'Lottie' Dean .... **Patricia Cutts**
Clive Hawksworth .... **Anthony Ainley**
Wallis Ackroyd .... **Veronica Carlson**
Albert Mason .... **Roger Lloyd Pack**

Creator **Richard Harris**
Producer **Dennis Vance**

International intrigue with three agents of a secret governmental unit.

The 'Web' of this programme's title is a top-secret, undercover, anti-espionage organization, and 'Spyder' refers to any of its agents. There are three prominent activists: Lottie Dean, Clive Hawksworth and Wallis Ackroyd. Individually or collectively, they investigate bizarre and complicated cases of infiltration and international deception. Albert Mason, Lottie's butler, is also seen. This light-hearted thriller was created by Richard Harris and penned mainly by comedy writer Roy Clarke.

Spyship ★★

UK (BBC) Spy Drama. BBC 1 1983

Martin Taylor .... **Tom Wilkinson**
Suzy Summerfield .... **Lesley Nightingale**
Sir Peter Hillmore .... **Michael Aldridge**
Francis Main .... **Peter Eyre**
Rokoff .... **David Burke**
Dr Dowdall .... **Thorley Walters**
Evans .... **Philip Hynd**
Simon .... **Paul Geoffrey**
Metcalfe .... **Jimmy Nail**
Mrs Metcalfe .... **Mandy Pickard**
Jean Williams .... **Christine Hargreaves**
Hoskins .... **Al Gillyon**
Sam .... **Joe Holmes**
Tom Silvers .... **Malcolm Hebden**
Erik Starvik .... **Bjorn Sundquist**

Writer **James Mitchell**
Producer **Colin Rogers**

A fisherman's son believes the sinking of his father's ship was no accident.

When a British trawler, the *Caistor*, is sunk in the Barents Sea – an area of known international espionage activity – the son of the chief engineer wants to know more. Martin Taylor discovers that his dad's boat was, in fact, equipped for surveillance, but the truth about its role has been suppressed. Taylor's efforts to expose the real reason for the trawler's demise lead him into trouble when an enemy agent, Evans, sets out to kill him, also attacking Martin's old schoolfriend, Suzy Summerfield. The six-part series was based on the novel of the same name by former Thames TV journalists Tom Keene and Brian Haynes.

Squirrels, The ★★

UK (ATV) Situation Comedy. ITV 1975–7

Mr Fletcher .... **Bernard Hepton**
Rex .... **Ken Jones**
Susan .... **Patsy Rowlands**
Harry .... **Alan David**
Burke .... **Ellis Jones**
Carol .... **Karin MacCarthy**

Creator **Eric Chappell**
Producer **Shaun O'Riordan**

Petty squabbles with the staff of a TV rental company.

Beginning as a one-off play in 1974, this comedy lifts the lid on the offices of International Rentals, a television hire firm. Head of the accounts staff is Mr Fletcher, and bickering beneath him are his hapless minions, Rex, Susan, Harry, Burke and Carol (played by Susan Tracy in the pilot). Joining creator Eric Chappell in scripting the series were writers like Kenneth Cope (of RANDALL AND HOPKIRK (DECEASED) fame) and BROOKSIDE's Phil Redmond. Chappell revamped the idea for another sitcom, FIDDLERS THREE.

Staff, Kathy

(Minnie Higginbottom; 1928–)

Northern actress, most familiar as the redoubtable Nora Batty in LAST OF THE SUMMER WINE. However, Staff has also been seen in both CORONATION STREET (corner shopkeeper Vera Hopkins) and CROSSROADS (Doris Luke), as well as a third soap, EMMERDALE FARM (Winnie Purvis). She was Mrs Blewitt, one of Arkwright's customers, in OPEN ALL HOURS and later played interfering grandmother Molly Bickerstaff in *No Frills*. Her other credits have included *Castle Haven*, HADLEIGH, *Sez Les*, *Dawson and Friends* and *The Benny Hill Show*.

Staggering Stories of Ferdinand De Bargos, The ★★★

UK (BBC) Comedy. BBC 2 1989; 1991; 1993; 1995

Voices **Enn Reitel, Jon Glover, Kate Robbins, Susie Blake, Jim Broadbent, Ann Bryson, Peter Bland, Caroline Leddy, Roger Blake, Joanna Brookes, Steve Steen, Ronni Ancona, Alistair McGowan**

Writers **Geoff Atkinson, Kim Fuller, Tony Garnett**
Producers **Geoff Atkinson, Kim Fuller**
Executive Producer **Tony Garnett**

Surreal collection of comic tales, featuring overdubbed old movie footage.

Taking a selection of bizarre clips from old (usually documentary) films and piecing them together to create a surreal story, *The Staggering Stories of Ferdinand de Bargos* featured comic dialogue from some of the best voice-over artists and impressionists of the 1990s. The stories often involved finding someone to narrate a tall tale, and featuring regularly in the action was a certain Dr Arnold MacFaddyan. Subjects explored included pandas, English village life, the Cold War, JFK, astronauts, the Wild West and time travel. As well as four series, spread over six years, there were specials in 1991 focusing on *The Staggering Story of Lime Grove* and *The Staggering Year of Ferdinand de Bargos*. Episodes generally ran to 20 minutes.

Stand Up, Nigel Barton/Vote, Vote, Vote for Nigel Barton ✶✶

UK (BBC) Drama. BBC 1 1965

Nigel Barton .... **Keith Barron**
Harry Barton .... **Jack Woolgar**
Mrs Taylor .... **Barbara Keogh**
Miss Tillings .... **Janet Henfrey**
Anne Barton .... **Valerie Gearon** *(Vote)*
Jack Hay .... **John Bailey** *(Vote)*
Archibald-Lake .... **Cyril Luckham** *(Vote)*

Writer **Dennis Potter**
Producer **James MacTaggart**

● ***A bright working-class lad makes a name for himself in politics.***

In *Stand Up, Nigel Barton*, the hero is a smart boy from an underprivileged background. Brought up in a mining family, he is one of the first generation locally to enjoy a decent education and everyone – including schoolteacher Miss Tillings – is sure he will do well. However, such a burden is not an easy one to carry as Nigel is torn between his tough, industrial heritage and the easy, prosperous life that seems to beckon. This WEDNESDAY PLAY was followed a week later by another, entitled *Vote, Vote, Vote for Nigel Barton*. By this stage, Barton has graduated from Oxford, is married to the beautiful Anne and is working as a journalist. He harbours political ambitions and is supported by his agent, Jack Hay, as he enters the race for a by-election. Regrettably, his past catches up with him and the newspapers have a field day as Barton's character is torn to shreds. Both plays (early autobiographic offerings from Dennis Potter) were directed by Gareth Davies.

Stanwyck, Barbara

(Ruby Stevens; 1907–90)

After a long and successful career in Hollywood, spanning nearly 40 years, Barbara Stanwyck at last ensured herself television posterity in 1965 when she was cast as Victoria Barkley, matriarch of the Barkley family, in THE BIG VALLEY. Her earlier excursions into TV had comprised guest spots in series like THE UNTOUCHABLES, RAWHIDE and WAGON TRAIN, in addition to her own short-lived anthology series, *The Barbara Stanwyck Show*. *The Big Valley* ran in the USA until 1969 and, after making a few TV movies, Stanwyck officially retired from the business in 1973. She was tempted back to the small screen on two occasions, however. In 1983 she played Mary Carson in THE THORN BIRDS and in 1985 was Constance Colby in THE COLBYS. Her second husband was actor Robert Taylor.

Stapleton, John

(1946–)

Oldham-born journalist and presenter of current affairs and lifestyle programmes, best remembered as host of NATIONWIDE, WATCHDOG, *The Time, the Place*, *My Favourite Hymns* and GMTV. Other contributions have been to PANORAMA, NEWSNIGHT and *Real Story*. He is married to fellow presenter Lynn Faulds Wood.

Star Cops ✶✶

UK (BBC) Science Fiction. BBC 2 1987

Nathan Spring .... **David Calder**
Pal Kenzy .... **Linda Newton**
David Theroux .... **Erick Ray Evans**
Colin Devis .... **Trevor Cooper**
Alexander Krivenko .... **Jonathan Adams**
Anna Shoun .... **Sayo Inaba**

Creator **Chris Boucher**
Writers **Chris Boucher, Philip Martin, John Collee**
Producer **Evgeny Gridneff**

● ***A grouchy, determined cop heads up a crime squad in space.***

Nathan Spring is a successful British detective but he is less than happy when he hears about his new job. Spring is to be head of the International Space Police Force, a team of Star Cops that patrol the Earth's various space stations keeping law and order. Reluctantly establishing his headquarters at a moonbase, Spring sets out to knock his team of part-time lawmen into shape as mysteries involving stranded spacemen, crashing rockets and possible hijackings demand his attention. Second in command is American David Theroux and also part of the head office team are Australian Pal Kenzy, sexist Brit Colin Devis, Russian moonbase chief Alexander Krivenko and later recruit Anna Shoun, a scientist from Japan. Free of aliens of all descriptions – these are essentially human crimes with a space dimension – the series was set in the year 2027. Justin Hayward of the Moody Blues provided the 'It Won't be Easy' theme song, but just nine episodes were produced.

Star Maidens ✶✶

UK/W. Germany (Scottish/Portman) Science Fiction. ITV 1976

Fulvia .... **Judy Geeson**
The President .... **Dawn Addams**
Adam .... **Pierre Brice**
Shem .... **Gareth Thomas**
Octavia .... **Christine Kruger**
Rudi .... **Christian Quadflieg**
Liz .... **Lisa Harrow**
Prof. Evans .... **Derek Farr**

Creators **Graf Von Hardenberg, Graefin Von Hardenberg**
Producer **James Gatward**

● ***Two male refugees from a female-dominated planet escape to Earth.***

Adam and Shem are male slaves on Mendusa, a planet ruled exclusively by women. There, men are no more than the subservient race, confined to a life of drudgery while their womenfolk live in luxury. Making a break for it, the two men steal a spaceship and flee to Earth, pursued by Adam's mistress, Supreme Councillor Fulvia, and her assistant, Octavia. Their arrival is monitored by Earth scientist Professor Evans, whose young colleagues, Rudi and Liz, are then taken hostage and whisked off into space when Fulvia fails to corner her escapees. With two Mendusans on Earth and two humans on Mendusa, the series follows the battle against the 'Star Maidens' on both worlds.

Thirteen episodes of *Star Maidens* were produced as a joint venture between British and West German companies, although the series (played mainly for laughs) was never very successful in the UK. A planned second series was quickly shelved.

Star Quality ✶✶

UK (BBC) Drama Anthology. BBC 1 1985

Producer **Alan Shallcross**

Noël Coward revisited.

Judi Dench, Susannah York, Tom Courtenay, Ian Richardson, Patricia Hayes, Nigel Havers and Ian Holm were among the names starring in this little collection of plays introducing a 1980s audience to the wit and wisdom of actor, writer and composer Noël Coward. The anthology consisted of *Star Quality, Mrs Capper's Birthday, What Mad Pursuit, Me and the Girls, Bon Voyage*, and *Mr and Mrs Edgehill*.

Star Trek ✶✶✶✶

US (Norway/Paramount/Desilu) Science Fiction. BBC 1 1969–71 (US: NBC 1966–9)

Capt. James T. Kirk .... **William Shatner**
Mr Spock .... **Leonard Nimoy**
Dr Leonard McCoy .... **DeForest Kelley**
Mr Sulu .... **George Takei**
Lt. Uhura .... **Nichelle Nichols**
Engineer Montgomery Scott .. **James Doohan**
Nurse Christine Chapel .... **Majel Barrett**
Ensign Pavel Chekov .... **Walter Koenig**
Yeoman Janice Rand .... **Grace Lee Whitney**

Creator/Executive Producer **Gene Roddenberry**
Producers **Gene L. Coon, John Meredyth Lucas, Fred Freiberger**

***The voyages of the starship* Enterprise.**

In the 23rd century, Earth has become a member of the United Federation of Planets, a galactic union that runs a joint defence organization, Starfleet. Its starships ply the cosmos, hoping to bring peace to other civilizations, or at least to discover more about alien life-forms. The USS *Enterprise* is one of these ships, and *Star Trek* follows its adventures on a five-year mission to 'boldly go where no man has gone before'.

The *Enterprise* is a massive exploration-cum-messenger craft which cruises at 'warp' speeds, all of which are faster than light. Protected by high-tech deflector shields and phasers, it whisks its crew of 428 from galaxy to galaxy and from one life-threatening adventure to another. The spaceship itself never lands: the crew are simply 'beamed down' on to the surface of a planet, to tackle new adversaries (with the minimum of special effects).

Commander of the ship is 34-year-old Captain James Tiberius Kirk, an American from Iowa. His Chief Navigator is Japanese Mr Sulu, assisted by a Russian, Chekov (added in the second season to provide international balance). Lt. Uhura, the communications officer, is a sultry African, and Chief Engineer is Montgomery 'Scotty' Scott. However, the key members of Kirk's team are his First Officer, Mr Spock, and the ship's doctor, 'Bones' McCoy. McCoy, an expert in space psychology from Georgia, USA, always considers himself to be a simple 'country' doctor. He is an emotional chap, quite unlike his perennial sparring partner, Spock, who, being half Vulcan, is devoid of human instincts. Green-blooded and pointy-eared, Spock is interested only in what is logical, his mind working through the facts like a computer. Kirk proves to be a mixture of the two, an often impetuous man with strong powers of leadership, a (sometimes) athletic frame and a firm belief in humanity as a force for overcoming evil. Consequently, *Star Trek* stories (beginning and ending with Kirk's vocal entry into the Captain's Log) usually have a moral theme, with the crew facing up to alien civilizations which echo the cruellest regimes our own world has seen, like the ancient Romans and the Nazis. Social issues of the day, such as civil rights and the Vietnamese war, are also reflected. The *Enterprise* has two main enemies, the militaristic Romulans and the greasy, barbarous Klingons, although all kinds of weird and wonderful foes are likely to turn up.

Star Trek was devised by Gene Roddenberry, previously scriptwriter on HAVE GUN WILL TRAVEL, and he perceived the programme as a sort of WAGON TRAIN in space. It was not an instant hit; in fact it flopped in the USA. In the UK it was eventually picked up by the BBC and screened only after the entire run had ended in America. However, reruns have ensured that the programme has gained a cult following, manifested in a legion of international fans known as 'Trekkies' for whom part of the attraction is the show's many clichés and sayings. A UK chart-topper from 1987, 'Star Trekkin', by a group called The Firm, parodied its classic lines like 'Klingons on the starboard bow', 'It's life, Jim, but not as we know it' and 'It's worse than that, he's dead, Jim'. In 2000, Sky One even produced a four-part *Star Trek* quiz called *Trekmasters*.

Star Trek's pilot episode, *The Cage*, starred Jeffrey Hunter as Christopher Pike, the first captain of the *Enterprise*, but it has been rarely seen, with some of its footage reworked into a later episode called *The Menagerie*. Only Leonard Nimoy and Majel Barrett from the main cast appeared in the pilot. A series of ten feature-length movies was made years after filming of the TV show finished in 1969, and a cartoon version was also issued. STAR TREK: THE NEXT GENERATION picked up the story again in 1989, and three further spin-offs, STAR TREK: DEEP SPACE NINE, STAR TREK: VOYAGER and STAR TREK: ENTERPRISE, have also now been produced.

Star Trek: Deep Space Nine ✶✶

US (Paramount) Science Fiction. BBC 2 1995–2001 (US Syndicated 1993–9)

Commander Benjamin Sisko .... **Avery Brooks**
Odo .... **René Auberjonois**
Dr Julian Bashir .... **Siddig El Fadil/Alexander Siddig**
Lt. Jadzia Dax .... **Terry Farrell**
Jake Sisko .... **Cirroc Lofton**
Chief Miles O'Brien .... **Colm Meaney**
Quark .... **Armin Shimerman**
Major Kira Nerys .... **Nana Visitor**
Lt. Commander Worf .... **Michael Dorn**
Ezri Dax .... **Nicole de Boer**
Gul Dukat .... **Marc Alaimo**
Nog .... **Aron Eisenberg**
Elim Garak .... **Andrew Robinson**
Rom .... **Max Grodénchik**
Leeta .... **Chase Masterson**
Gowron .... **Robert O'Reilly**

Creators **Rick Berman, Michael Piller**
Executive Producers **Rick Berman, Michael Piller, Ira Steven Behr**

Trouble and strife on an extreme outpost in the backyard of space.

Set, like STAR TREK: THE NEXT GENERATION, in the 24th century, this series, for once, does not feature a wandering USS spacecraft. Instead, the static setting is the eponymous *Deep Space Nine*, a run-down space station orbiting the wasted (by rival race the Cardassians) planet Bajor, way, way out in space. Its position close to a newly discovered 'wormhole' – a crack in space – means that it soon gains strategic importance and is a popular stopover for trans-galactic travellers using the wormhole to catapult across light years. This renders *DS9* akin to a Wild West frontier town, with visitors of all persuasions dropping by to wreak havoc with the station staff. The crew include the understandably disgruntled widower Commander Benjamin Sisko; his brattish teenage son, Jake; First Officer Major Kira Nerys, a patriotic Bajoran; Chief Miles O'Brien, the pessimistic operations director (ex of the USS *Enterprise*); and newly graduated medical man Dr Julian Bashir, who holds a torch for science officer Lt. Jadzia Dax, a Trill whose beautiful outer form conceals a 300-year-old slug-like symbiotic core. There are also the seedy Quark, a typically greedy Ferengi who specializes in dirty money (bars and holographic brothels); and Odo, a shape-shifting, naturally liquid creature who keeps his human form while on duty as a security officer. Odo's own race, the Founders of the Dominion, becomes one of Starfleet's new enemies, and to head them off *DS9* employs a prototype fighter spacecraft called the *Defiant*. Joining the crew later is Lt. Commander Worf, another *Next Generation* cross-over, who is the new Strategic Operations Officer.

Considerably darker than *Star Trek*'s two previous incarnations, *Deep Space Nine* is also grittier and far less optimistic, featuring characters who exhibit traits like distrust, spite and anger.

Star Trek: Enterprise ★★

US (Paramount) Science Fiction. Channel 4 2002–6
(US: UPN 2001–5)

Capt. Jonathan Archer .... **Scott Bakula**
Sub Commander T'Pol .... **Jolene Blalock**
Ensign Travis Mayweather ..... **Anthony Montgomery**
Commander Charles 'Trip' Tucker III .... **Connor Trinneer**
Ensign Hoshi Sato .... **Linda Park**
Dr Phlox .... **John Billingsley**
Lt. Malcolm Reed .... **Dominic Keating**

Creators/Executive Producers **Rick Berman, Brannon Braga, Manny Coto**

The early years of starship exploration.

Predating the original *Star Trek* series by more than 100 years, *Enterprise* is set in 2151. Its star is Captain Jonathan Archer, a man whose own father helped design the first starship, and it is he who boldly takes the *Enterprise* out into the cosmos for encounters with the Klingons and other races. Archer is supported by a team that consists of Vulcan science officer T'Pol; helmsman Travis Mayweather; Floridean chief engineer Charles 'Trip' Tucker III; multilingual communications officer Hoshi Sato; alien medical officer Phlox; and British tactical officer Malcolm Reed. The series – titled simply *Enterprise* until season three – aired first in the UK on Sky One.

Star Trek: The Next Generation ★★★

US (Paramount) Science Fiction. BBC 2 1990–6 (US: Syndicated 1987–94)

Capt. Jean-Luc Picard .... **Patrick Stewart**
Commander William T. Riker . **Jonathan Frakes**
Lt. Commander Geordi La Forge .... **LeVar Burton**
Lt. Worf .... **Michael Dorn**
Lt. Tasha Yar .... **Denise Crosby**
Dr Beverly Crusher .... **Gates McFadden**
Counsellor Deanna Troi .... **Marina Sirtis**
Lt. Commander Data .... **Brent Spiner**
Wesley Crusher .... **Wil Wheaton**
Dr Katherine Pulaski .... **Diana Muldaur**
Guinan .... **Whoopi Goldberg**
Ensign Ro Laren .... **Michelle Forbes**
Transporter Chief Miles O'Brien .... **Colm Meaney**
Q .... **John de Lancie**

Executive Producer **Gene Roddenberry**

The voyages of the starship Enterprise, resurrected.

In this *Star Trek* sequel, time has moved on to the 24th century, about 80 years after the exploits of Kirk and Co. The new *Enterprise* is much flashier – a Galaxy-class starship eight times as spacious as the original, with over 1,000 crew members (including families), and greatly advanced technology.

The ship's commander is stubborn Jean-Luc Picard, not as emotional or impetuous as his predecessor, Kirk, and less inclined to soil his hands. He delegates off-ship missions to his hard-working 'Number 1', the bearded Riker. Also on the bridge is Lt. Geordi La Forge, a blind black helmsman who can see by wearing a VISOR (Visual Instrument and Sight Organ Replacement) band. He later takes over as Chief Engineer. Deanna Troi, Riker's ex, is a half-Betazoid who works as an adviser, warning of impending danger by reading people's emotions (her mother, Lwaxana, is seen occasionally, played by *Star Trek* original Majel Barrett). Data, a pale-faced, encyclopaedic android, and Lt. Tasha Yar, the security chief who is killed by the alien Armus, also appear. Often violent Lt. Worf is a Klingon, from the race that was once Starfleet's enemy, and the ship's medical officer is widow Dr Beverly Crusher, later temporarily replaced by Dr Kate Pulaski. Crusher's kid-genius son, Wesley, is also on board, and Whoopi Goldberg drops in from time to time, playing the part of Guinan, bartender in the ship's Ten Forward lounge. Guest stars include Leonard Nimoy as Spock, James Doohan as Scotty and Stephen Hawking as himself.

Storylines, as in the original series, generally offer a moral, and the show was warmly received by 'Trekkies'. But *Star Trek: The Next Generation* was slow to come to the UK. It turned up first in video shops, before being bought by Sky. BBC 2 secured the rights for terrestrial transmission, but episodes were screened some time after premiering on satellite.

Star Trek: Voyager ★★★

US (Paramount) Science Fiction. BBC 2 1996–2002
(US: UPN 1995–2001)

Capt. Kathryn Janeway .... **Kate Mulgrew**

Chakotay .... **Robert Beltran**
B'Elanna Torres .... **Roxann Biggs-Dawson**
Kes .... **Jennifer Lien**
Lt. Tom Paris .... **Robert Duncan McNeill**
Neelix .... **Ethan Phillips**
Doctor .... **Robert Picardo**
Tuvok .... **Tim Russ**
Ensign Harry Kim .... **Garrett Wang**
Seven of Nine .... **Jeri Ryan**

Creators **Rick Berman, Michael Piller, Jeri Taylor**
Executive Producers **Rick Berman, Michael Piller, Jeri Taylor, Brannon Braga**

A Starfleet ship is lost in the outer reaches of the universe.
Some time in the 24th century, the USS *Voyager* (one of Starfleet's smaller ships) is hit by a wave of energy and sent hurtling 70,000 light years across the galaxies to the Gamma Quadrant. The efforts of its captain, Kathryn Janeway, and her team to return to parts of space that are more familiar form the basis of this LOST IN SPACE-like series.

Janeway's crew consists of an uneasy mix of Starfleet officers and Maquis terrorists who find themselves similarly marooned and reluctantly reliant on the *Voyager* for the hope of a journey home. Asian rookie communications officer Harry Kim, Vulcan security officer Tuvok, impetuous ex-pilot Lt. Tom Paris and Native American Chakotay (former Maquis leader) are key members of the team, along with half-Klingon B'Elanna Torres; an impatient holographic medical man known only as the Doctor; a treacherous Kazon named Seska; Neelix, a Talaxian cook-cum-handyman; and Neelix's Ocampan lover, Kes – the last three just some of the new species *Voyager* encounters in these uncharted regions of space. One notable later addition to the cast is stunning half-Borg Seven of Nine.

Stargate SG-1 ★★★

US (Double Secret/Gekko/MGM) Science Fiction. UK Channel 4 1999– (US: Showtime 1997–2002; Sci Fi 2002–)

Col. Jonathan 'Jack' O'Neill ..... **Richard Dean Anderson**
Capt./Major Samantha 'Sam' Carter .... **Amanda Tapping**
Dr Daniel Jackson .... **Michael Shanks**
Teal'c .... **Christopher Judge**
Gen. George Hammond .... **Don S. Davis**
Dr Janet Fraiser .... **Teryl Rothery**
Sgt Walter Harriman Davis .... **Gary Jones**
Jonas Quinn .... **Corin Nemec**
Vala Mal Doran .... **Claudia Black**

Creators **Brad Wright, Jonathan Glassner**
Executive Producers **Brad Wright, Jonathan Glassner, Michael Greenburg, Richard Dean Anderson, Robert C. Cooper, Joseph Mallozzi**

A team of action heroes travel the cosmos using an ancient space portal.
Following on from the 1994 cinema release *Stargate* (starring Kurt Russell and James Spader), this series centres on a space portal that allows access to other such 'Stargates' across the universe (the portal has been on Earth since the times of the ancient Egyptians). Ordered back into action by Texan General Hammond, Col. Jack O'Neill and his colleagues in the task force known as SG-1 make one final mission through the Stargate. On their return, they defy their superior's orders to bury the portal and use it again to thwart an attack they know is coming from the evil Goa'uld people. After this, the portal is left active for further missions, a specially constructed 'iris' being opened or closed to allow access. Joining O'Neill on his adventures are Dr Daniel Jackson, the man who knows how to decrypt and use the 39 hieroglyphic symbols surrounding each Stargate; blonde astrophysicist Sam Carter; and Teal'c, a big, warrior-like, but friendly alien (a Jaffa) they bring back on their first journey. Dr Janet Fraiser is the physician supporting the team back on Earth. Joining the crew in later seasons is Jonas Quinn, a human from another planet. With visuals that echo those used in THE TIME TUNNEL and the same 'will-they, won't-they get back in time' suspense, *Stargate SG-1* has similarities to that classic 1960s series. David Arnold wrote the theme music. Sky One has offered first-run transmissions for the UK since 1998.

Starkey, Dr David

(1945–)

Kendal-born TV historian, a former Cambridge don and lecturer at the London School of Economics. His programmes for Channel 5 on *Elizabeth I* and *The Six Wives of Henry VIII* helped re-establish history on television and prompted rumours that Starkey was the highest-paid presenter on British TV in 2002. More recently he has presented *Edward and Mary: the Unknown Tudors* and *Monarchy by David Starkey*.

Starr, Freddie

(Freddie Fowell; 1944–)

Unpredictable British comedian and impressionist with a cheeky grin, coming to the fore on OPPORTUNITY KNOCKS and establishing himself on WHO DO YOU DO? Starr's career has experienced several ups and downs, the ups including several series of his own, such as *The Freddie Starr Show* and *The Freddie Starr Showcase* (a talent show). In 1980 he shared the limelight with Russ Abbot in *Freddie Starr's Variety Madhouse* which, when Starr left, was renamed *Russ Abbot's Madhouse*. Starr has also been a popular variety show and panel game guest, and took to straight drama as Lance Izzard in SUPPLY AND DEMAND. In 1999 he fronted a Sky game show called *Beat the Crusher*.

Starr and Company ★★

UK (BBC) Soap Opera. BBC 1958

Megs Turner .... **Nancy Nevinson**
Gwyneth Turner .... **Gillian Gale**
Hughie Turner .... **Barry MacGregor**
Jim Turner .... **Philip Ray**
Tom Turner .... **Brian McDermott**
Robin Starr .... **Michael Murray**
Jane Starr .... **Deirdre Day**
Joseph Starr .... **William Sherwood**
Julia Starr .... **Pat Ann Key**
Edith Starr .... **Barbara Cavan**
Harry Crane .... **Arnold Ridley**
Mary Tennison .... **Patricia Mort**
Charlie .... **Barry Steele**
Steve Lacey .... **Harry Littlewood**
Joe Trimmer .... **George Roderick**
Rene Cremer .... **Katherine Parr**
Alec Cremer .... **Michael Bird**
Mrs Childs .... **Betty Cooper**

Allardyce .... **John Forbes-Robertson**
Bernard Kay .... **Denis Holmes**
Exton .... **Hugh Cross**
Isobel .... **Pamela Abbott**
Len Forbes .... **Glenn Williams**
Jennie .... **Stella Richman**
Arthur Gilbert .... **Graham Crowden**

Producers **Gerard Glaister, Barbara Burnham**

● ***The lives of workers and their families at an engineering factory near London.***

Having dispensed with THE GROVE FAMILY the year before, the BBC tried its hand at creating another soap in 1958. This time the setting was the suburban town of Sullbridge (population 30,000), less than 50 miles from London. Once a small market town, Sullbridge has, by the time we visit it, grown into a centre for light engineering, attracting skilled and semiskilled workers from all over the UK. One of the town's leading firms is Starr & Co., established in the 1850s by Joseph Starr to fabricate shipping buoys and famous for its 'Starr Buoy Light'. The present-day Joseph Starr is 54 and MD of the company. Like his naval ancestors, he likes to keep the business and its employees shipshape. Starr's family are at the forefront of the action: unflappable wife Edith (50); son Robin (28), a former apprentice and now deputy manager of the firm; daughter Julia (24), living and working in London as PR agent; and Robin's pregnant wife, Jane (25). The other major family in the series are the Turners, headed up by Lancastrian dad Jim, aged 56, a loyal Starr & Co. employee. Jim's family are impetuous Welsh wife Megs (45), elder son Tom (22), who works in the company's design office, younger son Hughie (19) and schoolgirl daughter Gwyneth (15). Apart from the interpersonal relationships of the two families and other key workers, plots revolve around the development of a revolutionary new buoy (the story ran parallel to such a development in a real engineering factory that advised the programme's production team). However, *Starr and Company* failed to provide enough excitement in its twice-weekly outings (Monday and Thursday) to survive beyond nine months.

Stars and Garters ✶✶

UK (Associated-Rediffusion) Variety. ITV 1963–6

Hosts **Ray Martine, Jill Browne, Willie Rushton**

Producers **Daphne Shadwell, John P. Hamilton, Rollo Gamble, Elkan Allan**

● ***Traditional pub entertainment presented from a fake hostelry.***

A cross between the earlier Café Continental and the later Wheeltappers' and Shunters' Social Club, *Stars and Garters* was a variety show dressed up as pub entertainment. Host Ray Martine and his pet mynah bird invited viewers to share in the pubby atmosphere and watch top acts, supported by resident performers like Kathy Kirby, Tommy Bruce, Clinton Ford, Kim Cordell, Vince Hill, Debbie Lee, Al Saxon, Queenie Watts and Julie Rayne. The Alan Braden and Peter Knight orchestras provided musical accompaniment. Martine was later replaced as host by EMERGENCY – WARD 10 star Jill Browne, who compered events with Willie Rushton. The title became *The New Stars and Garters* at the same time.

Stars in Their Eyes ✶✶✶

UK (Granada) Entertainment. ITV 1990–

Presenters **Leslie Crowther, Matthew Kelly, Davina McCall, Cat Deeley**

Executive Producers **Dianne Nelmes, Nigel Hall**
Producers **Jane Macnaught, Kieron Collins, Matthew Littleford, Nigel Hall, Andrew Wightman, Rachel Ashdown, Heather Coogan, Glen Middleham**

● ***Viewers impersonate their favourite singing stars.***

A cross between a talent show and a vehicle for impressionists, *Stars in Their Eyes* offers members of the public the chance to emulate their favourite musical performers. Togged up in appropriate gear by the wardrobe department and given the looks of their idols by make-up, the contestants then perform with the Ray Monk Orchestra to prove that they can sound like the real thing, too. A grand final (live) is held at the end of each series and in 1999 a *Champion of Champions* show pitched the first ten series' winners against each other, the winner (the 1999 series champion) impersonating Chris de Burgh. Also in 1999, editions of *Celebrity Stars in Their Eyes* were introduced, with showbiz names paying tribute to their heroes. Leslie Crowther was the series' original host, replaced after his tragic car accident immediately by Russ Abbot and then long term by Matthew Kelly, with Davina McCall taking over for some special editions in 2003. The same year *Stars in Their Eyes Kids* was hosted by Cat Deeley, who took over as presenter of the main series in 2005. A *Stars in Their Eyes – Families* special arrived in 2006.

Stars Look Down, The ✶✶

UK (Granada) Drama. ITV 1975

Martha Fenwick .... **Avril Elgar**
Robert Fenwick .... **Norman Jones**
Sammy Fenwick .... **James Bate**
Hughie Fenwick .... **Rod Culbertson**
David Fenwick .... **Ian Hastings**
Joe Gowlan .... **Alun Armstrong**
Richard Barras .... **Basil Dignam**
Annie Macer .... **Anne Raitt**
Hilda Barras .... **Barbara Hickmott**
Arthur Barras .... **Christian Rodska**
Jenny Sunley/Fenwick .... **Susan Tracy**
Hetty Todd .... **Adrienne Frank**
Adam Todd .... **David Markham**
Grace Barras/Teasdale .... **Catherine Terris**
Stanley Millington .... **Geoffrey Davien**
Laura Millington .... **Valerie Georgeson**
Jim Mawson .... **Ronald Herdman**
Tom Heddon .... **Ronald Radd**

Writer **Alan Plater**
Producer **Howard Baker**

● ***Grim times for the industrial heartland of the north-east.***

Adapted by Alan Plater from the 1935 novel by A. J. Cronin, the 13 episodes of *The Stars Look Down* tell of the depressed Northumbrian mining village of Sleescale. Beginning in March 1910, spanning 20 years and focusing on the Fenwick family, it paints a picture of a society ravaged by industrial unrest and growing violence. Families struggle to make a living and the young face a bleak future. Martha Fenwick is the prematurely aged matriarch, the stern mother of three sons (Sammy, Hughie and David – all miners), who finds herself pregnant again. Other key figures are Joe Gowlan, a fiercely ambitious lecher who quits the mines in favour of the iron foundry; his girlfriend Jenny, an innkeeper's daughter with ideas above her station who eventually leaves Joe for the politically hopeful David Fenwick; Annie Macer, who marries Sammy; Richard Barras, the unscrupulous owner of the local Neptune mine; and Barras's business partner, Adam Todd. Stanley Millington is Joe's boss in the metal industry and his wife, Laura, is just another to succumb to Joe's charms. Key events include David and Joe's migration to Newcastle, a major flood at the pit, and the outbreak of war and its effect on the community. The series, which took four years to complete, cost a sizeable £500,000 and was based on Cronin's own experiences as a colliery doctor.

Stars on Sunday **

UK (Yorkshire) Religion. ITV 1969–79

Presenter/Executive Producer **Jess Yates**

Cosy, Sunday-evening celebrity showcase with a religious slant.

Stars on Sunday, ITV's answer to SONGS OF PRAISE, specialized in attracting top showbusiness names into the studio to sing hymns or give Biblical readings. Masterminded and presented by Jess 'The Bishop' Yates (assumed father of Paula), its mixture of big stars and spiritual comforts made it extremely popular, and viewers' requests flooded in. Among the international celebrities to contribute were Bing Crosby, Princess Grace of Monaco, Johny Mathis, Raymond Burr and Howard Keel, while heading the home-grown talent were the Beverley Sisters, James Mason, Harry Secombe, Gracie Fields, John Gielgud, John Mills and Anna Neagle. The Archbishops of Canterbury and York also made appearances, as did a Prime Minister, Edward Heath. The resident singing troupe were The Poole Family, fronted by little Glyn Poole, and, as well as traditional hymns, moral modern pieces were also featured.

In 1974 the programme was rocked by the 'actress and the bishop' scandal, when Yates's relationship with Anita Kay, a showgirl more than 30 years his junior, was splashed over the tabloids. Yates was forced to leave the series and his career never recovered. His immediate short-term replacement as host was Anthony Valentine, but numerous personalities picked up the reins for the show's last five years on air. These included Moira Anderson, Wilfred Pickles, Robert Dougall, Cliff Michelmore and Gordon Jackson.

Starsky and Hutch ***

US (Spelling-Goldberg) Police Drama. BBC 1 1976–81 (US: ABC 1975–9)

Det. Dave Starsky	**Paul Michael Glaser**
Det. Ken ('Hutch') Hutchinson	**David Soul**
Capt. Harold Dobey	**Bernie Hamilton**
Huggy Bear	**Antonio Fargas**

Creator **William Blinn**
Executive Producers **Aaron Spelling, Leonard Goldberg**
Producer **Joseph T. Naar**

Two buddy-buddy undercover cops patrol the seedier areas of LA.

Dave Starsky and Ken 'Hutch' Hutchinson are cops. More than that, they are pals and it shows in their work. Hutch is blond, Starsky is dark-haired, and their lifestyles contrast just as sharply. Starsky enjoys junk food and streetlife; Hutch prefers health foods and the quiet life. But the main thing is that they know they can depend on each other, and this runs right to the heart of their working relationship.

Stationed in one of LA's seamiest districts, the casually dressed duo concentrate on only the most serious crimes, hustling drug-pushers, pimps and other society dregs, and apprehending muggers, rapists and racketeers. Screaming around the streets in Starsky's souped-up, red Ford Torino with a loud white strip along its side, they are hardly inconspicuous for undercover policemen. What's more, if they can enter a car through a window rather than a door, then they will, probably leaping on to the bonnet first. Yet they still get results, usually bending the rules along the way, but ultimately keeping their fiery boss, Captain Dobey (played by Richard Ward in the pilot), happy. Huggy Bear is their hip street-contact.

The show grew less aggressive over the years in response to anti-violence campaigns in the States, but it always enjoyed greater success in Britain, where the two principals were big stars. Paul Michael Glaser's chunky cardigans became fashion items and David Soul was able to reprise his recording career, notching up a string of middle-of-the-road hits, including a couple of number ones, 'Don't Give Up On Us' and 'Silver Lady'. In 2004 a new feature film, also called *Starsky and Hutch*, was released with Ben Stiller and Owen Wilson in the respective title roles, supported by Snoop Dogg as Huggy Bear.

State of Play ****

UK (Endor/BBC) Drama. BBC 1 2003
DVD: BBC

Stephen Collins	**David Morrissey**
Cal McCaffrey	**John Simm**
Della Smith	**Kelly Macdonald**
Cameron Foster	**Bill Nighy**
Anne Collins	**Polly Walker**
Dan Foster	**James McAvoy**
Helen Preger	**Amelia Bullmore**
Pete Cheng	**Benedict Wong**
Dominic Foy	**Marc Warren**
DCI Bell	**Philip Glenister**
Syd	**Tom Burke**
Liz	**Rebekah Staton**
Adam Greene	**Christopher Simpson**
Greer Thornton	**Deborah Findlay**
Andrew Wilson	**Michael Feast**
Det. Chief Constable Janson	**Nick Brimble**
George Fergus	**James Laurenson**
Yvonne Shaps	**Geraldine James**
Olicia Stagg	**Maureen Hibbert**
Sonny Stagg	**Johann Myers**

Writer **Paul Abbott**
Executive Producers **Paul Abbott, Gareth Neame, Laura Mackie**
Producer **Hilary Bevan Jones**

Dedicated, investigative journalists tackle spin and corruption in Westminster.

When rising MP Stephen Collins breaks down during a press conference called after the sudden death of his researcher, the press sniff a story. It turns out they are right: Collins has been having an affair with the girl, Sonia Baker, but this is just the tip of the iceberg. As Sonia's death – under a London tube train – is quickly assumed to be murder, Collins finds himself under the spotlight, although a team of broadsheet journalists from *The Herald* also uncovers evidence that she was being stalked by a hit man. The journos are headed up by Collins's old mate and former campaign manager, Cal McCaffrey. As the story develops into an account of political corruption and oil industry influence in high places, McCaffrey, supported by young assistants Della Smith and Dan Foster (estranged son of *The Herald*'s cool and wily editor, Cameron Foster), need to break the law and bend the rules to keep on the trail of the killer. Links to the murder of a black youth named Kelvin Stagg seem highly relevant, but matters are complicated by McCaffrey's ill-timed affair with Collins's angry wife, Anne. This acclaimed, six-part conspiracy thriller is directed by David Yates.

Staunton, Imelda

OBE (1956–)

Oscar-nominated British actress (for *Vera Drake*), married to actor Jim Carter. Imelda's major TV roles have included Izzy in UP THE GARDEN PATH, Bridget Bennet in *A Masculine Ending* and *Don't Leave Me This Way*, Muriel in IF YOU SEE GOD, TELL HIM, Stella in IS IT LEGAL?, Mrs Micawber in DAVID COPPERFIELD, DCI Billie Dory in *Murder*, Mrs Sucksby in *Fingersmith*, Queen Elizabeth in CAMBRIDGE SPIES, Polly in *A Midsummer Night's Dream* and Mrs Durrell in *My Family and Other Animals*. She has also featured in LADIES IN CHARGE, THE SINGING DETECTIVE, *Thompson*, FRANK STUBBS PROMOTES, *Look at the State We're In!*, MIDSOMER MURDERS, *Strange* and LITTLE BRITAIN, and provided voices for THE CANTERBURY TALES animation.

Stay Lucky ★★

UK (Yorkshire) Drama. ITV 1989–91; 1993

Thomas Gynn	**Dennis Waterman**
Sally Hardcastle	**Jan Francis**
Kevin	**Chris Jury**
Lively	**Niall Toibin**
Pippa	**Emma Wray**
Samantha Mansfield	**Susan George**
Franklyn Bysouth	**Ian McNeice**
Isabel	**Rula Lenska**
Jo	**Leslie Ash**

Creator **Geoff McQueen**
Executive Producer **Vernon Lawrence**
Producers **David Reynolds, Andrew Benson, Matthew Bird**

A Cockney wide-boy meanders between jobs, follows his heart and finds unlikely girlfriends.

On the run from the London underworld, Thomas Gynn bumps into recently widowed, northern businesswoman Sally Hardcastle at an A1 service station and, more by chance than design, the two reluctantly end up sharing a houseboat. At one point, Thomas – ducking and diving – drives minicabs in Newcastle, while headstrong Sally runs her narrowboat charter company in Yorkshire. By the third season, Thomas has spent time behind bars and Sally has long since left the scene. Thomas then saves the life of Samantha Mansfield, administrator of the Yorkshire Industrial Museum, who gives him a job and more besides, before he enjoys a fling in Eastern Europe with Isabel, a British trade official in Hungary. Finally, Jo, a dancer, becomes the new girl in his life. Pippa and Lively, two old friends, are usually on the scene, too, as is Franklyn Bysouth, Thomas's one-time cellmate. Now a dodgy businessman, he takes Thomas under his wing and offers him work.

Steadman, Alison

OBE (1946–)

Liverpool-born actress, for many years the wife of playwright Mike Leigh, in some of whose works (NUTS IN MAY and ABIGAIL'S PARTY) she has also been seen. Steadman's TV career opened in the early 1970s. She was WPC Bayliss in Z CARS, appeared in *Frost's Weekly* and took the part of Bernadette Clarkson in *The Wackers*. In the 1980s she played Mrs Marlow and Lili in THE SINGING DETECTIVE, and in the 1990s she was Edda Goering in SELLING HITLER, Lauren Patterson in GONE TO THE DOGS and Hilda Plant in its 'sequel', GONE TO SEED, Elinor Farr in *The Wimbledon Poisoner*, Mrs Bennet in PRIDE AND PREJUDICE, Evelyn Hamilton in NO BANANAS, Mrs Haynes in KARAOKE, Christine Peacock in *The Missing Postman*, and Madame de Plonge in *Let Them Eat Cake*. She played Betty Simpson in FAT FRIENDS and followed this with the roles of Pauline Mole in ADRIAN MOLE: THE CAPPUCCINO YEARS, Grandma in CELEB, Bronwen Race in *Happy Now* and Angela Cook in THE WORST WEEK OF MY LIFE. She also narrated *Love Town* and *Grumpy Old Women*, and provided voices for the animations CRAPSTON VILLAS, *Stressed Eric* and *Bosom Pals*. Her TV series have been underpinned by roles in single dramas like *Hard Labour*, *Through the Night*, *P'tang Yang Kipperbang*, *The Muscle Market* and *The Caucasian Chalk Circle*, and guest spots in series such as *Coogan's Run*, KAVANAGH QC, DALZIEL AND PASCOE and *Twisted Tales*.

Steel River Blues ★★

UK (Yorkshire) Drama. ITV 1 2004

Tony Barnes	**Daniel Casey**
Bill McGlinchy	**Stuart Graham**
George Barnes	**Charles Dale**
Julie Priestley	**Kelly Wenham**
Alan Priestley	**Steven Hillman**
Jeremy Lloyd	**Daniel Ainsleigh**
Sunil Gupta	**Satnam Bhogal**
Mick Hammond	**John Bowler**
Katy Bell	**Clare Buckfield**
Roger Hibbot	**Mark Cameron**
Sandra Harris	**Victoria Hawkins**
Dave Tanner	**Michael Nardone**
Andy Coulson	**Daniel Ryan**
Asif Hussain	**Nitin Kundra**
Sgt Moss	**Malcolm Scates**
Nicky Higgins	**Joanne Farrell**

Creators **Patrick Harbinson, Jonathan Critchley**
Writers **Patrick Harbinson, Charlie Fletcher, Alan Whiting, Patrick Melanaphy**
Producer **Ken Horn**

The stresses of life at a Middlesbrough fire station.

Inevitably inviting the descriptions of 'LONDON'S BURNING in the north' and 'Teesside's Burning', *Steel River Blues* centres on a team of firefighters based in Middlesbrough (the Tees being the 'Steel River' on account of its industrial heritage). The series kicks off with the arrival of new Station Officer Bill McGlinchy. He's been working in Belfast and brings plenty of personal baggage with him. Immediately there is conflict between the new boss and Tony Barnes, stalwart of the Blue Watch, who has just missed out on Bill's job. Other members of the unit are Tony's gentle giant brother George, soon to suffer a career-threatening accident in the line of duty; Julie Priestley, a control room operator who becomes the first female member of the firefighting team; her protective dad, Sub-Officer Alan Priestley, a father figure for the whole station; serial womanizer Dave Tanner; Jeremy Lloyd, a law school graduate, who runs the unit's book club; and caring family man Sunil Gupta. There's also Divisional Officer Mick Hammond, a rotary club man; Katy Bell, leading Fire Control Operator; Sandra, Katy's flighty colleague; mysterious Roger Hibbot, who keeps himself to himself; Asif Hussain, an Asian passionate about his ethnic roots, but comfortable in his Britishness, too; Andy Coulson, a hard man with a soft centre and a stutter; and feisty new female driver Nicky Higgins. Their beat is hazardous, in more ways than one, as Middlesbrough has more than its share of chemical plants, plus a nuclear power station close at hand. Their typical day's work combines a mix of the trivial and ludicrous (delivering smoke alarms to the community, rescuing a fat man stuck in a toilet window) to matters of life and death (a baby trapped above a burning chip shop, men stranded in a pit about to be flooded with water). Thankfully a combination of dark humour and high jinx help these brave men and women cope with their stressful occupation. Just one series of seven episodes was produced.

Stein, Rick

OBE (1947–)

Oxfordshire-born TV chef for whom media fame arrived after 20 years of running a seafood restaurant in Padstow, Cornwall. His landmark series was *Rick Stein's Taste of the Sea*, which he followed with *Rick Stein's Fruits of the Sea*, *Rick Stein's Seafood Odyssey*, *Fresh Food*, *Rick Stein's Seafood Lover's Guide*, *Rick Stein's Food Heroes* and *Rick Stein's French Odyssey*. On his travels he is often accompanied by his pet Jack Russell, Chalky. DJ Judge Jules is a nephew.

Stella Street ✳✳✳

UK (Tiger Aspect) Comedy. BBC 2 1997–8; 2000–1; 2004

John Sessions, Phil Cornwell

Writers **John Sessions, Phil Cornwell, Peter Richardson**
Producer **Ben Swaffer**

● ***A Surrey street is home to an array of comic celebrities.***

In this spoof soap, a quiet road in Surbiton (in reality a street in Chiswick) is where a host of major celebrities reside when not working. Employing the impersonation talents of stars John Sessions and Phil Cornwell to the full (supported by Sandra Cush and others), each ten- or 15-minute film features such names as Mick Jagger and Keith Richards (who run the corner shop), Jack Nicholson, Jimmy Hill, Dirk Bogarde, Al Pacino, Joe Pesci, Roger Moore, David Bowie, Patrick Moore and Marlon Brando, as well as numerous star 'visitors' and cleaning lady Mrs Huggett. It is left to Michael Caine to relate to the camera the latest absurd comings and goings in Stella Street. Four series were produced, which Peter Richardson directed. Three years after they ended, the team returned for a feature-length special.

Stephenson, Debra

(1972–)

Actress born in New Zealand but raised in Hull. She began her career as a teenage impressionist and reached the final of OPPORTUNITY KNOCKS. She later provided voices for SPITTING IMAGE and worked as a comedian, but decided to turn to drama. Major credits include *Cone Zone* (Corrie), PLAYING THE FIELD (Diane Powell), CATHERINE COOKSON'S *A Dinner of Herbs* (Kate Roystan), BAD GIRLS (Shell Dockley), *TV to Go*, MAD ABOUT ALICE (Kate) and CORONATION STREET (Frankie Baldwin), with guest spots in RECKLESS, MIDSOMER MURDERS, *Sam's Game*, SPOOKS, THE LAST DETECTIVE and WHERE THE HEART IS.

Stephenson, Pamela

(1949–)

Actress and comic born in New Zealand, a member of the NOT THE NINE O'CLOCK NEWS team from 1979. Her other credits have included appearances in WITHIN THESE WALLS, SPACE: 1999, TARGET, THE NEW AVENGERS, THE PROFESSIONALS, HAZELL (alongside her first husband, Nicholas Ball), *Funny Man*, *Lost Empires*, *Move Over Darling* and the American series *Saturday Night Live*. Stephenson now works as a psychotherapist in Los Angeles. Her second husband is Billy Connolly.

Steptoe and Son ✳✳✳✳

UK (BBC) Situation Comedy. BBC 1 1962–5; 1970; 1972–4

Albert Steptoe .... **Wilfrid Brambell**
Harold Steptoe .... **Harry H. Corbett**

Creators/Writers **Ray Galton, Alan Simpson**
Producers **Duncan Wood, John Howard Davies, Graeme Muir, Douglas Argent**

● ***A pretentious bachelor can't escape his grubby old father and the rag-and-bone business they share.***

There are few shows in the history of television which have reaped such wide appreciation as *Steptoe and Son*, Ray Galton and Alan Simpson's saga of a socially aspirant son and the dirty old dad who keeps him anchored to the mire of a scrapyard. Harold Steptoe, in his late 30s, dreams of a life away from the squalid, junk-filled house he shares with his father at 24 Oil Drum Lane, Shepherd's Bush. He longs to progress his cultural interests and to embark on some romantic journey but is always hauled back to sub-working-class grime by his disgusting, emaciated old man. His plans for soirées in gentrified circles usually collapse into nights at The Skinner's Arms or argumentative evenings in front of the box, thanks to the efforts of his seedy father. Albert Steptoe is vulgarity personified, a man who washes his socks only when taking a bath. He cooks and generally runs the house, while Harold does the rounds with Hercules (later Delilah) the carthorse, but Albert's idea of culinary finesse is edging a pie with his false teeth. Albert's greatest skill lies in scuppering his son's dreams of a better life. Whenever Harold makes a dash for freedom, the clinging, devious old man always stands in the way, using emotional blackmail to deny his son independence.

The gloriously coarse series – which is as much a tragedy as it is a comedy – ran in two bites, in the early 1960s (it first aired in 1962 as a COMEDY PLAYHOUSE episode called *The Offer*) and then in the early 1970s. A radio series was also produced, and the show spawned a US cover version, *Sanford and Son*, as well as two far less successful feature films, *Steptoe and Son* and *Steptoe and Son Ride Again*. In 2006 Jake Nightingale (Harold) and Harry Dickman (Albert) starred in a stage play based on the series. Called *Steptoe and Son in Murder at Oil Drum Lane*, it was penned by Ray Galton with John Antrobus.

Steven Spielberg's Amazing Stories ★★

US (Amblin/Universal) Science Fiction Anthology. BBC 1 1992–4 (US: NBC 1985–7)

Creators **Steven Spielberg, Joshua Brand, John Falsey**
Executive Producer **Steven Spielberg**

Lavish tales of the bizarre and the supernatural.

Movie giant Steven Spielberg was enticed back into television by the huge budget of this anthology series, which ran to 45 episodes. In the mould of THE TWILIGHT ZONE and THE OUTER LIMITS, *Amazing Stories* – with Spielberg scripting, directing and producing at various times – presents a collection of 30-minute fantasies and chillers. However, despite an array of star (or future star) names – Kevin Costner, Kiefer Sutherland, Harvey Keitel, Patrick Swayze and even Adam Ant – in front of the camera, and heavyweights like Clint Eastwood, Martin Scorsese, Burt Reynolds, Robert Zemeckis and Joe Dante behind it, it failed to capture the imagination of the public. This is no doubt part of the reason why the series did not materialize on UK TV until seven years after its US debut. More successful were Spielberg's supporting producers, Joshua Brand and John Falsey, who went on to create ST ELSEWHERE and NORTHERN EXPOSURE.

Stevens, Craig

(Gail Shikles; 1918–2000)

American actor popular at the turn of the 1960s, thanks to his portrayal of suave detective *Peter Gunn* and his role as photo journalist Mike Strait in MAN OF THE WORLD. A third series, *Mr Broadway*, proved less successful. In later years, he played David McCallum's boss, Walter Carlson, in THE INVISIBLE MAN, Asher Berg in RICH MAN, POOR MAN and, for a while, Craig Stewart in DALLAS.

Stevenson, Jessica

(1973–)

Brighton-born actress/writer best known as diet-dodging Cheryl Carroll in THE ROYLE FAMILY and as Daisy Steiner in SPACED (which she also co-wrote). Stevenson has also been seen in BOB AND ROSE (Holly Vance), *Tomorrow La Scala!* (Victoria) and *According to Bex* (Bex Atwell). Earlier appearances came alongside comedians Armstrong and Miller and in dramas like *Crown Prosecutor*, THE HOUSE OF ELIOTT and MIDSOMER MURDERS. She also featured in *Staying Alice* (Alice Timpson) and made guest appearances in RANDALL AND HOPKIRK (DECEASED) and AGATHA CHRISTIE'S MARPLE, as well as lending her voice to the animation *Bosom Pals*.

Stewart, Alastair

(1952–)

British journalist, presenter and newscaster. Stewart's initial TV work was for Southern Television in the late 1970s, before he joined ITN as its industrial correspondent in 1980. He was later Washington correspondent and anchor for various news bulletins, including NEWS *at Ten*, *News at 5.40* and *Channel 4 News*. He also worked on ITN specials, like election coverages, but left to launch *London Tonight*, Carlton TV's regional news programme in 1993. Since 1994 he has presented *The Sunday Programme* for GMTV and he has also hosted *Police, Camera, Action* and *Missing*.

Stewart, William G.

(1935–)

British comedy producer/director and latterly quiz show host. Stewart made his name in the late 1960s and early 1970s through programmes like MRS THURSDAY, *Send Foster*, FATHER, DEAR FATHER, BLESS THIS HOUSE, LOVE THY NEIGHBOUR, MY GOOD WOMAN, AND MOTHER MAKES FIVE, *Doctor Down Under*, *Down the Gate*, THE MANY WIVES OF PATRICK, *Paradise Island*, *My Name is Harry Worth*, SPOONER'S PATCH and THE RAG TRADE. In the 1980s he worked on the short-lived Alf Garnett revival *Till Death* ... and also the Channel 4 comedies THE LADY IS A TRAMP, *The Nineteenth Hole* and *The Bright Side*. Other credits include shows for comics like Frankie Howerd, Max Bygraves, Al Read, Larry Grayson, Tom O'Connor and Tommy Cooper, as well as the ITV game show THE PRICE IS RIGHT. From 1988 to 2003 he both produced and presented (very drily) the daily quiz show FIFTEEN TO ONE for Channel 4.

Stig of the Dump ★★

UK (Childsplay) Children's Drama. BBC 1 2002

Barney	**Thomas Sangster**
Robert	**Geoffrey Palmer**
Marjorie	**Phyllida Law**
Stig	**Robert Tannion**
Lou	**Perdita Weeks**
Caroline	**Saskia Wickham**
Billy Snarget	**Andrew Schofield**
Danny Snarget	**Andrew Mawdsley**
Kenny Snarget	**Craig Fitzpatrick**

Writer/Producer **Peter Tabern**

A young boy befriends a caveman he meets in a disused quarry.

This six-part Sunday teatime drama was broadly based on the 1963 children's novel of the same title by Clive King, although the story was brought up to modern times. It tells of young Barney, who, one summer, discovers a caveman living in a dump near his grandmother's house. In this version, the setting has been transferred from Kent to near Ashbourne, Derbyshire, Barney has acquired a grandfather (Robert) as well as a grandmother (Marjorie), and his single mother (Caroline) has more or less abandoned him and his sister (Lou) with the grandparents while she spends time with her new boyfriend. Also, for the first time, Stig is identified as belonging to a specific era and Barney and his pal Danny Snarget (one of three bullying brothers) ultimately help the sick man return to his own time, via an ancient rock arrangement. Otherwise, the premiss remains the same as in the book: a tale of friendship across the millennia as the modern boy helps the ingenuous caveman survive in an alien world. An earlier version was made by Thames Television (ITV 1981: Grant Ashley Warnock as Barney; Keith Jayne as Stig; adapted by Maggie Wadey and produced by Pamela Lonsdale).

Stilgoe, Richard

OBE (1943–)

Surrey-born humorist, musician and presenter. Cambridge Footlights graduate Stilgoe was a familiar face in the 1970s, writing topical ditties for THAT'S LIFE and NATIONWIDE. Later he was the front man on the sketch series A KICK UP THE EIGHTIES, and also appeared in *And Now the Good News*, the sketch shows *Psst!* and *Don't Ask Us*, and the sitcom *A Class by Himself*, which he also wrote. Stilgoe has also been involved in the theatre. Among his successes have been the musicals *Starlight Express* and *Phantom of the Opera*, for which he penned lyrics.

Stingray ***

UK (AP Films/ATV/ITC) Children's Science Fiction. ITV 1964–5

Voices:

Capt. Troy Tempest	**Don Mason**
George 'Phones' Sheridan	**Robert Easton**
Atlanta Shore	**Lois Maxwell**
Commander Sam Shore	**Ray Barrett**
Titan	**Ray Barrett**
Sub Lt. Fisher	**Ray Barrett**
X20	**Robert Easton**

Creators **Gerry Anderson, Sylvia Anderson**
Producer **Gerry Anderson**

● ***The crew of a supersub save the world.***

Stingray is the number-one craft of WASP, the World Aquanaut Security Patrol, which operates out of the city of Marineville, in the year 2000. With peace now established on land, the Earth's population has begun to harvest the minerals and other riches of the sea, which is where they encounter new enemies. WASP is the Earth's response to the dangers of the ocean.

Head of WASP is Commander Shore, a man crippled in a sea battle and now confined to a hoverchair. His assistant is Sub Lt. Fisher, and Shore's daughter, Atlanta, also lives and works in Marineville. Most of the action centres on the daring crew of *Stingray* itself, and in particular its fearless commander, Captain Troy Tempest. Voted 'Aquanaut of the Year', Tempest is the hero of the series, although he does have a juvenile tendency to sulk. His patrol partners are the amiable Phones (real name George Sheridan), who operates the craft's hydrophone sonar system, and Marina, a beautiful mute girl from the shell-like undersea world of Pacifica, where she grew up as the daughter of Emperor Aphony. Tempest saved her life and now she is in love with him. Back at Marineville, Marina owns a pet seal, Oink, and vies with Atlanta for Troy's attentions.

The arch-enemy of WASP is Titan, ruler of Titanica, who is assisted by his inept land-based agent, X20. Titan is also the power behind the evil Aquaphibians, who menace the ocean in mechanical Terror Fish, firing missiles from the large, fishy mouths. Stingray, a high-tech, blue-and-yellow supersub (with a number 3 on its tailfins), fires back Sting Missiles. Atomic-powered, the supersub can also leap from the waves like a salmon and dive deeper and travel faster than any other submarine.

Stingray was Gerry Anderson's third venture into Supermarionation. It was also the first British TV programme to be filmed in colour, even though it could only be shown in black and white on its initial run in the UK. Tension, for viewers, began to mount from Commander Shore's opening words at the start of each episode: 'Stand by for action. Anything can happen in the next half-hour!', but the closing theme song, 'Aquamarina', sung by Garry Miller, provided a soothing finish.

Stock, Nigel

(1919–86)

Malta-born, one-time child performer who grew into one of Britain's most prolific actors. His film career began in the 1930s, and he was also an early arrival on television. In 1947 he appeared in the Borstal play *Boys in Brown* and a farce, *The Happiest Days of Your Life*, and he continued to pop up in dramas for the next 30-odd years. In the 1950s–60s he made guest appearances in series like THE GAY CAVALIER, ESPIONAGE, THE SAINT, THE AVENGERS, DANGER MAN, THE TROUBLESHOOTERS and THE PRISONER and in 1965 took on the mantle of Dr Watson for the BBC's SHERLOCK HOLMES, a role he reprised three years later. Soon after, he joined THE DOCTORS as Thomas Owen, who then graduated to his own series, *Owen, MD*. In the 1970s he was Hoofd-Commissaris Samson in VAN DER VALK and appeared in series like COLDITZ and TINKER, TAILOR, SOLDIER, SPY. In 1981 he was cast as Wally James in TRIANGLE. Other appearances included parts in *And No Birds Sing*, *Churchill's People*, *A Tale of Two Cities*, *A Man Called Intrepid*, YES, MINISTER and *The Pickwick Papers*.

Stone Tape, The ***

UK (BBC) Drama. BBC 2 1972

Peter Brock	**Michael Bryant**
Jill	**Jane Asher**
Collinson	**Iain Cuthbertson**
Eddie	**Michael Bates**
Crawshaw	**Reginald Marsh**

Writer **Nigel Kneale**
Producer **Innes Lloyd**

● ***Tragedy awaits a team of ghostbusters in a mysterious mansion.***

An ultra-spooky, unseasonal offering for Christmas Day 1972. Nigel (QUATERMASS) Kneale's single drama tells of attempts by a scientific team led by Peter Brock to analyse the horrors that have taken place over the years in a Victorian house. With the latest technology, the crew intend to take readings from the walls, which may have absorbed various traumas, transferring the data onto a magnetic tape. Needless to say, all does not go to plan, with fateful consequences for Peter's colleague, Jill. Peter Sasdy directed; the BBC's Radiophonic Workshop added the atmospheric soundtrack.

Stoppard, Dr Miriam

(1937–)

British TV pop doctor who came to the fore in the 1970s as host and expert in YTV's science series DON'T ASK ME, *Don't Just Sit There* and WHERE THERE'S LIFE. Other credits have included *The Health Show* and *People Today*. She was formerly married to playwright Tom Stoppard.

Stoppard, Sir Tom

CBE (Thomas Strausler; 1937–)

Czech-born British playwright, a former freelance journalist who has contributed mainly to stage, radio and films, specializing in complex and intellectual productions. His *Professional Foul* (a 1977 *Play of the Week*) was an award winner. Among his other television offerings have been *Every Good*

Boy Deserves Favour (1979), an adaptation of *Three Men in a Boat* (1975) and the TV film *Squaring the Circle* (1984).

Storyboard ★★

UK (Thames) Drama Anthology. ITV 1983; 1985–6; 1989

● ***Intermittent series of drama pilots.***

Much in the style of COMEDY PLAYHOUSE, *Storyboard* was Thames TV's experimental drama anthology, giving airtime to assorted pilot episodes in the hope that some would turn into fully fledged series. Some, indeed, did. These were THE BILL (derived from the 1983 *Storyboard* episode entitled *Woodentop*), LYTTON'S DIARY, MR PALFREY OF WESTMINSTER (from a pilot called *The Traitor*), KING AND CASTLE and LADIES IN CHARGE.

Storyteller, The ★★★

UK (TVS/Jim Henson) Children's Entertainment. Channel 4 1988

The Storyteller .... **John Hurt**

● ***Classic European folktales brought to life with imaginative special effects.***

Using all the invention of Jim Henson's Creature Shop, *The Storyteller* was TVS's award-winning rendition of the great European fairytales. The Hobbit-like Storyteller related each tale in dramatic fashion at the side of his hearth, with his easily startled dog at his feet. Skilful animation by the Muppet team and complex special effects ensured that the series captured the imagination.

A follow-up series, *Jim Henson's Greek Myths* (Channel 4 1991), hosted by Michael Gambon, recalled the fabulous stories of ancient Greece concerning Theseus, Perseus, Orpheus and Eurydice, and Icarus and Daedalus.

Stott, Ken

(1955–)

Scottish actor whose best-known TV work has been as hospital radio DJ Eddie McKenna in TAKIN' OVER THE ASYLUM, Inspector Pat Chappel in THE VICE, Chief Inspector Red Metcalfe in MESSIAH and the second incarnation of Scottish detective REBUS. Stott also played Joe Hickey in *Bad Company*, fish farm manager McCaffrey in *A Mug's Game*, Barney Barnato in RHODES, Redfern in *Screen Two's Stone, Scissors, Paper*, striker Tommy Walton in DOCKERS, criminal Martin Cahill in *Vicious Circle*, Mike in *Promoted to Glory*, Adolf Hitler in *Uncle Adolf* and the Chancellor in *The Girl in the Café*. Other credits have come in TAGGART, THE SINGING DETECTIVE and SILENT WITNESS.

Stourton, Edward

(1957–)

Nigeria-born BBC newsreader, featuring in all the main bulletins in the 1990s and in current affairs programmes like PANORAMA, *Correspondent* and the religious series *Absolute Truth*, having previously worked for ITN and *Channel 4 News*.

Strachan, Michaela

(1966–)

Popular British children's presenter, seen first on TV-am hosting *Wide Awake Club* and *Wacaday*. Her other kids' series have included *Hey Hey It's Saturday*, *Michaela*, *Owl TV*, *But Can You Do It on TV?*, *Go-Getters*, *The Really Wild Show* and *Michaela's Wild Challenge*. Strachan has appeared regularly in *Countryfile* and presented *Elephant Diaries*, and was also seen with Pete Waterman in the late-night music show *The Hit Man and Her*.

Strange Report ★★

UK (Arena/ITC) Detective Drama. ITV 1969–70

Adam Strange .... **Anthony Quayle**
Hamlyn Gynt .... **Kaz Garas**
Evelyn McLean .... **Anneke Wills**
Prof. Marks .... **Charles Lloyd Pack**
Chief Supt. Cavanagh .... **Gerald Sim**

Creator/Executive Producer **Norman Felton**
Producer **Robert Buzz Berger**

● ***The adventures of a retired criminologist and his young assistants.***

Widower Adam Strange is a renowned expert on the criminal mind, a former Home Office criminologist. Although retired, he is called back into action whenever the authorities are baffled by a case or need help in sensitive areas. The investigations are complex and the crimes intricate, but Strange always has the answers, combining his vast experience with the latest techniques in a forensic laboratory at his Paddington flat. Assisted by a young museum researcher from Minnesota, Ham Gynt, and a model and artist neighbour, Evelyn McLean, Strange, rather unusually, races to the scenes of crime in an unlicensed black taxicab. Each episode is given a 'report' number: 'Report 4407 HEART – No Choice for the Donor', for instance, concerns an investigation into plans to use a live donor for a heart transplant, and 'Report 3906 COVER GIRLS – Last Year's Model' revolves around a mystery in the fashion world. Roger Webb supplies the music.

Strange World of Gurney Slade, The ★★★

UK (ATV) Situation Comedy. ITV 1960

Gurney Slade .... **Anthony Newley**

Creator **Anthony Newley**
Writers **Sid Green, Dick Hills**
Producer **Alan Tarrant**

● ***A young man wanders through life in a state of fantasy.***

In this bizarre, whimsical but short-lived series (only six episodes were made), the title character of Gurney Slade lives in a world of his own imagination. Talking to trees and animals, fantasizing about women, conjuring up unusual characters and bringing static beings to life, this young Londoner meanders his way through a number of weird situations.

Anthony Newley, the programme's creator and star, plucked the character's name from that of a Somerset village, and in devising this series he developed a concept that was simply too far ahead of its time. Audiences in 1960 were used to comfortable domestic comedies and that's what *The Strange*

World of Gurney Slade appeared to be, when it began by focusing on a family squabbling at home. But when Gurney suddenly stood up and walked off the set and into his own surreal world, he failed to take the bemused audience with him, and the series quickly drew to a close.

Stranger, The ★★

Australia (ABC) Science Fiction. BBC 1 1965–6

The Stranger (Adam Suisse) ... **Ron Haddrick**
Bernard Walsh ... **Bill Levis**
Jean Walsh ... **Janice Dinnen**
Peter Cannon ... **Michael Thomas**
Mr Walsh ... **John Fassen**
Mrs Walsh ... **Jessica Noad**
Prof. Mayer ... **Owen Weingott**
Varossa ... **Reginald Livermore**

Writer **G. K. Saunders**

An alien tries to create a new home for his people on Earth.

Shown as part of the *Tales From Overseas* strand, this six-part children's-hour drama is set in St Michael's School in southwest Australia. Bernie and Jean Walsh are the teenage offspring of headmaster Mr Walsh, and Peter Cannon is their schoolfriend. They are surprised one evening when a stranger turns up at the school, claiming to have lost his memory. Because of illness among the staff, the stranger – later known as Adam Suisse – is offered a post teaching languages and becomes a good friend of the pupils. However, when he keeps making long and frequent visits to the Blue Mountains, Bernie, Jean and Peter are intrigued. They follow him and discover his secret: he is actually an alien from the planet Soshuniss who has been sent to persuade the human race to share their planet with his people. The kids are taken to his home world and also meet Varossa, another alien visitor to Earth. Satellite expert Professor Mayer is drawn into events and finally government security services from Canberra are brought in to scupper the alien plans. In a six-part sequel, shown in 1966, Adam and Varossa are back on Earth preparing for the arrival of his compatriots but the world's media gets hold of the story and Peter finds himself taken captive on Soshuniss.

Strangers ★★

UK (Granada) Police Drama. ITV 1978–82

DS/DCI George Bulman ... **Don Henderson**
DC/DS Derek Willis ... **Dennis Blanch**
DS/DI David Singer ... **John Ronane**
WDC Linda Doran ... **Frances Tomelty**
WDC Vanessa Bennett ... **Fiona Mollison**
DCI Rainbow ... **David Hargreaves**
Det. Chief Supt. Jack Lambie .. **Mark McManus**
Insp. Pushkin ... **George Pravda**
William Dugdale ... **Thorley Walters**

Producer **Richard Everitt**

Scotland Yard detectives infiltrate crime rings in the North-West.

Notable for the return of the glove-wearing, inhaler-sniffing, Shakespeare-quoting Sgt Bulman, first seen in THE XYY MAN, *Strangers* once again teams the quirky detective with DC Derek Willis. This time they are based in Manchester, joined by WDC Linda Doran, an expert in self-defence who is later replaced by WDC Vanessa Bennett, a car fiend. They operate as Unit C23, literally 'strangers' in a neighbourhood where local police officers would be too well known. Assisted by DS Singer, who provides local knowledge, they take their assignments from the somewhat ineffective DCI Rainbow.

After two seasons, the format changes. The team moves back to London but can be given missions anywhere in the country. They become the 'Inner City Squad', under the command of Det. Chief Supt. Lambie, a tough, no-nonsense officer played by Mark McManus in a rehearsal for Taggart. Bulman is also introduced to William Dugdale, a university lecturer who has secret service connections and who is to assist him even more in the follow-up series, BULMAN. Willis is promoted to detective sergeant, and Bulman himself becomes a detective chief inspector in the penultimate season. The series ends with Bulman planning to marry Lambie's ex-wife. However, by the time *Bulman* reaches the screen, the engagement has clearly fallen through.

Strangers and Brothers ★★

UK (BBC) Drama. BBC 2 1984

Lewis Eliot ... **Shaughan Seymour**
Sheila Knight/Eliot ... **Sheila Ruskin**
Leonard March ... **Peter Sallis**
Roy Calvert ... **Nigel Havers**
Lady Muriel Royce ... **Elizabeth Spriggs**
Lord Boscastle ... **Tony Britton**
Lady Boscastle ... **Joan Greenwood**
Vernon Royce ... **Frederick Treves**
Charles March ... **Martyn Jacobs**
Ann March ... **Carmen du Sautoy**
Joan Royce ... **Kathryn Pogson**
Rosalind Wykes ... **Shirley Cassedy**
R. S. Robinson ... **Terence Alexander**
Francis Getliffe ... **Paul Hastings**
Margaret Davidson/Eliot ... **Cherie Lunghi**
Sir Hector Rose ... **Edward Hardwicke**
Geoffrey Hollis ... **Richard Heffer**
Roger Quaife ... **Anthony Hopkins**
Lady Caroline Quaife ... **Susan Fleetwood**
Austin Davidson ... **Christopher Casson**
Mr Knight ... **James Cossins**
Martin Eliot ... **Stephen Riddle**
Charles Eliot ... **Tony Hammond**
Irene Eliot ... **Tessa Peake-Jones**
Walter Luke ... **James Simmons**
Nora Luke ... **Vivienne Ritchie**
Arthur Mounteney ... **Gareth Thomas**

Writer **Julian Bond**
Producer **Philip Hinchcliffe**

A provincial boy makes his way through society and witnesses 'the corridors of power'.

Adapted from 11 somewhat autobiographical novels written over 30 years from 1940 by C. P. Snow, *Strangers and Brothers* tells of the life of Lewis Eliot, a Leicester boy who progresses through Cambridge and into the Establishment. Beginning in 1927, it follows his infatuation and eventual, short-lived, marriage to an unpredictable girl called Sheila Knight; his association at university with impetuous oriental specialist Roy Calvert; his post-graduation years at the Bar; and his wartime experience as a civil servant in Whitehall. It is there that he meets his second wife, Margaret Davidson, though she is already married at the time. In the Cold War years of the 1950s, Eliot fights for the cause of nuclear disarmament and becomes an associate of Tory minister Roger Quaife, whose scandalous life almost destroys Eliot's own career. In the 1960s, Eliot forgoes government in favour of writing but is tempted back by the offer of a job in the new Labour administration. Throughout the 13-part series, the concept of power, including those who wield it and how they do so, is a central theme (indeed Snow coined the phrase *The Corridors of Power* as the title for one of his books).

Strathblair ★★★

UK (BBC) Drama. BBC 1 1992–3

Alec Ritchie	**Derek Riddell**
Jennifer Ritchie	**Francesca Hunt**
Major Andrew Menzies	**David Robb**
Flora McInnes	**Kika Mirylees**
Sir James Menzies	**Ian Carmichael**
Pheemie Robertson	**Alison Peebles**
Alaistair McCrae	**Andrew Keir**
Robert Sinclair	**Neil McKinven**
Umberto Fabiani	**Urbano Barberini**
Mr Forbes	**Nicholas McArdle**

Creator **Bill Craig**
Executive Producer **Alex Gourlay**
Producers **Aileen Forsyth, Leonard White**

Newlywed, novice farmers struggle to make ends meet on a Scottish sheep farm.

In the early 1950s, Major Andrew Menzies returns home to Strathblair after military service with the Black Watch and walks straight into a row with his snooty dad, local laird Sir James. Against his father's wishes, Andrew has promised the tenancy of Corriebeg, a hill farm on the family's Perthshire estate, to one of his army men, Alec Ritchie. Ritchie promptly turns up to claim his gift with new wife Jennifer in tow. Despite initial wariness on all sides (not least because of the class difference between the working-class Ritchie and the Eton- and Sandhurst-educated Menzies), the newcomers proceed to make the farm work. They are assisted by a lazy sheepdog called Fly, local landgirl Pheemie Robertson and Pheemie's Italian ex-POW boyfriend, Umberto Fabiani. However, the relationship with resentful neighbouring farmer Alaistair McCrae (known to all as Balbuie, after the name of his farmstead, Wester Balbuie) is less harmonious. Also seen are Forbes, the cunning local grocer; McCrae's unreliable grandson, Robert Sinclair, who has given up his college place in Edinburgh to keep an eye on his inheritance in Strathblair; and the estate's factor, Flora McInnes, who has taken over the job after her husband's death at Anzio, and is now becoming close to Andrew. At the end of series one, Andrew has been called away to the Korean War and tragedy strikes at Strathblair, when Corriebeg burns to the ground. Series two picks up with the Ritchies temporarily living in a caravan while the croft is being rebuilt. Andrew, back from the war, turns to politics, standing against the local Conservative over plans for local land development. The two ten-part series of *Strathblair* – with their overdose of 1950s nostalgia and stunning scenery – were shot in the village of Blair Atholl and the surrounding countryside. Music was composed by Michael Gibbs.

Strauss, Peter

(1947–)

Largely seen in TV movies and blockbuster mini-series, American actor Peter Strauss made his TV name in the two RICH MAN, POOR MAN serials, playing Rudy Jordache. He was also Eleazar Ben Yair in MASADA, Dick Diver in TENDER IS THE NIGHT and Abel Rosnovski in *Kane and Abel*, as well as starring as *Peter Gunn* in a 1989 TV movie revival of the 1950s detective. In the 1990s he headlined in a US series called *Moloney* and provided the voice of Stoker for the cartoon series *Biker Mice from Mars*. In the new millennium he has starred as Dr Isaac Braun in *Body & Soul*.

Strauss Family, The ★★

UK (ATV) Historical Drama. ITV 1972

Johann Strauss	**Eric Woofe**
Johann Strauss Jr	**Stuart Wilson**
Anna Strauss	**Anne Stallybrass**
Adele Strauss	**Lynn Farleigh**
Emilie Trampusch	**Barbara Ferris**
Josef Lanner	**Derek Jacobi**
Eduard 'Edi' Strauss	**Tony Anholt**

Writers **Anthony Skene, David Butler**
Executive Producer **Cecil Clarke**
Producer **David Reid**

The life and times of Austria's famous musical family.

Spanning most of the 19th century and tracing 75 years of musical creativity from father and son Johann Strauss, Sr and Jr, this seven-part biopic wafts along to the strains of authentic Viennese waltzes, sweepingly performed by the London Symphony Orchestra. But, beyond the music, the duo's lives and loves are also explored. The series was made as part of ATV's historical drama spree in the mid-1970s.

Street-Porter, Janet

(1946–)

British presenter and TV executive. An architecture student and a former fashion journalist, Street-Porter came to the fore as a presenter for LWT, hosting, among other programmes, *Saturday Night People*, with Clive James and Russell Harty, and *After Midnight*. At the turn of the 1980s, she switched to behind-the-scenes work and then joined Channel 4, where she developed teenage output through *Network 7*. In 1988 she moved to the BBC to become Head of Youth Programming, which resulted in the DEF II programme strand and the commissioning of series like *Rough Guide to . . .* and *Rapido*. She was later the BBC's Head of Independent Entertainment Productions, bringing in series like *Paramount City*, *Ps and Qs* and HOW DO THEY DO THAT? In 1994 she joined Ffyona Campbell on the last leg of her global charity trek in *The Longest Walk*, and the same year left the BBC to be managing director of cable station L!ve TV, a post she quit after a year. Back in front of the camera, she has presented *Street-Porter's Men*, followed the work of art historian Nikolaus Pevsner in one of the *Travels With Pevsner* series, continued her walks in *As the Crow Flies*, made a series of *Cathedral Calls* and was one of the hosts of *Demolition*.

Streets of San Francisco, The ★★

US (Quinn Martin) Police Drama. ITV 1973–80 (US: ABC 1972–7)

Det. Lt. Mike Stone	**Karl Malden**
Insp. Steve Keller	**Michael Douglas**
Insp. Dan Robbins	**Richard Hatch**

Lt. Lessing .... **Lee Harris**
Sgt Sekulovich .... **Art Passarella**
Officer Haseejian .... **Vic Tayback**

Executive Producer **Quinn Martin**
Producers **William R. Yates, John Wilder, Cliff Gould**

● ***A veteran police officer and his young assistant tackle crime in the Bay Area.***

Detective Lt. Mike Stone is a widower with 23 years' experience in the force. He now works for the Bureau of Inspectors Division of the San Francisco Police Department, where he is paired with 28-year-old Insp. Steve Keller, a college graduate. Stone's tried-and-tested techniques are occasionally questioned by Keller, whose ideas are more modern, but they strike up an effective, wise-old-head/eager-younger-enthusiast partnership. When Keller leaves to take up teaching, he is replaced by another young cop, Dan Robbins, for the programme's last season.

For realism, some of the filming actually took place in the offices of the San Francisco Police Department, and the city's hilly streets were put to good use for the many car chases. The inspiration and the characters were drawn from Carolyn Weston's novel *Poor, Poor Ophelia*.

Strictly Come Dancing ★★★

UK (BBC) Entertainment. BBC 1 2004–

Presenters **Bruce Forsyth, Tess Daly, Natasha Kaplinsky**

Executive Producer **Karen Smith**
Producer **Izzi Pick**

● ***Celebrities put their best foot forward in a charity dancing contest.***

High-kicking new life into the televisually forgotten world of ballroom dancing, this celebrity showcase has proved remarkably popular with all ages. A bunch of celebrities are paired with professional dancing partners/tutors and coached each week in a couple of styles of dance. They then have to perform live on a Saturday and face the wrath of the assembled judges: Lorna Lee (series one only), Len Goodman, Craig Revel Horwood, Arlene Phillips and Bruno Tonioli. Next the phone lines are opened (profits going to Children in Need) and the public help decide who should live to dance another day, and who is shown the door.

The first batch of celebs taking to the floor were opera diva Lesley Garrett, rugby player Martin Offiah, actors Christopher Parker, Verona Joseph and Claire Sweeney, comedian Jason Wood, presenter David Dickinson, and the overall winner, BREAKFAST host Natasha Kaplinsky, who went on to co-host part of the second series with Bruce Forsyth. That series was contested by athletes Roger Black and Denise Lewis, comedian Julian Clary, gardener Diarmuid Gavin, singer Aled Jones, motoring expert Quentin Willson, THAT'S LIFE's Esther Rantzen, COUNTDOWN's Carol Vorderman and actresses Jill Halfpenny (the winner) and Sarah Manners. A Christmas special pitched the best couples of series one and two together, with Jill Halfpenny and her partner, Darren Bennet.

In series three, the winner was cricketer Darren Gough, who out-stepped athlete Colin Jackson, DJ Zoë Ball, chef James Martin, newsreader Bill Turnbull, snooker star Dennis Taylor, GMTV presenter Fiona Phillips, chat show host Gloria Hunniford and actors Will Thorp, Patsy Palmer, Jaye Jacobs and Siobhan Hayes. The 2005 Christmas special introduced rivalry from the US equivalent series, *Dancing with the Stars*, but Darren Gough and his partner, Lillia Kopylova, still triumphed.

The series has also generated spin-offs in the UK. In 2004 *Strictly Ice Dancing* and in 2005 *Strictly African Dancing* were two one-off specials, while a full series of *Strictly Dance Fever* (BBC 1 2005–), a non-celebrity event with a focus on salsa, swing, the lambada and other such styles, was hosted by Graham Norton.

Strictly Dance Fever

See *Strictly Come Dancing*.

Stride, John

(1936–)

British actor, star of THE MAIN CHANCE (solicitor David Main) and WILDE ALLIANCE (fiction writer/detective Rupert Wilde). He also played Julien Sorel in THE SCARLET AND THE BLACK and Lloyd George in *Number Ten*, and was seen in DIAMONDS (Frank Coleman), the BBC TELEVISION SHAKESPEARE production of *Henry VIII*, *Growing Rich* (Sir Bernard Bellamy), *The Old Devils* (Alun Weaver) and the dramatization of *The Trial of Klaus Barbie*. Other credits have included LOVE STORY, LYTTON'S DIARY (Wayne Munroe), *Imaginary Friends* (Prof. Tom McCann), JUMPING THE QUEUE (Tom), AGATHA CHRISTIE'S POIROT and THE INSPECTOR ALLEYN MYSTERIES.

Strike It Lucky/Strike It Rich ★★

UK (Thames/Central) Quiz. ITV 1986–94/1996–9

Presenter **Michael Barrymore**

Producer **Maurice Leonard**

● ***Easy-going game show involving quiz questions and a bank of illuminated TV screens.***

A game of general knowledge and chance, *Strike It Lucky* was a very effective vehicle for the talents of Michael Barrymore. His ease with the general public was highlighted in his dealings with (and gentle mockery of) the three pairs of contestants, and his manic, physical style of comedy was accommodated by a large, sprawling set.

The six contestants were divided up into question answerers and 'screen strikers'. By choosing to give two, three or four correct answers to questions in a given category (with a list of possible responses shown on a screen to help them), a contestant allowed his or her partner to advance the equivalent number of steps along a wide, raised stage. Each step housed a TV screen which, when 'struck', revealed a prize or a 'hot spot'. Contestants were able to stick with the prize or advance further along the stage. A hot spot cancelled all the prizes won in that turn, and attention then switched to the next pair of contestants.

The first contestants to cross the stage were offered a jackpot question which, if answered correctly, took them to the grand finale. For this finale the two contestants progressed along the stage together, striking screens, occasionally answering questions and hoping to avoid a set number of hot spots which would end their bid for the top cash prize. These prizes were significantly increased when the show was renamed *Strike It Rich* in 1996.

Stripping

A scheduling term meaning the transmission of the same programme on the same channel at the same time, five or more consecutive nights a week (as NEIGHBOURS has been in the UK, for instance).

Stritch, Elaine

(1926–)

American actress with a number of comedies and quizzes behind her in her native USA, as well as stage and film credits, but primarily known to UK viewers as writer Dorothy McNab, alongside Donald Sinden, in the culture-clash sitcom TWO'S COMPANY. She has also been seen in the UK in a 1973 adaptation of *Pollyanna* (Aunt Polly), the comedies *My Sister Eileen* (Ruth Sherwood) in 1964 and NOBODY'S PERFECT (Bill Hooper, also adapting the original US scripts herself) in 1980, plus series as diverse as TALES OF THE UNEXPECTED, THE COSBY SHOW and THIRD ROCK FROM THE SUN.

Strong, Gwyneth

(1959–)

London-born actress most familiar as Cassandra in ONLY FOOLS AND HORSES but seen in many other programmes, too. These have included THE FLOCKTON FLYER (Jan Carter), EDWARD THE SEVENTH (Minnie), *Bloody Kids*, PARADISE POSTPONED (Tina Fawcett/Kitson), THE KRYPTON FACTOR, *Nice Town* (Linda Thompson), *99–1* (Charlotte), *The Missing Postman* (WPC McMahon), REAL WOMEN (Janet), *Forgotten* (Denise Longden) and *Lucy Sullivan is Getting Married* (Hetty), with guest appearances in series such as MINDER, SILENT WITNESS, A TOUCH OF FROST, AN UNSUITABLE JOB FOR A WOMAN, CASUALTY, MURDER IN SUBURBIA and DOCTORS. She is married to actor Jesse Birdsall.

Strong, Mark

(Marco Salussolia; 1963–)

British actor of Italian/Austrian descent who shot to fame as Tosker Cox in OUR FRIENDS IN THE NORTH. Strong has also been seen in BETWEEN THE LINES, THE BUDDHA OF SUBURBIA, PRIME SUSPECT (Larry Hall), SHARPE, INSPECTOR MORSE, JANE AUSTEN'S EMMA (Mr Knightley), BIRTHS, MARRIAGES AND DEATHS (Terry), GOLD (Mr Smithson), *Trust* (Michael Mitcham), *In the Name of Love* (Chris Monroe), *Bomber* (Col. Chris Forsyth), ANNA KARENINA (Oblonsky), *The Jury* (Len Davies), *Fields of Gold* (Dr Tolkin) and *Falling Apart* (Pete). Other major roles have included Harry Starks in THE LONG FIRM, the Duke of Norfolk in *Henry VIII* and Andy Spader in *Walk Away and I Stumble*.

Stubbs, Una

(1937–)

British dancer and actress, first appearing in series like COOL FOR CATS, SUNDAY NIGHT AT THE LONDON PALLADIUM (in the chorus), *Moody in* . . . and NOT ONLY . . . BUT ALSO . . . In 1966 she began a nine-year (on-and-off) run as Alf Garnett's daughter, Rita, in TILL DEATH US DO PART, reprising the role occasionally in the follow-up series, *In Sickness and in Health*, in the 1980s. Stubbs was one of the team captains in the charades game GIVE US A CLUE, and played Aunt Sally in WORZEL GUMMIDGE. She appeared in the kids' comedies *Morris Minor's Marvellous Motors*, *The Worst Witch* and *Tricky Business*, and has been seen also in THE STRANGE WORLD OF GURNEY SLADE, FAWLTY TOWERS, HAPPY FAMILIES, *Delta Wave*, HEARTBEAT, MIDSOMER MURDERS, CASUALTY, BORN AND BRED, *Von Trapped* (Kath), *The Catherine Tate Show* and AGATHA CHRISTIE'S MARPLE, among other programmes. Her two husbands were both actors: Peter Gilmore and Nicky Henson.

STV

See *Scottish Television*.

Subtitle

Text superimposed on the screen (usually at the bottom) to provide a translation of foreign dialogue or to allow viewers with hearing difficulties to follow the action.

Suchet, David

OBE (1946–)

British actor, the brother of ITN newscaster John Suchet, undoubtedly best known for his work as AGATHA CHRISTIE'S POIROT, although he has enjoyed many other prominent roles. He played Blott in BLOTT ON THE LANDSCAPE, Edward Teller in OPPENHEIMER, Inspector Tsientsin in REILLY – ACE OF SPIES, Sigmund Freud in FREUD, Shakespeare's *Timon of Athens*, Adolf Verloc in *The Secret Agent*, Morris Price in *Seesaw*, Augustus Melmotte in THE WAY WE LIVE NOW, DI John Borne in NCS MANHUNT, Baron Stockmar in *Victoria and Albert*, George Carmen in *Get Carmen* and Cardinal Wolsey in HENRY VIII. He supplied the voice of the Phoenix for THE PHOENIX AND THE CARPET and narrated *Space Odyssey – Voyage to the Planets*, and among his other credits have been parts in dramas like PUBLIC EYE, THE PROTECTORS, THE PROFESSIONALS, OXBRIDGE BLUES, *Ulysses*, KING AND CASTLE, *Nobody Here But Us Chickens*, *Time to Die* and MURDER IN MIND.

Suchet, John

(1944–)

British journalist and newscaster, once with Reuters and the BBC but from 1972 to 2004 on ITN's staff. As well as working as ITN's Washington correspondent in the early 1980s, Suchet fronted most of the main news bulletins, including NEWS *at Ten*, *News at 5.40* and the lunchtime programmes. In 2006 he returned to news reading with a six-month assignment to *Five News*. Suchet is also a presenter of classical music on radio. His brother is actor David Suchet and he is the father of actor Damian Suchet.

Suddenly Susan ★★

US (Warner Brothers) Situation Comedy. Channel 4 1997–9 (US: NBC 1996–2000)

Susan Keane/Browne	**Brooke Shields**
Jack Richmond	**Judd Nelson**
Vicki Groener/Rubenstein	**Kathy Griffin**
Luis Rivera	**Nestor Carbonell**
Todd Stites	**David Strickland**
Helen Miller ('Nana')	**Barbara Barrie**

Maddy Piper .... **Andrea Bendewald**
Ian Maxtone-Graham .... **Eric Idle**
Nathan 'Nate' Neborsky .... **Currie Graham**
Miranda Charles .... **Sherri Shepherd**
Oliver Browne .... **Rob Estes**

Executive Producers **Gary Dontzig, Steven Peterman**

A girl ditches her rich but dull boyfriend and discovers a new lease of life.

Susan Keane 'suddenly' becomes a vibrant, interesting person when she dumps her ultra-rich fiancé on their wedding day. Now – egged on by her feisty Nana – she can start living and, to coincide with her liberation, she is promoted at work. A copy editor with a San Francisco magazine called *The Gate*, she is given her own lifestyle column ('Suddenly Susan'), which she fills with details of her nights out and the wacky people she encounters. At the mag, her supportive but slightly offbeat boss is Jack Richmond (brother of the tedious guy she has jilted and himself a romantic attachment for Susan in later episodes). Colleagues include sharp-tongued Vicki, the food and drink correspondent who marries a rabbi; Luis, a photographer; Todd, a rock music critic; and Maddy, a later addition to the writing staff who has an affair with Luis. When Jack eventually sells *The Gate*, Susan's new boss is Englishman Ian Maxtone-Graham and he upsets the staff by turning the publication into a men's magazine. Ian brings with him officious assistant Miranda Charles, sports writer Nate Neborsky and photographer Oliver Browne, the man who finally turns Susan's head for ever.

Sugden, Mollie

(1922–)

Yorkshire-born actress, the first choice of many producers when casting interfering, over-the-top mother figures. She played Mrs Clitheroe (Jimmy's mum) in JUST JIMMY, Mrs Hutchinson (Sandra's mum) in THE LIVER BIRDS, Mrs Waring (Duncan's mum) in *Doctor in Charge* (see DOCTOR IN THE HOUSE), Mrs Bassett (George's mum) in MY WIFE NEXT DOOR, Terry Scott's mum in *Son of the Bride* and Ida Willis (Robert Price's natural mum) in the adoption comedy THAT'S MY BOY. She was also Mrs Crispin in HUGH AND I, Flavia in UP POMPEII!, Mrs Noah in COME BACK MRS NOAH, Nora Powers in *My Husband and I* (opposite her late real-life husband, William Moore) and Nellie Harvey, landlady of The Laughing Donkey, in CORONATION STREET. Undoubtedly, her most popular character, however, has been Mrs Slocombe in ARE YOU BEING SERVED? and *Grace and Favour*. She has been seen also in other comedies, including PLEASE SIR!, FOR THE LOVE OF ADA, JUST WILLIAM and LITTLE BRITAIN, dramas like *Oliver's Travels* (Mrs Robson), the consumer show THAT'S LIFE, the *Revolver* sketch show and panel games such as WHODUNNIT? and CLUEDO.

Suez 1956 ★★★

UK (BBC) Drama. BBC 1 1979

Sir Anthony Eden .... **Michael Gough**
President Gamal Abdel Nasser .... **Robert Stephens**
Selwyn Lloyd .... **Peter Cellier**
Harold Macmillan .... **Richard Vernon**
Anthony Nutting .... **Richard Heffer**
Sir Winston Churchill .... **Wensley Pithey**
Anthony Head .... **Frederick Treves**
Earl of Home .... **Gerald Sim**
R. A. B. Butler .... **Lindsay Campbell**
Sir Walter Monckton .... **Patrick Troughton**
Hugh Gaitskell .... **Oscar Quitak**
Alfred Robens .... **Martin Wyldeck**
Denis Healey .... **Davyd Harries**
James Callaghan .... **Leon Sinden**
Gen. Mohammed Abdul Hakim Amer .... **Reginald Marsh**
Dr Mahmoud Fawzi .... **Edward Kelsey**
David Ben-Gurion .... **Edward Burnham**
Gen. Moshe Dayan .... **Jeremy Child**
Christian Pineau .... **Dudley Jones**
Guy Mollet .... **Lloyd Lambie**
Maurice Bourges-Maunoury .. **André Maranne**
Nikita Khrushchev .... **Aubrey Morris**
John Foster Dulles .... **Alexander Knox**
President Eisenhower .... **Michael Turner**
Robert Murphy .... **Robert Beatty**
Gen. Sir Gerald Templer .... **Mark Dignam**
Lt. Gen. Sir Hugh Stockwell .... **Douglas Wilmer**
Lt. Gen. Sir John Bagot Glubb **David Webb**
Admiral Earl Mountbatten ..... **Mark Brackenbury**
Lady Eden .... **Jennifer Daniel**
Sir Robert Menzies .... **Robert Raglan**
Dag Hammarskjøld .... **Seymour Green**

Writer **Ian Curteis**
Producer **Cedric Messina**

Epic account of how the Government dealt with the Suez Crisis of 1956.

Michael Darlow directs this detailed exploration of the Suez Crisis, which brought to an end the brief premiership of Sir Anthony Eden. Initially screened over three hours (with a short interval for the news), the play relates events taking place between March and November 1956, and the UK Government's response to the nationalization of the Suez Canal by new Egyptian president Nasser. It is a tale of diplomatic intrigue and brinkmanship, high-level resignations and intense international unease, as Britain, in alliance with France and Israel, opts for military intervention to secure the vital waterway. Apart from the major British politicians of the day, other key players include John Foster Dulles, US Secretary of State; Christian Pineau, French Foreign Minister; and David Ben-Gurion, Prime Minister of Israel.

In advance of the broadcast, writer Ian Curteis denied that his work was a reconstruction or a drama-documentary. He stressed that, although the facts were correct, the interpretation of those facts and other assumptions were his own. Such elements, he said, make up some three-quarters of the whole play.

Sullavan Brothers, The ★★

UK (ATV) Drama. ITV 1964–5

Paul Sullavan .... **Anthony Bate**
John Sullavan .... **Tenniel Evans**
Beth Sullavan .... **Mary Kenton**
Robert Sullavan QC .... **Hugh Manning**
Patrick Sullavan .... **David Summer**

Creator **Ted Willis**
Producer **Jack Williams**

Legal eagling with a family law team.

The Sullavan Brothers are three solicitors and a barrister who work in tandem for the benefit of their distressed clients. The barrister is Robert, a big, bulldozing type who takes on the most serious cases. The team administrator is Paul, a logical, level-headed thinker; John is the blind, cultured idealist; and youngest brother Patrick is a handsome, vintage car aficionado who does most of the leg work. Also involved is John's wife, Beth.

Sullivan, Ed

(1901–74)

The most famous of all variety show hosts. Ed Sullivan's background was in newspaper journalism, and it was as a Broadway columnist that he was introduced to the major showbusiness names of the 1930s, leading to his own immersion in radio and film work as an impresario and compere. When TV began to take off, Sullivan was quickly in the action, pioneering the variety show format with *The Toast of the Town* (soon renamed *The Ed Sullivan Show*) from 1948. In this legendary Sunday night American programme, Sullivan introduced to viewers many budding or emerging stars, and gave countless others their TV debut. They ranged from Dean Martin and Jerry Lewis (in the very first show) to Elvis Presley and The Beatles. The series ran until 1971. Never known for his ease in front of the camera, Sullivan, nicknamed 'The Great Stone Face', was nevertheless one of TV's early giants.

Sullivan, John

OBE (1946–)

London-born comedy writer, a former scene shifter at the BBC who knew he could write better scripts than the ones he was servicing. He talked producer Dennis Main Wilson into looking at his idea for a comedy based around a south London Marxist revolutionary and CITIZEN SMITH was born, initially as an episode of *Comedy Special*. Sullivan's next creation has been widely acclaimed as his greatest, namely ONLY FOOLS AND HORSES, although he has also entertained viewers with JUST GOOD FRIENDS, DEAR JOHN, SITTING PRETTY, ROGER ROGER, HEARTBURN HOTEL (with Steve Glover), MICAWBER, THE GREEN GREEN GRASS and the two-part wartime comedy-drama *Over Here*, as well as gags for THE TWO RONNIES. His London roots tend to show through in most of his work. Sullivan has also written (and sometimes performed) the theme songs for most of his own series.

Sullivans, The ★★★

Australia (Crawford) Drama. ITV 1977–82

David Sullivan .... **Paul Cronin**
Grace Sullivan .... **Lorraine Bayly**
John Sullivan .... **Andrew McFarlane**
Tom Sullivan .... **Steven Tandy**
Terry Sullivan .... **Richard Morgan**
Kitty Sullivan .... **Susan Hannaford**
Harry Sullivan .... **Michael Caton**
Geoff Sullivan .... **Jamie Higgins**
Jim Sullivan .... **Andy Anderson**
Maggie Hayward/Baker .... **Vikki Hammond**
Anna Kaufman/Sullivan .... **Ingrid Mason**
Lotte Kaufman .... **Marcella Burgoyne**
Hans Kaufman .... **Leon Lissek**
Jack Fletcher .... **Reg Gorman**
Magpie Haddern .... **Gary Sweet**
Rose Sullivan .... **Maggie Dence**
Mrs Jessup .... **Vivean Gray**
Major Barrington .... **Roger Oakley**
Melina .... **Chantal Contouri**
Bert Duggan .... **Peter Hehir**
Caroline O'Brien .... **Toni Vernon**
Michael Watkins .... **John Walton**
Alice Morgan .... **Megan Williams**
Norm Baker .... **Norman Yemm**

Executive Producers **Hector Crawford, Jock Blair**

● ***An Australian family struggles to come to terms with World War II.***

Beginning in 1939, *The Sullivans* relates the continuing story of the Melbourne-based Sullivan family, headed by engineering foreman dad Dave and devout Catholic mum Grace. They have four children: John is a medical student but also a pacifist, and he joins the army very reluctantly; his brother, Tom, is also recruited, while third son Terry is still only a freckle-faced youth when hostilities begin. The family's daughter is 13-year-old Kitty (played by 24-year-old actress Susan Hannaford). Anna Kaufman is John's girlfriend, a beautiful girl who suffers cruel abuse as anti-semitism spreads around the world.

Inspired by Granada's A FAMILY AT WAR, *The Sullivans* follows the family through thick and thin as the war takes a grip on the Antipodes. Scenes of desert and jungle conflicts, or action in Europe and North Africa, are combined with everyday domestic ups and downs, but many of the most poignant moments come after the war has ended. Terry's descent into petty crime is disturbing enough, but more shocking is Kitty's suicide following a visit to the devastation of Hiroshima with her photographer husband.

The Sullivans was a popular lunchtime offering in the UK, beginning just a year after its Australian première and conceived by ITV as a ready replacement for EMMERDALE FARM, which had been promoted to peak hours. In its native country, the series paved the way for later international hits like PRISONER: CELL BLOCK H, NEIGHBOURS and HOME AND AWAY, with many of *The Sullivans'* performers popping up in new guises in Wentworth, Erinsborough and Summer Bay.

Sunburn ★★

UK (BBC) Drama. BBC 1 1999–2000

Nicki Matthews .... **Michelle Collins**
Alan Brookes .... **George Layton**
Carol Simpson .... **Sharon Small**
Laura Hutchings .... **Rebecca Callard**
Julie Hill .... **Colette Brown**
Greg Patterson .... **James Buller**
Maria .... **Natalie Robb**
Yiannis Kyprianou .... **Peter Polycarpou**
Tassos .... **George Zenios**
Elena .... **Zeta Graff**
David Janus .... **Paul Nicholas**
Lee Wilson .... **Sean Maguire**

Creator **Mike Bullen**
Executive Producer **Antony Wood**
Producers **Kay Patrick, Julie Gardner**

● ***Professional and personal dilemmas for a team of holiday reps.***

Fun in the sun for winter Saturday evenings was the aim of this light-hearted drama, based around the lives of a group of package holiday reps. Nicki Matthews is the team leader, shepherding her clipboard-hugging associates through a long hot summer in the fictitious Cyprus resort of Limanaki. For Nicki, however, there is more on the menu than cheesy barbecues and plate smashing. She's currently estranged from her husband and now runs into Yiannis, a local with whom she had an affair some time ago. Love wires need to be untangled. Otherwise, the daily diet is based on keeping loutish lads in check, ensuring the safety and comfort of pensioners and selling excursions, although precious little help comes from inept area manager Alan Brookes. For series two, the setting shifts to the Algarve. Nicki has taken her crew of Laura, Carol and Greg along with her, augmented by new raw recruit Lee Wilson, who replaces the first series' Julie. Hapless Alan has also been transferred but new on the scene to oversee their efforts is David Janus, the man who owns the company and may just be interested in Nicki, too. Star Michelle Collins also sang the catchy title song – a minor UK hit in 1999. Fourteen episodes were made in all.

Sunday

See *Bloody Sunday*.

Sunday Night at the London Palladium ✶✶✶✶

UK (ATV) Variety. ITV 1955–67; 1973–4

Comperes **Tommy Trinder, Hughie Green, Alfred Marks, Robert Morley, Arthur Haynes, Dickie Henderson, Bruce Forsyth, Don Arrol, Bob Monkhouse, Dave Allen, Norman Vaughan, Jimmy Tarbuck, Des O'Connor, Roger Moore; Jim Dale**

Creator **Val Parnell**
Producers **Albert Locke, Francis Essex, Jon Scoffield, Colin Clews**

● ***Weekly showcase of international stars, at the world's number-one variety theatre.***

Sunday Night at the London Palladium was a British institution in the 1950s and 1960s. It was the show that everyone talked about the next day at work and it brought the world's most celebrated stars, plus the best of home-grown talent, into the living room of the ordinary citizen. The first ever show featured Gracie Fields and Guy Mitchell, and other stars appearing during its initial 12-year run included Judy Garland, Bob Hope, Johnny Ray, Liberace, Petula Clark, The Beatles and The Rolling Stones. The cheeky Italian mouse puppet Topo Gigio was a regular visitor. The programme's first host was music hall comedian Tommy Trinder, who set the tone with his sharp ad-libs and fast talk. Others are listed above with, apart from Trinder, the main presenters being Norman Vaughan, Jimmy Tarbuck and Bruce Forsyth. Forsyth, like Trinder before him, was the perfect compere for the show's games interlude, *Beat the Clock*, which was based on the American quiz show of the same name and involved couples performing silly tricks or stunts within a set time-period. Another feature was *The Word Game*, which called for words to be rearranged to make a sentence. Bruce kept order by yelling 'I'm in charge', and prizes were awarded to successful participants. THE GENERATION GAME was a logical progression.

The format of *Sunday Night at the London Palladium* seldom varied. Lasting an hour, it began with the high-kicking Tiller Girls and then a welcome from the compere. He introduced a couple of lesser acts, before launching into *Beat the Clock*. The second half of the show was devoted to the big name of the week, and the programme was rounded off with the entire cast waving goodbye from the famous revolving stage. Although cancelled in 1967, *Sunday Night at the London Palladium* was revived briefly in 1973, with Jim Dale as host, but its heyday had long gone and it survived only one year. However, that didn't stop another short-lived revival in 2000, with Bruce Forsyth in charge of *Tonight at the London Palladium*.

Sunnyside Farm ✶

UK (Granada) Situation Comedy. BBC 2 1997

Ray Sunnyside .... **Phil Daniels**
Ken Sunnyside .... **Mark Addy**
Ezekiel Letchworth .... **Michael Kitchen**
Mr Mills .... **Matt Lucas**
Wendy .... **Beth Goddard**
Justin .... **Tony Gardner**
Titania .... **Jennifer Leviston**
Oberon .... **Oliver Hamilton**

Writers **Richard Preddy, Gary Howe**
Producer **Spencer Campbell**

● ***Two brothers are stuck in the mire of their family farm.***

In the well-established tradition of situation comedy, *Sunnyside Farm* is anything but what its name suggests. This 40-acre dung heap is the home of brothers Ray and Ken Sunnyside. The self-absorbed Ray has no real interest in the place but is trapped in this rustic prison because of his brother. Ken is the brawnier sibling, sadly lacking a brain cell or two: he's the kind of farmer who can lose 15 cows on a bus. As we join the hapless pair, things appear to be looking up for Ray, with the arrival of new neighbours – or rather with the arrival of the lovely Wendy, for Ray seems rather blind to the fact that she has a husband and two kids. However, he is soon dismayed to find that these middle-class townies, who call their irritating brats Titania and Oberon, are really not his cup of tea after all. Adding colour to the boys' life are neighbours Mr Mills and Ezekiel Letchworth. Mills is an eccentric fellow farmer and part-time transvestite, while Letchworth is a smarmy, sarcastic, money-grabbing landowner. Critical acclaim not forthcoming, only one series of six episodes was produced.

Supercar ✶✶

UK (AP Films/ATV/ITC) Children's Science Fiction. ITV 1961–2

Voices:
Mike Mercury .... **Graydon Gould**
Prof. Popkiss .... **George Murcell**
Cyril Shaps
Jimmy Gibson .... **Sylvia Anderson**
Dr Beaker .... **David Graham**
Mitch .... **David Graham**
Masterspy .... **George Murcell**
Cyril Shaps
Zarin .... **David Graham**

Creators **Gerry Anderson, Reg Hill**
Writers **Martin Woodhouse, Hugh Woodhouse, Gerry Anderson, Sylvia Anderson**
Producer **Gerry Anderson**

● ***Adventures with the crew of an amazing land, sea and air vehicle.***

Gerry Anderson's first science-fiction series was based around a unique vehicle: a car, a plane and a submarine all rolled into one. Test pilot of Supercar is racing-driver-cum-airman-cum-deep-sea-diver Mike Mercury, who is joined on his missions by Professor Popkiss and the stammering Dr Beaker, co-inventors of the car. Also aboard are freckly ten-year-old Jimmy Gibson (one of two brothers whom Mike and Supercar rescued at sea) and Mitch, Jimmy's talking monkey. The Supercar team is based at a secret laboratory in an American desert, but their travels see them helping people and averting disasters all over the world. Their day-to-day enemies are the Sidney Greenstreet/Peter Lorre-type partnership of Masterspy and his sidekick, Zarin, who aim to steal Supercar and use it for their evil ends. Of course they never succeed.

Somewhat primitive by the standards of his later efforts, *Supercar* nevertheless was a breakthrough for Gerry Anderson, taking his puppet expertise to new levels and cementing his new partnership with Lew Grade's ITC production and distribution company. It was also the series that coined the term 'Supermarionation' to express the elaborate style of puppetry involved.

Supergran ✱✱

UK (Tyne-Tees) Children's Comedy. ITV 1985–7

Granny Smith ('Supergran') ... **Gudrun Ure**
The Scunner Campbell .... **Iain Cuthbertson**
Inventor Black .... **Bill Shine**
Insp. Muggins .... **Robert Austin**
Muscles .... **Alan Snell**
Dustin .... **Brian Lewis**
Edison .... **Holly English**
PC Leekie .... **Terry Joyce**
Tub .... **Lee Marshall**
Willard .... **Ian Towell**

Writer **Jenny McDade**
Producers **Keith Richardson, Graham C. Williams**

An old lady becomes a superheroine and uses her powers to help others.

Struck by a beam from a magic ray machine, gentle old Granny Smith finds herself accidentally endowed with superhuman powers. Adopting the guise of Supergran, she sets out on her amazing 'flycycle' to defend the good folk of Chisleton against baddies like The Scunner Campbell. Also in the action is Inventor Black, the man whose magic ray has transformed the old lady. Supergran was based on the books by Forrest Wilson. Billy Connolly co-wrote the programme's theme music.

Superman ✱✱

US (Lippert/National Periodical Publications) Science Fiction. ITV 1956–7 (US: Syndicated 1951–7)

Superman/Clark Kent .... **George Reeves**
Lois Lane .... **Phyllis Coates**
Noel Neill
Jimmy Olsen .... **Jack Larson**
Perry White .... **John Hamilton**
Insp. William Henderson .... **Robert Shayne**

Producers **Robert Maxwell, Bernard Luber, Whitney Ellsworth**

TV's first rendition of the comic-strip saga.

Created by Jerome Siegel and Joe Shuster in 1938, Superman is a refugee from the planet Krypton who lives on Earth and is endowed with superhuman powers. Under his *alter ego* of Clark Kent, he lives in Metropolis and works as a reporter for *The Daily Planet*, an ideal position for hearing about crime as it happens. Stripping off his spectacles and donning his tights and cape, Superman races to the rescue of helpless civilians, who often turn out to be his friends and colleagues. Demonstrating his superhuman strength by smashing down walls and bending iron bars, he is hailed as 'faster than a speeding bullet', once spectators have worked out that it is not a bird or a plane that has just flown past, but Superman himself. Those friends and colleagues include top reporter Lois Lane (in love with Superman, but disparaging of Clark Kent) and hapless trainee newshound Jimmy Olsen. His boss is pipe-smoking editor Perry White, often heard to exclaim, 'Great Caesar's ghost,' whenever anything startling happens, which is pretty often.

George Reeves, who had played Brent Tarleton in *Gone with the Wind*, suffered chronically from typecasting after this role, to the point where he was unable to work and eventually took his own life. Co-star Noel Neill reappeared briefly in the 1970s film version, this time as Superman's mother. See also THE NEW ADVENTURES OF SUPERMAN.

Supernatural [1] ✱✱

UK (BBC) Drama Anthology. BBC 1 1977

Writers **Robert Muller, Sue Lake**
Producer **Pieter Rogers**

Eight chilling stories hosted by a fictitious secret society.

Supernatural introduces viewers to the mysterious Club of the Damned and in particular the initiation rite it imposes on would-be members. To join this Victorian club you have to tell a spooky story that will make other members' spines tingle, but woe betide you if you fail. Eight such stories feature in this 1977 summertime substitute for MATCH OF THE DAY. Among the stars featuring in the 50-minute Gothic thrillers that resurrect werewolves, vampires, ghosts and other horror creations are Robert Hardy, Jeremy Brett, Denholm Elliott, Judy Cornwell, Gordon Jackson and Jeremy Clyde. Two stories focus on the same central character: Transylvanian Countess Ilona (Billie Whitelaw), whose guests don't quite receive the hospitality they expect. Another recurring character is Sir Francis, played by André Van Gyseghem. Seven of the stories were penned by Robert Muller, with Sue Lake contributing the eighth. Muller (who later became Billie Whitelaw's second husband) also edited an accompanying paperback book.

Supernatural [2]

See *Supersense*.

Supersense ✱✱✱

UK (BBC) Natural History. BBC 1 1988–9

Narrator **Andrew Sachs**

Writer/Producer **John Downer**

The remarkable use of senses by the creatures of the world.

This landmark documentary series explores the world of animal behaviour, focusing on extraordinary sensory perception that allows birds to navigate, certain creatures to predict natural disasters, fish to return to their spawning grounds, etc. Producer John Downer followed up with *Lifesense* (BBC 1 1991), which looks at the interaction between animals and humans from the animals' point of view. A third instalment, *Supernatural* (BBC 1 1999), employs the latest technology, and a certain amount of guile, to further explore the amazing world of animal senses and powers. Sharks that use electro-radiation to track down human swimmers, plants that summon help to fight off predators, creatures that somehow adapt to survive in extreme conditions and dolphins that employ ultrasound to investigate their environment are just some of the subjects covered.

Supersonic ★★

UK (LWT) Pop Music 1975–7

Creator/Producer **Mike Mansfield**

● ***State-of-the-art 1970s pop showcase.***

One of ITV's many attempts to match the success of TOP OF THE POPS, *Supersonic* suffered from the usual problem – networking (or lack of it), being shown at various times around the ITV regions (mostly Saturday mornings). The man behind the show was producer/director Mike Mansfield, who conceived the idea of a music show without a regular host. Instead, a camera was installed in the director's gallery and the acts were introduced simply by being cued in – along with the cameras, sound, etc. – by Mansfield himself ('Good luck, everybody, and roll *Supersonic*'). On the studio floor, the latest techniques were employed, such as roving cameras, stars perched on crane lifts over the audience, bubble machines, fireworks and the usual sea of dry ice and smoke. In his control box, Mansfield called up special effects like crazy wipes and multiple images. Four or five bands/artists appeared in each show, some performing more than once, and not just their current releases.

Superstars, The ★★★

UK (BBC/TWI) Sport. BBC 1 1975–82; 1985; 2003; 2005

Presenters **David Vine, Ron Pickering, Johnny Vaughan, Suzi Perry**

Producers **Ian Smith, Peter Hylton Cleaver, Cathy Jones**

● ***International sportsmen tackle representatives from other sports in a contest of fitness and skill.***

Beginning as a domestic event (initially entitled *Sporting Superstars*) but later going international, *The Superstars* was an innovative test of power, fitness, skill and adaptability. It aimed to discover which sports provided the best all-round athletes and competitors by pitting top names against each other in a series of contests. These ranged from gym tests (push-ups, squat thrusts, etc.), to disciplines like football control, rifle shooting, distance running, sprinting, cycling, basketball, archery, weightlifting, swimming and rowing. Competitors were not allowed to compete in their own sports or in sports akin to their own. The series made household names of lesser-known sportsmen like judo star Brian Jacks and rugby league's Keith Fielding. A spin-off series, *The Superteams*, matched team competitors from various sports. *Superstars* was exhumed for 2002's *Sport Relief* telethon, the winner being England rugby international Austin Healey, and a full series returned a year later. With events staged at the La Manga sports resort in Spain, and introduced by Johnny Vaughan and Suzi Perry, the winners were Du'aine Ladejo (athletics) for the men, and Zoe Baker (swimming) and Lesley McKenna (snowboarding) in a tie for the women. There was no event in 2004 but *Superstars* resumed in 2005, with Zoe Baker again claiming the female title and skier Alain Baxter taking the male honours.

Superted ★★

UK (Siriol/S4C) Animation. BBC 1 1983–6; 1990

Voices:

Superted .... **Derek Griffiths**
Spottyman .... **Jon Pertwee**
Texas Pete .... **Victor Spinetti**
Bulk .... **Roy Kinnear**
Skeleton .... **Melvyn Hayes**

Narrator **Peter Hawkins**

Writer **Robin Lyons**
Producer **Mike Young**

● ***A defective teddy bear becomes a superhero and saves the world.***

Airing first in Welsh on S4C, these colourful little adventures (directed by Dave Edwards) tell the tale of an unassuming teddy that was once cast aside because there was something wrong with him. Rescued and given superursine powers by a friendly alien called Spottyman, with the help of cosmic dust and Mother Nature, he becomes a force for good. From his treehouse or space station haunts, he flies in the face of evil Texas Pete and his sidekicks Skeleton and Bulk and scuppers their wicked ambitions. Music was provided by former Radio 2 presenter Chris Stuart and Mike Townend. Although Superted flew his last mission in 1986, the series returned in 1990 under the title *The Further Adventures of Superted*, a collection of episodes made for American consumption with US actors voicing.

Supply and Demand ★★

UK (La Plante/Yorkshire) Police Drama. ITV 1998

Simon Hughes .... **Larry Lamb**
Edna Colley .... **Miriam Margolyes**
DCI Jane Leyland .... **Stella Gonet**
DI Jake Brown .... **Eamonn Walker**
Sgt Carl Harrington .... **Ade Sapara**
DI Eddie McEwan .... **Martin Kemp**
Frankie Li .... **Benedict Wong**
Peter Harper .... **Terry O'Neill**
Da Souza .... **Christopher Simon**
Meryl .... **Susan Flynn**
Mike .... **Andrew Charleson**

Creator **Lynda La Plante**
Writers **Lynda La Plante, Paul Brodrick, Christine Harmer-Brown**
Producer **Lynda La Plante**

● ***The cases of a special undercover crime unit.***

Drugs, vice rings and business corruption are the targets when an experimental crime-busting team hits the streets. The covert activities squad is a mix of security agents and crack undercover police, and operates in the middle ground not properly covered by either MI5 or the police force. Heading up their investigations are mature lesbian Edna Colley, emotionally flawed Simon Hughes and laddish Jane Leyland. This six-part series (three stories) followed a pilot in 1997 in which Manchester drugs cop Jake Brown was paired with teetotal uniformed sergeant Carl Harrington to bust a villain played by comedian Freddie Starr.

Surgical Spirit ★★

UK (Humphrey Barclay/Granada) Situation Comedy. ITV 1989–95

Dr Sheila Sabatini	**Nichola McAuliffe**
Dr Jonathan Haslam	**Duncan Preston**
Joyce Watson	**Marji Campi**
George Hope-Wynne	**David Conville**
Neil Copeland	**Emlyn Price**
Simon Field	**Lyndam Gregory**
Giles Peake	**Simon Harrison**
Sister Cheryl Patching	**Suzette Llewellyn**
Dr Michael Sampson	**Beresford Le Roy**
Daniel Sabatini	**Andrew Groves**

Creator **Peter Learmouth**
Producer **Humphrey Barclay**

● ***A senior surgeon's tongue is as sharp as her scalpel.***

Sheila Sabatini is a hard-working surgeon at the Gillies Hospital. She is also hot-tempered, opinionated and sharp-tongued, but this doesn't prevent her anaesthetist colleague, Jonathan Haslam, from beginning a relationship with her (once her divorce has come through). Their on-off affair runs for six years amid weekly hospital crises and against a backdrop of open conflict in the operating theatre. Involved in matchmaking is the hospital's gossipy administrator, Joyce Watson, and her efforts pay off when the two are wed. Also seen are fellow surgeon Neil Copeland; houseman Giles Peake; sister Cheryl Patching; her live-in boyfriend, Dr Michael Sampson; George Hope-Wynne, a consultant surgeon with more interest in private medicine; and Sheila's teenage (later medical student) son, Daniel.

Surprise, Surprise ★★

UK (LWT) Entertainment. ITV 1984–2001

Presenters **Cilla Black, Christopher Biggins, Bob Carolgees, Gordon Burns**

Producers **Bob Merrilees, Brian Wesley, Linda Beadle, Colman Hutchinson, Nina Donaldson, Rob Clark, Chris O'Dell**

● ***Magic-wand show in which members of the public are given heart-warming surprises.***

Surprise, Surprise was created as a showcase for Cilla Black and was her first TV series for over eight years. It paired her initially with Christopher Biggins, but he left after the first series, to be replaced later by Bob Carolgees. The aim of the show was to make dreams come true in JIM'LL FIX IT fashion for members of the general public, acting on advice from relatives and friends. One segment, entitled *Searchline*, hosted for five years by Gordon Burns, hoped to re-establish contact between broken families and long-lost friends. Another feature was celebrities making unexpected visits to fans' homes. In true Cilla tradition there were a 'lorra lorra laffs', but plenty of tears, too. The programme only consisted of one-off specials after 1997.

Survival ★★★

UK (Anglia) Natural History. ITV 1961–2003

Creator **Aubrey Buxton**

● ***Long-running, award-winning wildlife series.***

Undoubtedly Anglia Television's greatest product, *Survival* has been seen all around the world (in some cases under the title of *The World of Survival*). Beginning in 1961 with a short series of films about London wildlife (with production assistance from Associated-Rediffusion), *Survival* has since expanded to cover nature stories all over the globe. Creator Aubrey Buxton was associated with the programme for many years and introduced some of the early episodes. His daughter, Cindy Buxton, has carried on the tradition, once famously being trapped on South Georgia during the 1982 Falklands conflict while filming for the series. Colin Willock has also been a major influence. The painstakingly made half-hour films (occasionally an hour in length, when they have been billed as *Survival Special*) have been narrated by the likes of David Niven, Peter Scott, Kenneth More, John Hedges, Brian Blessed, Duncan Carse, Ian Holm, Dennis Quilley, Andrew Sachs, T. P. McKenna, Robert Hardy, Robert Lindsay and David Suchet. Programmes have focused on the threat to wildlife, the environment and native peoples. Some of the best remembered have been *Tarantula!*, *The Painter and the Fighter* (African tribespeople) and *Polar Bear – Hunters on Ice*. John Forsythe has introduced the series for American viewers. Around 800 programmes have now been produced and *Survival* has picked up some 130 international awards.

Survivor ★★

UK (Planet 24) Game Show. ITV 2001–2

Presenters **Mark Austin, Mark Nicholas**

Creator **Charlie Parsons**
Executive Producers **Charlie Parsons, Ed Forsdick, Mary Durkan, Claudia Rosencrantz**
Producers **Nigel Lythgoe, Simon Tucker**

● ***Castaways on a remote island compete for a big cash prize.***

Already a smash in the USA, *Survivor* arrived in Britain as ITV's answer to BIG BROTHER. Here, however, the house/prison camp was swapped for a tropical island/prison camp, with the 16 contestants split into two 'tribes' and abandoned on an island (Pulua Tiga, off Borneo) in the South China Sea. The object: to cope with sparse food rations, meet challenges and 'survive' – in the physical sense and in the context of the programme, by avoiding being voted off by their colleagues as the 40-day test of endurance continued (John Leslie chatted to the dumped contenders). The prize for the ultimate 'Survivor' was a cool £1 million and it was Charlotte Hobrough who took it away, having defeated Jackie Carey in the finale. The series was renewed for 2002, with another bunch of castaways (this time 12) left to their own devices on an island off the coast of Panama. The big money went to Scottish policeman Jonny Gibb, edging out English teacher Susannah Moffat. Channel 4 cricket frontman Mark Nicholas replaced first host Mark Austin and John Leslie as host/narrator/interviewer.

Survivors ✳✳✳

UK (BBC) Science Fiction. BBC 1 1975–7

Abby Grant	**Carolyn Seymour**
Greg Preston	**Ian McCulloch**
Jenny Richards	**Lucy Fleming**
Charles Vaughan	**Denis Lill**
Dave Long	**Brian Peck**
Tom Price	**Talfryn Thomas**
John	**Stephen Dudley**
Lizzie	**Tanya Ronder**
	Angie Stevens
Vic Thatcher	**Terry Scully**
Paul Pitman	**Christopher Tranchell**
Mrs Emma Cohen	**Hana-Maria Pravda**
Charmian Wentworth	**Eileen Helsby**
Agnes	**Sally Osborn**
	Anna Pitt
Arthur Russell	**Michael Gover**
Alan	**Stephen Tate**
Seth	**Dan Meaden**
Pet Simpson	**Lorna Lewis**
Ruth Anderson	**Celia Gregory**
Hubert	**John Abineri**
Jack	**Gordon Salkilld**
Melanie	**Heather Wright**
Daniella	**Gigi Gatti**
Dave	**Peter Duncan**
Alec	**William Dysart**

Creator **Terry Nation**
Producer **Terence Dudley**

● ***The survivors of a killer plague struggle to rebuild civilization and establish a future for the world.***

Imagine a world that suddenly grinds to a halt. A world where 95 per cent of the population is wiped out in just a few weeks by a rogue virus and where the remaining 5 per cent has to battle to stay alive. Imagine a world where, for all the modern technology around him, man is forced to fall back on primitive skills to feed himself and to establish a pattern of law and order. This was the imagination of Terry Nation, the creator of the Daleks and the inspiration behind *Survivors*.

As graphically depicted in the programme's opening titles, the world has been gripped by a deadly virus, accidentally released when a scientist in the Far East smashes a test-tube. Inadvertently spread by jet-setting businessmen, the virus quickly reaches Britain, where *Survivors* takes up the story. It centres on a motley band of individuals, people who have either been immune to the plague or who have somehow recovered from it. At the forefront is suburban housewife Abby Grant, who watches her husband die in the first episode but who still hopes to find her lost son, Peter. Twenty-six-year-old secretary Jenny Richards, 38-year-old architect Charles Vaughan and the group's leader-elect, 35-year-old civil engineer Greg Preston, are also prominent. The first episodes reveal how they find each other as they wander around derelict towns and villages, seeking food, shelter and, above all, other people. After that, attention turns to their efforts to re-establish civilization and to harness whatever specialist talents remain in the survivors around them – the likes of doctors, electricians and teachers. Along the way, they encounter unpleasant characters, such as weaselly Welsh labourer Tom Price, and other communities which express their own perverse forms of law, order and justice.

Getting all the survivors to work in harmony proves impossible. Suspicion is rife and greed and power are two elements they find hard to subdue. Effectively, the Dark Ages have returned. The desperate need to reclaim society and to reinvent the skills needed to replenish supplies of food, medicine, transport, power and other essentials forms the backbone of the series, which, after three seasons, ends on a more optimistic note than it begins. Common sense and human spirit are beginning to shine through and, although the going remains tough, at least some kind of future is beckoning.

Susie

See *Private Secretary*.

Sutherland, Kiefer

(1966–)

Born in Britain and raised in Canada, Kiefer Sutherland is the actor/director son of actors Donald Sutherland and Shirley Douglas. His major TV role has been as counter terrorism agent Jack Bauer in 24, for which he has also been executive producer.

Sutherland's Law ✳✳

UK (BBC) Legal Drama. BBC 1 1973–6

John Sutherland	**Iain Cuthbertson**
Alec Duthie	**Gareth Thomas**
Christine Russell	**Maev Alexander**
Sgt McKechnie	**Don McKillop**
Dr Judith Roberts/ Sutherland	**Edith MacArthur**
Gail Munro	**Harriet Buchan**
Insp./Chief Insp. Menzies	**Victor Carin**
David Drummond	**Martin Cochrane**
Sheriff Derwent	**Moultrie Kelsall**
Helen Matheson	**Virginia Stark**
Kate Cameron	**Sarah Collier**

Creator **Lindsay Galloway**
Producers **Neil McCallum, Frank Cox**

● ***The cases of a procurator fiscal in a Scottish fishing town.***

In the small town of Glendoran, John Sutherland holds the post of procurator fiscal, a legal position somewhere between an investigative prosecuting lawyer, an American district attorney and a coroner. Under Scottish law, the police do not prosecute criminals themselves; they have to go to the procurator fiscal for action. So it was that Iain Cuthbertson, fresh from playing the rogue Charlie Endell in BUDGIE, became a reformed character and, as Sutherland, began to act on behalf of the people against the criminal fraternity, solving baffling mysteries along the way. Sutherland is supported at various times by Alec Duthie, Christine Russell, Gail Munro, David Drummond and Helen Matheson. The beautiful west coast views are a bonus. The series stemmed from a 1972 DRAMA PLAYHOUSE presentation.

Sutton, Shaun

OBE (1919–2004)

British actor, writer, producer and director, working mostly on children's comedies and dramas in the 1950s and 1960s such as *Thames Tug* (director), *The Cabin in the Clearing* (playing Silas Sutherland), *The Gordon Honour* (writer), *The Watch Tower* (writer/producer), *The Silver Sword* (producer), *Queen's*

Champion (writer/producer), *Paradise Walk* (writer/producer), BILLY BUNTER OF GREYFRIARS SCHOOL (producer), BONEHEAD (writer/producer), *The Great Detective* (producer) and ADVENTURE WEEKLY (writer), before becoming the BBC's Head of Drama, 1969–81. Among his other work was direction on THE TROUBLESHOOTERS, Z CARS, *Kipling* and DETECTIVE. He later produced many of THE BBC TELEVISION SHAKESPEARE presentations and another children's series, *Merlin of the Crystal Cave*.

S.W.A.T. ✶✶

US (Spelling Goldberg) Police Drama. ITV 1976 (US: ABC 1975–6)

Lt. Dan 'Hondo' Harrelson ...... **Steve Forrest**
Sgt David 'Deacon' Kay .... **Rod Perry**
Officer Jim Street .... **Robert Urich**
Officer Dominic Luca .... **Mark Shera**
Officer T. J. McCabe .... **James Coleman**
Betty Harrelson .... **Ellen Weston**
Matt Harrelson .... **Michael Harland**
Kevin Harrelson .... **David Adams**

Creator **Robert Hamner**
Executive Producers **Aaron Spelling, Leonard Goldberg**

● ***A crack team of army veterans lead the fight against urban crime.***

Charged with restoring order on the front line of violent inner cities, S.W.A.T. (Special Weapons And Tactics) squads were all the rage in the 1960s. TV's S.W.A.T. unit, based in California, consists of boss man 'Hondo' Harrelson, aided by his number two, 'Deacon' Kay, with other Vietnam veterans in support: Jim Street, Dominic Luca and T. J. McCabe. Fighting the cause of law and order as if they are engaging enemies on the battlefield, these men – armed to the hilt – hit hard and decisively, always happy to rain down bullets when a single one will suffice. Excessive violence, however, led to the show's early cancellation. The series was spun off from another police series, *The Rookies* (ABC 1972–6).

Sweeney, The ✶✶✶

UK (Euston Films/Thames) Police Drama. ITV 1975–6; 1978

DI Jack Regan .... **John Thaw**
DS George Carter .... **Dennis Waterman**
DCI Frank Haskins .... **Garfield Morgan**

Creator **Ian Kennedy Martin**
Executive Producers **Lloyd Shirley, George Taylor**
Producer **Ted Childs**

● ***Rough, tough and violent crime-busting with a no-nonsense pair of Flying Squad detectives.***

Taking its name from the Cockney rhyming slang for Flying Squad ('Sweeney Todd'), this is one of television's most physical cop shows. It features the investigations of door-smashing, crook-thumping, heavy-drinking DI Jack Regan and his junior partner, DS George Carter, who scream around London in a gold-coloured Ford Granada. Hard, and sometimes unquestioning, Regan has little time for rules and regulations. In his leather jacket and 1970s-style kipper ties, he is also a bit of a lad, found off-duty in the boozer, chatting to the local villains, or in bed with yet another woman (he is, not surprisingly, estranged from his wife). Carter is his loyal number two, learning the trade from his mentor and picking up bad habits along with good. Like his boss, he too is pretty useful with his fists. Supervising the operations, often in desperation at the tactics involved, is Chief Insp. Haskins.

The series began seven months after a pilot episode, *Regan*, part of the *Armchair Cinema* anthology, was screened in 1974, and it ended in 1978, when Regan was banged up for allegedly taking bribes. No charges were brought, but Regan had had enough and decided to call it a day. Through *The Sweeney*, the public was introduced to a new kind of policeman, one the authorities tried to deny existed but one that certain real-life lawmen privately acknowledged to be alive and kicking, especially kicking. Indeed, Jack Quarrie, a former Flying Squad officer, was the programme's technical adviser. But, for all its bad language and excessive violence, the series also has its humorous side, highlighted in the Regan-Carter Cockney repartee and an episode which features Morecambe and Wise as guest stars. Two feature films were also made. Harry South composed the theme music.

Sweeney, Claire

(1972–)

Liverpudlian actress, most prominent as Lindsey Corkhill in BROOKSIDE. A week in the *Celebrity Big Brother* house, however, helped propel her to West End stardom and she later presented A WEEK IN THE LIFE OF THE WEST END for television. An early TV appearance came in the talent show *Top Town*, and she has been seen more recently as Katrina in CLOCKING OFF, DS Roz Kelly in MERSEYBEAT, and as presenter of *Here Comes the Sun, Challenge of a Lifetime, 60-Minute Makeover* and *Chef v Britain*.

Sweet Sixteen ✶✶

UK (BBC) Situation Comedy. BBC 1 1983

Helen Walker .... **Penelope Keith**
Peter Morgan .... **Christopher Villiers**
James Walker .... **Matthew Solon**
Dr Ballantine .... **Mike Grady**
Arthur Poole .... **John Rapley**
Jane .... **Joan Blackham**
Tom Sherrin .... **Tony Millan**
Ken Green .... **Victor Spinetti**

Writer **Douglas Watkinson**
Producer **Gareth Gwenlan**

A hard-nosed businesswoman is softened up by a toy boy lover. Helen Walker is the plain-speaking, determined boss of a building firm, Carrington & Daughter. However, when one day she breaks her personal rule about mixing business with pleasure, and has a drink with architect Peter Morgan, her life changes for ever. Although Peter is 16 years her junior (hence the programme title), and despite all the pitfalls this generation gap promises, they fall in love, marry and soon a child is on the way. But, when Helen is left at home and Peter takes over the running of the family business, resentment begins to kick in. James is Helen's tactless son who eggs her into the romance in the first place. Just six episodes were produced.

Swift, Clive
(1936–)

British actor seen in numerous supporting roles, most prominently as the hen-pecked Richard Bucket in KEEPING UP APPEARANCES. He was DI Waugh in WAUGH ON CRIME (six *Thirty-Minute Theatre* productions in 1970), and was Mr Nesbitt in *The Nesbitts are Coming*. Among his many other credits have been parts in COMPACT, *Dig This Rhubarb*, CLAYHANGER (Albert Benbow), THE BROTHERS, LOVE STORY, THE LIVER BIRDS, SOUTH RIDING (Councillor Huggins), THE BARCHESTER CHRONICLES (Dr Proudie), TALES OF THE UNEXPECTED, 1990 (Tony Doran) and WINSTON CHURCHILL – THE WILDERNESS YEARS. Swift also appeared in *Beasts*, THE GENTLE TOUCH, SHELLEY, DOCTOR WHO, MINDER, A VERY PECULIAR PRACTICE, *Gentlemen and Players*, INSPECTOR MORSE, PEAK PRACTICE (Norman Shorthose), THE ARISTOCRATS (King George II), BORN AND BRED (Revd Brewer), HEARTBEAT, various adaptations of the classics, and more. He is the brother of actor David Swift and his first wife was author Margaret Drabble.

Swift, David
(1933–)

Liverpool-born actor with various acting connections: he is brother of Clive Swift, father of Julia Swift and father-in-law of David Bamber. He himself is probably mostly recognized as pompous newsreader Henry Davenport in DROP THE DEAD DONKEY, although he has been seen in countless other comedies and dramas. These have included CASANOVA (Valenglart), *Another Sunday and Sweet FA*, WAR AND PEACE (Napoleon), RISING DAMP, *Bloomers* (Dingley), THE PROFESSIONALS, *The Further Adventures of Oliver Twist*, THE DAY OF THE TRIFFIDS (Michael Beadley), FREUD (Joseph Breuer), COLD WARRIOR (Sir William Logie), BERGERAC, PRIVATE SCHULZ (Prof. Bodelschwingh), P. D. JAMES, *Operation Julie* (Det. Supt Gosling), VANITY FAIR, WISH ME LUCK, THE PARADISE CLUB, AGATHA CHRISTIE'S POIROT, *Couples*, HOLBY CITY and *Oscar Charlie* (Oscar Spinner). Do not confuse him with the American David Swift, a writer/producer.

Swiss Toni
See *The Fast Show*.

Swit, Loretta
(1937–)

Blonde American actress of Polish descent, M*A*S*H's Margaret 'Hotlips' Hoolihan, but also Christine Cagney in the pilot movie for CAGNEY AND LACEY (although not the series). She has since been seen in many other TV movies, with her earliest appearances coming in series like GUNSMOKE, HAWAII FIVE-O and MANNIX.

Sword of Freedom ✳

UK (Sapphire/ITC) Adventure. ITV 1958; 1960–1

Marco del Monte .... **Edmund Purdom**
Angelica .... **Adrienne Corri**
Sandro .... **Rowland Bartrop**
Duke de Medici .... **Martin Benson**
Francesca .... **Monica Stevenson**
Machiavelli .... **Kenneth Hyde**
Rodrigo .... **Derek Sydney**

Executive Producer **Hannah Weinstein**
Producer **Sidney Cole**

Robin Hood in an Italian Renaissance setting.

Marco del Monte is a 15th-century Florentine painter, much sickened by the excesses of the city-state's ruling family, the Medicis. Supported by Angelica, his former pickpocket model, and his broad-shouldered friend Sandro he constantly takes on the might of the authorities, displaying a flair for swordsmanship as well as art as he rides to the rescue of many an oppressed compatriot. In his sights are the Duke de Medici and his cruel sister, Francesca.

Sword of Honour ✳✳✳

UK (Talkback) Drama. Channel 4 2001

Guy Crouchback .... **Daniel Craig**
Gervase Crouchback .... **Leslie Phillips**
Virginia Troy .... **Megan Dodds**
Major Tickeridge .... **Malcolm Storry**
Angela Crouchback .... **Selina Cadell**
Frank De Souza .... **Stephen Mangan**
Brig. Ritchie-Hook .... **Robert Pugh**
Trimmer .... **Richard Coyle**
Ian Kilbannock .... **Julian Rhind-Tutt**
Kerstie Kilbannock .... **Abigail Cruttenden**
Ivor Claire .... **Tom Wisdom**
Tom Blackhouse .... **James Weber Brown**
Major Hound .... **Robert Daws**

Writer **William Boyd**
Producer **Gillian McNeill**

A disillusioned young man joins the army to find some meaning to life.

Guy Crouchback is the hero of this adaptation of Evelyn Waugh's wartime trilogy of novels. Crouchback enlists in the army as World War II gets underway and meets a collection of eccentric colleagues, not least the former hairdresser Trimmer, who resurfaces as a bogus officer in a Scottish regiment. Trimmer is also involved at some stage with Crouchback's society girl ex-wife, Virginia Troy, the woman Guy can never quite forget. Gervase is Guy's father. Crouchback travels overseas, including to France and Crete, all the while trying to make sense of the crazy events surrounding him and trying to uphold his own Catholic sense of morality. Humour and tragedy combine in this two-parter directed by Bill Anderson. The trilogy had previously been dramatized by the BBC as three successive plays in its *Theatre 625* anthology (BBC 2 1967: *Men at Arms, Officers and Gentlemen* and *Unconditional Surrender*, adapted by Giles Cooper with Edward Woodward as Guy Crouchback).

Syal, Meera
MBE (1963–)

Wolverhampton-born actress, writer, novelist and comedian, married to her regular co-star, Sanjeev Bhaskar. Together they have appeared in GOODNESS GRACIOUS ME and THE KUMARS AT NO. 42 (in which Meera played grandmother Sushila). She has also starred in *Kinsey* (Val), THE REAL MCCOY, *Degrees of Error* (Dr Jean Lowell), KEEPING MUM (Tina), *Forgive and Forget* (Judith Adams), BEDTIME (Ruby), *The All Star Comedy Show*,

ALL ABOUT ME (Rupinder Craddock), *Life Isn't All Ha Ha Hee Hee* (Sunita, also as writer), *The Secretary Who Stole £4 Million* (Joyti De-Laurey), MURDER INVESTIGATION TEAM (DCI Anita Wishart) and FAT FRIENDS (Aysha Kapoor). Smaller roles have been in BOON, ABSOLUTELY FABULOUS, SOLDIER, SOLDIER, *Screen Two's Crossing the Floor*, DROP THE DEAD DONKEY, THE MRS BRADLEY MYSTERIES and LINDA GREEN. Syal also narrated *Drama Connections* and wrote for *Tandoori Nights*.

Sykes ★★★

UK (BBC) Situation Comedy. BBC 1 1960–5; 1972–9

Eric	**Eric Sykes**
Hattie	**Hattie Jacques**
Mr Charles Brown	**Richard Wattis**
Corky	**Deryck Guyler**

Writers **Johnny Speight, Eric Sykes**
Producers **Dennis Main Wilson, Sydney Lotterby, Philip Barker, Roger Race**

● *A hapless brother and sister share a suburban home.*

Life at 24 Sebastopol Terrace, Acton, is seldom straightforward. Home to bachelor brother Eric and spinster sister Hattie, it plays host to countless domestic crises. With Eric constantly trying to better himself, misunderstandings are rife and often involve Eric and Hattie's snooty, interfering neighbour, Mr Brown, or Corky, the pompous neighbourhood bobby.

Initially, this long-running series went out under the title of *Sykes and . . .*, with the object, implement or creature that was about to cause chaos inserted into the title. Examples included *Sykes and a Telephone* and *Sykes and a Plank*. Some early episodes were scripted by Johny Speight, but the lion's share of programmes were penned by Eric Sykes himself. The title became simply *Sykes* when the series was revived in the 1970s.

Sykes, Eric

CBE (1923–)

British comedian and writer, who broke into radio after the war, penning scripts for *Educating Archie* and other series. He also wrote for television: *The Howerd Crowd* for Frankie Howerd in 1952, gags for Max Bygraves, Harry Secombe and Jimmy Logan, and Tony Hancock's first TV sketches, screened as *The Tony Hancock Show* by ITV in 1956. The Goonish *Idiot Weekly, Price 2d* was another of his early outlets, and he was also involved in the film world by the time his long-running sitcom SYKES began in 1960. Apart from a seven-year hiatus in the middle, the series ran until 1979. Originally, the *Sykes* scripts were written by Johnny Speight, but Eric soon took control himself, although his relationship with Speight was to resume in 1969, when Sykes played the liberal factory foreman in Speight's controversial CURRY AND CHIPS. He and Speight teamed up again in 1989 for another sitcom, *The Nineteenth Hole*. Sykes has been known also for his visual humour, exemplified in silent films like *The Plank*, *It's Your Move* and *Mr H is Late*. He also directed a TV film, *If You Go Down to the Woods Today*, in 1981 and other credits in his long career have included *Sykes versus ITV* (a mock court case), *Sykes and a Big Big Show* and guest spots in NOT ONLY . . . BUT ALSO . . . More recently, he provided the voice of the lion in TELETUBBIES, made guest appearances in THE RETURN OF SHERLOCK HOLMES, DINNERLADIES, HOLBY CITY, THE BILL, and DOCTORS, and appeared as Mollocks in GORMENGHAST and Stafford in *Stan the Man*.

Sylvania Waters ★★

Australia (BBC/Australian Broadcasting Company) Documentary. BBC 1 1993

Producer **Paul Watson**

● *Warts-and-all, 12-part documentary about the daily life of an Australian family.*

In the fly-on-the-wall tradition of his earlier programme, THE FAMILY, producer Paul Watson captured the domestic ups and downs of the Baker-Donaher family in one of Sydney's well-off suburbs. Heads of the family were rich divorcees Noeline Baker and Laurie Donaher, proud of the hard-working way in which they had built up their wealth and determined to enjoy it to the full. Intra-family squabbles added spice to the story, with running arguments between Noeline and her elder son, Paul, the unfolding drama of his wife Dione's pregnancy and the teenage trials of younger son Michael, who narrated the programme.

These real-life NEIGHBOURS caused a storm in their native Australia when they were criticized for their brash, bigoted behaviour and their heavy-drinking/smoking lifestyle.

Syms, Sylvia

(1934–)

Kent-born actress whose major TV roles have been as Sylvia Gibbons in MY GOOD WOMAN, Nanaire Langhorne in NANCY ASTOR, Harriet in *Natural Lies*, Lady Constance in CATHERINE COOKSON'S *The Glass Virgin*, Esme Carling in *Original Sin*, Mrs Champness in *Neville's Island*, Isabel de Gines in PEAK PRACTICE, Marion Riley in AT HOME WITH THE BRAITHWAITES and Elsie Beamish in *The Jury*. Syms also played Margaret Thatcher in ITV's *Thatcher – the Final Days*, a role she resumed in *Screen Two's Half the Picture*, and guest appearances have come in programmes as varied as THE SAINT, THE BARON, *It's Your Move*, MISS MARPLE, DOCTOR WHO, THE RUTH RENDELL MYSTERIES, HEARTBEAT, KAVANAGH QC, HOLBY CITY, WHERE THE HEART IS, DOCTORS and BORN AND BRED. Her daughter is actress Beatie Edney.

Syndication

An American term for the sale of programmes to independent stations (rather than the national networks) for screening locally. Old, repeat episodes of prime-time series are syndicated, as are new series which the major networks decline to take up. Some programmes are made specifically for syndication (low-budget features, game shows, etc.) and occasionally a major series begins or only airs in syndication (STAR TREK: THE NEXT GENERATION is one example). Many British series have been seen in the USA only in syndication.

T

Tab Hunter Show, The ✶

US (Famous Artists/Shunto) Situation Comedy. BBC 1961 (US: NBC 1960–1)

Paul Morgan .... **Tab Hunter**
Peter Fairfield III .... **Richard Erdman**
John Larsen .... **Jerome Cowan**
Thelma .... **Reta Shaw**

Producer **Norman Tokar**

● ***A young cartoonist makes his own life the subject of a popular strip.***

Tab Hunter is best remembered in the UK as a teen-movie actor and singer, performer of the 1957 hits 'Young Love' and '99 Ways'. Three years later, he was pitched into his own sitcom vehicle. Hunter plays Paul Morgan, a Californian cartoonist, creator of the comic strip *Bachelor at Large*, which is essentially a sketch of Morgan's own colourful life in Malibu Beach. Peter Fairfield is Morgan's affluent buddy, another bachelor, while John Larsen is Morgan's boss at Comics Inc. Thelma is Morgan's disapproving housekeeper.

Taggart ✶✶✶

UK (Scottish) Police Drama. ITV 1983; 1985–90; 1992–

DCI Jim Taggart .... **Mark McManus**
DS Peter Livingstone .... **Neil Duncan**
Supt. Jack McVitie .... **Iain Anders**
Supt. Murray .... **Tony Watson**
DC/DS/DI/DCI Mike Jardine .... **James Macpherson**
Jean Taggart .... **Harriet Buchan**
Alison Taggart .... **Geraldine Alexander**
Dr Stephen Andrews .... **Robert Robertson**
WDC/WDS Jackie Reid .... **Blythe Duff**
DC Stuart Fraser .... **Colin McCredie**
DI Robbie Ross .... **John Michie**
DCI Matt Burke .... **Alex Norton**
Det. Supt. Valerie Patterson ... **Anne-Marie Timoney**
Sheila Crombie .... **Tamara Kennedy**
Gemma Kerr .... **Lesley Harcourt**

Creator **Glenn Chandler**
Producers **Robert Love, Murray Ferguson, Paddy Higson, Bernard Krichefski, John G. Temple, Frank Cox, Richard Handford, Mike Dormer, Emma Hayter, Graeme Gordon**

● ***Gruesome murder investigations with a gritty Glaswegian detective.***

Jim Taggart works for the Glasgow CID. Covering the Northern Division, he is hard-nosed, firm and dedicated, yet saddened by his job to the point of cynicism. His wife, Jean, has been wheelchair-bound for over 20 years (since the birth of their daughter, Alison) and she is largely resigned to her husband's devotion to work, not that he has a lot to say when he does eventually return home. Working with the down-to-earth Taggart is university-educated DS Peter Livingstone, a man with quite different social roots. Livingstone is later replaced by Mike Jardine, a keen, young teetotaller (much to the disgust of Taggart, a malt whisky connoisseur) who works his way up from detective constable under his mentor's tutelage. Their cases involve the grisliest, most distressing and baffling murders, all set against the distinctive backdrop of Glasgow city, with a touch of wry Scottish humour to sugar the pill.

Combining one-off stories (most feature-length) with short serials, in a somewhat intermittent fashion, *Taggart* began with a thriller entitled *Killer* in 1983 and seemed likely to end with the premature death of its star, Mark McManus, in 1994. However, Taggart continued, with Jardine and DS Jackie Reid moving on to centre stage, until Jardine was murdered in 2002 and new boss Matt Burke began barking out the orders at Maryhill police station.

Take a Girl Like You ✶✶✶

UK (BBC/WGBH) Drama. BBC 1 2000

Patrick Standish .... **Rupert Graves**
Jenny Bunn .... **Sienna Guillory**
Julian Ormerod .... **Hugh Bonneville**
Dick Thompson .... **Robert Daws**
Martha Thompson .... **Emma Chambers**
Graham McClintoch .... **Ian Driver**
Anna Le Page .... **Kathy Kiera Clarke**
Horace Charlton .... **Jeff Rawle**
Sheila Torkingham .... **Amelia Warner**
Mr Bunn .... **Dave Hill**
Mrs Bunn .... **Jacki Piper**
Miss Sinclair .... **Bridget McConnel**
Lord Archie Edgerstone .... **Leslie Phillips**
Lady Dot Edgerstone .... **Marsha Fitzalan**
Susan .... **Deborah Cornelius**
Joan .... **Natalie Roles**
Horse .... **Simon Evans**
Wendy .... **Nina Young**

Writer **Andrew Davies**
Executive Producers **Jane Tranter, Rebecca Eaton**
Producer **Gareth Neame**

● ***An old-fashioned girl struggles with a new, promiscuous era.***

The year is 1959. A young northern girl heads south to take up her first job as a teacher. Twenty-year-old Jenny Bunn is still a virgin and clings desperately to her principle of 'no sex before marriage' as the randy vultures in her new world home in. Her clown of a landlord, Dick Thompson, is one such predator, as is upper-class twit Julian Ormerod. Lusty Lord Edgerstone is a third, but the man who presents the most difficulty is handsome rogue Patrick Standish. Britain stands on the cusp of a sexual revolution as the 1960s beckon and Jenny is on the brink with the rest of the country. This three-part drama, which regularly halts the action so that the personal thoughts of the main characters can be expressed, was based on the novel of the same name by Kingsley Amis and directed by Nick Hurran.

Take a Letter ✶

UK (Granada) Game Show. ITV 1962–4

Presenter **Bob Holness**

Producers **John Hamp, Max Morgan-Witts, Pamela Brown**

● ***Crossword-based family puzzle game.***

By solving clues and choosing letters to complete mystery words, the contestants in this popular programme attempted to win small cash prizes. The amount won depended on the number of letters selected before the correct answer was given. Future BLOCKBUSTERS host Bob Holness took charge of proceedings.

Take Hart

See *Vision On*.

Take Me Home ✶✶✶

UK (BBC) Drama. BBC 1 1989

Tom	**Keith Barron**
Kathy	**Maggie O'Neill**
Liz	**Annette Crosbie**
Martin	**Reece Dinsdale**
Ray	**Tim Preece**
Joyce	**Anne Carroll**
Salter	**Neil McCaul**
Colin	**Michael Crompton**

Writer **Tony Marchant**
Producer **David Snodin**

● ***A middle-aged cabbie begins a torrid affair with a younger woman.***

Tom is a set-in-his-ways minicab driver living and working in the new town of Woodleigh Abbots (Telford was used for filming). One night he is waved down by Kathy, a much younger bank clerk who has just had a bust-up in a restaurant with her computer programmer husband, Martin. Having at last rebelled against Martin's yuppie materialism, she is in great distress. Tom comforts her and she responds to his kindness. Before they know it, the unlikely couple are having an affair and Tom is behaving like an excited schoolboy. Inevitably, it ends in tears when Martin and Tom's frumpy wife, Liz, find out their sordid secret, with hurt a-plenty for all concerned. The emotionally charged three episodes provided an early insight into the work of award-winning writer Tony Marchant.

Take the High Road/High Road ✶✶

UK (Scottish) Drama. ITV 1980–2003

Elizabeth Cunningham	**Edith Macarthur**
Fiona Cunningham/Ryder	**Caroline Ashley**
Isabel Blair/Morgan	**Eileen McCallum**
Brian Blair	**Kenneth Watson**
Jimmy Blair	**Jimmy Chisholm**
Alice McEwan/Taylor	**Muriel Romanes**
Dougal Lachlan	**Alec Monteath**
Gladys Aitken/Lachlan	**Ginni Barlow**
Grace Lachlan	**Marjorie Thomson**
Donald Lachlan	**Steven Brown**
Alan McIntyre	**Martin Cochrane**
Davie Sneddon	**Derek Lord**
Mrs Mary Mack	**Gwyneth Guthrie**
Lorna Seton	**Joan Alcorn**
Mr Obadiah Arthur Murdoch	**Robert Trotter**
Alex Geddes	**James Cosmo**
Tom Kerr ('Inverdarroch')	**John Stahl**
Bob Taylor	**Iain Agnew**
Fergus Jamieson	**Frank Wylie**
Ken Calder	**Bill Henderson**
Dr Sandy Wallace	**Michael Elder**
Archie Menzies	**Paul Kermack**
Max Langemann	**Frederick Jaeger**
Jane Steedman	**Ingrid Hafner**
Sheila Lamont/Ramsay	**Lesley Fitz-Simons**
Sir John Ross-Gifford	**Michael Browning**
Lady Margaret Ross-Gifford	**Jan Waters**
Eric Ross-Gifford	**Richard Greenwood**
Joanna Simpson/Ross-Gifford	**Tamara Kennedy**
Emma Aitken	**Amanda Whitehead**
Greg Ryder	**Alan Hunter**
Sam Hagen	**Briony McRoberts**
Jockie McDonald	**Jackie Farrell**
Sadie McDonald	**Doreen Cameron**
Trish McDonald	**Natalie Robb**
Gary McDonald	**Joseph McFadden**
Carol McKay/Wilson	**Teri Lally**
Lynne McNeil	**Gillian McNeill**
Mr Ian McPherson	**John Young**
Effie MacInnes/McDonald	**Mary Riggans**
Jennifer Goudie	**Victoria Burton**
Paul Martin	**Peter Bruce**
Alun Morgan	**Mike Hayward**
Menna Morgan	**Manon Jones**
Nick Stapleton	**Stephen Hogan**
Sgt Murray	**James McDonald**
Revd Michael Ross	**Gordon MacArthur**
Morag Stewart/Kerr	**Jeannie Fisher**
Tee Jay Wilson	**Andrew Gillan**
Miss Symonds	**Harriet Buchan**
Eddie Ramsay	**Robin Cameron**
George Carradine	**Leon Sinden**
Sarah Gilchrist/McDonald	**Shonagh Pryce**
Callum Gilchrist	**Jim Webster**
Judith Crombie	**Anne Marie Timoney**
PC Douglas Kirk	**Graeme Robertson**
Phineas ('Fin') North	**William Tapley**
Tiffany Bowles	**Rachel Ogilvy**
Chic Cherry	**Andy Cameron**
Susan Duncan/Ross	**Jacqueline Gilbride**
Dominic Ramsay	**Gary Hollywood**
Paul Lafferty	**Simon Weir**
Lachie McIvor	**Alec Heggie**
Ewan Logan	**Gordon Brown**
PC Tony Piacentini	**Alan McHugh**
Victor Kemp	**Iain Andrew**
Sally McGann	**Catriona Evans**
Josh.	**Gary Cross**
Lilly	**Suzanne Dante**
Sharon	**Leni Harper**
Zoe Scoular	**Jo James**
Dr Douglas Clark	**John Kazek**
Mairi McNeil	**Anne Myatt**
Victor Spinetti	**Terry Vale**
Nigel Jenkins	**Keith Warwick**

Creator **Don Houghton**
Producers **Clarke Tait, Frank Cox, John G. Temple, Mark Grindle**

● ***Life in a rural Scottish community.***

A sort of EMMERDALE FARM north of the border, *Take the High Road* was the long-running saga of the good folk of Glendarroch and the next-door parish of Auchtarne. The main characters included local gossip Mrs Mack, shopkeepers Isabel and Brian Blair, their heart-throb son, Jimmy, and roguish Irish land-manager Davie Sneddon. Others to feature were hypocritical Mr Murdoch, postman Fergus Jamieson, farmer Inverdarroch, old-fashioned Dr Wallace, minister Mr McPherson, *Auchtarne Herald* reporter Sheila Ramsay and Ardvain crofter Dougal Lachlan, but the series also focused on the Lairds of Glendarroch House, to whose estate the village belonged. When the first Lady Laird, Elizabeth Cunningham, was dramatically killed in a car accident in 1987, and her daughter, Fiona, also left the house (she later married ruthless businessman Greg Ryder), Glendarroch gained new Lairds in the shape of Sir John and Lady Margaret Ross-Gifford. Being English, they were looked upon with distrust. Action took place in such settings as Blair's Store and the Ardnacraig Hotel, the latter run by the Ross-Giffords' son, Eric, and his wife, Joanna. The real-life village used for filming was Luss on Loch Lomond.

Despite enjoying large audiences in its native Scotland, *Take the High Road* only gained an afternoon time-slot elsewhere in the UK. The title was shortened to *High Road* in 1994, but ITV regions gradually lost interest and began dropping the series. Immediately before it was cancelled in 2003, only Ulster Television was still carrying the series outside Scotland.

Take Three Girls ✶✶

UK (BBC) Comedy Drama. BBC 1 1969–71

Kate .... **Susan Jameson**
Avril .... **Angela Down**
Victoria Edgecombe .... **Liza Goddard**
Mr Edgecombe .... **David Langton**
Jenny .... **Carolyn Seymour**
Lulie .... **Barra Grant**

Creator **Gerald Savory**
Producer **Michael Hayes**

● ***Ups and downs in the lives of three girl flatsharers.***

The three girls in question are cello-playing deb Victoria (one of life's losers), failed actress Kate (a struggling single parent) and Cockney art student Avril. Together they share a flat in London SW3 and with it their experiences of life as single women in the capital. Also seen is Victoria's mean dad, Mr Edgecombe. When the second series begins, only Victoria remains of the original trio, Kate having been married off and Avril leaving to work in Paris. Victoria is joined by new flatmates, 23-year-old Jenny, a journalist, and Lulie, an American psychology graduate. A four-part reunion special, entitled *Take Three Women* and featuring Victoria, Kate and Avril, was screened in 1982. Thirteen years on from the earliest episodes, it saw Victoria widowed and raising her young daughter alone, Kate living with the teacher of her 13-year-old son and Avril proprietress of an art gallery. Music for early and later episodes was performed by folk, jazz and blues band Pentangle.

Take Your Pick ✶✶

UK (Associated-Rediffusion/Arlington/Thames) Quiz. ITV 1955–68; 1992–8

Hosts **Michael Miles, Des O'Connor**
Announcer **Bob Danvers-Walker**

Producer **Brian Klein**

● ***Popular quiz game played for laughs.***

Hosted by New Zealander Michael Miles, billed as 'your quiz inquisitor', *Take Your Pick* took its place in the very first ITV schedules and stayed there (alongside its great rival, DOUBLE YOUR MONEY) for 13 years. Like *Double Your Money*, it graduated to television from Radio Luxembourg, where it had been a hit for three years. *Take Your Pick* involved contestants answering three general knowledge questions successfully in order to pick up a key to a numbered box. Each box contained details of a prize, although three of the prizes were worthless – a prune or a clothes peg, for example. Before the box was opened, Miles attempted to buy the key from the contestant, offering him or her ever-increasing sums of money. 'Take the money or open the box?' he asked, at the same time encouraging the audience to yell their advice. While some heads were turned by the prospect of cash in hand, others risked all on the turn of the key. To add to the excitement, there was also the mysterious Box 13, the contents of which were unknown even to Miles, and the additional prospect of winning the Treasure Chest of Money or 'Tonight's Star Prize'. The booming voice of Bob Danvers-Walker announced the prizes and Harold Smart gave a quick burst on the organ to add to the thrill.

To reach the questions stage, contestants – plucked from the studio audience just minutes before the show began – had to survive a gruelling ordeal in which Miles asked them questions about their life, work, hobbies, family, etc. Without hesitation, and without nodding or shaking their head, participants had to respond avoiding the use of the words 'yes' and 'no'. Those who lasted longest progressed to the general knowledge phase. The 'Yes/No Interlude', as it became known, was patrolled by Alec Dane, who banged a gong whenever the forbidden words were uttered.

A year after *Take Your Pick* ended, Michael Miles resurfaced with a similar concept entitled *Wheel of Fortune* (1969–71). Not to be confused with the later American import (hosted in the UK by Nicky Campbell and others; see separate entry), this *Wheel of Fortune* offered star and booby prizes just like *Take Your Pick*, only this time they were determined by the spin of a large wheel. Danvers-Walker and Smart were again in support. *Take Your Pick* itself was revived with some success in 1992. Des O'Connor took over from the late Miles and Jodie Wilson acted as his assistant and gong-mistress, before she gave way in 1994 to the Australian twins Gayle and Gillian Blakeney, once of NEIGHBOURS fame, then to Sarah Matravers and Sasha Lawrence.

Take Your Pick was briefly revived as one instalment of ANT & DEC's *Game Show Marathon* in 2005, a series that celebrated the best-loved game shows in ITV's 50-year history.

Takin' Over the Asylum ✶✶✶

UK (BBC) Drama. BBC 2 1994

Eddie McKenna .... **Ken Stott**
Francine .... **Katy Murphy**

Grandma .... **Elizabeth Spriggs**
Griffin .... **Roy Hanlon**
Campbell .... **David Tennant**
Fergus .... **Angus MacFadyen**
Rosalie .... **Ruth McCabe**
Isabel .... **Angela Bruce**
Stuart .... **Kenneth Bryans**
Paula .... **Arabella Weir**
MacAteer .... **Neil McKinven**

Writer **Donna Franceschild**
Producer **Chris Parr**

A radio station is a beacon of hope in a mental hospital.
Frustrated double-glazing salesman Eddie McKenna really wants to be a radio presenter, but has just been sacked from his training ground at Hospital Radio Glasgow. There is another outlet, however. The radio system at St Jude's Mental Hospital is in a bad state of repair, the record collection is archaic and the patients are clearly uninterested in its presence, but Eddie decides to get it up and running again. As he does so, he gathers around him a small but enthusiastic group of helpers. Each of these patients is then showcased in one of the six episodes (all titled after classic pop tracks: 'Hey Jude', 'Fly Like an Eagle', 'You Always Hurt the One You Love', 'Fool on the Hill', 'Rainy Night in Georgia' and 'Let It Be'). They include obsessive-compulsive Rosalie, schizophrenic Fergus, manic-depressive Campbell and sad Francine, to whom Eddie takes a shine. Together the team make a success of the station, raising money for new equipment and, in the process, finding direction in their own lives. The experience also proves to be a voyage of discovery for McKenna, who embarks on a battle with his own demon – booze. The series, directed by David Blair, was filmed by BBC Scotland at Gartloch Hospital near Glasgow.

Taking the Floor ✶✶

UK (Alomo) Situation Comedy. BBC 1 1991

Brian Wheeler .... **Matthew Cottle**
Karen Tranter .... **Barbara Durkin**
Mr Wheeler .... **Timothy Kightley**
Mrs Wheeler .... **Janet Dale**
Colin Wheeler .... **Dean Gatiss**
Mr Tranter .... **Christopher Godwin**
Mrs Tranter .... **Claire Nielson**

Creator **Paul Makin**
Writers **Paul Makin, Geoff Rowley**
Producers **Derek Goodwin**

An aspiring dancer falls for his pampered partner.
Brian Wheeler is a talented ballroom dancer and wants to turn professional. Regrettably, the young Midlander does not have a partner, until he discovers Karen Tranter. Snooty Karen is from quite a different background to that of the working-class Brian. Her parents are prosperous, her house has a swimming pool and, dancing apart, their personal interests don't seem to coincide. But they work well on the dance floor and, as they progress towards the final of an important Latin American competition, they become quite close. With humour coming from cross-class friction, the six-episode *Taking the Floor* was the first major TV role for Matthew Cottle, later star of GAME ON and A PERFECT STATE.

Tales from Europe ✶✶

Europe (various) Children's Drama Anthology. BBC 1 1964–9

Producer **(UK) Peggy Miller**

Anthology of Euro-fairytales with an English commentary.
Effectively a pooling of material, *Tales From Europe* was the umbrella title given to a collection of children's drama serials (mostly fairy stories like *Rumpelstiltskin*) produced by television companies all across the Continent. Each was shown in its native language, with an English narrative dubbed on top. Probably the best-remembered offering was a 1957 East German film produced by Alexander Lösche and directed by Francesco Stefani called *The Singing Ringing Tree*. In three parts it told of a beautiful but bad-tempered and spoilt princess (played by Christel Bodelstein) who demands a magic tree as a gift before she will wed a prince (Eckart Dux) who seeks her hand. The magical tree unfortunately belongs to a wicked dwarf, who turns the prince into a bear. The bear, in desperation, carries off the princess and, because she has been so cruel to all the other animals, no-one will assist her in her plight. Eventually, however, the princess learns the art of humility and kindness. She helps the bear build a cave home and starts to look after the other creatures the dwarf treats so badly, like the giant fish that lives in the nearby lake. Thus, she is able to help the Prince revert to his human form and defeat the dwarf (acquiring the tree in the process). They marry and, in the manner of such fables, live happily ever after. Despite growing into a cult hit in the UK, *The Singing Ringing Tree* was roundly condemned in its native, Communist country for being 'dangerously bourgeois' in focusing on royalty instead of the working classes. Antony Bilbow gave the English narrative.

Tales of Mystery ✶✶

UK (Associated-Rediffusion) Suspense Anthology. ITV 1961–3

Algernon Blackwood .... **John Laurie**

Executive Producer **John Frankau**
Producer **Peter Graham Scott**

Suspense anthology centring on the supernatural.
John Laurie, the rolling-eyed, spooky undertaker from DAD'S ARMY, was the host of this series of half-hour thrillers. He took on the guise of writer Algernon Blackwood, the author of many of the bizarre tales that were adapted for the programme. Laurie generally introduced ghost stories, but the base was extended in the second and third seasons to include other supernatural yarns with a twist in the tail. Plenty of established British actors filled the lead roles, including Harry H. Corbett, Patrick Cargill, Peter Barkworth, Francesca Annis and Dinsdale Landen.

Tales of Para Handy, The

See *Para Handy – Master Mariner.*

Tales of the Riverbank ✶✶

Canada (Dave Ellison/Ray Billings) Children's Entertainment. BBC 1960–4

Narrator (UK) **Johnny Morris**

Creators/Writers/Producers **Dave Ellison, Paul Sutherland**
Producer **(UK) Peggy Miller**

● ***Messing about on the water with a cute little hamster and his big friend, a white rat.***

Tales of the Riverbank – screened by the BBC as part of the WATCH WITH MOTHER lunch-time strand from 1963, but before that at around 5 p.m. – concerned the everyday affairs of busy Hammy Hamster, his friend Roderick the Rat and their wildlife associates, like GP the guinea-pig. The animals were real, with words put into their mouths by the whimsical Johnny Morris. Their homes were furnished as human homes and they enjoyed all human comforts, including musical instruments, cars, aeroplanes and even a little boat in which to travel up and down the river. Produced in Canada, the series was filmed at high speed, so that the rodents' movements appeared slower and more deliberate in playback. And, because hamsters lose their looks after about nine months, dozens of look-alikes were called up to play Hammy over the years. The series was repeated on BBC 1 until 1971 and also aired under the title of *Hammy Hamster's Adventures on the Riverbank* on ITV (1974–6). A sequel, entitled *Further Tales of the Riverbank*, was also seen on Channel 4 in the 1990s.

Tales of the Unexpected ✶✶

UK (Anglia) Suspense Anthology. ITV 1979–86; 1988

Executive Producer **John Woolf**
Producers **John Rosenberg**

● ***A collection of tales with a twist.***

Originally introduced by Roald Dahl, whose short stories formed the core of this anthology, *Tales of the Unexpected* (*Roald Dahl's Tales of the Unexpected* for the first series) offered a weekly carousel ride of suspense and black humour, always with a neat, unsuspected, quirky ending. Sinister fairground music played over the opening titles, which featured the slinky silhouette of a siren female dancer.

Some of Dahl's stories had already been treated to TV interpretation by ALFRED HITCHCOCK PRESENTS, but these mystery tales forwent Hitchcock's sardonic, oddball introductions, concentrating instead on a simple moral warning from the author. Even these were phased out when other writers were brought in. With a different cast for every episode, guest stars abounded, ranging from John Gielgud, Telly Savalas and Joan Collins to Joseph Cotton, Brian Blessed and Wendy Hiller. The series was a great export success for Anglia.

Tales of Wells Fargo

See *Wells Fargo*.

Talk Show

Although the term talk show can apply to all kinds of interview programmes, it is more precisely connected with American audience-participation shows like *Jerry Springer* and *The Oprah Winfrey Show* (and UK equivalents like *Kilroy* and *Trisha*), where selected members of the studio audience reveal their emotional hang-ups and particular points of pique. Because of their low production costs, talk shows are popular choices for daytime programming. The term can also apply to celebrity interviews in the *Parkinson* and *Wogan* vein, although these are generally known as chat shows in the UK.

Talking Heads/Talking Heads 2 ✶✶✶✶

UK (BBC) Drama. BBC 1 1988/BBC 2 1998

Writer **Alan Bennett**
Producers **Innes Lloyd, Mark Shivas**

● ***Two series of acclaimed monologues.***

Alan Bennett's 1988 series of six monologues – inspired by his success in scripting *A Woman of No Importance* for Patricia Routledge – was so well received (even finding its way on to A-level syllabuses) that it is something of a surprise that it was ten years before he served up another helping (he claimed he found it difficult to write such pieces). Written in his typically gossipy style, focusing (on the face of it) on parochial matters, each script, however, had great depth, spotlighting some truly sad, often pathetic, characters. Their depressing tales – emotional reflections on wasted lives with hints of dark secrets and obscure obsessions, all mixed up with tittle-tattle and talk of voluntary workers and the social services – were lightened by a generous sprinkling of Bennett's noted flair for social observation and moments of wry humour.

The first series consisted of the following monologues: *A Chip in the Sugar* (Alan Bennett himself in a tale of the relationship between a mother and her middle-aged son); *A Lady of Letters* (Patricia Routledge as a woman whose sole pleasure in life is correspondence); *Bed among the Lentils* (Maggie Smith as a vicar's wife with little time for God); *Soldiering On* (Stephanie Cole as a stockbroker's widow now bereft of her assets, including her memories); *Her Big Chance* (Julie Walters as an aspiring actress who lands a role in a porn film but makes out it's serious drama); and *A Cream Cracker under the Settee* (Thora Hird as the pensioner who suffers a fall and spots the eponymous item). The 1998 series was made up of: *Miss Fozzard Finds Her Feet* (Patricia Routledge as a spinster shop assistant whose home life is dominated by her stroke-victim brother and whose only pleasure is in a visit to the chiropodist); *The Hand of God* (Eileen Atkins as an antiques dealer who develops an unhealthy interest in the possessions of a sick acquaintance); *Playing Sandwiches* (David Haig as an efficient park-keeper with a mysterious past and a black secret to hide); *The Outside Dog* (Julie Walters as a hygiene-mad wife who despises her husband's dog); *Nights in the Gardens of Spain* (Penelope Wilton as a gardening-obsessed woman who befriends her murdering neighbour); and *Waiting for the Telegram* (Thora Hird as a pensioner awaiting 100th-birthday congratulations from the Queen and recalling a telegram of a more tragic nature that arrived during World War I).

In addition to Bennett's dialogue, the performances of the actors were highly acclaimed. Singled out particularly were Julie Walters and the BAFTA award-winning Thora Hird.

Tarbuck, Jimmy

OBE (1940–)

Liverpudlian comic turned TV quizmaster. A former Butlin's redcoat, Tarbuck arrived on our screens in 1963 in programmes like *Comedy Bandbox* and, more notably, SUNDAY NIGHT AT THE LONDON PALLADIUM, in which he proved so popular that he made a number of quick return visits and, just two years later, took over as the show's compere. In tandem with the Merseybeat boom, he swiftly grew into one of the biggest names of the 1960s and 1970s, a familiar face on various star-studded shows and launching numerous series of his own. These included *It's Tarbuck, Tarbuck at The Prince of Wales, Tarbuck's Back, The Jimmy Tarbuck Show, Tarbuck's Luck* and *Tell Tarby*. He later tried his hand at quizzes and chat shows. He hosted the gambling quiz WINNER TAKES ALL for many years and later presented *Tarby's Frame Game* and the golf game *Full Swing*. He was in the chair for *Tarby and Friends* and another talk show, *Tarbuck Late*, and appeared as Mr Belafonte in the single comedy *Brazen Hussies*, although he has not forgotten his variety roots, emceeing events like *Live from Her Majesty's* and *Live from the Palladium* in the 1980s. Actress/presenter Liza Tarbuck is his daughter and he made a guest appearance alongside her in LINDA GREEN.

Tarbuck, Liza

(1964–)

RADA-trained actress daughter of comic Jimmy Tarbuck. Liza Tarbuck gained her first major TV role as Pamela Wilson/Lynch in WATCHING. She had earlier appeared in TUMBLEDOWN and *Chimera*, and later hosted *She's Gotta Have It*, *Passport to the Sun*, THE BIG BREAKFAST and Sky's revival of BLOCKBUSTERS, before starring in the comedy-drama LINDA GREEN. Tarbuck was also seen in the BBC's 2002 version of *Hound of the Baskervilles* (Mrs Barrymore) and its 2005 adaptation of BLEAK HOUSE (Mrs Jellyby), and hosted more game shows in *Without Prejudice?* and *Win, Lose or Draw*. She has also made guest appearances in THE LEAGUE OF GENTLEMEN and *French and Saunders*, lent her voice to *Tractor Tom*, and taken over from John Nettles as narrator of AIRPORT.

Target ✱✱

UK (BBC) Police Drama. BBC 1977–8

Det. Supt. Steve Hackett	**Patrick Mower**
DS Louise Colbert	**Vivien Heilbron**
Det. Chief Supt. Tate	**Philip Madoc**
DS Frank Bonney	**Brendan Price**
DC Dukes	**Carl Rigg**

Producer **Philip Hinchcliffe**

The rough, tough tactics of a regional police force.

In *Target*, 1970s viewers were, for once, treated to a police series based outside the big cities. But this was no village bobby fantasy. Instead, it surveyed the hard-hitting tactics of a Hampshire regional crime squad, working in and around an unidentified major port. Seventies trendy Patrick Mower was the actor charged with bringing the series some sex appeal as it was pitched into rivalry with ITV's THE SWEENEY to see which cops could punch the hardest. *Target* probably won fists up, but was criticized for its excessive violence and for its lack of humour, which, for many, was *The Sweeney*'s saving grace. A second series followed, but with the action toned down somewhat, although its main man, 39-year-old divorced Liverpudlian Steve Hackett, was just as unscrupulous as ever. 'Target' was the name police gave to a person active in the commission of a serious crime.

Target Luna/Pathfinders in Space/Pathfinders to Mars/Pathfinders to Venus ✱✱

UK (ABC) Children's Science Fiction. ITV 1960/1960/1960–1/1961

Prof. Wedgwood	**David Markham** *(Target Luna)*
	Peter Williams
Conway Henderson	**Frank Finlay** *(Target Luna)*
	Gerald Flood
Geoffrey Wedgwood	**Michael Craze** *(Target Luna)*
	Stewart Guidotti
Valerie Wedgwood	**Sylvia Davies** *(Target Luna)*
	Gillian Ferguson
Jimmy Wedgwood	**Michael Hammond** *(Target Luna)*
	Richard Dean
Ian Murray	**John Cairney** *(Target Luna)*
	Hugh Evans
Dr O'Connell	**Harold Goldblatt**
Prof. Mary Meadows	**Pamela Barney**
Harcourt Brown	**George Coulouris**
Margaret Henderson	**Hester Cameron**
Capt. Wilson	**Graydon Gould**

Creators **Malcolm Hulke, Eric Paice**
Producer **Sydney Newman**

Escapades in outer space with the pioneering Wedgwood family.

The *Pathfinders* quartet of sci fi dramas begins with an adventure in six parts, which went out under the title of *Target Luna*. Its sequels, *Pathfinders in Space, Pathfinders to Mars* and *Pathfinders to Venus*, were all broadcast as part of ITV's Sunday *Family Hour*. In *Target Luna* (with a completely different cast), Professor Wedgwood successfully manages to send his son, Jimmy, and pet hamster, Hamlet, into lunar orbit and back. In the first of the *Pathfinders* stories, the scientist and his family go a step further and actually land on the moon. Despite being stranded on the surface and facing alien threats, they eventually escape back home. In the second story the destination is Mars. Again fraught with danger, and despite unexpected outside interference, the expedition is once more a success. The third tale picks up from the return journey to Earth and involves the rescue of a rival astronaut from the planet Venus under the gaze of menacing pterodactyls and an erupting volcano. As well as members of the Wedgwood family, the adventures rope in several other transient characters, in particular writer Conway Henderson and Professor Meadows, the leading female authority on space.

Pathfinders was produced by future DOCTOR WHO creator Sydney Newman and partly devised by Malcolm Hulke, writer of *Doctor Who* and CROSSROADS stories among other TV work. Although somewhat crude, the series was itself a pathfinder for children's science-fiction television.

Tarmey, William

(William Piddington; 1941–)

Mancunian actor, a former builder and shopkeeper who entered showbusiness as a part-time singer, gradually picking up 'extra' work in a number of TV series. He appeared in dramas like CROWN COURT, STRANGERS and THE GHOSTS OF MOTLEY HALL before, in 1979, he was given the chance to appear as Jack Duckworth in CORONATION STREET and, since becoming a regular cast member, has never looked back.

Tarrant, Chris

OBE (1946–)

British presenter, a former teacher who broke into television as a reporter with ATV in Birmingham. As host and producer of the anarchic TISWAS, he brought a new strain of children's television to the UK, making the show a cult favourite with adults, too. His attempt at a proper grown-up, late-night version, *OTT*, failed miserably, however, and was replaced by another Tarrant offering, *Saturday Stayback*, after one series. Tarrant then headed into radio, taking over as breakfast presenter on London's Capital Radio, while making a name for himself in the advert voice-over world and contributing to LWT's *The Six O'Clock Show*. He succeeded Clive James and Keith Floyd in the chair of what became *Tarrant on TV*, presented the 'help' show *Hotline*, and has also hosted numerous game shows, including *PSI*, CLUEDO, *Everybody's Equal*, *Lose a Million*, THE MAIN EVENT, *Pop Quiz*, *The Opposite Sex*, *Prove It*, *Man O Man* and the phenomenally successful WHO WANTS TO BE A MILLIONAIRE? Other credits include the sports retrospective *Starting Blocks*.

Tarzan ✶✶

US (Banner) Adventure. ITV 1967–70 (US: NBC 1966–8)

Tarzan	**Ron Ely**
Jai	**Manuel Padilla Jr**
Jason Flood	**Alan Caillou**
Rao	**Rockne Tarkington**
Tall Boys	**Stewart Raffill**

● ***More adventures with the apeman created by Edgar Rice Burroughs.***

In this television version, Tarzan (the Earl of Greystoke) returns from civilization to live once again among his animal friends. This time there is no Jane and no pidgin-English, but at least the Tarzan yodel is authentic (they used the Johnny Weissmuller original). Now Tarzan is accompanied by a chimpanzee called Cheetah and Jai, a young native orphan he has befriended. Tracking down illegal hunters and other *persona non grata*, the Lord of the Jungle becomes a kind of gamekeeper and animal doctor. Also seen are Jai's tutor, Jason Flood, Rao, the local vet, and Rao's assistant, Tall Boy. The show was shot in Mexico and Brazil.

Tate, Catherine

After roles in series such as THE BILL, BIG TRAIN, *That Peter Kay Thing*, *Barking*, *TV Go Home* and WILD WEST (Angela Phillips), London-born Catherine Tate exploded on to the comedy stage when the BBC offered her *The Catherine Tate Show* in 2004. This provided the versatile actress and writer with the chance to create some of the most popular comic characters of the era, most notably dismissive schoolgirl Lauren ('Am I bovvered?'), effeminate Derek, who takes extreme offence at being considered gay ('How very dare you!'), and the foul-mouthed, tactless East Ender pensioner, Nan. Tate has also been seen in AGATHA CHRISTIE'S MARPLE, *Twisted Tales* and BLEAK HOUSE (Mrs Chadband).

Taxi [1] ✶✶

UK (BBC) Comedy Drama. BBC 1963–4

Sid Stone	**Sid James**
Fred Cuddell	**Bill Owen**
Terry Mills	**Ray Brooks**
Madeleine	**Vanda Godsell**
Sandra	**Diane Aubrey**
Bert Stoker	**Toke Townley**
Dolly Stoker	**Clare Kelly**
Jean Stoker	**Janet Kelly**

Creator **Ted Willis**
Writers **Ted Willis, Harry Driver, Jack Rosenthal**
Producers **Michael Mills, Harry Carlisle, Douglas Moodie**

● ***A London taxi-driver involves himself with other people's problems.***

Driver Sid Stone owns his own cab and plies his trade on the streets of London. Unfortunately, Sid also has a flair for interfering in other people's business, be they his fare-paying customers, his partner, Fred Cuddell, or his young colleague, Terry Mills. The three drivers share rooms in a converted house and, in the second season, the upstairs neighbours, Bert and Dolly Stoker (with daughter Jean), are introduced. By this time, however, Fred has left the scene. Sid's girlfriends are Madeleine (in the first series) and Sandra (thereafter).

Taxi [2] ✶✶✶

US (Paramount/John Charles Walters) Situation Comedy. BBC 1 1980–5 (US: ABC 1978–82; NBC 1982–3)

Alex Reiger	**Judd Hirsch**
Bobby Wheeler	**Jeff Conaway**
Louie De Palma	**Danny De Vito**
Elaine Nardo	**Marilu Henner**
Tony Banta	**Tony Danza**
Latka Gravas	**Andy Kaufman**
John Burns	**Randall Carver**
'Revd' Jim 'Iggie' Ignatowski	**Christopher Lloyd**
Simka Dahblitz Gravas	**Carol Kane**
Jeff Bennett	**J. Alan Thomas**
Zena Sherman	**Rhea Perlman**

Creators/Writers/Executive Producers **James L. Brooks, Stan Daniels, Ed Weinberger, David Davis**
Producers **Glen Charles, Les Charles**

● ***The sad, frustrated lives of a team of New York cabbies.***

If you can't do the job you want, you can always drive a taxi until a suitable position becomes available. It'll only be for a while. Well, that is what the drivers at the Sunshine Cab Company believe. Here is a bunch of rainbow-chasers, dreamers hoping that the right door will open so they can leave the grubby garage and move on to their chosen career. Sadly, everyone knows that they are likely to be driving taxis for the rest of their lives.

Among the crew is Tony Banta, a boxer who has lost every fight, Bobby Wheeler, a failed actor, and Elaine Nardo, a single mother who longs to run an art gallery. More intriguing are Latka Gravas, an immigrant garage mechanic who can hardly speak English, and wacky Reverend Jim, a burned-out hippie who lives in a condemned flat and is oblivious to the world around him. While they plan their perfect futures they are hustled and hassled by the firm's lecherous dispatcher, the vicious, pint-sized Louie De Palma who barks out instructions from his 'cage'. He charges the cabbies for phone messages, spies on Elaine as she changes clothes and generally becomes their common enemy. Only one cabbie is happy with his lot. This is kind, thoughtful Alex Reiger, a man with limited horizons. He is number one driver, a father figure and the best friend of all his colleagues.

Other characters who appear are naïve, romantic student John Burns (a driver for one season), and Simka, a scatter-brained compatriot of Latka's who later becomes his wife. Also seen is Rhea Perlman as Louie's girlfriend, Zena, a vending-machine stocker. She and Danny De Vito were actually married during a *Taxi* lunchbreak and when the show's producers moved on to create CHEERS they took Perlman with them. De Vito and Christopher Lloyd soon became major Hollywood names, starring in films like *Romancing the Stone* and *Back to the Future* respectively, but Andy Kaufman, who played the zany Latka, tragically died of cancer in 1984.

Taylforth, Gillian
(1955–)

London-born actress becoming famous as Kathy Beale/ Mitchell in EASTENDERS, having previously been seen in the PLAY FOR TODAY *Eleanor* and series like *Zigger Zagger*, THE RAG TRADE (Lyn), *Watch This Space*, SINK OR SWIM, BIG JIM AND THE FIGARO CLUB and MINDER. Since leaving Albert Square, Taylforth has starred in *Big Cat* (Polly), FOOTBALLERS' WIVES (Jackie Pascoe), MESSIAH (Helen Warren) and *The House That Jack Built* (Maxine), and made guest appearances in OPERATION GOOD GUYS, CASUALTY, MCCREADY AND DAUGHTER and NEW TRICKS. Her sister is actress Kim Taylforth.

Taylor, Gwen
(Gwen Allsop; 1939–)

British actress seen mostly in comedy or light drama roles on television. Most prominent have been the parts of Amy Pearce in DUTY FREE, Rita Simcock in A BIT OF A DO, Liz in *Sob Sisters*, Celia Forrest in THE SHARP END, Annie in SCREAMING, Gen Masefield in *Conjugal Rites*, Tilly in PILGRIM'S REST, Barbara in BARBARA, Laura, the deputy mayor, in A PERFECT STATE, Margaret Lewis in BELONGING, Mrs Thompson in FAT FRIENDS and Peggy Armstrong in HEARTBEAT. Earlier credits included RUTLAND WEEKEND TELEVISION, *Took and Co.*, *Sounding Brass* and numerous single dramas, including Alan Plater's PLAY FOR TODAY *The Land of Green Ginger*. Guest appearances take in WITHIN THESE WALLS, THE SWEENEY, SPACE: 1999, THE NEW AVENGERS, INSPECTOR MORSE, MIDSOMER MURDERS and the shorts series *Table 12*.

Taylor, Ken
(1922–)

British writer responsible for dramas like *China Doll* (1960), *Into the Dark* (1963), *The Devil and John Brown* (1964) and a trilogy, *The Seekers* (also 1964). He adapted H. G. Wells's *Days to Come* in 1966 and was later co-writer of THE BORGIAS. Somewhat more successfully, Taylor wrote the screenplays for MANSFIELD PARK, THE JEWEL IN THE CROWN, THE CAMOMILE LAWN, *Cause Célèbre* and *Peacock Spring*. He also contributed to series like WHITE HUNTER, *Shoulder to Shoulder* and MISS MARPLE.

Taylor, Shaw
(1924–)

British presenter, most familiar urging viewers to 'keep 'em peeled' as host of POLICE FIVE (from 1962). Previously, Shaw had been quizmaster for DOTTO, and was later seen in ITV's motoring magazine, *Drive-In*.

TCM
(Turner Classic Movies)

Digital film channel making the most of the MGM, Warner Brothers and RKO movie libraries owned by its parent company, Time Warner. As its name suggests, Hollywood favourites abound.

Teachers ★★

UK (Tiger Aspect) Drama. Channel 4 2001–4
DVD: VCI

Simon Casey .... **Andrew Lincoln**
Kurt McKenna .... **Navin Chowdhry**
Brian Steadman .... **Adrian Bower**
Susan Gately .... **Raquel Cassidy**
Jenny Page .... **Nina Sosanya**
Clare Hunter .... **Gillian Bevan**
Geoff .... **Simon Chandler**
Carol Schickelgruber .... **Ursula Holden Gill**
Marcella .... **Anna Holkar**
Stephen .... **Bob Mason**
Bob Porter .... **Lloyd McGuire**
Maggie .... **Zoe Telford**
Liz Webb .... **Ellen Thomas**
Danny .... **Daniel Bliss**
Tanya .... **Kelly Brennan**
Jeremy .... **James Corden**
Arnie .... **Peter England**
Bev .... **Ashley Madekwe**
Teddy .... **Keir Mills**
Hayley .... **Lucy Shore**
Ian .... **Tim Smith**
Cheryl .... **Phoebe Thomas**
Pauline .... **Kara Tointon**
John Paul ('JP') Keating .... **Shaun Evans**
Penny Neville .... **Tamzin Malleson**
Matt Harvey .... **James Lance**
Lindsay Pearce .... **Vicky Hall**
Kayla .... **Marsha Crosby**
Adam Grint .... **Jason Boyd**
Curtis .... **Ed Browning**
Brandon .... **Tyrone Lewis**
Thomas .... **Max Dobbs**
Ben Birket .... **Mathew Horne**
Damien Wallace .... **Daon Broni**
Ewan Doherty .... **Lee Williams**
Anthony .... **Jonas Armstrong**
Ping .... **Su Bhoopongsa**

Producers **Tim Bradley, Rhonda Smith**

Behaviour at a West Country secondary school is out of control – and the kids are almost as bad.

At Summerdown Comprehensive in Bristol the teachers are more unruly than the pupils. Skiving, bad language, stupid pranks, drugs, affairs and petty rivalries are rife in and around the staffroom here, that's if the teachers aren't sneaking off to the toilets for a crafty smoke or nipping down the pub. Leading the gang is 27-year-old Simon, a feckless, unconventional teacher of English but adored nonetheless by his pupils. Maggie is his policewoman girlfriend and Susan, a psychiatry teacher, is his best friend at work. Jenny is the no-nonsense colleague in the English department Simon battles with most. Bob is head of English, but he is one of life's losers. Among the other staff members, Brian is a PE teacher, while Carol is a school secretary. Computer science teacher Kurt is Carol's boyfriend. Despite its heavy leaning on coarse language and situations (or perhaps because of it), *Teachers* quickly won a loyal fan base and became Channel 4's most successful drama series ever, running to an unprecedented four series. Snappily edited and fast-moving, with rock music built into the soundtrack, it offers echoes of star Andrew Lincoln's previous triumph in THIS LIFE, and yet proves to be also quirky and sometimes bizarre, such as when the Krankies show up for a parents' evening. There are surreal moments, too, epitomized by things the schoolkids do in the background of shots, or by the donkey seen wandering the school corridors. Thirty-nine episodes were produced, some (in series three) directed by Lincoln.

New teachers make their bow as episodes progress, teachers such as JP, the gay new languages master, self-centred blonde Penny, and Matt, who takes over Simon's job when he leaves at the end of series two. Lindsay is a new biology teacher in series three, while significant cast changes result in series four when Summerdown merges with Wattkins Comprehensive and a change of school is demanded. Out go Kurt, Brian and Matt and in come Ewan, the gullible new head of English, Ben, a hypochondriac RE master (an atheist), and Damien, a sarcastic food technology teacher. Another new arrival is Ping, Bob's new Asian girlfriend. Throughout, Clare is their headteacher.

Tears Before Bedtime ✶✶

UK (BBC) Situation Comedy. BBC 1 1983

Anne Dickens .... **Geraldine McEwan**
Geoffrey Dickens .... **Francis Matthews**

Writer **Richard Waring**
Producer **Harold Snoad**

Frustrated parents start a new life away from their annoying children.

If the kids won't leave home, then maybe the parents had better flee the nest themselves. That's the premiss of this short-lived sitcom. Anne and Geoffrey Dickens have had just about enough of the rowdy world of youth. Their three kids – aged 18, 19 and 20 – have driven them to distraction with their loud music, strange fashions and independent behaviour, so they decide to move out. They end up 70 miles from home, living in a run-down basement flat. However, their attempts to settle down and start a new life prove far from easy. Just seven episodes were produced.

Ted and Alice ✶✶

UK (Granada) Comedy Drama. BBC 1 2002

Alice Putkin .... **Dawn French**
Ted .... **Stephen Tompkinson**
Barry Branch .... **Owen Teale**
Shane .... **David Walliams**
Joy .... **Katy Cavanagh**
Stan .... **David Troughton**
Mark .... **Peter Serafinowicz**
Perdita Lowe .... **Eleanor Bron**
Karen .... **Geraldine McNulty**

Writer **Nick Vivian**
Executive Producers **Jon Plowman, Sita Williams**
Producer **Jacinta Peel**

A Lake District tourism officer falls in love with an alien.

Alice Putkin is unlucky in love – unlucky in loving boorish policeman Barry Branch, that is. After six years of courtship, he still hasn't proposed and, what's more, lies to her so he can play pool at the pub while she does his washing. Alice finally snaps, kicks Barry into touch and shortly afterwards meets Ted, a slightly odd but very pleasant stranger who rents her spare room. Romance blossoms and, even after Ted's revelation that he is in fact an alien, who really looks like a lizard and has come to Earth for sex, she finds it hard not to cling to her new lover. Complicating matters, however, are alien hunters Stan and Shane who are out to capture the new arrival for their secret organization, the Foundation, and, of course, Barry, who wants his girlfriend/skivvy back. Mark is another alien who masquerades as a barman in the local pub, Perdita is an experienced lover of aliens who teaches dance, and Joy is Alice's colleague at the tourist information centre. Steve Bendelack directed this three-part serial.

Telecine

A machine which allows films and film inserts to be shown on television by converting them into electronic signals. The system was largely abandoned in newsrooms with the advent of videotape and VCRs.

Telegoons, The ✶✶

UK (BBC/Grosvenor Films) Comedy. BBC 1963–4

Writers **Spike Milligan, Eric Sykes, Larry Stephens**
Producer **Tony Young**

***Animated, visual version of classic radio scripts from* The Goon Show.**

Although some new material was specially recorded, this puppet series essentially made use of archive radio programmes for its soundtrack. As in the radio days, *The Telegoons* were voiced by Peter Sellers, Harry Secombe and Spike Milligan, taking the parts of the characters Neddy Seagoon, Major Denis Bloodnok, Bluebottle, Eccles, Henry Crun, Moriarty, Minnie Bannister, Brigadier Grytpype-Thynne and others.

Teleplay

An old-fashioned word (used in the 1950s and 1960s) for the script of a fictional drama programme, equivalent to screenplay in the cinema.

Telerecording

A primitive means of recording TV pictures on to film, used in the days before videotape as a way of preserving live broadcasts. Effectively, the TV screen was filmed and a telecine machine was used for playback. The system was known as kinescope in the USA.

Teletext

A TV screen-based data system that conveys information about news, sports, weather, recipes, travel, etc. It also offers subtitles for hearing-impaired viewers on certain programmes. The viewer with a Teletext TV set can call up the information at the press of a button. For the technically minded, the information is carried in the blanking interval of the TV waveform (i.e. it uses the spare lines which make up the screen image). The BBC's text service is known as CEEFAX and was first made available in 1974. ITV's service was initially known as ORACLE (Optional Reception of Announcements by Coded Line Electronics) and run by a company jointly owned by the ITV companies. However, since 1993 the licence has been operated by Teletext Ltd and the service known simply as Teletext. Teletext Ltd also provides the service for Channel 4, S4C and Channel 5.

Telethon

The name given to a television broadcast marathon (lasting an entire evening or longer), specifically designed to draw attention to one or more causes and usually tied in with a charity appeal. The name was appropriated by ITV for their regular appeals in the late 1980s, although the best-known annual telethon is the BBC's CHILDREN IN NEED. Others have included COMIC RELIEF and *Sport Relief*.

Teletubbies ✱✱

UK (Ragdoll) Children's Entertainment. BBC 2 1997–2001

Tinky Winky	**Dave Thompson**
	Mark Heenehan
	Simon Shelton
Dipsy	**John Simmit**
Laa-Laa	**Nikky Smedley**
Po	**Pui Fan Lee**

Creators **Anne Wood, Andrew Davenport**
Writer **Andrew Davenport**

Hugely successful pre-school series featuring four colourful characters.

The Teletubbies live in Teletubbyland (actually a grassy hill in Warwickshire) along with some nibbling rabbits, talking flowers, a magic windmill and periscope-like voice-trumpets which surface to make announcements. Their home is the Tubbytronic Superdome, which they share with a vacuum-cleaner named the Noo-noo. Played by actors in costumes, the radiant, dancing, prancing stars – akin to giant alien babies – in descending order of size are Tinky Winky (a purple creature with a triangular aerial on his head; prone to falling over and carrying a handbag – a gay icon); Dipsy (green, with a spike aerial; sings 'Bptum, bptum, bptum, bptum'); Laa-Laa (yellow, with a curled aerial; the happiest of the bunch); and Po (red, with a loop aerial; easily worked up and sings in Cantonese). All have grey squares in the centre of the tummy on which at times are projected films of real-life activities. Their diet consists of Tubby Custard and Tubby Toast. Also seen are a toy lion and bear (voiced by Eric Sykes and Penelope Keith, respectively), and all is watched over by a giggling baby framed in the corona of the sun. Toyah Willcox provides the opening narration.

These bizarre creations caused quite a furore when they first appeared. Parents were up in arms over the way they shunned proper English for 'goo-goo' talk ('Eh-oh' for 'Hello', for example). The creators hit back, explaining that their mission was to encourage under-fives to learn through play, inspiring them to inter-react with the characters. Contact with the adult world was kept to a minimum or approached only through the eyes of a real toddler (in the deliberately repetitious filmed sequences). Toddlers immediately loved the *Teletubbies*, and not just in the UK. The series became one of the BBC's biggest exports and the source for some extremely lucrative merchandising, including the 1997 chart-topper 'Teletubbies Say Eh-Oh!' After the original series ended in 2001, production company Ragdoll turned their attention to *Teletubbies Everywhere*, an educational expansion of the idea that premiered on CBeebies in 2002. 'Time for Tubby Bye Bye!'

Television ✱✱✱

UK (Granada) Documentary. ITV 1984

Narrator **Ian Holm**

Producers **Leslie Woodhead, Norman Swallow**

The history of television, by television.

Tracing the development of the 20th century's major communications medium, right from the pioneering days of Logie Baird and others (although not in strict chronological order), this 13-part documentary squared up to the difficult task of evaluating the impact and style of television. Old footage, interviews, discussions, reconstructions and plenty of illustrative clips and flashbacks helped the producers to reflect on television's treatment of news, politics, drama, comedy, commercials, etc. Filming took place right across the globe, showing East Berliners watching West German TV, extracts from a Samurai drama in Japan, an outside broadcast in Indonesia and the transmission of Soviet news simultaneously in places as far apart as Tashkent and Siberia. An edited version was prepared for transmission in the USA, taking out certain British examples and adding American substitutes.

Television Dancing Club ✱✱

UK (BBC) Entertainment. BBC 1948–64

Producer **Richard Afton**

Long-running dance showcase.

Predating its sister programme, COME DANCING, by two years, *Television Dancing Club* was largely devoted to the dance music of Victor Sylvester and his Ballroom Orchestra. Sylvester also offered dance instruction and was assisted by hostesses Patti Morgan and Sylvia Peters. For the last season, 1963–4, the title was shortened to *Dancing Club*.

Television South

See *TVS*.

Television South West

See *TSW*.

Television Top of the Form ✶✶

UK (BBC) Quiz. BBC 1 1962–75

Presenters **Geoffrey Wheeler, David Dimbleby, Paddy Feeny, John Edmunds, John Dunn**

Producers **Innes Lloyd, Bill Wright, Mary Evans**

● ***General knowledge tournament for grammar school kids.***

Launched on radio in 1948 and emulated on television from 1962, *Top of the Form* was a contest for well-behaved high school children. Schools were invited to put forward a team of four pupils, of varying ages, to compete in a national tournament to find who really was 'Top of the Form'. In the early days, two questionmasters were employed, one in the assembly hall of one school and the other similarly housed at another. Geoffrey Wheeler and David Dimbleby were the first to fill these roles and Boswell Taylor was the programme's chief question-setter. In 1967 a special *Transworld Top of the Form* was seen. Linking teams in the UK and Australia, it was chaired by Aussie anchorman Bill Salmon.

Television Wales and West

See *TWW*.

Telewest

Cable television provider that began as a small operation known as Croydon Cable in 1984. Through various take-overs and mergers involving US media businesses, the company emerged as Telewest Communications in 1991. In 2000 Telewest merged with Flextech and in 2006 a merger with telecom giant NTL was completed. The combined company is now known as NTL Incorporated. See also FLEXTECH and NTL.

Telford's Change ✶✶✶

UK (BBC) Drama. BBC 1 1979

Mark Telford .... **Peter Barkworth**
Sylvia Telford .... **Hannah Gordon**
Keith Everley .... **Albert Welling**
Peter Telford .... **Michael Maloney**
Tim Hart .... **Keith Barron**
Maddox .... **Colin Douglas**
Helen Santon .... **Zena Walker**

Creator **Peter Barkworth**
Writer **Brian Clark**
Producer **Mark Shivas**

● ***A successful banker opts for the quiet life and, in so doing, puts his marriage on the line.***

High-flying, middle-aged international bank official Mark Telford has reached a crossroads in life. Should be continue in the fast lane or is it time to take things a little more easily? He opts for the latter, accepting an appointment as manager of a branch in Dover. His wife, Sylvia, however, refuses to be dragged away from London, where she is carving out a career in the theatre world. The result is a ten-episode soapy drama that focuses on the intriguing clients of the provincial bank and the various twists and turns of the Telfords' marriage, which is threatened by the intrusion of Sylvia's friend, Tim Hart. The series was based on an idea that star Peter Barkworth first conceived in 1968.

Tell It to the Marines ✶

UK (Associated-Rediffusion/Jack Hylton) Situation Comedy. ITV 1959–60

Leading Seaman White .... **Alan White**
Cpl Surtees .... **Ronald Hines**
Lt. Raleigh .... **Henry McGee**
Petty Officer Woodward .... **John Baskcomb**
Whittle .... **Ian Whittaker**
Kilmartin Dalrymple .... **Ian MacNaughton**
Commander Walters .... **Ian Colin**
Major Howard .... **Jack Allen**

Creator **Ted Willis**
Producer **Jack Hylton**

● ***The Navy and the Marines share a traditional rivalry.***

Exploiting the long-standing tensions between the men of the Royal Navy and those of the Royal Marines, *Tell It to the Marines* features petty squabbles, minor battles and endless joking between the two forces. Principal among the characters are Leading Seaman White and Marine Cpl Surtees, with superior officers like Lt. Raleigh and Major Howard also in the fray. The premiss is that the tensions between the forces have come to a head after a squabble over girls in a pub, leading to the top brass deciding to stamp out the animosity by arranging a series of 'friendly' sports events – an exercise that is doomed to failure.

Telly Addicts ✶✶

UK (BBC) Quiz. BBC 1 1985–98

Presenter **Noel Edmonds**

Producers **Juliet May, John King, Richard L. Lewis, Helen Lott**

● ***Teams of contestants test their knowledge of television.***

In this light-hearted quiz, two teams of four competed to show off their knowledge of television history. For the first nine years, the teams were made up of family members only, but in 1994 the rules were relaxed to allow friends, workmates, etc., to make up the numbers. (Also in 1994, *The Archers* actor Charles Collingwood was recruited to fool around while reading out the scores.) A knockout tournament unearthed each year's *Telly Addicts* champions. The first winning team was the Payne family from Swindon, but in that inaugural series the rules were different. Instead of progressing through a knockout, the winning family stayed on to meet new challengers week after week. In 1995, the series celebrated its tenth anniversary with *Champion Telly Addicts*, an additional tournament designed to find the best of the best. For the final season, in 1998, the couch potatoes were dragged from their armchairs as *Telly Addicts* was revamped into a quiz for three teams of two, played on a stage that required much moving around.

The origins of *Telly Addicts* lay in a series entitled *Telly Quiz*, presented by Jerry Stevens, which was seen on BBC 1 between Christmas Eve 1984 and 2 January 1985. In *Telly Quiz*, celebrities took on viewers, as they did in an early rival to *Telly Addicts*, ITV's *We Love TV*, which was hosted by Gloria Hunniford.

Tempo ✱✱

UK (ABC) Arts. ITV 1961–7

Presenters **Earl of Harewood, Clive Goodwin, Leonard Maguire, David Mahlowe**

Producers **Lloyd Shirley, Reginald Collin, Mike Hodges, Pamela Lonsdale**
Editors **Kenneth Tynan, Peter Luke, Peter Brinson, John Rodker, Clive Goodwin, John Kershaw**

● ***Fortnightly arts magazine.***

Conceived as a response to the BBC's successful MONITOR programme, *Tempo* was a 50-minute (later 25-minute) arts indulgence hosted first by the Earl of Harewood, then by Leonard Maguire and others. As well as the classic arts of painting, sculpture, ballet and music, *Tempo* also reviewed film, literature and drama, with the aim of allowing a mass audience to appreciate the artistic world without the intrusion of academic opinion.

10%ers, The ✱✱

UK (Grant Naylor/Carlton) Situation Comedy. ITV 1994; 1996

Dominic Eden	**Clive Francis**
Atin	**Benedict Taylor**
Gloria	**Irene Sutcliffe**
Enid	**Hilda Braid**
Tony	**Colin Stinton**
Helen	**Gabrielle Cowburn**
Joan	**Elizabeth Bennett**
Vanessa	**Emma Cunniffe**

Creators **Rob Grant, Doug Naylor**
Producers **Rob Grant, Doug Naylor, Marcus Mortimer, Ed Bye**

● ***The daily grind at a London theatrical agency.***

A quick spin-off from ITV's COMEDY PLAYHOUSE series of pilots, *The 10%ers* is set in Eden Management, a West End theatrical agency with a motley crew of employees (the series taking its name from the agent's traditional cut of clients' fees). Head of the agency Dominic Eden is always looking to woo new talent and he and his colleagues spend much of their time frantically nursing actors' delicate egos or fighting off the attentions of rival agents. The team consists of untrustworthy American Tony, self-centred Joan, obliging Helen, suave Atin and two doddery secretaries, Enid and Gloria (the latter played by Madge Ryan in the pilot). Vanessa is a new agent joining the team in place of Helen in series two (which, after only two episodes, was shunted from peak hours to a later time slot). Fourteen episodes in all followed the pilot, shown in 1993.

Tenafly ✱✱

US (Universal) Detective Drama. ITV 1974 (US: NBC 1973–4)

Harry Tenafly	**James McEachin**
Ruth Tenafly	**Lillian Lehman**
Herb Tenafly	**Paul Jackson**
Lt. Sam Church	**David Huddleston**
Lorrie	**Rosanna Huffman**

Executive Producers **Richard Levinson, William Link**
Producer **Jon Epstein**

● ***A detective, for once, puts his family first.***

Not many TV private eyes can claim to be family men, so Harry Tenafly is quite an exception. Bars and broads are simply not his style. He is also black, which was fairly remarkable at the time this series was made. Operating in and around Los Angeles, Tenafly makes sure he leads two separate lives: at work – an investigation company – and at home – where his wife is Ruth and his son is Herb. Lt. Sam Church is the police pal who helps out when the going gets tough. Lorrie is Harry's secretary. *Tenafly* formed part of the MYSTERY MOVIE sequence, but just four episodes were made after the pilot, which was simply called *Tenafly*.

Tenant of Wildfell Hall, The ✱✱✱

UK (BBC/WGBH) Drama. BBC 1 1996

Helen Graham	**Tara Fitzgerald**
Gilbert Markham	**Toby Stephens**
Arthur Huntingdon	**Robert Graves**
Frederick Lawrence	**James Purefoy**
Mrs Markham	**Pam Ferris**
Revd Millward	**Kenneth Cranham**
Annabella Wilmot	**Beatie Edney**
Rose Markham	**Paloma Baeza**
Arthur Graham	**Jackson Leach**
Eliza Millward	**Miranda Pleasence**
Hargrave	**Sean Gallagher**
Hattersley	**Jonathan Cake**
Rachel	**Sarah Badel**
Lowborough	**Dominic Rowan**
Miss Myers	**Cathy Murphy**

Writers **David Nokes, Janet Barron**
Producer **Suzan Harrison**

● ***The beautiful but mysterious new incumbent of a country house hides a dark secret.***

When Helen Graham arrives at Wildfell Hall tongues start to wag. She is a single mother, of five-year-old Arthur, and this is the middle of the 19th century. It is not the done thing by a long chalk. Helen meets handsome farmer Gilbert Markham and, despite her penurious position, romance begins to bloom, but the enigma of Helen's background just won't go away. Could it be that the despicable man known as Huntingdon has something to do with her past? Or Mr Lawrence, her landlord? Other key characters include Gilbert's protective mother, Mrs Markham; Reverend Millward, who attacks Helen's standards in his fiery sermons; and Annabella Wilmot, a possible romantic rival for Helen. Mike Barker directed this three-part adaptation of Anne Brontë's novel of 1848, which had been previously dramatized in 1968–9 (BBC 2: Janet Munro as Helen, Corin Redgrave as Huntingdon, Bryan Marshall as Gilbert and William Gaunt as Mr Lawrence).

Tender is the Night ✱✱

UK (BBC/Showtime) Drama. BBC 2 1985

Dick Diver	**Peter Strauss**
Nicole Warren	**Mary Steenburgen**
Devereux Warren	**Edward Asner**
Baby Warren	**Kate Harper**
Franz Gregorovius	**Jürgen Brügger**
Abe North	**John Heard**

Mary North	**Nancy Paul**
Rosemary Hoyt	**Sean Young**
Tommy Barban	**Joris Stuyck**
Hannah	**Joanna David**
Mr Morris	**Timothy West**

Writer **Dennis Potter**
Producer **Betty Willingale**

An aspiring psychiatrist is trapped by the love of a sick woman.

It is 1917 and ambitious young doctor Dick Diver is studying in Switzerland when he meets someone who will radically change his life. Nicole Warren is a beautiful and wealthy heiress who suffers from mental problems. She becomes Dick's patient and they fall in love. Soon – thanks to her money – they are living a hedonistic lifestyle on the French Riviera, where among their American expatriate cohorts is young film star Rosemary Hoyt, who has a crush on Dick. Diver later returns to Switzerland to take over a rich person's clinic with long-term associate Franz Gregorovius, but his life has already turned sour. Even a return to the Riviera can't restore Diver's spirits. The Depression is looming and he is trapped in a relationship with a dependent, schizophrenic woman. By the time of the sixth and final episode, the roles have been reversed. It is Nicole who is able to call the shots as she becomes stronger and happier, while Diver is a mental wreck, his life crumbling.

Robert Knights directs this Dennis Potter adaptation of F. Scott Fitzgerald's 1934 novel, which echoes the author's own topsy-turvy life with wife Zelda Sayre. Richard Rodney Bennett supplies the music.

Tenko ✶✶✶

UK (BBC) Drama. BBC 1 1981–2; 1984–5

Rose Millar	**Stephanie Beacham**
Marion Jefferson	**Ann Bell**
Sylvia Ashburton	**Renee Asherson**
Major Yamauchi	**Bert Kwouk**
Dr Beatrice Mason	**Stephanie Cole**
Kate Norris	**Claire Oberman**
Minah	**Pauline Peters**
Vicky Armstrong	**Wendy Williams**
Sally Markham	**Joanna Hole**
Nellie Keene	**Jeananne Crowley**
Gerda	**Maya Woolfe**
Mrs Domenica Van Meyer	**Elizabeth Chambers**
Christina Campbell	**Emily Bolton**
Blanche Simmons	**Louise Jameson**
Dorothy Bennett	**Veronica Roberts**
Joss Holbrook	**Jean Anderson**
Debbie Bowen	**Karin Foley**
Verna Johnson	**Rosemary Martin**
Maggie Thorpe	**Elizabeth Mickery**
Alice Courtenay	**Cindy Shelley**
Edna	**Edna Doré**
Col. Clifford Jefferson	**Jonathan Newth**
Bernard Webster	**Edmund Pegge**
Cpl Jackson	**Colin Dunn**
Major Sims	**David Gooderson**
Sister Ulrica	**Patricia Lawrence**
Miss Hassan	**Josephine Welcome**
Johnny Saunders	**Gregory de Polnay**
Harry Milne	**Andrew Sharp**
Father Lim	**Ric Young**
Tom Redburn	**Daniel Hill**
Jack Armstrong	**Ivor Danvers**
Simon Treves	**Jeffrey Hardy**
Dolah	**Ronald Eng**
Shinya	**Takashi Kawahara**
Kasaki	**Takahiro Oba**
Yukio	**Peter Silverleaf**
Sato	**Eiji Kusuhara**
Joan	**Dawn Keeler**
Timmy	**Nigel Harman**

Creator **Lavinia Warner**
Writers **Jill Hyem, Anne Valery, Paul Wheeler**
Producers **Ken Riddington, Vere Lorrimer**

The hardships of female prisoner-of-war camps in 1940s Malaya.

Following the invasion of Singapore by Japan in 1942, the expatriate women of Britain and Holland were torn from their menfolk and imprisoned in makeshift holding camps. *Tenko* – meaning 'roll call' in Japanese – tells the story of one such group of women, trapped in filthy conditions, abused, beaten and degraded, thousands of miles from home and out of reach of assistance. Their appalling living conditions, their relationships with their captors, and the relationships among the women themselves (where race and class became prominent issues) were documented in this hugely popular programme which ran for three seasons.

Appointed head of the women is Marion Jefferson, the wife of a colonel and obvious choice as leader. Around her are gathered the likes of rape victim Rose Millar; Beatrice Mason, a formidable doctor; nurses Kate Norris and Nellie Keene; ageing academic Joss Holbrook; Dorothy Bennett who, having lost both her husband and her child, turns to prostitution with the guards; tarty Cockney Blanche Simmons; and ladylike Verna Johnson. Formidable Sister Ulrica is head of the Dutch section, which also features the nauseatingly selfish Mrs Van Meyer. The cruelty of their captors is too underplayed, according to some viewers, but nevertheless the prisoners are subjected to enormous humiliation, torturous working conditions, malnutrition, disease, long marches to new camps and insufferable indignity beneath a baking Asian sun.

The first series depicts how the women struggle to adjust to captivity and how the hope of release lingers long in their minds. By the second season, that hope has largely disappeared, replaced by a determination to survive, as their personal values change dramatically. The last series concerns the end of the war and the efforts of the survivors to come to terms with life back in society, coping with estranged husbands and shattered lifestyles. A one-off reunion episode, played as a murder mystery and set in 1950, was produced in 1985.

The series was created by Lavinia Warner, who had researched the history of Japanese POW camps for a THIS IS YOUR LIFE programme on Margo Turner, a nursing corps officer who had once been held captive. Warner developed the idea into an OMNIBUS documentary before dramatizing the harrowing events in *Tenko*.

Tennant, David

(David McDonald; 1971–)

Scottish actor, now installed as the tenth DOCTOR WHO. Tennant's major break came when cast as Campbell in TAKIN' OVER THE ASYLUM. From this he moved on to *A Mug's Game* (Gavin), DUCK PATROL (Darwin) and *Love in the 21st Century*, with guest appearances in THE MRS BRADLEY MYSTERIES,

RANDALL AND HOPKIRK (DECEASED), *People Like Us*, FOYLE'S WAR and *Posh Nosh*. He then played Christopher Willans in *The Deputy*, Mr Gibson in HE KNEW HE WAS RIGHT, DI Peter Carlisle in BLACKPOOL, and the title role in CASANOVA, as well as appearing in a live revival of *The* QUATERMASS *Experiment* for BBC 4. Other roles have come in *Secret Smile* (Brendan Block) and *The Romantics* (Jean Jacques Rousseau) and earlier credits include small parts in THE BILL and HOLDING THE BABY.

Terrahawks ★★

UK (Anderson Burr/LWT) Children's Science Fiction. ITV 1983–4; 1986

Voices:

Zelda .... **Denise Bryer**
Sgt Major Zero .... **Windsor Davies**
Capt. Mary Falconer .... **Denise Bryer**
Dr Tiger Ninestein .... **Jeremy Hitcher**
Lt. Hiro .... **Jeremy Hitcher**
Lt. Hawkeye .... **Jeremy Hitcher**
Capt. Kate Kestrel .... **Anne Ridler**
Yung-Star .... **Ben Stevens**
Cy-Star .... **Anne Ridler**
Hudson .... **Ben Stevens**
Space Sgt 101 .... **Ben Stevens**

Creator **Gerry Anderson**
Writer **Tony Barwick**
Producers **Gerry Anderson, Christopher Burr**

A defence force protects the Earth from an ugly alien witch queen.

In Gerry Anderson's major contribution to television in the 1980s, his 'Supermarionation' progressed into 'Supermacromation', an advanced form of glove puppetry. However, following the tried and tested Anderson formula, the heroes were unsurprisingly familiar. This time they were the Terrahawks, an élite squad of dare-devils who risked life and limb to save the Earth from alien invasion in the year 2020.

Headed by Dr Tiger Ninestein, the ninth clone of Austrian-American scientist Gerhard Stein, the Terrahawks consist of ace pilot Mary Falconer; Hawkeye, an American with computer-aided vision; Lt. Hiro, the team's computer boffin; and pop-singer-turned-pilot Kate Kestrel. From Hawknest, a secret South American base, they face the cunning might of the cackling, prune-faced android Zelda and her equally hideous allies from the planet Guk. These include her useless son, Yung-Star, and her spiteful twin sister, Cy-Star. With the use of cube-shaped robots, and other agents like Yuri, the space bear, and MOID (Master of Infinite Disguise), Zelda aims to take over the planet. The Terrahawks, in their spaceship known as *Hawkwing*, cover her every move, assisted by round robots called Zeroids. These are controlled when on Earth by Sgt Major Zero and when in space by Space Sgt 101, pilot of the Zeroid spacecraft, *Spacehawk*. Also on display is Hudson, a Rolls-Royce with a mind of its own.

Terry and June ★★

UK (BBC) Situation Comedy. BBC 1 1979–83; 1985; 1987

Terry Medford .... **Terry Scott**
June Medford .... **June Whitfield**
Sir Dennis Hodge .... **Reginald Marsh**
Beattie .... **Rosemary Frankau**
Malcolm .... **Terence Alexander**
Tim Barrett
John Quayle

Creator **John Kane**
Producers **Peter Whitmore, Robin Nash, John B. Hobbs**

Mishaps and misunderstandings in the life of a typical suburban couple.

Terry and June Medford are an ordinary middle-class couple whiling away their middle age in suburban Purley – except that Terry is bumptious, ham-fisted, over-ambitious and helplessly accident-prone, and June is the archetypal long-suffering wife who has to pick up the pieces. Terry commutes into the city, where he works for Sir Dennis Hodge, a man likely to call at the Medfords' home just at the wrong moment, usually with farcical consequences.

Safe, silly and unspectacular, *Terry and June* was effectively a reworking of an early Scott/Whitfield sitcom, HAPPY EVER AFTER, but without the old lady, the mynah bird or occasional visits from grown-up children seen in the earlier outing.

Terry-Thomas

(Thomas Terry Hoar Stevens 1911–90)

Although largely known for his film work, gap-toothed, plummy comedian Terry-Thomas was one of TV's earliest stars, appearing on the BBC from the 1940s in programmes like *To Town with Terry*, *How Do You View?* and *Strictly T–T*. He later headed for the USA, where his 'frightfully-Englishness' led to more TV success (including guest appearances in series like BURKE'S LAW), but he found his better days behind him when he returned to the BBC in 1968 for a short-lived comedy entitled *The Old Campaigner*, in which he played travelling salesman James Franklin-Jones.

Tess of the D'Urbervilles ★★★

UK (LWT) Drama. ITV 1998

Tess Durbeyfield .... **Justine Waddell**
Alec D'Urberville .... **Jason Flemyng**
Angel Clare .... **Oliver Milburn**
Joan Durbeyfield .... **Lesley Dunlop**
Jack Durbeyfield .... **John McEnery**

Writer **Ted Whitehead**
Producer **Sarah Wilson**

An impoverished girl of noble descent is caught between two fallible men.

Tess Durbeyfield comes from a poor family. The D'Urbervilles, their distant relatives, are very wealthy and live nearby and there is no other option for the young girl than to take work on the D'Urberville estate. It is there that she is preyed upon by the cruel Alec D'Urberville and gives birth to his child, which dies in infancy. Later, working as a milkmaid, she falls in love with preacher's son Angel Clare, an idealistic young man who becomes her husband but disowns her when the truth of her relationship with Alec is revealed. The two men continue to play major roles in her tragic life and the emotional turmoil finally erupts in a famous climax staged at Stonehenge. Ian Sharp directed this two-part adaptation of Thomas Hardy's 1891 novel.

Test Card

A card marked with colours, shades, patterns and lines of various sizes and thicknesses, used by engineers to calibrate cameras and monitors for best performance. The test card was a familiar sight until daytime television arrived in the 1980s, with TV installers using it to set up and adjust receivers. The BBC colour test card featured a schoolgirl, a blackboard and some toys. The girl's name was Carole Hersee and she consequently holds the record for being the most-seen person on British television.

Testament of Youth ★★★

UK (BBC) Drama. BBC 2 1979

Vera Brittain	**Cheryl Campbell**
Mr Brittain	**Emrys James**
Mrs Brittain	**Jane Wenham**
Edward Brittain	**Rupert Frazer**
Roland Leighton	**Peter Woodward**
Victor Richardson	**Michael Troughton**
Miss Penrose	**Rosalie Crutchley**
Geoffrey	**Geoffrey Burridge**
Mrs Leighton	**June Tobin**
Mr Leighton	**Victor Lucas**

Writer **Elaine Morgan**
Producer **Jonathan Powell**

● ***Twelve formative years in the life of a devout pacifist.***

The autobiography (published 1933) of Vera Brittain (mother of politician Shirley Williams) was adapted by Elaine Morgan and directed in five parts by Moira Armstrong. It begins in 1913. In the Derbyshire town of Buxton, 18-year-old Vera lives with her well-to-do parents but, in this age of female emancipation, is already suffocating in provincial life. Thankfully, she earns herself a place at Somerville College, Oxford, but unfortunately war breaks out and Vera has to leave academia to sign up as a volunteer nurse. She becomes one of the brave young women nursing in London, in Malta and also at the front in France. The horrors of war are all around her (archive footage helps set the grim scene), compounded further by the deaths of her closest male companions. Fiancé Roland is killed in action, close friend Geoffrey also dies in France and her brother Edward is yet another casualty. Vera begins a relationship with Victor, a man who has been blinded in the war, but he, too, dies. Vera is then pulled out of the action by her parents, who insist she returns home to care for her mother, who has flu, and this part of her story winds up in 1925. However, the sickening experience was to haunt Brittain all her life. Indeed, the book was written as a reminder to all about the horror of warfare and the shocking impact it has on people's lives.

TFI Friday ★★★

UK (Ginger) Channel 4 1996–2000

Presenter **Chris Evans**

Producers **Suzie Aplin, David Granger, Will Macdonald, Stephen Joel**
Executive Producers **Chris Evans, John Revell**

● ***Lively, Friday teatime mix of entertainment and chat.***

Chris Evans bounced back on to the small screen, fresh from Radio 1 breakfast show success, with this youth-oriented show which majored on pop bands, showbiz gossip and daft stunts and games. The letters in the title standing for *Thank Four It's . . .*, the show was broadcast from the Riverside Studios in Hammersmith, with a set that conveyed the impression of a nightclub below and a manager's office (from where Evans anchored the show) above. Producer Will Macdonald joined Evans to present a series of intriguing 'pub tricks', involving matches, glasses, etc. Star guests dropped by for a chat, ugly people paraded their best features, and there were plenty of other similarly wacky competitions. The programme was repeated at around 11 p.m. the same evening. By the time of the final series, in autumn 2000, Chris Evans had left the show and the programme was fronted by different celebrity guests each week, winding up with Sir Elton John.

Chris Evans returned to mainstream television with the equally chaotic *OFI Sunday* (ITV 2005–).

Thames Television

Formed by the merger of two ITV contractors (ABC and Associated-Rediffusion) at the instigation of the ITA, Thames took over the London weekday franchise on 29 July 1968. Its franchise was retained during the 1980 reviews but was surprisingly taken away from the company in the 1991 auctions, when Thames was outbid by Carlton Communications. This decision, among others, seriously brought into question the logic of the new auction system, whereby the franchise was awarded to the highest bidder, providing the ITC was satisfied that business plans were viable and commitments to programme quality would be met. It effectively ignored Thames's remarkable programming record, which had brought many notable contributions to the ITV network. Among the company's biggest hits were THE SWEENEY, MINDER, MAN ABOUT THE HOUSE, THE WORLD AT WAR, ROCK FOLLIES, BLESS THIS HOUSE, THIS WEEK, THIS IS YOUR LIFE, WISH YOU WERE HERE . . . ? and THE WIND IN THE WILLOWS.

Thames subsequently concentrated on programme production and also helped establish the satellite channel, UK Gold. A consortium headed by Thames was the sole bidder for the proposed Channel 5 project when it was first touted but, with doubts about the viability of the new network and the company's business plan, the licence was not awarded by the ITC. In 1993 Thames was bought by Pearson plc, becoming part of Pearson Television, where it was joined by companies like Alomo, Witzend and Grundy (the group is now known as FremantleMedia). The company, now titled Talkback Thames and operating as Fremantle's UK production wing, continues to make programmes for BBC and commercial networks, including THE BILL and *Family Affairs*.

Thank Your Lucky Stars ★★

UK (ABC) Pop Music. ITV 1961–6

Presenters **Keith Fordyce, Brian Matthew, Jim Dale**

Producers **Philip Jones, Helen Standage, Keith Beckett, Milo Lewis**

● ***Successful Saturday-evening pop show.***

Planned as ITV's answer to JUKE BOX JURY, *Thank Your Lucky Stars* presented the pop sensations of the day miming to their latest tracks. Keith Fordyce and, later, Brian Matthew were the main frontmen, although in earlier programmes hosts included the likes of Jimmy Savile, Pete Murray, Alan Dell, Sam Costa, Barry Alldis, Kent Walton, Jimmy Young and Don Moss. The segment known as Spin a Disc (a shamelessly direct copy of *Juke Box Jury*) called on a panel of celebrities and local teenagers to give their views on record releases, and it was in this part of the programme that 16-year-old office clerk Janice Nicholls was discovered in 1962. Her broad Black Country accent, displayed when she declared 'Oi'll give it foive', made her an instant favourite and ensured she became a programme regular. *Thank Your Lucky Stars* also gave The Beatles their first national television exposure, in February 1963. Jim Dale took over as presenter in 1965, but the programme was cancelled a year later, just as the British beat boom was coming to a close. The summer programmes in 1963–5 went out under the title of *Lucky Stars Summer Spin*.

That was the Week That Was ★★★★

UK (BBC) Comedy. BBC 1962–3

David Frost, Millicent Martin, Lance Percival, Bernard Levin, William Rushton, Roy Kinnear, Timothy Birdsall, Kenneth Cope, David Kernan, Al Mancini, Robert Lang, Irwin Watson

Producer **Ned Sherrin**

● ***Hard-hitting, revolutionary satire, week by week.***

That was the Week That Was broke new ground for television. Airing on a Saturday night, it was a product of the BBC's current affairs department rather than its light entertainment crew, a fact reflected in its commitment to topicality and its biting tone. The programme looked at the major events of the previous week, ridiculed them, drew comment and exposed ironies. At the helm was a young David Frost who became host after Brian Redhead and John Bird had declined the position. (Bird reportedly suggested the title of the programme having seen a petrol slogan that read: 'That's Shell, that was'. He also recommended Frost for the job.) Frost's team included the likes of Willie Rushton, Roy Kinnear, Lance Percival, Bernard Levin and Millicent Martin, whose opening song recalled the week's news in its lyrics. The remainder of the programme was given over to sketches, interviews and guest spots, with scripts written by the likes of Kenneth Tynan, Dennis Potter and Keith Waterhouse. For the first time, sacred cows like racism, royalty, politics and religion were slaughtered in a humorous fashion, prompting much criticism from the Establishment. Individuals, such as the then Home Secretary, Henry Brooke, were also singled out for treatment. Bernard Levin upset many viewers with his forthright opinions (to the point where one night a member of the studio audience assaulted him on air). In addition, the programme adopted a technically *laissez faire* approach which allowed cameras to wander into shot and the studio audience to be seen, something which had seldom been experienced before on prim-and-proper British television.

The format and title also transferred to the USA, again with Frost in the chair. His Stateside collaborators included Alan Alda and Tom Bosley, but the show didn't really click. Back in the UK, *TW3* (as it became known), with 37 editions under its belt, was taken off before the election year of 1964 (in case it influenced voters) and was succeeded by two short-lived sequels, NOT SO MUCH A PROGRAMME, MORE A WAY OF LIFE and BBC-3.

That's Life ★★★

UK (BBC) Consumer Affairs. BBC 1 1973–94

Presenters **Esther Rantzen, George Layton, Bob Wellings, Kieran Prendiville, Glyn Worsnip, Cyril Fletcher, Paul Heiney, Chris Serle, Bill Buckley, Doc Cox, Gavin Campbell, Michael Groth, Joanna Munro, John Gould, Maev Alexander, Adrian Mills, Grant Baynham, Mollie Sugden, Howard Leader, Simon Fanshawe, Scott Sherrin, Kevin Devine**

Creator **John Lloyd**
Producers/Editors **Esther Rantzen, Henry Murray, Peter Chafer, Michael Bunce, Ron Neil, Gordon Watts, John Morrell, Bryher Scudamore, Shaun Woodward, John Getgood**

● ***Consumer/light entertainment magazine filled with silly stunts, painful puns and invaluable investigations.***

Originally planned for just a six-week run, *That's Life* continued instead for 21 years. The series was conceived as a follow-up to the Saturday night offering BRADEN'S WEEK, in which Bernard Braden and a team of reporters made people laugh and fought consumers' battles. One of those reporters was Esther Rantzen and, installed in the new *That's Life* format, she quickly made the series her own.

Rantzen was assisted by an ever-changing team of mostly male reporters, with George Layton and Bob Wellings her first co-stars. Cyril Fletcher joined in 1974 to recite his odd odes and to pick out funny misprints from newspapers (a job later done by Mollie Sugden and Doc Cox among others), and Richard Stilgoe, the Fivepenny Piece and Victoria Wood were recruited to provide witty songs. A weekly *vox pop* saw Esther out on the streets of London, challenging punters to sample strange items of food or drink. Invariably, she bumped into Annie, an elderly lady who became a stalwart of the programme.

That's Life also offered plenty of daft stories about talented pets and quirky pastimes, but its real merit was as a consumers' champion. It presented a 'Heap of the Week' award for shoddily made goods, dished out 'Jobsworth' and plain English accolades for excessive bureaucracy and tackled conmen on their doorsteps. More importantly still, the programme also campaigned heavily for the protection of children, a crusade which resulted in the establishment of the Childline charity.

In 1984 a story which moved every viewer concerned two-year-old Ben Hardwicke, a toddler suffering from an incurable liver disease. Ben sadly died, but not before the case for child organ transplants had been thoroughly aired. As part of the campaign, Marti Webb released a version of Michael Jackson's 'Ben', which reached the Top Five in 1985.

That's Life, with its careful balance of the silly and the serious, its brassy theme music and topical closing cartoons (drawn by Rod Jordan), became an intrinsic part of the weekend for many viewers. In 1979 there was also a version for younger fans, *Junior That's Life*, from the same team.

That's Love ★★

UK (TVS) Situation Comedy. ITV 1988–90; 1992

Donald Redfern .... **Jimmy Mulville**
Patsy Redfern .... **Diana Hardcastle**
Amanda Owen .... **Lynne Pearson**

Gary Owen .... **Rob Spendlove**
Olive .... **Vivienne McKone**
Babs .... **Phyllida Law**
Victor .... **Ralph Nossek**
Zoe Redfern .... **Zoe Hodges**
Matthew Redfern .... **Matthew Cole**
Laurel Manasotti .... **Liza Goddard**
Tristan Beasley .... **Tony Slattery**

Creator/Writer **Terence Frisby**
Executive Producers **John Kaye Cooper, Sarah Lawson, Gill Stribling-Wright**
Producer **Humphrey Barclay**

Domestic discord strikes a professional couple.

Lawyer Donald Redfern and his designer partner, Patsy, enjoy a happy relationship until skeletons from her distant past are unfortunately unearthed. The revelations introduce new tensions and suspicions into their lives that sustain this comedy for four series. Despite the fact that they have two children, Zoe and Matthew, Donald and Patsy now find themselves drifting apart. Visits from Patsy's mum, Babs, and her husband, Victor, do little to help the situation. Donald then embarks on an affair with wealthy widow Laurel Manasotti, and, in an effort to patch up their ailing marriage, the Redferns seek advice from counsellor Tristan Beasley. However, Beasley falls in love with Patsy and they begin a relationship, leaving the Redferns hurtling ever faster towards divorce. The Redferns' close friends are Amanda and Gary Owen, who have four kids and a turbulent relationship of their own. Olive is the Redferns' nanny. Writer Terence Frisby also guests in the series.

That's My Boy ★★

UK (Yorkshire) Situation Comedy. ITV 1981; 1983–6

Ida Willis .... **Mollie Sugden**
Dr Robert Price .... **Christopher Blake**
Angie Price .... **Jennifer Lonsdale**
Mrs Price .... **Clare Richards**
Wilfred Willis .... **Harold Goodwin**
Miss Parfitt .... **Deddie Davies**

Writers **Pam Valentine, Michael Ashton**
Producer **Graeme Muir**

A housekeeper discovers her employer is really her son.

After endlessly pestering a domestic employment agency, fearsome Ida Willis is finally installed in the position of housekeeper, taking up residence with young Dr Robert Price and his model wife, Angie. Gradually realizing that Robert is the son she gave away for adoption at birth, Ida becomes increasingly possessive of him, much to the despair of his adoptive mother. The young doctor is left to dither between the two. The family (and housekeeper) later move out of London to Yorkshire, where Ida gains a friend, Miss Parfitt, and also has her brother, Wilfred, to keep her occupied.

Thaw, John

CBE (1942–2002)

Characters as well defined as INSPECTOR MORSE, THE SWEENEY's Jack Regan, KAVANAGH QC and HOME TO ROOST's Henry Willows testify to the versatility of award-winning British actor John Thaw. Thaw's TV debut came in an anthology series called *The Younger Generation* in 1961 and his first starring role was in REDCAP in 1964, playing military policeman John Mann. Apart from the series listed above, he was also seen as Mark Paxton in Francis Durbridge's *Bat out of Hell*; Fast Jack in *Pretenders*; Stan in THICK AS THIEVES; Francis Drake in a 1980 TV movie *Drake's Venture*; crime reporter *Mitch*; wartime RAF supremo, BOMBER HARRIS; Stanley Duke in *Stanley and the Women*; Peter Mayle in A YEAR IN PROVENCE; Labour Party leader George Jones in *Screen Two's The Absence of War*; Harry Barnett in the murder mystery *Into the Blue*; Tom Oakley in the award-winning GOODNIGHT MR TOM; plastic surgeon Joe MacConnell in *Plastic Man*; legal clerk Joshua Mantle in the spy drama *The Waiting Time*; the title character in MONSIGNOR RENARD; Jim Proctor in *The Glass*; Peter Harris in *Killer Waiting*; and Harry Jenkins in *Buried Treasure*. Guest appearances in programmes like Z CARS, THE AVENGERS, STRANGE REPORT, BUDGIE, *The Morecambe and Wise Show* and THE ONEDIN LINE, and narration work on series such as *The Second World War in Colour*, added to his credits. Thaw was married to actress Sheila Hancock. He was the father of actress Abigail Thaw and step-father of actress Melanie Thaw.

Theakston, Jamie

(1970–)

Tall, youth TV presenter, the host of series like *The O Zone*, LIVE AND KICKING, TOP OF THE POPS, *The Priory*, *A Question of Pop*, The Games, Beg, Borrow or Steal, *UK Music Hall of Fame* and *With a Little Help from My Friends*. Theakston has also been seen hosting award ceremonies, featuring in *Rock Profiles*, MURDER IN MIND and *The Afternoon Play*, making guest appearances in LINDA GREEN, LITTLE BRITAIN and AGATHA CHRISTIE'S MARPLE, and starring as Doug in *Mad About Alice*. Voice-over work includes narration for *Trading Places*, *Traffic Cops* and *Car Wars*.

Therese Raquin ★★★

UK (BBC) Drama. BBC 2 1980

Thérèse Raquin .... **Kate Nelligan**
Madame Raquin .... **Mona Washbourne**
Camille Raquin .... **Kenneth Cranham**
Laurent .... **Brian Cox**
Michaud .... **Richard Pearson**
Grivet .... **Timothy Bateson**
Olivier Michaud .... **Philip Bowen**
Suzanne .... **Jenny Galloway**
Vidal .... **Alan Rickman**

Writer **Philip Mackie**
Producer **Jonathan Powell**

A neglected wife finds a lover but tragedy awaits.

Emile Zola's scandalous novel of 1867 was brought to BBC 2 in three parts, with Simon Langton directing. The tale now begins in 1875 when Thérèse Raquin is unhappily married and living with her feeble husband, Camille, and her mother-in-law in the Passage du Pont Neuf, in Paris. Although her life is dreary and unexciting, she cannot believe that it will ever change, until she meets Camille's friend, Laurent. They become lovers and murder the husband, but the wicked deed is not easy for either to live with. Patrick Gowers added the music.

Theroux, Louis

(1970–)

Reporter son of novelist Paul Theroux, specializing in unearthing secrets by befriending celebrities in his series *When Louis Met . . .* By spending time with people like Jimmy Savile, Paul Daniels and Debbie McGee, Neil and Christine Hamilton, Max Clifford and Ann Widdecombe, Theroux aimed to coax out the real people behind the public facades. His earlier series, *Louis Theroux's Weird Weekends*, brought him into contact with people with strange hobbies and preoccupations, the likes of neo-fascists, South African white supremacists, female bodybuilders and porn stars. Later documentaries included *Louis and the Brothel, Louis, Martin and Michael* (Bashir and Jackson) and *Louis and the Nazis*. Previously, Theroux, who was born in Singapore, brought up in Wandsworth and gained a First at Oxford, had been a reporter for Michael Moore's *TV Nation*.

They Think It's All Over ★★★

UK (Talkback/BBC) Comedy Quiz. BBC 1 1995–

Presenters **Nick Hancock, Lee Mack**

Producers **Harry Thompson, Jim Pullin, Simon Bullivant**
Executive Producer **Peter Fincham**

● ***Irreverent sports quiz.***

More akin to HAVE I GOT NEWS FOR YOU than its BBC 1 stablemate A QUESTION OF SPORT, *They Think It's All Over* features the talents of chairman Nick Hancock (giving way to Lee Mack in 2005) and resident comedians Rory McGrath and Jonathan Ross (initially Lee Hurst). Adding sporting authenticity to the mirth are team captains David Gower and Gary Lineker (later replaced by David Seaman and Phil Tufnell, both eventually replaced in turn by Ian Wright and Boris Becker), who become the butt of much of the humour. They are joined by varied sporting guests. Rounds include explaining bizarre goal celebrations, unravelling a photofit image of three personalities, 'Feel the Sportsman' (blindfolded reveal-the-identity) and guessing as many names of sports stars as possible from clues given by team colleagues within a time limit. The programme title (and part of its opening sequence) is taken from Kenneth Wolstenholme's famous closing commentary on the 1966 World Cup Final.

Thick as Thieves ★★★

UK (LWT) Situation Comedy. ITV 1974

George Dobbs .... **Bob Hoskins**
Stan .... **John Thaw**
Annie Dobbs .... **Pat Ashton**
Tommy Hollister .... **Trevor Peacock**
Daphne .... **Nell Curran**

Creators/Writers **Dick Clement, Ian La Frenais**
Producer **Derrick Goodwin**

● ***Two crooks share one house and one woman.***

When petty criminal George 'Dobbsie' Dobbs is released from prison after three years, he returns home to Fulham to discover his best pal, Stan, shacked up with his missus, Annie. Rather than punching each other's lights out, they reluctantly come to an agreement to share the house, with predictable consequences, especially when fellow jailbird Tommy Hollister, who's on the run, also moves in. Daphne is Annie's friend and much-needed confidante.

Only eight episodes were produced, although creators Dick Clement and Ian La Frenais had made plans to develop the series, sending its two main characters back inside. Instead, largely because actor John Thaw had been signed up for THE SWEENEY, they returned to the BBC, for whom they developed their Ronnie Barker pilot *Prisoner and Escort* into another old lag comedy – PORRIDGE.

Thick of It, The ★★★★

UK (BBC) Situation Comedy. BBC 2 2006–

Hugh Abbot .... **Chris Langham**
Malcolm Tucker .... **Peter Capaldi**
Olly Reeder .... **Chris Addison**
Terri Coverley .... **Joanna Scanlon**
Glenn Cullen .... **James Smith**
Robyn Murdoch .... **Polly Kemp**

Creator **Armando Iannucci**
Writers **Jesse Armstrong, Simon Blackwell, Tony Roche, Armando Iannucci**
Producer **Adam Tandy**

● ***A minister's ineptitude threatens to undermine the image of the Government.***

Filmed in documentary style, with no laugh track, this merciless send-up of the spin-doctored, image-conscious, cack-handed world of politics was a hit first on BBC 4, before transferring to BBC 2. Hugh Abbot is the newly appointed Minister for Social Affairs. Frankly, he's a liability, as Machiavellian Downing Street enforcer Malcolm Tucker knows only too well. It falls to Tucker to knock the hapless, out-of-touch, paranoid Abbot and his small team of bumblers into shape in each episode in a bid to prevent serious damage being done to the Government's reputation. Benefit fraud, media relations, housing bills, factory tours, reshuffles and obscene e-mail trouble are all traps that the dithering Abbot falls into and which leave the Rottweiler Tucker snarling. The language is strong throughout as the actors improvise the dialogue from a basic script. Creator Armando Iannucci also directs.

Thief Takers ★★

UK (Central/Carlton) Police Drama. ITV 1996–7

DI Charlie Scott .... **Reece Dinsdale**
DS Bob 'Bingo' Tate .... **Brendan Coyle**
DS Helen Ash .... **Lynda Steadman**
DC Alan Oxford .... **Gary McDonald**
DC Ted Donachie .... **Robert Willox**
DC Grace Harris .... **Pooky Quesnel**
DCI Frank Uttley .... **David Sterne**
Stephanie Scott .... **Kate McKenzie**
Bryony Oxford .... **Michelle Joseph**
David Ash .... **Glyn Grimstead**
DS Anna Dryden .... **Amanda Pays**
DI Glenn Matteo .... **Grant Masters**
DC Lucy McCarthy .... **Simone Lahbib**
DCI Nick Hall .... **Nicholas Ball**
Marilyn Parker .... **Cecilia Noble**

Creator **Roy Mitchell**
Producers **Gina Cronk, Colin McKeown**
Executive Producer **Ted Childs**

● THE SWEENEY *for the 90s, with a lick of* MIAMI VICE *gloss.*

Thief Takers revolves around the all-action exploits of the Metropolitan Police's Armed Robbery Squad (aka the Flying Squad). The heavily 'tooled up' team is led into action by DI Charlie Scott, a man haunted by the death of his infant son from leukaemia. His sergeants are 'Bingo' Tate and Helen Ash. Tate is a maverick, lone operator whose taste for danger takes him into the most precarious of situations, including an affair with a hardened villain's wife. Ash is an Irish blonde whose husband, David, resents her calls to duty (she is replaced in the second series by new DS Anna Dryden). The team is completed by quietly tough Scot Ted Donachie; Alan Oxford, who is able to infiltrate black clubs for the word on the street; and rookie Grace Harris, a brunette with experience in the vice squad. Back at base, grouchy DCI Frank Uttley calls the shots and takes the rap whenever the team fouls up. For the third series, the team has a new DI, Glenn Matteo, and a new DC, Lucy McCarthy (replacing Scott and Harris), with Uttley giving way to a new supremo, DCI Nick Hall, returning to London after 20 years in Hong Kong. Music was composed by Hal Lindes, and a Miami Vice-style rock beat underscored most of the action, which, as in that American series, was fast and stylishly shot. The series followed a pilot episode shown in 1995, in which there were several cast differences. In place of Scott, the squad was led by DI Mickey 'Jack' Dawes (played by Robert Reynolds); predating Harris was Angela Prudhoe (Sophie Dix); and Oxford was played by Lennie James. Executive producer Ted Childs also worked on TV's other major flying squad series, THE SWEENEY, in the 1970s.

Thin Air ★★

UK (BBC) Drama. BBC 1 1988

Rachel Hamilton .... **Kate Hardie**
Mark Gentian .... **Kevin McNally**
Henry Campbell .... **Sam Kelly**
Richard Hellier .... **Nicky Henson**
Samantha Graham .... **Sarah Jane Morris**
Zac Diamond .... **James Aubrey**
Joe Jeffries .... **Brian Bovell**
Michael Haig .... **Robert Pugh**
Leonard Draeger .... **Clive Merrison**
Susan Draeger .... **San Lee**
Pat .... **Linda Robson**
Max .... **Peter Lovstrom**
Mallet .... **Adam Robertson**
Brian .... **Andrew Johnson**
Colin .... **Philip Croskin**
Linda .... **June Page**
Terry .... **Kevin Walsh**
Rose Marie .... **Cristina Avery**
George Fletcher .... **James Snell**
Guang .... **Burt Kwouk**

Writers **Sarah Dunant, Peter Busby**
Producer **Caroline Oulton**

● ***An intrepid girl reporter trails crime and corruption in Docklands London.***

Rachel Hamilton works as a reporter for Urban Air, a London commercial radio station. Her investigations lead her to uncover corruption in a new property development called Riverside. The grubby world she stumbles into is mired in dirty deals, drug peddling, forced evictions and even murder, and it seems that people at the top in her own radio station may be involved. When Rachel produces a documentary programme entitled *Riverzone* to lift the lid on what's been going on, she finds her life is on the line. Among the other key players are Richard Hellier, local developer and owner of Urban Air; Samantha Graham, his mistress; Draeger and Haig, Hellier's dodgy partners; and Mark Gentian, a local activist. At the station Henry is the stressed-out news editor, Zac is a DJ who does drugs, and Joe presents the night-time slot.

This five-part thriller, redolent of the get-rich-quick 1980s, is directed by Antonia Bird, with music by Andy Roberts. Co-writer Sarah Dunant was a presenter of Radio 4's *Woman's Hour*, while Sarah Jane Morris, who plays Samantha, topped the singles chart with The Communards in 1986 with 'Don't Leave Me This Way'. Star Kate Hardie is daughter of THE GOODIES' Bill Oddie.

Thin Blue Line, The ★★

UK (Tiger Aspect) Comedy. BBC 1 1995–6

Insp. Raymond Fowler .... **Rowan Atkinson**
Sgt Patricia Dawkins .... **Serena Evans**
PC Maggie Habib .... **Mina Anwar**
PC Kevin Goody .... **James Dreyfus**
PC Frank Gladstone .... **Rudolph Walker**
DI Derek Grim .... **David Haig**
DC Kray .... **Kevin Allen**
DC Gary Boyle .... **Mark Addy**

Writer **Ben Elton**
Producers **Ben Elton, Geoffrey Perkins**

● ***The misadventures of an incompetent police inspector and his equally inept team.***

Ben Elton has often declared his admiration for the sitcom genius of DAD'S ARMY, and in *The Thin Blue Line* there is more than an echo of Captain Mainwaring and his bumbling platoon, albeit in a cruder, 1990s style. The setting is Gasforth police station, ruled over with a rod of plastic by stick-in-the-mud traditionalist Inspector Raymond Fowler. Joining him in the force is his eminently more sensible live-in girlfriend of ten years, Sgt Dawkins, and other members of the team are Constable Habib (an Asian from Accrington and another voice of womanly reason); languid West Indian Constable Gladstone (filled with irrelevant recollections of the old days); and jumpy, vain and decidedly effeminate (despite his lust for Habib) Constable Goody. Friction at the station comes from the CID division, headed by the angry, unscrupulous DI Grim (prone to mixed metaphors) and his right-hand men, initially the smirky Kray then the bluff Boyle.

Collectively, the Gasforth crew face such difficult situations as dealing with young offenders, martialling football hooligans, policing anti-road protesters, flushing out drug-dealers and making themselves attractive for a TV documentary. Two series were made.

Thin Man, The ★★

US (MGM) Detective Drama. BBC 1957–8 (US: NBC 1957–9)

Nick Charles .... **Peter Lawford**
Nora Charles .... **Phyllis Kirk**
Lt. Ralph Raines .... **Stafford Repp**
Lt. Steve King .... **Tol Avery**

● ***A husband, a wife and their dog are a team of amateur detectives.***

The first thing to forget about this series is the Thin Man.

There isn't one. That character appeared in the film from which the series was derived and in which our heroes, Nick and Nora Charles, made their debut. Played by William Powell and Myrna Loy, this pair of amateur sleuths appeared in five more cinema features before arriving on TV in the persons of Peter Lawford and Phyllis Kirk.

Nick used to be a private eye with the Trans American Detective Agency, but now, fabulously rich, he and his new wife, Nora, have retired to a swanky apartment on New York's Park Avenue and settled into a world of good living. However, Nick finds old habits die hard, and he soon returns to the detective game, this time with his devoted wife at his side. The couple's wire-haired fox-terrier, Asta, also plays a part, sniffing out clues like a bloodhound. What the plots lack in depth is compensated for by the sparkling husband-and-wife repartee.

These characters, created by novelist Dashiell Hammett, have proved highly influential. If you ever wondered where the likes of HART TO HART, MCMILLAN AND WIFE and WILDE ALLIANCE found their inspiration, look no further.

Third Man, The ★★

UK/US (BBC/National Telefilm/British Lion) Drama. BBC 1959–60; 1962–5

Harry Lime	**Michael Rennie**
Bradford Webster	**Jonathan Harris**
Arthur Shillings	**Rupert Davies**

Executive Producer **Vernon Burns**
Producer **Felix Jackson**

The further adventures of Graham Greene's treacherous Viennese double-dealer.

In a move away from the famous cinema version starring Orson Welles, the TV *Third Man* cast Michael Rennie as Harry Lime, a charming amateur sleuth – quite unlike the film character – officially running an import–export agency but travelling the world to pin down crooks and help people in trouble at the same time. Specializing in works of art, the suave, sophisticated Lime's companies include Harry Lime Ltd, in London, and its equivalent, Harry Lime Inc., in New York. In his work he is assisted by his treasurer-cum-manservant, Bradford Webster (played by a pre-LOST IN SPACE Jonathan Harris), and on his investigations he enjoys a close liaison with Scotland Yard's Arthur Shillings (Rupert Davies in training for his future role as MAIGRET). A joint UK/US production, filming took place in both Shepperton Studios and Hollywood.

3rd Rock From the Sun ★★★

US (Carsey-Werner) Situation Comedy. BBC 2 1996–2002 (US: NBC 1996–2001)

Dr Dick Solomon	**John Lithgow**
Sally Solomon	**Kristen Johnston**
Harry Solomon	**French Stewart**
Tommy Solomon	**Joseph Gordon-Levitt**
Dr Mary Albright	**Jane Curtin**
Nina Campbell	**Simbi Khali**
Alissa Strudwick	**Larisa Oleynik**
Mrs Mamie Dubcek	**Elmarie Wendel**
Vicki Dubcek	**Jan Hooks**
Officer Don Orville	**Wayne Knight**
Stone Philips	**William Shatner**

Creators **Bonnie Turner, Terry Turner**
Executive Producers **Marcy Carsey, Caryn Mandabach, Bonnie Turner, Terry Turner, Tom Werner**

Four aliens adopt human identities to study life on Earth.

There is more than an echo of MY FAVORITE MARTIAN and MORK AND MINDY in this wacky aliens-on-Earth sitcom. But, although this is, like its forebears, a space comedy of manners, it is noticeably less sickly. This time the rather prickly aliens shape up as a family, changing their appearances to look human but inevitably failing to grasp the nuances of human life and therefore always in danger of exposing their true identities. At the same time, they provide sharply observed comment on the less logical aspects of mankind's way of living. The aliens originally arrive for a planned two-week observation but stay much longer, taking up residence in fictitious Rutherford, a town 52 miles from Cleveland, Ohio. High Commander of the mission is gullible Dick Solomon, posing as a physics teacher at a third-rate university, where he shares an office with (and is attracted to) Dr Mary Albright. She is constantly bemused by her zany roommate who always accepts things at face value. Dick's stunning 'sister' is Sally Solomon, actually a decorated lieutenant (male) in the alien force. The male/female conflict is a running problem for Sally. Dick's 'son' is the pubescent and hormonally charged Tommy (really an intelligence specialist older than the others) and completing the family is Dick's offbeat 'brother', Harry, whose eyes are never fully opened. Harry is only along for the ride – there was a spare seat on the spacecraft. Nina is Dick and Mary's feisty secretary; Mrs Dubcek is the family's eccentric landlady (she rents them an attic). Mrs Dubcek's daughter, Vicki, later dates Harry. Also seen are Officer Don Orville, a chubby police boyfriend of Sally's; Alissa, a girlfriend of Tommy's and the daughter of Dick's university rival; and Jennifer, the new office-share girl (guest star Laurie Metcalf) who comes between Dick and Mary, after Mary is promoted to Dean. The aliens' boss back home is the Big Giant Head, who appears in the guise of earthling Stone Philips.

Filming of series four was disrupted in 1998, following the sudden death of actor Phil Hartman, who had been guesting as Vicki's psychotic former boyfriend, Randy. Cliffhanger scenes featuring Hartman had to be reshot with a new guest star. Another guest was Roseanne, who appeared as a 'wife' for Dick from the home planet. John Cleese also dropped by. The series was created by husband and wife Terry and Bonnie Turner, the brains behind *Wayne's World*. In the UK, episodes aired first on Sky One.

thirtysomething ★★★

US (MGM/United Artists) Drama. Channel 4 1989–92 (US: ABC 1987–91)

Michael Steadman	**Ken Olin**
Hope Steadman	**Mel Harris**
Elliot Weston	**Timothy Busfield**
Nancy Weston	**Patricia Wettig**
Melissa Steadman	**Melanie Mayron**
Ellyn Warren/Sidel	**Polly Draper**
Prof. Gary Shepherd	**Peter Horton**
Janey Steadman	**Brittany and Lacey Craven**
Ethan Weston	**Luke Rossi**
Brittany Weston	**Jordana 'Bink' Shapiro**
Miles Drentell	**David Clennon**
Susannah Hart/Shepherd	**Patricia Kalember**
Steve Woodman	**Terry Kinney**
Jeffrey Milgrom	**Richard Gilliland**
Lee Owens	**Corey Parker**

Billy Sidel .... **Erich Anderson**

Creators **Ed Zwick, Marshall Herskovitz**
Producers **Ed Zwick, Marshall Herskovitz, Paul Haggis**

Light-hearted drama about a group of upwardly mobile friends in Philadelphia.

Against a background of disappearing youth and unfulfilled careers, *thirtysomething* introduces viewers to seven professional people in their thirties, children of the baby-boomer generation, now adults in a yuppie world. There are two couples and three singles, and the programme traces their lives, their loves, their fears and their ambitions.

Michael and Elliot are colleagues at an advertising agency who branch out into their own business. Hope and Nancy are their respective wives. Hope is a Princeton graduate and writer who puts her own career on hold in order to raise little Janey (and, later, Leo); Nancy is a 1960s flower child with artistic pretensions who looks after her and Elliot's school-age children, Ethan and Brittany. The three other main characters are Gary Shepherd, a college classics lecturer; Melissa Steadman, Michael's photographer cousin; and Ellyn Warren (Hope's best friend), an administrator at the City Hall. Both Melissa and Ellyn drift in and out of affairs, before Ellyn eventually marries an old flame, Billy Sidel.

The series focuses on each of the characters as they approach the crossroads and crises that affect everyone's lives, like the death of a parent (Michael's father), marital problems (Nancy and Elliot go through a messy separation) and personal illness (Nancy is diagnosed as having ovarian cancer). Career matters are always under discussion, particularly when Michael and Elliot's business collapses and they are forced to work for the devious Miles Drentell. Romance is never far away, as when Gary marries Susannah Hart and they have baby Emma. Nor is death: Gary is then killed in a car accident.

It is not surprising to discover that most of the programme's audience were in their 30s themselves. Viewers clearly identified with the series, sharing the characters' childhood memories and facing up to the same challenges of maturity.

This is Your Life ★★

UK (BBC/Thames) Entertainment. BBC 1955–64; ITV 1969–94; BBC 1 1994–2003

Presenters **Eamonn Andrews, Michael Aspel**

Creator **Ralph Edwards**
Producers **T. Leslie Jackson, Vere Lorrimer, Robert Tyrrel, Malcolm Morris, Jack Crawshaw, John Graham, Sue Green**

The life story of an unsuspecting celebrity retold with the help of surprise guests.

Taking people unawares, surrounding them with friends and family, and reliving the major moments in their life is what this programme was all about. *This is Your Life* began on American TV in 1952, with Ralph Edwards, its creator, also acting as host. In the UK it meandered between channels, beginning first on the BBC in 1955 and running for nine years. After a five-year hiatus, Thames picked up the format for ITV, and the company continued to produce the show when it returned to the BBC in 1994.

The same formula was followed from the start. The unsuspecting victim was cornered by the presenter (usually in disguise) at a public event or at a contrived meeting, informed 'This is your life' and then whisked away to a nearby TV studio, where close family and friends welcomed the fêted one. Other guests were introduced as the host worked his way chronologically through the person's life, reading from a large red book. Mystery voices hidden behind closed doors gave way to forgotten faces and warm embraces. Amusing anecdotes were told and glowing tributes were paid. The final guest was usually someone special: a child from the other side of the world, an inspirational teacher from the distant past, a person who had saved the celebrity's life, or vice versa. Buckets of tears were shed.

The very first victim was Eamonn Andrews, who was already signed up to be the programme's regular host. Ralph Edwards had flown over from the USA to conduct the inaugural programme but, after the *Daily Sketch* had spoiled the launch by revealing that the subject was going to be Stanley Matthews, a new victim had to be found. Andrews expected boxer Freddie Mills to be the target. Instead, it was Andrews himself. When Thames revived the series, its first victim was Des O'Connor. Some celebrities refused outright to appear. Soccer star Danny Blanchflower was one; novelist Richard Gordon (of *Doctor in the House* fame) was another. To avoid such embarrassments, the programme was later prerecorded.

Not all those featured were famous. One or two guests per series came from the ranks of anonymous worthies – brave airmen, industrious charity workers, selfless foster-parents, etc. Probably the highest-profile victim was Lord Mountbatten, the subject of a *This is Your Life* special in the Jubilee Year of 1977.

When Eamonn Andrews died in 1987, Michael Aspel picked up the big red book. The one used on screen contained just the programme script, but a real biographical scrapbook was later presented as a memento to the featured guest. Regular consultants to the series were Roy Bottomley and Tom Brennand.

This Life ★★★★

UK (World/BBC) Drama. BBC 2 1996–7

Miles Stewart .... **Jack Davenport**
Djamila 'Milly' Nassim .... **Amita Dhiri**
Warren Jones .... **Jason Hughes**
Edgar 'Egg' Cook .... **Andrew Lincoln**
Anna Forbes .... **Daniela Nardini**
James Hooperman .... **Geoffrey Bateman**
Michael O'Donnell .... **David Mallinson**
Graham Enamejowa .... **Cyril Nri**
Jo .... **Steve John Shepherd**
Delilah .... **Charlotte Bicknell**
Kira .... **Luisa Bradshaw-White**
Kelly .... **Sacha Craise**
Dale Jones .... **Mark Lewis Jones**
Jerry Cook .... **Paul Copley**
Therapist .... **Gillian McCutcheon**
Rachel .... **Natasha Little**
Ferdinand 'Ferdy' Garcia .... **Ramon Tikaram**
Nicki .... **Juliet Cowan**
Montgomery Stewart .... **Michael Elwyn**
Paul .... **Paul J. Medford**
Sarah Newley .... **Clare Clifford**
Mrs Cochrane .... **Steph Bramwell**
George .... **Greg Prentice**
Lenny .... **Tony Curran**
Francesca Allington .... **Rachel Fielding**

Creators **Amy Jenkins, Tony Garnett**
Producer **Jane Fallon**
Executive Producer **Tony Garnett**

● ***The lifestyle of professional young Londoners, through the eyes of five housesharers.***

Quickly gathering cult status, *This Life* was the brainchild of BBC 2 controller Michael Jackson and was developed by award-winning producer Tony Garnett and writer Amy Jenkins. It features five young lawyers (Jenkins was herself a legal clerk) who are disillusioned with the restrictions of office work and lead turbulent social lives – casual sex, drugs and heavy language are par for the course.

Three of the five – Miles (slightly arrogant and homophobic ex-public schoolboy), Milly (hard-working and a perfectionist) and her immature boyfriend of five years, Egg (sensitive Manchester United worshipper) – were once good friends at university and now share a house at 13 Benjamin Street, Southwark. However, they need a couple more people to help with the rent and so bring in chain-smoking Scot Anna (brash, witty and impetuous), who is a 'squatter' at Miles's chambers and once slept with him – a perennial source of tension. They also take in gay Welshman Warren, a work colleague of Milly and Egg's at Moore, Spencer, Wright solicitors, who on the face of it is hyper-confident but who makes regular visits to a psychotherapist. Hand-held cameras follow them to work, to the wine bar, to the bathroom and to bed. Additional characters include bulimic coke-head Delilah, a tarty girlfriend of Miles; Warren's sparky cousin Kira, who discovers his homosexuality, a secret back in Wales; barrister's clerk Jo, one of Anna's one-night stands; half-Mexican motorbike courier Ferdy, Warren's new boyfriend and later his replacement in the house; Egg's recently separated dad, Jerry, who sleeps with Anna; and annoyingly pushy Rachel, who irritates Milly at work. Storylines concerning naïve Egg's uncertainty over his chosen career path (not being the type to stick at anything, he'd rather be a novelist, a football writer or a cook), Anna's frustration at work, Milly's affair with boss O'Donnell, and Miles and Anna's reluctance to admit mutual fondness allow a wide range of twentysomething troubles to come to the fore.

Two series were made, the second a mighty 21 episodes long. The theme music, written by Mark Anderson and Cliff Freeborn, was performed by The Way Out.

This Week ★★★

UK (Associated-Rediffusion/Thames) Current Affairs. ITV 1956–78; 1986–92

Presenters **Leslie Mitchell, René Cutforth, Michael Westmore, Ludovic Kennedy, Daniel Farson, Brian Connell, Alastair Burnet, Jonathan Dimbleby**

Editors/Producers **Caryl Doncaster, Peter Hunt, Cyril Bennett, Peter Morley, Jeremy Isaacs, Cliff Morgan, Phillip Whitehead, David Elstein**

● ***Award-winning weekly current affairs reports.***

ITV's answer to PANORAMA, *This Week* began life as a simple topical news magazine with the slogan 'A window on the world behind the headlines'. In the mid-1960s *This Week* changed to adopt the single-investigation format it employed until its demise in 1992. Among its celebrated crew were reporters like Desmond Wilcox, James Cameron, Robert Kee, Llew Gardner, future Liberal leader Jeremy Thorpe, and, later, Jonathan Dimbleby. For some reason, the programme was renamed *TV Eye* in 1978 (when one of its reporters was the temporarily unseated Labour MP Bryan Gould), but the original title was restored in 1986. *This Week*'s stirring theme music was an excerpt from Sibelius's *Karelia Suite*.

Thomas, Antony

(1940–)

Documentary and factual drama film-maker, raised in South Africa and known for passionate involvement in his work. His prize-winning trilogy *The South African Experience* aired in 1977, although infinitely more controversial was his DEATH OF A PRINCESS in 1980, a dramatized account of the execution of an Islamic princess who had adopted some Western ideas and so questioned the values of Islam. It led to an international row and the disruption of diplomatic relations between Britain and Saudi Arabia. Thomas also scripted the lavish drama series RHODES (appearing as MP Henry Labouchere, too). Other contributions have included *Where Harry Stood*, *The Japanese Experience* (both 1974), *The Arab Experience* (1975), *The Good, the Bad and the Indifferent* (1976) and *The Most Dangerous Man in the World* (1982).

Thomas, Gareth

(1945–)

Welsh Shakespearean actor who has enjoyed a number of popular roles on television. Probably his most prominent was as the rebel leader Roj Blake in BLAKE'S 7, even though he was a member of the cast for only the first two seasons. He was also DC Ron Radley in *Parkin's Patch*, the Reverend Mr Gruffydd in *How Green was My Valley*, Dr Philip Denny in THE CITADEL, Major General Horton in BY THE SWORD DIVIDED, scientist Adam Brake in CHILDREN OF THE STONES, Owen in KNIGHTS OF GOD, refugee Shem in STAR MAIDENS, Idris in *Emlyn's Moon*, Morgan in MORGAN'S BOY and Charles in DISTANT SHORES. Thomas has also appeared in PUBLIC EYE, SPECIAL BRANCH, *Shades of Darkness*, HAMMER HOUSE OF HORROR, THE ADVENTURES OF SHERLOCK HOLMES, MEDICS, *Crown Prosecutor*, LONDON'S BURNING, DOCTORS, CASUALTY, TAGGART, HEARTBEAT, and numerous single dramas like *Shipman*.

Thomas the Tank Engine and Friends/Thomas and Friends ★★

UK (Clearwater/Britt Allcroft/Central/Gullane/HIT) Animation. ITV 1984; 1986; 1992; 2003–

Narrators **Ringo Starr, Michael Angelis**

Writers **Britt Allcroft, David Mitton**
Executive Producer **Britt Allcroft**
Producers **Britt Allcroft, David Mitton, Robert Cardona, Phil Fehrle, Simon Spencer**

● ***The adventures of a steam railway engine and his fellow vehicles.***

Narrated initially by Beatle Ringo Starr and then in the same dry, Liverpudlian manner by Michael Angelis, *Thomas the Tank Engine and Friends* is the television incarnation of the Reverend Wilbert Awdry's children's stories from the 1940s. Star of the show is Thomas, the blue tank engine bearing the number 1. Unlike most children's characters, Thomas is not always a goodie and is prone to bouts of moodiness, depicted in his expressionful face and rolling eyes (painted on the front). All the same, he has become a hero for toddlers, and a massive merchandising business has been the result.

Joining Thomas in his scrapes on the island of Sodor are old Edward, the blue number 2 engine; Henry (green, number 3); Gordon (blue, number 4); James, the mixed traffic engine (red, number 5); Percy, the saddle tank (green, number 6); Toby, the tram engine (brown, number 7); Montague, a Great Western engine familiarly known as 'Duck' because he waddles (green, number 8); the twin black engines, Donald (number 9) and Douglas (number 10); and Oliver (green, number 11). Thomas's carriages are Annie and Clarabel, and also seen are Daisy, the diesel rail car, Diesel, a diesel engine, and Henrietta, another carriage. Several new engines and vehicles are added in later series. All operate under instructions from the Fat Controller (Sir Topham Hatt), who, like the drivers, firemen and other human characters, is simply seen as a static figurine. Thomas's other acquaintances are Terence the tractor, Harold the helicopter and Bertie the bus.

Thomas the Tank Engine and Friends, made using models, is one of the few British animations to be sold to the USA, where George Carlin, Alec Baldwin and Michael Brandon have taken turns at narrating since Ringo Starr quit the job. It also made it to feature film status when *Thomas and the Magic Railroad* was released in 2000. Further series arrived in the new millennium, with the name changing slightly, to *Thomas and Friends*, in 2005.

Thompson, Emma

(1959–)

Versatile British actress and all-purpose entertainer, the daughter of Eric 'MAGIC ROUNDABOUT' Thompson and former PLAY SCHOOL presenter Phyllida Law. Now an international film name, Emma, a Cambridge Footlights graduate, has also been acclaimed for her television work, which began with the comedy series ALFRESCO. She played Suzi Kettles in the musical drama TUTTI FRUTTI, and in FORTUNES OF WAR she starred as Harriet Pringle opposite her future husband, Kenneth Branagh (since divorced). Unfortunately, her adventurous sketch series, *Thompson*, a showcase for her multi-talents in 1988, was not so well received. More recently, she played Nurse Emily in *Angels in America*. Emma has also made guest appearances in THE YOUNG ONES and CHEERS, and appeared with Jasper Carrott in *Carrott's Lib*. Her sister is actress Sophie Thompson.

Thompson, Mark

(1957–)

London-born TV executive who became BBC Director-General in 2004. His television career began as a production trainee with the BBC in 1979, and he worked on programmes such as WATCHDOG, BREAKFAST TIME, NEWSNIGHT and other news programmes before being appointed editor of PANORAMA in 1990. He became the BBC's Head of Features in 1992, and Head of Factual Programmes two years later. From 1996 to 1998, he was Controller of BBC 2, taking over as Director of National and Regional Broadcasting in 1999 and then Director of Television in 2000. In 2001, he left the Corporation to become Chief Executive of Channel 4.

Thomson, John

(1969–)

British comedian and actor, coming to the fore as Fat Bob in Steve Coogan's Paul Calf programmes and as dim publican Ken in MEN BEHAVING BADLY. He has since supported Coogan in *Coogan's Run*, KNOWING ME, KNOWING YOU with Alan Partridge and DR TERRIBLE'S HOUSE OF HORRIBLE. Thomson was also a member of the FAST SHOW team and starred in ROGER ROGER (Barry), COLD FEET (Pete Gifford), PLAYING THE FIELD (Eddie), *Stan the Man* (Stan Tully) and BLACKPOOL (Terry Corlette), also appearing in dramas and comedies like MURDER MOST HORRID, IS IT LEGAL?, SOLDIER, SOLDIER, *The World of Lee Evans, Station Jim* (Harold), MURDER IN MIND, RANDALL AND HOPKIRK (DECEASED), *Monkey Trousers*, and the nativity short *It's a Girl*. In 2001, he provided the voice for Bill in the revival of FLOWER POT MEN.

Thorn Birds, The ✱✱✱

US (ABC) Drama. BBC 1 1984 (US: ABC 1983)

Father Ralph de Bricassart ...... **Richard Chamberlain**
Meggie Cleary .... **Sydney Penny**
Rachel Ward
Mary Carson .... **Barbara Stanwyck**
Fiona 'Fee' Cleary .... **Jean Simmons**
Archbishop Contini-Verchese . **Christopher Plummer**
Luke O'Neill .... **Bryan Brown**
Paddy Cleary .... **Richard Kiley**
Rainer Hartheim .... **Ken Howard**
Justine .... **Mare Winningham**
Luddie Mueller .... **Earl Holliman**
Anne Mueller .... **Piper Laurie**
Dane .... **Philip Anglim**

Writer **Carmen Culver**
Producers **David L. Wolper, Stan Margulies**

Forbidden love in the Australian outback.

The Thorn Birds is the story of ambitious and handsome Catholic priest Ralph de Bricassart who is dragged off the straight and narrow by Meggie Cleary, the beautiful daughter of an Australian sheep-farmer, a girl he has known from an early age (Sydney Penny plays Meggie as a child). Set between the years 1920 and 1962, the five-part serial chronicles the consequences of their illicit love affair, for the priest's conscience and his clerical career, and for Meggie, who gives birth to a son, Dane, who follows his father into the church. Hovering in the background is Meggie's matriarchal grandmother, Mary Carson, who herself has designs on the heart-throb churchman. *The Thorn Birds* was adapted by Carmen Culver from Colleen McCullough's steamy novel. Richard Chamberlain resumed the role of Ralph for a two-part sequel, *The Thorn Birds: the Missing Years*, in the 1990s.

Thorne, Angela

(1939–)

British actress, typically seen in upper-class parts, as characterized by her roles in TO THE MANOR BORN (Marjory Frobisher), THREE UP, TWO DOWN (Daphne Trenchard) and *Farrington of the F.O.* (Harriet Emily Farrington). She also appeared in ELIZABETH R (Lettice Knollys), *Ballet Shoes* (Sylvia), COLD COMFORT FARM (Mrs Hawk-Monitor), NOAH'S ARK (Valerie Kirby), the sketch show *World in Ferment*, and the kids' comedy *The Bagthorpe Saga* (Laura Bagthorpe), and other credits have included *The Canterville Ghost, Haunted*, WITHIN THESE WALLS, THE GOOD GUYS, HEARTBEAT, MIDSOMER MURDERS and FOYLE'S WAR. She is married to actor Peter Penry-Jones and is mother of actors Laurence and Rupert Penry-Jones.

Thornton, Frank

(Frank Thornton Ball; 1921–)

Staunch British comedy support, coming into his own in the guise of Captain Peacock in ARE YOU BEING SERVED? and *Grace and Favour*. Previously, Thornton had been seen largely as a straight man to many comics, including Tony Hancock (HANCOCK'S HALF HOUR), Michael Bentine (IT'S A SQUARE WORLD), Spike Milligan (*The World of Beachcomber*), Reg Varney, Gordon Peters and Harry Worth. Thornton was also Commander Fairweather of *HMS Paradise* in the 1964 sitcom of the same name, and has appeared in THE FOUR JUST MEN, WILLIAM TELL, THE AVENGERS, DANGER MAN, THE CHAMPIONS, STEPTOE AND SON, JANE, THE UPPER HAND and HOLBY CITY, among many other programmes. More recently, he played legal clerk Geoffrey Parker-Knoll in *All Rise for Julian Clary* and starred as Truly in LAST OF THE SUMMER WINE.

Thornton, Kate

(1973–)

British presenter of music, lifestyle and youth-oriented programmes such as *Straight Up, Dishes*, TOP OF THE POPS, *Don't Try This at Home, The Ideal Home Show, Pop Idol Extra*, HOLIDAY, THE X FACTOR and *Celebrity Wrestling*. She began her career as a music journalist, becoming the youngest ever editor of *Smash Hits* magazine in 1995, and still contributes to the national press.

Thorp, Richard

(1932–)

EMMERDALE's Alan Turner has, in fact, enjoyed a long career on TV. Surrey-born actor Richard Thorp first appeared on our screens back in the 1950s, when he played heart-throb Dr John Rennie in EMERGENCY – WARD 10, also starring in its spin-off, *Call Oxbridge 2000*. He was also seen in series like THE ADVENTURES OF ROBIN HOOD, THE FOUR JUST MEN, DANGER MAN, THE AVENGERS, HONEY LANE, A FAMILY AT WAR, TIMESLIP, CROSSROADS (Doug Randall), PUBLIC EYE, *The Cedar Tree*, STRANGERS and TO THE MANOR BORN before he joined *Emmerdale Farm* as 'Fatty' Turner, then boss of NY Estates, in 1982.

Threads ★★★

UK (BBC) Drama. BBC 2 1984

Ruth Beckett	**Karen Meagher**
Jimmy Kemp	**Reece Dinsdale**
Mr Beckett	**Henry Moxon**
Mrs Beckett	**June Broughton**
Granny Beckett	**Sylvia Stoker**
Mr Kemp	**David Brierley**
Mrs Kemp	**Rita May**
Michael Kemp	**Nicholas Lane**
Alison Kemp	**Jane Hazlegrove**
Clive Sutton	**Harry Beety**
Marjorie Sutton	**Ruth Holden**

Narrator **Paul Vaughan**

Writer **Barry Hines**
Executive Producers **Graham Massey, John Purdie**
Producer **Mike Jackson**

● ***Bleak portrayal of life in a post-holocaust Britain.***

For Ruth Beckett and Jimmy Kemp, girlfriend and boyfriend sitting in a Sheffield pub, the prospect of nuclear war seems a million miles away. The bubbling cauldron of the Middle East, where the catalyst for an atomic attack may be cooked up, is another world that barely concerns them. However, for Ruth and Jimmy, and millions of other British citizens, there's a rude awakening in store. The West and the Soviet Union are at loggerheads over Iran and the Russians make the first nuclear move, sending 200 megatons of missiles (ten times the amount used in Hiroshima) onto the UK. Two land on or near Sheffield and for Ruth, Jimmy and their families, life will never be the same again. *Threads*, a shocking single drama based on contemporary scientific knowledge, suggests what the outbreak of nuclear war could mean, focusing on the four weeks leading up to the attack and its hideous consequences during the next decade. Sheffield's peacetime civic leader, Clive Sutton, is appointed wartime controller and it is through his eyes, and those of the Beckett and Kemp families, that viewers witness the holocaust. The key question is: how strong are the threads that will keep society together in the wake of such devastation? Producer Mike Jackson also directs.

Three of a Kind ★★★

UK (BBC) Comedy. BBC 1 1981–3

Tracey Ullman, Lenny Henry, David Copperfield

Producer **Paul Jackson**

● ***Comedy sketch show featuring three promising performers.***

As a showcase for emerging talent, *Three of a Kind* certainly delivered the goods. Lenny Henry had already been seen on NEW FACES, THE FOSTERS and TISWAS, and Tracey Ullman had appeared in West End musicals. They were drawn into a team with fellow comic David Copperfield (not to be confused with the American illusionist) by producer Paul Jackson and presented two series of sketches and monologues which were well received. Everyone knows what happened to Henry and Ullman, but the fate of David Copperfield remains a mystery to many viewers (he moved into the world of cabaret).

Three of a Kind was also the title of another vehicle for up-and-coming talents, which was screened in 1967. The three in question then were Lulu (not that she was *that* new), Mike Yarwood and Ray Fell (the David Copperfield of the trio, who went on to appear on the Las Vegas cabaret circuit).

3-2-1 ★

UK (Yorkshire) Game Show. ITV 1978–87

Presenter **Ted Rogers**

Executive Producer **Alan Tarrant**
Producers **Derek Burrell-Davis, Mike Goddard, Ian Bolt, Terry Henebery, Graham Wetherell**

● ***Game show in which contestants decipher clues to win prizes.***

3-2-1 was based on the Spanish quiz *Uno, Dos, Tres* and focused on three married couples as they battled for the right to win valuable prizes. The first segment of the game was a quiz (often 'list' questions), after which the leading couple went away to return in the next programme. In early editions, a second round consisted of physical games and observation questions about a performed sketch, but the format employed for the rest of the show, devoted to a series of playlets, songs and sketches featuring surprise celebrity guests, was soon used from the end of round one onwards. Resident comics Chris Emmet, Dougie Brown and Debbie Arnold were known as 'The Disrepertory Company', and the Brian Rogers' Connection was the supporting dance troupe. The sketches all followed a theme: Arabian Nights, the circus, Merrie England, etc., and, following each skit, one of the performers read out a related riddle which referred to a prize. When the two remaining couples had been whittled down to one by an elimination question, the final couple then had to decide which of the cryptic clues to discard in the search for the best prize (usually a car). One prize they all wanted to avoid was the new metal rubbish-bin, representing the show's robotic mascot, Dusty Bin. Compere Ted Rogers fast-talked his way through each show, twirling his fingers in a *3–2–1* salute. He was supported by a team of hostesses known as The Gentle Secs.

Three Up, Two Down ✱✱✱

UK (BBC) Situation Comedy. BBC 1 1985–7; 1989

Sam Tyler .... **Michael Elphick**
Daphne Trenchard .... **Angela Thorne**
Nick Tyler .... **Ray Burdis**
Angie Tyler .... **Lysette Anthony**
Major Giles Bradshaw .... **Neil Stacy**
Wilf .... **John Grillo**
Rhonda .... **Vicki Woolf**

Creator/Writer **Richard Ommanney**
Producers **David Askey, John B. Hobbs**

● ***A stuck-up widow and a down-to-earth widower share a flat and a grandchild, but have little else in common.***

With a new son (Joe) to look after and finances stretched, photographer Nick Tyler and his model wife, Angie, decide to install one of the child's grandparents in their basement flat, as a live-in baby-sitter. This means that either Nick's working-class dad, Sam, or Angie's well-bred mum, Daphne, will take up residence, but, because of a mix-up, both are invited and both accept. Reluctantly agreeing to share the flat, in order to be near their grandchild, Cockney Sam and Cheltenham-raised Daphne become the worst of enemies, despite Sam's obviously warm feelings towards his cold, snooty flatmate. His easy-going, earthy manner frustrates her and his taxidermy hobby only makes matters worse, filling the flat with stuffed penguins and other dead creatures. However, after a disastrous fling with con-man Giles Bradshaw, Daphne finally realizes that kind-hearted Sam is really the man for her, despite their many differences, and the two embark on a rather more harmonious co-existence. Wilf is the theatrically minded zookeeper who provides animals for Sam to stuff, and also seen in later episodes is flirty neighbour Rhonda. Ronnie Hazlehurst composed the theme music.

Threlfall, David

(1953–)

Northern Shakespearean actor who took the part of Leslie Titmuss MP in John Mortimer's PARADISE POSTPONED and *Titmuss Regained*. He was also seen in the RSC's *The Life and Adventures of Nicholas Nickleby* (Smike), played Prince Charles in BSkyB's *Diana: Her True Story* and turned to comedy for the sitcoms NIGHTINGALES (security guard Bell) and MEN OF THE WORLD (travel agent Lenny Smart). In addition, Threlfall appeared with Sheila Hancock in JUMPING THE QUEUE and as devious fryer Norman Kershaw in SEX, CHIPS AND ROCK 'N' ROLL. More recently, he has starred as Frank Gallagher in SHAMELESS and Prince Philip in *The Queen's Sister*, and made guest appearances in THE KNOCK, CUTTING IT, THE LAST DETECTIVE and SPOOKS. Other credits have included *Scum*, *The Gathering Seed*, *A Murder of Quality*, *Clothes in the Wardrobe*, CONSPIRACY (Dr Friedrich Kritzinger) and *The Romantics* (William Wordsworth).

Thriller ✱✱

UK (ATV) Suspense Anthology. ITV 1973–6

Creator **Brian Clemens**

● ***Series of feature-length film thrillers.***

Created and largely written by Brian Clemens, *Thriller* offered a collection of twist-in-the-tail stories designed to keep the audience on the edge of their seats. The best-remembered contributions included *A Coffin for the Bride* (starring Helen Mirren), *Only a Scream Away* (Hayley Mills), *Nurse Will Make It Better* (Diana Dors) and *The Crazy Kill* (Denholm Elliott).

Through the Keyhole ✱

UK (Yorkshire/David Parradine) Game Show. ITV 1987–94; BBC 1 1997–2004; BBC 2 2006–

Presenters **David Frost, Loyd Grossman, Catherine Gee**

Executive Producer **Kevin Sim**
Producers **Ian Bolt, Chantal Rutherford Browne**

● ***Who-lives-where game show featuring celebrity panellists.***

In this easy-going, family panel game, derived from a slot in TV-am's programming, Loyd Grossman (replaced in 2003 by Catherine Gee) leads a camera team through the various rooms of a celebrity's house, pointing out features of décor, their style of living and evidence of hobbies and professions. Three famous guests then have to guess to whom the house belongs, taking note of extra clues from host David Frost. The householder subsequently strolls on to confront the panellists.

After being axed by ITV, *Through the Keyhole*, produced by David Frost's own production company, was picked up by the BBC for its daytime schedules.

Thrower, Debbie

(1957–)

British presenter and newsreader, born in Kenya. After working in newspapers and radio, Thrower joined BBC South as a reporter on the news magazine *South Today*, before going national and reading the main BBC news bulletins. At this time, she was also seen in programmes like *Out of Court*, *Lifeline* and action reports such as *Hospital Watch*, and as host of SONGS OF PRAISE. Returning to regional broadcasting, she took over as presenter of TVS's *Coast to Coast*, which evolved into *Meridian Tonight*. She has also presented other local programmes and Channel 4's *Collectors' Lot*.

Thrower, Percy

MBE (1913–88)

Percy Thrower, as host of GARDENING CLUB for 12 years from 1955 and its successor, GARDENERS' WORLD (filmed at his own home), from 1968, was the king of TV gardeners. But, as well as having green fingers, he proved to be a popular TV personality, popping up in numerous other programmes, including ITV's *Gardening My Way* and BLUE PETER (1974–88), for which he designed a famous Italian sunken garden in 1978.

Thunderbirds ★★★★

UK (AP Films/ATV/ITC) Children's Science Fiction. ITV 1965–6

Voices:

Jeff Tracy	**Peter Dyneley**
Scott Tracy	**Shane Rimmer**
Virgil Tracy	**David Holliday**
	Jeremy Wilkin
Alan Tracy	**Matt Zimmerman**
Gordon Tracy	**David Graham**
John Tracy	**Ray Barrett**
Lady Penelope Creighton-Ward	**Sylvia Anderson**
Brains	**David Graham**
Aloysius Parker	**David Graham**
The Hood	**Ray Barrett**
Tin-Tin Kyrano	**Christine Finn**
Kyrano	**David Graham**
Grandma	**Christine Finn**

Creators **Gerry Anderson, Sylvia Anderson**
Producers **Gerry Anderson, Reg Hill**

A 21st-century family runs a global rescue service, using advanced aircraft and technology.

In the year 2063 International Rescue (IR) is established by retired astronaut Jeff Tracy in a mountain refuge on his isolated Pacific island. Utilizing futuristic aircraft devised by Brains, a stammering, bespectacled genius, he sends into action a squad of brave, humanitarian rescuers – all his own sons, named after the first five Americans in space and dedicated to averting disasters.

The stars of the show are the Thunderbirds themselves, wonderfully high-tech vehicles capable of incredible speeds and amazing manoeuvres. Thunderbird 1 (with Scott, Jeff's eldest son and second-in-command, at the helm) is a combination of reconnaissance jet and rocket. Thunderbird 2 (piloted by the softly spoken, piano-playing Virgil) is the fleet's freighter, carrying machinery like the burrowing tool, The Mole, and the team's submarine, Thunderbird 4, in a series of six pods which can be inserted into its belly. Thunderbird 4, when called into use, is controlled by aquanaut Gordon Tracy, an enthusiastic practical-joker who is always keen for action. Their blond-haired, impetuous brother, Alan, pilots the rocket, Thunderbird 3, taking it into orbit to join the team's space-station, Thunderbird 5, manned by the fifth son, John, the loner of the family. John and Alan sometimes switch jobs.

The Thunderbirds (which Anderson named after Thunderbird airfield in Arizona) may be called out at any time. Usually the siren is sounded by Thunderbird 5, picking up distress messages from all around the globe. Thunderbird 1 is first on the scene, making full use of its 7,000 m.p.h. velocity, allowing Scott to liaise with base and advise the slower Thunderbird 2, following in its wake. The elaborate take-off procedures from Tracy Island are a highlight of the show. Swivelling walls and sinking sofas convey the pilots out of the luxurious Tracy home to the hangars beneath, with chutes and slides positioning them perfectly in their craft, before swimming pools retract and palm trees fall back to reveal hidden launch-pads. Once in action, the boys report back via a video intercom which superimposes their faces on to wall portraits. All messages are punctuated with the acknowledgement 'F.A.B.'

However, the whole International Rescue set-up remains a mystery to the rest of the world, and the identity of the Thunderbird pilots shrouded in secrecy. The only parties in the know are the Tracys themselves, their island staff and a special London agent and her butler. The staff are Kyrano, Jeff's oriental manservant, and his daughter, Tin-Tin (an electronics expert and Alan's romantic interest). The London agent is Lady Penelope Creighton-Ward, a true aristocrat with a cool, calm approach to dealing with thugs. She travels in a souped-up, well-armed, pink Rolls-Royce (registration FAB 1; FAB 2 is her luxury yacht), which is driven by her shifty-looking, safe-cracking butler, Parker, a Cockney best remembered for his loyal 'Yes, m'Lady'. Hounding the rescuers is the evil, bald-headed Hood. Kyrano's half-brother, he lives in a temple in a Thai jungle, but he is also a master of disguise and wanders the world trying to ensnare the Tracy brothers and their fabulous machines. He also has power over Kyrano, his eyes lighting up whenever he casts his 'hoodoo' spell.

The series has been widely acknowledged as Gerry Anderson's masterpiece. Filmed in 50-minute episodes to corner the prime-time market, the format provided plenty of scope for character development and tension-building. By this stage, the 'Supermarionation' production technique had almost reached perfection. The puppets' eye- and lip-movements were synchronized with the dialogue and their control wires were so thin (one 5,000th of an inch) that they were barely noticeable. With its stirring theme music by Barry Gray, sophisticated special effects and multitude of explosions, *Thunderbirds* captured an adult, as well as a children's, audience. A bandwagon rolled out in *Thunderbird* merchandise, and two feature films were also produced, *Thunderbirds are Go* and *Thunderbird Six*. A digitally remastered version of the series was screened on BBC 2 in 2000.

Tilbury, Peter

(1945–)

British writer and actor, the creator of SHELLEY and CHEF! His other writing credits have included episodes of NEVER THE TWAIN, BIRDS OF A FEATHER, DUCK PATROL and *Lee Evans – So What Now?*, and the sitcoms *Sorry, I'm a Stranger Here Myself* (with David Firth) and IT TAKES A WORRIED MAN (in which he also starred as Philip Roath). In addition, his acting career has taken in series like DIXON OF DOCK GREEN, THE EXPERT, C.A.T.S. EYES, FORTUNES OF WAR, FIRST BORN, CASUALTY and THE BILL.

Till Death Us Do Part/In Sickness and in Health ★★★★

UK (BBC) Situation Comedy. BBC 1 1966–8; 1972; 1974–5/BBC 1 1985–7; 1989–90; 1992

Alf Garnett	**Warren Mitchell**
Else Garnett	**Dandy Nichols**
Rita	**Una Stubbs**
Mike	**Anthony Booth** *(Till Death)*
Bert Reed	**Alfie Bass** *(Till Death)*
Min Reed	**Patricia Hayes** *(Till Death)*
Winston	**Eamonn Walker** *(In Sickness)*

Arthur .... **Arthur English** *(In Sickness)*
Fred Johnson .... **Ken Campbell** *(In Sickness)*
Mrs Hollingbery .... **Carmel McSharry** *(In Sickness)*
Michael .... **James Ellis** *(In Sickness)*

Creator/Writer **Johnny Speight**
Producers **Dennis Main Wilson, Brian Winston, David Croft**

● ***A bigoted East End docker shares his home with his dim wife, his liberal daughter and her left-wing husband.***

Alf Garnett remains one of TV's most memorable creations. He has been loved and he has been hated, but he is unlikely to be forgotten. The man who brought racist views and foul language into British living rooms is a hard act to follow. Although the 1980s' 'alternative' comedians aimed to shock, their impact was negligible in comparison with TV's first controversial loudmouth.

The Garnetts live in London's decaying East End, long before the Isle of Dogs is transformed into a yuppie paradise. Their little docker's terraced house is home to four adults: Alf, his wife, Else, daughter Rita and son-in-law Mike. Such close habitation induces claustrophobia and an endless amount of personal friction. On one side, there is Alf, a bald, bespectacled bigot, patriotically standing up for the Queen and cheerfully pushing the blame for the country's ills on to 'Darling Harold' Wilson and immigrants. Mind you, if he was to succeed in shipping out the immigrants and dislodging the Labour Party from government, Alf still wouldn't be happy with Edward Heath in charge – he being a grammar school boy, not a traditional Tory like Winston Churchill. On the other side is Mike, a long-haired, unemployed, Liverpudlian socialist, 'Shirley Temple' or 'randy Scouse git', as he becomes known. In between are the phlegmatic, rather dopey Else and the giggly Rita.

Alf's rantings were heavily criticized by the church, Mary Whitehouse and politicians, but his character has other sides to it, too. He is incredibly selfish, and extremely mean to his long-suffering wife. Yet Else takes it all in her rather sluggish stride, shrugging off insults like 'silly old moo' and conjuring up sharp retorts to put Alf firmly in his place. Whenever that happens, he dons his West Ham scarf and skulks off to the pub. When Dandy Nichols briefly leaves the series (Else went to visit her sister in Australia in the 1970s), Alf's invective is directed against his neighbours, Bert and Min.

Till Death Us Do Part began as an episode of COMEDY PLAYHOUSE in 1965. In this pilot, Warren Mitchell played Alf Ramsey (as in the football manager), with Gretchen Franklin (Ethel in EASTENDERS) as his maligned wife. The series proper ran from 1966 to 1968 and was exhumed for a new run in 1972. A short-lived 1981 version, *Till Death . . .* (produced by ATV), was followed by a new BBC revival in 1985. This time the title had been changed to *In Sickness and in Health*, sadly appropriate considering the obvious illness of Dandy Nichols. In this, the Garnetts have been rehoused in a new development, without Rita (only an occasional visitor) or Mike, and the antagonizer's role is filled by a gay, black home-help, provocatively named Winston. Arthur is his chief boozing buddy. This series continued even after Nichols's death in 1986 (Alf's neighbour, Mrs Hollingbery, played by Carmel McSharry, becomes his new sparring partner). However, by this time the political climate had changed. Even though Alf could slate the incumbent Tory government for being a bunch of spivs ruled over by a grocer's daughter, the bite had disappeared and the series was far less successful. Johnny Speight's monstrous creation had had his day. An American version of *Till Death Us Do Part*, ALL IN THE FAMILY, was just as big and controversial.

Tilt

The pivoting of a camera vertically up and down, as opposed to a pan, which involves horizontal movement from left to right or vice versa.

Time After Time ★★

UK (LWT) Situation Comedy. ITV 1994–5

Kenny Conway .... **Brian Conley**
Gillian Walcott .... **Samantha Beckinsale**
Jake Brewer .... **Richard Graham**
Ma Conway .... **Kate Williams**
Robbie Conway .... **David Shane**
Donna Strachan .... **Georgia Allen**
Mike Tredwell .... **Neil McCaul**
Auntie Dot .... **Deddie Davies**

Writers **Paul Minett, Brian Leveson**
Producer **John Kaye Cooper**

● ***A cockney car thief tries to go straight.***

Kenny Conway is a bad lot, although he plans to turn over a new leaf. Released from jail on parole, the chirpy Londoner decides it is time to go straight, but this is not so easy when the rest of your family – from dad Charlie (still behind bars), to committed crook Ma and teenage apprentice brother Robbie – plus your best mate, Jake, are all villains. At least he has the support of girlfriend Donna and Gillian, his probation officer, as he tries to keep to the straight and narrow, although having two women in his life is yet another complication for Kenny. Mr Tredwell is Gillian's less liberal colleague. The two series (14 episodes) followed a pilot in 1993 entitled *Outside Chance*, in which Gillian was played by Kim Thomson.

Time Team ★★★

UK (Videotext/Picture House) Archaeology. Channel 4 1994–
DVD: DD Home Entertainment

Presenter **Tony Robinson**

Producers **Tim Taylor, Simon Raikes, Mel Morpeth, Graham Dixon, Michael Douglas, Laurence Vulliamy**
Executive Producer **Philip Clarke**

● ***Unravelling history through race-against-time archaeological excavations.***

Time Team has become one of Channel 4's most durable, if unlikely, hits. The idea stemmed from a four-part series called *Time Signs*, screened by the channel in summer 1991 and presented by Mick Aston, Professor of Landscape Archaeology at Bristol University. Producer Tim Taylor returned to the idea of bringing archaeology to television a year later, when the pilot for *Time Team* was made, employing, on Mick's suggestion, Tony Robinson as host. Robinson's role was to ask the irritating questions that ensured experts explained clearly to viewers what was happening. Mick continued to lead the dig. The pilot was never screened and Robinson initially declined the offer of hosting a series, but he was persuaded back and the first run of programmes followed in January 1994. The first dig of the series took place at Athelney in Somerset as the team looked for clues that might explain how the Danes defeated Alfred the Great.

The premiss of *Time Team* is to demystify archaeology,

providing stories and explanations about objects that are unearthed. Each dig has a strict three-day deadline, so the experts are continually battling against the clock. Regular specialists are Aston (usually wearing a rainbow-coloured pullover), plus Phil Harding of the Trust for Wessex Archaeology (never without his battered old hat) and Carenza Lewis from University of Cambridge. Other experts joining the team have included Robin Bush, Margaret Cox, Victor Ambrus and Francis Pryor, and celebrities such as Sandi Toksvig have helped lighten the tone where necessary. The team's work has also seen them roam beyond the UK, to places such as Maryland (on the trail of early British settlers), Normandy (to find a missing World War II Spitfire) and Montana (in the hunt for dinosaurs). Various specials have been produced, including live excavations and *The Big Dig* mass participation events.

The 1998 series was accompanied by a separate programme called *Time Team Extra* in which presenter Robin Bush asked experts for their views on the latest finds. A further related series, *History Hunters*, aired on Channel 4 in 1998–9. Over six programmes, teams of amateur sleuths investigated the secret history of some of Britain's most famous buildings, like London's Crystal Palace, Burton Abbey and the ancient pubs of Nottingham. Tony Robinson again presented, assisted by Mick Aston and historian Carl Chinn.

Time Tunnel, The ✱✱

US (Twentieth Century Fox/Irwin Allen) Science Fiction. BBC 1 1968 (US: ABC 1966–7)

Dr Tony Newman .... **James Darren**
Dr Doug Phillips .... **Robert Colbert**
Dr Ann MacGregor .... **Lee Meriwether**
Lt. Gen. Heywood Kirk .... **Whit Bissel**
Dr Raymond Swain .... **John Zaremba**

Creator/Executive Producer **Irwin Allen**

Two scientists are trapped in a man-made 'time tunnel' and thrown into historical adventures.

Tony Newman and Doug Phillips work on a top-secret project to build a machine which can transport people backwards or forwards in time. When a penny-pinching government official arrives at their research centre, hidden beneath the Arizona desert, to demand evidence of progress, Tony is forced to enter the 'time tunnel' to prove it works. However, as he knows, the machine is not yet perfected and his risk backfires, leaving him swirling in the mists of time. He eventually materializes on the deck of the *Titanic* on the day before it sinks. Seeing him trapped, Doug volunteers to rescue him. Despite their best efforts to convince the ship's captain of the impending doom, he, of course, takes no notice and the pair have to be whisked away from the disaster just as it strikes.

This sets the pattern for other adventures. The team back at base (Drs Swain and MacGregor), while not able to retrieve the scientists, can, however, move them in and out of situations and occasionally catch glimpses of their lost colleagues. Tumbling through time, the travellers fall into adventure after adventure, always arriving at a key point in history – the Alamo before its capitulation, Krakatoa on the point of eruption, Pearl Harbor in advance of the Japanese attack. They also witness the French Revolution, the siege of Troy and the Battle of Gettysburg. (Ample use was made of old cinema footage to keep expenditure within the show's very limited budget.)

Time Warner

The world's largest media and entertainments group was formed in 2001 with the merger of Internet provider America Online and Time Warner, itself a 1989 merger of the Time magazine group – the founder, in 1972, of HBO (the Home Box Office pay-per-view channel) – and Warner Communications, a descendant of Warner Brothers. The group owns the WB Network, launched in 1995 to challenge the big three US TV networks and the fledgling Fox network, and also part of the corporation is the former Turner Broadcasting System network of stations, which Time Warner absorbed in 1996. TBS, founded by Ted Turner, was the parent company of CNN and CNN International. Part of the group's considerable assets are the film libraries of the MGM and Warner Brothers studios, which have been used to good effect in programming the TNT (Turner Network Television), TCM (Turner Classic Movies) and Cartoon Network channels.

Timeslip ✱✱✱

UK (ATV) Children's Science Fiction. ITV 1970–1

Liz Skinner .... **Cheryl Burfield**
Simon Randall .... **Spencer Banks**
Frank Skinner .... **Derek Benfield**
Jean Skinner .... **Iris Russell**
Commander Traynor .... **Denis Quilley**
Frank .... **John Alkin**
Morgan C. Devereaux .... **John Barron**
Beth Skinner .... **Mary Preston**
2957 .... **David Graham**

Creators **Ruth Boswell, James Boswell**
Writers **Bruce Stewart, Victor Pemberton**
Producer **John Cooper**

Two teenagers move backwards and forwards in time through an invisible time-barrier.

On holiday in the village of St Oswald with her parents, Liz Skinner and her friend Simon Randall are intrigued by the disappearance of a young girl at the site of an old wartime weapons base. Also interested is the mysterious Commander Traynor, Liz's dad's CO when the base was active. The teenagers discover an invisible fence and feel their way along it until they come to a hole. Squeezing through, they emerge in 1940 and embark upon an adventure in which they help a young Mr Skinner to dismantle a secret laser before it is stolen by the Germans. The job done, Liz and Simon return through the time-barrier to find themselves not in their original 1970 but in 1990, at an Antarctic research station called the Ice Box. Experiments are being performed there on human beings, using a longevity drug known as HA 57. They meet Beth, an unpleasant older version of Liz, and also discover her parents, with her father entombed in ice, the victim of an experiment. Leading the project is base director Morgan C. Devereaux, who, it transpires, is actually a clone. The kids escape back to their own time, only to be persuaded to return to the future once more by an anxious Commander Traynor.

On this occasion, they arrive again in 1990, but in a tropical, baking-hot Britain, the result of a failed experiment in climate control. They encounter a friendly Beth and also an older Simon, known simply by the number 2957, who is in charge of a team of clones. But this is not the last of their adventures, and they discover that Commander Traynor is not all he seems when they take another trip through the barrier and surface in 1965.

The first episode of this imaginative science-fiction series was introduced by ITN's science correspondent, Peter Fairley, who was called up to explain to the young audience the general concept of time travel. The fact that such a prologue was necessary indicated how complex the subsequent episodes were, as they followed the two friends backwards and forwards through time, recognizing the unavoidable interdependence of the past and the future, and of actions and consequences.

Timeslip's four adventures (*The Wrong End of Time*, *The Time of the Ice Box*, *The Year of the Burn-up* and *The Day of the Clone*) ran back to back, as one 26-week series. It is fondly remembered by science-fiction fans and was co-created by ITV sci-fi specialist Ruth Boswell, later producer of THE TOMORROW PEOPLE.

Timothy, Christopher

(1940–)

Welsh-born actor whose role as vet James Herriot in ALL CREATURES GREAT AND SMALL has dominated his TV career. However, Timothy has also been seen in series like UFO, VAN DER VALK, SOME MOTHERS DO 'AVE 'EM, KATE, JACKANORY *Playhouse*, MURDER MOST ENGLISH (DS Love), RETURN OF THE SAINT, HOLBY CITY and CASUALTY, plus single dramas and Shakespearean classics. Recently, he has played Dr Brendan McGuire in the daytime series DOCTORS, directing some episodes, too. He also narrated the docu-soaps *Vets' School* and *Vets in Practice*.

Tingha and Tucker

Jean Morton was an on-screen continuity announcer with ITV in the Midlands. One day some studio wag thought it would be funny to quietly set up two teddy bears so that they peered over her shoulder at the camera. Like a true professional, Morton carried on regardless and later turned the idea of appearing on screen with two stuffed animals into her own TV series. That's the legend behind the creation of Tingha and Tucker, a pair of twin koalas who were popular characters on children's TV in the 1960s. Early appearances for Jean and the puppets came in *The New Adventures of Pinocchio* (ITV 1961–2), but more popular was *The Tingha and Tucker Club* (ITV 1962–70), a short offering in which Auntie Jean opened her 'Once upon a Time Book' to deliver wholesome tales to her antipodean babies. Kids could join the club and they did so in droves. In this series (also produced by Morton), the koalas lived in Bears Cottage, Bearsville. They attended Bearsville Nursery School and read the Bearsworld newspaper. One of their friends was Willie Wombat who later branched out with Morton into his own Sunday evening religious series, *The Tree House Family*.

Tinker, Tailor, Soldier, Spy/Smiley's People ★★★

UK (BBC) Spy Drama. BBC 2 1979/1982

George Smiley .... **Alec Guinness**
Toby Esterhase .... **Bernard Hepton**
Roy Bland .... **Terence Rigby** *(Tinker, Tailor)*
Percy Alleline .... **Michael Aldridge** *(Tinker, Tailor)*
Bill Haydon .... **Ian Richardson** *(Tinker, Tailor)*
Peter Guillam .... **Michael Jayston** *(Tinker, Tailor)*
Michael Byrne *(Smiley's People)*
Sir Oliver Lacon .... **Anthony Bate**
Ricki Tarr .... **Hywel Bennett** *(Tinker, Tailor)*
Control .... **Alexander Knox** *(Tinker, Tailor)*
Insp. Mendel .... **George Sewell** *(Tinker, Tailor)*
Jim Prideaux .... **Ian Bannen** *(Tinker, Tailor)*
Connie Sachs .... **Beryl Reid**
Karla .... **Patrick Stewart**
Spikely .... **Daniel Beecher** *(Tinker, Tailor)*
Ann Smiley .... **Siân Phillips**
Gen. Vladimir .... **Curd Jürgens** *(Simley's People)*
Madame Ostrakova .... **Eileen Atkins** *(Smiley's People)*
Oleg Kirov .... **Dudley Sutton** *(Smiley's People)*
Mikhel .... **Michael Gough** *(Smiley's People)*
Lander Strickland .... **Bill Paterson** *(Smiley's People)*
Otto Leipzig .... **Vladek Sheybal** *(Smiley's People)*
Stella Craven .... **Maureen Lipman** *(Smiley's People)*
Elvira .... **Ingrid Pitt** *(Smiley's People)*
Claus Kretzschmar .... **Mario Adorf** *(Smiley's People)*
Saul Enderby .... **Barry Foster** *(Smiley's People)*
Grigoriev .... **Michael Lonsdale** *(Smiley's People)*
Mother Felicity .... **Rosalie Crutchley** *(Smiley's People)*

Writer **Arthur Hopcraft** *(Tinker, Tailor)*, **John Le Carré, John Hopkins** *(Smiley's People)*
Producer **Jonathan Powell**

A British spy-catcher is brought out of retirement to lead the hunt for a mole.

World-weary British intelligence agent George Smiley is suddenly dragged back into the field of international espionage when his help is needed in tracking down a mysterious double-agent. Back at the 'Circus' – as the intelligence agency in London's Cambridge Circus is known – Smiley discovers that some of the top men (Esterhase, Bland, Alleline and Haydon) are under suspicion, each being targeted for investigation under codenames like 'Tinker', 'Tailor', 'Soldier' and 'Poor Man'. Despite struggling with the humiliation of his wife's adultery, Smiley diligently sets about his task and painstakingly uncovers vital clues that put him on the road to unmasking the mole.

Based on John Le Carré's novel of the same name, *Tinker, Tailor, Soldier, Spy* was dramatized by Arthur Hopcraft in seven episodes and won enormous acclaim. It wasn't the end of Smiley's intelligence career, however. Three years later he resurfaced (again played by Alec Guinness) in another of Le Carré's offerings, *Smiley's People*. In this six-parter, Smiley is asked to resolve a major problem with an old general, but roads lead back to an old Russian adversary named Karla, already encountered in the earlier serial. The character reappeared once more in a 1991 two-hour Thames production called *A Murder of Quality*, in which he was played by Denholm Elliott.

Tintin

See *Hergé's Adventures of TinTin*.

Tipping the Velvet ★★★

UK (Sally Head) Drama. BBC 2 2002
DVD: Contender

Nancy 'Nan' Astley .... **Rachael Stirling**
Kitty Butler .... **Keeley Hawes**
Diana Lethaby .... **Anna Chancellor**

Florence Banner	**Jodhi May**
Alice Astley	**Monica Dolan**
Mr Astley	**Richard Hope**
Mrs Astley	**Annie Hulley**
Davy Astley	**Peter Kelly**
Freddy	**Benedict Cumberbatch**
Tony Reeves	**Dean Lennox Kelly**
Tricky Reeves	**Jim McManus**
Gully Sutherland	**Johnny Vegas**
Walter Bliss	**John Bowe**
Mrs Dendy	**Bernice Stegers**
Charles Frobisher	**Alexei Sayle**
Mrs Milne	**Tilly Vosburgh**
Mrs Jex	**Janet Henfrey**
Dickie	**Sara Stockbridge**
Corder	**Carl Chase**
Zena Blake	**Sally Hawkins**
Ralph Banner	**Hugh Bonneville**

Writer **Andrew Davies**
Executive Producers **Sally Head, Gareth Neame, Sally Woodward Gentle**
Producer **Georgina Lowe**

● ***A young Victorian girl experiences trauma in her lesbian love life.***

Sarah Water's novel of lesbian relationships in the 1890s was brought to television by Andrew Davies. With echoes of his earlier MOLL FLANDERS, this romping, at times whimsical, tale centres on 18-year-old Whitstable girl Nan Astley, who becomes infatuated with male impersonator Kitty Butler, member of Gully Sutherland's travelling music hall troupe. Nan decides to help out as Kitty's dresser and, when she is offered this job full time, she leaves home, her boyfriend, Freddy, and her job at the family oyster parlour. The show moves to London. Nan and Kitty share lodgings at Mrs Dendy's chaotic theatrical digs in Brixton and soon, adopting the stage name of Nan King, Nan joins Kitty as part of a double act, with songs about Bill and his shy brother, Bob. Their closeness eventually blossoms into what Nan has been dreaming of, a steamy romance, but rejection awaits her when Kitty accepts the advances of their manager, Walter Bliss. Passing off as a boy, Nan is forced to turn to prostitution to get by, eventually ending up as a sex slave to wealthy widow Diana Lethaby. Finally, after some two years of abuse, Nan breaks free and rediscovers an old friend, Florence Banner. She shares a house in Bethnal Green with Florence and her amiable, socialist brother, Ralph, before becoming Florence's lover. A successful return to the stage and a final rejection of Kitty, when she asks Nan to return to her, provide a happy ending. The various music hall songs were composed by Terry Davies. Adrian Johnston supplied the other music and the three-part drama was directed by Geoff Sax.

Tiswas ★★★★

UK (ATV/Central) Children's Entertainment. ITV 1974–82

Presenters **Chris Tarrant, John Asher, Trevor East, Sally James, Lenny Henry, John Gorman, Sylvester McCoy, Frank Carson, Bob Carolgees, Gordon Astley, Fogwell Flax, Den Hegarty, David Rappaport**

Producers **Peter Harris, Glyn Edwards, Chris Tarrant**

● ***Anarchic Saturday morning live entertainment***

Tiswas was the series that tore up the rulebooks of kids' TV. In contrast with MULTI-COLOURED SWAP SHOP, its BBC Saturday morning rival, *Tiswas* ditched goody-goody, wholesome fare in favour of raucous, get-stuck-in slapstick. Custard pies and buckets of water reigned supreme. Silly sketches featured the likes of Lenny Henry and Frank Carson, plus Bob Carolgees and his punk dog, Spit. Former Scaffold member John Gorman played the appropriately named Smello, but who was the Phantom Flan Flinger who terrorized the studio audience with his foaming pies? Anchors Trevor East, John Asher and particularly Chris Tarrant and Sally James made no attempt to restrain the erupting chaos as they struggled to introduce cartoons, interview pop stars and take competition calls on the Wellyphone (made of old gum boots).

Tiswas began as a regional show in the Midlands in 1974 and took a few years to gain full network coverage. ITV companies then opted out of various segments of the show in order to drop in their own cartoons and adventure series. Apart from its sheer anarchy, what made *Tiswas* such a cult series was the fact that adults loved it, too, and there were plenty of dubious, 'grown-up' gags thrown in for them to enjoy. There was even a waiting list of 'mature' viewers demanding to be trapped in 'The Cage' and subjected to regular dousings. This adult following eventually led to a late-night spin-off entitled *OTT* (*Over the Top*) in 1982, hosted by most of the *Tiswas* crew, with the addition of Helen Atkinson-Wood, Colette Hiller and Alexei Sayle. Sadly, crudeness took over and the series was quickly cancelled. *Tiswas*, too, suffered, largely from the loss of Chris Tarrant, and it soon followed *OTT* into the TV archives.

Tiswas (the name was said to be an acronym for Today Is Saturday, Watch And Smile) also generated a hit single when Tarrant, James, Carolgees and Gorman joined forces as The Four Bucketeers to enter the 1980 Top 30 with 'The Bucket of Water Song'.

Titchmarsh, Alan

MBE (1949–)

Yorkshire-born, Kew-trained gardening expert turned television presenter. In addition to green-fingered programming (fronting GARDENERS' WORLD, GROUND FORCE, *How to be a Gardener* and *Royal Gardeners*, in particular), Titchmarsh has become associated with SONGS OF PRAISE, PEBBLE MILL and other daytime programmes. Other credits have included NATIONWIDE, BREAKFAST TIME, POINTS OF VIEW, *Titchmarsh's Travels*, *British Isles: a Natural History*, *Last Night of the Proms*, *20th Century Roadshow*, *A Year at Kew* (narrator), *Gordon the Garden Gnome* (voice of Gordon) and even one edition of THE WORD. He is also a published novelist.

Titles

See *Closing Titles* and *Opening Titles*.

Titmuss Regained

See *Paradise Postponed*.

T. J. Hooker ★★

US (Spelling-Goldberg/Columbia) Police Drama. ITV 1983–5 (US: ABC 1982–5; CBS 1985–7)

Sgt T. J. Hooker	**William Shatner**
Officer Vince Romano	**Adrian Zmed**
Capt. Dennis Sheridan	**Richard Herd**

Fran Hooker	**Lee Bryant**
Vicki Taylor	**April Clough**
Officer Stacy Sheridan	**Heather Locklear**
Officer Jim Corrigan	**James Darren**

Creator **Rick Husky**
Executive Producers **Aaron Spelling, Leonard Goldberg**
Producer **Jeffrey Hayes**

An experienced police officer teaches rookies rights and wrongs.

Honest and decent, plain-clothes detective T. J. Hooker has grown tired of investigations and longs to return to the beat. Reverting to his former role of sergeant, he is assigned to the Academy Precinct of the LCPD, where his keen young partner is Vince Romano. While performing his duties in an exemplary fashion, Hooker becomes a role-model for trainee officers, educating them in the moral dimensions of policing, as well as the strategic and physical aspects. He has seen one of his partners killed in action and over the years has had plenty of time to contemplate the good and bad sides of law enforcement.

Hooker is divorced but is still friendly with his ex-wife, Fran, a nurse. His police family includes rookies Vicki Taylor and Stacy Sheridan, the latter the daughter of his hard-nosed boss, Captain Dennis Sheridan. She is later promoted to patrol officer and teams up with experienced Jim Corrigan. Cameo appearances from stars like the Beach Boys and Leonard Nimoy are common. The 'LC' of LCPD is never explained; nor are Hooker's initials, T. J.

To Play the King

See *House of Cards*.

To Serve Them All My Days ★★★

UK (BBC/Australian Broadcasting Commission) Drama. BBC 1 1980–1

David Powlett-Jones	**John Duttine**
Algy Herries	**Frank Middlemass**
Ellie Herries	**Patricia Lawrence**
Ian Howarth	**Alan MacNaughtan**
T. S. Carter	**Neil Stacy**
Judy Cordwainer	**John Welsh**
Chad Boyer	**Simon Gipps-Kent**
	Gene Foad
R. A. L. Dobson	**Nicholas Lyndhurst**
Emrys Powlett-Jones	**Phillip Joseph**
Beth Marwood/Powlett-Jones	**Belinda Lang**
Julia Derbyshire	**Kim Braden**
Sir Rufus Creighton	**Cyril Luckham**
Mr Alcock	**Charles Kay**
Christine Forster/Powlett-Jones	**Susan Jameson**
Barnaby	**David King**
Molyneux	**Alastair Wyllie**

Writer **Andrew Davies**
Producer **Ken Riddington**

A Welsh miner's son dedicates his working life to a public school.

Second Lieutenant David Powlett-Jones of the South Wales Borderers, the youngest son of a mining family from Pontnewydd, near Abergavenny, is invalided out of World War I, suffering from a leg wound and severe shell shock. In his early 20s, he applies – not without misgivings – for a position as a teacher of Modern History and English at Bamfylde School, an exclusive, fee-paying establishment on the fringe of Exmoor, Devon. To his surprise, he is given the job. The year is 1918 and little does David realize at the time that he will spend the best part of his life in love with the school and its crusty old environment. The proverbial fish out of water, Powlett-Jones is surrounded by ageing or sick masters who have been called out of retirement to fill vacancies left by men going to war. Among his staffroom colleagues are the gung-ho Carter, a science teacher who develops into a persistent right-wing opponent of David's sensitive socialism, and the more amenable, chain-smoking Howarth, the senior English master, who becomes a drinking companion and confidant. However, it is the influence of the genial headmaster, the Reverend Algy Herries, that shapes David's life and career. Herries fills the role of his mentor and it is inevitable that, one day, Powlett-Jones will rise through the ranks to become master of one of the houses (Havelock's) and eventually headmaster himself. For the reluctant hero – much respected by the boys – the years in between are not easy. His miner brother, Emrys, resents his escape from the pits and his comfortable social status; his first wife, Beth, and their twin baby daughters, Gracie and Joan, are killed in a car accident; and a fling with flighty former colleague Julia Derbyshire brings yet more heartache. David is then persecuted by malicious new headmaster Mr Alcock to the point of near-dismissal, and a second marriage to headstrong socialist Christine Forster is also turbulent, until she finds a constructive and challenging role within the school. As the series closes, another world war is already underway. The 13-part series, based on the novel by R. F. Delderfield, was filmed at Milton Abbey School in Dorset. Music was by Kenyon Emrys-Roberts. Radio 4 broadcast a new five-part adaptation of the novel in 2006, with Oliver Milburn voicing the part of Powlett-Jones.

To the Manor Born ★★★

UK (BBC) Situation Comedy. BBC 1 1979–81

Audrey fforbes-Hamilton	**Penelope Keith**
Richard DeVere	**Peter Bowles**
Marjory Frobisher	**Angela Thorne**
Brabinger	**John Rudling**
Mrs Polouvicka	**Daphne Heard**
Rector	**Gerald Sim**
Brigadier Lemington	**Anthony Sharp**
Ned	**Michael Bilton**
Mrs Patterson	**Daphne Oxenford**

Creator **Peter Spence**
Producer **Gareth Gwenlan**

A widow is forced to sell her stately home and move into more limited surroundings.

When Audrey fforbes-Hamilton's husband, Martin, dies, he leaves her his stately pile, Grantleigh Manor, but also a mound of death-duties to pay. Not being able to keep up the estate, Audrey is forced to sell the property (it fetches £876,000 at auction) to Richard DeVere, a former costermonger and now the tycoon head of supermarket and catering chain Cavendish Foods. She being strictly old money and he being *nouveau riche*, Audrey is desperate to keep an eye on his activities, to make sure he does not destroy the character of the estate. By moving into one of the manor's lodges with her ageing butler, Brabinger, and with the use of a pair of binoculars, at least she is able to monitor proceedings. But not even that is enough.

Distrusting the new Lord of the Manor, resenting his position and also fancying him quite a bit, Audrey is always meddling in DeVere's affairs. She guides him in the etiquette of lordship and ensures – as far as she can – that Grantleigh is still run on traditional lines. Audrey's old school chum, Marjory Frobisher, drops in regularly to keep her friend in her place, while Richard's Czech mother, Mrs Polouvicka, acts as a matchmaker for her son and Audrey, whom she considers perfect for each other. Her efforts bear fruit at the end of the series when the two are married – and Audrey is at last back in charge at the manor.

The series, filmed at Cricket St Thomas in Somerset and with music from Ronnie Hazlehurst, was originally devised for radio, and a pilot show was recorded, featuring Penelope Keith and Bernard Braden (as an American). However, it was never broadcast, although a radio version was produced in 1997, with Keith Barron slipping into the role of DeVere, alongside Penelope Keith.

Todd, Bob

(1921–92)

One of the UK's leading comic supports, Bob Todd played straight man to numerous comedians, including Dick Emery, Michael Bentine, Jimmy Tarbuck, Des O'Connor, Jim Davidson and, particularly, Benny Hill. Todd arrived in showbusiness late, having served in the RAF and worked as a cattle farmer. In addition to a marathon stint in *The Benny Hill Show*, he worked on series like *The Marty Feldman Comedy Machine*, *The Best Things in Life* (Mr Pollard), *Doctor at Sea* (Entertainments Officer), *What's on Next?*, JANE, *Funny Man*, *The Steam Video Company*, *Q8* and *Q9*, *Cribbins* and his own comedy *In for a Penny* (in which he starred as Dan, a lavatory supervisor). He was similarly well known for commercials, once advertising stock cubes with a cry of 'It's beef!'

Toddlers' truce

The historic one-hour gap in transmission, between 6 and 7 p.m., designed to allow mums to put children to bed (after children's programmes had finished) and to allow older children to get on with their homework. The Truce was respected by both BBC and ITV until February 1957. Commercial considerations then gained the upper hand. ITV filled the gap with action series like THE ADVENTURES OF ROBIN HOOD, while the BBC went for the news/current affairs audience with TONIGHT on weeknights and the youth market on Saturday with SIX-FIVE SPECIAL.

Todman, Bill

(1918–79)

See *Goodson, Mark*.

Toksvig, Sandi

(1958–)

Danish comedian, writer and presenter, raised in Zimbabwe and America. After graduating from Cambridge, Toksvig worked in children's television, most notably playing Ethel Davis in ITV's Saturday morning offering NO. 73. She then turned to alternative comedy, with appearances in WHOSE LINE IS IT ANYWAY? and in the sitcom THE BIG ONE, with Mike McShane (as Deddie Tobert and also as co-writer). She has also contributed regularly to TIME TEAM, hosted *Police Dog Academy* and *The Big Read*, and was a team captain for CALL MY BLUFF, as well as writing for *The Basil Brush Show*.

Tom and Jerry ★★★

US (MGM) Animation. BBC 1 1967 (US: CBS 1965–72)

Creators **William Hanna, Joseph Barbera**
Producer **Fred Quimby**

● ***A cat and a mouse are the worst of enemies, with violent consequences.***

Tom and Jerry have been playing cat and mouse since 1940, when these short theatrical cartoons were first screened. On television, they have become two of the most popular and enduring characters, with the BBC happily dropping in the five-minute episodes whenever programmes have run short or technical problems have delayed regular transmissions.

Each cartoon adopts the same format, effectively an extremely violent, breathtaking chase around a house, a garden, a ship, etc., with the cat (Tom) desperately trying to get even with the wily mouse (Jerry). Much flattening of faces, crumbling of teeth and crushing of tails has been witnessed, but viewers have also noticed various differences in animation styles from film to film. The first (and generally regarded as the best) selection came from the years up to 1958, when the characters' creators, Bill Hanna and Joe Barbera, were still employed on the project at MGM. The studio then decided to drop out of animation and Hanna and Barbera went their own successful way, developing the likes of HUCKLEBERRY HOUND, THE FLINTSTONES and SCOOBY DOO. MGM commissioned 13 more *Tom and Jerrys* from Czechoslovakia in 1961, and then more films were made by cult animator Chuck Jones with Les Goldman in the mid-1960s. Further episodes were made as part of a longer children's cartoon compilation in 1975, but received little acclaim.

Tom Brown's Schooldays ★★★

UK (Company Pictures) Drama. ITV 2005
DVD: Acorn Media

Dr Arnold	**Stephen Fry**
Tom Brown	**Alex Pettyfer**
Mary Arnold	**Jemma Redgrave**
Flashman	**Joseph Beattie**
East	**Harry Michell**
Tadpole	**Dane Carter**
Green	**Hugh Mitchell**
Mr Smith	**Stephen Boxer**
Matron	**Amanda Boxer**
Sally	**Georgina Moffett**
Speedicot	**Ben Tillett**
Squire Brown	**Julian Wadham**
Mr Lampard	**John Carlisle**
Arthur	**Harry Smith**

Writer **Ashley Pharoah**
Producer **Suzan Harrison**

● ***An innocent new pupil finds a public school is a place of savage cruelty.***

This two-hour retelling of Thomas Hughes's classic novel (1857) of life at Rugby School was ITV's first major drama of 2005. Young country boy Tom Brown discovers life to be tough in his new environment, where he struggles to conform to the routines of public school life – not least the fagging (taking on menial duties) demanded of younger pupils and the institutionalized bullying led by the sadistic fifth-former Flashman. Thankfully, a visionary new headteacher, Dr Arnold (based on a real-life Rugby headmaster), has designs on making mid-19th-century Rugby a more humane place to live and study, although his aspirations are not shared by some of the older boys or even the more entrenched staff. Support does come, however, from his loyal wife, Mary. While plucky Tom suffers for his refusal to be bullied, he does manage to form a few worthwhile friendships, most notably with the mischievous East. David Moore directs.

Tom Brown's Schooldays had previously been dramatized in four parts by Anthony Stevens (BBC 1 1971: with Iain Cuthbertson as Arnold, Richard Morant as Flashman and Anthony Murphy as Tom).

Tom Jones ★★★

UK (BBC/A&E) Drama. BBC 1 1997

Tom Jones	**Max Beesley**
Squire Allworthy	**Benjamin Whitrow**
Bridget Allworthy	**Tessa Peake-Jones**
Sophia Western	**Samantha Morton**
Squire Western	**Brian Blessed**
Aunt Western	**Frances de la Tour**
Henry Fielding	**John Sessions**
Blifil	**James D'Arcy**
Honour	**Kathy Burke**
Mr Square	**Christopher Fulford**
Revd Thwackum	**Richard Ridings**
George Seagrim	**Brian Hibbard**
Molly Seagrim	**Rachel Scorgie**
Betty Seagrim	**Jane Danson**
Goody Seagrim	**Mossie Smith**
Jenny Jones	**Camille Coduri**
Partridge	**Ron Cook**
Mrs Whitfield	**June Whitfield**
Mr Fitzpatrick	**Richard O'Callaghan**
Mrs Fitzpatrick	**Michelle Fairley**
Lady Bellaston	**Lindsay Duncan**
Lord Fellamar	**Peter Capaldi**
Parson Supple	**Brian Pettifer**
Mrs Miller	**Celia Imrie**
Nancy Miller	**Kelly Reilly**
Anderson	**Roger Lloyd-Pack**
Mr Dowling	**Sylvester McCoy**
Jack Nightingale	**Matt Bardock**

Writer **Simon Burke**
Producer **Suzan Harrison**

● ***The adventures of a young man with a zest for life and for women.***

When kindly Squire Allworthy discovers a new-born infant on his bed at Paradise Hall, he launches a tale of an 18th-century boy's rakish progress through life. The baby is christened Tom Jones and is brought up by the squire and his sister, Bridget, until it is contrived by his enemies that Tom is expelled from the house and has to make his own way in the world. Among their neighbours are Squire Western and his family – most notably for Tom daughter Sophia, who becomes the love of his life, though the path of true love in this case certainly does not run true. Among the other larger-than-life characters that Tom encounters on his journey are his tutors, Mr Square and Reverend Thwackum; the despicable Blifil family; gamekeeper's daughter Molly Seagrim (Tom's first conquest); wandering former schoolmaster Mr Partridge, who may well be Tom's real father; the selfish Lady Bellaston, who seeks to separate Tom and Sophia to keep him for her own; the foppish Lord Fellamar, who is Lady Bellaston's accomplice; and Honour, Sophia's scheming maid. This five-part adaptation of the great novel by Henry Fielding (played as on-screen narrator by John Sessions) was directed by Metin Huseyin.

Tom Tom ★★

UK (BBC) Children's Magazine. BBC 1 1965–70

Presenters **Jeremy Carrad, John Earle, Norman Tozer, Janet Kelly, Jan Leeming**

Producers **Hugh Duggan, Kenneth Savidge, Lawrence Wade**

● ***The wide and colourful world of technology and arts, presented for kids.***

Produced in Bristol by BBC West, *Tom Tom* was a mix of TOMORROW'S WORLD and BLUE PETER. In a weekly feast for anoraks and techno-nerds, science, technology, arts, sports and hobbies of all kinds were championed by initial hosts Jeremy Carrad (also of regional news magazine *Points West*) and John Earle. Norman Tozer and Janet Kelly added a more youthful touch from 1968, with Jan Leeming joining the team a year later. Hovertrains, yoga, Native American customs, sailing and especially Formula 1 Grand Prix reports were typical of the standard fare, presented – it was hoped – in an informative and entertaining fashion. The series also ran its own annual contest: the Tom Tom Inventors' Competition.

Tombstone Territory ★★

US (Ziv) Western. ITV 1957–9 (US: ABC 1957–9; Syndicated 1959–60)

Sheriff Clay Hollister	**Pat Conway**
Harris Claibourne	**Richard Eastham**
Deputy Charlie Riggs	**Gill Rankin**

Producers **Frank Pittman, Andy White**

● ***Actions speak louder than words for a Wild West sheriff.***

Clay Hollister is lawkeeper in the town of Tombstone, Arizona Territory (dubbed 'the town too tough to die'), back in the Old West. Supported by Harris Claibourne, editor of the local rag, *The Epitaph* (who also narrates the story), and initially his deputy, Charlie Riggs, Hollister saves the dusty frontier town from the clutches of assorted outlaws in typical Western fashion. Star Pat Conway, who was raised on a ranch, once attributed the appeal of the series to the fact that it 'takes the cowboy off the couch and puts him back on the horse, where he belongs'. William M. Backer's theme song was called 'Whistle Me Up a Memory'.

Tomlinson, Ricky

(Eric Tomlinson; 1939–)

Liverpudlian actor, a former construction worker, who has received greatest acclaim as Jim Royle in THE ROYLE FAMILY but was previously seen in UNITED KINGDOM (Dennis), BOYS FROM THE BLACKSTUFF and as Bobby Grant in BROOKSIDE, DCI Wise in CRACKER and Cinders the cook in ROUGHNECKS. Always in demand, Tomlinson has also starred in *The Fix* (Gordon), PLAYING THE FIELD (Jim Pratt), HILLSBOROUGH (John Glover),

DOCKERS (Macca Macaulay), *The Greatest Store in the World* (Santa), *Safe as Houses* (Lawrence Davidson), *My Beautiful Son* (Uncle Alfred), CLOCKING OFF (Ronnie Anderson), NICE GUY EDDIE (Eddie McMullen), DOWN TO EARTH (Tony Murphy) and MIKE BASSETT: MANAGER (title role). Guest roles have come in series like THE BILL, COLD FEET, DALZIEL AND PASCOE and the *All Star Comedy Show*.

Tomorrow People, The ★★★

UK (Thames/Tetra) Children's Science Fiction. ITV 1973–9; 1992; 1994–5

John	**Nicholas Young**
Stephen Jameson	**Peter Vaughan-Clarke**
Carol	**Sammie Winmill**
Kenny	**Steve Salmon**
Tim	**Philip Gilbert** *(voice only)*
Jedekiah	**Frances de Wolff**
	Roger Bizley
Prof. Cawston	**Brian Stanion**
Elizabeth	**Elizabeth Adare**
Tyso Boswell	**Dean Lawrence**
Mike Bell	**Mike Holloway**
Hsui Tai	**Misako Koba**
Andrew Forbes	**Nigel Rhodes**
Ginge	**Michael Standing**
Lefty	**Derek Crewe**
Adam	**Kristian Schmid** *(1992–5)*
Megabyte	**Christian Tessier** *(1992–5)*
Lisa	**Kristen Ariza** *(1992–5)*
Kevin	**Adam Pearce** *(1992–5)*
Ami	**Naomie Harris** *(1992–5)*

Creator **Roger Price**
Producers **Ruth Boswell, Roger Price, Vic Hughes**

● ***A team of telepathic teenagers use their powers to save the Earth.***

The Tomorrow People are homosuperions: the first exponents of the next stage in man's development after *Homo sapiens* (or 'saps', as they are known). They are teenagers endowed with powers of telepathy, telekinesis and ESP, and become Earth's first 'ambassadors' to the Galactic Empire. By employing their advanced minds, they are able to thwart malevolent aliens and protect the Earth from invasion and interference.

The first Tomorrow Person to become aware of his special powers and to come to terms with them is 17-year-old John, a lean, dark-haired, level-headed lad who is able to counsel and help other youngsters endure this painful transition, known as 'breaking out'. The next two are Carol and Kenny, who leave after the first series to work on the Galactic Trig (a Galactic Empire space-complex), but new Tomorrow People break out on a regular basis and take their places in the cast. They are Stephen (in the programme's first episode), Elizabeth, Tyso, Mike (played by Mike Holloway, the drummer in the teenage band Flintlock), Hsui Tai and Andrew. They travel by 'jaunting', a process of teleportation in which mind power alone takes them from place to place, and they even go back in time and into space to confront villains like the bearded Jedekiah, an evil alien robot. In and out of their secret hideout ('The Lab'), constructed in a disused London Underground station, using funds generated by John's inventions, they are assisted and guided by a deep-voiced, paternal, biological computer called Tim.

The Tomorrow People was touted as an ITV rival to DOCTOR WHO, filling the kids' fantasy slot vacated by ACE OF WANDS. At first it was intriguing and adventurous, but after a few seasons the plots thinned and the special effects became very weak. Its creator, Roger Price, pursued the idea yet again in a new version (1992–5), which cast NEIGHBOURS star Kristian Schmid as a Tomorrow Person. The original theme music was reused in 2002 for a Channel 5 quiz called *Topranko!*

Tomorrow's World ★★★

UK (BBC) Science. BBC 1 1965–2002

Presenters **Raymond Baxter, James Burke, William Woollard, Michael Rodd, Judith Hann, Anna Ford, Kieran Prendiville, Maggie Philbin, Su Ingle, Peter Macann, Howard Stableford, Kate Bellingham, Carmen Pryce, John Diamond, Carol Vorderman, Shahnaz Pakravan, Vivienne Parry, Rebecca Stephens, Richard Mabey, Monty Don, Philippa Forrester, Jez Nelson, Craig Doyle, Peter Snow, Anya Sitaram, Lindsey Fallow, Nick Baker, Adam Hart-Davis, Roger Black, Katie Knapman, David Bull**

Producers/Editors **Glyn Jones, Max Morgan-Witts, Michael Latham, Peter Bruce, Lawrence Wade, Dick Gilling, Michael Blakstad, David Filkin, Richard Reisz, Dana Purvis, Edward Briffa, Saul Nassé, Sally Dixon, Alison Gregory**

● ***A weekly look at new inventions and discoveries.***

Initially titled *Tomorrow's World . . . in the Making Today*, this long-running, popular science programme looked at the very latest innovations and discoveries over four decades, explaining how they work and describing how the new technology could be of use to mankind in major or minor ways. Among the many items introduced by the series were hole-in-the-wall cash machines, TV tennis (the earliest video game) and the compact disc. Studio experiments and dry runs illustrated proceedings.

For years, *Tomorrow's World*'s chief presenter was Raymond Baxter, supported by the likes of James Burke, William Woollard and Michael Rodd, although the number of participants increased significantly in the last two decades. An occasional inventors' insert was compiled by Bob Symes. Transmitted live for most of its existence (with hazardous consequences when experiments backfired), it was pretaped in latter years, allowing its reporters to travel the world in search of innovations. Annual fixtures included a visit from the Prince of Wales to present his *Award for Innovation*, and *Megalab*, a programme of live experiments in which viewers could participate.

In 1997 and 1998, a sister programme for summer, *TW Time Machine*, reported on inventions showcased in previous years and their relative success or failure. Although the series ended in summer 2002, there are plans to produce one-off science programmes under the *Tomorrow's World* banner.

Tompkinson, Stephen

(1965–)

British actor, born in Stockton-on-Tees and seen in a number of high-profile roles, from devious reporter Damien Day in DROP THE DEAD DONKEY to Father Peter Clifford in BALLYKISSANGEL. His career has also taken in THE MANAGERESS (Jim Wilson), CHANCER (Marcus Worton), MINDER (DC Park), DOWNWARDLY MOBILE (Mark), *The Deep Blue Sea* (Philip Welch), ALL QUIET ON THE PRESTON FRONT (Spock), *Black Cab*, *Oktober* (Jim Harper), GRAFTERS (Trevor Purvis), *The Flint Street Nativity* (Narrator), IN DEEP (Garth O'Hanlon), BEDTIME (Paul Newcombe), *Mr Charity* (Graham Templeton), TED AND ALICE (Ted),

LUCKY JIM (Jim Dixon), *In Denial of Murder* (Don Hale), *Marian, Again* (Chris Bevan), *The Taming of the Shrew* (Harry Kavanagh) and *Wild at Heart* (Danny Trevanion). Guest appearances have come in CASUALTY, BOON, FATHER TED, DAD, *Staying Up*, MY DAD'S THE PRIME MINISTER, AGATHA CHRISTIE'S MARPLE, THE LAST DETECTIVE and NEW TRICKS. Tompkinson has also provided the voice for BOB THE BUILDER's brother, Tom, and narrated the docu-soap *Dover*.

Tonight ✶✶✶

UK (BBC) Current Affairs. BBC 1957–65

Presenter **Cliff Michelmore**

Producers/Editors **Donald Baverstock, Alasdair Milne, Antony Jay, Peter Batty, Gordon Watkins, Derrick Amoore**

● ***Easy-going but influential nightly news magazine.***

Conceived as a means of filling the TODDLERS' TRUCE on weeknights, *Tonight* offered a review of the major events of the day, mixed with songs, unusual items and bits of humour. Presented by the unflappable Cliff Michelmore (whose closing remarks were 'The next *Tonight* will be tomorrow night'), *Tonight* numbered among its reporters Alan Whicker, Derek Hart, Fyfe Robertson, Geoffrey Johnson Smith, Trevor Philpott, Polly Elwes, Julian Pettifer, Macdonald Hastings, Kenneth Allsop, Brian Redhead and Magnus Magnusson. Robin Hall and Jimmie Macgregor were the resident folk singers who rounded off each show.

When *Tonight* ended in 1965, many of its crew were shunted off into its late-night replacement, 24 HOURS. Of its producers, Alasdair Milne went on to become BBC Director-General and Antony Jay later co-wrote the hugely successful comedy YES, MINISTER. *Tonight*, as a title, was revived in 1975, with presenters Sue Lawley, Donald MacCormick, Denis Tuohy and John Timpson hosting a show (again late in the evening) which was altogether less frivolous than the original early-evening show. It ran for four years on BBC 1.

Took, Barry

(1928–2002)

London-born comedy writer and performer, discovered on a Carroll Levis talent show in 1952. As well as performing stand-up routines, Took then went on to write for radio and television, scripting series like *Colonel Trumper's Private War* and various other comedies in collaboration with Marty Feldman (see Feldman's entry for joint credits). Took also produced Kenneth Horne's *Horne a Plenty*, wrote for the BOOTSIE AND SNUDGE follow-up, *Foreign Affairs*, created and produced the stand-up show *Grubstreet*, adapted *The World of Beachcomber* and *One-Upmanship*, devised and starred in the sketch show *N.U.T.S.*, and introduced comedy guests in *Took and Co.* His other work included a sitcom, *A Roof over My Head*, the drama *Scoop* (adapted from the Evelyn Waugh novel) and the illiteracy campaign series ON THE MOVE. As a consultant to the BBC comedy department in the late 1960s, he was instrumental in seeing that MONTY PYTHON'S FLYING CIRCUS reached the screen and helped THE GOODIES get off the ground. Took also brought his wry humour to bear from the chair of POINTS OF VIEW for many years, and among his other credits were the television magazine *TV Weekly* and UK Gold's chat show *Funny You Ask*.

Top Cat

See *Boss Cat*.

Top Gear ✶✶

UK (BBC) Motoring Magazine. BBC 2 1978–

Presenters **Angela Rippon, Barrie Gill, Noel Edmonds, William Woollard, Sue Baker, Jeremy Clarkson, Quentin Willson, Tiff Needell, Chris Goffey, Tony Mason, Janet Trewin, Michele Newman, Steve Berry, Andy Wilman, James May, Kate Humble, Jason Barlow, Vicki Butler-Henderson, Jason Dawe, Richard Hammond, James May**

Executive Producers **Dennis Adams, Andy Wilman**
Producers/Editors **Derek Smith, Tom Ross, John Bentley, Ken Pollock, John Wilcox, Chris Richards, Julie Clive, Richard Pearson, Andy Wilman, Gary Broadhurst, Pat Doyle**

● ***Long-running motoring magazine.***

Road-testing new models, highlighting innovations and generally keeping the motorist well informed, *Top Gear* was given a test drive in the BBC Midlands area in 1977 before being given the green light nationwide a year later. Its first hosts were Angela Rippon and Barrie Gill. Noel Edmonds was behind the wheel for a while, but Jeremy Clarkson held pole position for many years, returning after time away in 2002. Sister programmes, *Top Gear GTi*, *Top Gear Motorsport* and *Top Gear Waterworld*, were also screened in the late 1990s.

Top of the Form

See *Television Top of the Form*.

Top of the Pops ✶✶✶

UK (BBC) Pop Music. BBC 1 1964–2005; BBC 2 2005–6

Producers **Johnnie Stewart, Colin Charmey, Stanley Dorfman, Mel Cornish, Robin Nash, Brian Whitehouse, David G. Hillier, Stanley Appel, Michael Hurll, Paul Ciani, Ric Blaxill, Mark Wells, Chris Cowey, Lee Lodge, Michael Kelpie, Sally Wood**

● ***The UK's premier chart-music show.***

With the immortal words, 'It's Number One, it's Top of the Pops,' Britain's top pop programme made its bow on New Year's Day 1964 and quickly became the most influential music programme on air. From the start, record companies clamoured for their artists to appear, recognizing the boost the programme gave to new releases and to fledgling or fading careers.

The programme was unashamedly based around the Top 30/Top 40 singles chart, and albums never had much of a look-in. To emphasize this, each programme gave a rundown of the latest chart positions and ended with the number one song. Other contributions came from chart (or soon to be chart) artists, most appearing in the studio. For many years, when important artists were not available, the resident *Top of the Pops* dancers performed to the records. Pan's People (Babs – who married actor Robert Powell – Ruth, Dee Dee, Louise, Andrea, plus American choreographer Flick Colby and, later, Cherry and Sue) enjoyed this privilege for nine years up to 1976, breaking away from an earlier dance troupe called the

Go Jos. Ruby Flipper, Legs and Co. and finally Zoo replaced them, but dance troupes were abandoned in 1983, in favour of pop videos.

The very first presenter was Jimmy Savile, who hosted the show from its original home in a converted Manchester church. On that landmark programme were stars like The Rolling Stones, The Dave Clark Five, The Swinging Blue Jeans, Dusty Springfield and The Hollies. Savile and three other DJ colleagues, Pete Murray, David Jacobs and Alan Freeman, took turns to host the show during its formative years. Other radio personalities (mostly drawn from Radio 1) dominated the programme in later years. These included Tony Blackburn, Noel Edmonds, Dave Lee Travis, Ed Stewart, David 'Kid' Jensen, John Peel, David Hamilton, Peter Powell, Simon Bates, Tommy Vance, Mike Read, Andy Peebles, Gary Davies, Richard Skinner, Mike Smith, Steve Wright, Janice Long, Bruno Brookes, Simon Mayo, Mark Goodier, Nicky Campbell and Jakki Brambles. In 1991 the 'personality DJ' was abandoned in favour of lesser-known, younger hosts like Tony Dortie and Mark Franklin. At the same time *Top of the Pops* inherited a new home at BBC Elstree and began to focus more on live bands, for the first time wavering from its chart-only format. Later, celebrities, including pop stars like the Spice Girls and comedians like Jack Dee, shared the compering duties, before the Radio 1 DJ was reinstalled, in the form of presenters such as Mark Radcliffe and Marc Riley, Zoë Ball and Jo Whiley, joined by the likes of Jayne Middlemiss, Jamie Theakston, Kate Thornton, Gail Porter, Richard Blackwood, Sarah Cawood, Lisa Snowdon and Richard Bacon. A sister radio programme was added in 1997, featuring interviews with, and other music from, artists appearing in each week's show. In summer 1999, *Top of the Pops* left its Elstree home and headed out on a short tour of provincial cities and in 2001 production returned to BBC Television Centre. The first *Top of the Pops* Awards were handed out in the same year. In 2002 the 2,000th show was broadcast.

Before miming to records was officially outlawed by the Musicians' Union in 1966, records were visibly placed on a turntable and guests simply mouthed the words. Denise Sampey spun the discs in the earliest programmes, but model Samantha Juste (later wife of the MONKEES' Micky Dolenz) took over and is the girl older viewers remember at Jimmy Savile's side, even though she hardly ever spoke. When the mime ban came into force, artists had to prerecord their contributions or perform live. Accompaniment usually came from Johnny Pearson and his *Top of the Pops* Orchestra, with the Ladybirds providing backing vocals.

During the 1970s, CCS's version of Led Zeppelin's 'Whole Lotta Love' was used as the *Top of the Pops* theme music, and this was revamped and reintroduced in 1998. In 1981, 'Yellow Pearl' by Phil Lynott launched the show, followed by other theme tracks in the 1980s and 1990s.

In 1994, BBC 2 introduced a spin-off programme, *TOTP 2*, featuring highlights from the previous week's *Top of the Pops*, plus selections from the archives. Steve Wright was the (unseen) presenter. *Top of the Pops Saturday* was inaugurated in 2003 as competition for ITV 1's morning music show, *CD: UK*. In November the same year, *Top of the Pops* was given another major overhaul, under the guidance of the BBC's head of popular music, Andi Peters. Under the initial title *All New Top of the Pops*, along came live programmes, down went the number of studio-based acts and in came interviews, features and reports from the world of music. Tim Kash, a former MTV VJ, was installed as regular host, later joined by Reggie Yates and Fearne Cotton, who jointly took over when Kash left in 2004. In July 2005, more major changes were afoot when the programme left BBC 1 and moved to a new Sunday evening slot on BBC 2. Shortly after, the Saturday morning contribution was repackaged as *Top of the Pops Reloaded*. Audiences continued to decline, however, and the final *Top of the Pops* was broadcast on Sunday, 30 July 2006.

Top of the World ✶

UK (Thames) Quiz. ITV 1982

Presenter **Eamonn Andrews**

Executive Producer **Philip Jones**
Producer **Malcolm Morris**

Satellite quiz across three continents.

This ambitious quiz used two satellites to connect contestants in Britain, the USA and Australia, with the aim of finding the brainiest person in the English-speaking world. Eamonn Andrews conducted proceedings from a London studio, battling against numerous technical hitches as he questioned participants at home and in studios in Miami and Sydney. Answering questions about their own countries, their rivals' countries, a specialist subject and the rest of the world, contenders went head to head with their international opponents. In the grand final, the champions of each nation competed for the major prize of a vintage motor car (a 1924 Rolls-Royce 20).

Top Secret ✶

UK (Associated-Rediffusion) Spy Drama. ITV 1961 2

Peter Dallas .... **William Franklyn**
Miguel Garetta .... **Patrick Cargill**
Mike .... **Alan Rothwell**

Producer **Jordan Lawrence**

The all-action adventures of a pair of secret agents in South America.

Peter Dallas is a tough but likeable British intelligence agent based in Argentina. Given a year's secondment, he finds himself working for local businessman Miguel Garetta (who also has secret service connections) in a fight against crime and subversion. Delving into matters which the everyday law-enforcers cannot touch, Dallas heads undercover to undermine crooks and spies throughout South America and is joined on his assignments by Mike, Garetta's young nephew.

The show made a star out of William Franklyn (later the Schweppes 'Shh! You know who!' man), while Patrick Cargill moved on from this serious role to specialize in farces and sitcoms like FATHER, DEAR FATHER. Alan Rothwell is better remembered as David Barlow in CORONATION STREET. The show's theme tune, 'Sucu Sucu' by Laurie Johnson, was a hit in 1961 for several artists.

Top Secret Life of Edgar Briggs, The ✶✶

UK (LWT) Situation Comedy. ITV 1974

Edgar Briggs .... **David Jason**
The Commander .... **Noel Coleman**
Buxton .... **Michael Stainton**
Jennifer Briggs .... **Barbara Angell**
Spencer .... **Mark Eden**
Cathy .... **Elizabeth Counsell**

Creators **Bernard McKenna, Richard Laing**
Producer **Humphrey Barclay**

Counter-espionage capers with a bumbling British secret agent.

Edgar Briggs works for SIS, the Secret Intelligence Service, and is strangely successful at his job, considering that he is probably the most incapable agent British security has ever employed. It was a paperwork error that resulted in his transfer to the position of personal assistant to the Commander of SIS and the consequence is that the hapless Briggs is now involved in the most hush-hush undercover operations. Inevitably, he fouls up the best-laid plans – by shredding vital documents, inadvertently announcing secret tactics over a Tannoy system or handing over his holiday snaps instead of an important film. But, amazingly, Briggs has the knack of bringing matters to a satisfactory conclusion. This early starring role for David Jason lasted only 13 episodes.

Topper ✶✶

US (Loveton-Schubert) Situation Comedy. ITV 1955–7
(US: CBS 1953–5)

Marion Kerby .... **Anne Jeffreys**
George Kerby .... **Robert Sterling**
Cosmo Topper .... **Leo G. Carroll**
Henrietta Topper .... **Lee Patrick**
Mr Schuyler .... **Thurston Hall**
Katie .... **Kathleen Freeman**
Maggie .... **Edna Skinner**

A crusty old banker's new house is haunted by mischievous ghosts.

Cosmo Topper buys a country house in New York state and finds that it is haunted by the ghosts of its previous residents. Marion and George Kerby were a fun-loving couple who were killed in an avalanche while skiing in Switzerland on their fifth wedding anniversary. Now, in spirit form, they are back in their old home, accompanied by the ghost of the St Bernard dog, Neil (played by Buck), that had valiantly failed to rescue them and had died in the cause. Judging by Neil's penchant for brandy, perhaps this was not such a surprise in the world of canine rescue. The late Mr and Mrs Kerby take a shine to Topper, a stuffy old bank vice-president, and do their best to loosen him up. Gradually, he responds, much to the concern of his wife, Henrietta, who is very much a traditionalist. Initially, however, Topper is frustrated by the fact that only he can see the trio of ghosts, which makes things difficult when his overbearing boss, Mr Schuyler, comes to call. Katie and Maggie are the Toppers' housemaids.

The series, which starred Leo G. Carroll (later better known as Mr Waverly in THE MAN FROM U.N.C.L.E.),, and real-life husband and wife Robert Sterling and Anne Jeffries as his perky lodgers, was based on Thorne Smith's novel *The Jovial Ghosts*. This was made into a film, *Topper*, starring Cary Grant as George and Roland Young as Cosmo, in 1937, with sequels *Topper Takes a Trip* and *Topper Returns* following in 1939 and 1941, respectively. *Topper* was the forerunner of fantasy sitcoms like BEWITCHED, I DREAM OF JEANNIE and THE GHOST AND MRS MUIR and a couple of attempts have been made to resurrect the concept. In 1973 Roddy McDowall starred in a new pilot episode, *Topper Returns*, and in 1979 Jack Warden took the lead in a feature-length pilot called, simply, *Topper*. Neither progressed to series status.

Torchy, The Battery Boy ✶

UK (Pelham Films/AP Films/ABC) Children's Entertainment. ITV 1960

Voices **Olwyn Griffiths, Kenneth Connor, Jill Raymond, Patricia Somerset**

Creator/Writer/Producer **Roberta Leigh**

A battery-powered doll has fun at a toys' refuge in space.

Torchy, the battery boy, lives in Topsy Turvy Land, a haven in space where abused and neglected toys savour their freedom, and walk and talk like humans. The land (where the only rain is orange juice – a new kind of sticky weather, you might say) is ruled by King Dithers from his Orange Peel Palace and has its mixture of good and bad toys. These range from the pirate doll, Pongo, to Pom Pom the poodle, Sparky the baby dragon, Squish the space boy, Pilliwig the clown and Flopsy the rag doll, most living in the settlement of Fruitown (all the houses being made of fruit, with Torchy's a pineapple). Torchy, boarding his giant rocket, is also able to travel back to Earth, where he assists his friend, dear old Mr Bumbledrop, and runs into old adversaries like Bossy Boots, a domineering little girl, and Bogey, a particularly naughty boy. Only Torchy and Pom Pom are able to visit Earth, because they are *moving* toys; the others would revert to their static former selves. But even Torchy has his problems. Occasionally, he hits trouble when his battery fails and the magic beam from the lamp on his hat grows dim. Future puppetmaster Gerry Anderson directed some of the episodes.

Tors, Ivan

(1916–83)

Hungarian writer who moved to the USA and became a successful producer of wildlife adventure series, most notably SEA HUNT, FLIPPER, DAKTARI and GENTLE BEN, through his own Ivan Tors Productions. Among his other credits were action series like RIPCORD.

TOTP 2

See *Top of the Pops*.

Tottering Towers ✶✶

UK (Thames) Situation Comedy. ITV 1971–2

Clarence Emsworth Archibald Montmorency Maltravers (the 43rd Duke of Tottering) .... **William Mervyn**
Gabbidge .... **David Stoll**
Daffodil Primrose O'Kelly ('Daffy') .... **Stacey Gregg**
Dick .... **Tom Owen**
Mrs Daisy Pouncer .... **Avice Landon**
PC Poppy .... **David Lodge**

Creator **Paddy Manning**
Producers **Adrian Cooper, Vic Hughes**

A cranky old aristocrat invents oddball things to make ends meet.

The Duke of Tottering is a blue-blooded eccentric in the finest

English tradition. His wackiness exhibits itself in his crazy inventions, like a car that lays eggs or the automated suit of armour that greets visitors to his crumbling mansion, Tottering Towers. The genial old duke has been coming up with harebrained ideas all his life. He used to work for WOOSI (Weapons of Odd Strategic Ingenuity) and CRACKPOTS (Council for Research and Co-ordination of Potential Objectives Tactically Suitable), but now invents to keep the wolf from the door. Looking after the old buffer are his world-weary butler, Gabbidge, and housekeeper, Mrs Pouncer. Dick (Mrs Pouncer's nephew) is the odd-job boy at the haunted stately home, which gains a new resident with the arrival from the USA of the duke's distant relative, Daffy. Also involved in the slapstick is country copper PC Poppy, who has taken a shine to Mrs Pouncer and her hearty cooking. The 13 episodes were partly shot at Paxhill Park, a Tudor mansion in Sussex, which was at the time an old folks' home.

Touch of Frost, A ★★★

UK (Yorkshire/Excelsior) Drama. ITV 1992; 1994–7; 1999; 2001–

DI William Edward 'Jack' Frost .... **David Jason**
Supt. Mullett .... **Bruce Alexander**
DCI Allen .... **Neil Phillips**
DC Clive Barnard .... **Matt Bardock**
Shirley Fisher .... **Lindy Whiteford**
DS George Toolan .... **John Lyons**
Rosalie Martin .... **Isla Blair**
WPC/DS Hazel Wallace .... **Caroline Harker**
DS Liz Maud .... **Susannah Doyle**
Kitty Rayford .... **Gwyneth Powell**
Sgt Brady .... **James McKenna**
PC Ernie Trigg .... **Arthur White**
DS Terry Reid .... **Robert Glenister**
Dr McKenzie .... **David McKail**
DS Maureen Lawson .... **Sally Dexter**
DC Jasper Tranter .... **Nicholas Burns**

Executive Producers **Vernon Lawrence, Richard Bates, Philip Burley, David Jason**
Producers **Don Leaver, Simon Lewis, Martyn Auty, Lars Macfarlane, Richard Bates, David Reynolds**

The investigations of a lonely and rather disorganized detective.

Representing a change of career direction for comic star David Jason, the 'serious' role of DI Jack Frost of the Denton police revealed new talents in Britain's top sitcom actor (Jason's brother, Arthur White, also appears).

Frost, a moustached, greying little copper, is a terrier-like investigator. Despite being almost shambolically disorganized and having a grudge against both technology and authority (represented by the disapproving Supt. Mullett – 'Horn-rimmed Harry'), he proves himself to be perceptive and thorough, if old-fashioned in approach. The fact that his wife is terminally ill (she dies in the first episode) is not allowed to interfere with his work, but his irritability when trying to give up smoking does, however, shine through. Viewers instantly took to the sandwich-munching, curry-scoffing, George Cross-winning policeman who had once been shot on duty. Frost was the creation of novelist R. D. Wingfield.

Touching Evil ★★

UK (Anglia/Coastal) Police Drama. BBC 1997–9

DI Dave Creegan .... **Robson Green**
DI Susan Taylor .... **Nicola Walker**
DC Mark Rivers .... **Shaun Dingwall**
DS Jonathan Kreitman .... **Adam Kotz**
Commander Enright .... **Michael Feast**

Creator **Paul Abbott**
Executive Producers **Simon Lewis, Michele Buck, Damien Timmer, Sandra Jobling**
Producers **Jane Featherstone, Philip Leach**

A maverick cop joins an élite squad of detectives in tracking down serial criminals.

DI Dave Creegan is a member of the Organized and Serial Crime Unit (OSC), a rapid-response force of specially trained officers covering the whole of the UK (though based in London) and charged with tracking down serial killers, child abductors and the like. The unit has been pulled together by Commander Enright as a British equivalent of the FBI, in response to the increase in serial crime. Although his language is often rich and his temper quick, Creegan – a divorced father of two – is also a thoughtful copper, an intelligent detective quickly climbing the police ladder. Imbued with a deep sense of justice, Creegan has already fought his way back from mental illness, having been shot in the head on duty. Working closely with Creegan is 28-year-old Susan Taylor, another high-flyer who initially doubts his unorthodox methods but soon gives him full support. They are backed up by the youngest member of the squad, the seemingly confident DC Mark Rivers, and also by DS Jonathan Kreitman, a usually dependable family man who tends to be overtaken by events. For once, the action is well and truly focused on the cases in hand, with little attention paid to the characters' personal lives.

A US version, using the same title, stars Jeffrey Donovan and Vera Farmiga. It was first seen in the UK on ITV 3 in 2005.

Traffik ★★★

UK (Picture Partnership) Drama. Channel 4 1989

Jack Lithgow .... **Bill Paterson**
Helen .... **Lindsay Duncan**
Karl .... **George Kukura**
Dieter .... **Tilo Pruckner**
Ulli .... **Fritz Müller-Scherz**
Fazal .... **Jamal Shah**
Tariq Butt .... **Talat Hussain**
Caroline .... **Julia Ormond**
Rachel .... **Linda Bassett**
Henderson .... **Peter Bourke**

Writer **Simon Moore**
Producer **Brian Eastman**

Gritty thriller exposing the winners and losers in the global drugs game.

An intense story set in three separate locations, *Traffik* looks at the complicated and turbulent world of international drug movement. Crusading British politician Jack Lithgow is hell-bent on putting an end to opium shipments from the North-West Frontier Province of Pakistan, but there could be some tragic consequences should he prove successful. In Pakistan, Lithgow's mission could spell ruin for local farmer Fazal and his impoverished family. Meanwhile, in Germany, at the prosperous end of the narcotics market, there is a shock in store for Helen when her trafficker husband, Karl, is jailed after a major seizure. But, too comfortable in her own luxurious lifestyle, she decides to carry on the family business, with all its risks. Back home Lithgow battles with a customs strike and harrowing personal problems of his own.

Alastair Reid directed the five episodes. The story was refashioned into the 2000 movie *Traffik*, starring Michael Douglas and Catherine Zeta-Jones.

Train Now Standing . . ., The ★★

UK (LWT) Situation Comedy. ITV 1972–3

Hedley Green .... **Bill Fraser**
Peter Pringle .... **Hugh Walters**
Mr Potts .... **Denis Lill**
George .... **Norman Mitchell**
Rosie .... **Pamela Cundell**
Fred .... **Arthur White**
Bill .... **George Waring**
Charlie .... **Geoff L'Cise**
Mr Pitts .... **Garfield Morgan**
Ken .... **Ken Wynne**

Writers **John Watkins, John Swallow, Ian La Frenais, Geoff Rowley, Andy Baker**
Producer **Derrick Goodwin**

● ***A stationmaster longs for the good old days of steam railways.***

Burberry Halt is a long-forgotten station on the Milchester line. Somehow escaping Dr Beeching's sharpened axe, it now welcomes only three stopping trains a day. But Burberry remains a little piece of traditional England, thanks in no short measure to its stationmaster of 30 years' standing, Hedley Green. Green still sports a GWR uniform and thumbs a 1933 rule book. He is fiercely patriotic (especially when confronted by Germans) and despises change. The old chocolate machine on the platform is symptomatic of his love of the past. Helping him preserve this slice of living history is his easily bullied young porter, Peter Pringle, while Mr Potts (later replaced by Mr Pitts) is the area manager. After an initial early-evening time slot, which allowed younger viewers to share in the simple laughs, the second run, inexplicably, was screened at a much later time (around 9.30 p.m.). The series was shot at Bodiam station in Sussex, a long-redundant halt spruced up specifically for filming. Ron Grainer supplied the music.

Trainer ★★

UK (BBC) Drama. BBC 1 1991–2

Mike Hardy .... **Mark Greenstreet**
Rachel Ware .... **Susannah York**
John Grey .... **David McCallum**
James Brant .... **Nigel Davenport**
Hugo Latimer .... **Patrick Ryecart**
Joe Hogan .... **Des McAleer**
David Ware .... **Marcus D'Amico**
Kath Brant .... **Sarah Atkinson**
Frances Ross .... **Nicola King**
Jack Ross .... **Ken Farrington**
Nick Peters .... **Floyd Bevan**
Mo Ratcliffe .... **Audrey Jenkinson**
Alex Farrell .... **Claire Oberman**
Robert Firman .... **John Bowe**
Sue Lawrence .... **Melanie Thaw**

Creator/Producer **Gerald Glaister**

● ***A young trainer tries to succeed in the competitive world of horse racing.***

Mike Hardy is the lead character in this horse saga, set among the padded anoraks and green wellies of the Sport of Kings. Given the chance to set up as a trainer in his own right, Hardy secures the backing of grouchy businessman James Brant, who sends his best horses to Hardy's Arkenfield Stables. Also on Hardy's side is wealthy widow and stud owner Rachel Ware, local gambler John Grey and head lad Joe Hogan. However, Hardy also has his enemies, including his former boss, rival trainer Hugo Latimer, and he also battles with a drink problem. After an only moderately successful first season, *Trainer* rode on to a second series, which sees James Brant disappear and Hardy fall in love with Alex Farrell, the girl sent to administer Brant's estate.

Trainer was filmed on the Berkshire downs and on racecourses up and down the country. The village pub, The Dog & Gun, was actually The Crown & Horns at East Ilsley, just north of Newbury. The theme song, co-written by disc jockey Mike Read and Simon May, was performed by Cliff Richard.

Training Dogs the Woodhouse Way ★★

UK (BBC) Information. BBC 2 1980

Host **Barbara Woodhouse**

Producer **Peter Riding**

● ***Education for dog-owners.***

What was intended as a straightforward course for would-be dog-handlers turned into a cult TV hit, thanks to the eccentricities of its bossy, senior-citizen host. Barbara Woodhouse, aged 70, and a former horse trainer, had developed her own forceful techniques for teaching dogs obedience. Her snapped commands and shrill requests soon made her a household name, with her personality and character enhanced by a staid, woolly-kilt-and-sensible-shoes appearance. Her techniques received much criticism at the time and have continued to do so since her death in 1988, although it was always the nervous owners who looked terrified, not the hounds.

Transponder

The satellite component that collects signals beamed up from the ground, amplifies them and sends them back to dish receivers.

Travanti, Daniel J.

(1940–)

American actor who, after some 20 years of playing bit parts in series like *Route 66*, THE MAN FROM U.N.C.L.E., PERRY MASON, THE DEFENDERS, LOST IN SPACE, GUNSMOKE, KOJAK and HART TO HART, suddenly found fame as Captain Frank Furillo in HILL STREET BLUES in 1981. He has since been seen in the 1989 BBC political drama *Fellow Traveller* and in the US series *Missing Persons* and *Poltergeist: the Legacy*, as well as in numerous TV movies.

Traveller in Time, A ✱✱

UK (BBC) Science Fiction. BBC 1 1978

Penelope .... **Sophie Thompson**
Uncle Barnabas .... **Gerald James**
Aunt Tissie/Dame Cicely .... **Elizabeth Bradley**
Mistress Babington .... **Mary Maude**
Tabitha .... **Sarah Benfield**
Francis Babington .... **Simon Gipps-Kent**
Arabella Babington .... **Michele Copsey**
Jude .... **Lewis Hammond**
Anthony Babington .... **Charles Rogers**
Tom Snowball .... **Michael Greatorex**
Adam Deedick .... **Graham Rigby**
Mary, Queen of Scots .... **Heather Chasen**

Writer **Diana De Vere Cole**
Executive Producer **Anna Home**

● ***A journey to the past places a girl in the thick of a treasonous plot.***

Young Penelope leaves London and goes to stay at Thackers, the farmhouse home of her aunt and uncle in Derbyshire. In Elizabethan times, the house had been the residence of the Babington family, who were at the heart of the famous Babington plot to unseat Queen Elizabeth and release her prisoner, the ambitious Mary, Queen of Scots. Penelope finds herself drawn back in time to that dangerous era and is unwittingly embroiled in the murky goings-on of some 400 years earlier. Dorothea Brooking directed the five episodes, which were based on the novel of the same name by Alison Uttley, who herself grew up on a Derbyshire farm. The farm used for filming was, apparently, the one owned by the family of future BLUE PETER presenter Simon Groom.

Travelling Man ✱✱

UK (Granada) Drama. ITV 1984–5

Lomax .... **Leigh Lawson**
Robinson .... **Terry Taplin**

Creator **Roger Marshall**
Executive Producer **Richard Everitt**
Producer **Brian Armstrong**

● ***A former drug squad officer, freed from prison, sets out to find his son and track down the man who framed him.***

The life of Detective Inspector Lomax of the Metropolitan Police Drugs Squad has suddenly fallen apart. Framed for the theft of £100,000 after a drugs seizure went awry, he has spent two years behind bars for a crime he did not commit. On his release, he finds that his wife, Jan, has left him for Canada, and Steve, his drop-out son, is hiding away on Britain's canal network. To add to his worries, the police have placed him under surveillance (in case the money turns up), and the underworld is also on his tail. Almost as threatening is Robinson, an investigative reporter in pursuit of a story.

Stepping aboard his own narrowboat, named *Harmony*, Lomax heads off along the waterways and mixes with canal folk, hunting for the man who set him up and hoping to trace his missing son. The result was a sort of THE FUGITIVE for the 1980s.

Treacher, Bill

(1937–)

British actor best known as Arthur Fowler in EASTENDERS. Earlier credits included Z CARS, *Bold as Brass*, BLESS THIS HOUSE, THE SWEENEY, GRANGE HILL, ANGELS, THE PROFESSIONALS, THE AGATHA CHRISTIE HOUR, MAGGIE AND HER, SWEET SIXTEEN and *The Bright Side* (prisoner Chadwick). Radio fans will remember his voice as that of Sidney, the milkman, in *The Dales*.

Treasure Hunt ✱✱

UK (Chatsworth) Game Show. Channel 4 1982–9; BBC 2 2002–3

Presenters **Kenneth Kendall, Anneka Rice, Wincey Willis, Annabel Croft, Dermot Murnaghan, Suzi Perry**

Creator **Anne Meo**
Producers **Malcolm Heyworth, Peter Holmans, Hester Davies**

● ***Helicopter-oriented adventure game.***

In this all-action game show, two studio-bound contestants yelled directions to a 'runner' who darted around the countryside in a helicopter, looking for clues. Each treasure hunt took place within a 50-mile radius of its starting point and, by using maps and solving five riddles discovered on the way, the contestants aimed to claim the treasure (£1,000) within the 45-minute time-limit. Kenneth Kendall tried to keep calm in the studio along with adjudicator Anne Meo (replaced by Annette Lynton and then, for much of the series' run, Wincey Willis), while Anneka Rice (and, in 1989, ex-tennis star Annabel Croft) acted as runner, supported by an athletic roving camera team. Croft also appeared in the similarly styled *Interceptor* (1989–90), in which contestants attempted to avoid enemy agents.

Treasure Hunt was revived by the BBC in 2002, with Dermot Murnaghan in the studio and Suzi Perry out and about. The concept was based on the French game show *Chasse au trésor*.

Treats from the Edwardian Country House

See *1900 House, The*.

Trench, The ✱✱

UK (BBC) Documentary. BBC 2 2002

Narrator **Andrew Lincoln**

Producer **Dick Colthurst**

● ***Volunteers spend two weeks in the trenches to experience the horrors of World War I.***

In an effort to bring to life the misery that faced soldiers on the front line during World War I, this three-part series took 24 men from the city of Hull, gave them 11 days' basic military training at Catterick and then deposited them into a re-created trench system in France. Following closely the regimental diary of the 10th Battalion of the East Yorkshire Regiment, which served in the Somme in the last two weeks of October 1916, the volunteers were pitched into a world of fear, discomfort, bone-chilling cold, sleep deprivation and boredom.

The only thing missing from the actual events of 85 years earlier was the not insignificant dread of being killed or maimed. This was compensated for to a degree by quietly removing men from the experiment on a random basis – an admittedly unsatisfactory means of re-creating death and its traumas. Other details, however, were scrupulously followed, from the itchy woollen uniforms and basic latrines, to the inedible food, the right brand of tea to drink and even constant explosions that sent mud and earth showering down on the trenches and delivered inescapable constant noise. Overseeing the authenticity was a team of historical specialists known as the 'Khaki Chums'; the volunteers themselves were dubbed the 'Hull Pals', after the name given to the original regiment. The series was recorded in farmland near Flesquières, northern France. As a counterpoint to the reconstruction, veterans of the bloody conflict, now centenarians, provided their own memories of the horrific conditions they were forced to endure. Always conscious of appearing insensitive, the production team was at pains to ensure that this was no game show or gimmick but nevertheless still attracted a fair amount of criticism for their 'disrespect'.

Trethowan, Sir Ian

(1922–90)

British political journalist (*Daily Sketch*) who joined ITN in 1958, working as newscaster, diplomatic editor and political editor. He switched to the BBC in 1963, to contribute to PANORAMA and *Gallery*, then, between 1970 and 1975, was Managing Director of BBC Radio, on one occasion famously sacking Kenny Everett for making a joke about the wife of a politician. He became Managing Editor of BBC Television in 1976 and the BBC's Director-General in 1977, holding the position for five years. He was later Chairman of Thames Television. Trethowan was knighted in 1980.

Trevor, William

KBE (William Trevor Cox; 1928–)

Irish novelist and dramatist, known for his sensitive treatment of elderly folk and women. Among his offerings have been *The Baby Sitter* (1965), *The Mark-Two Wife* (1969), *O Fat White Woman* (1971), *The General's Day* (1972), *Eleanor* and *Love Affair* (1974), *Mrs Acland's Ghost* (1975), *Secret Orchards* (1980), *Matilda's England* (a trilogy, 1981), *Autumn Sunshine* and *The Ballroom of Romance* (both 1982), plus a 1979 adaptation of *The Old Curiosity Shop* and an episode of *Shades of Greene* (Graham Greene stories).

Trial and Retribution ★★★

UK (La Plante) Police Drama. ITV 1997–2000; 2002–4

Det. Supt./Chief Supt. Michael Walker .... **David Hayman**
DI Pat North .... **Kate Buffery**
DS Dave Satchell .... **Dorian Lough**
Robert Rylands QC .... **Corin Redgrave**
PC Brown .... **Daniel Ryan**
Rupert Halliday QC .... **Simon Callow**
DS/DI Jeff Batchley .... **Paul Kynman**
DC Jack Hutchens .... **George Asprey**
DC Vivien Watkins .... **Sandra James Young**
Lynn Walker .... **Jacqueline Tong**
DC Doug Collins .... **James Simmons**
DC Lisa WestN'Deaye Baa-Clements .... **Sarah Ozeke**
DCI Roisin Connor .... **Victoria Smurfit**
DS Taylor Matthews .... **Ben Cross**

Creator **Lynda La Plante**
Writers **Lynda La Plante, Vaughan Kinghan**
Producers **Lynda La Plante, Peter McAleese, Chris Clough**

● ***Major crime investigations seen through split-screen effects.***

Beginning in 1997 with a child murder case, and continuing with investigations into serial killers, a missing teenager, an eight-year-old murder case, and the discovery of a long-dead body, *Trial and Retribution*'s collection of two-part stories tackles some of the most heinous crimes. Fortunately, in its police leads, Mike Walker and Pat North, it also has two of the most reassuring cops, even if their progress to a conviction is not always smooth. Later after his own murder trial and acquittal, Walker has new colleagues in Roisin Connor and her sidekicks Matthews and, later, Satchell. The hook of the series is that it follows each case from crime discovery to the end of the trial, using split-screen technology (up to four images at a time) to reveal various aspects of the story and pack in more detail. The series was created and produced by Lynda La Plante, who was assisted in writing the courtroom scenes by Vaughan Kinghan.

Trials of Life, The ★★★★

UK (BBC) Natural History. BBC 1 1990

Presenter/Writer **David Attenborough**

Executive Producer **Peter Jones**
Producer **Keenan Smart**

● ***The survival of the fittest in the animal world.***

Produced by the BBC's Natural History Unit, *The Trials of Life* formed the third part of David Attenborough's epic wildlife documentary series, which had begun with LIFE ON EARTH and continued with THE LIVING PLANET. In this 12-part voyeuristic examination of animal behaviour, Attenborough turns his attention to the struggle for survival of the planet's many species, from birth to death, via feeding, reproduction, etc. The colourful and detailed footage was painstakingly shot over a three-year period, by over 30 cameramen, sometimes in truly life-threatening situations.

Triangle ★

UK (BBC) Drama. BBC 1 1981–3

Katherine Laker .... **Kate O'Mara**
John Anderson .... **Michael Craig**
Matt Taylor .... **Larry Lamb**
Tom Kelly .... **Scott Fredericks**
Wally James .... **Nigel Stock**
Nick Stevens .... **Tony Anholt**
Marion Terson .... **Diana Coupland**
George Larsen .... **Dennis Burgess**
Christine Harris .... **Sandra Payne**
Dougie Evans .... **Christopher Saul**
Charles Woodhouse .... **Paul Jerricho**
Jo Bailey .... **Elizabeth Larner**
Peter Nuttall .... **Jonathan Owen**

Tony Grant .... **Philip Hatton**
Judith Harper .... **Joan Greenwood**
Mrs Landers .... **Dawn Addams**
Sarah Hallam .... **Penelope Horner**
Penny Warrender .... **Sandra Dickinson**
Kevin Warrender .... **Peter Arne**
David West .... **George Baker**
Arthur Parker .... **Douglas Sheldon**
Sandy McCormick .... **Helena Breck**
Joe Francis .... **David Arlen**

Creator/Producer **Bill Sellars**

Drama with the passengers and crew of a North Sea ferry.

Triangle is one of those programmes its producers and participants probably want to forget, given the amount of flak fired in its direction. Indeed, the twice-weekly series lasted only three seasons, the last without its star (Kate O'Mara), who had already quit.

Action takes place aboard a ferry making the triangular journey of Felixstowe-Gothenburg-Rotterdam-Felixstowe. Initial intrigue follows the appointment of a new chief purser, Katherine Laker, who turns out to be the daughter of a Triangle Lines bigwig. Subsequently, there is much vying for position and numerous skulking visits to strange cabins in the dead of night.

Bravely experimenting with new lightweight equipment and actually filming aboard a moving ship (the *Tor Scandinavia*), the team, unfortunately, encountered all manner of unforeseen problems. Most daytime cabin shots had to be taken with the curtains drawn to avoid glare, and the movement of the North Sea upset the crew and performers alike. Worse still, there was little viewer interest. The bleak and icy waters of northern Europe just didn't have the appeal of the warm, azure Caribbean lagoons that made THE LOVE BOAT such a success.

Tribal Eye, The ★★★

UK (BBC) Documentary. BBC 2 1975

Presenter **David Attenborough**

Writer **David Attenborough**
Producers **David Collison, Michael MacIntyre**

In search of great ethnic artworks.

Leaving his executive's office at the BBC to return to programme making, David Attenborough made tribal art his theme in this seven-part series. Attenborough travelled the globe to try to relate masterpieces of indigenous culture to the people and places that created them. His journey took him to visit the Dogon people of Mali, the Indians of the north-west coast of America, the stamping ground of the Aztecs and Incas, the Obas of Benin, the Qashqa'i of Iran, south-west Pacific islanders, and the inhabitants of New Guinea and Hawaii.

Trigger Happy TV ★★

UK (Absolutely) Comedy. Channel 4 2000–1

Dom Joly

Producers **Alex Jackson-Long, Dom Joly**

Surreal stunts ensnare an unsuspecting public.

A combination of wind-ups, hidden-camera tricks and a little surrealism are the mainstays of this sketch show, wrapped up in a contemporary rock soundtrack. Dom Joly, former political journalist and researcher for Mark Thomas's comedy series for Channel 4, comes into the limelight as an arch-prankster in assorted disguises (traffic warden, park keeper, boy scout, etc.). Visual gags include a man shouting into a giant mobile phone. Twelve episodes were produced over two series (the second screened on the digital channel E4 before crossing to Channel 4), plus two Christmas specials in 2001.

Trinder, Tommy

CBE (1909–89)

Chirpy Cockney comedian who arrived on television after years of music hall and film work. In 1955 he was the first compere of SUNDAY NIGHT AT THE LONDON PALLADIUM, which benefited from his quick thinking and skill with the ad lib. His own series, *Trinder Box*, followed. 'You lucky people' became his catchphrase.

Trinity Tales ★★

UK (BBC) Drama. BBC 2 1975

Eric, the Prologue .... **Francis Matthews**
Stan, the Fryer .... **Bill Maynard**
Dave, the Joiner .... **Paul Copley**
Judy, the Judy .... **Susan Littler**
Nick, the Driver .... **Colin Farrell**
Smith, the Man of Law .... **John Stratton**
Alice, the Wife of Batley .... **Gaye Brown**

Creator/Writer **Alan Plater**
Producer **David Rose**

A group of rugby fans tell tall stories on the way to a cup final.

Writer Alan Plater took Chaucer's *Canterbury Tales* and placed them in a contemporary setting for this innovative six-part series. It concerns a minibus of Wakefield Trinity fans making their way down to Wembley for the Rugby League Challenge Cup Final. To while away the miles, they each tell a story (all of which are somewhat far-fetched, with slapstick elements). The six episodes are subtitled *The Driver's Tale, The Fryer's Tale, The Judy's Tale, The Joiner's Tale, The Wife of Batley's Tale* and *The Man of Law's Tale.*

Tripods, The ★★★

UK (BBC) Children's Science Fiction. BBC 1 1984–5

Will Parker .... **John Shackley**
Henry Parker .... **Jim Baker**
Beanpole (Jean-Paul) .... **Ceri Seel**
Duc de Sarlat .... **Robin Langford**
Count .... **Jeremy Young**
Countess .... **Pamela Salem**
Eloise .... **Charlotte Long**
Ozymandias .... **Roderick Horn**
Vichot .... **Stephen Marlowe**
Mme Vichot .... **Anni Lee Taylor**
Fritz .... **Robin Hayter**
Krull .... **Jeffrey Perry**

Ulf .... **Richard Beale**
Master 468 .... **John Woodvine**
Boll .... **Edward Highmore**
Borman .... **James Coyle**
Coggy .... **Christopher Guard**
Ali Pasha .... **Bruce Purchase**
Speyer .... **Alfred Hoffman**
Jeanne .... **Elizabeth McKechnie**

Writers **Alick Rowe, Christopher Penfold**
Producer **Richard Bates**

● ***Three youths flee tyrannical alien machines in a medieval world of the future.***

The Tripods was an adventurous exercise in science fiction by the BBC. Sadly, the ratings and expenses did not balance out and the series was cancelled two-thirds of the way through, leaving viewers stranded in mid-story.

The tale concerns a trio of youths living in the year 2089 at a time when the Earth has been ruled by ruthless, three-legged alien machines known as the Tripods for over 100 years. A medieval society has been restored to the planet, with all children 'capped' at the age of 16 to ensure complete subservience. Two English teenagers about to be processed (which involves attaching a metal plate to the head) decide to make a break for it in an attempt to reach the White Mountains of Switzerland, where the Free Men allegedly live. The two are cousins Will and Henry Parker. Making it as far as France, they are joined by a local youth, Beanpole, and together they lurch from danger to danger, progressing south to the safe lands.

Series two picks up in the year 2090 as the three boys and their Free Men hosts plot to overthrow the Tripods and free the human race. A newcomer, Fritz, replaces Henry, and the trio head for the Tripod Annual Games in the guise of competitors, in an attempt to infiltrate the Tripods' City of Gold. They encounter the Masters, the monsters from the planet Trion which devised the machines, and learn of their sinister plans for the Earth. And that is where the BBC leaves it – with the Tripods still in control and the boys back on the run.

Twenty-five episodes were made in total, although sci-fi fans were left crying out for a few more to set the story straight. Those keen enough will have turned to the original novels by John Christopher: *The White Mountains*, *The City of Gold and Lead* and *The Pool of Fire*.

Tripper's Day/Slinger's Day ✶

UK (Thames) Situation Comedy. ITV 1984/1986–7

Norman Tripper .... **Leonard Rossiter**
Hilda Rimmer .... **Pat Ashton**
Alf Battle .... **Gordon Gostelow**
Mr Christian .... **Paul Clarkson**
Hardie .... **Philip Bird**
Laurel .... **David John**
Higgins .... **Andrew Paul**
Sylvia .... **Liz Crowther**
Marlene .... **Charon Bourke**
Dottie .... **Vicky Licorish**
Cecil Slinger .... **Bruce Forsyth** *(Slinger's Day)*
Fred .... **David Kelly** *(Slinger's Day)*
Colin .... **Charlie Hawkins** *(Slinger's Day)*
Shirley .... **Jacqueline De Peza** *(Slinger's Day)*
Miss Foster .... **Suzanne Church** *(Slinger's Day)*

Creator **Brian Cooke**
Producers **Michael Mills, Anthony Parker** *(Tripper's Day)*, **Mark Stuart** *(Slinger's Day)*

● ***Days in the life of a harassed supermarket manager.***

This comedy series pitched Leonard Rossiter into the role of Norman Tripper, manager of the Supafare supermarket. Tripper marshals his staff like a US police chief, reflecting his fascination with American cop series, and flirts with canteen manageress Hilda Rimmer. Also seen are secretary Sylvia, elderly security guard Alf Battle, shop steward Hardie, management trainee Mr Christian and oafish staffer Higgins. The series proved to be Rossiter's last TV offering and, following his untimely death, the programme was retitled and recast. It became *Slinger's Day*, with Bruce Forsyth enrolled as Supafare's new manager, Cecil Slinger, but with only two members of Tripper's supporting staff maintained, namely Mr Christian and Hardie.

Don Adams, star of the 1960s comedy *Get Smart*, was enrolled for a Canadian version, entitled *Check It Out!*, in the mid-1980s.

Trodd, Kenith

Acclaimed British producer, closely associated with playwright Dennis Potter, working on *Double Dare*, *Brimstone and Treacle* (both 1976), PENNIES FROM HEAVEN (1978), BLUE REMEMBERED HILLS (1979), *Blade on the Feather*, *Rain in the Roof*, *Cream in My Coffee* (all 1980), THE SINGING DETECTIVE (1986), CHRISTABEL (1988) and Potter's final works, KARAOKE/COLD LAZARUS. Trodd, a campaigner for filmed, rather than videotaped, drama, has also been responsible for *Dinner at the Sporting Club* (1978), CAUGHT ON A TRAIN (1980), UNITED KINGDOM (1981), *Screen Two*'s *Femme Fatale* (1993), *The Fix* (1997) and *Promoted to Glory* (2003), among other dramas.

Troubleshooters, The

See *Mogul*.

Troughton, Patrick

(1920–87)

British Shakespearean actor who first worked on television as early as 1948. He appeared in *Toad of Toad Hall* in 1950, starred in a 1953 BBC version of *Robin Hood*, played Sir Andrew Ffoulkes in THE SCARLET PIMPERNEL in 1955 and was Captain Luke Settle in the 1960 Civil War drama *The Splendid Spur*. Troughton also took the small roles of George Barton in CORONATION STREET and Eddie Goldsmith in COMPACT, but it was as the second DOCTOR WHO (1966–9) that he became a household name. Later, he played the Duke of Norfolk in THE SIX WIVES OF HENRY VIII, Nasca in *The Feathered Serpent*, Clement Atlee in EDWARD AND MRS SIMPSON, journalist J. P. Schofield in FOXY LADY, Sextus in THE CLEOPATRAS and Perce (Nicholas Lyndhurst's grandad) in THE TWO OF US. Seldom away from the small screen, Troughton was also seen in many other productions, including THE COUNT OF MONTE CRISTO, THE ADVENTURES OF ROBIN HOOD, SWORD OF FREEDOM, THE INVISIBLE MAN, *Smuggler's Bay*, MAN OF THE WORLD, A FAMILY AT WAR (Harry Porter), SPECIAL BRANCH, THE PROTECTORS, THE SWEENEY, THE SAINT, THE GOODIES, DOOMWATCH, DR FINLAY'S CASEBOOK, COLDITZ, *Churchill's People*, MINDER, NANNY, Z CARS, SURVIVORS, *Sally Ann*, THE BOX OF DELIGHTS (Cole Hawlings), INSPECTOR MORSE, ALL CREATURES GREAT AND SMALL and assorted single dramas. One of his last roles was as the rebel,

Arthur, in KNIGHTS OF GOD in 1987. He was the father of actors David and Michael Troughton.

Trumpton

See *Camberwick Green.*

TSW

(Television South West)

The ITV contractor for South-west England from 12 August 1981 to 31 December 1992, TSW succeeded Westward Television on to the air. This was one of the more predictable changes of the 1980 franchise round, as Westward had suffered badly from boardroom turmoil in the run-up to the reallocations. TSW broadcast from a Plymouth base, but made little contribution to the ITV network during its 11-year franchise tenure, the most prominent being editions of HIGHWAY and *About Britain*, plus the canine quiz *That's My Dog*. In applying for the continuation of its licence in the 1991 franchise auctions, the company was deemed to have 'overbid' by the ITC, which then appointed Westcountry Television as the new contractor for the South-west region.

TTT

See *Tyne Tees Television.*

Tube, The ★★★

UK (Tyne Tees) Rock Magazine. Channel 4 1982–7

Presenters **Jools Holland, Paula Yates, Leslie Ash, Muriel Gray, Gary James, Felix Howard**

Producers **Malcolm Gerrie, Paul Corley, John Gwyn, Jill Sinclair**

● ***Influential 1980s rock magazine.***

The READY, STEADY, GO! of the 1980s, *The Tube* was presented live on a Friday teatime from the studios of Tyne Tees in Newcastle. Live bands, star interviews, reviews and reports were combined to produce an up-to-the-minute look at the rock music scene, and the programme became a launching pad for many of the decade's most prominent names, including Frankie Goes to Hollywood, Paul Young, U2 and The Eurythmics. Established stars like Elton John, David Bowie and Tina Turner also made appearances. Model and pop columnist Paula Yates was accompanied as host by former Squeeze keyboards man Jools Holland, and their flippant and controversial presentational style (Holland was once suspended for using a four-letter word in a programme trailer), combined with numerous technical fluffs, contrasted sharply with the slick patter of the fab DJs and the glossier presentation of TOP OF THE POPS. Muriel Gray, Gary James and, briefly, Leslie Ash also hosted proceedings, with nervous contributions from young Felix Howard.

In November 1999, Sky One re-created the series as a one-off show, *Apocalypse Tube*, broadcast from the same Newcastle studio, with hosts Chris Moyles and Donna Air.

Tucker's Luck

See *Grange Hill.*

Tugboat Annie

See *Adventures of Tugboat Annie, The*

Tully, Susan

(1967–)

London-born actress-director, on TV since her teens hosting Saturday morning series like *Our Show* and *The Saturday Banana*. She took the roles of Suzanne Ross in GRANGE HILL and Rosalie in *Why Can't I Go Home?*, and then joined EASTENDERS at its inception in 1985, playing Michelle Fowler until 1995. She has since returned to Albert Square as programme director. Other credits have included the documentary series *Genderquake* (presenter), *Holiday Reps* (narrator) and as director of LONDON'S BURNING, *Black Cab, The Story of Tracy Beaker*, THE BILL, MIT, *Twisted Tales*, 55 DEGREES NORTH and *Funland*.

Tumbledown ★★★

UK (BBC) Drama. BBC 1 1988

Robert Lawrence	**Colin Firth**
Hugh Mackessac	**Paul Rhys**
John Lawrence	**David Calder**
Jean Lawrence	**Barbara Leigh-Hunt**
Sophie	**Emma Harbour**
Nick Lawrence	**Rupert Baker**
Christopher Lawrence	**Jack Fortune**
George Stubbs	**Roddy Maude-Roxby**
Helen Stubbs	**Ann Bell**
Louise Stubbs	**Sophie Thompson**
Prothero	**Dan Hilderbrand**
Sgt Brodick	**Tam Dean Burn**
Lumpy	**Mark Williams**

Writer **Charles Wood**
Producer **Richard Broke**

● ***An invalided soldier is forgotten by the army.***

The Falklands, 1982. Number 3 Platoon of the Right Flank Company of the Scots Guards successfully wipes out an Argentinian machine gun position on Tumbledown hill. The war is nearly over. Lt. Robert Lawrence stands reflecting on the achievement, then a sniper strikes. Lawrence is shot in the back of the head and loses 40 per cent of his brain. He survives, but his world is understandably in pieces: his health devastated, his army career instantly terminated. This single film, through flashbacks, dramatizes Lawrence's true story, following his three years of rehabilitation, his personal battles and his disappointment at the lack of concern shown by the army about his welfare and that of other wounded soldiers. Not surprisingly, there were protests from the Establishment, even before the programme aired. Lawrence himself acted as consultant; Richard Eyre directed.

Turn Out the Lights

See *Pardon the Expression.*

Turner, Anthea

(1960–)

Staffordshire-born presenter, moving from radio to BLUE PETER and then on to GMTV, THE NATIONAL LOTTERY LIVE, *Pet Power, All You Need is Love, Change Your Life Forever*, TOP OF

THE POPS, WISH YOU WERE HERE . . . ? and *Turner Round the World*. She was once married to her manager, former DJ Peter Powell, and is the sister of presenter Wendy Turner Webster, with whom she hosted the game show *Your Kids are in Charge*.

Turner, Ted

(Robert Edward Turner; 1938–)

Flamboyant and ambitious American TV executive, head of Turner Broadcasting System (TBS) and one of the most influential TV magnates of the 1980s. Turner sold off his family's advertising business in the early 1970s, purchasing instead a small Atlanta television station, which he renamed WTBS. In 1976, by beaming its signal off a satellite to cable systems in other parts of the USA, Turner created one of the first 'superstations'. In 1980 he defied the advice of experts and set up a 24-hour cable news station. That was CNN, now globally relayed by satellite and one of the world's most watched channels, its reputation enhanced by coverage of the Gulf War (1991). TBS also launched the TNT channel (Turner Network Television) to screen old movies from the MGM and United Artists archives (also in Turner's ownership) and Cartoon Network. In 1996 TBS was sold to Time-Warner, with Turner joining the board as head of its cable TV divisions. He was later vice-chairman of AOL-Time Warner until 2003. He is now divorced from actress Jane Fonda.

Turner Broadcasting System

See *AOL-Time Warner*.

Turner Classic Movies

See *TCM*.

Turtle's Progress ★★

UK (ATV) Drama. ITV 1979–80

Turtle	**John Landry**
Razor Eddie	**Michael Attwell**
Supt. Rafferty	**James Grout**
	David Swift
Ethel Wagstaff	**Ruby Head**
WPC Andrews	**Jo Ross**

Creator **Edmund Ward**
Producer **Joan Brown, Nicholas Palmer**
Executive Producer **David Reid**

● ***A petty crook and his accomplice are troubled by both the police and other felons.***

Six months before viewers were treated to the dodgy dealings of Arthur Daley and his punchy sidekick, Terry, in MINDER, ITV launched this not too dissimilar light drama. The focus is on Turtle – a character first seen in the 1975 thriller serial THE HANGED MAN – a lovable, unrepentant, small-time crook who lives with his Aunt Ethel and is joined in his petty larceny by the big-eating Razor Eddie (a giant former hooligan, now 'bettering himself'). Indicative of this duo's criminal ambitions is the fact that they nick a van for the modest fee of £35. What they don't realize is that the van contains a hoard of stolen safety-deposit boxes, which their rightful and wrongful owners soon demand back. Keeping out of the reach of both police and fellow law-breakers, Turtle and Eddie discover that the boxes contain a fortune. They hide half in a safe in a scrapyard and the other half in a neighbour's loft, and set up a company, 'Guaranteed Security Inc.' (which specializes in murky underworld operations), with some of the lolly, taking a five-year lease on a high-rise office in Victoria. Unfortunately, each security box (one opened per episode) also contains a headache for the lads – top-secret documents, important chemical formulae – that they need to shake off. The setting is Fulham, and Turtle's local is The Robin Hood, where the redoubtable Aunt Ethel works as a barmaid, calling time while her husband is inside doing it.

The part of Turtle's nemesis, Supt. Rafferty, was taken over by David Swift after original incumbent James Grout broke a leg. Alan Price wrote and sang the theme song.

Tutti Frutti ★★★

UK (BBC) Comedy Drama. BBC 1 1987

Danny McGlone	**Robbie Coltrane**
Suzi Kettles	**Emma Thompson**
Eddie Clockerty	**Richard Wilson**
Vincent Diver	**Maurice Roëves**
Bomba MacAteer	**Stuart McGugan**
Fud O'Donnell	**Jake D'Arcy**
Dennis Sproul	**Ron Donachie**
Janice Toner	**Katy Murphy**

Creator/Writer **John Byrne**
Producer **Andy Park**

● ***On the road with a Scottish rock 'n' roll band.***

Returning home from New York for the funeral of his brother, Big Jazza ('The Beast of Rock'), who has been killed in a car crash, failed artist Danny McGlone stumbles into singer Suzi Kettles, an old flame. Donning drainpipes and crêpe soles, he finds himself enrolled alongside her into his late brother's rock 'n' roll band, The Majestics, billed as 'Scotland's Kings of Rock'. The Majestics comprise guitarist Vincent Diver, bass-player Fud O'Donnell and drummer Bomba MacAteer and are shakily managed by the staid Eddie Clockerty. As they set out on tour to celebrate 25 years in the business, their roadie is Dennis Sproul. The six-episode series follows the band as they travel from gig to gig, and watches the developing relationship between slobbish Danny and hard-nosed Suzi.

TV-am

TV-am won the franchise for the ITV breakfast slot in 1980 and went on air with its *Good Morning Britain* programme on 1 February 1983. This followed early difficulties that delayed the launch and allowed the BBC to get ahead of the game by presenting its own BREAKFAST TIME on 17 January the same year. TV-am's teething troubles were not over, however, as advertising problems and other matters continued to dog the early days.

The company ambitiously took to the air with a self-declared 'mission to explain'. Its 'Famous Five' presenters were all big names: Robert Kee (who hosted the earliest segment of the day, known as *Daybreak*), Angela Rippon, David Frost, Michael Parkinson and Anna Ford. Peter Jay was the company's chief executive. However, its formal, somewhat high-brow approach soon lost favour with viewers, who preferred the BBC's warmer, more casual style. As audiences shrank, changes needed to be made. Jay left after only six weeks. Rippon and Ford quickly followed, sacked by station boss Timothy Aitken, to make room for fresher presenters like Anne Diamond and Nick Owen. Greg Dyke was brought in from LWT as Editor-in-Chief to mastermind a revival, and he instigated a more lightweight style of programming. The station's fortunes were improved yet further in 1983 when a glove puppet named Roland Rat was introduced during school holidays. The streetwise rodent quickly built up a cult following and eventually transferred to his own series on BBC 1. A weekend segment for kids, *Wide Awake Club*, hosted by Timmy Mallett, was also added. When Greg Dyke left to become programme controller at TVS, he was succeeded by Bruce Gyngell, who was introduced by fellow Australian Kerry Packer, who had bought into TV-am. Gyngell, who had been the first person seen on Australian TV, ran the station for the rest of its time on air, shrugging off a walk-out of technical staff by handing out dismissal notices in 1987. On the studio couch new hosts Lorraine Kelly and Mike Morris took over from Diamond and Owen. By the time of the 1991 franchise renewals, TV-am was in good shape financially and enjoyed a sizeable audience. David Frost's and, later, Maya Even's Sunday programme was an important part of the political week. This was not enough, however. When the company was outbid by Sunrise Television (later renamed GMTV), the ITC awarded the franchise to their rivals, to the fury of all at TV-am. Even former premier Margaret Thatcher, whose Government had introduced the auction system, was contrite. She wrote to Gyngell apologizing for TV-am's downfall. TV-am's last day on air was 31 December 1992.

TV Eye

See *This Week*.

TVS

(Television South)

TVS was the company that controversially 'stole' the South and South-east of England ITV franchise from the well-established Southern Television during the 1980 licensing round. Making an application for the contract under the consortium name of South and South-East Communications, the company's strongest cards were its original personnel, which included notable broadcasting executives like Michael Blakstad (formerly of the BBC and Yorkshire Television) and Anna Home (from BBC children's programmes). Awarded the licence, it adopted the broadcasting name of TVS, bought the old Southern studios in Southampton and went on air on 1 January 1982. The company proceeded to open up new studios in Maidstone and split its regional news coverage into southern and south-eastern sectors. It made programmes like C.A.T.S. EYES, *Davro's Sketch Pad*, FRAGGLE ROCK, THE STORYTELLER, CATCHPHRASE and popular Saturday morning shows for the ITV network and expanded internationally, ambitiously taking over the MTM Entertainment company (producers of HILL STREET BLUES and LOU GRANT among other shows) in 1988, a move which unfortunately caused TVS some financial distress. When reapplying for its licence in 1991, TVS was deemed to have 'overbid' by the ITC and lost its franchise to Meridian Television, broadcasting finally on 31 December 1992. The TVS company and its Maidstone studios were subsequently bought by The Family Channel (now Challenge TV, part of Flextech).

TW3

See *That Was The Week That Was*.

Tweenies ★★

UK (Tell-Tale) Children's Entertainment. BBC 2/BBC 1 1999–2000

Producers **Iain Lauchlan, Will Brenton**

● ***Rainbow-coloured entertainment and advice for playgroup-age kids.***

Fun and games are liberally dosed with education in this highly colourful programme for toddlers. *The Tweenies* – live-action, costumed characters with animatronic heads and Kickers-style boots – are four youngsters who spend their days in the care of childminders Max and Judy. Imaginative Milo (aged four) is the purple one, with stubbly hair; energetic Fizz (nearly four) is the girl with the yellow face, dreadlocks and pink floral dress; bossy Bella (four and a half) has yellow hair, yellow dungarees and a blue face; and babyish, orange-faced Jake (still not three) has a splendid yellow Mohican hairstyle. In their games, they are joined by Doodles, a large red and yellow dog. The Tweenie Clock ('Where will it stop?') is pressed to decide the next activity, which could be story time, song time, messy time (making things), telly time (a film to watch) or news time (discussion of recent activity). While the Tweenies are kept busy with such activities, or having one of their many little arguments, snippets of practical advice about tying shoelaces or considering the feelings of others are dropped in by the kindly childminders. The characters proved such an immediate hit that the *Tweenies* show was taken on the road, where it played to thousands of adoring young fans in major concert venues. The preschool icons even had a special edition of TOP OF THE POPS devoted to their music at Christmas 2001.

24 ★★★★

US (Imagine/Twentieth Century-Fox) Secret Agent Drama. BBC 2 2002–3 (US: Fox 2001–)

Jack Bauer	**Kiefer Sutherland**
Teri Bauer	**Leslie Hope**
Kimberly Bauer	**Elisha Cuthbert**
Nina Myers	**Sarah Clarke**
Senator/President David Palmer	**Dennis Haysbert**
Sherry Palmer	**Penny Johnson Jerald**
Tony Almeida	**Carlos Bernard**
George Mason	**Xander Berkeley**
Rick	**Daniel Bess**
Richard Walsh	**Michael O'Neill**
Ira Gaines	**Michael Massee**
Mandy	**Mia Kirshner**
Alan York/Kevin Carroll	**Richard Burgi**
Jamey Farrell	**Karina Arroyave**
Mike Novick	**Jude Ciccolella**
Keith Palmer	**Vicellous Shannon**
Nicole Palmer	**Megalyn Echikunwoke**
Carl Webb	**Zach Grenier**
Alberta Green	**Tamara Tunie**
Andre Drazen	**Zeljko Ivanek**
Alexis Drazen	**Misha Collins**
Elizabeth Nash	**Kara Zediker**
Victor Drazen	**Dennis Hopper**
Patty Brooks	**Tanya Wright**
Kate Warner	**Sarah Wynter**
Bob Warner	**John Terry**

Marie Warner .... **Laura Harris**
Reza Naiyeer .... **Philip Rhys**
Lynne Kresge .... **Michelle Forbes**
Roger Stanton .... **Harris Yulin**
Michelle Dessler .... **Reiko Aylesworth**
Carrie Turner .... **Lourdes Benedicto**
Chase Edmunds .... **James Badge Dale**
Chloe O'Brian .... **Mary Lynn Rajskub**
Wayne Palmer .... **D. B. Woodside**
Aaron Pierce .... **Glenn Morshower**
Dr Sunny Macir .... **Christina Chang**
Adam Kaufman .... **Zachary Quinto**
Kyle Singer .... **Riley Smith**
Hector Salazar .... **Vincent Laresca**
Ramon Salazar .... **Joaquim de Almeda**
Gael Ortega .... **Jesse Borrego**
Dr Anne Packard .... **Wendy Crewson**
Michael Amador .... **Greg Ellis**
Alan Milliken .... **Albert Hall**
Julia Milliken .... **Gina Torres**
Senator/President John Keeler .... **Geoff Pierson**
Marcus Alvers .... **Lothaire Bluteau**
Ryan Chapelle .... **Paul Schulze**
Stephen Saunders .... **Paul Blackthorne**
Vice-President Jim Prescott .... **Alan Dale**
Secretary of Defense James Heller .... **William Devane**
Audrey Raines .... **Kim Raver**
Edgar Stiles .... **Louis Lombardi**
Erin Driscoll .... **Alberta Watson**
Curtis Manning .... **Roger Cross**
Dina Araz .... **Shohreh Aghdashloo**
Behrooz Araz .... **Jonathan Ahdout**
Navi Araz .... **Nestor Serrano**
Paul Raines .... **James Frain**
Richard Heller .... **Logan Marshall-Green**
Marianne Taylor .... **Aisha Tyler**
Habib Marwan .... **Arnold Vosloo**
Eric Richards .... **Butch Klein**
Bill Buchanan .... **James Morrison**
President Charles Logan .... **Gregory Itzin**
Martha Logan .... **Jean Smart**
Lynn McGill .... **Sean Astin**
Christopher Henderson .... **Peter Weller**
Vladimir Bierko .... **Julian Sands**
Vice-President Hal Gardner .... **Ray Wise**

Creators/Executive Producers **Joel Surnow, Robert Cochran, Brian Grazer, Ron Howard, Tony Kranz, Howard Gordon, Evan Katz**

● ***The day of the California Presidential Primary is the longest day in a government agent's life.***

'What a difference a day makes . . .' Jack Bauer is a secret-service agent working for the Los Angeles-based CTU (Counter Terrorist Unit). In the early hours of one morning he is called into action after a tip-off that the life of a leading politician is under threat. Senator David Palmer is well placed to become the first black president of the USA and this is the day of the influential California Primary, a contest that will go a long way towards deciding his future. Things rapidly become even more complicated for Jack. He is told that someone in his own team may be involved and then learns that his teenage daughter, Kimberly, has gone missing. When his wife, Teri, goes looking for her it only adds to the confusion and concern. Jack and Teri are just beginning a reconciliation after a period of estrangement and Jack's affair with colleague Nina Myers, so the situation is delicate emotionally, too. For target Palmer, life is equally stressful. While the electioneering appears to be going well, his marriage to the over-ambitious Sherry is on the rocks, and he learns that his son, Keith, may have to face trial for the murder of the man who raped Palmer's daughter, Nicole, seven years before. Masterminding the assassination bid is the icy-cool Ira Gaines, but is he merely an operative in a grander scheme? All is revealed as the series plays out in real time, one hour per episode over 24 weeks, covering from midnight to midnight on this fateful day. Using split screens to show contemporaneous action, and displaying a ticking digital clock at regular intervals, the widely acclaimed *24* offers a thrill a minute, and is chockful of twists and turns, red herrings and moments of high suspense.

A second series was broadcast in the USA from autumn 2002, reaching BBC 2 in spring 2003. This time the clock ticks onward from 8 a.m. as Bauer attempts to stop a nuclear bomb being exploded by terrorists in Los Angeles. Series three arrived in the UK via Sky One in 2004. Set three years later, it kicks off at 1 p.m. and sees Bauer returning to CTU to lead the fight to prevent the release of a deadly virus. Sky One also carried season four, with Bauer initially working as an aide to Secretary of Defense James Heller, but soon drawn into CTU work as a nuclear warhead goes missing, and season five, which starts with the assassination of a major figure and sees a presumed-dead Bauer drawn back into counter terrorism operations. Both these seasons start the clock ticking at 7 a.m.

24 Hours ★★

UK (BBC) Current Affairs. BBC 1 1965–72

Presenters **Cliff Michelmore, Kenneth Allsop, Ian Trethowan, Michael Barrett, Robert McKenzie, David Dimbleby, Ludovic Kennedy**

Producers/Editors **Derrick Amoore, Anthony Whitby, Anthony Smith, Peter Pagnamenta, Tony Summers, John Dekker, Gordon Watts, David Harrison, Michael Bukht, Michael Townson**

● ***Late-night current affairs series.***

The replacement for TONIGHT, *24 Hours* reviewed the day's news events from a late-night (10.30 p.m.) standpoint, rather than a teatime position. It inherited many members of the *Tonight* crew, including anchorman Cliff Michelmore, and ran for seven years, before giving way to *Midweek* in 1972. Among the reporting team were the likes of Michael Parkinson, Robin Day, David Lomax, Julian Pettifer, Fyfe Robertson, Leonard Parkin, Philip Tibenham, Denis Tuohy and Linda Blandford.

Its most controversial moment came in 1971 with a film entitled *Yesterday's Men*. Referring to a slogan used by the Labour Party about the Conservatives in the previous year's general election, it featured an interview with the ex-Prime Minister, Harold Wilson, in which reporter David Dimbleby quizzed him about the profits he received from his published memoirs. This angered Wilson and a cut was made, but the whole style of the film, with its satirical Gerald Scarfe cartoons and songs by The Scaffold, still caused a furore when broadcast. Matters were complicated by the following evening's *24 Hours* film about the Conservatives, a much kinder documentary entitled *Mr Heath's Quiet Revolution*. The BBC Programmes Complaints Commission was established as a consequence of this particular dispute.

29 Minutes of Fame ✶

UK (Angst) Comedy Quiz. BBC 1 2005

Presenter **Bob Mortimer**

Producers **Dan Patterson, Mark Leveson**

● ***Irreverent team quiz based around the world of celebrity.***

Jo Brand and Alistair McGowan are team captains in this celebrity-pokes-fun-at-celebrity game. Famous people of all backgrounds, from all eras, form the subject matter and provide plenty of scope for obscure facts, impressions, gags and one-liners from regular guest Sean Lock and other comedians like Stephen Fry, Ricky Tomlinson and Al Murray. The pilot show had a tighter remit, focusing only on the *Hello* celebrity set, but series producer Dan Patterson (formerly the brains behind WHOSE LINE IS IT ANYWAY?) saw the sense in broadening out the format so that absurd juxtapositions of celebrities could be introduced. Hence the possibility of Albert Einstein and Kylie Minogue appearing in the same sequence. In comedy panel game tradition, this isn't simply a question and answer quiz, but one with offbeat themed rounds, such as spotting the celebrity from what he or she would perhaps yell out in a frenzy of passion. For host Bob Mortimer, *29 Minutes of Fame* was a strange and, for many, disappointing move into the sort of game show that he parodied so brilliantly with Vic Reeves in SHOOTING STARS.

Twilight Zone, The ✶✶✶✶

US (Cayuga) Science Fiction. ITV 1963–6 (US: CBS 1959–64)

Host/Narrator **Rod Serling**

Creator/Writer/Executive Producer **Rod Serling**
Producers **Buck Houghton, Herbert Hirschman, Bert Granet, William Froug**

● ***Cult anthology of science-fiction thrillers.***

The Twilight Zone was a labour of love for one man, Rod Serling. An Emmy-winning TV playwright, Serling not only created and produced the series, he also wrote most of the episodes and appeared on screen as host and narrator. He developed a simple format of half-hour playlets (some one-hour episodes were also produced), which succinctly told a story with a curious, often shocking, twist in the tail. The storylines effectively merged illusion and reality, introduced intriguing concepts and ideas, and conveyed a moral message. Some episodes were subtle human parables; others were downright spooky. The black-and-white footage added a sinister tone, but special effects were virtually non-existent.

One classic episode concerns a bank clerk who loves to read. Sneaking away into a vault one lunchtime to delve into his book, he emerges to find that a nuclear disaster has destroyed all life on Earth. He is the only survivor. At last he can read to his heart's content. Then he drops and breaks his glasses . . . Another episode tells of an alien that arrives on Earth to offer help. It accidentally leaves behind a book called *To Serve Man*. By following the alien's advice, Earth is rid of hunger and war, and humans begin to pay visits to the alien's home planet. Then a translator finishes decoding the book, to find it is actually a cookery manual. And then there is the episode starring Agnes Moorehead as a woman whose home is invaded by miniature alien spacemen. Once she has fought them off, it is revealed that the spacemen were actually NASA astronauts who had landed on a planet of giants. It is she who is the alien.

The series played host to a horde of guest stars, ranging from William Shatner, Charles Bronson and Burt Reynolds to Mickey Rooney, Roddy McDowall and Robert Redford. Airing between 1959 and 1965 in its native USA, *The Twilight Zone* received only sporadic screenings in the UK. ITV first transmitted some episodes, but further runs (including previously unseen episodes) came on BBC 2 and Channel 4 in the 1980s.

The concept was picked up again for a 1983 cinema film, *Twilight Zone the Movie*, in which four directors (Steven Spielberg, John Landis, Joe Dante and George Miller) reworked three original TV scripts, plus one unused story by Serling. A second television version came along in 1985. Filmed in colour, in an hour-long format, featuring two or three stories per episode, it met with little success. There was no Rod Serling this time.

Twin Peaks ✶✶✶

US (Lynch/Frost/Spelling Entertainment/ABC) Drama. BBC 2 1990–1 (US: ABC 1990–1)

Agent Dale Cooper .... **Kyle MacLachlan**
Sheriff Harry S. Truman .... **Michael Ontkean**
Leland Palmer .... **Ray Wise**
Sarah Palmer .... **Grace Zabriskie**
Laura Palmer/Madeleine Ferguson .... **Sheryl Lee**
Jocelyn 'Josie' Packard .... **Joan Chen**
Catherine Martell .... **Piper Laurie**
Pete Martell .... **Jack Nance**
Major Garland Briggs .... **Don Davis**
Bobby Briggs .... **Dana Ashbrook**
Benjamin Horne .... **Richard Beymer**
Audrey Horne .... **Sherilyn Fenn**
Jerry Horne .... **David Patrick Kelly**
Shelly Johnson .... **Mädchen Amick**
Leo Johnson .... **Eric Da Re**
Dr William Hayward .... **Warren Frost**
Donna Hayward .... **Lara Flynn Boyle**
Eileen Hayward .... **Mary Jo Deschanel**
Big Ed Hurley .... **Everett McGill**
Nadine Hurley .... **Wendy Robie**
James Hurley .... **James Marshall**
Hank Jennings .... **Chris Mulkey**
Norma Jennings .... **Peggy Lipton**
Lucy Moran .... **Kimmy Robertson**
Dr Lawrence Jacoby .... **Russ Tamblyn**
Deputy Andy Brennan .... **Harry Goaz**
Deputy Tommy 'The Hawk' Hill .... **Michael Horse**
Mike Nelson .... **Gary Hershberger**
Richard Tremayne .... **Ian Buchanan**
Margaret .... **Catherine E. Coulson**
Windom Earle .... **Kenneth Welsh**
Annie Blackburne .... **Heather Graham**

Creators/Executive Producers **David Lynch, Mark Frost**

● ***Surreal mystery-cum-soap-opera set in the Pacific north-west of America.***

Twin Peaks exemplifies the power of hype. This bizarre series arrived with such a fanfare that the TV public around the world simply couldn't ignore it. Early episodes in the USA topped 35 million viewers and, despite its relegation to BBC 2, it attracted an extremely healthy audience in the UK.

However, for all the promotion and the merchandising that followed, the series failed to hang on to its viewers and it ended with a whimper rather than a bang.

At least partly responsible for its decline was its incredibly weird plot, which meandered in and out of minor tales without getting to the bottom of the main question: 'Who killed Laura Palmer?' That is the mystery that FBI agent Dale Cooper is hoping to resolve when he arrives in the sleepy lumber town of Twin Peaks, in pine-covered Washington State. Laura, a 17-year-old homecoming queen, has been fished out of the lake, her body naked and draped in a plastic sheet. Through his investigations, Cooper uncovers more and more about Laura's shady lifestyle, and about the dark secrets, skulduggery and sexual intrigue that go to make the town of Twin Peaks the PEYTON PLACE of the 1990s.

Cooper's detection methods are strange, to say the least. For a start, most of his leads come from ESP or from dreams involving midgets. His findings are then dictated to his never-seen assistant, Diane, via a microcassette recorder, between mouthfuls of his favourite cherry pie and 'damn fine coffee'. Of little help are local sheriff Harry S. Truman, a man of few words, and his tearful deputy, Andy Brennan. But, little by little, Cooper unearths the truth about this spooky, misty backwater. Illicit love triangles are revealed, nasty plots to take over the town's Packard Sawmill are exposed, and some of the strangest people keep cropping up – like a dwarf who talked backwards, like Margaret, the 'Log Lady', who nurses a piece of timber in her arms, and like Audrey Horne, the teenage seductress who ties knots in cherry stalks with her tongue. Yet, although the finger of suspicion points at most of the eccentric townsfolk, the identity of Laura's killer remains obscure. Eventually, to most viewers' relief, it is revealed to be Laura's own father, Leland, but only because he has become possessed by the so-called Killer BOB. Even then Cooper does not take the hint. He stays in Twin Peaks, investigating other murders, and the arty quirkiness of the series continues into a second season.

Criticized as being the proverbial triumph of style over substance, *Twin Peaks* was, at least initially, powerful viewing. A creation of cult film director David Lynch (of *Eraserhead*, *The Elephant Man* and *Blue Velvet* fame), and HILL STREET BLUES writer Mark Frost, its haunting, sinister atmosphere was skilfully manufactured. The dreamy, oddball feel and cinematic look were later echoed in the more successful NORTHERN EXPOSURE and the weird EERIE, INDIANA. The haunting theme music was by Angelo Badalamenti and location shooting took place in the once-peaceful, one-horse town of Snoqualmie Falls, Washington, a community now besieged by devoted fans.

Twizzle

See *Adventures of Twizzle, The.*

Two in Clover ★★

UK (Thames) Situation Comedy. ITV 1969–70

Sid Turner .... **Sid James**
Vic Evans .... **Victor Spinetti**

Creators/Writers **Vince Powell, Harry Driver**
Producer **Alan Tarrant**

Two City clerks move to the country and find it less appealing than they imagined.

Londoner Sid Turner and Welshman Vic Evans are clerks in a City insurance office and thoroughly fed up with their lot. Throwing in their jobs, they purchase Clover Farm, a small-holding in the country. However, with problematic livestock to look after, and the insular locals difficult to agree with, they soon realize that country life is not as calm and trouble-free as they first thought. Their rustic dream becomes more of a nightmare.

Two of Us, The ★★

UK (LWT) Situation Comedy. ITV 1986–90

Ashley Phillips .... **Nicholas Lyndhurst**
Elaine .... **Janet Dibley**
Perce .... **Patrick Troughton**
Tenniel Evans
Colin Phillips .... **Paul McDowell**
Lillian Phillips .... **Jennifer Piercey**

Creator/Writer **Alex Shearer**
Producers **Marcus Plantin, Robin Carr**

Two young people live together despite having different outlooks on life.

Computer programmer Ashley and his girlfriend, Elaine, don't always see eye to eye. In fact, they usually talk at cross-purposes. Nevertheless, they are happy to share a flat and a relationship of sorts. Ashley is keen on marriage, Elaine is not; but they do eventually tie the knot and settle down to a life of marital ups and downs. Ashley's parents and his widowed grandad, Perce, are also seen.

Two Pints of Lager and a Packet of Crisps ★★

UK (BBC) Situation Comedy. BBC 2 2001–4
DVD: BBC

Jonny .... **Ralf Little**
Janet .... **Sheridan Smith**
Donna .... **Natalie Casey**
Gaz .... **Will Mellor**
Louise .... **Kathryn Drysdale**
Flo Henshaw .... **Beverley Callard**
Munch .... **Lee Oakes**
David .... **Jonathon Dutton**
Kate .... **Alison Mac**

Creator **Susan Nickson**
Writers **Susan Nickson, Karen Laws, Danny Peak**
Producer **Stephen McCrum**

The sex- and booze-propelled, insecure world of five young northern friends.

Jonny and Janet are a boy- and girlfriend living in the Cheshire town of Runcorn (stars Ralf Little and Sheridan Smith reprising the on-screen relationship they first developed as Antony and Emma in THE ROYLE FAMILY, although taking it to a considerably coarser level). Like most young couples, they live for the moment, with lives revolving around lager, sex and cigarettes. Sharing their passion for the hedonistic in life are Gaz, Jonny's best mate, Man City fan and arch slob, and Donna, his mouthy girlfriend. There's also Louise, a more feminine friend, on the face of it intellectual but actually staggeringly dim. Their local hangout is The Archer Hotel – hence the title. Plots range around sexual fantasies, rows, insecurities and other issues important to the late-teen/early-twenties crowd. Setting a bad example is Donna's slutty mother, Flo. The title of the very first episode, *Fags, Shags and Kebabs*, says it all and hints at why the series was panned by older critics.

However, in keeping with the nature of the programme, its language, its scenarios and its target audience, series two aired first on the digital channel BBC Choice, with subsequent series debuting on Choice's successor, BBC 3 (only up to series four made the transfer to BBC 2). As a preamble to series four, a musical special was produced, revealing how Janet and Jonny met. For the climax of that series, viewers were able to choose the outcome to a plot by phoning or texting the producers. The decision was then revealed at the start of series five and resulted in the killing off of one of the major characters.

2 Point 4 Children ★★★

UK (BBC) Situation Comedy. BBC 1 1991–6; 1998–9

Bill Porter	**Belinda Lang**
Ben Porter	**Gary Olsen**
Rona Harris	**Julia Hills**
Jenny Porter	**Clare Woodgate**
	Clare Buckfield
David Porter	**John Pickard**
Gerry	**Leonard O'Malley**
Angelo Shepherd	**Ray Polhill**
Christine	**Kim Benson**
Bette/Aunt Belle	**Liz Smith**
Pearl	**Barbara Lott**
Tina	**Patricia Brake**
	Sandra Dickinson
Tony	**Tom Roberts**
Declan	**Alex Kew**

Creator **Andrew Marshall**
Producers **Richard Boden, Andrew Marshall, Marcus Mortimer, Rosemary McGowan**

A working mum struggles to balance professional and domestic responsibilities.

Centring around the Porter family of 142 Chepstow Road, Chiswick, *2 Point 4 Children* views (sometimes surreally) the life of a working mum, her easy-going, child-like husband and their two troublesome teenagers as they seek to make ends meet. Head of the household is Bill Porter, first seen working in Hanson's bakery with her man-hungry friend and neighbour, Rona. They later move to an airline meals factory, before setting up their own catering company, working from home. Bill's husband, Ben, is a central heating engineer who employs a Scot named Gerry, then the rebellious Christine, as his assistant. The Porters' two children are stroppy, boy-crazed Jenny and adolescent David, who is usually to be found dabbling in murky pursuits. Occasional visitors, much to everyone's dread, are Bill's mum, Bette (pally with Rona's Auntie Pearl), Bette's sister, Belle, and Ben's snooty sister, Tina. During early episodes, a mysterious biker named Angelo Shepherd haunts Bill's every move until his sudden death on the M25. A late addition to the family is Declan, a young boy the Porters foster when Jenny leaves for college.

Beginning very much like a UK version of Roseanne, *2 Point 4 Children* quickly found its own direction. With fantasy sequences becoming more and more the norm, it also gained in popularity and secured itself a run of Christmas spectaculars (including music and dance), in addition to regular series.

Two Ronnies, The ★★★★

UK (BBC) Comedy. BBC 1/BBC 2 1971–87

Ronnie Barker, Ronnie Corbett

Executive Producers **James Gilbert, Michael Hurll**
Producers **Terry Hughes, Peter Whitmore, Brian Penders, Paul Jackson, Marcus Plantin, Michael Hurll**

Gags and sketches from a long-standing comedy partnership.

Messers Barker and Corbett, the big and the small of TV comedy, had first worked together in the mid-1960s when contributing to various David Frost programmes. Although they each enjoyed individual opportunities to shine (such as SORRY! for Corbett and PORRIDGE for Barker), their joint efforts are equally well remembered.

The Two Ronnies ran for 16 years from 1971 and was hugely successful. Most programmes were shown on BBC 1, but some aired under the *Show of the Week* banner on BBC 2. Calling upon a host of talented scriptwriters (including the likes of David Nobbs, David Renwick and assorted Pythons – as well as Gerald Wiley, a pseudonym used by Barker himself), each show followed a simple format, opening and closing with mock news items. In between, 'in a packed programme', viewers were treated to cocktail party sketches, a boisterous costume musical, a meandering Corbett monologue delivered from a big chair, and doses of Barker's astounding pronunciation power, with a decent helping of gentle smut thrown in for good measure. There were also spoof serials like *The Phantom Raspberry Blower of Old London Town* (written by Spike Milligan), *The Worm That Turned* and the cases of private investigators Charley Farley and Piggy Malone. Regular musical guests broke up the humour. These included middle-of-the-road performers such as Barbara Dickson, Elaine Paige and the Nolan sisters. Finally, it was 'Goodnight from me, and goodnight from him', as the programme rounded off with some 'late news'.

As a postscript to their successful career together, Barker and Corbett returned to BBC 1 in 2005 to present *The Two Ronnies Sketchbook*, a package of highlights from the series, linked by new gags. Barker died later that year, but was seen in a Christmas special that had been recorded in the summer when he knew his health was failing.

Two Thousand Acres of Sky ★★

UK (Zenith) Drama. BBC 1 2001–3

Abby Wallace	**Michelle Collins**
Kenny Marsh	**Paul Kaye**
Alfie Wallace	**Phillip Dowling**
Charley Wallace	**Charlotte Graham**
Douglas Raeburn	**Michael Carter**
Gordon MacPhee	**Sean Scanlan**
Alistair MacLeod	**John Straiton**
Helen Kennedy	**Joanna Roth**
Big Jerry Kennedy	**Andy Gray**
Little Jerry Kennedy	**Jonny Smith**
Mary Fraser/Raeburn	**Monica Gibb**
Carolyn Fraser	**Karen Westwood**
Murdo Campbell	**Tom Watson**
Malcolm Campbell	**George Anton**
Elizabeth Campbell	**Mona Bruce**
Marjorie McGowan	**Elaine C. Smith**

Heather McGowan .... **Jenny Foulds**
Ida Macasaet .... **Sarah Lam**
Peter Macasaet .... **Jordan Gumayagay**
Dr Ewan Talbot .... **Henry Ian Cusick**
Colin Campbell .... **Paul Ireland**
Robbie Leonard .... **Michael Hodgson**
Hamish Raeburn .... **Gerald Lepkowski**
Angie Raeburn .... **Ashley Jensen**
Terry Marsh .... **Ray Brooks**

Writers **Timothy Prager, Sergio Casci**
Executive Producers **Adrian Bate, Barbara McKissack**
Producers **Tony Redston, Ros Anderson**

● ***A struggling mum tries to build a new home on a remote Scottish island.***

Life is pretty miserable for single mum Abby Wallace. Deserted by husband Robbie and stuck in a rut, she is desperate to find a way out of the grim world she inhabits. Home is a council tower block in London, work is behind the till in a mini-market and the future for her kids Alfie and Charley is none too rosy. She spots a newspaper advert asking for a young family to take up residence on the Hebridean island of Ronansay (population: 40) and persuades her best friend, Kenny Marsh, to pretend to be her husband for her application. Kenny is an unsuccessful rock musician who, despite harbouring more than platonic thoughts about his old schoolmate, is most uncertain about the prospect of living in the back of beyond. But his rough-and-ready exterior conceals a heart of gold and he decides to go along for the ride on the basis that should Abby settle in Scotland, he could always return to his life in the city.

Against all odds, Abby and Kenny are chosen by the islanders, who are desperate to have two more children in their community. This way, the island's school will be allowed to remain open. For their part of the deal, the people of Ronansay provide a bed-and-breakfast business for the Wallaces to run, but it is dilapidated to say the least and Abby and Kenny soon realize that, beautiful as their new home is, life on Ronansay is going to be no picnic. An initial snooty frostiness on the part of some islanders does not help, but gradually the Londoners win the locals around and become key members of the community. Among the prominent island folk are Douglas Raeburn, proprietor of the rival Raeburn Hotel; his girlfriend (later wife), schoolteacher Mary Fraser; Mary's daughter, Carolyn; Carolyn's boyfriend, Alistair MacLeod (later, Kenny's rival for Abby's attentions); ferryman Gordon MacPhee; shop worker Helen Kennedy (like the Wallaces an 'incomer' but now long assimilated), husband Jerry and son Little Jerry; and oddball father and son Murdo and Malcolm Campbell. The series was filmed – by the same company that produced HAMISH MACBETH – in the fishing town of Port Logan on Scotland's western coast.

Two's Company ✶✶

UK (LWT) Situation Comedy. ITV 1975–6; 1978–9

Dorothy McNab .... **Elaine Stritch**
Robert Hiller .... **Donald Sinden**

Creator **Bill MacIlwraith**
Producers **Stuart Allen, Humphrey Barclay**

● ***Friction between a brash American author and her staid British butler.***

American thriller-writer Dorothy McNab has taken up residence in London, employing traditional butler Robert Hiller to manage her household. As depicted by the bald eagle and proud lion in the programme's titles, this is no happy arrangement. For a start, Dorothy is one of the worst type of Americans, loud and rather uncouth, a cheroot-smoker with a pushy attitude to life. Hiller is very much of the old school, a champion of etiquette and decorum with impeccable manners. Their love-hate relationship provides the humour. An American version, *The Two of Us*, starring Peter Cook and Mimi Kennedy, followed in 1981 (ITV 1983).

TWW

(Television Wales and West)

TWW was the original ITV contractor for South Wales and the West of England, taking to the air on 14 January 1958 from studios in Cardiff and Bristol. Coverage of the northern and western parts of the Principality did not fall into its initial remit but was instead looked after by Wales West and North (WWN), which began broadcasting in 1962. However, when WWN folded a year later, TWW was allowed to absorb its territory. TWW's contributions to the national ITV network were few (most notable, probably, was *Land of Song*), but it did have the added obligation of producing a number of programmes in the Welsh language. TWW lost its franchise to Harlech Television in the 1967 reshuffle, eventually leaving the airwaves on 3 March 1968.

Tynan, Kenneth

(1927–80)

British theatre/film critic, infamous for being the first person to use the 'F' word on British television. The controversial utterance came not as a piece of thoughtless abuse but as part of a debate about theatre censorship taking place on the satirical programme, BBC-3, in 1965. Robert Robinson was the interviewer at the time. This has tended to overshadow Tynan's other television achievements, which included writing for THAT WAS THE WEEK THAT WAS, editing TEMPO – ITV's answer to MONITOR – and taking part in the 1950s quiz THE 64,000 QUESTION, in which he answered questions on jazz. He also made some programmes about method acting and contributed to the documentary series *One Pair of Eyes*.

Tyne Tees Television

(TTT)

Tyne Tees Television took to the air on 15 January 1959, to serve the far North-east of England from its Newcastle upon Tyne studios. Its successful consortium included film producer Sidney Box and *News Chronicle* impresarios George and Alfred Black.

Having one of the smallest ITV regions, the company's ambitions were always modest in the early days. However, horizons were raised in 1974 when its programmes were broadcast for the first time to most of North Yorkshire, following a transmitter swap with Yorkshire Television, which was instigated by the IBA. At the same time, in order to stabilize finances and maximize advertising potential, Tyne Tees and Yorkshire set up a joint holding company known as Trident Television. (The third 'prong' of Trident was intended to be Anglia Television, which had also exchanged transmitters with Yorkshire, but the IBA ruled out Anglia's involvement.) Trident was eventually disbanded on the instructions of the IBA when it reappointed both Tyne Tees and Yorkshire to their franchises in 1980. However, following successful bids by the two companies in the 1991 auctions, they again merged under the Trident name, before both being swallowed up by Granada, eventually becoming part of ITV plc.

Among Tyne Tees's best-remembered programmes have been daytime variety and game shows like *Those Wonderful TV Times*, the current affairs series *Face the Press*, the children's drama SUPERGRAN, the drama-documentary *Operation Julie*, and the pop shows *The Geordie Scene*, *Razzamatazz* and, for Channel 4, THE TUBE.

Tyzack, Margaret

(OBE; 1931–)

British actress, seen in a number of prominent roles in classic serials. She was Winifred Forsyte in THE FORSYTE SAGA, Bette Fischer in *Cousin Bette*, Princess Anne in THE FIRST CHURCHILLS, Antonia in I, CLAUDIUS and also appeared in the 1979 revival of QUATERMASS. More recent credits have included MISS MARPLE, THE INSPECTOR ALLEYN MYSTERIES, *The Young Indiana Jones Chronicles* (teacher Helen Seymour), *Family Money* (Delia), OUR MUTUAL FRIEND (Lady Tippins), DALZIEL AND PASCOE, MIDSOMER MURDERS, HEARTBEAT, DOC MARTIN, ROSEMARY AND THYME and *Wallis and Edward* (Queen Mary).

UFO ✶✶

UK (Century 21/ITC) Science Fiction. ITV 1970–1; 1973
DVD: Granada Ventures

Commander Edward Straker .... **Ed Bishop**
Col. Alec Freeman .... **George Sewell**
Capt. Peter Carlin .... **Peter Gordeno**
Lt. Gay Ellis .... **Gabrielle Drake**
Col. Paul Foster .... **Michael Billington**
Gen. Henderson .... **Grant Taylor**
Col. Virginia Lake .... **Wanda Ventham**
Dr Doug Jackson .... **Vladek Sheybal**
Joan Harrington .... **Antonia Ellis**
Nina Barry .... **Dolores Mantez**
Lt. Mark Bradley .... **Harry Baird**
Capt. Lew Waterman .... **Gary Myers**
Lt. Ford .... **Keith Alexander**
Skydiver navigator .... **Jeremy Wilkin**

Creators **Gerry Anderson, Sylvia Anderson**
Executive Producer **Gerry Anderson**
Producer **Reg Hill**

● ***A secret defence agency protects Earth from space invaders.***

UFO was puppet-specialists Gerry and Sylvia Anderson's first full attempt at real-life action. In the series Earth is pitted against a mysterious alien force, some time in the 1980s. Arriving in weird, pyramid-shaped spacecraft, the intruders are seldom seen. Viewers do learn, however, that they have green skin and breathe not air but liquid, and that they are a sterile race, having lost the power of reproduction. The only way for them to survive is by kidnapping humans and stealing their organs for transplantation.

The general public is not alerted to the threat, for fear of causing widespread panic. Instead, a secret global defence unit has been formed to anticipate UFO attacks and thwart any landings: SHADO (Supreme Headquarters, Alien Defence Organization), whose command centre, Control, housed deep beneath the Harlington-Straker film studios on the outskirts of London, is spearheaded by abrasive USAF officer Ed Straker, working under the cover of a film producer. Straker is assisted by amiable Col. Freeman; moody Capt. Carlin (who lost his sister to the intruders); dare-devil test pilot Col. Paul Foster; and Lt. Gay Ellis, shapely commander of the organization's futuristic Moonbase, the first line of defence (where, for some reason, all operatives wear white catsuits, string vests and purple wigs).

SHADO is well prepared for a UFO attack. Its Interceptor spacecraft, crewed by females and launched from the moon, are first into action, when alerted by the SID (Space Intruder Detector), a reconnaissance satellite. If this line is breached, Skydivers are called into play. These nuclear submarines are capable of underwater and aerial combat. If all else fails, and land defence is required, SHADO air-drops its SHADO-mobile supertanks into the fray.

UFO is clearly more adult-oriented than the Andersons' 'Supermarionation' series. The characters have fuller profiles, the plots have darker tones and the uniforms (being filled with real people, not woodentops) are certainly more provocative. One or two episodes touch on murky subjects such as hallucination, drugs and sex, and these contrived to give the series a falsely risqué reputation. As a result, it was denied a network screening on ITV and floated between Saturday mornings and late nights around the country. It seems schedulers could not make up their minds whether this was kids' or grown ups' fare.

UKTV

Digital channel provider, jointly owned by Telewest/NTL and BBC Worldwide and supplying UKTV Gold, UKTV Style, UKTV Drama, UKTV History, UKTV Food, UKTV People, UKTV Documentary, UKTV G2 and UKTV Bright Ideas. Its origins lie in the establishment of UK Gold in 1992, a joint venture by the BBC and Thames Television to transmit their archive material, plus some programmes from overseas.

Ullman, Tracey

(1959–)

British actress, comic and singer, a hit on both sides of the Atlantic. Ullman first came to light in 1981 in THREE OF A KIND, in which she shared the honours with Lenny Henry and David Copperfield. She also appeared in A KICK UP THE EIGHTIES and then became one of the GIRLS ON TOP (Candice) in 1985. After heading off to Hollywood, Ullman was given her own sketch programme, *The Tracey Ullman Show*, in 1987, which ran for three years, was a ratings success and won her an Emmy. It also helped launch the cartoon series THE SIMPSONS, but did not take off when screened in the UK, being deemed 'too American'. Back home, Ullman appeared in *A Class Act*, a satire in three parts, in 1993 for the new ITV company Meridian, of which her producer husband, Allan McKeown, was a director. This led to the one-off, three-part satire *Tracey Ullman Takes on New York*, which gave rise to a whole series of *Tracey Ullman Takes on* ... in the USA. More recently, she has been seen as psychiatrist Dr Tracey Clark in ALLY MCBEAL, in a series called *Visible Panty Line* and as a guest in WILL & GRACE.

Ulster Television

(UTV)

Ulster Television, or UTV as it is now known, has provided the Independent Television service for Northern Ireland since 31 October 1959. Always having to tread a fine line politically, because of the region's sensitivities, Ulster has had one of the more difficult tasks in the ITV network. Nevertheless, it has survived every franchise shake-up. Notable contributions to ITV's national output have been few, however.

Ultimate Force ✶✶

UK (Bentley) Drama. ITV 1 2002–3; 2005–
DVD: Granada Ventures

Sgt Henno Garvie .... **Ross Kemp**

Jamie Dow	**Jamie Draven**
Alex Leonard	**Sendhil Ramamurthy**
Sgt Pete Twamley	**Tony Curran**
Capt. Caroline Walshe	**Alex Reid**
Ricky Mann	**Danny Sapani**
Jem Poynton	**Elliot Cowan**
Lt. 'Dotsy' Doheny	**Jamie Bamber**
Col. Aidan Dempsey	**Miles Anderson**
Mrs Twamley	**Jackie Morrison**
Ricky Mann	**Danny Sapani**
Louis Hoffman	**Christopher Fox**
Pru Banks	**Lucy Akhurst**
Capt. Ian Macalwain	**Richard Armitage**
Sgt Sean Smith	**Derek Horne**
Becca Gallagher	**Heather Peace**
Cpl Dave Woolston	**Louis Decosta Johnson**
Ed Dwyer	**Liam Garrigan**
Kathy Crampton	**Hannah Yelland**
Capt. Patrick Fleming	**Sam Callis**
Cpl Finn Younger	**Jamie Michie**

Writers **Rob Heyland, Julian Jones, Len Collin, Charlie Fletcher**
Executive Producer **Brian True-May**
Producer **Peter Norris**

An SAS squad works and plays hard.

The arrival of new recruit Jamie Dow, a reformed car thief, introduces viewers to the 22 Regiment of the SAS. Under the command of Colonel Dempsey and his junior officer Lt. 'Dotsy' Doheny, the team is employed to deal with tasks that fall beyond the abilities of the regular forces or the police. These are hard, single-minded men, who won't let emotion affect their performance, as 'Red Troop' leader Sgt Henno Garvie constantly declares. Dow quickly realizes what a demanding life this is going to be and has to face up to the challenge or ship out. Another rookie is Jamie's friend Alex, the adopted brother of established team member Sam Leonard. When Sam is killed by a bank robber within days of his arrival, Alex, too, needs to get the measure of his new career. Along the way, missions include tackling a terrorist threat to a biochemical lab and protecting a Unionist politician in Northern Ireland.

More testosterone-fuelled carnage ensues in series two, shown in 2003. In series three, broadcast two years later, Red Troop takes in a new body of recruits. These include Becca Gallagher, the first ever female, whose arrival infuriates the diehards until she proves her worth in the field.

SAS veteran Chris Ryan was consultant to the series and made a cameo appearance.

Undermind ★★

UK (ABC) Adventure. ITV 1965

Drew Heriot	**Jeremy Wilkin**
Anne Heriot	**Rosemary Nicols**
Frank Heriot	**Jeremy Kemp**
Prof. Val Randolph	**Dennis Quilley**
Sir Geoffrey Tillinger	**John Barron**

Creator **Robert Banks Stewart**
Producer **Michael Chapman**

A man and his sister-in-law try to save Britain from alien subversion.

When normally dependable policeman Frank Heroit begins to act strangely, it is of grave concern to his brother, Drew, who has just flown in from Australia. With Frank's wife, Anne, he discovers that his brother has fallen foul of a menacing plot to undermine Britain's Establishment, by brainwashing stalwarts of the community, weakening the fabric of society and bringing anarchy to the country. The likes of writers, clergymen, scientists, accountants and doctors are all targets. Their minds are being taken over by an unseen alien force, which transmits high-frequency signals into their brains from space, leading them to wreak havoc with law, order and morale. Drew and Anne become marked people as they delve into the weird goings-on. The story unfolds over 11 episodes. Writers included DOCTOR WHO stalwarts David Whitaker and Robert Holmes.

Ungentlemanly Act, An ★★★

UK (Union Pictures/BBC/London Films) Drama. BBC 2 1992
DVD: Odyssey Video

Governor Rex Hunt	**Ian Richardson**
Mavis Hunt	**Rosemary Leach**
Dick Baker	**Ian McNeice**
Major Mike Norman	**Bob Peck**
Major Garry Noott	**Hugh Ross**
Vice Commodore Hector Gilobert	**Antonio Valero**
Chief of Police Ronnie Lamb	**Alex Norton**
Patrick Watts	**Mike Grady**
Simon Winchester	**Paul Geoffrey**

Writer **Stuart Urban**
Executive Producers **Michael Wearing, Franc Roddam**
Producer **Bradley Adams**

Dramatization of the first two days of the Falklands conflict.

Commissioned to mark the tenth anniversary of the war in the South Atlantic, this single drama relates key moments in the Argentinian invasion of the Falkland Islands in April 1982. At the centre of affairs is the islands' governor, Rex Hunt, who has just welcomed Major Mike Norman to Port Stanley. Norman is the new commander of the small group of Royal Marines stationed on the Falklands and has just taken over from Major Garry Noott, who is still in position to facilitate a smooth handover. Noott's strategic knowledge is soon called into use when news breaks that a large Argentinian fleet is hovering offshore. As the inevitability of invasion hits home, the drama follows Hunt and Norman's plans to protect both the local citizens and the sovereignty of the islands. Resistance against such overwhelming odds is futile, however, and despite a gutsy display of defiance from the Green Berets, with some help from the volunteers of the Falklands Islands Defence Force (FIDS), surrender of Government House ('GH') is the only logical option facing the British. The two-and-a-quarter-hour film ends with Hunt and his wife, Mavis, being flown off the island and a short pictorial resumé of the future battles to recapture the territory. Other key figures are Dick Baker, Hunt's right-hand man; Hector Gilobert, an officer in the Argentinian air force stationed on the islands; police officer Ronnie Lamb; Simon Winchester, a *Sunday Times* journalist caught up the whirlwind; and Patrick Watts, broadcaster with the local radio station, FIBS. Although the circumstances are anything but jovial, there is a current of humour running through the drama, reflecting the sheer bemusement of the locals ('kelpers') at this crazy incursion. One man is seen trying to walk to work through the gunfire, for instance, and, at another time, a lady offers cups of tea to soldiers under fire on the front line. The real-life Major Mike Norman acted as military adviser to the production team. Writer Stuart Urban also directed.

United! ✱✱

UK (BBC) Drama. BBC 1 1965–7

Gerry Barford	**David Lodge**
Jack Birkett	**Bryan Marshall**
Jimmy Stokes	**George Layton**
Kenny Craig	**Stephen Yardley**
Horace Martin	**Harold Goodwin**
Ted Dawson	**Robin Wentworth**
Frank Sibley	**Arnold Peters**
Mary Barford	**Ursula O'Leary**
Kevin Barford	**Peter Craze**
Dan Davis	**Arthur Pentelow**
Mick Dougall	**Robert Cross**
Curly Parker	**Ben Howard**
Jean Jones	**Mitzi Rogers**
Danny South	**Mark Kingston**
Dave Rockway	**Christopher Coll**
Bryn Morrison	**Derek Sherwin**
Mark Wilson	**Ronald Allen**
Dick Mitchell	**Tony Caunter**
Chris Wood	**Mike Redfern**

Creator **Brian Hayles**
Producers **Bernard Hepton, Anthony Cornish, David Conroy, John McRae**

● ***Life in and around a struggling soccer club.***

As one strand of the BBC's autumn 1965 soap offensive (the other strand was THE NEWCOMERS), *United!* was another attempt by the Corporation to break the popular drama stranglehold held by CORONATION STREET. Airing on Monday and Wednesday evenings, it focused on the struggling Second Division team of Brentwich United just as the new manager, Londoner Gerry Barford, was drafted in to keep the club afloat. Sadly, his best efforts failed to boost the team's affairs and, by 1966, another new boss, Mark Wilson, had succeeded him.

Most prominent among the team members were goalkeeper Kenny Craig and strikers Jimmy Stokes and Jack Birkett (the team captain). Club trainer was Horace Martin, Ted Dawson was the chairman and the secretary was Frank Sibley. Dan Davis was chairman of the supporters' club. Boardroom battles, personal problems and domestic friction combined with the soccer stories throughout, and also seen were Barford's wife, Mary, and their soccer-mad, 18-year-old son, Kevin. Jimmy Hill acted as technical adviser and match action was filmed at Stoke City's Victoria Ground. These efforts were all in vain, however, and *United!* left the screen in 1967.

United Kingdom ✱✱

UK (BBC) Drama. BBC 1 1981

Chief Constable James McBride	**Colin Welland**
Kath	**Val McLane**
Tony	**Bill Paterson**
MP	**Rosemary Martin**
Dennis	**Ricky Tomlinson**
Peter Connor	**Peter Kerrigan**

Writer **Jim Allen**
Producer **Kenith Trodd**

● ***A dispute between the government and a rebel council leads to trouble on the streets.***

When the right-wing government slashes council budgets, left-wing councillors rebel. A Labour council in the north-east agrees not to cut public services, force workers onto the dole or pay the surcharge that is consequently levied at them. Thus disqualified from office, they hamper the work of a commissioner appointed to run the local authority by stealing vital computer tapes relating to local affairs. It is therefore down to the police – increasingly seen as a vehicle of the state – to restore law and order as street battles begin. Stuck in the middle are housewife Kath, who decides to go out and fight for her family, and hard-line Chief Constable James McBride. Directed by Roland Joffe and including some improvised dialogue, this long single drama was screened as part of the PLAY FOR TODAY anthology.

University Challenge ✱✱✱

UK (Granada) Quiz. ITV 1962–87; BBC 2 1994–

Presenters **Bamber Gascoigne, Jeremy Paxman**

Creator **Don Reid**
Producers **Barrie Heads, Patricia Owtram, Douglas Terry, Peter Mullings, Kieran Roberts, Peter Gwyn, Irene Daniels**

● ***Long-running intellectual quiz for teams of university students.***

A decade before MASTERMIND made its debut, Granada's *University Challenge* had already cornered the market in highbrow trivia, becoming, like *Mastermind*, an unexpected success. No one could have anticipated that a programme which posed questions about nuclear physics or Renaissance artists would run for 25 years.

Scholarly questionmaster Bamber Gascoigne took delight in taxing Britain's brightest young brains and added a touch of personality to what was otherwise a drably presented programme. Two four-person teams from competing universities or colleges did battle for a half-hour in a bland set, with a split screen employed to impose one team above the other. A round of questions opened with a 'starter for ten' (which became a catchphrase), and continued with three bonus questions. There were no holds barred and topics ranged from the sublime to the ridiculous, from Rachmaninov's piano concertos to First Division goalkeepers. The winning team stayed on to face a new challenge the following week, hoping to achieve three consecutive wins and earn a place in the end-of-the-series knock-out. The first contest took place between the universities of Manchester and Leeds. In 1994 the programme was exhumed by Granada, who sold it to the BBC. Jeremy Paxman was installed as host and a somewhat jazzier set was employed. A straight knock-out tournament replaced the original 'challenge' format.

University Challenge was closely modelled on the US series *College Bowl*, and champion teams from both sides of the Atlantic occasionally faced off in a special match. A number of notable personalities appeared as contestants in their youthful days, including writers Clive James, Sebastian Faulkes and David Aaronovitch, actors Stephen Fry, Miriam Margolyes and Julian Fellowes, TV journalist John Simpson and Conservative politicians Malcolm Rifkind and David Mellor. In 2002, a special series reuniting victorious teams from the past was produced to commemorate the programme's 40th birthday. A year later *University Challenge – the Professionals* opened up the contest to teams of specialist workers like civil servants and architects.

Unsuitable Job for a Woman, An ✱✱

UK (Ecosse/HTV/WGBH Boston) Detective Drama 1997–9; 2001

Cordelia Gray .... **Helen Baxendale**
Edith Sparshott .... **Annette Crosbie**
Det. Chief Supt. Fergusson ..... **Struan Rodger**

Executive Producers **Douglas Rae, Rebecca Eaton**
Producers **Colin Ludlow, Debbie Shewell**

● ***A rookie detective inherits her boss's investigation agency.***

Cordelia Gray, in her late 20s, has worked for private eye Bernie Pryde for eight months, but his sudden suicide changes her life. His bequest to her of the ropey Pryde's Detective Agency in London's Brick Lane means she is no longer an apprentice private eye but the head of the firm, and she is thrown right in at the deep end when hired by a scientist to look into the suspicious death of his son, a Cambridge student. After this first three-part investigation, Gray never looks back, renaming the company Gray's Detective Agency. Intelligent and bookish, she hides her inexperience behind a dogged determination and a deep sense of natural justice. Adding not always welcome advice and lending a hand with the cases is matronly office manager Edith Sparshott. To coincide with star Helen Baxendale's own pregnancy, Gray is also shown expecting in later episodes.

The series was based on a character created by P. D. JAMES.

Untouchables, The ✱✱✱

US (Desilu/Langford) Police Drama. ITV 1966–9
(US: ABC 1959–63)

Eliot Ness .... **Robert Stack**
Agent Martin Flaherty .... **Jerry Paris**
Agent William Youngfellow ... **Abel Fernandez**
Agent Enrico Rossi .... **Nick Georgiade**
Agent Cam Allison .... **Anthony George**
Agent Lee Hobson .... **Paul Picerni**
Agent Jack Rossman .... **Steve London**
Frank ('The Enforcer') Nitti ..... **Bruce Gordon**
Al Capone .... **Neville Brand**
'Mad Dog' Coll .... **Clu Gallagher**
Narrator .... **Walter Winchell**

Executive Producers **Jerry Thorpe, Leonard Freeman, Quinn Martin**
Producers **Howard Hoffman, Alan A. Armer, Alvin Cooperman, Lloyd Richards, Charles Russell, Fred Freiberger**

● ***A US Treasury official and his incorruptible men home in on gangsters in Prohibition Chicago.***

Based on the life of the real Eliot Ness, who brought Al Capone to book in 1931 (for non-payment of taxes), *The Untouchables* tells the story of an honest, upright and dedicated Treasury man as he seeks to rid Chicago of organized crime. The dour, tight-lipped Ness and his whiter-than-white colleagues earn themselves the nickname 'The Untouchables' from the fact that they cannot be bribed or influenced in any way.

The capture of Capone had been portrayed in a two-part TV special starring Robert Stack as Eliot Ness, which was screened in the USA as part of the *Desilu Playhouse* anthology. It proved so successful that this series ensued, although fact quickly gave way to fiction as it took hold. Although it showed the agents rounding up the likes of Frank Nitti (Capone's right-hand man), Ma Barker, Bugs Moran, Dutch Schultz, Walter Legenza and 'Mad Dog' Coll, the real Ness had had nothing to do with these events. Criticism also came from Italianate Americans, who complained how their names were being dragged through the mud in every episode. In response, the producers added a disclaimer to the end of the show, admitting that much of the action was fictional, and also cut down the number of Italian criminals.

The Untouchables was a notably violent programme, filmed in stark, realistic black and white, with plenty of gunfire to keep its large audience enthralled. Kevin Costner took over the Ness role for a 1987 cinema version, directed by Brian De Palma. The series was remade in 1993, casting Tom Amandes as Ness, but with little impact.

Up Pompeii! ✱✱✱

UK (BBC) Situation Comedy. BBC 1 1970

Lurcio .... **Frankie Howerd**
Ludicrus Sextus .... **Max Adrian**
Wallas Eaton
Mark Dignam
Ammonia .... **Elizabeth Larner**
Erotica .... **Georgina Moon**
Jennifer Lonsdale
Nausius .... **Kerry Gardner**
Senna .... **Jeanne Mockford**
Plautus .... **William Rushton**

Creator **Talbot Rothwell**
Writers **Talbot Rothwell, Sid Collin**
Producers **David Croft, Sydney Lotterby**

● ***Innuendo and double entendre in old Pompeii.***

The centre of attention in this Roman farce is Lurcio, the weather-beaten slave of randy senator Ludicrus Sextus. Constantly diverted from his attempts to deliver 'The Prologue' to the viewing audience, Lurcio is obliged to act as a go-between for Ludicrus and the rest of his household and their friends as they all seek to bed one another. Lurcio keeps viewers informed about the goings-on through asides to the camera. Ammonia is Ludicrus's wanton wife, Erotica the appropriately named daughter and Nausius the wimpy son. Other characters (and numerous guest stars) float in and out of the action, not least batty old Senna, the soothsayer who foolishly predicts the destruction of the town.

Based on Frankie Howerd's stage success in the musical *A Funny Thing Happened on the Way to the Forum, Up Pompeii!* began life as a *Comedy Playhouse* pilot in 1969. It went on to spawn a feature film, leading to various other '*Up*' movies for Howerd, and also gained a TV sequel in 1973, *Whoops Baghdad!*, with the action transferred to the Middle East and Howerd adopting the guise of servant Ali Oopla. In addition, two revival specials were seen, both called *Further Up Pompeii!*, one in 1975 and the other (for ITV) in 1991. The programme's heavy innuendo was notably daring for the time.

Up Sunday ✱✱

UK (BBC) Comedy. BBC 2 1972–3

John Wells, James Cameron, Kenny Everett, William Rushton, Keith Dewhurst, John Fortune

Editor **Rowan Ayres**

Executive Producer **Mike Fentiman**
Producer **Ian Keill**

● ***Irreverent take on the week's affairs.***

Billed as 'a last look at the week', this late-night Sunday offering aired initially as part of BBC 2's LINE-UP strand. A THAT WAS THE WEEK THAT WAS for the 1970s, it featured an ever-changing crew of comics and writers in support of the main stars, among them Clive James, Roy Hudd, Jack Trevor Story, P. J. Kavanagh, Molly Parkin, Humphrey Lyttelton, Roger McGough, Don McLean, Alex Glasgow, Eric Idle, Vivian Stanshall, William Davis, Harvey Matusow, John Gorman, John Bird, Madeline Smith, Barry Humphries, Bill Barclay, Eleanor Bron and the folk band Gryphon. Bob Gale provided the animations.

Up the Elephant and Round the Castle ✶

UK (Thames) Situation Comedy. ITV 1983–5

Jim London .... **Jim Davidson**
Lois Tight .... **Anita Dobson**
Vera Spiggott .... **Sara Corper**
Ernie London .... **John Bardon**
Mum London .... **Rosalind Knight**
Councillor Bertram Allnutt ..... **Roger Sloman**
Wanda Pickles .... **Sue Nicholls**
Tosh Carey .... **Brian Capron**
Councillor Arnold Moggs .... **Nicholas Day**
Brian .... **Brian Hall**

Producer **Anthony Parker**

● ***A cockney bachelor inherits a house and plenty of troublesome neighbours.***

Unemployed Jim London thinks he's landed on his feet when he inherits a little terraced house from his late Aunt Min, but the reality is rather different. Number 17 Railway Terrace, Elephant and Castle, is a pleasant enough little Victorian gaff close to a viaduct, it's just that Jim's neighbours and friends don't give him enough peace to savour his new independence. Councillor Bertram Allnut is a particular pain, always finding fault and interfering in everything Jim does (Allnut is replaced by the equally irritating Councillor Arnie Moggs later), and the womenfolk also bring their share of woes. Jim fancies local looker Lois Tight but would have much more chance with pushy, 35-year-old next-door neighbour Wanda Pickles, whose husband, Stan, is conveniently tucked away in Parkhurst prison. On the other side of Jim, chubby Vera Spiggott lives with her dad and gazes longingly at her new neighbour through her unflattering glasses. Add in Mr Wilkins, the never-seen, often-heard sitting tenant upstairs, plus Jim's dad, Ernie, a frequent visitor, and life is anything but free and easy, as Jim often explains direct to camera. Lucky there's always the Freemasons Arms to escape to, where Brian is the barman, but even here life is never straightforward. After a couple of years of shattered tranquillity, the series closed, the character of Jim London transferring to another comedy, HOME JAMES.

Up the Garden Path ✶✶✶

UK (Humphrey Barclay/Granada) Situation Comedy. ITV 1990–1; 1993

Izzy Comyn .... **Imelda Staunton**
Dick .... **Mike Grady**
Maria .... **Tessa Peake-Jones**
Gwyn .... **Tom Mannion**
Michael .... **Nicholas Le Prevost**
Louise .... **Susan Kyd**
'Razors' .... **Rene Zagger**
Charles .... **David Robb**
Bill .... **Neil McCaul**

Writer **Sue Limb**
Producer **Humphrey Barclay**

● ***A dizzy teacher struggles to find Mr Right.***

Scatty and disorganized Izzy Comyn is a teacher in her 30s still looking for the right man in her life. She dallies with a number of unsuitable suitors, including womanizing Michael, posh Charles, thoughtful academic Bill and a former pupil, Razors, but can't seem to make the right choice. If she only knew it, Mr Right would probably be her teacher friend, Dick, but she fails to recognize his devotion. Apart from Dick, Izzy's best friend and confidante is Maria, married to Welshman Gwyn, though when all else fails, she falls back on the tried and tested comfort supplied by lots and lots of chocolate cake. This is something she needs to do quite often, thanks to her unfortunate habit of telling fibs to extract herself from a tricky situation. *Up the Garden Path* was initially a novel by Sue Limb, who adapted it for Radio 4 in 1987. A second radio series followed, then this TV adaptation, with a third and final collection of radio episodes airing after television had had its fill.

Up the Junction ✶✶

UK (BBC) Drama. BBC 1 1965

Sylvie .... **Carol White**
Eileen .... **Vickery Turner**
Rube .... **Geraldine Sherman**
Dave .... **Tony Selby**
Ron .... **Ray Barron**
Terry .... **Michael Standing**
Mrs Hardy .... **Rita Webb**
The Tallyman .... **George Sewell**

Writer **Nell Dunn**
Producer **James MacTaggart**

● ***Earthy portrayal of life among the south London working classes.***

Described by its production team as a mix of play, documentary and musical, *Up the Junction* focuses on three vibrant, down-to-earth girls who live and work in Battersea and have their fun by heading up the Junction (Clapham Junction). Regrettably, it all turns sour for one girl, who finds herself pregnant, alone and faced with abortion. Directed by Ken Loach, and shot largely on film, this controversial WEDNESDAY PLAY observes the bleak London streets the girls call home and their dead-end jobs, but ensures their coarse *joie-de-vivre* shines shockingly (for the time) through. It was dramatized, from her own 1963 novel, by Nell Dunn, and Paul Jones provided the theme song. A film version was made in 1967, starring Suzy Kendall and Dennis Waterman.

Up the Workers ✶✶

UK (ATV) Situation Comedy. ITV 1974; 1976

Bernard Peck .... **Lance Percival**

Richard 'Dicky' Bligh .... **Henry McGee**
Sid Stubbins .... **Norman Bird**
Bert Hamflitt .... **Dudley Sutton**
Deirdre .... **Trudi Van Doorn**
Mick Briggs .... **Charles Bolton**
Mavis .... **Vivienne Martin**
Fergy .... **Leon Vitali**
Fred Hamflitt .... **Victor Maddern**
Andrea .... **Lesley Duff**
Sir Charles .... **Charles Lloyd-Pack**

Creator **Lance Percival**
Writers **Tom Brennand, Roy Bottomley**
Producers **John Scholz-Conway, Alan Tarrant**

Labour unrest at a Midlands factory.

Sending up the widespread militancy of the 1970s, *Up the Workers* reports industrial relations at Cockers Components Ltd, a factory in the Midlands. In this battle of the classes the workers always have a grudge and the bosses are never sympathetic to shop-floor troubles. MD Dicky Bligh is the man at the top, trying to keep the wheels turning, while shop steward Sid Stubbins is ever ready to pull out the troops over issues big or small. In the middle is labour relations manager Bernard Peck. Also prominent are Bert Hamflitt, the maintenance man/first aider (later replaced by Fred Hamflitt), Deirdre, Bligh's glamorous secretary, and apprentice Mick Briggs. Two series followed a pilot episode in 1973 in which Hamflitt was played by Gordon Rollings and Deirdre by Lynn Smith. Music was by Jack Parnell

Upchat Line, The/The Upchat Connection ★★

UK (Thames) Situation Comedy. ITV 1977/1978

Mike Upchat .... **John Alderton**
Robin Nedwell *(Connection)*
Maggie .... **Susan Jameson** *(Connection)*
Polly .... **Bernadette Milnes** *(Connection)*

Writer **Keith Waterhouse**
Producer **Robert Reed**

A homeless writer sweet-talks a host of women.

Who Mike Upchat is, no one seems to know. For Upchat by name, upchat by nature is a lone wolf, a lovable rogue who lives out of a left-luggage locker at Marylebone station. A writer of little repute but abundant imagination, he uses the name of Mike Upchat in his everyday affairs, which concern plenty of pretty women providing beds for the night, and other flights of fancy. But it seems that you can have too much of a good thing, for our hero emigrates to Australia before the start of the second series, which aired as *The Upchat Connection*. With Robin Nedwell replacing John Alderton in the lead, 'Upchat' has bequeathed his pseudonym, his address book and his locker key to a new man – the winner of a raffle for the said prizes. The new 'Upchat' has to face a series of social challenges, some set by his friends, Maggie and Polly, which test his upchatting skills to the full. Mike Batt provided the theme music.

Upper Hand, The ★★

UK (Central) Situation Comedy. ITV 1990–3; 1995–6

Charlie Burrows .... **Joe McGann**
Caroline Wheatley .... **Diana Weston**
Laura West .... **Honor Blackman**
Joanna Burrows .... **Kellie Bright**
Tom Wheatley .... **William Puttock**
Michael Wheatley .... **Nicky Henson**

Executive Producer **Paul Spencer**
Producer **Christopher Walker**

A former footballer becomes housekeeper to a female advertising executive.

Injured soccer star Charlie Burrows needs a new vocation. A widower, he's also looking for a good environment in which to bring up his 11-year-old daughter, Joanna. So the Londoner applies for and is taken on as live-in housekeeper to Henley-based business executive Caroline Wheatley, mother of seven-year-old Tom and separated wife of Michael, a wildlife film-maker. Caroline's man-hungry mother, Laura West, her assistant at the Blake and Hunter advertising agency, is also on the scene.

Problems with the kids, as well as more mundane domestic matters, draw Charlie and Caroline into conflict but, at the same time, help foster their growing romance. After four seasons of amiable squabbling, love finally wins through and Charlie and Caroline are engaged to be married. A one-off, hour-long special in 1995 sees the dithering duo finally make it to the altar and, in the last series, they struggle to come to terms with their new status as man and wife.

The Upper Hand was based on the US sitcom *Who's the Boss* and largely followed the same scripts, adapted for UK audiences.

Upstairs, Downstairs ★★★★

UK (LWT/Sagitta) Drama. ITV 1971–5
DVD: Network

Mr Angus Hudson .... **Gordon Jackson**
Mrs Kate Bridges/Hudson .... **Angela Baddeley**
Rose Buck .... **Jean Marsh**
Lord Richard Bellamy .... **David Langton**
Lady Marjorie Bellamy .... **Rachel Gurney**
Capt. James Bellamy .... **Simon Williams**
Elizabeth Bellamy/Kirbridge .... **Nicola Pagett**
Georgina Worsley .... **Lesley-Anne Down**
Daisy .... **Jacqueline Tong**
Edward .... **Christopher Beeny**
Sarah .... **Pauline Collins**
Emily .... **Evin Crowley**
Alfred .... **George Innes**
Roberts .... **Patsy Smart**
Pearce .... **Brian Osborne**
Lawrence Kirbridge .... **Ian Ogilvy**
Hazel Forrest/Bellamy .... **Meg Wynn Owen**
Ruby .... **Jenny Tomasin**
Thomas Watkins .... **John Alderton**
Virginia Hamilton/Bellamy .... **Hannah Gordon**
Frederick .... **Gareth Hunt**
Alice .... **Anne Yarker**
William .... **Jonathan Seely**
Lily .... **Karen Dotrice**
Sir Geoffrey Dillon .... **Raymond Huntley**

Lady Prudence Fairfax .... **Joan Benham**
Marquis of Stockbridge .... **Anthony Andrews**
Violet .... **Angela Walker**

Creators **Jean Marsh, Eileen Atkins**
Executive Producer **Rex Firkin**
Producer **John Hawkesworth**

● ***Events in the lives of a turn-of-the-century London family and their loyal servants.***

Much praised, fondly remembered and hugely successful, *Upstairs, Downstairs* focuses on life at 165 Eaton Place, the Belgravia home of Tory MP Richard Bellamy, his lady wife, Marjorie, and their two children, James and Elizabeth. The family is rich, but not extravagantly so, with most of their wealth inherited on Lady Bellamy's side (she is the daughter of a prime minister). So Richard's career is vital to the upkeep of the family's home and its standing in society, something which the indiscretions of his wayward children continually place in jeopardy.

But, as the title suggests, the 'Upstairs' goings-on are only half the story, with the 'Downstairs' world of the Bellamys' domestic staff equally prominent. Head of the servants is Mr Hudson, the highly responsible, softly spoken but firm Scottish butler, a man who knows his place and makes sure other staff members know theirs. A father figure to the servants, he masterminds the team effort which keeps the house afloat, ably assisted by Mrs Bridges, the gruff, plump cook, and Rose, the level-headed chief housemaid. Beneath them work the younger staff – feisty, daydreaming under-parlourmaid Sarah, maturing footman Edward, loyal housemaid Daisy (later Edward's wife), pathetic maid Ruby, and, in later episodes, new footmen Thomas and Frederick.

The series opens in November 1903, shortly after the death of Queen Victoria, and runs through until 1930. Along the way, in cosy, soap opera fashion, it depicts the household's struggles to win through in times of adversity, whether social (such as a visit by the King for dinner) or real (when Rose's fiancé is tragically killed in the Great War). It reflects all the early fads and fashions of the 20th century, from the Suffragette movement to the jazz age, writing historical events into the plot. The General Strike is one example and the loss of Lady Marjorie on the *Titanic* another. Lord Bellamy remarries (to Scottish widow Virginia Hamilton), his ward Georgina moves in to replace the petulant Elizabeth, and other characters come and go, both above and below stairs, before disaster strikes at the end of the series. The family's wealth is lost in the 1929 Wall Street Crash, James commits suicide and the house has to be sold. The final episode sees Hudson marry Mrs Bridges and, together with Ruby, set off to run their own guest house. Edward and Daisy become butler and maid to Georgina and her new husband, the Marquis of Stockbridge, and Rose is the last to leave, wandering through the rooms and closing up the house, with voices from the past reminding her of events, happy and sad, that have dominated her life in Eaton Place.

Upstairs, Downstairs – widely acclaimed for its historical accuracy and shrewd social comment – was the brainchild of Jean Marsh and fellow actress Eileen Atkins (who had created the role of Sarah for herself but found herself committed to stage work when the programme began). They repeated the exercise in devising THE HOUSE OF ELIOTT in the 1990s. *Upstairs, Downstairs* enjoyed sales all across the world and led to a spin-off series, *Thomas and Sarah*, which followed the two young servants as they took up a new appointment in the country. An American version, *Beacon Hill*, set in 1920s Boston, was also attempted but didn't succeed.

Us Girls ✱✱

UK (BBC) Situation Comedy. BBC 1 1992–3

Grandma Pinnock .... **Mona Hammond**
Beverley .... **Joanne Campbell**
Nicola Blackman
Aisha .... **Marlaine Gordon**
Grandad Pinnock .... **Allister Bain**
Catherine .... **Kerry Potter**
Gail .... **Dona Croll**
Miss Mack .... **Anni Domingo**

Writer **Lisselle Kayla**
Producer **David Askey**

● ***Generation-gap humour with a West Indian family.***

'Us Girls' – a grandmother, daughter and granddaughter trio of Jamaican descent – live in London. Independent-minded daughter Bev is a freelance journalist who gives up her job at the local council to relaunch the lifestyle magazine *Shades* with her lazy editor colleague, Gail. Demanding granddaughter Aisha is still at school, and immersed in the usual ups and downs of teenage life with best friend Catherine, while Grandma – married for nearly 40 years to henpecked Grandad – is one of those people who just can't help interfering in the lives of the others. For Grandma, nearly everything the girls do is a 'fool fool' idea. Her ally in the cross-generation conflict is Miss Mack, a fellow Jamaican who works as a tea lady at the council.

UTV

See *Ulster Television*.

V ★★★

US (Daniel H. Blatt and Robert Singer/Warner Brothers) Science Fiction. ITV 1984–5 (US: NBC 1984–5)
DVD: Warner Home Video

Mike Donovan	**Marc Singer**
Dr Julie Parrish	**Faye Grant**
Diana	**Jane Badler**
Nathan Bates	**Lane Smith**
Robin Maxwell	**Blair Tefkin**
Elizabeth	**Jenny Beck**
	Jennifer Cooke
Ham Tyler	**Michael Ironside**
Willie	**Robert Englund**
Elias	**Michael Wright**
Kyle Bates	**Jeff Yagher**
Lydia	**June Chadwick**
Sean Donovan	**Nicky Katt**
Mr Chiang	**Aki Aleong**
Charles	**Duncan Regehr**
Martin/Philip	**Frank Ashmore**
Lt. James	**Judson Scott**
Howard K. Smith	**Himself**

Creator **Kenneth Johnson**
Executive Producers **Daniel H. Blatt, Robert Singer**

● ***Earth is taken over by Nazi lizards from outer space.***

V began as two successful mini-series (*V* and *V: The Final Battle*) and then expanded into a weekly run, which was never as popular. The 'V' in the title actually stood for 'Visitors' and 'Victory', with the storyline revolving around an alien invasion of Earth and the underground resistance to it.

The Visitors come from somewhere near the star Sirius, arriving in Los Angeles in the late 20th century in massive spacecraft, ranging in size from three to five miles wide. They ostensibly come in peace, offering advice and technical help to the Earth's population in return for some vital minerals. However, once the human race has been wooed, the Visitors begin to take over the planet, using subtle coercion and clever propaganda. If this sounds familiar, it is because *V* is modelled on the rise of fascism in Germany before World War II. But in case the metaphor passes some viewers by, there are some even more obvious references. The aliens dress in uniforms with swastika-type motifs. They form an élite squad of storm-troopers, like the SS, and round up all opposition, confining subversives in concentration camps. But, like the Nazis, they also meet resistance.

Working against them is TV journalist Mike Donovan, who has penetrated an alien spaceship and discovered their true intentions. He has learned that the Visitors are not humanoids at all but forked-tongued, giant, rodent-eating reptiles whose scaly skin is revealed whenever their flesh is torn. They have come to steal Earth's water and, more menacingly, to take back frozen humans as food. Pursued by the aliens, Mike teams up with scientist Julie Parrish (a concentration camp escapee); mercenary Ham Tyler; a friendly alien named Willie (played by the film world's future Freddie Kruger, Robert Englund); and young Robin Maxwell, who was seduced by a Visitor and gave birth to a hybrid child named Elizabeth. They hide out in the Club Creole and adopt the 'V for Victory' sign as their emblem. Thankfully, by the end of the mini-series, they have seen off the oppressors with the aid of a specially produced bacterial red dust.

When the weekly series begins, the Visitors soon regain the upper hand. Diana, their evil, duplicitous leader, is back in control, thanks to chemical magnate Nathan Bates (whose Scientific Frontiers Corporation had manufactured the lethal red dust). Bates springs her from a Nuremberg-style trial. The underground still battles valiantly and the half-alien Elizabeth rapidly develops into a teenager with special mental powers. When the climax comes, Diana and her cronies are thwarted by a mutual desire for peace between the two races.

V is well remembered for one classic scene in which Jane Badler, as Diana, swallows a mouse. It was actually done using chocolate mice, a mechanical jaw for close-ups and a false expandable throat, which showed the mouse slipping down, but it looked very realistic and upset the squeamish.

Valentine, Anthony

(1939–)

British actor, often cast in sinister, sneery roles. Among these have been the parts of Toby Meres in CALLAN and Major Mohn in COLDITZ. As a teenager in the 1950s Valentine was one of the actors to play Harry Wharton in BILLY BUNTER OF GREYFRIARS SCHOOL. He also appeared in WHIRLIGIG and the 1955 adaptation of *Children of the New Forest* and went on, in the 1960s, to pop up in DR FINLAY'S CASEBOOK, playing Bruce Cameron. Valentine was TV's RAFFLES in the 1970s and had prominent roles in JUSTICE and the thriller series *Codename*. As Maurice, he was an occasional visitor to MINDER and, as Simon De Belleme, he was a mystic sorcerer in ROBIN OF SHERWOOD. He has been seen in numerous single dramas and other parts have been in series like DEPARTMENT S, THE AVENGERS, SPACE: 1999, HAMMER HOUSE OF HORROR, TALES OF THE UNEXPECTED, BERGERAC, MASADA (Merovius), THE CASEBOOK OF SHERLOCK HOLMES, LOVEJOY, THE HOUSE OF ELIOTT (Victor Stride), *Body and Soul* (Stan Beattie), JILLY COOPER'S RIDERS (Col Carter), WAKING THE DEAD, JUDGE JOHN DEED, THE COMMANDER, NEW TRICKS and AGATHA CHRISTIE'S POIROT. In complete contrast, he also once hosted STARS ON SUNDAY.

Van Der Valk ★★

UK (Thames/Euston Films/Elmgate) Police Drama. ITV 1972–3; 1977; 1991–2
DVD: Clear Vision Video

Piet Van der Valk	**Barry Foster**
Arlette Van der Valk	**Susan Travers**
	Joanna Dunham
	Meg Davies
Kroon	**Michael Latimer**
Samson	**Martin Wyldeck**
	Nigel Stock
	Ronald Hines
Wim Van der Valk	**Richard Huw**

Creator **Nicholas Freeling**
Executive Producers **Lloyd Shirley, George Taylor, Brian Walcroft**

Producers **Michael Chapman, Robert Love, Geoffrey Gilbert, Chris Burt**

● ***The investigations of a Dutch detective.***

Set against the cosmopolitan backdrop of Amsterdam, with its reputation for drugs and prostitution, this series explores the world of local CID officer, Van der Valk. The blond, curly haired, impulsive detective scours the canals and polders of the Dutch city in his search for common criminals and those involved in more subversive activity.

After an initial two-year run, the series was brought back in 1977 by Euston Films, with Joanna Dunham now in the part of Arlette, Van der Valk's wife, and Nigel Stock taking over as his boss, Samson. It was revived yet again in 1991, cashing in on the INSPECTOR MORSE, P. D. JAMES's Dalgliesh, INSPECTOR WEXFORD and TAGGART success stories. In this two-hour-format series, yet another actress, Meg Davies, comes in to play Arlette, Ronald Hines plays Samson and Van der Valk now also has a policeman son, Wim. Van der Valk himself, greying and still rather uncharismatic, has been promoted to Commissaris.

The character of Van der Valk was created by author Nicholas Freeling in 1962. The programme's catchy theme music, 'Eye Level' by the Simon Park Orchestra, surprisingly topped the British singles chart in 1973.

Van Dyke, Dick

(1925–)

American entertainer whose showbusiness ambitions seemed limited when he worked as an announcer for southern TV stations, having already failed to make the grade in a mime act. But, moving to New York, he gained a foothold on Broadway, guested in THE PHIL SILVERS SHOW and then launched his own sitcom, THE DICK VAN DYKE SHOW, in 1961. The series, in which he played writer Rob Petrie, brought him international fame and a host of Emmy awards. Van Dyke then looked for greater achievements in the movies, but his material, by common consent, was not the best and he returned to television. His later series (such as *The New Dick Van Dyke Show*, with Dick as talk-show host Dick Preston, and *The Van Dyke Show*, with Dick as ex-Broadway star Dick Burgess) did not prove particularly successful, however, and he was largely seen in specials and TV movies until fighting back as doctor-detective Mark Sloan in DIAGNOSIS MURDER, in 1993. His brother, Jerry Van Dyke, is also an actor.

Van Outen, Denise

(Denise Outen; 1974–)

Basildon-born actress/presenter of Dutch descent, a former member of the Those 2 Girls pop group, who made her name as host of THE BIG BREAKFAST, having previously been seen in the programme's weather helicopter. Earlier, she had fronted the kids' series *Massive* and *Scratchy & Co.*, and featured in the children's sitcom *Kappatoo*. She has since starred in BABES IN THE WOOD (Leigh), WHERE THE HEART IS (Kim Blakeney) and the TV pantomime *Jack and the Beanstalk* (Jill). Denise has also narrated *When Will I be Famous?* and presented shows like *Something for the Weekend, Prickly Heat, The Record of the Year, The 100 Greatest Musicals* and *Johnny & Denise – Passport to Paradise* (with Johnny Vaughan). Guest appearances have been in THE BILL and MURDER IN MIND.

Vanishing Man, The ★★

UK (ABTV/Harbour Pictures) Science Fiction Drama. ITV 1998

Nick Cameron	**Neil Morrissey**
Alice Grant	**Lucy Akehurst**
Joe Cameron	**Mark Womack**
Moreau	**John Castle**
Michelle Peters	**Sheila Ruskin**
Jacob	**Razaaq Aqdoti**
Dr Jeffries	**Jill Baker**

Creators **Linda Agran, Anthony Horowitz**
Writers **Anthony Horowitz, Tony Jordan, David Fox**
Producer **Linda Agran**

● ***A wrongly imprisoned man, trapped in invisibility, becomes an undercover agent.***

Nick Cameron is an air-freight pilot who is convicted for a crime he did not commit. In his frustration at his predicament, he volunteers to take part in a scientific trial (the Gyges experiment), not knowing that the end result is invisibility. Consequently, every time Cameron gets wet, he fades from view – very handy if you intend to be up to no good but, for Nick, a severe inconvenience. Still, it does mean that Cameron is now of value to the authorities. They undertake to search for a cure to his ailment if he agrees to do little surveillance jobs in return. As he can hardly refuse, the scene is set for investigations into blackmail, ghosts, thieves, etc. Using computer graphics to deal with the hero's unusual attributes, this six-part, tongue-in-cheek series is a homage to the 1950s classic THE INVISIBLE MAN. It followed a pilot episode in 1997 in which Miss Jeffries, the naughty doctor who put Cameron into this predicament, was played by Barbara Flynn, and Moreau, the man who assigns the missions, by James Laurenson.

Vanity Fair ★★★

UK (BBC) Drama. BBC 1 1998
DVD: BBC

Becky Sharp/Crawley	**Natasha Little**
Amelia Sedley	**Frances Grey**
Miss Pinkerton	**Pat Keen**
Jemima Pinkerton	**Charlotte West-Oram**
Mrs Sedley	**Michele Dotrice**
Mr Sedley	**David Ross**
Jos Sedley	**Jeremy Swift**
George Osborne	**Tom Ward**
William Dobbin	**Philip Glenister**
Sir Pitt Crawley	**David Bradley**
Lady Crawley	**Joanna Scanlan**
Capt. Rawdon Crawley	**Nathaniel Parker**
Miss Crawley	**Miriam Margolyes**
Mr Pitt Crawley	**Anton Lesser**
Mrs Bute Crawley	**Janine Duvitski**
Bute Crawley	**Stephen Frost**
Samuel	**Felix Dexter**
Mr John Osborne	**Tim Woodward**
Jane Osborne	**Abigail Thaw**
Raggles	**Bryan Pringle**
Miss Briggs	**Janet Dale**
Mrs O'Dowd	**Frances Tomelty**
Major/Col. O'Dowd	**Mark Lambert**
Lady Jane Crawley	**Sylvestra Le Touzel**
Lady Bareacres	**Eleanor Bron**
Lord Bareacres	**Graham Crowden**

Lady Blanche	**Sarah Crowden**
Gen. Tufto	**Windsor Davies**
Lord Steyne	**Gerard Murphy**
Lady Steyne	**Siân Thomas**

Writer **Andrew Davies**
Producer **Gillian McNeill**

A lowly orphan schemes her way into the heart of high society.

The time is the early 19th century. The Napoleonic Wars are raging across Europe but a new battle is about to begin in England. Becky Sharp, a parentless, half-French girl, seems to have little to look forward to in life except perhaps a position as someone's governess. However, she has other ideas. She knows what she wants – money, power, fun – and intends to get it. In contrast, her dutiful young companion, Amelia Sedley, who leaves Miss Pinkerton's young ladies' academy at the same time, is completely passive. Her drippy, indifferent take on life provides a counterpoint to Becky's blinkered, go-getter attitude. It is Amelia's fat brother who is first on Becky's hit list. He's no looker but he is very rich. Sadly, her plans are upset. The ambitious Miss Sharp does find a husband later, in the shape of Rawdon Crawley, whom she meets when she becomes a governess at Queen's Crawley, a decaying country house owned by the mean Sir Pitt Crawley and home also to his bossy sister, Miss Crawley. The action also switches to Brussels at the time of the Battle of Waterloo before retreating to England and then moving on to Germany, where Becky's story is concluded. Throughout, the anti-heroine Sharp portrays a distinct lack of compassion. She cheats, she lies, she breaks hearts and even despises her own son. Her saving grace is that at least she is honest about her scheming. Andrew Davies adapted William Thackeray's 1847–8 satirical portrait of contemporary society in six parts. Marc Munden directed. Previous dramatizations were in 1956–7 (BBC: Joyce Redman as Becky), 1967 (BBC 2: Susan Hampshire as Becky) and 1987 (BBC 1: Eve Matheson as Becky).

Varney, Reg

(1916–)

London-born comic actor, initially working as a teenage singer and ragtime pianist in workingmen's clubs. He moved on to the music halls and, after the war, teamed up with Benny Hill, who acted as Reg's stooge. It wasn't until the turn of the 1960s that Varney began to make television inroads. He was cast as Reg, the foreman, in the very popular sitcom THE RAG TRADE, and followed it up with a children's series, *The Valiant Varneys*. He also starred in BEGGAR MY NEIGHBOUR in 1967, playing Harry Butt, before, in 1969, ON THE BUSES arrived. Hugely successful, it ran for four years and even had three film spin-offs. It was very much Varney's series, and his clippie-chasing Stan Butler character was always at the centre of the action. When *On the Buses* ended, Varney was given his own showcase programmes on ITV and starred in yet another sitcom, but *Down the Gate*, featuring Reg as fishmarket porter Reg Furnell, proved to be short lived. As a result of his working on stage elsewhere in the world, and convalescing after heart problems, UK viewers have seen little of Reg Varney in recent years.

Vaughan, Johnny

(1966–)

London-born comedian, DJ and presenter of light entertainment programmes, particularly *The Fall Guy*, *Here's Johnny*, *Moviewatch*, *The Johnny Vaughan Film Show* and THE BIG BREAKFAST (forming a successful on-screen partnership with Denise Van Outen in the last). Vaughan has also hosted *The Brit Awards* and fronted a number of celebrity interview specials, most notably with the stars of FRIENDS in *The One Where Johnny Makes Friends*. In 2001 he co-wrote and starred in the sitcom 'ORRIBLE, playing petty crook Paul Clark. Vaughan also scripted the comedy-drama *Dead Casual*, and in 2003, through his chat show, *Johnny Vaughan Tonight*, he was handed the honour of opening up the new digital channel BBC 3. Later credits have included hosting THE SUPERSTARS, *Johnny & Denise – Passport to Paradise* (again with Van Outen) and *Space Cadets*.

Vaughan, Norman

(1927–2002)

Liverpudlian entertainer who made his name as compere of SUNDAY NIGHT AT THE LONDON PALLADIUM in 1962. Vaughan, then a comparative unknown, had previously worked as a host of stage shows and had first been seen on TV in 1954, later appearing in *The Harry Secombe Show* and with Terry Scott in *Scott Free*. However, by the time his three-year spell at the Palladium ended, he was one of Britain's brightest stars. Along the way, he conjured up the thumbs-up, thumbs-down catchphrases of 'Swinging' and 'Dodgy'. Another catchphrase was 'Roses grow on you', taken from his commercials for chocolates. He was given his own series by both ITV (*A Touch of the Norman Vaughans*) and the BBC (*The Norman Vaughan Show*). In 1972, he took over from Bob Monkhouse as host of THE GOLDEN SHOT, but stayed with the programme for only one year. He hadn't finished with game shows, though, as he went on to co-devise BULLSEYE for Central Television. Working more on stage as an actor, Vaughan's later TV appearances were mostly in panel games and variety shows, although he did compere *Pebble Mill Showcase* in 1978.

Vaughan, Peter

(Peter Ohm; 1923–)

Silver-haired, Shropshire-born actor, one of whose best-remembered creations was that of pampered prison baron, 'Genial' Harry Grout, in PORRIDGE. He followed this with another sitcom success as Charlie Johnson, Wolfie's prospective father-in-law and class enemy in CITIZEN SMITH. However, Vaughan's TV career stretches back to the 1950s. One of his first starring roles was in the newspaper drama DEADLINE MIDNIGHT (Joe Dunn). He took the lead in 1969's THE GOLD ROBBERS (Det. Chief Supt. Cradock) and also starred as Billy Fox in the 1980 series FOX. He was David Kimber-Hutchinson in GAME, SET AND MATCH, Thomas Franklyn in CHANCER, Tom Hincks in *Dandelion Dead*, Frank Ashworth in *The Choir*, Delaney in *Oliver's Travels*, Gabriel Betteredge in *The Moonstone* and Alzheimer's victim Felix Hutchinson in OUR FRIENDS IN THE NORTH. More recently, he played George Graham in LONGITUDE, Ray Skinner in *The Thing about Vince . . .*, Sonny in *Face*, Michael Colchester in *The Jury*, Robbins in *Beauty* and Widdicombe in MALICE AFORETHOUGHT. Guest spots have included roles in OUR MAN FROM ST MARK'S, HORNBLOWER, SECOND SIGHT, CASUALTY, HEARTBEAT, IN DEEP,

MARGERY AND GLADYS, and SWEET MEDICINE. Vaughan has also been seen in mini-series and adaptations of the classics (Bill Sikes in the 1962 version of *Oliver Twist*, Long John Silver in a 1968 presentation of *Treasure Island*, Tulkinghorn in BLEAK HOUSE, Mr Boffin in OUR MUTUAL FRIEND and Sir Ensor Doone in *Lorna Doone*, for instance). Both his wives have been actresses: Billie Whitelaw and Lillias Walker.

Vaughn, Robert

(1932–)

One of TV's international stars of the 1960s, Robert Vaughn was Napoleon Solo, THE MAN FROM U.N.C.L.E. He remained a man undercover in the 1970s, when he returned to our screens as Harry Rule in THE PROTECTORS. Vaughn's first appearances came in the 1950s, when he took minor roles in series like DRAGNET, and his first prime-time lead arrived in 1963 in a US drama called *The Lieutenant*. For most of the 1970s, Vaughn was cast in TV movies and glossy mini-series, and he continued to be active in the cinema (he had been one of *The Magnificent Seven* back in 1960). He played Chief of Staff Frank Flaherty in WASHINGTON: BEHIND CLOSED DOORS in 1978 and resurfaced in 1986 to take the role of General Hunt Stockwell in THE A-TEAM. In the 1990s, he hosted the spoof adventure series *Danger Theatre* and featured in the TV series version of *The Magnificent Seven* (Judge Orin Travis). Of late, Vaughn has been seen in HUSTLE, playing con man Albert Stroller.

VCR

See *Videotape*.

Vega$ ✶✶

US (Spelling-Cramer) Detective Drama. ITV 1978–81
(US: ABC 1978–81)

Dan Tanna	**Robert Urich**
Philip Roth	**Tony Curtis**
Bobby Borso ('Binzer')	**Bart Braverman**
Beatrice Travis	**Phyllis Davis**
Angie Turner	**Judy Landers**
Sgt Bella Archer	**Naomi Stevens**
Lt. David Nelson	**Greg Morris**
Chief Harlon Two Leaf	**Will Sampson**

Creator **Michael Mann**
Executive Producers **Aaron Spelling, Douglas S. Cramer**

A private eye is hired by a Vegas casino baron.

Dan Tanna is a rebellious private investigator who plies his trade in the gaming rooms and bars of Las Vegas, when not cruising the Strip in a 1957 red Thunderbird convertible. He is employed by Philip Roth, a gambling magnate and owner of a number of Vegas hotels, at one of which – the Desert Inn – Tanna keeps an office. Though Roth – or 'Slick', as Tanna dubs him – is only occasionally seen, Tanna is often in the company of Binzer, a clumsy reformed crook, and two show girls who help him out: Angie is a rather dim receptionist and Beatrice a brighter secretary. Sgt Archer and later Lt. Nelson are Tanna's contacts with the Vegas police, and Chief Two Leaf is Dan's Native American buddy. Creator Michael Mann later scored a much bigger hit with MIAMI VICE.

Vegas, Johnny

(Michael Pennington; 1971–)

St Helens-born comedian and actor, a regular guest on panel games like SHOOTING STARS. Vegas was once a ceramics student and his early stage shows included a potter's wheel segment. He has since moved on to appear in dramas like *Staying Up*, TIPPING THE VELVET (Gully Sutherland), BLEAK HOUSE (Krook) and *A Midsummer Night's Dream* (Bottom), plus the comedies HAPPINESS (Charlie), DEAD MAN WEDS (Lewis Donat) and *Ideal* (Moz). He has also fronted his own series, *Johnny Vegas: 18 Stone of Idiot*.

Vernon, Richard

(1925–97)

Reading-born actor, often cast in upright, slightly aristocratic roles. One of his best remembered was as Oldenshaw in THE MAN IN ROOM 17 and THE FELLOWS, in the mid-1960s. Vernon also starred in THE DUCHESS OF DUKE STREET (Major Smith-Barton), EDWARD THE SEVENTH (Lord Salisbury), THE SANDBAGGERS ('C'), *A Gentlemen's Club* (George), L FOR LESTER (bank manager Mr Davies), LEAVING (Mr Chessington), ROLL OVER BEETHOVEN (crusty dad Oliver Purcell), THE HITCHHIKER'S GUIDE TO THE GALAXY (Slartibartfast), PARADISE POSTPONED (Sir Nicholas Fanner), THE BORROWERS (Mr Pott) and *Class Act* (Sir Horace Mainwaring). Other credits included Dick Emery's *Legacy of Murder*, *Something in Disguise*, YES, MINISTER, *Return of the Antelope* and numerous single dramas, including SUEZ 1956 (Harold Macmillan).

Vertue, Beryl

OBE

British independent producer who began her career as a theatrical agent, representing top comedians and comic writers including Spike Milligan, Eric Sykes, Johnny Speight, Frankie Howerd, Tony Hancock, and Galton and Simpson. In 1960 Beryl Vertue formed her own company, Associated London Films, which was to specialize in feature-film versions of top sitcoms like TILL DEATH US DO PART and STEPTOE AND SON. The company was merged into the Robert Stigwood Group in 1968 and Vertue, as a director, began making films and TV series for the USA, including *Beacon Hill* (an UPSTAIRS, DOWNSTAIRS clone), and the UK, including *The Prime of Miss Jean Brodie*. She also led the way in selling basic TV formats internationally, allowing an American version of *Steptoe and Son* to be made as *Sanford and Son*, and *Till Death Us Do Part* as ALL IN THE FAMILY. Vertue formed Hartswood Films in the 1980s, generating hit comedies like MEN BEHAVING BADLY, IS IT LEGAL?, MY GOOD FRIEND, BORDER CAFÉ, *Wonderful You*, COUPLING, THE SAVAGES, and CARRIE AND BARRY, plus dramas like *Codename Kyril*, *A Woman's Guide to Adultery* and *The English Wife*, and also documentaries such as *The War behind the Wire* and *The Welsh Great Escape*. Her producer daughter, Sue Vertue, is married to writer Steven Moffat.

Very Big Very Soon ✶✶

UK (Central) Situation Comedy. ITV 1991

Harry James	**Paul Shane**
Beattie	**Kate David**
Ernie Chester	**Tim Wylton**

Avril .... **Sheila White**
Matthew Kite .... **Andrew Maclean**
Vic .... **Shaun Curry**

Writer **Daniel Peacock**
Producer **Glen Cardno**

● ***An unreliable agent tries to find work for his troupe of no-hopers.***

'Very big, very soon': the sort of promise that seedy theatrical agents like Harry James always make to their prospective clients. Seldom, however, does such a prophecy prove accurate, and never in Harry's case. It's not surprising, though, when you consider the band of losers he tries to find work for on the northern clubs circuit. But Harry does try – with a ventriloquist, a memory man, and even his oldest client, Ernie Chester, a faded stand-up-comic-cum-bingo-caller – but the only person interested most of the time is the taxman. Matthew is another of Harry's hopefuls, Beattie is Harry's assistant and Vic is the guy who runs the local café. Although an obvious extension to Paul Shane's Ted Bovis character from HI-DE-HI!, *Very Big Very Soon* was nowhere near as successful and ran to only six episodes.

Very British Coup, A ★★★

UK (Skreba Films/Channel 4) Drama. Channel 4 1988
DVD: Quantum Leap Group

Harry Perkins .... **Ray McAnally**
Joan Cook .... **Marjorie Yates**
Newsome .... **Jim Carter**
Lawrence Wainwright .... **Geoffrey Beevers**
Andrews .... **Roger Brierley**
Sampson .... **Hugh Martin**
Fred Thompson .... **Keith Allen**
Horace Tweed .... **Oliver Ford Davies**
Insp. Page .... **Bernard Kay**
Sir Percy Browne .... **Alan MacNaughtan**
Fiennes .... **Tim McInnerny**
Liz Fain .... **Christine Kavanagh**
Sir James Robertson .... **David McKail**
US Secretary of State Morgan .... **Shane Rimmer**
Chambers .... **Erin Donovan**
Sir George Fison .... **Philip Madoc**
Reg Smith .... **Berwick Kaler**
Mr Patel .... **Harmage Singh Kalirai**
Lord Fain .... **Preston Lockwood**
Sir Montague Kowalsky .... **Oscar Quitak**
Helen Jarvis .... **Kika Markham**

Writer **Alan Plater**
Producers **Ann Skinner, Sally Hibbin**

● ***A Sheffield socialist becomes an embattled prime minister.***

Harry Perkins is a man of the people: a born-and-bred steelworker turned politician. As Labour member for a Sheffield constituency, he has worked his way up the ladder to become party leader. He is then overwhelmingly elected prime minister, much to the consternation of shady civil service figures who proceed to use covert means to destabilize his administration. The drama's title refers to this subtle attempt at revolution on the part of the Establishment, the press and even the USA. With a run on the pound and union unrest to contend with, too, Perkins needs every ounce of his unorthodox battling spirit, and the help of his press officer, Fred Thompson, to keep control of affairs. Other key figures include home secretary Joan Cook, head of the Secret Service Sir Percy Browne, secret-service operative Fiennes, newspaper baron Sir George Fison, and CIA agent Chambers. The three-part drama was based on the novel of the same name by Chris Mullin, who had been elected Labour MP for Sunderland a year before the serial was aired. Mick Jackson directed and music was by John Keane.

Very Merry Widow, The ★★

UK (BBC) Situation Comedy. BBC 1 1967–9

Jacqueline Villiers .... **Moira Lister**
Jennifer Villiers .... **Sally Thomsett**
Freddie Phillipson .... **Donald Hewlett**
Mrs Frayle .... **Molly Urquhart**
François .... **Georges Lambert**
Roger .... **Jimmy Thompson**
Francis .... **Jeffrey Gardiner**
Nicholas Parsons

Writer **Alan Melville**
Producers **Graeme Muir, Robin Nash, John Howard Davies**

● ***A glamorous young widow is determined to create a new life for herself.***

Poor Jacqui Villiers. Recently widowed and left £22,000 in debt by her sweet-talking husband, Charles (who died in a sailing accident off Cape Finisterre), she really ought to be distraught. But, on the contrary, Jacqui is glad to see the back of her womanizing, untrustworthy spouse and is happy to square up to the challenges presented by his abrupt departure. Firstly, she wants to keep her teenage daughter, Jennifer, at her good school; secondly, she is determined not to give up her fashionable flat in London's Charleston Mews. So out Jacqui goes to work, trying a succession of jobs that usually end in disaster – anything from running a meals-on-wheels service and selling china in Petticoat Lane, to acting and becoming a paid companion to an ageing dowager in the south of France. She also takes in a lodger, Freddie Phillipson. However, after two series of such fiascos, Jacqui changes tack, leaves her home and begins work as a researcher for *How* magazine, a consumer journal that calls on her to investigate such varied issues as London Transport, prams, slimming products and greasy spoon cafés. Her bosses at the magazine are Roger and Francis (the latter played mostly by Nicholas Parsons but for one initial episode by Jeffrey Gardiner). This third and final series aired under the title *The Very Merry Widow and How*.

Very Peculiar Practice, A ★★★★

UK (BBC) Comedy Drama. BBC 2 1986; 1988
DVD: Network

Dr Stephen Daker .... **Peter Davison**
Dr Bob Buzzard .... **David Troughton**
Dr Jock McCannon .... **Graham Crowden**
Dr Rose Marie .... **Barbara Flynn**
Lyn Turtle .... **Amanda Hillwood**
Chen Sung Yau .... **Takashi Kawahara**
Maureen Cahagan .... **Lindy Whiteford**
Mrs Carmen Kramer .... **Gillian Rainer**
Ernest Hemmingway .... **John Bird**
Dorothy Hampton .... **Frances White**
Dr Grete Grotowska .... **Joanna Kanska**
Jack B. Daniels .... **Michael J. Shannon**
Julie Daniels .... **Toria Fuller**

Sammy Limb .... **Dominic Arnold**
Prof. George Bunn .... **James Grout**
Nuns .... **Sonia Hart**
Elaine Turrell

Creator/Writer **Andrew Davies**
Producer **Ken Riddington**

Surreal tales of life at an ailing university medical practice.

Keen, idealistic, rather neurotic young doctor Stephen Daker is in for a rude awakening on his arrival at Lowlands University. Accepting a position in the medical centre, in the hope of starting a new life after a messy marital break-up in Walsall, he discovers anarchy and moral decline all around him and chiefly among his professional colleagues. His genial but boozy boss, Jock McCannon, has hopelessly lost control of the practice and spends most of his time dictating his forthcoming book, *The Sick University*. This leaves room for the cynical and amoral Bob Buzzard to introduce dubious money-making schemes and for the devious arch-feminist Dr Rose Marie (who believes that illness is something men inflict on women) to scheme against the male species. Daker at least finds humanity in the form of chirpy police student Lyn Turtle, and his Burmese mathematician flatmate, Chen Sung Yau.

In the second series, when Lyn has departed, prickly Pole Grete Grotowska, an art historian, becomes Daker's new girlfriend. At this time, sinister forces are on the move at Lowlands. An unscrupulous new American vice-chancellor (Jack B. Daniels) has been appointed and right-wing market forces are taking over. Throughout both series, two mysterious, silent nuns flit around the campus, rummaging in waste-bins, doing quirky things and generally becoming the programme's trademark. Elkie Brooks sang the theme song, which was written by Dave Greenslade.

In 1992 Andrew Davies followed up *A Very Peculiar Practice* with a *Screen One* presentation entitled *A Very Polish Practice*. Set in Warsaw amid decaying Communism and advancing capitalism, it features Stephen, Grete (now his wife) and Bob Buzzard, who is in town on a business trip and hoping, as ever, to make a fast buck.

VH1

See *MTV*.

VHS

Video cassette format established by JVC in Japan in 1976 and now the standard for domestic users. It was initially challenged in the marketplace by Sony's Betamax system, launched a year earlier, which some claimed provided a better image. However, although both systems use 1/2-inch-wide tape inside the cassette, the VHS tape recorded and played back longer and gradually saw off its rival. VHS stands for Video Home System.

Viacom

Major international media group whose television interests now include America's MTV channels (including VH1), Nickelodeon, Country Music Television, TV Land and Comedy Central. The company was formed in 1971 as an offshoot of CBS, dealing in programme syndication. CBS became part of the Viacom group in 2000, but was de-merged as CBS Corporation at the end of 2005.

Vicar of Dibley, The ★★★

UK (Tiger Aspect) Situation Comedy. BBC 1 1994; 1996–2000; 2004–5
DVD: Universal/Vision Video

Geraldine Granger .... **Dawn French**
David Horton .... **Gary Waldhorn**
Hugo Horton .... **James Fleet**
Alice Tinker/Horton .... **Emma Chambers**
Letitia Cropley .... **Liz Smith**
Frank Pickle .... **John Bluthal**
Jim Trott .... **Trevor Peacock**
Owen Newitt .... **Roger Lloyd Pack**
Simon Horton .... **Clive Mantle**

Writers **Richard Curtis, Paul Mayhew-Archer**
Producers **Jon Plowman, Sue Vertue, Margot Gavan Duffy, Phillipa Catt**

A new female vicar adds zest to life in a sleepy village.

When Pottle, the ancient vicar of St Barnabas in the rural village of Dibley, finally passes on, there is much speculation about his successor. What the villagers don't expect is a woman. The arrival of Geraldine Granger certainly raises a few eyebrows, especially those of the local squire, David Horton, who sets his face against her from the start. It isn't just that she is female, she has these crazy liberal values, too, not to mention a radical, almost flippant, approach to Christianity. A more favourable response comes from David's dozy son, Hugo, and the girl (later wife) he has his eye on, drippy, naïve, ultra-dim verger Alice Tinker – clearly a product of local inbreeding. The other villagers are also positive about the change: boring Frank Pickle, who goes on to stun the community by revealing his homosexuality; lavatorial farmer Owen Newitt; sexually liberated, stuttering pensioner Jim Trott ('No, no, no, no, no . . . yes'); and organist/flower arranger Letitia Cropley, who 'treats' the parish council meetings to her finest culinary creations, such as a cake iced with Marmite, before dying one Easter.

Geraldine herself is what she might call a small-time sinner – sex and chocolate her major vices – but by the time she is actually contemplating a move to a new parish (to chase after David's hunky brother, Simon), she has even won over Horton. Her boundless energy and novel ideas have not only encouraged larger congregations but fostered a new spirit in the village. A trademark of each episode is a post-credits ending in which Geraldine tries to explain a smutty joke to Alice, always without success.

When *The Vicar of Dibley* returned after nearly five years at Christmas/New Year 2004/2005, it was to celebrate Geraldine's tenth year in the inbreds' village. The New Year's Day episode, however, had a genuine surprise in store for viewers when it closed with a heart-rending, real-life scene of deprivation in Africa and the Dibley regulars showing their support for Third World relief by wearing white armbands.

Vice, The ★★★

UK (Carlton) Police Drama. ITV 1999–2003
DVD: Network

Insp. Pat Chappel .... **Ken Stott**
Dr Christina Weir .... **Anna Chancellor**
PC Cheryl Hutchins .... **Caroline Catz**
Sgt/Insp. Joe Robinson .... **David Harewood**
PC Dougie Raymond .... **Marc Warren**

Supt. Jeff Callard .... **Garry Cooper**
DI Greer .... **Valerie Edmond**
Shirley Robinson .... **Diane Parish**
PC Kirsty Morgan .... **Rosie Marcel**
DS/DCI Frank Vickers .... **Tim Pigott-Smith**
Jane .... **Sarah Parish**
Supt. Archer .... **Christopher Villiers**
PC Adam Parkes .... **Mel Raido**
PC Lorraine Johnstone .... **Tamzin Malleson**
Sgt Stuart Cole .... **Jake Nightingale**

Creators **Barry Simner, Rob Pursey**
Executive Producer **Rob Pursey**
Producer **Stephen Smallwood**

The grim and seedy world of a vice officer with a heavy heart.

Pat Chappel is an important member of the Metropolitan Police's vice squad. It is a position he has held for many years and the burden of his experience has begun to take its toll. Deeply committed to his work, he has little in the way of a personal life. With the exception of company from police psychiatrist Christina Weir (a married woman) and certain former prostitutes he has helped, the highlights of his evenings off are takeaway meals eaten from the carton. This said, it is a wonder that Chappel has any appetite at all after what he witnesses during a typical working day. Chappel's beat consists of illicit London sex and gambling dens, and the cruelty and depravity he encounters inevitably weighs heavily on his shoulders. Helping him battle the endless parade of pimps, rent boys, pornographers and worse is a small team of brave undercover officers, notably Joe Robinson and Cheryl Hutchins. The perils of being distracted by the 'glamour' surrounding them are starkly laid out in the disgrace that befalls another colleague, Dougie Raymond.

Glossily filmed, and sometimes very difficult to view, *The Vice* and the haunted presence of its thoroughly decent lead character make no bones about the iniquity of the sex trade. Rock band Portishead provides the theme music. Five series were produced, with Chappel bowing out in the final run, his grim work finally getting the better of him. He is replaced by obnoxious and duplicitous Frank Vickers as head of the team, with Robinson promoted to inspector to carry out the nauseating investigations.

Vickerage, Lesley

(1961–)

London-born actress seen in major roles in dramas and comedies like BETWEEN THE LINES (Jenny Dean), SOLDIER, SOLDIER (Kate Butler), ROGER ROGER (Chrissie), MY GOOD FRIEND (Ellie), *Get Real* (Francine), GRAFTERS (Viv Casey), *The Bench* (Katharine Tyrell) and THE INSPECTOR LYNLEY MYSTERIES (Helen Clyde). Guest roles have come in INSPECTOR MORSE, THE BILL, BUGS, MIDSOMER MURDERS, BADGER, SECOND SIGHT, *Spine Chillers*, P. D. JAMES and SEA OF SOULS.

Victory at Sea ★★★

US (NBC/Project 20) Documentary. BBC 1952–3 (US: NBC 1952–3)
DVD: Oracle Home Entertainment

Narrator **Leonard Graves**

Producer **Henry Saloman**

American history of World War II sea battles.

Introduced for British audiences by Michael Lewis, Professor of History at the Royal Naval College in Greenwich, this ground-breaking documentary examined the maritime context of the war effort. Using combat footage (from both sides of the conflict) in 26 parts, it discussed key events like the bombing of Pearl Harbor. The production team worked closely with the US Navy, and Richard Rodgers provided a rousing musical score. The series' award-winning status ensured plenty of reruns in the early 1950s.

Video Tape

Video Tape Recording or VTR – a means of translating television signals on to magnetic tape, for future playback – was first pioneered in the early 1950s, but the technology was primitive and the resolution poor. It wasn't until the Ampex Corporation launched a completely new system in 1956 that the industry began to take it seriously. Colour versions arrived two years later and the Ampex system remained in international use until the late 1970s, by which time simpler, cheaper and better-quality reel-to-reel systems had been introduced. Professionally, 2-inch and 1-inch Quad tape systems have been in use, though ¾-inch U-matic, ½-inch VHS and Betamax, and ¼-inch Quartercam have also been employed (the smaller tapes mostly by amateurs). Cassette-based systems (Video Cassette Recorders, or VCRs) are now commonplace and have provided more flexibility in news gathering. They have also enabled domestic viewers to enjoy record and playback facilities, of course. Sony's Video 8 (8 mm. tape) and its high-resolution sister, Hi-8, are popular with camcorder users.

Video Wall

A bank of television monitors, each showing different images or each contributing one part to a larger image.

View from Daniel Pike, The ★★

UK (BBC) Detective Drama. BBC 2 1971–3

Daniel Pike .... **Roddy McMillan**
Sam Sweet .... **Beth Robens**
Paperboy .... **David Gallacher**
Tarquin Halford .... **Robert Docherty**
Lady Halford .... **Lennox Milne**
DC Sanderson .... **James Cosmo**

Creator **Edward Boyd**
Producers **Anthony Coburn, Keith Williams**

A canny private detective works the Glaswegian underworld.

The View from Daniel Pike was based on a play called *Good Morning, Yesterday!*, shown as part of the *Menace* anthology in 1970. In this, Roddy McMillan played a character called Dan Britt who was trying to unravel a 15-year-old murder mystery. With a small name change, the same tough-nut Scottish detective returns in two mean and moody series to investigate murders, missing people, unpaid debts and suchlike dirty deeds in the grimy backwaters of Glasgow. An accompanying novel by Edward Boyd and Bill Knox was published by Arrow Books.

Vincent ★★★

UK (Granada) Detective Drama. ITV 1 2005–

Vincent Gallagher	**Ray Winstone**
Beth	**Suranne Jones**
Cathy	**Eva Pope**
DCI David Driscoll	**Philip Glenister**
Robert	**Joe Absolom**
John	**Ian Puleston-Davies**
Gillian	**Angel Coulby**
Lynn	**Lisa Millett**
Chris	**Jonathan Guy Lewis**

Creator/Writer **Stephen Butchard**
Producers **Rebecca Hodgson, John Rushton**

● ***A moody private detective is married to his work.***

Vincent Gallagher is a man dedicated to his job. He used to be a detective sergeant; now he's a private eye and has assembled a small team of assistants to help him with the cases he undertakes. Primarily, there's his business partner, Beth, mother of a seven-year-old boy who lives with his dad in America. She takes it upon herself to keep Vincent under control and also to prove her worth as an investigator in her own right. Vincent's right-hand man is John. He's the one who does all the bugging and the candid camerawork. Learning the ropes is young Robert, but he's also the team's techie. Gillian is the agency's receptionist. Although he's no longer in the force, Vincent leans heavily on it – or rather on his brother-in-law, Chris, a copper – for inside information. Meanwhile, Chris's wife, Lynn, is determined to find her brother a new woman to keep him out of trouble, after his true love, Cathy, left him because of his devotion to duty. She now lives with DCI Driscoll, the policeman Vincent loves to hate.

Just four episodes were broadcast in 2005, but a second series was commissioned even before filming of the first had been completed.

Vine, David

(1936–)

British sports frontman, a newspaper journalist who entered television with Westward TV but joined the BBC in 1966. He has focused largely on skiing (as host of *Ski Sunday*), show-jumping and snooker, but has been involved with most sports and most BBC sports programmes. He was the first questionmaster of A QUESTION OF SPORT (following on from hosting QUIZ BALL), and has introduced THE SUPERSTARS, IT'S A KNOCKOUT, MISS WORLD and the EUROVISION SONG CONTEST.

Vine, Jeremy

(1965–)

Surrey-born journalist and presenter of current affairs and other programmes, most notably NEWSNIGHT, *Jeremy Vine Meets . . .* , *Page Turners* and *The Politics Show*. He has also narrated *Time Machine*. Earlier in his career he was a BBC political correspondent and, later, the corporation's Africa correspondent. Comedian Tim Vine is his brother.

Virgin of the Secret Service ★★

UK (ATV) Spy Drama. ITV 1968

Capt. Robert Virgin	**Clinton Greyn**
Mrs Virginia Cortez	**Veronica Strong**
Doublett	**John Cater**
Karl Von Brauner	**Alexander Doré**
Klaus Striebeck	**Peter Swannick**
Col. Shaw-Camberley	**Noel Coleman**

Creator **Ted Willis**
Producer **Josephine Douglas**

● ***The dangerous assignments of a patriotic British agent in the early 1900s.***

Intrepid Captain Robert Virgin more than works for the British secret service: he lives and breathes to defend British honour at a time when the Empire is beginning to crumble. From the North-west Frontier of India to all parts of the Middle and Far East, and even South America, Virgin fights for his country, obeying the orders of his superior, Colonel Shaw-Camberley, protecting his lady assistant, Mrs Cortez, and physically fending off his ruthless opponents, Karl Von Brauner and Klaus Striebeck. Doublett is his loyal batman.

Virginian, The/The Men from Shiloh ★★★

US (Universal) Western. BBC 1 1964–73 (US: NBC 1962–71)

The Virginian	**James Drury**
Judge Henry Gath	**Lee J. Cobb**
Trampas	**Doug McClure**
Steve Hill	**Gary Clarke**
Molly Wood	**Pippa Scott**
Betsy Garth	**Roberta Shore**
Randy Garth	**Randy Boone**
Sheriff Brannon	**Harlan Wade**
Deputy Emmett Ryker	**Clu Gulager**
Belden	**L. Q. Jones**
Jennifer	**Diane Roter**
Starr	**John Dehner**
John Grainger	**Charles Bickford**
Stacy Grainger	**Don Quine**
Elizabeth Grainger	**Sara Lane**
Sheriff Abbott	**Ross Elliott**
Clay Grainger	**John McIntire**
Holly Grainger	**Jeanette Nolan**
David Sutton	**David Hartman**
Jim Horn	**Tim Matheson**
Col. Alan MacKenzie	**Stewart Granger** *(Shiloh)*
Roy Tate	**Lee Majors** *(Shiloh)*
Parker	**John McLiam** *(Shiloh)*

Executive Producer **Norman MacDonnell**
Producers **Howard Christie, Paul Freeman, Jim McAdams**

● ***An eastern ranch foreman brings new methods to a western cattle farm.***

This cowboy series is set on the Shiloh Ranch in Medicine Bow, Wyoming Territory. At the thick of the action is the ranch foreman, known only as 'The Virginian'. Little else is ever revealed about this mystery man of few words but, stern, level-headed and imbued with a strong sense of justice, he is a respected figurehead for the local community. His presence at Shiloh reflects how eastern influence and modern thinking spread across America in the 1880s, eroding primitive western ways.

The ranch is owned initially by Judge Garth, then by brothers John and Clay Grainger, and finally by Englishman Colonel McKenzie (by which time the era has moved on to the 1890s and the programme retitled *The Men from Shiloh*). On the range Trampas is The Virginian's impulsive young friend, one of a supporting cast of family members, ranch-hands and assorted lawmen. Many top stars are introduced in one-off supporting roles – Bette Davis, Ryan O'Neal, George C. Scott, Charles Bronson, Telly Savalas and Lee Marvin, to name but a handful – and, as in WAGON TRAIN, stories tend to focus on these visitors, rather than on the rather aloof members of the regular cast.

The Virginian was TV's first feature-length Western series, presenting virtually a movie a week. It was loosely based on the turn-of-the-century book of the same name by Owen Wister, which had also been covered three times for the cinema, most notably starring Gary Cooper in 1929.

Vision Mixer

The name given to the equipment that enables its operator (also known as a vision mixer) to select, mix, cut and fade different camera shots (or introduce visual effects) during recording or transmission on the instructions of the director.

Vision On **

UK (BBC) Children's Entertainment. BBC 1964–76

Presenters **Pat Keysell, Tony Hart, Larry Parker, Ben Benison, Wilf Lunn, Sylvester McCoy, David Cleveland**

Producers **Ursula Eason, Leonard Chase, Patrick Dowling**

● ***Juvenile entertainment accessible to youngsters with hearing impediments.***

Vision On was the more politically correct follow-up to a programme baldly entitled *For Deaf Children*, which had begun in 1952. Aiming to cater for children with hearing difficulties as well as those with adequate hearing, *Vision On* was, as its name suggested, a visual extravaganza. Arty features by Tony Hart, a former graphic artist, dominated the show and one regular feature was 'The Gallery', displaying drawings sent in by young viewers. There were also crazy inventions to look at, lots of sight gags and sketches, plus the misadventures of pipe-cleaner men Phil O'Pat and Pat O'Phil. Co-host Pat Keysell signed for those who could not hear and, in the first series, there was also an emphasis on lip-reading. From the second series, however, words became increasingly irrelevant, and the programme had little verbal content beyond a courteous hello and goodbye each week. However, lively music and weird and wonderful sounds remained important to the make-up as the producers recognized that deaf people could pick up vibrations and appreciate the feel of the programme in this way.

When *Vision On* ended in 1976, it was succeeded by a more obvious art programme, again hosted by Tony Hart and entitled *Take Hart* (1977–83), which itself was superseded by *Hartbeat* (1984–93). It was in *Take Hart* that the popular plasticine creature named Morph (created by Aardman Animations, future producers of the WALLACE & GROMIT films) made his debut.

Vital Spark, The

See *Para Handy – Master Mariner*.

Volume

The intensity of sound reproduction and the control on the receiver to adjust this.

Vorderman, Carol

MBE (1960–)

Brainy British presenter, coming to the fore as a number-crunching hostess on COUNTDOWN in 1982 but since seen on a variety of science-based or educational programmes, including HOW 2, NOTES AND QUERIES WITH CLIVE ANDERSON and TOMORROW'S WORLD. Her many other credits include *The Wide Awake Club, Entertainment Today, Out of This World, Put It to the Test, The Antiques Inspectors, Mysteries with Carol Vorderman*, THE NATIONAL LOTTERY LIVE, *Computers Don't Bite, Testing ... Testing, Hot Gadgets*, POINTS OF VIEW, *What Will They Think of Next?, Carol Vorderman's Better Homes, Dream House, Find a Fortune, Tested to Destruction, Britain's Brainiest, Soap Star Lives* and *The Golden Lot*, plus coverage of the World Chess Championship.

Vote, Vote, Vote for Nigel Barton

See *Stand Up, Nigel Barton*.

Vox Pop

The views of people in the street when stopped by a reporter, which are then edited into a sequence for use in current affairs or magazine programmes.

Voyage to the Bottom of the Sea **

US (Twentieth Century-Fox/Irwin Allen) Science Fiction. ITV 1964–6 (US: ABC 1964–8)

Admiral Harriman Nelson	**Richard Basehart**
Commander/Capt. Lee Crane	**David Hedison**
Lt. Commander Chip Morton	**Robert Dowdell**
CPO Curley Jones	**Henry Kulky**
CPO Francis Sharkey	**Terry Becker**
Stu Riley	**Allan Hunt**
Kowalsky	**Del Monroe**
Crewman Sparks	**Arch Whiting**
Crewman Patterson	**Paul Trinka**
Doctor	**Richard Bull**

Creator/Executive Producer **Irwin Allen**

● ***The crew of a super-submarine take on threats to the world.***

The *Seaview* is the world's most advanced nuclear submarine, created by its commander, Retired Admiral Harriman Nelson, and housed in a pen 200 feet down at his Nelson Institute of Marine Research, at Santa Barbara, California. Six hundred feet long, the supersub can dive deeper (4,450 feet) and travel faster (70 knots) than any of its rivals, and is equipped with all the latest devices, including atomic torpedoes. It carries a separate mini-sub, a diving bell, a snowcat and an innovative 'flying fish', a small vessel capable of both water and air travel.

The action is set 13 years in the future and, although their role is meant to be research, Nelson and his crew are constantly called upon to maintain peace below the waves, by thwarting aggressors, whether human, fish or alien. After a reasonably serious beginning, the storylines soon plummet to ridiculous depths. One of the most memorable villains is Professor Multiple, played by Vincent Price, who tries to take over the *Seaview* using life-like puppets. In addition, the ship confronts all manner of outrageous monsters from the deep: werewolves, enemy orchids, giant jellyfish, supersquids, even Nazis. One adventure takes place inside a whale. Valiantly assisting Nelson in his protection of our planet are the youngest submarine captain ever, Captain Lee Crane, and fellow officers Chip Morton, Francis Sharkey and Curley Jones.

The show was created by low-budget sci-fi specialist Irwin Allen (LOST IN SPACE, LAND OF THE GIANTS, etc.), and was spun off his 1961 cinema version starring Walter Pidgeon. Much of the film footage was reused in the TV series, and the sub itself was also a relic of the movie.

VTR

See *Videotape*.

Wacky Races ★★

US (Hanna-Barbera/Heatter-Quigley) Cartoon. BBC 1 1969–70 (US: CBS 1968–70)

Voices:

Dick Dastardly	**Paul Winchell**
Muttley	**Don Messick**
Peter Perfect	**Daws Butler**
Penelope Pitstop	**Janet Waldo**
Luke and Blubber Bear	**John Stephenson**
Rufus Ruffcut	**Daws Butler**
Rock and Gravel Slag	**Daws Butler**
Prof. Pat Pending	**Don Messick**
The General	**John Stephenson**
Clyde	**Paul Winchell**
Sgt Blast	**Daws Butler**
Pte Pinkley	**Paul Winchell**
Red Max	**Daws Butler**
The Ant Hill Mob	**Mel Blanc**
Big Gruesome	**Daws Butler**
Little Gruesome	**Don Messick**
Sawtooth	**Don Messick**
Ring a Ding Convert-a-Car	**Don Messick**
Narrator	**Dave Willock**

Creators/Executive Producers **William Hanna, Joseph Barbera**

Animated series of hair-raising contests between eccentric drivers and their weird vehicles.

Based loosely on the film *The Great Race, Wacky Races* draws together America's finest drivers, each behind the wheel of the strangest speed machines. In each episode, the 11 daredevil teams line up for a cross-country race, eager to claim the title of 'The World's Wackiest Racer'. In car No. 1, the Boulder Mobile, are the cavemen Slag brothers, Rock and Gravel, and they are joined on the starting grid by the Gruesome Twosome in the Creepy Coupé (No. 2); inventor Professor Pat Pending in his Ring-a-Ding Convert-a-Car (3); the Red Max in the Crimson Haybailer (4); girl racer Penelope Pitstop in the Compact Pussycat (5); the General, Sgt Blast and Private Pinkley in the Army Surplus Special (6); gangster Clyde and The Ant Hill Mob in the Bulletproof Bomb (7); Luke and Blubber Bear in the Arkansas Chugabug (8); the all-American Peter Perfect in his Turbo Terrific (9); and Rufus Ruffcut and Sawtooth in the Buzz Wagon (10). Villain of the piece is the appropriately named Dick Dastardly in the Mean Machine (00), whose sole aim is to win at all costs, especially if it means cheating. Thankfully, usually through the ineptitude of his sniggering dog sidekick, Muttley, Dastardly's attempts to impede his rivals always backfire.

The series, one of the most popular cartoons to come out of the prolific Hanna-Barbera studio, gave birth to two spin-offs, *The Perils of Penelope Pitstop* and *Dastardly and Muttley in their Flying Machines*, a clone of *Those Magnificent Men in Their Flying Machines*, in which Dastardly's hopeless Vulture Squadron tries in vain to stop Yankee Doodle Pigeon. 'Drat and triple drat,' Dastardly exclaims.

Wagner, Lindsay

(1949–)

TV's BIONIC WOMAN (Jaime Sommers), Lindsay Wagner's road to fame began with modelling and rock singing in the 1960s. Turning to acting, she appeared in shows like THE ROCKFORD FILES and MARCUS WELBY, MD, but her break came with an episode of THE SIX MILLION DOLLAR MAN, in which she played the girlfriend of bionic man Steve Austin. Despite the fact that she died in the episode, the producers liked her so much they spun her off into her own bionic series. Her later work has included US prime-time dramas *Jessie* and *A Peaceable Kingdom*, plus plenty of TV movies and mini-series.

Wagner, Robert

(1930–)

American actor who first came to light in the cinema in the 1950s. A decade later, movie work not proving so fruitful, Wagner moved into television, starring in the adventure series IT TAKES A THIEF, playing Alexander Mundy. He crossed the Atlantic to take the part of Flt Lt. Phil Carrington in COLDITZ but then returned to Hollywood to star in *Switch*. In 1979 he began possibly his most successful role, that of millionaire adventurer Jonathan Hart in HART TO HART. His most notable series since has been the drama series *Lime Street* (1985), which ran to only five episodes as a result of the death of one of his co-stars, Samantha Smith (the schoolgirl who had gained global fame by writing to Soviet leader Yuri Andropov to ask for peace). In recent times, Wagner has largely been seen in TV movies and glossy dramas. His wife – on two occasions – was the late Natalie Wood.

Wagon Train ★★★

US (Revue/Universal) Western. ITV 1958–62/BBC 1962–3 (US: NBC 1957–62; ABC 1962–5)

Major Seth Adams	**Ward Bond**
Flint McCullough	**Robert Horton**
Charlie Wooster	**Frank McGrath**
Bill Hawks	**Terry Wilson**
Christopher Hale	**John McIntire**
Duke Shannon	**Scott Miller**
Cooper Smith	**Robert Fuller**
Barnaby West	**Michael Burns**

Producer **Howard Christie**

The adventures of a wagon train as it crosses the West in the 1880s.

This wagon train, although studio-bound in reality, supposedly runs from St Joseph ('St Joe') in Missouri to California, echoing the hazardous journey across the plains and the Rocky Mountains endured by many 19th-century settlers. The train's leader is middle-aged father figure Major Seth Adams, who gives way to Chris Hale (when actor Ward Bond died in 1960). Ensuring that Indians do not impede progress is frontier scout Flint McCullough, later replaced by Duke Shannon and Cooper Smith. Other regulars are lead wagon driver Bill Hawks and cook Charlie Wooster. A 13-year-old orphan, Barnaby West, found wandering the trail alone, also joins the train.

In many ways, the regular cast merely provides the backdrop, for, while they sometimes have their own tale to tell, most of the action is introduced by travellers who come and go, briefly joining the train and then heading off again. They bring with them hopes and experiences, but usually trouble, ensuring a different story every week. Many episodes are simply known as *The ... Story*, with the name of the guest character filling the gap. John Wayne, James Coburn, Ernest Borgnine, Shelley Winters, Jane Wyman, Lee Van Cleef, Lou Costello, Bette Davis, Mickey Rooney and Ronald Reagan are all among the big names taking on these roles. *Wagon Train* also tries its hand at the classics, with a couple of episodes devoted to what are effectively revamps of *Great Expectations* and *Pride and Prejudice*.

The series, based on the 1950 John Ford movie *Wagonmaster* (in which Ward Bond had appeared, although not in the same role), was one of those oddity programmes that switched channels in the UK (from ITV to BBC) during its first showing. Most episodes were an hour long, but some feature-length films were also made. Actor Robert Horton left the show in 1962, allegedly fed up with Westerns. However, his next starring role came in another oater, A MAN CALLED SHENANDOAH, and co-star John McIntire also held on to his spurs, moving on next to THE VIRGINIAN.

Wait till Your Father Gets Home ✶✶

US (Hanna-Barbera) Cartoon. ITV 1973–5 (US: Syndicated 1972–4)

Voices:

Harry Boyle .... **Tom Bosley**
Irma Boyle .... **Joan Gerber**
Alice Boyle .... **Kristina Holland**
Chet Boyle .... **David Hayward**
Jamie Boyle .... **Jackie Haley**
Ralph .... **Jack Burns**

Executive Producers **William Hanna, Joseph Barbera**

● ***An all-American dad wages a generation-gap war with his kids.***

Wait Till Your Father Gets Home was ALL IN THE FAMILY in cartoon form, and an early inspiration for KING OF THE HILL. Harry Boyle is the Archie Bunker character. Harry is head of the Boyle Restaurant Supply Company, but when he returns home from work he is nettled by the easy morals of his daughter, Alice, and the pinko tendencies of his hippie son, Chet. Luckily, third child Jamie is on dad's side, as is fellow conservative neighbour Ralph (who marshals his family in readiness for the Communist invasion). In the middle sits Harry's long-suffering wife, Irma.

Waiting for God ✶✶

UK (BBC) Situation Comedy. BBC 1 1990–4

Diana Trent .... **Stephanie Cole**
Tom Ballard .... **Graham Crowden**
Harvey Bains .... **Daniel Hill**
Jane Edwards .... **Janine Duvitski**
Geoffrey Ballard .... **Andrew Tourell**
Marion Ballard .... **Sandy Payne**
Jenny .... **Dawn Hope**
Basil Makepeace .... **Michael Bilton**
Davey .... **Ross Thompson**
Jamie Edwards .... **Paddy Ward**
Revd Dennis Sparrow .... **Tim Preece**

Creator/Writer **Michael Aitkens**
Producer **Gareth Gwenlan**

● ***Two stroppy inmates keep the staff of an old folks' home on their toes.***

Tom Ballard and Diana Trent are neighbours at the Bayview Retirement Home in Bournemouth. Tom, a former accountant, is dumped in the home by his thoughtless son, Geoffrey, and grasping daughter-in-law, Marion, in the series' first episode, but remains philosophical about it all. His natural cheer, his eccentric sense of humour and his flair for adventure remain undiminished. He pairs up, to form a formidable, subversive geriatric duo, with the next-door resident, retired photo-journalist Diana Trent, for whom 'trout' would be a more appropriate surname. Domineering and dismissive, acid-tongued Diana had largely given up on enjoyment before Tom's arrival, but now they lead the home's cynical manager, Harvey Bains, and his fawning, drippy assistant, Jane Edwards, a merry dance. They scupper all Harvey's cost-cutting measures with threats of bad publicity and goad their fellow residents into demanding more from life. When finances become tight, Diana is forced to move in with Tom, but she fights tooth and nail against marriage. Also seen are Jenny, the good-natured waitress, OAP colleagues like Basil, Davey and Jamie, and, later, spaced-out vicar Dennis Sparrow.

Waking the Dead ✶✶✶

UK (BBC) Police Drama. BBC 1 2000–

DCI Peter Boyd .... **Trevor Eve**
Dr Grace Foley .... **Sue Johnston**
DC Amelia 'Mel' Silver .... **Claire Goose**
Dr Frankie Wharton .... **Holly Aird**
DS Spencer Jordan .... **Wil Johnson**
DAC Ralph Christie .... **Simon Kunz**
Felix Gibson .... **Esther Hall**
DC Stella Goodman .... **Félicité du Jeu**

Executive Producer **Mal Young**
Producers **Deborah Jones, Joy Spink, Victoria Fea, Richard Burrell**

● ***A team of experts tackles unsolved cases in police files.***

DCI Peter Boyd is head of the new Cold Case Squad, set up to investigate the Metropolitan Police's backlog of unresolved crimes. The belief behind the 12-month experiment is that new developments and the latest technology will provide a breakthrough where previous investigations have failed. The smartly presented Boyd is a quiet but firm leader, somewhat haunted by the mistakes of his past. Joining him in the new team, which is housed in a converted warehouse containing all the relevant crime archives, is Dr Grace Foley, a criminal psychologist employed to piece together personality profiles. Alongside them are plain-speaking pathologist Dr Frankie Wharton, and their regular police supporters, naïve Mel Silver and headstrong Spencer Jordan. As the series progresses, the team become increasingly integrated and we learn more about their pasts (if not their home lives), until one of their number is brutally murdered at the end of series four. For series five, there are two replacement members of the crew: new forensic pathologist Felix Gibson and fast-track DC Stella Goodman.

A mix of CRACKER and SILENT WITNESS, *Waking the Dead* is

occasionally gruesome and disturbing viewing, with stories broken over two episodes. Some have aired under BBC 1's *Crime Doubles* umbrella.

Walden, Brian

(1932–)

Brian Walden took over as host of the political programme WEEKEND WORLD in 1977 and gained a reputation as a relentless interviewer. He eventually relinquished the hot seat to Matthew Parris nine years later but, when the programme ended in 1988, he returned to interrogate parliamentarians in *The Walden Interview* (later retitled simply *Walden*). In the 1990s, he presented two series of unscripted, one-take lectures, *Walden on Heroes* and *Walden on Villains*. Prior to TV, he had been Labour MP for Birmingham All Saints and Birmingham Ladywood (1964–77). He is the father of actor Ben Walden.

Wales West and North

(WWN)

The short-lived ITV contractor for West and North Wales (TWW held South Wales) which came on air on 14 September 1962 but went out of business, because of low advertising revenue, on 26 January 1964. WWN was the only ITV franchise-holder to go broke. Appreciating that the transmission area was too small to support an independent station, the ITA amalgamated it into the South Wales and West of England ITV region, allowing TWW to expand its coverage across the whole of the Principality.

Walk On By: the Story of Popular Song ★★★

UK (BBC) Documentary. BBC 2 2001

Narrator **Clive Owen**

Executive Producer **Michael Poole**
Producer **Alan Lewens**

● ***The 20th century's greatest hits explored.***
Employing archive footage, interviews with experts and quotes from those involved (where possible), this eight-part retrospective charts the development of the popular song from its beginnings in the ghettos of New York City. It was here that the immigrants from Russia, Italy, Ireland and elsewhere ended up, bringing their musical heritage that somehow blended together to spark the rise of composers such as Gershwin and Berlin and the birth of the Broadway musical. The journey continues via the jazz age to rock 'n' roll and beyond: new writing partnerships of the 1960s like Bacharach and David and Goffin and King; The Beatles and their aftermath; the psychedelic and country rock eras; movie soundtracks; and finally an overview of the last three decades, from glam rock to Britney Spears by way of production line pop.

Walker, Clint

(Norman Eugene Walker; 1927–)

Massive American actor who became an overnight success in 1955 when cast as the mysterious wanderer CHEYENNE. Contractual wrangles led to his walking out for a while (Ty Hardin was introduced as Bronco Layne to fill the gap in production), but Walker eventually returned to the series. When his contract ended in 1962, he spent most of his time away from show business, making just a handful of cameo appearances. He made a comeback in the 1970s, but without much success. His TV movies were not particularly well received and a new prime-time drama, *Kodiak*, didn't make the grade.

Walker, Murray

OBE (1923–)

Veteran motor-racing commentator, for both BBC and ITV. The son of racer/commentator Graham Walker, he followed his father into broadcasting in 1949 and they worked together for 13 years. Like David Coleman, Walker is famous for his much-loved, over-excited commentaries and clangers such as 'Do my eyes deceive me or is Senna's Lotus sounding a bit rough', 'The boot is on the other Schumacher' and 'You can cut the tension with a cricket stump'. Walker retired from broadcasting at the end of the 2001 Formula 1 season.

Walker, Roy

(1940–)

Northern Irish entertainer, first seen on NEW FACES in 1977 and then as one of THE COMEDIANS, before hosting the guessing game CATCHPHRASE. He has also had his own series, *Licensed for Singing and Dancing*, and compered *Summertime Special*. His son Mark is also a TV presenter/musician.

Walking With Dinosaurs ★★★

UK (BBC) Natural History. BBC 1 1999

Narrator **Kenneth Branagh**

Executive Producer **John Lynch**
Producers **Tim Haines, Jasper James**

● ***Dinosaurs live, thanks to the latest computer software.***
Dinosaurs ruled the Earth for 170 million years and, through state-of-the-art computer animation, they are brought back to life and given the BBC natural history treatment in this six-part series. Generating images of the mighty beasts as they roam against the sort of backdrop that might have existed all those millennia ago (filmed in places as far afield as New Zealand and Chile), the series also uses large, hand-held animatronic heads for close-ups of feeding and interaction. Dinosaurs on land, in the sea and in the air are featured, covering their physiology, feeding habits, hunting regime, etc., starting 220 million years BC and ending some 65 million years ago with the end of the dinosaur dynasty. Three years in the making, the series cost around £6 million. At Christmas 2000, BBC 1 screened two *Walking With Dinosaurs* specials: *The Ballad of Big Al* and *Big Al Uncovered*, inspired by the discovery in Wyoming in 1991 of a fossilized skeleton of a 30-foot-long allosaurus. A follow-up series, *Walking With Beasts* (BBC 1 2001), from the same production team, looks at the amazing creatures that assumed control of the planet after the demise of the dinosaurs. This was followed in 2003 by *Walking With Cavemen*, presented by Professor Robert Winston.

Wall, Max

(Maxwell Lorimer; 1908–90)

British comedian, famed for his silly walks, pained expressions and ridiculous black tights and big boots. After years on the stage and in radio, Wall was given his own television show in the 1950s and continued to make guest appearances on variety shows in the following decades. He played Tommy Tonsley in the 1978 sitcom *Born and Bred*, and also made cameo appearances in CORONATION STREET (Harry Payne, a friend of Elsie Tanner), EMMERDALE FARM (Arthur Braithwaite), CROSSROADS (Walter Soper, a cousin of Arthur Brownlow), MINDER (Ernie Dodds, a jailbird) and the kids' series DANGER – MARMALADE AT WORK (a judge).

Wallace & Gromit ★★★★

UK (Aardman/Wallace & Gromit/BBC) Animation. Channel 4 1990; BBC 2 1993; 1995

Wallace .... **Peter Sallis** *(voice only)*

Writers **Nick Park, Bob Baker**
Producers **Christopher Moll, Michael Rose**

● ***An inventor and his dog tumble into a series of adventures.***

The multi-award-winning escapades of Wallace, a northern inventor with a lust for cheese, and his eccentric dog, Gromit, began in 1990 with the film *A Grand Day Out*. In this, the 'Claymation' models, animated into a 25-minute feature, decide that an appropriate destination for their annual picnic is the moon, where there is cheese a-plenty. After a tussle with an obstructive robot caretaker (an old cooker), the duo return to Earth to entertain us another day. That came in 1993 with the screening of *The Wrong Trousers*, in which a pair of automated trousers disturbs their domestic harmony at 62 West Wallaby Street, especially when a criminal-minded penguin named Feathers McGraw becomes their lodger and decides to use the trousers in one of his 'jobs'. The third outing for Wallace and Gromit came in *A Close Shave* in 1995, in which Wallace falls in love with a lady named Wendolene (voiced by Anne Reid), who runs a wool shop and has a dog named Preston. There is a devious plot afoot to rustle sheep and create a wool shortage (a disaster for keen knitter Gromit) and our heroes are assisted in their efforts to restore normality by a courageous sheep named Shaun. With regular reruns, the Plasticine duo became standard bank holiday fare in the 1990s. In 2005, man and dog turned to the cinema with a feature-length movie entitled *Wallace & Gromit and the Curse of Were-rabbit*.

Director Nick Park's previous success had come with *Creature Comforts*, part of the *Lip Synch* series (Channel 4 1990), which animated a collection of clay animals to soundbites from everyday people – a sort of zoological vox pop that was developed for a series of energy commercials. Aardman Animations, the production company, had previously created Morph for VISION ON.

Walliams, David

(1971–)

Best-known as one half of the LITTLE BRITAIN team, Surrey-born David Walliams has appeared with his co-star in that series, Matt Lucas, on more than one occasion. Together they wrote and performed *Rock Profiles*, *Sir Bernard's Stately Homes* and *Mash and Peas* for satellite TV. Earlier, Walliams was seen in Sky's computer games show *Games World*. Other comedy roles have been in SPACED, *Barking*, BLACK BOOKS, CRUISE OF THE GODS (Lurky), *The All Star Comedy Show*, FRENCH AND SAUNDERS, and LOOK AROUND YOU, among other series. Walliams has also made his mark as a straight actor, with appearances in ATTACHMENTS (Jake Plaskow), RANDALL AND HOPKIRK (DECEASED), TED AND ALICE (Shane), THE BILL, EASTENDERS, CASUALTY, HUSTLE, AGATHA CHRISTIE'S MARPLE, WAKING THE DEAD and *High Stakes* (Stephen Clay).

Walsh, Bradley

(1960–)

Watford-born comedian turned actor. A former Pontin's Blue Coat entertainer and a professional footballer with Brentford FC, Walsh initially appeared in numerous TV variety shows as a fast-talking stand-up comic. He also presented WHEEL OF FORTUNE and THE NATIONAL LOTTERY LIVE, plus *Sports Addicts* for Challenge TV, before turning to drama with *Lock, Stock . . .*, *The Thing about Vince*, *Night and Day* (Woody), *MIT* and *Murder City*, and then taking the role of Danny Baldwin in CORONATION STREET. Walsh has also stood in as a guest presenter of *Today with Des and Mel*.

Walter, Harriet

CBE (1950–)

British Shakespearean actress seen in such series as A DOROTHY L. SAYERS MYSTERY (Harriet Vane) and the Channel 4 kidnap thriller, *The Price* (Frances Carr), plus the play *Amy*, in which she starred as aviator Amy Johnson. More prominently, Walter played Charity Walton in the steamy academic serial, THE MEN'S ROOM, Giulia Lazzari in ASHENDEN, Rachel in a BBC Schools version of *Hard Times*, Amy in the sitcom *Unfinished Business*, Mildred in A DANCE TO THE MUSIC OF TIME, Felicity Normal in *Norman Ormal: a Very Political Turtle*, and the title role in *George Eliot: a Scandalous Life*. She was also Virginia Woolf in *London* and Professor Robb in MESSIAH, and featured in *Frankenstein: Birth of a Monster*, with guest roles coming in series like INSPECTOR MORSE, DALZIEL AND PASCOE, WAKING THE DEAD, *My Uncle Silas*, SPOOKS, MIDSOMER MURDERS, NEW TRICKS and AGATHA CHRISTIE'S MARPLE.

Walters, Julie

OBE (1950–)

Acclaimed British actress, known for her versatility. She appeared with Victoria Wood in *Wood and Walters*, and the two have worked together many times, in plays like *Talent*, the series *Victoria Wood – As Seen on TV* (charlady Mrs Overall in the CROSSROADS spoof *Acorn Antiques*) and *Victoria Wood*, and TV films like *Pat and Margaret*. Walters appeared in BOYS FROM THE BLACKSTUFF, played Pauline Mole (Adrian's young mum) in THE SECRET DIARY OF ADRIAN MOLE and Mrs Murray (Robert Lindsay's pensioner mum) in GBH. She also delivered some of Alan Bennett's TALKING HEADS monologues, starred in her own special, *Julie Walters and Friends*, and took the parts of Diana Longden and Alice in *Screen One's Wide-Eyed and Legless* and *Bambino Mio*, respectively; publican Maureen Hardcastle in the feature-length comedy *Brazen Hussies*; Julie Diadoni in *Jake's Progress*; Paula in *Melissa*; Petula, Bren's mother, in DINNERLADIES; Mrs Mann in OLIVER TWIST; both the girl and her grandmother in *Roald Dahl's Little Red Riding Hood*; Sheila Fitzpatrick in *My Beautiful Son*; and Angela

Maurer in *Murder*. More recently, she has been seen as Beth in CANTERBURY TALES, Lizzie Hunt in *The Return* and Marie Stubbs in *Ahead of the Class*.

Walton, Kent

(Kenneth Walton; 1917–2003)

Canadian sports commentator, for years ITV's voice of wrestling on Saturday afternoons, also contributing to THE INDOOR LEAGUE. In the late 1950s, however, Walton worked in a quite different field, that of pop music, as host of the teenage music show COOL FOR CATS, and DJ with Radio Luxembourg.

Waltons, The ★★★

US (Lorimar) Drama. BBC 2 1974–82 (US: CBS 1972–81)

John Walton	**Ralph Waite**
Olivia Walton	**Michael Learned**
Zeb (Grandpa) Walton	**Will Geer**
Esther (Grandma) Walton	**Ellen Corby**
John Boy Walton	**Richard Thomas**
	Robert Wightman
Mary Ellen Walton/Willard	**Judy Norton-Taylor**
Jason Walton	**Jon Walmsley**
Erin Walton	**Mary Elizabeth McDonough**
James Robert 'Jim-Bob' Walton	**David W. Harper**
Ben Walton	**Eric Scott**
Elizabeth Walton	**Kami Cotler**
Ike Godsey	**Joe Conley**
Corabeth Godsey	**Ronnie Claire Edwards**
Aimee Godsey	**Rachel Longaker**
Sheriff Ep Bridges	**John Crawford**
Mamie Baldwin	**Helen Kleeb**
Emily Baldwin	**Mary Jackson**
Verdie Foster	**Lynn Hamilton**
Revd Matthew Fordwick	**John Ritter**
Emily Hunter/Fordwick	**Mariclare Costello**
Yancy Tucker	**Robert Donner**
Flossie Brimmer	**Nora Marlowe**
Maude Gormsley	**Merie Earle**
Dr Curtis Willard	**Tom Bower**
Revd Hank Buchanan	**Peter Fox**
J. D. Pickett	**Lewis Arquette**
John Curtis Willard	**Marshall and Michael Reed**
Rose Burton	**Peggy Rea**
Serena Burton	**Martha Nix**
Jeffrey Burton	**Keith Mitchell**
Cindy Brunson/Walton	**Leslie Winston**
Toni Hazleton	**Lisa Harrison**
Arlington Wescott Jones ('Jonesy')	**Richard Gilliland**
Narrator	**Earl Hamner Jr**

Executive Producers **Lee Rich, Earl Hamner Jr**

Sentimental tales of a Virginian family during the Depression and World War II.

The Walton family live in the town of Walton's Mountain, in the Blue Ridge Mountains of Jefferson County, Virginia. Mom and Dad are Olivia and John, she a caring, devoted mother, he a solid father figure and part-owner of the family's sawmill, with Grandpa Walton.

The Waltons have seven children, plus a dog named Reckless. The eldest is John Boy, a fresh-faced youth with writing ambitions. He majors in English at Boatwright University, starts a local newspaper, *The Blue Ridge Chronicle*, has a novel published which takes him to New York, then works as a war correspondent during the hostilities. Next in line is Mary Ellen, who becomes a nurse, marries Dr Curtis Willard, gives birth to little John Curtis and then sees her husband die at Pearl Harbor (or so it is thought). When he resurfaces in Florida, he decides not to return to Virginia, leaving Mary Ellen with the new man in her life, a fellow pre-med student named Jonesy. The Waltons' other sons are Jim-Bob, Jason and Ben, and the two youngest daughters are Elizabeth and Erin. They don't play such prominent roles but are always on hand to help out during family crises, of which there are plenty.

Grandma is taken ill, then Grandpa dies (actor Will Geer passed away between seasons). Olivia suffers an attack of tuberculosis and is sent away to recuperate in a sanitarium, with her place as housekeeper given to her cousin, Rose. Then the war arrives and sees the boys taken off with the armed forces, leaving the sawmill short-staffed and forced into temporary closure. Meanwhile the other townsfolk also have their ups and downs. Most prominent are storekeeper Ike Godsey and his prim wife, Corabeth; the vicar, Reverend Fordwick, who marries schoolteacher Emily Hunter; and two fading spinster sisters, Mamie and Emily Baldwin.

The Waltons shuns sex and violence for human tragedy and family drama. It shows the children growing up and getting married, follows domestic upheaval after domestic upheaval, and portrays a good-natured family struggling to survive in one of America's poorest areas at a time of great deprivation. All stories are told through the moist eyes of John Boy.

The series was created by Earl Hamner Jr, who also acts as narrator. The stories were based on his own life, which had first been dramatized in a 1963 Henry Fonda film, *Spencer's Mountain. The Waltons* (which began as a TV movie called *The Homecoming*) was so squeaky-clean and wholesome that it attracted much parody, particularly for its closing sequence when the family, tucked up in bed, all called 'Goodnight' to each other as the household lights were dimmed one by one. After the series ended, three TV movie specials were produced to update events in Walton's Mountain.

Wanamaker, Zoë

CBE (Hon.) (1949–)

American-born actress, daughter of US actor/director Sam Wanamaker. She has been seen in EDGE OF DARKNESS (Clemmy), PARADISE POSTPONED (Charlotte Fanner), PRIME SUSPECT (Morya Henson), *Screen Two's Memento Mori* (Olive Mannering), *The Blackheath Poisonings* (Charlotte Collard), the *Performance* presentation of *The Widowing of Mrs Holroyd* (title character), *The English Wife* (Madame Griveau), A DANCE TO THE MUSIC OF TIME (Audrey Maclintick), DAVID COPPERFIELD (Miss Murdstone), GORMENGHAST (Clarice), *Johnny and the Bomb* (Mrs Tachyon) and other dramas, plus the sitcoms MY FAMILY (Susan Harper) and ADRIAN MOLE: THE CAPPUCCINO YEARS (Tania Braithwaite). Smaller roles and guest credits have come in JENNIE, LADY RANDOLPH CHURCHILL, TALES OF THE UNEXPECTED, INSPECTOR MORSE, AGATHA CHRISTIE'S MARPLE, DOCTOR WHO and AGATHA CHRISTIE'S POIROT. She has also narrated series like *Life Before Birth* and *Someone to Watch Over Me*. However, it was as Tessa Piggott alongside Adam Faith in LOVE HURTS that she became widely known. Wanamaker is married to actor Gawn Grainger.

War and Peace ✶✶

UK (BBC) Drama. BBC 2 1972–3
DVD: DD Home Entertainment

Count Rostov	**Rupert Davies**
Countess Rostova	**Faith Brook**
Natasha	**Morag Hood**
Nikolai	**Sylvester Morand**
Petya	**Barnaby Shaw**
	Rufus Frampton
Sonya	**Joanna David**
Pierre	**Anthony Hopkins**
Anatole Kuragin	**Colin Baker**
Vera	**Patricia Shakesby**
Boris Drubetskoy	**Neil Stacy**
Prince Vasili Kuragin	**Basil Henson**
Princess Lisa Bolkonskya	**Alison Frazer**
Princess Drubetskoya	**Anne Blake**
Prince Andrei Bolkonsky	**Alan Dobie**
Dolohov	**Donald Burton**
Princess Maria Bolkonskya	**Angela Down**
Prince Bolkonsky	**Anthony Jacobs**
Anna Scherer	**Barbara Young**
Madame Scherer	**Edith Sharpe**
Hélène Kuragina	**Fiona Gaunt**
Napoleon	**David Swift**
Kutuzov	**Frank Middlemass**
Denisov	**Gary Watson**
Prokofy	**Edmund Bailey**
Mlle Bourienne	**Athene Fielding**
Tsar Alexander	**Donald Douglas**
Marshal Berthier	**John Breslin**
Marshal Davout	**Tony Steedman**
Nikolenka	**Toby Bridge**
	Christopher Moran
Platon Karatayev	**Harry Locke**

Writer **Jack Pulman**
Producer **David Conroy**

● ***Complex dramatization of Tolstoy's epic masterpiece.***
Sprawling over 20 episodes and taking nearly two years to make, *War and Peace* begins in Moscow in 1805 with the rather chaotic Rostov family planning to celebrate the name-day of both Countess Rostova and her 13-year-old daughter, Natalia, nicknamed Natasha. One guest at the dinner, Pierre, the illegitimate son of the important Count Bezuhov, is called away to be at his deathbed. Pierre's best friend is the headstrong Prince Andrei Bolkonsky and, supported by a host of lesser characters, it is the lives of Natasha, Pierre and Andrei that take centre stage as the story unfolds. All the while, an unavoidable counterpoint to the personal dramas is Napoleon's invasion of Russia and the cruelty and bloodshed it brings. As the series progresses events move on some 20 years, with love, tragedy, triumph and disaster marching arm in arm with the leading figures, and war taking its grim toll on families and friends.

The drama was directed by John Howard Davies and filmed mostly in Yugoslavia, with interiors at BBC Television Centre. A special *Radio Times* illustrated guide to *War and Peace* was issued to accompany the production.

War and Peace had previously been adapted as a one-off play for television by Robert David MacDonald, for Granada (ITV 1963: Kenneth Griffith as Napoleon).

War and Remembrance

See *Winds of War, The.*

War Game, The ✶✶✶

UK (BBC) Drama. BBC 1 1985

Writer/Producer **Peter Watkins**

● ***Graphic portrayal of nuclear destruction.***
One of the BBC's most controversial projects, *The War Game* depicts in harrowing images the aftermath of an imaginary nuclear attack on the UK. Initially showing civilians preparing for the onslaught, the 50-minute film then reveals in stark black-and-white footage the horrors of the resulting chaos.

The War Game was made in drama-documentary style as a film for MONITOR in 1965 and producer Peter Watkins employed mostly non-professional actors to add to the realism. However, the overall effect was so startling and distressing that Director-General Sir Hugh Greene banned its transmission, fearing it would alarm or confuse the old and fretful in society. Although it was released for cinema showings, it was not televised until 20 years later, when it was screened as part of the BBC's 40th-anniversary commemoration of the bombing of Hiroshima.

War in the Air ✶✶

UK (BBC) Documentary. BBC 1954–5

Narrator **Robert Harris**

Writer/Producer **John Elliot**

● ***Analysis of the role of aircraft in combat.***
With Sir Philip Joubert as series adviser, *War in the Air* was a 15-part retrospective on the role played by air power before, during and immediately after World War II. The half-hour programmes, directed by Philip Dorté, were made in collaboration with the Air Ministry. Sir Arthur Bliss composed the theme music, which was performed by the London Symphony Orchestra under Muir Mathieson.

Ward, The

See *Children's Ward.*

Waring, Eddie

MBE (1910–86)

For many years Eddie Waring was the voice of rugby league on the BBC, and his excitable commentaries were as much a part of the entertainment as the match itself. His northern accent, novel approach and well-oiled catchphrases like 'early bath' and 'up and under' readily exposed him to the impressionists of the day. Waring gave his first TV commentary in 1946, having previously managed both Dewsbury and Leeds rugby league clubs. Additionally, he was one of the presenters of IT'S A KNOCKOUT and *Jeux Sans Frontières* (usually taking charge of the Mini-Marathon). Always game for a laugh, Eddie was also seen as a guest in THE GOODIES and *The Morecambe and Wise Show*. At one time, in complete contrast, he hosted SONGS OF PRAISE. He retired in 1981.

Waring, Richard

(Brian Barton-Chapple; 1925–94)

British comedy writer majoring on domestic sitcoms. Among his contributions were LIFE WITH THE LYONS, *On the Bright Side*, *The Eggheads*, MARRIAGE LINES, *The World of Wooster*, NOT IN FRONT OF THE CHILDREN, *Ukridge*, BACHELOR FATHER, AND MOTHER MAKES THREE/FIVE, MY WIFE NEXT DOOR, *Second Time Around*, THE MANY WIVES OF PATRICK, *My Honourable Mrs*, MISS JONES AND SON, RINGS ON THEIR FINGERS, *Partners* and TEARS BEFORE BEDTIME. Waring provided some early scripts for Richard Hearne, Charlie Drake and Tommy Cooper, wrote episodes of DIXON OF DOCK GREEN and was also seen as an actor. He played Henry Blagrove alongside Richard Briers in the 1962 comedy BROTHERS IN LAW (some episodes as writer as well), and was seen in SIX FACES OF JIM and EDWARD AND MRS SIMPSON, among other programmes. He was the brother of actor Derek Waring.

Wark, Kirsty

(1955–)

Kilmarnock-born journalist and current affairs presenter, a regular anchor of NEWSNIGHT and also host of *The Late Show*, *One Foot in the Past* and *Rough Justice*, as well as a political show for Scotland. She set up her own production company, Wark Clements, with her husband, Alan Clements. This is now part of IWC Media, formed from a merger in 2004 with Ideal World, a company run by fellow presenter Muriel Gray and her husband, Hamish Barbour.

Warner, Jack

OBE (Horace John Waters; 1896–1981)

As totally reliable copper George Dixon in DIXON OF DOCK GREEN, Jack Warner became a national institution. Born in London's East End, Warner, the brother of radio and stage entertainers Elsie and Doris Waters (otherwise known as Gert and Daisy), followed his sisters into showbusiness. He won fame on radio, 'Mind my bike' becoming his catchphrase in *Garrison Theatre* during the war, and he also played Joe Huggett, head of the Huggett family, in a series of films and radio programmes. In 1949 Warner played PC Dixon in the film *The Blue Lamp* and was shockingly shot dead. However, the character struck a chord with cinema audiences, and prolific writer Ted Willis was encouraged by the BBC to furnish Dixon with his own TV series. *Dixon of Dock Green* started in 1955 and ran for 21 years. Apart from occasional variety appearances, and the linkman's job on the BBC's CHRISTMAS NIGHT WITH THE STARS package, it was Warner's only major TV role. He was 80 when it ended.

Warriors ★★★

UK (BBC) Drama. BBC 1 1999

Pte Alan James	**Matthew Macfadyen**
Pte Peter Skeet	**Darren Morfitt**
Sgt Andre Sochanik	**Cal Macaninch**
Lt. John Feeley	**Ioan Gruffudd**
Lt. Neil Loughrey	**Damian Lewis**
Cpl Gary Sprague	**Joe Renton**
Pte 'Tommo' Redmond	**Steve Chaplin**
Minka	**Sheyla Shehovich**
Aida	**Jasmina Sijercic**
Capt. Richard Gurney	**Tom Ward**
Lt. Jonathan Engel	**Ifan Meredith**
Rik Langrubber	**Carsten Voigt**
Major 'Brick' Stone	**Simon Shepherd**
Pte John Hookway	**Shaun Dooley**
Pte Martin Rook	**Greg Chisholm**
Emma	**Jodhi May**

Writer **Leigh Jackson**
Producer **Nigel Stafford-Clark**

● ***British peacekeepers are forced to remain neutral in an ugly war.***

August 1992: leave is suddenly cancelled for a group of relaxing soldiers across the UK. Their battalion has just been called up for service as peacekeepers in Bosnia-Herzegovina. Donning the distinctive blue berets of the United Nations forces, the lads are pitched into an immediately harrowing situation. Arriving in Vitez, their role is to patrol the district in white armoured vehicles ('warriors') to ensure that locals do not starve, but they are under strict instructions never to take sides in this disgusting conflict and cannot fire their weapons unless their own lives are in danger. Seeing at first hand the barbarism man can inflict upon fellow-man, witnessing tragic, near-biblical scenes of exodus, and being frustrated at their impotence to prevent so-called ethnic cleansing make this tour of duty an experience that will change their lives for ever. Most prominent among the shocked troops are Scouser Alan James, whose best mate, Skeet, is killed soon after arrival in Bosnia; Sgt Andre Sochanik, a Scot of Polish and Serbian (which he is naturally keen to keep secret) descent; and lieutenants John Feeley and Neil Loughrey, who struggle to keep their emotions in check behind a calm exterior. Minka and Aida are the local interpreters whose safety preoccupies the officers' minds. With scenes of sickening brutality and harrowing tableaux of death and depravity, the two-part *Warriors* was, understandably, not comfortable viewing but reaped many accolades for its earnest insight into this most filthy of wars. Though the characters were fictitious, the story was based on real-life events and filming took place in the Czech Republic under the guidance of award-winning director Peter Kominsky.

Warship ★★

UK (BBC) Drama. BBC 1 1973–4; 1976–7

Commander Nialls	**Donald Burton**
Lt. Commander Beaumont	**David Savile**
Lt. Commander Kiley	**John Lee**
Lt. Last	**Norman Eshley**
Lt. Parry	**Richard Warwick**
MAA Heron	**Don Henderson**
Leading Regulator Fuller	**James Cosmo**
Commander 'Murky' Murton	**Malcolm Terris**
Lt. Boswall	**Christopher Coll**
Lt. Commander Junnion	**Rex Robinson**
Lt. Wakelin	**Graeme Eton**
Lt. Palfrey	**Michael Cochrane**
LMA Milner	**Colin Rix**
Lt. Peek	**Andrew Burt**
Commander Glenn	**Bryan Marshall**
Lt. Tagg	**James Leith**
MAA Burnett	**Frank Jarvis**
Capt. Edward Holt	**Derek Godfrey**

Lt. Commander James Napier	**Robert Morris**
L/Seaman Anderson	**Nigel Humphries**
Zoe Carter	**Prunella Ransome**

Creators **Ian MacKintosh, Anthony Coburn**
Producers **Anthony Coburn, Joe Waters**

Drama on the high seas with a Royal Navy frigate.

Routine and not-so-routine manoeuvres give rise to the action in this durable military soap opera. Amid much naval banter and a plethora of stiff upper lips, the crew of HMS *Hero*, a Royal Navy frigate (number F42), sticks loyally to its chores in places as far apart as the Mediterranean and the Far East, chores that involve anything from NATO exercises to Cold War face-offs, policing fishing wars or picking up defecting spies. Most of the attention focuses on the commissioned ranks. In the last series, journalist Zoe Carter is also featured. The BBC worked closely with the Navy on the series and the military collaboration even extended to the supply of a real warship for filming.

Washington: Behind Closed Doors ★★★

US (Paramount) Drama. BBC 1 1977–8 (US: ABC 1977)

President Richard Monckton	**Jason Robards**
William Martin	**Cliff Robertson**
Linda Martin	**Lois Nettleton**
Sally Whalen	**Stefanie Powers**
Frank Flaherty	**Robert Vaughn**
Esker Anderson	**Andy Griffith**
Bob Bailey	**Barry Nelson**
Myron Dunn	**John Houseman**
Carl Tessler	**Harold Gould**
Adam Gardiner	**Tony Bill**
Hank Ferris	**Nicholas Pryor**
Lars Haglund	**Skip Homeier**

Creator **David W. Rintels**
Executive Producer **Stan Kallis**
Producer **Norman Powell**

Fictional tale of intrigue in 1970s American politics.

Based on the novel *The Company*, by John Ehrlichman, a former aide to President Nixon, this six-part mini-series is essentially Watergate with the names changed. It doesn't take viewers long to realize that President Richard Monckton is meant to be Nixon, or that his predecessor, Esker Anderson, is Lyndon Johnson. Robert Vaughn plays Monckton's devious right-hand man, Frank Flaherty, as the White House manoeuvres to avoid being implicated in a political scandal.

Watch With Mother ★★★

UK (BBC) Children's Entertainment. BBC 1953–80

Programmes for pre-school-age children.

Watch With Mother was an umbrella title for various offerings from the BBC's children's department. In the immediate post-war years, its predecessor had been FOR THE CHILDREN (with Muffin the Mule, *et al.*), but in 1953 the title was changed to complement the radio series *Listen With Mother*, and new component programmes were introduced. Originally, *Watch With Mother* aired at around 3.45 in the afternoon, Tuesday-Thursday, as part of the *Children's Television* sequence, but more familiar is the 1.30 p.m. slot it occupied for most of its 27 years on air.

Running from Monday to Friday, the classic *Watch With Mother* line-up consisted of PICTURE BOOK on Mondays, ANDY PANDY on Tuesdays, FLOWER POT MEN on Wednesdays, RAG TAG AND BOBTAIL on Thursdays and THE WOODENTOPS on Fridays. Later additions in the 1960s were TALES OF THE RIVERBANK, CAMBERWICK GREEN/TRUMPTON/CHIGLEY, POGLES' WOOD, JOE, THE HERBS, BIZZY LIZZY, and MARY, MUNGO AND MIDGE. Among other favourites in the 1970s were MR BENN, BAGPUSS, FINGERBOBS, BARNABY and *The Mister Men* (1974–6). In 1980, the formula was maintained but, with occupational and viewing habits changing, the name *Watch With Mother* was discarded in favour of the less politically troublesome *See-Saw*.

Watchdog ★★★

UK (BBC) Consumer Affairs. BBC 1 1985–

Presenters **Nick Ross, Lynn Faulds Wood, John Stapleton, Anne Robinson, Alice Beer, Charlotte Hudson, Nicky Campbell**

Editors **Lino Ferrari, Nick Hayes, Sarah Caplin, Steve Anderson, Helen O'Rahilly, Mark Killick, Doug Carnegie**

Effective consumer-affairs programme.

Launched as a programme in its own right, having been a segment of the defunct NATIONWIDE (hosted by Hugh Scully) and its equally defunct successor, *Sixty Minutes*, *Watchdog* was initially presented by Nick Ross with Lynn Faulds Wood. Faulds Wood was later joined as co-host by her husband, John Stapleton. These were supported by reporters like Dina Gold, Fran Morrison, Malcolm Wilson, Nicholas Woolley, Mike Embley, Sarah Spiller, Michael Levin, Sue Bishop and Will Hanrahan.

Anne Robinson took over in 1993, assisted by Alice Beer, with, among other reporters in subsequent years, Chris Choi, Simon Walton, Johnathan Maitland, Denise Mahoney, Andy Webb, Liz Kershaw, John Nicolson, Beaky Evetts, Matt Allwright, Adrian Goldberg and David Bull. Nicky Campbell replaced Robinson in 2001, backed up by a team that has since included Kate Sanderson, Paul Heiney, Ashley Blake and Julia Bradbury. The aim of the series has been to expose con-men, lift the lid on shoddy workmanship and give the real facts about consumer goods. Viewers have been invited to write and ring in with their personal experiences.

In 1995, Judith Hann and Alice Beer presented *Watchdog Healthcheck*, which focused on medical matters, and other spin-offs have been *Watchdog: Face Value* (cosmetics consumerism), *Watchdog: Value for Money* (high street rip-offs), *Watchdog: the Big Dinner* (food and catering investigations), *Watchdog on the House* (DIY cons) and *Weekend Watchdog* (leisure industry concerns).

Watching ★★★

UK (Granda) Situation Comedy. ITV 1987–93

Malcolm Stoneway	**Paul Bown**
Brenda Wilson	**Emma Wray**
Mrs Marjorie Stoneway	**Patsy Byrne**
Mrs Joyce Wilson	**Noreen Kershaw**

Pamela Wilson/Lynch	**Liza Tarbuck**
Terry Milton	**Perry Fenwick**
David Lynch	**John Bowler**
Lucinda Stoneway	**Elizabeth Morton**
Harold	**Al T. Kossy**
Cedric	**Bill Moores**
Gerald Wilson	**Andrew Hilton**
Jonathan Macmillan	**Richard Good**

Creator/Writer **Jim Hitchmough**
Executive Producer **David Liddiment**
Producers **David Liddiment, Les Chatfield**

A couple struggle to keep their relationship on the rails.

Set in Merseyside, *Watching* takes its name from the diverse hobbies enjoyed by its dithering lead couple, men's outfitter Malcolm Stoneway and his sarcastic girlfriend, Brenda Wilson. Brenda, never the most modest dresser, lives in Liverpool with her secretary sister, Pamela, and frequents the local boozer, The Grapes, where they 'watch' the male talent and ponder their singles lifestyle. Malcolm – proud owner of a 1939 Norton 500 motorcycle and 1936 sidecar – lives across the Mersey, in the affluent district of Meols on the Wirral, with his mother. His pastime is bird watching.

As the series progresses, Malcolm opens his own motorcycle repair shop, Brenda goes to work as a barmaid at The Grapes for dopey landlord Harold, and Pamela marries social climber David Lynch and gives birth to two daughters (Sarah and Zelda). Also introduced are Brenda's potty mum, Joyce, and child-genius brother, the navy-fascinated Gerald, who live, regrettably for Malcolm's snooty mum, in deprived Toxteth. Unfortunately, Malcolm and Brenda's relationship is seldom stable and there is much to-ing and fro-ing across the Mersey to their respective mothers' homes as one tiff leads to another. When this happens, they spend more time watching each other than watching birds.

During one period of 'divorce', Malcolm marries Lucinda, a nursing sister from the Royal Hospital, but the marriage breaks down (she becomes pregnant by doctor Jonathan Macmillan) and he and Brenda are soon watching each other again. The Mersey-crossed lovers eventually marry in the final episode. The programme's theme song, 'What Does He See in Me?', by Charles Hart, is sung by star Emma Wray.

Water Margin, The ★★★

Japan (NTV) Drama. BBC 2 1976–8

Lin Chung	**Atsuo Nakamura**
Kao Chiu	**Kei Sato**
Wu Sung	**Hajime Hana**
Hu San-niang	**Sanae Tsuchida**
Hsiao Lan	**Yoshiyo Matuso**
Yang Chih	**Ko Sato**

Writer **David Weir**

Flailing swords and mystic magic in medieval China.

Adapted by David Weir from translations of the original Japanese script, *The Water Margin* tells of 108 chivalrous knights aroused from their graves to combat tyranny and corruption in the Orient, from their base in the water margins of Lian Shan Po. The hero is Lin Chung, with Hsiao his wife. This Japanese treatment of the 13th-century Chinese classic by Shih Nai-an proved surprisingly popular. Among those voicing the English version were Bert Kwouk and Miriam Margolyes. The theme song to the series was a bilingual, Japanese/English, double-A-side UK hit in 1977 for American vocalist Pete Mac Jr and Japanese band Godiego. In 1979 David Weir adapted another Japanese/Chinese serial, Wu Ch'eng-en's *Monkey*, which starred Masaaki Sakai as a Buddhist Pilgrim.

Waterfront Beat ★★

UK (New Media Age/BBC) Police Drama. BBC 1 1990–1

Chief Supt. Don Henderson	**John Ashton**
Det. Supt. Frank Mathews	**Geoffrey Leesley**
Supt. Peter Fallows	**Rupert Frazer**
PC Ronnie Barker	**Brian McCardie**
ACC (Ops)	**Denis Lill**
WDC Jane Long	**Helena Little**
DS Mike McCarthy	**Owen Teale**
Sgt Trevor Simon	**Stuart Golland**
PC Barry Smith	**Philip Middlemiss**
WPC Madeline Forest	**Jane Hazelgrove**
June Henderson	**Denise Stephenson**
Margaret Fallows	**Catriona MacColl**
PC Jacko Jackbridge	**Ray Polhill**
Denny Hagland	**Tommy Boyle**
DI Charlie Bush	**John Patrick**
PC Geoff Morgan	**Gordon Cameron**
DS 'Macker' McVay	**Mark Moraghan**
WDS Jackie Byrnes	**Eve Bland**
Chief Supt. Alan Briscoe	**Bruce Alexander**
DI Banston	**David Ashton**
DI Cyril Jacobs	**Roger Walker**
PC Bob 'Snake' Nelson	**Richard Good**
PC Ashir Malek	**Kulvinder Ghir**

Creator/Producer **Phil Redmond**
Writers **Phil Redmond, Andy Lynch**

The professional and personal problems of a team of big city police officers.

The Inner City and Waterfront Division of an urban police force (Liverpool) is the focus of this stylish series by GRANGE HILL and BROOKSIDE creator Phil Redmond. Instead of the usual rough-and-tumble cop antics, the emphasis falls on the internal workings of a city police force and the private worries of the officers involved. Forty-two-year-old Chief Supt. Don Henderson is the team leader, a bright, keen and caring cop with a dislike of bureaucracy. Henderson's rival is the arrogant Supt. Peter Fallows, and also prominent is naïve, 18-year-old recruit PC Ronnie Barker. Realism was intended as the key but office politics and backbiting were not to viewers' liking. Consequently, when the second series appeared, more action was introduced and attention turned to crime on and around the Mersey. Pepping up the series didn't work, however, and there was no third season. Music was by Steve Wright.

Waterhouse, Keith

CBE (1929–)

British newspaper journalist, novelist and TV scriptwriter. His series have generally involved humour or light drama and most have been in conjunction with Willis Hall (see Hall's entry for their joint credits). Alone, Waterhouse has also written *West End Tales*, ANDY CAPP, THE HAPPY APPLE, CHARTERS AND CALDICOTT, THE UPCHAT LINE/CONNECTION and the TV film *Charlie Muffin*.

Waterman, Dennis
(1948–)

British leading man, a one-time schoolboy actor, on TV since the late 1950s. In the 1970s he became familiar as tough nut George Carter in THE SWEENEY, but he has also taken on lighter roles, such as MINDER's Terry McCann, millionaire East Ender Tony Carpenter in ON THE UP, and wide-boy Thomas Gynn in STAY LUCKY. Waterman's TV career began with plays like *Member of the Wedding* (1959) and *All Summer Long* (1960), and the title role in *William* (an early JUST WILLIAM) in 1962. He appeared as Judy Carne's brother, Neville Finch, in the transatlantic sitcom *Fair Exchange* the same year and subsequently made guest appearances in series like JOURNEY TO THE UNKNOWN and MAN ABOUT THE HOUSE. He played King Harold in *Churchill's People* and was seen in Alan Plater's *Première* film *Give Us a Kiss, Christabel*. Waterman was instrumental in bringing the story of the victory of a Durham miners' football team in the first ever 'World Cup' to our screens in the drama *The World Cup – a Captain's Tale* (as co-producer and star) in 1982. (His love of football was manifested again later when he presented *Match of the Seventies*.) He was seen as Bobbo in THE LIFE AND LOVES OF A SHE DEVIL, SAS man John Neil in *Circles of Deceit* and villain John Danson in THE KNOCK. More recent credits have been in MURDER IN MIND, NEW TRICKS (Gerry Standing) and CANTERBURY TALES (John Crosby), with narration work on series like *Bad Lads' Army* and *Bailiffs*, and guest spots in DALZIEL AND PASCOE and WHERE THE HEART IS. His third wife was actress Rula Lenska and he is the father of actress Hannah Waterman.

Watkins, Peter
(1935–)

Pioneering British film-maker who employed documentary newsreel techniques and non-professional actors in his dramatic reconstructions. His CULLODEN in 1964 surprised viewers with its graphic depiction of the last battle to be fought on British soil, but more controversy followed THE WAR GAME, a year later. This account of the aftermath of a nuclear attack was banned from transmission by the then BBC Director-General, Sir Hugh Greene. It was eventually shown in 1985 as part of a season of programmes marking the 40th anniversary of the dropping of the atomic bomb on Hiroshima. Watkins later worked in Scandinavia, his Edvard Munch biopic being screened in the UK in 1976.

Watling, Jack
(1923–2001)

British actor familiar in the 1960s as Don Henderson in THE PLANE MAKERS/THE POWER GAME. Before that, he played Major Lockwood in THE WORLD OF TIM FRAZER and afterwards he was a late arrival in THE NEWCOMERS (Hugh Robertson). Watling, the father of actress Deborah Watling, and the stepfather of actress Dilys Watling, continued to work in television throughout the 1970s and 1980s. In 1972 he played Doc Saxon in the wartime RAF series *The Pathfinders*. In 1977 he appeared in *Lord Tramp* and in 1981 starred as Dr Carmichael in the sitcom *Doctor's Daughters*. Guest roles over his career took in series as varied as MARK SABER, THE ADVENTURES OF ROBIN HOOD, WILLIAM TELL, THE INVISIBLE MAN, DANGER MAN, GHOST SQUAD, DOCTOR WHO, NO HIDING PLACE, DIXON OF DOCK GREEN, HANCOCK'S HALF HOUR, BOYD QC, JASON KING, RUMPOLE OF THE BAILEY, FORTUNES OF WAR, HOT METAL, BERGERAC (Frank Blakemore), JEEVES AND WOOSTER, THE HOUSE OF ELIOTT and HEARTBEAT.

Waugh on Crime ★★

UK (BBC) Drama. BBC 2 1970–1

DI Waugh .... **Clive Swift**
PC White .... **Robin Chadwick**

Writer **Arden Winch**
Producer **Innes Lloyd**

● ***Cerebral detective work with an amiable CID man.***

The character of Detective Inspector Waugh, a chuckly copper in his 30s with a slightly flippant air, was first seen in 1968 in a *Thirty-Minute Theatre* story. In that three-part outing, Waugh was played by Charles Gray. His young sidekick, PC White, was played by Robin Chadwick, who resumes the role in this series, which sees Clive Swift take over the leading man's duties. Waugh is one of those brainy coppers, who enjoys the challenge of a tricky whodunnit. Tristan De Vere Cole and Philip Dudley share the directing duties through the six episodes, which were also screened under the *Thirty-Minute Theatre* umbrella.

Wax, Ruby
(Ruby Wachs; 1953–)

Illinois-born comic, actress and interviewer, the loud, intrusive host of *Don't Miss Wax, Wax on Wheels, Hit and Run, The Full Wax, Ruby's Health Quest, Ruby Does the Season, Ruby Wax Meets . . ., Ruby, Ruby's American Pie, Ruby Wax's Commercial Breakdown* and *Ruby Wax with* . . . Among her earliest work in the UK were sketches for NOT THE NINE O'CLOCK NEWS and the satire *For 4 Tonight*, and a small role in THE PROFESSIONALS. In 1985 she co-wrote and co-starred in GIRLS ON TOP (Shelley) and went on to be script editor for ABSOLUTELY FABULOUS (also making guest appearances) and write the Joan Collins one-off comedy *Mama's Back*. Wax has also appeared in THE COMIC STRIP PRESENTS, HAPPY FAMILIES and RED DWARF, and hosted *The Waiting Game* quiz. She is married to producer/director Ed Bye.

Way We Live Now, The ★★★

UK (BBC/WGBH) Drama. BBC 1 2001

Augustus Melmotte .... **David Suchet**
Marie Melmotte .... **Shirley Henderson**
Madame Melmotte .... **Helen Schlesinger**
Sir Felix Carbury .... **Matthew Macfadyen**
Hetta Carbury .... **Paloma Baeza**
Lady Carbury .... **Cheryl Campbell**
Paul Montague .... **Cillian Murphy**
Roger Carbury .... **Douglas Hodge**
Mrs Hurtle .... **Miranda Otto**
Mr Longestaffe .... **Oliver Ford Davies**
Adolphus 'Dolly' Longestaffe .... **Richard Cant**
Georgiana Longestaffe .... **Anne-Marie Duff**
Lady Pomona Longestaffe .... **Joanna David**
Mr Brehgert .... **Jim Carter**
Mr Alf .... **Rob Brydon**
Mr Broune .... **David Bradley**
Ruby Ruggles .... **Maxine Peake**

Mr Ruggles	**Trevor Peacock**
John Crumb	**Nicholas McGaughey**
Hamilton K. Fisker	**Michael Riley**
Croll	**Allan Corduner**
Lord Alfred Grendall	**Tony Britton**
Miles Grendall	**Angus Wright**
Marquis of Auld Reekie	**Graham Crowden**
Lord Nidderdale	**Stuart McQuarrie**
Mrs Pipkin	**Michele Dotrice**

Writer **Andrew Davies**
Producer **Nigel Stafford-Clark**

A European businessman with a mysterious past buys his way into London society.

Andrew Davies's four-part adaptation of Anthony Trollope's satirical novel was a resounding success in autumn 2001. Directed by David Yates, it told the story of foreign financier Augustus Melmotte, who arrives in London in the 1870s to claim a high place in society, after a period of murky dealings in Austria. He brings with him a subdued French wife and a headstrong daughter, Marie, whose hand is keenly sought for the dowry that it is thought to carry. Foremost among the suitors is wastrel Sir Felix Carbury, a baronet heir to no fortune, who deceitfully squanders the last remnants of his mother's money on wine and gambling. His sister, Hetta, is as determined as Marie Melmotte, though far less impulsive. She takes a shine to young railway architect Paul Montague, spurning the advances of her upright cousin Roger Carbury in favour of the younger man's sense of adventure. Paul has his own troubles, in the shape of Southern belle Mrs Hurtle, who has pursued him to London to hold him to his one-time promise of engagement. Such romantic entanglements are woven around the central plot in which Melmotte seeks to use Montague's plan for a new USA to Mexico railway as a basis for City fraud, taking advantage of the potential wealth it creates to buy his way into the nobility and into parliament. David Suchet's menacing performance as the manipulative fraudster was widely acclaimed (it was claimed he read biographies of Robert Maxwell for an insight into the role).

Wdyjsoytsagadslbi?

See *Why Don't You . . . ?*

We are the Champions ✱✱

UK (BBC) Children's Game Show. BBC 1 1973–87

Presenter **Ron Pickering**
Producer **Peter Charlton**

Long-running, inter-school sports contest.

The BBC's Mr Athletics, Ron Pickering, hosted this durable series which pitched school versus school (by region) in a sequence of physical contests and races. Competition was played down in favour of taking part and kids didn't need to be superb athletes to be involved. Games, held both on the field and in the pool, were often based around mini-assault courses. Star guests like Gary Sobers, Sebastian Coe, David Wilkie, Sharron Davies and Ian Rush egged on the youngsters. A special edition for children with disabilities was aired in 1987. The series ended the same year, but a number of one-off 'specials' were shown through to the mid-1990s.

Weakest Link, The ✱✱

UK (BBC) Quiz. BBC 2/BBC 1 2000–

Presenter **Anne Robinson**

Creators **Fintan Coyle, Cathy Dunning**
Producers **Ruth Davis, Phil Parsons, Andy Rowe**

Winner-takes-all quiz in which contestants themselves nominate the losers.

Designed as a late-afternoon offering on BBC 2, *The Weakest Link* quickly gained a cult following. Despite premiering only in August 2000, by October it had graduated to BBC 1 and a peak-hour evening slot. Anne Robinson hosts proceedings like a strict schoolmistress, chastizing contestants for performing poorly and brutally sending a loser down the so-called 'Walk of Shame' at the end of each round ('You are The Weakest Link: Goodbye!').

Nine contestants begin each programme, answering general knowledge questions in sequence over eight timed rounds, each question adding more money to the jackpot to be claimed by the eventual winner. Prize money jumps substantially for each consecutive correct answer, with a total of £1,000 available for stringing together nine correct answers in each round. Although contestants can 'bank' the money gained at any point, a wrong answer takes the total for the run of questions back to zero. Money gained in the eighth round is trebled, making a potential daily jackpot of £10,000. When each round is completed, the contestants each nominate the person they consider to be 'The Weakest Link' and the person with the most votes (whether or not he or she is actually the weakest in terms of correct answers or banked money) is evicted from the game. Their comments on being voted off are then recorded and edited in to the finished programme. In the final, the remaining two contestants are each asked five questions, with the higher scorer taking all the accumulated money. If scores are level after the five questions, 'sudden death' is employed, with the first wrong answer deciding the winner and loser.

The evening version, initially entitled *The Weakest Link: Champions' League*, introduced a studio audience, doubled the potential prize money to £20,000 and pitted previous winners against one another. Another evening show focused on 'Bad Losers', bringing back contestants who felt they were unjustly voted off during their previous afternoon performance. Celebrity editions have also been made. The show has successfully transferred all over the world, with Anne Robinson also acting as interrogator in the American version (also shown in the UK).

Weather

The world's first television weather forecast was broadcast by the BBC on 20 November 1936 at 4.01 p.m. and lasted six minutes. An anonymous hand sketched in the isobars on a weather chart, while an off-screen voice provided the forecast over a bed of light music – all somewhat different from today's world of computer graphics and personality weather-presenters. The first on-screen meteorology men appeared in Canada and the USA, quickly bringing a showbiz element to proceedings in an attempt to keep viewers switched on. In the UK no weather man was seen until 1954, when George Cowling gave the first in-view summary for the BBC on 11 January. Cowling, like his successors, was a Meteorological Office employee, not a BBC man. The first weather woman was

Barbara Edwards, who made her bow in 1974. Among other notable weather folk (on the BBC) have been Bert Foord, Graham Parker, Jack Scott, Keith Best, Michael Fish, Ian McCaskill, Jim Bacon, John Kettley, Bernard Davey, Suzanne Charlton, Peter Cockroft, Rob McElwee, Penny Tranter, Richard Edgar, Helen Young, David Lee, Isobel Lang, David Braine, Philip Avery, Peter Gibbs, Sarah Wilmshurst, Darren Bett, Helen Willetts, Alex Deakin, John Hammond, Dan Corbett and Francis Wilson (who worked on BREAKFAST TIME forecasts). Bill Giles took over as head of the BBC's team in 1983, a move that coincided with the introduction of flashy computer imagery and a new emphasis on the personalities of the presenters. ITV began its own national weather forecasts in 1989, with Alex Hill, Siân Lloyd, Trish Williamson, Martyn Davies, Laura Greene, Fiona Farrell, John Hammond (later with the BBC), Clare Nasir, Chrissie Reidy, Robin Lermitte, Becky Mantin and Jo Blythe the most prominent forecasters. BBC has also screened *The Weather Show* (1996–9), a lunchtime series of short programmes fronted by weather presenters, revealing how the weather affects people's lives. In the USA, the Weather Channel is a 24-hour cable service that reports on national and local conditions. In the 1990s, a sister channel for the UK proved very short-lived.

Weaver, Dennis

(1924–2006)

American actor whose earliest TV appearances came in the 1950s, in series like DRAGNET. Weaver went on to take the role of Matt Dillon's deputy, Chester Goode, in GUNSMOKE and stayed with the series for nine years. He left to star in his own vehicle, *Kentucky Jones*, but it failed to take and, instead, Weaver headed into children's adventures as family man Tom Wedloe in GENTLE BEN. He then found himself another durable role when he was cast as MCCLOUD, the backwaters sheriff who brought his Southern ways to New York City. When it ended in 1977, Weaver was still in demand and he later took parts in a host of prime-time US series and dramas such as *Buck James*, which did not, however, transfer to the UK. He was also seen in numerous TV movies.

Weavers Green ✶

UK (Anglia) Soap Opera. ITV 1966

Alan Armstrong .... **Grant Taylor**
Dorothy 'Dotty' Armstrong ..... **Megs Jenkins**
Tim Armstrong .... **Paul Anthony Martin**
Mick Armstrong .... **Kate O'Mara**
Geoffrey Toms .... **Eric Flynn**
Celia Toms .... **Georgina Ward**
Mrs Vincent .... **Susan Field**
Bert Vincent .... **Charles Lamb**
Milly Vincent .... **Vanessa Forsyth**
Derek Swan .... **Maurice Kaufmann**
Jack Royston .... **Richard Coleman**
Margaret Royston .... **Doreen Aris**
Hazel Westcott .... **Marjie Lawrence**
Colin Westcott .... **John Moulder-Brown**
Daniel Jessop .... **John Glyn-Jones**
Archibald Langley OBE .... **Gerald Young**
Ernie Arkwright .... **Frederick Piper**
Sue Patterson .... **Sheila Fearn**
Capt. Toby Patterson .... **Jack Melford**
Reg Hopgood .... **Denzil Ellis**
Mona Hopgood .... **Faith Kent**
Bobby Brent .... **Edward Underdown**
PC Sam Moneypenny .... **Peter Lawrence**
Paddy O'Connor .... **Gerry Duggan**
George Banham .... **Peter Tuddenham**
Col. Fielding .... **Lindsay Campbell**
Lord Norstead .... **Norman Wynne**
Bill Thorpe .... **Brian Cant**
Carol Thorpe .... **Clare Jenkins**
Harry Catchpole .... **Peter Reeves**
Mr Wooley .... **Leslie Anderson**
Samantha Dinwoodie .... **Helena Gloag**
Edina Dinwoodie .... **Margaret Lacey**

Creators **Peter Lambda, Betty Lambda**
Producer **John Jacobs**

Twice-weekly soap featuring the farmers and other folk of a small country town.

Alan Armstrong is an Australian who has worked as a vet in the UK for 28 years and it is life in and around his practice in the rural town of Weavers Green that provides the backbone of this short-lived, *Archers*-esque drama. Armstrong is married to Dotty and they have two kids: Mick (a daughter – an early role for Kate O'Mara) is 22 and a student vet at Cambridge; Tim (15) is away at boarding school. Alan joined his father-in-law's practice after the war and bought the old man out in 1952. He eventually signed up a junior partner, Geoffrey Toms, to help with the increasing workload. Toms, son of a Surrey farmer, is married to the aristocratic Celia, who struggles to fulfil her role as the ordinary wife of a country vet. Other major characters seen during the six-month run were Mrs Vincent, Dotty's daily; her husband Bert (a cowman) and their two daughters; Jack Royston, a go-ahead young farmer; Archibald Langley, a retired colonial official; horse trainer Toby Patterson; farm equipment salesman Derek Swan; and middle-aged playboy Bobby Brent. Also featuring were poacher Daniel Jessop; post office proprietor Mr Wooley; pensioner Ernie Arkwright; Hazel Westcott with her son, Colin; and the local bobby, Sam Moneypenny. Wilfred Josephs supplied the music.

Webb, Jack

(1920–82)

One of American TV's golden greats, former radio announcer Jack Webb made his mark as the glamourless, 'just the facts' policeman Joe Friday in the long-running crime series DRAGNET. It was, in effect, Jack Webb's show. It was he who created it for US radio in 1949, bringing a new realism into police series and using genuine police files as sources for his stories. Webb had previously played other cops on radio, but none with the down-to-earth character of Friday, and none with the same success. When it transferred to TV in 1952, Webb was also its producer. The series ran for seven years and was revived for another three years in 1967. He did very little acting otherwise, but his Mark VII production company did turn out a number of US series, including *The DA*, *Pete Kelly's Blues*, *Adam 12* and HEC RAMSEY. He also produced the final season of 77 SUNSET STRIP and was in charge of Warner TV for a while. Webb was once married to actress-singer Julie London.

Wednesday Play, The ★★★★

UK (BBC) Drama Anthology. BBC 1 1964–70

● ***Adventurous and influential vehicle for 1960s dramatic talent.***

Quickly gaining a reputation for breaking new ground in television drama, *The Wednesday Play* was a showcase for emerging playwrights. Taking its cue from ABC's ARMCHAIR THEATRE and the angry young men of the late 1950s, its gritty social commentaries also furnished it with a left-of-centre image. The first *Wednesday Play* was Nikolai Leskov's *A Crack in the Ice*, dramatized by Ronald Eyre, and among other notable offerings were Sartre's *In Camera*, adapted by Phillip Saville (1964), David Mercer's *And Did Those Feet?*, Dennis Potter's VOTE, VOTE, VOTE FOR NIGEL BARTON/ STAND UP, NIGEL BARTON, Nell Dunn's UP THE JUNCTION (all 1965) and Jim Allen's *The Lump* (1967). Probably the most controversial and important play was Jeremy Sandford's study of a homeless family in CATHY COME HOME (1966).

In addition to the writers listed, others like Peter Nichols, James Hanley, James O'Connor, Nigel Kneale and Michael Frayn also contributed memorable material, and production and direction were skilfully handled by the likes of Rudolph Cartier, Don Taylor, Tony Garnett, Ken Loach, Gilchrist Calder, Kenith Trodd, James MacTaggart, Waris Hussein, Jack Gold, Alan Bridges, Roger Smith, Irene Shubik and Charles Jarrott.

With a change of transmission day and the start of a new decade, *The Wednesday Play* eventually gave way to PLAY FOR TODAY.

Weekend World ★★★★

UK (LWT) Current Affairs. ITV 1972–88

Presenters **Peter Jay, John Torode, Mary Holland, Brian Walden, Matthew Parris**

Producers **John Birt, Barry Cox**

● ***Influential Sunday lunchtime political programme.***

Weekend World was the programme that introduced politics to Sunday lunchtimes. Launched as a means of filling the gap between news bulletins and current affairs series like THIS WEEK and WORLD IN ACTION, the series brought leading politicians and industrialists into the studio and quizzed them over the state of the nation, economic plans, foreign policies, etc. Major events in the week ahead were flagged up. John Torode and Mary Holland shared the presentation with Peter Jay in the early days, although Jay soon became sole frontman. When he left to take up an appointment as British Ambassador to the USA in 1977, he was replaced by former Labour MP, Brian Walden. Ex-Tory MP Matthew Parris was in charge for the final two years from 1986. The programme's powerful theme music was 'Nantucket Sleighride' by American rock band Mountain.

Weeks, Alan

(1923–96)

BBC sports commentator (from 1951), specializing in ice events in his latter years, but also heard over football matches, swimming, gymnastics and on other major occasions. He also fronted POT BLACK and GRANDSTAND. Prior to working in television (and sometimes during), Weeks publicized ice shows and the Brighton Tigers Ice Hockey Club.

Weinstein, Hannah

(Hannah Dorner, 1911–84)

American independent film-maker of the 1950s, formerly a *New York Herald Tribune* journalist and a publicist. Her interest in film began in the early 1950s and led to her joining forces with ATV to produce action series like THE ADVENTURES OF ROBIN HOOD, SWORD OF FREEDOM and THE BUCCANEERS. She also produced COLONEL MARCH OF SCOTLAND YARD and THE FOUR JUST MEN. Weinstein then returned to the USA, where she spoke out against racial discrimination in the film industry.

Welcome Back, Kotter ★★

US (Komack/Wolper) Situation Comedy. ITV 1981–3 (US: ABC 1975–9)

Gabe Kotter	**Gabriel Kaplan**
Julie Kotter	**Marcia Strassman**
Vinnie Barbarino	**John Travolta**
Freddie 'Boom Boom' Washington	**Lawrence Hilton-Jacobs**
Juan Luis Pedro Phillipo de Huevos Epstein	**Robert Hegyes**
Arnold Horshack	**Ron Palillo**
Mr Michael Woodman	**John Sylvester White**
Rosalie 'Hotzie' Totzie	**Debralee Scott**
Verna Jean	**Vernee Watson**
Judy Borden	**Helaine Lembeck**
Todd Ludlow	**Dennis Bowen**
Maria	**Catarina Cellino**
Angie Globagoski	**Melonie Haller**
Beau De Labarre	**Stephen Shortridge**
Mary Johnson	**Irene Arranga**

Creators **Gabriel Kaplan, Alan Sacks**
Executive Producer **James Kormack**

● ***An unorthodox teacher returns to his old school to work with underachievers.***

Although the inspiration came from creator/star Gabriel Kaplan's own experience, there was more than an element of the UK's PLEASE SIR! about this American high school comedy. It centres on young teacher Gabe Kotter, who takes a job at the John Buchanan High, a Brooklyn school he attended some ten years previously. His class is the most troublesome in the establishment, wise on the streets if dumb in the schoolroom. Unlike *Please Sir!*'s Bernard Hedges though, Kotter is able to mix readily with the kids, earning their respect and, by bending the rules, managing to shape them for the real world in ways that are not always academic. His unruly mob of pupils are the self-styled 'Sweathogs', primarily black 'Boom Boom' (catchphrase: 'Hi there!'), Jewish Puerto Rican Juan Epstein, nerdy Horshack and Italian ringleader Vinnie Barbarino (played by future superstar John Travolta). Other kids – including female Sweathog Angie Globagoski and Southerner Beau De Labarre – join and leave the class as the series advances. Also seen is Kotter's wife, Julie, who gives birth to twins, and the school's vice-principal, Mr Woodman. John Sebastian, former leader of the Lovin' Spoonful, topped the US charts in 1976 with his theme song, 'Welcome Back'.

Weldon, Fay

CBE (1931–)

British novelist and playwright noted for her feminist stance and her portrayal of women who dare to break free from men's shadows. Among her TV offerings have been the plays *The Fat Woman's Tale, A Catching Complaint* (both 1966), *Poor Cherry* (1967), *Splinter of Ice* (1972) and *Life for Christine* (1980). She also contributed episodes to THE DOCTORS, UPSTAIRS, DOWNSTAIRS (including the pilot) and the anthology series MENACE, and, in 1980, she adapted Jane Austen's *Pride and Prejudice*. Her novel THE LIFE AND LOVES OF A SHE DEVIL was dramatized to great acclaim by the BBC in 1986, and a year later *Heart of the Country* was also well received. In 1991 ITV produced her *The Cloning of Joanna May*, followed in 1992 by *Growing Rich* and in 1998 her series *Big Women* was shown on Channel 4. In an earlier job in advertising, she was credited with developing the slogan 'Go to work on an egg'.

We'll Meet Again ★★

UK (LWT) Drama. ITV 1982

Dr Helen Dereham	**Susannah York**
Major Ronald Dereham	**Ronald Hines**
Patricia Dereham	**Lise-Ann McLaughlin**
Major Jim Kiley	**Michael J. Shannon**
Albert Mundy	**Ray Smith**
Vera Mundy	**June Barry**
Letty Mundy	**Natalie Ogle**
Peter Mundy	**Patrick Pearson**
Jack Blair	**Patrick O'Connell**
Rosie Blair	**Lynne Pearson**
Violet Blair	**Kathryn Pogson**
Col. Rufus Krasnowici	**Ed Devereaux**
M/Sgt Joe 'Mac' McGraw	**Christopher Malcolm**
M/Sgt Chuck Ericson	**Joris Stuyck**

Creator **David Butler**
Writers **David Butler, David Crane, John Gorrie**
Producer **Tony Wharmby**

● ***An Englishwoman falls for an American major during the wartime 'invasion' of Britain by the USA.***

'Overpaid, oversexed and over here' was the familiar description applied to US military personnel stationed in the UK during World War II, and this 13-part drama sets out to prove its validity. Based around the sleepy Suffolk market town of Market Wetherby, *We'll Meet Again* focuses on the impact made on its residents by the arrival of 2,000 men from the US Eighth Air Force 525th Bomb Group in 1943. At the forefront of the action is hospital doctor Helen Dereham, wife of army man Ronald Dereham, who is drawn to the charms of suave Yank Jim Kiley, second-in-command at the US airbase. The Derehams' daughter, Patricia, is also present, having refused to return to her academic studies in Cambridge. Local resentment towards the 'intruders' is fuelled by grouchy grocer and ARP warden Albert Mundy, but there is more of a welcome at the pub, The Plough, run by Jack Blair and his two daughters, flighty Rosie and more sensible Violet. Chuck Ericson is the US NCO who saves Violet's life.

To keep within the show's modest budget, only one B-17 bomber is seen, with the rest of the action involving models or stock footage.

Welland, Colin

(Colin Williams; 1934–)

Lancashire-born actor and writer. In front of the camera his most familiar performances have been in Z CARS (PC David Graham), *Cowboys* (Geyser), Dennis Potter's BLUE REMEMBERED HILLS (Willie), *Screen Two's Femme Fatale* (Harty), *The Fix* (Harry Catterick), TRIAL AND RETRIBUTION (Mallory) and BRAMWELL. As a writer, he has contributed plays like *Bangelstein's Boys* (1969), *Slattery's Mounted Foot, Say Goodnight to Your Grandma, Roll On Four O'Clock* (all three 1970), *Kisses at Fifty, Jack Point* (both 1973), *Leeds – United!* (1974) and *Your Man from the Six Counties* (1976), plus the series *The Wild West Show* (1975). After winning an Oscar for *Chariots of Fire*, he eventually returned to television writing with a *Screen One* film, *Bambino Mio* (1994).

Wells Fargo ★★

US (Overland/Juggernaut/Universal) Western. BBC 1957–64 (US: NBC 1957–62)

Jim Hardie	**Dale Robertson**
Beau McCloud	**Jack Ging**
Jeb Gaine	**William Demarest**
Ovie	**Virginia Christine**
Mary Gee	**Mary Jane Saunders**
Tina	**Lory Patrick**

Producers **Earle Lyon, Nat Holt**

● ***The adventures of a stagecoach company troubleshooter in the Gold Rush days.***

In the 1860s Jim Hardie is a roaming agent for the passenger and shipping company of Wells Fargo, Incorporated, based in the Californian town of Gloribee. His duties extend from ironing out problems with employees to preventing the hijacking of coaches and the theft of the gold bullion they carry. The series, initially a half-hour in length, was expanded to full-hour episodes in 1961, when it switched production companies from Overland to Juggernaut. With the move, Hardie settles down a little, buys the Haymaker Farm ranch on the outskirts of San Francisco and is given a cast of co-stars. These are his ranch supervisor, Jeb Gaine; his young assistant, Beau McCloud; and a widowed neighbour, Ovie (who fancies Jeb), plus her two daughters, Mary Gee and Tina. Despite these distractions, Hardie still fulfils his duties for the company in exemplary fashion. Properly titled *Tales of Wells Fargo*, the series was known only as *Wells Fargo* in the UK.

West, Timothy

CBE (1934–)

Bradford-born actor, often seen in distinguished, hard-nosed or blustery roles, with probably his best-remembered portrayal that of EDWARD THE SEVENTH. That apart, West has taken major parts in very many series and plays. They include BIG BREADWINNER HOG (Lennox), *Churchill and the Generals* (Winston Churchill), THE EDWARDIANS (Horatio Bottomley), THE MONOCLED MUTINEER (Brigadier General Thomson), A VERY PECULIAR PRACTICE (the aptly named Dr Furie), CRIME AND PUNISHMENT (Inspector Porfiry), BRASS (Bradley Hardacre), *The Good Dr Bodkin Adams* (Adams), MASADA (Vespasian), *Framed* (DCI McKinnes), *Over Here* (Squadron Leader Archie Bunting), *Cuts* (TV magnate Lord Mellow), BEDTIME (Andrew Oldfield), *Station Jim* (Sir Christopher Ellis) and

Dickens (John Dickens). Among other important credits have been *Cottage to Let*, *Hard Times*, THE BBC TELEVISION SHAKESPEARE's *Henry VIII* (and other TV classics), *Harry's Kingdom*, *Shadow on the Sun*, *Screen One's Blore MP*, *The Alan Clark Diaries* (Sir Robert Armstrong), *London* (Henry Mayhew), COLDITZ (Bunny Warren) and BLEAK HOUSE (Sir Leicester Dedlock). Guest roles include parts in HINE, MISS MARPLE, CAMPION, GOODNIGHT SWEETHEART, MIDSOMER MURDERS, MURDER IN MIND, WAKING THE DEAD and NEW TRICKS. He is married to actress Prunella Scales, with whom he once made a guest appearance in AFTER HENRY and also starred in *Looking for Victoria*, and is the father of actor Sam West.

West Wing, The ★★★★

US (John Wells/Warner Brothers) Drama. Channel 4 2001–5 (US: NBC 1999–2006)

President Josiah Bartlet	**Martin Sheen**
Sam Seaborn	**Rob Lowe**
Leo McGarry	**John Spencer**
Josh Lyman	**Bradley Whitford**
Claudia Jean ('C. J.') Cregg	**Allison Janney**
Donna Moss	**Janel Moloney**
Toby Ziegler	**Richard Schiff**
Charlie Young	**Dulé Hill**
Mandy Hampton	**Moira Kelly**
Vice-President John Hoynes	**Tim Matheson**
Abigail 'Abby' Bartlet	**Stockard Channing**
Danny Concannon	**Timothy Busfield**
Zoey Bartlet	**Elisabeth Moss**
Cal Mathis	**Andy Umberger**
Ainsley Hayes	**Emily Procter**
Lionel Tribby	**John Larroquette**
Will Baily	**Joshua Malina**
Greg Brock	**Sam Robards**
Kate Harper	**Mary McCormack**
Congressman Matthew Santos	**Jimmy Smits**
Senator Arnold Vinick	**Alan Alda**
Annabeth Schott	**Kristin Chenoweth**

Creator **Aaron Sorkin**
Executive Producers **Aaron Sorkin, Thomas Schlamme, John Wells, Christopher Misiano, Alex Graves, Lawrence O'Donnell, Peter Noah**

● ***Political and personal drama behind the doors of the White House.***

Emmys galore and acclaim from the highest quarters: that was the critical story of *The West Wing*, a fast-moving, in-depth account of day-to-day operations around the Oval Office. Incumbent president is New Hampshire Democrat Josiah Bartlet, an easy-going, brilliant and dedicated politician with a folksy attitude but an incisive bite when required. Loyally supporting her husband, but never afraid to call him to account, is first lady Abby Bartlet, a doctor, but it is the extended family of advisers, press gurus and negotiators who absorb the spotlight most. Chief of staff is Leo McGarry, a man in touch with the people who keeps his team in order despite being a recovering alcoholic. Deputy chief of staff Josh Lyman is key member of the unit, a sharp strategist with strong liberal views that can get him into trouble, especially with his caustic number two, Donna Moss. Facing the probing questions of the media is tall press secretary C. J. Cregg, who works alongside cynical communications director Toby Ziegler and Toby's deputy, Sam Seaborn, an outstanding speech and slogan writer. Personal aide to the president is the straight-talking Charlie Young. The camera follows the sleep-deprived lives of the devoted administration team as they stroll the corridors of the West Wing or climb aboard *Air Force One*, reacting to political crises, weighing up least-worst options, juggling priorities and engaging in Washington horse-trading in order that the president's will be done. And meanwhile their personal lives go to pot. Ensuring attention to detail is a team of political advisers, some former White House executives themselves. As Bartlet's two terms in The White House draw to a close, later episodes focus on the race to become the new US President, with frontfronners being Californian Republican Arnold Vinick and Texan Democrat Matthew Santos. This change of emphasis, plus falling ratings after a scheduling change in the USA, and perhaps even the sudden death of John Spencer, who played Leo McGarry, led to the sixth season being declared the last.

For the UK, some episodes appeared on the digital channel E4, prior to switching to Channel 4. E4 also carried season five, which has yet to air on Channel 4, while another digital channel, More 4, ran season six in 2005–6.

Westcountry

The ITV franchise-holder for the South-west of England, Westcountry went on air on 1 January 1993, having outbid the existing service provider, TSW. A judicial review followed the ITC's move to award the contract to Westcountry, but the decision was upheld. From the start, Westcountry went for an entirely new approach to regional programming, bringing in the latest technology and a host of new faces. This initially alienated some viewers, but gradually audiences settled down. The company was later taken over by Carlton Communications and the station renamed Carlton Westcountry. It is now part of ITV plc. Its main studios are in Plymouth, but there are smaller studios across the region. There has been little contribution to the national network to date.

Westward

Serving South-west England, Westward took to the air on 29 April 1961 and remained the ITV contractor for the region until 11 August 1981. The company became indelibly linked to its outspoken executive chairman, Peter Cadbury, who campaigned vehemently for the South-west ITV region to be enlarged up as far as Bristol (the part of the West Country controlled by TWW and, later, HTV West). Cadbury also found himself involved in internal disputes, and a major boardroom tussle in 1980 helped seal Westward's fate as the franchise reappraisals loomed large. Even though programme standards were deemed to be good and there was local satisfaction with the service provided, the licence was awarded instead to TSW, which then purchased Westward's Plymouth studios. For many years, Westward was administratively joined to Channel Television, in an effort to maximize advertising potential for the two stations and keep down office costs. Westward produced few national programmes of note.

Westway ★★

UK (HTV) Children's Drama 1976

Len Saxby	**Ivor Salter**
Anna Saxby	**Chris Range**
Phil Saxby	**Ashley Knight**

Mark Saxby .... **Nigel Rhodes**
Pete Ryder .... **Donald Morley**
Jan Ryder .... **Ann Lynn**
Crispin Ryder .... **Simon Gipps-Kent**
Samantha Ryder .... **Sylvestra Le Touzel**
Paula Harvey .... **Jane Lowe**
Ron Harvey .... **Dean Lawrence**
Sue Harvey .... **Sarah Sutton**
Miss Marlbury .... **Daphne Heard**
Graham Lawrence .... **Tim Preece**

Writer **Guy Slater**
Executive Producer **Patrick Dromgoole**
Producer **Leonard White**

● ***The ups and downs of commune life in a spooky old house.***

Single parent Len Saxby decides he needs to build a better life for his three children – blossoming teenager Anna, bespectacled adolescent Phil and young, inquisitive Mark – and responds to an advertisement offering places at a commune. The Saxbys arrive at Westway and find the old house to be a forbidding place. Nevertheless, they knuckle down and start to build relationships with the other commune members, the Ryder and Harvey families. Lurking in the background is a disapproving 'sitting tenant', Miss Marlbury, an eccentric old woman with a mysterious past. The seven episodes revolve around the Saxbys settling in, trouble for all the kids at school (which leads to the adults setting up their own school at Westway) and Mark's endless quest for hidden treasure. At one point, it looks as if Westway is to be sold, rendering everyone homeless, but the threat is averted, with the kids pulling together when the grown-ups begin to fall out. In the final episode a feast is staged for all residents, including Miss Marlbury, who is assimilated into the throng after Mark discovers secret papers that reveal her true ancestry.

Whack-O! ✶✶

UK (BBC) Situation Comedy. BBC 1956–60; 1971–2

Prof. James Edwards .... **Jimmy Edwards**
Mr Oliver Pettigrew .... **Arthur Howard**
Julian Orchard *(1971–2)*
Mr F. D. Price Whittaker .... **Kenneth Cope**
Mr S. A. Smallpiece .... **Norman Bird**
Mr Lumley .... **John Stirling**
Mr R. P. Trench .... **Peter Glaze**
Mr Halliforth .... **Edwin Apps**
Peter Greene *(1971–2)*
Parker .... **David Langford**
Mr Forbes .... **Keith Smith**
Mr Proctor .... **Brian Rawlinson**
Mr Dinwiddie .... **Gordon Phillott**
Harold Bennett *(1971–2)*
Mr Cope-Willoughby .... **Frank Raymond**
Matron .... **Barbara Archer**
Elizabeth Fraser
Charlotte Mitchell
Taplow .... **Gary Warren** *(1971–2)*
Potter .... **Greg Smith** *(1971–2)*

Creators/Writers **Denis Norden, Frank Muir**
Producers **Douglas Moodie, Eric Fawcett, Douglas Argent**

● ***A school is tyrannized by its cane-swishing headmaster.***

Professor James Edwards, MA, is principal of Chiselbury School, an educational establishment that he rules with an iron cane. While the schoolboys are always easy targets for the bullying, manipulative headmaster, so, too, are his staff and in particular his weedy right-hand man, Mr Pettigrew (played by Leslie Howard's brother, Arthur). Other members of staff come and go during the programme's four-year run.

A spin-off film, *Bottoms Up*, was released in 1959, and *Whack-O!* was briefly revived on TV in 1971, with Julian Orchard in the role of Pettigrew and the indomitable Jimmy Edwards again donning the boozy principal's cap and gown.

What the Papers Say ✶✶

UK (Granada) Current Affairs. ITV 1956–82; Channel 4 1982–9; BBC 2 1990–

Presenters **Kingsley Martin, Brian Inglis, Stuart Hall**

● ***Weekly review of newspaper headlines.***

What the Papers Say is one of those programmes that have done the rounds of the channels, and yet it has been produced by the same company, Granada, since its inception in 1956. The first hosts were *New Statesman* editor Kingsley Martin and *The Spectator*'s assistant editor, Brian Inglis, who alternated appearances. Inglis eventually became sole host. Under the temporary title of *The Papers*, in 1969 Stuart Hall inherited the presenter's chair, and various other personalities and Fleet Street scribes have filled that seat since. The role of them all has been to consider the week's newspaper coverage, to discuss the headlines, to analyse the treatment of big issues and to follow lines of opinion and bias, often with a light and very humorous touch. Each edition has lasted 10–15 minutes.

What the Romans Did for Us/ What the Victorians Did for Us/ What the Tudors Did for Us/ What the Stuarts Did for Us/ What the Ancients Did for Us ✶✶✶

UK (BBC) History. BBC 2 2000/2001/2002/2002/2005

Presenter **Adam Hart-Davis**

Executive Producers **Caroline van den Bruel, Stephen Wilkinson, Martin Mortimore**
Producers **Martin Mortimore, Cameron Balbirnie, Paul Bradshaw, Ian Potts**

● ***Lively account of progress through the ages.***

Accessible history, that's Adam Hart-Davis's game. The energetic, silver-haired presenter darts around the centuries, exploring the lives of first the Romans, then the Victorians, the Tudors, the Stuarts, and finally the Ancients (assisted in this last series by various travelling helpers), examining the technological, artistic, sporting and fashionable legacies they bequeathed to the modern world. Never afraid to don period costumes and ham it up to make a point, the quirky Hart-Davis re-creates engineering triumphs of the past – be they musical instruments, printing presses or flushing toilets – visits places that played a role in shaping our lives today and generally buzzes with enthusiasm for the successes of our forebears.

Whately, Kevin
(1951–)

North-eastern actor who came to the fore as Neville in AUF WIEDERSEHEN, PET in 1983, but won even more acclaim for his subsequent performance as INSPECTOR MORSE's genial side-kick, Detective Sgt Lewis. The character resurfaced in a *Morse* spin-off, entitled *Lewis*, in 2006. Whately has also starred in PEAK PRACTICE (Dr Jack Kerruish), *Screen Two*'s *Skallagrigg* (Hopkins), *Screen One*'s *Trip Trap* (abusive husband Ian Armstrong) and *Gobble* (MAFF official Colin Worsfold), THE BROKER'S MAN (insurance investigator Jimmy Griffin), *Pure Wickedness* (Geoff Meadows), MURDER IN MIND and *Plain Jane* (David Bruce). Recent credits have included *Promoted to Glory* (Salvation Army Major Nigel Hurst), *Dad* (Oliver James), *The Legend of the Tamworth Two* (Wolf), *Belonging* (Jacob Copplestone) and *Footprints in the Snow* (Kevin Hill). One of his earliest TV appearances was as a miner in WHEN THE BOAT COMES IN and other supporting roles have come in ANGELS, SHOESTRING, STRANGERS, MISS MARPLE and MERSEYBEAT. He is married to actress Madelaine Newton.

Whatever Happened to the Likely Lads? ✶
See *Likely Lads, The.*

Whatever You Want ✶

UK (Hat Trick) Game Show. BBC 1 1997–2000

Presenter **Gaby Roslin**

Producers **David Young, Rob Clark, Clare Horton, Amanda Wilson**

Game show in which money can't buy the prizes on offer.

This JIM'LL FIX IT for the 1990s asked its participants to do more than just write a letter and ask for a dream to come true. In *Whatever You Want*, they had to earn it. Gaby Roslin put the hopefuls through their paces in a series of games and quizzes in a bid to secure a chance of a lifetime. This might be a slot in a major fashion show for would-be designers, tuition from a top coach for amateur golfers, a prize dalek for DOCTOR WHO buffs, or a night in a haunted house for some ghost hunters – effectively, the sort of treat that money cannot normally buy. Regular features included 'Locked in the Limo', the confined person or persons being celebrities prepared to spend some time with a successful fan, and the self-explanatory 'Wedding You Want'. The Status Quo track of the same title was used as the programme's theme music.

What's My Line? ✶✶

UK (BBC/Thames) Panel Game. BBC 1 1951–63; BBC 2 1973–4; ITV 1984–90

Hosts **Eamonn Andrews, David Jacobs, Penelope Keith, Angela Rippon**

Creators **Mark Goodson, Bill Todman**
Producers **T. Leslie Jackson, Dicky Leeman, Harry Carlisle, Dennis Main Wilson, Brian Tesler, John Warrington, Richard Evans, Ernest Maxin, Maurice Leonard**

A celebrity panel tries to guess contestants' occupations.

What's My Line? was one of the biggest successes in television history. Not only did it enjoy three runs on British television but it was also a hit in its native USA, where it eventually ran for 25 years. And yet the formula was remarkably simple. Contestants 'signed in', gave a brief mime to illustrate the work they did (or part of it), and four celebrity panellists then tried to guess the profession, by asking the contestant questions which elicited no more than a yes or no answer. If the occupation was not discovered by the time ten *nos* had been received, the contestant was declared the winner and took away a certificate to prove it. The host acted as adjudicator to ensure that fair questions were asked and that contestants always told the truth.

The first UK host was Eamonn Andrews and he chaired the quiz until its cancellation in 1963 (except for a short period when Australian Ron Randall took over in 1954 and a few other occasions when Gilbert Harding, Jerry Desmonde and Elizabeth Allen took charge of events). David Jacobs was frontman for the short-lived 1970s version and Andrews returned for an ITV revival in 1984. On Andrews's death in 1987, Penelope Keith and then, more permanently, Angela Rippon were drafted into the presenter's chair. Panellists varied, but the classic 1950s line-up was Barbara Kelly, David Nixon, Lady Isobel Barnett and the notoriously grouchy Gilbert Harding (the first ever panel comprised Kelly, Jerry Desmonde and Ted Kavanagh). Under the guidance of David Jacobs, the panel consisted of Lady Barnett, Kenneth Williams, William Franklyn and one other. Barbara Kelly returned in 1984, accompanied most often by Jilly Cooper and George Gale.

What's My Line? was revived yet again, this time as a regional programme (not fully networked) by Meridian Television (1994–6). Emma Forbes was installed as presenter and Roy Hudd, Kate Robbins, June Whitfield, Peter Smith and Denise Black were among the regular panellists.

Wheel of Fortune ✶

UK (Scottish) Quiz. ITV 1988–2001

Presenters **Nicky Campbell, Bradley Walsh, John Leslie, Paul Hendy**

Executive Producer **Sandy Ross**
Producers **Stephen Leahy, Anne Mason**

Colourful game show broadly based on Hangman.

Derived from the phenomenally popular American show of the same name, *Wheel of Fortune* gave Scottish Television its first big success in the world of networked game shows. Hosted initially by Radio 1 disc jockey Nicky Campbell, the programme invites three contestants to answer general knowledge questions, spin a large wheel marked with variously numbered segments and guess the missing letters of a mystery phrase. Whichever number is indicated by the pointer when the wheel stops is translated into points in the player's bank. Contestants correctly identifying the phrase pick up an extra prize, and the highest overall scorer attempts one more phrase in the grand finale, in the hope of collecting even bigger rewards – a car or a large cash sum. Angela Ekaette was the hostess/letter-turner in the early programmes, with Carol Smillie and then Jenny Powell taking over later. When Nicky Campbell left the show to concentrate on more cerebral TV and radio, he was succeeded by Bradley Walsh, who in turn soon gave way to John Leslie. In 1999 *Wheel of Fortune* was switched out of prime time and into the afternoon schedules. Paul Hendy took over as host in 2001.

Wheel of Fortune was also the name of a successor programme to TAKE YOUR PICK, offering star and booby prizes on the turn of a wheel, hosted by Michael Miles.

Wheeltappers' and Shunters' Social Club ★★

UK (Granada) Variety. ITV 1974–7

Presenters **Bernard Manning, Colin Crompton**

Creator/Producer **John Hamp**

● ***Variety show with a northern clubland atmosphere.***

Presented from the fictitious Wheeltappers' and Shunters' Social Club, this series offered a collection of decent acts from the northern club scene plus some international names, all performing in the smoky, noisy atmosphere of a mock-up club concert hall. Earthy comedian Bernard Manning was compere, competing for attention with bell-ringing 'concert chairman' Colin Crompton, who was forever interrupting to announce that the meat pies had arrived or that the bingo would start in half an hour. Reruns are worth watching to enjoy the tasteless 1970s fashions and hairstyles in the easily amused audience.

Wheldon, Sir Huw

OBE (1916–86)

Once described as 'the best Director-General the BBC never had', Welshman Huw Wheldon joined the Corporation in 1952 as a publicity officer. He then became a senior producer, working on programmes such as *Press Conference* and *Men in Battle*. Wheldon also appeared in front of the camera, conducting interviews for PANORAMA and hosting kids' shows such as ALL YOUR OWN. More famously, he became editor and presenter of the arts magazine MONITOR. Wheldon was subsequently promoted to the positions of Head of Documentary and Music Programmes (1963–5) and Controller of Programmes (1965–8). In 1968 he took over as Managing Director of Television, becoming Deputy Director-General in 1976. On leaving the boardroom, Wheldon returned to presenting, with the *Royal Heritage* series (timed to coincide with the Queen's Jubilee in 1977). From 1979 until shortly before his death in 1986, Sir Huw was President of the Royal Television Society.

When the Boat Comes In ★★★

UK (BBC) Drama. BBC 1 1976–7; 1981

Jack Ford .... **James Bolam**
Jessie Seaton/Ashton .... **Susan Jameson**
Bella Seaton .... **Jean Heywood**
Bill Seaton .... **James Garbutt**
Tom Seaton .... **John Nightingale**
Billy Seaton .... **Edward Wilson**
Dolly Headley/Ford .... **Madelaine Newton**
Matt Headley .... **Malcolm Terris**
Arthur Ashton .... **Geoffrey Rose**
Sir Horatio Manners .... **Basil Henson**
Mary .... **Michelle Newell**
Lady Caroline .... **Isla Blair**
Lois Baxter
Duke of Bedlington .... **William Fox**
'Geordie' Watson .... **Ian Cullen**
Miss Laidlaw .... **Catherine Terris**
Len Laidlaw .... **Peter McGowan**
Roddy .... **Martin Duncan**
Channing .... **Christopher Benjamin**
Mary Routledge/Seaton .... **Michelle Newell**
Sarah Headley .... **Rosalind Bailey**
Doughty .... **Bryan Pringle**
John Hartley .... **William Squire**
Tania Corley .... **Judy Loe**
Nigel Scott-Palliser .... **Clive Merrison**

Creator **James Mitchell**
Producers **Leonard Lewis, Andrew Osborn, David Maloney**

● ***Lives and loves in the depressed north-east.***

Centring on one Jack Ford, a shipyard fitter who dabbles in unionism and politics before working his way up the capitalist ladder, *When the Boat Comes In* depicts the hard days of the 1920s in the cobbled streets of Gallowshield (based on South Shields, where author James Mitchell's dad had once been mayor). Ford is a Jack the Lad-type figure, a rough diamond with a good heart who is closely allied to the Seaton family, especially attractive daughter Jessie, a schoolteacher. Her brother, Tom, is Jack's miner friend and her younger brother, Billy, becomes a doctor and brings free medicine to the local people. Dolly is the girl who becomes Ford's wife and Ashton is the po-faced teacher Jessie marries.

Using Ford, man of the people, as guide, and beginning in 1919 with his return from the Great War to a land rife with injustice, Mitchell effectively portrays the deep, grim poverty of this proud industrial region and the earthy but noble character of its people. After three series, the programme ends with Jack heading for a new life in the USA, only to return six years later in dubious circumstances, having made a fortune from bootlegging during Prohibition and then losing it all in the Wall Street Crash. This last season, set in the 1930s, sees our hero involved in the Jarrow marches and also taking part in the Spanish conflict.

Familiar through its jaunty 'Dance Ti Thi Daddy' theme song (written by David Fanshawe and sung by Alex Glasgow), *When the Boat Comes In* introduced viewers to the peculiarities of the lilting Geordie dialect and has since been fondly remembered as a poignant piece of social history.

Where the Heart Is ★★

UK (United/Anglia/Meridian) Drama 1997–

Margaret 'Peggy' Snow .... **Pam Ferris**
Ruth Goddard .... **Sarah Lancashire**
Vic Snow .... **Tony Haygarth**
Simon Goddard .... **Thomas Craig**
Stephen Snow .... **William Ash**
Jason Done
Lucy Snow .... **Jessica Baglow**
Wendy Atkins .... **Susannah Wise**
Patricia Illingworth .... **Maggie Wells**
Deborah Allis .... **Laura Crossley**
Dick Lampard .... **William Travis**
Henry .... **Andrew Knott**
Terry .... **Simon Ashley**
Jacqui Richards/Snow .... **Marsha Thomason**
Paulette Williams
Cheryl Lampard .... **Kathryn Hunt**
Sandra Harrison .... **Melanie Kilburn**
Keith Harrison .... **Neil McCaul**

Craig Harrison .... **Alex Carter**
Alison Storey .... **Katrina Levon**
Anna Kirkwall .... **Lesley Dunlop**
Luke Kirkwall .... **Christian Cooke**
Chris Eckersley .... **Vincenzo Pellegrino**
Karen Buckley .... **Leslie Ash**
David Buckley .... **Philip Middlemiss**
Jess Buckley .... **Kelly Wenham**
Beth Enright/Beresford .... **Kerrie Taylor**
Joe Beresford .... **Danny Seward**
Molly Beresford .... **Katie Riddoch**
Tom Beresford .... **Julian Lewis Jones**
Oscar Lampard .... **Joseph Aston**
Dean Pilsbury .... **Steve Chaplin**
Bella Scott .... **Rachel Leskovac**
Alan Boothe .... **Keith Barron**
Sally Boothe .... **Samantha Giles**
Billy Boothe .... **Andrew Paul**
Megan Boothe .... **Holly Grainger**
Samantha Boothe .... **Katy Clayton**
Nathan Boothe .... **Adam Paul Harvey**
Dr Kenworthy .... **Tom Chadbon**
Russell Naylor .... **Luke de Woolfson**
Ozias Harding .... **Brian Capron**
Alice Harding .... **Georgia Moffett**
Danny Flint .... **Richard Mylan**
Kim Blakeney .... **Denise Van Outen**
Callum Blakeney .... **Beans Balawi**

Creators **Ashley Pharoah, Vicky Featherstone**
Executive Producers **Simon Lewis, Michele Buck, Damien Timmer**
Producers **Kate Anthony, Simon Lewis, Avon Harpley, Richard Broke, Ian Hopkins**

Heartwarming tales concerning nurses at a Yorkshire health centre.

'A series about everyday things like living and dying', according to its early star, Pam Ferris, *Where the Heart Is* is the story of two sisters-in-law working as district nurses in the Yorkshire town of Skelthwaite. While committed to their work, they also recognize the responsibilities they face with their own families.

Kind-hearted, 48-year-old Peggy is the wife of Vic and mother of teenage son Stephen and young daughter Lucy. Ruth, wife of Peggy's astute businessman brother, Simon, is about to give birth to their first child, Alfie, as the series opens. Simon owns the toilet paper factory where Vic works. Action focuses more on wholesome, human stories rather than medical crises, with plenty of humour, a few pints of Chapstons down The Skelthwaite Arms, and a little sporting spice – through Vic's involvement as the ageing player-coach of the Skelthwaite Skorpions rugby league team – all thrown in for good measure. Featuring later are new nurse Jacqui Richards, an 'outsider' with new ideas who starts a relationship with Stephen and lodges with widow Maggie Wells, a member of the Skelthwaite Medical Centre team; Vic's sister, Sandra, and her new-in-town family; recently widowed mum, Anna Kirkwall (a nursing sister who replaces Ruth – who walks out on Simon and heads for Australia); and Chris Eckersley, the town's first male nurse. When tragedy strikes and Peggy is killed in a car accident involving a runaway horse, her place is taken by new nurse Karen Buckley, an old friend of Anna's who arrives with husband David and 17-year-old daughter Jess in tow. In later series, the Boothes are a new family in town while further recruits to the practice are nurses Beth Enright and Kim Blakeney. Ozias Harding is the businessman who becomes the new owner of the paper factory.

Paddy McAloon of the band Prefab Sprout wrote and performed the theme song.

Where There's Life ★★

UK (Yorkshire) Medical. ITV 1981–9

Presenters **Miriam Stoppard, Rob Buckman**

Executive Producer **Duncan Dallas**
Producers **John Fanshawe, David Taylor, Ian McFarlane, Derek Goodall, Irene Garrow, Anne Pivcevic, David Poyser, Paul Bader**

Discussion programme about medical matters.

Hosted by doctors Miriam Stoppard and Rob Buckman, the long-running *Where There's Life* talked to ordinary people about the medical traumas in their life and instigated debate about healthy lifestyles. It also considered new ideas and developments in the world of medicine.

Whicker, Alan

CBE (1925–)

Britain's most-travelled TV reporter, Alan Whicker, was born in Egypt. After entering journalism, he became a war correspondent and then joined the influential current affairs series TONIGHT when it began in 1957. His dry, distinctive delivery and his ability to play the ordinary Brit abroad led to his own series for the BBC, *Whicker's World*, in 1959. Initially a compilation of his *Tonight* reports, it soon broadened into new assignments, many under individual series titles, like *Whicker Down Under* in 1961. In 1968 he defected to the newly formed Yorkshire Television, where he continued to notch up air mile after air mile in the pursuit of oddities overseas and insights into other people's lifestyles. He later returned to the BBC and, in the 1980s, presented *Living with Uncle Sam* and *Living with Waltzing Matilda*, series about British expatriates in the USA and Australia. He then turned down the chance to emulate Phileas Fogg and go AROUND THE WORLD IN 80 DAYS (Michael Palin stepped in and reaped the rewards), preferring instead to take things rather more easily in *Around Whicker's World: the Ultimate Package*, in which he shadowed a wealthy tour party as they made their champagne circumnavigation. Among his other offerings have been *Whicker on Top of the World* (1962), *Whicker Down Mexico Way* (1963), *Whicker's New World*, *Whicker in Europe* (both 1969), *Whicker's Walkabout* (1970), *The World of Whicker* (1971), *Whicker's Orient*, *Whicker within a Woman's World* (both 1972), *Whicker's South Seas*, *Whicker Way Out West* (both 1973), *Around Whicker's World in 25 Years* (1982), *Whicker's World: a Taste of Spain* (1992) and *Whicker's War* (2004, retracing his own wartime footsteps). He also gained unexpected access to Haiti dictator Papa Doc Duvalier for a famous 1969 documentary, *Papa Doc – the Black Sheep*.

Whiplash ★★

UK (ATV) Western. ITV 1960–1

Christopher Cobb .... **Peter Graves**
Dan .... **Anthony Wickert**

A Western set not on the plains of America but in the Australian bush.

Chris Cobb is an American who arrives in Australia in the 1850s to establish Cobb & Co., the country's first stagecoach line. Even though he is based Down Under, and not in the Wild West, he faces the usual collection of cowboy outlaws. Thirty-four episodes were made, but star Peter Graves made more of an impression when he later appeared as Jim Phelps in MISSION: IMPOSSIBLE.

Whirligig ✶✶

UK (BBC) Children's Magazine. BBC 1950–6

Presenter **Humphrey Lestocq**

Creator **Michael Westmore**
Producers **Michael Westmore, Gilchrist Calder, Desmond O'Donovan**

● ***Early TV potpourri for younger viewers.***
Britain's first television magazine programme for children was a fortnightly affair fronted by Humphrey Lestocq with more than a little hindrance from string puppet Mr Turnip (activated by Joy Laurey and voiced by Peter Hawkins). Among the first regular features were *Box of Tricks* (a conjuring slot hosted by Geoffrey Robinson), a helicopter-themed travel quiz called *Flying Visit* (with Marcus Stellman), *Write It Yourself* (a chance for kids to pen the next instalment of a serial, hosted by Frank Coven) and a strip cartoon Western, *The Adventures of Hank* (renamed *Hank Rides Again*, with Francis Coudrill). Later contributions came from John Le Mesurier, who joined Marcus Stellman in *Mr Lumber's Shop*; Leslie Woodgate, who hosted *Sing Merrily, Sing!*; and Reginald Jacques, who fronted *Sing Song*. Robert Harbin briefly replaced Robinson as resident magician, Steve Race contributed *Room for Music*, Harry Corbett created *Magic and Mischief* with Sooty, and Rolf Harris was seen with Willoughby (his animated drawing board). Among the other serials included were *Stranger From Space, Big Top, The Highwayman's Bargain, Secrets of the Centuries, Jeremy Make-Believe* and *Can We Help You* (some scripted by Peter Ling and Hazel Adair, subsequently creators of CROSSROADS). *Whirligig* was screened on Saturday teatimes, alternating with programmes like *Telescope, Saturday Special* (later *SS Saturday Special*), *Sugar and Spice* and *All Your Own*.

Whirlybirds ✶✶

US (CBS/Desilu) Adventure. BBC 1958–62 (US: Syndicated 1957–9)

Chuck Martin .... **Ken Tobey**
Pete 'PT' Moore .... **Craig Hill**
Janet Culver .... **Sandra Spence**
Helen Carter .... **Nancy Hale**

Producer **N. Gayle Gitterman**

● ***Two helicopter pilots find adventure.***
Chuck Martin and PT Moore are two young pilots who found their own helicopter charter company, Whirlybird Service, based in Longwood Field, California. Every day proves to be an adventure, as the young daredevils fly their aircraft into tense and dangerous situations, hunting for missing folk or apprehending villains. With stunts aplenty, this is an all-action series that appealed to younger viewers and was produced by Lucille Ball and Desi Arnaz's Desilu company.

Whistle Test

See *Old Grey Whistle Test*.

White, Betty

(1922–)

American comic actress, a US hit as early as 1953 with her first sitcom, *Life With Elizabeth*, and successful throughout that decade in quizzes, variety shows and the comedy *Date with the Angels*. However, it wasn't until the 1970s that she began to attract the attention of viewers elsewhere in the world, having fallen out of the mainstream in the 1960s. As man-hungry Sue Ann Nivens in THE MARY TYLER MOORE SHOW her prime-time career took off again, and she followed it with game show appearances and her own comedy, *The Betty White Show*, in which she played Joyce Whitman. For most people, however, White is the naïve, dim-witted but caring Rose Nylund from THE GOLDEN GIRLS and *The Golden Palace*, a role she picked up in 1985 when in her 60s. Since these ended she has appeared in Bob Newhart's sitcom *Bob*, alongside Marie Osmond in *Maybe This Time* and Alfred Molina in *Ladies Man*, as well as in another US series called *Lionhearts*. Other recent credits include guest roles in *That '70s Show*, MALCOLM IN THE MIDDLE and JOEY, and a recurring role in *Boston Legal* (secretary Catherine Piper).

White, Carol

(Carole White; 1941–91)

British actress, a child film star in the 1950s, on TV in the mid-1960s and then quickly moving on to Hollywood. White's forte was the ingenue, the girl who was easily led, attracted by bright lights and ending up in trouble, as she exemplified in the powerful dramas UP THE JUNCTION (Sylvie) and CATHY COME HOME (Cathy).

White, Frances

(1938–)

Yorkshire-born actress, seen in many roles on TV since the 1970s. She was Andrea Warner in *A Raging Calm*, Julia in I, CLAUDIUS, Linda Clark in *A Little Bit of Wisdom*, Queen Charlotte in PRINCE REGENT, Sister May in I WOKE UP ONE MORNING, Molly Cramer in DANGERFIELD, and secretaries Dorothy Hampton in A VERY PECULIAR PRACTICE and Kate Hamilton in CROSSROADS. However, White is probably best known as Miss Flood in MAY TO DECEMBER. Smaller roles have come in series such as *Sanctuary*, THE RIVALS OF SHERLOCK HOLMES, HUNTER'S WALK, RUMPOLE OF THE BAILEY, PEAK PRACTICE, WYCLIFFE and *The Courtroom*, among other series.

White Heather Club, The ✶

UK (BBC) Variety. BBC 1 1958–68

Presenters **Robert Wilson, Andy Stewart, Robin Hall, Jimmie Macgregor**
Producer **Iain MacFadyan**

● ***Singing and dancing, Scottish style.***
An extension of the traditional Hogmanay parties, *The White Heather Club* was an excuse for Scottish performers to don their best kilts and jig around to the best folksongs and ballads

north of the border. Featuring stars like Moira Anderson, Duncan Macrae, Roddy McMillan, The Joe Gordon Folk Four, James Urquhart, Jimmy Logan, dancers Isobel James and Dixie Ingram and bandleaders Jimmy Shand and Ian Powrie, the series, produced by the BBC at its Springfield Road studio in Glasgow, ran and ran – for 285 editions. Tenor Robert Wilson was the first host, giving way after six programmes to Andy Stewart and the TONIGHT pairing of Robin Hall and Jimmie Macgregor.

White Horses, The ★★

Germany/Yugoslavia (Jugoslavija Film) Children's Drama. BBC 1 1968

Julia .... **Helga Anders**
Uncle Dimitri .... **Helmuth Schnider**
Hugo .... **Franz Muxeneder**

A teenage girl enjoys horsey adventures during her holidays.

Fifteen-year-old Julia lives in Belgrade but is given the chance to spend her holiday at the stud farm run by her Uncle Dimitri and his head groom, Hugo. Julia instantly falls in love with the farm's white Lippizaner horses, particularly one named Boris who leads the girl into a series of adventures.

Made on the Continent and dubbed into English, the series proved to be enchanting children's hour escapism. Its evocative theme song, also called 'White Horses', was a hit in 1968 for Jacky (later, as Jackie Lee, to record another theme song hit with 'Rupert').

White Hunter ★★

UK (Beaconsfield/ITP) Adventure. ITV 1958–60

John A. Hunter .... **Rhodes Reason**
Atimbu .... **Harry Baird**

Producer **Norman Williams**

Adventures in the African jungle with the appropriately named John Hunter.

This series was based on the true-life tales of John A. Hunter, author of the books *African Safari* and *Hunter's Tracks*. *White Hunter* is set in East Africa, with stories revolving around wildlife, rebellious locals and outsiders seeking to disrupt the natural harmony of the Dark Continent. Thirty-nine episodes were made.

White Rabbit, The ★★★

UK (BBC) Drama. BBC 2 1967

Wing Commander Forest Frederick Yeo-Thomas .... **Kenneth More**
Rudi .... **Alan MacNaughtan**
Barbara .... **Denise Buckley**
José Dupuis .... **Annette Crosbie**
Ernst .... **Stephen Bradley**
Pierre Brossolette .... **George Hagan**
Col. Brierley .... **Roy Purcell**
Col. Robinson .... **Robert Bruce**
Horace .... **David Collings**
Cadillac .... **Christopher Benjamin**

Writer **Michael Voysey**

Producer **David Conroy**

An RAF officer with close connections to France defies his Nazi torturers.

Based on Bruce Marshall's biography of 'Tommy' Yeo-Thomas GC, MC, a fashion house executive who linked up with the French resistance and was captured by the Gestapo, this four-part drama is directed by Peter Hammond. Yeo-Thomas's story is one of incredible human courage in the face of wartime atrocities. His family had lived in France since 1855 and he felt strong loyalties to France, hence we have an unconventional hero, but a hero all the same. Yeo-Thomas becomes an RAF officer, adopts the codename The White Rabbit and makes two hazardous journeys into France to maintain contact with the resistance. On a third visit, he is captured in Paris but manages to hold out under duress for 48 hours to allow his contacts to disperse. He is then imprisoned in Fresnes before being transported to Buchenwald concentration camp where he suffers at the hands of his adversaries. The Gestapo, headed up by interrogator Rudi, find that The White Rabbit is a stubborn man and hard to break. José is Tommy's resistance contact; Barbara is Tommy's girlfriend.

White Room, The ★★★

UK (Initial) Rock Music. Channel 4 1995–6

Presenter **Mark Radcliffe**

Producer **Chris Cowey**

Late-night, largely gimmick-free rock showcase.

Named after its bare white studio set (a metaphorical 'blank canvas' on which artists – encouraged to wear black and white – could paint), *The White Room* was a live music hour that featured established performers (Stevie Wonder, Little Richard, Lou Reed and others) plus the up and coming. The mid-1990s was a good time to launch the show as the Britpop wave was about to crash onto the sands of the record charts – bands like Oasis, Blur and Pulp all appeared. Pop and rock dominated, but with space also for jazz and hip hop. The three series followed a pilot in 1994 that was devoted to reggae.

Whitehouse, Mary

CBE (1910–2001)

Former schoolteacher who turned moral crusader when establishing her Clean-Up TV campaign in 1964 and formalizing it as The National Viewers' and Listeners' Association (now known as Mediawatch-UK) a year later. TILL DEATH US DO PART (not surprisingly) was one programme to raise her blood pressure, and she was particularly critical of the works of Dennis Potter. The regime of Sir Hugh Greene, the BBC's Director-General in the permissive 1960s, was blamed for contributing to moral decay. She formally retired from the campaign in 1994. Despite the flippant use of her name, she had nothing to do with the comedy sketch show called THE MARY WHITEHOUSE EXPERIENCE!

Whitehouse, Paul

(1958–)

South Wales-born, London-raised comedian, actor and writer. Whitehouse was part of the supporting crew on *Vic Reeves Big Night Out* but gained recognition as Harry Enfield's co-star (with Kathy Burke) in *Harry Enfield's Television Programme* and *Harry Enfield and Chums*, having already written material for Enfield's appearances on SATURDAY LIVE/FRIDAY NIGHT LIVE. From this, Whitehouse (with Charlie Higson) wrote and appeared in a *Comic Asides* pilot called *The Honeymoon's Over* (shown in 1994) but a series didn't follow. Instead, they created and starred in the hugely successful THE FAST SHOW, which led to spin-offs like *Ted and Ralph* and Sky's soccer quiz *Jumpers for Goalposts* (with Paul as Ron Manager). A new sitcom, HAPPINESS (with Whitehouse playing Danny Spencer and co-writing), followed and Whitehouse also appeared in the BBC's 1999 version of DAVID COPPERFIELD (pawnbroker). In 2005 he wrote and starred in *Help*, playing all the weird and wonderful patients who visit the psychotherapist played by Chris Langham. Whitehouse has also been seen in *The Smell of Reeves and Mortimer*, *The Catherine Tate Show* and *Fun at the Funeral Parlour*, and has provided voices for the *Robbie the Reindeer* animations. As a writer, he has contributed to RANDALL AND HOPKIRK (DECEASED).

Whitelaw, Billie

CBE (1932–)

Warwickshire-born actress who arrived on TV in the 1950s, appearing in dramas like *The Secret Garden* (Martha) and THE ADVENTURES OF ROBIN HOOD and playing Mary, the daughter of DIXON OF DOCK GREEN, soon to be married to Dixon's young colleague, Andy Crawford. She left *Dixon* after just one year but went on to support Bob Monkhouse in *My Pal Bob*, was Josephine in Thames TV's 1974 series *Napoleon and Love*, and, in 1981, she turned to comedy again, taking the role of Bertha Freyer in PRIVATE SCHULZ. Among her many notable performances have been parts in the ARMCHAIR THEATRE offerings *No Trams to Lime Street* and *Lena, O My Lena*, the SUPERNATURAL presentations *Countess Ilona* and *The Werewolf Reunion*, plus *Jamaica Inn*, *The Dressmaker*, *Imaginary Friends* (Elsie Novar), *Lorna Doone* (Sarah Ridd), *A Murder of Quality*, *The Cloning of Joanna May* (Mavis), *Firm Friends* (Rose Gutteridge), *Performance*'s presentation of *The Entertainer* (Phoebe Rice) and *Screen Two's Skallagrigg*. Whitelaw has been seen also in *Merlin* (Ambrosia), *Born to Run* (Lili Flitch), SHOOTING THE PAST (Veronica), THE LAST OF THE BLONDE BOMBSHELLS (Evelyn), CATHERINE COOKSON*'s The Fifteen Streets* (Beatrice Llewellyn) and *A Dinner of Herbs* (Kate Makepeace), and JUDGE JOHN DEED. Her first husband was actor Peter Vaughan and she later married writer Robert Muller.

Whiteley, Richard

CBE (1943–2005)

Yorkshire-born presenter, the first face seen on both Channel 4 (as the punning host of the long-running COUNTDOWN) and Yorkshire Television (spending no less than 30 years at the helm of the regional news magazine, *Calendar*, after an ITN traineeship). Whiteley also hosted *Richard Whiteley Unbriefed*, in which he bravely interviewed famous guests without being told who they were or given any research notes.

Whitfield, June

CBE (1925–)

RADA-trained, London-born comedy actress, the archetypal suburban sitcom wife, thanks to her long partnership with the late Terry Scott in HAPPY EVER AFTER (June Fletcher) and TERRY AND JUNE (June Medford). Whitfield had previously appeared with Scott in *Scott On ...* After success on radio in *Take It from Here* and other series, Whitfield's first TV appearances came in the 1950s, in shows like *Idiot Weekly, Price 2d*, *The Benny Hill Show* and then, in 1961, *Hancock* (see HANCOCK'S HALF-HOUR) (she was the nurse in *The Blood Donor*). She appeared again with Hancock in 1967, playing Esmeralda Stavely-Smythe, a waitress in his last TV series (also called *Hancock*). Whitfield was seen also in *The Arthur Askey Show* (and his earlier *Before Your Very Eyes*) and supported Jimmy Edwards in THE SEVEN FACES OF JIM and Stanley Baxter in *Baxter On ...* She later played Rose Garvey in BEGGAR MY NEIGHBOUR and starred as Mabel Pollard, Harry H. Corbett's fiancée, in *The Best Things in Life*. She has also gamely turned her hand to 'newer' comedy, making guest appearances with Julian Clary in *Terry and Julian* and *All Rise for Julian Clary*, and playing the part of Jennifer Saunders's mum in ABSOLUTELY FABULOUS (also appearing in Saunders's *Mirrorball*). Whitfield, who has featured in various sketch shows and panel games (including *Jokers Wild* and as Mrs White in CLUEDO), was also seen in THE PALLISERS (Mrs Bonteen), COMMON AS MUCK (Irene), TOM JONES (Mrs Whitfield) and *Time Keepers of the Millennium*. Additionally, she played Mrs Birkstead in CATHERINE COOKSON*'s The Secret*, Annie in LAST OF THE BLONDE BOMBSHELLS and Delphi and Nelly in LAST OF THE SUMMER WINE. More recently, she has provided voices for BOB THE BUILDER (Bob's mum) and *The World of Peter Rabbit and Friends*, and taken guest roles in *The Afternoon Play*, THE ROYAL, MIDSOMER MURDERS and AGATHA CHRISTIE'S MARPLE. Actress Suzy Aitchison in her daughter.

Whitney, John

(1930–)

British TV executive, a former writer and producer who scripted for 1950s and 1960s series like SHADOW SQUAD, *The Verdict is Yours*, CRIME SHEET, KNIGHT ERRANT, THE AVENGERS, GHOST SQUAD, HARPERS WEST ONE, *The Hidden Truth* and THE INFORMER, in collaboration with Geoffrey Bellman (the last three also as creators). He also wrote a sitcom, *In for a Penny*, with John Hawkesworth. Whitney was script editor for THE PLANE MAKERS and later became Head of LWT, before advancing to the position of Director-General of the IBA (1982–9). Recently he has been Chairman of RADA, the Royal Academy of Dramatic Art.

Who Dares, Wins ... ★★★

UK (Holmes) Comedy. Channel 4 1984–6; 1988

Rory McGrath, Philip Pope, Jimmy Mulville, Julia Hills, Tony Robinson

Producers **Denise O'Donoghue, Andy Hamilton**

Comedy sketch show featuring an up-and-coming team of writers/comedians.

In the view of most critics, the often satirical but not necessarily topical *Who Dares, Wins ...* succeeded where similar 'alternative' sketch shows failed, because it was innovative. Among the best-remembered items was a series on pandas plotting to escape from a zoo. Julia Hills played a tense, accident-prone TV interviewer and Tony Robinson spent two programmes totally naked. The series followed a one-off 'special' in 1983 and early episodes carried a sub-title, such as 'A Camping Holiday in Beirut' or 'A Ticket for the Cup Final'.

Who Do You Do? ★★

UK (LWT) Comedy. ITV 1972–6

Freddie Starr, Peter Goodwright, Faith Brown, Janet Brown, Margo Henderson, Roger Kitter, Barry Cryer, Johnny More, Jerry Stevens, Len Lowe, Dailey and Wayne, Paul Melba, Little and Large, Aiden J. Harvey

Creator/Producer **Jon Scoffield**

● ***Comedy sketches featuring top impressionists.***

Although leaning heavily on the talents of Freddie Starr and Peter Goodwright, *Who Do You Do?* also featured most of the other leading impressionists of the day in a series of gags and skits. Tightly editing together its various components, the programme offered a gag a second in the style of THE COMEDIANS. The series was renamed *New Who Do You Do?* in 1975 and *Now Who Do You Do?* in 1976 (when the cast incorporated new faces like Michael Barrymore, Les Dennis and Dustin Gee).

Who Pays the Ferryman? ★★★

UK (BBC) Drama. BBC 2 1977

Alan Haldane	**Jack Hedley**
Annika Zeferis	**Betty Arvaniti**
Babis Spiridakis	**Neil McCarthy**
Matheos Noukakis	**Takis Emmanuel**
Alexis Vassilakis	**Alexis Sergis**
Nikos Vassilakis	**Nikos Verlekis**
Elena Vassilakis	**Maria Sokali**
Katerina Matakis	**Patience Collier**
Xenophon Hasapis	**Nikos Kouros**
Major	**Stefan Gryff**

Writer **Michael J. Bird**
Producer **William Slater**

● ***A former resistance officer returns to Greece and finds the past is an obstacle to a happy life.***

When Alan Haldane, a one-time officer in the Greek resistance, leaves his boat-building business in the UK to return to Crete after an absence of 30 years, he stirs up a hornet's nest. With old passions and hatreds reignited, he discovers he has an illegitimate daughter on the island and that there is a vendetta against him in Elounda, where he takes up residence. He begins a relationship with local woman Annika, but, unknown to her, Haldane is haunted by memories of her dead sister. Tension mounts as old Greek traditions conflict with the ways of the modern world.

The programme title is derived from the legend of Charon, who demanded a fee to ferry passengers across the River Styx to the Underworld. Star Jack Hedley took on the role of Haldane after Peter Finch, who was first choice for the part, unexpectedly passed away. Writer Michael J. Bird had previously explored the mystic Greek islands in his earlier BBC series, THE LOTUS EATERS. Music for this eight-part drama was performed by Yannis Markopoulos and his orchestra, who scored a UK hit with the theme tune in 1977.

Who Wants to be a Millionaire? ★★★★

UK (Celador) Quiz. ITV 1998–

Presenter **Chris Tarrant**

Creators **David Briggs, Mike Whitehill, Steve Knight**
Producers **Guy Freeman, Colman Hutchinson, David Briggs**

● DOUBLE YOUR MONEY ***for the turn of the millennium.***

It's often the simplest programming that is the most successful, and *Who Wants to be a Millionaire?* is certainly successful, the format being sold all round the world. It also seems simple on the face of it: a contestant pitched into the hot seat, working his way up a ladder of cash prizes, having to decide whether to quit while ahead or gamble big money in the hope of an even bigger cash prize. However, this synopsis tends to ignore the planning that goes into staging the contest, so that the game is easy to follow and viewers are enthralled by the unfolding drama. A carefully lit set, the constant throbbing of background music and an edgy studio atmosphere are all key elements in lifting this quiz above the ordinary. Questionmaster Chris Tarrant's encouragement – repeating the options available, making sure they understand their situation ('Is that your final answer?') – also adds to the tension. However, it is the sheer magnitude of the prize money that proves the biggest draw.

Contestants progress from a £100 base to the possible jackpot of £1 million via a series of 15 questions. For each question, four possible answers are shown and the contestant even has the options of asking the audience for help, eliminating two of the answers by going '50/50', or phoning a friend for assistance. But questions become increasingly difficult and the pressure of gambling away many thousands of pounds deters all but the bravest from aiming for the top – even though the producers have built in guaranteed prizes of £1,000 and £32,000 for contestants who reach those levels. To take part in the show, viewers are invited to phone in and answer eliminator questions, the cost of the calls covering the show's prize money. Ten viewers are then selected for the programme and a place in the hot seat is won by answering a 'fastest finger first' question, involving placing four answers in the correct order in the quickest time.

The first person to go all the way to the jackpot came in the American version. John Carpenter scooped the $1 million prize in November 1999. A year later, Judith Keppel became the first £1 million winner in the UK. In 2003 another £1 million winner, Major Charles Ingram, was found guilty of attempting to defraud the show, along with his wife, Diana, and fellow contestant Tecwen Whittock.

Who-Dun-It ★★

UK (ATV) Mystery Anthology. ITV 1969

Jeremy Moon	**Gary Raymond**
DI Trubshaw	**Victor Platt**
Cynthia Park	**Amanda Reiss**

Creator **Lewis Greifer**
Producer **Jack Williams**

● ***Series of plays with a murder theme, offering viewers the chance to spot the culprit.***

This 13-episode series presented a different mystery each week and, after the discovery of a body – a Hollywood film star on a transatlantic liner, perhaps – viewers were invited to hazard a guess as to *Who-Dun-It*, before finally all was revealed. Recurring characters involved in the investigations were Jeremy Moon, Inspector Trubshaw and Cynthia Park.

Whodunnit? ✶✶

UK (Thames) Panel Game. ITV 1972–8

Hosts **Edward Woodward, Jon Pertwee**

Creators/Writers **Jeremy Lloyd, Lance Percival**
Producers **Malcolm Morris, Robert Reed, Dennis Kirkland, Anthony Parker, Leon Thau**

● ***Celebrity panellists attempt to spot the culprit in a series of half-hour mysteries.***

Hosted initially by Edward Woodward and then by Jon Pertwee, this light-hearted panel game offered celebrity guests the chance to find the killer in a mystery playlet. After seeing the action on tape, each celebrity was allowed to request a short action replay of a telling moment and then to question all the characters involved. Finally, they were called upon to name the guilty party, who would, in a great show of bravado, stand up to take the rap. The performers changed from week to week, but a handful of panellists became regulars, most notably Patrick Mower and Anouska Hempel. Created by comedians Jeremy Lloyd and Lance Percival, the formula was rehashed for CLUEDO in the 1990s.

Whoops Apocalypse ✶✶✶

UK (LWT) Comedy. ITV 1982

Johnny Cyclops	**Barry Morse**
Premier Dubienkin	**Richard Griffiths**
The Deacon	**John Barron**
Commissar Solzhenitsyn	**Alexei Sayle**
Kevin Pork	**Peter Jones**
Foreign Secretary	**Geoffrey Palmer**
Chancellor of the Exchequer	**Richard Davies**
Shah Mashiq Rassim	**Bruce Montague**
Lacrobat	**John Cleese**
Jay Garrick	**Ed Bishop**
Abdab	**David Kelly**

Creators/Writers **Andrew Marshall, David Renwick**
Producer **Humphrey Barclay**

● ***A world dominated by crackpot politicians rushes towards World War III.***

In this irreverent comedy, attempts to restore Shah Mashiq Rassim to the throne of Iran by the use of the nuclear Quark bomb prove disastrous when events run haywire and Israel is blown up. The world is spent spinning towards Armageddon, with the balance of power fought over by US President Johnny Cyclops (a lobotomized former actor from Omaha) and Soviet Premier Dubienkin. In the middle is the idiotic British Prime Minister, Kevin Pork. The Deacon is the USA's crazed security adviser, and also in the fray is an international terrorist named Lacrobat. A feature-film version, starring Peter Cook and Loretta Swit, was released in 1986.

Whoops Baghdad!

See *Up Pompeii!*

Whose Line is It Anyway? ✶✶✶

UK (Hat Trick) Comedy. Channel 4 1988–2000

Presenter **Clive Anderson**

Creators **Dan Patterson, Mark Leveson**
Producer **Dan Patterson**

● ***Celebrity improvisation game show.***

Transferring to television from Radio 4, *Whose Line is It Anyway?* brought the drama school discipline of improv – improvisation – into the world of mainstream comedy. Each programme featured four ad-libbing comedians working singly, in pairs or all together, to execute a series of parlour games. Host Clive Anderson asked the studio audience for suggestions for some games, others were predetermined, but all demanded instant response and imagination from the assembled performers. Favourite guests included Tony Slattery, John Sessions, Josie Lawrence, Greg Proops, Paul Merton, Sandi Toksvig, Mike McShane, Ryan Stiles, Stephen Fry, Caroline Quentin and Colin Mochrie. Music was supplied by Richard Vranch at the piano. Editions were also made in the USA for airing on both sides of the Atlantic.

A similar concept, entitled *Impromptu*, was shown on BBC 2 in 1964. Produced by David Croft, it called on a resident team of performers (Victor Spinetti, Lance Percival, Anne Cunningham, Peter Reeves and Betty Impey) to act out a whole programme, working from basic instructions given to them on cards by Jeremy Hawk.

Why Don't You . . . ? ✶✶

UK (BBC) Children's Entertainment. BBC 1 1973–95

Creator **Patrick Dowling**
Executive Producer **Molly Cox**
Producers **Patrick Dowling, Molly Cox, Patrick Charlton, Hilary Murphy, Catherine McFarlane, Brian Willis, Allan Cook, David J. Evans, Kirstie Fisher, Trevor Long**

● ***Ideas to fill school holiday hours.***

Billed initially in *Radio Times* as *Wdyjsoytsagadslbi?*, standing for *Why don't you just switch off your television set and go and do something less boring instead?*, *Why Don't You . . . ?* took a bunch of kids and a stack of letters from viewers and put them together to teach youngsters how to make the best of their time during school holidays. Crafts, cookery, sports and music were all touted as boredom busters and the show later moved from its original home in Bristol around the BBC regions – to Belfast, Glasgow, Cardiff, Liverpool, Newcastle (where Ant McPartlin was one of the team) and Manchester. Each region prided itself on its wacky studio set – a Bristol basement, a run-down church hall in Belfast, a Cardiff seaside café, the countryside around Glasgow – but these changed with the times, too. One short run in 1990 was presented as 'an adventure drama series'. The idea was launched at a time when BBC 1 still closed down for a couple of hours from 11 a.m., but the BBC bravely persevered with the concept later, despite the threat that kids really might turn off.

Whyton, Wally
(1929–97)

Former skiffle musician Wally Whyton was one of ITV's favourite children's entertainers from the 1950s to the 1970s. He began his showbiz career with The Vipers group (who notched up three hits in 1957) and found his way into television by sitting in for Rolf Harris on one show. Whyton was soon in demand for series like *Small Time*, *Musical Box*, *The Three Scampis* and FIVE O'CLOCK CLUB, where he worked with puppets like Pussy Cat Willum, Ollie Beak, Fred Barker, Joe Crow and Spike McPike. He was later seen in PLAY SCHOOL and as co-host of the pop show LIFT OFF.

Widescreen

Widescreen (pioneered in the UK by Channel 4 and S4C and now commonly available, thanks to digital broadcasting) is a means of displaying the TV picture so that it more natually fits the human eye. Widescreen imagery has a ratio of 16:9 (16 units high and nine units wide), as opposed to the picture on conventional TV screens which has a 4:3 ratio (or, to compare like with like, 12:9). The added width allows the new technology to assimilate more closely the human field of vision and is, therefore, reputedly more comfortable to watch. Viewers with old-style sets can use their digital control box to switch to widescreen format, which displays the whole widescreen picture but with black horizontal bars at the top and bottom. When programmes made in the old 4:3 ratio are viewed on a dedicated widescreen television, there are three options available to the viewer. The first involves allowing the picture to sit in the middle of the screen, with black bars vertically down each side. The second is for the set to crop the picture at the top and bottom, and then stretch the edges of the image to fill out the screen (stretching the whole image results in distorted figures). The third option zooms in on the image to fill out the screen, but the top and bottom of the image are then lost.

Widows/Widows II/She's Out ★★★

UK (Thames/Euston Films) Crime Drama. ITV 1983/1985/1995

Dolly Rawlins	**Ann Mitchell**
Linda Perelli	**Maureen O'Farrell**
Shirley Miller	**Fiona Hendley**
Bella O'Reilly	**Eva Mottley**
	Debby Bishop *(II)*
DI Resnick	**David Calder**
DS Fuller	**Paul Jesson**
Harry Rawlins	**Maurice O'Connell**
Audrey Withey	**Kate Williams**
DC Andrews	**Peter Machin**
Boxer Davis	**Dudley Sutton**
Kathleen Resnick	**Thelma Whiteley**
Trudie	**Catherine Neilson**
Arnie Fisher	**Jeffrey Chiswick**
Tony Fisher	**Chris Ellison**
Vic Morgan	**Stephen Yardley** *(II)*
Micky Tesco	**Andrew Kazamia** *(II)*
Ester Freeman	**Linda Marlowe** *(She's Out)*
Gloria Radford	**Maureen Sweeney** *(She's Out)*
Julia Lawson	**Anna Patrick** *(She's Out)*
Connie Stephens	**Zoe Heyes** *(She's Out)*
Angela Dunn	**Indra Ove** *(She's Out)*
Kathleen O'Reilly	**Maggie McCarthy** *(She's Out)*
DS Mike Withy	**Adrian Rawlins** *(She's Out)*
DCI Ron Craigh	**Hugh Quarshie** *(She's Out)*
DS John Palmer	**Douglas McFerran** *(She's Out)*

Creator/Writer **Lynda La Plante**
Executive Producers **Verity Lambert, Linda Agran, Johnny Goodman**
Producers **Linda Agran, Irving Teitelbaum, Verity Lambert**

● ***Four inexperienced female crooks pull off a daring armed robbery.***

When arch-villain Harry Rawlins is killed in an attempted hold-up, his wife, Dolly, inherits his well-laid plans for future robberies. One involves attacking a security van in a subway, and Dolly fancies her chances of pulling it off. She assembles around her three other widows: attractive, blonde Shirley Miller and dark-haired Linda Perelli (whose husbands are killed along with Harry), plus black stripper Bella O'Reilly, whose husband has died of a drugs overdose. Together they plan the raid meticulously, but with the Fisher brothers (Harry's old adversaries) lurking around, and Detective Inspector Resnick deeply suspicious, keeping their secret is not easy. Yet all goes swimmingly and the four girls fly off to Rio with suitcases full of cash.

It is in the sequel, two years later, that their troubles begin. Their tongues become loose and their behaviour invites comment. Most alarming is the fact that Harry is not dead after all, but has faked his death to live with another woman and is now out to regain the money that is rightly his. (In this second series, Bella was played by Debby Bishop, following the death of Eva Mottley.)

The story is picked up yet again in a second sequel entitled *She's Out*. This sees Dolly Rawlins released from an eight-year jail-term and hoping to set up a children's home, yet surrounded by a new troupe of female felons, as well as numerous other unsavoury characters, all of whom are after her stashed-away loot.

Creator Lynda La Plante scripted a new American version of *Widows* in 2000.

Wife Swap ★★★

UK (RDF Media) Documentary. Channel 4 2003–
DVD: VCI

Executive Producers **Stephen Lambert, Jenny Crowther**
Producers **Jenny Crowther, Helen Richards**

● ***Women from two families swap homes with startling consequences.***

Take the women out of two, rather different families, make them change places for two weeks, light the blue touchpaper and retire. That's the fairly simple premise of this reality series but one that has proved engrossing and hugely popular with viewers. In each episode two families swap wives/mothers, not for anything 'suspicious' but simply to reveal how people's domestic standards vary. The inter-reaction between the new partners is a particular highlight, as one or other party delivers some long-overdue home truths about diet, hygiene and general contributions to home life. Political views, budgets, the disciplining of children and other issues also bubble to the top. Of course, the producers engineer the scenarios to a degree by deliberately choosing families between whom there is likely to be friction, but the participants rarely let the side down with their bluntness and often downright hostility to each other.

Some follow-up programmes entitled *Wife Swap Changed Our Marriage* have also been screened. There was also a *Celebrity Wife Swap* in 2003, with ex-Big Brother 'star' Jade Goody swapping places with Diana Ingram, wife of disgraced Major Charles Ingram, who was convicted of cheating on WHO WANTS TO BE A MILLIONAIRE? The format has been sold around the world, including to the USA, and some of these American episodes have been aired on Channel 4.

Wilcox, Desmond

(1931–2000)

Award-winning British documentary-maker and current affairs reporter, married to Esther Rantzen, with whom he worked when co-editor of the long-running MAN ALIVE series and editor of BRADEN'S WEEK. In the early 1960s Wilcox was a reporter with THIS WEEK and he was later Head of General Features at the BBC, but he returned in front of the cameras in 1983 as anchor of *Sixty Minutes*, the short-lived successor to NATIONWIDE. That same year he began writing, presenting and producing *The Visit*, a series which accompanied people undertaking dramatic, life-changing journeys. The highlight was the story of *The Boy David*, a young Peruvian Indian receiving facial plastic surgery in the UK. Wilcox employed the same documentary techniques when following the wedding plans of a young couple from Cardiff in another 1980s series, *The Marriage*. Later contributions included *The Lost Children* (1991, about Colombian street-kids) and its follow-up, *Children of the Sewers* (1999).

Wilcox, Paula

(1949–)

Manchester-born actress, starring as Beryl in THE LOVERS, after appearances in series like THE DUSTBINMEN and CORONATION STREET (Ray Langton's sister, Janice). Around the same time, she popped up in another comedy, *On the House*, but enjoyed far more success as Chrissy in MAN ABOUT THE HOUSE. When this series ended, Wilcox was cast in her own sitcom, the daring (for the time) single-parent comedy MISS JONES AND SON (Elizabeth Jones). After a few quiet years, Wilcox resurfaced in the 1985 Channel 4 comedy *The Bright Side*, playing prison widow Cynthia Bright. In the 1990s she took the role of Ros West in FIDDLERS THREE and then appeared as Ivy in Frank Skinner's comedy, BLUE HEAVEN, Sylv in *Life After Birth*, Mrs Audrey Parker in the children's series *The Queen's Nose*, Mrs Walwyn in *The Stalker's Apprentice*, Marguerite Laslett in FOOTBALLERS' WIVES, and Lilian in THE SMOKING ROOM. Other credits over the years have included guest spots in THE ONEDIN LINE, THE LIVER BIRDS, HADLEIGH, KATE, BOON, BROOKSIDE, PEAK PRACTICE, HOLBY CITY, *The Afternoon Play*, ALL ABOUT ME, DOWN TO EARTH and MURDER IN SUBURBIA.

Wild Palms ★★★

US (Ixtlan/Greengrass) Science Fiction. BBC 2 1993
(US: ABC 1993)

Harry Wyckoff .... **James Belushi**
Grace Wyckoff .... **Dana Delany**
Senator Anton 'Tony' Kreutzer .... **Robert Loggia**
Paige Katz .... **Kim Cattrall**
Josie Ito .... **Angie Dickinson**
Tommy Laszlo .... **Ernie Hudson**
Tabba Schwartzkopf .... **Bebe Neuwirth**
Coty Wyckoff .... **Ben Savage**
Tully Woiwode .... **Nick Mancuso**
Eli Levitt .... **David Warner**
Chickie Levitt .... **Brad Dourif**

Creators/Executive Producers **Bruce Wagner, Oliver Stone**

● ***A TV executive fights plans to use virtual reality to control the world.***

The potential power of television lies at the core of this heavily hyped, five-part sci-fi thriller. The year is 2007 and in Los Angeles lawyer Harry Wyckoff is newly installed as an executive with Channel 3, a TV network owned by Senator Tony Kreutzner's Wild Palms Group. Kreutzner is, however, power-crazed and sees the development of 3D images (holosynths) and virtual reality broadcasts as an effective means of controlling the population, especially if used in conjunction with Mimezine, a mind-warping drug made by another of his companies. Kreutzner is also head of an agency known as The Fathers, who kidnap children and brainwash them into his 'New Realism' philosophy. Opposing The Fathers is the underground resistance, The Friends, headed up by Harry's father-in-law, Eli Levitt. Thus, Harry is caught in the midst of real and unreal worlds, trapped between good and evil with his own family under immediate threat. Key characters include the villainous Josie Ito, Kreutzner's sister and former wife of Levitt, and Paige Katz, Kreutzner's mistress and an old flame of Harry's. Harry's family consists of wife Grace, mute daughter Deirdre, and son Coty, who stars in Channel 3's 3D sitcom *Church Windows*, alongside actress Tabba Schwartzkopf. The serial was developed from the comic strip of the same name by Bruce Wagner in *Details* magazine and was film director Oliver Stone's first venture into television. Both men made cameo appearances. Stunning visuals – essential for making the concept work – included a memorable image of a rhino in a swimming pool.

Wild West ★★★

UK (BBC) Situation Comedy. BBC 1 2002; 2004
DVD: BBC

Mary Trewednack .... **Dawn French**
Angela Phillips .... **Catherine Tate**
Holly .... **Anne-Marie Duff**
Robin Weaver
Jeff .... **Sean Foley**
Jake .... **David Bradley**
Harry .... **Richard Mylan**
PC Alan .... **Stewart Wright**
Gilly .... **Liza Goddard**
Doug .... **Bill Bailey**

Creator/Writer **Simon Nye**
Executive Producer **Sophie Clarke-Jervoise**
Producers **Paul Schlesinger, Jacinta Peel**

● ***Two eccentric lesbians try to improve life in their sheltered village.***

Cornwall is an odd county: odd in the sense that it sticks out into the sea and is not on the road to anywhere. Simon Nye's *Wild West* also suggests that Cornwall is odd in other ways, not least in its quirky population. The setting is the tiny, fictitious village of St Gweep (real-life Portloe), home to Mary and Angela, two weird, frumpy women who are stuck together because no one else will have them. Mary is the dominant partner, constantly finding ways of keeping the neurotic

Angela in the village. They run and live above the grocery/post office and their day-to-day movements centre around the shop, the beach and the local pub, The Coach and Horses, where Jeff is the landlord with an interest in 'swinging'. Among the other barking villagers are Holly, who runs the Museum of Witchcraft, PC Alan, the ice-cream-addicted lawman, Harry, who lives in a campervan on the beach, and old sea dog Jake. Stories revolve around the problem of second-home buying, the plus/minus nature of tourism, the windy weather, efforts to revive the Cornish language, a decision to stop being lesbians (if they ever really were at all) and the arrival of a film crew in the village. Two series were produced, but failed to catch the viewers' imagination.

Wild, Wild West, The ★★★

US (CBS) Western/Secret Agent Drama. US (Michael Garrison/CBS) Western. ITV 1968 (US: CBS 1965–70)

Major James T. West .... **Robert Conrad**
Artemus 'Artie' Gordon .... **Ross Martin**
Dr Miguelito Loveless .... **Michael Dunn**

Creator **Michael Garrison**
Producers **Michael Garrison, Gene L. Coon, Fred Freiberger, Collier Young, John Mantley, Bruce Lansbury**

The adventures of a pair of secret agents in the Old West.

James T. West works for President Ulysses S. Grant, travelling the Wild West of the 1870s hunting terrorists, bandits and other enemies of the fledgling USA. On his assignments, he is assisted by undercover agent Artemus 'Artie' Gordon, a man of many faces and voices. The daring duo cross the prairies in a specially adapted railroad car, equipped with facilities for creating novel, ad hoc weapons (giving rise to James Bond-style special effects nearly 100 years before their time). Their arch-enemy is megalomaniac midget Dr Miguelito Loveless, a man short on stature but big on menace, a corrupt genius who even invents time travel to try to get the better of his adversaries. All 104 episodes of this tongue-in-cheek series are entitled 'The Night of the . . .' (fill in the blank). During one season, while co-star Ross Martin was ill, Robert Conrad briefly gained a new sidekick, Jeremy Pike, played by Charles Aidman. A couple of TV movie reunions were made at the turn of the 1980s and a feature film version, starring Will Smith as West and Kevin Kline as Gordon, was released in 1999.

Wilde, Brian

British actor, best known for his roles as starchy Foggy Dewhurst in LAST OF THE SUMMER WINE and gullible prison warder Mr Barrowclough in PORRIDGE. Earlier, Wilde had appeared in the dramas THE WORLD OF TIM FRAZER (Tupper) and *The Men from Room 13*, and the sitcoms *The Love of Mike* and *Room at the Bottom*, and also played Bloody Delilah in THE DUSTBINMEN and Edgar Ryder in THE MANY WIVES OF PATRICK. Other credits have included the parts of radio station boss Roland Simpson in THE KIT CURRAN RADIO SHOW and Major Wyatt in *Wyatt's Watchdogs*, with smaller roles in series like THE MAN IN ROOM 17, THE BARON, THE AVENGERS, CATWEAZLE, OUT OF THE UNKNOWN, ACE OF WANDS and CROWN COURT.

Wilde Alliance ★★

UK (Yorkshire) Detective Drama. ITV 1978

Rupert Wilde .... **John Stride**
Amy Wilde .... **Julia Foster**
Christopher Bridgewater .... **John Lee**
Bailey .... **Patrick Newell**

Executive Producer **David Cunliffe**
Producer **Ian MacKintosh**

A thriller-writer and his wife become involved in real-life intrigue.

Rupert Wilde is a successful author of detective novels and lives with his attractive wife, Amy, in a luxurious country mansion in Yorkshire. However, for the Wildes life imitates art, and the lively couple themselves become sleuths as they stumble into a series of investigations, any of which could have come from Rupert's books. Rupert's agent, Christopher Bridgewater, is also dragged into the action. *Wilde Alliance* was a short-lived British attempt at a MCMILLAN AND WIFE/HART TO HART/THE THIN MAN-type series: just 13 episodes were made.

Will & Grace ★★★

US (Komut/Three Sisters/NBC) Situation Comedy. Channel 4 2001– (US: NBC 1998–2006)

Will Truman .... **Eric McCormack**
Grace Adler .... **Debra Messing**
Karen Walker .... **Megan Mullally**
Jack McFarland .... **Sean Hayes**
Rosario .... **Shelley Morrison**

Creators **David Kohan, Max Mutchnik**
Executive Producers **James Burrows, David Kohan, Max Mutchnik, Jeff Greenstein, Alex Herschlag, Jhoni Marchinko, Tim Kaiser, Gary Janetti, Tracy Poust, Jon Kinnally, Bill Wrubel, Greg Malins**

Two yuppie friends share a flat – he is gay and she is straight.

Early-thirtysomethings Will Truman and Grace Adler share an apartment in Manhattan. But they are not 'living together' as such, because Will, a smart, successful lawyer, is gay. Not that you'd really notice, however. His homosexuality is quietly concealed and never flaunted – unlike the orientation of his best friend, the ultra-camp Jack (a John Inman for the 1990s), whom Will often has to bail out of trouble. Will and Grace – an interior designer – have a great platonic relationship. They share the same pastimes (French movies and poker games) and, knowing they will never find romance together, are content that they will always have each other to lean on. Grace, known for her wayward red hair, shares her office with squeaky assistant Karen, a girl of independent means who doesn't need to work, but does so to keep in touch with the world. Rosario is Karen's El Salvadorean maid, who at one time marries Jack in order to avoid being deported. The series was screened by various satellite and digital channels before making its UK terrestrial debut on Channel 4, to much acclaim.

Will Shakespeare ✶

UK (ATV) Drama. ITV 1978

Will Shakespeare	**Tim Curry**
Dick Burbage	**Paul Freeman**
Jack Rice	**Ron Cook**
Christopher Marlowe	**Ian McShane**
Edward Alleyn	**André Morell**
Earl of Southampton	**Nicholas Clay**
Hamnet Sadler	**John McEnery**
Sir Thomas Walsingham	**Simon MacCorkindale**
Anne Hathaway/ Shakespeare	**Meg Wyn Owen**
Ingram Frizer	**Simon Rouse**

Writer **John Mortimer**
Producer **Cecil Clarke**

The life of the Bard of Avon.

With historical facts rather thin on the ground, writer John Mortimer adds more than a touch of fiction to his dramatization of the life and times of William Shakespeare. This bustling six-part series follows young Will as he breaks through into theatrical circles and gradually establishes himself as the finest playwright of his generation. Viewers are treated to a new 'human' angle on the bard, with Tim Curry portraying him as a bawdy and romantic type, hovering around the Globe Theatre and mingling in the court of Queen Elizabeth.

William

See *Just William*.

William and Mary ✶✶

UK (Granada) Drama. ITV 1 2003–5
DVD: Granada Ventures

William Shawcross	**Martin Clunes**
Mary Gilcrest	**Julie Graham**
Molly Gilcrest/Straud	**Cheryl Campbell**
Kate Shawcross	**Peta Cornish**
Julia Shawcross	**Georgina Terry**
Rick Straud	**Michael Begley**
Doris	**Claire Hackett**
Brendan Gilcrest	**Ricci McLeod**
Terence Gilcrest	**Dominick Baron**
Mrs Ball	**June Watson**
Arnold McKinnon	**James Greene**
Mrs Jane Spalding	**Catherine Terris**
Billy Two Hats	**David Kennedy**
Reuben	**Paterson Joseph**
Thomas Shawcross	**Max Mills**
	Harvey Mills

Writer **Mick Ford**
Executive Producers **Michele Buck, Tim Vaughan**
Producer **Trevor Hopkins**

An undertaker and a midwife are brought together by a dating agency.

William and Mary is a soft-hearted, romantic wallow aimed firmly at the female viewer. It's a story of a fortysomething widower who's an undertaker by profession and passes his time singing in a choir and playing bass in a rock group called No Name. He's also the father of two teenage daughters. The one thing missing from his life, however, is love, so he signs up with a video dating agency. His courage is rewarded when he is put in touch with Mary Gilcrest, a sparky midwife also looking for love. She has two teenage sons. The two get together, and, while there's more than a hiccup in proceedings (often to do with the interference of Mary's eccentric mother, Molly – who has a younger lover of her own in handyman Rick), an engagement is soon on the cards. In series two, William has to set up a new funeral business after Shawcross & Son is sold behind his back, and Mary falls pregnant as their wedding day approaches (star Julie Graham's own pregnancy was written into the series). More turmoil arrives in series three, with the emotional professions of the main characters as ever impinging on their own private hopes and fears. The series is set in London and Brighton.

William Tell ✶

UK (ITP/National Telefilm) Adventure. ITV 1958–9
DVD: Network

William Tell	**Conrad Phillips**
Hedda Tell	**Jennifer Jayne**
Walter Tell	**Richard Rogers**
Landburgher Gessler	**Willoughby Goddard**
Fertog ('The Bear')	**Nigel Greene**

Executive Producer **Ralph Smart**
Producer **Leslie Arliss**

A 14th-century freedom fighter helps the poor people of Switzerland.

Loosely based on the original story by Johann von Schiller, this series relates the legend of William Tell, an Alpine hero from the settlement of Berglan, who fights for the oppressed people of Altdorf against the occupying Austrians. The first episode sees Tell challenged by Gessler (the hated Austrian leader) to display his crossbow marksmanship by shooting an apple off the head of his own son, Walter. This Tell duly achieves, but with a second arrow tucked away for Gessler in case his aim fails. Discovering this subterfuge, the tyrant attempts to arrest Tell, who flees to the mountains with Walter and his wife, Hedda. From here, assisted by a small band of followers, he sets about disrupting Austrian activities with clever and cunning forays, taking on the mantle of a Swiss Robin Hood. Gessler never gets his man, and in compensation eats vast amounts of food. Scene after scene sees him stuffing his face with meat.

The series (filmed partly in Snowdonia) features a theme song sung by David Whitfield and is punctuated by the appearance of numerous aspiring actors, including Michael Caine and Frazer Hines, and other notable guests such as Christopher Lee, John Le Mesurier, Patrick Troughton and Wilfrid Brambell. Many years later, star Conrad Phillips resurfaced in EMMERDALE FARM, playing Christopher Meadows, MD, of NY Estates. Later still (1989), an Anglo-French revamp of *William Tell* was made. This starred Will Lyman and Jeremy Clyde. Conrad Phillips appeared as a guest star.

Williams, Andy

(1927–)

Relaxed American singer, once a member of the Williams Brothers singing group, who hosted his own variety series in the USA through most of the 1960s and 1970s. The show was carried by the BBC in the UK and, among other things, introduced viewers to the Osmond Brothers.

Williams, Kenneth

(1926–88)

British comedian and comedy actor, well known from *Carry On* films and various radio series but also familiar on television, his catalogue of funny voices and shocked faces and his skill as a raconteur making him popular on chat shows and panel games. He supported Tony Hancock in the early days of HANCOCK'S HALF HOUR, hosted *International Cabaret* for several years, was given his own sketch show by the BBC and read on many occasions for JACKANORY. His last contributions included the kids' series *Whizzkid's Guide* and GALLOPING GALAXIES! (the voice of the computer, SID), and he also provided the voices for the WILLO THE WISP cartoon series and many commercials.

Williams, Mark

(1959–)

West Midlands-born Oxford University graduate most familiar as a member of THE FAST SHOW team, but also seen in TUMBLEDOWN (Lumpy), THE STORYTELLER, *Merlin of the Crystal Cave* (Cerdic), SEARCHING (Gerald), GORMENGHAST (Prof. Perch), SHACKLETON, GRASS, CARRIE AND BARRY (Kirk), THE ROTTERS CLUB (Sam Chase), *Help* and numerous single comedies, plus programmes about our industrial heritage for the Discovery channel. Guest spots have come in RED DWARF and HAPPINESS, among other series.

Williams, Michael

(1935–2001)

Versatile British actor, at home with both dramatic and comedy roles. In the former vein, he played The Duke of Alençon in ELIZABETH R, Philip Hart in *A Raging Calm*, Alan Crowe in THE HANGED MAN, William Essex in *My Son, My Son*, Uncle Davey in *Love in a Cold Climate*, Billy Balsam in SEPTEMBER SONG and Ted Jeavons in A DANCE TO THE MUSIC OF TIME. Comedy-wise, Williams was Mike Selway in A FINE ROMANCE (with his real-life wife, Judi Dench), N. V. Standish in DOUBLE FIRST and Barry Masefield in *Conjugal Rites*. He enjoyed many other credits, too, including TV Shakespeare, A FAMILY AT WAR and *Tracey Ullman Takes On New York*.

Williams, Robin

(1952–)

Energetic, quickfire, quirky American comedian who shot to fame in the 1970s when he was spotted playing LA nightclubs. A master of improvisation and ad-lib, he was given a role in the short-lived revival of ROWAN AND MARTIN'S LAUGH-IN and contributed to *The Richard Pryor Show*, but a bigger break came with a guest appearance in HAPPY DAYS. Cast as zany alien Mork from Ork, he proved such a hit that his own series, MORK AND MINDY, was soon on the screens. That took Williams into the cinema and he has since become one of Hollywood's biggest names.

Williams, Simon

(1946–)

British actor winning fans with his portrayal of Captain James Bellamy in UPSTAIRS, DOWNSTAIRS and later seen in the comedies AGONY (Laurence Lucas), KINVIG (Buddo) and DON'T WAIT UP (Dr Charles Cartwright). He also played Simon Company in the musical drama *Company and Co.*, was cast as Ken Hawkes in DEMOB and barrister Gerald Triggs in LAW AND DISORDER, took the lead in the pilot for THE INSPECTOR ALLEYN MYSTERIES, and played Lord Scott in *A Respectable Trade*, Prof. Rae in *Pig Heart Boy*, Terence Philip in THE GATHERING STORM, Father Raffe in CUTTING IT and Johan Strauss II in *Strauss – the Waltz King*. He has also featured in series like MAN IN A SUITCASE, THE REGIMENT, WODEHOUSE PLAYHOUSE, STRANGERS, DOCTOR WHO, BERGERAC, PILGRIM'S REST, DINNERLADIES, THE SCARLET PIMPERNEL, HOLBY CITY, KILLER NET, DALZIEL AND PASCOE, BAD GIRLS, THE INSPECTOR LYNLEY MYSTERIES, HEARTBEAT, DOCTORS and THE BILL. Williams is married to actress Lucy Fleming and his children, Tam and Amy, are both actors.

Willis, Bruce

(1955–)

American actor born in Germany who shot to fame as the jive-talking, ultra-casual detective David Addison in MOONLIGHTING in 1985, having previously acted on stage and made a few TV appearances in shows like HART TO HART and MIAMI VICE. He quickly turned his attention to the movie world and also notched up a few hit singles. He married actress Demi Moore. Other TV appearances include guest spots in FRIENDS.

Willis, Lord Ted

(1918–92)

One of TV's most prolific writers and programme creators, Ted Willis pioneered working-class, 'kitchen sink' dramas and social realism with his scriptwriting in the 1950s. Among his brainchildren – revealing a flair for both comedy and straight pieces – were DIXON OF DOCK GREEN, TELL IT TO THE MARINES, SERGEANT CORK, TAXI, THE SULLAVAN BROTHERS, MRS THURSDAY, VIRGIN OF THE SECRET SERVICE, COPPERS END and HUNTER'S WALK. In all, it is said he created 41 television series. In addition, his plays included *Woman in a Dressing Gown*, the ARMCHAIR THEATRE presentation HOT SUMMER NIGHT, and an adaptation of Richard Gordon's *Doctor in the House*. He was made a peer in 1963.

Willo the Wisp ★★

UK (Nicholas Cartoon Films) Children's Entertainment. BBC 1 1981

Narrator **Kenneth Williams**

Creator/Writer **Nicholas Spargo**

● ***Tittle-tattle and tales from a magical woodland.***

This pre-early-evening-news animation set out to charm both young and adult audiences with its surreal mix of characters from a strange fairy tale world (Doyley Woods). Narrator Kenneth Williams, as the gossipy spirit Willo the Wisp (who looks a good deal like Williams himself), leads viewers through the quirky adventures of creations like Arthur, the cynical caterpillar; the Moog, a dense dog; Carwash, a pretentious, myopic cat; and a confused creature known as the Beast. Also prominent are Evil Edna, a wicked witch in the form of a television set, and Mavis Cruet, a podgy fairy who never quite manages to take to the air. Twenty-six, five-minute episodes were made, with music by Tony Kinsey, and screened in 1981, but a new series, written by Jamie Rix and voiced by James Dreyfuss, was produced in 2003, with Evil Edna now upgraded to include her own digibox. Creator Nick Spargo had died in 1997 but his daughter, Bobbie, led the new team. It was not shown on terrestrial TV in the UK.

Wilson, Dennis Main

(1924–97)

Long-serving British light entertainment producer and occasional director, initially working in radio and on TV programmes like SIX-FIVE SPECIAL, but more obviously associated with sitcoms. These included *The Two Charleys*, SYKES, THE RAG TRADE, TILL DEATH US DO PART, *Scott On . . .*, *Them*, *Well Anyway*, CITIZEN SMITH, *Mr Big*, *Time of My Life*, L FOR LESTER, *Roger Doesn't Live Here Anymore* and THE LADY IS A TRAMP. Other comedies included *Lance at Large*, *A Series of Bird's*, *The Dick Emery Show*, *Marty* and countless programme pilots and single pieces.

Wilson, Donald

(1910–2002)

British screenwriter, script editor and producer, largely on BBC historical dramas (he was one of the Corporation's early contract-writers). In 1954 he became chief of the BBC's script department and then Head of Serials. Among his writing credits were *The Six Proud Walkers* (1954 and again in 1962), *The Royalty* (1957, with Michael Voysey), *No Wreath for the General* (1960), *The Flying Swan* (1965), THE FIRST CHURCHILLS (1969, as writer, director and producer), ANNA KARENINA (1977, as writer and producer) and, most celebrated of all, THE FORSYTE SAGA (1967, as producer and co-writer).

Wilson, Francis

(1949–)

Scottish weather-presenter, known for his relaxed, easy-going style which initially won him fans while he was working on *Thames News* (1978–82). Wilson then moved to the BBC's BREAKFAST TIME and *Breakfast News* before defecting to Sky News in 1992.

Wilson, Richard

OBE (Iain Wilson; 1936–)

Award-winning Scottish actor and director, a former scientist who, after years of supporting others, playing vicars, doctors and barristers, found his niche as the grumpy Victor Meldrew in ONE FOOT IN THE GRAVE. Otherwise, Wilson has played the Revd Martin Hooper in MY GOOD WOMAN, Jeremy Parsons QC in CROWN COURT, Dr Gordon Thorpe in ONLY WHEN I LAUGH, the TV chaplain in *Room at the Bottom*, newspaper managing editor Richard Lipton in HOT METAL, teacher Mr Ridley in *Andy Robson*, Eddie Clockerty, the manager of the Majestics, in TUTTI FRUTTI, bank manager Richard Talbot in HIGH AND DRY, and Hector Duff in *Unnatural Pursuits*. He was also seen as Mr Lichfield in *The Life and Times of Henry Pratt*, the Revd Green in CLUEDO, the Prime Minister, James Forth, in *Screenplay's The Vision Thing*, Ben Glazier in *Under the Hammer* (also as director), Bill Webster in *Screen One's The Lord of Misrule*, the Professor of Language in GULLIVER'S TRAVELS, Lord Tone in *In the Red* and river policeman Prof in DUCK PATROL. Other major roles include John Doone in *Life Support*, Alex Cameron in *Life as We Know It*, Sally the Cook in *Dick Whittington*, The Duke of Edinburgh in *Jeffrey Archer – the Truth*, Dr Donald Newman in BORN AND BRED, Frank in *King of Fridges* and Bruce Morton in *High Stakes*. In addition, he has narrated the docu-soap *The Zoo Keepers*, provided voices for *The World of Peter Rabbit and Friends*, and been seen in DR FINLAY'S CASEBOOK, A SHARP INTAKE OF BREATH, THE SWEENEY, THE ADVENTURES OF SHERLOCK HOLMES, INSPECTOR MORSE, *The Last Place on Earth*, WHOOPS APOCALYPSE, DOCTOR WHO and other series and single dramas.

Wilton, Penelope

OBE (1946–)

Yorkshire-born actress, probably best recalled as Ann, the long-suffering wife of pedantic Martin Bryce, in EVER DECREASING CIRCLES. However, Wilton was also a member of the cast of *The Norman Conquests* and played Beatrice in Carla Lane's SCREAMING and Homily in THE BORROWERS. She also appeared in THE MONOCLED MUTINEER (Lady Angela Forbes), WIVES AND DAUGHTERS (Mrs Hamley), *The Whistle-Blower* (Heather Graham), *Victoria and Albert* (Duchess of Kent), BOB AND ROSE (Monica Gossage) and LUCKY JIM (Mrs Welch), and has taken roles in dramas like *King Lear*, *The Widowing of Mrs Holroyd*, *The Sullen Sisters*, the *Performance* production of *The Deep Blue Sea* (Hester Collyer), TALKING HEADS 2 (Rosemary), FALLING (Daisy Langrish) and DOCTOR WHO (MP Harriet Jones). Guest roles include parts in C.A.T.S. EYES and KAVANAGH QC. Her two husbands have both been actors: the late Daniel Massey and Ian Holm.

Wind in the Willows, The ★★★

UK (Thames/Cosgrove Hall) Animation. ITV 1984–8

Voices:

Mole	**Richard Pearson**
Rat	**Peter Sallis**
Toad	**David Jason**
Badger	**Michael Hordern**
Narrator	**Ian Carmichael**

Writers **Brian Trueman, Rosemary Anne Sisson**
Executive Producer **John Hambley**
Producers **Mark Hall, Brian Cosgrove**

● ***Rural roving in Edwardian England with a motley band of creatures.***

Following the success the previous year of a 90-minute, animated musical adaptation of Kenneth Grahame's 1908 classic novel, Thames launched this series of additional rodent tales in 1984. Peter Sallis took over the role of Rat from Ian Carmichael, but otherwise the principal voicers remained in place. Ralph McTell sang the theme song. The success of the series lay chiefly in the quality of the animation, with each model reputedly costing around £5,000 to build.

Winds of War, The ★★★

US (ABC) Drama. ITV 1983 (US: ABC 1983)

Commander Victor 'Pug' Henry	**Robert Mitchum**
Natalie Jastrow	**Ali MacGraw**
Byron Henry	**Jan-Michael Vincent**
Warren Henry	**Ben Murphy**

Madeline Henry	**Lisa Eilbacher**
Rhoda Henry	**Polly Bergen**
Berel Jastrow	**Topol**
Aaron Jastrow	**John Houseman**
Palmer 'Fred' Kirby	**Peter Graves**
Pamela Tudsbury	**Victoria Tennant**
Alistair Tudsbury	**Michael Logan**
Leslie Slote	**David Dukes**
President Franklin D. Roosevelt	**Ralph Bellamy**
Winston Churchill	**Howard Lang**
Adolf Hitler	**Gunter Meisner**
Brigadier Gen. Armin Von Roon	**Jeremy Kemp**
Narrator	**William Woodson**

Writer **Herman Wouk**
Producer **Dan Curtis**

The globe-trotting escapades of an American military attaché in the early years of World War II.

Beginning with the German advance into Poland in 1939 and continuing through to the Japanese attack on Pearl Harbor in 1941, this mammoth drama is the story of one man's war. That man is 'Pug' Henry, an American naval officer who is sent around the world, meeting the likes of Churchill and Hitler, but encounters personal problems along the way. These come from his unfaithful wife, Rhoda, pilot son Warren, artistic son Byron and student daughter Madeline. More strife is discovered with an English rose named Pam, with whom he embarks on an affair, and an eccentric Jewish girl, Natalie, who finds herself in Poland as the Germans invade and becomes Byron's lover.

The Winds of War, adapted in eight parts from his own novel by Herman Wouk, cost £26 million to make and was heralded with a loud fanfare of publicity. However, viewers and critics were less than impressed on the whole. A sequel, *War and Remembrance*, which dramatized the remainder of Wouk's book and covered the final years of the war, was screened in 1989.

Windsor, Barbara
MBE (Barbara-Ann Deeks; 1937–)

Diminutive blonde actress, for many years a stalwart of the *Carry On* movies but reviving her career on television as Peggy Mitchell in EASTENDERS. Earlier she had appeared as Judy in THE RAG TRADE, Millie in *Wild, Wild Women*, Saucy Nancy in WORZEL GUMMIDGE and Myrtle in YOU RANG, M'LORD? She also provided voices for the *The Great Bong* cartoon and narrated *Disaster Masters*, while other credits take in DAD'S ARMY, UP POMPEII, FILTHY RICH AND CATFLAP, and ONE FOOT IN THE GRAVE.

Windsor, Frank
(1927–)

Frank Windsor, for most viewers, is John Watt, star of Z CARS and SOFTLY, SOFTLY. However, before arriving in Newtown, the Midlands-born actor had been seen in the Shakespearean anthology AN AGE OF KINGS and as scientist Dennis Bridger in A FOR ANDROMEDA. Among his later credits have been the title roles in *The Real Eddy English* and *Headmaster* (Tom Fisher), and the parts of Harry Bradley in the Rolls-Royce drama FLYING LADY, Cyril Wendage in SEPTEMBER SONG, Simon Armstrong in *Screen One's Trip Trap* and William in *Anchor Me*. Other performances have come in THE AVENGERS, RANDALL AND HOPKIRK (DECEASED), CROWN COURT, WHODUNNIT?, *Kidnapped*, *Into the Labyrinth*, DOCTOR WHO, BLEAK HOUSE, BOON, CHANCER, LOVEJOY, CATHERINE COOKSON'*s The Fifteen Streets* (James Llewellyn), MIDSOMER MURDERS, PEAK PRACTICE, SUNBURN, JUDGE JOHN DEED and CASUALTY, as well as a 1973 attempt to discover the truth behind *Jack the Ripper* (again in the guise of John Watt) and a follow-up series, looking at other controversial crimes, called SECOND VERDICT.

Winfrey, Oprah
(1954–)

American Oprah Winfrey was the first black woman to host a major US daytime talk show (*The Oprah Winfrey Show*, 1986) and proved so successful that she quickly became the richest woman on TV. Her career began as a teenager in Nashville, where she worked as a newsreader. Moving to Baltimore and then Chicago, she transferred into talk shows, rapidly outgunning her daytime rivals and soon being syndicated nationwide. Her shows (screened initially on Channel 4 in the UK) are highly charged emotionally and sometimes have a strong personal involvement from Oprah, such as her admission of childhood abuse and her well-publicized weight-watching regime. She now owns her own production company, Harpo Productions, and has several acting credits to her name, including in *Brewster Place* and ELLEN.

Wings ★★
UK (BBC) Drama. BBC 1 1977–8

Sgt/2nd Lt. Alan Farmer	**Tim Woodward**
Capt. Owen Triggers	**Nicholas Jones**
Lt./2nd Lt. Charles Gaylion	**Michael Cochrane**
Lt. Richard Bravington	**David Troughton**
Lt. Michael Starling	**Michael Jayes**
Sgt Mills	**Roger Elliott**
Harry Farmer	**John Hallam**
Molly Farmer	**Anne Kristen**
Lorna Collins	**Sarah Porter**
2nd Lt. Favell	**Simon Turner**
Tom	**Reg Lye**
Kate Gaylion	**Celia Bannerman**

Creator **Barry Thomas**
Producer **Peter Cregeen**

Stirring action in the skies during World War I.

Over two series, and beginning in February 1915, *Wings* focuses on the daring pilots of the Royal Flying Corps, the pioneers of air combat during the Great War. Tackling the Hun in their sheepskin jackets, leather hats and goggles are France-based aviators Farmer, Triggers, Gaylion, Bravington and others. Farmer is initially the odd man out, being a poorly educated blacksmith's son from Sussex who teaches himself to fly and subsequently gains promotion from the NCO ranks to join the snooty commissioned men. The series takes as its inspiration events in the lives of real RFC airmen and makes good use of numerous re-created old flying machines. Alexander Faris composed the sweeping period theme music. An accompanying book, by creator Barry Thomas, was published in 1977.

Winkler, Henry

(1945–)

American actor, producer and director, whose creation of Fonzie, the superhuman biker with the heart of gold, turned HAPPY DAYS from a ratings also-ran into America's number one show. Winkler was with the series for its entire run (1974–84), becoming a US institution in the process. When it ended, he moved behind the scenes, producing MACGYVER (with John Rich) and other projects. He has also been seen in a few TV movies and recently played lawyer Barry Zuckerkorn in *Arrested Development*.

Winner Takes All ✶

UK (Yorkshire) Quiz. ITV 1975–88

Presenters **Jimmy Tarbuck, Geoffrey Wheeler**

Creator **Geoffrey Wheeler**
Producers **Guy Caplan, Lawrie Higgins, Ian Bolt, Don Clayton, Terry Henebery, Graham Wetherell**

● ***Long-running quiz in which contestants gamble on the answers to questions.***

Jimmy Tarbuck welcomed the guests and the unseen Geoffrey Wheeler asked the questions in this popular general knowledge quiz show. The four contestants competed in a little knock-out tournament to find one winner who would 'take all', namely a big cash prize, at the end of each programme. The winner then stayed on the following week, risking a proportion of his winnings in the pursuit of more money.

Five questions were offered, one at a time, together with six possible answers. Each answer was accompanied by appropriate odds, ranging from even money, through 2–1, 3–1, 4–1 and 5–1 to the rank outsider at 10–1. The contestants had to select an answer and back it with a proportion of their points bank, losing the gambled points if the answer was wrong, but reaping the rewards if they gambled correctly. The contestant with the most points was the winner. In the final round, pounds replaced points, but only the winner could take away his final total. When Jimmy Tarbuck left the series in 1987 to present a new game show, *Tarby's Frame Game*, Geoffrey Wheeler (who was also the deviser of the series) was brought into vision as joint host and question master.

Winston, Lord Robert

(1940–)

Professor of Fertility Studies at Imperial College, London, and a Labour life peer, who specializes in presenting popular science programmes. His major contributions include YOUR LIFE IN THEIR HANDS (as narrator), *Making Babies*, THE HUMAN BODY, *The Secret Life of Twins*, *Superhuman*, *Threads of Life*, *Child of Our Time*, *Walking with Cavemen*, *The Human Mind*, *The Story of God*, *Frankenstein: Birth of a Monster* (narrator) and *How to Sleep Better*.

Winston Churchill – The Wilderness Years ✶✶

UK (Southern) Historical Drama. ITV 1981

Winston Churchill .... **Robert Hardy**
Clementine Churchill .... **Siân Phillips**
Randolph Churchill .... **Nigel Havers**
Stanley Baldwin .... **Peter Barkworth**
Neville Chamberlain .... **Eric Porter**
Sir Samuel Hoare .... **Edward Woodward**
Ralph Wigram .... **Paul Freeman**
Bernard Baruch .... **Sam Wanamaker**
Sir Thomas Inskip .... **Peter Vaughan**
Mrs Pearman .... **Sherrie Hewson**
Brenden Bracken .... **Tim Pigott-Smith**
Prof. Lindemann .... **David Swift**
Sarah .... **Chloe Salaman**
Ramsay MacDonald .... **Robert James**

Creators **Martin Gilbert, Richard Broke**
Executive Producer **Mark Shivas**
Producer **Richard Broke**

● ***Dramatization of Churchill's period of political 'exile'.***

After Churchill's meteoric rise to prominence in the early decades of the 20th century, his political career ground dramatically to a halt during the 1930s. A change in leadership in the Conservative Party and momentous movements on the world stage left the always outspoken Churchill sitting in the shadows, his voice singing out of tune with many of his own political colour. This drama looks back at those 'wilderness years', viewing how the great man bides his time, speaking out in vain on issues such as the rise of fascism and self-government for India, offering support for Edward VIII in the Abdication Crisis and waiting for the moment when the country would again call upon his services. The eight-part series was one of Southern Television's last productions. See also THE GATHERING STORM, which covers the same turbulent era.

Winstone, Ray

(1957–)

East London-born actor starring in programmes like GET BACK (Martin Sweet), *The Ghostbusters of East Finchley* (Thane), *Our Boy* (Woody), BIRTHS, MARRIAGES AND DEATHS (Alan) and *Last Christmas* (Neville). He also featured in the single drama *Scum* and appeared in series such as FOX (Kenny Fox), MINDER (Arnie), ROBIN OF SHERWOOD (Will Scarlet), PULASKI (DS Ford), FAIRLY SECRET ARMY (Stubby Collins), *Father Matthew's Daughter* (Father Charlie) and *Tough Love* and its sequel, *Lenny Blue* (DC Lenny Milton). He also played Dave in *Face*, the title role in *Henry VIII*, Harry Sands in *She's Gone*, Vincent Gallagher in VINCENT and the Demon Barber himself in *Sweeney Todd*. Among the many guest roles are parts in AUF WIEDERSEHEN, PET, BOON, BIRDS OF A FEATHER, BETWEEN THE LINES, CASUALTY, SPACE PRECINCT, THE BILL, *Sharman*, MURDER MOST HORRID, THIEF TAKERS, KAVANAGH QC, ONE FOOT IN THE GRAVE and AT HOME WITH THE BRAITHWAITES. One of his earliest TV roles was as a teenager in THE SWEENEY.

Winters:

MIKE (Michael Weinstein; 1930–) and BERNIE (Bernie Weinstein; 1932–91)

British comedy double-act of the 1950s–1970s, real-life brothers who originally worked together as part of a music and impressions band. After gaining radio experience, they were given regular exposure on SIX-FIVE SPECIAL in 1957 and, after a few ups and downs, were hosts of *Big Night Out* and *Blackpool Night Out* in the 1960s. They also starred in *Mike and Bernie's Show*, *Mike and Bernie's Scene* and their own sitcom, *Mike and Bernie*. Their act was essentially traditional music hall crosstalk, with Mike the straight man and Bernie the idiot who referred to his brother as 'Choochy Face'. However, differences came to the fore and the brothers split up in 1978. Mike became a businessman in Florida, while Bernie teamed up with Schnorbitz, his St Bernard dog, and starred in his own series, *Bernie*, and hosted the game show *Whose Baby?* He also perfected an impersonation of Bud Flanagan and performed it on stage and TV, with Leslie Crowther as his partner, Chesney Allen.

Winton, Dale

(1955–)

Light entertainment presenter, coming to the fore as host of the cult daytime game show *Supermarket Sweep*. He has since presented *Pets Win Prizes*, THE NATIONAL LOTTERY LIVE (and some of its various game shows), *The Other Half*, *Dale's All Stars*, *I'm the Answer*, *Stars Reunited* and *Celebrity Fit Club*, as well as fronting GMTV. The son of 1960s TV starlet Sheree Winton (who reportedly named him after actor Dale Robertson), Winton began his career in radio, with the United Biscuits Network and then Radio Trent in Nottingham. He moved into TV as presenter of *Pet Watch* in 1986, and worked on *Network 7*, *Home Today* and *Public Enemy Number One*, as well as satellite television, before *Supermarket Sweep* made him a star.

Wipe

A visual effect in which one camera shot displaces another on the screen, 'wiping' across from side to side, top to bottom or even breaking through in contrived patterns. The facility was much employed in 1970s pop-music programmes.

Wire in the Blood ★★

UK (Coastal) Police Drama. ITV 1 2002; 2004–5
DVD: Revelation

Dr Tony Hill .... **Robson Green**
DI Carol Jordan .... **Hermione Norris**
DS Don Merrick .... **Alan Stocks**
DS Kevin Geoffries .... **Mark Letheren**
DC Annie Reiss .... **Doreene Blackstock**
ACC John Brandon .... **Tom Chadbon**
Dr Ashley Vernon .... **Mark Penfold**
DC Paula McIntyre .... **Emma Handy**
ACC Paul Eden .... **Peter Sullivan**

Writers **Patrick Harbinson, Alan Whiting, Niall Leonard, Jeff Povey, Guy Burt**
Executive Producer **Sandra Joblin**
Producer **Phil Leach**

● ***A brilliant psychologist is the police's only hope in snaring mass murderers.***

Despite slating its far-fetched plots and some of television's most sickening scenes of violence, critics remain generally upbeat about *Wire in the Blood*. The drama is based on characters created by Val McDermid, with the first series adapting her original novels, and later episodes based on new storylines. Set in the north-east of England, in and around the town of Bradfield, the thrust of each episode is the hunt for a serial killer, someone so perverse and twisted as to have tortured and debased his/her victims to stomach-churning lengths. Heading the police inquiries is DI Carol Jordan, a steely, level-headed, ambitious detective who just can't manage without the assistance of clinical psychologist Dr Tony Hill. He's a rather eccentric university lecturer, who helps convicted serial killers in his spare time, but it is his moments of enlightenment and leaps of reason that provide the key to unlocking the case. As is the style of such intense detective dramas, the lead pairing fight a 'will-they-won't-they' romantic battle.

Wisdom, Sir Norman

OBE (1915–)

Acknowledged as one of Britain's great screen clowns, diminutive Norman Wisdom has made his mark in the story of television, too, even though his TV work generally fitted in and around his film career. London-born Wisdom was given his first TV series, *Wit and Wisdom*, in 1948, followed in 1953 by *It's Wisdom* and, in 1956, by *The Norman Wisdom Show*. On one famous TV occasion, he starred in SUNDAY NIGHT AT THE LONDON PALLADIUM, taking over the show, wallpapering the set and eventually being chased off by compere Bruce Forsyth. With his best cinema days behind him, he turned to sitcom in 1970 with *Norman*, a series about a taxman-turned-musician, and followed it with *Nobody is Norman Wisdom*, as Nobody, a daydreamer. His next series, *A Little Bit of Wisdom*, ran for three years, with various situations and characters. In contrast, his performance as a man dying of cancer in the 1981 drama GOING GENTLY drew much acclaim and, enjoying his switch to straight acting, he was later seen as a guest in BERGERAC, LAST OF THE SUMMER WINE, CASUALTY, DALZIEL AND PASCOE and THE LAST DETECTIVE, as well as in BETWEEN THE SHEETS (Maurice Hardy) and CORONATION STREET (Ernie Crabb).

Wise, Ernie

OBE (Ernest Wiseman; 1925–99)

See *Morecambe, Eric*.

Wise, Herbert

(1924–)

Austrian-born director responsible for I, CLAUDIUS and *The Norman Conquests*, plus episodes of such series as SHADOW SQUAD, KNIGHT ERRANT, *The Victorians*, Z CARS, *Six Shades of Black*, MAN IN A SUITCASE, UPSTAIRS, DOWNSTAIRS, THE SIX WIVES OF HENRY VIII, ELIZABETH R, HELEN – A WOMAN OF TODAY, THE BBC TELEVISION SHAKESPEARE, RUMPOLE OF THE BAILEY, TALES OF THE UNEXPECTED, *Number 10*, INSPECTOR MORSE, THE RUTH RENDELL MYSTERIES, CADFAEL, NOAH'S ARK and the P. D. JAMES Adam Dalgliesh story *Death of an Expert Witness*. Single dramas include *The Cruel Day*, *The Big Donkey*, *Walk With Destiny*, *The Woman in Black* and BREAKING THE CODE.

Wish Me Luck ★★★

UK (LWT) Drama. ITV 1988–90

Liz Grainger .... **Kate Buffery**
Mathilde 'Matty' Firman .... **Suzanna Hamilton**
Col. James 'Cad' Cadogan .... **Julian Glover**
Kit Vanston .... **Michael J. Jackson**

Faith Ashley .... **Jane Asher**
Colin Beale .... **Jeremy Northam**
Claudine de Valois .... **Shelagh McLeod**
Lois Mountjoy .... **Abigail McKern**
Col. Werner Krieger .... **Warren Clarke**
Laurence Grainger .... **Nigel Le Vaillant**
Vivien Ashton .... **Lynn Farleigh**
Emily Whitbread .... **Jane Snowden**
Gordon Stewart .... **Stuart McGugan**
Lewis .... **Jeremy Nicholas**
Virginia .... **Catherine Schell**
Renard .... **Trevor Peacock**
Nicole .... **Felicity Montagu**
Gen. Stuckler .... **Terrence Hardiman**
Col. Max Dubois .... **Damien Thomas**

Creators **Jill Hyem, Lavinia Warner**
Executive Producer **Nick Elliott**
Producers **Colin Shindler, Lavinia Warner, Michael Chaplin**

Brave men and women infiltrate German-occupied France.

Like the similarly styled MANHUNT and SECRET ARMY, *Wish Me Luck* is set in World War II and focuses on daring young people who risk life and limb to spy on the enemy and sabotage the Nazi advance. Two women in particular are highlighted, both fluent in French, with a local's knowledge of Normandy. One is well-bred blonde Liz Grainger from Devon, a twentysomething mother of a five-year-old daughter, who answers an appeal for pictures of Normandy and is duly recruited. Her brother has been killed in action and her husband, Laurence, is away with the forces. The other is earthy 22-year-old Cockney Matty Firman, whose mother is French and whose father is a London Jew. She is initially recruited as a wireless operator. Both work as agents of the Special Operations Executive (casually known as 'The Outfit'), run by Colonel James 'Cad' Cadogan, assisted by Oxford graduate Faith Ashley (dubbed 'The Snow Queen') and wireless receiver Lois Mountjoy (the teenage daughter of a vicar).

The unlikely duo operate together behind enemy lines, along with baronet's son and Oxford blue Kit Vanston (the chief intelligence officer in the area), fellow agent Colin Beale (naval experience) and Claudine (a wealthy former Sorbonne buddy of Liz's, now forced to work for a living: she takes an instant dislike to the 'common' Matty). Claudine develops a risky 'friendship' with the increasingly cruel local Nazi boss, Colonel Krieger, who is later replaced by General Stuckler. New agents are also introduced in later series, primarily Vivien (a recently widowed former dancer) and Emily (a Catholic doctor's daughter).

Wish You Were Here . . . ?

See *Holiday*.

Witchell, Nicholas

(1953–)

Red-haired BBC journalist, a former Northern Ireland reporter and foreign correspondent (Beirut and the Falklands) who joined the Corporation as a trainee in 1976. He has fronted all the main bulletins (especially *Breakfast News*), and contributed to PANORAMA. He was made diplomatic correspondent in 1995 and royal correspondent in 1998.

Within These Walls ★★

UK (LWT) Drama. ITV 1974–6; 1978

Faye Boswell .... **Googie Withers**
Charles Radley .... **Jerome Willis**
Chief Officer Mrs Armitage .... **Mona Bruce**
Dr Peter Mayes .... **Denys Hawthorne**
Miss Clarke .... **Beth Harris**
Martha Parrish .... **Sonia Graham**
Officer Spencer .... **Elaine Wells**
Helen Forrester .... **Katharine Blake**
Officer Parsons .... **Miranda Forbes**
Susan Marshall .... **Sarah Lawson**

Executive Producer **Rex Firkin**
Producer **Jack Williams**

Drama centring on the governor of a women's prison.

Set in HMP Stone Park, *Within These Walls* features its newly installed governor, Faye Boswell, as she sets out to liberalize the firmly run institution. Boswell quickly realizes that all is not going to be plain sailing and she meets resentment not only from inmates but from her staff, too. The impact on her personal life of this stressful job is also scrutinized. Boswell lasts three years before making way for a new governor, Helen Forrester, who is in turn succeeded by Susan Marshall in 1978. The series was the inspiration for the Australian soap PRISONER: CELL BLOCK H, which proved much more durable. Denis King provided the music.

Witt, Paul Junger

(1943–)

American producer, working on series like THE PARTRIDGE FAMILY in the early 1970s, before producing the comedies SOAP and BENSON (both written by his wife, Susan Harris), in partnership with Tony Thomas. Joining forces in Witt-Thomas-Harris Productions, they have since handled all Harris's other hits, including THE GOLDEN GIRLS, *The Golden Palace*, EMPTY NEST and NURSES. Witt and Thomas have also produced BEAUTY AND THE BEAST, BLOSSOM, *Herman's Head, Pearl, The Secret Lives of Men* and *Everything's Relative*.

Wives and Daughters ★★★

UK (BBC/WGBH) Drama. BBC 1 1999

Molly Gibson .... **Anna Maguire** *(young)*
Justine Waddell
Mr Gibson .... **Bill Paterson**
Mrs Hyacinth Clare Kirkpatrick .... **Francesca Annis**
Cynthia Kirkpatrick .... **Keeley Hawes**
Squire Hamley .... **Michael Gambon**
Mrs Hamley .... **Penelope Wilton**
Roger Hamley .... **Anthony Howell**
Osborne Hamley .... **Tom Hollander**
Miss Sally Browning .... **Barbara Flynn**
Miss Phoebe Browning .... **Deborah Findley**
Lady Cumnor .... **Barbara Leigh-Hunt**
Lord Cumnor .... **Ian Carmichael**
Lady Harriet Cumnor .... **Rosamund Pike**
Mr Robert Preston .... **Iain Glen**
Mr Coxe .... **Richard Coyle**
Robinson .... **Peter Copley**

Mrs Goodenough .... **Elizabeth Spriggs**
Lord Hollingford .... **Shaughan Seymour**

Writer **Andrew Davies**
Producer **Sue Birtwistle**

● ***Social skulduggery in a small English town.***

Elizabeth Gaskell's final (and unfinished) novel, published in book form in 1866, is a portrait of the petty rivalries, snobbery and affected customs that distinguished the middle classes of her era. The time is the 1820s and the setting is the little market town of Hollingford (filmed at Marshfield, Gloucestershire). At the heart of the story are widower Mr Gibson, the local doctor, and his young daughter, Molly. Keen for Molly to have a new mother, Gibson marries Mrs Kirkpatrick, a former governess who lives as a paid companion at Cumnor Towers, home of the aristocratic Cumnor family. His new wife is serene and superficially kind but her sugary exterior hides an inner cunning. Molly recognizes her scheming nature early but tries to make the relationship work, especially when her stepmother's daughter, Cynthia, arrives from school in France. But Cynthia is as mysterious and devious as her mother and eventually draws Molly into her subterfuge, which involves the enigmatic Mr Preston, the Cumnors' land agent. In the meantime, Molly has been almost adopted by Squire Hamley and his family at Hamley Hall, where she finds the warmth her life has needed. The squire is hot-headed but means well, even if he has been overtaken by the changes the Industrial Revolution has wreaked on his society. Number one son is the pretentious poet Osborne, but Molly falls for second son Roger, a scientist, and is heartbroken when he is betrothed to Cynthia. His expeditions take him to Africa, but Hollingford is home to almost as many secrets as the dark continent itself, as Molly discovers. Andrew Davies's four-part serial was directed by Nicholas Renton. The novel was previously dramatized by the BBC in 1971 (BBC 2: Zhivila Roche as Molly, Rosalind Lloyd as Cynthia, Alan MacNaughton as Gibson and Clive Morton as Squire Hamley).

WKRP in Cincinnati ★★★

US (MTM) Situation Comedy. ITV 1981–2/Channel 4 1983–4 (US: CBS 1978–82)

Andy Travis .... **Gary Sandy**
Arthur Carlson ('Big Guy') .... **Gordon Jump**
Jennifer Marlowe .... **Loni Anderson**
Les Nessman .... **Richard Sanders**
Herb Tarlek .... **Frank Bonner**
Gordon Sims (Venus Flytrap) .... **Tim Reid**
Bailey Quarters .... **Jan Smithers**
Johnny Caravella (Dr Johnny Fever) .... **Howard Hesseman**
Lillian 'Mama' Carlson .... **Carol Bruce**

Creator **Hugh Wilson**

● ***A dying radio station is kicked into life when a new programme director takes over.***

WKRP, one of Cincinnati's 18 radio stations, is losing money hand over fist. Its drab playlist attracts only a drab, ageing audience and drab advertising sponsors. But all that changes when new programme controller Andy Travis arrives. He encourages the station's elderly owner, Mama Carlson, and her son, Arthur, the incompetent station manager (commonly known as 'Big Guy'), to take a chance, make the switch to rock music and put some life back in the programming. Mrs Carlson buys the idea and ratings begin to take off. All the same, it is obvious that this radio station will never be a huge success.

The WKRP team consists of Les Nessman, a bumptious news, weather and farming reporter; Bailey Quarters, Andy's young assistant, who becomes a journalist; and the station's top two DJs, Dr Johnny Fever (real name Johnny Caravella), the laid-back, jive-talking morning presenter, and Venus Flytrap (Gordon Sims), a cool, black night-time jock. Holding the station together is busty, blonde secretary, Jennifer Marlowe, constantly pursued by obnoxious ad salesman Herb Tarlek.

Nine years after the series ended, a new version was produced for syndication in the USA. Only three members of the original cast were recalled: Arthur Carlson, Herb Tarlek and Les Nessman.

Wodehouse Playhouse ★★★

UK (BBC) Comedy. BBC 1 1975–6; 1978

John Alderton, Pauline Collins

Writer **David Climie**
Producers **David Askey, Michael Mills, Gareth Gwenlan**

● ***Anthology of P. G. Wodehouse comedies.***

Adapted by David Climie from the short stories of P. G. Wodehouse, this collection of 1920s high society farces stars the husband-and-wife pairing of John Alderton and Pauline Collins in a variety of different roles (Alderton only for the third and final series). Wodehouse himself introduces the earliest episodes.

Wogan, Terry

KBE (Hon.) (1938–)

Irish presenter and chat show host. A one-time bank clerk, then a presenter with RTE in Dublin, Wogan joined the BBC in the 1960s and was one of Radio 1's original team of presenters in 1967. His Radio 2 breakfast show in the 1970s and early 1980s gained a cult following and established his distinctively witty, self-effacing presentational style. Items like 'Fighting the Flab' and 'Wogan's Winner' characterized the show, and his constant digs at Dallas ensured that the soap became a hit in the UK. Although he had already hosted a chat show, *Lunchtime With Wogan*, for ATV in 1972, and the pop quiz *Disco* in 1975, it wasn't until 1979, when he began five years at the helm of the panel game BLANKETY BLANK, that his TV career began to take off. In 1980 he turned his hand to chat shows with *What's On Wogan*, a live Saturday teatime programme. Two years later, it metamorphosed into *Wogan* and was transmitted late on a Saturday night, before being promoted in 1985 to an early-evening, thrice-weekly live event. Terry quickly became *the* TV personality of the 1980s and was seldom off British screens. When *Wogan* ended to make way for ELDORADO in 1992, he returned to his old Radio 2 morning slot, saving room all the same for another music-and-chat show, *Wogan's Friday Night*, and the Ireland travelogue *Wogan's Island*. He has since presented POINTS OF VIEW, co-hosted CHILDREN IN NEED since 1980, shared *The Terry and Gaby Show* with Gaby Roslin, and can be heard every year genially rubbishing the entries on the EUROVISION SONG CONTEST. Among his other TV credits have been COME DANCING, MISS WORLD, *Do the Right Thing* and the bloopers programme *Auntie's Bloomers* and its spin-offs. More recently, he hosted

Wogan: Now and Then, a package of new and archive interviews, for UKTV Gold. He is the father of actress Katherine Wogan and chef Mark Wogan.

Wokenwell ★★★

UK (LWT) Police Drama. ITV 1997

Sgt Duncan Bonney .... **Ian McElhinney**
PC Brian Rainford .... **Jason Done**
PC Rudy Whiteside .... **Nicholas Gleaves**
June Bonney .... **Celia Imrie**
Lucky Whiteside .... **Lesley Dunlop**
Fran Rainford .... **Nicola Stephenson**
Natalie .... **Samantha Bishop**
Melissa .... **Kate Collings**
Barry Whiteside .... **Matthew Knowles**
Sadly Stan Potter .... **Bryan Pringle**

Writer **Bill Gallagher**
Producer **Paul Marcus**

● ***On the beat in a sleepy town that is home to some strange crimes.***

An unusual six-part series that marries laughter with tragedy, *Wokenwell* is set in the fictitious northern settlement of the same name (filming took place in the Yorkshire town of Marsden). Central to events are the police trio of Sgt Bonney and PCs Rainford and Whiteside, but equally pivotal to the action are their wives, June, Fran and Lucky. Their complicated relationships add a further dimension. Beginning with an investigation into a severed finger found outside a butcher's shop, the series covers an assortment of intrigues that strike the close-knit community – a place where the oddest things tend to happen.

Wolfe, Ronald

See *Chesney, Ronald*.

Wolstenholme, Kenneth

DFC (1920–2002)

British soccer commentator, a contributor to *Sports Special* in the 1950s and the voice of football with the BBC in the 1960s, thanks to his work on MATCH OF THE DAY. It was Wolstenholme who uttered the famous words, 'Some people are on the pitch – they think it's all over . . . it is now' at the end of the 1966 World Cup Final. He left the BBC in 1971 to make way for a new generation of commentators after 23 years with the Corporation, but continued to cover soccer for Tyne Tees before retiring. He later made numerous guest appearances and became something of a cult figure. Prior to entering broadcasting, Wolstenholme was a bomber pilot in the war and was awarded the DFC.

Woman in White, The ★★★

UK (Carlton/BBC) Drama. BBC 1 1997

Marian Halcombe .... **Tara Fitzgerald**
Laura Fairlie .... **Justine Waddell**
Sir Percival Glyde .... **James Wilby**
Count Fosco .... **Simon Callow**
Mr Frederick Fairlie .... **Ian Richardson**
Walter Hartright .... **Andrew Lincoln**
Mr Gilmore .... **John Standing**
Mrs Rideout .... **Ann Bell**
Anne Catherick .... **Susan Vidler**
Margaret Porcher .... **Adie Allen**
Dr Kidson .... **Corin Redgrave**
Madame Fosco .... **Kika Markham**

Writer **David Pirie**
Producer **Gareth Neame**

● ***The lives of two young girls and a mysterious woman seem interwined.***

Wilkie Collins's dark suspense story of 1860 was brought to television in two parts, directed by Tim Fywell. The tale is of two half-sisters, isolated in the home of their mean uncle, Mr Fairlie, whose hearts skip a beat when they hear a fascinating revelation from their new tutor, Walter Hartright. He has encountered a mysterious woman dressed in white, but is this merely an apparition? Was the lady a ghost or is there something even more sinister taking place close to their home at Blackwater Park? Laura's fiancé, Sir Percival Glyde, then arrives, to bring new misery into the girls' lives, aided and abetted by his creepy sidekick, Count Fosco. For Laura and Marian the future begins to look as bleak as it does for the enigmatic Woman in White. With major cuts made to the plot and characterization, to condense the story into just over two hours' viewing, the drama was applauded for its atmosphere but slammed by some for its distortion of the original work. Earlier TV versions were shown in 1957 (ITV single drama: Mary Mackenzie as Marian), 1966 (BBC 1: Alethea Charlton as Marian, Jennifer Hilary as Laura and Geoffrey Bayldon as Fairlie) and 1982 (BBC 2: Diana Quick as Marian, Jenny Seagrove as Laura and Ian Richardson, again, as Fairlie).

Woman of Substance, A ★★

UK (Portman Artemis) Drama. Channel 4 1985

Emma Harte .... **Jenny Seagrove**
Deborah Kerr
Henry Rossiter .... **John Mills**
Laura Spencer .... **Diane Baker**
Bruce McGill .... **George Baker**
Olivia .... **Gayle Hunnicutt**
Adele Fairley .... **Nicola Pagett**
Paula .... **Miranda Richardson**
Paul McGill .... **Barry Bostwick**
Shane O'Neill .... **Liam Neeson**
Murgatroyd .... **Barry Morse**

Writer **Lee Langley**
Producer **Diane Baker**

● ***An ambitious servant girl drives her way to the top.***

Told in flashback and beginning in 1905, *A Woman of Substance* is the rags-to-riches story of Emma Harte, a Yorkshire lass from the serving classes who makes her way up through society. Her ambitions lead her out of the scullery and into the world of business. She moves to the USA and becomes one of the world's wealthiest women, owning a major chain of department stores. Jenny Seagrove plays Emma up to the age of 49, with Deborah Kerr taking over for the heroine's later years. Adapted by Lee Langley from Barbara Taylor Bradford's romantic novel, this mini-series was shown on three consecutive nights on Channel 4 in 1985. A year later, a sequel made in America and entitled *Hold That Dream* once again saw Seagrove and Kerr in the role of Harte.

Wombles, The ✱✱

UK (Filmfair/Cinar Films) Children's Entertainment. BBC 1 1973; 1975; ITV 1990–1; 1998–2001

Narrator **Bernard Cribbins**

Creator/Writer **Elisabeth Beresford**

● ***A small colony of cuddly conservationists keeps Wimbledon Common free of litter.***

'Underground, overground, wombling free', the long-nosed, furry Wombles of Wimbledon Common were Britain's foremost ecologists in the 1970s. 'Making good use of the things that they find, things that the everyday folk leave behind', the incredibly devious Wombles turn trash into useful items – useful to a Womble at least. Their burrow is wallpapered in discarded newsprint and there is always some new contraption being conjured up. Headed by Great Uncle Bulgaria, the Wombles are Tomsk, Orinoco, Tobermory, Wellington, Bungo and their French housemaid, Mme Cholet.

Based on the stories by Elisabeth Beresford (who was once married to broadcaster Max Robertson), the five-minute Wombles tales, animated by Ivor Wood, are whimsically narrated by Bernard Cribbins. Mike Batt performs the theme music (which became a hit in 1974 and led to a spate of other Wombling pop pieces). A feature film, *Wombling Free*, was released in 1977, and the busy little creatures were resurrected by ITV for a couple of specials in 1990–1. In 1998 the Wombles were back, with four new members in the clan: Stepney (a Cockney), Obidos (a pan piper from Brazil), Shanshi (from China) and the skateboarding Alderney, who lived in a treehouse. Contemporary technology like womfaxes and the Internet made life easier for the fluffy recyclists, but, with a cast of actors to provide their voices, they now had to make do without the cheery commentary from Cribbins.

Wonder Woman ✱✱

US (Warner Brothers) Science Fiction. BBC 1 1978–80 (US: ABC 1976–7; CBS 1977–9)

Diana Prince/Wonder Woman	**Lynda Carter**
Steve Trevor	**Lyle Waggoner**
Joe Atkinson	**Normann Burton**
IRA	**Tom Kratochzil** *(voice only)*

Executive Producer **Douglas S. Cramer**
Producer **Bruce Lansbury**

● ***A superwoman uses her powers to fight subversion.***

Wonder Woman, a creation of cartoonist Charles Moulton, actually appeared in two different settings on TV in the 1970s. Firstly, in a series entitled *The New, Original Wonder Woman*, she lives in the 1940s. She is discovered among a race of Amazon women on Paradise Island, an uncharted piece of land somewhere in the Caribbean, by a crash-landed US major, Steve Trevor. The women, refugees from ancient Greece and Rome, have lived on the island since about 200 BC, having stumbled across a magical material called Feminum which, when moulded into bracelets or belts, gives them superhuman powers.

The future Wonder Woman is Princess Diana, daughter of Hippolyte, the Queen of the Amazons. Nursing the wounded soldier back to health, she falls in love and returns with him to civilization. There, she assumes the identity of Diana Prince and becomes his secretary in the War Department. However, whenever trouble beckons, she adopts the mantle of Wonder Woman, performing a quick change of clothes by spinning herself around and donning a patriotic red, white and blue costume, complete with Feminum belt to give her strength and Feminum bracelets to deflect bullets. The magical lasso she carries forces her enemies (usually Nazis) to tell the truth.

This series was not shown in the UK. We did catch up with her, however, in the second series, *The New Adventures of Wonder Woman*, in which the setting is 1970s America. Diana has once again returned from Paradise Island, showing no sign of ageing, to take up a post as an agent for the Inter-Agency Defense Command (IADC). Her boss is Joe Atkinson and her close colleague is the son of her former friend, Steve Trevor, conveniently the double of his father (and also called Steve). For the IADC, Diana fights against crazed scientists, saboteurs, terrorists and aliens, and, like all the agents, is assisted by a talking Internal Retrieval Associative computer (IRA). Only IRA knows Diana's *alter ego*.

The statuesque Lynda Carter was perfectly built to fill this Amazonian role – she had been Miss America in 1973. That said, a 1974 pilot film cast Cathy Lee Crosby in the title role.

Wonder Years, The ✱✱✱

US (Black/Marlens) Situation Comedy. Channel 4 1989–93 (US: ABC 1988–93)

Kevin Arnold	**Fred Savage**
Kevin Arnold (adult)	**Daniel Stern** *(voice only)*
Jack Arnold	**Dan Lauria**
Norma Arnold	**Alley Mills**
Wayne Arnold	**Jason Hervey**
Karen Arnold	**Olivia d'Abo**
Paul Pfeiffer	**Josh Saviano**
Gwendolyn 'Winnie' Cooper	**Danica McKellar**
Coach Ed Cutlip	**Robert Picardo**

Creators **Neal Marlens, Carol Black**
Executive Producers **Neal Marlens, Carol Black, Bob Brush**

● ***Nostalgic tales of growing up in suburban America in the late 1960s.***

The Wonder Years forms the memoirs of Kevin Arnold, a 12-year-old (at the programme's outset), just starting out at the Robert F. Kennedy Junior High School in 1968 and desperate to make the right impression with his peers, especially the girls. The adult Kevin (never seen) acts as narrator, telling viewers just what his younger self was thinking at the time. The result is a whimsical, poignant observation of adolescent woes in an era of social change.

Kevin is the youngest child of a typical suburban family. His mom and dad are 1940s teenagers turned parents and householders, overtaken somewhat by time and finding it difficult to relate to their children (especially after a hard day's work). Wayne, Kevin's obnoxious brother, teases him mercilessly, while his sister, Karen, is into every peace and protest movement of the day. Kevin's best friend is Paul, a gangly, nerdy type with glasses and a brace, and Winnie Cooper is the girl next door whom Kevin has his eye on.

Old newsreel clips add period atmosphere, as does music of the time (the show's theme is Joe Cocker's 'With a Little Help from My Friends'), but this is a programme whose success comes from the strength of its characterization and its scripts, not cheap, nostalgic in-fills.

Woobinda ✶

Australia (NLT) Children's Drama. ITV 1969

John Stevens .... **Don Pascoe**
Peter Fischer .... **Lutz Hochstraate**
Tiggie Stevens .... **Sonia Hofmann**
Jack Johnson .... **Slim De Grey**
Kevin Stevens .... **Bindi Williams**

Creator **Malcolm Hulke**
Producer **Roger Mirams**

● ***A vet works in the wild Australian bush.***

Subtitled 'Animal Doctor' after the aboriginal name for a vet, Woobinda features the day-to-day adventures of widower John Stevens, whose practice is deep in the mysterious and dangerous outback of Australia, home to all kinds of wild animals. In his DAKTARI-like adventures, the morally steadfast, cool-headed vet is assisted by his family – teenage daughter Tiggie and adopted aboriginal orphan Kevin – and young German colleague Peter Fischer – which ensured exposure for the series on German television at the time. Also seen is Jack Johnson, a close family friend.

Wood, Duncan

(1925–97)

BBC comedy producer of the 1950s–1970s, working with Benny Hill, Frankie Howerd and Ken Dodd, and also responsible for such classic sitcoms as HANCOCK'S HALF HOUR and STEPTOE AND SON. *Strictly T-T, Great Scott – It's Maynard!*, CITIZEN JAMES, THE BED-SIT GIRL, HUGH AND I, *Harry Worth*, OH BROTHER!, THE FURTHER ADVENTURES OF LUCKY JIM, *The World of Beachcomber* and *Now Take My Wife* were other notable production credits. He moved to Yorkshire Television in the 1970s as Head of Light Entertainment, where he commissioned series like RISING DAMP, *Hello Cheeky*, OH NO! IT'S SELWYN FROGGITT and 3-2-1.

Wood, Ivor

(1932–2004)

Leeds-born pioneer of stop-frame animation and the brains behind some of the most memorable children's series. Much of Wood's early life was spent in France, where he began making children's puppet programmes, working closely with Serge Danot in creating THE MAGIC ROUNDABOUT. He moved back to Britain to work for the Filmfair production company, painstakingly animating/directing THE HERBS, THE ADVENTURES OF PARSLEY, THE WOMBLES, PADDINGTON and *Simon in the Land of Chalk Drawings*. He later set up Woodlands Animations, a company responsible for series such as *Gran*, *Bertha* and, most popular of all, POSTMAN PAT.

Wood, Victoria

OBE (1953–)

Lancashire-born comic, musician and writer, coming to light in the NEW FACES talent show in 1975 and its spin-off, *The Summer Show*. A year later, she secured herself fortnightly work writing topical songs for THAT'S LIFE and by the end of the decade was moving into her own comic plays like *Talent*, *Nearly a Happy Ending* and *Happy Since I Met You*, usually with her regular partner, Julie Walters. Together they hosted a show for Granada entitled *Wood and Walters*, before Victoria switched to the BBC and began a run of successful comedies, among them *Victoria Wood – As Seen on TV* (a sketch and monologue show with a repertory cast of Walters, Celia Imrie, Duncan Preston and Susie Blake, and featuring the CROSSROADS spoof, *Acorn Antiques*), and the playlet series, *Victoria Wood*. In 1994 she starred again with Julie Walters in a *Screen One* comedy, *Pat and Margaret*, in 1996 took one of the *Great Railway Journeys* (see GREAT RAILWAY JOURNEYS OF THE WORLD), and in 1998 launched her own sitcom, DINNERLADIES, appearing herself as Bren. In 2000 she hosted *Don't Panic! The Dad's Army Story* and a year later fronted *Victoria Wood's Sketch Show Story*. In 2004, she presented the two-part *Victoria Wood's Big Fat Documentary* about obesity and its treatment in society. Wood married entertainer Geoffrey Durham (aka The Great Soprendo), but they have since separated.

Woodentops, The ✶✶

UK (BBC) Children's Entertainment. BBC 1955–8

Voices **Peter Hawkins, Eileen Brown, Josephina Ray**

Creators **Freda Lingstrom, Maria Bird**
Producer **Freda Lingstrom**
Writer **Maria Bird**

● ***Idyllic life down on the farm with an industrious puppet family.***

Friday's WATCH WITH MOTHER offering was brought to the screen by the same team responsible for Tuesday's (ANDY PANDY) and Wednesday's (FLOWER POT MEN). The Woodentops are Daddy Woodentop (seldom seen with a shirt on his back), Mummy Woodentop (so busy in the kitchen that she needs daily help from Mrs Scrubbitt), high-pitched twins Jenny and Willy Woodentop and, completing the family, Baby Woodentop, still in his mother's arms. Also seen is Sam, the man who helped Daddy Woodentop in the garden, as well as Buttercup the cow and a rascally hound by the appropriate name of Spotty Dog, in fact 'the biggest spotty dog you ever did see'. With action thin on the ground, the best that toddlers can hope for is Jenny or Willy getting into a scrape and being late for dinner, or Spotty taking the odd liberty with his caring owners. All ends well, however, and the whole cast waves goodbye over the closing credits. Audrey Atterbury and Molly Gibson pulled the strings.

Woodhouse, Barbara

(1910–88)

Irish-born doctor's wife and farmer who became an unlikely TV celebrity as an animal trainer. After years of supplying star animals for the media, Barbara Woodhouse's heyday arrived in 1980 when she hosted an educational series entitled TRAINING DOGS THE WOODHOUSE WAY, which was considered to be light entertainment of the first order by many viewers. The bossy granny in a Scottish kilt and sensible shoes pioneered 'quick training' methods for dogs, barking shrill orders and yanking them into submission with her much-criticized choke-chains. But she was equally tough on inept owners who failed to bring their pets into line. She later took her message around the country in *The Woodhouse Roadshow* and also hosted other canine and equine programmes.

Woodward, Edward

OBE (1930–)

British actor fond of tough, determined roles like that of secret agent CALLAN and avenging angel Robert McCall in THE EQUALIZER. Among his other credits have been DETECTIVE (Edgar Allan Poe's Auguste Dupin), SWORD OF HONOUR (Guy Crouchback), 1990 (journalist Jim Kyle), WINSTON CHURCHILL – THE WILDERNESS YEARS (Sir Samuel Hoare), *Nice Work* (labour official Edwin Thornfield), COMMON AS MUCK (Nev), an American crime series *Over My Dead Body* (detective-novelist Maxwell Becket), GULLIVER'S TRAVELS (Drunlo), *Marcie's Dowry* (Gus Wise), *Night Flight* (Vic Green) and MESSIAH (Revd Stephen Hedges). He also appeared in the 1977 drama *The Bass Player and the Blonde*, hosted the anthology series *In Suspicious Circumstances*, and has plenty of single plays in his portfolio. His earliest guest appearances came in 1960s series like SIR FRANCIS DRAKE, MOGUL, THE BARON, THE SAINT and MYSTERY AND IMAGINATION. More recent guest spots have been in MURDER IN SUBURBIA and WHERE THE HEART IS. The father of actors Tim, Peter and Sarah Woodward, and husband of actress Michele Dotrice, he also hosted the panel game WHODUNNIT?, and was occasionally heard singing in 1970s variety shows such as his own *The Edward Woodward Hour*.

Word, The ★★

UK (24 Hour/Planet 24) Channel 4 1990–5

Presenters **Terry Christian, Amanda de Cadanet, Kate Puckrik, Mark Lamarr, Dani Behr, Huffty, Jasmine Dottiwala, Andrew Connor**

Editors **Charlie Parsons, Sebastian Scott, Paul Ross, Duncan Grey**
Producers **Dele Oniya, Richard Godfrey, Tamsin Summers, Asif Zubairy**
Executive Producer **Charlie Parsons**

● ***Controversial, late-night music and chat show.***

For middle-aged critics *The Word* was everything that was bad about early 1990s television. A new generation of youth culture had finally arrived and, pre-empting even less disciplined programmes like *The Girlie Show*, this magazine led the way with its laddish approach, gossipy interviews and sometimes ignorant interviewees. One notorious slot was called The Hopefuls and featured members of the general public who would do, it seemed, absolutely anything to get on television, from outrageous stunts to revolting things with their bodies. The series started out in a 6 p.m. transmission slot but was soon moved to around 11 p.m. – indicative of its appeal to the post-pub crowd. But *The Word* was at least live and lively, with a buzzing audience milling around the guests, and among its achievements was providing Oasis with their first ever TV exposure. Paul Ross (brother of Jonathan) was editor for a time and Jo Whiley was music producer.

Worker, The ★★

UK (ATV) Situation Comedy. ITV 1965; 1969–70

Charlie	**Charlie Drake**
Mr Whittaker	**Percy Herbert**
Mr Pugh	**Henry McGee**

Writers **Charlie Drake, Lew Schwarz**
Producers **Alan Tarrant, Shaun O'Riordan**

● ***An unemployable nuisance is the scourge of the local labour exchange.***

Although he is known as the Worker, Charlie doesn't – work, that is, at least not for more than one day at a time, such is his inability to hold down a job. Apparently he has fouled up nearly 1,000 jobs in 20 years. As a result, the irrepressible, ginger-haired imp bangs on the counter of the Weybridge labour exchange every other morning, much to the frustration of the clerks, first Mr Whittaker then, more famously, Mr Pugh (or Mr Peooow, as our hero dubs him). Such antagonism unfailingly ends with Pugh grabbing Charlie by the throat and winching him off the ground. After a gap of four years, the series was brought back in 1969, and it was briefly revived once more in 1978 as part of *Bruce Forsyth's Big Night*, with Drake and McGee again doing battle in the job centre.

World about Us, The ★★★

UK (BBC) Natural History. BBC 2 1967–86

● ***Long-running series featuring the wonders of nature and assorted global explorations.***

Initially making use of amateur footage, but soon becoming fully professional in its contributions, *The World about Us* ran for nearly 20 years. It was commissioned by David Attenborough (then head of BBC 2) to illustrate the scope of colour television (which had just been introduced), the glorious hues of the natural world providing the perfect subject-matter. Major geographical expeditions were also featured (one went up the Orinoco and Amazon by hovercraft), and Jacques Cousteau's undersea explorations also formed part of the package. *The Natural World* has been its successor.

World at War, The ★★★★

UK (Thames) Historical Documentary. ITV 1973–4

Narrator **Laurence Olivier**

Producer **Jeremy Isaacs**

● ***Eye-opening account of World War II.***

Thoroughly researched (with historical accuracy monitored by Noble Frankland), *The World at War* looks at the 1939–45 conflict in 26 episodes. From the rise to power of Hitler to the bombing of Hiroshima, all the dramas and horrors of the war are documented using old film footage (some newly unearthed) and harrowing eye-witness accounts. The accompanying book sold half a million copies and the series won awards all round the world.

World in Action ★★★★

UK (Granada) Current Affairs. ITV 1963–98

Creator **Tim Hewat**
Producers **Tim Hewat, David Plowright, Leslie Woodhead, Jeremy Wallington, Gus McDonald, Denis Mitchell, Michael Apted, Mike Wooller, John Birt, Ray Fitzwalter, Alex Valentine, Brian Lapping, Nick Hayes, Charles Tremayne, Steve Boulton**

● ***Long-running, award-winning current affairs series.***

Launched with the intention of providing 'not simply the news but the full background story', *World in Action* became one of the world's most acclaimed public affairs series. From the first edition, when it focused on the nuclear arms race, the series was never afraid to confront authority. Its hard-hitting, in-depth investigations caused embarrassment to many politicians and industrialists, exposing scandals and unearthing hidden facts. Programmes were generally half an hour in length and aired on Monday evenings. Its cancellation in 1998 provided further evidence, for many critics, of the 'dumbing-down' of British television.

World of Sport ★★

UK (Various) Sport. ITV 1965–85

Presenters **Eamonn Andrews, Richard Davies**

● ***Four-and-a-half-hour Saturday sports marathon.***

ITV's answer to GRANDSTAND, *World of Sport* tried somewhat unsuccessfully to compete with its BBC rival for 20 years, before finally throwing in the towel. Although, as an overall package, it was never on terms with *Grandstand* (largely because the BBC controlled all the major events), *World of Sport* did enjoy a sizeable following for its minority sports, particularly horse racing and wrestling.

World of Sport was a team effort involving most ITV companies, with studio facilities and programme production provided by LWT in later years. Its first host was Eamonn Andrews, supported by a team of Fleet Street sub-editors who clattered around in the background, thrusting latest scores and other news items into his hand as he talked to camera. Richard 'Dickie' Davies took over in 1968 and remained in charge until the programme was cancelled in 1985. Fred Dinenage was Davies's relief presenter.

For many years the running order featured football to start, followed by horse racing and the likes of snooker, darts and motor sports, with wrestling taking over the second half of the programme and leading into the results service at about 4.45 p.m. Some events were screened under the umbrella subtitle of *International Sports Special*, which embraced anything from show-jumping and water skiing to Australian rules football and arm wrestling. In the early days, Fred Trueman and Ian Wooldridge were specialist contributors to the programme and Peter Lorenzo previewed the day's soccer. When the football slot was retitled *On the Ball*, Brian Moore and Jimmy Hill were drafted in as hosts. Ian St John and Jimmy Greaves were the last football pundits, and when *World of Sport* was cancelled their slot survived as a separate programme, entitled *Saint and Greavsie*. (*On the Ball* was revived as a programme in its own right in 1998, with presenters Gabby Yorath/Logan and Barry Venison.)

World of Sport was the pioneer of multi-course racing coverage, as an all-action alternative to one-card racing. Its *ITV Seven* (an accumulator built around the winners of all seven featured races) became a popular bet. Trilby-hatted John Rickman took charge of racing affairs for many years, and also seen were John Oaksey, Ken Butler, Brough Scott and Derek Thompson, with commentaries by Tony Cooke, John Penney, Raleigh Gilbert and Graham Goode and results from John Tyrrel. Wrestling was in the capable hands of former disc-jockey Kent Walton, and other commentators included Tony Green for darts, John Pulman for snooker, Adrian Metcalfe for athletics and Reg Gutteridge for boxing.

World of Tim Frazer, The ★★

UK (BBC) Drama. BBC 1960–1

Tim Frazer .... **Jack Hedley**
Charles Ross .... **Ralph Michael**
Helen Baker .... **Heather Chasen**
Dr Killick .... **Gerald Cross**
Crombie .... **Donald Morley**
Anya .... **Janina Faye**
Ruth Edwards .... **Barbara Couper**
Donald Edwards .... **Redmond Phillips**
Tupper .... **Brian Wilde**
Harry Denston .... **John Dearth**
Barbara Day .... **Patricia Haynes**
Vivien Gilmore .... **Patricia Marmont**
Arthur Fairlie .... **Michael Aldridge**
Lewis Richards .... **Francis Matthews**
Gordon Dempsey .... **Kenneth J. Warren**
Miss Thackeray/Eve Turner .... **Ellen McIntosh**
Major Lockwood .... **Jack Watling**
Roger Thornton .... **David Langton**
Elwyn Roberts .... **Laurence Hardy**
Laurence James .... **Patrick McAlinney**

Writers **Francis Durbridge, Clive Exton, Barry Thomas, Charles Hatton**
Producers **Alan Bromley, Terence Dudley, Richmond Harding**

● ***An inquisitive young bachelor helps the government solve crimes.***

At the time the longest-ever serial produced by the BBC (18 weeks), *The World of Tim Frazer* aired under the *Francis Durbridge Presents* . . . umbrella. The hero is a dashing young engineer with a penchant for fast cars and a nose for intrigue, and his curiosity leads him into three separate adventures during the course of the programme's run. We first meet him visiting an old friend and business partner, Harry Denston, in the fishing village of Henton. But Harry is nowhere to be seen and, out of the blue, Frazer is asked by Charles Ross, head of a government department, to find his old pal. Tim follows up this investigation with another concerning diamond smuggling in Amsterdam, in which a metronome and an enigmatic crime baron named 'Ericson' feature prominently. Finally, Frazer heads for Wales, to the town of Melynfforest, where one of Ross's agents has been murdered.

World's End ★★

UK (BBC) Drama. BBC 2 1981

Danny .... **Michael Angelis**
Jack .... **Tom Marshall**
Dodie .... **Eileen Pollock**
Stewart .... **Victor Lucas**
Brahms .... **Brian Vaughan**
Camille .... **Pam Scotcher**
Robin .... **Neville Smith**
Nicola .... **Primi Townsend**
Tim .... **Daniel Holender**
Lynn .... **Catherine Neilson**
Daley .... **Derek Martin**
Angela .... **Helen Bush**
Lord Arvin .... **Paul Brooke**
Andy .... **Harry Fowler**
Paddy .... **Chris Gannon**
Space .... **Bradley Lavelle**

Barney .... **Toby Salaman**
Jonathan .... **Peter Harlowe**
Antonia .... **Gillian Barge**
Else .... **Christina Paul**
Edwin .... **Sam Dastor**

Creator/Writer **Ted Whitehead**
Producer **Colin Tucker**

● ***Everyday drama in a cosmopolitan London village.***

In retrospect, *World's End* may be seen as a sort of *WestEnders*. But, as well as being scheduled for late-night viewing on BBC 2, the 13-part serial also differs from EASTENDERS in being socially inclusive, with characters from all walks of life seen to be getting along rather well.

The setting is the London 'village' of World's End (Chelsea), with The Mulberry pub at its hub, providing a meeting place and source of various sexual and political storylines. All human life is here, as the *News of the World* used to boast, with anyone from the labourer to the politician seen as very much part of the community. There's Camille, a single mum who runs a stall in the antique market; ex-Communist Nicola, who has just given up her job in personnel to return to college to study Humanities; and Lynn, a nightclub croupier who shares a house with Camille and Nicola. Then there's Robin, Nicola's boyfriend, a Cambridge graduate now working as a bricklayer. He greatly disapproves of Nicola's return to studies. Danny is the Liverpudlian tinker who wanders the local streets, while Angela is the new girl in town, suburban by upbringing and now a Mormon by religion. Representing both extremes of the political map are Lord Arvin, a 'caring Tory', and Andy, a militantly socialist handyman. Stewart is the pub's landlord, Dodie is the former model and Windmill girl who now washes the pub's pots (if not doting on her cat, Chivers), and Brahms is a playwright who works behind the bar (actor Brian Vaughan was spotted doing just the same in real life by series creator Ted Whitehead).

Whitehead developed the concept after living in Chelsea for seven years, basing his characters and storylines on personal experiences and the fact that Chelsea has the same mix of social types, with council estates just yards from the King's Road and posh peoples' mansions. His message was tolerance: social harmony can exist in spite of major differences between neighbours. Whitehead also wrote a companion novel of the same title. The programme's theme song, 'Down at the World's End', was provided by Alan Price.

Worst Week of My Life, The ★★★

UK (Hat Trick) Situation Comedy. BBC 1 2004–5
DVD: VCI

Howard Steel .... **Ben Miller**
Mel Cook/Steel .... **Sarah Alexander**
Angela Cook .... **Alison Steadman**
Dick Cook .... **Geoffrey Whitehead**
Sophie Cook .... **Emma Pierson**
Cassie .... **Raquel Cassidy**
Eve Whittle .... **Janine Duvitski**
Granny Cook .... **Hazel Douglas**
Dom .... **Dean Lennox Kelly**
Ron Steel .... **John Benfield**
Trish .... **Lizzie Roper**
Fraser .... **Ronald Pickup**
Nicola .... **Sian Thomas**
Cordelia Melville .... **Anastasia Griffith**
Gerard .... **Terrence Hardiman**

Creators/Writers/Producers **Mark Bussell, Justin Sbresni**

● ***The run-up to his wedding day is a minefield for a hapless publisher.***

With more than an echo of Jack Lemmon's classic *The Out of Towners* in its frantic, disaster-ridden plot, *The Worst Week of My Life* features Howard Steel, an amiable but hopelessly accident-prone editor with the Brooke Doyle publishing company. It's a big week, because he's getting married on Saturday, but from Monday onwards nothing runs according to plan. Howard does his best to make amends for all the mishaps but only succeeds in making things worse, much to the disdain of his snooty father-in-law-to-be, Dick Cook, the frustration of Dick's wife, Angela, and the weary resignation of feisty fiancée Mel, a vet. Somehow, despite Howard being haunted by deranged former (one-occasion) lover Cassie and, somewhat inevitably, losing the wedding ring, among other trials, they do manage to tie the knot and return for a second series set ten months on, in which Mel is about to deliver their first child. Once again, what should be a memorable occasion is turned into an unmitigated horror story as Howard falls victim to yet further mishaps and excruciating embarrassments. Refreshingly funny, if at times rather predictable, *The Worst Week of My Life* is a successful, fast-moving farce for the new millennium. The creative team of Mark Bussell and Justin Sbresni also direct series two.

Worth, Harry

(Harry Illingsworth; 1917–89)

Yorkshire-born comedian and comic actor, generally seen as a genial, bungling interferer who ends up confusing all and sundry. Breaking into showbiz as a ventriloquist, Worth, a former miner, abandoned his dummies reportedly on the advice of Stan Laurel and became a stand-up comic. In 1959 he began his first TV series, a sitcom called *The Trouble with Harry*, and less than a year later starred in HERE'S HARRY, in which he introduced his trademark shop-window routine, using his reflection to make it look as if he was waving all four limbs at once. *Here's Harry* ran for five years and was followed during the 1960s and 1970s by *Harry Worth, Thirty Minutes' Worth, My Name is Harry Worth* (titled after his catchphrase), HOW'S YOUR FATHER (as Harry Matthews, an out-of-touch widowed father of two teenagers) and OH HAPPY BAND! (playing himself as a brass band conductor). He was also seen as William Boot in the BBC's 1972 serialization of Evelyn Waugh's *Scoop*.

Worzel Gummidge ★★

UK (Southern) Children's Adventure. ITV 1979–81

Worzel Gummidge .... **Jon Pertwee**
Aunt Sally .... **Una Stubbs**
The Crowman .... **Geoffrey Bayldon**
John Peters .... **Jeremy Austin**
Sue Peters .... **Charlotte Coleman**
Mr Peters .... **Mike Berry**
Mrs Braithwaite .... **Megs Jenkins**
Mr Braithwaite .... **Norman Bird**
Saucy Nancy .... **Barbara Windsor**
Dolly Clothes-Peg .... **Lorraine Chase**
Mrs Bloomsbury-Barton .... **Joan Sims**
Mr Shepherd .... **Michael Ripper**

Writers **Keith Waterhouse, Willis Hall**
Executive Producer **Lewis Rudd**

Producer **James Hill**

● ***The adventures of a living scarecrow.***
Worzel Gummidge, a warty scarecrow with a turnip head, straggly straw hair and a unique line in yokelese, is a friend of young John and Sue Peters. They have just moved to the country, with their dad, having lost their mum, when they stumble across this mischievous character in Ten Acre Field of Scatterbrook Farm, and he transforms their life with his clumsy antics and good-natured humour. Wherever Worzel goes, disaster follows. His girlfriend is Aunt Sally, a skittle doll, although he also falls for Saucy Nancy, a ship's figurehead, and flirts with a tailor's dummy called Dolly Clothes-Peg. The Crowman is Worzel's creator and can fashion new heads for him to change his character, if required.

The series, written by Keith Waterhouse and Willis Hall, was based on the books of Barbara Euphan Todd and was largely the idea of star Jon Pertwee. In marked contrast to his role as DOCTOR WHO, this part gave him the chance to show off his comedy skills, which had been honed on BBC Radio for many years. When Southern Television lost its ITV franchise, production was halted, until the idea was picked up by a New Zealand company in 1987, with Worzel taking up residence in the Antipodes in a series called *Worzel Gummidge Down Under* (UK: Channel 4 1987; 1989). Jon Pertwee also had a minor chart hit with 'Worzel's Song' in 1980.

TV's first Worzel Gummidge was Frank Atkinson, who played the part in the 1953 series *Worzel Gummidge Turns Detective*.

Wrather, Jack
(1918–84)

Texan oil and TV executive who purchased the rights to LASSIE and THE LONE RANGER and reaped the benefits of his foresight when both proved to be perennial and global hits. His company, Wrather TV Productions, produced both series, plus other juvenile action series like SERGEANT PRESTON OF THE YUKON. He was also prominent in television sales and syndication, with Lew Grade forming the American wing of ITC, ITC Inc., to distribute Wrather and ITC programmes in the USA, although he was later bought out by Grade. He was married to actress Bonita Granville.

Wright, Ian
(1963–)

Former England football striker (33 caps) turned presenter of sports and light entertainment shows. Among the programmes he has fronted are *Friday Night's All Wright, Guinness World Records, Friends Like These, Spy TV, I'd Do Anything, Wright Here, Wright Now,* THE NATIONAL LOTTERY – *Wright around the World* and *What Kids Really Think*. He has also appeared as a team captain on THEY THINK IT'S ALL OVER and featured in the documentary *Ian Wright Surviving the Kalahari*. His stepson is current England international Shaun Wright-Phillips.

Wright, Steve
(1954–)

Greenwich-born Radio 2 presenter whose television CV covers such programmes as TOP OF THE POPS and *TOTP2* (which he wrote and narrated). Wright also hosted the game show *Home Truths*, his own chat/consumer programme, *Steve Wright's People Show*, and the nostalgic *Auntie's TV Favourites*. Wright also made a guest appearance in the sitcom HAPPINESS.

Wuthering Heights ✱✱
UK (LWT) Drama. ITV 1998

Cathy Earnshaw	**Kadie Savage** *(young)*
	Orla Brady
Heathcliff	**Terry Clynes** *(young)*
	Robert Cavanah
Joseph Lockwood	**Peter Davison**
Mr Earnshaw	**Ken Kitson**
Joseph	**Tom Georgeson**
Hindley Earnshaw	**Kevin Jones** *(young)*
	Ian Shaw
Hareton Earnshaw	**Jake Thornton** *(young)*
	Matthew Macfadyen
Nelly Dean	**Polly Hemingway**
Edgar Linton	**Crispin Bonham-Carter**
Isabella Linton	**Flora Montgomery**
Catherine Linton	**Sarah Smart**

Writer **Neil Mckay**
Executive Producer **Jo Wright**

● ***Passion and revenge on the Yorkshire moors.***
Emily Brontë's great romance of 1847 was brought to television in this single, 140-minute film directed by David Skynner. Largely true to the original novel and its structure, the drama follows childhood sweethearts Heathcliff and Cathy Earnshaw from their days at her home, Wuthering Heights, when he was but an orphan brought into the family fold. The story moves on to Cathy's apparent rejection of his affections and the passionate Heathcliff's climb to wealth and power. He becomes vengeful lord of Wuthering Heights and neighbouring Thrushcross Grange, the one-time home of the Linton family, whose affairs are destined to merge with those of the Earnshaws. Previous UK TV adaptations of the classic novel were in 1948 (BBC: Kieron Moore as Heathcliff, Katharine Blake as Cathy), 1953 (BBC: Richard Todd and Yvonne Mitchell), 1962 (BBC: Keith Michell and Claire Bloom), 1967 (BBC 2: Ian McShane and Angela Scoular) and 1978 (BBC 2: Ken Hutchison and Kay Adshead).

WWN
See *Wales West and North.*

Wyatt Earp
See *Life and Legend of Wyatt Earp, The.*

Wycliffe ✱✱
UK (HTV/Red Rooster) Police Drama. ITV 1994–8

Det. Supt. Charles Wycliffe	**Jack Shepherd**
DI Lucy Lane	**Helen Masters**
Helen Wycliffe	**Lynn Farleigh**
DI Doug Kersey	**Jimmy Yuill**
DS Andy Dixon	**Aaron Harris**
DC Ian Potter	**Adam Barker**
Franks	**Tim Wylton**
David Wycliffe	**Greg Chisholm**
Ruth Wycliffe	**Charlie Hayes**
DCC Stevens	**Michael Attwell**

Supt. Le Page .... **Sharon Duce**

Producers **Pennant Roberts, Geraint Morris, Michael Bartley**
Executive Producers **Jenny Reeks, Steve Matthews**

● ***The cases of a glum-looking Cornish detective.***

Based on the novels of W. J. Burley, this series follows the investigations of Det. Superintendent Charles Wycliffe – named by Burley after John Wycliffe, who translated the Bible back in the 1500s. This Wycliffe is a man who knows his own mind, is thoughtful and fairly tolerant but who doesn't suffer fools gladly. He is not a Cornishman himself and views local folk with a certain objectivity. He is assisted in his work (in and around Penzance, with excursions to picturesque coves, deserted tin mines and Bodmin Moor) by DIs Doug Kersey and Lucy Lane (the latter played by Carla Mendonça in the 1993 pilot episode, which was subtitled '. . . and the Cycle of Death').

Wycliffe's family is kept largely in the background for the first two series, then he is given a domestic dimension with more appearances from his wife, Helen (Lucy Fleming in the pilot), and the introduction of his teenage kids, David and Ruth. In a later series, Wycliffe is shot and badly injured, taking several episodes to make a full recovery. Star Jack Shepherd also directs some stories.

Wyman, Jane

(Sarah Jane Fulks; 1914–)

Oscar-winning American actress who has enjoyed two bites of the TV cherry. In the 1950s, on the back of her Hollywood success, Wyman was called up by US TV to host two series of drama anthologies. In the 1960s and 1970s, her small-screen appearances were relatively few, but she bounced back in 1981 when cast as Angela Channing, matriarch of the vineyards in FALCON CREST. She played the part for nine years and has also been seen in numerous TV movies. Wyman was married to Ronald Reagan in 1940–8.

Wymark, Patrick

(Patrick Cheeseman; 1926–70)

Popular British actor of the 1960s. Formerly a Shakespearean stage performer, Wymark took small roles in series such as DANGER MAN, SIR FRANCIS DRAKE and MAN OF THE WORLD before shooting to fame as John Wilder, the ruthless managing director in THE PLANE MAKERS/THE POWER GAME (the latter its sequel). Sadly, he had little time to capitalize on his success, dying suddenly at the age of 44, not long after the last series of *The Power Game* ended. Actress Jane Wymark is his daughter.

Wyndham-Goldie, Grace

OBE (1900–86)

Influential BBC current affairs producer of the 1950s. Moving into television from radio, she became Assistant Head of Talks in 1954 and, from this position, was responsible for shaking up and revamping PANORMA in 1955 and launching TONIGHT two years later, also handling coverage of elections. In 1962 Wyndham-Goldie was promoted to Head of Talks and Current Affairs. She retired in 1965.

Wyngarde, Peter

(1933–)

French-born actor whose earliest television appearances came in 1950s plays like *Rope* and *A Tale of Two Cities*. In subsequent years he starred in episodes of the anthology series *On Trial* and OUT OF THIS WORLD, and became a familiar guest face in ITC action series like SWORD OF FREEDOM, THE BARON, THE AVENGERS, THE SAINT, THE PRISONER and THE CHAMPIONS. In 1969 he was cast in his most famous role, that of flamboyant novelist/secret agent Jason King in DEPARTMENT S, and, although only one of a trio of agents, he proved so popular that he was brought back in his own spin-off, entitled simply JASON KING, in 1971. His TV work has been thin since, but he has been spotted in DOCTOR WHO, BULMAN, THE TWO RONNIES, THE COMIC STRIP PRESENTS and THE MEMOIRS OF SHERLOCK HOLMES.

X Factor, The ✳✳✳

UK (Thames/Syco) Talent Show. ITV 1 2004–
DVD: Sony

Presenter **Kate Thornton**

Executive Producers **Nigel Hall, Richard Holloway, Mark Wells, Siobhan Greene, Claire Horton**
Producer **Andrew Llinares**

● ***Singers of all ages do battle for a recording contract.***
Fuelled by the success of POPSTARS and POP IDOL, 'Mr Nasty' judge Simon Cowell came up with his own talent show for ITV 1. This time, however, the contest is open to all ages (above 16), not just young wannabes, with three categories established: solo acts under 25, solo acts over 25 and groups. Joining Cowell in the judging row are Sharon Osbourne and pop impresario Louis Walsh. The judges also fulfil the role of mentor for each category. Those successfully making it to the televised stages are put through a 'Boot Camp' where they are hard-coached in showbiz disciplines. At a later stage, the surviving candidates in each category are taken to the homes of their mentors, and finally the best of each section go head-to-head for the top prize, with the viewing public (as throughout) having the final say through phone voting. Around 50,000 hopefuls entered the first series, which was won by Steve Brookstein. Winner of series two in 2005 was Shayne Ward, who saw off challenges from 75,000 entrants.

A celebrity series, *The X Factor: Battle of the Stars*, was screened in 2006. It was won by actress Lucy Benjamin.

Xena: Warrior Princess ✳✳✳

US (Renaissance/MCA) Drama. Channel 5 1997–2001 (US: Syndicated 1995–2001)
DVD: Universal

Xena	**Lucy Lawless**
Gabrielle	**Renee O'Connor**
Joxer	**Ted Raimi**
Autolycus	**Bruce Campbell**
Ares	**Kevin Smith**
Callisto	**Hudson Leick**
Salmoneus	**Robert Trebor**

Executive Producers **Sam Raimi, Robert G. Tapert, R. J. Stewart**

● ***In ancient times, a battle-hardened maiden rescues folks in distress.***
Xena: Warrior Princess is a spin-off from another adventure series set in the ancient world of myths and magic entitled HERCULES: THE LEGENDARY JOURNEYS. In *Hercules*, Xena is portrayed as an evil warrior, but in her own series she turns to the side of good, roaming around the world on her horse, Argo, rescuing the underdog. At her side is blonde runaway village girl Gabrielle, who considers herself something of a bard, and occasionally the cack-handed but well-meaning Joxer. Ares, a war god, shows up from time to time, as do the thieving Autolycus and Xena's nemesis, Callisto. But the star of the show is the Amazonian Xena, her skimpy bodice and martial arts skills turning her into a lesbian icon among certain viewers as she kicks, fences and hurls her enemies into their places. The series was shot in New Zealand, star Lucy Lawless's home country, and in the UK was aired on Sky One prior to screening on the fledgling Channel 5.

X-Files, The ✳✳✳✳

US (Ten-Thirteen/Twentieth Century-Fox) Science Fiction. BBC 2 1994–5; BBC 1 1996–2000; BBC 2 2000–3 (US: Fox 1993–2002)
DVD: Fox

Agent Fox Mulder	**David Duchovny**
Agent Dana Scully	**Gillian Anderson**
Deep Throat	**Jerry Hardin**
Cigarette-Smoking Man	**William B. Davis**
X	**Steven Williams**
Assistant Director Walter Skinner	**Mitch Pileggi**
Alex Krycek	**Nicholas Lea**
Frohike	**Tom Braidwood**
Byers	**Bruce Harwood**
Langly	**Dean Haglund**
Well-Manicured Man	**John Neville**
Agent Jeffrey Spender	**Chris Owens**
Agent Diana Fowley	**Mimi Rogers**
Michael Kritschgau	**John Finn**
Agent John Doggett	**Robert Patrick**
Agent Monica Reyes	**Annabeth Gish**

Creator **Chris Carter**
Executive Producers **Chris Carter, Frank Spotnitz**

● ***Two FBI agents investigate paranormal cases.***
American Fox Mulder is an Oxford graduate in psychology who believes his eight-year-old sister was abducted by aliens when he was 12. He has joined the FBI, where he now puts his preoccupation with the paranormal to good use by delving into the 'X-Files', classified documents detailing unsolved investigations which seem to involve alien encounters or other weird occurrences. He is assisted in his work by red-haired Dana Scully, a doctor who has given up medicine for the challenges the FBI offers. After two years' experience with the agency, she has been given the job of Mulder's partner, largely to keep an eye on his activities and, using her scientific knowledge, to throw cold water on his extravagant theories. Shady figures like Deep Throat and the Cigarette-Smoking Man provide leads and advice in 'Watergate' fashion, while Mulder's chief, Skinner, is among those who contrive to cover up his discoveries. Gradually, however, as the parade of UFO sightings, out-of-body experiences, spontaneous combustions, etc. keeps rolling by – not to mention her own abduction by aliens – it crosses Scully's sceptical mind, too, that 'the truth' really is 'out there'. Eventually, the inevitable happens and Mulder himself goes missing. Former marine and New York cop John Doggett is assigned to Scully's side as the search gets underway to find the lost agent. In the ninth and final series, Doggett and Scully are joined by another operative, Monica Reyes.

A delight for conspiracy theorists, *The X-Files* was the creation of Chris Carter, at the time a writer for a surfing magazine. Filmed in Vancouver, it was undoubtedly the number one sci-fi show of the 1990s and enjoyed cult status across the globe. In the UK, Sky One was first off the mark, screening episodes well ahead of the BBC. An *X-Files* feature film was theatrically released in 1998.

XYY Man, The ✱✱

UK (Granada) Spy Drama. ITV 1976–7

William 'Spider' Scott .... **Stephen Yardley**
Maggie Parsons .... **Vivienne McKee**
DS George Bulman .... **Don Henderson**
DC Derek Willis .... **Dennis Blanch**
Fairfax .... **Mark Dignam**
Laidlaw .... **William Squire**

Producer **Richard Everitt**

● ***An unusual cat-burglar is recruited by British Intelligence.***

Spider Scott is different. In his cell structure he has a spare chromosome, an extra 'Y' chromosome which makes him noticeably tall and instills in him the urge to steal. He became a practised cat-burglar, one of the best, but has retired – until mysterious Fairfax of the British secret service entices him to commit a break-in at a foreign embassy. After the embassy affair and its drawn-out consequences, Spider finds it difficult to go straight again, especially when Fairfax reappears, asking him to spring a criminal from jail. On his trail at all times are Det. Sgt Bulman and DC Willis of Scotland Yard (and later of STRANGERS). This early incarnation of Bulman is quite unlike the quirky later model. Here he is far from sympathetic, and is rough and unstinting in his pursuit of the elusive Spider.

The series was based on the book by Scottish author Kenneth Royce and began with a three-part mini-drama in 1976.

Yardley, Stephen
(1942–)

British actor, now popular for the 'man you love to hate' type of role, thanks to his portrayal of slimy Ken Masters in HOWARDS' WAY. Previously, Yardley's most prominent credit had been as Spider Scott, the burglar with the genetic defect, in THE XYY MAN, although his TV appearances began in the 1960s in series like DR FINLAY'S CASEBOOK, UNITED! (goalkeeper Kenny Craig), DANGER MAN, THE CHAMPIONS and Z CARS (PC Alec May). Yardley was also in the cast of the BBC's 1981 version of THE DAY OF THE TRIFFIDS (John) and played Max Brocard in SECRET ARMY. He has been seen also in series like THE GUARDIANS, *Napoleon and Love*, THE RIVALS OF SHERLOCK HOLMES, CROWN COURT, HUNTER'S WALK, NEW SCOTLAND YARD, PUBLIC EYE, WITHIN THESE WALLS, THRILLER, THE GENTLE TOUCH, THE PROFESSIONALS, BLOOD MONEY (James Drew), MORGAN'S BOY (Alan), DOCTOR WHO, WIDOWS II (Vic Morgan), REMINGTON STEELE, *Virtual Murder* (Inspector Cadogan), HEARTBEAT, THE BILL and CORONATION STREET. More recently, he has played Vince Farmer in *Family Affairs* and made a guest appearance in HOLBY CITY.

Yarwood, Mike
OBE (1941–)

Britain's number one impressionist of the late 1960s–1970s. Mike Yarwood's career really took off in a 1964 edition of SUNDAY NIGHT AT THE LONDON PALLADIUM, when his impersonation of premier Harold Wilson, among others, put him on the map. Yarwood soon grew into one of TV's top attractions, hosting his own series and Christmas Day extravaganzas. Wilson remained probably his greatest success, although he also won applause for his general attention to detail (particularly for his victims' mannerisms) and for his mimicry of the likes of Brian Clough, Eddie Waring, Alf Garnett, Robin Day and Ted Heath. With such a political bias to his act, the arrival of the inimitable Mrs Thatcher at Number 10 contributed to his demise and his career sadly veered off course in the 1980s. At a time when comedy was demanding a harder edge, Yarwood quickly lost ground to Rory Bremner and a new breed of satirists. His cause was not helped by a run of personal problems and a few mini-comebacks since have failed to bring him back into the limelight. Yarwood's major series over the years have been THREE OF A KIND (with Lulu and Ray Fell), *Will the Real Mike Yarwood Stand Up?*, *Look – Mike Yarwood!* and *Mike Yarwood in Persons*.

Yates, Jess
(Jesse Yates; 1918–93)

British TV presenter and producer, generally associated with the long-running STARS ON SUNDAY showcase, through which he earned the nickname 'The Bishop'. However, Yates, a former cinema organist, worked in television from the early 1950s, climbing his way up from designer to writer, producer and director. Series like THE GOOD OLD DAYS, *Top Town* and COME DANCING gave him a grounding in light entertainment that he was to exploit when, after some years away from the business, he returned to TV with the fledgling Yorkshire Television in 1968. Under his auspices as Head of Children's Programmes, such series as JUNIOR SHOWTIME, THE FLAXTON BOYS, *The Boy Dominic*, ORIGAMI and the educational *How We Used to Live* reached the screen, before Yates turned his attention to religious programming with *Choirs on Sunday* and eventually *Stars on Sunday*. He was unceremoniously dropped from the show in the mid-1970s after disclosures about his private life and he never returned to television in a big way afterwards. Scandal continued to mark him even after his death, when it was revealed that he was not the father of model/presenter Paula Yates as was generally believed, the news breaking after the funeral of her real father, Hughie Green.

Yates, Paula
(1960–2000)

British model turned TV presenter whose troubled life often made the headlines. Yates was the daughter of actress/writer Heller Toren and her father was thought to have been Toren's husband, STARS ON SUNDAY host Jess Yates. However, it was later announced that her father was actually OPPORTUNITY KNOCKS frontman Hughie Green. Yates herself married Boomtown Rats singer Bob Geldof, but left him for Michael Hutchence of the band INXS, who was found dead in his hotel room in 1997. Yates herself was found dead in 2000. Her TV career highlights included fronting THE TUBE with Jools Holland and being part of the founding team of THE BIG BREAKFAST, for which she interviewed celebrities on a lavish double bed.

Year in Provence, A ★★

UK (BBC) Comedy Drama. BBC 1 1993
DVD: Prism Leisure

Peter Mayle	**John Thaw**
Annie Mayle	**Lindsay Duncan**
Colombani	**Jean-Pierre Delage**
Amedée Clément	**Jo Doumerg**
Antoine Rivière	**Marcel Champel**
Marcel	**Bernard Spiegel**
Madame Hermonville	**Annie Sinigalia**
Huguette Clément	**Francine Olivier**

Writer **Michael Sadler**
Producer **Ken Riddington**

● ***Twelve-part dramatization of Peter Mayle's best-seller about life in the south of France.***

Peter and Annie Mayle, an advertising executive and an accountant, bravely abandon their rat-race jobs to move to their farmhouse home in the Luberon where, they hope, a relaxing new world awaits them. However, things do not quite work out as planned. While the views are beautiful and the food glorious, the local French neighbours and workers prove totally unpredictable; petty disasters, plus the constant threat of British visitors, lurk around every corner. Mayle's attempts to settle into writing a novel prove fruitless and a far better book eventually emerges from the frustrating and complicated situations which unfold as they try to set up their new home.

Although much promoted by the BBC and supported by a serialized feature on *Peter Mayle's Provence* in *Radio Times*, *A Year in Provence* was considered by most critics to be one of the flops of 1993.

Year of the Sex Olympics, The ★★★

UK (BBC) Drama. BBC 2 1968
DVD: BFI Video Publishing

Co-ordinator Ugo Priest .... **Leonard Rossiter**
Deanie Webb .... **Suzanne Neve**
Nat Mender .... **Tony Vogel**
Keten Webb .... **Lesley Roach**
Misch .... **Vickery Turner**
Grels .... **George Murcell**
Lasar Opie .... **Brian Cox**
Kin Hodder .... **Martin Potter**

Writer **Nigel Kneale**
Producer **Ronald Travers**

In the bleak near future, TV controls every human emotion.

Michael Elliott directed this nightmare vision of a world dominated by television. Screened as part of the *Theatre 625* anthology, Nigel Kneale's play is set at a time when people are divided into two groups. 'Low-drive' people (98 percent of the population) no longer have any need to communicate with each other: they just react to television stimuli. 'High-drive' people (the other 2 per cent) make the TV programmes. As all 'tensions' in the world (love, hate, war, loyalty, etc.) have been removed, the only effective way to control population trends is through the medium of television. Hence programmes on gluttony put people off food and contrived pornography deters the populace from having sex. Such pornography is shaped into strands such as art-sex and even sports-sex, and, as the title reveals, this is the year of the sex Olympics. However, such a controlled world is not for everyone and one family, Deanie Webb, Nat Mender and their child, escape to a little island where TV, for once, is not king. However, with cameras following their every move, they themselves become part of a TV programme. Their *Live Life Show* becomes a ratings winner, but tragedy is about to strike.

Yellowthread Street ★★

UK (Yorkshire) Police Drama. ITV 1990

Chief Insp. Alex Vale .... **Ray Lonnen**
Det. C. J. Brady .... **Mark McGann**
Det. Kelly Lang .... **Catherine Neilson**
Det. Nick Eden .... **Bruce Payne**
Det. Eddie Pak .... **Tzi Ma**
Det. Peter Marenta .... **Robert Taylor**
Det. Jackie Wu .... **Doreen Chan**

Executive Producer **Keith Richardson**
Producer **Ranald Graham**

Crimebusting on the teeming streets of Hong Kong.

Based on the novel of the same name by ex-Hong Kong journalist William Marshall, *Yellowthread Street* was a 13-part drama centring on the activities of seven members of the Royal Hong Kong Police. With crime soaring, and the transfer of sovereignty only seven years away, law enforces in this colourful province at the time plodded a dangerous beat, impregnated with extortion, racketeering and drug-dealing. In the series, the team patrolling the Yellowthread Street patch is fronted by the sullen Chief Insp. Vale. Vale is supported by the eager C. J. Brady, one-time Vietnamese refugee Eddie Pak, tall Australian import Peter Marenta (played by former Australian swimming champion Robert Taylor), confident Nick Eden, attractive Kelly Lang and Jackie Wu, the determined daughter of a Triad family, who intends to show there is another way to the top other than through organized crime. Though filmed on location at great expense (£8 million), using cinematic 35 mm stock instead of the 16 mm normally employed for television, the programme failed to hold on to its Saturday night audience. Music was by Roger Bellon.

Yentob, Alan

(1947–)

London-born producer (a BBC trainee from 1968) who worked on series like OMNIBUS and ARENA (creator), which led to his appointment as the BBC's Head of Music and Arts in 1985. He became Controller of BBC 2 in 1988, and of BBC 1 in 1993, moving on to be the Corporation's Director of Programmes and Director of Television, before his appointment as Director of Drama, Entertainment and CBBC in 2000. In 2004, he was also made the BBC's Creative Director. In 2003, Yentob wrote and presented *Leonardo*, a biography of Leonardo da Vinci, and he has continued to combine his executive role with time in front of the camera as presenter of the arts magazine *Imagine*.

Yes – Honestly

See *No – Honestly*.

Yes, Minister/Yes, Prime Minister ★★★★

UK (BBC) Situation Comedy. BBC 2 1980–2; 1984/1986–8
DVD: BBC

Right Hon. James Hacker MP . **Paul Eddington**
Sir Humphrey Appleby .... **Nigel Hawthorne**
Bernard Woolley .... **Derek Fowlds**
Annie Hacker .... **Diana Hoddinott**
Sir Arnold Robinson .... **John Nettleton**

Creators/Writers **Antony Jay, Jonathan Lynn**
Producers **Stuart Allen, Sydney Lotterby, Peter Whitmore**

An ambitious government minister is put firmly in his place by his chief civil servant.

Yes, Minister follows the political career of one Jim Hacker, initially an MP for an unnamed party, but later divulged to be a Tory. It opens with Hacker taking up his first ministerial position (Administrative Affairs) and teaming up with Permanent Under-Secretary Sir Humphrey Appleby. Filled with bright ideas for cleaning up his department, Hacker begins to set the wheels in motion, only to find himself stymied by the career civil servant, who is intent on keeping power out of politicians' hands and firmly in the control of the permanent staff. And it is these concepts of idealism against political reality, and perceived power against real power, which underpin the entire series, with Hacker flying ambitious kites and Sir Humphrey cheerfully shooting them down.

While the persuasive Sir Humphrey bamboozles Hacker

with his tongue-twisting, jargon-loaded, over-stretched explanations, Hacker's genial Private Secretary, Bernard Woolley, hovers nervously in the middle, gently offering opinions on the implications and complications of this or that decision (especially if they affect Hacker's political future). But Hacker must heed their advice pretty well in the first three series, for a major career move quickly follows. When the incumbent prime minister resigns, three candidates stand for the top job – two extremists and the rather mundane Hacker. By stealing the middle ground, Hacker (somewhat by default) finds himself installed in Downing Street for the final two seasons (which went out under the title of *Yes, Prime Minister*).

The series was much acclaimed by real politicians, who enjoyed the show's cynical dismissal of Whitehall intrigue and its insight into the machinations of government. Even Margaret Thatcher dubbed it her favourite (before dubbing writer Antony Jay a knight in the Honours' List).

Yesterday's Men

See *24 Hours*.

Yogi Bear ✶✶

US (Hanna-Barbera) Cartoon. ITV 1961–4 (US: Syndicated 1961–3)
DVD: Warner Home Video (Region 1 only)

Voices:

Yogi Bear	**Daws Butler**
Boo Boo	**Don Messick**
Ranger John Smith	**Don Messick**
Cindy Bear	**Julie Bennett**
Snagglepuss	**Daws Butler**
Yakky Doodle	**Jimmy Weldon**
Chopper	**Vance Colvig**

Creators/Executive Producers **William Hanna, Joseph Barbera**

● ***A hungry bear preys on picnickers in a national park.***

Holidaying families are never safe when Yogi is around, for the crafty bear with the healthy appetite is always likely to talk them out of their lunch. Dressed in a tie and a pork-pie hat, Yogi, with his bear-cub sidekick, Boo Boo, prowls the expanses of Jellystone National Park, skilfully avoiding the attentions of Ranger John Smith. After all, as Yogi himself declares, he is 'smarter than the average bear'. Also seen at times is Yogi's Southern sweetheart, Cindy Bear, prone to cries of 'Ah do declare.'

Yogi Bear (named after New York Yankees pitcher, Yogi Berra) first appeared in THE HUCKLEBERRY HOUND SHOW, although he quickly outgrew his second-fiddle status. Awarded his own series, Yogi was himself then supported by other cartoons. These featured the theatrical lion, Snagglepuss (fond of thespian exclamations like 'Heavens to Murgatroyd'), and a garrulous duck, Yakky Doodle, who was closely guarded by his pal, Chopper the Bulldog. In the 1970s, in later series, Yogi moved out of Jellystone and into more adventurous situations, taking on environmental crusades and even risking space travel.

Yorkshire Television

(YTV)

Yorkshire Television became the ITV contractor for the region east of the Pennines in 1968, when previous incumbent Granada was obliged by the ITA to refocus its coverage on the North-west. A consortium known as Telefusion Yorkshire Ltd won the franchise in 1967 and, on 29 July a year later, Yorkshire Television (its chosen broadcasting name) went on air, hastily constructing purpose-designed studios in Leeds. Former BBC producer Donald Baverstock was its first Programme Controller and he was succeeded in 1973 by another BBC executive, Paul Fox. Alan Whicker was also a board member and major shareholder.

Yorkshire's initial 'trading' area was not just the county of Yorkshire, but also parts of Derbyshire and Nottinghamshire. However, changes were made in the early 1970s, when the company lost most of North Yorkshire to Tyne Tees (thanks to an IBA transmitter swap) and then gained Lincolnshire and Humberside from Anglia (another transmitter reallocation). To stabilize the three companies (Yorkshire, Tyne Tees and Anglia) and to maximize advertising revenue, a new holding company, known as Trident Television, was proposed. However, the IBA declined to allow Anglia to join, and Trident was formed out of Yorkshire and Tyne Tees only. When, in 1980, both companies' franchises were renewed, the IBA insisted on their leaving Trident and becoming independent once more. The Trident partnership was resumed after the 1991 franchise auctions, which were again successful for both companies. However, both Tyne Tees and Yorkshire were later taken over by Granada, which is now part of ITV plc.

From the start, Yorkshire was charged with the role of a network provider, that is being one of the big five companies that supply the bulk of ITV's national programmes. Its successes were many, including *Whicker's World*, THE SKY'S THE LIMIT, EMMERDALE FARM, WHERE THERE'S LIFE, WINNER TAKES ALL, HADLEIGH, THE MAIN CHANCE, RISING DAMP, THE BEIDERBECKE AFFAIR, DUTY FREE, 3–2–1, FOLLYFOOT, STARS ON SUNDAY, A BIT OF A DO and THE DARLING BUDS OF MAY.

You Bet! ✶✶

UK (LWT) Game Show. ITV 1988–96

Presenters **Bruce Forsyth, Matthew Kelly, Darren Day, Diane Youdale**

Executive Producer **Marcus Plantin**
Producers **Richard Hearsey, Alasdair Macmillan, Linda Beadle, Mark Linsey**

● ***Light-hearted panel game in which celebrities and the studio audience bet on the skills of a guest enthusiast.***

Hosted originally by Bruce Forsyth, then by Matthew Kelly from 1991, with Darren Day and Diane Youdale taking over for the final season, *You Bet!* was a showcase for the skills and talents of its many guests, who attempted to perform odd feats related to their hobbies or professions within a given time. Could three divers put up a tent underwater, for example? How much would politician Roy Hattersley know about his favourite programme, CORONATION STREET? Each guest was sponsored by one of the celebrity panellists and, if the guest failed in his task, the celebrity was forced to accept a forfeit. The studio audience, meanwhile, gambled on whether the guest would make the grade, and all profits were directed to charity. The series was originally based on a Dutch format.

You Must be Joking! ✱✱

UK (Thames) Children's Comedy. ITV 1975–6

Presenters **Ray Burdis, John Blundell, Pauline Quirke, Elvis Payne, Jim Bowen, Michael Holloway, Flintlock**

Producer **Roger Price**

● ***Fast-moving, youth-inspired topical comedy revue.***
With the aim of giving kids a more grown-up voice than traditionally heard in children's hour, Roger Price developed this collection of sketches, gags, thought-provoking songs and topical commentaries for a group of East End kids. Placing Jim Bowen as the token adult in the show, Price gave the stage to students at the Anna Scher drama club, who also wrote most of the material and offered a more sophisticated take on current affairs and humour than expected. Among the cast were 16-year-old Pauline Quirke and Elvis Payne, the former on her way to star status, the latter an Antiguan boy offering a cynical look at issues in the news. Also seen was 13-year-old Mike Holloway, drummer with the resident band Flintlock (otherwise Derek Pascoe, Jamie Stone, John Summerton and Bill Rice – who also appeared in sketches). Holloway was later seen in Price's THE TOMORROW PEOPLE. Among the up-and-coming guests were Linda Robson, Gary Kemp, Phil Daniels and Sylvestra Le Touzel. A follow-up series, *You Can't be Serious*, with a different cast, aired in 1978.

You Rang, M'Lord? ✱✱

UK (BBC) Situation Comedy. BBC 1 1990–1; 1993
DVD: Cinema Club

Alf Stokes	**Paul Shane**
Ivy Teasdale	**Su Pollard**
James Twelvetrees	**Jeffrey Holland**
Mrs Blanche Lipton	**Brenda Cowling**
Lord George Meldrum	**Donald Hewlett**
Hon. Teddy Meldrum	**Michael Knowles**
Poppy Meldrum	**Susie Brann**
Cecily 'Cissy' Meldrum	**Catherine Rabett**
Lady Lavender Meldrum	**Mavis Pugh**
Henry	**Perry Benson**
Mabel	**Barbara New**
PC Wilson	**Bill Pertwee**
Sir Ralph Shawcross	**John Horsley**
Lady Agatha Shawcross	**Angela Scoular**
Myrtle	**Barbara Windsor**

Creators/Writers **Jimmy Perry, David Croft**
Producer **David Croft**

● ***Life up- and downstairs in an eccentric 1920s household.***
An hour-long pilot, screened in 1988, sets the scene for this UPSTAIRS, DOWNSTAIRS send-up which has more than an echo of other Perry/Croft sitcoms, especially HI-DE-HI! It begins in 1918, in the trenches of World War I and with the discovery of the body of an army officer by two foot-soldiers. One of the soldiers, Alf Stokes, loots the officer's possessions, as the other, James Twelvetrees, vainly argues against the theft. However, discovering that the officer is not in fact dead, the two men carry him to safety. He turns out to be Captain Edward Meldrum, known to others as 'the Honourable Teddy', and in return for their life-saving efforts he promises the men a favour.

Back in civvy street, nine years later, Twelvetrees has cashed in his favour and been taken on as head of the household at the Meldrum residence, which is presided over by the well-meaning Lord Meldrum. When their butler dies, the bad penny Stokes arrives and, much to Twelvetrees's disgust, talks his way into the job. He brings with him as parlourmaid his daughter, Ivy, but keeps their relationship secret (she uses her mother's maiden name). Like all the parlourmaids employed before her, Ivy, despite her plain looks, is relentlessly pursued by the randy Teddy, a true upper-class twit, while his flighty sister, Poppy, takes a similar shine to Twelvetrees. Other Meldrum family members include socialist lesbian Cissy, who wears a monocle and dresses like a man, and bedridden, food-throwing Lady Lavender, the lord's batty and gin-sodden mother. Family friends are Sir Ralph and Lady Agatha Shawcross, Lady Agatha also being Lord Meldrum's secret lover.

The serving staff comprises cook Mrs Lipton, droll boot-boy Henry (regular recipient of clipped ears) and, lowest of the low, scullery maid Mabel. A regular visitor to the kitchen is scrounging local bobby, PC Wilson, a devotee of Mrs Lipton's culinary skills. While the upright Twelvetrees conducts his affairs in the most honest and decent fashion, the sly Stokes works on plans to swindle his betters and line his own pockets. And so the series continues (through 50-minute episodes – unusual for a sitcom), finally ending when the Meldrum family fall on desperate times and are forced to give up their home and staff.

The programme's theme song, written by Jimmy Perry and Roy Moore, was sung by Bob Monkhouse and Paul Shane.

Youens, Bernard

(Bernard Popley; 1914–84)

Remembered as the boozy, work-shy Stan Ogden in CORONATION STREET, one of TV's most lovable characters, Sussex born Bernard Youens was, in real life, a totally different person from the slob he played on screen. Far from only being able to garble, 'A pint and a pie, missus,' Youens was an eloquent, well-spoken performer. Indeed, one of his first jobs in television was as a continuity announcer at Granada. His first TV acting parts were also with Granada, in series like SHADOW SQUAD and KNIGHT ERRANT. He joined *Coronation Street* in 1964 and stayed with the series (through considerable restricting illness in later years) until his death in 1984.

You'll Never Get Rich

See *Phil Silvers Show, The.*

Young, Alan

(Angus Young; 1919–)

British-born actor/comedian, raised in Canada, who became a reasonable success in the USA. By far his most memorable role was as Wilbur Post, straight man to MISTER ED, the talking horse, in the early 1960s, although, by that time, Young had already picked up an Emmy and headlined in his own variety series, *The Alan Young Show*, and the USA's *Saturday Night Revue*. In the late 1950s and early 1960s he starred in his own ITV showcases, including *Personal Appearance*. In the 1980s he was cast in the retirement sitcom *Coming of Age*, and more recently has made a guest appearance in ER and provided the voice for Haggis MacHaggis in THE REN & STIMPY SHOW.

Young, Kirsty

(1968–)

Scottish presenter and newscaster, entering broadcasting with BBC Radio Scotland and then Scottish Television, on which she had her own chat show. After featuring in programmes like HOLIDAY, FILM 96 and *The Street*, Young was snapped up to front the new *Channel 5 News*, from which she was poached in 1999 to anchor ITN news bulletins. In 2000, she hosted the quiz *The People Versus* and *Ratrap*. She returned to *Channel 5 News* in 2002, but has also been seen as a guest presenter of HAVE I GOT NEWS FOR YOU.

Young, Mal

(1957–)

A former graphic designer, Liverpool-born Mal Young learned his television trade over many years alongside Phil Redmond at Mersey Television (BROOKSIDE, AND THE BEAT GOES ON). Later, as Head of Drama at Pearson Television 1996–7, he worked on THE BILL and created *Family Affairs* for Channel 5, before moving to the BBC as Head of Drama, switching to Head of Continuing Drama Series in 2001. This made him executive producer of the Corporation's most popular offerings, from EASTENDERS, CASUALTY and HOLBY CITY to SILENT WITNESS, MERSEYBEAT and DALZIEL AND PASCOE. In 2005 he switched to the independent sector, becoming Director of Drama with Simon Cowell's international production company, 19TV.

Young, Muriel

(1928–2001)

British presenter, one of Associated-Rediffusion's earliest continuity announcers and a DJ with Radio Luxembourg. However, it was as a star of kids' TV in the late 1950s and early 1960s, in series like *Small Time, Tuesday Rendezvous* and FIVE O'CLOCK CLUB, that she became known to viewers nationwide, working with puppets Ollie Beak, Fred Barker, Pussy Cat Willum and others. In the late 1960s she moved north to Granada to become Head of Children's Programmes. There, as producer, she established such favourites as CLAPPERBOARD, LIFT OFF WITH AYSHEA, *Get It Together* and other pop shows for stars such as the Bay City Rollers (*Shang-a-Lang*), Marc Bolan (*Marc*) and *The Arrows*. She retired from television in 1986.

Young, Robert

(1907–98)

American movie actor of the 1930s who never really found his niche until television arrived. There his homely, kindly features were put to good use in an award-winning domestic sitcom, *Father Knows Best* (dad Jim Anderson), that ran for six years (having already been a hit on radio). Unusually, it also enjoyed prime-time repeat showings until 1963, although the 1960s were generally leaner years for Young, and another comedy, *Window on Main Street*, didn't take. However, in 1968, his first TV movie, MARCUS WELBY, MD, sparked another long-running series, in which Young played a gentle, understanding family practitioner. It ended in 1976 and Young did little television afterwards, save the odd commercial, occasional TV movie, a couple of *Father Knows Best* reunions and some impressions in *Kopykats*.

Young Ones, The ★★★★

UK (BBC) Situation Comedy. BBC 2 1982; 1984

Rick .... **Rik Mayall**
Neil .... **Nigel Planer**
Vyvyan .... **Adrian Edmondson**
Mike .... **Christopher Ryan**
Jerzy Balowski (and his family) .... **Alexei Sayle**

Writers **Ben Elton, Rik Mayall, Lise Mayer**
Producer **Paul Jackson**

Four anarchic students share a decrepit house.

The Young Ones are Rick, Neil, Vyvyan and Mike. Sneering Rick is a Cliff Richard fan; long-haired Neil is a melancholic, vegetarian hippie; and stud-headed, gormlessly aggressive Vyvyan owns a pet hamster known as SPG (Special Patrol Group). Diminutive Mike is the most 'normal' of the bunch, although his wide-boy tendencies and moments of paranoia mark him out, too, from the rest of the public. In an atmosphere of absolute squalor (even the stale food begins to move), the four lead a life of mindless violence and brainless conversation, rebelling against the world outside. Storylines are vague and the comedy is heavily slapstick, usually involving the destruction of the house or of each other, but there are bizarre moments of surreal humour, too. The boys' Russian landlord, Jerzy Balowski (or other members of his family, all played by Alexei Sayle), has his own slot and, unusually for a comedy, contemporary pop groups (Madness, Motorhead, etc.) also perform their stuff. With Cliff's hit single of the same title as its theme song, the series ends with yet more allusions to the Peter Pan of pop: the lads symbolically drive a *Summer Holiday*-influenced double-decker bus over a 'cliff'.

Viewers tuned in to *The Young Ones* to be shocked. The younger generations loved it and felt the series was right on their wavelength. More 'mature' critics were appalled at the wanton violence, infantile jokes and total disrespect for society; but many of these, too, were won over as the series progressed. It was a series that certainly shook up television comedy and heralded the age of the 'alternative' comedian. Indeed, *The Young Ones* has continued well beyond its 12 episodes, with Mayall and Edmondson's later offerings, FILTHY RICH AND CATFLAP and BOTTOM, essentially extensions of the series. Nigel Planer, in the guise of Neil, also had a spin-off hit single in 1984, with a cover of Traffic's 'Hole in my Shoe', and the foul foursome joined Cliff Richard on a chart-topping remake of 'Living Doll' for charity in 1986.

Young Sherlock – The Mystery of the Manor House ★★

UK (Granda) Children's Detective Drama. ITV 1982
DVD: Goldhil (Region 1 only)

Sherlock Holmes .... **Guy Henry**
John Whitney .... **Tim Brierley**
Col. Turnbull .... **Donald Douglas**
Mrs Turnbull .... **June Barry**
Tom Hudson .... **Robert Grange**
Ranjeet .... **Lewis Fiander**
Capt. Cholmondeley .... **Andrew Johns**
Dr Sowerbutts .... **David Ryder-Futcher**
Aunt Rachel .... **Heather Chasen**

Writer **Gerald Frow**

Producer **Pieter Rogers**

● ***The great detective unravels a mystery in his formative years.***

This eight-part series, shown early on Sunday evenings, depicts Sherlock Holmes as a 16-year-old schoolboy (donning a deerstalker even then), assisted this time by friend John Whitney in an investigation at a manor house. It appeared three years before Steven Spielberg and Barry Levinson's cinema version of *Young Sherlock Holmes and the Pyramid of Fear*.

Your Cheatin' Heart ★★★

UK (BBC) Drama. BBC 1 1990

Frank McClusky .... **John Gordon-Sinclair**
Cissie Crouch .... **Tilda Swinton**
Fraser Boyle .... **Ken Stott**
Dorwood Crouch .... **Kevin McMonagle**
Billie McPhail .... **Katy Murphy**
Jolene Jowett .... **Eddi Reader**
David Cole .... **Guy Gregory**
Timberwold Tierney/Cherokee George/Eric the barber/Father Tierney/Aberdeen matron .... **Tom Watson**
Tamara MacAskill .... **Helen Atkinson-Wood**

Writer **John Byrne**
Producer **Peter Broughan**

● ***A Scottish reporter is dragged into the linked world of crime and country music.***

Following his success with TUTTI FRUTTI, John Byrne turned from rock 'n' roll to country and western for this six-part drama set in Glasgow. Local country singer Dorwood Crouch is in jail but his waitress wife, Cissie, believes in his innocence and sets out to prove it. She enlists journalist Frank McClusky to her cause and the two start to delve into the city's murky underside. One man to avoid is drug-pushing Elvis fan Fraser Boyle. Also prominent are Billie and Jolene, the singing McPhail Sisters who perform at the OK Corral country hangout. Michael Whyte directs, adding hints of *film noir* to the soundtrack's 1940s and 1950s country hits.

Your Life in Their Hands ★★★

UK (BBC) Documentary. BBC 1958–64; BBC 2 1980–6; 1991; BBC 1 2004–5

Producers **Bill Duncalf, Peter Bruce, Humphrey Fisher, John Mansfield, Fiona Holmes, Stephen Rose, Michael Houldey, Helen Thomas**

● ***The wonders of surgery explored in close detail.***

This innovative series was conceived with a tripartite purpose in mind: to investigate new medical techniques, to applaud the medical profession and to provide 'reassurance' for citizens at home. However, with its blood-and-guts visuals, *Your Life in Their Hands* excited some viewers and alarmed others.

The prerecorded programmes interviewed sick patients, watched their admission to hospital, heard the prognosis of the experts and learned of the action intended by the surgeon. Overhead mirrors, microscopes and numerous cameras were then used to capture events in the operating theatre, before the patient's recovery was monitored in the weeks and months that followed. Never before had gallstones been removed on British television. Open-heart surgery was even more dramatic, and Caesarean birth was demonstrated just as graphically. Predictably, there was an outcry from the Establishment. The British Medical Association criticized it for frightening, rather than reassuring, viewers and there were reports of sick people preferring suicide to treatment, having seen the programme. Other doctors warmly applauded the programme's frankness and its educational value.

When the series was revived in 1980, operations were shown for the first time in full, gory colour and were definitely not for the squeamish. For this series, surgeon Robert Winston acted as the informative narrator. Five more editions were screened in 1991. It was 13 more years before *Your Life in Their Hands* returned once more in all its gory, emotional detail, highlighting the highly skilled, dramatic work of some of the UK's top surgeons.

You're Only Young Twice ★

UK (Yorkshire) Situation Comedy. ITV 1977–81

Flora Petty .... **Peggy Mount**
Cissie Lupin .... **Pat Coombs**
Dolly Love .... **Lally Bowers**
Katy O'Rourke .... **Peggy Ledger**
Mildred Fanshaw .... **Diana King**
Miss 'Finchy' Finch .... **Georgina Moon**
Miss Milton .... **Charmian May**
Roger .... **Johnny Wade**

Writers **Pam Valentine, Michael Ashton**
Producer **Graeme Muir**

● ***A grumpy battleaxe leads the revolt in an old folks' home.***

Flora Petty is the dominant figure in this retirement home comedy. Bossy Flora lives at Paradise Lodge, a 'superior residence for retired gentlefolk', though nothing is ever to her satisfaction. Among her assorted cronies are dim Cissie, Dolly, Katy and motorcycling geriatric Mildred. Miss Milton is the proprietress of the home, helped by 'Finchy' Finch and odd-jobber Roger. Dennis Wilson provided the music for the programme, which ran to four series.

You've Been Framed ★★

UK (Granada) Comedy. ITV 1990–

Presenters **Jeremy Beadle, Lisa Riley, Jonathan Wilkes, Harry Hill**

Producers **Jane Macnaught, Kieran Roberts, Mark Gorton, Mark Wells, Nigel Hall, Kieron Collins, Denise Harrington-Harrop, Chris Thornton**

● ***Selections of home video howlers.***

You've Been Framed has ridden the wave of interest in home video bloopers that has swept around the world since the introduction of the camcorder. Emulating similar programmes in the USA, Japan and elsewhere, it has gathered together some of the most amusing clips of video footage, most of which have shown people falling over, children unwittingly misbehaving or pets displaying unusual talents. A contest for the best British clip was incorporated into early programmes but was later abandoned. EMMERDALE star Lisa Riley took over as presenter in 1998. She was succeeded by Jonathan Wilkes and then Harry Hill. Later episodes have been aired as *New You've Been Framed!* The BBC attempted to cash in with its own version, *Caught in the Act* (BBC 1, 1992), hosted by Shane Richie, but it failed to take off.

YTV

See *Yorkshire Television.*

Yus My Dear

See *Romany Jones.*

Z

Z Cars ★★★

UK (BBC) Police Drama. BBC 1 1962–5; 1967–78

DCI Charlie Barlow	**Stratford Johns**
DS/Det. Chief Supt. John Watt	**Frank Windsor**
PC William 'Fancy' Smith	**Brian Blessed**
PC John 'Jock' Weir	**Joseph Brady**
PC/DC/Sgt/Insp. Herbert 'Bert' Lynch	**James Ellis**
DI/Supt. Dunn	**Dudley Foster**
PC Bob Steele	**Jeremy Kemp**
PC Ian Sweet	**Terence Edmond**
Sgt Twentyman	**Leonard Williams**
Mary Watt	**Gwen Cherrell**
Sgt Blackitt	**Robert Keegan**
PC David Graham	**Colin Welland**
Det. Supt. Miller	**Leslie Sands**
DI Sam Hudson	**John Barrie**
Chief Supt. Robbins	**John Phillips**
PC Ken Baker	**Geoffrey Whitehead**
PC Raymond Walker	**Donald Gee**
DS Tom Stone	**John Slater**
PC Owen Culshaw	**David Daker**
PC Alec May	**Stephen Yardley**
WPC Jane Shepherd	**Luanshya Greer**
PC Steve Tate	**Sebastian Breaks**
PC Finch	**Christopher Denham**
DC Kane	**Christopher Coll**
PC Jackson	**John Wreford**
WPC Parkin	**Pauline Taylor**
PC Bannerman	**Paul Angelis**
PC Roach	**Ron Davies**
PC Horrocks	**Barry Lowe**
DS Cecil Haggar	**John Collin**
DC Scatliff	**Geoffrey Hayes**
PC Render	**Allan O'Keefe**
PC Covill	**Jack Carr**
PC/Sgt Bowman	**John Swindells**
DS Miller	**Geoffrey Whitehead**
PC Yates	**Nicholas Smith**
Insp. Ralph Pratt	**Graham Armitage**
DC Braithwaite	**David Jackson**
WPC Bayliss	**Alison Steadman**
DS/DI Terry Moffat	**Ray Lonnen**
DI Connor	**Gary Watson**
Sgt Culshaw	**John Challis**
WP Sgt Cameron	**June Watson**
Sgt Chubb	**Paul Stewart**
DC Bowker	**Brian Grellis**
PC Bill Newcombe	**Bernard Holley**
DI Brogan	**George Sewell**
DI Todd	**Joss Ackland**
DI Alan Witty	**John Woodvine**
PC/Sgt Quilley	**Douglas Fielding**
DI Neil Goss	**Derek Waring**
PC/DC Joe Skinner	**Ian Cullen**
WPC Jill Howarth	**Stephanie Turner**
DI Maddan	**Tommy Boyle**
WPC Jane Beck	**Victoria Plucknett**
PC Roger Stevens	**Ralph Watson**
BD girls	**Anjula Harman** **Jennie Goossens**

Creator **Troy Kennedy Martin**
Producers **David E. Rose, Colin Morris, Ronald Travers, Richard Beynon, Ron Craddock, Roderick Graham**

● ***Long-running and influential police drama series, highlighting the work of patrol car policemen.***

In 1962 the DIXON OF DOCK GREEN type of police series was already looking dated. The cosy life of a community copper had been lost for ever, certainly in the big cities at least, and it was time for television to reflect this change. However, it wasn't until writer Troy Kennedy Martin was ill in bed with mumps and, to while away the time, tuned into the police wavelengths that such a change became a possibility. Martin instantly recognized that what he was hearing was a world away from George Dixon's weekly homilies and decided to work his findings into an idea for a new programme. The result was *Z Cars*, a series that aimed to portray the *real* relationship between the police and the community.

Filled with northern grit and heavily influenced by contemporary 'kitchen sink' dramas, *Z Cars* was set on Merseyside, at a time when the Liverpool docklands were undergoing radical social change. Traditional streets, now designated slums, were making way for high-rise blocks of concrete flats, functional but soulless living spaces that rapidly turned into fertile breeding-grounds for unrest. The pace of life was quickening and crime was responding in its own unpleasant fashion. To combat this crime wave, police were taken off the beat and placed in patrol cars, with the aim of providing a swifter response. *Z Cars* depicted the efforts of one such patrol team as it roamed the streets of both the old district of Seaport and the modern development of Newtown.

The very first episode reveals how the death of a police officer has led to the formation of the team. Det. Insp. Barlow and DS Watt are invited to select their new élite squad, and it introduces viewers to the four patrolmen who are chosen. In the first patrol car, Z Victor 1, are burly northerner 'Fancy' Smith and a rugby-playing Scot, Jock Weir. In Z Victor 2 are Irishman Herbert Lynch and red-headed Bob Steele. Both cars are Ford Zephyrs, initially Mark 4s (later traded in for Mark 6s). Supervising events back at the station is old-fashioned Sgt Twentyman, replaced after a year by Sgt Blackitt (when actor Leonard Williams suddenly died).

However, *Z Cars* didn't just focus on the new type of crime in the early 1960s, or the police response to it, but, for the first time on British television, it actually dared to suggest that policemen were not as wholesome as they ought to be. Troy Kennedy Martin had wanted the crooks to win through now and again, to show that police were not infallible, but this was too much to ask of a staid BBC. However, he did get away with showing policemen as real human beings, with complicated home lives and vices of their own. Martin and his colleagues painted them as gamblers, drinkers and, most controversially of all, even wife-beaters. Real-life police withdrew their co-operation in response to such excesses.

Another innovation was the portrayal by Stratford Johns of Charlie Barlow as a nasty superior officer, not averse to dishing out aggression. Johns was tired of seeing bumbling, ineffective TV detectives. What he wanted was a police officer who actually made the running, was hard on his subordinates and was not afraid to pound suspects into submission. Together with the gentler John Watt, he offered the classic combination of the nice and the nasty; and such was their success, they headed off to the Regional Crime Squad after three years and a series of their own, SOFTLY, SOFTLY.

Watt and Barlow's departure in 1965 was intended to be the finale for *Z Cars*, but it returned to the screens in 1967, installing John Barrie and John Slater as DI Hudson and DS Stone, their replacements. New Panda cars roared into action and some fresh constables were added to the team, although continuity was maintained through Weir and Lynch (a man who was to rise steadily through the ranks). The format switched from 50-minute episodes to two 25-minute programmes a week, and continued in this vein until 1971, when the longer forms were reintroduced.

Other notable characters to come and go over the years are young PC Ian Sweet, who is tragically drowned in a heroic rescue attempt; Leigh-born PC David Graham, Lynch's second partner (an early break for actor/writer Colin Welland); sarcastic Insp. Dunn; and Geordie heart-throb PC Joe Skinner and his partner, PC Quilley. Indeed, future stars fared rather well, either as guests or as regulars. They included John Thaw, Judi Dench, Kenneth Cope, Alison Steadman, David Daker, Stephen Yardley, George Sewell, Joss Ackland, Patrick Troughton and Ralph Bates, whose character pulls a gun on Joe Skinner and shoots him dead.

Like *Dixon of Dock Green* before it, *Z Cars* found itself left behind by other cop shows in the 1970s. Not only were the likes of KOJAK and STARSKY AND HUTCH screaming on to British TV screens, but there was also our own THE SWEENEY to contend with. Still *Z Cars* rolled on, probably showing a more realistic image of 1970s policing than its contemporaries, until the end finally arrived in 1978.

Originally transmitted live, making use of crude techniques like back-projection for car scenes, *Z Cars* looks very dated today. However, the quality of writing, from the likes of Martin, Alan Plater, Elwyn Jones and John Hopkins, is still apparent in the few surviving episodes from those early days. The last episode, penned by Martin, brings the newly promoted Det. Chief Superintendent Watt back to Newtown and features cameo appearances from Joseph Brady, Brian Blessed, Jeremy Kemp and Colin Welland. Over the previous 16 years, the programme's unforgettable theme tune (based on the folk song 'Johnny Todd', with an ominous drumbeat intro) had become synonymous with TV policing.

Zero One ✶✶

UK (BBC/MGM) Adventure. BBC 1 1962–5

Alan Garnett	**Nigel Patrick**
Maya	**Katya Douglas**
Jim Delaney	**Bill Smith**

Producer **Lawrence P. Bachmann**

● ***The cases of an airline detective.***

Zero One is the call-sign of International Air Security, an organization dedicated to the safety of air travel all around the world. Its London agent is Alan Garnett and he is called up to combat hijackers, prevent disasters and generally preserve peace in the air and at airports. Jim Delaney is his assistant and Maya his secretary.

Zimbalist, Efrem, Jr

(1918–)

American actor, the son of classical music entertainers Efrem Zimbalist and Alma Gluck. Zimbalist Jr enjoyed two major starring roles between the late 1950s and mid-1970s. He was Ivy League-educated detective Stu Bailey in 77 SUNSET STRIP for six years from 1958 and then quickly donned the mantle of Inspector Lew Erskine of THE FBI, to ensure he remained on US TV screens until 1974. He has since appeared in *Hotel* (Charles Cabot), TV movies and mini-series, as well as a revival of *Zorro* (Don Alejandro). Among his numerous guest appearances over the years have been spots in THE PHIL SILVERS SHOW, MAVERICK (Dandy Jim Buckley), REMINGTON STEELE (alongside his daughter, Stephanie Zimbalist) and BABYLON 5.

Zodiac ✶✶

UK (Thames) Police Drama. ITV 1974

David Gradley	**Anton Rogers**
Esther Jones	**Anouska Hempel**

Writers **Roger Marshall, Pat Hoddinott, Peter Yeldham**
Executive Producer **Kim Mills**
Producer **Jacqueline Davis**

● ***A policeman finds astrology a useful tool in his work.***

Former Harrow public schoolboy David Gradley has little time for horoscopes – or his police work, come to that. However, his enthusiasm for both begins to change when he meets attractive astrologer Esther Jones, who tries to persuade him that, with a little help from the stars above, cracking crime can be an entertaining business. Six episodes of this light drama series were produced, each devoted to a different star sign and built around the premiss that, if only a certain person had consulted their horoscope that morning, things might have turned out differently.

Zoo Gang, The ✶✶

UK (ATV/ITC) Adventure. ITV 1974

Tommy Devon	**John Mills**
Stephen Halliday	**Brian Keith**
Alec Marlowe	**Barry Morse**
Manouche Roget	**Lilli Palmer**
Lt. Georges Roget	**Michael Petrovitch**
Jill Burton	**Seretta Wilson**

Creator **Paul Gallico**
Producer **Herbert Hirschman**

● ***Four French Resistance fighters reunite to maintain law and order on the Riviera.***

Nearly 30 years after disbanding at the end of the war, the so-called Zoo Gang are back in business. The members of this crack Resistance unit possess individual skills and operate under animal codenames. Team organizer is Tommy Devon, or Elephant, as he is known. When an old Nazi adversary walks into his jewellery shop on the French Riviera, he calls up surviving members of the squad to bring the war criminal to book. His colleagues are Stephen Halliday (a New York businessman and electronics expert, codenamed Fox), Canadian Alec Marlowe (Tiger, a mechanical genius), and Madame Manouche Roget (Leopard, the widow of another team member, Claude Roget – or Wolf – who was killed by the

Gestapo). Manouche runs a bar in Nice and is skilled in explosives. Her son, Georges, a French policeman, is also seen. Having nailed the Nazi, the four stay together to bring justice to the Côte d'Azur in Robin Hood fashion for five more episodes. The theme music was provided by Paul and Linda McCartney.

Zoo Quest ✶✶

UK (BBC) Natural History. BBC 1954–61

Producers **David Attenborough, Paul Johnstone**

Global expeditions in search of rare wildlife.

Zoo Quest, a six-series collaboration between the BBC Talks Department and London Zoo, recorded zoological searches for rare animals in the far corners of the world, such as the hunt for paradise birds in Madagascar. The aim was to bring examples back for exhibition and protection at the zoo. Individual series' titles reflected the nature of the expedition. They included *Zoo Quest to Guiana*, *Zoo Quest for a Dragon* (the komodo dragon) and *Zoo Quest in Paraguay*.

Zoo Time ✶✶

UK (Granada) Natural History. ITV 1956–68

Presenters **Desmond Morris, Harry Watt, Chris Kelly**

Producers **Milton Shulman, Derek Twist, David Warwick, Peter Mullings**

Studies of animal behaviour at London Zoo.

Initially introduced by animal watcher Desmond Morris, and aimed at the younger viewer, *Zoo Time* focused on the inmates of London Zoo and examined their innate behaviourial instincts. Harry Watt became host in 1960 and Chris Kelly took over in 1967, by which time the action had switched to Chester Zoo. Spin-off programmes like *A to Zoo*, *Breakthrough* and *Animal Story* were produced contemporaneously.

Zorro ✶✶

US (Walt Disney) Western. BBC 1 1976 (US: ABC 1957–9)

Don Diego de la Vega ('Zorro') .... **Guy Williams**
Don Alejandro de la Vega .... **George J. Lewis**
Bernardo .... **Gene Sheldon**
Capt. Monastario .... **Britt Lomond**
Sgt Garcia .... **Henry Calvin**
Cpl Reyes .... **Don Diamond**
Nacho Torres .... **Jan Arvan**
Elena Torres .... **Eugenia Paul**
Magistrate Galindo .... **Vinton Hayworth**
Anna Maria Verdugo .... **Jolene Brand**
Senor Gregorio Verdugo .... **Eduard Franz**

Executive Producer **Walt Disney**
Producer **William H. Anderson**

A mysterious masked cavalier always defeats a local despot.

In 1820 Don Diego de la Vega was summoned home from Spain to southern California by his father, Don Alejandro, to assist in the overthrow of a new local tyrant. Merciless Captain Monastario has taken control of the local Fortress de Los Angeles, and all the nobles of the area are under threat. Much is expected of the well-educated Don Diego. Sadly, it seems that their hopes are to be dashed, as the young nobleman turns out to be something of a fop. But, under the secret disguise of Zorro, a swashbuckling masked swordsman, he makes sure that the cruel Captain and his cronies – stupid, slobbish Sgt Garcia and Corporal Reyes – are put firmly in their place.

Everyone knows when Zorro has visited – he carves a distinctive 'Z' with the point of his sword – but only one man knows his true identity, his dumb servant, Bernardo, who also pretends to be deaf in order to spy for his master. Don Diego's two trusty steeds are the black Tornado (for use as himself) and the white Phantom (ridden by Zorro). Anna Maria Verdugo is Don Diego's romantic interest.

Zorro, meaning 'fox' in Spanish, was created by author Johnston McCulley in 1919. The character had already been played in the cinema by the likes of Douglas Fairbanks and Tyrone Power before Guy Williams took on the role. Williams himself is possibly better remembered as Professor John Robinson in LOST IN SPACE.

Zworykin, Vladimir K.

(1889–1982)

Russian-born American engineer, one of the pioneers of television. In the 1920s he produced an all-electronic television system that quickly found favour over Baird's electromechanical units. It was based on his development of the iconoscope (the cathode ray tube used in cameras) and the kinescope (the tube in the receiver).

Appendix A

The ITV Companies

Area	Programme company	On air	Off air
London (weekdays)	Associated-Rediffusion	22.9.55	29.7.68
	Thames Television	30.7.68	31.12.92
	Carlton Television	1.1.93	
London (weekends)	ATV	24.9.55	28.7.68
	London Weekend Television (LWT)	2.8.68	
Midlands (weekdays – and later all week)	ATV	17.2.56	31.12.81
	Central Independent Television	1.1.82	
Midlands (weekends)	ABC	18.2.56	28.7.68
North of England (weekdays)	Granada Television	3.5.56	26.7.68
North of England (weekends)	ABC	5.5.56	28.7.68
Central Scotland	Scottish Television	31.8.57	
Wales and the West of England	TWW	14.1.58	3.3.68
	HTV	4.3.68	
South of England (later South and South east England)	Southern Television	30.8.58	31.12.81
	TVS	1.1.82	31.12.92
	Meridian Broadcasting	1.1.93	
North-east England	Tyne Tees Television	15.1.59	
East of England	Anglia Television	27.10.59	
Northern Ireland	Ulster Television	31.10.59	
South-west England	Westward Television	29.4.61	11.8.81
	TSW	12.8.81	31.12.92
	Westcountry Television	1.1.93	
The Borders	Border Television	1.9.61	
North of Scotland	Grampian Television	30.9.61	
Channel Islands	Channel Television	1.9.62	
West and North Wales (later absorbed into Wales and the West of England)	Wales West and North	14.9.62	26.1.64
North-west England	Granada Television	29.7.68	
Yorkshire	Yorkshire Television	29.7.68	
National Breakfast Service	TV-am	1.2.83	31.12.92
	GMTV	1.1.93	

NB: The Midlands weekend franchise was amalgamated into the weekdays franchise in 1968. At the same time the North of England weekdays and weekend franchises were restructured into two new, all-week franchise areas, North-west England and Yorkshire. Following numerous takeovers and mergers, most of the ITV companies ended up in the hands of Granada and Carlton, who merged in 2004 to form ITV plc. However, the regions covered by Grampian and Scottish (owned by Scottish Media), Ulster and Channel remain independent.

Appendix B

Notable Dates in British Television History

1922 *18 October* British Broadcasting Company Ltd is established.

1923 *8 September* First edition of *Radio Times*.

1925 *30 October* First transmission of a human face (that of teenager William Taynton) by television, during an experiment by John Logie Baird in London.

1927 *1 January* British Broadcasting Corporation is established.

1929 *20 August* First BBC television trials, using Baird's 30-line equipment.

1932 *22 August* The BBC's experimental television service begins from Broadcasting House.

1936 *2 November* The world's first regular high-definition television service is launched by the BBC at Alexandra Palace. Baird's technology is eventually abandoned in favour of Marconi-EMI's 405-line system.

1939 *1 September* The BBC television service is closed down with the advent of war.

1946 *7 June* The television service is resumed.

1953 *2 June* The Coronation of Queen Elizabeth II – an occasion covered live by the BBC, which inspires thousands of citizens to purchase their first TV sets.

1954 *30 July* The Independent Television Authority (ITA) is inaugurated to oversee and regulate commercial television in the UK.

1955 *20 September* *TV Times* is first published (London area).

22 September ITV begins with broadcasts to the London area by Associated-Rediffusion.

10 October Test transmissions for colour television begin.

1957 *16 February* Toddlers' Truce is abandoned.

24 September BBC schools service is inaugurated.

1960 *29 June* BBC Television Centre at Shepherd's Bush is opened.

1962 *11 July* First live transatlantic broadcast, courtesy of the Telstar communications satellite.

1964 *20 April* BBC 2 begins transmissions on 625 lines, though much of the first night's output is blacked out by a power failure.

1967 *25 June* *Our World* – the first worldwide live satellite link-up – is broadcast.

1 July The UK's first regular colour transmissions begin on BBC 2.

1969 *21 July* Man first walks on the moon, watched by millions, thanks to television.

15 November Colour transmissions are extended to BBC 1 and ITV.

1971 *3 January* Open University broadcasts begin on the BBC.

1972 *12 June* The ITA takes control of independent radio as well as television and is renamed the Independent Broadcasting Authority (IBA).

1974 *23 September* CEEFAX, the BBC's teletext service, begins transmissions. ITV's answer, ORACLE, begins in July 1975.

1982 *1 November* S4C, the Welsh fourth channel, begins transmissions.

2 November Channel 4 takes to the air.

1983 *17 January* The BBC's breakfast television service (*Breakfast Time*) begins.

1 February ITV's breakfast television service (through TV-am) begins.

1984 *16 January* Sky television starts broadcasting via satellite and cable systems to selected conurbations in the UK.

1986 *27 October* The BBC begins daytime (all day) broadcasts.

1989 *5 February* Sky's direct-to-home satellite service begins, broadcasting from the Astra satellite, over a year before 'official' rival British Satellite Broadcasting (BSB) commences transmissions from the Marco Polo satellite.

1990 *2 November* Sky and BSB merge to form BSkyB.

1991 *1 January* The Independent Television Commission (ITC) replaces the IBA as regulator of ITV companies and their output.

15 April BBC World Service Television is inaugurated.

1997 *30 March* Channel 5 takes to the air.

9 November BBC News 24 begins broadcasting.

1998 *23 September* BBC launches BBC Choice, soon followed by other new digital channels.

1 October BSkyB is the first to offer digital television, by satellite.

15 November ONdigital (later ITV Digital) starts terrestrial digital transmissions.

7 December ITV 2 is launched.

2000 *1 August* ITN launches its digital, 24-hour ITN News Channel (now ITV News Channel).

2001 *11 August* ITV is rebranded ITV 1.

2002 *2 March* BBC 4 starts transmissions.

1 May ITV Digital collapses and goes off air.

16 September Channel 5 adopts a new identity as five.

30 October Freeview is launched as the replacement digital terrestrial service for ITV Digital.

2003 *9 February* BBC 3 takes to the air, replacing BBC Choice.

2004 *2 February* Shares in the newly created ITV plc are traded for the first time.

1 November ITV 3 is launched.

2005 *1 November* ITV 4 begins broadcasting.